Pub. No. 9

AMERICAN PRACTICAL NAVIGATOR

AN EPITOME OF NAVIGATION

ORIGINALLY BY

NATHANIEL BOWDITCH, LL.D.

2019 EDITION
Volume 2

Prepared and published by the
NATIONAL GEOSPATIAL-INTELLIGENCE AGENCY
Springfield, Virginia

Last painting by Gilbert Stuart (1828). Considered by the family of Bowditch to be the best of various paintings made, although it was unfinished when the artist died.

NATHANIEL BOWDITCH
(1773-1838)

Nathaniel Bowditch was born on March 26, 1773, in Salem, Massachusetts, fourth of the seven children of shipmaster Habakkuk Bowditch and his wife, Mary.

From the time William Bowditch migrated from England in the 17th century, the Bowditch family resided in Salem. Most of its sons, like those of other families in this New England seaport, had gone to sea, and many of them became shipmasters. Nathaniel Bowditch himself sailed as master on his last voyage, and two of his brothers met untimely deaths while pursuing careers at sea.

Nathaniel Bowditch's father, Habakkuk, was said to have lost two ships at sea, and by late Revolutionary days he was forced to return to the cooper trade that he had learned in his youth. Although cooper products such as the cask and barrel containers used for shipping flour, gunpowder, tobacco and liquids were in very high demand, this work delivered an insufficient income to properly provide for the needs of this growing family, who were often hungry and cold.

For many years the nearly destitute family received an annual grant of 15 to 20 dollars from the Salem Marine Society. By the time Nathaniel had reached the age of 10, the family's poverty forced him to leave school and join his father in the cooperage trade to help support the family.

Nathaniel was unsuccessful as a cooper, and when he was about 12 years of age, he entered the first of two ship-chandlery firms by which he was employed. It was during the nearly 10 years he was so employed that his great mind first attracted public attention. From the time he began school, Bowditch had an all-consuming interest in learning, particularly mathematics. By his middle teens he was recognized in Salem as an authority on that subject. Salem being primarily a shipping town, most of the inhabitants sooner or later found their way to the ship chandler, and news of the brilliant young clerk spread until eventually it came to the attention of the learned men of his day. Impressed by his desire to educate himself, they supplied him with books that he might learn of the discoveries of other men. Since many of the best books were written by Europeans, Bowditch first taught himself their languages, learning French, Spanish, Latin, Greek and German which were among the two dozen or more languages and dialects he studied during his life. At the age of 16 he began the study of Newton's *Principia*, translating parts of it from the Latin. He even found an error in that classic text, and though lacking the confidence to announce it at the time, he later published findings that were accepted by the scientific community.

During the Revolutionary War, a privateer out of Beverly, a neighboring town to Salem, had taken as one of its prizes an English vessel which was carrying the philosophical library of a famed Irish scholar, Dr. Richard Kirwan. The books were brought to the Colonies and there bought by a group of educated Salem men who used them to found the Philosophical Library Company, reputed to have been the best library north of Philadelphia at the time. In 1791, when Bowditch was 18, two Harvard-educated ministers, Rev. John Prince and Rev. William Bentley, persuaded the Company to allow Bowditch the use of its library. Encouraged by these two men and a third, Nathan Read, an apothecary who was also a Harvard man, Bowditch studied the works of the great men who had preceded him, especially the mathematicians and the astronomers. By the time he reached adulthood, this knowledge, acquired when not working long hours at the chandlery, had made young Nathaniel the outstanding mathematician in the Commonwealth, and perhaps even the country.

In the seafaring town of Salem, Bowditch was drawn to navigation early, learning the subject at the age of 13 from an old British sailor. A year later he began studying surveying, and in 1794 he assisted in a survey of the town. At 15 he devised an almanac reputed to have been of great accuracy. His other youthful accomplishments included the construction of a crude barometer and a sundial.

When Bowditch went to sea at the age of 21, it was as captain's writer and nominal second mate, the officer's berth being offered him because of his reputation as a scholar. Under Captain Henry Prince, the ship *Henry* sailed from Salem in the winter of 1795 on what was to be a year-long voyage to the Ile de Bourbon (now called Reunion) in the Indian Ocean.

Bowditch began his seagoing career when accurate time was not available to the average naval or merchant ship. A reliable marine chronometer had been invented some 60 years before, but the prohibitive cost, plus the long voyages without opportunity to check the error of the timepiece, made the large investment impractical. A system of determining longitude by "lunar distance," a method which did not require an accurate timepiece, was known, but this product of the minds of mathematicians and astronomers was so involved as to be beyond the capabilities of the uneducated seamen of that day. Consequently, ships were navigated by a combination of dead reckoning and parallel sailing (a system of sailing north or south to the latitude of the destination and then east or west to the destination). The navigational routine of the time was "lead, log, and lookout."

To Bowditch, the mathematical genius, computation of lunar distances was no mystery, of course, but he recognized the need for an easier method of working them in order to navigate ships more safely and efficiently.

Through analysis and observation, he derived a new and simplified formula during his first voyage.

John Hamilton Moore's *The Practical Navigator* was the leading navigational text when Bowditch first went to sea, and had been for many years. Early in his first voyage, however, the captain's writer-second mate began turning up errors in Moore's book, and before long he found it necessary to recompute some of the tables he most often used in working his sights. Bowditch recorded the errors he found, and by the end of his second voyage, made in the higher capacity of supercargo, the news of his findings in *The New Practical Navigator* had reached Edmund Blunt, a printer at Newburyport, Mass. At Blunt's request, Bowditch agreed to participate with other learned men in the preparation of an American edition of the thirteenth (1798) edition of Moore's work. The first American edition was published at Newburyport by Blunt in 1799. This edition corrected many of the errors that Moore had introduced.

Although most of the errors were of little significance to practical navigation because they were errors in the fifth and sixth places of logarithm tables, some errors were significant. The most significant mistake was listing the year 1800 as a leap year in the table of the sun's declination. The consequence was that Moore gave the declination for March 1, 1800, as 7°11'. Since the actual value was 7° 33', the calculation of a meridian altitude would be in error by 22 minutes of latitude, or 22 nautical miles. This infamous mathematical error would result in loss of life and at least two vessels, and contributed to numerous other hazardous situations. An outcome that Bowditch personally considered to be criminal.

Bowditch's principal contribution to the first American edition was his chapter "The Method of Finding the Longitude at Sea," which discussed his new method for computing lunar distances. Following publication of the first American edition, Blunt obtained Bowditch's services in checking the American and English editions for further errors. Blunt then published a second American edition of Moore's thirteenth edition in 1800. When preparing a third American edition for the press, Blunt decided that Bowditch had revised Moore's work to such an extent that Bowditch should be named as author. The title was changed to *The New American Practical Navigator* and the book was published in 1802 as a first edition. Bowditch vowed while writing this edition to "put down in the book nothing I can't teach the crew," and it is said that every member of his crew including the cook could take a lunar observation and plot the ship's position.

Bowditch made a total of five trips to sea, over a period of about nine years, his last as master and part owner of the three-masted *Putnam*. Homeward bound from a 13-month voyage to Sumatra and the Ile de France (now called Mauritius), the *Putnam* approached Salem Harbor on December 25, 1803, during a thick fog without having had a celestial observation since noon on the 24th. Relying upon his dead reckoning, Bowditch conned his wooden-hulled ship to the entrance of the rocky harbor, where he had the good fortune to get a momentary glimpse of Eastern Point, Cape Ann, enough to confirm his position. The *Putnam* proceeded in, past such hazards as "Bowditch's Ledge" (named after a great-grandfather who had wrecked his ship on the rock more than a century before) and anchored safely at 1900 that evening. Word of the daring feat, performed when other masters were hove-to outside the harbor, spread along the coast and added greatly to Bowditch's reputation. He was, indeed, the "practical navigator."

His standing as a mathematician and successful shipmaster earned him a well-paid position ashore within a matter of weeks after his last voyage. He was installed as president of a Salem fire and marine insurance company at the age of 30, and during the 20 years he held that position the company prospered. In 1823 he left Salem to take a similar position with a Boston insurance firm, serving that company with equal success until his death.

From the time he finished the "*Navigator*" until 1814, Bowditch's mathematical and scientific pursuits consisted of studies and papers on the orbits of comets, applications of Napier's rules, magnetic variation, eclipses, calculations on tides, and the charting of Salem Harbor. In that year, however, he turned to what he considered the greatest work of his life, the translation into English of *Mecanique Celeste*, by Pierre Laplace. *Mecanique Celeste* was a summary of all the then known facts about the workings of the heavens. Bowditch translated four of the five volumes before his death, and published them at his own expense. He gave many formula derivations which Laplace had not shown, and also included further discoveries following the time of publication. His work made this information available to American astronomers and enabled them to pursue their studies on the basis of that which was already known. Continuing his style of writing for the learner, Bowditch presented his English version of *Mecanique Celeste* in such a manner that the student of mathematics could easily trace the steps involved in reaching the most complicated conclusions.

Shortly after the publication of *The New American Practical Navigator*, Harvard College honored its author with the presentation of the honorary degree of Master of Arts, and in 1816 the college made him an honorary Doctor of Laws. From the time the Harvard graduates of Salem first assisted him in his studies, Bowditch had a great interest in that college, and in 1810 he was elected one of its Overseers, a position he held until 1826, when he was elected to the Corporation. During 1826-27 he was the leader of a small group of men who saved the school from financial disaster by forcing necessary economies on the college's reluctant president. At one time Bowditch was offered a Professorship in Mathematics at Harvard but this, as well as similar offers from West Point and the University of Virginia, he declined. In all his life he was never known to have made a public speech or to have addressed any large group of people.

Many other honors came to Bowditch in recognition of his astronomical, mathematical, and marine accomplishments. He became a member of the American Academy of Arts and Sciences, the East India Marine Society, the Royal Academy of Edinburgh, the Royal Society of London, the Royal Irish Academy, the American Philosophical Society, the Connecticut Academy of Arts and Sciences, the Boston Marine Society, the Royal Astronomical Society, the Palermo Academy of Science, and the Royal Academy of Berlin.

Nathaniel Bowditch outlived all of his brothers and sisters by nearly 30 years. He died on March 16, 1838, in his sixty-fifth year. The following eulogy by the Salem Marine Society indicates the regard in which this distinguished American was held by his contemporaries:

"In his death a public, a national, a human benefactor has departed. Not this community, nor our country only, but the whole world, has reason to do honor to his memory. When the voice of Eulogy shall be still, when the tear of Sorrow shall cease to flow, no monument will be needed to keep alive his memory among men; but as long as ships shall sail, the needle point to the north, and the stars go through their wonted courses in the heavens, the name of Dr. Bowditch will be revered as of one who helped his fellow-men in a time of need, who was and is a guide to them over the pathless ocean, and of one who forwarded the great interests of mankind."

Bowditch is buried in historic Mount Auburn Cemetery in Cambridge, Massachusetts. There is a bronze statue of Nathaniel Bowditch within the cemetery that marks his life.

THE NEW AMERICAN

PRACTICAL NAVIGATOR;

BEING AN

EPITOME OF NAVIGATION;

CONTAINING ALL THE TABLES NECESSARY TO BE USED WITH THE

NAUTICAL ALMANAC,

IN DETERMINING THE

LATITUDE;

AND THE

LONGITUDE BY LUNAR OBSERVATIONS;

AND

KEEPING A COMPLETE RECKONING AT SEA:

ILLUSTRATED BY

PROPER RULES AND EXAMPLES:

THE WHOLE EXEMPLIFIED IN A

JOURNAL,

KEPT FROM

BOSTON TO MADEIRA,

IN WHICH ALL THE RULES OF NAVIGATION ARE INTRODUCED:

ALSO

The Demonstration of the most useful Rules of Trigonometry: With many useful Problems in Mensuration, Surveying, and Gauging: And a Dictionary of Sea-Terms; with the Manner of performing the most common Evolutions at Sea.

TO WHICH ARE ADDED,

Some General Instructions and Information to Merchants, Masters of Vessels, and others concerned in Navigation, relative to Maritime Laws and Mercantile Customs.

FROM THE BEST AUTHORITIES.

ENRICHED WITH A NUMBER OF

NEW TABLES,

WITH ORIGINAL IMPROVEMENTS AND ADDITIONS, AND A LARGE VARIETY OF NEW AND IMPORTANT MATTER:

ALSO,

MANY THOUSAND ERRORS ARE CORRECTED,

WHICH HAVE APPEARED IN THE BEST SYSTEMS OF NAVIGATION YET PUBLISHED.

BY NATHANIEL BOWDITCH,

FELLOW OF THE AMERICAN ACADEMY OF ARTS AND SCIENCES.

ILLUSTRATED WITH COPPERPLATES.

First Edition.

PRINTED AT NEWBURYPORT, (MASS.) 1802,

BY

EDMUND M. BLUNT, (Proprietor)

FOR CUSHING & APPLETON, SALEM.

SOLD BY EVERY BOOKSELLER, SHIP-CHANDLER, AND MATHEMATICAL INSTRUMENT-MAKER, IN THE UNITED STATES AND WEST-INDIES.

Original title page of *The New American Practical Navigator*, First Edition, published in 1802.

PREFACE

The Naval Observatory library in Washington, D.C., is unnaturally quiet. It is a large circular room, filled with thousands of books. Its acoustics are perfect; a mere whisper from the room's open circular balcony can be easily heard by those standing on the ground floor. A fountain in the center of the ground floor softly breaks the room's silence as its water stream gently splashes into a small pool. From this serene room, a library clerk will lead you into an antechamber, beyond which is a vault containing the Observatory's most rare books. In this vault, one can find an original 1802 first edition of the *New American Practical Navigator*.

One cannot hold this small, delicate, slipcovered book without being impressed by the nearly 200-year unbroken chain of publication that it has enjoyed. It sailed on U.S. merchantmen and Navy ships shortly after the quasi-war with France and during British impressment of merchant seamen that led to the War of 1812. It sailed on U.S. Naval vessels during operations against Mexico in the 1840's, on ships of both the Union and Confederate fleets during the Civil War, and with the U.S. Navy in Cuba in 1898. It went around the world with the Great White Fleet, across the North Atlantic to Europe during both World Wars, to Asia during the Korean and Vietnam Wars, and to the Middle East during Operation Desert Storm. It has circled the globe with countless thousands of merchant ships for 200 years.

As navigational requirements and procedures have changed throughout the years, *Bowditch* has changed with them. Originally devoted almost exclusively to celestial navigation, it now also covers a host of modern topics. It is as practical today as it was when Nathaniel Bowditch, master of the *Putnam*, gathered the crew on deck and taught them the mathematics involved in calculating lunar distances. It is that practicality that has been the publication's greatest strength, and that makes the publication as useful today as it was in the age of sail.

Seafarers have long memories. In no other profession is tradition more closely guarded. Even the oldest and most cynical acknowledge the special bond that connects those who have made their livelihood plying the sea. This bond is not comprised of a single strand; rather, it is a rich and varied tapestry that stretches from the present back to the birth of our nation and its seafaring culture. As this book is a part of that tapestry, it should not be lightly regarded; rather, it should be preserved, as much for its historical importance as for its practical utility.

Since antiquity, mariners have gathered available navigation information and put it into a text for others to follow. One of the first attempts at this involved volumes of Spanish and Portuguese navigational manuals translated into English between about 1550 to 1750. Writers and translators of the time "borrowed" freely in compiling navigational texts, a practice which continues today with works such as Sailing Directions and Pilots.

Colonial and early American navigators depended exclusively on English navigation texts because there were no American editions. The first American navigational text, *Orthodoxal Navigation*, was completed by Benjamin Hubbard in 1656. The first American navigation text published in America was Captain Thomas Truxton's *Remarks, Instructions, and Examples Relating to the Latitude and Longitude; also the Variation of the Compass, Etc., Etc.*, published in 1794.

The most popular navigational text of the late 18th century was John Hamilton Moore's *The New Practical Navigator*. Edmund M. Blunt, a Newburyport publisher, decided to issue a revised copy of this work for American navigators. Blunt convinced Nathaniel Bowditch, a locally famous mariner and mathematician, to revise and update *The New Practical Navigator*. Several other learned men assisted in this revision. Blunt's *The New Practical Navigator* was published in 1799. Blunt also published a second American edition of Moore's book in 1800.

By 1802, when Blunt was ready to publish a third edition, Nathaniel Bowditch and others had corrected so many errors in Moore's work that Blunt decided to issue the work as a first edition of the *New American Practical Navigator*. It is to that 1802 work that the current edition of the *American Practical Navigator* traces its pedigree.

The *New American Practical Navigator* stayed in the Bowditch and Blunt family until the government bought the copyright in 1867. Edmund M. Blunt published the book until 1833; upon his retirement, his sons, Edmund and George, took over publication.The elder Blunt died in 1862; his son Edmund followed in 1866. The next year, 1867, George Blunt sold the copyright to the government for $25,000. The government has published *Bowditch* ever since. George Blunt died in 1878.

Nathaniel Bowditch continued to correct and revise the book until his death in 1838. Upon his death, the editorial responsibility for the *American Practical Navigator* passed to his son, J. Ingersoll Bowditch. Ingersoll Bowditch continued editing the *Navigator* until George Blunt sold the copyright to the government. He outlived all of the principals involved in publishing and editing the *Navigator*, dying in 1889.

The U.S. government has published numerous editions of the *American Practical Navigator* since acquiring the copyright. Over time the book has come to be known simply by its original author's name and by its year of publishing. Thus, this work represents the 2019 edition of *Bowditch.* Like the previous edition, this one is also composed of a two volume set.

Today, mariners can access the official "digital" version of *Pub No. 9 - American Practical Navigator - Bowditch,* free of charge, from NGA's Maritime Safety Information web portal. As with NGA's other nautical publications, the digital *online* edition eliminates the need "to print" new editions in order to convey new information to the marine navigation community. The *online* edition is under continuous maintenance and therefore represents the most up-to-date version of this text, unlike a printed edition which is only a static picture in time.

As much as it is a part of history, *Bowditch* is not a history book. In this edition, as in past editions, dated material was dropped and new methods, technologies and techniques added to keep pace with changes in the practice of navigation. The changes are intended to ensure *Bowditch* remains the premier reference work for modern, practical marine navigation. This edition replaces but does not cancel former editions, which may be retained and consulted as to historical navigation methods not discussed herein.

CHAPTER 1, MATHEMATICS once again includes sections on basic arithmetic including: expressing numbers, significant digits, addition, subtraction, rounding off, reciprocals, multiplication and division. Likewise, the expanded chapter includes discussions on calculus and differential equations. Though rarely used today, an in-depth discussion on logarithms returns to this chapter. This topic is supplemented by the inclusion of haversine tables (found in Appendix B), which makes this publication perhaps the last in existence to provide this esoteric data, should the need arise to perform complex calculation manually.

CHAPTER 2, INTERPOLATION includes discussion on single, double, triple and nonlinear interpolation (with Bessel's formula included).

CHAPTER 3, NAVIGATIONAL ERROR was greatly expanded and updated by Johns Hopkins University-Applied Physics Laboratory.

CHAPTER 4, CALCULATIONS AND CONVERSIONS summarizes the formulas the navigator depends upon during voyage planning, piloting, celestial navigation, and various related tasks.

CHAPTER 5, COMPASS CONVERSIONS contains information on magnetic compass error, deviation table, applying variation and deviation, along with several example problems.

CHAPTER 6, COMPASS ERROR examines the process for determining compass error using *Pub No. 229 - Sight Reduction Tables for Marine Navigation.*

NGA seeks and encourages critical feedback on this publication. Suggestions and comments for changes and additions may be sent to:

MARITIME SAFETY OFFICE
MAIL STOP N64-SFH
NGA
7500 GEOINT DRIVE
SPRINGFIELD, VIRGINIA, 22150-7500
UNITED STATES OF AMERICA
Email: mcdpubs@nga.mil
Website: https://msi.nga.mil

ACKNOWLEDGMENTS

This 2019 edition of *The American Practical Navigator (Bowditch), Pub No. 9,* exists to codify the latest body of marine navigation knowledge and practical application. Its publication success is a result of the dedicated efforts of many hands and voices from academia, science and seafaring experts. This edition has advanced from the judiciously shaped recommendations-some comprehensive, some minute, all indispensable-of a multitude of maritime and science professionals. At the same time, it was equally essential that those recommendations be compared, vetted, and applied in a consistent manner and with a clear vision, a challenging task performed in exemplary fashion by this edition's principal editor, **Dr. Gerard J. Clifford, Jr.**

Many institutions, organizations, groups and individuals directly contributed or assisted in the success of this edition of Bowditch. Of particular note, grateful acknowledgment of effort goes out to the following:

California State University Maritime Academy:
Captain Tuuli Messer-Bookman, Samuel R. Pecota, Captain Scott Powell

Carnegie Science/Observatory:
John Grula, Tina McDowell

Civilian mariners:
James Baldwin on board the HORIZON CONSUMER, Allan B. Campbell, John A. Graham on board the USNS ARCTIC, Michael J. Holliday on board the USNS SISLER, Christopher Moore, Jere M. St. Angelo

College of William and Mary:
Dr. Christopher M. Bailey

Defense Logistics Agency:
Mr. Albert Zamora

European Space Agency:
Dr. Avila Rodriguez

Hempstead Maritime Training LLC:
Christian Hempstead

Huntington Library:
Dr. Daniel Lewis

International Hydrographic Bureau/International Hydrographic Organization:
Tony Pharaoh, David Wyatt

International Maritime Organization:
Simone Leyers

Johns Hopkins University-Applied Physics Laboratory:
Mr. Ned A. Brokloff, Ms. Leah C. Campbell, Mr. Jeffrey L. Girsch, Ms. Michelle C. Greiner, Dr. Shannon M. H all, Dr. Daniel G. Jablonski, Mr. George H. Klaus III, Mr. Bradford J. Lapsansky, Mr. Andrew E. Love Jr., Dr. William R. Martin, Dr. David L. Porter, Mr. David R. Stark, Mr. Jonathan J. Thomas, Mr. Gregory L. Weaver

Maine Maritime Academy:
Captain Andy Chase, Captain Les Eadie, Captain Donald P. Eley, Captain Nathan D. Powers, Captain Adam Slazas, Captain Sam Teel

Maritime Institute of Technology and Graduate Studies:
Captain John Brennan, Mr. Glen Paine

Massachusetts Maritime Academy:
John L. Belle, Captain Michael R. Burns Jr., Captain Craig N. Dalton, Laurel Delong, David B. Mackey, Captain Patrick J. Modic, Linda Letourneau

NASA:
James White

Northrop Grumman Sperry Marine:
Michael R. Sawyer

Norwegian Coastal Administration:
Anne Grethe Nilson, John E. Hagen

Pennsylvania State University - Applied Research Laboratory:
Mr. Lee R. Insley

State University of New York Maritime College:
James Rogin

Teledyne RDI:
Blair Brumley, Paul Wanis

Texas A&M Maritime Academy:
Captain James P. Cleary, Captain Scott Putty, Captain Augusta "Gussie" D. Roth

U. S. Army Transportation Command:
Robert H. Brockman

U. S. Coast Guard:
LCDR Lawrence F. Ahlin, Mr. Jorge Arroyo, BMC Doug Bullock, Thomas R. Casey, BMCS Scott Cichoracki, LT Nick Cichucki (USN), LT Andrew Dennelly, George H. Detweiler, LT Brennan P. Dougherty, Mr. Clay Diamond (USCG Ret.), Mr. Paul Eulitt, LT Trip Fernandes, LT Nick Forni, LT Curt Gookin, LTJG Clay Haywood, CDR Michael Hicks, LT Mike Higbie, LT Eric W. Johnson, LT Taylor Kellogg, Mr. Robert D. Lewald, Mr. Vernon L. Mann, C.B. Mauro, CDR Gabrielle G. McGrath, USCG (Ret.), Mr. David Merrill, Mr. Russ Levin, BMC John C. Lobherr, CDR Stephen A. Love, LT Dan Miller, ENS Nickolette A. Morin, MST2 Daniel M. Morrisey, CAPT Steven W. Nerheim USN (Ret), LT Nathan Neuhardt, LT Andrew Norberg, Mr. Frank L. Parker, LCDR Michael A. Patterson, LT Patrick R. Powers, LT Eric Quigley, LT Jackie D. Ramirez, ET2 Chelsea Rasmussen, Mr. Bruce R. Riley, LT Sarah K. Shveda, CAPT Scott J. Smith, CDR John M. Stone, BMCM Tim Sullivan, E.J. Terminella, Mr. Robert

M. Trainor, Mr. Steve Tucker, BOSN Tim Tully, CDR Michael A. Turdo, LCDR Matthew J, Walter, CDR William C. Woityra

U.S. Government Publishing Office

Mr. Kenneth Kerns, Mr. John M. Carey

U. S. Maritime Administration:

Kevin Kolhman, Kevin M. Tokerski

U. S. National Oceanic and Atmospheric Administration:

Dr. Benjamin Albright, Eric Blake, Johan Booth, Tyra Brown, Hugh Cobb, RADM Samuel De Bow, NOAA (Ret.), Patrick A. Dixon, James Franklin, Megan Greenaway, Mark Griffin, Colby A. Harmon, Robert Heeley, Craig Hodan, Paul Lee, Rick Lumpkin, John Brent Macek, CDR Gabrielle G McGrath (USCG), Martin Nelson, Richard Pasch, LT Joseph T. Phillips, Julia Powell, Dr. Scott D. Rudlosky, Paula Rychtar, Joseph Sienkiewicz, Stacy Stewart, Dr. Rodney Viereck, LTJG Jason P. Wilson, Gregory Zwicker

U.S. National Geospatial-Intelligence Agency:

CAPT Brian D. Connon, USN (Ret.), Mr. Herman W. Dick, Mr. John A. Gandy, Ms. Dorthea Horne, LT Richard C. Johnson (USNR), CAPT Richard A. Kennedy Jr., USN, Dr. J.N. (Nikki) Markiel, Mr. Dennis J. McCleary, Dr. Terry Monroe, Mr. Daniel F. Mullaney, Ms. Elizabeth Neise, CAPT Philip J. Saltzman (USNR), Ms. Carling R. Uhler, Mr. Muridith W. Winder

U. S. Naval Academy:

LCDR Andrew Storey, Royal Navy

U. S. Naval Institute:

Thomas J. Cutler

U. S. Naval Oceanographic Office:

Scott Davison, Susan Sebastian

U. S. Naval Observatory:

Jennifer Bartlett, James L. Hilton, George H. Kaplan, Demetrios Mataskis, Dr. Nancy A. Oliverson, OMC Tim Sheedy (USN), Susan G. Stewart, Mark S. Stollberg, Sean E. Urban

U. S. Navy COMPACFLT:

Daniel G. Morris, LCDR Mark H. Schaff

U. S. Navy Military Sealift Command:

Patrick T. Christian

U. S. Navy Space and Naval Warfare Systems Command:

Robert A. Greer

U. S. Navy Surface Warfare Officer School:

QMC Robert P. Hoops, LT Andrew P. McCarthy, LT Kevin F. Mullins, LCDR Douglas E Raineault, QMCS David A. Rodriquez, Captain Bud Weeks

University Corporation for Atmospheric Research:

Christopher J. Kennedy

University of New Hampshire:

Dr. Lee Alexander, Colleen Mitchell, Tara Hicks Johnson

UrsaNav:

Chuck Schue

WR Systems Ltd:

CAPT Paul K. Heim, USN (Ret.)

Acknowledgment must also be extended to the following dedicated maritime navigation experts who examined the penultimate draft of this manuscript and meticulously analyzed, commented, proofread, edited and prepared it for publication:

Mr. Keith E. Alexander
Mr. David E. Allen
Mr. David W. Anderson
Ms. Jacqueline Barone
Captain Anthony G. Bastidas
LCDR Daniel E. Butler, USN
QMCM Randy L. Bryant, USN (Ret.)
Mr. Sebastian P. Carisio
Mr. Howard J. Cohen
Mr. Matthew M Cronin
Mr. Brian M. Drew
Mr. Peter M. Doherty
Mr. Keith E. Dominic
Mr. Patrick V. Dorr
QMC Philip Dorsainvil, USN (Ret.)
Mrs. Jenny R. Floyd
Mr. James D. Ford
Ms. Billie Jean Gooch
Captain LeeAnne E. Gordon
Mr. Joseph A. Grzymkowski III
Ms. Misty R. Harris
Ms. Donna M. Harrison
Mr. John J. Haumann Jr.
Mr. Brian R. Heap
Mr. Walter D. Holtgren
Mr. Matthew C. Hume
Mr. Jerome Hyman
Mrs. Jennifer Kearns
Mr. Carl G. Kaempfer
Mr. Virgil (Buddy) R. Klepper, Jr.
Mr. Michael S. Kushla
Ms. Prasnee K. Luebke
Ms. Ann M. Luken
Mr. Christopher J. Lonergan
Mr. Michael W. Mauceri
Ms. Sheryl L. McCash
Mr. Sean M. McGurgan
Mr. Philip Meeks
Mr. Ryan S. Milligan
Ms. Sara R. Mock
Mr. Eugene L. Moisan
ETC Robert J. Mueller, Jr., USN (Ret.)
Mr. Darryl R. Mulato
Mr. Mark E. Nueslein

Mr. Steven R. Offenback
Mr. Jason J. Otero-Torres
Captain Geoffrey J. Phelps
Mr. Robert J. Raffles
Mr. James E. Rogers, Jr.
LCDR Douglas L. Roush, USN (Ret.)
Mr. Frederick R. Sanders
LCDR Jared B. Shorter, USNR
Mr. Christopher W. Sisson
Ms. DanaAnn T. Sisson
Mr. Jason D. Strom
Mr. Jamison N. Stubbs
Mr. Andrew M. Sullivan
Mr. Michael A. Theberge
Mr. Stuart Vick
Mr. John W. von Rosenberg
Mr. Brian S. Walker
QMC James F. Witts II, USN (Ret.)
Mr. Jeffrey M. Whittaker
QMC Shane T. Wilson, USN (Ret.)
Ms. Rachael C. Wold
Mr. Paul C. Youngs

QMCM Michael G. Harrison, USN (Ret.)
Chief, Publications Branch
Maritime Safety Office
National Geospatial-Intelligence Agency
Springfield, Virginia

TABLE OF CONTENTS

PART 1

USEFUL TABLES

MATHEMATICAL TABLES

CARTOGRAPHIC TABLES

PILOTING TABLES

CELESTIAL NAVIGATION TABLES

METEOROLOGICAL TABLES

PART 2

MATHEMATICS FOR NAVIGATION

PART 3

APPENDICES

GLOSSARIES

INDEX

METEORLOGICAL TABLES (cont.)

EXPLANATION OF NAVIGATION TABLES

Mathematical Tables

Table 1. Logarithms of Numbers – The first page of this table gives the complete common logarithm (characteristic and mantissa) of numbers 1 through 250. Succeeding pages give the mantissa only of the common logarithm of any number. Values are given for four significant digits of entering values, the first three being in the left-hand column, and the fourth at the heading of one of the other columns. Thus, the mantissa of a three-digit number is given in the column headed 0, on the line with the given number; while the mantissa of a four-digit number is given in the column headed by the fourth digit, on the line with the first three digits. As an example, the mantissa of 328 is 51587, while that of 3.284 is 51640. For additional digits, interpolation should be used. The difference between each tabulated mantissa and the next larger tabulated mantissa is given in the "d" column to the right of the smaller mantissa. This difference can be used to enter the appropriate proportional parts ("Prop. parts") auxiliary table to interpolate for the fifth digit of the given number. If an accuracy of more than five significant digits is to be preserved in a computation, a table of logarithms to additional decimal places should be used. For a number of one or two digits, use the first page of the table or add zeros to make three digits. That is, the mantissa of 3, 30, and 300 is the same, 47712. Interpolation on the first page of the table is not recommended. The second part should be used for values not listed on the first page.

Table 2. Natural Trigonometric Functions – This table gives the values of natural sines, cosecants, tangents, cotangents, secants, and cosines of angles from 0° to 180°, at intervals of 1'. For angles between 0° and 45° use the column labels at the top and the minutes at the left; for angles between 45° and 90° use the column labels at the bottom and the minutes at the right; for angles between 90° and 135° use the column labels at the bottom and the minutes at the left; and for angles between 135° and 180° use the column labels at the top and the minutes at the right. These combinations are indicated by the arrows accompanying the figures representing the number of degrees. For angles between 180° and 360°, subtract 180° and proceed as indicated above to obtain the numerical values of the various functions.

Differences between consecutive entries are shown in the "Diff. 1'" column to the right of each column of values of a trigonometric function, as an aid to interpolation. These differences are one-half line out of step with the numbers to which they apply, as in a critical table. Each difference applies to the values half a line above and half a line below. To determine the correction to apply to the value for the smaller entering angle, multiply the difference by the number of tenths of a minute (or seconds ÷ 60) of the entering angle. Note whether the function is increasing or decreasing, and add or subtract the correction as appropriate, so that the interpolated value lies between the two values between which interpolation is made.

Table 3. Logarithms of Trigonometric Functions – This table gives the common logarithms (+10) of sines, cosecants, tangents, cotangents, secants, and cosines of angles from 0° to 180°, at intervals of 1'. For angles between 0° and 45° use the column labels at the top and the minutes at the left; for angles between 45° and 90° use the column labels at the bottom and the minutes at the right; for angles between 90° and 135° use the column labels at the bottom and the minutes at the left; and for angles between 135° and 180° use the column labels at the top and the minutes at the right. These combinations are indicated by the arrows accompanying the figures representing the number of degrees. For angles between 180° and 360°, subtract 180° and proceed as indicated above to obtain the numerical values of the various functions.

Differences between consecutive entries are shown in the "Diff. 1'" columns, except that one difference column is used for both sines and cosecants, another for both tangents and cotangents, and a third for both secants and cosines. These differences, given as an aid to interpolation, are one-half line out of step with the numbers to which they apply, as in a critical table. Each difference applies to the values half a line above and half a line below. To determine the correction to apply to the value for the smaller entering angle, multiply the difference by the number of tenths of a minute (or seconds ÷ 60) of the entering angle. Note whether the function is increasing or decreasing, and add or subtract the correction as appropriate, so that the interpolated value lies between the two values between which interpolation is made.

Table 4. Traverse Table – This table can be used in the solution of any of the sailings except great-circle and composite. In providing the values of the difference of latitude and departure corresponding to distances up to 600 miles and for courses for every degree of the compass, Table 4 is essentially a tabulation of the solutions of plane right triangles. Since the solutions are for integral values of the acute angle and the distance, interpolation for intermediate values may be required. Through appropriate interchanges of the headings of the columns, solutions for other than plane sailings can be made. The interchanges of the headings of the different columns are summarized at the foot of each table opening.

The distance, difference of latitude, and departure columns are labeled Dist., D. Lat., and Dep., respectively.

For solution of a plane right triangle, any number N in the distance column is the hypotenuse; the number opposite in the difference of latitude column is N times the cosine of the acute angle; and the other number opposite in the departure column is N times the sine of the acute angle. Or, the number in the column labeled D. Lat. is the value of the side adjacent and the number in the column labeled Dep. is the value of the side opposite the acute angle.

Appendix B. Haversines – These tables list the common logarithms (+10) of haversines and natural haversines of angles from 0° to 360°, at intervals of 1'. For angles between 0° and 180° use the degrees as given at the tops of the columns and the minutes at the left; for angles between 180° and 360° use the degrees as given at the bottom of the columns and the minutes at the right.

Cartographic Tables

Table 5. Natural and Numerical Chart Scales – This table gives the numerical scale equivalents for various natural or fractional chart scales. The scale of a chart is the ratio of a given distance on the chart to the actual distance which it represents on the earth. The scale may be expressed as a simple ratio or fraction, known as the **natural scale**. For example, 1:80,000 or $\frac{1}{80000}$ means that one unit (such as an inch) on the chart represents 80,000 of the same unit on the surface of the earth. The scale may also be expressed as a statement of that distance on the earth shown as one unit (usually an inch) on the chart, or vice versa. This is the **numerical scale**.

The table was computed using 72,913.39 inches per nautical mile and 63,360 inches per statute mile.

Table 6. Meridional Parts – In this table the meridional parts used in the construction of Mercator charts and in Mercator sailing are tabulated to one decimal place for each minute of latitude from the equator to the poles.

The table was computed using the formula:

$$M = a \log_e 10 \log \tan\left(45 + \frac{L}{2}\right) - a\left(e^2 \sin L + \frac{e^4}{3}\sin^3 L + \frac{e^6}{5}\sin^5 L + \ldots\right),$$

in which M is the number of meridional parts between the equator and the given latitude, a is the equatorial radius of the earth, expressed in minutes of arc of the equator, or

$$a = \frac{21600}{2\pi} = 3437.74677078 (\log = 3.5362739),$$

$\log_e$ is the natural (Naperian) logarithm, using the base e = 2.71828182846,

$$\log_e 10 = 2.3025851 \quad (\log = 0.36221569)$$

L is the latitude,

f is earth's flattening, or

$$f = \frac{1}{298.257223563}$$

$$= 3.35281066475 \cdot 10^{-3} \quad (\log = 7.474591 - 10)$$

the squared eccentricity of the earth, e^2 [not to be confused with Euler's constant, the base of natural logarithms] is

$$e^2 = 2f - f^2$$

$$= 6.694379990141 \cdot 10^{-3} \quad (\log = 7.1742896 - 10)$$

Using these values,

$$a \log_e 10 = 7915.7 \ (\log = 3.8984893)$$

$$ae^2 = 23.01358319 \ (\log = 1.3619842)$$

$$\frac{ae^4}{3} = 0.05135389 (\log = 8.2894349 - 10)$$

$$\frac{ae^6}{5} = 0.00020627 (\log = 6.6855639 - 10)$$

Hence, the formula becomes

$$M = 7915.7 \log \tan\left(45° + \frac{L}{2}\right) - 23.01358319 \sin L - 0.05135389 \sin^3 L - 0.00020627 \sin^5 L \ldots$$

The constants used in this derivation and in the table are based upon the World Geodetic System 1984 (WGS 84) ellipsoid.

Table 7. Length of a Degree of Latitude and Longitude – This table gives the length of one degree of latitude and longitude at intervals of 1° from the equator to the poles. In the case of latitude, the values given are the lengths of the arcs extending half a degree on each side of the tabulated latitudes. Lengths are given in nautical miles, statute miles, feet, and meters.

The values were computed in meters, using parameters of the World Geodetic System 1984 (WGS 84) ellipsoid, and converted to other units. The following formulas were used:

$$M = \left(\frac{\pi}{180}\right)\left[\frac{a(1-e^2)}{w^3}\right] \text{ where}$$

a = 6378137, the semi - major axis of the WGS 84 ellipsoid

$$e^2 = 2f - f^2 = 6.694379990141 \bullet 10^{-3}$$

$$w = \sqrt{1 - e^2 \sin^2 \varphi}$$

$$\varphi = \text{geodetic latitude}$$

And

$$P = \left(\frac{\pi}{180}\right)\left[\frac{a(\cos \varphi)}{w}\right]$$

Piloting Tables

Table 8. Conversion Table for Meters, Feet, and Fathoms – The number of feet and fathoms corresponding to a given number of meters, and vice versa, can be taken directly from this table for any value of the entering argument from 1 to 120. The entering value can be multiplied by any power of 10, including negative powers, if the corresponding values of the other units are multiplied by the same power. Thus, 420 meters are equivalent to 1378.0 feet, and 11.2 fathoms are equivalent to 20.483 meters.

The table was computed by means of the relationships:

1 meter = 39.370079 inches,

1 foot = 12 inches,

1 fathom = 6 feet.

Table 9. Conversion Table for Nautical and Statute Miles – This table gives the number of statute miles corresponding to any whole number of nautical miles from 1 to 100, and the number of nautical miles corresponding to any whole number of statute miles within the same range. The entering value can be multiplied by any power of 10, including negative powers, if the corresponding value of the other unit is multiplied by the same power. Thus, 2,700 nautical miles are equivalent to 3,107.1 statute miles, and 0.3 statute mile is equivalent to 0.2607 nautical mile.

The table was computed using the conversion factors:

1 nautical mile = 1.15077945 statute miles,

1 statute mile = 0.86897624 nautical mile.

Table 10. Speed Table for Measured Mile – To find the speed of a vessel on a measured nautical mile in a given number of minutes and seconds of time, enter this table at the top or bottom with the number of minutes, and at either side with the number of seconds. The number taken from the table is speed in knots. Accurate results can be obtained by interpolating to the nearest 0.1 second.

This table was computed by means of the formula:

$S = \frac{3600}{T}$, in which S is speed in knots, and T is elapsed time in seconds.

Table 11. Speed, Time, and Distance Table – To find the distance steamed at any given speed between 0.5 and 40 knots in any given number of minutes from 1 to 60, enter this table at the top with the speed, and at the left with the number of minutes. The number taken from the table is the distance in nautical miles. If hours are substituted for minutes, the tabulated distance should be multiplied by 60; if seconds are substituted for minutes, the tabulated distance should be divided by 60.

The table was computed by means of the formula:

$D = \frac{ST}{60}$, in which D is distance in nautical miles, S is speed in knots, and T is elapsed time in minutes.

Table 12. Distance of the Horizon – This table gives the distance in nautical and statute miles of the visible sea horizon for various heights of eye in feet and meters. The actual distance varies somewhat as refraction changes. However, the error is generally less than that introduced by nonstandard atmospheric conditions. Also the formula used contains an approximation which introduces a small error at the greatest heights tabulated.

The table was computed using the formula:

$$D = \sqrt{\frac{2r_o h_f}{6076.1\ \beta_o}}$$

in which D is the distance to the horizon in nautical miles; ro is the mean radius of the earth, 3440.1 nautical miles; h_f is the height of eye in feet; and β_o (0.8279) accounts for terrestrial refraction.

This formula simplifies to: $D\ (\text{nm}) = 1.169\sqrt{h_f}$

$$(\text{statute miles}) = 1.345\sqrt{h_f}$$

Table 13. Geographic Range – This table gives the geographic range or the maximum distance at which the curvature of the earth permits a light to be seen from a particular height of eye without regard to the luminous intensity of the light. The geographic range depends upon the height of both the light and the eye of the observer.

The table was computed using the formula:

$$D = 1.17\sqrt{H} + 1.17\sqrt{h},$$

in which D is the geographic range in nautical miles, H is the height in feet of the light above sea level, and h is the height in feet of the eye of the observer above sea level.

Table 14. Dip of the Sea Short of the Horizon – If land, another vessel, or other obstruction is between the observer and the sea horizon, use the waterline of the obstruction as the horizontal reference for altitude measurements, and substitute dip from this table for the dip of the horizon (height of eye correction) given in the *Nautical Almanac*. The values below the bold rules are for normal dip, the visible horizon being between the observer and the obstruction.

The table was computed with the formula:

$$D_s = 60 \tan^{-1}\left(\frac{h_f}{6076.1 d_s} + \frac{\beta_o d_s}{2 r_o}\right)$$

in which D_s is the dip short of the sea horizon, in minutes of arc; h_f is the height of eye of the observer above sea level in feet; β_o (0.8321) accounts for terrestrial refraction; r_o is the mean radius of the earth, 3440.1 nautical miles; and d_s is the distance to the waterline of the obstruction in nautical miles.

Table 15. Distance by Vertical Angle Measured Between Sea Horizon and Top of Object Beyond Sea Horizon – This table tabulates the distance to an object of known height above sea level when the object lies beyond the horizon. The vertical angle between the top of the object and the visible horizon is measured with a sextant and corrected for index error and dip only. The table is entered with the difference in the height of the object and the height of eye of the observer and the corrected vertical angle; and the distance in nautical miles is taken directly from the table. An error may be introduced if refraction differs from the standard value used in the computation of the table.

The table was computed using the formula:

$$D = \sqrt{\left(\frac{\tan\alpha}{0.0002419}\right)^2 + \frac{H-h}{0.7349}} - \frac{\tan\alpha}{0.0002419}$$

in which D is the distance in nautical miles, α is the corrected vertical angle, H is the height of the top of the object above sea level in feet, and h is the height of eye of the observer above sea level in feet. The constants 0.0002419 and 0.7349 account for terrestrial refraction.

Table 16. Distance by Vertical Angle Measured Between Waterline at Object and Top of Object – This table tabulates the angle subtended by an object of known height lying at a particular distance within the observer's visible horizon or vice versa.

The table provides the solution of a plane right triangle having its right angle at the base of the observed object and its altitude coincident with the vertical dimension of the observed object. The solutions are based upon the following simplifying assumptions: (1) the eye of the observer is at sea level, (2) the sea surface between the observer and the object is flat, (3) atmospheric refraction is negligible, and (4) the waterline at the object is vertically below the peak of the object. The error due to the height of eye of the observer does not exceed 3 percent of the distance-off for sextant angles less than 20° and heights of eye less than one-third of the object height. The error due to the waterline not being below the peak of the object does not exceed 3 percent of the distance-off when the height of eye is less than one-third of the object height and the offset of the waterline from the base of the object is less than one-tenth of the distance-off. Errors due to earth's curvature and atmospheric refraction are negligible for cases of practical interest.

Table 17. Distance by Vertical Angle Measured Between Waterline at Object and Sea Horizon Beyond Object – This table tabulates the distance to an object lying within or short of the horizon when the height of eye of the observer is known. The vertical angle between the waterline at the object and the visible (sea) horizon beyond is measured and corrected for index error. The table is entered with the corrected vertical angle and the height of eye of the observer in feet; the distance in yards is taken directly from the table

The table was computed from the formula:

$$\tan h_s = (A - B) \div (1 + AB) \text{ where}$$

$$A = \frac{h}{d_s} + \frac{\beta_o d_s}{2 r_o} \text{ and}$$

$$B = \sqrt{2\beta_o h / r_o}$$

in which β_o (0.8279) accounts for terrestrial refraction, r_o is the mean radius of the earth, 3440.1 nautical miles; h is the height of eye of the observer in feet; h_s is the observed vertical angle corrected for index error; and d_s is the distance to the waterline of the object in nautical miles.

Table 18. Distance of an Object by Two Bearings – To determine the distance of an object as a vessel on a steady course passes it, observe the difference between the course and two bearings of the object, and note the time interval between bearings. Enter this table with the two differences. Multiply the distance run between bearings by the number in the first column to find the distance of the object at the time of the second bearing, and by the number in the second column to find the distance when abeam.

The table was computed by solving plane oblique and right triangles.

Celestial Navigation Tables

Table 19. Table of Offsets – This table gives the corrections to the straight line of position (LOP) as drawn on a chart or plotting sheet to provide a closer approximation to the arc of the circle of equal altitude, a small circle of radius equal to the zenith distance.

In adjusting the straight LOP to obtain a closer approximation of the arc of the circle of equal altitude, points on the LOP are offset at right angles to the LOP in the direction of the celestial body. The arguments for entering the table are the distance from the DR to the foot of the perpendicular and the altitude of the body.

The table was computed using the formulas:

$$R = 3438' \cot h$$

$$\sin \theta = D/R$$

$$X = R(1 - \cos \theta),$$

in which X is the offset, R is the radius of a circle of equal altitude for altitude h, and D is the distance from the intercept to the point on the LOP to be offset.

Table 20. Meridian Angle and Altitude of a Body on the Prime Vertical Circle – A celestial body having a declination of contrary name to the latitude does not cross the prime vertical above the celestial horizon, its nearest approach being at rising or setting.

If the declination and latitude are of the same name, and the declination is numerically greater, the body does not cross the prime vertical, but makes its nearest approach (in azimuth) when its meridian angle, east or west, and altitude are as shown in this table, these values being given in italics above the heavy line. At this time the body is stationary in azimuth.

If the declination and latitude are of the same name and numerically equal, the body passes through the zenith as it crosses both the celestial meridian and the prime vertical, as shown in the table.

If the declination and latitude are of the same name, and the declination is numerically less, the body crosses the prime vertical when its meridian angle, east or west, and altitude are as tabulated in vertical type below the heavy line.

The table is entered with declination of the celestial body and the latitude of the observer. Computed altitudes are given, with no allowance made for refraction, dip, parallax, etc. The tabulated values apply to any celestial body, but values are not given for declination greater than 23° because the tabulated information is generally desired for the sun only.

The table was computed using the following formulas, derived by Napier's rules:

Nearest approach (in azimuth) to the prime vertical:

$$\csc h = \sin d \csc L$$

$$\sec t = \tan d \cot L$$

On the prime vertical:

$$\sin h = \sin d \csc L$$

$$\cos t = \tan d \cot L$$

In these formulas, h is the altitude, d is the declination, L is the latitude, t is the meridian angle.

Table 21. Latitude and Longitude Factors – The latitude obtained by an ex-meridian sight is inaccurate if the longitude used in determining the meridian angle is incorrect. Similarly, the longitude obtained by solution of a time sight is inaccurate if the latitude used in the solution is incorrect, unless the celestial body is on the prime vertical. This table gives the errors resulting from unit errors in the assumed values used in the computations. There are two columns for each tabulated value of latitude. The first gives the latitude factor, f, which is the error in minutes of latitude for a one-minute error of longitude. The second gives the longitude factor, F, which is the error in minutes of longitude for a one-minute error of latitude. In each case, the total error is the factor multiplied by the number of minutes error in the assumed value. Although the factors were originally intended for use in correcting ex-meridian altitudes and time-sight longitudes, they have other uses as well.

The azimuth angle used for entering the table can be measured from either the north or south, through 90°; or it may be measured from the elevated pole, through 180°. If the celestial body is in the southeast (090°– 180°) or northwest (270°– 360°) quadrant, the f correction is applied to the northward if the correct longitude is east of that used in the solution, and to the southward if the correct longitude is west of that used; while the F correction is applied to the eastward if the correct latitude is north of that used in the solution, and to the westward if the correct latitude is south of that used. If the body is in the northeast (000°– 090°) or southwest (180°– 270°) quadrant, the correction is applied in the opposite direction. These rules apply in both north and south latitude.

The table was computed using the formulas:

$$f = \cos L \tan Z = \frac{1}{\sec L \cot Z} = \frac{1}{F}$$

$$F = \sec L \cot Z = \frac{1}{\cos L \tan Z} = \frac{1}{f}$$

in which f is the tabulated latitude factor, L is the latitude, Z is the azimuth angle, and F is the tabulated longitude factor.

Table 22. Amplitudes – This table lists amplitudes of celestial bodies at rising and setting. Enter with the declination of the body and the latitude of the observer. The value taken from the table is the amplitude when the *center* of the body is on the *celestial* horizon. For the sun, this occurs when the lower limb is a little more than half a diameter above the visible horizon. For the moon it occurs when the upper limb is about on the horizon. Use the prefix E if the body is rising, and W if it is setting; use the suffix N or S to agree with the declination of the body. Table 23 can be used with reversed sign to correct the tabulations to the values for the visible horizon.

The table was computed using the following formula, derived by Napier's rules:

$$\sin A = \sec L \sin d$$

in which A is the amplitude, L is the latitude of the observer, and d is the declination of the celestial body.

Table 23. Correction of Amplitude Observed on the Visible Horizon – This table contains a correction to be applied to the amplitude observed when the center of a celestial body is on the visible horizon, to obtain the corresponding amplitude when the center of the body is on the celestial horizon. For the sun, a planet, or a star, apply the correction in the direction away from the elevated pole, thus *increasing* the *azimuth angle*. For the moon apply *half* the correction *toward* the elevated pole. This correction can be applied in the opposite direction to a value taken from Table 22 to find the corresponding amplitude when the center of a celestial body is on the visible horizon. The table was computed for a height of eye of 41 feet. For other heights normally encountered, the error is too small to be of practical significance in ordinary navigation.

The values in the table were determined by computing the azimuth angle when the center of the celestial body is on the visible horizon, converting this to amplitude, and determining the difference between this value and the corresponding value from Table 22. Computation of azimuth angle was made for an altitude of (–)0°42.0' determined as follows:

Azimuth angle was computed by means of the formula:

$$\cos Z = \frac{\sin d - \sin h \sin L}{\cos h \cos L}$$

in which Z is the azimuth angle, d is the declination of the celestial body, h is the altitude (–0°42.0'), and L is the latitude of the observer.

Table 24. Altitude Factors – In one minute of time from meridian transit the altitude of a celestial body changes by the amount shown in this table if the altitude is between 6° and 86°, the latitude is not more than 60°, and the declination is not more than 63°. The values taken from this table are used to enter Table 25 for solving reduction to the meridian (ex-meridian) problems.

For upper transit, use the left-hand pages if the declination and latitude are of the same name (both north or both south) and the right-hand pages if of contrary name. For lower transit, use the values below the heavy lines on the last three contrary-name pages. When a factor is taken from this part of the table, the correction from table 25 is *subtracted* from the observed altitude to obtain the corresponding meridian altitude. All other corrections are added.

The table was computed using the formula:

$$a = 1.9635'' \cos L \cos d \csc (L \sim d)$$

in which a is the change of altitude in one minute from meridian transit (the tabulated value), L is the latitude of the observer, and d is the declination of the celestial body.

This formula can be used to compute values outside the limits of the table, but is not accurate if the altitude is greater than 86°.

Table 25. Change of Altitude in Given Time from Meridian Transit – Enter this table with the altitude factor from table 24 and the meridian angle, in either arc or time units, and take out the difference between the altitude at the given time and the altitude at meridian transit. Enter the table separately with whole numbers and tenths of a, interpolating for t if necessary, and add the two values to obtain the total difference. This total can be applied as a correction to observed altitude to obtain the corresponding meridian altitude, adding for upper transit and subtracting for lower transit.

The table was computed using the formulas:

$$C = \frac{at^2}{60}$$

in which C is the tabulated difference to be used as a correction to observed altitude in minutes of arc; a is the altitude factor from table 24 in seconds of arc; and t is the meridian angle in minutes of time.

This formula should not be used for determining values beyond the limits of the table unless reduced accuracy is acceptable.

Table 26. Time Zones, Descriptions, and Suffixes – The zone description and the single letter of the alphabet designating a time zone and sometimes used as a suffix to zone time for all time zones are given in this table.

Table 27. Altitude Correction for Air Temperature – This table provides a correction to be applied to the altitude of a celestial body when the air temperature varies from the 50° F used for determining mean refraction with the *Nautical Almanac*. For maximum accuracy, apply index correction and dip to sextant altitude first, obtaining apparent (rectified) altitude for use in entering this table. Enter the table with altitude and air temperature in degrees Fahrenheit. Apply the correction in accordance with its tabulated sign to altitude.

The table was computed using formula:

$$\text{Correction} = R_m\left(1 - \frac{510}{460 + T}\right)$$

in which R_m is mean refraction and T is temperature in degrees Fahrenheit.

Table 28. Altitude Correction for Atmospheric Pressure – This table provides a correction to be applied to the altitude of a celestial body when the atmospheric pressure varies from the 29.83 inches (1010 millibars) used for determining mean refraction using the *Nautical Almanac*. For most accurate results, apply index correction and dip to sextant altitude first, obtaining apparent (rectified) altitude for use in entering this table. Enter the table with altitude and atmospheric pressure. Apply the correction to altitude, *adding* if the pressure is less than 29.83 inches and *subtracting* if it is more than 29.83 inches. The table was computed by means of the formula:

$$\text{Correction} = R_m\left(1 - \frac{P}{29.83}\right)$$

in which R_m is mean refraction and P is atmospheric pressure in inches of mercury.

Meteorological Tables

Table 29. Conversion Table for Thermometer Scales – Enter this table with temperature Fahrenheit, F; Celsius (centigrade), C; or Kelvin, K; and take out the corresponding readings on the other two temperature scales.

On the Fahrenheit scale, the freezing temperature of pure water at standard sea level pressure is 32°, and the boiling point under the same conditions is 212°. The corresponding temperatures are 0° and 100° on the Celsius scale and 273.15° and 373.15°, respectively, on the Kelvin scale. The value of (–) 273.15° C for absolute zero, the starting point of the Kelvin scale, is the value recognized officially by the National Institute of Standards and Technology (NIST).

The formulas are:

$$C = 5/9(F \times 32°) = K - 273.15°$$

$$F = 9/5C + 32° = 9/5\,K - 459.67°$$

$$K = 5/9(F + 459.67°) = C + 273.15°$$

Table 30. Direction and Speed of True Wind – This table converts apparent wind to true wind. To use the table, divide the apparent wind in knots by the vessel's speed in knots. This gives the apparent wind speed in units of ship's speed. Enter the table with this value and the difference between the heading and the apparent wind direction. The values taken from the table are (1) the difference between the heading and the true wind direction, and (2) the speed of the true wind in units of ship's speed. The true wind is on the same side as the apparent wind, and from a point farther aft.

To convert wind speed in units of ship's speed to speed in knots, multiply by the vessel's speed in knots. The steadiness of the wind and the accuracy of its measurement are seldom sufficient to warrant interpolation in this table. If speed of the true wind and relative direction of the apparent wind are known, enter the column for direction of the apparent wind, and find the speed of the true wind in units of ship's speed. The number to the left is the relative direction of the true wind. The number on the same line in the side columns is the speed of the apparent wind in units of ship's speed. Two solutions are possible if speed of the true wind is less than ship's speed.

The table was computed by solving the triangle involved in a graphical solution, using the formulas:

$$\tan \alpha = \frac{\sin B_A}{S_A - \cos B_A}$$

$$B_T = B_A + \alpha$$

$$S_T = \frac{\sin B_A}{\sin \alpha}$$

in which α is an auxiliary angle, B_A is the difference between the heading and the apparent wind direction, S_A is the speed of the apparent wind in units of ship's speed, B_T is the difference between the heading and the true wind direction, and S_T is the speed of the true wind in units of ship's speed.

Table 31. Correction of Barometer Reading for Height Above Sea Level – If simultaneous barometer readings at different heights are to be of maximum value in weather analysis, they should be converted to the corresponding readings at a standard height, usually sea level. To convert the observed barometer reading to this level, enter this table with the outside temperature and the height of the barometer above sea level. The height of a barometer is the height of its sensitive element; in the case of a mercurial barometer, this is the height of the free surface of mercury in the cistern. The correction taken from this table applies to the readings of any type barometer, and is always *added* to the observed readings, unless the barometer is below sea level.

The table was computed using the formula:

$$C = 29.92126\left(1 - \frac{1}{\text{antilog}\left(\frac{0.0081350H}{T + 0.00178308H}\right)}\right)$$

in which C is the correction in inches of mercury, H is the height of the barometer above sea level in feet, and T is the mean temperature, in degrees Rankine (degrees Fahrenheit plus 459.67°), of the air between the barometer and sea level. At sea the outside air temperature is sufficiently accurate for this purpose.

Table 32. Correction of Barometer Reading for Gravity – The height of the column of a mercury barometer is affected by the force of gravity, which changes with latitude and is approximately equal along any parallel of latitude. The average gravitational force at latitude 45°32'40" is used as the standard for calibration. This table provides a correction to convert the observed reading at any other latitude to the corresponding value at latitude 45°32'40". Enter the table with the latitude, take out the correction, and apply in accordance with the sign given. This correction does not apply to aneroid barometers.

The correction was computed using the formula:

$$C = B(-0.002637 \cos 2L + 0.000006 \cos^2 2L - 0.000050)\ .$$

in which C is the correction in inches, B is the observed reading of the barometer (corrected for temperature and instrumental errors) in inches of mercury, and L is the latitude. This table was computed for a standard height of 30 inches.

Table 33. Correction of Barometer Reading for Temperature – Because of the difference in expansion of the mercury column of a mercurial barometer and that of the brass scale by which the height is measured, a correction should be applied to the reading when the temperature differs from the standard used for calibration of the instrument. To find the correction, enter this table with the temperature in degrees Fahrenheit and the barometer reading. Apply the correction in accordance with the sign given. This correction does not apply to aneroid barometers.

The standard temperature used for calibration is 32° F for the mercury, and 62° F for the brass. The correction was computed using the formula:

$$C = -B\frac{m(T - 32°) - l(T - 62°)}{1 + m(T - 32°)}$$

in which C is the correction in inches, B is the observed reading of the barometer in inches of mercury, m is the coefficient of cubical expansion of mercury = 0.0001010 cubic inches per degree F, l is the coefficient of linear expansion of brass = 0.0000102 inches per degree F, and T is the temperature of the attached thermometer in degrees F. Substituting the values for m and l and simplifying:

$$C = -B\frac{T - 28.630°}{1.1123T + 10978°}$$

The minus sign before B indicates that the correction is negative if the temperature is more than 28.630°.

Table 34. Conversion Table for hecto-Pascals (Millibars), Inches of Mercury, and Millimeters of Mercury – The reading of a barometer in inches or millimeters of mercury corresponding to a given reading in hecto-Pascals can be found directly from this table.

The formula for the pressure in hecto-Pascals is:

$$P = \frac{B_m D_g}{1000}$$

in which P is the atmospheric pressure in hecto-Pascals, B_m is the height of the column of mercury in millimeters, D is the density of mercury = 13.5951 grams per cubic centimeter, and g is the standard value of gravity = 980.665 dynes. Substituting numerical values:

$$P = 1.33322B_m,\ \text{and}$$

$$B_m = \frac{P}{1.33322} = 0.750064P$$

Since one millimeter = 0.750064inches

$$B_i = \frac{0.03937P}{1.33322} = 0.0295300P,$$

in which B_i is the height of the column of mercury in inches.

Table 35. Relative Humidity – To determine the relative humidity of the atmosphere, enter this table with the dry-bulb (air) temperature (F), and the *difference* between the dry-bulb and wet-bulb temperatures (F). The value taken from the table is the approximate percentage of relative humidity. If the dry-bulb and wet-bulb temperatures are the same, relative humidity is 100 percent.

The table was computed using the formula:

$$R= \frac{100_e}{e_w}$$

in which R is the approximate relative humidity in percent, e is the ambient vapor pressure, and e_w is the saturation vapor pressure over water at dry-bulb temperature. Professor Ferrel's psychrometric formula was used for computation of e:

$$e' - \left(0.000367P(t - t') \left(1 + \frac{t - 32^\circ}{1571}\right)\right)$$

in which e is the ambient vapor pressure in millibars, e' is the saturation vapor pressure in millibars at wet-bulb temperature with respect to water, P is the atmospheric pressure (the millibar equivalent of 30 inches of mercury is used for this table), t is the dry-bulb temperature in degrees Fahrenheit, and t' is the wet-bulb temperature in degrees Fahrenheit.

The values of e_w were taken from the International Meteorological Organization Publication Number 79, 1951, table 2, pages 82–83.

Table 36. Dew Point – To determine the dew point, enter this table with the dry-bulb (air) temperature (F), and the *difference* between the dry-bulb and wet-bulb temperatures (F). The value taken from the table is the dew point in degrees Fahrenheit. If the dry-bulb and wet-bulb temperatures are the same, the air is at or below the dew point.

TABLE 1
Logarithms of Numbers

1–250

No.	Log	No.	Log	No.	Log	No.	Log	No.	Log
1	0.00000	51	1.70757	101	2.00432	151	2.17898	201	2.30320
2	0.30103	52	1.71600	102	2.00860	152	2.18184	202	2.30535
3	0.47712	53	1.72428	103	2.01284	153	2.18469	203	2.30750
4	0.60206	54	1.73239	104	2.01703	154	2.18752	204	2.30963
5	0.69897	55	1.74036	105	2.02119	155	2.19033	205	2.31175
6	0.77815	56	1.74819	106	2.02531	156	2.19312	206	2.31387
7	0.84510	57	1.75587	107	2.02938	157	2.19590	207	2.31597
8	0.90309	58	1.76343	108	2.03342	158	2.19866	208	2.31806
9	0.95424	59	1.77085	109	2.03743	159	2.20140	209	2.32015
10	1.00000	60	1.77815	110	2.04139	160	2.20412	210	2.32222
11	1.04139	61	1.78533	111	2.04532	161	2.20683	211	2.32428
12	1.07918	62	1.79239	112	2.04922	162	2.20952	212	2.32634
13	1.11394	63	1.79934	113	2.05308	163	2.21219	213	2.32838
14	1.14613	64	1.80618	114	2.05690	164	2.21484	214	2.33041
15	1.17609	65	1.81291	115	2.06070	165	2.21748	215	2.33244
16	1.20412	66	1.81954	116	2.06446	166	2.22011	216	2.33445
17	1.23045	67	1.82607	117	2.06819	167	2.22272	217	2.33646
18	1.25527	68	1.83251	118	2.07188	168	2.22531	218	2.33846
19	1.27875	69	1.83885	119	2.07555	169	2.22789	219	2.34044
20	1.30103	70	1.84510	120	2.07918	170	2.23045	220	2.34242
21	1.32222	71	1.85126	121	2.08279	171	2.23300	221	2.34439
22	1.34242	72	1.85733	122	2.08636	172	2.23553	222	2.34635
23	1.36173	73	1.86332	123	2.08991	173	2.23805	223	2.34830
24	1.38021	74	1.86923	124	2.09342	174	2.24055	224	2.35025
25	1.39794	75	1.87506	125	2.09691	175	2.24304	225	2.35218
26	1.41497	76	1.88081	126	2.10037	176	2.24551	226	2.35411
27	1.43136	77	1.88649	127	2.10380	177	2.24797	227	2.35603
28	1.44716	78	1.89209	128	2.10721	178	2.25042	228	2.35793
29	1.46240	79	1.89763	129	2.11059	179	2.25285	229	2.35984
30	1.47712	80	1.90309	130	2.11394	180	2.25527	230	2.36173
31	1.49136	81	1.90849	131	2.11727	181	2.25768	231	2.36361
32	1.50515	82	1.91381	132	2.12057	182	2.26007	232	2.36549
33	1.51851	83	1.91908	133	2.12385	183	2.26245	233	2.36736
34	1.53148	84	1.92428	134	2.12710	184	2.26482	234	2.36922
35	1.54407	85	1.92942	135	2.13033	185	2.26717	235	2.37107
36	1.55630	86	1.93450	136	2.13354	186	2.26951	236	2.37291
37	1.56820	87	1.93952	137	2.13672	187	2.27184	237	2.37475
38	1.57978	88	1.94448	138	2.13988	188	2.27416	238	2.37658
39	1.59106	89	1.94939	139	2.14301	189	2.27646	239	2.37840
40	1.60206	90	1.95424	140	2.14613	190	2.27875	240	2.38021
41	1.61278	91	1.95904	141	2.14922	191	2.28103	241	2.38202
42	1.62325	92	1.96379	142	2.15229	192	2.28330	242	2.38382
43	1.63347	93	1.96848	143	2.15534	193	2.28556	243	2.38561
44	1.64345	94	1.97313	144	2.15836	194	2.28780	244	2.38739
45	1.65321	95	1.97772	145	2.16137	195	2.29003	245	2.38917
46	1.66276	96	1.98227	146	2.16435	196	2.29226	246	2.39094
47	1.67210	97	1.98677	147	2.16732	197	2.29447	247	2.39270
48	1.68124	98	1.99123	148	2.17026	198	2.29667	248	2.39445
49	1.69020	99	1.99564	149	2.17319	199	2.29885	249	2.39620
50	1.69897	100	2.00000	150	2.17609	200	2.30103	250	2.39794

TABLE 1
Logarithms of Numbers

1000–1500

No.	0	d	1	d	2	d	3	d	4	d	5	d	6	d	7	d	8	d	9	d
100	00000	43	00043	44	00087	43	00130	43	00173	44	00217	43	00260	43	00303	43	00346	43	00389	43
101	00432	43	00475	43	00518	43	00561	43	00604	43	00647	42	00689	43	00732	43	00775	42	00817	43
102	00860	43	00903	42	00945	43	00988	42	01030	42	01072	43	01115	42	01157	42	01199	43	01242	42
103	01284	42	01326	42	01368	42	01410	42	01452	42	01494	42	01536	42	01578	42	01620	42	01662	41
104	01703	42	01745	42	01787	41	01828	42	01870	42	01912	41	01953	42	01995	41	02036	42	02078	41
105	02119	41	02160	42	02202	41	02243	41	02284	41	02325	41	02366	41	02407	42	02449	41	02490	41
106	02531	41	02572	40	02612	41	02653	41	02694	41	02735	41	02776	40	02816	41	02857	41	02898	40
107	02938	41	02979	40	03019	41	03060	40	03100	41	03141	40	03181	41	03222	40	03262	40	03302	40
108	03342	41	03383	40	03423	40	03463	40	03503	40	03543	40	03583	40	03623	40	03663	40	03703	40
109	03743	39	03782	40	03822	40	03862	40	03902	39	03941	40	03981	40	04021	39	04060	40	04100	39
110	04139	40	04179	39	04218	40	04258	39	04297	39	04336	40	04376	39	04415	39	04454	39	04493	39
111	04532	39	04571	39	04610	40	04650	39	04689	38	04727	39	04766	39	04805	39	04844	39	04883	39
112	04922	39	04961	38	04999	39	05038	39	05077	38	05115	39	05154	38	05192	39	05231	38	05269	39
113	05308	38	05346	39	05385	38	05423	38	05461	39	05500	38	05538	38	05576	38	05614	38	05652	38
114	05690	39	05729	38	05767	38	05805	38	05843	38	05881	37	05918	38	05956	38	05994	38	06032	38
115	06070	38	06108	37	06145	38	06183	38	06221	37	06258	38	06296	37	06333	38	06371	37	06408	38
116	06446	37	06483	38	06521	37	06558	37	06595	38	06633	37	06670	37	06707	37	06744	37	06781	38
117	06819	37	06856	37	06893	37	06930	37	06967	37	07004	37	07041	37	07078	37	07115	36	07151	37
118	07188	37	07225	37	07262	36	07298	37	07335	37	07372	36	07408	37	07445	37	07482	36	07518	37
119	07555	36	07591	37	07628	36	07664	36	07700	37	07737	36	07773	36	07809	37	07846	36	07882	36
120	07918	36	07954	36	07990	37	08027	36	08063	36	08099	36	08135	36	08171	36	08207	36	08243	36
121	08279	35	08314	36	08350	36	08386	36	08422	36	08458	35	08493	36	08529	36	08565	35	08600	36
122	08636	36	08672	35	08707	36	08743	35	08778	36	08814	35	08849	35	08884	36	08920	35	08955	36
123	08991	35	09026	35	09061	35	09096	36	09132	35	09167	35	09202	35	09237	35	09272	35	09307	35
124	09342	35	09377	35	09412	35	09447	35	09482	35	09517	35	09552	35	09587	34	09621	35	09656	35
125	09691	35	09726	34	09760	35	09795	35	09830	34	09864	35	09899	35	09934	34	09968	35	10003	34
126	10037	35	10072	34	10106	34	10140	35	10175	34	10209	34	10243	35	10278	34	10312	34	10346	34
127	10380	35	10415	34	10449	34	10483	34	10517	34	10551	34	10585	34	10619	34	10653	34	10687	34
128	10721	34	10755	34	10789	34	10823	34	10857	33	10890	34	10924	34	10958	34	10992	33	11025	34
129	11059	34	11093	33	11126	34	11160	33	11193	34	11227	34	11261	33	11294	33	11327	34	11361	33
130	11394	34	11428	33	11461	33	11494	34	11528	33	11561	33	11594	34	11628	33	11661	33	11694	33
131	11727	33	11760	33	11793	33	11826	34	11860	33	11893	33	11926	33	11959	33	11992	32	12024	33
132	12057	33	12090	33	12123	33	12156	33	12189	33	12222	32	12254	33	12287	33	12320	32	12352	33
133	12385	33	12418	32	12450	33	12483	33	12516	32	12548	33	12581	32	12613	33	12646	32	12678	32
134	12710	33	12743	32	12775	33	12808	32	12840	32	12872	33	12905	32	12937	32	12969	32	13001	32
135	13033	33	13066	32	13098	32	13130	32	13162	32	13194	32	13226	32	13258	32	13290	32	13322	32
136	13354	32	13386	32	13418	32	13450	31	13481	32	13513	32	13545	32	13577	32	13609	31	13640	32
137	13672	32	13704	31	13735	32	13767	32	13799	31	13830	32	13862	31	13893	32	13925	31	13956	32
138	13988	31	14019	32	14051	31	14082	32	14114	31	14145	31	14176	32	14208	31	14239	31	14270	31
139	14301	32	14333	31	14364	31	14395	31	14426	31	14457	32	14489	31	14520	31	14551	31	14582	31
140	14613	31	14644	31	14675	31	14706	31	14737	31	14768	31	14799	30	14829	31	14860	31	14891	31
141	14922	31	14953	30	14983	31	15014	31	15045	31	15076	30	15106	31	15137	31	15168	30	15198	31
142	15229	30	15259	31	15290	30	15320	31	15351	30	15381	31	15412	30	15442	31	15473	30	15503	31
143	15534	30	15564	30	15594	31	15625	30	15655	30	15685	30	15715	31	15746	30	15776	30	15806	30
144	15836	30	15866	31	15897	30	15927	30	15957	30	15987	30	16017	30	16047	30	16077	30	16107	30
145	16137	30	16167	30	16197	30	16227	29	16256	30	16286	30	16316	30	16346	30	16376	30	16406	29
146	16435	30	16465	30	16495	29	16524	30	16554	30	16584	29	16613	30	16643	30	16673	29	16702	30
147	16732	29	16761	30	16791	29	16820	30	16850	29	16879	30	16909	29	16938	29	16967	30	16997	29
148	17026	30	17056	29	17085	29	17114	29	17143	30	17173	29	17202	29	17231	29	17260	29	17289	30
149	17319	29	17348	29	17377	29	17406	29	17435	29	17464	29	17493	29	17522	29	17551	29	17580	29
150	17609	29	17638	29	17667	29	17696	29	17725	29	17754	28	17782	29	17811	29	17840	29	17869	29
No.	0	d	1	d	2	d	3	d	4	d	5	d	6	d	7	d	8	d	9	d

Prop. parts

	44	43	42	41	40	39	38	37	36	35	34	33
1	4	4	4	4	4	4	4	4	4	4	3	3
2	9	9	8	8	8	8	8	7	7	7	7	7
3	13	13	13	12	12	12	11	11	11	10	10	10
4	18	17	17	16	16	16	15	15	14	14	14	13
5	22	22	21	20	20	20	19	18	18	18	17	16
6	26	26	25	25	24	23	23	22	22	21	20	20
7	31	30	29	29	28	27	27	26	25	24	24	23
8	35	34	34	33	32	31	30	30	29	28	27	26
9	40	39	38	37	36	35	34	33	32	32	31	30

TABLE 1
Logarithms of Numbers

1500–2000

No.	0	d	1	d	2	d	3	d	4	d	5	d	6	d	7	d	8	d	9	d
150	17609	29	17638	29	17667	29	17696	29	17725	29	17754	28	17782	29	17811	29	17840	29	17869	29
151	17898	28	17926	29	17955	29	17984	29	18013	28	18041	29	18070	29	18099	28	18127	29	18156	28
152	18184	29	18213	28	18241	29	18270	28	18298	29	18327	28	18355	29	18384	28	18412	29	18441	28
153	18469	29	18498	28	18526	28	18554	29	18583	28	18611	28	18639	28	18667	29	18696	28	18724	28
154	18752	28	18780	28	18808	29	18837	28	18865	28	18893	28	18921	28	18949	28	18977	28	19005	28
155	19033	28	19061	28	19089	28	19117	28	19145	28	19173	28	19201	28	19229	28	19257	28	19285	27
156	19312	28	19340	28	19368	28	19396	28	19424	27	19451	28	19479	28	19507	28	19535	27	19562	28
157	19590	28	19618	27	19645	28	19673	27	19700	28	19728	28	19756	27	19783	28	19811	27	19838	28
158	19866	27	19893	28	19921	27	19948	28	19976	27	20003	27	20030	28	20058	27	20085	27	20112	28
159	20140	27	20167	27	20194	28	20222	27	20249	27	20276	27	20303	27	20330	28	20358	27	20385	27
160	20412	27	20439	27	20466	27	20493	27	20520	28	20548	27	20575	27	20602	27	20629	27	20656	27
161	20683	27	20710	27	20737	26	20763	27	20790	27	20817	27	20844	27	20871	27	20898	27	20925	27
162	20952	26	20978	27	21005	27	21032	27	21059	26	21085	27	21112	27	21139	26	21165	27	21192	27
163	21219	26	21245	27	21272	27	21299	26	21325	27	21352	26	21378	27	21405	26	21431	27	21458	26
164	21484	27	21511	26	21537	27	21564	26	21590	27	21617	26	21643	26	21669	27	21696	26	21722	26
165	21748	27	21775	26	21801	26	21827	27	21854	26	21880	26	21906	26	21932	26	21958	27	21985	26
166	22011	26	22037	26	22063	26	22089	26	22115	26	22141	26	22167	27	22194	26	22220	26	22246	26
167	22272	26	22298	26	22324	26	22350	26	22376	25	22401	26	22427	26	22453	26	22479	26	22505	26
168	22531	26	22557	26	22583	25	22608	26	22634	26	22660	26	22686	26	22712	25	22737	26	22763	26
169	22789	25	22814	26	22840	26	22866	25	22891	26	22917	26	22943	25	22968	26	22994	25	23019	26
170	23045	25	23070	26	23096	25	23121	26	23147	25	23172	26	23198	25	23223	26	23249	25	23274	26
171	23300	25	23325	25	23350	26	23376	25	23401	25	23426	26	23452	25	23477	25	23502	26	23528	25
172	23553	25	23578	25	23603	26	23629	25	23654	25	23679	25	23704	25	23729	25	23754	25	23779	26
173	23805	25	23830	25	23855	25	23880	25	23905	25	23930	25	23955	25	23980	25	24005	25	24030	25
174	24055	25	24080	25	24105	25	24130	25	24155	25	24180	24	24204	25	24229	25	24254	25	24279	25
175	24304	25	24329	24	24353	25	24378	25	24403	25	24428	24	24452	25	24477	25	24502	25	24527	24
176	24551	25	24576	25	24601	24	24625	25	24650	24	24674	25	24699	25	24724	24	24748	25	24773	24
177	24797	25	24822	24	24846	25	24871	24	24895	25	24920	24	24944	25	24969	24	24993	25	25018	24
178	25042	24	25066	25	25091	24	25115	24	25139	25	25164	24	25188	24	25212	25	25237	24	25261	24
179	25285	25	25310	24	25334	24	25358	24	25382	24	25406	25	25431	24	25455	24	25479	24	25503	24
180	25527	24	25551	24	25575	25	25600	24	25624	24	25648	24	25672	24	25696	24	25720	24	25744	24
181	25768	24	25792	24	25816	24	25840	24	25864	24	25888	24	25912	23	25935	24	25959	24	25983	24
182	26007	24	26031	24	26055	24	26079	23	26102	24	26126	24	26150	24	26174	24	26198	23	26221	24
183	26245	24	26269	24	26293	23	26316	24	26340	24	26364	23	26387	24	26411	24	26435	23	26458	24
184	26482	23	26505	24	26529	24	26553	23	26576	24	26600	23	26623	24	26647	23	26670	24	26694	23
185	26717	24	26741	23	26764	24	26788	23	26811	23	26834	24	26858	23	26881	24	26905	23	26928	23
186	26951	24	26975	23	26998	23	27021	24	27045	23	27068	23	27091	23	27114	24	27138	23	27161	23
187	27184	23	27207	24	27231	23	27254	23	27277	23	27300	23	27323	23	27346	24	27370	23	27393	23
188	27416	23	27439	23	27462	23	27485	23	27508	23	27531	23	27554	23	27577	23	27600	23	27623	23
189	27646	23	27669	23	27692	23	27715	23	27738	23	27761	23	27784	23	27807	23	27830	22	27852	23
190	27875	23	27898	23	27921	23	27944	23	27967	22	27989	23	28012	23	28035	23	28058	23	28081	22
191	28103	23	28126	23	28149	22	28171	23	28194	23	28217	23	28240	22	28262	23	28285	22	28307	23
192	28330	23	28353	22	28375	23	28398	23	28421	22	28443	23	28466	22	28488	23	28511	22	28533	23
193	28556	22	28578	23	28601	22	28623	23	28646	22	28668	23	28691	22	28713	22	28735	23	28758	22
194	28780	23	28803	22	28825	22	28847	23	28870	22	28892	22	28914	23	28937	22	28959	22	28981	22
195	29003	23	29026	22	29048	22	29070	22	29092	23	29115	22	29137	22	29159	22	29181	22	29203	23
196	29226	22	29248	22	29270	22	29292	22	29314	22	29336	22	29358	22	29380	23	29403	22	29425	22
197	29447	22	29469	22	29491	22	29513	22	29535	22	29557	22	29579	22	29601	22	29623	22	29645	22
198	29667	21	29688	22	29710	22	29732	22	29754	22	29776	22	29798	22	29820	22	29842	21	29863	22
199	29885	22	29907	22	29929	22	29951	22	29973	21	29994	22	30016	22	30038	22	30060	21	30081	22
200	30103	22	30125	21	30146	22	30168	22	30190	21	30211	22	30233	22	30255	21	30276	22	30298	22
No.	0	d	1	d	2	d	3	d	4	d	5	d	6	d	7	d	8	d	9	d

Prop. parts

	32	31		30	29		28	27		26	25		24	23		22	21
1	3	3	1	3	3	1	3	3	1	3	2	1	2	2	1	2	2
2	6	6	2	6	6	2	6	5	2	5	5	2	5	5	2	4	4
3	10	9	3	9	9	3	8	8	3	8	8	3	7	7	3	7	6
4	13	12	4	12	12	4	11	11	4	10	10	4	10	9	4	9	8
5	16	16	5	15	14	5	14	14	5	13	12	5	12	12	5	11	10
6	19	19	6	18	17	6	17	16	6	16	15	6	14	14	6	13	13
7	22	22	7	21	20	7	20	19	7	18	18	7	17	16	7	15	15
8	26	25	8	24	23	8	22	22	8	21	20	8	19	18	8	18	17
9	29	28	9	27	26	9	25	24	9	23	22	9	22	21	9	20	19

TABLE 1
Logarithms of Numbers

2000–2500

No.	0	d	1	d	2	d	3	d	4	d	5	d	6	d	7	d	8	d	9	d
200	30103	22	30125	21	30146	22	30168	22	30190	21	30211	22	30233	22	30255	21	30276	22	30298	22
201	30320	21	30341	22	30363	21	30384	22	30406	22	30428	21	30449	22	30471	21	30492	22	30514	21
202	30535	22	30557	21	30578	22	30600	21	30621	22	30643	21	30664	21	30685	22	30707	21	30728	22
203	30750	21	30771	21	30792	22	30814	21	30835	21	30856	22	30878	21	30899	21	30920	22	30942	21
204	30963	21	30984	22	31006	21	31027	21	31048	21	31069	22	31091	21	31112	21	31133	21	31154	21
205	31175	22	31197	21	31218	21	31239	21	31260	21	31281	21	31302	21	31323	22	31345	21	31366	21
206	31387	21	31408	21	31429	21	31450	21	31471	21	31492	21	31513	21	31534	21	31555	21	31576	21
207	31597	21	31618	21	31639	21	31660	21	31681	21	31702	21	31723	21	31744	21	31765	20	31785	21
208	31806	21	31827	21	31848	21	31869	21	31890	21	31911	20	31931	21	31952	21	31973	21	31994	21
209	32015	20	32035	21	32056	21	32077	21	32098	20	32118	21	32139	21	32160	21	32181	20	32201	21
210	32222	21	32243	20	32263	21	32284	21	32305	20	32325	21	32346	20	32366	21	32387	21	32408	20
211	32428	21	32449	20	32469	21	32490	20	32510	21	32531	21	32552	20	32572	21	32593	20	32613	21
212	32634	20	32654	21	32675	20	32695	20	32715	21	32736	20	32756	21	32777	20	32797	21	32818	20
213	32838	20	32858	21	32879	20	32899	20	32919	21	32940	20	32960	20	32980	21	33001	20	33021	20
214	33041	21	33062	20	33082	20	33102	20	33122	21	33143	20	33163	20	33183	20	33203	21	33224	20
215	33244	20	33264	20	33284	20	33304	21	33325	20	33345	20	33365	20	33385	20	33405	20	33425	20
216	33445	20	33465	21	33486	20	33506	20	33526	20	33546	20	33566	20	33586	20	33606	20	33626	20
217	33646	20	33666	20	33686	20	33706	20	33726	20	33746	20	33766	20	33786	20	33806	20	33826	20
218	33846	20	33866	19	33885	20	33905	20	33925	20	33945	20	33965	20	33985	20	34005	20	34025	19
219	34044	20	34064	20	34084	20	34104	20	34124	19	34143	20	34163	20	34183	20	34203	20	34223	19
220	34242	20	34262	20	34282	19	34301	20	34321	20	34341	20	34361	19	34380	20	34400	20	34420	19
221	34439	20	34459	20	34479	19	34498	20	34518	19	34537	20	34557	20	34577	19	34596	20	34616	19
222	34635	20	34655	19	34674	20	34694	19	34713	20	34733	20	34753	19	34772	20	34792	19	34811	19
223	34830	20	34850	19	34869	20	34889	19	34908	20	34928	19	34947	20	34967	19	34986	19	35005	20
224	35025	19	35044	20	35064	19	35083	19	35102	20	35122	19	35141	19	35160	20	35180	19	35199	19
225	35218	20	35238	19	35257	19	35276	19	35295	20	35315	19	35334	19	35353	19	35372	20	35392	19
226	35411	19	35430	19	35449	19	35468	20	35488	19	35507	19	35526	19	35545	19	35564	19	35583	20
227	35603	19	35622	19	35641	19	35660	19	35679	19	35698	19	35717	19	35736	19	35755	19	35774	19
228	35793	20	35813	19	35832	19	35851	19	35870	19	35889	19	35908	19	35927	19	35946	19	35965	19
229	35984	19	36003	18	36021	19	36040	19	36059	19	36078	19	36097	19	36116	19	36135	19	36154	19
230	36173	19	36192	19	36211	18	36229	19	36248	19	36267	19	36286	19	36305	19	36324	18	36342	19
231	36361	19	36380	19	36399	19	36418	18	36436	19	36455	19	36474	19	36493	18	36511	19	36530	19
232	36549	19	36568	18	36586	19	36605	19	36624	18	36642	19	36661	19	36680	18	36698	19	36717	19
233	36736	18	36754	19	36773	18	36791	19	36810	19	36829	18	36847	19	36866	18	36884	19	36903	19
234	36922	18	36940	19	36959	18	36977	19	36996	18	37014	19	37033	18	37051	19	37070	18	37088	19
235	37107	18	37125	19	37144	18	37162	19	37181	18	37199	19	37218	18	37236	18	37254	19	37273	18
236	37291	19	37310	18	37328	18	37346	19	37365	18	37383	18	37401	19	37420	18	37438	19	37457	18
237	37475	18	37493	18	37511	19	37530	18	37548	18	37566	19	37585	18	37603	18	37621	18	37639	19
238	37658	18	37676	18	37694	18	37712	19	37731	18	37749	18	37767	18	37785	18	37803	19	37822	18
239	37840	18	37858	18	37876	18	37894	18	37912	19	37931	18	37949	18	37967	18	37985	18	38003	18
240	38021	18	38039	18	38057	18	38075	18	38093	19	38112	18	38130	18	38148	18	38166	18	38184	18
241	38202	18	38220	18	38238	18	38256	18	38274	18	38292	18	38310	18	38328	18	38346	18	38364	18
242	38382	17	38399	18	38417	18	38435	18	38453	18	38471	18	38489	18	38507	18	38525	18	38543	18
243	38561	17	38578	18	38596	18	38614	18	38632	18	38650	18	38668	18	38686	17	38703	18	38721	18
244	38739	18	38757	18	38775	17	38792	18	38810	18	38828	18	38846	17	38863	18	38881	18	38899	18
245	38917	17	38934	18	38952	18	38970	17	38987	18	39005	18	39023	18	39041	17	39058	18	39076	18
246	39094	17	39111	18	39129	17	39146	18	39164	18	39182	17	39199	18	39217	18	39235	17	39252	18
247	39270	17	39287	18	39305	17	39322	18	39340	18	39358	17	39375	18	39393	17	39410	18	39428	17
248	39445	18	39463	17	39480	18	39498	17	39515	18	39533	17	39550	18	39568	17	39585	17	39602	18
249	39620	17	39637	18	39655	17	39672	18	39690	17	39707	17	39724	18	39742	17	39759	18	39777	17
250	39794	17	39811	18	39829	17	39846	17	39863	18	39881	17	39898	17	39915	18	39933	17	39950	17
No.	0	d	1	d	2	d	3	d	4	d	5	d	6	d	7	d	8	d	9	d

Prop. parts

	22		21		20		19		18		17
1	2	1	2	1	2	1	2	1	2	1	2
2	4	2	4	2	4	2	4	2	4	2	3
3	7	3	6	3	6	3	6	3	5	3	5
4	9	4	8	4	8	4	8	4	7	4	7
5	11	5	10	5	10	5	10	5	9	5	8
6	13	6	13	6	12	6	11	6	11	6	10
7	15	7	15	7	14	7	13	7	13	7	12
8	18	8	17	8	16	8	15	8	14	8	14
9	20	9	19	9	18	9	17	9	16	9	15

TABLE 1
Logarithms of Numbers

2500–3000

No.	0	d	1	d	2	d	3	d	4	d	5	d	6	d	7	d	8	d	9	d
250	39794	17	39811	18	39829	17	39846	17	39863	18	39881	17	39898	17	39915	18	39933	17	39950	17
251	39967	18	39985	17	40002	17	40019	18	40037	17	40054	17	40071	17	40088	18	40106	17	40123	17
252	40140	17	40157	18	40175	17	40192	17	40209	17	40226	17	40243	18	40261	17	40278	17	40295	17
253	40312	17	40329	17	40346	18	40364	17	40381	17	40398	17	40415	17	40432	17	40449	17	40466	17
254	40483	17	40500	18	40518	17	40535	17	40552	17	40569	17	40586	17	40603	17	40620	17	40637	17
255	40654	17	40671	17	40688	17	40705	17	40722	17	40739	17	40756	17	40773	17	40790	17	40807	17
256	40824	17	40841	17	40858	17	40875	17	40892	17	40909	17	40926	17	40943	17	40960	16	40976	17
257	40993	17	41010	17	41027	17	41044	17	41061	17	41078	17	41095	16	41111	17	41128	17	41145	17
258	41162	17	41179	17	41196	16	41212	17	41229	17	41246	17	41263	17	41280	16	41296	17	41313	17
259	41330	17	41347	16	41363	17	41380	17	41397	17	41414	16	41430	17	41447	17	41464	17	41481	16
260	41497	17	41514	17	41531	16	41547	17	41564	17	41581	16	41597	17	41614	17	41631	16	41647	17
261	41664	17	41681	16	41697	17	41714	17	41731	16	41747	17	41764	16	41780	17	41797	17	41814	16
262	41830	17	41847	16	41863	17	41880	16	41896	17	41913	16	41929	17	41946	17	41963	16	41979	17
263	41996	16	42012	17	42029	16	42045	17	42062	16	42078	17	42095	16	42111	16	42127	17	42144	16
264	42160	17	42177	16	42193	17	42210	16	42226	17	42243	16	42259	16	42275	17	42292	16	42308	17
265	42325	16	42341	16	42357	17	42374	16	42390	16	42406	17	42423	16	42439	16	42455	17	42472	16
266	42488	16	42504	17	42521	16	42537	16	42553	17	42570	16	42586	16	42602	17	42619	16	42635	16
267	42651	16	42667	17	42684	16	42700	16	42716	16	42732	17	42749	16	42765	16	42781	16	42797	16
268	42813	17	42830	16	42846	16	42862	16	42878	16	42894	17	42911	16	42927	16	42943	16	42959	16
269	42975	16	42991	17	43008	16	43024	16	43040	16	43056	16	43072	16	43088	16	43104	16	43120	16
270	43136	16	43152	17	43169	16	43185	16	43201	16	43217	16	43233	16	43249	16	43265	16	43281	16
271	43297	16	43313	16	43329	16	43345	16	43361	16	43377	16	43393	16	43409	16	43425	16	43441	16
272	43457	16	43473	16	43489	16	43505	16	43521	16	43537	16	43553	16	43569	15	43584	16	43600	16
273	43616	16	43632	16	43648	16	43664	16	43680	16	43696	16	43712	15	43727	16	43743	16	43759	16
274	43775	16	43791	16	43807	16	43823	15	43838	16	43854	16	43870	16	43886	16	43902	15	43917	16
275	43933	16	43949	16	43965	16	43981	15	43996	16	44012	16	44028	16	44044	15	44059	16	44075	16
276	44091	16	44107	15	44122	16	44138	16	44154	16	44170	15	44185	16	44201	16	44217	15	44232	16
277	44248	16	44264	15	44279	16	44295	16	44311	15	44326	16	44342	16	44358	15	44373	16	44389	15
278	44404	16	44420	16	44436	15	44451	16	44467	16	44483	15	44498	16	44514	15	44529	16	44545	15
279	44560	16	44576	16	44592	15	44607	16	44623	15	44638	16	44654	15	44669	16	44685	15	44700	16
280	44716	15	44731	16	44747	15	44762	16	44778	15	44793	16	44809	15	44824	16	44840	15	44855	16
281	44871	15	44886	16	44902	15	44917	15	44932	16	44948	15	44963	16	44979	15	44994	16	45010	15
282	45025	15	45040	16	45056	15	45071	15	45086	16	45102	15	45117	16	45133	15	45148	15	45163	16
283	45179	15	45194	15	45209	16	45225	15	45240	15	45255	16	45271	15	45286	15	45301	16	45317	15
284	45332	15	45347	15	45362	16	45378	15	45393	15	45408	15	45423	16	45439	15	45454	15	45469	15
285	45484	16	45500	15	45515	15	45530	15	45545	16	45561	15	45576	15	45591	15	45606	15	45621	16
286	45637	15	45652	15	45667	15	45682	15	45697	15	45712	16	45728	15	45743	15	45758	15	45773	15
287	45788	15	45803	15	45818	16	45834	15	45849	15	45864	15	45879	15	45894	15	45909	15	45924	15
288	45939	15	45954	15	45969	15	45984	16	46000	15	46015	15	46030	15	46045	15	46060	15	46075	15
289	46090	15	46105	15	46120	15	46135	15	46150	15	46165	15	46180	15	46195	15	46210	15	46225	15
290	46240	15	46255	15	46270	15	46285	15	46300	15	46315	15	46330	15	46345	14	46359	15	46374	15
291	46389	15	46404	15	46419	15	46434	15	46449	15	46464	15	46479	15	46494	15	46509	14	46523	15
292	46538	15	46553	15	46568	15	46583	15	46598	15	46613	14	46627	15	46642	15	46657	15	46672	15
293	46687	15	46702	14	46716	15	46731	15	46746	15	46761	15	46776	14	46790	15	46805	15	46820	15
294	46835	15	46850	14	46864	15	46879	15	46894	15	46909	14	46923	15	46938	15	46953	14	46967	15
295	46982	15	46997	15	47012	14	47026	15	47041	15	47056	14	47070	15	47085	15	47100	14	47114	15
296	47129	15	47144	15	47159	14	47173	15	47188	14	47202	15	47217	15	47232	14	47246	15	47261	15
297	47276	14	47290	15	47305	14	47319	15	47334	15	47349	14	47363	15	47378	14	47392	15	47407	15
298	47422	14	47436	15	47451	14	47465	15	47480	14	47494	15	47509	15	47524	14	47538	15	47553	14
299	47567	15	47582	14	47596	15	47611	14	47625	15	47640	14	47654	15	47669	14	47683	15	47698	14
300	47712	15	47727	14	47741	15	47756	14	47770	14	47784	15	47799	14	47813	15	47828	14	47842	15
No.	0	d	1	d	2	d	3	d	4	d	5	d	6	d	7	d	8	d	9	d

Prop. parts

	18
1	2
2	4
3	5
4	7
5	9
6	11
7	13
8	14
9	16

	17
1	2
2	3
3	5
4	7
5	8
6	10
7	12
8	14
9	15

	16
1	2
2	3
3	5
4	6
5	8
6	10
7	11
8	13
9	14

	15
1	2
2	3
3	4
4	6
5	8
6	9
7	10
8	12
9	14

	14
1	1
2	3
3	4
4	6
5	7
6	8
7	10
8	11
9	13

TABLE 1
Logarithms of Numbers

3000–3500

No.	0	d	1	d	2	d	3	d	4	d	5	d	6	d	7	d	8	d	9	d
300	47712	15	47727	14	47741	15	47756	14	47770	14	47784	15	47799	14	47813	15	47828	14	47842	15
301	47857	14	47871	14	47885	15	47900	14	47914	15	47929	14	47943	15	47958	14	47972	14	47986	15
302	48001	14	48015	14	48029	15	48044	14	48058	15	48073	14	48087	14	48101	15	48116	14	48130	14
303	48144	15	48159	14	48173	14	48187	15	48202	14	48216	14	48230	14	48244	15	48259	14	48273	14
304	48287	15	48302	14	48316	14	48330	14	48344	15	48359	14	48373	14	48387	14	48401	15	48416	14
305	48430	14	48444	14	48458	15	48473	14	48487	14	48501	14	48515	15	48530	14	48544	14	48558	14
306	48572	14	48586	15	48601	14	48615	14	48629	14	48643	14	48657	14	48671	15	48686	14	48700	14
307	48714	14	48728	14	48742	14	48756	14	48770	15	48785	14	48799	14	48813	14	48827	14	48841	14
308	48855	14	48869	14	48883	14	48897	14	48911	15	48926	14	48940	14	48954	14	48968	14	48982	14
309	48996	14	49010	14	49024	14	49038	14	49052	14	49066	14	49080	14	49094	14	49108	14	49122	14
310	49136	14	49150	14	49164	14	49178	14	49192	14	49206	14	49220	14	49234	14	49248	14	49262	14
311	49276	14	49290	14	49304	14	49318	14	49332	14	49346	14	49360	14	49374	14	49388	14	49402	13
312	49415	14	49429	14	49443	14	49457	14	49471	14	49485	14	49499	14	49513	14	49527	14	49541	13
313	49554	14	49568	14	49582	14	49596	14	49610	14	49624	14	49638	13	49651	14	49665	14	49679	14
314	49693	14	49707	14	49721	13	49734	14	49748	14	49762	14	49776	14	49790	13	49803	14	49817	14
315	49831	14	49845	14	49859	13	49872	14	49886	14	49900	14	49914	13	49927	14	49941	14	49955	14
316	49969	13	49982	14	49996	14	50010	14	50024	13	50037	14	50051	14	50065	14	50079	13	50092	14
317	50106	14	50120	13	50133	14	50147	14	50161	13	50174	14	50188	14	50202	13	50215	14	50229	14
318	50243	13	50256	14	50270	14	50284	13	50297	14	50311	14	50325	13	50338	14	50352	13	50365	14
319	50379	14	50393	13	50406	14	50420	13	50433	14	50447	14	50461	13	50474	14	50488	13	50501	14
320	50515	14	50529	13	50542	14	50556	13	50569	14	50583	13	50596	14	50610	13	50623	14	50637	14
321	50651	13	50664	14	50678	13	50691	14	50705	13	50718	14	50732	13	50745	14	50759	13	50772	14
322	50786	13	50799	14	50813	13	50826	14	50840	13	50853	13	50866	14	50880	13	50893	14	50907	13
323	50920	14	50934	13	50947	14	50961	13	50974	13	50987	14	51001	13	51014	14	51028	13	51041	14
324	51055	13	51068	13	51081	14	51095	13	51108	13	51121	14	51135	13	51148	14	51162	13	51175	13
325	51188	14	51202	13	51215	13	51228	14	51242	13	51255	13	51268	14	51282	13	51295	13	51308	14
326	51322	13	51335	13	51348	14	51362	13	51375	13	51388	14	51402	13	51415	13	51428	13	51441	14
327	51455	13	51468	13	51481	14	51495	13	51508	13	51521	13	51534	14	51548	13	51561	13	51574	13
328	51587	14	51601	13	51614	13	51627	13	51640	14	51654	13	51667	13	51680	13	51693	13	51706	14
329	51720	13	51733	13	51746	13	51759	13	51772	14	51786	13	51799	13	51812	13	51825	13	51838	13
330	51851	14	51865	13	51878	13	51891	13	51904	13	51917	13	51930	13	51943	14	51957	13	51970	13
331	51983	13	51996	13	52009	13	52022	13	52035	13	52048	13	52061	14	52075	13	52088	13	52101	13
332	52114	13	52127	13	52140	13	52153	13	52166	13	52179	13	52192	13	52205	13	52218	13	52231	13
333	52244	13	52257	13	52270	14	52284	13	52297	13	52310	13	52323	13	52336	13	52349	13	52362	13
334	52375	13	52388	13	52401	13	52414	13	52427	13	52440	13	52453	13	52466	13	52479	13	52492	12
335	52504	13	52517	13	52530	13	52543	13	52556	13	52569	13	52582	13	52595	13	52608	13	52621	13
336	52634	13	52647	13	52660	13	52673	13	52686	13	52699	12	52711	13	52724	13	52737	13	52750	13
337	52763	13	52776	13	52789	13	52802	13	52815	12	52827	13	52840	13	52853	13	52866	13	52879	13
338	52892	13	52905	12	52917	13	52930	13	52943	13	52956	13	52969	13	52982	12	52994	13	53007	13
339	53020	13	53033	13	53046	12	53058	13	53071	13	53084	13	53097	13	53110	12	53122	13	53135	13
340	53148	13	53161	12	53173	13	53186	13	53199	13	53212	12	53224	13	53237	13	53250	13	53263	12
341	53275	13	53288	13	53301	13	53314	12	53326	13	53339	13	53352	12	53364	13	53377	13	53390	13
342	53403	12	53415	13	53428	13	53441	12	53453	13	53466	13	53479	12	53491	13	53504	13	53517	12
343	53529	13	53542	13	53555	12	53567	13	53580	13	53593	12	53605	13	53618	13	53631	12	53643	13
344	53656	12	53668	13	53681	13	53694	12	53706	13	53719	13	53732	12	53744	13	53757	12	53769	13
345	53782	12	53794	13	53807	13	53820	12	53832	13	53845	12	53857	13	53870	12	53882	13	53895	13
346	53908	12	53920	13	53933	12	53945	13	53958	12	53970	13	53983	12	53995	13	54008	12	54020	13
347	54033	12	54045	13	54058	12	54070	13	54083	12	54095	13	54108	12	54120	13	54133	12	54145	13
348	54158	12	54170	13	54183	12	54195	13	54208	12	54220	13	54233	12	54245	13	54258	12	54270	13
349	54283	12	54295	12	54307	13	54320	12	54332	13	54345	12	54357	13	54370	12	54382	12	54394	13
350	54407	12	54419	13	54432	12	54444	12	54456	13	54469	12	54481	13	54494	12	54506	12	54518	13
No.	0	d	1	d	2	d	3	d	4	d	5	d	6	d	7	d	8	d	9	d

Prop. parts

	15
1	2
2	3
3	4
4	6
5	8
6	9
7	10
8	12
9	14

	14
1	1
2	3
3	4
4	6
5	7
6	8
7	10
8	11
9	13

	13
1	1
2	3
3	4
4	5
5	6
6	8
7	9
8	10
9	12

	12
1	1
2	2
3	4
4	5
5	6
6	7
7	8
8	10
9	11

TABLE 1
Logarithms of Numbers

3500–4000

No.	0	d	1	d	2	d	3	d	4	d	5	d	6	d	7	d	8	d	9	d
350	54407	12	54419	13	54432	12	54444	12	54456	13	54469	12	54481	13	54494	12	54506	12	54518	13
351	54531	12	54543	12	54555	13	54568	12	54580	13	54593	12	54605	12	54617	13	54630	12	54642	12
352	54654	13	54667	12	54679	12	54691	13	54704	12	54716	12	54728	13	54741	12	54753	12	54765	12
353	54777	13	54790	12	54802	12	54814	13	54827	12	54839	12	54851	13	54864	12	54876	12	54888	12
354	54900	13	54913	12	54925	12	54937	12	54949	13	54962	12	54974	12	54986	12	54998	13	55011	12
355	55023	12	55035	12	55047	13	55060	12	55072	12	55084	12	55096	12	55108	13	55121	12	55133	12
356	55145	12	55157	12	55169	13	55182	12	55194	12	55206	12	55218	12	55230	12	55242	13	55255	12
357	55267	12	55279	12	55291	12	55303	12	55315	13	55328	12	55340	12	55352	12	55364	12	55376	12
358	55388	12	55400	13	55413	12	55425	12	55437	12	55449	12	55461	12	55473	12	55485	12	55497	12
359	55509	13	55522	12	55534	12	55546	12	55558	12	55570	12	55582	12	55594	12	55606	12	55618	12
360	55630	12	55642	12	55654	12	55666	12	55678	13	55691	12	55703	12	55715	12	55727	12	55739	12
361	55751	12	55763	12	55775	12	55787	12	55799	12	55811	12	55823	12	55835	12	55847	12	55859	12
362	55871	12	55883	12	55895	12	55907	12	55919	12	55931	12	55943	12	55955	12	55967	12	55979	12
363	55991	12	56003	12	56015	12	56027	11	56038	12	56050	12	56062	12	56074	12	56086	12	56098	12
364	56110	12	56122	12	56134	12	56146	12	56158	12	56170	12	56182	12	56194	11	56205	12	56217	12
365	56229	12	56241	12	56253	12	56265	12	56277	12	56289	12	56301	11	56312	12	56324	12	56336	12
366	56348	12	56360	12	56372	12	56384	12	56396	11	56407	12	56419	12	56431	12	56443	12	56455	12
367	56467	11	56478	12	56490	12	56502	12	56514	12	56526	12	56538	11	56549	12	56561	12	56573	12
368	56585	12	56597	11	56608	12	56620	12	56632	12	56644	12	56656	11	56667	12	56679	12	56691	12
369	56703	11	56714	12	56726	12	56738	12	56750	11	56761	12	56773	12	56785	12	56797	11	56808	12
370	56820	12	56832	12	56844	11	56855	12	56867	12	56879	12	56891	11	56902	12	56914	12	56926	11
371	56937	12	56949	12	56961	11	56972	12	56984	12	56996	12	57008	11	57019	12	57031	12	57043	11
372	57054	12	57066	12	57078	11	57089	12	57101	12	57113	11	57124	12	57136	12	57148	11	57159	12
373	57171	12	57183	11	57194	12	57206	11	57217	12	57229	12	57241	11	57252	12	57264	12	57276	11
374	57287	12	57299	11	57310	12	57322	12	57334	11	57345	12	57357	11	57368	12	57380	12	57392	11
375	57403	12	57415	11	57426	12	57438	11	57449	12	57461	12	57473	11	57484	12	57496	11	57507	12
376	57519	11	57530	12	57542	11	57553	12	57565	11	57576	12	57588	12	57600	11	57611	12	57623	11
377	57634	12	57646	11	57657	12	57669	11	57680	12	57692	11	57703	12	57715	11	57726	12	57738	11
378	57749	12	57761	11	57772	12	57784	11	57795	12	57807	11	57818	12	57830	11	57841	11	57852	12
379	57864	11	57875	12	57887	11	57898	12	57910	11	57921	12	57933	11	57944	11	57955	12	57967	11
380	57978	12	57990	11	58001	12	58013	11	58024	11	58035	12	58047	11	58058	12	58070	11	58081	11
381	58092	12	58104	11	58115	12	58127	11	58138	11	58149	12	58161	11	58172	12	58184	11	58195	11
382	58206	12	58218	11	58229	11	58240	12	58252	11	58263	11	58274	12	58286	11	58297	12	58309	11
383	58320	11	58331	12	58343	11	58354	11	58365	12	58377	11	58388	11	58399	11	58410	12	58422	11
384	58433	11	58444	12	58456	11	58467	11	58478	12	58490	11	58501	11	58512	12	58524	11	58535	11
385	58546	11	58557	12	58569	11	58580	11	58591	11	58602	12	58614	11	58625	11	58636	11	58647	12
386	58659	11	58670	11	58681	11	58692	12	58704	11	58715	11	58726	11	58737	12	58749	11	58760	11
387	58771	11	58782	12	58794	11	58805	11	58816	11	58827	11	58838	12	58850	11	58861	11	58872	11
388	58883	11	58894	12	58906	11	58917	11	58928	11	58939	11	58950	11	58961	12	58973	11	58984	11
389	58995	11	59006	11	59017	11	59028	12	59040	11	59051	11	59062	11	59073	11	59084	11	59095	11
390	59106	12	59118	11	59129	11	59140	11	59151	11	59162	11	59173	11	59184	11	59195	12	59207	11
391	59218	11	59229	11	59240	11	59251	11	59262	11	59273	11	59284	11	59295	11	59306	12	59318	11
392	59329	11	59340	11	59351	11	59362	11	59373	11	59384	11	59395	11	59406	11	59417	11	59428	11
393	59439	11	59450	11	59461	11	59472	11	59483	11	59494	12	59506	11	59517	11	59528	11	59539	11
394	59550	11	59561	11	59572	11	59583	11	59594	11	59605	11	59616	11	59627	11	59638	11	59649	11
395	59660	11	59671	11	59682	11	59693	11	59704	11	59715	11	59726	11	59737	11	59748	11	59759	11
396	59770	10	59780	11	59791	11	59802	11	59813	11	59824	11	59835	11	59846	11	59857	11	59868	11
397	59879	11	59890	11	59901	11	59912	11	59923	11	59934	11	59945	11	59956	10	59966	11	59977	11
398	59988	11	59999	11	60010	11	60021	11	60032	11	60043	11	60054	11	60065	11	60076	10	60086	11
399	60097	11	60108	11	60119	11	60130	11	60141	11	60152	11	60163	10	60173	11	60184	11	60195	11
400	60206	11	60217	11	60228	11	60239	10	60249	11	60260	11	60271	11	60282	11	60293	11	60304	10
No.	0	d	1	d	2	d	3	d	4	d	5	d	6	d	7	d	8	d	9	d

Prop. parts

	13	12	11	10
1	1	1	1	1
2	3	2	2	2
3	4	4	3	3
4	5	5	4	4
5	6	6	6	5
6	8	7	7	6
7	9	8	8	7
8	10	10	9	8
9	12	11	10	9

TABLE 1
Logarithms of Numbers

4000–4500

No.	0	d	1	d	2	d	3	d	4	d	5	d	6	d	7	d	8	d	9	d
400	60206	11	60217	11	60228	11	60239	10	60249	11	60260	11	60271	11	60282	11	60293	11	60304	10
401	60314	11	60325	11	60336	11	60347	11	60358	11	60369	10	60379	11	60390	11	60401	11	60412	11
402	60423	10	60433	11	60444	11	60455	11	60466	11	60477	10	60487	11	60498	11	60509	11	60520	11
403	60531	10	60541	11	60552	11	60563	11	60574	10	60584	11	60595	11	60606	11	60617	10	60627	11
404	60638	11	60649	11	60660	10	60670	11	60681	11	60692	11	60703	10	60713	11	60724	11	60735	11
405	60746	10	60756	11	60767	11	60778	10	60788	11	60799	11	60810	11	60821	10	60831	11	60842	11
406	60853	10	60863	11	60874	11	60885	10	60895	11	60906	11	60917	10	60927	11	60938	11	60949	10
407	60959	11	60970	11	60981	10	60991	11	61002	11	61013	10	61023	11	61034	11	61045	10	61055	11
408	61066	11	61077	10	61087	11	61098	11	61109	10	61119	11	61130	10	61140	11	61151	11	61162	10
409	61172	11	61183	11	61194	10	61204	11	61215	10	61225	11	61236	11	61247	10	61257	11	61268	10
410	61278	11	61289	11	61300	10	61310	11	61321	10	61331	11	61342	10	61352	11	61363	11	61374	10
411	61384	11	61395	10	61405	11	61416	10	61426	11	61437	11	61448	10	61458	11	61469	10	61479	11
412	61490	10	61500	11	61511	10	61521	11	61532	10	61542	11	61553	10	61563	11	61574	10	61584	11
413	61595	11	61606	10	61616	11	61627	10	61637	11	61648	10	61658	11	61669	10	61679	11	61690	10
414	61700	11	61711	10	61721	10	61731	11	61742	10	61752	11	61763	10	61773	11	61784	10	61794	11
415	61805	10	61815	11	61826	10	61836	11	61847	10	61857	11	61868	10	61878	10	61888	11	61899	10
416	61909	11	61920	10	61930	11	61941	10	61951	11	61962	10	61972	10	61982	11	61993	10	62003	11
417	62014	10	62024	10	62034	11	62045	10	62055	11	62066	10	62076	10	62086	11	62097	10	62107	11
418	62118	10	62128	10	62138	11	62149	10	62159	11	62170	10	62180	10	62190	11	62201	10	62211	10
419	62221	11	62232	10	62242	10	62252	11	62263	10	62273	11	62284	10	62294	10	62304	11	62315	10
420	62325	10	62335	11	62346	10	62356	10	62366	11	62377	10	62387	10	62397	11	62408	10	62418	10
421	62428	11	62439	10	62449	10	62459	10	62469	11	62480	10	62490	10	62500	11	62511	10	62521	10
422	62531	11	62542	10	62552	10	62562	10	62572	11	62583	10	62593	10	62603	10	62613	11	62624	10
423	62634	10	62644	11	62655	10	62665	10	62675	10	62685	11	62696	10	62706	10	62716	10	62726	11
424	62737	10	62747	10	62757	10	62767	11	62778	10	62788	10	62798	10	62808	10	62818	11	62829	10
425	62839	10	62849	10	62859	11	62870	10	62880	10	62890	10	62900	10	62910	11	62921	10	62931	10
426	62941	10	62951	10	62961	11	62972	10	62982	10	62992	10	63002	10	63012	10	63022	11	63033	10
427	63043	10	63053	10	63063	10	63073	10	63083	11	63094	10	63104	10	63114	10	63124	10	63134	10
428	63144	11	63155	10	63165	10	63175	10	63185	10	63195	10	63205	10	63215	10	63225	11	63236	10
429	63246	10	63256	10	63266	10	63276	10	63286	10	63296	10	63306	11	63317	10	63327	10	63337	10
430	63347	10	63357	10	63367	10	63377	10	63387	10	63397	10	63407	10	63417	11	63428	10	63438	10
431	63448	10	63458	10	63468	10	63478	10	63488	10	63498	10	63508	10	63518	10	63528	10	63538	10
432	63548	10	63558	10	63568	11	63579	10	63589	10	63599	10	63609	10	63619	10	63629	10	63639	10
433	63649	10	63659	10	63669	10	63679	10	63689	10	63699	10	63709	10	63719	10	63729	10	63739	10
434	63749	10	63759	10	63769	10	63779	10	63789	10	63799	10	63809	10	63819	10	63829	10	63839	10
435	63849	10	63859	10	63869	10	63879	10	63889	10	63899	10	63909	10	63919	10	63929	10	63939	10
436	63949	10	63959	10	63969	10	63979	9	63988	10	63998	10	64008	10	64018	10	64028	10	64038	10
437	64048	10	64058	10	64068	10	64078	10	64088	10	64098	10	64108	10	64118	10	64128	9	64137	10
438	64147	10	64157	10	64167	10	64177	10	64187	10	64197	10	64207	10	64217	10	64227	10	64237	9
439	64246	10	64256	10	64266	10	64276	10	64286	10	64296	10	64306	10	64316	10	64326	9	64335	10
440	64345	10	64355	10	64365	10	64375	10	64385	10	64395	9	64404	10	64414	10	64424	10	64434	10
441	64444	10	64454	10	64464	9	64473	10	64483	10	64493	10	64503	10	64513	10	64523	9	64532	10
442	64542	10	64552	10	64562	10	64572	10	64582	9	64591	10	64601	10	64611	10	64621	10	64631	9
443	64640	10	64650	10	64660	10	64670	10	64680	9	64689	10	64699	10	64709	10	64719	10	64729	9
444	64738	10	64748	10	64758	10	64768	9	64777	10	64787	10	64797	10	64807	9	64816	10	64826	10
445	64836	10	64846	10	64856	9	64865	10	64875	10	64885	10	64895	9	64904	10	64914	10	64924	9
446	64933	10	64943	10	64953	10	64963	9	64972	10	64982	10	64992	10	65002	9	65011	10	65021	10
447	65031	9	65040	10	65050	10	65060	10	65070	9	65079	10	65089	10	65099	9	65108	10	65118	10
448	65128	9	65137	10	65147	10	65157	10	65167	9	65176	10	65186	10	65196	9	65205	10	65215	10
449	65225	9	65234	10	65244	10	65254	9	65263	10	65273	10	65283	9	65292	10	65302	10	65312	9
450	65321	10	65331	10	65341	9	65350	10	65360	9	65369	10	65379	10	65389	9	65398	10	65408	10
No.	0	d	1	d	2	d	3	d	4	d	5	d	6	d	7	d	8	d	9	d

Prop. parts

	11	10	9
1	1	1	1
2	2	2	2
3	3	3	3
4	4	4	4
5	6	5	4
6	7	6	5
7	8	7	6
8	9	8	7
9	10	9	8

TABLE 1
Logarithms of Numbers

4500–5000

No.	0	d	1	d	2	d	3	d	4	d	5	d	6	d	7	d	8	d	9	d
450	65321	10	65331	10	65341	9	65350	10	65360	9	65369	10	65379	10	65389	9	65398	10	65408	10
451	65418	9	65427	10	65437	10	65447	9	65456	10	65466	9	65475	10	65485	10	65495	9	65504	10
452	65514	9	65523	10	65533	10	65543	9	65552	10	65562	9	65571	10	65581	10	65591	9	65600	10
453	65610	9	65619	10	65629	10	65639	9	65648	10	65658	9	65667	10	65677	9	65686	10	65696	10
454	65706	9	65715	10	65725	9	65734	10	65744	9	65753	10	65763	9	65772	10	65782	10	65792	9
455	65801	10	65811	9	65820	10	65830	9	65839	10	65849	9	65858	10	65868	9	65877	10	65887	9
456	65896	10	65906	10	65916	9	65925	10	65935	9	65944	10	65954	9	65963	10	65973	9	65982	10
457	65992	9	66001	10	66011	9	66020	10	66030	9	66039	10	66049	9	66058	10	66068	9	66077	10
458	66087	9	66096	10	66106	9	66115	9	66124	10	66134	9	66143	10	66153	9	66162	10	66172	9
459	66181	10	66191	9	66200	10	66210	9	66219	10	66229	9	66238	9	66247	10	66257	9	66266	10
460	66276	9	66285	10	66295	9	66304	10	66314	9	66323	9	66332	10	66342	9	66351	10	66361	9
461	66370	10	66380	9	66389	9	66398	10	66408	9	66417	10	66427	9	66436	9	66445	10	66455	9
462	66464	10	66474	9	66483	9	66492	10	66502	9	66511	10	66521	9	66530	9	66539	10	66549	9
463	66558	9	66567	10	66577	9	66586	10	66596	9	66605	9	66614	10	66624	9	66633	9	66642	10
464	66652	9	66661	10	66671	9	66680	9	66689	10	66699	9	66708	9	66717	10	66727	9	66736	9
465	66745	10	66755	9	66764	9	66773	10	66783	9	66792	9	66801	10	66811	9	66820	9	66829	10
466	66839	9	66848	9	66857	10	66867	9	66876	9	66885	9	66894	10	66904	9	66913	9	66922	10
467	66932	9	66941	9	66950	10	66960	9	66969	9	66978	9	66987	10	66997	9	67006	9	67015	10
468	67025	9	67034	9	67043	9	67052	10	67062	9	67071	9	67080	9	67089	10	67099	9	67108	9
469	67117	10	67127	9	67136	9	67145	9	67154	10	67164	9	67173	9	67182	9	67191	10	67201	9
470	67210	9	67219	9	67228	9	67237	10	67247	9	67256	9	67265	9	67274	10	67284	9	67293	9
471	67302	9	67311	10	67321	9	67330	9	67339	9	67348	9	67357	10	67367	9	67376	9	67385	9
472	67394	9	67403	10	67413	9	67422	9	67431	9	67440	9	67449	10	67459	9	67468	9	67477	9
473	67486	9	67495	9	67504	10	67514	9	67523	9	67532	9	67541	9	67550	10	67560	9	67569	9
474	67578	9	67587	9	67596	9	67605	9	67614	10	67624	9	67633	9	67642	9	67651	9	67660	9
475	67669	10	67679	9	67688	9	67697	9	67706	9	67715	9	67724	9	67733	9	67742	10	67752	9
476	67761	9	67770	9	67779	9	67788	9	67797	9	67806	9	67815	10	67825	9	67834	9	67843	9
477	67852	9	67861	9	67870	9	67879	9	67888	9	67897	9	67906	10	67916	9	67925	9	67934	9
478	67943	9	67952	9	67961	9	67970	9	67979	9	67988	9	67997	9	68006	9	68015	9	68024	10
479	68034	9	68043	9	68052	9	68061	9	68070	9	68079	9	68088	9	68097	9	68106	9	68115	9
480	68124	9	68133	9	68142	9	68151	9	68160	9	68169	9	68178	9	68187	9	68196	9	68205	10
481	68215	9	68224	9	68233	9	68242	9	68251	9	68260	9	68269	9	68278	9	68287	9	68296	9
482	68305	9	68314	9	68323	9	68332	9	68341	9	68350	9	68359	9	68368	9	68377	9	68386	9
483	68395	9	68404	9	68413	9	68422	9	68431	9	68440	9	68449	9	68458	9	68467	9	68476	9
484	68485	9	68494	8	68502	9	68511	9	68520	9	68529	9	68538	9	68547	9	68556	9	68565	9
485	68574	9	68583	9	68592	9	68601	9	68610	9	68619	9	68628	9	68637	9	68646	9	68655	9
486	68664	9	68673	8	68681	9	68690	9	68699	9	68708	9	68717	9	68726	9	68735	9	68744	9
487	68753	9	68762	9	68771	9	68780	9	68789	8	68797	9	68806	9	68815	9	68824	9	68833	9
488	68842	9	68851	9	68860	9	68869	9	68878	8	68886	9	68895	9	68904	9	68913	9	68922	9
489	68931	9	68940	9	68949	9	68958	8	68966	9	68975	9	68984	9	68993	9	69002	9	69011	9
490	69020	8	69028	9	69037	9	69046	9	69055	9	69064	9	69073	9	69082	8	69090	9	69099	9
491	69108	9	69117	9	69126	9	69135	9	69144	8	69152	9	69161	9	69170	9	69179	9	69188	9
492	69197	8	69205	9	69214	9	69223	9	69232	9	69241	8	69249	9	69258	9	69267	9	69276	9
493	69285	9	69294	8	69302	9	69311	9	69320	9	69329	9	69338	8	69346	9	69355	9	69364	9
494	69373	8	69381	9	69390	9	69399	9	69408	9	69417	8	69425	9	69434	9	69443	9	69452	9
495	69461	8	69469	9	69478	9	69487	9	69496	8	69504	9	69513	9	69522	9	69531	8	69539	9
496	69548	9	69557	9	69566	8	69574	9	69583	9	69592	9	69601	8	69609	9	69618	9	69627	9
497	69636	8	69644	9	69653	9	69662	9	69671	8	69679	9	69688	9	69697	8	69705	9	69714	9
498	69723	9	69732	8	69740	9	69749	9	69758	9	69767	8	69775	9	69784	9	69793	8	69801	9
499	69810	9	69819	8	69827	9	69836	9	69845	9	69854	8	69862	9	69871	9	69880	8	69888	9
500	69897	9	69906	8	69914	9	69923	9	69932	8	69940	9	69949	9	69958	8	69966	9	69975	9
No.	0	d	1	d	2	d	3	d	4	d	5	d	6	d	7	d	8	d	9	d

Prop. parts

	10		9		8
1	1	1	1	1	1
2	2	2	2	2	2
3	3	3	3	3	2
4	4	4	4	4	3
5	5	5	4	5	4
6	6	6	5	6	5
7	7	7	6	7	6
8	8	8	7	8	6
9	9	9	8	9	7

TABLE 1
Logarithms of Numbers

5000–5500

No.	0	d	1	d	2	d	3	d	4	d	5	d	6	d	7	d	8	d	9	d
500	69897	9	69906	8	69914	9	69923	9	69932	8	69940	9	69949	9	69958	8	69966	9	69975	9
501	69984	8	69992	9	70001	9	70010	8	70018	9	70027	9	70036	8	70044	9	70053	9	70062	8
502	70070	9	70079	9	70088	8	70096	9	70105	9	70114	8	70122	9	70131	9	70140	8	70148	9
503	70157	8	70165	9	70174	9	70183	8	70191	9	70200	9	70209	8	70217	9	70226	8	70234	9
504	70243	9	70252	8	70260	9	70269	9	70278	8	70286	9	70295	8	70303	9	70312	9	70321	8
505	70329	9	70338	8	70346	9	70355	9	70364	8	70372	9	70381	8	70389	9	70398	8	70406	9
506	70415	9	70424	8	70432	9	70441	8	70449	9	70458	9	70467	8	70475	9	70484	8	70492	9
507	70501	8	70509	9	70518	8	70526	9	70535	9	70544	8	70552	9	70561	8	70569	9	70578	8
508	70586	9	70595	8	70603	9	70612	9	70621	8	70629	9	70638	8	70646	9	70655	8	70663	9
509	70672	8	70680	9	70689	8	70697	9	70706	8	70714	9	70723	8	70731	9	70740	9	70749	8
510	70757	9	70766	8	70774	9	70783	8	70791	9	70800	8	70808	9	70817	8	70825	9	70834	8
511	70842	9	70851	8	70859	9	70868	8	70876	9	70885	8	70893	9	70902	8	70910	9	70919	8
512	70927	8	70935	9	70944	8	70952	9	70961	8	70969	9	70978	8	70986	9	70995	8	71003	9
513	71012	8	71020	9	71029	8	71037	9	71046	8	71054	9	71063	8	71071	8	71079	9	71088	8
514	71096	9	71105	8	71113	9	71122	8	71130	9	71139	8	71147	8	71155	9	71164	8	71172	9
515	71181	8	71189	9	71198	8	71206	8	71214	9	71223	8	71231	9	71240	8	71248	9	71257	8
516	71265	8	71273	9	71282	8	71290	9	71299	8	71307	8	71315	9	71324	8	71332	9	71341	8
517	71349	8	71357	9	71366	8	71374	9	71383	8	71391	8	71399	9	71408	8	71416	9	71425	8
518	71433	8	71441	9	71450	8	71458	8	71466	9	71475	8	71483	9	71492	8	71500	8	71508	9
519	71517	8	71525	8	71533	9	71542	8	71550	9	71559	8	71567	8	71575	9	71584	8	71592	8
520	71600	9	71609	8	71617	8	71625	9	71634	8	71642	8	71650	9	71659	8	71667	8	71675	9
521	71684	8	71692	8	71700	9	71709	8	71717	8	71725	9	71734	8	71742	8	71750	9	71759	8
522	71767	8	71775	9	71784	8	71792	8	71800	9	71809	8	71817	8	71825	9	71834	8	71842	8
523	71850	8	71858	9	71867	8	71875	8	71883	9	71892	8	71900	8	71908	9	71917	8	71925	8
524	71933	8	71941	9	71950	8	71958	8	71966	9	71975	8	71983	8	71991	8	71999	9	72008	8
525	72016	8	72024	8	72032	9	72041	8	72049	8	72057	9	72066	8	72074	8	72082	8	72090	9
526	72099	8	72107	8	72115	8	72123	9	72132	8	72140	8	72148	8	72156	9	72165	8	72173	8
527	72181	8	72189	9	72198	8	72206	8	72214	8	72222	8	72230	9	72239	8	72247	8	72255	8
528	72263	9	72272	8	72280	8	72288	8	72296	8	72304	9	72313	8	72321	8	72329	8	72337	9
529	72346	8	72354	8	72362	8	72370	8	72378	9	72387	8	72395	8	72403	8	72411	8	72419	9
530	72428	8	72436	8	72444	8	72452	8	72460	9	72469	8	72477	8	72485	8	72493	8	72501	8
531	72509	9	72518	8	72526	8	72534	8	72542	8	72550	8	72558	9	72567	8	72575	8	72583	8
532	72591	8	72599	8	72607	9	72616	8	72624	8	72632	8	72640	8	72648	8	72656	9	72665	8
533	72673	8	72681	8	72689	8	72697	8	72705	8	72713	9	72722	8	72730	8	72738	8	72746	8
534	72754	8	72762	8	72770	9	72779	8	72787	8	72795	8	72803	8	72811	8	72819	8	72827	8
535	72835	8	72843	9	72852	8	72860	8	72868	8	72876	8	72884	8	72892	8	72900	8	72908	8
536	72916	9	72925	8	72933	8	72941	8	72949	8	72957	8	72965	8	72973	8	72981	8	72989	8
537	72997	9	73006	8	73014	8	73022	8	73030	8	73038	8	73046	8	73054	8	73062	8	73070	8
538	73078	8	73086	8	73094	8	73102	9	73111	8	73119	8	73127	8	73135	8	73143	8	73151	8
539	73159	8	73167	8	73175	8	73183	8	73191	8	73199	8	73207	8	73215	8	73223	8	73231	8
540	73239	8	73247	8	73255	8	73263	9	73272	8	73280	8	73288	8	73296	8	73304	8	73312	8
541	73320	8	73328	8	73336	8	73344	8	73352	8	73360	8	73368	8	73376	8	73384	8	73392	8
542	73400	8	73408	8	73416	8	73424	8	73432	8	73440	8	73448	8	73456	8	73464	8	73472	8
543	73480	8	73488	8	73496	8	73504	8	73512	8	73520	8	73528	8	73536	8	73544	8	73552	8
544	73560	8	73568	8	73576	8	73584	8	73592	8	73600	8	73608	8	73616	8	73624	8	73632	8
545	73640	8	73648	8	73656	8	73664	8	73672	7	73679	8	73687	8	73695	8	73703	8	73711	8
546	73719	8	73727	8	73735	8	73743	8	73751	8	73759	8	73767	8	73775	8	73783	8	73791	8
547	73799	8	73807	8	73815	8	73823	7	73830	8	73838	8	73846	8	73854	8	73862	8	73870	8
548	73878	8	73886	8	73894	8	73902	8	73910	8	73918	8	73926	7	73933	8	73941	8	73949	8
549	73957	8	73965	8	73973	8	73981	8	73989	8	73997	8	74005	8	74013	7	74020	8	74028	8
550	74036	8	74044	8	74052	8	74060	8	74068	8	74076	8	74084	8	74092	7	74099	8	74107	8
No.	0	d	1	d	2	d	3	d	4	d	5	d	6	d	7	d	8	d	9	d

Prop. parts

	9		8		7
1	1	1	1	1	1
2	2	2	2	2	1
3	3	3	2	3	2
4	4	4	3	4	3
5	4	5	4	5	4
6	5	6	5	6	4
7	6	7	6	7	5
8	7	8	6	8	6
9	8	9	7	9	6

TABLE 1
Logarithms of Numbers

5500–6000

No.	0	d	1	d	2	d	3	d	4	d	5	d	6	d	7	d	8	d	9	d
550	74036	8	74044	8	74052	8	74060	8	74068	8	74076	8	74084	8	74092	7	74099	8	74107	8
551	74115	8	74123	8	74131	8	74139	8	74147	8	74155	7	74162	8	74170	8	74178	8	74186	8
552	74194	8	74202	8	74210	8	74218	7	74225	8	74233	8	74241	8	74249	8	74257	8	74265	8
553	74273	7	74280	8	74288	8	74296	8	74304	8	74312	8	74320	7	74327	8	74335	8	74343	8
554	74351	8	74359	8	74367	7	74374	8	74382	8	74390	8	74398	8	74406	8	74414	7	74421	8
555	74429	8	74437	8	74445	8	74453	8	74461	7	74468	8	74476	8	74484	8	74492	8	74500	7
556	74507	8	74515	8	74523	8	74531	8	74539	8	74547	7	74554	8	74562	8	74570	8	74578	8
557	74586	7	74593	8	74601	8	74609	8	74617	7	74624	8	74632	8	74640	8	74648	8	74656	7
558	74663	8	74671	8	74679	8	74687	8	74695	7	74702	8	74710	8	74718	8	74726	7	74733	8
559	74741	8	74749	8	74757	7	74764	8	74772	8	74780	8	74788	8	74796	7	74803	8	74811	8
560	74819	8	74827	7	74834	8	74842	8	74850	8	74858	7	74865	8	74873	8	74881	8	74889	7
561	74896	8	74904	8	74912	8	74920	7	74927	8	74935	8	74943	7	74950	8	74958	8	74966	8
562	74974	7	74981	8	74989	8	74997	8	75005	7	75012	8	75020	8	75028	7	75035	8	75043	8
563	75051	8	75059	7	75066	8	75074	8	75082	7	75089	8	75097	8	75105	8	75113	7	75120	8
564	75128	8	75136	7	75143	8	75151	8	75159	7	75166	8	75174	8	75182	7	75189	8	75197	8
565	75205	8	75213	7	75220	8	75228	8	75236	7	75243	8	75251	8	75259	7	75266	8	75274	8
566	75282	7	75289	8	75297	8	75305	7	75312	8	75320	8	75328	7	75335	8	75343	8	75351	7
567	75358	8	75366	8	75374	7	75381	8	75389	8	75397	7	75404	8	75412	8	75420	7	75427	8
568	75435	7	75442	8	75450	8	75458	7	75465	8	75473	8	75481	7	75488	8	75496	8	75504	7
569	75511	8	75519	7	75526	8	75534	8	75542	7	75549	8	75557	8	75565	7	75572	8	75580	7
570	75587	8	75595	8	75603	7	75610	8	75618	8	75626	7	75633	8	75641	7	75648	8	75656	8
571	75664	7	75671	8	75679	7	75686	8	75694	8	75702	7	75709	8	75717	7	75724	8	75732	8
572	75740	7	75747	8	75755	7	75762	8	75770	8	75778	7	75785	8	75793	7	75800	8	75808	7
573	75815	8	75823	8	75831	7	75838	8	75846	7	75853	8	75861	7	75868	8	75876	8	75884	7
574	75891	8	75899	7	75906	8	75914	7	75921	8	75929	8	75937	7	75944	8	75952	7	75959	8
575	75967	7	75974	8	75982	7	75989	8	75997	8	76005	7	76012	8	76020	7	76027	8	76035	7
576	76042	8	76050	7	76057	8	76065	7	76072	8	76080	7	76087	8	76095	8	76103	7	76110	8
577	76118	7	76125	8	76133	7	76140	8	76148	7	76155	8	76163	7	76170	8	76178	7	76185	8
578	76193	7	76200	8	76208	7	76215	8	76223	7	76230	8	76238	7	76245	8	76253	7	76260	8
579	76268	7	76275	8	76283	7	76290	8	76298	7	76305	8	76313	7	76320	8	76328	7	76335	8
580	76343	7	76350	8	76358	7	76365	8	76373	7	76380	8	76388	7	76395	8	76403	7	76410	8
581	76418	7	76425	8	76433	7	76440	8	76448	7	76455	7	76462	8	76470	7	76477	8	76485	7
582	76492	8	76500	7	76507	8	76515	7	76522	8	76530	7	76537	8	76545	7	76552	7	76559	8
583	76567	7	76574	8	76582	7	76589	8	76597	7	76604	8	76612	7	76619	7	76626	8	76634	7
584	76641	8	76649	7	76656	8	76664	7	76671	7	76678	8	76686	7	76693	8	76701	7	76708	8
585	76716	7	76723	7	76730	8	76738	7	76745	8	76753	7	76760	8	76768	7	76775	7	76782	8
586	76790	7	76797	8	76805	7	76812	7	76819	8	76827	7	76834	8	76842	7	76849	7	76856	8
587	76864	7	76871	8	76879	7	76886	7	76893	8	76901	7	76908	8	76916	7	76923	7	76930	8
588	76938	7	76945	8	76953	7	76960	7	76967	8	76975	7	76982	7	76989	8	76997	7	77004	8
589	77012	7	77019	7	77026	8	77034	7	77041	7	77048	8	77056	7	77063	7	77070	8	77078	7
590	77085	8	77093	7	77100	7	77107	8	77115	7	77122	7	77129	8	77137	7	77144	7	77151	8
591	77159	7	77166	7	77173	8	77181	7	77188	7	77195	8	77203	7	77210	7	77217	8	77225	7
592	77232	8	77240	7	77247	7	77254	8	77262	7	77269	7	77276	7	77283	8	77291	7	77298	7
593	77305	8	77313	7	77320	7	77327	8	77335	7	77342	7	77349	8	77357	7	77364	7	77371	8
594	77379	7	77386	7	77393	8	77401	7	77408	7	77415	7	77422	8	77430	7	77437	7	77444	8
595	77452	7	77459	7	77466	8	77474	7	77481	7	77488	7	77495	8	77503	7	77510	7	77517	8
596	77525	7	77532	7	77539	7	77546	8	77554	7	77561	7	77568	8	77576	7	77583	7	77590	7
597	77597	8	77605	7	77612	7	77619	8	77627	7	77634	7	77641	7	77648	8	77656	7	77663	7
598	77670	7	77677	8	77685	7	77692	7	77699	7	77706	8	77714	7	77721	7	77728	7	77735	8
599	77743	7	77750	7	77757	7	77764	8	77772	7	77779	7	77786	7	77793	8	77801	7	77808	7
600	77815	7	77822	8	77830	7	77837	7	77844	7	77851	8	77859	7	77866	7	77873	7	77880	7
No.	0	d	1	d	2	d	3	d	4	d	5	d	6	d	7	d	8	d	9	d

Prop. parts

	8
1	1
2	2
3	2
4	3
5	4
6	5
7	6
8	6
9	7

	7
1	1
2	1
3	2
4	3
5	4
6	4
7	5
8	6
9	6

TABLE 1
Logarithms of Numbers

6000–6500

No.	0	d	1	d	2	d	3	d	4	d	5	d	6	d	7	d	8	d	9	d
600	77815	7	77822	8	77830	7	77837	7	77844	7	77851	8	77859	7	77866	7	77873	7	77880	7
601	77887	8	77895	7	77902	7	77909	7	77916	8	77924	7	77931	7	77938	7	77945	7	77952	8
602	77960	7	77967	7	77974	7	77981	7	77988	8	77996	7	78003	7	78010	7	78017	8	78025	7
603	78032	7	78039	7	78046	7	78053	8	78061	7	78068	7	78075	7	78082	7	78089	8	78097	7
604	78104	7	78111	7	78118	7	78125	7	78132	8	78140	7	78147	7	78154	7	78161	7	78168	8
605	78176	7	78183	7	78190	7	78197	7	78204	7	78211	8	78219	7	78226	7	78233	7	78240	7
606	78247	7	78254	8	78262	7	78269	7	78276	7	78283	7	78290	7	78297	8	78305	7	78312	7
607	78319	7	78326	7	78333	7	78340	7	78347	8	78355	7	78362	7	78369	7	78376	7	78383	7
608	78390	8	78398	7	78405	7	78412	7	78419	7	78426	7	78433	7	78440	7	78447	8	78455	7
609	78462	7	78469	7	78476	7	78483	7	78490	7	78497	7	78504	8	78512	7	78519	7	78526	7
610	78533	7	78540	7	78547	7	78554	7	78561	8	78569	7	78576	7	78583	7	78590	7	78597	7
611	78604	7	78611	7	78618	7	78625	8	78633	7	78640	7	78647	7	78654	7	78661	7	78668	7
612	78675	7	78682	7	78689	7	78696	8	78704	7	78711	7	78718	7	78725	7	78732	7	78739	7
613	78746	7	78753	7	78760	7	78767	7	78774	7	78781	8	78789	7	78796	7	78803	7	78810	7
614	78817	7	78824	7	78831	7	78838	7	78845	7	78852	7	78859	7	78866	7	78873	7	78880	8
615	78888	7	78895	7	78902	7	78909	7	78916	7	78923	7	78930	7	78937	7	78944	7	78951	7
616	78958	7	78965	7	78972	7	78979	7	78986	7	78993	7	79000	7	79007	7	79014	7	79021	8
617	79029	7	79036	7	79043	7	79050	7	79057	7	79064	7	79071	7	79078	7	79085	7	79092	7
618	79099	7	79106	7	79113	7	79120	7	79127	7	79134	7	79141	7	79148	7	79155	7	79162	7
619	79169	7	79176	7	79183	7	79190	7	79197	7	79204	7	79211	7	79218	7	79225	7	79232	7
620	79239	7	79246	7	79253	7	79260	7	79267	7	79274	7	79281	7	79288	7	79295	7	79302	7
621	79309	7	79316	7	79323	7	79330	7	79337	7	79344	7	79351	7	79358	7	79365	7	79372	7
622	79379	7	79386	7	79393	7	79400	7	79407	7	79414	7	79421	7	79428	7	79435	7	79442	7
623	79449	7	79456	7	79463	7	79470	7	79477	7	79484	7	79491	7	79498	7	79505	6	79511	7
624	79518	7	79525	7	79532	7	79539	7	79546	7	79553	7	79560	7	79567	7	79574	7	79581	7
625	79588	7	79595	7	79602	7	79609	7	79616	7	79623	7	79630	7	79637	7	79644	6	79650	7
626	79657	7	79664	7	79671	7	79678	7	79685	7	79692	7	79699	7	79706	7	79713	7	79720	7
627	79727	7	79734	7	79741	7	79748	6	79754	7	79761	7	79768	7	79775	7	79782	7	79789	7
628	79796	7	79803	7	79810	7	79817	7	79824	7	79831	6	79837	7	79844	7	79851	7	79858	7
629	79865	7	79872	7	79879	7	79886	7	79893	7	79900	6	79906	7	79913	7	79920	7	79927	7
630	79934	7	79941	7	79948	7	79955	7	79962	7	79969	6	79975	7	79982	7	79989	7	79996	7
631	80003	7	80010	7	80017	7	80024	6	80030	7	80037	7	80044	7	80051	7	80058	7	80065	7
632	80072	7	80079	6	80085	7	80092	7	80099	7	80106	7	80113	7	80120	7	80127	7	80134	6
633	80140	7	80147	7	80154	7	80161	7	80168	7	80175	7	80182	6	80188	7	80195	7	80202	7
634	80209	7	80216	7	80223	6	80229	7	80236	7	80243	7	80250	7	80257	7	80264	7	80271	6
635	80277	7	80284	7	80291	7	80298	7	80305	7	80312	6	80318	7	80325	7	80332	7	80339	7
636	80346	7	80353	6	80359	7	80366	7	80373	7	80380	7	80387	6	80393	7	80400	7	80407	7
637	80414	7	80421	7	80428	6	80434	7	80441	7	80448	7	80455	7	80462	6	80468	7	80475	7
638	80482	7	80489	7	80496	6	80502	7	80509	7	80516	7	80523	7	80530	6	80536	7	80543	7
639	80550	7	80557	7	80564	6	80570	7	80577	7	80584	7	80591	7	80598	6	80604	7	80611	7
640	80618	7	80625	7	80632	6	80638	7	80645	7	80652	7	80659	6	80665	7	80672	7	80679	7
641	80686	7	80693	6	80699	7	80706	7	80713	7	80720	6	80726	7	80733	7	80740	7	80747	7
642	80754	6	80760	7	80767	7	80774	7	80781	6	80787	7	80794	7	80801	7	80808	6	80814	7
643	80821	7	80828	7	80835	6	80841	7	80848	7	80855	7	80862	6	80868	7	80875	7	80882	7
644	80889	6	80895	7	80902	7	80909	7	80916	6	80922	7	80929	7	80936	7	80943	6	80949	7
645	80956	7	80963	6	80969	7	80976	7	80983	7	80990	6	80996	7	81003	7	81010	7	81017	6
646	81023	7	81030	7	81037	6	81043	7	81050	7	81057	7	81064	6	81070	7	81077	7	81084	6
647	81090	7	81097	7	81104	7	81111	6	81117	7	81124	7	81131	6	81137	7	81144	7	81151	7
648	81158	6	81164	7	81171	7	81178	6	81184	7	81191	7	81198	6	81204	7	81211	7	81218	6
649	81224	7	81231	7	81238	7	81245	6	81251	7	81258	7	81265	6	81271	7	81278	7	81285	6
650	81291	7	81298	7	81305	6	81311	7	81318	7	81325	6	81331	7	81338	7	81345	6	81351	7
No.	0	d	1	d	2	d	3	d	4	d	5	d	6	d	7	d	8	d	9	d

Prop. parts

	8
1	1
2	2
3	2
4	3
5	4
6	5
7	6
8	6
9	7

	7
1	1
2	1
3	2
4	3
5	4
6	4
7	5
8	6
9	6

	6
1	1
2	1
3	2
4	2
5	3
6	4
7	4
8	5
9	5

TABLE 1
Logarithms of Numbers

6500–7000

No.	0	d	1	d	2	d	3	d	4	d	5	d	6	d	7	d	8	d	9	d
650	81291	7	81298	7	81305	6	81311	7	81318	7	81325	6	81331	7	81338	7	81345	6	81351	7
651	81358	7	81365	6	81371	7	81378	7	81385	6	81391	7	81398	7	81405	6	81411	7	81418	7
652	81425	6	81431	7	81438	7	81445	6	81451	7	81458	7	81465	6	81471	7	81478	7	81485	6
653	81491	7	81498	7	81505	6	81511	7	81518	7	81525	6	81531	7	81538	6	81544	7	81551	7
654	81558	6	81564	7	81571	7	81578	6	81584	7	81591	7	81598	6	81604	7	81611	6	81617	7
655	81624	7	81631	6	81637	7	81644	7	81651	6	81657	7	81664	7	81671	6	81677	7	81684	6
656	81690	7	81697	7	81704	6	81710	7	81717	6	81723	7	81730	7	81737	6	81743	7	81750	7
657	81757	6	81763	7	81770	6	81776	7	81783	7	81790	6	81796	7	81803	6	81809	7	81816	7
658	81823	6	81829	7	81836	6	81842	7	81849	7	81856	6	81862	7	81869	6	81875	7	81882	7
659	81889	6	81895	7	81902	6	81908	7	81915	6	81921	7	81928	7	81935	6	81941	7	81948	6
660	81954	7	81961	7	81968	6	81974	7	81981	6	81987	7	81994	6	82000	7	82007	7	82014	6
661	82020	7	82027	6	82033	7	82040	6	82046	7	82053	7	82060	6	82066	7	82073	6	82079	7
662	82086	6	82092	7	82099	6	82105	7	82112	7	82119	6	82125	7	82132	6	82138	7	82145	6
663	82151	7	82158	6	82164	7	82171	7	82178	6	82184	7	82191	6	82197	7	82204	6	82210	7
664	82217	6	82223	7	82230	6	82236	7	82243	6	82249	7	82256	7	82263	6	82269	7	82276	6
665	82282	7	82289	6	82295	7	82302	6	82308	7	82315	6	82321	7	82328	6	82334	7	82341	6
666	82347	7	82354	6	82360	7	82367	6	82373	7	82380	7	82387	6	82393	7	82400	6	82406	7
667	82413	6	82419	7	82426	6	82432	7	82439	6	82445	7	82452	6	82458	7	82465	6	82471	7
668	82478	6	82484	7	82491	6	82497	7	82504	6	82510	7	82517	6	82523	7	82530	6	82536	7
669	82543	6	82549	7	82556	6	82562	7	82569	6	82575	7	82582	6	82588	7	82595	6	82601	6
670	82607	7	82614	6	82620	7	82627	6	82633	7	82640	6	82646	7	82653	6	82659	7	82666	6
671	82672	7	82679	6	82685	7	82692	6	82698	7	82705	6	82711	7	82718	6	82724	6	82730	7
672	82737	6	82743	7	82750	6	82756	7	82763	6	82769	7	82776	6	82782	7	82789	6	82795	7
673	82802	6	82808	6	82814	7	82821	6	82827	7	82834	6	82840	7	82847	6	82853	7	82860	6
674	82866	6	82872	7	82879	6	82885	7	82892	6	82898	7	82905	6	82911	7	82918	6	82924	6
675	82930	7	82937	6	82943	7	82950	6	82956	7	82963	6	82969	6	82975	7	82982	6	82988	7
676	82995	6	83001	7	83008	6	83014	6	83020	7	83027	6	83033	7	83040	6	83046	6	83052	7
677	83059	6	83065	7	83072	6	83078	7	83085	6	83091	6	83097	7	83104	6	83110	7	83117	6
678	83123	6	83129	7	83136	6	83142	7	83149	6	83155	6	83161	7	83168	6	83174	7	83181	6
679	83187	6	83193	7	83200	6	83206	7	83213	6	83219	6	83225	7	83232	6	83238	7	83245	6
680	83251	6	83257	7	83264	6	83270	6	83276	7	83283	6	83289	7	83296	6	83302	6	83308	7
681	83315	6	83321	6	83327	7	83334	6	83340	7	83347	6	83353	6	83359	7	83366	6	83372	6
682	83378	7	83385	6	83391	7	83398	6	83404	6	83410	7	83417	6	83423	6	83429	7	83436	6
683	83442	6	83448	7	83455	6	83461	6	83467	7	83474	6	83480	7	83487	6	83493	6	83499	7
684	83506	6	83512	6	83518	7	83525	6	83531	6	83537	7	83544	6	83550	6	83556	7	83563	6
685	83569	6	83575	7	83582	6	83588	6	83594	7	83601	6	83607	6	83613	7	83620	6	83626	6
686	83632	7	83639	6	83645	6	83651	7	83658	6	83664	6	83670	7	83677	6	83683	6	83689	7
687	83696	6	83702	6	83708	7	83715	6	83721	6	83727	7	83734	6	83740	6	83746	7	83753	6
688	83759	6	83765	6	83771	7	83778	6	83784	6	83790	7	83797	6	83803	6	83809	7	83816	6
689	83822	6	83828	7	83835	6	83841	6	83847	6	83853	7	83860	6	83866	6	83872	7	83879	6
690	83885	6	83891	6	83897	7	83904	6	83910	6	83916	7	83923	6	83929	6	83935	7	83942	6
691	83948	6	83954	6	83960	7	83967	6	83973	6	83979	6	83985	7	83992	6	83998	6	84004	7
692	84011	6	84017	6	84023	6	84029	7	84036	6	84042	6	84048	7	84055	6	84061	6	84067	6
693	84073	7	84080	6	84086	6	84092	6	84098	7	84105	6	84111	6	84117	6	84123	7	84130	6
694	84136	6	84142	6	84148	7	84155	6	84161	6	84167	6	84173	7	84180	6	84186	6	84192	6
695	84198	7	84205	6	84211	6	84217	6	84223	7	84230	6	84236	6	84242	6	84248	7	84255	6
696	84261	6	84267	6	84273	7	84280	6	84286	6	84292	6	84298	7	84305	6	84311	6	84317	6
697	84323	7	84330	6	84336	6	84342	6	84348	6	84354	7	84361	6	84367	6	84373	6	84379	7
698	84386	6	84392	6	84398	6	84404	6	84410	7	84417	6	84423	6	84429	6	84435	7	84442	6
699	84448	6	84454	6	84460	6	84466	7	84473	6	84479	6	84485	6	84491	6	84497	7	84504	6
700	84510	6	84516	6	84522	6	84528	7	84535	6	84541	6	84547	6	84553	6	84559	7	84566	6
No.	0	d	1	d	2	d	3	d	4	d	5	d	6	d	7	d	8	d	9	d

Prop. parts

	7
1	1
2	1
3	2
4	3
5	4
6	4
7	5
8	6
9	6

	6
1	1
2	1
3	2
4	2
5	3
6	4
7	4
8	5
9	5

TABLE 1
Logarithms of Numbers

7000–7500

No.	0	d	1	d	2	d	3	d	4	d	5	d	6	d	7	d	8	d	9	d
700	84510	6	84516	6	84522	6	84528	7	84535	6	84541	6	84547	6	84553	6	84559	7	84566	6
701	84572	6	84578	6	84584	6	84590	7	84597	6	84603	6	84609	6	84615	6	84621	7	84628	6
702	84634	6	84640	6	84646	6	84652	6	84658	7	84665	6	84671	6	84677	6	84683	6	84689	7
703	84696	6	84702	6	84708	6	84714	6	84720	6	84726	7	84733	6	84739	6	84745	6	84751	6
704	84757	6	84763	7	84770	6	84776	6	84782	6	84788	6	84794	6	84800	7	84807	6	84813	6
705	84819	6	84825	6	84831	6	84837	7	84844	6	84850	6	84856	6	84862	6	84868	6	84874	6
706	84880	7	84887	6	84893	6	84899	6	84905	6	84911	6	84917	7	84924	6	84930	6	84936	6
707	84942	6	84948	6	84954	6	84960	7	84967	6	84973	6	84979	6	84985	6	84991	6	84997	6
708	85003	6	85009	7	85016	6	85022	6	85028	6	85034	6	85040	6	85046	6	85052	6	85058	7
709	85065	6	85071	6	85077	6	85083	6	85089	6	85095	6	85101	6	85107	7	85114	6	85120	6
710	85126	6	85132	6	85138	6	85144	6	85150	6	85156	7	85163	6	85169	6	85175	6	85181	6
711	85187	6	85193	6	85199	6	85205	6	85211	6	85217	7	85224	6	85230	6	85236	6	85242	6
712	85248	6	85254	6	85260	6	85266	6	85272	6	85278	7	85285	6	85291	6	85297	6	85303	6
713	85309	6	85315	6	85321	6	85327	6	85333	6	85339	6	85345	7	85352	6	85358	6	85364	6
714	85370	6	85376	6	85382	6	85388	6	85394	6	85400	6	85406	6	85412	6	85418	7	85425	6
715	85431	6	85437	6	85443	6	85449	6	85455	6	85461	6	85467	6	85473	6	85479	6	85485	6
716	85491	6	85497	6	85503	6	85509	7	85516	6	85522	6	85528	6	85534	6	85540	6	85546	6
717	85552	6	85558	6	85564	6	85570	6	85576	6	85582	6	85588	6	85594	6	85600	6	85606	6
718	85612	6	85618	7	85625	6	85631	6	85637	6	85643	6	85649	6	85655	6	85661	6	85667	6
719	85673	6	85679	6	85685	6	85691	6	85697	6	85703	6	85709	6	85715	6	85721	6	85727	6
720	85733	6	85739	6	85745	6	85751	6	85757	6	85763	6	85769	6	85775	6	85781	7	85788	6
721	85794	6	85800	6	85806	6	85812	6	85818	6	85824	6	85830	6	85836	6	85842	6	85848	6
722	85854	6	85860	6	85866	6	85872	6	85878	6	85884	6	85890	6	85896	6	85902	6	85908	6
723	85914	6	85920	6	85926	6	85932	6	85938	6	85944	6	85950	6	85956	6	85962	6	85968	6
724	85974	6	85980	6	85986	6	85992	6	85998	6	86004	6	86010	6	86016	6	86022	6	86028	6
725	86034	6	86040	6	86046	6	86052	6	86058	6	86064	6	86070	6	86076	6	86082	6	86088	6
726	86094	6	86100	6	86106	6	86112	6	86118	6	86124	6	86130	6	86136	5	86141	6	86147	6
727	86153	6	86159	6	86165	6	86171	6	86177	6	86183	6	86189	6	86195	6	86201	6	86207	6
728	86213	6	86219	6	86225	6	86231	6	86237	6	86243	6	86249	6	86255	6	86261	6	86267	6
729	86273	6	86279	6	86285	6	86291	6	86297	6	86303	5	86308	6	86314	6	86320	6	86326	6
730	86332	6	86338	6	86344	6	86350	6	86356	6	86362	6	86368	6	86374	6	86380	6	86386	6
731	86392	6	86398	6	86404	6	86410	5	86415	6	86421	6	86427	6	86433	6	86439	6	86445	6
732	86451	6	86457	6	86463	6	86469	6	86475	6	86481	6	86487	6	86493	6	86499	5	86504	6
733	86510	6	86516	6	86522	6	86528	6	86534	6	86540	6	86546	6	86552	6	86558	6	86564	6
734	86570	6	86576	5	86581	6	86587	6	86593	6	86599	6	86605	6	86611	6	86617	6	86623	6
735	86629	6	86635	6	86641	5	86646	6	86652	6	86658	6	86664	6	86670	6	86676	6	86682	6
736	86688	6	86694	6	86700	5	86705	6	86711	6	86717	6	86723	6	86729	6	86735	6	86741	6
737	86747	6	86753	6	86759	5	86764	6	86770	6	86776	6	86782	6	86788	6	86794	6	86800	6
738	86806	6	86812	5	86817	6	86823	6	86829	6	86835	6	86841	6	86847	6	86853	6	86859	5
739	86864	6	86870	6	86876	6	86882	6	86888	6	86894	6	86900	6	86906	5	86911	6	86917	6
740	86923	6	86929	6	86935	6	86941	6	86947	6	86953	5	86958	6	86964	6	86970	6	86976	6
741	86982	6	86988	6	86994	5	86999	6	87005	6	87011	6	87017	6	87023	6	87029	6	87035	5
742	87040	6	87046	6	87052	6	87058	6	87064	6	87070	5	87075	6	87081	6	87087	6	87093	6
743	87099	6	87105	6	87111	5	87116	6	87122	6	87128	6	87134	6	87140	6	87146	5	87151	6
744	87157	6	87163	6	87169	6	87175	6	87181	5	87186	6	87192	6	87198	6	87204	6	87210	6
745	87216	5	87221	6	87227	6	87233	6	87239	6	87245	6	87251	5	87256	6	87262	6	87268	6
746	87274	6	87280	6	87286	5	87291	6	87297	6	87303	6	87309	6	87315	5	87320	6	87326	6
747	87332	6	87338	6	87344	5	87349	6	87355	6	87361	6	87367	6	87373	6	87379	5	87384	6
748	87390	6	87396	6	87402	6	87408	5	87413	6	87419	6	87425	6	87431	6	87437	5	87442	6
749	87448	6	87454	6	87460	6	87466	5	87471	6	87477	6	87483	6	87489	6	87495	5	87500	6
750	87506	6	87512	6	87518	5	87523	6	87529	6	87535	6	87541	6	87547	5	87552	6	87558	6
No.	0	d	1	d	2	d	3	d	4	d	5	d	6	d	7	d	8	d	9	d

Prop. parts

	7
1	1
2	1
3	2
4	3
5	4
6	4
7	5
8	6
9	6

	6
1	1
2	1
3	2
4	2
5	3
6	4
7	4
8	5
9	5

	5
1	0
2	1
3	2
4	2
5	2
6	3
7	4
8	4
9	4

TABLE 1
Logarithms of Numbers

7500–8000

No.	0	d	1	d	2	d	3	d	4	d	5	d	6	d	7	d	8	d	9	d
750	87506	6	87512	6	87518	5	87523	6	87529	6	87535	6	87541	6	87547	5	87552	6	87558	6
751	87564	6	87570	6	87576	5	87581	6	87587	6	87593	6	87599	5	87604	6	87610	6	87616	6
752	87622	6	87628	5	87633	6	87639	6	87645	6	87651	5	87656	6	87662	6	87668	6	87674	5
753	87679	6	87685	6	87691	6	87697	6	87703	5	87708	6	87714	6	87720	6	87726	5	87731	6
754	87737	6	87743	6	87749	5	87754	6	87760	6	87766	6	87772	5	87777	6	87783	6	87789	6
755	87795	5	87800	6	87806	6	87812	6	87818	5	87823	6	87829	6	87835	6	87841	5	87846	6
756	87852	6	87858	6	87864	5	87869	6	87875	6	87881	6	87887	5	87892	6	87898	6	87904	6
757	87910	5	87915	6	87921	6	87927	6	87933	5	87938	6	87944	6	87950	5	87955	6	87961	6
758	87967	6	87973	5	87978	6	87984	6	87990	6	87996	5	88001	6	88007	6	88013	5	88018	6
759	88024	6	88030	6	88036	5	88041	6	88047	6	88053	5	88058	6	88064	6	88070	6	88076	5
760	88081	6	88087	6	88093	5	88098	6	88104	6	88110	6	88116	5	88121	6	88127	6	88133	5
761	88138	6	88144	6	88150	6	88156	5	88161	6	88167	6	88173	5	88178	6	88184	6	88190	5
762	88195	6	88201	6	88207	6	88213	5	88218	6	88224	6	88230	5	88235	6	88241	6	88247	5
763	88252	6	88258	6	88264	6	88270	5	88275	6	88281	6	88287	5	88292	6	88298	6	88304	5
764	88309	6	88315	6	88321	5	88326	6	88332	6	88338	5	88343	6	88349	6	88355	5	88360	6
765	88366	6	88372	5	88377	6	88383	6	88389	6	88395	5	88400	6	88406	6	88412	5	88417	6
766	88423	6	88429	5	88434	6	88440	6	88446	5	88451	6	88457	6	88463	5	88468	6	88474	6
767	88480	5	88485	6	88491	6	88497	5	88502	6	88508	5	88513	6	88519	6	88525	5	88530	6
768	88536	6	88542	5	88547	6	88553	6	88559	5	88564	6	88570	6	88576	5	88581	6	88587	6
769	88593	5	88598	6	88604	6	88610	5	88615	6	88621	6	88627	5	88632	6	88638	5	88643	6
770	88649	6	88655	5	88660	6	88666	6	88672	5	88677	6	88683	6	88689	5	88694	6	88700	5
771	88705	6	88711	6	88717	5	88722	6	88728	6	88734	5	88739	6	88745	5	88750	6	88756	6
772	88762	5	88767	6	88773	6	88779	5	88784	6	88790	5	88795	6	88801	6	88807	5	88812	6
773	88818	6	88824	5	88829	6	88835	5	88840	6	88846	6	88852	5	88857	6	88863	5	88868	6
774	88874	6	88880	5	88885	6	88891	6	88897	5	88902	6	88908	5	88913	6	88919	6	88925	5
775	88930	6	88936	5	88941	6	88947	6	88953	5	88958	6	88964	5	88969	6	88975	6	88981	5
776	88986	6	88992	5	88997	6	89003	6	89009	5	89014	6	89020	5	89025	6	89031	6	89037	5
777	89042	6	89048	5	89053	6	89059	5	89064	6	89070	6	89076	5	89081	6	89087	5	89092	6
778	89098	6	89104	5	89109	6	89115	5	89120	6	89126	5	89131	6	89137	6	89143	5	89148	6
779	89154	5	89159	6	89165	5	89170	6	89176	6	89182	5	89187	6	89193	5	89198	6	89204	5
780	89209	6	89215	6	89221	5	89226	6	89232	5	89237	6	89243	5	89248	6	89254	6	89260	5
781	89265	6	89271	5	89276	6	89282	5	89287	6	89293	5	89298	6	89304	6	89310	5	89315	6
782	89321	5	89326	6	89332	5	89337	6	89343	5	89348	6	89354	6	89360	5	89365	6	89371	5
783	89376	6	89382	5	89387	6	89393	5	89398	6	89404	5	89409	6	89415	6	89421	5	89426	6
784	89432	5	89437	6	89443	5	89448	6	89454	5	89459	6	89465	5	89470	6	89476	5	89481	6
785	89487	5	89492	6	89498	6	89504	5	89509	6	89515	5	89520	6	89526	5	89531	6	89537	5
786	89542	6	89548	5	89553	6	89559	5	89564	6	89570	5	89575	6	89581	5	89586	6	89592	5
787	89597	6	89603	6	89609	5	89614	6	89620	5	89625	6	89631	5	89636	6	89642	5	89647	6
788	89653	5	89658	6	89664	5	89669	6	89675	5	89680	6	89686	5	89691	6	89697	5	89702	6
789	89708	5	89713	6	89719	5	89724	6	89730	5	89735	6	89741	5	89746	6	89752	5	89757	6
790	89763	5	89768	6	89774	5	89779	6	89785	5	89790	6	89796	5	89801	6	89807	5	89812	6
791	89818	5	89823	6	89829	5	89834	6	89840	5	89845	6	89851	5	89856	6	89862	5	89867	6
792	89873	5	89878	5	89883	6	89889	5	89894	6	89900	5	89905	6	89911	5	89916	6	89922	5
793	89927	6	89933	5	89938	6	89944	5	89949	6	89955	5	89960	6	89966	5	89971	6	89977	5
794	89982	6	89988	5	89993	5	89998	6	90004	5	90009	6	90015	5	90020	6	90026	5	90031	6
795	90037	5	90042	6	90048	5	90053	6	90059	5	90064	5	90069	6	90075	5	90080	6	90086	5
796	90091	6	90097	5	90102	6	90108	5	90113	6	90119	5	90124	5	90129	6	90135	5	90140	6
797	90146	5	90151	6	90157	5	90162	6	90168	5	90173	6	90179	5	90184	5	90189	6	90195	5
798	90200	6	90206	5	90211	6	90217	5	90222	5	90227	6	90233	5	90238	6	90244	5	90249	6
799	90255	5	90260	6	90266	5	90271	5	90276	6	90282	5	90287	6	90293	5	90298	6	90304	5
800	90309	5	90314	6	90320	5	90325	6	90331	5	90336	6	90342	5	90347	5	90352	6	90358	5
No.	0	d	1	d	2	d	3	d	4	d	5	d	6	d	7	d	8	d	9	d

Prop. parts

	6
1	1
2	1
3	2
4	2
5	3
6	4
7	4
8	5
9	5

	5
1	0
2	1
3	2
4	2
5	2
6	3
7	4
8	4
9	4

TABLE 1
Logarithms of Numbers

8000–8500

No.	0	d	1	d	2	d	3	d	4	d	5	d	6	d	7	d	8	d	9	d
800	90309	5	90314	6	90320	5	90325	6	90331	5	90336	6	90342	5	90347	5	90352	6	90358	5
801	90363	6	90369	5	90374	6	90380	5	90385	5	90390	6	90396	5	90401	6	90407	5	90412	5
802	90417	6	90423	5	90428	6	90434	5	90439	6	90445	5	90450	5	90455	6	90461	5	90466	6
803	90472	5	90477	5	90482	6	90488	5	90493	6	90499	5	90504	5	90509	6	90515	5	90520	6
804	90526	5	90531	5	90536	6	90542	5	90547	6	90553	5	90558	5	90563	6	90569	5	90574	6
805	90580	5	90585	5	90590	6	90596	5	90601	6	90607	5	90612	5	90617	6	90623	5	90628	6
806	90634	5	90639	5	90644	6	90650	5	90655	5	90660	6	90666	5	90671	6	90677	5	90682	5
807	90687	6	90693	5	90698	5	90703	6	90709	5	90714	6	90720	5	90725	5	90730	6	90736	5
808	90741	6	90747	5	90752	5	90757	6	90763	5	90768	5	90773	6	90779	5	90784	5	90789	6
809	90795	5	90800	6	90806	5	90811	5	90816	6	90822	5	90827	5	90832	6	90838	5	90843	6
810	90849	5	90854	5	90859	6	90865	5	90870	5	90875	6	90881	5	90886	5	90891	6	90897	5
811	90902	5	90907	6	90913	5	90918	6	90924	5	90929	5	90934	6	90940	5	90945	5	90950	6
812	90956	5	90961	5	90966	6	90972	5	90977	5	90982	6	90988	5	90993	5	90998	6	91004	5
813	91009	5	91014	6	91020	5	91025	5	91030	6	91036	5	91041	5	91046	6	91052	5	91057	5
814	91062	6	91068	5	91073	5	91078	6	91084	5	91089	5	91094	6	91100	5	91105	5	91110	6
815	91116	5	91121	5	91126	6	91132	5	91137	5	91142	6	91148	5	91153	5	91158	6	91164	5
816	91169	5	91174	6	91180	5	91185	5	91190	6	91196	5	91201	5	91206	6	91212	5	91217	5
817	91222	6	91228	5	91233	5	91238	5	91243	6	91249	5	91254	5	91259	6	91265	5	91270	5
818	91275	6	91281	5	91286	5	91291	6	91297	5	91302	5	91307	5	91312	6	91318	5	91323	5
819	91328	6	91334	5	91339	5	91344	6	91350	5	91355	5	91360	5	91365	6	91371	5	91376	5
820	91381	6	91387	5	91392	5	91397	6	91403	5	91408	5	91413	5	91418	6	91424	5	91429	5
821	91434	6	91440	5	91445	5	91450	5	91455	6	91461	5	91466	5	91471	6	91477	5	91482	5
822	91487	5	91492	6	91498	5	91503	5	91508	6	91514	5	91519	5	91524	5	91529	6	91535	5
823	91540	5	91545	6	91551	5	91556	5	91561	5	91566	6	91572	5	91577	5	91582	5	91587	6
824	91593	5	91598	5	91603	6	91609	5	91614	5	91619	5	91624	6	91630	5	91635	5	91640	5
825	91645	6	91651	5	91656	5	91661	5	91666	6	91672	5	91677	5	91682	5	91687	6	91693	5
826	91698	5	91703	6	91709	5	91714	5	91719	5	91724	6	91730	5	91735	5	91740	5	91745	6
827	91751	5	91756	5	91761	5	91766	6	91772	5	91777	5	91782	5	91787	6	91793	5	91798	5
828	91803	5	91808	6	91814	5	91819	5	91824	5	91829	5	91834	6	91840	5	91845	5	91850	5
829	91855	6	91861	5	91866	5	91871	5	91876	6	91882	5	91887	5	91892	5	91897	6	91903	5
830	91908	5	91913	5	91918	6	91924	5	91929	5	91934	5	91939	5	91944	6	91950	5	91955	5
831	91960	5	91965	6	91971	5	91976	5	91981	5	91986	5	91991	6	91997	5	92002	5	92007	5
832	92012	6	92018	5	92023	5	92028	5	92033	5	92038	6	92044	5	92049	5	92054	5	92059	6
833	92065	5	92070	5	92075	5	92080	5	92085	6	92091	5	92096	5	92101	5	92106	5	92111	6
834	92117	5	92122	5	92127	5	92132	5	92137	6	92143	5	92148	5	92153	5	92158	5	92163	6
835	92169	5	92174	5	92179	5	92184	5	92189	6	92195	5	92200	5	92205	5	92210	5	92215	6
836	92221	5	92226	5	92231	5	92236	5	92241	6	92247	5	92252	5	92257	5	92262	5	92267	6
837	92273	5	92278	5	92283	5	92288	5	92293	5	92298	6	92304	5	92309	5	92314	5	92319	5
838	92324	6	92330	5	92335	5	92340	5	92345	5	92350	5	92355	6	92361	5	92366	5	92371	5
839	92376	5	92381	6	92387	5	92392	5	92397	5	92402	5	92407	5	92412	6	92418	5	92423	5
840	92428	5	92433	5	92438	5	92443	6	92449	5	92454	5	92459	5	92464	5	92469	5	92474	6
841	92480	5	92485	5	92490	5	92495	5	92500	5	92505	6	92511	5	92516	5	92521	5	92526	5
842	92531	5	92536	6	92542	5	92547	5	92552	5	92557	5	92562	5	92567	5	92572	6	92578	5
843	92583	5	92588	5	92593	5	92598	5	92603	6	92609	5	92614	5	92619	5	92624	5	92629	5
844	92634	5	92639	6	92645	5	92650	5	92655	5	92660	5	92665	5	92670	5	92675	6	92681	5
845	92686	5	92691	5	92696	5	92701	5	92706	5	92711	5	92716	6	92722	5	92727	5	92732	5
846	92737	5	92742	5	92747	5	92752	6	92758	5	92763	5	92768	5	92773	5	92778	5	92783	5
847	92788	5	92793	6	92799	5	92804	5	92809	5	92814	5	92819	5	92824	5	92829	5	92834	6
848	92840	5	92845	5	92850	5	92855	5	92860	5	92865	5	92870	5	92875	6	92881	5	92886	5
849	92891	5	92896	5	92901	5	92906	5	92911	5	92916	5	92921	6	92927	5	92932	5	92937	5
850	92942	5	92947	5	92952	5	92957	5	92962	5	92967	6	92973	5	92978	5	92983	5	92988	5
No.	0	d	1	d	2	d	3	d	4	d	5	d	6	d	7	d	8	d	9	d

Prop. parts

	6
1	1
2	1
3	2
4	2
5	3
6	4
7	4
8	5
9	5

	5
1	0
2	1
3	2
4	2
5	2
6	3
7	4
8	4
9	4

TABLE 1
Logarithms of Numbers

8500–9000

No.	0	d	1	d	2	d	3	d	4	d	5	d	6	d	7	d	8	d	9	d
850	92942	5	92947	5	92952	5	92957	5	92962	5	92967	6	92973	5	92978	5	92983	5	92988	5
851	92993	5	92998	5	93003	5	93008	5	93013	5	93018	6	93024	5	93029	5	93034	5	93039	5
852	93044	5	93049	5	93054	5	93059	5	93064	5	93069	6	93075	5	93080	5	93085	5	93090	5
853	93095	5	93100	5	93105	5	93110	5	93115	5	93120	5	93125	6	93131	5	93136	5	93141	5
854	93146	5	93151	5	93156	5	93161	5	93166	5	93171	5	93176	5	93181	5	93186	6	93192	5
855	93197	5	93202	5	93207	5	93212	5	93217	5	93222	5	93227	5	93232	5	93237	5	93242	5
856	93247	5	93252	6	93258	5	93263	5	93268	5	93273	5	93278	5	93283	5	93288	5	93293	5
857	93298	5	93303	5	93308	5	93313	5	93318	5	93323	5	93328	6	93334	5	93339	5	93344	5
858	93349	5	93354	5	93359	5	93364	5	93369	5	93374	5	93379	5	93384	5	93389	5	93394	5
859	93399	5	93404	5	93409	5	93414	6	93420	5	93425	5	93430	5	93435	5	93440	5	93445	5
860	93450	5	93455	5	93460	5	93465	5	93470	5	93475	5	93480	5	93485	5	93490	5	93495	5
861	93500	5	93505	5	93510	5	93515	5	93520	6	93526	5	93531	5	93536	5	93541	5	93546	5
862	93551	5	93556	5	93561	5	93566	5	93571	5	93576	5	93581	5	93586	5	93591	5	93596	5
863	93601	5	93606	5	93611	5	93616	5	93621	5	93626	5	93631	5	93636	5	93641	5	93646	5
864	93651	5	93656	5	93661	5	93666	5	93671	5	93676	6	93682	5	93687	5	93692	5	93697	5
865	93702	5	93707	5	93712	5	93717	5	93722	5	93727	5	93732	5	93737	5	93742	5	93747	5
866	93752	5	93757	5	93762	5	93767	5	93772	5	93777	5	93782	5	93787	5	93792	5	93797	5
867	93802	5	93807	5	93812	5	93817	5	93822	5	93827	5	93832	5	93837	5	93842	5	93847	5
868	93852	5	93857	5	93862	5	93867	5	93872	5	93877	5	93882	5	93887	5	93892	5	93897	5
869	93902	5	93907	5	93912	5	93917	5	93922	5	93927	5	93932	5	93937	5	93942	5	93947	5
870	93952	5	93957	5	93962	5	93967	5	93972	5	93977	5	93982	5	93987	5	93992	5	93997	5
871	94002	5	94007	5	94012	5	94017	5	94022	5	94027	5	94032	5	94037	5	94042	5	94047	5
872	94052	5	94057	5	94062	5	94067	5	94072	5	94077	5	94082	4	94086	5	94091	5	94096	5
873	94101	5	94106	5	94111	5	94116	5	94121	5	94126	5	94131	5	94136	5	94141	5	94146	5
874	94151	5	94156	5	94161	5	94166	5	94171	5	94176	5	94181	5	94186	5	94191	5	94196	5
875	94201	5	94206	5	94211	5	94216	5	94221	5	94226	5	94231	5	94236	4	94240	5	94245	5
876	94250	5	94255	5	94260	5	94265	5	94270	5	94275	5	94280	5	94285	5	94290	5	94295	5
877	94300	5	94305	5	94310	5	94315	5	94320	5	94325	5	94330	5	94335	5	94340	5	94345	4
878	94349	5	94354	5	94359	5	94364	5	94369	5	94374	5	94379	5	94384	5	94389	5	94394	5
879	94399	5	94404	5	94409	5	94414	5	94419	5	94424	5	94429	4	94433	5	94438	5	94443	5
880	94448	5	94453	5	94458	5	94463	5	94468	5	94473	5	94478	5	94483	5	94488	5	94493	5
881	94498	5	94503	4	94507	5	94512	5	94517	5	94522	5	94527	5	94532	5	94537	5	94542	5
882	94547	5	94552	5	94557	5	94562	5	94567	4	94571	5	94576	5	94581	5	94586	5	94591	5
883	94596	5	94601	5	94606	5	94611	5	94616	5	94621	5	94626	4	94630	5	94635	5	94640	5
884	94645	5	94650	5	94655	5	94660	5	94665	5	94670	5	94675	5	94680	5	94685	4	94689	5
885	94694	5	94699	5	94704	5	94709	5	94714	5	94719	5	94724	5	94729	5	94734	4	94738	5
886	94743	5	94748	5	94753	5	94758	5	94763	5	94768	5	94773	5	94778	5	94783	4	94787	5
887	94792	5	94797	5	94802	5	94807	5	94812	5	94817	5	94822	5	94827	5	94832	4	94836	5
888	94841	5	94846	5	94851	5	94856	5	94861	5	94866	5	94871	5	94876	4	94880	5	94885	5
889	94890	5	94895	5	94900	5	94905	5	94910	5	94915	4	94919	5	94924	5	94929	5	94934	5
890	94939	5	94944	5	94949	5	94954	5	94959	4	94963	5	94968	5	94973	5	94978	5	94983	5
891	94988	5	94993	5	94998	4	95002	5	95007	5	95012	5	95017	5	95022	5	95027	5	95032	4
892	95036	5	95041	5	95046	5	95051	5	95056	5	95061	5	95066	5	95071	4	95075	5	95080	5
893	95085	5	95090	5	95095	5	95100	5	95105	4	95109	5	95114	5	95119	5	95124	5	95129	5
894	95134	5	95139	4	95143	5	95148	5	95153	5	95158	5	95163	5	95168	5	95173	4	95177	5
895	95182	5	95187	5	95192	5	95197	5	95202	5	95207	4	95211	5	95216	5	95221	5	95226	5
896	95231	5	95236	4	95240	5	95245	5	95250	5	95255	5	95260	5	95265	5	95270	4	95274	5
897	95279	5	95284	5	95289	5	95294	5	95299	4	95303	5	95308	5	95313	5	95318	5	95323	5
898	95328	4	95332	5	95337	5	95342	5	95347	5	95352	5	95357	4	95361	5	95366	5	95371	5
899	95376	5	95381	5	95386	4	95390	5	95395	5	95400	5	95405	5	95410	5	95415	4	95419	5
900	95424	5	95429	5	95434	5	95439	5	95444	4	95448	5	95453	5	95458	5	95463	5	95468	4
No.	0	d	1	d	2	d	3	d	4	d	5	d	6	d	7	d	8	d	9	d

Prop. parts

	6
1	1
2	1
3	2
4	2
5	3
6	4
7	4
8	5
9	5

	5
1	0
2	1
3	2
4	2
5	2
6	3
7	4
8	4
9	4

	4
1	0
2	1
3	1
4	2
5	2
6	2
7	3
8	3
9	4

TABLE 1
Logarithms of Numbers

9000–9500

No.	0	d	1	d	2	d	3	d	4	d	5	d	6	d	7	d	8	d	9	d
900	95424	5	95429	5	95434	5	95439	5	95444	4	95448	5	95453	5	95458	5	95463	5	95468	4
901	95472	5	95477	5	95482	5	95487	5	95492	5	95497	4	95501	5	95506	5	95511	5	95516	5
902	95521	4	95525	5	95530	5	95535	5	95540	5	95545	5	95550	4	95554	5	95559	5	95564	5
903	95569	5	95574	4	95578	5	95583	5	95588	5	95593	5	95598	4	95602	5	95607	5	95612	5
904	95617	5	95622	4	95626	5	95631	5	95636	5	95641	5	95646	4	95650	5	95655	5	95660	5
905	95665	5	95670	4	95674	5	95679	5	95684	5	95689	5	95694	4	95698	5	95703	5	95708	5
906	95713	5	95718	4	95722	5	95727	5	95732	5	95737	5	95742	4	95746	5	95751	5	95756	5
907	95761	5	95766	4	95770	5	95775	5	95780	5	95785	4	95789	5	95794	5	95799	5	95804	5
908	95809	4	95813	5	95818	5	95823	5	95828	4	95832	5	95837	5	95842	5	95847	5	95852	4
909	95856	5	95861	5	95866	5	95871	4	95875	5	95880	5	95885	5	95890	5	95895	4	95899	5
910	95904	5	95909	5	95914	4	95918	5	95923	5	95928	5	95933	5	95938	4	95942	5	95947	5
911	95952	5	95957	4	95961	5	95966	5	95971	5	95976	4	95980	5	95985	5	95990	5	95995	4
912	95999	5	96004	5	96009	5	96014	5	96019	4	96023	5	96028	5	96033	5	96038	4	96042	5
913	96047	5	96052	5	96057	4	96061	5	96066	5	96071	5	96076	4	96080	5	96085	5	96090	5
914	96095	4	96099	5	96104	5	96109	5	96114	4	96118	5	96123	5	96128	5	96133	4	96137	5
915	96142	5	96147	5	96152	4	96156	5	96161	5	96166	5	96171	4	96175	5	96180	5	96185	5
916	96190	4	96194	5	96199	5	96204	5	96209	4	96213	5	96218	5	96223	4	96227	5	96232	5
917	96237	5	96242	4	96246	5	96251	5	96256	5	96261	4	96265	5	96270	5	96275	5	96280	4
918	96284	5	96289	5	96294	4	96298	5	96303	5	96308	5	96313	4	96317	5	96322	5	96327	5
919	96332	4	96336	5	96341	5	96346	4	96350	5	96355	5	96360	5	96365	4	96369	5	96374	5
920	96379	5	96384	4	96388	5	96393	5	96398	4	96402	5	96407	5	96412	5	96417	4	96421	5
921	96426	5	96431	4	96435	5	96440	5	96445	5	96450	4	96454	5	96459	5	96464	4	96468	5
922	96473	5	96478	5	96483	4	96487	5	96492	5	96497	4	96501	5	96506	5	96511	4	96515	5
923	96520	5	96525	5	96530	4	96534	5	96539	5	96544	4	96548	5	96553	5	96558	4	96562	5
924	96567	5	96572	5	96577	4	96581	5	96586	5	96591	4	96595	5	96600	5	96605	4	96609	5
925	96614	5	96619	5	96624	4	96628	5	96633	5	96638	4	96642	5	96647	5	96652	4	96656	5
926	96661	5	96666	4	96670	5	96675	5	96680	5	96685	4	96689	5	96694	5	96699	4	96703	5
927	96708	5	96713	4	96717	5	96722	5	96727	4	96731	5	96736	5	96741	4	96745	5	96750	5
928	96755	4	96759	5	96764	5	96769	5	96774	4	96778	5	96783	5	96788	4	96792	5	96797	5
929	96802	4	96806	5	96811	5	96816	4	96820	5	96825	5	96830	4	96834	5	96839	5	96844	4
930	96848	5	96853	5	96858	4	96862	5	96867	5	96872	4	96876	5	96881	5	96886	4	96890	5
931	96895	5	96900	4	96904	5	96909	5	96914	4	96918	5	96923	5	96928	4	96932	5	96937	5
932	96942	4	96946	5	96951	5	96956	4	96960	5	96965	5	96970	4	96974	5	96979	5	96984	4
933	96988	5	96993	4	96997	5	97002	5	97007	4	97011	5	97016	5	97021	4	97025	5	97030	5
934	97035	4	97039	5	97044	5	97049	4	97053	5	97058	5	97063	4	97067	5	97072	5	97077	4
935	97081	5	97086	4	97090	5	97095	5	97100	4	97104	5	97109	5	97114	4	97118	5	97123	5
936	97128	4	97132	5	97137	5	97142	4	97146	5	97151	4	97155	5	97160	5	97165	4	97169	5
937	97174	5	97179	4	97183	5	97188	4	97192	5	97197	5	97202	4	97206	5	97211	5	97216	4
938	97220	5	97225	5	97230	4	97234	5	97239	4	97243	5	97248	5	97253	4	97257	5	97262	5
939	97267	4	97271	5	97276	4	97280	5	97285	5	97290	4	97294	5	97299	5	97304	4	97308	5
940	97313	4	97317	5	97322	5	97327	4	97331	5	97336	4	97340	5	97345	5	97350	4	97354	5
941	97359	5	97364	4	97368	5	97373	4	97377	5	97382	5	97387	4	97391	5	97396	4	97400	5
942	97405	5	97410	4	97414	5	97419	5	97424	4	97428	5	97433	4	97437	5	97442	5	97447	4
943	97451	5	97456	4	97460	5	97465	5	97470	4	97474	5	97479	4	97483	5	97488	5	97493	4
944	97497	5	97502	4	97506	5	97511	5	97516	4	97520	5	97525	4	97529	5	97534	5	97539	4
945	97543	5	97548	4	97552	5	97557	5	97562	4	97566	5	97571	4	97575	5	97580	5	97585	4
946	97589	5	97594	4	97598	5	97603	4	97607	5	97612	5	97617	4	97621	5	97626	4	97630	5
947	97635	5	97640	4	97644	5	97649	4	97653	5	97658	5	97663	4	97667	5	97672	4	97676	5
948	97681	4	97685	5	97690	5	97695	4	97699	5	97704	4	97708	5	97713	4	97717	5	97722	5
949	97727	4	97731	5	97736	4	97740	5	97745	4	97749	5	97754	5	97759	4	97763	5	97768	4
950	97772	5	97777	5	97782	4	97786	5	97791	4	97795	5	97800	4	97804	5	97809	4	97813	5
No.	0	d	1	d	2	d	3	d	4	d	5	d	6	d	7	d	8	d	9	d

Prop. parts

	5
1	0
2	1
3	2
4	2
5	2
6	3
7	4
8	4
9	4

	4
1	0
2	1
3	1
4	2
5	2
6	2
7	3
8	3
9	4

TABLE 1
Logarithms of Numbers

9500–10000

No.	0	d	1	d	2	d	3	d	4	d	5	d	6	d	7	d	8	d	9	d
950	97772	5	97777	5	97782	4	97786	5	97791	4	97795	5	97800	4	97804	5	97809	4	97813	5
951	97818	5	97823	4	97827	5	97832	4	97836	5	97841	4	97845	5	97850	5	97855	4	97859	5
952	97864	4	97868	5	97873	4	97877	5	97882	4	97886	5	97891	5	97896	4	97900	5	97905	4
953	97909	5	97914	4	97918	5	97923	5	97928	4	97932	5	97937	4	97941	5	97946	4	97950	5
954	97955	4	97959	5	97964	4	97968	5	97973	5	97978	4	97982	5	97987	4	97991	5	97996	4
955	98000	5	98005	4	98009	5	98014	5	98019	4	98023	5	98028	4	98032	5	98037	4	98041	5
956	98046	4	98050	5	98055	4	98059	5	98064	4	98068	5	98073	5	98078	4	98082	5	98087	4
957	98091	5	98096	4	98100	5	98105	4	98109	5	98114	4	98118	5	98123	4	98127	5	98132	5
958	98137	4	98141	5	98146	4	98150	5	98155	4	98159	5	98164	4	98168	5	98173	4	98177	5
959	98182	4	98186	5	98191	4	98195	5	98200	4	98204	5	98209	5	98214	4	98218	5	98223	4
960	98227	5	98232	4	98236	5	98241	4	98245	5	98250	4	98254	5	98259	4	98263	5	98268	4
961	98272	5	98277	4	98281	5	98286	4	98290	5	98295	4	98299	5	98304	4	98308	5	98313	5
962	98318	4	98322	5	98327	4	98331	5	98336	4	98340	5	98345	4	98349	5	98354	4	98358	5
963	98363	4	98367	5	98372	4	98376	5	98381	4	98385	5	98390	4	98394	5	98399	4	98403	5
964	98408	4	98412	5	98417	4	98421	5	98426	4	98430	5	98435	4	98439	5	98444	4	98448	5
965	98453	4	98457	5	98462	4	98466	5	98471	4	98475	5	98480	4	98484	5	98489	4	98493	5
966	98498	4	98502	5	98507	4	98511	5	98516	4	98520	5	98525	4	98529	5	98534	4	98538	5
967	98543	4	98547	5	98552	4	98556	5	98561	4	98565	5	98570	4	98574	5	98579	4	98583	5
968	98588	4	98592	5	98597	4	98601	4	98605	5	98610	4	98614	5	98619	4	98623	5	98628	4
969	98632	5	98637	4	98641	5	98646	4	98650	5	98655	4	98659	5	98664	4	98668	5	98673	4
970	98677	5	98682	4	98686	5	98691	4	98695	5	98700	4	98704	5	98709	4	98713	4	98717	5
971	98722	4	98726	5	98731	4	98735	5	98740	4	98744	5	98749	4	98753	5	98758	4	98762	5
972	98767	4	98771	5	98776	4	98780	4	98784	5	98789	4	98793	5	98798	4	98802	5	98807	4
973	98811	5	98816	4	98820	5	98825	4	98829	5	98834	4	98838	5	98843	4	98847	4	98851	5
974	98856	4	98860	5	98865	4	98869	5	98874	4	98878	5	98883	4	98887	5	98892	4	98896	4
975	98900	5	98905	4	98909	5	98914	4	98918	5	98923	4	98927	5	98932	4	98936	5	98941	4
976	98945	4	98949	5	98954	4	98958	5	98963	4	98967	5	98972	4	98976	5	98981	4	98985	4
977	98989	5	98994	4	98998	5	99003	4	99007	5	99012	4	99016	5	99021	4	99025	4	99029	5
978	99034	4	99038	5	99043	4	99047	5	99052	4	99056	5	99061	4	99065	4	99069	5	99074	4
979	99078	5	99083	4	99087	5	99092	4	99096	4	99100	5	99105	4	99109	5	99114	4	99118	5
980	99123	4	99127	4	99131	5	99136	4	99140	5	99145	4	99149	5	99154	4	99158	4	99162	5
981	99167	4	99171	5	99176	4	99180	5	99185	4	99189	4	99193	5	99198	4	99202	5	99207	4
982	99211	5	99216	4	99220	4	99224	5	99229	4	99233	5	99238	4	99242	5	99247	4	99251	4
983	99255	5	99260	4	99264	5	99269	4	99273	4	99277	5	99282	4	99286	5	99291	4	99295	5
984	99300	4	99304	4	99308	5	99313	4	99317	5	99322	4	99326	4	99330	5	99335	4	99339	5
985	99344	4	99348	4	99352	5	99357	4	99361	5	99366	4	99370	4	99374	5	99379	4	99383	5
986	99388	4	99392	4	99396	5	99401	4	99405	5	99410	4	99414	5	99419	4	99423	4	99427	5
987	99432	4	99436	5	99441	4	99445	4	99449	5	99454	4	99458	5	99463	4	99467	4	99471	5
988	99476	4	99480	4	99484	5	99489	4	99493	5	99498	4	99502	4	99506	5	99511	4	99515	5
989	99520	4	99524	4	99528	5	99533	4	99537	5	99542	4	99546	4	99550	5	99555	4	99559	5
990	99564	4	99568	4	99572	5	99577	4	99581	4	99585	5	99590	4	99594	5	99599	4	99603	4
991	99607	5	99612	4	99616	5	99621	4	99625	4	99629	5	99634	4	99638	4	99642	5	99647	4
992	99651	5	99656	4	99660	4	99664	5	99669	4	99673	4	99677	5	99682	4	99686	5	99691	4
993	99695	4	99699	5	99704	4	99708	4	99712	5	99717	4	99721	5	99726	4	99730	4	99734	5
994	99739	4	99743	4	99747	5	99752	4	99756	4	99760	5	99765	4	99769	5	99774	4	99778	4
995	99782	5	99787	4	99791	4	99795	5	99800	4	99804	4	99808	5	99813	4	99817	5	99822	4
996	99826	4	99830	5	99835	4	99839	4	99843	5	99848	4	99852	4	99856	5	99861	4	99865	5
997	99870	4	99874	4	99878	5	99883	4	99887	4	99891	5	99896	4	99900	4	99904	5	99909	4
998	99913	4	99917	5	99922	4	99926	4	99930	5	99935	4	99939	5	99944	4	99948	4	99952	5
999	99957	4	99961	4	99965	5	99970	4	99974	4	99978	5	99983	4	99987	4	99991	5	99996	4
1000	00000	4	00004	5	00009	4	00013	4	00017	5	00022	4	00026	4	00030	5	00035	4	00039	4
No.	0	d	1	d	2	d	3	d	4	d	5	d	6	d	7	d	8	d	9	d

Prop. parts

	5
1	0
2	1
3	2
4	2
5	2
6	3
7	4
8	4
9	4

	4
1	0
2	1
3	1
4	2
5	2
6	2
7	3
8	3
9	4

TABLE 2

Natural Trigonometric Functions

0° → ↓ ′	sin	Diff. 1′	csc	Diff. 1′	tan	Diff. 1′	cot	Diff. 1′	sec	Diff. 1′	cos	Diff. 1′	← 179° ↓ ′
0	0.00000		∞		0.00000		∞		1.00000		1.00000		60
1	.00029	29	3437.75	— —	.00029	29	3437.75	— —	.00000	0	.00000	0	59
2	.00058	29	1718.87	1718.88	.00058	29	1718.87	1718.88	.00000	0	.00000	0	58
3	.00087	29	1145.92	572.958	.00087	29	1145.92	572.958	.00000	0	.00000	0	57
4	.00116	29	859.437	286.479	.00116	29	859.436	286.479	.00000	0	.00000	0	56
5	0.00145	29	687.550	171.887	0.00145	29	687.549	171.887	1.00000	0	1.00000	0	55
6	.00175	30	572.958	114.592	.00175	30	572.957	114.592	.00000	0	.00000	0	54
7	.00204	29	491.107	81.851	.00204	29	491.106	81.851	.00000	0	.00000	0	53
8	.00233	29	429.719	61.388	.00233	29	429.718	61.388	.00000	0	.00000	0	52
9	.00262	29	381.972	47.746	.00262	29	381.971	47.747	.00000	0	.00000	0	51
10	0.00291	29	343.775	38.197	0.00291	29	343.774	38.197	1.00000	0	1.00000	0	50
11	.00320	29	312.523	31.252	.00320	29	312.521	31.252	.00001	1	.99999	1	49
12	.00349	29	286.479	26.043	.00349	29	286.478	26.044	.00001	0	.99999	0	48
13	.00378	29	264.443	22.037	.00378	29	264.441	22.037	.00001	0	.99999	0	47
14	.00407	29	245.554	18.889	.00407	29	245.552	18.889	.00001	0	.99999	0	46
15	0.00436	29	229.184	16.370	0.00436	29	229.182	16.370	1.00001	0	0.99999	0	45
16	.00465	29	214.860	14.324	.00465	29	214.858	14.324	.00001	0	.99999	0	44
17	.00495	30	202.221	12.639	.00495	30	202.219	12.639	.00001	0	.99999	0	43
18	.00524	29	190.987	11.234	.00524	29	190.984	11.235	.00001	0	.99999	0	42
19	.00553	29	180.935	10.052	.00553	29	180.932	10.052	.00002	1	.99998	1	41
20	0.00582	29	171.888	9.047	0.00582	29	171.885	9.047	1.00002	0	0.99998	0	40
21	.00611	29	163.703	8.185	.00611	29	163.700	8.185	.00002	0	.99998	0	39
22	.00640	29	156.262	7.441	.00640	29	156.259	7.441	.00002	0	.99998	0	38
23	.00669	29	149.468	6.794	.00669	29	149.465	6.794	.00002	0	.99998	0	37
24	.00698	29	143.241	6.228	.00698	29	143.237	6.228	.00002	0	.99998	0	36
25	0.00727	29	137.511	5.730	0.00727	29	137.507	5.730	1.00003	1	0.99997	1	35
26	.00756	29	132.222	5.289	.00756	29	132.219	5.289	.00003	0	.99997	0	34
27	.00785	29	127.325	4.897	.00785	29	127.321	4.897	.00003	0	.99997	0	33
28	.00814	29	122.778	4.547	.00815	30	122.774	4.547	.00003	0	.99997	0	32
29	.00844	30	118.544	4.234	.00844	29	118.540	4.234	.00004	1	.99996	1	31
30	0.00873	29	114.593	3.951	0.00873	29	114.589	3.952	1.00004	0	0.99996	0	30
31	.00902	29	110.897	3.696	.00902	29	110.892	3.697	.00004	0	.99996	0	29
32	.00931	29	107.431	3.465	.00931	29	107.426	3.466	.00004	0	.99996	0	28
33	.00960	29	104.176	3.255	.00960	29	104.171	3.256	.00005	1	.99995	1	27
34	.00989	29	101.112	3.064	.00989	29	101.107	3.064	.00005	0	.99995	0	26
35	0.01018	29	98.2230	2.8888	0.01018	29	98.2179	2.8890	1.00005	0	0.99995	0	25
36	.01047	29	95.4947	2.7283	.01047	29	95.4895	2.7285	.00005	0	.99995	0	24
37	.01076	29	92.9139	2.5808	.01076	29	92.9085	2.5810	.00006	1	.99994	1	23
38	.01105	29	90.4689	2.4450	.01105	29	90.4633	2.4452	.00006	0	.99994	0	22
39	.01134	29	88.1492	2.3196	.01135	30	88.1436	2.3198	.00006	0	.99994	0	21
40	0.01164	30	85.9456	2.2036	0.01164	29	85.9398	2.2038	1.00007	1	0.99993	1	20
41	.01193	29	83.8495	2.0961	.01193	29	83.8435	2.0963	.00007	0	.99993	0	19
42	.01222	29	81.8531	1.9963	.01222	29	81.8470	1.9965	.00007	0	.99993	0	18
43	.01251	29	79.9497	1.9035	.01251	29	79.9434	1.9036	.00008	1	.99992	1	17
44	.01280	29	78.1327	1.8169	.01280	29	78.1263	1.8171	.00008	0	.99992	0	16
45	0.01309	29	76.3966	1.7362	0.01309	29	76.3900	1.7363	1.00009	1	0.99991	1	15
46	.01338	29	74.7359	1.6607	.01338	29	74.7292	1.6608	.00009	0	.99991	0	14
47	.01367	29	73.1458	1.5900	.01367	29	73.1390	1.5902	.00009	0	.99991	0	13
48	.01396	29	71.6221	1.5238	.01396	29	71.6151	1.5239	.00010	1	.99990	1	12
49	.01425	29	70.1605	1.4616	.01425	29	70.1533	1.4617	.00010	0	.99990	0	11
50	0.01454	29	68.7574	1.4031	0.01455	30	68.7501	1.4033	1.00011	1	0.99989	1	10
51	.01483	29	67.4093	1.3481	.01484	29	67.4019	1.3482	.00011	0	.99989	0	9
52	.01513	30	66.1130	1.2962	.01513	29	66.1055	1.2964	.00011	0	.99989	0	8
53	.01542	29	64.8657	1.2473	.01542	29	64.8580	1.2475	.00012	1	.99988	1	7
54	.01571	29	63.6646	1.2011	.01571	29	63.6567	1.2013	.00012	0	.99988	0	6
55	0.01600	29	62.5072	1.1574	0.01600	29	62.4992	1.1576	1.00013	1	0.99987	1	5
56	.01629	29	61.3911	1.1161	.01629	29	61.3829	1.1162	.00013	0	.99987	0	4
57	.01658	29	60.3141	1.0769	.01658	29	60.3058	1.0771	.00014	1	.99986	1	3
58	.01687	29	59.2743	1.0398	.01687	29	59.2659	1.0399	.00014	0	.99986	0	2
59	.01716	29	58.2698	1.0046	.01716	29	58.2612	1.0047	.00015	1	.99985	1	1
60	0.01745	29	57.2987	0.9711	0.01746	30	57.2900	0.9712	1.00015	0	0.99985	0	0
↑ 90° →	cos	Diff. 1′	sec	Diff. 1′	cot	Diff. 1′	tan	Diff. 1′	csc	Diff. 1′	sin	Diff. 1′ ← 89°	↑

TABLE 2

Natural Trigonometric Functions

1° → ↓ ′	sin	Diff. 1′	csc	Diff. 1′	tan	Diff. 1′	cot	Diff. 1′	sec	Diff. 1′	cos	Diff. 1′	← 178° ↓ ′
0	0.01745		57.2987		0.01746		57.2900		1.00015		0.99985		60
1	.01774	29	56.3595	9392	.01775	29	56.3506	9394	.00016	1	.99984	1	59
2	.01803	29	55.4505	9089	.01804	29	55.4415	9091	.00016	0	.99984	0	58
3	.01832	29	54.5705	8801	.01833	29	54.5613	8802	.00017	1	.99983	1	57
4	.01862	30	53.7179	8526	.01862	29	53.7086	8527	.00017	0	.99983	0	56
5	0.01891	29	52.8916	8263	0.01891	29	52.8821	8265	1.00018	1	0.99982	1	55
6	.01920	29	52.0903	8013	.01920	29	52.0807	8014	.00018	0	.99982	0	54
7	.01949	29	51.3129	7774	.01949	29	51.3032	7775	.00019	1	.99981	1	53
8	.01978	29	50.5584	7545	.01978	29	50.5485	7547	.00020	1	.99980	1	52
9	.02007	29	49.8258	7326	.02007	29	49.8157	7328	.00020	0	.99980	0	51
10	0.02036	29	49.1141	7117	0.02036	29	49.1039	7118	1.00021	1	0.99979	1	50
11	.02065	29	48.4224	6917	.02066	30	48.4121	6918	.00021	0	.99979	0	49
12	.02094	29	47.7500	6724	.02095	29	47.7395	6726	.00022	1	.99978	1	48
13	.02123	29	47.0960	6540	.02124	29	47.0853	6542	.00023	1	.99977	1	47
14	.02152	29	46.4596	6363	.02153	29	46.4489	6365	.00023	0	.99977	0	46
15	0.02181	29	45.8403	6194	0.02182	29	45.8294	6195	1.00024	1	0.99976	1	45
16	.02211	30	45.2372	6031	.02211	29	45.2261	6032	.00024	0	.99976	0	44
17	.02240	29	44.6498	5874	.02240	29	44.6386	5875	.00025	1	.99975	1	43
18	.02269	29	44.0775	5723	.02269	29	44.0661	5725	.00026	1	.99974	1	42
19	.02298	29	43.5196	5578	.02298	29	43.5081	5580	.00026	0	.99974	0	41
20	0.02327	29	42.9757	5439	0.02328	30	42.9641	5440	1.00027	1	0.99973	1	40
21	.02356	29	42.4452	5305	.02357	29	42.4335	5306	.00028	1	.99972	1	39
22	.02385	29	41.9277	5175	.02386	29	41.9158	5177	.00028	0	.99972	0	38
23	.02414	29	41.4227	5051	.02415	29	41.4106	5052	.00029	1	.99971	1	37
24	.02443	29	40.9296	4930	.02444	29	40.9174	4932	.00030	1	.99970	1	36
25	0.02472	29	40.4482	4814	0.02473	29	40.4358	4816	1.00031	1	0.99969	1	35
26	.02501	29	39.9780	4702	.02502	29	39.9655	4704	.00031	0	.99969	0	34
27	.02530	29	.5185	4594	.02531	29	.5059	4596	.00032	1	.99968	1	33
28	.02560	30	39.0696	4490	.02560	29	39.0568	4491	.00033	1	.99967	1	32
29	.02589	29	38.6307	4389	.02589	29	38.6177	4390	.00034	1	.99966	1	31
30	0.02618	29	38.2016	4291	0.02619	30	38.1885	4293	1.00034	0	0.99966	0	30
31	.02647	29	37.7818	4197	.02648	29	37.7686	4198	.00035	1	.99965	1	29
32	.02676	29	37.3713	4106	.02677	29	37.3579	4107	.00036	1	.99964	1	28
33	.02705	29	36.9695	4017	.02706	29	36.9560	4019	.00037	1	.99963	1	27
34	.02734	29	.5763	3932	.02735	29	.5627	3933	.00037	0	.99963	0	26
35	0.02763	29	36.1914	3849	0.02764	29	36.1776	3851	1.00038	1	0.99962	1	25
36	.02792	29	35.8145	3769	.02793	29	35.8006	3770	.00039	1	.99961	1	24
37	.02821	29	.4454	3691	.02822	29	.4313	3693	.00040	1	.99960	1	23
38	.02850	29	35.0838	3616	.02851	29	35.0695	3617	.00041	1	.99959	1	22
39	.02879	29	34.7295	3543	.02881	30	34.7151	3544	.00041	0	.99959	0	21
40	0.02908	29	34.3823	3472	0.02910	29	34.3678	3473	1.00042	1	0.99958	1	20
41	.02938	30	34.0420	3403	.02939	29	34.0273	3405	.00043	1	.99957	1	19
42	.02967	29	33.7083	3336	.02968	29	33.6935	3338	.00044	1	.99956	1	18
43	.02996	29	.3812	3272	.02997	29	.3662	3273	.00045	1	.99955	1	17
44	.03025	29	33.0603	3209	.03026	29	33.0452	3210	.00046	1	.99954	1	16
45	0.03054	29	32.7455	3148	0.03055	29	32.7303	3149	1.00047	1	0.99953	1	15
46	.03083	29	.4367	3088	.03084	29	.4213	3090	.00048	1	.99952	1	14
47	.03112	29	32.1337	3031	.03114	30	32.1181	3032	.00048	0	.99952	0	13
48	.03141	29	31.8362	2974	.03143	29	31.8205	2976	.00049	1	.99951	1	12
49	.03170	29	.5442	2920	.03172	29	.5284	2921	.00050	1	.99950	1	11
50	0.03199	29	31.2576	2867	0.03201	29	31.2416	2868	1.00051	1	0.99949	1	10
51	.03228	29	30.9761	2815	.03230	29	30.9599	2816	.00052	1	.99948	1	9
52	.03257	29	.6996	2765	.03259	29	.6833	2766	.00053	1	.99947	1	8
53	.03286	29	.4280	2716	.03288	29	.4116	2717	.00054	1	.99946	1	7
54	.03316	30	30.1612	2668	.03317	29	30.1446	2670	.00055	1	.99945	1	6
55	0.03345	29	29.8990	2622	0.03346	29	29.8823	2623	1.00056	1	0.99944	1	5
56	.03374	29	.6414	2577	.03376	30	.6245	2578	.00057	1	.99943	1	4
57	.03403	29	.3881	2532	.03405	29	.3711	2534	.00058	1	.99942	1	3
58	.03432	29	29.1392	2490	.03434	29	29.1220	2491	.00059	1	.99941	1	2
59	.03461	29	28.8944	2448	.03463	29	28.8771	2449	.00060	1	.99940	1	1
60	0.03490	29	28.6537	2407	0.03492	29	28.6363	2408	1.00061	1	0.99939	1	0
↑ 91° →	cos	Diff. 1′	sec	Diff. 1′	cot	Diff. 1′	tan	Diff. 1′	csc	Diff. 1′	sin	Diff. 1′ ← 88°	↑

TABLE 2
Natural Trigonometric Functions

2° → ′	sin	Diff. 1′	csc	Diff. 1′	tan	Diff. 1′	cot	Diff. 1′	sec	Diff. 1′	cos	Diff. 1′	← 177° ′
0	0.03490		28.6537		0.03492		28.6363		1.00061		0.99939		60
1	.03519	29	.4170	2367	.03521	29	.3994	2369	.00062	1	.99938	1	59
2	.03548	29	28.1842	2328	.03550	29	28.1664	2330	.00063	1	.99937	1	58
3	.03577	29	27.9551	2290	.03579	29	27.9372	2292	.00064	1	.99936	1	57
4	.03606	29	.7298	2253	.03609	30	.7117	2255	.00065	1	.99935	1	56
5	0.03635	29	27.5080	2217	0.03638	29	27.4899	2219	1.00066	1	0.99934	1	55
6	.03664	29	.2898	2182	.03667	29	.2715	2184	.00067	1	.99933	1	54
7	.03693	29	27.0750	2148	.03696	29	27.0566	2149	.00068	1	.99932	1	53
8	.03723	30	26.8636	2114	.03725	29	26.8450	2116	.00069	1	.99931	1	52
9	.03752	29	.6555	2081	.03754	29	.6367	2083	.00070	1	.99930	1	51
10	0.03781	29	26.4505	2049	0.03783	29	26.4316	2051	1.00072	2	0.99929	1	50
11	.03810	29	.2487	2018	.03812	29	.2296	2020	.00073	1	.99927	2	49
12	.03839	29	26.0499	1988	.03842	30	26.0307	1989	.00074	1	.99926	1	48
13	.03868	29	25.8542	1958	.03871	29	25.8348	1959	.00075	1	.99925	1	47
14	.03897	29	.6613	1928	.03900	29	.6418	1930	.00076	1	.99924	1	46
15	0.03926	29	25.4713	1900	0.03929	29	25.4517	1901	1.00077	1	0.99923	1	45
16	.03955	29	.2841	1872	.03958	29	.2644	1873	.00078	1	.99922	1	44
17	.03984	29	25.0997	1845	.03987	29	25.0798	1846	.00079	1	.99921	1	43
18	.04013	29	24.9179	1818	.04016	29	24.8978	1819	.00081	2	.99919	2	42
19	.04042	29	.7387	1792	.04046	30	.7185	1793	.00082	1	.99918	1	41
20	0.04071	29	24.5621	1766	0.04075	29	24.5418	1768	1.00083	1	0.99917	1	40
21	.04100	29	.3880	1741	.04104	29	.3675	1742	.00084	1	.99916	1	39
22	.04129	29	.2164	1716	.04133	29	.1957	1718	.00085	1	.99915	1	38
23	.04159	30	24.0471	1692	.04162	29	24.0263	1694	.00087	2	.99913	2	37
24	.04188	29	23.8802	1669	.04191	29	23.8593	1670	.00088	1	.99912	1	36
25	0.04217	29	23.7156	1646	0.04220	29	23.6945	1647	1.00089	1	0.99911	1	35
26	.04246	29	.5533	1623	.04250	30	.5321	1625	.00090	1	.99910	1	34
27	.04275	29	.3932	1601	.04279	29	.3718	1603	.00091	1	.99909	1	33
28	.04304	29	.2352	1580	.04308	29	.2137	1581	.00093	2	.99907	2	32
29	.04333	29	23.0794	1558	.04337	29	23.0577	1560	.00094	1	.99906	1	31
30	0.04362	29	22.9256	1538	0.04366	29	22.9038	1539	1.00095	1	0.99905	1	30
31	.04391	29	.7739	1517	.04395	29	.7519	1519	.00097	2	.99904	1	29
32	.04420	29	.6241	1497	.04424	29	.6020	1499	.00098	1	.99902	2	28
33	.04449	29	.4764	1478	.04454	30	.4541	1479	.00099	1	.99901	1	27
34	.04478	29	.3305	1459	.04483	29	.3081	1460	.00100	1	.99900	1	26
35	0.04507	29	22.1865	1440	0.04512	29	22.1640	1441	1.00102	2	0.99898	2	25
36	.04536	29	22.0444	1421	.04541	29	22.0217	1423	.00103	1	.99897	1	24
37	.04565	29	21.9041	1403	.04570	29	21.8813	1405	.00104	1	.99896	1	23
38	.04594	29	.7656	1385	.04599	29	.7426	1387	.00106	2	.99894	2	22
39	.04623	29	.6288	1368	.04628	29	.6056	1369	.00107	1	.99893	1	21
40	0.04653	30	21.4937	1351	0.04658	30	21.4704	1352	1.00108	1	0.99892	1	20
41	.04682	29	.3603	1334	.04687	29	.3369	1335	.00110	2	.99890	2	19
42	.04711	29	.2285	1318	.04716	29	.2049	1319	.00111	1	.99889	1	18
43	.04740	29	21.0984	1301	.04745	29	21.0747	1303	.00113	2	.99888	1	17
44	.04769	29	20.9698	1286	.04774	29	20.9460	1287	.00114	1	.99886	2	16
45	0.04798	29	20.8428	1270	0.04803	29	20.8188	1271	1.00115	1	0.99885	1	15
46	.04827	29	.7174	1255	.04833	30	.6932	1256	.00117	2	.99883	2	14
47	.04856	29	.5934	1240	.04862	29	.5691	1241	.00118	1	.99882	1	13
48	.04885	29	.4709	1225	.04891	29	.4465	1226	.00120	2	.99881	1	12
49	.04914	29	.3499	1210	.04920	29	.3253	1212	.00121	1	.99879	2	11
50	0.04943	29	20.2303	1196	0.04949	29	20.2056	1198	1.00122	1	0.99878	1	10
51	.04972	29	20.1121	1182	.04978	29	20.0872	1184	.00124	2	.99876	2	9
52	.05001	29	19.9952	1168	.05007	29	19.9702	1170	.00125	1	.99875	1	8
53	.05030	29	.8798	1155	.05037	30	.8546	1156	.00127	2	.99873	2	7
54	.05059	29	.7656	1142	.05066	29	.7403	1143	.00128	1	.99872	1	6
55	0.05088	29	19.6528	1128	0.05095	29	19.6273	1130	1.00130	2	0.99870	2	5
56	.05117	29	.5412	1116	.05124	29	.5156	1117	.00131	1	.99869	1	4
57	.05146	29	.4309	1103	.05153	29	.4051	1105	.00133	2	.99867	2	3
58	.05175	29	.3218	1091	.05182	29	.2959	1092	.00134	1	.99866	1	2
59	.05205	30	.2140	1078	.05212	30	.1879	1080	.00136	2	.99864	2	1
60	0.05234	29	19.1073	1066	0.05241	29	19.0811	1068	1.00137	1	0.99863	1	0
92° →	cos	Diff. 1′	sec	Diff. 1′	cot	Diff. 1′	tan	Diff. 1′	csc	Diff. 1′	sin	Diff. 1′	← 87°

TABLE 2
Natural Trigonometric Functions

3° → ′	sin	Diff. 1′	csc	Diff. 1′	tan	Diff. 1′	cot	Diff. 1′	sec	Diff. 1′	cos	Diff. 1′	← 176° ′
0	0.05234		19.1073		0.05241		19.0811		1.00137		0.99863		60
1	.05263	29	19.0019	1055	.05270	29	18.9755	1056	.00139	2	.99861	2	59
2	.05292	29	18.8975	1043	.05299	29	.8711	1045	.00140	1	.99860	1	58
3	.05321	29	.7944	1032	.05328	29	.7678	1033	.00142	2	.99858	2	57
4	.05350	29	.6923	1020	.05357	29	.6656	1022	.00143	1	.99857	1	56
5	0.05379	29	18.5914	1009	0.05387	30	18.5645	1011	1.00145	2	0.99855	2	55
6	.05408	29	.4915	999	.05416	29	.4645	1000	.00147	2	.99854	1	54
7	.05437	29	.3927	988	.05445	29	.3655	989	.00148	1	.99852	2	53
8	.05466	29	.2950	977	.05474	29	.2677	979	.00150	2	.99851	1	52
9	.05495	29	.1983	967	.05503	29	.1708	968	.00151	1	.99849	2	51
10	0.05524	29	18.1026	957	0.05533	30	18.0750	958	1.00153	2	0.99847	2	50
11	.05553	29	18.0079	947	.05562	29	17.9802	948	.00155	2	.99846	1	49
12	.05582	29	17.9142	937	.05591	29	.8863	938	.00156	1	.99844	2	48
13	.05611	29	.8215	927	.05620	29	.7934	929	.00158	2	.99842	2	47
14	.05640	29	.7298	918	.05649	29	.7015	919	.00159	1	.99841	1	46
15	0.05669	29	17.6389	908	0.05678	29	17.6106	910	1.00161	2	0.99839	2	45
16	.05698	29	.5490	899	.05708	30	.5205	900	.00163	2	.99838	1	44
17	.05727	29	.4600	890	.05737	29	.4314	891	.00164	1	.99836	2	43
18	.05756	29	.3720	881	.05766	29	.3432	882	.00166	2	.99834	2	42
19	.05785	29	.2848	872	.05795	29	.2558	873	.00168	2	.99833	1	41
20	0.05814	29	17.1984	863	0.05824	29	17.1693	865	1.00169	1	0.99831	2	40
21	.05844	30	.1130	855	.05854	30	17.0837	856	.00171	2	.99829	2	39
22	.05873	29	17.0283	846	.05883	29	16.9990	848	.00173	2	.99827	2	38
23	.05902	29	16.9446	838	.05912	29	.9150	839	.00175	2	.99826	1	37
24	.05931	29	.8616	830	.05941	29	.8319	831	.00176	1	.99824	2	36
25	0.05960	29	16.7794	822	0.05970	29	16.7496	823	1.00178	2	0.99822	2	35
26	.05989	29	.6981	814	.05999	29	.6681	815	.00180	2	.99821	1	34
27	.06018	29	.6175	806	.06029	30	.5874	807	.00182	2	.99819	2	33
28	.06047	29	.5377	798	.06058	29	.5075	799	.00183	1	.99817	2	32
29	.06076	29	.4587	790	.06087	29	.4283	792	.00185	2	.99815	2	31
30	0.06105	29	16.3804	783	0.06116	29	16.3499	784	1.00187	2	0.99813	2	30
31	.06134	29	.3029	775	.06145	29	.2722	777	.00189	2	.99812	1	29
32	.06163	29	.2261	768	.06175	30	.1952	769	.00190	1	.99810	2	28
33	.06192	29	.1500	761	.06204	29	.1190	762	.00192	2	.99808	2	27
34	.06221	29	16.0746	754	.06233	29	16.0435	755	.00194	2	.99806	2	26
35	0.06250	29	15.9999	747	0.06262	29	15.9687	748	1.00196	2	0.99804	2	25
36	.06279	29	.9260	740	.06291	29	.8945	741	.00198	2	.99803	1	24
37	.06308	29	.8527	733	.06321	30	.8211	734	.00200	2	.99801	2	23
38	.06337	29	.7801	726	.06350	29	.7483	728	.00201	1	.99799	2	22
39	.06366	29	.7081	720	.06379	29	.6762	721	.00203	2	.99797	2	21
40	0.06395	29	15.6368	713	0.06408	29	15.6048	714	1.00205	2	0.99795	2	20
41	.06424	29	.5661	707	.06437	29	.5340	708	.00207	2	.99793	2	19
42	.06453	29	.4961	700	.06467	30	.4638	702	.00209	2	.99792	1	18
43	.06482	29	.4267	694	.06496	29	.3943	695	.00211	2	.99790	2	17
44	.06511	29	.3579	688	.06525	29	.3254	689	.00213	2	.99788	2	16
45	0.06540	29	15.2898	682	0.06554	29	15.2571	683	1.00215	2	0.99786	2	15
46	.06569	29	.2222	676	.06584	30	.1893	677	.00216	1	.99784	2	14
47	.06598	29	.1553	670	.06613	29	.1222	671	.00218	2	.99782	2	13
48	.06627	29	.0889	664	.06642	29	15.0557	665	.00220	2	.99780	2	12
49	.06656	29	15.0231	658	.06671	29	14.9898	659	.00222	2	.99778	2	11
50	0.06685	29	14.9579	652	0.06700	29	14.9244	654	1.00224	2	0.99776	2	10
51	.06714	29	.8932	647	.06730	30	.8596	648	.00226	2	.99774	2	9
52	.06743	29	.8291	641	.06759	29	.7954	642	.00228	2	.99772	2	8
53	.06773	30	.7656	635	.06788	29	.7317	637	.00230	2	.99770	2	7
54	.06802	29	.7026	630	.06817	29	.6685	631	.00232	2	.99768	2	6
55	0.06831	29	14.6401	625	0.06847	30	14.6059	626	1.00234	2	0.99766	2	5
56	.06860	29	.5782	619	.06876	29	.5438	621	.00236	2	.99764	2	4
57	.06889	29	.5168	614	.06905	29	.4823	616	.00238	2	.99762	2	3
58	.06918	29	.4559	609	.06934	29	.4212	610	.00240	2	.99760	2	2
59	.06947	29	.3955	604	.06963	29	.3607	605	.00242	2	.99758	2	1
60	0.06976	29	14.3356	599	0.06993	30	14.3007	600	1.00244	2	0.99756	2	0
93° →	cos	Diff. 1′	sec	Diff. 1′	cot	Diff. 1′	tan	Diff. 1′	csc	Diff. 1′	sin	Diff. 1′	← 86°

TABLE 2
Natural Trigonometric Functions

4°→ ↓ ′	sin	Diff. 1′	csc	Diff. 1′	tan	Diff. 1′	cot	Diff. 1′	sec	Diff. 1′	cos	Diff. 1′	← 175° ↓ ′
0	0.06976		14.3356		0.06993		14.3007		1.00244		0.99756		60
1	.07005	29	.2762	594	.07022	29	.2411	595	.00246	2	.99754	2	59
2	.07034	29	.2173	589	.07051	29	.1821	590	.00248	2	.99752	2	58
3	.07063	29	.1589	584	.07080	29	.1235	586	.00250	2	.99750	2	57
4	.07092	29	.1010	579	.07110	30	.0655	581	.00252	2	.99748	2	56
5	0.07121	29	14.0435	575	0.07139	29	14.0079	576	1.00254	2	0.99746	2	55
6	.07150	29	13.9865	570	.07168	29	13.9507	571	.00257	3	.99744	2	54
7	.07179	29	.9300	565	.07197	29	.8940	567	.00259	2	.99742	2	53
8	.07208	29	.8739	561	.07227	30	.8378	562	.00261	2	.99740	2	52
9	.07237	29	.8183	556	.07256	29	.7821	558	.00263	2	.99738	2	51
10	0.07266	29	13.7631	552	0.07285	29	13.7267	553	1.00265	2	0.99736	2	50
11	.07295	29	.7084	547	.07314	29	.6719	549	.00267	2	.99734	2	49
12	.07324	29	.6541	543	.07344	30	.6174	544	.00269	2	.99731	3	48
13	.07353	29	.6002	539	.07373	29	.5634	540	.00271	2	.99729	2	47
14	.07382	29	.5468	534	.07402	29	.5098	536	.00274	3	.99727	2	46
15	0.07411	29	13.4937	530	0.07431	29	13.4566	532	1.00276	2	0.99725	2	45
16	.07440	29	.4411	526	.07461	30	.4039	528	.00278	2	.99723	2	44
17	.07469	29	.3889	522	.07490	29	.3515	523	.00280	2	.99721	2	43
18	.07498	29	.3371	518	.07519	29	.2996	519	.00282	2	.99719	2	42
19	.07527	29	.2857	514	.07548	29	.2480	515	.00284	2	.99716	3	41
20	0.07556	29	13.2347	510	0.07578	30	13.1969	511	1.00287	3	0.99714	2	40
21	.07585	29	.1841	506	.07607	29	.1461	508	.00289	2	.99712	2	39
22	.07614	29	.1339	502	.07636	29	.0958	504	.00291	2	.99710	2	38
23	.07643	29	.0840	498	.07665	29	13.0458	500	.00293	2	.99708	2	37
24	.07672	29	13.0346	495	.07695	30	12.9962	496	.00296	3	.99705	3	36
25	0.07701	29	12.9855	491	0.07724	29	12.9469	492	1.00298	2	0.99703	2	35
26	.07730	29	.9368	487	.07753	29	.8981	489	.00300	2	.99701	2	34
27	.07759	29	.8884	484	.07782	29	.8496	485	.00302	2	.99699	2	33
28	.07788	29	.8404	480	.07812	30	.8014	481	.00305	3	.99696	3	32
29	.07817	29	.7928	476	.07841	29	.7536	478	.00307	2	.99694	2	31
30	0.07846	29	12.7455	473	0.07870	29	12.7062	474	1.00309	2	0.99692	2	30
31	.07875	29	.6986	469	.07899	29	.6591	471	.00312	3	.99689	3	29
32	.07904	29	.6520	466	.07929	30	.6124	467	.00314	2	.99687	2	28
33	.07933	29	.6057	462	.07958	29	.5660	464	.00316	2	.99685	2	27
34	.07962	29	.5598	459	.07987	29	.5199	461	.00318	2	.99683	2	26
35	0.07991	29	12.5142	456	0.08017	30	12.4742	457	1.00321	3	0.99680	3	25
36	.08020	29	.4690	452	.08046	29	.4288	454	.00323	2	.99678	2	24
37	.08049	29	.4241	449	.08075	29	.3838	451	.00326	3	.99676	2	23
38	.08078	29	.3795	446	.08104	29	.3390	447	.00328	2	.99673	3	22
39	.08107	29	.3352	443	.08134	30	.2946	444	.00330	2	.99671	2	21
40	0.08136	29	12.2913	440	0.08163	29	12.2505	441	1.00333	3	0.99668	3	20
41	.08165	29	.2476	436	.08192	29	.2067	438	.00335	2	.99666	2	19
42	.08194	29	.2043	433	.08221	29	.1632	435	.00337	2	.99664	2	18
43	.08223	29	.1612	430	.08251	30	.1201	432	.00340	3	.99661	3	17
44	.08252	29	.1185	427	.08280	29	.0772	429	.00342	2	.99659	2	16
45	0.08281	29	12.0761	424	0.08309	29	12.0346	426	1.00345	3	0.99657	2	15
46	.08310	29	12.0340	421	.08339	30	11.9923	423	.00347	2	.99654	3	14
47	.08339	29	11.9921	418	.08368	29	.9504	420	.00350	3	.99652	2	13
48	.08368	29	.9506	415	.08397	29	.9087	417	.00352	2	.99649	3	12
49	.08397	29	.9093	413	.08427	30	.8673	414	.00354	2	.99647	2	11
50	0.08426	29	11.8684	410	0.08456	29	11.8262	411	1.00357	3	0.99644	3	10
51	.08455	29	.8277	407	.08485	29	.7853	408	.00359	2	.99642	2	9
52	.08484	29	.7873	404	.08514	29	.7448	406	.00362	3	.99639	3	8
53	.08513	29	.7471	401	.08544	30	.7045	403	.00364	2	.99637	2	7
54	.08542	29	.7073	399	.08573	29	.6645	400	.00367	3	.99635	2	6
55	0.08571	29	11.6677	396	0.08602	29	11.6248	397	1.00369	2	0.99632	3	5
56	.08600	29	.6284	393	.08632	30	.5853	395	.00372	3	.99630	2	4
57	.08629	29	.5893	391	.08661	29	.5461	392	.00374	2	.99627	3	3
58	.08658	29	.5505	388	.08690	29	.5072	389	.00377	3	.99625	2	2
59	.08687	29	.5120	385	.08720	30	.4685	387	.00379	2	.99622	3	1
60	0.08716	29	11.4737	383	0.08749	29	11.4301	384	1.00382	3	0.99619	3	0
↑ 94°→	cos	Diff. 1′	sec	Diff. 1′	cot	Diff. 1′	tan	Diff. 1′	csc	Diff. 1′	sin	Diff. 1′	↑ ←85°

TABLE 2
Natural Trigonometric Functions

5°→ ↓ ′	sin	Diff. 1′	csc	Diff. 1′	tan	Diff. 1′	cot	Diff. 1′	sec	Diff. 1′	cos	Diff. 1′	← 174° ↓ ′
0	0.08716		11.4737		0.08749		11.4301		1.00382		0.99619		60
1	.08745	29	.4357	380	.08778	29	.3919	382	.00385	3	.99617	2	59
2	.08774	29	.3979	378	.08807	29	.3540	379	.00387	2	.99614	3	58
3	.08803	29	.3604	375	.08837	30	.3163	377	.00390	3	.99612	2	57
4	.08831	28	.3231	373	.08866	29	.2789	374	.00392	2	.99609	3	56
5	0.08860	29	11.2861	370	0.08895	29	11.2417	372	1.00395	3	0.99607	2	55
6	.08889	29	.2493	368	.08925	30	.2048	369	.00397	2	.99604	3	54
7	.08918	29	.2128	365	.08954	29	.1681	367	.00400	3	.99602	2	53
8	.08947	29	.1765	363	.08983	29	.1316	365	.00403	3	.99599	3	52
9	.08976	29	.1404	361	.09013	30	.0954	362	.00405	2	.99596	3	51
10	0.09005	29	11.1045	358	0.09042	29	11.0594	360	1.00408	3	0.99594	2	50
11	.09034	29	.0689	356	.09071	29	11.0237	358	.00411	3	.99591	3	49
12	.09063	29	11.0336	354	.09101	30	10.9882	355	.00413	2	.99588	3	48
13	.09092	29	10.9984	352	.09130	29	.9529	353	.00416	3	.99586	2	47
14	.09121	29	.9635	349	.09159	29	.9178	351	.00419	3	.99583	3	46
15	0.09150	29	10.9288	347	0.09189	30	10.8829	349	1.00421	2	0.99580	3	45
16	.09179	29	.8943	345	.09218	29	.8483	346	.00424	3	.99578	2	44
17	.09208	29	.8600	343	.09247	29	.8139	344	.00427	3	.99575	3	43
18	.09237	29	.8260	341	.09277	30	.7797	342	.00429	2	.99572	3	42
19	.09266	29	.7921	338	.09306	29	.7457	340	.00432	3	.99570	2	41
20	0.09295	29	10.7585	336	0.09335	29	10.7119	338	1.00435	3	0.99567	3	40
21	.09324	29	.7251	334	.09365	30	.6783	336	.00438	3	.99564	3	39
22	.09353	29	.6919	332	.09394	29	.6450	334	.00440	2	.99562	2	38
23	.09382	29	.6589	330	.09423	29	.6118	332	.00443	3	.99559	3	37
24	.09411	29	.6261	328	.09453	30	.5789	329	.00446	3	.99556	3	36
25	0.09440	29	10.5935	326	0.09482	29	10.5462	327	1.00449	3	0.99553	3	35
26	.09469	29	.5611	324	.09511	29	.5136	325	.00451	2	.99551	2	34
27	.09498	29	.5289	322	.09541	30	.4813	323	.00454	3	.99548	3	33
28	.09527	29	.4969	320	.09570	29	.4491	321	.00457	3	.99545	3	32
29	.09556	29	.4650	318	.09600	30	.4172	320	.00460	3	.99542	3	31
30	0.09585	29	10.4334	316	0.09629	29	10.3854	318	1.00463	3	0.99540	2	30
31	.09614	29	.4020	314	.09658	29	.3538	316	.00465	2	.99537	3	29
32	.09642	28	.3708	312	.09688	30	.3224	314	.00468	3	.99534	3	28
33	.09671	29	.3397	310	.09717	29	.2913	312	.00471	3	.99531	3	27
34	.09700	29	.3089	309	.09746	29	.2602	310	.00474	3	.99528	3	26
35	0.09729	29	10.2782	307	0.09776	30	10.2294	308	1.00477	3	0.99526	2	25
36	.09758	29	.2477	305	.09805	29	.1988	306	.00480	3	.99523	3	24
37	.09787	29	.2174	303	.09834	29	.1683	305	.00482	2	.99520	3	23
38	.09816	29	.1873	301	.09864	30	.1381	303	.00485	3	.99517	3	22
39	.09845	29	.1573	300	.09893	29	.1080	301	.00488	3	.99514	3	21
40	0.09874	29	10.1275	298	0.09923	30	10.0780	299	1.00491	3	0.99511	3	20
41	.09903	29	.0979	296	.09952	29	.0483	297	.00494	3	.99508	3	19
42	.09932	29	.0685	294	.09981	29	10.0187	296	.00497	3	.99506	2	18
43	.09961	29	.0392	293	.10011	30	9.98931	2940	.00500	3	.99503	3	17
44	.09990	29	10.0101	291	.10040	29	.96007	2923	.00503	3	.99500	3	16
45	0.10019	29	9.98123	2891	0.10069	29	9.93101	2907	1.00506	3	0.99497	3	15
46	.10048	29	.95248	2876	.10099	30	.90211	2890	.00509	3	.99494	3	14
47	.10077	29	.92389	2859	.10128	29	.87338	2873	.00512	3	.99491	3	13
48	.10106	29	.89547	2841	.10158	30	.84482	2857	.00515	3	.99488	3	12
49	.10135	29	.86722	2826	.10187	29	.81641	2840	.00518	3	.99485	3	11
50	0.10164	29	9.83912	2810	0.10216	29	9.78817	2824	1.00521	3	0.99482	3	10
51	.10192	28	.81119	2793	.10246	30	.76009	2809	.00524	3	.99479	3	9
52	.10221	29	.78341	2778	.10275	29	.73217	2792	.00527	3	.99476	3	8
53	.10250	29	.75579	2761	.10305	30	.70441	2777	.00530	3	.99473	3	7
54	.10279	29	.72833	2747	.10334	29	.67680	2760	.00533	3	.99470	3	6
55	0.10308	29	9.70103	2730	0.10363	29	9.64935	2746	1.00536	3	0.99467	3	5
56	.10337	29	.67387	2716	.10393	30	.62205	2730	.00539	3	.99464	3	4
57	.10366	29	.64687	2700	.10422	29	.59490	2714	.00542	3	.99461	3	3
58	.10395	29	.62002	2684	.10452	30	.56791	2700	.00545	3	.99458	3	2
59	.10424	29	.59332	2670	.10481	29	.54106	2684	.00548	3	.99455	3	1
60	0.10453	29	9.56677	2656	0.10510	29	9.51436	2670	1.00551	3	0.99452	3	0
↑ 95°→	cos	Diff. 1′	sec	Diff. 1′	cot	Diff. 1′	tan	Diff. 1′	csc	Diff. 1′	sin	Diff. 1′	↑ ←84°

TABLE 2
Natural Trigonometric Functions

6°→ ↓ ′	sin	Diff. 1′	csc	Diff. 1′	tan	Diff. 1′	cot	Diff. 1′	sec	Diff. 1′	cos	Diff. 1′	← 173° ↓ ′
0	0.10453		9.56677		0.10510		9.51436		1.00551		0.99452		60
1	.10482	29	.54037	2640	.10540	30	.48781	2654	.00554	3	.99449	3	59
2	.10511	29	.51411	2626	.10569	29	.46141	2640	.00557	3	.99446	3	58
3	.10540	29	.48800	2611	.10599	30	.43515	2626	.00560	3	.99443	3	57
4	.10569	29	.46203	2597	.10628	29	.40904	2611	.00563	3	.99440	3	56
5	0.10597	28	9.43620	2582	0.10657	29	9.38307	2598	1.00566	3	0.99437	3	55
6	.10626	29	.41052	2569	.10687	30	.35724	2583	.00569	3	.99434	3	54
7	.10655	29	.38497	2554	.10716	29	.33155	2570	.00573	4	.99431	3	53
8	.10684	29	.35957	2540	.10746	30	.30599	2556	.00576	3	.99428	3	52
9	.10713	29	.33430	2527	.10775	29	.28058	2541	.00579	3	.99424	4	51
10	0.10742	29	9.30917	2513	0.10805	30	9.25530	2528	1.00582	3	0.99421	3	50
11	.10771	29	.28417	2500	.10834	29	.23016	2514	.00585	3	.99418	3	49
12	.10800	29	.25931	2487	.10863	29	.20516	2500	.00588	3	.99415	3	48
13	.10829	29	.23459	2472	.10893	30	.18028	2488	.00592	4	.99412	3	47
14	.10858	29	.20999	2460	.10922	29	.15554	2474	.00595	3	.99409	3	46
15	0.10887	29	9.18553	2447	0.10952	30	9.13093	2460	1.00598	3	0.99406	3	45
16	.10916	29	.16120	2433	.10981	29	.10646	2448	.00601	3	.99402	4	44
17	.10945	29	.13699	2420	.11011	30	.08211	2434	.00604	3	.99399	3	43
18	.10973	28	.11292	2408	.11040	29	.05789	2422	.00608	4	.99396	3	42
19	.11002	29	.08897	2394	.11070	30	.03379	2410	.00611	3	.99393	3	41
20	0.11031	29	9.06515	2382	0.11099	29	9.00983	2397	1.00614	3	0.99390	3	40
21	.11060	29	.04146	2370	.11128	29	8.98598	2384	.00617	3	.99386	4	39
22	.11089	29	9.01788	2358	.11158	30	.96227	2371	.00621	4	.99383	3	38
23	.11118	29	8.99444	2344	.11187	29	.93867	2360	.00624	3	.99380	3	37
24	.11147	29	.97111	2332	.11217	30	.91520	2348	.00627	3	.99377	3	36
25	0.11176	29	8.94791	2320	0.11246	29	8.89185	2336	1.00630	3	0.99374	3	35
26	.11205	29	.92482	2309	.11276	30	.86862	2322	.00634	4	.99370	4	34
27	.11234	29	.90186	2297	.11305	29	.84551	2311	.00637	3	.99367	3	33
28	.11263	29	.87901	2284	.11335	30	.82252	2300	.00640	3	.99364	3	32
29	.11291	28	.85628	2272	.11364	29	.79964	2288	.00644	4	.99360	4	31
30	0.11320	29	8.83367	2261	0.11394	30	8.77689	2276	1.00647	3	0.99357	3	30
31	.11349	29	.81118	2250	.11423	29	.75425	2264	.00650	3	.99354	3	29
32	.11378	29	.78880	2239	.11452	29	.73172	2252	.00654	4	.99351	3	28
33	.11407	29	.76653	2227	.11482	30	.70931	2241	.00657	3	.99347	4	27
34	.11436	29	.74438	2216	.11511	29	.68701	2230	.00660	3	.99344	3	26
35	0.11465	29	8.72234	2204	0.11541	30	8.66482	2219	1.00664	4	0.99341	3	25
36	.11494	29	.70041	2192	.11570	29	.64275	2208	.00667	3	.99337	4	24
37	.11523	29	.67859	2181	.11600	30	.62078	2197	.00671	4	.99334	3	23
38	.11552	29	.65688	2170	.11629	29	.59893	2186	.00674	3	.99331	3	22
39	.11580	28	.63528	2160	.11659	30	.57718	2174	.00677	3	.99327	4	21
40	0.11609	29	8.61379	2150	0.11688	29	8.55555	2163	1.00681	4	0.99324	3	20
41	.11638	29	.59241	2139	.11718	30	.53402	2152	.00684	3	.99320	4	19
42	.11667	29	.57113	2128	.11747	29	.51259	2142	.00688	4	.99317	3	18
43	.11696	29	.54996	2118	.11777	30	.49128	2131	.00691	3	.99314	3	17
44	.11725	29	.52889	2107	.11806	29	.47007	2121	.00695	4	.99310	4	16
45	0.11754	29	8.50793	2097	0.11836	30	8.44896	2110	1.00698	3	0.99307	3	15
46	.11783	29	.48707	2086	.11865	29	.42795	2100	.00701	3	.99303	4	14
47	.11812	29	.46632	2076	.11895	30	.40705	2090	.00705	4	.99300	3	13
48	.11840	28	.44566	2066	.11924	29	.38625	2080	.00708	3	.99297	3	12
49	.11869	29	.42511	2056	.11954	30	.36555	2070	.00712	4	.99293	4	11
50	0.11898	29	8.40466	2046	0.11983	29	8.34496	2060	1.00715	3	0.99290	3	10
51	.11927	29	.38431	2036	.12013	30	.32446	2050	.00719	4	.99286	4	9
52	.11956	29	.36405	2026	.12042	29	.30406	2040	.00722	3	.99283	3	8
53	.11985	29	.34390	2016	.12072	30	.28376	2030	.00726	4	.99279	4	7
54	.12014	29	.32384	2006	.12101	29	.26355	2020	.00730	4	.99276	3	6
55	0.12043	29	8.30388	1997	0.12131	30	8.24345	2010	1.00733	3	0.99272	4	5
56	.12071	28	.28402	1987	.12160	29	.22344	2001	.00737	4	.99269	3	4
57	.12100	29	.26425	1977	.12190	30	.20352	1991	.00740	3	.99265	4	3
58	.12129	29	.24457	1968	.12219	29	.18370	1981	.00744	4	.99262	3	2
59	.12158	29	.22500	1958	.12249	30	.16398	1972	.00747	3	.99258	4	1
60	0.12187	29	8.20551	1949	0.12278	29	8.14435	1963	1.00751	4	0.99255	3	0
↑ 96°→	cos	Diff. 1′	sec	Diff. 1′	cot	Diff. 1′	tan	Diff. 1′	csc	Diff. 1′	sin	Diff. 1′←	↑ 83°

TABLE 2
Natural Trigonometric Functions

7°→ ↓ ′	sin	Diff. 1′	csc	Diff. 1′	tan	Diff. 1′	cot	Diff. 1′	sec	Diff. 1′	cos	Diff. 1′	← 172° ↓ ′
0	0.12187		8.20551		0.12278		8.14435		1.00751		0.99255		60
1	.12216	29	.18612	1940	.12308	30	.12481	1953	.00755	4	.99251	4	59
2	.12245	29	.16681	1930	.12338	30	.10536	1944	.00758	3	.99248	3	58
3	.12274	29	.14760	1920	.12367	29	.08600	1936	.00762	4	.99244	4	57
4	.12302	28	.12849	1911	.12397	30	.06674	1927	.00765	3	.99240	4	56
5	0.12331	29	8.10946	1902	0.12426	29	8.04756	1918	1.00769	4	0.99237	3	55
6	.12360	29	.09052	1893	.12456	30	.02848	1909	.00773	4	.99233	4	54
7	.12389	29	.07167	1886	.12485	29	8.00948	1900	.00776	3	.99230	3	53
8	.12418	29	.05291	1877	.12515	30	7.99058	1890	.00780	4	.99226	4	52
9	.12447	29	.03423	1868	.12544	29	.97176	1882	.00784	4	.99222	4	51
10	0.12476	29	8.01565	1859	0.12574	30	7.95302	1873	1.00787	3	0.99219	3	50
11	.12504	28	7.99714	1850	.12603	29	.93438	1864	.00791	4	.99215	4	49
12	.12533	29	.97873	1841	.12633	30	.91582	1857	.00795	4	.99211	4	48
13	.12562	29	.96040	1832	.12662	29	.89734	1848	.00799	4	.99208	3	47
14	.12591	29	.94216	1824	.12692	30	.87895	1840	.00802	3	.99204	4	46
15	0.12620	29	7.92399	1817	0.12722	30	7.86064	1830	1.00806	4	0.99200	4	45
16	.12649	29	.90592	1808	.12751	29	.84242	1822	.00810	4	.99197	3	44
17	.12678	29	.88792	1800	.12781	30	.82428	1814	.00813	3	.99193	4	43
18	.12706	28	.87001	1791	.12810	29	.80622	1806	.00817	4	.99189	4	42
19	.12735	29	.85218	1782	.12840	30	.78825	1798	.00821	4	.99186	3	41
20	0.12764	29	7.83443	1774	0.12869	29	7.77035	1790	1.00825	4	0.99182	4	40
21	.12793	29	.81677	1767	.12899	30	.75254	1781	.00828	3	.99178	4	39
22	.12822	29	.79918	1759	.12929	30	.73480	1773	.00832	4	.99175	3	38
23	.12851	29	.78167	1750	.12958	29	.71715	1766	.00836	4	.99171	4	37
24	.12880	29	.76424	1742	.12988	30	.69957	1758	.00840	4	.99167	4	36
25	0.12908	28	7.74689	1736	0.13017	29	7.68208	1750	1.00844	4	0.99163	4	35
26	.12937	29	.72962	1728	.13047	30	.66466	1741	.00848	4	.99160	3	34
27	.12966	29	.71242	1720	.13076	29	.64732	1734	.00851	3	.99156	4	33
28	.12995	29	.69530	1711	.13106	30	.63005	1727	.00855	4	.99152	4	32
29	.13024	29	.67826	1704	.13136	30	.61287	1719	.00859	4	.99148	4	31
30	0.13053	29	7.66130	1697	0.13165	29	7.59575	1711	1.00863	4	0.99144	4	30
31	.13081	28	.64441	1690	.13195	30	.57872	1703	.00867	4	.99141	3	29
32	.13110	29	.62759	1681	.13224	29	.56176	1697	.00871	4	.99137	4	28
33	.13139	29	.61085	1674	.13254	30	.54487	1689	.00875	4	.99133	4	27
34	.13168	29	.59418	1667	.13284	30	.52806	1681	.00878	3	.99129	4	26
35	0.13197	29	7.57759	1660	0.13313	29	7.51132	1673	1.00882	4	0.99125	4	25
36	.13226	29	.56107	1652	.13343	30	.49465	1667	.00886	4	.99122	3	24
37	.13254	28	.54462	1644	.13372	29	.47806	1660	.00890	4	.99118	4	23
38	.13283	29	.52825	1638	.13402	30	.46154	1652	.00894	4	.99114	4	22
39	.13312	29	.51194	1630	.13432	30	.44509	1646	.00898	4	.99110	4	21
40	0.13341	29	7.49571	1623	0.13461	29	7.42871	1638	1.00902	4	0.99106	4	20
41	.13370	29	.47955	1617	.13491	30	.41240	1630	.00906	4	.99102	4	19
42	.13399	29	.46346	1610	.13521	30	.39616	1623	.00910	4	.99098	4	18
43	.13427	28	.44743	1602	.13550	29	.37999	1617	.00914	4	.99094	4	17
44	.13456	29	.43148	1596	.13580	30	.36389	1610	.00918	4	.99091	3	16
45	0.13485	29	7.41560	1589	0.13609	29	7.34786	1603	1.00922	4	0.99087	4	15
46	.13514	29	.39978	1581	.13639	30	.33190	1597	.00926	4	.99083	4	14
47	.13543	29	.38403	1574	.13669	30	.31600	1590	.00930	4	.99079	4	13
48	.13572	29	.36835	1569	.13698	29	.30018	1582	.00934	4	.99075	4	12
49	.13600	28	.35274	1561	.13728	30	.28442	1576	.00938	4	.99071	4	11
50	0.13629	29	7.33719	1554	0.13758	30	7.26873	1570	1.00942	4	0.99067	4	10
51	.13658	29	.32171	1549	.13787	29	.25310	1562	.00946	4	.99063	4	9
52	.13687	29	.30630	1541	.13817	30	.23754	1557	.00950	4	.99059	4	8
53	.13716	29	.29095	1534	.13846	29	.22204	1550	.00954	4	.99055	4	7
54	.13744	28	.27566	1529	.13876	30	.20661	1543	.00958	4	.99051	4	6
55	0.13773	29	7.26044	1521	0.13906	30	7.19125	1537	1.00962	4	0.99047	4	5
56	.13802	29	.24529	1516	.13935	29	.17594	1530	.00966	4	.99043	4	4
57	.13831	29	.23019	1510	.13965	30	.16071	1523	.00970	4	.99039	4	3
58	.13860	29	.21517	1502	.13995	30	.14553	1518	.00975	5	.99035	4	2
59	.13889	29	.20020	1497	.14024	29	.13042	1511	.00979	4	.99031	4	1
60	0.13917	28	7.18530	1490	0.14054	30	7.11537	1504	1.00983	4	0.99027	4	0
↑ 97°→	cos	Diff. 1′	sec	Diff. 1′	cot	Diff. 1′	tan	Diff. 1′	csc	Diff. 1′	sin	Diff. 1′←	↑ 82°

TABLE 2

Natural Trigonometric Functions

8° → ↓ ′	sin	Diff. 1′	csc	Diff. 1′	tan	Diff. 1′	cot	Diff. 1′	sec	Diff. 1′	cos	Diff. 1′	← 171° ↓ ′
0	0.13917		7.18530		0.14054		7.11537		1.00983		0.99027		60
1	.13946	29	.17046	1484	.14084	30	.10038	1499	.00987	4	.99023	4	59
2	.13975	29	.15568	1478	.14113	29	.08546	1492	.00991	4	.99019	4	58
3	.14004	29	.14096	1471	.14143	30	.07059	1487	.00995	4	.99015	4	57
4	.14033	29	.12630	1466	.14173	30	.05579	1480	.00999	4	.99011	4	56
5	0.14061	28	7.11171	1460	0.14202	29	7.04105	1474	1.01004	5	0.99006	5	55
6	.14090	29	.09717	1453	.14232	30	.02637	1469	.01008	4	.99002	4	54
7	.14119	29	.08269	1448	.14262	30	7.01174	1462	.01012	4	.98998	4	53
8	.14148	29	.06828	1441	.14291	29	6.99718	1457	.01016	4	.98994	4	52
9	.14177	29	.05392	1436	.14321	30	.98268	1450	.01020	4	.98990	4	51
10	0.14205	28	7.03962	1430	0.14351	30	6.96823	1444	1.01024	4	0.98986	4	50
11	.14234	29	.02538	1423	.14381	30	.95385	1439	.01029	5	.98982	4	49
12	.14263	29	7.01120	1419	.14410	29	.93952	1432	.01033	4	.98978	4	48
13	.14292	29	6.99708	1412	.14440	30	.92525	1428	.01037	4	.98973	5	47
14	.14320	28	.98301	1407	.14470	30	.91104	1421	.01041	4	.98969	4	46
15	0.14349	29	6.96900	1400	0.14499	29	6.89688	1416	1.01046	5	0.98965	4	45
16	.14378	29	.95505	1396	.14529	30	.88278	1410	.01050	4	.98961	4	44
17	.14407	29	.94115	1390	.14559	30	.86874	1404	.01054	4	.98957	4	43
18	.14436	29	.92731	1384	.14588	29	.85475	1399	.01059	5	.98953	4	42
19	.14464	28	.91352	1379	.14618	30	.84082	1393	.01063	4	.98948	5	41
20	0.14493	29	6.89979	1372	0.14648	30	6.82694	1388	1.01067	4	0.98944	4	40
21	.14522	29	.88612	1368	.14678	30	.81312	1382	.01071	4	.98940	4	39
22	.14551	29	.87250	1362	.14707	29	.79936	1377	.01076	5	.98936	4	38
23	.14580	29	.85893	1357	.14737	30	.78564	1371	.01080	4	.98931	5	37
24	.14608	28	.84542	1351	.14767	30	.77199	1366	.01084	4	.98927	4	36
25	0.14637	29	6.83196	1346	0.14796	29	6.75838	1360	1.01089	5	0.98923	4	35
26	.14666	29	.81856	1340	.14826	30	.74483	1356	.01093	4	.98919	4	34
27	.14695	29	.80521	1336	.14856	30	.73133	1350	.01097	4	.98914	5	33
28	.14723	28	.79191	1330	.14886	30	.71789	1344	.01102	5	.98910	4	32
29	.14752	29	.77866	1324	.14915	29	.70450	1340	.01106	4	.98906	4	31
30	0.14781	29	6.76547	1320	0.14945	30	6.69116	1334	1.01111	5	0.98902	4	30
31	.14810	29	.75233	1314	.14975	30	.67787	1329	.01115	4	.98897	5	29
32	.14838	28	.73924	1310	.15005	30	.66463	1323	.01119	4	.98893	4	28
33	.14867	29	.72620	1303	.15034	29	.65144	1319	.01124	5	.98889	4	27
34	.14896	29	.71321	1299	.15064	30	.63831	1313	.01128	4	.98884	5	26
35	0.14925	29	6.70027	1293	0.15094	30	6.62523	1309	1.01133	5	0.98880	4	25
36	.14954	29	.68738	1289	.15124	30	.61219	1303	.01137	4	.98876	4	24
37	.14982	28	.67454	1283	.15153	29	.59921	1299	.01142	5	.98871	5	23
38	.15011	29	.66176	1279	.15183	30	.58627	1293	.01146	4	.98867	4	22
39	.15040	29	.64902	1273	.15213	30	.57339	1289	.01151	5	.98863	4	21
40	0.15069	29	6.63633	1269	0.15243	30	6.56055	1283	1.01155	4	0.98858	5	20
41	.15097	28	.62369	1264	.15272	29	.54777	1279	.01160	5	.98854	4	19
42	.15126	29	.61110	1260	.15302	30	.53503	1273	.01164	4	.98849	5	18
43	.15155	29	.59855	1254	.15332	30	.52234	1269	.01169	5	.98845	4	17
44	.15184	29	.58606	1250	.15362	30	.50970	1264	.01173	4	.98841	4	16
45	0.15212	28	6.57361	1244	0.15391	29	6.49710	1260	1.01178	5	0.98836	5	15
46	.15241	29	.56121	1240	.15421	30	.48456	1254	.01182	4	.98832	4	14
47	.15270	29	.54886	1236	.15451	30	.47206	1250	.01187	5	.98827	5	13
48	.15299	29	.53655	1230	.15481	30	.45961	1246	.01191	4	.98823	4	12
49	.15327	28	.52429	1226	.15511	30	.44720	1240	.01196	5	.98818	5	11
50	0.15356	29	6.51208	1221	0.15540	29	6.43484	1236	1.01200	4	0.98814	4	10
51	.15385	29	.49991	1217	.15570	30	.42253	1231	.01205	5	.98809	5	9
52	.15414	29	.48779	1212	.15600	30	.41026	1227	.01209	4	.98805	4	8
53	.15442	28	.47572	1208	.15630	30	.39804	1222	.01214	5	.98800	5	7
54	.15471	29	.46369	1202	.15660	30	.38587	1218	.01219	5	.98796	4	6
55	0.15500	29	6.45171	1199	0.15689	29	6.37374	1213	1.01223	4	0.98791	5	5
56	.15529	29	.43977	1193	.15719	30	.36165	1209	.01228	5	.98787	4	4
57	.15557	28	.42787	1190	.15749	30	.34961	1204	.01233	5	.98782	5	3
58	.15586	29	.41602	1186	.15779	30	.33761	1200	.01237	4	.98778	4	2
59	.15615	29	.40422	1180	.15809	30	.32566	1196	.01242	5	.98773	5	1
60	0.15643	28	6.39245	1177	0.15838	29	6.31375	1190	1.01247	5	0.98769	4	0
↑ 98° →	cos	Diff. 1′	sec	Diff. 1′	cot	Diff. 1′	tan	Diff. 1′	csc	Diff. 1′	sin	Diff. 1′ ←	81° ↑

TABLE 2

Natural Trigonometric Functions

9° → ↓ ′	sin	Diff. 1′	csc	Diff. 1′	tan	Diff. 1′	cot	Diff. 1′	sec	Diff. 1′	cos	Diff. 1′	← 170° ↓ ′
0	0.15643		6.39245		0.15838		6.31375		1.01247		0.98769		60
1	.15672	29	.38073	1171	.15868	30	.30189	1187	.01251	4	.98764	5	59
2	.15701	29	.36906	1168	.15898	30	.29007	1182	.01256	5	.98760	4	58
3	.15730	29	.35743	1163	.15928	30	.27829	1178	.01261	5	.98755	5	57
4	.15758	28	.34584	1159	.15958	30	.26655	1173	.01265	4	.98751	4	56
5	0.15787	29	6.33429	1154	0.15988	30	6.25486	1170	1.01270	5	0.98746	5	55
6	.15816	29	.32279	1150	.16017	29	.24321	1166	.01275	5	.98741	5	54
7	.15845	29	.31133	1147	.16047	30	.23160	1160	.01279	4	.98737	4	53
8	.15873	28	.29991	1141	.16077	30	.22003	1157	.01284	5	.98732	5	52
9	.15902	29	.28853	1138	.16107	30	.20851	1152	.01289	5	.98728	4	51
10	0.15931	29	6.27719	1133	0.16137	30	6.19703	1149	1.01294	5	0.98723	5	50
11	.15959	28	.26590	1130	.16167	30	.18559	1144	.01298	4	.98718	5	49
12	.15988	29	.25464	1126	.16196	29	.17419	1140	.01303	5	.98714	4	48
13	.16017	29	.24343	1121	.16226	30	.16283	1136	.01308	5	.98709	5	47
14	.16046	29	.23226	1118	.16256	30	.15151	1131	.01313	5	.98704	5	46
15	0.16074	28	6.22113	1113	0.16286	30	6.14023	1128	1.01317	4	0.98700	4	45
16	.16103	29	.21004	1110	.16316	30	.12899	1123	.01322	5	.98695	5	44
17	.16132	29	.19898	1106	.16346	30	.11779	1120	.01327	5	.98690	5	43
18	.16160	28	.18797	1101	.16376	30	.10664	1116	.01332	5	.98686	4	42
19	.16189	29	.17700	1098	.16405	29	.09552	1111	.01337	5	.98681	5	41
20	0.16218	29	6.16607	1093	0.16435	30	6.08444	1108	1.01342	5	0.98676	5	40
21	.16246	28	.15517	1090	.16465	30	.07340	1104	.01346	4	.98671	5	39
22	.16275	29	.14432	1086	.16495	30	.06240	1100	.01351	5	.98667	4	38
23	.16304	29	.13350	1081	.16525	30	.05143	1097	.01356	5	.98662	5	37
24	.16333	29	.12273	1078	.16555	30	.04051	1092	.01361	5	.98657	5	36
25	0.16361	28	6.11199	1073	0.16585	30	6.02962	1089	1.01366	5	0.98652	5	35
26	.16390	29	.10129	1070	.16615	30	.01878	1084	.01371	5	.98648	4	34
27	.16419	29	.09062	1067	.16645	30	6.00797	1080	.01376	5	.98643	5	33
28	.16447	28	.08000	1062	.16674	29	5.99720	1078	.01381	5	.98638	5	32
29	.16476	29	.06941	1059	.16704	30	.98646	1073	.01386	5	.98633	5	31
30	0.16505	29	6.05886	1056	0.16734	30	5.97576	1070	1.01391	5	0.98629	4	30
31	.16533	28	.04834	1051	.16764	30	.96510	1066	.01395	4	.98624	5	29
32	.16562	29	.03787	1048	.16794	30	.95448	1062	.01400	5	.98619	5	28
33	.16591	29	.02743	1043	.16824	30	.94390	1059	.01405	5	.98614	5	27
34	.16620	29	.01702	1040	.16854	30	.93335	1054	.01410	5	.98609	5	26
35	0.16648	28	6.00666	1037	0.16884	30	5.92283	1051	1.01415	5	0.98604	5	25
36	.16677	29	5.99633	1033	.16914	30	.91236	1048	.01420	5	.98600	4	24
37	.16706	29	.98603	1030	.16944	30	.90191	1044	.01425	5	.98595	5	23
38	.16734	28	.97577	1026	.16974	30	.89151	1040	.01430	5	.98590	5	22
39	.16763	29	.96555	1022	.17004	30	.88114	1037	.01435	5	.98585	5	21
40	0.16792	29	5.95536	1019	0.17033	29	5.87080	1033	1.01440	5	0.98580	5	20
41	.16820	28	.94521	1016	.17063	30	.86051	1030	.01445	5	.98575	5	19
42	.16849	29	.93509	1011	.17093	30	.85024	1027	.01450	5	.98570	5	18
43	.16878	29	.92501	1009	.17123	30	.84001	1022	.01455	5	.98565	5	17
44	.16906	28	.91496	1004	.17153	30	.82982	1020	.01460	5	.98561	4	16
45	0.16935	29	5.90495	1001	0.17183	30	5.81966	1017	1.01466	6	0.98556	5	15
46	.16964	29	.89497	998	.17213	30	.80953	1012	.01471	5	.98551	5	14
47	.16992	28	.88502	994	.17243	30	.79944	1010	.01476	5	.98546	5	13
48	.17021	29	.87511	991	.17273	30	.78938	1006	.01481	5	.98541	5	12
49	.17050	29	.86524	988	.17303	30	.77936	1002	.01486	5	.98536	5	11
50	0.17078	28	5.85539	984	0.17333	30	5.76937	1000	1.01491	5	0.98531	5	10
51	.17107	29	.84558	981	.17363	30	.75941	996	.01496	5	.98526	5	9
52	.17136	29	.83581	978	.17393	30	.74949	992	.01501	5	.98521	5	8
53	.17164	28	.82606	974	.17423	30	.73960	990	.01506	5	.98516	5	7
54	.17193	29	.81635	971	.17453	30	.72974	986	.01512	6	.98511	5	6
55	0.17222	29	5.80667	968	0.17483	30	5.71992	982	1.01517	5	0.98506	5	5
56	.17250	28	.79703	964	.17513	30	.71013	980	.01522	5	.98501	5	4
57	.17279	29	.78742	961	.17543	30	.70037	976	.01527	5	.98496	5	3
58	.17308	29	.77783	959	.17573	30	.69064	972	.01532	5	.98491	5	2
59	.17336	28	.76829	954	.17603	30	.68094	970	.01537	5	.98486	5	1
60	0.17365	29	5.75877	951	0.17633	30	5.67128	967	1.01543	6	0.98481	5	0
↑ 99° →	cos	Diff. 1′	sec	Diff. 1′	cot	Diff. 1′	tan	Diff. 1′	csc	Diff. 1′	sin	Diff. 1′ ←	80° ↑

TABLE 2
Natural Trigonometric Functions

10°→ ↓ ′	sin	Diff. 1′	csc	Diff. 1′	tan	Diff. 1′	cot	Diff. 1′	sec	Diff. 1′	cos	Diff. 1′	← 169° ↓ ′
0	0.17365		5.75877		0.17633		5.67128		1.01543		0.98481		60
1	.17393	28	.74929	949	.17663	30	.66165	963	.01548	5	.98476	5	59
2	.17422	29	.73983	946	.17693	30	.65205	960	.01553	5	.98471	5	58
3	.17451	29	.73041	942	.17723	30	.64248	957	.01558	5	.98466	5	57
4	.17479	28	.72102	939	.17753	30	.63295	953	.01564	6	.98461	5	56
5	0.17508	29	5.71166	936	0.17783	30	5.62344	950	1.01569	5	0.98455	6	55
6	.17537	29	.70234	932	.17813	30	.61397	948	.01574	5	.98450	5	54
7	.17565	28	.69304	930	.17843	30	.60452	944	.01579	5	.98445	5	53
8	.17594	29	.68377	927	.17873	30	.59511	941	.01585	6	.98440	5	52
9	.17623	29	.67454	923	.17903	30	.58573	939	.01590	5	.98435	5	51
10	0.17651	28	5.66533	920	0.17933	30	5.57638	936	1.01595	5	0.98430	5	50
11	.17680	29	.65616	918	.17963	30	.56706	932	.01601	6	.98425	5	49
12	.17708	28	.64701	914	.17993	30	.55777	930	.01606	5	.98420	5	48
13	.17737	29	.63790	911	.18023	30	.54851	927	.01611	5	.98414	6	47
14	.17766	29	.62881	909	.18053	30	.53927	923	.01616	5	.98409	5	46
15	0.17794	28	5.61976	906	0.18083	30	5.53007	920	1.01622	6	0.98404	5	45
16	.17823	29	.61073	902	.18113	30	.52090	918	.01627	5	.98399	5	44
17	.17852	29	.60174	900	.18143	30	.51176	914	.01633	6	.98394	5	43
18	.17880	28	.59277	897	.18173	30	.50264	911	.01638	5	.98389	5	42
19	.17909	29	.58383	893	.18203	30	.49356	909	.01643	5	.98383	6	41
20	0.17937	28	5.57493	890	0.18233	30	5.48451	906	1.01649	6	0.98378	5	40
21	.17966	29	.56605	888	.18263	30	.47548	902	.01654	5	.98373	5	39
22	.17995	29	.55720	886	.18293	30	.46648	900	.01659	5	.98368	5	38
23	.18023	28	.54837	882	.18323	30	.45751	897	.01665	6	.98362	6	37
24	.18052	29	.53958	880	.18353	30	.44857	894	.01670	5	.98357	5	36
25	0.18081	29	5.53081	877	0.18384	31	5.43966	891	1.01676	6	0.98352	5	35
26	.18109	28	.52208	873	.18414	30	.43077	889	.01681	5	.98347	5	34
27	.18138	29	.51337	870	.18444	30	.42192	886	.01687	6	.98341	6	33
28	.18166	28	.50468	869	.18474	30	.41309	882	.01692	5	.98336	5	32
29	.18195	29	.49603	866	.18504	30	.40429	880	.01698	6	.98331	5	31
30	0.18224	29	5.48740	862	0.18534	30	5.39552	878	1.01703	5	0.98325	6	30
31	.18252	28	.47881	860	.18564	30	.38677	874	.01709	6	.98320	5	29
32	.18281	29	.47023	858	.18594	30	.37805	871	.01714	5	.98315	5	28
33	.18309	28	.46169	854	.18624	30	.36936	870	.01720	6	.98310	5	27
34	.18338	29	.45317	851	.18654	30	.36070	867	.01725	5	.98304	6	26
35	0.18367	29	5.44468	850	0.18684	30	5.35206	863	1.01731	6	0.98299	5	25
36	.18395	28	.43622	847	.18714	30	.34345	860	.01736	5	.98294	5	24
37	.18424	29	.42778	843	.18745	31	.33487	859	.01742	6	.98288	6	23
38	.18452	28	.41937	840	.18775	30	.32631	856	.01747	5	.98283	5	22
39	.18481	29	.41099	839	.18805	30	.31778	853	.01753	6	.98277	6	21
40	0.18509	28	5.40263	836	0.18835	30	5.30928	850	1.01758	5	0.98272	5	20
41	.18538	29	.39430	833	.18865	30	.30080	848	.01764	6	.98267	5	19
42	.18567	29	.38600	830	.18895	30	.29235	846	.01769	5	.98261	6	18
43	.18595	28	.37772	828	.18925	30	.28393	842	.01775	6	.98256	5	17
44	.18624	29	.36947	826	.18955	30	.27553	840	.01781	6	.98250	6	16
45	0.18652	28	5.36124	822	0.18986	31	5.26715	838	1.01786	5	0.98245	5	15
46	.18681	29	.35304	820	.19016	30	.25880	834	.01792	6	.98240	5	14
47	.18710	29	.34486	818	.19046	30	.25048	832	.01798	6	.98234	6	13
48	.18738	28	.33671	816	.19076	30	.24218	830	.01803	5	.98229	5	12
49	.18767	29	.32859	812	.19106	30	.23391	828	.01809	6	.98223	6	11
50	0.18795	28	5.32049	810	0.19136	30	5.22566	824	1.01815	6	0.98218	5	10
51	.18824	29	.31241	808	.19166	30	.21744	822	.01820	5	.98212	6	9
52	.18852	28	.30436	806	.19197	31	.20925	820	.01826	6	.98207	5	8
53	.18881	29	.29634	802	.19227	30	.20107	818	.01832	6	.98201	6	7
54	.18910	29	.28833	800	.19257	30	.19293	814	.01837	5	.98196	5	6
55	0.18938	28	5.28036	798	0.19287	30	5.18480	812	1.01843	6	0.98190	6	5
56	.18967	29	.27241	796	.19317	30	.17671	810	.01849	6	.98185	5	4
57	.18995	28	.26448	792	.19347	30	.16863	808	.01854	5	.98179	6	3
58	.19024	29	.25658	790	.19378	31	.16058	804	.01860	6	.98174	5	2
59	.19052	28	.24870	788	.19408	30	.15256	802	.01866	6	.98168	6	1
60	0.19081	29	5.24084	786	0.19438	30	5.14455	800	1.01872	6	0.98163	5	0
↑ 100°→	cos	Diff. 1′	sec	Diff. 1′	cot	Diff. 1′	tan	Diff. 1′	csc	Diff. 1′	sin	Diff. 1′← 79°	↑

TABLE 2
Natural Trigonometric Functions

11°→ ↓ ′	sin	Diff. 1′	csc	Diff. 1′	tan	Diff. 1′	cot	Diff. 1′	sec	Diff. 1′	cos	Diff. 1′	← 168° ↓ ′
0	0.19081		5.24084		0.19438		5.14455		1.01872		0.98163		60
1	.19109	28	.23301	783	.19468	30	.13658	798	.01877	5	.98157	6	59
2	.19138	29	.22521	780	.19498	30	.12862	796	.01883	6	.98152	5	58
3	.19167	29	.21742	779	.19529	31	.12069	793	.01889	6	.98146	6	57
4	.19195	28	.20966	776	.19559	30	.11279	790	.01895	6	.98140	6	56
5	0.19224	29	5.20193	773	0.19589	30	5.10490	789	1.01901	6	0.98135	5	55
6	.19252	28	.19421	771	.19619	30	.09704	786	.01906	5	.98129	6	54
7	.19281	29	.18652	769	.19649	30	.08921	783	.01912	6	.98124	5	53
8	.19309	28	.17886	767	.19680	31	.08139	781	.01918	6	.98118	6	52
9	.19338	29	.17121	764	.19710	30	.07360	780	.01924	6	.98112	6	51
10	0.19366	28	5.16359	762	0.19740	30	5.06584	777	1.01930	6	0.98107	5	50
11	.19395	29	.15599	760	.19770	30	.05809	774	.01936	6	.98101	6	49
12	.19423	28	.14842	758	.19801	31	.05037	772	.01941	5	.98096	5	48
13	.19452	29	.14087	756	.19831	30	.04267	770	.01947	6	.98090	6	47
14	.19481	29	.13334	752	.19861	30	.03499	768	.01953	6	.98084	6	46
15	0.19509	28	5.12583	750	0.19891	30	5.02734	766	1.01959	6	0.98079	5	45
16	.19538	29	.11835	749	.19921	30	.01971	763	.01965	6	.98073	6	44
17	.19566	28	.11088	747	.19952	31	.01210	760	.01971	6	.98067	6	43
18	.19595	29	.10344	744	.19982	30	5.00451	759	.01977	6	.98061	6	42
19	.19623	28	.09602	741	.20012	30	4.99695	757	.01983	6	.98056	5	41
20	0.19652	29	5.08863	740	0.20042	30	4.98940	754	1.01989	6	0.98050	6	40
21	.19680	28	.08125	738	.20073	31	.98188	752	.01995	6	.98044	6	39
22	.19709	29	.07390	736	.20103	30	.97438	750	.02001	6	.98039	5	38
23	.19737	28	.06657	733	.20133	30	.96690	748	.02007	6	.98033	6	37
24	.19766	29	.05926	730	.20164	31	.95945	746	.02013	6	.98027	6	36
25	0.19794	28	5.05197	729	0.20194	30	4.95201	743	1.02019	6	0.98021	6	35
26	.19823	29	.04471	727	.20224	30	.94460	741	.02025	6	.98016	5	34
27	.19851	28	.03746	724	.20254	30	.93721	740	.02031	6	.98010	6	33
28	.19880	29	.03024	722	.20285	31	.92984	738	.02037	6	.98004	6	32
29	.19908	28	.02303	720	.20315	30	.92249	734	.02043	6	.97998	6	31
30	0.19937	29	5.01585	719	0.20345	30	4.91516	732	1.02049	6	0.97992	6	30
31	.19965	28	.00869	717	.20376	31	.90785	730	.02055	6	.97987	5	29
32	.19994	29	5.00155	714	.20406	30	.90056	729	.02061	6	.97981	6	28
33	.20022	28	4.99443	711	.20436	30	.89330	727	.02067	6	.97975	6	27
34	.20051	29	.98733	710	.20466	30	.88605	724	.02073	6	.97969	6	26
35	0.20079	28	4.98025	708	0.20497	31	4.87882	722	1.02079	6	0.97963	6	25
36	.20108	29	.97320	706	.20527	30	.87162	720	.02085	6	.97958	5	24
37	.20136	28	.96616	703	.20557	30	.86444	719	.02091	6	.97952	6	23
38	.20165	29	.95914	701	.20588	31	.85727	717	.02097	6	.97946	6	22
39	.20193	28	.95215	700	.20618	30	.85013	714	.02103	6	.97940	6	21
40	0.20222	29	4.94517	698	0.20648	30	4.84300	712	1.02110	7	0.97934	6	20
41	.20250	28	.93821	696	.20679	31	.83590	710	.02116	6	.97928	6	19
42	.20279	29	.93128	693	.20709	30	.82882	709	.02122	6	.97922	6	18
43	.20307	28	.92436	691	.20739	30	.82175	707	.02128	6	.97916	6	17
44	.20336	29	.91746	690	.20770	31	.81471	704	.02134	6	.97910	6	16
45	0.20364	28	4.91058	688	0.20800	30	4.80769	702	1.02140	6	0.97905	5	15
46	.20393	29	.90373	686	.20830	30	.80068	700	.02146	6	.97899	6	14
47	.20421	28	.89689	683	.20861	31	.79370	699	.02153	7	.97893	6	13
48	.20450	29	.89007	681	.20891	30	.78673	697	.02159	6	.97887	6	12
49	.20478	28	.88327	680	.20921	30	.77978	694	.02165	6	.97881	6	11
50	0.20507	29	4.87649	678	0.20952	31	4.77286	692	1.02171	6	0.97875	6	10
51	.20535	28	.86973	677	.20982	30	.76595	690	.02178	7	.97869	6	9
52	.20563	28	.86299	674	.21013	31	.75906	689	.02184	6	.97863	6	8
53	.20592	29	.85627	672	.21043	30	.75219	687	.02190	6	.97857	6	7
54	.20620	28	.84956	670	.21073	30	.74534	686	.02196	6	.97851	6	6
55	0.20649	29	4.84288	669	0.21104	31	4.73851	683	1.02203	7	0.97845	6	5
56	.20677	28	.83621	667	.21134	30	.73170	681	.02209	6	.97839	6	4
57	.20706	29	.82956	664	.21164	30	.72490	680	.02215	6	.97833	6	3
58	.20734	28	.82294	662	.21195	31	.71813	678	.02221	6	.97827	6	2
59	.20763	29	.81633	660	.21225	30	.71137	676	.02228	7	.97821	6	1
60	0.20791	28	4.80973	660	0.21256	31	4.70463	673	1.02234	6	0.97815	6	0
↑ 101°→	cos	Diff. 1′	sec	Diff. 1′	cot	Diff. 1′	tan	Diff. 1′	csc	Diff. 1′	sin	Diff. 1′← 78°	↑

TABLE 2
Natural Trigonometric Functions

12° → ↓ ′	sin	Diff. 1′	csc	Diff. 1′	tan	Diff. 1′	cot	Diff. 1′	sec	Diff. 1′	cos	Diff. 1′	← 167° ↓ ′
0	0.20791		4.80973		0.21256		4.70463		1.02234		0.97815		60
1	.20820	29	.80316	658	.21286	30	.69791	672	.02240	6	.97809	6	59
2	.20848	28	.79661	656	.21316	30	.69121	670	.02247	7	.97803	6	58
3	.20877	29	.79007	653	.21347	31	.68452	669	.02253	6	.97797	6	57
4	.20905	28	.78355	651	.21377	30	.67786	667	.02259	6	.97791	6	56
5	0.20933	28	4.77705	650	0.21408	31	4.67121	664	1.02266	7	0.97784	7	55
6	.20962	29	.77057	649	.21438	30	.66458	662	.02272	6	.97778	6	54
7	.20990	28	.76411	647	.21469	31	.65797	661	.02279	7	.97772	6	53
8	.21019	29	.75766	644	.21499	30	.65138	660	.02285	6	.97766	6	52
9	.21047	28	.75123	642	.21529	30	.64480	658	.02291	6	.97760	6	51
10	0.21076	29	4.74482	641	0.21560	31	4.63825	656	1.02298	7	0.97754	6	50
11	.21104	28	.73843	640	.21590	30	.63171	654	.02304	6	.97748	6	49
12	.21132	28	.73205	638	.21621	31	.62518	652	.02311	7	.97742	6	48
13	.21161	29	.72569	636	.21651	30	.61868	650	.02317	6	.97735	7	47
14	.21189	28	.71935	634	.21682	31	.61219	649	.02323	6	.97729	6	46
15	0.21218	29	4.71303	632	0.21712	30	4.60572	648	1.02330	7	0.97723	6	45
16	.21246	28	.70673	630	.21743	31	.59927	646	.02336	6	.97717	6	44
17	.21275	29	.70044	629	.21773	30	.59283	643	.02343	7	.97711	6	43
18	.21303	28	.69417	628	.21804	31	.58641	641	.02349	6	.97705	6	42
19	.21331	28	.68791	626	.21834	30	.58001	640	.02356	7	.97698	7	41
20	0.21360	29	4.68167	623	0.21864	30	4.57363	639	1.02362	6	0.97692	6	40
21	.21388	28	.67545	622	.21895	31	.56726	637	.02369	7	.97686	6	39
22	.21417	29	.66925	620	.21925	30	.56091	636	.02375	6	.97680	6	38
23	.21445	28	.66307	619	.21956	31	.55458	633	.02382	7	.97673	7	37
24	.21474	29	.65690	617	.21986	30	.54826	631	.02388	6	.97667	6	36
25	0.21502	28	4.65074	616	0.22017	31	4.54196	630	1.02395	7	0.97661	6	35
26	.21530	28	.64461	613	.22047	30	.53568	629	.02402	7	.97655	6	34
27	.21559	29	.63849	611	.22078	31	.52941	627	.02408	6	.97648	7	33
28	.21587	28	.63238	610	.22108	30	.52316	626	.02415	7	.97642	6	32
29	.21616	29	.62630	609	.22139	31	.51693	623	.02421	6	.97636	6	31
30	0.21644	28	4.62023	608	0.22169	30	4.51071	621	1.02428	7	0.97630	6	30
31	.21672	28	.61417	606	.22200	31	.50451	620	.02435	7	.97623	7	29
32	.21701	29	.60813	603	.22231	31	.49832	619	.02441	6	.97617	6	28
33	.21729	28	.60211	602	.22261	30	.49215	617	.02448	7	.97611	6	27
34	.21758	29	.59611	600	.22292	31	.48600	616	.02454	6	.97604	7	26
35	0.21786	28	4.59012	599	0.22322	30	4.47986	613	1.02461	7	0.97598	6	25
36	.21814	28	.58414	598	.22353	31	.47374	612	.02468	7	.97592	6	24
37	.21843	29	.57819	596	.22383	30	.46764	610	.02474	6	.97585	7	23
38	.21871	28	.57224	594	.22414	31	.46155	609	.02481	7	.97579	6	22
39	.21899	28	.56632	592	.22444	30	.45548	608	.02488	7	.97573	6	21
40	0.21928	29	4.56041	591	0.22475	31	4.44942	606	1.02494	6	0.97566	7	20
41	.21956	28	.55451	590	.22505	30	.44338	604	.02501	7	.97560	6	19
42	.21985	29	.54863	588	.22536	31	.43735	602	.02508	7	.97553	7	18
43	.22013	28	.54277	587	.22567	31	.43134	601	.02515	7	.97547	6	17
44	.22041	28	.53692	584	.22597	30	.42534	600	.02521	6	.97541	6	16
45	0.22070	29	4.53109	583	0.22628	31	4.41936	598	1.02528	7	0.97534	7	15
46	.22098	28	.52527	581	.22658	30	.41340	597	.02535	7	.97528	6	14
47	.22126	28	.51947	580	.22689	31	.40745	594	.02542	7	.97521	7	13
48	.22155	29	.51368	579	.22719	30	.40152	593	.02548	6	.97515	6	12
49	.22183	28	.50791	578	.22750	31	.39560	591	.02555	7	.97508	7	11
50	0.22212	29	4.50216	576	0.22781	31	4.38969	590	1.02562	7	0.97502	6	10
51	.22240	28	.49642	574	.22811	30	.38381	589	.02569	7	.97496	6	9
52	.22268	28	.49069	572	.22842	31	.37793	588	.02576	7	.97489	7	8
53	.22297	29	.48498	571	.22872	30	.37207	586	.02582	6	.97483	6	7
54	.22325	28	.47928	570	.22903	31	.36623	584	.02589	7	.97476	7	6
55	0.22353	28	4.47360	569	0.22934	31	4.36040	582	1.02596	7	0.97470	6	5
56	.22382	29	.46793	567	.22964	30	.35459	581	.02603	7	.97463	7	4
57	.22410	28	.46228	566	.22995	31	.34879	580	.02610	7	.97457	6	3
58	.22438	28	.45664	563	.23026	31	.34300	579	.02617	7	.97450	7	2
59	.22467	29	.45102	562	.23056	30	.33723	578	.02624	7	.97444	6	1
60	0.22495	28	4.44541	560	0.23087	31	4.33148	576	1.02630	6	0.97437	7	0
↑ 102° →	cos	Diff. 1′	sec	Diff. 1′	cot	Diff. 1′	tan	Diff. 1′	csc	Diff. 1′	sin	Diff. 1′	↑ ← 77°

TABLE 2
Natural Trigonometric Functions

13° → ↓ ′	sin	Diff. 1′	csc	Diff. 1′	tan	Diff. 1′	cot	Diff. 1′	sec	Diff. 1′	cos	Diff. 1′	← 166° ↓ ′
0	0.22495		4.44541		0.23087		4.33148		1.02630		0.97437		60
1	.22523	28	.43982	560	.23117	30	.32573	574	.02637	7	.97430	7	59
2	.22552	29	.43424	558	.23148	31	.32001	572	.02644	7	.97424	6	58
3	.22580	28	.42867	557	.23179	31	.31430	571	.02651	7	.97417	7	57
4	.22608	28	.42312	556	.23209	30	.30860	570	.02658	7	.97411	6	56
5	0.22637	29	4.41759	553	0.23240	31	4.30291	569	1.02665	7	0.97404	7	55
6	.22665	28	.41206	552	.23271	31	.29724	567	.02672	7	.97398	6	54
7	.22693	28	.40656	550	.23301	30	.29159	566	.02679	7	.97391	7	53
8	.22722	29	.40106	550	.23332	31	.28595	564	.02686	7	.97384	7	52
9	.22750	28	.39558	548	.23363	31	.28032	562	.02693	7	.97378	6	51
10	0.22778	28	4.39012	547	0.23393	30	4.27471	561	1.02700	7	0.97371	7	50
11	.22807	29	.38466	546	.23424	31	.26911	560	.02707	7	.97365	6	49
12	.22835	28	.37923	543	.23455	31	.26352	559	.02714	7	.97358	7	48
13	.22863	28	.37380	542	.23485	30	.25795	558	.02721	7	.97351	7	47
14	.22892	29	.36839	541	.23516	31	.25239	556	.02728	7	.97345	6	46
15	0.22920	28	4.36299	540	0.23547	31	4.24685	554	1.02735	7	0.97338	7	45
16	.22948	28	.35761	539	.23578	31	.24132	553	.02742	7	.97331	7	44
17	.22977	29	.35224	537	.23608	30	.23580	551	.02749	7	.97325	6	43
18	.23005	28	.34689	536	.23639	31	.23030	550	.02756	7	.97318	7	42
19	.23033	28	.34154	534	.23670	31	.22481	549	.02763	7	.97311	7	41
20	0.23062	29	4.33622	532	0.23700	30	4.21933	548	1.02770	7	0.97304	7	40
21	.23090	28	.33090	531	.23731	31	.21387	547	.02777	7	.97298	6	39
22	.23118	28	.32560	530	.23762	31	.20842	544	.02784	7	.97291	7	38
23	.23146	28	.32031	529	.23793	31	.20298	543	.02791	7	.97284	7	37
24	.23175	29	.31503	528	.23823	30	.19756	542	.02799	8	.97278	6	36
25	0.23203	28	4.30977	527	0.23854	31	4.19215	540	1.02806	7	0.97271	7	35
26	.23231	28	.30452	524	.23885	31	.18675	540	.02813	7	.97264	7	34
27	.23260	29	.29929	523	.23916	31	.18137	539	.02820	7	.97257	7	33
28	.23288	28	.29406	522	.23946	30	.17600	538	.02827	7	.97251	6	32
29	.23316	28	.28885	520	.23977	31	.17064	536	.02834	7	.97244	7	31
30	0.23345	29	4.28366	520	0.24008	31	4.16530	534	1.02842	8	0.97237	7	30
31	.23373	28	.27847	519	.24039	31	.15997	533	.02849	7	.97230	7	29
32	.23401	28	.27330	518	.24069	30	.15465	531	.02856	7	.97223	7	28
33	.23429	28	.26814	516	.24100	31	.14934	530	.02863	7	.97217	6	27
34	.23458	29	.26300	514	.24131	31	.14405	530	.02870	7	.97210	7	26
35	0.23486	28	4.25787	513	0.24162	31	4.13877	528	1.02878	8	0.97203	7	25
36	.23514	28	.25275	511	.24193	31	.13350	527	.02885	7	.97196	7	24
37	.23542	28	.24764	510	.24223	30	.12825	526	.02892	7	.97189	7	23
38	.23571	29	.24255	510	.24254	31	.12301	524	.02899	7	.97182	7	22
39	.23599	28	.23746	509	.24285	31	.11778	522	.02907	8	.97176	6	21
40	0.23627	28	4.23239	507	0.24316	31	4.11256	521	1.02914	7	0.97169	7	20
41	.23656	29	.22734	506	.24347	31	.10736	520	.02921	7	.97162	7	19
42	.23684	28	.22229	504	.24377	30	.10216	520	.02928	7	.97155	7	18
43	.23712	28	.21726	503	.24408	31	.09699	518	.02936	8	.97148	7	17
44	.23740	28	.21224	501	.24439	31	.09182	517	.02943	7	.97141	7	16
45	0.23769	29	4.20723	500	0.24470	31	4.08666	516	1.02950	7	0.97134	7	15
46	.23797	28	.20224	500	.24501	31	.08152	514	.02958	8	.97127	7	14
47	.23825	28	.19725	499	.24532	31	.07639	513	.02965	7	.97120	7	13
48	.23853	28	.19228	498	.24562	30	.07127	511	.02972	7	.97113	7	12
49	.23882	29	.18733	496	.24593	31	.06616	510	.02980	8	.97106	7	11
50	0.23910	28	4.18238	494	0.24624	31	4.06107	510	1.02987	7	0.97100	6	10
51	.23938	28	.17744	493	.24655	31	.05599	509	.02994	7	.97093	7	9
52	.23966	28	.17252	492	.24686	31	.05092	508	.03002	8	.97086	7	8
53	.23995	29	.16761	491	.24717	31	.04586	506	.03009	7	.97079	7	7
54	.24023	28	.16271	490	.24747	30	.04081	504	.03017	8	.97072	7	6
55	0.24051	28	4.15782	489	0.24778	31	4.03578	503	1.03024	7	0.97065	7	5
56	.24079	28	.15295	488	.24809	31	.03076	502	.03032	8	.97058	7	4
57	.24108	29	.14809	487	.24840	31	.02574	501	.03039	7	.97051	7	3
58	.24136	28	.14323	486	.24871	31	.02074	500	.03046	7	.97044	7	2
59	.24164	28	.13839	484	.24902	31	.01576	499	.03054	8	.97037	7	1
60	0.24192	28	4.13357	482	0.24933	31	4.01078	498	1.03061	7	0.97030	7	0
↑ 103° →	cos	Diff. 1′	sec	Diff. 1′	cot	Diff. 1′	tan	Diff. 1′	csc	Diff. 1′	sin	Diff. 1′	↑ ← 76°

TABLE 2
Natural Trigonometric Functions

14° → ↓ ′	sin	Diff. 1′	csc	Diff. 1′	tan	Diff. 1′	cot	Diff. 1′	sec	Diff. 1′	cos	Diff. 1′	← 165° ↓ ′
0	0.24192		4.13357		0.24933		4.01078		1.03061		0.97030		60
1	.24220	28	.12875	481	.24964	31	.00582	497	.03069	8	.97023	7	59
2	.24249	29	.12394	480	.24995	31	4.00086	496	.03076	7	.97015	8	58
3	.24277	28	.11915	480	.25026	31	3.99592	494	.03084	8	.97008	7	57
4	.24305	28	.11437	479	.25056	30	.99099	492	.03091	7	.97001	7	56
5	0.24333	28	4.10960	478	0.25087	31	3.98607	491	1.03099	8	0.96994	7	55
6	.24362	29	.10484	476	.25118	31	.98117	490	.03106	7	.96987	7	54
7	.24390	28	.10009	474	.25149	31	.97627	490	.03114	8	.96980	7	53
8	.24418	28	.09535	473	.25180	31	.97139	489	.03121	7	.96973	7	52
9	.24446	28	.09063	472	.25211	31	.96651	488	.03129	8	.96966	7	51
10	0.24474	28	4.08591	471	0.25242	31	3.96165	487	1.03137	8	0.96959	7	50
11	.24503	29	.08121	470	.25273	31	.95680	486	.03144	7	.96952	7	49
12	.24531	28	.07652	470	.25304	31	.95196	483	.03152	8	.96945	7	48
13	.24559	28	.07184	469	.25335	31	.94713	482	.03159	7	.96937	8	47
14	.24587	28	.06717	467	.25366	31	.94232	481	.03167	8	.96930	7	46
15	0.24615	28	4.06251	466	0.25397	31	3.93751	480	1.03175	8	0.96923	7	45
16	.24644	29	.05786	464	.25428	31	.93271	480	.03182	7	.96916	7	44
17	.24672	28	.05322	463	.25459	31	.92793	479	.03190	8	.96909	7	43
18	.24700	28	.04860	462	.25490	31	.92316	478	.03197	7	.96902	7	42
19	.24728	28	.04398	461	.25521	31	.91839	477	.03205	8	.96894	8	41
20	0.24756	28	4.03938	460	0.25552	31	3.91364	476	1.03213	8	0.96887	7	40
21	.24784	28	.03479	460	.25583	31	.90890	474	.03220	7	.96880	7	39
22	.24813	29	.03020	459	.25614	31	.90417	473	.03228	8	.96873	7	38
23	.24841	28	.02563	458	.25645	31	.89945	471	.03236	8	.96866	7	37
24	.24869	28	.02107	457	.25676	31	.89474	470	.03244	8	.96858	8	36
25	0.24897	28	4.01652	456	0.25707	31	3.89004	470	1.03251	7	0.96851	7	35
26	.24925	28	.01198	453	.25738	31	.88536	469	.03259	8	.96844	7	34
27	.24954	29	.00745	452	.25769	31	.88068	468	.03267	8	.96837	7	33
28	.24982	28	4.00293	451	.25800	31	.87601	467	.03275	8	.96829	8	32
29	.25010	28	3.99843	450	.25831	31	.87136	466	.03282	7	.96822	7	31
30	0.25038	28	3.99393	450	0.25862	31	3.86671	464	1.03290	8	0.96815	7	30
31	.25066	28	.98944	449	.25893	31	.86208	463	.03298	8	.96807	8	29
32	.25094	28	.98497	448	.25924	31	.85745	462	.03306	8	.96800	7	28
33	.25122	28	.98050	447	.25955	31	.85284	461	.03313	7	.96793	7	27
34	.25151	29	.97604	446	.25986	31	.84824	460	.03321	8	.96786	7	26
35	0.25179	28	3.97160	444	0.26017	31	3.84364	460	1.03329	8	0.96778	8	25
36	.25207	28	.96716	443	.26048	31	.83906	459	.03337	8	.96771	7	24
37	.25235	28	.96274	442	.26079	31	.83449	458	.03345	8	.96764	7	23
38	.25263	28	.95832	441	.26110	31	.82992	457	.03353	8	.96756	8	22
39	.25291	28	.95392	440	.26141	31	.82537	456	.03360	7	.96749	7	21
40	0.25320	29	3.94952	440	0.26172	31	3.82083	454	1.03368	8	0.96742	7	20
41	.25348	28	.94514	439	.26203	31	.81630	453	.03376	8	.96734	8	19
42	.25376	28	.94076	438	.26235	32	.81177	452	.03384	8	.96727	7	18
43	.25404	28	.93640	437	.26266	31	.80726	451	.03392	8	.96719	8	17
44	.25432	28	.93204	436	.26297	31	.80276	450	.03400	8	.96712	7	16
45	0.25460	28	3.92770	434	0.26328	31	3.79827	450	1.03408	8	0.96705	7	15
46	.25488	28	.92337	433	.26359	31	.79378	449	.03416	8	.96697	8	14
47	.25516	28	.91904	432	.26390	31	.78931	448	.03424	8	.96690	7	13
48	.25545	29	.91473	431	.26421	31	.78485	447	.03432	8	.96682	8	12
49	.25573	28	.91042	430	.26452	31	.78040	446	.03439	7	.96675	7	11
50	0.25601	28	3.90613	430	0.26483	31	3.77595	444	1.03447	8	0.96667	8	10
51	.25629	28	.90184	429	.26515	32	.77152	443	.03455	8	.96660	7	9
52	.25657	28	.89756	428	.26546	31	.76709	442	.03463	8	.96653	7	8
53	.25685	28	.89330	427	.26577	31	.76268	441	.03471	8	.96645	8	7
54	.25713	28	.88904	426	.26608	31	.75828	440	.03479	8	.96638	7	6
55	0.25741	28	3.88479	424	0.26639	31	3.75388	440	1.03487	8	0.96630	8	5
56	.25769	28	.88056	423	.26670	31	.74950	439	.03495	8	.96623	7	4
57	.25798	29	.87633	422	.26701	31	.74512	438	.03503	8	.96615	8	3
58	.25826	28	.87211	421	.26733	32	.74075	437	.03511	8	.96608	7	2
59	.25854	28	.86790	420	.26764	31	.73640	436	.03520	9	.96600	8	1
60	0.25882	28	3.86370	420	0.26795	31	3.73205	434	1.03528	8	0.96593	7	0
↑ 104° →	cos	Diff. 1′	sec	Diff. 1′	cot	Diff. 1′	tan	Diff. 1′	csc	Diff. 1′	sin	Diff. 1′	← 75° ↑

TABLE 2
Natural Trigonometric Functions

15° → ↓ ′	sin	Diff. 1′	csc	Diff. 1′	tan	Diff. 1′	cot	Diff. 1′	sec	Diff. 1′	cos	Diff. 1′	← 164° ↓ ′
0	0.25882		3.86370		0.26795		3.73205		1.03528		0.96593		60
1	.25910	28	.85951	419	.26826	31	.72771	433	.03536	8	.96585	8	59
2	.25938	28	.85533	419	.26857	31	.72338	432	.03544	8	.96578	7	58
3	.25966	28	.85116	418	.26888	31	.71907	431	.03552	8	.96570	8	57
4	.25994	28	.84700	417	.26920	32	.71476	430	.03560	8	.96562	8	56
5	0.26022	28	3.84285	416	0.26951	31	3.71046	430	1.03568	8	0.96555	7	55
6	.26050	28	.83871	414	.26982	31	.70616	430	.03576	8	.96547	8	54
7	.26079	29	.83457	413	.27013	31	.70188	429	.03584	8	.96540	7	53
8	.26107	28	.83045	412	.27044	31	.69761	428	.03592	8	.96532	8	52
9	.26135	28	.82633	411	.27076	32	.69335	427	.03601	9	.96524	8	51
10	0.26163	28	3.82223	410	0.27107	31	3.68909	426	1.03609	8	0.96517	7	50
11	.26191	28	.81813	410	.27138	31	.68485	424	.03617	8	.96509	8	49
12	.26219	28	.81404	409	.27169	31	.68061	423	.03625	8	.96502	7	48
13	.26247	28	.80996	408	.27201	32	.67638	422	.03633	8	.96494	8	47
14	.26275	28	.80589	407	.27232	31	.67217	421	.03642	9	.96486	8	46
15	0.26303	28	3.80183	407	0.27263	31	3.66796	420	1.03650	8	0.96479	7	45
16	.26331	28	.79778	406	.27294	31	.66376	420	.03658	8	.96471	8	44
17	.26359	28	.79374	404	.27326	32	.65957	420	.03666	8	.96463	8	43
18	.26387	28	.78970	403	.27357	31	.65538	419	.03674	8	.96456	7	42
19	.26415	28	.78568	402	.27388	31	.65121	418	.03683	9	.96448	8	41
20	0.26443	28	3.78166	401	0.27419	31	3.64705	417	1.03691	8	0.96440	8	40
21	.26471	28	.77765	400	.27451	32	.64289	416	.03699	8	.96433	7	39
22	.26500	29	.77365	400	.27482	31	.63874	414	.03708	9	.96425	8	38
23	.26528	28	.76966	399	.27513	31	.63461	413	.03716	8	.96417	8	37
24	.26556	28	.76568	399	.27545	32	.63048	412	.03724	8	.96410	7	36
25	0.26584	28	3.76171	398	0.27576	31	3.62636	412	1.03732	8	0.96402	8	35
26	.26612	28	.75775	397	.27607	31	.62224	411	.03741	9	.96394	8	34
27	.26640	28	.75379	396	.27638	31	.61814	410	.03749	8	.96386	8	33
28	.26668	28	.74984	394	.27670	32	.61405	410	.03757	8	.96379	7	32
29	.26696	28	.74591	393	.27701	31	.60996	409	.03766	9	.96371	8	31
30	0.26724	28	3.74198	392	0.27732	31	3.60588	408	1.03774	8	0.96363	8	30
31	.26752	28	.73806	392	.27764	32	.60181	407	.03783	9	.96355	8	29
32	.26780	28	.73414	391	.27795	31	.59775	407	.03791	8	.96347	8	28
33	.26808	28	.73024	390	.27826	31	.59370	406	.03799	8	.96340	7	27
34	.26836	28	.72635	390	.27858	32	.58966	404	.03808	9	.96332	8	26
35	0.26864	28	3.72246	389	0.27889	31	3.58562	403	1.03816	8	0.96324	8	25
36	.26892	28	.71858	388	.27921	32	.58160	402	.03825	9	.96316	8	24
37	.26920	28	.71471	387	.27952	31	.57758	401	.03833	8	.96308	8	23
38	.26948	28	.71085	387	.27983	31	.57357	400	.03842	9	.96301	7	22
39	.26976	28	.70700	386	.28015	32	.56957	400	.03850	8	.96293	8	21
40	0.27004	28	3.70315	384	0.28046	31	3.56557	400	1.03858	8	0.96285	8	20
41	.27032	28	.69931	383	.28077	31	.56159	399	.03867	9	.96277	8	19
42	.27060	28	.69549	382	.28109	32	.55761	398	.03875	8	.96269	8	18
43	.27088	28	.69167	382	.28140	31	.55364	397	.03884	9	.96261	8	17
44	.27116	28	.68785	381	.28172	32	.54968	397	.03892	8	.96253	8	16
45	0.27144	28	3.68405	380	0.28203	31	3.54573	396	1.03901	9	0.96246	7	15
46	.27172	28	.68025	380	.28234	31	.54179	394	.03909	8	.96238	8	14
47	.27200	28	.67647	379	.28266	32	.53785	393	.03918	9	.96230	8	13
48	.27228	28	.67269	378	.28297	31	.53393	392	.03927	9	.96222	8	12
49	.27256	28	.66892	378	.28329	32	.53001	391	.03935	8	.96214	8	11
50	0.27284	28	3.66515	377	0.28360	31	3.52609	391	1.03944	9	0.96206	8	10
51	.27312	28	.66140	376	.28391	31	.52219	390	.03952	8	.96198	8	9
52	.27340	28	.65765	374	.28423	32	.51829	390	.03961	9	.96190	8	8
53	.27368	28	.65391	373	.28454	31	.51441	389	.03969	8	.96182	8	7
54	.27396	28	.65018	373	.28486	32	.51053	388	.03978	9	.96174	8	6
55	0.27424	28	3.64645	372	0.28517	31	3.50666	388	1.03987	9	0.96166	8	5
56	.27452	28	.64274	371	.28549	32	.50279	387	.03995	8	.96158	8	4
57	.27480	28	.63903	370	.28580	31	.49894	386	.04004	9	.96150	8	3
58	.27508	28	.63533	370	.28612	32	.49509	384	.04013	9	.96142	8	2
59	.27536	28	.63164	370	.28643	31	.49125	384	.04021	8	.96134	8	1
60	0.27564	28	3.62796	369	0.28675	32	3.48741	383	1.04030	9	0.96126	8	0
↑ 105° →	cos	Diff. 1′	sec	Diff. 1′	cot	Diff. 1′	tan	Diff. 1′	csc	Diff. 1′	sin	Diff. 1′	← 74° ↑

TABLE 2

Natural Trigonometric Functions

16° → ↓ ′	sin	Diff. 1′	csc	Diff. 1′	tan	Diff. 1′	cot	Diff. 1′	sec	Diff. 1′	cos	Diff. 1′	← 163° ↓ ′
0	0.27564		3.62796		0.28675		3.48741		1.04030		0.96126		60
1	.27592	28	.62428	368	.28706	31	.48359	382	.04039	9	.96118	8	59
2	.27620	28	.62061	367	.28738	32	.47977	381	.04047	8	.96110	8	58
3	.27648	28	.61695	367	.28769	31	.47596	380	.04056	9	.96102	8	57
4	.27676	28	.61330	366	.28801	32	.47216	380	.04065	9	.96094	8	56
5	0.27704	28	3.60965	364	0.28832	31	3.46837	380	1.04073	8	0.96086	8	55
6	.27731	27	.60601	363	.28864	32	.46458	379	.04082	9	.96078	8	54
7	.27759	28	.60238	363	.28895	31	.46080	378	.04091	9	.96070	8	53
8	.27787	28	.59876	362	.28927	32	.45703	378	.04100	9	.96062	8	52
9	.27815	28	.59514	361	.28958	31	.45327	377	.04108	8	.96054	8	51
10	0.27843	28	3.59154	360	0.28990	32	3.44951	376	1.04117	9	0.96046	8	50
11	.27871	28	.58794	360	.29021	31	.44576	374	.04126	9	.96037	9	49
12	.27899	28	.58434	360	.29053	32	.44202	374	.04135	9	.96029	8	48
13	.27927	28	.58076	359	.29084	31	.43829	373	.04144	9	.96021	8	47
14	.27955	28	.57718	358	.29116	32	.43456	372	.04152	8	.96013	8	46
15	0.27983	28	3.57361	358	0.29147	31	3.43084	371	1.04161	9	0.96005	8	45
16	.28011	28	.57005	357	.29179	32	.42713	371	.04170	9	.95997	8	44
17	.28039	28	.56649	356	.29210	31	.42343	370	.04179	9	.95989	8	43
18	.28067	28	.56294	354	.29242	32	.41973	370	.04188	9	.95981	8	42
19	.28095	28	.55940	354	.29274	32	.41604	369	.04197	9	.95972	9	41
20	0.28123	28	3.55587	353	0.29305	31	3.41236	369	1.04206	9	0.95964	8	40
21	.28150	27	.55234	352	.29337	32	.40869	368	.04214	8	.95956	8	39
22	.28178	28	.54883	351	.29368	31	.40502	367	.04223	9	.95948	8	38
23	.28206	28	.54531	351	.29400	32	.40136	366	.04232	9	.95940	8	37
24	.28234	28	.54181	350	.29432	32	.39771	366	.04241	9	.95931	9	36
25	0.28262	28	3.53831	350	0.29463	31	3.39406	364	1.04250	9	0.95923	8	35
26	.28290	28	.53482	349	.29495	32	.39042	363	.04259	9	.95915	8	34
27	.28318	28	.53134	349	.29526	31	.38679	363	.04268	9	.95907	8	33
28	.28346	28	.52787	348	.29558	32	.38317	362	.04277	9	.95898	9	32
29	.28374	28	.52440	347	.29590	32	.37955	361	.04286	9	.95890	8	31
30	0.28402	28	3.52094	347	0.29621	31	3.37594	360	1.04295	9	0.95882	8	30
31	.28429	27	.51748	346	.29653	32	.37234	360	.04304	9	.95874	8	29
32	.28457	28	.51404	344	.29685	32	.36875	360	.04313	9	.95865	9	28
33	.28485	28	.51060	343	.29716	31	.36516	359	.04322	9	.95857	8	27
34	.28513	28	.50716	343	.29748	32	.36158	359	.04331	9	.95849	8	26
35	0.28541	28	3.50374	342	0.29780	32	3.35800	358	1.04340	9	0.95841	8	25
36	.28569	28	.50032	341	.29811	31	.35443	357	.04349	9	.95832	9	24
37	.28597	28	.49691	341	.29843	32	.35087	357	.04358	9	.95824	8	23
38	.28625	28	.49350	340	.29875	32	.34732	356	.04367	9	.95816	8	22
39	.28652	27	.49010	340	.29906	31	.34377	354	.04376	9	.95807	9	21
40	0.28680	28	3.48671	340	0.29938	32	3.34023	353	1.04385	9	0.95799	8	20
41	.28708	28	.48333	339	.29970	32	.33670	353	.04394	9	.95791	8	19
42	.28736	28	.47995	338	.30001	31	.33317	352	.04403	9	.95782	9	18
43	.28764	28	.47658	338	.30033	32	.32965	351	.04413	10	.95774	8	17
44	.28792	28	.47321	337	.30065	32	.32614	351	.04422	9	.95766	8	16
45	0.28820	28	3.46986	336	0.30097	32	3.32264	350	1.04431	9	0.95757	9	15
46	.28847	27	.46651	336	.30128	31	.31914	350	.04440	9	.95749	8	14
47	.28875	28	.46316	334	.30160	32	.31565	350	.04449	9	.95740	9	13
48	.28903	28	.45983	333	.30192	32	.31216	349	.04458	9	.95732	8	12
49	.28931	28	.45650	333	.30224	32	.30868	348	.04468	10	.95724	8	11
50	0.28959	28	3.45317	332	0.30255	31	3.30521	348	1.04477	9	0.95715	9	10
51	.28987	28	.44986	331	.30287	32	.30174	347	.04486	9	.95707	8	9
52	.29015	28	.44655	331	.30319	32	.29829	346	.04495	9	.95698	9	8
53	.29042	27	.44324	330	.30351	32	.29483	346	.04504	9	.95690	8	7
54	.29070	28	.43995	330	.30382	31	.29139	344	.04514	10	.95681	9	6
55	0.29098	28	3.43666	330	0.30414	32	3.28795	343	1.04523	9	0.95673	8	5
56	.29126	28	.43337	329	.30446	32	.28452	343	.04532	9	.95664	9	4
57	.29154	28	.43010	328	.30478	32	.28109	342	.04541	9	.95656	8	3
58	.29182	28	.42683	328	.30509	31	.27767	341	.04551	10	.95647	9	2
59	.29209	27	.42356	327	.30541	32	.27426	341	.04560	9	.95639	8	1
60	0.29237	28	3.42030	326	0.30573	32	3.27085	340	1.04569	9	0.95630	9	0
↑ 106° →	cos	Diff. 1′	sec	Diff. 1′	cot	Diff. 1′	tan	Diff. 1′	csc	Diff. 1′	sin	Diff. 1′	↑ ← 73°

TABLE 2

Natural Trigonometric Functions

17° → ↓ ′	sin	Diff. 1′	csc	Diff. 1′	tan	Diff. 1′	cot	Diff. 1′	sec	Diff. 1′	cos	Diff. 1′	← 162° ↓ ′
0	0.29237		3.42030		0.30573		3.27085		1.04569		0.95630		60
1	.29265	28	.41705	326	.30605	32	.26745	340	.04578	9	.95622	8	59
2	.29293	28	.41381	324	.30637	32	.26406	340	.04588	10	.95613	9	58
3	.29321	28	.41057	323	.30669	32	.26067	339	.04597	9	.95605	8	57
4	.29348	27	.40734	323	.30700	31	.25729	339	.04606	9	.95596	9	56
5	0.29376	28	3.40411	322	0.30732	32	3.25392	338	1.04616	10	0.95588	8	55
6	.29404	28	.40089	321	.30764	32	.25055	337	.04625	9	.95579	9	54
7	.29432	28	.39768	321	.30796	32	.24719	337	.04635	10	.95571	8	53
8	.29460	28	.39448	320	.30828	32	.24383	336	.04644	9	.95562	9	52
9	.29487	27	.39128	320	.30860	32	.24049	334	.04653	9	.95554	8	51
10	0.29515	28	3.38808	320	0.30891	31	3.23714	334	1.04663	10	0.95545	9	50
11	.29543	28	.38489	319	.30923	32	.23381	333	.04672	9	.95536	9	49
12	.29571	28	.38171	319	.30955	32	.23048	332	.04682	10	.95528	8	48
13	.29599	28	.37854	318	.30987	32	.22715	332	.04691	9	.95519	9	47
14	.29626	27	.37537	317	.31019	32	.22384	331	.04700	9	.95511	8	46
15	0.29654	28	3.37221	317	0.31051	32	3.22053	331	1.04710	10	0.95502	9	45
16	.29682	28	.36905	316	.31083	32	.21722	330	.04719	9	.95493	9	44
17	.29710	28	.36590	314	.31115	32	.21392	330	.04729	10	.95485	8	43
18	.29737	27	.36276	314	.31147	32	.21063	330	.04738	9	.95476	9	42
19	.29765	28	.35962	313	.31178	31	.20734	329	.04748	10	.95467	9	41
20	0.29793	28	3.35649	313	0.31210	32	3.20406	329	1.04757	9	0.95459	8	40
21	.29821	28	.35336	312	.31242	32	.20079	328	.04767	10	.95450	9	39
22	.29849	28	.35025	311	.31274	32	.19752	327	.04776	9	.95441	9	38
23	.29876	27	.34713	311	.31306	32	.19426	327	.04786	10	.95433	8	37
24	.29904	28	.34403	310	.31338	32	.19100	326	.04795	9	.95424	9	36
25	0.29932	28	3.34092	310	0.31370	32	3.18775	324	1.04805	10	0.95415	9	35
26	.29960	28	.33783	310	.31402	32	.18451	324	.04815	10	.95407	8	34
27	.29987	27	.33474	309	.31434	32	.18127	323	.04824	9	.95398	9	33
28	.30015	28	.33166	309	.31466	32	.17804	323	.04834	10	.95389	9	32
29	.30043	28	.32858	308	.31498	32	.17481	322	.04843	9	.95380	9	31
30	0.30071	28	3.32551	308	0.31530	32	3.17159	321	1.04853	10	0.95372	8	30
31	.30098	27	.32244	307	.31562	32	.16838	321	.04863	10	.95363	9	29
32	.30126	28	.31939	306	.31594	32	.16517	320	.04872	9	.95354	9	28
33	.30154	28	.31633	306	.31626	32	.16197	320	.04882	10	.95345	9	27
34	.30182	28	.31328	304	.31658	32	.15877	320	.04891	9	.95337	8	26
35	0.30209	27	3.31024	304	0.31690	32	3.15558	320	1.04901	10	0.95328	9	25
36	.30237	28	.30721	303	.31722	32	.15240	319	.04911	10	.95319	9	24
37	.30265	28	.30418	302	.31754	32	.14922	318	.04920	9	.95310	9	23
38	.30292	27	.30115	302	.31786	32	.14605	318	.04930	10	.95301	9	22
39	.30320	28	.29814	301	.31818	32	.14288	317	.04940	10	.95293	8	21
40	0.30348	28	3.29512	301	0.31850	32	3.13972	317	1.04950	10	0.95284	9	20
41	.30376	28	.29212	300	.31882	32	.13656	316	.04959	9	.95275	9	19
42	.30403	27	.28912	300	.31914	32	.13341	314	.04969	10	.95266	9	18
43	.30431	28	.28612	300	.31946	32	.13027	314	.04979	10	.95257	9	17
44	.30459	28	.28313	299	.31978	32	.12713	313	.04989	10	.95248	9	16
45	0.30486	27	3.28015	299	0.32010	32	3.12400	313	1.04998	9	0.95240	8	15
46	.30514	28	.27717	298	.32042	32	.12087	312	.05008	10	.95231	9	14
47	.30542	28	.27420	298	.32074	32	.11775	312	.05018	10	.95222	9	13
48	.30570	28	.27123	297	.32106	32	.11464	311	.05028	10	.95213	9	12
49	.30597	27	.26827	297	.32139	33	.11153	310	.05038	10	.95204	9	11
50	0.30625	28	3.26531	296	0.32171	32	3.10842	310	1.05047	9	0.95195	9	10
51	.30653	28	.26237	294	.32203	32	.10532	310	.05057	10	.95186	9	9
52	.30680	27	.25942	294	.32235	32	.10223	310	.05067	10	.95177	9	8
53	.30708	28	.25648	293	.32267	32	.09914	309	.05077	10	.95168	9	7
54	.30736	28	.25355	293	.32299	32	.09606	309	.05087	10	.95159	9	6
55	0.30763	27	3.25062	292	0.32331	32	3.09298	308	1.05097	10	0.95150	9	5
56	.30791	28	.24770	292	.32363	32	.08991	308	.05107	10	.95142	8	4
57	.30819	28	.24478	291	.32396	33	.08685	307	.05116	9	.95133	9	3
58	.30846	27	.24187	291	.32428	32	.08379	306	.05126	10	.95124	9	2
59	.30874	28	.23897	290	.32460	32	.08073	306	.05136	10	.95115	9	1
60	0.30902	28	3.23607	290	0.32492	32	3.07768	304	1.05146	10	0.95106	9	0
↑ 107° →	cos	Diff. 1′	sec	Diff. 1′	cot	Diff. 1′	tan	Diff. 1′	csc	Diff. 1′	sin	Diff. 1′	↑ ← 72°

TABLE 2
Natural Trigonometric Functions

18° → ↓	sin	Diff. 1′	csc	Diff. 1′	tan	Diff. 1′	cot	Diff. 1′	sec	Diff. 1′	cos	Diff. 1′	← 161° ↓
′													′
0	0.30902		3.23607		0.32492		3.07768		1.05146		0.95106		60
1	.30929	27	.23317	290	.32524	32	.07464	304	.05156	10	.95097	9	59
2	.30957	28	.23028	289	.32556	32	.07160	303	.05166	10	.95088	9	58
3	.30985	28	.22740	289	.32588	32	.06857	303	.05176	10	.95079	9	57
4	.31012	27	.22452	288	.32621	33	.06554	302	.05186	10	.95070	9	56
5	0.31040	28	3.22165	288	0.32653	32	3.06252	302	1.05196	10	0.95061	9	55
6	.31068	28	.21878	287	.32685	32	.05950	301	.05206	10	.95052	9	54
7	.31095	27	.21592	287	.32717	32	.05649	301	.05216	10	.95043	9	53
8	.31123	28	.21306	286	.32749	32	.05349	300	.05226	10	.95033	10	52
9	.31151	28	.21021	286	.32782	33	.05049	300	.05236	10	.95024	9	51
10	0.31178	27	3.20737	284	0.32814	32	3.04749	300	1.05246	10	0.95015	9	50
11	.31206	28	.20453	284	.32846	32	.04450	299	.05256	10	.95006	9	49
12	.31233	27	.20169	283	.32878	32	.04152	299	.05266	10	.94997	9	48
13	.31261	28	.19886	283	.32911	33	.03854	298	.05276	10	.94988	9	47
14	.31289	28	.19604	282	.32943	32	.03556	298	.05286	10	.94979	9	46
15	0.31316	27	3.19322	281	0.32975	32	3.03260	297	1.05297	11	0.94970	9	45
16	.31344	28	.19040	281	.33007	32	.02963	297	.05307	10	.94961	9	44
17	.31372	28	.18759	280	.33040	33	.02667	296	.05317	10	.94952	9	43
18	.31399	27	.18479	280	.33072	32	.02372	296	.05327	10	.94943	9	42
19	.31427	28	.18199	280	.33104	32	.02077	294	.05337	10	.94933	10	41
20	0.31454	27	3.17920	280	0.33136	32	3.01783	294	1.05347	10	0.94924	9	40
21	.31482	28	.17641	279	.33169	33	.01489	293	.05357	10	.94915	9	39
22	.31510	28	.17363	279	.33201	32	.01196	293	.05367	10	.94906	9	38
23	.31537	27	.17085	278	.33233	32	.00903	292	.05378	11	.94897	9	37
24	.31565	28	.16808	278	.33266	33	.00611	292	.05388	10	.94888	9	36
25	0.31593	28	3.16531	277	0.33298	32	3.00319	291	1.05398	10	0.94878	10	35
26	.31620	27	.16255	277	.33330	32	3.00028	291	.05408	10	.94869	9	34
27	.31648	28	.15979	276	.33363	33	2.99738	290	.05418	10	.94860	9	33
28	.31675	27	.15704	276	.33395	32	.99447	290	.05429	11	.94851	9	32
29	.31703	28	.15429	274	.33427	32	.99158	290	.05439	10	.94842	9	31
30	0.31730	27	3.15155	274	0.33460	33	2.98868	290	1.05449	10	0.94832	10	30
31	.31758	28	.14881	273	.33492	32	.98580	289	.05459	10	.94823	9	29
32	.31786	28	.14608	273	.33524	32	.98292	289	.05470	11	.94814	9	28
33	.31813	27	.14335	272	.33557	33	.98004	288	.05480	10	.94805	9	27
34	.31841	28	.14063	272	.33589	32	.97717	288	.05490	10	.94795	10	26
35	0.31868	27	3.13791	271	0.33621	32	2.97430	287	1.05501	11	0.94786	9	25
36	.31896	28	.13520	271	.33654	33	.97144	287	.05511	10	.94777	9	24
37	.31923	27	.13249	270	.33686	32	.96858	286	.05521	10	.94768	9	23
38	.31951	28	.12979	270	.33718	32	.96573	286	.05532	11	.94758	10	22
39	.31979	28	.12709	270	.33751	33	.96288	284	.05542	10	.94749	9	21
40	0.32006	27	3.12440	270	0.33783	32	2.96004	284	1.05552	10	0.94740	9	20
41	.32034	28	.12171	269	.33816	33	.95721	283	.05563	11	.94730	10	19
42	.32061	27	.11903	269	.33848	32	.95437	283	.05573	10	.94721	9	18
43	.32089	28	.11635	268	.33881	33	.95155	282	.05584	11	.94712	9	17
44	.32116	27	.11367	268	.33913	32	.94872	282	.05594	10	.94702	10	16
45	0.32144	28	3.11101	267	0.33945	32	2.94591	281	1.05604	10	0.94693	9	15
46	.32171	27	.10834	267	.33978	33	.94309	281	.05615	11	.94684	9	14
47	.32199	28	.10568	266	.34010	32	.94028	280	.05625	10	.94674	10	13
48	.32227	28	.10303	266	.34043	33	.93748	280	.05636	11	.94665	9	12
49	.32254	27	.10038	264	.34075	32	.93468	280	.05646	10	.94656	9	11
50	0.32282	28	3.09774	264	0.34108	33	2.93189	280	1.05657	11	0.94646	10	10
51	.32309	27	.09510	263	.34140	32	.92910	279	.05667	10	.94637	9	9
52	.32337	28	.09246	263	.34173	33	.92632	279	.05678	11	.94627	10	8
53	.32364	27	.08983	263	.34205	32	.92354	278	.05688	10	.94618	9	7
54	.32392	28	.08721	262	.34238	33	.92076	278	.05699	11	.94609	9	6
55	0.32419	27	3.08459	262	0.34270	32	2.91799	278	1.05709	10	0.94599	10	5
56	.32447	28	.08197	261	.34303	33	.91523	277	.05720	11	.94590	9	4
57	.32474	27	.07936	261	.34335	32	.91246	277	.05730	10	.94580	10	3
58	.32502	28	.07675	260	.34368	33	.90971	276	.05741	11	.94571	9	2
59	.32529	27	.07415	260	.34400	32	.90696	276	.05751	10	.94561	10	1
60	0.32557	28	3.07155	260	0.34433	33	2.90421	274	1.05762	11	0.94552	9	0
↑ 108° →	cos	Diff. 1′	sec	Diff. 1′	cot	Diff. 1′	tan	Diff. 1′	csc	Diff. 1′	sin	Diff. 1′ ←	↑ 71°

TABLE 2
Natural Trigonometric Functions

19° → ↓	sin	Diff. 1′	csc	Diff. 1′	tan	Diff. 1′	cot	Diff. 1′	sec	Diff. 1′	cos	Diff. 1′	← 160° ↓
′													′
0	0.32557		3.07155		0.34433		2.90421		1.05762		0.94552		60
1	.32584	27	.06896	260	.34465	32	.90147	274	.05773	11	.94542	10	59
2	.32612	28	.06637	259	.34498	33	.89873	273	.05783	10	.94533	9	58
3	.32639	27	.06379	259	.34530	32	.89600	273	.05794	11	.94523	10	57
4	.32667	28	.06121	258	.34563	33	.89327	272	.05805	11	.94514	9	56
5	0.32694	27	3.05864	258	0.34596	33	2.89055	272	1.05815	10	0.94504	10	55
6	.32722	28	.05607	257	.34628	32	.88783	271	.05826	11	.94495	9	54
7	.32749	27	.05350	257	.34661	33	.88511	271	.05836	10	.94485	10	53
8	.32777	28	.05094	256	.34693	32	.88240	270	.05847	11	.94476	9	52
9	.32804	27	.04839	256	.34726	33	.87970	270	.05858	11	.94466	10	51
10	0.32832	28	3.04584	256	0.34758	32	2.87700	270	1.05869	11	0.94457	9	50
11	.32859	27	.04329	254	.34791	33	.87430	270	.05879	10	.94447	10	49
12	.32887	28	.04075	254	.34824	33	.87161	270	.05890	11	.94438	9	48
13	.32914	27	.03821	253	.34856	32	.86892	269	.05901	11	.94428	10	47
14	.32942	28	.03568	253	.34889	33	.86624	269	.05911	10	.94418	10	46
15	0.32969	27	3.03315	252	0.34922	33	2.86356	268	1.05922	11	0.94409	9	45
16	.32997	28	.03062	252	.34954	32	.86089	268	.05933	11	.94399	10	44
17	.33024	27	.02810	251	.34987	33	.85822	267	.05944	11	.94390	9	43
18	.33051	27	.02559	251	.35020	33	.85555	267	.05955	11	.94380	10	42
19	.33079	28	.02308	251	.35052	32	.85289	267	.05965	10	.94370	10	41
20	0.33106	27	3.02057	250	0.35085	33	2.85023	266	1.05976	11	0.94361	9	40
21	.33134	28	.01807	250	.35118	33	.84758	266	.05987	11	.94351	10	39
22	.33161	27	.01557	250	.35150	32	.84494	264	.05998	11	.94342	9	38
23	.33189	28	.01308	250	.35183	33	.84229	264	.06009	11	.94332	10	37
24	.33216	27	.01059	249	.35216	33	.83965	263	.06020	11	.94322	10	36
25	0.33244	28	3.00810	249	0.35248	32	2.83702	263	1.06030	10	0.94313	9	35
26	.33271	27	.00562	249	.35281	33	.83439	262	.06041	11	.94303	10	34
27	.33298	27	.00315	248	.35314	33	.83176	262	.06052	11	.94293	10	33
28	.33326	28	3.00067	248	.35346	32	.82914	262	.06063	11	.94284	9	32
29	.33353	27	2.99821	247	.35379	33	.82653	261	.06074	11	.94274	10	31
30	0.33381	28	2.99574	247	0.35412	33	2.82391	261	1.06085	11	0.94264	10	30
31	.33408	27	.99329	246	.35445	33	.82130	260	.06096	11	.94254	10	29
32	.33436	28	.99083	246	.35477	32	.81870	260	.06107	11	.94245	9	28
33	.33463	27	.98838	246	.35510	33	.81610	260	.06118	11	.94235	10	27
34	.33490	27	.98594	244	.35543	33	.81350	260	.06129	11	.94225	10	26
35	0.33518	28	2.98349	244	0.35576	33	2.81091	260	1.06140	11	0.94215	10	25
36	.33545	27	.98106	243	.35608	32	.80833	259	.06151	11	.94206	9	24
37	.33573	28	.97862	243	.35641	33	.80574	259	.06162	11	.94196	10	23
38	.33600	27	.97619	242	.35674	33	.80316	258	.06173	11	.94186	10	22
39	.33627	27	.97377	242	.35707	33	.80059	258	.06184	11	.94176	10	21
40	0.33655	28	2.97135	242	0.35740	33	2.79802	258	1.06195	11	0.94167	9	20
41	.33682	27	.96893	241	.35772	32	.79545	257	.06206	11	.94157	10	19
42	.33710	28	.96652	241	.35805	33	.79289	257	.06217	11	.94147	10	18
43	.33737	27	.96411	240	.35838	33	.79033	256	.06228	11	.94137	10	17
44	.33764	27	.96171	240	.35871	33	.78778	256	.06239	11	.94127	10	16
45	0.33792	28	2.95931	240	0.35904	33	2.78523	254	1.06250	11	0.94118	9	15
46	.33819	27	.95691	240	.35937	33	.78269	254	.06261	11	.94108	10	14
47	.33846	27	.95452	240	.35969	32	.78014	254	.06272	11	.94098	10	13
48	.33874	28	.95213	239	.36002	33	.77761	253	.06283	11	.94088	10	12
49	.33901	27	.94975	239	.36035	33	.77507	253	.06295	12	.94078	10	11
50	0.33929	28	2.94737	238	0.36068	33	2.77254	252	1.06306	11	0.94068	10	10
51	.33956	27	.94500	238	.36101	33	.77002	252	.06317	11	.94058	10	9
52	.33983	27	.94263	238	.36134	33	.76750	252	.06328	11	.94049	9	8
53	.34011	28	.94026	237	.36167	33	.76498	251	.06339	11	.94039	10	7
54	.34038	27	.93790	237	.36199	32	.76247	251	.06350	11	.94029	10	6
55	0.34065	27	2.93554	236	0.36232	33	2.75996	250	1.06362	12	0.94019	10	5
56	.34093	28	.93318	236	.36265	33	.75746	250	.06373	11	.94009	10	4
57	.34120	27	.93083	236	.36298	33	.75496	250	.06384	11	.93999	10	3
58	.34147	27	.92849	234	.36331	33	.75246	250	.06395	11	.93989	10	2
59	.34175	28	.92614	234	.36364	33	.74997	250	.06407	12	.93979	10	1
60	0.34202	27	2.92380	233	0.36397	33	2.74748	249	1.06418	11	0.93969	10	0
↑ 109° →	cos	Diff. 1′	sec	Diff. 1′	cot	Diff. 1′	tan	Diff. 1′	csc	Diff. 1′	sin	Diff. 1′ ←	↑ 70°

TABLE 2

Natural Trigonometric Functions

20°→ ↓	sin	Diff. 1′	csc	Diff. 1′	tan	Diff. 1′	cot	Diff. 1′	sec	Diff. 1′	cos	Diff. 1′	← 159° ↓
′													′
0	0.34202		2.92380		0.36397		2.74748		1.06418		0.93969		60
1	.34229	27	.92147	233	.36430	33	.74499	249	.06429	11	.93959	10	59
2	.34257	28	.91914	233	.36463	33	.74251	249	.06440	11	.93949	10	58
3	.34284	27	.91681	232	.36496	33	.74004	248	.06452	12	.93939	10	57
4	.34311	27	.91449	232	.36529	33	.73756	248	.06463	11	.93929	10	56
5	0.34339	28	2.91217	231	0.36562	33	2.73509	247	1.06474	11	0.93919	10	55
6	.34366	27	.90986	231	.36595	33	.73263	247	.06486	12	.93909	10	54
7	.34393	27	.90754	231	.36628	33	.73017	247	.06497	11	.93899	10	53
8	.34421	28	.90524	230	.36661	33	.72771	246	.06508	11	.93889	10	52
9	.34448	27	.90293	230	.36694	33	.72526	246	.06520	12	.93879	10	51
10	0.34475	27	2.90063	230	0.36727	33	2.72281	244	1.06531	11	0.93869	10	50
11	.34503	28	.89834	230	.36760	33	.72036	244	.06542	11	.93859	10	49
12	.34530	27	.89605	230	.36793	33	.71792	244	.06554	12	.93849	10	48
13	.34557	27	.89376	229	.36826	33	.71548	243	.06565	11	.93839	10	47
14	.34584	27	.89148	229	.36859	33	.71305	243	.06577	12	.93829	10	46
15	0.34612	28	2.88920	229	0.36892	33	2.71062	243	1.06588	11	0.93819	10	45
16	.34639	27	.88692	228	.36925	33	.70819	242	.06600	12	.93809	10	44
17	.34666	27	.88465	228	.36958	33	.70577	242	.06611	11	.93799	10	43
18	.34694	28	.88238	227	.36991	33	.70335	241	.06622	11	.93789	10	42
19	.34721	27	.88011	227	.37024	33	.70094	241	.06634	12	.93779	10	41
20	0.34748	27	2.87785	227	0.37057	33	2.69853	241	1.06645	11	0.93769	10	40
21	.34775	27	.87560	226	.37090	33	.69612	240	.06657	12	.93759	10	39
22	.34803	28	.87334	226	.37123	33	.69371	240	.06668	11	.93748	11	38
23	.34830	27	.87109	224	.37157	34	.69131	240	.06680	12	.93738	10	37
24	.34857	27	.86885	224	.37190	33	.68892	240	.06691	11	.93728	10	36
25	0.34884	27	2.86661	224	0.37223	33	2.68653	240	1.06703	12	0.93718	10	35
26	.34912	28	.86437	223	.37256	33	.68414	239	.06715	12	.93708	10	34
27	.34939	27	.86213	223	.37289	33	.68175	239	.06726	11	.93698	10	33
28	.34966	27	.85990	223	.37322	33	.67937	239	.06738	12	.93688	10	32
29	.34993	27	.85767	222	.37355	33	.67700	238	.06749	11	.93677	11	31
30	0.35021	28	2.85545	222	0.37388	33	2.67462	238	1.06761	12	0.93667	10	30
31	.35048	27	.85323	221	.37422	34	.67225	237	.06773	12	.93657	10	29
32	.35075	27	.85102	221	.37455	33	.66989	237	.06784	11	.93647	10	28
33	.35102	27	.84880	221	.37488	33	.66752	237	.06796	12	.93637	10	27
34	.35130	28	.84659	220	.37521	33	.66516	236	.06807	11	.93626	11	26
35	0.35157	27	2.84439	220	0.37554	33	2.66281	236	1.06819	12	0.93616	10	25
36	.35184	27	.84219	220	.37588	34	.66046	236	.06831	12	.93606	10	24
37	.35211	27	.83999	220	.37621	33	.65811	234	.06842	11	.93596	10	23
38	.35239	28	.83780	220	.37654	33	.65576	234	.06854	12	.93585	11	22
39	.35266	27	.83561	220	.37687	33	.65342	234	.06866	12	.93575	10	21
40	0.35293	27	2.83342	219	0.37720	33	2.65109	233	1.06878	12	0.93565	10	20
41	.35320	27	.83124	219	.37754	34	.64875	233	.06889	11	.93555	10	19
42	.35347	27	.82906	218	.37787	33	.64642	232	.06901	12	.93544	11	18
43	.35375	28	.82688	218	.37820	33	.64410	232	.06913	12	.93534	10	17
44	.35402	27	.82471	218	.37853	33	.64177	232	.06925	12	.93524	10	16
45	0.35429	27	2.82254	217	0.37887	34	2.63945	231	1.06936	11	0.93514	10	15
46	.35456	27	.82037	217	.37920	33	.63714	231	.06948	12	.93503	11	14
47	.35484	28	.81821	217	.37953	33	.63483	231	.06960	12	.93493	10	13
48	.35511	27	.81605	216	.37986	33	.63252	230	.06972	12	.93483	10	12
49	.35538	27	.81390	216	.38020	34	.63021	230	.06984	12	.93472	11	11
50	0.35565	27	2.81175	216	0.38053	33	2.62791	230	1.06995	11	0.93462	10	10
51	.35592	27	.80960	214	.38086	33	.62561	230	.07007	12	.93452	10	9
52	.35619	27	.80746	214	.38120	34	.62332	230	.07019	12	.93441	11	8
53	.35647	28	.80531	214	.38153	33	.62103	230	.07031	12	.93431	10	7
54	.35674	27	.80318	213	.38186	33	.61874	229	.07043	12	.93420	11	6
55	0.35701	27	2.80104	213	0.38220	34	2.61646	229	1.07055	12	0.93410	10	5
56	.35728	27	.79891	213	.38253	33	.61418	229	.07067	12	.93400	10	4
57	.35755	27	.79679	212	.38286	33	.61190	228	.07079	12	.93389	11	3
58	.35782	27	.79466	212	.38320	34	.60963	228	.07091	12	.93379	10	2
59	.35810	28	.79254	211	.38353	33	.60736	228	.07103	12	.93368	11	1
60	0.35837	27	2.79043	211	0.38386	33	2.60509	227	1.07114	11	0.93358	10	0
↑ 110°→	cos	Diff. 1′	sec	Diff. 1′	cot	Diff. 1′	tan	Diff. 1′	csc	Diff. 1′	sin	Diff. 1′	← 69° ↑

TABLE 2

Natural Trigonometric Functions

21°→ ↓	sin	Diff. 1′	csc	Diff. 1′	tan	Diff. 1′	cot	Diff. 1′	sec	Diff. 1′	cos	Diff. 1′	← 158° ↓
′													′
0	0.35837		2.79043		0.38386		2.60509		1.07114		0.93358		60
1	.35864	27	.78832	211	.38420	34	.60283	227	.07126	12	.93348	10	59
2	.35891	27	.78621	210	.38453	33	.60057	226	.07138	12	.93337	11	58
3	.35918	27	.78410	210	.38487	34	.59831	226	.07150	12	.93327	10	57
4	.35945	27	.78200	210	.38520	33	.59606	226	.07162	12	.93316	11	56
5	0.35973	28	2.77990	210	0.38553	33	2.59381	224	1.07174	12	0.93306	10	55
6	.36000	27	.77780	210	.38587	34	.59156	224	.07186	12	.93295	11	54
7	.36027	27	.77571	210	.38620	33	.58932	224	.07199	13	.93285	10	53
8	.36054	27	.77362	209	.38654	34	.58708	223	.07211	12	.93274	11	52
9	.36081	27	.77154	209	.38687	33	.58484	223	.07223	12	.93264	10	51
10	0.36108	27	2.76945	209	0.38721	34	2.58261	223	1.07235	12	0.93253	11	50
11	.36135	27	.76737	208	.38754	33	.58038	222	.07247	12	.93243	10	49
12	.36162	27	.76530	208	.38787	33	.57815	222	.07259	12	.93232	11	48
13	.36190	28	.76323	208	.38821	34	.57593	222	.07271	12	.93222	10	47
14	.36217	27	.76116	207	.38854	33	.57371	221	.07283	12	.93211	11	46
15	0.36244	27	2.75909	207	0.38888	34	2.57150	221	1.07295	12	0.93201	10	45
16	.36271	27	.75703	207	.38921	33	.56928	221	.07307	12	.93190	11	44
17	.36298	27	.75497	206	.38955	34	.56707	220	.07320	13	.93180	10	43
18	.36325	27	.75292	206	.38988	33	.56487	220	.07332	12	.93169	11	42
19	.36352	27	.75086	206	.39022	34	.56266	220	.07344	12	.93159	10	41
20	0.36379	27	2.74881	204	0.39055	33	2.56046	220	1.07356	12	0.93148	11	40
21	.36406	27	.74677	204	.39089	34	.55827	220	.07368	12	.93137	11	39
22	.36434	28	.74473	204	.39122	33	.55608	220	.07380	12	.93127	10	38
23	.36461	27	.74269	203	.39156	34	.55389	219	.07393	13	.93116	11	37
24	.36488	27	.74065	203	.39190	34	.55170	219	.07405	12	.93106	10	36
25	0.36515	27	2.73862	203	0.39223	33	2.54952	219	1.07417	12	0.93095	11	35
26	.36542	27	.73659	202	.39257	34	.54734	219	.07429	12	.93084	11	34
27	.36569	27	.73456	202	.39290	33	.54516	218	.07442	13	.93074	10	33
28	.36596	27	.73254	202	.39324	34	.54299	218	.07454	12	.93063	11	32
29	.36623	27	.73052	201	.39357	33	.54082	218	.07466	12	.93052	11	31
30	0.36650	27	2.72850	201	0.39391	34	2.53865	217	1.07479	13	0.93042	10	30
31	.36677	27	.72649	201	.39425	34	.53648	217	.07491	12	.93031	11	29
32	.36704	27	.72448	201	.39458	33	.53432	217	.07503	12	.93020	11	28
33	.36731	27	.72247	200	.39492	34	.53217	216	.07516	13	.93010	10	27
34	.36758	27	.72047	200	.39526	34	.53001	216	.07528	12	.92999	11	26
35	0.36785	27	2.71847	200	0.39559	33	2.52786	216	1.07540	12	0.92988	11	25
36	.36812	27	.71647	200	.39593	34	.52571	214	.07553	13	.92978	10	24
37	.36839	27	.71448	200	.39626	33	.52357	214	.07565	12	.92967	11	23
38	.36867	28	.71249	200	.39660	34	.52142	214	.07578	13	.92956	11	22
39	.36894	27	.71050	199	.39694	34	.51929	213	.07590	12	.92945	11	21
40	0.36921	27	2.70851	199	0.39727	33	2.51715	213	1.07602	12	0.92935	10	20
41	.36948	27	.70653	199	.39761	34	.51502	213	.07615	13	.92924	11	19
42	.36975	27	.70455	198	.39795	34	.51289	212	.07627	12	.92913	11	18
43	.37002	27	.70258	198	.39829	34	.51076	212	.07640	13	.92902	11	17
44	.37029	27	.70061	198	.39862	33	.50864	212	.07652	12	.92892	10	16
45	0.37056	27	2.69864	197	0.39896	34	2.50652	211	1.07665	13	0.92881	11	15
46	.37083	27	.69667	197	.39930	34	.50440	211	.07677	12	.92870	11	14
47	.37110	27	.69471	197	.39963	33	.50229	211	.07690	13	.92859	11	13
48	.37137	27	.69275	196	.39997	34	.50018	211	.07702	12	.92849	10	12
49	.37164	27	.69079	196	.40031	34	.49807	210	.07715	13	.92838	11	11
50	0.37191	27	2.68884	196	0.40065	34	2.49597	210	1.07727	12	0.92827	11	10
51	.37218	27	.68689	196	.40098	33	.49386	210	.07740	13	.92816	11	9
52	.37245	27	.68494	194	.40132	34	.49177	210	.07752	12	.92805	11	8
53	.37272	27	.68299	194	.40166	34	.48967	210	.07765	13	.92794	11	7
54	.37299	27	.68105	194	.40200	34	.48758	210	.07778	13	.92784	10	6
55	0.37326	27	2.67911	193	0.40234	34	2.48549	209	1.07790	12	0.92773	11	5
56	.37353	27	.67718	193	.40267	33	.48340	209	.07803	13	.92762	11	4
57	.37380	27	.67525	193	.40301	34	.48132	209	.07816	13	.92751	11	3
58	.37407	27	.67332	192	.40335	34	.47924	209	.07828	12	.92740	11	2
59	.37434	27	.67139	192	.40369	34	.47716	208	.07841	13	.92729	11	1
60	0.37461	27	2.66947	192	0.40403	34	2.47509	208	1.07853	12	0.92718	11	0
↑ 111°→	cos	Diff. 1′	sec	Diff. 1′	cot	Diff. 1′	tan	Diff. 1′	csc	Diff. 1′	sin	Diff. 1′	← 68° ↑

TABLE 2
Natural Trigonometric Functions

22°→ ↓ ′	sin	Diff. 1′	csc	Diff. 1′	tan	Diff. 1′	cot	Diff. 1′	sec	Diff. 1′	cos	Diff. 1′	← 157° ↓ ′
0	0.37461		2.66947		0.40403		2.47509		1.07853		0.92718		60
1	.37488	27	.66755	192	.40436	33	.47302	208	.07866	13	.92707	11	59
2	.37515	27	.66563	191	.40470	34	.47095	207	.07879	13	.92697	10	58
3	.37542	27	.66371	191	.40504	34	.46888	207	.07892	13	.92686	11	57
4	.37569	27	.66180	191	.40538	34	.46682	207	.07904	12	.92675	11	56
5	0.37595	26	2.65989	190	0.40572	34	2.46476	206	1.07917	13	0.92664	11	55
6	.37622	27	.65799	190	.40606	34	.46270	206	.07930	13	.92653	11	54
7	.37649	27	.65609	190	.40640	34	.46065	206	.07943	13	.92642	11	53
8	.37676	27	.65419	190	.40674	34	.45860	206	.07955	12	.92631	11	52
9	.37703	27	.65229	190	.40707	33	.45655	204	.07968	13	.92620	11	51
10	0.37730	27	2.65040	190	0.40741	34	2.45451	204	1.07981	13	0.92609	11	50
11	.37757	27	.64851	190	.40775	34	.45246	204	.07994	13	.92598	11	49
12	.37784	27	.64662	189	.40809	34	.45043	203	.08006	12	.92587	11	48
13	.37811	27	.64473	189	.40843	34	.44839	203	.08019	13	.92576	11	47
14	.37838	27	.64285	189	.40877	34	.44636	203	.08032	13	.92565	11	46
15	0.37865	27	2.64097	188	0.40911	34	2.44433	203	1.08045	13	0.92554	11	45
16	.37892	27	.63909	188	.40945	34	.44230	202	.08058	13	.92543	11	44
17	.37919	27	.63722	188	.40979	34	.44027	202	.08071	13	.92532	11	43
18	.37946	27	.63535	188	.41013	34	.43825	202	.08084	13	.92521	11	42
19	.37973	27	.63348	187	.41047	34	.43623	201	.08097	13	.92510	11	41
20	0.37999	26	2.63162	187	0.41081	34	2.43422	201	1.08109	12	0.92499	11	40
21	.38026	27	.62976	187	.41115	34	.43220	201	.08122	13	.92488	11	39
22	.38053	27	.62790	186	.41149	34	.43019	201	.08135	13	.92477	11	38
23	.38080	27	.62604	186	.41183	34	.42819	200	.08148	13	.92466	11	37
24	.38107	27	.62419	186	.41217	34	.42618	200	.08161	13	.92455	11	36
25	0.38134	27	2.62234	186	0.41251	34	2.42418	200	1.08174	13	0.92444	11	35
26	.38161	27	.62049	184	.41285	34	.42218	200	.08187	13	.92432	12	34
27	.38188	27	.61864	184	.41319	34	.42019	200	.08200	13	.92421	11	33
28	.38215	27	.61680	184	.41353	34	.41819	200	.08213	13	.92410	11	32
29	.38241	26	.61496	183	.41387	34	.41620	200	.08226	13	.92399	11	31
30	0.38268	27	2.61313	183	0.41421	34	2.41421	199	1.08239	13	0.92388	11	30
31	.38295	27	.61129	183	.41455	34	.41223	199	.08252	13	.92377	11	29
32	.38322	27	.60946	183	.41490	35	.41025	199	.08265	13	.92366	11	28
33	.38349	27	.60763	182	.41524	34	.40827	198	.08278	13	.92355	11	27
34	.38376	27	.60581	182	.41558	34	.40629	198	.08291	13	.92343	12	26
35	0.38403	27	2.60399	182	0.41592	34	2.40432	198	1.08305	14	0.92332	11	25
36	.38430	27	.60217	181	.41626	34	.40235	198	.08318	13	.92321	11	24
37	.38456	26	.60035	181	.41660	34	.40038	197	.08331	13	.92310	11	23
38	.38483	27	.59853	181	.41694	34	.39841	197	.08344	13	.92299	11	22
39	.38510	27	.59672	181	.41728	34	.39645	197	.08357	13	.92287	12	21
40	0.38537	27	2.59491	180	0.41763	35	2.39449	197	1.08370	13	0.92276	11	20
41	.38564	27	.59311	180	.41797	34	.39253	196	.08383	13	.92265	11	19
42	.38591	27	.59130	180	.41831	34	.39058	196	.08397	14	.92254	11	18
43	.38617	26	.58950	180	.41865	34	.38863	196	.08410	13	.92243	11	17
44	.38644	27	.58771	180	.41899	34	.38668	194	.08423	13	.92231	12	16
45	0.38671	27	2.58591	180	0.41933	34	2.38473	194	1.08436	13	0.92220	11	15
46	.38698	27	.58412	180	.41968	35	.38279	194	.08449	13	.92209	11	14
47	.38725	27	.58233	179	.42002	34	.38084	194	.08463	14	.92198	11	13
48	.38752	27	.58054	179	.42036	34	.37891	193	.08476	13	.92186	12	12
49	.38778	26	.57876	179	.42070	34	.37697	193	.08489	13	.92175	11	11
50	0.38805	27	2.57698	179	0.42105	35	2.37504	193	1.08503	14	0.92164	11	10
51	.38832	27	.57520	178	.42139	34	.37311	193	.08516	13	.92152	12	9
52	.38859	27	.57342	178	.42173	34	.37118	192	.08529	13	.92141	11	8
53	.38886	27	.57165	178	.42207	34	.36925	192	.08542	13	.92130	11	7
54	.38912	26	.56988	178	.42242	35	.36733	192	.08556	14	.92119	11	6
55	0.38939	27	2.56811	177	0.42276	34	2.36541	191	1.08569	13	0.92107	12	5
56	.38966	27	.56634	177	.42310	34	.36349	191	.08582	13	.92096	11	4
57	.38993	27	.56458	177	.42345	35	.36158	191	.08596	14	.92085	11	3
58	.39020	27	.56282	177	.42379	34	.35967	191	.08609	13	.92073	12	2
59	.39046	26	.56106	176	.42413	34	.35776	190	.08623	14	.92062	11	1
60	0.39073	27	2.55930	176	0.42447	34	2.35585	190	1.08636	13	0.92050	12	0
↑ 112°→	cos	Diff. 1′	sec	Diff. 1′	cot	Diff. 1′	tan	Diff. 1′	csc	Diff. 1′	sin	Diff. 1′ ← 67°	↑

TABLE 2
Natural Trigonometric Functions

23°→ ↓ ′	sin	Diff. 1′	csc	Diff. 1′	tan	Diff. 1′	cot	Diff. 1′	sec	Diff. 1′	cos	Diff. 1′	← 156° ↓ ′
0	0.39073		2.55930		0.42447		2.35585		1.08636		0.92050		60
1	.39100	27	.55755	176	.42482	35	.35395	190	.08649	13	.92039	11	59
2	.39127	27	.55580	174	.42516	34	.35205	190	.08663	14	.92028	11	58
3	.39153	26	.55405	174	.42551	35	.35015	190	.08676	13	.92016	12	57
4	.39180	27	.55231	174	.42585	34	.34825	190	.08690	14	.92005	11	56
5	0.39207	27	2.55057	174	0.42619	34	2.34636	190	1.08703	13	0.91994	11	55
6	.39234	27	.54883	173	.42654	35	.34447	190	.08717	14	.91982	12	54
7	.39260	26	.54709	173	.42688	34	.34258	189	.08730	13	.91971	11	53
8	.39287	27	.54536	173	.42722	34	.34069	189	.08744	14	.91959	12	52
9	.39314	27	.54363	173	.42757	35	.33881	189	.08757	13	.91948	11	51
10	0.39341	27	2.54190	172	0.42791	34	2.33693	189	1.08771	14	0.91936	12	50
11	.39367	26	.54017	172	.42826	35	.33505	188	.08784	13	.91925	11	49
12	.39394	27	.53845	172	.42860	34	.33317	188	.08798	14	.91914	11	48
13	.39421	27	.53672	172	.42894	34	.33130	188	.08811	13	.91902	12	47
14	.39448	27	.53500	171	.42929	35	.32943	188	.08825	14	.91891	11	46
15	0.39474	26	2.53329	171	0.42963	34	2.32756	187	1.08839	14	0.91879	12	45
16	.39501	27	.53157	171	.42998	35	.32570	187	.08852	13	.91868	11	44
17	.39528	27	.52986	171	.43032	34	.32383	187	.08866	14	.91856	12	43
18	.39555	27	.52815	170	.43067	35	.32197	187	.08880	14	.91845	11	42
19	.39581	26	.52645	170	.43101	34	.32012	186	.08893	13	.91833	12	41
20	0.39608	27	2.52474	170	0.43136	35	2.31826	186	1.08907	14	0.91822	11	40
21	.39635	27	.52304	170	.43170	34	.31641	186	.08920	13	.91810	12	39
22	.39661	26	.52134	170	.43205	35	.31456	186	.08934	14	.91799	11	38
23	.39688	27	.51965	170	.43239	34	.31271	184	.08948	14	.91787	12	37
24	.39715	27	.51795	170	.43274	35	.31086	184	.08962	14	.91775	12	36
25	0.39741	26	2.51626	170	0.43308	34	2.30902	184	1.08975	13	0.91764	11	35
26	.39768	27	.51457	169	.43343	35	.30718	184	.08989	14	.91752	12	34
27	.39795	27	.51289	169	.43378	35	.30534	183	.09003	14	.91741	11	33
28	.39822	27	.51120	169	.43412	34	.30351	183	.09017	14	.91729	12	32
29	.39848	26	.50952	169	.43447	35	.30167	183	.09030	13	.91718	11	31
30	0.39875	27	2.50784	168	0.43481	34	2.29984	183	1.09044	14	0.91706	12	30
31	.39902	27	.50617	168	.43516	35	.29801	182	.09058	14	.91694	12	29
32	.39928	26	.50449	168	.43550	34	.29619	182	.09072	14	.91683	11	28
33	.39955	27	.50282	168	.43585	35	.29437	182	.09086	14	.91671	12	27
34	.39982	27	.50115	167	.43620	35	.29254	182	.09099	13	.91660	11	26
35	0.40008	26	2.49948	167	0.43654	34	2.29073	181	1.09113	14	0.91648	12	25
36	.40035	27	.49782	167	.43689	35	.28891	181	.09127	14	.91636	12	24
37	.40062	27	.49616	167	.43724	35	.28710	181	.09141	14	.91625	11	23
38	.40088	26	.49450	166	.43758	34	.28528	181	.09155	14	.91613	12	22
39	.40115	27	.49284	166	.43793	35	.28348	180	.09169	14	.91601	12	21
40	0.40141	26	2.49119	166	0.43828	35	2.28167	180	1.09183	14	0.91590	11	20
41	.40168	27	.48954	166	.43862	34	.27987	180	.09197	14	.91578	12	19
42	.40195	27	.48789	164	.43897	35	.27806	180	.09211	14	.91566	12	18
43	.40221	26	.48624	164	.43932	35	.27626	180	.09224	13	.91555	11	17
44	.40248	27	.48459	164	.43966	34	.27447	180	.09238	14	.91543	12	16
45	0.40275	27	2.48295	164	0.44001	35	2.27267	180	1.09252	14	0.91531	12	15
46	.40301	26	.48131	164	.44036	35	.27088	180	.09266	14	.91519	12	14
47	.40328	27	.47967	163	.44071	35	.26909	179	.09280	14	.91508	11	13
48	.40355	27	.47804	163	.44105	34	.26730	179	.09294	14	.91496	12	12
49	.40381	26	.47640	163	.44140	35	.26552	179	.09308	14	.91484	12	11
50	0.40408	27	2.47477	163	0.44175	35	2.26374	179	1.09323	15	0.91472	12	10
51	.40434	26	.47314	162	.44210	35	.26196	179	.09337	14	.91461	11	9
52	.40461	27	.47152	162	.44244	34	.26018	178	.09351	14	.91449	12	8
53	.40488	27	.46989	162	.44279	35	.25840	178	.09365	14	.91437	12	7
54	.40514	26	.46827	162	.44314	35	.25663	178	.09379	14	.91425	12	6
55	0.40541	27	2.46665	161	0.44349	35	2.25486	178	1.09393	14	0.91414	11	5
56	.40567	26	.46504	161	.44384	35	.25309	177	.09407	14	.91402	12	4
57	.40594	27	.46342	161	.44418	34	.25132	177	.09421	14	.91390	12	3
58	.40621	27	.46181	161	.44453	35	.24956	177	.09435	14	.91378	12	2
59	.40647	26	.46020	160	.44488	35	.24780	177	.09449	14	.91366	12	1
60	0.40674	27	2.45859	160	0.44523	35	2.24604	176	1.09464	15	0.91355	11	0
↑ 113°→	cos	Diff. 1′	sec	Diff. 1′	cot	Diff. 1′	tan	Diff. 1′	csc	Diff. 1′	sin	Diff. 1′ ← 66°	↑

TABLE 2
Natural Trigonometric Functions

24° → ↓ ′	sin	Diff. 1′	csc	Diff. 1′	tan	Diff. 1′	cot	Diff. 1′	sec	Diff. 1′	cos	Diff. 1′	← 155° ↓ ′
0	0.40674		2.45859		0.44523		2.24604		1.09464		0.91355		60
1	.40700	26	.45699	160	.44558	35	.24428	176	.09478	14	.91343	12	59
2	.40727	27	.45539	160	.44593	35	.24252	176	.09492	14	.91331	12	58
3	.40753	26	.45378	160	.44627	34	.24077	176	.09506	14	.91319	12	57
4	.40780	27	.45219	160	.44662	35	.23902	176	.09520	14	.91307	12	56
5	0.40806	26	2.45059	160	0.44697	35	2.23727	174	1.09535	15	0.91295	12	55
6	.40833	27	.44900	160	.44732	35	.23553	174	.09549	14	.91283	12	54
7	.40860	27	.44741	160	.44767	35	.23378	174	.09563	14	.91272	11	53
8	.40886	26	.44582	159	.44802	35	.23204	174	.09577	14	.91260	12	52
9	.40913	27	.44423	159	.44837	35	.23030	173	.09592	15	.91248	12	51
10	0.40939	26	2.44264	159	0.44872	35	2.22857	173	1.09606	14	0.91236	12	50
11	.40966	27	.44106	159	.44907	35	.22683	173	.09620	14	.91224	12	49
12	.40992	26	.43948	159	.44942	35	.22510	173	.09635	15	.91212	12	48
13	.41019	27	.43790	158	.44977	35	.22337	172	.09649	14	.91200	12	47
14	.41045	26	.43633	158	.45012	35	.22164	172	.09663	14	.91188	12	46
15	0.41072	27	2.43476	158	0.45047	35	2.21992	172	1.09678	15	0.91176	12	45
16	.41098	26	.43318	158	.45082	35	.21819	172	.09692	14	.91164	12	44
17	.41125	27	.43162	157	.45117	35	.21647	172	.09707	15	.91152	12	43
18	.41151	26	.43005	157	.45152	35	.21475	171	.09721	14	.91140	12	42
19	.41178	27	.42848	157	.45187	35	.21304	171	.09735	14	.91128	12	41
20	0.41204	26	2.42692	157	0.45222	35	2.21132	171	1.09750	15	0.91116	12	40
21	.41231	27	.42536	157	.45257	35	.20961	171	.09764	14	.91104	12	39
22	.41257	26	.42380	156	.45292	35	.20790	171	.09779	15	.91092	12	38
23	.41284	27	.42225	156	.45327	35	.20619	170	.09793	14	.91080	12	37
24	.41310	26	.42070	156	.45362	35	.20449	170	.09808	15	.91068	12	36
25	0.41337	27	2.41914	156	0.45397	35	2.20278	170	1.09822	14	0.91056	12	35
26	.41363	26	.41760	154	.45432	35	.20108	170	.09837	15	.91044	12	34
27	.41390	27	.41605	154	.45467	35	.19938	170	.09851	14	.91032	12	33
28	.41416	26	.41450	154	.45502	35	.19769	170	.09866	15	.91020	12	32
29	.41443	27	.41296	154	.45538	36	.19599	170	.09880	14	.91008	12	31
30	0.41469	26	2.41142	154	0.45573	35	2.19430	170	1.09895	15	0.90996	12	30
31	.41496	27	.40988	153	.45608	35	.19261	170	.09909	14	.90984	12	29
32	.41522	26	.40835	153	.45643	35	.19092	169	.09924	15	.90972	12	28
33	.41549	27	.40681	153	.45678	35	.18923	169	.09939	15	.90960	12	27
34	.41575	26	.40528	153	.45713	35	.18755	169	.09953	14	.90948	12	26
35	0.41602	27	2.40375	152	0.45748	35	2.18587	169	1.09968	15	0.90936	12	25
36	.41628	26	.40222	152	.45784	36	.18419	168	.09982	14	.90924	12	24
37	.41655	27	.40070	152	.45819	35	.18251	168	.09997	15	.90911	13	23
38	.41681	26	.39918	152	.45854	35	.18084	168	.10012	15	.90899	12	22
39	.41707	26	.39766	152	.45889	35	.17916	168	.10026	14	.90887	12	21
40	0.41734	27	2.39614	151	0.45924	35	2.17749	168	1.10041	15	0.90875	12	20
41	.41760	26	.39462	151	.45960	36	.17582	167	.10056	15	.90863	12	19
42	.41787	27	.39311	151	.45995	35	.17416	167	.10071	15	.90851	12	18
43	.41813	26	.39159	151	.46030	35	.17249	167	.10085	14	.90839	12	17
44	.41840	27	.39008	150	.46065	35	.17083	167	.10100	15	.90826	13	16
45	0.41866	26	2.38857	150	0.46101	36	2.16917	167	1.10115	15	0.90814	12	15
46	.41892	26	.38707	150	.46136	35	.16751	166	.10130	15	.90802	12	14
47	.41919	27	.38556	150	.46171	35	.16585	166	.10144	14	.90790	12	13
48	.41945	26	.38406	150	.46206	35	.16420	166	.10159	15	.90778	12	12
49	.41972	27	.38256	150	.46242	36	.16255	166	.10174	15	.90766	12	11
50	0.41998	26	2.38107	150	0.46277	35	2.16090	166	1.10189	15	0.90753	13	10
51	.42024	26	.37957	150	.46312	35	.15925	164	.10204	15	.90741	12	9
52	.42051	27	.37808	150	.46348	36	.15760	164	.10218	14	.90729	12	8
53	.42077	26	.37658	150	.46383	35	.15596	164	.10233	15	.90717	12	7
54	.42104	27	.37509	149	.46418	35	.15432	164	.10248	15	.90704	13	6
55	0.42130	26	2.37361	149	0.46454	36	2.15268	163	1.10263	15	0.90692	12	5
56	.42156	26	.37212	149	.46489	35	.15104	163	.10278	15	.90680	12	4
57	.42183	27	.37064	149	.46525	36	.14940	163	.10293	15	.90668	12	3
58	.42209	26	.36916	149	.46560	35	.14777	163	.10308	15	.90655	13	2
59	.42235	26	.36768	148	.46595	35	.14614	163	.10323	15	.90643	12	1
60	0.42262	27	2.36620	148	0.46631	36	2.14451	162	1.10338	15	0.90631	12	0
↑ 114° →	cos	Diff. 1′	sec	Diff. 1′	cot	Diff. 1′	tan	Diff. 1′	csc	Diff. 1′	sin	Diff. 1′	↑ ← 65°

TABLE 2
Natural Trigonometric Functions

25° → ↓ ′	sin	Diff. 1′	csc	Diff. 1′	tan	Diff. 1′	cot	Diff. 1′	sec	Diff. 1′	cos	Diff. 1′	← 154° ↓ ′
0	0.42262		2.36620		0.46631		2.14451		1.10338		0.90631		60
1	.42288	26	.36473	148	.46666	35	.14288	162	.10353	15	.90618	13	59
2	.42315	27	.36325	148	.46702	36	.14125	162	.10368	15	.90606	12	58
3	.42341	26	.36178	148	.46737	35	.13963	162	.10383	15	.90594	12	57
4	.42367	26	.36031	147	.46772	35	.13801	162	.10398	15	.90582	12	56
5	0.42394	27	2.35885	147	0.46808	36	2.13639	161	1.10413	15	0.90569	13	55
6	.42420	26	.35738	147	.46843	35	.13477	161	.10428	15	.90557	12	54
7	.42446	26	.35592	147	.46879	36	.13316	161	.10443	15	.90545	12	53
8	.42473	27	.35446	147	.46914	35	.13154	161	.10458	15	.90532	13	52
9	.42499	26	.35300	146	.46950	36	.12993	161	.10473	15	.90520	12	51
10	0.42525	26	2.35154	146	0.46985	35	2.12832	160	1.10488	15	0.90507	13	50
11	.42552	27	.35009	146	.47021	36	.12671	160	.10503	15	.90495	12	49
12	.42578	26	.34863	146	.47056	35	.12511	160	.10518	15	.90483	12	48
13	.42604	26	.34718	146	.47092	36	.12350	160	.10533	15	.90470	13	47
14	.42631	27	.34573	144	.47128	36	.12190	160	.10549	16	.90458	12	46
15	0.42657	26	2.34429	144	0.47163	35	2.12030	160	1.10564	15	0.90446	12	45
16	.42683	26	.34284	144	.47199	36	.11871	160	.10579	15	.90433	13	44
17	.42709	26	.34140	144	.47234	35	.11711	160	.10594	15	.90421	12	43
18	.42736	27	.33996	144	.47270	36	.11552	160	.10609	15	.90408	13	42
19	.42762	26	.33852	143	.47305	35	.11392	160	.10625	16	.90396	12	41
20	0.42788	26	2.33708	143	0.47341	36	2.11233	159	1.10640	15	0.90383	13	40
21	.42815	27	.33565	143	.47377	36	.11075	159	.10655	15	.90371	12	39
22	.42841	26	.33422	143	.47412	35	.10916	159	.10670	15	.90358	13	38
23	.42867	26	.33278	143	.47448	36	.10758	159	.10686	16	.90346	12	37
24	.42894	27	.33135	142	.47483	35	.10600	159	.10701	15	.90334	12	36
25	0.42920	26	2.32993	142	0.47519	36	2.10442	159	1.10716	15	0.90321	13	35
26	.42946	26	.32850	142	.47555	36	.10284	158	.10731	15	.90309	12	34
27	.42972	26	.32708	142	.47590	35	.10126	158	.10747	16	.90296	13	33
28	.42999	27	.32566	142	.47626	36	.09969	158	.10762	15	.90284	12	32
29	.43025	26	.32424	141	.47662	36	.09811	158	.10777	15	.90271	13	31
30	0.43051	26	2.32282	141	0.47698	36	2.09654	158	1.10793	16	0.90259	12	30
31	.43077	26	.32140	141	.47733	35	.09498	157	.10808	15	.90246	13	29
32	.43104	27	.31999	141	.47769	36	.09341	157	.10824	16	.90233	13	28
33	.43130	26	.31858	141	.47805	36	.09184	157	.10839	15	.90221	12	27
34	.43156	26	.31717	140	.47840	35	.09028	157	.10854	15	.90208	13	26
35	0.43182	26	2.31576	140	0.47876	36	2.08872	157	1.10870	16	0.90196	12	25
36	.43209	27	.31436	140	.47912	36	.08716	156	.10885	15	.90183	13	24
37	.43235	26	.31295	140	.47948	36	.08560	156	.10901	16	.90171	12	23
38	.43261	26	.31155	140	.47984	36	.08405	156	.10916	15	.90158	13	22
39	.43287	26	.31015	140	.48019	35	.08250	156	.10932	16	.90146	12	21
40	0.43313	26	2.30875	140	0.48055	36	2.08094	156	1.10947	15	0.90133	13	20
41	.43340	27	.30735	140	.48091	36	.07939	154	.10963	16	.90120	13	19
42	.43366	26	.30596	140	.48127	36	.07785	154	.10978	15	.90108	12	18
43	.43392	26	.30457	140	.48163	36	.07630	154	.10994	16	.90095	13	17
44	.43418	26	.30318	140	.48198	35	.07476	154	.11009	15	.90082	13	16
45	0.43445	27	2.30179	139	0.48234	36	2.07321	154	1.11025	16	0.90070	12	15
46	.43471	26	.30040	139	.48270	36	.07167	154	.11041	16	.90057	13	14
47	.43497	26	.29901	139	.48306	36	.07014	153	.11056	15	.90045	12	13
48	.43523	26	.29763	139	.48342	36	.06860	153	.11072	16	.90032	13	12
49	.43549	26	.29625	139	.48378	36	.06706	153	.11087	15	.90019	13	11
50	0.43575	26	2.29487	138	0.48414	36	2.06553	153	1.11103	16	0.90007	12	10
51	.43602	27	.29349	138	.48450	36	.06400	153	.11119	16	.89994	13	9
52	.43628	26	.29211	138	.48486	36	.06247	152	.11134	15	.89981	13	8
53	.43654	26	.29074	138	.48521	35	.06094	152	.11150	16	.89968	13	7
54	.43680	26	.28937	138	.48557	36	.05942	152	.11166	16	.89956	12	6
55	0.43706	26	2.28800	138	0.48593	36	2.05790	152	1.11181	15	0.89943	13	5
56	.43733	27	.28663	137	.48629	36	.05637	152	.11197	16	.89930	13	4
57	.43759	26	.28526	137	.48665	36	.05485	152	.11213	16	.89918	12	3
58	.43785	26	.28390	137	.48701	36	.05333	151	.11229	16	.89905	13	2
59	.43811	26	.28253	137	.48737	36	.05182	151	.11244	15	.89892	13	1
60	0.43837	26	2.28117	137	0.48773	36	2.05030	151	1.11260	16	0.89879	13	0
↑ 115° →	cos	Diff. 1′	sec	Diff. 1′	cot	Diff. 1′	tan	Diff. 1′	csc	Diff. 1′	sin	Diff. 1′	↑ ← 64°

TABLE 2
Natural Trigonometric Functions

26°→ ↓	sin	Diff. 1′	csc	Diff. 1′	tan	Diff. 1′	cot	Diff. 1′	sec	Diff. 1′	cos	Diff. 1′	← 153° ↓
′													′
0	0.43837		2.28117		0.48773		2.05030		1.11260		0.89879		60
1	.43863	26	.27981	136	.48809	36	.04879	151	.11276	16	.89867	12	59
2	.43889	26	.27845	136	.48845	36	.04728	151	.11292	16	.89854	13	58
3	.43916	27	.27710	136	.48881	36	.04577	150	.11308	16	.89841	13	57
4	.43942	26	.27574	136	.48917	36	.04426	150	.11323	15	.89828	13	56
5	0.43968	26	2.27439	136	0.48953	36	2.04276	150	1.11339	16	0.89816	12	55
6	.43994	26	.27304	136	.48989	36	.04125	150	.11355	16	.89803	13	54
7	.44020	26	.27169	134	.49026	37	.03975	150	.11371	16	.89790	13	53
8	.44046	26	.27035	134	.49062	36	.03825	150	.11387	16	.89777	13	52
9	.44072	26	.26900	134	.49098	36	.03675	150	.11403	16	.89764	13	51
10	0.44098	26	2.26766	134	0.49134	36	2.03526	150	1.11419	16	0.89752	12	50
11	.44124	26	.26632	134	.49170	36	.03376	150	.11435	16	.89739	13	49
12	.44151	27	.26498	133	.49206	36	.03227	150	.11451	16	.89726	13	48
13	.44177	26	.26364	133	.49242	36	.03078	150	.11467	16	.89713	13	47
14	.44203	26	.26230	133	.49278	36	.02929	149	.11483	16	.89700	13	46
15	0.44229	26	2.26097	133	0.49315	37	2.02780	149	1.11499	16	0.89687	13	45
16	.44255	26	.25963	133	.49351	36	.02631	149	.11515	16	.89674	13	44
17	.44281	26	.25830	133	.49387	36	.02483	149	.11531	16	.89662	12	43
18	.44307	26	.25697	132	.49423	36	.02335	149	.11547	16	.89649	13	42
19	.44333	26	.25565	132	.49459	36	.02187	149	.11563	16	.89636	13	41
20	0.44359	26	2.25432	132	0.49495	36	2.02039	148	1.11579	16	0.89623	13	40
21	.44385	26	.25300	132	.49532	37	.01891	148	.11595	16	.89610	13	39
22	.44411	26	.25167	132	.49568	36	.01743	148	.11611	16	.89597	13	38
23	.44437	26	.25035	132	.49604	36	.01596	148	.11627	16	.89584	13	37
24	.44464	27	.24903	131	.49640	36	.01449	148	.11643	16	.89571	13	36
25	0.44490	26	2.24772	131	0.49677	37	2.01302	148	1.11659	16	0.89558	13	35
26	.44516	26	.24640	131	.49713	36	.01155	147	.11675	16	.89545	13	34
27	.44542	26	.24509	131	.49749	36	.01008	147	.11691	16	.89532	13	33
28	.44568	26	.24378	131	.49786	37	.00862	147	.11708	17	.89519	13	32
29	.44594	26	.24247	131	.49822	36	.00715	147	.11724	16	.89506	13	31
30	0.44620	26	2.24116	130	0.49858	36	2.00569	147	1.11740	16	0.89493	13	30
31	.44646	26	.23985	130	.49894	36	.00423	147	.11756	16	.89480	13	29
32	.44672	26	.23855	130	.49931	37	.00277	146	.11772	16	.89467	13	28
33	.44698	26	.23724	130	.49967	36	2.00131	146	.11789	17	.89454	13	27
34	.44724	26	.23594	130	.50004	37	1.99986	146	.11805	16	.89441	13	26
35	0.44750	26	2.23464	130	0.50040	36	1.99841	146	1.11821	16	0.89428	13	25
36	.44776	26	.23334	130	.50076	36	.99695	146	.11838	17	.89415	13	24
37	.44802	26	.23205	130	.50113	37	.99550	146	.11854	16	.89402	13	23
38	.44828	26	.23075	130	.50149	36	.99406	144	.11870	16	.89389	13	22
39	.44854	26	.22946	130	.50185	36	.99261	144	.11886	16	.89376	13	21
40	0.44880	26	2.22817	130	0.50222	37	1.99116	144	1.11903	17	0.89363	13	20
41	.44906	26	.22688	129	.50258	36	.98972	144	.11919	16	.89350	13	19
42	.44932	26	.22559	129	.50295	37	.98828	144	.11936	17	.89337	13	18
43	.44958	26	.22430	129	.50331	36	.98684	144	.11952	16	.89324	13	17
44	.44984	26	.22302	129	.50368	37	.98540	143	.11968	16	.89311	13	16
45	0.45010	26	2.22174	129	0.50404	36	1.98396	143	1.11985	17	0.89298	13	15
46	.45036	26	.22045	129	.50441	37	.98253	143	.12001	16	.89285	13	14
47	.45062	26	.21918	128	.50477	36	.98110	143	.12018	17	.89272	13	13
48	.45088	26	.21790	128	.50514	37	.97966	143	.12034	16	.89259	13	12
49	.45114	26	.21662	128	.50550	36	.97823	143	.12051	17	.89245	14	11
50	0.45140	26	2.21535	128	0.50587	37	1.97681	142	1.12067	16	0.89232	13	10
51	.45166	26	.21407	128	.50623	36	.97538	142	.12083	16	.89219	13	9
52	.45192	26	.21280	128	.50660	37	.97395	142	.12100	17	.89206	13	8
53	.45218	26	.21153	127	.50696	36	.97253	142	.12117	17	.89193	13	7
54	.45243	25	.21026	127	.50733	37	.97111	142	.12133	16	.89180	13	6
55	0.45269	26	2.20900	127	0.50769	36	1.96969	142	1.12150	17	0.89167	13	5
56	.45295	26	.20773	127	.50806	37	.96827	141	.12166	16	.89153	14	4
57	.45321	26	.20647	127	.50843	37	.96685	141	.12183	17	.89140	13	3
58	.45347	26	.20521	127	.50879	36	.96544	141	.12199	16	.89127	13	2
59	.45373	26	.20395	126	.50916	37	.96402	141	.12216	17	.89114	13	1
60	0.45399	26	2.20269	126	0.50953	37	1.96261	141	1.12233	17	0.89101	13	0
↑ 116°→	cos	Diff. 1′	sec	Diff. 1′	cot	Diff. 1′	tan	Diff. 1′	csc	Diff. 1′	sin	Diff. 1′ ← 63°	↑

TABLE 2
Natural Trigonometric Functions

27°→ ↓	sin	Diff. 1′	csc	Diff. 1′	tan	Diff. 1′	cot	Diff. 1′	sec	Diff. 1′	cos	Diff. 1′	← 152° ↓
′													′
0	0.45399		2.20269		0.50953		1.96261		1.12233		0.89101		60
1	.45425	26	.20143	126	.50989	36	.96120	141	.12249	16	.89087	14	59
2	.45451	26	.20018	126	.51026	37	.95979	140	.12266	17	.89074	13	58
3	.45477	26	.19892	126	.51063	37	.95838	140	.12283	17	.89061	13	57
4	.45503	26	.19767	126	.51099	36	.95698	140	.12299	16	.89048	13	56
5	0.45529	26	2.19642	126	0.51136	37	1.95557	140	1.12316	17	0.89035	13	55
6	.45554	25	.19517	124	.51173	37	.95417	140	.12333	17	.89021	14	54
7	.45580	26	.19393	124	.51209	36	.95277	140	.12349	16	.89008	13	53
8	.45606	26	.19268	124	.51246	37	.95137	140	.12366	17	.88995	13	52
9	.45632	26	.19144	124	.51283	37	.94997	140	.12383	17	.88981	14	51
10	0.45658	26	2.19019	124	0.51319	36	1.94858	140	1.12400	17	0.88968	13	50
11	.45684	26	.18895	124	.51356	37	.94718	140	.12416	16	.88955	13	49
12	.45710	26	.18772	123	.51393	37	.94579	140	.12433	17	.88942	13	48
13	.45736	26	.18648	123	.51430	37	.94440	140	.12450	17	.88928	14	47
14	.45762	26	.18524	123	.51467	37	.94301	139	.12467	17	.88915	13	46
15	0.45787	25	2.18401	123	0.51503	36	1.94162	139	1.12484	17	0.88902	13	45
16	.45813	26	.18277	123	.51540	37	.94023	139	.12501	17	.88888	14	44
17	.45839	26	.18154	123	.51577	37	.93885	139	.12518	17	.88875	13	43
18	.45865	26	.18031	122	.51614	37	.93746	139	.12534	16	.88862	13	42
19	.45891	26	.17909	122	.51651	37	.93608	139	.12551	17	.88848	14	41
20	0.45917	26	2.17786	122	0.51688	37	1.93470	139	1.12568	17	0.88835	13	40
21	.45942	25	.17663	122	.51724	36	.93332	138	.12585	17	.88822	13	39
22	.45968	26	.17541	122	.51761	37	.93195	138	.12602	17	.88808	14	38
23	.45994	26	.17419	122	.51798	37	.93057	138	.12619	17	.88795	13	37
24	.46020	26	.17297	122	.51835	37	.92920	138	.12636	17	.88782	13	36
25	0.46046	26	2.17175	121	0.51872	37	1.92782	138	1.12653	17	0.88768	14	35
26	.46072	26	.17053	121	.51909	37	.92645	138	.12670	17	.88755	13	34
27	.46097	25	.16932	121	.51946	37	.92508	137	.12687	17	.88741	14	33
28	.46123	26	.16810	121	.51983	37	.92371	137	.12704	17	.88728	13	32
29	.46149	26	.16689	121	.52020	37	.92235	137	.12721	17	.88715	13	31
30	0.46175	26	2.16568	121	0.52057	37	1.92098	137	1.12738	17	0.88701	14	30
31	.46201	26	.16447	120	.52094	37	.91962	137	.12755	17	.88688	13	29
32	.46226	25	.16326	120	.52131	37	.91826	137	.12772	17	.88674	14	28
33	.46252	26	.16206	120	.52168	37	.91690	137	.12789	17	.88661	13	27
34	.46278	26	.16085	120	.52205	37	.91554	136	.12807	18	.88647	14	26
35	0.46304	26	2.15965	120	0.52242	37	1.91418	136	1.12824	17	0.88634	13	25
36	.46330	26	.15845	120	.52279	37	.91282	136	.12841	17	.88620	14	24
37	.46355	25	.15725	120	.52316	37	.91147	136	.12858	17	.88607	13	23
38	.46381	26	.15605	120	.52353	37	.91012	136	.12875	17	.88593	14	22
39	.46407	26	.15485	120	.52390	37	.90876	136	.12892	17	.88580	13	21
40	0.46433	26	2.15366	120	0.52427	37	1.90741	134	1.12910	18	0.88566	14	20
41	.46458	25	.15246	120	.52464	37	.90607	134	.12927	17	.88553	13	19
42	.46484	26	.15127	120	.52501	37	.90472	134	.12944	17	.88539	14	18
43	.46510	26	.15008	120	.52538	37	.90337	134	.12961	17	.88526	13	17
44	.46536	26	.14889	119	.52575	37	.90203	134	.12979	18	.88512	14	16
45	0.46561	25	2.14770	119	0.52613	38	1.90069	134	1.12996	17	0.88499	13	15
46	.46587	26	.14651	119	.52650	37	.89935	134	.13013	17	.88485	14	14
47	.46613	26	.14533	119	.52687	37	.89801	133	.13031	18	.88472	13	13
48	.46639	26	.14414	119	.52724	37	.89667	133	.13048	17	.88458	14	12
49	.46664	25	.14296	119	.52761	37	.89533	133	.13065	17	.88445	13	11
50	0.46690	26	2.14178	119	0.52798	37	1.89400	133	1.13083	18	0.88431	14	10
51	.46716	26	.14060	118	.52836	38	.89266	133	.13100	17	.88417	14	9
52	.46742	26	.13942	118	.52873	37	.89133	133	.13117	17	.88404	13	8
53	.46767	25	.13825	118	.52910	37	.89000	133	.13135	18	.88390	14	7
54	.46793	26	.13707	118	.52947	37	.88867	132	.13152	17	.88377	13	6
55	0.46819	26	2.13590	118	0.52985	38	1.88734	132	1.13170	18	0.88363	14	5
56	.46844	25	.13473	118	.53022	37	.88602	132	.13187	17	.88349	14	4
57	.46870	26	.13356	118	.53059	37	.88469	132	.13205	18	.88336	13	3
58	.46896	26	.13239	117	.53096	37	.88337	132	.13222	17	.88322	14	2
59	.46921	25	.13122	117	.53134	38	.88205	132	.13239	17	.88308	14	1
60	0.46947	26	2.13005	117	0.53171	37	1.88073	132	1.13257	18	0.88295	13	0
↑ 117°→	cos	Diff. 1′	sec	Diff. 1′	cot	Diff. 1′	tan	Diff. 1′	csc	Diff. 1′	sin	Diff. 1′ ← 62°	↑

TABLE 2
Natural Trigonometric Functions

28°→ ↓ ′	sin	Diff. 1′	csc	Diff. 1′	tan	Diff. 1′	cot	Diff. 1′	sec	Diff. 1′	cos	Diff. 1′	← 151° ↓ ′
0	0.46947		2.13005		0.53171		1.88073		1.13257		0.88295		60
1	.46973	26	.12889	117	.53208	37	.87941	131	.13275	18	.88281	14	59
2	.46999	26	.12773	117	.53246	38	.87809	131	.13292	17	.88267	14	58
3	.47024	25	.12657	117	.53283	37	.87677	131	.13310	18	.88254	13	57
4	.47050	26	.12540	117	.53320	37	.87546	131	.13327	17	.88240	14	56
5	0.47076	26	2.12425	116	0.53358	38	1.87415	131	1.13345	18	0.88226	14	55
6	.47101	25	.12309	116	.53395	37	.87283	131	.13362	17	.88213	13	54
7	.47127	26	.12193	116	.53432	37	.87152	131	.13380	18	.88199	14	53
8	.47153	26	.12078	116	.53470	38	.87021	130	.13398	18	.88185	14	52
9	.47178	25	.11963	116	.53507	37	.86891	130	.13415	17	.88172	13	51
10	0.47204	26	2.11847	116	0.53545	38	1.86760	130	1.13433	18	0.88158	14	50
11	.47229	25	.11732	116	.53582	37	.86630	130	.13451	18	.88144	14	49
12	.47255	26	.11617	114	.53620	38	.86499	130	.13468	17	.88130	14	48
13	.47281	26	.11503	114	.53657	37	.86369	130	.13486	18	.88117	13	47
14	.47306	25	.11388	114	.53694	37	.86239	130	.13504	18	.88103	14	46
15	0.47332	26	2.11274	114	0.53732	38	1.86109	130	1.13521	17	0.88089	14	45
16	.47358	26	.11159	114	.53769	37	.85979	130	.13539	18	.88075	14	44
17	.47383	25	.11045	114	.53807	38	.85850	130	.13557	18	.88062	13	43
18	.47409	26	.10931	114	.53844	37	.85720	130	.13575	18	.88048	14	42
19	.47434	25	.10817	113	.53882	38	.85591	130	.13593	18	.88034	14	41
20	0.47460	26	2.10704	113	0.53920	38	1.85462	130	1.13610	17	0.88020	14	40
21	.47486	26	.10590	113	.53957	37	.85333	130	.13628	18	.88006	14	39
22	.47511	25	.10477	113	.53995	38	.85204	129	.13646	18	.87993	13	38
23	.47537	26	.10363	113	.54032	37	.85075	129	.13664	18	.87979	14	37
24	.47562	25	.10250	113	.54070	38	.84946	129	.13682	18	.87965	14	36
25	0.47588	26	2.10137	113	0.54107	37	1.84818	129	1.13700	18	0.87951	14	35
26	.47614	26	.10024	112	.54145	38	.84689	129	.13718	18	.87937	14	34
27	.47639	25	.09911	112	.54183	38	.84561	129	.13735	17	.87923	14	33
28	.47665	26	.09799	112	.54220	37	.84433	129	.13753	18	.87909	14	32
29	.47690	25	.09686	112	.54258	38	.84305	128	.13771	18	.87896	13	31
30	0.47716	26	2.09574	112	0.54296	38	1.84177	128	1.13789	18	0.87882	14	30
31	.47741	25	.09462	112	.54333	37	.84049	128	.13807	18	.87868	14	29
32	.47767	26	.09350	112	.54371	38	.83922	128	.13825	18	.87854	14	28
33	.47793	26	.09238	111	.54409	38	.83794	128	.13843	18	.87840	14	27
34	.47818	25	.09126	111	.54446	37	.83667	128	.13861	18	.87826	14	26
35	0.47844	26	2.09014	111	0.54484	38	1.83540	128	1.13879	18	0.87812	14	25
36	.47869	25	.08903	111	.54522	38	.83413	128	.13897	18	.87798	14	24
37	.47895	26	.08791	111	.54560	38	.83286	127	.13915	18	.87784	14	23
38	.47920	25	.08680	111	.54597	37	.83159	127	.13934	19	.87770	14	22
39	.47946	26	.08569	111	.54635	38	.83033	127	.13952	18	.87756	14	21
40	0.47971	25	2.08458	110	0.54673	38	1.82906	127	1.13970	18	0.87743	13	20
41	.47997	26	.08347	110	.54711	38	.82780	127	.13988	18	.87729	14	19
42	.48022	25	.08236	110	.54748	37	.82654	127	.14006	18	.87715	14	18
43	.48048	26	.08126	110	.54786	38	.82528	127	.14024	18	.87701	14	17
44	.48073	25	.08015	110	.54824	38	.82402	126	.14042	18	.87687	14	16
45	0.48099	26	2.07905	110	0.54862	38	1.82276	126	1.14061	19	0.87673	14	15
46	.48124	25	.07795	110	.54900	38	.82150	126	.14079	18	.87659	14	14
47	.48150	26	.07685	110	.54938	38	.82025	126	.14097	18	.87645	14	13
48	.48175	25	.07575	110	.54975	37	.81899	126	.14115	18	.87631	14	12
49	.48201	26	.07465	110	.55013	38	.81774	126	.14134	19	.87617	14	11
50	0.48226	25	2.07356	110	0.55051	38	1.81649	126	1.14152	18	0.87603	14	10
51	.48252	26	.07246	110	.55089	38	.81524	126	.14170	18	.87589	14	9
52	.48277	25	.07137	110	.55127	38	.81399	124	.14188	18	.87575	14	8
53	.48303	26	.07027	110	.55165	38	.81274	124	.14207	19	.87561	14	7
54	.48328	25	.06918	110	.55203	38	.81150	124	.14225	18	.87546	15	6
55	0.48354	26	2.06809	109	0.55241	38	1.81025	124	1.14243	18	0.87532	14	5
56	.48379	25	.06701	109	.55279	38	.80901	124	.14262	19	.87518	14	4
57	.48405	26	.06592	109	.55317	38	.80777	124	.14280	18	.87504	14	3
58	.48430	25	.06483	109	.55355	38	.80653	124	.14299	19	.87490	14	2
59	.48456	26	.06375	109	.55393	38	.80529	123	.14317	18	.87476	14	1
60	0.48481	25	2.06267	109	0.55431	38	1.80405	123	1.14335	18	0.87462	14	0
↑ 118°→	cos	Diff. 1′	sec	Diff. 1′	cot	Diff. 1′	tan	Diff. 1′	csc	Diff. 1′	sin	Diff. 1′← 61°	↑

TABLE 2
Natural Trigonometric Functions

29°→ ↓ ′	sin	Diff. 1′	csc	Diff. 1′	tan	Diff. 1′	cot	Diff. 1′	sec	Diff. 1′	cos	Diff. 1′	← 150° ↓ ′
0	0.48481		2.06267		0.55431		1.80405		1.14335		0.87462		60
1	.48506	25	.06158	109	.55469	38	.80281	123	.14354	19	.87448	14	59
2	.48532	26	.06050	109	.55507	38	.80158	123	.14372	18	.87434	14	58
3	.48557	25	.05942	108	.55545	38	.80034	123	.14391	19	.87420	14	57
4	.48583	26	.05835	108	.55583	38	.79911	123	.14409	18	.87406	14	56
5	0.48608	25	2.05727	108	0.55621	38	1.79788	123	1.14428	19	0.87391	15	55
6	.48634	26	.05619	108	.55659	38	.79665	123	.14446	18	.87377	14	54
7	.48659	25	.05512	108	.55697	38	.79542	122	.14465	19	.87363	14	53
8	.48684	25	.05405	108	.55736	39	.79419	122	.14483	18	.87349	14	52
9	.48710	26	.05298	108	.55774	38	.79296	122	.14502	19	.87335	14	51
10	0.48735	25	2.05191	108	0.55812	38	1.79174	122	1.14521	19	0.87321	14	50
11	.48761	26	.05084	107	.55850	38	.79051	122	.14539	18	.87306	15	49
12	.48786	25	.04977	107	.55888	38	.78929	122	.14558	19	.87292	14	48
13	.48811	25	.04870	107	.55926	38	.78807	122	.14576	18	.87278	14	47
14	.48837	26	.04764	107	.55964	38	.78685	122	.14595	19	.87264	14	46
15	0.48862	25	2.04657	107	0.56003	39	1.78563	121	1.14614	19	0.87250	14	45
16	.48888	26	.04551	107	.56041	38	.78441	121	.14632	18	.87235	15	44
17	.48913	25	.04445	107	.56079	38	.78319	121	.14651	19	.87221	14	43
18	.48938	25	.04339	106	.56117	38	.78198	121	.14670	19	.87207	14	42
19	.48964	26	.04233	106	.56156	39	.78077	121	.14689	19	.87193	14	41
20	0.48989	25	2.04128	106	0.56194	38	1.77955	121	1.14707	18	0.87178	15	40
21	.49014	25	.04022	106	.56232	38	.77834	121	.14726	19	.87164	14	39
22	.49040	26	.03916	106	.56270	38	.77713	121	.14745	19	.87150	14	38
23	.49065	25	.03811	106	.56309	39	.77592	120	.14764	19	.87136	14	37
24	.49090	25	.03706	106	.56347	38	.77471	120	.14782	18	.87121	15	36
25	0.49116	26	2.03601	106	0.56385	38	1.77351	120	1.14801	19	0.87107	14	35
26	.49141	25	.03496	104	.56424	39	.77230	120	.14820	19	.87093	14	34
27	.49166	25	.03391	104	.56462	38	.77110	120	.14839	19	.87079	14	33
28	.49192	26	.03286	104	.56501	39	.76990	120	.14858	19	.87064	15	32
29	.49217	25	.03182	104	.56539	38	.76869	120	.14877	19	.87050	14	31
30	0.49242	25	2.03077	104	0.56577	38	1.76749	120	1.14896	19	0.87036	14	30
31	.49268	26	.02973	104	.56616	39	.76629	120	.14914	18	.87021	15	29
32	.49293	25	.02869	104	.56654	38	.76510	120	.14933	19	.87007	14	28
33	.49318	25	.02765	104	.56693	39	.76390	120	.14952	19	.86993	14	27
34	.49344	26	.02661	103	.56731	38	.76271	120	.14971	19	.86978	15	26
35	0.49369	25	2.02557	103	0.56769	38	1.76151	120	1.14990	19	0.86964	14	25
36	.49394	25	.02453	103	.56808	39	.76032	120	.15009	19	.86949	15	24
37	.49419	25	.02349	103	.56846	38	.75913	120	.15028	19	.86935	14	23
38	.49445	26	.02246	103	.56885	39	.75794	120	.15047	19	.86921	14	22
39	.49470	25	.02143	103	.56923	38	.75675	119	.15066	19	.86906	15	21
40	0.49495	25	2.02039	103	0.56962	39	1.75556	119	1.15085	19	0.86892	14	20
41	.49521	26	.01936	103	.57000	38	.75437	119	.15105	20	.86878	14	19
42	.49546	25	.01833	102	.57039	39	.75319	119	.15124	19	.86863	15	18
43	.49571	25	.01730	102	.57078	39	.75200	119	.15143	19	.86849	14	17
44	.49596	25	.01628	102	.57116	38	.75082	119	.15162	19	.86834	15	16
45	0.49622	26	2.01525	102	0.57155	39	1.74964	119	1.15181	19	0.86820	14	15
46	.49647	25	.01422	102	.57193	38	.74846	119	.15200	19	.86805	15	14
47	.49672	25	.01320	102	.57232	39	.74728	118	.15219	19	.86791	14	13
48	.49697	25	.01218	102	.57271	39	.74610	118	.15239	20	.86777	14	12
49	.49723	26	.01116	102	.57309	38	.74492	118	.15258	19	.86762	15	11
50	0.49748	25	2.01014	102	0.57348	39	1.74375	118	1.15277	19	0.86748	14	10
51	.49773	25	.00912	101	.57386	38	.74257	118	.15296	19	.86733	15	9
52	.49798	25	.00810	101	.57425	39	.74140	118	.15315	19	.86719	14	8
53	.49824	26	.00708	101	.57464	39	.74022	118	.15335	20	.86704	15	7
54	.49849	25	.00607	101	.57503	39	.73905	118	.15354	19	.86690	14	6
55	0.49874	25	2.00505	101	0.57541	38	1.73788	118	1.15373	19	0.86675	15	5
56	.49899	25	.00404	101	.57580	39	.73671	117	.15393	20	.86661	14	4
57	.49924	25	.00303	101	.57619	39	.73555	117	.15412	19	.86646	15	3
58	.49950	26	.00202	101	.57657	38	.73438	117	.15431	19	.86632	14	2
59	.49975	25	.00101	100	.57696	39	.73321	117	.15451	20	.86617	15	1
60	0.50000	25	2.00000	100	0.57735	39	1.73205	117	1.15470	19	0.86603	14	0
↑ 119°→	cos	Diff. 1′	sec	Diff. 1′	cot	Diff. 1′	tan	Diff. 1′	csc	Diff. 1′	sin	Diff. 1′← 60°	↑

TABLE 2
Natural Trigonometric Functions

30°→ ↓ ′	sin	Diff. 1′	csc	Diff. 1′	tan	Diff. 1′	cot	Diff. 1′	sec	Diff. 1′	cos	Diff. 1′	← 149° ↓ ′
0	0.50000		2.00000		0.57735		1.73205		1.15470		0.86603		60
1	.50025	25	1.99899	100	.57774	39	.73089	117	.15489	19	.86588	15	59
2	.50050	25	.99799	100	.57813	39	.72973	117	.15509	20	.86573	15	58
3	.50076	26	.99698	100	.57851	38	.72857	117	.15528	19	.86559	14	57
4	.50101	25	.99598	100	.57890	39	.72741	116	.15548	20	.86544	15	56
5	0.50126	25	1.99498	100	0.57929	39	1.72625	116	1.15567	19	0.86530	14	55
6	.50151	25	.99398	100	.57968	39	.72509	116	.15587	20	.86515	15	54
7	.50176	25	.99298	100	.58007	39	.72393	116	.15606	19	.86501	14	53
8	.50201	25	.99198	100	.58046	39	.72278	116	.15626	20	.86486	15	52
9	.50227	26	.99098	100	.58085	39	.72163	116	.15645	19	.86471	15	51
10	0.50252	25	1.98998	100	0.58124	39	1.72047	116	1.15665	20	0.86457	14	50
11	.50277	25	.98899	100	.58162	38	.71932	116	.15684	19	.86442	15	49
12	.50302	25	.98799	100	.58201	39	.71817	116	.15704	20	.86427	15	48
13	.50327	25	.98700	100	.58240	39	.71702	114	.15724	20	.86413	14	47
14	.50352	25	.98601	100	.58279	39	.71588	114	.15743	19	.86398	15	46
15	0.50377	25	1.98502	100	0.58318	39	1.71473	114	1.15763	20	0.86384	14	45
16	.50403	26	.98403	99	.58357	39	.71358	114	.15782	19	.86369	15	44
17	.50428	25	.98304	99	.58396	39	.71244	114	.15802	20	.86354	15	43
18	.50453	25	.98205	99	.58435	39	.71129	114	.15822	20	.86340	14	42
19	.50478	25	.98107	99	.58474	39	.71015	114	.15841	19	.86325	15	41
20	0.50503	25	1.98008	99	0.58513	39	1.70901	114	1.15861	20	0.86310	15	40
21	.50528	25	.97910	99	.58552	39	.70787	113	.15881	20	.86295	15	39
22	.50553	25	.97811	99	.58591	39	.70673	113	.15901	20	.86281	14	38
23	.50578	25	.97713	99	.58631	40	.70560	113	.15920	19	.86266	15	37
24	.50603	25	.97615	99	.58670	39	.70446	113	.15940	20	.86251	15	36
25	0.50628	25	1.97517	98	0.58709	39	1.70332	113	1.15960	20	0.86237	14	35
26	.50654	26	.97420	98	.58748	39	.70219	113	.15980	20	.86222	15	34
27	.50679	25	.97322	98	.58787	39	.70106	113	.16000	20	.86207	15	33
28	.50704	25	.97224	98	.58826	39	.69992	113	.16019	19	.86192	15	32
29	.50729	25	.97127	98	.58865	39	.69879	113	.16039	20	.86178	14	31
30	0.50754	25	1.97029	98	0.58905	40	1.69766	112	1.16059	20	0.86163	15	30
31	.50779	25	.96932	98	.58944	39	.69653	112	.16079	20	.86148	15	29
32	.50804	25	.96835	98	.58983	39	.69541	112	.16099	20	.86133	15	28
33	.50829	25	.96738	98	.59022	39	.69428	112	.16119	20	.86119	14	27
34	.50854	25	.96641	97	.59061	39	.69316	112	.16139	20	.86104	15	26
35	0.50879	25	1.96544	97	0.59101	40	1.69203	112	1.16159	20	0.86089	15	25
36	.50904	25	.96448	97	.59140	39	.69091	112	.16179	20	.86074	15	24
37	.50929	25	.96351	97	.59179	39	.68979	112	.16199	20	.86059	15	23
38	.50954	25	.96255	97	.59218	39	.68866	112	.16219	20	.86045	14	22
39	.50979	25	.96158	97	.59258	40	.68754	111	.16239	20	.86030	15	21
40	0.51004	25	1.96062	97	0.59297	39	1.68643	111	1.16259	20	0.86015	15	20
41	.51029	25	.95966	97	.59336	39	.68531	111	.16279	20	.86000	15	19
42	.51054	25	.95870	97	.59376	40	.68419	111	.16299	20	.85985	15	18
43	.51079	25	.95774	96	.59415	39	.68308	111	.16319	20	.85970	15	17
44	.51104	25	.95678	96	.59454	39	.68196	111	.16339	20	.85956	14	16
45	0.51129	25	1.95583	96	0.59494	40	1.68085	111	1.16359	20	0.85941	15	15
46	.51154	25	.95487	96	.59533	39	.67974	111	.16380	21	.85926	15	14
47	.51179	25	.95392	96	.59573	40	.67863	111	.16400	20	.85911	15	13
48	.51204	25	.95296	96	.59612	39	.67752	111	.16420	20	.85896	15	12
49	.51229	25	.95201	96	.59651	39	.67641	110	.16440	20	.85881	15	11
50	0.51254	25	1.95106	96	0.59691	40	1.67530	110	1.16460	20	0.85866	15	10
51	.51279	25	.95011	96	.59730	39	.67419	110	.16481	21	.85851	15	9
52	.51304	25	.94916	94	.59770	40	.67309	110	.16501	20	.85836	15	8
53	.51329	25	.94821	94	.59809	39	.67198	110	.16521	20	.85821	15	7
54	.51354	25	.94726	94	.59849	40	.67088	110	.16541	20	.85806	15	6
55	0.51379	25	1.94632	94	0.59888	39	1.66978	110	1.16562	21	0.85792	14	5
56	.51404	25	.94537	94	.59928	40	.66867	110	.16582	20	.85777	15	4
57	.51429	25	.94443	94	.59967	39	.66757	110	.16602	20	.85762	15	3
58	.51454	25	.94349	94	.60007	40	.66647	110	.16623	21	.85747	15	2
59	.51479	25	.94254	94	.60046	39	.66538	110	.16643	20	.85732	15	1
60	0.51504	25	1.94160	94	0.60086	40	1.66428	110	1.16663	20	0.85717	15	0
↑ 120°→	cos	Diff. 1′	sec	Diff. 1′	cot	Diff. 1′	tan	Diff. 1′	csc	Diff. 1′	sin	Diff. 1′	↑ ←59°

TABLE 2
Natural Trigonometric Functions

31°→ ↓ ′	sin	Diff. 1′	csc	Diff. 1′	tan	Diff. 1′	cot	Diff. 1′	sec	Diff. 1′	cos	Diff. 1′	← 148° ↓ ′
0	0.51504		1.94160		0.60086		1.66428		1.16663		0.85717		60
1	.51529	25	.94066	93	.60126	40	.66318	110	.16684	21	.85702	15	59
2	.51554	25	.93973	93	.60165	39	.66209	110	.16704	20	.85687	15	58
3	.51579	25	.93879	93	.60205	40	.66099	110	.16725	21	.85672	15	57
4	.51604	25	.93785	93	.60245	40	.65990	110	.16745	20	.85657	15	56
5	0.51628	24	1.93692	93	0.60284	39	1.65881	110	1.16766	21	0.85642	15	55
6	.51653	25	.93598	93	.60324	40	.65772	110	.16786	20	.85627	15	54
7	.51678	25	.93505	93	.60364	40	.65663	109	.16806	20	.85612	15	53
8	.51703	25	.93412	93	.60403	39	.65554	109	.16827	21	.85597	15	52
9	.51728	25	.93319	93	.60443	40	.65445	109	.16848	21	.85582	15	51
10	0.51753	25	1.93226	92	0.60483	40	1.65337	109	1.16868	20	0.85567	15	50
11	.51778	25	.93133	92	.60522	39	.65228	109	.16889	21	.85551	16	49
12	.51803	25	.93040	92	.60562	40	.65120	109	.16909	20	.85536	15	48
13	.51828	25	.92947	92	.60602	40	.65011	109	.16930	21	.85521	15	47
14	.51852	24	.92855	92	.60642	40	.64903	109	.16950	20	.85506	15	46
15	0.51877	25	1.92762	92	0.60681	39	1.64795	109	1.16971	21	0.85491	15	45
16	.51902	25	.92670	92	.60721	40	.64687	109	.16992	21	.85476	15	44
17	.51927	25	.92578	92	.60761	40	.64579	108	.17012	20	.85461	15	43
18	.51952	25	.92486	92	.60801	40	.64471	108	.17033	21	.85446	15	42
19	.51977	25	.92394	92	.60841	40	.64363	108	.17054	21	.85431	15	41
20	0.52002	25	1.92302	91	0.60881	40	1.64256	108	1.17075	21	0.85416	15	40
21	.52026	24	.92210	91	.60921	40	.64148	108	.17095	20	.85401	15	39
22	.52051	25	.92118	91	.60960	39	.64041	108	.17116	21	.85385	16	38
23	.52076	25	.92027	91	.61000	40	.63934	108	.17137	21	.85370	15	37
24	.52101	25	.91935	91	.61040	40	.63826	108	.17158	21	.85355	15	36
25	0.52126	25	1.91844	91	0.61080	40	1.63719	108	1.17178	20	0.85340	15	35
26	.52151	25	.91752	91	.61120	40	.63612	108	.17199	21	.85325	15	34
27	.52175	24	.91661	91	.61160	40	.63505	107	.17220	21	.85310	15	33
28	.52200	25	.91570	91	.61200	40	.63398	107	.17241	21	.85294	16	32
29	.52225	25	.91479	91	.61240	40	.63292	107	.17262	21	.85279	15	31
30	0.52250	25	1.91388	90	0.61280	40	1.63185	107	1.17283	21	0.85264	15	30
31	.52275	25	.91297	90	.61320	40	.63079	107	.17304	21	.85249	15	29
32	.52299	24	.91207	90	.61360	40	.62972	107	.17325	21	.85234	15	28
33	.52324	25	.91116	90	.61400	40	.62866	107	.17346	21	.85218	16	27
34	.52349	25	.91026	90	.61440	40	.62760	107	.17367	21	.85203	15	26
35	0.52374	25	1.90935	90	0.61480	40	1.62654	107	1.17388	21	0.85188	15	25
36	.52399	25	.90845	90	.61520	40	.62548	106	.17409	21	.85173	15	24
37	.52423	24	.90755	90	.61561	41	.62442	106	.17430	21	.85157	16	23
38	.52448	25	.90665	90	.61601	40	.62336	106	.17451	21	.85142	15	22
39	.52473	25	.90575	90	.61641	40	.62230	106	.17472	21	.85127	15	21
40	0.52498	25	1.90485	90	0.61681	40	1.62125	106	1.17493	21	0.85112	15	20
41	.52522	24	.90395	90	.61721	40	.62019	106	.17514	21	.85096	16	19
42	.52547	25	.90305	90	.61761	40	.61914	106	.17535	21	.85081	15	18
43	.52572	25	.90216	90	.61801	40	.61808	106	.17556	21	.85066	15	17
44	.52597	25	.90126	90	.61842	41	.61703	106	.17577	21	.85051	15	16
45	0.52621	24	1.90037	90	0.61882	40	1.61598	106	1.17598	21	0.85035	16	15
46	.52646	25	.89948	90	.61922	40	.61493	106	.17620	22	.85020	15	14
47	.52671	25	.89858	90	.61962	40	.61388	104	.17641	21	.85005	15	13
48	.52696	25	.89769	90	.62003	41	.61283	104	.17662	21	.84989	16	12
49	.52720	24	.89680	89	.62043	40	.61179	104	.17683	21	.84974	15	11
50	0.52745	25	1.89591	89	0.62083	40	1.61074	104	1.17704	21	0.84959	15	10
51	.52770	25	.89503	89	.62124	41	.60970	104	.17726	22	.84943	16	9
52	.52794	24	.89414	89	.62164	40	.60865	104	.17747	21	.84928	15	8
53	.52819	25	.89325	89	.62204	40	.60761	104	.17768	21	.84913	15	7
54	.52844	25	.89237	89	.62245	41	.60657	104	.17790	22	.84897	16	6
55	0.52869	25	1.89148	89	0.62285	40	1.60553	104	1.17811	21	0.84882	15	5
56	.52893	24	.89060	89	.62325	40	.60449	104	.17832	21	.84866	16	4
57	.52918	25	.88972	89	.62366	41	.60345	103	.17854	22	.84851	15	3
58	.52943	25	.88884	89	.62406	40	.60241	103	.17875	21	.84836	15	2
59	.52967	24	.88796	88	.62446	40	.60137	103	.17896	21	.84820	16	1
60	0.52992	25	1.88708	88	0.62487	41	1.60033	103	1.17918	22	0.84805	15	0
↑ 121°→	cos	Diff. 1′	sec	Diff. 1′	cot	Diff. 1′	tan	Diff. 1′	csc	Diff. 1′	sin	Diff. 1′	↑ ←58°

TABLE 2
Natural Trigonometric Functions

32° → ↓ ′	sin	Diff. 1′	csc	Diff. 1′	tan	Diff. 1′	cot	Diff. 1′	sec	Diff. 1′	cos	← 147° Diff. 1′	↓ ′
0	0.52992		1.88708		0.62487		1.60033		1.17918		0.84805		60
1	.53017	25	.88620	88	.62527	40	.59930	103	.17939	21	.84789	16	59
2	.53041	24	.88532	88	.62568	41	.59826	103	.17961	22	.84774	15	58
3	.53066	25	.88445	88	.62608	40	.59723	103	.17982	21	.84759	15	57
4	.53091	25	.88357	88	.62649	41	.59620	103	.18004	22	.84743	16	56
5	0.53115	24	1.88270	88	0.62689	40	1.59517	103	1.18025	21	0.84728	15	55
6	.53140	25	.88183	88	.62730	41	.59414	103	.18047	22	.84712	16	54
7	.53164	24	.88095	88	.62770	40	.59311	102	.18068	21	.84697	15	53
8	.53189	25	.88008	88	.62811	41	.59208	102	.18090	22	.84681	16	52
9	.53214	25	.87921	88	.62852	41	.59105	102	.18111	21	.84666	15	51
10	0.53238	24	1.87834	87	0.62892	40	1.59002	102	1.18133	22	0.84650	16	50
11	.53263	25	.87748	87	.62933	41	.58900	102	.18155	22	.84635	15	49
12	.53288	25	.87661	87	.62973	40	.58797	102	.18176	21	.84619	16	48
13	.53312	24	.87574	87	.63014	41	.58695	102	.18198	22	.84604	15	47
14	.53337	25	.87488	87	.63055	41	.58593	102	.18220	22	.84588	16	46
15	0.53361	24	1.87401	87	0.63095	40	1.58490	102	1.18241	21	0.84573	15	45
16	.53386	25	.87315	87	.63136	41	.58388	102	.18263	22	.84557	16	44
17	.53411	25	.87229	87	.63177	41	.58286	102	.18285	22	.84542	15	43
18	.53435	24	.87142	87	.63217	40	.58184	101	.18307	22	.84526	16	42
19	.53460	25	.87056	87	.63258	41	.58083	101	.18328	21	.84511	15	41
20	0.53484	24	1.86970	86	0.63299	41	1.57981	101	1.18350	22	0.84495	16	40
21	.53509	25	.86885	86	.63340	41	.57879	101	.18372	22	.84480	15	39
22	.53534	25	.86799	86	.63380	40	.57778	101	.18394	22	.84464	16	38
23	.53558	24	.86713	86	.63421	41	.57676	101	.18416	22	.84448	16	37
24	.53583	25	.86627	86	.63462	41	.57575	101	.18437	21	.84433	15	36
25	0.53607	24	1.86542	86	0.63503	41	1.57474	101	1.18459	22	0.84417	16	35
26	.53632	25	.86457	86	.63544	41	.57372	101	.18481	22	.84402	15	34
27	.53656	24	.86371	86	.63584	40	.57271	101	.18503	22	.84386	16	33
28	.53681	25	.86286	86	.63625	41	.57170	100	.18525	22	.84370	16	32
29	.53705	24	.86201	86	.63666	41	.57069	100	.18547	22	.84355	15	31
30	0.53730	25	1.86116	86	0.63707	41	1.56969	100	1.18569	22	0.84339	16	30
31	.53754	24	.86031	84	.63748	41	.56868	100	.18591	22	.84324	15	29
32	.53779	25	.85946	84	.63789	41	.56767	100	.18613	22	.84308	16	28
33	.53804	25	.85861	84	.63830	41	.56667	100	.18635	22	.84292	16	27
34	.53828	24	.85777	84	.63871	41	.56566	100	.18657	22	.84277	15	26
35	0.53853	25	1.85692	84	0.63912	41	1.56466	100	1.18679	22	0.84261	16	25
36	.53877	24	.85608	84	.63953	41	.56366	100	.18701	22	.84245	16	24
37	.53902	25	.85523	84	.63994	41	.56265	100	.18723	22	.84230	15	23
38	.53926	24	.85439	84	.64035	41	.56165	100	.18745	22	.84214	16	22
39	.53951	25	.85355	84	.64076	41	.56065	100	.18767	22	.84198	16	21
40	0.53975	24	1.85271	84	0.64117	41	1.55966	100	1.18790	23	0.84182	16	20
41	.54000	25	.85187	84	.64158	41	.55866	100	.18812	22	.84167	15	19
42	.54024	24	.85103	83	.64199	41	.55766	100	.18834	22	.84151	16	18
43	.54049	25	.85019	83	.64240	41	.55666	100	.18856	22	.84135	16	17
44	.54073	24	.84935	83	.64281	41	.55567	100	.18878	22	.84120	15	16
45	0.54097	24	1.84852	83	0.64322	41	1.55467	100	1.18901	23	0.84104	16	15
46	.54122	25	.84768	83	.64363	41	.55368	100	.18923	22	.84088	16	14
47	.54146	24	.84685	83	.64404	41	.55269	100	.18945	22	.84072	16	13
48	.54171	25	.84601	83	.64446	42	.55170	100	.18967	22	.84057	15	12
49	.54195	24	.84518	83	.64487	41	.55071	100	.18990	23	.84041	16	11
50	0.54220	25	1.84435	83	0.64528	41	1.54972	99	1.19012	22	0.84025	16	10
51	.54244	24	.84352	83	.64569	41	.54873	99	.19034	22	.84009	16	9
52	.54269	25	.84269	83	.64610	41	.54774	99	.19057	23	.83994	15	8
53	.54293	24	.84186	82	.64652	42	.54675	99	.19079	22	.83978	16	7
54	.54317	24	.84103	82	.64693	41	.54576	99	.19102	23	.83962	16	6
55	0.54342	25	1.84020	82	0.64734	41	1.54478	99	1.19124	22	0.83946	16	5
56	.54366	24	.83938	82	.64775	41	.54379	99	.19146	22	.83930	16	4
57	.54391	25	.83855	82	.64817	42	.54281	99	.19169	23	.83915	15	3
58	.54415	24	.83773	82	.64858	41	.54183	99	.19191	22	.83899	16	2
59	.54440	25	.83690	82	.64899	41	.54085	99	.19214	23	.83883	16	1
60	0.54464	24	1.83608	82	0.64941	42	1.53986	99	1.19236	22	0.83867	16	0
↑ 122° →	cos	Diff. 1′	sec	Diff. 1′	cot	Diff. 1′	tan	Diff. 1′	csc	Diff. 1′	sin	Diff. 1′ ← 57°	↑

TABLE 2
Natural Trigonometric Functions

33° → ↓ ′	sin	Diff. 1′	csc	Diff. 1′	tan	Diff. 1′	cot	Diff. 1′	sec	Diff. 1′	cos	← 146° Diff. 1′	↓ ′
0	0.54464		1.83608		0.64941		1.53986		1.19236		0.83867		60
1	.54488	24	.83526	82	.64982	41	.53888	99	.19259	23	.83851	16	59
2	.54513	25	.83444	82	.65024	42	.53791	98	.19281	22	.83835	16	58
3	.54537	24	.83362	82	.65065	41	.53693	98	.19304	23	.83819	16	57
4	.54561	24	.83280	81	.65106	41	.53595	98	.19327	23	.83804	15	56
5	0.54586	25	1.83198	81	0.65148	42	1.53497	98	1.19349	22	0.83788	16	55
6	.54610	24	.83116	81	.65189	41	.53400	98	.19372	23	.83772	16	54
7	.54635	25	.83034	81	.65231	42	.53302	98	.19394	22	.83756	16	53
8	.54659	24	.82953	81	.65272	41	.53205	98	.19417	23	.83740	16	52
9	.54683	24	.82871	81	.65314	42	.53107	98	.19440	23	.83724	16	51
10	0.54708	25	1.82790	81	0.65355	41	1.53010	98	1.19463	23	0.83708	16	50
11	.54732	24	.82709	81	.65397	42	.52913	98	.19485	22	.83692	16	49
12	.54756	24	.82627	81	.65438	41	.52816	98	.19508	23	.83676	16	48
13	.54781	25	.82546	81	.65480	42	.52719	97	.19531	23	.83660	16	47
14	.54805	24	.82465	81	.65521	41	.52622	97	.19553	22	.83645	15	46
15	0.54829	24	1.82384	80	0.65563	42	1.52525	97	1.19576	23	0.83629	16	45
16	.54854	25	.82303	80	.65604	41	.52429	97	.19599	23	.83613	16	44
17	.54878	24	.82222	80	.65646	42	.52332	97	.19622	23	.83597	16	43
18	.54902	24	.82142	80	.65688	42	.52235	97	.19645	23	.83581	16	42
19	.54927	25	.82061	80	.65729	41	.52139	97	.19668	23	.83565	16	41
20	0.54951	24	1.81981	80	0.65771	42	1.52043	97	1.19691	23	0.83549	16	40
21	.54975	24	.81900	80	.65813	42	.51946	97	.19713	22	.83533	16	39
22	.54999	24	.81820	80	.65854	41	.51850	97	.19736	23	.83517	16	38
23	.55024	25	.81740	80	.65896	42	.51754	97	.19759	23	.83501	16	37
24	.55048	24	.81659	80	.65938	42	.51658	97	.19782	23	.83485	16	36
25	0.55072	24	1.81579	80	0.65980	42	1.51562	96	1.19805	23	0.83469	16	35
26	.55097	25	.81499	80	.66021	41	.51466	96	.19828	23	.83453	16	34
27	.55121	24	.81419	80	.66063	42	.51370	96	.19851	23	.83437	16	33
28	.55145	24	.81340	80	.66105	42	.51275	96	.19874	23	.83421	16	32
29	.55169	24	.81260	80	.66147	42	.51179	96	.19897	23	.83405	16	31
30	0.55194	25	1.81180	80	0.66189	42	1.51084	96	1.19920	23	0.83389	16	30
31	.55218	24	.81101	80	.66230	41	.50988	96	.19944	24	.83373	16	29
32	.55242	24	.81021	80	.66272	42	.50893	96	.19967	23	.83356	17	28
33	.55266	24	.80942	80	.66314	42	.50797	96	.19990	23	.83340	16	27
34	.55291	25	.80862	80	.66356	42	.50702	96	.20013	23	.83324	16	26
35	0.55315	24	1.80783	80	0.66398	42	1.50607	96	1.20036	23	0.83308	16	25
36	.55339	24	.80704	80	.66440	42	.50512	96	.20059	23	.83292	16	24
37	.55363	24	.80625	80	.66482	42	.50417	94	.20083	24	.83276	16	23
38	.55388	25	.80546	79	.66524	42	.50322	94	.20106	23	.83260	16	22
39	.55412	24	.80467	79	.66566	42	.50228	94	.20129	23	.83244	16	21
40	0.55436	24	1.80388	79	0.66608	42	1.50133	94	1.20152	23	0.83228	16	20
41	.55460	24	.80309	79	.66650	42	.50038	94	.20176	24	.83212	16	19
42	.55484	24	.80231	79	.66692	42	.49944	94	.20199	23	.83195	17	18
43	.55509	25	.80152	79	.66734	42	.49849	94	.20222	23	.83179	16	17
44	.55533	24	.80074	79	.66776	42	.49755	94	.20246	24	.83163	16	16
45	0.55557	24	1.79995	79	0.66818	42	1.49661	94	1.20269	23	0.83147	16	15
46	.55581	24	.79917	79	.66860	42	.49566	94	.20292	23	.83131	16	14
47	.55605	24	.79839	79	.66902	42	.49472	94	.20316	24	.83115	16	13
48	.55630	25	.79761	79	.66944	42	.49378	94	.20339	23	.83098	17	12
49	.55654	24	.79682	79	.66986	42	.49284	93	.20363	24	.83082	16	11
50	0.55678	24	1.79604	78	0.67028	42	1.49190	93	1.20386	23	0.83066	16	10
51	.55702	24	.79527	78	.67071	43	.49097	93	.20410	24	.83050	16	9
52	.55726	24	.79449	78	.67113	42	.49003	93	.20433	23	.83034	16	8
53	.55750	24	.79371	78	.67155	42	.48909	93	.20457	24	.83017	17	7
54	.55775	25	.79293	78	.67197	42	.48816	93	.20480	23	.83001	16	6
55	0.55799	24	1.79216	78	0.67239	42	1.48722	93	1.20504	24	0.82985	16	5
56	.55823	24	.79138	78	.67282	43	.48629	93	.20527	23	.82969	16	4
57	.55847	24	.79061	78	.67324	42	.48536	93	.20551	24	.82953	16	3
58	.55871	24	.78984	78	.67366	42	.48442	93	.20575	24	.82936	17	2
59	.55895	24	.78906	78	.67409	43	.48349	93	.20598	23	.82920	16	1
60	0.55919	24	1.78829	78	0.67451	42	1.48256	93	1.20622	24	0.82904	16	0
↑ 123° →	cos	Diff. 1′	sec	Diff. 1′	cot	Diff. 1′	tan	Diff. 1′	csc	Diff. 1′	sin	Diff. 1′ ← 56°	↑

TABLE 2
Natural Trigonometric Functions

34°→ ↓ ′	sin	Diff. 1′	csc	Diff. 1′	tan	Diff. 1′	cot	Diff. 1′	sec	Diff. 1′	cos	Diff. 1′	← 145° ↓ ′
0	0.55919		1.78829		0.67451		1.48256		1.20622		0.82904		60
1	.55943	24	.78752	78	.67493	42	.48163	92	.20645	23	.82887	17	59
2	.55968	25	.78675	77	.67536	43	.48070	92	.20669	24	.82871	16	58
3	.55992	24	.78598	77	.67578	42	.47977	92	.20693	24	.82855	16	57
4	.56016	24	.78521	77	.67620	42	.47885	92	.20717	24	.82839	16	56
5	0.56040	24	1.78445	77	0.67663	43	1.47792	92	1.20740	23	0.82822	17	55
6	.56064	24	.78368	77	.67705	42	.47699	92	.20764	24	.82806	16	54
7	.56088	24	.78291	77	.67748	43	.47607	92	.20788	24	.82790	16	53
8	.56112	24	.78215	77	.67790	42	.47514	92	.20812	24	.82773	17	52
9	.56136	24	.78138	77	.67832	42	.47422	92	.20836	24	.82757	16	51
10	0.56160	24	1.78062	77	0.67875	43	1.47330	92	1.20859	23	0.82741	16	50
11	.56184	24	.77986	77	.67917	42	.47238	92	.20883	24	.82724	17	49
12	.56208	24	.77910	77	.67960	43	.47146	92	.20907	24	.82708	16	48
13	.56232	24	.77833	77	.68002	42	.47053	92	.20931	24	.82692	16	47
14	.56256	24	.77757	77	.68045	43	.46962	91	.20955	24	.82675	17	46
15	0.56280	24	1.77681	76	0.68088	43	1.46870	91	1.20979	24	0.82659	16	45
16	.56305	25	.77606	76	.68130	42	.46778	91	.21003	24	.82643	16	44
17	.56329	24	.77530	76	.68173	43	.46686	91	.21027	24	.82626	17	43
18	.56353	24	.77454	76	.68215	42	.46595	91	.21051	24	.82610	16	42
19	.56377	24	.77378	76	.68258	43	.46503	91	.21075	24	.82593	17	41
20	0.56401	24	1.77303	76	0.68301	43	1.46411	91	1.21099	24	0.82577	16	40
21	.56425	24	.77227	76	.68343	42	.46320	91	.21123	24	.82561	16	39
22	.56449	24	.77152	76	.68386	43	.46229	91	.21147	24	.82544	17	38
23	.56473	24	.77077	76	.68429	43	.46137	91	.21171	24	.82528	16	37
24	.56497	24	.77001	76	.68471	42	.46046	91	.21195	24	.82511	17	36
25	0.56521	24	1.76926	76	0.68514	43	1.45955	91	1.21220	25	0.82495	16	35
26	.56545	24	.76851	76	.68557	43	.45864	91	.21244	24	.82478	17	34
27	.56569	24	.76776	74	.68600	43	.45773	90	.21268	24	.82462	16	33
28	.56593	24	.76701	74	.68642	42	.45682	90	.21292	24	.82446	16	32
29	.56617	24	.76626	74	.68685	43	.45592	90	.21316	24	.82429	17	31
30	0.56641	24	1.76552	74	0.68728	43	1.45501	90	1.21341	25	0.82413	16	30
31	.56665	24	.76477	74	.68771	43	.45410	90	.21365	24	.82396	17	29
32	.56689	24	.76402	74	.68814	43	.45320	90	.21389	24	.82380	16	28
33	.56713	24	.76328	74	.68857	43	.45229	90	.21414	25	.82363	17	27
34	.56736	23	.76253	74	.68900	43	.45139	90	.21438	24	.82347	16	26
35	0.56760	24	1.76179	74	0.68942	42	1.45049	90	1.21462	24	0.82330	17	25
36	.56784	24	.76105	74	.68985	43	.44958	90	.21487	25	.82314	16	24
37	.56808	24	.76031	74	.69028	43	.44868	90	.21511	24	.82297	17	23
38	.56832	24	.75956	74	.69071	43	.44778	90	.21535	24	.82281	16	22
39	.56856	24	.75882	74	.69114	43	.44688	90	.21560	25	.82264	17	21
40	0.56880	24	1.75808	73	0.69157	43	1.44598	90	1.21584	24	0.82248	16	20
41	.56904	24	.75734	73	.69200	43	.44508	90	.21609	25	.82231	17	19
42	.56928	24	.75661	73	.69243	43	.44418	90	.21633	24	.82214	17	18
43	.56952	24	.75587	73	.69286	43	.44329	90	.21658	25	.82198	16	17
44	.56976	24	.75513	73	.69329	43	.44239	90	.21682	24	.82181	17	16
45	0.57000	24	1.75440	73	0.69372	43	1.44149	90	1.21707	25	0.82165	16	15
46	.57024	24	.75366	73	.69416	44	.44060	90	.21731	24	.82148	17	14
47	.57047	23	.75293	73	.69459	43	.43970	90	.21756	25	.82132	16	13
48	.57071	24	.75219	73	.69502	43	.43881	90	.21781	25	.82115	17	12
49	.57095	24	.75146	73	.69545	43	.43792	90	.21805	24	.82098	17	11
50	0.57119	24	1.75073	73	0.69588	43	1.43703	90	1.21830	25	0.82082	16	10
51	.57143	24	.75000	73	.69631	43	.43614	90	.21855	25	.82065	17	9
52	.57167	24	.74927	73	.69675	44	.43525	90	.21879	24	.82048	17	8
53	.57191	24	.74854	72	.69718	43	.43436	89	.21904	25	.82032	16	7
54	.57215	24	.74781	72	.69761	43	.43347	89	.21929	25	.82015	17	6
55	0.57238	23	1.74708	72	0.69804	43	1.43258	89	1.21953	24	0.81999	16	5
56	.57262	24	.74635	72	.69847	43	.43169	89	.21978	25	.81982	17	4
57	.57286	24	.74562	72	.69891	44	.43080	89	.22003	25	.81965	17	3
58	.57310	24	.74490	72	.69934	43	.42992	89	.22028	25	.81949	16	2
59	.57334	24	.74417	72	.69977	43	.42903	89	.22053	25	.81932	17	1
60	0.57358	24	1.74345	72	0.70021	44	1.42815	89	1.22077	24	0.81915	17	0
↑ 124°→	cos	Diff. 1′	sec	Diff. 1′	cot	Diff. 1′	tan	Diff. 1′	csc	Diff. 1′	sin	Diff. 1′	1′← 55° ↑

TABLE 2
Natural Trigonometric Functions

35°→ ↓ ′	sin	Diff. 1′	csc	Diff. 1′	tan	Diff. 1′	cot	Diff. 1′	sec	Diff. 1′	cos	Diff. 1′	← 144° ↓ ′
0	0.57358		1.74345		0.70021		1.42815		1.22077		0.81915		60
1	.57381	23	.74272	72	.70064	43	.42726	89	.22102	25	.81899	16	59
2	.57405	24	.74200	72	.70107	43	.42638	89	.22127	25	.81882	17	58
3	.57429	24	.74128	72	.70151	44	.42550	89	.22152	25	.81865	17	57
4	.57453	24	.74056	72	.70194	43	.42462	89	.22177	25	.81848	17	56
5	0.57477	24	1.73983	72	0.70238	44	1.42374	89	1.22202	25	0.81832	16	55
6	.57501	24	.73911	72	.70281	43	.42286	89	.22227	25	.81815	17	54
7	.57524	23	.73840	71	.70325	44	.42198	88	.22252	25	.81798	17	53
8	.57548	24	.73768	71	.70368	43	.42110	88	.22277	25	.81782	16	52
9	.57572	24	.73696	71	.70412	44	.42022	88	.22302	25	.81765	17	51
10	0.57596	24	1.73624	71	0.70455	43	1.41934	88	1.22327	25	0.81748	17	50
11	.57619	23	.73552	71	.70499	44	.41847	88	.22352	25	.81731	17	49
12	.57643	24	.73481	71	.70542	43	.41759	88	.22377	25	.81714	17	48
13	.57667	24	.73409	71	.70586	44	.41672	88	.22402	25	.81698	16	47
14	.57691	24	.73338	71	.70629	43	.41584	88	.22428	26	.81681	17	46
15	0.57715	24	1.73267	71	0.70673	44	1.41497	88	1.22453	25	0.81664	17	45
16	.57738	23	.73195	71	.70717	44	.41409	88	.22478	25	.81647	17	44
17	.57762	24	.73124	71	.70760	43	.41322	88	.22503	25	.81631	16	43
18	.57786	24	.73053	71	.70804	44	.41235	88	.22528	25	.81614	17	42
19	.57810	24	.72982	71	.70848	44	.41148	88	.22554	26	.81597	17	41
20	0.57833	23	1.72911	70	0.70891	43	1.41061	88	1.22579	25	0.81580	17	40
21	.57857	24	.72840	70	.70935	44	.40974	87	.22604	25	.81563	17	39
22	.57881	24	.72769	70	.70979	44	.40887	87	.22629	25	.81546	17	38
23	.57904	23	.72698	70	.71023	44	.40800	87	.22655	26	.81530	16	37
24	.57928	24	.72628	70	.71066	43	.40714	87	.22680	25	.81513	17	36
25	0.57952	24	1.72557	70	0.71110	44	1.40627	87	1.22706	26	0.81496	17	35
26	.57976	24	.72487	70	.71154	44	.40540	87	.22731	25	.81479	17	34
27	.57999	23	.72416	70	.71198	44	.40454	87	.22756	25	.81462	17	33
28	.58023	24	.72346	70	.71242	44	.40367	87	.22782	26	.81445	17	32
29	.58047	24	.72275	70	.71285	43	.40281	87	.22807	25	.81428	17	31
30	0.58070	23	1.72205	70	0.71329	44	1.40195	87	1.22833	26	0.81412	16	30
31	.58094	24	.72135	70	.71373	44	.40109	87	.22858	25	.81395	17	29
32	.58118	24	.72065	70	.71417	44	.40022	87	.22884	26	.81378	17	28
33	.58141	23	.71995	70	.71461	44	.39936	87	.22909	25	.81361	17	27
34	.58165	24	.71925	70	.71505	44	.39850	87	.22935	26	.81344	17	26
35	0.58189	24	1.71855	70	0.71549	44	1.39764	86	1.22960	25	0.81327	17	25
36	.58212	23	.71785	70	.71593	44	.39679	86	.22986	26	.81310	17	24
37	.58236	24	.71715	70	.71637	44	.39593	86	.23012	26	.81293	17	23
38	.58260	24	.71646	70	.71681	44	.39507	86	.23037	25	.81276	17	22
39	.58283	23	.71576	70	.71725	44	.39421	86	.23063	26	.81259	17	21
40	0.58307	24	1.71506	70	0.71769	44	1.39336	86	1.23089	26	0.81242	17	20
41	.58330	23	.71437	70	.71813	44	.39250	86	.23114	25	.81225	17	19
42	.58354	24	.71368	70	.71857	44	.39165	86	.23140	26	.81208	17	18
43	.58378	24	.71298	70	.71901	44	.39079	86	.23166	26	.81191	17	17
44	.58401	23	.71229	70	.71946	45	.38994	86	.23192	26	.81174	17	16
45	0.58425	24	1.71160	70	0.71990	44	1.38909	86	1.23217	25	0.81157	17	15
46	.58449	24	.71091	70	.72034	44	.38824	86	.23243	26	.81140	17	14
47	.58472	23	.71022	70	.72078	44	.38738	86	.23269	26	.81123	17	13
48	.58496	24	.70953	69	.72122	44	.38653	86	.23295	26	.81106	17	12
49	.58519	23	.70884	69	.72167	45	.38568	84	.23321	26	.81089	17	11
50	0.58543	24	1.70815	69	0.72211	44	1.38484	84	1.23347	26	0.81072	17	10
51	.58567	24	.70746	69	.72255	44	.38399	84	.23373	26	.81055	17	9
52	.58590	23	.70677	69	.72299	44	.38314	84	.23398	25	.81038	17	8
53	.58614	24	.70609	69	.72344	45	.38229	84	.23424	26	.81021	17	7
54	.58637	23	.70540	69	.72388	44	.38145	84	.23450	26	.81004	17	6
55	0.58661	24	1.70472	69	0.72432	44	1.38060	84	1.23476	26	0.80987	17	5
56	.58684	23	.70403	69	.72477	45	.37976	84	.23502	26	.80970	17	4
57	.58708	24	.70335	69	.72521	44	.37891	84	.23529	27	.80953	17	3
58	.58731	23	.70267	69	.72565	44	.37807	84	.23555	26	.80936	17	2
59	.58755	24	.70198	69	.72610	45	.37722	84	.23581	26	.80919	17	1
60	0.58779	24	1.70130	69	0.72654	44	1.37638	84	1.23607	26	0.80902	17	0
↑ 125°→	cos	Diff. 1′	sec	Diff. 1′	cot	Diff. 1′	tan	Diff. 1′	csc	Diff. 1′	sin	Diff. 1′	1′← 54° ↑

TABLE 2
Natural Trigonometric Functions

36°→ ↓ ′	sin	Diff. 1′	csc	Diff. 1′	tan	Diff. 1′	cot	Diff. 1′	sec	Diff. 1′	cos	Diff. 1′	← 143° ↓ ′
0	0.58779		1.70130		0.72654		1.37638		1.23607		0.80902		60
1	.58802	23	.70062	69	.72699	45	.37554	84	.23633	26	.80885	17	59
2	.58826	24	.69994	69	.72743	44	.37470	84	.23659	26	.80867	18	58
3	.58849	23	.69926	68	.72788	45	.37386	84	.23685	26	.80850	17	57
4	.58873	24	.69858	68	.72832	44	.37302	83	.23711	26	.80833	17	56
5	0.58896	23	1.69790	68	0.72877	45	1.37218	83	1.23738	27	0.80816	17	55
6	.58920	24	.69723	68	.72921	44	.37134	83	.23764	26	.80799	17	54
7	.58943	23	.69655	68	.72966	45	.37050	83	.23790	26	.80782	17	53
8	.58967	24	.69587	68	.73010	44	.36967	83	.23816	26	.80765	17	52
9	.58990	23	.69520	68	.73055	45	.36883	83	.23843	27	.80748	17	51
10	0.59014	24	1.69452	68	0.73100	45	1.36800	83	1.23869	26	0.80730	18	50
11	.59037	23	.69385	68	.73144	44	.36716	83	.23895	26	.80713	17	49
12	.59061	24	.69318	68	.73189	45	.36633	83	.23922	27	.80696	17	48
13	.59084	23	.69250	68	.73234	45	.36549	83	.23948	26	.80679	17	47
14	.59108	24	.69183	68	.73278	44	.36466	83	.23975	27	.80662	17	46
15	0.59131	23	1.69116	68	0.73323	45	1.36383	83	1.24001	26	0.80644	18	45
16	.59154	23	.69049	68	.73368	45	.36300	83	.24028	27	.80627	17	44
17	.59178	24	.68982	67	.73413	45	.36217	83	.24054	26	.80610	17	43
18	.59201	23	.68915	67	.73457	44	.36134	83	.24081	27	.80593	17	42
19	.59225	24	.68848	67	.73502	45	.36051	82	.24107	26	.80576	17	41
20	0.59248	23	1.68782	67	0.73547	45	1.35968	82	1.24134	27	0.80558	18	40
21	.59272	24	.68715	67	.73592	45	.35885	82	.24160	26	.80541	17	39
22	.59295	23	.68648	67	.73637	45	.35802	82	.24187	27	.80524	17	38
23	.59318	23	.68582	67	.73681	44	.35719	82	.24213	26	.80507	17	37
24	.59342	24	.68515	67	.73726	45	.35637	82	.24240	27	.80489	18	36
25	0.59365	23	1.68449	67	0.73771	45	1.35554	82	1.24267	27	0.80472	17	35
26	.59389	24	.68382	67	.73816	45	.35472	82	.24293	26	.80455	17	34
27	.59412	23	.68316	67	.73861	45	.35389	82	.24320	27	.80438	17	33
28	.59436	24	.68250	67	.73906	45	.35307	82	.24347	27	.80420	18	32
29	.59459	23	.68183	67	.73951	45	.35224	82	.24373	26	.80403	17	31
30	0.59482	23	1.68117	67	0.73996	45	1.35142	82	1.24400	27	0.80386	17	30
31	.59506	24	.68051	67	.74041	45	.35060	82	.24427	27	.80368	18	29
32	.59529	23	.67985	66	.74086	45	.34978	82	.24454	27	.80351	17	28
33	.59552	23	.67919	66	.74131	45	.34896	82	.24481	27	.80334	17	27
34	.59576	24	.67853	66	.74176	45	.34814	81	.24508	27	.80316	18	26
35	0.59599	23	1.67788	66	0.74221	45	1.34732	81	1.24534	26	0.80299	17	25
36	.59622	23	.67722	66	.74267	46	.34650	81	.24561	27	.80282	17	24
37	.59646	24	.67656	66	.74312	45	.34568	81	.24588	27	.80264	18	23
38	.59669	23	.67591	66	.74357	45	.34487	81	.24615	27	.80247	17	22
39	.59693	24	.67525	66	.74402	45	.34405	81	.24642	27	.80230	17	21
40	0.59716	23	1.67460	66	0.74447	45	1.34323	81	1.24669	27	0.80212	18	20
41	.59739	23	.67394	66	.74492	45	.34242	81	.24696	27	.80195	17	19
42	.59763	24	.67329	66	.74538	46	.34160	81	.24723	27	.80178	17	18
43	.59786	23	.67264	66	.74583	45	.34079	81	.24750	27	.80160	18	17
44	.59809	23	.67198	66	.74628	45	.33998	81	.24777	27	.80143	17	16
45	0.59832	23	1.67133	66	0.74674	46	1.33916	81	1.24804	27	0.80125	18	15
46	.59856	24	.67068	66	.74719	45	.33835	81	.24832	28	.80108	17	14
47	.59879	23	.67003	66	.74764	45	.33754	81	.24859	27	.80091	17	13
48	.59902	23	.66938	64	.74810	46	.33673	81	.24886	27	.80073	18	12
49	.59926	24	.66873	64	.74855	45	.33592	81	.24913	27	.80056	17	11
50	0.59949	23	1.66809	64	0.74900	45	1.33511	80	1.24940	27	0.80038	18	10
51	.59972	23	.66744	64	.74946	46	.33430	80	.24967	27	.80021	17	9
52	.59995	23	.66679	64	.74991	45	.33349	80	.24995	28	.80003	18	8
53	.60019	24	.66615	64	.75037	46	.33268	80	.25022	27	.79986	17	7
54	.60042	23	.66550	64	.75082	45	.33187	80	.25049	27	.79968	18	6
55	0.60065	23	1.66486	64	0.75128	46	1.33107	80	1.25077	28	0.79951	17	5
56	.60089	24	.66421	64	.75173	45	.33026	80	.25104	27	.79934	17	4
57	.60112	23	.66357	64	.75219	46	.32946	80	.25131	27	.79916	18	3
58	.60135	23	.66292	64	.75264	45	.32865	80	.25159	28	.79899	17	2
59	.60158	23	.66228	64	.75310	46	.32785	80	.25186	27	.79881	18	1
60	0.60182	24	1.66164	64	0.75355	45	1.32704	80	1.25214	28	0.79864	17	0
↑ 126°→	cos	Diff. 1′	sec	Diff. 1′	cot	Diff. 1′	tan	Diff. 1′	csc	Diff. 1′	sin	Diff. 1′ ← 53°	↑

TABLE 2
Natural Trigonometric Functions

37°→ ↓ ′	sin	Diff. 1′	csc	Diff. 1′	tan	Diff. 1′	cot	Diff. 1′	sec	Diff. 1′	cos	Diff. 1′	← 142° ↓ ′
0	0.60182		1.66164		0.75355		1.32704		1.25214		0.79864		60
1	.60205	23	.66100	64	.75401	46	.32624	80	.25241	27	.79846	18	59
2	.60228	23	.66036	64	.75447	46	.32544	80	.25269	28	.79829	17	58
3	.60251	23	.65972	63	.75492	45	.32464	80	.25296	27	.79811	18	57
4	.60274	23	.65908	63	.75538	46	.32384	80	.25324	28	.79793	18	56
5	0.60298	24	1.65844	63	0.75584	46	1.32304	80	1.25351	27	0.79776	17	55
6	.60321	23	.65780	63	.75629	45	.32224	80	.25379	28	.79758	18	54
7	.60344	23	.65717	63	.75675	46	.32144	80	.25406	27	.79741	17	53
8	.60367	23	.65653	63	.75721	46	.32064	80	.25434	28	.79723	18	52
9	.60390	23	.65589	63	.75767	46	.31984	80	.25462	28	.79706	17	51
10	0.60414	24	1.65526	63	0.75812	45	1.31904	80	1.25489	27	0.79688	18	50
11	.60437	23	.65462	63	.75858	46	.31825	80	.25517	28	.79671	17	49
12	.60460	23	.65399	63	.75904	46	.31745	80	.25545	28	.79653	18	48
13	.60483	23	.65335	63	.75950	46	.31666	80	.25572	27	.79635	18	47
14	.60506	23	.65272	63	.75996	46	.31586	80	.25600	28	.79618	17	46
15	0.60529	23	1.65209	63	0.76042	46	1.31507	80	1.25628	28	0.79600	18	45
16	.60553	24	.65146	63	.76088	46	.31427	80	.25656	28	.79583	17	44
17	.60576	23	.65083	63	.76134	46	.31348	80	.25683	27	.79565	18	43
18	.60599	23	.65020	63	.76180	46	.31269	80	.25711	28	.79547	18	42
19	.60622	23	.64957	62	.76226	46	.31190	80	.25739	28	.79530	17	41
20	0.60645	23	1.64894	62	0.76272	46	1.31110	80	1.25767	28	0.79512	18	40
21	.60668	23	.64831	62	.76318	46	.31031	80	.25795	28	.79494	18	39
22	.60691	23	.64768	62	.76364	46	.30952	80	.25823	28	.79477	17	38
23	.60714	23	.64705	62	.76410	46	.30873	79	.25851	28	.79459	18	37
24	.60738	24	.64643	62	.76456	46	.30795	79	.25879	28	.79441	18	36
25	0.60761	23	1.64580	62	0.76502	46	1.30716	79	1.25907	28	0.79424	17	35
26	.60784	23	.64518	62	.76548	46	.30637	79	.25935	28	.79406	18	34
27	.60807	23	.64455	62	.76594	46	.30558	79	.25963	28	.79388	18	33
28	.60830	23	.64393	62	.76640	46	.30480	79	.25991	28	.79371	17	32
29	.60853	23	.64330	62	.76686	46	.30401	79	.26019	28	.79353	18	31
30	0.60876	23	1.64268	62	0.76733	47	1.30323	79	1.26047	28	0.79335	18	30
31	.60899	23	.64206	62	.76779	46	.30244	79	.26075	28	.79318	17	29
32	.60922	23	.64144	62	.76825	46	.30166	79	.26104	29	.79300	18	28
33	.60945	23	.64081	62	.76871	46	.30087	79	.26132	28	.79282	18	27
34	.60968	23	.64019	62	.76918	47	.30009	79	.26160	28	.79264	18	26
35	0.60991	23	1.63957	61	0.76964	46	1.29931	79	1.26188	28	0.79247	17	25
36	.61015	24	.63895	61	.77010	46	.29853	79	.26216	28	.79229	18	24
37	.61038	23	.63834	61	.77057	47	.29775	79	.26245	29	.79211	18	23
38	.61061	23	.63772	61	.77103	46	.29696	79	.26273	28	.79193	18	22
39	.61084	23	.63710	61	.77149	46	.29618	78	.26301	28	.79176	17	21
40	0.61107	23	1.63648	61	0.77196	47	1.29541	78	1.26330	29	0.79158	18	20
41	.61130	23	.63587	61	.77242	46	.29463	78	.26358	28	.79140	18	19
42	.61153	23	.63525	61	.77289	47	.29385	78	.26387	29	.79122	18	18
43	.61176	23	.63464	61	.77335	46	.29307	78	.26415	28	.79105	17	17
44	.61199	23	.63402	61	.77382	47	.29229	78	.26443	28	.79087	18	16
45	0.61222	23	1.63341	61	0.77428	46	1.29152	78	1.26472	29	0.79069	18	15
46	.61245	23	.63279	61	.77475	47	.29074	78	.26500	28	.79051	18	14
47	.61268	23	.63218	61	.77521	46	.28997	78	.26529	29	.79033	18	13
48	.61291	23	.63157	61	.77568	47	.28919	78	.26557	28	.79016	17	12
49	.61314	23	.63096	61	.77615	47	.28842	78	.26586	29	.78998	18	11
50	0.61337	23	1.63035	61	0.77661	46	1.28764	78	1.26615	29	0.78980	18	10
51	.61360	23	.62974	61	.77708	47	.28687	78	.26643	28	.78962	18	9
52	.61383	23	.62913	60	.77754	46	.28610	78	.26672	29	.78944	18	8
53	.61406	23	.62852	60	.77801	47	.28533	78	.26701	29	.78926	18	7
54	.61429	23	.62791	60	.77848	47	.28456	78	.26729	28	.78908	18	6
55	0.61451	22	1.62730	60	0.77895	47	1.28379	78	1.26758	29	0.78891	17	5
56	.61474	23	.62669	60	.77941	46	.28302	78	.26787	29	.78873	18	4
57	.61497	23	.62609	60	.77988	47	.28225	77	.26815	28	.78855	18	3
58	.61520	23	.62548	60	.78035	47	.28148	77	.26844	29	.78837	18	2
59	.61543	23	.62487	60	.78082	47	.28071	77	.26873	29	.78819	18	1
60	0.61566	23	1.62427	60	0.78129	47	1.27994	77	1.26902	29	0.78801	18	0
↑ 127°→	cos	Diff. 1′	sec	Diff. 1′	cot	Diff. 1′	tan	Diff. 1′	csc	Diff. 1′	sin	Diff. 1′ ← 52°	↑

TABLE 2
Natural Trigonometric Functions

38°→ ↓ ′	sin	Diff. 1′	csc	Diff. 1′	tan	Diff. 1′	cot	Diff. 1′	sec	Diff. 1′	cos	Diff. 1′	← 141° ↓ ′
0	0.61566		1.62427		0.78129		1.27994		1.26902		0.78801		60
1	.61589	23	.62366	60	.78175	46	.27917	77	.26931	29	.78783	18	59
2	.61612	23	.62306	60	.78222	47	.27841	77	.26960	29	.78765	18	58
3	.61635	23	.62246	60	.78269	47	.27764	77	.26988	28	.78747	18	57
4	.61658	23	.62185	60	.78316	47	.27688	77	.27017	29	.78729	18	56
5	0.61681	23	1.62125	60	0.78363	47	1.27611	77	1.27046	29	0.78711	18	55
6	.61704	23	.62065	60	.78410	47	.27535	77	.27075	29	.78694	17	54
7	.61726	22	.62005	60	.78457	47	.27458	77	.27104	29	.78676	18	53
8	.61749	23	.61945	60	.78504	47	.27382	77	.27133	29	.78658	18	52
9	.61772	23	.61885	60	.78551	47	.27306	77	.27162	29	.78640	18	51
10	0.61795	23	1.61825	60	0.78598	47	1.27230	77	1.27191	29	0.78622	18	50
11	.61818	23	.61765	60	.78645	47	.27153	77	.27221	30	.78604	18	49
12	.61841	23	.61705	60	.78692	47	.27077	77	.27250	29	.78586	18	48
13	.61864	23	.61646	60	.78739	47	.27001	77	.27279	29	.78568	18	47
14	.61887	23	.61586	60	.78786	47	.26925	76	.27308	29	.78550	18	46
15	0.61909	22	1.61526	60	0.78834	48	1.26849	76	1.27337	29	0.78532	18	45
16	.61932	23	.61467	60	.78881	47	.26774	76	.27366	29	.78514	18	44
17	.61955	23	.61407	60	.78928	47	.26698	76	.27396	30	.78496	18	43
18	.61978	23	.61348	60	.78975	47	.26622	76	.27425	29	.78478	18	42
19	.62001	23	.61288	60	.79022	47	.26546	76	.27454	29	.78460	18	41
20	0.62024	23	1.61229	60	0.79070	48	1.26471	76	1.27483	29	0.78442	18	40
21	.62046	22	.61170	60	.79117	47	.26395	76	.27513	30	.78424	18	39
22	.62069	23	.61111	60	.79164	47	.26319	76	.27542	29	.78405	19	38
23	.62092	23	.61051	60	.79212	48	.26244	76	.27572	30	.78387	18	37
24	.62115	23	.60992	60	.79259	47	.26169	76	.27601	29	.78369	18	36
25	0.62138	23	1.60933	60	0.79306	47	1.26093	76	1.27630	29	0.78351	18	35
26	.62160	22	.60874	60	.79354	48	.26018	76	.27660	30	.78333	18	34
27	.62183	23	.60815	59	.79401	47	.25943	76	.27689	29	.78315	18	33
28	.62206	23	.60756	59	.79449	48	.25867	76	.27719	30	.78297	18	32
29	.62229	23	.60698	59	.79496	47	.25792	76	.27748	29	.78279	18	31
30	0.62251	22	1.60639	59	0.79544	48	1.25717	76	1.27778	30	0.78261	18	30
31	.62274	23	.60580	59	.79591	47	.25642	76	.27807	29	.78243	18	29
32	.62297	23	.60521	59	.79639	48	.25567	74	.27837	30	.78225	18	28
33	.62320	23	.60463	59	.79686	47	.25492	74	.27867	30	.78206	19	27
34	.62342	22	.60404	59	.79734	48	.25417	74	.27896	29	.78188	18	26
35	0.62365	23	1.60346	59	0.79781	47	1.25343	74	1.27926	30	0.78170	18	25
36	.62388	23	.60287	59	.79829	48	.25268	74	.27956	30	.78152	18	24
37	.62411	23	.60229	59	.79877	48	.25193	74	.27985	29	.78134	18	23
38	.62433	22	.60171	59	.79924	47	.25118	74	.28015	30	.78116	18	22
39	.62456	23	.60112	59	.79972	48	.25044	74	.28045	30	.78098	18	21
40	0.62479	23	1.60054	59	0.80020	48	1.24969	74	1.28075	30	0.78079	19	20
41	.62502	23	.59996	59	.80067	47	.24895	74	.28105	30	.78061	18	19
42	.62524	22	.59938	59	.80115	48	.24820	74	.28134	29	.78043	18	18
43	.62547	23	.59880	59	.80163	48	.24746	74	.28164	30	.78025	18	17
44	.62570	23	.59822	58	.80211	48	.24672	74	.28194	30	.78007	18	16
45	0.62592	22	1.59764	58	0.80258	47	1.24597	74	1.28224	30	0.77988	19	15
46	.62615	23	.59706	58	.80306	48	.24523	74	.28254	30	.77970	18	14
47	.62638	23	.59648	58	.80354	48	.24449	74	.28284	30	.77952	18	13
48	.62660	22	.59590	58	.80402	48	.24375	74	.28314	30	.77934	18	12
49	.62683	23	.59533	58	.80450	48	.24301	74	.28344	30	.77916	18	11
50	0.62706	23	1.59475	58	0.80498	48	1.24227	74	1.28374	30	0.77897	19	10
51	.62728	22	.59418	58	.80546	48	.24153	73	.28404	30	.77879	18	9
52	.62751	23	.59360	58	.80594	48	.24079	73	.28434	30	.77861	18	8
53	.62774	23	.59302	58	.80642	48	.24005	73	.28464	30	.77843	18	7
54	.62796	22	.59245	58	.80690	48	.23931	73	.28495	31	.77824	19	6
55	0.62819	23	1.59188	58	0.80738	48	1.23858	73	1.28525	30	0.77806	18	5
56	.62842	23	.59130	58	.80786	48	.23784	73	.28555	30	.77788	18	4
57	.62864	22	.59073	58	.80834	48	.23710	73	.28585	30	.77769	19	3
58	.62887	23	.59016	58	.80882	48	.23637	73	.28615	30	.77751	18	2
59	.62909	22	.58959	58	.80930	48	.23563	73	.28646	31	.77733	18	1
60	0.62932	23	1.58902	58	0.80978	48	1.23490	73	1.28676	30	0.77715	18	0
↑ 128°→	cos	Diff. 1′	sec	Diff. 1′	cot	Diff. 1′	tan	Diff. 1′	csc	Diff. 1′	sin	Diff. 1′	← 51° ↑

TABLE 2
Natural Trigonometric Functions

39°→ ↓ ′	sin	Diff. 1′	csc	Diff. 1′	tan	Diff. 1′	cot	Diff. 1′	sec	Diff. 1′	cos	Diff. 1′	← 140° ↓ ′
0	0.62932		1.58902		0.80978		1.23490		1.28676		0.77715		60
1	.62955	23	.58845	58	.81027	49	.23416	73	.28706	30	.77696	19	59
2	.62977	22	.58788	57	.81075	48	.23343	73	.28737	31	.77678	18	58
3	.63000	23	.58731	57	.81123	48	.23270	73	.28767	30	.77660	18	57
4	.63022	22	.58674	57	.81171	48	.23196	73	.28797	30	.77641	19	56
5	0.63045	23	1.58617	57	0.81220	49	1.23123	73	1.28828	31	0.77623	18	55
6	.63068	23	.58560	57	.81268	48	.23050	73	.28858	30	.77605	18	54
7	.63090	22	.58503	57	.81316	48	.22977	73	.28889	31	.77586	19	53
8	.63113	23	.58447	57	.81364	48	.22904	73	.28919	30	.77568	18	52
9	.63135	22	.58390	57	.81413	49	.22831	73	.28950	31	.77550	18	51
10	0.63158	23	1.58333	57	0.81461	48	1.22758	72	1.28980	30	0.77531	19	50
11	.63180	22	.58277	57	.81510	49	.22685	72	.29011	31	.77513	18	49
12	.63203	23	.58221	57	.81558	48	.22612	72	.29042	31	.77494	19	48
13	.63225	22	.58164	57	.81606	48	.22539	72	.29072	30	.77476	18	47
14	.63248	23	.58108	57	.81655	49	.22467	72	.29103	31	.77458	18	46
15	0.63271	23	1.58051	57	0.81703	48	1.22394	72	1.29133	30	0.77439	19	45
16	.63293	22	.57995	57	.81752	49	.22321	72	.29164	31	.77421	18	44
17	.63316	23	.57939	57	.81800	48	.22249	72	.29195	31	.77402	19	43
18	.63338	22	.57883	57	.81849	49	.22176	72	.29226	31	.77384	18	42
19	.63361	23	.57827	57	.81898	49	.22104	72	.29256	30	.77366	18	41
20	0.63383	22	1.57771	57	0.81946	48	1.22031	72	1.29287	31	0.77347	19	40
21	.63406	23	.57715	56	.81995	49	.21959	72	.29318	31	.77329	18	39
22	.63428	22	.57659	56	.82044	49	.21886	72	.29349	31	.77310	19	38
23	.63451	23	.57603	56	.82092	48	.21814	72	.29380	31	.77292	18	37
24	.63473	22	.57547	56	.82141	49	.21742	72	.29411	31	.77273	19	36
25	0.63496	23	1.57491	56	0.82190	49	1.21670	72	1.29442	31	0.77255	18	35
26	.63518	22	.57436	56	.82238	48	.21598	72	.29473	31	.77236	19	34
27	.63540	22	.57380	56	.82287	49	.21526	72	.29504	31	.77218	18	33
28	.63563	23	.57324	56	.82336	49	.21454	72	.29535	31	.77199	19	32
29	.63585	22	.57269	56	.82385	49	.21382	71	.29566	31	.77181	18	31
30	0.63608	23	1.57213	56	0.82434	49	1.21310	71	1.29597	31	0.77162	19	30
31	.63630	22	.57158	56	.82483	49	.21238	71	.29628	31	.77144	18	29
32	.63653	23	.57103	56	.82531	48	.21166	71	.29659	31	.77125	19	28
33	.63675	22	.57047	56	.82580	49	.21094	71	.29690	31	.77107	18	27
34	.63698	23	.56992	56	.82629	49	.21023	71	.29721	31	.77088	19	26
35	0.63720	22	1.56937	56	0.82678	49	1.20951	71	1.29752	31	0.77070	18	25
36	.63742	22	.56881	56	.82727	49	.20879	71	.29784	32	.77051	19	24
37	.63765	23	.56826	56	.82776	49	.20808	71	.29815	31	.77033	18	23
38	.63787	22	.56771	56	.82825	49	.20736	71	.29846	31	.77014	19	22
39	.63810	23	.56716	56	.82874	49	.20665	71	.29877	31	.76996	18	21
40	0.63832	22	1.56661	54	0.82923	49	1.20593	71	1.29909	32	0.76977	19	20
41	.63854	22	.56606	54	.82972	49	.20522	71	.29940	31	.76959	18	19
42	.63877	23	.56551	54	.83022	50	.20451	71	.29971	31	.76940	19	18
43	.63899	22	.56497	54	.83071	49	.20379	71	.30003	32	.76921	19	17
44	.63922	23	.56442	54	.83120	49	.20308	71	.30034	31	.76903	18	16
45	0.63944	22	1.56387	54	0.83169	49	1.20237	71	1.30066	32	0.76884	19	15
46	.63966	22	.56332	54	.83218	49	.20166	71	.30097	31	.76866	18	14
47	.63989	23	.56278	54	.83268	50	.20095	71	.30129	32	.76847	19	13
48	.64011	22	.56223	54	.83317	49	.20024	71	.30160	31	.76828	19	12
49	.64033	22	.56169	54	.83366	49	.19953	70	.30192	32	.76810	18	11
50	0.64056	23	1.56114	54	0.83415	49	1.19882	70	1.30223	31	0.76791	19	10
51	.64078	22	.56060	54	.83465	50	.19811	70	.30255	32	.76772	19	9
52	.64100	22	.56005	54	.83514	49	.19740	70	.30287	32	.76754	18	8
53	.64123	23	.55951	54	.83564	50	.19669	70	.30318	31	.76735	19	7
54	.64145	22	.55897	54	.83613	49	.19599	70	.30350	32	.76717	18	6
55	0.64167	22	1.55843	54	0.83662	49	1.19528	70	1.30382	32	0.76698	19	5
56	.64190	23	.55789	54	.83712	50	.19457	70	.30413	31	.76679	19	4
57	.64212	22	.55734	54	.83761	49	.19387	70	.30445	32	.76661	18	3
58	.64234	22	.55680	54	.83811	50	.19316	70	.30477	32	.76642	19	2
59	.64256	22	.55626	54	.83860	49	.19246	70	.30509	32	.76623	19	1
60	0.64279	23	1.55572	53	0.83910	50	1.19175	70	1.30541	32	0.76604	19	0
↑ 129°→	cos	Diff. 1′	sec	Diff. 1′	cot	Diff. 1′	tan	Diff. 1′	csc	Diff. 1′	sin	Diff. 1′	← 50° ↑

TABLE 2

Natural Trigonometric Functions

40°→ ↓ ′	sin	Diff. 1′	csc	Diff. 1′	tan	Diff. 1′	cot	Diff. 1′	sec	Diff. 1′	cos	Diff. 1′	← 139° ↓ ′
0	0.64279		1.55572		0.83910		1.19175		1.30541		0.76604		60
1	.64301	22	.55518	53	.83960	50	.19105	70	.30573	32	.76586	18	59
2	.64323	22	.55465	53	.84009	49	.19035	70	.30605	32	.76567	19	58
3	.64346	23	.55411	53	.84059	50	.18964	70	.30636	31	.76548	19	57
4	.64368	22	.55357	53	.84108	49	.18894	70	.30668	32	.76530	18	56
5	0.64390	22	1.55303	53	0.84158	50	1.18824	70	1.30700	32	0.76511	19	55
6	.64412	22	.55250	53	.84208	50	.18754	70	.30732	32	.76492	19	54
7	.64435	23	.55196	53	.84258	50	.18684	70	.30764	32	.76473	19	53
8	.64457	22	.55143	53	.84307	49	.18614	70	.30796	32	.76455	18	52
9	.64479	22	.55089	53	.84357	50	.18544	70	.30829	33	.76436	19	51
10	0.64501	22	1.55036	53	0.84407	50	1.18474	70	1.30861	32	0.76417	19	50
11	.64524	23	.54982	53	.84457	50	.18404	70	.30893	32	.76398	19	49
12	.64546	22	.54929	53	.84507	50	.18334	70	.30925	32	.76380	18	48
13	.64568	22	.54876	53	.84556	49	.18264	70	.30957	32	.76361	19	47
14	.64590	22	.54822	53	.84606	50	.18194	70	.30989	32	.76342	19	46
15	0.64612	22	1.54769	53	0.84656	50	1.18125	70	1.31022	33	0.76323	19	45
16	.64635	23	.54716	53	.84706	50	.18055	70	.31054	32	.76304	19	44
17	.64657	22	.54663	53	.84756	50	.17986	70	.31086	32	.76286	18	43
18	.64679	22	.54610	53	.84806	50	.17916	70	.31119	33	.76267	19	42
19	.64701	22	.54557	53	.84856	50	.17846	70	.31151	32	.76248	19	41
20	0.64723	22	1.54504	52	0.84906	50	1.17777	70	1.31183	32	0.76229	19	40
21	.64746	23	.54451	52	.84956	50	.17708	70	.31216	33	.76210	19	39
22	.64768	22	.54398	52	.85006	50	.17638	70	.31248	32	.76192	18	38
23	.64790	22	.54345	52	.85057	51	.17569	70	.31281	33	.76173	19	37
24	.64812	22	.54292	52	.85107	50	.17500	70	.31313	32	.76154	19	36
25	0.64834	22	1.54240	52	0.85157	50	1.17430	70	1.31346	33	0.76135	19	35
26	.64856	22	.54187	52	.85207	50	.17361	70	.31378	32	.76116	19	34
27	.64878	22	.54134	52	.85257	50	.17292	70	.31411	33	.76097	19	33
28	.64901	23	.54082	52	.85308	51	.17223	70	.31443	32	.76078	19	32
29	.64923	22	.54029	52	.85358	50	.17154	70	.31476	33	.76059	19	31
30	0.64945	22	1.53977	52	0.85408	50	1.17085	69	1.31509	33	0.76041	18	30
31	.64967	22	.53924	52	.85458	50	.17016	69	.31541	32	.76022	19	29
32	.64989	22	.53872	52	.85509	51	.16947	69	.31574	33	.76003	19	28
33	.65011	22	.53820	52	.85559	50	.16878	69	.31607	33	.75984	19	27
34	.65033	22	.53768	52	.85609	50	.16809	69	.31640	33	.75965	19	26
35	0.65055	22	1.53715	52	0.85660	51	1.16741	69	1.31672	32	0.75946	19	25
36	.65077	22	.53663	52	.85710	50	.16672	69	.31705	33	.75927	19	24
37	.65100	23	.53611	52	.85761	51	.16603	69	.31738	33	.75908	19	23
38	.65122	22	.53559	52	.85811	50	.16535	69	.31771	33	.75889	19	22
39	.65144	22	.53507	52	.85862	51	.16466	69	.31804	33	.75870	19	21
40	0.65166	22	1.53455	51	0.85912	50	1.16398	69	1.31837	33	0.75851	19	20
41	.65188	22	.53403	51	.85963	51	.16329	69	.31870	33	.75832	19	19
42	.65210	22	.53351	51	.86014	51	.16261	69	.31903	33	.75813	19	18
43	.65232	22	.53299	51	.86064	50	.16192	69	.31936	33	.75794	19	17
44	.65254	22	.53247	51	.86115	51	.16124	69	.31969	33	.75775	19	16
45	0.65276	22	1.53196	51	0.86166	51	1.16056	69	1.32002	33	0.75756	19	15
46	.65298	22	.53144	51	.86216	50	.15987	69	.32035	33	.75738	18	14
47	.65320	22	.53092	51	.86267	51	.15919	69	.32068	33	.75719	19	13
48	.65342	22	.53041	51	.86318	51	.15851	69	.32101	33	.75700	19	12
49	.65364	22	.52989	51	.86368	50	.15783	69	.32134	33	.75680	20	11
50	0.65386	22	1.52938	51	0.86419	51	1.15715	69	1.32168	34	0.75661	19	10
51	.65408	22	.52886	51	.86470	51	.15647	69	.32201	33	.75642	19	9
52	.65430	22	.52835	51	.86521	51	.15579	68	.32234	33	.75623	19	8
53	.65452	22	.52784	51	.86572	51	.15511	68	.32267	33	.75604	19	7
54	.65474	22	.52732	51	.86623	51	.15443	68	.32301	34	.75585	19	6
55	0.65496	22	1.52681	51	0.86674	51	1.15375	68	1.32334	33	0.75566	19	5
56	.65518	22	.52630	51	.86725	51	.15308	68	.32368	34	.75547	19	4
57	.65540	22	.52579	51	.86776	51	.15240	68	.32401	33	.75528	19	3
58	.65562	22	.52527	51	.86827	51	.15172	68	.32434	33	.75509	19	2
59	.65584	22	.52476	51	.86878	51	.15104	68	.32468	34	.75490	19	1
60	0.65606	22	1.52425	51	0.86929	51	1.15037	68	1.32501	33	0.75471	19	0
↑ 130°→	cos	Diff. 1′	sec	Diff. 1′	cot	Diff. 1′	tan	Diff. 1′	csc	Diff. 1′	sin	Diff. 1′	↑ ←49°

TABLE 2

Natural Trigonometric Functions

41°→ ↓ ′	sin	Diff. 1′	csc	Diff. 1′	tan	Diff. 1′	cot	Diff. 1′	sec	Diff. 1′	cos	Diff. 1′	← 138° ↓ ′
0	0.65606		1.52425		0.86929		1.15037		1.32501		0.75471		60
1	.65628	22	.52374	50	.86980	51	.14969	68	.32535	34	.75452	19	59
2	.65650	22	.52323	50	.87031	51	.14902	68	.32568	33	.75433	19	58
3	.65672	22	.52273	50	.87082	51	.14834	68	.32602	34	.75414	19	57
4	.65694	22	.52222	50	.87133	51	.14767	68	.32636	34	.75395	19	56
5	0.65716	22	1.52171	50	0.87184	51	1.14699	68	1.32669	33	0.75375	20	55
6	.65738	22	.52120	50	.87236	52	.14632	68	.32703	34	.75356	19	54
7	.65759	21	.52069	50	.87287	51	.14565	68	.32737	34	.75337	19	53
8	.65781	22	.52019	50	.87338	51	.14498	68	.32770	33	.75318	19	52
9	.65803	22	.51968	50	.87389	51	.14430	68	.32804	34	.75299	19	51
10	0.65825	22	1.51918	50	0.87441	52	1.14363	68	1.32838	34	0.75280	19	50
11	.65847	22	.51867	50	.87492	51	.14296	68	.32872	34	.75261	19	49
12	.65869	22	.51817	50	.87543	51	.14229	68	.32905	33	.75241	20	48
13	.65891	22	.51766	50	.87595	52	.14162	68	.32939	34	.75222	19	47
14	.65913	22	.51716	50	.87646	51	.14095	67	.32973	34	.75203	19	46
15	0.65935	22	1.51665	50	0.87698	52	1.14028	67	1.33007	34	0.75184	19	45
16	.65956	21	.51615	50	.87749	51	.13961	67	.33041	34	.75165	19	44
17	.65978	22	.51565	50	.87801	52	.13894	67	.33075	34	.75146	19	43
18	.66000	22	.51515	50	.87852	51	.13828	67	.33109	34	.75126	20	42
19	.66022	22	.51465	50	.87904	52	.13761	67	.33143	34	.75107	19	41
20	0.66044	22	1.51415	50	0.87955	51	1.13694	67	1.33177	34	0.75088	19	40
21	.66066	22	.51364	50	.88007	52	.13627	67	.33211	34	.75069	19	39
22	.66088	22	.51314	50	.88059	52	.13561	67	.33245	34	.75050	19	38
23	.66109	21	.51265	50	.88110	51	.13494	67	.33279	34	.75030	20	37
24	.66131	22	.51215	50	.88162	52	.13428	67	.33314	35	.75011	19	36
25	0.66153	22	1.51165	50	0.88214	52	1.13361	67	1.33348	34	0.74992	19	35
26	.66175	22	.51115	50	.88265	51	.13295	67	.33382	34	.74973	19	34
27	.66197	22	.51065	50	.88317	52	.13228	67	.33416	34	.74953	20	33
28	.66218	21	.51015	50	.88369	52	.13162	67	.33451	35	.74934	19	32
29	.66240	22	.50966	50	.88421	52	.13096	67	.33485	34	.74915	19	31
30	0.66262	22	1.50916	50	0.88473	52	1.13029	67	1.33519	34	0.74896	19	30
31	.66284	22	.50866	50	.88524	51	.12963	67	.33554	35	.74876	20	29
32	.66306	22	.50817	50	.88576	52	.12897	67	.33588	34	.74857	19	28
33	.66327	21	.50767	50	.88628	52	.12831	67	.33622	34	.74838	19	27
34	.66349	22	.50718	50	.88680	52	.12765	67	.33657	35	.74818	20	26
35	0.66371	22	1.50669	50	0.88732	52	1.12699	67	1.33691	34	0.74799	19	25
36	.66393	22	.50619	50	.88784	52	.12633	67	.33726	35	.74780	19	24
37	.66414	21	.50570	50	.88836	52	.12567	66	.33760	34	.74760	20	23
38	.66436	22	.50521	50	.88888	52	.12501	66	.33795	35	.74741	19	22
39	.66458	22	.50471	50	.88940	52	.12435	66	.33830	35	.74722	19	21
40	0.66480	22	1.50422	50	0.88992	52	1.12369	66	1.33864	34	0.74703	19	20
41	.66501	21	.50373	50	.89045	53	.12303	66	.33899	35	.74683	20	19
42	.66523	22	.50324	50	.89097	52	.12238	66	.33934	35	.74664	19	18
43	.66545	22	.50275	50	.89149	52	.12172	66	.33968	34	.74644	20	17
44	.66566	21	.50226	50	.89201	52	.12106	66	.34003	35	.74625	19	16
45	0.66588	22	1.50177	49	0.89253	52	1.12041	66	1.34038	35	0.74606	19	15
46	.66610	22	.50128	49	.89306	53	.11975	66	.34073	35	.74586	20	14
47	.66632	22	.50079	49	.89358	52	.11909	66	.34108	35	.74567	19	13
48	.66653	21	.50030	49	.89410	52	.11844	66	.34142	34	.74548	19	12
49	.66675	22	.49981	49	.89463	53	.11778	66	.34177	35	.74528	20	11
50	0.66697	22	1.49933	49	0.89515	52	1.11713	66	1.34212	35	0.74509	19	10
51	.66718	21	.49884	49	.89567	52	.11648	66	.34247	35	.74489	20	9
52	.66740	22	.49835	49	.89620	53	.11582	66	.34282	35	.74470	19	8
53	.66762	22	.49787	49	.89672	52	.11517	66	.34317	35	.74451	19	7
54	.66783	21	.49738	49	.89725	53	.11452	66	.34352	35	.74431	20	6
55	0.66805	22	1.49690	49	0.89777	52	1.11387	66	1.34387	35	0.74412	19	5
56	.66827	22	.49641	49	.89830	53	.11321	66	.34423	36	.74392	20	4
57	.66848	21	.49593	49	.89883	53	.11256	66	.34458	35	.74373	19	3
58	.66870	22	.49544	49	.89935	52	.11191	66	.34493	35	.74353	20	2
59	.66891	21	.49496	49	.89988	53	.11126	66	.34528	35	.74334	19	1
60	0.66913	22	1.49448	49	0.90040	52	1.11061	64	1.34563	35	0.74314	20	0
↑ 131°→	cos	Diff. 1′	sec	Diff. 1′	cot	Diff. 1′	tan	Diff. 1′	csc	Diff. 1′	sin	Diff. 1′	↑ ←48°

TABLE 2
Natural Trigonometric Functions

42°→ ↓ ′	sin	Diff. 1′	csc	Diff. 1′	tan	Diff. 1′	cot	Diff. 1′	sec	Diff. 1′	cos	Diff. 1′	← 137° ↓ ′
0	0.66913		1.49448		0.90040		1.11061		1.34563		0.74314		60
1	.66935	22	.49399	49	.90093	53	.10996	64	.34599	36	.74295	19	59
2	.66956	21	.49351	49	.90146	53	.10931	64	.34634	35	.74276	19	58
3	.66978	22	.49303	49	.90199	53	.10867	64	.34669	35	.74256	20	57
4	.66999	21	.49255	49	.90251	52	.10802	64	.34704	35	.74237	19	56
5	0.67021	22	1.49207	49	0.90304	53	1.10737	64	1.34740	36	0.74217	20	55
6	.67043	22	.49159	49	.90357	53	.10672	64	.34775	35	.74198	19	54
7	.67064	21	.49111	48	.90410	53	.10607	64	.34811	36	.74178	20	53
8	.67086	22	.49063	48	.90463	53	.10543	64	.34846	35	.74159	19	52
9	.67107	21	.49015	48	.90516	53	.10478	64	.34882	36	.74139	20	51
10	0.67129	22	1.48967	48	0.90569	53	1.10414	64	1.34917	35	0.74120	19	50
11	.67151	22	.48919	48	.90621	52	.10349	64	.34953	36	.74100	20	49
12	.67172	21	.48871	48	.90674	53	.10285	64	.34988	35	.74080	20	48
13	.67194	22	.48824	48	.90727	53	.10220	64	.35024	36	.74061	19	47
14	.67215	21	.48776	48	.90781	54	.10156	64	.35060	36	.74041	20	46
15	0.67237	22	1.48728	48	0.90834	53	1.10091	64	1.35095	35	0.74022	19	45
16	.67258	21	.48681	48	.90887	53	.10027	64	.35131	36	.74002	20	44
17	.67280	22	.48633	48	.90940	53	.09963	64	.35167	36	.73983	19	43
18	.67301	21	.48586	48	.90993	53	.09899	64	.35203	36	.73963	20	42
19	.67323	22	.48538	48	.91046	53	.09834	64	.35238	35	.73944	19	41
20	0.67344	21	1.48491	48	0.91099	53	1.09770	64	1.35274	36	0.73924	20	40
21	.67366	22	.48443	48	.91153	54	.09706	64	.35310	36	.73904	20	39
22	.67387	21	.48396	48	.91206	53	.09642	64	.35346	36	.73885	19	38
23	.67409	22	.48349	48	.91259	53	.09578	64	.35382	36	.73865	20	37
24	.67430	21	.48301	48	.91313	54	.09514	63	.35418	36	.73846	19	36
25	0.67452	22	1.48254	48	0.91366	53	1.09450	63	1.35454	36	0.73826	20	35
26	.67473	21	.48207	48	.91419	53	.09386	63	.35490	36	.73806	20	34
27	.67495	22	.48160	48	.91473	54	.09322	63	.35526	36	.73787	19	33
28	.67516	21	.48113	48	.91526	53	.09258	63	.35562	36	.73767	20	32
29	.67538	22	.48066	48	.91580	54	.09195	63	.35598	36	.73747	20	31
30	0.67559	21	1.48019	48	0.91633	53	1.09131	63	1.35634	36	0.73728	19	30
31	.67580	21	.47972	47	.91687	54	.09067	63	.35670	36	.73708	20	29
32	.67602	22	.47925	47	.91740	53	.09003	63	.35707	37	.73688	20	28
33	.67623	21	.47878	47	.91794	54	.08940	63	.35743	36	.73669	19	27
34	.67645	22	.47831	47	.91847	53	.08876	63	.35779	36	.73649	20	26
35	0.67666	21	1.47784	47	0.91901	54	1.08813	63	1.35815	36	0.73629	20	25
36	.67688	22	.47738	47	.91955	54	.08749	63	.35852	37	.73610	19	24
37	.67709	21	.47691	47	.92008	53	.08686	63	.35888	36	.73590	20	23
38	.67730	21	.47644	47	.92062	54	.08622	63	.35924	36	.73570	20	22
39	.67752	22	.47598	47	.92116	54	.08559	63	.35961	37	.73551	19	21
40	0.67773	21	1.47551	47	0.92170	54	1.08496	63	1.35997	36	0.73531	20	20
41	.67795	22	.47504	47	.92224	54	.08432	63	.36034	37	.73511	20	19
42	.67816	21	.47458	47	.92277	53	.08369	63	.36070	36	.73491	20	18
43	.67837	21	.47411	47	.92331	54	.08306	63	.36107	37	.73472	19	17
44	.67859	22	.47365	47	.92385	54	.08243	63	.36143	36	.73452	20	16
45	0.67880	21	1.47319	47	0.92439	54	1.08179	63	1.36180	37	0.73432	20	15
46	.67901	21	.47272	47	.92493	54	.08116	63	.36217	37	.73413	19	14
47	.67923	22	.47226	47	.92547	54	.08053	63	.36253	36	.73393	20	13
48	.67944	21	.47180	47	.92601	54	.07990	63	.36290	37	.73373	20	12
49	.67965	21	.47134	47	.92655	54	.07927	62	.36327	37	.73353	20	11
50	0.67987	22	1.47087	47	0.92709	54	1.07864	62	1.36363	36	0.73333	20	10
51	.68008	21	.47041	47	.92763	54	.07801	62	.36400	37	.73314	19	9
52	.68029	21	.46995	47	.92817	54	.07738	62	.36437	37	.73294	20	8
53	.68051	22	.46949	47	.92872	55	.07676	62	.36474	37	.73274	20	7
54	.68072	21	.46903	47	.92926	54	.07613	62	.36511	37	.73254	20	6
55	0.68093	21	1.46857	46	0.92980	54	1.07550	62	1.36548	37	0.73234	20	5
56	.68115	22	.46811	46	.93034	54	.07487	62	.36585	37	.73215	19	4
57	.68136	21	.46765	46	.93088	54	.07425	62	.36622	37	.73195	20	3
58	.68157	21	.46719	46	.93143	55	.07362	62	.36659	37	.73175	20	2
59	.68179	22	.46674	46	.93197	54	.07299	62	.36696	37	.73155	20	1
60	0.68200	21	1.46628	46	0.93252	55	1.07237	62	1.36733	37	0.73135	20	0
↑ 132°→	cos	Diff. 1′	sec	Diff. 1′	cot	Diff. 1′	tan	Diff. 1′	csc	Diff. 1′	sin	Diff. 1′←	↑ 47°

TABLE 2
Natural Trigonometric Functions

43°→ ↓ ′	sin	Diff. 1′	csc	Diff. 1′	tan	Diff. 1′	cot	Diff. 1′	sec	Diff. 1′	cos	Diff. 1′	← 136° ↓ ′
0	0.68200		1.46628		0.93252		1.07237		1.36733		0.73135		60
1	.68221	21	.46582	46	.93306	54	.07174	62	.36770	37	.73116	19	59
2	.68242	21	.46537	46	.93360	54	.07112	62	.36807	37	.73096	20	58
3	.68264	22	.46491	46	.93415	55	.07049	62	.36844	37	.73076	20	57
4	.68285	21	.46445	46	.93469	54	.06987	62	.36881	37	.73056	20	56
5	0.68306	21	1.46400	46	0.93524	55	1.06925	62	1.36919	38	0.73036	20	55
6	.68327	21	.46354	46	.93578	54	.06862	62	.36956	37	.73016	20	54
7	.68349	22	.46309	46	.93633	55	.06800	62	.36993	37	.72996	20	53
8	.68370	21	.46263	46	.93688	55	.06738	62	.37030	37	.72976	20	52
9	.68391	21	.46218	46	.93742	54	.06676	62	.37068	38	.72957	19	51
10	0.68412	21	1.46173	46	0.93797	55	1.06613	62	1.37105	37	0.72937	20	50
11	.68434	22	.46127	46	.93852	55	.06551	62	.37143	38	.72917	20	49
12	.68455	21	.46082	46	.93906	54	.06489	62	.37180	37	.72897	20	48
13	.68476	21	.46037	46	.93961	55	.06427	62	.37218	38	.72877	20	47
14	.68497	21	.45992	46	.94016	55	.06365	62	.37255	37	.72857	20	46
15	0.68518	21	1.45946	46	0.94071	55	1.06303	61	1.37293	38	0.72837	20	45
16	.68539	21	.45901	46	.94125	54	.06241	61	.37330	37	.72817	20	44
17	.68561	22	.45856	46	.94180	55	.06179	61	.37368	38	.72797	20	43
18	.68582	21	.45811	46	.94235	55	.06117	61	.37406	38	.72777	20	42
19	.68603	21	.45766	44	.94290	55	.06056	61	.37443	37	.72757	20	41
20	0.68624	21	1.45721	44	0.94345	55	1.05994	61	1.37481	38	0.72737	20	40
21	.68645	21	.45676	44	.94400	55	.05932	61	.37519	38	.72717	20	39
22	.68666	21	.45631	44	.94455	55	.05870	61	.37556	37	.72697	20	38
23	.68688	22	.45587	44	.94510	55	.05809	61	.37594	38	.72677	20	37
24	.68709	21	.45542	44	.94565	55	.05747	61	.37632	38	.72657	20	36
25	0.68730	21	1.45497	44	0.94620	55	1.05685	61	1.37670	38	0.72637	20	35
26	.68751	21	.45452	44	.94676	56	.05624	61	.37708	38	.72617	20	34
27	.68772	21	.45408	44	.94731	55	.05562	61	.37746	38	.72597	20	33
28	.68793	21	.45363	44	.94786	55	.05501	61	.37784	38	.72577	20	32
29	.68814	21	.45319	44	.94841	55	.05439	61	.37822	38	.72557	20	31
30	0.68835	21	1.45274	44	0.94896	55	1.05378	61	1.37860	38	0.72537	20	30
31	.68857	22	.45229	44	.94952	56	.05317	61	.37898	38	.72517	20	29
32	.68878	21	.45185	44	.95007	55	.05255	61	.37936	38	.72497	20	28
33	.68899	21	.45141	44	.95062	55	.05194	61	.37974	38	.72477	20	27
34	.68920	21	.45096	44	.95118	56	.05133	61	.38012	38	.72457	20	26
35	0.68941	21	1.45052	44	0.95173	55	1.05072	61	1.38051	39	0.72437	20	25
36	.68962	21	.45007	44	.95229	56	.05010	61	.38089	38	.72417	20	24
37	.68983	21	.44963	44	.95284	55	.04949	61	.38127	38	.72397	20	23
38	.69004	21	.44919	44	.95340	56	.04888	61	.38165	38	.72377	20	22
39	.69025	21	.44875	44	.95395	55	.04827	61	.38204	39	.72357	20	21
40	0.69046	21	1.44831	44	0.95451	56	1.04766	61	1.38242	38	0.72337	20	20
41	.69067	21	.44787	44	.95506	55	.04705	60	.38280	38	.72317	20	19
42	.69088	21	.44742	44	.95562	56	.04644	60	.38319	39	.72297	20	18
43	.69109	21	.44698	44	.95618	56	.04583	60	.38357	38	.72277	20	17
44	.69130	21	.44654	44	.95673	55	.04522	60	.38396	39	.72257	20	16
45	0.69151	21	1.44610	43	0.95729	56	1.04461	60	1.38434	38	0.72236	21	15
46	.69172	21	.44567	43	.95785	56	.04401	60	.38473	39	.72216	20	14
47	.69193	21	.44523	43	.95841	56	.04340	60	.38512	39	.72196	20	13
48	.69214	21	.44479	43	.95897	56	.04279	60	.38550	38	.72176	20	12
49	.69235	21	.44435	43	.95952	55	.04218	60	.38589	39	.72156	20	11
50	0.69256	21	1.44391	43	0.96008	56	1.04158	60	1.38628	39	0.72136	20	10
51	.69277	21	.44347	43	.96064	56	.04097	60	.38666	38	.72116	20	9
52	.69298	21	.44304	43	.96120	56	.04036	60	.38705	39	.72095	21	8
53	.69319	21	.44260	43	.96176	56	.03976	60	.38744	39	.72075	20	7
54	.69340	21	.44217	43	.96232	56	.03915	60	.38783	39	.72055	20	6
55	0.69361	21	1.44173	43	0.96288	56	1.03855	60	1.38822	39	0.72035	20	5
56	.69382	21	.44129	43	.96344	56	.03794	60	.38860	38	.72015	20	4
57	.69403	21	.44086	43	.96400	56	.03734	60	.38899	39	.71995	20	3
58	.69424	21	.44042	43	.96457	57	.03674	60	.38938	39	.71974	21	2
59	.69445	21	.43999	43	.96513	56	.03613	60	.38977	39	.71954	20	1
60	0.69466	21	1.43956	43	0.96569	56	1.03553	60	1.39016	39	0.71934	20	0
↑ 133°→	cos	Diff. 1′	sec	Diff. 1′	cot	Diff. 1′	tan	Diff. 1′	csc	Diff. 1′	sin	Diff. 1′←	↑ 46°

TABLE 2
Natural Trigonometric Functions

44°→ ↓ ′	sin	Diff. 1′	csc	Diff. 1′	tan	Diff. 1′	cot	Diff. 1′	sec	Diff. 1′	cos	← 135° Diff. 1′	↓ ′
0	0.69466		1.43956		0.96569		1.03553		1.39016		0.71934		60
1	.69487	21	.43912	43	.96625	56	.03493	60	.39055	39	.71914	20	59
2	.69508	21	.43869	43	.96681	56	.03433	60	.39095	40	.71894	20	58
3	.69529	21	.43826	43	.96738	57	.03372	60	.39134	39	.71873	21	57
4	.69549	20	.43783	43	.96794	56	.03312	60	.39173	39	.71853	20	56
5	0.69570	21	1.43739	43	0.96850	56	1.03252	60	1.39212	39	0.71833	20	55
6	.69591	21	.43696	43	.96907	57	.03192	60	.39251	39	.71813	20	54
7	.69612	21	.43653	43	.96963	56	.03132	60	.39291	40	.71792	21	53
8	.69633	21	.43610	43	.97020	57	.03072	60	.39330	39	.71772	20	52
9	.69654	21	.43567	43	.97076	56	.03012	60	.39369	39	.71752	20	51
10	0.69675	21	1.43524	43	0.97133	57	1.02952	60	1.39409	40	0.71732	20	50
11	.69696	21	.43481	42	.97189	56	.02892	60	.39448	39	.71711	21	49
12	.69717	21	.43438	42	.97246	57	.02832	60	.39487	39	.71691	20	48
13	.69737	20	.43395	42	.97302	56	.02772	60	.39527	40	.71671	20	47
14	.69758	21	.43352	42	.97359	57	.02713	60	.39566	39	.71650	21	46
15	0.69779	21	1.43309	42	0.97416	57	1.02653	60	1.39606	40	0.71630	20	45
16	.69800	21	.43267	42	.97472	56	.02593	60	.39646	40	.71610	20	44
17	.69821	21	.43224	42	.97529	57	.02533	60	.39685	39	.71590	20	43
18	.69842	21	.43181	42	.97586	57	.02474	60	.39725	40	.71569	21	42
19	.69862	20	.43139	42	.97643	57	.02414	60	.39764	39	.71549	20	41
20	0.69883	21	1.43096	42	0.97700	57	1.02355	60	1.39804	40	0.71529	20	40
21	.69904	21	.43053	42	.97756	56	.02295	60	.39844	40	.71508	21	39
22	.69925	21	.43011	42	.97813	57	.02236	60	.39884	40	.71488	20	38
23	.69946	21	.42968	42	.97870	57	.02176	60	.39924	40	.71468	20	37
24	.69966	20	.42926	42	.97927	57	.02117	60	.39963	39	.71447	21	36
25	0.69987	21	1.42883	42	0.97984	57	1.02057	60	1.40003	40	0.71427	20	35
26	.70008	21	.42841	42	.98041	57	.01998	60	.40043	40	.71407	20	34
27	.70029	21	.42799	42	.98098	57	.01939	60	.40083	40	.71386	21	33
28	.70049	20	.42756	42	.98155	57	.01879	60	.40123	40	.71366	20	32
29	.70070	21	.42714	42	.98213	58	.01820	60	.40163	40	.71345	21	31
30	0.70091	21	1.42672	42	0.98270	57	1.01761	60	1.40203	40	0.71325	20	30
31	.70112	21	.42630	42	.98327	57	.01702	60	.40243	40	.71305	20	29
32	.70132	20	.42587	42	.98384	57	.01642	60	.40283	40	.71284	21	28
33	.70153	21	.42545	42	.98441	57	.01583	60	.40324	41	.71264	20	27
34	.70174	21	.42503	42	.98499	58	.01524	60	.40364	40	.71243	21	26
35	0.70195	21	1.42461	42	0.98556	57	1.01465	60	1.40404	40	0.71223	20	25
36	.70215	20	.42419	42	.98613	57	.01406	60	.40444	40	.71203	20	24
37	.70236	21	.42377	41	.98671	58	.01347	59	.40485	41	.71182	21	23
38	.70257	21	.42335	41	.98728	57	.01288	59	.40525	40	.71162	20	22
39	.70277	20	.42293	41	.98786	58	.01229	59	.40565	40	.71141	21	21
40	0.70298	21	1.42251	41	0.98843	57	1.01170	59	1.40606	41	0.71121	20	20
41	.70319	21	.42209	41	.98901	58	.01112	59	.40646	40	.71100	21	19
42	.70339	20	.42168	41	.98958	57	.01053	59	.40687	41	.71080	20	18
43	.70360	21	.42126	41	.99016	58	.00994	59	.40727	40	.71059	21	17
44	.70381	21	.42084	41	.99073	57	.00935	59	.40768	41	.71039	20	16
45	0.70401	20	1.42042	41	0.99131	58	1.00876	59	1.40808	40	0.71019	20	15
46	.70422	21	.42001	41	.99189	58	.00818	59	.40849	41	.70998	21	14
47	.70443	21	.41959	41	.99247	58	.00759	59	.40890	41	.70978	20	13
48	.70463	20	.41918	41	.99304	57	.00701	59	.40930	40	.70957	21	12
49	.70484	21	.41876	41	.99362	58	.00642	59	.40971	41	.70937	20	11
50	0.70505	21	1.41835	41	0.99420	58	1.00583	59	1.41012	41	0.70916	21	10
51	.70525	20	.41793	41	.99478	58	.00525	59	.41053	41	.70896	20	9
52	.70546	21	.41752	41	.99536	58	.00467	59	.41093	40	.70875	21	8
53	.70567	21	.41710	41	.99594	58	.00408	59	.41134	41	.70855	20	7
54	.70587	20	.41669	41	.99652	58	.00350	59	.41175	41	.70834	21	6
55	0.70608	21	1.41627	41	0.99710	58	1.00291	59	1.41216	41	0.70813	21	5
56	.70628	20	.41586	41	.99768	58	.00233	59	.41257	41	.70793	20	4
57	.70649	21	.41545	41	.99826	58	.00175	59	.41298	41	.70772	21	3
58	.70670	21	.41504	41	.99884	58	.00116	59	.41339	41	.70752	20	2
59	.70690	20	.41463	41	.99942	58	.00058	59	.41380	41	.70731	21	1
60	0.70711	21	1.41421	41	1.00000	58	1.00000	59	1.41421	41	0.70711	20	0
↑ 134°→	cos	Diff. 1′	sec	Diff. 1′	cot	Diff. 1′	tan	Diff. 1′	csc	Diff. 1′	sin	Diff. 1′←	↑ 45°

TABLE 3

Common Logarithms of Trigonometric Functions (offset +10)

0°→ ′	sin	Diff. 1′	csc	tan	Diff. 1′	cot	sec	Diff. 1′	cos ←179°	′
0	∞	— —	∞	∞	— —	∞	10.00000	0	10.00000	60
1	6.46373	30103	13.53627	6.46373	30103	13.53627	.00000	0	.00000	59
2	.76476	17609	.23524	.76476	17609	.23524	.00000	0	.00000	58
3	6.94085	12494	.05915	6.94085	12494	.05915	.00000	0	.00000	57
4	7.06579	9691	.93421	7.06579	9691	.93421	.00000	0	.00000	56
5	7.16270	7918	12.83730	7.16270	7918	12.83730	10.00000	0	10.00000	55
6	.24188	6694	.75812	.24188	6694	.75812	.00000	0	.00000	54
7	.30882	5800	.69118	.30882	5800	.69118	.00000	0	.00000	53
8	.36682	5115	.63318	.36682	5115	.63318	.00000	0	.00000	52
9	.41797	4576	.58203	.41797	4576	.58203	.00000	0	.00000	51
10	7.46373	4139	12.53627	7.46373	4139	12.53627	10.00000	0	10.00000	50
11	.50512	3779	.49488	.50512	3779	.49488	.00000	0	.00000	49
12	.54291	3476	.45709	.54291	3476	.45709	.00000	0	.00000	48
13	.57767	3218	.42233	.57767	3219	.42233	.00000	0	.00000	47
14	.60985	2997	.39015	.60986	2996	.39014	.00000	0	.00000	46
15	7.63982	2802	12.36018	7.63982	2803	12.36018	10.00000	0	10.00000	45
16	.66784	2633	.33216	.66785	2633	.33215	.00000	1	.00000	44
17	.69417	2483	.30583	.69418	2482	.30582	.00001	0	.99999	43
18	.71900	2348	.28100	.71900	2348	.28100	.00001	0	.99999	42
19	.74248	2227	.25752	.74248	2228	.25752	.00001	0	.99999	41
20	7.76475	2119	12.23525	7.76476	2119	12.23524	10.00001	0	9.99999	40
21	.78594	2021	.21406	.78595	2020	.21405	.00001	0	.99999	39
22	.80615	1930	.19385	.80615	1931	.19385	.00001	0	.99999	38
23	.82545	1848	.17455	.82546	1848	.17454	.00001	0	.99999	37
24	.84393	1773	.15607	.84394	1773	.15606	.00001	0	.99999	36
25	7.86166	1704	12.13834	7.86167	1704	12.13833	10.00001	0	9.99999	35
26	.87870	1639	.12130	.87871	1639	.12129	.00001	0	.99999	34
27	.89509	1579	.10491	.89510	1579	.10490	.00001	0	.99999	33
28	.91088	1524	.08912	.91089	1524	.08911	.00001	1	.99999	32
29	.92612	1472	.07388	.92613	1473	.07387	.00002	0	.99998	31
30	7.94084	1424	12.05916	7.94086	1424	12.05914	10.00002	0	9.99998	30
31	.95508	1379	.04492	.95510	1379	.04490	.00002	0	.99998	29
32	.96887	1336	.03113	.96889	1336	.03111	.00002	0	.99998	28
33	.98223	1297	.01777	.98225	1297	.01775	.00002	0	.99998	27
34	7.99520	1259	.00480	7.99522	1259	.00478	.00002	0	.99998	26
35	8.00779	1223	11.99221	8.00781	1223	11.99219	10.00002	0	9.99998	25
36	.02002	1190	.97998	.02004	1190	.97996	.00002	1	.99998	24
37	.03192	1158	.96808	.03194	1159	.96806	.00003	0	.99997	23
38	.04350	1128	.95650	.04353	1128	.95647	.00003	0	.99997	22
39	.05478	1100	.94522	.05481	1100	.94519	.00003	0	.99997	21
40	8.06578	1072	11.93422	8.06581	1072	11.93419	10.00003	0	9.99997	20
41	.07650	1046	.92350	.07653	1047	.92347	.00003	0	.99997	19
42	.08696	1022	.91304	.08700	1022	.91300	.00003	0	.99997	18
43	.09718	999	.90282	.09722	998	.90278	.00003	1	.99997	17
44	.10717	976	.89283	.10720	976	.89280	.00004	0	.99996	16
45	8.11693	954	11.88307	8.11696	955	11.88304	10.00004	0	9.99996	15
46	.12647	934	.87353	.12651	934	.87349	.00004	0	.99996	14
47	.13581	914	.86419	.13585	915	.86415	.00004	0	.99996	13
48	.14495	896	.85505	.14500	895	.85500	.00004	0	.99996	12
49	.15391	877	.84609	.15395	878	.84605	.00004	1	.99996	11
50	8.16268	860	11.83732	8.16273	860	11.83727	10.00005	0	9.99995	10
51	.17128	843	.82872	.17133	843	.82867	.00005	0	.99995	9
52	.17971	827	.82029	.17976	828	.82024	.00005	0	.99995	8
53	.18798	812	.81202	.18804	812	.81196	.00005	0	.99995	7
54	.19610	797	.80390	.19616	797	.80384	.00005	1	.99995	6
55	8.20407	782	11.79593	8.20413	782	11.79587	10.00006	0	9.99994	5
56	.21189	769	.78811	.21195	769	.78805	.00006	0	.99994	4
57	.21958	755	.78042	.21964	756	.78036	.00006	0	.99994	3
58	.22713	743	.77287	.22720	742	.77280	.00006	0	.99994	2
59	.23456	730	.76544	.23462	730	.76538	.00006	1	.99994	1
60	8.24186		11.75814	8.24192		11.75808	10.00007		9.99993	0
90°→	cos	Diff. 1′	sec	cot	Diff. 1′	tan	csc	Diff. 1′	sin ← 89°	

TABLE 3

Common Logarithms of Trigonometric Functions (offset +10)

1°→ ′	sin	Diff. 1′	csc	tan	Diff. 1′	cot	sec	Diff. 1′	cos ←178°	′
0	8.24186	717	11.75814	8.24192	718	11.75808	10.00007	0	9.99993	60
1	.24903	706	.75097	.24910	706	.75090	.00007	0	.99993	59
2	.25609	695	.74391	.25616	696	.74384	.00007	0	.99993	58
3	.26304	684	.73696	.26312	684	.73688	.00007	1	.99993	57
4	.26988	673	.73012	.26996	673	.73004	.00008	0	.99992	56
5	8.27661	663	11.72339	8.27669	663	11.72331	10.00008	0	9.99992	55
6	.28324	653	.71676	.28332	654	.71668	.00008	0	.99992	54
7	.28977	644	.71023	.28986	643	.71014	.00008	0	.99992	53
8	.29621	634	.70379	.29629	634	.70371	.00008	1	.99992	52
9	.30255	624	.69745	.30263	625	.69737	.00009	0	.99991	51
10	8.30879	616	11.69121	8.30888	617	11.69112	10.00009	0	9.99991	50
11	.31495	608	.68505	.31505	607	.68495	.00009	1	.99991	49
12	.32103	599	.67897	.32112	599	.67888	.00010	0	.99990	48
13	.32702	590	.67298	.32711	591	.67289	.00010	0	.99990	47
14	.33292	583	.66708	.33302	584	.66698	.00010	0	.99990	46
15	8.33875	575	11.66125	8.33886	575	11.66114	10.00010	1	9.99990	45
16	.34450	568	.65550	.34461	568	.65539	.00011	0	.99989	44
17	.35018	560	.64982	.35029	561	.64971	.00011	0	.99989	43
18	.35578	553	.64422	.35590	553	.64410	.00011	0	.99989	42
19	.36131	547	.63869	.36143	546	.63857	.00011	1	.99989	41
20	8.36678	539	11.63322	8.36689	540	11.63311	10.00012	0	9.99988	40
21	.37217	533	.62783	.37229	533	.62771	.00012	0	.99988	39
22	.37750	526	.62250	.37762	527	.62238	.00012	1	.99988	38
23	.38276	520	.61724	.38289	520	.61711	.00013	0	.99987	37
24	.38796	514	.61204	.38809	514	.61191	.00013	0	.99987	36
25	8.39310	508	11.60690	8.39323	509	11.60677	10.00013	1	9.99987	35
26	.39818	502	.60182	.39832	502	.60168	.00014	0	.99986	34
27	.40320	496	.59680	.40334	496	.59666	.00014	0	.99986	33
28	.40816	491	.59184	.40830	491	.59170	.00014	1	.99986	32
29	.41307	485	.58693	.41321	486	.58679	.00015	0	.99985	31
30	8.41792	480	11.58208	8.41807	480	11.58193	10.00015	0	9.99985	30
31	.42272	474	.57728	.42287	475	.57713	.00015	1	.99985	29
32	.42746	470	.57254	.42762	470	.57238	.00016	0	.99984	28
33	.43216	464	.56784	.43232	464	.56768	.00016	0	.99984	27
34	.43680	459	.56320	.43696	460	.56304	.00016	1	.99984	26
35	8.44139	455	11.55861	8.44156	455	11.55844	10.00017	0	9.99983	25
36	.44594	450	.55406	.44611	450	.55389	.00017	0	.99983	24
37	.45044	445	.54956	.45061	446	.54939	.00017	1	.99983	23
38	.45489	441	.54511	.45507	441	.54493	.00018	0	.99982	22
39	.45930	436	.54070	.45948	437	.54052	.00018	0	.99982	21
40	8.46366	433	11.53634	8.46385	432	11.53615	10.00018	1	9.99982	20
41	.46799	427	.53201	.46817	428	.53183	.00019	0	.99981	19
42	.47226	424	.52774	.47245	424	.52755	.00019	0	.99981	18
43	.47650	419	.52350	.47669	420	.52331	.00019	1	.99981	17
44	.48069	416	.51931	.48089	416	.51911	.00020	0	.99980	16
45	8.48485	411	11.51515	8.48505	412	11.51495	10.00020	1	9.99980	15
46	.48896	408	.51104	.48917	408	.51083	.00021	0	.99979	14
47	.49304	404	.50696	.49325	404	.50675	.00021	0	.99979	13
48	.49708	400	.50292	.49729	401	.50271	.00021	1	.99979	12
49	.50108	396	.49892	.50130	397	.49870	.00022	0	.99978	11
50	8.50504	393	11.49496	8.50527	393	11.49473	10.00022	1	9.99978	10
51	.50897	390	.49103	.50920	390	.49080	.00023	0	.99977	9
52	.51287	386	.48713	.51310	386	.48690	.00023	0	.99977	8
53	.51673	382	.48327	.51696	383	.48304	.00023	1	.99977	7
54	.52055	379	.47945	.52079	380	.47921	.00024	0	.99976	6
55	8.52434	376	11.47566	8.52459	376	11.47541	10.00024	1	9.99976	5
56	.52810	373	.47190	.52835	373	.47165	.00025	0	.99975	4
57	.53183	369	.46817	.53208	370	.46792	.00025	1	.99975	3
58	.53552	367	.46448	.53578	367	.46422	.00026	0	.99974	2
59	.53919	363	.46081	.53945	363	.46055	.00026	0	.99974	1
60	8.54282		11.45718	8.54308		11.45692	10.00026		9.99974	0
91°→	cos	Diff. 1′	sec	cot	Diff. 1′	tan	csc	Diff. 1′	sin ← 88°	

TABLE 3

Common Logarithms of Trigonometric Functions (offset +10)

2° → ↓	sin	Diff. 1′	csc	tan	Diff. 1′	cot	sec	Diff. 1′	cos ← 177°	↓
′										′
0	8.54282	360	11.45718	8.54308	361	11.45692	10.00026	1	9.99974	60
1	.54642	357	.45358	.54669	358	.45331	.00027	0	.99973	59
2	.54999	355	.45001	.55027	355	.44973	.00027	1	.99973	58
3	.55354	351	.44646	.55382	352	.44618	.00028	0	.99972	57
4	.55705	349	.44295	.55734	349	.44266	.00028	1	.99972	56
5	8.56054	346	11.43946	8.56083	346	11.43917	10.00029	0	9.99971	55
6	.56400	343	.43600	.56429	344	.43571	.00029	1	.99971	54
7	.56743	341	.43257	.56773	341	.43227	.00030	0	.99970	53
8	.57084	337	.42916	.57114	338	.42886	.00030	1	.99970	52
9	.57421	336	.42579	.57452	336	.42548	.00031	0	.99969	51
10	8.57757	332	11.42243	8.57788	333	11.42212	10.00031	1	9.99969	50
11	.58089	330	.41911	.58121	330	.41879	.00032	0	.99968	49
12	.58419	328	.41581	.58451	328	.41549	.00032	1	.99968	48
13	.58747	325	.41253	.58779	326	.41221	.00033	0	.99967	47
14	.59072	323	.40928	.59105	323	.40895	.00033	0	.99967	46
15	8.59395	320	11.40605	8.59428	321	11.40572	10.00033	1	9.99967	45
16	.59715	318	.40285	.59749	319	.40251	.00034	0	.99966	44
17	.60033	316	.39967	.60068	316	.39932	.00034	1	.99966	43
18	.60349	313	.39651	.60384	314	.39616	.00035	1	.99965	42
19	.60662	311	.39338	.60698	311	.39302	.00036	0	.99964	41
20	8.60973	309	11.39027	8.61009	310	11.38991	10.00036	1	9.99964	40
21	.61282	307	.38718	.61319	307	.38681	.00037	0	.99963	39
22	.61589	305	.38411	.61626	305	.38374	.00037	1	.99963	38
23	.61894	302	.38106	.61931	303	.38069	.00038	0	.99962	37
24	.62196	301	.37804	.62234	301	.37766	.00038	1	.99962	36
25	8.62497	298	11.37503	8.62535	299	11.37465	10.00039	0	9.99961	35
26	.62795	296	.37205	.62834	297	.37166	.00039	1	.99961	34
27	.63091	294	.36909	.63131	295	.36869	.00040	0	.99960	33
28	.63385	293	.36615	.63426	292	.36574	.00040	1	.99960	32
29	.63678	290	.36322	.63718	291	.36282	.00041	0	.99959	31
30	8.63968	288	11.36032	8.64009	289	11.35991	10.00041	1	9.99959	30
31	.64256	287	.35744	.64298	287	.35702	.00042	0	.99958	29
32	.64543	284	.35457	.64585	285	.35415	.00042	1	.99958	28
33	.64827	283	.35173	.64870	284	.35130	.00043	1	.99957	27
34	.65110	281	.34890	.65154	281	.34846	.00044	0	.99956	26
35	8.65391	279	11.34609	8.65435	280	11.34565	10.00044	1	9.99956	25
36	.65670	277	.34330	.65715	278	.34285	.00045	0	.99955	24
37	.65947	276	.34053	.65993	276	.34007	.00045	1	.99955	23
38	.66223	274	.33777	.66269	274	.33731	.00046	0	.99954	22
39	.66497	272	.33503	.66543	273	.33457	.00046	1	.99954	21
40	8.66769	270	11.33231	8.66816	271	11.33184	10.00047	1	9.99953	20
41	.67039	269	.32961	.67087	269	.32913	.00048	0	.99952	19
42	.67308	267	.32692	.67356	268	.32644	.00048	1	.99952	18
43	.67575	266	.32425	.67624	266	.32376	.00049	0	.99951	17
44	.67841	263	.32159	.67890	264	.32110	.00049	1	.99951	16
45	8.68104	263	11.31896	8.68154	263	11.31846	10.00050	1	9.99950	15
46	.68367	260	.31633	.68417	261	.31583	.00051	0	.99949	14
47	.68627	259	.31373	.68678	260	.31322	.00051	1	.99949	13
48	.68886	258	.31114	.68938	258	.31062	.00052	0	.99948	12
49	.69144	256	.30856	.69196	257	.30804	.00052	1	.99948	11
50	8.69400	254	11.30600	8.69453	255	11.30547	10.00053	1	9.99947	10
51	.69654	253	.30346	.69708	254	.30292	.00054	0	.99946	9
52	.69907	252	.30093	.69962	252	.30038	.00054	1	.99946	8
53	.70159	250	.29841	.70214	251	.29786	.00055	1	.99945	7
54	.70409	249	.29591	.70465	249	.29535	.00056	0	.99944	6
55	8.70658	247	11.29342	8.70714	248	11.29286	10.00056	1	9.99944	5
56	.70905	246	.29095	.70962	246	.29038	.00057	1	.99943	4
57	.71151	244	.28849	.71208	245	.28792	.00058	0	.99942	3
58	.71395	243	.28605	.71453	244	.28547	.00058	1	.99942	2
59	.71638	242	.28362	.71697	243	.28303	.00059	1	.99941	1
60	8.71880		11.28120	8.71940		11.28060	10.00060		9.99940	0
↑ 92° →	cos	Diff. 1′	sec	cot	Diff. 1′	tan	csc	Diff. 1′	sin ← 87°	↑

TABLE 3

Common Logarithms of Trigonometric Functions (offset +10)

3° → ↓	sin	Diff. 1′	csc	tan	Diff. 1′	cot	sec	Diff. 1′	cos ← 176°	↓
′										′
0	8.71880	240	11.28120	8.71940	241	11.28060	10.00060	0	9.99940	60
1	.72120	239	.27880	.72181	239	.27819	.00060	1	.99940	59
2	.72359	238	.27641	.72420	239	.27580	.00061	1	.99939	58
3	.72597	237	.27403	.72659	237	.27341	.00062	0	.99938	57
4	.72834	235	.27166	.72896	236	.27104	.00062	1	.99938	56
5	8.73069	234	11.26931	8.73132	234	11.26868	10.00063	1	9.99937	55
6	.73303	232	.26697	.73366	234	.26634	.00064	0	.99936	54
7	.73535	232	.26465	.73600	232	.26400	.00064	1	.99936	53
8	.73767	230	.26233	.73832	231	.26168	.00065	1	.99935	52
9	.73997	229	.26003	.74063	229	.25937	.00066	0	.99934	51
10	8.74226	228	11.25774	8.74292	229	11.25708	10.00066	1	9.99934	50
11	.74454	226	.25546	.74521	227	.25479	.00067	1	.99933	49
12	.74680	226	.25320	.74748	226	.25252	.00068	0	.99932	48
13	.74906	224	.25094	.74974	225	.25026	.00068	1	.99932	47
14	.75130	223	.24870	.75199	224	.24801	.00069	1	.99931	46
15	8.75353	222	11.24647	8.75423	222	11.24577	10.00070	1	9.99930	45
16	.75575	220	.24425	.75645	222	.24355	.00071	0	.99929	44
17	.75795	220	.24205	.75867	220	.24133	.00071	1	.99929	43
18	.76015	219	.23985	.76087	219	.23913	.00072	1	.99928	42
19	.76234	217	.23766	.76306	219	.23694	.00073	1	.99927	41
20	8.76451	216	11.23549	8.76525	217	11.23475	10.00074	0	9.99926	40
21	.76667	216	.23333	.76742	216	.23258	.00074	1	.99926	39
22	.76883	214	.23117	.76958	215	.23042	.00075	1	.99925	38
23	.77097	213	.22903	.77173	214	.22827	.00076	1	.99924	37
24	.77310	212	.22690	.77387	213	.22613	.00077	0	.99923	36
25	8.77522	211	11.22478	8.77600	211	11.22400	10.00077	1	9.99923	35
26	.77733	210	.22267	.77811	211	.22189	.00078	1	.99922	34
27	.77943	209	.22057	.78022	210	.21978	.00079	1	.99921	33
28	.78152	208	.21848	.78232	209	.21768	.00080	0	.99920	32
29	.78360	208	.21640	.78441	208	.21559	.00080	1	.99920	31
30	8.78568	206	11.21432	8.78649	206	11.21351	10.00081	1	9.99919	30
31	.78774	205	.21226	.78855	206	.21145	.00082	1	.99918	29
32	.78979	204	.21021	.79061	205	.20939	.00083	0	.99917	28
33	.79183	203	.20817	.79266	204	.20734	.00083	1	.99917	27
34	.79386	202	.20614	.79470	203	.20530	.00084	1	.99916	26
35	8.79588	201	11.20412	8.79673	202	11.20327	10.00085	1	9.99915	25
36	.79789	201	.20211	.79875	201	.20125	.00086	1	.99914	24
37	.79990	199	.20010	.80076	201	.19924	.00087	0	.99913	23
38	.80189	199	.19811	.80277	199	.19723	.00087	1	.99913	22
39	.80388	197	.19612	.80476	198	.19524	.00088	1	.99912	21
40	8.80585	197	11.19415	8.80674	198	11.19326	10.00089	1	9.99911	20
41	.80782	196	.19218	.80872	196	.19128	.00090	1	.99910	19
42	.80978	195	.19022	.81068	196	.18932	.00091	0	.99909	18
43	.81173	194	.18827	.81264	195	.18736	.00091	1	.99909	17
44	.81367	193	.18633	.81459	194	.18541	.00092	1	.99908	16
45	8.81560	192	11.18440	8.81653	193	11.18347	10.00093	1	9.99907	15
46	.81752	192	.18248	.81846	192	.18154	.00094	1	.99906	14
47	.81944	190	.18056	.82038	192	.17962	.00095	1	.99905	13
48	.82134	190	.17866	.82230	190	.17770	.00096	0	.99904	12
49	.82324	189	.17676	.82420	190	.17580	.00096	1	.99904	11
50	8.82513	188	11.17487	8.82610	189	11.17390	10.00097	1	9.99903	10
51	.82701	187	.17299	.82799	188	.17201	.00098	1	.99902	9
52	.82888	187	.17112	.82987	188	.17013	.00099	1	.99901	8
53	.83075	186	.16925	.83175	186	.16825	.00100	1	.99900	7
54	.83261	185	.16739	.83361	186	.16639	.00101	1	.99899	6
55	8.83446	184	11.16554	8.83547	185	11.16453	10.00102	0	9.99898	5
56	.83630	183	.16370	.83732	184	.16268	.00102	1	.99898	4
57	.83813	183	.16187	.83916	184	.16084	.00103	1	.99897	3
58	.83996	181	.16004	.84100	182	.15900	.00104	1	.99896	2
59	.84177	181	.15823	.84282	182	.15718	.00105	1	.99895	1
60	8.84358		11.15642	8.84464		11.15536	10.00106		9.99894	0
↑ 93° →	cos	Diff. 1′	sec	cot	Diff. 1′	tan	csc	Diff. 1′	sin ← 86°	↑

TABLE 3

Common Logarithms of Trigonometric Functions (offset +10)

4° → ↓ ′	sin	Diff. 1′	csc	tan	Diff. 1′	cot	sec	Diff. 1′	cos	← 175° ↓ ′
0	8.84358	181	11.15642	8.84464	182	11.15536	10.00106	1	9.99894	60
1	.84539	179	.15461	.84646	180	.15354	.00107	1	.99893	59
2	.84718	179	.15282	.84826	180	.15174	.00108	1	.99892	58
3	.84897	178	.15103	.85006	179	.14994	.00109	0	.99891	57
4	.85075	177	.14925	.85185	178	.14815	.00109	1	.99891	56
5	8.85252	177	11.14748	8.85363	177	11.14637	10.00110	1	9.99890	55
6	.85429	176	.14571	.85540	177	.14460	.00111	1	.99889	54
7	.85605	175	.14395	.85717	176	.14283	.00112	1	.99888	53
8	.85780	175	.14220	.85893	176	.14107	.00113	1	.99887	52
9	.85955	173	.14045	.86069	174	.13931	.00114	1	.99886	51
10	8.86128	173	11.13872	8.86243	174	11.13757	10.00115	1	9.99885	50
11	.86301	173	.13699	.86417	174	.13583	.00116	1	.99884	49
12	.86474	171	.13526	.86591	172	.13409	.00117	1	.99883	48
13	.86645	171	.13355	.86763	172	.13237	.00118	1	.99882	47
14	.86816	171	.13184	.86935	171	.13065	.00119	1	.99881	46
15	8.86987	169	11.13013	8.87106	171	11.12894	10.00120	1	9.99880	45
16	.87156	169	.12844	.87277	170	.12723	.00121	0	.99879	44
17	.87325	169	.12675	.87447	169	.12553	.00121	1	.99879	43
18	.87494	167	.12506	.87616	169	.12384	.00122	1	.99878	42
19	.87661	168	.12339	.87785	168	.12215	.00123	1	.99877	41
20	8.87829	166	11.12171	8.87953	167	11.12047	10.00124	1	9.99876	40
21	.87995	166	.12005	.88120	167	.11880	.00125	1	.99875	39
22	.88161	165	.11839	.88287	166	.11713	.00126	1	.99874	38
23	.88326	164	.11674	.88453	165	.11547	.00127	1	.99873	37
24	.88490	164	.11510	.88618	165	.11382	.00128	1	.99872	36
25	8.88654	163	11.11346	8.88783	165	11.11217	10.00129	1	9.99871	35
26	.88817	163	.11183	.88948	163	.11052	.00130	1	.99870	34
27	.88980	162	.11020	.89111	163	.10889	.00131	1	.99869	33
28	.89142	162	.10858	.89274	163	.10726	.00132	1	.99868	32
29	.89304	160	.10696	.89437	161	.10563	.00133	1	.99867	31
30	8.89464	161	11.10536	8.89598	162	11.10402	10.00134	1	9.99866	30
31	.89625	159	.10375	.89760	160	.10240	.00135	1	.99865	29
32	.89784	159	.10216	.89920	160	.10080	.00136	1	.99864	28
33	.89943	159	.10057	.90080	160	.09920	.00137	1	.99863	27
34	.90102	158	.09898	.90240	159	.09760	.00138	1	.99862	26
35	8.90260	157	11.09740	8.90399	158	11.09601	10.00139	1	9.99861	25
36	.90417	157	.09583	.90557	158	.09443	.00140	1	.99860	24
37	.90574	156	.09426	.90715	157	.09285	.00141	1	.99859	23
38	.90730	155	.09270	.90872	157	.09128	.00142	1	.99858	22
39	.90885	155	.09115	.91029	156	.08971	.00143	1	.99857	21
40	8.91040	155	11.08960	8.91185	155	11.08815	10.00144	1	9.99856	20
41	.91195	154	.08805	.91340	155	.08660	.00145	1	.99855	19
42	.91349	153	.08651	.91495	155	.08505	.00146	1	.99854	18
43	.91502	153	.08498	.91650	153	.08350	.00147	1	.99853	17
44	.91655	152	.08345	.91803	154	.08197	.00148	1	.99852	16
45	8.91807	152	11.08193	8.91957	153	11.08043	10.00149	1	9.99851	15
46	.91959	151	.08041	.92110	152	.07890	.00150	2	.99850	14
47	.92110	151	.07890	.92262	152	.07738	.00152	1	.99848	13
48	.92261	150	.07739	.92414	151	.07586	.00153	1	.99847	12
49	.92411	150	.07589	.92565	151	.07435	.00154	1	.99846	11
50	8.92561	149	11.07439	8.92716	150	11.07284	10.00155	1	9.99845	10
51	.92710	149	.07290	.92866	150	.07134	.00156	1	.99844	9
52	.92859	148	.07141	.93016	149	.06984	.00157	1	.99843	8
53	.93007	147	.06993	.93165	148	.06835	.00158	1	.99842	7
54	.93154	147	.06846	.93313	149	.06687	.00159	1	.99841	6
55	8.93301	147	11.06699	8.93462	147	11.06538	10.00160	1	9.99840	5
56	.93448	146	.06552	.93609	147	.06391	.00161	1	.99839	4
57	.93594	146	.06406	.93756	147	.06244	.00162	1	.99838	3
58	.93740	145	.06260	.93903	146	.06097	.00163	1	.99837	2
59	.93885	145	.06115	.94049	146	.05951	.00164	2	.99836	1
60	8.94030		11.05970	8.94195		11.05805	10.00166		9.99834	0
↑ 94° →	cos	Diff. 1′	sec	cot	Diff. 1′	tan	csc	Diff. 1′	sin	← 85° ↑

TABLE 3

Common Logarithms of Trigonometric Functions (offset +10)

5° → ↓ ′	sin	Diff. 1′	csc	tan	Diff. 1′	cot	sec	Diff. 1′	cos	← 174° ↓ ′
0	8.94030	144	11.05970	8.94195	145	11.05805	10.00166	1	9.99834	60
1	.94174	143	.05826	.94340	145	.05660	.00167	1	.99833	59
2	.94317	144	.05683	.94485	145	.05515	.00168	1	.99832	58
3	.94461	142	.05539	.94630	143	.05370	.00169	1	.99831	57
4	.94603	143	.05397	.94773	144	.05227	.00170	1	.99830	56
5	8.94746	141	11.05254	8.94917	143	11.05083	10.00171	1	9.99829	55
6	.94887	142	.05113	.95060	142	.04940	.00172	1	.99828	54
7	.95029	141	.04971	.95202	142	.04798	.00173	2	.99827	53
8	.95170	140	.04830	.95344	142	.04656	.00175	1	.99825	52
9	.95310	140	.04690	.95486	141	.04514	.00176	1	.99824	51
10	8.95450	139	11.04550	8.95627	140	11.04373	10.00177	1	9.99823	50
11	.95589	139	.04411	.95767	141	.04233	.00178	1	.99822	49
12	.95728	139	.04272	.95908	139	.04092	.00179	1	.99821	48
13	.95867	138	.04133	.96047	140	.03953	.00180	1	.99820	47
14	.96005	138	.03995	.96187	138	.03813	.00181	2	.99819	46
15	8.96143	137	11.03857	8.96325	139	11.03675	10.00183	1	9.99817	45
16	.96280	137	.03720	.96464	138	.03536	.00184	1	.99816	44
17	.96417	136	.03583	.96602	137	.03398	.00185	1	.99815	43
18	.96553	136	.03447	.96739	138	.03261	.00186	1	.99814	42
19	.96689	136	.03311	.96877	136	.03123	.00187	1	.99813	41
20	8.96825	135	11.03175	8.97013	137	11.02987	10.00188	2	9.99812	40
21	.96960	135	.03040	.97150	135	.02850	.00190	1	.99810	39
22	.97095	134	.02905	.97285	136	.02715	.00191	1	.99809	38
23	.97229	134	.02771	.97421	135	.02579	.00192	1	.99808	37
24	.97363	133	.02637	.97556	135	.02444	.00193	1	.99807	36
25	8.97496	133	11.02504	8.97691	134	11.02309	10.00194	2	9.99806	35
26	.97629	133	.02371	.97825	134	.02175	.00196	1	.99804	34
27	.97762	132	.02238	.97959	133	.02041	.00197	1	.99803	33
28	.97894	132	.02106	.98092	133	.01908	.00198	1	.99802	32
29	.98026	131	.01974	.98225	133	.01775	.00199	1	.99801	31
30	8.98157	131	11.01843	8.98358	132	11.01642	10.00200	2	9.99800	30
31	.98288	131	.01712	.98490	132	.01510	.00202	1	.99798	29
32	.98419	130	.01581	.98622	131	.01378	.00203	1	.99797	28
33	.98549	130	.01451	.98753	131	.01247	.00204	1	.99796	27
34	.98679	129	.01321	.98884	131	.01116	.00205	2	.99795	26
35	8.98808	129	11.01192	8.99015	130	11.00985	10.00207	1	9.99793	25
36	.98937	129	.01063	.99145	130	.00855	.00208	1	.99792	24
37	.99066	128	.00934	.99275	130	.00725	.00209	1	.99791	23
38	.99194	128	.00806	.99405	129	.00595	.00210	2	.99790	22
39	.99322	128	.00678	.99534	128	.00466	.00212	1	.99788	21
40	8.99450	127	11.00550	8.99662	129	11.00338	10.00213	1	9.99787	20
41	.99577	127	.00423	.99791	128	.00209	.00214	1	.99786	19
42	.99704	126	.00296	8.99919	127	.00081	.00215	2	.99785	18
43	.99830	126	.00170	9.00046	128	.99954	.00217	1	.99783	17
44	8.99956	126	.00044	.00174	127	.99826	.00218	1	.99782	16
45	9.00082	125	10.99918	9.00301	126	10.99699	10.00219	1	9.99781	15
46	.00207	125	.99793	.00427	126	.99573	.00220	2	.99780	14
47	.00332	124	.99668	.00553	126	.99447	.00222	1	.99778	13
48	.00456	125	.99544	.00679	126	.99321	.00223	1	.99777	12
49	.00581	123	.99419	.00805	125	.99195	.00224	1	.99776	11
50	9.00704	124	10.99296	9.00930	125	10.99070	10.00225	2	9.99775	10
51	.00828	123	.99172	.01055	124	.98945	.00227	1	.99773	9
52	.00951	123	.99049	.01179	124	.98821	.00228	1	.99772	8
53	.01074	122	.98926	.01303	124	.98697	.00229	2	.99771	7
54	.01196	122	.98804	.01427	123	.98573	.00231	1	.99769	6
55	9.01318	122	10.98682	9.01550	123	10.98450	10.00232	1	9.99768	5
56	.01440	121	.98560	.01673	123	.98327	.00233	2	.99767	4
57	.01561	121	.98439	.01796	122	.98204	.00235	1	.99765	3
58	.01682	121	.98318	.01918	122	.98082	.00236	1	.99764	2
59	.01803	120	.98197	.02040	122	.97960	.00237	2	.99763	1
60	9.01923		10.98077	9.02162		10.97838	10.00239		9.99761	0
↑ 95° →	cos	Diff. 1′	sec	cot	Diff. 1′	tan	csc	Diff. 1′	sin	← 84° ↑

TABLE 3

Common Logarithms of Trigonometric Functions (offset +10)

6° → ′ ↓	sin	Diff. 1′	csc	tan	Diff. 1′	cot	sec	Diff. 1′	cos	← 173° ′ ↓
0	9.01923	120	10.98077	9.02162	121	10.97838	10.00239	1	9.99761	60
1	.02043	120	.97957	.02283	121	.97717	.00240	1	.99760	59
2	.02163	120	.97837	.02404	121	.97596	.00241	2	.99759	58
3	.02283	119	.97717	.02525	120	.97475	.00243	1	.99757	57
4	.02402	118	.97598	.02645	121	.97355	.00244	1	.99756	56
5	9.02520	119	10.97480	9.02766	119	10.97234	10.00245	2	9.99755	55
6	.02639	118	.97361	.02885	120	.97115	.00247	1	.99753	54
7	.02757	117	.97243	.03005	119	.96995	.00248	1	.99752	53
8	.02874	118	.97126	.03124	118	.96876	.00249	2	.99751	52
9	.02992	117	.97008	.03242	119	.96758	.00251	1	.99749	51
10	9.03109	117	10.96891	9.03361	118	10.96639	10.00252	1	9.99748	50
11	.03226	116	.96774	.03479	118	.96521	.00253	2	.99747	49
12	.03342	116	.96658	.03597	117	.96403	.00255	1	.99745	48
13	.03458	116	.96542	.03714	118	.96286	.00256	2	.99744	47
14	.03574	116	.96426	.03832	116	.96168	.00258	1	.99742	46
15	9.03690	115	10.96310	9.03948	117	10.96052	10.00259	1	9.99741	45
16	.03805	115	.96195	.04065	116	.95935	.00260	2	.99740	44
17	.03920	114	.96080	.04181	116	.95819	.00262	1	.99738	43
18	.04034	115	.95966	.04297	116	.95703	.00263	1	.99737	42
19	.04149	113	.95851	.04413	115	.95587	.00264	2	.99736	41
20	9.04262	114	10.95738	9.04528	115	10.95472	10.00266	1	9.99734	40
21	.04376	114	.95624	.04643	115	.95357	.00267	2	.99733	39
22	.04490	113	.95510	.04758	115	.95242	.00269	1	.99731	38
23	.04603	112	.95397	.04873	114	.95127	.00270	2	.99730	37
24	.04715	113	.95285	.04987	114	.95013	.00272	1	.99728	36
25	9.04828	112	10.95172	9.05101	113	10.94899	10.00273	1	9.99727	35
26	.04940	112	.95060	.05214	114	.94786	.00274	2	.99726	34
27	.05052	112	.94948	.05328	113	.94672	.00276	1	.99724	33
28	.05164	111	.94836	.05441	112	.94559	.00277	2	.99723	32
29	.05275	111	.94725	.05553	113	.94447	.00279	1	.99721	31
30	9.05386	111	10.94614	9.05666	112	10.94334	10.00280	2	9.99720	30
31	.05497	110	.94503	.05778	112	.94222	.00282	1	.99718	29
32	.05607	110	.94393	.05890	112	.94110	.00283	1	.99717	28
33	.05717	110	.94283	.06002	111	.93998	.00284	2	.99716	27
34	.05827	110	.94173	.06113	111	.93887	.00286	1	.99714	26
35	9.05937	109	10.94063	9.06224	111	10.93776	10.00287	2	9.99713	25
36	.06046	109	.93954	.06335	110	.93665	.00289	1	.99711	24
37	.06155	109	.93845	.06445	111	.93555	.00290	2	.99710	23
38	.06264	108	.93736	.06556	110	.93444	.00292	1	.99708	22
39	.06372	109	.93628	.06666	109	.93334	.00293	2	.99707	21
40	9.06481	108	10.93519	9.06775	110	10.93225	10.00295	1	9.99705	20
41	.06589	107	.93411	.06885	109	.93115	.00296	2	.99704	19
42	.06696	108	.93304	.06994	109	.93006	.00298	1	.99702	18
43	.06804	107	.93196	.07103	108	.92897	.00299	2	.99701	17
44	.06911	107	.93089	.07211	109	.92789	.00301	1	.99699	16
45	9.07018	106	10.92982	9.07320	108	10.92680	10.00302	2	9.99698	15
46	.07124	107	.92876	.07428	108	.92572	.00304	1	.99696	14
47	.07231	106	.92769	.07536	107	.92464	.00305	2	.99695	13
48	.07337	105	.92663	.07643	108	.92357	.00307	1	.99693	12
49	.07442	106	.92558	.07751	107	.92249	.00308	2	.99692	11
50	9.07548	105	10.92452	9.07858	106	10.92142	10.00310	1	9.99690	10
51	.07653	105	.92347	.07964	107	.92036	.00311	2	.99689	9
52	.07758	105	.92242	.08071	106	.91929	.00313	1	.99687	8
53	.07863	105	.92137	.08177	106	.91823	.00314	2	.99686	7
54	.07968	104	.92032	.08283	106	.91717	.00316	1	.99684	6
55	9.08072	104	10.91928	9.08389	106	10.91611	10.00317	2	9.99683	5
56	.08176	104	.91824	.08495	105	.91505	.00319	1	.99681	4
57	.08280	103	.91720	.08600	105	.91400	.00320	2	.99680	3
58	.08383	103	.91617	.08705	105	.91295	.00322	1	.99678	2
59	.08486	103	.91514	.08810	104	.91190	.00323	2	.99677	1
60	9.08589		10.91411	9.08914		10.91086	10.00325		9.99675	0
↑ 96° →	cos	Diff. 1′	sec	cot	Diff. 1′	tan	csc	Diff. 1′	sin ←	↑ 83°

TABLE 3

Common Logarithms of Trigonometric Functions (offset +10)

7° → ′ ↓	sin	Diff. 1′	csc	tan	Diff. 1′	cot	sec	Diff. 1′	cos	← 172° ′ ↓
0	9.08589	103	10.91411	9.08914	105	10.91086	10.00325	1	9.99675	60
1	.08692	103	.91308	.09019	104	.90981	.00326	2	.99674	59
2	.08795	102	.91205	.09123	104	.90877	.00328	2	.99672	58
3	.08897	102	.91103	.09227	103	.90773	.00330	1	.99670	57
4	.08999	102	.91001	.09330	104	.90670	.00331	2	.99669	56
5	9.09101	101	10.90899	9.09434	103	10.90566	10.00333	1	9.99667	55
6	.09202	102	.90798	.09537	103	.90463	.00334	2	.99666	54
7	.09304	101	.90696	.09640	102	.90360	.00336	1	.99664	53
8	.09405	101	.90595	.09742	103	.90258	.00337	2	.99663	52
9	.09506	100	.90494	.09845	102	.90155	.00339	2	.99661	51
10	9.09606	101	10.90394	9.09947	102	10.90053	10.00341	1	9.99659	50
11	.09707	100	.90293	.10049	101	.89951	.00342	2	.99658	49
12	.09807	100	.90193	.10150	102	.89850	.00344	1	.99656	48
13	.09907	99	.90093	.10252	101	.89748	.00345	2	.99655	47
14	.10006	100	.89994	.10353	101	.89647	.00347	2	.99653	46
15	9.10106	99	10.89894	9.10454	101	10.89546	10.00349	1	9.99651	45
16	.10205	99	.89795	.10555	101	.89445	.00350	2	.99650	44
17	.10304	98	.89696	.10656	100	.89344	.00352	1	.99648	43
18	.10402	99	.89598	.10756	100	.89244	.00353	2	.99647	42
19	.10501	98	.89499	.10856	100	.89144	.00355	2	.99645	41
20	9.10599	98	10.89401	9.10956	100	10.89044	10.00357	1	9.99643	40
21	.10697	98	.89303	.11056	99	.88944	.00358	2	.99642	39
22	.10795	98	.89205	.11155	99	.88845	.00360	2	.99640	38
23	.10893	97	.89107	.11254	99	.88746	.00362	1	.99638	37
24	.10990	97	.89010	.11353	99	.88647	.00363	2	.99637	36
25	9.11087	97	10.88913	9.11452	99	10.88548	10.00365	2	9.99635	35
26	.11184	97	.88816	.11551	98	.88449	.00367	1	.99633	34
27	.11281	96	.88719	.11649	98	.88351	.00368	2	.99632	33
28	.11377	97	.88623	.11747	98	.88253	.00370	1	.99630	32
29	.11474	96	.88526	.11845	98	.88155	.00371	2	.99629	31
30	9.11570	96	10.88430	9.11943	97	10.88057	10.00373	2	9.99627	30
31	.11666	95	.88334	.12040	98	.87960	.00375	1	.99625	29
32	.11761	96	.88239	.12138	97	.87862	.00376	2	.99624	28
33	.11857	95	.88143	.12235	97	.87765	.00378	2	.99622	27
34	.11952	95	.88048	.12332	96	.87668	.00380	2	.99620	26
35	9.12047	95	10.87953	9.12428	97	10.87572	10.00382	1	9.99618	25
36	.12142	94	.87858	.12525	96	.87475	.00383	2	.99617	24
37	.12236	95	.87764	.12621	96	.87379	.00385	2	.99615	23
38	.12331	94	.87669	.12717	96	.87283	.00387	1	.99613	22
39	.12425	94	.87575	.12813	96	.87187	.00388	2	.99612	21
40	9.12519	93	10.87481	9.12909	95	10.87091	10.00390	2	9.99610	20
41	.12612	94	.87388	.13004	95	.86996	.00392	1	.99608	19
42	.12706	93	.87294	.13099	95	.86901	.00393	2	.99607	18
43	.12799	93	.87201	.13194	95	.86806	.00395	2	.99605	17
44	.12892	93	.87108	.13289	95	.86711	.00397	2	.99603	16
45	9.12985	93	10.87015	9.13384	94	10.86616	10.00399	1	9.99601	15
46	.13078	93	.86922	.13478	95	.86522	.00400	2	.99600	14
47	.13171	92	.86829	.13573	94	.86427	.00402	2	.99598	13
48	.13263	92	.86737	.13667	94	.86333	.00404	1	.99596	12
49	.13355	92	.86645	.13761	93	.86239	.00405	2	.99595	11
50	9.13447	92	10.86553	9.13854	94	10.86146	10.00407	2	9.99593	10
51	.13539	91	.86461	.13948	93	.86052	.00409	2	.99591	9
52	.13630	92	.86370	.14041	93	.85959	.00411	1	.99589	8
53	.13722	91	.86278	.14134	93	.85866	.00412	2	.99588	7
54	.13813	91	.86187	.14227	93	.85773	.00414	2	.99586	6
55	9.13904	90	10.86096	9.14320	92	10.85680	10.00416	2	9.99584	5
56	.13994	91	.86006	.14412	92	.85588	.00418	1	.99582	4
57	.14085	90	.85915	.14504	93	.85496	.00419	2	.99581	3
58	.14175	91	.85825	.14597	91	.85403	.00421	2	.99579	2
59	.14266	90	.85734	.14688	92	.85312	.00423	2	.99577	1
60	9.14356		10.85644	9.14780		10.85220	10.00425		9.99575	0
↑ 97° →	cos	Diff. 1′	sec	cot	Diff. 1′	tan	csc	Diff. 1′	sin ←	↑ 82°

TABLE 3

Common Logarithms of Trigonometric Functions (offset +10)

8° → ↓ ′	sin	Diff. 1′	csc	tan	Diff. 1′	cot	sec	Diff. 1′	cos	← 171° ↓ ′
0	9.14356	89	10.85644	9.14780	92	10.85220	10.00425	1	9.99575	60
1	.14445	90	.85555	.14872	91	.85128	.00426	2	.99574	59
2	.14535	89	.85465	.14963	91	.85037	.00428	2	.99572	58
3	.14624	90	.85376	.15054	91	.84946	.00430	2	.99570	57
4	.14714	89	.85286	.15145	91	.84855	.00432	2	.99568	56
5	9.14803	88	10.85197	9.15236	91	10.84764	10.00434	1	9.99566	55
6	.14891	89	.85109	.15327	90	.84673	.00435	2	.99565	54
7	.14980	89	.85020	.15417	91	.84583	.00437	2	.99563	53
8	.15069	88	.84931	.15508	90	.84492	.00439	2	.99561	52
9	.15157	88	.84843	.15598	90	.84402	.00441	2	.99559	51
10	9.15245	88	10.84755	9.15688	89	10.84312	10.00443	1	9.99557	50
11	.15333	88	.84667	.15777	90	.84223	.00444	2	.99556	49
12	.15421	87	.84579	.15867	89	.84133	.00446	2	.99554	48
13	.15508	88	.84492	.15956	90	.84044	.00448	2	.99552	47
14	.15596	87	.84404	.16046	89	.83954	.00450	2	.99550	46
15	9.15683	87	10.84317	9.16135	89	10.83865	10.00452	2	9.99548	45
16	.15770	87	.84230	.16224	88	.83776	.00454	1	.99546	44
17	.15857	87	.84143	.16312	89	.83688	.00455	2	.99545	43
18	.15944	86	.84056	.16401	88	.83599	.00457	2	.99543	42
19	.16030	86	.83970	.16489	88	.83511	.00459	2	.99541	41
20	9.16116	87	10.83884	9.16577	88	10.83423	10.00461	2	9.99539	40
21	.16203	86	.83797	.16665	88	.83335	.00463	2	.99537	39
22	.16289	85	.83711	.16753	88	.83247	.00465	2	.99535	38
23	.16374	86	.83626	.16841	87	.83159	.00467	1	.99533	37
24	.16460	85	.83540	.16928	88	.83072	.00468	2	.99532	36
25	9.16545	86	10.83455	9.17016	87	10.82984	10.00470	2	9.99530	35
26	.16631	85	.83369	.17103	87	.82897	.00472	2	.99528	34
27	.16716	85	.83284	.17190	87	.82810	.00474	2	.99526	33
28	.16801	85	.83199	.17277	86	.82723	.00476	2	.99524	32
29	.16886	84	.83114	.17363	87	.82637	.00478	2	.99522	31
30	9.16970	85	10.83030	9.17450	86	10.82550	10.00480	2	9.99520	30
31	.17055	84	.82945	.17536	86	.82464	.00482	1	.99518	29
32	.17139	84	.82861	.17622	86	.82378	.00483	2	.99517	28
33	.17223	84	.82777	.17708	86	.82292	.00485	2	.99515	27
34	.17307	84	.82693	.17794	86	.82206	.00487	2	.99513	26
35	9.17391	83	10.82609	9.17880	85	10.82120	10.00489	2	9.99511	25
36	.17474	84	.82526	.17965	86	.82035	.00491	2	.99509	24
37	.17558	83	.82442	.18051	85	.81949	.00493	2	.99507	23
38	.17641	83	.82359	.18136	85	.81864	.00495	2	.99505	22
39	.17724	83	.82276	.18221	85	.81779	.00497	2	.99503	21
40	9.17807	83	10.82193	9.18306	85	10.81694	10.00499	2	9.99501	20
41	.17890	83	.82110	.18391	84	.81609	.00501	2	.99499	19
42	.17973	82	.82027	.18475	85	.81525	.00503	2	.99497	18
43	.18055	82	.81945	.18560	84	.81440	.00505	1	.99495	17
44	.18137	83	.81863	.18644	84	.81356	.00506	2	.99494	16
45	9.18220	82	10.81780	9.18728	84	10.81272	10.00508	2	9.99492	15
46	.18302	81	.81698	.18812	84	.81188	.00510	2	.99490	14
47	.18383	82	.81617	.18896	83	.81104	.00512	2	.99488	13
48	.18465	82	.81535	.18979	84	.81021	.00514	2	.99486	12
49	.18547	81	.81453	.19063	83	.80937	.00516	2	.99484	11
50	9.18628	81	10.81372	9.19146	83	10.80854	10.00518	2	9.99482	10
51	.18709	81	.81291	.19229	83	.80771	.00520	2	.99480	9
52	.18790	81	.81210	.19312	83	.80688	.00522	2	.99478	8
53	.18871	81	.81129	.19395	83	.80605	.00524	2	.99476	7
54	.18952	81	.81048	.19478	83	.80522	.00526	2	.99474	6
55	9.19033	80	10.80967	9.19561	82	10.80439	10.00528	2	9.99472	5
56	.19113	80	.80887	.19643	82	.80357	.00530	2	.99470	4
57	.19193	80	.80807	.19725	82	.80275	.00532	2	.99468	3
58	.19273	80	.80727	.19807	82	.80193	.00534	2	.99466	2
59	.19353	80	.80647	.19889	82	.80111	.00536	2	.99464	1
60	9.19433		10.80567	9.19971		10.80029	10.00538		9.99462	0
↑ 98° →	cos	Diff. 1′	sec	cot	Diff. 1′	tan	csc	Diff. 1′	sin ← 81° ↑	

TABLE 3

Common Logarithms of Trigonometric Functions (offset +10)

9° → ↓ ′	sin	Diff. 1′	csc	tan	Diff. 1′	cot	sec	Diff. 1′	cos	← 170° ↓ ′
0	9.19433	80	10.80567	9.19971	82	10.80029	10.00538	2	9.99462	60
1	.19513	79	.80487	.20053	81	.79947	.00540	2	.99460	59
2	.19592	80	.80408	.20134	82	.79866	.00542	2	.99458	58
3	.19672	79	.80328	.20216	81	.79784	.00544	2	.99456	57
4	.19751	79	.80249	.20297	81	.79703	.00546	2	.99454	56
5	9.19830	79	10.80170	9.20378	81	10.79622	10.00548	2	9.99452	55
6	.19909	79	.80091	.20459	81	.79541	.00550	2	.99450	54
7	.19988	79	.80012	.20540	81	.79460	.00552	2	.99448	53
8	.20067	78	.79933	.20621	80	.79379	.00554	2	.99446	52
9	.20145	78	.79855	.20701	81	.79299	.00556	2	.99444	51
10	9.20223	79	10.79777	9.20782	80	10.79218	10.00558	2	9.99442	50
11	.20302	78	.79698	.20862	80	.79138	.00560	2	.99440	49
12	.20380	78	.79620	.20942	80	.79058	.00562	2	.99438	48
13	.20458	77	.79542	.21022	80	.78978	.00564	2	.99436	47
14	.20535	78	.79465	.21102	80	.78898	.00566	2	.99434	46
15	9.20613	78	10.79387	9.21182	79	10.78818	10.00568	3	9.99432	45
16	.20691	77	.79309	.21261	80	.78739	.00571	2	.99429	44
17	.20768	77	.79232	.21341	79	.78659	.00573	2	.99427	43
18	.20845	77	.79155	.21420	79	.78580	.00575	2	.99425	42
19	.20922	77	.79078	.21499	79	.78501	.00577	2	.99423	41
20	9.20999	77	10.79001	9.21578	79	10.78422	10.00579	2	9.99421	40
21	.21076	77	.78924	.21657	79	.78343	.00581	2	.99419	39
22	.21153	76	.78847	.21736	78	.78264	.00583	2	.99417	38
23	.21229	77	.78771	.21814	79	.78186	.00585	2	.99415	37
24	.21306	76	.78694	.21893	78	.78107	.00587	2	.99413	36
25	9.21382	76	10.78618	9.21971	78	10.78029	10.00589	2	9.99411	35
26	.21458	76	.78542	.22049	78	.77951	.00591	2	.99409	34
27	.21534	76	.78466	.22127	78	.77873	.00593	3	.99407	33
28	.21610	75	.78390	.22205	78	.77795	.00596	2	.99404	32
29	.21685	76	.78315	.22283	78	.77717	.00598	2	.99402	31
30	9.21761	75	10.78239	9.22361	77	10.77639	10.00600	2	9.99400	30
31	.21836	76	.78164	.22438	78	.77562	.00602	2	.99398	29
32	.21912	75	.78088	.22516	77	.77484	.00604	2	.99396	28
33	.21987	75	.78013	.22593	77	.77407	.00606	2	.99394	27
34	.22062	75	.77938	.22670	77	.77330	.00608	2	.99392	26
35	9.22137	74	10.77863	9.22747	77	10.77253	10.00610	2	9.99390	25
36	.22211	75	.77789	.22824	77	.77176	.00612	3	.99388	24
37	.22286	75	.77714	.22901	76	.77099	.00615	2	.99385	23
38	.22361	74	.77639	.22977	77	.77023	.00617	2	.99383	22
39	.22435	74	.77565	.23054	76	.76946	.00619	2	.99381	21
40	9.22509	74	10.77491	9.23130	76	10.76870	10.00621	2	9.99379	20
41	.22583	74	.77417	.23206	77	.76794	.00623	2	.99377	19
42	.22657	74	.77343	.23283	76	.76717	.00625	3	.99375	18
43	.22731	74	.77269	.23359	76	.76641	.00628	2	.99372	17
44	.22805	73	.77195	.23435	75	.76565	.00630	2	.99370	16
45	9.22878	74	10.77122	9.23510	76	10.76490	10.00632	2	9.99368	15
46	.22952	73	.77048	.23586	75	.76414	.00634	2	.99366	14
47	.23025	73	.76975	.23661	76	.76339	.00636	2	.99364	13
48	.23098	73	.76902	.23737	75	.76263	.00638	3	.99362	12
49	.23171	73	.76829	.23812	75	.76188	.00641	2	.99359	11
50	9.23244	73	10.76756	9.23887	75	10.76113	10.00643	2	9.99357	10
51	.23317	73	.76683	.23962	75	.76038	.00645	2	.99355	9
52	.23390	72	.76610	.24037	75	.75963	.00647	2	.99353	8
53	.23462	73	.76538	.24112	74	.75888	.00649	3	.99351	7
54	.23535	72	.76465	.24186	75	.75814	.00652	2	.99348	6
55	9.23607	72	10.76393	9.24261	74	10.75739	10.00654	2	9.99346	5
56	.23679	73	.76321	.24335	75	.75665	.00656	2	.99344	4
57	.23752	71	.76248	.24410	74	.75590	.00658	2	.99342	3
58	.23823	72	.76177	.24484	74	.75516	.00660	3	.99340	2
59	.23895	72	.76105	.24558	74	.75442	.00663	2	.99337	1
60	9.23967		10.76033	9.24632		10.75368	10.00665		9.99335	0
↑ 99° →	cos	Diff. 1′	sec	cot	Diff. 1′	tan	csc	Diff. 1′	sin ← 80° ↑	

TABLE 3

Common Logarithms of Trigonometric Functions (offset +10)

10°→ ↓ ′	sin	Diff. 1′	csc	tan	Diff. 1′	cot	sec	Diff. 1′	cos ←169°	↓ ′
0	9.23967	72	10.76033	9.24632	74	10.75368	10.00665	2	9.99335	60
1	.24039	71	.75961	.24706	73	.75294	.00667	2	.99333	59
2	.24110	71	.75890	.24779	74	.75221	.00669	3	.99331	58
3	.24181	72	.75819	.24853	73	.75147	.00672	2	.99328	57
4	.24253	71	.75747	.24926	74	.75074	.00674	2	.99326	56
5	9.24324	71	10.75676	9.25000	73	10.75000	10.00676	2	9.99324	55
6	.24395	71	.75605	.25073	73	.74927	.00678	3	.99322	54
7	.24466	70	.75534	.25146	73	.74854	.00681	2	.99319	53
8	.24536	71	.75464	.25219	73	.74781	.00683	2	.99317	52
9	.24607	70	.75393	.25292	73	.74708	.00685	2	.99315	51
10	9.24677	71	10.75323	9.25365	72	10.74635	10.00687	3	9.99313	50
11	.24748	70	.75252	.25437	73	.74563	.00690	2	.99310	49
12	.24818	70	.75182	.25510	72	.74490	.00692	2	.99308	48
13	.24888	70	.75112	.25582	73	.74418	.00694	2	.99306	47
14	.24958	70	.75042	.25655	72	.74345	.00696	3	.99304	46
15	9.25028	70	10.74972	9.25727	72	10.74273	10.00699	2	9.99301	45
16	.25098	70	.74902	.25799	72	.74201	.00701	2	.99299	44
17	.25168	69	.74832	.25871	72	.74129	.00703	3	.99297	43
18	.25237	70	.74763	.25943	72	.74057	.00706	2	.99294	42
19	.25307	69	.74693	.26015	71	.73985	.00708	2	.99292	41
20	9.25376	69	10.74624	9.26086	72	10.73914	10.00710	2	9.99290	40
21	.25445	69	.74555	.26158	71	.73842	.00712	3	.99288	39
22	.25514	69	.74486	.26229	72	.73771	.00715	2	.99285	38
23	.25583	69	.74417	.26301	71	.73699	.00717	2	.99283	37
24	.25652	69	.74348	.26372	71	.73628	.00719	3	.99281	36
25	9.25721	69	10.74279	9.26443	71	10.73557	10.00722	2	9.99278	35
26	.25790	68	.74210	.26514	71	.73486	.00724	2	.99276	34
27	.25858	69	.74142	.26585	70	.73415	.00726	3	.99274	33
28	.25927	68	.74073	.26655	71	.73345	.00729	2	.99271	32
29	.25995	68	.74005	.26726	71	.73274	.00731	2	.99269	31
30	9.26063	68	10.73937	9.26797	70	10.73203	10.00733	3	9.99267	30
31	.26131	68	.73869	.26867	70	.73133	.00736	2	.99264	29
32	.26199	68	.73801	.26937	71	.73063	.00738	2	.99262	28
33	.26267	68	.73733	.27008	70	.72992	.00740	3	.99260	27
34	.26335	68	.73665	.27078	70	.72922	.00743	2	.99257	26
35	9.26403	67	10.73597	9.27148	70	10.72852	10.00745	3	9.99255	25
36	.26470	68	.73530	.27218	70	.72782	.00748	2	.99252	24
37	.26538	67	.73462	.27288	69	.72712	.00750	2	.99250	23
38	.26605	67	.73395	.27357	70	.72643	.00752	3	.99248	22
39	.26672	67	.73328	.27427	69	.72573	.00755	2	.99245	21
40	9.26739	67	10.73261	9.27496	70	10.72504	10.00757	2	9.99243	20
41	.26806	67	.73194	.27566	69	.72434	.00759	3	.99241	19
42	.26873	67	.73127	.27635	69	.72365	.00762	2	.99238	18
43	.26940	67	.73060	.27704	69	.72296	.00764	3	.99236	17
44	.27007	66	.72993	.27773	69	.72227	.00767	2	.99233	16
45	9.27073	67	10.72927	9.27842	69	10.72158	10.00769	2	9.99231	15
46	.27140	66	.72860	.27911	69	.72089	.00771	3	.99229	14
47	.27206	67	.72794	.27980	69	.72020	.00774	2	.99226	13
48	.27273	66	.72727	.28049	68	.71951	.00776	3	.99224	12
49	.27339	66	.72661	.28117	69	.71883	.00779	2	.99221	11
50	9.27405	66	10.72595	9.28186	68	10.71814	10.00781	2	9.99219	10
51	.27471	66	.72529	.28254	69	.71746	.00783	3	.99217	9
52	.27537	65	.72463	.28323	68	.71677	.00786	2	.99214	8
53	.27602	66	.72398	.28391	68	.71609	.00788	3	.99212	7
54	.27668	66	.72332	.28459	68	.71541	.00791	2	.99209	6
55	9.27734	65	10.72266	9.28527	68	10.71473	10.00793	3	9.99207	5
56	.27799	65	.72201	.28595	67	.71405	.00796	2	.99204	4
57	.27864	66	.72136	.28662	68	.71338	.00798	2	.99202	3
58	.27930	65	.72070	.28730	68	.71270	.00800	3	.99200	2
59	.27995	65	.72005	.28798	67	.71202	.00803	2	.99197	1
60	9.28060		10.71940	9.28865		10.71135	10.00805		9.99195	0
↑ 100°→	cos	Diff. 1′	sec	cot	Diff. 1′	tan	csc	Diff. 1′	sin ← 79°	↑

TABLE 3

Common Logarithms of Trigonometric Functions (offset +10)

11°→ ↓ ′	sin	Diff. 1′	csc	tan	Diff. 1′	cot	sec	Diff. 1′	cos ←168°	↓ ′
0	9.28060	65	10.71940	9.28865	68	10.71135	10.00805	3	9.99195	60
1	.28125	65	.71875	.28933	67	.71067	.00808	2	.99192	59
2	.28190	64	.71810	.29000	67	.71000	.00810	3	.99190	58
3	.28254	65	.71746	.29067	67	.70933	.00813	2	.99187	57
4	.28319	65	.71681	.29134	67	.70866	.00815	3	.99185	56
5	9.28384	64	10.71616	9.29201	67	10.70799	10.00818	2	9.99182	55
6	.28448	64	.71552	.29268	67	.70732	.00820	3	.99180	54
7	.28512	65	.71488	.29335	67	.70665	.00823	2	.99177	53
8	.28577	64	.71423	.29402	66	.70598	.00825	3	.99175	52
9	.28641	64	.71359	.29468	67	.70532	.00828	2	.99172	51
10	9.28705	64	10.71295	9.29535	66	10.70465	10.00830	3	9.99170	50
11	.28769	64	.71231	.29601	67	.70399	.00833	2	.99167	49
12	.28833	63	.71167	.29668	66	.70332	.00835	3	.99165	48
13	.28896	64	.71104	.29734	66	.70266	.00838	2	.99162	47
14	.28960	64	.71040	.29800	66	.70200	.00840	3	.99160	46
15	9.29024	63	10.70976	9.29866	66	10.70134	10.00843	2	9.99157	45
16	.29087	63	.70913	.29932	66	.70068	.00845	3	.99155	44
17	.29150	64	.70850	.29998	66	.70002	.00848	2	.99152	43
18	.29214	63	.70786	.30064	66	.69936	.00850	3	.99150	42
19	.29277	63	.70723	.30130	65	.69870	.00853	2	.99147	41
20	9.29340	63	10.70660	9.30195	66	10.69805	10.00855	3	9.99145	40
21	.29403	63	.70597	.30261	65	.69739	.00858	2	.99142	39
22	.29466	63	.70534	.30326	65	.69674	.00860	3	.99140	38
23	.29529	62	.70471	.30391	66	.69609	.00863	2	.99137	37
24	.29591	63	.70409	.30457	65	.69543	.00865	3	.99135	36
25	9.29654	62	10.70346	9.30522	65	10.69478	10.00868	2	9.99132	35
26	.29716	63	.70284	.30587	65	.69413	.00870	3	.99130	34
27	.29779	62	.70221	.30652	65	.69348	.00873	3	.99127	33
28	.29841	62	.70159	.30717	65	.69283	.00876	2	.99124	32
29	.29903	63	.70097	.30782	64	.69218	.00878	3	.99122	31
30	9.29966	62	10.70034	9.30846	65	10.69154	10.00881	2	9.99119	30
31	.30028	62	.69972	.30911	64	.69089	.00883	3	.99117	29
32	.30090	61	.69910	.30975	65	.69025	.00886	2	.99114	28
33	.30151	62	.69849	.31040	64	.68960	.00888	3	.99112	27
34	.30213	62	.69787	.31104	64	.68896	.00891	3	.99109	26
35	9.30275	61	10.69725	9.31168	65	10.68832	10.00894	2	9.99106	25
36	.30336	62	.69664	.31233	64	.68767	.00896	3	.99104	24
37	.30398	61	.69602	.31297	64	.68703	.00899	2	.99101	23
38	.30459	62	.69541	.31361	64	.68639	.00901	3	.99099	22
39	.30521	61	.69479	.31425	64	.68575	.00904	3	.99096	21
40	9.30582	61	10.69418	9.31489	63	10.68511	10.00907	2	9.99093	20
41	.30643	61	.69357	.31552	64	.68448	.00909	3	.99091	19
42	.30704	61	.69296	.31616	63	.68384	.00912	2	.99088	18
43	.30765	61	.69235	.31679	64	.68321	.00914	3	.99086	17
44	.30826	61	.69174	.31743	63	.68257	.00917	3	.99083	16
45	9.30887	60	10.69113	9.31806	64	10.68194	10.00920	2	9.99080	15
46	.30947	61	.69053	.31870	63	.68130	.00922	3	.99078	14
47	.31008	60	.68992	.31933	63	.68067	.00925	3	.99075	13
48	.31068	61	.68932	.31996	63	.68004	.00928	2	.99072	12
49	.31129	60	.68871	.32059	63	.67941	.00930	3	.99070	11
50	9.31189	61	10.68811	9.32122	63	10.67878	10.00933	3	9.99067	10
51	.31250	60	.68750	.32185	63	.67815	.00936	2	.99064	9
52	.31310	60	.68690	.32248	63	.67752	.00938	3	.99062	8
53	.31370	60	.68630	.32311	62	.67689	.00941	3	.99059	7
54	.31430	60	.68570	.32373	63	.67627	.00944	2	.99056	6
55	9.31490	59	10.68510	9.32436	62	10.67564	10.00946	3	9.99054	5
56	.31549	60	.68451	.32498	63	.67502	.00949	3	.99051	4
57	.31609	60	.68391	.32561	62	.67439	.00952	2	.99048	3
58	.31669	59	.68331	.32623	62	.67377	.00954	3	.99046	2
59	.31728	60	.68272	.32685	62	.67315	.00957	3	.99043	1
60	9.31788		10.68212	9.32747		10.67253	10.00960		9.99040	0
↑ 101°→	cos	Diff. 1′	sec	cot	Diff. 1′	tan	csc	Diff. 1′	sin ← 78°	↑

TABLE 3

Common Logarithms of Trigonometric Functions (offset +10)

12°→ ↓ ′	sin	Diff. 1′	csc	tan	Diff. 1′	cot	sec	Diff. 1′	cos	←167° ↓ ′
0	9.31788	59	10.68212	9.32747	63	10.67253	10.00960	2	9.99040	60
1	.31847	60	.68153	.32810	62	.67190	.00962	3	.99038	59
2	.31907	59	.68093	.32872	61	.67128	.00965	3	.99035	58
3	.31966	59	.68034	.32933	62	.67067	.00968	2	.99032	57
4	.32025	59	.67975	.32995	62	.67005	.00970	3	.99030	56
5	9.32084	59	10.67916	9.33057	62	10.66943	10.00973	3	9.99027	55
6	.32143	59	.67857	.33119	61	.66881	.00976	2	.99024	54
7	.32202	59	.67798	.33180	62	.66820	.00978	3	.99022	53
8	.32261	58	.67739	.33242	61	.66758	.00981	3	.99019	52
9	.32319	59	.67681	.33303	62	.66697	.00984	3	.99016	51
10	9.32378	59	10.67622	9.33365	61	10.66635	10.00987	2	9.99013	50
11	.32437	58	.67563	.33426	61	.66574	.00989	3	.99011	49
12	.32495	58	.67505	.33487	61	.66513	.00992	3	.99008	48
13	.32553	59	.67447	.33548	61	.66452	.00995	3	.99005	47
14	.32612	58	.67388	.33609	61	.66391	.00998	2	.99002	46
15	9.32670	58	10.67330	9.33670	61	10.66330	10.01000	3	9.99000	45
16	.32728	58	.67272	.33731	61	.66269	.01003	3	.98997	44
17	.32786	58	.67214	.33792	61	.66208	.01006	3	.98994	43
18	.32844	58	.67156	.33853	60	.66147	.01009	2	.98991	42
19	.32902	58	.67098	.33913	61	.66087	.01011	3	.98989	41
20	9.32960	58	10.67040	9.33974	60	10.66026	10.01014	3	9.98986	40
21	.33018	57	.66982	.34034	61	.65966	.01017	3	.98983	39
22	.33075	58	.66925	.34095	60	.65905	.01020	2	.98980	38
23	.33133	57	.66867	.34155	60	.65845	.01022	3	.98978	37
24	.33190	58	.66810	.34215	61	.65785	.01025	3	.98975	36
25	9.33248	57	10.66752	9.34276	60	10.65724	10.01028	3	9.98972	35
26	.33305	57	.66695	.34336	60	.65664	.01031	2	.98969	34
27	.33362	58	.66638	.34396	60	.65604	.01033	3	.98967	33
28	.33420	57	.66580	.34456	60	.65544	.01036	3	.98964	32
29	.33477	57	.66523	.34516	60	.65484	.01039	3	.98961	31
30	9.33534	57	10.66466	9.34576	59	10.65424	10.01042	3	9.98958	30
31	.33591	56	.66409	.34635	60	.65365	.01045	2	.98955	29
32	.33647	57	.66353	.34695	60	.65305	.01047	3	.98953	28
33	.33704	57	.66296	.34755	59	.65245	.01050	3	.98950	27
34	.33761	57	.66239	.34814	60	.65186	.01053	3	.98947	26
35	9.33818	56	10.66182	9.34874	59	10.65126	10.01056	3	9.98944	25
36	.33874	57	.66126	.34933	59	.65067	.01059	3	.98941	24
37	.33931	56	.66069	.34992	59	.65008	.01062	2	.98938	23
38	.33987	56	.66013	.35051	60	.64949	.01064	3	.98936	22
39	.34043	57	.65957	.35111	59	.64889	.01067	3	.98933	21
40	9.34100	56	10.65900	9.35170	59	10.64830	10.01070	3	9.98930	20
41	.34156	56	.65844	.35229	59	.64771	.01073	3	.98927	19
42	.34212	56	.65788	.35288	59	.64712	.01076	3	.98924	18
43	.34268	56	.65732	.35347	58	.64653	.01079	2	.98921	17
44	.34324	56	.65676	.35405	59	.64595	.01081	3	.98919	16
45	9.34380	56	10.65620	9.35464	59	10.64536	10.01084	3	9.98916	15
46	.34436	55	.65564	.35523	58	.64477	.01087	3	.98913	14
47	.34491	56	.65509	.35581	59	.64419	.01090	3	.98910	13
48	.34547	55	.65453	.35640	58	.64360	.01093	3	.98907	12
49	.34602	56	.65398	.35698	59	.64302	.01096	3	.98904	11
50	9.34658	55	10.65342	9.35757	58	10.64243	10.01099	3	9.98901	10
51	.34713	56	.65287	.35815	58	.64185	.01102	2	.98898	9
52	.34769	55	.65231	.35873	58	.64127	.01104	3	.98896	8
53	.34824	55	.65176	.35931	58	.64069	.01107	3	.98893	7
54	.34879	55	.65121	.35989	58	.64011	.01110	3	.98890	6
55	9.34934	55	10.65066	9.36047	58	10.63953	10.01113	3	9.98887	5
56	.34989	55	.65011	.36105	58	.63895	.01116	3	.98884	4
57	.35044	55	.64956	.36163	58	.63837	.01119	3	.98881	3
58	.35099	55	.64901	.36221	58	.63779	.01122	3	.98878	2
59	.35154	55	.64846	.36279	57	.63721	.01125	3	.98875	1
60	9.35209		10.64791	9.36336		10.63664	10.01128		9.98872	0
↑ 102°→	cos	Diff. 1′	sec	cot	Diff. 1′	tan	csc	Diff. 1′	sin ←	77° ↑

TABLE 3

Common Logarithms of Trigonometric Functions (offset +10)

13°→ ↓ ′	sin	Diff. 1′	csc	tan	Diff. 1′	cot	sec	Diff. 1′	cos	←166° ↓ ′
0	9.35209	54	10.64791	9.36336	58	10.63664	10.01128	3	9.98872	60
1	.35263	55	.64737	.36394	58	.63606	.01131	2	.98869	59
2	.35318	55	.64682	.36452	57	.63548	.01133	3	.98867	58
3	.35373	54	.64627	.36509	57	.63491	.01136	3	.98864	57
4	.35427	54	.64573	.36566	58	.63434	.01139	3	.98861	56
5	9.35481	55	10.64519	9.36624	57	10.63376	10.01142	3	9.98858	55
6	.35536	54	.64464	.36681	57	.63319	.01145	3	.98855	54
7	.35590	54	.64410	.36738	57	.63262	.01148	3	.98852	53
8	.35644	54	.64356	.36795	57	.63205	.01151	3	.98849	52
9	.35698	54	.64302	.36852	57	.63148	.01154	3	.98846	51
10	9.35752	54	10.64248	9.36909	57	10.63091	10.01157	3	9.98843	50
11	.35806	54	.64194	.36966	57	.63034	.01160	3	.98840	49
12	.35860	54	.64140	.37023	57	.62977	.01163	3	.98837	48
13	.35914	54	.64086	.37080	57	.62920	.01166	3	.98834	47
14	.35968	54	.64032	.37137	56	.62863	.01169	3	.98831	46
15	9.36022	53	10.63978	9.37193	57	10.62807	10.01172	3	9.98828	45
16	.36075	54	.63925	.37250	56	.62750	.01175	3	.98825	44
17	.36129	53	.63871	.37306	57	.62694	.01178	3	.98822	43
18	.36182	54	.63818	.37363	56	.62637	.01181	3	.98819	42
19	.36236	53	.63764	.37419	57	.62581	.01184	3	.98816	41
20	9.36289	53	10.63711	9.37476	56	10.62524	10.01187	3	9.98813	40
21	.36342	53	.63658	.37532	56	.62468	.01190	3	.98810	39
22	.36395	54	.63605	.37588	56	.62412	.01193	3	.98807	38
23	.36449	53	.63551	.37644	56	.62356	.01196	3	.98804	37
24	.36502	53	.63498	.37700	56	.62300	.01199	3	.98801	36
25	9.36555	53	10.63445	9.37756	56	10.62244	10.01202	3	9.98798	35
26	.36608	52	.63392	.37812	56	.62188	.01205	3	.98795	34
27	.36660	53	.63340	.37868	56	.62132	.01208	3	.98792	33
28	.36713	53	.63287	.37924	56	.62076	.01211	3	.98789	32
29	.36766	53	.63234	.37980	55	.62020	.01214	3	.98786	31
30	9.36819	52	10.63181	9.38035	56	10.61965	10.01217	3	9.98783	30
31	.36871	53	.63129	.38091	56	.61909	.01220	3	.98780	29
32	.36924	52	.63076	.38147	55	.61853	.01223	3	.98777	28
33	.36976	52	.63024	.38202	55	.61798	.01226	3	.98774	27
34	.37028	53	.62972	.38257	56	.61743	.01229	3	.98771	26
35	9.37081	52	10.62919	9.38313	55	10.61687	10.01232	3	9.98768	25
36	.37133	52	.62867	.38368	55	.61632	.01235	3	.98765	24
37	.37185	52	.62815	.38423	56	.61577	.01238	3	.98762	23
38	.37237	52	.62763	.38479	55	.61521	.01241	3	.98759	22
39	.37289	52	.62711	.38534	55	.61466	.01244	3	.98756	21
40	9.37341	52	10.62659	9.38589	55	10.61411	10.01247	3	9.98753	20
41	.37393	52	.62607	.38644	55	.61356	.01250	4	.98750	19
42	.37445	52	.62555	.38699	55	.61301	.01254	3	.98746	18
43	.37497	52	.62503	.38754	54	.61246	.01257	3	.98743	17
44	.37549	51	.62451	.38808	55	.61192	.01260	3	.98740	16
45	9.37600	52	10.62400	9.38863	55	10.61137	10.01263	3	9.98737	15
46	.37652	51	.62348	.38918	54	.61082	.01266	3	.98734	14
47	.37703	52	.62297	.38972	55	.61028	.01269	3	.98731	13
48	.37755	51	.62245	.39027	55	.60973	.01272	3	.98728	12
49	.37806	52	.62194	.39082	54	.60918	.01275	3	.98725	11
50	9.37858	51	10.62142	9.39136	54	10.60864	10.01278	3	9.98722	10
51	.37909	51	.62091	.39190	55	.60810	.01281	4	.98719	9
52	.37960	51	.62040	.39245	54	.60755	.01285	3	.98715	8
53	.38011	51	.61989	.39299	54	.60701	.01288	3	.98712	7
54	.38062	51	.61938	.39353	54	.60647	.01291	3	.98709	6
55	9.38113	51	10.61887	9.39407	54	10.60593	10.01294	3	9.98706	5
56	.38164	51	.61836	.39461	54	.60539	.01297	3	.98703	4
57	.38215	51	.61785	.39515	54	.60485	.01300	3	.98700	3
58	.38266	51	.61734	.39569	54	.60431	.01303	3	.98697	2
59	.38317	51	.61683	.39623	54	.60377	.01306	4	.98694	1
60	9.38368		10.61632	9.39677		10.60323	10.01310		9.98690	0
↑ 103°→	cos	Diff. 1′	sec	cot	Diff. 1′	tan	csc	Diff. 1′	sin ←	76° ↑

TABLE 3

Common Logarithms of Trigonometric Functions (offset +10)

14°→ ↓ ′	sin	Diff. 1′	csc	tan	Diff. 1′	cot	sec	Diff. 1′	cos	←165° ↓ ′
0	9.38368	50	10.61632	9.39677	54	10.60323	10.01310	3	9.98690	60
1	.38418	51	.61582	.39731	54	.60269	.01313	3	.98687	59
2	.38469	50	.61531	.39785	53	.60215	.01316	3	.98684	58
3	.38519	51	.61481	.39838	54	.60162	.01319	3	.98681	57
4	.38570	50	.61430	.39892	53	.60108	.01322	3	.98678	56
5	9.38620	50	10.61380	9.39945	54	10.60055	10.01325	4	9.98675	55
6	.38670	51	.61330	.39999	53	.60001	.01329	3	.98671	54
7	.38721	50	.61279	.40052	54	.59948	.01332	3	.98668	53
8	.38771	50	.61229	.40106	53	.59894	.01335	3	.98665	52
9	.38821	50	.61179	.40159	53	.59841	.01338	3	.98662	51
10	9.38871	50	10.61129	9.40212	54	10.59788	10.01341	3	9.98659	50
11	.38921	50	.61079	.40266	53	.59734	.01344	4	.98656	49
12	.38971	50	.61029	.40319	53	.59681	.01348	3	.98652	48
13	.39021	50	.60979	.40372	53	.59628	.01351	3	.98649	47
14	.39071	50	.60929	.40425	53	.59575	.01354	3	.98646	46
15	9.39121	49	10.60879	9.40478	53	10.59522	10.01357	3	9.98643	45
16	.39170	50	.60830	.40531	53	.59469	.01360	4	.98640	44
17	.39220	50	.60780	.40584	52	.59416	.01364	3	.98636	43
18	.39270	49	.60730	.40636	53	.59364	.01367	3	.98633	42
19	.39319	50	.60681	.40689	53	.59311	.01370	3	.98630	41
20	9.39369	49	10.60631	9.40742	53	10.59258	10.01373	4	9.98627	40
21	.39418	49	.60582	.40795	52	.59205	.01377	3	.98623	39
22	.39467	50	.60533	.40847	53	.59153	.01380	3	.98620	38
23	.39517	49	.60483	.40900	52	.59100	.01383	3	.98617	37
24	.39566	49	.60434	.40952	53	.59048	.01386	4	.98614	36
25	9.39615	49	10.60385	9.41005	52	10.58995	10.01390	3	9.98610	35
26	.39664	49	.60336	.41057	52	.58943	.01393	3	.98607	34
27	.39713	49	.60287	.41109	52	.58891	.01396	3	.98604	33
28	.39762	49	.60238	.41161	53	.58839	.01399	4	.98601	32
29	.39811	49	.60189	.41214	52	.58786	.01403	3	.98597	31
30	9.39860	49	10.60140	9.41266	52	10.58734	10.01406	3	9.98594	30
31	.39909	49	.60091	.41318	52	.58682	.01409	3	.98591	29
32	.39958	48	.60042	.41370	52	.58630	.01412	4	.98588	28
33	.40006	49	.59994	.41422	52	.58578	.01416	3	.98584	27
34	.40055	48	.59945	.41474	52	.58526	.01419	3	.98581	26
35	9.40103	49	10.59897	9.41526	52	10.58474	10.01422	4	9.98578	25
36	.40152	48	.59848	.41578	51	.58422	.01426	3	.98574	24
37	.40200	49	.59800	.41629	52	.58371	.01429	3	.98571	23
38	.40249	48	.59751	.41681	52	.58319	.01432	3	.98568	22
39	.40297	49	.59703	.41733	51	.58267	.01435	4	.98565	21
40	9.40346	48	10.59654	9.41784	52	10.58216	10.01439	3	9.98561	20
41	.40394	48	.59606	.41836	51	.58164	.01442	3	.98558	19
42	.40442	48	.59558	.41887	52	.58113	.01445	4	.98555	18
43	.40490	48	.59510	.41939	51	.58061	.01449	3	.98551	17
44	.40538	48	.59462	.41990	51	.58010	.01452	3	.98548	16
45	9.40586	48	10.59414	9.42041	52	10.57959	10.01455	4	9.98545	15
46	.40634	48	.59366	.42093	51	.57907	.01459	3	.98541	14
47	.40682	48	.59318	.42144	51	.57856	.01462	3	.98538	13
48	.40730	48	.59270	.42195	51	.57805	.01465	4	.98535	12
49	.40778	47	.59222	.42246	51	.57754	.01469	3	.98531	11
50	9.40825	48	10.59175	9.42297	51	10.57703	10.01472	3	9.98528	10
51	.40873	48	.59127	.42348	51	.57652	.01475	4	.98525	9
52	.40921	47	.59079	.42399	51	.57601	.01479	3	.98521	8
53	.40968	48	.59032	.42450	51	.57550	.01482	3	.98518	7
54	.41016	47	.58984	.42501	51	.57499	.01485	4	.98515	6
55	9.41063	48	10.58937	9.42552	51	10.57448	10.01489	3	9.98511	5
56	.41111	47	.58889	.42603	50	.57397	.01492	3	.98508	4
57	.41158	47	.58842	.42653	51	.57347	.01495	4	.98505	3
58	.41205	47	.58795	.42704	51	.57296	.01499	3	.98501	2
59	.41252	48	.58748	.42755	50	.57245	.01502	4	.98498	1
60	9.41300		10.58700	9.42805		10.57195	10.01506		9.98494	0
↑ 104°→	cos	Diff. 1′	sec	cot	Diff. 1′	tan	csc	Diff. 1′	sin ← 75°	↑

TABLE 3

Common Logarithms of Trigonometric Functions (offset +10)

15°→ ↓ ′	sin	Diff. 1′	csc	tan	Diff. 1′	cot	sec	Diff. 1′	cos	←164° ↓ ′
0	9.41300	47	10.58700	9.42805	51	10.57195	10.01506	3	9.98494	60
1	.41347	47	.58653	.42856	50	.57144	.01509	3	.98491	59
2	.41394	47	.58606	.42906	51	.57094	.01512	4	.98488	58
3	.41441	47	.58559	.42957	50	.57043	.01516	3	.98484	57
4	.41488	47	.58512	.43007	50	.56993	.01519	4	.98481	56
5	9.41535	47	10.58465	9.43057	51	10.56943	10.01523	3	9.98477	55
6	.41582	46	.58418	.43108	50	.56892	.01526	3	.98474	54
7	.41628	47	.58372	.43158	50	.56842	.01529	4	.98471	53
8	.41675	47	.58325	.43208	50	.56792	.01533	3	.98467	52
9	.41722	46	.58278	.43258	50	.56742	.01536	4	.98464	51
10	9.41768	47	10.58232	9.43308	50	10.56692	10.01540	3	9.98460	50
11	.41815	46	.58185	.43358	50	.56642	.01543	4	.98457	49
12	.41861	47	.58139	.43408	50	.56592	.01547	3	.98453	48
13	.41908	46	.58092	.43458	50	.56542	.01550	3	.98450	47
14	.41954	47	.58046	.43508	50	.56492	.01553	4	.98447	46
15	9.42001	46	10.57999	9.43558	49	10.56442	10.01557	3	9.98443	45
16	.42047	46	.57953	.43607	50	.56393	.01560	4	.98440	44
17	.42093	47	.57907	.43657	50	.56343	.01564	3	.98436	43
18	.42140	46	.57860	.43707	49	.56293	.01567	4	.98433	42
19	.42186	46	.57814	.43756	50	.56244	.01571	3	.98429	41
20	9.42232	46	10.57768	9.43806	49	10.56194	10.01574	4	9.98426	40
21	.42278	46	.57722	.43855	50	.56145	.01578	3	.98422	39
22	.42324	46	.57676	.43905	49	.56095	.01581	4	.98419	38
23	.42370	46	.57630	.43954	50	.56046	.01585	3	.98415	37
24	.42416	45	.57584	.44004	49	.55996	.01588	3	.98412	36
25	9.42461	46	10.57539	9.44053	49	10.55947	10.01591	4	9.98409	35
26	.42507	46	.57493	.44102	49	.55898	.01595	3	.98405	34
27	.42553	46	.57447	.44151	50	.55849	.01598	4	.98402	33
28	.42599	45	.57401	.44201	49	.55799	.01602	3	.98398	32
29	.42644	46	.57356	.44250	49	.55750	.01605	4	.98395	31
30	9.42690	45	10.57310	9.44299	49	10.55701	10.01609	3	9.98391	30
31	.42735	46	.57265	.44348	49	.55652	.01612	4	.98388	29
32	.42781	45	.57219	.44397	49	.55603	.01616	3	.98384	28
33	.42826	46	.57174	.44446	49	.55554	.01619	4	.98381	27
34	.42872	45	.57128	.44495	49	.55505	.01623	4	.98377	26
35	9.42917	45	10.57083	9.44544	48	10.55456	10.01627	3	9.98373	25
36	.42962	46	.57038	.44592	49	.55408	.01630	4	.98370	24
37	.43008	45	.56992	.44641	49	.55359	.01634	3	.98366	23
38	.43053	45	.56947	.44690	48	.55310	.01637	4	.98363	22
39	.43098	45	.56902	.44738	49	.55262	.01641	3	.98359	21
40	9.43143	45	10.56857	9.44787	49	10.55213	10.01644	4	9.98356	20
41	.43188	45	.56812	.44836	48	.55164	.01648	3	.98352	19
42	.43233	45	.56767	.44884	49	.55116	.01651	4	.98349	18
43	.43278	45	.56722	.44933	48	.55067	.01655	3	.98345	17
44	.43323	44	.56677	.44981	48	.55019	.01658	4	.98342	16
45	9.43367	45	10.56633	9.45029	49	10.54971	10.01662	4	9.98338	15
46	.43412	45	.56588	.45078	48	.54922	.01666	3	.98334	14
47	.43457	45	.56543	.45126	48	.54874	.01669	4	.98331	13
48	.43502	44	.56498	.45174	48	.54826	.01673	3	.98327	12
49	.43546	45	.56454	.45222	49	.54778	.01676	4	.98324	11
50	9.43591	44	10.56409	9.45271	48	10.54729	10.01680	3	9.98320	10
51	.43635	45	.56365	.45319	48	.54681	.01683	4	.98317	9
52	.43680	44	.56320	.45367	48	.54633	.01687	4	.98313	8
53	.43724	45	.56276	.45415	48	.54585	.01691	3	.98309	7
54	.43769	44	.56231	.45463	48	.54537	.01694	4	.98306	6
55	9.43813	44	10.56187	9.45511	48	10.54489	10.01698	3	9.98302	5
56	.43857	44	.56143	.45559	47	.54441	.01701	4	.98299	4
57	.43901	45	.56099	.45606	48	.54394	.01705	4	.98295	3
58	.43946	44	.56054	.45654	48	.54346	.01709	3	.98291	2
59	.43990	44	.56010	.45702	48	.54298	.01712	4	.98288	1
60	9.44034		10.55966	9.45750		10.54250	10.01716		9.98284	0
↑ 105°→	cos	Diff. 1′	sec	cot	Diff. 1′	tan	csc	Diff. 1′	sin ← 74°	↑

TABLE 3

Common Logarithms of Trigonometric Functions (offset +10)

16°→ ↓ ′	sin	Diff. 1′	csc	tan	Diff. 1′	cot	sec	Diff. 1′	cos	←163° ↓ ′
0	9.44034	44	10.55966	9.45750	47	10.54250	10.01716	3	9.98284	60
1	.44078	44	.55922	.45797	48	.54203	.01719	4	.98281	59
2	.44122	44	.55878	.45845	47	.54155	.01723	4	.98277	58
3	.44166	44	.55834	.45892	48	.54108	.01727	3	.98273	57
4	.44210	43	.55790	.45940	47	.54060	.01730	4	.98270	56
5	9.44253	44	10.55747	9.45987	48	10.54013	10.01734	4	9.98266	55
6	.44297	44	.55703	.46035	47	.53965	.01738	3	.98262	54
7	.44341	44	.55659	.46082	48	.53918	.01741	4	.98259	53
8	.44385	43	.55615	.46130	47	.53870	.01745	4	.98255	52
9	.44428	44	.55572	.46177	47	.53823	.01749	3	.98251	51
10	9.44472	44	10.55528	9.46224	47	10.53776	10.01752	4	9.98248	50
11	.44516	43	.55484	.46271	48	.53729	.01756	4	.98244	49
12	.44559	43	.55441	.46319	47	.53681	.01760	3	.98240	48
13	.44602	44	.55398	.46366	47	.53634	.01763	4	.98237	47
14	.44646	43	.55354	.46413	47	.53587	.01767	4	.98233	46
15	9.44689	44	10.55311	9.46460	47	10.53540	10.01771	3	9.98229	45
16	.44733	43	.55267	.46507	47	.53493	.01774	4	.98226	44
17	.44776	43	.55224	.46554	47	.53446	.01778	4	.98222	43
18	.44819	43	.55181	.46601	47	.53399	.01782	3	.98218	42
19	.44862	43	.55138	.46648	46	.53352	.01785	4	.98215	41
20	9.44905	43	10.55095	9.46694	47	10.53306	10.01789	4	9.98211	40
21	.44948	44	.55052	.46741	47	.53259	.01793	3	.98207	39
22	.44992	43	.55008	.46788	47	.53212	.01796	4	.98204	38
23	.45035	42	.54965	.46835	46	.53165	.01800	4	.98200	37
24	.45077	43	.54923	.46881	47	.53119	.01804	4	.98196	36
25	9.45120	43	10.54880	9.46928	47	10.53072	10.01808	3	9.98192	35
26	.45163	43	.54837	.46975	46	.53025	.01811	4	.98189	34
27	.45206	43	.54794	.47021	47	.52979	.01815	4	.98185	33
28	.45249	43	.54751	.47068	46	.52932	.01819	4	.98181	32
29	.45292	42	.54708	.47114	46	.52886	.01823	3	.98177	31
30	9.45334	43	10.54666	9.47160	47	10.52840	10.01826	4	9.98174	30
31	.45377	42	.54623	.47207	46	.52793	.01830	4	.98170	29
32	.45419	43	.54581	.47253	46	.52747	.01834	4	.98166	28
33	.45462	42	.54538	.47299	47	.52701	.01838	3	.98162	27
34	.45504	43	.54496	.47346	46	.52654	.01841	4	.98159	26
35	9.45547	42	10.54453	9.47392	46	10.52608	10.01845	4	9.98155	25
36	.45589	43	.54411	.47438	46	.52562	.01849	4	.98151	24
37	.45632	42	.54368	.47484	46	.52516	.01853	3	.98147	23
38	.45674	42	.54326	.47530	46	.52470	.01856	4	.98144	22
39	.45716	42	.54284	.47576	46	.52424	.01860	4	.98140	21
40	9.45758	43	10.54242	9.47622	46	10.52378	10.01864	4	9.98136	20
41	.45801	42	.54199	.47668	46	.52332	.01868	3	.98132	19
42	.45843	42	.54157	.47714	46	.52286	.01871	4	.98129	18
43	.45885	42	.54115	.47760	46	.52240	.01875	4	.98125	17
44	.45927	42	.54073	.47806	46	.52194	.01879	4	.98121	16
45	9.45969	42	10.54031	9.47852	45	10.52148	10.01883	4	9.98117	15
46	.46011	42	.53989	.47897	46	.52103	.01887	3	.98113	14
47	.46053	42	.53947	.47943	46	.52057	.01890	4	.98110	13
48	.46095	41	.53905	.47989	46	.52011	.01894	4	.98106	12
49	.46136	42	.53864	.48035	45	.51965	.01898	4	.98102	11
50	9.46178	42	10.53822	9.48080	46	10.51920	10.01902	4	9.98098	10
51	.46220	42	.53780	.48126	45	.51874	.01906	4	.98094	9
52	.46262	41	.53738	.48171	46	.51829	.01910	3	.98090	8
53	.46303	42	.53697	.48217	45	.51783	.01913	4	.98087	7
54	.46345	41	.53655	.48262	45	.51738	.01917	4	.98083	6
55	9.46386	42	10.53614	9.48307	46	10.51693	10.01921	4	9.98079	5
56	.46428	41	.53572	.48353	45	.51647	.01925	4	.98075	4
57	.46469	42	.53531	.48398	45	.51602	.01929	4	.98071	3
58	.46511	41	.53489	.48443	46	.51557	.01933	4	.98067	2
59	.46552	42	.53448	.48489	45	.51511	.01937	3	.98063	1
60	9.46594		10.53406	9.48534		10.51466	10.01940		9.98060	0
↑ 106°→	cos	Diff. 1′	sec	cot	Diff. 1′	tan	csc	Diff. 1′	sin	← 73° ↑

TABLE 3

Common Logarithms of Trigonometric Functions (offset +10)

17°→ ↓ ′	sin	Diff. 1′	csc	tan	Diff. 1′	cot	sec	Diff. 1′	cos	←162° ↓ ′
0	9.46594	41	10.53406	9.48534	45	10.51466	10.01940	4	9.98060	60
1	.46635	41	.53365	.48579	45	.51421	.01944	4	.98056	59
2	.46676	41	.53324	.48624	45	.51376	.01948	4	.98052	58
3	.46717	41	.53283	.48669	45	.51331	.01952	4	.98048	57
4	.46758	42	.53242	.48714	45	.51286	.01956	4	.98044	56
5	9.46800	41	10.53200	9.48759	45	10.51241	10.01960	4	9.98040	55
6	.46841	41	.53159	.48804	45	.51196	.01964	4	.98036	54
7	.46882	41	.53118	.48849	45	.51151	.01968	3	.98032	53
8	.46923	41	.53077	.48894	45	.51106	.01971	4	.98029	52
9	.46964	41	.53036	.48939	45	.51061	.01975	4	.98025	51
10	9.47005	40	10.52995	9.48984	45	10.51016	10.01979	4	9.98021	50
11	.47045	41	.52955	.49029	44	.50971	.01983	4	.98017	49
12	.47086	41	.52914	.49073	45	.50927	.01987	4	.98013	48
13	.47127	41	.52873	.49118	45	.50882	.01991	4	.98009	47
14	.47168	41	.52832	.49163	44	.50837	.01995	4	.98005	46
15	9.47209	40	10.52791	9.49207	45	10.50793	10.01999	4	9.98001	45
16	.47249	41	.52751	.49252	44	.50748	.02003	4	.97997	44
17	.47290	40	.52710	.49296	45	.50704	.02007	4	.97993	43
18	.47330	41	.52670	.49341	44	.50659	.02011	3	.97989	42
19	.47371	40	.52629	.49385	45	.50615	.02014	4	.97986	41
20	9.47411	41	10.52589	9.49430	44	10.50570	10.02018	4	9.97982	40
21	.47452	40	.52548	.49474	45	.50526	.02022	4	.97978	39
22	.47492	41	.52508	.49519	44	.50481	.02026	4	.97974	38
23	.47533	40	.52467	.49563	44	.50437	.02030	4	.97970	37
24	.47573	40	.52427	.49607	45	.50393	.02034	4	.97966	36
25	9.47613	41	10.52387	9.49652	44	10.50348	10.02038	4	9.97962	35
26	.47654	40	.52346	.49696	44	.50304	.02042	4	.97958	34
27	.47694	40	.52306	.49740	44	.50260	.02046	4	.97954	33
28	.47734	40	.52266	.49784	44	.50216	.02050	4	.97950	32
29	.47774	40	.52226	.49828	44	.50172	.02054	4	.97946	31
30	9.47814	40	10.52186	9.49872	44	10.50128	10.02058	4	9.97942	30
31	.47854	40	.52146	.49916	44	.50084	.02062	4	.97938	29
32	.47894	40	.52106	.49960	44	.50040	.02066	4	.97934	28
33	.47934	40	.52066	.50004	44	.49996	.02070	4	.97930	27
34	.47974	40	.52026	.50048	44	.49952	.02074	4	.97926	26
35	9.48014	40	10.51986	9.50092	44	10.49908	10.02078	4	9.97922	25
36	.48054	40	.51946	.50136	44	.49864	.02082	4	.97918	24
37	.48094	39	.51906	.50180	43	.49820	.02086	4	.97914	23
38	.48133	40	.51867	.50223	44	.49777	.02090	4	.97910	22
39	.48173	40	.51827	.50267	44	.49733	.02094	4	.97906	21
40	9.48213	39	10.51787	9.50311	44	10.49689	10.02098	4	9.97902	20
41	.48252	40	.51748	.50355	43	.49645	.02102	4	.97898	19
42	.48292	40	.51708	.50398	44	.49602	.02106	4	.97894	18
43	.48332	39	.51668	.50442	43	.49558	.02110	4	.97890	17
44	.48371	40	.51629	.50485	44	.49515	.02114	4	.97886	16
45	9.48411	39	10.51589	9.50529	43	10.49471	10.02118	4	9.97882	15
46	.48450	40	.51550	.50572	44	.49428	.02122	4	.97878	14
47	.48490	39	.51510	.50616	43	.49384	.02126	4	.97874	13
48	.48529	39	.51471	.50659	44	.49341	.02130	4	.97870	12
49	.48568	39	.51432	.50703	43	.49297	.02134	5	.97866	11
50	9.48607	40	10.51393	9.50746	43	10.49254	10.02139	4	9.97861	10
51	.48647	39	.51353	.50789	44	.49211	.02143	4	.97857	9
52	.48686	39	.51314	.50833	43	.49167	.02147	4	.97853	8
53	.48725	39	.51275	.50876	43	.49124	.02151	4	.97849	7
54	.48764	39	.51236	.50919	43	.49081	.02155	4	.97845	6
55	9.48803	39	10.51197	9.50962	43	10.49038	10.02159	4	9.97841	5
56	.48842	39	.51158	.51005	43	.48995	.02163	4	.97837	4
57	.48881	39	.51119	.51048	44	.48952	.02167	4	.97833	3
58	.48920	39	.51080	.51092	43	.48908	.02171	4	.97829	2
59	.48959	39	.51041	.51135	43	.48865	.02175	4	.97825	1
60	9.48998		10.51002	9.51178		10.48822	10.02179		9.97821	0
↑ 107°→	cos	Diff. 1′	sec	cot	Diff. 1′	tan	csc	Diff. 1′	sin	← 72° ↑

TABLE 3

Common Logarithms of Trigonometric Functions (offset +10)

18° → ↓ ′	sin	Diff. 1′	csc	tan	Diff. 1′	cot	sec	Diff. 1′	cos	← 161° ↓ ′
0	9.48998	39	10.51002	9.51178	43	10.48822	10.02179	4	9.97821	60
1	.49037	39	.50963	.51221	43	.48779	.02183	5	.97817	59
2	.49076	39	.50924	.51264	42	.48736	.02188	4	.97812	58
3	.49115	38	.50885	.51306	43	.48694	.02192	4	.97808	57
4	.49153	39	.50847	.51349	43	.48651	.02196	4	.97804	56
5	9.49192	39	10.50808	9.51392	43	10.48608	10.02200	4	9.97800	55
6	.49231	38	.50769	.51435	43	.48565	.02204	4	.97796	54
7	.49269	39	.50731	.51478	42	.48522	.02208	4	.97792	53
8	.49308	39	.50692	.51520	43	.48480	.02212	4	.97788	52
9	.49347	38	.50653	.51563	43	.48437	.02216	5	.97784	51
10	9.49385	39	10.50615	9.51606	42	10.48394	10.02221	4	9.97779	50
11	.49424	38	.50576	.51648	43	.48352	.02225	4	.97775	49
12	.49462	38	.50538	.51691	43	.48309	.02229	4	.97771	48
13	.49500	39	.50500	.51734	42	.48266	.02233	4	.97767	47
14	.49539	38	.50461	.51776	43	.48224	.02237	4	.97763	46
15	9.49577	38	10.50423	9.51819	42	10.48181	10.02241	5	9.97759	45
16	.49615	39	.50385	.51861	42	.48139	.02246	4	.97754	44
17	.49654	38	.50346	.51903	43	.48097	.02250	4	.97750	43
18	.49692	38	.50308	.51946	42	.48054	.02254	4	.97746	42
19	.49730	38	.50270	.51988	43	.48012	.02258	4	.97742	41
20	9.49768	38	10.50232	9.52031	42	10.47969	10.02262	4	9.97738	40
21	.49806	38	.50194	.52073	42	.47927	.02266	5	.97734	39
22	.49844	38	.50156	.52115	42	.47885	.02271	4	.97729	38
23	.49882	38	.50118	.52157	43	.47843	.02275	4	.97725	37
24	.49920	38	.50080	.52200	42	.47800	.02279	4	.97721	36
25	9.49958	38	10.50042	9.52242	42	10.47758	10.02283	4	9.97717	35
26	.49996	38	.50004	.52284	42	.47716	.02287	5	.97713	34
27	.50034	38	.49966	.52326	42	.47674	.02292	4	.97708	33
28	.50072	38	.49928	.52368	42	.47632	.02296	4	.97704	32
29	.50110	38	.49890	.52410	42	.47590	.02300	4	.97700	31
30	9.50148	37	10.49852	9.52452	42	10.47548	10.02304	5	9.97696	30
31	.50185	38	.49815	.52494	42	.47506	.02309	4	.97691	29
32	.50223	38	.49777	.52536	42	.47464	.02313	4	.97687	28
33	.50261	37	.49739	.52578	42	.47422	.02317	4	.97683	27
34	.50298	38	.49702	.52620	41	.47380	.02321	5	.97679	26
35	9.50336	38	10.49664	9.52661	42	10.47339	10.02326	4	9.97674	25
36	.50374	37	.49626	.52703	42	.47297	.02330	4	.97670	24
37	.50411	38	.49589	.52745	42	.47255	.02334	4	.97666	23
38	.50449	37	.49551	.52787	42	.47213	.02338	5	.97662	22
39	.50486	37	.49514	.52829	41	.47171	.02343	4	.97657	21
40	9.50523	38	10.49477	9.52870	42	10.47130	10.02347	4	9.97653	20
41	.50561	37	.49439	.52912	41	.47088	.02351	4	.97649	19
42	.50598	37	.49402	.52953	42	.47047	.02355	5	.97645	18
43	.50635	38	.49365	.52995	42	.47005	.02360	4	.97640	17
44	.50673	37	.49327	.53037	41	.46963	.02364	4	.97636	16
45	9.50710	37	10.49290	9.53078	42	10.46922	10.02368	4	9.97632	15
46	.50747	37	.49253	.53120	41	.46880	.02372	5	.97628	14
47	.50784	37	.49216	.53161	41	.46839	.02377	4	.97623	13
48	.50821	37	.49179	.53202	42	.46798	.02381	4	.97619	12
49	.50858	38	.49142	.53244	41	.46756	.02385	5	.97615	11
50	9.50896	37	10.49104	9.53285	42	10.46715	10.02390	4	9.97610	10
51	.50933	37	.49067	.53327	41	.46673	.02394	4	.97606	9
52	.50970	37	.49030	.53368	41	.46632	.02398	5	.97602	8
53	.51007	36	.48993	.53409	41	.46591	.02403	4	.97597	7
54	.51043	37	.48957	.53450	42	.46550	.02407	4	.97593	6
55	9.51080	37	10.48920	9.53492	41	10.46508	10.02411	5	9.97589	5
56	.51117	37	.48883	.53533	41	.46467	.02416	4	.97584	4
57	.51154	37	.48846	.53574	41	.46426	.02420	4	.97580	3
58	.51191	36	.48809	.53615	41	.46385	.02424	5	.97576	2
59	.51227	37	.48773	.53656	41	.46344	.02429	4	.97571	1
60	9.51264		10.48736	9.53697		10.46303	10.02433		9.97567	0
↑ 108° →	cos	Diff. 1′	sec	cot	Diff. 1′	tan	csc	Diff. 1′	sin	← 71° ↑

TABLE 3

Common Logarithms of Trigonometric Functions (offset +10)

19° → ↓ ′	sin	Diff. 1′	csc	tan	Diff. 1′	cot	sec	Diff. 1′	cos	← 160° ↓ ′
0	9.51264	37	10.48736	9.53697	41	10.46303	10.02433	4	9.97567	60
1	.51301	37	.48699	.53738	41	.46262	.02437	5	.97563	59
2	.51338	36	.48662	.53779	41	.46221	.02442	4	.97558	58
3	.51374	37	.48626	.53820	41	.46180	.02446	4	.97554	57
4	.51411	36	.48589	.53861	41	.46139	.02450	5	.97550	56
5	9.51447	37	10.48553	9.53902	41	10.46098	10.02455	4	9.97545	55
6	.51484	36	.48516	.53943	41	.46057	.02459	5	.97541	54
7	.51520	37	.48480	.53984	41	.46016	.02464	4	.97536	53
8	.51557	36	.48443	.54025	40	.45975	.02468	4	.97532	52
9	.51593	36	.48407	.54065	41	.45935	.02472	5	.97528	51
10	9.51629	37	10.48371	9.54106	41	10.45894	10.02477	4	9.97523	50
11	.51666	36	.48334	.54147	40	.45853	.02481	4	.97519	49
12	.51702	36	.48298	.54187	41	.45813	.02485	5	.97515	48
13	.51738	36	.48262	.54228	41	.45772	.02490	4	.97510	47
14	.51774	37	.48226	.54269	40	.45731	.02494	5	.97506	46
15	9.51811	36	10.48189	9.54309	41	10.45691	10.02499	4	9.97501	45
16	.51847	36	.48153	.54350	40	.45650	.02503	5	.97497	44
17	.51883	36	.48117	.54390	41	.45610	.02508	4	.97492	43
18	.51919	36	.48081	.54431	40	.45569	.02512	4	.97488	42
19	.51955	36	.48045	.54471	41	.45529	.02516	5	.97484	41
20	9.51991	36	10.48009	9.54512	40	10.45488	10.02521	4	9.97479	40
21	.52027	36	.47973	.54552	41	.45448	.02525	5	.97475	39
22	.52063	36	.47937	.54593	40	.45407	.02530	4	.97470	38
23	.52099	36	.47901	.54633	40	.45367	.02534	5	.97466	37
24	.52135	36	.47865	.54673	41	.45327	.02539	4	.97461	36
25	9.52171	36	10.47829	9.54714	40	10.45286	10.02543	4	9.97457	35
26	.52207	35	.47793	.54754	40	.45246	.02547	5	.97453	34
27	.52242	36	.47758	.54794	41	.45206	.02552	4	.97448	33
28	.52278	36	.47722	.54835	40	.45165	.02556	5	.97444	32
29	.52314	36	.47686	.54875	40	.45125	.02561	4	.97439	31
30	9.52350	35	10.47650	9.54915	40	10.45085	10.02565	5	9.97435	30
31	.52385	36	.47615	.54955	40	.45045	.02570	4	.97430	29
32	.52421	35	.47579	.54995	40	.45005	.02574	5	.97426	28
33	.52456	36	.47544	.55035	40	.44965	.02579	4	.97421	27
34	.52492	35	.47508	.55075	40	.44925	.02583	5	.97417	26
35	9.52527	36	10.47473	9.55115	40	10.44885	10.02588	4	9.97412	25
36	.52563	35	.47437	.55155	40	.44845	.02592	5	.97408	24
37	.52598	36	.47402	.55195	40	.44805	.02597	4	.97403	23
38	.52634	35	.47366	.55235	40	.44765	.02601	5	.97399	22
39	.52669	36	.47331	.55275	40	.44725	.02606	4	.97394	21
40	9.52705	35	10.47295	9.55315	40	10.44685	10.02610	5	9.97390	20
41	.52740	35	.47260	.55355	40	.44645	.02615	4	.97385	19
42	.52775	36	.47225	.55395	39	.44605	.02619	5	.97381	18
43	.52811	35	.47189	.55434	40	.44566	.02624	4	.97376	17
44	.52846	35	.47154	.55474	40	.44526	.02628	5	.97372	16
45	9.52881	35	10.47119	9.55514	40	10.44486	10.02633	4	9.97367	15
46	.52916	35	.47084	.55554	39	.44446	.02637	5	.97363	14
47	.52951	35	.47049	.55593	40	.44407	.02642	5	.97358	13
48	.52986	35	.47014	.55633	40	.44367	.02647	4	.97353	12
49	.53021	35	.46979	.55673	39	.44327	.02651	5	.97349	11
50	9.53056	36	10.46944	9.55712	40	10.44288	10.02656	4	9.97344	10
51	.53092	34	.46908	.55752	39	.44248	.02660	5	.97340	9
52	.53126	35	.46874	.55791	40	.44209	.02665	4	.97335	8
53	.53161	35	.46839	.55831	39	.44169	.02669	5	.97331	7
54	.53196	35	.46804	.55870	40	.44130	.02674	4	.97326	6
55	9.53231	35	10.46769	9.55910	39	10.44090	10.02678	5	9.97322	5
56	.53266	35	.46734	.55949	40	.44051	.02683	5	.97317	4
57	.53301	35	.46699	.55989	39	.44011	.02688	4	.97312	3
58	.53336	34	.46664	.56028	39	.43972	.02692	5	.97308	2
59	.53370	35	.46630	.56067	40	.43933	.02697	4	.97303	1
60	9.53405		10.46595	9.56107		10.43893	10.02701		9.97299	0
↑ 109° →	cos	Diff. 1′	sec	cot	Diff. 1′	tan	csc	Diff. 1′	sin	← 70° ↑

TABLE 3

Common Logarithms of Trigonometric Functions (offset +10)

20° → ′	sin	Diff. 1′	csc	tan	Diff. 1′	cot	sec	Diff. 1′	cos	← 159° ′
0	9.53405	35	10.46595	9.56107	39	10.43893	10.02701	5	9.97299	60
1	.53440	35	.46560	.56146	39	.43854	.02706	5	.97294	59
2	.53475	34	.46525	.56185	39	.43815	.02711	4	.97289	58
3	.53509	35	.46491	.56224	40	.43776	.02715	5	.97285	57
4	.53544	34	.46456	.56264	39	.43736	.02720	4	.97280	56
5	9.53578	35	10.46422	9.56303	39	10.43697	10.02724	5	9.97276	55
6	.53613	34	.46387	.56342	39	.43658	.02729	5	.97271	54
7	.53647	35	.46353	.56381	39	.43619	.02734	4	.97266	53
8	.53682	34	.46318	.56420	39	.43580	.02738	5	.97262	52
9	.53716	35	.46284	.56459	39	.43541	.02743	5	.97257	51
10	9.53751	34	10.46249	9.56498	39	10.43502	10.02748	4	9.97252	50
11	.53785	34	.46215	.56537	39	.43463	.02752	5	.97248	49
12	.53819	35	.46181	.56576	39	.43424	.02757	5	.97243	48
13	.53854	34	.46146	.56615	39	.43385	.02762	4	.97238	47
14	.53888	34	.46112	.56654	39	.43346	.02766	5	.97234	46
15	9.53922	35	10.46078	9.56693	39	10.43307	10.02771	5	9.97229	45
16	.53957	34	.46043	.56732	39	.43268	.02776	4	.97224	44
17	.53991	34	.46009	.56771	39	.43229	.02780	5	.97220	43
18	.54025	34	.45975	.56810	39	.43190	.02785	5	.97215	42
19	.54059	34	.45941	.56849	38	.43151	.02790	4	.97210	41
20	9.54093	34	10.45907	9.56887	39	10.43113	10.02794	5	9.97206	40
21	.54127	34	.45873	.56926	39	.43074	.02799	5	.97201	39
22	.54161	34	.45839	.56965	39	.43035	.02804	4	.97196	38
23	.54195	34	.45805	.57004	38	.42996	.02808	5	.97192	37
24	.54229	34	.45771	.57042	39	.42958	.02813	5	.97187	36
25	9.54263	34	10.45737	9.57081	39	10.42919	10.02818	4	9.97182	35
26	.54297	34	.45703	.57120	38	.42880	.02822	5	.97178	34
27	.54331	34	.45669	.57158	39	.42842	.02827	5	.97173	33
28	.54365	34	.45635	.57197	38	.42803	.02832	5	.97168	32
29	.54399	34	.45601	.57235	39	.42765	.02837	4	.97163	31
30	9.54433	33	10.45567	9.57274	38	10.42726	10.02841	5	9.97159	30
31	.54466	34	.45534	.57312	39	.42688	.02846	5	.97154	29
32	.54500	34	.45500	.57351	38	.42649	.02851	4	.97149	28
33	.54534	33	.45466	.57389	39	.42611	.02855	5	.97145	27
34	.54567	34	.45433	.57428	38	.42572	.02860	5	.97140	26
35	9.54601	34	10.45399	9.57466	38	10.42534	10.02865	5	9.97135	25
36	.54635	33	.45365	.57504	39	.42496	.02870	4	.97130	24
37	.54668	34	.45332	.57543	38	.42457	.02874	5	.97126	23
38	.54702	33	.45298	.57581	38	.42419	.02879	5	.97121	22
39	.54735	34	.45265	.57619	39	.42381	.02884	5	.97116	21
40	9.54769	33	10.45231	9.57658	38	10.42342	10.02889	4	9.97111	20
41	.54802	34	.45198	.57696	38	.42304	.02893	5	.97107	19
42	.54836	33	.45164	.57734	38	.42266	.02898	5	.97102	18
43	.54869	34	.45131	.57772	38	.42228	.02903	5	.97097	17
44	.54903	33	.45097	.57810	39	.42190	.02908	5	.97092	16
45	9.54936	33	10.45064	9.57849	38	10.42151	10.02913	4	9.97087	15
46	.54969	34	.45031	.57887	38	.42113	.02917	5	.97083	14
47	.55003	33	.44997	.57925	38	.42075	.02922	5	.97078	13
48	.55036	33	.44964	.57963	38	.42037	.02927	5	.97073	12
49	.55069	33	.44931	.58001	38	.41999	.02932	5	.97068	11
50	9.55102	34	10.44898	9.58039	38	10.41961	10.02937	4	9.97063	10
51	.55136	33	.44864	.58077	38	.41923	.02941	5	.97059	9
52	.55169	33	.44831	.58115	38	.41885	.02946	5	.97054	8
53	.55202	33	.44798	.58153	38	.41847	.02951	5	.97049	7
54	.55235	33	.44765	.58191	38	.41809	.02956	5	.97044	6
55	9.55268	33	10.44732	9.58229	38	10.41771	10.02961	4	9.97039	5
56	.55301	33	.44699	.58267	37	.41733	.02965	5	.97035	4
57	.55334	33	.44666	.58304	38	.41696	.02970	5	.97030	3
58	.55367	33	.44633	.58342	38	.41658	.02975	5	.97025	2
59	.55400	33	.44600	.58380	38	.41620	.02980	5	.97020	1
60	9.55433		10.44567	9.58418		10.41582	10.02985		9.97015	0
↑ 110° →	cos	Diff. 1′	sec	cot	Diff. 1′	tan	csc	Diff. 1′	sin	← 69° ↑

TABLE 3

Common Logarithms of Trigonometric Functions (offset +10)

21° → ′	sin	Diff. 1′	csc	tan	Diff. 1′	cot	sec	Diff. 1′	cos	← 158° ′
0	9.55433	33	10.44567	9.58418	37	10.41582	10.02985	5	9.97015	60
1	.55466	33	.44534	.58455	38	.41545	.02990	5	.97010	59
2	.55499	33	.44501	.58493	38	.41507	.02995	4	.97005	58
3	.55532	32	.44468	.58531	38	.41469	.02999	5	.97001	57
4	.55564	33	.44436	.58569	37	.41431	.03004	5	.96996	56
5	9.55597	33	10.44403	9.58606	38	10.41394	10.03009	5	9.96991	55
6	.55630	33	.44370	.58644	37	.41356	.03014	5	.96986	54
7	.55663	32	.44337	.58681	38	.41319	.03019	5	.96981	53
8	.55695	33	.44305	.58719	38	.41281	.03024	5	.96976	52
9	.55728	33	.44272	.58757	37	.41243	.03029	5	.96971	51
10	9.55761	32	10.44239	9.58794	38	10.41206	10.03034	4	9.96966	50
11	.55793	33	.44207	.58832	37	.41168	.03038	5	.96962	49
12	.55826	32	.44174	.58869	38	.41131	.03043	5	.96957	48
13	.55858	33	.44142	.58907	37	.41093	.03048	5	.96952	47
14	.55891	32	.44109	.58944	37	.41056	.03053	5	.96947	46
15	9.55923	33	10.44077	9.58981	38	10.41019	10.03058	5	9.96942	45
16	.55956	32	.44044	.59019	37	.40981	.03063	5	.96937	44
17	.55988	33	.44012	.59056	38	.40944	.03068	5	.96932	43
18	.56021	32	.43979	.59094	37	.40906	.03073	5	.96927	42
19	.56053	32	.43947	.59131	37	.40869	.03078	5	.96922	41
20	9.56085	33	10.43915	9.59168	37	10.40832	10.03083	5	9.96917	40
21	.56118	32	.43882	.59205	38	.40795	.03088	5	.96912	39
22	.56150	32	.43850	.59243	37	.40757	.03093	4	.96907	38
23	.56182	33	.43818	.59280	37	.40720	.03097	5	.96903	37
24	.56215	32	.43785	.59317	37	.40683	.03102	5	.96898	36
25	9.56247	32	10.43753	9.59354	37	10.40646	10.03107	5	9.96893	35
26	.56279	32	.43721	.59391	38	.40609	.03112	5	.96888	34
27	.56311	32	.43689	.59429	37	.40571	.03117	5	.96883	33
28	.56343	32	.43657	.59466	37	.40534	.03122	5	.96878	32
29	.56375	33	.43625	.59503	37	.40497	.03127	5	.96873	31
30	9.56408	32	10.43592	9.59540	37	10.40460	10.03132	5	9.96868	30
31	.56440	32	.43560	.59577	37	.40423	.03137	5	.96863	29
32	.56472	32	.43528	.59614	37	.40386	.03142	5	.96858	28
33	.56504	32	.43496	.59651	37	.40349	.03147	5	.96853	27
34	.56536	32	.43464	.59688	37	.40312	.03152	5	.96848	26
35	9.56568	31	10.43432	9.59725	37	10.40275	10.03157	5	9.96843	25
36	.56599	32	.43401	.59762	37	.40238	.03162	5	.96838	24
37	.56631	32	.43369	.59799	36	.40201	.03167	5	.96833	23
38	.56663	32	.43337	.59835	37	.40165	.03172	5	.96828	22
39	.56695	32	.43305	.59872	37	.40128	.03177	5	.96823	21
40	9.56727	32	10.43273	9.59909	37	10.40091	10.03182	5	9.96818	20
41	.56759	31	.43241	.59946	37	.40054	.03187	5	.96813	19
42	.56790	32	.43210	.59983	36	.40017	.03192	5	.96808	18
43	.56822	32	.43178	.60019	37	.39981	.03197	5	.96803	17
44	.56854	32	.43146	.60056	37	.39944	.03202	5	.96798	16
45	9.56886	31	10.43114	9.60093	37	10.39907	10.03207	5	9.96793	15
46	.56917	32	.43083	.60130	36	.39870	.03212	5	.96788	14
47	.56949	31	.43051	.60166	37	.39834	.03217	5	.96783	13
48	.56980	32	.43020	.60203	37	.39797	.03222	6	.96778	12
49	.57012	32	.42988	.60240	36	.39760	.03228	5	.96772	11
50	9.57044	31	10.42956	9.60276	37	10.39724	10.03233	5	9.96767	10
51	.57075	32	.42925	.60313	36	.39687	.03238	5	.96762	9
52	.57107	31	.42893	.60349	37	.39651	.03243	5	.96757	8
53	.57138	31	.42862	.60386	36	.39614	.03248	5	.96752	7
54	.57169	32	.42831	.60422	37	.39578	.03253	5	.96747	6
55	9.57201	31	10.42799	9.60459	36	10.39541	10.03258	5	9.96742	5
56	.57232	32	.42768	.60495	37	.39505	.03263	5	.96737	4
57	.57264	31	.42736	.60532	36	.39468	.03268	5	.96732	3
58	.57295	31	.42705	.60568	37	.39432	.03273	5	.96727	2
59	.57326	32	.42674	.60605	36	.39395	.03278	5	.96722	1
60	9.57358		10.42642	9.60641		10.39359	10.03283		9.96717	0
↑ 111° →	cos	Diff. 1′	sec	cot	Diff. 1′	tan	csc	Diff. 1′	sin	← 68° ↑

TABLE 3
Common Logarithms of Trigonometric Functions (offset +10)

22°→ ′ ↓	sin	Diff. 1′	csc	tan	Diff. 1′	cot	sec	Diff. 1′	cos	←157° ′ ↓
0	9.57358	31	10.42642	9.60641	36	10.39359	10.03283	6	9.96717	60
1	.57389	31	.42611	.60677	37	.39323	.03289	5	.96711	59
2	.57420	31	.42580	.60714	36	.39286	.03294	5	.96706	58
3	.57451	31	.42549	.60750	36	.39250	.03299	5	.96701	57
4	.57482	32	.42518	.60786	37	.39214	.03304	5	.96696	56
5	9.57514	31	10.42486	9.60823	36	10.39177	10.03309	5	9.96691	55
6	.57545	31	.42455	.60859	36	.39141	.03314	5	.96686	54
7	.57576	31	.42424	.60895	36	.39105	.03319	5	.96681	53
8	.57607	31	.42393	.60931	36	.39069	.03324	6	.96676	52
9	.57638	31	.42362	.60967	37	.39033	.03330	5	.96670	51
10	9.57669	31	10.42331	9.61004	36	10.38996	10.03335	5	9.96665	50
11	.57700	31	.42300	.61040	36	.38960	.03340	5	.96660	49
12	.57731	31	.42269	.61076	36	.38924	.03345	5	.96655	48
13	.57762	31	.42238	.61112	36	.38888	.03350	5	.96650	47
14	.57793	31	.42207	.61148	36	.38852	.03355	5	.96645	46
15	9.57824	31	10.42176	9.61184	36	10.38816	10.03360	6	9.96640	45
16	.57855	30	.42145	.61220	36	.38780	.03366	5	.96634	44
17	.57885	31	.42115	.61256	36	.38744	.03371	5	.96629	43
18	.57916	31	.42084	.61292	36	.38708	.03376	5	.96624	42
19	.57947	31	.42053	.61328	36	.38672	.03381	5	.96619	41
20	9.57978	30	10.42022	9.61364	36	10.38636	10.03386	6	9.96614	40
21	.58008	31	.41992	.61400	36	.38600	.03392	5	.96608	39
22	.58039	31	.41961	.61436	36	.38564	.03397	5	.96603	38
23	.58070	31	.41930	.61472	36	.38528	.03402	5	.96598	37
24	.58101	30	.41899	.61508	36	.38492	.03407	5	.96593	36
25	9.58131	31	10.41869	9.61544	35	10.38456	10.03412	6	9.96588	35
26	.58162	30	.41838	.61579	36	.38421	.03418	5	.96582	34
27	.58192	31	.41808	.61615	36	.38385	.03423	5	.96577	33
28	.58223	30	.41777	.61651	36	.38349	.03428	5	.96572	32
29	.58253	31	.41747	.61687	35	.38313	.03433	5	.96567	31
30	9.58284	30	10.41716	9.61722	36	10.38278	10.03438	6	9.96562	30
31	.58314	31	.41686	.61758	36	.38242	.03444	5	.96556	29
32	.58345	30	.41655	.61794	36	.38206	.03449	5	.96551	28
33	.58375	31	.41625	.61830	35	.38170	.03454	5	.96546	27
34	.58406	30	.41594	.61865	36	.38135	.03459	6	.96541	26
35	9.58436	31	10.41564	9.61901	35	10.38099	10.03465	5	9.96535	25
36	.58467	30	.41533	.61936	36	.38064	.03470	5	.96530	24
37	.58497	30	.41503	.61972	36	.38028	.03475	5	.96525	23
38	.58527	30	.41473	.62008	35	.37992	.03480	6	.96520	22
39	.58557	31	.41443	.62043	36	.37957	.03486	5	.96514	21
40	9.58588	30	10.41412	9.62079	35	10.37921	10.03491	5	9.96509	20
41	.58618	30	.41382	.62114	36	.37886	.03496	6	.96504	19
42	.58648	30	.41352	.62150	35	.37850	.03502	5	.96498	18
43	.58678	31	.41322	.62185	36	.37815	.03507	5	.96493	17
44	.58709	30	.41291	.62221	35	.37779	.03512	5	.96488	16
45	9.58739	30	10.41261	9.62256	36	10.37744	10.03517	6	9.96483	15
46	.58769	30	.41231	.62292	35	.37708	.03523	5	.96477	14
47	.58799	30	.41201	.62327	35	.37673	.03528	5	.96472	13
48	.58829	30	.41171	.62362	36	.37638	.03533	6	.96467	12
49	.58859	30	.41141	.62398	35	.37602	.03539	5	.96461	11
50	9.58889	30	10.41111	9.62433	35	10.37567	10.03544	5	9.96456	10
51	.58919	30	.41081	.62468	36	.37532	.03549	6	.96451	9
52	.58949	30	.41051	.62504	35	.37496	.03555	5	.96445	8
53	.58979	30	.41021	.62539	35	.37461	.03560	5	.96440	7
54	.59009	30	.40991	.62574	35	.37426	.03565	6	.96435	6
55	9.59039	30	10.40961	9.62609	36	10.37391	10.03571	5	9.96429	5
56	.59069	29	.40931	.62645	35	.37355	.03576	5	.96424	4
57	.59098	30	.40902	.62680	35	.37320	.03581	6	.96419	3
58	.59128	30	.40872	.62715	35	.37285	.03587	5	.96413	2
59	.59158	30	.40842	.62750	35	.37250	.03592	5	.96408	1
60	9.59188		10.40812	9.62785		10.37215	10.03597		9.96403	0
↑ 112°→	cos	Diff. 1′	sec	cot	Diff. 1′	tan	csc	Diff. 1′	sin	← 67° ↑

TABLE 3
Common Logarithms of Trigonometric Functions (offset +10)

23°→ ′ ↓	sin	Diff. 1′	csc	tan	Diff. 1′	cot	sec	Diff. 1′	cos	←156° ′ ↓
0	9.59188	30	10.40812	9.62785	35	10.37215	10.03597	6	9.96403	60
1	.59218	29	.40782	.62820	35	.37180	.03603	5	.96397	59
2	.59247	30	.40753	.62855	35	.37145	.03608	5	.96392	58
3	.59277	30	.40723	.62890	36	.37110	.03613	6	.96387	57
4	.59307	29	.40693	.62926	35	.37074	.03619	5	.96381	56
5	9.59336	30	10.40664	9.62961	35	10.37039	10.03624	6	9.96376	55
6	.59366	30	.40634	.62996	35	.37004	.03630	5	.96370	54
7	.59396	29	.40604	.63031	35	.36969	.03635	5	.96365	53
8	.59425	30	.40575	.63066	35	.36934	.03640	6	.96360	52
9	.59455	29	.40545	.63101	34	.36899	.03646	5	.96354	51
10	9.59484	30	10.40516	9.63135	35	10.36865	10.03651	6	9.96349	50
11	.59514	29	.40486	.63170	35	.36830	.03657	5	.96343	49
12	.59543	30	.40457	.63205	35	.36795	.03662	5	.96338	48
13	.59573	29	.40427	.63240	35	.36760	.03667	6	.96333	47
14	.59602	30	.40398	.63275	35	.36725	.03673	5	.96327	46
15	9.59632	29	10.40368	9.63310	35	10.36690	10.03678	6	9.96322	45
16	.59661	29	.40339	.63345	34	.36655	.03684	5	.96316	44
17	.59690	30	.40310	.63379	35	.36621	.03689	6	.96311	43
18	.59720	29	.40280	.63414	35	.36586	.03695	5	.96305	42
19	.59749	29	.40251	.63449	35	.36551	.03700	6	.96300	41
20	9.59778	30	10.40222	9.63484	35	10.36516	10.03706	5	9.96294	40
21	.59808	29	.40192	.63519	34	.36481	.03711	5	.96289	39
22	.59837	29	.40163	.63553	35	.36447	.03716	6	.96284	38
23	.59866	29	.40134	.63588	35	.36412	.03722	5	.96278	37
24	.59895	29	.40105	.63623	34	.36377	.03727	6	.96273	36
25	9.59924	30	10.40076	9.63657	35	10.36343	10.03733	5	9.96267	35
26	.59954	29	.40046	.63692	34	.36308	.03738	6	.96262	34
27	.59983	29	.40017	.63726	35	.36274	.03744	5	.96256	33
28	.60012	29	.39988	.63761	35	.36239	.03749	6	.96251	32
29	.60041	29	.39959	.63796	34	.36204	.03755	5	.96245	31
30	9.60070	29	10.39930	9.63830	35	10.36170	10.03760	6	9.96240	30
31	.60099	29	.39901	.63865	34	.36135	.03766	5	.96234	29
32	.60128	29	.39872	.63899	35	.36101	.03771	6	.96229	28
33	.60157	29	.39843	.63934	34	.36066	.03777	5	.96223	27
34	.60186	29	.39814	.63968	35	.36032	.03782	6	.96218	26
35	9.60215	29	10.39785	9.64003	34	10.35997	10.03788	5	9.96212	25
36	.60244	29	.39756	.64037	35	.35963	.03793	6	.96207	24
37	.60273	29	.39727	.64072	34	.35928	.03799	5	.96201	23
38	.60302	29	.39698	.64106	34	.35894	.03804	6	.96196	22
39	.60331	28	.39669	.64140	35	.35860	.03810	5	.96190	21
40	9.60359	29	10.39641	9.64175	34	10.35825	10.03815	6	9.96185	20
41	.60388	29	.39612	.64209	34	.35791	.03821	5	.96179	19
42	.60417	29	.39583	.64243	35	.35757	.03826	6	.96174	18
43	.60446	28	.39554	.64278	34	.35722	.03832	6	.96168	17
44	.60474	29	.39526	.64312	34	.35688	.03838	5	.96162	16
45	9.60503	29	10.39497	9.64346	35	10.35654	10.03843	6	9.96157	15
46	.60532	29	.39468	.64381	34	.35619	.03849	5	.96151	14
47	.60561	28	.39439	.64415	34	.35585	.03854	6	.96146	13
48	.60589	29	.39411	.64449	34	.35551	.03860	5	.96140	12
49	.60618	28	.39382	.64483	34	.35517	.03865	6	.96135	11
50	9.60646	29	10.39354	9.64517	35	10.35483	10.03871	6	9.96129	10
51	.60675	29	.39325	.64552	34	.35448	.03877	5	.96123	9
52	.60704	28	.39296	.64586	34	.35414	.03882	6	.96118	8
53	.60732	29	.39268	.64620	34	.35380	.03888	5	.96112	7
54	.60761	28	.39239	.64654	34	.35346	.03893	6	.96107	6
55	9.60789	29	10.39211	9.64688	34	10.35312	10.03899	6	9.96101	5
56	.60818	28	.39182	.64722	34	.35278	.03905	5	.96095	4
57	.60846	29	.39154	.64756	34	.35244	.03910	6	.96090	3
58	.60875	28	.39125	.64790	34	.35210	.03916	5	.96084	2
59	.60903	28	.39097	.64824	34	.35176	.03921	6	.96079	1
60	9.60931		10.39069	9.64858		10.35142	10.03927		9.96073	0
↑ 113°→	cos	Diff. 1′	sec	cot	Diff. 1′	tan	csc	Diff. 1′	sin	← 66° ↑

TABLE 3

Common Logarithms of Trigonometric Functions (offset +10)

24° → ↓	sin	Diff. 1′	csc	tan	Diff. 1′	cot	sec	Diff. 1′	cos	← 155° ↓
′										′
0	9.60931	29	10.39069	9.64858	34	10.35142	10.03927	6	9.96073	60
1	.60960	28	.39040	.64892	34	.35108	.03933	5	.96067	59
2	.60988	28	.39012	.64926	34	.35074	.03938	6	.96062	58
3	.61016	29	.38984	.64960	34	.35040	.03944	6	.96056	57
4	.61045	28	.38955	.64994	34	.35006	.03950	5	.96050	56
5	9.61073	28	10.38927	9.65028	34	10.34972	10.03955	6	9.96045	55
6	.61101	28	.38899	.65062	34	.34938	.03961	5	.96039	54
7	.61129	29	.38871	.65096	34	.34904	.03966	6	.96034	53
8	.61158	28	.38842	.65130	34	.34870	.03972	6	.96028	52
9	.61186	28	.38814	.65164	33	.34836	.03978	5	.96022	51
10	9.61214	28	10.38786	9.65197	34	10.34803	10.03983	6	9.96017	50
11	.61242	28	.38758	.65231	34	.34769	.03989	6	.96011	49
12	.61270	28	.38730	.65265	34	.34735	.03995	5	.96005	48
13	.61298	28	.38702	.65299	34	.34701	.04000	6	.96000	47
14	.61326	28	.38674	.65333	33	.34667	.04006	6	.95994	46
15	9.61354	28	10.38646	9.65366	34	10.34634	10.04012	6	9.95988	45
16	.61382	29	.38618	.65400	34	.34600	.04018	5	.95982	44
17	.61411	27	.38589	.65434	33	.34566	.04023	6	.95977	43
18	.61438	28	.38562	.65467	34	.34533	.04029	6	.95971	42
19	.61466	28	.38534	.65501	34	.34499	.04035	5	.95965	41
20	9.61494	28	10.38506	9.65535	33	10.34465	10.04040	6	9.95960	40
21	.61522	28	.38478	.65568	34	.34432	.04046	6	.95954	39
22	.61550	28	.38450	.65602	34	.34398	.04052	6	.95948	38
23	.61578	28	.38422	.65636	33	.34364	.04058	5	.95942	37
24	.61606	28	.38394	.65669	34	.34331	.04063	6	.95937	36
25	9.61634	28	10.38366	9.65703	33	10.34297	10.04069	6	9.95931	35
26	.61662	27	.38338	.65736	34	.34264	.04075	5	.95925	34
27	.61689	28	.38311	.65770	33	.34230	.04080	6	.95920	33
28	.61717	28	.38283	.65803	34	.34197	.04086	6	.95914	32
29	.61745	28	.38255	.65837	33	.34163	.04092	6	.95908	31
30	9.61773	27	10.38227	9.65870	34	10.34130	10.04098	5	9.95902	30
31	.61800	28	.38200	.65904	33	.34096	.04103	6	.95897	29
32	.61828	28	.38172	.65937	34	.34063	.04109	6	.95891	28
33	.61856	27	.38144	.65971	33	.34029	.04115	6	.95885	27
34	.61883	28	.38117	.66004	34	.33996	.04121	6	.95879	26
35	9.61911	28	10.38089	9.66038	33	10.33962	10.04127	5	9.95873	25
36	.61939	27	.38061	.66071	33	.33929	.04132	6	.95868	24
37	.61966	28	.38034	.66104	34	.33896	.04138	6	.95862	23
38	.61994	27	.38006	.66138	33	.33862	.04144	6	.95856	22
39	.62021	28	.37979	.66171	33	.33829	.04150	6	.95850	21
40	9.62049	27	10.37951	9.66204	34	10.33796	10.04156	5	9.95844	20
41	.62076	28	.37924	.66238	33	.33762	.04161	6	.95839	19
42	.62104	27	.37896	.66271	33	.33729	.04167	6	.95833	18
43	.62131	28	.37869	.66304	33	.33696	.04173	6	.95827	17
44	.62159	27	.37841	.66337	34	.33663	.04179	6	.95821	16
45	9.62186	28	10.37814	9.66371	33	10.33629	10.04185	5	9.95815	15
46	.62214	27	.37786	.66404	33	.33596	.04190	6	.95810	14
47	.62241	27	.37759	.66437	33	.33563	.04196	6	.95804	13
48	.62268	28	.37732	.66470	33	.33530	.04202	6	.95798	12
49	.62296	27	.37704	.66503	34	.33497	.04208	6	.95792	11
50	9.62323	27	10.37677	9.66537	33	10.33463	10.04214	6	9.95786	10
51	.62350	27	.37650	.66570	33	.33430	.04220	5	.95780	9
52	.62377	28	.37623	.66603	33	.33397	.04225	6	.95775	8
53	.62405	27	.37595	.66636	33	.33364	.04231	6	.95769	7
54	.62432	27	.37568	.66669	33	.33331	.04237	6	.95763	6
55	9.62459	27	10.37541	9.66702	33	10.33298	10.04243	6	9.95757	5
56	.62486	27	.37514	.66735	33	.33265	.04249	6	.95751	4
57	.62513	28	.37487	.66768	33	.33232	.04255	6	.95745	3
58	.62541	27	.37459	.66801	33	.33199	.04261	6	.95739	2
59	.62568	27	.37432	.66834	33	.33166	.04267	5	.95733	1
60	9.62595		10.37405	9.66867		10.33133	10.04272		9.95728	0
↑ 114° →	cos	Diff. 1′	sec	cot	Diff. 1′	tan	csc	Diff. 1′	sin	← 65° ↑

TABLE 3

Common Logarithms of Trigonometric Functions (offset +10)

25° → ↓	sin	Diff. 1′	csc	tan	Diff. 1′	cot	sec	Diff. 1′	cos	← 154° ↓
′										′
0	9.62595	27	10.37405	9.66867	33	10.33133	10.04272	6	9.95728	60
1	.62622	27	.37378	.66900	33	.33100	.04278	6	.95722	59
2	.62649	27	.37351	.66933	33	.33067	.04284	6	.95716	58
3	.62676	27	.37324	.66966	33	.33034	.04290	6	.95710	57
4	.62703	27	.37297	.66999	33	.33001	.04296	6	.95704	56
5	9.62730	27	10.37270	9.67032	33	10.32968	10.04302	6	9.95698	55
6	.62757	27	.37243	.67065	33	.32935	.04308	6	.95692	54
7	.62784	27	.37216	.67098	33	.32902	.04314	6	.95686	53
8	.62811	27	.37189	.67131	32	.32869	.04320	6	.95680	52
9	.62838	27	.37162	.67163	33	.32837	.04326	6	.95674	51
10	9.62865	27	10.37135	9.67196	33	10.32804	10.04332	5	9.95668	50
11	.62892	26	.37108	.67229	33	.32771	.04337	6	.95663	49
12	.62918	27	.37082	.67262	33	.32738	.04343	6	.95657	48
13	.62945	27	.37055	.67295	32	.32705	.04349	6	.95651	47
14	.62972	27	.37028	.67327	33	.32673	.04355	6	.95645	46
15	9.62999	27	10.37001	9.67360	33	10.32640	10.04361	6	9.95639	45
16	.63026	26	.36974	.67393	33	.32607	.04367	6	.95633	44
17	.63052	27	.36948	.67426	32	.32574	.04373	6	.95627	43
18	.63079	27	.36921	.67458	33	.32542	.04379	6	.95621	42
19	.63106	27	.36894	.67491	33	.32509	.04385	6	.95615	41
20	9.63133	26	10.36867	9.67524	32	10.32476	10.04391	6	9.95609	40
21	.63159	27	.36841	.67556	33	.32444	.04397	6	.95603	39
22	.63186	27	.36814	.67589	33	.32411	.04403	6	.95597	38
23	.63213	26	.36787	.67622	32	.32378	.04409	6	.95591	37
24	.63239	27	.36761	.67654	33	.32346	.04415	6	.95585	36
25	9.63266	26	10.36734	9.67687	32	10.32313	10.04421	6	9.95579	35
26	.63292	27	.36708	.67719	33	.32281	.04427	6	.95573	34
27	.63319	26	.36681	.67752	33	.32248	.04433	6	.95567	33
28	.63345	27	.36655	.67785	32	.32215	.04439	6	.95561	32
29	.63372	26	.36628	.67817	33	.32183	.04445	6	.95555	31
30	9.63398	27	10.36602	9.67850	32	10.32150	10.04451	6	9.95549	30
31	.63425	26	.36575	.67882	33	.32118	.04457	6	.95543	29
32	.63451	27	.36549	.67915	32	.32085	.04463	6	.95537	28
33	.63478	26	.36522	.67947	33	.32053	.04469	6	.95531	27
34	.63504	27	.36496	.67980	32	.32020	.04475	6	.95525	26
35	9.63531	26	10.36469	9.68012	32	10.31988	10.04481	6	9.95519	25
36	.63557	26	.36443	.68044	33	.31956	.04487	6	.95513	24
37	.63583	27	.36417	.68077	32	.31923	.04493	7	.95507	23
38	.63610	26	.36390	.68109	33	.31891	.04500	6	.95500	22
39	.63636	26	.36364	.68142	32	.31858	.04506	6	.95494	21
40	9.63662	27	10.36338	9.68174	32	10.31826	10.04512	6	9.95488	20
41	.63689	26	.36311	.68206	33	.31794	.04518	6	.95482	19
42	.63715	26	.36285	.68239	32	.31761	.04524	6	.95476	18
43	.63741	26	.36259	.68271	32	.31729	.04530	6	.95470	17
44	.63767	27	.36233	.68303	33	.31697	.04536	6	.95464	16
45	9.63794	26	10.36206	9.68336	32	10.31664	10.04542	6	9.95458	15
46	.63820	26	.36180	.68368	32	.31632	.04548	6	.95452	14
47	.63846	26	.36154	.68400	32	.31600	.04554	6	.95446	13
48	.63872	26	.36128	.68432	33	.31568	.04560	6	.95440	12
49	.63898	26	.36102	.68465	32	.31535	.04566	7	.95434	11
50	9.63924	26	10.36076	9.68497	32	10.31503	10.04573	6	9.95427	10
51	.63950	26	.36050	.68529	32	.31471	.04579	6	.95421	9
52	.63976	26	.36024	.68561	32	.31439	.04585	6	.95415	8
53	.64002	26	.35998	.68593	33	.31407	.04591	6	.95409	7
54	.64028	26	.35972	.68626	32	.31374	.04597	6	.95403	6
55	9.64054	26	10.35946	9.68658	32	10.31342	10.04603	6	9.95397	5
56	.64080	26	.35920	.68690	32	.31310	.04609	7	.95391	4
57	.64106	26	.35894	.68722	32	.31278	.04616	6	.95384	3
58	.64132	26	.35868	.68754	32	.31246	.04622	6	.95378	2
59	.64158	26	.35842	.68786	32	.31214	.04628	6	.95372	1
60	9.64184		10.35816	9.68818		10.31182	10.04634		9.95366	0
↑ 115° →	cos	Diff. 1′	sec	cot	Diff. 1′	tan	csc	Diff. 1′	sin	← 64° ↑

TABLE 3

Common Logarithms of Trigonometric Functions (offset +10)

26°→ ↓ ′	sin	Diff. 1′	csc	tan	Diff. 1′	cot	sec	Diff. 1′	cos ←153°	↓ ′
0	9.64184	26	10.35816	9.68818	32	10.31182	10.04634	6	9.95366	60
1	.64210	26	.35790	.68850	32	.31150	.04640	6	.95360	59
2	.64236	26	.35764	.68882	32	.31118	.04646	6	.95354	58
3	.64262	26	.35738	.68914	32	.31086	.04652	7	.95348	57
4	.64288	25	.35712	.68946	32	.31054	.04659	6	.95341	56
5	9.64313	26	10.35687	9.68978	32	10.31022	10.04665	6	9.95335	55
6	.64339	26	.35661	.69010	32	.30990	.04671	6	.95329	54
7	.64365	26	.35635	.69042	32	.30958	.04677	6	.95323	53
8	.64391	26	.35609	.69074	32	.30926	.04683	7	.95317	52
9	.64417	25	.35583	.69106	32	.30894	.04690	6	.95310	51
10	9.64442	26	10.35558	9.69138	32	10.30862	10.04696	6	9.95304	50
11	.64468	26	.35532	.69170	32	.30830	.04702	6	.95298	49
12	.64494	25	.35506	.69202	32	.30798	.04708	6	.95292	48
13	.64519	26	.35481	.69234	32	.30766	.04714	7	.95286	47
14	.64545	26	.35455	.69266	32	.30734	.04721	6	.95279	46
15	9.64571	25	10.35429	9.69298	31	10.30702	10.04727	6	9.95273	45
16	.64596	26	.35404	.69329	32	.30671	.04733	6	.95267	44
17	.64622	25	.35378	.69361	32	.30639	.04739	7	.95261	43
18	.64647	26	.35353	.69393	32	.30607	.04746	6	.95254	42
19	.64673	25	.35327	.69425	32	.30575	.04752	6	.95248	41
20	9.64698	26	10.35302	9.69457	31	10.30543	10.04758	6	9.95242	40
21	.64724	25	.35276	.69488	32	.30512	.04764	7	.95236	39
22	.64749	26	.35251	.69520	32	.30480	.04771	6	.95229	38
23	.64775	25	.35225	.69552	32	.30448	.04777	6	.95223	37
24	.64800	26	.35200	.69584	31	.30416	.04783	6	.95217	36
25	9.64826	25	10.35174	9.69615	32	10.30385	10.04789	7	9.95211	35
26	.64851	26	.35149	.69647	32	.30353	.04796	6	.95204	34
27	.64877	25	.35123	.69679	31	.30321	.04802	6	.95198	33
28	.64902	25	.35098	.69710	32	.30290	.04808	7	.95192	32
29	.64927	26	.35073	.69742	32	.30258	.04815	6	.95185	31
30	9.64953	25	10.35047	9.69774	31	10.30226	10.04821	6	9.95179	30
31	.64978	25	.35022	.69805	32	.30195	.04827	6	.95173	29
32	.65003	26	.34997	.69837	31	.30163	.04833	7	.95167	28
33	.65029	25	.34971	.69868	32	.30132	.04840	6	.95160	27
34	.65054	25	.34946	.69900	32	.30100	.04846	6	.95154	26
35	9.65079	25	10.34921	9.69932	31	10.30068	10.04852	7	9.95148	25
36	.65104	26	.34896	.69963	32	.30037	.04859	6	.95141	24
37	.65130	25	.34870	.69995	31	.30005	.04865	6	.95135	23
38	.65155	25	.34845	.70026	32	.29974	.04871	7	.95129	22
39	.65180	25	.34820	.70058	31	.29942	.04878	6	.95122	21
40	9.65205	25	10.34795	9.70089	32	10.29911	10.04884	6	9.95116	20
41	.65230	25	.34770	.70121	31	.29879	.04890	7	.95110	19
42	.65255	26	.34745	.70152	32	.29848	.04897	6	.95103	18
43	.65281	25	.34719	.70184	31	.29816	.04903	7	.95097	17
44	.65306	25	.34694	.70215	32	.29785	.04910	6	.95090	16
45	9.65331	25	10.34669	9.70247	31	10.29753	10.04916	6	9.95084	15
46	.65356	25	.34644	.70278	31	.29722	.04922	7	.95078	14
47	.65381	25	.34619	.70309	32	.29691	.04929	6	.95071	13
48	.65406	25	.34594	.70341	31	.29659	.04935	6	.95065	12
49	.65431	25	.34569	.70372	32	.29628	.04941	7	.95059	11
50	9.65456	25	10.34544	9.70404	31	10.29596	10.04948	6	9.95052	10
51	.65481	25	.34519	.70435	31	.29565	.04954	7	.95046	9
52	.65506	25	.34494	.70466	32	.29534	.04961	6	.95039	8
53	.65531	25	.34469	.70498	31	.29502	.04967	6	.95033	7
54	.65556	24	.34444	.70529	31	.29471	.04973	7	.95027	6
55	9.65580	25	10.34420	9.70560	32	10.29440	10.04980	6	9.95020	5
56	.65605	25	.34395	.70592	31	.29408	.04986	7	.95014	4
57	.65630	25	.34370	.70623	31	.29377	.04993	6	.95007	3
58	.65655	25	.34345	.70654	31	.29346	.04999	6	.95001	2
59	.65680	25	.34320	.70685	32	.29315	.05005	7	.94995	1
60	9.65705		10.34295	9.70717		10.29283	10.05012		9.94988	0
↑ 116°→	cos	Diff. 1′	sec	cot	Diff. 1′	tan	csc	Diff. 1′	sin ←	↑ 63°

TABLE 3

Common Logarithms of Trigonometric Functions (offset +10)

27°→ ↓ ′	sin	Diff. 1′	csc	tan	Diff. 1′	cot	sec	Diff. 1′	cos ←152°	↓ ′
0	9.65705	24	10.34295	9.70717	31	10.29283	10.05012	6	9.94988	60
1	.65729	25	.34271	.70748	31	.29252	.05018	7	.94982	59
2	.65754	25	.34246	.70779	31	.29221	.05025	6	.94975	58
3	.65779	25	.34221	.70810	31	.29190	.05031	7	.94969	57
4	.65804	24	.34196	.70841	32	.29159	.05038	6	.94962	56
5	9.65828	25	10.34172	9.70873	31	10.29127	10.05044	7	9.94956	55
6	.65853	25	.34147	.70904	31	.29096	.05051	6	.94949	54
7	.65878	24	.34122	.70935	31	.29065	.05057	7	.94943	53
8	.65902	25	.34098	.70966	31	.29034	.05064	6	.94936	52
9	.65927	25	.34073	.70997	31	.29003	.05070	7	.94930	51
10	9.65952	24	10.34048	9.71028	31	10.28972	10.05077	6	9.94923	50
11	.65976	25	.34024	.71059	31	.28941	.05083	6	.94917	49
12	.66001	24	.33999	.71090	31	.28910	.05089	7	.94911	48
13	.66025	25	.33975	.71121	32	.28879	.05096	6	.94904	47
14	.66050	25	.33950	.71153	31	.28847	.05102	7	.94898	46
15	9.66075	24	10.33925	9.71184	31	10.28816	10.05109	6	9.94891	45
16	.66099	25	.33901	.71215	31	.28785	.05115	7	.94885	44
17	.66124	24	.33876	.71246	31	.28754	.05122	7	.94878	43
18	.66148	25	.33852	.71277	31	.28723	.05129	6	.94871	42
19	.66173	24	.33827	.71308	31	.28692	.05135	7	.94865	41
20	9.66197	24	10.33803	9.71339	31	10.28661	10.05142	6	9.94858	40
21	.66221	25	.33779	.71370	31	.28630	.05148	7	.94852	39
22	.66246	24	.33754	.71401	30	.28599	.05155	6	.94845	38
23	.66270	25	.33730	.71431	31	.28569	.05161	7	.94839	37
24	.66295	24	.33705	.71462	31	.28538	.05168	6	.94832	36
25	9.66319	24	10.33681	9.71493	31	10.28507	10.05174	7	9.94826	35
26	.66343	25	.33657	.71524	31	.28476	.05181	6	.94819	34
27	.66368	24	.33632	.71555	31	.28445	.05187	7	.94813	33
28	.66392	24	.33608	.71586	31	.28414	.05194	7	.94806	32
29	.66416	25	.33584	.71617	31	.28383	.05201	6	.94799	31
30	9.66441	24	10.33559	9.71648	31	10.28352	10.05207	7	9.94793	30
31	.66465	24	.33535	.71679	30	.28321	.05214	6	.94786	29
32	.66489	24	.33511	.71709	31	.28291	.05220	7	.94780	28
33	.66513	24	.33487	.71740	31	.28260	.05227	6	.94773	27
34	.66537	25	.33463	.71771	31	.28229	.05233	7	.94767	26
35	9.66562	24	10.33438	9.71802	31	10.28198	10.05240	7	9.94760	25
36	.66586	24	.33414	.71833	30	.28167	.05247	6	.94753	24
37	.66610	24	.33390	.71863	31	.28137	.05253	7	.94747	23
38	.66634	24	.33366	.71894	31	.28106	.05260	6	.94740	22
39	.66658	24	.33342	.71925	30	.28075	.05266	7	.94734	21
40	9.66682	24	10.33318	9.71955	31	10.28045	10.05273	7	9.94727	20
41	.66706	25	.33294	.71986	31	.28014	.05280	6	.94720	19
42	.66731	24	.33269	.72017	31	.27983	.05286	7	.94714	18
43	.66755	24	.33245	.72048	30	.27952	.05293	7	.94707	17
44	.66779	24	.33221	.72078	31	.27922	.05300	6	.94700	16
45	9.66803	24	10.33197	9.72109	31	10.27891	10.05306	7	9.94694	15
46	.66827	24	.33173	.72140	30	.27860	.05313	7	.94687	14
47	.66851	24	.33149	.72170	31	.27830	.05320	6	.94680	13
48	.66875	24	.33125	.72201	30	.27799	.05326	7	.94674	12
49	.66899	23	.33101	.72231	31	.27769	.05333	7	.94667	11
50	9.66922	24	10.33078	9.72262	31	10.27738	10.05340	6	9.94660	10
51	.66946	24	.33054	.72293	30	.27707	.05346	7	.94654	9
52	.66970	24	.33030	.72323	31	.27677	.05353	7	.94647	8
53	.66994	24	.33006	.72354	30	.27646	.05360	6	.94640	7
54	.67018	24	.32982	.72384	31	.27616	.05366	7	.94634	6
55	9.67042	24	10.32958	9.72415	30	10.27585	10.05373	7	9.94627	5
56	.67066	24	.32934	.72445	31	.27555	.05380	6	.94620	4
57	.67090	23	.32910	.72476	30	.27524	.05386	7	.94614	3
58	.67113	24	.32887	.72506	31	.27494	.05393	7	.94607	2
59	.67137	24	.32863	.72537	30	.27463	.05400	7	.94600	1
60	9.67161		10.32839	9.72567		10.27433	10.05407		9.94593	0
↑ 117°→	cos	Diff. 1′	sec	cot	Diff. 1′	tan	csc	Diff. 1′	sin ←	↑ 62°

TABLE 3
Common Logarithms of Trigonometric Functions (offset +10)

28° → ↓ ′	sin	Diff. 1′	csc	tan	Diff. 1′	cot	sec	Diff. 1′	cos	← 151° ↓ ′
0	9.67161	24	10.32839	9.72567	31	10.27433	10.05407	6	9.94593	60
1	.67185	23	.32815	.72598	30	.27402	.05413	7	.94587	59
2	.67208	24	.32792	.72628	31	.27372	.05420	7	.94580	58
3	.67232	24	.32768	.72659	30	.27341	.05427	6	.94573	57
4	.67256	24	.32744	.72689	31	.27311	.05433	7	.94567	56
5	9.67280	23	10.32720	9.72720	30	10.27280	10.05440	7	9.94560	55
6	.67303	24	.32697	.72750	30	.27250	.05447	7	.94553	54
7	.67327	23	.32673	.72780	31	.27220	.05454	6	.94546	53
8	.67350	24	.32650	.72811	30	.27189	.05460	7	.94540	52
9	.67374	24	.32626	.72841	31	.27159	.05467	7	.94533	51
10	9.67398	23	10.32602	9.72872	30	10.27128	10.05474	7	9.94526	50
11	.67421	24	.32579	.72902	30	.27098	.05481	6	.94519	49
12	.67445	23	.32555	.72932	31	.27068	.05487	7	.94513	48
13	.67468	24	.32532	.72963	30	.27037	.05494	7	.94506	47
14	.67492	23	.32508	.72993	30	.27007	.05501	7	.94499	46
15	9.67515	24	10.32485	9.73023	31	10.26977	10.05508	7	9.94492	45
16	.67539	23	.32461	.73054	30	.26946	.05515	6	.94485	44
17	.67562	24	.32438	.73084	30	.26916	.05521	7	.94479	43
18	.67586	23	.32414	.73114	30	.26886	.05528	7	.94472	42
19	.67609	24	.32391	.73144	31	.26856	.05535	7	.94465	41
20	9.67633	23	10.32367	9.73175	30	10.26825	10.05542	7	9.94458	40
21	.67656	24	.32344	.73205	30	.26795	.05549	6	.94451	39
22	.67680	23	.32320	.73235	30	.26765	.05555	7	.94445	38
23	.67703	23	.32297	.73265	30	.26735	.05562	7	.94438	37
24	.67726	24	.32274	.73295	31	.26705	.05569	7	.94431	36
25	9.67750	23	10.32250	9.73326	30	10.26674	10.05576	7	9.94424	35
26	.67773	23	.32227	.73356	30	.26644	.05583	7	.94417	34
27	.67796	24	.32204	.73386	30	.26614	.05590	6	.94410	33
28	.67820	23	.32180	.73416	30	.26584	.05596	7	.94404	32
29	.67843	23	.32157	.73446	30	.26554	.05603	7	.94397	31
30	9.67866	24	10.32134	9.73476	31	10.26524	10.05610	7	9.94390	30
31	.67890	23	.32110	.73507	30	.26493	.05617	7	.94383	29
32	.67913	23	.32087	.73537	30	.26463	.05624	7	.94376	28
33	.67936	23	.32064	.73567	30	.26433	.05631	7	.94369	27
34	.67959	23	.32041	.73597	30	.26403	.05638	7	.94362	26
35	9.67982	24	10.32018	9.73627	30	10.26373	10.05645	6	9.94355	25
36	.68006	23	.31994	.73657	30	.26343	.05651	7	.94349	24
37	.68029	23	.31971	.73687	30	.26313	.05658	7	.94342	23
38	.68052	23	.31948	.73717	30	.26283	.05665	7	.94335	22
39	.68075	23	.31925	.73747	30	.26253	.05672	7	.94328	21
40	9.68098	23	10.31902	9.73777	30	10.26223	10.05679	7	9.94321	20
41	.68121	23	.31879	.73807	30	.26193	.05686	7	.94314	19
42	.68144	23	.31856	.73837	30	.26163	.05693	7	.94307	18
43	.68167	23	.31833	.73867	30	.26133	.05700	7	.94300	17
44	.68190	23	.31810	.73897	30	.26103	.05707	7	.94293	16
45	9.68213	24	10.31787	9.73927	30	10.26073	10.05714	7	9.94286	15
46	.68237	23	.31763	.73957	30	.26043	.05721	6	.94279	14
47	.68260	23	.31740	.73987	30	.26013	.05727	7	.94273	13
48	.68283	22	.31717	.74017	30	.25983	.05734	7	.94266	12
49	.68305	23	.31695	.74047	30	.25953	.05741	7	.94259	11
50	9.68328	23	10.31672	9.74077	30	10.25923	10.05748	7	9.94252	10
51	.68351	23	.31649	.74107	30	.25893	.05755	7	.94245	9
52	.68374	23	.31626	.74137	29	.25863	.05762	7	.94238	8
53	.68397	23	.31603	.74166	30	.25834	.05769	7	.94231	7
54	.68420	23	.31580	.74196	30	.25804	.05776	7	.94224	6
55	9.68443	23	10.31557	9.74226	30	10.25774	10.05783	7	9.94217	5
56	.68466	23	.31534	.74256	30	.25744	.05790	7	.94210	4
57	.68489	23	.31511	.74286	30	.25714	.05797	7	.94203	3
58	.68512	22	.31488	.74316	29	.25684	.05804	7	.94196	2
59	.68534	23	.31466	.74345	30	.25655	.05811	7	.94189	1
60	9.68557		10.31443	9.74375		10.25625	10.05818		9.94182	0
↑ 118° →	cos	Diff. 1′	sec	cot	Diff. 1′	tan	csc	Diff. 1′	sin	← 61° ↑

TABLE 3
Common Logarithms of Trigonometric Functions (offset +10)

29° → ↓ ′	sin	Diff. 1′	csc	tan	Diff. 1′	cot	sec	Diff. 1′	cos	← 150° ↓ ′
0	9.68557	23	10.31443	9.74375	30	10.25625	10.05818	7	9.94182	60
1	.68580	23	.31420	.74405	30	.25595	.05825	7	.94175	59
2	.68603	22	.31397	.74435	30	.25565	.05832	7	.94168	58
3	.68625	23	.31375	.74465	29	.25535	.05839	7	.94161	57
4	.68648	23	.31352	.74494	30	.25506	.05846	7	.94154	56
5	9.68671	23	10.31329	9.74524	30	10.25476	10.05853	7	9.94147	55
6	.68694	22	.31306	.74554	29	.25446	.05860	7	.94140	54
7	.68716	23	.31284	.74583	30	.25417	.05867	7	.94133	53
8	.68739	23	.31261	.74613	30	.25387	.05874	7	.94126	52
9	.68762	22	.31238	.74643	30	.25357	.05881	7	.94119	51
10	9.68784	23	10.31216	9.74673	29	10.25327	10.05888	7	9.94112	50
11	.68807	22	.31193	.74702	30	.25298	.05895	7	.94105	49
12	.68829	23	.31171	.74732	30	.25268	.05902	8	.94098	48
13	.68852	23	.31148	.74762	29	.25238	.05910	7	.94090	47
14	.68875	22	.31125	.74791	30	.25209	.05917	7	.94083	46
15	9.68897	23	10.31103	9.74821	30	10.25179	10.05924	7	9.94076	45
16	.68920	22	.31080	.74851	29	.25149	.05931	7	.94069	44
17	.68942	23	.31058	.74880	30	.25120	.05938	7	.94062	43
18	.68965	22	.31035	.74910	29	.25090	.05945	7	.94055	42
19	.68987	23	.31013	.74939	30	.25061	.05952	7	.94048	41
20	9.69010	22	10.30990	9.74969	29	10.25031	10.05959	7	9.94041	40
21	.69032	23	.30968	.74998	30	.25002	.05966	7	.94034	39
22	.69055	22	.30945	.75028	30	.24972	.05973	7	.94027	38
23	.69077	23	.30923	.75058	29	.24942	.05980	8	.94020	37
24	.69100	22	.30900	.75087	30	.24913	.05988	7	.94012	36
25	9.69122	22	10.30878	9.75117	29	10.24883	10.05995	7	9.94005	35
26	.69144	23	.30856	.75146	30	.24854	.06002	7	.93998	34
27	.69167	22	.30833	.75176	29	.24824	.06009	7	.93991	33
28	.69189	23	.30811	.75205	30	.24795	.06016	7	.93984	32
29	.69212	22	.30788	.75235	29	.24765	.06023	7	.93977	31
30	9.69234	22	10.30766	9.75264	30	10.24736	10.06030	7	9.93970	30
31	.69256	23	.30744	.75294	29	.24706	.06037	8	.93963	29
32	.69279	22	.30721	.75323	30	.24677	.06045	7	.93955	28
33	.69301	22	.30699	.75353	29	.24647	.06052	7	.93948	27
34	.69323	22	.30677	.75382	29	.24618	.06059	7	.93941	26
35	9.69345	23	10.30655	9.75411	30	10.24589	10.06066	7	9.93934	25
36	.69368	22	.30632	.75441	29	.24559	.06073	7	.93927	24
37	.69390	22	.30610	.75470	30	.24530	.06080	8	.93920	23
38	.69412	22	.30588	.75500	29	.24500	.06088	7	.93912	22
39	.69434	22	.30566	.75529	29	.24471	.06095	7	.93905	21
40	9.69456	23	10.30544	9.75558	30	10.24442	10.06102	7	9.93898	20
41	.69479	22	.30521	.75588	29	.24412	.06109	7	.93891	19
42	.69501	22	.30499	.75617	30	.24383	.06116	8	.93884	18
43	.69523	22	.30477	.75647	29	.24353	.06124	7	.93876	17
44	.69545	22	.30455	.75676	29	.24324	.06131	7	.93869	16
45	9.69567	22	10.30433	9.75705	30	10.24295	10.06138	7	9.93862	15
46	.69589	22	.30411	.75735	29	.24265	.06145	8	.93855	14
47	.69611	22	.30389	.75764	29	.24236	.06153	7	.93847	13
48	.69633	22	.30367	.75793	29	.24207	.06160	7	.93840	12
49	.69655	22	.30345	.75822	30	.24178	.06167	7	.93833	11
50	9.69677	22	10.30323	9.75852	29	10.24148	10.06174	7	9.93826	10
51	.69699	22	.30301	.75881	29	.24119	.06181	8	.93819	9
52	.69721	22	.30279	.75910	29	.24090	.06189	7	.93811	8
53	.69743	22	.30257	.75939	30	.24061	.06196	7	.93804	7
54	.69765	22	.30235	.75969	29	.24031	.06203	8	.93797	6
55	9.69787	22	10.30213	9.75998	29	10.24002	10.06211	7	9.93789	5
56	.69809	22	.30191	.76027	29	.23973	.06218	7	.93782	4
57	.69831	22	.30169	.76056	30	.23944	.06225	7	.93775	3
58	.69853	22	.30147	.76086	29	.23914	.06232	8	.93768	2
59	.69875	22	.30125	.76115	29	.23885	.06240	7	.93760	1
60	9.69897		10.30103	9.76144		10.23856	10.06247		9.93753	0
↑ 119° →	cos	Diff. 1′	sec	cot	Diff. 1′	tan	csc	Diff. 1′	sin	← 60° ↑

TABLE 3

Common Logarithms of Trigonometric Functions (offset +10)

30° → ′	sin	Diff. 1′	csc	tan	Diff. 1′	cot	sec	Diff. 1′	cos	← 149° ′
0	9.69897	22	10.30103	9.76144	29	10.23856	10.06247	7	9.93753	60
1	.69919	22	.30081	.76173	29	.23827	.06254	8	.93746	59
2	.69941	22	.30059	.76202	29	.23798	.06262	7	.93738	58
3	.69963	21	.30037	.76231	30	.23769	.06269	7	.93731	57
4	.69984	22	.30016	.76261	29	.23739	.06276	7	.93724	56
5	9.70006	22	10.29994	9.76290	29	10.23710	10.06283	8	9.93717	55
6	.70028	22	.29972	.76319	29	.23681	.06291	7	.93709	54
7	.70050	22	.29950	.76348	29	.23652	.06298	7	.93702	53
8	.70072	21	.29928	.76377	29	.23623	.06305	8	.93695	52
9	.70093	22	.29907	.76406	29	.23594	.06313	7	.93687	51
10	9.70115	22	10.29885	9.76435	29	10.23565	10.06320	7	9.93680	50
11	.70137	22	.29863	.76464	29	.23536	.06327	8	.93673	49
12	.70159	21	.29841	.76493	29	.23507	.06335	7	.93665	48
13	.70180	22	.29820	.76522	29	.23478	.06342	8	.93658	47
14	.70202	22	.29798	.76551	29	.23449	.06350	7	.93650	46
15	9.70224	21	10.29776	9.76580	29	10.23420	10.06357	7	9.93643	45
16	.70245	22	.29755	.76609	30	.23391	.06364	8	.93636	44
17	.70267	21	.29733	.76639	29	.23361	.06372	7	.93628	43
18	.70288	22	.29712	.76668	29	.23332	.06379	7	.93621	42
19	.70310	22	.29690	.76697	28	.23303	.06386	8	.93614	41
20	9.70332	21	10.29668	9.76725	29	10.23275	10.06394	7	9.93606	40
21	.70353	22	.29647	.76754	29	.23246	.06401	8	.93599	39
22	.70375	21	.29625	.76783	29	.23217	.06409	7	.93591	38
23	.70396	22	.29604	.76812	29	.23188	.06416	7	.93584	37
24	.70418	21	.29582	.76841	29	.23159	.06423	8	.93577	36
25	9.70439	22	10.29561	9.76870	29	10.23130	10.06431	7	9.93569	35
26	.70461	21	.29539	.76899	29	.23101	.06438	8	.93562	34
27	.70482	22	.29518	.76928	29	.23072	.06446	7	.93554	33
28	.70504	21	.29496	.76957	29	.23043	.06453	8	.93547	32
29	.70525	22	.29475	.76986	29	.23014	.06461	7	.93539	31
30	9.70547	21	10.29453	9.77015	29	10.22985	10.06468	7	9.93532	30
31	.70568	22	.29432	.77044	29	.22956	.06475	8	.93525	29
32	.70590	21	.29410	.77073	28	.22927	.06483	7	.93517	28
33	.70611	22	.29389	.77101	29	.22899	.06490	8	.93510	27
34	.70633	21	.29367	.77130	29	.22870	.06498	7	.93502	26
35	9.70654	21	10.29346	9.77159	29	10.22841	10.06505	8	9.93495	25
36	.70675	22	.29325	.77188	29	.22812	.06513	7	.93487	24
37	.70697	21	.29303	.77217	29	.22783	.06520	8	.93480	23
38	.70718	21	.29282	.77246	28	.22754	.06528	7	.93472	22
39	.70739	22	.29261	.77274	29	.22726	.06535	8	.93465	21
40	9.70761	21	10.29239	9.77303	29	10.22697	10.06543	7	9.93457	20
41	.70782	21	.29218	.77332	29	.22668	.06550	8	.93450	19
42	.70803	21	.29197	.77361	29	.22639	.06558	7	.93442	18
43	.70824	22	.29176	.77390	28	.22610	.06565	8	.93435	17
44	.70846	21	.29154	.77418	29	.22582	.06573	7	.93427	16
45	9.70867	21	10.29133	9.77447	29	10.22553	10.06580	8	9.93420	15
46	.70888	21	.29112	.77476	29	.22524	.06588	7	.93412	14
47	.70909	22	.29091	.77505	28	.22495	.06595	8	.93405	13
48	.70931	21	.29069	.77533	29	.22467	.06603	7	.93397	12
49	.70952	21	.29048	.77562	29	.22438	.06610	8	.93390	11
50	9.70973	21	10.29027	9.77591	28	10.22409	10.06618	7	9.93382	10
51	.70994	21	.29006	.77619	29	.22381	.06625	8	.93375	9
52	.71015	21	.28985	.77648	29	.22352	.06633	7	.93367	8
53	.71036	22	.28964	.77677	29	.22323	.06640	8	.93360	7
54	.71058	21	.28942	.77706	28	.22294	.06648	8	.93352	6
55	9.71079	21	10.28921	9.77734	29	10.22266	10.06656	7	9.93344	5
56	.71100	21	.28900	.77763	28	.22237	.06663	8	.93337	4
57	.71121	21	.28879	.77791	29	.22209	.06671	7	.93329	3
58	.71142	21	.28858	.77820	29	.22180	.06678	8	.93322	2
59	.71163	21	.28837	.77849	28	.22151	.06686	7	.93314	1
60	9.71184		10.28816	9.77877		10.22123	10.06693		9.93307	0
120° →	cos	Diff. 1′	sec	cot	Diff. 1′	tan	csc	Diff. 1′	sin	← 59°

TABLE 3

Common Logarithms of Trigonometric Functions (offset +10)

31° → ′	sin	Diff. 1′	csc	tan	Diff. 1′	cot	sec	Diff. 1′	cos	← 148° ′
0	9.71184	21	10.28816	9.77877	29	10.22123	10.06693	8	9.93307	60
1	.71205	21	.28795	.77906	29	.22094	.06701	8	.93299	59
2	.71226	21	.28774	.77935	28	.22065	.06709	7	.93291	58
3	.71247	21	.28753	.77963	29	.22037	.06716	8	.93284	57
4	.71268	21	.28732	.77992	28	.22008	.06724	7	.93276	56
5	9.71289	21	10.28711	9.78020	29	10.21980	10.06731	8	9.93269	55
6	.71310	21	.28690	.78049	28	.21951	.06739	8	.93261	54
7	.71331	21	.28669	.78077	29	.21923	.06747	7	.93253	53
8	.71352	21	.28648	.78106	29	.21894	.06754	8	.93246	52
9	.71373	20	.28627	.78135	28	.21865	.06762	8	.93238	51
10	9.71393	21	10.28607	9.78163	29	10.21837	10.06770	7	9.93230	50
11	.71414	21	.28586	.78192	28	.21808	.06777	8	.93223	49
12	.71435	21	.28565	.78220	29	.21780	.06785	8	.93215	48
13	.71456	21	.28544	.78249	28	.21751	.06793	7	.93207	47
14	.71477	21	.28523	.78277	29	.21723	.06800	8	.93200	46
15	9.71498	21	10.28502	9.78306	28	10.21694	10.06808	8	9.93192	45
16	.71519	20	.28481	.78334	29	.21666	.06816	7	.93184	44
17	.71539	21	.28461	.78363	28	.21637	.06823	8	.93177	43
18	.71560	21	.28440	.78391	28	.21609	.06831	8	.93169	42
19	.71581	21	.28419	.78419	29	.21581	.06839	7	.93161	41
20	9.71602	20	10.28398	9.78448	28	10.21552	10.06846	8	9.93154	40
21	.71622	21	.28378	.78476	29	.21524	.06854	8	.93146	39
22	.71643	21	.28357	.78505	28	.21495	.06862	7	.93138	38
23	.71664	21	.28336	.78533	29	.21467	.06869	8	.93131	37
24	.71685	20	.28315	.78562	28	.21438	.06877	8	.93123	36
25	9.71705	21	10.28295	9.78590	28	10.21410	10.06885	7	9.93115	35
26	.71726	21	.28274	.78618	29	.21382	.06892	8	.93108	34
27	.71747	20	.28253	.78647	28	.21353	.06900	8	.93100	33
28	.71767	21	.28233	.78675	29	.21325	.06908	8	.93092	32
29	.71788	21	.28212	.78704	28	.21296	.06916	7	.93084	31
30	9.71809	20	10.28191	9.78732	28	10.21268	10.06923	8	9.93077	30
31	.71829	21	.28171	.78760	29	.21240	.06931	8	.93069	29
32	.71850	20	.28150	.78789	28	.21211	.06939	8	.93061	28
33	.71870	21	.28130	.78817	28	.21183	.06947	7	.93053	27
34	.71891	20	.28109	.78845	29	.21155	.06954	8	.93046	26
35	9.71911	21	10.28089	9.78874	28	10.21126	10.06962	8	9.93038	25
36	.71932	20	.28068	.78902	28	.21098	.06970	8	.93030	24
37	.71952	21	.28048	.78930	29	.21070	.06978	8	.93022	23
38	.71973	21	.28027	.78959	28	.21041	.06986	7	.93014	22
39	.71994	20	.28006	.78987	28	.21013	.06993	8	.93007	21
40	9.72014	20	10.27986	9.79015	28	10.20985	10.07001	8	9.92999	20
41	.72034	21	.27966	.79043	29	.20957	.07009	8	.92991	19
42	.72055	20	.27945	.79072	28	.20928	.07017	7	.92983	18
43	.72075	21	.27925	.79100	28	.20900	.07024	8	.92976	17
44	.72096	20	.27904	.79128	28	.20872	.07032	8	.92968	16
45	9.72116	21	10.27884	9.79156	29	10.20844	10.07040	8	9.92960	15
46	.72137	20	.27863	.79185	28	.20815	.07048	8	.92952	14
47	.72157	20	.27843	.79213	28	.20787	.07056	8	.92944	13
48	.72177	21	.27823	.79241	28	.20759	.07064	7	.92936	12
49	.72198	20	.27802	.79269	28	.20731	.07071	8	.92929	11
50	9.72218	20	10.27782	9.79297	29	10.20703	10.07079	8	9.92921	10
51	.72238	21	.27762	.79326	28	.20674	.07087	8	.92913	9
52	.72259	20	.27741	.79354	28	.20646	.07095	8	.92905	8
53	.72279	20	.27721	.79382	28	.20618	.07103	8	.92897	7
54	.72299	21	.27701	.79410	28	.20590	.07111	8	.92889	6
55	9.72320	20	10.27680	9.79438	28	10.20562	10.07119	7	9.92881	5
56	.72340	20	.27660	.79466	29	.20534	.07126	8	.92874	4
57	.72360	21	.27640	.79495	28	.20505	.07134	8	.92866	3
58	.72381	20	.27619	.79523	28	.20477	.07142	8	.92858	2
59	.72401	20	.27599	.79551	28	.20449	.07150	8	.92850	1
60	9.72421		10.27579	9.79579		10.20421	10.07158		9.92842	0
121° →	cos	Diff. 1′	sec	cot	Diff. 1′	tan	csc	Diff. 1′	sin	← 58°

TABLE 3
Common Logarithms of Trigonometric Functions (offset +10)

32° → ′	sin	Diff. 1′	csc	tan	Diff. 1′	cot	sec	Diff. 1′	cos ← 147° ′	
0	9.72421	20	10.27579	9.79579	28	10.20421	10.07158	8	9.92842	60
1	.72441	20	.27559	.79607	28	.20393	.07166	8	.92834	59
2	.72461	21	.27539	.79635	28	.20365	.07174	8	.92826	58
3	.72482	20	.27518	.79663	28	.20337	.07182	8	.92818	57
4	.72502	20	.27498	.79691	28	.20309	.07190	7	.92810	56
5	9.72522	20	10.27478	9.79719	28	10.20281	10.07197	8	9.92803	55
6	.72542	20	.27458	.79747	29	.20253	.07205	8	.92795	54
7	.72562	20	.27438	.79776	28	.20224	.07213	8	.92787	53
8	.72582	20	.27418	.79804	28	.20196	.07221	8	.92779	52
9	.72602	20	.27398	.79832	28	.20168	.07229	8	.92771	51
10	9.72622	21	10.27378	9.79860	28	10.20140	10.07237	8	9.92763	50
11	.72643	20	.27357	.79888	28	.20112	.07245	8	.92755	49
12	.72663	20	.27337	.79916	28	.20084	.07253	8	.92747	48
13	.72683	20	.27317	.79944	28	.20056	.07261	8	.92739	47
14	.72703	20	.27297	.79972	28	.20028	.07269	8	.92731	46
15	9.72723	20	10.27277	9.80000	28	10.20000	10.07277	8	9.92723	45
16	.72743	20	.27257	.80028	28	.19972	.07285	8	.92715	44
17	.72763	20	.27237	.80056	28	.19944	.07293	8	.92707	43
18	.72783	20	.27217	.80084	28	.19916	.07301	8	.92699	42
19	.72803	20	.27197	.80112	28	.19888	.07309	8	.92691	41
20	9.72823	20	10.27177	9.80140	28	10.19860	10.07317	8	9.92683	40
21	.72843	20	.27157	.80168	27	.19832	.07325	8	.92675	39
22	.72863	20	.27137	.80195	28	.19805	.07333	8	.92667	38
23	.72883	19	.27117	.80223	28	.19777	.07341	8	.92659	37
24	.72902	20	.27098	.80251	28	.19749	.07349	8	.92651	36
25	9.72922	20	10.27078	9.80279	28	10.19721	10.07357	8	9.92643	35
26	.72942	20	.27058	.80307	28	.19693	.07365	8	.92635	34
27	.72962	20	.27038	.80335	28	.19665	.07373	8	.92627	33
28	.72982	20	.27018	.80363	28	.19637	.07381	8	.92619	32
29	.73002	20	.26998	.80391	28	.19609	.07389	8	.92611	31
30	9.73022	19	10.26978	9.80419	28	10.19581	10.07397	8	9.92603	30
31	.73041	20	.26959	.80447	27	.19553	.07405	8	.92595	29
32	.73061	20	.26939	.80474	28	.19526	.07413	8	.92587	28
33	.73081	20	.26919	.80502	28	.19498	.07421	8	.92579	27
34	.73101	20	.26899	.80530	28	.19470	.07429	8	.92571	26
35	9.73121	19	10.26879	9.80558	28	10.19442	10.07437	8	9.92563	25
36	.73140	20	.26860	.80586	28	.19414	.07445	9	.92555	24
37	.73160	20	.26840	.80614	28	.19386	.07454	8	.92546	23
38	.73180	20	.26820	.80642	27	.19358	.07462	8	.92538	22
39	.73200	19	.26800	.80669	28	.19331	.07470	8	.92530	21
40	9.73219	20	10.26781	9.80697	28	10.19303	10.07478	8	9.92522	20
41	.73239	20	.26761	.80725	28	.19275	.07486	8	.92514	19
42	.73259	19	.26741	.80753	28	.19247	.07494	8	.92506	18
43	.73278	20	.26722	.80781	27	.19219	.07502	8	.92498	17
44	.73298	20	.26702	.80808	28	.19192	.07510	8	.92490	16
45	9.73318	19	10.26682	9.80836	28	10.19164	10.07518	9	9.92482	15
46	.73337	20	.26663	.80864	28	.19136	.07527	8	.92473	14
47	.73357	20	.26643	.80892	27	.19108	.07535	8	.92465	13
48	.73377	19	.26623	.80919	28	.19081	.07543	8	.92457	12
49	.73396	20	.26604	.80947	28	.19053	.07551	8	.92449	11
50	9.73416	19	10.26584	9.80975	28	10.19025	10.07559	8	9.92441	10
51	.73435	20	.26565	.81003	27	.18997	.07567	8	.92433	9
52	.73455	19	.26545	.81030	28	.18970	.07575	9	.92425	8
53	.73474	20	.26526	.81058	28	.18942	.07584	8	.92416	7
54	.73494	19	.26506	.81086	27	.18914	.07592	8	.92408	6
55	9.73513	20	10.26487	9.81113	28	10.18887	10.07600	8	9.92400	5
56	.73533	19	.26467	.81141	28	.18859	.07608	8	.92392	4
57	.73552	20	.26448	.81169	27	.18831	.07616	8	.92384	3
58	.73572	19	.26428	.81196	28	.18804	.07624	9	.92376	2
59	.73591	20	.26409	.81224	28	.18776	.07633	8	.92367	1
60	9.73611		10.26389	9.81252		10.18748	10.07641		9.92359	0
↑ 122° →	cos	Diff. 1′	sec	cot	Diff. 1′	tan	csc	Diff. 1′	sin ←	↑ 57°

TABLE 3
Common Logarithms of Trigonometric Functions (offset +10)

33° → ′	sin	Diff. 1′	csc	tan	Diff. 1′	cot	sec	Diff. 1′	cos ← 146° ′	
0	9.73611	19	10.26389	9.81252	27	10.18748	10.07641	8	9.92359	60
1	.73630	20	.26370	.81279	28	.18721	.07649	8	.92351	59
2	.73650	19	.26350	.81307	28	.18693	.07657	8	.92343	58
3	.73669	20	.26331	.81335	27	.18665	.07665	9	.92335	57
4	.73689	19	.26311	.81362	28	.18638	.07674	8	.92326	56
5	9.73708	19	10.26292	9.81390	28	10.18610	10.07682	8	9.92318	55
6	.73727	20	.26273	.81418	27	.18582	.07690	8	.92310	54
7	.73747	19	.26253	.81445	28	.18555	.07698	9	.92302	53
8	.73766	19	.26234	.81473	27	.18527	.07707	8	.92293	52
9	.73785	20	.26215	.81500	28	.18500	.07715	8	.92285	51
10	9.73805	19	10.26195	9.81528	28	10.18472	10.07723	8	9.92277	50
11	.73824	19	.26176	.81556	27	.18444	.07731	9	.92269	49
12	.73843	20	.26157	.81583	28	.18417	.07740	8	.92260	48
13	.73863	19	.26137	.81611	27	.18389	.07748	8	.92252	47
14	.73882	19	.26118	.81638	28	.18362	.07756	9	.92244	46
15	9.73901	20	10.26099	9.81666	27	10.18334	10.07765	8	9.92235	45
16	.73921	19	.26079	.81693	28	.18307	.07773	8	.92227	44
17	.73940	19	.26060	.81721	27	.18279	.07781	8	.92219	43
18	.73959	19	.26041	.81748	28	.18252	.07789	9	.92211	42
19	.73978	19	.26022	.81776	27	.18224	.07798	8	.92202	41
20	9.73997	20	10.26003	9.81803	28	10.18197	10.07806	8	9.92194	40
21	.74017	19	.25983	.81831	27	.18169	.07814	9	.92186	39
22	.74036	19	.25964	.81858	28	.18142	.07823	8	.92177	38
23	.74055	19	.25945	.81886	27	.18114	.07831	8	.92169	37
24	.74074	19	.25926	.81913	28	.18087	.07839	9	.92161	36
25	9.74093	20	10.25907	9.81941	27	10.18059	10.07848	8	9.92152	35
26	.74113	19	.25887	.81968	28	.18032	.07856	8	.92144	34
27	.74132	19	.25868	.81996	27	.18004	.07864	9	.92136	33
28	.74151	19	.25849	.82023	28	.17977	.07873	8	.92127	32
29	.74170	19	.25830	.82051	27	.17949	.07881	8	.92119	31
30	9.74189	19	10.25811	9.82078	28	10.17922	10.07889	9	9.92111	30
31	.74208	19	.25792	.82106	27	.17894	.07898	8	.92102	29
32	.74227	19	.25773	.82133	28	.17867	.07906	8	.92094	28
33	.74246	19	.25754	.82161	27	.17839	.07914	9	.92086	27
34	.74265	19	.25735	.82188	27	.17812	.07923	8	.92077	26
35	9.74284	19	10.25716	9.82215	28	10.17785	10.07931	9	9.92069	25
36	.74303	19	.25697	.82243	27	.17757	.07940	8	.92060	24
37	.74322	19	.25678	.82270	28	.17730	.07948	8	.92052	23
38	.74341	19	.25659	.82298	27	.17702	.07956	9	.92044	22
39	.74360	19	.25640	.82325	27	.17675	.07965	8	.92035	21
40	9.74379	19	10.25621	9.82352	28	10.17648	10.07973	9	9.92027	20
41	.74398	19	.25602	.82380	27	.17620	.07982	8	.92018	19
42	.74417	19	.25583	.82407	28	.17593	.07990	8	.92010	18
43	.74436	19	.25564	.82435	27	.17565	.07998	9	.92002	17
44	.74455	19	.25545	.82462	27	.17538	.08007	8	.91993	16
45	9.74474	19	10.25526	9.82489	28	10.17511	10.08015	9	9.91985	15
46	.74493	19	.25507	.82517	27	.17483	.08024	8	.91976	14
47	.74512	19	.25488	.82544	27	.17456	.08032	9	.91968	13
48	.74531	18	.25469	.82571	28	.17429	.08041	8	.91959	12
49	.74549	19	.25451	.82599	27	.17401	.08049	9	.91951	11
50	9.74568	19	10.25432	9.82626	27	10.17374	10.08058	8	9.91942	10
51	.74587	19	.25413	.82653	28	.17347	.08066	9	.91934	9
52	.74606	19	.25394	.82681	27	.17319	.08075	8	.91925	8
53	.74625	19	.25375	.82708	27	.17292	.08083	9	.91917	7
54	.74644	18	.25356	.82735	27	.17265	.08092	8	.91908	6
55	9.74662	19	10.25338	9.82762	28	10.17238	10.08100	9	9.91900	5
56	.74681	19	.25319	.82790	27	.17210	.08109	8	.91891	4
57	.74700	19	.25300	.82817	27	.17183	.08117	9	.91883	3
58	.74719	18	.25281	.82844	27	.17156	.08126	8	.91874	2
59	.74737	19	.25263	.82871	28	.17129	.08134	9	.91866	1
60	9.74756		10.25244	9.82899		10.17101	10.08143		9.91857	0
↑ 123° →	cos	Diff. 1′	sec	cot	Diff. 1′	tan	csc	Diff. 1′	sin ←	↑ 56°

TABLE 3

Common Logarithms of Trigonometric Functions (offset +10)

34° → ′	sin	Diff. 1′	csc	tan	Diff. 1′	cot	sec	Diff. 1′	cos	← 145° ′
0	9.74756	19	10.25244	9.82899	27	10.17101	10.08143	8	9.91857	60
1	.74775	19	.25225	.82926	27	.17074	.08151	9	.91849	59
2	.74794	18	.25206	.82953	27	.17047	.08160	8	.91840	58
3	.74812	19	.25188	.82980	28	.17020	.08168	9	.91832	57
4	.74831	19	.25169	.83008	27	.16992	.08177	8	.91823	56
5	9.74850	18	10.25150	9.83035	27	10.16965	10.08185	9	9.91815	55
6	.74868	19	.25132	.83062	27	.16938	.08194	8	.91806	54
7	.74887	19	.25113	.83089	28	.16911	.08202	9	.91798	53
8	.74906	18	.25094	.83117	27	.16883	.08211	8	.91789	52
9	.74924	19	.25076	.83144	27	.16856	.08219	9	.91781	51
10	9.74943	18	10.25057	9.83171	27	10.16829	10.08228	9	9.91772	50
11	.74961	19	.25039	.83198	27	.16802	.08237	8	.91763	49
12	.74980	19	.25020	.83225	27	.16775	.08245	9	.91755	48
13	.74999	18	.25001	.83252	28	.16748	.08254	8	.91746	47
14	.75017	19	.24983	.83280	27	.16720	.08262	9	.91738	46
15	9.75036	18	10.24964	9.83307	27	10.16693	10.08271	9	9.91729	45
16	.75054	19	.24946	.83334	27	.16666	.08280	8	.91720	44
17	.75073	18	.24927	.83361	27	.16639	.08288	9	.91712	43
18	.75091	19	.24909	.83388	27	.16612	.08297	8	.91703	42
19	.75110	18	.24890	.83415	27	.16585	.08305	9	.91695	41
20	9.75128	19	10.24872	9.83442	28	10.16558	10.08314	9	9.91686	40
21	.75147	18	.24853	.83470	27	.16530	.08323	8	.91677	39
22	.75165	19	.24835	.83497	27	.16503	.08331	9	.91669	38
23	.75184	18	.24816	.83524	27	.16476	.08340	9	.91660	37
24	.75202	19	.24798	.83551	27	.16449	.08349	8	.91651	36
25	9.75221	18	10.24779	9.83578	27	10.16422	10.08357	9	9.91643	35
26	.75239	19	.24761	.83605	27	.16395	.08366	9	.91634	34
27	.75258	18	.24742	.83632	27	.16368	.08375	8	.91625	33
28	.75276	18	.24724	.83659	27	.16341	.08383	9	.91617	32
29	.75294	19	.24706	.83686	27	.16314	.08392	9	.91608	31
30	9.75313	18	10.24687	9.83713	27	10.16287	10.08401	8	9.91599	30
31	.75331	19	.24669	.83740	28	.16260	.08409	9	.91591	29
32	.75350	18	.24650	.83768	27	.16232	.08418	9	.91582	28
33	.75368	18	.24632	.83795	27	.16205	.08427	8	.91573	27
34	.75386	19	.24614	.83822	27	.16178	.08435	9	.91565	26
35	9.75405	18	10.24595	9.83849	27	10.16151	10.08444	9	9.91556	25
36	.75423	18	.24577	.83876	27	.16124	.08453	9	.91547	24
37	.75441	18	.24559	.83903	27	.16097	.08462	8	.91538	23
38	.75459	19	.24541	.83930	27	.16070	.08470	9	.91530	22
39	.75478	18	.24522	.83957	27	.16043	.08479	9	.91521	21
40	9.75496	18	10.24504	9.83984	27	10.16016	10.08488	8	9.91512	20
41	.75514	19	.24486	.84011	27	.15989	.08496	9	.91504	19
42	.75533	18	.24467	.84038	27	.15962	.08505	9	.91495	18
43	.75551	18	.24449	.84065	27	.15935	.08514	9	.91486	17
44	.75569	18	.24431	.84092	27	.15908	.08523	8	.91477	16
45	9.75587	18	10.24413	9.84119	27	10.15881	10.08531	9	9.91469	15
46	.75605	19	.24395	.84146	27	.15854	.08540	9	.91460	14
47	.75624	18	.24376	.84173	27	.15827	.08549	9	.91451	13
48	.75642	18	.24358	.84200	27	.15800	.08558	9	.91442	12
49	.75660	18	.24340	.84227	27	.15773	.08567	8	.91433	11
50	9.75678	18	10.24322	9.84254	26	10.15746	10.08575	9	9.91425	10
51	.75696	18	.24304	.84280	27	.15720	.08584	9	.91416	9
52	.75714	19	.24286	.84307	27	.15693	.08593	9	.91407	8
53	.75733	18	.24267	.84334	27	.15666	.08602	9	.91398	7
54	.75751	18	.24249	.84361	27	.15639	.08611	8	.91389	6
55	9.75769	18	10.24231	9.84388	27	10.15612	10.08619	9	9.91381	5
56	.75787	18	.24213	.84415	27	.15585	.08628	9	.91372	4
57	.75805	18	.24195	.84442	27	.15558	.08637	9	.91363	3
58	.75823	18	.24177	.84469	27	.15531	.08646	9	.91354	2
59	.75841	18	.24159	.84496	27	.15504	.08655	9	.91345	1
60	9.75859		10.24141	9.84523		10.15477	10.08664		9.91336	0
↑ 124° →	cos	Diff. 1′	sec	cot	Diff. 1′	tan	csc	Diff. 1′	sin ←	55° ↑

TABLE 3

Common Logarithms of Trigonometric Functions (offset +10)

35° → ′	sin	Diff. 1′	csc	tan	Diff. 1′	cot	sec	Diff. 1′	cos	← 144° ′
0	9.75859	18	10.24141	9.84523	27	10.15477	10.08664	8	9.91336	60
1	.75877	18	.24123	.84550	26	.15450	.08672	9	.91328	59
2	.75895	18	.24105	.84576	27	.15424	.08681	9	.91319	58
3	.75913	18	.24087	.84603	27	.15397	.08690	9	.91310	57
4	.75931	18	.24069	.84630	27	.15370	.08699	9	.91301	56
5	9.75949	18	10.24051	9.84657	27	10.15343	10.08708	9	9.91292	55
6	.75967	18	.24033	.84684	27	.15316	.08717	9	.91283	54
7	.75985	18	.24015	.84711	27	.15289	.08726	8	.91274	53
8	.76003	18	.23997	.84738	26	.15262	.08734	9	.91266	52
9	.76021	18	.23979	.84764	27	.15236	.08743	9	.91257	51
10	9.76039	18	10.23961	9.84791	27	10.15209	10.08752	9	9.91248	50
11	.76057	18	.23943	.84818	27	.15182	.08761	9	.91239	49
12	.76075	18	.23925	.84845	27	.15155	.08770	9	.91230	48
13	.76093	18	.23907	.84872	27	.15128	.08779	9	.91221	47
14	.76111	18	.23889	.84899	26	.15101	.08788	9	.91212	46
15	9.76129	17	10.23871	9.84925	27	10.15075	10.08797	9	9.91203	45
16	.76146	18	.23854	.84952	27	.15048	.08806	9	.91194	44
17	.76164	18	.23836	.84979	27	.15021	.08815	9	.91185	43
18	.76182	18	.23818	.85006	27	.14994	.08824	9	.91176	42
19	.76200	18	.23800	.85033	26	.14967	.08833	9	.91167	41
20	9.76218	18	10.23782	9.85059	27	10.14941	10.08842	9	9.91158	40
21	.76236	17	.23764	.85086	27	.14914	.08851	8	.91149	39
22	.76253	18	.23747	.85113	27	.14887	.08859	9	.91141	38
23	.76271	18	.23729	.85140	26	.14860	.08868	9	.91132	37
24	.76289	18	.23711	.85166	27	.14834	.08877	9	.91123	36
25	9.76307	17	10.23693	9.85193	27	10.14807	10.08886	9	9.91114	35
26	.76324	18	.23676	.85220	27	.14780	.08895	9	.91105	34
27	.76342	18	.23658	.85247	26	.14753	.08904	9	.91096	33
28	.76360	18	.23640	.85273	27	.14727	.08913	9	.91087	32
29	.76378	17	.23622	.85300	27	.14700	.08922	9	.91078	31
30	9.76395	18	10.23605	9.85327	27	10.14673	10.08931	9	9.91069	30
31	.76413	18	.23587	.85354	26	.14646	.08940	9	.91060	29
32	.76431	17	.23569	.85380	27	.14620	.08949	9	.91051	28
33	.76448	18	.23552	.85407	27	.14593	.08958	9	.91042	27
34	.76466	18	.23534	.85434	26	.14566	.08967	10	.91033	26
35	9.76484	17	10.23516	9.85460	27	10.14540	10.08977	9	9.91023	25
36	.76501	18	.23499	.85487	27	.14513	.08986	9	.91014	24
37	.76519	18	.23481	.85514	26	.14486	.08995	9	.91005	23
38	.76537	17	.23463	.85540	27	.14460	.09004	9	.90996	22
39	.76554	18	.23446	.85567	27	.14433	.09013	9	.90987	21
40	9.76572	18	10.23428	9.85594	26	10.14406	10.09022	9	9.90978	20
41	.76590	17	.23410	.85620	27	.14380	.09031	9	.90969	19
42	.76607	18	.23393	.85647	27	.14353	.09040	9	.90960	18
43	.76625	17	.23375	.85674	26	.14326	.09049	9	.90951	17
44	.76642	18	.23358	.85700	27	.14300	.09058	9	.90942	16
45	9.76660	17	10.23340	9.85727	27	10.14273	10.09067	9	9.90933	15
46	.76677	18	.23323	.85754	26	.14246	.09076	9	.90924	14
47	.76695	17	.23305	.85780	27	.14220	.09085	9	.90915	13
48	.76712	18	.23288	.85807	27	.14193	.09094	10	.90906	12
49	.76730	17	.23270	.85834	26	.14166	.09104	9	.90896	11
50	9.76747	18	10.23253	9.85860	27	10.14140	10.09113	9	9.90887	10
51	.76765	17	.23235	.85887	26	.14113	.09122	9	.90878	9
52	.76782	18	.23218	.85913	27	.14087	.09131	9	.90869	8
53	.76800	17	.23200	.85940	27	.14060	.09140	9	.90860	7
54	.76817	18	.23183	.85967	26	.14033	.09149	9	.90851	6
55	9.76835	17	10.23165	9.85993	27	10.14007	10.09158	10	9.90842	5
56	.76852	18	.23148	.86020	26	.13980	.09168	9	.90832	4
57	.76870	17	.23130	.86046	27	.13954	.09177	9	.90823	3
58	.76887	17	.23113	.86073	27	.13927	.09186	9	.90814	2
59	.76904	18	.23096	.86100	26	.13900	.09195	9	.90805	1
60	9.76922		10.23078	9.86126		10.13874	10.09204		9.90796	0
↑ 125° →	cos	Diff. 1′	sec	cot	Diff. 1′	tan	csc	Diff. 1′	sin ←	54° ↑

TABLE 3

Common Logarithms of Trigonometric Functions (offset +10)

36°→ ↓ ′	sin	Diff. 1′	csc	tan	Diff. 1′	cot	sec	Diff. 1′	cos ←143°	↓ ′
0	9.76922	17	10.23078	9.86126	27	10.13874	10.09204	9	9.90796	60
1	.76939	18	.23061	.86153	26	.13847	.09213	10	.90787	59
2	.76957	17	.23043	.86179	27	.13821	.09223	9	.90777	58
3	.76974	17	.23026	.86206	26	.13794	.09232	9	.90768	57
4	.76991	18	.23009	.86232	27	.13768	.09241	9	.90759	56
5	9.77009	17	10.22991	9.86259	26	10.13741	10.09250	9	9.90750	55
6	.77026	17	.22974	.86285	27	.13715	.09259	10	.90741	54
7	.77043	18	.22957	.86312	26	.13688	.09269	9	.90731	53
8	.77061	17	.22939	.86338	27	.13662	.09278	9	.90722	52
9	.77078	17	.22922	.86365	27	.13635	.09287	9	.90713	51
10	9.77095	17	10.22905	9.86392	26	10.13608	10.09296	10	9.90704	50
11	.77112	18	.22888	.86418	27	.13582	.09306	9	.90694	49
12	.77130	17	.22870	.86445	26	.13555	.09315	9	.90685	48
13	.77147	17	.22853	.86471	27	.13529	.09324	9	.90676	47
14	.77164	17	.22836	.86498	26	.13502	.09333	10	.90667	46
15	9.77181	18	10.22819	9.86524	27	10.13476	10.09343	9	9.90657	45
16	.77199	17	.22801	.86551	26	.13449	.09352	9	.90648	44
17	.77216	17	.22784	.86577	26	.13423	.09361	9	.90639	43
18	.77233	17	.22767	.86603	27	.13397	.09370	10	.90630	42
19	.77250	18	.22750	.86630	26	.13370	.09380	9	.90620	41
20	9.77268	17	10.22732	9.86656	27	10.13344	10.09389	9	9.90611	40
21	.77285	17	.22715	.86683	26	.13317	.09398	10	.90602	39
22	.77302	17	.22698	.86709	27	.13291	.09408	9	.90592	38
23	.77319	17	.22681	.86736	26	.13264	.09417	9	.90583	37
24	.77336	17	.22664	.86762	27	.13238	.09426	9	.90574	36
25	9.77353	17	10.22647	9.86789	26	10.13211	10.09435	10	9.90565	35
26	.77370	17	.22630	.86815	27	.13185	.09445	9	.90555	34
27	.77387	18	.22613	.86842	26	.13158	.09454	9	.90546	33
28	.77405	17	.22595	.86868	26	.13132	.09463	10	.90537	32
29	.77422	17	.22578	.86894	27	.13106	.09473	9	.90527	31
30	9.77439	17	10.22561	9.86921	26	10.13079	10.09482	9	9.90518	30
31	.77456	17	.22544	.86947	27	.13053	.09491	10	.90509	29
32	.77473	17	.22527	.86974	26	.13026	.09501	9	.90499	28
33	.77490	17	.22510	.87000	27	.13000	.09510	10	.90490	27
34	.77507	17	.22493	.87027	26	.12973	.09520	9	.90480	26
35	9.77524	17	10.22476	9.87053	26	10.12947	10.09529	9	9.90471	25
36	.77541	17	.22459	.87079	27	.12921	.09538	10	.90462	24
37	.77558	17	.22442	.87106	26	.12894	.09548	9	.90452	23
38	.77575	17	.22425	.87132	26	.12868	.09557	9	.90443	22
39	.77592	17	.22408	.87158	27	.12842	.09566	10	.90434	21
40	9.77609	17	10.22391	9.87185	26	10.12815	10.09576	9	9.90424	20
41	.77626	17	.22374	.87211	27	.12789	.09585	10	.90415	19
42	.77643	17	.22357	.87238	26	.12762	.09595	9	.90405	18
43	.77660	17	.22340	.87264	26	.12736	.09604	10	.90396	17
44	.77677	17	.22323	.87290	27	.12710	.09614	9	.90386	16
45	9.77694	17	10.22306	9.87317	26	10.12683	10.09623	9	9.90377	15
46	.77711	17	.22289	.87343	26	.12657	.09632	10	.90368	14
47	.77728	16	.22272	.87369	27	.12631	.09642	9	.90358	13
48	.77744	17	.22256	.87396	26	.12604	.09651	10	.90349	12
49	.77761	17	.22239	.87422	26	.12578	.09661	9	.90339	11
50	9.77778	17	10.22222	9.87448	27	10.12552	10.09670	10	9.90330	10
51	.77795	17	.22205	.87475	26	.12525	.09680	9	.90320	9
52	.77812	17	.22188	.87501	26	.12499	.09689	10	.90311	8
53	.77829	17	.22171	.87527	27	.12473	.09699	9	.90301	7
54	.77846	16	.22154	.87554	26	.12446	.09708	10	.90292	6
55	9.77862	17	10.22138	9.87580	26	10.12420	10.09718	9	9.90282	5
56	.77879	17	.22121	.87606	27	.12394	.09727	10	.90273	4
57	.77896	17	.22104	.87633	26	.12367	.09737	9	.90263	3
58	.77913	17	.22087	.87659	26	.12341	.09746	10	.90254	2
59	.77930	16	.22070	.87685	26	.12315	.09756	9	.90244	1
60	9.77946		10.22054	9.87711		10.12289	10.09765		9.90235	0
↑ 126°→	cos	Diff. 1′	sec	cot	Diff. 1′	tan	csc	Diff. 1′	sin ← 53°	↑

TABLE 3

Common Logarithms of Trigonometric Functions (offset +10)

37°→ ↓ ′	sin	Diff. 1′	csc	tan	Diff. 1′	cot	sec	Diff. 1′	cos ←142°	↓ ′
0	9.77946	17	10.22054	9.87711	27	10.12289	10.09765	10	9.90235	60
1	.77963	17	.22037	.87738	26	.12262	.09775	9	.90225	59
2	.77980	17	.22020	.87764	26	.12236	.09784	10	.90216	58
3	.77997	16	.22003	.87790	27	.12210	.09794	9	.90206	57
4	.78013	17	.21987	.87817	26	.12183	.09803	10	.90197	56
5	9.78030	17	10.21970	9.87843	26	10.12157	10.09813	9	9.90187	55
6	.78047	16	.21953	.87869	26	.12131	.09822	10	.90178	54
7	.78063	17	.21937	.87895	27	.12105	.09832	9	.90168	53
8	.78080	17	.21920	.87922	26	.12078	.09841	10	.90159	52
9	.78097	16	.21903	.87948	26	.12052	.09851	10	.90149	51
10	9.78113	17	10.21887	9.87974	26	10.12026	10.09861	9	9.90139	50
11	.78130	17	.21870	.88000	27	.12000	.09870	10	.90130	49
12	.78147	16	.21853	.88027	26	.11973	.09880	9	.90120	48
13	.78163	17	.21837	.88053	26	.11947	.09889	10	.90111	47
14	.78180	17	.21820	.88079	26	.11921	.09899	10	.90101	46
15	9.78197	16	10.21803	9.88105	26	10.11895	10.09909	9	9.90091	45
16	.78213	17	.21787	.88131	27	.11869	.09918	10	.90082	44
17	.78230	16	.21770	.88158	26	.11842	.09928	9	.90072	43
18	.78246	17	.21754	.88184	26	.11816	.09937	10	.90063	42
19	.78263	17	.21737	.88210	26	.11790	.09947	10	.90053	41
20	9.78280	16	10.21720	9.88236	26	10.11764	10.09957	9	9.90043	40
21	.78296	17	.21704	.88262	27	.11738	.09966	10	.90034	39
22	.78313	16	.21687	.88289	26	.11711	.09976	10	.90024	38
23	.78329	17	.21671	.88315	26	.11685	.09986	9	.90014	37
24	.78346	16	.21654	.88341	26	.11659	.09995	10	.90005	36
25	9.78362	17	10.21638	9.88367	26	10.11633	10.10005	10	9.89995	35
26	.78379	16	.21621	.88393	27	.11607	.10015	9	.89985	34
27	.78395	17	.21605	.88420	26	.11580	.10024	10	.89976	33
28	.78412	16	.21588	.88446	26	.11554	.10034	10	.89966	32
29	.78428	17	.21572	.88472	26	.11528	.10044	9	.89956	31
30	9.78445	16	10.21555	9.88498	26	10.11502	10.10053	10	9.89947	30
31	.78461	17	.21539	.88524	26	.11476	.10063	10	.89937	29
32	.78478	16	.21522	.88550	27	.11450	.10073	9	.89927	28
33	.78494	16	.21506	.88577	26	.11423	.10082	10	.89918	27
34	.78510	17	.21490	.88603	26	.11397	.10092	10	.89908	26
35	9.78527	16	10.21473	9.88629	26	10.11371	10.10102	10	9.89898	25
36	.78543	17	.21457	.88655	26	.11345	.10112	9	.89888	24
37	.78560	16	.21440	.88681	26	.11319	.10121	10	.89879	23
38	.78576	16	.21424	.88707	26	.11293	.10131	10	.89869	22
39	.78592	17	.21408	.88733	26	.11267	.10141	10	.89859	21
40	9.78609	16	10.21391	9.88759	27	10.11241	10.10151	9	9.89849	20
41	.78625	17	.21375	.88786	26	.11214	.10160	10	.89840	19
42	.78642	16	.21358	.88812	26	.11188	.10170	10	.89830	18
43	.78658	16	.21342	.88838	26	.11162	.10180	10	.89820	17
44	.78674	17	.21326	.88864	26	.11136	.10190	9	.89810	16
45	9.78691	16	10.21309	9.88890	26	10.11110	10.10199	10	9.89801	15
46	.78707	16	.21293	.88916	26	.11084	.10209	10	.89791	14
47	.78723	16	.21277	.88942	26	.11058	.10219	10	.89781	13
48	.78739	17	.21261	.88968	26	.11032	.10229	10	.89771	12
49	.78756	16	.21244	.88994	26	.11006	.10239	9	.89761	11
50	9.78772	16	10.21228	9.89020	26	10.10980	10.10248	10	9.89752	10
51	.78788	17	.21212	.89046	27	.10954	.10258	10	.89742	9
52	.78805	16	.21195	.89073	26	.10927	.10268	10	.89732	8
53	.78821	16	.21179	.89099	26	.10901	.10278	10	.89722	7
54	.78837	16	.21163	.89125	26	.10875	.10288	10	.89712	6
55	9.78853	16	10.21147	9.89151	26	10.10849	10.10298	9	9.89702	5
56	.78869	17	.21131	.89177	26	.10823	.10307	10	.89693	4
57	.78886	16	.21114	.89203	26	.10797	.10317	10	.89683	3
58	.78902	16	.21098	.89229	26	.10771	.10327	10	.89673	2
59	.78918	16	.21082	.89255	26	.10745	.10337	10	.89663	1
60	9.78934		10.21066	9.89281		10.10719	10.10347		9.89653	0
↑ 127°→	cos	Diff. 1′	sec	cot	Diff. 1′	tan	csc	Diff. 1′	sin ← 52°	↑

TABLE 3

Common Logarithms of Trigonometric Functions (offset +10)

38° → ′	sin	Diff. 1′	csc	tan	Diff. 1′	cot	sec	Diff. 1′	cos	← 141° ′
0	9.78934	16	10.21066	9.89281	26	10.10719	10.10347	10	9.89653	60
1	.78950	17	.21050	.89307	26	.10693	.10357	10	.89643	59
2	.78967	16	.21033	.89333	26	.10667	.10367	9	.89633	58
3	.78983	16	.21017	.89359	26	.10641	.10376	10	.89624	57
4	.78999	16	.21001	.89385	26	.10615	.10386	10	.89614	56
5	9.79015	16	10.20985	9.89411	26	10.10589	10.10396	10	9.89604	55
6	.79031	16	.20969	.89437	26	.10563	.10406	10	.89594	54
7	.79047	16	.20953	.89463	26	.10537	.10416	10	.89584	53
8	.79063	16	.20937	.89489	26	.10511	.10426	10	.89574	52
9	.79079	16	.20921	.89515	26	.10485	.10436	10	.89564	51
10	9.79095	16	10.20905	9.89541	26	10.10459	10.10446	10	9.89554	50
11	.79111	17	.20889	.89567	26	.10433	.10456	10	.89544	49
12	.79128	16	.20872	.89593	26	.10407	.10466	10	.89534	48
13	.79144	16	.20856	.89619	26	.10381	.10476	10	.89524	47
14	.79160	16	.20840	.89645	26	.10355	.10486	10	.89514	46
15	9.79176	16	10.20824	9.89671	26	10.10329	10.10496	9	9.89504	45
16	.79192	16	.20808	.89697	26	.10303	.10505	10	.89495	44
17	.79208	16	.20792	.89723	26	.10277	.10515	10	.89485	43
18	.79224	16	.20776	.89749	26	.10251	.10525	10	.89475	42
19	.79240	16	.20760	.89775	26	.10225	.10535	10	.89465	41
20	9.79256	16	10.20744	9.89801	26	10.10199	10.10545	10	9.89455	40
21	.79272	16	.20728	.89827	26	.10173	.10555	10	.89445	39
22	.79288	16	.20712	.89853	26	.10147	.10565	10	.89435	38
23	.79304	15	.20696	.89879	26	.10121	.10575	10	.89425	37
24	.79319	16	.20681	.89905	26	.10095	.10585	10	.89415	36
25	9.79335	16	10.20665	9.89931	26	10.10069	10.10595	10	9.89405	35
26	.79351	16	.20649	.89957	26	.10043	.10605	10	.89395	34
27	.79367	16	.20633	.89983	26	.10017	.10615	10	.89385	33
28	.79383	16	.20617	.90009	26	.09991	.10625	11	.89375	32
29	.79399	16	.20601	.90035	26	.09965	.10636	10	.89364	31
30	9.79415	16	10.20585	9.90061	25	10.09939	10.10646	10	9.89354	30
31	.79431	16	.20569	.90086	26	.09914	.10656	10	.89344	29
32	.79447	16	.20553	.90112	26	.09888	.10666	10	.89334	28
33	.79463	15	.20537	.90138	26	.09862	.10676	10	.89324	27
34	.79478	16	.20522	.90164	26	.09836	.10686	10	.89314	26
35	9.79494	16	10.20506	9.90190	26	10.09810	10.10696	10	9.89304	25
36	.79510	16	.20490	.90216	26	.09784	.10706	10	.89294	24
37	.79526	16	.20474	.90242	26	.09758	.10716	10	.89284	23
38	.79542	16	.20458	.90268	26	.09732	.10726	10	.89274	22
39	.79558	15	.20442	.90294	26	.09706	.10736	10	.89264	21
40	9.79573	16	10.20427	9.90320	26	10.09680	10.10746	10	9.89254	20
41	.79589	16	.20411	.90346	25	.09654	.10756	11	.89244	19
42	.79605	16	.20395	.90371	26	.09629	.10767	10	.89233	18
43	.79621	15	.20379	.90397	26	.09603	.10777	10	.89223	17
44	.79636	16	.20364	.90423	26	.09577	.10787	10	.89213	16
45	9.79652	16	10.20348	9.90449	26	10.09551	10.10797	10	9.89203	15
46	.79668	16	.20332	.90475	26	.09525	.10807	10	.89193	14
47	.79684	15	.20316	.90501	26	.09499	.10817	10	.89183	13
48	.79699	16	.20301	.90527	26	.09473	.10827	11	.89173	12
49	.79715	16	.20285	.90553	25	.09447	.10838	10	.89162	11
50	9.79731	15	10.20269	9.90578	26	10.09422	10.10848	10	9.89152	10
51	.79746	16	.20254	.90604	26	.09396	.10858	10	.89142	9
52	.79762	16	.20238	.90630	26	.09370	.10868	10	.89132	8
53	.79778	15	.20222	.90656	26	.09344	.10878	10	.89122	7
54	.79793	16	.20207	.90682	26	.09318	.10888	11	.89112	6
55	9.79809	16	10.20191	9.90708	26	10.09292	10.10899	10	9.89101	5
56	.79825	15	.20175	.90734	25	.09266	.10909	10	.89091	4
57	.79840	16	.20160	.90759	26	.09241	.10919	10	.89081	3
58	.79856	16	.20144	.90785	26	.09215	.10929	11	.89071	2
59	.79872	15	.20128	.90811	26	.09189	.10940	10	.89060	1
60	9.79887		10.20113	9.90837		10.09163	10.10950		9.89050	0
128° →	cos	Diff. 1′	sec	cot	Diff. 1′	tan	csc	Diff. 1′	sin	← 51°

TABLE 3

Common Logarithms of Trigonometric Functions (offset +10)

39° → ′	sin	Diff. 1′	csc	tan	Diff. 1′	cot	sec	Diff. 1′	cos	← 140° ′
0	9.79887	16	10.20113	9.90837	26	10.09163	10.10950	10	9.89050	60
1	.79903	15	.20097	.90863	26	.09137	.10960	10	.89040	59
2	.79918	16	.20082	.90889	25	.09111	.10970	10	.89030	58
3	.79934	16	.20066	.90914	26	.09086	.10980	11	.89020	57
4	.79950	15	.20050	.90940	26	.09060	.10991	10	.89009	56
5	9.79965	16	10.20035	9.90966	26	10.09034	10.11001	10	9.88999	55
6	.79981	15	.20019	.90992	26	.09008	.11011	11	.88989	54
7	.79996	16	.20004	.91018	25	.08982	.11022	10	.88978	53
8	.80012	15	.19988	.91043	26	.08957	.11032	10	.88968	52
9	.80027	16	.19973	.91069	26	.08931	.11042	10	.88958	51
10	9.80043	15	10.19957	9.91095	26	10.08905	10.11052	11	9.88948	50
11	.80058	16	.19942	.91121	26	.08879	.11063	10	.88937	49
12	.80074	15	.19926	.91147	25	.08853	.11073	10	.88927	48
13	.80089	16	.19911	.91172	26	.08828	.11083	11	.88917	47
14	.80105	15	.19895	.91198	26	.08802	.11094	10	.88906	46
15	9.80120	16	10.19880	9.91224	26	10.08776	10.11104	10	9.88896	45
16	.80136	15	.19864	.91250	26	.08750	.11114	11	.88886	44
17	.80151	15	.19849	.91276	25	.08724	.11125	10	.88875	43
18	.80166	16	.19834	.91301	26	.08699	.11135	10	.88865	42
19	.80182	15	.19818	.91327	26	.08673	.11145	11	.88855	41
20	9.80197	16	10.19803	9.91353	26	10.08647	10.11156	10	9.88844	40
21	.80213	15	.19787	.91379	25	.08621	.11166	10	.88834	39
22	.80228	16	.19772	.91404	26	.08596	.11176	11	.88824	38
23	.80244	15	.19756	.91430	26	.08570	.11187	10	.88813	37
24	.80259	15	.19741	.91456	26	.08544	.11197	10	.88803	36
25	9.80274	16	10.19726	9.91482	25	10.08518	10.11207	11	9.88793	35
26	.80290	15	.19710	.91507	26	.08493	.11218	10	.88782	34
27	.80305	15	.19695	.91533	26	.08467	.11228	11	.88772	33
28	.80320	16	.19680	.91559	26	.08441	.11239	10	.88761	32
29	.80336	15	.19664	.91585	25	.08415	.11249	10	.88751	31
30	9.80351	15	10.19649	9.91610	26	10.08390	10.11259	11	9.88741	30
31	.80366	16	.19634	.91636	26	.08364	.11270	10	.88730	29
32	.80382	15	.19618	.91662	26	.08338	.11280	11	.88720	28
33	.80397	15	.19603	.91688	25	.08312	.11291	10	.88709	27
34	.80412	16	.19588	.91713	26	.08287	.11301	11	.88699	26
35	9.80428	15	10.19572	9.91739	26	10.08261	10.11312	10	9.88688	25
36	.80443	15	.19557	.91765	26	.08235	.11322	10	.88678	24
37	.80458	15	.19542	.91791	25	.08209	.11332	11	.88668	23
38	.80473	16	.19527	.91816	26	.08184	.11343	10	.88657	22
39	.80489	15	.19511	.91842	26	.08158	.11353	11	.88647	21
40	9.80504	15	10.19496	9.91868	25	10.08132	10.11364	10	9.88636	20
41	.80519	15	.19481	.91893	26	.08107	.11374	11	.88626	19
42	.80534	16	.19466	.91919	26	.08081	.11385	10	.88615	18
43	.80550	15	.19450	.91945	26	.08055	.11395	11	.88605	17
44	.80565	15	.19435	.91971	25	.08029	.11406	10	.88594	16
45	9.80580	15	10.19420	9.91996	26	10.08004	10.11416	11	9.88584	15
46	.80595	15	.19405	.92022	26	.07978	.11427	10	.88573	14
47	.80610	15	.19390	.92048	25	.07952	.11437	11	.88563	13
48	.80625	16	.19375	.92073	26	.07927	.11448	10	.88552	12
49	.80641	15	.19359	.92099	26	.07901	.11458	11	.88542	11
50	9.80656	15	10.19344	9.92125	25	10.07875	10.11469	10	9.88531	10
51	.80671	15	.19329	.92150	26	.07850	.11479	11	.88521	9
52	.80686	15	.19314	.92176	26	.07824	.11490	11	.88510	8
53	.80701	15	.19299	.92202	25	.07798	.11501	10	.88499	7
54	.80716	15	.19284	.92227	26	.07773	.11511	11	.88489	6
55	9.80731	15	10.19269	9.92253	26	10.07747	10.11522	10	9.88478	5
56	.80746	16	.19254	.92279	25	.07721	.11532	11	.88468	4
57	.80762	15	.19238	.92304	26	.07696	.11543	10	.88457	3
58	.80777	15	.19223	.92330	26	.07670	.11553	11	.88447	2
59	.80792	15	.19208	.92356	25	.07644	.11564	11	.88436	1
60	9.80807		10.19193	9.92381		10.07619	10.11575		9.88425	0
129° →	cos	Diff. 1′	sec	cot	Diff. 1′	tan	csc	Diff. 1′	sin	← 50°

TABLE 3

Common Logarithms of Trigonometric Functions (offset +10)

40° → ′ ↓	sin	Diff. 1′	csc	tan	Diff. 1′	cot	sec	Diff. 1′	cos	← 139° ′ ↓
0	9.80807	15	10.19193	9.92381	26	10.07619	10.11575	10	9.88425	60
1	.80822	15	.19178	.92407	26	.07593	.11585	11	.88415	59
2	.80837	15	.19163	.92433	25	.07567	.11596	10	.88404	58
3	.80852	15	.19148	.92458	26	.07542	.11606	11	.88394	57
4	.80867	15	.19133	.92484	26	.07516	.11617	11	.88383	56
5	9.80882	15	10.19118	9.92510	25	10.07490	10.11628	10	9.88372	55
6	.80897	15	.19103	.92535	26	.07465	.11638	11	.88362	54
7	.80912	15	.19088	.92561	26	.07439	.11649	11	.88351	53
8	.80927	15	.19073	.92587	25	.07413	.11660	10	.88340	52
9	.80942	15	.19058	.92612	26	.07388	.11670	11	.88330	51
10	9.80957	15	10.19043	9.92638	25	10.07362	10.11681	11	9.88319	50
11	.80972	15	.19028	.92663	26	.07337	.11692	10	.88308	49
12	.80987	15	.19013	.92689	26	.07311	.11702	11	.88298	48
13	.81002	15	.18998	.92715	25	.07285	.11713	11	.88287	47
14	.81017	15	.18983	.92740	26	.07260	.11724	10	.88276	46
15	9.81032	15	10.18968	9.92766	26	10.07234	10.11734	11	9.88266	45
16	.81047	14	.18953	.92792	25	.07208	.11745	11	.88255	44
17	.81061	15	.18939	.92817	26	.07183	.11756	10	.88244	43
18	.81076	15	.18924	.92843	25	.07157	.11766	11	.88234	42
19	.81091	15	.18909	.92868	26	.07132	.11777	11	.88223	41
20	9.81106	15	10.18894	9.92894	26	10.07106	10.11788	11	9.88212	40
21	.81121	15	.18879	.92920	25	.07080	.11799	10	.88201	39
22	.81136	15	.18864	.92945	26	.07055	.11809	11	.88191	38
23	.81151	15	.18849	.92971	25	.07029	.11820	11	.88180	37
24	.81166	14	.18834	.92996	26	.07004	.11831	11	.88169	36
25	9.81180	15	10.18820	9.93022	26	10.06978	10.11842	10	9.88158	35
26	.81195	15	.18805	.93048	25	.06952	.11852	11	.88148	34
27	.81210	15	.18790	.93073	26	.06927	.11863	11	.88137	33
28	.81225	15	.18775	.93099	25	.06901	.11874	11	.88126	32
29	.81240	14	.18760	.93124	26	.06876	.11885	10	.88115	31
30	9.81254	15	10.18746	9.93150	25	10.06850	10.11895	11	9.88105	30
31	.81269	15	.18731	.93175	26	.06825	.11906	11	.88094	29
32	.81284	15	.18716	.93201	26	.06799	.11917	11	.88083	28
33	.81299	15	.18701	.93227	25	.06773	.11928	11	.88072	27
34	.81314	14	.18686	.93252	26	.06748	.11939	10	.88061	26
35	9.81328	15	10.18672	9.93278	25	10.06722	10.11949	11	9.88051	25
36	.81343	15	.18657	.93303	26	.06697	.11960	11	.88040	24
37	.81358	14	.18642	.93329	25	.06671	.11971	11	.88029	23
38	.81372	15	.18628	.93354	26	.06646	.11982	11	.88018	22
39	.81387	15	.18613	.93380	26	.06620	.11993	11	.88007	21
40	9.81402	15	10.18598	9.93406	25	10.06594	10.12004	11	9.87996	20
41	.81417	14	.18583	.93431	26	.06569	.12015	10	.87985	19
42	.81431	15	.18569	.93457	25	.06543	.12025	11	.87975	18
43	.81446	15	.18554	.93482	26	.06518	.12036	11	.87964	17
44	.81461	14	.18539	.93508	25	.06492	.12047	11	.87953	16
45	9.81475	15	10.18525	9.93533	26	10.06467	10.12058	11	9.87942	15
46	.81490	15	.18510	.93559	25	.06441	.12069	11	.87931	14
47	.81505	14	.18495	.93584	26	.06416	.12080	11	.87920	13
48	.81519	15	.18481	.93610	26	.06390	.12091	11	.87909	12
49	.81534	15	.18466	.93636	25	.06364	.12102	11	.87898	11
50	9.81549	14	10.18451	9.93661	26	10.06339	10.12113	10	9.87887	10
51	.81563	15	.18437	.93687	25	.06313	.12123	11	.87877	9
52	.81578	14	.18422	.93712	26	.06288	.12134	11	.87866	8
53	.81592	15	.18408	.93738	25	.06262	.12145	11	.87855	7
54	.81607	15	.18393	.93763	26	.06237	.12156	11	.87844	6
55	9.81622	14	10.18378	9.93789	25	10.06211	10.12167	11	9.87833	5
56	.81636	15	.18364	.93814	26	.06186	.12178	11	.87822	4
57	.81651	14	.18349	.93840	25	.06160	.12189	11	.87811	3
58	.81665	15	.18335	.93865	26	.06135	.12200	11	.87800	2
59	.81680	14	.18320	.93891	25	.06109	.12211	11	.87789	1
60	9.81694		10.18306	9.93916		10.06084	10.12222		9.87778	0
↑ 130° →	cos	Diff. 1′	sec	cot	Diff. 1′	tan	csc	Diff. 1′	sin	← 49° ↑

TABLE 3

Common Logarithms of Trigonometric Functions (offset +10)

41° → ′ ↓	sin	Diff. 1′	csc	tan	Diff. 1′	cot	sec	Diff. 1′	cos	← 138° ′ ↓
0	9.81694	15	10.18306	9.93916	26	10.06084	10.12222	11	9.87778	60
1	.81709	14	.18291	.93942	25	.06058	.12233	11	.87767	59
2	.81723	15	.18277	.93967	26	.06033	.12244	11	.87756	58
3	.81738	14	.18262	.93993	25	.06007	.12255	11	.87745	57
4	.81752	15	.18248	.94018	26	.05982	.12266	11	.87734	56
5	9.81767	14	10.18233	9.94044	25	10.05956	10.12277	11	9.87723	55
6	.81781	15	.18219	.94069	26	.05931	.12288	11	.87712	54
7	.81796	14	.18204	.94095	25	.05905	.12299	11	.87701	53
8	.81810	15	.18190	.94120	26	.05880	.12310	11	.87690	52
9	.81825	14	.18175	.94146	25	.05854	.12321	11	.87679	51
10	9.81839	15	10.18161	9.94171	26	10.05829	10.12332	11	9.87668	50
11	.81854	14	.18146	.94197	25	.05803	.12343	11	.87657	49
12	.81868	14	.18132	.94222	26	.05778	.12354	11	.87646	48
13	.81882	15	.18118	.94248	25	.05752	.12365	11	.87635	47
14	.81897	14	.18103	.94273	26	.05727	.12376	11	.87624	46
15	9.81911	15	10.18089	9.94299	25	10.05701	10.12387	12	9.87613	45
16	.81926	14	.18074	.94324	26	.05676	.12399	11	.87601	44
17	.81940	15	.18060	.94350	25	.05650	.12410	11	.87590	43
18	.81955	14	.18045	.94375	26	.05625	.12421	11	.87579	42
19	.81969	14	.18031	.94401	25	.05599	.12432	11	.87568	41
20	9.81983	15	10.18017	9.94426	26	10.05574	10.12443	11	9.87557	40
21	.81998	14	.18002	.94452	25	.05548	.12454	11	.87546	39
22	.82012	14	.17988	.94477	26	.05523	.12465	11	.87535	38
23	.82026	15	.17974	.94503	25	.05497	.12476	11	.87524	37
24	.82041	14	.17959	.94528	26	.05472	.12487	12	.87513	36
25	9.82055	14	10.17945	9.94554	25	10.05446	10.12499	11	9.87501	35
26	.82069	15	.17931	.94579	25	.05421	.12510	11	.87490	34
27	.82084	14	.17916	.94604	26	.05396	.12521	11	.87479	33
28	.82098	14	.17902	.94630	25	.05370	.12532	11	.87468	32
29	.82112	14	.17888	.94655	26	.05345	.12543	11	.87457	31
30	9.82126	15	10.17874	9.94681	25	10.05319	10.12554	12	9.87446	30
31	.82141	14	.17859	.94706	26	.05294	.12566	11	.87434	29
32	.82155	14	.17845	.94732	25	.05268	.12577	11	.87423	28
33	.82169	15	.17831	.94757	26	.05243	.12588	11	.87412	27
34	.82184	14	.17816	.94783	25	.05217	.12599	11	.87401	26
35	9.82198	14	10.17802	9.94808	26	10.05192	10.12610	12	9.87390	25
36	.82212	14	.17788	.94834	25	.05166	.12622	11	.87378	24
37	.82226	14	.17774	.94859	25	.05141	.12633	11	.87367	23
38	.82240	15	.17760	.94884	26	.05116	.12644	11	.87356	22
39	.82255	14	.17745	.94910	25	.05090	.12655	11	.87345	21
40	9.82269	14	10.17731	9.94935	26	10.05065	10.12666	12	9.87334	20
41	.82283	14	.17717	.94961	25	.05039	.12678	11	.87322	19
42	.82297	14	.17703	.94986	26	.05014	.12689	11	.87311	18
43	.82311	15	.17689	.95012	25	.04988	.12700	12	.87300	17
44	.82326	14	.17674	.95037	25	.04963	.12712	11	.87288	16
45	9.82340	14	10.17660	9.95062	26	10.04938	10.12723	11	9.87277	15
46	.82354	14	.17646	.95088	25	.04912	.12734	11	.87266	14
47	.82368	14	.17632	.95113	26	.04887	.12745	12	.87255	13
48	.82382	14	.17618	.95139	25	.04861	.12757	11	.87243	12
49	.82396	14	.17604	.95164	26	.04836	.12768	11	.87232	11
50	9.82410	14	10.17590	9.95190	25	10.04810	10.12779	12	9.87221	10
51	.82424	15	.17576	.95215	25	.04785	.12791	11	.87209	9
52	.82439	14	.17561	.95240	26	.04760	.12802	11	.87198	8
53	.82453	14	.17547	.95266	25	.04734	.12813	12	.87187	7
54	.82467	14	.17533	.95291	26	.04709	.12825	11	.87175	6
55	9.82481	14	10.17519	9.95317	25	10.04683	10.12836	11	9.87164	5
56	.82495	14	.17505	.95342	26	.04658	.12847	12	.87153	4
57	.82509	14	.17491	.95368	25	.04632	.12859	11	.87141	3
58	.82523	14	.17477	.95393	25	.04607	.12870	11	.87130	2
59	.82537	14	.17463	.95418	26	.04582	.12881	12	.87119	1
60	9.82551		10.17449	9.95444		10.04556	10.12893		9.87107	0
↑ 131° →	cos	Diff. 1′	sec	cot	Diff. 1′	tan	csc	Diff. 1′	sin	← 48° ↑

TABLE 3

Common Logarithms of Trigonometric Functions (offset +10)

42°→ ′ ↓	sin	Diff. 1′	csc	tan	Diff. 1′	cot	sec	Diff. 1′	cos	←137° ′ ↓
0	9.82551	14	10.17449	9.95444	25	10.04556	10.12893	11	9.87107	60
1	.82565	14	.17435	.95469	26	.04531	.12904	11	.87096	59
2	.82579	14	.17421	.95495	25	.04505	.12915	12	.87085	58
3	.82593	14	.17407	.95520	25	.04480	.12927	11	.87073	57
4	.82607	14	.17393	.95545	26	.04455	.12938	12	.87062	56
5	9.82621	14	10.17379	9.95571	25	10.04429	10.12950	11	9.87050	55
6	.82635	14	.17365	.95596	26	.04404	.12961	11	.87039	54
7	.82649	14	.17351	.95622	25	.04378	.12972	12	.87028	53
8	.82663	14	.17337	.95647	25	.04353	.12984	11	.87016	52
9	.82677	14	.17323	.95672	26	.04328	.12995	12	.87005	51
10	9.82691	14	10.17309	9.95698	25	10.04302	10.13007	11	9.86993	50
11	.82705	14	.17295	.95723	25	.04277	.13018	12	.86982	49
12	.82719	14	.17281	.95748	26	.04252	.13030	11	.86970	48
13	.82733	14	.17267	.95774	25	.04226	.13041	12	.86959	47
14	.82747	14	.17253	.95799	26	.04201	.13053	11	.86947	46
15	9.82761	14	10.17239	9.95825	25	10.04175	10.13064	12	9.86936	45
16	.82775	13	.17225	.95850	25	.04150	.13076	11	.86924	44
17	.82788	14	.17212	.95875	26	.04125	.13087	11	.86913	43
18	.82802	14	.17198	.95901	25	.04099	.13098	12	.86902	42
19	.82816	14	.17184	.95926	26	.04074	.13110	11	.86890	41
20	9.82830	14	10.17170	9.95952	25	10.04048	10.13121	12	9.86879	40
21	.82844	14	.17156	.95977	25	.04023	.13133	12	.86867	39
22	.82858	14	.17142	.96002	26	.03998	.13145	11	.86855	38
23	.82872	13	.17128	.96028	25	.03972	.13156	12	.86844	37
24	.82885	14	.17115	.96053	25	.03947	.13168	11	.86832	36
25	9.82899	14	10.17101	9.96078	26	10.03922	10.13179	12	9.86821	35
26	.82913	14	.17087	.96104	25	.03896	.13191	11	.86809	34
27	.82927	14	.17073	.96129	26	.03871	.13202	12	.86798	33
28	.82941	14	.17059	.96155	25	.03845	.13214	11	.86786	32
29	.82955	13	.17045	.96180	25	.03820	.13225	12	.86775	31
30	9.82968	14	10.17032	9.96205	26	10.03795	10.13237	11	9.86763	30
31	.82982	14	.17018	.96231	25	.03769	.13248	12	.86752	29
32	.82996	14	.17004	.96256	25	.03744	.13260	12	.86740	28
33	.83010	13	.16990	.96281	26	.03719	.13272	11	.86728	27
34	.83023	14	.16977	.96307	25	.03693	.13283	12	.86717	26
35	9.83037	14	10.16963	9.96332	25	10.03668	10.13295	11	9.86705	25
36	.83051	14	.16949	.96357	26	.03643	.13306	12	.86694	24
37	.83065	13	.16935	.96383	25	.03617	.13318	12	.86682	23
38	.83078	14	.16922	.96408	25	.03592	.13330	11	.86670	22
39	.83092	14	.16908	.96433	26	.03567	.13341	12	.86659	21
40	9.83106	14	10.16894	9.96459	25	10.03541	10.13353	12	9.86647	20
41	.83120	13	.16880	.96484	26	.03516	.13365	11	.86635	19
42	.83133	14	.16867	.96510	25	.03490	.13376	12	.86624	18
43	.83147	14	.16853	.96535	25	.03465	.13388	12	.86612	17
44	.83161	13	.16839	.96560	26	.03440	.13400	11	.86600	16
45	9.83174	14	10.16826	9.96586	25	10.03414	10.13411	12	9.86589	15
46	.83188	14	.16812	.96611	25	.03389	.13423	12	.86577	14
47	.83202	13	.16798	.96636	26	.03364	.13435	11	.86565	13
48	.83215	14	.16785	.96662	25	.03338	.13446	12	.86554	12
49	.83229	13	.16771	.96687	25	.03313	.13458	12	.86542	11
50	9.83242	14	10.16758	9.96712	26	10.03288	10.13470	12	9.86530	10
51	.83256	14	.16744	.96738	25	.03262	.13482	11	.86518	9
52	.83270	13	.16730	.96763	25	.03237	.13493	12	.86507	8
53	.83283	14	.16717	.96788	26	.03212	.13505	12	.86495	7
54	.83297	13	.16703	.96814	25	.03186	.13517	11	.86483	6
55	9.83310	14	10.16690	9.96839	25	10.03161	10.13528	12	9.86472	5
56	.83324	14	.16676	.96864	26	.03136	.13540	12	.86460	4
57	.83338	13	.16662	.96890	25	.03110	.13552	12	.86448	3
58	.83351	14	.16649	.96915	25	.03085	.13564	11	.86436	2
59	.83365	13	.16635	.96940	26	.03060	.13575	12	.86425	1
60	9.83378		10.16622	9.96966		10.03034	10.13587		9.86413	0
↑ 132°→	cos	Diff. 1′	sec	cot	Diff. 1′	tan	csc	Diff. 1′	sin	← 47° ↑

TABLE 3

Common Logarithms of Trigonometric Functions (offset +10)

43°→ ′ ↓	sin	Diff. 1′	csc	tan	Diff. 1′	cot	sec	Diff. 1′	cos	←136° ′ ↓
0	9.83378	14	10.16622	9.96966	25	10.03034	10.13587	12	9.86413	60
1	.83392	13	.16608	.96991	25	.03009	.13599	12	.86401	59
2	.83405	14	.16595	.97016	26	.02984	.13611	12	.86389	58
3	.83419	13	.16581	.97042	25	.02958	.13623	11	.86377	57
4	.83432	14	.16568	.97067	25	.02933	.13634	12	.86366	56
5	9.83446	13	10.16554	9.97092	26	10.02908	10.13646	12	9.86354	55
6	.83459	14	.16541	.97118	25	.02882	.13658	12	.86342	54
7	.83473	13	.16527	.97143	25	.02857	.13670	12	.86330	53
8	.83486	14	.16514	.97168	25	.02832	.13682	12	.86318	52
9	.83500	13	.16500	.97193	26	.02807	.13694	11	.86306	51
10	9.83513	14	10.16487	9.97219	25	10.02781	10.13705	12	9.86295	50
11	.83527	13	.16473	.97244	25	.02756	.13717	12	.86283	49
12	.83540	14	.16460	.97269	26	.02731	.13729	12	.86271	48
13	.83554	13	.16446	.97295	25	.02705	.13741	12	.86259	47
14	.83567	14	.16433	.97320	25	.02680	.13753	12	.86247	46
15	9.83581	13	10.16419	9.97345	26	10.02655	10.13765	12	9.86235	45
16	.83594	14	.16406	.97371	25	.02629	.13777	12	.86223	44
17	.83608	13	.16392	.97396	25	.02604	.13789	11	.86211	43
18	.83621	13	.16379	.97421	26	.02579	.13800	12	.86200	42
19	.83634	14	.16366	.97447	25	.02553	.13812	12	.86188	41
20	9.83648	13	10.16352	9.97472	25	10.02528	10.13824	12	9.86176	40
21	.83661	13	.16339	.97497	26	.02503	.13836	12	.86164	39
22	.83674	14	.16326	.97523	25	.02477	.13848	12	.86152	38
23	.83688	13	.16312	.97548	25	.02452	.13860	12	.86140	37
24	.83701	14	.16299	.97573	25	.02427	.13872	12	.86128	36
25	9.83715	13	10.16285	9.97598	26	10.02402	10.13884	12	9.86116	35
26	.83728	13	.16272	.97624	25	.02376	.13896	12	.86104	34
27	.83741	14	.16259	.97649	25	.02351	.13908	12	.86092	33
28	.83755	13	.16245	.97674	26	.02326	.13920	12	.86080	32
29	.83768	13	.16232	.97700	25	.02300	.13932	12	.86068	31
30	9.83781	14	10.16219	9.97725	25	10.02275	10.13944	12	9.86056	30
31	.83795	13	.16205	.97750	26	.02250	.13956	12	.86044	29
32	.83808	13	.16192	.97776	25	.02224	.13968	12	.86032	28
33	.83821	13	.16179	.97801	25	.02199	.13980	12	.86020	27
34	.83834	14	.16166	.97826	25	.02174	.13992	12	.86008	26
35	9.83848	13	10.16152	9.97851	26	10.02149	10.14004	12	9.85996	25
36	.83861	13	.16139	.97877	25	.02123	.14016	12	.85984	24
37	.83874	13	.16126	.97902	25	.02098	.14028	12	.85972	23
38	.83887	14	.16113	.97927	26	.02073	.14040	12	.85960	22
39	.83901	13	.16099	.97953	25	.02047	.14052	12	.85948	21
40	9.83914	13	10.16086	9.97978	25	10.02022	10.14064	12	9.85936	20
41	.83927	13	.16073	.98003	26	.01997	.14076	12	.85924	19
42	.83940	14	.16060	.98029	25	.01971	.14088	12	.85912	18
43	.83954	13	.16046	.98054	25	.01946	.14100	12	.85900	17
44	.83967	13	.16033	.98079	25	.01921	.14112	12	.85888	16
45	9.83980	13	10.16020	9.98104	26	10.01896	10.14124	12	9.85876	15
46	.83993	13	.16007	.98130	25	.01870	.14136	13	.85864	14
47	.84006	14	.15994	.98155	25	.01845	.14149	12	.85851	13
48	.84020	13	.15980	.98180	26	.01820	.14161	12	.85839	12
49	.84033	13	.15967	.98206	25	.01794	.14173	12	.85827	11
50	9.84046	13	10.15954	9.98231	25	10.01769	10.14185	12	9.85815	10
51	.84059	13	.15941	.98256	25	.01744	.14197	12	.85803	9
52	.84072	13	.15928	.98281	26	.01719	.14209	12	.85791	8
53	.84085	13	.15915	.98307	25	.01693	.14221	13	.85779	7
54	.84098	14	.15902	.98332	25	.01668	.14234	12	.85766	6
55	9.84112	13	10.15888	9.98357	26	10.01643	10.14246	12	9.85754	5
56	.84125	13	.15875	.98383	25	.01617	.14258	12	.85742	4
57	.84138	13	.15862	.98408	25	.01592	.14270	12	.85730	3
58	.84151	13	.15849	.98433	25	.01567	.14282	12	.85718	2
59	.84164	13	.15836	.98458	26	.01542	.14294	13	.85706	1
60	9.84177		10.15823	9.98484		10.01516	10.14307		9.85693	0
↑ 133°→	cos	Diff. 1′	sec	cot	Diff. 1′	tan	csc	Diff. 1′	sin	← 46° ↑

TABLE 3

Common Logarithms of Trigonometric Functions (offset +10)

44° → ↓ ′	sin	Diff. 1′	csc	tan	Diff. 1′	cot	sec	Diff. 1′	cos	← 135° ↓ ′
0	9.84177	13	10.15823	9.98484	25	10.01516	10.14307	12	9.85693	60
1	.84190	13	.15810	.98509	25	.01491	.14319	12	.85681	59
2	.84203	13	.15797	.98534	26	.01466	.14331	12	.85669	58
3	.84216	13	.15784	.98560	25	.01440	.14343	12	.85657	57
4	.84229	13	.15771	.98585	25	.01415	.14355	13	.85645	56
5	9.84242	13	10.15758	9.98610	25	10.01390	10.14368	12	9.85632	55
6	.84255	14	.15745	.98635	26	.01365	.14380	12	.85620	54
7	.84269	13	.15731	.98661	25	.01339	.14392	12	.85608	53
8	.84282	13	.15718	.98686	25	.01314	.14404	13	.85596	52
9	.84295	13	.15705	.98711	26	.01289	.14417	12	.85583	51
10	9.84308	13	10.15692	9.98737	25	10.01263	10.14429	12	9.85571	50
11	.84321	13	.15679	.98762	25	.01238	.14441	12	.85559	49
12	.84334	13	.15666	.98787	25	.01213	.14453	13	.85547	48
13	.84347	13	.15653	.98812	26	.01188	.14466	12	.85534	47
14	.84360	13	.15640	.98838	25	.01162	.14478	12	.85522	46
15	9.84373	12	10.15627	9.98863	25	10.01137	10.14490	13	9.85510	45
16	.84385	13	.15615	.98888	25	.01112	.14503	12	.85497	44
17	.84398	13	.15602	.98913	26	.01087	.14515	12	.85485	43
18	.84411	13	.15589	.98939	25	.01061	.14527	13	.85473	42
19	.84424	13	.15576	.98964	25	.01036	.14540	12	.85460	41
20	9.84437	13	10.15563	9.98989	26	10.01011	10.14552	12	9.85448	40
21	.84450	13	.15550	.99015	25	.00985	.14564	13	.85436	39
22	.84463	13	.15537	.99040	25	.00960	.14577	12	.85423	38
23	.84476	13	.15524	.99065	25	.00935	.14589	12	.85411	37
24	.84489	13	.15511	.99090	26	.00910	.14601	13	.85399	36
25	9.84502	13	10.15498	9.99116	25	10.00884	10.14614	12	9.85386	35
26	.84515	13	.15485	.99141	25	.00859	.14626	13	.85374	34
27	.84528	12	.15472	.99166	25	.00834	.14639	12	.85361	33
28	.84540	13	.15460	.99191	26	.00809	.14651	12	.85349	32
29	.84553	13	.15447	.99217	25	.00783	.14663	13	.85337	31
30	9.84566	13	10.15434	9.99242	25	10.00758	10.14676	12	9.85324	30
31	.84579	13	.15421	.99267	26	.00733	.14688	13	.85312	29
32	.84592	13	.15408	.99293	25	.00707	.14701	12	.85299	28
33	.84605	13	.15395	.99318	25	.00682	.14713	13	.85287	27
34	.84618	12	.15382	.99343	25	.00657	.14726	12	.85274	26
35	9.84630	13	10.15370	9.99368	26	10.00632	10.14738	12	9.85262	25
36	.84643	13	.15357	.99394	25	.00606	.14750	13	.85250	24
37	.84656	13	.15344	.99419	25	.00581	.14763	12	.85237	23
38	.84669	13	.15331	.99444	25	.00556	.14775	13	.85225	22
39	.84682	12	.15318	.99469	26	.00531	.14788	12	.85212	21
40	9.84694	13	10.15306	9.99495	25	10.00505	10.14800	13	9.85200	20
41	.84707	13	.15293	.99520	25	.00480	.14813	12	.85187	19
42	.84720	13	.15280	.99545	25	.00455	.14825	13	.85175	18
43	.84733	12	.15267	.99570	26	.00430	.14838	12	.85162	17
44	.84745	13	.15255	.99596	25	.00404	.14850	13	.85150	16
45	9.84758	13	10.15242	9.99621	25	10.00379	10.14863	12	9.85137	15
46	.84771	13	.15229	.99646	26	.00354	.14875	13	.85125	14
47	.84784	12	.15216	.99672	25	.00328	.14888	12	.85112	13
48	.84796	13	.15204	.99697	25	.00303	.14900	13	.85100	12
49	.84809	13	.15191	.99722	25	.00278	.14913	13	.85087	11
50	9.84822	13	10.15178	9.99747	26	10.00253	10.14926	12	9.85074	10
51	.84835	12	.15165	.99773	25	.00227	.14938	13	.85062	9
52	.84847	13	.15153	.99798	25	.00202	.14951	12	.85049	8
53	.84860	13	.15140	.99823	25	.00177	.14963	13	.85037	7
54	.84873	12	.15127	.99848	26	.00152	.14976	12	.85024	6
55	9.84885	13	10.15115	9.99874	25	10.00126	10.14988	13	9.85012	5
56	.84898	13	.15102	.99899	25	.00101	.15001	13	.84999	4
57	.84911	12	.15089	.99924	25	.00076	.15014	12	.84986	3
58	.84923	13	.15077	.99949	26	.00051	.15026	13	.84974	2
59	.84936	13	.15064	.99975	25	.00025	.15039	12	.84961	1
60	9.84949		10.15051	10.00000		10.00000	10.15051		9.84949	0
↑ 134° →	cos	Diff. 1′	sec	cot	Diff. 1′	tan	csc	Diff. 1′	sin ←	↑ 45°

TABLE 4

359° | 001°
181° | 179°

Traverse **1°** Table

Dist.	D. Lat.	Dep.	Dist.	D. Lat.	Dep.	Dist.	D. Lat.	Dep.	Dist.	D. Lat.	Dep.	Dist.	D. Lat.	Dep.
1	1.0	0.0	61	61.0	1.1	121	121.0	2.1	181	181.0	3.2	241	241.0	4.2
2	2.0	0.0	62	62.0	1.1	22	122.0	2.1	82	182.0	3.2	42	242.0	4.2
3	3.0	0.1	63	63.0	1.1	23	123.0	2.1	83	183.0	3.2	43	243.0	4.2
4	4.0	0.1	64	64.0	1.1	24	124.0	2.2	84	184.0	3.2	44	244.0	4.3
5	5.0	0.1	65	65.0	1.1	25	125.0	2.2	85	185.0	3.2	45	245.0	4.3
6	6.0	0.1	66	66.0	1.2	26	126.0	2.2	86	186.0	3.2	46	246.0	4.3
7	7.0	0.1	67	67.0	1.2	27	127.0	2.2	87	187.0	3.3	47	247.0	4.3
8	8.0	0.1	68	68.0	1.2	28	128.0	2.2	88	188.0	3.3	48	248.0	4.3
9	9.0	0.2	69	69.0	1.2	29	129.0	2.3	89	189.0	3.3	49	249.0	4.3
10	10.0	0.2	70	70.0	1.2	30	130.0	2.3	90	190.0	3.3	50	250.0	4.4
11	11.0	0.2	71	71.0	1.2	131	131.0	2.3	191	191.0	3.3	251	251.0	4.4
12	12.0	0.2	72	72.0	1.3	32	132.0	2.3	92	192.0	3.4	52	252.0	4.4
13	13.0	0.2	73	73.0	1.3	33	133.0	2.3	93	193.0	3.4	53	253.0	4.4
14	14.0	0.2	74	74.0	1.3	34	134.0	2.3	94	194.0	3.4	54	254.0	4.4
15	15.0	0.3	75	75.0	1.3	35	135.0	2.4	95	195.0	3.4	55	255.0	4.5
16	16.0	0.3	76	76.0	1.3	36	136.0	2.4	96	196.0	3.4	56	256.0	4.5
17	17.0	0.3	77	77.0	1.3	37	137.0	2.4	97	197.0	3.4	57	257.0	4.5
18	18.0	0.3	78	78.0	1.4	38	138.0	2.4	98	198.0	3.5	58	258.0	4.5
19	19.0	0.3	79	79.0	1.4	39	139.0	2.4	99	199.0	3.5	59	259.0	4.5
20	20.0	0.3	80	80.0	1.4	40	140.0	2.4	200	200.0	3.5	60	260.0	4.5
21	21.0	0.4	81	81.0	1.4	141	141.0	2.5	201	201.0	3.5	261	261.0	4.6
22	22.0	0.4	82	82.0	1.4	42	142.0	2.5	02	202.0	3.5	62	262.0	4.6
23	23.0	0.4	83	83.0	1.4	43	143.0	2.5	03	203.0	3.5	63	263.0	4.6
24	24.0	0.4	84	84.0	1.5	44	144.0	2.5	04	204.0	3.6	64	264.0	4.6
25	25.0	0.4	85	85.0	1.5	45	145.0	2.5	05	205.0	3.6	65	265.0	4.6
26	26.0	0.5	86	86.0	1.5	46	146.0	2.5	06	206.0	3.6	66	266.0	4.6
27	27.0	0.5	87	87.0	1.5	47	147.0	2.6	07	207.0	3.6	67	267.0	4.7
28	28.0	0.5	88	88.0	1.5	48	148.0	2.6	08	208.0	3.6	68	268.0	4.7
29	29.0	0.5	89	89.0	1.6	49	149.0	2.6	09	209.0	3.6	69	269.0	4.7
30	30.0	0.5	90	90.0	1.6	50	150.0	2.6	10	210.0	3.7	70	270.0	4.7
31	31.0	0.5	91	91.0	1.6	151	151.0	2.6	211	211.0	3.7	271	271.0	4.7
32	32.0	0.6	92	92.0	1.6	52	152.0	2.7	12	212.0	3.7	72	272.0	4.7
33	33.0	0.6	93	93.0	1.6	53	153.0	2.7	13	213.0	3.7	73	273.0	4.8
34	34.0	0.6	94	94.0	1.6	54	154.0	2.7	14	214.0	3.7	74	274.0	4.8
35	35.0	0.6	95	95.0	1.7	55	155.0	2.7	15	215.0	3.8	75	275.0	4.8
36	36.0	0.6	96	96.0	1.7	56	156.0	2.7	16	216.0	3.8	76	276.0	4.8
37	37.0	0.6	97	97.0	1.7	57	157.0	2.7	17	217.0	3.8	77	277.0	4.8
38	38.0	0.7	98	98.0	1.7	58	158.0	2.8	18	218.0	3.8	78	278.0	4.9
39	39.0	0.7	99	99.0	1.7	59	159.0	2.8	19	219.0	3.8	79	279.0	4.9
40	40.0	0.7	100	100.0	1.7	60	160.0	2.8	20	220.0	3.8	80	280.0	4.9
41	41.0	0.7	101	101.0	1.8	161	161.0	2.8	221	221.0	3.9	281	281.0	4.9
42	42.0	0.7	02	102.0	1.8	62	162.0	2.8	22	222.0	3.9	82	282.0	4.9
43	43.0	0.8	03	103.0	1.8	63	163.0	2.8	23	223.0	3.9	83	283.0	4.9
44	44.0	0.8	04	104.0	1.8	64	164.0	2.9	24	224.0	3.9	84	284.0	5.0
45	45.0	0.8	05	105.0	1.8	65	165.0	2.9	25	225.0	3.9	85	285.0	5.0
46	46.0	0.8	06	106.0	1.8	66	166.0	2.9	26	226.0	3.9	86	286.0	5.0
47	47.0	0.8	07	107.0	1.9	67	167.0	2.9	27	227.0	4.0	87	287.0	5.0
48	48.0	0.8	08	108.0	1.9	68	168.0	2.9	28	228.0	4.0	88	288.0	5.0
49	49.0	0.9	09	109.0	1.9	69	169.0	2.9	29	229.0	4.0	89	289.0	5.0
50	50.0	0.9	10	110.0	1.9	70	170.0	3.0	30	230.0	4.0	90	290.0	5.1
51	51.0	0.9	111	111.0	1.9	171	171.0	3.0	231	231.0	4.0	291	291.0	5.1
52	52.0	0.9	12	112.0	2.0	72	172.0	3.0	32	232.0	4.0	92	292.0	5.1
53	53.0	0.9	13	113.0	2.0	73	173.0	3.0	33	233.0	4.1	93	293.0	5.1
54	54.0	0.9	14	114.0	2.0	74	174.0	3.0	34	234.0	4.1	94	294.0	5.1
55	55.0	1.0	15	115.0	2.0	75	175.0	3.1	35	235.0	4.1	95	295.0	5.1
56	56.0	1.0	16	116.0	2.0	76	176.0	3.1	36	236.0	4.1	96	296.0	5.2
57	57.0	1.0	17	117.0	2.0	77	177.0	3.1	37	237.0	4.1	97	297.0	5.2
58	58.0	1.0	18	118.0	2.1	78	178.0	3.1	38	238.0	4.2	98	298.0	5.2
59	59.0	1.0	19	119.0	2.1	79	179.0	3.1	39	239.0	4.2	99	299.0	5.2
60	60.0	1.0	20	120.0	2.1	80	180.0	3.1	40	240.0	4.2	300	300.0	5.2
Dist.	Dep.	D. Lat.	Dist.	Dep.	D. Lat.	Dist.	Dep.	D. Lat.	Dist.	Dep.	D. Lat.	Dist.	Dep.	D. Lat.

271° | 089°
269° | 091°

89°

Dist.	D. Lat.	Dep.
N.	N x Cos.	N x Sin.
Hypotenuse	Side Adj.	Side Opp.

TABLE 4

359° | 001°
181° | 179°

Traverse **1°** Table

Dist.	D. Lat.	Dep.	Dist.	D. Lat.	Dep.	Dist.	D. Lat.	Dep.	Dist.	D. Lat.	Dep.	Dist.	D. Lat.	Dep.
301	301.0	5.3	361	360.9	6.3	421	420.9	7.3	481	480.9	8.4	541	540.9	9.4
02	302.0	5.3	62	361.9	6.3	22	421.9	7.4	82	481.9	8.4	42	541.9	9.5
03	303.0	5.3	63	362.9	6.3	23	422.9	7.4	83	482.9	8.4	43	542.9	9.5
04	304.0	5.3	64	363.9	6.4	24	423.9	7.4	84	483.9	8.4	44	543.9	9.5
05	305.0	5.3	65	364.9	6.4	25	424.9	7.4	85	484.9	8.5	45	544.9	9.5
06	306.0	5.3	66	365.9	6.4	26	425.9	7.4	86	485.9	8.5	46	545.9	9.5
07	307.0	5.4	67	366.9	6.4	27	426.9	7.5	87	486.9	8.5	47	546.9	9.5
08	308.0	5.4	68	367.9	6.4	28	427.9	7.5	88	487.9	8.5	48	547.9	9.6
09	309.0	5.4	69	368.9	6.4	29	428.9	7.5	89	488.9	8.5	49	548.9	9.6
10	310.0	5.4	70	369.9	6.5	30	429.9	7.5	90	489.9	8.6	50	549.9	9.6
311	311.0	5.4	371	370.9	6.5	431	430.9	7.5	491	490.9	8.6	551	550.9	9.6
12	312.0	5.4	72	371.9	6.5	32	431.9	7.5	92	491.9	8.6	52	551.9	9.6
13	313.0	5.5	73	372.9	6.5	33	432.9	7.6	93	492.9	8.6	53	552.9	9.7
14	314.0	5.5	74	373.9	6.5	34	433.9	7.6	94	493.9	8.6	54	553.9	9.7
15	315.0	5.5	75	374.9	6.5	35	434.9	7.6	95	494.9	8.6	55	554.9	9.7
16	316.0	5.5	76	375.9	6.6	36	435.9	7.6	96	495.9	8.7	56	555.9	9.7
17	317.0	5.5	77	376.9	6.6	37	436.9	7.6	97	496.9	8.7	57	556.9	9.7
18	318.0	5.5	78	377.9	6.6	38	437.9	7.6	98	497.9	8.7	58	557.9	9.7
19	319.0	5.6	79	378.9	6.6	39	438.9	7.7	99	498.9	8.7	59	558.9	9.8
20	320.0	5.6	80	379.9	6.6	40	439.9	7.7	500	499.9	8.7	60	559.9	9.8
321	321.0	5.6	381	380.9	6.6	441	440.9	7.7	501	500.9	8.7	561	560.9	9.8
22	322.0	5.6	82	381.9	6.7	42	441.9	7.7	02	501.9	8.8	62	561.9	9.8
23	323.0	5.6	83	382.9	6.7	43	442.9	7.7	03	502.9	8.8	63	562.9	9.8
24	324.0	5.7	84	383.9	6.7	44	443.9	7.7	04	503.9	8.8	64	563.9	9.8
25	325.0	5.7	85	384.9	6.7	45	444.9	7.8	05	504.9	8.8	65	564.9	9.9
26	326.0	5.7	86	385.9	6.7	46	445.9	7.8	06	505.9	8.8	66	565.9	9.9
27	327.0	5.7	87	386.9	6.8	47	446.9	7.8	07	506.9	8.8	67	566.9	9.9
28	328.0	5.7	88	387.9	6.8	48	447.9	7.8	08	507.9	8.9	68	567.9	9.9
29	328.9	5.7	89	388.9	6.8	49	448.9	7.8	09	508.9	8.9	69	568.9	9.9
30	329.9	5.8	90	389.9	6.8	50	449.9	7.9	10	509.9	8.9	70	569.9	9.9
331	330.9	5.8	391	390.9	6.8	451	450.9	7.9	511	510.9	8.9	571	570.9	10.0
32	331.9	5.8	92	391.9	6.8	52	451.9	7.9	12	511.9	8.9	72	571.9	10.0
33	332.9	5.8	93	392.9	6.9	53	452.9	7.9	13	512.9	9.0	73	572.9	10.0
34	333.9	5.8	94	393.9	6.9	54	453.9	7.9	14	513.9	9.0	74	573.9	10.0
35	334.9	5.8	95	394.9	6.9	55	454.9	7.9	15	514.9	9.0	75	574.9	10.0
36	335.9	5.9	96	395.9	6.9	56	455.9	8.0	16	515.9	9.0	76	575.9	10.1
37	336.9	5.9	97	396.9	6.9	57	456.9	8.0	17	516.9	9.0	77	576.9	10.1
38	337.9	5.9	98	397.9	6.9	58	457.9	8.0	18	517.9	9.0	78	577.9	10.1
39	338.9	5.9	99	398.9	7.0	59	458.9	8.0	19	518.9	9.1	79	578.9	10.1
40	339.9	5.9	400	399.9	7.0	60	459.9	8.0	20	519.9	9.1	80	579.9	10.1
341	340.9	6.0	401	400.9	7.0	461	460.9	8.0	521	520.9	9.1	581	580.9	10.1
42	341.9	6.0	02	401.9	7.0	62	461.9	8.1	22	521.9	9.1	82	581.9	10.2
43	342.9	6.0	03	402.9	7.0	63	462.9	8.1	23	522.9	9.1	83	582.9	10.2
44	343.9	6.0	04	403.9	7.1	64	463.9	8.1	24	523.9	9.1	84	583.9	10.2
45	344.9	6.0	05	404.9	7.1	65	464.9	8.1	25	524.9	9.2	85	584.9	10.2
46	345.9	6.0	06	405.9	7.1	66	465.9	8.1	26	525.9	9.2	86	585.9	10.2
47	346.9	6.1	07	406.9	7.1	67	466.9	8.2	27	526.9	9.2	87	586.9	10.2
48	347.9	6.1	08	407.9	7.1	68	467.9	8.2	28	527.9	9.2	88	587.9	10.3
49	348.9	6.1	09	408.9	7.1	69	468.9	8.2	29	528.9	9.2	89	588.9	10.3
50	349.9	6.1	10	409.9	7.2	70	469.9	8.2	30	529.9	9.2	90	589.9	10.3
351	350.9	6.1	411	410.9	7.2	471	470.9	8.2	531	530.9	9.3	591	590.9	10.3
52	351.9	6.1	12	411.9	7.2	72	471.9	8.2	32	531.9	9.3	92	591.9	10.3
53	352.9	6.2	13	412.9	7.2	73	472.9	8.3	33	532.9	9.3	93	592.9	10.3
54	353.9	6.2	14	413.9	7.2	74	473.9	8.3	34	533.9	9.3	94	593.9	10.4
55	354.9	6.2	15	414.9	7.2	75	474.9	8.3	35	534.9	9.3	95	594.9	10.4
56	355.9	6.2	16	415.9	7.3	76	475.9	8.3	36	535.9	9.4	96	595.9	10.4
57	356.9	6.2	17	416.9	7.3	77	476.9	8.3	37	536.9	9.4	97	596.9	10.4
58	357.9	6.2	18	417.9	7.3	78	477.9	8.3	38	537.9	9.4	98	597.9	10.4
59	358.9	6.3	19	418.9	7.3	79	478.9	8.4	39	538.9	9.4	99	598.9	10.5
60	359.9	6.3	20	419.9	7.3	80	479.9	8.4	40	539.9	9.4	600	599.9	10.5
Dist.	Dep.	D. Lat.	Dist.	Dep.	D. Lat.	Dist.	Dep.	D. Lat.	Dist.	Dep.	D. Lat.	Dist.	Dep.	D. Lat.

Dist.	D. Lat.	Dep.
D Lo	Dep.	
	m	D Lo

89°

271° | 089°
269° | 091°

TABLE 4

Traverse 2° Table

358° | 002° — 182° | 178°

Dist.	D. Lat.	Dep.	Dist.	D. Lat.	Dep.	Dist.	D. Lat.	Dep.	Dist.	D. Lat.	Dep.	Dist.	D. Lat.	Dep.
1	1.0	0.0	61	61.0	2.1	121	120.9	4.2	181	180.9	6.3	241	240.9	8.4
2	2.0	0.1	62	62.0	2.2	22	121.9	4.3	82	181.9	6.4	42	241.9	8.4
3	3.0	0.1	63	63.0	2.2	23	122.9	4.3	83	182.9	6.4	43	242.9	8.5
4	4.0	0.1	64	64.0	2.2	24	123.9	4.3	84	183.9	6.4	44	243.9	8.5
5	5.0	0.2	65	65.0	2.3	25	124.9	4.4	85	184.9	6.5	45	244.9	8.6
6	6.0	0.2	66	66.0	2.3	26	125.9	4.4	86	185.9	6.5	46	245.9	8.6
7	7.0	0.2	67	67.0	2.3	27	126.9	4.4	87	186.9	6.5	47	246.8	8.6
8	8.0	0.3	68	68.0	2.4	28	127.9	4.5	88	187.9	6.6	48	247.8	8.7
9	9.0	0.3	69	69.0	2.4	29	128.9	4.5	89	188.9	6.6	49	248.8	8.7
10	10.0	0.3	70	70.0	2.4	30	129.9	4.5	90	189.9	6.6	50	249.8	8.7
11	11.0	0.4	71	71.0	2.5	131	130.9	4.6	191	190.9	6.7	251	250.8	8.8
12	12.0	0.4	72	72.0	2.5	32	131.9	4.6	92	191.9	6.7	52	251.8	8.8
13	13.0	0.5	73	73.0	2.5	33	132.9	4.6	93	192.9	6.7	53	252.8	8.8
14	14.0	0.5	74	74.0	2.6	34	133.9	4.7	94	193.9	6.8	54	253.8	8.9
15	15.0	0.5	75	75.0	2.6	35	134.9	4.7	95	194.9	6.8	55	254.8	8.9
16	16.0	0.6	76	76.0	2.7	36	135.9	4.7	96	195.9	6.8	56	255.8	8.9
17	17.0	0.6	77	77.0	2.7	37	136.9	4.8	97	196.9	6.9	57	256.8	9.0
18	18.0	0.6	78	78.0	2.7	38	137.9	4.8	98	197.9	6.9	58	257.8	9.0
19	19.0	0.7	79	79.0	2.8	39	138.9	4.9	99	198.9	6.9	59	258.8	9.0
20	20.0	0.7	80	80.0	2.8	40	139.9	4.9	200	199.9	7.0	60	259.8	9.1
21	21.0	0.7	81	81.0	2.8	141	140.9	4.9	201	200.9	7.0	261	260.8	9.1
22	22.0	0.8	82	82.0	2.9	42	141.9	5.0	02	201.9	7.0	62	261.8	9.1
23	23.0	0.8	83	82.9	2.9	43	142.9	5.0	03	202.9	7.1	63	262.8	9.2
24	24.0	0.8	84	83.9	2.9	44	143.9	5.0	04	203.9	7.1	64	263.8	9.2
25	25.0	0.9	85	84.9	3.0	45	144.9	5.1	05	204.9	7.2	65	264.8	9.2
26	26.0	0.9	86	85.9	3.0	46	145.9	5.1	06	205.9	7.2	66	265.8	9.3
27	27.0	0.9	87	86.9	3.0	47	146.9	5.1	07	206.9	7.2	67	266.8	9.3
28	28.0	1.0	88	87.9	3.1	48	147.9	5.2	08	207.9	7.3	68	267.8	9.4
29	29.0	1.0	89	88.9	3.1	49	148.9	5.2	09	208.9	7.3	69	268.8	9.4
30	30.0	1.0	90	89.9	3.1	50	149.9	5.2	10	209.9	7.3	70	269.8	9.4
31	31.0	1.1	91	90.9	3.2	151	150.9	5.3	211	210.9	7.4	271	270.8	9.5
32	32.0	1.1	92	91.9	3.2	52	151.9	5.3	12	211.9	7.4	72	271.8	9.5
33	33.0	1.2	93	92.9	3.2	53	152.9	5.3	13	212.9	7.4	73	272.8	9.5
34	34.0	1.2	94	93.9	3.3	54	153.9	5.4	14	213.9	7.5	74	273.8	9.6
35	35.0	1.2	95	94.9	3.3	55	154.9	5.4	15	214.9	7.5	75	274.8	9.6
36	36.0	1.3	96	95.9	3.4	56	155.9	5.4	16	215.9	7.5	76	275.8	9.6
37	37.0	1.3	97	96.9	3.4	57	156.9	5.5	17	216.9	7.6	77	276.8	9.7
38	38.0	1.3	98	97.9	3.4	58	157.9	5.5	18	217.9	7.6	78	277.8	9.7
39	39.0	1.4	99	98.9	3.5	59	158.9	5.5	19	218.9	7.6	79	278.8	9.7
40	40.0	1.4	100	99.9	3.5	60	159.9	5.6	20	219.9	7.7	80	279.8	9.8
41	41.0	1.4	101	100.9	3.5	161	160.9	5.6	221	220.9	7.7	281	280.8	9.8
42	42.0	1.5	02	101.9	3.6	62	161.9	5.7	22	221.9	7.7	82	281.8	9.8
43	43.0	1.5	03	102.9	3.6	63	162.9	5.7	23	222.9	7.8	83	282.8	9.9
44	44.0	1.5	04	103.9	3.6	64	163.9	5.7	24	223.9	7.8	84	283.8	9.9
45	45.0	1.6	05	104.9	3.7	65	164.9	5.8	25	224.9	7.9	85	284.8	9.9
46	46.0	1.6	06	105.9	3.7	66	165.9	5.8	26	225.9	7.9	86	285.8	10.0
47	47.0	1.6	07	106.9	3.7	67	166.9	5.8	27	226.9	7.9	87	286.8	10.0
48	48.0	1.7	08	107.9	3.8	68	167.9	5.9	28	227.9	8.0	88	287.8	10.1
49	49.0	1.7	09	108.9	3.8	69	168.9	5.9	29	228.9	8.0	89	288.8	10.1
50	50.0	1.7	10	109.9	3.8	70	169.9	5.9	30	229.9	8.0	90	289.8	10.1
51	51.0	1.8	111	110.9	3.9	171	170.9	6.0	231	230.9	8.1	291	290.8	10.2
52	52.0	1.8	12	111.9	3.9	72	171.9	6.0	32	231.9	8.1	92	291.8	10.2
53	53.0	1.8	13	112.9	3.9	73	172.9	6.0	33	232.9	8.1	93	292.8	10.2
54	54.0	1.9	14	113.9	4.0	74	173.9	6.1	34	233.9	8.2	94	293.8	10.3
55	55.0	1.9	15	114.9	4.0	75	174.9	6.1	35	234.9	8.2	95	294.8	10.3
56	56.0	2.0	16	115.9	4.0	76	175.9	6.1	36	235.9	8.2	96	295.8	10.3
57	57.0	2.0	17	116.9	4.1	77	176.9	6.2	37	236.9	8.3	97	296.8	10.4
58	58.0	2.0	18	117.9	4.1	78	177.9	6.2	38	237.9	8.3	98	297.8	10.4
59	59.0	2.1	19	118.9	4.2	79	178.9	6.2	39	238.9	8.3	99	298.8	10.4
60	60.0	2.1	20	119.9	4.2	80	179.9	6.3	40	239.9	8.4	300	299.8	10.5
Dist.	Dep.	D. Lat.	Dist.	Dep.	D. Lat.	Dist.	Dep.	D. Lat.	Dist.	Dep.	D. Lat.	Dist.	Dep.	D. Lat.

272° | 088° — 268° | 092°

88°

Dist.	D. Lat.	Dep.
N.	N x Cos.	N x Sin.
Hypotenuse	Side Adj.	Side Opp.

TABLE 4

Traverse 2° Table

358° | 002° — 182° | 178°

Dist.	D. Lat.	Dep.	Dist.	D. Lat.	Dep.	Dist.	D. Lat.	Dep.	Dist.	D. Lat.	Dep.	Dist.	D. Lat.	Dep.
301	300.8	10.5	361	360.8	12.6	421	420.7	14.7	481	480.7	16.8	541	540.7	18.9
02	301.8	10.5	62	361.8	12.6	22	421.7	14.7	82	481.7	16.8	42	541.7	18.9
03	302.8	10.6	63	362.8	12.7	23	422.7	14.8	83	482.7	16.9	43	542.7	19.0
04	303.8	10.6	64	363.8	12.7	24	423.7	14.8	84	483.7	16.9	44	543.7	19.0
05	304.8	10.6	65	364.8	12.7	25	424.7	14.8	85	484.7	16.9	45	544.7	19.0
06	305.8	10.7	66	365.8	12.8	26	425.7	14.9	86	485.7	17.0	46	545.7	19.1
07	306.8	10.7	67	366.8	12.8	27	426.7	14.9	87	486.7	17.0	47	546.7	19.1
08	307.8	10.7	68	367.8	12.8	28	427.7	14.9	88	487.7	17.0	48	547.7	19.1
09	308.8	10.8	69	368.8	12.9	29	428.7	15.0	89	488.7	17.1	49	548.7	19.2
10	309.8	10.8	70	369.8	12.9	30	429.7	15.0	90	489.7	17.1	50	549.7	19.2
311	310.8	10.9	371	370.8	12.9	431	430.7	15.0	491	490.7	17.1	551	550.7	19.2
12	311.8	10.9	72	371.8	13.0	32	431.7	15.1	92	491.7	17.2	52	551.7	19.3
13	312.8	10.9	73	372.8	13.0	33	432.7	15.1	93	492.7	17.2	53	552.7	19.3
14	313.8	11.0	74	373.8	13.1	34	433.7	15.1	94	493.7	17.2	54	553.7	19.3
15	314.8	11.0	75	374.8	13.1	35	434.7	15.2	95	494.7	17.3	55	554.7	19.4
16	315.8	11.0	76	375.8	13.1	36	435.7	15.2	96	495.7	17.3	56	555.7	19.4
17	316.8	11.1	77	376.8	13.2	37	436.7	15.3	97	496.7	17.3	57	556.7	19.4
18	317.8	11.1	78	377.8	13.2	38	437.7	15.3	98	497.7	17.4	58	557.7	19.5
19	318.8	11.1	79	378.8	13.2	39	438.7	15.3	99	498.7	17.4	59	558.7	19.5
20	319.8	11.2	80	379.8	13.3	40	439.7	15.4	500	499.7	17.4	60	559.7	19.5
321	320.8	11.2	381	380.8	13.3	441	440.7	15.4	501	500.7	17.5	561	560.7	19.6
22	321.8	11.2	82	381.8	13.3	42	441.7	15.4	02	501.7	17.5	62	561.7	19.6
23	322.8	11.3	83	382.8	13.4	43	442.7	15.5	03	502.7	17.6	63	562.7	19.6
24	323.8	11.3	84	383.8	13.4	44	443.7	15.5	04	503.7	17.6	64	563.7	19.7
25	324.8	11.3	85	384.8	13.4	45	444.7	15.5	05	504.7	17.6	65	564.7	19.7
26	325.8	11.4	86	385.8	13.5	46	445.7	15.6	06	505.7	17.7	66	565.7	19.8
27	326.8	11.4	87	386.8	13.5	47	446.7	15.6	07	506.7	17.7	67	566.7	19.8
28	327.8	11.4	88	387.8	13.5	48	447.7	15.6	08	507.7	17.7	68	567.7	19.8
29	328.8	11.5	89	388.8	13.6	49	448.7	15.7	09	508.7	17.8	69	568.7	19.9
30	329.8	11.5	90	389.8	13.6	50	449.7	15.7	10	509.7	17.8	70	569.7	19.9
331	330.8	11.6	391	390.8	13.6	451	450.7	15.7	511	510.7	17.8	571	570.7	19.9
32	331.8	11.6	92	391.8	13.7	52	451.7	15.8	12	511.7	17.9	72	571.7	20.0
33	332.8	11.6	93	392.8	13.7	53	452.7	15.8	13	512.7	17.9	73	572.7	20.0
34	333.8	11.7	94	393.8	13.8	54	453.7	15.8	14	513.7	17.9	74	573.7	20.0
35	334.8	11.7	95	394.8	13.8	55	454.7	15.9	15	514.7	18.0	75	574.6	20.1
36	335.8	11.7	96	395.8	13.8	56	455.7	15.9	16	515.7	18.0	76	575.6	20.1
37	336.8	11.8	97	396.8	13.9	57	456.7	15.9	17	516.7	18.0	77	576.6	20.1
38	337.8	11.8	98	397.8	13.9	58	457.7	16.0	18	517.7	18.1	78	577.6	20.2
39	338.8	11.8	99	398.8	13.9	59	458.7	16.0	19	518.7	18.1	79	578.6	20.2
40	339.8	11.9	400	399.8	14.0	60	459.7	16.1	20	519.7	18.1	80	579.6	20.2
341	340.8	11.9	401	400.8	14.0	461	460.7	16.1	521	520.7	18.2	581	580.6	20.3
42	341.8	11.9	02	401.8	14.0	62	461.7	16.1	22	521.7	18.2	82	581.6	20.3
43	342.8	12.0	03	402.8	14.1	63	462.7	16.2	23	522.7	18.3	83	582.6	20.3
44	343.8	12.0	04	403.8	14.1	64	463.7	16.2	24	523.7	18.3	84	583.6	20.4
45	344.8	12.0	05	404.8	14.1	65	464.7	16.2	25	524.7	18.3	85	584.6	20.4
46	345.8	12.1	06	405.8	14.2	66	465.7	16.3	26	525.7	18.4	86	585.6	20.5
47	346.8	12.1	07	406.8	14.2	67	466.7	16.3	27	526.7	18.4	87	586.6	20.5
48	347.8	12.1	08	407.8	14.2	68	467.7	16.3	28	527.7	18.4	88	587.6	20.5
49	348.8	12.2	09	408.8	14.3	69	468.7	16.4	29	528.7	18.5	89	588.6	20.6
50	349.8	12.2	10	409.8	14.3	70	469.7	16.4	30	529.7	18.5	90	589.6	20.6
351	350.8	12.2	411	410.7	14.3	471	470.7	16.4	531	530.7	18.5	591	590.6	20.6
52	351.8	12.3	12	411.7	14.4	72	471.7	16.5	32	531.7	18.6	92	591.6	20.7
53	352.8	12.3	13	412.7	14.4	73	472.7	16.5	33	532.7	18.6	93	592.6	20.7
54	353.8	12.4	14	413.7	14.4	74	473.7	16.5	34	533.7	18.6	94	593.6	20.7
55	354.8	12.4	15	414.7	14.5	75	474.7	16.6	35	534.7	18.7	95	594.6	20.8
56	355.8	12.4	16	415.7	14.5	76	475.7	16.6	36	535.7	18.7	96	595.6	20.8
57	356.8	12.5	17	416.7	14.6	77	476.7	16.6	37	536.7	18.7	97	596.6	20.8
58	357.8	12.5	18	417.7	14.6	78	477.7	16.7	38	537.7	18.8	98	597.6	20.9
59	358.8	12.5	19	418.7	14.6	79	478.7	16.7	39	538.7	18.8	99	598.6	20.9
60	359.8	12.6	20	419.7	14.7	80	479.7	16.8	40	539.7	18.8	600	599.6	20.9
Dist.	Dep.	D. Lat.	Dist.	Dep.	D. Lat.	Dist.	Dep.	D. Lat.	Dist.	Dep.	D. Lat.	Dist.	Dep.	D. Lat.

Dist.	D. Lat.	Dep.
D Lo	Dep.	
	m	D Lo

88°

272° | 088° — 268° | 092°

TABLE 4
3°
Traverse Table

357° | 003° / 183° | 177°														357° | 003° / 183° | 177°
Dist.	D. Lat.	Dep.	Dist.	D. Lat.	Dep.	Dist.	D. Lat.	Dep.	Dist.	D. Lat.	Dep.	Dist.	D. Lat.	Dep.
1	1.0	0.1	61	60.9	3.2	121	120.8	6.3	181	180.8	9.5	241	240.7	12.6
2	2.0	0.1	62	61.9	3.2	22	121.8	6.4	82	181.8	9.5	42	241.7	12.7
3	3.0	0.2	63	62.9	3.3	23	122.8	6.4	83	182.7	9.6	43	242.7	12.7
4	4.0	0.2	64	63.9	3.3	24	123.8	6.5	84	183.7	9.6	44	243.7	12.8
5	5.0	0.3	65	64.9	3.4	25	124.8	6.5	85	184.7	9.7	45	244.7	12.8
6	6.0	0.3	66	65.9	3.5	26	125.8	6.6	86	185.7	9.7	46	245.7	12.9
7	7.0	0.4	67	66.9	3.5	27	126.8	6.6	87	186.7	9.8	47	246.7	12.9
8	8.0	0.4	68	67.9	3.6	28	127.8	6.7	88	187.7	9.8	48	247.7	13.0
9	9.0	0.5	69	68.9	3.6	29	128.8	6.8	89	188.7	9.9	49	248.7	13.0
10	10.0	0.5	70	69.9	3.7	30	129.8	6.8	90	189.7	9.9	50	249.7	13.1
11	11.0	0.6	71	70.9	3.7	131	130.8	6.9	191	190.7	10.0	251	250.7	13.1
12	12.0	0.6	72	71.9	3.8	32	131.8	6.9	92	191.7	10.0	52	251.7	13.2
13	13.0	0.7	73	72.9	3.8	33	132.8	7.0	93	192.7	10.1	53	252.7	13.2
14	14.0	0.7	74	73.9	3.9	34	133.8	7.0	94	193.7	10.2	54	253.7	13.3
15	15.0	0.8	75	74.9	3.9	35	134.8	7.1	95	194.7	10.2	55	254.7	13.3
16	16.0	0.8	76	75.9	4.0	36	135.8	7.1	96	195.7	10.3	56	255.6	13.4
17	17.0	0.9	77	76.9	4.0	37	136.8	7.2	97	196.7	10.3	57	256.6	13.5
18	18.0	0.9	78	77.9	4.1	38	137.8	7.2	98	197.7	10.4	58	257.6	13.5
19	19.0	1.0	79	78.9	4.1	39	138.8	7.3	99	198.7	10.4	59	258.6	13.6
20	20.0	1.0	80	79.9	4.2	40	139.8	7.3	200	199.7	10.5	60	259.6	13.6
21	21.0	1.1	81	80.9	4.2	141	140.8	7.4	201	200.7	10.5	261	260.6	13.7
22	22.0	1.2	82	81.9	4.3	42	141.8	7.4	02	201.7	10.6	62	261.6	13.7
23	23.0	1.2	83	82.9	4.3	43	142.8	7.5	03	202.7	10.6	63	262.6	13.8
24	24.0	1.3	84	83.9	4.4	44	143.8	7.5	04	203.7	10.7	64	263.6	13.8
25	25.0	1.3	85	84.9	4.4	45	144.8	7.6	05	204.7	10.7	65	264.6	13.9
26	26.0	1.4	86	85.9	4.5	46	145.8	7.6	06	205.7	10.8	66	265.6	13.9
27	27.0	1.4	87	86.9	4.6	47	146.8	7.7	07	206.7	10.8	67	266.6	14.0
28	28.0	1.5	88	87.9	4.6	48	147.8	7.7	08	207.7	10.9	68	267.6	14.0
29	29.0	1.5	89	88.9	4.7	49	148.8	7.8	09	208.7	10.9	69	268.6	14.1
30	30.0	1.6	90	89.9	4.7	50	149.8	7.9	10	209.7	11.0	70	269.6	14.1
31	31.0	1.6	91	90.9	4.8	151	150.8	7.9	211	210.7	11.0	271	270.6	14.2
32	32.0	1.7	92	91.9	4.8	52	151.8	8.0	12	211.7	11.1	72	271.6	14.2
33	33.0	1.7	93	92.9	4.9	53	152.8	8.0	13	212.7	11.1	73	272.6	14.3
34	34.0	1.8	94	93.9	4.9	54	153.8	8.1	14	213.7	11.2	74	273.6	14.3
35	35.0	1.8	95	94.9	5.0	55	154.8	8.1	15	214.7	11.3	75	274.6	14.4
36	36.0	1.9	96	95.9	5.0	56	155.8	8.2	16	215.7	11.3	76	275.6	14.4
37	36.9	1.9	97	96.9	5.1	57	156.8	8.2	17	216.7	11.4	77	276.6	14.5
38	37.9	2.0	98	97.9	5.1	58	157.8	8.3	18	217.7	11.4	78	277.6	14.5
39	38.9	2.0	99	98.9	5.2	59	158.8	8.3	19	218.7	11.5	79	278.6	14.6
40	39.9	2.1	100	99.9	5.2	60	159.8	8.4	20	219.7	11.5	80	279.6	14.7
41	40.9	2.1	101	100.9	5.3	161	160.8	8.4	221	220.7	11.6	281	280.6	14.7
42	41.9	2.2	02	101.9	5.3	62	161.8	8.5	22	221.7	11.6	82	281.6	14.8
43	42.9	2.3	03	102.9	5.4	63	162.8	8.5	23	222.7	11.7	83	282.6	14.8
44	43.9	2.3	04	103.9	5.4	64	163.8	8.6	24	223.7	11.7	84	283.6	14.9
45	44.9	2.4	05	104.9	5.5	65	164.8	8.6	25	224.7	11.8	85	284.6	14.9
46	45.9	2.4	06	105.9	5.5	66	165.8	8.7	26	225.7	11.8	86	285.6	15.0
47	46.9	2.5	07	106.9	5.6	67	166.8	8.7	27	226.7	11.9	87	286.6	15.0
48	47.9	2.5	08	107.9	5.7	68	167.8	8.8	28	227.7	11.9	88	287.6	15.1
49	48.9	2.6	09	108.9	5.7	69	168.8	8.8	29	228.7	12.0	89	288.6	15.1
50	49.9	2.6	10	109.8	5.8	70	169.8	8.9	30	229.7	12.0	90	289.6	15.2
51	50.9	2.7	111	110.8	5.8	171	170.8	8.9	231	230.7	12.1	291	290.6	15.2
52	51.9	2.7	12	111.8	5.9	72	171.8	9.0	32	231.7	12.1	92	291.6	15.3
53	52.9	2.8	13	112.8	5.9	73	172.8	9.1	33	232.7	12.2	93	292.6	15.3
54	53.9	2.8	14	113.8	6.0	74	173.8	9.1	34	233.7	12.2	94	293.6	15.4
55	54.9	2.9	15	114.8	6.0	75	174.8	9.2	35	234.7	12.3	95	294.6	15.4
56	55.9	2.9	16	115.8	6.1	76	175.8	9.2	36	235.7	12.4	96	295.6	15.5
57	56.9	3.0	17	116.8	6.1	77	176.8	9.3	37	236.7	12.4	97	296.6	15.5
58	57.9	3.0	18	117.8	6.2	78	177.8	9.3	38	237.7	12.5	98	297.6	15.6
59	58.9	3.1	19	118.8	6.2	79	178.8	9.4	39	238.7	12.5	99	298.6	15.6
60	59.9	3.1	20	119.8	6.3	80	179.8	9.4	40	239.7	12.6	300	299.6	15.7
Dist.	Dep.	D. Lat.	Dist.	Dep.	D. Lat.	Dist.	Dep.	D. Lat.	Dist.	Dep.	D. Lat.	Dist.	Dep.	D. Lat.

273° | 087°
267° | 093°

87°

Dist.	D. Lat.	Dep.
N.	N x Cos.	N x Sin.
Hypotenuse	Side Adj.	Side Opp.

TABLE 4
3°
Traverse Table

357° | 003° / 183° | 177°														357° | 003° / 183° | 177°
Dist.	D. Lat.	Dep.	Dist.	D. Lat.	Dep.	Dist.	D. Lat.	Dep.	Dist.	D. Lat.	Dep.	Dist.	D. Lat.	Dep.
301	300.6	15.8	361	360.5	18.9	421	420.4	22.0	481	480.3	25.2	541	540.3	28.3
02	301.6	15.8	62	361.5	18.9	22	421.4	22.1	82	481.3	25.2	42	541.3	28.4
03	302.6	15.9	63	362.5	19.0	23	422.4	22.1	83	482.3	25.3	43	542.3	28.4
04	303.6	15.9	64	363.5	19.1	24	423.4	22.2	84	483.3	25.3	44	543.3	28.5
05	304.6	16.0	65	364.5	19.1	25	424.4	22.2	85	484.3	25.4	45	544.3	28.5
06	305.6	16.0	66	365.5	19.2	26	425.4	22.3	86	485.3	25.4	46	545.3	28.6
07	306.6	16.1	67	366.5	19.2	27	426.4	22.3	87	486.3	25.5	47	546.3	28.6
08	307.6	16.1	68	367.5	19.3	28	427.4	22.4	88	487.3	25.5	48	547.2	28.7
09	308.6	16.2	69	368.5	19.3	29	428.4	22.5	89	488.3	25.6	49	548.2	28.7
10	309.6	16.2	70	369.5	19.4	30	429.4	22.5	90	489.3	25.6	50	549.2	28.8
311	310.6	16.3	371	370.5	19.4	431	430.4	22.6	491	490.3	25.7	551	550.2	28.8
12	311.6	16.3	72	371.5	19.5	32	431.4	22.6	92	491.3	25.7	52	551.2	28.9
13	312.6	16.4	73	372.5	19.5	33	432.4	22.7	93	492.3	25.8	53	552.2	28.9
14	313.6	16.4	74	373.5	19.6	34	433.4	22.7	94	493.3	25.9	54	553.2	29.0
15	314.6	16.5	75	374.5	19.6	35	434.4	22.8	95	494.3	25.9	55	554.2	29.0
16	315.6	16.5	76	375.5	19.7	36	435.4	22.8	96	495.3	26.0	56	555.2	29.1
17	316.6	16.6	77	376.5	19.7	37	436.4	22.9	97	496.3	26.0	57	556.2	29.2
18	317.6	16.6	78	377.5	19.8	38	437.4	22.9	98	497.3	26.1	58	557.2	29.2
19	318.6	16.7	79	378.5	19.8	39	438.4	23.0	99	498.3	26.1	59	558.2	29.3
20	319.6	16.7	80	379.5	19.9	40	439.4	23.0	500	499.3	26.2	60	559.2	29.3
321	320.6	16.8	381	380.5	19.9	441	440.4	23.1	501	500.3	26.2	561	560.2	29.4
22	321.6	16.9	82	381.5	20.0	42	441.4	23.1	02	501.3	26.3	62	561.2	29.4
23	322.6	16.9	83	382.5	20.0	43	442.4	23.2	03	502.3	26.3	63	562.2	29.5
24	323.6	17.0	84	383.5	20.1	44	443.4	23.2	04	503.3	26.4	64	563.2	29.5
25	324.6	17.0	85	384.5	20.1	45	444.4	23.3	05	504.3	26.4	65	564.2	29.6
26	325.6	17.1	86	385.5	20.2	46	445.4	23.3	06	505.3	26.5	66	565.2	29.6
27	326.6	17.1	87	386.5	20.3	47	446.4	23.4	07	506.3	26.5	67	566.2	29.7
28	327.6	17.2	88	387.5	20.3	48	447.4	23.4	08	507.3	26.6	68	567.2	29.7
29	328.5	17.2	89	388.5	20.4	49	448.4	23.5	09	508.3	26.6	69	568.2	29.8
30	329.5	17.3	90	389.5	20.4	50	449.4	23.6	10	509.3	26.7	70	569.2	29.8
331	330.5	17.3	391	390.5	20.5	451	450.4	23.6	511	510.3	26.7	571	570.2	29.9
32	331.5	17.4	92	391.5	20.5	52	451.4	23.7	12	511.3	26.8	72	571.2	29.9
33	332.5	17.4	93	392.5	20.6	53	452.4	23.7	13	512.3	26.8	73	572.2	30.0
34	333.5	17.5	94	393.5	20.6	54	453.4	23.8	14	513.3	26.9	74	573.2	30.0
35	334.5	17.5	95	394.5	20.7	55	454.4	23.8	15	514.3	27.0	75	574.2	30.1
36	335.5	17.6	96	395.5	20.7	56	455.4	23.9	16	515.3	27.0	76	575.2	30.1
37	336.5	17.6	97	396.5	20.8	57	456.4	23.9	17	516.3	27.1	77	576.2	30.2
38	337.5	17.7	98	397.5	20.8	58	457.4	24.0	18	517.3	27.1	78	577.2	30.3
39	338.5	17.7	99	398.5	20.9	59	458.4	24.0	19	518.3	27.2	79	578.2	30.3
40	339.5	17.8	400	399.5	20.9	60	459.4	24.1	20	519.3	27.2	80	579.2	30.4
341	340.5	17.8	401	400.5	21.0	461	460.4	24.1	521	520.3	27.3	581	580.2	30.4
42	341.5	17.9	02	401.4	21.0	62	461.4	24.2	22	521.3	27.3	82	581.2	30.5
43	342.5	18.0	03	402.4	21.1	63	462.4	24.2	23	522.3	27.4	83	582.2	30.5
44	343.5	18.0	04	403.4	21.1	64	463.4	24.3	24	523.3	27.4	84	583.2	30.6
45	344.5	18.1	05	404.4	21.2	65	464.4	24.3	25	524.3	27.5	85	584.2	30.6
46	345.5	18.1	06	405.4	21.2	66	465.4	24.4	26	525.3	27.5	86	585.2	30.7
47	346.5	18.2	07	406.4	21.3	67	466.4	24.4	27	526.3	27.6	87	586.2	30.7
48	347.5	18.2	08	407.4	21.4	68	467.4	24.5	28	527.3	27.6	88	587.2	30.8
49	348.5	18.3	09	408.4	21.4	69	468.4	24.5	29	528.3	27.7	89	588.2	30.8
50	349.5	18.3	10	409.4	21.5	70	469.4	24.6	30	529.3	27.7	90	589.2	30.9
351	350.5	18.4	411	410.4	21.5	471	470.4	24.7	531	530.3	27.8	591	590.2	30.9
52	351.5	18.4	12	411.4	21.6	72	471.4	24.7	32	531.3	27.8	92	591.2	31.0
53	352.5	18.5	13	412.4	21.6	73	472.4	24.8	33	532.3	27.9	93	592.2	31.0
54	353.5	18.5	14	413.4	21.7	74	473.4	24.8	34	533.3	27.9	94	593.2	31.1
55	354.5	18.6	15	414.4	21.7	75	474.3	24.9	35	534.3	28.0	95	594.2	31.1
56	355.5	18.6	16	415.4	21.8	76	475.3	24.9	36	535.3	28.1	96	595.2	31.2
57	356.5	18.7	17	416.4	21.8	77	476.3	25.0	37	536.3	28.1	97	596.2	31.2
58	357.5	18.7	18	417.4	21.9	78	477.3	25.0	38	537.3	28.2	98	597.2	31.3
59	358.5	18.8	19	418.4	21.9	79	478.3	25.1	39	538.3	28.2	99	598.2	31.3
60	359.5	18.8	20	419.4	22.0	80	479.3	25.1	40	539.3	28.3	600	599.2	31.4
Dist.	Dep.	D. Lat.	Dist.	Dep.	D. Lat.	Dist.	Dep.	D. Lat.	Dist.	Dep.	D. Lat.	Dist.	Dep.	D. Lat.

Dist.	D. Lat.	Dep.
D Lo	Dep.	
	m	D Lo

87°

273° | 087°
267° | 093°

TABLE 4

356° | 004°
184° | 176°

Traverse **4°** Table

Dist.	D. Lat.	Dep.	Dist.	D. Lat.	Dep.	Dist.	D. Lat.	Dep.	Dist.	D. Lat.	Dep.	Dist.	D. Lat.	Dep.
1	1.0	0.1	61	60.9	4.3	121	120.7	8.4	181	180.6	12.6	241	240.4	16.8
2	2.0	0.1	62	61.8	4.3	22	121.7	8.5	82	181.6	12.7	42	241.4	16.9
3	3.0	0.2	63	62.8	4.4	23	122.7	8.6	83	182.6	12.8	43	242.4	17.0
4	4.0	0.3	64	63.8	4.5	24	123.7	8.6	84	183.6	12.8	44	243.4	17.0
5	5.0	0.3	65	64.8	4.5	25	124.7	8.7	85	184.5	12.9	45	244.4	17.1
6	6.0	0.4	66	65.8	4.6	26	125.7	8.8	86	185.5	13.0	46	245.4	17.2
7	7.0	0.5	67	66.8	4.7	27	126.7	8.9	87	186.5	13.0	47	246.4	17.2
8	8.0	0.6	68	67.8	4.7	28	127.7	8.9	88	187.5	13.1	48	247.4	17.3
9	9.0	0.6	69	68.8	4.8	29	128.7	9.0	89	188.5	13.2	49	248.4	17.4
10	10.0	0.7	70	69.8	4.9	30	129.7	9.1	90	189.5	13.3	50	249.4	17.4
11	11.0	0.8	71	70.8	5.0	131	130.7	9.1	191	190.5	13.3	251	250.4	17.5
12	12.0	0.8	72	71.8	5.0	32	131.7	9.2	92	191.5	13.4	52	251.4	17.6
13	13.0	0.9	73	72.8	5.1	33	132.7	9.3	93	192.5	13.5	53	252.4	17.6
14	14.0	1.0	74	73.8	5.2	34	133.7	9.3	94	193.5	13.5	54	253.4	17.7
15	15.0	1.0	75	74.8	5.2	35	134.7	9.4	95	194.5	13.6	55	254.4	17.8
16	16.0	1.1	76	75.8	5.3	36	135.7	9.5	96	195.5	13.7	56	255.4	17.9
17	17.0	1.2	77	76.8	5.4	37	136.7	9.6	97	196.5	13.7	57	256.4	17.9
18	18.0	1.3	78	77.8	5.4	38	137.7	9.6	98	197.5	13.8	58	257.4	18.0
19	19.0	1.3	79	78.8	5.5	39	138.7	9.7	99	198.5	13.9	59	258.4	18.1
20	20.0	1.4	80	79.8	5.6	40	139.7	9.8	200	199.5	14.0	60	259.4	18.1
21	20.9	1.5	81	80.8	5.7	141	140.7	9.8	201	200.5	14.0	261	260.4	18.2
22	21.9	1.5	82	81.8	5.7	42	141.7	9.9	02	201.5	14.1	62	261.4	18.3
23	22.9	1.6	83	82.8	5.8	43	142.7	10.0	03	202.5	14.2	63	262.4	18.3
24	23.9	1.7	84	83.8	5.9	44	143.6	10.0	04	203.5	14.2	64	263.4	18.4
25	24.9	1.7	85	84.8	5.9	45	144.6	10.1	05	204.5	14.3	65	264.4	18.5
26	25.9	1.8	86	85.8	6.0	46	145.6	10.2	06	205.5	14.4	66	265.4	18.6
27	26.9	1.9	87	86.8	6.1	47	146.6	10.3	07	206.5	14.4	67	266.3	18.6
28	27.9	2.0	88	87.8	6.1	48	147.6	10.3	08	207.5	14.5	68	267.3	18.7
29	28.9	2.0	89	88.8	6.2	49	148.6	10.4	09	208.5	14.6	69	268.3	18.8
30	29.9	2.1	90	89.8	6.3	50	149.6	10.5	10	209.5	14.6	70	269.3	18.8
31	30.9	2.2	91	90.8	6.3	151	150.6	10.5	211	210.5	14.7	271	270.3	18.9
32	31.9	2.2	92	91.8	6.4	52	151.6	10.6	12	211.5	14.8	72	271.3	19.0
33	32.9	2.3	93	92.8	6.5	53	152.6	10.7	13	212.5	14.9	73	272.3	19.0
34	33.9	2.4	94	93.8	6.6	54	153.6	10.7	14	213.5	14.9	74	273.3	19.1
35	34.9	2.4	95	94.8	6.6	55	154.6	10.8	15	214.5	15.0	75	274.3	19.2
36	35.9	2.5	96	95.8	6.7	56	155.6	10.9	16	215.5	15.1	76	275.3	19.3
37	36.9	2.6	97	96.8	6.8	57	156.6	11.0	17	216.5	15.1	77	276.3	19.3
38	37.9	2.7	98	97.8	6.8	58	157.6	11.0	18	217.5	15.2	78	277.3	19.4
39	38.9	2.7	99	98.8	6.9	59	158.6	11.1	19	218.5	15.3	79	278.3	19.5
40	39.9	2.8	100	99.8	7.0	60	159.6	11.2	20	219.5	15.3	80	279.3	19.5
41	40.9	2.9	101	100.8	7.0	161	160.6	11.2	221	220.5	15.4	281	280.3	19.6
42	41.9	2.9	02	101.8	7.1	62	161.6	11.3	22	221.5	15.5	82	281.3	19.7
43	42.9	3.0	03	102.7	7.2	63	162.6	11.4	23	222.5	15.6	83	282.3	19.7
44	43.9	3.1	04	103.7	7.3	64	163.6	11.4	24	223.5	15.6	84	283.3	19.8
45	44.9	3.1	05	104.7	7.3	65	164.6	11.5	25	224.5	15.7	85	284.3	19.9
46	45.9	3.2	06	105.7	7.4	66	165.6	11.6	26	225.4	15.8	86	285.3	20.0
47	46.9	3.3	07	106.7	7.5	67	166.6	11.6	27	226.4	15.8	87	286.3	20.0
48	47.9	3.3	08	107.7	7.5	68	167.6	11.7	28	227.4	15.9	88	287.3	20.1
49	48.9	3.4	09	108.7	7.6	69	168.6	11.8	29	228.4	16.0	89	288.3	20.2
50	49.9	3.5	10	109.7	7.7	70	169.6	11.9	30	229.4	16.0	90	289.3	20.2
51	50.9	3.6	111	110.7	7.7	171	170.6	11.9	231	230.4	16.1	291	290.3	20.3
52	51.9	3.6	12	111.7	7.8	72	171.6	12.0	32	231.4	16.2	92	291.3	20.4
53	52.9	3.7	13	112.7	7.9	73	172.6	12.1	33	232.4	16.3	93	292.3	20.4
54	53.9	3.8	14	113.7	8.0	74	173.6	12.1	34	233.4	16.3	94	293.3	20.5
55	54.9	3.8	15	114.7	8.0	75	174.6	12.2	35	234.4	16.4	95	294.3	20.6
56	55.9	3.9	16	115.7	8.1	76	175.6	12.3	36	235.4	16.5	96	295.3	20.6
57	56.9	4.0	17	116.7	8.2	77	176.6	12.3	37	236.4	16.5	97	296.3	20.7
58	57.9	4.0	18	117.7	8.2	78	177.6	12.4	38	237.4	16.6	98	297.3	20.8
59	58.9	4.1	19	118.7	8.3	79	178.6	12.5	39	238.4	16.7	99	298.3	20.9
60	59.9	4.2	20	119.7	8.4	80	179.6	12.6	40	239.4	16.7	300	299.3	20.9
Dist.	Dep.	D. Lat.	Dist.	Dep.	D. Lat.	Dist.	Dep.	D. Lat.	Dist.	Dep.	D. Lat.	Dist.	Dep.	D. Lat.

274° | 086°
266° | 094°

86°

Dist.	D. Lat.	Dep.
N.	N x Cos.	N x Sin.
Hypotenuse	Side Adj.	Side Opp.

TABLE 4

356° | 004°
184° | 176°

Traverse **4°** Table

Dist.	D. Lat.	Dep.	Dist.	D. Lat.	Dep.	Dist.	D. Lat.	Dep.	Dist.	D. Lat.	Dep.	Dist.	D. Lat.	Dep.
301	300.3	21.0	361	360.1	25.2	421	420.0	29.4	481	479.8	33.6	541	539.7	37.7
02	301.3	21.1	62	361.1	25.3	22	421.0	29.4	82	480.8	33.6	42	540.7	37.8
03	302.3	21.1	63	362.1	25.3	23	422.0	29.5	83	481.8	33.7	43	541.7	37.9
04	303.3	21.2	64	363.1	25.4	24	423.0	29.6	84	482.8	33.8	44	542.7	37.9
05	304.3	21.3	65	364.1	25.5	25	424.0	29.6	85	483.8	33.8	45	543.7	38.0
06	305.3	21.3	66	365.1	25.5	26	425.0	29.7	86	484.8	33.9	46	544.7	38.1
07	306.3	21.4	67	366.1	25.6	27	426.0	29.8	87	485.8	34.0	47	545.7	38.2
08	307.2	21.5	68	367.1	25.7	28	427.0	29.9	88	486.8	34.0	48	546.7	38.2
09	308.2	21.6	69	368.1	25.7	29	428.0	29.9	89	487.8	34.1	49	547.7	38.3
10	309.2	21.6	70	369.1	25.8	30	429.0	30.0	90	488.8	34.2	50	548.7	38.4
311	310.2	21.7	371	370.1	25.9	431	430.0	30.1	491	489.8	34.3	551	549.7	38.4
12	311.2	21.8	72	371.1	25.9	32	430.9	30.1	92	490.8	34.3	52	550.7	38.5
13	312.2	21.8	73	372.1	26.0	33	431.9	30.2	93	491.8	34.4	53	551.7	38.6
14	313.2	21.9	74	373.1	26.1	34	432.9	30.3	94	492.8	34.5	54	552.7	38.6
15	314.2	22.0	75	374.1	26.2	35	433.9	30.3	95	493.8	34.5	55	553.6	38.7
16	315.2	22.0	76	375.1	26.2	36	434.9	30.4	96	494.8	34.6	56	554.6	38.8
17	316.2	22.1	77	376.1	26.3	37	435.9	30.5	97	495.8	34.7	57	555.6	38.9
18	317.2	22.2	78	377.1	26.4	38	436.9	30.6	98	496.8	34.7	58	556.6	38.9
19	318.2	22.3	79	378.1	26.4	39	437.9	30.6	99	497.8	34.8	59	557.6	39.0
20	319.2	22.3	80	379.1	26.5	40	438.9	30.7	500	498.8	34.9	60	558.6	39.1
321	320.2	22.4	381	380.1	26.6	441	439.9	30.8	501	499.8	34.9	561	559.6	39.1
22	321.2	22.5	82	381.1	26.6	42	440.9	30.8	02	500.8	35.0	62	560.6	39.2
23	322.2	22.5	83	382.1	26.7	43	441.9	30.9	03	501.8	35.1	63	561.6	39.3
24	323.2	22.6	84	383.1	26.8	44	442.9	31.0	04	502.8	35.2	64	562.6	39.3
25	324.2	22.7	85	384.1	26.9	45	443.9	31.0	05	503.8	35.2	65	563.6	39.4
26	325.2	22.7	86	385.1	26.9	46	444.9	31.1	06	504.8	35.3	66	564.6	39.5
27	326.2	22.8	87	386.1	27.0	47	445.9	31.2	07	505.8	35.4	67	565.6	39.6
28	327.2	22.9	88	387.1	27.1	48	446.9	31.3	08	506.8	35.4	68	566.6	39.6
29	328.2	22.9	89	388.1	27.1	49	447.9	31.3	09	507.8	35.5	69	567.6	39.7
30	329.2	23.0	90	389.0	27.2	50	448.9	31.4	10	508.8	35.6	70	568.6	39.8
331	330.2	23.1	391	390.0	27.3	451	449.9	31.5	511	509.8	35.6	571	569.6	39.8
32	331.2	23.2	92	391.0	27.3	52	450.9	31.5	12	510.8	35.7	72	570.6	39.9
33	332.2	23.2	93	392.0	27.4	53	451.9	31.6	13	511.8	35.8	73	571.6	40.0
34	333.2	23.3	94	393.0	27.5	54	452.9	31.7	14	512.7	35.9	74	572.6	40.0
35	334.2	23.4	95	394.0	27.6	55	453.9	31.7	15	513.7	35.9	75	573.6	40.1
36	335.2	23.4	96	395.0	27.6	56	454.9	31.8	16	514.7	36.0	76	574.6	40.2
37	336.2	23.5	97	396.0	27.7	57	455.9	31.9	17	515.7	36.1	77	575.6	40.2
38	337.2	23.6	98	397.0	27.8	58	456.9	31.9	18	516.7	36.1	78	576.6	40.3
39	338.2	23.6	99	398.0	27.8	59	457.9	32.0	19	517.7	36.2	79	577.6	40.4
40	339.2	23.7	400	399.0	27.9	60	458.9	32.1	20	518.7	36.3	80	578.6	40.5
341	340.2	23.8	401	400.0	28.0	461	459.9	32.2	521	519.7	36.3	581	579.6	40.5
42	341.2	23.9	02	401.0	28.0	62	460.9	32.2	22	520.7	36.4	82	580.6	40.6
43	342.2	23.9	03	402.0	28.1	63	461.9	32.3	23	521.7	36.5	83	581.6	40.7
44	343.2	24.0	04	403.0	28.2	64	462.9	32.4	24	522.7	36.6	84	582.6	40.7
45	344.2	24.1	05	404.0	28.3	65	463.9	32.4	25	523.7	36.6	85	583.6	40.8
46	345.2	24.1	06	405.0	28.3	66	464.9	32.5	26	524.7	36.7	86	584.6	40.9
47	346.2	24.2	07	406.0	28.4	67	465.9	32.6	27	525.7	36.8	87	585.6	40.9
48	347.2	24.3	08	407.0	28.5	68	466.9	32.6	28	526.7	36.8	88	586.6	41.0
49	348.1	24.3	09	408.0	28.5	69	467.9	32.7	29	527.7	36.9	89	587.6	41.1
50	349.1	24.4	10	409.0	28.6	70	468.9	32.8	30	528.7	37.0	90	588.6	41.2
351	350.1	24.5	411	410.0	28.7	471	469.9	32.9	531	529.7	37.0	591	589.6	41.2
52	351.1	24.6	12	411.0	28.7	72	470.9	32.9	32	530.7	37.1	92	590.6	41.3
53	352.1	24.6	13	412.0	28.8	73	471.8	33.0	33	531.7	37.2	93	591.6	41.4
54	353.1	24.7	14	413.0	28.9	74	472.8	33.1	34	532.7	37.2	94	592.6	41.4
55	354.1	24.8	15	414.0	28.9	75	473.8	33.1	35	533.7	37.3	95	593.6	41.5
56	355.1	24.8	16	415.0	29.0	76	474.8	33.2	36	534.7	37.4	96	594.5	41.6
57	356.1	24.9	17	416.0	29.1	77	475.8	33.3	37	535.7	37.5	97	595.5	41.6
58	357.1	25.0	18	417.0	29.2	78	476.8	33.3	38	536.7	37.5	98	596.5	41.7
59	358.1	25.0	19	418.0	29.2	79	477.8	33.4	39	537.7	37.6	99	597.5	41.8
60	359.1	25.1	20	419.0	29.3	80	478.8	33.5	40	538.7	37.7	600	598.5	41.9
Dist.	Dep.	D. Lat.	Dist.	Dep.	D. Lat.	Dist.	Dep.	D. Lat.	Dist.	Dep.	D. Lat.	Dist.	Dep.	D. Lat.

Dist.	D. Lat.	Dep.
D Lo	Dep.	
	m	D Lo

86°

274° | 086°
266° | 094°

TABLE 4

5° Traverse Table

355° | 005° — 185° | 175°

Dist.	D. Lat.	Dep.	Dist.	D. Lat.	Dep.	Dist.	D. Lat.	Dep.	Dist.	D. Lat.	Dep.	Dist.	D. Lat.	Dep.
1	1.0	0.1	61	60.8	5.3	121	120.5	10.5	181	180.3	15.8	241	240.1	21.0
2	2.0	0.2	62	61.8	5.4	22	121.5	10.6	82	181.3	15.9	42	241.1	21.1
3	3.0	0.3	63	62.8	5.5	23	122.5	10.7	83	182.3	15.9	43	242.1	21.2
4	4.0	0.3	64	63.8	5.6	24	123.5	10.8	84	183.3	16.0	44	243.1	21.3
5	5.0	0.4	65	64.8	5.7	25	124.5	10.9	85	184.3	16.1	45	244.1	21.4
6	6.0	0.5	66	65.7	5.8	26	125.5	11.0	86	185.3	16.2	46	245.1	21.4
7	7.0	0.6	67	66.7	5.8	27	126.5	11.1	87	186.3	16.3	47	246.1	21.5
8	8.0	0.7	68	67.7	5.9	28	127.5	11.2	88	187.3	16.4	48	247.1	21.6
9	9.0	0.8	69	68.7	6.0	29	128.5	11.2	89	188.3	16.5	49	248.1	21.7
10	10.0	0.9	70	69.7	6.1	30	129.5	11.3	90	189.3	16.6	50	249.0	21.8
11	11.0	1.0	71	70.7	6.2	131	130.5	11.4	191	190.3	16.6	251	250.0	21.9
12	12.0	1.0	72	71.7	6.3	32	131.5	11.5	92	191.3	16.7	52	251.0	22.0
13	13.0	1.1	73	72.7	6.4	33	132.5	11.6	93	192.3	16.8	53	252.0	22.1
14	13.9	1.2	74	73.7	6.4	34	133.5	11.7	94	193.3	16.9	54	253.0	22.1
15	14.9	1.3	75	74.7	6.5	35	134.5	11.8	95	194.3	17.0	55	254.0	22.2
16	15.9	1.4	76	75.7	6.6	36	135.5	11.9	96	195.3	17.1	56	255.0	22.3
17	16.9	1.5	77	76.7	6.7	37	136.5	11.9	97	196.3	17.2	57	256.0	22.4
18	17.9	1.6	78	77.7	6.8	38	137.5	12.0	98	197.2	17.3	58	257.0	22.5
19	18.9	1.7	79	78.7	6.9	39	138.5	12.1	99	198.2	17.3	59	258.0	22.6
20	19.9	1.7	80	79.7	7.0	40	139.5	12.2	200	199.2	17.4	60	259.0	22.7
21	20.9	1.8	81	80.7	7.1	141	140.5	12.3	201	200.2	17.5	261	260.0	22.7
22	21.9	1.9	82	81.7	7.1	42	141.5	12.4	02	201.2	17.6	62	261.0	22.8
23	22.9	2.0	83	82.7	7.2	43	142.5	12.5	03	202.2	17.7	63	262.0	22.9
24	23.9	2.1	84	83.7	7.3	44	143.5	12.6	04	203.2	17.8	64	263.0	23.0
25	24.9	2.2	85	84.7	7.4	45	144.4	12.6	05	204.2	17.9	65	264.0	23.1
26	25.9	2.3	86	85.7	7.5	46	145.4	12.7	06	205.2	18.0	66	265.0	23.2
27	26.9	2.4	87	86.7	7.6	47	146.4	12.8	07	206.2	18.0	67	266.0	23.3
28	27.9	2.4	88	87.7	7.7	48	147.4	12.9	08	207.2	18.1	68	267.0	23.4
29	28.9	2.5	89	88.7	7.8	49	148.4	13.0	09	208.2	18.2	69	268.0	23.4
30	29.9	2.6	90	89.7	7.8	50	149.4	13.1	10	209.2	18.3	70	269.0	23.5
31	30.9	2.7	91	90.7	7.9	151	150.4	13.2	211	210.2	18.4	271	270.0	23.6
32	31.9	2.8	92	91.6	8.0	52	151.4	13.2	12	211.2	18.5	72	271.0	23.7
33	32.9	2.9	93	92.6	8.1	53	152.4	13.3	13	212.2	18.6	73	272.0	23.8
34	33.9	3.0	94	93.6	8.2	54	153.4	13.4	14	213.2	18.7	74	273.0	23.9
35	34.9	3.1	95	94.6	8.3	55	154.4	13.5	15	214.2	18.7	75	274.0	24.0
36	35.9	3.1	96	95.6	8.4	56	155.4	13.6	16	215.2	18.8	76	274.9	24.1
37	36.9	3.2	97	96.6	8.5	57	156.4	13.7	17	216.2	18.9	77	275.9	24.1
38	37.9	3.3	98	97.6	8.5	58	157.4	13.8	18	217.2	19.0	78	276.9	24.2
39	38.9	3.4	99	98.6	8.6	59	158.4	13.9	19	218.2	19.1	79	277.9	24.3
40	39.8	3.5	100	99.6	8.7	60	159.4	13.9	20	219.2	19.2	80	278.9	24.4
41	40.8	3.6	101	100.6	8.8	161	160.4	14.0	221	220.2	19.3	281	279.9	24.5
42	41.8	3.7	02	101.6	8.9	62	161.4	14.1	22	221.2	19.3	82	280.9	24.6
43	42.8	3.7	03	102.6	9.0	63	162.4	14.2	23	222.2	19.4	83	281.9	24.7
44	43.8	3.8	04	103.6	9.1	64	163.4	14.3	24	223.1	19.5	84	282.9	24.8
45	44.8	3.9	05	104.6	9.2	65	164.4	14.4	25	224.1	19.6	85	283.9	24.8
46	45.8	4.0	06	105.6	9.2	66	165.4	14.5	26	225.1	19.7	86	284.9	24.9
47	46.8	4.1	07	106.6	9.3	67	166.4	14.6	27	226.1	19.8	87	285.9	25.0
48	47.8	4.2	08	107.6	9.4	68	167.4	14.6	28	227.1	19.9	88	286.9	25.1
49	48.8	4.3	09	108.6	9.5	69	168.4	14.7	29	228.1	20.0	89	287.9	25.2
50	49.8	4.4	10	109.6	9.6	70	169.4	14.8	30	229.1	20.0	90	288.9	25.3
51	50.8	4.4	111	110.6	9.7	171	170.3	14.9	231	230.1	20.1	291	289.9	25.4
52	51.8	4.5	12	111.6	9.8	72	171.3	15.0	32	231.1	20.2	92	290.9	25.4
53	52.8	4.6	13	112.6	9.8	73	172.3	15.1	33	232.1	20.3	93	291.9	25.5
54	53.8	4.7	14	113.6	9.9	74	173.3	15.2	34	233.1	20.4	94	292.9	25.6
55	54.8	4.8	15	114.6	10.0	75	174.3	15.3	35	234.1	20.5	95	293.9	25.7
56	55.8	4.9	16	115.6	10.1	76	175.3	15.3	36	235.1	20.6	96	294.9	25.8
57	56.8	5.0	17	116.6	10.2	77	176.3	15.4	37	236.1	20.7	97	295.9	25.9
58	57.8	5.1	18	117.6	10.3	78	177.3	15.5	38	237.1	20.7	98	296.9	26.0
59	58.8	5.1	19	118.5	10.4	79	178.3	15.6	39	238.1	20.8	99	297.9	26.1
60	59.8	5.2	20	119.5	10.5	80	179.3	15.7	40	239.1	20.9	300	298.9	26.1
Dist.	Dep.	D. Lat.	Dist.	Dep.	D. Lat.	Dist.	Dep.	D. Lat.	Dist.	Dep.	D. Lat.	Dist.	Dep.	D. Lat.

275° | 085° — 265° | 095°

85°

Dist.	D. Lat.	Dep.
N.	N x Cos.	N x Sin.
Hypotenuse	Side Adj.	Side Opp.

TABLE 4

5° Traverse Table

355° | 005° — 185° | 175°

Dist.	D. Lat.	Dep.	Dist.	D. Lat.	Dep.	Dist.	D. Lat.	Dep.	Dist.	D. Lat.	Dep.	Dist.	D. Lat.	Dep.
301	299.9	26.2	361	359.6	31.5	421	419.4	36.7	481	479.2	41.9	541	538.9	47.2
02	300.9	26.3	62	360.6	31.6	22	420.4	36.8	82	480.2	42.0	42	539.9	47.2
03	301.8	26.4	63	361.6	31.6	23	421.4	36.9	83	481.2	42.1	43	540.9	47.3
04	302.8	26.5	64	362.6	31.7	24	422.4	37.0	84	482.2	42.2	44	541.9	47.4
05	303.8	26.6	65	363.6	31.8	25	423.4	37.0	85	483.2	42.3	45	542.9	47.5
06	304.8	26.7	66	364.6	31.9	26	424.4	37.1	86	484.2	42.4	46	543.9	47.6
07	305.8	26.8	67	365.6	32.0	27	425.4	37.2	87	485.1	42.4	47	544.9	47.7
08	306.8	26.8	68	366.6	32.1	28	426.4	37.3	88	486.1	42.5	48	545.9	47.8
09	307.8	26.9	69	367.6	32.2	29	427.4	37.4	89	487.1	42.6	49	546.9	47.8
10	308.8	27.0	70	368.6	32.2	30	428.4	37.5	90	488.1	42.7	50	547.9	47.9
311	309.8	27.1	371	369.6	32.3	431	429.4	37.6	491	489.1	42.8	551	548.9	48.0
12	310.8	27.2	72	370.6	32.4	32	430.4	37.7	92	490.1	42.9	52	549.9	48.1
13	311.8	27.3	73	371.6	32.5	33	431.4	37.7	93	491.1	43.0	53	550.9	48.2
14	312.8	27.4	74	372.6	32.6	34	432.3	37.8	94	492.1	43.1	54	551.9	48.3
15	313.8	27.5	75	373.6	32.7	35	433.3	37.9	95	493.1	43.1	55	552.9	48.4
16	314.8	27.5	76	374.6	32.8	36	434.3	38.0	96	494.1	43.2	56	553.9	48.5
17	315.8	27.6	77	375.6	32.9	37	435.3	38.1	97	495.1	43.3	57	554.9	48.5
18	316.8	27.7	78	376.6	32.9	38	436.3	38.2	98	496.1	43.4	58	555.9	48.6
19	317.8	27.8	79	377.6	33.0	39	437.3	38.3	99	497.1	43.5	59	556.9	48.7
20	318.8	27.9	80	378.6	33.1	40	438.3	38.3	500	498.1	43.6	60	557.9	48.8
321	319.8	28.0	381	379.6	33.2	441	439.3	38.4	501	499.1	43.7	561	558.9	48.9
22	320.8	28.1	82	380.5	33.3	42	440.3	38.5	02	500.1	43.8	62	559.9	49.0
23	321.8	28.2	83	381.5	33.4	43	441.3	38.6	03	501.1	43.8	63	560.9	49.1
24	322.8	28.2	84	382.5	33.5	44	442.3	38.7	04	502.1	43.9	64	561.9	49.2
25	323.8	28.3	85	383.5	33.6	45	443.3	38.8	05	503.1	44.0	65	562.9	49.2
26	324.8	28.4	86	384.5	33.6	46	444.3	38.9	06	504.1	44.1	66	563.8	49.3
27	325.8	28.5	87	385.5	33.7	47	445.3	39.0	07	505.1	44.2	67	564.8	49.4
28	326.8	28.6	88	386.5	33.8	48	446.3	39.0	08	506.1	44.3	68	565.8	49.5
29	327.7	28.7	89	387.5	33.9	49	447.3	39.1	09	507.1	44.4	69	566.8	49.6
30	328.7	28.8	90	388.5	34.0	50	448.3	39.2	10	508.1	44.4	70	567.8	49.7
331	329.7	28.8	391	389.5	34.1	451	449.3	39.3	511	509.1	44.5	571	568.8	49.8
32	330.7	28.9	92	390.5	34.2	52	450.3	39.4	12	510.1	44.6	72	569.8	49.9
33	331.7	29.0	93	391.5	34.3	53	451.3	39.5	13	511.0	44.7	73	570.8	49.9
34	332.7	29.1	94	392.5	34.3	54	452.3	39.6	14	512.0	44.8	74	571.8	50.0
35	333.7	29.2	95	393.5	34.4	55	453.3	39.7	15	513.0	44.9	75	572.8	50.1
36	334.7	29.3	96	394.5	34.5	56	454.3	39.7	16	514.0	45.0	76	573.8	50.2
37	335.7	29.4	97	395.5	34.6	57	455.3	39.8	17	515.0	45.1	77	574.8	50.3
38	336.7	29.5	98	396.5	34.7	58	456.3	39.9	18	516.0	45.1	78	575.8	50.4
39	337.7	29.5	99	397.5	34.8	59	457.3	40.0	19	517.0	45.2	79	576.8	50.5
40	338.7	29.6	400	398.5	34.9	60	458.2	40.1	20	518.0	45.3	80	577.8	50.6
341	339.7	29.7	401	399.5	34.9	461	459.2	40.2	521	519.0	45.4	581	578.8	50.6
42	340.7	29.8	02	400.5	35.0	62	460.2	40.3	22	520.0	45.5	82	579.8	50.7
43	341.7	29.9	03	401.5	35.1	63	461.2	40.4	23	521.0	45.6	83	580.8	50.8
44	342.7	30.0	04	402.5	35.2	64	462.2	40.4	24	522.0	45.7	84	581.8	50.9
45	343.7	30.1	05	403.5	35.3	65	463.2	40.5	25	523.0	45.8	85	582.8	51.0
46	344.7	30.2	06	404.5	35.4	66	464.2	40.6	26	524.0	45.8	86	583.8	51.1
47	345.7	30.2	07	405.5	35.5	67	465.2	40.7	27	525.0	45.9	87	584.8	51.2
48	346.7	30.3	08	406.4	35.6	68	466.2	40.8	28	526.0	46.0	88	585.8	51.2
49	347.7	30.4	09	407.4	35.6	69	467.2	40.9	29	527.0	46.1	89	586.8	51.3
50	348.7	30.5	10	408.4	35.7	70	468.2	41.0	30	528.0	46.2	90	587.8	51.4
351	349.7	30.6	411	409.4	35.8	471	469.2	41.1	531	529.0	46.3	591	588.8	51.5
52	350.7	30.7	12	410.4	35.9	72	470.2	41.1	32	530.0	46.4	92	589.7	51.6
53	351.7	30.8	13	411.4	36.0	73	471.2	41.2	33	531.0	46.5	93	590.7	51.7
54	352.7	30.9	14	412.4	36.1	74	472.2	41.3	34	532.0	46.5	94	591.7	51.8
55	353.6	30.9	15	413.4	36.2	75	473.2	41.4	35	533.0	46.6	95	592.7	51.9
56	354.6	31.0	16	414.4	36.3	76	474.2	41.5	36	534.0	46.7	96	593.7	51.9
57	355.6	31.1	17	415.4	36.3	77	475.2	41.6	37	535.0	46.8	97	594.7	52.0
58	356.6	31.2	18	416.4	36.4	78	476.2	41.7	38	536.0	46.9	98	595.7	52.1
59	357.6	31.3	19	417.4	36.5	79	477.2	41.7	39	536.9	47.0	99	596.7	52.2
60	358.6	31.4	20	418.4	36.6	80	478.2	41.8	40	537.9	47.1	600	597.7	52.3
Dist.	Dep.	D. Lat.	Dist.	Dep.	D. Lat.	Dist.	Dep.	D. Lat.	Dist.	Dep.	D. Lat.	Dist.	Dep.	D. Lat.

Dist.	D. Lat.	Dep.
D Lo	Dep.	
	m	D Lo

85°

275° | 085° — 265° | 095°

TABLE 4

Traverse 6° Table

354° | 006°
186° | 174°

Dist.	D. Lat.	Dep.	Dist.	D. Lat.	Dep.	Dist.	D. Lat.	Dep.	Dist.	D. Lat.	Dep.	Dist.	D. Lat.	Dep.
1	1.0	0.1	61	60.7	6.4	121	120.3	12.6	181	180.0	18.9	241	239.7	25.2
2	2.0	0.2	62	61.7	6.5	22	121.3	12.8	82	181.0	19.0	42	240.7	25.3
3	3.0	0.3	63	62.7	6.6	23	122.3	12.9	83	182.0	19.1	43	241.7	25.4
4	4.0	0.4	64	63.6	6.7	24	123.3	13.0	84	183.0	19.2	44	242.7	25.5
5	5.0	0.5	65	64.6	6.8	25	124.3	13.1	85	184.0	19.3	45	243.7	25.6
6	6.0	0.6	66	65.6	6.9	26	125.3	13.2	86	185.0	19.4	46	244.7	25.7
7	7.0	0.7	67	66.6	7.0	27	126.3	13.3	87	186.0	19.5	47	245.6	25.8
8	8.0	0.8	68	67.6	7.1	28	127.3	13.4	88	187.0	19.7	48	246.6	25.9
9	9.0	0.9	69	68.6	7.2	29	128.3	13.5	89	188.0	19.8	49	247.6	26.0
10	9.9	1.0	70	69.6	7.3	30	129.3	13.6	90	189.0	19.9	50	248.6	26.1
11	10.9	1.1	71	70.6	7.4	131	130.3	13.7	191	190.0	20.0	251	249.6	26.2
12	11.9	1.3	72	71.6	7.5	32	131.3	13.8	92	190.9	20.1	52	250.6	26.3
13	12.9	1.4	73	72.6	7.6	33	132.3	13.9	93	191.9	20.2	53	251.6	26.4
14	13.9	1.5	74	73.6	7.7	34	133.3	14.0	94	192.9	20.3	54	252.6	26.6
15	14.9	1.6	75	74.6	7.8	35	134.3	14.1	95	193.9	20.4	55	253.6	26.7
16	15.9	1.7	76	75.6	7.9	36	135.3	14.2	96	194.9	20.5	56	254.6	26.8
17	16.9	1.8	77	76.6	8.0	37	136.2	14.3	97	195.9	20.6	57	255.6	26.9
18	17.9	1.9	78	77.6	8.2	38	137.2	14.4	98	196.9	20.7	58	256.6	27.0
19	18.9	2.0	79	78.6	8.3	39	138.2	14.5	99	197.9	20.8	59	257.6	27.1
20	19.9	2.1	80	79.6	8.4	40	139.2	14.6	200	198.9	20.9	60	258.6	27.2
21	20.9	2.2	81	80.6	8.5	141	140.2	14.7	201	199.9	21.0	261	259.6	27.3
22	21.9	2.3	82	81.6	8.6	42	141.2	14.8	02	200.9	21.1	62	260.6	27.4
23	22.9	2.4	83	82.5	8.7	43	142.2	14.9	03	201.9	21.2	63	261.6	27.5
24	23.9	2.5	84	83.5	8.8	44	143.2	15.1	04	202.9	21.3	64	262.6	27.6
25	24.9	2.6	85	84.5	8.9	45	144.2	15.2	05	203.9	21.4	65	263.5	27.7
26	25.9	2.7	86	85.5	9.0	46	145.2	15.3	06	204.9	21.5	66	264.5	27.8
27	26.9	2.8	87	86.5	9.1	47	146.2	15.4	07	205.9	21.6	67	265.5	27.9
28	27.8	2.9	88	87.5	9.2	48	147.2	15.5	08	206.9	21.7	68	266.5	28.0
29	28.8	3.0	89	88.5	9.3	49	148.2	15.6	09	207.9	21.8	69	267.5	28.1
30	29.8	3.1	90	89.5	9.4	50	149.2	15.7	10	208.8	22.0	70	268.5	28.2
31	30.8	3.2	91	90.5	9.5	151	150.2	15.8	211	209.8	22.1	271	269.5	28.3
32	31.8	3.3	92	91.5	9.6	52	151.2	15.9	12	210.8	22.2	72	270.5	28.4
33	32.8	3.4	93	92.5	9.7	53	152.2	16.0	13	211.8	22.3	73	271.5	28.5
34	33.8	3.6	94	93.5	9.8	54	153.2	16.1	14	212.8	22.4	74	272.5	28.6
35	34.8	3.7	95	94.5	9.9	55	154.2	16.2	15	213.8	22.5	75	273.5	28.7
36	35.8	3.8	96	95.5	10.0	56	155.1	16.3	16	214.8	22.6	76	274.5	28.8
37	36.8	3.9	97	96.5	10.1	57	156.1	16.4	17	215.8	22.7	77	275.5	29.0
38	37.8	4.0	98	97.5	10.2	58	157.1	16.5	18	216.8	22.8	78	276.5	29.1
39	38.8	4.1	99	98.5	10.3	59	158.1	16.6	19	217.8	22.9	79	277.5	29.2
40	39.8	4.2	100	99.5	10.5	60	159.1	16.7	20	218.8	23.0	80	278.5	29.3
41	40.8	4.3	101	100.4	10.6	161	160.1	16.8	221	219.8	23.1	281	279.5	29.4
42	41.8	4.4	02	101.4	10.7	62	161.1	16.9	22	220.8	23.2	82	280.5	29.5
43	42.8	4.5	03	102.4	10.8	63	162.1	17.0	23	221.8	23.3	83	281.4	29.6
44	43.8	4.6	04	103.4	10.9	64	163.1	17.1	24	222.8	23.4	84	282.4	29.7
45	44.8	4.7	05	104.4	11.0	65	164.1	17.2	25	223.8	23.5	85	283.4	29.8
46	45.7	4.8	06	105.4	11.1	66	165.1	17.4	26	224.8	23.6	86	284.4	29.9
47	46.7	4.9	07	106.4	11.2	67	166.1	17.5	27	225.8	23.7	87	285.4	30.0
48	47.7	5.0	08	107.4	11.3	68	167.1	17.6	28	226.8	23.8	88	286.4	30.1
49	48.7	5.1	09	108.4	11.4	69	168.1	17.7	29	227.7	23.9	89	287.4	30.2
50	49.7	5.2	10	109.4	11.5	70	169.1	17.8	30	228.7	24.0	90	288.4	30.3
51	50.7	5.3	111	110.4	11.6	171	170.1	17.9	231	229.7	24.1	291	289.4	30.4
52	51.7	5.4	12	111.4	11.7	72	171.1	18.0	32	230.7	24.3	92	290.4	30.5
53	52.7	5.5	13	112.4	11.8	73	172.1	18.1	33	231.7	24.4	93	291.4	30.6
54	53.7	5.6	14	113.4	11.9	74	173.0	18.2	34	232.7	24.5	94	292.4	30.7
55	54.7	5.7	15	114.4	12.0	75	174.0	18.3	35	233.7	24.6	95	293.4	30.8
56	55.7	5.9	16	115.4	12.1	76	175.0	18.4	36	234.7	24.7	96	294.4	30.9
57	56.7	6.0	17	116.4	12.2	77	176.0	18.5	37	235.7	24.8	97	295.4	31.0
58	57.7	6.1	18	117.4	12.3	78	177.0	18.6	38	236.7	24.9	98	296.4	31.1
59	58.7	6.2	19	118.3	12.4	79	178.0	18.7	39	237.7	25.0	99	297.4	31.3
60	59.7	6.3	20	119.3	12.5	80	179.0	18.8	40	238.7	25.1	300	298.4	31.4
Dist.	Dep.	D. Lat.	Dist.	Dep.	D. Lat.	Dist.	Dep.	D. Lat.	Dist.	Dep.	D. Lat.	Dist.	Dep.	D. Lat.

276° | 084°
264° | 096°

84°

Dist.	D. Lat.	Dep.
N.	N x Cos.	N x Sin.
Hypotenuse	Side Adj.	Side Opp.

TABLE 4

Traverse 6° Table

354° | 006°
186° | 174°

Dist.	D. Lat.	Dep.	Dist.	D. Lat.	Dep.	Dist.	D. Lat.	Dep.	Dist.	D. Lat.	Dep.	Dist.	D. Lat.	Dep.
301	299.4	31.5	361	359.0	37.7	421	418.7	44.0	481	478.4	50.3	541	538.0	56.5
02	300.3	31.6	62	360.0	37.8	22	419.7	44.1	82	479.4	50.4	42	539.0	56.7
03	301.3	31.7	63	361.0	37.9	23	420.7	44.2	83	480.4	50.5	43	540.0	56.8
04	302.3	31.8	64	362.0	38.0	24	421.7	44.3	84	481.3	50.6	44	541.0	56.9
05	303.3	31.9	65	363.0	38.2	25	422.7	44.4	85	482.3	50.7	45	542.0	57.0
06	304.3	32.0	66	364.0	38.3	26	423.7	44.5	86	483.3	50.8	46	543.0	57.1
07	305.3	32.1	67	365.0	38.4	27	424.7	44.6	87	484.3	50.9	47	544.0	57.2
08	306.3	32.2	68	366.0	38.5	28	425.7	44.7	88	485.3	51.0	48	545.0	57.3
09	307.3	32.3	69	367.0	38.6	29	426.6	44.8	89	486.3	51.1	49	546.0	57.4
10	308.3	32.4	70	368.0	38.7	30	427.6	44.9	90	487.3	51.2	50	547.0	57.5
311	309.3	32.5	371	369.0	38.8	431	428.6	45.1	491	488.3	51.3	551	548.0	57.6
12	310.3	32.6	72	370.0	38.9	32	429.6	45.2	92	489.3	51.4	52	549.0	57.7
13	311.3	32.7	73	371.0	39.0	33	430.6	45.3	93	490.3	51.5	53	550.0	57.8
14	312.3	32.8	74	372.0	39.1	34	431.6	45.4	94	491.3	51.6	54	551.0	57.9
15	313.3	32.9	75	372.9	39.2	35	432.6	45.5	95	492.3	51.7	55	552.0	58.0
16	314.3	33.0	76	373.9	39.3	36	433.6	45.6	96	493.3	51.8	56	553.0	58.1
17	315.3	33.1	77	374.9	39.4	37	434.6	45.7	97	494.3	52.0	57	553.9	58.2
18	316.3	33.2	78	375.9	39.5	38	435.6	45.8	98	495.3	52.1	58	554.9	58.3
19	317.3	33.3	79	376.9	39.6	39	436.6	45.9	99	496.3	52.2	59	555.9	58.4
20	318.2	33.4	80	377.9	39.7	40	437.6	46.0	500	497.3	52.3	60	556.9	58.5
321	319.2	33.6	381	378.9	39.8	441	438.6	46.1	501	498.3	52.4	561	557.9	58.6
22	320.2	33.7	82	379.9	39.9	42	439.6	46.2	02	499.2	52.5	62	558.9	58.7
23	321.2	33.8	83	380.9	40.0	43	440.6	46.3	03	500.2	52.6	63	559.9	58.8
24	322.2	33.9	84	381.9	40.1	44	441.6	46.4	04	501.2	52.7	64	560.9	59.0
25	323.2	34.0	85	382.9	40.2	45	442.6	46.5	05	502.2	52.8	65	561.9	59.1
26	324.2	34.1	86	383.9	40.3	46	443.6	46.6	06	503.2	52.9	66	562.9	59.2
27	325.2	34.2	87	384.9	40.5	47	444.6	46.7	07	504.2	53.0	67	563.9	59.3
28	326.2	34.3	88	385.9	40.6	48	445.5	46.8	08	505.2	53.1	68	564.9	59.4
29	327.2	34.4	89	386.9	40.7	49	446.5	46.9	09	506.2	53.2	69	565.9	59.5
30	328.2	34.5	90	387.9	40.8	50	447.5	47.0	10	507.2	53.3	70	566.9	59.6
331	329.2	34.6	391	388.9	40.9	451	448.5	47.1	511	508.2	53.4	571	567.9	59.7
32	330.2	34.7	92	389.9	41.0	52	449.5	47.2	12	509.2	53.5	72	568.9	59.8
33	331.2	34.8	93	390.8	41.1	53	450.5	47.4	13	510.2	53.6	73	569.9	59.9
34	332.2	34.9	94	391.8	41.2	54	451.5	47.5	14	511.2	53.7	74	570.9	60.0
35	333.2	35.0	95	392.8	41.3	55	452.5	47.6	15	512.2	53.8	75	571.9	60.1
36	334.2	35.1	96	393.8	41.4	56	453.5	47.7	16	513.2	53.9	76	572.8	60.2
37	335.2	35.2	97	394.8	41.5	57	454.5	47.8	17	514.2	54.0	77	573.8	60.3
38	336.1	35.3	98	395.8	41.6	58	455.5	47.9	18	515.2	54.1	78	574.8	60.4
39	337.1	35.4	99	396.8	41.7	59	456.5	48.0	19	516.2	54.3	79	575.8	60.5
40	338.1	35.5	400	397.8	41.8	60	457.5	48.1	20	517.2	54.4	80	576.8	60.6
341	339.1	35.6	401	398.8	41.9	461	458.5	48.2	521	518.1	54.5	581	577.8	60.7
42	340.1	35.7	02	399.8	42.0	62	459.5	48.3	22	519.1	54.6	82	578.8	60.8
43	341.1	35.9	03	400.8	42.1	63	460.5	48.4	23	520.1	54.7	83	579.8	60.9
44	342.1	36.0	04	401.8	42.2	64	461.5	48.5	24	521.1	54.8	84	580.8	61.0
45	343.1	36.1	05	402.8	42.3	65	462.5	48.6	25	522.1	54.9	85	581.8	61.1
46	344.1	36.2	06	403.8	42.4	66	463.4	48.7	26	523.1	55.0	86	582.8	61.3
47	345.1	36.3	07	404.8	42.5	67	464.4	48.8	27	524.1	55.1	87	583.8	61.4
48	346.1	36.4	08	405.8	42.6	68	465.4	48.9	28	525.1	55.2	88	584.8	61.5
49	347.1	36.5	09	406.8	42.8	69	466.4	49.0	29	526.1	55.3	89	585.8	61.6
50	348.1	36.6	10	407.8	42.9	70	467.4	49.1	30	527.1	55.4	90	586.8	61.7
351	349.1	36.7	411	408.7	43.0	471	468.4	49.2	531	528.1	55.5	591	587.8	61.8
52	350.1	36.8	12	409.7	43.1	72	469.4	49.3	32	529.1	55.6	92	588.8	61.9
53	351.1	36.9	13	410.7	43.2	73	470.4	49.4	33	530.1	55.7	93	589.8	62.0
54	352.1	37.0	14	411.7	43.3	74	471.4	49.5	34	531.1	55.8	94	590.7	62.1
55	353.1	37.1	15	412.7	43.4	75	472.4	49.7	35	532.1	55.9	95	591.7	62.2
56	354.0	37.2	16	413.7	43.5	76	473.4	49.8	36	533.1	56.0	96	592.7	62.3
57	355.0	37.3	17	414.7	43.6	77	474.4	49.9	37	534.1	56.1	97	593.7	62.4
58	356.0	37.4	18	415.7	43.7	78	475.4	50.0	38	535.1	56.2	98	594.7	62.5
59	357.0	37.5	19	416.7	43.8	79	476.4	50.1	39	536.0	56.3	99	595.7	62.6
60	358.0	37.6	20	417.7	43.9	80	477.4	50.2	40	537.0	56.4	600	596.7	62.7
Dist.	Dep.	D. Lat.	Dist.	Dep.	D. Lat.	Dist.	Dep.	D. Lat.	Dist.	Dep.	D. Lat.	Dist.	Dep.	D. Lat.

Dist.	D. Lat.	Dep.
D Lo	Dep.	
	m	D Lo

84°

276° | 084°
264° | 096°

TABLE 4
7° Traverse Table

353° | 007° — 187° | 173°

Dist.	D. Lat.	Dep.	Dist.	D. Lat.	Dep.	Dist.	D. Lat.	Dep.	Dist.	D. Lat.	Dep.	Dist.	D. Lat.	Dep.
1	1.0	0.1	61	60.5	7.4	121	120.1	14.7	181	179.7	22.1	241	239.2	29.4
2	2.0	0.2	62	61.5	7.6	22	121.1	14.9	82	180.6	22.2	42	240.2	29.5
3	3.0	0.4	63	62.5	7.7	23	122.1	15.0	83	181.6	22.3	43	241.2	29.6
4	4.0	0.5	64	63.5	7.8	24	123.1	15.1	84	182.6	22.4	44	242.2	29.7
5	5.0	0.6	65	64.5	7.9	25	124.1	15.2	85	183.6	22.5	45	243.2	29.9
6	6.0	0.7	66	65.5	8.0	26	125.1	15.4	86	184.6	22.7	46	244.2	30.0
7	6.9	0.9	67	66.5	8.2	27	126.1	15.5	87	185.6	22.8	47	245.2	30.1
8	7.9	1.0	68	67.5	8.3	28	127.0	15.6	88	186.6	22.9	48	246.2	30.2
9	8.9	1.1	69	68.5	8.4	29	128.0	15.7	89	187.6	23.0	49	247.1	30.3
10	9.9	1.2	70	69.5	8.5	30	129.0	15.8	90	188.6	23.2	50	248.1	30.5
11	10.9	1.3	71	70.5	8.7	131	130.0	16.0	191	189.6	23.3	251	249.1	30.6
12	11.9	1.5	72	71.5	8.8	32	131.0	16.1	92	190.6	23.4	52	250.1	30.7
13	12.9	1.6	73	72.5	8.9	33	132.0	16.2	93	191.6	23.5	53	251.1	30.8
14	13.9	1.7	74	73.4	9.0	34	133.0	16.3	94	192.6	23.6	54	252.1	31.0
15	14.9	1.8	75	74.4	9.1	35	134.0	16.5	95	193.5	23.8	55	253.1	31.1
16	15.9	1.9	76	75.4	9.3	36	135.0	16.6	96	194.5	23.9	56	254.1	31.2
17	16.9	2.1	77	76.4	9.4	37	136.0	16.7	97	195.5	24.0	57	255.1	31.3
18	17.9	2.2	78	77.4	9.5	38	137.0	16.8	98	196.5	24.1	58	256.1	31.4
19	18.9	2.3	79	78.4	9.6	39	138.0	16.9	99	197.5	24.3	59	257.1	31.6
20	19.9	2.4	80	79.4	9.7	40	139.0	17.1	200	198.5	24.4	60	258.1	31.7
21	20.8	2.6	81	80.4	9.9	141	139.9	17.2	201	199.5	24.5	261	259.1	31.8
22	21.8	2.7	82	81.4	10.0	42	140.9	17.3	02	200.5	24.6	62	260.0	31.9
23	22.8	2.8	83	82.4	10.1	43	141.9	17.4	03	201.5	24.7	63	261.0	32.1
24	23.8	2.9	84	83.4	10.2	44	142.9	17.5	04	202.5	24.9	64	262.0	32.2
25	24.8	3.0	85	84.4	10.4	45	143.9	17.7	05	203.5	25.0	65	263.0	32.3
26	25.8	3.2	86	85.4	10.5	46	144.9	17.8	06	204.5	25.1	66	264.0	32.4
27	26.8	3.3	87	86.4	10.6	47	145.9	17.9	07	205.5	25.2	67	265.0	32.5
28	27.8	3.4	88	87.3	10.7	48	146.9	18.0	08	206.4	25.3	68	266.0	32.7
29	28.8	3.5	89	88.3	10.8	49	147.9	18.2	09	207.4	25.5	69	267.0	32.8
30	29.8	3.7	90	89.3	11.0	50	148.9	18.3	10	208.4	25.6	70	268.0	32.9
31	30.8	3.8	91	90.3	11.1	151	149.9	18.4	211	209.4	25.7	271	269.0	33.0
32	31.8	3.9	92	91.3	11.2	52	150.9	18.5	12	210.4	25.8	72	270.0	33.1
33	32.8	4.0	93	92.3	11.3	53	151.9	18.6	13	211.4	26.0	73	271.0	33.3
34	33.7	4.1	94	93.3	11.5	54	152.9	18.8	14	212.4	26.1	74	272.0	33.4
35	34.7	4.3	95	94.3	11.6	55	153.8	18.9	15	213.4	26.2	75	273.0	33.5
36	35.7	4.4	96	95.3	11.7	56	154.8	19.0	16	214.4	26.3	76	273.9	33.6
37	36.7	4.5	97	96.3	11.8	57	155.8	19.1	17	215.4	26.4	77	274.9	33.8
38	37.7	4.6	98	97.3	11.9	58	156.8	19.3	18	216.4	26.6	78	275.9	33.9
39	38.7	4.8	99	98.3	12.1	59	157.8	19.4	19	217.4	26.7	79	276.9	34.0
40	39.7	4.9	100	99.3	12.2	60	158.8	19.5	20	218.4	26.8	80	277.9	34.1
41	40.7	5.0	101	100.2	12.3	161	159.8	19.6	221	219.4	26.9	281	278.9	34.2
42	41.7	5.1	02	101.2	12.4	62	160.8	19.7	22	220.3	27.1	82	279.9	34.4
43	42.7	5.2	03	102.2	12.6	63	161.8	19.9	23	221.3	27.2	83	280.9	34.5
44	43.7	5.4	04	103.2	12.7	64	162.8	20.0	24	222.3	27.3	84	281.9	34.6
45	44.7	5.5	05	104.2	12.8	65	163.8	20.1	25	223.3	27.4	85	282.9	34.7
46	45.7	5.6	06	105.2	12.9	66	164.8	20.2	26	224.3	27.5	86	283.9	34.9
47	46.6	5.7	07	106.2	13.0	67	165.8	20.4	27	225.3	27.7	87	284.9	35.0
48	47.6	5.8	08	107.2	13.2	68	166.7	20.5	28	226.3	27.8	88	285.9	35.1
49	48.6	6.0	09	108.2	13.3	69	167.7	20.6	29	227.3	27.9	89	286.8	35.2
50	49.6	6.1	10	109.2	13.4	70	168.7	20.7	30	228.3	28.0	90	287.8	35.3
51	50.6	6.2	111	110.2	13.5	171	169.7	20.8	231	229.3	28.2	291	288.8	35.5
52	51.6	6.3	12	111.2	13.6	72	170.7	21.0	32	230.3	28.3	92	289.8	35.6
53	52.6	6.5	13	112.2	13.8	73	171.7	21.1	33	231.3	28.4	93	290.8	35.7
54	53.6	6.6	14	113.2	13.9	74	172.7	21.2	34	232.3	28.5	94	291.8	35.8
55	54.6	6.7	15	114.1	14.0	75	173.7	21.3	35	233.2	28.6	95	292.8	36.0
56	55.6	6.8	16	115.1	14.1	76	174.7	21.4	36	234.2	28.8	96	293.8	36.1
57	56.6	6.9	17	116.1	14.3	77	175.7	21.6	37	235.2	28.9	97	294.8	36.2
58	57.6	7.1	18	117.1	14.4	78	176.7	21.7	38	236.2	29.0	98	295.8	36.3
59	58.6	7.2	19	118.1	14.5	79	177.7	21.8	39	237.2	29.1	99	296.8	36.4
60	59.6	7.3	20	119.1	14.6	80	178.7	21.9	40	238.2	29.2	300	297.8	36.6
Dist.	Dep.	D. Lat.	Dist.	Dep.	D. Lat.	Dist.	Dep.	D. Lat.	Dist.	Dep.	D. Lat.	Dist.	Dep.	D. Lat.

277° | 083° — 263° | 097°

83°

Dist.	D. Lat.	Dep.
N.	N x Cos.	N x Sin.
Hypotenuse	Side Adj.	Side Opp.

TABLE 4
7° Traverse Table

353° | 007° — 187° | 173°

Dist.	D. Lat.	Dep.	Dist.	D. Lat.	Dep.	Dist.	D. Lat.	Dep.	Dist.	D. Lat.	Dep.	Dist.	D. Lat.	Dep.
301	298.8	36.7	361	358.3	44.0	421	417.9	51.3	481	477.4	58.6	541	537.0	65.9
02	299.7	36.8	62	359.3	44.1	22	418.9	51.4	82	478.4	58.7	42	538.0	66.1
03	300.7	36.9	63	360.3	44.2	23	419.8	51.6	83	479.4	58.9	43	539.0	66.2
04	301.7	37.0	64	361.3	44.4	24	420.8	51.7	84	480.4	59.0	44	539.9	66.3
05	302.7	37.2	65	362.3	44.5	25	421.8	51.8	85	481.4	59.1	45	540.9	66.4
06	303.7	37.3	66	363.3	44.6	26	422.8	51.9	86	482.4	59.2	46	541.9	66.5
07	304.7	37.4	67	364.3	44.7	27	423.8	52.0	87	483.4	59.4	47	542.9	66.7
08	305.7	37.5	68	365.3	44.8	28	424.8	52.2	88	484.4	59.5	48	543.9	66.8
09	306.7	37.7	69	366.2	45.0	29	425.8	52.3	89	485.4	59.6	49	544.9	66.9
10	307.7	37.8	70	367.2	45.1	30	426.8	52.4	90	486.3	59.7	50	545.9	67.0
311	308.7	37.9	371	368.2	45.2	431	427.8	52.5	491	487.3	59.8	551	546.9	67.2
12	309.7	38.0	72	369.2	45.3	32	428.8	52.6	92	488.3	60.0	52	547.9	67.3
13	310.7	38.1	73	370.2	45.5	33	429.8	52.8	93	489.3	60.1	53	548.9	67.4
14	311.7	38.3	74	371.2	45.6	34	430.8	52.9	94	490.3	60.2	54	549.9	67.5
15	312.7	38.4	75	372.2	45.7	35	431.8	53.0	95	491.3	60.3	55	550.9	67.6
16	313.6	38.5	76	373.2	45.8	36	432.8	53.1	96	492.3	60.4	56	551.9	67.8
17	314.6	38.6	77	374.2	45.9	37	433.7	53.3	97	493.3	60.6	57	552.8	67.9
18	315.6	38.8	78	375.2	46.1	38	434.7	53.4	98	494.3	60.7	58	553.8	68.0
19	316.6	38.9	79	376.2	46.2	39	435.7	53.5	99	495.3	60.8	59	554.8	68.1
20	317.6	39.0	80	377.2	46.3	40	436.7	53.6	500	496.3	60.9	60	555.8	68.2
321	318.6	39.1	381	378.2	46.4	441	437.7	53.7	501	497.3	61.1	561	556.8	68.4
22	319.6	39.2	82	379.2	46.6	42	438.7	53.9	02	498.3	61.2	62	557.8	68.5
23	320.6	39.4	83	380.1	46.7	43	439.7	54.0	03	499.3	61.3	63	558.8	68.6
24	321.6	39.5	84	381.1	46.8	44	440.7	54.1	04	500.2	61.4	64	559.8	68.7
25	322.6	39.6	85	382.1	46.9	45	441.7	54.2	05	501.2	61.5	65	560.8	68.9
26	323.6	39.7	86	383.1	47.0	46	442.7	54.4	06	502.2	61.7	66	561.8	69.0
27	324.6	39.9	87	384.1	47.2	47	443.7	54.5	07	503.2	61.8	67	562.8	69.1
28	325.6	40.0	88	385.1	47.3	48	444.7	54.6	08	504.2	61.9	68	563.8	69.2
29	326.5	40.1	89	386.1	47.4	49	445.7	54.7	09	505.2	62.0	69	564.8	69.3
30	327.5	40.2	90	387.1	47.5	50	446.6	54.8	10	506.2	62.2	70	565.8	69.5
331	328.5	40.3	391	388.1	47.7	451	447.6	55.0	511	507.2	62.3	571	566.7	69.6
32	329.5	40.5	92	389.1	47.8	52	448.6	55.1	12	508.2	62.4	72	567.7	69.7
33	330.5	40.6	93	390.1	47.9	53	449.6	55.2	13	509.2	62.5	73	568.7	69.8
34	331.5	40.7	94	391.1	48.0	54	450.6	55.3	14	510.2	62.6	74	569.7	70.0
35	332.5	40.8	95	392.1	48.1	55	451.6	55.5	15	511.2	62.8	75	570.7	70.1
36	333.5	40.9	96	393.0	48.3	56	452.6	55.6	16	512.2	62.9	76	571.7	70.2
37	334.5	41.1	97	394.0	48.4	57	453.6	55.7	17	513.1	63.0	77	572.7	70.3
38	335.5	41.2	98	395.0	48.5	58	454.6	55.8	18	514.1	63.1	78	573.7	70.4
39	336.5	41.3	99	396.0	48.6	59	455.6	55.9	19	515.1	63.3	79	574.7	70.6
40	337.5	41.4	400	397.0	48.7	60	456.6	56.1	20	516.1	63.4	80	575.7	70.7
341	338.5	41.6	401	398.0	48.9	461	457.6	56.2	521	517.1	63.5	581	576.7	70.8
42	339.5	41.7	02	399.0	49.0	62	458.6	56.3	22	518.1	63.6	82	577.7	70.9
43	340.4	41.8	03	400.0	49.1	63	459.5	56.4	23	519.1	63.7	83	578.7	71.0
44	341.4	41.9	04	401.0	49.2	64	460.5	56.5	24	520.1	63.9	84	579.6	71.2
45	342.4	42.0	05	402.0	49.4	65	461.5	56.7	25	521.1	64.0	85	580.6	71.3
46	343.4	42.2	06	403.0	49.5	66	462.5	56.8	26	522.1	64.1	86	581.6	71.4
47	344.4	42.3	07	404.0	49.6	67	463.5	56.9	27	523.1	64.2	87	582.6	71.5
48	345.4	42.4	08	405.0	49.7	68	464.5	57.0	28	524.1	64.3	88	583.6	71.7
49	346.4	42.5	09	406.0	49.8	69	465.5	57.2	29	525.1	64.5	89	584.6	71.8
50	347.4	42.7	10	406.9	50.0	70	466.5	57.3	30	526.0	64.6	90	585.6	71.9
351	348.4	42.8	411	407.9	50.1	471	467.5	57.4	531	527.0	64.7	591	586.6	72.0
52	349.4	42.9	12	408.9	50.2	72	468.5	57.5	32	528.0	64.8	92	587.6	72.1
53	350.4	43.0	13	409.9	50.3	73	469.5	57.6	33	529.0	65.0	93	588.6	72.3
54	351.4	43.1	14	410.9	50.5	74	470.5	57.8	34	530.0	65.1	94	589.6	72.4
55	352.4	43.3	15	411.9	50.6	75	471.5	57.9	35	531.0	65.2	95	590.6	72.5
56	353.3	43.4	16	412.9	50.7	76	472.5	58.0	36	532.0	65.3	96	591.6	72.6
57	354.3	43.5	17	413.9	50.8	77	473.4	58.1	37	533.0	65.4	97	592.6	72.8
58	355.3	43.6	18	414.9	50.9	78	474.4	58.3	38	534.0	65.6	98	593.5	72.9
59	356.3	43.8	19	415.9	51.1	79	475.4	58.4	39	535.0	65.7	99	594.5	73.0
60	357.3	43.9	20	416.9	51.2	80	476.4	58.5	40	536.0	65.8	600	595.5	73.1
Dist.	Dep.	D. Lat.	Dist.	Dep.	D. Lat.	Dist.	Dep.	D. Lat.	Dist.	Dep.	D. Lat.	Dist.	Dep.	D. Lat.

Dist.	D. Lat.	Dep.
D Lo	Dep.	
	m	D Lo

83°

277° | 083° — 263° | 097°

TABLE 4

Traverse 8° Table

352° 188°	008° 172°

Dist.	D. Lat.	Dep.	Dist.	D. Lat.	Dep.	Dist.	D. Lat.	Dep.	Dist.	D. Lat.	Dep.	Dist.	D. Lat.	Dep.
1	1.0	0.1	61	60.4	8.5	121	119.8	16.8	181	179.2	25.2	241	238.7	33.5
2	2.0	0.3	62	61.4	8.6	22	120.8	17.0	82	180.2	25.3	42	239.6	33.7
3	3.0	0.4	63	62.4	8.8	23	121.8	17.1	83	181.2	25.5	43	240.6	33.8
4	4.0	0.6	64	63.4	8.9	24	122.8	17.3	84	182.2	25.6	44	241.6	34.0
5	5.0	0.7	65	64.4	9.0	25	123.8	17.4	85	183.2	25.7	45	242.6	34.1
6	5.9	0.8	66	65.4	9.2	26	124.8	17.5	86	184.2	25.9	46	243.6	34.2
7	6.9	1.0	67	66.3	9.3	27	125.8	17.7	87	185.2	26.0	47	244.6	34.4
8	7.9	1.1	68	67.3	9.5	28	126.8	17.8	88	186.2	26.2	48	245.6	34.5
9	8.9	1.3	69	68.3	9.6	29	127.7	18.0	89	187.2	26.3	49	246.6	34.7
10	9.9	1.4	70	69.3	9.7	30	128.7	18.1	90	188.2	26.4	50	247.6	34.8
11	10.9	1.5	71	70.3	9.9	131	129.7	18.2	191	189.1	26.6	251	248.6	34.9
12	11.9	1.7	72	71.3	10.0	32	130.7	18.4	92	190.1	26.7	52	249.5	35.1
13	12.9	1.8	73	72.3	10.2	33	131.7	18.5	93	191.1	26.9	53	250.5	35.2
14	13.9	1.9	74	73.3	10.3	34	132.7	18.6	94	192.1	27.0	54	251.5	35.3
15	14.9	2.1	75	74.3	10.4	35	133.7	18.8	95	193.1	27.1	55	252.5	35.5
16	15.8	2.2	76	75.3	10.6	36	134.7	18.9	96	194.1	27.3	56	253.5	35.6
17	16.8	2.4	77	76.3	10.7	37	135.7	19.1	97	195.1	27.4	57	254.5	35.8
18	17.8	2.5	78	77.2	10.9	38	136.7	19.2	98	196.1	27.6	58	255.5	35.9
19	18.8	2.6	79	78.2	11.0	39	137.6	19.3	99	197.1	27.7	59	256.5	36.0
20	19.8	2.8	80	79.2	11.1	40	138.6	19.5	200	198.1	27.8	60	257.5	36.2
21	20.8	2.9	81	80.2	11.3	141	139.6	19.6	201	199.0	28.0	261	258.5	36.3
22	21.8	3.1	82	81.2	11.4	42	140.6	19.8	02	200.0	28.1	62	259.5	36.5
23	22.8	3.2	83	82.2	11.6	43	141.6	19.9	03	201.0	28.3	63	260.4	36.6
24	23.8	3.3	84	83.2	11.7	44	142.6	20.0	04	202.0	28.4	64	261.4	36.7
25	24.8	3.5	85	84.2	11.8	45	143.6	20.2	05	203.0	28.5	65	262.4	36.9
26	25.7	3.6	86	85.2	12.0	46	144.6	20.3	06	204.0	28.7	66	263.4	37.0
27	26.7	3.8	87	86.2	12.1	47	145.6	20.5	07	205.0	28.8	67	264.4	37.2
28	27.7	3.9	88	87.1	12.2	48	146.6	20.6	08	206.0	28.9	68	265.4	37.3
29	28.7	4.0	89	88.1	12.4	49	147.5	20.7	09	207.0	29.1	69	266.4	37.4
30	29.7	4.2	90	89.1	12.5	50	148.5	20.9	10	208.0	29.2	70	267.4	37.6
31	30.7	4.3	91	90.1	12.7	151	149.5	21.0	211	208.9	29.4	271	268.4	37.7
32	31.7	4.5	92	91.1	12.8	52	150.5	21.2	12	209.9	29.5	72	269.4	37.9
33	32.7	4.6	93	92.1	12.9	53	151.5	21.3	13	210.9	29.6	73	270.3	38.0
34	33.7	4.7	94	93.1	13.1	54	152.5	21.4	14	211.9	29.8	74	271.3	38.1
35	34.7	4.9	95	94.1	13.2	55	153.5	21.6	15	212.9	29.9	75	272.3	38.3
36	35.6	5.0	96	95.1	13.4	56	154.5	21.7	16	213.9	30.1	76	273.3	38.4
37	36.6	5.1	97	96.1	13.5	57	155.5	21.9	17	214.9	30.2	77	274.3	38.6
38	37.6	5.3	98	97.0	13.6	58	156.5	22.0	18	215.9	30.3	78	275.3	38.7
39	38.6	5.4	99	98.0	13.8	59	157.5	22.1	19	216.9	30.5	79	276.3	38.8
40	39.6	5.6	100	99.0	13.9	60	158.4	22.3	20	217.9	30.6	80	277.3	39.0
41	40.6	5.7	101	100.0	14.1	161	159.4	22.4	221	218.8	30.8	281	278.3	39.1
42	41.6	5.8	02	101.0	14.2	62	160.4	22.5	22	219.8	30.9	82	279.3	39.2
43	42.6	6.0	03	102.0	14.3	63	161.4	22.7	23	220.8	31.0	83	280.2	39.4
44	43.6	6.1	04	103.0	14.5	64	162.4	22.8	24	221.8	31.2	84	281.2	39.5
45	44.6	6.3	05	104.0	14.6	65	163.4	23.0	25	222.8	31.3	85	282.2	39.7
46	45.6	6.4	06	105.0	14.8	66	164.4	23.1	26	223.8	31.5	86	283.2	39.8
47	46.5	6.5	07	106.0	14.9	67	165.4	23.2	27	224.8	31.6	87	284.2	39.9
48	47.5	6.7	08	106.9	15.0	68	166.4	23.4	28	225.8	31.7	88	285.2	40.1
49	48.5	6.8	09	107.9	15.2	69	167.4	23.5	29	226.8	31.9	89	286.2	40.2
50	49.5	7.0	10	108.9	15.3	70	168.3	23.7	30	227.8	32.0	90	287.2	40.4
51	50.5	7.1	111	109.9	15.4	171	169.3	23.8	231	228.8	32.1	291	288.2	40.5
52	51.5	7.2	12	110.9	15.6	72	170.3	23.9	32	229.7	32.3	92	289.2	40.6
53	52.5	7.4	13	111.9	15.7	73	171.3	24.1	33	230.7	32.4	93	290.1	40.8
54	53.5	7.5	14	112.9	15.9	74	172.3	24.2	34	231.7	32.6	94	291.1	40.9
55	54.5	7.7	15	113.9	16.0	75	173.3	24.4	35	232.7	32.7	95	292.1	41.1
56	55.5	7.8	16	114.9	16.1	76	174.3	24.5	36	233.7	32.8	96	293.1	41.2
57	56.4	7.9	17	115.9	16.3	77	175.3	24.6	37	234.7	33.0	97	294.1	41.3
58	57.4	8.1	18	116.9	16.4	78	176.3	24.8	38	235.7	33.1	98	295.1	41.5
59	58.4	8.2	19	117.8	16.6	79	177.3	24.9	39	236.7	33.3	99	296.1	41.6
60	59.4	8.4	20	118.8	16.7	80	178.2	25.1	40	237.7	33.4	300	297.1	41.8
Dist.	Dep.	D. Lat.	Dist.	Dep.	D. Lat.	Dist.	Dep.	D. Lat.	Dist.	Dep.	D. Lat.	Dist.	Dep.	D. Lat.

278° 262°	082° 098°

82°

Dist.	D. Lat.	Dep.
N.	N x Cos.	N x Sin.
Hypotenuse	Side Adj.	Side Opp.

TABLE 4

Traverse 8° Table

352° 188°	008° 172°

Dist.	D. Lat.	Dep.	Dist.	D. Lat.	Dep.	Dist.	D. Lat.	Dep.	Dist.	D. Lat.	Dep.	Dist.	D. Lat.	Dep.
301	298.1	41.9	361	357.5	50.2	421	416.9	58.6	481	476.3	66.9	541	535.7	75.3
02	299.1	42.0	62	358.5	50.4	22	417.9	58.7	82	477.3	67.1	42	536.7	75.4
03	300.1	42.2	63	359.5	50.5	23	418.9	58.9	83	478.3	67.2	43	537.7	75.6
04	301.0	42.3	64	360.5	50.7	24	419.9	59.0	84	479.3	67.4	44	538.7	75.7
05	302.0	42.4	65	361.4	50.8	25	420.9	59.1	85	480.3	67.5	45	539.7	75.8
06	303.0	42.6	66	362.4	50.9	26	421.9	59.3	86	481.3	67.6	46	540.7	76.0
07	304.0	42.7	67	363.4	51.1	27	422.8	59.4	87	482.3	67.8	47	541.7	76.1
08	305.0	42.9	68	364.4	51.2	28	423.8	59.6	88	483.3	67.9	48	542.7	76.3
09	306.0	43.0	69	365.4	51.4	29	424.8	59.7	89	484.2	68.1	49	543.7	76.4
10	307.0	43.1	70	366.4	51.5	30	425.8	59.8	90	485.2	68.2	50	544.6	76.5
311	308.0	43.3	371	367.4	51.6	431	426.8	60.0	491	486.2	68.3	551	545.6	76.7
12	309.0	43.4	72	368.4	51.8	32	427.8	60.1	92	487.2	68.5	52	546.6	76.8
13	310.0	43.6	73	369.4	51.9	33	428.8	60.3	93	488.2	68.6	53	547.6	77.0
14	310.9	43.7	74	370.4	52.1	34	429.8	60.4	94	489.2	68.8	54	548.6	77.1
15	311.9	43.8	75	371.4	52.2	35	430.8	60.5	95	490.2	68.9	55	549.6	77.2
16	312.9	44.0	76	372.3	52.3	36	431.8	60.7	96	491.2	69.0	56	550.6	77.4
17	313.9	44.1	77	373.3	52.5	37	432.7	60.8	97	492.2	69.2	57	551.6	77.5
18	314.9	44.3	78	374.3	52.6	38	433.7	61.0	98	493.2	69.3	58	552.6	77.7
19	315.9	44.4	79	375.3	52.7	39	434.7	61.1	99	494.1	69.4	59	553.6	77.8
20	316.9	44.5	80	376.3	52.9	40	435.7	61.2	500	495.1	69.6	60	554.6	77.9
321	317.9	44.7	381	377.3	53.0	441	436.7	61.4	501	496.1	69.7	561	555.5	78.1
22	318.9	44.8	82	378.3	53.2	42	437.7	61.5	02	497.1	69.9	62	556.5	78.2
23	319.9	45.0	83	379.3	53.3	43	438.7	61.7	03	498.1	70.0	63	557.5	78.4
24	320.8	45.1	84	380.3	53.4	44	439.7	61.8	04	499.1	70.1	64	558.5	78.5
25	321.8	45.2	85	381.3	53.6	45	440.7	61.9	05	500.1	70.3	65	559.5	78.6
26	322.8	45.4	86	382.2	53.7	46	441.7	62.1	06	501.1	70.4	66	560.5	78.8
27	323.8	45.5	87	383.2	53.9	47	442.6	62.2	07	502.1	70.6	67	561.5	78.9
28	324.8	45.6	88	384.2	54.0	48	443.6	62.3	08	503.1	70.7	68	562.5	79.1
29	325.8	45.8	89	385.2	54.1	49	444.6	62.5	09	504.0	70.8	69	563.5	79.2
30	326.8	45.9	90	386.2	54.3	50	445.6	62.6	10	505.0	71.0	70	564.5	79.3
331	327.8	46.1	391	387.2	54.4	451	446.6	62.8	511	506.0	71.1	571	565.4	79.5
32	328.8	46.2	92	388.2	54.6	52	447.6	62.9	12	507.0	71.3	72	566.4	79.6
33	329.8	46.3	93	389.2	54.7	53	448.6	63.0	13	508.0	71.4	73	567.4	79.7
34	330.7	46.5	94	390.2	54.8	54	449.6	63.2	14	509.0	71.5	74	568.4	79.9
35	331.7	46.6	95	391.2	55.0	55	450.6	63.3	15	510.0	71.7	75	569.4	80.0
36	332.7	46.8	96	392.1	55.1	56	451.6	63.5	16	511.0	71.8	76	570.4	80.2
37	333.7	46.9	97	393.1	55.3	57	452.6	63.6	17	512.0	72.0	77	571.4	80.3
38	334.7	47.0	98	394.1	55.4	58	453.5	63.7	18	513.0	72.1	78	572.4	80.4
39	335.7	47.2	99	395.1	55.5	59	454.5	63.9	19	513.9	72.2	79	573.4	80.6
40	336.7	47.3	400	396.1	55.7	60	455.5	64.0	20	514.9	72.4	80	574.4	80.7
341	337.7	47.5	401	397.1	55.8	461	456.5	64.2	521	515.9	72.5	581	575.3	80.9
42	338.7	47.6	02	398.1	55.9	62	457.5	64.3	22	516.9	72.6	82	576.3	81.0
43	339.7	47.7	03	399.1	56.1	63	458.5	64.4	23	517.9	72.8	83	577.3	81.1
44	340.7	47.9	04	400.1	56.2	64	459.5	64.6	24	518.9	72.9	84	578.3	81.3
45	341.6	48.0	05	401.1	56.4	65	460.5	64.7	25	519.9	73.1	85	579.3	81.4
46	342.6	48.2	06	402.0	56.5	66	461.5	64.9	26	520.9	73.2	86	580.3	81.6
47	343.6	48.3	07	403.0	56.6	67	462.5	65.0	27	521.9	73.3	87	581.3	81.7
48	344.6	48.4	08	404.0	56.8	68	463.4	65.1	28	522.9	73.5	88	582.3	81.8
49	345.6	48.6	09	405.0	56.9	69	464.4	65.3	29	523.9	73.6	89	583.3	82.0
50	346.6	48.7	10	406.0	57.1	70	465.4	65.4	30	524.8	73.8	90	584.3	82.1
351	347.6	48.8	411	407.0	57.2	471	466.4	65.6	531	525.8	73.9	591	585.2	82.3
52	348.6	49.0	12	408.0	57.3	72	467.4	65.7	32	526.8	74.0	92	586.2	82.4
53	349.6	49.1	13	409.0	57.5	73	468.4	65.8	33	527.8	74.2	93	587.2	82.5
54	350.6	49.3	14	410.0	57.6	74	469.4	66.0	34	528.8	74.3	94	588.2	82.7
55	351.5	49.4	15	411.0	57.8	75	470.4	66.1	35	529.8	74.5	95	589.2	82.8
56	352.5	49.5	16	412.0	57.9	76	471.4	66.2	36	530.8	74.6	96	590.2	82.9
57	353.5	49.7	17	412.9	58.0	77	472.4	66.4	37	531.8	74.7	97	591.2	83.1
58	354.5	49.8	18	413.9	58.2	78	473.3	66.5	38	532.8	74.9	98	592.2	83.2
59	355.5	50.0	19	414.9	58.3	79	474.3	66.7	39	533.8	75.0	99	593.2	83.4
60	356.5	50.1	20	415.9	58.5	80	475.3	66.8	40	534.7	75.2	600	594.2	83.5
Dist.	Dep.	D. Lat.	Dist.	Dep.	D. Lat.	Dist.	Dep.	D. Lat.	Dist.	Dep.	D. Lat.	Dist.	Dep.	D. Lat.

Dist.	D. Lat.	Dep.
D Lo	Dep.	
	m	D Lo

82°

278° 262°	082° 098°

TABLE 4

351° | 009° — 189° | 171°

Traverse **9°** Table

Dist.	D. Lat.	Dep.	Dist.	D. Lat.	Dep.	Dist.	D. Lat.	Dep.	Dist.	D. Lat.	Dep.	Dist.	D. Lat.	Dep.
1	1.0	0.2	61	60.2	9.5	121	119.5	18.9	181	178.8	28.3	241	238.0	37.7
2	2.0	0.3	62	61.2	9.7	22	120.5	19.1	82	179.8	28.5	42	239.0	37.9
3	3.0	0.5	63	62.2	9.9	23	121.5	19.2	83	180.7	28.6	43	240.0	38.0
4	4.0	0.6	64	63.2	10.0	24	122.5	19.4	84	181.7	28.8	44	241.0	38.2
5	4.9	0.8	65	64.2	10.2	25	123.5	19.6	85	182.7	28.9	45	242.0	38.3
6	5.9	0.9	66	65.2	10.3	26	124.4	19.7	86	183.7	29.1	46	243.0	38.5
7	6.9	1.1	67	66.2	10.5	27	125.4	19.9	87	184.7	29.3	47	244.0	38.6
8	7.9	1.3	68	67.2	10.6	28	126.4	20.0	88	185.7	29.4	48	244.9	38.8
9	8.9	1.4	69	68.2	10.8	29	127.4	20.2	89	186.7	29.6	49	245.9	39.0
10	9.9	1.6	70	69.1	11.0	30	128.4	20.3	90	187.7	29.7	50	246.9	39.1
11	10.9	1.7	71	70.1	11.1	131	129.4	20.5	191	188.6	29.9	251	247.9	39.3
12	11.9	1.9	72	71.1	11.3	32	130.4	20.6	92	189.6	30.0	52	248.9	39.4
13	12.8	2.0	73	72.1	11.4	33	131.4	20.8	93	190.6	30.2	53	249.9	39.6
14	13.8	2.2	74	73.1	11.6	34	132.4	21.0	94	191.6	30.3	54	250.9	39.7
15	14.8	2.3	75	74.1	11.7	35	133.3	21.1	95	192.6	30.5	55	251.9	39.9
16	15.8	2.5	76	75.1	11.9	36	134.3	21.3	96	193.6	30.7	56	252.8	40.0
17	16.8	2.7	77	76.1	12.0	37	135.3	21.4	97	194.6	30.8	57	253.8	40.2
18	17.8	2.8	78	77.0	12.2	38	136.3	21.6	98	195.6	31.0	58	254.8	40.4
19	18.8	3.0	79	78.0	12.4	39	137.3	21.7	99	196.5	31.1	59	255.8	40.5
20	19.8	3.1	80	79.0	12.5	40	138.3	21.9	200	197.5	31.3	60	256.8	40.7
21	20.7	3.3	81	80.0	12.7	141	139.3	22.1	201	198.5	31.4	261	257.8	40.8
22	21.7	3.4	82	81.0	12.8	42	140.3	22.2	02	199.5	31.6	62	258.8	41.0
23	22.7	3.6	83	82.0	13.0	43	141.2	22.4	03	200.5	31.8	63	259.8	41.1
24	23.7	3.8	84	83.0	13.1	44	142.2	22.5	04	201.5	31.9	64	260.7	41.3
25	24.7	3.9	85	84.0	13.3	45	143.2	22.7	05	202.5	32.1	65	261.7	41.5
26	25.7	4.1	86	84.9	13.5	46	144.2	22.8	06	203.5	32.2	66	262.7	41.6
27	26.7	4.2	87	85.9	13.6	47	145.2	23.0	07	204.5	32.4	67	263.7	41.8
28	27.7	4.4	88	86.9	13.8	48	146.2	23.2	08	205.4	32.5	68	264.7	41.9
29	28.6	4.5	89	87.9	13.9	49	147.2	23.3	09	206.4	32.7	69	265.7	42.1
30	29.6	4.7	90	88.9	14.1	50	148.2	23.5	10	207.4	32.9	70	266.7	42.2
31	30.6	4.8	91	89.9	14.2	151	149.1	23.6	211	208.4	33.0	271	267.7	42.4
32	31.6	5.0	92	90.9	14.4	52	150.1	23.8	12	209.4	33.2	72	268.7	42.6
33	32.6	5.2	93	91.9	14.5	53	151.1	23.9	13	210.4	33.3	73	269.6	42.7
34	33.6	5.3	94	92.8	14.7	54	152.1	24.1	14	211.4	33.5	74	270.6	42.9
35	34.6	5.5	95	93.8	14.9	55	153.1	24.2	15	212.4	33.6	75	271.6	43.0
36	35.6	5.6	96	94.8	15.0	56	154.1	24.4	16	213.3	33.8	76	272.6	43.2
37	36.5	5.8	97	95.8	15.2	57	155.1	24.6	17	214.3	33.9	77	273.6	43.3
38	37.5	5.9	98	96.8	15.3	58	156.1	24.7	18	215.3	34.1	78	274.6	43.5
39	38.5	6.1	99	97.8	15.5	59	157.0	24.9	19	216.3	34.3	79	275.6	43.6
40	39.5	6.3	100	98.8	15.6	60	158.0	25.0	20	217.3	34.4	80	276.6	43.8
41	40.5	6.4	101	99.8	15.8	161	159.0	25.2	221	218.3	34.6	281	277.5	44.0
42	41.5	6.6	02	100.7	16.0	62	160.0	25.3	22	219.3	34.7	82	278.5	44.1
43	42.5	6.7	03	101.7	16.1	63	161.0	25.5	23	220.3	34.9	83	279.5	44.3
44	43.5	6.9	04	102.7	16.3	64	162.0	25.7	24	221.2	35.0	84	280.5	44.4
45	44.4	7.0	05	103.7	16.4	65	163.0	25.8	25	222.2	35.2	85	281.5	44.6
46	45.4	7.2	06	104.7	16.6	66	164.0	26.0	26	223.2	35.4	86	282.5	44.7
47	46.4	7.4	07	105.7	16.7	67	164.9	26.1	27	224.2	35.5	87	283.5	44.9
48	47.4	7.5	08	106.7	16.9	68	165.9	26.3	28	225.2	35.7	88	284.5	45.1
49	48.4	7.7	09	107.7	17.1	69	166.9	26.4	29	226.2	35.8	89	285.4	45.2
50	49.4	7.8	10	108.6	17.2	70	167.9	26.6	30	227.2	36.0	90	286.4	45.4
51	50.4	8.0	111	109.6	17.4	171	168.9	26.8	231	228.2	36.1	291	287.4	45.5
52	51.4	8.1	12	110.6	17.5	72	169.9	26.9	32	229.1	36.3	92	288.4	45.7
53	52.3	8.3	13	111.6	17.7	73	170.9	27.1	33	230.1	36.4	93	289.4	45.8
54	53.3	8.4	14	112.6	17.8	74	171.9	27.2	34	231.1	36.6	94	290.4	46.0
55	54.3	8.6	15	113.6	18.0	75	172.8	27.4	35	232.1	36.8	95	291.4	46.1
56	55.3	8.8	16	114.6	18.1	76	173.8	27.5	36	233.1	36.9	96	292.4	46.3
57	56.3	8.9	17	115.6	18.3	77	174.8	27.7	37	234.1	37.1	97	293.3	46.5
58	57.3	9.1	18	116.5	18.5	78	175.8	27.8	38	235.1	37.2	98	294.3	46.6
59	58.3	9.2	19	117.5	18.6	79	176.8	28.0	39	236.1	37.4	99	295.3	46.8
60	59.3	9.4	20	118.5	18.8	80	177.8	28.2	40	237.0	37.5	300	296.3	46.9
Dist.	Dep.	D. Lat.	Dist.	Dep.	D. Lat.	Dist.	Dep.	D. Lat.	Dist.	Dep.	D. Lat.	Dist.	Dep.	D. Lat.

279° | 081° — 261° | 099°

81°

Dist.	D. Lat.	Dep.
N.	N x Cos.	N x Sin.
Hypotenuse	Side Adj.	Side Opp.

TABLE 4

351° | 009° — 189° | 171°

Traverse **9°** Table

Dist.	D. Lat.	Dep.	Dist.	D. Lat.	Dep.	Dist.	D. Lat.	Dep.	Dist.	D. Lat.	Dep.	Dist.	D. Lat.	Dep.
301	297.3	47.1	361	356.6	56.5	421	415.8	65.9	481	475.1	75.2	541	534.3	84.6
02	298.3	47.2	62	357.5	56.6	22	416.8	66.0	82	476.1	75.4	42	535.3	84.8
03	299.3	47.4	63	358.5	56.8	23	417.8	66.2	83	477.1	75.6	43	536.3	84.9
04	300.3	47.6	64	359.5	56.9	24	418.8	66.3	84	478.0	75.7	44	537.3	85.1
05	301.2	47.7	65	360.5	57.1	25	419.8	66.5	85	479.0	75.9	45	538.3	85.3
06	302.2	47.9	66	361.5	57.3	26	420.8	66.6	86	480.0	76.0	46	539.3	85.4
07	303.2	48.0	67	362.5	57.4	27	421.7	66.8	87	481.0	76.2	47	540.3	85.6
08	304.2	48.2	68	363.5	57.6	28	422.7	67.0	88	482.0	76.3	48	541.3	85.7
09	305.2	48.3	69	364.5	57.7	29	423.7	67.1	89	483.0	76.5	49	542.2	85.9
10	306.2	48.5	70	365.4	57.9	30	424.7	67.3	90	484.0	76.7	50	543.2	86.0
311	307.2	48.7	371	366.4	58.0	431	425.7	67.4	491	485.0	76.8	551	544.2	86.2
12	308.2	48.8	72	367.4	58.2	32	426.7	67.6	92	485.9	77.0	52	545.2	86.4
13	309.1	49.0	73	368.4	58.4	33	427.7	67.7	93	486.9	77.1	53	546.2	86.5
14	310.1	49.1	74	369.4	58.5	34	428.7	67.9	94	487.9	77.3	54	547.2	86.7
15	311.1	49.3	75	370.4	58.7	35	429.6	68.0	95	488.9	77.4	55	548.2	86.8
16	312.1	49.4	76	371.4	58.8	36	430.6	68.2	96	489.9	77.6	56	549.2	87.0
17	313.1	49.6	77	372.4	59.0	37	431.6	68.4	97	490.9	77.7	57	550.1	87.1
18	314.1	49.7	78	373.3	59.1	38	432.6	68.5	98	491.9	77.9	58	551.1	87.3
19	315.1	49.9	79	374.3	59.3	39	433.6	68.7	99	492.9	78.1	59	552.1	87.4
20	316.1	50.1	80	375.3	59.4	40	434.6	68.8	500	493.8	78.2	60	553.1	87.6
321	317.0	50.2	381	376.3	59.6	441	435.6	69.0	501	494.8	78.4	561	554.1	87.8
22	318.0	50.4	82	377.3	59.8	42	436.6	69.1	02	495.8	78.5	62	555.1	87.9
23	319.0	50.5	83	378.3	59.9	43	437.5	69.3	03	496.8	78.7	63	556.1	88.1
24	320.0	50.7	84	379.3	60.1	44	438.5	69.5	04	497.8	78.8	64	557.1	88.2
25	321.0	50.8	85	380.3	60.2	45	439.5	69.6	05	498.8	79.0	65	558.0	88.4
26	322.0	51.0	86	381.2	60.4	46	440.5	69.8	06	499.8	79.2	66	559.0	88.5
27	323.0	51.2	87	382.2	60.5	47	441.5	69.9	07	500.8	79.3	67	560.0	88.7
28	324.0	51.3	88	383.2	60.7	48	442.5	70.1	08	501.7	79.5	68	561.0	88.9
29	324.9	51.5	89	384.2	60.9	49	443.5	70.2	09	502.7	79.6	69	562.0	89.0
30	325.9	51.6	90	385.2	61.0	50	444.5	70.4	10	503.7	79.8	70	563.0	89.2
331	326.9	51.8	391	386.2	61.2	451	445.4	70.6	511	504.7	79.9	571	564.0	89.3
32	327.9	51.9	92	387.2	61.3	52	446.4	70.7	12	505.7	80.1	72	565.0	89.5
33	328.9	52.1	93	388.2	61.5	53	447.4	70.9	13	506.7	80.3	73	565.9	89.6
34	329.9	52.2	94	389.1	61.6	54	448.4	71.0	14	507.7	80.4	74	566.9	89.8
35	330.9	52.4	95	390.1	61.8	55	449.4	71.2	15	508.7	80.6	75	567.9	89.9
36	331.9	52.6	96	391.1	61.9	56	450.4	71.3	16	509.6	80.7	76	568.9	90.1
37	332.9	52.7	97	392.1	62.1	57	451.4	71.5	17	510.6	80.9	77	569.9	90.3
38	333.8	52.9	98	393.1	62.3	58	452.4	71.6	18	511.6	81.0	78	570.9	90.4
39	334.8	53.0	99	394.1	62.4	59	453.3	71.8	19	512.6	81.2	79	571.9	90.6
40	335.8	53.2	400	395.1	62.6	60	454.3	72.0	20	513.6	81.3	80	572.9	90.7
341	336.8	53.3	401	396.1	62.7	461	455.3	72.1	521	514.6	81.5	581	573.8	90.9
42	337.8	53.5	02	397.1	62.9	62	456.3	72.3	22	515.6	81.7	82	574.8	91.0
43	338.8	53.7	03	398.0	63.0	63	457.3	72.4	23	516.6	81.8	83	575.8	91.2
44	339.8	53.8	04	399.0	63.2	64	458.3	72.6	24	517.5	82.0	84	576.8	91.4
45	340.8	54.0	05	400.0	63.4	65	459.3	72.7	25	518.5	82.1	85	577.8	91.5
46	341.7	54.1	06	401.0	63.5	66	460.3	72.9	26	519.5	82.3	86	578.8	91.7
47	342.7	54.3	07	402.0	63.7	67	461.3	73.1	27	520.5	82.4	87	579.8	91.8
48	343.7	54.4	08	403.0	63.8	68	462.2	73.2	28	521.5	82.6	88	580.8	92.0
49	344.7	54.6	09	404.0	64.0	69	463.2	73.4	29	522.5	82.8	89	581.7	92.1
50	345.7	54.8	10	405.0	64.1	70	464.2	73.5	30	523.5	82.9	90	582.7	92.3
351	346.7	54.9	411	405.9	64.3	471	465.2	73.7	531	524.5	83.1	591	583.7	92.5
52	347.7	55.1	12	406.9	64.5	72	466.2	73.8	32	525.5	83.2	92	584.7	92.6
53	348.7	55.2	13	407.9	64.6	73	467.2	74.0	33	526.4	83.4	93	585.7	92.8
54	349.6	55.4	14	408.9	64.8	74	468.2	74.1	34	527.4	83.5	94	586.7	92.9
55	350.6	55.5	15	409.9	64.9	75	469.2	74.3	35	528.4	83.7	95	587.7	93.1
56	351.6	55.7	16	410.9	65.1	76	470.1	74.5	36	529.4	83.8	96	588.7	93.2
57	352.6	55.8	17	411.9	65.2	77	471.1	74.6	37	530.4	84.0	97	589.6	93.4
58	353.6	56.0	18	412.9	65.4	78	472.1	74.8	38	531.4	84.2	98	590.6	93.5
59	354.6	56.2	19	413.8	65.5	79	473.1	74.9	39	532.4	84.3	99	591.6	93.7
60	355.6	56.3	20	414.8	65.7	80	474.1	75.1	40	533.4	84.5	600	592.6	93.9
Dist.	Dep.	D. Lat.	Dist.	Dep.	D. Lat.	Dist.	Dep.	D. Lat.	Dist.	Dep.	D. Lat.	Dist.	Dep.	D. Lat.

Dist.	D. Lat.	Dep.
D Lo	Dep.	
	m	D Lo

81°

279° | 081° — 261° | 099°

TABLE 4

350° | 010°
190° | 170°

Traverse **10°** Table

350° | 010°
190° | 170°

Dist.	D. Lat.	Dep.	Dist.	D. Lat.	Dep.	Dist.	D. Lat.	Dep.	Dist.	D. Lat.	Dep.	Dist.	D. Lat.	Dep.
1	1.0	0.2	61	60.1	10.6	121	119.2	21.0	181	178.3	31.4	241	237.3	41.8
2	2.0	0.3	62	61.1	10.8	22	120.1	21.2	82	179.2	31.6	42	238.3	42.0
3	3.0	0.5	63	62.0	10.9	23	121.1	21.4	83	180.2	31.8	43	239.3	42.2
4	3.9	0.7	64	63.0	11.1	24	122.1	21.5	84	181.2	32.0	44	240.3	42.4
5	4.9	0.9	65	64.0	11.3	25	123.1	21.7	85	182.2	32.1	45	241.3	42.5
6	5.9	1.0	66	65.0	11.5	26	124.1	21.9	86	183.2	32.3	46	242.3	42.7
7	6.9	1.2	67	66.0	11.6	27	125.1	22.1	87	184.2	32.5	47	243.2	42.9
8	7.9	1.4	68	67.0	11.8	28	126.1	22.2	88	185.1	32.6	48	244.2	43.1
9	8.9	1.6	69	68.0	12.0	29	127.0	22.4	89	186.1	32.8	49	245.2	43.2
10	9.8	1.7	70	68.9	12.2	30	128.0	22.6	90	187.1	33.0	50	246.2	43.4
11	10.8	1.9	71	69.9	12.3	131	129.0	22.7	191	188.1	33.2	251	247.2	43.6
12	11.8	2.1	72	70.9	12.5	32	130.0	22.9	92	189.1	33.3	52	248.2	43.8
13	12.8	2.3	73	71.9	12.7	33	131.0	23.1	93	190.1	33.5	53	249.2	43.9
14	13.8	2.4	74	72.9	12.8	34	132.0	23.3	94	191.1	33.7	54	250.1	44.1
15	14.8	2.6	75	73.9	13.0	35	132.9	23.4	95	192.0	33.9	55	251.1	44.3
16	15.8	2.8	76	74.8	13.2	36	133.9	23.6	96	193.0	34.0	56	252.1	44.5
17	16.7	3.0	77	75.8	13.4	37	134.9	23.8	97	194.0	34.2	57	253.1	44.6
18	17.7	3.1	78	76.8	13.5	38	135.9	24.0	98	195.0	34.4	58	254.1	44.8
19	18.7	3.3	79	77.8	13.7	39	136.9	24.1	99	196.0	34.6	59	255.1	45.0
20	19.7	3.5	80	78.8	13.9	40	137.9	24.3	200	197.0	34.7	60	256.1	45.1
21	20.7	3.6	81	79.8	14.1	141	138.9	24.5	201	197.9	34.9	261	257.0	45.3
22	21.7	3.8	82	80.8	14.2	42	139.8	24.7	02	198.9	35.1	62	258.0	45.5
23	22.7	4.0	83	81.7	14.4	43	140.8	24.8	03	199.9	35.3	63	259.0	45.7
24	23.6	4.2	84	82.7	14.6	44	141.8	25.0	04	200.9	35.4	64	260.0	45.8
25	24.6	4.3	85	83.7	14.8	45	142.8	25.2	05	201.9	35.6	65	261.0	46.0
26	25.6	4.5	86	84.7	14.9	46	143.8	25.4	06	202.9	35.8	66	262.0	46.2
27	26.6	4.7	87	85.7	15.1	47	144.8	25.5	07	203.9	35.9	67	262.9	46.4
28	27.6	4.9	88	86.7	15.3	48	145.8	25.7	08	204.8	36.1	68	263.9	46.5
29	28.6	5.0	89	87.6	15.5	49	146.7	25.9	09	205.8	36.3	69	264.9	46.7
30	29.5	5.2	90	88.6	15.6	50	147.7	26.0	10	206.8	36.5	70	265.9	46.9
31	30.5	5.4	91	89.6	15.8	151	148.7	26.2	211	207.8	36.6	271	266.9	47.1
32	31.5	5.6	92	90.6	16.0	52	149.7	26.4	12	208.8	36.8	72	267.9	47.2
33	32.5	5.7	93	91.6	16.1	53	150.7	26.6	13	209.8	37.0	73	268.9	47.4
34	33.5	5.9	94	92.6	16.3	54	151.7	26.7	14	210.7	37.2	74	269.8	47.6
35	34.5	6.1	95	93.6	16.5	55	152.6	26.9	15	211.7	37.3	75	270.8	47.8
36	35.5	6.3	96	94.5	16.7	56	153.6	27.1	16	212.7	37.5	76	271.8	47.9
37	36.4	6.4	97	95.5	16.8	57	154.6	27.3	17	213.7	37.7	77	272.8	48.1
38	37.4	6.6	98	96.5	17.0	58	155.6	27.4	18	214.7	37.9	78	273.8	48.3
39	38.4	6.8	99	97.5	17.2	59	156.6	27.6	19	215.7	38.0	79	274.8	48.4
40	39.4	6.9	100	98.5	17.4	60	157.6	27.8	20	216.7	38.2	80	275.7	48.6
41	40.4	7.1	101	99.5	17.5	161	158.6	28.0	221	217.6	38.4	281	276.7	48.8
42	41.4	7.3	02	100.5	17.7	62	159.5	28.1	22	218.6	38.5	82	277.7	49.0
43	42.3	7.5	03	101.4	17.9	63	160.5	28.3	23	219.6	38.7	83	278.7	49.1
44	43.3	7.6	04	102.4	18.1	64	161.5	28.5	24	220.6	38.9	84	279.7	49.3
45	44.3	7.8	05	103.4	18.2	65	162.5	28.7	25	221.6	39.1	85	280.7	49.5
46	45.3	8.0	06	104.4	18.4	66	163.5	28.8	26	222.6	39.2	86	281.7	49.7
47	46.3	8.2	07	105.4	18.6	67	164.5	29.0	27	223.6	39.4	87	282.6	49.8
48	47.3	8.3	08	106.4	18.8	68	165.4	29.2	28	224.5	39.6	88	283.6	50.0
49	48.3	8.5	09	107.3	18.9	69	166.4	29.3	29	225.5	39.8	89	284.6	50.2
50	49.2	8.7	10	108.3	19.1	70	167.4	29.5	30	226.5	39.9	90	285.6	50.4
51	50.2	8.9	111	109.3	19.3	171	168.4	29.7	231	227.5	40.1	291	286.6	50.5
52	51.2	9.0	12	110.3	19.4	72	169.4	29.9	32	228.5	40.3	92	287.6	50.7
53	52.2	9.2	13	111.3	19.6	73	170.4	30.0	33	229.5	40.5	93	288.5	50.9
54	53.2	9.4	14	112.3	19.8	74	171.4	30.2	34	230.4	40.6	94	289.5	51.1
55	54.2	9.6	15	113.3	20.0	75	172.3	30.4	35	231.4	40.8	95	290.5	51.2
56	55.1	9.7	16	114.2	20.1	76	173.3	30.6	36	232.4	41.0	96	291.5	51.4
57	56.1	9.9	17	115.2	20.3	77	174.3	30.7	37	233.4	41.2	97	292.5	51.6
58	57.1	10.1	18	116.2	20.5	78	175.3	30.9	38	234.4	41.3	98	293.5	51.7
59	58.1	10.2	19	117.2	20.7	79	176.3	31.1	39	235.4	41.5	99	294.5	51.9
60	59.1	10.4	20	118.2	20.8	80	177.3	31.3	40	236.4	41.7	300	295.4	52.1
Dist.	Dep.	D. Lat.	Dist.	Dep.	D. Lat.	Dist.	Dep.	D. Lat.	Dist.	Dep.	D. Lat.	Dist.	Dep.	D. Lat.

280° | 080°
260° | 100°

80°

Dist.	D. Lat.	Dep.
N.	N x Cos.	N x Sin.
Hypotenuse	Side Adj.	Side Opp.

TABLE 4

350° | 010°
190° | 170°

Traverse **10°** Table

350° | 010°
190° | 170°

Dist.	D. Lat.	Dep.	Dist.	D. Lat.	Dep.	Dist.	D. Lat.	Dep.	Dist.	D. Lat.	Dep.	Dist.	D. Lat.	Dep.
301	296.4	52.3	361	355.5	62.7	421	414.6	73.1	481	473.7	83.5	541	532.8	93.9
02	297.4	52.4	62	356.5	62.9	22	415.6	73.3	82	474.7	83.7	42	533.8	94.1
03	298.4	52.6	63	357.5	63.0	23	416.6	73.5	83	475.7	83.9	43	534.8	94.3
04	299.4	52.8	64	358.5	63.2	24	417.6	73.6	84	476.6	84.0	44	535.7	94.5
05	300.4	53.0	65	359.5	63.4	25	418.5	73.8	85	477.6	84.2	45	536.7	94.6
06	301.4	53.1	66	360.4	63.6	26	419.5	74.0	86	478.6	84.4	46	537.7	94.8
07	302.3	53.3	67	361.4	63.7	27	420.5	74.1	87	479.6	84.6	47	538.7	95.0
08	303.3	53.5	68	362.4	63.9	28	421.5	74.3	88	480.6	84.7	48	539.7	95.2
09	304.3	53.7	69	363.4	64.1	29	422.5	74.5	89	481.6	84.9	49	540.7	95.3
10	305.3	53.8	70	364.4	64.2	30	423.5	74.7	90	482.6	85.1	50	541.6	95.5
311	306.3	54.0	371	365.4	64.4	431	424.5	74.8	491	483.5	85.3	551	542.6	95.7
12	307.3	54.2	72	366.3	64.6	32	425.4	75.0	92	484.5	85.4	52	543.6	95.9
13	308.2	54.4	73	367.3	64.8	33	426.4	75.2	93	485.5	85.6	53	544.6	96.0
14	309.2	54.5	74	368.3	64.9	34	427.4	75.4	94	486.5	85.8	54	545.6	96.2
15	310.2	54.7	75	369.3	65.1	35	428.4	75.5	95	487.5	86.0	55	546.6	96.4
16	311.2	54.9	76	370.3	65.3	36	429.4	75.7	96	488.5	86.1	56	547.6	96.5
17	312.2	55.0	77	371.3	65.5	37	430.4	75.9	97	489.4	86.3	57	548.5	96.7
18	313.2	55.2	78	372.3	65.6	38	431.3	76.1	98	490.4	86.5	58	549.5	96.9
19	314.2	55.4	79	373.2	65.8	39	432.3	76.2	99	491.4	86.7	59	550.5	97.1
20	315.1	55.6	80	374.2	66.0	40	433.3	76.4	500	492.4	86.8	60	551.5	97.2
321	316.1	55.7	381	375.2	66.2	441	434.3	76.6	501	493.4	87.0	561	552.5	97.4
22	317.1	55.9	82	376.2	66.3	42	435.3	76.8	02	494.4	87.2	62	553.5	97.6
23	318.1	56.1	83	377.2	66.5	43	436.3	76.9	03	495.4	87.3	63	554.4	97.8
24	319.1	56.3	84	378.2	66.7	44	437.3	77.1	04	496.3	87.5	64	555.4	97.9
25	320.1	56.4	85	379.2	66.9	45	438.2	77.3	05	497.3	87.7	65	556.4	98.1
26	321.0	56.6	86	380.1	67.0	46	439.2	77.4	06	498.3	87.9	66	557.4	98.3
27	322.0	56.8	87	381.1	67.2	47	440.2	77.6	07	499.3	88.0	67	558.4	98.5
28	323.0	57.0	88	382.1	67.4	48	441.2	77.8	08	500.3	88.2	68	559.4	98.6
29	324.0	57.1	89	383.1	67.5	49	442.2	78.0	09	501.3	88.4	69	560.4	98.8
30	325.0	57.3	90	384.1	67.7	50	443.2	78.1	10	502.3	88.6	70	561.3	99.0
331	326.0	57.5	391	385.1	67.9	451	444.1	78.3	511	503.2	88.7	571	562.3	99.2
32	327.0	57.7	92	386.0	68.1	52	445.1	78.5	12	504.2	88.9	72	563.3	99.3
33	327.9	57.8	93	387.0	68.2	53	446.1	78.7	13	505.2	89.1	73	564.3	99.5
34	328.9	58.0	94	388.0	68.4	54	447.1	78.8	14	506.2	89.3	74	565.3	99.7
35	329.9	58.2	95	389.0	68.6	55	448.1	79.0	15	507.2	89.4	75	566.3	99.8
36	330.9	58.3	96	390.0	68.8	56	449.1	79.2	16	508.2	89.6	76	567.2	100.0
37	331.9	58.5	97	391.0	68.9	57	450.1	79.4	17	509.1	89.8	77	568.2	100.2
38	332.9	58.7	98	392.0	69.1	58	451.0	79.5	18	510.1	89.9	78	569.2	100.4
39	333.8	58.9	99	392.9	69.3	59	452.0	79.7	19	511.1	90.1	79	570.2	100.5
40	334.8	59.0	400	393.9	69.5	60	453.0	79.9	20	512.1	90.3	80	571.2	100.7
341	335.8	59.2	401	394.9	69.6	461	454.0	80.1	521	513.1	90.5	581	572.2	100.9
42	336.8	59.4	02	395.9	69.8	62	455.0	80.2	22	514.1	90.6	82	573.2	101.1
43	337.8	59.6	03	396.9	70.0	63	456.0	80.4	23	515.1	90.8	83	574.1	101.2
44	338.8	59.7	04	397.9	70.2	64	457.0	80.6	24	516.0	91.0	84	575.1	101.4
45	339.8	59.9	05	398.8	70.3	65	457.9	80.7	25	517.0	91.2	85	576.1	101.6
46	340.7	60.1	06	399.8	70.5	66	458.9	80.9	26	518.0	91.3	86	577.1	101.8
47	341.7	60.3	07	400.8	70.7	67	459.9	81.1	27	519.0	91.5	87	578.1	101.9
48	342.7	60.4	08	401.8	70.8	68	460.9	81.3	28	520.0	91.7	88	579.1	102.1
49	343.7	60.6	09	402.8	71.0	69	461.9	81.4	29	521.0	91.9	89	580.1	102.3
50	344.7	60.8	10	403.8	71.2	70	462.9	81.6	30	521.9	92.0	90	581.0	102.5
351	345.7	61.0	411	404.8	71.4	471	463.8	81.8	531	522.9	92.2	591	582.0	102.6
52	346.7	61.1	12	405.7	71.5	72	464.8	82.0	32	523.9	92.4	92	583.0	102.8
53	347.6	61.3	13	406.7	71.7	73	465.8	82.1	33	524.9	92.6	93	584.0	103.0
54	348.6	61.5	14	407.7	71.9	74	466.8	82.3	34	525.9	92.7	94	585.0	103.1
55	349.6	61.6	15	408.7	72.1	75	467.8	82.5	35	526.9	92.9	95	586.0	103.3
56	350.6	61.8	16	409.7	72.2	76	468.8	82.7	36	527.9	93.1	96	586.9	103.5
57	351.6	62.0	17	410.7	72.4	77	469.8	82.8	37	528.8	93.2	97	587.9	103.7
58	352.6	62.2	18	411.6	72.6	78	470.7	83.0	38	529.8	93.4	98	588.9	103.8
59	353.5	62.3	19	412.6	72.8	79	471.7	83.2	39	530.8	93.6	99	589.9	104.0
60	354.5	62.5	20	413.6	72.9	80	472.7	83.4	40	531.8	93.8	600	590.9	104.2
Dist.	Dep.	D. Lat.	Dist.	Dep.	D. Lat.	Dist.	Dep.	D. Lat.	Dist.	Dep.	D. Lat.	Dist.	Dep.	D. Lat.

Dist.	D. Lat.	Dep.
D Lo	Dep.	
	m	D Lo

80°

280° | 080°
260° | 100°

TABLE 4

11°

Traverse Table

349° | 011°
191° | 169°

Dist.	D. Lat.	Dep.	Dist.	D. Lat.	Dep.	Dist.	D. Lat.	Dep.	Dist.	D. Lat.	Dep.	Dist.	D. Lat.	Dep.
1	1.0	0.2	61	59.9	11.6	121	118.8	23.1	181	177.7	34.5	241	236.6	46.0
2	2.0	0.4	62	60.9	11.8	22	119.8	23.3	82	178.7	34.7	42	237.6	46.2
3	2.9	0.6	63	61.8	12.0	23	120.7	23.5	83	179.6	34.9	43	238.5	46.4
4	3.9	0.8	64	62.8	12.2	24	121.7	23.7	84	180.6	35.1	44	239.5	46.6
5	4.9	1.0	65	63.8	12.4	25	122.7	23.9	85	181.6	35.3	45	240.5	46.7
6	5.9	1.1	66	64.8	12.6	26	123.7	24.0	86	182.6	35.5	46	241.5	46.9
7	6.9	1.3	67	65.8	12.8	27	124.7	24.2	87	183.6	35.7	47	242.5	47.1
8	7.9	1.5	68	66.8	13.0	28	125.6	24.4	88	184.5	35.9	48	243.4	47.3
9	8.8	1.7	69	67.7	13.2	29	126.6	24.6	89	185.5	36.1	49	244.4	47.5
10	9.8	1.9	70	68.7	13.4	30	127.6	24.8	90	186.5	36.3	50	245.4	47.7
11	10.8	2.1	71	69.7	13.5	131	128.6	25.0	191	187.5	36.4	251	246.4	47.9
12	11.8	2.3	72	70.7	13.7	32	129.6	25.2	92	188.5	36.6	52	247.4	48.1
13	12.8	2.5	73	71.7	13.9	33	130.6	25.4	93	189.5	36.8	53	248.4	48.3
14	13.7	2.7	74	72.6	14.1	34	131.5	25.6	94	190.4	37.0	54	249.3	48.5
15	14.7	2.9	75	73.6	14.3	35	132.5	25.8	95	191.4	37.2	55	250.3	48.7
16	15.7	3.1	76	74.6	14.5	36	133.5	26.0	96	192.4	37.4	56	251.3	48.8
17	16.7	3.2	77	75.6	14.7	37	134.5	26.1	97	193.4	37.6	57	252.3	49.0
18	17.7	3.4	78	76.6	14.9	38	135.5	26.3	98	194.4	37.8	58	253.3	49.2
19	18.7	3.6	79	77.5	15.1	39	136.4	26.5	99	195.3	38.0	59	254.2	49.4
20	19.6	3.8	80	78.5	15.3	40	137.4	26.7	200	196.3	38.2	60	255.2	49.6
21	20.6	4.0	81	79.5	15.5	141	138.4	26.9	201	197.3	38.4	261	256.2	49.8
22	21.6	4.2	82	80.5	15.6	42	139.4	27.1	02	198.3	38.5	62	257.2	50.0
23	22.6	4.4	83	81.5	15.8	43	140.4	27.3	03	199.3	38.7	63	258.2	50.2
24	23.6	4.6	84	82.5	16.0	44	141.4	27.5	04	200.3	38.9	64	259.1	50.4
25	24.5	4.8	85	83.4	16.2	45	142.3	27.7	05	201.2	39.1	65	260.1	50.6
26	25.5	5.0	86	84.4	16.4	46	143.3	27.9	06	202.2	39.3	66	261.1	50.8
27	26.5	5.2	87	85.4	16.6	47	144.3	28.0	07	203.2	39.5	67	262.1	50.9
28	27.5	5.3	88	86.4	16.8	48	145.3	28.2	08	204.2	39.7	68	263.1	51.1
29	28.5	5.5	89	87.4	17.0	49	146.3	28.4	09	205.2	39.9	69	264.1	51.3
30	29.4	5.7	90	88.3	17.2	50	147.2	28.6	10	206.1	40.1	70	265.0	51.5
31	30.4	5.9	91	89.3	17.4	151	148.2	28.8	211	207.1	40.3	271	266.0	51.7
32	31.4	6.1	92	90.3	17.6	52	149.2	29.0	12	208.1	40.5	72	267.0	51.9
33	32.4	6.3	93	91.3	17.7	53	150.2	29.2	13	209.1	40.6	73	268.0	52.1
34	33.4	6.5	94	92.3	17.9	54	151.2	29.4	14	210.1	40.8	74	269.0	52.3
35	34.4	6.7	95	93.3	18.1	55	152.2	29.6	15	211.0	41.0	75	269.9	52.5
36	35.3	6.9	96	94.2	18.3	56	153.1	29.8	16	212.0	41.2	76	270.9	52.7
37	36.3	7.1	97	95.2	18.5	57	154.1	30.0	17	213.0	41.4	77	271.9	52.9
38	37.3	7.3	98	96.2	18.7	58	155.1	30.1	18	214.0	41.6	78	272.9	53.0
39	38.3	7.4	99	97.2	18.9	59	156.1	30.3	19	215.0	41.8	79	273.9	53.2
40	39.3	7.6	100	98.2	19.1	60	157.1	30.5	20	216.0	42.0	80	274.9	53.4
41	40.2	7.8	101	99.1	19.3	161	158.0	30.7	221	216.9	42.2	281	275.8	53.6
42	41.2	8.0	02	100.1	19.5	62	159.0	30.9	22	217.9	42.4	82	276.8	53.8
43	42.2	8.2	03	101.1	19.7	63	160.0	31.1	23	218.9	42.6	83	277.8	54.0
44	43.2	8.4	04	102.1	19.8	64	161.0	31.3	24	219.9	42.7	84	278.8	54.2
45	44.2	8.6	05	103.1	20.0	65	162.0	31.5	25	220.9	42.9	85	279.8	54.4
46	45.2	8.8	06	104.1	20.2	66	163.0	31.7	26	221.8	43.1	86	280.7	54.6
47	46.1	9.0	07	105.0	20.4	67	163.9	31.9	27	222.8	43.3	87	281.7	54.8
48	47.1	9.2	08	106.0	20.6	68	164.9	32.1	28	223.8	43.5	88	282.7	55.0
49	48.1	9.3	09	107.0	20.8	69	165.9	32.2	29	224.8	43.7	89	283.7	55.1
50	49.1	9.5	10	108.0	21.0	70	166.9	32.4	30	225.8	43.9	90	284.7	55.3
51	50.1	9.7	111	109.0	21.2	171	167.9	32.6	231	226.8	44.1	291	285.7	55.5
52	51.0	9.9	12	109.9	21.4	72	168.8	32.8	32	227.7	44.3	92	286.6	55.7
53	52.0	10.1	13	110.9	21.6	73	169.8	33.0	33	228.7	44.5	93	287.6	55.9
54	53.0	10.3	14	111.9	21.8	74	170.8	33.2	34	229.7	44.6	94	288.6	56.1
55	54.0	10.5	15	112.9	21.9	75	171.8	33.4	35	230.7	44.8	95	289.6	56.3
56	55.0	10.7	16	113.9	22.1	76	172.8	33.6	36	231.7	45.0	96	290.6	56.5
57	56.0	10.9	17	114.9	22.3	77	173.7	33.8	37	232.6	45.2	97	291.5	56.7
58	56.9	11.1	18	115.8	22.5	78	174.7	34.0	38	233.6	45.4	98	292.5	56.9
59	57.9	11.3	19	116.8	22.7	79	175.7	34.2	39	234.6	45.6	99	293.5	57.1
60	58.9	11.4	20	117.8	22.9	80	176.7	34.3	40	235.6	45.8	300	294.5	57.2
Dist.	Dep.	D. Lat.	Dist.	Dep.	D. Lat.	Dist.	Dep.	D. Lat.	Dist.	Dep.	D. Lat.	Dist.	Dep.	D. Lat.

281° | 079°
259° | 101°

79°

Dist.	D. Lat.	Dep.
N.	N x Cos.	N x Sin.
Hypotenuse	Side Adj.	Side Opp.

TABLE 4

11°

Traverse Table

349° | 011°
191° | 169°

Dist.	D. Lat.	Dep.	Dist.	D. Lat.	Dep.	Dist.	D. Lat.	Dep.	Dist.	D. Lat.	Dep.	Dist.	D. Lat.	Dep.
301	295.5	57.4	361	354.4	68.9	421	413.3	80.3	481	472.2	91.8	541	531.1	103.2
02	296.5	57.6	62	355.3	69.1	22	414.2	80.5	82	473.1	92.0	42	532.0	103.4
03	297.4	57.8	63	356.3	69.3	23	415.2	80.7	83	474.1	92.2	43	533.0	103.6
04	298.4	58.0	64	357.3	69.5	24	416.2	80.9	84	475.1	92.4	44	534.0	103.8
05	299.4	58.2	65	358.3	69.6	25	417.2	81.1	85	476.1	92.5	45	535.0	104.0
06	300.4	58.4	66	359.3	69.8	26	418.2	81.3	86	477.1	92.7	46	536.0	104.2
07	301.4	58.6	67	360.3	70.0	27	419.2	81.5	87	478.1	92.9	47	537.0	104.4
08	302.3	58.8	68	361.2	70.2	28	420.1	81.7	88	479.0	93.1	48	537.9	104.6
09	303.3	59.0	69	362.2	70.4	29	421.1	81.9	89	480.0	93.3	49	538.9	104.8
10	304.3	59.2	70	363.2	70.6	30	422.1	82.0	90	481.0	93.5	50	539.9	104.9
311	305.3	59.3	371	364.2	70.8	431	423.1	82.2	491	482.0	93.7	551	540.9	105.1
12	306.3	59.5	72	365.2	71.0	32	424.1	82.4	92	483.0	93.9	52	541.9	105.3
13	307.2	59.7	73	366.1	71.2	33	425.0	82.6	93	483.9	94.1	53	542.8	105.5
14	308.2	59.9	74	367.1	71.4	34	426.0	82.8	94	484.9	94.3	54	543.8	105.7
15	309.2	60.1	75	368.1	71.6	35	427.0	83.0	95	485.9	94.5	55	544.8	105.9
16	310.2	60.3	76	369.1	71.7	36	428.0	83.2	96	486.9	94.6	56	545.8	106.1
17	311.2	60.5	77	370.1	71.9	37	429.0	83.4	97	487.9	94.8	57	546.8	106.3
18	312.2	60.7	78	371.1	72.1	38	430.0	83.6	98	488.9	95.0	58	547.7	106.5
19	313.1	60.9	79	372.0	72.3	39	430.9	83.8	99	489.8	95.2	59	548.7	106.7
20	314.1	61.1	80	373.0	72.5	40	431.9	84.0	500	490.8	95.4	60	549.7	106.9
321	315.1	61.2	381	374.0	72.7	441	432.9	84.1	501	491.8	95.6	561	550.7	107.0
22	316.1	61.4	82	375.0	72.9	42	433.9	84.3	02	492.8	95.8	62	551.7	107.2
23	317.1	61.6	83	376.0	73.1	43	434.9	84.5	03	493.8	96.0	63	552.7	107.4
24	318.0	61.8	84	376.9	73.3	44	435.8	84.7	04	494.7	96.2	64	553.6	107.6
25	319.0	62.0	85	377.9	73.5	45	436.8	84.9	05	495.7	96.4	65	554.6	107.8
26	320.0	62.2	86	378.9	73.7	46	437.8	85.1	06	496.7	96.5	66	555.6	108.0
27	321.0	62.4	87	379.9	73.8	47	438.8	85.3	07	497.7	96.7	67	556.6	108.2
28	322.0	62.6	88	380.9	74.0	48	439.8	85.5	08	498.7	96.9	68	557.6	108.4
29	323.0	62.8	89	381.9	74.2	49	440.8	85.7	09	499.6	97.1	69	558.5	108.6
30	323.9	63.0	90	382.8	74.4	50	441.7	85.9	10	500.6	97.3	70	559.5	108.8
331	324.9	63.2	391	383.8	74.6	451	442.7	86.1	511	501.6	97.5	571	560.5	109.0
32	325.9	63.3	92	384.8	74.8	52	443.7	86.2	12	502.6	97.7	72	561.5	109.1
33	326.9	63.5	93	385.8	75.0	53	444.7	86.4	13	503.6	97.9	73	562.5	109.3
34	327.9	63.7	94	386.8	75.2	54	445.7	86.6	14	504.6	98.1	74	563.5	109.5
35	328.8	63.9	95	387.7	75.4	55	446.6	86.8	15	505.5	98.3	75	564.4	109.7
36	329.8	64.1	96	388.7	75.6	56	447.6	87.0	16	506.5	98.5	76	565.4	109.9
37	330.8	64.3	97	389.7	75.8	57	448.6	87.2	17	507.5	98.6	77	566.4	110.1
38	331.8	64.5	98	390.7	75.9	58	449.6	87.4	18	508.5	98.8	78	567.4	110.3
39	332.8	64.7	99	391.7	76.1	59	450.6	87.6	19	509.5	99.0	79	568.4	110.5
40	333.8	64.9	400	392.7	76.3	60	451.5	87.8	20	510.4	99.2	80	569.3	110.7
341	334.7	65.1	401	393.6	76.5	461	452.5	88.0	521	511.4	99.4	581	570.3	110.9
42	335.7	65.3	02	394.6	76.7	62	453.5	88.2	22	512.4	99.6	82	571.3	111.1
43	336.7	65.4	03	395.6	76.9	63	454.5	88.3	23	513.4	99.8	83	572.3	111.2
44	337.7	65.6	04	396.6	77.1	64	455.5	88.5	24	514.4	100.0	84	573.3	111.4
45	338.7	65.8	05	397.6	77.3	65	456.5	88.7	25	515.4	100.2	85	574.3	111.6
46	339.6	66.0	06	398.5	77.5	66	457.4	88.9	26	516.3	100.4	86	575.2	111.8
47	340.6	66.2	07	399.5	77.7	67	458.4	89.1	27	517.3	100.6	87	576.2	112.0
48	341.6	66.4	08	400.5	77.9	68	459.4	89.3	28	518.3	100.7	88	577.2	112.2
49	342.6	66.6	09	401.5	78.0	69	460.4	89.5	29	519.3	100.9	89	578.2	112.4
50	343.6	66.8	10	402.5	78.2	70	461.4	89.7	30	520.3	101.1	90	579.2	112.6
351	344.6	67.0	411	403.4	78.4	471	462.3	89.9	531	521.2	101.3	591	580.1	112.8
52	345.5	67.2	12	404.4	78.6	72	463.3	90.1	32	522.2	101.5	92	581.1	113.0
53	346.5	67.4	13	405.4	78.8	73	464.3	90.3	33	523.2	101.7	93	582.1	113.1
54	347.5	67.5	14	406.4	79.0	74	465.3	90.4	34	524.2	101.9	94	583.1	113.3
55	348.5	67.7	15	407.4	79.2	75	466.3	90.6	35	525.2	102.1	95	584.1	113.5
56	349.5	67.9	16	408.4	79.4	76	467.3	90.8	36	526.2	102.3	96	585.0	113.7
57	350.4	68.1	17	409.3	79.6	77	468.2	91.0	37	527.1	102.5	97	586.0	113.9
58	351.4	68.3	18	410.3	79.8	78	469.2	91.2	38	528.1	102.7	98	587.0	114.1
59	352.4	68.5	19	411.3	79.9	79	470.2	91.4	39	529.1	102.8	99	588.0	114.3
60	353.4	68.7	20	412.3	80.1	80	471.2	91.6	40	530.1	103.0	600	589.0	114.5
Dist.	Dep.	D. Lat.	Dist.	Dep.	D. Lat.	Dist.	Dep.	D. Lat.	Dist.	Dep.	D. Lat.	Dist.	Dep.	D. Lat.

Dist.	D. Lat.	Dep.
D Lo	Dep.	
	m	D Lo

79°

281° | 079°
259° | 101°

TABLE 4

Traverse 12° Table

348° | 012° / 192° | 168°

Dist.	D. Lat.	Dep.	Dist.	D. Lat.	Dep.	Dist.	D. Lat.	Dep.	Dist.	D. Lat.	Dep.	Dist.	D. Lat.	Dep.
1	1.0	0.2	61	59.7	12.7	121	118.4	25.2	181	177.0	37.6	241	235.7	50.1
2	2.0	0.4	62	60.6	12.9	22	119.3	25.4	82	178.0	37.8	42	236.7	50.3
3	2.9	0.6	63	61.6	13.1	23	120.3	25.6	83	179.0	38.0	43	237.7	50.5
4	3.9	0.8	64	62.6	13.3	24	121.3	25.8	84	180.0	38.3	44	238.7	50.7
5	4.9	1.0	65	63.6	13.5	25	122.3	26.0	85	181.0	38.5	45	239.6	50.9
6	5.9	1.2	66	64.6	13.7	26	123.2	26.2	86	181.9	38.7	46	240.6	51.1
7	6.8	1.5	67	65.5	13.9	27	124.2	26.4	87	182.9	38.9	47	241.6	51.4
8	7.8	1.7	68	66.5	14.1	28	125.2	26.6	88	183.9	39.1	48	242.6	51.6
9	8.8	1.9	69	67.5	14.3	29	126.2	26.8	89	184.9	39.3	49	243.6	51.8
10	9.8	2.1	70	68.5	14.6	30	127.2	27.0	90	185.8	39.5	50	244.5	52.0
11	10.8	2.3	71	69.4	14.8	131	128.1	27.2	191	186.8	39.7	251	245.5	52.2
12	11.7	2.5	72	70.4	15.0	32	129.1	27.4	92	187.8	39.9	52	246.5	52.4
13	12.7	2.7	73	71.4	15.2	33	130.1	27.7	93	188.8	40.1	53	247.5	52.6
14	13.7	2.9	74	72.4	15.4	34	131.1	27.9	94	189.8	40.3	54	248.4	52.8
15	14.7	3.1	75	73.4	15.6	35	132.0	28.1	95	190.7	40.5	55	249.4	53.0
16	15.7	3.3	76	74.3	15.8	36	133.0	28.3	96	191.7	40.8	56	250.4	53.2
17	16.6	3.5	77	75.3	16.0	37	134.0	28.5	97	192.7	41.0	57	251.4	53.4
18	17.6	3.7	78	76.3	16.2	38	135.0	28.7	98	193.7	41.2	58	252.4	53.6
19	18.6	4.0	79	77.3	16.4	39	136.0	28.9	99	194.7	41.4	59	253.3	53.8
20	19.6	4.2	80	78.3	16.6	40	136.9	29.1	200	195.6	41.6	60	254.3	54.1
21	20.5	4.4	81	79.2	16.8	141	137.9	29.3	201	196.6	41.8	261	255.3	54.3
22	21.5	4.6	82	80.2	17.0	42	138.9	29.5	02	197.6	42.0	62	256.3	54.5
23	22.5	4.8	83	81.2	17.3	43	139.9	29.7	03	198.6	42.2	63	257.3	54.7
24	23.5	5.0	84	82.2	17.5	44	140.9	29.9	04	199.5	42.4	64	258.2	54.9
25	24.5	5.2	85	83.1	17.7	45	141.8	30.1	05	200.5	42.6	65	259.2	55.1
26	25.4	5.4	86	84.1	17.9	46	142.8	30.4	06	201.5	42.8	66	260.2	55.3
27	26.4	5.6	87	85.1	18.1	47	143.8	30.6	07	202.5	43.0	67	261.2	55.5
28	27.4	5.8	88	86.1	18.3	48	144.8	30.8	08	203.5	43.2	68	262.1	55.7
29	28.4	6.0	89	87.1	18.5	49	145.7	31.0	09	204.4	43.5	69	263.1	55.9
30	29.3	6.2	90	88.0	18.7	50	146.7	31.2	10	205.4	43.7	70	264.1	56.1
31	30.3	6.4	91	89.0	18.9	151	147.7	31.4	211	206.4	43.9	271	265.1	56.3
32	31.3	6.7	92	90.0	19.1	52	148.7	31.6	12	207.4	44.1	72	266.1	56.6
33	32.3	6.9	93	91.0	19.3	53	149.7	31.8	13	208.3	44.3	73	267.0	56.8
34	33.3	7.1	94	91.9	19.5	54	150.6	32.0	14	209.3	44.5	74	268.0	57.0
35	34.2	7.3	95	92.9	19.8	55	151.6	32.2	15	210.3	44.7	75	269.0	57.2
36	35.2	7.5	96	93.9	20.0	56	152.6	32.4	16	211.3	44.9	76	270.0	57.4
37	36.2	7.7	97	94.9	20.2	57	153.6	32.6	17	212.3	45.1	77	270.9	57.6
38	37.2	7.9	98	95.9	20.4	58	154.5	32.9	18	213.2	45.3	78	271.9	57.8
39	38.1	8.1	99	96.8	20.6	59	155.5	33.1	19	214.2	45.5	79	272.9	58.0
40	39.1	8.3	100	97.8	20.8	60	156.5	33.3	20	215.2	45.7	80	273.9	58.2
41	40.1	8.5	101	98.8	21.0	161	157.5	33.5	221	216.2	45.9	281	274.9	58.4
42	41.1	8.7	02	99.8	21.2	62	158.5	33.7	22	217.1	46.2	82	275.8	58.6
43	42.1	8.9	03	100.7	21.4	63	159.4	33.9	23	218.1	46.4	83	276.8	58.8
44	43.0	9.1	04	101.7	21.6	64	160.4	34.1	24	219.1	46.6	84	277.8	59.0
45	44.0	9.4	05	102.7	21.8	65	161.4	34.3	25	220.1	46.8	85	278.8	59.3
46	45.0	9.6	06	103.7	22.0	66	162.4	34.5	26	221.1	47.0	86	279.8	59.5
47	46.0	9.8	07	104.7	22.2	67	163.4	34.7	27	222.0	47.2	87	280.7	59.7
48	47.0	10.0	08	105.6	22.5	68	164.3	34.9	28	223.0	47.4	88	281.7	59.9
49	47.9	10.2	09	106.6	22.7	69	165.3	35.1	29	224.0	47.6	89	282.7	60.1
50	48.9	10.4	10	107.6	22.9	70	166.3	35.3	30	225.0	47.8	90	283.7	60.3
51	49.9	10.6	111	108.6	23.1	171	167.3	35.6	231	226.0	48.0	291	284.6	60.5
52	50.9	10.8	12	109.6	23.3	72	168.2	35.8	32	226.9	48.2	92	285.6	60.7
53	51.8	11.0	13	110.5	23.5	73	169.2	36.0	33	227.9	48.4	93	286.6	60.9
54	52.8	11.2	14	111.5	23.7	74	170.2	36.2	34	228.9	48.7	94	287.6	61.1
55	53.8	11.4	15	112.5	23.9	75	171.2	36.4	35	229.9	48.9	95	288.6	61.3
56	54.8	11.6	16	113.5	24.1	76	172.2	36.6	36	230.8	49.1	96	289.5	61.5
57	55.8	11.9	17	114.4	24.3	77	173.1	36.8	37	231.8	49.3	97	290.5	61.7
58	56.7	12.1	18	115.4	24.5	78	174.1	37.0	38	232.8	49.5	98	291.5	62.0
59	57.7	12.3	19	116.4	24.7	79	175.1	37.2	39	233.8	49.7	99	292.5	62.2
60	58.7	12.5	20	117.4	24.9	80	176.1	37.4	40	234.8	49.9	300	293.4	62.4
Dist.	Dep.	D. Lat.	Dist.	Dep.	D. Lat.	Dist.	Dep.	D. Lat.	Dist.	Dep.	D. Lat.	Dist.	Dep.	D. Lat.

282° | 078° / 258° | 102°

78°

Dist.	D. Lat.	Dep.
N.	N x Cos.	N x Sin.
Hypotenuse	Side Adj.	Side Opp.

TABLE 4

Traverse 12° Table

348° | 012° / 192° | 168°

Dist.	D. Lat.	Dep.	Dist.	D. Lat.	Dep.	Dist.	D. Lat.	Dep.	Dist.	D. Lat.	Dep.	Dist.	D. Lat.	Dep.
301	294.4	62.6	361	353.1	75.1	421	411.8	87.5	481	470.5	100.0	541	529.2	112.5
02	295.4	62.8	62	354.1	75.3	22	412.8	87.7	82	471.5	100.2	42	530.2	112.7
03	296.4	63.0	63	355.1	75.5	23	413.8	87.9	83	472.4	100.4	43	531.1	112.9
04	297.4	63.2	64	356.0	75.7	24	414.7	88.2	84	473.4	100.6	44	532.1	113.1
05	298.3	63.4	65	357.0	75.9	25	415.7	88.4	85	474.4	100.8	45	533.1	113.3
06	299.3	63.6	66	358.0	76.1	26	416.7	88.6	86	475.4	101.0	46	534.1	113.5
07	300.3	63.8	67	359.0	76.3	27	417.7	88.8	87	476.4	101.3	47	535.0	113.7
08	301.3	64.0	68	360.0	76.5	28	418.6	89.0	88	477.3	101.5	48	536.0	113.9
09	302.2	64.2	69	360.9	76.7	29	419.6	89.2	89	478.3	101.7	49	537.0	114.1
10	303.2	64.5	70	361.9	76.9	30	420.6	89.4	90	479.3	101.9	50	538.0	114.4
311	304.2	64.7	371	362.9	77.1	431	421.6	89.6	491	480.3	102.1	551	539.0	114.6
12	305.2	64.9	72	363.9	77.3	32	422.6	89.8	92	481.2	102.3	52	539.9	114.8
13	306.2	65.1	73	364.8	77.6	33	423.5	90.0	93	482.2	102.5	53	540.9	115.0
14	307.1	65.3	74	365.8	77.8	34	424.5	90.2	94	483.2	102.7	54	541.9	115.2
15	308.1	65.5	75	366.8	78.0	35	425.5	90.4	95	484.2	102.9	55	542.9	115.4
16	309.1	65.7	76	367.8	78.2	36	426.5	90.6	96	485.2	103.1	56	543.9	115.6
17	310.1	65.9	77	368.8	78.4	37	427.5	90.9	97	486.1	103.3	57	544.8	115.8
18	311.1	66.1	78	369.7	78.6	38	428.4	91.1	98	487.1	103.5	58	545.8	116.0
19	312.0	66.3	79	370.7	78.8	39	429.4	91.3	99	488.1	103.7	59	546.8	116.2
20	313.0	66.5	80	371.7	79.0	40	430.4	91.5	500	489.1	104.0	60	547.8	116.4
321	314.0	66.7	381	372.7	79.2	441	431.4	91.7	501	490.1	104.2	561	548.7	116.6
22	315.0	66.9	82	373.7	79.4	42	432.3	91.9	02	491.0	104.4	62	549.7	116.8
23	315.9	67.2	83	374.6	79.6	43	433.3	92.1	03	492.0	104.6	63	550.7	117.1
24	316.9	67.4	84	375.6	79.8	44	434.3	92.3	04	493.0	104.8	64	551.7	117.3
25	317.9	67.6	85	376.6	80.0	45	435.3	92.5	05	494.0	105.0	65	552.7	117.5
26	318.9	67.8	86	377.6	80.3	46	436.3	92.7	06	494.9	105.2	66	553.6	117.7
27	319.9	68.0	87	378.5	80.5	47	437.2	92.9	07	495.9	105.4	67	554.6	117.9
28	320.8	68.2	88	379.5	80.7	48	438.2	93.1	08	496.9	105.6	68	555.6	118.1
29	321.8	68.4	89	380.5	80.9	49	439.2	93.4	09	497.9	105.8	69	556.6	118.3
30	322.8	68.6	90	381.5	81.1	50	440.2	93.6	10	498.9	106.0	70	557.5	118.5
331	323.8	68.8	391	382.5	81.3	451	441.1	93.8	511	499.8	106.2	571	558.5	118.7
32	324.7	69.0	92	383.4	81.5	52	442.1	94.0	12	500.8	106.5	72	559.5	118.9
33	325.7	69.2	93	384.4	81.7	53	443.1	94.2	13	501.8	106.7	73	560.5	119.1
34	326.7	69.4	94	385.4	81.9	54	444.1	94.4	14	502.8	106.9	74	561.5	119.3
35	327.7	69.7	95	386.4	82.1	55	445.1	94.6	15	503.7	107.1	75	562.4	119.5
36	328.7	69.9	96	387.3	82.3	56	446.0	94.8	16	504.7	107.3	76	563.4	119.8
37	329.6	70.1	97	388.3	82.5	57	447.0	95.0	17	505.7	107.5	77	564.4	120.0
38	330.6	70.3	98	389.3	82.7	58	448.0	95.2	18	506.7	107.7	78	565.4	120.2
39	331.6	70.5	99	390.3	83.0	59	449.0	95.4	19	507.7	107.9	79	566.3	120.4
40	332.6	70.7	400	391.3	83.2	60	449.9	95.6	20	508.6	108.1	80	567.3	120.6
341	333.5	70.9	401	392.2	83.4	461	450.9	95.8	521	509.6	108.3	581	568.3	120.8
42	334.5	71.1	02	393.2	83.6	62	451.9	96.1	22	510.6	108.5	82	569.3	121.0
43	335.5	71.3	03	394.2	83.8	63	452.9	96.3	23	511.6	108.7	83	570.3	121.2
44	336.5	71.5	04	395.2	84.0	64	453.9	96.5	24	512.5	108.9	84	571.2	121.4
45	337.5	71.7	05	396.1	84.2	65	454.8	96.7	25	513.5	109.2	85	572.2	121.6
46	338.4	71.9	06	397.1	84.4	66	455.8	96.9	26	514.5	109.4	86	573.2	121.8
47	339.4	72.1	07	398.1	84.6	67	456.8	97.1	27	515.5	109.6	87	574.2	122.0
48	340.4	72.4	08	399.1	84.8	68	457.8	97.3	28	516.5	109.8	88	575.2	122.3
49	341.4	72.6	09	400.1	85.0	69	458.8	97.5	29	517.4	110.0	89	576.1	122.5
50	342.4	72.8	10	401.0	85.2	70	459.7	97.7	30	518.4	110.2	90	577.1	122.7
351	343.3	73.0	411	402.0	85.5	471	460.7	97.9	531	519.4	110.4	591	578.1	122.9
52	344.3	73.2	12	403.0	85.7	72	461.7	98.1	32	520.4	110.6	92	579.1	123.1
53	345.3	73.4	13	404.0	85.9	73	462.7	98.3	33	521.4	110.8	93	580.0	123.3
54	346.3	73.6	14	405.0	86.1	74	463.6	98.6	34	522.3	111.0	94	581.0	123.5
55	347.2	73.8	15	405.9	86.3	75	464.6	98.8	35	523.3	111.2	95	582.0	123.7
56	348.2	74.0	16	406.9	86.5	76	465.6	99.0	36	524.3	111.4	96	583.0	123.9
57	349.2	74.2	17	407.9	86.7	77	466.6	99.2	37	525.3	111.6	97	584.0	124.1
58	350.2	74.4	18	408.9	86.9	78	467.6	99.4	38	526.2	111.9	98	584.9	124.3
59	351.2	74.6	19	409.8	87.1	79	468.5	99.6	39	527.2	112.1	99	585.9	124.5
60	352.1	74.8	20	410.8	87.3	80	469.5	99.8	40	528.2	112.3	600	586.9	124.7
Dist.	Dep.	D. Lat.	Dist.	Dep.	D. Lat.	Dist.	Dep.	D. Lat.	Dist.	Dep.	D. Lat.	Dist.	Dep.	D. Lat.

Dist.	D. Lat.	Dep.
D Lo	Dep.	
	m	D Lo

78°

282° | 078° / 258° | 102°

TABLE 4

13°

Traverse Table

347° | 013°
193° | 167°

Dist.	D. Lat.	Dep.	Dist.	D. Lat.	Dep.	Dist.	D. Lat.	Dep.	Dist.	D. Lat.	Dep.	Dist.	D. Lat.	Dep.
1	1.0	0.2	61	59.4	13.7	121	117.9	27.2	181	176.4	40.7	241	234.8	54.2
2	1.9	0.4	62	60.4	13.9	22	118.9	27.4	82	177.3	40.9	42	235.8	54.4
3	2.9	0.7	63	61.4	14.2	23	119.8	27.7	83	178.3	41.2	43	236.8	54.7
4	3.9	0.9	64	62.4	14.4	24	120.8	27.9	84	179.3	41.4	44	237.7	54.9
5	4.9	1.1	65	63.3	14.6	25	121.8	28.1	85	180.3	41.6	45	238.7	55.1
6	5.8	1.3	66	64.3	14.8	26	122.8	28.3	86	181.2	41.8	46	239.7	55.3
7	6.8	1.6	67	65.3	15.1	27	123.7	28.6	87	182.2	42.1	47	240.7	55.6
8	7.8	1.8	68	66.3	15.3	28	124.7	28.8	88	183.2	42.3	48	241.6	55.8
9	8.8	2.0	69	67.2	15.5	29	125.7	29.0	89	184.2	42.5	49	242.6	56.0
10	9.7	2.2	70	68.2	15.7	30	126.7	29.2	90	185.1	42.7	50	243.6	56.2
11	10.7	2.5	71	69.2	16.0	131	127.6	29.5	191	186.1	43.0	251	244.6	56.5
12	11.7	2.7	72	70.2	16.2	32	128.6	29.7	92	187.1	43.2	52	245.5	56.7
13	12.7	2.9	73	71.1	16.4	33	129.6	29.9	93	188.1	43.4	53	246.5	56.9
14	13.6	3.1	74	72.1	16.6	34	130.6	30.1	94	189.0	43.6	54	247.5	57.1
15	14.6	3.4	75	73.1	16.9	35	131.5	30.4	95	190.0	43.9	55	248.5	57.4
16	15.6	3.6	76	74.1	17.1	36	132.5	30.6	96	191.0	44.1	56	249.4	57.6
17	16.6	3.8	77	75.0	17.3	37	133.5	30.8	97	192.0	44.3	57	250.4	57.8
18	17.5	4.0	78	76.0	17.5	38	134.5	31.0	98	192.9	44.5	58	251.4	58.0
19	18.5	4.3	79	77.0	17.8	39	135.4	31.3	99	193.9	44.8	59	252.4	58.3
20	19.5	4.5	80	77.9	18.0	40	136.4	31.5	200	194.9	45.0	60	253.3	58.5
21	20.5	4.7	81	78.9	18.2	141	137.4	31.7	201	195.8	45.2	261	254.3	58.7
22	21.4	4.9	82	79.9	18.4	42	138.4	31.9	02	196.8	45.4	62	255.3	58.9
23	22.4	5.2	83	80.9	18.7	43	139.3	32.2	03	197.8	45.7	63	256.3	59.2
24	23.4	5.4	84	81.8	18.9	44	140.3	32.4	04	198.8	45.9	64	257.2	59.4
25	24.4	5.6	85	82.8	19.1	45	141.3	32.6	05	199.7	46.1	65	258.2	59.6
26	25.3	5.8	86	83.8	19.3	46	142.3	32.8	06	200.7	46.3	66	259.2	59.8
27	26.3	6.1	87	84.8	19.6	47	143.2	33.1	07	201.7	46.6	67	260.2	60.1
28	27.3	6.3	88	85.7	19.8	48	144.2	33.3	08	202.7	46.8	68	261.1	60.3
29	28.3	6.5	89	86.7	20.0	49	145.2	33.5	09	203.6	47.0	69	262.1	60.5
30	29.2	6.7	90	87.7	20.2	50	146.2	33.7	10	204.6	47.2	70	263.1	60.7
31	30.2	7.0	91	88.7	20.5	151	147.1	34.0	211	205.6	47.5	271	264.1	61.0
32	31.2	7.2	92	89.6	20.7	52	148.1	34.2	12	206.6	47.7	72	265.0	61.2
33	32.2	7.4	93	90.6	20.9	53	149.1	34.4	13	207.5	47.9	73	266.0	61.4
34	33.1	7.6	94	91.6	21.1	54	150.1	34.6	14	208.5	48.1	74	267.0	61.6
35	34.1	7.9	95	92.6	21.4	55	151.0	34.9	15	209.5	48.4	75	268.0	61.9
36	35.1	8.1	96	93.5	21.6	56	152.0	35.1	16	210.5	48.6	76	268.9	62.1
37	36.1	8.3	97	94.5	21.8	57	153.0	35.3	17	211.4	48.8	77	269.9	62.3
38	37.0	8.5	98	95.5	22.0	58	154.0	35.5	18	212.4	49.0	78	270.9	62.5
39	38.0	8.8	99	96.5	22.3	59	154.9	35.8	19	213.4	49.3	79	271.8	62.8
40	39.0	9.0	100	97.4	22.5	60	155.9	36.0	20	214.4	49.5	80	272.8	63.0
41	39.9	9.2	101	98.4	22.7	161	156.9	36.2	221	215.3	49.7	281	273.8	63.2
42	40.9	9.4	02	99.4	22.9	62	157.8	36.4	22	216.3	49.9	82	274.8	63.4
43	41.9	9.7	03	100.4	23.2	63	158.8	36.7	23	217.3	50.2	83	275.7	63.7
44	42.9	9.9	04	101.3	23.4	64	159.8	36.9	24	218.3	50.4	84	276.7	63.9
45	43.8	10.1	05	102.3	23.6	65	160.8	37.1	25	219.2	50.6	85	277.7	64.1
46	44.8	10.3	06	103.3	23.8	66	161.7	37.3	26	220.2	50.8	86	278.7	64.3
47	45.8	10.6	07	104.3	24.1	67	162.7	37.6	27	221.2	51.1	87	279.6	64.6
48	46.8	10.8	08	105.2	24.3	68	163.7	37.8	28	222.2	51.3	88	280.6	64.8
49	47.7	11.0	09	106.2	24.5	69	164.7	38.0	29	223.1	51.5	89	281.6	65.0
50	48.7	11.2	10	107.2	24.7	70	165.6	38.2	30	224.1	51.7	90	282.6	65.2
51	49.7	11.5	111	108.2	25.0	171	166.6	38.5	231	225.1	52.0	291	283.5	65.5
52	50.7	11.7	12	109.1	25.2	72	167.6	38.7	32	226.1	52.2	92	284.5	65.7
53	51.6	11.9	13	110.1	25.4	73	168.6	38.9	33	227.0	52.4	93	285.5	65.9
54	52.6	12.1	14	111.1	25.6	74	169.5	39.1	34	228.0	52.6	94	286.5	66.1
55	53.6	12.4	15	112.1	25.9	75	170.5	39.4	35	229.0	52.9	95	287.4	66.4
56	54.6	12.6	16	113.0	26.1	76	171.5	39.6	36	230.0	53.1	96	288.4	66.6
57	55.5	12.8	17	114.0	26.3	77	172.5	39.8	37	230.9	53.3	97	289.4	66.8
58	56.5	13.0	18	115.0	26.5	78	173.4	40.0	38	231.9	53.5	98	290.4	67.0
59	57.5	13.3	19	116.0	26.8	79	174.4	40.3	39	232.9	53.8	99	291.3	67.3
60	58.5	13.5	20	116.9	27.0	80	175.4	40.5	40	233.8	54.0	300	292.3	67.5
Dist.	Dep.	D. Lat.	Dist.	Dep.	D. Lat.	Dist.	Dep.	D. Lat.	Dist.	Dep.	D. Lat.	Dist.	Dep.	D. Lat.

283° | 077°
257° | 103°

77°

Dist.	D. Lat.	Dep.
N.	N x Cos.	N x Sin.
Hypotenuse	Side Adj.	Side Opp.

TABLE 4

13°

Traverse Table

347° | 013°
193° | 167°

Dist.	D. Lat.	Dep.	Dist.	D. Lat.	Dep.	Dist.	D. Lat.	Dep.	Dist.	D. Lat.	Dep.	Dist.	D. Lat.	Dep.
301	293.3	67.7	361	351.7	81.2	421	410.2	94.7	481	468.7	108.2	541	527.1	121.7
02	294.3	67.9	62	352.7	81.4	22	411.2	94.9	82	469.6	108.4	42	528.1	121.9
03	295.2	68.2	63	353.7	81.7	23	412.2	95.2	83	470.6	108.7	43	529.1	122.1
04	296.2	68.4	64	354.7	81.9	24	413.1	95.4	84	471.6	108.9	44	530.1	122.4
05	297.2	68.6	65	355.6	82.1	25	414.1	95.6	85	472.6	109.1	45	531.0	122.6
06	298.2	68.8	66	356.6	82.3	26	415.1	95.8	86	473.5	109.3	46	532.0	122.8
07	299.1	69.1	67	357.6	82.6	27	416.1	96.1	87	474.5	109.6	47	533.0	123.0
08	300.1	69.3	68	358.6	82.8	28	417.0	96.3	88	475.5	109.8	48	534.0	123.3
09	301.1	69.5	69	359.5	83.0	29	418.0	96.5	89	476.5	110.0	49	534.9	123.5
10	302.1	69.7	70	360.5	83.2	30	419.0	96.7	90	477.4	110.2	50	535.9	123.7
311	303.0	70.0	371	361.5	83.5	431	420.0	97.0	491	478.4	110.5	551	536.9	123.9
12	304.0	70.2	72	362.5	83.7	32	420.9	97.2	92	479.4	110.7	52	537.9	124.2
13	305.0	70.4	73	363.4	83.9	33	421.9	97.4	93	480.4	110.9	53	538.8	124.4
14	306.0	70.6	74	364.4	84.1	34	422.9	97.6	94	481.3	111.1	54	539.8	124.6
15	306.9	70.9	75	365.4	84.4	35	423.9	97.9	95	482.3	111.4	55	540.8	124.8
16	307.9	71.1	76	366.4	84.6	36	424.8	98.1	96	483.3	111.6	56	541.7	125.1
17	308.9	71.3	77	367.3	84.8	37	425.8	98.3	97	484.3	111.8	57	542.7	125.3
18	309.8	71.5	78	368.3	85.0	38	426.8	98.5	98	485.2	112.0	58	543.7	125.5
19	310.8	71.8	79	369.3	85.3	39	427.7	98.8	99	486.2	112.3	59	544.7	125.7
20	311.8	72.0	80	370.3	85.5	40	428.7	99.0	500	487.2	112.5	60	545.6	126.0
321	312.8	72.2	381	371.2	85.7	441	429.7	99.2	501	488.2	112.7	561	546.6	126.2
22	313.7	72.4	82	372.2	85.9	42	430.7	99.4	02	489.1	112.9	62	547.6	126.4
23	314.7	72.7	83	373.2	86.2	43	431.6	99.7	03	490.1	113.2	63	548.6	126.6
24	315.7	72.9	84	374.2	86.4	44	432.6	99.9	04	491.1	113.4	64	549.5	126.9
25	316.7	73.1	85	375.1	86.6	45	433.6	100.1	05	492.1	113.6	65	550.5	127.1
26	317.6	73.3	86	376.1	86.8	46	434.6	100.3	06	493.0	113.8	66	551.5	127.3
27	318.6	73.6	87	377.1	87.1	47	435.5	100.6	07	494.0	114.1	67	552.5	127.5
28	319.6	73.8	88	378.1	87.3	48	436.5	100.8	08	495.0	114.3	68	553.4	127.8
29	320.6	74.0	89	379.0	87.5	49	437.5	101.0	09	496.0	114.5	69	554.4	128.0
30	321.5	74.2	90	380.0	87.7	50	438.5	101.2	10	496.9	114.7	70	555.4	128.2
331	322.5	74.5	391	381.0	88.0	451	439.4	101.5	511	497.9	114.9	571	556.4	128.4
32	323.5	74.7	92	382.0	88.2	52	440.4	101.7	12	498.9	115.2	72	557.3	128.7
33	324.5	74.9	93	382.9	88.4	53	441.4	101.9	13	499.9	115.4	73	558.3	128.9
34	325.4	75.1	94	383.9	88.6	54	442.4	102.1	14	500.8	115.6	74	559.3	129.1
35	326.4	75.4	95	384.9	88.9	55	443.3	102.4	15	501.8	115.8	75	560.3	129.3
36	327.4	75.6	96	385.9	89.1	56	444.3	102.6	16	502.8	116.1	76	561.2	129.6
37	328.4	75.8	97	386.8	89.3	57	445.3	102.8	17	503.7	116.3	77	562.2	129.8
38	329.3	76.0	98	387.8	89.5	58	446.3	103.0	18	504.7	116.5	78	563.2	130.0
39	330.3	76.3	99	388.8	89.8	59	447.2	103.3	19	505.7	116.7	79	564.2	130.2
40	331.3	76.5	400	389.7	90.0	60	448.2	103.5	20	506.7	117.0	80	565.1	130.5
341	332.3	76.7	401	390.7	90.2	461	449.2	103.7	521	507.6	117.2	581	566.1	130.7
42	333.2	76.9	02	391.7	90.4	62	450.2	103.9	22	508.6	117.4	82	567.1	130.9
43	334.2	77.2	03	392.7	90.7	63	451.1	104.2	23	509.6	117.6	83	568.1	131.1
44	335.2	77.4	04	393.6	90.9	64	452.1	104.4	24	510.6	117.9	84	569.0	131.4
45	336.2	77.6	05	394.6	91.1	65	453.1	104.6	25	511.5	118.1	85	570.0	131.6
46	337.1	77.8	06	395.6	91.3	66	454.1	104.8	26	512.5	118.3	86	571.0	131.8
47	338.1	78.1	07	396.6	91.6	67	455.0	105.1	27	513.5	118.5	87	572.0	132.0
48	339.1	78.3	08	397.5	91.8	68	456.0	105.3	28	514.5	118.8	88	572.9	132.3
49	340.1	78.5	09	398.5	92.0	69	457.0	105.5	29	515.4	119.0	89	573.9	132.5
50	341.0	78.7	10	399.5	92.2	70	458.0	105.7	30	516.4	119.2	90	574.9	132.7
351	342.0	79.0	411	400.5	92.5	471	458.9	106.0	531	517.4	119.4	591	575.9	132.9
52	343.0	79.2	12	401.4	92.7	72	459.9	106.2	32	518.4	119.7	92	576.8	133.2
53	344.0	79.4	13	402.4	92.9	73	460.9	106.4	33	519.3	119.9	93	577.8	133.4
54	344.9	79.6	14	403.4	93.1	74	461.9	106.6	34	520.3	120.1	94	578.8	133.6
55	345.9	79.9	15	404.4	93.4	75	462.8	106.9	35	521.3	120.3	95	579.8	133.8
56	346.9	80.1	16	405.3	93.6	76	463.8	107.1	36	522.3	120.6	96	580.7	134.1
57	347.9	80.3	17	406.3	93.8	77	464.8	107.3	37	523.2	120.8	97	581.7	134.3
58	348.8	80.5	18	407.3	94.0	78	465.7	107.5	38	524.2	121.0	98	582.7	134.5
59	349.8	80.8	19	408.3	94.3	79	466.7	107.8	39	525.2	121.2	99	583.6	134.7
60	350.8	81.0	20	409.2	94.5	80	467.7	108.0	40	526.2	121.5	600	584.6	135.0
Dist.	Dep.	D. Lat.	Dist.	Dep.	D. Lat.	Dist.	Dep.	D. Lat.	Dist.	Dep.	D. Lat.	Dist.	Dep.	D. Lat.

Dist.	D. Lat.	Dep.
D Lo	Dep.	
	m	D Lo

77°

283° | 077°
257° | 103°

TABLE 4

Traverse 14° Table

346° / 194°	014° / 166°													
Dist.	D. Lat.	Dep.	Dist.	D. Lat.	Dep.	Dist.	D. Lat.	Dep.	Dist.	D. Lat.	Dep.	Dist.	D. Lat.	Dep.
1	1.0	0.2	61	59.2	14.8	121	117.4	29.3	181	175.6	43.8	241	233.8	58.3
2	1.9	0.5	62	60.2	15.0	22	118.4	29.5	82	176.6	44.0	42	234.8	58.5
3	2.9	0.7	63	61.1	15.2	23	119.3	29.8	83	177.6	44.3	43	235.8	58.8
4	3.9	1.0	64	62.1	15.5	24	120.3	30.0	84	178.5	44.5	44	236.8	59.0
5	4.9	1.2	65	63.1	15.7	25	121.3	30.2	85	179.5	44.8	45	237.7	59.3
6	5.8	1.5	66	64.0	16.0	26	122.3	30.5	86	180.5	45.0	46	238.7	59.5
7	6.8	1.7	67	65.0	16.2	27	123.2	30.7	87	181.4	45.2	47	239.7	59.8
8	7.8	1.9	68	66.0	16.5	28	124.2	31.0	88	182.4	45.5	48	240.6	60.0
9	8.7	2.2	69	67.0	16.7	29	125.2	31.2	89	183.4	45.7	49	241.6	60.2
10	9.7	2.4	70	67.9	16.9	30	126.1	31.4	90	184.4	46.0	50	242.6	60.5
11	10.7	2.7	71	68.9	17.2	131	127.1	31.7	191	185.3	46.2	251	243.5	60.7
12	11.6	2.9	72	69.9	17.4	32	128.1	31.9	92	186.3	46.4	52	244.5	61.0
13	12.6	3.1	73	70.8	17.7	33	129.0	32.2	93	187.3	46.7	53	245.5	61.2
14	13.6	3.4	74	71.8	17.9	34	130.0	32.4	94	188.2	46.9	54	246.5	61.4
15	14.6	3.6	75	72.8	18.1	35	131.0	32.7	95	189.2	47.2	55	247.4	61.7
16	15.5	3.9	76	73.7	18.4	36	132.0	32.9	96	190.2	47.4	56	248.4	61.9
17	16.5	4.1	77	74.7	18.6	37	132.9	33.1	97	191.1	47.7	57	249.4	62.2
18	17.5	4.4	78	75.7	18.9	38	133.9	33.4	98	192.1	47.9	58	250.3	62.4
19	18.4	4.6	79	76.7	19.1	39	134.9	33.6	99	193.1	48.1	59	251.3	62.7
20	19.4	4.8	80	77.6	19.4	40	135.8	33.9	200	194.1	48.4	60	252.3	62.9
21	20.4	5.1	81	78.6	19.6	141	136.8	34.1	201	195.0	48.6	261	253.2	63.1
22	21.3	5.3	82	79.6	19.8	42	137.8	34.4	02	196.0	48.9	62	254.2	63.4
23	22.3	5.6	83	80.5	20.1	43	138.8	34.6	03	197.0	49.1	63	255.2	63.6
24	23.3	5.8	84	81.5	20.3	44	139.7	34.8	04	197.9	49.4	64	256.2	63.9
25	24.3	6.0	85	82.5	20.6	45	140.7	35.1	05	198.9	49.6	65	257.1	64.1
26	25.2	6.3	86	83.4	20.8	46	141.7	35.3	06	199.9	49.8	66	258.1	64.4
27	26.2	6.5	87	84.4	21.0	47	142.6	35.6	07	200.9	50.1	67	259.1	64.6
28	27.2	6.8	88	85.4	21.3	48	143.6	35.8	08	201.8	50.3	68	260.0	64.8
29	28.1	7.0	89	86.4	21.5	49	144.6	36.0	09	202.8	50.6	69	261.0	65.1
30	29.1	7.3	90	87.3	21.8	50	145.5	36.3	10	203.8	50.8	70	262.0	65.3
31	30.1	7.5	91	88.3	22.0	151	146.5	36.5	211	204.7	51.0	271	263.0	65.6
32	31.0	7.7	92	89.3	22.3	52	147.5	36.8	12	205.7	51.3	72	263.9	65.8
33	32.0	8.0	93	90.2	22.5	53	148.5	37.0	13	206.7	51.5	73	264.9	66.0
34	33.0	8.2	94	91.2	22.7	54	149.4	37.3	14	207.6	51.8	74	265.9	66.3
35	34.0	8.5	95	92.2	23.0	55	150.4	37.5	15	208.6	52.0	75	266.8	66.5
36	34.9	8.7	96	93.1	23.2	56	151.4	37.7	16	209.6	52.3	76	267.8	66.8
37	35.9	9.0	97	94.1	23.5	57	152.3	38.0	17	210.6	52.5	77	268.8	67.0
38	36.9	9.2	98	95.1	23.7	58	153.3	38.2	18	211.5	52.7	78	269.7	67.3
39	37.8	9.4	99	96.1	24.0	59	154.3	38.5	19	212.5	53.0	79	270.7	67.5
40	38.8	9.7	100	97.0	24.2	60	155.2	38.7	20	213.5	53.2	80	271.7	67.7
41	39.8	9.9	101	98.0	24.4	161	156.2	38.9	221	214.4	53.5	281	272.7	68.0
42	40.8	10.2	02	99.0	24.7	62	157.2	39.2	22	215.4	53.7	82	273.6	68.2
43	41.7	10.4	03	99.9	24.9	63	158.2	39.4	23	216.4	53.9	83	274.6	68.5
44	42.7	10.6	04	100.9	25.2	64	159.1	39.7	24	217.3	54.2	84	275.6	68.7
45	43.7	10.9	05	101.9	25.4	65	160.1	39.9	25	218.3	54.4	85	276.5	68.9
46	44.6	11.1	06	102.9	25.6	66	161.1	40.2	26	219.3	54.7	86	277.5	69.2
47	45.6	11.4	07	103.8	25.9	67	162.0	40.4	27	220.3	54.9	87	278.5	69.4
48	46.6	11.6	08	104.8	26.1	68	163.0	40.6	28	221.2	55.2	88	279.4	69.7
49	47.5	11.9	09	105.8	26.4	69	164.0	40.9	29	222.2	55.4	89	280.4	69.9
50	48.5	12.1	10	106.7	26.6	70	165.0	41.1	30	223.2	55.6	90	281.4	70.2
51	49.5	12.3	111	107.7	26.9	171	165.9	41.4	231	224.1	55.9	291	282.4	70.4
52	50.5	12.6	12	108.7	27.1	72	166.9	41.6	32	225.1	56.1	92	283.3	70.6
53	51.4	12.8	13	109.6	27.3	73	167.9	41.9	33	226.1	56.4	93	284.3	70.9
54	52.4	13.1	14	110.6	27.6	74	168.8	42.1	34	227.0	56.6	94	285.3	71.1
55	53.4	13.3	15	111.6	27.8	75	169.8	42.3	35	228.0	56.9	95	286.2	71.4
56	54.3	13.5	16	112.6	28.1	76	170.8	42.6	36	229.0	57.1	96	287.2	71.6
57	55.3	13.8	17	113.5	28.3	77	171.7	42.8	37	230.0	57.3	97	288.2	71.9
58	56.3	14.0	18	114.5	28.5	78	172.7	43.1	38	230.9	57.6	98	289.1	72.1
59	57.2	14.3	19	115.5	28.8	79	173.7	43.3	39	231.9	57.8	99	290.1	72.3
60	58.2	14.5	20	116.4	29.0	80	174.7	43.5	40	232.9	58.1	300	291.1	72.6
Dist.	Dep.	D. Lat.	Dist.	Dep.	D. Lat.	Dist.	Dep.	D. Lat.	Dist.	Dep.	D. Lat.	Dist.	Dep.	D. Lat.
284° / 256°	076° / 104°													

76°

Dist.	D. Lat.	Dep.
N.	N x Cos.	N x Sin.
Hypotenuse	Side Adj.	Side Opp.

TABLE 4

Traverse 14° Table

346° / 194°	014° / 166°													
Dist.	D. Lat.	Dep.	Dist.	D. Lat.	Dep.	Dist.	D. Lat.	Dep.	Dist.	D. Lat.	Dep.	Dist.	D. Lat.	Dep.
301	292.1	72.8	361	350.3	87.3	421	408.5	101.8	481	466.7	116.4	541	524.9	130.9
02	293.0	73.1	62	351.2	87.6	22	409.5	102.1	82	467.7	116.6	42	525.9	131.1
03	294.0	73.3	63	352.2	87.8	23	410.4	102.3	83	468.7	116.8	43	526.9	131.4
04	295.0	73.5	64	353.2	88.1	24	411.4	102.6	84	469.6	117.1	44	527.8	131.6
05	295.9	73.8	65	354.2	88.3	25	412.4	102.8	85	470.6	117.3	45	528.8	131.8
06	296.9	74.0	66	355.1	88.5	26	413.3	103.1	86	471.6	117.6	46	529.8	132.1
07	297.9	74.3	67	356.1	88.8	27	414.3	103.3	87	472.5	117.8	47	530.8	132.3
08	298.9	74.5	68	357.1	89.0	28	415.3	103.5	88	473.5	118.1	48	531.7	132.6
09	299.8	74.8	69	358.0	89.3	29	416.3	103.8	89	474.5	118.3	49	532.7	132.8
10	300.8	75.0	70	359.0	89.5	30	417.2	104.0	90	475.4	118.5	50	533.7	133.1
311	301.8	75.2	371	360.0	89.8	431	418.2	104.3	491	476.4	118.8	551	534.6	133.3
12	302.7	75.5	72	361.0	90.0	32	419.2	104.5	92	477.4	119.0	52	535.6	133.5
13	303.7	75.7	73	361.9	90.2	33	420.1	104.8	93	478.4	119.3	53	536.6	133.8
14	304.7	76.0	74	362.9	90.5	34	421.1	105.0	94	479.3	119.5	54	537.5	134.0
15	305.6	76.2	75	363.9	90.7	35	422.1	105.2	95	480.3	119.8	55	538.5	134.3
16	306.6	76.4	76	364.8	91.0	36	423.0	105.5	96	481.3	120.0	56	539.5	134.5
17	307.6	76.7	77	365.8	91.2	37	424.0	105.7	97	482.2	120.2	57	540.5	134.8
18	308.6	76.9	78	366.8	91.4	38	425.0	106.0	98	483.2	120.5	58	541.4	135.0
19	309.5	77.2	79	367.7	91.7	39	426.0	106.2	99	484.2	120.7	59	542.4	135.2
20	310.5	77.4	80	368.7	91.9	40	426.9	106.4	500	485.1	121.0	60	543.4	135.5
321	311.5	77.7	381	369.7	92.2	441	427.9	106.7	501	486.1	121.2	561	544.3	135.7
22	312.4	77.9	82	370.7	92.4	42	428.9	106.9	02	487.1	121.4	62	545.3	136.0
23	313.4	78.1	83	371.6	92.7	43	429.8	107.2	03	488.1	121.7	63	546.3	136.2
24	314.4	78.4	84	372.6	92.9	44	430.8	107.4	04	489.0	121.9	64	547.2	136.4
25	315.3	78.6	85	373.6	93.1	45	431.8	107.7	05	490.0	122.2	65	548.2	136.7
26	316.3	78.9	86	374.5	93.4	46	432.8	107.9	06	491.0	122.4	66	549.2	136.9
27	317.3	79.1	87	375.5	93.6	47	433.7	108.1	07	491.9	122.7	67	550.2	137.2
28	318.3	79.4	88	376.5	93.9	48	434.7	108.4	08	492.9	122.9	68	551.1	137.4
29	319.2	79.6	89	377.4	94.1	49	435.7	108.6	09	493.9	123.1	69	552.1	137.7
30	320.2	79.8	90	378.4	94.3	50	436.6	108.9	10	494.9	123.4	70	553.1	137.9
331	321.2	80.1	391	379.4	94.6	451	437.6	109.1	511	495.8	123.6	571	554.0	138.1
32	322.1	80.3	92	380.4	94.8	52	438.6	109.3	12	496.8	123.9	72	555.0	138.4
33	323.1	80.6	93	381.3	95.1	53	439.5	109.6	13	497.8	124.1	73	556.0	138.6
34	324.1	80.8	94	382.3	95.3	54	440.5	109.8	14	498.7	124.3	74	556.9	138.9
35	325.0	81.0	95	383.3	95.6	55	441.5	110.1	15	499.7	124.6	75	557.9	139.1
36	326.0	81.3	96	384.2	95.8	56	442.5	110.3	16	500.7	124.8	76	558.9	139.3
37	327.0	81.5	97	385.2	96.0	57	443.4	110.6	17	501.6	125.1	77	559.9	139.6
38	328.0	81.8	98	386.2	96.3	58	444.4	110.8	18	502.6	125.3	78	560.8	139.8
39	328.9	82.0	99	387.1	96.5	59	445.4	111.0	19	503.6	125.6	79	561.8	140.1
40	329.9	82.3	400	388.1	96.8	60	446.3	111.3	20	504.6	125.8	80	562.8	140.3
341	330.9	82.5	401	389.1	97.0	461	447.3	111.5	521	505.5	126.0	581	563.7	140.6
42	331.8	82.7	02	390.1	97.3	62	448.3	111.8	22	506.5	126.3	82	564.7	140.8
43	332.8	83.0	03	391.0	97.5	63	449.2	112.0	23	507.5	126.5	83	565.7	141.0
44	333.8	83.2	04	392.0	97.7	64	450.2	112.3	24	508.4	126.8	84	566.7	141.3
45	334.8	83.5	05	393.0	98.0	65	451.2	112.5	25	509.4	127.0	85	567.6	141.5
46	335.7	83.7	06	393.9	98.2	66	452.2	112.7	26	510.4	127.3	86	568.6	141.8
47	336.7	83.9	07	394.9	98.5	67	453.1	113.0	27	511.3	127.5	87	569.6	142.0
48	337.7	84.2	08	395.9	98.7	68	454.1	113.2	28	512.3	127.7	88	570.5	142.3
49	338.6	84.4	09	396.9	98.9	69	455.1	113.5	29	513.3	128.0	89	571.5	142.5
50	339.6	84.7	10	397.8	99.2	70	456.0	113.7	30	514.3	128.2	90	572.5	142.7
351	340.6	84.9	411	398.8	99.4	471	457.0	113.9	531	515.2	128.5	591	573.4	143.0
52	341.5	85.2	12	399.8	99.7	72	458.0	114.2	32	516.2	128.7	92	574.4	143.2
53	342.5	85.4	13	400.7	99.9	73	458.9	114.4	33	517.2	128.9	93	575.4	143.5
54	343.5	85.6	14	401.7	100.2	74	459.9	114.7	34	518.1	129.2	94	576.4	143.7
55	344.5	85.9	15	402.7	100.4	75	460.9	114.9	35	519.1	129.4	95	577.3	143.9
56	345.4	86.1	16	403.6	100.6	76	461.9	115.2	36	520.1	129.7	96	578.3	144.2
57	346.4	86.4	17	404.6	100.9	77	462.8	115.4	37	521.0	129.9	97	579.3	144.4
58	347.4	86.6	18	405.6	101.1	78	463.8	115.6	38	522.0	130.2	98	580.2	144.7
59	348.3	86.8	19	406.6	101.4	79	464.8	115.9	39	523.0	130.4	99	581.2	144.9
60	349.3	87.1	20	407.5	101.6	80	465.7	116.1	40	524.0	130.6	600	582.2	145.2
Dist.	Dep.	D. Lat.	Dist.	Dep.	D. Lat.	Dist.	Dep.	D. Lat.	Dist.	Dep.	D. Lat.	Dist.	Dep.	D. Lat.
												284° / 256°	076° / 104°	

Dist.	D. Lat.	Dep.
D Lo	Dep.	
	m	D Lo

76°

TABLE 4

Traverse 15° Table

345° / 195°	015° / 165°													
Dist.	D. Lat.	Dep.	Dist.	D. Lat.	Dep.	Dist.	D. Lat.	Dep.	Dist.	D. Lat.	Dep.	Dist.	D. Lat.	Dep.
1	1.0	0.3	61	58.9	15.8	121	116.9	31.3	181	174.8	46.8	241	232.8	62.4
2	1.9	0.5	62	59.9	16.0	22	117.8	31.6	82	175.8	47.1	42	233.8	62.6
3	2.9	0.8	63	60.9	16.3	23	118.8	31.8	83	176.8	47.4	43	234.7	62.9
4	3.9	1.0	64	61.8	16.6	24	119.8	32.1	84	177.7	47.6	44	235.7	63.2
5	4.8	1.3	65	62.8	16.8	25	120.7	32.4	85	178.7	47.9	45	236.7	63.4
6	5.8	1.6	66	63.8	17.1	26	121.7	32.6	86	179.7	48.1	46	237.6	63.7
7	6.8	1.8	67	64.7	17.3	27	122.7	32.9	87	180.6	48.4	47	238.6	63.9
8	7.7	2.1	68	65.7	17.6	28	123.6	33.1	88	181.6	48.7	48	239.5	64.2
9	8.7	2.3	69	66.6	17.9	29	124.6	33.4	89	182.6	48.9	49	240.5	64.4
10	9.7	2.6	70	67.6	18.1	30	125.6	33.6	90	183.5	49.2	50	241.5	64.7
11	10.6	2.8	71	68.6	18.4	131	126.5	33.9	191	184.5	49.4	251	242.4	65.0
12	11.6	3.1	72	69.5	18.6	32	127.5	34.2	92	185.5	49.7	52	243.4	65.2
13	12.6	3.4	73	70.5	18.9	33	128.5	34.4	93	186.4	50.0	53	244.4	65.5
14	13.5	3.6	74	71.5	19.2	34	129.4	34.7	94	187.4	50.2	54	245.3	65.7
15	14.5	3.9	75	72.4	19.4	35	130.4	34.9	95	188.4	50.5	55	246.3	66.0
16	15.5	4.1	76	73.4	19.7	36	131.4	35.2	96	189.3	50.7	56	247.3	66.3
17	16.4	4.4	77	74.4	19.9	37	132.3	35.5	97	190.3	51.0	57	248.2	66.5
18	17.4	4.7	78	75.3	20.2	38	133.3	35.7	98	191.3	51.2	58	249.2	66.8
19	18.4	4.9	79	76.3	20.4	39	134.3	36.0	99	192.2	51.5	59	250.2	67.0
20	19.3	5.2	80	77.3	20.7	40	135.2	36.2	200	193.2	51.8	60	251.1	67.3
21	20.3	5.4	81	78.2	21.0	141	136.2	36.5	201	194.2	52.0	261	252.1	67.6
22	21.3	5.7	82	79.2	21.2	42	137.2	36.8	02	195.1	52.3	62	253.1	67.8
23	22.2	6.0	83	80.2	21.5	43	138.1	37.0	03	196.1	52.5	63	254.0	68.1
24	23.2	6.2	84	81.1	21.7	44	139.1	37.3	04	197.0	52.8	64	255.0	68.3
25	24.1	6.5	85	82.1	22.0	45	140.1	37.5	05	198.0	53.1	65	256.0	68.6
26	25.1	6.7	86	83.1	22.3	46	141.0	37.8	06	199.0	53.3	66	256.9	68.8
27	26.1	7.0	87	84.0	22.5	47	142.0	38.0	07	199.9	53.6	67	257.9	69.1
28	27.0	7.2	88	85.0	22.8	48	143.0	38.3	08	200.9	53.8	68	258.9	69.4
29	28.0	7.5	89	86.0	23.0	49	143.9	38.6	09	201.9	54.1	69	259.8	69.6
30	29.0	7.8	90	86.9	23.3	50	144.9	38.8	10	202.8	54.4	70	260.8	69.9
31	29.9	8.0	91	87.9	23.6	151	145.9	39.1	211	203.8	54.6	271	261.8	70.1
32	30.9	8.3	92	88.9	23.8	52	146.8	39.3	12	204.8	54.9	72	262.7	70.4
33	31.9	8.5	93	89.8	24.1	53	147.8	39.6	13	205.7	55.1	73	263.7	70.7
34	32.8	8.8	94	90.8	24.3	54	148.8	39.9	14	206.7	55.4	74	264.7	70.9
35	33.8	9.1	95	91.8	24.6	55	149.7	40.1	15	207.7	55.6	75	265.6	71.2
36	34.8	9.3	96	92.7	24.8	56	150.7	40.4	16	208.6	55.9	76	266.6	71.4
37	35.7	9.6	97	93.7	25.1	57	151.7	40.6	17	209.6	56.2	77	267.6	71.7
38	36.7	9.8	98	94.7	25.4	58	152.6	40.9	18	210.6	56.4	78	268.5	72.0
39	37.7	10.1	99	95.6	25.6	59	153.6	41.2	19	211.5	56.7	79	269.5	72.2
40	38.6	10.4	100	96.6	25.9	60	154.5	41.4	20	212.5	56.9	80	270.5	72.5
41	39.6	10.6	101	97.6	26.1	161	155.5	41.7	221	213.5	57.2	281	271.4	72.7
42	40.6	10.9	02	98.5	26.4	62	156.5	41.9	22	214.4	57.5	82	272.4	73.0
43	41.5	11.1	03	99.5	26.7	63	157.4	42.2	23	215.4	57.7	83	273.4	73.2
44	42.5	11.4	04	100.5	26.9	64	158.4	42.4	24	216.4	58.0	84	274.3	73.5
45	43.5	11.6	05	101.4	27.2	65	159.4	42.7	25	217.3	58.2	85	275.3	73.8
46	44.4	11.9	06	102.4	27.4	66	160.3	43.0	26	218.3	58.5	86	276.3	74.0
47	45.4	12.2	07	103.4	27.7	67	161.3	43.2	27	219.3	58.8	87	277.2	74.3
48	46.4	12.4	08	104.3	28.0	68	162.3	43.5	28	220.2	59.0	88	278.2	74.5
49	47.3	12.7	09	105.3	28.2	69	163.2	43.7	29	221.2	59.3	89	279.2	74.8
50	48.3	12.9	10	106.3	28.5	70	164.2	44.0	30	222.2	59.5	90	280.1	75.1
51	49.3	13.2	111	107.2	28.7	171	165.2	44.3	231	223.1	59.8	291	281.1	75.3
52	50.2	13.5	12	108.2	29.0	72	166.1	44.5	32	224.1	60.0	92	282.1	75.6
53	51.2	13.7	13	109.1	29.2	73	167.1	44.8	33	225.1	60.3	93	283.0	75.8
54	52.2	14.0	14	110.1	29.5	74	168.1	45.0	34	226.0	60.6	94	284.0	76.1
55	53.1	14.2	15	111.1	29.8	75	169.0	45.3	35	227.0	60.8	95	284.9	76.4
56	54.1	14.5	16	112.0	30.0	76	170.0	45.6	36	228.0	61.1	96	285.9	76.6
57	55.1	14.8	17	113.0	30.3	77	171.0	45.8	37	228.9	61.3	97	286.9	76.9
58	56.0	15.0	18	114.0	30.5	78	171.9	46.1	38	229.9	61.6	98	287.8	77.1
59	57.0	15.3	19	114.9	30.8	79	172.9	46.3	39	230.9	61.9	99	288.8	77.4
60	58.0	15.5	20	115.9	31.1	80	173.9	46.6	40	231.8	62.1	300	289.8	77.6
Dist.	Dep.	D. Lat.	Dist.	Dep.	D. Lat.	Dist.	Dep.	D. Lat.	Dist.	Dep.	D. Lat.	Dist.	Dep.	D. Lat.
285° / 255°	075° / 105°													

75°

Dist.	D. Lat.	Dep.
N.	N x Cos.	N x Sin.
Hypotenuse	Side Adj.	Side Opp.

TABLE 4

Traverse 15° Table

345° / 195°	015° / 165°													
Dist.	D. Lat.	Dep.	Dist.	D. Lat.	Dep.	Dist.	D. Lat.	Dep.	Dist.	D. Lat.	Dep.	Dist.	D. Lat.	Dep.
301	290.7	77.9	361	348.7	93.4	421	406.7	109.0	481	464.6	124.5	541	522.6	140.0
02	291.7	78.2	62	349.7	93.7	22	407.6	109.2	82	465.6	124.8	42	523.5	140.3
03	292.7	78.4	63	350.6	94.0	23	408.6	109.5	83	466.5	125.0	43	524.5	140.5
04	293.6	78.7	64	351.6	94.2	24	409.6	109.7	84	467.5	125.3	44	525.5	140.8
05	294.6	78.9	65	352.6	94.5	25	410.5	110.0	85	468.5	125.5	45	526.4	141.1
06	295.6	79.2	66	353.5	94.7	26	411.5	110.3	86	469.4	125.8	46	527.4	141.3
07	296.5	79.5	67	354.5	95.0	27	412.5	110.5	87	470.4	126.0	47	528.4	141.6
08	297.5	79.7	68	355.5	95.2	28	413.4	110.8	88	471.4	126.3	48	529.3	141.8
09	298.5	80.0	69	356.4	95.5	29	414.4	111.0	89	472.3	126.6	49	530.3	142.1
10	299.4	80.2	70	357.4	95.8	30	415.3	111.3	90	473.3	126.8	50	531.3	142.4
311	300.4	80.5	371	358.4	96.0	431	416.3	111.6	491	474.3	127.1	551	532.2	142.6
12	301.4	80.8	72	359.3	96.3	32	417.3	111.8	92	475.2	127.3	52	533.2	142.9
13	302.3	81.0	73	360.3	96.5	33	418.2	112.1	93	476.2	127.6	53	534.2	143.1
14	303.3	81.3	74	361.3	96.8	34	419.2	112.3	94	477.2	127.9	54	535.1	143.4
15	304.3	81.5	75	362.2	97.1	35	420.2	112.6	95	478.1	128.1	55	536.1	143.6
16	305.2	81.8	76	363.2	97.3	36	421.1	112.8	96	479.1	128.4	56	537.1	143.9
17	306.2	82.0	77	364.2	97.6	37	422.1	113.1	97	480.1	128.6	57	538.0	144.2
18	307.2	82.3	78	365.1	97.8	38	423.1	113.4	98	481.0	128.9	58	539.0	144.4
19	308.1	82.6	79	366.1	98.1	39	424.0	113.6	99	482.0	129.2	59	540.0	144.7
20	309.1	82.8	80	367.1	98.4	40	425.0	113.9	500	483.0	129.4	60	540.9	144.9
321	310.1	83.1	381	368.0	98.6	441	426.0	114.1	501	483.9	129.7	561	541.9	145.2
22	311.0	83.3	82	369.0	98.9	42	426.9	114.4	02	484.9	129.9	62	542.9	145.5
23	312.0	83.6	83	369.9	99.1	43	427.9	114.7	03	485.9	130.2	63	543.8	145.7
24	313.0	83.9	84	370.9	99.4	44	428.9	114.9	04	486.8	130.4	64	544.8	146.0
25	313.9	84.1	85	371.9	99.6	45	429.8	115.2	05	487.8	130.7	65	545.7	146.2
26	314.9	84.4	86	372.8	99.9	46	430.8	115.4	06	488.8	131.0	66	546.7	146.5
27	315.9	84.6	87	373.8	100.2	47	431.8	115.7	07	489.7	131.2	67	547.7	146.8
28	316.8	84.9	88	374.8	100.4	48	432.7	116.0	08	490.7	131.5	68	548.6	147.0
29	317.8	85.2	89	375.7	100.7	49	433.7	116.2	09	491.7	131.7	69	549.6	147.3
30	318.8	85.4	90	376.7	100.9	50	434.7	116.5	10	492.6	132.0	70	550.6	147.5
331	319.7	85.7	391	377.7	101.2	451	435.6	116.7	511	493.6	132.3	571	551.5	147.8
32	320.7	85.9	92	378.6	101.5	52	436.6	117.0	12	494.6	132.5	72	552.5	148.0
33	321.7	86.2	93	379.6	101.7	53	437.6	117.2	13	495.5	132.8	73	553.5	148.3
34	322.6	86.4	94	380.6	102.0	54	438.5	117.5	14	496.5	133.0	74	554.4	148.6
35	323.6	86.7	95	381.5	102.2	55	439.5	117.8	15	497.5	133.3	75	555.4	148.8
36	324.6	87.0	96	382.5	102.5	56	440.5	118.0	16	498.4	133.6	76	556.4	149.1
37	325.5	87.2	97	383.5	102.8	57	441.4	118.3	17	499.4	133.8	77	557.3	149.3
38	326.5	87.5	98	384.4	103.0	58	442.4	118.5	18	500.3	134.1	78	558.3	149.6
39	327.4	87.7	99	385.4	103.3	59	443.4	118.8	19	501.3	134.3	79	559.3	149.9
40	328.4	88.0	400	386.4	103.5	60	444.3	119.1	20	502.3	134.6	80	560.2	150.1
341	329.4	88.3	401	387.3	103.8	461	445.3	119.3	521	503.2	134.8	581	561.2	150.4
42	330.3	88.5	02	388.3	104.0	62	446.3	119.6	22	504.2	135.1	82	562.2	150.6
43	331.3	88.8	03	389.3	104.3	63	447.2	119.8	23	505.2	135.4	83	563.1	150.9
44	332.3	89.0	04	390.2	104.6	64	448.2	120.1	24	506.1	135.6	84	564.1	151.2
45	333.2	89.3	05	391.2	104.8	65	449.2	120.4	25	507.1	135.9	85	565.1	151.4
46	334.2	89.6	06	392.2	105.1	66	450.1	120.6	26	508.1	136.1	86	566.0	151.7
47	335.2	89.8	07	393.1	105.3	67	451.1	120.9	27	509.0	136.4	87	567.0	151.9
48	336.1	90.1	08	394.1	105.6	68	452.1	121.1	28	510.0	136.7	88	568.0	152.2
49	337.1	90.3	09	395.1	105.9	69	453.0	121.4	29	511.0	136.9	89	568.9	152.4
50	338.1	90.6	10	396.0	106.1	70	454.0	121.6	30	511.9	137.2	90	569.9	152.7
351	339.0	90.8	411	397.0	106.4	471	455.0	121.9	531	512.9	137.4	591	570.9	153.0
52	340.0	91.1	12	398.0	106.6	72	455.9	122.2	32	513.9	137.7	92	571.8	153.2
53	341.0	91.4	13	398.9	106.9	73	456.9	122.4	33	514.8	138.0	93	572.8	153.5
54	341.9	91.6	14	399.9	107.2	74	457.8	122.7	34	515.8	138.2	94	573.8	153.7
55	342.9	91.9	15	400.9	107.4	75	458.8	122.9	35	516.8	138.5	95	574.7	154.0
56	343.9	92.1	16	401.8	107.7	76	459.8	123.2	36	517.7	138.7	96	575.7	154.3
57	344.8	92.4	17	402.8	107.9	77	460.7	123.5	37	518.7	139.0	97	576.7	154.5
58	345.8	92.7	18	403.8	108.2	78	461.7	123.7	38	519.7	139.2	98	577.6	154.8
59	346.8	92.9	19	404.7	108.4	79	462.7	124.0	39	520.6	139.5	99	578.6	155.0
60	347.7	93.2	20	405.7	108.7	80	463.6	124.2	40	521.6	139.8	600	579.6	155.3
Dist.	Dep.	D. Lat.	Dist.	Dep.	D. Lat.	Dist.	Dep.	D. Lat.	Dist.	Dep.	D. Lat.	Dist.	Dep.	D. Lat.
285° / 255°	075° / 105°													

Dist.	D. Lat.	Dep.
D Lo	Dep.	
	m	D Lo

75°

TABLE 4

Traverse 16° Table

344° 196°	016° 164°

Dist.	D. Lat.	Dep.	Dist.	D. Lat.	Dep.	Dist.	D. Lat.	Dep.	Dist.	D. Lat.	Dep.	Dist.	D. Lat.	Dep.
1	1.0	0.3	61	58.6	16.8	121	116.3	33.4	181	174.0	49.9	241	231.7	66.4
2	1.9	0.6	62	59.6	17.1	22	117.3	33.6	82	174.9	50.2	42	232.6	66.7
3	2.9	0.8	63	60.6	17.4	23	118.2	33.9	83	175.9	50.4	43	233.6	67.0
4	3.8	1.1	64	61.5	17.6	24	119.2	34.2	84	176.9	50.7	44	234.5	67.3
5	4.8	1.4	65	62.5	17.9	25	120.2	34.5	85	177.8	51.0	45	235.5	67.5
6	5.8	1.7	66	63.4	18.2	26	121.1	34.7	86	178.8	51.3	46	236.5	67.8
7	6.7	1.9	67	64.4	18.5	27	122.1	35.0	87	179.8	51.5	47	237.4	68.1
8	7.7	2.2	68	65.4	18.7	28	123.0	35.3	88	180.7	51.8	48	238.4	68.4
9	8.7	2.5	69	66.3	19.0	29	124.0	35.6	89	181.7	52.1	49	239.4	68.6
10	9.6	2.8	70	67.3	19.3	30	125.0	35.8	90	182.6	52.4	50	240.3	68.9
11	10.6	3.0	71	68.2	19.6	131	125.9	36.1	191	183.6	52.6	251	241.3	69.2
12	11.5	3.3	72	69.2	19.8	32	126.9	36.4	92	184.6	52.9	52	242.2	69.5
13	12.5	3.6	73	70.2	20.1	33	127.8	36.7	93	185.5	53.2	53	243.2	69.7
14	13.5	3.9	74	71.1	20.4	34	128.8	36.9	94	186.5	53.5	54	244.2	70.0
15	14.4	4.1	75	72.1	20.7	35	129.8	37.2	95	187.4	53.7	55	245.1	70.3
16	15.4	4.4	76	73.1	20.9	36	130.7	37.5	96	188.4	54.0	56	246.1	70.6
17	16.3	4.7	77	74.0	21.2	37	131.7	37.8	97	189.4	54.3	57	247.0	70.8
18	17.3	5.0	78	75.0	21.5	38	132.7	38.0	98	190.3	54.6	58	248.0	71.1
19	18.3	5.2	79	75.9	21.8	39	133.6	38.3	99	191.3	54.9	59	249.0	71.4
20	19.2	5.5	80	76.9	22.1	40	134.6	38.6	200	192.3	55.1	60	249.9	71.7
21	20.2	5.8	81	77.9	22.3	141	135.5	38.9	201	193.2	55.4	261	250.9	71.9
22	21.1	6.1	82	78.8	22.6	42	136.5	39.1	02	194.2	55.7	62	251.9	72.2
23	22.1	6.3	83	79.8	22.9	43	137.5	39.4	03	195.1	56.0	63	252.8	72.5
24	23.1	6.6	84	80.7	23.2	44	138.4	39.7	04	196.1	56.2	64	253.8	72.8
25	24.0	6.9	85	81.7	23.4	45	139.4	40.0	05	197.1	56.5	65	254.7	73.0
26	25.0	7.2	86	82.7	23.7	46	140.3	40.2	06	198.0	56.8	66	255.7	73.3
27	26.0	7.4	87	83.6	24.0	47	141.3	40.5	07	199.0	57.1	67	256.7	73.6
28	26.9	7.7	88	84.6	24.3	48	142.3	40.8	08	199.9	57.3	68	257.6	73.9
29	27.9	8.0	89	85.6	24.5	49	143.2	41.1	09	200.9	57.6	69	258.6	74.1
30	28.8	8.3	90	86.5	24.8	50	144.2	41.3	10	201.9	57.9	70	259.5	74.4
31	29.8	8.5	91	87.5	25.1	151	145.2	41.6	211	202.8	58.2	271	260.5	74.7
32	30.8	8.8	92	88.4	25.4	52	146.1	41.9	12	203.8	58.4	72	261.5	75.0
33	31.7	9.1	93	89.4	25.6	53	147.1	42.2	13	204.7	58.7	73	262.4	75.2
34	32.7	9.4	94	90.4	25.9	54	148.0	42.4	14	205.7	59.0	74	263.4	75.5
35	33.6	9.6	95	91.3	26.2	55	149.0	42.7	15	206.7	59.3	75	264.3	75.8
36	34.6	9.9	96	92.3	26.5	56	150.0	43.0	16	207.6	59.5	76	265.3	76.1
37	35.6	10.2	97	93.2	26.7	57	150.9	43.3	17	208.6	59.8	77	266.3	76.4
38	36.5	10.5	98	94.2	27.0	58	151.9	43.6	18	209.6	60.1	78	267.2	76.6
39	37.5	10.7	99	95.2	27.3	59	152.8	43.8	19	210.5	60.4	79	268.2	76.9
40	38.5	11.0	100	96.1	27.6	60	153.8	44.1	20	211.5	60.6	80	269.2	77.2
41	39.4	11.3	101	97.1	27.8	161	154.8	44.4	221	212.4	60.9	281	270.1	77.5
42	40.4	11.6	02	98.0	28.1	62	155.7	44.7	22	213.4	61.2	82	271.1	77.7
43	41.3	11.9	03	99.0	28.4	63	156.7	44.9	23	214.4	61.5	83	272.0	78.0
44	42.3	12.1	04	100.0	28.7	64	157.6	45.2	24	215.3	61.7	84	273.0	78.3
45	43.3	12.4	05	100.9	28.9	65	158.6	45.5	25	216.3	62.0	85	274.0	78.6
46	44.2	12.7	06	101.9	29.2	66	159.6	45.8	26	217.2	62.3	86	274.9	78.8
47	45.2	13.0	07	102.9	29.5	67	160.5	46.0	27	218.2	62.6	87	275.9	79.1
48	46.1	13.2	08	103.8	29.8	68	161.5	46.3	28	219.2	62.8	88	276.8	79.4
49	47.1	13.5	09	104.8	30.0	69	162.5	46.6	29	220.1	63.1	89	277.8	79.7
50	48.1	13.8	10	105.7	30.3	70	163.4	46.9	30	221.1	63.4	90	278.8	79.9
51	49.0	14.1	111	106.7	30.6	171	164.4	47.1	231	222.1	63.7	291	279.7	80.2
52	50.0	14.3	12	107.7	30.9	72	165.3	47.4	32	223.0	63.9	92	280.7	80.5
53	50.9	14.6	13	108.6	31.1	73	166.3	47.7	33	224.0	64.2	93	281.6	80.8
54	51.9	14.9	14	109.6	31.4	74	167.3	48.0	34	224.9	64.5	94	282.6	81.0
55	52.9	15.2	15	110.5	31.7	75	168.2	48.2	35	225.9	64.8	95	283.6	81.3
56	53.8	15.4	16	111.5	32.0	76	169.2	48.5	36	226.9	65.1	96	284.5	81.6
57	54.8	15.7	17	112.5	32.2	77	170.1	48.8	37	227.8	65.3	97	285.5	81.9
58	55.8	16.0	18	113.4	32.5	78	171.1	49.1	38	228.8	65.6	98	286.5	82.1
59	56.7	16.3	19	114.4	32.8	79	172.1	49.3	39	229.7	65.9	99	287.4	82.4
60	57.7	16.5	20	115.4	33.1	80	173.0	49.6	40	230.7	66.2	300	288.4	82.7
Dist.	Dep.	D. Lat.	Dist.	Dep.	D. Lat.	Dist.	Dep.	D. Lat.	Dist.	Dep.	D. Lat.	Dist.	Dep.	D. Lat.

286° 254°	074° 106°

74°

Dist.	D. Lat.	Dep.
N.	N x Cos.	N x Sin.
Hypotenuse	Side Adj.	Side Opp.

TABLE 4

Traverse 16° Table

344° 196°	016° 164°

Dist.	D. Lat.	Dep.	Dist.	D. Lat.	Dep.	Dist.	D. Lat.	Dep.	Dist.	D. Lat.	Dep.	Dist.	D. Lat.	Dep.
301	289.3	83.0	361	347.0	99.5	421	404.7	116.0	481	462.4	132.6	541	520.0	149.1
02	290.3	83.2	62	348.0	99.8	22	405.7	116.3	82	463.3	132.9	42	521.0	149.4
03	291.3	83.5	63	348.9	100.1	23	406.6	116.6	83	464.3	133.1	43	522.0	149.7
04	292.2	83.8	64	349.9	100.3	24	407.6	116.9	84	465.3	133.4	44	522.9	149.9
05	293.2	84.1	65	350.9	100.6	25	408.5	117.1	85	466.2	133.7	45	523.9	150.2
06	294.1	84.3	66	351.8	100.9	26	409.5	117.4	86	467.2	134.0	46	524.8	150.5
07	295.1	84.6	67	352.8	101.2	27	410.5	117.7	87	468.1	134.2	47	525.8	150.8
08	296.1	84.9	68	353.7	101.4	28	411.4	118.0	88	469.1	134.5	48	526.8	151.0
09	297.0	85.2	69	354.7	101.7	29	412.4	118.2	89	470.1	134.8	49	527.7	151.3
10	298.0	85.4	70	355.7	102.0	30	413.3	118.5	90	471.0	135.1	50	528.7	151.6
311	299.0	85.7	371	356.6	102.3	431	414.3	118.8	491	472.0	135.3	551	529.7	151.9
12	299.9	86.0	72	357.6	102.5	32	415.3	119.1	92	472.9	135.6	52	530.6	152.2
13	300.9	86.3	73	358.6	102.8	33	416.2	119.4	93	473.9	135.9	53	531.6	152.4
14	301.8	86.6	74	359.5	103.1	34	417.2	119.6	94	474.9	136.2	54	532.5	152.7
15	302.8	86.8	75	360.5	103.4	35	418.1	119.9	95	475.8	136.4	55	533.5	153.0
16	303.8	87.1	76	361.4	103.6	36	419.1	120.2	96	476.8	136.7	56	534.5	153.3
17	304.7	87.4	77	362.4	103.9	37	420.1	120.5	97	477.7	137.0	57	535.4	153.5
18	305.7	87.7	78	363.4	104.2	38	421.0	120.7	98	478.7	137.3	58	536.4	153.8
19	306.6	87.9	79	364.3	104.5	39	422.0	121.0	99	479.7	137.5	59	537.3	154.1
20	307.6	88.2	80	365.3	104.7	40	423.0	121.3	500	480.6	137.8	60	538.3	154.4
321	308.6	88.5	381	366.2	105.0	441	423.9	121.6	501	481.6	138.1	561	539.3	154.6
22	309.5	88.8	82	367.2	105.3	42	424.9	121.8	02	482.6	138.4	62	540.2	154.9
23	310.5	89.0	83	368.2	105.6	43	425.8	122.1	03	483.5	138.6	63	541.2	155.2
24	311.4	89.3	84	369.1	105.8	44	426.8	122.4	04	484.5	138.9	64	542.2	155.5
25	312.4	89.6	85	370.1	106.1	45	427.8	122.7	05	485.4	139.2	65	543.1	155.7
26	313.4	89.9	86	371.0	106.4	46	428.7	122.9	06	486.4	139.5	66	544.1	156.0
27	314.3	90.1	87	372.0	106.7	47	429.7	123.2	07	487.4	139.7	67	545.0	156.3
28	315.3	90.4	88	373.0	106.9	48	430.6	123.5	08	488.3	140.0	68	546.0	156.6
29	316.3	90.7	89	373.9	107.2	49	431.6	123.8	09	489.3	140.3	69	547.0	156.8
30	317.2	91.0	90	374.9	107.5	50	432.6	124.0	10	490.2	140.6	70	547.9	157.1
331	318.2	91.2	391	375.9	107.8	451	433.5	124.3	511	491.2	140.9	571	548.9	157.4
32	319.1	91.5	92	376.8	108.0	52	434.5	124.6	12	492.2	141.1	72	549.8	157.7
33	320.1	91.8	93	377.8	108.3	53	435.5	124.9	13	493.1	141.4	73	550.8	157.9
34	321.1	92.1	94	378.7	108.6	54	436.4	125.1	14	494.1	141.7	74	551.8	158.2
35	322.0	92.3	95	379.7	108.9	55	437.4	125.4	15	495.0	142.0	75	552.7	158.5
36	323.0	92.6	96	380.7	109.2	56	438.3	125.7	16	496.0	142.2	76	553.7	158.8
37	323.9	92.9	97	381.6	109.4	57	439.3	126.0	17	497.0	142.5	77	554.6	159.0
38	324.9	93.2	98	382.6	109.7	58	440.3	126.2	18	497.9	142.8	78	555.6	159.3
39	325.9	93.4	99	383.5	110.0	59	441.2	126.5	19	498.9	143.1	79	556.6	159.6
40	326.8	93.7	400	384.5	110.3	60	442.2	126.8	20	499.9	143.3	80	557.5	159.9
341	327.8	94.0	401	385.5	110.5	461	443.1	127.1	521	500.8	143.6	581	558.5	160.1
42	328.8	94.3	02	386.4	110.8	62	444.1	127.3	22	501.8	143.9	82	559.5	160.4
43	329.7	94.5	03	387.4	111.1	63	445.1	127.6	23	502.7	144.2	83	560.4	160.7
44	330.7	94.8	04	388.3	111.4	64	446.0	127.9	24	503.7	144.4	84	561.4	161.0
45	331.6	95.1	05	389.3	111.6	65	447.0	128.2	25	504.7	144.7	85	562.3	161.2
46	332.6	95.4	06	390.3	111.9	66	447.9	128.4	26	505.6	145.0	86	563.3	161.5
47	333.6	95.6	07	391.2	112.2	67	448.9	128.7	27	506.6	145.3	87	564.3	161.8
48	334.5	95.9	08	392.2	112.5	68	449.9	129.0	28	507.5	145.5	88	565.2	162.1
49	335.5	96.2	09	393.2	112.7	69	450.8	129.3	29	508.5	145.8	89	566.2	162.4
50	336.4	96.5	10	394.1	113.0	70	451.8	129.5	30	509.5	146.1	90	567.1	162.6
351	337.4	96.7	411	395.1	113.3	471	452.8	129.8	531	510.4	146.4	591	568.1	162.9
52	338.4	97.0	12	396.0	113.6	72	453.7	130.1	32	511.4	146.6	92	569.1	163.2
53	339.3	97.3	13	397.0	113.8	73	454.7	130.4	33	512.4	146.9	93	570.0	163.5
54	340.3	97.6	14	398.0	114.1	74	455.6	130.7	34	513.3	147.2	94	571.0	163.7
55	341.2	97.9	15	398.9	114.4	75	456.6	130.9	35	514.3	147.5	95	572.0	164.0
56	342.2	98.1	16	399.9	114.7	76	457.6	131.2	36	515.2	147.7	96	572.9	164.3
57	343.2	98.4	17	400.8	114.9	77	458.5	131.5	37	516.2	148.0	97	573.9	164.6
58	344.1	98.7	18	401.8	115.2	78	459.5	131.8	38	517.2	148.3	98	574.8	164.8
59	345.1	99.0	19	402.8	115.5	79	460.4	132.0	39	518.1	148.6	99	575.8	165.1
60	346.1	99.2	20	403.7	115.8	80	461.4	132.3	40	519.1	148.8	600	576.8	165.4
Dist.	Dep.	D. Lat.	Dist.	Dep.	D. Lat.	Dist.	Dep.	D. Lat.	Dist.	Dep.	D. Lat.	Dist.	Dep.	D. Lat.

Dist.	D. Lat.	Dep.
D Lo	Dep.	
	m	D Lo

74°

286° 254°	074° 106°

TABLE 4

Traverse 17° Table

343° | 017° — 197° | 163°

Dist.	D. Lat.	Dep.	Dist.	D. Lat.	Dep.	Dist.	D. Lat.	Dep.	Dist.	D. Lat.	Dep.	Dist.	D. Lat.	Dep.
1	1.0	0.3	61	58.3	17.8	121	115.7	35.4	181	173.1	52.9	241	230.5	70.5
2	1.9	0.6	62	59.3	18.1	22	116.7	35.7	82	174.0	53.2	42	231.4	70.8
3	2.9	0.9	63	60.2	18.4	23	117.6	36.0	83	175.0	53.5	43	232.4	71.0
4	3.8	1.2	64	61.2	18.7	24	118.6	36.3	84	176.0	53.8	44	233.3	71.3
5	4.8	1.5	65	62.2	19.0	25	119.5	36.5	85	176.9	54.1	45	234.3	71.6
6	5.7	1.8	66	63.1	19.3	26	120.5	36.8	86	177.9	54.4	46	235.3	71.9
7	6.7	2.0	67	64.1	19.6	27	121.5	37.1	87	178.8	54.7	47	236.2	72.2
8	7.7	2.3	68	65.0	19.9	28	122.4	37.4	88	179.8	55.0	48	237.2	72.5
9	8.6	2.6	69	66.0	20.2	29	123.4	37.7	89	180.7	55.3	49	238.1	72.8
10	9.6	2.9	70	66.9	20.5	30	124.3	38.0	90	181.7	55.6	50	239.1	73.1
11	10.5	3.2	71	67.9	20.8	131	125.3	38.3	191	182.7	55.8	251	240.0	73.4
12	11.5	3.5	72	68.9	21.1	32	126.2	38.6	92	183.6	56.1	52	241.0	73.7
13	12.4	3.8	73	69.8	21.3	33	127.2	38.9	93	184.6	56.4	53	241.9	74.0
14	13.4	4.1	74	70.8	21.6	34	128.1	39.2	94	185.5	56.7	54	242.9	74.3
15	14.3	4.4	75	71.7	21.9	35	129.1	39.5	95	186.5	57.0	55	243.9	74.6
16	15.3	4.7	76	72.7	22.2	36	130.1	39.8	96	187.4	57.3	56	244.8	74.8
17	16.3	5.0	77	73.6	22.5	37	131.0	40.1	97	188.4	57.6	57	245.8	75.1
18	17.2	5.3	78	74.6	22.8	38	132.0	40.3	98	189.3	57.9	58	246.7	75.4
19	18.2	5.6	79	75.5	23.1	39	132.9	40.6	99	190.3	58.2	59	247.7	75.7
20	19.1	5.8	80	76.5	23.4	40	133.9	40.9	200	191.3	58.5	60	248.6	76.0
21	20.1	6.1	81	77.5	23.7	141	134.8	41.2	201	192.2	58.8	261	249.6	76.3
22	21.0	6.4	82	78.4	24.0	42	135.8	41.5	02	193.2	59.1	62	250.6	76.6
23	22.0	6.7	83	79.4	24.3	43	136.8	41.8	03	194.1	59.4	63	251.5	76.9
24	23.0	7.0	84	80.3	24.6	44	137.7	42.1	04	195.1	59.6	64	252.5	77.2
25	23.9	7.3	85	81.3	24.9	45	138.7	42.4	05	196.0	59.9	65	253.4	77.5
26	24.9	7.6	86	82.2	25.1	46	139.6	42.7	06	197.0	60.2	66	254.4	77.8
27	25.8	7.9	87	83.2	25.4	47	140.6	43.0	07	198.0	60.5	67	255.3	78.1
28	26.8	8.2	88	84.2	25.7	48	141.5	43.3	08	198.9	60.8	68	256.3	78.4
29	27.7	8.5	89	85.1	26.0	49	142.5	43.6	09	199.9	61.1	69	257.2	78.6
30	28.7	8.8	90	86.1	26.3	50	143.4	43.9	10	200.8	61.4	70	258.2	78.9
31	29.6	9.1	91	87.0	26.6	151	144.4	44.1	211	201.8	61.7	271	259.2	79.2
32	30.6	9.4	92	88.0	26.9	52	145.4	44.4	12	202.7	62.0	72	260.1	79.5
33	31.6	9.6	93	88.9	27.2	53	146.3	44.7	13	203.7	62.3	73	261.1	79.8
34	32.5	9.9	94	89.9	27.5	54	147.3	45.0	14	204.6	62.6	74	262.0	80.1
35	33.5	10.2	95	90.8	27.8	55	148.2	45.3	15	205.6	62.9	75	263.0	80.4
36	34.4	10.5	96	91.8	28.1	56	149.2	45.6	16	206.6	63.2	76	263.9	80.7
37	35.4	10.8	97	92.8	28.4	57	150.1	45.9	17	207.5	63.4	77	264.9	81.0
38	36.3	11.1	98	93.7	28.7	58	151.1	46.2	18	208.5	63.7	78	265.9	81.3
39	37.3	11.4	99	94.7	28.9	59	152.1	46.5	19	209.4	64.0	79	266.8	81.6
40	38.3	11.7	100	95.6	29.2	60	153.0	46.8	20	210.4	64.3	80	267.8	81.9
41	39.2	12.0	101	96.6	29.5	161	154.0	47.1	221	211.3	64.6	281	268.7	82.2
42	40.2	12.3	02	97.5	29.8	62	154.9	47.4	22	212.3	64.9	82	269.7	82.4
43	41.1	12.6	03	98.5	30.1	63	155.9	47.7	23	213.3	65.2	83	270.6	82.7
44	42.1	12.9	04	99.5	30.4	64	156.8	47.9	24	214.2	65.5	84	271.6	83.0
45	43.0	13.2	05	100.4	30.7	65	157.8	48.2	25	215.2	65.8	85	272.5	83.3
46	44.0	13.4	06	101.4	31.0	66	158.7	48.5	26	216.1	66.1	86	273.5	83.6
47	44.9	13.7	07	102.3	31.3	67	159.7	48.8	27	217.1	66.4	87	274.5	83.9
48	45.9	14.0	08	103.3	31.6	68	160.7	49.1	28	218.0	66.7	88	275.4	84.2
49	46.9	14.3	09	104.2	31.9	69	161.6	49.4	29	219.0	67.0	89	276.4	84.5
50	47.8	14.6	10	105.2	32.2	70	162.6	49.7	30	220.0	67.2	90	277.3	84.8
51	48.8	14.9	111	106.1	32.5	171	163.5	50.0	231	220.9	67.5	291	278.3	85.1
52	49.7	15.2	12	107.1	32.7	72	164.5	50.3	32	221.9	67.8	92	279.2	85.4
53	50.7	15.5	13	108.1	33.0	73	165.4	50.6	33	222.8	68.1	93	280.2	85.7
54	51.6	15.8	14	109.0	33.3	74	166.4	50.9	34	223.8	68.4	94	281.2	86.0
55	52.6	16.1	15	110.0	33.6	75	167.4	51.2	35	224.7	68.7	95	282.1	86.2
56	53.6	16.4	16	110.9	33.9	76	168.3	51.5	36	225.7	69.0	96	283.1	86.5
57	54.5	16.7	17	111.9	34.2	77	169.3	51.7	37	226.6	69.3	97	284.0	86.8
58	55.5	17.0	18	112.8	34.5	78	170.2	52.0	38	227.6	69.6	98	285.0	87.1
59	56.4	17.2	19	113.8	34.8	79	171.2	52.3	39	228.6	69.9	99	285.9	87.4
60	57.4	17.5	20	114.8	35.1	80	172.1	52.6	40	229.5	70.2	300	286.9	87.7
Dist.	Dep.	D. Lat.	Dist.	Dep.	D. Lat.	Dist.	Dep.	D. Lat.	Dist.	Dep.	D. Lat.	Dist.	Dep.	D. Lat.

287° | 073° — 253° | 107°

73°

Dist.	D. Lat.	Dep.
N.	N x Cos.	N x Sin.
Hypotenuse	Side Adj.	Side Opp.

TABLE 4

Traverse 17° Table

343° | 017° — 197° | 163°

Dist.	D. Lat.	Dep.	Dist.	D. Lat.	Dep.	Dist.	D. Lat.	Dep.	Dist.	D. Lat.	Dep.	Dist.	D. Lat.	Dep.
301	287.8	88.0	361	345.2	105.5	421	402.6	123.1	481	460.0	140.6	541	517.4	158.2
02	288.8	88.3	62	346.2	105.8	22	403.6	123.4	82	460.9	140.9	42	518.3	158.5
03	289.8	88.6	63	347.1	106.1	23	404.5	123.7	83	461.9	141.2	43	519.3	158.8
04	290.7	88.9	64	348.1	106.4	24	405.5	124.0	84	462.9	141.5	44	520.2	159.1
05	291.7	89.2	65	349.1	106.7	25	406.4	124.3	85	463.8	141.8	45	521.2	159.3
06	292.6	89.5	66	350.0	107.0	26	407.4	124.6	86	464.8	142.1	46	522.1	159.6
07	293.6	89.8	67	351.0	107.3	27	408.3	124.8	87	465.7	142.4	47	523.1	159.9
08	294.5	90.1	68	351.9	107.6	28	409.3	125.1	88	466.7	142.7	48	524.1	160.2
09	295.5	90.3	69	352.9	107.9	29	410.3	125.4	89	467.6	143.0	49	525.0	160.5
10	296.5	90.6	70	353.8	108.2	30	411.2	125.7	90	468.6	143.3	50	526.0	160.8
311	297.4	90.9	371	354.8	108.5	431	412.2	126.0	491	469.5	143.6	551	526.9	161.1
12	298.4	91.2	72	355.7	108.8	32	413.1	126.3	92	470.5	143.8	52	527.9	161.4
13	299.3	91.5	73	356.7	109.1	33	414.1	126.6	93	471.5	144.1	53	528.8	161.7
14	300.3	91.8	74	357.7	109.3	34	415.0	126.9	94	472.4	144.4	54	529.8	162.0
15	301.2	92.1	75	358.6	109.6	35	416.0	127.2	95	473.4	144.7	55	530.7	162.3
16	302.2	92.4	76	359.6	109.9	36	416.9	127.5	96	474.3	145.0	56	531.7	162.6
17	303.1	92.7	77	360.5	110.2	37	417.9	127.8	97	475.3	145.3	57	532.7	162.9
18	304.1	93.0	78	361.5	110.5	38	418.9	128.1	98	476.2	145.6	58	533.6	163.1
19	305.1	93.3	79	362.4	110.8	39	419.8	128.4	99	477.2	145.9	59	534.6	163.4
20	306.0	93.6	80	363.4	111.1	40	420.8	128.6	500	478.2	146.2	60	535.5	163.7
321	307.0	93.9	381	364.4	111.4	441	421.7	128.9	501	479.1	146.5	561	536.5	164.0
22	307.9	94.1	82	365.3	111.7	42	422.7	129.2	02	480.1	146.8	62	537.4	164.3
23	308.9	94.4	83	366.3	112.0	43	423.6	129.5	03	481.0	147.1	63	538.4	164.6
24	309.8	94.7	84	367.2	112.3	44	424.6	129.8	04	482.0	147.4	64	539.4	164.9
25	310.8	95.0	85	368.2	112.6	45	425.6	130.1	05	482.9	147.6	65	540.3	165.2
26	311.8	95.3	86	369.1	112.9	46	426.5	130.4	06	483.9	147.9	66	541.3	165.5
27	312.7	95.6	87	370.1	113.1	47	427.5	130.7	07	484.8	148.2	67	542.2	165.8
28	313.7	95.9	88	371.0	113.4	48	428.4	131.0	08	485.8	148.5	68	543.2	166.1
29	314.6	96.2	89	372.0	113.7	49	429.4	131.3	09	486.8	148.8	69	544.1	166.4
30	315.6	96.5	90	373.0	114.0	50	430.3	131.6	10	487.7	149.1	70	545.1	166.7
331	316.5	96.8	391	373.9	114.3	451	431.3	131.9	511	488.7	149.4	571	546.1	166.9
32	317.5	97.1	92	374.9	114.6	52	432.2	132.2	12	489.6	149.7	72	547.0	167.2
33	318.4	97.4	93	375.8	114.9	53	433.2	132.4	13	490.6	150.0	73	548.0	167.5
34	319.4	97.7	94	376.8	115.2	54	434.2	132.7	14	491.5	150.3	74	548.9	167.8
35	320.4	97.9	95	377.7	115.5	55	435.1	133.0	15	492.5	150.6	75	549.9	168.1
36	321.3	98.2	96	378.7	115.8	56	436.1	133.3	16	493.5	150.9	76	550.8	168.4
37	322.3	98.5	97	379.7	116.1	57	437.0	133.6	17	494.4	151.2	77	551.8	168.7
38	323.2	98.8	98	380.6	116.4	58	438.0	133.9	18	495.4	151.4	78	552.7	169.0
39	324.2	99.1	99	381.6	116.7	59	438.9	134.2	19	496.3	151.7	79	553.7	169.3
40	325.1	99.4	400	382.5	116.9	60	439.9	134.5	20	497.3	152.0	80	554.7	169.6
341	326.1	99.7	401	383.5	117.2	461	440.9	134.8	521	498.2	152.3	581	555.6	169.9
42	327.1	100.0	02	384.4	117.5	62	441.8	135.1	22	499.2	152.6	82	556.6	170.2
43	328.0	100.3	03	385.4	117.8	63	442.8	135.4	23	500.1	152.9	83	557.5	170.5
44	329.0	100.6	04	386.3	118.1	64	443.7	135.7	24	501.1	153.2	84	558.5	170.7
45	329.9	100.9	05	387.3	118.4	65	444.7	136.0	25	502.1	153.5	85	559.4	171.0
46	330.9	101.2	06	388.3	118.7	66	445.6	136.2	26	503.0	153.8	86	560.4	171.3
47	331.8	101.5	07	389.2	119.0	67	446.6	136.5	27	504.0	154.1	87	561.4	171.6
48	332.8	101.7	08	390.2	119.3	68	447.6	136.8	28	504.9	154.4	88	562.3	171.9
49	333.8	102.0	09	391.1	119.6	69	448.5	137.1	29	505.9	154.7	89	563.3	172.2
50	334.7	102.3	10	392.1	119.9	70	449.5	137.4	30	506.8	155.0	90	564.2	172.5
351	335.7	102.6	411	393.0	120.2	471	450.4	137.7	531	507.8	155.2	591	565.2	172.8
52	336.6	102.9	12	394.0	120.5	72	451.4	138.0	32	508.8	155.5	92	566.1	173.1
53	337.6	103.2	13	395.0	120.7	73	452.3	138.3	33	509.7	155.8	93	567.1	173.4
54	338.5	103.5	14	395.9	121.0	74	453.3	138.6	34	510.7	156.1	94	568.0	173.7
55	339.5	103.8	15	396.9	121.3	75	454.2	138.9	35	511.6	156.4	95	569.0	174.0
56	340.4	104.1	16	397.8	121.6	76	455.2	139.2	36	512.6	156.7	96	570.0	174.3
57	341.4	104.4	17	398.8	121.9	77	456.2	139.5	37	513.5	157.0	97	570.9	174.5
58	342.4	104.7	18	399.7	122.2	78	457.1	139.8	38	514.5	157.3	98	571.9	174.8
59	343.3	105.0	19	400.7	122.5	79	458.1	140.0	39	515.4	157.6	99	572.8	175.1
60	344.3	105.3	20	401.6	122.8	80	459.0	140.3	40	516.4	157.9	600	573.8	175.4
Dist.	Dep.	D. Lat.	Dist.	Dep.	D. Lat.	Dist.	Dep.	D. Lat.	Dist.	Dep.	D. Lat.	Dist.	Dep.	D. Lat.

Dist.	D. Lat.	Dep.
D Lo	Dep.	
	m	D Lo

73°

287° | 073° — 253° | 107°

TABLE 4

Traverse **18°** Table

342°	018°
198°	162°

Dist.	D. Lat.	Dep.	Dist.	D. Lat.	Dep.	Dist.	D. Lat.	Dep.	Dist.	D. Lat.	Dep.	Dist.	D. Lat.	Dep.
1	1.0	0.3	61	58.0	18.9	121	115.1	37.4	181	172.1	55.9	241	229.2	74.5
2	1.9	0.6	62	59.0	19.2	22	116.0	37.7	82	173.1	56.2	42	230.2	74.8
3	2.9	0.9	63	59.9	19.5	23	117.0	38.0	83	174.0	56.6	43	231.1	75.1
4	3.8	1.2	64	60.9	19.8	24	117.9	38.3	84	175.0	56.9	44	232.1	75.4
5	4.8	1.5	65	61.8	20.1	25	118.9	38.6	85	175.9	57.2	45	233.0	75.7
6	5.7	1.9	66	62.8	20.4	26	119.8	38.9	86	176.9	57.5	46	234.0	76.0
7	6.7	2.2	67	63.7	20.7	27	120.8	39.2	87	177.8	57.8	47	234.9	76.3
8	7.6	2.5	68	64.7	21.0	28	121.7	39.6	88	178.8	58.1	48	235.9	76.6
9	8.6	2.8	69	65.6	21.3	29	122.7	39.9	89	179.7	58.4	49	236.8	76.9
10	9.5	3.1	70	66.6	21.6	30	123.6	40.2	90	180.7	58.7	50	237.8	77.3
11	10.5	3.4	71	67.5	21.9	131	124.6	40.5	191	181.7	59.0	251	238.7	77.6
12	11.4	3.7	72	68.5	22.2	32	125.5	40.8	92	182.6	59.3	52	239.7	77.9
13	12.4	4.0	73	69.4	22.6	33	126.5	41.1	93	183.6	59.6	53	240.6	78.2
14	13.3	4.3	74	70.4	22.9	34	127.4	41.4	94	184.5	59.9	54	241.6	78.5
15	14.3	4.6	75	71.3	23.2	35	128.4	41.7	95	185.5	60.3	55	242.5	78.8
16	15.2	4.9	76	72.3	23.5	36	129.3	42.0	96	186.4	60.6	56	243.5	79.1
17	16.2	5.3	77	73.2	23.8	37	130.3	42.3	97	187.4	60.9	57	244.4	79.4
18	17.1	5.6	78	74.2	24.1	38	131.2	42.6	98	188.3	61.2	58	245.4	79.7
19	18.1	5.9	79	75.1	24.4	39	132.2	43.0	99	189.3	61.5	59	246.3	80.0
20	19.0	6.2	80	76.1	24.7	40	133.1	43.3	200	190.2	61.8	60	247.3	80.3
21	20.0	6.5	81	77.0	25.0	141	134.1	43.6	201	191.2	62.1	261	248.2	80.7
22	20.9	6.8	82	78.0	25.3	42	135.1	43.9	02	192.1	62.4	62	249.2	81.0
23	21.9	7.1	83	78.9	25.6	43	136.0	44.2	03	193.1	62.7	63	250.1	81.3
24	22.8	7.4	84	79.9	26.0	44	137.0	44.5	04	194.0	63.0	64	251.1	81.6
25	23.8	7.7	85	80.8	26.3	45	137.9	44.8	05	195.0	63.3	65	252.0	81.9
26	24.7	8.0	86	81.8	26.6	46	138.9	45.1	06	195.9	63.7	66	253.0	82.2
27	25.7	8.3	87	82.7	26.9	47	139.8	45.4	07	196.9	64.0	67	253.9	82.5
28	26.6	8.7	88	83.7	27.2	48	140.8	45.7	08	197.8	64.3	68	254.9	82.8
29	27.6	9.0	89	84.6	27.5	49	141.7	46.0	09	198.8	64.6	69	255.8	83.1
30	28.5	9.3	90	85.6	27.8	50	142.7	46.4	10	199.7	64.9	70	256.8	83.4
31	29.5	9.6	91	86.5	28.1	151	143.6	46.7	211	200.7	65.2	271	257.7	83.7
32	30.4	9.9	92	87.5	28.4	52	144.6	47.0	12	201.6	65.5	72	258.7	84.1
33	31.4	10.2	93	88.4	28.7	53	145.5	47.3	13	202.6	65.8	73	259.6	84.4
34	32.3	10.5	94	89.4	29.0	54	146.5	47.6	14	203.5	66.1	74	260.6	84.7
35	33.3	10.8	95	90.4	29.4	55	147.4	47.9	15	204.5	66.4	75	261.5	85.0
36	34.2	11.1	96	91.3	29.7	56	148.4	48.2	16	205.4	66.7	76	262.5	85.3
37	35.2	11.4	97	92.3	30.0	57	149.3	48.5	17	206.4	67.1	77	263.4	85.6
38	36.1	11.7	98	93.2	30.3	58	150.3	48.8	18	207.3	67.4	78	264.4	85.9
39	37.1	12.1	99	94.2	30.6	59	151.2	49.1	19	208.3	67.7	79	265.3	86.2
40	38.0	12.4	100	95.1	30.9	60	152.2	49.4	20	209.2	68.0	80	266.3	86.5
41	39.0	12.7	101	96.1	31.2	161	153.1	49.8	221	210.2	68.3	281	267.2	86.8
42	39.9	13.0	02	97.0	31.5	62	154.1	50.1	22	211.1	68.6	82	268.2	87.1
43	40.9	13.3	03	98.0	31.8	63	155.0	50.4	23	212.1	68.9	83	269.1	87.5
44	41.8	13.6	04	98.9	32.1	64	156.0	50.7	24	213.0	69.2	84	270.1	87.8
45	42.8	13.9	05	99.9	32.4	65	156.9	51.0	25	214.0	69.5	85	271.1	88.1
46	43.7	14.2	06	100.8	32.8	66	157.9	51.3	26	214.9	69.8	86	272.0	88.4
47	44.7	14.5	07	101.8	33.1	67	158.8	51.6	27	215.9	70.1	87	273.0	88.7
48	45.7	14.8	08	102.7	33.4	68	159.8	51.9	28	216.8	70.5	88	273.9	89.0
49	46.6	15.1	09	103.7	33.7	69	160.7	52.2	29	217.8	70.8	89	274.9	89.3
50	47.6	15.5	10	104.6	34.0	70	161.7	52.5	30	218.7	71.1	90	275.8	89.6
51	48.5	15.8	111	105.6	34.3	171	162.6	52.8	231	219.7	71.4	291	276.8	89.9
52	49.5	16.1	12	106.5	34.6	72	163.6	53.2	32	220.6	71.7	92	277.7	90.2
53	50.4	16.4	13	107.5	34.9	73	164.5	53.5	33	221.6	72.0	93	278.7	90.5
54	51.4	16.7	14	108.4	35.2	74	165.5	53.8	34	222.5	72.3	94	279.6	90.9
55	52.3	17.0	15	109.4	35.5	75	166.4	54.1	35	223.5	72.6	95	280.6	91.2
56	53.3	17.3	16	110.3	35.8	76	167.4	54.4	36	224.4	72.9	96	281.5	91.5
57	54.2	17.6	17	111.3	36.2	77	168.3	54.7	37	225.4	73.2	97	282.5	91.8
58	55.2	17.9	18	112.2	36.5	78	169.3	55.0	38	226.4	73.5	98	283.4	92.1
59	56.1	18.2	19	113.2	36.8	79	170.2	55.3	39	227.3	73.9	99	284.4	92.4
60	57.1	18.5	20	114.1	37.1	80	171.2	55.6	40	228.3	74.2	300	285.3	92.7
Dist.	Dep.	D. Lat.	Dist.	Dep.	D. Lat.	Dist.	Dep.	D. Lat.	Dist.	Dep.	D. Lat.	Dist.	Dep.	D. Lat.

288°	072°
252°	108°

72°

Dist.	D. Lat.	Dep.
N.	N x Cos.	N x Sin.
Hypotenuse	Side Adj.	Side Opp.

TABLE 4

Traverse **18°** Table

342°	018°
198°	162°

Dist.	D. Lat.	Dep.	Dist.	D. Lat.	Dep.	Dist.	D. Lat.	Dep.	Dist.	D. Lat.	Dep.	Dist.	D. Lat.	Dep.
301	286.3	93.0	361	343.3	111.6	421	400.4	130.1	481	457.5	148.6	541	514.5	167.2
02	287.2	93.3	62	344.3	111.9	22	401.3	130.4	82	458.4	148.9	42	515.5	167.5
03	288.2	93.6	63	345.2	112.2	23	402.3	130.7	83	459.4	149.3	43	516.4	167.8
04	289.1	93.9	64	346.2	112.5	24	403.2	131.0	84	460.3	149.6	44	517.4	168.1
05	290.1	94.3	65	347.1	112.8	25	404.2	131.3	85	461.3	149.9	45	518.3	168.4
06	291.0	94.6	66	348.1	113.1	26	405.2	131.6	86	462.2	150.2	46	519.3	168.7
07	292.0	94.9	67	349.0	113.4	27	406.1	132.0	87	463.2	150.5	47	520.2	169.0
08	292.9	95.2	68	350.0	113.7	28	407.1	132.3	88	464.1	150.8	48	521.2	169.3
09	293.9	95.5	69	350.9	114.0	29	408.0	132.6	89	465.1	151.1	49	522.1	169.7
10	294.8	95.8	70	351.9	114.3	30	409.0	132.9	90	466.0	151.4	50	523.1	170.0
311	295.8	96.1	371	352.8	114.6	431	409.9	133.2	491	467.0	151.7	551	524.0	170.3
12	296.7	96.4	72	353.8	115.0	32	410.9	133.5	92	467.9	152.0	52	525.0	170.6
13	297.7	96.7	73	354.7	115.3	33	411.8	133.8	93	468.9	152.3	53	525.9	170.9
14	298.6	97.0	74	355.7	115.6	34	412.8	134.1	94	469.8	152.7	54	526.9	171.2
15	299.6	97.3	75	356.6	115.9	35	413.7	134.4	95	470.8	153.0	55	527.8	171.5
16	300.5	97.6	76	357.6	116.2	36	414.7	134.7	96	471.7	153.3	56	528.8	171.8
17	301.5	98.0	77	358.5	116.5	37	415.6	135.0	97	472.7	153.6	57	529.7	172.1
18	302.4	98.3	78	359.5	116.8	38	416.6	135.3	98	473.6	153.9	58	530.7	172.4
19	303.4	98.6	79	360.5	117.1	39	417.5	135.7	99	474.6	154.2	59	531.6	172.7
20	304.3	98.9	80	361.4	117.4	40	418.5	136.0	500	475.5	154.5	60	532.6	173.0
321	305.3	99.2	381	362.4	117.7	441	419.4	136.3	501	476.5	154.8	561	533.5	173.4
22	306.2	99.5	82	363.3	118.0	42	420.4	136.6	02	477.4	155.1	62	534.5	173.7
23	307.2	99.8	83	364.3	118.4	43	421.3	136.9	03	478.4	155.4	63	535.4	174.0
24	308.1	100.1	84	365.2	118.7	44	422.3	137.2	04	479.3	155.7	64	536.4	174.3
25	309.1	100.4	85	366.2	119.0	45	423.2	137.5	05	480.3	156.1	65	537.3	174.6
26	310.0	100.7	86	367.1	119.3	46	424.2	137.8	06	481.2	156.4	66	538.3	174.9
27	311.0	101.0	87	368.1	119.6	47	425.1	138.1	07	482.2	156.7	67	539.2	175.2
28	311.9	101.4	88	369.0	119.9	48	426.1	138.4	08	483.1	157.0	68	540.2	175.5
29	312.9	101.7	89	370.0	120.2	49	427.0	138.7	09	484.1	157.3	69	541.2	175.8
30	313.8	102.0	90	370.9	120.5	50	428.0	139.1	10	485.0	157.6	70	542.1	176.1
331	314.8	102.3	391	371.9	120.8	451	428.9	139.4	511	486.0	157.9	571	543.1	176.4
32	315.8	102.6	92	372.8	121.1	52	429.9	139.7	12	486.9	158.2	72	544.0	176.8
33	316.7	102.9	93	373.8	121.4	53	430.8	140.0	13	487.9	158.5	73	545.0	177.1
34	317.7	103.2	94	374.7	121.8	54	431.8	140.3	14	488.8	158.8	74	545.9	177.4
35	318.6	103.5	95	375.7	122.1	55	432.7	140.6	15	489.8	159.1	75	546.9	177.7
36	319.6	103.8	96	376.6	122.4	56	433.7	140.9	16	490.7	159.5	76	547.8	178.0
37	320.5	104.1	97	377.6	122.7	57	434.6	141.2	17	491.7	159.8	77	548.8	178.3
38	321.5	104.4	98	378.5	123.0	58	435.6	141.5	18	492.6	160.1	78	549.7	178.6
39	322.4	104.8	99	379.5	123.3	59	436.5	141.8	19	493.6	160.4	79	550.7	178.9
40	323.4	105.1	400	380.4	123.6	60	437.5	142.1	20	494.5	160.7	80	551.6	179.2
341	324.3	105.4	401	381.4	123.9	461	438.4	142.5	521	495.5	161.0	581	552.6	179.5
42	325.3	105.7	02	382.3	124.2	62	439.4	142.8	22	496.5	161.3	82	553.5	179.8
43	326.2	106.0	03	383.3	124.5	63	440.3	143.1	23	497.4	161.6	83	554.5	180.2
44	327.2	106.3	04	384.2	124.8	64	441.3	143.4	24	498.4	161.9	84	555.4	180.5
45	328.1	106.6	05	385.2	125.2	65	442.2	143.7	25	499.3	162.2	85	556.4	180.8
46	329.1	106.9	06	386.1	125.5	66	443.2	144.0	26	500.3	162.5	86	557.3	181.1
47	330.0	107.2	07	387.1	125.8	67	444.1	144.3	27	501.2	162.9	87	558.3	181.4
48	331.0	107.5	08	388.0	126.1	68	445.1	144.6	28	502.2	163.2	88	559.2	181.7
49	331.9	107.8	09	389.0	126.4	69	446.0	144.9	29	503.1	163.5	89	560.2	182.0
50	332.9	108.2	10	389.9	126.7	70	447.0	145.2	30	504.1	163.8	90	561.1	182.3
351	333.8	108.5	411	390.9	127.0	471	447.9	145.5	531	505.0	164.1	591	562.1	182.6
52	334.8	108.8	12	391.8	127.3	72	448.9	145.9	32	506.0	164.4	92	563.0	182.9
53	335.7	109.1	13	392.8	127.6	73	449.8	146.2	33	506.9	164.7	93	564.0	183.2
54	336.7	109.4	14	393.7	127.9	74	450.8	146.5	34	507.9	165.0	94	564.9	183.6
55	337.6	109.7	15	394.7	128.2	75	451.8	146.8	35	508.8	165.3	95	565.9	183.9
56	338.6	110.0	16	395.6	128.6	76	452.7	147.1	36	509.8	165.6	96	566.8	184.2
57	339.5	110.3	17	396.6	128.9	77	453.7	147.4	37	510.7	165.9	97	567.8	184.5
58	340.5	110.6	18	397.5	129.2	78	454.6	147.7	38	511.7	166.3	98	568.7	184.8
59	341.4	110.9	19	398.5	129.5	79	455.6	148.0	39	512.6	166.6	99	569.7	185.1
60	342.4	111.2	20	399.4	129.8	80	456.5	148.3	40	513.6	166.9	600	570.6	185.4
Dist.	Dep.	D. Lat.	Dist.	Dep.	D. Lat.	Dist.	Dep.	D. Lat.	Dist.	Dep.	D. Lat.	Dist.	Dep.	D. Lat.

Dist.	D. Lat.	Dep.
D Lo	Dep.	
	m	D Lo

72°

288°	072°
252°	108°

TABLE 4

19°

Traverse Table

341° | 019° / 199° | 161°														341° | 019° / 199° | 161°
Dist.	D. Lat.	Dep.	Dist.	D. Lat.	Dep.	Dist.	D. Lat.	Dep.	Dist.	D. Lat.	Dep.	Dist.	D. Lat.	Dep.
1	0.9	0.3	61	57.7	19.9	121	114.4	39.4	181	171.1	58.9	241	227.9	78.5
2	1.9	0.7	62	58.6	20.2	22	115.4	39.7	82	172.1	59.3	42	228.8	78.8
3	2.8	1.0	63	59.6	20.5	23	116.3	40.0	83	173.0	59.6	43	229.8	79.1
4	3.8	1.3	64	60.5	20.8	24	117.2	40.4	84	174.0	59.9	44	230.7	79.4
5	4.7	1.6	65	61.5	21.2	25	118.2	40.7	85	174.9	60.2	45	231.7	79.8
6	5.7	2.0	66	62.4	21.5	26	119.1	41.0	86	175.9	60.6	46	232.6	80.1
7	6.6	2.3	67	63.3	21.8	27	120.1	41.3	87	176.8	60.9	47	233.5	80.4
8	7.6	2.6	68	64.3	22.1	28	121.0	41.7	88	177.8	61.2	48	234.5	80.7
9	8.5	2.9	69	65.2	22.5	29	122.0	42.0	89	178.7	61.5	49	235.4	81.1
10	9.5	3.3	70	66.2	22.8	30	122.9	42.3	90	179.6	61.9	50	236.4	81.4
11	10.4	3.6	71	67.1	23.1	131	123.9	42.6	191	180.6	62.2	251	237.3	81.7
12	11.3	3.9	72	68.1	23.4	32	124.8	43.0	92	181.5	62.5	52	238.3	82.0
13	12.3	4.2	73	69.0	23.8	33	125.8	43.3	93	182.5	62.8	53	239.2	82.4
14	13.2	4.6	74	70.0	24.1	34	126.7	43.6	94	183.4	63.2	54	240.2	82.7
15	14.2	4.9	75	70.9	24.4	35	127.6	44.0	95	184.4	63.5	55	241.1	83.0
16	15.1	5.2	76	71.9	24.7	36	128.6	44.3	96	185.3	63.8	56	242.1	83.3
17	16.1	5.5	77	72.8	25.1	37	129.5	44.6	97	186.3	64.1	57	243.0	83.7
18	17.0	5.9	78	73.8	25.4	38	130.5	44.9	98	187.2	64.5	58	243.9	84.0
19	18.0	6.2	79	74.7	25.7	39	131.4	45.3	99	188.2	64.8	59	244.9	84.3
20	18.9	6.5	80	75.6	26.0	40	132.4	45.6	200	189.1	65.1	60	245.8	84.6
21	19.9	6.8	81	76.6	26.4	141	133.3	45.9	201	190.0	65.4	261	246.8	85.0
22	20.8	7.2	82	77.5	26.7	42	134.3	46.2	02	191.0	65.8	62	247.7	85.3
23	21.7	7.5	83	78.5	27.0	43	135.2	46.6	03	191.9	66.1	63	248.7	85.6
24	22.7	7.8	84	79.4	27.3	44	136.2	46.9	04	192.9	66.4	64	249.6	85.9
25	23.6	8.1	85	80.4	27.7	45	137.1	47.2	05	193.8	66.7	65	250.6	86.3
26	24.6	8.5	86	81.3	28.0	46	138.0	47.5	06	194.8	67.1	66	251.5	86.6
27	25.5	8.8	87	82.3	28.3	47	139.0	47.9	07	195.7	67.4	67	252.5	86.9
28	26.5	9.1	88	83.2	28.6	48	139.9	48.2	08	196.7	67.7	68	253.4	87.3
29	27.4	9.4	89	84.2	29.0	49	140.9	48.5	09	197.6	68.0	69	254.3	87.6
30	28.4	9.8	90	85.1	29.3	50	141.8	48.8	10	198.6	68.4	70	255.3	87.9
31	29.3	10.1	91	86.0	29.6	151	142.8	49.2	211	199.5	68.7	271	256.2	88.2
32	30.3	10.4	92	87.0	30.0	52	143.7	49.5	12	200.4	69.0	72	257.2	88.6
33	31.2	10.7	93	87.9	30.3	53	144.7	49.8	13	201.4	69.3	73	258.1	88.9
34	32.1	11.1	94	88.9	30.6	54	145.6	50.1	14	202.3	69.7	74	259.1	89.2
35	33.1	11.4	95	89.8	30.9	55	146.6	50.5	15	203.3	70.0	75	260.0	89.5
36	34.0	11.7	96	90.8	31.3	56	147.5	50.8	16	204.2	70.3	76	261.0	89.9
37	35.0	12.0	97	91.7	31.6	57	148.4	51.1	17	205.2	70.6	77	261.9	90.2
38	35.9	12.4	98	92.7	31.9	58	149.4	51.4	18	206.1	71.0	78	262.9	90.5
39	36.9	12.7	99	93.6	32.2	59	150.3	51.8	19	207.1	71.3	79	263.8	90.8
40	37.8	13.0	100	94.6	32.6	60	151.3	52.1	20	208.0	71.6	80	264.7	91.2
41	38.8	13.3	101	95.5	32.9	161	152.2	52.4	221	209.0	72.0	281	265.7	91.5
42	39.7	13.7	02	96.4	33.2	62	153.2	52.7	22	209.9	72.3	82	266.6	91.8
43	40.7	14.0	03	97.4	33.5	63	154.1	53.1	23	210.9	72.6	83	267.6	92.1
44	41.6	14.3	04	98.3	33.9	64	155.1	53.4	24	211.8	72.9	84	268.5	92.5
45	42.5	14.7	05	99.3	34.2	65	156.0	53.7	25	212.7	73.3	85	269.5	92.8
46	43.5	15.0	06	100.2	34.5	66	157.0	54.0	26	213.7	73.6	86	270.4	93.1
47	44.4	15.3	07	101.2	34.8	67	157.9	54.4	27	214.6	73.9	87	271.4	93.4
48	45.4	15.6	08	102.1	35.2	68	158.8	54.7	28	215.6	74.2	88	272.3	93.8
49	46.3	16.0	09	103.1	35.5	69	159.8	55.0	29	216.5	74.6	89	273.3	94.1
50	47.3	16.3	10	104.0	35.8	70	160.7	55.3	30	217.5	74.9	90	274.2	94.4
51	48.2	16.6	111	105.0	36.1	171	161.7	55.7	231	218.4	75.2	291	275.1	94.7
52	49.2	16.9	12	105.9	36.5	72	162.6	56.0	32	219.4	75.5	92	276.1	95.1
53	50.1	17.3	13	106.8	36.8	73	163.6	56.3	33	220.3	75.9	93	277.0	95.4
54	51.1	17.6	14	107.8	37.1	74	164.5	56.6	34	221.3	76.2	94	278.0	95.7
55	52.0	17.9	15	108.7	37.4	75	165.5	57.0	35	222.2	76.5	95	278.9	96.0
56	52.9	18.2	16	109.7	37.8	76	166.4	57.3	36	223.1	76.8	96	279.9	96.4
57	53.9	18.6	17	110.6	38.1	77	167.4	57.6	37	224.1	77.2	97	280.8	96.7
58	54.8	18.9	18	111.6	38.4	78	168.3	58.0	38	225.0	77.5	98	281.8	97.0
59	55.8	19.2	19	112.5	38.7	79	169.2	58.3	39	226.0	77.8	99	282.7	97.3
60	56.7	19.5	20	113.5	39.1	80	170.2	58.6	40	226.9	78.1	300	283.7	97.7
Dist.	Dep.	D. Lat.	Dist.	Dep.	D. Lat.	Dist.	Dep.	D. Lat.	Dist.	Dep.	D. Lat.	Dist.	Dep.	D. Lat.

289° | 071°
251° | 109°

71°

Dist.	D. Lat.	Dep.
N.	N x Cos.	N x Sin.
Hypotenuse	Side Adj.	Side Opp.

TABLE 4

19°

Traverse Table

341° | 019° / 199° | 161°														341° | 019° / 199° | 161°
Dist.	D. Lat.	Dep.	Dist.	D. Lat.	Dep.	Dist.	D. Lat.	Dep.	Dist.	D. Lat.	Dep.	Dist.	D. Lat.	Dep.
301	284.6	98.0	361	341.3	117.5	421	398.1	137.1	481	454.8	156.6	541	511.5	176.1
02	285.5	98.3	62	342.3	117.9	22	399.0	137.4	82	455.7	156.9	42	512.5	176.5
03	286.5	98.6	63	343.2	118.2	23	400.0	137.7	83	456.7	157.2	43	513.4	176.8
04	287.4	99.0	64	344.2	118.5	24	400.9	138.0	84	457.6	157.6	44	514.4	177.1
05	288.4	99.3	65	345.1	118.8	25	401.8	138.4	85	458.6	157.9	45	515.3	177.4
06	289.3	99.6	66	346.1	119.2	26	402.8	138.7	86	459.5	158.2	46	516.3	177.8
07	290.3	99.9	67	347.0	119.5	27	403.7	139.0	87	460.5	158.6	47	517.2	178.1
08	291.2	100.3	68	348.0	119.8	28	404.7	139.3	88	461.4	158.9	48	518.1	178.4
09	292.2	100.6	69	348.9	120.1	29	405.6	139.7	89	462.4	159.2	49	519.1	178.7
10	293.1	100.9	70	349.8	120.5	30	406.6	140.0	90	463.3	159.5	50	520.0	179.1
311	294.1	101.3	371	350.8	120.8	431	407.5	140.3	491	464.2	159.9	551	521.0	179.4
12	295.0	101.6	72	351.7	121.1	32	408.5	140.6	92	465.2	160.2	52	521.9	179.7
13	295.9	101.9	73	352.7	121.4	33	409.4	141.0	93	466.1	160.5	53	522.9	180.0
14	296.9	102.2	74	353.6	121.8	34	410.4	141.3	94	467.1	160.8	54	523.8	180.4
15	297.8	102.6	75	354.6	122.1	35	411.3	141.6	95	468.0	161.2	55	524.8	180.7
16	298.8	102.9	76	355.5	122.4	36	412.2	141.9	96	469.0	161.5	56	525.7	181.0
17	299.7	103.2	77	356.5	122.7	37	413.2	142.3	97	469.9	161.8	57	526.7	181.3
18	300.7	103.5	78	357.4	123.1	38	414.1	142.6	98	470.9	162.1	58	527.6	181.7
19	301.6	103.9	79	358.4	123.4	39	415.1	142.9	99	471.8	162.5	59	528.5	182.0
20	302.6	104.2	80	359.3	123.7	40	416.0	143.2	500	472.8	162.8	60	529.5	182.3
321	303.5	104.5	381	360.2	124.0	441	417.0	143.6	501	473.7	163.1	561	530.4	182.6
22	304.5	104.8	82	361.2	124.4	42	417.9	143.9	02	474.7	163.4	62	531.4	183.0
23	305.4	105.2	83	362.1	124.7	43	418.9	144.2	03	475.6	163.8	63	532.3	183.3
24	306.3	105.5	84	363.1	125.0	44	419.8	144.6	04	476.5	164.1	64	533.3	183.6
25	307.3	105.8	85	364.0	125.3	45	420.8	144.9	05	477.5	164.4	65	534.2	183.9
26	308.2	106.1	86	365.0	125.7	46	421.7	145.2	06	478.4	164.7	66	535.2	184.3
27	309.2	106.5	87	365.9	126.0	47	422.6	145.5	07	479.4	165.1	67	536.1	184.6
28	310.1	106.8	88	366.9	126.3	48	423.6	145.9	08	480.3	165.4	68	537.1	184.9
29	311.1	107.1	89	367.8	126.6	49	424.5	146.2	09	481.3	165.7	69	538.0	185.2
30	312.0	107.4	90	368.8	127.0	50	425.5	146.5	10	482.2	166.0	70	538.9	185.6
331	313.0	107.8	391	369.7	127.3	451	426.4	146.8	511	483.2	166.4	571	539.9	185.9
32	313.9	108.1	92	370.6	127.6	52	427.4	147.2	12	484.1	166.7	72	540.8	186.2
33	314.9	108.4	93	371.6	127.9	53	428.3	147.5	13	485.1	167.0	73	541.8	186.6
34	315.8	108.7	94	372.5	128.3	54	429.3	147.8	14	486.0	167.3	74	542.7	186.9
35	316.7	109.1	95	373.5	128.6	55	430.2	148.1	15	486.9	167.7	75	543.7	187.2
36	317.7	109.4	96	374.4	128.9	56	431.2	148.5	16	487.9	168.0	76	544.6	187.5
37	318.6	109.7	97	375.4	129.3	57	432.1	148.8	17	488.8	168.3	77	545.6	187.9
38	319.6	110.0	98	376.3	129.6	58	433.0	149.1	18	489.8	168.6	78	546.5	188.2
39	320.5	110.4	99	377.3	129.9	59	434.0	149.4	19	490.7	169.0	79	547.5	188.5
40	321.5	110.7	400	378.2	130.2	60	434.9	149.8	20	491.7	169.3	80	548.4	188.8
341	322.4	111.0	401	379.2	130.6	461	435.9	150.1	521	492.6	169.6	581	549.3	189.2
42	323.4	111.3	02	380.1	130.9	62	436.8	150.4	22	493.6	169.9	82	550.3	189.5
43	324.3	111.7	03	381.0	131.2	63	437.8	150.7	23	494.5	170.3	83	551.2	189.8
44	325.3	112.0	04	382.0	131.5	64	438.7	151.1	24	495.5	170.6	84	552.2	190.1
45	326.2	112.3	05	382.9	131.9	65	439.7	151.4	25	496.4	170.9	85	553.1	190.5
46	327.1	112.6	06	383.9	132.2	66	440.6	151.7	26	497.3	171.2	86	554.1	190.8
47	328.1	113.0	07	384.8	132.5	67	441.6	152.0	27	498.3	171.6	87	555.0	191.1
48	329.0	113.3	08	385.8	132.8	68	442.5	152.4	28	499.2	171.9	88	556.0	191.4
49	330.0	113.6	09	386.7	133.2	69	443.4	152.7	29	500.2	172.2	89	556.9	191.8
50	330.9	113.9	10	387.7	133.5	70	444.4	153.0	30	501.1	172.6	90	557.9	192.1
351	331.9	114.3	411	388.6	133.8	471	445.3	153.3	531	502.1	172.9	591	558.8	192.4
52	332.8	114.6	12	389.6	134.1	72	446.3	153.7	32	503.0	173.2	92	559.7	192.7
53	333.8	114.9	13	390.5	134.5	73	447.2	154.0	33	504.0	173.5	93	560.7	193.1
54	334.7	115.3	14	391.4	134.8	74	448.2	154.3	34	504.9	173.9	94	561.6	193.4
55	335.7	115.6	15	392.4	135.1	75	449.1	154.6	35	505.9	174.2	95	562.6	193.7
56	336.6	115.9	16	393.3	135.4	76	450.1	155.0	36	506.8	174.5	96	563.5	194.0
57	337.6	116.2	17	394.3	135.8	77	451.0	155.3	37	507.7	174.8	97	564.5	194.4
58	338.5	116.6	18	395.2	136.1	78	452.0	155.6	38	508.7	175.2	98	565.4	194.7
59	339.4	116.9	19	396.2	136.4	79	452.9	155.9	39	509.6	175.5	99	566.4	195.0
60	340.4	117.2	20	397.1	136.7	80	453.8	156.3	40	510.6	175.8	600	567.3	195.3
Dist.	Dep.	D. Lat.	Dist.	Dep.	D. Lat.	Dist.	Dep.	D. Lat.	Dist.	Dep.	D. Lat.	Dist.	Dep.	D. Lat.

Dist.	D. Lat.	Dep.
D Lo	Dep.	
	m	D Lo

71°

289° | 071°
251° | 109°

TABLE 4

20° Traverse Table

340° | 020° — 200° | 160°

Dist.	D. Lat.	Dep.	Dist.	D. Lat.	Dep.	Dist.	D. Lat.	Dep.	Dist.	D. Lat.	Dep.	Dist.	D. Lat.	Dep.
1	0.9	0.3	61	57.3	20.9	121	113.7	41.4	181	170.1	61.9	241	226.5	82.4
2	1.9	0.7	62	58.3	21.2	22	114.6	41.7	82	171.0	62.2	42	227.4	82.8
3	2.8	1.0	63	59.2	21.5	23	115.6	42.1	83	172.0	62.6	43	228.3	83.1
4	3.8	1.4	64	60.1	21.9	24	116.5	42.4	84	172.9	62.9	44	229.3	83.5
5	4.7	1.7	65	61.1	22.2	25	117.5	42.8	85	173.8	63.3	45	230.2	83.8
6	5.6	2.1	66	62.0	22.6	26	118.4	43.1	86	174.8	63.6	46	231.2	84.1
7	6.6	2.4	67	63.0	22.9	27	119.3	43.4	87	175.7	64.0	47	232.1	84.5
8	7.5	2.7	68	63.9	23.3	28	120.3	43.8	88	176.7	64.3	48	233.0	84.8
9	8.5	3.1	69	64.8	23.6	29	121.2	44.1	89	177.6	64.6	49	234.0	85.2
10	9.4	3.4	70	65.8	23.9	30	122.2	44.5	90	178.5	65.0	50	234.9	85.5
11	10.3	3.8	71	66.7	24.3	131	123.1	44.8	191	179.5	65.3	251	235.9	85.8
12	11.3	4.1	72	67.7	24.6	32	124.0	45.1	92	180.4	65.7	52	236.8	86.2
13	12.2	4.4	73	68.6	25.0	33	125.0	45.5	93	181.4	66.0	53	237.7	86.5
14	13.2	4.8	74	69.5	25.3	34	125.9	45.8	94	182.3	66.4	54	238.7	86.9
15	14.1	5.1	75	70.5	25.7	35	126.9	46.2	95	183.2	66.7	55	239.6	87.2
16	15.0	5.5	76	71.4	26.0	36	127.8	46.5	96	184.2	67.0	56	240.6	87.6
17	16.0	5.8	77	72.4	26.3	37	128.7	46.9	97	185.1	67.4	57	241.5	87.9
18	16.9	6.2	78	73.3	26.7	38	129.7	47.2	98	186.1	67.7	58	242.4	88.2
19	17.9	6.5	79	74.2	27.0	39	130.6	47.5	99	187.0	68.1	59	243.4	88.6
20	18.8	6.8	80	75.2	27.4	40	131.6	47.9	200	187.9	68.4	60	244.3	88.9
21	19.7	7.2	81	76.1	27.7	141	132.5	48.2	201	188.9	68.7	261	245.3	89.3
22	20.7	7.5	82	77.1	28.0	42	133.4	48.6	02	189.8	69.1	62	246.2	89.6
23	21.6	7.9	83	78.0	28.4	43	134.4	48.9	03	190.8	69.4	63	247.1	90.0
24	22.6	8.2	84	78.9	28.7	44	135.3	49.3	04	191.7	69.8	64	248.1	90.3
25	23.5	8.6	85	79.9	29.1	45	136.3	49.6	05	192.6	70.1	65	249.0	90.6
26	24.4	8.9	86	80.8	29.4	46	137.2	49.9	06	193.6	70.5	66	250.0	91.0
27	25.4	9.2	87	81.8	29.8	47	138.1	50.3	07	194.5	70.8	67	250.9	91.3
28	26.3	9.6	88	82.7	30.1	48	139.1	50.6	08	195.5	71.1	68	251.8	91.7
29	27.3	9.9	89	83.6	30.4	49	140.0	51.0	09	196.4	71.5	69	252.8	92.0
30	28.2	10.3	90	84.6	30.8	50	141.0	51.3	10	197.3	71.8	70	253.7	92.3
31	29.1	10.6	91	85.5	31.1	151	141.9	51.6	211	198.3	72.2	271	254.7	92.7
32	30.1	10.9	92	86.5	31.5	52	142.8	52.0	12	199.2	72.5	72	255.6	93.0
33	31.0	11.3	93	87.4	31.8	53	143.8	52.3	13	200.2	72.9	73	256.5	93.4
34	31.9	11.6	94	88.3	32.1	54	144.7	52.7	14	201.1	73.2	74	257.5	93.7
35	32.9	12.0	95	89.3	32.5	55	145.7	53.0	15	202.0	73.5	75	258.4	94.1
36	33.8	12.3	96	90.2	32.8	56	146.6	53.4	16	203.0	73.9	76	259.4	94.4
37	34.8	12.7	97	91.2	33.2	57	147.5	53.7	17	203.9	74.2	77	260.3	94.7
38	35.7	13.0	98	92.1	33.5	58	148.5	54.0	18	204.9	74.6	78	261.2	95.1
39	36.6	13.3	99	93.0	33.9	59	149.4	54.4	19	205.8	74.9	79	262.2	95.4
40	37.6	13.7	100	94.0	34.2	60	150.4	54.7	20	206.7	75.2	80	263.1	95.8
41	38.5	14.0	101	94.9	34.5	161	151.3	55.1	221	207.7	75.6	281	264.1	96.1
42	39.5	14.4	02	95.8	34.9	62	152.2	55.4	22	208.6	75.9	82	265.0	96.4
43	40.4	14.7	03	96.8	35.2	63	153.2	55.7	23	209.6	76.3	83	265.9	96.8
44	41.3	15.0	04	97.7	35.6	64	154.1	56.1	24	210.5	76.6	84	266.9	97.1
45	42.3	15.4	05	98.7	35.9	65	155.0	56.4	25	211.4	77.0	85	267.8	97.5
46	43.2	15.7	06	99.6	36.3	66	156.0	56.8	26	212.4	77.3	86	268.8	97.8
47	44.2	16.1	07	100.5	36.6	67	156.9	57.1	27	213.3	77.6	87	269.7	98.2
48	45.1	16.4	08	101.5	36.9	68	157.9	57.5	28	214.2	78.0	88	270.6	98.5
49	46.0	16.8	09	102.4	37.3	69	158.8	57.8	29	215.2	78.3	89	271.6	98.8
50	47.0	17.1	10	103.4	37.6	70	159.7	58.1	30	216.1	78.7	90	272.5	99.2
51	47.9	17.4	111	104.3	38.0	171	160.7	58.5	231	217.1	79.0	291	273.5	99.5
52	48.9	17.8	12	105.2	38.3	72	161.6	58.8	32	218.0	79.3	92	274.4	99.9
53	49.8	18.1	13	106.2	38.6	73	162.6	59.2	33	218.9	79.7	93	275.3	100.2
54	50.7	18.5	14	107.1	39.0	74	163.5	59.5	34	219.9	80.0	94	276.3	100.6
55	51.7	18.8	15	108.1	39.3	75	164.4	59.9	35	220.8	80.4	95	277.2	100.9
56	52.6	19.2	16	109.0	39.7	76	165.4	60.2	36	221.8	80.7	96	278.1	101.2
57	53.6	19.5	17	109.9	40.0	77	166.3	60.5	37	222.7	81.1	97	279.1	101.6
58	54.5	19.8	18	110.9	40.4	78	167.3	60.9	38	223.6	81.4	98	280.0	101.9
59	55.4	20.2	19	111.8	40.7	79	168.2	61.2	39	224.6	81.7	99	281.0	102.3
60	56.4	20.5	20	112.8	41.0	80	169.1	61.6	40	225.5	82.1	300	281.9	102.6
Dist.	Dep.	D. Lat.	Dist.	Dep.	D. Lat.	Dist.	Dep.	D. Lat.	Dist.	Dep.	D. Lat.	Dist.	Dep.	D. Lat.

290° | 070° — 250° | 110°

70°

Dist.	D. Lat.	Dep.
N.	N x Cos.	N x Sin.
Hypotenuse	Side Adj.	Side Opp.

TABLE 4

20° Traverse Table

340° | 020° — 200° | 160°

Dist.	D. Lat.	Dep.	Dist.	D. Lat.	Dep.	Dist.	D. Lat.	Dep.	Dist.	D. Lat.	Dep.	Dist.	D. Lat.	Dep.
301	282.8	102.9	361	339.2	123.5	421	395.6	144.0	481	452.0	164.5	541	508.4	185.0
02	283.8	103.3	62	340.2	123.8	22	396.6	144.3	82	452.9	164.9	42	509.3	185.4
03	284.7	103.6	63	341.1	124.2	23	397.5	144.7	83	453.9	165.2	43	510.3	185.7
04	285.7	104.0	64	342.0	124.5	24	398.4	145.0	84	454.8	165.5	44	511.2	186.1
05	286.6	104.3	65	343.0	124.8	25	399.4	145.4	85	455.8	165.9	45	512.1	186.4
06	287.5	104.7	66	343.9	125.2	26	400.3	145.7	86	456.7	166.2	46	513.1	186.7
07	288.5	105.0	67	344.9	125.5	27	401.2	146.0	87	457.6	166.6	47	514.0	187.1
08	289.4	105.3	68	345.8	125.9	28	402.2	146.4	88	458.6	166.9	48	515.0	187.4
09	290.4	105.7	69	346.7	126.2	29	403.1	146.7	89	459.5	167.2	49	515.9	187.8
10	291.3	106.0	70	347.7	126.5	30	404.1	147.1	90	460.4	167.6	50	516.8	188.1
311	292.2	106.4	371	348.6	126.9	431	405.0	147.4	491	461.4	167.9	551	517.8	188.5
12	293.2	106.7	72	349.6	127.2	32	405.9	147.8	92	462.3	168.3	52	518.7	188.8
13	294.1	107.1	73	350.5	127.6	33	406.9	148.1	93	463.3	168.6	53	519.7	189.1
14	295.1	107.4	74	351.4	127.9	34	407.8	148.4	94	464.2	169.0	54	520.6	189.5
15	296.0	107.7	75	352.4	128.3	35	408.8	148.8	95	465.1	169.3	55	521.5	189.8
16	296.9	108.1	76	353.3	128.6	36	409.7	149.1	96	466.1	169.6	56	522.5	190.2
17	297.9	108.4	77	354.3	128.9	37	410.6	149.5	97	467.0	170.0	57	523.4	190.5
18	298.8	108.8	78	355.2	129.3	38	411.6	149.8	98	468.0	170.3	58	524.3	190.8
19	299.8	109.1	79	356.1	129.6	39	412.5	150.1	99	468.9	170.7	59	525.3	191.2
20	300.7	109.4	80	357.1	130.0	40	413.5	150.5	500	469.8	171.0	60	526.2	191.5
321	301.6	109.8	381	358.0	130.3	441	414.4	150.8	501	470.8	171.4	561	527.2	191.9
22	302.6	110.1	82	359.0	130.7	42	415.3	151.2	02	471.7	171.7	62	528.1	192.2
23	303.5	110.5	83	359.9	131.0	43	416.3	151.5	03	472.7	172.0	63	529.0	192.6
24	304.5	110.8	84	360.8	131.3	44	417.2	151.9	04	473.6	172.4	64	530.0	192.9
25	305.4	111.2	85	361.8	131.7	45	418.2	152.2	05	474.5	172.7	65	530.9	193.2
26	306.3	111.5	86	362.7	132.0	46	419.1	152.5	06	475.5	173.1	66	531.9	193.6
27	307.3	111.8	87	363.7	132.4	47	420.0	152.9	07	476.4	173.4	67	532.8	193.9
28	308.2	112.2	88	364.6	132.7	48	421.0	153.2	08	477.4	173.7	68	533.7	194.3
29	309.2	112.5	89	365.5	133.0	49	421.9	153.6	09	478.3	174.1	69	534.7	194.6
30	310.1	112.9	90	366.5	133.4	50	422.9	153.9	10	479.2	174.4	70	535.6	195.0
331	311.0	113.2	391	367.4	133.7	451	423.8	154.3	511	480.2	174.8	571	536.6	195.3
32	312.0	113.6	92	368.4	134.1	52	424.7	154.6	12	481.1	175.1	72	537.5	195.6
33	312.9	113.9	93	369.3	134.4	53	425.7	154.9	13	482.1	175.5	73	538.4	196.0
34	313.9	114.2	94	370.2	134.8	54	426.6	155.3	14	483.0	175.8	74	539.4	196.3
35	314.8	114.6	95	371.2	135.1	55	427.6	155.6	15	483.9	176.1	75	540.3	196.7
36	315.7	114.9	96	372.1	135.4	56	428.5	156.0	16	484.9	176.5	76	541.3	197.0
37	316.7	115.3	97	373.1	135.8	57	429.4	156.3	17	485.8	176.8	77	542.2	197.3
38	317.6	115.6	98	374.0	136.1	58	430.4	156.6	18	486.8	177.2	78	543.1	197.7
39	318.6	115.9	99	374.9	136.5	59	431.3	157.0	19	487.7	177.5	79	544.1	198.0
40	319.5	116.3	400	375.9	136.8	60	432.3	157.3	20	488.6	177.9	80	545.0	198.4
341	320.4	116.6	401	376.8	137.2	461	433.2	157.7	521	489.6	178.2	581	546.0	198.7
42	321.4	117.0	02	377.8	137.5	62	434.1	158.0	22	490.5	178.5	82	546.9	199.1
43	322.3	117.3	03	378.7	137.8	63	435.1	158.4	23	491.5	178.9	83	547.8	199.4
44	323.3	117.7	04	379.6	138.2	64	436.0	158.7	24	492.4	179.2	84	548.8	199.7
45	324.2	118.0	05	380.6	138.5	65	437.0	159.0	25	493.3	179.6	85	549.7	200.1
46	325.1	118.3	06	381.5	138.9	66	437.9	159.4	26	494.3	179.9	86	550.7	200.4
47	326.1	118.7	07	382.5	139.2	67	438.8	159.7	27	495.2	180.2	87	551.6	200.8
48	327.0	119.0	08	383.4	139.5	68	439.8	160.1	28	496.2	180.6	88	552.5	201.1
49	328.0	119.4	09	384.3	139.9	69	440.7	160.4	29	497.1	180.9	89	553.5	201.4
50	328.9	119.7	10	385.3	140.2	70	441.7	160.7	30	498.0	181.3	90	554.4	201.8
351	329.8	120.0	411	386.2	140.6	471	442.6	161.1	531	499.0	181.6	591	555.4	202.1
52	330.8	120.4	12	387.2	140.9	72	443.5	161.4	32	499.9	182.0	92	556.3	202.5
53	331.7	120.7	13	388.1	141.3	73	444.5	161.8	33	500.9	182.3	93	557.2	202.8
54	332.7	121.1	14	389.0	141.6	74	445.4	162.1	34	501.8	182.6	94	558.2	203.2
55	333.6	121.4	15	390.0	141.9	75	446.4	162.5	35	502.7	183.0	95	559.1	203.5
56	334.5	121.8	16	390.9	142.3	76	447.3	162.8	36	503.7	183.3	96	560.1	203.8
57	335.5	122.1	17	391.9	142.6	77	448.2	163.1	37	504.6	183.7	97	561.0	204.2
58	336.4	122.4	18	392.8	143.0	78	449.2	163.5	38	505.6	184.0	98	561.9	204.5
59	337.3	122.8	19	393.7	143.3	79	450.1	163.8	39	506.5	184.3	99	562.9	204.9
60	338.3	123.1	20	394.7	143.6	80	451.1	164.2	40	507.4	184.7	600	563.8	205.2
Dist.	Dep.	D. Lat.	Dist.	Dep.	D. Lat.	Dist.	Dep.	D. Lat.	Dist.	Dep.	D. Lat.	Dist.	Dep.	D. Lat.

Dist.	D. Lat.	Dep.
D Lo	Dep.	
	m	D Lo

70°

290° | 070° — 250° | 110°

TABLE 4

Traverse 21° Table

339° | 021° — 201° | 159°

Dist.	D. Lat.	Dep.	Dist.	D. Lat.	Dep.	Dist.	D. Lat.	Dep.	Dist.	D. Lat.	Dep.	Dist.	D. Lat.	Dep.
1	0.9	0.4	61	56.9	21.9	121	113.0	43.4	181	169.0	64.9	241	225.0	86.4
2	1.9	0.7	62	57.9	22.2	22	113.9	43.7	82	169.9	65.2	42	225.9	86.7
3	2.8	1.1	63	58.8	22.6	23	114.8	44.1	83	170.8	65.6	43	226.9	87.1
4	3.7	1.4	64	59.7	22.9	24	115.8	44.4	84	171.8	65.9	44	227.8	87.4
5	4.7	1.8	65	60.7	23.3	25	116.7	44.8	85	172.7	66.3	45	228.7	87.8
6	5.6	2.2	66	61.6	23.7	26	117.6	45.2	86	173.6	66.7	46	229.7	88.2
7	6.5	2.5	67	62.5	24.0	27	118.6	45.5	87	174.6	67.0	47	230.6	88.5
8	7.5	2.9	68	63.5	24.4	28	119.5	45.9	88	175.5	67.4	48	231.5	88.9
9	8.4	3.2	69	64.4	24.7	29	120.4	46.2	89	176.4	67.7	49	232.5	89.2
10	9.3	3.6	70	65.4	25.1	30	121.4	46.6	90	177.4	68.1	50	233.4	89.6
11	10.3	3.9	71	66.3	25.4	131	122.3	46.9	191	178.3	68.4	251	234.3	90.0
12	11.2	4.3	72	67.2	25.8	32	123.2	47.3	92	179.2	68.8	52	235.3	90.3
13	12.1	4.7	73	68.2	26.2	33	124.2	47.7	93	180.2	69.2	53	236.2	90.7
14	13.1	5.0	74	69.1	26.5	34	125.1	48.0	94	181.1	69.5	54	237.1	91.0
15	14.0	5.4	75	70.0	26.9	35	126.0	48.4	95	182.0	69.9	55	238.1	91.4
16	14.9	5.7	76	71.0	27.2	36	127.0	48.7	96	183.0	70.2	56	239.0	91.7
17	15.9	6.1	77	71.9	27.6	37	127.9	49.1	97	183.9	70.6	57	239.9	92.1
18	16.8	6.5	78	72.8	28.0	38	128.8	49.5	98	184.8	71.0	58	240.9	92.5
19	17.7	6.8	79	73.8	28.3	39	129.8	49.8	99	185.8	71.3	59	241.8	92.8
20	18.7	7.2	80	74.7	28.7	40	130.7	50.2	200	186.7	71.7	60	242.7	93.2
21	19.6	7.5	81	75.6	29.0	141	131.6	50.5	201	187.6	72.0	261	243.7	93.5
22	20.5	7.9	82	76.6	29.4	42	132.6	50.9	02	188.6	72.4	62	244.6	93.9
23	21.5	8.2	83	77.5	29.7	43	133.5	51.2	03	189.5	72.7	63	245.5	94.3
24	22.4	8.6	84	78.4	30.1	44	134.4	51.6	04	190.5	73.1	64	246.5	94.6
25	23.3	9.0	85	79.4	30.5	45	135.4	52.0	05	191.4	73.5	65	247.4	95.0
26	24.3	9.3	86	80.3	30.8	46	136.3	52.3	06	192.3	73.8	66	248.3	95.3
27	25.2	9.7	87	81.2	31.2	47	137.2	52.7	07	193.3	74.2	67	249.3	95.7
28	26.1	10.0	88	82.2	31.5	48	138.2	53.0	08	194.2	74.5	68	250.2	96.0
29	27.1	10.4	89	83.1	31.9	49	139.1	53.4	09	195.1	74.9	69	251.1	96.4
30	28.0	10.8	90	84.0	32.3	50	140.0	53.8	10	196.1	75.3	70	252.1	96.8
31	28.9	11.1	91	85.0	32.6	151	141.0	54.1	211	197.0	75.6	271	253.0	97.1
32	29.9	11.5	92	85.9	33.0	52	141.9	54.5	12	197.9	76.0	72	253.9	97.5
33	30.8	11.8	93	86.8	33.3	53	142.8	54.8	13	198.9	76.3	73	254.9	97.8
34	31.7	12.2	94	87.8	33.7	54	143.8	55.2	14	199.8	76.7	74	255.8	98.2
35	32.7	12.5	95	88.7	34.0	55	144.7	55.5	15	200.7	77.0	75	256.7	98.6
36	33.6	12.9	96	89.6	34.4	56	145.6	55.9	16	201.7	77.4	76	257.7	98.9
37	34.5	13.3	97	90.6	34.8	57	146.6	56.3	17	202.6	77.8	77	258.6	99.3
38	35.5	13.6	98	91.5	35.1	58	147.5	56.6	18	203.5	78.1	78	259.5	99.6
39	36.4	14.0	99	92.4	35.5	59	148.4	57.0	19	204.5	78.5	79	260.5	100.0
40	37.3	14.3	100	93.4	35.8	60	149.4	57.3	20	205.4	78.8	80	261.4	100.3
41	38.3	14.7	101	94.3	36.2	161	150.3	57.7	221	206.3	79.2	281	262.3	100.7
42	39.2	15.1	02	95.2	36.6	62	151.2	58.1	22	207.3	79.6	82	263.3	101.1
43	40.1	15.4	03	96.2	36.9	63	152.2	58.4	23	208.2	79.9	83	264.2	101.4
44	41.1	15.8	04	97.1	37.3	64	153.1	58.8	24	209.1	80.3	84	265.1	101.8
45	42.0	16.1	05	98.0	37.6	65	154.0	59.1	25	210.1	80.6	85	266.1	102.1
46	42.9	16.5	06	99.0	38.0	66	155.0	59.5	26	211.0	81.0	86	267.0	102.5
47	43.9	16.8	07	99.9	38.3	67	155.9	59.8	27	211.9	81.3	87	267.9	102.9
48	44.8	17.2	08	100.8	38.7	68	156.8	60.2	28	212.9	81.7	88	268.9	103.2
49	45.7	17.6	09	101.8	39.1	69	157.8	60.6	29	213.8	82.1	89	269.8	103.6
50	46.7	17.9	10	102.7	39.4	70	158.7	60.9	30	214.7	82.4	90	270.7	103.9
51	47.6	18.3	111	103.6	39.8	171	159.6	61.3	231	215.7	82.8	291	271.7	104.3
52	48.5	18.6	12	104.6	40.1	72	160.6	61.6	32	216.6	83.1	92	272.6	104.6
53	49.5	19.0	13	105.5	40.5	73	161.5	62.0	33	217.5	83.5	93	273.5	105.0
54	50.4	19.4	14	106.4	40.9	74	162.4	62.4	34	218.5	83.9	94	274.5	105.4
55	51.3	19.7	15	107.4	41.2	75	163.4	62.7	35	219.4	84.2	95	275.4	105.7
56	52.3	20.1	16	108.3	41.6	76	164.3	63.1	36	220.3	84.6	96	276.3	106.1
57	53.2	20.4	17	109.2	41.9	77	165.2	63.4	37	221.3	84.9	97	277.3	106.4
58	54.1	20.8	18	110.2	42.3	78	166.2	63.8	38	222.2	85.3	98	278.2	106.8
59	55.1	21.1	19	111.1	42.6	79	167.1	64.1	39	223.1	85.6	99	279.1	107.2
60	56.0	21.5	20	112.0	43.0	80	168.0	64.5	40	224.1	86.0	300	280.1	107.5
Dist.	Dep.	D. Lat.	Dist.	Dep.	D. Lat.	Dist.	Dep.	D. Lat.	Dist.	Dep.	D. Lat.	Dist.	Dep.	D. Lat.

291° | 069° — 249° | 111°

69°

Dist.	D. Lat.	Dep.
N.	N x Cos.	N x Sin.
Hypotenuse	Side Adj.	Side Opp.

TABLE 4

Traverse 21° Table

339° | 021° — 201° | 159°

Dist.	D. Lat.	Dep.	Dist.	D. Lat.	Dep.	Dist.	D. Lat.	Dep.	Dist.	D. Lat.	Dep.	Dist.	D. Lat.	Dep.
301	281.0	107.9	361	337.0	129.4	421	393.0	150.9	481	449.1	172.4	541	505.1	193.9
02	281.9	108.2	62	338.0	129.7	22	394.0	151.2	82	450.0	172.7	42	506.0	194.2
03	282.9	108.6	63	338.9	130.1	23	394.9	151.6	83	450.9	173.1	43	506.9	194.6
04	283.8	108.9	64	339.8	130.4	24	395.8	151.9	84	451.9	173.5	44	507.9	195.0
05	284.7	109.3	65	340.8	130.8	25	396.8	152.3	85	452.8	173.8	45	508.8	195.3
06	285.7	109.7	66	341.7	131.2	26	397.7	152.7	86	453.7	174.2	46	509.7	195.7
07	286.6	110.0	67	342.6	131.5	27	398.6	153.0	87	454.7	174.5	47	510.7	196.0
08	287.5	110.4	68	343.6	131.9	28	399.6	153.4	88	455.6	174.9	48	511.6	196.4
09	288.5	110.7	69	344.5	132.2	29	400.5	153.7	89	456.5	175.2	49	512.5	196.7
10	289.4	111.1	70	345.4	132.6	30	401.4	154.1	90	457.5	175.6	50	513.5	197.1
311	290.3	111.5	371	346.4	133.0	431	402.4	154.5	491	458.4	176.0	551	514.4	197.5
12	291.3	111.8	72	347.3	133.3	32	403.3	154.8	92	459.3	176.3	52	515.3	197.8
13	292.2	112.2	73	348.2	133.7	33	404.2	155.2	93	460.3	176.7	53	516.3	198.2
14	293.1	112.5	74	349.2	134.0	34	405.2	155.5	94	461.2	177.0	54	517.2	198.5
15	294.1	112.9	75	350.1	134.4	35	406.1	155.9	95	462.1	177.4	55	518.1	198.9
16	295.0	113.2	76	351.0	134.7	36	407.0	156.2	96	463.1	177.8	56	519.1	199.3
17	295.9	113.6	77	352.0	135.1	37	408.0	156.6	97	464.0	178.1	57	520.0	199.6
18	296.9	114.0	78	352.9	135.5	38	408.9	157.0	98	464.9	178.5	58	520.9	200.0
19	297.8	114.3	79	353.8	135.8	39	409.8	157.3	99	465.9	178.8	59	521.9	200.3
20	298.7	114.7	80	354.8	136.2	40	410.8	157.7	500	466.8	179.2	60	522.8	200.7
321	299.7	115.0	381	355.7	136.5	441	411.7	158.0	501	467.7	179.5	561	523.7	201.0
22	300.6	115.4	82	356.6	136.9	42	412.6	158.4	02	468.7	179.9	62	524.7	201.4
23	301.5	115.8	83	357.6	137.3	43	413.6	158.8	03	469.6	180.3	63	525.6	201.8
24	302.5	116.1	84	358.5	137.6	44	414.5	159.1	04	470.5	180.6	64	526.5	202.1
25	303.4	116.5	85	359.4	138.0	45	415.4	159.5	05	471.5	181.0	65	527.5	202.5
26	304.3	116.8	86	360.4	138.3	46	416.4	159.8	06	472.4	181.3	66	528.4	202.8
27	305.3	117.2	87	361.3	138.7	47	417.3	160.2	07	473.3	181.7	67	529.3	203.2
28	306.2	117.5	88	362.2	139.0	48	418.2	160.5	08	474.3	182.1	68	530.3	203.6
29	307.1	117.9	89	363.2	139.4	49	419.2	160.9	09	475.2	182.4	69	531.2	203.9
30	308.1	118.3	90	364.1	139.8	50	420.1	161.3	10	476.1	182.8	70	532.1	204.3
331	309.0	118.6	391	365.0	140.1	451	421.0	161.6	511	477.1	183.1	571	533.1	204.6
32	309.9	119.0	92	366.0	140.5	52	422.0	162.0	12	478.0	183.5	72	534.0	205.0
33	310.9	119.3	93	366.9	140.8	53	422.9	162.3	13	478.9	183.8	73	534.9	205.3
34	311.8	119.7	94	367.8	141.2	54	423.8	162.7	14	479.9	184.2	74	535.9	205.7
35	312.7	120.1	95	368.8	141.6	55	424.8	163.1	15	480.8	184.6	75	536.8	206.1
36	313.7	120.4	96	369.7	141.9	56	425.7	163.4	16	481.7	184.9	76	537.7	206.4
37	314.6	120.8	97	370.6	142.3	57	426.6	163.8	17	482.7	185.3	77	538.7	206.8
38	315.6	121.1	98	371.6	142.6	58	427.6	164.1	18	483.6	185.6	78	539.6	207.1
39	316.5	121.5	99	372.5	143.0	59	428.5	164.5	19	484.5	186.0	79	540.5	207.5
40	317.4	121.8	400	373.4	143.3	60	429.4	164.8	20	485.5	186.4	80	541.5	207.9
341	318.4	122.2	401	374.4	143.7	461	430.4	165.2	521	486.4	186.7	581	542.4	208.2
42	319.3	122.6	02	375.3	144.1	62	431.3	165.6	22	487.3	187.1	82	543.3	208.6
43	320.2	122.9	03	376.2	144.4	63	432.2	165.9	23	488.3	187.4	83	544.3	208.9
44	321.2	123.3	04	377.2	144.8	64	433.2	166.3	24	489.2	187.8	84	545.2	209.3
45	322.1	123.6	05	378.1	145.1	65	434.1	166.6	25	490.1	188.1	85	546.1	209.6
46	323.0	124.0	06	379.0	145.5	66	435.0	167.0	26	491.1	188.5	86	547.1	210.0
47	324.0	124.4	07	380.0	145.9	67	436.0	167.4	27	492.0	188.9	87	548.0	210.4
48	324.9	124.7	08	380.9	146.2	68	436.9	167.7	28	492.9	189.2	88	548.9	210.7
49	325.8	125.1	09	381.8	146.6	69	437.8	168.1	29	493.9	189.6	89	549.9	211.1
50	326.8	125.4	10	382.8	146.9	70	438.8	168.4	30	494.8	189.9	90	550.8	211.4
351	327.7	125.8	411	383.7	147.3	471	439.7	168.8	531	495.7	190.3	591	551.7	211.8
52	328.6	126.1	12	384.6	147.6	72	440.6	169.1	32	496.7	190.7	92	552.7	212.2
53	329.6	126.5	13	385.6	148.0	73	441.6	169.5	33	497.6	191.0	93	553.6	212.5
54	330.5	126.9	14	386.5	148.4	74	442.5	169.9	34	498.5	191.4	94	554.5	212.9
55	331.4	127.2	15	387.4	148.7	75	443.5	170.2	35	499.5	191.7	95	555.5	213.2
56	332.4	127.6	16	388.4	149.1	76	444.4	170.6	36	500.4	192.1	96	556.4	213.6
57	333.3	127.9	17	389.3	149.4	77	445.3	170.9	37	501.3	192.4	97	557.3	213.9
58	334.2	128.3	18	390.2	149.8	78	446.3	171.3	38	502.3	192.8	98	558.3	214.3
59	335.2	128.7	19	391.2	150.2	79	447.2	171.7	39	503.2	193.2	99	559.2	214.7
60	336.1	129.0	20	392.1	150.5	80	448.1	172.0	40	504.1	193.5	600	560.1	215.0
Dist.	Dep.	D. Lat.	Dist.	Dep.	D. Lat.	Dist.	Dep.	D. Lat.	Dist.	Dep.	D. Lat.	Dist.	Dep.	D. Lat.

Dist.	D. Lat.	Dep.
D Lo	Dep.	
	m	D Lo

69°

291° | 069° — 249° | 111°

TABLE 4

Traverse 22° Table

338° / 202°	022° / 158°												338° / 202°	022° / 158°
Dist.	D. Lat.	Dep.	Dist.	D. Lat.	Dep.	Dist.	D. Lat.	Dep.	Dist.	D. Lat.	Dep.	Dist.	D. Lat.	Dep.
1	0.9	0.4	61	56.6	22.9	121	112.2	45.3	181	167.8	67.8	241	223.5	90.3
2	1.9	0.7	62	57.5	23.2	22	113.1	45.7	82	168.7	68.2	42	224.4	90.7
3	2.8	1.1	63	58.4	23.6	23	114.0	46.1	83	169.7	68.6	43	225.3	91.0
4	3.7	1.5	64	59.3	24.0	24	115.0	46.5	84	170.6	68.9	44	226.2	91.4
5	4.6	1.9	65	60.3	24.3	25	115.9	46.8	85	171.5	69.3	45	227.2	91.8
6	5.6	2.2	66	61.2	24.7	26	116.8	47.2	86	172.5	69.7	46	228.1	92.2
7	6.5	2.6	67	62.1	25.1	27	117.8	47.6	87	173.4	70.1	47	229.0	92.5
8	7.4	3.0	68	63.0	25.5	28	118.7	47.9	88	174.3	70.4	48	229.9	92.9
9	8.3	3.4	69	64.0	25.8	29	119.6	48.3	89	175.2	70.8	49	230.9	93.3
10	9.3	3.7	70	64.9	26.2	30	120.5	48.7	90	176.2	71.2	50	231.8	93.7
11	10.2	4.1	71	65.8	26.6	131	121.5	49.1	191	177.1	71.5	251	232.7	94.0
12	11.1	4.5	72	66.8	27.0	32	122.4	49.4	92	178.0	71.9	52	233.7	94.4
13	12.1	4.9	73	67.7	27.3	33	123.3	49.8	93	178.9	72.3	53	234.6	94.8
14	13.0	5.2	74	68.6	27.7	34	124.2	50.2	94	179.9	72.7	54	235.5	95.2
15	13.9	5.6	75	69.5	28.1	35	125.2	50.6	95	180.8	73.0	55	236.4	95.5
16	14.8	6.0	76	70.5	28.5	36	126.1	50.9	96	181.7	73.4	56	237.4	95.9
17	15.8	6.4	77	71.4	28.8	37	127.0	51.3	97	182.7	73.8	57	238.3	96.3
18	16.7	6.7	78	72.3	29.2	38	128.0	51.7	98	183.6	74.2	58	239.2	96.6
19	17.6	7.1	79	73.2	29.6	39	128.9	52.1	99	184.5	74.5	59	240.1	97.0
20	18.5	7.5	80	74.2	30.0	40	129.8	52.4	200	185.4	74.9	60	241.1	97.4
21	19.5	7.9	81	75.1	30.3	141	130.7	52.8	201	186.4	75.3	261	242.0	97.8
22	20.4	8.2	82	76.0	30.7	42	131.7	53.2	02	187.3	75.7	62	242.9	98.1
23	21.3	8.6	83	77.0	31.1	43	132.6	53.6	03	188.2	76.0	63	243.8	98.5
24	22.3	9.0	84	77.9	31.5	44	133.5	53.9	04	189.1	76.4	64	244.8	98.9
25	23.2	9.4	85	78.8	31.8	45	134.4	54.3	05	190.1	76.8	65	245.7	99.3
26	24.1	9.7	86	79.7	32.2	46	135.4	54.7	06	191.0	77.2	66	246.6	99.6
27	25.0	10.1	87	80.7	32.6	47	136.3	55.1	07	191.9	77.5	67	247.6	100.0
28	26.0	10.5	88	81.6	33.0	48	137.2	55.4	08	192.9	77.9	68	248.5	100.4
29	26.9	10.9	89	82.5	33.3	49	138.2	55.8	09	193.8	78.3	69	249.4	100.8
30	27.8	11.2	90	83.4	33.7	50	139.1	56.2	10	194.7	78.7	70	250.3	101.1
31	28.7	11.6	91	84.4	34.1	151	140.0	56.6	211	195.6	79.0	271	251.3	101.5
32	29.7	12.0	92	85.3	34.5	52	140.9	56.9	12	196.6	79.4	72	252.2	101.9
33	30.6	12.4	93	86.2	34.8	53	141.9	57.3	13	197.5	79.8	73	253.1	102.3
34	31.5	12.7	94	87.2	35.2	54	142.8	57.7	14	198.4	80.2	74	254.0	102.6
35	32.5	13.1	95	88.1	35.6	55	143.7	58.1	15	199.3	80.5	75	255.0	103.0
36	33.4	13.5	96	89.0	36.0	56	144.6	58.4	16	200.3	80.9	76	255.9	103.4
37	34.3	13.9	97	89.9	36.3	57	145.6	58.8	17	201.2	81.3	77	256.8	103.8
38	35.2	14.2	98	90.9	36.7	58	146.5	59.2	18	202.1	81.7	78	257.8	104.1
39	36.2	14.6	99	91.8	37.1	59	147.4	59.6	19	203.1	82.0	79	258.7	104.5
40	37.1	15.0	100	92.7	37.5	60	148.3	59.9	20	204.0	82.4	80	259.6	104.9
41	38.0	15.4	101	93.6	37.8	161	149.3	60.3	221	204.9	82.8	281	260.5	105.3
42	38.9	15.7	02	94.6	38.2	62	150.2	60.7	22	205.8	83.2	82	261.5	105.6
43	39.9	16.1	03	95.5	38.6	63	151.1	61.1	23	206.8	83.5	83	262.4	106.0
44	40.8	16.5	04	96.4	39.0	64	152.1	61.4	24	207.7	83.9	84	263.3	106.4
45	41.7	16.9	05	97.4	39.3	65	153.0	61.8	25	208.6	84.3	85	264.2	106.8
46	42.7	17.2	06	98.3	39.7	66	153.9	62.2	26	209.5	84.7	86	265.2	107.1
47	43.6	17.6	07	99.2	40.1	67	154.8	62.6	27	210.5	85.0	87	266.1	107.5
48	44.5	18.0	08	100.1	40.5	68	155.8	62.9	28	211.4	85.4	88	267.0	107.9
49	45.4	18.4	09	101.1	40.8	69	156.7	63.3	29	212.3	85.8	89	268.0	108.3
50	46.4	18.7	10	102.0	41.2	70	157.6	63.7	30	213.3	86.2	90	268.9	108.6
51	47.3	19.1	111	102.9	41.6	171	158.5	64.1	231	214.2	86.5	291	269.8	109.0
52	48.2	19.5	12	103.8	42.0	72	159.5	64.4	32	215.1	86.9	92	270.7	109.4
53	49.1	19.9	13	104.8	42.3	73	160.4	64.8	33	216.0	87.3	93	271.7	109.8
54	50.1	20.2	14	105.7	42.7	74	161.3	65.2	34	217.0	87.7	94	272.6	110.1
55	51.0	20.6	15	106.6	43.1	75	162.3	65.6	35	217.9	88.0	95	273.5	110.5
56	51.9	21.0	16	107.6	43.5	76	163.2	65.9	36	218.8	88.4	96	274.4	110.9
57	52.8	21.4	17	108.5	43.8	77	164.1	66.3	37	219.7	88.8	97	275.4	111.3
58	53.8	21.7	18	109.4	44.2	78	165.0	66.7	38	220.7	89.2	98	276.3	111.6
59	54.7	22.1	19	110.3	44.6	79	166.0	67.1	39	221.6	89.5	99	277.2	112.0
60	55.6	22.5	20	111.3	45.0	80	166.9	67.4	40	222.5	89.9	300	278.2	112.4
Dist.	Dep.	D. Lat.	Dist.	Dep.	D. Lat.	Dist.	Dep.	D. Lat.	Dist.	Dep.	D. Lat.	Dist.	Dep.	D. Lat.
292° / 248°	068° / 112°													

68°

Dist.	D. Lat.	Dep.
N.	N x Cos.	N x Sin.
Hypotenuse	Side Adj.	Side Opp.

TABLE 4

Traverse 22° Table

338° / 202°	022° / 158°												338° / 202°	022° / 158°
Dist.	D. Lat.	Dep.	Dist.	D. Lat.	Dep.	Dist.	D. Lat.	Dep.	Dist.	D. Lat.	Dep.	Dist.	D. Lat.	Dep.
301	279.1	112.8	361	334.7	135.2	421	390.3	157.7	481	446.0	180.2	541	501.6	202.7
02	280.0	113.1	62	335.6	135.6	22	391.3	158.1	82	446.9	180.6	42	502.5	203.0
03	280.9	113.5	63	336.6	136.0	23	392.2	158.5	83	447.8	180.9	43	503.5	203.4
04	281.9	113.9	64	337.5	136.4	24	393.1	158.8	84	448.8	181.3	44	504.4	203.8
05	282.8	114.3	65	338.4	136.7	25	394.1	159.2	85	449.7	181.7	45	505.3	204.2
06	283.7	114.6	66	339.3	137.1	26	395.0	159.6	86	450.6	182.1	46	506.2	204.5
07	284.6	115.0	67	340.3	137.5	27	395.9	160.0	87	451.5	182.4	47	507.2	204.9
08	285.6	115.4	68	341.2	137.9	28	396.8	160.3	88	452.5	182.8	48	508.1	205.3
09	286.5	115.8	69	342.1	138.2	29	397.8	160.7	89	453.4	183.2	49	509.0	205.7
10	287.4	116.1	70	343.1	138.6	30	398.7	161.1	90	454.3	183.6	50	510.0	206.0
311	288.4	116.5	371	344.0	139.0	431	399.6	161.5	491	455.2	183.9	551	510.9	206.4
12	289.3	116.9	72	344.9	139.4	32	400.5	161.8	92	456.2	184.3	52	511.8	206.8
13	290.2	117.3	73	345.8	139.7	33	401.5	162.2	93	457.1	184.7	53	512.7	207.2
14	291.1	117.6	74	346.8	140.1	34	402.4	162.6	94	458.0	185.1	54	513.7	207.5
15	292.1	118.0	75	347.7	140.5	35	403.3	163.0	95	459.0	185.4	55	514.6	207.9
16	293.0	118.4	76	348.6	140.9	36	404.3	163.3	96	459.9	185.8	56	515.5	208.3
17	293.9	118.8	77	349.5	141.2	37	405.2	163.7	97	460.8	186.2	57	516.4	208.7
18	294.8	119.1	78	350.5	141.6	38	406.1	164.1	98	461.7	186.6	58	517.4	209.0
19	295.8	119.5	79	351.4	142.0	39	407.0	164.5	99	462.7	186.9	59	518.3	209.4
20	296.7	119.9	80	352.3	142.4	40	408.0	164.8	500	463.6	187.3	60	519.2	209.8
321	297.6	120.2	381	353.3	142.7	441	408.9	165.2	501	464.5	187.7	561	520.2	210.2
22	298.6	120.6	82	354.2	143.1	42	409.8	165.6	02	465.4	188.1	62	521.1	210.5
23	299.5	121.0	83	355.1	143.5	43	410.7	166.0	03	466.4	188.4	63	522.0	210.9
24	300.4	121.4	84	356.0	143.8	44	411.7	166.3	04	467.3	188.8	64	522.9	211.3
25	301.3	121.7	85	357.0	144.2	45	412.6	166.7	05	468.2	189.2	65	523.9	211.7
26	302.3	122.1	86	357.9	144.6	46	413.5	167.1	06	469.2	189.6	66	524.8	212.0
27	303.2	122.5	87	358.8	145.0	47	414.5	167.4	07	470.1	189.9	67	525.7	212.4
28	304.1	122.9	88	359.7	145.3	48	415.4	167.8	08	471.0	190.3	68	526.6	212.8
29	305.0	123.2	89	360.7	145.7	49	416.3	168.2	09	471.9	190.7	69	527.6	213.2
30	306.0	123.6	90	361.6	146.1	50	417.2	168.6	10	472.9	191.0	70	528.5	213.5
331	306.9	124.0	391	362.5	146.5	451	418.2	168.9	511	473.8	191.4	571	529.4	213.9
32	307.8	124.4	92	363.5	146.8	52	419.1	169.3	12	474.7	191.8	72	530.3	214.3
33	308.8	124.7	93	364.4	147.2	53	420.0	169.7	13	475.6	192.2	73	531.3	214.6
34	309.7	125.1	94	365.3	147.6	54	420.9	170.1	14	476.6	192.5	74	532.2	215.0
35	310.6	125.5	95	366.2	148.0	55	421.9	170.4	15	477.5	192.9	75	533.1	215.4
36	311.5	125.9	96	367.2	148.3	56	422.8	170.8	16	478.4	193.3	76	534.1	215.8
37	312.5	126.2	97	368.1	148.7	57	423.7	171.2	17	479.4	193.7	77	535.0	216.1
38	313.4	126.6	98	369.0	149.1	58	424.7	171.6	18	480.3	194.0	78	535.9	216.5
39	314.3	127.0	99	369.9	149.5	59	425.6	171.9	19	481.2	194.4	79	536.8	216.9
40	315.2	127.4	400	370.9	149.8	60	426.5	172.3	20	482.1	194.8	80	537.8	217.3
341	316.2	127.7	401	371.8	150.2	461	427.4	172.7	521	483.1	195.2	581	538.7	217.6
42	317.1	128.1	02	372.7	150.6	62	428.4	173.1	22	484.0	195.5	82	539.6	218.0
43	318.0	128.5	03	373.7	151.0	63	429.3	173.4	23	484.9	195.9	83	540.5	218.4
44	319.0	128.9	04	374.6	151.3	64	430.2	173.8	24	485.8	196.3	84	541.5	218.8
45	319.9	129.2	05	375.5	151.7	65	431.1	174.2	25	486.8	196.7	85	542.4	219.1
46	320.8	129.6	06	376.4	152.1	66	432.1	174.6	26	487.7	197.0	86	543.3	219.5
47	321.7	130.0	07	377.4	152.5	67	433.0	174.9	27	488.6	197.4	87	544.3	219.9
48	322.7	130.4	08	378.3	152.8	68	433.9	175.3	28	489.6	197.8	88	545.2	220.3
49	323.6	130.7	09	379.2	153.2	69	434.8	175.7	29	490.5	198.2	89	546.1	220.6
50	324.5	131.1	10	380.1	153.6	70	435.8	176.1	30	491.4	198.5	90	547.0	221.0
351	325.4	131.5	411	381.1	154.0	471	436.7	176.4	531	492.3	198.9	591	548.0	221.4
52	326.4	131.9	12	382.0	154.3	72	437.6	176.8	32	493.3	199.3	92	548.9	221.8
53	327.3	132.2	13	382.9	154.7	73	438.6	177.2	33	494.2	199.7	93	549.8	222.1
54	328.2	132.6	14	383.9	155.1	74	439.5	177.6	34	495.1	200.0	94	550.7	222.5
55	329.2	133.0	15	384.8	155.5	75	440.4	177.9	35	496.0	200.4	95	551.7	222.9
56	330.1	133.4	16	385.7	155.8	76	441.3	178.3	36	497.0	200.8	96	552.6	223.3
57	331.0	133.7	17	386.6	156.2	77	442.3	178.7	37	497.9	201.2	97	553.5	223.6
58	331.9	134.1	18	387.6	156.6	78	443.2	179.1	38	498.8	201.5	98	554.5	224.0
59	332.9	134.5	19	388.5	157.0	79	444.1	179.4	39	499.8	201.9	99	555.4	224.4
60	333.8	134.9	20	389.4	157.3	80	445.0	179.8	40	500.7	202.3	600	556.3	224.8
Dist.	Dep.	D. Lat.	Dist.	Dep.	D. Lat.	Dist.	Dep.	D. Lat.	Dist.	Dep.	D. Lat.	Dist.	Dep.	D. Lat.
													292° / 248°	068° / 112°

Dist.	D. Lat.	Dep.
D Lo	Dep.	
	m	D Lo

68°

TABLE 4

Traverse 23° Table

337° | 023° / 203° | 157°

Dist.	D. Lat.	Dep.	Dist.	D. Lat.	Dep.	Dist.	D. Lat.	Dep.	Dist.	D. Lat.	Dep.	Dist.	D. Lat.	Dep.
1	0.9	0.4	61	56.2	23.8	121	111.4	47.3	181	166.6	70.7	241	221.8	94.2
2	1.8	0.8	62	57.1	24.2	22	112.3	47.7	82	167.5	71.1	42	222.8	94.6
3	2.8	1.2	63	58.0	24.6	23	113.2	48.1	83	168.5	71.5	43	223.7	94.9
4	3.7	1.6	64	58.9	25.0	24	114.1	48.5	84	169.4	71.9	44	224.6	95.3
5	4.6	2.0	65	59.8	25.4	25	115.1	48.8	85	170.3	72.3	45	225.5	95.7
6	5.5	2.3	66	60.8	25.8	26	116.0	49.2	86	171.2	72.7	46	226.4	96.1
7	6.4	2.7	67	61.7	26.2	27	116.9	49.6	87	172.1	73.1	47	227.4	96.5
8	7.4	3.1	68	62.6	26.6	28	117.8	50.0	88	173.1	73.5	48	228.3	96.9
9	8.3	3.5	69	63.5	27.0	29	118.7	50.4	89	174.0	73.8	49	229.2	97.3
10	9.2	3.9	70	64.4	27.4	30	119.7	50.8	90	174.9	74.2	50	230.1	97.7
11	10.1	4.3	71	65.4	27.7	131	120.6	51.2	191	175.8	74.6	251	231.0	98.1
12	11.0	4.7	72	66.3	28.1	32	121.5	51.6	92	176.7	75.0	52	232.0	98.5
13	12.0	5.1	73	67.2	28.5	33	122.4	52.0	93	177.7	75.4	53	232.9	98.9
14	12.9	5.5	74	68.1	28.9	34	123.3	52.4	94	178.6	75.8	54	233.8	99.2
15	13.8	5.9	75	69.0	29.3	35	124.3	52.7	95	179.5	76.2	55	234.7	99.6
16	14.7	6.3	76	70.0	29.7	36	125.2	53.1	96	180.4	76.6	56	235.6	100.0
17	15.6	6.6	77	70.9	30.1	37	126.1	53.5	97	181.3	77.0	57	236.6	100.4
18	16.6	7.0	78	71.8	30.5	38	127.0	53.9	98	182.3	77.4	58	237.5	100.8
19	17.5	7.4	79	72.7	30.9	39	128.0	54.3	99	183.2	77.8	59	238.4	101.2
20	18.4	7.8	80	73.6	31.3	40	128.9	54.7	200	184.1	78.1	60	239.3	101.6
21	19.3	8.2	81	74.6	31.6	141	129.8	55.1	201	185.0	78.5	261	240.3	102.0
22	20.3	8.6	82	75.5	32.0	42	130.7	55.5	02	185.9	78.9	62	241.2	102.4
23	21.2	9.0	83	76.4	32.4	43	131.6	55.9	03	186.9	79.3	63	242.1	102.8
24	22.1	9.4	84	77.3	32.8	44	132.6	56.3	04	187.8	79.7	64	243.0	103.2
25	23.0	9.8	85	78.2	33.2	45	133.5	56.7	05	188.7	80.1	65	243.9	103.5
26	23.9	10.2	86	79.2	33.6	46	134.4	57.0	06	189.6	80.5	66	244.9	103.9
27	24.9	10.5	87	80.1	34.0	47	135.3	57.4	07	190.5	80.9	67	245.8	104.3
28	25.8	10.9	88	81.0	34.4	48	136.2	57.8	08	191.5	81.3	68	246.7	104.7
29	26.7	11.3	89	81.9	34.8	49	137.2	58.2	09	192.4	81.7	69	247.6	105.1
30	27.6	11.7	90	82.8	35.2	50	138.1	58.6	10	193.3	82.1	70	248.5	105.5
31	28.5	12.1	91	83.8	35.6	151	139.0	59.0	211	194.2	82.4	271	249.5	105.9
32	29.5	12.5	92	84.7	35.9	52	139.9	59.4	12	195.1	82.8	72	250.4	106.3
33	30.4	12.9	93	85.6	36.3	53	140.8	59.8	13	196.1	83.2	73	251.3	106.7
34	31.3	13.3	94	86.5	36.7	54	141.8	60.2	14	197.0	83.6	74	252.2	107.1
35	32.2	13.7	95	87.4	37.1	55	142.7	60.6	15	197.9	84.0	75	253.1	107.5
36	33.1	14.1	96	88.4	37.5	56	143.6	61.0	16	198.8	84.4	76	254.1	107.8
37	34.1	14.5	97	89.3	37.9	57	144.5	61.3	17	199.7	84.8	77	255.0	108.2
38	35.0	14.8	98	90.2	38.3	58	145.4	61.7	18	200.7	85.2	78	255.9	108.6
39	35.9	15.2	99	91.1	38.7	59	146.4	62.1	19	201.6	85.6	79	256.8	109.0
40	36.8	15.6	100	92.1	39.1	60	147.3	62.5	20	202.5	86.0	80	257.7	109.4
41	37.7	16.0	101	93.0	39.5	161	148.2	62.9	221	203.4	86.4	281	258.7	109.8
42	38.7	16.4	02	93.9	39.9	62	149.1	63.3	22	204.4	86.7	82	259.6	110.2
43	39.6	16.8	03	94.8	40.2	63	150.0	63.7	23	205.3	87.1	83	260.5	110.6
44	40.5	17.2	04	95.7	40.6	64	151.0	64.1	24	206.2	87.5	84	261.4	111.0
45	41.4	17.6	05	96.7	41.0	65	151.9	64.5	25	207.1	87.9	85	262.3	111.4
46	42.3	18.0	06	97.6	41.4	66	152.8	64.9	26	208.0	88.3	86	263.3	111.7
47	43.3	18.4	07	98.5	41.8	67	153.7	65.3	27	209.0	88.7	87	264.2	112.1
48	44.2	18.8	08	99.4	42.2	68	154.6	65.6	28	209.9	89.1	88	265.1	112.5
49	45.1	19.1	09	100.3	42.6	69	155.6	66.0	29	210.8	89.5	89	266.0	112.9
50	46.0	19.5	10	101.3	43.0	70	156.5	66.4	30	211.7	89.9	90	266.9	113.3
51	46.9	19.9	111	102.2	43.4	171	157.4	66.8	231	212.6	90.3	291	267.9	113.7
52	47.9	20.3	12	103.1	43.8	72	158.3	67.2	32	213.6	90.6	92	268.8	114.1
53	48.8	20.7	13	104.0	44.2	73	159.2	67.6	33	214.5	91.0	93	269.7	114.5
54	49.7	21.1	14	104.9	44.5	74	160.2	68.0	34	215.4	91.4	94	270.6	114.9
55	50.6	21.5	15	105.9	44.9	75	161.1	68.4	35	216.3	91.8	95	271.5	115.3
56	51.5	21.9	16	106.8	45.3	76	162.0	68.8	36	217.2	92.2	96	272.5	115.7
57	52.5	22.3	17	107.7	45.7	77	162.9	69.2	37	218.2	92.6	97	273.4	116.0
58	53.4	22.7	18	108.6	46.1	78	163.8	69.6	38	219.1	93.0	98	274.3	116.4
59	54.3	23.1	19	109.5	46.5	79	164.8	69.9	39	220.0	93.4	99	275.2	116.8
60	55.2	23.4	20	110.5	46.9	80	165.7	70.3	40	220.9	93.8	300	276.2	117.2
Dist.	Dep.	D. Lat.	Dist.	Dep.	D. Lat.	Dist.	Dep.	D. Lat.	Dist.	Dep.	D. Lat.	Dist.	Dep.	D. Lat.

293° | 067° / 247° | 113°

67°

Dist.	D. Lat.	Dep.
N.	N x Cos.	N x Sin.
Hypotenuse	Side Adj.	Side Opp.

TABLE 4

Traverse 23° Table

337° | 023° / 203° | 157°

Dist.	D. Lat.	Dep.	Dist.	D. Lat.	Dep.	Dist.	D. Lat.	Dep.	Dist.	D. Lat.	Dep.	Dist.	D. Lat.	Dep.
301	277.1	117.6	361	332.3	141.1	421	387.5	164.5	481	442.8	187.9	541	498.0	211.4
02	278.0	118.0	62	333.2	141.4	22	388.5	164.9	82	443.7	188.3	42	498.9	211.8
03	278.9	118.4	63	334.1	141.8	23	389.4	165.3	83	444.6	188.7	43	499.8	212.2
04	279.8	118.8	64	335.1	142.2	24	390.3	165.7	84	445.5	189.1	44	500.8	212.6
05	280.8	119.2	65	336.0	142.6	25	391.2	166.1	85	446.4	189.5	45	501.7	212.9
06	281.7	119.6	66	336.9	143.0	26	392.1	166.5	86	447.4	189.9	46	502.6	213.3
07	282.6	120.0	67	337.8	143.4	27	393.1	166.8	87	448.3	190.3	47	503.5	213.7
08	283.5	120.3	68	338.7	143.8	28	394.0	167.2	88	449.2	190.7	48	504.4	214.1
09	284.4	120.7	69	339.7	144.2	29	394.9	167.6	89	450.1	191.1	49	505.4	214.5
10	285.4	121.1	70	340.6	144.6	30	395.8	168.0	90	451.0	191.5	50	506.3	214.9
311	286.3	121.5	371	341.5	145.0	431	396.7	168.4	491	452.0	191.8	551	507.2	215.3
12	287.2	121.9	72	342.4	145.4	32	397.7	168.8	92	452.9	192.2	52	508.1	215.7
13	288.1	122.3	73	343.3	145.7	33	398.6	169.2	93	453.8	192.6	53	509.0	216.1
14	289.0	122.7	74	344.3	146.1	34	399.5	169.6	94	454.7	193.0	54	510.0	216.5
15	290.0	123.1	75	345.2	146.5	35	400.4	170.0	95	455.6	193.4	55	510.9	216.9
16	290.9	123.5	76	346.1	146.9	36	401.3	170.4	96	456.6	193.8	56	511.8	217.2
17	291.8	123.9	77	347.0	147.3	37	402.3	170.7	97	457.5	194.2	57	512.7	217.6
18	292.7	124.3	78	348.0	147.7	38	403.2	171.1	98	458.4	194.6	58	513.6	218.0
19	293.6	124.6	79	348.9	148.1	39	404.1	171.5	99	459.3	195.0	59	514.6	218.4
20	294.6	125.0	80	349.8	148.5	40	405.0	171.9	500	460.3	195.4	60	515.5	218.8
321	295.5	125.4	381	350.7	148.9	441	405.9	172.3	501	461.2	195.8	561	516.4	219.2
22	296.4	125.8	82	351.6	149.3	42	406.9	172.7	02	462.1	196.1	62	517.3	219.6
23	297.3	126.2	83	352.6	149.7	43	407.8	173.1	03	463.0	196.5	63	518.2	220.0
24	298.2	126.6	84	353.5	150.0	44	408.7	173.5	04	463.9	196.9	64	519.2	220.4
25	299.2	127.0	85	354.4	150.4	45	409.6	173.9	05	464.9	197.3	65	520.1	220.8
26	300.1	127.4	86	355.3	150.8	46	410.5	174.3	06	465.8	197.7	66	521.0	221.2
27	301.0	127.8	87	356.2	151.2	47	411.5	174.7	07	466.7	198.1	67	521.9	221.5
28	301.9	128.2	88	357.2	151.6	48	412.4	175.0	08	467.6	198.5	68	522.8	221.9
29	302.8	128.6	89	358.1	152.0	49	413.3	175.4	09	468.5	198.9	69	523.8	222.3
30	303.8	128.9	90	359.0	152.4	50	414.2	175.8	10	469.5	199.3	70	524.7	222.7
331	304.7	129.3	391	359.9	152.8	451	415.1	176.2	511	470.4	199.7	571	525.6	223.1
32	305.6	129.7	92	360.8	153.2	52	416.1	176.6	12	471.3	200.1	72	526.5	223.5
33	306.5	130.1	93	361.8	153.6	53	417.0	177.0	13	472.2	200.4	73	527.4	223.9
34	307.4	130.5	94	362.7	153.9	54	417.9	177.4	14	473.1	200.8	74	528.4	224.3
35	308.4	130.9	95	363.6	154.3	55	418.8	177.8	15	474.1	201.2	75	529.3	224.7
36	309.3	131.3	96	364.5	154.7	56	419.8	178.2	16	475.0	201.6	76	530.2	225.1
37	310.2	131.7	97	365.4	155.1	57	420.7	178.6	17	475.9	202.0	77	531.1	225.5
38	311.1	132.1	98	366.4	155.5	58	421.6	179.0	18	476.8	202.4	78	532.1	225.8
39	312.1	132.5	99	367.3	155.9	59	422.5	179.3	19	477.7	202.8	79	533.0	226.2
40	313.0	132.8	400	368.2	156.3	60	423.4	179.7	20	478.7	203.2	80	533.9	226.6
341	313.9	133.2	401	369.1	156.7	461	424.4	180.1	521	479.6	203.6	581	534.8	227.0
42	314.8	133.6	02	370.0	157.1	62	425.3	180.5	22	480.5	204.0	82	535.7	227.4
43	315.7	134.0	03	371.0	157.5	63	426.2	180.9	23	481.4	204.4	83	536.7	227.8
44	316.7	134.4	04	371.9	157.9	64	427.1	181.3	24	482.3	204.7	84	537.6	228.2
45	317.6	134.8	05	372.8	158.2	65	428.0	181.7	25	483.3	205.1	85	538.5	228.6
46	318.5	135.2	06	373.7	158.6	66	429.0	182.1	26	484.2	205.5	86	539.4	229.0
47	319.4	135.6	07	374.6	159.0	67	429.9	182.5	27	485.1	205.9	87	540.3	229.4
48	320.3	136.0	08	375.6	159.4	68	430.8	182.9	28	486.0	206.3	88	541.3	229.7
49	321.3	136.4	09	376.5	159.8	69	431.7	183.3	29	486.9	206.7	89	542.2	230.1
50	322.2	136.8	10	377.4	160.2	70	432.6	183.6	30	487.9	207.1	90	543.1	230.5
351	323.1	137.1	411	378.3	160.6	471	433.6	184.0	531	488.8	207.5	591	544.0	230.9
52	324.0	137.5	12	379.2	161.0	72	434.5	184.4	32	489.7	207.9	92	544.9	231.3
53	324.9	137.9	13	380.2	161.4	73	435.4	184.8	33	490.6	208.3	93	545.9	231.7
54	325.9	138.3	14	381.1	161.8	74	436.3	185.2	34	491.5	208.7	94	546.8	232.1
55	326.8	138.7	15	382.0	162.2	75	437.2	185.6	35	492.5	209.0	95	547.7	232.5
56	327.7	139.1	16	382.9	162.5	76	438.2	186.0	36	493.4	209.4	96	548.6	232.9
57	328.6	139.5	17	383.9	162.9	77	439.1	186.4	37	494.3	209.8	97	549.5	233.3
58	329.5	139.9	18	384.8	163.3	78	440.0	186.8	38	495.2	210.2	98	550.5	233.7
59	330.5	140.3	19	385.7	163.7	79	440.9	187.2	39	496.2	210.6	99	551.4	234.0
60	331.4	140.7	20	386.6	164.1	80	441.8	187.6	40	497.1	211.0	600	552.3	234.4
Dist.	Dep.	D. Lat.	Dist.	Dep.	D. Lat.	Dist.	Dep.	D. Lat.	Dist.	Dep.	D. Lat.	Dist.	Dep.	D. Lat.

Dist.	D. Lat.	Dep.
D Lo	Dep.	
	m	D Lo

67°

293° | 067° / 247° | 113°

TABLE 4

Traverse 24° Table

336° / 204°	024° / 156°												336° / 204°	024° / 156°
Dist.	D. Lat.	Dep.	Dist.	D. Lat.	Dep.	Dist.	D. Lat.	Dep.	Dist.	D. Lat.	Dep.	Dist.	D. Lat.	Dep.
1	0.9	0.4	61	55.7	24.8	121	110.5	49.2	181	165.4	73.6	241	220.2	98.0
2	1.8	0.8	62	56.6	25.2	22	111.5	49.6	82	166.3	74.0	42	221.1	98.4
3	2.7	1.2	63	57.6	25.6	23	112.4	50.0	83	167.2	74.4	43	222.0	98.8
4	3.7	1.6	64	58.5	26.0	24	113.3	50.4	84	168.1	74.8	44	222.9	99.2
5	4.6	2.0	65	59.4	26.4	25	114.2	50.8	85	169.0	75.2	45	223.8	99.7
6	5.5	2.4	66	60.3	26.8	26	115.1	51.2	86	169.9	75.7	46	224.7	100.1
7	6.4	2.8	67	61.2	27.3	27	116.0	51.7	87	170.8	76.1	47	225.6	100.5
8	7.3	3.3	68	62.1	27.7	28	116.9	52.1	88	171.7	76.5	48	226.6	100.9
9	8.2	3.7	69	63.0	28.1	29	117.8	52.5	89	172.7	76.9	49	227.5	101.3
10	9.1	4.1	70	63.9	28.5	30	118.8	52.9	90	173.6	77.3	50	228.4	101.7
11	10.0	4.5	71	64.9	28.9	131	119.7	53.3	191	174.5	77.7	251	229.3	102.1
12	11.0	4.9	72	65.8	29.3	32	120.6	53.7	92	175.4	78.1	52	230.2	102.5
13	11.9	5.3	73	66.7	29.7	33	121.5	54.1	93	176.3	78.5	53	231.1	102.9
14	12.8	5.7	74	67.6	30.1	34	122.4	54.5	94	177.2	78.9	54	232.0	103.3
15	13.7	6.1	75	68.5	30.5	35	123.3	54.9	95	178.1	79.3	55	233.0	103.7
16	14.6	6.5	76	69.4	30.9	36	124.2	55.3	96	179.1	79.7	56	233.9	104.1
17	15.5	6.9	77	70.3	31.3	37	125.2	55.7	97	180.0	80.1	57	234.8	104.5
18	16.4	7.3	78	71.3	31.7	38	126.1	56.1	98	180.9	80.5	58	235.7	104.9
19	17.4	7.7	79	72.2	32.1	39	127.0	56.5	99	181.8	80.9	59	236.6	105.3
20	18.3	8.1	80	73.1	32.5	40	127.9	56.9	200	182.7	81.3	60	237.5	105.8
21	19.2	8.5	81	74.0	32.9	141	128.8	57.3	201	183.6	81.8	261	238.4	106.2
22	20.1	8.9	82	74.9	33.4	42	129.7	57.8	02	184.5	82.2	62	239.3	106.6
23	21.0	9.4	83	75.8	33.8	43	130.6	58.2	03	185.4	82.6	63	240.3	107.0
24	21.9	9.8	84	76.7	34.2	44	131.6	58.6	04	186.4	83.0	64	241.2	107.4
25	22.8	10.2	85	77.7	34.6	45	132.5	59.0	05	187.3	83.4	65	242.1	107.8
26	23.8	10.6	86	78.6	35.0	46	133.4	59.4	06	188.2	83.8	66	243.0	108.2
27	24.7	11.0	87	79.5	35.4	47	134.3	59.8	07	189.1	84.2	67	243.9	108.6
28	25.6	11.4	88	80.4	35.8	48	135.2	60.2	08	190.0	84.6	68	244.8	109.0
29	26.5	11.8	89	81.3	36.2	49	136.1	60.6	09	190.9	85.0	69	245.7	109.4
30	27.4	12.2	90	82.2	36.6	50	137.0	61.0	10	191.8	85.4	70	246.7	109.8
31	28.3	12.6	91	83.1	37.0	151	137.9	61.4	211	192.8	85.8	271	247.6	110.2
32	29.2	13.0	92	84.0	37.4	52	138.9	61.8	12	193.7	86.2	72	248.5	110.6
33	30.1	13.4	93	85.0	37.8	53	139.8	62.2	13	194.6	86.6	73	249.4	111.0
34	31.1	13.8	94	85.9	38.2	54	140.7	62.6	14	195.5	87.0	74	250.3	111.4
35	32.0	14.2	95	86.8	38.6	55	141.6	63.0	15	196.4	87.4	75	251.2	111.9
36	32.9	14.6	96	87.7	39.0	56	142.5	63.5	16	197.3	87.9	76	252.1	112.3
37	33.8	15.0	97	88.6	39.5	57	143.4	63.9	17	198.2	88.3	77	253.1	112.7
38	34.7	15.5	98	89.5	39.9	58	144.3	64.3	18	199.2	88.7	78	254.0	113.1
39	35.6	15.9	99	90.4	40.3	59	145.3	64.7	19	200.1	89.1	79	254.9	113.5
40	36.5	16.3	100	91.4	40.7	60	146.2	65.1	20	201.0	89.5	80	255.8	113.9
41	37.5	16.7	101	92.3	41.1	161	147.1	65.5	221	201.9	89.9	281	256.7	114.3
42	38.4	17.1	02	93.2	41.5	62	148.0	65.9	22	202.8	90.3	82	257.6	114.7
43	39.3	17.5	03	94.1	41.9	63	148.9	66.3	23	203.7	90.7	83	258.5	115.1
44	40.2	17.9	04	95.0	42.3	64	149.8	66.7	24	204.6	91.1	84	259.4	115.5
45	41.1	18.3	05	95.9	42.7	65	150.7	67.1	25	205.5	91.5	85	260.4	115.9
46	42.0	18.7	06	96.8	43.1	66	151.6	67.5	26	206.5	91.9	86	261.3	116.3
47	42.9	19.1	07	97.7	43.5	67	152.6	67.9	27	207.4	92.3	87	262.2	116.7
48	43.9	19.5	08	98.7	43.9	68	153.5	68.3	28	208.3	92.7	88	263.1	117.1
49	44.8	19.9	09	99.6	44.3	69	154.4	68.7	29	209.2	93.1	89	264.0	117.5
50	45.7	20.3	10	100.5	44.7	70	155.3	69.1	30	210.1	93.5	90	264.9	118.0
51	46.6	20.7	111	101.4	45.1	171	156.2	69.6	231	211.0	94.0	291	265.8	118.4
52	47.5	21.2	12	102.3	45.6	72	157.1	70.0	32	211.9	94.4	92	266.8	118.8
53	48.4	21.6	13	103.2	46.0	73	158.0	70.4	33	212.9	94.8	93	267.7	119.2
54	49.3	22.0	14	104.1	46.4	74	159.0	70.8	34	213.8	95.2	94	268.6	119.6
55	50.2	22.4	15	105.1	46.8	75	159.9	71.2	35	214.7	95.6	95	269.5	120.0
56	51.2	22.8	16	106.0	47.2	76	160.8	71.6	36	215.6	96.0	96	270.4	120.4
57	52.1	23.2	17	106.9	47.6	77	161.7	72.0	37	216.5	96.4	97	271.3	120.8
58	53.0	23.6	18	107.8	48.0	78	162.6	72.4	38	217.4	96.8	98	272.2	121.2
59	53.9	24.0	19	108.7	48.4	79	163.5	72.8	39	218.3	97.2	99	273.2	121.6
60	54.8	24.4	20	109.6	48.8	80	164.4	73.2	40	219.3	97.6	300	274.1	122.0
Dist.	Dep.	D. Lat.	Dist.	Dep.	D. Lat.	Dist.	Dep.	D. Lat.	Dist.	Dep.	D. Lat.	Dist.	Dep.	D. Lat.
294° / 246°	066° / 114°													

66°

Dist.	D. Lat.	Dep.
N.	N x Cos.	N x Sin.
Hypotenuse	Side Adj.	Side Opp.

TABLE 4

Traverse 24° Table

336° / 204°	024° / 156°												336° / 204°	024° / 156°
Dist.	D. Lat.	Dep.	Dist.	D. Lat.	Dep.	Dist.	D. Lat.	Dep.	Dist.	D. Lat.	Dep.	Dist.	D. Lat.	Dep.
301	275.0	122.4	361	329.8	146.8	421	384.6	171.2	481	439.4	195.6	541	494.2	220.0
02	275.9	122.8	62	330.7	147.2	22	385.5	171.6	82	440.3	196.0	42	495.1	220.5
03	276.8	123.2	63	331.6	147.6	23	386.4	172.0	83	441.2	196.5	43	496.1	220.9
04	277.7	123.6	64	332.5	148.1	24	387.3	172.5	84	442.2	196.9	44	497.0	221.3
05	278.6	124.1	65	333.4	148.5	25	388.3	172.9	85	443.1	197.3	45	497.9	221.7
06	279.5	124.5	66	334.4	148.9	26	389.2	173.3	86	444.0	197.7	46	498.8	222.1
07	280.5	124.9	67	335.3	149.3	27	390.1	173.7	87	444.9	198.1	47	499.7	222.5
08	281.4	125.3	68	336.2	149.7	28	391.0	174.1	88	445.8	198.5	48	500.6	222.9
09	282.3	125.7	69	337.1	150.1	29	391.9	174.5	89	446.7	198.9	49	501.5	223.3
10	283.2	126.1	70	338.0	150.5	30	392.8	174.9	90	447.6	199.3	50	502.5	223.7
311	284.1	126.5	371	338.9	150.9	431	393.7	175.3	491	448.6	199.7	551	503.4	224.1
12	285.0	126.9	72	339.8	151.3	32	394.7	175.7	92	449.5	200.1	52	504.3	224.5
13	285.9	127.3	73	340.8	151.7	33	395.6	176.1	93	450.4	200.5	53	505.2	224.9
14	286.9	127.7	74	341.7	152.1	34	396.5	176.5	94	451.3	200.9	54	506.1	225.3
15	287.8	128.1	75	342.6	152.5	35	397.4	176.9	95	452.2	201.3	55	507.0	225.7
16	288.7	128.5	76	343.5	152.9	36	398.3	177.3	96	453.1	201.7	56	507.9	226.1
17	289.6	128.9	77	344.4	153.3	37	399.2	177.7	97	454.0	202.1	57	508.8	226.6
18	290.5	129.3	78	345.3	153.7	38	400.1	178.2	98	454.9	202.6	58	509.8	227.0
19	291.4	129.7	79	346.2	154.2	39	401.0	178.6	99	455.9	203.0	59	510.7	227.4
20	292.3	130.2	80	347.1	154.6	40	402.0	179.0	500	456.8	203.4	60	511.6	227.8
321	293.2	130.6	381	348.1	155.0	441	402.9	179.4	501	457.7	203.8	561	512.5	228.2
22	294.2	131.0	82	349.0	155.4	42	403.8	179.8	02	458.6	204.2	62	513.4	228.6
23	295.1	131.4	83	349.9	155.8	43	404.7	180.2	03	459.5	204.6	63	514.3	229.0
24	296.0	131.8	84	350.8	156.2	44	405.6	180.6	04	460.4	205.0	64	515.2	229.4
25	296.9	132.2	85	351.7	156.6	45	406.5	181.0	05	461.3	205.4	65	516.2	229.8
26	297.8	132.6	86	352.6	157.0	46	407.4	181.4	06	462.3	205.8	66	517.1	230.2
27	298.7	133.0	87	353.5	157.4	47	408.4	181.8	07	463.2	206.2	67	518.0	230.6
28	299.6	133.4	88	354.5	157.8	48	409.3	182.2	08	464.1	206.6	68	518.9	231.0
29	300.6	133.8	89	355.4	158.2	49	410.2	182.6	09	465.0	207.0	69	519.8	231.4
30	301.5	134.2	90	356.3	158.6	50	411.1	183.0	10	465.9	207.4	70	520.7	231.8
331	302.4	134.6	391	357.2	159.0	451	412.0	183.4	511	466.8	207.8	571	521.6	232.2
32	303.3	135.0	92	358.1	159.4	52	412.9	183.8	12	467.7	208.2	72	522.5	232.7
33	304.2	135.4	93	359.0	159.8	53	413.8	184.3	13	468.6	208.7	73	523.5	233.1
34	305.1	135.9	94	359.9	160.3	54	414.7	184.7	14	469.6	209.1	74	524.4	233.5
35	306.0	136.3	95	360.9	160.7	55	415.7	185.1	15	470.5	209.5	75	525.3	233.9
36	307.0	136.7	96	361.8	161.1	56	416.6	185.5	16	471.4	209.9	76	526.2	234.3
37	307.9	137.1	97	362.7	161.5	57	417.5	185.9	17	472.3	210.3	77	527.1	234.7
38	308.8	137.5	98	363.6	161.9	58	418.4	186.3	18	473.2	210.7	78	528.0	235.1
39	309.7	137.9	99	364.5	162.3	59	419.3	186.7	19	474.1	211.1	79	528.9	235.5
40	310.6	138.3	400	365.4	162.7	60	420.2	187.1	20	475.0	211.5	80	529.9	235.9
341	311.5	138.7	401	366.3	163.1	461	421.1	187.5	521	476.0	211.9	581	530.8	236.3
42	312.4	139.1	02	367.2	163.5	62	422.1	187.9	22	476.9	212.3	82	531.7	236.7
43	313.3	139.5	03	368.2	163.9	63	423.0	188.3	23	477.8	212.7	83	532.6	237.1
44	314.3	139.9	04	369.1	164.3	64	423.9	188.7	24	478.7	213.1	84	533.5	237.5
45	315.2	140.3	05	370.0	164.7	65	424.8	189.1	25	479.6	213.5	85	534.4	237.9
46	316.1	140.7	06	370.9	165.1	66	425.7	189.5	26	480.5	213.9	86	535.3	238.3
47	317.0	141.1	07	371.8	165.5	67	426.6	189.9	27	481.4	214.4	87	536.3	238.8
48	317.9	141.5	08	372.7	165.9	68	427.5	190.4	28	482.4	214.8	88	537.2	239.2
49	318.8	142.0	09	373.6	166.4	69	428.5	190.8	29	483.3	215.2	89	538.1	239.6
50	319.7	142.4	10	374.6	166.8	70	429.4	191.2	30	484.2	215.6	90	539.0	240.0
351	320.7	142.8	411	375.5	167.2	471	430.3	191.6	531	485.1	216.0	591	539.9	240.4
52	321.6	143.2	12	376.4	167.6	72	431.2	192.0	32	486.0	216.4	92	540.8	240.8
53	322.5	143.6	13	377.3	168.0	73	432.1	192.4	33	486.9	216.8	93	541.7	241.2
54	323.4	144.0	14	378.2	168.4	74	433.0	192.8	34	487.8	217.2	94	542.6	241.6
55	324.3	144.4	15	379.1	168.8	75	433.9	193.2	35	488.7	217.6	95	543.6	242.0
56	325.2	144.8	16	380.0	169.2	76	434.8	193.6	36	489.7	218.0	96	544.5	242.4
57	326.1	145.2	17	380.9	169.6	77	435.8	194.0	37	490.6	218.4	97	545.4	242.8
58	327.0	145.6	18	381.9	170.0	78	436.7	194.4	38	491.5	218.8	98	546.3	243.2
59	328.0	146.0	19	382.8	170.4	79	437.6	194.8	39	492.4	219.2	99	547.2	243.6
60	328.9	146.4	20	383.7	170.8	80	438.5	195.2	40	493.3	219.6	600	548.1	244.0
Dist.	Dep.	D. Lat.	Dist.	Dep.	D. Lat.	Dist.	Dep.	D. Lat.	Dist.	Dep.	D. Lat.	Dist.	Dep.	D. Lat.
												294° / 246°	066° / 114°	

Dist.	D. Lat.	Dep.
D Lo	Dep.	
	m	D Lo

66°

TABLE 4

335° | 025° / 205° | 155°

Traverse 25° Table

Dist.	D. Lat.	Dep.	Dist.	D. Lat.	Dep.	Dist.	D. Lat.	Dep.	Dist.	D. Lat.	Dep.	Dist.	D. Lat.	Dep.
1	0.9	0.4	61	55.3	25.8	121	109.7	51.1	181	164.0	76.5	241	218.4	101.9
2	1.8	0.8	62	56.2	26.2	22	110.6	51.6	82	164.9	76.9	42	219.3	102.3
3	2.7	1.3	63	57.1	26.6	23	111.5	52.0	83	165.9	77.3	43	220.2	102.7
4	3.6	1.7	64	58.0	27.0	24	112.4	52.4	84	166.8	77.8	44	221.1	103.1
5	4.5	2.1	65	58.9	27.5	25	113.3	52.8	85	167.7	78.2	45	222.0	103.5
6	5.4	2.5	66	59.8	27.9	26	114.2	53.2	86	168.6	78.6	46	223.0	104.0
7	6.3	3.0	67	60.7	28.3	27	115.1	53.7	87	169.5	79.0	47	223.9	104.4
8	7.3	3.4	68	61.6	28.7	28	116.0	54.1	88	170.4	79.5	48	224.8	104.8
9	8.2	3.8	69	62.5	29.2	29	116.9	54.5	89	171.3	79.9	49	225.7	105.2
10	9.1	4.2	70	63.4	29.6	30	117.8	54.9	90	172.2	80.3	50	226.6	105.7
11	10.0	4.6	71	64.3	30.0	131	118.7	55.4	191	173.1	80.7	251	227.5	106.1
12	10.9	5.1	72	65.3	30.4	32	119.6	55.8	92	174.0	81.1	52	228.4	106.5
13	11.8	5.5	73	66.2	30.9	33	120.5	56.2	93	174.9	81.6	53	229.3	106.9
14	12.7	5.9	74	67.1	31.3	34	121.4	56.6	94	175.8	82.0	54	230.2	107.3
15	13.6	6.3	75	68.0	31.7	35	122.4	57.1	95	176.7	82.4	55	231.1	107.8
16	14.5	6.8	76	68.9	32.1	36	123.3	57.5	96	177.6	82.8	56	232.0	108.2
17	15.4	7.2	77	69.8	32.5	37	124.2	57.9	97	178.5	83.3	57	232.9	108.6
18	16.3	7.6	78	70.7	33.0	38	125.1	58.3	98	179.4	83.7	58	233.8	109.0
19	17.2	8.0	79	71.6	33.4	39	126.0	58.7	99	180.4	84.1	59	234.7	109.5
20	18.1	8.5	80	72.5	33.8	40	126.9	59.2	200	181.3	84.5	60	235.6	109.9
21	19.0	8.9	81	73.4	34.2	141	127.8	59.6	201	182.2	84.9	261	236.5	110.3
22	19.9	9.3	82	74.3	34.7	42	128.7	60.0	02	183.1	85.4	62	237.5	110.7
23	20.8	9.7	83	75.2	35.1	43	129.6	60.4	03	184.0	85.8	63	238.4	111.1
24	21.8	10.1	84	76.1	35.5	44	130.5	60.9	04	184.9	86.2	64	239.3	111.6
25	22.7	10.6	85	77.0	35.9	45	131.4	61.3	05	185.8	86.6	65	240.2	112.0
26	23.6	11.0	86	77.9	36.3	46	132.3	61.7	06	186.7	87.1	66	241.1	112.4
27	24.5	11.4	87	78.8	36.8	47	133.2	62.1	07	187.6	87.5	67	242.0	112.8
28	25.4	11.8	88	79.8	37.2	48	134.1	62.5	08	188.5	87.9	68	242.9	113.3
29	26.3	12.3	89	80.7	37.6	49	135.0	63.0	09	189.4	88.3	69	243.8	113.7
30	27.2	12.7	90	81.6	38.0	50	135.9	63.4	10	190.3	88.7	70	244.7	114.1
31	28.1	13.1	91	82.5	38.5	151	136.9	63.8	211	191.2	89.2	271	245.6	114.5
32	29.0	13.5	92	83.4	38.9	52	137.8	64.2	12	192.1	89.6	72	246.5	115.0
33	29.9	13.9	93	84.3	39.3	53	138.7	64.7	13	193.0	90.0	73	247.4	115.4
34	30.8	14.4	94	85.2	39.7	54	139.6	65.1	14	193.9	90.4	74	248.3	115.8
35	31.7	14.8	95	86.1	40.1	55	140.5	65.5	15	194.9	90.9	75	249.2	116.2
36	32.6	15.2	96	87.0	40.6	56	141.4	65.9	16	195.8	91.3	76	250.1	116.6
37	33.5	15.6	97	87.9	41.0	57	142.3	66.4	17	196.7	91.7	77	251.0	117.1
38	34.4	16.1	98	88.8	41.4	58	143.2	66.8	18	197.6	92.1	78	252.0	117.5
39	35.3	16.5	99	89.7	41.8	59	144.1	67.2	19	198.5	92.6	79	252.9	117.9
40	36.3	16.9	100	90.6	42.3	60	145.0	67.6	20	199.4	93.0	80	253.8	118.3
41	37.2	17.3	101	91.5	42.7	161	145.9	68.0	221	200.3	93.4	281	254.7	118.8
42	38.1	17.7	02	92.4	43.1	62	146.8	68.5	22	201.2	93.8	82	255.6	119.2
43	39.0	18.2	03	93.3	43.5	63	147.7	68.9	23	202.1	94.2	83	256.5	119.6
44	39.9	18.6	04	94.3	44.0	64	148.6	69.3	24	203.0	94.7	84	257.4	120.0
45	40.8	19.0	05	95.2	44.4	65	149.5	69.7	25	203.9	95.1	85	258.3	120.4
46	41.7	19.4	06	96.1	44.8	66	150.4	70.2	26	204.8	95.5	86	259.2	120.9
47	42.6	19.9	07	97.0	45.2	67	151.4	70.6	27	205.7	95.9	87	260.1	121.3
48	43.5	20.3	08	97.9	45.6	68	152.3	71.0	28	206.6	96.4	88	261.0	121.7
49	44.4	20.7	09	98.8	46.1	69	153.2	71.4	29	207.5	96.8	89	261.9	122.1
50	45.3	21.1	10	99.7	46.5	70	154.1	71.8	30	208.5	97.2	90	262.8	122.6
51	46.2	21.6	111	100.6	46.9	171	155.0	72.3	231	209.4	97.6	291	263.7	123.0
52	47.1	22.0	12	101.5	47.3	72	155.9	72.7	32	210.3	98.0	92	264.6	123.4
53	48.0	22.4	13	102.4	47.8	73	156.8	73.1	33	211.2	98.5	93	265.5	123.8
54	48.9	22.8	14	103.3	48.2	74	157.7	73.5	34	212.1	98.9	94	266.5	124.2
55	49.8	23.2	15	104.2	48.6	75	158.6	74.0	35	213.0	99.3	95	267.4	124.7
56	50.8	23.7	16	105.1	49.0	76	159.5	74.4	36	213.9	99.7	96	268.3	125.1
57	51.7	24.1	17	106.0	49.4	77	160.4	74.8	37	214.8	100.2	97	269.2	125.5
58	52.6	24.5	18	106.9	49.9	78	161.3	75.2	38	215.7	100.6	98	270.1	125.9
59	53.5	24.9	19	107.9	50.3	79	162.2	75.6	39	216.6	101.0	99	271.0	126.4
60	54.4	25.4	20	108.8	50.7	80	163.1	76.1	40	217.5	101.4	300	271.9	126.8
Dist.	Dep.	D. Lat.	Dist.	Dep.	D. Lat.	Dist.	Dep.	D. Lat.	Dist.	Dep.	D. Lat.	Dist.	Dep.	D. Lat.

295° | 065° / 245° | 115°

65°

Dist.	D. Lat.	Dep.
N.	N x Cos.	N x Sin.
Hypotenuse	Side Adj.	Side Opp.

TABLE 4

335° | 025° / 205° | 155°

Traverse 25° Table

Dist.	D. Lat.	Dep.	Dist.	D. Lat.	Dep.	Dist.	D. Lat.	Dep.	Dist.	D. Lat.	Dep.	Dist.	D. Lat.	Dep.
301	272.8	127.2	361	327.2	152.6	421	381.6	177.9	481	435.9	203.3	541	490.3	228.6
02	273.7	127.6	62	328.1	153.0	22	382.5	178.3	82	436.8	203.7	42	491.2	229.1
03	274.6	128.1	63	329.0	153.4	23	383.4	178.8	83	437.7	204.1	43	492.1	229.5
04	275.5	128.5	64	329.9	153.8	24	384.3	179.2	84	438.7	204.5	44	493.0	229.9
05	276.4	128.9	65	330.8	154.3	25	385.2	179.6	85	439.6	205.0	45	493.9	230.3
06	277.3	129.3	66	331.7	154.7	26	386.1	180.0	86	440.5	205.4	46	494.8	230.7
07	278.2	129.7	67	332.6	155.1	27	387.0	180.5	87	441.4	205.8	47	495.8	231.2
08	279.1	130.2	68	333.5	155.5	28	387.9	180.9	88	442.3	206.2	48	496.7	231.6
09	280.0	130.6	69	334.4	155.9	29	388.8	181.3	89	443.2	206.7	49	497.6	232.0
10	281.0	131.0	70	335.3	156.4	30	389.7	181.7	90	444.1	207.1	50	498.5	232.4
311	281.9	131.4	371	336.2	156.8	431	390.6	182.1	491	445.0	207.5	551	499.4	232.9
12	282.8	131.9	72	337.1	157.2	32	391.5	182.6	92	445.9	207.9	52	500.3	233.3
13	283.7	132.3	73	338.1	157.6	33	392.4	183.0	93	446.8	208.4	53	501.2	233.7
14	284.6	132.7	74	339.0	158.1	34	393.3	183.4	94	447.7	208.8	54	502.1	234.1
15	285.5	133.1	75	339.9	158.5	35	394.2	183.8	95	448.6	209.2	55	503.0	234.6
16	286.4	133.5	76	340.8	158.9	36	395.2	184.3	96	449.5	209.6	56	503.9	235.0
17	287.3	134.0	77	341.7	159.3	37	396.1	184.7	97	450.4	210.0	57	504.8	235.4
18	288.2	134.4	78	342.6	159.7	38	397.0	185.1	98	451.3	210.5	58	505.7	235.8
19	289.1	134.8	79	343.5	160.2	39	397.9	185.5	99	452.2	210.9	59	506.6	236.2
20	290.0	135.2	80	344.4	160.6	40	398.8	186.0	500	453.2	211.3	60	507.5	236.7
321	290.9	135.7	381	345.3	161.0	441	399.7	186.4	501	454.1	211.7	561	508.4	237.1
22	291.8	136.1	82	346.2	161.4	42	400.6	186.8	02	455.0	212.2	62	509.3	237.5
23	292.7	136.5	83	347.1	161.9	43	401.5	187.2	03	455.9	212.6	63	510.3	237.9
24	293.6	136.9	84	348.0	162.3	44	402.4	187.6	04	456.8	213.0	64	511.2	238.4
25	294.6	137.4	85	348.9	162.7	45	403.3	188.1	05	457.7	213.4	65	512.1	238.8
26	295.5	137.8	86	349.8	163.1	46	404.2	188.5	06	458.6	213.8	66	513.0	239.2
27	296.4	138.2	87	350.7	163.6	47	405.1	188.9	07	459.5	214.3	67	513.9	239.6
28	297.3	138.6	88	351.6	164.0	48	406.0	189.3	08	460.4	214.7	68	514.8	240.0
29	298.2	139.0	89	352.6	164.4	49	406.9	189.8	09	461.3	215.1	69	515.7	240.5
30	299.1	139.5	90	353.5	164.8	50	407.8	190.2	10	462.2	215.5	70	516.6	240.9
331	300.0	139.9	391	354.4	165.2	451	408.7	190.6	511	463.1	216.0	571	517.5	241.3
32	300.9	140.3	92	355.3	165.7	52	409.7	191.0	12	464.0	216.4	72	518.4	241.7
33	301.8	140.7	93	356.2	166.1	53	410.6	191.4	13	464.9	216.8	73	519.3	242.2
34	302.7	141.2	94	357.1	166.5	54	411.5	191.9	14	465.8	217.2	74	520.2	242.6
35	303.6	141.6	95	358.0	166.9	55	412.4	192.3	15	466.7	217.6	75	521.1	243.0
36	304.5	142.0	96	358.9	167.4	56	413.3	192.7	16	467.7	218.1	76	522.0	243.4
37	305.4	142.4	97	359.8	167.8	57	414.2	193.1	17	468.6	218.5	77	522.9	243.9
38	306.3	142.8	98	360.7	168.2	58	415.1	193.6	18	469.5	218.9	78	523.8	244.3
39	307.2	143.3	99	361.6	168.6	59	416.0	194.0	19	470.4	219.3	79	524.8	244.7
40	308.1	143.7	400	362.5	169.0	60	416.9	194.4	20	471.3	219.8	80	525.7	245.1
341	309.1	144.1	401	363.4	169.5	461	417.8	194.8	521	472.2	220.2	581	526.6	245.5
42	310.0	144.5	02	364.3	169.9	62	418.7	195.2	22	473.1	220.6	82	527.5	246.0
43	310.9	145.0	03	365.2	170.3	63	419.6	195.7	23	474.0	221.0	83	528.4	246.4
44	311.8	145.4	04	366.1	170.7	64	420.5	196.1	24	474.9	221.5	84	529.3	246.8
45	312.7	145.8	05	367.1	171.2	65	421.4	196.5	25	475.8	221.9	85	530.2	247.2
46	313.6	146.2	06	368.0	171.6	66	422.3	196.9	26	476.7	222.3	86	531.1	247.7
47	314.5	146.6	07	368.9	172.0	67	423.2	197.4	27	477.6	222.7	87	532.0	248.1
48	315.4	147.1	08	369.8	172.4	68	424.2	197.8	28	478.5	223.1	88	532.9	248.5
49	316.3	147.5	09	370.7	172.9	69	425.1	198.2	29	479.4	223.6	89	533.8	248.9
50	317.2	147.9	10	371.6	173.3	70	426.0	198.6	30	480.3	224.0	90	534.7	249.3
351	318.1	148.3	411	372.5	173.7	471	426.9	199.1	531	481.2	224.4	591	535.6	249.8
52	319.0	148.8	12	373.4	174.1	72	427.8	199.5	32	482.2	224.8	92	536.5	250.2
53	319.9	149.2	13	374.3	174.5	73	428.7	199.9	33	483.1	225.3	93	537.4	250.6
54	320.8	149.6	14	375.2	175.0	74	429.6	200.3	34	484.0	225.7	94	538.3	251.0
55	321.7	150.0	15	376.1	175.4	75	430.5	200.7	35	484.9	226.1	95	539.3	251.5
56	322.6	150.5	16	377.0	175.8	76	431.4	201.2	36	485.8	226.5	96	540.2	251.9
57	323.6	150.9	17	377.9	176.2	77	432.3	201.6	37	486.7	226.9	97	541.1	252.3
58	324.5	151.3	18	378.8	176.7	78	433.2	202.0	38	487.6	227.4	98	542.0	252.7
59	325.4	151.7	19	379.7	177.1	79	434.1	202.4	39	488.5	227.8	99	542.9	253.1
60	326.3	152.1	20	380.6	177.5	80	435.0	202.9	40	489.4	228.2	600	543.8	253.6
Dist.	Dep.	D. Lat.	Dist.	Dep.	D. Lat.	Dist.	Dep.	D. Lat.	Dist.	Dep.	D. Lat.	Dist.	Dep.	D. Lat.

Dist.	D. Lat.	Dep.
D Lo	Dep.	
	m	D Lo

65°

295° | 065° / 245° | 115°

TABLE 4

Traverse 26° Table

334° | 026°
206° | 154°

Dist.	D. Lat.	Dep.	Dist.	D. Lat.	Dep.	Dist.	D. Lat.	Dep.	Dist.	D. Lat.	Dep.	Dist.	D. Lat.	Dep.
1	0.9	0.4	61	54.8	26.7	121	108.8	53.0	181	162.7	79.3	241	216.6	105.6
2	1.8	0.9	62	55.7	27.2	22	109.7	53.5	82	163.6	79.8	42	217.5	106.1
3	2.7	1.3	63	56.6	27.6	23	110.6	53.9	83	164.5	80.2	43	218.4	106.5
4	3.6	1.8	64	57.5	28.1	24	111.5	54.4	84	165.4	80.7	44	219.3	107.0
5	4.5	2.2	65	58.4	28.5	25	112.3	54.8	85	166.3	81.1	45	220.2	107.4
6	5.4	2.6	66	59.3	28.9	26	113.2	55.2	86	167.2	81.5	46	221.1	107.8
7	6.3	3.1	67	60.2	29.4	27	114.1	55.7	87	168.1	82.0	47	222.0	108.3
8	7.2	3.5	68	61.1	29.8	28	115.0	56.1	88	169.0	82.4	48	222.9	108.7
9	8.1	3.9	69	62.0	30.2	29	115.9	56.5	89	169.9	82.9	49	223.8	109.2
10	9.0	4.4	70	62.9	30.7	30	116.8	57.0	90	170.8	83.3	50	224.7	109.6
11	9.9	4.8	71	63.8	31.1	131	117.7	57.4	191	171.7	83.7	251	225.6	110.0
12	10.8	5.3	72	64.7	31.6	32	118.6	57.9	92	172.6	84.2	52	226.5	110.5
13	11.7	5.7	73	65.6	32.0	33	119.5	58.3	93	173.5	84.6	53	227.4	110.9
14	12.6	6.1	74	66.5	32.4	34	120.4	58.7	94	174.4	85.0	54	228.3	111.3
15	13.5	6.6	75	67.4	32.9	35	121.3	59.2	95	175.3	85.5	55	229.2	111.8
16	14.4	7.0	76	68.3	33.3	36	122.2	59.6	96	176.2	85.9	56	230.1	112.2
17	15.3	7.5	77	69.2	33.8	37	123.1	60.1	97	177.1	86.4	57	231.0	112.7
18	16.2	7.9	78	70.1	34.2	38	124.0	60.5	98	178.0	86.8	58	231.9	113.1
19	17.1	8.3	79	71.0	34.6	39	124.9	60.9	99	178.9	87.2	59	232.8	113.5
20	18.0	8.8	80	71.9	35.1	40	125.8	61.4	200	179.8	87.7	60	233.7	114.0
21	18.9	9.2	81	72.8	35.5	141	126.7	61.8	201	180.7	88.1	261	234.6	114.4
22	19.8	9.6	82	73.7	35.9	42	127.6	62.2	02	181.6	88.6	62	235.5	114.9
23	20.7	10.1	83	74.6	36.4	43	128.5	62.7	03	182.5	89.0	63	236.4	115.3
24	21.6	10.5	84	75.5	36.8	44	129.4	63.1	04	183.4	89.4	64	237.3	115.7
25	22.5	11.0	85	76.4	37.3	45	130.3	63.6	05	184.3	89.9	65	238.2	116.2
26	23.4	11.4	86	77.3	37.7	46	131.2	64.0	06	185.2	90.3	66	239.1	116.6
27	24.3	11.8	87	78.2	38.1	47	132.1	64.4	07	186.1	90.7	67	240.0	117.0
28	25.2	12.3	88	79.1	38.6	48	133.0	64.9	08	186.9	91.2	68	240.9	117.5
29	26.1	12.7	89	80.0	39.0	49	133.9	65.3	09	187.8	91.6	69	241.8	117.9
30	27.0	13.2	90	80.9	39.5	50	134.8	65.8	10	188.7	92.1	70	242.7	118.4
31	27.9	13.6	91	81.8	39.9	151	135.7	66.2	211	189.6	92.5	271	243.6	118.8
32	28.8	14.0	92	82.7	40.3	52	136.6	66.6	12	190.5	92.9	72	244.5	119.2
33	29.7	14.5	93	83.6	40.8	53	137.5	67.1	13	191.4	93.4	73	245.4	119.7
34	30.6	14.9	94	84.5	41.2	54	138.4	67.5	14	192.3	93.8	74	246.3	120.1
35	31.5	15.3	95	85.4	41.6	55	139.3	67.9	15	193.2	94.2	75	247.2	120.6
36	32.4	15.8	96	86.3	42.1	56	140.2	68.4	16	194.1	94.7	76	248.1	121.0
37	33.3	16.2	97	87.2	42.5	57	141.1	68.8	17	195.0	95.1	77	249.0	121.4
38	34.2	16.7	98	88.1	43.0	58	142.0	69.3	18	195.9	95.6	78	249.9	121.9
39	35.1	17.1	99	89.0	43.4	59	142.9	69.7	19	196.8	96.0	79	250.8	122.3
40	36.0	17.5	100	89.9	43.8	60	143.8	70.1	20	197.7	96.4	80	251.7	122.7
41	36.9	18.0	101	90.8	44.3	161	144.7	70.6	221	198.6	96.9	281	252.6	123.2
42	37.7	18.4	02	91.7	44.7	62	145.6	71.0	22	199.5	97.3	82	253.5	123.6
43	38.6	18.8	03	92.6	45.2	63	146.5	71.5	23	200.4	97.8	83	254.4	124.1
44	39.5	19.3	04	93.5	45.6	64	147.4	71.9	24	201.3	98.2	84	255.3	124.5
45	40.4	19.7	05	94.4	46.0	65	148.3	72.3	25	202.2	98.6	85	256.2	124.9
46	41.3	20.2	06	95.3	46.5	66	149.2	72.8	26	203.1	99.1	86	257.1	125.4
47	42.2	20.6	07	96.2	46.9	67	150.1	73.2	27	204.0	99.5	87	258.0	125.8
48	43.1	21.0	08	97.1	47.3	68	151.0	73.6	28	204.9	99.9	88	258.9	126.3
49	44.0	21.5	09	98.0	47.8	69	151.9	74.1	29	205.8	100.4	89	259.8	126.7
50	44.9	21.9	10	98.9	48.2	70	152.8	74.5	30	206.7	100.8	90	260.7	127.1
51	45.8	22.4	111	99.8	48.7	171	153.7	75.0	231	207.6	101.3	291	261.5	127.6
52	46.7	22.8	12	100.7	49.1	72	154.6	75.4	32	208.5	101.7	92	262.4	128.0
53	47.6	23.2	13	101.6	49.5	73	155.5	75.8	33	209.4	102.1	93	263.3	128.4
54	48.5	23.7	14	102.5	50.0	74	156.4	76.3	34	210.3	102.6	94	264.2	128.9
55	49.4	24.1	15	103.4	50.4	75	157.3	76.7	35	211.2	103.0	95	265.1	129.3
56	50.3	24.5	16	104.3	50.9	76	158.2	77.2	36	212.1	103.5	96	266.0	129.8
57	51.2	25.0	17	105.2	51.3	77	159.1	77.6	37	213.0	103.9	97	266.9	130.2
58	52.1	25.4	18	106.1	51.7	78	160.0	78.0	38	213.9	104.3	98	267.8	130.6
59	53.0	25.9	19	107.0	52.2	79	160.9	78.5	39	214.8	104.8	99	268.7	131.1
60	53.9	26.3	20	107.9	52.6	80	161.8	78.9	40	215.7	105.2	300	269.6	131.5
Dist.	Dep.	D. Lat.	Dist.	Dep.	D. Lat.	Dist.	Dep.	D. Lat.	Dist.	Dep.	D. Lat.	Dist.	Dep.	D. Lat.

296° | 064°
244° | 116°

64°

Dist.	D. Lat.	Dep.
N.	N x Cos.	N x Sin.
Hypotenuse	Side Adj.	Side Opp.

TABLE 4

Traverse 26° Table

334° | 026°
206° | 154°

Dist.	D. Lat.	Dep.	Dist.	D. Lat.	Dep.	Dist.	D. Lat.	Dep.	Dist.	D. Lat.	Dep.	Dist.	D. Lat.	Dep.
301	270.5	131.9	361	324.5	158.3	421	378.4	184.6	481	432.3	210.9	541	486.2	237.2
02	271.4	132.4	62	325.4	158.7	22	379.3	185.0	82	433.2	211.3	42	487.1	237.6
03	272.3	132.8	63	326.3	159.1	23	380.2	185.4	83	434.1	211.7	43	488.0	238.0
04	273.2	133.3	64	327.2	159.6	24	381.1	185.9	84	435.0	212.2	44	488.9	238.5
05	274.1	133.7	65	328.1	160.0	25	382.0	186.3	85	435.9	212.6	45	489.8	238.9
06	275.0	134.1	66	329.0	160.4	26	382.9	186.7	86	436.8	213.0	46	490.7	239.4
07	275.9	134.6	67	329.9	160.9	27	383.8	187.2	87	437.7	213.5	47	491.6	239.8
08	276.8	135.0	68	330.8	161.3	28	384.7	187.6	88	438.6	213.9	48	492.5	240.2
09	277.7	135.5	69	331.7	161.8	29	385.6	188.1	89	439.5	214.4	49	493.4	240.7
10	278.6	135.9	70	332.6	162.2	30	386.5	188.5	90	440.4	214.8	50	494.3	241.1
311	279.5	136.3	371	333.5	162.6	431	387.4	188.9	491	441.3	215.2	551	495.2	241.5
12	280.4	136.8	72	334.4	163.1	32	388.3	189.4	92	442.2	215.7	52	496.1	242.0
13	281.3	137.2	73	335.3	163.5	33	389.2	189.8	93	443.1	216.1	53	497.0	242.4
14	282.2	137.6	74	336.1	164.0	34	390.1	190.3	94	444.0	216.6	54	497.9	242.9
15	283.1	138.1	75	337.0	164.4	35	391.0	190.7	95	444.9	217.0	55	498.8	243.3
16	284.0	138.5	76	337.9	164.8	36	391.9	191.1	96	445.8	217.4	56	499.7	243.7
17	284.9	139.0	77	338.8	165.3	37	392.8	191.6	97	446.7	217.9	57	500.6	244.2
18	285.8	139.4	78	339.7	165.7	38	393.7	192.0	98	447.6	218.3	58	501.5	244.6
19	286.7	139.8	79	340.6	166.1	39	394.6	192.4	99	448.5	218.7	59	502.4	245.0
20	287.6	140.3	80	341.5	166.6	40	395.5	192.9	500	449.4	219.2	60	503.3	245.5
321	288.5	140.7	381	342.4	167.0	441	396.4	193.3	501	450.3	219.6	561	504.2	245.9
22	289.4	141.2	82	343.3	167.5	42	397.3	193.8	02	451.2	220.1	62	505.1	246.4
23	290.3	141.6	83	344.2	167.9	43	398.2	194.2	03	452.1	220.5	63	506.0	246.8
24	291.2	142.0	84	345.1	168.3	44	399.1	194.6	04	453.0	220.9	64	506.9	247.2
25	292.1	142.5	85	346.0	168.8	45	400.0	195.1	05	453.9	221.4	65	507.8	247.7
26	293.0	142.9	86	346.9	169.2	46	400.9	195.5	06	454.8	221.8	66	508.7	248.1
27	293.9	143.3	87	347.8	169.6	47	401.8	196.0	07	455.7	222.3	67	509.6	248.6
28	294.8	143.8	88	348.7	170.1	48	402.7	196.4	08	456.6	222.7	68	510.5	249.0
29	295.7	144.2	89	349.6	170.5	49	403.6	196.8	09	457.5	223.1	69	511.4	249.4
30	296.6	144.7	90	350.5	171.0	50	404.5	197.3	10	458.4	223.6	70	512.3	249.9
331	297.5	145.1	391	351.4	171.4	451	405.4	197.7	511	459.3	224.0	571	513.2	250.3
32	298.4	145.5	92	352.3	171.8	52	406.3	198.1	12	460.2	224.4	72	514.1	250.7
33	299.3	146.0	93	353.2	172.3	53	407.2	198.6	13	461.1	224.9	73	515.0	251.2
34	300.2	146.4	94	354.1	172.7	54	408.1	199.0	14	462.0	225.3	74	515.9	251.6
35	301.1	146.9	95	355.0	173.2	55	409.0	199.5	15	462.9	225.8	75	516.8	252.1
36	302.0	147.3	96	355.9	173.6	56	409.9	199.9	16	463.8	226.2	76	517.7	252.5
37	302.9	147.7	97	356.8	174.0	57	410.7	200.3	17	464.7	226.6	77	518.6	252.9
38	303.8	148.2	98	357.7	174.5	58	411.6	200.8	18	465.6	227.1	78	519.5	253.4
39	304.7	148.6	99	358.6	174.9	59	412.5	201.2	19	466.5	227.5	79	520.4	253.8
40	305.6	149.0	400	359.5	175.3	60	413.4	201.7	20	467.4	228.0	80	521.3	254.3
341	306.5	149.5	401	360.4	175.8	461	414.3	202.1	521	468.3	228.4	581	522.2	254.7
42	307.4	149.9	02	361.3	176.2	62	415.2	202.5	22	469.2	228.8	82	523.1	255.1
43	308.3	150.4	03	362.2	176.7	63	416.1	203.0	23	470.1	229.3	83	524.0	255.6
44	309.2	150.8	04	363.1	177.1	64	417.0	203.4	24	471.0	229.7	84	524.9	256.0
45	310.1	151.2	05	364.0	177.5	65	417.9	203.8	25	471.9	230.1	85	525.8	256.4
46	311.0	151.7	06	364.9	178.0	66	418.8	204.3	26	472.8	230.6	86	526.7	256.9
47	311.9	152.1	07	365.8	178.4	67	419.7	204.7	27	473.7	231.0	87	527.6	257.3
48	312.8	152.6	08	366.7	178.9	68	420.6	205.2	28	474.6	231.5	88	528.5	257.8
49	313.7	153.0	09	367.6	179.3	69	421.5	205.6	29	475.5	231.9	89	529.4	258.2
50	314.6	153.4	10	368.5	179.7	70	422.4	206.0	30	476.4	232.3	90	530.3	258.6
351	315.5	153.9	411	369.4	180.2	471	423.3	206.5	531	477.3	232.8	591	531.2	259.1
52	316.4	154.3	12	370.3	180.6	72	424.2	206.9	32	478.2	233.2	92	532.1	259.5
53	317.3	154.7	13	371.2	181.0	73	425.1	207.3	33	479.1	233.7	93	533.0	260.0
54	318.2	155.2	14	372.1	181.5	74	426.0	207.8	34	480.0	234.1	94	533.9	260.4
55	319.1	155.6	15	373.0	181.9	75	426.9	208.2	35	480.9	234.5	95	534.8	260.8
56	320.0	156.1	16	373.9	182.4	76	427.8	208.7	36	481.8	235.0	96	535.7	261.3
57	320.9	156.5	17	374.8	182.8	77	428.7	209.1	37	482.7	235.4	97	536.6	261.7
58	321.8	156.9	18	375.7	183.2	78	429.6	209.5	38	483.6	235.8	98	537.5	262.1
59	322.7	157.4	19	376.6	183.7	79	430.5	210.0	39	484.4	236.3	99	538.4	262.6
60	323.6	157.8	20	377.5	184.1	80	431.4	210.4	40	485.3	236.7	600	539.3	263.0
Dist.	Dep.	D. Lat.	Dist.	Dep.	D. Lat.	Dist.	Dep.	D. Lat.	Dist.	Dep.	D. Lat.	Dist.	Dep.	D. Lat.

Dist.	D. Lat.	Dep.
D Lo	Dep.	
	m	D Lo

64°

296° | 064°
244° | 116°

TABLE 4

27° Traverse Table

333° | 027° — 207° | 153°

Dist.	D. Lat.	Dep.	Dist.	D. Lat.	Dep.	Dist.	D. Lat.	Dep.	Dist.	D. Lat.	Dep.	Dist.	D. Lat.	Dep.
1	0.9	0.5	61	54.4	27.7	121	107.8	54.9	181	161.3	82.2	241	214.7	109.4
2	1.8	0.9	62	55.2	28.1	22	108.7	55.4	82	162.2	82.6	42	215.6	109.9
3	2.7	1.4	63	56.1	28.6	23	109.6	55.8	83	163.1	83.1	43	216.5	110.3
4	3.6	1.8	64	57.0	29.1	24	110.5	56.3	84	163.9	83.5	44	217.4	110.8
5	4.5	2.3	65	57.9	29.5	25	111.4	56.7	85	164.8	84.0	45	218.3	111.2
6	5.3	2.7	66	58.8	30.0	26	112.3	57.2	86	165.7	84.4	46	219.2	111.7
7	6.2	3.2	67	59.7	30.4	27	113.2	57.7	87	166.6	84.9	47	220.1	112.1
8	7.1	3.6	68	60.6	30.9	28	114.0	58.1	88	167.5	85.4	48	221.0	112.6
9	8.0	4.1	69	61.5	31.3	29	114.9	58.6	89	168.4	85.8	49	221.9	113.0
10	8.9	4.5	70	62.4	31.8	30	115.8	59.0	90	169.3	86.3	50	222.8	113.5
11	9.8	5.0	71	63.3	32.2	131	116.7	59.5	191	170.2	86.7	251	223.6	114.0
12	10.7	5.4	72	64.2	32.7	32	117.6	59.9	92	171.1	87.2	52	224.5	114.4
13	11.6	5.9	73	65.0	33.1	33	118.5	60.4	93	172.0	87.6	53	225.4	114.9
14	12.5	6.4	74	65.9	33.6	34	119.4	60.8	94	172.9	88.1	54	226.3	115.3
15	13.4	6.8	75	66.8	34.0	35	120.3	61.3	95	173.7	88.5	55	227.2	115.8
16	14.3	7.3	76	67.7	34.5	36	121.2	61.7	96	174.6	89.0	56	228.1	116.2
17	15.1	7.7	77	68.6	35.0	37	122.1	62.2	97	175.5	89.4	57	229.0	116.7
18	16.0	8.2	78	69.5	35.4	38	123.0	62.7	98	176.4	89.9	58	229.9	117.1
19	16.9	8.6	79	70.4	35.9	39	123.8	63.1	99	177.3	90.3	59	230.8	117.6
20	17.8	9.1	80	71.3	36.3	40	124.7	63.6	200	178.2	90.8	60	231.7	118.0
21	18.7	9.5	81	72.2	36.8	141	125.6	64.0	201	179.1	91.3	261	232.6	118.5
22	19.6	10.0	82	73.1	37.2	42	126.5	64.5	02	180.0	91.7	62	233.4	118.9
23	20.5	10.4	83	74.0	37.7	43	127.4	64.9	03	180.9	92.2	63	234.3	119.4
24	21.4	10.9	84	74.8	38.1	44	128.3	65.4	04	181.8	92.6	64	235.2	119.9
25	22.3	11.3	85	75.7	38.6	45	129.2	65.8	05	182.7	93.1	65	236.1	120.3
26	23.2	11.8	86	76.6	39.0	46	130.1	66.3	06	183.5	93.5	66	237.0	120.8
27	24.1	12.3	87	77.5	39.5	47	131.0	66.7	07	184.4	94.0	67	237.9	121.2
28	24.9	12.7	88	78.4	40.0	48	131.9	67.2	08	185.3	94.4	68	238.8	121.7
29	25.8	13.2	89	79.3	40.4	49	132.8	67.6	09	186.2	94.9	69	239.7	122.1
30	26.7	13.6	90	80.2	40.9	50	133.7	68.1	10	187.1	95.3	70	240.6	122.6
31	27.6	14.1	91	81.1	41.3	151	134.5	68.6	211	188.0	95.8	271	241.5	123.0
32	28.5	14.5	92	82.0	41.8	52	135.4	69.0	12	188.9	96.2	72	242.4	123.5
33	29.4	15.0	93	82.9	42.2	53	136.3	69.5	13	189.8	96.7	73	243.2	123.9
34	30.3	15.4	94	83.8	42.7	54	137.2	69.9	14	190.7	97.2	74	244.1	124.4
35	31.2	15.9	95	84.6	43.1	55	138.1	70.4	15	191.6	97.6	75	245.0	124.8
36	32.1	16.3	96	85.5	43.6	56	139.0	70.8	16	192.5	98.1	76	245.9	125.3
37	33.0	16.8	97	86.4	44.0	57	139.9	71.3	17	193.3	98.5	77	246.8	125.8
38	33.9	17.3	98	87.3	44.5	58	140.8	71.7	18	194.2	99.0	78	247.7	126.2
39	34.7	17.7	99	88.2	44.9	59	141.7	72.2	19	195.1	99.4	79	248.6	126.7
40	35.6	18.2	100	89.1	45.4	60	142.6	72.6	20	196.0	99.9	80	249.5	127.1
41	36.5	18.6	101	90.0	45.9	161	143.5	73.1	221	196.9	100.3	281	250.4	127.6
42	37.4	19.1	02	90.9	46.3	62	144.3	73.5	22	197.8	100.8	82	251.3	128.0
43	38.3	19.5	03	91.8	46.8	63	145.2	74.0	23	198.7	101.2	83	252.2	128.5
44	39.2	20.0	04	92.7	47.2	64	146.1	74.5	24	199.6	101.7	84	253.0	128.9
45	40.1	20.4	05	93.6	47.7	65	147.0	74.9	25	200.5	102.1	85	253.9	129.4
46	41.0	20.9	06	94.4	48.1	66	147.9	75.4	26	201.4	102.6	86	254.8	129.8
47	41.9	21.3	07	95.3	48.6	67	148.8	75.8	27	202.3	103.1	87	255.7	130.3
48	42.8	21.8	08	96.2	49.0	68	149.7	76.3	28	203.1	103.5	88	256.6	130.7
49	43.7	22.2	09	97.1	49.5	69	150.6	76.7	29	204.0	104.0	89	257.5	131.2
50	44.6	22.7	10	98.0	49.9	70	151.5	77.2	30	204.9	104.4	90	258.4	131.7
51	45.4	23.2	111	98.9	50.4	171	152.4	77.6	231	205.8	104.9	291	259.3	132.1
52	46.3	23.6	12	99.8	50.8	72	153.3	78.1	32	206.7	105.3	92	260.2	132.6
53	47.2	24.1	13	100.7	51.3	73	154.1	78.5	33	207.6	105.8	93	261.1	133.0
54	48.1	24.5	14	101.6	51.8	74	155.0	79.0	34	208.5	106.2	94	262.0	133.5
55	49.0	25.0	15	102.5	52.2	75	155.9	79.4	35	209.4	106.7	95	262.8	133.9
56	49.9	25.4	16	103.4	52.7	76	156.8	79.9	36	210.3	107.1	96	263.7	134.4
57	50.8	25.9	17	104.2	53.1	77	157.7	80.4	37	211.2	107.6	97	264.6	134.8
58	51.7	26.3	18	105.1	53.6	78	158.6	80.8	38	212.1	108.0	98	265.5	135.3
59	52.6	26.8	19	106.0	54.0	79	159.5	81.3	39	213.0	108.5	99	266.4	135.7
60	53.5	27.2	20	106.9	54.5	80	160.4	81.7	40	213.8	109.0	300	267.3	136.2
Dist.	Dep.	D. Lat.	Dist.	Dep.	D. Lat.	Dist.	Dep.	D. Lat.	Dist.	Dep.	D. Lat.	Dist.	Dep.	D. Lat.

297° | 063° — 243° | 117°

63°

Dist.	D. Lat.	Dep.
N.	N x Cos.	N x Sin.
Hypotenuse	Side Adj.	Side Opp.

TABLE 4

27° Traverse Table

333° | 027° — 207° | 153°

Dist.	D. Lat.	Dep.	Dist.	D. Lat.	Dep.	Dist.	D. Lat.	Dep.	Dist.	D. Lat.	Dep.	Dist.	D. Lat.	Dep.
301	268.2	136.7	361	321.7	163.9	421	375.1	191.1	481	428.6	218.4	541	482.0	245.6
02	269.1	137.1	62	322.5	164.3	22	376.0	191.6	82	429.5	218.8	42	482.9	246.1
03	270.0	137.6	63	323.4	164.8	23	376.9	192.0	83	430.4	219.3	43	483.8	246.5
04	270.9	138.0	64	324.3	165.3	24	377.8	192.5	84	431.2	219.7	44	484.7	247.0
05	271.8	138.5	65	325.2	165.7	25	378.7	192.9	85	432.1	220.2	45	485.6	247.4
06	272.6	138.9	66	326.1	166.2	26	379.6	193.4	86	433.0	220.6	46	486.5	247.9
07	273.5	139.4	67	327.0	166.6	27	380.5	193.9	87	433.9	221.1	47	487.4	248.3
08	274.4	139.8	68	327.9	167.1	28	381.4	194.3	88	434.8	221.5	48	488.3	248.8
09	275.3	140.3	69	328.8	167.5	29	382.2	194.8	89	435.7	222.0	49	489.2	249.2
10	276.2	140.7	70	329.7	168.0	30	383.1	195.2	90	436.6	222.5	50	490.1	249.7
311	277.1	141.2	371	330.6	168.4	431	384.0	195.7	491	437.5	222.9	551	490.9	250.1
12	278.0	141.6	72	331.5	168.9	32	384.9	196.1	92	438.4	223.4	52	491.8	250.6
13	278.9	142.1	73	332.3	169.3	33	385.8	196.6	93	439.3	223.8	53	492.7	251.1
14	279.8	142.6	74	333.2	169.8	34	386.7	197.0	94	440.2	224.3	54	493.6	251.5
15	280.7	143.0	75	334.1	170.2	35	387.6	197.5	95	441.0	224.7	55	494.5	252.0
16	281.6	143.5	76	335.0	170.7	36	388.5	197.9	96	441.9	225.2	56	495.4	252.4
17	282.4	143.9	77	335.9	171.2	37	389.4	198.4	97	442.8	225.6	57	496.3	252.9
18	283.3	144.4	78	336.8	171.6	38	390.3	198.8	98	443.7	226.1	58	497.2	253.3
19	284.2	144.8	79	337.7	172.1	39	391.2	199.3	99	444.6	226.5	59	498.1	253.8
20	285.1	145.3	80	338.6	172.5	40	392.0	199.8	500	445.5	227.0	60	499.0	254.2
321	286.0	145.7	381	339.5	173.0	441	392.9	200.2	501	446.4	227.4	561	499.9	254.7
22	286.9	146.2	82	340.4	173.4	42	393.8	200.7	02	447.3	227.9	62	500.7	255.1
23	287.8	146.6	83	341.3	173.9	43	394.7	201.1	03	448.2	228.4	63	501.6	255.6
24	288.7	147.1	84	342.1	174.3	44	395.6	201.6	04	449.1	228.8	64	502.5	256.1
25	289.6	147.5	85	343.0	174.8	45	396.5	202.0	05	450.0	229.3	65	503.4	256.5
26	290.5	148.0	86	343.9	175.2	46	397.4	202.5	06	450.8	229.7	66	504.3	257.0
27	291.4	148.5	87	344.8	175.7	47	398.3	202.9	07	451.7	230.2	67	505.2	257.4
28	292.3	148.9	88	345.7	176.1	48	399.2	203.4	08	452.6	230.6	68	506.1	257.9
29	293.1	149.4	89	346.6	176.6	49	400.1	203.8	09	453.5	231.1	69	507.0	258.3
30	294.0	149.8	90	347.5	177.1	50	401.0	204.3	10	454.4	231.5	70	507.9	258.8
331	294.9	150.3	391	348.4	177.5	451	401.8	204.7	511	455.3	232.0	571	508.8	259.2
32	295.8	150.7	92	349.3	178.0	52	402.7	205.2	12	456.2	232.4	72	509.7	259.7
33	296.7	151.2	93	350.2	178.4	53	403.6	205.7	13	457.1	232.9	73	510.5	260.1
34	297.6	151.6	94	351.1	178.9	54	404.5	206.1	14	458.0	233.4	74	511.4	260.6
35	298.5	152.1	95	351.9	179.3	55	405.4	206.6	15	458.9	233.8	75	512.3	261.0
36	299.4	152.5	96	352.8	179.8	56	406.3	207.0	16	459.8	234.3	76	513.2	261.5
37	300.3	153.0	97	353.7	180.2	57	407.2	207.5	17	460.7	234.7	77	514.1	262.0
38	301.2	153.4	98	354.6	180.7	58	408.1	207.9	18	461.5	235.2	78	515.0	262.4
39	302.1	153.9	99	355.5	181.1	59	409.0	208.4	19	462.4	235.6	79	515.9	262.9
40	302.9	154.4	400	356.4	181.6	60	409.9	208.8	20	463.3	236.1	80	516.8	263.3
341	303.8	154.8	401	357.3	182.1	461	410.8	209.3	521	464.2	236.5	581	517.7	263.8
42	304.7	155.3	02	358.2	182.5	62	411.6	209.7	22	465.1	237.0	82	518.6	264.2
43	305.6	155.7	03	359.1	183.0	63	412.5	210.2	23	466.0	237.4	83	519.5	264.7
44	306.5	156.2	04	360.0	183.4	64	413.4	210.7	24	466.9	237.9	84	520.3	265.1
45	307.4	156.6	05	360.9	183.9	65	414.3	211.1	25	467.8	238.3	85	521.2	265.6
46	308.3	157.1	06	361.7	184.3	66	415.2	211.6	26	468.7	238.8	86	522.1	266.0
47	309.2	157.5	07	362.6	184.8	67	416.1	212.0	27	469.6	239.3	87	523.0	266.5
48	310.1	158.0	08	363.5	185.2	68	417.0	212.5	28	470.5	239.7	88	523.9	266.9
49	311.0	158.4	09	364.4	185.7	69	417.9	212.9	29	471.3	240.2	89	524.8	267.4
50	311.9	158.9	10	365.3	186.1	70	418.8	213.4	30	472.2	240.6	90	525.7	267.9
351	312.7	159.4	411	366.2	186.6	471	419.7	213.8	531	473.1	241.1	591	526.6	268.3
52	313.6	159.8	12	367.1	187.0	72	420.6	214.3	32	474.0	241.5	92	527.5	268.8
53	314.5	160.3	13	368.0	187.5	73	421.4	214.7	33	474.9	242.0	93	528.4	269.2
54	315.4	160.7	14	368.9	188.0	74	422.3	215.2	34	475.8	242.4	94	529.3	269.7
55	316.3	161.2	15	369.8	188.4	75	423.2	215.6	35	476.7	242.9	95	530.1	270.1
56	317.2	161.6	16	370.7	188.9	76	424.1	216.1	36	477.6	243.3	96	531.0	270.6
57	318.1	162.1	17	371.5	189.3	77	425.0	216.6	37	478.5	243.8	97	531.9	271.0
58	319.0	162.5	18	372.4	189.8	78	425.9	217.0	38	479.4	244.2	98	532.8	271.5
59	319.9	163.0	19	373.3	190.2	79	426.8	217.5	39	480.3	244.7	99	533.7	271.9
60	320.8	163.4	20	374.2	190.7	80	427.7	217.9	40	481.1	245.2	600	534.6	272.4
Dist.	Dep.	D. Lat.	Dist.	Dep.	D. Lat.	Dist.	Dep.	D. Lat.	Dist.	Dep.	D. Lat.	Dist.	Dep.	D. Lat.

Dist.	D. Lat.	Dep.
D Lo	Dep.	
	m	D Lo

63°

297° | 063° — 243° | 117°

TABLE 4

332° | 028° / 208° | 152° — Traverse **28°** Table — 332° | 028° / 208° | 152°

Dist.	D. Lat.	Dep.	Dist.	D. Lat.	Dep.	Dist.	D. Lat.	Dep.	Dist.	D. Lat.	Dep.	Dist.	D. Lat.	Dep.
1	0.9	0.5	61	53.9	28.6	121	106.8	56.8	181	159.8	85.0	241	212.8	113.1
2	1.8	0.9	62	54.7	29.1	22	107.7	57.3	82	160.7	85.4	42	213.7	113.6
3	2.6	1.4	63	55.6	29.6	23	108.6	57.7	83	161.6	85.9	43	214.6	114.1
4	3.5	1.9	64	56.5	30.0	24	109.5	58.2	84	162.5	86.4	44	215.4	114.6
5	4.4	2.3	65	57.4	30.5	25	110.4	58.7	85	163.3	86.9	45	216.3	115.0
6	5.3	2.8	66	58.3	31.0	26	111.3	59.2	86	164.2	87.3	46	217.2	115.5
7	6.2	3.3	67	59.2	31.5	27	112.1	59.6	87	165.1	87.8	47	218.1	116.0
8	7.1	3.8	68	60.0	31.9	28	113.0	60.1	88	166.0	88.3	48	219.0	116.4
9	7.9	4.2	69	60.9	32.4	29	113.9	60.6	89	166.9	88.7	49	219.9	116.9
10	8.8	4.7	70	61.8	32.9	30	114.8	61.0	90	167.8	89.2	50	220.7	117.4
11	9.7	5.2	71	62.7	33.3	131	115.7	61.5	191	168.6	89.7	251	221.6	117.8
12	10.6	5.6	72	63.6	33.8	32	116.5	62.0	92	169.5	90.1	52	222.5	118.3
13	11.5	6.1	73	64.5	34.3	33	117.4	62.4	93	170.4	90.6	53	223.4	118.8
14	12.4	6.6	74	65.3	34.7	34	118.3	62.9	94	171.3	91.1	54	224.3	119.2
15	13.2	7.0	75	66.2	35.2	35	119.2	63.4	95	172.2	91.5	55	225.2	119.7
16	14.1	7.5	76	67.1	35.7	36	120.1	63.8	96	173.1	92.0	56	226.0	120.2
17	15.0	8.0	77	68.0	36.1	37	121.0	64.3	97	173.9	92.5	57	226.9	120.7
18	15.9	8.5	78	68.9	36.6	38	121.8	64.8	98	174.8	93.0	58	227.8	121.1
19	16.8	8.9	79	69.8	37.1	39	122.7	65.3	99	175.7	93.4	59	228.7	121.6
20	17.7	9.4	80	70.6	37.6	40	123.6	65.7	200	176.6	93.9	60	229.6	122.1
21	18.5	9.9	81	71.5	38.0	141	124.5	66.2	201	177.5	94.4	261	230.4	122.5
22	19.4	10.3	82	72.4	38.5	42	125.4	66.7	02	178.4	94.8	62	231.3	123.0
23	20.3	10.8	83	73.3	39.0	43	126.3	67.1	03	179.2	95.3	63	232.2	123.5
24	21.2	11.3	84	74.2	39.4	44	127.1	67.6	04	180.1	95.8	64	233.1	123.9
25	22.1	11.7	85	75.1	39.9	45	128.0	68.1	05	181.0	96.2	65	234.0	124.4
26	23.0	12.2	86	75.9	40.4	46	128.9	68.5	06	181.9	96.7	66	234.9	124.9
27	23.8	12.7	87	76.8	40.8	47	129.8	69.0	07	182.8	97.2	67	235.7	125.3
28	24.7	13.1	88	77.7	41.3	48	130.7	69.5	08	183.7	97.7	68	236.6	125.8
29	25.6	13.6	89	78.6	41.8	49	131.6	70.0	09	184.5	98.1	69	237.5	126.3
30	26.5	14.1	90	79.5	42.3	50	132.4	70.4	10	185.4	98.6	70	238.4	126.8
31	27.4	14.6	91	80.3	42.7	151	133.3	70.9	211	186.3	99.1	271	239.3	127.2
32	28.3	15.0	92	81.2	43.2	52	134.2	71.4	12	187.2	99.5	72	240.2	127.7
33	29.1	15.5	93	82.1	43.7	53	135.1	71.8	13	188.1	100.0	73	241.0	128.2
34	30.0	16.0	94	83.0	44.1	54	136.0	72.3	14	189.0	100.5	74	241.9	128.6
35	30.9	16.4	95	83.9	44.6	55	136.9	72.8	15	189.8	100.9	75	242.8	129.1
36	31.8	16.9	96	84.8	45.1	56	137.7	73.2	16	190.7	101.4	76	243.7	129.6
37	32.7	17.4	97	85.6	45.5	57	138.6	73.7	17	191.6	101.9	77	244.6	130.0
38	33.6	17.8	98	86.5	46.0	58	139.5	74.2	18	192.5	102.3	78	245.5	130.5
39	34.4	18.3	99	87.4	46.5	59	140.4	74.6	19	193.4	102.8	79	246.3	131.0
40	35.3	18.8	100	88.3	46.9	60	141.3	75.1	20	194.2	103.3	80	247.2	131.5
41	36.2	19.2	101	89.2	47.4	161	142.2	75.6	221	195.1	103.8	281	248.1	131.9
42	37.1	19.7	02	90.1	47.9	62	143.0	76.1	22	196.0	104.2	82	249.0	132.4
43	38.0	20.2	03	90.9	48.4	63	143.9	76.5	23	196.9	104.7	83	249.9	132.9
44	38.8	20.7	04	91.8	48.8	64	144.8	77.0	24	197.8	105.2	84	250.8	133.3
45	39.7	21.1	05	92.7	49.3	65	145.7	77.5	25	198.7	105.6	85	251.6	133.8
46	40.6	21.6	06	93.6	49.8	66	146.6	77.9	26	199.5	106.1	86	252.5	134.3
47	41.5	22.1	07	94.5	50.2	67	147.5	78.4	27	200.4	106.6	87	253.4	134.7
48	42.4	22.5	08	95.4	50.7	68	148.3	78.9	28	201.3	107.0	88	254.3	135.2
49	43.3	23.0	09	96.2	51.2	69	149.2	79.3	29	202.2	107.5	89	255.2	135.7
50	44.1	23.5	10	97.1	51.6	70	150.1	79.8	30	203.1	108.0	90	256.1	136.1
51	45.0	23.9	111	98.0	52.1	171	151.0	80.3	231	204.0	108.4	291	256.9	136.6
52	45.9	24.4	12	98.9	52.6	72	151.9	80.7	32	204.8	108.9	92	257.8	137.1
53	46.8	24.9	13	99.8	53.1	73	152.7	81.2	33	205.7	109.4	93	258.7	137.6
54	47.7	25.4	14	100.7	53.5	74	153.6	81.7	34	206.6	109.9	94	259.6	138.0
55	48.6	25.8	15	101.5	54.0	75	154.5	82.2	35	207.5	110.3	95	260.5	138.5
56	49.4	26.3	16	102.4	54.5	76	155.4	82.6	36	208.4	110.8	96	261.4	139.0
57	50.3	26.8	17	103.3	54.9	77	156.3	83.1	37	209.3	111.3	97	262.2	139.4
58	51.2	27.2	18	104.2	55.4	78	157.2	83.6	38	210.1	111.7	98	263.1	139.9
59	52.1	27.7	19	105.1	55.9	79	158.0	84.0	39	211.0	112.2	99	264.0	140.4
60	53.0	28.2	20	106.0	56.3	80	158.9	84.5	40	211.9	112.7	300	264.9	140.8
Dist.	Dep.	D. Lat.	Dist.	Dep.	D. Lat.	Dist.	Dep.	D. Lat.	Dist.	Dep.	D. Lat.	Dist.	Dep.	D. Lat.

298° | 062° / 242° | 118° — **62°**

Dist.	D. Lat.	Dep.
N.	N x Cos.	N x Sin.
Hypotenuse	Side Adj.	Side Opp.

TABLE 4

332° | 028° / 208° | 152° — Traverse **28°** Table — 332° | 028° / 208° | 152°

Dist.	D. Lat.	Dep.	Dist.	D. Lat.	Dep.	Dist.	D. Lat.	Dep.	Dist.	D. Lat.	Dep.	Dist.	D. Lat.	Dep.
301	265.8	141.3	361	318.7	169.5	421	371.7	197.6	481	424.7	225.8	541	477.7	254.0
02	266.7	141.8	62	319.6	169.9	22	372.6	198.1	82	425.6	226.3	42	478.6	254.5
03	267.5	142.2	63	320.5	170.4	23	373.5	198.6	83	426.5	226.8	43	479.4	254.9
04	268.4	142.7	64	321.4	170.9	24	374.4	199.1	84	427.3	227.2	44	480.3	255.4
05	269.3	143.2	65	322.3	171.4	25	375.3	199.5	85	428.2	227.7	45	481.2	255.9
06	270.2	143.7	66	323.2	171.8	26	376.1	200.0	86	429.1	228.2	46	482.1	256.3
07	271.1	144.1	67	324.0	172.3	27	377.0	200.5	87	430.0	228.6	47	483.0	256.8
08	271.9	144.6	68	324.9	172.8	28	377.9	200.9	88	430.9	229.1	48	483.9	257.3
09	272.8	145.1	69	325.8	173.2	29	378.8	201.4	89	431.8	229.6	49	484.7	257.7
10	273.7	145.5	70	326.7	173.7	30	379.7	201.9	90	432.6	230.0	50	485.6	258.2
311	274.6	146.0	371	327.6	174.2	431	380.6	202.3	491	433.5	230.5	551	486.5	258.7
12	275.5	146.5	72	328.5	174.6	32	381.4	202.8	92	434.4	231.0	52	487.4	259.1
13	276.4	146.9	73	329.3	175.1	33	382.3	203.3	93	435.3	231.4	53	488.3	259.6
14	277.2	147.4	74	330.2	175.6	34	383.2	203.8	94	436.2	231.9	54	489.2	260.1
15	278.1	147.9	75	331.1	176.1	35	384.1	204.2	95	437.1	232.4	55	490.0	260.6
16	279.0	148.4	76	332.0	176.5	36	385.0	204.7	96	437.9	232.9	56	490.9	261.0
17	279.9	148.8	77	332.9	177.0	37	385.8	205.2	97	438.8	233.3	57	491.8	261.5
18	280.8	149.3	78	333.8	177.5	38	386.7	205.6	98	439.7	233.8	58	492.7	262.0
19	281.7	149.8	79	334.6	177.9	39	387.6	206.1	99	440.6	234.3	59	493.6	262.4
20	282.5	150.2	80	335.5	178.4	40	388.5	206.6	500	441.5	234.7	60	494.5	262.9
321	283.4	150.7	381	336.4	178.9	441	389.4	207.0	501	442.4	235.2	561	495.3	263.4
22	284.3	151.2	82	337.3	179.3	42	390.3	207.5	02	443.2	235.7	62	496.2	263.8
23	285.2	151.6	83	338.2	179.8	43	391.1	208.0	03	444.1	236.1	63	497.1	264.3
24	286.1	152.1	84	339.1	180.3	44	392.0	208.4	04	445.0	236.6	64	498.0	264.8
25	287.0	152.6	85	339.9	180.7	45	392.9	208.9	05	445.9	237.1	65	498.9	265.3
26	287.8	153.0	86	340.8	181.2	46	393.8	209.4	06	446.8	237.6	66	499.7	265.7
27	288.7	153.5	87	341.7	181.7	47	394.7	209.9	07	447.7	238.0	67	500.6	266.2
28	289.6	154.0	88	342.6	182.2	48	395.6	210.3	08	448.5	238.5	68	501.5	266.7
29	290.5	154.5	89	343.5	182.6	49	396.4	210.8	09	449.4	239.0	69	502.4	267.1
30	291.4	154.9	90	344.3	183.1	50	397.3	211.3	10	450.3	239.4	70	503.3	267.6
331	292.3	155.4	391	345.2	183.6	451	398.2	211.7	511	451.2	239.9	571	504.2	268.1
32	293.1	155.9	92	346.1	184.0	52	399.1	212.2	12	452.1	240.4	72	505.0	268.5
33	294.0	156.3	93	347.0	184.5	53	400.0	212.7	13	453.0	240.8	73	505.9	269.0
34	294.9	156.8	94	347.9	185.0	54	400.9	213.1	14	453.8	241.3	74	506.8	269.5
35	295.8	157.3	95	348.8	185.4	55	401.7	213.6	15	454.7	241.8	75	507.7	269.9
36	296.7	157.7	96	349.6	185.9	56	402.6	214.1	16	455.6	242.2	76	508.6	270.4
37	297.6	158.2	97	350.5	186.4	57	403.5	214.5	17	456.5	242.7	77	509.5	270.9
38	298.4	158.7	98	351.4	186.8	58	404.4	215.0	18	457.4	243.2	78	510.3	271.4
39	299.3	159.2	99	352.3	187.3	59	405.3	215.5	19	458.2	243.7	79	511.2	271.8
40	300.2	159.6	400	353.2	187.8	60	406.2	216.0	20	459.1	244.1	80	512.1	272.3
341	301.1	160.1	401	354.1	188.3	461	407.0	216.4	521	460.0	244.6	581	513.0	272.8
42	302.0	160.6	02	354.9	188.7	62	407.9	216.9	22	460.9	245.1	82	513.9	273.2
43	302.9	161.0	03	355.8	189.2	63	408.8	217.4	23	461.8	245.5	83	514.8	273.7
44	303.7	161.5	04	356.7	189.7	64	409.7	217.8	24	462.7	246.0	84	515.6	274.2
45	304.6	162.0	05	357.6	190.1	65	410.6	218.3	25	463.5	246.5	85	516.5	274.6
46	305.5	162.4	06	358.5	190.6	66	411.5	218.8	26	464.4	246.9	86	517.4	275.1
47	306.4	162.9	07	359.4	191.1	67	412.3	219.2	27	465.3	247.4	87	518.3	275.6
48	307.3	163.4	08	360.2	191.5	68	413.2	219.7	28	466.2	247.9	88	519.2	276.0
49	308.1	163.8	09	361.1	192.0	69	414.1	220.2	29	467.1	248.4	89	520.1	276.5
50	309.0	164.3	10	362.0	192.5	70	415.0	220.7	30	468.0	248.8	90	520.9	277.0
351	309.9	164.8	411	362.9	193.0	471	415.9	221.1	531	468.8	249.3	591	521.8	277.5
52	310.8	165.3	12	363.8	193.4	72	416.8	221.6	32	469.7	249.8	92	522.7	277.9
53	311.7	165.7	13	364.7	193.9	73	417.6	222.1	33	470.6	250.2	93	523.6	278.4
54	312.6	166.2	14	365.5	194.4	74	418.5	222.5	34	471.5	250.7	94	524.5	278.9
55	313.4	166.7	15	366.4	194.8	75	419.4	223.0	35	472.4	251.2	95	525.4	279.3
56	314.3	167.1	16	367.3	195.3	76	420.3	223.5	36	473.3	251.6	96	526.2	279.8
57	315.2	167.6	17	368.2	195.8	77	421.2	223.9	37	474.1	252.1	97	527.1	280.3
58	316.1	168.1	18	369.1	196.2	78	422.0	224.4	38	475.0	252.6	98	528.0	280.7
59	317.0	168.5	19	370.0	196.7	79	422.9	224.9	39	475.9	253.0	99	528.9	281.2
60	317.9	169.0	20	370.8	197.2	80	423.8	225.3	40	476.8	253.5	600	529.8	281.7
Dist.	Dep.	D. Lat.	Dist.	Dep.	D. Lat.	Dist.	Dep.	D. Lat.	Dist.	Dep.	D. Lat.	Dist.	Dep.	D. Lat.

Dist.	D. Lat.	Dep.
D Lo	Dep.	
	m	D Lo

62° — 298° | 062° / 242° | 118°

TABLE 4

331° | 029° / 209° | 151°

Traverse **29°** Table

331° | 029° / 209° | 151°

Dist.	D. Lat.	Dep.	Dist.	D. Lat.	Dep.	Dist.	D. Lat.	Dep.	Dist.	D. Lat.	Dep.	Dist.	D. Lat.	Dep.
1	0.9	0.5	61	53.4	29.6	121	105.8	58.7	181	158.3	87.8	241	210.8	116.8
2	1.7	1.0	62	54.2	30.1	22	106.7	59.1	82	159.2	88.2	42	211.7	117.3
3	2.6	1.5	63	55.1	30.5	23	107.6	59.6	83	160.1	88.7	43	212.5	117.8
4	3.5	1.9	64	56.0	31.0	24	108.5	60.1	84	160.9	89.2	44	213.4	118.3
5	4.4	2.4	65	56.9	31.5	25	109.3	60.6	85	161.8	89.7	45	214.3	118.8
6	5.2	2.9	66	57.7	32.0	26	110.2	61.1	86	162.7	90.2	46	215.2	119.3
7	6.1	3.4	67	58.6	32.5	27	111.1	61.6	87	163.6	90.7	47	216.0	119.7
8	7.0	3.9	68	59.5	33.0	28	112.0	62.1	88	164.4	91.1	48	216.9	120.2
9	7.9	4.4	69	60.3	33.5	29	112.8	62.5	89	165.3	91.6	49	217.8	120.7
10	8.7	4.8	70	61.2	33.9	30	113.7	63.0	90	166.2	92.1	50	218.7	121.2
11	9.6	5.3	71	62.1	34.4	131	114.6	63.5	191	167.1	92.6	251	219.5	121.7
12	10.5	5.8	72	63.0	34.9	32	115.4	64.0	92	167.9	93.1	52	220.4	122.2
13	11.4	6.3	73	63.8	35.4	33	116.3	64.5	93	168.8	93.6	53	221.3	122.7
14	12.2	6.8	74	64.7	35.9	34	117.2	65.0	94	169.7	94.1	54	222.2	123.1
15	13.1	7.3	75	65.6	36.4	35	118.1	65.4	95	170.6	94.5	55	223.0	123.6
16	14.0	7.8	76	66.5	36.8	36	118.9	65.9	96	171.4	95.0	56	223.9	124.1
17	14.9	8.2	77	67.3	37.3	37	119.8	66.4	97	172.3	95.5	57	224.8	124.6
18	15.7	8.7	78	68.2	37.8	38	120.7	66.9	98	173.2	96.0	58	225.7	125.1
19	16.6	9.2	79	69.1	38.3	39	121.6	67.4	99	174.0	96.5	59	226.5	125.6
20	17.5	9.7	80	70.0	38.8	40	122.4	67.9	200	174.9	97.0	60	227.4	126.1
21	18.4	10.2	81	70.8	39.3	141	123.3	68.4	201	175.8	97.4	261	228.3	126.5
22	19.2	10.7	82	71.7	39.8	42	124.2	68.8	02	176.7	97.9	62	229.2	127.0
23	20.1	11.2	83	72.6	40.2	43	125.1	69.3	03	177.5	98.4	63	230.0	127.5
24	21.0	11.6	84	73.5	40.7	44	125.9	69.8	04	178.4	98.9	64	230.9	128.0
25	21.9	12.1	85	74.3	41.2	45	126.8	70.3	05	179.3	99.4	65	231.8	128.5
26	22.7	12.6	86	75.2	41.7	46	127.7	70.8	06	180.2	99.9	66	232.6	129.0
27	23.6	13.1	87	76.1	42.2	47	128.6	71.3	07	181.0	100.4	67	233.5	129.4
28	24.5	13.6	88	77.0	42.7	48	129.4	71.8	08	181.9	100.8	68	234.4	129.9
29	25.4	14.1	89	77.8	43.1	49	130.3	72.2	09	182.8	101.3	69	235.3	130.4
30	26.2	14.5	90	78.7	43.6	50	131.2	72.7	10	183.7	101.8	70	236.1	130.9
31	27.1	15.0	91	79.6	44.1	151	132.1	73.2	211	184.5	102.3	271	237.0	131.4
32	28.0	15.5	92	80.5	44.6	52	132.9	73.7	12	185.4	102.8	72	237.9	131.9
33	28.9	16.0	93	81.3	45.1	53	133.8	74.2	13	186.3	103.3	73	238.8	132.4
34	29.7	16.5	94	82.2	45.6	54	134.7	74.7	14	187.2	103.7	74	239.6	132.8
35	30.6	17.0	95	83.1	46.1	55	135.6	75.1	15	188.0	104.2	75	240.5	133.3
36	31.5	17.5	96	84.0	46.5	56	136.4	75.6	16	188.9	104.7	76	241.4	133.8
37	32.4	17.9	97	84.8	47.0	57	137.3	76.1	17	189.8	105.2	77	242.3	134.3
38	33.2	18.4	98	85.7	47.5	58	138.2	76.6	18	190.7	105.7	78	243.1	134.8
39	34.1	18.9	99	86.6	48.0	59	139.1	77.1	19	191.5	106.2	79	244.0	135.3
40	35.0	19.4	100	87.5	48.5	60	139.9	77.6	20	192.4	106.7	80	244.9	135.7
41	35.9	19.9	101	88.3	49.0	161	140.8	78.1	221	193.3	107.1	281	245.8	136.2
42	36.7	20.4	02	89.2	49.5	62	141.7	78.5	22	194.2	107.6	82	246.6	136.7
43	37.6	20.8	03	90.1	49.9	63	142.6	79.0	23	195.0	108.1	83	247.5	137.2
44	38.5	21.3	04	91.0	50.4	64	143.4	79.5	24	195.9	108.6	84	248.4	137.7
45	39.4	21.8	05	91.8	50.9	65	144.3	80.0	25	196.8	109.1	85	249.3	138.2
46	40.2	22.3	06	92.7	51.4	66	145.2	80.5	26	197.7	109.6	86	250.1	138.7
47	41.1	22.8	07	93.6	51.9	67	146.1	81.0	27	198.5	110.1	87	251.0	139.1
48	42.0	23.3	08	94.5	52.4	68	146.9	81.4	28	199.4	110.5	88	251.9	139.6
49	42.9	23.8	09	95.3	52.8	69	147.8	81.9	29	200.3	111.0	89	252.8	140.1
50	43.7	24.2	10	96.2	53.3	70	148.7	82.4	30	201.2	111.5	90	253.6	140.6
51	44.6	24.7	111	97.1	53.8	171	149.6	82.9	231	202.0	112.0	291	254.5	141.1
52	45.5	25.2	12	98.0	54.3	72	150.4	83.4	32	202.9	112.5	92	255.4	141.6
53	46.4	25.7	13	98.8	54.8	73	151.3	83.9	33	203.8	113.0	93	256.3	142.0
54	47.2	26.2	14	99.7	55.3	74	152.2	84.4	34	204.7	113.4	94	257.1	142.5
55	48.1	26.7	15	100.6	55.8	75	153.1	84.8	35	205.5	113.9	95	258.0	143.0
56	49.0	27.1	16	101.5	56.2	76	153.9	85.3	36	206.4	114.4	96	258.9	143.5
57	49.9	27.6	17	102.3	56.7	77	154.8	85.8	37	207.3	114.9	97	259.8	144.0
58	50.7	28.1	18	103.2	57.2	78	155.7	86.3	38	208.2	115.4	98	260.6	144.5
59	51.6	28.6	19	104.1	57.7	79	156.6	86.8	39	209.0	115.9	99	261.5	145.0
60	52.5	29.1	20	105.0	58.2	80	157.4	87.3	40	209.9	116.4	300	262.4	145.4
Dist.	Dep.	D. Lat.	Dist.	Dep.	D. Lat.	Dist.	Dep.	D. Lat.	Dist.	Dep.	D. Lat.	Dist.	Dep.	D. Lat.

299° | 061° / 241° | 119°

61°

Dist.	D. Lat.	Dep.
N.	N x Cos.	N x Sin.
Hypotenuse	Side Adj.	Side Opp.

TABLE 4

331° | 029° / 209° | 151°

Traverse **29°** Table

331° | 029° / 209° | 151°

Dist.	D. Lat.	Dep.	Dist.	D. Lat.	Dep.	Dist.	D. Lat.	Dep.	Dist.	D. Lat.	Dep.	Dist.	D. Lat.	Dep.
301	263.3	145.9	361	315.7	175.0	421	368.2	204.1	481	420.7	233.2	541	473.2	262.3
02	264.1	146.4	62	316.6	175.5	22	369.1	204.6	82	421.6	233.7	42	474.0	262.8
03	265.0	146.9	63	317.5	176.0	23	370.0	205.1	83	422.4	234.2	43	474.9	263.3
04	265.9	147.4	64	318.4	176.5	24	370.8	205.6	84	423.3	234.6	44	475.8	263.7
05	266.8	147.9	65	319.2	177.0	25	371.7	206.0	85	424.2	235.1	45	476.7	264.2
06	267.6	148.4	66	320.1	177.4	26	372.6	206.5	86	425.1	235.6	46	477.5	264.7
07	268.5	148.8	67	321.0	177.9	27	373.5	207.0	87	425.9	236.1	47	478.4	265.2
08	269.4	149.3	68	321.9	178.4	28	374.3	207.5	88	426.8	236.6	48	479.3	265.7
09	270.3	149.8	69	322.7	178.9	29	375.2	208.0	89	427.7	237.1	49	480.2	266.2
10	271.1	150.3	70	323.6	179.4	30	376.1	208.5	90	428.6	237.6	50	481.0	266.6
311	272.0	150.8	371	324.5	179.9	431	377.0	209.0	491	429.4	238.0	551	481.9	267.1
12	272.9	151.3	72	325.4	180.3	32	377.8	209.4	92	430.3	238.5	52	482.8	267.6
13	273.8	151.7	73	326.2	180.8	33	378.7	209.9	93	431.2	239.0	53	483.7	268.1
14	274.6	152.2	74	327.1	181.3	34	379.6	210.4	94	432.1	239.5	54	484.5	268.6
15	275.5	152.7	75	328.0	181.8	35	380.5	210.9	95	432.9	240.0	55	485.4	269.1
16	276.4	153.2	76	328.9	182.3	36	381.3	211.4	96	433.8	240.5	56	486.3	269.6
17	277.3	153.7	77	329.7	182.8	37	382.2	211.9	97	434.7	241.0	57	487.2	270.0
18	278.1	154.2	78	330.6	183.3	38	383.1	212.3	98	435.6	241.4	58	488.0	270.5
19	279.0	154.7	79	331.5	183.7	39	384.0	212.8	99	436.4	241.9	59	488.9	271.0
20	279.9	155.1	80	332.4	184.2	40	384.8	213.3	500	437.3	242.4	60	489.8	271.5
321	280.8	155.6	381	333.2	184.7	441	385.7	213.8	501	438.2	242.9	561	490.7	272.0
22	281.6	156.1	82	334.1	185.2	42	386.6	214.3	02	439.1	243.4	62	491.5	272.5
23	282.5	156.6	83	335.0	185.7	43	387.5	214.8	03	439.9	243.9	63	492.4	272.9
24	283.4	157.1	84	335.9	186.2	44	388.3	215.3	04	440.8	244.3	64	493.3	273.4
25	284.3	157.6	85	336.7	186.7	45	389.2	215.7	05	441.7	244.8	65	494.2	273.9
26	285.1	158.0	86	337.6	187.1	46	390.1	216.2	06	442.6	245.3	66	495.0	274.4
27	286.0	158.5	87	338.5	187.6	47	391.0	216.7	07	443.4	245.8	67	495.9	274.9
28	286.9	159.0	88	339.4	188.1	48	391.8	217.2	08	444.3	246.3	68	496.8	275.4
29	287.7	159.5	89	340.2	188.6	49	392.7	217.7	09	445.2	246.8	69	497.7	275.9
30	288.6	160.0	90	341.1	189.1	50	393.6	218.2	10	446.1	247.3	70	498.5	276.3
331	289.5	160.5	391	342.0	189.6	451	394.5	218.6	511	446.9	247.7	571	499.4	276.8
32	290.4	161.0	92	342.9	190.0	52	395.3	219.1	12	447.8	248.2	72	500.3	277.3
33	291.2	161.4	93	343.7	190.5	53	396.2	219.6	13	448.7	248.7	73	501.2	277.8
34	292.1	161.9	94	344.6	191.0	54	397.1	220.1	14	449.6	249.2	74	502.0	278.3
35	293.0	162.4	95	345.5	191.5	55	398.0	220.6	15	450.4	249.7	75	502.9	278.8
36	293.9	162.9	96	346.3	192.0	56	398.8	221.1	16	451.3	250.2	76	503.8	279.3
37	294.7	163.4	97	347.2	192.5	57	399.7	221.6	17	452.2	250.6	77	504.7	279.7
38	295.6	163.9	98	348.1	193.0	58	400.6	222.0	18	453.1	251.1	78	505.5	280.2
39	296.5	164.4	99	349.0	193.4	59	401.5	222.5	19	453.9	251.6	79	506.4	280.7
40	297.4	164.8	400	349.8	193.9	60	402.3	223.0	20	454.8	252.1	80	507.3	281.2
341	298.2	165.3	401	350.7	194.4	461	403.2	223.5	521	455.7	252.6	581	508.2	281.7
42	299.1	165.8	02	351.6	194.9	62	404.1	224.0	22	456.6	253.1	82	509.0	282.2
43	300.0	166.3	03	352.5	195.4	63	404.9	224.5	23	457.4	253.6	83	509.9	282.6
44	300.9	166.8	04	353.3	195.9	64	405.8	225.0	24	458.3	254.0	84	510.8	283.1
45	301.7	167.3	05	354.2	196.3	65	406.7	225.4	25	459.2	254.5	85	511.7	283.6
46	302.6	167.7	06	355.1	196.8	66	407.6	225.9	26	460.0	255.0	86	512.5	284.1
47	303.5	168.2	07	356.0	197.3	67	408.4	226.4	27	460.9	255.5	87	513.4	284.6
48	304.4	168.7	08	356.8	197.8	68	409.3	226.9	28	461.8	256.0	88	514.3	285.1
49	305.2	169.2	09	357.7	198.3	69	410.2	227.4	29	462.7	256.5	89	515.2	285.6
50	306.1	169.7	10	358.6	198.8	70	411.1	227.9	30	463.5	256.9	90	516.0	286.0
351	307.0	170.2	411	359.5	199.3	471	411.9	228.3	531	464.4	257.4	591	516.9	286.5
52	307.9	170.7	12	360.3	199.7	72	412.8	228.8	32	465.3	257.9	92	517.8	287.0
53	308.7	171.1	13	361.2	200.2	73	413.7	229.3	33	466.2	258.4	93	518.6	287.5
54	309.6	171.6	14	362.1	200.7	74	414.6	229.8	34	467.0	258.9	94	519.5	288.0
55	310.5	172.1	15	363.0	201.2	75	415.4	230.3	35	467.9	259.4	95	520.4	288.5
56	311.4	172.6	16	363.8	201.7	76	416.3	230.8	36	468.8	259.9	96	521.3	288.9
57	312.2	173.1	17	364.7	202.2	77	417.2	231.3	37	469.7	260.3	97	522.1	289.4
58	313.1	173.6	18	365.6	202.7	78	418.1	231.7	38	470.5	260.8	98	523.0	289.9
59	314.0	174.0	19	366.5	203.1	79	418.9	232.2	39	471.4	261.3	99	523.9	290.4
60	314.9	174.5	20	367.3	203.6	80	419.8	232.7	40	472.3	261.8	600	524.8	290.9
Dist.	Dep.	D. Lat.	Dist.	Dep.	D. Lat.	Dist.	Dep.	D. Lat.	Dist.	Dep.	D. Lat.	Dist.	Dep.	D. Lat.

Dist.	D. Lat.	Dep.
D Lo	Dep.	
	m	D Lo

61°

299° | 061° / 241° | 119°

TABLE 4

330° 210°	030° 150°				Traverse 30° Table								330° 210°	030° 150°
Dist.	D. Lat.	Dep.	Dist.	D. Lat.	Dep.	Dist.	D. Lat.	Dep.	Dist.	D. Lat.	Dep.	Dist.	D. Lat.	Dep.
1	0.9	0.5	61	52.8	30.5	121	104.8	60.5	181	156.8	90.5	241	208.7	120.5
2	1.7	1.0	62	53.7	31.0	22	105.7	61.0	82	157.6	91.0	42	209.6	121.0
3	2.6	1.5	63	54.6	31.5	23	106.5	61.5	83	158.5	91.5	43	210.4	121.5
4	3.5	2.0	64	55.4	32.0	24	107.4	62.0	84	159.3	92.0	44	211.3	122.0
5	4.3	2.5	65	56.3	32.5	25	108.3	62.5	85	160.2	92.5	45	212.2	122.5
6	5.2	3.0	66	57.2	33.0	26	109.1	63.0	86	161.1	93.0	46	213.0	123.0
7	6.1	3.5	67	58.0	33.5	27	110.0	63.5	87	161.9	93.5	47	213.9	123.5
8	6.9	4.0	68	58.9	34.0	28	110.9	64.0	88	162.8	94.0	48	214.8	124.0
9	7.8	4.5	69	59.8	34.5	29	111.7	64.5	89	163.7	94.5	49	215.6	124.5
10	8.7	5.0	70	60.6	35.0	30	112.6	65.0	90	164.5	95.0	50	216.5	125.0
11	9.5	5.5	71	61.5	35.5	131	113.4	65.5	191	165.4	95.5	251	217.4	125.5
12	10.4	6.0	72	62.4	36.0	32	114.3	66.0	92	166.3	96.0	52	218.2	126.0
13	11.3	6.5	73	63.2	36.5	33	115.2	66.5	93	167.1	96.5	53	219.1	126.5
14	12.1	7.0	74	64.1	37.0	34	116.0	67.0	94	168.0	97.0	54	220.0	127.0
15	13.0	7.5	75	65.0	37.5	35	116.9	67.5	95	168.9	97.5	55	220.8	127.5
16	13.9	8.0	76	65.8	38.0	36	117.8	68.0	96	169.7	98.0	56	221.7	128.0
17	14.7	8.5	77	66.7	38.5	37	118.6	68.5	97	170.6	98.5	57	222.6	128.5
18	15.6	9.0	78	67.5	39.0	38	119.5	69.0	98	171.5	99.0	58	223.4	129.0
19	16.5	9.5	79	68.4	39.5	39	120.4	69.5	99	172.3	99.5	59	224.3	129.5
20	17.3	10.0	80	69.3	40.0	40	121.2	70.0	200	173.2	100.0	60	225.2	130.0
21	18.2	10.5	81	70.1	40.5	141	122.1	70.5	201	174.1	100.5	261	226.0	130.5
22	19.1	11.0	82	71.0	41.0	42	123.0	71.0	02	174.9	101.0	62	226.9	131.0
23	19.9	11.5	83	71.9	41.5	43	123.8	71.5	03	175.8	101.5	63	227.8	131.5
24	20.8	12.0	84	72.7	42.0	44	124.7	72.0	04	176.7	102.0	64	228.6	132.0
25	21.7	12.5	85	73.6	42.5	45	125.6	72.5	05	177.5	102.5	65	229.5	132.5
26	22.5	13.0	86	74.5	43.0	46	126.4	73.0	06	178.4	103.0	66	230.4	133.0
27	23.4	13.5	87	75.3	43.5	47	127.3	73.5	07	179.3	103.5	67	231.2	133.5
28	24.2	14.0	88	76.2	44.0	48	128.2	74.0	08	180.1	104.0	68	232.1	134.0
29	25.1	14.5	89	77.1	44.5	49	129.0	74.5	09	181.0	104.5	69	233.0	134.5
30	26.0	15.0	90	77.9	45.0	50	129.9	75.0	10	181.9	105.0	70	233.8	135.0
31	26.8	15.5	91	78.8	45.5	151	130.8	75.5	211	182.7	105.5	271	234.7	135.5
32	27.7	16.0	92	79.7	46.0	52	131.6	76.0	12	183.6	106.0	72	235.6	136.0
33	28.6	16.5	93	80.5	46.5	53	132.5	76.5	13	184.5	106.5	73	236.4	136.5
34	29.4	17.0	94	81.4	47.0	54	133.4	77.0	14	185.3	107.0	74	237.3	137.0
35	30.3	17.5	95	82.3	47.5	55	134.2	77.5	15	186.2	107.5	75	238.2	137.5
36	31.2	18.0	96	83.1	48.0	56	135.1	78.0	16	187.1	108.0	76	239.0	138.0
37	32.0	18.5	97	84.0	48.5	57	136.0	78.5	17	187.9	108.5	77	239.9	138.5
38	32.9	19.0	98	84.9	49.0	58	136.8	79.0	18	188.8	109.0	78	240.8	139.0
39	33.8	19.5	99	85.7	49.5	59	137.7	79.5	19	189.7	109.5	79	241.6	139.5
40	34.6	20.0	100	86.6	50.0	60	138.6	80.0	20	190.5	110.0	80	242.5	140.0
41	35.5	20.5	101	87.5	50.5	161	139.4	80.5	221	191.4	110.5	281	243.4	140.5
42	36.4	21.0	02	88.3	51.0	62	140.3	81.0	22	192.3	111.0	82	244.2	141.0
43	37.2	21.5	03	89.2	51.5	63	141.2	81.5	23	193.1	111.5	83	245.1	141.5
44	38.1	22.0	04	90.1	52.0	64	142.0	82.0	24	194.0	112.0	84	246.0	142.0
45	39.0	22.5	05	90.9	52.5	65	142.9	82.5	25	194.9	112.5	85	246.8	142.5
46	39.8	23.0	06	91.8	53.0	66	143.8	83.0	26	195.7	113.0	86	247.7	143.0
47	40.7	23.5	07	92.7	53.5	67	144.6	83.5	27	196.6	113.5	87	248.5	143.5
48	41.6	24.0	08	93.5	54.0	68	145.5	84.0	28	197.5	114.0	88	249.4	144.0
49	42.4	24.5	09	94.4	54.5	69	146.4	84.5	29	198.3	114.5	89	250.3	144.5
50	43.3	25.0	10	95.3	55.0	70	147.2	85.0	30	199.2	115.0	90	251.1	145.0
51	44.2	25.5	111	96.1	55.5	171	148.1	85.5	231	200.1	115.5	291	252.0	145.5
52	45.0	26.0	12	97.0	56.0	72	149.0	86.0	32	200.9	116.0	92	252.9	146.0
53	45.9	26.5	13	97.9	56.5	73	149.8	86.5	33	201.8	116.5	93	253.7	146.5
54	46.8	27.0	14	98.7	57.0	74	150.7	87.0	34	202.6	117.0	94	254.6	147.0
55	47.6	27.5	15	99.6	57.5	75	151.6	87.5	35	203.5	117.5	95	255.5	147.5
56	48.5	28.0	16	100.5	58.0	76	152.4	88.0	36	204.4	118.0	96	256.3	148.0
57	49.4	28.5	17	101.3	58.5	77	153.3	88.5	37	205.2	118.5	97	257.2	148.5
58	50.2	29.0	18	102.2	59.0	78	154.2	89.0	38	206.1	119.0	98	258.1	149.0
59	51.1	29.5	19	103.1	59.5	79	155.0	89.5	39	207.0	119.5	99	258.9	149.5
60	52.0	30.0	20	103.9	60.0	80	155.9	90.0	40	207.8	120.0	300	259.8	150.0
Dist.	Dep.	D. Lat.	Dist.	Dep.	D. Lat.	Dist.	Dep.	D. Lat.	Dist.	Dep.	D. Lat.	Dist.	Dep.	D. Lat.
300° 240°	060° 120°				60°									

Dist.	D. Lat.	Dep.
N.	N x Cos.	N x Sin.
Hypotenuse	Side Adj.	Side Opp.

TABLE 4

330° 210°	030° 150°				Traverse 30° Table								330° 210°	030° 150°
Dist.	D. Lat.	Dep.	Dist.	D. Lat.	Dep.	Dist.	D. Lat.	Dep.	Dist.	D. Lat.	Dep.	Dist.	D. Lat.	Dep.
301	260.7	150.5	361	312.6	180.5	421	364.6	210.5	481	416.6	240.5	541	468.5	270.5
02	261.5	151.0	62	313.5	181.0	22	365.5	211.0	82	417.4	241.0	42	469.4	271.0
03	262.4	151.5	63	314.4	181.5	23	366.3	211.5	83	418.3	241.5	43	470.3	271.5
04	263.3	152.0	64	315.2	182.0	24	367.2	212.0	84	419.2	242.0	44	471.1	272.0
05	264.1	152.5	65	316.1	182.5	25	368.1	212.5	85	420.0	242.5	45	472.0	272.5
06	265.0	153.0	66	317.0	183.0	26	368.9	213.0	86	420.9	243.0	46	472.8	273.0
07	265.9	153.5	67	317.8	183.5	27	369.8	213.5	87	421.8	243.5	47	473.7	273.5
08	266.7	154.0	68	318.7	184.0	28	370.7	214.0	88	422.6	244.0	48	474.6	274.0
09	267.6	154.5	69	319.6	184.5	29	371.5	214.5	89	423.5	244.5	49	475.4	274.5
10	268.5	155.0	70	320.4	185.0	30	372.4	215.0	90	424.4	245.0	50	476.3	275.0
311	269.3	155.5	371	321.3	185.5	431	373.3	215.5	491	425.2	245.5	551	477.2	275.5
12	270.2	156.0	72	322.2	186.0	32	374.1	216.0	92	426.1	246.0	52	478.0	276.0
13	271.1	156.5	73	323.0	186.5	33	375.0	216.5	93	427.0	246.5	53	478.9	276.5
14	271.9	157.0	74	323.9	187.0	34	375.9	217.0	94	427.8	247.0	54	479.8	277.0
15	272.8	157.5	75	324.8	187.5	35	376.7	217.5	95	428.7	247.5	55	480.6	277.5
16	273.7	158.0	76	325.6	188.0	36	377.6	218.0	96	429.5	248.0	56	481.5	278.0
17	274.5	158.5	77	326.5	188.5	37	378.5	218.5	97	430.4	248.5	57	482.4	278.5
18	275.4	159.0	78	327.4	189.0	38	379.3	219.0	98	431.3	249.0	58	483.2	279.0
19	276.3	159.5	79	328.2	189.5	39	380.2	219.5	99	432.1	249.5	59	484.1	279.5
20	277.1	160.0	80	329.1	190.0	40	381.1	220.0	500	433.0	250.0	60	485.0	280.0
321	278.0	160.5	381	330.0	190.5	441	381.9	220.5	501	433.9	250.5	561	485.8	280.5
22	278.9	161.0	82	330.8	191.0	42	382.8	221.0	02	434.7	251.0	62	486.7	281.0
23	279.7	161.5	83	331.7	191.5	43	383.6	221.5	03	435.6	251.5	63	487.6	281.5
24	280.6	162.0	84	332.6	192.0	44	384.5	222.0	04	436.5	252.0	64	488.4	282.0
25	281.5	162.5	85	333.4	192.5	45	385.4	222.5	05	437.3	252.5	65	489.3	282.5
26	282.3	163.0	86	334.3	193.0	46	386.2	223.0	06	438.2	253.0	66	490.2	283.0
27	283.2	163.5	87	335.2	193.5	47	387.1	223.5	07	439.1	253.5	67	491.0	283.5
28	284.1	164.0	88	336.0	194.0	48	388.0	224.0	08	439.9	254.0	68	491.9	284.0
29	284.9	164.5	89	336.9	194.5	49	388.8	224.5	09	440.8	254.5	69	492.8	284.5
30	285.8	165.0	90	337.7	195.0	50	389.7	225.0	10	441.7	255.0	70	493.6	285.0
331	286.7	165.5	391	338.6	195.5	451	390.6	225.5	511	442.5	255.5	571	494.5	285.5
32	287.5	166.0	92	339.5	196.0	52	391.4	226.0	12	443.4	256.0	72	495.4	286.0
33	288.4	166.5	93	340.3	196.5	53	392.3	226.5	13	444.3	256.5	73	496.2	286.5
34	289.3	167.0	94	341.2	197.0	54	393.2	227.0	14	445.1	257.0	74	497.1	287.0
35	290.1	167.5	95	342.1	197.5	55	394.0	227.5	15	446.0	257.5	75	498.0	287.5
36	291.0	168.0	96	342.9	198.0	56	394.9	228.0	16	446.9	258.0	76	498.8	288.0
37	291.9	168.5	97	343.8	198.5	57	395.8	228.5	17	447.7	258.5	77	499.7	288.5
38	292.7	169.0	98	344.7	199.0	58	396.6	229.0	18	448.6	259.0	78	500.6	289.0
39	293.6	169.5	99	345.5	199.5	59	397.5	229.5	19	449.5	259.5	79	501.4	289.5
40	294.4	170.0	400	346.4	200.0	60	398.4	230.0	20	450.3	260.0	80	502.3	290.0
341	295.3	170.5	401	347.3	200.5	461	399.2	230.5	521	451.2	260.5	581	503.2	290.5
42	296.2	171.0	02	348.1	201.0	62	400.1	231.0	22	452.1	261.0	82	504.0	291.0
43	297.0	171.5	03	349.0	201.5	63	401.0	231.5	23	452.9	261.5	83	504.9	291.5
44	297.9	172.0	04	349.9	202.0	64	401.8	232.0	24	453.8	262.0	84	505.8	292.0
45	298.8	172.5	05	350.7	202.5	65	402.7	232.5	25	454.7	262.5	85	506.6	292.5
46	299.6	173.0	06	351.6	203.0	66	403.6	233.0	26	455.5	263.0	86	507.5	293.0
47	300.5	173.5	07	352.5	203.5	67	404.4	233.5	27	456.4	263.5	87	508.4	293.5
48	301.4	174.0	08	353.3	204.0	68	405.3	234.0	28	457.3	264.0	88	509.2	294.0
49	302.2	174.5	09	354.2	204.5	69	406.2	234.5	29	458.1	264.5	89	510.1	294.5
50	303.1	175.0	10	355.1	205.0	70	407.0	235.0	30	459.0	265.0	90	511.0	295.0
351	304.0	175.5	411	355.9	205.5	471	407.9	235.5	531	459.9	265.5	591	511.8	295.5
52	304.8	176.0	12	356.8	206.0	72	408.8	236.0	32	460.7	266.0	92	512.7	296.0
53	305.7	176.5	13	357.7	206.5	73	409.6	236.5	33	461.6	266.5	93	513.6	296.5
54	306.6	177.0	14	358.5	207.0	74	410.5	237.0	34	462.5	267.0	94	514.4	297.0
55	307.4	177.5	15	359.4	207.5	75	411.4	237.5	35	463.3	267.5	95	515.3	297.5
56	308.3	178.0	16	360.3	208.0	76	412.2	238.0	36	464.2	268.0	96	516.2	298.0
57	309.2	178.5	17	361.1	208.5	77	413.1	238.5	37	465.1	268.5	97	517.0	298.5
58	310.0	179.0	18	362.0	209.0	78	414.0	239.0	38	465.9	269.0	98	517.9	299.0
59	310.9	179.5	19	362.9	209.5	79	414.8	239.5	39	466.8	269.5	99	518.7	299.5
60	311.8	180.0	20	363.7	210.0	80	415.7	240.0	40	467.7	270.0	600	519.6	300.0
Dist.	Dep.	D. Lat.	Dist.	Dep.	D. Lat.	Dist.	Dep.	D. Lat.	Dist.	Dep.	D. Lat.	Dist.	Dep.	D. Lat.
					60°								300° 240°	060° 120°

Dist.	D. Lat.	Dep.
D Lo	Dep.	
	m	D Lo

TABLE 4

31° Traverse Table

329° 211°	031° 149°												329° 211°	031° 149°
Dist.	D. Lat.	Dep.	Dist.	D. Lat.	Dep.	Dist.	D. Lat.	Dep.	Dist.	D. Lat.	Dep.	Dist.	D. Lat.	Dep.
1	0.9	0.5	61	52.3	31.4	121	103.7	62.3	181	155.1	93.2	241	206.6	124.1
2	1.7	1.0	62	53.1	31.9	22	104.6	62.8	82	156.0	93.7	42	207.4	124.6
3	2.6	1.5	63	54.0	32.4	23	105.4	63.3	83	156.9	94.3	43	208.3	125.2
4	3.4	2.1	64	54.9	33.0	24	106.3	63.9	84	157.7	94.8	44	209.1	125.7
5	4.3	2.6	65	55.7	33.5	25	107.1	64.4	85	158.6	95.3	45	210.0	126.2
6	5.1	3.1	66	56.6	34.0	26	108.0	64.9	86	159.4	95.8	46	210.9	126.7
7	6.0	3.6	67	57.4	34.5	27	108.9	65.4	87	160.3	96.3	47	211.7	127.2
8	6.9	4.1	68	58.3	35.0	28	109.7	65.9	88	161.1	96.8	48	212.6	127.7
9	7.7	4.6	69	59.1	35.5	29	110.6	66.4	89	162.0	97.3	49	213.4	128.2
10	8.6	5.2	70	60.0	36.1	30	111.4	67.0	90	162.9	97.9	50	214.3	128.8
11	9.4	5.7	71	60.9	36.6	131	112.3	67.5	191	163.7	98.4	251	215.1	129.3
12	10.3	6.2	72	61.7	37.1	32	113.1	68.0	92	164.6	98.9	52	216.0	129.8
13	11.1	6.7	73	62.6	37.6	33	114.0	68.5	93	165.4	99.4	53	216.9	130.3
14	12.0	7.2	74	63.4	38.1	34	114.9	69.0	94	166.3	99.9	54	217.7	130.8
15	12.9	7.7	75	64.3	38.6	35	115.7	69.5	95	167.1	100.4	55	218.6	131.3
16	13.7	8.2	76	65.1	39.1	36	116.6	70.0	96	168.0	100.9	56	219.4	131.8
17	14.6	8.8	77	66.0	39.7	37	117.4	70.6	97	168.9	101.5	57	220.3	132.4
18	15.4	9.3	78	66.9	40.2	38	118.3	71.1	98	169.7	102.0	58	221.1	132.9
19	16.3	9.8	79	67.7	40.7	39	119.1	71.6	99	170.6	102.5	59	222.0	133.4
20	17.1	10.3	80	68.6	41.2	40	120.0	72.1	200	171.4	103.0	60	222.9	133.9
21	18.0	10.8	81	69.4	41.7	141	120.9	72.6	201	172.3	103.5	261	223.7	134.4
22	18.9	11.3	82	70.3	42.2	42	121.7	73.1	02	173.1	104.0	62	224.6	134.9
23	19.7	11.8	83	71.1	42.7	43	122.6	73.7	03	174.0	104.6	63	225.4	135.5
24	20.6	12.4	84	72.0	43.3	44	123.4	74.2	04	174.9	105.1	64	226.3	136.0
25	21.4	12.9	85	72.9	43.8	45	124.3	74.7	05	175.7	105.6	65	227.1	136.5
26	22.3	13.4	86	73.7	44.3	46	125.1	75.2	06	176.6	106.1	66	228.0	137.0
27	23.1	13.9	87	74.6	44.8	47	126.0	75.7	07	177.4	106.6	67	228.9	137.5
28	24.0	14.4	88	75.4	45.3	48	126.9	76.2	08	178.3	107.1	68	229.7	138.0
29	24.9	14.9	89	76.3	45.8	49	127.7	76.7	09	179.1	107.6	69	230.6	138.5
30	25.7	15.5	90	77.1	46.4	50	128.6	77.3	10	180.0	108.2	70	231.4	139.1
31	26.6	16.0	91	78.0	46.9	151	129.4	77.8	211	180.9	108.7	271	232.3	139.6
32	27.4	16.5	92	78.9	47.4	52	130.3	78.3	12	181.7	109.2	72	233.1	140.1
33	28.3	17.0	93	79.7	47.9	53	131.1	78.8	13	182.6	109.7	73	234.0	140.6
34	29.1	17.5	94	80.6	48.4	54	132.0	79.3	14	183.4	110.2	74	234.9	141.1
35	30.0	18.0	95	81.4	48.9	55	132.9	79.8	15	184.3	110.7	75	235.7	141.6
36	30.9	18.5	96	82.3	49.4	56	133.7	80.3	16	185.1	111.2	76	236.6	142.2
37	31.7	19.1	97	83.1	50.0	57	134.6	80.9	17	186.0	111.8	77	237.4	142.7
38	32.6	19.6	98	84.0	50.5	58	135.4	81.4	18	186.9	112.3	78	238.3	143.2
39	33.4	20.1	99	84.9	51.0	59	136.3	81.9	19	187.7	112.8	79	239.1	143.7
40	34.3	20.6	100	85.7	51.5	60	137.1	82.4	20	188.6	113.3	80	240.0	144.2
41	35.1	21.1	101	86.6	52.0	161	138.0	82.9	221	189.4	113.8	281	240.9	144.7
42	36.0	21.6	02	87.4	52.5	62	138.9	83.4	22	190.3	114.3	82	241.7	145.2
43	36.9	22.1	03	88.3	53.0	63	139.7	84.0	23	191.1	114.9	83	242.6	145.8
44	37.7	22.7	04	89.1	53.6	64	140.6	84.5	24	192.0	115.4	84	243.4	146.3
45	38.6	23.2	05	90.0	54.1	65	141.4	85.0	25	192.9	115.9	85	244.3	146.8
46	39.4	23.7	06	90.9	54.6	66	142.3	85.5	26	193.7	116.4	86	245.1	147.3
47	40.3	24.2	07	91.7	55.1	67	143.1	86.0	27	194.6	116.9	87	246.0	147.8
48	41.1	24.7	08	92.6	55.6	68	144.0	86.5	28	195.4	117.4	88	246.9	148.3
49	42.0	25.2	09	93.4	56.1	69	144.9	87.0	29	196.3	117.9	89	247.7	148.8
50	42.9	25.8	10	94.3	56.7	70	145.7	87.6	30	197.1	118.5	90	248.6	149.4
51	43.7	26.3	111	95.1	57.2	171	146.6	88.1	231	198.0	119.0	291	249.4	149.9
52	44.6	26.8	12	96.0	57.7	72	147.4	88.6	32	198.9	119.5	92	250.3	150.4
53	45.4	27.3	13	96.9	58.2	73	148.3	89.1	33	199.7	120.0	93	251.2	150.9
54	46.3	27.8	14	97.7	58.7	74	149.1	89.6	34	200.6	120.5	94	252.0	151.4
55	47.1	28.3	15	98.6	59.2	75	150.0	90.1	35	201.4	121.0	95	252.9	151.9
56	48.0	28.8	16	99.4	59.7	76	150.9	90.6	36	202.3	121.5	96	253.7	152.5
57	48.9	29.4	17	100.3	60.3	77	151.7	91.2	37	203.1	122.1	97	254.6	153.0
58	49.7	29.9	18	101.1	60.8	78	152.6	91.7	38	204.0	122.6	98	255.4	153.5
59	50.6	30.4	19	102.0	61.3	79	153.4	92.2	39	204.9	123.1	99	256.3	154.0
60	51.4	30.9	20	102.9	61.8	80	154.3	92.7	40	205.7	123.6	300	257.2	154.5
Dist.	Dep.	D. Lat.	Dist.	Dep.	D. Lat.	Dist.	Dep.	D. Lat.	Dist.	Dep.	D. Lat.	Dist.	Dep.	D. Lat.
301° 239°	059° 121°													

59°

Dist.	D. Lat.	Dep.
N.	N x Cos.	N x Sin.
Hypotenuse	Side Adj.	Side Opp.

TABLE 4

31° Traverse Table

329° 211°	031° 149°												329° 211°	031° 149°
Dist.	D. Lat.	Dep.	Dist.	D. Lat.	Dep.	Dist.	D. Lat.	Dep.	Dist.	D. Lat.	Dep.	Dist.	D. Lat.	Dep.
301	258.0	155.0	361	309.4	185.9	421	360.9	216.8	481	412.3	247.7	541	463.7	278.6
02	258.9	155.5	62	310.3	186.4	22	361.7	217.3	82	413.2	248.2	42	464.6	279.2
03	259.7	156.1	63	311.2	187.0	23	362.6	217.9	83	414.0	248.8	43	465.4	279.7
04	260.6	156.6	64	312.0	187.5	24	363.4	218.4	84	414.9	249.3	44	466.3	280.2
05	261.4	157.1	65	312.9	188.0	25	364.3	218.9	85	415.7	249.8	45	467.2	280.7
06	262.3	157.6	66	313.7	188.5	26	365.2	219.4	86	416.6	250.3	46	468.0	281.2
07	263.2	158.1	67	314.6	189.0	27	366.0	219.9	87	417.4	250.8	47	468.9	281.7
08	264.0	158.6	68	315.4	189.5	28	366.9	220.4	88	418.3	251.3	48	469.7	282.2
09	264.9	159.1	69	316.3	190.0	29	367.7	221.0	89	419.2	251.9	49	470.6	282.8
10	265.7	159.7	70	317.2	190.6	30	368.6	221.5	90	420.0	252.4	50	471.4	283.3
311	266.6	160.2	371	318.0	191.1	431	369.4	222.0	491	420.9	252.9	551	472.3	283.8
12	267.4	160.7	72	318.9	191.6	32	370.3	222.5	92	421.7	253.4	52	473.2	284.3
13	268.3	161.2	73	319.7	192.1	33	371.2	223.0	93	422.6	253.9	53	474.0	284.8
14	269.2	161.7	74	320.6	192.6	34	372.0	223.5	94	423.4	254.4	54	474.9	285.3
15	270.0	162.2	75	321.4	193.1	35	372.9	224.0	95	424.3	254.9	55	475.7	285.8
16	270.9	162.8	76	322.3	193.7	36	373.7	224.6	96	425.2	255.5	56	476.6	286.4
17	271.7	163.3	77	323.2	194.2	37	374.6	225.1	97	426.0	256.0	57	477.4	286.9
18	272.6	163.8	78	324.0	194.7	38	375.4	225.6	98	426.9	256.5	58	478.3	287.4
19	273.4	164.3	79	324.9	195.2	39	376.3	226.1	99	427.7	257.0	59	479.2	287.9
20	274.3	164.8	80	325.7	195.7	40	377.2	226.6	500	428.6	257.5	60	480.0	288.4
321	275.2	165.3	381	326.6	196.2	441	378.0	227.1	501	429.4	258.0	561	480.9	288.9
22	276.0	165.8	82	327.4	196.7	42	378.9	227.6	02	430.3	258.5	62	481.7	289.5
23	276.9	166.4	83	328.3	197.3	43	379.7	228.2	03	431.2	259.1	63	482.6	290.0
24	277.7	166.9	84	329.2	197.8	44	380.6	228.7	04	432.0	259.6	64	483.4	290.5
25	278.6	167.4	85	330.0	198.3	45	381.4	229.2	05	432.9	260.1	65	484.3	291.0
26	279.4	167.9	86	330.9	198.8	46	382.3	229.7	06	433.7	260.6	66	485.2	291.5
27	280.3	168.4	87	331.7	199.3	47	383.2	230.2	07	434.6	261.1	67	486.0	292.0
28	281.2	168.9	88	332.6	199.8	48	384.0	230.7	08	435.4	261.6	68	486.9	292.5
29	282.0	169.4	89	333.4	200.3	49	384.9	231.3	09	436.3	262.2	69	487.7	293.1
30	282.9	170.0	90	334.3	200.9	50	385.7	231.8	10	437.2	262.7	70	488.6	293.6
331	283.7	170.5	391	335.2	201.4	451	386.6	232.3	511	438.0	263.2	571	489.4	294.1
32	284.6	171.0	92	336.0	201.9	52	387.4	232.8	12	438.9	263.7	72	490.3	294.6
33	285.4	171.5	93	336.9	202.4	53	388.3	233.3	13	439.7	264.2	73	491.2	295.1
34	286.3	172.0	94	337.7	202.9	54	389.2	233.8	14	440.6	264.7	74	492.0	295.6
35	287.2	172.5	95	338.6	203.4	55	390.0	234.3	15	441.4	265.2	75	492.9	296.1
36	288.0	173.1	96	339.4	204.0	56	390.9	234.9	16	442.3	265.8	76	493.7	296.7
37	288.9	173.6	97	340.3	204.5	57	391.7	235.4	17	443.2	266.3	77	494.6	297.2
38	289.7	174.1	98	341.2	205.0	58	392.6	235.9	18	444.0	266.8	78	495.4	297.7
39	290.6	174.6	99	342.0	205.5	59	393.4	236.4	19	444.9	267.3	79	496.3	298.2
40	291.4	175.1	400	342.9	206.0	60	394.3	236.9	20	445.7	267.8	80	497.2	298.7
341	292.3	175.6	401	343.7	206.5	461	395.2	237.4	521	446.6	268.3	581	498.0	299.2
42	293.2	176.1	02	344.6	207.0	62	396.0	237.9	22	447.4	268.8	82	498.9	299.8
43	294.0	176.7	03	345.4	207.6	63	396.9	238.5	23	448.3	269.4	83	499.7	300.3
44	294.9	177.2	04	346.3	208.1	64	397.7	239.0	24	449.2	269.9	84	500.6	300.8
45	295.7	177.7	05	347.2	208.6	65	398.6	239.5	25	450.0	270.4	85	501.4	301.3
46	296.6	178.2	06	348.0	209.1	66	399.4	240.0	26	450.9	270.9	86	502.3	301.8
47	297.4	178.7	07	348.9	209.6	67	400.3	240.5	27	451.7	271.4	87	503.2	302.3
48	298.3	179.2	08	349.7	210.1	68	401.2	241.0	28	452.6	271.9	88	504.0	302.8
49	299.2	179.7	09	350.6	210.7	69	402.0	241.6	29	453.4	272.5	89	504.9	303.4
50	300.0	180.3	10	351.4	211.2	70	402.9	242.1	30	454.3	273.0	90	505.7	303.9
351	300.9	180.8	411	352.3	211.7	471	403.7	242.6	531	455.2	273.5	591	506.6	304.4
52	301.7	181.3	12	353.2	212.2	72	404.6	243.1	32	456.0	274.0	92	507.4	304.9
53	302.6	181.8	13	354.0	212.7	73	405.4	243.6	33	456.9	274.5	93	508.3	305.4
54	303.4	182.3	14	354.9	213.2	74	406.3	244.1	34	457.7	275.0	94	509.2	305.9
55	304.3	182.8	15	355.7	213.7	75	407.2	244.6	35	458.6	275.5	95	510.0	306.4
56	305.2	183.4	16	356.6	214.3	76	408.0	245.2	36	459.4	276.1	96	510.9	307.0
57	306.0	183.9	17	357.4	214.8	77	408.9	245.7	37	460.3	276.6	97	511.7	307.5
58	306.9	184.4	18	358.3	215.3	78	409.7	246.2	38	461.2	277.1	98	512.6	308.0
59	307.7	184.9	19	359.2	215.8	79	410.6	246.7	39	462.0	277.6	99	513.4	308.5
60	308.6	185.4	20	360.0	216.3	80	411.4	247.2	40	462.9	278.1	600	514.3	309.0
Dist.	Dep.	D. Lat.	Dist.	Dep.	D. Lat.	Dist.	Dep.	D. Lat.	Dist.	Dep.	D. Lat.	Dist.	Dep.	D. Lat.
													301° 239°	059° 121°

Dist.	D. Lat.	Dep.
D Lo	Dep.	
	m	D Lo

59°

TABLE 4

Traverse 32° Table

328° | 032° / 212° | 148°

Dist.	D. Lat.	Dep.	Dist.	D. Lat.	Dep.	Dist.	D. Lat.	Dep.	Dist.	D. Lat.	Dep.	Dist.	D. Lat.	Dep.
1	0.8	0.5	61	51.7	32.3	121	102.6	64.1	181	153.5	95.9	241	204.4	127.7
2	1.7	1.1	62	52.6	32.9	22	103.5	64.7	82	154.3	96.4	42	205.2	128.2
3	2.5	1.6	63	53.4	33.4	23	104.3	65.2	83	155.2	97.0	43	206.1	128.8
4	3.4	2.1	64	54.3	33.9	24	105.2	65.7	84	156.0	97.5	44	206.9	129.3
5	4.2	2.6	65	55.1	34.4	25	106.0	66.2	85	156.9	98.0	45	207.8	129.8
6	5.1	3.2	66	56.0	35.0	26	106.9	66.8	86	157.7	98.6	46	208.6	130.4
7	5.9	3.7	67	56.8	35.5	27	107.7	67.3	87	158.6	99.1	47	209.5	130.9
8	6.8	4.2	68	57.7	36.0	28	108.6	67.8	88	159.4	99.6	48	210.3	131.4
9	7.6	4.8	69	58.5	36.6	29	109.4	68.4	89	160.3	100.2	49	211.2	131.9
10	8.5	5.3	70	59.4	37.1	30	110.2	68.9	90	161.1	100.7	50	212.0	132.5
11	9.3	5.8	71	60.2	37.6	131	111.1	69.4	191	162.0	101.2	251	212.9	133.0
12	10.2	6.4	72	61.1	38.2	32	111.9	69.9	92	162.8	101.7	52	213.7	133.5
13	11.0	6.9	73	61.9	38.7	33	112.8	70.5	93	163.7	102.3	53	214.6	134.1
14	11.9	7.4	74	62.8	39.2	34	113.6	71.0	94	164.5	102.8	54	215.4	134.6
15	12.7	7.9	75	63.6	39.7	35	114.5	71.5	95	165.4	103.3	55	216.3	135.1
16	13.6	8.5	76	64.5	40.3	36	115.3	72.1	96	166.2	103.9	56	217.1	135.7
17	14.4	9.0	77	65.3	40.8	37	116.2	72.6	97	167.1	104.4	57	217.9	136.2
18	15.3	9.5	78	66.1	41.3	38	117.0	73.1	98	167.9	104.9	58	218.8	136.7
19	16.1	10.1	79	67.0	41.9	39	117.9	73.7	99	168.8	105.5	59	219.6	137.2
20	17.0	10.6	80	67.8	42.4	40	118.7	74.2	200	169.6	106.0	60	220.5	137.8
21	17.8	11.1	81	68.7	42.9	141	119.6	74.7	201	170.5	106.5	261	221.3	138.3
22	18.7	11.7	82	69.5	43.5	42	120.4	75.2	02	171.3	107.0	62	222.2	138.8
23	19.5	12.2	83	70.4	44.0	43	121.3	75.8	03	172.2	107.6	63	223.0	139.4
24	20.4	12.7	84	71.2	44.5	44	122.1	76.3	04	173.0	108.1	64	223.9	139.9
25	21.2	13.2	85	72.1	45.0	45	123.0	76.8	05	173.8	108.6	65	224.7	140.4
26	22.0	13.8	86	72.9	45.6	46	123.8	77.4	06	174.7	109.2	66	225.6	141.0
27	22.9	14.3	87	73.8	46.1	47	124.7	77.9	07	175.5	109.7	67	226.4	141.5
28	23.7	14.8	88	74.6	46.6	48	125.5	78.4	08	176.4	110.2	68	227.3	142.0
29	24.6	15.4	89	75.5	47.2	49	126.4	79.0	09	177.2	110.8	69	228.1	142.5
30	25.4	15.9	90	76.3	47.7	50	127.2	79.5	10	178.1	111.3	70	229.0	143.1
31	26.3	16.4	91	77.2	48.2	151	128.1	80.0	211	178.9	111.8	271	229.8	143.6
32	27.1	17.0	92	78.0	48.8	52	128.9	80.5	12	179.8	112.3	72	230.7	144.1
33	28.0	17.5	93	78.9	49.3	53	129.8	81.1	13	180.6	112.9	73	231.5	144.7
34	28.8	18.0	94	79.7	49.8	54	130.6	81.6	14	181.5	113.4	74	232.4	145.2
35	29.7	18.5	95	80.6	50.3	55	131.4	82.1	15	182.3	113.9	75	233.2	145.7
36	30.5	19.1	96	81.4	50.9	56	132.3	82.7	16	183.2	114.5	76	234.1	146.3
37	31.4	19.6	97	82.3	51.4	57	133.1	83.2	17	184.0	115.0	77	234.9	146.8
38	32.2	20.1	98	83.1	51.9	58	134.0	83.7	18	184.9	115.5	78	235.8	147.3
39	33.1	20.7	99	84.0	52.5	59	134.8	84.3	19	185.7	116.1	79	236.6	147.8
40	33.9	21.2	100	84.8	53.0	60	135.7	84.8	20	186.6	116.6	80	237.5	148.4
41	34.8	21.7	101	85.7	53.5	161	136.5	85.3	221	187.4	117.1	281	238.3	148.9
42	35.6	22.3	02	86.5	54.1	62	137.4	85.8	22	188.3	117.6	82	239.1	149.4
43	36.5	22.8	03	87.3	54.6	63	138.2	86.4	23	189.1	118.2	83	240.0	150.0
44	37.3	23.3	04	88.2	55.1	64	139.1	86.9	24	190.0	118.7	84	240.8	150.5
45	38.2	23.8	05	89.0	55.6	65	139.9	87.4	25	190.8	119.2	85	241.7	151.0
46	39.0	24.4	06	89.9	56.2	66	140.8	88.0	26	191.7	119.8	86	242.5	151.6
47	39.9	24.9	07	90.7	56.7	67	141.6	88.5	27	192.5	120.3	87	243.4	152.1
48	40.7	25.4	08	91.6	57.2	68	142.5	89.0	28	193.4	120.8	88	244.2	152.6
49	41.6	26.0	09	92.4	57.8	69	143.3	89.6	29	194.2	121.4	89	245.1	153.1
50	42.4	26.5	10	93.3	58.3	70	144.2	90.1	30	195.1	121.9	90	245.9	153.7
51	43.3	27.0	111	94.1	58.8	171	145.0	90.6	231	195.9	122.4	291	246.8	154.2
52	44.1	27.6	12	95.0	59.4	72	145.9	91.1	32	196.7	122.9	92	247.6	154.7
53	44.9	28.1	13	95.8	59.9	73	146.7	91.7	33	197.6	123.5	93	248.5	155.3
54	45.8	28.6	14	96.7	60.4	74	147.6	92.2	34	198.4	124.0	94	249.3	155.8
55	46.6	29.1	15	97.5	60.9	75	148.4	92.7	35	199.3	124.5	95	250.2	156.3
56	47.5	29.7	16	98.4	61.5	76	149.3	93.3	36	200.1	125.1	96	251.0	156.9
57	48.3	30.2	17	99.2	62.0	77	150.1	93.8	37	201.0	125.6	97	251.9	157.4
58	49.2	30.7	18	100.1	62.5	78	151.0	94.3	38	201.8	126.1	98	252.7	157.9
59	50.0	31.3	19	100.9	63.1	79	151.8	94.9	39	202.7	126.7	99	253.6	158.4
60	50.9	31.8	20	101.8	63.6	80	152.6	95.4	40	203.5	127.2	300	254.4	159.0
Dist.	Dep.	D. Lat.	Dist.	Dep.	D. Lat.	Dist.	Dep.	D. Lat.	Dist.	Dep.	D. Lat.	Dist.	Dep.	D. Lat.

302° | 058° / 238° | 122°

58°

Dist.	D. Lat.	Dep.
N.	N x Cos.	N x Sin.
Hypotenuse	Side Adj.	Side Opp.

TABLE 4

Traverse 32° Table

328° | 032° / 212° | 148°

Dist.	D. Lat.	Dep.	Dist.	D. Lat.	Dep.	Dist.	D. Lat.	Dep.	Dist.	D. Lat.	Dep.	Dist.	D. Lat.	Dep.
301	255.3	159.5	361	306.1	191.3	421	357.0	223.1	481	407.9	254.9	541	458.8	286.7
02	256.1	160.0	62	307.0	191.8	22	357.9	223.6	82	408.8	255.4	42	459.6	287.2
03	257.0	160.6	63	307.8	192.4	23	358.7	224.2	83	409.6	256.0	43	460.5	287.7
04	257.8	161.1	64	308.7	192.9	24	359.6	224.7	84	410.5	256.5	44	461.3	288.3
05	258.7	161.6	65	309.5	193.4	25	360.4	225.2	85	411.3	257.0	45	462.2	288.8
06	259.5	162.2	66	310.4	194.0	26	361.3	225.7	86	412.2	257.5	46	463.0	289.3
07	260.4	162.7	67	311.2	194.5	27	362.1	226.3	87	413.0	258.1	47	463.9	289.9
08	261.2	163.2	68	312.1	195.0	28	363.0	226.8	88	413.8	258.6	48	464.7	290.4
09	262.0	163.7	69	312.9	195.5	29	363.8	227.3	89	414.7	259.1	49	465.6	290.9
10	262.9	164.3	70	313.8	196.1	30	364.7	227.9	90	415.5	259.7	50	466.4	291.5
311	263.7	164.8	371	314.6	196.6	431	365.5	228.4	491	416.4	260.2	551	467.3	292.0
12	264.6	165.3	72	315.5	197.1	32	366.4	228.9	92	417.2	260.7	52	468.1	292.5
13	265.4	165.9	73	316.3	197.7	33	367.2	229.5	93	418.1	261.3	53	469.0	293.0
14	266.3	166.4	74	317.2	198.2	34	368.1	230.0	94	418.9	261.8	54	469.8	293.6
15	267.1	166.9	75	318.0	198.7	35	368.9	230.5	95	419.8	262.3	55	470.7	294.1
16	268.0	167.5	76	318.9	199.2	36	369.7	231.0	96	420.6	262.8	56	471.5	294.6
17	268.8	168.0	77	319.7	199.8	37	370.6	231.6	97	421.5	263.4	57	472.4	295.2
18	269.7	168.5	78	320.6	200.3	38	371.4	232.1	98	422.3	263.9	58	473.2	295.7
19	270.5	169.0	79	321.4	200.8	39	372.3	232.6	99	423.2	264.4	59	474.1	296.2
20	271.4	169.6	80	322.3	201.4	40	373.1	233.2	500	424.0	265.0	60	474.9	296.8
321	272.2	170.1	381	323.1	201.9	441	374.0	233.7	501	424.9	265.5	561	475.8	297.3
22	273.1	170.6	82	324.0	202.4	42	374.8	234.2	02	425.7	266.0	62	476.6	297.8
23	273.9	171.2	83	324.8	203.0	43	375.7	234.8	03	426.6	266.5	63	477.5	298.3
24	274.8	171.7	84	325.7	203.5	44	376.5	235.3	04	427.4	267.1	64	478.3	298.9
25	275.6	172.2	85	326.5	204.0	45	377.4	235.8	05	428.3	267.6	65	479.1	299.4
26	276.5	172.8	86	327.3	204.5	46	378.2	236.3	06	429.1	268.1	66	480.0	299.9
27	277.3	173.3	87	328.2	205.1	47	379.1	236.9	07	430.0	268.7	67	480.8	300.5
28	278.2	173.8	88	329.0	205.6	48	379.9	237.4	08	430.8	269.2	68	481.7	301.0
29	279.0	174.3	89	329.9	206.1	49	380.8	237.9	09	431.7	269.7	69	482.5	301.5
30	279.9	174.9	90	330.7	206.7	50	381.6	238.5	10	432.5	270.3	70	483.4	302.1
331	280.7	175.4	391	331.6	207.2	451	382.5	239.0	511	433.4	270.8	571	484.2	302.6
32	281.6	175.9	92	332.4	207.7	52	383.3	239.5	12	434.2	271.3	72	485.1	303.1
33	282.4	176.5	93	333.3	208.3	53	384.2	240.1	13	435.0	271.8	73	485.9	303.6
34	283.2	177.0	94	334.1	208.8	54	385.0	240.6	14	435.9	272.4	74	486.8	304.2
35	284.1	177.5	95	335.0	209.3	55	385.9	241.1	15	436.7	272.9	75	487.6	304.7
36	284.9	178.1	96	335.8	209.8	56	386.7	241.6	16	437.6	273.4	76	488.5	305.2
37	285.8	178.6	97	336.7	210.4	57	387.6	242.2	17	438.4	274.0	77	489.3	305.8
38	286.6	179.1	98	337.5	210.9	58	388.4	242.7	18	439.3	274.5	78	490.2	306.3
39	287.5	179.6	99	338.4	211.4	59	389.3	243.2	19	440.1	275.0	79	491.0	306.8
40	288.3	180.2	400	339.2	212.0	60	390.1	243.8	20	441.0	275.6	80	491.9	307.4
341	289.2	180.7	401	340.1	212.5	461	391.0	244.3	521	441.8	276.1	581	492.7	307.9
42	290.0	181.2	02	340.9	213.0	62	391.8	244.8	22	442.7	276.6	82	493.6	308.4
43	290.9	181.8	03	341.8	213.6	63	392.6	245.4	23	443.5	277.1	83	494.4	308.9
44	291.7	182.3	04	342.6	214.1	64	393.5	245.9	24	444.4	277.7	84	495.3	309.5
45	292.6	182.8	05	343.5	214.6	65	394.3	246.4	25	445.2	278.2	85	496.1	310.0
46	293.4	183.4	06	344.3	215.1	66	395.2	246.9	26	446.1	278.7	86	497.0	310.5
47	294.3	183.9	07	345.2	215.7	67	396.0	247.5	27	446.9	279.3	87	497.8	311.1
48	295.1	184.4	08	346.0	216.2	68	396.9	248.0	28	447.8	279.8	88	498.7	311.6
49	296.0	184.9	09	346.9	216.7	69	397.7	248.5	29	448.6	280.3	89	499.5	312.1
50	296.8	185.5	10	347.7	217.3	70	398.6	249.1	30	449.5	280.9	90	500.3	312.7
351	297.7	186.0	411	348.5	217.8	471	399.4	249.6	531	450.3	281.4	591	501.2	313.2
52	298.5	186.5	12	349.4	218.3	72	400.3	250.1	32	451.2	281.9	92	502.0	313.7
53	299.4	187.1	13	350.2	218.9	73	401.1	250.7	33	452.0	282.4	93	502.9	314.2
54	300.2	187.6	14	351.1	219.4	74	402.0	251.2	34	452.9	283.0	94	503.7	314.8
55	301.1	188.1	15	351.9	219.9	75	402.8	251.7	35	453.7	283.5	95	504.6	315.3
56	301.9	188.7	16	352.8	220.4	76	403.7	252.2	36	454.6	284.0	96	505.4	315.8
57	302.8	189.2	17	353.6	221.0	77	404.5	252.8	37	455.4	284.6	97	506.3	316.4
58	303.6	189.7	18	354.5	221.5	78	405.4	253.3	38	456.2	285.1	98	507.1	316.9
59	304.4	190.2	19	355.3	222.0	79	406.2	253.8	39	457.1	285.6	99	508.0	317.4
60	305.3	190.8	20	356.2	222.6	80	407.1	254.4	40	457.9	286.2	600	508.8	318.0
Dist.	Dep.	D. Lat.	Dist.	Dep.	D. Lat.	Dist.	Dep.	D. Lat.	Dist.	Dep.	D. Lat.	Dist.	Dep.	D. Lat.

Dist.	D. Lat.	Dep.
D Lo	Dep.	
	m	D Lo

58°

302° | 058° / 238° | 122°

TABLE 4

Traverse 33° Table

327° | 033°
213° | 147°

Dist.	D. Lat.	Dep.	Dist.	D. Lat.	Dep.	Dist.	D. Lat.	Dep.	Dist.	D. Lat.	Dep.	Dist.	D. Lat.	Dep.
1	0.8	0.5	61	51.2	33.2	121	101.5	65.9	181	151.8	98.6	241	202.1	131.3
2	1.7	1.1	62	52.0	33.8	22	102.3	66.4	82	152.6	99.1	42	203.0	131.8
3	2.5	1.6	63	52.8	34.3	23	103.2	67.0	83	153.5	99.7	43	203.8	132.3
4	3.4	2.2	64	53.7	34.9	24	104.0	67.5	84	154.3	100.2	44	204.6	132.9
5	4.2	2.7	65	54.5	35.4	25	104.8	68.1	85	155.2	100.8	45	205.5	133.4
6	5.0	3.3	66	55.4	35.9	26	105.7	68.6	86	156.0	101.3	46	206.3	134.0
7	5.9	3.8	67	56.2	36.5	27	106.5	69.2	87	156.8	101.8	47	207.2	134.5
8	6.7	4.4	68	57.0	37.0	28	107.3	69.7	88	157.7	102.4	48	208.0	135.1
9	7.5	4.9	69	57.9	37.6	29	108.2	70.3	89	158.5	102.9	49	208.8	135.6
10	8.4	5.4	70	58.7	38.1	30	109.0	70.8	90	159.3	103.5	50	209.7	136.2
11	9.2	6.0	71	59.5	38.7	131	109.9	71.3	191	160.2	104.0	251	210.5	136.7
12	10.1	6.5	72	60.4	39.2	32	110.7	71.9	92	161.0	104.6	52	211.3	137.2
13	10.9	7.1	73	61.2	39.8	33	111.5	72.4	93	161.9	105.1	53	212.2	137.8
14	11.7	7.6	74	62.1	40.3	34	112.4	73.0	94	162.7	105.7	54	213.0	138.3
15	12.6	8.2	75	62.9	40.8	35	113.2	73.5	95	163.5	106.2	55	213.9	138.9
16	13.4	8.7	76	63.7	41.4	36	114.1	74.1	96	164.4	106.7	56	214.7	139.4
17	14.3	9.3	77	64.6	41.9	37	114.9	74.6	97	165.2	107.3	57	215.5	140.0
18	15.1	9.8	78	65.4	42.5	38	115.7	75.2	98	166.1	107.8	58	216.4	140.5
19	15.9	10.3	79	66.3	43.0	39	116.6	75.7	99	166.9	108.4	59	217.2	141.1
20	16.8	10.9	80	67.1	43.6	40	117.4	76.2	200	167.7	108.9	60	218.1	141.6
21	17.6	11.4	81	67.9	44.1	141	118.3	76.8	201	168.6	109.5	261	218.9	142.2
22	18.5	12.0	82	68.8	44.7	42	119.1	77.3	02	169.4	110.0	62	219.7	142.7
23	19.3	12.5	83	69.6	45.2	43	119.9	77.9	03	170.3	110.6	63	220.6	143.2
24	20.1	13.1	84	70.4	45.7	44	120.8	78.4	04	171.1	111.1	64	221.4	143.8
25	21.0	13.6	85	71.3	46.3	45	121.6	79.0	05	171.9	111.7	65	222.2	144.3
26	21.8	14.2	86	72.1	46.8	46	122.4	79.5	06	172.8	112.2	66	223.1	144.9
27	22.6	14.7	87	73.0	47.4	47	123.3	80.1	07	173.6	112.7	67	223.9	145.4
28	23.5	15.2	88	73.8	47.9	48	124.1	80.6	08	174.4	113.3	68	224.8	146.0
29	24.3	15.8	89	74.6	48.5	49	125.0	81.2	09	175.3	113.8	69	225.6	146.5
30	25.2	16.3	90	75.5	49.0	50	125.8	81.7	10	176.1	114.4	70	226.4	147.1
31	26.0	16.9	91	76.3	49.6	151	126.6	82.2	211	177.0	114.9	271	227.3	147.6
32	26.8	17.4	92	77.2	50.1	52	127.5	82.8	12	177.8	115.5	72	228.1	148.1
33	27.7	18.0	93	78.0	50.7	53	128.3	83.3	13	178.6	116.0	73	229.0	148.7
34	28.5	18.5	94	78.8	51.2	54	129.2	83.9	14	179.5	116.6	74	229.8	149.2
35	29.4	19.1	95	79.7	51.7	55	130.0	84.4	15	180.3	117.1	75	230.6	149.8
36	30.2	19.6	96	80.5	52.3	56	130.8	85.0	16	181.2	117.6	76	231.5	150.3
37	31.0	20.2	97	81.4	52.8	57	131.7	85.5	17	182.0	118.2	77	232.3	150.9
38	31.9	20.7	98	82.2	53.4	58	132.5	86.1	18	182.8	118.7	78	233.2	151.4
39	32.7	21.2	99	83.0	53.9	59	133.3	86.6	19	183.7	119.3	79	234.0	152.0
40	33.5	21.8	100	83.9	54.5	60	134.2	87.1	20	184.5	119.8	80	234.8	152.5
41	34.4	22.3	101	84.7	55.0	161	135.0	87.7	221	185.3	120.4	281	235.7	153.0
42	35.2	22.9	02	85.5	55.6	62	135.9	88.2	22	186.2	120.9	82	236.5	153.6
43	36.1	23.4	03	86.4	56.1	63	136.7	88.8	23	187.0	121.5	83	237.3	154.1
44	36.9	24.0	04	87.2	56.6	64	137.5	89.3	24	187.9	122.0	84	238.2	154.7
45	37.7	24.5	05	88.1	57.2	65	138.4	89.9	25	188.7	122.5	85	239.0	155.2
46	38.6	25.1	06	88.9	57.7	66	139.2	90.4	26	189.5	123.1	86	239.9	155.8
47	39.4	25.6	07	89.7	58.3	67	140.1	91.0	27	190.4	123.6	87	240.7	156.3
48	40.3	26.1	08	90.6	58.8	68	140.9	91.5	28	191.2	124.2	88	241.5	156.9
49	41.1	26.7	09	91.4	59.4	69	141.7	92.0	29	192.1	124.7	89	242.4	157.4
50	41.9	27.2	10	92.3	59.9	70	142.6	92.6	30	192.9	125.3	90	243.2	157.9
51	42.8	27.8	111	93.1	60.5	171	143.4	93.1	231	193.7	125.8	291	244.1	158.5
52	43.6	28.3	12	93.9	61.0	72	144.3	93.7	32	194.6	126.4	92	244.9	159.0
53	44.4	28.9	13	94.8	61.5	73	145.1	94.2	33	195.4	126.9	93	245.7	159.6
54	45.3	29.4	14	95.6	62.1	74	145.9	94.8	34	196.2	127.4	94	246.6	160.1
55	46.1	30.0	15	96.4	62.6	75	146.8	95.3	35	197.1	128.0	95	247.4	160.7
56	47.0	30.5	16	97.3	63.2	76	147.6	95.9	36	197.9	128.5	96	248.2	161.2
57	47.8	31.0	17	98.1	63.7	77	148.4	96.4	37	198.8	129.1	97	249.1	161.8
58	48.6	31.6	18	99.0	64.3	78	149.3	96.9	38	199.6	129.6	98	249.9	162.3
59	49.5	32.1	19	99.8	64.8	79	150.1	97.5	39	200.4	130.2	99	250.8	162.8
60	50.3	32.7	20	100.6	65.4	80	151.0	98.0	40	201.3	130.7	300	251.6	163.4
Dist.	Dep.	D. Lat.	Dist.	Dep.	D. Lat.	Dist.	Dep.	D. Lat.	Dist.	Dep.	D. Lat.	Dist.	Dep.	D. Lat.

303° | 057°
237° | 123°

57°

Dist.	D. Lat.	Dep.
N.	N x Cos.	N x Sin.
Hypotenuse	Side Adj.	Side Opp.

TABLE 4

Traverse 33° Table

327° | 033°
213° | 147°

Dist.	D. Lat.	Dep.	Dist.	D. Lat.	Dep.	Dist.	D. Lat.	Dep.	Dist.	D. Lat.	Dep.	Dist.	D. Lat.	Dep.
301	252.4	163.9	361	302.8	196.6	421	353.1	229.3	481	403.4	262.0	541	453.7	294.6
02	253.3	164.5	62	303.6	197.2	22	353.9	229.8	82	404.2	262.5	42	454.6	295.2
03	254.1	165.0	63	304.4	197.7	23	354.8	230.4	83	405.1	263.1	43	455.4	295.7
04	255.0	165.6	64	305.3	198.2	24	355.6	230.9	84	405.9	263.6	44	456.2	296.3
05	255.8	166.1	65	306.1	198.8	25	356.4	231.5	85	406.8	264.1	45	457.1	296.8
06	256.6	166.7	66	307.0	199.3	26	357.3	232.0	86	407.6	264.7	46	457.9	297.4
07	257.5	167.2	67	307.8	199.9	27	358.1	232.6	87	408.4	265.2	47	458.8	297.9
08	258.3	167.7	68	308.6	200.4	28	359.0	233.1	88	409.3	265.8	48	459.6	298.5
09	259.1	168.3	69	309.5	201.0	29	359.8	233.7	89	410.1	266.3	49	460.4	299.0
10	260.0	168.8	70	310.3	201.5	30	360.6	234.2	90	410.9	266.9	50	461.3	299.6
311	260.8	169.4	371	311.1	202.1	431	361.5	234.7	491	411.8	267.4	551	462.1	300.1
12	261.7	169.9	72	312.0	202.6	32	362.3	235.3	92	412.6	268.0	52	462.9	300.6
13	262.5	170.5	73	312.8	203.2	33	363.1	235.8	93	413.5	268.5	53	463.8	301.2
14	263.3	171.0	74	313.7	203.7	34	364.0	236.4	94	414.3	269.1	54	464.6	301.7
15	264.2	171.6	75	314.5	204.2	35	364.8	236.9	95	415.1	269.6	55	465.5	302.3
16	265.0	172.1	76	315.3	204.8	36	365.7	237.5	96	416.0	270.1	56	466.3	302.8
17	265.9	172.7	77	316.2	205.3	37	366.5	238.0	97	416.8	270.7	57	467.1	303.4
18	266.7	173.2	78	317.0	205.9	38	367.3	238.6	98	417.7	271.2	58	468.0	303.9
19	267.5	173.7	79	317.9	206.4	39	368.2	239.1	99	418.5	271.8	59	468.8	304.5
20	268.4	174.3	80	318.7	207.0	40	369.0	239.6	500	419.3	272.3	60	469.7	305.0
321	269.2	174.8	381	319.5	207.5	441	369.9	240.2	501	420.2	272.9	561	470.5	305.5
22	270.1	175.4	82	320.4	208.1	42	370.7	240.7	02	421.0	273.4	62	471.3	306.1
23	270.9	175.9	83	321.2	208.6	43	371.5	241.3	03	421.9	274.0	63	472.2	306.6
24	271.7	176.5	84	322.0	209.1	44	372.4	241.8	04	422.7	274.5	64	473.0	307.2
25	272.6	177.0	85	322.9	209.7	45	373.2	242.4	05	423.5	275.0	65	473.8	307.7
26	273.4	177.6	86	323.7	210.2	46	374.0	242.9	06	424.4	275.6	66	474.7	308.3
27	274.2	178.1	87	324.6	210.8	47	374.9	243.5	07	425.2	276.1	67	475.5	308.8
28	275.1	178.6	88	325.4	211.3	48	375.7	244.0	08	426.0	276.7	68	476.4	309.4
29	275.9	179.2	89	326.2	211.9	49	376.6	244.5	09	426.9	277.2	69	477.2	309.9
30	276.8	179.7	90	327.1	212.4	50	377.4	245.1	10	427.7	277.8	70	478.0	310.4
331	277.6	180.3	391	327.9	213.0	451	378.2	245.6	511	428.6	278.3	571	478.9	311.0
32	278.4	180.8	92	328.8	213.5	52	379.1	246.2	12	429.4	278.9	72	479.7	311.5
33	279.3	181.4	93	329.6	214.0	53	379.9	246.7	13	430.2	279.4	73	480.6	312.1
34	280.1	181.9	94	330.4	214.6	54	380.8	247.3	14	431.1	279.9	74	481.4	312.6
35	281.0	182.5	95	331.3	215.1	55	381.6	247.8	15	431.9	280.5	75	482.2	313.2
36	281.8	183.0	96	332.1	215.7	56	382.4	248.4	16	432.8	281.0	76	483.1	313.7
37	282.6	183.5	97	333.0	216.2	57	383.3	248.9	17	433.6	281.6	77	483.9	314.3
38	283.5	184.1	98	333.8	216.8	58	384.1	249.4	18	434.4	282.1	78	484.8	314.8
39	284.3	184.6	99	334.6	217.3	59	384.9	250.0	19	435.3	282.7	79	485.6	315.3
40	285.1	185.2	400	335.5	217.9	60	385.8	250.5	20	436.1	283.2	80	486.4	315.9
341	286.0	185.7	401	336.3	218.4	461	386.6	251.1	521	436.9	283.8	581	487.3	316.4
42	286.8	186.3	02	337.1	218.9	62	387.5	251.6	22	437.8	284.3	82	488.1	317.0
43	287.7	186.8	03	338.0	219.5	63	388.3	252.2	23	438.6	284.8	83	488.9	317.5
44	288.5	187.4	04	338.8	220.0	64	389.1	252.7	24	439.5	285.4	84	489.8	318.1
45	289.3	187.9	05	339.7	220.6	65	390.0	253.3	25	440.3	285.9	85	490.6	318.6
46	290.2	188.4	06	340.5	221.1	66	390.8	253.8	26	441.1	286.5	86	491.5	319.2
47	291.0	189.0	07	341.3	221.7	67	391.7	254.3	27	442.0	287.0	87	492.3	319.7
48	291.9	189.5	08	342.2	222.2	68	392.5	254.9	28	442.8	287.6	88	493.1	320.2
49	292.7	190.1	09	343.0	222.8	69	393.3	255.4	29	443.7	288.1	89	494.0	320.8
50	293.5	190.6	10	343.9	223.3	70	394.2	256.0	30	444.5	288.7	90	494.8	321.3
351	294.4	191.2	411	344.7	223.8	471	395.0	256.5	531	445.3	289.2	591	495.7	321.9
52	295.2	191.7	12	345.5	224.4	72	395.9	257.1	32	446.2	289.7	92	496.5	322.4
53	296.1	192.3	13	346.4	224.9	73	396.7	257.6	33	447.0	290.3	93	497.3	323.0
54	296.9	192.8	14	347.2	225.5	74	397.5	258.2	34	447.9	290.8	94	498.2	323.5
55	297.7	193.3	15	348.0	226.0	75	398.4	258.7	35	448.7	291.4	95	499.0	324.1
56	298.6	193.9	16	348.9	226.6	76	399.2	259.2	36	449.5	291.9	96	499.8	324.6
57	299.4	194.4	17	349.7	227.1	77	400.0	259.8	37	450.4	292.5	97	500.7	325.1
58	300.2	195.0	18	350.6	227.7	78	400.9	260.3	38	451.2	293.0	98	501.5	325.7
59	301.1	195.5	19	351.4	228.2	79	401.7	260.9	39	452.0	293.6	99	502.4	326.2
60	301.9	196.1	20	352.2	228.7	80	402.6	261.4	40	452.9	294.1	600	503.2	326.8
Dist.	Dep.	D. Lat.	Dist.	Dep.	D. Lat.	Dist.	Dep.	D. Lat.	Dist.	Dep.	D. Lat.	Dist.	Dep.	D. Lat.

Dist.	D. Lat.	Dep.
D Lo	Dep.	
	m	D Lo

57°

303° | 057°
237° | 123°

TABLE 4

Traverse 34° Table

326° | 034° / 214° | 146°

Dist.	D. Lat.	Dep.	Dist.	D. Lat.	Dep.	Dist.	D. Lat.	Dep.	Dist.	D. Lat.	Dep.	Dist.	D. Lat.	Dep.
1	0.8	0.6	61	50.6	34.1	121	100.3	67.7	181	150.1	101.2	241	199.8	134.8
2	1.7	1.1	62	51.4	34.7	22	101.1	68.2	82	150.9	101.8	42	200.6	135.3
3	2.5	1.7	63	52.2	35.2	23	102.0	68.8	83	151.7	102.3	43	201.5	135.9
4	3.3	2.2	64	53.1	35.8	24	102.8	69.3	84	152.5	102.9	44	202.3	136.4
5	4.1	2.8	65	53.9	36.3	25	103.6	69.9	85	153.4	103.5	45	203.1	137.0
6	5.0	3.4	66	54.7	36.9	26	104.5	70.5	86	154.2	104.0	46	203.9	137.6
7	5.8	3.9	67	55.5	37.5	27	105.3	71.0	87	155.0	104.6	47	204.8	138.1
8	6.6	4.5	68	56.4	38.0	28	106.1	71.6	88	155.9	105.1	48	205.6	138.7
9	7.5	5.0	69	57.2	38.6	29	106.9	72.1	89	156.7	105.7	49	206.4	139.2
10	8.3	5.6	70	58.0	39.1	30	107.8	72.7	90	157.5	106.2	50	207.3	139.8
11	9.1	6.2	71	58.9	39.7	131	108.6	73.3	191	158.3	106.8	251	208.1	140.4
12	9.9	6.7	72	59.7	40.3	32	109.4	73.8	92	159.2	107.4	52	208.9	140.9
13	10.8	7.3	73	60.5	40.8	33	110.3	74.4	93	160.0	107.9	53	209.7	141.5
14	11.6	7.8	74	61.3	41.4	34	111.1	74.9	94	160.8	108.5	54	210.6	142.0
15	12.4	8.4	75	62.2	41.9	35	111.9	75.5	95	161.7	109.0	55	211.4	142.6
16	13.3	8.9	76	63.0	42.5	36	112.7	76.1	96	162.5	109.6	56	212.2	143.2
17	14.1	9.5	77	63.8	43.1	37	113.6	76.6	97	163.3	110.2	57	213.1	143.7
18	14.9	10.1	78	64.7	43.6	38	114.4	77.2	98	164.1	110.7	58	213.9	144.3
19	15.8	10.6	79	65.5	44.2	39	115.2	77.7	99	165.0	111.3	59	214.7	144.8
20	16.6	11.2	80	66.3	44.7	40	116.1	78.3	200	165.8	111.8	60	215.5	145.4
21	17.4	11.7	81	67.2	45.3	141	116.9	78.8	201	166.6	112.4	261	216.4	145.9
22	18.2	12.3	82	68.0	45.9	42	117.7	79.4	02	167.5	113.0	62	217.2	146.5
23	19.1	12.9	83	68.8	46.4	43	118.6	80.0	03	168.3	113.5	63	218.0	147.1
24	19.9	13.4	84	69.6	47.0	44	119.4	80.5	04	169.1	114.1	64	218.9	147.6
25	20.7	14.0	85	70.5	47.5	45	120.2	81.1	05	170.0	114.6	65	219.7	148.2
26	21.6	14.5	86	71.3	48.1	46	121.0	81.6	06	170.8	115.2	66	220.5	148.7
27	22.4	15.1	87	72.1	48.6	47	121.9	82.2	07	171.6	115.8	67	221.4	149.3
28	23.2	15.7	88	73.0	49.2	48	122.7	82.8	08	172.4	116.3	68	222.2	149.9
29	24.0	16.2	89	73.8	49.8	49	123.5	83.3	09	173.3	116.9	69	223.0	150.4
30	24.9	16.8	90	74.6	50.3	50	124.4	83.9	10	174.1	117.4	70	223.8	151.0
31	25.7	17.3	91	75.4	50.9	151	125.2	84.4	211	174.9	118.0	271	224.7	151.5
32	26.5	17.9	92	76.3	51.4	52	126.0	85.0	12	175.8	118.5	72	225.5	152.1
33	27.4	18.5	93	77.1	52.0	53	126.8	85.6	13	176.6	119.1	73	226.3	152.7
34	28.2	19.0	94	77.9	52.6	54	127.7	86.1	14	177.4	119.7	74	227.2	153.2
35	29.0	19.6	95	78.8	53.1	55	128.5	86.7	15	178.2	120.2	75	228.0	153.8
36	29.8	20.1	96	79.6	53.7	56	129.3	87.2	16	179.1	120.8	76	228.8	154.3
37	30.7	20.7	97	80.4	54.2	57	130.2	87.8	17	179.9	121.3	77	229.6	154.9
38	31.5	21.2	98	81.2	54.8	58	131.0	88.4	18	180.7	121.9	78	230.5	155.5
39	32.3	21.8	99	82.1	55.4	59	131.8	88.9	19	181.6	122.5	79	231.3	156.0
40	33.2	22.4	100	82.9	55.9	60	132.6	89.5	20	182.4	123.0	80	232.1	156.6
41	34.0	22.9	101	83.7	56.5	161	133.5	90.0	221	183.2	123.6	281	233.0	157.1
42	34.8	23.5	02	84.6	57.0	62	134.3	90.6	22	184.0	124.1	82	233.8	157.7
43	35.6	24.0	03	85.4	57.6	63	135.1	91.1	23	184.9	124.7	83	234.6	158.3
44	36.5	24.6	04	86.2	58.2	64	136.0	91.7	24	185.7	125.3	84	235.4	158.8
45	37.3	25.2	05	87.0	58.7	65	136.8	92.3	25	186.5	125.8	85	236.3	159.4
46	38.1	25.7	06	87.9	59.3	66	137.6	92.8	26	187.4	126.4	86	237.1	159.9
47	39.0	26.3	07	88.7	59.8	67	138.4	93.4	27	188.2	126.9	87	237.9	160.5
48	39.8	26.8	08	89.5	60.4	68	139.3	93.9	28	189.0	127.5	88	238.8	161.0
49	40.6	27.4	09	90.4	61.0	69	140.1	94.5	29	189.8	128.1	89	239.6	161.6
50	41.5	28.0	10	91.2	61.5	70	140.9	95.1	30	190.7	128.6	90	240.4	162.2
51	42.3	28.5	111	92.0	62.1	171	141.8	95.6	231	191.5	129.2	291	241.2	162.7
52	43.1	29.1	12	92.9	62.6	72	142.6	96.2	32	192.3	129.7	92	242.1	163.3
53	43.9	29.6	13	93.7	63.2	73	143.4	96.7	33	193.2	130.3	93	242.9	163.8
54	44.8	30.2	14	94.5	63.7	74	144.3	97.3	34	194.0	130.9	94	243.7	164.4
55	45.6	30.8	15	95.3	64.3	75	145.1	97.9	35	194.8	131.4	95	244.6	165.0
56	46.4	31.3	16	96.2	64.9	76	145.9	98.4	36	195.7	132.0	96	245.4	165.5
57	47.3	31.9	17	97.0	65.4	77	146.7	99.0	37	196.5	132.5	97	246.2	166.1
58	48.1	32.4	18	97.8	66.0	78	147.6	99.5	38	197.3	133.1	98	247.1	166.6
59	48.9	33.0	19	98.7	66.5	79	148.4	100.1	39	198.1	133.6	99	247.9	167.2
60	49.7	33.6	20	99.5	67.1	80	149.2	100.7	40	199.0	134.2	300	248.7	167.8
Dist.	Dep.	D. Lat.	Dist.	Dep.	D. Lat.	Dist.	Dep.	D. Lat.	Dist.	Dep.	D. Lat.	Dist.	Dep.	D. Lat.

304° | 056° / 236° | 124°

56°

Dist.	D. Lat.	Dep.
N.	N x Cos.	N x Sin.
Hypotenuse	Side Adj.	Side Opp.

TABLE 4

Traverse 34° Table

326° | 034° / 214° | 146°

Dist.	D. Lat.	Dep.	Dist.	D. Lat.	Dep.	Dist.	D. Lat.	Dep.	Dist.	D. Lat.	Dep.	Dist.	D. Lat.	Dep.
301	249.5	168.3	361	299.3	201.9	421	349.0	235.4	481	398.8	269.0	541	448.5	302.5
02	250.4	168.9	62	300.1	202.4	22	349.9	236.0	82	399.6	269.5	42	449.3	303.1
03	251.2	169.4	63	300.9	203.0	23	350.7	236.5	83	400.4	270.1	43	450.2	303.6
04	252.0	170.0	64	301.8	203.5	24	351.5	237.1	84	401.3	270.6	44	451.0	304.2
05	252.9	170.6	65	302.6	204.1	25	352.3	237.7	85	402.1	271.2	45	451.8	304.8
06	253.7	171.1	66	303.4	204.7	26	353.2	238.2	86	402.9	271.8	46	452.7	305.3
07	254.5	171.7	67	304.3	205.2	27	354.0	238.8	87	403.7	272.3	47	453.5	305.9
08	255.3	172.2	68	305.1	205.8	28	354.8	239.3	88	404.6	272.9	48	454.3	306.4
09	256.2	172.8	69	305.9	206.3	29	355.7	239.9	89	405.4	273.4	49	455.1	307.0
10	257.0	173.3	70	306.7	206.9	30	356.5	240.5	90	406.2	274.0	50	456.0	307.6
311	257.8	173.9	371	307.6	207.5	431	357.3	241.0	491	407.1	274.6	551	456.8	308.1
12	258.7	174.5	72	308.4	208.0	32	358.1	241.6	92	407.9	275.1	52	457.6	308.7
13	259.5	175.0	73	309.2	208.6	33	359.0	242.1	93	408.7	275.7	53	458.5	309.2
14	260.3	175.6	74	310.1	209.1	34	359.8	242.7	94	409.5	276.2	54	459.3	309.8
15	261.1	176.1	75	310.9	209.7	35	360.6	243.2	95	410.4	276.8	55	460.1	310.4
16	262.0	176.7	76	311.7	210.3	36	361.5	243.8	96	411.2	277.4	56	460.9	310.9
17	262.8	177.3	77	312.5	210.8	37	362.3	244.4	97	412.0	277.9	57	461.8	311.5
18	263.6	177.8	78	313.4	211.4	38	363.1	244.9	98	412.9	278.5	58	462.6	312.0
19	264.5	178.4	79	314.2	211.9	39	363.9	245.5	99	413.7	279.0	59	463.4	312.6
20	265.3	178.9	80	315.0	212.5	40	364.8	246.0	500	414.5	279.6	60	464.3	313.1
321	266.1	179.5	381	315.9	213.1	441	365.6	246.6	501	415.3	280.2	561	465.1	313.7
22	267.0	180.1	82	316.7	213.6	42	366.4	247.2	02	416.2	280.7	62	465.9	314.3
23	267.8	180.6	83	317.5	214.2	43	367.3	247.7	03	417.0	281.3	63	466.7	314.8
24	268.6	181.2	84	318.4	214.7	44	368.1	248.3	04	417.8	281.8	64	467.6	315.4
25	269.4	181.7	85	319.2	215.3	45	368.9	248.8	05	418.7	282.4	65	468.4	315.9
26	270.3	182.3	86	320.0	215.8	46	369.8	249.4	06	419.5	283.0	66	469.2	316.5
27	271.1	182.9	87	320.8	216.4	47	370.6	250.0	07	420.3	283.5	67	470.1	317.1
28	271.9	183.4	88	321.7	217.0	48	371.4	250.5	08	421.2	284.1	68	470.9	317.6
29	272.8	184.0	89	322.5	217.5	49	372.2	251.1	09	422.0	284.6	69	471.7	318.2
30	273.6	184.5	90	323.3	218.1	50	373.1	251.6	10	422.8	285.2	70	472.6	318.7
331	274.4	185.1	391	324.2	218.6	451	373.9	252.2	511	423.6	285.7	571	473.4	319.3
32	275.2	185.7	92	325.0	219.2	52	374.7	252.8	12	424.5	286.3	72	474.2	319.9
33	276.1	186.2	93	325.8	219.8	53	375.6	253.3	13	425.3	286.9	73	475.0	320.4
34	276.9	186.8	94	326.6	220.3	54	376.4	253.9	14	426.1	287.4	74	475.9	321.0
35	277.7	187.3	95	327.5	220.9	55	377.2	254.4	15	427.0	288.0	75	476.7	321.5
36	278.6	187.9	96	328.3	221.4	56	378.0	255.0	16	427.8	288.5	76	477.5	322.1
37	279.4	188.4	97	329.1	222.0	57	378.9	255.6	17	428.6	289.1	77	478.4	322.7
38	280.2	189.0	98	330.0	222.6	58	379.7	256.1	18	429.4	289.7	78	479.2	323.2
39	281.0	189.6	99	330.8	223.1	59	380.5	256.7	19	430.3	290.2	79	480.0	323.8
40	281.9	190.1	400	331.6	223.7	60	381.4	257.2	20	431.1	290.8	80	480.8	324.3
341	282.7	190.7	401	332.4	224.2	461	382.2	257.8	521	431.9	291.3	581	481.7	324.9
42	283.5	191.2	02	333.3	224.8	62	383.0	258.3	22	432.8	291.9	82	482.5	325.5
43	284.4	191.8	03	334.1	225.4	63	383.8	258.9	23	433.6	292.5	83	483.3	326.0
44	285.2	192.4	04	334.9	225.9	64	384.7	259.5	24	434.4	293.0	84	484.2	326.6
45	286.0	192.9	05	335.8	226.5	65	385.5	260.0	25	435.2	293.6	85	485.0	327.1
46	286.8	193.5	06	336.6	227.0	66	386.3	260.6	26	436.1	294.1	86	485.8	327.7
47	287.7	194.0	07	337.4	227.6	67	387.2	261.1	27	436.9	294.7	87	486.6	328.2
48	288.5	194.6	08	338.2	228.2	68	388.0	261.7	28	437.7	295.3	88	487.5	328.8
49	289.3	195.2	09	339.1	228.7	69	388.8	262.3	29	438.6	295.8	89	488.3	329.4
50	290.2	195.7	10	339.9	229.3	70	389.6	262.8	30	439.4	296.4	90	489.1	329.9
351	291.0	196.3	411	340.7	229.8	471	390.5	263.4	531	440.2	296.9	591	490.0	330.5
52	291.8	196.8	12	341.6	230.4	72	391.3	263.9	32	441.0	297.5	92	490.8	331.0
53	292.7	197.4	13	342.4	230.9	73	392.1	264.5	33	441.9	298.0	93	491.6	331.6
54	293.5	198.0	14	343.2	231.5	74	393.0	265.1	34	442.7	298.6	94	492.4	332.2
55	294.3	198.5	15	344.1	232.1	75	393.8	265.6	35	443.5	299.2	95	493.3	332.7
56	295.1	199.1	16	344.9	232.6	76	394.6	266.2	36	444.4	299.7	96	494.1	333.3
57	296.0	199.6	17	345.7	233.2	77	395.5	266.7	37	445.2	300.3	97	494.9	333.8
58	296.8	200.2	18	346.5	233.7	78	396.3	267.3	38	446.0	300.8	98	495.8	334.4
59	297.6	200.8	19	347.4	234.3	79	397.1	267.9	39	446.9	301.4	99	496.6	335.0
60	298.5	201.3	20	348.2	234.9	80	397.9	268.4	40	447.7	302.0	600	497.4	335.5
Dist.	Dep.	D. Lat.	Dist.	Dep.	D. Lat.	Dist.	Dep.	D. Lat.	Dist.	Dep.	D. Lat.	Dist.	Dep.	D. Lat.

Dist.	D. Lat.	Dep.
D Lo	Dep.	
	m	D Lo

56°

304° | 056° / 236° | 124°

TABLE 4

325° | 035°	215° | 145°	Traverse	35°	Table	325° | 035°	215° | 145°

Dist.	D. Lat.	Dep.	Dist.	D. Lat.	Dep.	Dist.	D. Lat.	Dep.	Dist.	D. Lat.	Dep.	Dist.	D. Lat.	Dep.
1	0.8	0.6	61	50.0	35.0	121	99.1	69.4	181	148.3	103.8	241	197.4	138.2
2	1.6	1.1	62	50.8	35.6	22	99.9	70.0	82	149.1	104.4	42	198.2	138.8
3	2.5	1.7	63	51.6	36.1	23	100.8	70.5	83	149.9	105.0	43	199.1	139.4
4	3.3	2.3	64	52.4	36.7	24	101.6	71.1	84	150.7	105.5	44	199.9	140.0
5	4.1	2.9	65	53.2	37.3	25	102.4	71.7	85	151.5	106.1	45	200.7	140.5
6	4.9	3.4	66	54.1	37.9	26	103.2	72.3	86	152.4	106.7	46	201.5	141.1
7	5.7	4.0	67	54.9	38.4	27	104.0	72.8	87	153.2	107.3	47	202.3	141.7
8	6.6	4.6	68	55.7	39.0	28	104.9	73.4	88	154.0	107.8	48	203.1	142.2
9	7.4	5.2	69	56.5	39.6	29	105.7	74.0	89	154.8	108.4	49	204.0	142.8
10	8.2	5.7	70	57.3	40.2	30	106.5	74.6	90	155.6	109.0	50	204.8	143.4
11	9.0	6.3	71	58.2	40.7	131	107.3	75.1	191	156.5	109.6	251	205.6	144.0
12	9.8	6.9	72	59.0	41.3	32	108.1	75.7	92	157.3	110.1	52	206.4	144.5
13	10.6	7.5	73	59.8	41.9	33	108.9	76.3	93	158.1	110.7	53	207.2	145.1
14	11.5	8.0	74	60.6	42.4	34	109.8	76.9	94	158.9	111.3	54	208.1	145.7
15	12.3	8.6	75	61.4	43.0	35	110.6	77.4	95	159.7	111.8	55	208.9	146.3
16	13.1	9.2	76	62.3	43.6	36	111.4	78.0	96	160.6	112.4	56	209.7	146.8
17	13.9	9.8	77	63.1	44.2	37	112.2	78.6	97	161.4	113.0	57	210.5	147.4
18	14.7	10.3	78	63.9	44.7	38	113.0	79.2	98	162.2	113.6	58	211.3	148.0
19	15.6	10.9	79	64.7	45.3	39	113.9	79.7	99	163.0	114.1	59	212.2	148.6
20	16.4	11.5	80	65.5	45.9	40	114.7	80.3	200	163.8	114.7	60	213.0	149.1
21	17.2	12.0	81	66.4	46.5	141	115.5	80.9	201	164.6	115.3	261	213.8	149.7
22	18.0	12.6	82	67.2	47.0	42	116.3	81.4	02	165.5	115.9	62	214.6	150.3
23	18.8	13.2	83	68.0	47.6	43	117.1	82.0	03	166.3	116.4	63	215.4	150.9
24	19.7	13.8	84	68.8	48.2	44	118.0	82.6	04	167.1	117.0	64	216.3	151.4
25	20.5	14.3	85	69.6	48.8	45	118.8	83.2	05	167.9	117.6	65	217.1	152.0
26	21.3	14.9	86	70.4	49.3	46	119.6	83.7	06	168.7	118.2	66	217.9	152.6
27	22.1	15.5	87	71.3	49.9	47	120.4	84.3	07	169.6	118.7	67	218.7	153.1
28	22.9	16.1	88	72.1	50.5	48	121.2	84.9	08	170.4	119.3	68	219.5	153.7
29	23.8	16.6	89	72.9	51.0	49	122.1	85.5	09	171.2	119.9	69	220.4	154.3
30	24.6	17.2	90	73.7	51.6	50	122.9	86.0	10	172.0	120.5	70	221.2	154.9
31	25.4	17.8	91	74.5	52.2	151	123.7	86.6	211	172.8	121.0	271	222.0	155.4
32	26.2	18.4	92	75.4	52.8	52	124.5	87.2	12	173.7	121.6	72	222.8	156.0
33	27.0	18.9	93	76.2	53.3	53	125.3	87.8	13	174.5	122.2	73	223.6	156.6
34	27.9	19.5	94	77.0	53.9	54	126.1	88.3	14	175.3	122.7	74	224.4	157.2
35	28.7	20.1	95	77.8	54.5	55	127.0	88.9	15	176.1	123.3	75	225.3	157.7
36	29.5	20.6	96	78.6	55.1	56	127.8	89.5	16	176.9	123.9	76	226.1	158.3
37	30.3	21.2	97	79.5	55.6	57	128.6	90.1	17	177.8	124.5	77	226.9	158.9
38	31.1	21.8	98	80.3	56.2	58	129.4	90.6	18	178.6	125.0	78	227.7	159.5
39	31.9	22.4	99	81.1	56.8	59	130.2	91.2	19	179.4	125.6	79	228.5	160.0
40	32.8	22.9	100	81.9	57.4	60	131.1	91.8	20	180.2	126.2	80	229.4	160.6
41	33.6	23.5	101	82.7	57.9	161	131.9	92.3	221	181.0	126.8	281	230.2	161.2
42	34.4	24.1	02	83.6	58.5	62	132.7	92.9	22	181.9	127.3	82	231.0	161.7
43	35.2	24.7	03	84.4	59.1	63	133.5	93.5	23	182.7	127.9	83	231.8	162.3
44	36.0	25.2	04	85.2	59.7	64	134.3	94.1	24	183.5	128.5	84	232.6	162.9
45	36.9	25.8	05	86.0	60.2	65	135.2	94.6	25	184.3	129.1	85	233.5	163.5
46	37.7	26.4	06	86.8	60.8	66	136.0	95.2	26	185.1	129.6	86	234.3	164.0
47	38.5	27.0	07	87.6	61.4	67	136.8	95.8	27	185.9	130.2	87	235.1	164.6
48	39.3	27.5	08	88.5	61.9	68	137.6	96.4	28	186.8	130.8	88	235.9	165.2
49	40.1	28.1	09	89.3	62.5	69	138.4	96.9	29	187.6	131.3	89	236.7	165.8
50	41.0	28.7	10	90.1	63.1	70	139.3	97.5	30	188.4	131.9	90	237.6	166.3
51	41.8	29.3	111	90.9	63.7	171	140.1	98.1	231	189.2	132.5	291	238.4	166.9
52	42.6	29.8	12	91.7	64.2	72	140.9	98.7	32	190.0	133.1	92	239.2	167.5
53	43.4	30.4	13	92.6	64.8	73	141.7	99.2	33	190.9	133.6	93	240.0	168.1
54	44.2	31.0	14	93.4	65.4	74	142.5	99.8	34	191.7	134.2	94	240.8	168.6
55	45.1	31.5	15	94.2	66.0	75	143.4	100.4	35	192.5	134.8	95	241.6	169.2
56	45.9	32.1	16	95.0	66.5	76	144.2	100.9	36	193.3	135.4	96	242.5	169.8
57	46.7	32.7	17	95.8	67.1	77	145.0	101.5	37	194.1	135.9	97	243.3	170.4
58	47.5	33.3	18	96.7	67.7	78	145.8	102.1	38	195.0	136.5	98	244.1	170.9
59	48.3	33.8	19	97.5	68.3	79	146.6	102.7	39	195.8	137.1	99	244.9	171.5
60	49.1	34.4	20	98.3	68.8	80	147.4	103.2	40	196.6	137.7	300	245.7	172.1
Dist.	Dep.	D. Lat.	Dist.	Dep.	D. Lat.	Dist.	Dep.	D. Lat.	Dist.	Dep.	D. Lat.	Dist.	Dep.	D. Lat.

305° | 055°	235° | 125°	55°

Dist.	D. Lat.	Dep.
N.	N x Cos.	N x Sin.
Hypotenuse	Side Adj.	Side Opp.

TABLE 4

325° | 035°	215° | 145°	Traverse	35°	Table	325° | 035°	215° | 145°

Dist.	D. Lat.	Dep.	Dist.	D. Lat.	Dep.	Dist.	D. Lat.	Dep.	Dist.	D. Lat.	Dep.	Dist.	D. Lat.	Dep.
301	246.6	172.6	361	295.7	207.1	421	344.9	241.5	481	394.0	275.9	541	443.2	310.3
02	247.4	173.2	62	296.5	207.6	22	345.7	242.0	82	394.8	276.5	42	444.0	310.9
03	248.2	173.8	63	297.4	208.2	23	346.5	242.6	83	395.7	277.0	43	444.8	311.5
04	249.0	174.4	64	298.2	208.8	24	347.3	243.2	84	396.5	277.6	44	445.6	312.0
05	249.8	174.9	65	299.0	209.4	25	348.1	243.8	85	397.3	278.2	45	446.4	312.6
06	250.7	175.5	66	299.8	209.9	26	349.0	244.3	86	398.1	278.8	46	447.3	313.2
07	251.5	176.1	67	300.6	210.5	27	349.8	244.9	87	398.9	279.3	47	448.1	313.7
08	252.3	176.7	68	301.4	211.1	28	350.6	245.5	88	399.7	279.9	48	448.9	314.3
09	253.1	177.2	69	302.3	211.6	29	351.4	246.1	89	400.6	280.5	49	449.7	314.9
10	253.9	177.8	70	303.1	212.2	30	352.2	246.6	90	401.4	281.1	50	450.5	315.5
311	254.8	178.4	371	303.9	212.8	431	353.1	247.2	491	402.2	281.6	551	451.4	316.0
12	255.6	179.0	72	304.7	213.4	32	353.9	247.8	92	403.0	282.2	52	452.2	316.6
13	256.4	179.5	73	305.5	213.9	33	354.7	248.4	93	403.8	282.8	53	453.0	317.2
14	257.2	180.1	74	306.4	214.5	34	355.5	248.9	94	404.7	283.3	54	453.8	317.8
15	258.0	180.7	75	307.2	215.1	35	356.3	249.5	95	405.5	283.9	55	454.6	318.3
16	258.9	181.3	76	308.0	215.7	36	357.2	250.1	96	406.3	284.5	56	455.4	318.9
17	259.7	181.8	77	308.8	216.2	37	358.0	250.7	97	407.1	285.1	57	456.3	319.5
18	260.5	182.4	78	309.6	216.8	38	358.8	251.2	98	407.9	285.6	58	457.1	320.1
19	261.3	183.0	79	310.5	217.4	39	359.6	251.8	99	408.8	286.2	59	457.9	320.6
20	262.1	183.5	80	311.3	218.0	40	360.4	252.4	500	409.6	286.8	60	458.7	321.2
321	262.9	184.1	381	312.1	218.5	441	361.2	252.9	501	410.4	287.4	561	459.5	321.8
22	263.8	184.7	82	312.9	219.1	42	362.1	253.5	02	411.2	287.9	62	460.4	322.3
23	264.6	185.3	83	313.7	219.7	43	362.9	254.1	03	412.0	288.5	63	461.2	322.9
24	265.4	185.8	84	314.6	220.3	44	363.7	254.7	04	412.9	289.1	64	462.0	323.5
25	266.2	186.4	85	315.4	220.8	45	364.5	255.2	05	413.7	289.7	65	462.8	324.1
26	267.0	187.0	86	316.2	221.4	46	365.3	255.8	06	414.5	290.2	66	463.6	324.6
27	267.9	187.6	87	317.0	222.0	47	366.2	256.4	07	415.3	290.8	67	464.5	325.2
28	268.7	188.1	88	317.8	222.5	48	367.0	257.0	08	416.1	291.4	68	465.3	325.8
29	269.5	188.7	89	318.7	223.1	49	367.8	257.5	09	416.9	292.0	69	466.1	326.4
30	270.3	189.3	90	319.5	223.7	50	368.6	258.1	10	417.8	292.5	70	466.9	326.9
331	271.1	189.9	391	320.3	224.3	451	369.4	258.7	511	418.6	293.1	571	467.7	327.5
32	272.0	190.4	92	321.1	224.8	52	370.3	259.3	12	419.4	293.7	72	468.6	328.1
33	272.8	191.0	93	321.9	225.4	53	371.1	259.8	13	420.2	294.2	73	469.4	328.7
34	273.6	191.6	94	322.7	226.0	54	371.9	260.4	14	421.0	294.8	74	470.2	329.2
35	274.4	192.1	95	323.6	226.6	55	372.7	261.0	15	421.9	295.4	75	471.0	329.8
36	275.2	192.7	96	324.4	227.1	56	373.5	261.6	16	422.7	296.0	76	471.8	330.4
37	276.1	193.3	97	325.2	227.7	57	374.4	262.1	17	423.5	296.5	77	472.7	331.0
38	276.9	193.9	98	326.0	228.3	58	375.2	262.7	18	424.3	297.1	78	473.5	331.5
39	277.7	194.4	99	326.8	228.9	59	376.0	263.3	19	425.1	297.7	79	474.3	332.1
40	278.5	195.0	400	327.7	229.4	60	376.8	263.8	20	426.0	298.3	80	475.1	332.7
341	279.3	195.6	401	328.5	230.0	461	377.6	264.4	521	426.8	298.8	581	475.9	333.2
42	280.1	196.2	02	329.3	230.6	62	378.4	265.0	22	427.6	299.4	82	476.7	333.8
43	281.0	196.7	03	330.1	231.2	63	379.3	265.6	23	428.4	300.0	83	477.6	334.4
44	281.8	197.3	04	330.9	231.7	64	380.1	266.1	24	429.2	300.6	84	478.4	335.0
45	282.6	197.9	05	331.8	232.3	65	380.9	266.7	25	430.1	301.1	85	479.2	335.5
46	283.4	198.5	06	332.6	232.9	66	381.7	267.3	26	430.9	301.7	86	480.0	336.1
47	284.2	199.0	07	333.4	233.4	67	382.5	267.9	27	431.7	302.3	87	480.8	336.7
48	285.1	199.6	08	334.2	234.0	68	383.4	268.4	28	432.5	302.8	88	481.7	337.3
49	285.9	200.2	09	335.0	234.6	69	384.2	269.0	29	433.3	303.4	89	482.5	337.8
50	286.7	200.8	10	335.9	235.2	70	385.0	269.6	30	434.2	304.0	90	483.3	338.4
351	287.5	201.3	411	336.7	235.7	471	385.8	270.2	531	435.0	304.6	591	484.1	339.0
52	288.3	201.9	12	337.5	236.3	72	386.6	270.7	32	435.8	305.1	92	484.9	339.6
53	289.2	202.5	13	338.3	236.9	73	387.5	271.3	33	436.6	305.7	93	485.8	340.1
54	290.0	203.0	14	339.1	237.5	74	388.3	271.9	34	437.4	306.3	94	486.6	340.7
55	290.8	203.6	15	339.9	238.0	75	389.1	272.4	35	438.2	306.9	95	487.4	341.3
56	291.6	204.2	16	340.8	238.6	76	389.9	273.0	36	439.1	307.4	96	488.2	341.9
57	292.4	204.8	17	341.6	239.2	77	390.7	273.6	37	439.9	308.0	97	489.0	342.4
58	293.3	205.3	18	342.4	239.8	78	391.6	274.2	38	440.7	308.6	98	489.9	343.0
59	294.1	205.9	19	343.2	240.3	79	392.4	274.7	39	441.5	309.2	99	490.7	343.6
60	294.9	206.5	20	344.0	240.9	80	393.2	275.3	40	442.3	309.7	600	491.5	344.1
Dist.	Dep.	D. Lat.	Dist.	Dep.	D. Lat.	Dist.	Dep.	D. Lat.	Dist.	Dep.	D. Lat.	Dist.	Dep.	D. Lat.

Dist.	D. Lat.	Dep.
D Lo	Dep.	
	m	D Lo

55°	305° | 055°	235° | 125°

TABLE 4

Traverse 36° Table

324° | 036°
216° | 144°

Dist.	D. Lat.	Dep.	Dist.	D. Lat.	Dep.	Dist.	D. Lat.	Dep.	Dist.	D. Lat.	Dep.	Dist.	D. Lat.	Dep.
1	0.8	0.6	61	49.4	35.9	121	97.9	71.1	181	146.4	106.4	241	195.0	141.7
2	1.6	1.2	62	50.2	36.4	22	98.7	71.7	82	147.2	107.0	42	195.8	142.2
3	2.4	1.8	63	51.0	37.0	23	99.5	72.3	83	148.1	107.6	43	196.6	142.8
4	3.2	2.4	64	51.8	37.6	24	100.3	72.9	84	148.9	108.2	44	197.4	143.4
5	4.0	2.9	65	52.6	38.2	25	101.1	73.5	85	149.7	108.7	45	198.2	144.0
6	4.9	3.5	66	53.4	38.8	26	101.9	74.1	86	150.5	109.3	46	199.0	144.6
7	5.7	4.1	67	54.2	39.4	27	102.7	74.6	87	151.3	109.9	47	199.8	145.2
8	6.5	4.7	68	55.0	40.0	28	103.6	75.2	88	152.1	110.5	48	200.6	145.8
9	7.3	5.3	69	55.8	40.6	29	104.4	75.8	89	152.9	111.1	49	201.4	146.4
10	8.1	5.9	70	56.6	41.1	30	105.2	76.4	90	153.7	111.7	50	202.3	146.9
11	8.9	6.5	71	57.4	41.7	131	106.0	77.0	191	154.5	112.3	251	203.1	147.5
12	9.7	7.1	72	58.2	42.3	32	106.8	77.6	92	155.3	112.9	52	203.9	148.1
13	10.5	7.6	73	59.1	42.9	33	107.6	78.2	93	156.1	113.4	53	204.7	148.7
14	11.3	8.2	74	59.9	43.5	34	108.4	78.8	94	156.9	114.0	54	205.5	149.3
15	12.1	8.8	75	60.7	44.1	35	109.2	79.4	95	157.8	114.6	55	206.3	149.9
16	12.9	9.4	76	61.5	44.7	36	110.0	79.9	96	158.6	115.2	56	207.1	150.5
17	13.8	10.0	77	62.3	45.3	37	110.8	80.5	97	159.4	115.8	57	207.9	151.1
18	14.6	10.6	78	63.1	45.8	38	111.6	81.1	98	160.2	116.4	58	208.7	151.6
19	15.4	11.2	79	63.9	46.4	39	112.5	81.7	99	161.0	117.0	59	209.5	152.2
20	16.2	11.8	80	64.7	47.0	40	113.3	82.3	200	161.8	117.6	60	210.3	152.8
21	17.0	12.3	81	65.5	47.6	141	114.1	82.9	201	162.6	118.1	261	211.2	153.4
22	17.8	12.9	82	66.3	48.2	42	114.9	83.5	02	163.4	118.7	62	212.0	154.0
23	18.6	13.5	83	67.1	48.8	43	115.7	84.1	03	164.2	119.3	63	212.8	154.6
24	19.4	14.1	84	68.0	49.4	44	116.5	84.6	04	165.0	119.9	64	213.6	155.2
25	20.2	14.7	85	68.8	50.0	45	117.3	85.2	05	165.8	120.5	65	214.4	155.8
26	21.0	15.3	86	69.6	50.5	46	118.1	85.8	06	166.7	121.1	66	215.2	156.4
27	21.8	15.9	87	70.4	51.1	47	118.9	86.4	07	167.5	121.7	67	216.0	156.9
28	22.7	16.5	88	71.2	51.7	48	119.7	87.0	08	168.3	122.3	68	216.8	157.5
29	23.5	17.0	89	72.0	52.3	49	120.5	87.6	09	169.1	122.8	69	217.6	158.1
30	24.3	17.6	90	72.8	52.9	50	121.4	88.2	10	169.9	123.4	70	218.4	158.7
31	25.1	18.2	91	73.6	53.5	151	122.2	88.8	211	170.7	124.0	271	219.2	159.3
32	25.9	18.8	92	74.4	54.1	52	123.0	89.3	12	171.5	124.6	72	220.1	159.9
33	26.7	19.4	93	75.2	54.7	53	123.8	89.9	13	172.3	125.2	73	220.9	160.5
34	27.5	20.0	94	76.0	55.3	54	124.6	90.5	14	173.1	125.8	74	221.7	161.1
35	28.3	20.6	95	76.9	55.8	55	125.4	91.1	15	173.9	126.4	75	222.5	161.6
36	29.1	21.2	96	77.7	56.4	56	126.2	91.7	16	174.7	127.0	76	223.3	162.2
37	29.9	21.7	97	78.5	57.0	57	127.0	92.3	17	175.6	127.5	77	224.1	162.8
38	30.7	22.3	98	79.3	57.6	58	127.8	92.9	18	176.4	128.1	78	224.9	163.4
39	31.6	22.9	99	80.1	58.2	59	128.6	93.5	19	177.2	128.7	79	225.7	164.0
40	32.4	23.5	100	80.9	58.8	60	129.4	94.0	20	178.0	129.3	80	226.5	164.6
41	33.2	24.1	101	81.7	59.4	161	130.3	94.6	221	178.8	129.9	281	227.3	165.2
42	34.0	24.7	02	82.5	60.0	62	131.1	95.2	22	179.6	130.5	82	228.1	165.8
43	34.8	25.3	03	83.3	60.5	63	131.9	95.8	23	180.4	131.1	83	229.0	166.3
44	35.6	25.9	04	84.1	61.1	64	132.7	96.4	24	181.2	131.7	84	229.8	166.9
45	36.4	26.5	05	84.9	61.7	65	133.5	97.0	25	182.0	132.3	85	230.6	167.5
46	37.2	27.0	06	85.8	62.3	66	134.3	97.6	26	182.8	132.8	86	231.4	168.1
47	38.0	27.6	07	86.6	62.9	67	135.1	98.2	27	183.6	133.4	87	232.2	168.7
48	38.8	28.2	08	87.4	63.5	68	135.9	98.7	28	184.5	134.0	88	233.0	169.3
49	39.6	28.8	09	88.2	64.1	69	136.7	99.3	29	185.3	134.6	89	233.8	169.9
50	40.5	29.4	10	89.0	64.7	70	137.5	99.9	30	186.1	135.2	90	234.6	170.5
51	41.3	30.0	111	89.8	65.2	171	138.3	100.5	231	186.9	135.8	291	235.4	171.0
52	42.1	30.6	12	90.6	65.8	72	139.2	101.1	32	187.7	136.4	92	236.2	171.6
53	42.9	31.2	13	91.4	66.4	73	140.0	101.7	33	188.5	137.0	93	237.0	172.2
54	43.7	31.7	14	92.2	67.0	74	140.8	102.3	34	189.3	137.5	94	237.9	172.8
55	44.5	32.3	15	93.0	67.6	75	141.6	102.9	35	190.1	138.1	95	238.7	173.4
56	45.3	32.9	16	93.8	68.2	76	142.4	103.5	36	190.9	138.7	96	239.5	174.0
57	46.1	33.5	17	94.7	68.8	77	143.2	104.0	37	191.7	139.3	97	240.3	174.6
58	46.9	34.1	18	95.5	69.4	78	144.0	104.6	38	192.5	139.9	98	241.1	175.2
59	47.7	34.7	19	96.3	69.9	79	144.8	105.2	39	193.4	140.5	99	241.9	175.7
60	48.5	35.3	20	97.1	70.5	80	145.6	105.8	40	194.2	141.1	300	242.7	176.3
Dist.	Dep.	D. Lat.	Dist.	Dep.	D. Lat.	Dist.	Dep.	D. Lat.	Dist.	Dep.	D. Lat.	Dist.	Dep.	D. Lat.

306° | 054°
234° | 126°

54°

Dist.	D. Lat.	Dep.
N.	N x Cos.	N x Sin.
Hypotenuse	Side Adj.	Side Opp.

TABLE 4

Traverse 36° Table

324° | 036°
216° | 144°

Dist.	D. Lat.	Dep.	Dist.	D. Lat.	Dep.	Dist.	D. Lat.	Dep.	Dist.	D. Lat.	Dep.	Dist.	D. Lat.	Dep.
301	243.5	176.9	361	292.1	212.2	421	340.6	247.5	481	389.1	282.7	541	437.7	318.0
02	244.3	177.5	62	292.9	212.8	22	341.4	248.0	82	389.9	283.3	42	438.5	318.6
03	245.1	178.1	63	293.7	213.4	23	342.2	248.6	83	390.8	283.9	43	439.3	319.2
04	245.9	178.7	64	294.5	214.0	24	343.0	249.2	84	391.6	284.5	44	440.1	319.8
05	246.8	179.3	65	295.3	214.5	25	343.8	249.8	85	392.4	285.1	45	440.9	320.3
06	247.6	179.9	66	296.1	215.1	26	344.6	250.4	86	393.2	285.7	46	441.7	320.9
07	248.4	180.5	67	296.9	215.7	27	345.5	251.0	87	394.0	286.3	47	442.5	321.5
08	249.2	181.0	68	297.7	216.3	28	346.3	251.6	88	394.8	286.8	48	443.3	322.1
09	250.0	181.6	69	298.5	216.9	29	347.1	252.2	89	395.6	287.4	49	444.2	322.7
10	250.8	182.2	70	299.3	217.5	30	347.9	252.7	90	396.4	288.0	50	445.0	323.3
311	251.6	182.8	371	300.1	218.1	431	348.7	253.3	491	397.2	288.6	551	445.8	323.9
12	252.4	183.4	72	301.0	218.7	32	349.5	253.9	92	398.0	289.2	52	446.6	324.5
13	253.2	184.0	73	301.8	219.2	33	350.3	254.5	93	398.8	289.8	53	447.4	325.0
14	254.0	184.6	74	302.6	219.8	34	351.1	255.1	94	399.7	290.4	54	448.2	325.6
15	254.8	185.2	75	303.4	220.4	35	351.9	255.7	95	400.5	291.0	55	449.0	326.2
16	255.6	185.7	76	304.2	221.0	36	352.7	256.3	96	401.3	291.5	56	449.8	326.8
17	256.5	186.3	77	305.0	221.6	37	353.5	256.9	97	402.1	292.1	57	450.6	327.4
18	257.3	186.9	78	305.8	222.2	38	354.3	257.4	98	402.9	292.7	58	451.4	328.0
19	258.1	187.5	79	306.6	222.8	39	355.2	258.0	99	403.7	293.3	59	452.2	328.6
20	258.9	188.1	80	307.4	223.4	40	356.0	258.6	500	404.5	293.9	60	453.0	329.2
321	259.7	188.7	381	308.2	223.9	441	356.8	259.2	501	405.3	294.5	561	453.9	329.7
22	260.5	189.3	82	309.0	224.5	42	357.6	259.8	02	406.1	295.1	62	454.7	330.3
23	261.3	189.9	83	309.9	225.1	43	358.4	260.4	03	406.9	295.7	63	455.5	330.9
24	262.1	190.4	84	310.7	225.7	44	359.2	261.0	04	407.7	296.2	64	456.3	331.5
25	262.9	191.0	85	311.5	226.3	45	360.0	261.6	05	408.6	296.8	65	457.1	332.1
26	263.7	191.6	86	312.3	226.9	46	360.8	262.2	06	409.4	297.4	66	457.9	332.7
27	264.5	192.2	87	313.1	227.5	47	361.6	262.7	07	410.2	298.0	67	458.7	333.3
28	265.4	192.8	88	313.9	228.1	48	362.4	263.3	08	411.0	298.6	68	459.5	333.9
29	266.2	193.4	89	314.7	228.6	49	363.2	263.9	09	411.8	299.2	69	460.3	334.4
30	267.0	194.0	90	315.5	229.2	50	364.1	264.5	10	412.6	299.8	70	461.1	335.0
331	267.8	194.6	391	316.3	229.8	451	364.9	265.1	511	413.4	300.4	571	461.9	335.6
32	268.6	195.1	92	317.1	230.4	52	365.7	265.7	12	414.2	300.9	72	462.8	336.2
33	269.4	195.7	93	317.9	231.0	53	366.5	266.3	13	415.0	301.5	73	463.6	336.8
34	270.2	196.3	94	318.8	231.6	54	367.3	266.9	14	415.8	302.1	74	464.4	337.4
35	271.0	196.9	95	319.6	232.2	55	368.1	267.4	15	416.6	302.7	75	465.2	338.0
36	271.8	197.5	96	320.4	232.8	56	368.9	268.0	16	417.5	303.3	76	466.0	338.6
37	272.6	198.1	97	321.2	233.4	57	369.7	268.6	17	418.3	303.9	77	466.8	339.2
38	273.4	198.7	98	322.0	233.9	58	370.5	269.2	18	419.1	304.5	78	467.6	339.7
39	274.3	199.3	99	322.8	234.5	59	371.3	269.8	19	419.9	305.1	79	468.4	340.3
40	275.1	199.8	400	323.6	235.1	60	372.1	270.4	20	420.7	305.6	80	469.2	340.9
341	275.9	200.4	401	324.4	235.7	461	373.0	271.0	521	421.5	306.2	581	470.0	341.5
42	276.7	201.0	02	325.2	236.3	62	373.8	271.6	22	422.3	306.8	82	470.8	342.1
43	277.5	201.6	03	326.0	236.9	63	374.6	272.1	23	423.1	307.4	83	471.7	342.7
44	278.3	202.2	04	326.8	237.5	64	375.4	272.7	24	423.9	308.0	84	472.5	343.3
45	279.1	202.8	05	327.7	238.1	65	376.2	273.3	25	424.7	308.6	85	473.3	343.9
46	279.9	203.4	06	328.5	238.6	66	377.0	273.9	26	425.5	309.2	86	474.1	344.4
47	280.7	204.0	07	329.3	239.2	67	377.8	274.5	27	426.4	309.8	87	474.9	345.0
48	281.5	204.5	08	330.1	239.8	68	378.6	275.1	28	427.2	310.4	88	475.7	345.6
49	282.3	205.1	09	330.9	240.4	69	379.4	275.7	29	428.0	310.9	89	476.5	346.2
50	283.2	205.7	10	331.7	241.0	70	380.2	276.3	30	428.8	311.5	90	477.3	346.8
351	284.0	206.3	411	332.5	241.6	471	381.0	276.8	531	429.6	312.1	591	478.1	347.4
52	284.8	206.9	12	333.3	242.2	72	381.9	277.4	32	430.4	312.7	92	478.9	348.0
53	285.6	207.5	13	334.1	242.8	73	382.7	278.0	33	431.2	313.3	93	479.7	348.6
54	286.4	208.1	14	334.9	243.3	74	383.5	278.6	34	432.0	313.9	94	480.6	349.1
55	287.2	208.7	15	335.7	243.9	75	384.3	279.2	35	432.8	314.5	95	481.4	349.7
56	288.0	209.3	16	336.6	244.5	76	385.1	279.8	36	433.6	315.1	96	482.2	350.3
57	288.8	209.8	17	337.4	245.1	77	385.9	280.4	37	434.4	315.6	97	483.0	350.9
58	289.6	210.4	18	338.2	245.7	78	386.7	281.0	38	435.3	316.2	98	483.8	351.5
59	290.4	211.0	19	339.0	246.3	79	387.5	281.5	39	436.1	316.8	99	484.6	352.1
60	291.2	211.6	20	339.8	246.9	80	388.3	282.1	40	436.9	317.4	600	485.4	352.7
Dist.	Dep.	D. Lat.	Dist.	Dep.	D. Lat.	Dist.	Dep.	D. Lat.	Dist.	Dep.	D. Lat.	Dist.	Dep.	D. Lat.

Dist.	D. Lat.	Dep.
D Lo	Dep.	
	m	D Lo

54°

306° | 054°
234° | 126°

TABLE 4

Traverse 37° Table

323° | 037° / 217° | 143°

Dist.	D. Lat.	Dep.	Dist.	D. Lat.	Dep.	Dist.	D. Lat.	Dep.	Dist.	D. Lat.	Dep.	Dist.	D. Lat.	Dep.
1	0.8	0.6	61	48.7	36.7	121	96.6	72.8	181	144.6	108.9	241	192.5	145.0
2	1.6	1.2	62	49.5	37.3	22	97.4	73.4	82	145.4	109.5	42	193.3	145.6
3	2.4	1.8	63	50.3	37.9	23	98.2	74.0	83	146.2	110.1	43	194.1	146.2
4	3.2	2.4	64	51.1	38.5	24	99.0	74.6	84	146.9	110.7	44	194.9	146.8
5	4.0	3.0	65	51.9	39.1	25	99.8	75.2	85	147.7	111.3	45	195.7	147.4
6	4.8	3.6	66	52.7	39.7	26	100.6	75.8	86	148.5	111.9	46	196.5	148.0
7	5.6	4.2	67	53.5	40.3	27	101.4	76.4	87	149.3	112.5	47	197.3	148.6
8	6.4	4.8	68	54.3	40.9	28	102.2	77.0	88	150.1	113.1	48	198.1	149.3
9	7.2	5.4	69	55.1	41.5	29	103.0	77.6	89	150.9	113.7	49	198.9	149.9
10	8.0	6.0	70	55.9	42.1	30	103.8	78.2	90	151.7	114.3	50	199.7	150.5
11	8.8	6.6	71	56.7	42.7	131	104.6	78.8	191	152.5	114.9	251	200.5	151.1
12	9.6	7.2	72	57.5	43.3	32	105.4	79.4	92	153.3	115.5	52	201.3	151.7
13	10.4	7.8	73	58.3	43.9	33	106.2	80.0	93	154.1	116.2	53	202.1	152.3
14	11.2	8.4	74	59.1	44.5	34	107.0	80.6	94	154.9	116.8	54	202.9	152.9
15	12.0	9.0	75	59.9	45.1	35	107.8	81.2	95	155.7	117.4	55	203.7	153.5
16	12.8	9.6	76	60.7	45.7	36	108.6	81.8	96	156.5	118.0	56	204.5	154.1
17	13.6	10.2	77	61.5	46.3	37	109.4	82.4	97	157.3	118.6	57	205.2	154.7
18	14.4	10.8	78	62.3	46.9	38	110.2	83.1	98	158.1	119.2	58	206.0	155.3
19	15.2	11.4	79	63.1	47.5	39	111.0	83.7	99	158.9	119.8	59	206.8	155.9
20	16.0	12.0	80	63.9	48.1	40	111.8	84.3	200	159.7	120.4	60	207.6	156.5
21	16.8	12.6	81	64.7	48.7	141	112.6	84.9	201	160.5	121.0	261	208.4	157.1
22	17.6	13.2	82	65.5	49.3	42	113.4	85.5	02	161.3	121.6	62	209.2	157.7
23	18.4	13.8	83	66.3	50.0	43	114.2	86.1	03	162.1	122.2	63	210.0	158.3
24	19.2	14.4	84	67.1	50.6	44	115.0	86.7	04	162.9	122.8	64	210.8	158.9
25	20.0	15.0	85	67.9	51.2	45	115.8	87.3	05	163.7	123.4	65	211.6	159.5
26	20.8	15.6	86	68.7	51.8	46	116.6	87.9	06	164.5	124.0	66	212.4	160.1
27	21.6	16.2	87	69.5	52.4	47	117.4	88.5	07	165.3	124.6	67	213.2	160.7
28	22.4	16.9	88	70.3	53.0	48	118.2	89.1	08	166.1	125.2	68	214.0	161.3
29	23.2	17.5	89	71.1	53.6	49	119.0	89.7	09	166.9	125.8	69	214.8	161.9
30	24.0	18.1	90	71.9	54.2	50	119.8	90.3	10	167.7	126.4	70	215.6	162.5
31	24.8	18.7	91	72.7	54.8	151	120.6	90.9	211	168.5	127.0	271	216.4	163.1
32	25.6	19.3	92	73.5	55.4	52	121.4	91.5	12	169.3	127.6	72	217.2	163.7
33	26.4	19.9	93	74.3	56.0	53	122.2	92.1	13	170.1	128.2	73	218.0	164.3
34	27.2	20.5	94	75.1	56.6	54	123.0	92.7	14	170.9	128.8	74	218.8	164.9
35	28.0	21.1	95	75.9	57.2	55	123.8	93.3	15	171.7	129.4	75	219.6	165.5
36	28.8	21.7	96	76.7	57.8	56	124.6	93.9	16	172.5	130.0	76	220.4	166.1
37	29.5	22.3	97	77.5	58.4	57	125.4	94.5	17	173.3	130.6	77	221.2	166.7
38	30.3	22.9	98	78.3	59.0	58	126.2	95.1	18	174.1	131.2	78	222.0	167.3
39	31.1	23.5	99	79.1	59.6	59	127.0	95.7	19	174.9	131.8	79	222.8	167.9
40	31.9	24.1	100	79.9	60.2	60	127.8	96.3	20	175.7	132.4	80	223.6	168.5
41	32.7	24.7	101	80.7	60.8	161	128.6	96.9	221	176.5	133.0	281	224.4	169.1
42	33.5	25.3	02	81.5	61.4	62	129.4	97.5	22	177.3	133.6	82	225.2	169.7
43	34.3	25.9	03	82.3	62.0	63	130.2	98.1	23	178.1	134.2	83	226.0	170.3
44	35.1	26.5	04	83.1	62.6	64	131.0	98.7	24	178.9	134.8	84	226.8	170.9
45	35.9	27.1	05	83.9	63.2	65	131.8	99.3	25	179.7	135.4	85	227.6	171.5
46	36.7	27.7	06	84.7	63.8	66	132.6	99.9	26	180.5	136.0	86	228.4	172.1
47	37.5	28.3	07	85.5	64.4	67	133.4	100.5	27	181.3	136.6	87	229.2	172.7
48	38.3	28.9	08	86.3	65.0	68	134.2	101.1	28	182.1	137.2	88	230.0	173.3
49	39.1	29.5	09	87.1	65.6	69	135.0	101.7	29	182.9	137.8	89	230.8	173.9
50	39.9	30.1	10	87.8	66.2	70	135.8	102.3	30	183.7	138.4	90	231.6	174.5
51	40.7	30.7	111	88.6	66.8	171	136.6	102.9	231	184.5	139.0	291	232.4	175.1
52	41.5	31.3	12	89.4	67.4	72	137.4	103.5	32	185.3	139.6	92	233.2	175.7
53	42.3	31.9	13	90.2	68.0	73	138.2	104.1	33	186.1	140.2	93	234.0	176.3
54	43.1	32.5	14	91.0	68.6	74	139.0	104.7	34	186.9	140.8	94	234.8	176.9
55	43.9	33.1	15	91.8	69.2	75	139.8	105.3	35	187.7	141.4	95	235.6	177.5
56	44.7	33.7	16	92.6	69.8	76	140.6	105.9	36	188.5	142.0	96	236.4	178.1
57	45.5	34.3	17	93.4	70.4	77	141.4	106.5	37	189.3	142.6	97	237.2	178.7
58	46.3	34.9	18	94.2	71.0	78	142.2	107.1	38	190.1	143.2	98	238.0	179.3
59	47.1	35.5	19	95.0	71.6	79	143.0	107.7	39	190.9	143.8	99	238.8	179.9
60	47.9	36.1	20	95.8	72.2	80	143.8	108.3	40	191.7	144.4	300	239.6	180.5
Dist.	Dep.	D. Lat.	Dist.	Dep.	D. Lat.	Dist.	Dep.	D. Lat.	Dist.	Dep.	D. Lat.	Dist.	Dep.	D. Lat.

307° | 053° / 233° | 127°

53°

Dist.	D. Lat.	Dep.
N.	N x Cos.	N x Sin.
Hypotenuse	Side Adj.	Side Opp.

TABLE 4

Traverse 37° Table

323° | 037° / 217° | 143°

Dist.	D. Lat.	Dep.	Dist.	D. Lat.	Dep.	Dist.	D. Lat.	Dep.	Dist.	D. Lat.	Dep.	Dist.	D. Lat.	Dep.
301	240.4	181.1	361	288.3	217.3	421	336.2	253.4	481	384.1	289.5	541	432.1	325.6
02	241.2	181.7	62	289.1	217.9	22	337.0	254.0	82	384.9	290.1	42	432.9	326.2
03	242.0	182.3	63	289.9	218.5	23	337.8	254.6	83	385.7	290.7	43	433.7	326.8
04	242.8	183.0	64	290.7	219.1	24	338.6	255.2	84	386.5	291.3	44	434.5	327.4
05	243.6	183.6	65	291.5	219.7	25	339.4	255.8	85	387.3	291.9	45	435.3	328.0
06	244.4	184.2	66	292.3	220.3	26	340.2	256.4	86	388.1	292.5	46	436.1	328.6
07	245.2	184.8	67	293.1	220.9	27	341.0	257.0	87	388.9	293.1	47	436.9	329.2
08	246.0	185.4	68	293.9	221.5	28	341.8	257.6	88	389.7	293.7	48	437.7	329.8
09	246.8	186.0	69	294.7	222.1	29	342.6	258.2	89	390.5	294.3	49	438.5	330.4
10	247.6	186.6	70	295.5	222.7	30	343.4	258.8	90	391.3	294.9	50	439.2	331.0
311	248.4	187.2	371	296.3	223.3	431	344.2	259.4	491	392.1	295.5	551	440.0	331.6
12	249.2	187.8	72	297.1	223.9	32	345.0	260.0	92	392.9	296.1	52	440.8	332.2
13	250.0	188.4	73	297.9	224.5	33	345.8	260.6	93	393.7	296.7	53	441.6	332.8
14	250.8	189.0	74	298.7	225.1	34	346.6	261.2	94	394.5	297.3	54	442.4	333.4
15	251.6	189.6	75	299.5	225.7	35	347.4	261.8	95	395.3	297.9	55	443.2	334.0
16	252.4	190.2	76	300.3	226.3	36	348.2	262.4	96	396.1	298.5	56	444.0	334.6
17	253.2	190.8	77	301.1	226.9	37	349.0	263.0	97	396.9	299.1	57	444.8	335.2
18	254.0	191.4	78	301.9	227.5	38	349.8	263.6	98	397.7	299.7	58	445.6	335.8
19	254.8	192.0	79	302.7	228.1	39	350.6	264.2	99	398.5	300.3	59	446.4	336.4
20	255.6	192.6	80	303.5	228.7	40	351.4	264.8	500	399.3	300.9	60	447.2	337.0
321	256.4	193.2	381	304.3	229.3	441	352.2	265.4	501	400.1	301.5	561	448.0	337.6
22	257.2	193.8	82	305.1	229.9	42	353.0	266.0	02	400.9	302.1	62	448.8	338.2
23	258.0	194.4	83	305.9	230.5	43	353.8	266.6	03	401.7	302.7	63	449.6	338.8
24	258.8	195.0	84	306.7	231.1	44	354.6	267.2	04	402.5	303.3	64	450.4	339.4
25	259.6	195.6	85	307.5	231.7	45	355.4	267.8	05	403.3	303.9	65	451.2	340.0
26	260.4	196.2	86	308.3	232.3	46	356.2	268.4	06	404.1	304.5	66	452.0	340.6
27	261.2	196.8	87	309.1	232.9	47	357.0	269.0	07	404.9	305.1	67	452.8	341.2
28	262.0	197.4	88	309.9	233.5	48	357.8	269.6	08	405.7	305.7	68	453.6	341.8
29	262.8	198.0	89	310.7	234.1	49	358.6	270.2	09	406.5	306.3	69	454.4	342.4
30	263.5	198.6	90	311.5	234.7	50	359.4	270.8	10	407.3	306.9	70	455.2	343.0
331	264.3	199.2	391	312.3	235.3	451	360.2	271.4	511	408.1	307.5	571	456.0	343.6
32	265.1	199.8	92	313.1	235.9	52	361.0	272.0	12	408.9	308.1	72	456.8	344.2
33	265.9	200.4	93	313.9	236.5	53	361.8	272.6	13	409.7	308.7	73	457.6	344.8
34	266.7	201.0	94	314.7	237.1	54	362.6	273.2	14	410.5	309.3	74	458.4	345.4
35	267.5	201.6	95	315.5	237.7	55	363.4	273.8	15	411.3	309.9	75	459.2	346.0
36	268.3	202.2	96	316.3	238.3	56	364.2	274.4	16	412.1	310.5	76	460.0	346.6
37	269.1	202.8	97	317.1	238.9	57	365.0	275.0	17	412.9	311.1	77	460.8	347.2
38	269.9	203.4	98	317.9	239.5	58	365.8	275.6	18	413.7	311.7	78	461.6	347.8
39	270.7	204.0	99	318.7	240.1	59	366.6	276.2	19	414.5	312.3	79	462.4	348.5
40	271.5	204.6	400	319.5	240.7	60	367.4	276.8	20	415.3	312.9	80	463.2	349.1
341	272.3	205.2	401	320.3	241.3	461	368.2	277.4	521	416.1	313.5	581	464.0	349.7
42	273.1	205.8	02	321.1	241.9	62	369.0	278.0	22	416.9	314.1	82	464.8	350.3
43	273.9	206.4	03	321.9	242.5	63	369.8	278.6	23	417.7	314.7	83	465.6	350.9
44	274.7	207.0	04	322.6	243.1	64	370.6	279.2	24	418.5	315.4	84	466.4	351.5
45	275.5	207.6	05	323.4	243.7	65	371.4	279.8	25	419.3	316.0	85	467.2	352.1
46	276.3	208.2	06	324.2	244.3	66	372.2	280.4	26	420.1	316.6	86	468.0	352.7
47	277.1	208.8	07	325.0	244.9	67	373.0	281.0	27	420.9	317.2	87	468.8	353.3
48	277.9	209.4	08	325.8	245.5	68	373.8	281.6	28	421.7	317.8	88	469.6	353.9
49	278.7	210.0	09	326.6	246.1	69	374.6	282.3	29	422.5	318.4	89	470.4	354.5
50	279.5	210.6	10	327.4	246.7	70	375.4	282.9	30	423.3	319.0	90	471.2	355.1
351	280.3	211.2	411	328.2	247.3	471	376.2	283.5	531	424.1	319.6	591	472.0	355.7
52	281.1	211.8	12	329.0	247.9	72	377.0	284.1	32	424.9	320.2	92	472.8	356.3
53	281.9	212.4	13	329.8	248.5	73	377.8	284.7	33	425.7	320.8	93	473.6	356.9
54	282.7	213.0	14	330.6	249.2	74	378.6	285.3	34	426.5	321.4	94	474.4	357.5
55	283.5	213.6	15	331.4	249.8	75	379.4	285.9	35	427.3	322.0	95	475.2	358.1
56	284.3	214.2	16	332.2	250.4	76	380.2	286.5	36	428.1	322.6	96	476.0	358.7
57	285.1	214.8	17	333.0	251.0	77	380.9	287.1	37	428.9	323.2	97	476.8	359.3
58	285.9	215.4	18	333.8	251.6	78	381.7	287.7	38	429.7	323.8	98	477.6	359.9
59	286.7	216.1	19	334.6	252.2	79	382.5	288.3	39	430.5	324.4	99	478.4	360.5
60	287.5	216.7	20	335.4	252.8	80	383.3	288.9	40	431.3	325.0	600	479.2	361.1
Dist.	Dep.	D. Lat.	Dist.	Dep.	D. Lat.	Dist.	Dep.	D. Lat.	Dist.	Dep.	D. Lat.	Dist.	Dep.	D. Lat.

Dist.	D. Lat.	Dep.
D Lo	Dep.	
	m	D Lo

53°

307° | 053° / 233° | 127°

TABLE 4

Traverse 38° Table

322° | 038°
218° | 142°

Dist.	D. Lat.	Dep.	Dist.	D. Lat.	Dep.	Dist.	D. Lat.	Dep.	Dist.	D. Lat.	Dep.	Dist.	D. Lat.	Dep.
1	0.8	0.6	61	48.1	37.6	121	95.3	74.5	181	142.6	111.4	241	189.9	148.4
2	1.6	1.2	62	48.9	38.2	22	96.1	75.1	82	143.4	112.1	42	190.7	149.0
3	2.4	1.8	63	49.6	38.8	23	96.9	75.7	83	144.2	112.7	43	191.5	149.6
4	3.2	2.5	64	50.4	39.4	24	97.7	76.3	84	145.0	113.3	44	192.3	150.2
5	3.9	3.1	65	51.2	40.0	25	98.5	77.0	85	145.8	113.9	45	193.1	150.8
6	4.7	3.7	66	52.0	40.6	26	99.3	77.6	86	146.6	114.5	46	193.9	151.5
7	5.5	4.3	67	52.8	41.2	27	100.1	78.2	87	147.4	115.1	47	194.6	152.1
8	6.3	4.9	68	53.6	41.9	28	100.9	78.8	88	148.1	115.7	48	195.4	152.7
9	7.1	5.5	69	54.4	42.5	29	101.7	79.4	89	148.9	116.4	49	196.2	153.3
10	7.9	6.2	70	55.2	43.1	30	102.4	80.0	90	149.7	117.0	50	197.0	153.9
11	8.7	6.8	71	55.9	43.7	131	103.2	80.7	191	150.5	117.6	251	197.8	154.5
12	9.5	7.4	72	56.7	44.3	32	104.0	81.3	92	151.3	118.2	52	198.6	155.1
13	10.2	8.0	73	57.5	44.9	33	104.8	81.9	93	152.1	118.8	53	199.4	155.8
14	11.0	8.6	74	58.3	45.6	34	105.6	82.5	94	152.9	119.4	54	200.2	156.4
15	11.8	9.2	75	59.1	46.2	35	106.4	83.1	95	153.7	120.1	55	200.9	157.0
16	12.6	9.9	76	59.9	46.8	36	107.2	83.7	96	154.5	120.7	56	201.7	157.6
17	13.4	10.5	77	60.7	47.4	37	108.0	84.3	97	155.2	121.3	57	202.5	158.2
18	14.2	11.1	78	61.5	48.0	38	108.7	85.0	98	156.0	121.9	58	203.3	158.8
19	15.0	11.7	79	62.3	48.6	39	109.5	85.6	99	156.8	122.5	59	204.1	159.5
20	15.8	12.3	80	63.0	49.3	40	110.3	86.2	200	157.6	123.1	60	204.9	160.1
21	16.5	12.9	81	63.8	49.9	141	111.1	86.8	201	158.4	123.7	261	205.7	160.7
22	17.3	13.5	82	64.6	50.5	42	111.9	87.4	02	159.2	124.4	62	206.5	161.3
23	18.1	14.2	83	65.4	51.1	43	112.7	88.0	03	160.0	125.0	63	207.2	161.9
24	18.9	14.8	84	66.2	51.7	44	113.5	88.7	04	160.8	125.6	64	208.0	162.5
25	19.7	15.4	85	67.0	52.3	45	114.3	89.3	05	161.5	126.2	65	208.8	163.2
26	20.5	16.0	86	67.8	52.9	46	115.0	89.9	06	162.3	126.8	66	209.6	163.8
27	21.3	16.6	87	68.6	53.6	47	115.8	90.5	07	163.1	127.4	67	210.4	164.4
28	22.1	17.2	88	69.3	54.2	48	116.6	91.1	08	163.9	128.1	68	211.2	165.0
29	22.9	17.9	89	70.1	54.8	49	117.4	91.7	09	164.7	128.7	69	212.0	165.6
30	23.6	18.5	90	70.9	55.4	50	118.2	92.3	10	165.5	129.3	70	212.8	166.2
31	24.4	19.1	91	71.7	56.0	151	119.0	93.0	211	166.3	129.9	271	213.6	166.8
32	25.2	19.7	92	72.5	56.6	52	119.8	93.6	12	167.1	130.5	72	214.3	167.5
33	26.0	20.3	93	73.3	57.3	53	120.6	94.2	13	167.8	131.1	73	215.1	168.1
34	26.8	20.9	94	74.1	57.9	54	121.4	94.8	14	168.6	131.8	74	215.9	168.7
35	27.6	21.5	95	74.9	58.5	55	122.1	95.4	15	169.4	132.4	75	216.7	169.3
36	28.4	22.2	96	75.6	59.1	56	122.9	96.0	16	170.2	133.0	76	217.5	169.9
37	29.2	22.8	97	76.4	59.7	57	123.7	96.7	17	171.0	133.6	77	218.3	170.5
38	29.9	23.4	98	77.2	60.3	58	124.5	97.3	18	171.8	134.2	78	219.1	171.2
39	30.7	24.0	99	78.0	61.0	59	125.3	97.9	19	172.6	134.8	79	219.9	171.8
40	31.5	24.6	100	78.8	61.6	60	126.1	98.5	20	173.4	135.4	80	220.6	172.4
41	32.3	25.2	101	79.6	62.2	161	126.9	99.1	221	174.2	136.1	281	221.4	173.0
42	33.1	25.9	02	80.4	62.8	62	127.7	99.7	22	174.9	136.7	82	222.2	173.6
43	33.9	26.5	03	81.2	63.4	63	128.4	100.4	23	175.7	137.3	83	223.0	174.2
44	34.7	27.1	04	82.0	64.0	64	129.2	101.0	24	176.5	137.9	84	223.8	174.8
45	35.5	27.7	05	82.7	64.6	65	130.0	101.6	25	177.3	138.5	85	224.6	175.5
46	36.2	28.3	06	83.5	65.3	66	130.8	102.2	26	178.1	139.1	86	225.4	176.1
47	37.0	28.9	07	84.3	65.9	67	131.6	102.8	27	178.9	139.8	87	226.2	176.7
48	37.8	29.6	08	85.1	66.5	68	132.4	103.4	28	179.7	140.4	88	226.9	177.3
49	38.6	30.2	09	85.9	67.1	69	133.2	104.0	29	180.5	141.0	89	227.7	177.9
50	39.4	30.8	10	86.7	67.7	70	134.0	104.7	30	181.2	141.6	90	228.5	178.5
51	40.2	31.4	111	87.5	68.3	171	134.7	105.3	231	182.0	142.2	291	229.3	179.2
52	41.0	32.0	12	88.3	69.0	72	135.5	105.9	32	182.8	142.8	92	230.1	179.8
53	41.8	32.6	13	89.0	69.6	73	136.3	106.5	33	183.6	143.4	93	230.9	180.4
54	42.6	33.2	14	89.8	70.2	74	137.1	107.1	34	184.4	144.1	94	231.7	181.0
55	43.3	33.9	15	90.6	70.8	75	137.9	107.7	35	185.2	144.7	95	232.5	181.6
56	44.1	34.5	16	91.4	71.4	76	138.7	108.4	36	186.0	145.3	96	233.3	182.2
57	44.9	35.1	17	92.2	72.0	77	139.5	109.0	37	186.8	145.9	97	234.0	182.9
58	45.7	35.7	18	93.0	72.6	78	140.3	109.6	38	187.5	146.5	98	234.8	183.5
59	46.5	36.3	19	93.8	73.3	79	141.1	110.2	39	188.3	147.1	99	235.6	184.1
60	47.3	36.9	20	94.6	73.9	80	141.8	110.8	40	189.1	147.8	300	236.4	184.7
Dist.	Dep.	D. Lat.	Dist.	Dep.	D. Lat.	Dist.	Dep.	D. Lat.	Dist.	Dep.	D. Lat.	Dist.	Dep.	D. Lat.

308° | 052°
232° | 128°

52°

Dist.	D. Lat.	Dep.
N.	N x Cos.	N x Sin.
Hypotenuse	Side Adj.	Side Opp.

TABLE 4

Traverse 38° Table

322° | 038°
218° | 142°

Dist.	D. Lat.	Dep.	Dist.	D. Lat.	Dep.	Dist.	D. Lat.	Dep.	Dist.	D. Lat.	Dep.	Dist.	D. Lat.	Dep.
301	237.2	185.3	361	284.5	222.3	421	331.8	259.2	481	379.0	296.1	541	426.3	333.1
02	238.0	185.9	62	285.3	222.9	22	332.5	259.8	82	379.8	296.7	42	427.1	333.7
03	238.8	186.5	63	286.0	223.5	23	333.3	260.4	83	380.6	297.4	43	427.9	334.3
04	239.6	187.2	64	286.8	224.1	24	334.1	261.0	84	381.4	298.0	44	428.7	334.9
05	240.3	187.8	65	287.6	224.7	25	334.9	261.7	85	382.2	298.6	45	429.5	335.5
06	241.1	188.4	66	288.4	225.3	26	335.7	262.3	86	383.0	299.2	46	430.3	336.2
07	241.9	189.0	67	289.2	225.9	27	336.5	262.9	87	383.8	299.8	47	431.0	336.8
08	242.7	189.6	68	290.0	226.6	28	337.3	263.5	88	384.5	300.4	48	431.8	337.4
09	243.5	190.2	69	290.8	227.2	29	338.1	264.1	89	385.3	301.1	49	432.6	338.0
10	244.3	190.9	70	291.6	227.8	30	338.8	264.7	90	386.1	301.7	50	433.4	338.6
311	245.1	191.5	371	292.4	228.4	431	339.6	265.4	491	386.9	302.3	551	434.2	339.2
12	245.9	192.1	72	293.1	229.0	32	340.4	266.0	92	387.7	302.9	52	435.0	339.8
13	246.6	192.7	73	293.9	229.6	33	341.2	266.6	93	388.5	303.5	53	435.8	340.5
14	247.4	193.3	74	294.7	230.3	34	342.0	267.2	94	389.3	304.1	54	436.6	341.1
15	248.2	193.9	75	295.5	230.9	35	342.8	267.8	95	390.1	304.8	55	437.3	341.7
16	249.0	194.5	76	296.3	231.5	36	343.6	268.4	96	390.9	305.4	56	438.1	342.3
17	249.8	195.2	77	297.1	232.1	37	344.4	269.0	97	391.6	306.0	57	438.9	342.9
18	250.6	195.8	78	297.9	232.7	38	345.1	269.7	98	392.4	306.6	58	439.7	343.5
19	251.4	196.4	79	298.7	233.3	39	345.9	270.3	99	393.2	307.2	59	440.5	344.2
20	252.2	197.0	80	299.4	234.0	40	346.7	270.9	500	394.0	307.8	60	441.3	344.8
321	253.0	197.6	381	300.2	234.6	441	347.5	271.5	501	394.8	308.4	561	442.1	345.4
22	253.7	198.2	82	301.0	235.2	42	348.3	272.1	02	395.6	309.1	62	442.9	346.0
23	254.5	198.9	83	301.8	235.8	43	349.1	272.7	03	396.4	309.7	63	443.7	346.6
24	255.3	199.5	84	302.6	236.4	44	349.9	273.4	04	397.2	310.3	64	444.4	347.2
25	256.1	200.1	85	303.4	237.0	45	350.7	274.0	05	397.9	310.9	65	445.2	347.8
26	256.9	200.7	86	304.2	237.6	46	351.5	274.6	06	398.7	311.5	66	446.0	348.5
27	257.7	201.3	87	305.0	238.3	47	352.2	275.2	07	399.5	312.1	67	446.8	349.1
28	258.5	201.9	88	305.7	238.9	48	353.0	275.8	08	400.3	312.8	68	447.6	349.7
29	259.3	202.6	89	306.5	239.5	49	353.8	276.4	09	401.1	313.4	69	448.4	350.3
30	260.0	203.2	90	307.3	240.1	50	354.6	277.0	10	401.9	314.0	70	449.2	350.9
331	260.8	203.8	391	308.1	240.7	451	355.4	277.7	511	402.7	314.6	571	450.0	351.5
32	261.6	204.4	92	308.9	241.3	52	356.2	278.3	12	403.5	315.2	72	450.7	352.2
33	262.4	205.0	93	309.7	242.0	53	357.0	278.9	13	404.2	315.8	73	451.5	352.8
34	263.2	205.6	94	310.5	242.6	54	357.8	279.5	14	405.0	316.4	74	452.3	353.4
35	264.0	206.2	95	311.3	243.2	55	358.5	280.1	15	405.8	317.1	75	453.1	354.0
36	264.8	206.9	96	312.1	243.8	56	359.3	280.7	16	406.6	317.7	76	453.9	354.6
37	265.6	207.5	97	312.8	244.4	57	360.1	281.4	17	407.4	318.3	77	454.7	355.2
38	266.3	208.1	98	313.6	245.0	58	360.9	282.0	18	408.2	318.9	78	455.5	355.9
39	267.1	208.7	99	314.4	245.6	59	361.7	282.6	19	409.0	319.5	79	456.3	356.5
40	267.9	209.3	400	315.2	246.3	60	362.5	283.2	20	409.8	320.1	80	457.0	357.1
341	268.7	209.9	401	316.0	246.9	461	363.3	283.8	521	410.6	320.8	581	457.8	357.7
42	269.5	210.6	02	316.8	247.5	62	364.1	284.4	22	411.3	321.4	82	458.6	358.3
43	270.3	211.2	03	317.6	248.1	63	364.8	285.1	23	412.1	322.0	83	459.4	358.9
44	271.1	211.8	04	318.4	248.7	64	365.6	285.7	24	412.9	322.6	84	460.2	359.5
45	271.9	212.4	05	319.1	249.3	65	366.4	286.3	25	413.7	323.2	85	461.0	360.2
46	272.7	213.0	06	319.9	250.0	66	367.2	286.9	26	414.5	323.8	86	461.8	360.8
47	273.4	213.6	07	320.7	250.6	67	368.0	287.5	27	415.3	324.5	87	462.6	361.4
48	274.2	214.3	08	321.5	251.2	68	368.8	288.1	28	416.1	325.1	88	463.4	362.0
49	275.0	214.9	09	322.3	251.8	69	369.6	288.7	29	416.9	325.7	89	464.1	362.6
50	275.8	215.5	10	323.1	252.4	70	370.4	289.4	30	417.6	326.3	90	464.9	363.2
351	276.6	216.1	411	323.9	253.0	471	371.2	290.0	531	418.4	326.9	591	465.7	363.9
52	277.4	216.7	12	324.7	253.7	72	371.9	290.6	32	419.2	327.5	92	466.5	364.5
53	278.2	217.3	13	325.4	254.3	73	372.7	291.2	33	420.0	328.1	93	467.3	365.1
54	279.0	217.9	14	326.2	254.9	74	373.5	291.8	34	420.8	328.8	94	468.1	365.7
55	279.7	218.6	15	327.0	255.5	75	374.3	292.4	35	421.6	329.4	95	468.9	366.3
56	280.5	219.2	16	327.8	256.1	76	375.1	293.1	36	422.4	330.0	96	469.7	366.9
57	281.3	219.8	17	328.6	256.7	77	375.9	293.7	37	423.2	330.6	97	470.4	367.5
58	282.1	220.4	18	329.4	257.3	78	376.7	294.3	38	423.9	331.2	98	471.2	368.2
59	282.9	221.0	19	330.2	258.0	79	377.5	294.9	39	424.7	331.8	99	472.0	368.8
60	283.7	221.6	20	331.0	258.6	80	378.2	295.5	40	425.5	332.5	600	472.8	369.4
Dist.	Dep.	D. Lat.	Dist.	Dep.	D. Lat.	Dist.	Dep.	D. Lat.	Dist.	Dep.	D. Lat.	Dist.	Dep.	D. Lat.

Dist.	D. Lat.	Dep.
D Lo	Dep.	
	m	D Lo

52°

308° | 052°
232° | 128°

TABLE 4

321° | 039° — 219° | 141°

Traverse 39° Table

Dist.	D. Lat.	Dep.	Dist.	D. Lat.	Dep.	Dist.	D. Lat.	Dep.	Dist.	D. Lat.	Dep.	Dist.	D. Lat.	Dep.
1	0.8	0.6	61	47.4	38.4	121	94.0	76.1	181	140.7	113.9	241	187.3	151.7
2	1.6	1.3	62	48.2	39.0	22	94.8	76.8	82	141.4	114.5	42	188.1	152.3
3	2.3	1.9	63	49.0	39.6	23	95.6	77.4	83	142.2	115.2	43	188.8	152.9
4	3.1	2.5	64	49.7	40.3	24	96.4	78.0	84	143.0	115.8	44	189.6	153.6
5	3.9	3.1	65	50.5	40.9	25	97.1	78.7	85	143.8	116.4	45	190.4	154.2
6	4.7	3.8	66	51.3	41.5	26	97.9	79.3	86	144.5	117.1	46	191.2	154.8
7	5.4	4.4	67	52.1	42.2	27	98.7	79.9	87	145.3	117.7	47	192.0	155.4
8	6.2	5.0	68	52.8	42.8	28	99.5	80.6	88	146.1	118.3	48	192.7	156.1
9	7.0	5.7	69	53.6	43.4	29	100.3	81.2	89	146.9	118.9	49	193.5	156.7
10	7.8	6.3	70	54.4	44.1	30	101.0	81.8	90	147.7	119.6	50	194.3	157.3
11	8.5	6.9	71	55.2	44.7	131	101.8	82.4	191	148.4	120.2	251	195.1	158.0
12	9.3	7.6	72	56.0	45.3	32	102.6	83.1	92	149.2	120.8	52	195.8	158.6
13	10.1	8.2	73	56.7	45.9	33	103.4	83.7	93	150.0	121.5	53	196.6	159.2
14	10.9	8.8	74	57.5	46.6	34	104.1	84.3	94	150.8	122.1	54	197.4	159.8
15	11.7	9.4	75	58.3	47.2	35	104.9	85.0	95	151.5	122.7	55	198.2	160.5
16	12.4	10.1	76	59.1	47.8	36	105.7	85.6	96	152.3	123.3	56	198.9	161.1
17	13.2	10.7	77	59.8	48.5	37	106.5	86.2	97	153.1	124.0	57	199.7	161.7
18	14.0	11.3	78	60.6	49.1	38	107.2	86.8	98	153.9	124.6	58	200.5	162.4
19	14.8	12.0	79	61.4	49.7	39	108.0	87.5	99	154.7	125.2	59	201.3	163.0
20	15.5	12.6	80	62.2	50.3	40	108.8	88.1	200	155.4	125.9	60	202.1	163.6
21	16.3	13.2	81	62.9	51.0	141	109.6	88.7	201	156.2	126.5	261	202.8	164.3
22	17.1	13.8	82	63.7	51.6	42	110.4	89.4	02	157.0	127.1	62	203.6	164.9
23	17.9	14.5	83	64.5	52.2	43	111.1	90.0	03	157.8	127.8	63	204.4	165.5
24	18.7	15.1	84	65.3	52.9	44	111.9	90.6	04	158.5	128.4	64	205.2	166.1
25	19.4	15.7	85	66.1	53.5	45	112.7	91.3	05	159.3	129.0	65	205.9	166.8
26	20.2	16.4	86	66.8	54.1	46	113.5	91.9	06	160.1	129.6	66	206.7	167.4
27	21.0	17.0	87	67.6	54.8	47	114.2	92.5	07	160.9	130.3	67	207.5	168.0
28	21.8	17.6	88	68.4	55.4	48	115.0	93.1	08	161.6	130.9	68	208.3	168.7
29	22.5	18.3	89	69.2	56.0	49	115.8	93.8	09	162.4	131.5	69	209.1	169.3
30	23.3	18.9	90	69.9	56.6	50	116.6	94.4	10	163.2	132.2	70	209.8	169.9
31	24.1	19.5	91	70.7	57.3	151	117.3	95.0	211	164.0	132.8	271	210.6	170.5
32	24.9	20.1	92	71.5	57.9	52	118.1	95.7	12	164.8	133.4	72	211.4	171.2
33	25.6	20.8	93	72.3	58.5	53	118.9	96.3	13	165.5	134.0	73	212.2	171.8
34	26.4	21.4	94	73.1	59.2	54	119.7	96.9	14	166.3	134.7	74	212.9	172.4
35	27.2	22.0	95	73.8	59.8	55	120.5	97.5	15	167.1	135.3	75	213.7	173.1
36	28.0	22.7	96	74.6	60.4	56	121.2	98.2	16	167.9	135.9	76	214.5	173.7
37	28.8	23.3	97	75.4	61.0	57	122.0	98.8	17	168.6	136.6	77	215.3	174.3
38	29.5	23.9	98	76.2	61.7	58	122.8	99.4	18	169.4	137.2	78	216.0	175.0
39	30.3	24.5	99	76.9	62.3	59	123.6	100.1	19	170.2	137.8	79	216.8	175.6
40	31.1	25.2	100	77.7	62.9	60	124.3	100.7	20	171.0	138.5	80	217.6	176.2
41	31.9	25.8	101	78.5	63.6	161	125.1	101.3	221	171.7	139.1	281	218.4	176.8
42	32.6	26.4	02	79.3	64.2	62	125.9	101.9	22	172.5	139.7	82	219.2	177.5
43	33.4	27.1	03	80.0	64.8	63	126.7	102.6	23	173.3	140.3	83	219.9	178.1
44	34.2	27.7	04	80.8	65.4	64	127.5	103.2	24	174.1	141.0	84	220.7	178.7
45	35.0	28.3	05	81.6	66.1	65	128.2	103.8	25	174.9	141.6	85	221.5	179.4
46	35.7	28.9	06	82.4	66.7	66	129.0	104.5	26	175.6	142.2	86	222.3	180.0
47	36.5	29.6	07	83.2	67.3	67	129.8	105.1	27	176.4	142.9	87	223.0	180.6
48	37.3	30.2	08	83.9	68.0	68	130.6	105.7	28	177.2	143.5	88	223.8	181.2
49	38.1	30.8	09	84.7	68.6	69	131.3	106.4	29	178.0	144.1	89	224.6	181.9
50	38.9	31.5	10	85.5	69.2	70	132.1	107.0	30	178.7	144.7	90	225.4	182.5
51	39.6	32.1	111	86.3	69.9	171	132.9	107.6	231	179.5	145.4	291	226.1	183.1
52	40.4	32.7	12	87.0	70.5	72	133.7	108.2	32	180.3	146.0	92	226.9	183.8
53	41.2	33.4	13	87.8	71.1	73	134.4	108.9	33	181.1	146.6	93	227.7	184.4
54	42.0	34.0	14	88.6	71.7	74	135.2	109.5	34	181.9	147.3	94	228.5	185.0
55	42.7	34.6	15	89.4	72.4	75	136.0	110.1	35	182.6	147.9	95	229.3	185.6
56	43.5	35.2	16	90.1	73.0	76	136.8	110.8	36	183.4	148.5	96	230.0	186.3
57	44.3	35.9	17	90.9	73.6	77	137.6	111.4	37	184.2	149.1	97	230.8	186.9
58	45.1	36.5	18	91.7	74.3	78	138.3	112.0	38	185.0	149.8	98	231.6	187.5
59	45.9	37.1	19	92.5	74.9	79	139.1	112.6	39	185.7	150.4	99	232.4	188.2
60	46.6	37.8	20	93.3	75.5	80	139.9	113.3	40	186.5	151.0	300	233.1	188.8
Dist.	Dep.	D. Lat.	Dist.	Dep.	D. Lat.	Dist.	Dep.	D. Lat.	Dist.	Dep.	D. Lat.	Dist.	Dep.	D. Lat.

309° | 051° — 231° | 129°

51°

Dist.	D. Lat.	Dep.
N.	N x Cos.	N x Sin.
Hypotenuse	Side Adj.	Side Opp.

TABLE 4

321° | 039° — 219° | 141°

Traverse 39° Table

Dist.	D. Lat.	Dep.	Dist.	D. Lat.	Dep.	Dist.	D. Lat.	Dep.	Dist.	D. Lat.	Dep.	Dist.	D. Lat.	Dep.
301	233.9	189.4	361	280.5	227.2	421	327.2	264.9	481	373.8	302.7	541	420.4	340.5
02	234.7	190.1	62	281.3	227.8	22	328.0	265.6	82	374.6	303.3	42	421.2	341.1
03	235.5	190.7	63	282.1	228.4	23	328.7	266.2	83	375.4	304.0	43	422.0	341.7
04	236.3	191.3	64	282.9	229.1	24	329.5	266.8	84	376.1	304.6	44	422.8	342.4
05	237.0	191.9	65	283.7	229.7	25	330.3	267.5	85	376.9	305.2	45	423.5	343.0
06	237.8	192.6	66	284.4	230.3	26	331.1	268.1	86	377.7	305.8	46	424.3	343.6
07	238.6	193.2	67	285.2	231.0	27	331.8	268.7	87	378.5	306.5	47	425.1	344.2
08	239.4	193.8	68	286.0	231.6	28	332.6	269.3	88	379.2	307.1	48	425.9	344.9
09	240.1	194.5	69	286.8	232.2	29	333.4	270.0	89	380.0	307.7	49	426.7	345.5
10	240.9	195.1	70	287.5	232.8	30	334.2	270.6	90	380.8	308.4	50	427.4	346.1
311	241.7	195.7	371	288.3	233.5	431	334.9	271.2	491	381.6	309.0	551	428.2	346.8
12	242.5	196.3	72	289.1	234.1	32	335.7	271.9	92	382.4	309.6	52	429.0	347.4
13	243.2	197.0	73	289.9	234.7	33	336.5	272.5	93	383.1	310.3	53	429.8	348.0
14	244.0	197.6	74	290.7	235.4	34	337.3	273.1	94	383.9	310.9	54	430.5	348.6
15	244.8	198.2	75	291.4	236.0	35	338.1	273.8	95	384.7	311.5	55	431.3	349.3
16	245.6	198.9	76	292.2	236.6	36	338.8	274.4	96	385.5	312.1	56	432.1	349.9
17	246.4	199.5	77	293.0	237.3	37	339.6	275.0	97	386.2	312.8	57	432.9	350.5
18	247.1	200.1	78	293.8	237.9	38	340.4	275.6	98	387.0	313.4	58	433.6	351.2
19	247.9	200.8	79	294.5	238.5	39	341.2	276.3	99	387.8	314.0	59	434.4	351.8
20	248.7	201.4	80	295.3	239.1	40	341.9	276.9	500	388.6	314.7	60	435.2	352.4
321	249.5	202.0	381	296.1	239.8	441	342.7	277.5	501	389.4	315.3	561	436.0	353.0
22	250.2	202.6	82	296.9	240.4	42	343.5	278.2	02	390.1	315.9	62	436.8	353.7
23	251.0	203.3	83	297.6	241.0	43	344.3	278.8	03	390.9	316.5	63	437.5	354.3
24	251.8	203.9	84	298.4	241.7	44	345.1	279.4	04	391.7	317.2	64	438.3	354.9
25	252.6	204.5	85	299.2	242.3	45	345.8	280.0	05	392.5	317.8	65	439.1	355.6
26	253.3	205.2	86	300.0	242.9	46	346.6	280.7	06	393.2	318.4	66	439.9	356.2
27	254.1	205.8	87	300.8	243.5	47	347.4	281.3	07	394.0	319.1	67	440.6	356.8
28	254.9	206.4	88	301.5	244.2	48	348.2	281.9	08	394.8	319.7	68	441.4	357.5
29	255.7	207.0	89	302.3	244.8	49	348.9	282.6	09	395.6	320.3	69	442.2	358.1
30	256.5	207.7	90	303.1	245.4	50	349.7	283.2	10	396.3	321.0	70	443.0	358.7
331	257.2	208.3	391	303.9	246.1	451	350.5	283.8	511	397.1	321.6	571	443.8	359.3
32	258.0	208.9	92	304.6	246.7	52	351.3	284.5	12	397.9	322.2	72	444.5	360.0
33	258.8	209.6	93	305.4	247.3	53	352.0	285.1	13	398.7	322.8	73	445.3	360.6
34	259.6	210.2	94	306.2	248.0	54	352.8	285.7	14	399.5	323.5	74	446.1	361.2
35	260.3	210.8	95	307.0	248.6	55	353.6	286.3	15	400.2	324.1	75	446.9	361.9
36	261.1	211.5	96	307.7	249.2	56	354.4	287.0	16	401.0	324.7	76	447.6	362.5
37	261.9	212.1	97	308.5	249.8	57	355.2	287.6	17	401.8	325.4	77	448.4	363.1
38	262.7	212.7	98	309.3	250.5	58	355.9	288.2	18	402.6	326.0	78	449.2	363.7
39	263.5	213.3	99	310.1	251.1	59	356.7	288.9	19	403.3	326.6	79	450.0	364.4
40	264.2	214.0	400	310.9	251.7	60	357.5	289.5	20	404.1	327.2	80	450.7	365.0
341	265.0	214.6	401	311.6	252.4	461	358.3	290.1	521	404.9	327.9	581	451.5	365.6
42	265.8	215.2	02	312.4	253.0	62	359.0	290.7	22	405.7	328.5	82	452.3	366.3
43	266.6	215.9	03	313.2	253.6	63	359.8	291.4	23	406.4	329.1	83	453.1	366.9
44	267.3	216.5	04	314.0	254.2	64	360.6	292.0	24	407.2	329.8	84	453.9	367.5
45	268.1	217.1	05	314.7	254.9	65	361.4	292.6	25	408.0	330.4	85	454.6	368.2
46	268.9	217.7	06	315.5	255.5	66	362.2	293.3	26	408.8	331.0	86	455.4	368.8
47	269.7	218.4	07	316.3	256.1	67	362.9	293.9	27	409.6	331.7	87	456.2	369.4
48	270.4	219.0	08	317.1	256.8	68	363.7	294.5	28	410.3	332.3	88	457.0	370.0
49	271.2	219.6	09	317.9	257.4	69	364.5	295.2	29	411.1	332.9	89	457.7	370.7
50	272.0	220.3	10	318.6	258.0	70	365.3	295.8	30	411.9	333.5	90	458.5	371.3
351	272.8	220.9	411	319.4	258.7	471	366.0	296.4	531	412.7	334.2	591	459.3	371.9
52	273.6	221.5	12	320.2	259.3	72	366.8	297.0	32	413.4	334.8	92	460.1	372.6
53	274.3	222.2	13	321.0	259.9	73	367.6	297.7	33	414.2	335.4	93	460.8	373.2
54	275.1	222.8	14	321.7	260.5	74	368.4	298.3	34	415.0	336.1	94	461.6	373.8
55	275.9	223.4	15	322.5	261.2	75	369.1	298.9	35	415.8	336.7	95	462.4	374.4
56	276.7	224.0	16	323.3	261.8	76	369.9	299.6	36	416.6	337.3	96	463.2	375.1
57	277.4	224.7	17	324.1	262.4	77	370.7	300.2	37	417.3	337.9	97	464.0	375.7
58	278.2	225.3	18	324.8	263.1	78	371.5	300.8	38	418.1	338.6	98	464.7	376.3
59	279.0	225.9	19	325.6	263.7	79	372.3	301.4	39	418.9	339.2	99	465.5	377.0
60	279.8	226.6	20	326.4	264.3	80	373.0	302.1	40	419.7	339.8	600	466.3	377.6
Dist.	Dep.	D. Lat.	Dist.	Dep.	D. Lat.	Dist.	Dep.	D. Lat.	Dist.	Dep.	D. Lat.	Dist.	Dep.	D. Lat.

Dist.	D. Lat.	Dep.
D Lo	Dep.	
	m	D Lo

51°

309° | 051° — 231° | 129°

TABLE 4

Traverse **40°** Table

320° | 040° — 220° | 140°

Dist.	D. Lat.	Dep.	Dist.	D. Lat.	Dep.	Dist.	D. Lat.	Dep.	Dist.	D. Lat.	Dep.	Dist.	D. Lat.	Dep.
1	0.8	0.6	61	46.7	39.2	121	92.7	77.8	181	138.7	116.3	241	184.6	154.9
2	1.5	1.3	62	47.5	39.9	22	93.5	78.4	82	139.4	117.0	42	185.4	155.6
3	2.3	1.9	63	48.3	40.5	23	94.2	79.1	83	140.2	117.6	43	186.1	156.2
4	3.1	2.6	64	49.0	41.1	24	95.0	79.7	84	141.0	118.3	44	186.9	156.8
5	3.8	3.2	65	49.8	41.8	25	95.8	80.3	85	141.7	118.9	45	187.7	157.5
6	4.6	3.9	66	50.6	42.4	26	96.5	81.0	86	142.5	119.6	46	188.4	158.1
7	5.4	4.5	67	51.3	43.1	27	97.3	81.6	87	143.3	120.2	47	189.2	158.8
8	6.1	5.1	68	52.1	43.7	28	98.1	82.3	88	144.0	120.8	48	190.0	159.4
9	6.9	5.8	69	52.9	44.4	29	98.8	82.9	89	144.8	121.5	49	190.7	160.1
10	7.7	6.4	70	53.6	45.0	30	99.6	83.6	90	145.5	122.1	50	191.5	160.7
11	8.4	7.1	71	54.4	45.6	131	100.4	84.2	191	146.3	122.8	251	192.3	161.3
12	9.2	7.7	72	55.2	46.3	32	101.1	84.8	92	147.1	123.4	52	193.0	162.0
13	10.0	8.4	73	55.9	46.9	33	101.9	85.5	93	147.8	124.1	53	193.8	162.6
14	10.7	9.0	74	56.7	47.6	34	102.6	86.1	94	148.6	124.7	54	194.6	163.3
15	11.5	9.6	75	57.5	48.2	35	103.4	86.8	95	149.4	125.3	55	195.3	163.9
16	12.3	10.3	76	58.2	48.9	36	104.2	87.4	96	150.1	126.0	56	196.1	164.6
17	13.0	10.9	77	59.0	49.5	37	104.9	88.1	97	150.9	126.6	57	196.9	165.2
18	13.8	11.6	78	59.8	50.1	38	105.7	88.7	98	151.7	127.3	58	197.6	165.8
19	14.6	12.2	79	60.5	50.8	39	106.5	89.3	99	152.4	127.9	59	198.4	166.5
20	15.3	12.9	80	61.3	51.4	40	107.2	90.0	200	153.2	128.6	60	199.2	167.1
21	16.1	13.5	81	62.0	52.1	141	108.0	90.6	201	154.0	129.2	261	199.9	167.8
22	16.9	14.1	82	62.8	52.7	42	108.8	91.3	02	154.7	129.8	62	200.7	168.4
23	17.6	14.8	83	63.6	53.4	43	109.5	91.9	03	155.5	130.5	63	201.5	169.1
24	18.4	15.4	84	64.3	54.0	44	110.3	92.6	04	156.3	131.1	64	202.2	169.7
25	19.2	16.1	85	65.1	54.6	45	111.1	93.2	05	157.0	131.8	65	203.0	170.3
26	19.9	16.7	86	65.9	55.3	46	111.8	93.8	06	157.8	132.4	66	203.8	171.0
27	20.7	17.4	87	66.6	55.9	47	112.6	94.5	07	158.6	133.1	67	204.5	171.6
28	21.4	18.0	88	67.4	56.6	48	113.4	95.1	08	159.3	133.7	68	205.3	172.3
29	22.2	18.6	89	68.2	57.2	49	114.1	95.8	09	160.1	134.3	69	206.1	172.9
30	23.0	19.3	90	68.9	57.9	50	114.9	96.4	10	160.9	135.0	70	206.8	173.6
31	23.7	19.9	91	69.7	58.5	151	115.7	97.1	211	161.6	135.6	271	207.6	174.2
32	24.5	20.6	92	70.5	59.1	52	116.4	97.7	12	162.4	136.3	72	208.4	174.8
33	25.3	21.2	93	71.2	59.8	53	117.2	98.3	13	163.2	136.9	73	209.1	175.5
34	26.0	21.9	94	72.0	60.4	54	118.0	99.0	14	163.9	137.6	74	209.9	176.1
35	26.8	22.5	95	72.8	61.1	55	118.7	99.6	15	164.7	138.2	75	210.7	176.8
36	27.6	23.1	96	73.5	61.7	56	119.5	100.3	16	165.5	138.8	76	211.4	177.4
37	28.3	23.8	97	74.3	62.4	57	120.3	100.9	17	166.2	139.5	77	212.2	178.1
38	29.1	24.4	98	75.1	63.0	58	121.0	101.6	18	167.0	140.1	78	213.0	178.7
39	29.9	25.1	99	75.8	63.6	59	121.8	102.2	19	167.8	140.8	79	213.7	179.3
40	30.6	25.7	100	76.6	64.3	60	122.6	102.8	20	168.5	141.4	80	214.5	180.0
41	31.4	26.4	101	77.4	64.9	161	123.3	103.5	221	169.3	142.1	281	215.3	180.6
42	32.2	27.0	02	78.1	65.6	62	124.1	104.1	22	170.1	142.7	82	216.0	181.3
43	32.9	27.6	03	78.9	66.2	63	124.9	104.8	23	170.8	143.3	83	216.8	181.9
44	33.7	28.3	04	79.7	66.8	64	125.6	105.4	24	171.6	144.0	84	217.6	182.6
45	34.5	28.9	05	80.4	67.5	65	126.4	106.1	25	172.4	144.6	85	218.3	183.2
46	35.2	29.6	06	81.2	68.1	66	127.2	106.7	26	173.1	145.3	86	219.1	183.8
47	36.0	30.2	07	82.0	68.8	67	127.9	107.3	27	173.9	145.9	87	219.9	184.5
48	36.8	30.9	08	82.7	69.4	68	128.7	108.0	28	174.7	146.6	88	220.6	185.1
49	37.5	31.5	09	83.5	70.1	69	129.5	108.6	29	175.4	147.2	89	221.4	185.8
50	38.3	32.1	10	84.3	70.7	70	130.2	109.3	30	176.2	147.8	90	222.2	186.4
51	39.1	32.8	111	85.0	71.3	171	131.0	109.9	231	177.0	148.5	291	222.9	187.1
52	39.8	33.4	12	85.8	72.0	72	131.8	110.6	32	177.7	149.1	92	223.7	187.7
53	40.6	34.1	13	86.6	72.6	73	132.5	111.2	33	178.5	149.8	93	224.5	188.3
54	41.4	34.7	14	87.3	73.3	74	133.3	111.8	34	179.3	150.4	94	225.2	189.0
55	42.1	35.4	15	88.1	73.9	75	134.1	112.5	35	180.0	151.1	95	226.0	189.6
56	42.9	36.0	16	88.9	74.6	76	134.8	113.1	36	180.8	151.7	96	226.7	190.3
57	43.7	36.6	17	89.6	75.2	77	135.6	113.8	37	181.6	152.3	97	227.5	190.9
58	44.4	37.3	18	90.4	75.8	78	136.4	114.4	38	182.3	153.0	98	228.3	191.6
59	45.2	37.9	19	91.2	76.5	79	137.1	115.1	39	183.1	153.6	99	229.0	192.2
60	46.0	38.6	20	91.9	77.1	80	137.9	115.7	40	183.9	154.3	300	229.8	192.8
Dist.	Dep.	D. Lat.	Dist.	Dep.	D. Lat.	Dist.	Dep.	D. Lat.	Dist.	Dep.	D. Lat.	Dist.	Dep.	D. Lat.

310° | 050° — 230° | 130°

50°

Dist.	D. Lat.	Dep.
N.	N x Cos.	N x Sin.
Hypotenuse	Side Adj.	Side Opp.

TABLE 4

Traverse **40°** Table

320° | 040° — 220° | 140°

Dist.	D. Lat.	Dep.	Dist.	D. Lat.	Dep.	Dist.	D. Lat.	Dep.	Dist.	D. Lat.	Dep.	Dist.	D. Lat.	Dep.
301	230.6	193.5	361	276.5	232.0	421	322.5	270.6	481	368.5	309.2	541	414.4	347.7
02	231.3	194.1	62	277.3	232.7	22	323.3	271.3	82	369.2	309.8	42	415.2	348.4
03	232.1	194.8	63	278.1	233.3	23	324.0	271.9	83	370.0	310.5	43	416.0	349.0
04	232.9	195.4	64	278.8	234.0	24	324.8	272.5	84	370.8	311.1	44	416.7	349.7
05	233.6	196.1	65	279.6	234.6	25	325.6	273.2	85	371.5	311.8	45	417.5	350.3
06	234.4	196.7	66	280.4	235.3	26	326.3	273.8	86	372.3	312.4	46	418.3	351.0
07	235.2	197.3	67	281.1	235.9	27	327.1	274.5	87	373.1	313.0	47	419.0	351.6
08	235.9	198.0	68	281.9	236.5	28	327.9	275.1	88	373.8	313.7	48	419.8	352.2
09	236.7	198.6	69	282.7	237.2	29	328.6	275.8	89	374.6	314.3	49	420.6	352.9
10	237.5	199.3	70	283.4	237.8	30	329.4	276.4	90	375.4	315.0	50	421.3	353.5
311	238.2	199.9	371	284.2	238.5	431	330.2	277.0	491	376.1	315.6	551	422.1	354.2
12	239.0	200.5	72	285.0	239.1	32	330.9	277.7	92	376.9	316.3	52	422.9	354.8
13	239.8	201.2	73	285.7	239.8	33	331.7	278.3	93	377.7	316.9	53	423.6	355.5
14	240.5	201.8	74	286.5	240.4	34	332.5	279.0	94	378.4	317.5	54	424.4	356.1
15	241.3	202.5	75	287.3	241.0	35	333.2	279.6	95	379.2	318.2	55	425.2	356.7
16	242.1	203.1	76	288.0	241.7	36	334.0	280.3	96	380.0	318.8	56	425.9	357.4
17	242.8	203.8	77	288.8	242.3	37	334.8	280.9	97	380.7	319.5	57	426.7	358.0
18	243.6	204.4	78	289.6	243.0	38	335.5	281.5	98	381.5	320.1	58	427.5	358.7
19	244.4	205.0	79	290.3	243.6	39	336.3	282.2	99	382.3	320.8	59	428.2	359.3
20	245.1	205.7	80	291.1	244.3	40	337.1	282.8	500	383.0	321.4	60	429.0	360.0
321	245.9	206.3	381	291.9	244.9	441	337.8	283.5	501	383.8	322.0	561	429.8	360.6
22	246.7	207.0	82	292.6	245.5	42	338.6	284.1	02	384.6	322.7	62	430.5	361.2
23	247.4	207.6	83	293.4	246.2	43	339.4	284.8	03	385.3	323.3	63	431.3	361.9
24	248.2	208.3	84	294.2	246.8	44	340.1	285.4	04	386.1	324.0	64	432.0	362.5
25	249.0	208.9	85	294.9	247.5	45	340.9	286.0	05	386.9	324.6	65	432.8	363.2
26	249.7	209.5	86	295.7	248.1	46	341.7	286.7	06	387.6	325.3	66	433.6	363.8
27	250.5	210.2	87	296.5	248.8	47	342.4	287.3	07	388.4	325.9	67	434.3	364.5
28	251.3	210.8	88	297.2	249.4	48	343.2	288.0	08	389.2	326.5	68	435.1	365.1
29	252.0	211.5	89	298.0	250.0	49	344.0	288.6	09	389.9	327.2	69	435.9	365.7
30	252.8	212.1	90	298.8	250.7	50	344.7	289.3	10	390.7	327.8	70	436.6	366.4
331	253.6	212.8	391	299.5	251.3	451	345.5	289.9	511	391.4	328.5	571	437.4	367.0
32	254.3	213.4	92	300.3	252.0	52	346.3	290.5	12	392.2	329.1	72	438.2	367.7
33	255.1	214.0	93	301.1	252.6	53	347.0	291.2	13	393.0	329.8	73	438.9	368.3
34	255.9	214.7	94	301.8	253.3	54	347.8	291.8	14	393.7	330.4	74	439.7	369.0
35	256.6	215.3	95	302.6	253.9	55	348.6	292.5	15	394.5	331.0	75	440.5	369.6
36	257.4	216.0	96	303.4	254.5	56	349.3	293.1	16	395.3	331.7	76	441.2	370.2
37	258.2	216.6	97	304.1	255.2	57	350.1	293.8	17	396.0	332.3	77	442.0	370.9
38	258.9	217.3	98	304.9	255.8	58	350.8	294.4	18	396.8	333.0	78	442.8	371.5
39	259.7	217.9	99	305.7	256.5	59	351.6	295.0	19	397.6	333.6	79	443.5	372.2
40	260.5	218.5	400	306.4	257.1	60	352.4	295.7	20	398.3	334.2	80	444.3	372.8
341	261.2	219.2	401	307.2	257.8	461	353.1	296.3	521	399.1	334.9	581	445.1	373.5
42	262.0	219.8	02	307.9	258.4	62	353.9	297.0	22	399.9	335.5	82	445.8	374.1
43	262.8	220.5	03	308.7	259.0	63	354.7	297.6	23	400.6	336.2	83	446.6	374.7
44	263.5	221.1	04	309.5	259.7	64	355.4	298.3	24	401.4	336.8	84	447.4	375.4
45	264.3	221.8	05	310.2	260.3	65	356.2	298.9	25	402.2	337.5	85	448.1	376.0
46	265.1	222.4	06	311.0	261.0	66	357.0	299.5	26	402.9	338.1	86	448.9	376.7
47	265.8	223.0	07	311.8	261.6	67	357.7	300.2	27	403.7	338.7	87	449.7	377.3
48	266.6	223.7	08	312.5	262.3	68	358.5	300.8	28	404.5	339.4	88	450.4	378.0
49	267.3	224.3	09	313.3	262.9	69	359.3	301.5	29	405.2	340.0	89	451.2	378.6
50	268.1	225.0	10	314.1	263.5	70	360.0	302.1	30	406.0	340.7	90	452.0	379.2
351	268.9	225.6	411	314.8	264.2	471	360.8	302.8	531	406.8	341.3	591	452.7	379.9
52	269.6	226.3	12	315.6	264.8	72	361.6	303.4	32	407.5	342.0	92	453.5	380.5
53	270.4	226.9	13	316.4	265.5	73	362.3	304.0	33	408.3	342.6	93	454.3	381.2
54	271.2	227.5	14	317.1	266.1	74	363.1	304.7	34	409.1	343.2	94	455.0	381.8
55	271.9	228.2	15	317.9	266.8	75	363.9	305.3	35	409.8	343.9	95	455.8	382.5
56	272.7	228.8	16	318.7	267.4	76	364.6	306.0	36	410.6	344.5	96	456.6	383.1
57	273.5	229.5	17	319.4	268.0	77	365.4	306.6	37	411.4	345.2	97	457.3	383.7
58	274.2	230.1	18	320.2	268.7	78	366.2	307.3	38	412.1	345.8	98	458.1	384.4
59	275.0	230.8	19	321.0	269.3	79	366.9	307.9	39	412.9	346.5	99	458.9	385.0
60	275.8	231.4	20	321.7	270.0	80	367.7	308.5	40	413.7	347.1	600	459.6	385.7
Dist.	Dep.	D. Lat.	Dist.	Dep.	D. Lat.	Dist.	Dep.	D. Lat.	Dist.	Dep.	D. Lat.	Dist.	Dep.	D. Lat.

Dist.	D. Lat.	Dep.
D Lo	Dep.	
	m	D Lo

50°

310° | 050° — 230° | 130°

TABLE 4

41°

Traverse Table

319°	041°
221°	139°

Dist.	D. Lat.	Dep.	Dist.	D. Lat.	Dep.	Dist.	D. Lat.	Dep.	Dist.	D. Lat.	Dep.	Dist.	D. Lat.	Dep.
1	0.8	0.7	61	46.0	40.0	121	91.3	79.4	181	136.6	118.7	241	181.9	158.1
2	1.5	1.3	62	46.8	40.7	22	92.1	80.0	82	137.4	119.4	42	182.6	158.8
3	2.3	2.0	63	47.5	41.3	23	92.8	80.7	83	138.1	120.1	43	183.4	159.4
4	3.0	2.6	64	48.3	42.0	24	93.6	81.4	84	138.9	120.7	44	184.1	160.1
5	3.8	3.3	65	49.1	42.6	25	94.3	82.0	85	139.6	121.4	45	184.9	160.7
6	4.5	3.9	66	49.8	43.3	26	95.1	82.7	86	140.4	122.0	46	185.7	161.4
7	5.3	4.6	67	50.6	44.0	27	95.8	83.3	87	141.1	122.7	47	186.4	162.0
8	6.0	5.2	68	51.3	44.6	28	96.6	84.0	88	141.9	123.3	48	187.2	162.7
9	6.8	5.9	69	52.1	45.3	29	97.4	84.6	89	142.6	124.0	49	187.9	163.4
10	7.5	6.6	70	52.8	45.9	30	98.1	85.3	90	143.4	124.7	50	188.7	164.0
11	8.3	7.2	71	53.6	46.6	131	98.9	85.9	191	144.1	125.3	251	189.4	164.7
12	9.1	7.9	72	54.3	47.2	32	99.6	86.6	92	144.9	126.0	52	190.2	165.3
13	9.8	8.5	73	55.1	47.9	33	100.4	87.3	93	145.7	126.6	53	190.9	166.0
14	10.6	9.2	74	55.8	48.5	34	101.1	87.9	94	146.4	127.3	54	191.7	166.6
15	11.3	9.8	75	56.6	49.2	35	101.9	88.6	95	147.2	127.9	55	192.5	167.3
16	12.1	10.5	76	57.4	49.9	36	102.6	89.2	96	147.9	128.6	56	193.2	168.0
17	12.8	11.2	77	58.1	50.5	37	103.4	89.9	97	148.7	129.2	57	194.0	168.6
18	13.6	11.8	78	58.9	51.2	38	104.1	90.5	98	149.4	129.9	58	194.7	169.3
19	14.3	12.5	79	59.6	51.8	39	104.9	91.2	99	150.2	130.6	59	195.5	169.9
20	15.1	13.1	80	60.4	52.5	40	105.7	91.8	200	150.9	131.2	60	196.2	170.6
21	15.8	13.8	81	61.1	53.1	141	106.4	92.5	201	151.7	131.9	261	197.0	171.2
22	16.6	14.4	82	61.9	53.8	42	107.2	93.2	02	152.5	132.5	62	197.7	171.9
23	17.4	15.1	83	62.6	54.5	43	107.9	93.8	03	153.2	133.2	63	198.5	172.5
24	18.1	15.7	84	63.4	55.1	44	108.7	94.5	04	154.0	133.8	64	199.2	173.2
25	18.9	16.4	85	64.2	55.8	45	109.4	95.1	05	154.7	134.5	65	200.0	173.9
26	19.6	17.1	86	64.9	56.4	46	110.2	95.8	06	155.5	135.1	66	200.8	174.5
27	20.4	17.7	87	65.7	57.1	47	110.9	96.4	07	156.2	135.8	67	201.5	175.2
28	21.1	18.4	88	66.4	57.7	48	111.7	97.1	08	157.0	136.5	68	202.3	175.8
29	21.9	19.0	89	67.2	58.4	49	112.5	97.8	09	157.7	137.1	69	203.0	176.5
30	22.6	19.7	90	67.9	59.0	50	113.2	98.4	10	158.5	137.8	70	203.8	177.1
31	23.4	20.3	91	68.7	59.7	151	114.0	99.1	211	159.2	138.4	271	204.5	177.8
32	24.2	21.0	92	69.4	60.4	52	114.7	99.7	12	160.0	139.1	72	205.3	178.4
33	24.9	21.6	93	70.2	61.0	53	115.5	100.4	13	160.8	139.7	73	206.0	179.1
34	25.7	22.3	94	70.9	61.7	54	116.2	101.0	14	161.5	140.4	74	206.8	179.8
35	26.4	23.0	95	71.7	62.3	55	117.0	101.7	15	162.3	141.1	75	207.5	180.4
36	27.2	23.6	96	72.5	63.0	56	117.7	102.3	16	163.0	141.7	76	208.3	181.1
37	27.9	24.3	97	73.2	63.6	57	118.5	103.0	17	163.8	142.4	77	209.1	181.7
38	28.7	24.9	98	74.0	64.3	58	119.2	103.7	18	164.5	143.0	78	209.8	182.4
39	29.4	25.6	99	74.7	64.9	59	120.0	104.3	19	165.3	143.7	79	210.6	183.0
40	30.2	26.2	100	75.5	65.6	60	120.8	105.0	20	166.0	144.3	80	211.3	183.7
41	30.9	26.9	101	76.2	66.3	161	121.5	105.6	221	166.8	145.0	281	212.1	184.4
42	31.7	27.6	02	77.0	66.9	62	122.3	106.3	22	167.5	145.6	82	212.8	185.0
43	32.5	28.2	03	77.7	67.6	63	123.0	106.9	23	168.3	146.3	83	213.6	185.7
44	33.2	28.9	04	78.5	68.2	64	123.8	107.6	24	169.1	147.0	84	214.3	186.3
45	34.0	29.5	05	79.2	68.9	65	124.5	108.2	25	169.8	147.6	85	215.1	187.0
46	34.7	30.2	06	80.0	69.5	66	125.3	108.9	26	170.6	148.3	86	215.8	187.6
47	35.5	30.8	07	80.8	70.2	67	126.0	109.6	27	171.3	148.9	87	216.6	188.3
48	36.2	31.5	08	81.5	70.9	68	126.8	110.2	28	172.1	149.6	88	217.4	188.9
49	37.0	32.1	09	82.3	71.5	69	127.5	110.9	29	172.8	150.2	89	218.1	189.6
50	37.7	32.8	10	83.0	72.2	70	128.3	111.5	30	173.6	150.9	90	218.9	190.3
51	38.5	33.5	111	83.8	72.8	171	129.1	112.2	231	174.3	151.5	291	219.6	190.9
52	39.2	34.1	12	84.5	73.5	72	129.8	112.8	32	175.1	152.2	92	220.4	191.6
53	40.0	34.8	13	85.3	74.1	73	130.6	113.5	33	175.8	152.9	93	221.1	192.2
54	40.8	35.4	14	86.0	74.8	74	131.3	114.2	34	176.6	153.5	94	221.9	192.9
55	41.5	36.1	15	86.8	75.4	75	132.1	114.8	35	177.4	154.2	95	222.6	193.5
56	42.3	36.7	16	87.5	76.1	76	132.8	115.5	36	178.1	154.8	96	223.4	194.2
57	43.0	37.4	17	88.3	76.8	77	133.6	116.1	37	178.9	155.5	97	224.1	194.8
58	43.8	38.1	18	89.1	77.4	78	134.3	116.8	38	179.6	156.1	98	224.9	195.5
59	44.5	38.7	19	89.8	78.1	79	135.1	117.4	39	180.4	156.8	99	225.7	196.2
60	45.3	39.4	20	90.6	78.7	80	135.8	118.1	40	181.1	157.5	300	226.4	196.8
Dist.	Dep.	D. Lat.	Dist.	Dep.	D. Lat.	Dist.	Dep.	D. Lat.	Dist.	Dep.	D. Lat.	Dist.	Dep.	D. Lat.

311°	049°
229°	131°

49°

Dist.	D. Lat.	Dep.
N.	N x Cos.	N x Sin.
Hypotenuse	Side Adj.	Side Opp.

TABLE 4

41°

Traverse Table

319°	041°
221°	139°

Dist.	D. Lat.	Dep.	Dist.	D. Lat.	Dep.	Dist.	D. Lat.	Dep.	Dist.	D. Lat.	Dep.	Dist.	D. Lat.	Dep.
301	227.2	197.5	361	272.5	236.8	421	317.7	276.2	481	363.0	315.6	541	408.3	354.9
02	227.9	198.1	62	273.2	237.5	22	318.5	276.9	82	363.8	316.2	42	409.1	355.6
03	228.7	198.8	63	274.0	238.1	23	319.2	277.5	83	364.5	316.9	43	409.8	356.2
04	229.4	199.4	64	274.7	238.8	24	320.0	278.2	84	365.3	317.5	44	410.6	356.9
05	230.2	200.1	65	275.5	239.5	25	320.8	278.8	85	366.0	318.2	45	411.3	357.6
06	230.9	200.8	66	276.2	240.1	26	321.5	279.5	86	366.8	318.8	46	412.1	358.2
07	231.7	201.4	67	277.0	240.8	27	322.3	280.1	87	367.5	319.5	47	412.8	358.9
08	232.5	202.1	68	277.7	241.4	28	323.0	280.8	88	368.3	320.2	48	413.6	359.5
09	233.2	202.7	69	278.5	242.1	29	323.8	281.4	89	369.1	320.8	49	414.3	360.2
10	234.0	203.4	70	279.2	242.7	30	324.5	282.1	90	369.8	321.5	50	415.1	360.8
311	234.7	204.0	371	280.0	243.4	431	325.3	282.8	491	370.6	322.1	551	415.8	361.5
12	235.5	204.7	72	280.8	244.1	32	326.0	283.4	92	371.3	322.8	52	416.6	362.1
13	236.2	205.3	73	281.5	244.7	33	326.8	284.1	93	372.1	323.4	53	417.4	362.8
14	237.0	206.0	74	282.3	245.4	34	327.5	284.7	94	372.8	324.1	54	418.1	363.5
15	237.7	206.7	75	283.0	246.0	35	328.3	285.4	95	373.6	324.7	55	418.9	364.1
16	238.5	207.3	76	283.8	246.7	36	329.1	286.0	96	374.3	325.4	56	419.6	364.8
17	239.2	208.0	77	284.5	247.3	37	329.8	286.7	97	375.1	326.1	57	420.4	365.4
18	240.0	208.6	78	285.3	248.0	38	330.6	287.4	98	375.8	326.7	58	421.1	366.1
19	240.8	209.3	79	286.0	248.6	39	331.3	288.0	99	376.6	327.4	59	421.9	366.7
20	241.5	209.9	80	286.8	249.3	40	332.1	288.7	500	377.4	328.0	60	422.6	367.4
321	242.3	210.6	381	287.5	250.0	441	332.8	289.3	501	378.1	328.7	561	423.4	368.0
22	243.0	211.3	82	288.3	250.6	42	333.6	290.0	02	378.9	329.3	62	424.1	368.7
23	243.8	211.9	83	289.1	251.3	43	334.3	290.6	03	379.6	330.0	63	424.9	369.4
24	244.5	212.6	84	289.8	251.9	44	335.1	291.3	04	380.4	330.7	64	425.7	370.0
25	245.3	213.2	85	290.6	252.6	45	335.8	291.9	05	381.1	331.3	65	426.4	370.7
26	246.0	213.9	86	291.3	253.2	46	336.6	292.6	06	381.9	332.0	66	427.2	371.3
27	246.8	214.5	87	292.1	253.9	47	337.4	293.3	07	382.6	332.6	67	427.9	372.0
28	247.5	215.2	88	292.8	254.6	48	338.1	293.9	08	383.4	333.3	68	428.7	372.6
29	248.3	215.8	89	293.6	255.2	49	338.9	294.6	09	384.1	333.9	69	429.4	373.3
30	249.1	216.5	90	294.3	255.9	50	339.6	295.2	10	384.9	334.6	70	430.2	374.0
331	249.8	217.2	391	295.1	256.5	451	340.4	295.9	511	385.7	335.2	571	430.9	374.6
32	250.6	217.8	92	295.8	257.2	52	341.1	296.5	12	386.4	335.9	72	431.7	375.3
33	251.3	218.5	93	296.6	257.8	53	341.9	297.2	13	387.2	336.6	73	432.4	375.9
34	252.1	219.1	94	297.4	258.5	54	342.6	297.9	14	387.9	337.2	74	433.2	376.6
35	252.8	219.8	95	298.1	259.1	55	343.4	298.5	15	388.7	337.9	75	434.0	377.2
36	253.6	220.4	96	298.9	259.8	56	344.1	299.2	16	389.4	338.5	76	434.7	377.9
37	254.3	221.1	97	299.6	260.5	57	344.9	299.8	17	390.2	339.2	77	435.5	378.5
38	255.1	221.7	98	300.4	261.1	58	345.7	300.5	18	390.9	339.8	78	436.2	379.2
39	255.8	222.4	99	301.1	261.8	59	346.4	301.1	19	391.7	340.5	79	437.0	379.9
40	256.6	223.1	400	301.9	262.4	60	347.2	301.8	20	392.4	341.2	80	437.7	380.5
341	257.4	223.7	401	302.6	263.1	461	347.9	302.4	521	393.2	341.8	581	438.5	381.2
42	258.1	224.4	02	303.4	263.7	62	348.7	303.1	22	394.0	342.5	82	439.2	381.8
43	258.9	225.0	03	304.1	264.4	63	349.4	303.8	23	394.7	343.1	83	440.0	382.5
44	259.6	225.7	04	304.9	265.0	64	350.2	304.4	24	395.5	343.8	84	440.8	383.1
45	260.4	226.3	05	305.7	265.7	65	350.9	305.1	25	396.2	344.4	85	441.5	383.8
46	261.1	227.0	06	306.4	266.4	66	351.7	305.7	26	397.0	345.1	86	442.3	384.5
47	261.9	227.7	07	307.2	267.0	67	352.4	306.4	27	397.7	345.7	87	443.0	385.1
48	262.6	228.3	08	307.9	267.7	68	353.2	307.0	28	398.5	346.4	88	443.8	385.8
49	263.4	229.0	09	308.7	268.3	69	354.0	307.7	29	399.2	347.1	89	444.5	386.4
50	264.1	229.6	10	309.4	269.0	70	354.7	308.3	30	400.0	347.7	90	445.3	387.1
351	264.9	230.3	411	310.2	269.6	471	355.5	309.0	531	400.8	348.4	591	446.0	387.7
52	265.7	230.9	12	310.9	270.3	72	356.2	309.7	32	401.5	349.0	92	446.8	388.4
53	266.4	231.6	13	311.7	271.0	73	357.0	310.3	33	402.3	349.7	93	447.5	389.0
54	267.2	232.2	14	312.4	271.6	74	357.7	311.0	34	403.0	350.3	94	448.3	389.7
55	267.9	232.9	15	313.2	272.3	75	358.5	311.6	35	403.8	351.0	95	449.1	390.4
56	268.7	233.6	16	314.0	272.9	76	359.2	312.3	36	404.5	351.6	96	449.8	391.0
57	269.4	234.2	17	314.7	273.6	77	360.0	312.9	37	405.3	352.3	97	450.6	391.7
58	270.2	234.9	18	315.5	274.2	78	360.8	313.6	38	406.0	353.0	98	451.3	392.3
59	270.9	235.5	19	316.2	274.9	79	361.5	314.3	39	406.8	353.6	99	452.1	393.0
60	271.7	236.2	20	317.0	275.5	80	362.3	314.9	40	407.5	354.3	600	452.8	393.6
Dist.	Dep.	D. Lat.	Dist.	Dep.	D. Lat.	Dist.	Dep.	D. Lat.	Dist.	Dep.	D. Lat.	Dist.	Dep.	D. Lat.

Dist.	D. Lat.	Dep.
D Lo	Dep.	
	m	D Lo

49°

311°	049°
229°	131°

TABLE 4

318° | 042°
222° | 138°

Traverse **42°** Table

318° | 042°
222° | 138°

Dist.	D. Lat.	Dep.	Dist.	D. Lat.	Dep.	Dist.	D. Lat.	Dep.	Dist.	D. Lat.	Dep.	Dist.	D. Lat.	Dep.
1	0.7	0.7	61	45.3	40.8	121	89.9	81.0	181	134.5	121.1	241	179.1	161.3
2	1.5	1.3	62	46.1	41.5	22	90.7	81.6	82	135.3	121.8	42	179.8	161.9
3	2.2	2.0	63	46.8	42.2	23	91.4	82.3	83	136.0	122.5	43	180.6	162.6
4	3.0	2.7	64	47.6	42.8	24	92.1	83.0	84	136.7	123.1	44	181.3	163.3
5	3.7	3.3	65	48.3	43.5	25	92.9	83.6	85	137.5	123.8	45	182.1	163.9
6	4.5	4.0	66	49.0	44.2	26	93.6	84.3	86	138.2	124.5	46	182.8	164.6
7	5.2	4.7	67	49.8	44.8	27	94.4	85.0	87	139.0	125.1	47	183.6	165.3
8	5.9	5.4	68	50.5	45.5	28	95.1	85.6	88	139.7	125.8	48	184.3	165.9
9	6.7	6.0	69	51.3	46.2	29	95.9	86.3	89	140.5	126.5	49	185.0	166.6
10	7.4	6.7	70	52.0	46.8	30	96.6	87.0	90	141.2	127.1	50	185.8	167.3
11	8.2	7.4	71	52.8	47.5	131	97.4	87.7	191	141.9	127.8	251	186.5	168.0
12	8.9	8.0	72	53.5	48.2	32	98.1	88.3	92	142.7	128.5	52	187.3	168.6
13	9.7	8.7	73	54.2	48.8	33	98.8	89.0	93	143.4	129.1	53	188.0	169.3
14	10.4	9.4	74	55.0	49.5	34	99.6	89.7	94	144.2	129.8	54	188.8	170.0
15	11.1	10.0	75	55.7	50.2	35	100.3	90.3	95	144.9	130.5	55	189.5	170.6
16	11.9	10.7	76	56.5	50.9	36	101.1	91.0	96	145.7	131.1	56	190.2	171.3
17	12.6	11.4	77	57.2	51.5	37	101.8	91.7	97	146.4	131.8	57	191.0	172.0
18	13.4	12.0	78	58.0	52.2	38	102.6	92.3	98	147.1	132.5	58	191.7	172.6
19	14.1	12.7	79	58.7	52.9	39	103.3	93.0	99	147.9	133.2	59	192.5	173.3
20	14.9	13.4	80	59.5	53.5	40	104.0	93.7	200	148.6	133.8	60	193.2	174.0
21	15.6	14.1	81	60.2	54.2	141	104.8	94.3	201	149.4	134.5	261	194.0	174.6
22	16.3	14.7	82	60.9	54.9	42	105.5	95.0	02	150.1	135.2	62	194.7	175.3
23	17.1	15.4	83	61.7	55.5	43	106.3	95.7	03	150.9	135.8	63	195.4	176.0
24	17.8	16.1	84	62.4	56.2	44	107.0	96.4	04	151.6	136.5	64	196.2	176.7
25	18.6	16.7	85	63.2	56.9	45	107.8	97.0	05	152.3	137.2	65	196.9	177.3
26	19.3	17.4	86	63.9	57.5	46	108.5	97.7	06	153.1	137.8	66	197.7	178.0
27	20.1	18.1	87	64.7	58.2	47	109.2	98.4	07	153.8	138.5	67	198.4	178.7
28	20.8	18.7	88	65.4	58.9	48	110.0	99.0	08	154.6	139.2	68	199.2	179.3
29	21.6	19.4	89	66.1	59.6	49	110.7	99.7	09	155.3	139.8	69	199.9	180.0
30	22.3	20.1	90	66.9	60.2	50	111.5	100.4	10	156.1	140.5	70	200.6	180.7
31	23.0	20.7	91	67.6	60.9	151	112.2	101.0	211	156.8	141.2	271	201.4	181.3
32	23.8	21.4	92	68.4	61.6	52	113.0	101.7	12	157.5	141.9	72	202.1	182.0
33	24.5	22.1	93	69.1	62.2	53	113.7	102.4	13	158.3	142.5	73	202.9	182.7
34	25.3	22.8	94	69.9	62.9	54	114.4	103.0	14	159.0	143.2	74	203.6	183.3
35	26.0	23.4	95	70.6	63.6	55	115.2	103.7	15	159.8	143.9	75	204.4	184.0
36	26.8	24.1	96	71.3	64.2	56	115.9	104.4	16	160.5	144.5	76	205.1	184.7
37	27.5	24.8	97	72.1	64.9	57	116.7	105.1	17	161.3	145.2	77	205.9	185.3
38	28.2	25.4	98	72.8	65.6	58	117.4	105.7	18	162.0	145.9	78	206.6	186.0
39	29.0	26.1	99	73.6	66.2	59	118.2	106.4	19	162.7	146.5	79	207.3	186.7
40	29.7	26.8	100	74.3	66.9	60	118.9	107.1	20	163.5	147.2	80	208.1	187.4
41	30.5	27.4	101	75.1	67.6	161	119.6	107.7	221	164.2	147.9	281	208.8	188.0
42	31.2	28.1	02	75.8	68.3	62	120.4	108.4	22	165.0	148.5	82	209.6	188.7
43	32.0	28.8	03	76.5	68.9	63	121.1	109.1	23	165.7	149.2	83	210.3	189.4
44	32.7	29.4	04	77.3	69.6	64	121.9	109.7	24	166.5	149.9	84	211.1	190.0
45	33.4	30.1	05	78.0	70.3	65	122.6	110.4	25	167.2	150.6	85	211.8	190.7
46	34.2	30.8	06	78.8	70.9	66	123.4	111.1	26	168.0	151.2	86	212.5	191.4
47	34.9	31.4	07	79.5	71.6	67	124.1	111.7	27	168.7	151.9	87	213.3	192.0
48	35.7	32.1	08	80.3	72.3	68	124.8	112.4	28	169.4	152.6	88	214.0	192.7
49	36.4	32.8	09	81.0	72.9	69	125.6	113.1	29	170.2	153.2	89	214.8	193.4
50	37.2	33.5	10	81.7	73.6	70	126.3	113.8	30	170.9	153.9	90	215.5	194.0
51	37.9	34.1	111	82.5	74.3	171	127.1	114.4	231	171.7	154.6	291	216.3	194.7
52	38.6	34.8	12	83.2	74.9	72	127.8	115.1	32	172.4	155.2	92	217.0	195.4
53	39.4	35.5	13	84.0	75.6	73	128.6	115.8	33	173.2	155.9	93	217.7	196.1
54	40.1	36.1	14	84.7	76.3	74	129.3	116.4	34	173.9	156.6	94	218.5	196.7
55	40.9	36.8	15	85.5	77.0	75	130.1	117.1	35	174.6	157.2	95	219.2	197.4
56	41.6	37.5	16	86.2	77.6	76	130.8	117.8	36	175.4	157.9	96	220.0	198.1
57	42.4	38.1	17	86.9	78.3	77	131.5	118.4	37	176.1	158.6	97	220.7	198.7
58	43.1	38.8	18	87.7	79.0	78	132.3	119.1	38	176.9	159.3	98	221.5	199.4
59	43.8	39.5	19	88.4	79.6	79	133.0	119.8	39	177.6	159.9	99	222.2	200.1
60	44.6	40.1	20	89.2	80.3	80	133.8	120.4	40	178.4	160.6	300	222.9	200.7
Dist.	Dep.	D. Lat.	Dist.	Dep.	D. Lat.	Dist.	Dep.	D. Lat.	Dist.	Dep.	D. Lat.	Dist.	Dep.	D. Lat.

312° | 048°
228° | 132°

48°

Dist.	D. Lat.	Dep.
N.	N x Cos.	N x Sin.
Hypotenuse	Side Adj.	Side Opp.

TABLE 4

318° | 042°
222° | 138°

Traverse **42°** Table

318° | 042°
222° | 138°

Dist.	D. Lat.	Dep.	Dist.	D. Lat.	Dep.	Dist.	D. Lat.	Dep.	Dist.	D. Lat.	Dep.	Dist.	D. Lat.	Dep.
301	223.7	201.4	361	268.3	241.6	421	312.9	281.7	481	357.5	321.9	541	402.0	362.0
02	224.4	202.1	62	269.0	242.2	22	313.6	282.4	82	358.2	322.5	42	402.8	362.7
03	225.2	202.7	63	269.8	242.9	23	314.4	283.0	83	358.9	323.2	43	403.5	363.3
04	225.9	203.4	64	270.5	243.6	24	315.1	283.7	84	359.7	323.9	44	404.3	364.0
05	226.7	204.1	65	271.2	244.2	25	315.8	284.4	85	360.4	324.5	45	405.0	364.7
06	227.4	204.8	66	272.0	244.9	26	316.6	285.0	86	361.2	325.2	46	405.8	365.3
07	228.1	205.4	67	272.7	245.6	27	317.3	285.7	87	361.9	325.9	47	406.5	366.0
08	228.9	206.1	68	273.5	246.2	28	318.1	286.4	88	362.7	326.5	48	407.2	366.7
09	229.6	206.8	69	274.2	246.9	29	318.8	287.1	89	363.4	327.2	49	408.0	367.4
10	230.4	207.4	70	275.0	247.6	30	319.6	287.7	90	364.1	327.9	50	408.7	368.0
311	231.1	208.1	371	275.7	248.2	431	320.3	288.4	491	364.9	328.5	551	409.5	368.7
12	231.9	208.8	72	276.4	248.9	32	321.0	289.1	92	365.6	329.2	52	410.2	369.4
13	232.6	209.4	73	277.2	249.6	33	321.8	289.7	93	366.4	329.9	53	411.0	370.0
14	233.3	210.1	74	277.9	250.3	34	322.5	290.4	94	367.1	330.6	54	411.7	370.7
15	234.1	210.8	75	278.7	250.9	35	323.3	291.1	95	367.9	331.2	55	412.4	371.4
16	234.8	211.4	76	279.4	251.6	36	324.0	291.7	96	368.6	331.9	56	413.2	372.0
17	235.6	212.1	77	280.2	252.3	37	324.8	292.4	97	369.3	332.6	57	413.9	372.7
18	236.3	212.8	78	280.9	252.9	38	325.5	293.1	98	370.1	333.2	58	414.7	373.4
19	237.1	213.5	79	281.7	253.6	39	326.2	293.7	99	370.8	333.9	59	415.4	374.0
20	237.8	214.1	80	282.4	254.3	40	327.0	294.4	500	371.6	334.6	60	416.2	374.7
321	238.5	214.8	381	283.1	254.9	441	327.7	295.1	501	372.3	335.2	561	416.9	375.4
22	239.3	215.5	82	283.9	255.6	42	328.5	295.8	02	373.1	335.9	62	417.6	376.1
23	240.0	216.1	83	284.6	256.3	43	329.2	296.4	03	373.8	336.6	63	418.4	376.7
24	240.8	216.8	84	285.4	256.9	44	330.0	297.1	04	374.5	337.2	64	419.1	377.4
25	241.5	217.5	85	286.1	257.6	45	330.7	297.8	05	375.3	337.9	65	419.9	378.1
26	242.3	218.1	86	286.9	258.3	46	331.4	298.4	06	376.0	338.6	66	420.6	378.7
27	243.0	218.8	87	287.6	259.0	47	332.2	299.1	07	376.8	339.2	67	421.4	379.4
28	243.8	219.5	88	288.3	259.6	48	332.9	299.8	08	377.5	339.9	68	422.1	380.1
29	244.5	220.1	89	289.1	260.3	49	333.7	300.4	09	378.3	340.6	69	422.8	380.7
30	245.2	220.8	90	289.8	261.0	50	334.4	301.1	10	379.0	341.3	70	423.6	381.4
331	246.0	221.5	391	290.6	261.6	451	335.2	301.8	511	379.7	341.9	571	424.3	382.1
32	246.7	222.2	92	291.3	262.3	52	335.9	302.4	12	380.5	342.6	72	425.1	382.7
33	247.5	222.8	93	292.1	263.0	53	336.6	303.1	13	381.2	343.3	73	425.8	383.4
34	248.2	223.5	94	292.8	263.6	54	337.4	303.8	14	382.0	343.9	74	426.6	384.1
35	249.0	224.2	95	293.5	264.3	55	338.1	304.5	15	382.7	344.6	75	427.3	384.8
36	249.7	224.8	96	294.3	265.0	56	338.9	305.1	16	383.5	345.3	76	428.1	385.4
37	250.4	225.5	97	295.0	265.6	57	339.6	305.8	17	384.2	345.9	77	428.8	386.1
38	251.2	226.2	98	295.8	266.3	58	340.4	306.5	18	384.9	346.6	78	429.5	386.8
39	251.9	226.8	99	296.5	267.0	59	341.1	307.1	19	385.7	347.3	79	430.3	387.4
40	252.7	227.5	400	297.3	267.7	60	341.8	307.8	20	386.4	347.9	80	431.0	388.1
341	253.4	228.2	401	298.0	268.3	461	342.6	308.5	521	387.2	348.6	581	431.8	388.8
42	254.2	228.8	02	298.7	269.0	62	343.3	309.1	22	387.9	349.3	82	432.5	389.4
43	254.9	229.5	03	299.5	269.7	63	344.1	309.8	23	388.7	350.0	83	433.3	390.1
44	255.6	230.2	04	300.2	270.3	64	344.8	310.5	24	389.4	350.6	84	434.0	390.8
45	256.4	230.9	05	301.0	271.0	65	345.6	311.1	25	390.2	351.3	85	434.7	391.4
46	257.1	231.5	06	301.7	271.7	66	346.3	311.8	26	390.9	352.0	86	435.5	392.1
47	257.9	232.2	07	302.5	272.3	67	347.0	312.5	27	391.6	352.6	87	436.2	392.8
48	258.6	232.9	08	303.2	273.0	68	347.8	313.2	28	392.4	353.3	88	437.0	393.4
49	259.4	233.5	09	303.9	273.7	69	348.5	313.8	29	393.1	354.0	89	437.7	394.1
50	260.1	234.2	10	304.7	274.3	70	349.3	314.5	30	393.9	354.6	90	438.5	394.8
351	260.8	234.9	411	305.4	275.0	471	350.0	315.2	531	394.6	355.3	591	439.2	395.5
52	261.6	235.5	12	306.2	275.7	72	350.8	315.8	32	395.4	356.0	92	439.9	396.1
53	262.3	236.2	13	306.9	276.4	73	351.5	316.5	33	396.1	356.6	93	440.7	396.8
54	263.1	236.9	14	307.7	277.0	74	352.3	317.2	34	396.8	357.3	94	441.4	397.5
55	263.8	237.5	15	308.4	277.7	75	353.0	317.8	35	397.6	358.0	95	442.2	398.1
56	264.6	238.2	16	309.1	278.4	76	353.7	318.5	36	398.3	358.7	96	442.9	398.8
57	265.3	238.9	17	309.9	279.0	77	354.5	319.2	37	399.1	359.3	97	443.7	399.5
58	266.0	239.5	18	310.6	279.7	78	355.2	319.8	38	399.8	360.0	98	444.4	400.1
59	266.8	240.2	19	311.4	280.4	79	356.0	320.5	39	400.6	360.7	99	445.1	400.8
60	267.5	240.9	20	312.1	281.0	80	356.7	321.2	40	401.3	361.3	600	445.9	401.5
Dist.	Dep.	D. Lat.	Dist.	Dep.	D. Lat.	Dist.	Dep.	D. Lat.	Dist.	Dep.	D. Lat.	Dist.	Dep.	D. Lat.

Dist.	D. Lat.	Dep.
D Lo	Dep.	
	m	D Lo

48°

312° | 048°
228° | 132°

TABLE 4

317° | 043°
223° | 137°

Traverse **43°** Table

Dist.	D. Lat.	Dep.	Dist.	D. Lat.	Dep.	Dist.	D. Lat.	Dep.	Dist.	D. Lat.	Dep.	Dist.	D. Lat.	Dep.
1	0.7	0.7	61	44.6	41.6	121	88.5	82.5	181	132.4	123.4	241	176.3	164.4
2	1.5	1.4	62	45.3	42.3	22	89.2	83.2	82	133.1	124.1	42	177.0	165.0
3	2.2	2.0	63	46.1	43.0	23	90.0	83.9	83	133.8	124.8	43	177.7	165.7
4	2.9	2.7	64	46.8	43.6	24	90.7	84.6	84	134.6	125.5	44	178.5	166.4
5	3.7	3.4	65	47.5	44.3	25	91.4	85.2	85	135.3	126.2	45	179.2	167.1
6	4.4	4.1	66	48.3	45.0	26	92.2	85.9	86	136.0	126.9	46	179.9	167.8
7	5.1	4.8	67	49.0	45.7	27	92.9	86.6	87	136.8	127.5	47	180.6	168.5
8	5.9	5.5	68	49.7	46.4	28	93.6	87.3	88	137.5	128.2	48	181.4	169.1
9	6.6	6.1	69	50.5	47.1	29	94.3	88.0	89	138.2	128.9	49	182.1	169.8
10	7.3	6.8	70	51.2	47.7	30	95.1	88.7	90	139.0	129.6	50	182.8	170.5
11	8.0	7.5	71	51.9	48.4	131	95.8	89.3	191	139.7	130.3	251	183.6	171.2
12	8.8	8.2	72	52.7	49.1	32	96.5	90.0	92	140.4	130.9	52	184.3	171.9
13	9.5	8.9	73	53.4	49.8	33	97.3	90.7	93	141.2	131.6	53	185.0	172.5
14	10.2	9.5	74	54.1	50.5	34	98.0	91.4	94	141.9	132.3	54	185.8	173.2
15	11.0	10.2	75	54.9	51.1	35	98.7	92.1	95	142.6	133.0	55	186.5	173.9
16	11.7	10.9	76	55.6	51.8	36	99.5	92.8	96	143.3	133.7	56	187.2	174.6
17	12.4	11.6	77	56.3	52.5	37	100.2	93.4	97	144.1	134.4	57	188.0	175.3
18	13.2	12.3	78	57.0	53.2	38	100.9	94.1	98	144.8	135.0	58	188.7	176.0
19	13.9	13.0	79	57.8	53.9	39	101.7	94.8	99	145.5	135.7	59	189.4	176.6
20	14.6	13.6	80	58.5	54.6	40	102.4	95.5	200	146.3	136.4	60	190.2	177.3
21	15.4	14.3	81	59.2	55.2	141	103.1	96.2	201	147.0	137.1	261	190.9	178.0
22	16.1	15.0	82	60.0	55.9	42	103.9	96.8	02	147.7	137.8	62	191.6	178.7
23	16.8	15.7	83	60.7	56.6	43	104.6	97.5	03	148.5	138.4	63	192.3	179.4
24	17.6	16.4	84	61.4	57.3	44	105.3	98.2	04	149.2	139.1	64	193.1	180.0
25	18.3	17.0	85	62.2	58.0	45	106.0	98.9	05	149.9	139.8	65	193.8	180.7
26	19.0	17.7	86	62.9	58.7	46	106.8	99.6	06	150.7	140.5	66	194.5	181.4
27	19.7	18.4	87	63.6	59.3	47	107.5	100.3	07	151.4	141.2	67	195.3	182.1
28	20.5	19.1	88	64.4	60.0	48	108.2	100.9	08	152.1	141.9	68	196.0	182.8
29	21.2	19.8	89	65.1	60.7	49	109.0	101.6	09	152.9	142.5	69	196.7	183.5
30	21.9	20.5	90	65.8	61.4	50	109.7	102.3	10	153.6	143.2	70	197.5	184.1
31	22.7	21.1	91	66.6	62.1	151	110.4	103.0	211	154.3	143.9	271	198.2	184.8
32	23.4	21.8	92	67.3	62.7	52	111.2	103.7	12	155.0	144.6	72	198.9	185.5
33	24.1	22.5	93	68.0	63.4	53	111.9	104.3	13	155.8	145.3	73	199.7	186.2
34	24.9	23.2	94	68.7	64.1	54	112.6	105.0	14	156.5	145.9	74	200.4	186.9
35	25.6	23.9	95	69.5	64.8	55	113.4	105.7	15	157.2	146.6	75	201.1	187.5
36	26.3	24.6	96	70.2	65.5	56	114.1	106.4	16	158.0	147.3	76	201.9	188.2
37	27.1	25.2	97	70.9	66.2	57	114.8	107.1	17	158.7	148.0	77	202.6	188.9
38	27.8	25.9	98	71.7	66.8	58	115.6	107.8	18	159.4	148.7	78	203.3	189.6
39	28.5	26.6	99	72.4	67.5	59	116.3	108.4	19	160.2	149.4	79	204.0	190.3
40	29.3	27.3	100	73.1	68.2	60	117.0	109.1	20	160.9	150.0	80	204.8	191.0
41	30.0	28.0	101	73.9	68.9	161	117.7	109.8	221	161.6	150.7	281	205.5	191.6
42	30.7	28.6	02	74.6	69.6	62	118.5	110.5	22	162.4	151.4	82	206.2	192.3
43	31.4	29.3	03	75.3	70.2	63	119.2	111.2	23	163.1	152.1	83	207.0	193.0
44	32.2	30.0	04	76.1	70.9	64	119.9	111.8	24	163.8	152.8	84	207.7	193.7
45	32.9	30.7	05	76.8	71.6	65	120.7	112.5	25	164.6	153.4	85	208.4	194.4
46	33.6	31.4	06	77.5	72.3	66	121.4	113.2	26	165.3	154.1	86	209.2	195.1
47	34.4	32.1	07	78.3	73.0	67	122.1	113.9	27	166.0	154.8	87	209.9	195.7
48	35.1	32.7	08	79.0	73.7	68	122.9	114.6	28	166.7	155.5	88	210.6	196.4
49	35.8	33.4	09	79.7	74.3	69	123.6	115.3	29	167.5	156.2	89	211.4	197.1
50	36.6	34.1	10	80.4	75.0	70	124.3	115.9	30	168.2	156.9	90	212.1	197.8
51	37.3	34.8	111	81.2	75.7	171	125.1	116.6	231	168.9	157.5	291	212.8	198.5
52	38.0	35.5	12	81.9	76.4	72	125.8	117.3	32	169.7	158.2	92	213.6	199.1
53	38.8	36.1	13	82.6	77.1	73	126.5	118.0	33	170.4	158.9	93	214.3	199.8
54	39.5	36.8	14	83.4	77.7	74	127.3	118.7	34	171.1	159.6	94	215.0	200.5
55	40.2	37.5	15	84.1	78.4	75	128.0	119.3	35	171.9	160.3	95	215.7	201.2
56	41.0	38.2	16	84.8	79.1	76	128.7	120.0	36	172.6	161.0	96	216.5	201.9
57	41.7	38.9	17	85.6	79.8	77	129.4	120.7	37	173.3	161.6	97	217.2	202.6
58	42.4	39.6	18	86.3	80.5	78	130.2	121.4	38	174.1	162.3	98	217.9	203.2
59	43.1	40.2	19	87.0	81.2	79	130.9	122.1	39	174.8	163.0	99	218.7	203.9
60	43.9	40.9	20	87.8	81.8	80	131.6	122.8	40	175.5	163.7	300	219.4	204.6
Dist.	Dep.	D. Lat.	Dist.	Dep.	D. Lat.	Dist.	Dep.	D. Lat.	Dist.	Dep.	D. Lat.	Dist.	Dep.	D. Lat.

313° | 047°
227° | 133°

47°

Dist.	D. Lat.	Dep.
N.	N x Cos.	N x Sin.
Hypotenuse	Side Adj.	Side Opp.

TABLE 4

317° | 043°
223° | 137°

Traverse **43°** Table

Dist.	D. Lat.	Dep.	Dist.	D. Lat.	Dep.	Dist.	D. Lat.	Dep.	Dist.	D. Lat.	Dep.	Dist.	D. Lat.	Dep.
301	220.1	205.3	361	264.0	246.2	421	307.9	287.1	481	351.8	328.0	541	395.7	369.0
02	220.9	206.0	62	264.8	246.9	22	308.6	287.8	82	352.5	328.7	42	396.4	369.6
03	221.6	206.6	63	265.5	247.6	23	309.4	288.5	83	353.2	329.4	43	397.1	370.3
04	222.3	207.3	64	266.2	248.2	24	310.1	289.2	84	354.0	330.1	44	397.9	371.0
05	223.1	208.0	65	266.9	248.9	25	310.8	289.8	85	354.7	330.8	45	398.6	371.7
06	223.8	208.7	66	267.7	249.6	26	311.6	290.5	86	355.4	331.5	46	399.3	372.4
07	224.5	209.4	67	268.4	250.3	27	312.3	291.2	87	356.2	332.1	47	400.1	373.1
08	225.3	210.1	68	269.1	251.0	28	313.0	291.9	88	356.9	332.8	48	400.8	373.7
09	226.0	210.7	69	269.9	251.7	29	313.8	292.6	89	357.6	333.5	49	401.5	374.4
10	226.7	211.4	70	270.6	252.3	30	314.5	293.3	90	358.4	334.2	50	402.2	375.1
311	227.5	212.1	371	271.3	253.0	431	315.2	293.9	491	359.1	334.9	551	403.0	375.8
12	228.2	212.8	72	272.1	253.7	32	315.9	294.6	92	359.8	335.5	52	403.7	376.5
13	228.9	213.5	73	272.8	254.4	33	316.7	295.3	93	360.6	336.2	53	404.4	377.1
14	229.6	214.1	74	273.5	255.1	34	317.4	296.0	94	361.3	336.9	54	405.2	377.8
15	230.4	214.8	75	274.3	255.7	35	318.1	296.7	95	362.0	337.6	55	405.9	378.5
16	231.1	215.5	76	275.0	256.4	36	318.9	297.4	96	362.8	338.3	56	406.6	379.2
17	231.8	216.2	77	275.7	257.1	37	319.6	298.0	97	363.5	339.0	57	407.4	379.9
18	232.6	216.9	78	276.5	257.8	38	320.3	298.7	98	364.2	339.6	58	408.1	380.6
19	233.3	217.6	79	277.2	258.5	39	321.1	299.4	99	364.9	340.3	59	408.8	381.2
20	234.0	218.2	80	277.9	259.2	40	321.8	300.1	500	365.7	341.0	60	409.6	381.9
321	234.8	218.9	381	278.6	259.8	441	322.5	300.8	501	366.4	341.7	561	410.3	382.6
22	235.5	219.6	82	279.4	260.5	42	323.3	301.4	02	367.1	342.4	62	411.0	383.3
23	236.2	220.3	83	280.1	261.2	43	324.0	302.1	03	367.9	343.0	63	411.8	384.0
24	237.0	221.0	84	280.8	261.9	44	324.7	302.8	04	368.6	343.7	64	412.5	384.6
25	237.7	221.6	85	281.6	262.6	45	325.5	303.5	05	369.3	344.4	65	413.2	385.3
26	238.4	222.3	86	282.3	263.3	46	326.2	304.2	06	370.1	345.1	66	413.9	386.0
27	239.2	223.0	87	283.0	263.9	47	326.9	304.9	07	370.8	345.8	67	414.7	386.7
28	239.9	223.7	88	283.8	264.6	48	327.6	305.5	08	371.5	346.5	68	415.4	387.4
29	240.6	224.4	89	284.5	265.3	49	328.4	306.2	09	372.3	347.1	69	416.1	388.1
30	241.3	225.1	90	285.2	266.0	50	329.1	306.9	10	373.0	347.8	70	416.9	388.7
331	242.1	225.7	391	286.0	266.7	451	329.8	307.6	511	373.7	348.5	571	417.6	389.4
32	242.8	226.4	92	286.7	267.3	52	330.6	308.3	12	374.5	349.2	72	418.3	390.1
33	243.5	227.1	93	287.4	268.0	53	331.3	308.9	13	375.2	349.9	73	419.1	390.8
34	244.3	227.8	94	288.2	268.7	54	332.0	309.6	14	375.9	350.5	74	419.8	391.5
35	245.0	228.5	95	288.9	269.4	55	332.8	310.3	15	376.6	351.2	75	420.5	392.1
36	245.7	229.2	96	289.6	270.1	56	333.5	311.0	16	377.4	351.9	76	421.3	392.8
37	246.5	229.8	97	290.3	270.8	57	334.2	311.7	17	378.1	352.6	77	422.0	393.5
38	247.2	230.5	98	291.1	271.4	58	335.0	312.4	18	378.8	353.3	78	422.7	394.2
39	247.9	231.2	99	291.8	272.1	59	335.7	313.0	19	379.6	354.0	79	423.5	394.9
40	248.7	231.9	400	292.5	272.8	60	336.4	313.7	20	380.3	354.6	80	424.2	395.6
341	249.4	232.6	401	293.3	273.5	461	337.2	314.4	521	381.0	355.3	581	424.9	396.2
42	250.1	233.2	02	294.0	274.2	62	337.9	315.1	22	381.8	356.0	82	425.6	396.9
43	250.9	233.9	03	294.7	274.8	63	338.6	315.8	23	382.5	356.7	83	426.4	397.6
44	251.6	234.6	04	295.5	275.5	64	339.3	316.4	24	383.2	357.4	84	427.1	398.3
45	252.3	235.3	05	296.2	276.2	65	340.1	317.1	25	384.0	358.0	85	427.8	399.0
46	253.0	236.0	06	296.9	276.9	66	340.8	317.8	26	384.7	358.7	86	428.6	399.7
47	253.8	236.7	07	297.7	277.6	67	341.5	318.5	27	385.4	359.4	87	429.3	400.3
48	254.5	237.3	08	298.4	278.3	68	342.3	319.2	28	386.2	360.1	88	430.0	401.0
49	255.2	238.0	09	299.1	278.9	69	343.0	319.9	29	386.9	360.8	89	430.8	401.7
50	256.0	238.7	10	299.9	279.6	70	343.7	320.5	30	387.6	361.5	90	431.5	402.4
351	256.7	239.4	411	300.6	280.3	471	344.5	321.2	531	388.3	362.1	591	432.2	403.1
52	257.4	240.1	12	301.3	281.0	72	345.2	321.9	32	389.1	362.8	92	433.0	403.7
53	258.2	240.7	13	302.0	281.7	73	345.9	322.6	33	389.8	363.5	93	433.7	404.4
54	258.9	241.4	14	302.8	282.3	74	346.7	323.3	34	390.5	364.2	94	434.4	405.1
55	259.6	242.1	15	303.5	283.0	75	347.4	323.9	35	391.3	364.9	95	435.2	405.8
56	260.4	242.8	16	304.2	283.7	76	348.1	324.6	36	392.0	365.6	96	435.9	406.5
57	261.1	243.5	17	305.0	284.4	77	348.9	325.3	37	392.7	366.2	97	436.6	407.2
58	261.8	244.2	18	305.7	285.1	78	349.6	326.0	38	393.5	366.9	98	437.3	407.8
59	262.6	244.8	19	306.4	285.8	79	350.3	326.7	39	394.2	367.6	99	438.1	408.5
60	263.3	245.5	20	307.2	286.4	80	351.0	327.4	40	394.9	368.3	600	438.8	409.2
Dist.	Dep.	D. Lat.	Dist.	Dep.	D. Lat.	Dist.	Dep.	D. Lat.	Dist.	Dep.	D. Lat.	Dist.	Dep.	D. Lat.

Dist.	D. Lat.	Dep.
D Lo	Dep.	
	m	D Lo

47°

313° | 047°
227° | 133°

TABLE 4

Traverse 44° Table

316° | 044° / 224° | 136°

Dist.	D. Lat.	Dep.	Dist.	D. Lat.	Dep.	Dist.	D. Lat.	Dep.	Dist.	D. Lat.	Dep.	Dist.	D. Lat.	Dep.
1	0.7	0.7	61	43.9	42.4	121	87.0	84.1	181	130.2	125.7	241	173.4	167.4
2	1.4	1.4	62	44.6	43.1	22	87.8	84.7	82	130.9	126.4	42	174.1	168.1
3	2.2	2.1	63	45.3	43.8	23	88.5	85.4	83	131.6	127.1	43	174.8	168.8
4	2.9	2.8	64	46.0	44.5	24	89.2	86.1	84	132.4	127.8	44	175.5	169.5
5	3.6	3.5	65	46.8	45.2	25	89.9	86.8	85	133.1	128.5	45	176.2	170.2
6	4.3	4.2	66	47.5	45.8	26	90.6	87.5	86	133.8	129.2	46	177.0	170.9
7	5.0	4.9	67	48.2	46.5	27	91.4	88.2	87	134.5	129.9	47	177.7	171.6
8	5.8	5.6	68	48.9	47.2	28	92.1	88.9	88	135.2	130.6	48	178.4	172.3
9	6.5	6.3	69	49.6	47.9	29	92.8	89.6	89	136.0	131.3	49	179.1	173.0
10	7.2	6.9	70	50.4	48.6	30	93.5	90.3	90	136.7	132.0	50	179.8	173.7
11	7.9	7.6	71	51.1	49.3	131	94.2	91.0	191	137.4	132.7	251	180.6	174.4
12	8.6	8.3	72	51.8	50.0	32	95.0	91.7	92	138.1	133.4	52	181.3	175.1
13	9.4	9.0	73	52.5	50.7	33	95.7	92.4	93	138.8	134.1	53	182.0	175.7
14	10.1	9.7	74	53.2	51.4	34	96.4	93.1	94	139.6	134.8	54	182.7	176.4
15	10.8	10.4	75	54.0	52.1	35	97.1	93.8	95	140.3	135.5	55	183.4	177.1
16	11.5	11.1	76	54.7	52.8	36	97.8	94.5	96	141.0	136.2	56	184.2	177.8
17	12.2	11.8	77	55.4	53.5	37	98.5	95.2	97	141.7	136.8	57	184.9	178.5
18	12.9	12.5	78	56.1	54.2	38	99.3	95.9	98	142.4	137.5	58	185.6	179.2
19	13.7	13.2	79	56.8	54.9	39	100.0	96.6	99	143.1	138.2	59	186.3	179.9
20	14.4	13.9	80	57.5	55.6	40	100.7	97.3	200	143.9	138.9	60	187.0	180.6
21	15.1	14.6	81	58.3	56.3	141	101.4	97.9	201	144.6	139.6	261	187.7	181.3
22	15.8	15.3	82	59.0	57.0	42	102.1	98.6	02	145.3	140.3	62	188.5	182.0
23	16.5	16.0	83	59.7	57.7	43	102.9	99.3	03	146.0	141.0	63	189.2	182.7
24	17.3	16.7	84	60.4	58.4	44	103.6	100.0	04	146.7	141.7	64	189.9	183.4
25	18.0	17.4	85	61.1	59.0	45	104.3	100.7	05	147.5	142.4	65	190.6	184.1
26	18.7	18.1	86	61.9	59.7	46	105.0	101.4	06	148.2	143.1	66	191.3	184.8
27	19.4	18.8	87	62.6	60.4	47	105.7	102.1	07	148.9	143.8	67	192.1	185.5
28	20.1	19.5	88	63.3	61.1	48	106.5	102.8	08	149.6	144.5	68	192.8	186.2
29	20.9	20.1	89	64.0	61.8	49	107.2	103.5	09	150.3	145.2	69	193.5	186.9
30	21.6	20.8	90	64.7	62.5	50	107.9	104.2	10	151.1	145.9	70	194.2	187.6
31	22.3	21.5	91	65.5	63.2	151	108.6	104.9	211	151.8	146.6	271	194.9	188.3
32	23.0	22.2	92	66.2	63.9	52	109.3	105.6	12	152.5	147.3	72	195.7	188.9
33	23.7	22.9	93	66.9	64.6	53	110.1	106.3	13	153.2	148.0	73	196.4	189.6
34	24.5	23.6	94	67.6	65.3	54	110.8	107.0	14	153.9	148.7	74	197.1	190.3
35	25.2	24.3	95	68.3	66.0	55	111.5	107.7	15	154.7	149.4	75	197.8	191.0
36	25.9	25.0	96	69.1	66.7	56	112.2	108.4	16	155.4	150.0	76	198.5	191.7
37	26.6	25.7	97	69.8	67.4	57	112.9	109.1	17	156.1	150.7	77	199.3	192.4
38	27.3	26.4	98	70.5	68.1	58	113.7	109.8	18	156.8	151.4	78	200.0	193.1
39	28.1	27.1	99	71.2	68.8	59	114.4	110.5	19	157.5	152.1	79	200.7	193.8
40	28.8	27.8	100	71.9	69.5	60	115.1	111.1	20	158.3	152.8	80	201.4	194.5
41	29.5	28.5	101	72.7	70.2	161	115.8	111.8	221	159.0	153.5	281	202.1	195.2
42	30.2	29.2	02	73.4	70.9	62	116.5	112.5	22	159.7	154.2	82	202.9	195.9
43	30.9	29.9	03	74.1	71.5	63	117.3	113.2	23	160.4	154.9	83	203.6	196.6
44	31.7	30.6	04	74.8	72.2	64	118.0	113.9	24	161.1	155.6	84	204.3	197.3
45	32.4	31.3	05	75.5	72.9	65	118.7	114.6	25	161.9	156.3	85	205.0	198.0
46	33.1	32.0	06	76.3	73.6	66	119.4	115.3	26	162.6	157.0	86	205.7	198.7
47	33.8	32.6	07	77.0	74.3	67	120.1	116.0	27	163.3	157.7	87	206.5	199.4
48	34.5	33.3	08	77.7	75.0	68	120.8	116.7	28	164.0	158.4	88	207.2	200.1
49	35.2	34.0	09	78.4	75.7	69	121.6	117.4	29	164.7	159.1	89	207.9	200.8
50	36.0	34.7	10	79.1	76.4	70	122.3	118.1	30	165.4	159.8	90	208.6	201.5
51	36.7	35.4	111	79.8	77.1	171	123.0	118.8	231	166.2	160.5	291	209.3	202.1
52	37.4	36.1	12	80.6	77.8	72	123.7	119.5	32	166.9	161.2	92	210.0	202.8
53	38.1	36.8	13	81.3	78.5	73	124.4	120.2	33	167.6	161.9	93	210.8	203.5
54	38.8	37.5	14	82.0	79.2	74	125.2	120.9	34	168.3	162.6	94	211.5	204.2
55	39.6	38.2	15	82.7	79.9	75	125.9	121.6	35	169.0	163.2	95	212.2	204.9
56	40.3	38.9	16	83.4	80.6	76	126.6	122.3	36	169.8	163.9	96	212.9	205.6
57	41.0	39.6	17	84.2	81.3	77	127.3	123.0	37	170.5	164.6	97	213.6	206.3
58	41.7	40.3	18	84.9	82.0	78	128.0	123.6	38	171.2	165.3	98	214.4	207.0
59	42.4	41.0	19	85.6	82.7	79	128.8	124.3	39	171.9	166.0	99	215.1	207.7
60	43.2	41.7	20	86.3	83.4	80	129.5	125.0	40	172.6	166.7	300	215.8	208.4
Dist.	Dep.	D. Lat.	Dist.	Dep.	D. Lat.	Dist.	Dep.	D. Lat.	Dist.	Dep.	D. Lat.	Dist.	Dep.	D. Lat.

314° | 046° / 226° | 134°

46°

Dist.	D. Lat.	Dep.
N.	N x Cos.	N x Sin.
Hypotenuse	Side Adj.	Side Opp.

TABLE 4

Traverse 44° Table

316° | 044° / 224° | 136°

Dist.	D. Lat.	Dep.	Dist.	D. Lat.	Dep.	Dist.	D. Lat.	Dep.	Dist.	D. Lat.	Dep.	Dist.	D. Lat.	Dep.
301	216.5	209.1	361	259.7	250.8	421	302.8	292.5	481	346.0	334.1	541	389.2	375.8
02	217.2	209.8	62	260.4	251.5	22	303.6	293.1	82	346.7	334.8	42	389.9	376.5
03	218.0	210.5	63	261.1	252.2	23	304.3	293.8	83	347.4	335.5	43	390.6	377.2
04	218.7	211.2	64	261.8	252.9	24	305.0	294.5	84	348.2	336.2	44	391.3	377.9
05	219.4	211.9	65	262.6	253.6	25	305.7	295.2	85	348.9	336.9	45	392.0	378.6
06	220.1	212.6	66	263.3	254.2	26	306.4	295.9	86	349.6	337.6	46	392.8	379.3
07	220.8	213.3	67	264.0	254.9	27	307.2	296.6	87	350.3	338.3	47	393.5	380.0
08	221.6	214.0	68	264.7	255.6	28	307.9	297.3	88	351.0	339.0	48	394.2	380.7
09	222.3	214.6	69	265.4	256.3	29	308.6	298.0	89	351.8	339.7	49	394.9	381.4
10	223.0	215.3	70	266.2	257.0	30	309.3	298.7	90	352.5	340.4	50	395.6	382.1
311	223.7	216.0	371	266.9	257.7	431	310.0	299.4	491	353.2	341.1	551	396.4	382.8
12	224.4	216.7	72	267.6	258.4	32	310.8	300.1	92	353.9	341.8	52	397.1	383.5
13	225.2	217.4	73	268.3	259.1	33	311.5	300.8	93	354.6	342.5	53	397.8	384.1
14	225.9	218.1	74	269.0	259.8	34	312.2	301.5	94	355.4	343.2	54	398.5	384.8
15	226.6	218.8	75	269.8	260.5	35	312.9	302.2	95	356.1	343.9	55	399.2	385.5
16	227.3	219.5	76	270.5	261.2	36	313.6	302.9	96	356.8	344.6	56	400.0	386.2
17	228.0	220.2	77	271.2	261.9	37	314.4	303.6	97	357.5	345.2	57	400.7	386.9
18	228.8	220.9	78	271.9	262.6	38	315.1	304.3	98	358.2	345.9	58	401.4	387.6
19	229.5	221.6	79	272.6	263.3	39	315.8	305.0	99	359.0	346.6	59	402.1	388.3
20	230.2	222.3	80	273.3	264.0	40	316.5	305.6	500	359.7	347.3	60	402.8	389.0
321	230.9	223.0	381	274.1	264.7	441	317.2	306.3	501	360.4	348.0	561	403.5	389.7
22	231.6	223.7	82	274.8	265.4	42	317.9	307.0	02	361.1	348.7	62	404.3	390.4
23	232.3	224.4	83	275.5	266.1	43	318.7	307.7	03	361.8	349.4	63	405.0	391.1
24	233.1	225.1	84	276.2	266.7	44	319.4	308.4	04	362.5	350.1	64	405.7	391.8
25	233.8	225.8	85	276.9	267.4	45	320.1	309.1	05	363.3	350.8	65	406.4	392.5
26	234.5	226.5	86	277.7	268.1	46	320.8	309.8	06	364.0	351.5	66	407.1	393.2
27	235.2	227.2	87	278.4	268.8	47	321.5	310.5	07	364.7	352.2	67	407.9	393.9
28	235.9	227.8	88	279.1	269.5	48	322.3	311.2	08	365.4	352.9	68	408.6	394.6
29	236.7	228.5	89	279.8	270.2	49	323.0	311.9	09	366.1	353.6	69	409.3	395.3
30	237.4	229.2	90	280.5	270.9	50	323.7	312.6	10	366.9	354.3	70	410.0	396.0
331	238.1	229.9	391	281.3	271.6	451	324.4	313.3	511	367.6	355.0	571	410.7	396.6
32	238.8	230.6	92	282.0	272.3	52	325.1	314.0	12	368.3	355.7	72	411.5	397.3
33	239.5	231.3	93	282.7	273.0	53	325.9	314.7	13	369.0	356.4	73	412.2	398.0
34	240.3	232.0	94	283.4	273.7	54	326.6	315.4	14	369.7	357.1	74	412.9	398.7
35	241.0	232.7	95	284.1	274.4	55	327.3	316.1	15	370.5	357.7	75	413.6	399.4
36	241.7	233.4	96	284.9	275.1	56	328.0	316.8	16	371.2	358.4	76	414.3	400.1
37	242.4	234.1	97	285.6	275.8	57	328.7	317.5	17	371.9	359.1	77	415.1	400.8
38	243.1	234.8	98	286.3	276.5	58	329.5	318.2	18	372.6	359.8	78	415.8	401.5
39	243.9	235.5	99	287.0	277.2	59	330.2	318.8	19	373.3	360.5	79	416.5	402.2
40	244.6	236.2	400	287.7	277.9	60	330.9	319.5	20	374.1	361.2	80	417.2	402.9
341	245.3	236.9	401	288.5	278.6	461	331.6	320.2	521	374.8	361.9	581	417.9	403.6
42	246.0	237.6	02	289.2	279.3	62	332.3	320.9	22	375.5	362.6	82	418.7	404.3
43	246.7	238.3	03	289.9	279.9	63	333.1	321.6	23	376.2	363.3	83	419.4	405.0
44	247.5	239.0	04	290.6	280.6	64	333.8	322.3	24	376.9	364.0	84	420.1	405.7
45	248.2	239.7	05	291.3	281.3	65	334.5	323.0	25	377.7	364.7	85	420.8	406.4
46	248.9	240.4	06	292.1	282.0	66	335.2	323.7	26	378.4	365.4	86	421.5	407.1
47	249.6	241.0	07	292.8	282.7	67	335.9	324.4	27	379.1	366.1	87	422.3	407.8
48	250.3	241.7	08	293.5	283.4	68	336.7	325.1	28	379.8	366.8	88	423.0	408.5
49	251.0	242.4	09	294.2	284.1	69	337.4	325.8	29	380.5	367.5	89	423.7	409.2
50	251.8	243.1	10	294.9	284.8	70	338.1	326.5	30	381.3	368.2	90	424.4	409.8
351	252.5	243.8	411	295.6	285.5	471	338.8	327.2	531	382.0	368.9	591	425.1	410.5
52	253.2	244.5	12	296.4	286.2	72	339.5	327.9	32	382.7	369.6	92	425.8	411.2
53	253.9	245.2	13	297.1	286.9	73	340.2	328.6	33	383.4	370.3	93	426.6	411.9
54	254.6	245.9	14	297.8	287.6	74	341.0	329.3	34	384.1	370.9	94	427.3	412.6
55	255.4	246.6	15	298.5	288.3	75	341.7	330.0	35	384.8	371.6	95	428.0	413.3
56	256.1	247.3	16	299.2	289.0	76	342.4	330.7	36	385.6	372.3	96	428.7	414.0
57	256.8	248.0	17	300.0	289.7	77	343.1	331.4	37	386.3	373.0	97	429.4	414.7
58	257.5	248.7	18	300.7	290.4	78	343.8	332.0	38	387.0	373.7	98	430.2	415.4
59	258.2	249.4	19	301.4	291.1	79	344.6	332.7	39	387.7	374.4	99	430.9	416.1
60	259.0	250.1	20	302.1	291.8	80	345.3	333.4	40	388.4	375.1	600	431.6	416.8
Dist.	Dep.	D. Lat.	Dist.	Dep.	D. Lat.	Dist.	Dep.	D. Lat.	Dist.	Dep.	D. Lat.	Dist.	Dep.	D. Lat.

Dist.	D. Lat.	Dep.
D Lo	Dep.	
	m	D Lo

46°

314° | 046° / 226° | 134°

TABLE 4

315° | 045° / 225° | 135° — Traverse **45°** Table — 315° | 045° / 225° | 135°

Dist.	D. Lat.	Dep.	Dist.	D. Lat.	Dep.	Dist.	D. Lat.	Dep.	Dist.	D. Lat.	Dep.	Dist.	D. Lat.	Dep.
1	0.7	0.7	61	43.1	43.1	121	85.6	85.6	181	128.0	128.0	241	170.4	170.4
2	1.4	1.4	62	43.8	43.8	22	86.3	86.3	82	128.7	128.7	42	171.1	171.1
3	2.1	2.1	63	44.5	44.5	23	87.0	87.0	83	129.4	129.4	43	171.8	171.8
4	2.8	2.8	64	45.3	45.3	24	87.7	87.7	84	130.1	130.1	44	172.5	172.5
5	3.5	3.5	65	46.0	46.0	25	88.4	88.4	85	130.8	130.8	45	173.2	173.2
6	4.2	4.2	66	46.7	46.7	26	89.1	89.1	86	131.5	131.5	46	173.9	173.9
7	4.9	4.9	67	47.4	47.4	27	89.8	89.8	87	132.2	132.2	47	174.7	174.7
8	5.7	5.7	68	48.1	48.1	28	90.5	90.5	88	132.9	132.9	48	175.4	175.4
9	6.4	6.4	69	48.8	48.8	29	91.2	91.2	89	133.6	133.6	49	176.1	176.1
10	7.1	7.1	70	49.5	49.5	30	91.9	91.9	90	134.4	134.4	50	176.8	176.8
11	7.8	7.8	71	50.2	50.2	131	92.6	92.6	191	135.1	135.1	251	177.5	177.5
12	8.5	8.5	72	50.9	50.9	32	93.3	93.3	92	135.8	135.8	52	178.2	178.2
13	9.2	9.2	73	51.6	51.6	33	94.0	94.0	93	136.5	136.5	53	178.9	178.9
14	9.9	9.9	74	52.3	52.3	34	94.8	94.8	94	137.2	137.2	54	179.6	179.6
15	10.6	10.6	75	53.0	53.0	35	95.5	95.5	95	137.9	137.9	55	180.3	180.3
16	11.3	11.3	76	53.7	53.7	36	96.2	96.2	96	138.6	138.6	56	181.0	181.0
17	12.0	12.0	77	54.4	54.4	37	96.9	96.9	97	139.3	139.3	57	181.7	181.7
18	12.7	12.7	78	55.2	55.2	38	97.6	97.6	98	140.0	140.0	58	182.4	182.4
19	13.4	13.4	79	55.9	55.9	39	98.3	98.3	99	140.7	140.7	59	183.1	183.1
20	14.1	14.1	80	56.6	56.6	40	99.0	99.0	200	141.4	141.4	60	183.8	183.8
21	14.8	14.8	81	57.3	57.3	141	99.7	99.7	201	142.1	142.1	261	184.6	184.6
22	15.6	15.6	82	58.0	58.0	42	100.4	100.4	02	142.8	142.8	62	185.3	185.3
23	16.3	16.3	83	58.7	58.7	43	101.1	101.1	03	143.5	143.5	63	186.0	186.0
24	17.0	17.0	84	59.4	59.4	44	101.8	101.8	04	144.2	144.2	64	186.7	186.7
25	17.7	17.7	85	60.1	60.1	45	102.5	102.5	05	145.0	145.0	65	187.4	187.4
26	18.4	18.4	86	60.8	60.8	46	103.2	103.2	06	145.7	145.7	66	188.1	188.1
27	19.1	19.1	87	61.5	61.5	47	103.9	103.9	07	146.4	146.4	67	188.8	188.8
28	19.8	19.8	88	62.2	62.2	48	104.7	104.7	08	147.1	147.1	68	189.5	189.5
29	20.5	20.5	89	62.9	62.9	49	105.4	105.4	09	147.8	147.8	69	190.2	190.2
30	21.2	21.2	90	63.6	63.6	50	106.1	106.1	10	148.5	148.5	70	190.9	190.9
31	21.9	21.9	91	64.3	64.3	151	106.8	106.8	211	149.2	149.2	271	191.6	191.6
32	22.6	22.6	92	65.1	65.1	52	107.5	107.5	12	149.9	149.9	72	192.3	192.3
33	23.3	23.3	93	65.8	65.8	53	108.2	108.2	13	150.6	150.6	73	193.0	193.0
34	24.0	24.0	94	66.5	66.5	54	108.9	108.9	14	151.3	151.3	74	193.7	193.7
35	24.7	24.7	95	67.2	67.2	55	109.6	109.6	15	152.0	152.0	75	194.5	194.5
36	25.5	25.5	96	67.9	67.9	56	110.3	110.3	16	152.7	152.7	76	195.2	195.2
37	26.2	26.2	97	68.6	68.6	57	111.0	111.0	17	153.4	153.4	77	195.9	195.9
38	26.9	26.9	98	69.3	69.3	58	111.7	111.7	18	154.1	154.1	78	196.6	196.6
39	27.6	27.6	99	70.0	70.0	59	112.4	112.4	19	154.9	154.9	79	197.3	197.3
40	28.3	28.3	100	70.7	70.7	60	113.1	113.1	20	155.6	155.6	80	198.0	198.0
41	29.0	29.0	101	71.4	71.4	161	113.8	113.8	221	156.3	156.3	281	198.7	198.7
42	29.7	29.7	02	72.1	72.1	62	114.6	114.6	22	157.0	157.0	82	199.4	199.4
43	30.4	30.4	03	72.8	72.8	63	115.3	115.3	23	157.7	157.7	83	200.1	200.1
44	31.1	31.1	04	73.5	73.5	64	116.0	116.0	24	158.4	158.4	84	200.8	200.8
45	31.8	31.8	05	74.2	74.2	65	116.7	116.7	25	159.1	159.1	85	201.5	201.5
46	32.5	32.5	06	75.0	75.0	66	117.4	117.4	26	159.8	159.8	86	202.2	202.2
47	33.2	33.2	07	75.7	75.7	67	118.1	118.1	27	160.5	160.5	87	202.9	202.9
48	33.9	33.9	08	76.4	76.4	68	118.8	118.8	28	161.2	161.2	88	203.6	203.6
49	34.6	34.6	09	77.1	77.1	69	119.5	119.5	29	161.9	161.9	89	204.4	204.4
50	35.4	35.4	10	77.8	77.8	70	120.2	120.2	30	162.6	162.6	90	205.1	205.1
51	36.1	36.1	111	78.5	78.5	171	120.9	120.9	231	163.3	163.3	291	205.8	205.8
52	36.8	36.8	12	79.2	79.2	72	121.6	121.6	32	164.0	164.0	92	206.5	206.5
53	37.5	37.5	13	79.9	79.9	73	122.3	122.3	33	164.8	164.8	93	207.2	207.2
54	38.2	38.2	14	80.6	80.6	74	123.0	123.0	34	165.5	165.5	94	207.9	207.9
55	38.9	38.9	15	81.3	81.3	75	123.7	123.7	35	166.2	166.2	95	208.6	208.6
56	39.6	39.6	16	82.0	82.0	76	124.5	124.5	36	166.9	166.9	96	209.3	209.3
57	40.3	40.3	17	82.7	82.7	77	125.2	125.2	37	167.6	167.6	97	210.0	210.0
58	41.0	41.0	18	83.4	83.4	78	125.9	125.9	38	168.3	168.3	98	210.7	210.7
59	41.7	41.7	19	84.1	84.1	79	126.6	126.6	39	169.0	169.0	99	211.4	211.4
60	42.4	42.4	20	84.9	84.9	80	127.3	127.3	40	169.7	169.7	300	212.1	212.1
Dist.	Dep.	D. Lat.	Dist.	Dep.	D. Lat.	Dist.	Dep.	D. Lat.	Dist.	Dep.	D. Lat.	Dist.	Dep.	D. Lat.

315° | 045° / 225° | 135° — **45°**

Dist.	D. Lat.	Dep.
N.	N x Cos.	N x Sin.
Hypotenuse	Side Adj.	Side Opp.

TABLE 4

315° | 045° / 225° | 135° — Traverse **45°** Table — 315° | 045° / 225° | 135°

Dist.	D. Lat.	Dep.	Dist.	D. Lat.	Dep.	Dist.	D. Lat.	Dep.	Dist.	D. Lat.	Dep.	Dist.	D. Lat.	Dep.
301	212.8	212.8	361	255.3	255.3	421	297.7	297.7	481	340.1	340.1	541	382.5	382.5
02	213.5	213.5	62	256.0	256.0	22	298.4	298.4	82	340.8	340.8	42	383.3	383.3
03	214.3	214.3	63	256.7	256.7	23	299.1	299.1	83	341.5	341.5	43	384.0	384.0
04	215.0	215.0	64	257.4	257.4	24	299.8	299.8	84	342.2	342.2	44	384.7	384.7
05	215.7	215.7	65	258.1	258.1	25	300.5	300.5	85	342.9	342.9	45	385.4	385.4
06	216.4	216.4	66	258.8	258.8	26	301.2	301.2	86	343.7	343.7	46	386.1	386.1
07	217.1	217.1	67	259.5	259.5	27	301.9	301.9	87	344.4	344.4	47	386.8	386.8
08	217.8	217.8	68	260.2	260.2	28	302.6	302.6	88	345.1	345.1	48	387.5	387.5
09	218.5	218.5	69	260.9	260.9	29	303.3	303.3	89	345.8	345.8	49	388.2	388.2
10	219.2	219.2	70	261.6	261.6	30	304.1	304.1	90	346.5	346.5	50	388.9	388.9
311	219.9	219.9	371	262.3	262.3	431	304.8	304.8	491	347.2	347.2	551	389.6	389.6
12	220.6	220.6	72	263.0	263.0	32	305.5	305.5	92	347.9	347.9	52	390.3	390.3
13	221.3	221.3	73	263.8	263.8	33	306.2	306.2	93	348.6	348.6	53	391.0	391.0
14	222.0	222.0	74	264.5	264.5	34	306.9	306.9	94	349.3	349.3	54	391.7	391.7
15	222.7	222.7	75	265.2	265.2	35	307.6	307.6	95	350.0	350.0	55	392.4	392.4
16	223.4	223.4	76	265.9	265.9	36	308.3	308.3	96	350.7	350.7	56	393.2	393.2
17	224.2	224.2	77	266.6	266.6	37	309.0	309.0	97	351.4	351.4	57	393.9	393.9
18	224.9	224.9	78	267.3	267.3	38	309.7	309.7	98	352.1	352.1	58	394.6	394.6
19	225.6	225.6	79	268.0	268.0	39	310.4	310.4	99	352.8	352.8	59	395.3	395.3
20	226.3	226.3	80	268.7	268.7	40	311.1	311.1	500	353.6	353.6	60	396.0	396.0
321	227.0	227.0	381	269.4	269.4	441	311.8	311.8	501	354.3	354.3	561	396.7	396.7
22	227.7	227.7	82	270.1	270.1	42	312.5	312.5	02	355.0	355.0	62	397.4	397.4
23	228.4	228.4	83	270.8	270.8	43	313.2	313.2	03	355.7	355.7	63	398.1	398.1
24	229.1	229.1	84	271.5	271.5	44	314.0	314.0	04	356.4	356.4	64	398.8	398.8
25	229.8	229.8	85	272.2	272.2	45	314.7	314.7	05	357.1	357.1	65	399.5	399.5
26	230.5	230.5	86	272.9	272.9	46	315.4	315.4	06	357.8	357.8	66	400.2	400.2
27	231.2	231.2	87	273.7	273.7	47	316.1	316.1	07	358.5	358.5	67	400.9	400.9
28	231.9	231.9	88	274.4	274.4	48	316.8	316.8	08	359.2	359.2	68	401.6	401.6
29	232.6	232.6	89	275.1	275.1	49	317.5	317.5	09	359.9	359.9	69	402.3	402.3
30	233.3	233.3	90	275.8	275.8	50	318.2	318.2	10	360.6	360.6	70	403.1	403.1
331	234.1	234.1	391	276.5	276.5	451	318.9	318.9	511	361.3	361.3	571	403.8	403.8
32	234.8	234.8	92	277.2	277.2	52	319.6	319.6	12	362.0	362.0	72	404.5	404.5
33	235.5	235.5	93	277.9	277.9	53	320.3	320.3	13	362.7	362.7	73	405.2	405.2
34	236.2	236.2	94	278.6	278.6	54	321.0	321.0	14	363.5	363.5	74	405.9	405.9
35	236.9	236.9	95	279.3	279.3	55	321.7	321.7	15	364.2	364.2	75	406.6	406.6
36	237.6	237.6	96	280.0	280.0	56	322.4	322.4	16	364.9	364.9	76	407.3	407.3
37	238.3	238.3	97	280.7	280.7	57	323.1	323.1	17	365.6	365.6	77	408.0	408.0
38	239.0	239.0	98	281.4	281.4	58	323.9	323.9	18	366.3	366.3	78	408.7	408.7
39	239.7	239.7	99	282.1	282.1	59	324.6	324.6	19	367.0	367.0	79	409.4	409.4
40	240.4	240.4	400	282.8	282.8	60	325.3	325.3	20	367.7	367.7	80	410.1	410.1
341	241.1	241.1	401	283.5	283.5	461	326.0	326.0	521	368.4	368.4	581	410.8	410.8
42	241.8	241.8	02	284.3	284.3	62	326.7	326.7	22	369.1	369.1	82	411.5	411.5
43	242.5	242.5	03	285.0	285.0	63	327.4	327.4	23	369.8	369.8	83	412.2	412.2
44	243.2	243.2	04	285.7	285.7	64	328.1	328.1	24	370.5	370.5	84	413.0	413.0
45	244.0	244.0	05	286.4	286.4	65	328.8	328.8	25	371.2	371.2	85	413.7	413.7
46	244.7	244.7	06	287.1	287.1	66	329.5	329.5	26	371.9	371.9	86	414.4	414.4
47	245.4	245.4	07	287.8	287.8	67	330.2	330.2	27	372.6	372.6	87	415.1	415.1
48	246.1	246.1	08	288.5	288.5	68	330.9	330.9	28	373.4	373.4	88	415.8	415.8
49	246.8	246.8	09	289.2	289.2	69	331.6	331.6	29	374.1	374.1	89	416.5	416.5
50	247.5	247.5	10	289.9	289.9	70	332.3	332.3	30	374.8	374.8	90	417.2	417.2
351	248.2	248.2	411	290.6	290.6	471	333.0	333.0	531	375.5	375.5	591	417.9	417.9
52	248.9	248.9	12	291.3	291.3	72	333.8	333.8	32	376.2	376.2	92	418.6	418.6
53	249.6	249.6	13	292.0	292.0	73	334.5	334.5	33	376.9	376.9	93	419.3	419.3
54	250.3	250.3	14	292.7	292.7	74	335.2	335.2	34	377.6	377.6	94	420.0	420.0
55	251.0	251.0	15	293.4	293.4	75	335.9	335.9	35	378.3	378.3	95	420.7	420.7
56	251.7	251.7	16	294.2	294.2	76	336.6	336.6	36	379.0	379.0	96	421.4	421.4
57	252.4	252.4	17	294.9	294.9	77	337.3	337.3	37	379.7	379.7	97	422.1	422.1
58	253.1	253.1	18	295.6	295.6	78	338.0	338.0	38	380.4	380.4	98	422.8	422.8
59	253.9	253.9	19	296.3	296.3	79	338.7	338.7	39	381.1	381.1	99	423.6	423.6
60	254.6	254.6	20	297.0	297.0	80	339.4	339.4	40	381.8	381.8	600	424.3	424.3
Dist.	Dep.	D. Lat.	Dist.	Dep.	D. Lat.	Dist.	Dep.	D. Lat.	Dist.	Dep.	D. Lat.	Dist.	Dep.	D. Lat.

Dist.	D. Lat.	Dep.
D Lo	Dep.	
	m	D Lo

45° — 315° | 045° / 225° | 135°

TABLE 5

Natural and Numerical Chart Scales

Natural Scale	Miles Per Inch		Inches Per Mile		Feet Per Inch
	Nautical	Statute	Nautical	Statute	
1:500	0.007	0.008	145.83	126.72	41.67
1:600	0.008	0.009	121.52	105.60	50.00
1:1,000	0.014	0.016	72.91	63.36	83.33
1:1,200	0.016	0.019	60.76	52.80	100.00
1:1,500	0.021	0.024	48.61	42.24	125.00
1:2,000	0.027	0.032	36.46	31.68	166.67
1:2,400	0.033	0.038	30.38	26.40	200.00
1:2,500	0.034	0.039	29.17	25.34	208.33
1:3,000	0.041	0.047	24.30	21.12	250.00
1:3,600	0.049	0.057	20.25	17.60	300.00
1:4,000	0.055	0.063	18.23	15.84	333.33
1:4,800	0.066	0.076	15.19	13.20	400.00
1:5,000	0.069	0.079	14.58	12.67	416.67
1:6,000	0.082	0.095	12.15	10.56	500.00
1:7,000	0.096	0.110	10.42	9.05	583.33
1:7,200	0.099	0.114	10.13	8.80	600.00
1:7,920	0.109	0.125	9.21	8.00	660.00
1:8,000	0.110	0.126	9.11	7.92	666.67
1:8,400	0.115	0.133	8.68	7.54	700.00
1:9,000	0.123	0.142	8.10	7.04	750.00
1:9,600	0.132	0.152	7.60	6.60	800.00
1:10,000	0.137	0.158	7.29	6.34	833.33
1:10,800	0.148	0.170	6.75	5.87	900.00
1:12,000	0.165	0.189	6.08	5.28	1,000.00
1:13,200	0.181	0.208	5.52	4.80	1,100.00
1:14,400	0.197	0.227	5.06	4.40	1,200.00
1:15,000	0.206	0.237	4.86	4.22	1,250.00
1:15,600	0.214	0.246	4.67	4.06	1,300.00
1:15,840	0.217	0.250	4.60	4.00	1,320.00
1:16,000	0.219	0.253	4.56	3.96	1,333.33
1:16,800	0.230	0.265	4.34	3.77	1,400.00
1:18,000	0.247	0.284	4.05	3.52	1,500.00
1:19,200	0.263	0.303	3.80	3.30	1,600.00
1:20,000	0.274	0.316	3.65	3.17	1,666.67
1:20,400	0.280	0.322	3.57	3.11	1,700.00
1:21,120	0.290	0.333	3.45	3.00	1,760.00
1:21,600	0.296	0.341	3.38	2.93	1,800.00
1:22,800	0.313	0.360	3.20	2.78	1,900.00
1:24,000	0.329	0.379	3.04	2.64	2,000.00
1:25,000	0.343	0.395	2.92	2.53	2,083.33
1:40,000	0.549	0.631	1.82	1.58	3,333.33
1:48,000	0.658	0.758	1.52	1.32	4,000.00
1:50,000	0.686	0.789	1.46	1.27	4,166.67
1:62,500	0.857	0.986	1.17	1.01	5,208.33
1:63,360	0.869	1.000	1.15	1.00	5,280.00
1:75,000	1.029	1.184	0.97	0.85	6,250.00
1:80,000	1.097	1.263	0.91	0.79	6,666.67
1:100,000	1.371	1.578	0.73	0.63	8,333.33
1:125,000	1.714	1.973	0.58	0.51	10,416.67
1:200,000	2.743	3.157	0.36	0.32	16,666.67
1:250,000	3.429	3.946	0.29	0.25	20,833.33
1:400,000	5.486	6.313	0.18	0.16	33,333.33
1:500,000	6.857	7.891	0.15	0.13	41,666.67
1:750,000	10.286	11.837	0.10	0.08	62,500.00
1:1,000,000	13.715	15.783	0.07	0.06	83,333.33
FORMULAS	$\frac{SCALE}{72,913.39}$	$\frac{SCALE}{63,360}$	$\frac{72,913.39}{SCALE}$	$\frac{63,360}{SCALE}$	$\frac{SCALE}{12}$

TABLE 6

Meridional Parts

Lat.	0°	1°	2°	3°	4°	5°	6°	7°	8°	9°	Lat.
′											′
0	0.0	59.6	119.2	178.9	238.6	298.4	358.3	418.2	478.4	538.6	0
1	01.0	60.6	20.2	79.9	39.6	299.4	59.3	19.2	79.4	39.6	1
2	02.0	61.6	21.2	80.9	40.6	300.4	60.3	20.2	80.4	40.6	2
3	03.0	62.6	22.2	81.9	41.6	01.4	61.3	21.2	81.4	41.7	3
4	04.0	63.6	23.2	82.9	42.6	02.4	62.2	22.2	82.4	42.7	4
5	5.0	64.6	124.2	183.9	243.6	303.4	363.2	423.2	483.4	543.7	5
6	06.0	65.6	25.2	84.8	44.6	04.4	64.2	24.2	84.4	44.7	6
7	07.0	66.6	26.2	85.8	45.6	05.4	65.2	25.3	85.4	45.7	7
8	07.9	67.5	27.2	86.8	46.6	06.4	66.2	26.3	86.4	46.7	8
9	08.9	68.5	28.2	87.8	47.6	07.4	67.2	27.3	87.4	47.7	9
10	9.9	69.5	129.2	188.8	248.5	308.3	368.2	428.3	488.4	548.7	10
11	10.9	70.5	30.2	89.8	49.5	09.3	69.2	29.3	89.4	49.7	11
12	11.9	71.5	31.1	90.8	50.5	10.3	70.2	30.3	90.4	50.7	12
13	12.9	72.5	32.1	91.8	51.5	11.3	71.2	31.3	91.4	51.7	13
14	13.9	73.5	33.1	92.8	52.5	12.3	72.2	32.3	92.4	52.7	14
15	14.9	74.5	134.1	193.8	253.5	313.3	373.2	433.3	493.4	553.7	15
16	15.9	75.5	35.1	94.8	54.5	14.3	74.2	34.3	94.4	54.7	16
17	16.9	76.5	36.1	95.8	55.5	15.3	75.2	35.3	95.4	55.7	17
18	17.9	77.5	37.1	96.8	56.5	16.3	76.2	36.3	96.4	56.7	18
19	18.9	78.5	38.1	97.8	57.5	17.3	77.2	37.3	97.4	57.8	19
20	19.9	79.5	139.1	198.8	258.5	318.3	378.2	438.3	498.4	558.8	20
21	20.9	80.5	40.1	199.8	59.5	19.3	79.2	39.3	499.4	59.8	21
22	21.9	81.5	41.1	200.8	60.5	20.3	80.2	40.3	500.4	60.8	22
23	22.8	82.5	42.1	01.8	61.5	21.3	81.2	41.3	01.4	61.8	23
24	23.8	83.4	43.1	02.8	62.5	22.3	82.2	42.3	02.5	62.8	24
25	24.8	84.4	144.1	203.8	263.5	323.3	383.2	443.3	503.5	563.8	25
26	25.8	85.4	45.1	04.7	64.5	24.3	84.2	44.3	04.5	64.8	26
27	26.8	86.4	46.1	05.7	65.5	25.3	85.2	45.3	05.5	65.8	27
28	27.8	87.4	47.1	06.7	66.5	26.3	86.2	46.3	06.5	66.8	28
29	28.8	88.4	48.0	07.7	67.5	27.3	87.2	47.3	07.5	67.8	29
30	29.8	89.4	149.0	208.7	268.5	328.3	388.2	448.3	508.5	568.8	30
31	30.8	90.4	50.0	09.7	69.5	29.3	89.2	49.3	09.5	69.8	31
32	31.8	91.4	51.0	10.7	70.5	30.3	90.2	50.3	10.5	70.8	32
33	32.8	92.4	52.0	11.7	71.5	31.3	91.2	51.3	11.5	71.9	33
34	33.8	93.4	53.0	12.7	72.5	32.3	92.2	52.3	12.5	72.9	34
35	34.8	94.4	154.0	213.7	273.5	333.3	393.2	453.3	513.5	573.9	35
36	35.8	95.4	55.0	14.7	74.5	34.3	94.2	54.3	14.5	74.9	36
37	36.8	96.4	56.0	15.7	75.4	35.3	95.2	55.3	15.5	75.9	37
38	37.7	97.4	57.0	16.7	76.4	36.3	96.2	56.3	16.5	76.9	38
39	38.7	98.4	58.0	17.7	77.4	37.3	97.2	57.3	17.5	77.9	39
40	39.7	99.3	159.0	218.7	278.4	338.3	398.2	458.3	518.5	578.9	40
41	40.7	100.3	60.0	19.7	79.4	39.3	399.2	59.3	19.5	79.9	41
42	41.7	01.3	61.0	20.7	80.4	40.3	400.2	60.3	20.5	80.9	42
43	42.7	02.3	62.0	21.7	81.4	41.3	01.2	61.3	21.5	81.9	43
44	43.7	03.3	63.0	22.7	82.4	42.3	02.2	62.3	22.5	82.9	44
45	44.7	104.3	164.0	223.7	283.4	343.3	403.2	463.3	523.6	583.9	45
46	45.7	05.3	65.0	24.7	84.4	44.3	04.2	64.3	24.6	85.0	46
47	46.7	06.3	65.9	25.6	85.4	45.3	05.2	65.3	25.6	86.0	47
48	47.7	07.3	66.9	26.6	86.4	46.3	06.2	66.3	26.6	87.0	48
49	48.7	08.3	67.9	27.6	87.4	47.3	07.2	67.3	27.6	88.0	49
50	49.7	109.3	168.9	228.6	288.4	348.3	408.2	468.3	528.6	589.0	50
51	50.7	10.3	69.9	29.6	89.4	49.3	09.2	69.3	29.6	90.0	51
52	51.7	11.3	70.9	30.6	90.4	50.3	10.2	70.3	30.6	91.0	52
53	52.6	12.3	71.9	31.6	91.4	51.3	11.2	71.3	31.6	92.0	53
54	53.6	13.3	72.9	32.6	92.4	52.3	12.2	72.3	32.6	93.0	54
55	54.6	114.3	173.9	233.6	293.4	353.3	413.2	473.3	533.6	594.0	55
56	55.6	15.2	74.9	34.6	94.4	54.3	14.2	74.4	34.6	95.0	56
57	56.6	16.2	75.9	35.6	95.4	55.3	15.2	75.4	35.6	96.0	57
58	57.6	17.2	76.9	36.6	96.4	56.3	16.2	76.4	36.6	97.1	58
59	58.6	18.2	77.9	37.6	97.4	57.3	17.2	77.4	37.6	98.1	59
60	59.6	119.2	178.9	238.6	298.4	358.3	418.2	478.4	538.6	599.1	60
Lat.	0°	1°	2°	3°	4°	5°	6°	7°	8°	9°	Lat.

TABLE 6

Meridional Parts

Lat.	10°	11°	12°	13°	14°	15°	16°	17°	18°	19°	Lat.
′											′
0	599.1	659.7	720.5	781.6	842.9	904.5	966.4	1028.6	1091.1	1154.0	0
1	600.1	60.7	21.6	82.6	43.9	05.5	67.4	29.6	92.1	55.0	1
2	01.1	61.7	22.6	83.6	45.0	06.6	68.4	30.7	93.2	56.1	2
3	02.1	62.7	23.6	84.7	46.0	07.6	69.5	31.7	94.2	57.1	3
4	03.1	63.7	24.6	85.7	47.0	08.6	70.5	32.7	95.3	58.2	4
5	604.1	664.8	725.6	786.7	848.0	909.6	971.6	1033.8	1096.3	1159.3	5
6	05.1	65.8	26.6	87.7	49.1	10.7	72.6	34.8	97.4	60.3	6
7	06.1	66.8	27.6	88.7	50.1	11.7	73.6	35.9	98.4	61.4	7
8	07.1	67.8	28.7	89.8	51.1	12.7	74.7	36.9	1099.5	62.4	8
9	08.2	68.8	29.7	90.8	52.1	13.8	75.7	37.9	1100.5	63.5	9
10	609.2	669.8	730.7	791.8	853.2	914.8	976.7	1039.0	1101.6	1164.5	10
11	10.2	70.8	31.7	92.8	54.2	15.8	77.8	40.0	02.6	65.6	11
12	11.2	71.9	32.7	93.8	55.2	16.9	78.8	41.1	03.7	66.6	12
13	12.2	72.9	33.7	94.9	56.2	17.9	79.8	42.1	04.7	67.7	13
14	13.2	73.9	34.8	95.9	57.3	18.9	80.9	43.1	05.7	68.7	14
15	614.2	674.9	735.8	796.9	858.3	919.9	981.9	1044.2	1106.8	1169.8	15
16	15.2	75.9	36.8	97.9	59.3	21.0	82.9	45.2	07.8	70.8	16
17	16.2	76.9	37.8	798.9	60.3	22.0	84.0	46.3	08.9	71.9	17
18	17.2	77.9	38.8	800.0	61.4	23.0	85.0	47.3	09.9	72.9	18
19	18.3	78.9	39.8	01.0	62.4	24.1	86.0	48.3	11.0	74.0	19
20	619.3	680.0	740.9	802.0	863.4	925.1	987.1	1049.4	1112.0	1175.0	20
21	20.3	81.0	41.9	03.0	64.4	26.1	88.1	50.4	13.1	76.1	21
22	21.3	82.0	42.9	04.1	65.5	27.2	89.1	51.5	14.1	77.1	22
23	22.3	83.0	43.9	05.1	66.5	28.2	90.2	52.5	15.2	78.2	23
24	23.3	84.0	44.9	06.1	67.5	29.2	91.2	53.5	16.2	79.3	24
25	624.3	685.0	746.0	807.1	868.5	930.2	992.3	1054.6	1117.3	1180.3	25
26	25.3	86.0	47.0	08.1	69.6	31.3	93.3	55.6	18.3	81.4	26
27	26.3	87.1	48.0	09.2	70.6	32.3	94.3	56.7	19.4	82.4	27
28	27.3	88.1	49.0	10.2	71.6	33.3	95.4	57.7	20.4	83.5	28
29	28.4	89.1	50.0	11.2	72.6	34.4	96.4	58.8	21.5	84.5	29
30	629.4	690.1	751.0	812.2	873.7	935.4	997.4	1059.8	1122.5	1185.6	30
31	30.4	91.1	52.1	13.2	74.7	36.4	98.5	60.8	23.5	86.6	31
32	31.4	92.1	53.1	14.3	75.7	37.5	999.5	61.9	24.6	87.7	32
33	32.4	93.1	54.1	15.3	76.8	38.5	1000.5	62.9	25.6	88.7	33
34	33.4	94.1	55.1	16.3	77.8	39.5	01.6	64.0	26.7	89.8	34
35	634.4	695.2	756.1	817.3	878.8	940.6	1002.6	1065.0	1127.7	1190.9	35
36	35.4	96.2	57.1	18.4	79.8	41.6	03.7	66.0	28.8	91.9	36
37	36.4	97.2	58.2	19.4	80.9	42.6	04.7	67.1	29.8	93.0	37
38	37.4	98.2	59.2	20.4	81.9	43.7	05.7	68.1	30.9	94.0	38
39	38.5	99.2	60.2	21.4	82.9	44.7	06.8	69.2	31.9	95.1	39
40	639.5	700.2	761.2	822.5	883.9	945.7	1007.8	1070.2	1133.0	1196.1	40
41	40.5	01.2	62.2	23.5	85.0	46.8	08.8	71.3	34.0	97.2	41
42	41.5	02.3	63.3	24.5	86.0	47.8	09.9	72.3	35.1	98.2	42
43	42.5	03.3	64.3	25.5	87.0	48.8	10.9	73.4	36.1	1199.3	43
44	43.5	04.3	65.3	26.5	88.1	49.9	12.0	74.4	37.2	1200.4	44
45	644.5	705.3	766.3	827.6	889.1	950.9	1013.0	1075.4	1138.2	1201.4	45
46	45.5	06.3	67.3	28.6	90.1	51.9	14.0	76.5	39.3	02.5	46
47	46.5	07.3	68.4	29.6	91.1	52.9	15.1	77.5	40.3	03.5	47
48	47.6	08.4	69.4	30.6	92.2	54.0	16.1	78.6	41.4	04.6	48
49	48.6	09.4	70.4	31.7	93.2	55.0	17.1	79.6	42.4	05.6	49
50	649.6	710.4	771.4	832.7	894.2	956.0	1018.2	1080.7	1143.5	1206.7	50
51	50.6	11.4	72.4	33.7	95.2	57.1	19.2	81.7	44.5	07.7	51
52	51.6	12.4	73.4	34.7	96.3	58.1	20.3	82.7	45.6	08.8	52
53	52.6	13.4	74.5	35.8	97.3	59.1	21.3	83.8	46.6	09.9	53
54	53.6	14.4	75.5	36.8	98.3	60.2	22.3	84.8	47.7	10.9	54
55	654.6	715.5	776.5	837.8	899.4	961.2	1023.4	1085.9	1148.7	1212.0	55
56	55.7	16.5	77.5	38.8	900.4	62.2	24.4	86.9	49.8	13.0	56
57	56.7	17.5	78.5	39.8	01.4	63.3	25.5	88.0	50.8	14.1	57
58	57.7	18.5	79.6	40.9	02.4	64.3	26.5	89.0	51.9	15.2	58
59	58.7	19.5	80.6	41.9	03.5	65.3	27.5	90.1	52.9	16.2	59
60	659.7	720.5	781.6	842.9	904.5	966.4	1028.6	1091.1	1154.0	1217.3	60
Lat.	10°	11°	12°	13°	14°	15°	16°	17°	18°	19°	Lat.

TABLE 6
Meridional Parts

Lat.	20°	21°	22°	23°	24°	25°	26°	27°	28°	29°	Lat.
′											′
0	1217.3	1280.9	1345.1	1409.6	1474.7	1540.3	1606.4	1673.1	1740.4	1808.3	0
1	18.3	82.0	46.1	10.7	75.8	41.4	07.5	74.2	41.5	09.4	1
2	19.4	83.1	47.2	11.8	76.9	42.5	08.6	75.3	42.6	10.5	2
3	20.4	84.1	48.3	12.9	78.0	43.6	09.7	76.4	43.7	11.7	3
4	21.5	85.2	49.4	14.0	79.0	44.7	10.8	77.5	44.9	12.8	4
5	1222.6	1286.3	1350.4	1415.0	1480.1	1545.8	1611.9	1678.6	1746.0	1814.0	5
6	23.6	87.3	51.5	16.1	81.2	46.9	13.0	79.8	47.1	15.1	6
7	24.7	88.4	52.6	17.2	82.3	48.0	14.1	80.9	48.2	16.2	7
8	25.7	89.5	53.6	18.3	83.4	49.0	15.2	82.0	49.4	17.4	8
9	26.8	90.5	54.7	19.4	84.5	50.1	16.3	83.1	50.5	18.5	9
10	1227.9	1291.6	1355.8	1420.4	1485.6	1551.2	1617.5	1684.2	1751.6	1819.7	10
11	28.9	92.7	56.9	21.5	86.7	52.3	18.6	85.4	52.8	20.8	11
12	30.0	93.7	57.9	22.6	87.8	53.4	19.7	86.5	53.9	21.9	12
13	31.0	94.8	59.0	23.7	88.9	54.5	20.8	87.6	55.0	23.1	13
14	32.1	95.9	60.1	24.8	89.9	55.6	21.9	88.7	56.1	24.2	14
15	1233.1	1296.9	1361.2	1425.9	1491.0	1556.7	1623.0	1689.8	1757.3	1825.4	15
16	34.2	98.0	62.2	26.9	92.1	57.8	24.1	90.9	58.4	26.5	16
17	35.3	1299.1	63.3	28.0	93.2	58.9	25.2	92.1	59.5	27.6	17
18	36.3	1300.1	64.4	29.1	94.3	60.0	26.3	93.2	60.7	28.8	18
19	37.4	01.2	65.5	30.2	95.4	61.1	27.4	94.3	61.8	29.9	19
20	1238.4	1302.3	1366.5	1431.3	1496.5	1562.2	1628.5	1695.4	1762.9	1831.1	20
21	39.5	03.3	67.6	32.3	97.6	63.3	29.7	96.5	64.1	32.2	21
22	40.6	04.4	68.7	33.4	98.7	64.4	30.8	97.7	65.2	33.3	22
23	41.6	05.5	69.8	34.5	1499.8	65.5	31.9	98.8	66.3	34.5	23
24	42.7	06.5	70.8	35.6	1500.9	66.6	33.0	1699.9	67.4	35.6	24
25	1243.7	1307.6	1371.9	1436.7	1502.0	1567.7	1634.1	1701.0	1768.6	1836.8	25
26	44.8	08.7	73.0	37.8	03.0	68.8	35.2	02.1	69.7	37.9	26
27	45.9	09.7	74.1	38.8	04.1	69.9	36.3	03.3	70.8	39.1	27
28	46.9	10.8	75.1	39.9	05.2	71.0	37.4	04.4	72.0	40.2	28
29	48.0	11.9	76.2	41.0	06.3	72.2	38.5	05.5	73.1	41.3	29
30	1249.1	1312.9	1377.3	1442.1	1507.4	1573.3	1639.6	1706.6	1774.2	1842.5	30
31	50.1	14.0	78.4	43.2	08.5	74.4	40.8	07.8	75.4	43.6	31
32	51.2	15.1	79.4	44.3	09.6	75.5	41.9	08.9	76.5	44.8	32
33	52.2	16.2	80.5	45.4	10.7	76.6	43.0	010.0	77.6	45.9	33
34	53.3	17.2	81.6	46.4	11.8	77.7	44.1	11.1	78.8	47.1	34
35	1254.4	1318.3	1382.7	1447.5	1512.9	1578.8	1645.2	1712.2	1779.9	1848.2	35
36	55.4	19.4	83.7	48.6	14.0	79.9	46.3	13.4	81.0	49.3	36
37	56.5	20.4	84.8	49.7	15.1	81.0	47.4	14.5	82.2	50.5	37
38	57.5	21.5	85.9	50.8	16.2	82.1	48.5	15.6	83.3	51.6	38
39	58.6	22.6	87.0	51.9	17.3	83.2	49.7	16.7	84.4	52.8	39
40	1259.7	1323.6	1388.1	1453.0	1518.3	1584.3	1650.8	1717.9	1785.6	1853.9	40
41	60.7	24.7	89.1	54.0	19.4	85.4	51.9	19.0	86.7	55.1	41
42	61.8	25.8	90.2	55.1	20.5	86.5	53.0	20.1	87.8	56.2	42
43	62.9	26.9	91.3	56.2	21.6	87.6	54.1	21.2	89.0	57.4	43
44	63.9	27.9	92.4	57.3	22.7	88.7	55.2	22.3	90.1	58.5	44
45	1265.0	1329.0	1393.4	1458.4	1523.8	1589.8	1656.3	1723.5	1791.2	1859.7	45
46	66.1	30.1	94.5	59.5	24.9	90.9	57.5	24.6	92.4	60.8	46
47	67.1	31.1	95.6	60.6	26.0	92.0	58.6	25.7	93.5	61.9	47
48	68.2	32.2	96.7	61.6	27.1	93.1	59.7	26.8	94.6	63.1	48
49	69.2	33.3	97.8	62.7	28.2	94.2	60.8	28.0	95.8	64.2	49
50	1270.3	1334.3	1398.8	1463.8	1529.3	1595.3	1661.9	1729.1	1796.9	1865.4	50
51	71.4	35.4	1399.9	64.9	30.4	96.4	63.0	30.2	98.0	66.5	51
52	72.4	36.5	1401.0	66.0	31.5	97.5	64.1	31.3	1799.2	67.7	52
53	73.5	37.6	02.1	67.1	32.6	98.6	65.3	32.5	1800.3	68.8	53
54	74.6	38.6	03.2	68.2	33.7	1599.7	66.4	33.6	01.5	70.0	54
55	1275.6	1339.7	1404.2	1469.3	1534.8	1600.8	1667.5	1734.7	1802.6	1871.1	55
56	76.7	40.8	05.3	70.3	35.9	02.0	68.6	35.8	03.7	72.3	56
57	77.8	41.8	06.4	71.4	37.0	03.1	69.7	37.0	04.9	73.4	57
58	78.8	42.9	07.5	72.5	38.1	04.2	70.8	38.1	06.0	74.6	58
59	79.9	44.0	08.6	73.6	39.2	05.3	71.9	39.2	07.1	75.7	59
60	1280.9	1345.1	1409.6	1474.7	1540.3	1606.4	1673.1	1740.4	1808.3	1876.9	60
Lat.	20°	21°	22°	23°	24°	25°	26°	27°	28°	29°	Lat.

TABLE 6
Meridional Parts

Lat.	30°	31°	32°	33°	34°	35°	36°	37°	38°	39°	Lat.
′											′
0	1876.9	1946.2	2016.2	2087.0	2158.6	2231.1	2304.5	2378.8	2454.1	2530.4	0
1	78.0	47.3	17.4	88.2	59.8	32.3	05.7	80.0	55.3	31.7	1
2	79.2	48.5	18.5	89.4	61.0	33.5	06.9	81.3	56.6	33.0	2
3	80.3	49.6	19.7	90.5	62.2	34.7	08.1	82.5	57.9	34.3	3
4	81.5	50.8	20.9	91.7	63.4	35.9	09.4	83.8	59.1	35.6	4
5	1882.6	1952.0	2022.1	2092.9	2164.6	2237.2	2310.6	2385.0	2460.4	2536.8	5
6	83.8	53.1	23.2	94.1	65.8	38.4	11.8	86.3	61.7	38.1	6
7	84.9	54.3	24.4	95.3	67.0	39.6	13.1	87.5	62.9	39.4	7
8	86.1	55.4	25.6	96.5	68.2	40.8	14.3	88.8	64.2	40.7	8
9	87.2	56.6	26.8	97.7	69.4	42.0	15.5	90.0	65.5	42.0	9
10	1888.4	1957.8	2027.9	2098.9	2170.6	2243.2	2316.8	2391.3	2466.7	2543.3	10
11	89.5	58.9	29.1	2100.1	71.8	44.5	18.0	92.5	68.0	44.5	11
12	90.7	60.1	30.3	01.2	73.0	45.7	19.2	93.8	69.3	45.8	12
13	91.8	61.3	31.5	02.4	74.2	46.9	20.5	95.0	70.5	47.1	13
14	93.0	62.4	32.6	03.6	75.4	48.1	21.7	96.3	71.8	48.4	14
15	1894.1	1963.6	2033.8	2104.8	2176.6	2249.3	2322.9	2397.5	2473.1	2549.7	15
16	95.3	64.8	35.0	06.0	77.8	50.6	24.2	2398.8	74.3	51.0	16
17	96.4	65.9	36.2	07.2	79.0	51.8	25.4	2400.0	75.6	52.3	17
18	97.6	67.1	37.3	08.4	80.3	53.0	26.6	01.3	76.9	53.6	18
19	98.7	68.2	38.5	09.6	81.5	54.2	27.9	02.5	78.1	54.8	19
20	1899.9	1969.4	2039.7	2110.8	2182.7	2255.4	2329.1	2403.8	2479.4	2556.1	20
21	1901.0	70.6	40.9	12.0	83.9	56.7	30.4	05.0	80.7	57.4	21
22	02.2	71.7	42.1	13.1	85.1	57.9	31.6	06.3	82.0	58.7	22
23	03.3	72.9	43.2	14.3	86.3	59.1	32.8	07.5	83.2	60.0	23
24	04.5	74.1	44.4	15.5	87.5	60.3	34.1	08.8	84.5	61.3	24
25	1905.6	1975.2	2045.6	2116.7	2188.7	2261.5	2335.3	2410.0	2485.8	2562.6	25
26	06.8	76.4	46.8	17.9	89.9	62.8	36.5	11.3	87.0	63.9	26
27	08.0	77.6	47.9	19.1	91.1	64.0	37.8	12.5	88.3	65.1	27
28	09.1	78.7	49.1	20.3	92.3	65.2	39.0	13.8	89.6	66.4	28
29	10.3	79.9	50.3	21.5	93.5	66.4	40.3	15.0	90.9	67.7	29
30	1911.4	1981.1	2051.5	2122.7	2194.7	2267.6	2341.5	2416.3	2492.1	2569.0	30
31	12.6	82.2	52.7	23.9	95.9	68.9	42.7	17.6	93.4	70.3	31
32	13.7	83.4	53.8	25.1	97.1	70.1	44.0	18.8	94.7	71.6	32
33	14.9	84.6	55.0	26.3	98.4	71.3	45.2	20.1	95.9	72.9	33
34	16.0	85.7	56.2	27.5	2199.6	72.5	46.4	21.3	97.2	74.2	34
35	1917.2	1986.9	2057.4	2128.7	2200.8	2273.8	2347.7	2422.6	2498.5	2575.5	35
36	18.4	88.1	58.6	29.9	02.0	75.0	48.9	23.8	2499.8	76.8	36
37	19.5	89.2	59.7	31.1	03.2	76.2	50.2	25.1	2501.0	78.1	37
38	20.7	90.4	60.9	32.2	04.4	77.4	51.4	26.3	02.3	79.4	38
39	21.8	91.6	62.1	33.4	05.6	78.7	52.6	27.6	03.6	80.6	39
40	1923.0	1992.8	2063.3	2134.6	2206.8	2279.9	2353.9	2428.9	2504.9	2581.9	40
41	24.1	93.9	64.5	35.8	08.0	81.1	55.1	30.1	06.1	83.2	41
42	25.3	95.1	65.7	37.0	09.2	82.3	56.4	31.4	07.4	84.5	42
43	26.4	96.3	66.8	38.2	10.5	83.6	57.6	32.6	08.7	85.8	43
44	27.6	97.4	68.0	39.4	11.7	84.8	58.9	33.9	010.0	87.1	44
45	1928.8	1998.6	2069.2	2140.6	2212.9	2286.0	2360.1	2435.2	2511.2	2588.4	45
46	29.9	1999.8	70.4	41.8	14.1	87.2	61.3	36.4	12.5	89.7	46
47	31.1	2000.9	71.6	43.0	15.3	88.5	62.6	37.7	13.8	91.0	47
48	32.2	02.1	72.8	44.2	16.5	89.7	63.8	38.9	15.1	92.3	48
49	33.4	03.3	73.9	45.4	17.7	90.9	65.1	40.2	16.4	93.6	49
50	1934.6	2004.5	2075.1	2146.6	2218.9	2292.2	2366.3	2441.5	2517.6	2594.9	50
51	35.7	05.6	76.3	47.8	20.1	93.4	67.6	42.7	18.9	96.2	51
52	36.9	06.8	77.5	49.0	21.4	94.6	68.8	44.0	20.2	97.5	52
53	38.0	08.0	78.7	50.2	22.6	95.8	70.0	45.2	21.5	2598.8	53
54	39.2	09.1	79.9	51.4	23.8	97.1	71.2	46.5	22.8	2600.1	54
55	1940.4	2010.3	2081.1	2152.6	2225.0	2298.3	2372.5	2447.8	2524.0	2601.4	55
56	41.5	11.5	82.2	53.8	26.2	2299.5	73.8	49.0	25.3	02.7	56
57	42.7	12.7	83.4	55.0	27.4	2300.8	75.0	50.3	26.6	04.0	57
58	43.8	13.8	84.6	56.2	28.6	02.0	76.3	51.6	27.9	05.3	58
59	45.0	15.0	85.8	57.4	29.9	03.2	77.5	52.8	29.2	06.6	59
60	1946.2	2016.2	2087.0	2158.6	2231.1	2304.5	2378.8	2454.1	2530.4	2607.9	60
Lat.	30°	31°	32°	33°	34°	35°	36°	37°	38°	39°	Lat.

TABLE 6

Meridional Parts

Lat. ′	40°	41°	42°	43°	44°	45°	46°	47°	48°	49°	Lat. ′
0	2607.9	2686.5	2766.3	2847.4	2929.8	3013.6	3099.0	3185.9	3274.4	3364.7	0
1	09.2	87.8	67.6	48.7	31.2	15.1	3100.4	87.3	75.9	66.2	1
2	10.5	89.1	69.0	50.1	32.6	16.5	01.8	88.8	77.4	67.7	2
3	11.8	90.4	70.3	51.5	34.0	17.9	03.3	90.2	78.9	69.3	3
4	13.1	91.8	71.7	52.8	35.4	19.3	04.7	91.7	80.4	70.8	4
5	2614.4	2693.1	2773.0	2854.2	2936.7	3020.7	3106.2	3193.2	3281.9	3372.3	5
6	15.7	94.4	74.3	55.6	38.1	22.1	07.6	94.6	83.4	73.8	6
7	17.0	95.7	75.7	56.9	39.5	23.5	09.0	96.1	84.8	75.3	7
8	18.3	97.1	77.0	58.3	40.9	24.9	10.5	97.6	86.3	76.9	8
9	19.6	98.4	78.4	59.7	42.3	26.4	11.9	3199.0	87.8	78.4	9
10	2620.9	2699.7	2779.7	2861.0	2943.7	3027.8	3113.3	3200.5	3289.3	3379.9	10
11	22.2	2701.0	81.1	62.4	45.1	29.2	14.8	02.0	90.8	81.4	11
12	23.5	02.3	82.4	63.8	46.5	30.6	16.2	03.4	92.3	83.0	12
13	24.8	03.7	83.8	65.1	47.9	32.0	17.7	04.9	93.8	84.5	13
14	26.1	05.0	85.1	66.5	49.2	33.4	19.1	06.4	95.3	86.0	14
15	2627.4	2706.3	2786.4	2867.9	2950.6	3034.8	3120.5	3207.8	3296.8	3387.5	15
16	28.7	07.6	87.8	69.2	52.0	36.3	22.0	09.3	98.3	89.1	16
17	30.0	09.0	89.1	70.6	53.4	37.7	23.4	10.8	3299.8	90.6	17
18	31.3	10.3	90.5	72.0	54.8	39.1	24.9	12.2	3301.3	92.1	18
19	32.6	11.6	91.8	73.3	56.2	40.5	26.3	13.7	02.8	93.7	19
20	2634.0	2713.0	2793.2	2874.7	2957.6	3041.9	3127.8	3215.2	3304.3	3395.2	20
21	35.3	14.3	94.5	76.1	59.0	43.3	29.2	16.7	05.8	96.7	21
22	36.6	15.6	95.9	77.4	60.4	44.8	30.6	18.1	07.3	98.3	22
23	37.9	16.9	97.2	78.8	61.8	46.2	32.1	19.6	08.8	3399.8	23
24	39.2	18.3	98.6	80.2	63.2	47.6	33.5	21.1	10.3	3401.3	24
25	2640.5	2719.6	2799.9	2881.6	2964.6	3049.0	3135.0	3222.5	3311.8	3402.8	25
26	41.8	20.9	2801.3	82.9	66.0	50.4	36.4	24.0	13.3	04.4	26
27	43.1	22.2	02.6	84.3	67.4	51.9	37.9	25.5	14.8	05.9	27
28	44.4	23.6	04.0	85.7	68.8	53.3	39.3	27.0	16.3	07.4	28
29	45.7	24.9	05.3	87.1	70.2	54.7	40.8	28.4	17.8	09.0	29
30	2647.0	2726.2	2806.7	2888.4	2971.5	3056.1	3142.2	3229.9	3319.3	3410.5	30
31	48.3	27.6	08.0	89.8	72.9	57.5	43.7	31.4	20.8	12.1	31
32	49.7	28.9	09.4	91.2	74.3	59.0	45.1	32.9	22.3	13.6	32
33	51.0	30.2	10.7	92.5	75.7	60.4	46.6	34.4	23.8	15.1	33
34	52.3	31.6	12.1	93.9	77.1	61.8	48.0	35.8	25.3	16.7	34
35	2653.6	2732.9	2813.4	2895.3	2978.5	3063.2	3149.5	3237.3	3326.9	3418.2	35
36	54.9	34.2	14.8	96.7	79.9	64.7	50.9	38.8	28.4	19.7	36
37	56.2	35.6	16.1	98.1	81.3	66.1	52.4	40.3	29.9	21.3	37
38	57.5	36.9	17.5	2899.4	82.7	67.5	53.8	41.7	31.4	22.8	38
39	58.8	38.2	18.9	2900.8	84.1	68.9	55.3	43.2	32.9	24.4	39
40	2660.2	2739.6	2820.2	2902.2	2985.5	3070.4	3156.7	3244.7	3334.4	3425.9	40
41	61.5	40.9	21.6	03.6	86.9	71.8	58.2	46.2	35.9	27.4	41
42	62.8	42.2	22.9	04.9	88.3	73.2	59.6	47.7	37.4	29.0	42
43	64.1	43.6	24.3	06.3	89.7	74.6	61.1	49.1	38.9	30.5	43
44	65.4	44.9	25.6	07.7	91.1	76.1	62.5	50.6	40.4	32.1	44
45	2666.7	2746.2	2827.0	2909.1	2992.6	3077.5	3164.0	3252.1	3342.0	3433.6	45
46	68.0	47.6	28.3	10.5	94.0	78.9	65.4	53.6	43.5	35.2	46
47	69.4	48.9	29.7	11.8	95.4	80.4	66.9	55.1	45.0	36.7	47
48	70.7	50.2	31.1	13.2	96.8	81.8	68.4	56.6	46.5	38.2	48
49	72.0	51.6	32.4	14.6	98.2	83.2	69.8	58.0	48.0	39.8	49
50	2673.3	2752.9	2833.8	2916.0	2999.6	3084.6	3171.3	3259.5	3349.5	3441.3	50
51	74.6	54.2	35.1	17.4	3001.0	86.1	72.7	61.0	51.0	42.9	51
52	75.9	55.6	36.5	18.7	02.4	87.5	74.2	62.5	52.5	44.4	52
53	77.3	56.9	37.9	20.1	03.8	88.9	75.6	64.0	54.1	46.0	53
54	78.6	58.3	39.2	21.5	05.2	90.4	77.1	65.5	55.6	47.5	54
55	2679.9	2759.6	2840.6	2922.9	3006.6	3091.8	3178.6	3267.0	3357.1	3449.1	55
56	81.2	60.9	41.9	24.3	08.0	93.2	80.0	68.4	58.6	50.6	56
57	82.5	62.3	43.3	25.7	09.4	94.7	81.5	69.9	60.1	52.2	57
58	83.8	63.6	44.7	27.0	10.8	96.1	82.9	71.4	61.7	53.7	58
59	85.2	65.0	46.0	28.4	12.2	97.5	84.4	72.9	63.2	55.3	59
60	2686.5	2766.3	2847.4	2929.8	3013.6	3099.0	3185.9	3274.4	3364.7	3456.8	60
Lat.	40°	41°	42°	43°	44°	45°	46°	47°	48°	49°	Lat.

TABLE 6

Meridional Parts

Lat. ′	50°	51°	52°	53°	54°	55°	56°	57°	58°	59°	Lat. ′
0	3456.8	3550.9	3647.0	3745.4	3846.0	3949.1	4054.8	4163.3	4274.8	4389.4	0
1	58.4	52.5	48.7	47.0	47.7	50.8	56.6	65.1	76.6	91.3	1
2	59.9	54.1	50.3	48.7	49.4	52.6	58.4	67.0	78.5	93.3	2
3	61.5	55.7	51.9	50.3	51.1	54.3	60.2	68.8	80.4	95.2	3
4	63.0	57.2	53.5	52.0	52.8	56.1	61.9	70.6	82.3	97.1	4
5	3464.6	3558.8	3655.1	3753.7	3854.5	3957.8	4063.7	4172.5	4284.2	4399.1	5
6	66.1	60.4	56.8	55.3	56.2	59.5	65.5	74.3	86.1	4401.0	6
7	67.7	62.0	58.4	57.0	57.9	61.3	67.3	76.1	88.0	03.0	7
8	69.2	63.6	60.0	58.6	59.6	63.0	69.1	78.0	89.8	04.9	8
9	70.8	65.2	61.6	60.3	61.3	64.8	70.9	79.8	91.7	06.9	9
10	3472.4	3566.8	3663.3	3762.0	3863.0	3966.5	4072.7	4181.7	4293.6	4408.8	10
11	73.9	68.4	64.9	63.6	64.7	68.3	74.5	83.5	95.5	10.8	11
12	75.5	70.0	66.5	65.3	66.4	70.0	76.3	85.3	97.4	12.7	12
13	77.0	71.5	68.1	67.0	68.1	71.8	78.1	87.2	4299.3	14.7	13
14	78.6	73.1	69.8	68.6	69.8	73.5	79.9	89.0	4301.2	16.6	14
15	3480.2	3574.7	3671.4	3770.3	3871.5	3975.3	4081.7	4190.9	4303.1	4418.6	15
16	81.7	76.3	73.0	72.0	73.2	77.0	83.4	92.7	05.0	20.5	16
17	83.3	77.9	74.7	73.6	74.9	78.8	85.2	94.6	06.9	22.5	17
18	84.8	79.5	76.3	75.3	76.7	80.5	87.0	96.4	08.8	24.4	18
19	86.4	81.1	77.9	77.0	78.4	82.3	88.8	98.3	10.7	26.4	19
20	3488.0	3582.7	3679.6	3778.6	3880.1	3984.0	4090.6	4200.1	4312.6	4428.3	20
21	89.5	84.3	81.2	80.3	81.8	85.8	92.4	02.0	14.5	30.3	21
22	91.1	85.9	82.8	82.0	83.5	87.5	94.2	03.8	16.4	32.3	22
23	92.6	87.5	84.5	83.7	85.2	89.3	96.0	05.7	18.3	34.2	23
24	94.2	89.1	86.1	85.3	86.9	91.0	97.8	07.5	20.2	36.2	24
25	3495.8	3590.7	3687.7	3787.0	3888.6	3992.8	4099.7	4209.4	4322.1	4438.1	25
26	97.3	92.3	89.4	88.7	90.4	94.6	4101.5	11.2	24.0	40.1	26
27	3498.9	93.9	91.0	90.3	92.1	96.3	03.3	13.1	25.9	42.1	27
28	3500.5	95.5	92.6	92.0	93.8	98.1	05.1	14.9	27.8	44.0	28
29	02.0	97.1	94.3	93.7	95.5	3999.8	06.9	16.8	29.7	46.0	29
30	3503.6	3598.7	3695.9	3795.4	3897.2	4001.6	4108.7	4218.6	4331.7	4448.0	30
31	05.2	3600.3	97.6	97.1	3898.9	03.4	10.5	20.5	33.6	49.9	31
32	06.7	01.9	3699.2	3798.7	3900.7	05.1	12.3	22.4	35.5	51.9	32
33	08.3	03.5	3700.8	3800.4	02.4	06.9	14.1	24.2	37.4	53.9	33
34	09.9	05.1	02.5	02.1	04.1	08.7	15.9	26.1	39.3	55.8	34
35	3511.5	3606.7	3704.1	3803.8	3905.8	4010.4	4117.7	4227.9	4341.2	4457.8	35
36	13.0	08.3	05.8	05.4	07.5	12.2	19.5	29.8	43.1	59.8	36
37	14.6	09.9	07.4	07.1	09.3	14.0	21.4	31.7	45.1	61.7	37
38	16.2	11.5	09.0	08.8	11.0	15.7	23.2	33.5	47.0	63.7	38
39	17.7	13.1	10.7	10.5	12.7	17.5	25.0	35.4	48.9	65.7	39
40	3519.3	3614.8	3712.3	3812.2	3914.4	4019.3	4126.8	4237.3	4350.8	4467.7	40
41	20.9	16.4	14.0	13.9	16.2	21.0	28.6	39.1	52.7	69.6	41
42	22.5	18.0	15.6	15.5	17.9	22.8	30.4	41.0	54.6	71.6	42
43	24.0	19.6	17.3	17.2	19.6	24.6	32.3	42.9	56.6	73.6	43
44	25.6	21.2	18.9	18.9	21.3	26.3	34.1	44.7	58.5	75.6	44
45	3527.2	3622.8	3720.6	3820.6	3923.1	4028.1	4135.9	4246.6	4360.4	4477.6	45
46	28.8	24.4	22.2	22.3	24.8	29.9	37.7	48.5	62.3	79.5	46
47	30.3	26.0	23.9	24.0	26.5	31.7	39.5	50.3	64.3	81.5	47
48	31.9	27.6	25.5	25.7	28.3	33.4	41.4	52.2	66.2	83.5	48
49	33.5	29.2	27.2	27.4	30.0	35.2	43.2	54.1	68.1	85.5	49
50	3535.1	3630.9	3728.8	3829.1	3931.7	4037.0	4145.0	4256.0	4370.0	4487.5	50
51	36.7	32.5	30.5	30.7	33.5	38.8	46.8	57.8	72.0	89.5	51
52	38.2	34.1	32.1	32.4	35.2	40.5	48.7	59.7	73.9	91.5	52
53	39.8	35.7	33.8	34.1	36.9	42.3	50.5	61.6	75.8	93.5	53
54	41.4	37.3	35.4	35.8	38.7	44.1	52.3	63.5	77.8	95.4	54
55	3543.0	3638.9	3737.1	3837.5	3940.4	4045.9	4154.1	4265.3	4379.7	4497.4	55
56	44.6	40.6	38.7	39.2	42.1	47.7	56.0	67.2	81.6	4499.4	56
57	46.1	42.2	40.4	40.9	43.9	49.4	57.8	69.1	83.6	4501.4	57
58	47.7	43.8	42.0	42.6	45.6	51.2	59.6	71.0	85.5	03.4	58
59	49.3	45.4	43.7	44.3	47.3	53.0	61.5	72.9	87.4	05.4	59
60	3550.9	3647.0	3745.4	3846.0	3949.1	4054.8	4163.3	4274.8	4389.4	4507.4	60
Lat.	50°	51°	52°	53°	54°	55°	56°	57°	58°	59°	Lat.

TABLE 6

Meridional Parts

Lat.	60°	61°	62°	63°	64°	65°	66°	67°	68°	69°	Lat.
′											′
0	4507.4	4629.1	4754.6	4884.4	5018.7	5157.9	5302.4	5452.8	5609.4	5773.0	0
1	09.4	31.1	56.8	86.6	21.0	60.3	04.9	55.3	12.1	75.8	1
2	11.4	33.2	58.9	88.8	23.3	62.6	07.4	57.9	14.8	78.6	2
3	13.4	35.2	61.0	91.0	25.5	65.0	09.8	60.5	17.4	81.4	3
4	15.4	37.3	63.1	93.2	27.8	67.4	12.3	63.0	20.1	84.2	4
5	4517.4	4639.4	4765.3	4895.4	5030.1	5169.7	5314.7	5465.6	5622.8	5787.0	5
6	19.4	41.4	67.4	97.6	32.4	72.1	17.2	68.2	25.5	89.8	6
7	21.4	43.5	69.5	4899.8	34.7	74.5	19.7	70.7	28.2	92.6	7
8	23.4	45.6	71.7	4902.0	37.0	76.9	22.1	73.3	30.8	95.4	8
9	25.4	47.6	73.8	04.2	39.3	79.2	24.6	75.9	33.5	5798.2	9
10	4527.4	4649.7	4776.0	4906.5	5041.6	5181.6	5327.1	5478.4	5636.2	5801.0	10
11	29.4	51.8	78.1	08.7	43.8	84.0	29.6	81.0	38.9	03.8	11
12	31.4	53.9	80.2	10.9	46.1	86.4	32.0	83.6	41.6	06.6	12
13	33.4	55.9	82.4	13.1	48.4	88.8	34.5	86.2	44.3	09.5	13
14	35.5	58.0	84.5	15.3	50.7	99.1	37.0	88.7	47.0	12.3	14
15	4537.5	4660.1	4786.7	4917.5	5053.0	5193.5	5339.5	5491.3	5649.7	5815.1	15
16	39.5	62.2	88.8	19.8	55.3	95.9	42.0	93.9	52.4	17.9	16
17	41.5	64.2	91.0	22.0	57.6	5198.3	44.4	96.5	55.1	20.7	17
18	43.5	66.3	93.1	24.2	59.9	5200.7	46.9	5499.1	57.8	23.6	18
19	45.5	68.4	95.3	26.4	62.2	03.1	49.4	5501.7	60.5	26.4	19
20	4547.5	4670.5	4797.4	4928.6	5064.5	5205.5	5351.9	5504.3	5663.2	5829.2	20
21	49.6	72.6	4799.6	30.9	66.8	07.9	54.4	06.9	65.9	32.1	21
22	51.6	74.6	4801.7	33.1	69.2	10.3	56.9	09.5	68.6	34.9	22
23	53.6	76.7	03.9	35.3	71.5	12.7	59.4	12.1	71.3	37.7	23
24	55.6	78.8	06.0	37.6	73.8	15.1	61.9	14.7	74.0	40.6	24
25	4557.6	4680.9	4808.2	4939.8	5076.1	5217.5	5364.4	5517.3	5676.7	5843.4	25
26	59.7	83.0	10.3	42.0	78.4	19.9	66.9	19.9	79.4	46.2	26
27	61.7	85.1	12.5	44.2	80.7	22.3	69.4	22.5	82.2	49.1	27
28	63.7	87.2	14.6	46.5	83.0	24.7	71.9	25.1	84.9	51.9	28
29	65.7	89.2	16.8	48.7	85.3	27.1	74.4	27.7	87.6	54.8	29
30	4567.8	4691.3	4819.0	4951.0	5087.7	5229.5	5376.9	5530.3	5690.3	5857.6	30
31	69.8	93.4	21.1	53.2	90.0	31.9	79.4	32.9	93.1	60.5	31
32	71.8	95.5	23.3	55.4	92.3	34.3	81.9	35.5	95.8	63.3	32
33	73.8	97.6	25.5	57.7	94.6	36.7	84.4	38.1	5698.5	66.2	33
34	75.9	4699.7	27.6	59.9	97.0	39.1	86.9	40.7	5701.2	69.1	34
35	4577.9	4701.8	4829.8	4962.2	5099.3	5241.6	5389.4	5543.6	5704.0	5871.9	35
36	79.9	03.9	32.0	64.4	5101.6	44.0	91.9	46.0	06.7	74.8	36
37	82.0	06.0	34.1	66.7	03.9	46.4	94.4	48.6	09.5	77.7	37
38	84.0	08.1	36.3	68.9	06.3	48.8	97.0	51.2	12.2	80.5	38
39	86.1	10.2	38.5	71.2	08.6	51.2	5399.5	53.9	14.9	83.4	39
40	4588.1	4712.3	4840.7	4973.4	5110.9	5253.7	5402.0	5556.5	5717.7	5886.3	40
41	90.1	14.4	42.8	75.7	13.3	56.1	04.5	59.1	20.4	89.2	41
42	92.2	16.5	45.0	77.9	15.6	58.5	07.0	61.7	23.2	92.0	42
43	94.2	18.6	47.2	80.2	17.9	60.9	09.6	64.4	25.9	94.9	43
44	96.3	20.7	49.4	82.4	20.3	63.4	12.1	67.0	28.7	5897.8	44
45	4598.3	4722.9	4851.5	4984.7	5122.6	5265.8	5414.6	5569.7	5731.4	5900.7	45
46	4600.3	25.0	53.7	86.9	25.0	68.2	17.2	72.3	34.2	03.6	46
47	02.4	27.1	55.9	89.2	27.3	70.7	19.7	74.9	37.0	06.5	47
48	04.4	29.2	58.1	91.5	29.7	73.1	22.2	77.6	39.7	09.4	48
49	06.5	31.3	60.3	93.7	32.0	75.5	24.8	80.2	42.5	12.3	49
50	4608.5	4733.4	4862.5	4996.0	5134.4	5278.0	5427.3	5582.9	5745.3	5915.2	50
51	10.6	35.5	64.6	4998.3	36.7	80.4	29.8	85.5	48.0	18.1	51
52	12.6	37.6	66.8	5000.5	39.1	82.9	32.4	88.2	50.8	21.0	52
53	14.7	39.8	69.0	02.8	41.4	85.3	34.9	90.8	53.6	23.9	53
54	16.7	41.9	71.2	05.1	43.8	87.7	37.5	93.5	56.3	26.8	54
55	4618.8	4744.0	4873.4	5007.3	5146.1	5290.2	5440.0	5596.1	5759.1	5929.7	55
56	20.8	46.1	75.6	09.6	48.5	92.6	42.6	5598.8	61.9	32.6	56
57	22.9	48.3	77.8	11.9	50.8	95.1	45.1	5601.4	64.7	35.5	57
58	24.9	50.4	80.0	14.1	53.2	5297.5	47.7	04.1	67.5	38.4	58
59	27.0	52.5	82.2	16.4	55.5	5300.0	50.2	06.8	70.2	41.3	59
60	4629.1	4754.6	4884.4	5018.7	5157.9	5302.4	5452.8	5609.4	5773.0	5944.2	60
Lat.	60°	61°	62°	63°	64°	65°	66°	67°	68°	69°	Lat.

TABLE 6

Meridional Parts

Lat.	70°	71°	72°	73°	74°	75°	76°	77°	78°	79°	Lat.
′											′
0	5944.2	6123.9	6312.9	6512.4	6723.6	6948.1	7187.7	7444.7	7722.0	8023.1	0
1	47.2	27.0	16.1	15.8	27.2	51.9	91.8	49.2	26.8	28.3	1
2	50.1	30.0	19.4	19.2	30.8	55.8	7196.0	53.6	31.6	33.6	2
3	53.0	33.1	22.6	22.6	34.5	59.7	7200.1	58.1	36.5	38.8	3
4	56.0	36.2	25.9	26.1	38.1	63.5	04.3	62.6	41.3	44.1	4
5	5958.9	6139.3	6329.1	6529.5	6741.8	6967.4	7208.4	7467.0	7746.1	8049.4	5
6	61.8	42.4	32.4	32.9	45.4	71.3	12.6	71.5	51.0	54.6	6
7	64.8	45.4	35.6	36.4	49.0	75.2	16.7	76.0	55.8	59.9	7
8	67.7	48.5	38.9	39.8	52.7	79.1	20.9	80.5	60.7	65.2	8
9	70.6	51.6	42.1	43.3	56.4	83.0	25.1	85.0	65.6	70.5	9
10	5973.6	6154.7	6345.4	6546.7	6760.0	6986.9	7229.3	7489.5	7770.4	8075.9	10
11	76.5	57.8	48.7	50.2	63.7	90.8	33.4	94.0	75.3	81.2	11
12	79.5	60.9	51.9	53.6	67.4	94.7	37.6	7498.5	80.2	86.5	12
13	82.4	64.0	55.2	57.1	71.0	6998.6	41.8	7503.0	85.1	91.9	13
14	85.4	67.1	58.5	60.5	74.7	7002.5	46.0	07.5	90.0	8097.2	14
15	5988.3	6170.2	6361.7	6564.0	6778.4	7006.5	7250.2	7512.0	7794.9	8102.6	15
16	91.3	73.3	65.0	67.5	82.1	10.4	54.4	16.6	7799.8	07.9	16
17	94.3	76.5	68.3	71.0	85.8	14.3	58.6	21.1	7804.7	13.3	17
18	5997.2	79.6	71.6	74.4	89.4	18.3	62.9	25.6	09.6	18.7	18
19	6000.2	82.7	74.9	77.9	93.1	22.2	67.1	30.2	14.6	24.1	19
20	6003.2	6185.8	6378.2	6581.4	6796.8	7026.2	7271.3	7534.8	7819.5	8129.5	20
21	06.1	88.9	81.5	84.9	6800.5	30.1	75.5	39.3	24.5	34.9	21
22	09.1	92.1	84.8	88.4	04.3	34.1	79.8	43.9	29.4	40.3	22
23	12.1	95.2	88.1	91.9	08.0	38.0	84.0	48.5	34.4	45.7	23
24	15.0	6198.3	91.4	95.4	11.7	42.0	88.3	53.0	39.3	51.1	24
25	6018.0	6201.5	6394.7	6598.9	6815.4	7045.9	7292.5	7557.6	7844.3	8156.6	25
26	21.0	04.6	6398.0	6602.4	19.1	49.9	7296.8	62.2	49.3	62.0	26
27	24.0	07.7	6401.3	05.9	22.8	53.9	7301.1	66.8	54.3	67.5	27
28	27.0	10.9	04.6	09.4	26.6	57.9	05.3	71.4	59.3	72.9	28
29	30.0	14.0	07.9	12.9	30.3	61.9	09.6	76.0	64.3	78.4	29
30	6033.0	6217.2	6411.3	6616.4	6834.1	7065.9	7313.9	7580.6	7869.3	8183.9	30
31	36.0	20.3	14.6	19.9	37.8	69.8	18.2	85.3	74.3	89.4	31
32	39.0	23.5	17.9	23.5	41.5	73.8	22.4	89.9	79.3	8194.9	32
33	42.0	26.6	21.2	27.0	45.3	77.9	26.7	94.5	84.4	8200.4	33
34	45.0	29.8	24.6	30.5	49.0	81.9	31.0	7599.2	89.4	05.9	34
35	6048.0	6233.0	6427.9	6634.1	6852.8	7085.9	7335.4	7603.8	7894.5	8211.4	35
36	51.0	36.1	31.3	37.6	56.6	89.9	39.7	08.5	7899.5	17.0	36
37	54.0	39.3	34.6	41.1	60.3	93.9	44.0	13.1	7904.6	22.5	37
38	57.0	42.5	37.9	44.7	64.1	7097.9	48.3	17.8	09.7	28.1	38
39	60.0	45.6	41.3	48.2	67.9	7102.0	52.6	22.5	14.7	33.6	39
40	6063.0	6248.8	6444.6	6651.8	6871.7	7106.0	7357.0	7627.1	7919.8	8239.2	40
41	66.0	52.0	48.0	55.3	75.4	10.0	61.3	31.8	24.9	44.8	41
42	69.1	55.2	51.4	58.9	79.2	14.1	65.6	36.5	30.0	50.4	42
43	72.1	58.3	54.7	62.5	83.0	18.1	70.0	41.2	35.1	56.0	43
44	75.1	61.5	58.1	66.0	86.8	22.2	74.3	45.9	40.2	61.6	44
45	6078.1	6264.7	6461.5	6669.6	6890.6	7126.2	7378.7	7650.6	7945.3	8267.2	45
46	81.2	67.9	64.8	73.2	94.4	30.3	83.1	55.3	50.5	72.8	46
47	84.2	71.1	68.2	76.7	6898.2	34.4	87.4	60.0	55.6	78.4	47
48	87.3	74.3	71.6	80.3	6902.0	38.5	91.8	64.8	60.7	84.1	48
49	90.3	77.5	75.0	83.9	05.8	42.5	7396.2	69.5	65.9	89.7	49
50	6093.3	6280.7	6478.3	6687.5	6909.7	7146.6	7400.6	7674.2	7971.1	8295.4	50
51	96.4	83.9	81.7	91.1	13.5	50.7	05.0	79.0	76.2	8301.0	51
52	6099.4	87.1	85.1	94.7	17.3	54.8	09.4	83.7	81.4	06.7	52
53	6102.5	90.3	88.5	6698.3	21.1	58.9	13.8	88.5	86.6	12.4	53
54	05.5	93.6	91.9	6701.9	25.0	63.0	18.2	93.3	91.8	18.1	54
55	6108.6	6296.8	6495.3	6705.5	6928.8	7167.1	7422.6	7698.0	7997.0	8323.8	55
56	11.6	6300.0	6498.7	09.1	32.6	71.2	27.0	7702.8	8002.2	29.5	56
57	14.7	03.2	6502.1	12.7	36.5	75.3	31.4	07.6	07.4	35.3	57
58	17.8	06.4	05.5	16.3	40.3	79.4	35.9	12.4	12.6	41.0	58
59	20.8	09.7	09.0	20.0	44.2	83.6	40.3	17.2	17.8	46.7	59
60	6123.9	6312.9	6512.4	6723.6	6948.1	7187.7	7444.7	7722.0	8023.1	8352.5	60
Lat.	70°	71°	72°	73°	74°	75°	76°	77°	78°	79°	Lat.

TABLE 6

Meridional Parts

Lat.	80°	81°	82°	83°	84°	85°	86°	87°	88°	89°	Lat.
′											′
0	8352.5	8716.3	9122.6	9582.9	10113.9	10741.6	11509.5	12499.1	13893.4	16276.5	0
1	58.2	22.7	29.8	91.1	123.5	753.1	523.9	518.2	922.2	334.3	1
2	64.0	29.1	37.0	9599.4	133.1	764.7	538.3	537.5	951.2	393.0	2
3	69.8	35.5	44.2	9607.6	142.8	776.2	552.8	556.9	13980.4	452.8	3
4	75.6	41.9	51.5	15.9	152.4	787.8	567.3	576.4	14009.9	513.7	4
5	8381.4	8748.4	9158.7	9624.2	10162.1	10799.5	11581.9	12596.0	14039.7	16575.6	5
6	87.2	54.8	66.0	32.5	171.8	811.2	596.6	615.7	069.7	638.7	6
7	93.0	61.3	73.3	40.8	181.6	822.9	611.3	635.5	100.0	703.0	7
8	8398.9	67.8	80.6	49.2	191.3	834.7	626.1	655.4	130.6	768.5	8
9	8404.7	74.3	87.9	57.6	201.1	846.5	641.0	675.5	161.4	835.2	9
10	8410.5	8780.8	9195.2	9666.0	10211.0	10858.3	11655.9	12695.7	14192.6	16903.3	10
11	16.4	87.3	9202.6	74.4	220.8	870.2	670.9	715.9	224.0	16972.8	11
12	22.3	8793.8	09.9	82.8	230.7	882.1	686.0	736.4	255.6	17043.6	12
13	28.1	8800.4	17.3	91.3	240.6	894.1	701.1	756.9	287.6	116.0	13
14	34.0	06.9	24.7	9699.7	250.5	906.1	716.3	777.5	319.9	189.9	14
15	8439.9	8813.5	9232.1	9708.2	10260.5	10918.2	11731.5	12798.3	14352.5	17265.5	15
16	45.8	20.1	39.5	16.8	270.5	930.3	746.9	819.2	385.4	342.8	16
17	51.8	26.7	47.0	25.3	280.5	942.4	762.3	840.3	418.6	421.8	17
18	57.7	33.3	54.4	33.9	290.6	954.6	777.7	861.4	452.2	502.7	18
19	63.6	39.9	61.9	42.4	300.7	966.8	793.2	882.7	486.0	585.5	19
20	8469.6	8846.5	9269.4	9751.0	10310.8	10979.1	11808.8	12904.1	14520.3	17670.4	20
21	75.5	53.2	76.9	59.7	320.9	10991.4	824.5	925.7	554.8	757.5	21
22	81.5	59.8	84.4	68.3	331.1	11003.8	840.3	947.4	589.7	846.8	22
23	87.5	66.5	91.9	77.0	341.3	016.2	856.1	969.2	625.0	17938.4	23
24	93.5	73.2	9299.5	85.7	351.5	028.6	872.0	12991.2	660.6	18032.6	24
25	8499.5	8879.9	9307.0	9794.4	10361.8	11041.1	11887.9	13013.3	14696.6	18129.5	25
26	8505.5	86.6	14.6	9803.1	372.1	053.6	904.0	035.6	733.0	229.1	26
27	11.5	8893.3	22.2	11.9	382.4	066.2	920.1	058.0	769.8	331.8	27
28	17.5	8900.0	29.8	20.6	392.7	078.8	936.3	080.5	806.9	437.6	28
29	23.6	06.8	37.5	29.4	403.1	091.5	952.5	103.2	844.5	546.7	29
30	8529.6	8913.5	9345.1	9838.3	10413.6	11104.2	11968.9	13126.1	14882.5	18659.4	30
31	35.7	20.3	52.8	47.1	424.0	117.0	11985.3	149.1	920.9	776.0	31
32	41.8	27.1	60.5	56.0	434.5	129.8	12001.8	172.2	959.8	18896.6	32
33	47.9	33.9	68.2	64.9	445.0	142.7	018.4	195.6	14999.1	19021.6	33
34	54.0	40.7	75.9	73.8	455.5	155.6	035.0	219.0	15038.8	151.4	34
35	8560.1	8947.5	9383.7	9882.7	10466.1	11168.6	12051.8	13242.7	15079.0	19286.2	35
36	66.2	54.3	91.4	9891.7	476.7	181.6	068.6	266.5	119.7	426.5	36
37	72.3	61.2	9399.2	9900.6	487.4	194.6	085.5	290.4	160.9	572.9	37
38	78.4	68.1	9407.0	09.7	498.0	207.7	102.5	314.6	202.6	725.7	38
39	84.6	74.9	14.8	18.7	508.7	220.9	119.5	338.9	244.7	19885.6	39
40	8590.7	8981.8	9422.6	9927.7	10519.5	11234.1	12136.7	13363.3	15287.5	20053.3	40
41	8596.9	88.7	30.4	36.8	530.3	247.4	153.9	388.0	330.7	229.7	41
42	8603.1	8995.7	38.3	45.9	541.1	260.7	171.3	412.8	374.5	415.5	42
43	09.3	9002.6	46.2	55.0	551.9	274.0	188.7	437.8	418.9	612.0	43
44	15.5	09.5	54.1	64.2	562.8	287.5	206.2	463.0	463.8	20820.4	44
45	8621.7	9016.5	9462.0	9973.4	10573.7	11300.9	12223.8	13488.4	15509.3	21042.3	45
46	27.9	23.5	69.9	82.6	584.6	314.4	241.5	513.9	555.5	279.5	46
47	34.2	30.5	77.9	9991.8	595.6	328.0	259.2	539.7	602.3	534.2	47
48	40.4	37.5	85.8	10001.0	606.6	341.6	277.1	565.7	649.7	21809.4	48
49	46.7	44.5	9493.8	010.3	617.7	355.3	295.1	591.8	697.8	22108.5	49
50	8652.9	9051.5	9501.8	10019.6	10628.8	11369.1	12313.1	13618.2	15746.5	22436.2	50
51	59.2	58.6	09.9	028.9	639.9	382.8	331.3	644.7	796.0	22798.4	51
52	65.5	65.6	17.9	038.3	651.1	396.7	349.5	671.5	846.2	23203.3	52
53	71.8	72.7	26.0	047.6	662.3	410.6	367.9	698.4	897.1	23662.4	53
54	78.1	79.8	34.0	057.0	673.5	424.6	386.3	725.6	15948.8	24192.3	54
55	8684.5	9086.9	9542.1	10066.4	10684.8	11438.6	12404.8	13753.0	16001.3	24819.1	55
56	90.8	9094.0	50.3	075.9	696.1	452.6	423.5	780.6	054.6	25586.2	56
57	8697.2	9101.1	58.4	085.4	707.4	466.8	442.2	808.5	108.8	26575.1	57
58	8703.5	08.3	66.6	094.9	718.8	481.0	461.1	836.5	163.8	27969.8	58
59	09.9	15.4	74.7	10104.4	730.2	495.2	480.0	864.8	219.7	30351.6	59
60	8716.3	9122.6	9582.9	10113.9	10741.6	11509.5	12499.1	13893.4	16276.5	- - - - -	60
Lat.	80°	81°	82°	83°	84°	85°	86°	87°	88°	89°	Lat.

TABLE 7

Length of a Degree of Latitude and Longitude

Lat.	Degree of latitude				Degree of longitude				Lat.
	Nautical Miles	Statute Miles	Feet	Meters	Nautical Miles	Statute Miles	Feet	Meters	
°									°
0	59. 705	68. 708	362 776	110 574	60. 108	69. 171	365 221	111 319	0
1	. 706	. 708	778	575	60. 099	69. 160	365 166	111 303	1
2	. 706	. 709	781	576	60. 071	69. 129	365 000	111 252	2
3	. 707	. 710	786	577	60. 026	69. 077	364 724	111 168	3
4	. 708	. 711	794	580	59. 962	69. 003	364 338	111 050	4
5	59. 710	68. 713	362 804	110 583	59. 880	68. 909	363 841	110 899	5
6	. 712	. 715	816	586	59. 781	68. 794	363 234	110 714	6
7	. 714	. 718	831	591	59. 663	68. 659	362 517	110 495	7
8	. 717	. 721	847	596	59. 527	68. 502	361 690	110 243	8
9	. 720	. 725	866	601	59. 373	68. 325	360 754	109 958	9
10	59. 723	68. 728	362 886	110 608	59. 201	68. 127	359 709	109 639	10
11	. 727	. 733	909	615	59. 011	67. 908	358 555	109 288	11
12	. 731	. 738	934	622	58. 803	67. 669	357 292	108 903	12
13	. 736	. 743	961	630	58. 577	67. 409	355 921	108 485	13
14	. 740	. 748	990	639	58. 334	67. 129	354 442	108 034	14
15	59. 746	68. 754	363 021	110 649	58. 073	66. 829	352 856	107 550	15
16	. 751	. 760	053	659	57. 794	66. 508	351 163	107 034	16
17	. 757	. 767	088	669	57. 498	66. 167	349 363	106 486	17
18	. 763	. 774	125	680	57. 184	65. 806	347 457	105 905	18
19	. 769	. 781	163	692	56. 853	65. 425	345 446	105 292	19
20	59. 776	68. 788	363 203	110 704	56. 505	65. 025	343 330	104 647	20
21	. 782	. 796	245	717	56. 140	64. 604	341 110	103 970	21
22	. 790	. 805	288	730	55. 757	64. 164	338 786	103 262	22
23	. 797	. 813	333	744	55. 358	63. 705	336 360	102 523	23
24	. 805	. 822	380	758	54. 942	63. 226	333 831	101 752	24
25	59. 813	68. 831	363 428	110 773	54. 509	62. 727	331 201	100 950	25
26	. 821	. 840	478	788	54. 059	62. 210	328 470	100 118	26
27	. 829	. 850	529	804	53. 593	61. 674	325 639	99 255	27
28	. 838	. 860	581	819	53. 111	61. 119	322 709	98 362	28
29	. 847	. 870	634	836	52. 613	60. 546	319 681	97 439	29
30	59. 856	68. 881	363 689	110 852	52. 098	59. 954	316 556	96 486	30
31	. 865	. 891	745	869	51. 568	59. 344	313 334	95 504	31
32	. 874	. 902	802	887	51. 022	58. 715	310 017	94 493	32
33	. 884	. 913	860	904	50. 461	58. 069	306 605	93 453	33
34	. 893	. 924	919	922	49. 884	57. 405	303 100	92 385	34
35	59. 903	68. 935	363 978	110 941	49. 292	56. 724	299 502	91 288	35
36	. 913	. 947	364 039	959	48. 684	56. 025	295 813	90 164	36
37	. 923	. 958	100	978	48. 062	55. 309	292 033	89 012	37
38	. 933	. 970	162	996	47. 426	54. 577	288 164	87 832	38
39	. 944	. 982	224	111 015	46. 774	53. 827	284 207	86 626	39
40	59. 954	68. 994	364 287	111 035	46. 109	53. 061	280 163	85 394	40
41	. 964	69. 006	350	054	45. 429	52. 279	276 034	84 135	41
42	. 975	. 018	414	073	44. 736	51. 481	271 820	82 851	42
43	. 985	. 030	477	093	44. 029	50. 667	267 523	81 541	43
44	. 996	. 042	541	112	43. 308	49. 838	263 144	80 206	44
45	60. 006	69. 054	364 605	111 132	42. 574	48. 993	258 684	78 847	45

TABLE 7

Length of a Degree of Latitude and Longitude

Lat.	Degree of latitude				Degree of longitude				Lat.
	Nautical Miles	Statute Miles	Feet	Meters	Nautical Miles	Statute Miles	Feet	Meters	
°									°
45	60. 006	69. 054	364 605	111 132	42. 574	48. 993	258 684	78 847	45
46	. 017	. 066	670	151	41. 827	48. 133	254 145	77 463	46
47	. 027	. 078	734	171	41. 067	47. 259	249 527	76 056	47
48	. 038	. 090	798	190	40. 294	46. 370	244 834	74 625	48
49	. 048	. 103	861	210	39. 510	45. 467	240 065	73 172	49
50	60. 059	69. 115	364 925	111 229	38. 713	44. 550	235 222	71 696	50
51	. 069	. 126	988	248	37. 904	43. 619	230 307	70 198	51
52	. 080	. 138	365 050	267	37. 083	42. 675	225 321	68 678	52
53	. 090	. 150	112	286	36. 251	41. 717	220 266	67 137	53
54	. 100	. 162	174	305	35. 408	40. 747	215 144	65 576	54
55	60. 110	69. 173	365 235	111 323	34. 554	39. 764	209 954	63 994	55
56	. 120	. 185	295	342	33. 689	38. 769	204 701	62 393	56
57	. 129	. 196	354	360	32. 814	37. 762	199 384	60 772	57
58	. 139	. 207	412	378	31. 929	36. 743	194 005	59 133	58
59	. 149	. 218	469	395	31. 034	35. 713	188 567	57 475	59
60	60. 158	69. 228	365 526	111 412	30. 130	34. 672	183 071	55 800	60
61	. 167	. 239	581	429	29. 216	33. 621	177 518	54 107	61
62	. 176	. 249	635	446	28. 293	32. 559	171 910	52 398	62
63	. 184	. 259	688	462	27. 361	31. 487	166 249	50 673	63
64	. 193	. 269	739	477	26. 421	30. 405	160 537	48 932	64
65	60. 201	69. 278	365 789	111 493	25. 473	29. 314	154 775	47 176	65
66	. 209	. 287	838	507	24. 517	28. 213	148 966	45 405	66
67	. 217	. 296	885	522	23. 553	27. 104	143 110	43 620	67
68	. 224	. 305	931	536	22. 582	25. 987	137 210	41 822	68
69	. 232	. 313	975	549	21. 604	24. 861	131 267	40 010	69
70	60. 239	69. 321	366 017	111 562	20. 619	23. 728	125 284	38 187	70
71	. 245	. 329	058	574	19. 628	22. 587	119 262	36 351	71
72	. 252	. 336	096	586	18. 631	21. 440	113 203	34 504	72
73	. 258	. 343	133	597	17. 628	20. 286	107 109	32 647	73
74	. 264	. 350	169	608	16. 619	19. 125	100 981	30 779	74
75	60. 269	69. 356	366 202	111 618	15. 606	17. 959	94 823	28 902	75
76	. 274	. 362	233	628	14. 587	16. 787	88 635	27 016	76
77	. 279	. 368	262	637	13. 564	15. 610	82 419	25 121	77
78	. 284	. 373	290	645	12. 537	14. 428	76 178	23 219	78
79	. 288	. 378	315	653	11. 506	13. 241	69 913	21 310	79
80	60. 292	69. 382	366 338	111 660	10. 472	12. 051	63 627	19 393	80
81	. 295	. 386	359	666	9. 434	10. 856	57 321	17 471	81
82	. 298	. 390	378	672	8. 393	9. 658	50 997	15 544	82
83	. 301	. 393	395	677	7. 350	8. 458	44 657	13 611	83
84	. 303	. 396	409	682	6. 304	7. 254	38 303	11 675	84
85	60. 305	69. 398	366 422	111 685	5. 256	6. 049	31 937	9 735	85
86	. 307	. 400	432	688	4. 207	4. 841	25 562	7 791	86
87	. 308	. 401	440	691	3. 156	3. 632	19 178	5 846	87
88	. 309	. 403	445	693	2. 105	2. 422	12 789	3 898	88
89	. 310	. 403	449	694	1. 053	1. 211	6 395	1 949	89
90	60. 310	69. 403	366 450	111 694	0. 000	0. 000	0	0	90

TABLE 8

Conversion Table for Meters, Feet, and Fathoms

Meters	Feet	Fathoms	Meters	Feet	Fathoms	Feet	Meters	Feet	Meters	Fathoms	Meters	Fathoms	Meters
1	3.28	0.55	61	200.13	33.36	1	0.30	61	18.59	1	1.83	61	111.56
2	6.56	1.09	62	203.41	33.90	2	0.61	62	18.90	2	3.66	62	113.39
3	9.84	1.64	63	206.69	34.45	3	0.91	63	19.20	3	5.49	63	115.21
4	13.12	2.19	64	209.97	35.00	4	1.22	64	19.51	4	7.32	64	117.04
5	16.40	2.73	65	213.25	35.54	5	1.52	65	19.81	5	9.14	65	118.87
6	19.69	3.28	66	216.54	36.09	6	1.83	66	20.12	6	10.97	66	120.70
7	22.97	3.83	67	219.82	36.64	7	2.13	67	20.42	7	12.80	67	122.53
8	26.25	4.37	68	223.10	37.18	8	2.44	68	20.73	8	14.63	68	124.36
9	29.53	4.92	69	226.38	37.73	9	2.74	69	21.03	9	16.46	69	126.19
10	32.81	5.47	70	229.66	38.28	10	3.05	70	21.34	10	18.29	70	128.02
11	36.09	6.01	71	232.94	38.82	11	3.35	71	21.64	11	20.12	71	129.84
12	39.37	6.56	72	236.22	39.37	12	3.66	72	21.95	12	21.95	72	131.67
13	42.65	7.11	73	239.50	39.92	13	3.96	73	22.25	13	23.77	73	133.50
14	45.93	7.66	74	242.78	40.46	14	4.27	74	22.56	14	25.60	74	135.33
15	49.21	8.20	75	246.06	41.01	15	4.57	75	22.86	15	27.43	75	137.16
16	52.49	8.75	76	249.34	41.56	16	4.88	76	23.16	16	29.26	76	138.99
17	55.77	9.30	77	252.62	42.10	17	5.18	77	23.47	17	31.09	77	140.82
18	59.06	9.84	78	255.91	42.65	18	5.49	78	23.77	18	32.92	78	142.65
19	62.34	10.39	79	259.19	43.20	19	5.79	79	24.08	19	34.75	79	144.48
20	65.62	10.94	80	262.47	43.74	20	6.10	80	24.38	20	36.58	80	146.30
21	68.90	11.48	81	265.75	44.29	21	6.40	81	24.69	21	38.40	81	148.13
22	72.18	12.03	82	269.03	44.84	22	6.71	82	24.99	22	40.23	82	149.96
23	75.46	12.58	83	272.31	45.38	23	7.01	83	25.30	23	42.06	83	151.79
24	78.74	13.12	84	275.59	45.93	24	7.32	84	25.60	24	43.89	84	153.62
25	82.02	13.67	85	278.87	46.48	25	7.62	85	25.91	25	45.72	85	155.45
26	85.30	14.22	86	282.15	47.03	26	7.92	86	26.21	26	47.55	86	157.28
27	88.58	14.76	87	285.43	47.57	27	8.23	87	26.52	27	49.38	87	159.11
28	91.86	15.31	88	288.71	48.12	28	8.53	88	26.82	28	51.21	88	160.93
29	95.14	15.86	89	291.99	48.67	29	8.84	89	27.13	29	53.04	89	162.76
30	98.43	16.40	90	295.28	49.21	30	9.14	90	27.43	30	54.86	90	164.59
31	101.71	16.95	91	298.56	49.76	31	9.45	91	27.74	31	56.69	91	166.42
32	104.99	17.50	92	301.84	50.31	32	9.75	92	28.04	32	58.52	92	168.25
33	108.27	18.04	93	305.12	50.85	33	10.06	93	28.35	33	60.35	93	170.08
34	111.55	18.59	94	308.40	51.40	34	10.36	94	28.65	34	62.18	94	171.91
35	114.83	19.14	95	311.68	51.95	35	10.67	95	28.96	35	64.01	95	173.74
36	118.11	19.69	96	314.96	52.49	36	10.97	96	29.26	36	65.84	96	175.56
37	121.39	20.23	97	318.24	53.04	37	11.28	97	29.57	37	67.67	97	177.39
38	124.67	20.78	98	321.52	53.59	38	11.58	98	29.87	38	69.49	98	179.22
39	127.95	21.33	99	324.80	54.13	39	11.89	99	30.18	39	71.32	99	181.05
40	131.23	21.87	100	328.08	54.68	40	12.19	100	30.48	40	73.15	100	182.88
41	134.51	22.42	101	331.36	55.23	41	12.50	101	30.78	41	74.98	101	184.71
42	137.80	22.97	102	334.65	55.77	42	12.80	102	31.09	42	76.81	102	186.54
43	141.08	23.51	103	337.93	56.32	43	13.11	103	31.39	43	78.64	103	188.37
44	144.36	24.06	104	341.21	56.87	44	13.41	104	31.70	44	80.47	104	190.20
45	147.64	24.61	105	344.49	57.41	45	13.72	105	32.00	45	82.30	105	192.02
46	150.92	25.15	106	347.77	57.96	46	14.02	106	32.31	46	84.12	106	193.85
47	154.20	25.70	107	351.05	58.51	47	14.33	107	32.61	47	85.95	107	195.68
48	157.48	26.25	108	354.33	59.06	48	14.63	108	32.92	48	87.78	108	197.51
49	160.76	26.79	109	357.61	59.60	49	14.94	109	33.22	49	89.61	109	199.34
50	164.04	27.34	110	360.89	60.15	50	15.24	110	33.53	50	91.44	110	201.17
51	167.32	27.89	111	364.17	60.70	51	15.54	111	33.83	51	93.27	111	203.00
52	170.60	28.43	112	367.45	61.24	52	15.85	112	34.14	52	95.10	112	204.83
53	173.88	28.98	113	370.73	61.79	53	16.15	113	34.44	53	96.93	113	206.65
54	177.17	29.53	114	374.02	62.34	54	16.46	114	34.75	54	98.76	114	208.48
55	180.45	30.07	115	377.30	62.88	55	16.76	115	35.05	55	100.58	115	210.31
56	183.73	30.62	116	380.58	63.43	56	17.07	116	35.36	56	102.41	116	212.14
57	187.01	31.17	117	383.86	63.98	57	17.37	117	35.66	57	104.24	117	213.97
58	190.29	31.71	118	387.14	64.52	58	17.68	118	35.97	58	106.07	118	215.80
59	193.57	32.26	119	390.42	65.07	59	17.98	119	36.27	59	107.90	119	217.63
60	196.85	32.81	120	393.70	65.62	60	18.29	120	36.58	60	109.73	120	219.46

TABLE 9

Conversion Table for Nautical and Statute Miles

1 nautical mile = 6,076.11548 . . . feet

1 statute mile = 5,280 feet

Nautical miles to statute miles				Statute miles to nautical miles			
Nautical miles	Statute miles	Nautical miles	Statute miles	Statute miles	Nautical miles	Statute miles	Nautical miles
1	1. 151	51	58. 690	1	0. 869	51	44. 318
2	2. 302	52	59. 841	2	1. 738	52	45. 187
3	3. 452	53	60. 991	3	2. 607	53	46. 056
4	4. 603	54	62. 142	4	3. 476	54	46. 925
5	5. 754	55	63. 293	5	4. 345	55	47. 794
6	6. 905	56	64. 444	6	5. 214	56	48. 663
7	8. 055	57	65. 594	7	6. 083	57	49. 532
8	9. 206	58	66. 745	8	6. 952	58	50. 401
9	10. 357	59	67. 896	9	7. 821	59	51. 270
10	11. 508	60	69. 047	10	8. 690	60	52. 139
11	12. 659	61	70. 198	11	9. 559	61	53. 008
12	13. 809	62	71. 348	12	10. 428	62	53. 877
13	14. 960	63	72. 499	13	11. 297	63	54. 746
14	16. 111	64	73. 650	14	12. 166	64	55. 614
15	17. 262	65	74. 801	15	13. 035	65	56. 483
16	18. 412	66	75. 951	16	13. 904	66	57. 352
17	19. 563	67	77. 102	17	14. 773	67	58. 221
18	20. 714	68	78. 253	18	15. 642	68	59. 090
19	21. 865	69	79. 404	19	16. 511	69	59. 959
20	23. 016	70	80. 555	20	17. 380	70	60. 828
21	24. 166	71	81. 705	21	18. 249	71	61. 697
22	25. 317	72	82. 856	22	19. 117	72	62. 566
23	26. 468	73	84. 007	23	19. 986	73	63. 435
24	27. 619	74	85. 158	24	20. 855	74	64. 304
25	28. 769	75	86. 308	25	21. 724	75	65. 173
26	29. 920	76	87. 459	26	22. 593	76	66. 042
27	31. 071	77	88. 610	27	23. 462	77	66. 911
28	32. 222	78	89. 761	28	24. 331	78	67. 780
29	33. 373	79	90. 912	29	25. 200	79	68. 649
30	34. 523	80	92. 062	30	26. 069	80	69. 518
31	35. 674	81	93. 213	31	26. 938	81	70. 387
32	36. 825	82	94. 364	32	27. 807	82	71. 256
33	37. 976	83	95. 515	33	28. 676	83	72. 125
34	39. 127	84	96. 665	34	29. 545	84	72. 994
35	40. 277	85	97. 816	35	30. 414	85	73. 863
36	41. 428	86	98. 967	36	31. 283	86	74. 732
37	42. 579	87	100. 118	37	32. 152	87	75. 601
38	43. 730	88	101. 269	38	33. 021	88	76. 470
39	44. 880	89	102. 419	39	33. 890	89	77. 339
40	46. 031	90	103. 570	40	34. 759	90	78. 208
41	47. 182	91	104. 721	41	35. 628	91	79. 077
42	48. 333	92	105. 872	42	36. 497	92	79. 946
43	49. 484	93	107. 022	43	37. 366	93	80. 815
44	50. 634	94	108. 173	44	38. 235	94	81. 684
45	51. 785	95	109. 324	45	39. 104	95	82. 553
46	52. 936	96	110. 475	46	39. 973	96	83. 422
47	54. 087	97	111. 626	47	40. 842	97	84. 291
48	55. 237	98	112. 776	48	41. 711	98	85. 160
49	56. 388	99	113. 927	49	42. 580	99	86. 029
50	57. 539	100	115. 078	50	43. 449	100	86. 898

TABLE 10

Speed Table for Measured Mile

Sec.	Minutes 1	2	3	4	5	6	7	8	9	10	11	12	Sec.
	Knots	*Knots*	*Knots*	*Knots*	*Knots*	*Knots*	*Knots*	*Knots*	*Knots*	*Knots*	*Knots*	*Knots*	
0	60.000	30.000	20.000	15.000	12.000	10.000	8.571	7.500	6.667	6.000	5.455	5.000	0
1	59.016	29.752	19.890	14.938	11.960	9.972	8.551	7.484	6.654	5.990	5.446	4.993	1
2	58.065	29.508	19.780	14.876	11.921	9.945	8.531	7.469	6.642	5.980	5.438	4.986	2
3	57.143	29.268	19.672	14.815	11.881	9.917	8.511	7.453	6.630	5.970	5.430	4.979	3
4	56.250	29.032	19.565	14.754	11.842	9.890	8.491	7.438	6.618	5.960	5.422	4.972	4
5	55.385	28.800	19.459	14.694	11.803	9.863	8.471	7.423	6.606	5.950	5.414	4.966	5
6	54.545	28.571	19.355	14.634	11.765	9.836	8.451	7.407	6.593	5.941	5.405	4.959	6
7	53.731	28.346	19.251	14.575	11.726	9.809	8.431	7.392	6.581	5.931	5.397	4.952	7
8	52.941	28.125	19.149	14.516	11.688	9.783	8.411	7.377	6.569	5.921	5.389	4.945	8
9	52.174	27.907	19.048	14.458	11.650	9.756	8.392	7.362	6.557	5.911	5.381	4.938	9
10	51.429	27.692	18.947	14.400	11.613	9.730	8.372	7.347	6.545	5.902	5.373	4.932	10
11	50.704	27.481	18.848	14.343	11.576	9.704	8.353	7.332	6.534	5.892	5.365	4.925	11
12	50.000	27.273	18.750	14.286	11.538	9.677	8.333	7.317	6.522	5.882	5.357	4.918	12
13	49.315	27.068	18.653	14.229	11.502	9.651	8.314	7.302	6.510	5.873	5.349	4.911	13
14	48.649	26.866	18.557	14.173	11.465	9.626	8.295	7.287	6.498	5.863	5.341	4.905	14
15	48.000	26.667	18.462	14.118	11.429	9.600	8.276	7.273	6.486	5.854	5.333	4.898	15
16	47.368	26.471	18.367	14.062	11.392	9.574	8.257	7.258	6.475	5.844	5.325	4.891	16
17	46.753	26.277	18.274	14.008	11.356	9.549	8.238	7.243	6.463	5.835	5.318	4.885	17
18	46.154	26.087	18.182	13.953	11.321	9.524	8.219	7.229	6.452	5.825	5.310	4.878	18
19	45.570	25.899	18.090	13.900	11.285	9.499	8.200	7.214	6.440	5.816	5.302	4.871	19
20	45.000	25.714	18.000	13.846	11.250	9.474	8.182	7.200	6.429	5.806	5.294	4.865	20
21	44.444	25.532	17.910	13.793	11.215	9.449	8.163	7.186	6.417	5.797	5.286	4.858	21
22	43.902	25.352	17.822	13.740	11.180	9.424	8.145	7.171	6.406	5.788	5.279	4.852	22
23	43.373	25.175	17.734	13.688	11.146	9.399	8.126	7.157	6.394	5.778	5.271	4.845	23
24	42.857	25.000	17.647	13.636	11.111	9.375	8.108	7.143	6.383	5.769	5.263	4.839	24
25	42.353	24.828	17.561	13.585	11.077	9.351	8.090	7.129	6.372	5.760	5.255	4.832	25
26	41.860	24.658	17.476	13.534	11.043	9.326	8.072	7.115	6.360	5.751	5.248	4.826	26
27	41.379	24.490	17.391	13.483	11.009	9.302	8.054	7.101	6.349	5.742	5.240	4.819	27
28	40.909	24.324	17.308	13.433	10.976	9.278	8.036	7.087	6.338	5.732	5.233	4.813	28
29	40.449	24.161	17.225	13.383	10.942	9.254	8.018	7.073	6.327	5.723	5.225	4.806	29
30	40.000	24.000	17.143	13.333	10.909	9.231	8.000	7.059	6.316	5.714	5.217	4.800	30
31	39.560	23.841	17.062	13.284	10.876	9.207	7.982	7.045	6.305	5.705	5.210	4.794	31
32	39.130	23.684	16.981	13.235	10.843	9.184	7.965	7.031	6.294	5.696	5.202	4.787	32
33	38.710	23.529	16.901	13.187	10.811	9.160	7.947	7.018	6.283	5.687	5.195	4.781	33
34	38.298	23.377	16.822	13.139	10.778	9.137	7.930	7.004	6.272	5.678	5.187	4.775	34
35	37.895	23.226	16.744	13.091	10.746	9.114	7.912	6.990	6.261	5.669	5.180	4.768	35
36	37.500	23.077	16.667	13.043	10.714	9.091	7.895	6.977	6.250	5.660	5.172	4.762	36
37	37.113	22.930	16.590	12.996	10.682	9.068	7.877	6.963	6.239	5.651	5.165	4.756	37
38	36.735	22.785	16.514	12.950	10.651	9.045	7.860	6.950	6.228	5.643	5.158	4.749	38
39	36.364	22.642	16.438	12.903	10.619	9.023	7.843	6.936	6.218	5.634	5.150	4.743	39
40	36.000	22.500	16.364	12.857	10.588	9.000	7.826	6.923	6.207	5.625	5.143	4.737	40
41	35.644	22.360	16.290	12.811	10.557	8.978	7.809	6.910	6.196	5.616	5.136	4.731	41
42	35.294	22.222	16.216	12.766	10.526	8.955	7.792	6.897	6.186	5.607	5.128	4.724	42
43	34.951	22.086	16.143	12.721	10.496	8.933	7.775	6.883	6.175	5.599	5.121	4.718	43
44	34.615	21.951	16.071	12.676	10.465	8.911	7.759	6.870	6.164	5.590	5.114	4.712	44
45	34.286	21.818	16.000	12.632	10.435	8.889	7.742	6.857	6.154	5.581	5.106	4.706	45
46	33.962	21.687	15.929	12.587	10.405	8.867	7.725	6.844	6.143	5.573	5.099	4.700	46
47	33.645	21.557	15.859	12.544	10.375	8.845	7.709	6.831	6.133	5.564	5.092	4.694	47
48	33.333	21.429	15.789	12.500	10.345	8.824	7.692	6.818	6.122	5.556	5.085	4.688	48
49	33.028	21.302	15.721	12.457	10.315	8.802	7.676	6.805	6.112	5.547	5.078	4.681	49
50	32.727	21.176	15.652	12.414	10.286	8.780	7.660	6.792	6.102	5.538	5.070	4.675	50
51	32.432	21.053	15.584	12.371	10.256	8.759	7.643	6.780	6.091	5.530	5.063	4.669	51
52	32.143	20.930	15.517	12.329	10.227	8.738	7.627	6.767	6.081	5.521	5.056	4.663	52
53	31.858	20.809	15.451	12.287	10.198	8.717	7.611	6.754	6.071	5.513	5.049	4.657	53
54	31.579	20.690	15.385	12.245	10.169	8.696	7.595	6.742	6.061	5.505	5.042	4.651	54
55	31.304	20.571	15.319	12.203	10.141	8.675	7.579	6.729	6.050	5.496	5.035	4.645	55
56	31.034	20.455	15.254	12.162	10.112	8.654	7.563	6.716	6.040	5.488	5.028	4.639	56
57	30.769	20.339	15.190	12.121	10.084	8.633	7.547	6.704	6.030	5.479	5.021	4.633	57
58	30.508	20.225	15.126	12.081	10.056	8.612	7.531	6.691	6.020	5.471	5.014	4.627	58
59	30.252	20.112	15.063	12.040	10.028	8.592	7.516	6.679	6.010	5.463	5.007	4.621	59
60	30.000	20.000	15.000	12.000	10.000	8.571	7.500	6.667	6.000	5.455	5.000	4.615	60
Sec.	1	2	3	4	5	6	7	8	9	10	11	12	Sec.

TABLE 11
Speed, Time, and Distance

Minutes	0.5	1.0	1.5	2.0	2.5	3.0	3.5	4.0	4.5	5.0	5.5	6.0	6.5	7.0	7.5	8.0	Minutes
	Speed in knots																
	Miles	Miles	Miles	Miles	Miles	Miles	Miles	Miles	Miles	Miles	Miles	Miles	Miles	Miles	Miles	Miles	
1	0.0	0.0	0.0	0.0	0.0	0.0	0.1	0.1	0.1	0.1	0.1	0.1	0.1	0.1	0.1	0.1	1
2	0.0	0.0	0.0	0.1	0.1	0.1	0.1	0.1	0.2	0.2	0.2	0.2	0.2	0.2	0.2	0.3	2
3	0.0	0.0	0.1	0.1	0.1	0.2	0.2	0.2	0.2	0.2	0.3	0.3	0.3	0.4	0.4	0.4	3
4	0.0	0.1	0.1	0.1	0.2	0.2	0.2	0.3	0.3	0.3	0.4	0.4	0.4	0.5	0.5	0.5	4
5	0.0	0.1	0.1	0.2	0.2	0.2	0.3	0.3	0.4	0.4	0.5	0.5	0.5	0.6	0.6	0.7	5
6	0.0	0.1	0.2	0.2	0.2	0.3	0.4	0.4	0.4	0.5	0.6	0.6	0.6	0.7	0.8	0.8	6
7	0.1	0.1	0.2	0.2	0.3	0.4	0.4	0.5	0.5	0.6	0.6	0.7	0.8	0.8	0.9	0.9	7
8	0.1	0.1	0.2	0.3	0.3	0.4	0.5	0.5	0.6	0.7	0.7	0.8	0.9	0.9	1.0	1.1	8
9	0.1	0.2	0.2	0.3	0.4	0.4	0.5	0.6	0.7	0.8	0.8	0.9	1.0	1.0	1.1	1.2	9
10	0.1	0.2	0.2	0.3	0.4	0.5	0.6	0.7	0.8	0.8	0.9	1.0	1.1	1.2	1.2	1.3	10
11	0.1	0.2	0.3	0.4	0.5	0.6	0.6	0.7	0.8	0.9	1.0	1.1	1.2	1.3	1.4	1.5	11
12	0.1	0.2	0.3	0.4	0.5	0.6	0.7	0.8	0.9	1.0	1.1	1.2	1.3	1.4	1.5	1.6	12
13	0.1	0.2	0.3	0.4	0.5	0.6	0.8	0.9	1.0	1.1	1.2	1.3	1.4	1.5	1.6	1.7	13
14	0.1	0.2	0.4	0.5	0.6	0.7	0.8	0.9	1.0	1.2	1.3	1.4	1.5	1.6	1.8	1.9	14
15	0.1	0.2	0.4	0.5	0.6	0.8	0.9	1.0	1.1	1.2	1.4	1.5	1.6	1.8	1.9	2.0	15
16	0.1	0.3	0.4	0.5	0.7	0.8	0.9	1.1	1.2	1.3	1.5	1.6	1.7	1.9	2.0	2.1	16
17	0.1	0.3	0.4	0.6	0.7	0.8	1.0	1.1	1.3	1.4	1.6	1.7	1.8	2.0	2.1	2.3	17
18	0.2	0.3	0.4	0.6	0.8	0.9	1.0	1.2	1.4	1.5	1.6	1.8	2.0	2.1	2.2	2.4	18
19	0.2	0.3	0.5	0.6	0.8	1.0	1.1	1.3	1.4	1.6	1.7	1.9	2.1	2.2	2.4	2.5	19
20	0.2	0.3	0.5	0.7	0.8	1.0	1.2	1.3	1.5	1.7	1.8	2.0	2.2	2.3	2.5	2.7	20
21	0.2	0.4	0.5	0.7	0.9	1.0	1.2	1.4	1.6	1.8	1.9	2.1	2.3	2.4	2.6	2.8	21
22	0.2	0.4	0.6	0.7	0.9	1.1	1.3	1.5	1.6	1.8	2.0	2.2	2.4	2.6	2.8	2.9	22
23	0.2	0.4	0.6	0.8	1.0	1.2	1.3	1.5	1.7	1.9	2.1	2.3	2.5	2.7	2.9	3.1	23
24	0.2	0.4	0.6	0.8	1.0	1.2	1.4	1.6	1.8	2.0	2.2	2.4	2.6	2.8	3.0	3.2	24
25	0.2	0.4	0.6	0.8	1.0	1.2	1.5	1.7	1.9	2.1	2.3	2.5	2.7	2.9	3.1	3.3	25
26	0.2	0.4	0.6	0.9	1.1	1.3	1.5	1.7	2.0	2.2	2.4	2.6	2.8	3.0	3.2	3.5	26
27	0.2	0.4	0.7	0.9	1.1	1.4	1.6	1.8	2.0	2.2	2.5	2.7	2.9	3.2	3.4	3.6	27
28	0.2	0.5	0.7	0.9	1.2	1.4	1.6	1.9	2.1	2.3	2.6	2.8	3.0	3.3	3.5	3.7	28
29	0.2	0.5	0.7	1.0	1.2	1.4	1.7	1.9	2.2	2.4	2.7	2.9	3.1	3.4	3.6	3.9	29
30	0.2	0.5	0.8	1.0	1.2	1.5	1.8	2.0	2.2	2.5	2.8	3.0	3.2	3.5	3.8	4.0	30
31	0.3	0.5	0.8	1.0	1.3	1.6	1.8	2.1	2.3	2.6	2.8	3.1	3.4	3.6	3.9	4.1	31
32	0.3	0.5	0.8	1.1	1.3	1.6	1.9	2.1	2.4	2.7	2.9	3.2	3.5	3.7	4.0	4.3	32
33	0.3	0.6	0.8	1.1	1.4	1.6	1.9	2.2	2.5	2.8	3.0	3.3	3.6	3.8	4.1	4.4	33
34	0.3	0.6	0.8	1.1	1.4	1.7	2.0	2.3	2.6	2.8	3.1	3.4	3.7	4.0	4.2	4.5	34
35	0.3	0.6	0.9	1.2	1.5	1.8	2.0	2.3	2.6	2.9	3.2	3.5	3.8	4.1	4.4	4.7	35
36	0.3	0.6	0.9	1.2	1.5	1.8	2.1	2.4	2.7	3.0	3.3	3.6	3.9	4.2	4.5	4.8	36
37	0.3	0.6	0.9	1.2	1.5	1.8	2.2	2.5	2.8	3.1	3.4	3.7	4.0	4.3	4.6	4.9	37
38	0.3	0.6	1.0	1.3	1.6	1.9	2.2	2.5	2.8	3.2	3.5	3.8	4.1	4.4	4.8	5.1	38
39	0.3	0.6	1.0	1.3	1.6	2.0	2.3	2.6	2.9	3.2	3.6	3.9	4.2	4.6	4.9	5.2	39
40	0.3	0.7	1.0	1.3	1.7	2.0	2.3	2.7	3.0	3.3	3.7	4.0	4.3	4.7	5.0	5.3	40
41	0.3	0.7	1.0	1.4	1.7	2.0	2.4	2.7	3.1	3.4	3.8	4.1	4.4	4.8	5.1	5.5	41
42	0.4	0.7	1.0	1.4	1.8	2.1	2.4	2.8	3.2	3.5	3.8	4.2	4.6	4.9	5.2	5.6	42
43	0.4	0.7	1.1	1.4	1.8	2.2	2.5	2.9	3.2	3.6	3.9	4.3	4.7	5.0	5.4	5.7	43
44	0.4	0.7	1.1	1.5	1.8	2.2	2.6	2.9	3.3	3.7	4.0	4.4	4.8	5.1	5.5	5.9	44
45	0.4	0.8	1.1	1.5	1.9	2.2	2.6	3.0	3.4	3.8	4.1	4.5	4.9	5.2	5.6	6.0	45
46	0.4	0.8	1.2	1.5	1.9	2.3	2.7	3.1	3.4	3.8	4.2	4.6	5.0	5.4	5.8	6.1	46
47	0.4	0.8	1.2	1.6	2.0	2.4	2.7	3.1	3.5	3.9	4.3	4.7	5.1	5.5	5.9	6.3	47
48	0.4	0.8	1.2	1.6	2.0	2.4	2.8	3.2	3.6	4.0	4.4	4.8	5.2	5.6	6.0	6.4	48
49	0.4	0.8	1.2	1.6	2.0	2.4	2.9	3.3	3.7	4.1	4.5	4.9	5.3	5.7	6.1	6.5	49
50	0.4	0.8	1.2	1.7	2.1	2.5	2.9	3.3	3.8	4.2	4.6	5.0	5.4	5.8	6.2	6.7	50
51	0.4	0.8	1.3	1.7	2.1	2.6	3.0	3.4	3.8	4.2	4.7	5.1	5.5	6.0	6.4	6.8	51
52	0.4	0.9	1.3	1.7	2.2	2.6	3.0	3.5	3.9	4.3	4.8	5.2	5.6	6.1	6.5	6.9	52
53	0.4	0.9	1.3	1.8	2.2	2.6	3.1	3.5	4.0	4.4	4.9	5.3	5.7	6.2	6.6	7.1	53
54	0.4	0.9	1.4	1.8	2.2	2.7	3.2	3.6	4.1	4.5	5.0	5.4	5.8	6.3	6.8	7.2	54
55	0.5	0.9	1.4	1.8	2.3	2.8	3.2	3.7	4.1	4.6	5.0	5.5	6.0	6.4	6.9	7.3	55
56	0.5	0.9	1.4	1.9	2.3	2.8	3.3	3.7	4.2	4.7	5.1	5.6	6.1	6.5	7.0	7.5	56
57	0.5	1.0	1.4	1.9	2.4	2.8	3.3	3.8	4.3	4.8	5.2	5.7	6.2	6.6	7.1	7.6	57
58	0.5	1.0	1.4	1.9	2.4	2.9	3.4	3.9	4.4	4.8	5.3	5.8	6.3	6.8	7.2	7.7	58
59	0.5	1.0	1.5	2.0	2.5	3.0	3.4	3.9	4.4	4.9	5.4	5.9	6.4	6.9	7.4	7.9	59
60	0.5	1.0	1.5	2.0	2.5	3.0	3.5	4.0	4.5	5.0	5.5	6.0	6.5	7.0	7.5	8.0	60

TABLE 11
Speed, Time, and Distance

Minutes	8.5	9.0	9.5	10.0	10.5	11.0	11.5	12.0	12.5	13.0	13.5	14.0	14.5	15.0	15.5	16.0	Minutes
	Speed in knots																
	Miles	Miles	Miles	Miles	Miles	Miles	Miles	Miles	Miles	Miles	Miles	Miles	Miles	Miles	Miles	Miles	
1	0.1	0.2	0.2	0.2	0.2	0.2	0.2	0.2	0.2	0.2	0.2	0.2	0.2	0.2	0.3	0.3	1
2	0.3	0.3	0.3	0.3	0.4	0.4	0.4	0.4	0.4	0.4	0.4	0.5	0.5	0.5	0.5	0.5	2
3	0.4	0.4	0.5	0.5	0.5	0.6	0.6	0.6	0.6	0.6	0.7	0.7	0.7	0.8	0.8	0.8	3
4	0.6	0.6	0.6	0.7	0.7	0.7	0.8	0.8	0.8	0.9	0.9	0.9	1.0	1.0	1.0	1.1	4
5	0.7	0.8	0.8	0.8	0.9	0.9	1.0	1.0	1.0	1.1	1.1	1.2	1.2	1.2	1.3	1.3	5
6	0.9	0.9	1.0	1.0	1.0	1.1	1.2	1.2	1.2	1.3	1.4	1.4	1.4	1.5	1.6	1.6	6
7	1.0	1.0	1.1	1.2	1.2	1.3	1.3	1.4	1.5	1.5	1.6	1.6	1.7	1.8	1.8	1.9	7
8	1.1	1.2	1.3	1.3	1.4	1.5	1.5	1.6	1.7	1.7	1.8	1.9	1.9	2.0	2.1	2.1	8
9	1.3	1.4	1.4	1.5	1.6	1.6	1.7	1.8	1.9	2.0	2.0	2.1	2.2	2.2	2.3	2.4	9
10	1.4	1.5	1.6	1.7	1.8	1.8	1.9	2.0	2.1	2.2	2.2	2.3	2.4	2.5	2.6	2.7	10
11	1.6	1.6	1.7	1.8	1.9	2.0	2.1	2.2	2.3	2.4	2.5	2.6	2.7	2.8	2.8	2.9	11
12	1.7	1.8	1.9	2.0	2.1	2.2	2.3	2.4	2.5	2.6	2.7	2.8	2.9	3.0	3.1	3.2	12
13	1.8	2.0	2.1	2.2	2.3	2.4	2.5	2.6	2.7	2.8	2.9	3.0	3.1	3.2	3.4	3.5	13
14	2.0	2.1	2.2	2.3	2.4	2.6	2.7	2.8	2.9	3.0	3.2	3.3	3.4	3.5	3.6	3.7	14
15	2.1	2.2	2.4	2.5	2.6	2.8	2.9	3.0	3.1	3.2	3.4	3.5	3.6	3.8	3.9	4.0	15
16	2.3	2.4	2.5	2.7	2.8	2.9	3.1	3.2	3.3	3.5	3.6	3.7	3.9	4.0	4.1	4.3	16
17	2.4	2.5	2.7	2.8	3.0	3.1	3.3	3.4	3.5	3.7	3.8	4.0	4.1	4.2	4.4	4.5	17
18	2.6	2.7	2.8	3.0	3.2	3.3	3.4	3.6	3.8	3.9	4.0	4.2	4.4	4.5	4.6	4.8	18
19	2.7	2.8	3.0	3.2	3.3	3.5	3.6	3.8	4.0	4.1	4.3	4.4	4.6	4.8	4.9	5.1	19
20	2.8	3.0	3.2	3.3	3.5	3.7	3.8	4.0	4.2	4.3	4.5	4.7	4.8	5.0	5.2	5.3	20
21	3.0	3.2	3.3	3.5	3.7	3.8	4.0	4.2	4.4	4.6	4.7	4.9	5.1	5.2	5.4	5.6	21
22	3.1	3.3	3.5	3.7	3.8	4.0	4.2	4.4	4.6	4.8	5.0	5.1	5.3	5.5	5.7	5.9	22
23	3.3	3.4	3.6	3.8	4.0	4.2	4.4	4.6	4.8	5.0	5.2	5.4	5.6	5.8	5.9	6.1	23
24	3.4	3.6	3.8	4.0	4.2	4.4	4.6	4.8	5.0	5.2	5.4	5.6	5.8	6.0	6.2	6.4	24
25	3.5	3.8	4.0	4.2	4.4	4.6	4.8	5.0	5.2	5.4	5.6	5.8	6.0	6.2	6.5	6.7	25
26	3.7	3.9	4.1	4.3	4.6	4.8	5.0	5.2	5.4	5.6	5.8	6.1	6.3	6.5	6.7	6.9	26
27	3.8	4.0	4.3	4.5	4.7	5.0	5.2	5.4	5.6	5.8	6.1	6.3	6.5	6.8	7.0	7.2	27
28	4.0	4.2	4.4	4.7	4.9	5.1	5.4	5.6	5.8	6.1	6.3	6.5	6.8	7.0	7.2	7.5	28
29	4.1	4.4	4.6	4.8	5.1	5.3	5.6	5.8	6.0	6.3	6.5	6.8	7.0	7.2	7.5	7.7	29
30	4.2	4.5	4.8	5.0	5.2	5.5	5.8	6.0	6.2	6.5	6.8	7.0	7.2	7.5	7.8	8.0	30
31	4.4	4.6	4.9	5.2	5.4	5.7	5.9	6.2	6.5	6.7	7.0	7.2	7.5	7.8	8.0	8.3	31
32	4.5	4.8	5.1	5.3	5.6	5.9	6.1	6.4	6.7	6.9	7.2	7.5	7.7	8.0	8.3	8.5	32
33	4.7	5.0	5.2	5.5	5.8	6.0	6.3	6.6	6.9	7.2	7.4	7.7	8.0	8.2	8.5	8.8	33
34	4.8	5.1	5.4	5.7	6.0	6.2	6.5	6.8	7.1	7.4	7.6	7.9	8.2	8.5	8.8	9.1	34
35	5.0	5.2	5.5	5.8	6.1	6.4	6.7	7.0	7.3	7.6	7.9	8.2	8.5	8.8	9.0	9.3	35
36	5.1	5.4	5.7	6.0	6.3	6.6	6.9	7.2	7.5	7.8	8.1	8.4	8.7	9.0	9.3	9.6	36
37	5.2	5.6	5.9	6.2	6.5	6.8	7.1	7.4	7.7	8.0	8.3	8.6	8.9	9.2	9.6	9.9	37
38	5.4	5.7	6.0	6.3	6.8	7.0	7.3	7.6	7.9	8.2	8.6	8.9	9.2	9.5	9.8	10.1	38
39	5.5	5.8	6.2	6.5	6.8	7.2	7.5	7.8	8.1	8.4	8.8	9.1	9.4	9.8	10.1	10.4	39
40	5.7	6.0	6.3	6.7	7.0	7.3	7.7	8.0	8.3	8.7	9.0	9.3	9.7	10.0	10.3	10.7	40
41	5.8	6.2	6.5	6.8	7.2	7.5	7.9	8.2	8.5	8.9	9.2	9.6	9.9	10.2	10.6	10.9	41
42	6.0	6.3	6.6	7.0	7.4	7.7	8.0	8.4	8.8	9.1	9.4	9.8	10.2	10.5	10.9	11.2	42
43	6.1	6.4	6.8	7.2	7.5	7.9	8.2	8.6	9.0	9.3	9.7	10.0	10.4	10.8	11.1	11.5	43
44	6.2	6.6	7.0	7.3	7.7	8.1	8.4	8.8	9.2	9.5	9.9	10.3	10.6	11.0	11.4	11.7	44
45	6.4	6.8	7.1	7.5	7.9	8.2	8.6	9.0	9.4	9.8	10.1	10.5	10.9	11.2	11.6	12.0	45
46	6.5	6.9	7.3	7.7	8.0	8.4	8.8	9.2	9.6	10.0	10.4	10.7	11.1	11.5	11.9	12.3	46
47	6.7	7.0	7.4	7.8	8.2	8.6	9.0	9.4	9.8	10.2	10.6	11.0	11.4	11.8	12.1	12.5	47
48	6.8	7.2	7.6	8.0	8.4	8.8	9.2	9.6	10.0	10.4	10.8	11.2	11.6	12.0	12.4	12.8	48
49	6.9	7.3	7.8	8.2	8.6	9.0	9.4	9.8	10.2	10.6	11.0	11.4	11.8	12.2	12.7	13.1	49
50	7.1	7.5	7.9	8.3	8.8	9.2	9.6	10.0	10.4	10.8	11.2	11.7	12.1	12.5	12.9	13.3	50
51	7.2	7.6	8.1	8.5	8.9	9.4	9.8	10.2	10.6	11.1	11.5	11.9	12.3	12.8	13.2	13.6	51
52	7.4	7.8	8.2	8.7	9.1	9.5	10.0	10.4	10.8	11.3	11.7	12.1	12.6	13.0	13.4	13.9	52
53	7.5	8.0	8.4	8.8	9.3	9.7	10.2	10.6	11.0	11.5	11.9	12.4	12.8	13.2	13.7	14.1	53
54	7.6	8.1	8.6	9.0	9.4	9.9	10.4	10.8	11.2	11.7	12.1	12.6	13.0	13.5	14.0	14.4	54
55	7.8	8.2	8.7	9.2	9.6	10.1	10.5	11.0	11.5	11.9	12.4	12.8	13.3	13.8	14.2	14.7	55
56	7.9	8.4	8.9	9.3	9.8	10.3	10.7	11.2	11.7	12.1	12.6	13.1	13.5	14.0	14.5	14.9	56
57	8.1	8.6	9.0	9.5	10.0	10.4	10.9	11.4	11.9	12.4	12.8	13.3	13.8	14.2	14.7	15.2	57
58	8.2	8.7	9.2	9.7	10.2	10.6	11.1	11.6	12.1	12.6	13.0	13.5	14.0	14.5	15.0	15.5	58
59	8.4	8.9	9.3	9.8	10.3	10.8	11.3	11.8	12.3	12.8	13.3	13.8	14.3	14.8	15.2	15.7	59
60	8.5	9.0	9.5	10.0	10.5	11.0	11.5	12.0	12.5	13.0	13.5	14.0	14.5	15.0	15.5	16.0	60

TABLE 11
Speed, Time, and Distance

Minutes	16.5	17.0	17.5	18.0	18.5	19.0	19.5	20.0	20.5	21.0	21.5	22.0	22.5	23.0	23.5	24.0	Minutes
	Speed in knots																
	Miles	Miles	Miles	Miles	Miles	Miles	Miles	Miles	Miles	Miles	Miles	Miles	Miles	Miles	Miles	Miles	
1	0.3	0.3	0.3	0.3	0.3	0.3	0.3	0.3	0.3	0.4	0.4	0.4	0.4	0.4	0.4	0.4	1
2	0.6	0.6	0.6	0.6	0.6	0.6	0.6	0.7	0.7	0.7	0.7	0.7	0.8	0.8	0.8	0.8	2
3	0.8	0.8	0.9	0.9	0.9	1.0	1.0	1.0	1.0	1.0	1.1	1.1	1.1	1.1	1.2	1.2	3
4	1.1	1.1	1.2	1.2	1.2	1.3	1.3	1.3	1.4	1.4	1.4	1.5	1.5	1.5	1.6	1.6	4
5	1.4	1.4	1.5	1.5	1.5	1.6	1.6	1.7	1.7	1.8	1.8	1.8	1.9	1.9	2.0	2.0	5
6	1.6	1.7	1.8	1.8	1.8	1.9	2.0	2.0	2.0	2.1	2.2	2.2	2.2	2.3	2.4	2.4	6
7	1.9	2.0	2.0	2.1	2.2	2.2	2.3	2.3	2.4	2.4	2.5	2.6	2.6	2.7	2.7	2.8	7
8	2.2	2.3	2.3	2.4	2.5	2.5	2.6	2.7	2.7	2.8	2.9	2.9	3.0	3.1	3.1	3.2	8
9	2.5	2.6	2.6	2.7	2.8	2.8	2.9	3.0	3.1	3.2	3.2	3.3	3.4	3.4	3.5	3.6	9
10	2.8	2.8	2.9	3.0	3.1	3.2	3.2	3.3	3.4	3.5	3.6	3.7	3.8	3.8	3.9	4.0	10
11	3.0	3.1	3.2	3.3	3.4	3.5	3.6	3.7	3.8	3.8	3.9	4.0	4.1	4.2	4.3	4.4	11
12	3.3	3.4	3.5	3.6	3.7	3.8	3.9	4.0	4.1	4.2	4.3	4.4	4.5	4.6	4.7	4.8	12
13	3.6	3.7	3.8	3.9	4.0	4.1	4.2	4.3	4.4	4.6	4.7	4.8	4.9	5.0	5.1	5.2	13
14	3.8	4.0	4.1	4.2	4.3	4.4	4.6	4.7	4.8	4.9	5.0	5.1	5.2	5.4	5.5	5.6	14
15	4.1	4.2	4.4	4.5	4.6	4.8	4.9	5.0	5.1	5.2	5.4	5.5	5.6	5.8	5.9	6.0	15
16	4.4	4.5	4.7	4.8	4.9	5.1	5.2	5.3	5.5	5.6	5.7	5.9	6.0	6.1	6.3	6.4	16
17	4.7	4.8	5.0	5.1	5.2	5.4	5.5	5.7	5.8	6.0	6.1	6.2	6.4	6.5	6.7	6.8	17
18	5.0	5.1	5.2	5.4	5.6	5.7	5.8	6.0	6.2	6.3	6.4	6.6	6.8	6.9	7.0	7.2	18
19	5.2	5.4	5.5	5.7	5.9	6.0	6.2	6.3	6.5	6.6	6.8	7.0	7.1	7.3	7.4	7.6	19
20	5.5	5.7	5.8	6.0	6.2	6.3	6.5	6.7	6.8	7.0	7.2	7.3	7.5	7.7	7.8	8.0	20
21	5.8	6.0	6.1	6.3	6.5	6.6	6.8	7.0	7.2	7.4	7.5	7.7	7.9	8.0	8.2	8.4	21
22	6.0	6.2	6.4	6.6	6.8	7.0	7.2	7.3	7.5	7.7	7.9	8.1	8.2	8.4	8.6	8.8	22
23	6.3	6.5	6.7	6.9	7.1	7.3	7.5	7.7	7.9	8.0	8.2	8.4	8.6	8.8	9.0	9.2	23
24	6.6	6.8	7.0	7.2	7.4	7.6	7.8	8.0	8.2	8.4	8.6	8.8	9.0	9.2	9.4	9.6	24
25	6.9	7.1	7.3	7.5	7.7	7.9	8.1	8.3	8.5	8.8	9.0	9.2	9.4	9.6	9.8	10.0	25
26	7.2	7.4	7.6	7.8	8.0	8.2	8.4	8.7	8.9	9.1	9.3	9.5	9.8	10.0	10.2	10.4	26
27	7.4	7.6	7.9	8.1	8.3	8.6	8.8	9.0	9.2	9.4	9.7	9.9	10.1	10.4	10.6	10.8	27
28	7.7	7.9	8.2	8.4	8.6	8.9	9.1	9.3	9.6	9.8	10.0	10.3	10.5	10.7	11.0	11.2	28
29	8.0	8.2	8.5	8.7	8.9	9.2	9.4	9.7	9.9	10.2	10.4	10.6	10.9	11.1	11.4	11.6	29
30	8.2	8.5	8.8	9.0	9.2	9.5	9.8	10.0	10.2	10.5	10.8	11.0	11.2	11.5	11.8	12.0	30
31	8.5	8.8	9.0	9.3	9.6	9.8	10.1	10.3	10.6	10.8	11.1	11.4	11.6	11.9	12.1	12.4	31
32	8.8	9.1	9.3	9.6	9.9	10.1	10.4	10.7	10.9	11.2	11.5	11.7	12.0	12.3	12.5	12.8	32
33	9.1	9.4	9.6	9.9	10.2	10.4	10.7	11.0	11.3	11.6	11.8	12.1	12.4	12.6	12.9	13.2	33
34	9.4	9.6	9.9	10.2	10.5	10.8	11.0	11.3	11.6	11.9	12.2	12.5	12.8	13.0	13.3	13.6	34
35	9.6	9.9	10.2	10.5	10.8	11.1	11.4	11.7	12.0	12.2	12.5	12.8	13.1	13.4	13.7	14.0	35
36	9.9	10.2	10.5	10.8	11.1	11.4	11.7	12.0	12.3	12.6	12.9	13.2	13.5	13.8	14.1	14.4	36
37	10.2	10.5	10.8	11.1	11.4	11.7	12.0	12.3	12.6	13.0	13.3	13.6	13.9	14.2	14.5	14.8	37
38	10.4	10.8	11.1	11.4	11.7	12.0	12.4	12.7	13.0	13.3	13.6	13.9	14.2	14.6	14.9	15.2	38
39	10.7	11.0	11.4	11.7	12.0	12.4	12.7	13.0	13.3	13.6	14.0	14.3	14.6	15.0	15.3	15.6	39
40	11.0	11.3	11.7	12.0	12.3	12.7	13.0	13.3	13.7	14.0	14.3	14.7	15.0	15.3	15.7	16.0	40
41	11.3	11.6	12.0	12.3	12.6	13.0	13.3	13.7	14.0	14.4	14.7	15.0	15.4	15.7	16.1	16.4	41
42	11.6	11.9	12.2	12.6	13.0	13.3	13.6	14.0	14.4	14.7	15.0	15.4	15.8	16.1	16.4	16.8	42
43	11.8	12.2	12.5	12.9	13.3	13.6	14.0	14.3	14.7	15.0	15.4	15.8	16.1	16.5	16.8	17.2	43
44	12.1	12.5	12.8	13.2	13.6	13.9	14.3	14.7	15.0	15.4	15.8	16.1	16.5	16.9	17.2	17.6	44
45	12.4	12.8	13.1	13.5	13.9	14.2	14.6	15.0	15.4	15.8	16.1	16.5	16.9	17.2	17.6	18.0	45
46	12.6	13.0	13.4	13.8	14.2	14.6	15.0	15.3	15.7	16.1	16.5	16.9	17.2	17.6	18.0	18.4	46
47	12.9	13.3	13.7	14.1	14.5	14.9	15.3	15.7	16.1	16.4	16.8	17.2	17.6	18.0	18.4	18.8	47
48	13.2	13.6	14.0	14.4	14.8	15.2	15.6	16.0	16.4	16.8	17.2	17.6	18.0	18.4	18.8	19.2	48
49	13.5	13.9	14.3	14.7	15.1	15.5	15.9	16.3	16.7	17.2	17.6	18.0	18.4	18.8	19.2	19.6	49
50	13.8	14.2	14.6	15.0	15.4	15.8	16.2	16.7	17.1	17.5	17.9	18.3	18.8	19.2	19.6	20.0	50
51	14.0	14.4	14.9	15.3	15.7	16.2	16.6	17.0	17.4	17.8	18.3	18.7	19.1	19.6	20.0	20.4	51
52	14.3	14.7	15.2	15.6	16.0	16.5	16.9	17.3	17.8	18.2	18.6	19.1	19.5	19.9	20.4	20.8	52
53	14.6	15.0	15.5	15.9	16.3	16.8	17.2	17.7	18.1	18.6	19.0	19.4	19.9	20.3	20.8	21.2	53
54	14.8	15.3	15.8	16.2	16.6	17.1	17.6	18.0	18.4	18.9	19.4	19.8	20.2	20.7	21.2	21.6	54
55	15.1	15.6	16.0	16.5	17.0	17.4	17.9	18.3	18.8	19.2	19.7	20.2	20.6	21.1	21.5	22.0	55
56	15.4	15.9	16.3	16.8	17.3	17.7	18.2	18.7	19.1	19.6	20.1	20.5	21.0	21.5	21.9	22.4	56
57	15.7	16.2	16.6	17.1	17.6	18.0	18.5	19.0	19.5	20.0	20.4	20.9	21.4	21.8	22.3	22.8	57
58	16.0	16.4	16.9	17.4	17.9	18.4	18.8	19.3	19.8	20.3	20.8	21.3	21.8	22.2	22.7	23.2	58
59	16.2	16.7	17.2	17.7	18.2	18.7	19.2	19.7	20.2	20.6	21.1	21.6	22.1	22.6	23.1	23.6	59
60	16.5	17.0	17.5	18.0	18.5	19.0	19.5	20.0	20.5	21.0	21.5	22.0	22.5	23.0	23.5	24.0	60

TABLE 11
Speed, Time, and Distance

Minutes	24.5	25.0	25.5	26.0	26.5	27.0	27.5	28.0	28.5	29.0	29.5	30.0	30.5	31.0	31.5	32.0	Minutes
	Speed in knots																
	Miles	Miles	Miles	Miles	Miles	Miles	Miles	Miles	Miles	Miles	Miles	Miles	Miles	Miles	Miles	Miles	
1	0.4	0.4	0.4	0.4	0.4	0.4	0.5	0.5	0.5	0.5	0.5	0.5	0.5	0.5	0.5	0.5	1
2	0.8	0.8	0.8	0.9	0.9	0.9	0.9	0.9	1.0	1.0	1.0	1.0	1.0	1.0	1.0	1.1	2
3	1.2	1.2	1.3	1.3	1.3	1.4	1.4	1.4	1.4	1.4	1.5	1.5	1.5	1.6	1.6	1.6	3
4	1.6	1.7	1.7	1.7	1.8	1.8	1.8	1.9	1.9	1.9	2.0	2.0	2.0	2.1	2.1	2.1	4
5	2.0	2.1	2.1	2.2	2.2	2.2	2.3	2.3	2.4	2.4	2.5	2.5	2.5	2.6	2.6	2.7	5
6	2.4	2.5	2.6	2.6	2.6	2.7	2.8	2.8	2.8	2.9	3.0	3.0	3.0	3.1	3.2	3.2	6
7	2.9	2.9	3.0	3.0	3.1	3.2	3.2	3.3	3.3	3.4	3.4	3.5	3.6	3.6	3.7	3.7	7
8	3.3	3.3	3.4	3.5	3.5	3.6	3.7	3.7	3.8	3.9	3.9	4.0	4.1	4.1	4.2	4.3	8
9	3.7	3.8	3.8	3.9	4.0	4.0	4.1	4.2	4.3	4.4	4.4	4.5	4.6	4.6	4.7	4.8	9
10	4.1	4.2	4.2	4.3	4.4	4.5	4.6	4.7	4.8	4.8	4.9	5.0	5.1	5.2	5.2	5.3	10
11	4.5	4.6	4.7	4.8	4.9	5.0	5.0	5.1	5.2	5.3	5.4	5.5	5.6	5.7	5.8	5.9	11
12	4.9	5.0	5.1	5.2	5.3	5.4	5.5	5.6	5.7	5.8	5.9	6.0	6.1	6.2	6.3	6.4	12
13	5.3	5.4	5.5	5.6	5.7	5.8	6.0	6.1	6.2	6.3	6.4	6.5	6.6	6.7	6.8	6.9	13
14	5.7	5.8	6.0	6.1	6.2	6.3	6.4	6.5	6.6	6.8	6.9	7.0	7.1	7.2	7.4	7.5	14
15	6.1	6.2	6.4	6.5	6.6	6.8	6.9	7.0	7.1	7.2	7.4	7.5	7.6	7.8	7.9	8.0	15
16	6.5	6.7	6.8	6.9	7.1	7.2	7.3	7.5	7.6	7.7	7.9	8.0	8.1	8.3	8.4	8.5	16
17	6.9	7.1	7.2	7.4	7.5	7.6	7.8	7.9	8.1	8.2	8.4	8.5	8.6	8.8	8.9	9.1	17
18	7.4	7.5	7.6	7.8	8.0	8.1	8.2	8.4	8.6	8.7	8.8	9.0	9.2	9.3	9.4	9.6	18
19	7.8	7.9	8.1	8.2	8.4	8.6	8.7	8.9	9.0	9.2	9.3	9.5	9.7	9.8	10.0	10.1	19
20	8.2	8.3	8.5	8.7	8.8	9.0	9.2	9.3	9.5	9.7	9.8	10.0	10.2	10.3	10.5	10.7	20
21	8.6	8.8	8.9	9.1	9.3	9.4	9.6	9.8	10.0	10.2	10.3	10.5	10.7	10.8	11.0	11.2	21
22	9.0	9.2	9.4	9.5	9.7	9.9	10.1	10.3	10.4	10.6	10.8	11.0	11.2	11.4	11.6	11.7	22
23	9.4	9.6	9.8	10.0	10.2	10.4	10.5	10.7	10.9	11.1	11.3	11.5	11.7	11.9	12.1	12.3	23
24	9.8	10.0	10.2	10.4	10.6	10.8	11.0	11.2	11.4	11.6	11.8	12.0	12.2	12.4	12.6	12.8	24
25	10.2	10.4	10.6	10.8	11.0	11.2	11.5	11.7	11.9	12.1	12.3	12.5	12.7	12.9	13.1	13.3	25
26	10.6	10.8	11.0	11.3	11.5	11.7	11.9	12.1	12.4	12.6	12.8	13.0	13.2	13.4	13.6	13.9	26
27	11.0	11.2	11.5	11.7	11.9	12.2	12.4	12.6	12.8	13.0	13.3	13.5	13.7	14.0	14.2	14.4	27
28	11.4	11.7	11.9	12.1	12.4	12.6	12.8	13.1	13.3	13.5	13.8	14.0	14.2	14.5	14.7	14.9	28
29	11.8	12.1	12.3	12.6	12.8	13.0	13.3	13.5	13.8	14.0	14.3	14.5	14.7	15.0	15.2	15.5	29
30	12.2	12.5	12.8	13.0	13.2	13.5	13.8	14.0	14.2	14.5	14.8	15.0	15.2	15.5	15.8	16.0	30
31	12.7	12.9	13.2	13.4	13.7	14.0	14.2	14.5	14.7	15.0	15.2	15.5	15.8	16.0	16.3	16.5	31
32	13.1	13.3	13.6	13.9	14.1	14.4	14.7	14.9	15.2	15.5	15.7	16.0	16.3	16.5	16.8	17.1	32
33	13.5	13.8	14.0	14.3	14.6	14.8	15.1	15.4	15.7	16.0	16.2	16.5	16.8	17.0	17.3	17.6	33
34	13.9	14.2	14.4	14.7	15.0	15.3	15.6	15.9	16.2	16.4	16.7	17.0	17.3	17.6	17.8	18.1	34
35	14.3	14.6	14.9	15.2	15.5	15.8	16.0	16.3	16.6	16.9	17.2	17.5	17.8	18.1	18.4	18.7	35
36	14.7	15.0	15.3	15.6	15.9	16.2	16.5	16.8	17.1	17.4	17.7	18.0	18.3	18.6	18.9	19.2	36
37	15.1	15.4	15.7	16.0	16.3	16.6	17.0	17.3	17.6	17.9	18.2	18.5	18.8	19.1	19.4	19.7	37
38	15.5	15.8	16.2	16.5	16.8	17.1	17.4	17.7	18.0	18.4	18.7	19.0	19.3	19.6	20.0	20.3	38
39	15.9	16.2	16.6	16.9	17.2	17.6	17.9	18.2	18.5	18.8	19.2	19.5	19.8	20.2	20.5	20.8	39
40	16.3	16.7	17.0	17.3	17.7	18.0	18.3	18.7	19.0	19.3	19.7	20.0	20.3	20.7	21.0	21.3	40
41	16.7	17.1	17.4	17.8	18.1	18.4	18.8	19.1	19.5	19.8	20.2	20.5	20.8	21.2	21.5	21.9	41
42	17.2	17.5	17.8	18.2	18.6	18.9	19.2	19.6	20.0	20.3	20.6	21.0	21.4	21.7	22.0	22.4	42
43	17.6	17.9	18.3	18.6	19.0	19.4	19.7	20.1	20.4	20.8	21.1	21.5	21.9	22.2	22.6	22.9	43
44	18.0	18.3	18.7	19.1	19.4	19.8	20.2	20.5	20.9	21.3	21.6	22.0	22.4	22.7	23.1	23.5	44
45	18.4	18.8	19.1	19.5	19.9	20.2	20.6	21.0	21.4	21.8	22.1	22.5	22.9	23.2	23.6	24.0	45
46	18.8	19.2	19.6	19.9	20.3	20.7	21.1	21.5	21.8	22.2	22.6	23.0	23.4	23.8	24.2	24.5	46
47	19.2	19.6	20.0	20.4	20.8	21.2	21.5	21.9	22.3	22.7	23.1	23.5	23.9	24.3	24.7	25.1	47
48	19.6	20.0	20.4	20.8	21.2	21.6	22.0	22.4	22.8	23.2	23.6	24.0	24.4	24.8	25.2	25.6	48
49	20.0	20.4	20.8	21.2	21.6	22.0	22.5	22.9	23.3	23.7	24.1	24.5	24.9	25.3	25.7	26.1	49
50	20.4	20.8	21.2	21.7	22.1	22.5	22.9	23.3	23.8	24.2	24.6	25.0	25.4	25.8	26.2	26.7	50
51	20.8	21.2	21.7	22.1	22.5	23.0	23.4	23.8	24.2	24.6	25.1	25.5	25.9	26.4	26.8	27.2	51
52	21.2	21.7	22.1	22.5	23.0	23.4	23.8	24.3	24.7	25.1	25.6	26.0	26.4	26.9	27.3	27.7	52
53	21.6	22.1	22.5	23.0	23.4	23.8	24.3	24.7	25.2	25.6	26.1	26.5	26.9	27.4	27.8	28.3	53
54	22.0	22.5	23.0	23.4	23.8	24.3	24.8	25.2	25.6	26.1	26.6	27.0	27.4	27.9	28.4	28.8	54
55	22.5	22.9	23.4	23.8	24.3	24.8	25.2	25.7	26.1	26.6	27.0	27.5	28.0	28.4	28.9	29.3	55
56	22.9	23.3	23.8	24.3	24.7	25.2	25.7	26.1	26.6	27.1	27.5	28.0	28.5	28.9	29.4	29.9	56
57	23.3	23.8	24.2	24.7	25.2	25.6	26.1	26.6	27.1	27.6	28.0	28.5	29.0	29.4	29.9	30.4	57
58	23.7	24.2	24.6	25.1	25.6	26.1	26.6	27.1	27.6	28.0	28.5	29.0	29.5	30.0	30.4	30.9	58
59	24.1	24.6	25.1	25.6	26.1	26.6	27.0	27.5	28.0	28.5	29.0	29.5	30.0	30.5	31.0	31.5	59
60	24.5	25.0	25.5	26.0	26.5	27.0	27.5	28.0	28.5	29.0	29.5	30.0	30.5	31.0	31.5	32.0	60

TABLE 11

Speed, Time, and Distance

Min-utes	Speed in knots																Min-utes
	32.5	33.0	33.5	34.0	34.5	35.0	35.5	36.0	36.5	37.0	37.5	38.0	38.5	39.0	39.5	40.0	
	Miles	*Miles*	*Miles*	*Miles*	*Miles*	*Miles*	*Miles*	*Miles*	*Miles*	*Miles*	*Miles*	*Miles*	*Miles*	*Miles*	*Miles*	*Miles*	
1	0.5	0.6	0.6	0.6	0.6	0.6	0.6	0.6	0.6	0.6	0.6	0.6	0.6	0.6	0.7	0.7	1
2	1.1	1.1	1.1	1.1	1.1	1.2	1.2	1.2	1.2	1.2	1.2	1.3	1.3	1.3	1.3	1.3	2
3	1.6	1.6	1.7	1.7	1.7	1.8	1.8	1.8	1.8	1.8	1.9	1.9	1.9	2.0	2.0	2.0	3
4	2.2	2.2	2.2	2.3	2.3	2.3	2.4	2.4	2.4	2.5	2.5	2.5	2.6	2.6	2.6	2.7	4
5	2.7	2.8	2.8	2.8	2.9	2.9	3.0	3.0	3.0	3.1	3.1	3.2	3.2	3.2	3.3	3.3	5
6	3.2	3.3	3.4	3.4	3.4	3.5	3.6	3.6	3.6	3.7	3.8	3.8	3.8	3.9	4.0	4.0	6
7	3.8	3.8	3.9	4.0	4.0	4.1	4.1	4.2	4.3	4.3	4.4	4.4	4.5	4.6	4.6	4.7	7
8	4.3	4.4	4.5	4.5	4.6	4.7	4.7	4.8	4.9	4.9	5.0	5.1	5.1	5.2	5.3	5.3	8
9	4.9	5.0	5.0	5.1	5.2	5.2	5.3	5.4	5.5	5.6	5.6	5.7	5.8	5.8	5.9	6.0	9
10	5.4	5.5	5.6	5.7	5.8	5.8	5.9	6.0	6.1	6.2	6.2	6.3	6.4	6.5	6.6	6.7	10
11	6.0	6.0	6.1	6.2	6.3	6.4	6.5	6.6	6.7	6.8	6.9	7.0	7.1	7.2	7.2	7.3	11
12	6.5	6.6	6.7	6.8	6.9	7.0	7.1	7.2	7.3	7.4	7.5	7.6	7.7	7.8	7.9	8.0	12
13	7.0	7.2	7.3	7.4	7.5	7.6	7.7	7.8	7.9	8.0	8.1	8.2	8.3	8.4	8.6	8.7	13
14	7.6	7.7	7.8	7.9	8.0	8.2	8.3	8.4	8.5	8.6	8.8	8.9	9.0	9.1	9.2	9.3	14
15	8.1	8.2	8.4	8.5	8.6	8.8	8.9	9.0	9.1	9.2	9.4	9.5	9.6	9.8	9.9	10.0	15
16	8.7	8.8	8.9	9.1	9.2	9.3	9.5	9.6	9.7	9.9	10.0	10.1	10.3	10.4	10.5	10.7	16
17	9.2	9.4	9.5	9.6	9.8	9.9	10.1	10.2	10.3	10.5	10.6	10.8	10.9	11.0	11.2	11.3	17
18	9.8	9.9	10.1	10.2	10.4	10.5	10.6	10.8	11..0	11.1	11.2	11.4	11.6	11.7	11.8	12.0	18
19	10.3	10.4	10.6	10.8	10.9	11.1	11.2	11.4	11.6	11.7	11.9	12.0	12.2	12.4	12.5	12.7	19
20	10.8	11.0	11.2	11.3	11.5	11.7	11.8	12.0	12.2	12.3	12.5	12.7	12.8	13.0	13.2	13.3	20
21	11.4	11.6	11.7	11.9	12.1	12.2	12.4	12.6	12.8	13.0	13.1	13.3	13.5	13.6	13.8	14.0	21
22	11.9	12.1	12.3	12.5	12.6	12.8	13.0	13.2	13.4	13.6	13.8	13.9	14.1	14.3	14.5	14.7	22
23	12.5	12.6	12.8	13.0	13.2	13.4	13.6	13.8	14.0	14.2	14.4	14.6	14.8	15.0	15.1	15.3	23
24	13.0	13.2	13.4	13.6	13.8	14.0	14.2	14.4	14.6	14.8	15.0	15.2	15.4	15.6	15.8	16.0	24
25	13.5	13.8	14.0	14.2	14.4	14.6	14.8	15.0	15.2	15.4	15.6	15.8	16.0	16.2	16.5	16.7	25
26	14.1	14.3	14.5	14.7	15.0	15.2	15.4	15.6	15.8	16.0	16.2	16.5	16.7	16.9	17.1	17.3	26
27	14.6	14.8	15.1	15.3	15.5	15.8	16.0	16.2	16.4	16.6	16.9	17.1	17.3	17.6	17.8	18.0	27
28	15.2	15.4	15.6	15.9	16.1	16.3	16.6	16.8	17.0	17.3	17.5	17.7	18.0	18.2	18.4	18.7	28
29	15.7	16.0	16.2	16.4	16.7	16.9	17.2	17.4	17.6	17.9	18.1	18.4	18.6	18.9	19.1	19.3	29
30	16.2	16.5	16.8	17.0	17.2	17.5	17.8	18.0	18.2	18.5	18.8	19.0	19.2	19.5	19.8	20.0	30
31	16.8	17.0	17.3	17.6	17.8	18.1	18.3	18.6	18.9	19.1	19.4	19.6	19.9	20.2	20.4	20.7	31
32	17.3	17.6	17.9	18.1	18.4	18.7	18.9	19.2	19.5	19.7	20.0	20.3	20.5	20.8	21.1	21.3	32
33	17.9	18.2	18.4	18.7	19.0	19.2	19.5	19.8	20.1	20.4	20.6	20.9	21.2	21.4	21.7	22.0	33
34	18.4	18.7	19.0	19.3	19.6	19.8	20.1	20.4	20.7	21.0	21.2	21.5	21.8	22.1	22.4	22.7	34
35	19.0	19.2	19.5	19.8	20.1	20.4	20.7	21.0	21.3	21.6	21.9	22.2	22.5	22.8	23.0	23.3	35
36	19.5	19.8	20.1	20.4	20.7	21.0	21.3	21.6	21.9	22.2	22.5	22.8	23.1	23.4	23.7	24.0	36
37	20.0	20.4	20.7	21.0	21.3	21.6	21.9	22.2	22.5	22.8	23.1	23.4	23.7	24.0	24.4	24.7	37
38	20.6	20.9	21.2	21.5	21.8	22.2	22.5	22.8	23.1	23.4	23.8	24.1	24.4	24.7	25.0	25.3	38
39	21.1	21.4	21.8	22.1	22.4	22.8	23.1	23.4	23.7	24.0	24.4	24.7	25.0	25.4	25.7	26.0	39
40	21.7	22.0	22.3	22.7	23.0	23.3	23.7	24.0	24.3	24.7	25.0	25.3	25.7	26.0	26.3	26.7	40
41	22.2	22.6	22.9	23.2	23.6	23.9	24.3	24.6	24.9	25.3	25.6	26.0	26.3	26.6	27.0	27.3	41
42	22.8	23.1	23.4	23.8	24.2	24.5	24.8	25.2	25.6	25.9	26.2	26.6	27.0	27.3	27.6	28.0	42
43	23.3	23.6	24.0	24.4	24.7	25.1	25.4	25.8	26.2	26.5	26.9	27.2	27.6	28.0	28.3	28.7	43
44	23.8	24.2	24.6	24.9	25.3	25.7	26.0	26.4	26.8	27.1	27.5	27.9	28.2	28.6	29.0	29.3	44
45	24.4	24.8	25.1	25.5	25.9	26.2	26.6	27.0	27.4	27.8	28.1	28.5	28.9	29.2	29.6	30.0	45
46	24.9	25.3	25.7	26.1	26.4	26.8	27.2	27.6	28.0	28.4	28.8	29.1	29.5	29.9	30.3	30.7	46
47	25.5	25.8	26.2	26.6	27.0	27.4	27.8	28.2	28.6	29.0	29.4	29.8	30.2	30.6	30.9	31.3	47
48	26.0	26.4	26.8	27.2	27.6	28.0	28.4	28.8	29.2	29.6	30.0	30.4	30.8	31.2	31.6	32.0	48
49	26.5	27.0	27.4	27.8	28.2	28.6	29.0	29.4	29.8	30.2	30.6	31.0	31.4	31.8	32.3	32.7	49
50	27.1	27.5	27.9	28.3	28.8	29.2	29.6	30.0	30.4	30.8	31.2	31.7	32.1	32.5	32.9	33.3	50
51	27.6	28.0	28.5	28.9	29.3	29.8	30.2	30.6	31.0	31.4	31.9	32.3	32.7	33.2	33.6	34.0	51
52	28.2	28.6	29.0	29.5	29.9	30.3	30.8	31.2	31.6	32.1	32.5	32.9	33.4	33.8	34.2	34.7	52
53	28.7	29.2	29.6	30.0	30.5	30.9	31.4	31.8	32.2	32.7	33.1	33.6	34.0	34.4	34.9	35.3	53
54	29.2	29.7	30.2	30.6	31.0	31.5	32.0	32.4	32.8	33.3	33.8	34.2	34.6	35.1	35.6	36.0	54
55	29.8	30.2	30.7	31.2	31.6	32.1	32.5	33.0	33.5	33.9	34.4	34.8	35.3	35.8	36.2	36.7	55
56	30.3	30.8	31.3	31.7	32.2	32.7	33.1	33.6	34.1	34.5	35.0	35.5	35.9	36.4	36.9	37.3	56
57	30.9	31.4	31.8	32.3	32.8	33.2	33.7	34.2	34.7	35.2	35.6	36.1	36.6	37.0	37.5	38.0	57
58	31.4	31.9	32.4	32.9	33.4	33.8	34.3	34.8	35.3	35.8	36.2	36.7	37.2	37.7	38.2	38.7	58
59	32.0	32.4	32.9	33.4	33.9	34.4	34.9	35.4	35.9	36.4	36.9	37.4	37.9	38.4	38.8	39.3	59
60	32.5	33.0	33.5	34.0	34.5	35.0	35.5	36.0	36.5	37.0	37.5	38.0	38.5	39.0	39.5	40.0	60

TABLE 12

Distance of the Horizon

Height Feet	Nautical Miles	Statute Miles	Height *meters*	Height Feet	Nautical Miles	Statute Miles	Height *meters*
1	1.2	1.3	.30	120	12.8	14.7	36.58
2	1.7	1.9	.61	125	13.1	15.1	38.10
3	2.0	2.3	.91	130	13.3	15.4	39.62
4	2.3	2.7	1.22	135	13.6	15.6	41.15
5	2.6	3.0	1.52	140	13.8	15.9	42.67
6	2.9	3.3	1.83	145	14.1	16.2	44.20
7	3.1	3.6	2.13	150	14.3	16.5	45.72
8	3.3	3.8	2.44	160	14.8	17.0	48.77
9	3.5	4.0	2.74	170	15.3	17.6	51.82
10	3.7	4.3	3.05	180	15.7	18.1	54.86
11	3.9	4.5	3.35	190	16.1	18.6	57.91
12	4.1	4.7	3.66	200	16.5	19.0	60.96
13	4.2	4.9	3.96	210	17.0	19.5	64.01
14	4.4	5.0	4.27	220	17.4	20.0	67.06
15	4.5	5.2	4.57	230	17.7	20.4	70.10
16	4.7	5.4	4.88	240	18.1	20.9	73.15
17	4.8	5.6	5.18	250	18.5	21.3	76.20
18	5.0	5.7	5.49	260	18.9	21.7	79.25
19	5.1	5.9	5.79	270	19.2	22.1	82.30
20	5.2	6.0	6.10	280	19.6	22.5	85.34
21	5.4	6.2	6.40	290	19.9	22.9	88.39
22	5.5	6.3	6.71	300	20.3	23.3	91.44
23	5.6	6.5	7.01	310	20.6	23.7	94.49
24	5.7	6.6	7.32	320	20.9	24.1	97.54
25	5.9	6.7	7.62	330	21.3	24.5	100.58
26	6.0	6.9	7.92	340	21.6	24.8	103.63
27	6.1	7.0	8.23	350	21.9	25.2	106.68
28	6.2	7.1	8.53	360	22.2	25.5	109.73
29	6.3	7.3	8.84	370	22.5	25.9	112.78
30	6.4	7.4	9.14	380	22.8	26.2	115.82
31	6.5	7.5	9.45	390	23.1	26.6	118.87
32	6.6	7.6	9.75	400	23.4	26.9	121.92
33	6.7	7.7	10.06	410	23.7	27.3	124.97
34	6.8	7.9	10.36	420	24.0	27.6	128.02
35	6.9	8.0	10.67	430	24.3	27.9	131.06
36	7.0	8.1	10.97	440	24.5	28.2	134.11
37	7.1	8.2	11.28	450	24.8	28.6	137.16
38	7.2	8.3	11.58	460	25.1	28.9	140.21
39	7.3	8.4	11.89	470	25.4	29.2	143.26
40	7.4	8.5	12.19	480	25.6	29.5	146.30
41	7.5	8.6	12.50	490	25.9	29.8	149.35
42	7.6	8.7	12.80	500	26.2	30.1	152.40
43	7.7	8.8	13.11	510	26.4	30.4	155.45
44	7.8	8.9	13.41	520	26.7	30.7	158.50
45	7.8	9.0	13.72	530	26.9	31.0	161.54
46	7.9	9.1	14.02	540	27.2	31.3	164.59
47	8.0	9.2	14.33	550	27.4	31.6	167.64
48	8.1	9.3	14.63	560	27.7	31.9	170.69
49	8.2	9.4	14.94	570	27.9	32.1	173.74
50	8.3	9.5	15.24	580	28.2	32.4	176.78
55	8.7	10.0	16.76	590	28.4	32.7	179.83
60	9.1	10.4	18.29	600	28.7	33.0	182.88
65	9.4	10.9	19.81	620	29.1	33.5	188.98
70	9.8	11.3	21.34	640	29.5	34.1	195.07
75	10.1	11.7	22.86	660	30.1	34.6	201.17
80	10.5	12.0	24.38	680	30.5	35.1	207.26
85	10.8	12.4	25.91	700	31.0	35.6	213.36
90	11.1	12.8	27.43	720	31.4	36.1	219.46
95	11.4	13.1	28.96	740	31.8	36.6	225.55
100	11.7	13.5	30.48	760	32.3	37.1	231.65
105	12.0	13.8	32.00	780	32.7	37.6	237.74
110	12.3	14.1	33.53	800	33.1	38.1	243.84
115	12.5	14.4	35.05	820	33.5	38.6	249.94

TABLE 13
Geographic Range

Object Height Feet	Object Height Meters	7 ft / 2 m	10 ft / 3 m	13 ft / 4 m	16 ft / 5 m	20 ft / 6 m	23 ft / 7 m	26 ft / 8 m	30 ft / 9 m	33 ft / 10 m	36 ft / 11 m	Object Height Meters	Object Height Feet
		Miles	Miles	Miles	Miles	Miles	Miles	Miles	Miles	Miles	Miles		
0	0	3.1	3.7	4.2	4.7	5.2	5.6	6.0	6.4	6.7	7.0	0	0
3	1	5.1	5.7	6.2	6.7	7.3	7.6	8.0	8.4	8.7	9.0	1	3
7	2	6.2	6.8	7.3	7.8	8.3	8.7	9.1	9.5	9.8	10.1	2	7
10	3	6.8	7.4	7.9	8.4	8.9	9.3	9.7	10.1	10.4	10.7	3	10
13	4	7.3	7.9	8.4	8.9	9.5	9.8	10.2	10.6	10.9	11.2	4	13
16	5	7.8	8.4	8.9	9.4	9.9	10.3	10.6	11.1	11.4	11.7	5	16
20	6	8.3	8.9	9.5	9.9	10.5	10.8	11.2	11.6	12.0	12.3	6	20
23	7	8.7	9.3	9.8	10.3	10.8	11.2	11.6	12.0	12.3	12.6	7	23
26	8	9.1	9.7	10.2	10.6	11.2	11.6	11.9	12.4	12.7	13.0	8	26
30	9	9.5	10.1	10.6	11.1	11.6	12.0	12.4	12.8	13.1	13.4	9	30
33	10	9.8	10.4	10.9	11.4	12.0	12.3	12.7	13.1	13.4	13.7	10	33
36	11	10.1	10.7	11.2	11.7	12.3	12.6	13.0	13.4	13.7	14.0	11	36
39	12	10.4	11.0	11.5	12.0	12.5	12.9	13.3	13.7	14.0	14.3	12	39
43	13	10.8	11.4	11.9	12.4	12.9	13.3	13.6	14.1	14.4	14.7	13	43
46	14	11.0	11.6	12.2	12.6	13.2	13.5	13.9	14.3	14.7	15.0	14	46
49	15	11.3	11.9	12.4	12.9	13.4	13.8	14.2	14.6	14.9	15.2	15	49
52	16	11.5	12.1	12.7	13.1	13.7	14.0	14.4	14.8	15.2	15.5	16	52
56	17	11.9	12.5	13.0	13.4	14.0	14.4	14.7	15.2	15.5	15.8	17	56
59	18	12.1	12.7	13.2	13.7	14.2	14.6	15.0	15.4	15.7	16.0	18	59
62	19	12.3	12.9	13.4	13.9	14.4	14.8	15.2	15.6	15.9	16.2	19	62
66	20	12.6	13.2	13.7	14.2	14.7	15.1	15.5	15.9	16.2	16.5	20	66
72	22	13.0	13.6	14.1	14.6	15.2	15.5	15.9	16.3	16.6	16.9	22	72
79	24	13.5	14.1	14.6	15.1	15.6	16.0	16.4	16.8	17.1	17.4	24	79
85	26	13.9	14.5	15.0	15.5	16.0	16.4	16.8	17.2	17.5	17.8	26	85
92	28	14.3	14.9	15.4	15.9	16.5	16.8	17.2	17.6	17.9	18.2	28	92
98	30	14.7	15.3	15.8	16.3	16.8	17.2	17.5	18.0	18.3	18.6	30	98
115	35	15.6	16.2	16.8	17.2	17.8	18.2	18.5	19.0	19.3	19.6	35	115
131	40	16.5	17.1	17.6	18.1	18.6	19.0	19.4	19.8	20.1	20.4	40	131
148	45	17.3	17.9	18.5	18.9	19.5	19.8	20.2	20.6	21.0	21.3	45	148
164	50	18.1	18.7	19.2	19.7	20.2	20.6	20.9	21.4	21.7	22.0	50	164
180	55	18.8	19.4	19.9	20.4	20.9	21.3	21.7	22.1	22.4	22.7	55	180
197	60	19.5	20.1	20.6	21.1	21.7	22.0	22.4	22.8	23.1	23.4	60	197
213	65	20.2	20.8	21.3	21.8	22.3	22.7	23.0	23.5	23.8	24.1	65	213
230	70	20.8	21.4	22.0	22.4	23.0	23.4	23.7	24.2	24.5	24.8	70	230
246	75	21.4	22.1	22.6	23.0	23.6	24.0	24.3	24.8	25.1	25.4	75	246
262	80	22.0	22.6	23.2	23.6	24.2	24.5	24.9	25.3	25.7	26.0	80	262
279	85	22.6	23.2	23.8	24.2	24.8	25.2	25.5	26.0	26.3	26.6	85	279
295	90	23.2	23.8	24.3	24.8	25.3	25.7	26.1	26.5	26.8	27.1	90	295
312	95	23.8	24.4	24.9	25.3	25.9	26.3	26.6	27.1	27.4	27.7	95	312
328	100	24.3	24.9	25.4	25.9	26.4	26.8	27.2	27.6	27.9	28.2	100	328
361	110	25.3	25.9	26.4	26.9	27.5	27.8	28.2	28.6	29.0	29.3	110	361
394	120	26.3	26.9	27.4	27.9	28.5	28.8	29.2	29.6	29.9	30.2	120	394
427	130	27.3	27.9	28.4	28.9	29.4	29.8	30.1	30.6	30.9	31.2	130	427
459	140	28.2	28.8	29.3	29.7	30.3	30.7	31.0	31.5	31.8	32.1	140	459
492	150	29.0	29.7	30.2	30.6	31.2	31.6	31.9	32.4	32.7	33.0	150	492
525	160	29.9	30.5	31.0	31.5	32.0	32.4	32.8	33.2	33.5	33.8	160	525
558	170	30.7	31.3	31.9	32.3	32.9	33.2	33.6	34.0	34.4	34.7	170	558
591	180	31.5	32.1	32.7	33.1	33.7	34.1	34.4	34.9	35.2	35.5	180	591
623	190	32.3	32.9	33.4	33.9	34.4	34.8	35.2	35.6	35.9	36.2	190	623
656	200	33.1	33.7	34.2	34.6	35.2	35.6	35.9	36.4	36.7	37.0	200	656
722	220	34.5	35.1	35.7	36.1	36.7	37.0	37.4	37.8	38.2	38.5	220	722
787	240	35.9	36.5	37.0	37.5	38.1	38.4	38.8	39.2	39.5	39.8	240	787
853	260	37.3	37.9	38.4	38.9	39.4	39.8	40.1	40.6	40.9	41.2	260	853
919	280	38.6	39.2	39.7	40.1	40.7	41.1	41.4	41.9	42.2	42.5	280	919
984	300	39.8	40.4	40.9	41.4	41.9	42.3	42.7	43.1	43.4	43.7	300	984

TABLE 13
Geographic Range

Object Height Feet	Object Height Meters	39 ft / 12 m	43 ft / 13 m	46 ft / 14 m	49 ft / 15 m	52 ft / 16 m	56 ft / 17 m	59 ft / 18 m	62 ft / 19 m	66 ft / 20 m	69 ft / 21 m	Object Height Meters	Object Height Feet
		Miles	Miles	Miles	Miles	Miles	Miles	Miles	Miles	Miles	Miles		
0	0	7.3	7.7	7.9	8.2	8.4	8.8	9.0	9.2	9.5	9.7	0	0
3	1	9.3	9.7	10.0	10.2	10.5	10.8	11.0	11.2	11.5	11.7	1	3
7	2	10.4	10.8	11.0	11.3	11.5	11.9	12.1	12.3	12.6	12.8	2	7
10	3	11.0	11.4	11.6	11.9	12.1	12.5	12.7	12.9	13.2	13.4	3	10
13	4	11.5	11.9	12.2	12.4	12.7	13.0	13.2	13.4	13.7	13.9	4	13
16	5	12.0	12.4	12.6	12.9	13.1	13.4	13.7	13.9	14.2	14.4	5	16
20	6	12.5	12.9	13.2	13.4	13.7	14.0	14.2	14.4	14.7	15.0	6	20
23	7	12.9	13.3	13.5	13.8	14.0	14.4	14.6	14.8	15.1	15.3	7	23
26	8	13.3	13.6	13.9	14.2	14.4	14.7	15.0	15.2	15.5	15.7	8	26
30	9	13.7	14.1	14.3	14.6	14.8	15.2	15.4	15.6	15.9	16.1	9	30
33	10	14.0	14.4	14.7	14.9	15.2	15.5	15.7	15.9	16.2	16.4	10	33
36	11	14.3	14.7	15.0	15.2	15.5	15.8	16.0	16.2	16.5	16.7	11	36
39	12	14.6	15.0	15.2	15.5	15.7	16.1	16.3	16.5	16.8	17.0	12	39
43	13	15.0	15.3	15.6	15.9	16.1	16.4	16.7	16.9	17.2	17.4	13	43
46	14	15.2	15.6	15.9	16.1	16.4	16.7	16.9	17.1	17.4	17.7	14	46
49	15	15.5	15.9	16.1	16.4	16.6	16.9	17.2	17.4	17.7	17.9	15	49
52	16	15.7	16.1	16.4	16.6	16.9	17.2	17.4	17.6	17.9	18.2	16	52
56	17	16.1	16.4	16.7	16.9	17.2	17.5	17.7	18.0	18.3	18.5	17	56
59	18	16.3	16.7	16.9	17.2	17.4	17.7	18.0	18.2	18.5	18.7	18	59
62	19	16.5	16.9	17.1	17.4	17.6	18.0	18.2	18.4	18.7	18.9	19	62
66	20	16.8	17.2	17.4	17.7	17.9	18.3	18.5	18.7	19.0	19.2	20	66
72	22	17.2	17.6	17.9	18.1	18.4	18.7	18.9	19.1	19.4	19.6	22	72
79	24	17.7	18.1	18.3	18.6	18.8	19.2	19.4	19.6	19.9	20.1	24	79
85	26	18.1	18.5	18.7	19.0	19.2	19.5	19.8	20.0	20.3	20.5	26	85
92	28	18.5	18.9	19.2	19.4	19.7	20.0	20.2	20.4	20.7	20.9	28	92
98	30	18.9	19.3	19.5	19.8	20.0	20.3	20.6	20.8	21.1	21.3	30	98
115	35	19.9	20.2	20.5	20.7	21.0	21.3	21.5	21.8	22.1	22.3	35	115
131	40	20.7	21.1	21.3	21.6	21.8	22.1	22.4	22.6	22.9	23.1	40	131
148	45	21.5	21.9	22.2	22.4	22.7	23.0	23.2	23.4	23.7	24.0	45	148
164	50	22.3	22.7	22.9	23.2	23.4	23.7	24.0	24.2	24.5	24.7	50	164
180	55	23.0	23.4	23.6	23.9	24.1	24.5	24.7	24.9	25.2	25.4	55	180
197	60	23.7	24.1	24.4	24.6	24.9	25.2	25.4	25.6	25.9	26.1	60	197
213	65	24.4	24.7	25.0	25.3	25.5	25.8	26.1	26.3	26.6	26.8	65	213
230	70	25.1	25.4	25.7	25.9	26.2	26.5	26.7	27.0	27.2	27.5	70	230
246	75	25.7	26.0	26.3	26.5	26.8	27.1	27.3	27.6	27.9	28.1	75	246
262	80	26.2	26.6	26.9	27.1	27.4	27.7	27.9	28.2	28.4	28.7	80	262
279	85	26.8	27.2	27.5	27.7	28.0	28.3	28.5	28.8	29.0	29.3	85	279
295	90	27.4	27.8	28.0	28.3	28.5	28.9	29.1	29.3	29.6	29.8	90	295
312	95	28.0	28.3	28.6	28.9	29.1	29.4	29.7	29.9	30.2	30.4	95	312
328	100	28.5	28.9	29.1	29.4	29.6	29.9	30.2	30.4	30.7	30.9	100	328
361	110	29.5	29.9	30.2	30.4	30.7	31.0	31.2	31.4	31.7	31.9	110	361
394	120	30.5	30.9	31.2	31.4	31.7	32.0	32.2	32.4	32.7	32.9	120	394
427	130	31.5	31.8	32.1	32.4	32.6	32.9	33.2	33.4	33.7	33.9	130	427
459	140	32.4	32.7	33.0	33.3	33.5	33.8	34.1	34.3	34.6	34.8	140	459
492	150	33.3	33.6	33.9	34.1	34.4	34.7	34.9	35.2	35.5	35.7	150	492
525	160	34.1	34.5	34.7	35.0	35.2	35.6	35.8	36.0	36.3	36.5	160	525
558	170	34.9	35.3	35.6	35.8	36.1	36.4	36.6	36.9	37.1	37.4	170	558
591	180	35.7	36.1	36.4	36.6	36.9	37.2	37.4	37.7	37.9	38.2	180	591
623	190	36.5	36.9	37.1	37.4	37.6	38.0	38.2	38.4	38.7	38.9	190	623
656	200	37.3	37.6	37.9	38.2	38.4	38.7	39.0	39.2	39.5	39.7	200	656
722	220	38.7	39.1	39.4	39.6	39.9	40.2	40.4	40.7	40.9	41.2	220	722
787	240	40.1	40.5	40.8	41.0	41.3	41.6	41.8	42.0	42.3	42.5	240	787
853	260	41.5	41.8	42.1	42.4	42.6	42.9	43.2	43.4	43.7	43.9	260	853
919	280	42.8	43.1	43.4	43.7	43.9	44.2	44.5	44.7	45.0	45.2	280	919
984	300	44.0	44.4	44.6	44.9	45.1	45.5	45.7	45.9	46.2	46.4	300	984

TABLE 13

Geographic Range

Object Height		Height of eye of observer in feet and meters										Object Height	
Feet		72	75	79	82	85	89	92	95	98	115		Feet
	Meters	22	23	24	25	26	27	28	29	30	35	Meters	
		Miles	Miles	Miles	Miles	Miles	Miles	Miles	Miles	Miles	Miles		
0	0	9.9	10.2	10.4	10.6	10.8	11.0	11.2	11.4	11.6	12.5	0	0
3	1	12.0	12.2	12.4	12.6	12.8	13.1	13.2	13.4	13.6	14.6	1	3
7	2	13.0	13.3	13.5	13.7	13.9	14.1	14.3	14.5	14.7	15.6	2	7
10	3	13.6	13.9	14.1	14.3	14.5	14.7	14.9	15.1	15.3	16.2	3	10
13	4	14.1	14.4	14.6	14.8	15.0	15.3	15.4	15.6	15.8	16.8	4	13
16	5	14.6	14.9	15.1	15.3	15.5	15.7	15.9	16.1	16.3	17.2	5	16
20	6	15.2	15.4	15.6	15.8	16.0	16.3	16.5	16.6	16.8	17.8	6	20
23	7	15.5	15.8	16.0	16.2	16.4	16.6	16.8	17.0	17.2	18.2	7	23
26	8	15.9	16.2	16.4	16.6	16.8	17.0	17.2	17.4	17.5	18.5	8	26
30	9	16.3	16.6	16.8	17.0	17.2	17.4	17.6	17.8	18.0	19.0	9	30
33	10	16.6	16.9	17.1	17.3	17.5	17.8	17.9	18.1	18.3	19.3	10	33
36	11	16.9	17.2	17.4	17.6	17.8	18.1	18.2	18.4	18.6	19.6	11	36
39	12	17.2	17.5	17.7	17.9	18.1	18.3	18.5	18.7	18.9	19.8	12	39
43	13	17.6	17.9	18.1	18.3	18.5	18.7	18.9	19.1	19.3	20.2	13	43
46	14	17.9	18.1	18.3	18.5	18.7	19.0	19.2	19.3	19.5	20.5	14	46
49	15	18.1	18.4	18.6	18.8	19.0	19.2	19.4	19.6	19.8	20.7	15	49
52	16	18.4	18.6	18.8	19.0	19.2	19.5	19.7	19.8	20.0	21.0	16	52
56	17	18.7	19.0	19.2	19.4	19.5	19.8	20.0	20.2	20.3	21.3	17	56
59	18	18.9	19.2	19.4	19.6	19.8	20.0	20.2	20.4	20.6	21.5	18	59
62	19	19.1	19.4	19.6	19.8	20.0	20.3	20.4	20.6	20.8	21.8	19	62
66	20	19.4	19.7	19.9	20.1	20.3	20.5	20.7	20.9	21.1	22.0	20	66
72	22	19.9	20.1	20.3	20.5	20.7	21.0	21.2	21.3	21.5	22.5	22	72
79	24	20.3	20.6	20.8	21.0	21.2	21.4	21.6	21.8	22.0	22.9	24	79
85	26	20.7	21.0	21.2	21.4	21.6	21.8	22.0	22.2	22.4	23.3	26	85
92	28	21.2	21.4	21.6	21.8	22.0	22.3	22.4	22.6	22.8	23.8	28	92
98	30	21.5	21.8	22.0	22.2	22.4	22.6	22.8	23.0	23.2	24.1	30	98
115	35	22.5	22.7	22.9	23.1	23.3	23.6	23.8	24.0	24.1	25.1	35	115
131	40	23.3	23.6	23.8	24.0	24.2	24.4	24.6	24.8	25.0	25.9	40	131
148	45	24.2	24.4	24.6	24.8	25.0	25.3	25.5	25.6	25.8	26.8	45	148
164	50	24.9	25.2	25.4	25.6	25.8	26.0	26.2	26.4	26.6	27.5	50	164
180	55	25.6	25.9	26.1	26.3	26.5	26.7	26.9	27.1	27.3	28.2	55	180
197	60	26.3	26.6	26.8	27.0	27.2	27.5	27.6	27.8	28.0	29.0	60	197
213	65	27.0	27.3	27.5	27.7	27.9	28.1	28.3	28.5	28.7	29.6	65	213
230	70	27.7	27.9	28.1	28.3	28.5	28.8	29.0	29.1	29.3	30.3	70	230
246	75	28.3	28.6	28.7	28.9	29.1	29.4	29.6	29.7	29.9	30.9	75	246
262	80	28.9	29.1	29.3	29.5	29.7	30.0	30.1	30.3	30.5	31.5	80	262
279	85	29.5	29.7	29.9	30.1	30.3	30.6	30.8	30.9	31.1	32.1	85	279
295	90	30.0	30.3	30.5	30.7	30.9	31.1	31.3	31.5	31.7	32.6	90	295
312	95	30.6	30.9	31.1	31.3	31.4	31.7	31.9	32.1	32.2	33.2	95	312
328	100	31.1	31.4	31.6	31.8	32.0	32.2	32.4	32.6	32.8	33.7	100	328
361	110	32.2	32.4	32.6	32.8	33.0	33.3	33.5	33.6	33.8	34.8	110	361
394	120	33.2	33.4	33.6	33.8	34.0	34.3	34.4	34.6	34.8	35.8	120	394
427	130	34.1	34.4	34.6	34.8	35.0	35.2	35.4	35.6	35.8	36.7	130	427
459	140	35.0	35.3	35.5	35.7	35.9	36.1	36.3	36.5	36.6	37.6	140	459
492	150	35.9	36.2	36.4	36.5	36.7	37.0	37.2	37.3	37.5	38.5	150	492
525	160	36.7	37.0	37.2	37.4	37.6	37.8	38.0	38.2	38.4	39.4	160	525
558	170	37.6	37.8	38.0	38.2	38.4	38.7	38.9	39.0	39.2	40.2	170	558
591	180	38.4	38.6	38.8	39.0	39.2	39.5	39.7	39.8	40.0	41.0	180	591
623	190	39.1	39.4	39.6	39.8	40.0	40.2	40.4	40.6	40.8	41.8	190	623
656	200	39.9	40.2	40.4	40.6	40.8	41.0	41.2	41.4	41.5	42.5	200	656
722	220	41.4	41.6	41.8	42.0	42.2	42.5	42.7	42.8	43.0	44.0	220	722
787	240	42.8	43.0	43.2	43.4	43.6	43.9	44.0	44.2	44.4	45.4	240	787
853	260	44.1	44.4	44.6	44.8	45.0	45.2	45.4	45.6	45.8	46.7	260	853
919	280	45.4	45.7	45.9	46.1	46.3	46.5	46.7	46.9	47.1	48.0	280	919
984	300	46.6	46.9	47.1	47.3	47.5	47.7	47.9	48.1	48.3	49.2	300	984

TABLE 14
Dip of the Sea Short of the Horizon

Dis-tance	Height of eye above the sea, in feet and (meters)										Dis-tance
	5 (1.5)	10 (3.0)	15 (4.6)	20 (6.1)	25 (7.6)	30 (9.1)	35 (10.7)	40 (12.2)	45 (13.7)	50 (15.2)	
Miles	′	′	′	′	′	′	′	′	′	′	*Miles*
0.2	14.2	28.4	42.5	56.7	70.8	84.9	99.1	113.2	127.3	141.5	0.2
0.3	9.6	19.0	28.4	37.8	47.3	56.7	66.1	75.6	85.0	94.4	0.3
0.4	7.2	14.3	21.4	28.5	35.5	42.6	49.7	56.7	63.8	70.9	0.4
0.5	5.9	11.5	17.2	22.8	28.5	34.2	39.8	45.5	51.1	56.8	0.5
0.6	5.0	9.7	14.4	19.1	23.8	28.5	33.3	38.0	42.7	47.4	0.6
0.7	4.3	8.4	12.4	16.5	20.5	24.5	28.6	32.6	36.7	40.7	0.7
0.8	3.9	7.4	10.9	14.5	18.0	21.5	25.1	28.6	32.2	35.7	0.8
0.9	3.5	6.7	9.8	12.9	16.1	19.2	22.4	25.5	28.7	31.8	0.9
1.0	3.2	6.1	8.9	11.7	14.6	17.4	20.2	23.0	25.9	28.7	1.0
1.1	3.0	5.6	8.2	10.7	13.3	15.9	18.5	21.0	23.6	26.2	1.1
1.2	2.9	5.2	7.6	9.9	12.3	14.6	17.0	19.4	21.7	24.1	1.2
1.3	2.7	4.9	7.1	9.2	11.4	13.6	15.8	17.9	20.1	22.3	1.3
1.4	2.6	4.6	6.6	8.7	10.7	12.7	14.7	16.7	18.8	20.8	1.4
1.5	2.5	4.4	6.3	8.2	10.1	11.9	13.8	15.7	17.6	19.5	1.5
1.6	2.4	4.2	6.0	7.7	9.5	11.3	13.0	14.8	16.6	18.3	1.6
1.7	2.4	4.0	5.7	7.4	9.0	10.7	12.4	14.0	15.7	17.3	1.7
1.8	2.3	3.9	5.5	7.0	8.6	10.2	11.7	13.3	14.9	16.5	1.8
1.9	2.3	3.8	5.3	6.7	8.2	9.7	11.2	12.7	14.2	15.7	1.9
2.0	2.2	3.7	5.1	6.5	7.9	9.3	10.7	12.1	13.6	15.0	2.0
2.1	2.2	3.6	4.9	6.3	7.6	9.0	10.3	11.7	13.0	14.3	2.1
2.2	2.2	3.5	4.8	6.1	7.3	8.6	9.9	11.2	12.5	13.8	2.2
2.3	2.2	3.4	4.6	5.9	7.1	8.3	9.6	10.8	12.0	13.3	2.3
2.4	2.2	3.4	4.5	5.7	6.9	8.1	9.2	10.4	11.6	12.8	2.4
2.5	2.2	3.3	4.4	5.6	6.7	7.8	9.0	10.1	11.2	12.4	2.5
2.6	2.2	3.3	4.3	5.4	6.5	7.6	8.7	9.8	10.9	12.0	2.6
2.7	2.2	3.2	4.3	5.3	6.4	7.4	8.5	9.5	10.6	11.6	2.7
2.8	2.2	3.2	4.2	5.2	6.2	7.2	8.2	9.2	10.3	11.3	2.8
2.9	2.2	3.2	4.1	5.1	6.1	7.1	8.0	9.0	10.0	11.0	2.9
3.0	2.2	3.1	4.1	5.0	6.0	6.9	7.8	8.8	9.7	10.7	3.0
3.1	2.2	3.1	4.0	4.9	5.9	6.8	7.7	8.6	9.5	10.4	3.1
3.2	2.2	3.1	4.0	4.9	5.8	6.6	7.5	8.4	9.3	10.2	3.2
3.3	2.2	3.1	3.9	4.8	5.7	6.5	7.4	8.2	9.1	9.9	3.3
3.4	2.2	3.1	3.9	4.7	5.6	6.4	7.2	8.1	8.9	9.7	3.4
3.5	2.2	3.1	3.9	4.7	5.5	6.3	7.1	7.9	8.7	9.5	3.5
3.6	2.2	3.1	3.9	4.6	5.4	6.2	7.0	7.8	8.6	9.4	3.6
3.7	2.2	3.1	3.8	4.6	5.4	6.1	6.9	7.7	8.4	9.2	3.7
3.8	2.2	3.1	3.8	4.6	5.3	6.0	6.8	7.5	8.3	9.0	3.8
3.9	2.2	3.1	3.8	4.5	5.2	6.0	6.7	7.4	8.2	8.9	3.9
4.0	2.2	3.1	3.8	4.5	5.2	5.9	6.6	7.3	8.0	8.7	4.0
4.1	2.2	3.1	3.8	4.5	5.2	5.8	6.5	7.2	7.9	8.6	4.1
4.2	2.2	3.1	3.8	4.4	5.1	5.8	6.5	7.1	7.8	8.5	4.2
4.3	2.2	3.1	3.8	4.4	5.1	5.7	6.4	7.1	7.7	8.4	4.3
4.4	2.2	3.1	3.8	4.4	5.0	5.7	6.3	7.0	7.6	8.3	4.4
4.5	2.2	3.1	3.8	4.4	5.0	5.6	6.3	6.9	7.5	8.2	4.5
4.6	2.2	3.1	3.8	4.4	5.0	5.6	6.2	6.8	7.4	8.1	4.6
4.7	2.2	3.1	3.8	4.4	5.0	5.6	6.2	6.8	7.4	8.0	4.7
4.8	2.2	3.1	3.8	4.4	4.9	5.5	6.1	6.7	7.3	7.9	4.8
4.9	2.2	3.1	3.8	4.3	4.9	5.5	6.1	6.7	7.2	7.8	4.9
5.0	2.2	3.1	3.8	4.3	4.9	5.5	6.0	6.6	7.2	7.7	5.0
5.5	2.2	3.1	3.8	4.3	4.9	5.4	5.9	6.4	6.9	7.4	5.5
6.0	2.2	3.1	3.8	4.3	4.9	5.3	5.8	6.3	6.7	7.2	6.0
6.5	2.2	3.1	3.8	4.3	4.9	5.3	5.7	6.2	6.6	7.1	6.5
7.0	2.2	3.1	3.8	4.3	4.9	5.3	5.7	6.1	6.5	7.0	7.0
7.5	2.2	3.1	3.8	4.3	4.9	5.3	5.7	6.1	6.5	6.9	7.5
8.0	2.2	3.1	3.8	4.3	4.9	5.3	5.7	6.1	6.5	6.9	8.0
8.5	2.2	3.1	3.8	4.3	4.9	5.3	5.7	6.1	6.5	6.9	8.5
9.0	2.2	3.1	3.8	4.3	4.9	5.3	5.7	6.1	6.5	6.9	9.0
9.5	2.2	3.1	3.8	4.3	4.9	5.3	5.7	6.1	6.5	6.9	9.5
10.0	2.2	3.1	3.8	4.3	4.9	5.3	5.7	6.1	6.5	6.9	10.0

TABLE 14
Dip of the Sea Short of the Horizon

Dis-tance	Height of eye above the sea, in feet and (meters)										Dis-tance
	55 (16.8)	60 (18.3)	65 (19.8)	70 (21.3)	75 (22.9)	80 (24.4)	85 (25.9)	90 (27.4)	95 (29.0)	100 (30.5)	
Miles	′	′	′	′	′	′	′	′	′	′	*Miles*
0.2	155.6	169.7	183.3	197.9	212.0	226.1	240.2	254.2	268.3	282.3	0.2
0.3	103.8	113.3	122.7	132.1	141.6	151.0	160.4	169.9	179.3	188.7	0.3
0.4	77.9	85.0	92.1	99.2	106.2	113.3	120.3	127.4	134.5	141.5	0.4
0.5	62.4	68.1	73.8	79.4	85.1	90.7	96.4	102.0	107.7	113.3	0.5
0.6	52.1	56.8	61.5	66.3	71.0	75.7	80.4	85.1	89.8	94.5	0.6
0.7	44.7	48.8	52.8	56.9	60.9	64.9	69.0	73.0	77.1	81.1	0.7
0.8	39.2	42.8	46.3	49.8	53.4	56.9	60.4	64.0	67.5	71.1	0.8
0.9	34.9	38.1	41.2	44.4	47.5	50.7	53.8	56.9	60.1	63.2	0.9
1.0	31.5	34.4	37.2	40.0	42.8	45.7	48.5	51.3	54.2	57.0	1.0
1.1	28.7	31.3	33.9	36.5	39.0	41.6	44.2	46.7	49.3	51.9	1.1
1.2	26.4	28.8	31.1	33.5	35.9	38.2	40.6	42.9	45.3	47.6	1.2
1.3	24.5	26.7	28.8	31.0	33.2	35.4	37.5	39.7	41.9	44.1	1.3
1.4	22.8	24.8	26.8	28.9	30.9	32.9	34.9	37.0	39.0	41.0	1.4
1.5	21.4	23.3	25.1	27.0	28.9	30.8	32.7	34.6	36.5	38.3	1.5
1.6	20.1	21.9	23.6	25.4	27.2	29.0	30.7	32.5	34.3	36.0	1.6
1.7	19.0	20.7	22.3	24.0	25.7	27.3	29.0	30.7	32.3	34.0	1.7
1.8	18.0	19.6	21.2	22.8	24.3	25.9	27.5	29.0	30.6	32.2	1.8
1.9	17.2	18.7	20.1	21.6	23.1	24.6	26.1	27.6	29.1	30.6	1.9
2.0	16.4	17.8	19.2	20.6	22.0	23.5	24.9	26.3	27.7	29.1	2.0
2.1	15.7	17.0	18.4	19.7	21.1	22.4	23.8	25.1	26.5	27.8	2.1
2.2	15.1	16.3	17.6	18.9	20.2	21.5	22.8	24.1	25.3	26.6	2.2
2.3	14.5	15.7	16.9	18.2	19.4	20.6	21.9	23.1	24.3	25.6	2.3
2.4	14.0	15.1	16.3	17.5	18.7	19.9	21.0	22.2	23.4	24.6	2.4
2.5	13.5	14.6	15.8	16.9	18.0	19.1	20.3	21.4	22.5	23.7	2.5
2.6	13.0	14.1	15.2	16.3	17.4	18.5	19.6	20.7	21.8	22.8	2.6
2.7	12.6	13.7	14.7	15.8	16.8	17.9	18.9	20.0	21.0	22.1	2.7
2.8	12.3	13.3	14.3	15.3	16.3	17.3	18.3	19.3	20.4	21.4	2.8
2.9	11.9	12.9	13.9	14.9	15.8	16.8	17.8	18.8	19.7	20.7	2.9
3.0	11.6	12.6	13.5	14.4	15.4	16.3	17.3	18.2	19.2	20.1	3.0
3.1	11.3	12.2	13.2	14.1	15.0	15.9	16.8	17.7	18.6	19.5	3.1
3.2	11.1	11.9	12.8	13.7	14.6	15.5	16.4	17.2	18.1	19.0	3.2
3.3	10.8	11.7	12.5	13.4	14.2	15.1	15.9	16.8	17.7	18.5	3.3
3.4	10.6	11.4	12.2	13.1	13.9	14.7	15.6	16.4	17.2	18.1	3.4
3.5	10.3	11.2	12.0	12.8	13.6	14.4	15.2	16.0	16.8	17.6	3.5
3.6	10.1	10.9	11.7	12.5	13.3	14.1	14.9	15.6	16.4	17.2	3.6
3.7	9.9	10.7	11.5	12.2	13.0	13.8	14.5	15.3	16.1	16.8	3.7
3.8	9.8	10.5	11.3	12.0	12.7	13.5	14.2	15.0	15.7	16.5	3.8
3.9	9.6	10.3	11.1	11.8	12.5	13.2	14.0	14.7	15.4	16.1	3.9
4.0	9.4	10.1	10.9	11.6	12.3	13.0	13.7	14.4	15.1	15.8	4.0
4.1	9.3	10.0	10.7	11.4	12.1	12.7	13.4	14.1	14.8	15.5	4.1
4.2	9.2	9.8	10.5	11.2	11.8	12.5	13.2	13.9	14.5	15.2	4.2
4.3	9.0	9.7	10.3	11.0	11.7	12.3	13.0	13.6	14.3	14.9	4.3
4.4	8.9	9.5	10.2	10.8	11.5	12.1	12.8	13.4	14.0	14.7	4.4
4.5	8.8	9.4	10.0	10.7	11.3	11.9	12.6	13.2	13.8	14.4	4.5
4.6	8.7	9.3	9.9	10.5	11.1	11.8	12.4	13.0	13.6	14.2	4.6
4.7	8.6	9.2	9.8	10.4	11.0	11.6	12.2	12.8	13.4	14.0	4.7
4.8	8.5	9.1	9.7	10.2	10.8	11.4	12.0	12.6	13.2	13.8	4.8
4.9	8.4	9.0	9.5	10.1	10.7	11.3	11.9	12.4	13.0	13.6	4.9
5.0	8.3	8.9	9.4	10.0	10.6	11.1	11.7	12.3	12.8	13.4	5.0
5.5	7.9	8.5	9.0	9.5	10.0	10.5	11.0	11.5	12.1	12.6	5.5
6.0	7.7	8.2	8.6	9.1	9.6	10.0	10.5	11.0	11.5	11.9	6.0
6.5	7.5	7.9	8.4	8.8	9.2	9.7	10.1	10.5	11.0	11.4	6.5
7.0	7.4	7.8	8.2	8.6	9.0	9.4	9.8	10.2	10.6	11.0	7.0
7.5	7.3	7.6	8.0	8.4	8.8	9.2	9.5	9.9	10.3	10.7	7.5
8.0	7.2	7.6	7.9	8.3	8.6	9.0	9.3	9.7	10.0	10.4	8.0
8.5	7.2	7.5	7.9	8.2	8.5	8.9	9.2	9.5	9.9	10.2	8.5
9.0	7.2	7.5	7.8	8.1	8.5	8.8	9.1	9.4	9.7	10.0	9.0
9.5	7.2	7.5	7.8	8.1	8.4	8.7	9.0	9.3	9.6	9.9	9.5
10.0	7.2	7.5	7.8	8.1	8.4	8.7	9.0	9.3	9.5	9.8	10.0

TABLE 15
Distance by Vertical Angle
Measured Between Sea Horizon and Top of Object Beyond Sea Horizon

Difference in feet between height of object and height of eye of observer

Angle	25	30	35	40	45	50	60	70	80	90	Angle
° ′	*Miles*	*Miles*	*Miles*	*Miles*	*Miles*	*Miles*	*Miles*	*Miles*	*Miles*	*Miles*	° ′
–0 04	12. 4	12. 8	13. 2	13. 6	14. 0	14. 4	15. 0	15. 7	16. 3	16. 9	–0 04
–0 03	10. 5	10. 9	11. 4	11. 8	12. 2	12. 6	13. 3	14. 0	14. 6	15. 2	–0 03
–0 02	8. 7	9. 2	9. 7	10. 2	10. 6	11. 0	11. 8	12. 5	13. 1	13. 7	–0 02
–0 01	7. 2	7. 7	8. 2	8. 7	9. 1	9. 5	10. 3	11. 0	11. 7	12. 3	–0 01
0 00	5. 8	6. 4	6. 9	7. 4	7. 8	8. 2	9. 0	9. 7	10. 4	11. 1	0 00
0 01	4. 8	5. 3	5. 8	6. 3	6. 7	7. 1	7. 9	8. 6	9. 3	9. 9	0 01
0 02	3. 9	4. 4	4. 9	5. 4	5. 8	6. 2	6. 9	7. 6	8. 3	8. 9	0 02
0 03	3. 3	3. 7	4. 2	4. 6	5. 0	5. 4	6. 1	6. 8	7. 4	8. 0	0 03
0 04	2. 8	3. 2	3. 6	4. 0	4. 4	4. 7	5. 4	6. 1	6. 7	7. 3	0 04
0 05	2. 4	2. 8	3. 1	3. 5	3. 9	4. 2	4. 8	5. 5	6. 0	6. 6	0 05
0 06	2. 1	2. 4	2. 8	3. 1	3. 4	3. 7	4. 3	4. 9	5. 5	6. 0	0 06
0 07	1. 8	2. 2	2. 5	2. 8	3. 1	3. 4	3. 9	4. 5	5. 0	5. 5	0 07
0 08	1. 6	1. 9	2. 2	2. 5	2. 8	3. 1	3. 6	4. 1	4. 6	5. 0	0 08
0 09	1. 5	1. 7	2. 0	2. 3	2. 5	2. 8	3. 3	3. 8	4. 2	4. 7	0 09
0 10	1. 3	1. 6	1. 8	2. 1	2. 3	2. 6	3. 0	3. 5	3. 9	4. 3	0 10
0 15	0. 9	1. 1	1. 3	1. 5	1. 6	1. 8	2. 1	2. 5	2. 8	3. 1	0 15
0 20	0. 7	0. 8	1. 0	1. 1	1. 2	1. 4	1. 6	1. 9	2. 2	2. 4	0 20
0 25	0. 6	0. 7	0. 8	0. 9	1. 0	1. 1	1. 3	1. 5	1. 8	2. 0	0 25
0 30	0. 5	0. 6	0. 7	0. 7	0. 8	0. 9	1. 1	1. 3	1. 5	1. 7	0 30
0 35		0. 5	0. 6	0. 6	0. 7	0. 8	1. 0	1. 1	1. 3	1. 4	0 35
0 40			0. 5	0. 6	0. 6	0. 7	0. 8	1. 0	1. 1	1. 3	0 40
0 45				0. 5	0. 6	0. 6	0. 7	0. 9	1. 0	1. 1	0 45
0 50				0. 5	0. 5	0. 6	0. 7	0. 8	0. 9	1. 0	0 50
0 55					0. 5	0. 5	0. 6	0. 7	0. 8	0. 9	0 55
1 00						0. 5	0. 6	0. 7	0. 8	0. 8	1 00
1 10							0. 5	0. 6	0. 6	0. 7	1 10
1 20								0. 5	0. 6	0. 6	1 20
1 30									0. 5	0. 6	1 30
1 40									0. 5	0. 5	1 40
1 50										0. 5	1 50

TABLE 15
Distance by Vertical Angle
Measured Between Sea Horizon and Top of Object Beyond Sea Horizon

Difference in feet between height of object and height of eye of observer

Angle	100	120	140	160	180	200	250	300	350	400	450	Angle
° ′	*Miles*	*Miles*	*Miles*	*Miles*	*Miles*	*Miles*	*Miles*	*Miles*	*Miles*	*Miles*	*Miles*	° ′
0 00	11. 7	12. 8	13. 8	14. 8	15. 7	16. 5	18. 4	20. 2	21. 8	23. 3	24. 7	0 00
0 01	10. 5	11. 6	12. 7	13. 6	14. 5	15. 3	17. 3	19. 0	20. 7	22. 2	23. 6	0 01
0 02	9. 5	10. 6	11. 6	12. 5	13. 4	14. 3	16. 2	17. 9	19. 6	21. 0	22. 5	0 02
0 03	8. 6	9. 7	10. 7	11. 6	12. 5	13. 3	15. 2	16. 9	18. 5	20. 0	21. 4	0 03
0 04	7. 8	8. 8	9. 8	10. 7	11. 6	12. 4	14. 3	16. 0	17. 5	19. 0	20. 4	0 04
0 05	7. 1	8. 1	9. 0	9. 9	10. 8	11. 5	13. 4	15. 1	16. 6	18. 1	19. 5	0 05
0 06	6. 5	7. 5	8. 4	9. 2	10. 0	10. 8	12. 6	14. 2	15. 8	17. 2	18. 6	0 06
0 07	6. 0	6. 9	7. 7	8. 6	9. 4	10. 1	11. 9	13. 5	15. 0	16. 4	17. 7	0 07
0 08	5. 5	6. 4	7. 2	8. 0	8. 8	9. 5	11. 2	12. 8	14. 2	15. 6	16. 9	0 08
0 09	5. 1	5. 9	6. 7	7. 5	8. 2	8. 9	10. 6	12. 1	13. 5	14. 9	16. 2	0 09
0 10	4. 7	5. 5	6. 3	7. 0	7. 7	8. 4	10. 0	11. 5	12. 9	14. 2	15. 5	0 10
0 11	4. 4	5. 2	5. 9	6. 6	7. 3	7. 9	9. 5	10. 9	12. 3	13. 6	14. 8	0 11
0 12	4. 1	4. 8	5. 5	6. 2	6. 9	7. 5	9. 0	10. 4	11. 7	13. 0	14. 2	0 12
0 13	3. 9	4. 6	5. 2	5. 9	6. 5	7. 1	8. 5	9. 9	11. 2	12. 5	13. 6	0 13
0 14	3. 6	4. 3	4. 9	5. 6	6. 2	6. 7	8. 1	9. 5	10. 7	11. 9	13. 1	0 14
0 15	3. 4	4. 1	4. 7	5. 3	5. 8	6. 4	7. 8	9. 0	10. 3	11. 5	12. 6	0 15
0 20	2. 7	3. 2	3. 7	4. 2	4. 6	5. 1	6. 3	7. 4	8. 4	9. 5	10. 5	0 20
0 25	2. 2	2. 6	3. 0	3. 4	3. 8	4. 2	5. 2	6. 2	7. 1	8. 0	8. 9	0 25
0 30	1. 8	2. 2	2. 6	2. 9	3. 2	3. 6	4. 4	5. 3	6. 1	6. 9	7. 7	0 30
0 35	1. 6	1. 9	2. 2	2. 5	2. 8	3. 1	3. 9	4. 6	5. 3	6. 0	6. 7	0 35
0 40	1. 4	1. 7	1. 9	2. 2	2. 5	2. 8	3. 4	4. 1	4. 7	5. 4	6. 0	0 40
0 45	1. 2	1. 5	1. 7	2. 0	2. 2	2. 5	3. 1	3. 6	4. 2	4. 8	5. 4	0 45
0 50	1. 1	1. 3	1. 6	1. 8	2. 0	2. 2	2. 8	3. 3	3. 8	4. 4	4. 9	0 50
0 55	1. 0	1. 2	1. 4	1. 6	1. 8	2. 0	2. 5	3. 0	3. 5	4. 0	4. 5	0 55
1 00	0. 9	1. 1	1. 3	1. 5	1. 7	1. 9	2. 3	2. 8	3. 2	3. 7	4. 1	1 00
1 10	0. 8	1. 0	1. 1	1. 3	1. 4	1. 6	2. 0	2. 4	2. 8	3. 2	3. 6	1 10
1 20	0. 7	0. 8	1. 0	1. 1	1. 3	1. 4	1. 8	2. 1	2. 4	2. 8	3. 1	1 20
1 30	0. 6	0. 8	0. 9	1. 0	1. 1	1. 2	1. 6	1. 9	2. 2	2. 5	2. 8	1 30
1 40	0. 6	0. 7	0. 8	0. 9	1. 0	1. 1	1. 4	1. 7	2. 0	2. 2	2. 5	1 40
1 50	0. 5	0. 6	0. 7	0. 8	0. 9	1. 0	1. 3	1. 5	1. 8	2. 0	2. 3	1 50
2 00	0. 5	0. 6	0. 7	0. 8	0. 8	0. 9	1. 2	1. 4	1. 6	1. 9	2. 1	2 00
2 30		0. 5	0. 5	0. 6	0. 7	0. 8	0. 9	1. 1	1. 3	1. 5	1. 7	2 30
3 00				0. 5	0. 6	0. 6	0. 8	0. 9	1. 1	1. 3	1. 4	3 00
3 30					0. 5	0. 5	0. 7	0. 8	0. 9	1. 1	1. 2	3 30
4 00						0. 5	0. 6	0. 7	0. 8	0. 9	1. 1	4 00
4 30							0. 5	0. 6	0. 7	0. 8	0. 9	4 30
5 00							0. 5	0. 6	0. 7	0. 8	0. 8	5 00
6 00								0. 5	0. 5	0. 6	0. 7	6 00
7 00									0. 5	0. 5	0. 6	7 00
8 00										0. 5	0. 5	8 00
10 00												10 00

TABLE 15

Distance by Vertical Angle

Measured Between Sea Horizon and Top of Object Beyond Sea Horizon

Angle	Difference in feet between height of object and height of eye of observer											Angle
	500	600	700	800	900	1000	1200	1400	1600	1800	2000	
° ′	*Miles*	*Miles*	*Miles*	*Miles*	*Miles*	*Miles*	*Miles*	*Miles*	*Miles*	*Miles*	*Miles*	° ′
0 05	20.8	23.2	25.4	27.5	29.5	31.4	34.8	38.0	41.0	43.8	46.5	0 05
0 06	19.8	22.3	24.5	26.6	28.5	30.4	33.8	37.0	40.0	42.8	45.4	0 06
0 07	19.0	21.4	23.6	25.6	27.6	29.4	32.9	36.0	39.0	41.8	44.4	0 07
0 08	18.2	20.5	22.7	24.7	26.7	28.5	31.9	35.1	38.0	40.8	43.4	0 08
0 09	17.4	19.7	21.9	23.9	25.8	27.6	31.0	34.1	37.0	39.8	42.5	0 09
0 10	16.7	19.0	21.1	23.1	25.0	26.8	30.1	33.2	36.2	38.9	41.5	0 10
0 11	16.0	18.3	20.4	22.3	24.2	26.0	29.3	32.4	35.3	38.0	40.6	0 11
0 12	15.4	17.6	19.6	21.6	23.4	25.2	28.5	31.5	34.4	37.1	39.7	0 12
0 13	14.8	16.9	19.0	20.9	22.7	24.4	27.7	30.7	33.6	36.3	38.8	0 13
0 14	14.2	16.3	18.3	20.2	22.0	23.7	26.9	30.0	32.8	35.4	38.0	0 14
0 15	13.7	15.8	17.7	19.6	21.3	23.0	26.2	29.2	32.0	34.6	37.2	0 15
0 17	12.7	14.7	16.6	18.4	20.1	21.7	24.8	27.8	30.5	33.1	35.6	0 17
0 20	11.4	13.3	15.1	16.8	18.4	20.0	23.0	25.8	28.4	31.0	33.4	0 20
0 25	9.7	11.4	13.0	14.6	16.1	17.5	20.3	22.9	25.4	27.8	30.1	0 25
0 30	8.4	9.9	11.4	12.8	14.2	15.5	18.1	20.5	22.9	25.2	27.4	0 30
0 35	7.4	8.8	10.1	11.4	12.6	13.9	16.3	18.5	20.7	22.9	24.9	0 35
0 40	6.6	7.8	9.0	10.2	11.4	12.5	14.7	16.9	18.9	20.9	22.9	0 40
0 45	6.0	7.1	8.2	9.3	10.3	11.4	13.4	15.4	17.3	19.2	21.1	0 45
0 50	5.4	6.4	7.5	8.5	9.4	10.4	12.3	14.2	16.0	17.7	19.5	0 50
0 55	5.0	5.9	6.8	7.8	8.7	9.6	11.4	13.1	14.8	16.5	18.1	0 55
1 00	4.6	5.5	6.3	7.2	8.0	8.9	10.5	12.2	13.8	15.3	16.9	1 00
1 10	3.9	4.7	5.5	6.2	7.0	7.7	9.2	10.6	12.1	13.5	14.9	1 10
1 20	3.5	4.2	4.8	5.5	6.2	6.8	8.1	9.4	10.7	12.0	13.2	1 20
1 30	3.1	3.7	4.3	4.9	5.5	6.1	7.3	8.5	9.6	10.8	11.9	1 30
1 40	2.8	3.3	3.9	4.4	5.0	5.5	6.6	7.7	8.7	9.8	10.8	1 40
1 50	2.5	3.0	3.6	4.1	4.5	5.0	6.0	7.0	8.0	9.0	9.9	1 50
2 00	2.3	2.8	3.3	3.7	4.2	4.6	5.5	6.5	7.4	8.2	9.1	2 00
2 30	1.9	2.2	2.6	3.0	3.4	3.7	4.5	5.2	5.9	6.7	7.4	2 30
3 00	1.6	1.9	2.2	2.5	2.8	3.1	3.7	4.4	5.0	5.6	6.2	3 00
3 30	1.3	1.6	1.9	2.1	2.4	2.7	3.2	3.7	4.3	4.8	5.3	3 30
4 00	1.2	1.4	1.6	1.9	2.1	2.3	2.8	3.3	3.7	4.2	4.7	4 00
5 00	0.9	1.1	1.3	1.5	1.7	1.9	2.3	2.6	3.0	3.4	3.7	5 00
6 00	0.8	0.9	1.1	1.3	1.4	1.6	1.9	2.2	2.5	2.8	3.1	6 00
7 00	0.7	0.8	0.9	1.1	1.2	1.3	1.6	1.9	2.1	2.4	2.7	7 00
8 00	0.6	0.7	0.8	0.9	1.1	1.2	1.4	1.6	1.9	2.1	2.3	8 00
10 00	0.5	0.6	0.7	0.7	0.8	0.9	1.1	1.3	1.5	1.7	1.9	10 00
12 00		0.5	0.5	0.6	0.7	0.8	0.9	1.1	1.2	1.4	1.5	12 00
15 00				0.5	0.6	0.6	0.7	0.9	1.0	1.1	1.2	15 00
20 00						0.5	0.5	0.6	0.7	0.8	0.9	20 00
25 00								0.5	0.6	0.6	0.7	25 00
30 00									0.5	0.5	0.6	30 00

TABLE 16

Distance by Vertical Angle
Measured Between Waterline at Object and Top of Object

Angle	Height of object above the sea, in **feet** and (meters)										Angle
	10 (3.0)	**15** (4.6)	**20** (6.1)	**25** (7.6)	**30** (9.1)	**35** (10.7)	**40** (12.2)	**45** (13.7)	**50** (15.2)	**55** (16.8)	
° ′	*Miles*	*Miles*	*Miles*	*Miles*	*Miles*	*Miles*	*Miles*	*Miles*	*Miles*	*Miles*	° ′
0 10	0.57	0.85	1.13	1.41	1.70	1.98	2.26	2.55	2.83	3.11	0 10
0 11	0.51	0.77	1.03	1.29	1.54	1.80	2.06	2.31	2.57	2.83	0 11
0 12	0.47	0.71	0.94	1.18	1.41	1.65	1.89	2.12	2.36	2.59	0 12
0 13	0.44	0.65	0.87	1.09	1.31	1.52	1.74	1.96	2.18	2.39	0 13
0 14	0.40	0.61	0.81	1.01	1.21	1.41	1.62	1.82	2.02	2.22	0 14
0 15	0.38	0.57	0.75	0.94	1.18	1.32	1.51	1.70	1.89	2.07	0 15
0 20	0.28	0.42	0.57	0.71	0.85	0.99	1.13	1.27	1.41	1.56	0 20
0 25	0.23	0.34	0.45	0.57	0.68	0.79	0.91	1.02	1.13	1.24	0 25
0 30	0.19	0.28	0.38	0.47	0.57	0.66	0.75	0.85	0.94	1.04	0 30
0 35	0.16	0.24	0.32	0.40	0.46	0.57	0.65	0.73	0.81	0.89	0 35
0 40	0.14	0.21	0.28	0.35	0.42	0.50	0.57	0.64	0.71	0.78	0 40
0 45	0.13	0.19	0.25	0.31	0.38	0.44	0.50	0.57	0.63	0.69	0 45
0 50	0.11	0.17	0.23	0.28	0.34	0.40	0.45	0.51	0.57	0.62	0 50
0 55	0.10	0.15	0.21	0.26	0.31	0.36	0.41	0.46	0.51	0.57	0 55
1 00		0.14	0.19	0.24	0.28	0.33	0.38	0.42	0.47	0.52	1 00
1 10		0.12	0.16	0.20	0.24	0.28	0.32	0.36	0.40	0.44	1 10
1 20		0.11	0.14	0.18	0.21	0.25	0.28	0.32	0.35	0.39	1 20
1 30		0.09	0.13	0.16	0.19	0.22	0.25	0.28	0.31	0.35	1 30
1 40			0.11	0.14	0.17	0.20	0.23	0.25	0.28	0.31	1 40
1 50			0.10	0.13	0.15	0.18	0.21	0.23	0.26	0.28	1 50
2 00				0.12	0.14	0.16	0.19	0.21	0.24	0.26	2 00
2 15				0.10	0.13	0.15	0.17	0.19	0.21	0.23	2 15
2 30					0.11	0.13	0.15	0.17	0.19	0.21	2 30
2 45					0.10	0.12	0.14	0.15	0.17	0.19	2 45
3 00						0.11	0.13	0.14	0.16	0.17	3 00
3 20						0.10	0.11	0.13	0.14	0.16	3 20
3 40							0.10	0.12	0.13	0.14	3 40
4 00								0.11	0.12	0.13	4 00
4 20								0.10	0.11	0.12	4 20
4 40									0.10	0.11	4 40
5 00										0.10	5 00

TABLE 16

Distance by Vertical Angle
Measured Between Waterline at Object and Top of Object

Angle	Height of object above the sea, in **feet** and (meters)										Angle
	60 (18.3)	**65** (19.8)	**70** (21.3)	**75** (22. 9)	**80** (24.4)	**85** (25.9)	**90** (27.4)	**95** (29.0)	**100** (30.5)	**105** (32.0)	
° ′	*Miles*	*Miles*	*Miles*	*Miles*	*Miles*	*Miles*	*Miles*	*Miles*	*Miles*	*Miles*	° ′
0 10	3.39	3.68	3.96	4.24	4.53	4.81					0 10
0 11	3.09	3.34	3.60	3.86	4.11	4.37	4.63	4.89			0 11
0 12	2.83	3.06	3.30	3.54	3.77	4.01	4.24	4.48	4.71	4.95	0 12
0 13	2.61	2.83	3.05	3.26	3.48	3.70	3.92	4.13	4.35	4.57	0 13
0 14	2.42	2.63	2.83	3.03	3.23	3.44	3.64	3.84	4.04	4.24	0 14
0 15	2.26	2.45	2.64	2.83	3.02	3.21	3.39	3.58	3.77	3.96	0 15
0 20	1.70	1.84	1.98	2.12	2.26	2.40	2.55	2.69	2.83	2.97	0 20
0 25	1.36	1.47	1.58	1.70	1.81	1.92	2.04	2.15	2.26	2.38	0 25
0 30	1.13	1.23	1.32	1.41	1.51	1.60	1.70	1.79	1.89	1.98	0 30
0 35	0.97	1.05	1.13	1.21	1.29	1.37	1.45	1.54	1.62	1.70	0 35
0 40	0.85	0.92	0.99	1.06	1.13	1.20	1.27	1.34	1.41	1.49	0 40
0 45	0.75	0.82	0.88	0.94	1.01	1.07	1.13	1.19	1.26	1.32	0 45
0 50	0.68	0.74	0.79	0.85	0.91	0.96	1.02	1.07	1.13	1.19	0 50
0 55	0.62	0.67	0.72	0.77	0.82	0.87	0.93	0.98	1.03	1.08	0 55
1 00	0.57	0.61	0.66	0.71	0.75	0.80	0.85	0.90	0.94	0.99	1 00
1 10	0.48	0.53	0.57	0.61	0.65	0.69	0.73	0.77	0.81	0.85	1 10
1 20	0.42	0.46	0.49	0.53	0.57	0.60	0.64	0.67	0.71	0.74	1 20
1 30	0.38	0.41	0.44	0.47	0.50	0.53	0.57	0.60	0.63	0.66	1 30
1 40	0.34	0.37	0.40	0.42	0.45	0.48	0.51	0.54	0.57	0.59	1 40
1 50	0.31	0.33	0.36	0.39	0.41	0.44	0.46	0.49	0.51	0.54	1 50
2 00	0.28	0.31	0.33	0.35	0.38	0.40	0.42	0.45	0.47	0.49	2 00
2 15	0.25	0.27	0.29	0.31	0.34	0.36	0.38	0.40	0.42	0.44	2 15
2 30	0.23	0.25	0.26	0.28	0.30	0.32	0.34	0.36	0.38	0.40	2 30
2 45	0.21	0.22	0.24	0.26	0.27	0.29	0.31	0.33	0.34	0.36	2 45
3 00	0.19	0.20	0.22	0.24	0.25	0.27	0.28	0.30	0.31	0.33	3 00
3 20	0.17	0.18	0.20	0.21	0.23	0.24	0.25	0.27	0.28	0.30	3 20
3 40	0.15	0.17	0.18	0.19	0.21	0.22	0.23	0.24	0.26	0.27	3 40
4 00	0.14	0.15	0.16	0.18	0.19	0.20	0.21	0.22	0.24	0.25	4 00
4 20	0.13	0.14	0.15	0.16	0.17	0.18	0.20	0.21	0.22	0.23	4 20
4 40	0.12	0.13	0.14	0.15	0.16	0.17	0.18	0.19	0.20	0.21	4 40
5 00	0.11	0.12	0.13	0.14	0.15	0.16	0.17	0.18	0.19	0.20	5 00
5 20	0.11	0.11	0.12	0.13	0.14	0.15	0.16	0.17	0.18	0.19	5 20
5 40	0.10	0.11	0.12	0.12	0.13	0.14	0.15	0.16	0.17	0.17	5 40
6 00		0.10	0.11	0.12	0.13	0.13	0.14	0.15	0.16	0.16	6 00
6 20			0.10	0.11	0.12	0.13	0.13	0.14	0.15	0.16	6 20
6 40				0.11	0.11	0.12	0.13	0.13	0.14	0.15	6 40
7 00				0.10	0.11	0.11	0.12	0.13	0.13	0.14	7 00
7 20					0.10	0.11	0.12	0.12	0.13	0.13	7 20
7 40						0.10	0.11	0.12	0.12	0.13	7 40
8 00							0.11	0.11	0.12	0.12	8 00
8 20							0.10	0.11	0.11	0.12	8 20
8 40								0.10	0.11	0.11	8 40
9 00									0.10	0.11	9 00
9 30										0.10	9 30
10 00											10 00

TABLE 16

Distance by Vertical Angle
Measured Between Waterline at Object and Top of Object

Angle	Height of object above the sea, in **feet** and (meters)										Angle
	110 (33.5)	115 (35.1)	120 (36.6)	125 (38.1)	130 (39.6)	135 (41.1)	140 (42.7)	145 (44.2)	150 (45.7)	155 (47.2)	
° ′	*Miles*	*Miles*	*Miles*	*Miles*	*Miles*	*Miles*	*Miles*	*Miles*	*Miles*	*Miles*	° ′
0 10											0 10
0 11											0 11
0 12											0 12
0 13	4.79	5.00									0 13
0 14	4.45	4.65	4.85								0 14
0 15	4.15	4.34	4.53	4.71	4.90						0 15
0 20	3.11	3.25	3.39	3.54	3.68	3.82	3.96	4.10	4.24	4.38	0 20
0 25	2.49	2.60	2.72	2.83	2.94	3.06	3.17	3.28	3.30	3.51	0 25
0 30	2.07	2.17	2.26	2.36	2.45	2.55	2.64	2.73	2.83	2.92	0 30
0 35	1.78	1.86	1.94	2.02	2.10	2.18	2.26	2.34	2.42	2.51	0 35
0 40	1.56	1.63	1.70	1.77	1.84	1.91	1.98	2.05	2.12	2.19	0 40
0 45	1.30	1.45	1.51	1.57	1.63	1.70	1.76	1.82	1.89	1.95	0 45
0 50	1.24	1.30	1.36	1.41	1.47	1.53	1.58	1.64	1.70	1.75	0 50
0 55	1.13	1.18	1.23	1.29	1.34	1.39	1.44	1.49	1.54	1.59	0 55
1 00	1.04	1.08	1.13	1.18	1.23	1.27	1.32	1.37	1.41	1.46	1 00
1 10	0.89	0.93	0.97	1.01	1.05	1.09	1.13	1.17	1.21	1.25	1 10
1 20	0.78	0.81	0.85	0.88	0.92	0.95	0.99	1.03	1.06	1.10	1 20
1 30	0.69	0.72	0.75	0.79	0.82	0.85	0.88	0.91	0.94	0.97	1 30
1 40	0.62	0.65	0.66	0.71	0.74	0.76	0.79	0.82	0.85	0.88	1 40
1 50	0.57	0.59	0.62	0.64	0.67	0.69	0.72	0.75	0.77	0.80	1 50
2 00	0.52	0.54	0.57	0.59	0.61	0.64	0.66	0.68	0.71	0.73	2 00
2 15	0.46	0.48	0.50	0.52	0.54	0.57	0.59	0.61	0.63	0.65	2 15
2 30	0.41	0.43	0.45	0.47	0.49	0.51	0.53	0.55	0.57	0.58	2 30
2 45	0.38	0.39	0.41	0.43	0.45	0.46	0.48	0.50	0.51	0.53	2 45
3 00	0.35	0.36	0.38	0.39	0.41	0.42	0.44	0.46	0.47	0.49	3 00
3 20	0.31	0.32	0.34	0.35	0.37	0.38	0.40	0.41	0.42	0.44	3 20
3 40	0.28	0.30	0.31	0.32	0.33	0.35	0.36	0.37	0.39	0.40	3 40
4 00	0.26	0.27	0.28	0.29	0.31	0.32	0.33	0.34	0.35	0.36	4 00
4 20	0.24	0.25	0.26	0.27	0.28	0.29	0.30	0.31	0.33	0.34	4 20
4 40	0.22	0.23	0.24	0.25	0.26	0.27	0.28	0.29	0.30	0.31	4 40
5 00	0.21	0.22	0.23	0.24	0.24	0.25	0.26	0.27	0.28	0.29	5 00
5 20	0.19	0.20	0.21	0.22	0.23	0.24	0.25	0.26	0.26	0.27	5 20
5 40	0.18	0.19	0.20	0.21	0.22	0.22	0.23	0.24	0.25	0.26	5 40
6 00	0.17	0.18	0.19	0.20	0.20	0.21	0.22	0.23	0.23	0.24	6 00
6 20	0.16	0.17	0.18	0.19	0.19	0.20	0.21	0.22	0.22	0.23	6 20
6 40	0.15	0.17	0.17	0.18	0.18	0.19	0.20	0.20	0.21	0.22	6 40
7 00	0.15	0.15	0.16	0.17	0.17	0.18	0.19	0.19	0.20	0.21	7 00
7 20	0.14	0.15	0.15	0.16	0.17	0.17	0.18	0.19	0.19	0.20	7 20
7 40	0.13	0.14	0.15	0.15	0.16	0.17	0.17	0.18	0.18	0.19	7 40
8 00	0.13	0.13	0.14	0.15	0.15	0.16	0.16	0.17	0.18	0.18	8 00
8 20	0.12	0.13	0.13	0.14	0.15	0.15	0.16	0.16	0.17	0.17	8 20
8 40	0.12	0.12	0.13	0.13	0.14	0.15	0.15	0.16	0.16	0.17	8 40
9 00	0.11	0.12	0.12	0.13	0.14	0.14	0.15	0.15	0.16	0.16	9 00
9 30	0.11	0.11	0.12	0.13	0.13	0.13	0.14	0.14	0.15	0.15	9 30
10 00	0.10	0.11	0.11	0.12	0.12	0.13	0.13	0.14	0.14	0.14	10 00
10 30		0.10	0.11	0.11	0.12	0.12	0.12	0.13	0.13	0.14	10 30
11 00			0.10	0.11	0.11	0.11	0.12	0.12	0.13	0.13	11 00
11 30				0.10	0.11	0.11	0.11	0.12	0.12	0.13	11 30
12 00					0.10	0.10	0.11	0.11	0.12	0.12	12 00
12 30							0.10	0.11	0.11	0.12	12 30
13 00								0.10	0.11	0.11	13 00
13 30									0.10	0.11	13 30
14 00										0.10	14 00

TABLE 16

Distance by Vertical Angle
Measured Between Waterline at Object and Top of Object

Angle	Height of object above the sea, in **feet** and (meters)										Angle
	160 (48.8)	165 (50.3)	175 (53.3)	185 (56.4)	195 (59.4)	200 (61.0)	225 (68.6)	250 (76.2)	275 (83.8)	300 (91.4)	
° ′	*Miles*	*Miles*	*Miles*	*Miles*	*Miles*	*Miles*	*Miles*	*Miles*	*Miles*	*Miles*	° ′
0 15											0 15
0 20	4.53	4.67	4.95								0 20
0 25	3.62	3.73	3.96	4.19	4.41	4.53					0 25
0 30	3.02	3.11	3.30	3.49	3.68	3.77	4.24	4.71			0 30
0 35	2.59	2.67	2.83	2.99	3.15	3.23	3.64	4.04	4.45	4.85	0 35
0 40	2.26	2.33	2.48	2.62	2.76	2.83	3.18	3.54	3.89	4.24	0 40
0 45	2.01	2.07	2.20	2.33	2.45	2.51	2.83	3.14	3.46	3.77	0 45
0 50	1.81	1.87	1.98	2.09	2.21	2.26	2.55	2.83	3.11	3.39	0 50
0 55	1.65	1.70	1.80	1.90	2.01	2.06	2.31	2.57	2.83	3.09	0 55
1 00	1.51	1.56	1.65	1.74	1.84	1.89	2.12	2.36	2.59	2.83	1 00
1 10	1.20	1.33	1.41	1.50	1.58	1.62	1.82	2.02	2.22	2.42	1 10
1 20	1.13	1.17	1.24	1.31	1.38	1.41	1.59	1.77	1.94	2.12	1 20
1 30	1.01	1.04	1.10	1.16	1.23	1.26	1.41	1.57	1.73	1.89	1 30
1 40	0.91	0.93	0.99	1.05	1.10	1.13	1.27	1.41	1.56	1.70	1 40
1 50	0.82	0.85	0.90	0.95	1.00	1.03	1.16	1.29	1.41	1.54	1 50
2 00	0.75	0.78	0.82	0.87	0.92	0.94	1.06	1.18	1.30	1.41	2 00
2 15	0.67	0.69	0.73	0.77	0.82	0.84	0.94	1.05	1.15	1.26	2 15
2 30	0.60	0.62	0.66	0.70	0.74	0.75	0.85	0.94	1.04	1.13	2 30
2 45	0.55	0.57	0.60	0.63	0.67	0.69	0.77	0.86	0.94	1.03	2 45
3 00	0.50	0.52	0.55	0.58	0.61	0.63	0.71	0.79	0.86	0.94	3 00
3 20	0.45	0.47	0.49	0.52	0.55	0.57	0.64	0.71	0.78	0.85	3 20
3 40	0.41	0.42	0.45	0.48	0.50	0.51	0.58	0.64	0.71	0.77	3 40
4 00	0.38	0.39	0.41	0.44	0.46	0.47	0.53	0.59	0.65	0.71	4 00
4 20	0.35	0.36	0.38	0.40	0.42	0.43	0.49	0.54	0.60	0.65	4 20
4 40	0.32	0.33	0.35	0.37	0.39	0.40	0.45	0.50	0.55	0.60	4 40
5 00	0.30	0.31	0.33	0.35	0.37	0.38	0.42	0.47	0.52	0.56	5 00
5 20	0.28	0.29	0.31	0.33	0.34	0.35	0.40	0.44	0.48	0.53	5 20
5 40	0.27	0.27	0.29	0.31	0.32	0.33	0.37	0.41	0.46	0.50	5 40
6 00	0.25	0.26	0.27	0.29	0.31	0.31	0.35	0.39	0.43	0.47	6 00
6 20	0.24	0.24	0.26	0.27	0.29	0.30	0.33	0.37	0.41	0.44	6 20
6 40	0.23	0.23	0.25	0.26	0.27	0.28	0.32	0.35	0.39	0.42	6 40
7 00	0.21	0.22	0.23	0.25	0.26	0.27	0.30	0.34	0.37	0.40	7 00
7 20	0.20	0.21	0.22	0.24	0.25	0.26	0.29	0.32	0.35	0.38	7 20
7 40	0.20	0.20	0.21	0.23	0.24	0.24	0.28	0.31	0.34	0.37	7 40
8 00	0.19	0.19	0.20	0.22	0.23	0.23	0.26	0.29	0.32	0.35	8 00
8 20	0.18	0.19	0.20	0.21	0.22	0.22	0.25	0.28	0.31	0.34	8 20
8 40	0.17	0.19	0.19	0.20	0.21	0.22	0.24	0.27	0.30	0.32	8 40
9 00	0.17	0.17	0.18	0.19	0.20	0.21	0.23	0.26	0.29	0.31	9 00
9 30	0.16	0.16	0.17	0.18	0.19	0.20	0.22	0.25	0.27	0.30	9 30
10 00	0.15	0.15	0.16	0.17	0.18	0.19	0.21	0.23	0.26	0.28	10 00
10 30	0.14	0.15	0.16	0.16	0.17	0.18	0.20	0.22	0.24	0.27	10 30
11 00	0.14	0.14	0.15	0.16	0.17	0.17	0.19	0.21	0.23	0.25	11 00
11 30	0.13	0.13	0.14	0.15	0.16	0.16	0.18	0.20	0.22	0.24	11 30
12 00	0.12	0.13	0.14	0.14	0.15	0.15	0.17	0.19	0.21	0.23	12 00
12 30	0.12	0.12	0.13	0.14	0.14	0.15	0.17	0.19	0.20	0.22	12 30
13 00	0.11	0.11	0.12	0.13	0.14	0.14	0.16	0.18	0.20	0.21	13 00
13 30	0.11	0.11	0.12	0.13	0.13	0.14	0.15	0.17	0.19	0.21	13 30
14 00	0.11	0.11	0.12	0.12	0.13	0.13	0.15	0.17	0.18	0.20	14 00
14 30	0.10	0.10	0.11	0.12	0.12	0.13	0.14	0.16	0.18	0.19	14 30
15 00			0.11	0.11	0.12	0.12	0.14	0.15	0.17	0.18	15 00
16 00			0.10	0.11	0.11	0.11	0.13	0.14	0.16	0.17	16 00
17 00				0.10	0.10	0.11	0.12	0.13	0.15	0.16	17 00
18 00						0.10	0.11	0.13	0.14	0.15	18 00
19 00							0.11	0.12	0.13	0.14	19 00
20 00							0.10	0.11	0.12	0.14	20 00

TABLE 17

Distance by Vertical Angle

Measured Between Waterline at Object and Sea Horizon Beyond Object

Distance	Height of eye above the sea, in feet										Distance
	5	10	15	20	25	30	35	40	45	50	
Yards	° ′	° ′	° ′	° ′	° ′	° ′	° ′	° ′	° ′	° ′	*Yards*
100	0 55	1 52	2 48	3 45	4 41	5 37	6 34	7 30	8 26	9 21	100
200	27	0 54	1 22	1 50	2 18	2 46	3 15	3 43	4 11	4 39	200
300	17	35	0 54	1 12	1 31	1 49	2 08	2 27	2 45	3 04	300
400	12	26	39	0 53	1 07	1 21	1 35	1 49	2 02	2 16	400
500	9	20	31	42	0 53	1 04	1 15	1 26	1 37	1 48	500
600		16	25	34	43	0 52	1 01	1 10	1 20	1 29	600
700		13	21	29	36	44	0 52	0 59	1 07	1 15	700
800		11	18	24	31	38	45	51	0 58	1 05	800
900		10	16	21	27	33	39	45	51	0 57	900
1, 000			14	19	24	29	35	40	45	51	1, 000
1, 100			12	17	21	26	31	36	41	45	1, 100
1, 200			11	15	19	24	28	32	37	41	1, 200
1, 300			10	14	17	21	25	29	33	37	1, 300
1, 400				12	16	20	23	27	31	34	1, 400
1, 500				11	15	18	21	25	28	32	1, 500
1, 600				10	13	17	20	23	26	29	1, 600
1, 700					12	15	18	21	24	27	1, 700
1, 800					11	14	17	20	23	25	1, 800
1, 900					11	13	16	18	21	24	1, 900
2, 000					10	12	15	17	20	22	2, 000
2, 100						11	14	16	18	21	2, 100
2, 200						11	13	15	17	20	2, 200
2, 300						10	12	14	16	19	2, 300
2, 400							11	13	15	18	2, 400
2, 500							11	13	15	17	2, 500
2, 600							10	12	14	16	2, 600
2, 700								11	13	15	2, 700
2, 800								11	12	14	2, 800
2, 900								10	12	14	2, 900
3, 000									11	13	3, 000
3, 100									11	12	3, 100
3, 200									10	12	3, 200
3, 300										11	3, 300
3, 400										11	3, 400
3, 500										10	3, 500

TABLE 17

Distance by Vertical Angle

Measured Between Waterline at Object and Sea Horizon Beyond Object

Distance	Height of eye above the sea, in feet										Distance
	55	60	65	70	75	80	85	90	95	100	
Yards	° ′	° ′	° ′	° ′	° ′	° ′	° ′	° ′	° ′	° ′	*Yards*
100	10 16	11 11	12 06	13 00	13 54	14 48	15 41	16 34	17 26	18 17	100
200	5 07	5 35	6 03	6 31	6 59	7 27	7 55	8 23	8 51	9 18	200
300	3 23	3 41	4 00	4 19	4 38	4 56	5 15	5 34	5 52	6 11	300
400	2 30	2 44	2 58	3 12	3 26	3 40	3 54	4 08	4 22	4 36	400
500	1 59	2 10	2 21	2 32	2 43	2 55	3 06	3 17	3 28	3 39	500
600	1 38	1 47	1 56	2 06	2 15	2 24	2 33	2 43	2 52	3 01	600
700	1 23	1 31	1 39	1 47	1 54	2 02	2 10	2 18	2 26	2 34	700
800	1 12	1 19	1 25	1 32	1 39	1 46	1 53	2 00	2 07	2 14	800
900	1 03	1 09	1 15	1 21	1 27	1 33	1 39	1 46	1 52	1 58	900
1, 000	0 56	1 01	1 07	1 12	1 18	1 23	1 29	1 34	1 40	1 45	1, 000
1, 100	50	0 55	1 00	1 05	1 10	1 15	1 20	1 25	1 30	1 35	1, 100
1, 200	46	50	0 55	0 59	1 03	1 08	1 12	1 17	1 22	1 26	1, 200
1, 300	42	46	50	54	0 58	1 02	1 06	1 10	1 15	1 19	1, 300
1, 400	38	42	46	49	53	0 57	1 01	1 05	1 09	1 12	1, 400
1, 500	35	39	42	46	49	53	0 56	1 00	1 03	1 07	1, 500
1, 600	33	36	39	42	46	49	52	0 56	0 59	1 02	1, 600
1, 700	30	33	36	39	43	46	49	52	55	0 58	1, 700
1, 800	28	31	34	37	40	43	46	48	51	54	1, 800
1, 900	26	29	32	35	37	40	43	45	48	51	1, 900
2, 000	25	27	30	32	35	38	40	43	45	48	2, 000
2, 100	23	26	28	31	33	35	38	40	43	45	2, 100
2, 200	22	24	27	29	31	33	36	38	40	43	2, 200
2, 300	21	23	25	27	29	32	34	36	38	41	2, 300
2, 400	20	22	24	26	28	30	32	34	36	39	2, 400
2, 500	19	21	23	25	27	29	31	33	35	37	2, 500
2, 600	18	19	21	23	25	27	29	31	33	35	2, 600
2, 700	17	19	20	22	24	26	28	30	31	33	2, 700
2, 800	16	18	19	21	23	25	26	28	30	32	2, 800
2, 900	15	17	18	20	22	24	25	27	29	30	2, 900
3, 000	14	16	18	19	21	23	24	26	27	29	3, 000
3, 100	14	15	17	18	20	22	23	25	26	28	3, 100
3, 200	13	15	16	18	19	21	22	24	25	27	3, 200
3, 300	13	14	15	17	18	20	21	23	24	26	3, 300
3, 400	12	13	15	16	18	19	20	22	23	25	3, 400
3, 500	12	13	14	16	17	18	20	21	22	24	3, 500
3, 600	11	12	14	15	16	18	19	20	22	23	3, 600
3, 700	11	12	13	14	16	17	18	19	21	22	3, 700
3, 800	10	11	13	14	15	16	17	19	20	21	3, 800
3, 900		11	12	13	14	16	17	18	19	21	3, 900
4, 000		11	12	13	14	15	16	17	19	20	4, 000
4, 100		10	11	12	13	15	16	17	18	19	4, 100
4, 200			11	12	13	14	15	16	17	18	4, 200
4, 300			10	11	12	14	15	16	17	18	4, 300
4, 400			10	11	12	13	14	15	16	17	4, 400
4, 500			10	11	12	13	14	15	16	17	4, 500
4, 600				10	11	12	13	14	15	16	4, 600
4, 700					11	12	13	14	15	16	4, 700
4, 800					11	11	12	13	14	15	4, 800
4, 900					10	11	12	13	14	15	4, 900
5, 000					10	11	12	12	13	14	5, 000

TABLE 18

Distance of an Object by Two Bearings

Difference between the course and second bearing	Difference between the course and first bearing													
	20°		22°		24°		26°		28°		30°		32°	
°														
30	1.97	0.98												
32	1.64	0.87	2.16	1.14										
34	1.41	0.79	1.80	1.01	2.34	1.31								
36	1.24	0.73	1.55	0.91	1.96	1.15	2.52	1.48						
38	1.11	0.68	1.36	0.84	1.68	1.04	2.11	1.30	2.70	1.66				
40	1.00	0.64	1.21	0.78	1.48	0.95	1.81	1.16	2.26	1.45	2.88	1.85		
42	0.91	0.61	1.10	0.73	1.32	0.88	1.59	1.06	1.94	1.30	2.40	1.61	3.05	2.04
44	0.84	0.58	1.00	0.69	1.19	0.83	1.42	0.98	1.70	1.18	2.07	1.44	2.55	1.77
46	0.78	0.56	0.92	0.66	1.09	0.78	1.28	0.92	1.52	1.09	1.81	1.30	2.19	1.58
48	0.73	0.54	0.85	0.64	1.00	0.74	1.17	0.87	1.37	1.02	1.62	1.20	1.92	1.43
50	0.68	0.52	0.80	0.61	0.93	0.71	1.08	0.83	1.25	0.96	1.46	1.12	1.71	1.31
52	0.65	0.51	0.75	0.59	0.87	0.68	1.00	0.79	1.15	0.91	1.33	1.05	1.55	1.22
54	0.61	0.49	0.71	0.57	0.81	0.66	0.93	0.76	1.07	0.87	1.23	0.99	1.41	1.14
56	0.58	0.48	0.67	0.56	0.77	0.64	0.88	0.73	1.00	0.83	1.14	0.95	1.30	1.08
58	0.56	0.47	0.64	0.54	0.73	0.62	0.83	0.70	0.94	0.80	1.07	0.90	1.21	1.03
60	0.53	0.46	0.61	0.53	0.69	0.60	0.78	0.68	0.89	0.77	1.00	0.87	1.13	0.98
62	0.51	0.45	0.58	0.51	0.66	0.58	0.75	0.66	0.84	0.74	0.94	0.83	1.06	0.94
64	0.49	0.44	0.56	0.50	0.63	0.57	0.71	0.64	0.80	0.72	0.89	0.80	1.00	0.90
66	0.48	0.43	0.54	0.49	0.61	0.56	0.68	0.62	0.76	0.70	0.85	0.78	0.95	0.87
68	0.46	0.43	0.52	0.48	0.59	0.54	0.66	0.61	0.73	0.68	0.81	0.75	0.90	0.84
70	0.45	0.42	0.50	0.47	0.57	0.53	0.63	0.59	0.70	0.66	0.78	0.73	0.86	0.81
72	0.43	0.41	0.49	0.47	0.55	0.52	0.61	0.58	0.68	0.64	0.75	0.71	0.82	0.78
74	0.42	0.41	0.48	0.46	0.53	0.51	0.59	0.57	0.65	0.63	0.72	0.69	0.79	0.76
76	0.41	0.40	0.46	0.45	0.52	0.50	0.57	0.56	0.63	0.61	0.70	0.67	0.76	0.74
78	0.40	0.39	0.45	0.44	0.50	0.49	0.56	0.54	0.61	0.60	0.67	0.66	0.74	0.72
80	0.39	0.39	0.44	0.44	0.49	0.48	0.54	0.53	0.60	0.59	0.65	0.64	0.71	0.70
82	0.39	0.38	0.43	0.43	0.48	0.47	0.53	0.52	0.58	0.57	0.63	0.63	0.69	0.69
84	0.38	0.38	0.42	0.42	0.47	0.47	0.52	0.51	0.57	0.56	0.62	0.61	0.67	0.67
86	0.37	0.37	0.42	0.42	0.46	0.46	0.51	0.50	0.55	0.55	0.60	0.60	0.66	0.65
88	0.37	0.37	0.41	0.41	0.45	0.45	0.50	0.50	0.54	0.54	0.59	0.59	0.64	0.64
90	0.36	0.36	0.40	0.40	0.45	0.45	0.49	0.49	0.53	0.53	0.58	0.58	0.62	0.62
92	0.36	0.36	0.40	0.40	0.44	0.44	0.48	0.48	0.52	0.52	0.57	0.57	0.61	0.61
94	0.36	0.35	0.39	0.39	0.43	0.43	0.47	0.47	0.51	0.51	0.56	0.55	0.60	0.60
96	0.35	0.35	0.39	0.39	0.43	0.43	0.47	0.46	0.51	0.50	0.55	0.54	0.59	0.59
98	0.35	0.35	0.39	0.38	0.42	0.42	0.46	0.46	0.50	0.50	0.54	0.53	0.58	0.57
100	0.35	0.34	0.38	0.38	0.42	0.41	0.46	0.45	0.49	0.49	0.53	0.52	0.57	0.56
102	0.35	0.34	0.38	0.37	0.42	0.41	0.45	0.44	0.49	0.48	0.53	0.51	0.56	0.55
104	0.34	0.33	0.38	0.37	0.41	0.40	0.45	0.43	0.48	0.47	0.52	0.50	0.56	0.54
106	0.34	0.33	0.38	0.36	0.41	0.39	0.45	0.43	0.48	0.46	0.52	0.50	0.55	0.53
108	0.34	0.32	0.38	0.36	0.41	0.39	0.44	0.42	0.48	0.45	0.51	0.49	0.55	0.52
110	0.34	0.32	0.37	0.35	0.41	0.38	0.44	0.41	0.47	0.44	0.51	0.48	0.54	0.51
112	0.34	0.32	0.37	0.35	0.41	0.38	0.44	0.41	0.47	0.44	0.50	0.47	0.54	0.50
114	0.34	0.31	0.37	0.34	0.41	0.37	0.44	0.40	0.47	0.43	0.50	0.46	0.54	0.49
116	0.34	0.31	0.38	0.34	0.41	0.37	0.44	0.39	0.47	0.42	0.50	0.45	0.53	0.48
118	0.35	0.31	0.38	0.33	0.41	0.36	0.44	0.39	0.47	0.41	0.50	0.44	0.53	0.47
120	0.35	0.30	0.38	0.33	0.41	0.36	0.44	0.38	0.47	0.41	0.50	0.43	0.53	0.46
122	0.35	0.30	0.38	0.32	0.41	0.35	0.44	0.37	0.47	0.40	0.50	0.42	0.53	0.45
124	0.35	0.29	0.38	0.32	0.41	0.34	0.44	0.37	0.47	0.39	0.50	0.42	0.53	0.44
126	0.36	0.29	0.39	0.31	0.42	0.34	0.45	0.36	0.47	0.38	0.50	0.41	0.53	0.43
128	0.36	0.28	0.39	0.31	0.42	0.33	0.45	0.35	0.48	0.38	0.50	0.40	0.53	0.42
130	0.36	0.28	0.39	0.30	0.42	0.32	0.45	0.35	0.48	0.37	0.51	0.39	0.54	0.41
132	0.37	0.27	0.40	0.30	0.43	0.32	0.46	0.34	0.48	0.36	0.51	0.38	0.54	0.40
134	0.37	0.27	0.40	0.29	0.43	0.31	0.46	0.33	0.49	0.35	0.52	0.37	0.54	0.39
136	0.38	0.26	0.41	0.28	0.44	0.30	0.47	0.32	0.49	0.34	0.52	0.36	0.55	0.38
138	0.39	0.26	0.42	0.28	0.45	0.30	0.47	0.32	0.50	0.33	0.53	0.35	0.55	0.37
140	0.39	0.25	0.42	0.27	0.45	0.29	0.48	0.31	0.51	0.33	0.53	0.34	0.56	0.36
142	0.40	0.25	0.43	0.27	0.46	0.28	0.49	0.30	0.51	0.32	0.54	0.33	0.56	0.35
144	0.41	0.24	0.44	0.26	0.47	0.28	0.50	0.29	0.52	0.31	0.55	0.32	0.57	0.34
146	0.42	0.24	0.45	0.25	0.48	0.27	0.51	0.28	0.53	0.30	0.56	0.31	0.58	0.32
148	0.43	0.23	0.46	0.25	0.49	0.26	0.52	0.27	0.54	0.29	0.57	0.30	0.59	0.31
150	0.45	0.22	0.48	0.24	0.50	0.25	0.53	0.26	0.55	0.28	0.58	0.29	0.60	0.30
152	0.46	0.22	0.49	0.23	0.52	0.24	0.54	0.25	0.57	0.27	0.59	0.28	0.61	0.29
154	0.48	0.21	0.50	0.22	0.53	0.23	0.56	0.24	0.58	0.25	0.60	0.26	0.62	0.27
156	0.49	0.20	0.52	0.21	0.55	0.22	0.57	0.23	0.60	0.24	0.62	0.25	0.64	0.26
158	0.51	0.19	0.54	0.20	0.57	0.21	0.59	0.22	0.61	0.23	0.63	0.24	0.66	0.25
160	0.53	0.18	0.56	0.19	0.59	0.20	0.61	0.21	0.63	0.22	0.65	0.22	0.67	0.23

TABLE 18

Distance of an Object by Two Bearings

Difference between the course and second bearing	Difference between the course and first bearing													
	34°		36°		38°		40°		42°		44°		46°	
°														
44	3.22	2.24												
46	2.69	1.93	3.39	2.43										
48	2.31	1.72	2.83	2.10	3.55	2.63								
50	2.03	1.55	2.43	1.86	2.96	2.27	3.70	2.84						
52	1.81	1.43	2.13	1.68	2.54	2.01	3.09	2.44	3.85	3.04				
54	1.63	1.32	1.90	1.54	2.23	1.81	2.66	2.15	3.22	2.60	4.00	3.24		
56	1.49	1.24	1.72	1.42	1.99	1.65	2.33	1.93	2.77	2.29	3.34	2.77	4.14	3.43
58	1.37	1.17	1.57	1.33	1.80	1.53	2.08	1.76	2.43	2.06	2.87	2.44	3.46	2.93
60	1.28	1.10	1.45	1.25	1.64	1.42	1.88	1.63	2.17	1.88	2.52	2.18	2.97	2.57
62	1.19	1.05	1.34	1.18	1.51	1.34	1.72	1.52	1.96	1.73	2.25	1.98	2.61	2.30
64	1.12	1.01	1.25	1.13	1.40	1.26	1.58	1.42	1.79	1.61	2.03	1.83	2.33	2.09
66	1.06	0.96	1.18	1.07	1.31	1.20	1.47	1.34	1.65	1.51	1.85	1.69	2.10	1.92
68	1.00	0.93	1.11	1.03	1.23	1.14	1.37	1.27	1.53	1.42	1.71	1.58	1.92	1.78
70	0.95	0.89	1.05	0.99	1.16	1.09	1.29	1.21	1.43	1.34	1.58	1.49	1.77	1.66
72	0.91	0.86	1.00	0.95	1.10	1.05	1.21	1.15	1.34	1.27	1.48	1.41	1.64	1.56
74	0.87	0.84	0.95	0.92	1.05	1.01	1.15	1.10	1.26	1.21	1.39	1.34	1.53	1.47
76	0.84	0.81	0.91	0.89	1.00	0.97	1.09	1.06	1.20	1.16	1.31	1.27	1.44	1.40
78	0.80	0.79	0.88	0.86	0.96	0.94	1.04	1.02	1.14	1.11	1.24	1.22	1.36	1.33
80	0.78	0.77	0.85	0.83	0.92	0.91	1.00	0.98	1.09	1.07	1.18	1.16	1.28	1.27
82	0.75	0.75	0.82	0.81	0.89	0.88	0.96	0.95	1.04	1.03	1.13	1.12	1.22	1.21
84	0.73	0.73	0.79	0.79	0.86	0.85	0.93	0.92	1.00	0.99	1.08	1.07	1.17	1.16
86	0.71	0.71	0.77	0.77	0.83	0.83	0.89	0.89	0.96	0.96	1.04	1.04	1.12	1.12
88	0.69	0.69	0.75	0.75	0.80	0.80	0.86	0.86	0.93	0.93	1.00	1.00	1.08	1.07
90	0.67	0.67	0.73	0.73	0.78	0.78	0.84	0.84	0.90	0.90	0.97	0.97	1.04	1.04
92	0.66	0.66	0.71	0.71	0.76	0.76	0.82	0.82	0.87	0.87	0.93	0.93	1.00	1.00
94	0.65	0.64	0.69	0.69	0.74	0.74	0.79	0.79	0.85	0.85	0.91	0.90	0.97	0.97
96	0.63	0.63	0.68	0.67	0.73	0.72	0.78	0.77	0.83	0.82	0.88	0.88	0.94	0.93
98	0.62	0.62	0.67	0.66	0.71	0.70	0.76	0.75	0.81	0.80	0.86	0.85	0.91	0.90
100	0.61	0.60	0.65	0.64	0.70	0.69	0.74	0.73	0.79	0.78	0.84	0.83	0.89	0.88
102	0.60	0.59	0.64	0.63	0.68	0.67	0.73	0.71	0.77	0.76	0.82	0.80	0.87	0.85
104	0.60	0.58	0.63	0.61	0.67	0.65	0.72	0.69	0.76	0.74	0.80	0.78	0.85	0.82
106	0.59	0.57	0.63	0.60	0.66	0.64	0.70	0.68	0.74	0.72	0.79	0.76	0.83	0.80
108	0.58	0.55	0.62	0.59	0.66	0.62	0.69	0.66	0.73	0.70	0.77	0.74	0.81	0.77
110	0.58	0.54	0.61	0.57	0.65	0.61	0.68	0.64	0.72	0.68	0.76	0.71	0.80	0.75
112	0.57	0.53	0.61	0.56	0.64	0.59	0.68	0.63	0.71	0.66	0.75	0.69	0.79	0.73
114	0.57	0.52	0.60	0.55	0.63	0.58	0.67	0.61	0.70	0.64	0.74	0.68	0.78	0.71
116	0.56	0.51	0.60	0.54	0.63	0.57	0.66	0.60	0.70	0.63	0.73	0.66	0.77	0.69
118	0.56	0.50	0.59	0.52	0.63	0.55	0.66	0.58	0.69	0.61	0.72	0.64	0.76	0.67
120	0.56	0.49	0.59	0.51	0.62	0.54	0.65	0.57	0.68	0.59	0.72	0.62	0.75	0.65
122	0.56	0.47	0.59	0.50	0.62	0.53	0.65	0.55	0.68	0.58	0.71	0.60	0.74	0.63
124	0.56	0.46	0.59	0.49	0.62	0.51	0.65	0.54	0.68	0.56	0.71	0.58	0.74	0.61
126	0.56	0.45	0.59	0.48	0.62	0.50	0.64	0.52	0.67	0.54	0.70	0.57	0.73	0.59
128	0.56	0.44	0.59	0.46	0.62	0.49	0.64	0.51	0.67	0.53	0.70	0.55	0.73	0.57
130	0.56	0.43	0.59	0.45	0.62	0.47	0.64	0.49	0.67	0.51	0.70	0.53	0.72	0.55
132	0.56	0.42	0.59	0.44	0.62	0.46	0.64	0.48	0.67	0.50	0.70	0.52	0.72	0.54
134	0.57	0.41	0.59	0.43	0.62	0.45	0.64	0.46	0.67	0.48	0.69	0.50	0.72	0.52
136	0.57	0.40	0.60	0.41	0.62	0.43	0.65	0.45	0.67	0.47	0.70	0.48	0.72	0.50
138	0.58	0.39	0.60	0.40	0.63	0.42	0.65	0.43	0.67	0.45	0.70	0.47	0.72	0.48
140	0.58	0.37	0.61	0.39	0.63	0.40	0.65	0.42	0.68	0.43	0.70	0.45	0.72	0.46
142	0.59	0.36	0.61	0.38	0.63	0.39	0.66	0.41	0.68	0.42	0.70	0.43	0.72	0.45
144	0.60	0.35	0.62	0.36	0.64	0.38	0.66	0.39	0.68	0.40	0.71	0.41	0.73	0.43
146	0.60	0.34	0.63	0.35	0.65	0.36	0.67	0.37	0.69	0.39	0.71	0.40	0.73	0.41
148	0.61	0.32	0.63	0.34	0.66	0.35	0.68	0.36	0.70	0.37	0.72	0.38	0.74	0.39
150	0.62	0.31	0.64	0.32	0.66	0.33	0.68	0.34	0.70	0.35	0.72	0.36	0.74	0.37
152	0.63	0.30	0.65	0.31	0.67	0.32	0.69	0.33	0.71	0.33	0.73	0.34	0.75	0.35
154	0.65	0.28	0.67	0.29	0.68	0.30	0.70	0.31	0.72	0.32	0.74	0.32	0.76	0.33
156	0.66	0.27	0.68	0.28	0.70	0.28	0.72	0.29	0.73	0.30	0.75	0.30	0.77	0.31
158	0.67	0.25	0.69	0.26	0.71	0.27	0.73	0.27	0.74	0.28	0.76	0.28	0.78	0.29
160	0.69	0.24	0.71	0.24	0.73	0.25	0.74	0.25	0.76	0.26	0.77	0.26	0.79	0.27

TABLE 18
Distance of an Object by Two Bearings

Difference between the course and second bearing °	Difference between the course and first bearing													
	48°		50°		52°		54°		56°		58°		60°	
58	4.28	3.63												
60	3.57	3.10	4.41	3.82										
62	3.07	2.71	3.68	3.25	4.54	4.01								
64	2.70	2.42	3.17	2.85	3.79	3.41	4.66	4.19						
66	2.40	2.20	2.78	2.54	3.26	2.98	3.89	3.55	4.77	4.36				
68	2.17	2.01	2.48	2.30	2.86	2.65	3.34	3.10	3.99	3.71	4.88	4.53		
70	1.98	1.86	2.24	2.10	2.55	2.39	2.94	2.76	3.43	3.22	4.08	3.83	4.99	4.69
72	1.83	1.74	2.04	1.94	2.30	2.19	2.62	2.49	3.01	2.86	3.51	3.33	4.17	3.96
74	1.70	1.63	1.88	1.81	2.10	2.02	2.37	2.27	2.68	2.58	3.08	2.96	3.58	3.44
76	1.58	1.54	1.75	1.70	1.94	1.88	2.16	2.10	2.42	2.35	2.74	2.66	3.14	3.05
78	1.49	1.45	1.63	1.60	1.80	1.76	1.99	1.95	2.21	2.16	2.48	2.43	2.80	2.74
80	1.40	1.38	1.53	1.51	1.68	1.65	1.85	1.82	2.04	2.01	2.26	2.23	2.53	2.49
82	1.33	1.32	1.45	1.43	1.58	1.56	1.72	1.71	1.89	1.87	2.08	2.06	2.31	2.29
84	1.26	1.26	1.37	1.36	1.49	1.48	1.62	1.61	1.77	1.76	1.93	1.92	2.13	2.12
86	1.21	1.20	1.30	1.30	1.41	1.41	1.53	1.52	1.66	1.65	1.81	1.80	1.98	1.97
88	1.16	1.16	1.24	1.24	1.34	1.34	1.45	1.45	1.56	1.56	1.70	1.70	1.84	1.84
90	1.11	1.11	1.19	1.19	1.28	1.28	1.38	1.38	1.48	1.48	1.60	1.60	1.73	1.73
92	1.07	1.07	1.14	1.14	1.23	1.23	1.31	1.31	1.41	1.41	1.52	1.52	1.63	1.63
94	1.03	1.03	1.10	1.10	1.18	1.17	1.26	1.26	1.35	1.34	1.44	1.44	1.55	1.54
96	1.00	0.99	1.06	1.06	1.13	1.13	1.21	1.20	1.29	1.28	1.38	1.37	1.47	1.47
98	0.97	0.96	1.03	1.02	1.10	1.08	1.16	1.15	1.24	1.23	1.32	1.31	1.41	1.39
100	0.94	0.93	1.00	0.98	1.06	1.04	1.12	1.11	1.19	1.18	1.27	1.25	1.35	1.33
102	0.92	0.90	0.97	0.95	1.03	1.01	1.09	1.06	1.15	1.13	1.22	1.19	1.29	1.27
104	0.90	0.87	0.95	0.92	1.00	0.97	1.06	1.02	1.12	1.08	1.18	1.14	1.25	1.21
106	0.88	0.84	0.92	0.89	0.97	0.94	1.03	0.99	1.09	1.04	1.14	1.10	1.20	1.16
108	0.86	0.82	0.90	0.86	0.95	0.90	1.00	0.95	1.05	1.00	1.11	1.05	1.17	1.11
110	0.84	0.79	0.88	0.83	0.93	0.87	0.98	0.92	1.02	0.96	1.08	1.01	1.13	1.06
112	0.83	0.77	0.87	0.80	0.91	0.84	0.95	0.88	1.00	0.93	1.05	0.97	1.10	1.02
114	0.81	0.74	0.85	0.78	0.89	0.82	0.93	0.85	0.98	0.89	1.02	0.93	1.07	0.98
116	0.80	0.72	0.84	0.75	0.88	0.79	0.92	0.82	0.96	0.85	1.00	0.90	1.04	0.94
118	0.79	0.70	0.83	0.73	0.86	0.76	0.90	0.79	0.94	0.83	0.98	0.86	1.02	0.90
120	0.78	0.68	0.82	0.71	0.85	0.74	0.89	0.77	0.91	0.80	0.96	0.83	1.00	0.87
122	0.77	0.66	0.81	0.68	0.84	0.71	0.87	0.74	0.90	0.77	0.95	0.80	0.98	0.83
124	0.77	0.63	0.80	0.66	0.83	0.69	0.86	0.71	0.90	0.74	0.93	0.77	0.96	0.80
126	0.76	0.61	0.79	0.64	0.82	0.66	0.85	0.69	0.88	0.71	0.91	0.74	0.95	0.77
128	0.75	0.59	0.78	0.62	0.81	0.64	0.84	0.66	0.87	0.69	0.90	0.71	0.93	0.74
130	0.75	0.57	0.78	0.60	0.81	0.62	0.83	0.64	0.86	0.66	0.89	0.68	0.92	0.71
132	0.75	0.56	0.77	0.57	0.80	0.59	0.83	0.61	0.85	0.64	0.88	0.66	0.91	0.68
134	0.74	0.54	0.77	0.55	0.80	0.57	0.82	0.59	0.85	0.61	0.87	0.63	0.90	0.65
136	0.74	0.52	0.77	0.53	0.80	0.55	0.82	0.57	0.84	0.58	0.87	0.60	0.89	0.62
138	0.74	0.50	0.77	0.51	0.79	0.53	0.81	0.54	0.84	0.56	0.86	0.58	0.89	0.59
140	0.74	0.48	0.77	0.49	0.79	0.51	0.81	0.52	0.83	0.54	0.86	0.55	0.88	0.57
142	0.74	0.46	0.77	0.47	0.79	0.49	0.81	0.50	0.83	0.51	0.85	0.52	0.87	0.54
144	0.75	0.44	0.77	0.45	0.79	0.46	0.81	0.48	0.83	0.49	0.85	0.50	0.87	0.51
146	0.75	0.42	0.77	0.43	0.79	0.44	0.81	0.45	0.83	0.46	0.85	0.47	0.87	0.49
148	0.76	0.40	0.77	0.41	0.79	0.42	0.81	0.43	0.83	0.44	0.85	0.45	0.87	0.46
150	0.76	0.38	0.78	0.39	0.80	0.40	0.81	0.41	0.83	0.42	0.85	0.42	0.87	0.43
152	0.77	0.36	0.78	0.37	0.80	0.38	0.82	0.38	0.83	0.39	0.85	0.40	0.87	0.41
154	0.77	0.34	0.79	0.35	0.81	0.35	0.82	0.36	0.84	0.37	0.85	0.37	0.87	0.38
156	0.78	0.32	0.80	0.32	0.81	0.33	0.83	0.34	0.84	0.34	0.86	0.35	0.87	0.35
158	0.79	0.30	0.81	0.30	0.82	0.31	0.83	0.31	0.85	0.32	0.86	0.32	0.87	0.33
160	0.80	0.27	0.82	0.28	0.83	0.28	0.84	0.29	0.85	0.29	0.86	0.30	0.88	0.30

TABLE 18
Distance of an Object by Two Bearings

Difference between the course and second bearing °	Difference between the course and first bearing															
	62°		64°		66°		68°		70°		72°		74°		76°	
72	5.08	4.84														
74	4.25	4.08	5.18	4.98												
76	3.65	3.54	4.32	4.19	5.26	5.10										
78	3.20	3.13	3.72	3.63	4.39	4.30	5.34	5.22								
80	2.86	2.81	3.26	3.21	3.78	3.72	4.46	4.39	5.41	5.33						
82	2.58	2.56	2.91	2.88	3.31	3.28	3.83	3.80	4.52	4.48	5.48	5.42				
84	2.36	2.34	2.63	2.61	2.96	2.94	3.36	3.35	3.88	3.86	4.57	4.55	5.54	5.51		
86	2.17	2.17	2.40	2.39	2.67	2.66	3.00	2.99	3.41	3.40	3.93	3.92	4.62	4.61	5.59	5.57
88	2.01	2.01	2.21	2.21	2.44	2.44	2.71	2.71	3.04	3.04	3.45	3.45	3.97	3.97	4.67	4.66
90	1.88	1.88	2.05	2.05	2.25	2.25	2.48	2.48	2.75	2.75	3.08	3.08	3.49	3.49	4.01	4.01
92	1.77	1.76	1.91	1.91	2.08	2.08	2.28	2.28	2.51	2.51	2.78	2.78	3.11	3.11	3.52	3.52
94	1.67	1.66	1.80	1.79	1.95	1.94	2.12	2.11	2.31	2.30	2.54	2.53	2.81	2.80	3.14	3.13
96	1.58	1.57	1.70	1.69	1.83	1.82	1.97	1.96	2.14	2.13	2.34	2.33	2.57	2.55	2.84	2.82
98	1.50	1.49	1.61	1.59	1.72	1.71	1.85	1.84	2.00	1.98	2.17	2.15	2.36	2.34	2.59	2.56
100	1.43	1.41	1.53	1.51	1.63	1.61	1.75	1.72	1.88	1.85	2.03	2.00	2.19	2.16	2.39	2.35
102	1.37	1.34	1.46	1.43	1.55	1.52	1.66	1.62	1.77	1.73	1.90	1.86	2.05	2.00	2.21	2.16
104	1.32	1.28	1.40	1.36	1.48	1.44	1.58	1.53	1.68	1.63	1.79	1.74	1.92	1.87	2.07	2.01
106	1.27	1.22	1.34	1.29	1.42	1.37	1.51	1.45	1.60	1.54	1.70	1.63	1.81	1.74	1.94	1.87
108	1.23	1.17	1.29	1.23	1.37	1.30	1.44	1.37	1.53	1.45	1.62	1.54	1.72	1.63	1.83	1.74
110	1.19	1.12	1.25	1.17	1.32	1.24	1.39	1.30	1.46	1.37	1.54	1.45	1.64	1.54	1.74	1.63
112	1.15	1.07	1.21	1.12	1.27	1.18	1.33	1.24	1.40	1.30	1.48	1.37	1.56	1.45	1.65	1.53
114	1.12	1.02	1.17	1.07	1.23	1.12	1.29	1.18	1.35	1.24	1.42	1.30	1.50	1.37	1.58	1.44
116	1.09	0.98	1.14	1.03	1.19	1.07	1.25	1.12	1.31	1.17	1.37	1.23	1.44	1.29	1.51	1.36
118	1.07	0.94	1.11	0.98	1.16	1.02	1.21	1.07	1.26	1.12	1.32	1.17	1.38	1.22	1.45	1.28
120	1.04	0.90	1.08	0.94	1.13	0.98	1.18	1.02	1.23	1.06	1.28	1.11	1.34	1.16	1.40	1.21
122	1.02	0.86	1.06	0.90	1.10	0.93	1.15	0.97	1.19	1.01	1.24	1.05	1.29	1.10	1.35	1.14
124	1.00	0.83	1.04	0.86	1.08	0.89	1.12	0.93	1.16	0.96	1.21	1.00	1.25	1.04	1.31	1.08
126	0.98	0.79	1.02	0.82	1.05	0.85	1.09	0.88	1.13	0.92	1.18	0.95	1.22	0.99	1.27	1.02
128	0.97	0.76	1.00	0.79	1.03	0.82	1.07	0.84	1.11	0.87	1.15	0.90	1.19	0.94	1.23	0.97
130	0.95	0.73	0.98	0.75	1.02	0.78	1.05	0.80	1.09	0.83	1.12	0.86	1.16	0.89	1.20	0.92
132	0.94	0.70	0.97	0.72	1.00	0.74	1.03	0.77	1.06	0.79	1.10	0.82	1.13	0.84	1.17	0.87
134	0.93	0.67	0.96	0.69	0.99	0.71	1.01	0.73	1.04	0.75	1.08	0.77	1.11	0.80	1.14	0.82
136	0.92	0.64	0.95	0.66	0.97	0.68	1.00	0.69	1.03	0.71	1.06	0.74	1.09	0.76	1.12	0.78
138	0.91	0.61	0.94	0.63	0.96	0.64	0.99	0.66	1.01	0.68	1.04	0.70	1.07	0.72	1.10	0.74
140	0.90	0.58	0.93	0.60	0.95	0.61	0.97	0.63	1.00	0.64	1.03	0.66	1.05	0.68	1.08	0.69
142	0.90	0.55	0.92	0.57	0.94	0.58	0.96	0.59	0.99	0.61	1.01	0.62	1.04	0.64	1.06	0.65
144	0.89	0.52	0.91	0.54	0.93	0.55	0.96	0.56	0.98	0.57	1.00	0.59	1.02	0.60	1.05	0.62
146	0.89	0.50	0.91	0.51	0.93	0.52	0.95	0.53	0.97	0.54	0.99	0.55	1.01	0.57	1.03	0.58
148	0.89	0.47	0.90	0.48	0.92	0.49	0.94	0.50	0.96	0.51	0.98	0.52	1.00	0.53	1.02	0.54
150	0.88	0.44	0.90	0.45	0.92	0.46	0.94	0.47	0.95	0.48	0.97	0.49	0.99	0.50	1.01	0.50
152	0.88	0.41	0.90	0.42	0.92	0.43	0.93	0.44	0.95	0.45	0.97	0.45	0.98	0.46	1.00	0.47
154	0.88	0.39	0.90	0.39	0.91	0.40	0.93	0.41	0.94	0.41	0.96	0.42	0.98	0.43	0.99	0.43
156	0.89	0.36	0.90	0.37	0.91	0.37	0.93	0.38	0.94	0.38	0.96	0.39	0.97	0.39	0.99	0.40
158	0.89	0.33	0.90	0.34	0.91	0.34	0.93	0.35	0.94	0.35	0.95	0.36	0.97	0.36	0.98	0.37
160	0.89	0.30	0.90	0.31	0.91	0.31	0.93	0.32	0.94	0.32	0.95	0.33	0.96	0.33	0.98	0.33

TABLE 18

Distance of an Object by Two Bearings

Difference between the course and second bearing	Difference between the course and first bearing															
	78°		80°		82°		84°		86°		88°		90°		92°	
°																
88	5.63	5.63														
90	4.70	4.70	5.67	5.67												
92	4.04	4.04	4.74	4.73	5.70	5.70										
94	3.55	3.54	4.07	4.06	4.76	4.75	5.73	5.71								
96	3.17	3.15	3.57	3.55	4.09	4.07	4.78	4.76	5.74	5.71						
98	2.86	2.83	3.19	3.16	3.59	3.56	4.11	4.07	4.80	4.75	5.76	5.70				
100	2.61	2.57	2.88	2.84	3.20	3.16	3.61	3.55	4.12	4.06	4.81	4.73	5.76	5.67		
102	2.40	2.35	2.63	2.57	2.90	2.83	3.22	3.15	3.62	3.54	4.13	4.04	4.81	4.70	5.76	5.63
104	2.23	2.16	2.42	2.35	2.64	2.56	2.91	2.82	3.23	3.13	3.63	3.52	4.13	4.01	4.81	4.66
106	2.08	2.00	2.25	2.16	2.43	2.34	2.65	2.55	2.92	2.80	3.23	3.11	3.63	3.49	4.13	3.97
108	1.96	1.86	2.10	2.00	2.26	2.15	2.45	2.33	2.66	2.53	2.92	2.78	3.24	3.08	3.63	3.45
110	1.85	1.73	1.97	1.85	2.11	1.98	2.27	2.13	2.45	2.31	2.67	2.51	2.92	2.75	3.23	3.04
112	1.75	1.62	1.86	1.72	1.98	1.83	2.12	1.96	2.28	2.11	2.46	2.28	2.67	2.48	2.92	2.71
114	1.66	1.52	1.76	1.61	1.87	1.71	1.99	1.82	2.12	1.94	2.28	2.08	2.46	2.25	2.67	2.44
116	1.59	1.43	1.68	1.51	1.77	1.59	1.88	1.69	2.00	1.79	2.13	1.91	2.28	2.05	2.46	2.21
118	1.52	1.34	1.60	1.41	1.68	1.49	1.78	1.57	1.88	1.66	2.00	1.76	2.13	1.88	2.28	2.01
120	1.46	1.27	1.53	1.33	1.61	1.39	1.69	1.47	1.78	1.54	1.89	1.63	2.00	1.73	2.13	1.84
122	1.41	1.19	1.47	1.25	1.54	1.31	1.62	1.37	1.70	1.44	1.79	1.52	1.89	1.60	2.00	1.70
124	1.36	1.13	1.42	1.18	1.48	1.23	1.55	1.28	1.62	1.34	1.70	1.41	1.79	1.48	1.89	1.56
126	1.32	1.06	1.37	1.11	1.43	1.15	1.48	1.20	1.55	1.26	1.62	1.31	1.70	1.38	1.79	1.45
128	1.28	1.01	1.33	1.04	1.38	1.08	1.43	1.13	1.49	1.17	1.55	1.23	1.62	1.28	1.70	1.34
130	1.24	0.95	1.29	0.98	1.33	1.02	1.38	1.06	1.44	1.10	1.49	1.14	1.56	1.19	1.62	1.24
132	1.21	0.90	1.25	0.93	1.29	0.96	1.34	0.99	1.39	1.03	1.44	1.07	1.49	1.11	1.55	1.16
134	1.18	0.85	1.22	0.88	1.26	0.90	1.30	0.93	1.34	0.97	1.39	1.00	1.44	1.04	1.49	1.07
136	1.15	0.80	1.19	0.83	1.22	0.85	1.26	0.88	1.30	0.90	1.34	0.93	1.39	0.97	1.44	1.00
138	1.13	0.76	1.16	0.78	1.19	0.80	1.23	0.82	1.27	0.85	1.30	0.87	1.35	0.90	1.39	0.93
140	1.11	0.71	1.14	0.73	1.17	0.75	1.20	0.77	1.23	0.79	1.27	0.82	1.31	0.84	1.34	0.86
142	1.09	0.67	1.12	0.69	1.14	0.70	1.17	0.72	1.20	0.74	1.24	0.76	1.27	0.78	1.30	0.80
144	1.07	0.63	1.10	0.64	1.12	0.66	1.15	0.67	1.18	0.69	1.21	0.71	1.24	0.73	1.27	0.75
146	1.05	0.59	1.08	0.60	1.10	0.62	1.13	0.63	1.15	0.64	1.18	0.66	1.21	0.67	1.24	0.69
148	1.04	0.55	1.06	0.56	1.08	0.57	1.11	0.59	1.13	0.60	1.15	0.61	1.18	0.62	1.21	0.64
150	1.03	0.51	1.05	0.52	1.07	0.53	1.09	0.54	1.11	0.55	1.13	0.57	1.15	0.58	1.18	0.59
152	1.02	0.48	1.04	0.49	1.05	0.49	1.07	0.50	1.09	0.51	1.11	0.52	1.13	0.53	1.15	0.54
154	1.01	0.44	1.02	0.45	1.04	0.46	1.06	0.46	1.08	0.47	1.09	0.48	1.11	0.49	1.13	0.50
156	1.00	0.41	1.01	0.41	1.03	0.42	1.05	0.43	1.06	0.43	1.08	0.44	1.09	0.45	1.11	0.45
158	0.99	0.37	1.01	0.38	1.02	0.38	1.03	0.39	1.05	0.39	1.06	0.40	1.08	0.40	1.09	0.41
160	0.99	0.34	1.00	0.34	1.01	0.35	1.02	0.35	1.04	0.35	1.05	0.36	1.06	0.36	1.08	0.37
	94°		96°		98°		100°		102°		104°		106°		108°	
°																
104	5.74	5.57														
106	4.80	4.61	5.73	5.51												
108	4.12	3.92	4.78	4.55	5.70	5.42										
110	3.62	3.40	4.11	3.86	4.76	4.48	5.67	5.33								
112	3.23	2.99	3.61	3.35	4.09	3.80	4.74	4.40	5.63	5.22						
114	2.92	2.66	3.22	2.94	3.59	3.28	4.07	3.72	4.70	4.30	5.59	5.10				
116	2.66	2.39	2.91	2.61	3.20	2.88	3.57	3.21	4.04	3.63	4.67	4.19	5.54	4.98		
118	2.45	2.17	2.65	2.34	2.90	2.56	3.19	2.81	3.55	3.13	4.01	3.54	4.62	4.08	5.48	4.84
120	2.28	1.97	2.45	2.12	2.64	2.29	2.88	2.49	3.17	2.74	3.52	3.05	3.97	3.44	4.57	3.96
122	2.12	1.80	2.27	1.92	2.43	2.06	2.63	2.23	2.86	2.43	3.14	2.66	3.49	2.96	3.93	3.33
124	2.00	1.65	2.12	1.76	2.26	1.87	2.42	2.01	2.61	2.16	2.84	2.35	3.11	2.58	3.45	2.86
126	1.88	1.52	1.99	1.61	2.11	1.71	2.25	1.82	2.40	1.95	2.59	2.10	2.81	2.27	3.08	2.49
128	1.78	1.41	1.88	1.48	1.98	1.56	2.10	1.65	2.23	1.76	2.39	1.88	2.57	2.02	2.78	2.19
130	1.70	1.30	1.78	1.36	1.87	1.43	1.97	1.51	2.08	1.60	2.21	1.70	2.36	1.81	2.54	1.94
132	1.62	1.20	1.69	1.26	1.77	1.32	1.86	1.38	1.96	1.45	2.07	1.54	2.19	1.63	2.34	1.74
134	1.55	1.12	1.62	1.16	1.68	1.21	1.76	1.27	1.85	1.33	1.94	1.40	2.05	1.47	2.17	1.56
136	1.49	1.04	1.55	1.07	1.61	1.12	1.68	1.16	1.75	1.22	1.83	1.27	1.92	1.34	2.03	1.41
138	1.44	0.96	1.49	0.99	1.54	1.03	1.60	1.07	1.66	1.11	1.74	1.16	1.81	1.21	1.90	1.27
140	1.39	0.89	1.43	0.92	1.48	0.95	1.53	0.98	1.59	1.02	1.65	1.06	1.72	1.10	1.79	1.15
142	1.34	0.83	1.38	0.85	1.43	0.88	1.47	0.91	1.52	0.94	1.58	0.97	1.64	1.01	1.70	1.05
144	1.30	0.77	1.34	0.79	1.38	0.81	1.42	0.83	1.46	0.86	1.51	0.89	1.56	0.92	1.62	0.95
146	1.27	0.71	1.30	0.73	1.33	0.75	1.37	0.77	1.41	0.79	1.45	0.81	1.50	0.84	1.54	0.86
148	1.23	0.65	1.26	0.67	1.29	0.69	1.33	0.70	1.36	0.72	1.40	0.74	1.44	0.76	1.48	0.78
150	1.20	0.60	1.23	0.61	1.26	0.63	1.29	0.64	1.32	0.66	1.35	0.67	1.38	0.69	1.42	0.71
152	1.18	0.55	1.20	0.56	1.22	0.57	1.25	0.59	1.28	0.60	1.31	0.61	1.34	0.63	1.37	0.64
154	1.15	0.50	1.17	0.51	1.19	0.52	1.22	0.53	1.24	0.54	1.27	0.56	1.29	0.57	1.32	0.58
156	1.13	0.46	1.15	0.47	1.17	0.47	1.19	0.48	1.21	0.49	1.23	0.50	1.25	0.51	1.28	0.52
158	1.11	0.42	1.13	0.42	1.14	0.43	1.16	0.44	1.18	0.44	1.20	0.45	1.22	0.46	1.24	0.47
160	1.09	0.37	1.11	0.38	1.12	0.38	1.14	0.39	1.15	0.39	1.17	0.40	1.19	0.41	1.21	0.41

TABLE 18

Distance of an Object by Two Bearings

Difference between the course and second bearing	Difference between the course and first bearing													
	110°		112°		114°		116°		118°		120°		122°	
°														
120	5.41	4.69												
122	4.52	3.83	5.34	4.53										
124	3.88	3.22	4.46	3.70	5.26	4.36								
126	3.41	2.76	3.83	3.10	4.39	3.55	5.18	4.19						
128	3.04	2.40	3.36	2.65	3.78	2.98	4.32	3.41	5.08	4.01				
130	2.75	2.10	3.00	2.30	3.31	2.54	3.72	2.85	4.25	3.25	4.99	3.82		
132	2.51	1.86	2.71	2.01	2.96	2.20	3.26	2.42	3.65	2.71	4.17	3.10	4.88	3.63
134	2.31	1.66	2.48	1.78	2.67	1.92	2.91	2.09	3.20	2.30	3.58	2.57	4.08	2.93
136	2.14	1.49	2.28	1.58	2.44	1.69	2.63	1.83	2.86	1.98	3.14	2.18	3.51	2.44
138	2.00	1.34	2.12	1.42	2.25	1.50	2.40	1.61	2.58	1.73	2.80	1.88	3.08	2.06
140	1.88	1.21	1.97	1.27	2.08	1.34	2.21	1.42	2.36	1.52	2.53	1.63	2.74	1.76
142	1.77	1.09	1.85	1.14	1.95	1.20	2.05	1.26	2.17	1.34	2.31	1.42	2.48	1.53
144	1.68	0.99	1.75	1.03	1.83	1.07	1.91	1.13	2.01	1.18	2.13	1.25	2.26	1.33
146	1.60	0.89	1.66	0.93	1.72	0.96	1.80	1.01	1.88	1.05	1.98	1.10	2.08	1.17
148	1.53	0.81	1.58	0.84	1.63	0.87	1.70	0.90	1.77	0.94	1.84	0.98	1.93	1.03
150	1.46	0.73	1.51	0.75	1.55	0.78	1.61	0.80	1.67	0.83	1.73	0.87	1.81	0.90
152	1.40	0.66	1.44	0.68	1.48	0.70	1.53	0.72	1.58	0.74	1.63	0.77	1.70	0.80
154	1.35	0.59	1.39	0.61	1.42	0.62	1.46	0.64	1.50	0.66	1.55	0.68	1.60	0.70
156	1.31	0.53	1.33	0.54	1.37	0.56	1.40	0.57	1.43	0.58	1.47	0.60	1.52	0.62
158	1.26	0.47	1.29	0.48	1.32	0.49	1.34	0.50	1.37	0.51	1.41	0.53	1.44	0.54
160	1.23	0.42	1.25	0.43	1.27	0.43	1.29	0.44	1.32	0.45	1.35	0.46	1.38	0.47
	124°		126°		128°		130°		132°		134°		136°	
134	4.77	3.43												
136	3.99	2.77	4.66	3.24										
138	3.43	2.29	3.89	2.60	4.54	3.04								
140	3.01	1.93	3.34	2.15	3.79	2.44	4.41	2.84						
142	2.68	1.65	2.94	1.81	3.26	2.01	3.68	2.27	4.28	2.63				
144	2.42	1.42	2.62	1.54	2.86	1.68	3.17	1.86	3.57	2.10	4.14	2.43		
146	2.21	1.24	2.37	1.32	2.55	1.43	2.78	1.55	3.07	1.72	3.46	1.93	4.00	2.24
148	2.04	1.08	2.16	1.14	2.30	1.22	2.48	1.31	2.70	1.43	2.97	1.58	3.34	1.77
150	1.89	0.95	1.99	0.99	2.10	1.05	2.24	1.12	2.40	1.20	2.61	1.30	2.87	1.44
152	1.77	0.83	1.85	0.87	1.94	0.91	2.04	0.96	2.17	1.02	2.33	1.09	2.52	1.18
154	1.66	0.73	1.72	0.76	1.80	0.79	1.88	0.83	1.98	0.87	2.10	0.92	2.25	0.99
156	1.56	0.64	1.62	0.66	1.68	0.68	1.75	0.71	1.83	0.74	1.92	0.78	2.03	0.83
158	1.48	0.56	1.53	0.57	1.58	0.59	1.63	0.61	1.70	0.64	1.77	0.66	1.85	0.69
160	1.41	0.48	1.45	0.49	1.49	0.51	1.53	0.52	1.58	0.54	1.64	0.56	1.71	0.58
	138°		140°		142°		144°		146°		148°		150°	
148	3.85	2.04												
150	3.22	1.61	3.70	1.85										
152	2.77	1.30	3.09	1.45	3.55	1.66								
154	2.43	1.06	2.66	1.16	2.96	1.30	3.38	1.48						
156	2.17	0.88	2.33	0.95	2.54	1.04	2.83	1.15	3.22	1.31				
158	1.96	0.73	2.08	0.78	2.23	0.84	2.43	0.91	2.69	1.01	3.05	1.14		
160	1.79	0.61	1.88	0.64	1.99	0.68	2.13	0.73	2.31	0.79	2.55	0.87	2.88	0.98

TABLE 19

Table of Offsets

ALT.	00′	05′	10′	15′	20′	25′	30′	35′	40′	45′	ALT.
	DISTANCE ALONG POSITION LINE FROM INTERCEPT										
	OFFSETS										
0°	0′.0	0′.0	0′.0	0′.0	0′.0	0′.0	0′.0	0′.0	0′.0	0′.0	0°
30	0.0	0.0	0.0	0.0	0.0	0.1	0.1	0.1	0.1	0.2	30
40	0.0	0.0	0.0	0.0	0.1	0.1	0.1	0.2	0.2	0.3	40
50	0.0	0.0	0.0	0.0	0.1	0.1	0.2	0.2	0.3	0.3	50
55	0.0	0.0	0.0	0.0	0.1	0.1	0.2	0.3	0.3	0.4	55
60	0.0	0.0	0.0	0.1	0.1	0.2	0.2	0.3	0.4	0.5	60
62	0.0	0.0	0.0	0.1	0.1	0.2	0.2	0.3	0.4	0.5	62
64	0.0	0.0	0.0	0.1	0.1	0.2	0.3	0.4	0.5	0.6	64
66	0.0	0.0	0.0	0.1	0.1	0.2	0.3	0.4	0.5	0.7	66
68	0.0	0.0	0.0	0.1	0.1	0.2	0.3	0.4	0.6	0.7	68
70	0.0	0.0	0.0	0.1	0.2	0.2	0.4	0.5	0.6	0.8	70
71	0.0	0.0	0.0	0.1	0.2	0.3	0.4	0.5	0.7	0.9	71
72	0.0	0.0	0.0	0.1	0.2	0.3	0.4	0.5	0.7	0.9	72
73	0.0	0.0	0.0	0.1	0.2	0.3	0.4	0.6	0.8	1.0	73
74	0.0	0.0	0.1	0.1	0.2	0.3	0.5	0.6	0.8	1.0	74
75	0.0	0.0	0.1	0.1	0.2	0.3	0.5	0.7	0.9	1.1	75
76	0.0	0.0	0.1	0.1	0.2	0.4	0.5	0.7	0.9	1.2	76
77	0.0	0.0	0.1	0.1	0.3	0.4	0.6	0.8	1.0	1.3	77
78	0.0	0.0	0.1	0.2	0.3	0.4	0.6	0.8	1.1	1.4	78
79	0.0	0.0	0.1	0.2	0.3	0.5	0.7	0.9	1.2	1.5	79
80.0	0.0	0.0	0.1	0.2	0.3	0.5	0.7	1.0	1.3	1.7	80.0
80.5	0.0	0.0	0.1	0.2	0.3	0.5	0.8	1.1	1.4	1.8	80.5
81.0	0.0	0.0	0.1	0.2	0.4	0.6	0.8	1.1	1.5	1.9	81.0
81.5	0.0	0.0	0.1	0.2	0.4	0.6	0.9	1.2	1.6	2.0	81.5
82.0	0.0	0.0	0.1	0.2	0.4	0.6	0.9	1.3	1.7	2.1	82.0
82.5	0.0	0.0	0.1	0.2	0.4	0.7	1.0	1.4	1.8	2.2	82.5
83.0	0.0	0.0	0.1	0.3	0.5	0.7	1.1	1.5	1.9	2.4	83.0
83.5	0.0	0.0	0.1	0.3	0.5	0.8	1.2	1.6	2.0	2.6	83.5
84.0	0.0	0.0	0.1	0.3	0.5	0.9	1.2	1.7	2.2	2.8	84.0
84.5	0.0	0.0	0.2	0.3	0.6	1.0	1.4	1.9	2.4	3.1	84.5
85.0	0.0	0.0	0.2	0.4	0.7	1.0	1.5	2.1	2.7	3.4	85.0
85.5	0.0	0.0	0.2	0.4	0.7	1.2	1.7	2.3	3.0	3.8	85.5
86.0	0.0	0.1	0.2	0.5	0.8	1.3	1.9	2.6	3.4	4.3	86.0
86.5	0.0	0.1	0.2	0.5	1.0	1.5	2.2	2.9	3.8	4.9	86.5
87.0	0.0	0.1	0.3	0.6	1.1	1.7	2.5	3.4	4.5	5.7	87.0
87.5	0.0	0.1	0.3	0.8	1.3	2.1	3.0	4.1	5.4	6.9	87.5
88.0	0.0	0.1	0.4	0.9	1.7	2.7	3.8	5.2	6.9	8.8	88.0
88.5	0.0	0.2	0.6	1.3	2.3	3.5	5.1	7.1	9.4	12.1	88.5
89.0	0.0	0.3	0.8	1.9	3.4	5.5	8.0	11.3	15.3	20.3	89.0

TABLE 20

Meridian Angle and Altitude of a Body on the Prime Vertical Circle

Latitude	Declination (same name as Latitude)												Latitude
	0°		1°		2°		3°		4°		5°		
	t	Alt.	t	Alt.	t	Alt.	t	Alt.	t	Alt.	t	Alt.	
°	°	°	°	°	°	°	°	°	°	°	°	°	°
0	—	—	*90.0*	*0.0*	*90.0*	*0.0*	*90.0*	*0.0*	*90.0*	*0.0*	*90.0*	*0.0*	0
1	90.0	0.0	0.0	90.0	*60.0*	*30.0*	*70.5*	*19.5*	*75.5*	*14.5*	*78.5*	*11.6*	1
2	90.0	0.0	60.0	30.0	0.0	90.0	*48.2*	*41.8*	*60.0*	*30.0*	*66.5*	*23.6*	2
3	90.0	0.0	70.5	19.5	48.2	41.8	0.0	90.0	*41.5*	*48.6*	*53.2*	*36.9*	3
4	90.0	0.0	75.5	14.5	60.0	30.0	41.5	48.6	0.0	90.0	*36.9*	*53.2*	4
5	90.0	0.0	78.5	11.6	66.5	23.6	53.2	36.9	36.9	53.2	0.0	90.0	5
6	90.0	0.0	80.4	9.6	70.6	19.5	60.1	30.0	48.3	41.9	33.7	56.5	6
7	90.0	0.0	81.8	8.2	73.5	16.6	64.7	25.4	55.3	34.9	44.6	45.7	7
8	90.0	0.0	82.9	7.2	75.6	14.5	68.1	22.1	60.2	30.1	51.5	38.8	8
9	90.0	0.0	83.7	6.4	77.3	12.9	70.7	19.5	63.8	26.5	56.5	33.9	9
10	90.0	0.0	84.3	5.8	78.6	11.6	72.7	17.5	66.6	23.7	60.3	30.1	10
11	90.0	0.0	84.8	5.2	79.7	10.5	74.4	15.9	68.9	21.4	63.3	27.2	11
12	90.0	0.0	85.3	4.8	80.5	9.7	75.7	14.6	70.8	19.6	65.7	24.8	12
13	90.0	0.0	85.7	4.4	81.3	8.9	76.9	13.5	72.4	18.1	67.7	22.8	13
14	90.0	0.0	86.0	4.1	81.9	8.3	77.9	12.5	73.7	16.8	69.5	21.1	14
15	90.0	0.0	86.3	3.9	82.5	7.7	78.7	11.7	74.9	15.6	70.9	19.7	15
16	90.0	0.0	86.5	3.6	83.0	7.3	79.5	10.9	75.9	14.7	72.2	18.4	16
17	90.0	0.0	86.7	3.4	83.4	6.9	80.1	10.3	76.8	13.8	73.4	17.3	17
18	90.0	0.0	86.9	3.2	83.8	6.5	80.7	9.8	77.6	13.0	74.4	16.4	18
19	90.0	0.0	87.1	3.1	84.2	6.2	81.2	9.3	78.3	12.4	75.3	15.5	19
20	90.0	0.0	87.3	2.9	84.5	5.9	81.7	8.8	78.9	11.8	76.1	14.8	20
21	90.0	0.0	87.4	2.8	84.8	5.6	82.2	8.4	79.5	11.2	76.8	14.1	21
22	90.0	0.0	87.5	2.7	85.0	5.3	82.5	8.0	80.0	10.7	77.5	13.5	22
23	90.0	0.0	87.6	2.6	85.3	5.1	82.9	7.7	80.5	10.3	78.1	12.9	23
24	90.0	0.0	87.8	2.5	85.5	4.9	83.2	7.4	81.0	9.9	78.7	12.4	24
25	90.0	0.0	87.9	2.4	85.7	4.7	83.5	7.1	81.4	9.5	79.2	11.9	25
26	90.0	0.0	87.9	2.3	85.9	4.6	83.8	6.9	81.8	9.2	79.7	11.5	26
27	90.0	0.0	88.0	2.2	86.1	4.4	84.1	6.6	82.1	8.8	80.1	11.1	27
28	90.0	0.0	88.1	2.1	86.2	4.3	84.3	6.4	82.4	8.5	80.5	10.7	28
29	90.0	0.0	88.2	2.1	86.4	4.1	84.6	6.2	82.8	8.3	80.9	10.4	29
30	90.0	0.0	88.3	2.0	86.5	4.0	84.8	6.0	83.0	8.0	81.3	10.0	30
31	90.0	0.0	88.3	1.9	86.7	3.9	85.0	5.8	83.3	7.8	81.6	9.7	31
32	90.0	0.0	88.4	1.9	86.8	3.8	85.2	5.7	83.6	7.6	82.0	9.5	32
33	90.0	0.0	88.5	1.8	86.9	3.7	85.4	5.5	83.8	7.4	82.3	9.2	33
34	90.0	0.0	88.5	1.8	87.0	3.6	85.5	5.4	84.0	7.2	82.5	9.0	34
35	90.0	0.0	88.6	1.7	87.1	3.5	85.7	5.2	84.3	7.0	82.8	8.7	35
36	90.0	0.0	88.6	1.7	87.2	3.4	85.9	5.1	84.5	6.8	83.1	8.5	36
37	90.0	0.0	88.7	1.7	87.3	3.3	86.0	5.0	84.7	6.7	83.3	8.3	37
38	90.0	0.0	88.7	1.6	87.4	3.2	86.2	4.9	84.9	6.5	83.6	8.1	38
39	90.0	0.0	88.8	1.6	87.5	3.2	86.3	4.8	85.0	6.4	83.8	8.0	39
40	90.0	0.0	88.8	1.6	87.6	3.1	86.4	4.7	85.2	6.2	84.0	7.8	40
41	90.0	0.0	88.8	1.5	87.7	3.0	86.5	4.6	85.4	6.1	84.2	7.6	41
42	90.0	0.0	88.9	1.5	87.8	3.0	86.7	4.5	85.5	6.0	84.4	7.5	42
43	90.0	0.0	88.9	1.5	87.9	2.9	86.8	4.4	85.7	5.9	84.6	7.3	43
44	90.0	0.0	89.0	1.4	87.9	2.9	86.9	4.3	85.8	5.8	84.8	7.2	44
45	90.0	0.0	89.0	1.4	88.0	2.8	87.0	4.2	86.0	5.7	85.0	7.1	45
46	90.0	0.0	89.0	1.4	88.1	2.8	87.1	4.2	86.1	5.6	85.2	7.0	46
47	90.0	0.0	89.1	1.4	88.1	2.7	87.2	4.1	86.3	5.5	85.3	6.8	47
48	90.0	0.0	89.1	1.3	88.2	2.7	87.3	4.0	86.4	5.4	85.5	6.7	48
49	90.0	0.0	89.1	1.3	88.3	2.7	87.4	4.0	86.5	5.3	85.6	6.6	49
50	90.0	0.0	89.2	1.3	88.3	2.6	87.5	3.9	86.6	5.2	85.8	6.5	50
52	90.0	0.0	89.2	1.3	88.4	2.5	87.7	3.8	86.9	5.1	86.1	6.4	52
54	90.0	0.0	89.3	1.2	88.5	2.5	87.8	3.7	87.1	4.9	86.4	6.2	54
56	90.0	0.0	89.3	1.2	88.7	2.4	88.0	3.6	87.3	4.8	86.6	6.0	56
58	90.0	0.0	89.4	1.2	88.7	2.4	88.1	3.5	87.5	4.7	86.9	5.9	58
60	90.0	0.0	89.4	1.2	88.8	2.3	88.3	3.5	87.7	4.6	87.1	5.8	60
65	90.0	0.0	89.5	1.1	89.1	2.2	88.6	3.3	88.1	4.4	87.7	5.5	65
70	90.0	0.0	89.6	1.1	89.3	2.1	88.9	3.2	88.5	4.3	88.2	5.3	70
75	90.0	0.0	89.7	1.0	89.5	2.1	89.2	3.1	88.9	4.1	88.7	5.2	75
80	90.0	0.0	89.8	1.0	89.6	2.0	89.5	3.0	89.3	4.1	89.1	5.1	80
85	90.0	0.0	89.9	1.0	89.8	2.0	89.7	3.0	89.6	4.0	89.6	5.0	85

Numbers in *italics* indicate nearest approach to prime vertical

TABLE 20

Meridian Angle and Altitude of a Body on the Prime Vertical Circle

Latitude	Declination (same name as Latitude)												Latitude
	6°		7°		8°		9°		10°		11°		
	t	Alt.	t	Alt.	t	Alt.	t	Alt.	t	Alt.	t	Alt.	
°	°	°	°	°	°	°	°	°	°	°	°	°	°
0	*90.0*	*0.0*	*90.0*	*0.0*	*90.0*	*0.0*	*90.0*	*0.0*	*90.0*	*0.0*	*90.0*	*0.0*	0
1	*80.4*	*9.6*	*81.8*	*8.2*	*82.9*	*7.2*	*83.7*	*6.4*	*84.3*	*5.8*	*84.8*	*5.2*	1
2	*70.6*	*19.5*	*73.5*	*16.6*	*75.6*	*14.5*	*77.3*	*12.9*	*78.6*	*11.6*	*79.7*	*10.5*	2
3	*60.1*	*30.0*	*64.7*	*25.4*	*68.1*	*22.1*	*70.7*	*19.5*	*72.7*	*17.5*	*74.4*	*15.9*	3
4	*48.3*	*41.9*	*55.3*	*34.9*	*60.2*	*30.1*	*63.8*	*26.5*	*66.6*	*23.7*	*68.9*	*21.4*	4
5	*33.7*	*56.5*	*44.6*	*45.7*	*51.5*	*38.8*	*56.5*	*33.9*	*60.3*	*30.1*	*63.3*	*27.2*	5
6	0.0	90.0	*31.1*	*59.1*	*41.6*	*48.7*	*48.4*	*41.9*	*53.4*	*37.0*	*57.3*	*33.2*	6
7	31.1	59.1	0.0	90.0	*29.1*	*61.1*	*39.2*	*51.2*	*45.9*	*44.6*	*50.8*	*39.7*	7
8	41.6	48.7	29.1	61.1	0.0	90.0	*27.5*	*62.8*	*37.2*	*53.3*	*43.7*	*46.8*	8
9	48.4	41.9	39.2	51.2	27.5	62.8	0.0	90.0	*26.1*	*64.3*	*35.4*	*55.1*	9
10	53.4	37.0	45.9	44.6	37.2	53.3	26.1	64.3	0.0	90.0	*24.9*	*65.5*	10
11	57.3	33.2	50.8	39.7	43.7	46.8	35.4	55.1	24.9	65.5	0.0	90.0	11
12	60.4	30.2	54.7	35.9	48.6	42.0	41.8	48.8	33.9	56.6	23.9	66.6	12
13	62.9	27.7	57.9	32.8	52.5	38.2	46.7	44.1	40.2	50.5	32.7	58.0	13
14	65.1	25.6	60.5	30.2	55.7	35.1	50.6	40.3	45.0	45.9	38.8	52.1	14
15	66.9	23.8	62.7	28.1	58.4	32.5	53.8	37.2	48.8	42.1	43.5	47.5	15
16	68.5	22.3	64.6	26.2	60.7	30.3	56.5	34.6	52.1	39.0	47.3	43.8	16
17	69.9	20.9	66.3	24.6	62.6	28.4	58.8	32.3	54.8	36.4	50.5	40.7	17
18	71.1	19.8	67.8	23.2	64.4	26.8	60.8	30.4	57.1	34.2	53.3	38.1	18
19	72.2	18.7	69.1	22.0	65.9	25.3	62.6	28.7	59.2	32.2	55.6	35.9	19
20	73.2	17.8	70.3	20.9	67.3	24.0	64.2	27.2	61.0	30.5	57.7	33.9	20
21	74.1	17.0	71.3	19.9	68.5	22.9	65.6	25.9	62.7	29.0	59.6	32.2	21
22	74.9	16.2	72.3	19.0	69.6	21.8	66.9	24.7	64.1	27.6	61.2	30.6	22
23	75.7	15.5	73.2	18.2	70.7	20.9	68.1	23.6	65.5	26.4	62.7	29.2	23
24	76.3	14.9	74.0	17.4	71.6	20.0	69.2	22.6	66.7	25.3	64.1	28.0	24
25	77.0	14.3	74.7	16.8	72.5	19.2	70.1	21.7	67.8	24.3	65.4	26.8	25
26	77.6	13.8	75.4	16.1	73.3	18.5	71.1	20.9	68.8	23.3	66.5	25.8	26
27	78.1	13.3	76.1	15.6	74.0	17.9	71.9	20.2	69.8	22.5	67.6	24.9	27
28	78.6	12.9	76.6	15.0	74.7	17.2	72.7	19.5	70.6	21.7	68.6	24.0	28
29	79.1	12.5	77.2	14.6	75.3	16.7	73.4	18.8	71.5	21.0	69.5	23.2	29
30	79.5	12.1	77.7	14.1	75.9	16.2	74.1	18.2	72.2	20.3	70.3	22.4	30
31	79.9	11.7	78.2	13.7	76.5	15.7	74.7	17.7	72.9	19.7	71.1	21.7	31
32	80.3	11.4	78.7	13.3	77.0	15.2	75.3	17.2	73.6	19.1	71.9	21.1	32
33	80.7	11.1	79.1	12.9	77.5	14.8	75.9	16.7	74.2	18.6	72.6	20.5	33
34	81.0	10.8	79.5	12.6	78.0	14.4	76.4	16.2	74.8	18.1	73.3	20.0	34
35	81.4	10.5	79.9	12.3	78.4	14.0	76.9	15.8	75.4	17.6	73.9	19.4	35
36	81.7	10.2	80.3	12.0	78.8	13.7	77.4	15.4	76.0	17.2	74.5	18.9	36
37	82.0	10.0	80.6	11.7	79.3	13.4	77.9	15.1	76.5	16.8	75.1	18.5	37
38	82.3	9.8	81.0	11.4	79.6	13.1	78.3	14.7	77.0	16.4	75.6	18.1	38
39	82.5	9.6	81.3	11.2	80.0	12.8	78.7	14.4	77.4	16.0	76.1	17.6	39
40	82.8	9.4	81.6	10.9	80.4	12.5	79.1	14.1	77.9	15.7	76.6	17.3	40
41	83.1	9.2	81.9	10.7	80.7	12.2	79.5	13.8	78.3	15.3	77.1	16.9	41
42	83.3	9.0	82.2	10.5	81.0	12.0	79.9	13.5	78.7	15.0	77.5	16.6	42
43	83.5	8.8	82.4	10.3	81.3	11.8	80.2	13.3	79.1	14.8	78.0	16.2	43
44	83.8	8.7	82.7	10.1	81.6	11.6	80.6	13.0	79.5	14.5	78.4	15.9	44
45	84.0	8.5	82.9	9.9	81.9	11.4	80.9	12.8	79.8	14.2	78.8	15.7	45
46	84.2	8.4	83.2	9.8	82.2	11.2	81.2	12.6	80.2	14.0	79.2	15.4	46
47	84.4	8.2	83.4	9.6	82.5	11.0	81.5	12.4	80.5	13.7	79.6	15.1	47
48	84.6	8.1	83.7	9.4	82.7	10.8	81.8	12.2	80.9	13.5	79.9	14.9	48
49	84.8	8.0	83.9	9.3	83.0	10.6	82.1	12.0	81.2	13.3	80.3	14.6	49
50	84.9	7.8	84.1	9.2	83.2	10.5	82.4	11.8	81.5	13.1	80.6	14.4	50
52	85.3	7.6	84.5	8.9	83.7	10.2	82.9	11.5	82.1	12.7	81.3	14.0	52
54	85.6	7.4	84.9	8.7	84.1	9.9	83.4	11.1	82.6	12.4	81.9	13.6	54
56	85.9	7.2	85.2	8.5	84.6	9.7	83.9	10.9	83.2	12.1	82.5	13.3	56
58	86.2	7.1	85.6	8.3	85.0	9.4	84.3	10.6	83.7	11.8	83.0	13.0	58
60	86.5	6.9	85.9	8.1	85.3	9.2	84.8	10.4	84.2	11.6	83.6	12.7	60
65	87.2	6.6	86.7	7.7	86.2	8.8	85.8	9.9	85.3	11.0	84.8	12.2	65
70	87.8	6.4	87.4	7.5	87.1	8.5	86.7	9.6	86.3	10.6	85.9	11.7	70
75	88.4	6.2	88.1	7.2	87.8	8.3	87.6	9.3	87.3	10.4	87.0	11.4	75
80	88.9	6.1	88.8	7.1	88.6	8.1	88.4	9.1	88.2	10.2	88.0	11.2	80
85	89.5	6.0	89.4	7.0	89.3	8.0	89.2	9.0	89.1	10.0	89.0	11.0	85

Numbers in *italics* indicate nearest approach to prime vertical

TABLE 20

Meridian Angle and Altitude of a Body on the Prime Vertical Circle

Latitude	Declination (same name as Latitude) 12° t	12° Alt.	13° t	13° Alt.	14° t	14° Alt.	15° t	15° Alt.	16° t	16° Alt.	17° t	17° Alt.	Latitude
°	°	°	°	°	°	°	°	°	°	°	°	°	°
0	90.0	0.0	90.0	0.0	90.0	0.0	90.0	0.0	90.0	0.0	90.0	0.0	0
1	*85.3*	*4.8*	*85.7*	*4.4*	*86.0*	*4.1*	*86.3*	*3.9*	*86.5*	*3.6*	*86.7*	*3.4*	1
2	*80.5*	*9.7*	*81.3*	*8.9*	*81.9*	*8.3*	*82.5*	*7.7*	*83.0*	*7.3*	*83.4*	*6.9*	2
3	*75.7*	*14.6*	*76.9*	*13.5*	*77.9*	*12.5*	*78.7*	*11.7*	*79.5*	*10.9*	*80.1*	*10.3*	3
4	*70.8*	*19.6*	*72.4*	*18.1*	*73.7*	*16.8*	*74.9*	*15.6*	*75.9*	*14.7*	*76.8*	*13.8*	4
5	*65.7*	*24.8*	*67.7*	*22.8*	*69.5*	*21.1*	*70.9*	*19.7*	*72.2*	*18.4*	*73.4*	*17.3*	5
6	*60.4*	*30.2*	*62.9*	*27.7*	*65.1*	*25.6*	*66.9*	*23.8*	*68.5*	*22.3*	*69.9*	*20.9*	6
7	*54.7*	*35.9*	*57.9*	*32.8*	*60.5*	*30.2*	*62.7*	*28.1*	*64.6*	*26.2*	*66.3*	*24.6*	7
8	*48.6*	*42.0*	*52.5*	*38.2*	*55.7*	*35.1*	*58.4*	*32.5*	*60.7*	*30.3*	*62.6*	*28.4*	8
9	*41.8*	*48.8*	*46.7*	*44.1*	*50.6*	*40.3*	*53.8*	*37.2*	*56.5*	*34.6*	*58.8*	*32.3*	9
10	*33.9*	*56.6*	*40.2*	*50.5*	*45.0*	*45.9*	*48.8*	*42.1*	*52.1*	*39.0*	*54.8*	*36.4*	10
11	*23.9*	*66.6*	*32.7*	*58.0*	*38.8*	*52.1*	*43.5*	*47.5*	*47.3*	*43.8*	*50.5*	*40.7*	11
12	0.0	90.0	*23.0*	*67.6*	*31.5*	*59.3*	*37.5*	*53.4*	*42.2*	*49.0*	*46.0*	*45.3*	12
13	23.0	67.6	0.0	90.0	*22.2*	*68.4*	*30.5*	*60.4*	*36.4*	*54.7*	*41.0*	*50.3*	13
14	31.5	59.3	22.2	68.4	0.0	90.0	*21.5*	*69.2*	*29.6*	*61.4*	*35.4*	*55.8*	14
15	37.5	53.4	30.5	60.4	21.5	69.2	0.0	90.0	*20.9*	*69.9*	*28.8*	*62.3*	15
16	42.2	49.0	36.4	54.7	29.6	61.4	20.9	69.9	0.0	90.0	*20.3*	*70.5*	16
17	46.0	45.3	41.0	50.3	35.4	55.8	28.8	62.3	20.3	70.5	0.0	90.0	17
18	49.1	42.3	44.7	46.7	39.9	51.5	34.4	56.9	28.1	63.1	19.8	71.1	18
19	51.9	39.7	47.9	43.7	43.6	48.0	38.9	52.7	33.6	57.8	27.4	63.9	19
20	54.3	37.4	50.6	41.1	46.8	45.0	42.6	49.2	38.0	53.7	32.9	58.7	20
21	56.4	35.5	53.0	38.9	49.5	42.5	45.7	46.2	41.7	50.3	37.2	54.7	21
22	58.3	33.7	55.2	36.9	51.9	40.2	48.5	43.7	44.8	47.4	40.8	51.3	22
23	60.0	32.1	57.1	35.1	54.0	38.3	50.9	41.5	47.5	44.9	43.9	48.4	23
24	61.5	30.7	58.8	33.6	55.9	36.5	53.0	39.5	49.9	42.7	46.6	46.0	24
25	62.9	29.5	60.3	32.2	57.7	34.9	54.9	37.8	52.1	40.7	49.0	43.8	25
26	64.2	28.3	61.7	30.9	59.3	33.5	56.7	36.2	54.0	39.0	51.2	41.8	26
27	65.3	27.3	63.1	29.7	60.7	32.2	58.3	34.8	55.8	37.4	53.1	40.1	27
28	66.4	26.3	64.3	28.6	62.0	31.0	59.7	33.5	57.4	36.0	54.9	38.5	28
29	67.5	25.4	65.4	27.6	63.3	29.9	61.1	32.3	58.8	34.6	56.5	37.1	29
30	68.4	24.6	66.4	26.7	64.4	28.9	62.3	31.2	60.2	33.5	58.0	35.8	30
31	69.3	23.8	67.4	25.9	65.5	28.0	63.5	30.2	61.5	32.4	59.4	34.6	31
32	70.1	23.1	68.3	25.1	66.5	27.2	64.6	29.2	62.7	31.3	60.7	33.5	32
33	70.9	22.4	69.2	24.4	67.4	26.4	65.6	28.4	63.8	30.4	61.9	32.5	33
34	71.6	21.8	70.0	23.7	68.3	25.6	66.6	27.6	64.8	29.5	63.0	31.5	34
35	72.3	21.3	70.7	23.1	69.1	24.9	67.5	26.8	65.8	28.7	64.1	30.6	35
36	73.0	20.7	71.5	22.5	69.9	24.3	68.4	26.1	66.8	28.0	65.1	29.8	36
37	73.6	20.2	72.2	21.9	70.7	23.7	69.2	25.5	67.6	27.3	66.1	29.1	37
38	74.2	19.7	72.8	21.4	71.4	23.1	69.9	24.9	68.5	26.6	67.0	28.4	38
39	74.8	19.3	73.4	20.9	72.1	22.6	70.7	24.3	69.3	26.0	67.8	27.7	39
40	75.3	18.9	74.0	20.5	72.7	22.1	71.4	23.7	70.0	25.4	68.6	27.1	40
41	75.8	18.5	74.6	20.1	73.3	21.6	72.0	23.2	70.7	24.8	69.4	26.5	41
42	76.3	18.1	75.1	19.6	73.9	21.2	72.7	22.8	71.4	24.3	70.2	25.9	42
43	76.8	17.7	75.7	19.3	74.5	20.8	73.3	22.3	72.1	23.8	70.9	25.4	43
44	77.3	17.4	76.2	18.9	75.0	20.4	73.9	21.9	72.7	23.4	71.5	24.9	44
45	77.7	17.1	76.7	18.5	75.6	20.0	74.5	21.5	73.3	22.9	72.2	24.4	45
46	78.2	16.8	77.1	18.2	76.1	19.7	75.0	21.1	73.9	22.5	72.8	24.0	46
47	78.6	16.5	77.6	17.9	76.6	19.3	75.5	20.7	74.5	22.1	73.4	23.6	47
48	79.0	16.2	78.0	17.6	77.0	19.0	76.0	20.4	75.0	21.8	74.0	23.2	48
49	79.4	16.0	78.4	17.3	77.5	18.7	76.5	20.1	75.6	21.4	74.6	22.8	49
50	79.7	15.7	78.8	17.1	77.9	18.4	77.0	19.7	76.1	21.1	75.1	22.4	50
52	80.4	15.3	79.6	16.6	78.8	17.9	77.9	19.2	77.1	20.5	76.2	21.8	52
54	81.1	14.9	80.3	16.1	79.6	17.4	78.8	18.7	78.0	19.9	77.2	21.2	54
56	81.8	14.5	81.0	15.7	80.3	17.0	79.6	18.2	78.8	19.4	78.1	20.7	56
58	82.4	14.2	81.7	15.4	81.0	16.6	80.4	17.8	79.7	19.0	79.0	20.2	58
60	83.0	13.9	82.3	15.1	81.7	16.2	81.1	17.4	80.5	18.6	79.8	19.7	60
65	84.3	13.3	83.8	14.4	83.3	15.5	82.8	16.6	82.3	17.7	81.8	18.8	65
70	85.6	12.8	85.2	13.8	84.8	14.9	84.4	16.0	84.0	17.1	83.6	18.1	70
75	86.7	12.4	86.5	13.5	86.2	14.5	85.9	15.5	85.6	16.6	85.3	17.6	75
80	87.9	12.2	87.7	13.2	87.5	14.2	87.3	15.2	87.1	16.3	86.9	17.3	80
85	88.9	12.0	88.8	13.1	88.8	14.1	88.7	15.1	88.6	16.1	88.5	17.1	85

Numbers in *italics* indicate nearest approach to prime vertical

TABLE 20

Meridian Angle and Altitude of a Body on the Prime Vertical Circle

Latitude	Declination (same name as Latitude) 18° t	18° Alt.	19° t	19° Alt.	20° t	20° Alt.	21° t	21° Alt.	22° t	22° Alt.	23° t	23° Alt.	Latitude
°	°	°	°	°	°	°	°	°	°	°	°	°	°
0	*90.0*	*0.0*	90.0	*0.0*	90.0	*0.0*	90.0	*0.0*	90.0	*0.0*	90.0	*0.0*	0
1	*86.9*	*3.2*	*87.1*	*3.1*	*87.3*	*2.9*	*87.4*	*2.8*	*87.5*	*2.7*	*87.6*	*2.6*	1
2	*83.8*	*6.5*	*84.2*	*6.2*	*84.5*	*5.9*	*84.8*	*5.6*	*85.0*	*5.3*	*85.3*	*5.1*	2
3	*80.7*	*9.8*	*81.2*	*9.3*	*81.7*	*8.8*	*82.2*	*8.4*	*82.5*	*8.0*	*82.9*	*7.7*	3
4	*77.6*	*13.0*	*78.3*	*12.4*	*78.9*	*11.8*	*79.5*	*11.2*	*80.0*	*10.7*	*80.5*	*10.3*	4
5	*74.4*	*16.4*	*75.3*	*15.5*	*76.1*	*14.8*	*76.8*	*14.1*	*77.5*	*13.5*	*78.1*	*12.9*	5
6	*71.1*	*19.8*	*72.2*	*18.7*	*73.2*	*17.8*	*74.1*	*17.0*	*74.9*	*16.2*	*75.7*	*15.5*	6
7	*67.8*	*23.2*	*69.1*	*22.0*	*70.3*	*20.9*	*71.3*	*19.9*	*72.3*	*19.0*	*73.2*	*18.2*	7
8	*64.4*	*26.8*	*65.9*	*25.3*	*67.3*	*24.0*	*68.5*	*22.9*	*69.6*	*21.8*	*70.7*	*20.9*	8
9	*60.8*	*30.4*	*62.6*	*28.7*	*64.2*	*27.2*	*65.6*	*25.9*	*66.9*	*24.7*	*68.1*	*23.6*	9
10	*57.1*	*34.2*	*59.2*	*32.2*	*61.0*	*30.5*	*62.7*	*29.0*	*64.1*	*27.6*	*65.5*	*26.4*	10
11	*53.3*	*38.1*	*55.6*	*35.9*	*57.7*	*33.9*	*59.6*	*32.2*	*61.2*	*30.6*	*62.7*	*29.2*	11
12	*49.1*	*42.3*	*51.9*	*39.7*	*54.3*	*37.4*	*56.4*	*35.5*	*58.3*	*33.7*	*60.0*	*32.1*	12
13	*44.7*	*46.7*	*47.9*	*43.7*	*50.6*	*41.1*	*53.0*	*38.9*	*55.2*	*36.9*	*57.1*	*35.1*	13
14	*39.9*	*51.5*	*43.6*	*48.0*	*46.8*	*45.0*	*49.5*	*42.5*	*51.9*	*40.2*	*54.0*	*38.3*	14
15	*34.4*	*56.9*	*38.9*	*52.7*	*42.6*	*49.2*	*45.7*	*46.2*	*48.5*	*43.7*	*50.9*	*41.5*	15
16	*28.1*	*63.1*	*33.6*	*57.8*	*38.0*	*53.7*	*41.7*	*50.3*	*44.8*	*47.4*	*47.5*	*44.9*	16
17	*19.8*	*71.1*	*27.4*	*63.9*	*32.9*	*58.7*	*37.2*	*54.7*	*40.8*	*51.3*	*43.9*	*48.4*	17
18	0.0	90.0	*19.3*	*71.7*	*26.8*	*64.6*	*32.2*	*59.6*	*36.5*	*55.6*	*40.1*	*52.3*	18
19	19.3	71.7	0.0	90.0	*18.9*	*72.2*	*26.2*	*65.3*	*31.5*	*60.4*	*35.8*	*56.4*	19
20	26.8	64.6	18.9	72.2	0.0	90.0	*18.5*	*72.6*	*25.7*	*65.9*	*31.0*	*61.1*	20
21	32.2	59.6	26.2	65.3	18.5	72.6	0.0	90.0	*18.2*	*73.1*	*25.3*	*66.5*	21
22	36.5	55.6	31.5	60.4	25.7	65.9	18.2	73.1	0.0	90.0	*17.9*	*73.5*	22
23	40.1	52.3	35.8	56.4	31.0	61.1	25.3	66.5	17.9	73.5	0.0	90.0	23
24	43.1	49.4	39.3	53.2	35.2	57.2	30.4	61.8	24.8	67.1	17.6	73.9	24
25	45.8	47.0	42.4	50.4	38.7	54.0	34.6	58.0	30.0	62.4	24.5	67.6	25
26	48.2	44.8	45.1	48.0	41.7	51.3	38.1	54.8	34.1	58.7	29.5	63.0	26
27	50.4	42.9	47.5	45.8	44.4	48.9	41.1	52.1	37.5	55.6	33.6	59.4	27
28	52.3	41.2	49.6	43.9	46.8	46.8	43.8	49.8	40.5	52.9	37.0	56.3	28
29	54.1	39.6	51.6	42.2	49.0	44.9	46.2	47.7	43.2	50.6	40.0	53.7	29
30	55.8	38.2	53.4	40.6	50.9	43.2	48.3	45.8	45.6	48.5	42.7	51.4	30
31	57.3	36.9	55.0	39.2	52.7	41.6	50.3	44.1	47.7	46.7	45.1	49.3	31
32	58.7	35.7	56.6	37.9	54.4	40.2	52.1	42.6	49.7	45.0	47.2	47.5	32
33	60.0	34.6	58.0	36.7	55.9	38.9	53.8	41.1	51.5	43.5	49.2	45.8	33
34	61.2	33.5	59.3	35.6	57.3	37.7	55.3	39.9	53.2	42.1	51.0	44.3	34
35	62.4	32.6	60.5	34.6	58.7	36.6	56.8	38.7	54.8	40.8	52.7	42.9	35
36	63.4	31.7	61.7	33.6	59.9	35.6	58.1	37.6	56.2	39.6	54.3	41.7	36
37	64.5	30.9	62.8	32.8	61.1	34.6	59.4	36.5	57.6	38.5	55.7	40.5	37
38	65.4	30.1	63.9	31.9	62.2	33.7	60.6	35.6	58.9	37.5	57.1	39.4	38
39	66.3	29.4	64.8	31.2	63.3	32.9	61.7	34.7	60.1	36.5	58.4	38.4	39
40	67.2	28.7	65.8	30.4	64.3	32.1	62.8	33.9	61.2	35.6	59.6	37.4	40
41	68.1	28.1	66.7	29.8	65.2	31.4	63.8	33.1	62.3	34.8	60.8	36.6	41
42	68.8	27.5	67.5	29.1	66.2	30.7	64.8	32.4	63.3	34.0	61.9	35.7	42
43	69.6	26.9	68.3	28.5	67.0	30.1	65.7	31.7	64.3	33.3	62.9	35.0	43
44	70.3	26.4	69.1	27.9	67.9	29.5	66.6	31.1	65.3	32.6	63.9	34.2	44
45	71.0	25.9	69.9	27.4	68.7	28.9	67.4	30.5	66.2	32.0	64.9	33.5	45
46	71.7	25.4	70.6	26.9	69.4	28.4	68.2	29.9	67.0	31.4	65.8	32.9	46
47	72.4	25.0	71.3	26.4	70.2	27.9	69.0	29.3	67.9	30.8	66.7	32.3	47
48	73.0	24.6	71.9	26.0	70.9	27.4	69.8	28.8	68.7	30.3	67.5	31.7	48
49	73.6	24.2	72.6	25.6	71.6	26.9	70.5	28.3	69.4	29.8	68.3	31.2	49
50	74.2	23.8	73.2	25.2	72.2	26.5	71.2	27.9	70.2	29.3	69.1	30.7	50
52	75.3	23.1	74.4	24.4	73.5	25.7	72.5	27.1	71.6	28.4	70.6	29.7	52
54	76.3	22.5	75.5	23.7	74.7	25.0	73.8	26.3	72.9	27.6	72.0	28.9	54
56	77.3	21.9	76.6	23.1	75.8	24.4	75.0	25.6	74.2	26.9	73.4	28.1	56
58	78.3	21.4	77.6	22.6	76.9	23.8	76.1	25.0	75.4	26.2	74.6	27.4	58
60	79.2	20.9	78.5	22.1	77.9	23.3	77.2	24.4	76.5	25.6	75.8	26.8	60
65	81.3	19.9	80.8	21.1	80.2	22.2	79.7	23.3	79.1	24.4	78.6	25.5	65
70	83.2	19.2	82.8	20.3	82.4	21.3	82.0	22.4	81.5	23.5	81.1	24.6	70
75	85.0	18.7	84.7	19.7	84.4	20.7	84.1	21.8	83.8	22.8	83.5	23.9	75
80	86.7	18.3	86.5	19.3	86.3	20.3	86.1	21.3	85.9	22.4	85.7	23.4	80
85	88.4	18.1	88.3	19.1	88.2	20.1	88.1	21.1	88.0	22.1	87.9	23.1	85

Numbers in *italics* indicate nearest approach to prime vertical

TABLE 21

Latitude and Longitude Factors

f, the change of latitude for a unit change in longitude
F, the change of longitude for a unit change in latitude

Azimuth angle	Latitude 0° f	0° F	2° f	2° F	4° f	4° F	6° f	6° F	8° f	8° F	Azimuth angle
°											°
0	0.00	—	0.00	—	0.00	—	0.00	—	0.00	—	180
1	0.02	57.29	0.02	57.32	0.02	57.43	0.02	57.61	0.02	57.85	179
2	0.03	28.64	0.03	28.65	0.03	28.71	0.03	28.79	0.03	28.92	178
3	0.05	19.08	0.05	19.09	0.05	19.13	0.05	19.19	0.05	19.27	177
4	0.07	14.30	0.07	14.31	0.07	14.34	0.07	14.38	0.07	14.44	176
5	0.09	11.43	0.09	11.44	0.09	11.46	0.09	11.49	0.09	11.54	175
6	0.11	9.51	0.11	9.52	0.10	9.54	0.10	9.57	0.10	9.61	174
7	0.12	8.14	0.12	8.15	0.12	8.16	0.12	8.19	0.12	8.22	173
8	0.14	7.12	0.14	7.12	0.14	7.13	0.14	7.15	0.14	7.18	172
9	0.16	6.31	0.16	6.32	0.16	6.33	0.16	6.35	0.16	6.38	171
10	0.18	5.67	0.18	5.68	0.18	5.69	0.18	5.70	0.17	5.73	170
12	0.21	4.70	0.21	4.71	0.21	4.72	0.21	4.73	0.21	4.75	168
14	0.25	4.01	0.25	4.01	0.25	4.02	0.25	4.03	0.25	4.05	166
16	0.29	3.49	0.29	3.49	0.29	3.50	0.28	3.51	0.28	3.52	164
18	0.32	3.08	0.32	3.08	0.32	3.08	0.32	3.10	0.32	3.11	162
20	0.36	2.75	0.36	2.75	0.36	2.75	0.36	2.76	0.36	2.77	160
22	0.40	2.48	0.40	2.48	0.40	2.48	0.40	2.49	0.40	2.50	158
24	0.45	2.25	0.44	2.25	0.44	2.25	0.44	2.26	0.44	2.27	156
26	0.49	2.05	0.49	2.06	0.49	2.06	0.49	2.06	0.48	2.07	154
28	0.53	1.88	0.53	1.88	0.53	1.88	0.53	1.89	0.53	1.90	152
30	0.58	1.73	0.58	1.73	0.57	1.74	0.57	1.74	0.57	1.75	150
32	0.62	1.60	0.62	1.60	0.62	1.60	0.62	1.61	0.62	1.62	148
34	0.67	1.48	0.67	1.48	0.67	1.49	0.67	1.49	0.67	1.50	146
36	0.73	1.38	0.73	1.38	0.72	1.38	0.72	1.38	0.72	1.39	144
38	0.78	1.28	0.78	1.28	0.78	1.28	0.78	1.29	0.78	1.29	142
40	0.84	1.19	0.84	1.19	0.84	1.19	0.83	1.20	0.83	1.20	140
42	0.90	1.11	0.90	1.11	0.90	1.11	0.90	1.12	0.89	1.12	138
44	0.97	1.04	0.97	1.04	0.96	1.04	0.96	1.04	0.96	1.05	136
46	1.04	0.97	1.04	0.97	1.03	0.97	1.03	0.97	1.03	0.98	134
48	1.11	0.90	1.11	0.90	1.11	0.90	1.11	0.90	1.10	0.91	132
50	1.19	0.84	1.19	0.84	1.19	0.84	1.19	0.84	1.18	0.85	130
52	1.28	0.78	1.28	0.78	1.28	0.78	1.27	0.79	1.27	0.79	128
54	1.38	0.73	1.38	0.73	1.37	0.73	1.37	0.73	1.36	0.73	126
56	1.48	0.67	1.48	0.67	1.48	0.68	1.47	0.68	1.47	0.68	124
58	1.60	0.62	1.60	0.63	1.60	0.63	1.59	0.63	1.58	0.63	122
60	1.73	0.58	1.73	0.58	1.73	0.58	1.72	0.58	1.72	0.58	120
62	1.88	0.53	1.88	0.53	1.88	0.53	1.87	0.53	1.86	0.54	118
64	2.05	0.49	2.05	0.49	2.05	0.49	2.04	0.49	2.03	0.49	116
66	2.25	0.45	2.24	0.45	2.24	0.45	2.23	0.45	2.22	0.45	114
68	2.48	0.40	2.47	0.40	2.47	0.40	2.46	0.40	2.45	0.41	112
70	2.75	0.36	2.75	0.36	2.74	0.36	2.73	0.37	2.72	0.37	110
72	3.08	0.32	3.08	0.33	3.07	0.33	3.06	0.33	3.05	0.33	108
74	3.49	0.29	3.49	0.29	3.48	0.29	3.47	0.29	3.45	0.29	106
76	4.01	0.25	4.01	0.25	4.00	0.25	3.99	0.25	3.97	0.25	104
78	4.70	0.21	4.70	0.21	4.69	0.21	4.68	0.21	4.66	0.21	102
80	5.67	0.18	5.67	0.18	5.66	0.18	5.64	0.18	5.62	0.18	100
81	6.31	0.16	6.31	0.16	6.30	0.16	6.28	0.16	6.25	0.16	99
82	7.12	0.14	7.11	0.14	7.10	0.14	7.07	0.14	7.05	0.14	98
83	8.14	0.12	8.14	0.12	8.12	0.12	8.10	0.12	8.07	0.12	97
84	9.51	0.11	9.51	0.11	9.49	0.11	9.46	0.11	9.42	0.11	96
85	11.43	0.09	11.42	0.09	11.40	0.09	11.37	0.09	11.32	0.09	95
86	14.30	0.07	14.29	0.07	14.27	0.07	14.22	0.07	14.16	0.07	94
87	19.08	0.05	19.07	0.05	19.03	0.05	18.98	0.05	18.91	0.05	93
88	28.64	0.03	28.62	0.03	28.57	0.03	28.48	0.03	28.36	0.03	92
89	57.29	0.02	57.26	0.02	57.15	0.02	56.98	0.02	56.73	0.02	91
90	—	0.00	—	0.00	—	0.00	—	0.00	—	0.00	90
	0°		2°		4°		6°		8°		

Correction to latitude = f × error in longitude | Correction to longitude = F × error in latitude

TABLE 21

Latitude and Longitude Factors

f, the change of latitude for a unit change in longitude
F, the change of longitude for a unit change in latitude

Azimuth angle	Latitude 10° f	10° F	12° f	12° F	14° f	14° F	16° f	16° F	18° f	18° F	Azimuth angle
°											°
0	0.00	—	0.00	—	0.00	—	0.00	—	0.00	—	180
1	0.02	58.17	0.02	58.57	0.02	59.04	0.02	59.60	0.02	60.24	179
2	0.03	29.08	0.03	29.28	0.03	29.51	0.03	29.79	0.03	30.11	178
3	0.05	19.38	0.05	19.51	0.05	19.67	0.05	19.85	0.05	20.06	177
4	0.07	14.52	0.07	14.62	0.07	14.74	0.07	14.88	0.07	15.04	176
5	0.09	11.61	0.09	11.69	0.08	11.78	0.08	11.89	0.08	12.02	175
6	0.10	9.66	0.10	9.73	0.10	9.81	0.10	9.90	0.10	10.00	174
7	0.12	8.27	0.12	8.33	0.12	8.39	0.12	8.47	0.12	8.56	173
8	0.14	7.22	0.14	7.27	0.14	7.33	0.14	7.40	0.13	7.48	172
9	0.16	6.41	0.15	6.45	0.15	6.51	0.15	6.57	0.15	6.64	171
10	0.17	5.76	0.17	5.80	0.17	5.85	0.17	5.90	0.17	5.96	170
12	0.21	4.78	0.21	4.81	0.21	4.85	0.20	4.89	0.20	4.95	168
14	0.25	4.07	0.24	4.10	0.24	4.13	0.24	4.17	0.24	4.22	166
16	0.28	3.54	0.28	3.56	0.28	3.59	0.28	3.63	0.27	3.67	164
18	0.32	3.13	0.32	3.15	0.32	3.17	0.31	3.20	0.31	3.24	162
20	0.36	2.79	0.36	2.81	0.35	2.83	0.35	2.86	0.35	2.89	160
22	0.40	2.51	0.40	2.53	0.39	2.55	0.39	2.57	0.38	2.60	158
24	0.44	2.28	0.44	2.30	0.43	2.32	0.43	2.34	0.42	2.36	156
26	0.48	2.08	0.48	2.10	0.47	2.11	0.47	2.13	0.46	2.16	154
28	0.52	1.91	0.52	1.92	0.52	1.94	0.51	1.96	0.51	1.98	152
30	0.57	1.76	0.56	1.77	0.56	1.78	0.56	1.80	0.55	1.82	150
32	0.62	1.63	0.61	1.64	0.61	1.65	0.60	1.66	0.59	1.68	148
34	0.66	1.50	0.66	1.52	0.65	1.53	0.65	1.54	0.64	1.56	146
36	0.72	1.40	0.71	1.41	0.70	1.42	0.70	1.43	0.69	1.45	144
38	0.77	1.30	0.76	1.31	0.76	1.32	0.75	1.33	0.74	1.35	142
40	0.83	1.21	0.82	1.22	0.81	1.23	0.81	1.24	0.80	1.25	140
42	0.88	1.13	0.88	1.14	0.88	1.14	0.87	1.15	0.85	1.17	138
44	0.95	1.05	0.94	1.06	0.94	1.07	0.93	1.08	0.92	1.09	136
46	1.02	0.98	1.01	0.99	1.01	1.00	1.00	1.01	0.99	1.02	134
48	1.10	0.91	1.09	0.92	1.08	0.93	1.07	0.94	1.06	0.95	132
50	1.17	0.85	1.17	0.86	1.16	0.87	1.15	0.87	1.13	0.88	130
52	1.26	0.79	1.25	0.80	1.24	0.80	1.23	0.81	1.22	0.82	128
54	1.36	0.74	1.35	0.74	1.34	0.75	1.32	0.76	1.31	0.76	126
56	1.46	0.68	1.45	0.69	1.44	0.69	1.43	0.70	1.41	0.71	124
58	1.58	0.63	1.57	0.64	1.55	0.64	1.54	0.65	1.52	0.66	122
60	1.71	0.59	1.69	0.59	1.68	0.60	1.67	0.60	1.65	0.61	120
62	1.85	0.54	1.84	0.54	1.83	0.55	1.81	0.55	1.79	0.56	118
64	2.02	0.50	2.01	0.50	1.99	0.50	1.97	0.51	1.95	0.51	116
66	2.21	0.45	2.20	0.46	2.18	0.46	2.16	0.46	2.14	0.47	114
68	2.44	0.41	2.42	0.41	2.40	0.42	2.38	0.42	2.35	0.42	112
70	2.71	0.37	2.69	0.37	2.67	0.37	2.64	0.38	2.61	0.38	110
72	3.03	0.33	3.01	0.33	2.99	0.33	2.96	0.34	2.93	0.34	108
74	3.43	0.29	3.41	0.29	3.38	0.30	3.35	0.30	3.32	0.30	106
76	3.95	0.25	3.92	0.25	3.89	0.26	3.86	0.26	3.81	0.26	104
78	4.63	0.22	4.60	0.22	4.56	0.22	4.52	0.22	4.47	0.22	102
80	5.59	0.18	5.55	0.18	5.50	0.18	5.45	0.18	5.39	0.18	100
81	6.22	0.16	6.18	0.16	6.13	0.16	6.07	0.16	6.01	0.17	99
82	7.01	0.14	6.96	0.14	6.90	0.14	6.84	0.15	6.77	0.15	98
83	8.02	0.12	7.97	0.13	7.90	0.13	7.83	0.13	7.75	0.13	97
84	9.37	0.11	9.31	0.11	9.23	0.11	9.15	0.11	9.05	0.11	96
85	11.25	0.09	11.18	0.09	11.09	0.09	10.99	0.09	10.87	0.09	95
86	14.08	0.07	13.99	0.07	13.88	0.07	13.75	0.07	13.60	0.07	94
87	18.79	0.05	18.66	0.05	18.51	0.05	18.34	0.05	18.15	0.05	93
88	28.20	0.03	28.01	0.04	27.79	0.04	27.53	0.04	27.23	0.04	92
89	56.42	0.02	56.04	0.02	55.59	0.02	55.07	0.02	54.49	0.02	91
90	—	0.00	—	0.00	—	0.00	—	0.00	—	0.00	90
	10°		12°		14°		16°		18°		

Correction to latitude = f × error in longitude | Correction to longitude = F × error in latitude

TABLE 21

Latitude and Longitude Factors

f, the change of latitude for a unit change in longitude
F, the change of longitude for a unit change in latitude

Azimuth angle	Latitude 20° f	20° F	22° f	22° F	24° f	24° F	26° f	26° F	28° f	28° F	Azimuth angle
°											°
0	0.00	—	0.00	—	0.00	—	0.00	—	0.00	—	180
1	0.02	60.97	0.02	61.79	0.02	62.71	0.02	63.74	0.02	64.88	179
2	0.03	30.47	0.03	30.89	0.03	31.35	0.03	31.86	0.03	32.43	178
3	0.05	20.31	0.05	20.58	0.05	20.89	0.05	21.23	0.05	21.61	177
4	0.07	15.22	0.06	15.42	0.06	15.65	0.06	15.91	0.06	16.20	176
5	0.08	12.16	0.08	12.33	0.08	12.51	0.08	12.72	0.08	12.95	175
6	0.10	10.12	0.10	10.26	0.10	10.41	0.09	10.59	0.09	10.78	174
7	0.12	8.67	0.11	8.78	0.11	8.91	0.11	9.06	0.11	9.22	173
8	0.13	7.57	0.13	7.67	0.13	7.79	0.13	7.92	0.12	8.06	172
9	0.15	6.72	0.15	6.81	0.14	6.91	0.14	7.02	0.14	7.15	171
10	0.17	6.03	0.16	6.12	0.16	6.21	0.16	6.31	0.16	6.42	170
12	0.20	5.01	0.20	5.07	0.19	5.15	0.19	5.23	0.19	5.33	168
14	0.23	4.27	0.23	4.33	0.23	4.39	0.22	4.46	0.22	4.54	166
16	0.27	3.71	0.27	3.76	0.26	3.82	0.26	3.88	0.25	3.95	164
18	0.30	3.28	0.30	3.32	0.30	3.37	0.29	3.42	0.29	3.49	162
20	0.34	2.92	0.34	2.96	0.33	3.01	0.33	3.06	0.32	3.11	160
22	0.38	2.63	0.38	2.67	0.37	2.71	0.36	2.75	0.36	2.80	158
24	0.42	2.39	0.41	2.42	0.41	2.46	0.40	2.50	0.39	2.54	156
26	0.46	2.18	0.45	2.21	0.45	2.24	0.44	2.28	0.43	2.32	154
28	0.50	2.00	0.49	2.03	0.49	2.06	0.48	2.09	0.47	2.13	152
30	0.54	1.84	0.53	1.87	0.53	1.90	0.52	1.93	0.51	1.96	150
32	0.59	1.70	0.58	1.73	0.57	1.75	0.56	1.78	0.55	1.81	148
34	0.63	1.58	0.63	1.60	0.62	1.62	0.61	1.65	0.60	1.68	146
36	0.68	1.47	0.67	1.48	0.66	1.51	0.65	1.53	0.64	1.56	144
38	0.74	1.36	0.72	1.38	0.71	1.40	0.70	1.42	0.69	1.45	142
40	0.79	1.27	0.78	1.28	0.77	1.30	0.75	1.33	0.74	1.35	140
42	0.85	1.18	0.83	1.20	0.82	1.22	0.81	1.24	0.80	1.26	138
44	0.91	1.10	0.90	1.12	0.88	1.13	0.87	1.15	0.85	1.17	136
46	0.97	1.03	0.96	1.04	0.95	1.06	0.93	1.07	0.91	1.09	134
48	1.04	0.96	1.03	0.97	1.02	0.99	1.00	1.00	0.98	1.02	132
50	1.12	0.89	1.10	0.91	1.09	0.92	1.07	0.93	1.05	0.95	130
52	1.20	0.83	1.19	0.84	1.17	0.85	1.15	0.87	1.13	0.88	128
54	1.29	0.77	1.28	0.78	1.26	0.79	1.24	0.81	1.22	0.82	126
56	1.39	0.72	1.38	0.73	1.35	0.74	1.33	0.75	1.31	0.76	124
58	1.50	0.66	1.48	0.67	1.46	0.68	1.44	0.70	1.41	0.71	122
60	1.63	0.61	1.61	0.62	1.58	0.63	1.56	0.64	1.53	0.65	120
62	1.77	0.57	1.74	0.57	1.72	0.58	1.69	0.59	1.66	0.60	118
64	1.93	0.52	1.90	0.53	1.87	0.53	1.84	0.54	1.81	0.55	116
66	2.11	0.47	2.08	0.48	2.05	0.49	2.02	0.50	1.98	0.50	114
68	2.33	0.43	2.30	0.44	2.26	0.44	2.23	0.45	2.18	0.46	112
70	2.58	0.39	2.55	0.39	2.51	0.40	2.47	0.40	2.43	0.41	110
72	2.89	0.35	2.85	0.35	2.81	0.36	2.77	0.36	2.72	0.37	108
74	3.28	0.31	3.23	0.31	3.19	0.31	3.14	0.32	3.08	0.33	106
76	3.77	0.27	3.72	0.27	3.66	0.27	3.61	0.28	3.54	0.28	104
78	4.42	0.23	4.36	0.23	4.30	0.23	4.23	0.24	4.15	0.24	102
80	5.33	0.19	5.26	0.19	5.18	0.19	5.10	0.20	5.01	0.20	100
81	5.93	0.17	5.86	0.17	5.77	0.17	5.68	0.18	5.58	0.18	99
82	6.69	0.15	6.60	0.15	6.50	0.15	6.40	0.16	6.28	0.16	98
83	7.65	0.13	7.55	0.13	7.44	0.13	7.32	0.14	7.19	0.14	97
84	8.94	0.11	8.82	0.11	8.69	0.12	8.55	0.12	8.40	0.12	96
85	10.74	0.09	10.60	0.09	10.44	0.10	10.26	0.10	10.09	0.10	95
86	13.44	0.07	13.26	0.08	13.07	0.08	12.86	0.08	12.63	0.08	94
87	17.93	0.06	17.69	0.06	17.43	0.06	17.15	0.06	16.85	0.06	93
88	26.91	0.04	26.55	0.04	26.16	0.04	25.74	0.04	25.28	0.04	92
89	53.84	0.02	53.12	0.02	52.33	0.02	51.50	0.02	50.58	0.02	91
90	—	0.00	—	0.00	—	0.00	—	0.00	—	0.00	90
	20°		22°		24°		26°		28°		

Correction to latitude = f × error in longitude | Correction to longitude = F × error in latitude

TABLE 21

Latitude and Longitude Factors

f, the change of latitude for a unit change in longitude
F, the change of longitude for a unit change in latitude

Azimuth angle	Latitude 30° f	30° F	32° f	32° F	34° f	34° F	36° f	36° F	38° f	38° F	Azimuth angle
°											°
0	0.00	—	0.00	—	0.00	—	0.00	—	0.00	—	180
1	0.02	66.15	0.01	67.56	0.01	69.10	0.01	70.81	0.01	72.70	179
2	0.03	33.07	0.03	33.77	0.03	34.54	0.03	35.40	0.03	36.34	178
3	0.05	22.03	0.05	22.50	0.04	23.02	0.04	23.59	0.04	24.21	177
4	0.06	16.51	0.06	16.86	0.06	17.25	0.06	17.68	0.06	18.15	176
5	0.08	13.20	0.07	13.48	0.07	13.79	0.07	14.13	0.07	14.50	175
6	0.09	10.99	0.09	11.22	0.09	11.48	0.09	11.76	0.08	12.07	174
7	0.11	9.40	0.10	9.60	0.10	9.82	0.10	10.07	0.10	10.34	173
8	0.12	8.22	0.12	8.39	0.12	8.58	0.11	8.79	0.11	9.03	172
9	0.14	7.29	0.13	7.45	0.13	7.62	0.13	7.80	0.12	8.01	171
10	0.15	6.55	0.15	6.69	0.15	6.84	0.14	7.01	0.14	7.20	170
12	0.18	5.43	0.18	5.55	0.18	5.67	0.17	5.82	0.17	5.97	168
14	0.22	4.63	0.21	4.73	0.21	4.84	0.20	4.96	0.20	5.09	166
16	0.25	4.03	0.24	4.11	0.24	4.21	0.23	4.31	0.23	4.43	164
18	0.28	3.55	0.28	3.63	0.27	3.71	0.26	3.80	0.26	3.91	162
20	0.32	3.17	0.31	3.24	0.30	3.31	0.29	3.40	0.29	3.49	160
22	0.35	2.86	0.34	2.92	0.34	2.99	0.33	3.06	0.32	3.14	158
24	0.39	2.59	0.38	2.65	0.37	2.71	0.36	2.78	0.35	2.85	156
26	0.42	2.37	0.41	2.42	0.40	2.47	0.40	2.53	0.38	2.60	154
28	0.46	2.17	0.45	2.22	0.44	2.27	0.43	2.32	0.42	2.39	152
30	0.50	2.00	0.49	2.04	0.48	2.09	0.47	2.14	0.45	2.20	150
32	0.54	1.85	0.53	1.89	0.52	1.93	0.51	1.98	0.49	2.03	148
34	0.58	1.71	0.57	1.75	0.56	1.79	0.55	1.83	0.53	1.88	146
36	0.63	1.59	0.62	1.62	0.60	1.66	0.59	1.70	0.57	1.75	144
38	0.68	1.48	0.66	1.51	0.65	1.54	0.63	1.58	0.62	1.62	142
40	0.72	1.38	0.71	1.41	0.69	1.44	0.68	1.47	0.66	1.51	140
42	0.78	1.28	0.76	1.31	0.75	1.34	0.73	1.37	0.71	1.41	138
44	0.84	1.20	0.82	1.22	0.80	1.25	0.78	1.28	0.76	1.31	136
46	0.90	1.11	0.88	1.14	0.86	1.16	0.84	1.19	0.82	1.23	134
48	0.96	1.04	0.94	1.06	0.92	1.09	0.90	1.11	0.88	1.14	132
50	1.03	0.97	1.01	0.99	0.99	1.01	0.96	1.04	0.94	1.06	130
52	1.11	0.90	1.09	0.92	1.06	0.94	1.04	0.97	1.01	0.99	128
54	1.19	0.84	1.16	0.86	1.14	0.88	1.11	0.90	1.08	0.92	126
56	1.28	0.78	1.26	0.79	1.23	0.81	1.20	0.83	1.17	0.86	124
58	1.39	0.72	1.36	0.74	1.33	0.75	1.30	0.77	1.26	0.79	122
60	1.49	0.67	1.47	0.68	1.44	0.70	1.40	0.71	1.37	0.73	120
62	1.63	0.61	1.59	0.63	1.56	0.64	1.52	0.66	1.48	0.67	118
64	1.78	0.56	1.74	0.57	1.70	0.59	1.66	0.60	1.62	0.62	116
66	1.95	0.51	1.91	0.52	1.85	0.54	1.82	0.55	1.77	0.56	114
68	2.14	0.47	2.10	0.48	2.05	0.49	2.00	0.50	1.95	0.51	112
70	2.38	0.42	2.33	0.43	2.28	0.44	2.22	0.45	2.17	0.46	110
72	2.67	0.38	2.61	0.38	2.55	0.39	2.50	0.40	2.43	0.41	108
74	3.02	0.33	2.96	0.34	2.89	0.35	2.82	0.35	2.75	0.36	106
76	3.47	0.29	3.40	0.29	3.33	0.30	3.25	0.31	3.16	0.32	104
78	4.07	0.24	3.99	0.25	3.90	0.26	3.81	0.26	3.71	0.27	102
80	4.91	0.20	4.81	0.21	4.70	0.21	4.59	0.22	4.47	0.22	100
81	5.47	0.18	5.35	0.19	5.24	0.19	5.11	0.20	4.98	0.20	99
82	6.16	0.16	6.03	0.17	5.90	0.17	5.76	0.17	5.61	0.18	98
83	7.05	0.14	6.91	0.14	6.75	0.15	6.59	0.15	6.42	0.16	97
84	8.24	0.12	8.07	0.12	7.89	0.13	7.70	0.13	7.50	0.13	96
85	9.90	0.10	9.69	0.10	9.48	0.11	9.25	0.11	9.01	0.11	95
86	12.39	0.08	12.13	0.08	11.86	0.08	11.57	0.09	11.27	0.09	94
87	16.52	0.06	16.18	0.06	15.82	0.06	15.44	0.06	15.04	0.07	93
88	24.80	0.04	24.28	0.04	23.74	0.04	23.17	0.04	22.57	0.04	92
89	49.61	0.02	48.58	0.02	47.50	0.02	46.36	0.02	45.14	0.02	91
90	—	0.00	—	0.00	—	0.00	—	0.00	—	0.00	90
	30°		32°		34°		36°		38°		

Correction to latitude = f × error in longitude | Correction to longitude = F × error in latitude

TABLE 21
Latitude and Longitude Factors

f, the change of latitude for a unit change in longitude
F, the change of longitude for a unit change in latitude

Azimuth angle	Latitude 40° f	40° F	42° f	42° F	44° f	44° F	46° f	46° F	48° f	48° F	Azimuth angle
°											°
0	0.00	—	0.00	—	0.00	—	0.00	—	0.00	—	180
1	0.01	74.79	0.01	77.09	0.01	79.64	0.01	82.47	0.01	85.62	179
2	0.03	37.38	0.03	38.53	0.03	39.81	0.02	41.22	0.02	42.80	178
3	0.04	24.91	0.04	25.68	0.04	26.53	0.04	27.47	0.03	28.52	177
4	0.05	18.67	0.05	19.24	0.05	19.88	0.05	20.59	0.05	21.37	176
5	0.07	14.92	0.07	15.38	0.06	15.89	0.06	16.45	0.06	17.08	175
6	0.08	12.42	0.08	12.80	0.08	13.23	0.07	13.70	0.07	14.22	174
7	0.09	10.63	0.09	10.96	0.09	11.32	0.08	11.72	0.08	12.17	173
8	0.11	9.29	0.10	9.57	0.10	9.89	0.10	10.24	0.09	10.63	172
9	0.12	8.24	0.12	8.50	0.11	8.78	0.11	9.09	0.11	9.44	171
10	0.14	7.40	0.13	7.63	0.13	7.88	0.12	8.16	0.12	8.48	170
12	0.16	6.14	0.16	6.33	0.15	6.54	0.15	6.77	0.14	7.03	168
14	0.19	5.24	0.19	5.40	0.18	5.58	0.17	5.77	0.17	5.99	166
16	0.22	4.55	0.21	4.69	0.21	4.85	0.20	5.02	0.19	5.21	164
18	0.25	4.02	0.24	4.14	0.23	4.28	0.23	4.43	0.22	4.60	162
20	0.28	3.59	0.27	3.70	0.26	3.82	0.25	3.95	0.24	4.11	160
22	0.31	3.23	0.30	3.33	0.29	3.44	0.28	3.56	0.27	3.70	158
24	0.34	2.93	0.33	3.02	0.32	3.12	0.31	3.23	0.30	3.36	156
26	0.37	2.68	0.36	2.76	0.35	2.85	0.34	2.95	0.33	3.06	154
28	0.41	2.45	0.40	2.53	0.38	2.61	0.37	2.71	0.36	2.81	152
30	0.44	2.26	0.43	2.33	0.41	2.41	0.40	2.49	0.39	2.59	150
32	0.48	2.09	0.46	2.15	0.45	2.22	0.43	2.30	0.42	2.39	148
34	0.52	1.93	0.50	1.99	0.49	2.06	0.47	2.13	0.45	2.22	146
36	0.56	1.80	0.54	1.85	0.52	1.91	0.50	1.98	0.49	2.06	144
38	0.60	1.67	0.58	1.72	0.56	1.78	0.54	1.84	0.52	1.91	142
40	0.64	1.56	0.63	1.60	0.60	1.66	0.58	1.71	0.56	1.78	140
42	0.69	1.45	0.67	1.49	0.65	1.54	0.63	1.60	0.60	1.66	138
44	0.74	1.35	0.72	1.39	0.69	1.44	0.67	1.49	0.65	1.55	136
46	0.79	1.26	0.77	1.30	0.74	1.34	0.72	1.39	0.69	1.44	134
48	0.85	1.17	0.83	1.21	0.80	1.25	0.77	1.30	0.74	1.35	132
50	0.91	1.09	0.88	1.13	0.86	1.17	0.83	1.21	0.80	1.25	130
52	0.98	1.02	0.95	1.05	0.92	1.09	0.89	1.12	0.86	1.17	128
54	1.05	0.95	1.02	0.98	0.99	1.01	0.96	1.05	0.92	1.09	126
56	1.14	0.88	1.10	0.91	1.07	0.94	1.03	0.97	0.99	1.01	124
58	1.23	0.82	1.19	0.84	1.15	0.87	1.11	0.90	1.07	0.93	122
60	1.33	0.75	1.29	0.78	1.25	0.80	1.20	0.83	1.16	0.86	120
62	1.44	0.69	1.40	0.72	1.35	0.74	1.31	0.77	1.26	0.79	118
64	1.57	0.64	1.52	0.66	1.48	0.68	1.42	0.70	1.37	0.73	116
66	1.72	0.58	1.67	0.60	1.62	0.62	1.56	0.64	1.50	0.66	114
68	1.90	0.53	1.84	0.54	1.78	0.56	1.72	0.58	1.66	0.60	112
70	2.10	0.47	2.04	0.49	1.98	0.51	1.91	0.52	1.84	0.54	110
72	2.36	0.42	2.29	0.44	2.21	0.45	2.14	0.47	2.06	0.49	108
74	2.67	0.37	2.59	0.39	2.51	0.40	2.42	0.41	2.33	0.43	106
76	3.07	0.32	2.98	0.34	2.89	0.35	2.79	0.36	2.68	0.37	104
78	3.60	0.28	3.50	0.29	3.38	0.29	3.27	0.31	3.15	0.32	102
80	4.34	0.23	4.22	0.24	4.08	0.24	3.94	0.25	3.80	0.26	100
81	4.84	0.21	4.69	0.21	4.54	0.22	4.39	0.23	4.23	0.24	99
82	5.45	0.18	5.29	0.19	5.12	0.20	4.94	0.20	4.76	0.21	98
83	6.24	0.16	6.05	0.16	5.86	0.17	5.66	0.18	5.45	0.18	97
84	7.29	0.14	7.07	0.14	6.84	0.15	6.61	0.15	6.37	0.16	96
85	8.75	0.11	8.49	0.12	8.22	0.12	7.94	0.13	7.65	0.13	95
86	10.95	0.09	10.63	0.09	10.29	0.10	9.94	0.10	9.57	0.10	94
87	14.62	0.07	14.18	0.07	13.73	0.07	13.26	0.08	12.77	0.08	93
88	21.94	0.05	21.28	0.05	20.60	0.05	19.89	0.05	19.16	0.05	92
89	43.98	0.02	42.58	0.02	41.21	0.02	39.80	0.02	38.34	0.03	91
90	—	0.00	—	0.00	—	0.00	—	0.00	—	0.00	90
	40°		42°		44°		46°		48°		

Correction to latitude = f × error in longitude | Correction to longitude = F × error in latitude

TABLE 21
Latitude and Longitude Factors

f, the change of latitude for a unit change in longitude
F, the change of longitude for a unit change in latitude

Azimuth angle	Latitude 50° f	50° F	52° f	52° F	54° f	54° F	56° f	56° F	58° f	58° F	Azimuth angle
°											°
0	0.00	—	0.00	—	0.00	—	0.00	—	0.00	—	180
1	0.01	89.13	0.01	93.05	0.01	97.47	0.01	102.45	0.01	108.11	179
2	0.02	44.55	0.02	46.51	0.02	48.72	0.02	51.21	0.02	54.04	178
3	0.03	29.68	0.03	30.99	0.03	32.46	0.03	34.12	0.03	36.01	177
4	0.04	22.25	0.04	23.23	0.04	24.33	0.04	25.57	0.04	26.99	176
5	0.06	17.78	0.05	18.57	0.05	19.45	0.05	20.44	0.05	21.57	175
6	0.07	14.80	0.06	15.45	0.06	16.19	0.06	17.01	0.06	17.95	174
7	0.08	12.67	0.08	13.23	0.07	13.86	0.07	14.56	0.06	15.37	173
8	0.09	11.07	0.08	11.56	0.08	12.11	0.08	12.72	0.07	13.43	172
9	0.10	9.82	0.10	10.26	0.09	10.74	0.09	11.29	0.08	11.91	171
10	0.11	8.82	0.11	9.21	0.10	9.65	0.10	10.14	0.09	10.70	170
12	0.14	7.32	0.13	7.64	0.13	8.00	0.12	8.41	0.11	8.88	168
14	0.16	6.24	0.15	6.51	0.15	6.82	0.14	7.17	0.13	7.57	166
16	0.18	5.42	0.18	5.66	0.17	5.93	0.16	6.24	0.15	6.58	164
18	0.21	4.79	0.20	5.00	0.19	5.24	0.18	5.50	0.17	5.81	162
20	0.23	4.27	0.22	4.46	0.21	4.67	0.20	4.91	0.19	5.19	160
22	0.26	3.85	0.25	4.02	0.24	4.21	0.23	4.43	0.21	4.67	158
24	0.29	3.49	0.27	3.65	0.26	3.82	0.25	4.02	0.24	4.24	156
26	0.31	3.19	0.30	3.33	0.29	3.49	0.27	3.66	0.26	3.87	154
28	0.34	2.93	0.33	3.05	0.31	3.20	0.30	3.36	0.28	3.55	152
30	0.37	2.69	0.36	2.81	0.34	2.95	0.32	3.10	0.31	3.27	150
32	0.40	2.49	0.38	2.60	0.37	2.72	0.35	2.86	0.33	3.02	148
34	0.43	2.31	0.42	2.41	0.40	2.52	0.38	2.65	0.36	2.80	146
36	0.47	2.14	0.45	2.24	0.43	2.34	0.41	2.46	0.39	2.60	144
38	0.50	1.99	0.48	2.08	0.46	2.18	0.44	2.29	0.41	2.41	142
40	0.54	1.85	0.52	1.94	0.49	2.03	0.47	2.13	0.44	2.25	140
42	0.58	1.73	0.56	1.80	0.53	1.89	0.50	1.99	0.48	2.09	138
44	0.62	1.61	0.59	1.68	0.57	1.76	0.54	1.85	0.51	1.95	136
46	0.67	1.50	0.64	1.57	0.61	1.64	0.58	1.73	0.55	1.82	134
48	0.71	1.40	0.68	1.46	0.65	1.53	0.62	1.61	0.59	1.70	132
50	0.77	1.31	0.73	1.36	0.70	1.43	0.67	1.50	0.63	1.58	130
52	0.82	1.22	0.79	1.27	0.75	1.33	0.72	1.40	0.68	1.47	128
54	0.88	1.13	0.85	1.18	0.81	1.23	0.77	1.30	0.73	1.37	126
56	0.95	1.05	0.91	1.10	0.87	1.15	0.83	1.21	0.79	1.27	124
58	1.03	0.97	0.99	1.01	0.94	1.06	0.89	1.12	0.85	1.18	122
60	1.11	0.90	1.07	0.94	1.02	0.98	0.97	1.03	0.92	1.09	120
62	1.21	0.83	1.16	0.86	1.11	0.90	1.05	0.95	1.00	1.00	118
64	1.32	0.76	1.26	0.79	1.20	0.83	1.15	0.87	1.09	0.92	116
66	1.44	0.69	1.38	0.72	1.32	0.76	1.26	0.79	1.19	0.84	114
68	1.59	0.63	1.52	0.65	1.45	0.69	1.38	0.72	1.31	0.76	112
70	1.77	0.57	1.69	0.59	1.61	0.62	1.54	0.65	1.45	0.68	110
72	1.98	0.51	1.89	0.53	1.81	0.55	1.72	0.58	1.63	0.61	108
74	2.24	0.45	2.15	0.46	2.05	0.49	1.95	0.51	1.85	0.54	106
76	2.58	0.39	2.47	0.40	2.36	0.42	2.24	0.45	2.13	0.47	104
78	3.02	0.33	2.90	0.34	2.77	0.36	2.63	0.38	2.49	0.40	102
80	3.65	0.27	3.49	0.29	3.33	0.30	3.17	0.31	3.01	0.33	100
81	4.06	0.25	3.89	0.26	3.71	0.27	3.53	0.28	3.35	0.30	99
82	4.57	0.22	4.38	0.23	4.18	0.24	3.98	0.25	3.77	0.26	98
83	5.24	0.19	5.01	0.20	4.79	0.21	4.55	0.22	4.32	0.23	97
84	6.12	0.16	5.86	0.17	5.59	0.18	5.32	0.19	5.04	0.20	96
85	7.35	0.14	7.04	0.14	6.72	0.15	6.39	0.16	6.06	0.16	95
86	9.19	0.11	8.81	0.11	8.41	0.12	8.00	0.12	7.58	0.13	94
87	12.27	0.08	11.75	0.08	11.22	0.09	10.67	0.09	10.11	0.10	93
88	18.41	0.05	17.63	0.06	16.83	0.06	16.01	0.06	15.17	0.07	92
89	36.83	0.03	35.27	0.03	33.68	0.03	32.04	0.03	30.36	0.03	91
90	—	0.00	—	0.00	—	0.00	—	0.00	—	0.00	90
	50°		52°		54°		56°		58°		

Correction to latitude = f × error in longitude | Correction to longitude = F × error in latitude

TABLE 21

Latitude and Longitude Factors

f, the change of latitude for a unit change in longitude
F, the change of longitude for a unit change in latitude

Azimuth angle	Latitude 60°		62°		64°		66°		68°		Azimuth angle
	f	F	f	F	f	F	f	F	f	F	
°											°
0	0.00	—	0.00	—	0.00	—	0.00	—	0.00	—	180
1	0.01	114.58	0.01	122.03	0.01	130.69	0.01	140.85	0.01	152.93	179
2	0.02	57.27	0.02	61.00	0.02	65.32	0.01	70.40	0.01	76.44	178
3	0.03	38.16	0.02	40.64	0.02	43.53	0.02	46.91	0.02	50.94	177
4	0.03	28.60	0.03	30.46	0.03	32.62	0.03	35.16	0.03	38.18	176
5	0.04	22.86	0.04	24.35	0.04	26.07	0.04	28.10	0.03	30.51	175
6	0.05	19.03	0.05	20.27	0.05	21.70	0.04	23.39	0.04	25.40	174
7	0.06	16.29	0.06	17.35	0.05	18.58	0.05	20.02	0.05	21.74	173
8	0.07	14.23	0.07	15.16	0.06	16.23	0.06	17.49	0.05	18.99	172
9	0.08	12.63	0.07	13.45	0.07	14.40	0.06	15.52	0.06	16.85	171
10	0.09	11.34	0.08	12.08	0.08	12.94	0.07	13.94	0.07	15.14	170
12	0.11	9.41	0.10	10.02	0.09	10.73	0.09	11.57	0.08	12.56	168
14	0.12	8.02	0.12	8.54	0.11	9.15	0.10	9.86	0.09	10.71	166
16	0.14	6.97	0.13	7.43	0.13	7.96	0.12	8.57	0.11	9.31	164
18	0.16	6.15	0.15	6.56	0.14	7.02	0.13	7.57	0.12	8.22	162
20	0.18	5.49	0.17	5.85	0.16	6.27	0.15	6.75	0.14	7.33	160
22	0.20	4.95	0.19	5.27	0.18	5.65	0.16	6.09	0.15	6.61	158
24	0.22	4.49	0.21	4.78	0.20	5.12	0.18	5.52	0.17	6.00	156
26	0.24	4.10	0.23	4.37	0.21	4.68	0.20	5.04	0.18	5.47	154
28	0.27	3.76	0.25	4.01	0.23	4.29	0.22	4.62	0.20	5.02	152
30	0.29	3.46	0.27	3.69	0.25	3.95	0.23	4.26	0.22	4.62	150
32	0.31	3.20	0.29	3.41	0.27	3.65	0.25	3.93	0.23	4.27	148
34	0.34	2.96	0.32	3.16	0.30	3.38	0.27	3.65	0.25	3.96	146
36	0.36	2.75	0.34	2.93	0.32	3.14	0.30	3.38	0.27	3.67	144
38	0.39	2.56	0.37	2.73	0.34	2.92	0.32	3.15	0.29	3.42	142
40	0.42	2.38	0.39	2.54	0.37	2.72	0.34	2.93	0.31	3.18	140
42	0.45	2.22	0.42	2.37	0.39	2.53	0.37	2.73	0.34	2.96	138
44	0.48	2.07	0.45	2.21	0.42	2.36	0.39	2.55	0.36	2.76	136
46	0.52	1.93	0.49	2.06	0.45	2.20	0.42	2.37	0.39	2.58	134
48	0.56	1.80	0.52	1.92	0.49	2.05	0.45	2.21	0.42	2.40	132
50	0.60	1.68	0.56	1.79	0.52	1.91	0.48	2.06	0.45	2.24	130
52	0.64	1.56	0.60	1.66	0.56	1.78	0.52	1.92	0.48	2.09	128
54	0.69	1.45	0.65	1.55	0.60	1.66	0.56	1.79	0.52	1.94	126
56	0.74	1.35	0.70	1.44	0.65	1.54	0.60	1.66	0.56	1.80	124
58	0.80	1.25	0.75	1.33	0.70	1.43	0.65	1.54	0.60	1.67	122
60	0.87	1.15	0.81	1.23	0.76	1.32	0.70	1.42	0.65	1.54	120
62	0.94	1.06	0.88	1.13	0.82	1.21	0.76	1.31	0.70	1.42	118
64	1.03	0.97	0.96	1.04	0.90	1.11	0.83	1.20	0.77	1.30	116
66	1.12	0.89	1.05	0.95	0.98	1.02	0.91	1.09	0.84	1.19	114
68	1.24	0.81	1.16	0.86	1.09	0.92	1.01	0.99	0.93	1.08	112
70	1.37	0.73	1.29	0.78	1.20	0.83	1.12	0.89	1.03	0.97	110
72	1.54	0.65	1.44	0.69	1.35	0.74	1.25	0.80	1.15	0.87	108
74	1.74	0.57	1.64	0.61	1.53	0.65	1.42	0.70	1.31	0.77	106
76	2.01	0.50	1.88	0.53	1.76	0.57	1.63	0.61	1.50	0.67	104
78	2.35	0.42	2.21	0.45	2.06	0.48	1.91	0.52	1.76	0.57	102
80	2.84	0.35	2.66	0.38	2.49	0.40	2.31	0.43	2.12	0.47	100
81	3.16	0.32	2.96	0.34	2.77	0.36	2.57	0.39	2.37	0.42	99
82	3.56	0.28	3.34	0.30	3.12	0.32	2.89	0.35	2.67	0.38	98
83	4.07	0.25	3.82	0.26	3.57	0.28	3.31	0.30	3.05	0.33	97
84	4.76	0.21	4.47	0.22	4.17	0.24	3.87	0.26	3.56	0.28	96
85	5.72	0.17	5.37	0.19	5.01	0.20	4.65	0.22	4.28	0.23	95
86	7.15	0.14	6.71	0.15	6.27	0.16	5.82	0.17	5.36	0.19	94
87	9.54	0.10	8.96	0.11	8.36	0.12	7.76	0.13	7.15	0.14	93
88	14.32	0.07	13.44	0.07	12.55	0.08	11.65	0.09	10.73	0.09	92
89	28.65	0.03	26.90	0.04	25.11	0.04	23.30	0.04	21.46	0.05	91
90	—	0.00	—	0.00	—	0.00	—	0.00	—	0.00	90
	60°		62°		64°		66°		68°		

Correction to latitude = f × error in longitude

Correction to longitude = F × error in latitude

TABLE 22
Amplitudes

Latitude	Declination 0°0 Z	0°5 Z	1°0 Z	1°5 Z	2°0 Z	2°5 Z	3°0 Z	3°5 Z	4°0 Z	4°5 Z	5°0 Z	5°5 Z	6°0 Z	Latitude
°	°	°	°	°	°	°	°	°	°	°	°	°	°	°
0	0.0	0.5	1.0	1.5	2.0	2.5	3.0	3.5	4.0	4.5	5.0	5.5	6.0	0
10	0.0	0.5	1.0	1.5	2.0	2.5	3.0	3.6	4.1	4.6	5.1	5.6	6.1	10
15	0.0	0.5	1.0	1.6	2.1	2.6	3.1	3.6	4.1	4.7	5.2	5.7	6.2	15
20	0.0	0.5	1.1	1.6	2.1	2.7	3.2	3.7	4.3	4.8	5.3	5.9	6.4	20
25	0.0	0.6	1.1	1.7	2.2	2.8	3.3	3.9	4.4	5.0	5.5	6.1	6.6	25
30	0.0	0.6	1.2	1.7	2.3	2.9	3.5	4.0	4.6	5.2	5.8	6.4	6.9	30
32	0.0	0.6	1.2	1.8	2.4	2.9	3.5	4.1	4.7	5.3	5.9	6.5	7.1	32
34	0.0	0.6	1.2	1.8	2.4	3.0	3.6	4.2	4.8	5.4	6.0	6.6	7.2	34
36	0.0	0.6	1.2	1.9	2.5	3.1	3.7	4.3	4.9	5.6	6.2	6.8	7.4	36
38	0.0	0.6	1.3	1.9	2.5	3.2	3.8	4.4	5.1	5.7	6.4	7.0	7.6	38
40	0.0	0.7	1.3	2.0	2.6	3.3	3.9	4.6	5.2	5.9	6.5	7.2	7.8	40
42	0.0	0.7	1.3	2.0	2.7	3.4	4.0	4.7	5.4	6.1	6.7	7.4	8.1	42
44	0.0	0.7	1.4	2.1	2.8	3.5	4.2	4.9	5.6	6.3	7.0	7.7	8.4	44
46	0.0	0.7	1.4	2.2	2.9	3.6	4.3	5.0	5.8	6.5	7.2	7.9	8.7	46
48	0.0	0.7	1.5	2.2	3.0	3.7	4.5	5.2	6.0	6.7	7.5	8.2	9.0	48
50	0.0	0.8	1.6	2.3	3.1	3.9	4.7	5.4	6.2	7.0	7.8	8.6	9.4	50
51	0.0	0.8	1.6	2.4	3.2	4.0	4.8	5.6	6.4	7.2	8.0	8.8	9.6	51
52	0.0	0.8	1.6	2.4	3.2	4.1	4.9	5.7	6.5	7.3	8.1	9.0	9.8	52
53	0.0	0.8	1.7	2.5	3.3	4.2	5.0	5.8	6.7	7.5	8.3	9.2	10.0	53
54	0.0	0.9	1.7	2.6	3.4	4.3	5.1	6.0	6.8	7.7	8.5	9.4	10.2	54
55	0.0	0.9	1.7	2.6	3.5	4.4	5.2	6.1	7.0	7.9	8.7	9.6	10.5	55
56	0.0	0.9	1.8	2.7	3.6	4.5	5.4	6.3	7.2	8.1	9.0	9.9	10.8	56
57	0.0	0.9	1.8	2.8	3.7	4.6	5.5	6.4	7.4	8.3	9.2	10.1	11.1	57
58	0.0	0.9	1.9	2.8	3.8	4.7	5.7	6.6	7.6	8.5	9.5	10.4	11.4	58
59	0.0	1.0	1.9	2.9	3.9	4.9	5.8	6.8	7.8	8.8	9.7	10.7	11.7	59
60	0.0	1.0	2.0	3.0	4.0	5.0	6.0	7.0	8.0	9.0	10.0	11.1	12.1	60
61	0.0	1.0	2.1	3.1	4.1	5.2	6.2	7.2	8.3	9.3	10.3	11.4	12.5	61
62	0.0	1.1	2.1	3.2	4.3	5.3	6.4	7.5	8.5	9.6	10.7	11.8	12.9	62
63	0.0	1.1	2.2	3.3	4.4	5.5	6.6	7.7	8.8	10.0	11.1	12.2	13.3	63
64	0.0	1.1	2.3	3.4	4.6	5.7	6.9	8.0	9.2	10.3	11.5	12.6	13.8	64
65.0	0.0	1.2	2.4	3.6	4.7	5.9	7.1	8.3	9.5	10.7	11.9	13.1	14.3	65.0
65.5	0.0	1.2	2.4	3.6	4.8	6.0	7.3	8.5	9.7	10.9	12.1	13.4	14.6	65.5
66.0	0.0	1.2	2.5	3.7	4.9	6.2	7.4	8.6	9.9	11.1	12.4	13.6	14.9	66.0
66.5	0.0	1.3	2.5	3.8	5.0	6.3	7.5	8.8	10.1	11.3	12.6	13.9	15.2	66.5
67.0	0.0	1.3	2.6	3.8	5.1	6.4	7.7	9.0	10.3	11.6	12.9	14.2	15.5	67.0
67.5	0.0	1.3	2.6	3.9	5.2	6.5	7.9	9.2	10.5	11.8	13.2	14.5	15.9	67.5
68.0	0.0	1.3	2.7	4.0	5.3	6.7	8.0	9.4	10.7	12.1	13.5	14.8	16.2	68.0
68.5	0.0	1.4	2.7	4.1	5.5	6.8	8.2	9.6	11.0	12.4	13.8	15.2	16.6	68.5
69.0	0.0	1.4	2.8	4.2	5.6	7.0	8.4	9.8	11.2	12.6	14.1	15.5	17.0	69.0
69.5	0.0	1.4	2.9	4.3	5.7	7.2	8.6	10.0	11.5	12.9	14.4	15.9	17.4	69.5
70.0	0.0	1.5	2.9	4.4	5.9	7.3	8.8	10.3	11.8	13.3	14.8	16.3	17.8	70.0
70.5	0.0	1.5	3.0	4.5	6.0	7.5	9.0	10.5	12.1	13.6	15.1	16.7	18.2	70.5
71.0	0.0	1.5	3.1	4.6	6.2	7.7	9.3	10.8	12.4	13.9	15.5	17.1	18.7	71.0
71.5	0.0	1.6	3.2	4.7	6.3	7.9	9.5	11.1	12.7	14.3	15.9	17.6	19.2	71.5
72.0	0.0	1.6	3.2	4.9	6.5	8.1	9.8	11.4	13.0	14.7	16.4	18.1	19.8	72.0
72.5	0.0	1.7	3.3	5.0	6.7	8.3	10.0	11.7	13.4	15.1	16.8	18.6	20.3	72.5
73.0	0.0	1.7	3.4	5.1	6.9	8.6	10.3	12.1	13.8	15.6	17.3	19.1	20.9	73.0
73.5	0.0	1.8	3.5	5.3	7.1	8.8	10.6	12.4	14.2	16.0	17.9	19.7	21.6	73.5
74.0	0.0	1.8	3.6	5.4	7.3	9.1	10.9	12.8	14.7	16.5	18.4	20.3	22.3	74.0
74.5	0.0	1.9	3.7	5.6	7.5	9.4	11.3	13.2	15.1	17.1	19.0	21.0	23.0	74.5
75.0	0.0	1.9	3.9	5.8	7.7	9.7	11.7	13.6	15.6	17.6	19.7	21.7	23.8	75.0
75.5	0.0	2.0	4.0	6.0	8.0	10.0	12.1	14.1	16.2	18.3	20.4	22.5	24.7	75.5
76.0	0.0	2.1	4.1	6.2	8.3	10.4	12.5	14.6	16.8	18.9	21.1	23.3	25.6	76.0
76.5	0.0	2.1	4.3	6.4	8.6	10.8	13.0	15.2	17.4	19.6	21.9	24.2	26.6	76.5
77.0	0.0	2.2	4.4	6.7	8.9	11.2	13.5	15.7	18.1	20.4	22.8	25.2	27.7	77.0

TABLE 22
Amplitudes

Latitude	Declination 6°0 Z	6°5 Z	7°0 Z	7°5 Z	8°0 Z	8°5 Z	9°0 Z	9°5 Z	10°0 Z	10°5 Z	11°0 Z	11°5 Z	12°0 Z	Latitude
°	°	°	°	°	°	°	°	°	°	°	°	°	°	°
0	6.0	6.5	7.0	7.5	8.0	8.5	9.0	9.5	10.0	10.5	11.0	11.5	12.0	0
10	6.1	6.6	7.1	7.6	8.1	8.6	9.1	9.6	10.2	10.7	11.2	11.7	12.2	10
15	6.2	6.7	7.2	7.8	8.3	8.8	9.3	9.8	10.4	10.9	11.4	11.9	12.4	15
20	6.4	6.9	7.5	8.0	8.5	9.0	9.6	10.1	10.6	11.2	11.7	12.2	12.8	20
25	6.6	7.2	7.7	8.3	8.8	9.4	9.9	10.5	11.0	11.6	12.2	12.7	13.3	25
30	6.9	7.5	8.1	8.7	9.2	9.8	10.4	11.0	11.6	12.1	12.7	13.3	13.9	30
32	7.1	7.7	8.3	8.9	9.4	10.0	10.6	11.2	11.8	12.4	13.0	13.6	14.2	32
34	7.2	7.8	8.5	9.1	9.7	10.3	10.9	11.5	12.1	12.7	13.3	13.9	14.5	34
36	7.4	8.0	8.7	9.3	9.9	10.5	11.1	11.8	12.4	13.0	13.6	14.3	14.9	36
38	7.6	8.3	8.9	9.5	10.2	10.8	11.5	12.1	12.7	13.4	14.0	14.7	15.3	38
40	7.8	8.5	9.2	9.8	10.5	11.1	11.8	12.4	13.1	13.8	14.4	15.1	15.7	40
42	8.1	8.8	9.4	10.1	10.8	11.5	12.1	12.8	13.5	14.2	14.9	15.6	16.2	42
44	8.4	9.1	9.8	10.5	11.2	11.9	12.6	13.3	14.0	14.7	15.4	16.1	16.8	44
46	8.7	9.4	10.1	10.8	11.6	12.3	13.0	13.7	14.5	15.2	15.9	16.7	17.4	46
48	9.0	9.7	10.5	11.2	12.0	12.8	13.5	14.3	15.0	15.8	16.6	17.3	18.1	48
50	9.4	10.1	10.9	11.7	12.5	13.3	14.1	14.9	15.7	16.5	17.3	18.1	18.9	50
51	9.6	10.4	11.2	12.0	12.8	13.6	14.4	15.2	16.0	16.8	17.7	18.5	19.3	51
52	9.8	10.6	11.4	12.2	13.1	13.9	14.7	15.6	16.4	17.2	18.1	18.9	19.7	52
53	10.0	10.8	11.7	12.5	13.4	14.2	15.1	15.9	16.8	17.6	18.5	19.3	20.2	53
54	10.2	11.1	12.0	12.8	13.7	14.6	15.4	16.3	17.2	18.1	18.9	19.8	20.7	54
55	10.5	11.4	12.3	13.2	14.0	14.9	15.8	16.7	17.6	18.5	19.4	20.3	21.3	55
56	10.8	11.7	12.6	13.5	14.4	15.3	16.2	17.2	18.1	19.0	20.0	20.9	21.8	56
57	11.1	12.0	12.9	13.9	14.8	15.7	16.7	17.6	18.6	19.6	20.5	21.5	22.4	57
58	11.4	12.3	13.3	14.3	15.2	16.2	17.2	18.1	19.1	20.1	21.1	22.1	23.1	58
59	11.7	12.7	13.7	14.7	15.7	16.7	17.7	18.7	19.7	20.7	21.7	22.8	23.8	59
60	12.1	13.1	14.1	15.1	16.2	17.2	18.2	19.3	20.3	21.4	22.4	23.5	24.6	60
61	12.5	13.5	14.6	15.6	16.7	17.8	18.8	19.9	21.0	22.1	23.2	24.3	25.4	61
62	12.9	14.0	15.0	16.1	17.2	18.4	19.5	20.6	21.7	22.8	24.0	25.1	26.3	62
63	13.3	14.4	15.6	16.7	17.9	19.0	20.2	21.3	22.5	23.7	24.9	26.0	27.3	63
64	13.8	15.0	16.2	17.3	18.5	19.7	20.9	22.1	23.3	24.6	25.8	27.1	28.3	64
65.0	14.3	15.5	16.8	18.0	19.2	20.5	21.7	23.0	24.3	25.5	26.8	28.1	29.5	65.0
65.5	14.6	15.8	17.1	18.3	19.6	20.9	22.2	23.5	24.8	26.1	27.4	28.7	30.1	65.5
66.0	14.9	16.2	17.4	18.7	20.0	21.3	22.6	23.9	25.3	26.6	28.0	29.4	30.7	66.0
66.5	15.2	16.5	17.8	19.1	20.4	21.8	23.1	24.5	25.8	27.2	28.6	30.0	31.4	66.5
67.0	15.5	16.8	18.2	19.5	20.9	22.2	23.6	25.0	26.4	27.8	29.2	30.7	32.1	67.0
67.5	15.9	17.2	18.6	19.9	21.3	22.7	24.1	25.5	27.0	28.4	29.9	31.4	32.9	67.5
68.0	16.2	17.6	19.0	20.4	21.8	23.2	24.7	26.1	27.6	29.1	30.6	32.2	33.7	68.0
68.5	16.6	18.0	19.4	20.9	22.3	23.8	25.3	26.8	28.3	29.8	31.4	33.0	34.6	68.5
69.0	17.0	18.4	19.9	21.4	22.9	24.4	25.9	27.4	29.0	30.6	32.2	33.8	35.5	69.0
69.5	17.4	18.9	20.4	21.9	23.4	25.0	26.5	28.1	29.7	31.4	33.0	34.7	36.4	69.5
70.0	17.8	19.3	20.9	22.4	24.0	25.6	27.2	28.9	30.5	32.2	33.9	35.7	37.4	70.0
70.5	18.2	19.8	21.4	23.0	24.6	26.3	27.9	29.6	31.3	33.1	34.9	36.7	38.5	70.5
71.0	18.7	20.3	22.0	23.6	25.3	27.0	28.7	30.5	32.2	34.0	35.9	37.8	39.7	71.0
71.5	19.2	20.9	22.6	24.3	26.0	27.8	29.5	31.3	33.2	35.1	37.0	38.9	40.9	71.5
72.0	19.8	21.5	23.2	25.0	26.8	28.6	30.4	32.3	34.2	36.1	38.1	40.2	42.3	72.0
72.5	20.3	22.1	23.9	25.7	27.6	29.4	31.3	33.3	35.3	37.3	39.4	41.5	43.7	72.5
73.0	20.9	22.8	24.6	26.5	28.4	30.4	32.3	34.4	36.4	38.6	40.7	43.0	45.3	73.0
73.5	21.6	23.5	25.4	27.4	29.3	31.4	33.4	35.5	37.7	39.9	42.2	44.6	47.1	73.5
74.0	22.3	24.2	26.2	28.3	30.3	32.4	34.6	36.8	39.0	41.4	43.8	46.3	49.0	74.0
74.5	23.0	25.1	27.1	29.3	31.4	33.6	35.8	38.1	40.5	43.0	45.6	48.2	51.1	74.5
75.0	23.8	25.9	28.1	30.3	32.5	34.8	37.2	39.6	42.1	44.8	47.5	50.4	53.4	75.0
75.5	24.7	26.9	29.1	31.4	33.8	36.2	38.7	41.2	43.9	46.7	49.6	52.8	56.1	75.5
76.0	25.6	27.9	30.2	32.7	35.1	37.7	40.3	43.0	45.9	48.9	52.1	55.5	59.3	76.0
76.5	26.6	29.0	31.5	34.0	36.6	39.3	42.1	45.0	48.1	51.3	54.8	58.7	63.0	76.5
77.0	27.7	30.2	32.8	35.5	38.2	41.1	44.1	47.2	50.5	54.1	58.0	62.4	67.6	77.0

TABLE 22
Amplitudes

Latitude	Declination 12°0 Z	12°5 Z	13°0 Z	13°5 Z	14°0 Z	14°5 Z	15°0 Z	15°5 Z	16°0 Z	16°5 Z	17°0 Z	17°5 Z	18°0 Z	Latitude
°	°	°	°	°	°	°	°	°	°	°	°	°	°	°
0	12.0	12.5	13.0	13.5	14.0	14.5	15.0	15.5	16.0	16.5	17.0	17.5	18.0	0
10	12.2	12.7	13.2	13.7	14.2	14.7	15.2	15.7	16.3	16.8	17.3	17.8	18.3	10
15	12.4	12.9	13.5	14.0	14.5	15.0	15.5	16.1	16.6	17.1	17.6	18.1	18.7	15
20	12.8	13.3	13.9	14.4	14.9	15.5	16.0	16.5	17.1	17.6	18.1	18.7	19.2	20
25	13.3	13.8	14.4	14.9	15.5	16.0	16.6	17.1	17.7	18.3	18.8	19.4	19.9	25
30	13.9	14.5	15.1	15.6	16.2	16.8	17.4	18.0	18.6	19.1	19.7	20.3	20.9	30
32	14.2	14.8	15.4	16.0	16.6	17.2	17.8	18.4	19.0	19.6	20.2	20.8	21.4	32
34	14.5	15.1	15.7	16.4	17.0	17.6	18.2	18.8	19.4	20.0	20.7	21.3	21.9	34
36	14.9	15.5	16.1	16.8	17.4	18.0	18.7	19.3	19.9	20.6	21.2	21.8	22.5	36
38	15.3	15.9	16.6	17.2	17.9	18.5	19.2	19.8	20.5	21.1	21.8	22.4	23.1	38
40	15.7	16.4	17.1	17.7	18.4	19.1	19.7	20.4	21.1	21.8	22.4	23.1	23.8	40
41	16.0	16.7	17.3	18.0	18.7	19.4	20.1	20.8	21.4	22.1	22.8	23.5	24.2	41
42	16.2	16.9	17.6	18.3	19.0	19.7	20.4	21.1	21.8	22.5	23.2	23.9	24.6	42
43	16.5	17.2	17.9	18.6	19.3	20.0	20.7	21.4	22.1	22.9	23.6	24.3	25.0	43
44	16.8	17.5	18.2	18.9	19.7	20.4	21.1	21.8	22.5	23.3	24.0	24.7	25.4	44
45	17.1	17.8	18.5	19.3	20.0	20.7	21.5	22.2	22.9	23.7	24.4	25.2	25.9	45
46	17.4	18.2	18.9	19.6	20.4	21.1	21.9	22.6	23.4	24.1	24.9	25.7	26.4	46
47	17.7	18.5	19.3	20.0	20.8	21.5	22.3	23.1	23.8	24.6	25.4	26.2	26.9	47
48	18.1	18.9	19.6	20.4	21.2	22.0	22.8	23.5	24.3	25.1	25.9	26.7	27.5	48
49	18.5	19.3	20.1	20.8	21.6	22.4	23.2	24.0	24.8	25.7	26.5	27.3	28.1	49
50	18.9	19.7	20.5	21.3	22.1	22.9	23.7	24.6	25.4	26.2	27.1	27.9	28.7	50
51	19.3	20.1	20.9	21.8	22.6	23.4	24.3	25.1	26.0	26.8	27.7	28.5	29.4	51
52	19.7	20.6	21.4	22.3	23.1	24.0	24.9	25.7	26.6	27.5	28.3	29.2	30.1	52
53	20.2	21.1	21.9	22.8	23.7	24.6	25.5	26.4	27.3	28.2	29.1	30.0	30.9	53
54	20.7	21.6	22.5	23.4	24.3	25.2	26.1	27.0	28.0	28.9	29.8	30.8	31.7	54
55	21.3	22.2	23.1	24.0	24.9	25.9	26.8	27.8	28.7	29.7	30.6	31.6	32.6	55
56	21.8	22.8	23.7	24.7	25.6	26.6	27.6	28.5	29.5	30.5	31.5	32.5	33.5	56
57	22.4	23.4	24.4	25.4	26.4	27.4	28.4	29.4	30.4	31.4	32.5	33.5	34.6	57
58	23.1	24.1	25.1	26.1	27.2	28.2	29.2	30.3	31.3	32.4	33.5	34.6	35.7	58
59	23.8	24.8	25.9	27.0	28.0	29.1	30.2	31.3	32.4	33.5	34.6	35.7	36.9	59
60	24.6	25.7	26.7	27.8	28.9	30.1	31.2	32.3	33.5	34.6	35.8	37.0	38.2	60
61	25.4	26.5	27.6	28.8	29.9	31.1	32.3	33.5	34.6	35.9	37.1	38.3	39.6	61
62	26.3	27.5	28.6	29.8	31.0	32.2	33.5	34.7	36.0	37.2	38.5	39.8	41.2	62
63	27.3	28.5	29.7	30.9	32.2	33.5	34.8	36.1	37.4	38.7	40.1	41.5	42.9	63
64	28.3	29.6	30.9	32.2	33.5	34.8	36.2	37.6	39.0	40.4	41.8	43.3	44.8	64
65.0	29.5	30.8	32.2	33.5	34.9	36.3	37.8	39.2	40.7	42.2	43.8	45.4	47.0	65.0
65.5	30.1	31.5	32.9	34.3	35.7	37.1	38.6	40.1	41.7	43.2	44.8	46.5	48.2	65.5
66.0	30.7	32.1	33.6	35.0	36.5	38.0	39.5	41.1	42.7	44.3	46.0	47.7	49.4	66.0
66.5	31.4	32.9	34.3	35.8	37.3	38.9	40.5	42.1	43.7	45.4	47.2	48.9	50.8	66.5
67.0	32.1	33.6	35.1	36.7	38.3	39.9	41.5	43.2	44.9	46.6	48.4	50.3	52.3	67.0
67.5	32.9	34.4	36.0	37.6	39.2	40.9	42.6	44.3	46.1	47.9	49.8	51.8	53.9	67.5
68.0	33.7	35.3	36.9	38.6	40.2	41.9	43.7	45.5	47.4	49.3	51.3	53.4	55.6	68.0
68.5	34.6	36.2	37.9	39.6	41.3	43.1	44.9	46.8	48.8	50.8	52.9	55.1	57.5	68.5
69.0	35.5	37.2	38.9	40.6	42.5	44.3	46.2	48.2	50.3	52.4	54.7	57.0	59.6	69.0
69.5	36.4	38.2	40.0	41.8	43.7	45.6	47.7	49.7	51.9	54.2	56.6	59.2	61.9	69.5
70.0	37.4	39.3	41.1	43.0	45.0	47.1	49.2	51.4	53.7	56.1	58.7	61.5	64.6	70.0
70.5	38.5	40.4	42.4	44.4	46.4	48.6	50.8	53.2	55.7	58.3	61.1	64.3	67.8	70.5
71.0	39.7	41.7	43.7	45.8	48.0	50.3	52.7	55.2	57.8	60.7	63.9	67.5	71.7	71.0
71.5	40.9	43.0	45.1	47.4	49.7	52.1	54.7	57.4	60.3	63.5	67.1	71.4	76.9	71.5
72.0	42.3	44.5	46.7	49.1	51.5	54.1	56.9	59.9	63.1	66.8	71.1	76.7	90.0	72.0
72.5	43.7	46.0	48.4	50.9	53.6	56.4	59.4	62.7	66.4	70.8	76.5	90.0		72.5
73.0	45.3	47.8	50.3	53.0	55.8	58.9	62.3	66.1	70.5	76.3	90.0			73.0
73.5	47.1	49.6	52.4	55.3	58.4	61.8	65.7	70.2	76.0	90.0				73.5
74.0	49.0	51.7	54.7	57.9	61.4	65.3	69.9	75.8	90.0					74.0
74.5	51.1	54.1	57.3	60.9	64.9	69.5	75.6	90.0						74.5

TABLE 22
Amplitudes

Latitude	Declination 18°0 Z	18°5 Z	19°0 Z	19°5 Z	20°0 Z	20°5 Z	21°0 Z	21°5 Z	22°0 Z	22°5 Z	23°0 Z	23°5 Z	24°0 Z	Latitude
°	°	°	°	°	°	°	°	°	°	°	°	°	°	°
0	18.0	18.5	19.0	19.5	20.0	20.5	21.0	21.5	22.0	22.5	23.0	23.5	24.0	0
10	18.3	18.8	19.3	19.8	20.3	20.8	21.3	21.8	22.4	22.9	23.4	23.9	24.4	10
15	18.7	19.2	19.7	20.2	20.7	21.3	21.8	22.3	22.8	23.3	23.9	24.4	24.9	15
20	19.2	19.7	20.3	20.8	21.3	21.9	22.4	23.0	23.5	24.0	24.6	25.1	25.6	20
25	19.9	20.5	21.1	21.6	22.2	22.7	23.3	23.9	24.4	25.0	25.5	26.1	26.7	25
30	20.9	21.5	22.1	22.7	23.3	23.9	24.4	25.0	25.6	26.2	26.8	27.4	28.0	30
32	21.4	22.0	22.6	23.2	23.8	24.4	25.0	25.6	26.2	26.8	27.4	28.0	28.7	32
34	21.9	22.5	23.1	23.7	24.4	25.0	25.6	26.2	26.9	27.5	28.1	28.7	29.4	34
36	22.5	23.1	23.7	24.4	25.0	25.7	26.3	26.9	27.6	28.2	28.9	29.5	30.2	36
38	23.1	23.7	24.4	25.1	25.7	26.4	27.1	27.7	28.4	29.1	29.7	30.4	31.1	38
40	23.8	24.5	25.2	25.8	26.5	27.2	27.9	28.6	29.3	30.0	30.7	31.4	32.1	40
41	24.2	24.9	25.6	26.3	26.9	27.6	28.3	29.1	29.8	30.5	31.2	31.9	32.6	41
42	24.6	25.3	26.0	26.7	27.4	28.1	28.8	29.5	30.3	31.0	31.7	32.5	33.2	42
43	25.0	25.7	26.4	27.2	27.9	28.6	29.3	30.1	30.8	31.6	32.3	33.0	33.8	43
44	25.4	26.2	26.9	27.6	28.4	29.1	29.9	30.6	31.4	32.1	32.9	33.7	34.4	44
45	25.9	26.7	27.4	28.2	28.9	29.7	30.5	31.2	32.0	32.8	33.5	34.3	35.1	45
46	26.4	27.2	27.9	28.7	29.5	30.3	31.1	31.8	32.6	33.4	34.2	35.0	35.8	46
47	26.9	27.7	28.5	29.3	30.1	30.9	31.7	32.5	33.3	34.1	35.0	35.8	36.6	47
48	27.5	28.3	29.1	29.9	30.7	31.6	32.4	33.2	34.0	34.9	35.7	36.6	37.4	48
49	28.1	28.9	29.8	30.6	31.4	32.3	33.1	34.0	34.8	35.7	36.6	37.4	38.3	49
50	28.7	29.6	30.4	31.3	32.1	33.0	33.9	34.8	35.6	36.5	37.4	38.3	39.3	50
51	29.4	30.3	31.2	32.0	32.9	33.8	34.7	35.6	36.5	37.5	38.4	39.3	40.3	51
52	30.1	31.0	31.9	32.8	33.7	34.7	35.6	36.5	37.5	38.4	39.4	40.4	41.3	52
53	30.9	31.8	32.8	33.7	34.6	35.6	36.5	37.5	38.5	39.5	40.5	41.5	42.5	53
54	31.7	32.7	33.6	34.6	35.6	36.6	37.6	38.6	39.6	40.6	41.7	42.7	43.8	54
55	32.6	33.6	34.6	35.6	36.6	37.6	38.7	39.7	40.8	41.9	42.9	44.0	45.2	55
56	33.5	34.6	35.6	36.7	37.7	38.8	39.9	41.0	42.1	43.2	44.3	45.5	46.7	56
57	34.6	35.6	36.7	37.8	38.9	40.0	41.1	42.3	43.5	44.6	45.8	47.1	48.3	57
58	35.7	36.8	37.9	39.1	40.2	41.4	42.6	43.8	45.0	46.2	47.5	48.8	50.1	58
59	36.9	38.0	39.2	40.4	41.6	42.8	44.1	45.4	46.7	48.0	49.3	50.7	52.2	59
60.0	38.2	39.4	40.6	41.9	43.2	44.5	45.8	47.1	48.5	49.9	51.4	52.9	54.4	60.0
60.5	38.9	40.1	41.4	42.7	44.0	45.3	46.7	48.1	49.5	51.0	52.5	54.1	55.7	60.5
61.0	39.6	40.9	42.2	43.5	44.9	46.3	47.7	49.1	50.6	52.1	53.7	55.3	57.0	61.0
61.5	40.4	41.7	43.0	44.4	45.8	47.2	48.7	50.2	51.7	53.3	55.0	56.7	58.5	61.5
62.0	41.2	42.5	43.9	45.3	46.8	48.2	49.8	51.3	52.9	54.6	56.3	58.1	60.0	62.0
62.5	42.0	43.4	44.8	46.3	47.8	49.3	50.9	52.5	54.2	56.0	57.8	59.7	61.7	62.5
63.0	42.9	44.3	45.8	47.3	48.9	50.5	52.1	53.8	55.6	57.5	59.4	61.4	63.6	63.0
63.5	43.8	45.3	46.9	48.4	50.0	51.7	53.4	55.2	57.1	59.1	61.1	63.4	65.7	63.5
64.0	44.8	46.4	48.0	49.6	51.3	53.0	54.8	56.7	58.7	60.8	63.0	65.5	68.1	64.0
64.5	45.9	47.5	49.1	50.8	52.6	54.4	56.3	58.4	60.5	62.7	65.2	67.9	70.9	64.5
65.0	47.0	48.7	50.4	52.2	54.0	56.0	58.0	60.1	62.4	64.9	67.6	70.7	74.2	65.0
65.5	48.2	49.9	51.7	53.6	55.6	57.6	59.8	62.1	64.6	67.3	70.4	74.1	78.8	65.5
66.0	49.4	51.3	53.2	55.2	57.2	59.4	61.8	64.3	67.1	70.2	73.9	78.6	90.0	66.0
66.5	50.8	52.7	54.7	56.8	59.1	61.4	64.0	66.8	70.0	73.7	78.5	90.0		66.5
67.0	52.3	54.3	56.4	58.7	61.1	63.7	66.5	69.7	73.5	78.4	90.0			67.0
67.5	53.9	56.0	58.3	60.7	63.3	66.2	69.5	73.3	78.2	90.0				67.5
68.0	55.6	57.9	60.4	63.0	65.9	69.2	73.1	78.1	90.0					68.0
68.5	57.5	60.0	62.7	65.6	68.9	72.9	77.9	90.0						68.5
69.0	59.6	62.3	65.3	68.7	72.6	77.7	90.0							69.0
69.5	61.9	65.0	68.4	72.4	77.6	90.0								69.5
70.0	64.6	68.1	72.2	77.4	90.0									70.0
70.5	67.8	71.9	77.2	90.0										70.5
71.0	71.7	77.1	90.0											71.0
71.5	76.9	90.0												71.5
72.0	90.0													72.0

TABLE 23

Correction of Amplitude as Observed on the Visible Horizon

Latitude	Declination													Latitude
	0°	2°	4°	6°	8°	10°	12°	14°	16°	18°	20°	22°	24°	
°	°	°	°	°	°	°	°	°	°	°	°	°	°	°
0	0.0	0.0	0.0	0.0	0.0	0.0	0.0	0.0	0.0	0.0	0.0	0.0	0.0	0
10	0.1	0.1	0.1	0.1	0.1	0.1	0.1	0.1	0.1	0.1	0.1	0.1	0.1	10
15	0.2	0.2	0.2	0.2	0.2	0.2	0.2	0.2	0.2	0.2	0.2	0.2	0.2	15
20	0.3	0.3	0.3	0.3	0.3	0.3	0.3	0.3	0.3	0.3	0.3	0.3	0.3	20
25	0.3	0.3	0.3	0.3	0.3	0.4	0.3	0.3	0.3	0.3	0.3	0.3	0.3	25
30	0.4	0.4	0.4	0.4	0.5	0.4	0.4	0.4	0.4	0.4	0.4	0.5	0.5	30
32	0.4	0.4	0.4	0.4	0.5	0.4	0.4	0.4	0.4	0.4	0.5	0.5	0.5	32
34	0.5	0.5	0.5	0.5	0.5	0.5	0.5	0.5	0.5	0.5	0.5	0.5	0.5	34
36	0.5	0.5	0.5	0.5	0.5	0.5	0.5	0.5	0.6	0.5	0.6	0.6	0.6	36
38	0.6	0.6	0.6	0.6	0.6	0.6	0.6	0.6	0.6	0.6	0.6	0.6	0.6	38
40	0.6	0.6	0.6	0.6	0.6	0.6	0.6	0.6	0.6	0.6	0.7	0.7	0.7	40
42	0.6	0.6	0.6	0.6	0.7	0.7	0.7	0.7	0.7	0.7	0.7	0.7	0.7	42
44	0.7	0.7	0.7	0.6	0.6	0.7	0.7	0.7	0.8	0.8	0.8	0.8	0.9	44
46	0.7	0.7	0.7	0.7	0.7	0.8	0.8	0.8	0.8	0.8	0.8	0.9	0.9	46
48	0.8	0.8	0.8	0.8	0.8	0.8	0.8	0.8	0.9	0.9	1.0	1.0	1.0	48
50	0.8	0.8	0.8	0.8	0.9	0.9	0.9	0.9	0.9	1.0	1.0	1.1	1.0	50
51	0.8	0.8	0.8	0.8	0.9	0.9	0.9	0.9	0.9	1.0	1.1	1.1	1.1	51
52	0.9	0.9	0.9	0.9	0.9	0.9	1.0	1.0	1.0	1.1	1.1	1.1	1.3	52
53	0.9	0.9	0.9	0.9	0.9	0.9	1.0	1.0	1.0	1.1	1.2	1.2	1.3	53
54	1.0	1.0	1.0	1.0	1.0	1.0	1.1	1.1	1.1	1.2	1.2	1.3	1.3	54
55	1.0	1.0	1.0	1.0	1.1	1.1	1.0	1.2	1.2	1.2	1.3	1.3	1.4	55
56	1.0	1.0	1.0	1.0	1.1	1.1	1.2	1.2	1.2	1.3	1.3	1.4	1.5	56
57	1.1	1.1	1.1	1.1	1.1	1.1	1.2	1.2	1.3	1.3	1.4	1.5	1.7	57
58	1.1	1.1	1.1	1.1	1.2	1.2	1.2	1.2	1.4	1.4	1.5	1.6	1.8	58
59	1.2	1.2	1.2	1.2	1.2	1.2	1.3	1.3	1.3	1.4	1.6	1.7	1.9	59
60	1.2	1.2	1.2	1.2	1.2	1.3	1.3	1.4	1.4	1.5	1.7	1.9	2.2	60
61	1.3	1.3	1.3	1.3	1.3	1.3	1.4	1.5	1.6	1.7	1.8	2.0	2.4	61
62	1.3	1.3	1.3	1.3	1.4	1.4	1.5	1.6	1.6	1.7	1.9	2.3	2.6	62
63	1.3	1.4	1.4	1.4	1.4	1.5	1.5	1.6	1.7	1.9	2.1	2.5	3.3	63
64	1.4	1.4	1.4	1.5	1.5	1.6	1.7	1.7	1.8	2.1	2.3	2.9	4.3	64
65.0	1.5	1.5	1.5	1.6	1.6	1.6	1.7	1.9	2.0	2.2	2.7	3.5	7.2	65.0
65.5	1.5	1.5	1.5	1.6	1.6	1.7	1.8	1.9	2.1	2.3	2.8	3.9		65.5
66.0	1.6	1.6	1.6	1.6	1.7	1.7	1.9	2.0	2.1	2.5	3.1	4.4		66.0
66.5	1.6	1.6	1.6	1.7	1.7	1.8	1.9	2.1	2.3	2.6	3.3	5.4		66.5
67.0	1.7	1.7	1.7	1.7	1.7	1.8	2.0	2.1	2.3	2.8	3.6	7.5		67.0
67.5	1.7	1.7	1.7	1.7	1.8	1.9	2.0	2.2	2.5	2.9	4.1			67.5
68.0	1.7	1.8	1.8	1.8	1.9	2.0	2.1	2.3	2.6	3.2	4.7			68.0
68.5	1.8	1.8	1.8	1.8	2.0	2.0	2.2	2.4	2.8	3.5	5.7			68.5
69.0	1.8	1.9	1.9	1.9	1.9	2.1	2.2	2.5	2.9	3.8	7.9			69.0
69.5	1.9	1.9	1.9	1.9	2.1	2.2	2.4	2.6	3.2	4.3				69.5
70.0	1.9	1.9	1.9	2.0	2.1	2.3	2.5	2.8	3.4	5.0				70.0
70.5	2.0	2.0	2.0	2.2	2.2	2.4	2.6	3.0	3.6	6.0				70.5
71.0	2.0	2.0	2.1	2.2	2.3	2.5	2.7	3.1	4.1	8.3				71.0
71.5	2.1	2.1	2.2	2.3	2.4	2.5	2.9	3.3	4.6					71.5
72.0	2.2	2.2	2.3	2.3	2.4	2.6	3.0	3.6	5.3					72.0
72.5	2.2	2.2	2.3	2.4	2.5	2.7	3.2	3.9	6.4					72.5
73.0	2.3	2.3	2.4	2.5	2.7	2.9	3.4	4.4	8.9					73.0
73.5	2.4	2.4	2.5	2.6	2.8	3.0	3.6	4.9						73.5
74.0	2.4	2.4	2.5	2.7	2.9	3.3	3.8	5.6						74.0
74.5	2.5	2.6	2.7	2.8	3.0	3.4	4.2	6.8						74.5
75.0	2.6	2.7	2.8	2.9	3.2	3.7	4.7	9.3						75.0
75.5	2.7	2.8	2.8	3.0	3.3	3.9	5.3							75.5
76.0	2.8	2.8	2.9	3.2	3.5	4.2	5.6							76.0
76.5	2.9	3.0	3.1	3.3	3.7	4.5	7.3							76.5
77.0	3.0	3.1	3.2	3.5	4.0	5.1	10.2							77.0

For the **sun, a planet,** or a **star,** apply the correction to the observed amplitude in the direction **away** from the elevated pole. For the **moon** apply **half** the correction **toward** the elevated pole.

TABLE 24
Altitude Factor

a, the change of altitude in one minute from meridian transit.

Latitude	0°	1°	2°	3°	4°	5°	6°	7°	8°	9°	10°	11°	Latitude
	Declination **same** name to latitude, **upper** transit: **add** correction to observed altitude												
°	″	″	″	″	″	″	″	″	″	″	″	″	°
0					28.1	22.4	18.7	16.0	14.0	12.4	11.1	10.1	0
1						28.0	22.4	18.6	16.0	13.9	12.4	11.1	1
2							28.0	22.3	18.6	15.9	13.9	12.3	2
3								27.9	22.3	18.5	15.8	13.8	3
4	28.1								27.8	22.2	18.5	15.8	4
5	22.4	28.0								27.7	22.1	18.4	5
6	18.7	22.4	28.0								27.6	22.0	6
7	16.0	18.6	22.3	27.9								27.4	7
8	14.0	16.0	18.6	22.3	27.8								8
9	12.4	13.9	15.9	18.5	22.2	27.7							9
10	11.1	12.4	13.9	15.8	18.5	22.1	27.6						10
11	10.1	11.1	12.3	13.8	15.8	18.4	22.0	27.4					11
12	9.2	10.1	11.1	12.3	13.8	15.7	18.3	21.9	27.3				12
13	8.5	9.2	10.0	11.0	12.2	13.7	15.6	18.2	21.7	27.1			13
14	7.9	8.5	9.2	10.0	10.9	12.1	13.6	15.5	18.0	21.6	26.9		14
15	7.3	7.8	8.4	9.1	9.9	10.9	12.1	13.5	15.4	17.9	21.4	26.7	15
16	6.8	7.3	7.8	8.4	9.1	9.8	10.8	12.0	13.4	15.3	17.8	21.3	16
17	6.4	6.8	7.2	7.8	8.3	9.0	9.8	10.7	11.9	13.3	15.2	17.6	17
18	6.0	6.4	6.8	7.2	7.7	8.3	8.9	9.7	10.6	11.8	13.2	15.0	18
19	5.7	6.0	6.3	6.7	7.2	7.6	8.2	8.9	9.6	10.6	11.7	13.1	19
20	5.4	5.7	6.0	6.3	6.7	7.1	7.6	8.1	8.8	9.5	10.5	11.6	20
21	5.1	5.4	5.6	5.9	6.3	6.6	7.0	7.5	8.1	8.7	9.5	10.4	21
22	4.9	5.1	5.3	5.6	5.9	6.2	6.6	7.0	7.5	8.0	8.6	9.4	22
23	4.6	4.8	5.0	5.3	5.5	5.8	6.1	6.5	6.9	7.4	7.9	8.5	23
24	4.4	4.6	4.8	5.0	5.2	5.5	5.8	6.1	6.4	6.8	7.3	7.8	24
25	4.2	4.4	4.6	4.7	5.0	5.2	5.4	5.7	6.0	6.4	6.8	7.2	25
26	4.0	4.2	4.3	4.5	4.7	4.9	5.1	5.4	5.7	6.0	6.3	6.7	26
27	3.9	4.0	4.1	4.3	4.5	4.7	4.9	5.1	5.3	5.6	5.9	6.2	27
28	3.7	3.8	4.0	4.1	4.3	4.4	4.6	4.8	5.0	5.3	5.5	5.8	28
29	3.5	3.7	3.8	3.9	4.1	4.2	4.4	4.6	4.7	5.0	5.2	5.5	29
30	3.4	3.5	3.6	3.7	3.9	4.0	4.2	4.3	4.5	4.7	4.9	5.1	30
31	3.3	3.4	3.5	3.6	3.7	3.8	4.0	4.1	4.3	4.4	4.6	4.8	31
32	3.1	3.2	3.3	3.4	3.5	3.7	3.8	3.9	4.1	4.2	4.4	4.6	32
33	3.0	3.1	3.2	3.3	3.4	3.5	3.6	3.7	3.9	4.0	4.2	4.3	33
34	2.9	3.0	3.1	3.2	3.2	3.3	3.4	3.6	3.7	3.8	3.9	4.1	34
35	2.8	2.9	3.0	3.0	3.1	3.2	3.3	3.4	3.5	3.6	3.7	3.9	35
36	2.7	2.8	2.8	2.9	3.0	3.1	3.2	3.3	3.4	3.5	3.6	3.7	36
37	2.6	2.7	2.7	2.8	2.9	2.9	3.0	3.1	3.2	3.3	3.4	3.5	37
38	2.5	2.6	2.6	2.7	2.8	2.8	2.9	3.0	3.0	3.2	3.2	3.3	38
39	2.4	2.5	2.5	2.6	2.7	2.7	2.8	2.9	2.9	3.0	3.1	3.2	39
40	2.3	2.4	2.4	2.5	2.6	2.6	2.7	2.7	2.8	2.9	3.0	3.0	40
41	2.3	2.3	2.4	2.4	2.5	2.5	2.6	2.6	2.7	2.8	2.8	2.9	41
42	2.2	2.2	2.3	2.3	2.4	2.4	2.5	2.5	2.6	2.6	2.7	2.8	42
43	2.1	2.1	2.2	2.2	2.3	2.3	2.4	2.4	2.5	2.5	2.6	2.7	43
44	2.0	2.1	2.1	2.1	2.2	2.2	2.3	2.3	2.4	2.4	2.5	2.5	44
45	2.0	2.0	2.0	2.1	2.1	2.2	2.2	2.2	2.3	2.3	2.4	2.4	45
46	1.9	1.9	2.0	2.0	2.0	2.1	2.1	2.2	2.2	2.2	2.3	2.3	46
47	1.8	1.9	1.9	1.9	2.0	2.0	2.0	2.1	2.1	2.1	2.2	2.2	47
48	1.8	1.8	1.8	1.9	1.9	1.9	2.0	2.0	2.0	2.1	2.1	2.1	48
49	1.7	1.7	1.8	1.8	1.8	1.8	1.9	1.9	1.9	2.0	2.0	2.1	49
50	1.6	1.7	1.7	1.7	1.8	1.8	1.8	1.8	1.9	1.9	1.9	2.0	50
51	1.6	1.6	1.6	1.7	1.7	1.7	1.7	1.8	1.8	1.8	1.9	1.9	51
52	1.5	1.6	1.6	1.6	1.6	1.6	1.7	1.7	1.7	1.8	1.8	1.8	52
53	1.5	1.5	1.5	1.5	1.6	1.6	1.6	1.6	1.7	1.7	1.7	1.7	53
54	1.4	1.4	1.5	1.5	1.5	1.5	1.5	1.6	1.6	1.6	1.6	1.7	54
55	1.4	1.4	1.4	1.4	1.5	1.5	1.5	1.5	1.5	1.6	1.6	1.6	55
56	1.3	1.3	1.4	1.4	1.4	1.4	1.4	1.4	1.5	1.5	1.5	1.5	56
57	1.3	1.3	1.3	1.3	1.3	1.4	1.4	1.4	1.4	1.4	1.4	1.5	57
58	1.2	1.2	1.3	1.3	1.3	1.3	1.3	1.3	1.3	1.4	1.4	1.4	58
59	1.2	1.2	1.2	1.2	1.2	1.3	1.3	1.3	1.3	1.3	1.3	1.3	59
60	1.1	1.1	1.2	1.2	1.2	1.2	1.2	1.2	1.2	1.2	1.3	1.3	60
Latitude	0°	1°	2°	3°	4°	5°	6°	7°	8°	9°	10°	11°	Latitude
	Declination **same** name to latitude, **upper** transit: **add** correction to observed altitude												

TABLE 24
Altitude Factor

a, the change of altitude in one minute from meridian transit.

Latitude	0°	1°	2°	3°	4°	5°	6°	7°	8°	9°	10°	11°	Latitude
	Declination **contrary** name to latitude, **upper** transit: **add** correction to observed altitude												
°	″	″	″	″	″	″	″	″	″	″	″	″	°
0					28.1	22.4	18.7	16.0	14.0	12.4	11.1	10.1	0
1				28.1	22.4	18.7	16.0	14.0	12.4	11.2	10.1	9.3	1
2			28.1	22.4	18.7	16.0	14.0	12.5	11.2	10.2	9.3	8.6	2
3		28.1	22.4	18.7	16.0	14.0	12.5	11.2	10.2	9.3	8.6	8.0	3
4	28.1	22.4	18.7	16.0	14.0	12.5	11.2	10.2	9.3	8.6	8.0	7.4	4
5	22.4	18.7	16.0	14.0	12.5	11.2	10.2	9.3	8.6	8.0	7.4	7.0	5
6	18.7	16.0	14.0	12.5	11.2	10.2	9.3	8.6	8.0	7.5	7.0	6.6	6
7	16.0	14.0	12.4	11.2	10.2	9.3	8.6	8.0	7.5	7.0	6.6	6.2	7
8	14.0	12.4	11.2	10.2	9.3	8.6	8.0	7.5	7.0	6.6	6.2	5.9	8
9	12.4	11.2	10.2	9.3	8.6	8.0	7.5	7.0	6.6	6.2	5.9	5.6	9
10	11.1	10.1	9.3	8.6	8.0	7.4	7.0	6.6	6.2	5.9	5.6	5.3	10
11	10.1	9.3	8.6	8.0	7.4	7.0	6.6	6.2	5.9	5.6	5.3	5.1	11
12	9.2	8.5	7.9	7.4	7.0	6.5	6.2	5.9	5.6	5.3	5.0	4.8	12
13	8.5	7.9	7.4	6.9	6.5	6.2	5.8	5.6	5.3	5.0	4.8	4.6	13
14	7.9	7.4	6.9	6.5	6.2	5.8	5.5	5.3	5.0	4.8	4.6	4.4	14
15	7.3	6.9	6.5	6.1	5.8	5.5	5.3	5.0	4.8	4.6	4.4	4.2	15
16	6.8	6.5	6.1	5.8	5.5	5.2	5.0	4.8	4.6	4.4	4.2	4.1	16
17	6.4	6.1	5.8	5.5	5.2	5.0	4.8	4.6	4.4	4.2	4.1	3.9	17
18	6.0	5.7	5.5	5.2	5.0	4.8	4.6	4.4	4.2	4.1	3.9	3.8	18
19	5.7	5.4	5.2	4.9	4.7	4.5	4.4	4.2	4.0	3.9	3.8	3.6	19
20	5.4	5.1	4.9	4.7	4.5	4.3	4.2	4.0	3.9	3.8	3.6	3.5	20
21	5.1	4.9	4.7	4.5	4.3	4.2	4.0	3.9	3.7	3.6	3.5	3.4	21
22	4.9	4.7	4.5	4.3	4.1	4.0	3.9	3.7	3.6	3.5	3.4	3.3	22
23	4.6	4.4	4.3	4.1	4.0	3.8	3.7	3.6	3.5	3.4	3.3	3.2	23
24	4.4	4.2	4.1	3.9	3.8	3.7	3.6	3.5	3.4	3.3	3.2	3.1	24
25	4.2	4.1	3.9	3.8	3.7	3.5	3.4	3.3	3.2	3.1	3.1	3.0	25
26	4.0	3.9	3.8	3.6	3.5	3.4	3.3	3.2	3.1	3.0	3.0	2.9	26
27	3.9	3.7	3.6	3.5	3.4	3.3	3.2	3.1	3.0	2.9	2.9	2.8	27
28	3.7	3.6	3.5	3.4	3.3	3.2	3.1	3.0	2.9	2.8	2.8	2.7	28
29	3.5	3.4	3.3	3.2	3.1	3.1	3.0	2.9	2.8	2.8	2.7	2.6	29
30	3.4	3.3	3.2	3.1	3.0	3.0	2.9	2.8	2.7	2.7	2.6	2.5	30
31	3.3	3.2	3.1	3.0	2.9	2.9	2.8	2.7	2.6	2.6	2.5	2.5	31
32	3.2	3.1	3.0	2.9	2.8	2.8	2.7	2.6	2.6	2.5	2.5	2.4	32
33	3.0	2.9	2.9	2.8	2.7	2.7	2.6	2.5	2.5	2.4	2.4	2.3	33
34	2.9	2.8	2.8	2.7	2.6	2.6	2.5	2.5	2.4	2.4	2.3	2.3	34
35	2.8	2.7	2.7	2.6	2.5	2.5	2.4	2.4	2.3	2.3	2.2	2.2	35
36	2.7	2.6	2.6	2.5	2.5	2.4	2.4	2.3	2.3	2.2	2.2	2.1	36
37	2.6	2.5	2.5	2.4	2.4	2.3	2.3	2.2	2.2	2.2	2.1	2.1	37
38	2.5	2.5	2.4	2.4	2.3	2.3	2.2	2.2	2.1	2.1	2.1	2.0	38
39	2.4	2.4	2.3	2.3	2.2	2.2	2.1	2.1	2.1	2.0	2.0	2.0	39
40	2.3	2.3	2.2	2.2	2.2	2.1	2.1	2.0	2.0	2.0	1.9	1.9	40
41	2.3	2.2	2.2	2.1	2.1	2.1	2.0	2.0	1.9	1.9	1.9	1.8	41
42	2.2	2.1	2.1	2.1	2.0	2.0	2.0	1.9	1.9	1.9	1.8	1.8	42
43	2.1	2.1	2.0	2.0	2.0	1.9	1.9	1.9	1.8	1.8	1.8	1.7	43
44	2.0	2.0	2.0	1.9	1.9	1.9	1.8	1.8	1.8	1.7	1.7	1.7	44
45	2.0	1.9	1.9	1.9	1.8	1.8	1.8	1.7	1.7	1.7	1.7	1.6	45
46	1.9	1.9	1.8	1.8	1.8	1.7	1.7	1.7	1.7	1.6	1.6	1.6	46
47	1.8	1.8	1.8	1.7	1.7	1.7	1.7	1.6	1.6	1.6	1.6	1.6	47
48	1.8	1.7	1.7	1.7	1.7	1.6	1.6	1.6	1.6	1.6	1.5	1.5	48
49	1.7	1.7	1.7	1.6	1.6	1.6	1.6	1.5	1.5	1.5	1.5	1.5	49
50	1.6	1.6	1.6	1.6	1.6	1.5	1.5	1.5	1.5	1.5	1.4	1.4	50
51	1.6	1.6	1.6	1.5	1.5	1.5	1.5	1.5	1.4	1.4	1.4	1.4	51
52	1.5	1.5	1.5	1.5	1.5	1.4	1.4	1.4	1.4	1.4	1.4	1.3	52
53	1.5	1.5	1.4	1.4	1.4	1.4	1.4	1.4	1.3	1.3	1.3	1.3	53
54	1.4	1.4	1.4	1.4	1.4	1.3	1.3	1.3	1.3	1.3	1.3	1.3	54
55	1.4	1.4	1.3	1.3	1.3	1.3	1.3	1.3	1.3	1.2	1.2	1.2	55
56	1.3	1.3	1.3	1.3	1.3	1.3	1.2	1.2	1.2	1.2	1.2	1.2	56
57	1.3	1.3	1.3	1.2	1.2	1.2	1.2	1.2	1.2	1.2	1.1	1.1	57
58	1.2	1.2	1.2	1.2	1.2	1.2	1.2	1.1	1.1	1.1	1.1	1.1	58
59	1.2	1.2	1.2	1.2	1.1	1.1	1.1	1.1	1.1	1.1	1.1	1.1	59
60	1.1	1.1	1.1	1.1	1.1	1.1	1.1	1.1	1.0	1.0	1.0	1.0	60
Latitude	0°	1°	2°	3°	4°	5°	6°	7°	8°	9°	10°	11°	Latitude
	Declination **contrary** name to latitude, **upper** transit: **add** correction to observed altitude												

TABLE 24

Altitude Factor

a, the change of altitude in one minute from meridian transit.

Lati- tude	12°	13°	14°	15°	16°	17°	18°	19°	20°	21°	22°	23°	24°	Lati- tude
	Declination **same** name as latitude, **upper** transit: **add** correction to observed altitude													
°	″	″	″	″	″	″	″	″	″	″	″	″	″	°
0	9.2	8.5	7.9	7.3	6.8	6.4	6.0	5.7	5.4	5.1	4.9	4.6	4.4	0
1	10.1	9.2	8.5	7.8	7.3	6.8	6.4	6.0	5.7	5.4	5.1	4.8	4.6	1
2	11.1	10.0	9.2	8.4	7.8	7.2	6.8	6.3	6.0	5.6	5.3	5.0	4.8	2
3	12.3	11.0	10.0	9.1	8.4	7.8	7.2	6.7	6.3	5.9	5.6	5.3	5.0	3
4	13.8	12.2	10.9	9.9	9.1	8.3	7.7	7.2	6.7	6.3	5.9	5.5	5.2	4
5	15.7	13.7	12.1	10.9	9.8	9.0	8.3	7.6	7.1	6.6	6.2	5.8	5.5	5
6	18.3	15.6	13.6	12.1	10.8	9.8	8.9	8.2	7.6	7.0	6.6	6.1	5.8	6
7	21.9	18.2	15.5	13.5	12.0	10.7	9.7	8.9	8.1	7.5	7.0	6.5	6.1	7
8	27.3	21.7	18.0	15.4	13.4	11.9	10.6	9.6	8.8	8.1	7.5	6.9	6.4	8
9		27.1	21.6	17.9	15.3	13.3	11.8	10.6	9.5	8.7	8.0	7.4	6.8	9
10			26.9	21.4	17.8	15.2	13.2	11.7	10.5	9.5	8.6	7.9	7.3	10
11				26.7	21.3	17.6	15.0	13.1	11.6	10.4	9.4	8.5	7.8	11
12					26.5	21.1	17.5	14.9	13.0	11.5	10.3	9.3	8.4	12
13						26.2	20.9	17.3	14.8	12.8	11.3	10.1	9.2	13
14							26.0	20.7	17.1	14.6	12.7	11.2	10.0	14
15								25.7	20.4	16.9	14.4	12.5	11.1	15
16	26.5								25.4	20.2	16.7	14.3	12.4	16
17	21.1	26.2								25.1	20.0	16.5	14.1	17
18	17.5	20.9	26.0								24.8	19.7	16.3	18
19	14.9	17.3	20.7	25.7								24.5	19.5	19
20	13.0	14.8	17.1	20.4	25.4								24.2	20
21	11.5	12.8	14.6	16.9	20.2	25.1								21
22	10.3	11.3	12.7	14.4	16.7	20.0	24.8							22
23	9.3	10.1	11.2	12.5	14.3	16.5	19.7	24.5						23
24	8.4	9.2	10.0	11.1	12.4	14.1	16.3	19.5	24.2					24
25	7.7	8.3	9.0	9.9	10.9	12.2	13.9	16.1	19.2	23.8				25
26	7.1	7.6	8.2	8.9	9.8	10.8	12.1	13.7	15.9	18.9	23.5			26
27	6.6	7.0	7.5	8.1	8.8	9.6	10.6	11.9	13.5	15.6	18.6	23.1		27
28	6.2	6.5	7.0	7.4	8.0	8.7	9.5	10.5	11.7	13.3	15.4	18.3	22.7	28
29	5.7	6.1	6.4	6.9	7.3	7.9	8.6	9.4	10.3	11.5	13.1	15.1	18.0	29
30	5.4	5.7	6.0	6.4	6.8	7.2	7.8	8.4	9.2	10.1	11.3	12.8	14.9	30
31	5.1	5.3	5.6	5.9	6.3	6.7	7.1	7.7	8.3	9.0	10.0	11.1	12.6	31
32	4.8	5.0	5.2	5.5	5.8	6.2	6.5	7.0	7.5	8.1	8.9	9.8	10.9	32
33	4.5	4.7	4.9	5.1	5.4	5.7	6.1	6.4	6.9	7.4	8.0	8.7	9.6	33
34	4.3	4.4	4.6	4.8	5.1	5.3	5.6	5.9	6.3	6.8	7.3	7.8	8.6	34
35	4.0	4.2	4.4	4.5	4.7	5.0	5.2	5.5	5.8	6.2	6.6	7.1	7.7	35
36	3.8	4.0	4.1	4.3	4.5	4.7	4.9	5.1	5.4	5.7	6.1	6.5	7.0	36
37	3.6	3.8	3.9	4.0	4.2	4.4	4.6	4.8	5.0	5.3	5.6	6.0	6.4	37
38	3.4	3.6	3.7	3.8	4.0	4.1	4.3	4.5	4.7	4.9	5.2	5.5	5.8	38
39	3.3	3.4	3.5	3.6	3.8	3.9	4.0	4.2	4.4	4.6	4.8	5.1	5.4	39
40	3.1	3.2	3.3	3.4	3.6	3.7	3.8	4.0	4.1	4.3	4.5	4.7	5.0	40
41	3.0	3.1	3.2	3.3	3.4	3.5	3.6	3.7	3.9	4.0	4.2	4.4	4.6	41
42	2.9	2.9	3.0	3.1	3.2	3.3	3.4	3.5	3.7	3.8	4.0	4.1	4.3	42
43	2.7	2.8	2.9	3.0	3.0	3.1	3.2	3.3	3.5	3.6	3.7	3.9	4.0	43
44	2.6	2.7	2.7	2.8	2.9	3.0	3.1	3.2	3.3	3.4	3.5	3.6	3.8	44
45	2.5	2.6	2.6	2.7	2.8	2.8	2.9	3.0	3.1	3.2	3.3	3.4	3.5	45
46	2.4	2.4	2.5	2.6	2.6	2.7	2.8	2.8	2.9	3.0	3.1	3.2	3.3	46
47	2.3	2.3	2.4	2.4	2.5	2.6	2.6	2.7	2.8	2.9	2.9	3.0	3.1	47
48	2.2	2.2	2.3	2.3	2.4	2.4	2.5	2.6	2.6	2.7	2.8	2.9	3.0	48
49	2.1	2.1	2.2	2.2	2.3	2.3	2.4	2.4	2.5	2.6	2.6	2.7	2.8	49
50	2.0	2.0	2.1	2.1	2.2	2.2	2.3	2.3	2.4	2.4	2.5	2.6	2.6	50
51	1.9	2.0	2.0	2.0	2.1	2.1	2.2	2.2	2.3	2.3	2.4	2.4	2.5	51
52	1.8	1.9	1.9	1.9	2.0	2.0	2.1	2.1	2.1	2.2	2.2	2.3	2.4	52
53	1.8	1.8	1.8	1.9	1.9	1.9	2.0	2.0	2.0	2.1	2.1	2.2	2.2	53
54	1.7	1.7	1.7	1.8	1.8	1.8	1.9	1.9	1.9	2.0	2.0	2.1	2.1	54
55	1.6	1.6	1.7	1.7	1.7	1.8	1.8	1.8	1.9	1.9	1.9	2.0	2.0	55
56	1.5	1.6	1.6	1.6	1.6	1.7	1.7	1.7	1.8	1.8	1.8	1.9	1.9	56
57	1.5	1.5	1.5	1.5	1.6	1.6	1.6	1.6	1.7	1.7	1.7	1.8	1.8	57
58	1.4	1.4	1.5	1.5	1.5	1.5	1.5	1.6	1.6	1.6	1.6	1.7	1.7	58
59	1.4	1.4	1.4	1.4	1.4	1.5	1.5	1.5	1.5	1.5	1.6	1.6	1.6	59
60	1.3	1.3	1.3	1.3	1.4	1.4	1.4	1.4	1.4	1.5	1.5	1.5	1.5	60
Lati- tude	12°	13°	14°	15°	16°	17°	18°	19°	20°	21°	22°	23°	24°	Lati- tude
	Declination **same** name as latitude, **upper** transit: **add** correction to observed altitude													

TABLE 24

Altitude Factor

a, the change of altitude in one minute from meridian transit.

Lati- tude	12°	13°	14°	15°	16°	17°	18°	19°	20°	21°	22°	23°	24°	Lati- tude
	Declination **contrary** name to latitude, **upper** transit: **add** correction to observed altitude													
°	″	″	″	″	″	″	″	″	″	″	″	″	″	°
0	9.2	8.5	7.9	7.3	6.8	6.4	6.0	5.7	5.4	5.1	4.9	4.6	4.4	0
1	8.5	7.9	7.4	6.9	6.5	6.1	5.7	5.4	5.1	4.9	4.7	4.4	4.2	1
2	7.9	7.4	6.9	6.5	6.1	5.8	5.5	5.2	4.9	4.7	4.5	4.3	4.1	2
3	7.4	6.9	6.5	6.1	5.8	5.5	5.2	4.9	4.7	4.5	4.3	4.1	3.9	3
4	7.0	6.5	6.2	5.8	5.5	5.2	5.0	4.7	4.5	4.3	4.1	4.0	3.8	4
5	6.5	6.2	5.8	5.5	5.2	5.0	4.8	4.5	4.3	4.2	4.0	3.8	3.7	5
6	6.2	5.8	5.5	5.3	5.0	4.8	4.6	4.4	4.2	4.0	3.9	3.7	3.6	6
7	5.9	5.6	5.3	5.0	4.8	4.6	4.4	4.2	4.0	3.9	3.7	3.6	3.5	7
8	5.6	5.3	5.0	4.8	4.6	4.4	4.2	4.0	3.9	3.7	3.6	3.5	3.4	8
9	5.3	5.0	4.8	4.6	4.4	4.2	4.1	3.9	3.8	3.6	3.5	3.4	3.3	9
10	5.0	4.8	4.6	4.4	4.2	4.1	3.9	3.8	3.6	3.5	3.4	3.3	3.2	10
11	4.8	4.6	4.4	4.2	4.1	3.9	3.8	3.6	3.5	3.4	3.3	3.2	3.1	11
12	4.6	4.4	4.3	4.1	3.9	3.8	3.7	3.5	3.4	3.3	3.2	3.1	3.0	12
13	4.4	4.3	4.1	3.9	3.8	3.7	3.5	3.4	3.3	3.2	3.1	3.0	2.9	13
14	4.2	4.1	3.9	3.8	3.7	3.5	3.4	3.3	3.2	3.1	3.0	2.9	2.8	14
15	4.1	3.9	3.8	3.7	3.5	3.4	3.3	3.2	3.1	3.0	2.9	2.8	2.8	15
16	3.9	3.8	3.7	3.5	3.4	3.3	3.2	3.1	3.0	2.9	2.8	2.8	2.7	16
17	3.8	3.7	3.5	3.4	3.3	3.2	3.1	3.0	2.9	2.8	2.8	2.7	2.6	17
18	3.7	3.5	3.4	3.3	3.2	3.1	3.0	2.9	2.9	2.8	2.7	2.6	2.5	18
19	3.5	3.4	3.3	3.2	3.1	3.0	2.9	2.9	2.8	2.7	2.6	2.6	2.5	19
20	3.4	3.3	3.2	3.1	3.0	2.9	2.9	2.8	2.7	2.6	2.6	2.5	2.4	20
21	3.3	3.2	3.1	3.0	2.9	2.8	2.8	2.7	2.6	2.6	2.5	2.4	2.4	21
22	3.2	3.1	3.0	2.9	2.8	2.8	2.7	2.6	2.6	2.5	2.4	2.4	2.3	22
23	3.1	3.0	2.9	2.8	2.8	2.7	2.6	2.6	2.5	2.4	2.4	2.3	2.3	23
24	3.0	2.9	2.8	2.8	2.7	2.6	2.5	2.5	2.4	2.4	2.3	2.3	2.2	24
25	2.9	2.8	2.7	2.7	2.6	2.5	2.5	2.4	2.4	2.3	2.3	2.2	2.2	25
26	2.8	2.7	2.7	2.6	2.5	2.5	2.4	2.4	2.3	2.3	2.2	2.1	2.1	26
27	2.7	2.7	2.6	2.5	2.5	2.4	2.4	2.3	2.2	2.2	2.1	2.1	2.1	27
28	2.6	2.6	2.5	2.5	2.4	2.3	2.3	2.2	2.2	2.1	2.1	2.1	2.0	28
29	2.6	2.5	2.4	2.4	2.3	2.3	2.2	2.2	2.1	2.1	2.0	2.0	2.0	29
30	2.5	2.4	2.4	2.3	2.3	2.2	2.2	2.1	2.1	2.0	2.0	2.0	1.9	30
31	2.4	2.4	2.3	2.3	2.2	2.2	2.1	2.1	2.0	2.0	2.0	1.9	1.9	31
32	2.3	2.3	2.2	2.2	2.2	2.1	2.1	2.0	2.0	1.9	1.9	1.9	1.8	32
33	2.3	2.2	2.2	2.1	2.1	2.1	2.0	2.0	1.9	1.9	1.9	1.8	1.8	33
34	2.2	2.2	2.1	2.1	2.0	2.0	2.0	1.9	1.9	1.9	1.8	1.8	1.8	34
35	2.2	2.1	2.1	2.0	2.0	2.0	1.9	1.9	1.8	1.8	1.8	1.7	1.7	35
36	2.1	2.1	2.0	2.0	1.9	1.9	1.9	1.8	1.8	1.8	1.7	1.7	1.7	36
37	2.0	2.0	2.0	1.9	1.9	1.9	1.8	1.8	1.8	1.7	1.7	1.7	1.6	37
38	2.0	1.9	1.9	1.9	1.8	1.8	1.8	1.7	1.7	1.7	1.7	1.6	1.6	38
39	1.9	1.9	1.9	1.8	1.8	1.8	1.7	1.7	1.7	1.6	1.6	1.6	1.6	39
40	1.9	1.8	1.8	1.8	1.7	1.7	1.7	1.7	1.6	1.6	1.6	1.6	1.5	40
41	1.8	1.8	1.8	1.7	1.7	1.7	1.6	1.6	1.6	1.6	1.5	1.5	1.5	41
42	1.8	1.7	1.7	1.7	1.7	1.6	1.6	1.6	1.6	1.5	1.5	1.5	1.5	42
43	1.7	1.7	1.7	1.6	1.6	1.6	1.6	1.5	1.5	1.5	1.5	1.4	1.4	43
44	1.7	1.6	1.6	1.6	1.6	1.5	1.5	1.5	1.5	1.5	1.4	1.4	1.4	44
45	1.6	1.6	1.6	1.5	1.5	1.5	1.5	1.5	1.4	1.4	1.4	1.4	1.4	45
46	1.6	1.6	1.5	1.5	1.5	1.5	1.4	1.4	1.4	1.4	1.4	1.3	1.3	46
47	1.5	1.5	1.5	1.5	1.4	1.4	1.4	1.4	1.4	1.3	1.3	1.3	1.3	47
48	1.5	1.5	1.4	1.4	1.4	1.4	1.4	1.3	1.3	1.3	1.3	1.3	1.3	48
49	1.4	1.4	1.4	1.4	1.4	1.3	1.3	1.3	1.3	1.3	1.3	1.2	1.2	49
50	1.4	1.4	1.4	1.3	1.3	1.3	1.3	1.3	1.3	1.3	1.2	1.2	1.2	50
51	1.4	1.3	1.3	1.3	1.3	1.3	1.3	1.2	1.2	1.2	1.2	1.2	1.2	51
52	1.3	1.3	1.3	1.3	1.3	1.3	1.2	1.2	1.2	1.2	1.2	1.1	1.1	52
53	1.3	1.3	1.3	1.2	1.2	1.2	1.2	1.2	1.2	1.2	1.1	1.1	1.1	53
54	1.2	1.2	1.2	1.2	1.2	1.2	1.2	1.1	1.1	1.1	1.1	1.1	1.1	54
55	1.2	1.2	1.2	1.2	1.1	1.1	1.1	1.1	1.1	1.1	1.1	1.1	1.1	55
56	1.2	1.1	1.1	1.1	1.1	1.1	1.1	1.1	1.1	1.1	1.0	1.0	1.0	56
57	1.1	1.1	1.1	1.1	1.1	1.1	1.1	1.0	1.0	1.0	1.0	1.0	1.0	57
58	1.1	1.1	1.1	1.1	1.0	1.0	1.0	1.0	1.0	1.0	1.0	1.0	1.0	58
59	1.0	1.0	1.0	1.0	1.0	1.0	1.0	1.0	1.0	1.0	1.0	0.9	0.9	59
60	1.0	1.0	1.0	1.0	1.0	1.0	1.0	0.9	0.9	0.9	0.9	0.9	0.9	60
Lati- tude	12°	13°	14°	15°	16°	17°	18°	19°	20°	21°	22°	23°	24°	Lati- tude
	Declination **contrary** name to latitude, **upper** transit: **add** correction to observed altitude													

TABLE 24
Altitude Factor

a, the change of altitude in one minute from meridian transit.

Latitude	25°	26°	27°	28°	29°	30°	31°	32°	33°	34°	35°	36°	37°	Latitude
	Declination **same** name as latitude, **upper** transit: **add** correction to observed altitude													
°	″	″	″	″	″	″	″	″	″	″	″	″	″	°
0	4.2	4.0	3.9	3.7	3.5	3.4	3.3	3.1	3.0	2.9	2.8	2.7	2.6	0
1	4.4	4.2	4.0	3.8	3.7	3.5	3.4	3.2	3.1	3.0	2.9	2.8	2.7	1
2	4.6	4.3	4.1	4.0	3.8	3.6	3.5	3.3	3.2	3.1	3.0	2.8	2.7	2
3	4.7	4.5	4.3	4.1	3.9	3.7	3.6	3.4	3.3	3.2	3.0	2.9	2.8	3
4	5.0	4.7	4.5	4.3	4.1	3.9	3.7	3.5	3.4	3.2	3.1	3.0	2.9	4
5	5.2	4.9	4.7	4.4	4.2	4.0	3.8	3.7	3.5	3.3	3.2	3.1	3.0	5
6	5.4	5.1	4.9	4.6	4.4	4.2	4.0	3.8	3.6	3.5	3.3	3.2	3.0	6
7	5.7	5.4	5.1	4.8	4.6	4.3	4.1	3.9	3.7	3.6	3.4	3.3	3.1	7
8	6.0	5.7	5.3	5.0	4.8	4.5	4.3	4.1	3.9	3.7	3.5	3.4	3.2	8
9	6.4	6.0	5.6	5.3	5.0	4.7	4.4	4.2	4.0	3.8	3.6	3.5	3.3	9
10	6.8	6.3	5.9	5.5	5.2	4.9	4.6	4.4	4.2	3.9	3.7	3.6	3.4	10
11	7.2	6.7	6.2	5.8	5.5	5.1	4.8	4.6	4.3	4.1	3.9	3.7	3.5	11
12	7.7	7.1	6.6	6.2	5.8	5.4	5.1	4.8	4.5	4.3	4.0	3.8	3.6	12
13	8.3	7.6	7.1	6.5	6.1	5.7	5.3	5.0	4.7	4.4	4.2	4.0	3.8	13
14	9.1	8.2	7.6	7.0	6.4	6.0	5.6	5.2	4.9	4.6	4.4	4.1	3.9	14
15	9.9	8.9	8.1	7.4	6.9	6.4	5.9	5.5	5.2	4.8	4.5	4.3	4.0	15
16	10.9	9.8	8.8	8.0	7.3	6.8	6.3	5.8	5.4	5.1	4.8	4.5	4.2	16
17	12.2	10.8	9.6	8.7	7.9	7.2	6.7	6.2	5.7	5.3	5.0	4.7	4.4	17
18	13.9	12.1	10.6	9.5	8.6	7.8	7.1	6.6	6.1	5.6	5.2	4.9	4.6	18
19	16.1	13.7	11.9	10.5	9.4	8.4	7.7	7.0	6.4	6.0	5.5	5.1	4.8	19
20	19.2	15.9	13.5	11.7	10.3	9.2	8.3	7.5	6.9	6.3	5.8	5.4	5.0	20
21	23.8	18.9	15.6	13.3	11.5	10.1	9.1	8.2	7.4	6.8	6.2	5.7	5.3	21
22		23.5	18.6	15.4	13.1	11.3	10.0	8.9	8.0	7.3	6.6	6.1	5.6	22
23			23.1	18.3	15.1	12.8	11.1	9.8	8.7	7.9	7.1	6.5	6.0	23
24				22.7	18.0	14.9	12.6	10.9	9.6	8.6	7.7	7.0	6.4	24
25					22.3	17.7	14.6	12.4	10.7	9.4	8.4	7.5	6.8	25
26						21.9	17.4	14.3	12.1	10.5	9.2	8.2	7.4	26
27							21.5	17.0	14.0	11.9	10.3	9.1	8.1	27
28								21.1	16.7	13.8	11.7	10.1	8.9	28
29	22.3								20.6	16.3	13.5	11.4	9.9	29
30	17.7	21.9								20.2	16.0	13.2	11.1	30
31	14.6	17.4	21.5								19.8	15.6	12.9	31
32	12.4	14.3	17.0	21.1								19.3	15.3	32
33	10.7	12.1	14.0	16.7	20.6								18.9	33
34	9.4	10.5	11.9	13.8	16.3	20.2								34
35	8.4	9.2	10.3	11.7	13.5	16.0	19.8							35
36	7.5	8.2	9.1	10.1	11.4	13.2	15.6	19.3						36
37	6.8	7.4	8.1	8.9	9.9	11.1	12.9	15.3	18.9					37
38	6.2	6.7	7.2	7.9	8.7	9.6	10.9	12.6	14.9	18.4				38
39	5.7	6.1	6.5	7.1	7.7	8.5	9.4	10.6	12.2	14.5	17.9			39
40	5.3	5.6	6.0	6.4	6.9	7.5	8.2	9.2	10.4	11.9	14.1	17.4		40
41	4.9	5.2	5.5	5.8	6.2	6.7	7.3	8.0	8.9	10.1	11.6	13.8	17.0	41
42	4.5	4.8	5.0	5.3	5.7	6.1	6.6	7.1	7.8	8.7	9.8	11.3	13.4	42
43	4.2	4.4	4.6	4.9	5.2	5.5	5.9	6.4	6.9	7.6	8.5	9.5	11.0	43
44	3.9	4.1	4.3	4.5	4.8	5.1	5.4	5.8	6.2	6.7	7.4	8.2	9.3	44
45	3.7	3.8	4.0	4.2	4.4	4.7	4.9	5.2	5.6	6.0	6.6	7.2	8.0	45
46	3.5	3.6	3.7	3.9	4.1	4.3	4.5	4.8	5.1	5.4	5.9	6.4	7.0	46
47	3.3	3.4	3.5	3.6	3.8	4.0	4.2	4.4	4.6	4.9	5.3	5.7	6.2	47
48	3.1	3.2	3.3	3.4	3.5	3.7	3.9	4.0	4.3	4.5	4.8	5.1	5.5	48
49	2.9	3.0	3.1	3.2	3.3	3.4	3.6	3.7	3.9	4.1	4.4	4.6	5.0	49
50	2.7	2.8	2.9	3.0	3.1	3.2	3.3	3.5	3.6	3.8	4.0	4.2	4.5	50
51	2.6	2.6	2.7	2.8	2.9	3.0	3.1	3.2	3.4	3.5	3.7	3.9	4.1	51
52	2.4	2.5	2.6	2.6	2.7	2.8	2.9	3.0	3.1	3.2	3.4	3.6	3.7	52
53	2.3	2.3	2.4	2.5	2.5	2.6	2.7	2.8	2.9	3.0	3.1	3.3	3.4	53
54	2.2	2.2	2.3	2.3	2.4	2.5	2.5	2.6	2.7	2.8	2.9	3.0	3.2	54
55	2.0	2.1	2.1	2.2	2.2	2.3	2.4	2.4	2.5	2.6	2.7	2.8	2.9	55
56	1.9	2.0	2.0	2.1	2.1	2.2	2.2	2.3	2.4	2.4	2.5	2.6	2.7	56
57	1.8	1.9	1.9	2.0	2.0	2.0	2.1	2.2	2.2	2.3	2.3	2.4	2.5	57
58	1.7	1.8	1.8	1.8	1.9	1.9	2.0	2.0	2.1	2.1	2.2	2.3	2.3	58
59	1.6	1.7	1.7	1.7	1.8	1.8	1.9	1.9	1.9	2.0	2.0	2.1	2.2	59
60	1.6	1.6	1.6	1.6	1.7	1.7	1.7	1.8	1.8	1.9	1.9	2.0	2.0	60
Latitude	25°	26°	27°	28°	29°	30°	31°	32°	33°	34°	35°	36°	37°	Latitude
	Declination **same** name as latitude, **upper** transit: **add** correction to observed altitude													

TABLE 24
Altitude Factor

a, the change of altitude in one minute from meridian transit.

Latitude	25°	26°	27°	28°	29°	30°	31°	32°	33°	34°	35°	36°	37°	Latitude
	Declination **contrary** name to latitude **upper** transit: **add** correction to observed altitude													
°	″	″	″	″	″	″	″	″	″	″	″	″	″	°
0	4.2	4.0	3.9	3.7	3.5	3.4	3.3	3.1	3.0	2.9	2.8	2.7	2.6	0
1	4.1	3.9	3.7	3.6	3.4	3.3	3.2	3.1	2.9	2.8	2.7	2.6	2.6	1
2	3.9	3.8	3.6	3.5	3.3	3.2	3.1	3.0	2.9	2.8	2.7	2.6	2.5	2
3	3.8	3.6	3.5	3.4	3.2	3.1	3.0	2.9	2.8	2.7	2.6	2.5	2.4	3
4	3.7	3.5	3.4	3.3	3.2	3.0	2.9	2.8	2.7	2.6	2.5	2.5	2.4	4
5	3.6	3.4	3.3	3.2	3.1	3.0	2.9	2.8	2.7	2.6	2.5	2.4	2.3	5
6	3.4	3.3	3.2	3.1	3.0	2.9	2.8	2.7	2.6	2.5	2.4	2.4	2.3	6
7	3.3	3.2	3.1	3.0	2.9	2.8	2.7	2.6	2.5	2.5	2.4	2.3	2.2	7
8	3.2	3.1	3.0	2.9	2.8	2.7	2.7	2.6	2.5	2.4	2.3	2.3	2.2	8
9	3.1	3.0	2.9	2.8	2.8	2.7	2.6	2.5	2.4	2.4	2.3	2.2	2.2	9
10	3.1	3.0	2.9	2.8	2.7	2.6	2.5	2.5	2.4	2.3	2.2	2.2	2.1	10
11	3.0	2.9	2.8	2.7	2.6	2.5	2.5	2.4	2.3	2.3	2.2	2.1	2.1	11
12	2.9	2.8	2.7	2.6	2.6	2.5	2.4	2.3	2.3	2.2	2.2	2.1	2.0	12
13	2.8	2.7	2.7	2.6	2.5	2.4	2.4	2.3	2.2	2.2	2.1	2.1	2.0	13
14	2.7	2.7	2.6	2.5	2.4	2.4	2.3	2.3	2.2	2.1	2.1	2.0	2.0	14
15	2.7	2.6	2.5	2.5	2.4	2.3	2.3	2.2	2.1	2.1	2.0	2.0	1.9	15
16	2.6	2.5	2.5	2.4	2.3	2.3	2.2	2.2	2.1	2.0	2.0	1.9	1.9	16
17	2.5	2.5	2.4	2.3	2.3	2.2	2.2	2.1	2.1	2.0	2.0	1.9	1.9	17
18	2.5	2.4	2.4	2.3	2.2	2.2	2.1	2.1	2.0	2.0	1.9	1.9	1.8	18
19	2.4	2.4	2.3	2.2	2.2	2.1	2.1	2.0	2.0	1.9	1.9	1.8	1.8	19
20	2.4	2.3	2.3	2.2	2.1	2.1	2.0	2.0	1.9	1.9	1.9	1.8	1.8	20
21	2.3	2.3	2.2	2.1	2.1	2.0	2.0	2.0	1.9	1.9	1.8	1.8	1.7	21
22	2.3	2.2	2.2	2.1	2.1	2.0	2.0	1.9	1.9	1.8	1.8	1.7	1.7	22
23	2.2	2.2	2.1	2.1	2.0	2.0	1.9	1.9	1.8	1.8	1.8	1.7	1.7	23
24	2.2	2.1	2.1	2.0	2.0	1.9	1.9	1.8	1.8	1.8	1.7	1.7	1.6	24
25	2.1	2.1	2.0	2.0	1.9	1.9	1.8	1.8	1.8	1.7	1.7	1.6	1.6	25
26	2.1	2.0	2.0	1.9	1.9	1.8	1.8	1.8	1.7	1.7	1.7	1.6	1.6	26
27	2.0	2.0	1.9	1.9	1.9	1.8	1.8	1.7	1.7	1.7	1.6	1.6	1.6	27
28	2.0	1.9	1.9	1.8	1.8	1.8	1.7	1.7	1.7	1.6	1.6	1.6	1.5	28
29	1.9	1.9	1.9	1.8	1.8	1.7	1.7	1.7	1.6	1.6	1.6	1.5	1.5	29
30	1.9	1.8	1.8	1.8	1.7	1.7	1.7	1.6	1.6	1.6	1.5	1.5	1.5	30
31	1.8	1.8	1.8	1.7	1.7	1.7	1.6	1.6	1.6	1.5	1.5	1.5	1.5	31
32	1.8	1.8	1.7	1.7	1.7	1.6	1.6	1.6	1.5	1.5	1.5	1.5	1.4	32
33	1.8	1.7	1.7	1.7	1.6	1.6	1.6	1.5	1.5	1.5	1.5	1.4	1.4	33
34	1.7	1.7	1.7	1.6	1.6	1.6	1.5	1.5	1.5	1.5	1.4	1.4	1.4	34
35	1.7	1.7	1.6	1.6	1.6	1.5	1.5	1.5	1.5	1.4	1.4	1.4	1.4	35
36	1.6	1.6	1.6	1.6	1.5	1.5	1.5	1.5	1.4	1.4	1.4	1.4	1.3	36
37	1.6	1.6	1.6	1.5	1.5	1.5	1.5	1.4	1.4	1.4	1.4	1.3	1.3	37
38	1.6	1.5	1.5	1.5	1.5	1.5	1.4	1.4	1.4	1.4	1.3	1.3	1.3	38
39	1.5	1.5	1.5	1.5	1.4	1.4	1.4	1.4	1.4	1.3	1.3	1.3	1.3	39
40	1.5	1.5	1.5	1.4	1.4	1.4	1.4	1.3	1.3	1.3	1.3	1.3	1.2	40
41	1.5	1.4	1.4	1.4	1.4	1.4	1.3	1.3	1.3	1.3	1.3	1.2	1.2	41
42	1.4	1.4	1.4	1.4	1.4	1.3	1.3	1.3	1.3	1.2	1.2	1.2	1.2	42
43	1.4	1.4	1.4	1.3	1.3	1.3	1.3	1.3	1.2	1.2	1.2	1.2	1.2	43
44	1.4	1.4	1.3	1.3	1.3	1.3	1.3	1.2	1.2	1.2	1.2	1.2	1.2	44
45	1.3	1.3	1.3	1.3	1.3	1.2	1.2	1.2	1.2	1.2	1.2	1.1	1.1	45
46	1.3	1.3	1.3	1.3	1.2	1.2	1.2	1.2	1.2	1.2	1.1	1.1	1.1	46
47	1.3	1.3	1.2	1.2	1.2	1.2	1.2	1.2	1.1	1.1	1.1	1.1	1.1	47
48	1.2	1.2	1.2	1.2	1.2	1.2	1.1	1.1	1.1	1.1	1.1	1.1		48
49	1.2	1.2	1.2	1.2	1.2	1.1	1.1	1.1	1.1	1.1	1.1			49
50	1.2	1.2	1.2	1.1	1.1	1.1	1.1	1.1	1.1	1.1				50
51	1.2	1.1	1.1	1.1	1.1	1.1	1.1	1.1	1.0					51
52	1.1	1.1	1.1	1.1	1.1	1.1	1.0	1.0						52
53	1.1	1.1	1.1	1.1	1.0	1.0	1.0							53
54	1.1	1.1	1.0	1.0	1.0	1.0								54
55	1.0	1.0	1.0	1.0	1.0									55
56	1.0	1.0	1.0	1.0										56
57	1.0	1.0	1.0											57
58	1.0	0.9												58
59	0.9												0.8	59
60												0.8	0.8	60
Latitude	25°	26°	27°	28°	29°	30°	31°	32°	33°	34°	35°	36°	37°	Latitude
	Declination **contrary** name to latitude, **upper** transit: **add** correction to observed altitude													

TABLE 24

Altitude Factor

a, the change of altitude in one minute from meridian transit.

Latitude	Declination same name as latitude, upper transit: add correction to observed altitude													Latitude
	38°	39°	40°	41°	42°	43°	44°	45°	46°	47°	48°	49°	50°	
°	″	″	″	″	″	″	″	″	″	″	″	″	″	°
0	2.5	2.4	2.3	2.3	2.2	2.1	2.0	2.0	1.9	1.8	1.8	1.7	1.7	0
1	2.6	2.5	2.4	2.3	2.2	2.2	2.1	2.0	1.9	1.9	1.8	1.7	1.7	1
2	2.6	2.5	2.4	2.4	2.3	2.2	2.1	2.0	2.0	1.9	1.8	1.8	1.7	2
3	2.7	2.6	2.5	2.4	2.3	2.2	2.2	2.1	2.0	1.9	1.9	1.8	1.7	3
4	2.8	2.7	2.6	2.5	2.4	2.3	2.2	2.1	2.0	2.0	1.9	1.8	1.8	4
5	2.8	2.7	2.6	2.5	2.4	2.3	2.2	2.2	2.1	2.0	1.9	1.9	1.8	5
6	2.9	2.8	2.7	2.6	2.5	2.4	2.3	2.2	2.1	2.0	2.0	1.9	1.8	6
7	3.0	2.9	2.7	2.6	2.5	2.4	2.3	2.2	2.2	2.1	2.0	1.9	1.8	7
8	3.1	2.9	2.8	2.7	2.6	2.5	2.4	2.3	2.2	2.1	2.0	1.9	1.9	8
9	3.2	3.0	2.9	2.8	2.6	2.5	2.4	2.3	2.2	2.2	2.1	2.0	1.9	9
10	3.2	3.1	3.0	2.8	2.7	2.6	2.5	2.4	2.3	2.2	2.1	2.0	1.9	10
11	3.4	3.2	3.1	2.9	2.8	2.7	2.6	2.4	2.3	2.2	2.1	2.1	2.0	11
12	3.5	3.3	3.1	3.0	2.9	2.7	2.6	2.5	2.4	2.3	2.2	2.1	2.0	12
13	3.6	3.4	3.2	3.1	2.9	2.8	2.7	2.6	2.4	2.3	2.2	2.1	2.0	13
14	3.7	3.5	3.3	3.2	3.0	2.9	2.7	2.6	2.5	2.4	2.3	2.2	2.1	14
15	3.8	3.6	3.4	3.3	3.1	3.0	2.8	2.7	2.6	2.4	2.3	2.2	2.1	15
16	4.0	3.8	3.6	3.4	3.2	3.0	2.9	2.8	2.6	2.5	2.4	2.3	2.2	16
17	4.1	3.9	3.7	3.5	3.3	3.1	3.0	2.8	2.7	2.6	2.4	2.3	2.2	17
18	4.3	4.1	3.8	3.6	3.4	3.2	3.1	2.9	2.8	2.6	2.5	2.4	2.3	18
19	4.5	4.2	4.0	3.7	3.5	3.3	3.2	3.0	2.8	2.7	2.6	2.4	2.3	19
20	4.7	4.4	4.1	3.9	3.7	3.5	3.3	3.1	2.9	2.8	2.6	2.5	2.4	20
21	4.9	4.6	4.3	4.0	3.8	3.6	3.4	3.2	3.0	2.9	2.7	2.6	2.4	21
22	5.2	4.8	4.5	4.2	4.0	3.7	3.5	3.3	3.1	2.9	2.8	2.6	2.5	22
23	5.5	5.1	4.7	4.4	4.1	3.9	3.6	3.4	3.2	3.0	2.9	2.7	2.6	23
24	5.8	5.4	5.0	4.6	4.3	4.0	3.8	3.5	3.3	3.1	3.0	2.8	2.6	24
25	6.2	5.7	5.3	4.9	4.5	4.2	3.9	3.7	3.5	3.3	3.1	2.9	2.7	25
26	6.7	6.1	5.6	5.2	4.8	4.4	4.1	3.8	3.6	3.4	3.2	3.0	2.8	26
27	7.2	6.5	6.0	5.5	5.0	4.6	4.3	4.0	3.7	3.5	3.3	3.1	2.9	27
28	7.9	7.1	6.4	5.8	5.3	4.9	4.5	4.2	3.9	3.6	3.4	3.2	3.0	28
29	8.7	7.7	6.9	6.2	5.7	5.2	4.8	4.4	4.1	3.8	3.5	3.3	3.1	29
30	9.6	8.5	7.5	6.7	6.1	5.5	5.1	4.7	4.3	4.0	3.7	3.4	3.2	30
31	10.9	9.4	8.2	7.3	6.6	5.9	5.4	4.9	4.5	4.2	3.9	3.6	3.3	31
32	12.6	10.6	9.2	8.0	7.1	6.4	5.8	5.2	4.8	4.4	4.0	3.7	3.5	32
33	14.9	12.2	10.4	8.9	7.8	6.9	6.2	5.6	5.1	4.6	4.3	3.9	3.6	33
34	18.4	14.5	11.9	10.1	8.7	7.6	6.7	6.0	5.4	4.9	4.5	4.1	3.8	34
35		17.9	14.1	11.6	9.8	8.5	7.4	6.6	5.9	5.3	4.8	4.4	4.0	35
36			17.4	13.8	11.3	9.5	8.2	7.2	6.4	5.7	5.1	4.6	4.2	36
37				17.0	13.4	11.0	9.3	8.0	7.0	6.2	5.5	5.0	4.5	37
38					16.5	13.0	10.7	9.0	7.7	6.8	6.0	5.3	4.8	38
39						16.0	12.6	10.3	8.7	7.5	6.5	5.8	5.1	39
40							15.5	12.2	10.0	8.4	7.2	6.3	5.6	40
41								15.0	11.8	9.7	8.1	7.0	6.1	41
42	16.5								14.5	11.4	9.3	7.9	6.7	42
43	13.0	16.0								14.0	11.0	9.0	7.6	43
44	10.6	12.6	15.5								13.6	10.6	8.7	44
45	9.0	10.3	12.2	15.0								13.1	10.2	45
46	7.7	8.7	10.0	11.8	14.5								12.6	46
47	6.8	7.5	8.4	9.7	11.4	14.0								47
48	6.0	6.5	7.2	8.1	9.3	11.0	13.6							48
49	5.3	5.8	6.3	7.0	7.9	9.0	10.6	13.1						49
50	4.8	5.1	5.6	6.1	6.7	7.6	8.7	10.2	12.6					50
51	4.3	4.6	5.0	5.4	5.9	6.5	7.3	8.4	9.9	12.1				51
52	3.9	4.2	4.5	4.8	5.2	5.7	6.3	7.0	8.0	9.5	11.6			52
53	3.6	3.8	4.0	4.3	4.6	5.0	5.4	6.0	6.7	7.7	9.1	11.1		53
54	3.3	3.5	3.7	3.9	4.1	4.4	4.8	5.2	5.8	6.5	7.4	8.7	10.6	54
55	3.0	3.2	3.3	3.5	3.7	4.0	4.3	4.6	5.0	5.5	6.2	7.1	8.3	55
56	2.8	2.9	3.1	3.2	3.4	3.6	3.8	4.1	4.4	4.8	5.3	5.9	6.8	56
57	2.6	2.7	2.8	2.9	3.1	3.2	3.4	3.6	3.9	4.2	4.6	5.0	5.6	57
58	2.4	2.5	2.6	2.7	2.8	2.9	3.1	3.3	3.5	3.7	4.0	4.4	4.8	58
59	2.2	2.3	2.4	2.5	2.6	2.7	2.8	3.0	3.1	3.3	3.6	3.8	4.2	59
60	2.1	2.1	2.2	2.3	2.4	2.5	2.6	2.7	2.8	3.0	3.2	3.4	3.6	60
Latitude	38°	39°	40°	41°	42°	43°	44°	45°	46°	47°	48°	49°	50°	Latitude
	Declination same name as latitude, upper transit: add correction to observed altitude													

TABLE 24

Altitude Factor

a, the change of altitude in one minute from meridian transit.

Latitude	Declination contrary name to latitude, upper transit: add correction to observed altitude													Latitude
	38°	39°	40°	41°	42°	43°	44°	45°	46°	47°	48°	49°	50°	
°	″	″	″	″	″	″	″	″	″	″	″	″	″	°
0	2.5	2.4	2.3	2.3	2.2	2.1	2.0	2.0	1.9	1.8	1.8	1.7	1.7	0
1	2.5	2.4	2.3	2.2	2.1	2.1	2.0	1.9	1.9	1.8	1.7	1.7	1.6	1
2	2.4	2.3	2.3	2.2	2.1	2.0	2.0	1.9	1.8	1.8	1.7	1.7	1.6	2
3	2.4	2.3	2.2	2.1	2.1	2.0	1.9	1.9	1.8	1.8	1.7	1.6	1.6	3
4	2.3	2.2	2.2	2.1	2.0	2.0	1.9	1.8	1.8	1.7	1.7	1.6	1.6	4
5	2.3	2.2	2.1	2.1	2.0	1.9	1.9	1.8	1.8	1.7	1.6	1.6	1.5	5
6	2.2	2.2	2.1	2.0	2.0	1.9	1.8	1.8	1.7	1.7	1.6	1.6	1.5	6
7	2.2	2.1	2.0	2.0	1.9	1.9	1.8	1.8	1.7	1.6	1.6	1.5	1.5	7
8	2.1	2.1	2.0	1.9	1.9	1.8	1.8	1.7	1.7	1.6	1.6	1.5	1.5	8
9	2.1	2.0	2.0	1.9	1.9	1.8	1.8	1.7	1.6	1.6	1.6	1.5	1.5	9
10	2.1	2.0	1.9	1.9	1.8	1.8	1.7	1.7	1.6	1.6	1.5	1.5	1.4	10
11	2.0	2.0	1.9	1.8	1.8	1.7	1.7	1.6	1.6	1.6	1.5	1.5	1.4	11
12	2.0	1.9	1.9	1.8	1.8	1.7	1.7	1.6	1.6	1.5	1.5	1.4	1.4	12
13	1.9	1.9	1.8	1.8	1.7	1.7	1.6	1.6	1.6	1.5	1.5	1.4	1.4	13
14	1.9	1.9	1.8	1.8	1.7	1.7	1.6	1.6	1.5	1.5	1.4	1.4	1.4	14
15	1.9	1.8	1.8	1.7	1.7	1.6	1.6	1.6	1.5	1.5	1.4	1.4	1.4	15
16	1.8	1.8	1.7	1.7	1.7	1.6	1.6	1.5	1.5	1.4	1.4	1.4	1.3	16
17	1.8	1.8	1.7	1.7	1.6	1.6	1.5	1.5	1.5	1.4	1.4	1.4	1.3	17
18	1.8	1.7	1.7	1.6	1.6	1.6	1.5	1.5	1.4	1.4	1.4	1.3	1.3	18
19	1.7	1.7	1.7	1.6	1.6	1.5	1.5	1.5	1.4	1.4	1.4	1.3	1.3	19
20	1.7	1.7	1.6	1.6	1.6	1.5	1.5	1.4	1.4	1.4	1.3	1.3	1.3	20
21	1.7	1.6	1.6	1.6	1.5	1.5	1.5	1.4	1.4	1.4	1.3	1.3	1.3	21
22	1.7	1.6	1.6	1.5	1.5	1.5	1.4	1.4	1.4	1.3	1.3	1.3	1.2	22
23	1.6	1.6	1.6	1.5	1.5	1.4	1.4	1.4	1.3	1.3	1.3	1.3	1.2	23
24	1.6	1.6	1.5	1.5	1.5	1.4	1.4	1.4	1.3	1.3	1.3	1.2	1.2	24
25	1.6	1.5	1.5	1.5	1.4	1.4	1.4	1.3	1.3	1.3	1.2	1.2	1.2	25
26	1.6	1.5	1.5	1.5	1.4	1.4	1.4	1.3	1.3	1.3	1.2	1.2	1.2	26
27	1.5	1.5	1.5	1.4	1.4	1.4	1.3	1.3	1.3	1.2	1.2	1.2	1.2	27
28	1.5	1.5	1.4	1.4	1.4	1.3	1.3	1.3	1.3	1.2	1.2	1.2	1.1	28
29	1.5	1.4	1.4	1.4	1.4	1.3	1.3	1.3	1.2	1.2	1.2	1.2	1.1	29
30	1.5	1.4	1.4	1.4	1.3	1.3	1.3	1.2	1.2	1.2	1.2	1.1	1.1	30
31	1.4	1.4	1.4	1.3	1.3	1.3	1.3	1.2	1.2	1.2	1.2	1.1	1.1	31
32	1.4	1.4	1.3	1.3	1.3	1.3	1.2	1.2	1.2	1.2	1.1	1.1	1.1	32
33	1.4	1.4	1.3	1.3	1.3	1.2	1.2	1.2	1.2	1.1	1.1	1.1	1.1	33
34	1.4	1.3	1.3	1.3	1.3	1.2	1.2	1.2	1.2	1.1	1.1	1.1	1.1	34
35	1.3	1.3	1.3	1.3	1.2	1.2	1.2	1.2	1.1	1.1	1.1	1.1		35
36	1.3	1.3	1.3	1.2	1.2	1.2	1.2	1.1	1.1	1.1	1.1			36
37	1.3	1.3	1.2	1.2	1.2	1.2	1.2	1.1	1.1	1.1				37
38	1.3	1.2	1.2	1.2	1.2	1.2	1.1	1.1	1.1					38
39	1.2	1.2	1.2	1.2	1.2	1.1	1.1	1.1						39
40	1.2	1.2	1.2	1.2	1.1	1.1	1.1							40
41	1.2	1.2	1.2	1.1	1.1	1.1								41
42	1.2	1.2	1.1	1.1	1.1									42
43	1.2	1.1	1.1	1.1										43
44	1.1	1.1	1.1											44
45	1.1	1.1												45
46	1.1												0.9	46
47												0.9	0.9	47
48											0.9	0.9	0.9	48
49										0.9	0.9	0.9	0.8	49
50									0.9	0.9	0.9	0.8	0.8	50
51								0.9	0.9	0.9	0.8	0.8	0.8	51
52							0.9	0.9	0.9	0.8	0.8	0.8	0.8	52
53						0.9	0.9	0.8	0.8	0.8	0.8	0.8	0.8	53
54					0.9	0.9	0.8	0.8	0.8	0.8	0.8	0.8	0.8	54
55				0.9	0.8	0.8	0.8	0.8	0.8	0.8	0.8	0.8	0.7	55
56			0.8	0.8	0.8	0.8	0.8	0.8	0.8	0.8	0.8	0.7	0.7	56
57		0.8	0.8	0.8	0.8	0.8	0.8	0.8	0.8	0.8	0.7	0.7	0.7	57
58	0.8	0.8	0.8	0.8	0.8	0.8	0.8	0.8	0.8	0.7	0.7	0.7	0.7	58
59	0.8	0.8	0.8	0.8	0.8	0.8	0.8	0.7	0.7	0.7	0.7	0.7	0.7	59
60	0.8	0.8	0.8	0.8	0.8	0.7	0.7	0.7	0.7	0.7	0.7	0.7	0.7	60
Latitude	38°	39°	40°	41°	42°	43°	44°	45°	46°	47°	48°	49°	50°	Latitude
	Declination contrary name to latitude, upper transit: add correction to observed altitude													

TABLE 24

Altitude Factor

a, the change of altitude in one minute from meridian transit.

Latitude	Declination same name as latitude, upper transit: add correction to observed altitude													Latitude
	51°	52°	53°	54°	55°	56°	57°	58°	59°	60°	61°	62°	63°	
°	″	″	″	″	″	″	″	″	″	″	″	″	″	°
0	1.6	1.5	1.5	1.4	1.4	1.3	1.3	1.2	1.2	1.1	1.1	1.0	1.0	0
1	1.6	1.6	1.5	1.4	1.4	1.3	1.3	1.2	1.2	1.2	1.1	1.1	1.0	1
2	1.6	1.6	1.5	1.5	1.4	1.4	1.3	1.3	1.2	1.2	1.1	1.1	1.0	2
3	1.7	1.6	1.5	1.5	1.4	1.4	1.3	1.3	1.2	1.2	1.1	1.1	1.0	3
4	1.7	1.6	1.6	1.5	1.5	1.4	1.3	1.3	1.2	1.2	1.1	1.1	1.0	4
5	1.7	1.7	1.6	1.5	1.5	1.4	1.4	1.3	1.3	1.2	1.1	1.1	1.1	5
6	1.7	1.7	1.6	1.5	1.5	1.4	1.4	1.3	1.3	1.2	1.2	1.1	1.1	6
7	1.8	1.7	1.6	1.6	1.5	1.4	1.4	1.3	1.3	1.2	1.2	1.1	1.1	7
8	1.8	1.7	1.7	1.6	1.5	1.5	1.4	1.4	1.3	1.2	1.2	1.1	1.1	8
9	1.8	1.8	1.7	1.6	1.6	1.5	1.4	1.4	1.3	1.3	1.2	1.1	1.1	9
10	1.9	1.8	1.7	1.6	1.6	1.5	1.4	1.4	1.3	1.3	1.2	1.2	1.1	10
11	1.9	1.8	1.7	1.7	1.6	1.5	1.5	1.4	1.3	1.3	1.2	1.2	1.1	11
12	1.9	1.8	1.8	1.7	1.6	1.6	1.5	1.4	1.4	1.3	1.2	1.2	1.1	12
13	2.0	1.9	1.8	1.7	1.6	1.6	1.5	1.4	1.4	1.3	1.3	1.2	1.1	13
14	2.0	1.9	1.8	1.7	1.7	1.6	1.5	1.5	1.4	1.3	1.3	1.2	1.2	14
15	2.0	1.9	1.9	1.8	1.7	1.6	1.5	1.5	1.4	1.3	1.3	1.2	1.2	15
16	2.1	2.0	1.9	1.8	1.7	1.6	1.6	1.5	1.4	1.4	1.3	1.2	1.2	16
17	2.1	2.0	1.9	1.8	1.8	1.7	1.6	1.5	1.5	1.4	1.3	1.3	1.2	17
18	2.2	2.1	2.0	1.9	1.8	1.7	1.6	1.5	1.5	1.4	1.3	1.3	1.2	18
19	2.2	2.1	2.0	1.9	1.8	1.7	1.6	1.6	1.5	1.4	1.3	1.3	1.2	19
20	2.3	2.1	2.0	1.9	1.9	1.8	1.7	1.6	1.5	1.4	1.4	1.3	1.2	20
21	2.3	2.2	2.1	2.0	1.9	1.8	1.7	1.6	1.5	1.5	1.4	1.3	1.2	21
22	2.4	2.2	2.1	2.0	1.9	1.8	1.7	1.6	1.6	1.5	1.4	1.3	1.3	22
23	2.4	2.3	2.2	2.1	2.0	1.9	1.8	1.7	1.6	1.5	1.4	1.4	1.3	23
24	2.5	2.4	2.2	2.1	2.0	1.9	1.8	1.7	1.6	1.5	1.5	1.4	1.3	24
25	2.6	2.4	2.3	2.2	2.0	1.9	1.8	1.7	1.6	1.6	1.5	1.4	1.3	25
26	2.6	2.5	2.3	2.2	2.1	2.0	1.9	1.8	1.7	1.6	1.5	1.4	1.3	26
27	2.7	2.6	2.4	2.3	2.1	2.0	1.9	1.8	1.7	1.6	1.5	1.4	1.4	27
28	2.8	2.6	2.5	2.3	2.2	2.1	2.0	1.8	1.7	1.6	1.5	1.5	1.4	28
29	2.9	2.7	2.5	2.4	2.3	2.1	2.0	1.9	1.8	1.7	1.6	1.5	1.4	29
30	3.0	2.8	2.6	2.5	2.3	2.2	2.0	1.9	1.8	1.7	1.6	1.5	1.4	30
31	3.1	2.9	2.7	2.5	2.4	2.2	2.1	2.0	1.9	1.7	1.6	1.5	1.4	31
32	3.2	3.0	2.8	2.6	2.4	2.3	2.2	2.0	1.9	1.8	1.7	1.6	1.5	32
33	3.4	3.1	2.9	2.7	2.5	2.4	2.2	2.1	1.9	1.8	1.7	1.6	1.5	33
34	3.5	3.2	3.0	2.8	2.6	2.4	2.3	2.1	2.0	1.9	1.7	1.6	1.5	34
35	3.7	3.4	3.1	2.9	2.7	2.5	2.3	2.2	2.0	1.9	1.8	1.7	1.6	35
36	3.9	3.6	3.3	3.0	2.8	2.6	2.4	2.3	2.1	2.0	1.8	1.7	1.6	36
37	4.1	3.7	3.4	3.2	2.9	2.7	2.5	2.3	2.2	2.0	1.9	1.7	1.6	37
38	4.3	3.9	3.6	3.3	3.0	2.8	2.6	2.4	2.2	2.1	1.9	1.8	1.7	38
39	4.6	4.2	3.8	3.5	3.2	2.9	2.7	2.5	2.3	2.1	2.0	1.8	1.7	39
40	5.0	4.5	4.0	3.7	3.3	3.1	2.8	2.6	2.4	2.2	2.0	1.9	1.8	40
41	5.4	4.8	4.3	3.9	3.5	3.2	2.9	2.7	2.5	2.3	2.1	1.9	1.8	41
42	5.9	5.2	4.6	4.1	3.7	3.4	3.1	2.8	2.6	2.4	2.2	2.0	1.9	42
43	6.5	5.7	5.0	4.4	4.0	3.6	3.2	2.9	2.7	2.5	2.3	2.1	1.9	43
44	7.3	6.3	5.4	4.8	4.3	3.8	3.4	3.1	2.8	2.6	2.3	2.2	2.0	44
45	8.4	7.0	6.0	5.2	4.6	4.1	3.6	3.3	3.0	2.7	2.4	2.2	2.0	45
46	9.9	8.0	6.7	5.8	5.0	4.4	3.9	3.5	3.1	2.8	2.6	2.3	2.1	46
47	12.1	9.5	7.7	6.5	5.5	4.8	4.2	3.7	3.3	3.0	2.7	2.4	2.2	47
48		11.6	9.1	7.4	6.2	5.3	4.6	4.0	3.6	3.2	2.8	2.6	2.3	48
49			11.1	8.7	7.1	5.9	5.0	4.4	3.8	3.4	3.0	2.7	2.4	49
50				10.6	8.3	6.8	5.6	4.8	4.2	3.6	3.2	2.9	2.6	50
51					10.2	7.9	6.4	5.4	4.6	4.0	3.5	3.0	2.7	51
52						9.7	7.6	6.1	5.1	4.3	3.8	3.3	2.9	52
53							9.2	7.2	5.9	4.9	4.1	3.6	3.1	53
54								8.8	6.8	5.5	4.6	3.9	3.4	54
55	10.2								8.3	6.5	5.3	4.3	3.7	55
56	7.9	9.7								7.9	6.1	5.0	4.1	56
57	6.4	7.6	9.2								7.4	5.8	4.7	57
58	5.4	6.1	7.2	8.8								7.0	5.4	58
59	4.6	5.1	5.9	6.8	8.3								6.6	59
60	4.0	4.3	4.9	5.5	6.5	7.9								60
Latitude	51°	52°	53°	54°	55°	56°	57°	58°	59°	60°	61°	62°	63°	Latitude
	Declination same name as latitude, upper transit: add correction to observed altitude													

TABLE 24

Altitude Factor

a, the change of altitude in one minute from meridian transit.

Latitude	Declination contrary name to latitude, upper transit: add correction to observed altitude													Latitude
	51°	52°	53°	54°	55°	56°	57°	58°	59°	60°	61°	62°	63°	
°	″	″	″	″	″	″	″	″	″	″	″	″	″	°
0	1.6	1.5	1.5	1.4	1.4	1.3	1.3	1.2	1.2	1.1	1.1	1.0	1.0	0
1	1.6	1.5	1.5	1.4	1.4	1.3	1.3	1.2	1.2	1.1	1.1	1.0	1.0	1
2	1.5	1.5	1.4	1.4	1.3	1.3	1.3	1.2	1.2	1.1	1.1	1.0	1.0	2
3	1.5	1.5	1.4	1.4	1.3	1.3	1.2	1.2	1.1	1.1	1.1	1.0	1.0	3
4	1.5	1.5	1.4	1.4	1.3	1.3	1.2	1.2	1.1	1.1	1.1	1.0	1.0	4
5	1.5	1.4	1.4	1.3	1.3	1.3	1.2	1.2	1.1	1.1	1.0	1.0	1.0	5
6	1.5	1.4	1.4	1.3	1.3	1.2	1.2	1.2	1.1	1.1	1.0	1.0	1.0	6
7	1.4	1.4	1.4	1.3	1.3	1.2	1.2	1.1	1.1	1.1	1.0	1.0	0.9	7
8	1.4	1.4	1.3	1.3	1.3	1.2	1.2	1.1	1.1	1.1	1.0	1.0	0.9	8
9	1.4	1.4	1.3	1.3	1.2	1.2	1.2	1.1	1.1	1.0	1.0	1.0	0.9	9
10	1.4	1.4	1.3	1.3	1.2	1.2	1.1	1.1	1.1	1.0	1.0	1.0	0.9	10
11	1.4	1.3	1.3	1.3	1.2	1.2	1.1	1.1	1.1	1.0	1.0	1.0	0.9	11
12	1.4	1.3	1.3	1.2	1.2	1.2	1.1	1.1	1.1	1.0	1.0	0.9	0.9	12
13	1.3	1.3	1.3	1.2	1.2	1.2	1.1	1.1	1.0	1.0	1.0	0.9	0.9	13
14	1.3	1.3	1.3	1.2	1.2	1.1	1.1	1.1	1.0	1.0	1.0	0.9	0.9	14
15	1.3	1.3	1.2	1.2	1.2	1.1	1.1	1.1	1.0	1.0	1.0	0.9	0.9	15
16	1.3	1.3	1.2	1.2	1.1	1.1	1.1	1.0	1.0	1.0	0.9	0.9	0.9	16
17	1.3	1.2	1.2	1.2	1.1	1.1	1.1	1.0	1.0	1.0	0.9	0.9	0.9	17
18	1.3	1.2	1.2	1.2	1.1	1.1	1.1	1.0	1.0	1.0	0.9	0.9	0.9	18
19	1.2	1.2	1.2	1.1	1.1	1.1	1.0	1.0	1.0	1.0	0.9	0.9	0.9	19
20	1.2	1.2	1.2	1.1	1.1	1.1	1.0	1.0	1.0	0.9	0.9	0.9	0.8	20
21	1.2	1.2	1.2	1.1	1.1	1.1	1.0	1.0	1.0	0.9	0.9	0.9	0.8	21
22	1.2	1.2	1.1	1.1	1.1	1.0	1.0	1.0	1.0	0.9	0.9	0.9		22
23	1.2	1.2	1.1	1.1	1.1	1.0	1.0	1.0	0.9	0.9	0.9			23
24	1.2	1.1	1.1	1.1	1.1	1.0	1.0	1.0	0.9	0.9				24
25	1.2	1.1	1.1	1.1	1.0	1.0	1.0	1.0	0.9					25
26	1.1	1.1	1.1	1.1	1.0	1.0	1.0	0.9						26
27	1.1	1.1	1.1	1.0	1.0	1.0	1.0							27
28	1.1	1.1	1.1	1.0	1.0	1.0								28
29	1.1	1.1	1.0	1.0	1.0									29
30	1.1	1.1	1.0	1.0										30
31	1.1	1.0	1.0											31
32	1.1	1.0												32
33	1.1												0.8	33
34												0.8	0.7	34
35											0.8	0.8	0.7	35
36										0.8	0.8	0.8	0.7	36
37									0.8	0.8	0.8	0.7	0.7	37
38								0.8	0.8	0.8	0.8	0.7	0.7	38
39							0.8	0.8	0.8	0.8	0.8	0.7	0.7	39
40						0.8	0.8	0.8	0.8	0.8	0.8	0.7	0.7	40
41					0.9	0.8	0.8	0.8	0.8	0.8	0.7	0.7	0.7	41
42				0.9	0.8	0.8	0.8	0.8	0.8	0.8	0.7	0.7	0.7	42
43			0.9	0.9	0.8	0.8	0.8	0.8	0.8	0.7	0.7	0.7	0.7	43
44		0.9	0.9	0.8	0.8	0.8	0.8	0.8	0.8	0.7	0.7	0.7	0.7	44
45	0.9	0.9	0.8	0.8	0.8	0.8	0.8	0.8	0.7	0.7	0.7	0.7	0.7	45
46	0.9	0.9	0.8	0.8	0.8	0.8	0.8	0.8	0.7	0.7	0.7	0.7	0.7	46
47	0.9	0.8	0.8	0.8	0.8	0.8	0.8	0.7	0.7	0.7	0.7	0.7	0.6	47
48	0.8	0.8	0.8	0.8	0.8	0.8	0.7	0.7	0.7	0.7	0.7	0.7	0.6	48
49	0.8	0.8	0.8	0.8	0.8	0.7	0.7	0.7	0.7	0.7	0.7	0.6	0.6	49
50	0.8	0.8	0.8	0.8	0.7	0.7	0.7	0.7	0.7	0.7	0.7	0.6	0.6	50
51	0.8	0.8	0.8	0.8	0.7	0.7	0.7	0.7	0.7	0.7	0.7	0.6	0.6	51
52	0.8	0.8	0.8	0.7	0.7	0.7	0.7	0.7	0.7	0.7	0.6	0.6	0.6	52
53	0.8	0.8	0.7	0.7	0.7	0.7	0.7	0.7	0.7	0.6	0.6	0.6	0.6	53
54	0.8	0.7	0.7	0.7	0.7	0.7	0.7	0.7	0.6	0.6	0.6	0.6	0.6	54
55	0.7	0.7	0.7	0.7	0.7	0.7	0.7	0.7	0.6	0.6	0.6	0.6	0.6	55
56	0.7	0.7	0.7	0.7	0.7	0.7	0.7	0.6	0.6	0.6	0.6	0.6	0.6	56
57	0.7	0.7	0.7	0.7	0.7	0.7	0.6	0.6	0.6	0.6	0.6	0.6	0.6	57
58	0.7	0.7	0.7	0.7	0.7	0.6	0.6	0.6	0.6	0.6	0.6	0.6	0.6	58
59	0.7	0.7	0.7	0.6	0.6	0.6	0.6	0.6	0.6	0.6	0.6	0.6	0.5	59
60	0.7	0.7	0.6	0.6	0.6	0.6	0.6	0.6	0.6	0.6	0.6	0.6	0.5	60
Latitude	51°	52°	53°	54°	55°	56°	57°	58°	59°	60°	61°	62°	63°	Latitude
	Declination contrary name to latitude, upper transit: add correction to observed altitude													

TABLE 25

Change of Altitude in Given Time from Meridian Transit

a (table 24)	5′	10′	15′	20′	25′	30′	35′	40′	45′	50′	55′	1° 00′	1° 05′	1° 10′	a (table 24)
	t, meridian angle														
	$0^{m}20^{s}$	$0^{m}40^{s}$	$1^{m}00^{s}$	$1^{m}20^{s}$	$1^{m}40^{s}$	$2^{m}00^{s}$	$2^{m}20^{s}$	$2^{m}40^{s}$	$3^{m}00^{s}$	$3^{m}20^{s}$	$3^{m}40^{s}$	$4^{m}00^{s}$	$4^{m}20^{s}$	$4^{m}40^{s}$	
″	′	′	′	′	′	′	′	′	′	′	′	′	′	′	″
0.1	0.0	0.0	0.0	0.0	0.0	0.0	0.0	0.0	0.0	0.0	0.0	0.0	0.0	0.0	0.1
0.2	0.0	0.0	0.0	0.0	0.0	0.0	0.0	0.0	0.0	0.0	0.0	0.1	0.1	0.1	0.2
0.3	0.0	0.0	0.0	0.0	0.0	0.0	0.0	0.0	0.0	0.1	0.1	0.1	0.1	0.1	0.3
0.4	0.0	0.0	0.0	0.0	0.0	0.0	0.0	0.0	0.1	0.1	0.1	0.1	0.1	0.1	0.4
0.5	0.0	0.0	0.0	0.0	0.0	0.0	0.0	0.1	0.1	0.1	0.1	0.1	0.2	0.2	0.5
0.6	0.0	0.0	0.0	0.0	0.0	0.0	0.1	0.1	0.1	0.1	0.1	0.2	0.2	0.2	0.6
0.7	0.0	0.0	0.0	0.0	0.0	0.0	0.1	0.1	0.1	0.1	0.2	0.2	0.2	0.3	0.7
0.8	0.0	0.0	0.0	0.0	0.0	0.1	0.1	0.1	0.1	0.1	0.2	0.2	0.3	0.3	0.8
0.9	0.0	0.0	0.0	0.0	0.0	0.1	0.1	0.1	0.1	0.2	0.2	0.2	0.3	0.3	0.9
1.0	0.0	0.0	0.0	0.0	0.0	0.1	0.1	0.1	0.2	0.2	0.2	0.3	0.3	0.4	1.0
2.0	0.0	0.0	0.0	0.1	0.1	0.1	0.2	0.2	0.3	0.4	0.4	0.5	0.6	0.7	2.0
3.0	0.0	0.0	0.1	0.1	0.1	0.2	0.3	0.4	0.4	0.6	0.7	0.8	0.9	1.1	3.0
4.0	0.0	0.0	0.1	0.1	0.2	0.3	0.4	0.5	0.6	0.7	0.9	1.1	1.3	1.5	4.0
5.0	0.0	0.0	0.1	0.1	0.2	0.3	0.5	0.6	0.8	0.9	1.1	1.3	1.6	1.8	5.0
6.0	0.0	0.0	0.1	0.2	0.3	0.4	0.5	0.7	0.9	1.1	1.3	1.6	1.9	2.2	6.0
7.0	0.0	0.1	0.1	0.2	0.3	0.5	0.6	0.8	1.0	1.3	1.6	1.9	2.2	2.5	7.0
8.0	0.0	0.1	0.1	0.2	0.4	0.5	0.7	0.9	1.2	1.5	1.8	2.1	2.5	2.9	8.0
9.0	0.0	0.1	0.2	0.3	0.4	0.6	0.8	1.1	1.4	1.7	2.0	2.4	2.8	3.3	9.0
10.0	0.0	0.1	0.2	0.3	0.5	0.7	0.9	1.2	1.5	1.9	2.2	2.7	3.1	3.6	10.0
11.0	0.0	0.1	0.2	0.3	0.5	0.7	1.0	1.3	1.6	2.0	2.5	2.9	3.4	4.0	11.0
12.0	0.0	0.1	0.2	0.4	0.6	0.8	1.1	1.4	1.8	2.2	2.7	3.2	3.8	4.4	12.0
13.0	0.0	0.1	0.2	0.4	0.6	0.9	1.2	1.5	2.0	2.4	2.9	3.5	4.1	4.7	13.0
14.0	0.0	0.1	0.2	0.4	0.6	0.9	1.3	1.7	2.1	2.6	3.1	3.7	4.4	5.1	14.0
15.0	0.0	0.1	0.3	0.4	0.7	1.0	1.4	1.8	2.2	2.8	3.4	4.0	4.7	5.4	15.0
16.0	0.0	0.1	0.3	0.5	0.7	1.1	1.5	1.9	2.4	3.0	3.6	4.3	5.0	5.8	16.0
17.0	0.0	0.1	0.3	0.5	0.8	1.1	1.5	2.0	2.6	3.1	3.8	4.5	5.3	6.2	17.0
18.0	0.0	0.1	0.3	0.5	0.8	1.2	1.6	2.1	2.7	3.3	4.0	4.8	5.6	6.5	18.0
19.0	0.0	0.1	0.3	0.6	0.9	1.3	1.7	2.3	2.8	3.5	4.3	5.1	5.9	6.9	19.0
20.0	0.0	0.1	0.3	0.6	0.9	1.3	1.8	2.4	3.0	3.7	4.5	5.3	6.3	7.3	20.0
21.0	0.0	0.2	0.4	0.6	1.0	1.4	1.9	2.5	3.2	3.9	4.7	5.6	6.6	7.6	21.0
22.0	0.0	0.2	0.4	0.7	1.0	1.5	2.0	2.6	3.3	4.1	4.9	5.9	6.9	8.0	22.0
23.0	0.0	0.2	0.4	0.7	1.1	1.5	2.1	2.7	3.4	4.3	5.2	6.1	7.2	8.3	23.0
24.0	0.0	0.2	0.4	0.7	1.1	1.6	2.2	2.8	3.6	4.4	5.4	6.4	7.5	8.7	24.0
25.0	0.0	0.2	0.4	0.7	1.2	1.7	2.3	3.0	3.8	4.6	5.6	6.7	7.8	9.1	25.0
26.0	0.0	0.2	0.4	0.8	1.2	1.7	2.4	3.1	3.9	4.8	5.8	6.9	8.1	9.4	26.0
27.0	0.0	0.2	0.4	0.8	1.2	1.8	2.4	3.2	4.0	5.0	6.0	7.2	8.5	9.8	27.0
28.0	0.1	0.2	0.5	0.8	1.3	1.9	2.5	3.3	4.2	5.2	6.3	7.5	8.8	10.2	28.0

Caution. —If this table is entered with the meridian angle of the Moon in arc units, such units should correspond to the meridian angle in time units as given in the Increments and Corrections section of the *Nautical Almanac.*

TABLE 25

Change of Altitude in Given Time from Meridian Transit

a (table 24)	1° 15′	1° 20′	1° 25′	1° 30′	1° 35′	1° 40′	1° 45′	1° 50′	1° 55′	2° 00′	2° 05′	2° 10′	2° 15′	2° 20′	a (table 24)
	t, meridian angle														
	$5^{m}00^{s}$	$5^{m}20^{s}$	$5^{m}40^{s}$	$6^{m}00^{s}$	$6^{m}20^{s}$	$6^{m}40^{s}$	$7^{m}00^{s}$	$7^{m}20^{s}$	$7^{m}40^{s}$	$8^{m}00^{s}$	$8^{m}20^{s}$	$8^{m}40^{s}$	$9^{m}00^{s}$	$9^{m}20^{s}$	
″	′	′	′	′	′	′	′	′	′	′	′	′	′	′	″
0.1	0.0	0.0	0.1	0.1	0.1	0.1	0.1	0.1	0.1	0.1	0.1	0.1	0.1	0.1	0.1
0.2	0.1	0.1	0.1	0.1	0.1	0.1	0.2	0.2	0.2	0.2	0.2	0.3	0.3	0.3	0.2
0.3	0.1	0.1	0.2	0.2	0.2	0.2	0.2	0.3	0.3	0.3	0.3	0.4	0.4	0.4	0.3
0.4	0.2	0.2	0.2	0.2	0.3	0.3	0.3	0.4	0.4	0.4	0.5	0.5	0.5	0.6	0.4
0.5	0.2	0.2	0.3	0.3	0.3	0.4	0.4	0.5	0.5	0.5	0.6	0.6	0.7	0.7	0.5
0.6	0.2	0.3	0.3	0.4	0.4	0.4	0.5	0.5	0.6	0.6	0.7	0.8	0.8	0.9	0.6
0.7	0.3	0.3	0.4	0.4	0.5	0.5	0.6	0.6	0.7	0.7	0.8	0.9	0.9	1.0	0.7
0.8	0.3	0.4	0.4	0.5	0.5	0.6	0.7	0.7	0.8	0.9	0.9	1.0	1.1	1.2	0.8
0.9	0.4	0.4	0.5	0.5	0.6	0.7	0.7	0.8	0.9	1.0	1.0	1.1	1.2	1.3	0.9
1.0	0.4	0.5	0.5	0.6	0.7	0.7	0.8	0.9	1.0	1.1	1.2	1.3	1.4	1.5	1.0
2.0	0.8	0.9	1.1	1.2	1.3	1.5	1.6	1.8	2.0	2.1	2.3	2.5	2.7	2.9	2.0
3.0	1.2	1.4	1.6	1.8	2.0	2.2	2.4	2.7	2.9	3.2	3.5	3.8	4.0	4.4	3.0
4.0	1.7	1.9	2.1	2.4	2.7	3.0	3.3	3.6	3.9	4.3	4.6	5.0	5.4	5.8	4.0
5.0	2.1	2.4	2.7	3.0	3.3	3.7	4.1	4.5	4.9	5.3	5.8	6.3	6.8	7.3	5.0
6.0	2.5	2.8	3.2	3.6	4.0	4.4	4.9	5.4	5.9	6.4	6.9	7.5	8.1	8.7	6.0
7.0	2.9	3.3	3.7	4.2	4.7	5.2	5.7	6.3	6.9	7.5	8.1	8.8	9.4	10.2	7.0
8.0	3.3	3.8	4.3	4.8	5.3	5.9	6.5	7.2	7.8	8.5	9.3	10.0	10.8	11.6	8.0
9.0	3.8	4.3	4.8	5.4	6.0	6.7	7.4	8.1	8.8	9.6	10.4	11.3	12.2	13.1	9.0
10.0	4.2	4.7	5.4	6.0	6.7	7.4	8.2	9.0	9.8	10.7	11.6	12.5	13.5	14.5	10.0
11.0	4.6	5.2	5.9	6.6	7.4	8.1	9.0	9.9	10.8	11.7	12.7	13.8	14.8	16.0	11.0
12.0	5.0	5.7	6.4	7.2	8.0	8.9	9.8	10.8	11.8	12.8	13.9	15.0	16.2	17.4	12.0
13.0	5.4	6.2	7.0	7.8	8.7	9.6	10.6	11.7	12.7	13.9	15.0	16.3	17.6	18.9	13.0
14.0	5.8	6.6	7.5	8.4	9.4	10.4	11.4	12.5	13.7	14.9	16.2	17.5	18.9	20.3	14.0
15.0	6.2	7.1	8.0	9.0	10.0	11.1	12.2	13.4	14.7	16.0	17.4	18.8	20.2	21.8	15.0
16.0	6.7	7.6	8.6	9.6	10.7	11.9	13.1	14.3	15.7	17.1	18.5	20.0	21.6	23.2	16.0
17.0	7.1	8.1	9.1	10.2	11.4	12.6	13.9	15.2	16.7	18.1	19.7	21.3	23.0	24.7	17.0
18.0	7.5	8.5	9.6	10.8	12.0	13.3	14.7	16.1	17.6	19.2	20.8	22.5	24.3	26.1	18.0
19.0	7.9	9.0	10.2	11.4	12.7	14.1	15.5	17.0	18.6	20.3	22.0	23.8			19.0
20.0	8.3	9.5	10.7	12.0	13.4	14.8	16.3	17.9	19.6	21.3	23.1				20.0
21.0	8.8	10.0	11.2	12.6	14.0	15.6	17.2	18.8	20.6						21.0
22.0	9.2	10.4	11.8	13.2	14.7	16.3	18.0	19.7	21.6						22.0
23.0	9.6	10.9	12.3	13.8	15.4	17.0	18.8	20.6							23.0
24.0	10.0	11.4	12.8	14.4	16.0	17.8	19.6	21.5							24.0
25.0	10.4	11.9	13.4	15.0	16.7	18.5	20.4								25.0
26.0	10.8	12.3	13.9	15.6	17.4	19.3									26.0
27.0	11.2	12.8	14.4	16.2	18.0	20.0									27.0

Caution. —If this table is entered with the meridian angle of the Moon in arc units, such units should correspond to the meridian angle in time units as given in the Increments and Corrections section of the *Nautical Almanac.*

TABLE 25

Change of Altitude in Given Time from Meridian Transit

a (table 24)	t, meridian angle														*a* (table 24)
	2° 25′	2° 30′	2° 35′	2° 40′	2° 45′	2° 50′	2° 55′	3° 00′	3° 05′	3° 10′	3° 15′	3° 20′	3° 25′	3° 30′	
	9ᵐ 40ˢ	10ᵐ 00ˢ	10ᵐ 20ˢ	10ᵐ 40ˢ	11ᵐ 00ˢ	11ᵐ 20ˢ	11ᵐ 40ˢ	12ᵐ 00ˢ	12ᵐ 20ˢ	12ᵐ 40ˢ	13ᵐ 00ˢ	13ᵐ 20ˢ	13ᵐ 40ˢ	14ᵐ 00ˢ	
″	′	′	′	′	′	′	′	′	′	′	′	′	′	′	″
0.1	0.2	0.2	0.2	0.2	0.2	0.2	0.2	0.2	0.3	0.3	0.3	0.3	0.3	0.3	0.1
0.2	0.3	0.3	0.4	0.4	0.4	0.4	0.5	0.5	0.5	0.5	0.6	0.6	0.6	0.7	0.2
0.3	0.5	0.5	0.5	0.6	0.6	0.6	0.7	0.7	0.8	0.8	0.8	0.9	0.9	1.0	0.3
0.4	0.6	0.7	0.7	0.8	0.8	0.9	0.9	1.0	1.0	1.1	1.1	1.2	1.2	1.3	0.4
0.5	0.8	0.8	0.9	0.9	1.0	1.1	1.1	1.2	1.3	1.3	1.4	1.5	1.6	1.6	0.5
0.6	0.9	1.0	1.1	1.1	1.2	1.3	1.4	1.4	1.5	1.6	1.7	1.8	1.9	2.0	0.6
0.7	1.1	1.2	1.2	1.3	1.4	1.5	1.6	1.7	1.8	1.9	2.0	2.1	2.2	2.3	0.7
0.8	1.2	1.3	1.4	1.5	1.6	1.7	1.8	1.9	2.0	2.1	2.3	2.4	2.5	2.6	0.8
0.9	1.4	1.5	1.6	1.7	1.8	1.9	2.0	2.2	2.3	2.4	2.5	2.7	2.8	2.9	0.9
1.0	1.6	1.7	1.8	1.9	2.0	2.1	2.3	2.4	2.5	2.7	2.8	3.0	3.1	3.3	1.0
2.0	3.1	3.3	3.6	3.8	4.0	4.3	4.5	4.8	5.1	5.3	5.6	5.9	6.2	6.5	2.0
3.0	4.7	5.0	5.3	5.7	6.0	6.4	6.8	7.2	7.6	8.0	8.4	8.9	9.3	9.8	3.0
4.0	6.2	6.7	7.1	7.6	8.1	8.6	9.1	9.6	10.1	10.7	11.3	11.9	12.5	13.1	4.0
5.0	7.8	8.3	8.9	9.5	10.1	10.7	11.3	12.0	12.7	13.4	14.1	14.8	15.6	16.3	5.0
6.0	9.3	10.0	10.7	11.4	12.1	12.8	13.6	14.4	15.2	16.0	16.9	17.8	18.7	19.6	6.0
7.0	10.9	11.7	12.5	13.3	14.1	15.0	15.9	16.8	17.7	18.7	19.7	20.7	21.8	22.9	7.0
8.0	12.5	13.3	14.2	15.2	16.1	17.1	18.1	19.2	20.3	21.4	22.5	23.7	24.9	26.1	8.0
9.0	14.0	15.0	16.0	17.1	18.2	19.3	20.4	21.6	22.8	24.1	25.4	26.7	28.0	29.4	9.0
10.0	15.6	16.7	17.8	19.0	20.2	21.4	22.7	24.0	25.4	26.7	28.2	29.6			10.0
11.0	17.1	18.3	19.6	20.9	22.2	23.5	25.0	26.4	27.9	29.4					11.0
12.0	18.7	20.0	21.4	22.8	24.2	25.7	27.2	28.8							12.0
13.0	20.2	21.7	23.1	24.7	26.2	27.8	29.5								13.0
14.0	21.8	23.3	24.9	26.6	28.2	30.0									14.0
15.0	23.4	25.0	26.7	28.5	30.2										15.0
16.0	24.9	26.7	28.5	30.3											16.0
17.0	26.5	28.3	30.3												17.0

a (table 24)	t, meridian angle														*a* (table 24)
	3° 35′	3° 40′	3° 45′	3° 50′	3° 55′	4° 00′	4° 05′	4° 10′	4° 15′	4° 20′	4° 25′	4° 30′	4° 35′	4° 40′	
	14ᵐ 20ˢ	14ᵐ 40ˢ	15ᵐ 00ˢ	15ᵐ 20ˢ	15ᵐ 40ˢ	16ᵐ 00ˢ	16ᵐ 20ˢ	16ᵐ 40ˢ	17ᵐ 00ˢ	17ᵐ 20ˢ	17ᵐ 40ˢ	18ᵐ 00ˢ	18ᵐ 20ˢ	18ᵐ 40ˢ	
″	′	′	′	′	′	′	′	′	′	′	′	′	′	′	″
0.1	0.3	0.4	0.4	0.4	0.4	0.4	0.4	0.5	0.5	0.5	0.5	0.5	0.6	0.6	0.1
0.2	0.7	0.7	0.8	0.8	0.8	0.9	0.9	0.9	1.0	1.0	1.0	1.1	1.1	1.2	0.2
0.3	1.0	1.1	1.1	1.2	1.2	1.3	1.3	1.4	1.4	1.5	1.6	1.6	1.7	1.7	0.3
0.4	1.4	1.4	1.5	1.6	1.6	1.7	1.8	1.9	1.9	2.0	2.1	2.2	2.2	2.3	0.4
0.5	1.7	1.8	1.9	2.0	2.0	2.1	2.2	2.3	2.4	2.5	2.6	2.7	2.8	2.9	0.5
0.6	2.1	2.2	2.2	2.4	2.5	2.6	2.7	2.8	2.9	3.0	3.1	3.2	3.4	3.5	0.6
0.7	2.4	2.5	2.6	2.7	2.9	3.0	3.1	3.2	3.4	3.5	3.6	3.8	3.9	4.1	0.7
0.8	2.7	2.9	3.0	3.1	3.3	3.4	3.6	3.7	3.9	4.0	4.2	4.3	4.5	4.6	0.8
0.9	3.1	3.2	3.4	3.5	3.7	3.8	4.0	4.2	4.3	4.5	4.7	4.9	5.0	5.2	0.9
1.0	3.4	3.6	3.8	3.9	4.1	4.3	4.4	4.6	4.8	5.0	5.2	5.4	5.6	5.8	1.0
2.0	6.8	7.2	7.5	7.8	8.2	8.5	8.9	9.3	9.6	10.0	10.4	10.8	11.2	11.6	2.0
3.0	10.3	10.8	11.3	11.8	12.3	12.8	13.3	13.9	14.4	15.0	15.6	16.2	16.8	17.4	3.0
4.0	13.7	14.3	15.0	15.7	16.4	17.1	17.8	18.5	19.3	20.0	20.8	21.6	22.4	23.2	4.0
5.0	17.1	17.9	18.8	19.6	20.5	21.3	22.2	23.1	24.1	25.0	26.0	27.0	28.0	29.0	5.0
6.0	20.5	21.5	22.5	23.5	24.5	25.6	26.7	27.8							6.0
7.0	24.0	25.1	26.3	27.4											7.0
8.0	27.4	28.7	30.0												8.0

Caution. —If this table is entered with the meridian angle of the Moon in arc units, such units should correspond to the meridian angle in time units as given in the Increments and Corrections section of the *Nautical Almanac*.

TABLE 25

Change of Altitude in Given Time from Meridian Transit

a (table 24)	t, meridian angle														*a* (table 24)
	4° 45′	4° 50′	4° 55′	5° 00′	5° 05′	5° 10′	5° 15′	5° 20′	5° 25′	5° 30′	5° 35′	5° 40′	5° 45′	5° 50′	
	19ᵐ 00ˢ	19ᵐ 20ˢ	19ᵐ 40ˢ	20ᵐ 00ˢ	20ᵐ 20ˢ	20ᵐ 40ˢ	21ᵐ 00ˢ	21ᵐ 20ˢ	21ᵐ 40ˢ	22ᵐ 00ˢ	22ᵐ 20ˢ	22ᵐ 40ˢ	23ᵐ 00ˢ	23ᵐ 20ˢ	
″	′	′	′	′	′	′	′	′	′	′	′	′	′	′	″
0.1	0.6	0.6	0.6	0.7	0.7	0.7	0.7	0.8	0.8	0.8	0.8	0.9	0.9	0.9	0.1
0.2	1.2	1.2	1.3	1.3	1.4	1.4	1.5	1.5	1.6	1.6	1.7	1.7	1.8	1.8	0.2
0.3	1.8	1.9	1.9	2.0	2.1	2.1	2.2	2.3	2.3	2.4	2.5	2.6	2.6	2.7	0.3
0.4	2.4	2.5	2.6	2.7	2.8	2.8	2.9	3.0	3.1	3.2	3.3	3.4	3.5	3.6	0.4
0.5	3.0	3.1	3.2	3.3	3.4	3.6	3.7	3.8	3.9	4.0	4.2	4.3	4.4	4.5	0.5
0.6	3.6	3.7	3.9	4.0	4.1	4.3	4.4	4.6	4.7	4.8	5.0	5.1	5.3	5.4	0.6
0.7	4.2	4.4	4.5	4.7	4.8	5.0	5.1	5.3	5.5	5.6	5.8	6.0	6.2	6.4	0.7
0.8	4.8	5.0	5.2	5.3	5.5	5.7	5.9	6.1	6.3	6.5	6.7	6.9	7.1	7.3	0.8
0.9	5.4	5.6	5.8	6.0	6.2	6.4	6.6	6.8	7.0	7.3	7.5	7.7	7.9	8.2	0.9
1.0	6.0	6.2	6.4	6.7	6.9	7.1	7.4	7.6	7.8	8.1	8.3	8.6	8.8	9.1	1.0
2.0	12.0	12.5	12.9	13.3	13.8	14.2	14.7	15.2	15.6	16.1	16.6	17.1	17.6	18.1	2.0
3.0	18.0	18.7	19.3	20.0	20.7	21.4	22.0	22.8	23.5	24.2	24.9	25.7	26.4	27.2	3.0
4.0	24.1	24.9	25.8	26.7	27.6	28.5	29.4	30.3	31.3						4.0

a (table 24)	t, meridian angle														*a* (table 24)
	5° 55′	6° 00′	6° 05′	6° 10′	6° 15′	6° 20′	6° 25′	6° 30′	6° 35′	6° 40′	6° 45′	6° 50′	6° 55′	7° 00′	
	23ᵐ 40ˢ	24ᵐ 00ˢ	24ᵐ 20ˢ	24ᵐ 40ˢ	25ᵐ 00ˢ	25ᵐ 20ˢ	25ᵐ 40ˢ	26ᵐ 00ˢ	26ᵐ 20ˢ	26ᵐ 40ˢ	27ᵐ 00ˢ	27ᵐ 20ˢ	27ᵐ 40ˢ	28ᵐ 20ˢ	
″	′	′	′	′	′	′	′	′	′	′	′	′	′	′	″
0.1	0.9	1.0	1.0	1.0	1.0	1.1	1.1	1.1	1.2	1.2	1.2	1.2	1.3	1.3	0.1
0.2	1.9	1.9	2.0	2.0	2.1	2.1	2.2	2.3	2.3	2.4	2.4	2.5	2.6	2.6	0.2
0.3	2.8	2.9	3.0	3.0	3.1	3.2	3.3	3.4	3.5	3.6	3.6	3.7	3.8	3.9	0.3
0.4	3.7	3.8	3.9	4.1	4.2	4.3	4.4	4.5	4.6	4.7	4.9	5.0	5.1	5.2	0.4
0.5	4.7	4.8	4.9	5.1	5.2	5.3	5.5	5.6	5.8	5.9	6.1	6.2	6.4	6.5	0.5
0.6	5.6	5.8	5.9	6.1	6.2	6.4	6.6	6.8	6.9	7.1	7.3	7.5	7.7	7.8	0.6
0.7	6.5	6.7	6.9	7.1	7.3	7.5	7.7	7.9	8.1	8.3	8.5	8.7	8.9	9.1	0.7
0.8	7.5	7.7	7.9	8.1	8.3	8.6	8.8	9.0	9.2	9.5	9.7	10.0	10.2	10.5	0.8
0.9	8.4	8.6	8.9	9.1	9.4	9.6	9.9	10.1	10.4	10.7	10.9	11.2	11.5	11.8	0.9
1.0	9.3	9.6	9.9	10.1	10.4	10.7	11.0	11.3	11.6	11.9	12.2	12.5	12.8	13.1	1.0
2.0	18.7	19.2	19.7	20.3	20.8	21.4	22.0	22.5	23.1	23.7	24.3	24.9	25.5	26.1	2.0
3.0	28.0	28.8	29.6	30.4											3.0

Caution. —If this table is entered with the meridian angle of the Moon in arc units, such units should correspond to the meridian angle in time units as given in the Increments and Corrections section of the *Nautical Almanac*.

TABLE 26

Time Zones, Zone Descriptions, and Suffixes

ZONE	ZD	SUFFIX	ZONE	ZD	SUFFIX
7½°W to 7½°E.	0	Z	7½° W. to 22½° W.	+ 1	N
7½° E. to 22½°E.	– 1	A	22½° W. to 37½° W.	+ 2	O
22½° E. to 37½°E.	– 2	B	37½° W. to 52½° W.	+ 3	P
37½° E. to 52½°E.	– 3	C	52½° W. to 67½° W.	+ 4	Q
52½° E. to 67½°E.	– 4	D	67½° W. to 82½° W.	+ 5	R
67½° E. to 82½°E.	– 5	E	82½° W. to 97½° W.	+ 6	S
82½° E. to 97½°E.	– 6	F	97½° W. to 112½° W.	+ 7	T
97½° E. to 112½°E.	– 7	G	112½° W. to 127½° W.	+ 8	U
112½° E. to 127½°E.	– 8	H	127½° W. to 142½° W.	+ 9	V
127½° E. to 142½°E.	– 9	I	142½° W. to 157½° W.	+ 10	W
142½° E. to 157½°E.	– 10	K	157½° W. to 172½° W.	+ 11	X
157½° E. to 172½°E.	– 11	L	172½° W. to 180°	+ 12	Y
172½° E. to 180 °E.	– 12	M			

NOTE. – G M T is indicated by suffix Z. Standard times as kept in various places or countries are listed in *The Nautical Almanac* and *The Air Almanac.*

TABLE 27

Altitude Correction for Air Temperature

Altitude	Temperature—degrees Fahrenheit								Altitude
	− 40	− 30	− 20	− 10	0	+ 10	+ 20	+ 30	
° ′	′	′	′	′	′	′	′	′	° ′
− 0 10	− 7.9	− 6.8	− 5.8	− 4.9	− 4.0	− 3.1	− 2.3	− 1.5	− 0 10
0 00	7.4	6.4	5.5	4.6	3.8	2.9	2.2	1.4	0 00
+ 0 10	6.9	6.0	5.2	4.3	3.5	2.8	2.0	1.3	+ 0 10
0 20	6.6	5.7	4.9	4.1	3.3	2.6	1.9	1.2	0 20
0 30	6.1	5.3	4.6	3.8	3.1	2.4	1.8	1.2	0 30
+ 0 45	− 5.7	− 4.9	− 4.2	− 3.5	− 2.9	− 2.2	− 1.6	− 1.1	+ 0 45
1 00	5.2	4.5	3.9	3.2	2.6	2.1	1.5	1.0	1 00
1 20	4.7	4.1	3.5	2.9	2.4	1.9	1.4	0.9	1 20
1 40	4.3	3.7	3.2	2.7	2.2	1.7	1.2	0.8	1 40
2 00	3.9	3.4	2.9	2.4	2.0	1.6	1.1	0.7	2 00
+ 2 30	− 3.4	− 3.0	− 2.6	− 2.1	− 1.8	− 1.4	− 1.0	− 0.7	+ 2 30
3 00	3.1	2.7	2.3	1.9	1.6	1.2	0.9	0.6	3 00
4	2.5	2.2	1.9	1.6	1.3	1.0	0.7	0.5	4
5	2.1	1.8	1.6	1.3	1.1	0.8	0.6	0.4	5
6	1.8	1.6	1.4	1.1	0.9	0.7	0.5	0.3	6
+ 7	− 1.6	− 1.4	− 1.2	− 1.0	− 0.8	− 0.6	− 0.5	− 0.3	+ 7
8	1.4	1.2	1.0	0.9	0.7	0.6	0.4	0.3	8
9	1.3	1.1	0.9	0.8	0.6	0.5	0.4	0.2	9
10	1.1	1.0	0.8	0.7	0.6	0.5	0.3	0.2	10
15	0.8	0.7	0.6	0.5	0.4	0.3	0.2	0.1	15
+ 20	− 0.6	− 0.5	− 0.4	− 0.3	− 0.3	− 0.2	− 0.2	− 0.1	+ 20
30	0.4	0.3	0.3	0.2	0.2	0.1	0.1	0.1	30
50	0.2	0.1	0.1	0.1	0.1	0.1	0.0	0.0	50
70	0.1	0.1	0.1	0.1	0.0	0.0	0.0	0.0	70
+ 90	0.0	0.0	0.0	0.0	0.0	0.0	0.0	0.0	+ 90

Altitude	Temperature—degrees Fahrenheit								Altitude
	+ 40	+ 50	+ 60	+ 70	+ 80	+ 90	+ 100	+ 110	
° ′	′	′	′	′	′	′	′	′	° ′
− 0 10	− 0.7	0.0	+ 0.7	+ 1.4	+ 2.0	+ 2.7	+ 3.3	+ 3.9	− 0 10
0 00	0.7	0.0	0.7	1.3	1.9	2.5	3.1	3.6	0 00
+ 0 10	0.6	0.0	0.6	1.2	1.8	2.4	2.9	3.4	+ 0 10
0 20	0.6	0.0	0.6	1.2	1.7	2.2	2.7	3.2	0 20
0 30	0.6	0.0	0.6	1.1	1.6	2.1	2.6	3.0	0 30
+ 0 45	− 0.5	0.0	+ 0.5	+ 1.0	+ 1.5	+ 1.9	+ 2.4	+ 2.8	+ 0 45
1 00	0.5	0.0	0.5	0.9	1.4	1.8	2.2	2.6	1 00
1 20	0.4	0.0	0.4	0.8	1.2	1.6	2.0	2.3	1 20
1 40	0.4	0.0	0.4	0.8	1.1	1.5	1.8	2.1	1 40
2 00	0.4	0.0	0.4	0.7	1.0	1.3	1.6	1.9	2 00
+ 2 30	− 0.3	0.0	+ 0.3	+ 0.6	+ 0.9	+ 1.2	+ 1.4	+ 1.7	+ 2 30
3 00	0.3	0.0	0.3	0.5	0.8	1.0	1.3	1.5	3 00
4	0.2	0.0	0.2	0.4	0.7	0.9	1.1	1.2	4
5	0.2	0.0	0.2	0.4	0.6	0.7	0.9	1.0	5
6	0.2	0.0	0.2	0.3	0.5	0.6	0.8	0.9	6
+ 7	− 0.1	0.0	+ 0.1	+ 0.3	+ 0.4	+ 0.5	+ 0.7	+ 0.8	+ 7
8	0.1	0.0	0.1	0.2	0.4	0.5	0.6	0.7	8
9	0.1	0.0	0.1	0.2	0.3	0.4	0.5	0.6	9
10	0.1	0.0	0.1	0.2	0.3	0.4	0.5	0.6	10
15	0.1	0.0	0.1	0.1	0.2	0.3	0.3	0.4	15
+ 20	− 0.1	0.0	+ 0.1	+ 0.1	+ 0.1	+ 0.2	+ 0.2	+ 0.3	+ 20
30	0.0	0.0	0.0	0.1	0.1	0.1	0.2	0.2	30
50	0.0	0.0	0.0	0.0	0.0	0.1	0.1	0.1	50
70	0.0	0.0	0.0	0.0	0.0	0.0	0.0	0.0	70
+ 90	0.0	0.0	0.0	0.0	0.0	0.0	0.0	0.0	+ 90

TABLE 28

Altitude Correction for Atmospheric Pressure

Altitude	Pressure in inches or millibars— **Subtract** correction from sextant or rectified altitude								Altitude
	31.2	31.0	30.8	30.6	30.4	30.2	30.0	29.8	
	1056.56	1049.78	1043.01	1036.24	1029.46	1022.69	1015.92	1009.15	
° ′	′	′	′	′	′	′	′	′	° ′
− 0 10	− 1.7	− 1.4	− 1.2	− 1.0	− 0.7	− 0.5	− 0.2	0.0	− 0 10
0 00	1.6	1.4	1.1	0.9	0.7	0.4	0.2	0.0	0 00
+ 0 10	1.5	1.3	1.1	0.8	0.6	0.4	0.2	0.0	+ 0 10
0 20	1.4	1.2	1.0	0.8	0.6	0.4	0.2	0.0	0 20
0 30	1.3	1.1	0.9	0.7	0.6	0.4	0.2	0.0	0 30
+ 0 45	− 1.2	− 1.0	− 0.9	− 0.7	− 0.5	− 0.3	− 0.2	− 0.0	+ 0 45
1 00	1.1	1.0	0.8	0.6	0.5	0.3	0.1	0.0	1 00
1 20	1.0	0.9	0.7	0.6	0.4	0.3	0.1	0.0	1 20
1 40	0.9	0.8	0.7	0.5	0.4	0.3	0.1	0.0	1 40
2 00	0.8	0.7	0.6	0.5	0.4	0.2	0.1	0.0	2 00
+ 2 30	− 0.7	− 0.6	− 0.5	− 0.4	− 0.3	− 0.2	− 0.1	0.0	+ 2 30
3 00	0.7	0.6	0.5	0.4	0.3	0.2	0.1	0.0	3 00
4	0.5	0.5	0.4	0.3	0.2	0.1	0.1	0.0	4
5	0.5	0.4	0.3	0.3	0.2	0.1	0.0	0.0	5
6	0.4	0.3	0.3	0.2	0.2	0.1	0.0	0.0	6
+ 7	− 0.3	− 0.3	− 0.2	− 0.2	− 0.1	− 0.1	− 0.0	− 0.0	+ 7
8	0.3	0.3	0.2	0.2	0.1	0.1	0.0	0.0	8
9	0.3	0.2	0.2	0.2	0.1	0.1	0.0	0.0	9
10	0.2	0.2	0.2	0.1	0.1	0.1	0.0	0.0	10
15	0.2	0.1	0.1	0.1	0.1	0.0	0.0	0.0	15
+ 20	− 0.1	− 0.1	− 0.1	− 0.1	− 0.1	− 0.0	− 0.0	− 0.0	+ 20
30	0.1	0.1	0.1	0.0	0.0	0.0	0.0	0.0	30
50	0.0	0.0	0.0	0.0	0.0	0.0	0.0	0.0	50
70	0.0	0.0	0.0	0.0	0.0	0.0	0.0	0.0	70
+ 90	0.0	0.0	0.0	0.0	0.0	0.0	0.0	0.0	+ 90

Altitude	Pressure in inches or millibars— **Add** correction to sextant or rectified altitude								Altitude
	29.6	29.4	29.2	29.0	28.8	28.6	28.4	28.2	
	1002.37	995.60	988.83	982.05	975.28	968.51	961.74	954.96	
° ′	′	′	′	′	′	′	′	′	° ′
− 0 10	+ 0.3	+ 0.5	+ 0.8	+ 1.0	+ 1.3	+ 1.5	+ 1.8	+ 2.0	− 0 10
0 00	0.3	0.5	0.7	1.0	1.2	1.4	1.6	1.9	0 00
+ 0 10	0.2	0.5	0.7	0.9	1.1	1.3	1.5	1.8	+ 0 10
0 20	0.2	0.4	0.6	0.8	1.1	1.3	1.5	1.7	0 20
0 30	0.2	0.4	0.6	0.8	1.0	1.2	1.4	1.6	0 30
+ 0 45	+ 0.2	+ 0.4	+ 0.6	+ 0.7	+ 0.9	+ 1.1	+ 1.3	+ 1.4	+ 0 45
1 00	0.2	0.3	0.5	0.7	0.8	1.0	1.2	1.3	1 00
1 20	0.2	0.3	0.5	0.6	0.8	0.9	1.1	1.2	1 20
1 40	0.2	0.3	0.4	0.6	0.7	0.8	1.0	1.1	1 40
2 00	0.1	0.3	0.4	0.5	0.6	0.8	0.9	1.0	2 00
+ 2 30	+ 0.1	+ 0.2	+ 0.3	+ 0.4	+ 0.6	+ 0.7	+ 0.8	+ 0.9	+ 2 30
3 00	0.1	0.2	0.3	0.4	0.5	0.6	0.7	0.8	3 00
4	0.1	0.2	0.2	0.3	0.4	0.5	0.6	0.6	4
5	0.1	0.1	0.2	0.3	0.3	0.4	0.5	0.5	5
6	0.1	0.1	0.2	0.2	0.3	0.3	0.4	0.5	6
+ 7	+ 0.1	+ 0.1	+ 0.2	+ 0.2	+ 0.3	+ 0.3	+ 0.4	+ 0.4	+ 7
8	0.0	0.1	0.1	0.2	0.2	0.3	0.3	0.4	8
9	0.0	0.1	0.1	0.2	0.2	0.2	0.3	0.3	9
10	0.0	0.1	0.1	0.1	0.2	0.2	0.3	0.3	10
15	0.0	0.1	0.1	0.1	0.1	0.1	0.2	0.2	15
+ 20	+ 0.0	+ 0.0	+ 0.1	+ 0.1	+ 0.1	+ 0.1	+ 0.1	+ 0.1	+ 20
30	0.0	0.0	0.0	0.0	0.1	0.1	0.1	0.1	30
50	0.0	0.0	0.0	0.0	0.0	0.0	0.0	0.0	50
70	0.0	0.0	0.0	0.0	0.0	0.0	0.0	0.0	70
+ 90	0.0	0.0	0.0	0.0	0.0	0.0	0.0	0.0	+ 90

TABLE 29

Conversion Tables for Thermometer Scales

F = Fahrenheit, C = Celsius (centigrade), K = Kelvin

F	C	K	F	C	K	C	F	K	K	F	C
°	°	°	°	°	°	°	°	°	°	°	°
−20	−28.9	244.3	+40	+4.4	277.6	−25	−13.0	248.2	250	−9.7	−23.2
19	28.3	244.8	41	5.0	278.2	24	11.2	249.2	251	7.9	22.2
18	27.8	245.4	42	5.6	278.7	23	9.4	250.2	252	6.1	21.2
17	27.2	245.9	43	6.1	279.3	22	7.6	251.2	253	4.3	20.2
16	26.7	246.5	44	6.7	279.8	21	5.8	252.2	254	2.5	19.2
−15	−26.1	247.0	+45	+7.2	280.4	−20	−4.0	253.2	255	−0.7	−18.2
14	25.6	247.6	46	7.8	280.9	19	2.2	254.2	256	+1.1	17.2
13	25.0	248.2	47	8.3	281.5	18	−0.4	255.2	257	2.9	16.2
12	24.4	248.7	48	8.9	282.0	17	+1.4	256.2	258	4.7	15.2
11	23.9	249.3	49	9.4	282.6	16	3.2	257.2	259	6.5	14.2
−10	−23.3	249.8	+50	+10.0	283.2	−15	+5.0	258.2	260	+8.3	−13.2
9	22.8	250.4	51	10.6	283.7	14	6.8	259.2	261	10.1	12.2
8	22.2	250.9	52	11.1	284.3	13	8.6	260.2	262	11.9	11.2
7	21.7	251.5	53	11.7	284.8	12	10.4	261.2	263	13.7	10.2
6	21.1	252.0	54	12.2	285.4	11	12.2	262.2	264	15.5	9.2
−5	−20.6	252.6	+55	+12.8	285.9	−10	+14.0	263.2	265	+17.3	−8.2
4	20.0	253.2	56	13.3	286.5	9	15.8	264.2	266	19.1	7.2
3	19.4	253.7	57	13.9	287.0	8	17.6	265.2	267	20.9	6.2
2	18.9	254.3	58	14.4	287.6	7	19.4	266.2	268	22.7	5.2
−1	18.3	254.8	59	15.0	288.2	6	21.2	267.2	269	24.5	4.2
0	−17.8	255.4	+60	+15.6	288.7	−5	+23.0	268.2	270	+26.3	−3.2
+1	17.2	255.9	61	16.1	289.3	4	24.8	269.2	271	28.1	2.2
2	16.7	256.5	62	16.7	289.8	3	26.6	270.2	272	29.9	1.2
3	16.1	257.0	63	17.2	290.4	2	28.4	271.2	273	31.7	−0.2
4	15.6	257.6	64	17.8	290.9	−1	30.2	272.2	274	33.5	+0.8
+5	−15.0	258.2	+65	+18.3	291.5	0	+32.0	273.2	275	+35.3	+1.8
6	14.4	258.7	66	18.9	292.0	+1	33.8	274.2	276	37.1	2.8
7	13.9	259.3	67	19.4	292.6	2	35.6	275.2	277	38.9	3.8
8	13.3	259.8	68	20.0	293.2	3	37.4	276.2	278	40.7	4.8
9	12.8	260.4	69	20.6	293.7	4	39.2	277.2	279	42.5	5.8
+10	−12.2	260.9	+70	+21.1	294.3	+5	+41.0	278.2	280	+44.3	+6.8
11	11.7	261.5	71	21.7	294.8	6	42.8	279.2	281	46.1	7.8
12	11.1	262.0	72	22.2	295.4	7	44.6	280.2	282	47.9	8.8
13	10.6	262.6	73	22.8	295.9	8	46.4	281.2	283	49.7	9.8
14	10.0	263.2	74	23.3	296.5	9	48.2	282.2	284	51.5	10.8
+15	−9.4	263.7	+75	+23.9	297.0	+10	+50.0	283.2	285	+53.3	+11.8
16	8.9	264.3	76	24.4	297.6	11	51.8	284.2	286	55.1	12.8
17	8.3	264.8	77	25.0	298.2	12	53.6	285.2	287	56.9	13.8
18	7.8	265.4	78	25.6	298.7	13	55.4	286.2	288	58.7	14.8
19	7.2	265.9	79	26.1	299.3	14	57.2	287.2	289	60.5	15.8
+20	−6.7	266.5	+80	+26.7	299.8	+15	+59.0	288.2	290	+62.3	+16.8
21	6.1	267.0	81	27.2	300.4	16	60.8	289.2	291	64.1	17.8
22	5.6	267.6	82	27.8	300.9	17	62.6	290.2	292	65.9	18.8
23	5.0	268.2	83	28.3	301.5	18	64.4	291.2	293	67.7	19.8
24	4.4	268.7	84	28.9	302.0	19	66.2	292.2	294	69.5	20.8
+25	−3.9	269.3	+85	+29.4	302.6	+20	+68.0	293.2	295	+71.3	+21.8
26	3.3	269.8	86	30.0	303.2	21	69.8	294.2	296	73.1	22.8
27	2.8	270.4	87	30.6	303.7	22	71.6	295.2	297	74.9	23.8
28	2.2	270.9	88	31.1	304.3	23	73.4	296.2	298	76.7	24.8
29	1.7	271.5	89	31.7	304.8	24	75.2	297.2	299	78.5	25.8
+30	−1.1	272.0	+90	+32.2	305.4	+25	+77.0	298.2	300	+80.3	+26.8
31	0.6	272.6	91	32.8	305.9	26	78.8	299.2	301	82.1	27.8
32	0.0	273.2	92	33.3	306.5	27	80.6	300.2	302	83.9	28.8
33	+0.6	273.7	93	33.9	307.0	28	82.4	301.2	303	85.7	29.8
34	1.1	274.3	94	34.4	307.6	29	84.2	302.2	304	87.5	30.8
+35	+1.7	274.8	+95	+35.0	308.2	+30	+86.0	303.2	305	+89.3	+31.8
36	2.2	275.4	96	35.6	308.7	31	87.8	304.2	306	91.1	32.8
37	2.8	275.9	97	36.1	309.3	32	89.6	305.2	307	92.9	33.8
38	3.3	276.5	98	36.7	309.8	33	91.4	306.2	308	94.7	34.8
39	3.9	277.0	99	37.2	310.4	34	93.2	307.2	309	96.5	35.8
+40	+4.4	277.6	+100	+37.8	310.9	+35	+95.0	308.2	310	+98.3	+36.8

TABLE 30

Direction and Speed of True Wind in Units of Ship's Speed

Apparent wind speed	Difference between the heading and apparent wind direction										Apparent wind speed
	0°		10°		20°		30°		40°		
	°		°		°		°		°		
0.0	180	1.00	180	1.00	180	1.00	180	1.00	180	1.00	0.0
0.1	180	0.90	179	0.90	178	0.91	177	0.91	176	0.93	0.1
0.2	180	0.80	178	0.80	175	0.81	173	0.83	171	0.86	0.2
0.3	180	0.70	176	0.71	172	0.73	169	0.76	166	0.79	0.3
0.4	180	0.60	173	0.61	168	0.64	163	0.68	160	0.74	0.4
0.5	180	0.50	170	0.51	162	0.56	156	0.62	152	0.70	0.5
0.6	180	0.40	166	0.42	155	0.48	148	0.57	144	0.66	0.6
0.7	180	0.30	159	0.33	145	0.42	138	0.53	136	0.65	0.7
0.8	180	0.20	147	0.25	132	0.37	128	0.50	127	0.64	0.8
0.9	180	0.10	126	0.19	117	0.34	116	0.50	118	0.66	0.9
1.0	calm	0.00	95	0.17	100	0.35	105	0.52	110	0.68	1.0
1.1	0	0.10	66	0.21	85	0.38	95	0.55	103	0.72	1.1
1.2	0	0.20	49	0.28	73	0.43	86	0.60	96	0.78	1.2
1.3	0	0.30	39	0.36	64	0.50	79	0.66	90	0.84	1.3
1.4	0	0.40	33	0.45	57	0.57	73	0.73	85	0.90	1.4
1.5	0	0.50	29	0.54	51	0.66	68	0.81	81	0.98	1.5
1.6	0	0.60	26	0.64	47	0.74	64	0.89	78	1.05	1.6
1.7	0	0.70	24	0.74	44	0.83	61	0.97	75	1.13	1.7
1.8	0	0.80	22	0.83	42	0.93	58	1.06	72	1.22	1.8
1.9	0	0.90	21	0.93	40	1.02	56	1.15	70	1.30	1.9
2.0	0	1.00	20	1.03	38	1.11	54	1.24	68	1.39	2.0
2.5	0	1.50	17	1.52	32	1.60	47	1.71	60	1.85	2.5
3.0	0	2.00	15	2.02	29	2.09	43	2.19	56	2.32	3.0
3.5	0	2.50	14	2.52	28	2.58	41	2.68	53	2.81	3.5
4.0	0	3.00	13	3.02	26	3.08	39	3.17	51	3.30	4.0
4.5	0	3.50	13	3.52	25	3.58	38	3.67	50	3.79	4.5
5.0	0	4.00	12	4.02	25	4.08	37	4.16	49	4.28	5.0
6.0	0	5.00	12	5.02	24	5.07	36	5.16	47	5.27	6.0
7.0	0	6.00	12	6.02	23	6.07	35	6.15	46	6.27	7.0
8.0	0	7.00	11	7.02	23	7.07	34	7.15	45	7.26	8.0
9.0	0	8.00	11	8.02	22	8.07	34	8.15	44	8.26	9.0
10.0	0	9.00	11	9.02	22	9.06	33	9.15	44	9.26	10.0

Apparent wind speed	50°		60°		70°		80°		90°		Apparent wind speed
	°		°		°		°		°		
0.0	180	1.00	180	1.00	180	1.00	180	1.00	180	1.00	0.0
0.1	175	0.94	175	0.95	174	0.97	174	0.99	174	1.00	0.1
0.2	170	0.88	169	0.92	169	0.95	168	0.99	169	1.02	0.2
0.3	164	0.84	163	0.89	163	0.94	163	0.99	163	1.04	0.3
0.4	158	0.80	157	0.87	156	0.94	157	1.01	158	1.08	0.4
0.5	151	0.78	150	0.87	150	0.95	152	1.04	153	1.12	0.5
0.6	143	0.77	143	0.87	145	0.97	147	1.07	149	1.17	0.6
0.7	136	0.77	137	0.89	139	1.01	142	1.12	145	1.22	0.7
0.8	128	0.78	131	0.92	134	1.05	138	1.17	141	1.28	0.8
0.9	121	0.81	125	0.95	129	1.09	134	1.22	138	1.35	0.9
1.0	115	0.85	120	1.00	125	1.15	130	1.29	135	1.41	1.0
1.1	109	0.89	115	1.05	121	1.21	127	1.35	132	1.49	1.1
1.2	104	0.95	111	1.11	118	1.27	124	1.42	130	1.56	1.2
1.3	99	1.01	107	1.18	114	1.34	121	1.50	128	1.64	1.3
1.4	95	1.08	104	1.25	112	1.42	119	1.57	126	1.72	1.4
1.5	92	1.15	101	1.32	109	1.49	117	1.65	124	1.80	1.5
1.6	89	1.23	98	1.40	107	1.57	115	1.73	122	1.89	1.6
1.7	86	1.31	96	1.48	105	1.65	113	1.82	120	1.97	1.7
1.8	84	1.39	94	1.56	103	1.73	111	1.90	119	2.06	1.8
1.9	81	1.47	92	1.65	101	1.82	110	1.99	118	2.15	1.9
2.0	79	1.56	90	1.73	100	1.91	108	2.07	117	2.24	2.0
2.5	72	2.01	83	2.18	94	2.35	103	2.53	112	2.69	2.5
3.0	68	2.48	79	2.65	89	2.82	99	2.99	108	3.16	3.0
3.5	65	2.96	76	3.12	87	3.29	96	3.47	106	3.64	3.5
4.0	63	3.44	74	3.61	84	3.78	94	3.95	104	4.12	4.0
4.5	61	3.93	72	4.09	83	4.26	93	4.44	103	4.61	4.5
5.0	60	4.42	71	4.58	81	4.75	92	4.93	101	5.10	5.0
6.0	58	5.41	69	5.57	79	5.74	90	5.91	99	6.08	6.0
7.0	57	6.40	68	6.56	78	6.72	88	6.90	98	7.07	7.0
8.0	56	7.40	67	7.55	77	7.72	87	7.89	97	8.06	8.0
9.0	55	8.39	66	8.54	76	8.71	86	8.88	96	9.06	9.0
10.0	55	9.39	65	9.54	76	9.70	86	9.88	96	10.01	10.0

TABLE 30

Direction and Speed of True Wind in Units of Ship's Speed

Apparent wind speed	Difference between the heading and apparent wind direction										Apparent wind speed
	90°		100°		110°		120°		130°		
	°		°		°		°		°		
0.0	180	1.00	180	1.00	180	1.00	180	1.00	180	1.00	0.0
0.1	174	1.00	174	1.02	175	1.04	175	1.05	176	1.07	0.1
0.2	169	1.02	169	1.05	170	1.08	171	1.11	172	1.14	0.2
0.3	163	1.04	164	1.09	166	1.14	167	1.18	169	1.21	0.3
0.4	158	1.08	160	1.14	162	1.20	164	1.25	166	1.29	0.4
0.5	153	1.12	156	1.19	158	1.26	161	1.32	164	1.38	0.5
0.6	149	1.17	152	1.25	155	1.33	158	1.40	162	1.46	0.6
0.7	145	1.22	148	1.32	152	1.40	156	1.48	160	1.55	0.7
0.8	141	1.28	145	1.38	149	1.48	154	1.56	158	1.63	0.8
0.9	138	1.35	143	1.46	147	1.56	152	1.65	156	1.72	0.9
1.0	135	1.41	140	1.53	145	1.64	150	1.73	155	1.81	1.0
1.1	132	1.49	138	1.61	143	1.72	148	1.82	154	1.90	1.1
1.2	130	1.56	136	1.69	141	1.81	147	1.91	153	2.00	1.2
1.3	128	1.64	134	1.77	140	1.89	146	2.00	152	2.09	1.3
1.4	126	1.72	132	1.86	138	1.98	145	2.09	151	2.18	1.4
1.5	124	1.80	130	1.94	137	2.07	143	2.18	150	2.28	1.5
1.6	122	1.89	129	2.03	136	2.16	142	2.27	149	2.37	1.6
1.7	120	1.97	128	2.12	135	2.25	141	2.36	148	2.46	1.7
1.8	119	2.06	127	2.21	134	2.34	141	2.46	147	2.56	1.8
1.9	118	2.15	125	2.30	133	2.43	140	2.55	147	2.66	1.9
2.0	117	2.24	124	2.39	132	2.52	139	2.65	146	2.75	2.0
2.5	112	2.69	120	2.85	128	2.99	136	3.12	144	3.23	2.5
3.0	108	3.16	117	3.32	126	3.47	134	3.61	142	3.72	3.0
3.5	106	3.64	115	3.80	124	3.96	132	4.09	140	4.21	3.5
4.0	104	4.12	113	4.29	122	4.44	131	4.58	139	4.71	4.0
4.5	103	4.61	112	4.78	121	4.93	130	5.07	138	5.20	4.5
5.0	101	5.10	111	5.27	120	5.42	129	5.57	138	5.69	5.0
6.0	99	6.08	109	6.25	118	6.41	128	6.56	137	6.69	6.0
7.0	98	7.07	108	7.24	117	7.40	127	7.55	136	7.68	7.0
8.0	97	8.06	107	8.23	116	8.39	126	8.54	135	8.68	8.0
9.0	96	9.06	106	9.23	116	9.39	125	9.54	135	9.67	9.0
10.0	96	10.01	106	10.22	115	10.39	125	10.54	134	10.67	10.0

Apparent wind speed	140°		150°		160°		170°		180°		Apparent wind speed
	°		°		°		°		°		
0.0	180	1.00	180	1.00	180	1.00	180	1.00	180	1.00	0.0
0.1	177	1.08	177	1.09	178	1.09	179	1.10	180	1.10	0.1
0.2	174	1.16	175	1.18	177	1.19	178	1.20	180	1.20	0.2
0.3	171	1.24	173	1.27	175	1.29	178	1.30	180	1.30	0.3
0.4	169	1.33	172	1.36	174	1.38	177	1.40	180	1.40	0.4
0.5	167	1.42	170	1.45	173	1.48	177	1.50	180	1.50	0.5
0.6	165	1.51	169	1.55	173	1.58	176	1.60	180	1.60	0.6
0.7	164	1.60	168	1.64	172	1.68	176	1.69	180	1.70	0.7
0.8	162	1.69	167	1.74	171	1.77	176	1.79	180	1.80	0.8
0.9	161	1.79	166	1.84	171	1.87	175	1.89	180	1.90	0.9
1.0	160	1.88	165	1.93	170	1.97	175	1.99	180	2.00	1.0
1.1	159	1.97	164	2.03	170	2.07	175	2.09	180	2.10	1.1
1.2	158	2.07	164	2.13	169	2.17	175	2.19	180	2.20	1.2
1.3	157	2.16	163	2.22	169	2.27	174	2.29	180	2.30	1.3
1.4	157	2.26	162	2.32	168	2.36	174	2.39	180	2.40	1.4
1.5	156	2.36	162	2.42	168	2.46	174	2.49	180	2.50	1.5
1.6	155	2.45	161	2.52	168	2.56	174	2.59	180	2.60	1.6
1.7	155	2.55	161	2.61	167	2.66	174	2.69	180	2.70	1.7
1.8	154	2.65	161	2.71	167	2.76	174	2.79	180	2.80	1.8
1.9	154	2.74	160	2.81	167	2.86	173	2.89	180	2.90	1.9
2.0	153	2.84	160	2.91	167	2.96	173	2.99	180	3.00	2.0
2.5	151	3.33	158	3.40	166	3.46	173	3.49	180	3.50	2.5
3.0	150	3.82	157	3.90	165	3.95	172	3.99	180	4.00	3.0
3.5	149	4.31	157	4.39	164	4.45	172	4.49	180	4.50	3.5
4.0	148	4.81	156	4.89	164	4.95	172	4.99	180	5.00	4.0
4.5	147	5.31	155	5.39	164	5.45	172	5.49	180	5.50	4.5
5.0	146	5.80	155	5.89	163	5.95	172	5.99	180	6.00	5.0
6.0	145	6.80	154	6.88	163	6.95	171	6.99	180	7.00	6.0
7.0	145	7.79	154	7.88	162	7.95	171	7.99	180	8.00	7.0
8.0	144	8.79	153	8.88	162	8.95	171	8.99	180	9.00	8.0
9.0	144	9.79	153	9.88	162	9.95	171	9.99	180	10.00	9.0
10.0	143	10.78	153	10.88	162	10.95	171	10.98	180	11.00	10.0

TABLE 31

Correction of Barometer Reading for Height Above Sea Level

All barometers. All values positive.

Height in Feet	Outside temperature in degrees Fahrenheit													Height in Feet
	– 20°	– 10°	0°	10°	20°	30°	40°	50°	60°	70°	80°	90°	100°	
	Inches	*Inches*	*Inches*	*Inches*	*Inches*	*Inches*	*Inches*	*Inches*	*Inches*	*Inches*	*Inches*	*Inches*	*Inches*	
5	0.01	0.01	0.01	0.01	0.01	0.01	0.01	0.01	0.01	0.01	0.01	0.01	0.01	5
10	0.01	0.01	0.01	0.01	0.01	0.01	0.01	0.01	0.01	0.01	0.01	0.01	0.01	10
15	0.02	0.02	0.02	0.02	0.02	0.02	0.02	0.02	0.02	0.02	0.02	0.02	0.02	15
20	0.03	0.02	0.02	0.02	0.02	0.02	0.02	0.02	0.02	0.02	0.02	0.02	0.02	20
25	0.03	0.03	0.03	0.03	0.03	0.03	0.03	0.03	0.03	0.03	0.03	0.03	0.03	25
30	0.04	0.04	0.04	0.04	0.04	0.03	0.03	0.03	0.03	0.03	0.03	0.03	0.03	30
35	0.04	0.04	0.04	0.04	0.04	0.04	0.04	0.04	0.04	0.04	0.04	0.04	0.04	35
40	0.05	0.05	0.05	0.05	0.05	0.05	0.04	0.04	0.04	0.04	0.04	0.04	0.04	40
45	0.06	0.06	0.05	0.05	0.05	0.05	0.05	0.05	0.05	0.05	0.05	0.05	0.05	45
50	0.06	0.06	0.06	0.06	0.06	0.06	0.06	0.06	0.05	0.05	0.05	0.05	0.05	50
55	0.07	0.07	0.07	0.07	0.06	0.06	0.06	0.06	0.06	0.06	0.06	0.06	0.06	55
60	0.08	0.07	0.07	0.07	0.07	0.07	0.07	0.07	0.06	0.06	0.06	0.06	0.06	60
65	0.08	0.08	0.08	0.08	0.08	0.07	0.07	0.07	0.07	0.07	0.07	0.07	0.07	65
70	0.09	0.09	0.09	0.08	0.08	0.08	0.08	0.08	0.08	0.07	0.07	0.07	0.07	70
75	0.10	0.09	0.09	0.09	0.09	0.09	0.08	0.08	0.08	0.08	0.08	0.08	0.08	75
80	0.10	0.10	0.10	0.10	0.09	0.09	0.09	0.09	0.09	0.08	0.08	0.08	0.08	80
85	0.11	0.11	0.10	0.10	0.10	0.10	0.10	0.09	0.09	0.09	0.09	0.09	0.09	85
90	0.11	0.11	0.11	0.11	0.11	0.10	0.10	0.10	0.10	0.10	0.09	0.09	0.09	90
95	0.12	0.12	0.12	0.11	0.11	0.11	0.11	0.10	0.10	0.10	0.10	0.10	0.10	95
100	0.13	0.12	0.12	0.12	0.12	0.11	0.11	0.11	0.11	0.11	0.10	0.10	0.10	100
105	0.13	0.13	0.13	0.13	0.12	0.12	0.12	0.12	0.11	0.11	0.11	0.11	0.11	105
110	0.14	0.14	0.13	0.13	0.13	0.13	0.12	0.12	0.12	0.12	0.11	0.11	0.11	110
115	0.15	0.14	0.14	0.14	0.13	0.13	0.13	0.13	0.12	0.12	0.12	0.12	0.12	115
120	0.15	0.15	0.15	0.14	0.14	0.14	0.13	0.13	0.13	0.13	0.12	0.12	0.12	120
125	0.16	0.16	0.15	0.15	0.15	0.14	0.14	0.14	0.13	0.13	0.13	0.13	0.12	125

TABLE 32

Correction of Barometer Reading for Gravity

Mercurial barometers only.

Latitude	Correction	Latitude	Correction	Latitude	Correction	Latitude	Correction
°	*Inches*	°	*Inches*	°	*Inches*	°	*Inches*
0	– 0. 08	25	– 0. 05	50	+ 0. 01	75	+ 0. 07
5	– 0. 08	30	– 0. 04	55	+ 0. 03	80	+ 0. 07
10	– 0. 08	35	– 0. 03	60	+ 0. 04	85	+ 0. 08
15	– 0. 07	40	– 0. 02	65	+ 0. 05	90	+ 0. 08
20	– 0. 06	45	0. 00	70	+ 0. 06		

TABLE 33

Correction of Barometer Reading for Temperature

Mercurial barometers only.

Temp. F	Height of Barometers in inches								Temp. F
	27.5	28.0	28.5	29.0	29.5	30.0	30.5	31.0	
°	*Inches*	*Inches*	*Inches*	*Inches*	*Inches*	*Inches*	*Inches*	*Inches*	°
– 20	+ 0.12	+ 0.12	+ 0.13	+ 0.13	+ 0.13	+ 0.13	+ 0.14	+ 0.14	– 20
18	0.12	0.12	0.12	0.12	0.13	0.13	0.13	0.13	18
16	0.11	0.11	0.12	0.12	0.12	0.12	0.12	0.13	16
14	0.11	0.11	0.11	0.11	0.11	0.12	0.12	0.12	14
12	0.10	0.10	0.11	0.11	0.11	0.11	0.11	0.11	12
– 10	+ 0.10	+ 0.10	+ 0.10	+ 0.10	+ 0.10	+ 0.11	+ 0.11	+ 0.11	– 10
8	0.09	0.09	0.10	0.10	0.10	0.10	0.10	0.10	8
6	0.09	0.09	0.09	0.09	0.09	0.09	0.10	0.10	6
4	0.08	0.08	0.08	0.09	0.09	0.09	0.09	0.09	4
– 2	0.08	0.08	0.08	0.08	0.08	0.08	0.09	0.09	– 2
0	+ 0.07	+ 0.07	+ 0.07	+ 0.08	+ 0.08	+ 0.08	+ 0.08	+ 0.08	0
+ 2	0.07	0.07	0.07	0.07	0.07	0.07	0.07	0.08	+ 2
4	0.06	0.06	0.06	0.07	0.07	0.07	0.07	0.07	4
6	0.06	0.06	0.06	0.06	0.06	0.06	0.06	0.06	6
8	0.05	0.05	0.05	0.05	0.06	0.06	0.06	0.06	8
+ 10	+ 0.05	+ 0.05	+ 0.05	+ 0.05	+ 0.05	+ 0.05	+ 0.05	+ 0.05	+ 10
12	0.04	0.04	0.04	0.04	0.04	0.05	0.05	0.05	12
14	0.04	0.04	0.04	0.04	0.04	0.04	0.04	0.04	14
16	0.03	0.03	0.03	0.03	0.03	0.03	0.03	0.04	16
18	0.03	0.03	0.03	0.03	0.03	0.03	0.03	0.03	18
+ 20	+ 0.02	+ 0.02	+ 0.02	+ 0.02	+ 0.02	+ 0.02	+ 0.02	+ 0.02	+ 20
22	0.02	0.02	0.02	0.02	0.02	0.02	0.02	0.02	22
24	0.01	0.01	0.01	0.01	0.01	0.01	0.01	0.01	24
26	+ 0.01	+ 0.01	+ 0.01	+ 0.01	+ 0.01	+ 0.01	+ 0.01	+ 0.01	26
28	0.00	0.00	0.00	0.00	0.00	0.00	0.00	0.00	28
+ 30	0.00	0.00	0.00	0.00	0.00	0.00	0.00	0.00	+ 30
32	– 0.01	– 0.01	– 0.01	– 0.01	– 0.01	– 0.01	– 0.01	– 0.01	32
34	0.01	0.01	0.01	0.01	0.01	0.01	0.01	0.02	34
36	0.02	0.02	0.02	0.02	0.02	0.02	0.02	0.02	36
38	0.02	0.02	0.02	0.02	0.03	0.03	0.03	0.03	38
+ 40	– 0.03	– 0.03	– 0.03	– 0.03	– 0.03	– 0.03	– 0.03	– 0.03	+ 40
42	0.03	0.03	0.03	0.04	0.04	0.04	0.04	0.04	42
44	0.04	0.04	0.04	0.04	0.04	0.04	0.04	0.04	44
46	0.04	0.04	0.04	0.05	0.05	0.05	0.05	0.05	46
48	0.05	0.05	0.05	0.05	0.05	0.05	0.05	0.05	48
+ 50	– 0.05	– 0.05	– 0.06	– 0.06	– 0.06	– 0.06	– 0.06	– 0.06	+ 50
52	0.06	0.06	0.06	0.06	0.06	0.06	0.06	0.07	52
54	0.06	0.06	0.07	0.07	0.07	0.07	0.07	0.07	54
56	0.07	0.07	0.07	0.07	0.07	0.07	0.08	0.08	56
58	0.07	0.07	0.08	0.08	0.08	0.08	0.08	0.08	58
+ 60	– 0.08	– 0.08	– 0.08	– 0.08	– 0.08	– 0.09	– 0.09	– 0.09	+ 60
62	0.08	0.08	0.09	0.09	0.09	0.09	0.09	0.09	62
64	0.09	0.09	0.09	0.09	0.09	0.10	0.10	0.10	64
66	0.09	0.09	0.10	0.10	0.10	0.10	0.10	0.10	66
68	0.10	0.10	0.10	0.10	0.11	0.11	0.11	0.11	68
+ 70	– 0.10	– 0.10	– 0.11	– 0.11	– 0.11	– 0.11	– 0.11	– 0.12	+ 70
72	0.11	0.11	0.11	0.11	0.12	0.12	0.12	0.12	72
74	0.11	0.11	0.12	0.12	0.12	0.12	0.13	0.13	74
76	0.12	0.12	0.12	0.12	0.13	0.13	0.13	0.13	76
78	0.12	0.12	0.13	0.13	0.13	0.13	0.14	0.14	78
+ 80	– 0.13	– 0.13	– 0.13	– 0.13	– 0.14	– 0.14	– 0.14	– 0.14	+ 80
82	0.13	0.14	0.14	0.14	0.14	0.14	0.15	0.15	82
84	0.14	0.14	0.14	0.15	0.15	0.15	0.15	0.16	84
86	0.14	0.15	0.15	0.15	0.15	0.16	0.16	0.16	86
88	0.15	0.15	0.15	0.16	0.16	0.16	0.16	0.17	88
+ 90	– 0.15	– 0.16	– 0.16	– 0.16	– 0.16	– 0.17	– 0.17	– 0.17	+ 90
92	0.16	0.16	0.16	0.17	0.17	0.17	0.17	0.18	92
94	0.16	0.17	0.17	0.17	0.17	0.18	0.18	0.18	94
96	0.17	0.17	0.17	0.18	0.18	0.18	0.19	0.19	96
98	0.17	0.18	0.18	0.18	0.18	0.19	0.19	0.19	98
100	– 0.18	– 0.18	– 0.18	– 0.19	– 0.19	– 0.19	– 0.20	– 0.20	100

TABLE 34

Conversion Table for hecto-Pascals (millibars), Inches of Mercury, and Millimeters of Mercury

hPa	Inches	Millimeters	hPa	Inches	Millimeters	hPa	Inches	Millimeters
900	26.58	675.1	960	28.35	720.1	1020	30.12	765.1
901	26.61	675.8	961	28.38	720.8	1021	30.15	765.8
902	26.64	676.6	962	28.41	721.6	1022	30.18	766.6
903	26.67	677.3	963	28.44	722.3	1023	30.21	767.3
904	26.70	678.1	964	28.47	723.1	1024	30.24	768.1
905	26.72	678.8	965	28.50	723.8	1025	30.27	768.8
906	26.75	679.6	966	28.53	724.6	1026	30.30	769.6
907	26.78	680.3	967	28.56	725.3	1027	30.33	770.3
908	26.81	681.1	968	28.58	726.1	1028	30.36	771.1
909	26.84	681.8	969	28.61	726.8	1029	30.39	771.8
910	26.87	682.6	970	28.64	727.6	1030	30.42	772.6
911	26.90	683.3	971	28.67	728.3	1031	30.45	773.3
912	26.93	684.1	972	28.70	729.1	1032	30.47	774.1
913	26.96	684.8	973	28.73	729.8	1033	30.50	774.8
914	26.99	685.6	974	28.76	730.6	1034	30.53	775.6
915	27.02	686.3	975	28.79	731.3	1035	30.56	776.3
916	27.05	687.1	976	28.82	732.1	1036	30.59	777.1
917	27.08	687.8	977	28.85	732.8	1037	30.62	777.8
918	27.11	688.6	978	28.88	733.6	1038	30.65	778.6
919	27.14	689.3	979	28.91	734.3	1039	30.68	779.3
920	27.17	690.1	980	28.94	735.1	1040	30.71	780.1
921	27.20	690.8	981	28.97	735.8	1041	30.74	780.8
922	27.23	691.6	982	29.00	736.6	1042	30.77	781.6
923	27.26	692.3	983	29.03	737.3	1043	30.80	782.3
924	27.29	693.1	984	29.06	738.1	1044	30.83	783.1
925	27.32	693.8	985	29.09	738.8	1045	30.86	783.8
926	27.34	694.6	986	29.12	739.6	1046	30.89	784.6
927	27.37	695.3	987	29.15	740.3	1047	30.92	785.3
928	27.40	696.1	988	29.18	741.1	1048	30.95	786.1
929	27.43	696.8	989	29.21	741.8	1049	30.98	786.8
930	27.46	697.6	990	29.23	742.6	1050	31.01	787.6
931	27.49	698.3	991	29.26	743.3	1051	31.04	788.3
932	27.52	699.1	992	29.29	744.1	1052	31.07	789.1
933	27.55	699.8	993	29.32	744.8	1053	31.10	789.8
934	27.58	700.6	994	29.35	745.6	1054	31.12	790.6
935	27.61	701.3	995	29.38	746.3	1055	31.15	791.3
936	27.64	702.1	996	29.41	747.1	1056	31.18	792.1
937	27.67	702.8	997	29.44	747.8	1057	31.21	792.8
938	27.70	703.6	998	29.47	748.6	1058	31.24	793.6
939	27.73	704.3	999	29.50	749.3	1059	31.27	794.3
940	27.76	705.1	1000	29.53	750.1	1060	31.30	795.1
941	27.79	705.8	1001	29.56	750.8	1061	31.33	795.8
942	27.82	706.6	1002	29.59	751.6	1062	31.36	796.6
943	27.85	707.3	1003	29.62	752.3	1063	31.39	797.3
944	27.88	708.1	1004	29.65	753.1	1064	31.42	798.1
945	27.91	708.8	1005	29.68	753.8	1065	31.45	798.8
946	27.94	709.6	1006	29.71	754.6	1066	31.48	799.6
947	27.96	710.3	1007	29.74	755.3	1067	31.51	800.3
948	27.99	711.1	1008	29.77	756.1	1068	31.54	801.1
949	28.02	711.8	1009	29.80	756.8	1069	31.57	801.8
950	28.05	712.6	1010	29.83	757.6	1070	31.60	802.6
951	28.08	713.3	1011	29.85	758.3	1071	31.63	803.3
952	28.11	714.1	1012	29.88	759.1	1072	31.66	804.1
953	28.14	714.8	1013	29.91	759.8	1073	31.69	804.8
954	28.17	715.6	1014	29.94	760.6	1074	31.72	805.6
955	28.20	716.3	1015	29.97	761.3	1075	31.74	806.3
956	28.23	717.1	1016	30.00	762.1	1076	31.77	807.1
957	28.26	717.8	1017	30.03	762.8	1077	31.80	807.8
958	28.29	718.6	1018	30.06	763.6	1078	31.83	808.6
959	28.32	719.3	1019	30.09	764.3	1079	31.86	809.3
960	28.35	720.1	1020	30.12	765.1	1080	31.89	810.1

TABLE 35
Relative Humidity

Dry-bulb temp. F	1°	2°	3°	4°	5°	6°	7°	8°	9°	10°	11°	12°	13°	14°	Dry-bulb temp. F
°	%	%	%	%	%	%	%	%	%	%	%	%	%	%	°
− 20	7														− 20
18	14														18
16	21														16
14	27														14
12	32														12
− 10	37														− 10
8	41	2													8
6	45	9													6
4	49	16													4
− 2	52	22													− 2
0	56	28													0
+ 2	59	33	7												+ 2
4	62	37	14												4
6	64	42	20												6
8	67	46	25	5											8
+ 10	69	50	30	11											+ 10
12	71	53	35	17											12
14	73	56	40	23	7										14
16	76	60	44	28	13										16
18	77	62	48	33	19	4									18
+ 20	79	65	51	37	24	10									+ 20
22	81	68	55	42	29	16	4								22
24	83	70	58	45	33	21	10								24
26	85	73	61	49	38	26	15	4							26
28	86	75	64	53	42	31	20	10							28
+ 30	88	77	66	56	45	35	25	15	6						+ 30
32	89	79	69	59	49	39	30	20	11	2					32
34	90	81	71	62	52	43	34	25	16	8					34
36	91	82	73	64	55	47	38	29	21	13	5				36
38	91	83	74	66	58	50	42	33	25	18	10	2			38
+ 40	92	84	76	68	60	52	45	37	30	22	15	7			+ 40
42	92	84	77	69	62	54	47	40	33	26	19	12	5		42
44	92	85	78	70	63	56	49	43	36	29	23	17	10	4	44
46	93	86	79	72	65	58	52	45	39	32	26	20	14	8	46
48	93	86	79	73	66	60	54	47	41	35	29	24	18	12	48
+ 50	93	87	80	74	68	61	55	49	44	38	32	27	21	16	+ 50
52	94	87	81	75	69	63	57	51	46	40	35	29	24	19	52
54	94	88	82	76	70	64	59	53	48	42	37	32	27	22	54
56	94	88	82	77	71	65	60	55	50	44	39	35	30	25	56
58	94	88	83	77	72	67	61	56	51	46	42	37	32	28	58
+ 60	94	89	83	78	73	68	63	58	53	48	43	39	34	30	+ 60
62	95	89	84	79	74	69	64	59	54	50	45	41	37	32	62
64	95	89	84	79	74	70	65	60	56	51	47	43	38	34	64
66	95	90	85	80	75	71	66	61	57	53	49	44	40	36	66
68	95	90	85	81	76	71	67	63	58	54	50	46	42	38	68
+ 70	95	90	86	81	77	72	68	64	59	55	51	48	44	40	+ 70
72	95	91	86	82	77	73	69	65	61	57	53	49	45	42	72
74	95	91	86	82	78	74	69	65	62	58	54	50	47	43	74
76	95	91	87	82	78	74	70	66	63	59	55	51	48	45	76
78	96	91	87	83	79	75	71	67	63	60	56	53	49	46	78
+ 80	96	91	87	83	79	75	72	68	64	61	57	54	50	47	+ 80
82	96	92	88	84	80	76	72	69	65	62	58	55	52	48	82
84	96	92	88	84	80	76	73	69	66	62	59	56	53	49	84
86	96	92	88	84	81	77	73	70	67	63	60	57	54	51	86
88	96	92	88	85	81	77	74	71	67	64	61	58	55	52	88
+ 90	96	92	89	85	81	78	74	71	68	65	61	58	55	52	+ 90
92	96	92	89	85	82	78	75	72	68	65	62	59	56	53	92
94	96	93	89	85	82	79	75	72	69	66	63	60	57	54	94
96	96	93	89	86	82	79	76	73	70	67	64	61	58	55	96
98	96	93	89	86	83	79	76	73	70	67	64	61	59	56	98
+ 100	96	93	90	86	83	80	77	74	71	68	65	62	59	57	+ 100

Difference between dry-bulb and wet-bulb temperatures

TABLE 35
Relative Humidity

Dry-bulb temp. F	15°	16°	17°	18°	19°	20°	21°	22°	23°	24°	25°	26°	27°	28°	Dry-bulb temp. F
°	%	%	%	%	%	%	%	%	%	%	%	%	%	%	°
+ 46	2														+ 46
48	7	1													48
+ 50	10	5													+ 50
52	14	9	4												52
54	17	12	7	3											54
56	20	16	11	7	2										56
58	23	19	14	10	6	2									58
+ 60	26	21	17	13	9	5	1								+ 60
62	28	24	20	16	12	8	4	1							62
64	30	26	22	19	15	11	8	4							64
66	32	29	25	21	17	14	10	7	4						66
68	34	31	27	23	20	16	13	10	7	3					68
+ 70	36	33	29	26	22	19	16	12	9	6	3				+ 70
72	38	34	31	28	24	21	18	15	12	9	6	3			72
74	40	36	33	30	26	23	20	17	14	11	8	6	3		74
76	41	38	35	31	28	25	22	19	16	14	11	8	5	3	76
78	43	39	36	33	30	27	24	21	18	16	13	10	8	5	78
+ 80	44	41	38	35	32	29	26	23	20	18	15	13	10	8	+ 80
82	45	42	39	36	33	30	28	25	22	20	17	15	12	10	82
84	46	43	40	38	35	32	29	27	24	21	19	17	14	12	84
86	48	45	42	39	36	33	31	28	26	23	21	18	16	14	86
88	49	46	43	40	37	35	32	30	27	25	22	20	18	16	88
+ 90	50	47	44	41	39	36	34	31	29	26	24	22	19	17	+ 90
92	51	48	45	42	40	37	35	32	30	28	25	23	21	19	92
94	51	49	46	44	41	39	36	34	31	29	27	25	23	20	94
96	52	50	47	45	42	40	37	35	33	30	28	26	24	22	96
98	53	51	48	45	43	41	38	36	34	32	29	27	25	23	98
+ 100	54	51	49	46	44	42	39	37	35	33	31	29	27	25	+ 100

Difference between dry-bulb and wet-bulb temperatures

Dry-bulb temp. F	29°	30°	31°	32°	33°	34°	35°	36°	37°	38°	39°	40°	41°	42°	Dry-bulb temp. F
°	%	%	%	%	%	%	%	%	%	%	%	%	%	%	°
+ 78	3														+ 78
+ 80	5	3													+ 80
82	7	5	3	1											82
84	10	7	5	3	1										84
86	11	9	7	5	3	1									86
88	13	11	9	7	5	3	1								88
+ 90	15	13	11	9	7	5	3	1							+ 90
92	17	15	13	11	9	7	5	3	1						92
94	18	16	14	12	11	9	7	5	3	2					94
96	20	18	16	14	12	10	9	7	5	4	2				96
98	21	19	17	16	14	12	10	9	7	5	4	2	1		98
+ 100	23	21	19	17	15	14	12	10	9	7	5	4	2	1	+ 100

TABLE 36
Dew Point

Dry-bulb temp. F	Difference between dry-bulb and wet-bulb temperatures														Dry-bulb temp. F
	1°	2°	3°	4°	5°	6°	7°	8°	9°	10°	11°	12°	13°	14°	
°	°	°	°	°	°	°	°	°	°	°	°	°	°	°	°
−20															−20
18	−52														18
16	45														16
14	39														14
12	34														12
−10	−29														−10
8	25	−75													8
6	22	50													6
4	18	39													4
−2	15	32													−2
0	−12	−26													0
+2	9	21	−49												+2
4	6	16	35												4
6	3	12	27												6
8	−1	9	20	−50											8
+10	+2	−5	−15	−34											+10
12	5	−2	10	24											12
14	7	+1	6	17											14
16	10	4	−2	11											16
18	12	7	+1	6											18
+20	+15	+10	+5	−2											+20
22	17	13	8	+2											22
24	20	16	11	6											24
26	22	18	14	10	+4	−4									26
28	24	21	17	13	8	+1	−8	−22							28
+30	+27	+24	+20	+16	+11	+6	−1	−12	−31						+30
32	29	26	23	19	15	10	+4	−4	16	−47					32
34	32	29	26	22	18	14	9	+2	−7	22					34
36	34	31	28	25	22	18	13	7	0	11	−30				36
38	36	33	31	28	25	21	17	12	+6	−2	14	−42			38
+40	+38	+35	+33	+30	+27	+24	+20	+16	+11	+4	−4	−18	−79		+40
42	40	38	35	33	30	27	23	19	15	10	+3	−7	23		42
44	42	40	37	35	32	29	26	23	19	14	9	+2	−9	−29	44
46	44	42	40	37	35	32	29	26	22	18	13	7	0	11	46
48	46	44	42	40	37	35	32	29	26	22	18	13	+6	−2	48
+50	+48	+46	+44	+42	+40	+37	+35	+32	+29	+25	+21	+17	+12	+5	+50
52	50	48	46	44	42	40	37	35	32	29	25	21	17	11	52
54	52	50	49	47	44	42	40	37	35	32	28	25	21	16	54
56	54	53	51	49	47	45	42	40	37	35	32	28	25	21	56
58	56	55	53	51	49	47	45	43	40	38	35	32	28	25	58
+60	+58	+57	+55	+53	+51	+49	+47	+45	+43	+40	+38	+35	+32	+28	+60
62	60	59	57	55	54	52	50	48	45	43	41	38	35	32	62
64	62	61	59	57	56	54	52	50	48	46	43	41	38	35	64
66	64	63	61	60	58	56	54	52	50	48	46	44	41	39	66
68	67	65	63	62	60	58	57	55	53	51	49	46	44	42	68
+70	+69	+67	+66	+64	+62	+61	+59	+57	+55	+53	+51	+49	+47	+45	+70
72	71	69	68	66	64	63	61	59	58	56	54	52	50	47	72
74	73	71	70	68	67	65	63	62	60	58	56	54	52	50	74
76	75	73	72	70	69	67	66	64	62	61	59	57	55	53	76
78	77	75	74	72	71	69	68	66	65	63	61	59	57	55	78
+80	+79	+77	+76	+74	+73	+72	+70	+68	+67	+65	+64	+62	+60	+58	+80
82	81	79	78	77	75	74	72	71	69	67	66	64	62	61	82
84	83	81	80	79	77	76	74	73	71	70	68	67	65	63	84
86	85	83	82	81	79	78	76	75	74	72	70	69	67	66	86
88	87	85	84	83	81	80	79	77	76	74	73	71	70	68	88
+90	+89	+87	+86	+85	+84	+82	+81	+79	+78	+76	+75	+73	+72	+70	+90
92	91	89	88	87	86	84	83	82	80	79	77	76	74	73	92
94	93	92	90	89	88	86	85	84	82	81	79	78	76	75	94
96	95	94	92	91	90	88	87	86	84	83	82	80	79	77	96
98	97	96	94	93	92	91	89	88	87	85	84	82	81	80	98
+100	+99	+98	+96	+95	+94	+93	+91	+90	+89	+87	+86	+85	+83	+82	+100

TABLE 36
Dew Point

Dry-bulb temp. F	Difference between dry-bulb and wet-bulb temperatures														Dry-bulb temp. F
	15°	16°	17°	18°	19°	20°	21°	22°	23°	24°	25°	26°	27°	28°	
°	°	°	°	°	°	°	°	°	°	°	°	°	°	°	°
+46	−36														+46
48	14	−45													48
+50	−3	−17	−78												+50
52	+4	−5	21												52
54	10	+3	−7	−25											54
56	16	10	+2	−8	−29										56
58	20	16	10	+2	−10	−34									58
+60	+25	+20	+15	+9	+1	−11	−39								+60
62	29	25	20	15	9	+1	−12	−45							62
64	32	29	25	20	15	9	0	−13	−52						64
66	36	33	29	25	21	15	+9	0	−14	−59					66
68	39	36	33	29	25	21	16	+9	0	−14	−68				68
+70	+42	+39	+36	+33	+30	+26	+21	+16	+9	0	−14	−76			+70
72	45	43	40	37	34	30	26	22	16	+10	+1	−14	−77		72
74	48	46	43	40	37	34	31	27	22	17	10	+1	−13	−70	74
76	51	48	46	44	41	38	35	31	27	23	17	11	+2	−12	76
78	53	51	49	47	44	41	38	35	32	28	23	18	11	+3	78
+80	+56	+54	+52	+50	+47	+45	+42	+39	+36	+32	+28	+24	+19	+12	+80
82	59	57	55	53	50	48	45	43	40	37	33	29	25	20	82
84	61	59	57	55	53	51	49	46	43	41	37	34	30	26	84
86	64	62	60	58	56	54	52	49	47	44	41	38	35	31	86
88	66	64	63	61	59	57	55	52	50	48	45	42	39	36	88
+90	+69	+67	+65	+63	+62	+60	+58	+55	+53	+51	+48	+46	+43	+40	+90
92	71	69	68	66	64	62	60	58	56	54	52	49	47	44	92
94	73	72	70	68	67	65	63	61	59	57	55	52	50	47	94
96	76	74	73	71	69	67	66	64	62	60	58	56	53	51	96
98	78	77	75	73	72	70	68	67	65	63	61	59	57	54	98
+100	+80	+79	+77	+76	+74	+73	+71	+69	+67	+66	+64	+62	+60	+57	+100

Dry-bulb temp. F	Difference between dry-bulb and wet-bulb temperatures														Dry-bulb temp. F
	29°	30°	31°	32°	33°	34°	35°	36°	37°	38°	39°	40°	41°	42°	
°	°	°	°	°	°	°	°	°	°	°	°	°	°	°	°
+76	−61														+76
78	−11	−53													78
+80	+4	−10	−45												+80
82	13	+5	−8	−39											82
84	20	14	+6	−6	−33										84
86	27	21	15	+7	−4	−28									86
88	32	27	22	16	+9	−2	−23								88
+90	+36	+33	+28	+24	+18	+10	0	−18							+90
92	41	37	34	30	25	19	+12	+2	−14						92
94	45	42	38	35	31	26	20	13	+4	−10					94
96	48	46	43	39	36	32	27	22	15	+6	−7	−43			96
98	52	49	47	44	40	37	33	28	23	17	+9	−4	−30		98
+100	+55	+53	+50	+47	+45	+41	+38	+34	+30	+25	+19	+11	0	−21	+100

CHAPTER 1

MATHEMATICS

ARITHMETIC

100. Definition

Arithmetic is that branch of mathematics dealing with computation by numbers. The principal processes involved are addition, subtraction, multiplication, and division. A number consisting of a single symbol (1, 2, 3, etc.) is **a digit**. Any number that can be stated or indicated, however large or small, is called a **finite number**; one too large to be stated or indicated is called an **infinite number**; and one too small to be stated or indicated is called an **infinitesimal number**.

The **sign** of a number is the indication of whether it is positive (+) or negative (-). This may sometimes be indicated in another way. Thus, latitude is usually indicated as *north* (N) or *south* (S), but if north is considered positive, south is then negative with respect to north. In navigation, the north or south designation of latitude and declination is often called the "name" of the latitude or declination. A **positive number** is one having a positive sign (+); a **negative number** is one having a negative sign (-). The **absolute value** of a number is that number without regard to sign. Thus, the absolute value of both (+) 8 and (-) 8 is 8. Generally, a number without a sign can be considered positive.

101. Significant Digits

Significant digits are those digits of a number which have a significance. Zeros at the left of the number and sometimes those at the right are excluded. Thus, 1,325, 1,001, 1.408, 0.00005926, 625.0, and 0.4009 have four significant digits each. But in the number 186,000 there may be three, four, five, or six significant digits depending upon the accuracy with which the number has been determined. If the quantity has only been determined to the nearest thousand then there are three significant digits, the zeros at the right not being counted. If the number has been determined to the nearest one hundred, there are four significant digits, the first zero at the right being counted. If the number has been determined to the nearest ten, there are five significant digits, the first two zeros on the right being counted. If the quantity has been determined to the nearest unit, there are six significant digits, the three zeros at the right being counted.

This ambiguity is sometimes avoided by expressing numbers in powers of 10. Thus, 18.6×10^4 (18.6 x 10,000) indicates accuracy to the nearest thousand, 18.60×10^4 to the nearest hundred, 18.600×10^4 to the nearest ten, and 18.6000×10^4 to the nearest unit. The position of the decimal is not important if the correct power of 10 is given. For example, 18.6×10^4 is the same as 1.86×10^6, 186×10^3, etc. The small number above and to the right of 10 (the **exponent**) indicates the number of places the decimal point is to be moved to the right. If the exponent is negative, it indicates a reciprocal, and the decimal point is moved to the left. Thus, 1.86×10^{-6} is the same as 0.00000186. This system is called **scientific notation**.

102. Expressing Numbers

In navigation, fractions are usually expressed as decimals. Thus, $1/4$ is expressed as 0.25 and $1/3$ as 0.33. To determine the decimal equivalent of a fraction, divide the **numerator** (the number above the line) by the **denominator** (the number below the line). When a decimal is less than 1, as in the examples above, it is good practice to show the zero at the left of the decimal point (0.25, not .25).

A number should not be expressed using more significant digits than justified. The *implied* accuracy of a decimal is indicated by the number of digits shown to the right of the decimal point. Thus, the expression "14 miles" implies accuracy to the nearest whole mile, or any value between 13.5 and 14.5 miles. The expression "14.0 miles" implies accuracy of a tenth of a mile, or any value between 13.95 and 14.05 miles.

A quantity may be expressed to a greater implied accuracy than is justified by the accuracy of the information from which the quantity is derived. For instance, if a ship steams 1 mile in 3^m21^s, its speed is $60^m\div3^m21^s = 60\div3.35 = 17.910447761194$ knots, approximately. The division can be carried to as many places as desired, but if the time is measured only to the nearest second, the speed is accurate only to one decimal place in this example, because an error of 0.5 second introduces an error of more than 0.05 knot in the speed. Hence, the additional places are meaningless and possibly misleading, unless more accurate time is available. In general, it is not good practice to state a quantity to imply accuracy greater than what is justified. However, in marine navigation the accuracy of information is often unknown, and it is customary to give positions as if they were accurate to 0.1' of latitude and longitude, although they *may* not be accurate even to the nearest whole minute.

If there are no more significant digits, regardless of how far a computation is carried, this may be indicated by use of the word "exactly." Thus, 12÷4=3 exactly and 1 nautical mile = 1,852 meters exactly; but 12÷7=1.7 approximately, the word "approximately" indicating that additional decimal places might be computed. Another way of indicating an approximate relationship is by placing a positive or negative sign after the number. Thus, 12÷7=1.7+, and 11÷7=1.6-. This system has the advantage of showing whether the approximation is too great or too small.

In any arithmetical computation the answer is no more accurate than the least accurate value used. Thus, if it is desired to add 16.4 and 1.88, the answer might be given as 18.28, but since the first term might be anything from 16.35 to 16.45; the answer is anything from 18.23 to 18.33. Hence, to retain the second decimal place in the answer is to give a false indication of accuracy, for the number 18.28 indicates a value between 18.275 and 18.285. However, additional places are sometimes retained until the end of a computation to avoid an accumulation of small errors due to rounding off. In marine navigation it is customary to give most values to an accuracy of 0.1, even though some uncertainty may exist as to the accuracy of the last place. Examples are the dip and refraction corrections of sextant altitudes.

In general, a value obtained by interpolation in a table should not be expressed to more decimal places than given in the table.

Unless all numbers are exact, doubt exists as to the accuracy of the last digit in a computation. Thus, 12.3+9.4+4.6=26.3. But if the three terms to be added have been rounded off from 12.26, 9.38, and 4.57, the correct answer is 26.2, obtained by rounding off the answer of 26.21 found by retaining the second decimal place until the end. It is good practice to work with one more place than needed in the answer, when the information is available. In computations involving a large number of terms, or if greater accuracy is desired, it is sometimes advisable to retain two or more additional places until the end.

103. Rounding Off

In **rounding off** numbers to the number of places desired, one should take the nearest value. T the number 6.5049 is rounded to 6.505, 6.50, 6.5, or 7, depending upon the number of places desired. If the number to be rounded off ends in 5, the nearer even number is taken. Thus, 1.55 and 1.65 are both rounded to 1.6. Likewise, 12.750 is rounded to 12.8 if only one decimal place is desired. However, 12.749 is rounded to 12.7. That is, 12.749 is not first rounded to 12.75 and then to 12.8, but the entire number is rounded in one operation. When a number ends in 5, the computation can sometimes be carried to additional places to determine whether the correct value is more or less than 5.

104. Reciprocals

The **reciprocal** of a number is 1 divided by that number. The reciprocal of a fraction is obtained by interchanging the numerator and denominator. Thus, the reciprocal of $3/5$ is $5/3$. A whole number may be considered a fraction with 1 as the denominator. Thus, 54 is the same as $54/1$, and its reciprocal is $1/54$. Division by a number produces the same result as multiplying by its reciprocal, or vice versa. Thus, $12 \div 2 = 12 \times 1/2 = 6$, and $12 \times 2 = 12 \div 1/2 = 24$.

105. Addition

When two or more numbers are to be added, it is generally most convenient to write them in a column, with the decimal points in line. Thus, if 31.2, 0.8874, and 168.14 are to be added, this may be indicated by means of the addition sign (+): 31.2+0.8874+168.14=200.2. But the addition can be performed more conveniently by arranging the numbers as follows:

$$\begin{array}{r} 31.2 \\ 0.8874 \\ 168.14 \\ \hline 200.2 \end{array}$$

The answer is given only to the first decimal place, because the answer is no more accurate than the least precise number among those to be added, as indicated previously. Often it is preferable to state all numbers in a problem to the same precision before starting the addition, although this may introduce a small error:

$$\begin{array}{r} 31.2 \\ 0.9 \\ 168.1 \\ \hline 200.2 \end{array}$$

If there are no decimals, the last digit to the right is aligned:

$$\begin{array}{r} 166 \\ 2 \\ 96,758 \\ \hline 96,926 \end{array}$$

Numbers to be added should be given to the same absolute accuracy, when available, to avoid a false impression of accuracy in the result. Consider the following:

$$\begin{array}{r} 186,000 \\ 71,832 \\ 9,614 \\ 728 \\ \hline 268,174 \end{array}$$

The answer would imply accuracy to six places. If the first number given is accurate to only three places, or to the nearest 1,000, the answer is not more accurate, and hence the answer should be given as 268,000. Approximately the same answer would be obtained by rounding off at the start:

$$\begin{array}{r} 186,000 \\ 72,000 \\ 10,000 \\ 1,000 \\ \hline 269,000 \end{array}$$

If numbers are **added arithmetically**, their absolute values are added without regard to signs; but if they are **added algebraically**, due regard is given to signs. If two numbers to be added algebraically have the same sign, their absolute values are added and given their common sign. If two numbers to be added algebraically have unlike signs, the smaller absolute value is subtracted from the larger, and the sign of the value having the larger absolute value is given to the result. Thus, if +8 and -7 are added arithmetically, the answer is 15, but if they are added algebraically, the answer is + 1.

An answer obtained by addition is called a **sum**.

106. Subtraction

Subtraction is the inverse of addition. Stated differently, the *addition* of a *negative* number is the same as the *subtraction* of a *positive* number. That is, if a number is to be subtracted from another, the sign (+ or -) of the **subtrahend** (the number to be subtracted) is reversed and the result added algebraically to the **minuend** (the number from which the subtrahend is to be subtracted). Thus, 6-4=2. This may be written +6-(+4)=+2, which yields the same result as +6+ (-4). For solution, larger numbers are often conveniently arranged in a column with decimal points in a vertical column, as in addition. Thus, 3,728.41-1,861.16 may be written:

(+)3,728.41
(+)1,861.16 (subtract)
(+)1,867.25

This is the same as:

(+)3,728.41
(-)1,861.16 (add algebraically)
(+)1,867.25

The rule of sign reversal applies likewise to negative numbers. Thus, if -3 is to be *subtracted* from +5, this may be written +5- (-3) =5+3=8. In the algebraic addition of two numbers of opposite sign (numerical subtraction), the smaller number is subtracted from the larger and the result is given the sign of the larger number. Thus, +7 -4= +3, and -7 +4= -3, which is the same as +4 -7=-3.

In navigation, numbers to be numerically subtracted are usually marked (-), and those to be numerically added are marked (+) or the sign is not indicated. However, when a sign is part of a designation, and the reverse process is to be used, the word "reversed" (rev.) is written after the number. Thus, if GMT is known and ZT in the (+) 5 zone is to be found (by subtraction), the problem may be written:

$$\begin{array}{rl} GMT & 1754 \\ ZD & (+)5 \ \text{(rev.)} \\ ZT & 1254 \end{array}$$

The symbol ~ indicates that an absolute difference is required without regard to sign of the answer. Thus, 28~13=15, and 13~28=15. In both of these solutions 13 and 28 are positive and 15 is an absolute value without sign. If the signs or names of both numbers are the same, either positive or negative, the smaller is subtracted from the larger, but if they are of opposite sign or name, they are numerically added. Thus, (+)16~(+)21=5 and (-)16~(-)21=5, but (+)16~ (-)21=37 and (-)16~(+)21 =37. Similarly, the difference of latitude between 15°N and 20°N, or between 15°S and 20°S, is 5°, but the difference of latitude between 15°N and 20°S, or between15°S and 20°N, is 35°. If motion from one latitude to another is involved, the difference may be given a sign to indicate the direction of travel, or the location of one place with respect to another. Thus, if B is 50 miles west of A, and C is 125 miles west of A, B and C are 75 miles apart regardless of the direction of travel. However, B is 75 miles east of C, and C is 75 miles west of B. When direction is indicated, an algebraic difference is given, rather than an absolute difference, and the symbol ~ is not appropriate.

It is sometimes desirable to consider all addition and subtraction problems as addition, with negative signs (-) given before those numbers to be subtracted; so that there can be no question of which process is intended. The words "add" and "subtract" may be used instead of signs. In navigation, "names" (usually north, south, east, and west) are often used, and the relationship involved in a certain problem may need to be understood to determine whether to add or subtract. Thus, LHA=GHA-λ (west) and LHA=GHA+ λ (east). This is the same as saying LHA=GHA-λ if west longitude is considered positive, for in this case, LHA=GHA-(-λ) or LHA=GHA+λ in east longitude, the same as before.

If numbers are **subtracted arithmetically**, they are subtracted without regard to sign; but if they are **subtracted algebraically**, positive (+) numbers are *subtracted* and negative (-) numbers are *added.*

An answer obtained by subtraction is called a **difference**.

107. Multiplication

Multiplication may be indicated by the multiplication sign (×), as 154×28=4,312. For solution, the problem is conveniently arranged thus:

```
   154
(x)28
  1232
  308
  4312.
```

Either number may be given first, but it is generally more convenient to perform the multiplication if the larger number is placed on top, as shown. In this problem, 154 is first multiplied by 8 and then by 2. The second answer is placed under the first, but set one **place** to the left, so that the right-hand digit is directly below the 2 of the multiplier. These steps might be reversed, multiplication by 2 being performed first. This procedure is sometimes used in estimating.

When one number is placed below another for multiplication, as shown above, it is usually best to align the right-hand digits without regard for the position of the decimal point. The number of decimal places in the answer is the sum of the decimal places in the **multiplicand** (the number to be multiplied) and the **multiplier** (the second number):

```
    163.27
(x) 263.9
    146943
    48981
   97962
  32654
  43086.953
```

However, when a number ends in one or more zeros, these may be ignored until the end and then added on to the number:

```
   1924
(x)1800
  15392
  1924
  3463200
```

This is also true if both multiplicand and multiplier end in zeros:

```
   1924000
(x)1800
 15392
 1924
 3463200000
```

When negative values are to be multiplied, the sign of the answer is positive if an *even* number of negative signs appear, and negative if there are an *odd* number. Thus, 2×3=6, 2×(-3)=-6, -2×3=-6, -2× (-3)=(+)6. Also, 2×3×8× (-2)×5=-480, 2×(-3)×8×(-2)×5=480, 2×(-3)×(-8)×(-2) ×5=-480, 2×(-3)×(-8)×(-2)×(-5)=480, and (-2)×(-3)×(-8)×(-2)×(-5)=-480.

An answer obtained by multiplication is called a **product**. Any number multiplied by 1 is the number itself. Thus, 125×1=125. Any number multiplied by 0 is 0. Thus, 125×0=0 and l×0=0.

To multiply a number by itself is to **square** the number. This may be indicated by the **exponent** 2 placed to the right of the number and above the line as a **superior**. Thus, 15×15 may be written 15^2. Similarly, 15×I5×I5= 15^3, and 15×15×15×15= 15^4, etc. The exponent (2, 3, 4, etc.) indicates the **power** to which a number is to be **raised**, or how many times the number is to be used in multiplication. The expression 15^2 is usually read "15 squared", 15^3 is read "15 cubed" or "15 to the third power," 15^4 (or higher power) is read "15 to the fourth (or higher) power." The answer obtained by **raising to a power** is called the "square," "cube" etc., or the ... "power" of the number. Thus, 225 is the "square of 15", 3,375 is the "cube of 15" or the "third power of 15," etc. The zero power of any number except zero (if zero is considered a number) is 1. The zero power of zero is zero. Thus, 15^0 =1 and 0^0 =0.

Parentheses may be used to eliminate doubt as to what part of an expression is to be raised to a power. Thus, -32 may mean either -(3×3)=-9 or -3×-3=(+)9. To remove the ambiguity, the expression may be written -(3)2 if the first meaning is intended, and $-(3)^2$ if the second meaning is intended.

108. Division

Division is the inverse of multiplication. It may be indicated by the division sign (÷), as 376÷21=18 approximately; or by placing the number to be divided, called the **dividend** (376), over the other number, called the **divisor** (21), as $\frac{376}{21}$ =18 approximately. The expression $\frac{376}{21}$ may be written 376/21 with the same meaning. Such a problem is conveniently arranged for solution as follows:

```
     17
  21|376
     21
     166
     147
      19.
```

Since the **remainder** is 19, or more than half of the divisor (21), the answer is 18 to the nearest whole number.

An answer obtained by division is called a **quotient**. Any number divided by 1 is the number itself. Thus, 65÷1=65. A number cannot be divided by 0.

If the numbers involved are accurate only to the number of places given, the answer should not be carried to additional places. However, if the numbers are exact, the answer might be carried to as many decimal places as desired. Thus, 374÷21 =17.809523809523809523809523. . . When a series of digits repeat themselves with the same remainder, as 809523 (with remainder 17) in the example given above, an exact answer will not be obtained regardless of the number of places to which the division is carried. The series of dots (...) indicates a **repeating decimal**. In a non-repeating decimal, a plus sign (+) may be given to indicate a remainder, and a minus sign (-) to indicate that the last digit has been rounded to the next higher value. Thus, 18.68761 may be written 18.6876+ or 18.688-. If the last digit given is rounded off, the word "approximately" may be used instead of dots or a plus or minus sign.

If the divisor is a whole number, the decimal point in the quotient is directly above that of the dividend when the work form shown above is used. Thus, in the example given above, if the dividend had been 37.6 instead of 376, the quotient would have been 1.8 approximately. If the divisor is a decimal, both it and the dividend are multiplied by the power of 10 having an exponent equal to the number of decimal places in the divisor, and the division is then carried out as explained above. Thus, if there are two decimal places in the divisor, both divisor and dividend are multiplied by $10^2 = 100$. This is done by moving the decimal to the right until the divisor is a whole number. If necessary, zeros are added to the dividend. Thus, if 3.7 is to be divided by 2.11, both quantities are first multiplied by 10^2, and 370 is divided by 211. This is usually performed as follows:

```
        1.75
2.11 |3.7000
      211
      1590
      1477
       1130
       1055
         75.
```

If *both* the dividend and divisor are positive, or if *both* are negative, the quotient is positive; but if *either* is negative, the quotient is negative. Thus, 6÷3=2, (- 6)÷(-3)=+2, (-6)÷3=-2, and 6÷(-3)=-2.

The **square root** of a number is that number which, multiplied by itself, equals the given number. Thus, $15 \times 15 = 15^2 = 225$, and $\sqrt{225} = 225^{1/2} = 15$. The square root symbol $\sqrt{\ }$ is called the **radical sign**, or the exponent ½ indicates square root. Also, $\sqrt[3]{\ }$ or 1/3 as an exponent, indicates **cube root.** Fourth, fifth, or any root is indicated similarly, using the appropriate number. Nearly any arithmetic book explains the process of extracting roots, but this process is most easily performed by table, logarithms, or calculator. If no other means are available, it can be done by trial and error. The process of finding a root of a number is called **extracting a root.**

109. Logarithms

Though rarely used today, **logarithms** ("logs") provide an easy way to multiply, divide, raise numbers to powers, and extract roots. The logarithm of a number is the power to which a fixed number, called the base, must be raised to produce the value to which the logarithm corresponds. The base of **common logarithm**, (given in Tables 1 and 3) is 10. Hence, since $10^{1.8} = 63$ approximately, 1.8 is the logarithm, approximately, of 63 to the base 10. In table 1 logarithms of numbers are given to five decimal **places.** This is sufficient for most purposes of the navigator. For greater precision, a table having additional places should be used. In general, the number of *significant digits* which are correct in an answer obtained by logarithms is the same as the number of *places* in the logarithms used.

A logarithm is composed of two parts. That part to the left of the decimal point is called the **characteristic**. That part to the right of the decimal point is called the **mantissa**. The principal advantage of using 10 as the base is that any given combination of digits has the same mantissa regardless of the position of the decimal point. Hence, only the mantissa is given in the main tabulation of table 1. Thus, the logarithm (mantissa) of 2,374 is given as 37548. This is correct for 2,374,000,000; 2,374; 23.74; 2.374; 0.2374; 0.000002374; or for any other position of the decimal point.

The position of the decimal point determines the characteristic, which is not affected by the actual digits involved. The characteristic of a whole number is one less than the number of digits. The characteristic of a **mixed decimal** (one greater than 1) is one less than the number of digits to the left of the decimal point. Thus, in the example given above, the characteristic of the logarithm of 2,374,000,000 is 9; that of 2,374 is 3; that of 23.74 is 1; and that of 2.374 is 0. The complete logarithms of these numbers are:

log 2,374,000,000=9.37548
log 2,374 =3.37548
log 23.74 =1.37548
log 2.374 =0.37548

Since the mantissa of the logarithm of any multiple of ten is zero, the main table starts with 1,000. This can be considered 100, 10, 1, etc. Since the mantissa of these logarithms is zero, the logarithms consist of the characteristic only, and are whole numbers. Hence, the logarithm of 1 is 0 (0.00000), that of 10 is 1 (1.00000), that of 100 is 2 (2.00000), that of 1,000 is 3 (3.00000), etc.

The characteristic of the logarithm of a number less than 1 is negative. However, it is usually more conveniently indicated in a positive form, as follows: the characteristic is found by subtracting the number of zeros immediately to the right of the decimal point from 9 (or 19, 29, etc.) and following this by -10 (or -20, -30, etc.). Thus, the characteristic of the logarithm of 0.2374 is 9-10; that of 0.000002374 is 4-10; and that of 0:00000000002374 is 8-20. The complete logarithms of these numbers are:

log 2.374 =9.37548 - 10
log 0.000002374 =4.37548 - 10
log 0.00000000002374=8.37548 - 20

When there is no question of the meaning, the -10 may be omitted. This is usually done when using logarithms of trigonometric functions, as shown in table 3. Thus, if there is no reasonable possibility of confusion, the logarithm of 0.2374 may be written 9.37548.

Occasionally, the logarithm of a number less than 1 is shown by giving the negative characteristic with a minus sign above it (since only the characteristic is negative, the mantissa being positive). Thus, the logarithms of the numbers given above might be shown thus:

$$\log 0.2374 = \bar{1}.37548$$
$$\log 0.000002374 = \bar{6}.37548$$
$$\log 0.00000000002374 = \overline{12}.37548$$

In each case, the negative characteristic is one more than the number of zeros immediately to the right of the decimal point.

There is no real logarithm of 0, since there is no *finite* power to which *any* number can be raised to produce 0. As numbers approach 0, their logarithms approach negative infinity.

To find the number corresponding to a given logarithm, called finding the **antilogarithm** ("antilog"); enter the table with the mantissa of the given logarithm and determine the corresponding number, interpolating if necessary. Locate the position of the decimal point by means of the characteristic of the logarithm, in accordance with the rules given above.

110. Multiplication by Logarithms

To *multiply* one number by another, *add* their logarithms and find the antilogarithm of the sum. Thus, to multiply 1,635.8 by 0.0362 by logarithms:

log 1635.8= 3.21373
log 0.0362= 8.55871-10 (add)
log 59.216=11.77244-10 or 1.77244

Thus, 1,635.8×0.0362=59.216. In navigation it is customary to use a slightly modified form, and to omit the -10 where there is no reasonable possibility of confusion, as follows:

1635.8 log 3.21373
0.0362 log 8.55871
59.216 log 1.77244

To *raise a number to a power*, multiply the logarithm of that number by the power indicated, and find the antilogarithm of the product. Thus, to find 13.156^3 by logarithms, using the navigational form:

13.156 log 1.11913
x 3 (multiply)
2277.2 log 3.35739

111. Division by Logarithms

To *divide* one number by another, subtract the logarithm of the divisor from that of the dividend, and find the antilogarithm of the remainder. Thus, to find 0.4637÷28.03 by logarithms, using the navigational form:

0.4637 log 9.66624
28.03 log (-) 1.44762 (subtract)
0.016543 log 8.21862

It is sometimes necessary to modify the first logarithm before the subtraction can be made. This would occur in the example given above, for instance, if the divisor and dividend were reversed, so that the problem became 28.03÷0.4637. In this case 10-10 would be added to the logarithm of the dividend, becoming 11.44762-10:

28.03 log 11.44762 - 10
0.4637 log (-) 9.66624 - 10
60.448 log 1.78138

One experienced in the use of logarithms usually carries this change mentally, without showing it in his or her work form:

28.03 log 1.44762
0.4637 log (-) 9.66624
60.448 log 1.78138

Any number can be added to the characteristic as long as that same number is also subtracted. Conversely, any number can be subtracted from the characteristic as long as that same number is also added.

To *extract a root* of a number, divide the logarithm of that number by the root indicated, and find the antilogarithm of the quotient. Thus, to find $\sqrt{7}$ by logarithms:

7 log 0.84510 (÷2)
2.6458 log 0.42255

To divide a negative logarithm by the root indicated, first modify the logarithm so that the quotient will have a -10.

Thus, to find $\sqrt[3]{0.7}$ by logarithms:

$$\begin{array}{ll} 7 & \log \underline{29.84510} - 30\ (\div 3) \\ 0.88792 & \log 09.94837 - 10 \end{array}$$

or, carrying the -30 and -10 mentally,

$$\begin{array}{ll} 0.7 & \log \underline{29.84510}\ (\div 3) \\ 0.88792 & \log 9.94837 \end{array}$$

112. Cologarithms

The **cologarithm** ("colog") of a number is the value obtained by subtracting the logarithm of that number from zero, usually in the form 10-10. Thus, the logarithm of 18.615 is 1.26987. The cologarithm is:

$$\begin{array}{r} 10.00000-10 \\ (-)1.26987 \\ 8.73013-10 \end{array}$$

Similarly, the logarithm of 0.0018615 is 7.26987 -10, and its cologarithm is:

$$\begin{array}{r} 10.00000-10 \\ (-)\underline{7.26987-10} \\ 2.73013 \end{array}$$

The *cologarithm* of a number is the *logarithm* of the reciprocal of that number. Thus, the cologarithm of 2 is the logarithm of ½. Since division by a number is the same as multiplication by its reciprocal, the use of cologarithms permits division problems to be converted to problems of multiplication, eliminating the need for subtraction of logarithms. This is particularly useful when both multiplication and division are involved in the same problem. Thus, to find $\frac{92.732 \times 0.0137 \times 724.3}{0.516 \times 3941.1}$ by logarithm, one might *add* the logarithms of the three numbers in the numerator, and *subtract* the logarithms of the two numbers in the denominator. If cologarithms are used for the numbers in the denominator, all logarithmic values are added. Thus, the solution might be made as follows:

92.732		log 1.96723
0.0137		log 8.13672
724.3		log 2.85992
0.516	log 9.71265	colog 0.28735
3941.1	log 3.59562	colog 6.40438
0.45248		log 9.65560

113. Various Kinds of Logarithms

As indicated above, **common logarithms** use 10 as the base. These are also called **Brigg's logarithms**. For some purposes, it is convenient to use 2.7182818 approximately (designated e) as the base for logarithms. These are called **natural logarithms** or **Naperian logarithms** ($\log_e$). Common logarithms are shown as $\log_{10}$ when the base might otherwise be in doubt.

Addition and subtraction logarithms are logarithms of the sum and difference of two numbers. They are used when the logarithms of two numbers to be added or subtracted are known, making it unnecessary to find the numbers themselves.

114. Slide Rule

A **slide rule** is a mechanical analog computer. The slide rule is used primarily for multiplication and division, and also for functions such as roots, logarithms and trigonometry. The device is now obsolete with the advent of the hand held electronic calculator in the mid-1970's. Figure 114 depicts a typical slide rule.

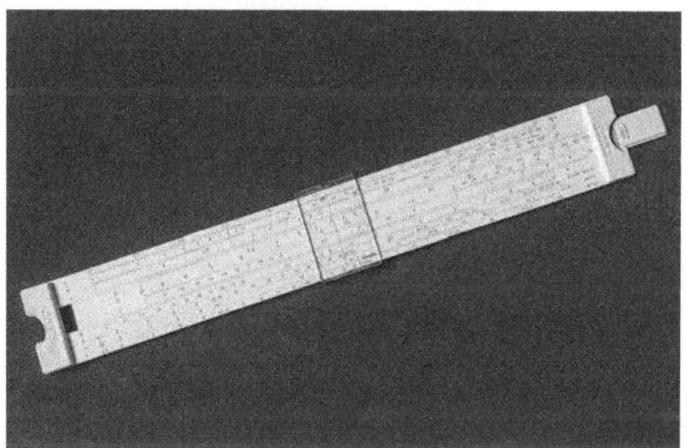

Figure 114. Slide rule. By Jan1959 (own work) via Wikimedia Commons

Slide rules come in many types and sizes, some designed for specific purposes. The most common form consists of an outer "body" or "frame" with grooves to permit a "slide" to be moved back and forth between the two outer parts, so that any graduation of a scale on the slide can be brought opposite any graduation of a scale on the body. A cursor called an "indicator" or "runner" is provided to assist in aligning the desired graduations. In a **circular slide rule** the "slide" is an inner disk surrounded by a larger one, both pivoted at their common center. The scales of a slide rule are *logarithmic.* That is, they increase proportionally to the logarithms of the numbers indicated, rather than to the numbers themselves. This permits addition and subtraction of logarithms by simply measuring off part of the length of the slide from a graduated point on the body, or vice versa. Two or three complete scales within the length of the rule may be provided for finding squares, cubes, square roots, and cube roots.

Properly used, a slide rule can provide quick answers to many of the problems of navigation. However, its precision is usually limited to from two to four significant digits, and should not be used if greater precision is desired.

Great care should be used in placing the decimal point in an answer obtained by slide rule, as the correct location often is not immediately apparent. Its position is usually determined by making a very rough mental solution. Thus, 2.93×8.3 is *about* 3×8=24. Hence, when the answer by slide rule is determined to be "243," it is known that the correct value is 24.3, not 2.43 or 243.

115. Mental Arithmetic

Many of the problems of the navigator can be solved mentally. The following are a few examples.

If the speed is a number divisible into 60 a whole number of times, distance problems can be solved by a simple relationship. Thus, at 10 knots a ship steams 1 mile in $\frac{60}{10}$ = 6 minutes. At 12 knots it requires 5 minutes, at 15 knots 4 minutes, etc. As an example of the use of such a relationship, a vessel steaming at 12 knots travels 5.6 miles in 28 minutes, since $\frac{28}{5}=5+\frac{3}{5}=5.6$, or 0.1 mile every half minute.

For relatively short distances, one nautical mile can be considered equal to 6,000 feet. Since one hour has 60 minutes, the speed in hundreds of feet per minute is equal to the speed in knots. Thus, a vessel steaming at 15 knots is moving at the rate of 1,500 feet per minute.

With respect to time, 6 minutes=0.1 hour, and 3 minutes = 0.05 hour. Hence, a ship steaming at 13 knots travels 3.9 miles in 18 minutes (13×0.3), and 5.8 miles in 27 minutes (13×0.45).

In arc units, 6' = 0.1° and 6" = 0.1'. This relationship is useful in rounding off values given in arc units. Thus, 17°23'44"=17°23.7' to the nearest 0.1', and 17.4° to the nearest 0.1°. A thorough knowledge of the six multiplication table is valuable. The 15 multiplication table is also useful, since $15° = 1^h$. Hence, $16^h = 16×15 = 240°$. This is particularly helpful in quick determination of zone description. Pencil and paper or a table should not be needed, for instance, to decide that a ship at sea in longitude 157°18.4' W is in the (+)10 zone.

It is also helpful to remember that $1° = 4^m$ and $1' = 4^s$. In converting the LMT of sunset to ZT, for instance, a quick mental solution can be made without reference to a table. Since this correction is usually desired only to the nearest whole minute, it is necessary only to multiply the longitude difference in degrees (to the nearest quarter degree) by four.

VECTORS

116. Scalars and Vector Quantities

A **scalar** is a quantity which has *magnitude* only; a **vector quantity** has both *magnitude* and *direction.* If a vessel is said to have a tank of 5,000 gallons capacity, the number 5,000 is a scalar. As used in this book, *speed* alone is considered a scalar, while *speed* and *direction* are considered to constitute *velocity*, a vector quantity. Thus, if a vessel is said to be steaming at 18 knots, without regard to direction, the number 18 is considered a scalar; but if the vessel is said to be steaming at 18 knots on course 157°, the combination of 18 knots, and 157° constitutes a vector quantity. *Distance* and *direction* also constitute a vector quantity.

A *scalar* can be represented fully by a number. A *vector quantity* vector requires, in addition, an indication of direction. This is conveniently done graphically by means of a straight line, the length of which indicates the *magnitude*, and the direction of which indicates the *direction* of application of the magnitude. Such a line is called a **vector**. Since a straight line has two directions, reciprocals of each other, an arrowhead is placed along or at one end of a vector to indicate the direction represented, unless this is apparent or indicated in some other manner.

117. Addition and Subtraction of Vectors

Two vectors can be *added* by *starting* the second at the termination (rather than the origin) of the first. A common navigational use of vectors is the dead reckoning plot of a vessel. Refer to Figure 117 depicting the addition and subtraction of vectors. If a ship starts at *A* and steams 18 miles on course 090° and then 12 miles on course 060°, it arrives by dead reckoning at *C*. The line *AB* is the vector for the first run, and *BC* is the vector for the second. Point *C* is the position found by *adding* vectors *AB* and *BC*. The vector *AC*, in this case the *course and distance made good*, is the **resultant**. Its value, both in direction and amount, can be determined by measurement. Lines *AB*, *BC*, and *AC* are all **distance vectors**. **Velocity vectors** are used when determining the effect of, or allowing for, current, interconverting true and apparent wind, and solving relative motion problems.

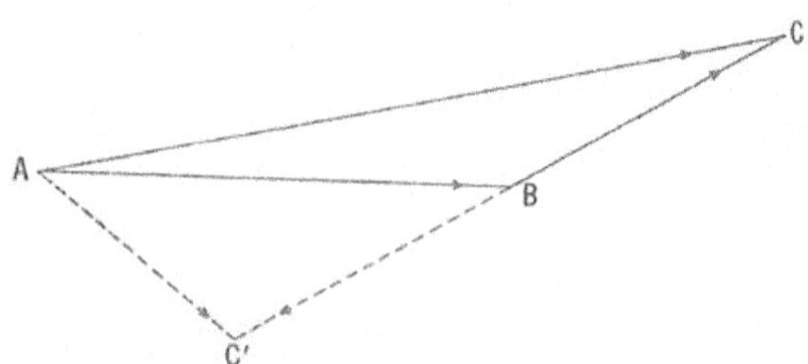

Figure 117. Addition and subtraction of vectors.

The **reciprocal** of a vector has the same magnitude but opposite direction of the vector. To *subtract* a vector, *add* it's reciprocal. This is indicated by the broken lines in Figure 117, in which the vector *BC'* is drawn in the opposite direction to *BC*. In this case the resultant is *AC'*. Subtraction of vectors is involved in some current and wind problems.

ALGEBRA

118. Definitions

Algebra is that branch of mathematics dealing with computation by letters and symbols. It permits the mathematical statement of certain relationships between variables. When numbers are substituted for the letters, algebra becomes arithmetic. Thus if $a=2b$, any value may be assigned to b, and a can be found by multiplying the assigned value by 2. Any statement of equality (as $a=2b$) is an **equation**. Any combination of numbers, letters, and symbols (as $2b$) is a **mathematical expression**.

119. Symbols

As in arithmetic, plus (+) and minus (-) signs are used, and with the same meaning. Multiplication (×) and division (÷) signs are seldom used. In algebra, $a\times b$ is usually written ab, or sometimes $a \cdot b$. For division $a \div b$ is usually written $\frac{a}{b}$ or a/b. The symbol > means "greater than" and < means "less than." Thus, $a > b$ means "a is greater than b," and $a \geq b$ means "a is equal to or greater than b."

The order of performing the operations indicated in an equation should be observed carefully. Consider the equation $a=b+cd-e/f$. If the equation is to be solved for a, the value cd should be determined by multiplication and e/f by division *before* the addition and subtraction, as each of these is to be considered a single quantity in making the addition and subtraction. Thus, if $cd=g$ and $e/f=h$, the formula can be written $a=b+g-h$.

If an equation including both multiplication and division between plus or minus signs is not carefully written, some doubt may arise as to which process to perform first. Thus, $a \div b \times c$ or $a/b \times c$ may be interpreted to mean either that a/b is to be multiplied by c or that a is to be divided by $b \times c$. Such an equation is better written ac/b if the first meaning is intended, or a/bc if the second meaning is intended.

Parentheses, ( ), may be used for the same purpose or to indicate any group of quantities that is to be considered a single quantity. Thus, a(b+c) is an indication that the sum of b and c is to be multiplied by a. Similarly, a+(b-c)2 indicates that c is first to be subtracted from b, and then the result is to be squared and the value thus obtained added to a. When an expression within parentheses is part of a larger expression which should also be in parentheses, brackets, [ ], are used in place of the outer parentheses. If yet another set is needed, braces, { }, are used.

A quantity written $\sqrt{3}\,ab$ is better written $ab\sqrt{3}$ to remove any suggestion that the square root of $3ab$ is to be found.

120. Addition and Subtraction

Addition and subtraction.-A plus sign before an expression in parentheses means that each term retains its sign as given. Thus, $a + (b + c - d)$ is the same as $a + b + c - d$. A minus sign preceding the parentheses means that each sign within the parentheses is to be reversed. For example, $a - (b + c - d) = a - b - c + d$.

In any equation involving addition and subtraction, similar terms can be combined. Thus, $a+b+c+b-2c-d=a+2b-c-d$. Also, $a+3ab+a^2-b-ab=a+2ab+a^2-b$. That is, to be combined, the terms must be truly alike, for a cannot be combined with ab, or with a^2.

Equal quantities can be added to or subtracted from both members of an equation without disturbing the equality. Thus, if $a=b$, $a+2=b+2$, or $a+x=b+x$. If $x=y$, then $a+x=b+y$.

121. Multiplication and Division

When an expression in parentheses is to be multiplied by a quantity outside the parentheses, each quantity separated by a plus or minus sign within the parentheses should be multiplied separately. Thus, $a(b+cd-e/f)$ may be written $ab+acd-ae/f$. Any quantity appearing in *every* term of one member of an equation can be separated out by **factoring**, or dividing each term by the common quantity. Thus, if $a = bc + \frac{bd}{e} - b^2 + b$, the equation may be written $a = b\left(c + \frac{d}{e} - b + 1\right)$.

Note that $\frac{b}{b}$ = and $\frac{b^2}{b} = b$. This is the inverse of multiplication: $a \times 1 = a$, but $a \times a = a^2$. Also, $a^2 \times a^3 = a^5$; and $\frac{a^7}{a^2} = a^5$. Thus, in multiplying a power of a number by a power of the same number, the powers are added, or, stated mathematically, $a^m \times a^n = a^{m+n}$. In division, $\frac{a^m}{a^n} = a^{m-n}$, or the exponents are subtracted. If n is greater than m, a *negative* exponent results. A value with a negative exponent is equal to the reciprocal of the same value with a positive exponent. Thus, $a^{-n} = \frac{1}{a^n}$ and $\frac{a^2b^{-3}}{c} = \frac{a^2}{b^3c}$.

In raising to a power a number with an exponent, the two exponents are multiplied. Thus, $(a^2)^3 = a^{2\times3} = a^6$, or $(a^n)^m = a^{nm}$. The inverse is true in extracting a root. Thus, $\sqrt[3]{a^2} = a^{\frac{2}{3}} = a^{0.667}$, or $\sqrt[m]{a^n} = a^{\frac{n}{m}}$.

Both members of an equation can be multiplied or divided by equal quantities without disturbing the equality, excluding division by zero or some expression equal to zero. Thus, if $a=b+c$, $2a=2(b+c)$, or if $x=y$, $ax=y(b+c)$ and $\frac{a}{x} = \frac{b+c}{y}$. Sometimes there is more than one answer to an equation. Division by one of the unknowns may eliminate one of the answers.

Both members of an equation can be raised to the same power, and like roots of both members can be taken, without disturbing the equality. Thus, if $a=b+c$, $a^2=(b+c)^2$, or if $x=y$, $a^x=(b+c)^y$. This is *not* the same as $a^x=b^y+c^y$. Similarly, if $a=b+c$, $\sqrt{a} = \sqrt{b+c}$, or if $x=y$, $\sqrt[x]{a} = \sqrt[y]{b+c}$. Again, $\sqrt[y]{b+c}$ is *not* equal to $\sqrt[y]{b} + \sqrt[y]{c}$, as a numerical example will indicate: $\sqrt{100} = \sqrt{64+36}$, but $\sqrt{100}$ does not equal $\sqrt{64} + \sqrt{36}$.

If two quantities to be multiplied or divided are both positive or both negative, the result is positive. Thus, $(+a)x(+b)=ab$ and $\frac{-a}{-b}=+\frac{a}{b}$. But if, the signs are opposite, the answer is negative. Thus, $(+a)x(-b)=-ab$, and $\frac{-a}{+b}=-\frac{a}{b}$; also, $(-a)x(+b)=-ab$, and $\frac{+a}{-b}=-\frac{a}{b}$.

In expressions containing both parentheses and brackets, or both of these and braces, the innermost symbols are removed first. Thus, $-\left\{6z - \frac{x(x+4)-5y}{y}\right\}=-\left\{6z - \frac{[x^2+4x-5y]}{y}\right\}=-\left\{6z - \frac{x^2}{y} - \frac{4x}{y} + 5\right\}=-6z + \frac{x^2}{y} + \frac{4x}{y} - 5.$

122. Fractions

To add or subtract two or more fractions, convert each to an expression having the same denominator, and then add the numerators.

Thus, $\frac{a}{b}+\frac{c}{d}+\frac{e}{f}=\frac{adf}{bdf}+\frac{cbf}{bdf}+\frac{ebd}{bdf}=\frac{adf+cbf+ebd}{bdf}$. That is, both numerator and denominator of each fraction are multiplied by the denominator of the other remaining fractions.

To multiply two or more fractions, multiply the numerators by each other, and also multiply the denominators by each other. Thus, $\frac{a}{b}\times\frac{c}{d}\times\frac{e}{f}=\frac{ace}{bdf}$.

To divide two fractions, invert the divisor and multiply. Thus, $\frac{a}{b}\div\frac{c}{d}=\frac{a}{b}\times\frac{d}{c}=\frac{ad}{bc}$.

If the same factor appears in all terms of a fraction, it can be factored out without changing the value of the fraction. Thus, $\frac{ab+ac+ad}{ae-af} = \frac{b+c+d}{e-f}$. This is the same as factoring a from the numerator and denominator separately. That is, $\frac{ab+ac+ad}{ae-af} = \frac{a(b+c+d)}{a(e-f)}$, but since $\frac{a}{a}=1$, this part can be removed, and the fraction appears as above.

123. Transposition

It is sometimes desirable to move terms of an expression from one side of the equals sign (=) to the other. This is called **transposition**, and to move one term is to **transpose** it. If the term to be moved is preceded by a plus or a minus sign, this sign is reversed when the term is transposed. Thus, if $a = b+c$, then $a-b=c$, $a-c=b$, $-b = c-a$, $-b-c=-a$, $-b-c=-a$, etc. Note that the signs of all terms can be reversed without destroying the equality, for if $a = b$, $b = a$. Thus, if all terms to the left of the equals sign are exchanged for all those to the right, no change in sign need take place, yet if each is moved individually, the signs reverse. For instance, if $a = b+c$, $-b-c=-a$. If each term is multiplied by -1, this becomes $b+c=a$.

A term which is to be multiplied or divided by *all* other terms on its side of the equation can be transposed if it is also moved from the numerator to the denominator, or vice versa. Thus, if $a = \frac{b}{c}$, then $ac = b$, $c = \frac{b}{a}$, $\frac{1}{b} = \frac{1}{ac}$, $\frac{c}{b} = \frac{1}{a}$, etc. (Note that $a = \frac{a}{1}$.) The same result could be obtained by multiplying both sides of an equation by the same quantity. For instance, if both sides of $a = \frac{b}{c}$ are multiplied by c, the equation becomes $ac = \frac{bc}{c}$ and since any number (except zero) divided by itself is unity, $\frac{c}{c} = 1$, and the equation becomes $ac = b$, as given above. Note, also, that *both* sides of an equation can be *inverted* without destroying the relationship, for if $a = b$, $\frac{a}{1} = \frac{b}{1}$, and $\frac{1}{b} = \frac{1}{a}$ or $\frac{1}{a} = \frac{1}{b}$. This is accomplished by transposing *all* terms of an equation.

Note that in the case of transposition by changing the plus or minus sign, an entire expression must be changed, and not a part of it. Thus, if $a = bc+d$, $a-bc=d$, but it is not true that $a+b = c+d$. Similarly, a term to be transposed by reversing its multiplication-division relationship must bear that relationship to *all* other terms on its side of the equation. That is, if $a = bc+d$, it is *not* true that $\frac{a}{b} = c+d$, or that $\frac{a}{bc} = d$, but $\frac{a}{bc+d} = 1$, if $a = b(cd+e)$.

124. Ratio and Proportions

If the relationship of a to b is the same as that of c to d, this fact can be written $a : b :: c : d$, or $\frac{a}{b} = \frac{c}{d}$. Either side of this equation, $\frac{a}{b}$ or $\frac{c}{d}$ is called a **ratio** and the whole equation is called a **proportion**. When a ratio is given a numerical value, it is often expressed as a decimal or as a percentage. Thus, if $\frac{a}{b} = \frac{1}{4}$ (that is, $a = 1$, $b = 4$), the ratio might be expressed as 0.25 or as 25 percent.

Since a ratio is a fraction, it can be handled as any other fraction.

GEOMETRY

125. Definition

Geometry deals with the properties, relations, and measurement of lines, surfaces, solids, and angles. **Plane geometry** deals with plane figures, and **solid geometry** deals with three–dimensional figures.

A **point**, considered mathematically, is a place having position but no extent. It has no length, breadth, or thickness. A point in motion produces a **line**, which has length, but neither breadth nor thickness. A **straight or right line** is the shortest distance between two points in space. A line in motion in any direction except along itself produces a **surface**, which has length and breadth, but not thickness. A **plane surface** or **plane** is a surface without curvature. A straight line connecting any two of its points lies wholly within the plane. A plane surface in motion in any direction except within its plane produces a **solid**, which has length, breadth, and thickness. **Parallel lines** or surfaces are those which are everywhere equidistant. **Perpendicular lines** or surfaces are those which meet at right or 90° angles. A perpendicular may be called a **normal**, particularly when it is perpendicular to the tangent to a curved line or surface at the point of tangency. All points equidistant from the ends of a straight line are on the perpendicular bisector of that line. The shortest distance from a point to a line is the length of the perpendicular between them.

126. Angles

An **angle** is formed by two straight lines which meet at a point. It is measured by the arc of a circle intercepted between the two lines forming the angle, the center of the circle being at the point of intersection. In Figure 126a, the angle formed by lines AB and BC, may be designated "angle B," "angle ABC," or "angle CBA"; or by Greek letter as "angle α." The three letter designation is preferred if there is more than one angle at the point. When three letters are used, the middle one should always be that at the **vertex** of the angle.

An **acute angle** is one less than a right angle (90°).

A **right angle** is one whose sides are perpendicular (90°).

An **obtuse angle** is one greater than a right angle (90°) but less than 180°.

A **straight angle** is one whose sides form a continuous straight line (180°).

A **reflex angle** is one greater than a straight angle (180°) but less than a circle (360°). Any two lines meeting at a point form two angles, one less than a straight angle of 180° (unless exactly a straight angle) and the other greater than a straight angle.

An **oblique angle** is any angle not a multiple of 90°.

Two angles whose sum is a right angle (90°) are **complementary angles**, and either is the **complement** of the other.

Two angles whose sum is a straight angle (180°) are **supplementary angles**, and either is the **supplement** of the other.

Two angles whose sum is a circle (360°) are **explementary angles**, and either is the **explement** of the other. The two angles formed when any two lines terminate at a common point are explementary.

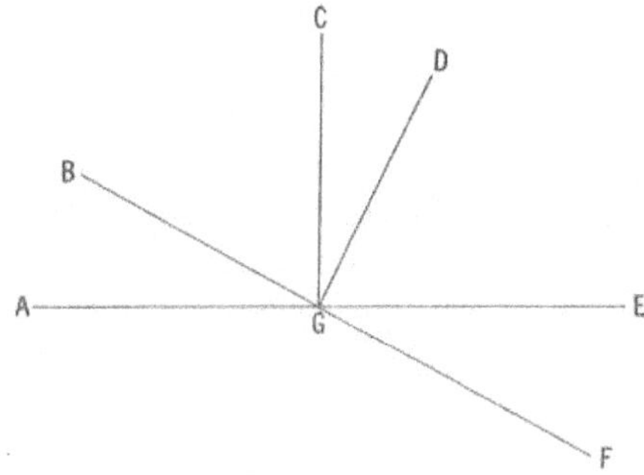

Figure 126a. Acute, right, and obtuse angles.

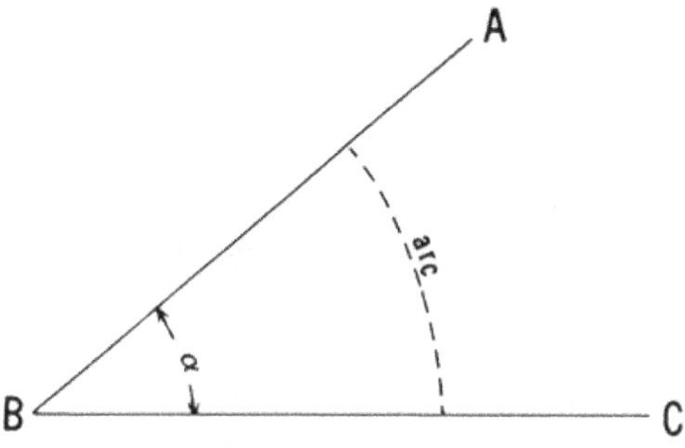

Figure 126b. An angle.

If the sides of one angle are perpendicular to those of another, the two angles are either equal or supplementary. Also, if the sides of one angle are parallel to those

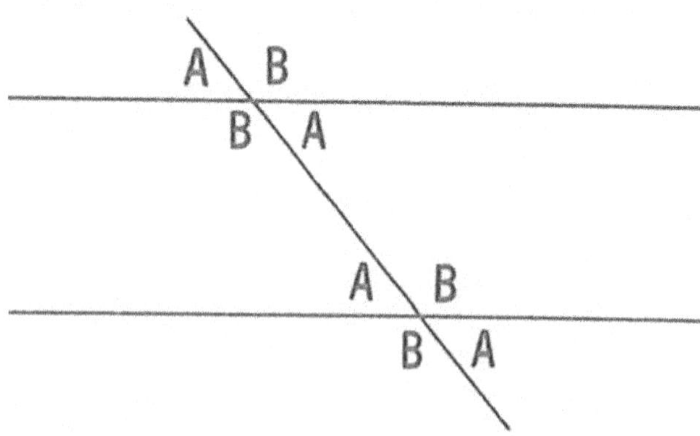

Figure 126c. Angles formed by a transversal.

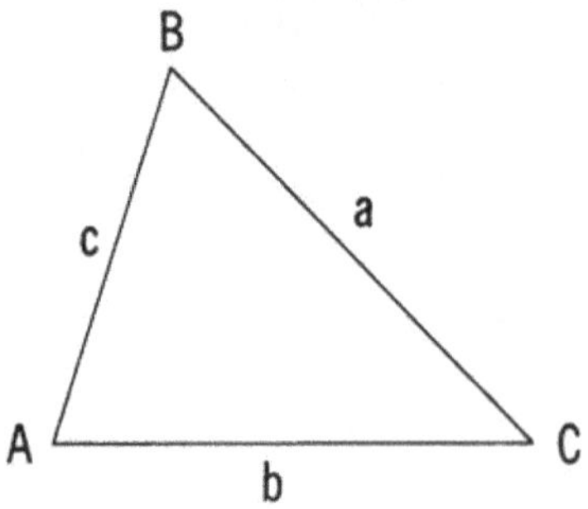

Figure 127a. A triangle.

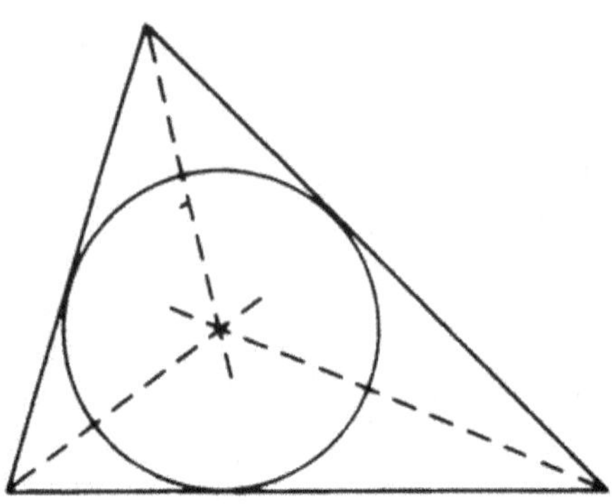

Figure 127b. A circle inscribed in a triangle.

of another, the two angles are either equal or supplementary.

When two straight lines intersect, forming four angles, the two opposite angles, called **vertical angles**, are equal. Angles which have the same vertex and lie on opposite sides of a common side are **adjacent angles**. Adjacent angles formed by intersecting lines are supplementary, since each pair of adjacent angles forms a straight angle. Thus, in Figure 126a, lines *AE* and BF intersect at *G*. Angles *AGB* and *EGF* form a pair of equal acute vertical angles, and *BGE* and *AGF* form a pair of equal obtuse vertical angles.

A **transversal** is a line that intersects two or more other lines. If two or more parallel lines are cut by a transversal, groups of adjacent and vertical angles are formed, as shown in Figure 126c. In this situation, all acute angles (*A*) are equal, all obtuse angles (*B*) are equal, and each acute angle is supplementary to each obtuse angle.

A **dihedral angle** is the angle between two intersecting planes.

127. Triangles

A **plane triangle** is a closed figure formed by three straight lines, called **sides**, which meet at three points called **vertices**. The vertices are labeled with capital letters and the sides with lowercase letters, as shown in Figure 127a, which depicts a triangle.

An **equilateral triangle** is one with its three sides equal in length. It must also be **equiangular**, with its three angles equal.

An **isosceles triangle** is one with two equal sides, called **legs**. The angles opposite the legs are equal. A line which **bisects** (divides into two equal parts) the unequal angle of an isosceles triangle is the perpendicular bisector of the opposite side, and divides the triangle into two equal right triangles.

A **scalene triangle** is one with no two sides equal. In such a triangle, no two angles are equal.

An **acute triangle** is one with three acute angles.

A **right triangle** is one having a right angle. The side opposite the right angle is called the **hypotenuse**. The other two sides may be called **legs**. A plane triangle can have only one right angle.

An **obtuse triangle** is one with an obtuse angle. A plane triangle can have only one obtuse angle.

An **oblique triangle** is one which does not contain a right angle.

The **altitude** of a triangle is a line or the distance from any vertex perpendicular to the opposite side.

A **median** of a triangle is a line from any vertex to the center of the opposite side. The three medians of a triangle meet at a point called the **centroid** of the triangle. This point divides each median into two parts, that part between the centroid and the vertex being twice as long as the other part.

Lines bisecting the three *angles* of a triangle meet at a point which is equidistant from the three sides, which is the center of the **inscribed circle**, as shown in Figure 127b. This point is of particular interest to navigators because it is the point theoretically taken as the fix when three lines of position of equal weight and having only random errors do not meet at a common point. In practical navigation, the point is found visually, not by construction, and other factors often influence the chosen fix position.

The perpendicular bisectors of the three *sides* of a triangle meet at a point which is equidistant from the three vertices, which is the center of the **circumscribed circle**, the circle through the three vertices and the smallest circle

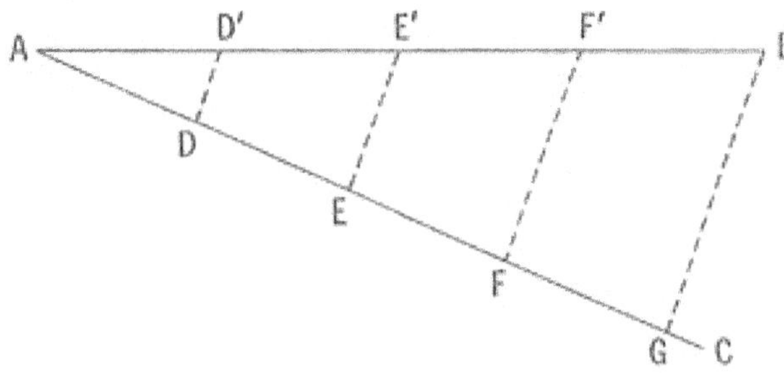

Figure 127c. Dividing a line into equal parts.

which can be drawn enclosing the triangle. The center of a circumscribed circle is *within* an acute triangle, *on the hypotenuse* of a right triangle, and *outside* an obtuse triangle.

A line connecting the mid–points of two sides of a triangle is always parallel to the third side and half as long. Also, a line parallel to one side of a triangle and intersecting the other two sides divides these sides proportionally. This principle can be used to divide a line into any number of equal or proportional parts. Refer to Figure 127c, which depicts dividing a line into equal parts. Suppose it is desired to divide line *AB* into four equal parts. From *A* draw any line *AC*. Along *C* measure four equal parts of any convenient lengths (*AD, DE, EF,* and *FG*). Draw *GB*, and through *F, E,* and *D* draw lines parallel to *GB* and intersecting *AB*. Then *AD', D' E', E' F'*, and *F' B* are equal and *AB* is divided into four equal parts.

The sum of the angles of a plane triangle is always 180°. Therefore, the sum of the acute angles of a right triangle is 90°, and the angles are complementary. If one side of a triangle is extended, the **exterior angle** thus formed is supplementary to the adjacent **interior angle** and is therefore equal to the sum of the two non adjacent angles. If two angles of one triangle are equal to two angles of another triangle, the third angles are also equal, and the triangles are **similar**. If the area of one triangle is equal to the area of another, the triangles are **equal**. Triangles having equal bases and altitudes also have equal areas. Two figures are **congruent** if one can be placed over the other to make an exact fit. Congruent figures are both similar and equal. If any side of one triangle is equal to any side of a similar triangle, the triangles are congruent. For example, if two right triangles have equal sides, they are congruent; if two right triangles have two corresponding sides equal, they are congruent. Triangles are congruent only if the sides and angles are equal.

The sum of two sides of a plane triangle is always greater than the third side; their difference is always less than the third side.

The area of a triangle is equal to 1/2 of the area of the polygon formed from its base and height. If *A* = area, *b* = one of the legs of a right triangle or the base of any plane triangle, *h* = altitude, *c* = the hypotenuse of a right triangle, *a* = the other leg of a right triangle, and *S* = the sum of the interior angles:

$$\text{Area of plane triangle } A = \frac{bh}{2}$$

Sum of interior angles of plane triangle: S = 180°

The square of the hypotenuse of a right triangle is equal to the sum of the squares of the other two sides, or $a^2 + b^2 = c^2$. Therefore the length of the hypotenuse of plane right triangle can be found by the formula:

$$c = \sqrt{a^2 + b^2}$$

128. Polygons

A **polygon** is a closed plane figure made up of three or more straight lines called **sides.** A polygon with three sides is a **triangle**, one with four sides is a **quadrilateral**, one with five sides is a **pentagon**, one with six sides is a **hexagon**, and one with eight sides is an **octagon**. An **equilateral polygon** has equal sides. An **equiangular polygon** has equal interior angles. A **regular polygon** is both equilateral and equiangular. As the number of sides of a regular polygon increases, the figure approaches a circle.

A **trapezoid** is a quadrilateral with one pair of opposite sides parallel and the other pair not parallel. A **parallelogram** is a quadrilateral with both pairs of opposite sides parallel. Any side of a parallelogram, or either of the parallel sides of a trapezoid, is the **base** of the figure. The perpendicular distance from the base to the opposite side is the altitude. A **rectangle** is a parallelogram with four right angles. (If anyone is a right angle, the other three must be, also.) A **square** is a rectangle with equal sides. A **rhomboid** is a parallelogram with oblique angles. A **rhombus** is a rhomboid with equal sides.

The sum of the exterior angles of a convex polygon (one having no interior reflex angles), made by extending each side in one direction only (consistently), is 360°.

A **diagonal** of a polygon is a straight line connecting any two vertices which are not adjacent. The diagonals of a parallelogram bisect each other.

The **perimeter** of a polygon is the sum of the lengths of its sides.

If *A* = area, *s* = the side of a square, *a* = that side of a rectangle adjacent to the base or that side of a trapezoid parallel to the base, *b* = the base of a quadrilateral, *h* = the altitude of a parallelogram or trapezoid, *S* = the sum of the angles of a polygon, and n = the number of sides of a polygon:

Area of a square: $A = s^2$

Area if a rectangle: $A = ab$

Area of a parallelogram: $A = bh$

Area of a trapezoid: $A = \frac{(a+b)h}{2}$

Sum of angles in convex polygon: $S = (n-2)180°$.

129. Circles

A **circle** is a plane, closed curve, all points of which are equidistant from a point within, called the **center**. See Figure 129 depicting elements of a circle.

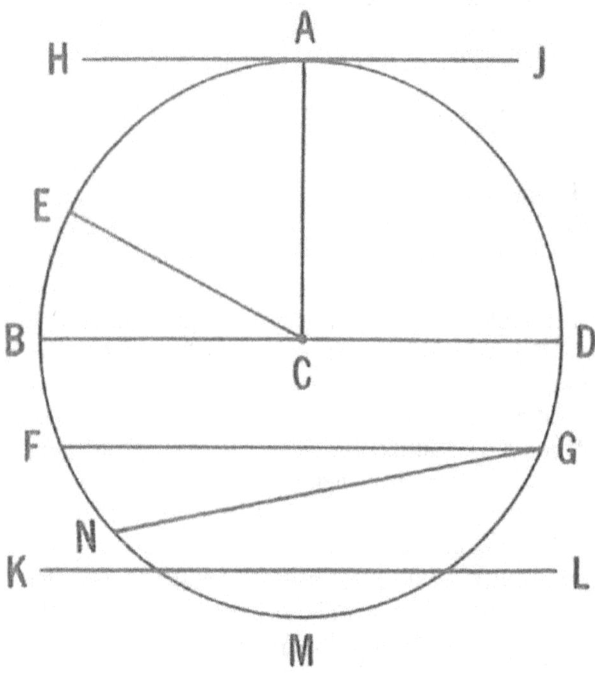

Figure 129. Elements of a circle.

The distance around a circle is called the **circumference**. Technically the length of this line is the **perimeter**, although the term "circumference" is often used. An arc is part of a circumference. A **major arc** is more than a semicircle (180°), a **minor arc** is less than a semicircle (180°). A **semi–circle** is half a circle (180°), a **quadrant** is a quarter of a circle (90°), a **quintant** is a fifth of a circle (72°), a **sextant** is a sixth of a circle (60°), an **octant** is an eighth of a circle (45°). Some of these names have been applied to instruments used by navigators for measuring altitudes of celestial bodies because of the part of a circle used for the length of the arc of the instrument.

Concentric circles have a common center. A **radius** (plural **radii**) or **semidiameter** is a straight line connecting the center of a circle with any point on its circumference. In Figure 129, *CA, CB, CD,* and *CE* are radii

A **diameter** of a circle is a straight line passing through its center and terminating at opposite sides of the circumference, or two radii in opposite directions (*BCD*, Figure 129). It divides a circle into two equal parts. The ratio of the length of the circumference of any circle to the length of its diameter is 3.14159+, or π (the Greek letter pi), a relationship that has many useful applications.

A **sector** is that part of a circle bounded by two radii and an arc. In Figure 129, *BCE, ECA, ACD, BCA,* and *ECD* are sectors.The angle formed by two radii is called a **central angle**. Any pair of radii divides a circle into sectors, one less than a semicircle (180°) and the other greater than a semicircle (unless the two radii form a diameter).

A **chord** is a straight line connecting any two points on the circumference of a circle (*FG, GN* in Figure 129). Chords equidistant from the center of a circle are equal in length.

A **segment** is the part of a circle bounded by a chord and the intercepted arc (*FGMF, NGMN* in Figure 129). A chord divides a circle into two segments, one less than a semicircle (180°), and the other greater than a semicircle (unless the chord is a diameter). A diameter perpendicular to a chord bisects it, its arc, and its segments. Either pair of vertical angles formed by intersecting chords has a combined number of degrees equal to the sum of the number of degrees in the two arcs intercepted by the two angles.

An **inscribed angle** is one whose vertex is on the circumference of a circle and whose sides are chords (*FGN* in Figure 129). It has half as many degrees as the arc it intercepts. Hence, an angle inscribed in a semicircle is a right angle if its sides terminate at the ends of the diameter forming the semicircle.

A **secant** of a circle is a line intersecting the circle, or a chord extended beyond the circumference (*KL* in Figure 129).

A **tangent** to a circle is a straight line, in the plane of the circle, which has only one point in common with the circumference (*HJ* in Figure 129). A tangent is perpendicular to the radius at the **point of tangency** (A in Figure 129). Two tangents from a common point to opposite sides of a circle are equal in length, and a line from the point to the center of the circle bisects the angle formed by the two tangents. An angle formed outside a circle by the intersection of two tangents, a tangent and a secant, or two secants has *half* as many degrees as the *difference* between the two intercepted arcs. An angle formed by a tangent and a chord, with the apex at the point of tangency, has half as many degrees as the arc it intercepts. A **common tangent** is one tangent to more than one circle. Two circles are tangent to each other if they touch at one point only. If of different sizes, the smaller circle may be either inside or outside the larger one.

Parallel lines intersecting a circle intercept equal arcs.

If A = area; r = radius; d = diameter; C = circumference; s = linear length of an arc; a = angular length of an arc, or the angle it subtends at the center of a circle, in degrees; b = angular length of an arc, or the angle it subtends at the center of a circle, in radians; *rad* = radians and *sin* = sine:

Circumference of a circle $C = 2\pi r = \pi d = 2\pi \text{ rad}$

Area of circle $A = \pi r^2 = \frac{\pi d^2}{4}$

Area of sector $= \frac{\pi r^2 a}{360} = \frac{r^2 b}{2} = \frac{rs}{2}$

Area of segment $= \frac{r^2(b - \sin a)}{2}$

130. Polyhedrons

A **polyhedron** is a solid having plane sides or faces.

A **cube** is a polyhedron having six square sides.

A **prism** is a solid having parallel, similar, equal, plane geometric figures as bases, and parallelograms as sides. By extension, the term is also applied to a similar solid having nonparallel bases, and trapezoids or a combination of trapezoids and parallelograms as sides. The **axis** of a prism is the straight line connecting the centers of its bases. A **right prism** is one having bases perpendicular to the axis. The sides of a right prism are rectangles. A **regular prism** is a right prism having regular polygons as bases. The **altitude** of a prism is the perpendicular distance between the planes of its bases. In the case of a right prism it is measured along the axis.

A **pyramid** is a polyhedron having a polygon as one end, the **base**; and a point, the **apex**, as the other; the two ends being connected by a number of triangular sides or **faces**. The **axis** of a pyramid is the straight line connecting the apex and the center of the base. A **right pyramid** is one having its base perpendicular to its axis. A **regular pyramid** is a right pyramid having a regular polygon as its base. The altitude of a pyramid is the perpendicular distance from its apex to the plane of its base. A **truncated pyramid** is that portion of a pyramid between its base and a plane intersecting all of the faces of the pyramid.

If A = area, s = edge of a cube or slant height of a regular pyramid (from the center of one side of its base to the apex), V = volume, a = side of a polygon, h = altitude, P = perimeter of base, n = number of sides of polygon, B = area of base, and r = perpendicular distance from the center of side of a polygon to the center of the polygon:

Cube:

Area of each face: $A = s^2$

Total area of all faces: $A = 6s^2$

Volume: $V = s^3$

Regular prism:

Area of each face: $A = ah$

Total area of all faces: $A = Ph = nah$

Area of each base: $B = \frac{nar}{2}$

Total area of both bases: $A = nar$

Volume: $V = Bh = \frac{narh}{2}$

Regular pyramid:

Area of each face: $A = \frac{as}{2}$

Total area of all faces: $A = \frac{nas}{2}$

Area of base: $B = \frac{nar}{2}$

Volume: $V = \frac{Bh}{3} = \frac{narh}{6}$

131. Cylinders

A **cylinder** is a solid having two parallel plane **bases** bounded by closed congruent curves, and a surface formed by an infinite number of parallel lines, called **elements**, connecting similar points on the two curves. A cylinder is similar to a prism, but with a curved lateral surface, instead of a number of flat sides connecting the bases. The axis of a cylinder is the straight line connecting the centers of the bases. A **right cylinder** is one having bases perpendicular to the axis. A **circular cylinder** is one having circular bases. The **altitude** of a cylinder is the perpendicular distance between the planes of its bases. The **perimeter** of a base is the length of the curve bounding it.

If A = area, P = perimeter of base, h = altitude, r = radius of a circular base, B = area of base, and V = volume, then for a right circular cylinder:

Lateral area: $A = Ph = 2\pi rh$

Area of each base: $B = \pi r^2$

Total area, both bases: $A = 2\pi r^2$

Volume: $V = Bh = \pi r^2 h$

132. Cones

A **cone** is a solid having a plane **base** bounded by a closed curve, and a surface formed by lines, called **elements**, from every point on the curve to a common point called the **apex**. A cone is similar to a pyramid, but with a curved surface connecting the base and apex, instead of a number of flat sides. The **axis** of a cone is the straight line connecting the apex and the center of the base. A **right cone** is one having its base perpendicular to its axis. A **circular cone** is one having a circular base. The **altitude** of a cone is the perpendicular distance from its apex to the plane of its base. A **frustum** of a cone is that portion of the cone between its base and any parallel plane intersecting all elements of the cone. A **truncated cone** is that portion of a cone between its base and any nonparallel plane which intersects all elements of the cone but does not intersect the base.

If A = area, r = radius of base, s = slant height or length of element, B = area of base, h = altitude, and V = volume, then for a right circular cone:

Lateral area: $A = \pi rs$

Area of base: $B = \pi r^2$

Slant height: $s = \sqrt{r^2 + h^2}$

Volume: $V = \frac{Bh}{3} = \frac{\pi r^2 h}{3}$

133. Conic Sections

If a right circular cone of indefinite extent is intersected by a plane perpendicular to the axis of the cone the line of intersection of the plane and the surface of the cone is a circle. Refer to Figure 133a for a depiction of conic sections.

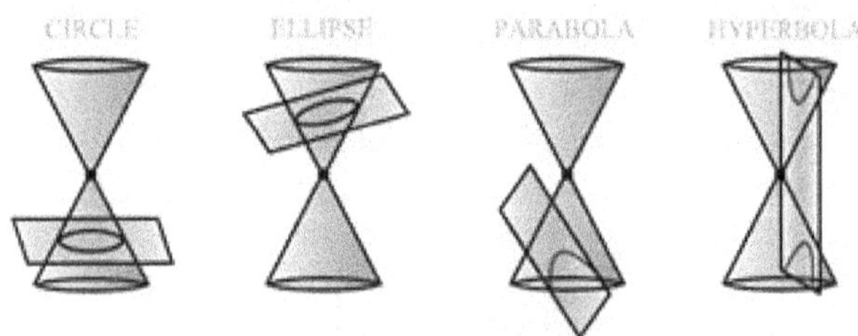

Figure 133a. Conic sections.

If an intersecting plane is tilted to some position, the intersection is an **ellipse** or flattened circle, see Figure 133b. The longest diameter of an ellipse is called its **major axis,** and half of this is its **semimajor axis,** which is identified by the letter "**a**" in Figure 133b. The shortest diameter of an ellipse is called its **minor axis,** and half of this is its semiminor axis, which is identified by the letter "**b**" in figure Figure 133b. Two points, F and F', called **foci** (singular **focus**) or **focal points,** on the major axis are so located that the sum of their distances from any point P on the curve is equal to the length of the major axis. That is $PF + PF' = 2a$ (Figure 133b). The **eccentricity** (**e**) of an ellipse is equal to $\frac{c}{a}$, where c is the distance from the center to one of the foci ($c = CF = CF'$). It is always greater than 0 but less than 1.

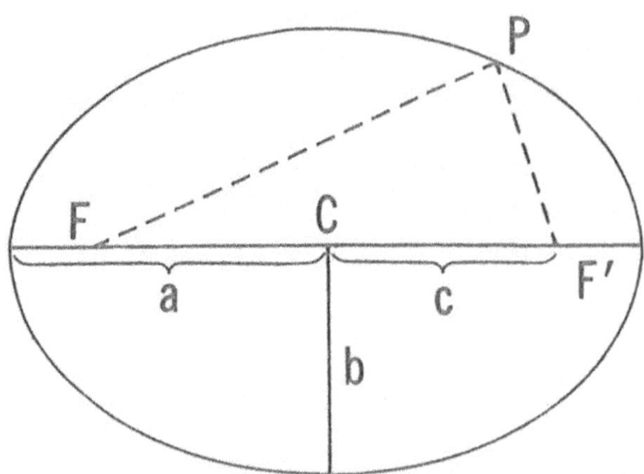

Figure 133b. An ellipse.

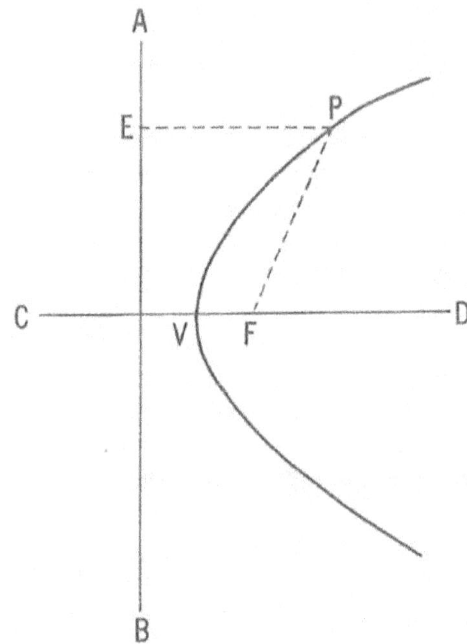

Figure 133c. A parabola.

If an intersecting plane is parallel to one element of the cone the intersection is a **parabola**, see Figure 133c. Any point P on a parabola is equidistant from a fixed point F, called the **focus** or **focal point**, and a fixed straight line, AB, called the **directrix**. Thus, for any point P, $PF = PE$. The point midway between the focus F and the directrix AB is called the **vertex**, V. The straight line through F and V is called the **axis,** CD. This line is perpendicular to the directrix AB. The **eccentricity** (e) of a parabola is 1.

If the elements of the cone are extended to form a second cone having the same axis and apex but extending in the opposite direction, and the intersecting plane is tilted beyond the position forming a parabola, so that it intersects both curves, the intersections of the plane with the cones is a **hyperbola**, see Figure 133d. There are two intersections or branches of a hyperbola, as shown. At any point P on either branch, the difference in the distance from two fixed points called **foci** or **focal points**, F and F', is constant and equal to the shortest distance between the two branches. That is, $PF - PF' = 2a$ (Figure 133d). The straight line through F and F' is called the **axis**. The **eccentricity** (**e**) of a hyperbola is the ratio $\frac{c}{a}$ (Figure 133d). It is always greater than 1.

Each branch of a hyperbola approaches ever closer to, but never reaches, a pair of intersecting straight lines, AB and CD, called **asymptotes**. These intersect at G.

The various conic sections bear an eccentricity relationship to each other. The eccentricity of a circle is 0, that of an ellipse is greater than 0 but less than 1; that of a parabola or straight line (a limiting case of a parabola) is 1, and that of a hyperbola is greater than 1.

If e = eccentricity, A = area, a = semimajor axis of an ellipse or half the shortest distance between the two branches of a hyperbola, b = the semiminor axis of an ellipse, and c = the distance between the center of an ellipse and one of its focal points or the distance between the focal point of a hyperbola and the intersection of its asymptotes:

Circle:

Eccentricity: $e = 0$

Ellipse:

Area: $A = \pi ab$

Eccentricity: $e = \frac{c}{a}$, greater that 0, but less than 1.

Parabola:

Eccentricity: $e = 1$

Hyperbola:

Eccentricity: $e = \frac{c}{a}$, greater than 1.

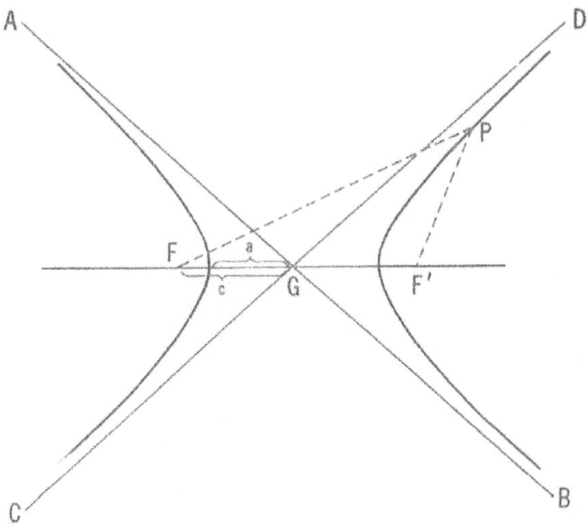

Figure 133d. A hyperbola.

When cones are intersected by some surface other than a plane, as the curved surface of the earth, the resulting sections do not follow the relationships given above, the amount of divergence therefrom depending upon the individual circumstances.

134. Spheres

A **sphere** is a solid bounded by a surface every point of which is equidistant from a point within called the **center**. It may also be formed by rotating a circle about any diameter.

A **radius** or **semidiameter of a sphere** is a straight line connecting its center with any point on its surface. A **diameter** of a sphere is a straight line through its center and terminated at both ends by the surface of the sphere. The poles of a sphere are the ends of a diameter.

The intersection of a plane and the surface of a sphere is a circle, a **great circle** if the plane passes through the center of the sphere, and a **small circle** if it does not. The shorter arc of the great circle between two points on the surface of a sphere is the shortest distance, on the surface of the sphere, between the points. Every great circle of a sphere bisects every other great circle of that sphere. The **poles** of a circle on a sphere are the extremities of the sphere's diameter which is perpendicular to the plane of the circle. All points on the circumference of the circle are equidistant from either of its poles. In the ease of a great circle, *both* poles are 90° from any point on the circumference of the circle. Any great circle may be considered a **primary**, particularly when it serves as the origin of measurement of a coordinate. The great circles through its poles are called **secondary**. Secondaries are perpendicular to their primary.

A **spherical triangle** is the figure formed on the surface of a sphere by the intersection of three great circles. The lengths of the sides of a spherical triangle are measured in degrees, minutes, and seconds, as the angular lengths of the arcs forming them. The sum of the three sides is always less than 360°. The sum of the three angles is always *more* than 180° and *less* than 540°.

A **lune** is the part of the surface of a sphere bounded by halves of two great circles.

A **spheroid** is a flattened sphere, which may be formed by rotating an ellipse about one of its axes. An **oblate spheroid**, such as the earth, is formed when an ellipse is rotated about its minor axis. In this case the diameter along the axis of rotation is less than the major axis. A **prolate spheroid** is formed when an ellipse is rotated about its major axis. In this case the diameter along the axis of rotation is greater than the minor axis.

If A = area, r = radius, d = diameter, and V = volume of a sphere:

Area: $A = 4\pi r^2 = \pi d^2$

Volume: $V = \frac{4\pi r^3}{3} = \frac{\pi d^3}{6}$

If A = area, a = semimajor axis, b = semiminor axis, e = eccentricity, and V = volume of an oblate spheroid:

$$\text{Area: } A = 4\pi a^2\left(1 - \frac{e^2}{3} - \frac{e^4}{15} - \frac{e^6}{35} - \ldots\right)$$

$$\text{Eccentricity: } e = \sqrt{\frac{a^2 - b^2}{a^2}}$$

$$\text{Volume: } V = \frac{4\pi a^2 b}{3}$$

135. Coordinates

Coordinates are magnitudes used to define a position. Many different types of coordinates are used. Important navigational ones are described below.

If a position is known to be at a stated point, no magnitudes are needed to identify the position, although they may be required to locate the point. Thus, if a vessel is at port A, its position is known if the location of port A is known, but latitude and, longitude may be needed to locate port A.

If a position is known to be on a given line, a single magnitude (coordinate) is needed to identify the position if an origin is stated or understood. Thus, if a vessel is known to be *south* of port B, it is known to be on a line extending southward from port B. If its distance from port B is known, and the position of port B is known, the position of the vessel is uniquely defined.

If a position is known to be on a given surface, two magnitudes (coordinates) are needed to define the position. Thus, if a vessel is known to be on the surface of the earth, its position can be identified by means of latitude and longitude. Latitude indicates its angular distance north or south of the equator, and longitude its angular distance east or west of the prime meridian.

If nothing is known regarding a position other than that it exists in space, three magnitudes (coordinates) are needed to define its position. Thus, the position of a submarine may be defined by means of latitude, longitude, and depth below the surface.

Each coordinate requires an origin, either stated or implied. If a position is known to be on a given plane, it might be defined by means of its distance from each of two intersecting lines, called **axes**. These are called **rectangular coordinates**. In Figure 135a, OY is called the **ordinate**, and OX is called the **abscissa**. Point O is the **origin**, and lines OX and OY the axes (called the X and Y axes, respectively). Point A is at position x, y. If the axes are not perpendicular but the lines x and y are drawn parallel to the axes, **oblique coordinates** result. Either type are called **Cartesian coordinates**. A three–dimensional system of Cartesian coordinates, with X, Y, and Z axes, is called **space coordinates.**

Another system of plane coordinates in common usage consists of the *direction* and *distance* from the origin (called the **pole**), as shown in Figure 135b. A line extending in the direction indicated is called a **radius vector**. Direction and distance from a fixed point constitute **polar coordinates**, sometimes called the rho– (the Greek ρ, to indicate distance) theta (the Greek θ, to indicate direction) system. An example of its use is the radar scope.

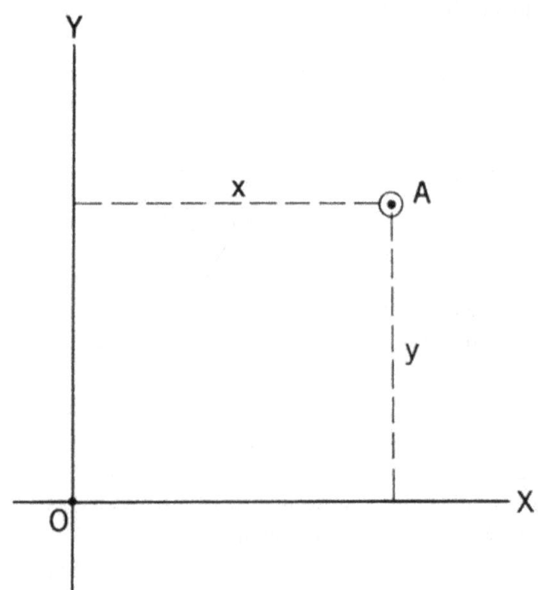

Figure 135a. Rectangular coordinates.

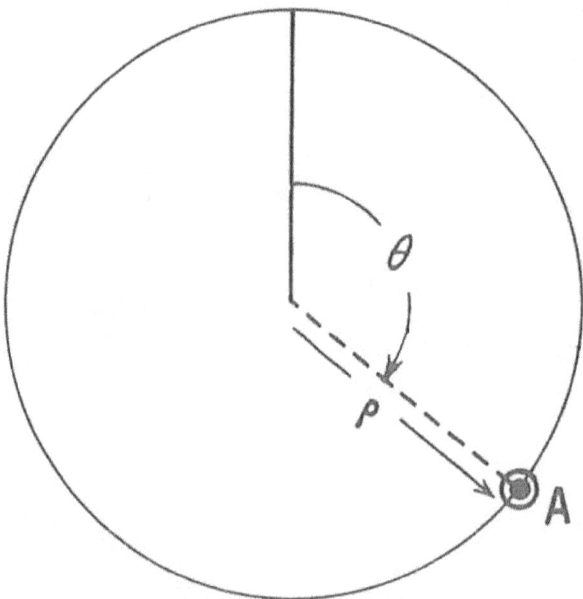

Figure 135b. Polar coordinates.

Spherical coordinates are used to define a position on the surface of a sphere or spheroid by indicating angular distance from a primary great circle and a reference secondary great circle. Examples used in navigation are latitude and longitude, altitude and azimuth, and declination and hour angle.

TRIGONOMETRY

136. Definitions

Trigonometry deals with the relations among the angles and sides of triangles. **Plane trigonometry** deals with plane triangles, those on a plane surface. **Spherical trigonometry** deals with spherical triangles, which are drawn on the surface of a sphere. In navigation, the common methods of celestial sight reduction use spherical triangles on the surface of the Earth. For most navigational purposes, the Earth is assumed to be a sphere, though it is somewhat flattened.

137. Angular Measure

A circle may be divided into 360 **degrees** (°), which is the **angular length** of its circumference. Each degree may be divided into 60 **minutes** ('), and each minute into 60 **seconds** ("). The angular measure of an arc is usually expressed in these units. By this system a right angle or quadrant has 90° and a straight angle or semicircle 180°. In marine navigation, altitudes, latitudes, and longitudes are usually expressed in degrees, minutes, and tenths (27°14.4'). Azimuths are usually expressed in degrees and tenths (164.7°). The system of degrees, minutes, and seconds indicated above is the **sexagesimal system**. In the **centesimal system,** used chiefly in France, the circle is divided into 400 **centesimal degrees** (sometimes called **grades**) each of which is divided into 100 centesimal minutes of 100 **centesimal seconds** each.

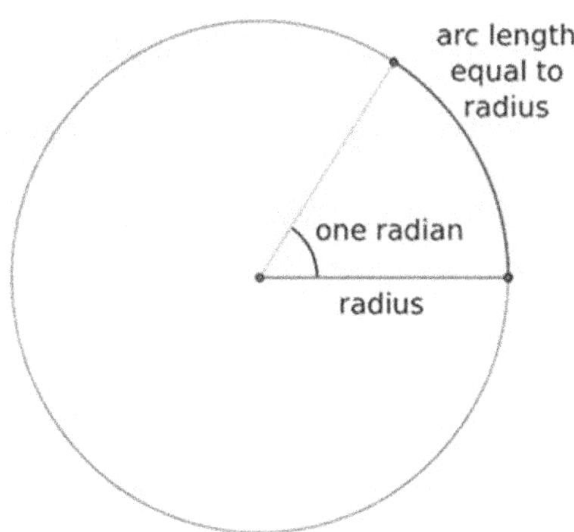

Figure 137. Image depicting one radian.

A **radian** is the angle subtended at the center of a circle by an arc having a linear length equal to the radius of the circle. A radian is equal to 57.2957795131° approximately, or 57°17'44.80625" approximately. The radian is sometimes used as a unit of angular measure. See Figure 137. A circle (360°) = 2π radians, a semicircle (180°) = π radians, a right angle measure (90°) = $\frac{\pi}{2}$ radians, and 1' = 0.0002908882 radians approximately.The length of the arc of a circle is equal to the radius multiplied by the angle subtended in radians.

138. Trigonometric Functions

Trigonometric functions are the various proportions or ratios of the sides of a plane right triangle, defined in relation to one of the acute angles. In Figure 138a, let θ be any acute angle. From any point R on line OA, draw a line perpendicular to OB at F. From any other point R' on OA, draw a line perpendicular to OB at F'. Then triangles OFR and OF'R' are similar right triangles because all their corresponding *angles* are equal. Since in any pair of similar triangles the ratio of any two sides of one triangle is equal to the ratio of the corresponding two sides of the other triangle.

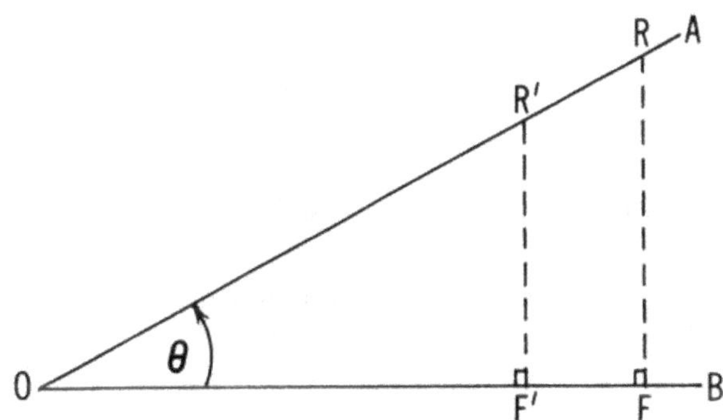

Figure 138a. Similar right triangles.

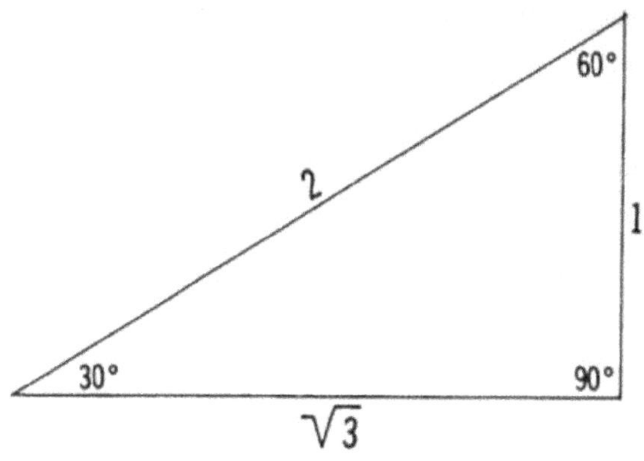

Figure 138b. *Numerical relationship of sides of a 30°-60°-90° triangle.*

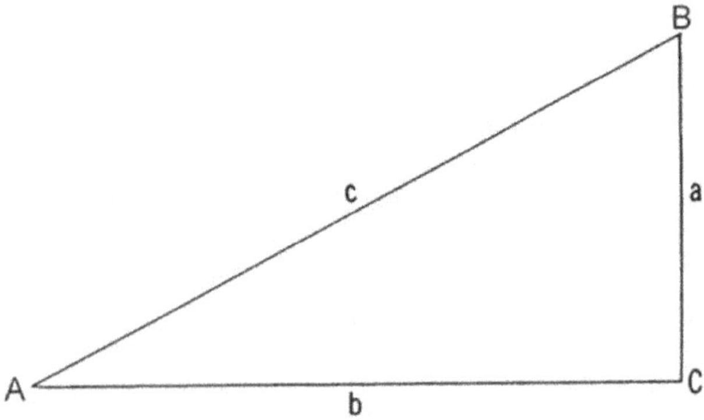

Figure 138c. A right triangle.

$$\frac{RF}{OF} = \frac{R'F'}{OF'}, \frac{RF}{OR} = \frac{R'F'}{OR'}, \text{ and } \frac{OF}{OR} = \frac{OF'}{OR'}$$

No matter where the point R is located on OA, the ratio between the lengths of any two sides in the triangle OFR has a constant value. Hence, for any value of the acute angle θ, there is a fixed set of values for the ratios of the various sides of the triangle. These ratios are defined as follows:

$$\text{sine } \theta = \sin\theta = \frac{\text{side opposite}}{\text{hypotenuse}}$$

$$\text{cosine } \theta = \cos\theta = \frac{\text{side adjacent}}{\text{hypotenuse}}$$

$$\text{tangent } \theta = \tan\theta = \frac{\text{side opposite}}{\text{side adjacent}}$$

$$\text{cosecant } \theta = \csc\theta = \frac{\text{hypotenuse}}{\text{side opposite}}$$

$$\text{secant } \theta = \sec\theta = \frac{\text{hypotenuse}}{\text{side adjacent}}$$

$$\text{cotangent } \theta = \cot\theta = \frac{\text{side adjacent}}{\text{side opposite}}$$

Of these six principal functions, the second three are the reciprocals of the first three; therefore

$$\sin\theta = \frac{1}{\csc\theta} \qquad \csc\theta = \frac{1}{\sin\theta}$$

$$\cos\theta = \frac{1}{\sec\theta} \qquad \sec\theta = \frac{1}{\cos\theta}$$

$$\tan\theta = \frac{1}{\cot\theta} \qquad \cot\theta = \frac{1}{\tan\theta}$$

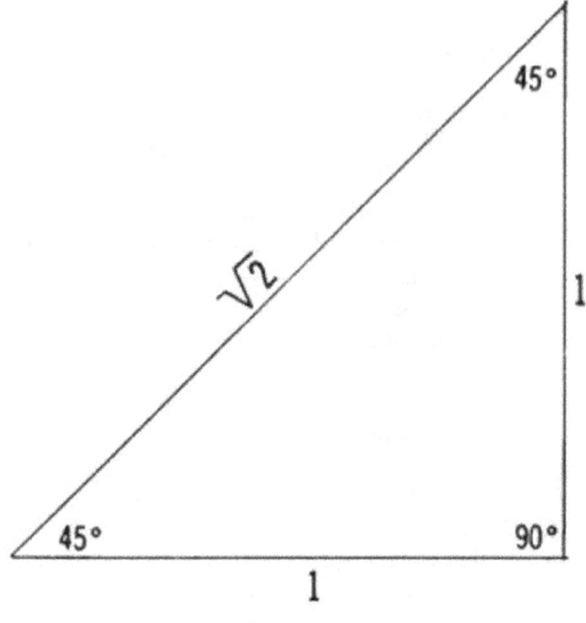

Figure 138d. Numerical relationship of sides of a 45°- 45° - 90° triangle.

In Figure 138c, *A*, *B*, and *C* are the angles of a plane right triangle, with the right angle at *C*. The sides are labeled *a*, *b*, *c*, with opposite angles labeled *A*, *B*, and *C* respectively.

The six principal trigonometric functions of angle *B* are:

$$\sin B = \frac{b}{c} = \cos A = \cos(90° - B)$$

$$\cos B = \frac{a}{c} = \sin A = \sin(90° - B)$$

$$\tan B = \frac{b}{a} = \cot A = \cot(90° - B)$$

$$\cot B = \frac{a}{b} = \tan A = \tan(90° - B)$$

$$\sec B = \frac{c}{a} = \csc A = \csc(90° - B)$$

$$\csc B = \frac{c}{b} = \sec A = \sec(90° - B)$$

Function	*30°*	*45°*	*60°*
sine	$\frac{1}{2}$	$\frac{1}{\sqrt{2}} = \frac{1}{2}\sqrt{2}$	$\frac{\sqrt{3}}{2} = \frac{1}{2}\sqrt{3}$
cosine	$\frac{\sqrt{3}}{2} = \frac{1}{2}\sqrt{3}$	$\frac{1}{\sqrt{2}} = \frac{1}{2}\sqrt{2}$	$\frac{1}{2}$
tangent	$\frac{1}{\sqrt{3}} = \frac{1}{3}\sqrt{3}$	$\frac{1}{1} = 1$	$\frac{\sqrt{3}}{1} = \sqrt{3}$
cotangent	$\frac{\sqrt{3}}{1} = \sqrt{3}$	$\frac{1}{1} = 1$	$\frac{1}{\sqrt{3}} = \frac{1}{3}\sqrt{3}$
secant	$\frac{2}{\sqrt{3}} = \frac{2}{3}\sqrt{3}$	$\frac{\sqrt{2}}{1} = \sqrt{2}$	$\frac{2}{1} = 2$
cosecant	$\frac{2}{1} = 2$	$\frac{\sqrt{2}}{1} = \sqrt{2}$	$\frac{2}{\sqrt{3}} = \frac{2}{3}\sqrt{3}$

Table 138e. Values of various trigonometric functions for angles 30°, 45°, and 60°.

Since *A* and *B* are *complementary*, these relations show that the sine of an angle is the cosine of its complement, the tangent of an angle is the cotangent of its complement, and the secant of an angle is the cosecant of its complement. Thus, the **co**-function of an angle is the function of its complement.

$$\sin(90° - A) = \cos A$$

$$\cos(90° - A) = \sin A$$

$$\tan(90° - A) = \cot A$$

$$\cot(90° - A) = \tan A$$

$$\sec(90° - A) = \csc A$$

$$\csc(90° - A) = \sec A$$

Certain additional relations are also classed as trigonometric functions:

versed sine θ = versine θ = vers θ = ver θ = $1 - \cos\theta$

versed cosine θ = coversed sine θ

(therefore) coversed sine θ = coversine θ

(therefore) coversine θ = covers θ

(therefore) covers θ = cov θ

(therefore) cov $\theta = 1 - \sin\theta$

haversine θ = hav θ = $1/2$ ver θ = $(1/2)(1 - \cos\theta)$.

The numerical value of a trigonometric function is sometimes called the **natural function** to distinguish it from the logarithm of the function, called the **logarithmic function**. Numerical values of the six principal functions are given at 1' intervals in Table 2 - Natural Trigonometric Functions. Logarithms are given at the same intervals in Table 3 - Common Logarithms of Trigonometric Functions.

Since the relationships of 30°, 60°, and 45° right triangles are as shown in Figure 138c and Figure 138b, certain values of the basic functions can be stated exactly, as shown in Table 138e.

All trigonometric functions can be shown as lengths of lines in a unit circle. See Figure 138f for a depiction of the following equations:

$$\sin\theta = RF$$
$$\cot\theta = AB$$
$$\cos\theta = OF$$
$$\sec\theta = OD$$
$$\tan\theta = DE$$
$$\csc\theta = OA$$
$$\text{ver}\,\theta = FE$$
$$\text{cov}\,\theta = BC.$$

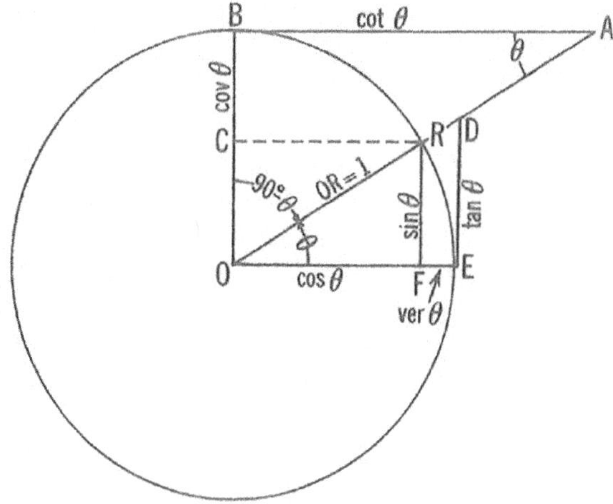

Figure 138f. Line definitions of trigonometric functions.

139. Functions in Various Quadrants

To make the definitions of the trigonometric functions more general to include those angles greater than 90°, the functions are defined in terms of the rectangular Cartesian coordinates of point R of Figure 138a, due regard being giv-

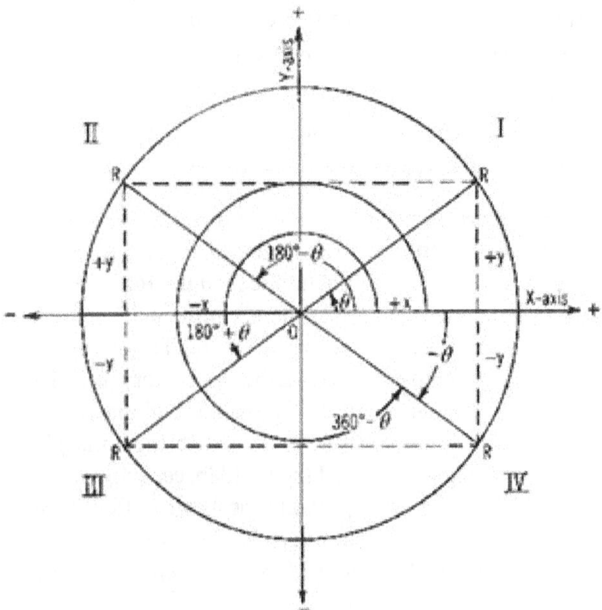

Figure 139a. The functions in various quadrants, mathematical convention.

en to the sign of the function. In Figure 139a, OR is assumed to be a *unit* radius. By convention the sign of OR is always positive. This radius is imagined to rotate in a counterclockwise direction through 360° from the horizontal position at 0°, the positive direction along the X axis. Ninety degrees (90°) is the positive direction along the Y axis. The angle between the original position of the radius and its position at any time increases from 0° to 90° in the *first quadrant* (I), 90° to 180° in the *second quadrant* (II), 180° to 270° in the *third quadrant* (III), and 270° to 360° in the *fourth quadrant* (IV).

The numerical value of the sine of an angle is equal to the projection of the unit radius on the Y–axis. According to the definition given in Section138, the sine of angle in the first quadrant of Figure 139a is $\frac{+y}{+OR}$. If the radius OR is equal to one, sin θ =+y. Since +y is equal to the projection of the unit radius OR on the Y axis, the sine function of an angle in the first quadrant defined in terms of rectangular Cartesian coordinates does not contradict the definition in Section 138. In Figure 139a,

$$\sin\theta = +y$$

$$\sin(180°-\theta) = +y = \sin\theta$$

$$\sin(180°+\theta) = -y = -\sin\theta$$

$$\sin(360°-\theta) = -y = \sin(-\theta) = -\sin\theta$$

The numerical value of the cosine of an angle is equal to the projection of the unit radius on the X axis. In Figure 139a,

$$\cos\theta = +x$$
$$\cos(180°-\theta) = -x = -\cos\theta$$
$$\cos(180°+\theta) = -x = -\cos\theta$$
$$\cos(360°-\theta) = +x = \cos(-\theta) = \cos\theta$$

The numerical value of the tangent of an angle is equal to the ratio of the projections of the unit radius on the Y and X axes. In Figure 139a,

$$\tan\theta = \frac{+y}{+x}$$

$$(180°-\theta) = \frac{+y}{-x} = -\tan\theta$$

$$\tan(180°+\theta) = \frac{-y}{-x} = \tan\theta$$

$$\tan(360°-\theta) = \frac{-y}{+x} = \tan(-\theta) = -\tan\theta$$

The cosecant, secant, and cotangent functions of angles in the various quadrants are similarly determined:

$$\csc\theta = \frac{1}{+y}$$

$$\csc(180°-\theta) = \frac{1}{+y} = \csc\theta$$

$$\csc(180°+\theta) = \frac{1}{-y} = -\csc\theta$$

$$\csc(360°-\theta) = \frac{1}{-y} = \csc(-\theta) = -\csc\theta$$

$$\sec\theta = \frac{1}{+x}$$

$$\sec(180°-\theta) = \frac{1}{-x} = -\sec\theta$$

$$\sec(180°+\theta) = \frac{1}{-x} = -\sec\theta$$

$$\sec(360°-\theta) = \frac{1}{+x} = \sec(-\theta) = \sec\theta$$

$$\cot\theta = \frac{+x}{+y}$$

$$\cot(180°-\theta) = \frac{-x}{+y} = -\cot\theta$$

$$\cot(180°+\theta) = \frac{-x}{-y} = \cot\theta$$

$$\cot(360°-\theta) = \frac{+x}{-y} = \cot(-\theta) = -\cot\theta.$$

The signs of the functions in the four different quadrants are shown below in Table 139b.

	I	II	III	IV
sine and cosecant	+	+	-	-
cosine and secant	+	-	-	+
tangent and cotangent	+	-	+	-

Table 139b. Signs of trigonometric functions by quadrants.

These relationships are shown in Table 139c and graphically in Figure 139d through Figure 139g.

	I	II	III	IV
sin	0 to +1	+1 to 0	0 to –1	–1 to 0
csc	+∞ to +1	+1 to 0	–∞ to –1	–1 to –∞
cos	+1 to 0	0 to –1	–1 to 0	0 to +1
sec	+1 to +∞	–∞ to –1	–1 to –∞	+∞ to +1
tan	0 to +∞	–∞ to 0	0 to +∞	–∞ to 0
cot	+∞ to 0	0 to –∞	+∞ to 0	0 to –∞

Table 139c. Values of trigonometric functions in various quadrants.

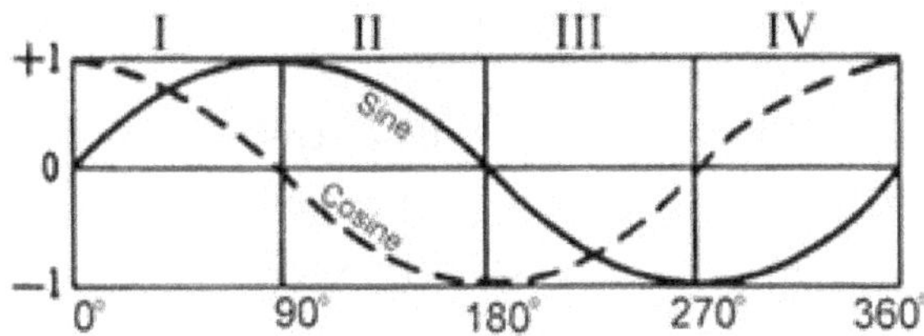

Figure 139d. Sine and cosine functions in various quadrants.

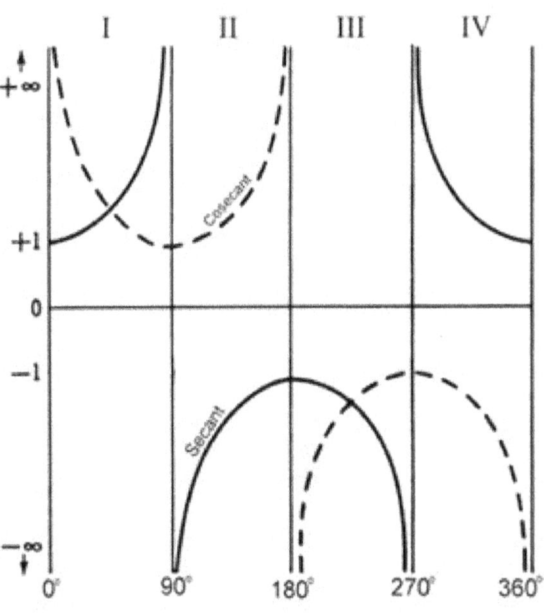

Figure 139e. Secant and cosecant functions in various quadrants.

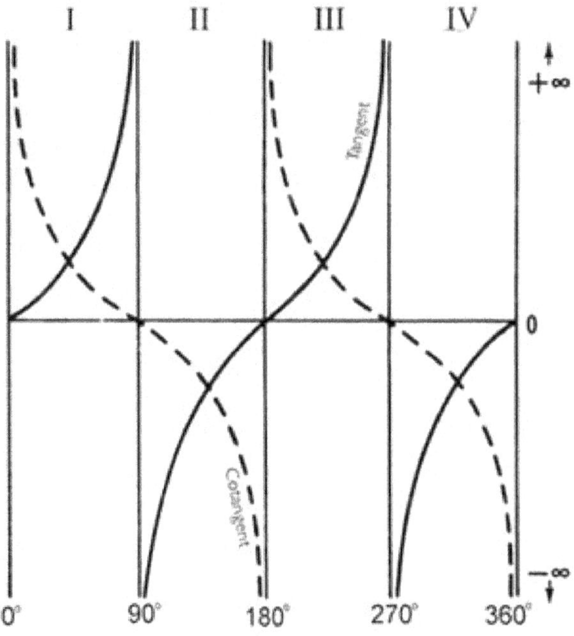

Figure 139f. Tangent and cotangent functions in various quadrants.

The numerical values vary by quadrant as shown above.

As shown in Figure 139a and Table 139b, the sign (+ or -) of the functions varies with the quadrant of an angle. In Figure 139a radius OR is imagined to rotate in a counter-

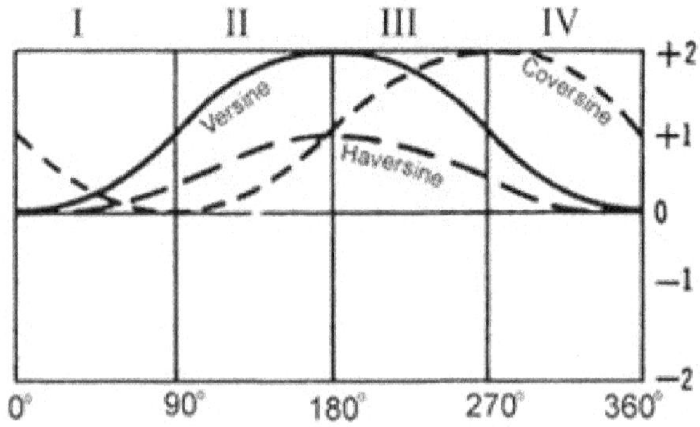

Figure 139g. Versine, coversine and haversine functions in various quadrants.

clockwise direction through 360° from the horizontal position at 0°. This is the **mathematical convention.** In Figure 139h this concept is shown in the usual **navigational convention** of a compass rose, starting with 000° at the top and rotating clockwise. In either diagram the angle θ between the original position of the radius and its position at any time increases from 0° to 90° in the *first quadrant* (I), 90° to 180° in the *second quadrant* (II), 180° to 270° in the *third quadrant* (III), and 270° to 360° in the *fourth quadrant* (IV). Also in either diagram, 0° is the positive direction along the X-axis. Ninety degrees (90°) is the positive direction along the Y-axis. Therefore, the projections of the unit radius OR on the X- and Y-axes, as appropriate, produce the same values of the trigonometric functions.

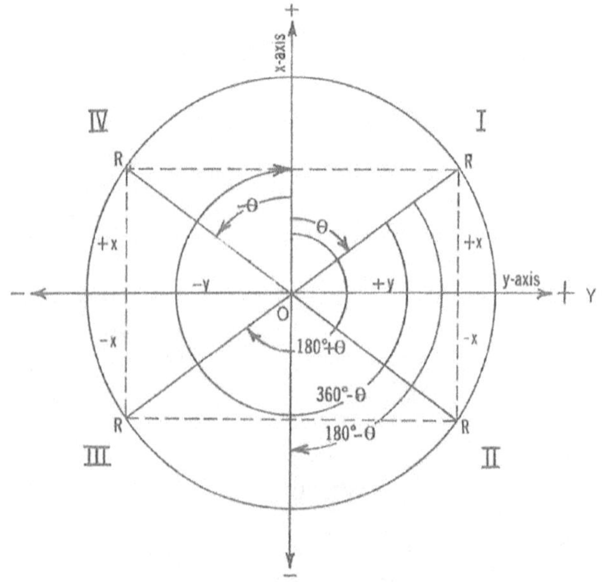

Figure 139h. The functions in various quadrants.

A negative angle (-θ) is an angle measured in a clockwise direction (mathematical convention) or in a direction opposite to that of a positive angle. The functions of a negative angle and the corresponding functions of a positive angle are as follows:

$$\sin(-\theta) = -\sin\theta$$

$$\cos(-\theta) = \cos\theta$$

$$\tan-\theta = -\tan\theta$$

$$\tan(-\theta) = \tan(360° - \theta)$$

140. Trigonometric Identities

A **trigonometric identity** is an equality involving trigonometric functions of θ which is true for all values of θ, except those values for which one of the functions is not defined or for which a denominator in the equality is equal to zero. The **fundamental identities** are those identities from which other identities can be derived.

$$\sin\theta = \frac{1}{\csc\theta} \qquad \csc\theta = \frac{1}{\sin\theta}$$

$$\cos\theta = \frac{1}{\sec\theta} \qquad \sec\theta = \frac{1}{\cos\theta}$$

$$\tan\theta = \frac{1}{\cot\theta} \qquad \cot\theta = \frac{1}{\tan\theta}$$

$$\tan\theta = \frac{\sin\theta}{\cos\theta} \qquad \cot\theta = \frac{\cos\theta}{\sin\theta}$$

$$\sin^2\theta + \cos^2\theta = 1 \qquad \tan^2\theta + 1 = \sec^2\theta$$

$$1 + \cot^2\theta = \csc^2\theta$$

141. Reduction Formulas

$$\sin(90° - \theta) = \cos\theta \qquad \csc(90° - \theta) = \sec\theta$$

$$\cos(90° - \theta) = \sin\theta \qquad \sec(90° - \theta) = \csc\theta$$

$$\tan(90° - \theta) = \cot\theta \qquad \cot(90° - \theta) = \tan\theta$$

$$\sin(-\theta) = -\sin\theta \qquad \csc(-\theta) = -\csc\theta$$

$$\cos(-\theta) = \cos\theta \qquad \sec(-\theta) = \sec\theta$$

$$\tan(-\theta) = -\tan\theta \qquad \cot(-\theta) = -\cot\theta$$

$$\sin(90+\theta) = \cos\theta \qquad \csc(90+\theta) = \sec\theta$$

$$\cos(90+\theta) = -\sin\theta \qquad \sec(90+\theta) = -\csc\theta$$

$$\tan(90+\theta) = -\cot\theta \qquad \cot(90+\theta) = -\tan\theta$$

$\sin(180°+\theta) = -\sin\theta$ $\csc(180°+\theta) = -\csc\theta$

$\cos(180°+\theta) = -\cos\theta$ $\sec(180°+\theta) = -\sec\theta$

$\tan(180°+\theta) = \tan\theta$ $\cot(180°+\theta) = \cot\theta$

$\sin(360° - \theta) = -\sin\theta$ $\csc(360° - \theta) = -\csc\theta$

$\cos(360° - \theta) = \cos\theta$ $\sec(360° - \theta) = \sec\theta$

$\tan(360° - \theta) = -\tan\theta$ $\cot(360° - \theta) = -\cot\theta$

142. Inverse Trigonometric Functions

An angle having a given trigonometric function may be indicated in any of several ways. Thus, $\sin y = x$, $y = \text{arc} \sin x$, and $y = \sin^{-1} x$ have the same meaning. The superior "–1" is not an exponent in this case. In each case, y is "the angle whose sine is x." In this case, y is the **inverse sine** of x. Similar relationships hold for all trigonometric functions.

SOLVING TRIANGLES

Solution of triangles. A triangle is composed of six parts: three angles and three sides. The angles may be designated *A*, *B*, and *C*; and the sides opposite these angles as *a*, *b*, and *c*, respectively. In general, when any three parts are known, the other three parts can be found, unless the known parts are the three angles of a plane triangle.

143. Right Plane Triangles

In a **right plane triangle** it is only necessary to substitute numerical values in the appropriate formulas representing the basic trigonometric functions and solve. Thus, if *a* and *b* are known,

$$\tan A = \frac{a}{b}$$
$$B = 90° - A$$
$$c = a \csc A$$

Similarly, if *c* and *B* are given,

$$A = 90° - B$$
$$a = c \sin A$$
$$b = c \cos A$$

144. Oblique Plane Triangles

When solving an **oblique plane triangle**, it is often desirable to draw a rough sketch of the triangle approximately to scale, as shown in Figure 144. The following laws are helpful in solving such triangles:

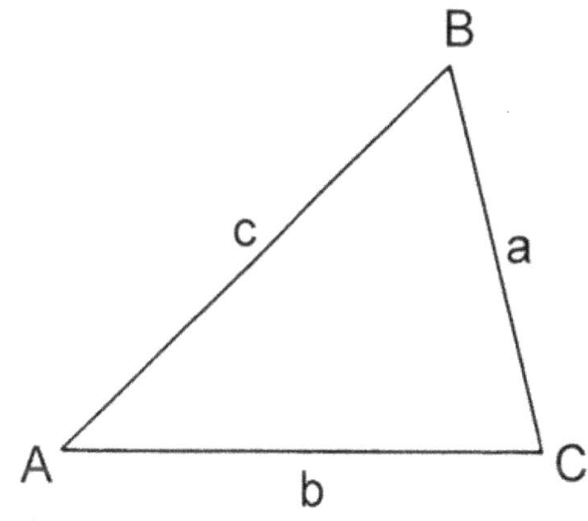

Figure 144. An oblique plane triangle.

Known	*To find*	*Formula*	*Comments*
a, b, c	*A*	$\cos A = \frac{c^2 + b^2 - a^2}{2bc}$	Cosine law
a, b, A	*B*	$\sin B = \frac{b \sin A}{a}$	Sine law. Two solutions if *b>a*
	C	$C = 180° - (A + B)$	$A + B + C = 180°$
	c	$c = \frac{a \sin C}{\sin A}$	Sine law
a, b, C	*A*	$\tan A = \frac{a \sin C}{b - a \cos C}$	

Table 144. Formulas for solving oblique plane triangles.

Known	*To find*	*Formula*	*Comments*
	B	$B = 180° - (A + C)$	$A + B + C = 180°$
	c	$c = \frac{a \sin C}{\sin A}$	Sine law
a, A, B	b	$b = \frac{a \sin B}{\sin A}$	Sine law
	C	$C = 180° - (A + B)$	$A + B + C = 180°$
	c	$c = \frac{a \sin C}{\sin A}$	Sine law

Table 144. Formulas for solving oblique plane triangles.

Law of sines: $\frac{a}{\sin A} = \frac{b}{\sin B} = \frac{c}{\sin C}$

Law of cosines: $a^2 = b^2 + c^2 - 2bc \cos A.$

The unknown parts of oblique plane triangles can be computed by the formulas in Table 144, among others. By reassignment of letters to sides and angles, these formulas can be used to solve for all unknown parts of oblique plane triangles.

SPHERICAL TRIGONOMETRY

145. Napier's Rules

Right spherical triangles can be solved with the aid of **Napier's Rules of Circular Parts.** If the right angle is omitted, the triangle has five parts: two angles and three sides, as shown in Figure 145a. Since the right angle is already known, the triangle can be solved if any two other parts are known. If the two sides forming the right angle, and the *complements* of the other three parts are used, these elements (called "parts" in the rules) can be arranged in five sectors of a circle in the same order in which they occur in the triangle, as shown in Figure 145b. Considering any part as the middle part, the two parts nearest it in the diagram are considered the adjacent parts, and the two farthest from it the opposite parts.

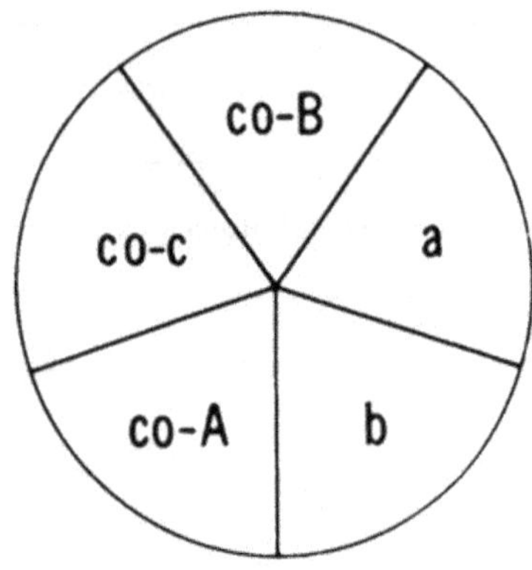

Figure 145b. Diagram for Napier's Rules of Circular Parts.

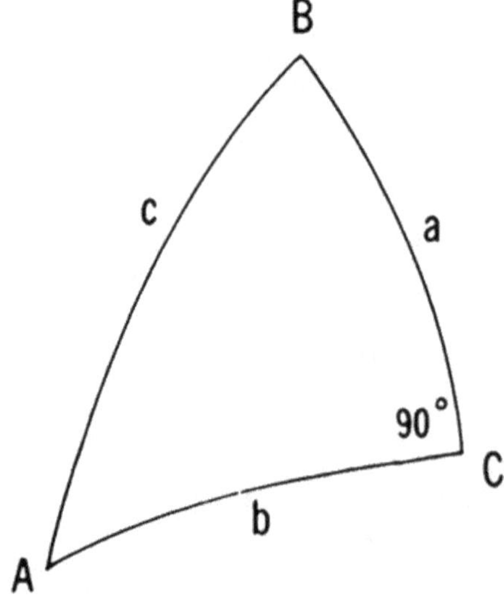

Figure 145a. Parts of a right spherical triangle as used in Napier's rules.

The following rules apply:

Napier's Rules state: The sine of a middle part equals the product of (1) the tangents of the adjacent parts or (2) the cosines of the opposite parts.

In the use of these rules, the co-function of a complement can be given as the function of the element. Thus, the cosine of co–A is the same as the sine of A. From these rules the following formulas can be derived:

$$\sin a = \tan b \cot B = \sin c \sin A$$

$$\sin b = \tan a \cot A = \sin c \sin B$$

$$\cos c = \cot A \cot B = \cos a \cos b$$

$$\cos A = \tan b \cot c = \cos a \sin B$$

$$\cos B = \tan a \cot c = \cos b \sin A$$

1. An oblique angle and the side opposite are in the same quadrant.

2. Side c (the hypotenuse) is less then 90° when a and b are in the same quadrant, and more than 90° when a and b are in different quadrants.

If the known parts are an angle and its opposite side, two solutions are possible.

A **quadrantal spherical triangle** is one having one side of 90°. A **biquadrantal spherical triangle** has two sides of 90°. A **triquadrantal spherical triangle** has three sides of 90°. A biquadrantal spherical triangle is isosceles and has two right angles opposite the 90° sides. A triquadrantal spherical triangle is equilateral, has three right angles, and bounds an octant (one–eighth) of the surface of the sphere. A quadrantal spherical triangle can be solved by Napier's rules provided any two elements in addition to the 90° side are known. The 90° side is omitted and the other parts are arranged in order in a five–sectored circle, using the complements of the three parts farthest from the 90° side. In the case of a quadrantal triangle, rule 1 above is used, and rule 2 restated: angle C (the angle opposite the side of 90°) is *more* than 90° when A and B are in the same quadrant, and *less* than 90° when A and B are in different quadrants. If the rule requires an angle of more than 90° and the solution produces an angle of less than 90°, subtract the solved angle from 180°.

146. Oblique Spherical Triangles

An **oblique spherical triangle** can be solved by dropping a perpendicular from one of the apexes to the opposite side, subtended if necessary, to form two right spherical triangles. It can also be solved by the following formulas in Table 146, reassigning the letters as necessary.

Known	*To find*	*Formula*	*Comments*
a, b, C	A	$\tan A = \dfrac{\sin D \tan C}{\sin(b - D)}$	$\tan D = \tan a \cos C$
	B	$\sin B = \dfrac{\sin C \sin b}{\sin c}$	
c, A, B	C	$\cos C = \sin A \sin B \cos c - \cos A \cos B$	
	a	$\tan a = \dfrac{\tan c \sin E}{\sin(B + E)}$	$\tan E = \tan A \cos c$
	b	$\tan b = \dfrac{\tan c \sin F}{\sin(A + F)}$	$\tan F = \tan B \cos c$
a, b, A	c	$\sin(c + G) = \dfrac{\cos a \sin G}{\cos b}$	$\cot G = \cos A \tan b$ Two solutions
	B	$\sin B = \dfrac{\sin A \sin b}{\sin a}$	Two solutions
	C	$\sin(C + H) = \sin H \tan b \cot a$	$\tan H = \tan A \cos b$ Two solutions
a, A, B	C	$\sin(C - K) = \dfrac{\cos A \sin K}{\cos B}$	$\cot K = \tan B \cos a$ Two solutions

Table 146. Formulas for solving oblique spherical triangles.

Known	*To find*	*Formula*	*Comments*
	b	$\sin b = \frac{\sin a\ \sin \mathrm{B}}{\sin \mathrm{A}}$	Two solutions
	c	$\sin(c-M) = \cot \mathrm{A}\ \tan \mathrm{B}\ \sin M$	$\tan M = \cos \mathrm{B}\ \tan a$ Two solutions

Table 146. Formulas for solving oblique spherical triangles.

147. Other Useful Formulas

In addition to the fundamental trigonometric identities and reduction formulas given in Section 139, the following formulas apply to plane and spherical trigonometry:

Addition and Subtraction Formulas

$$\sin(\theta+\phi) = \sin\theta\cos\phi + \cos\theta\sin\phi$$

$$\cos(\theta+\phi) = \cos\theta\cos\phi - \sin\theta\sin\phi$$

$$\sin(\theta-\phi) = \sin\theta\cos\phi - \cos\theta\sin\phi$$

$$\cos(\theta-\phi) = \cos\theta\cos\phi + \sin\theta\sin\phi$$

$$\tan(\theta+\phi) = \frac{\tan\theta + \tan\phi}{1 - \tan\theta\tan\phi}.$$

Double-Angle Formulas

$$\sin 2\theta = 2\sin\theta\cos\theta$$

$$\cos 2\theta = \cos^2\theta - \sin^2\theta$$

$$\tan 2\theta = \frac{2\tan\theta}{1-\tan^2\theta}.$$

Half-Angle Formulas

$$\sin\frac{\theta}{2} = \pm\sqrt{\frac{1-\cos\theta}{2}}$$

$$\cos\frac{\theta}{2} = \pm\sqrt{\frac{1+\cos\theta}{2}}$$

$$\tan\frac{\theta}{2} = \pm\sqrt{\frac{1-\cos\theta}{1+\cos\theta}}.$$

The following are useful formulas of spherical trigonometry:

Law of Cosines for Sides

$$\cos a = \cos b \cos c + \sin b \sin c \cos A$$

$$\cos b = \cos c \cos a + \sin c \sin a \cos B$$

$$\cos c = \cos a \cos b + \sin a \sin b \cos C$$

Law of Cosines for Angles

$$\cos A = -\cos B \cos C + \sin B \sin C \cos a$$

$$\cos B = -\cos C \cos A + \sin C \sin A \cos b$$

$$\cos C = -\cos A \cos B + \sin A \sin B \cos c.$$

Law of Sines

$$\frac{\sin a}{\sin A} = \frac{\sin b}{\sin B} = \frac{\sin c}{\sin C}.$$

Napier's Analogies

$$\tan\frac{1}{2}(A+B) = \frac{\cos\frac{1}{2}(a-b)}{\cos\frac{1}{2}(a+b)}\cot\frac{1}{2}C$$

$$\tan\frac{1}{2}(A-B) = \frac{\sin\frac{1}{2}(a-b)}{\sin\frac{1}{2}(a+b)}\cot\frac{1}{2}C$$

$$\tan\frac{1}{2}(a+b) = \frac{\cos\frac{1}{2}(A-B)}{\cos\frac{1}{2}(A+B)}\tan\frac{1}{2}c$$

$$\tan\frac{1}{2}(a-b) = \frac{\sin\frac{1}{2}(A-B)}{\sin\frac{1}{2}(A+B)}\tan\frac{1}{2}c.$$

Five Parts Formulas

$\sin a \cos B = \cos b \sin c - \sin b \cos c \cos A$

$\sin b \cos C = \cos c \sin a - \sin c \cos a \cos B$

$\sin c \cos A = \cos a \sin b - \sin a \cos b \cos C.$

Haversine Formulas

$\text{hav } a = \text{hav } (b \sim c) + \sin b \sin c \text{ hav } A$

$\text{hav } b = \text{hav } (a \sim c) + \sin a \sin c \text{ hav } B$

$\text{hav } c = \text{hav } (a \sim b) + \sin a \sin b \text{ hav } C$

$\text{hav } A = [\text{hav } a - \text{hav } (b \sim c)] \csc b \csc c$

$\text{hav } B = [\text{hav } b - \text{hav } (a \sim c)] \csc a \csc c$

$\text{hav } C = [\text{hav } c - \text{hav } (a \sim b)] \csc a \csc b.$

148. Functions of a Small Angle

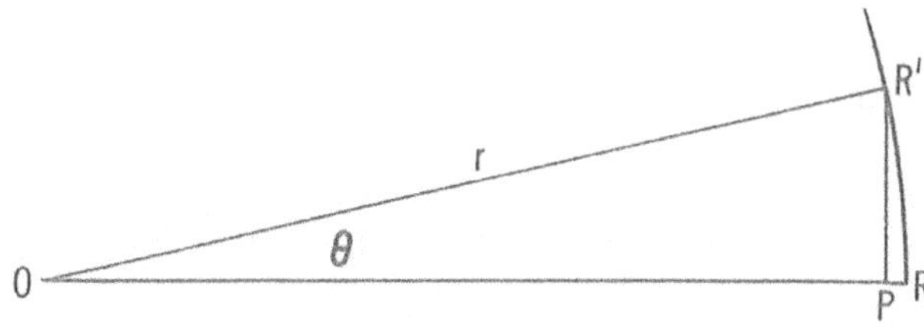

Figure 148. A small angle.

Functions of a small angle: In Figure 148, small angle θ, measured in radians, is subtended by the arc RR' of a circle. The radius of the circle is r, and $R'P$ is perpendicular to OR at P. Since the length of the arc of a circle is equal to the radius multiplied by the angle subtended in radians:

$$RR' = r \times \theta .$$

When θ is sufficiently small for $R'P$ to approximate RR',

$$\sin\theta = \theta$$

$$\text{since } \theta = \frac{RR'}{r} \text{ and } \sin\theta = \frac{R'P}{r}.$$

For small angles, it can also be shown that

$$\tan\theta = \theta .$$

If there are x minutes of arc (x') in a small angle of θ radians,

$$\sin x' = x \sin 1' .$$

Figure 148 also shows that when θ is small, OP is approximately equal to the radius. Therefore, $\cos\theta$ can be taken as equal to 1.

Another approximation can be obtained if $\cos\theta$ is expressed in terms of the half-angle:

$$\cos\theta = 1 - 2\sin^2\frac{1}{2}\theta$$

$$\cos\theta = 1 - 2\left(\frac{1}{2}\theta\right)^2$$

$$\cos\theta = 1 - \frac{1}{2}\theta^2 .$$

CALCULUS

149. Calculus

Calculus is that branch of mathematics dealing with the rate of change of one quantity with respect to another.

A **constant** is a quantity which does not change. If a vessel is making good a course of 090°, the latitude does not change and is therefore a constant.

A **variable**, where continuous, is a quantity which can have an infinite number of values, although there may be limits to the maximum and minimum. Thus, from latitude 30° to latitude 31 ° there are an infinite number of latitudes, if infinitesimally small units are taken, but no value is less than 30° nor more than 31°. If two variables are so related that for every value of one there is a corresponding value of the other, one of the values is known as a **function** of the other. Thus, if speed is constant, the distance a vessel steams depends upon the elapsed time. Since elapsed time does not depend upon any other quantity, it is called an **independent variable**. The distance depends upon the elapsed time, and therefore is called a **dependent variable**. If it is required to find the time needed to travel any given distance at constant speed, distance is the independent variable and time is the dependent variable.

The principal processes of calculus are differentiation and integration.

150. Differentiation

Differentiation is the process of finding the rate of change of one variable with respect to another. If x is an independent variable, y is a dependent variable, and y is a function of x, this relationship may be written $y = f(x)$. Since for every value of x there is a corresponding value of y, the relationship can be plotted as a curve, Figure 150. In this figure, A and B are any two points on the curve, a short distance apart.

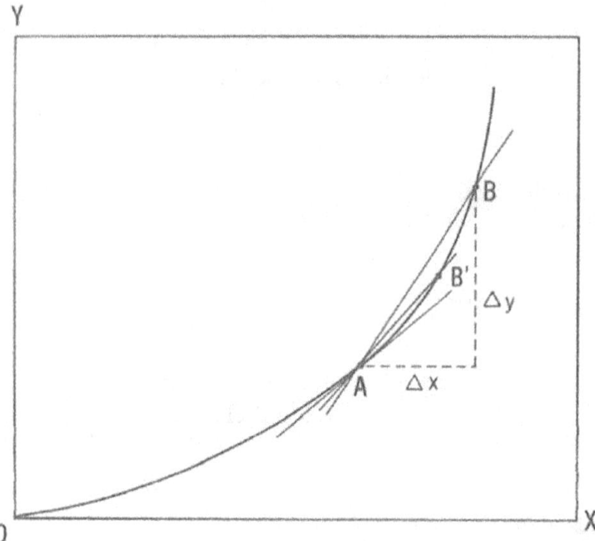

Figure 150. Differentiation.

The difference between the value of x at A and at B is Δx (delta x), and the corresponding difference in the value of y is Δy (delta y). The straight line through points A and B is a **secant** of the curve. It represents the rate of change between A and B for anywhere along this line the change of y is proportional to the change of x.

As B moves closer to A, as shown at B', both Δx and Δy become smaller, but at a different rate, and $\frac{\Delta y}{\Delta x}$ changes. This is indicated by the difference in the slope of the secant. Also, that part of the secant between A and B moves closer to the curve and becomes a better approximation of it. The limiting case occurs when B reaches A or is at an infinitesimal distance from it. As the distance becomes infinitesimal, both Δy and Δx become infinitely small, and are designated dy and dx, respectively. The straight line becomes tangent to the curve, and represents the rate of change, or slope, of the curve at that point. This is indicated by the expression $\frac{dy}{dx}$, called the **derivative** of y with respect to x.

The process of finding the value of the derivative is called **differentiation**. It depends upon the ability to connect x and y by an equation. For instance, if $y = x^n$, $\frac{dy}{dx} = nx^{n-1}$. If $n = 2$, $y = x^2$, and $\frac{dy}{dx} = 2x$. This is derived as follows: If point A on the curve is x, y; point B can be considered $x + \Delta x$, $y + \Delta y$. Since the relation $y = x^2$ is true anywhere on the curve, at B:

$$y + \Delta y = (x + \Delta x)^2 = x^2 + 2x\Delta x + (\Delta x)^2.$$

Since $y = x^2$, and equal quantities can be subtracted from both sides of an equation without destroying the equality:

$$\Delta y = 2x\Delta x + (\Delta x)^2.$$

Dividing by Δx:

$$\frac{\Delta y}{\Delta x} = 2x + \Delta x.$$

As B approaches A, Δx becomes infinitesimally small, approaching 0 as a limit, Therefore $\frac{\Delta y}{\Delta x}$ approached $2x$ as a limit.

This can be demonstrated by means of a numerical example. Let $y = x^2$. Suppose at A, $x = 2$ and $y = 4$, and at B, $x = 2.1$ and $y = 4.41$. In this case $\Delta x = 0.1$ and $\Delta y = 0.41$, and

$$\frac{\Delta y}{\Delta x} = \frac{0.41}{0.1} = 4.1.$$

From the other side of the equation:

$$2x + \Delta x = 2 \times 2 + 0.1 = 4.1.$$

If Δx is 0.01 and Δy is 0.0401, $\frac{\Delta y}{\Delta x} = 4.01$. If Δx is 0.001, $\frac{\Delta y}{\Delta x} = 4.001$; and if Δx is 0.0001, $\frac{\Delta y}{\Delta x} = 4.0001$. As Δx approaches 0 as a limit, $\frac{\Delta y}{\Delta x}$ approaches 4, which is therefore the value $\frac{dy}{dx}$. Therefore, at point A the *rate* of change of y with respect to x is 4, or y is increasing in value 4 times as fast as x.

151. Integration

Integration is the inverse of differentiation. Unlike the latter, however, it is not a direct process, but involves the recognition of a mathematical expression as the differential of a known function. The function sought is the **integral** of the given expression. Most functions can be differentiated, but many cannot be integrated.

Integration can be considered the summation of an infinite number of infinitesimally small quantities, between specified limits. Consider, for instance, the problem of finding an area below a specified part of a curve for which a mathematical expression can be written. Suppose it is desired to find the area $ABCD$ of Figure 151. If vertical lines are drawn dividing the area into a number of vertical strips, each Δx wide, and if y is the height of each strip at the midpoint of Δx, the area of each strip is approximately $y\Delta x$; and the approximate total area of all strips is the sum of the areas of the individual strips. This may be written $\sum_{x1}^{x2} y\Delta x$, meaning the sum of all $y\ \Delta x$ values between x_1 and x_2. The symbol Σ is the Greek letter *sigma*, the equivalent of the English *S*. If Δx is made progressively smaller, the sum of the small areas becomes ever closer to the true total area. If Δx becomes infinitely small, the summation expression is written $\int_{x1}^{x2} ydx$, the symbol dx denoting an infinitely small Δx. The symbol $\int$, called the "integral sign," is a distorted *S*.

An expression such as $\int_{x1}^{x2} ydx$ is called a **definite integral** because limits are specified (x_1 and x_2). If limits are not specified, as in $\int ydx$, the expression is called an **indefinite integral**.

A navigational application of integration is the finding of meridional parts, Table 6. The *rate* of change of meridional parts with respect to latitude changes progressively. The formula given in the explanation of the table is the equivalent of an integral representing the sum of the meridional parts from the equator to any given latitude.

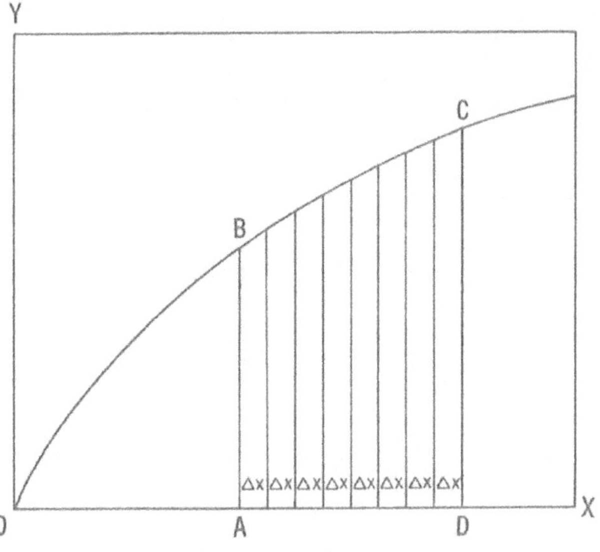

Figure 151. Integration.

152. Differential Equations

An expression such as *dy* or *dx* is called a **differential.** An equation involving a differential or a derivative is called a **differential equation**.

As shown in Section 150, if $y = x^2$, $\frac{dy}{dx} = 2x$. Neither *dy* nor *dx* is a finite quantity, but both are limits to which Δy and Δx approach as they are made progressively smaller. Therefore $\frac{dy}{dx}$ is merely a ratio, the limiting value of $\frac{\Delta y}{\Delta x}$, and not one finite number divided by another. However, since the ratio is the same as would be obtained by using finite quantities, it is possible to use the two differentials *dy* and *dx* independently in certain relationships. Differential equations involve such relationships.

Other examples of differential equations are:

$d \sin x = \cos x\ dx$ $\quad d \csc x = - \cot x \csc x\ dx$

$d \cos x = - \sin x\ dx$ $\quad d \sec x = \tan x \sec x\ dx$

$d \tan x = \sec^2 x\ dx$ $\quad d \cot x = - \csc^2 x\ dx$.

Some differential equations indicating the variations in the astronomical triangle are:

$dh = - \cos L \sin Z\ dt$; L and d constant

$dh = \cos Z\ dL$; d and t constant

$dh = - \cos h \tan M\ dZ$; L and d constant

$dZ = - \sec L \cot t\ dL$; d and h constant

$dZ = \tan h \sin Z\ dL$; d and t constant

$dt = - \sec L \cot Z\ dL$; d and h constant

$dZ = \cos d \sec h \cos M\ dt$; L and d constant

$dd = \cos d \tan M\ dt$; L and h constant

$dd = \cos L \sin t\ dZ$; L and h constant,

where h is the altitude, L is the latitude, Z is the azimuth angle, d is the declination, t is the meridian angle, and M is the parallactic angle.

CHAPTER 2

INTERPOLATION

FINDING THE VALUE BETWEEN TABULATED ENTRIES

200. Introduction

When one quantity varies with changing values of a second quantity, and the mathematical relationship of the two is known, a curve can be drawn to represent the values of one corresponding to various values of the other. To find the value of either quantity corresponding to a given value of the other, one finds that point, on the curve defined by the given value, and reads the answer on the scale relating to the other quantity. This assumes, of course, that for each value of one quantity, there is only one value of the other quantity.

Information of this kind can also be tabulated. Each entry represents one point on the curve. The finding of value *between* tabulated entries is called **interpolation**. The extending of tabulated values to find values *beyond* the limits of the table is called **extrapolation**.

Thus, the *Nautical Almanac* tabulates values of declination of the sun for each hour of Coordinated Universal Time (UTC) or Universal Time (UT). The finding of declination for a time between two whole hours requires interpolation. Since there is only one entering **argument** (in this case UT), **single interpolation** is involved.

Table 11 gives the distance traveled in various times at certain speeds. In this table there are two entering arguments. If both given values are between tabulated values, **double interpolation** is needed.

In *Pub. No. 229*, azimuth angle varies with a change in any of the three variables: latitude, declination, and local hour angle. With intermediate values of all three, **triple interpolation** is needed.

Interpolation can sometimes be avoided. A table having a single entering argument can be arranged as a **critical table**. An example is the dip (height of eye) correction on the inside front cover of the *Nautical Almanac*. Interpolation is avoided through dividing the argument into intervals so chosen that successive intervals correspond to successive values of the required quantity, the respondent. For any value of the argument within these intervals, the respondent can be extracted from the table without interpolation. The lower and upper limits (critical values) of the argument correspond to half-way values of the respondent and, by convention, are chosen so that when the argument is equal to one of the critical values, the respondent corresponding to the preceding (upper) interval is to be used. Another way of avoiding interpolation would be to include every possible entering argument. If this were done for *Pub. No. 229*, interpolation being eliminated for declination only, and assuming declination values to 0'.1, the number of volumes would be increased from six to more than 3,600. If interpolation for meridian angle and latitude, to 0'.1, were also to be avoided, a total of more than 1,296,000,000 volumes would be needed. A more practical method is to select an assumed position to avoid the need for interpolation for two of the variables.

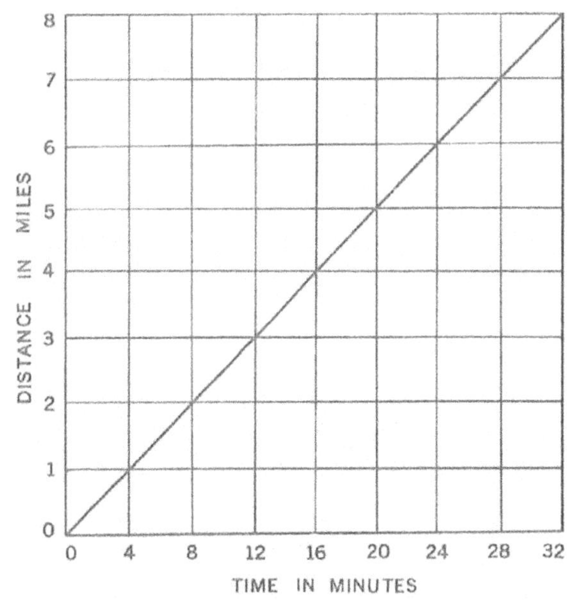

Figure 201a. Plot of $D = t / 4$.

201. Single Interpolation

The accurate determination of intermediate values requires knowledge of the nature of the change between tabulated values. The simplest relationship is linear, the change in the tabulated value being directly proportional to the change in the entering argument. Thus, if a vessel is proceeding at 15 knots, the distance traveled is directly proportional to the time, as shown in Figure 201a. The same information might be given in tabular form, as shown in table 201b. Mathematically, this relationship for 15 knots is written $D = \frac{15t}{60} = \frac{t}{4}$, where D is distance in nautical miles, and t is time in minutes.

In such a table, interpolation can be accomplished by simple proportion. Suppose, for example, that the distance is desired for a time of 15 minutes. It will be some value between 3.0 and 4.0 miles, because these are the distances for 12 and 16 minutes, respectively, the tabulated times on each side of the desired time.

Minutes	Miles
0	0.0
4	1.0
8	2.0
12	3.0
16	4.0
20	5.0
24	6.0
28	7.0
32	8.0

Table 201a. Table of D = t / 4

The proportion might be formed as follows:

$$\left.\begin{array}{l} 3\left[\begin{array}{c}12\\15\end{array}\right. \\ \quad 16\end{array}\right]4$$

$$\left.\begin{array}{l} x\left[\begin{array}{c}3.0\\y\end{array}\right. \\ \quad 4.0\end{array}\right]1.0$$

$$\frac{3}{4} = \frac{x}{1.0}$$

$$x = \frac{3 \times 1.0}{4} = 0.75 \text{ (0.8 to the nearest 0.1 mi.)}$$

$$y = 3.0 + x = 3.0 + 0.8 = 3.8 \text{ mi.}$$

A simple interpolation such as this should be performed mentally. During the four-minute interval between 12 and 16 minutes, the distance *increases* 1.0 mile from 3.0 to 4.0 miles. At 15 minutes, 3/4 of the interval has elapsed, and so the distance Increases 3/4 of 1.0 mile, or 0.75 mile, and is therefore 3.0+0.8=3.8, to the nearest 0.1 mile.

This might also have been performed by starting with 16 minutes, as follows:

$$\left.\begin{array}{l} \quad 12 \\ 1\left[\begin{array}{c}15\\16\end{array}\right.\end{array}\right]4$$

$$\left.\begin{array}{l} \quad 3.0 \\ (\text{-})x\left[\begin{array}{c}y\\4.0\end{array}\right.\end{array}\right]1.0$$

$$\frac{1}{4} = \frac{(\text{-})x}{1.0}$$

$$x = (\text{-})0.25 \text{ (-0.2 to the nearest 0.1 mi.)}$$

$$y = 4.0 - 0.2 = 3.8$$

Mentally, 15 is one quarter of the way from 16 to 12, and therefore the distance is 1/4 the way between 4.0 and 3.0, or 3.8.

This interpolation might have been performed by noting that if distance changes 1.0 mile in four minutes, it must change $\frac{1.0}{10} = 0.1$ mile in $\frac{4}{10} = 0.4$ minute, or 24 seconds.

This relationship can be used for mental interpolation in situations which might seem to require pencil and paper. Thus, if distance to the nearest 0.1 mile is desired for 13m 15s, the answer is 3.3 miles, determined as follows: The time 13^m15^s is 1^m15^s (1.2^m approx.) more than 12^m. If 1.2 is divided by 0.4, the quotient is 3, to the nearest whole number. Therefore, $3 \times 0.1 = 0.3$ is added to 3, the tabulated value for 12 minutes. Alternatively, 13^m15^s is 2^m45^s (2.8m approx.) less than 16^m, and $2.8 \div 0.4 = 7$, and therefore the interpolated value is $7 \times 0.1 = 0.7$ *less* than 4, the tabulated value for 16^m. In either case, the interpolated value is 3.3 miles,

A common mistake in single interpolation is to apply the correction (x) with the wrong sign, particularly when it should be negative (-). This mistake can be avoided by always checking to be certain that the interpolated value lies between the two values used in the interpolation.

When the curve representing the values of a table is a straight line, as in a, the process of finding intermediate values in the manner described above is called **linear interpolation.** If tabulated values of such a line are exact (not approximations), as in Table 201a, the interpolation can be carried to any degree of precision without sacrificing accuracy. Thus, in 21.5 minutes the distance is $5.0 + \frac{1.5}{4} \times 1.0 = 5.375$ miles. Similarly, for 29.9364 minutes the distance is $7.0 + \frac{1.9364}{4} \times 1.0 = 7.4841$ miles, a value which has little or no significance in practical navigation. If one had occasion to find such a value, it could most easily be done by dividing the time, in minutes, by 4, since the distance increases at the rate of one mile each four minutes. This would be a case of avoiding interpolation by solving the equation connecting the two quantities. For a simple relationship such as that involved here, such a solution might be easier than interpolation.

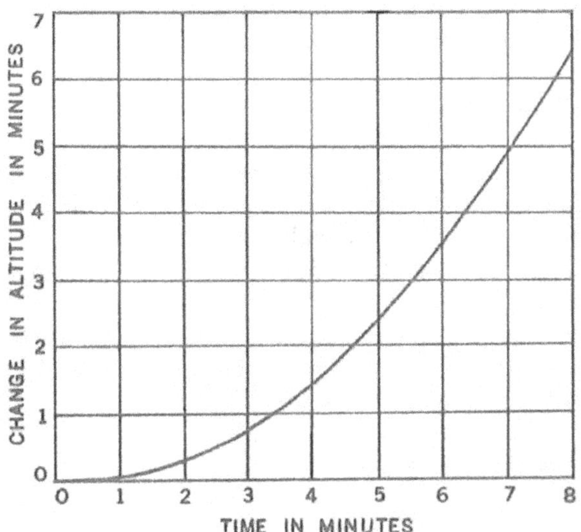

Figure 201b. Plot of altitude change = at^2.

Many of the tables of navigation are not linear. Consider Figure 201b. From Table 24 (Altitude Factors) it is found that for latitude 25° and declination 8°, same name, the variation of altitude in one minute of time from meridian transit (the altitude factor) is 6.0" (0.1'). For limited angular distance on each side of the celestial meridian, the change in altitude is approximately equal to at^2, where a is the altitude factor (Table 24) and t is the time in minutes from meridian transit. Figure 201b is the plot of change in altitude against time. The same information is shown in tabular form in Table 201c.

Minutes	*Miles*
0	0.0
1	0.1
2	0.4
3	0.9
4	1.6
5	2.5
6	3.6
7	4.9
8	6.4

Table 201c. Table of altitude change = at^2, where a=0.1'.

To be strictly accurate in interpolating in such a table, one should consider the curvature of the line. However, in most navigational tables the points on the curve selected for tabulation are sufficiently close that the portion of the curve between entries can be considered a straight line without introducing a significant error. This is similar to considering the line of position from a celestial observation as a part of the circle of equal altitude. Thus, to the nearest 0.1', the change of altitude for 3.4 minutes is $0.9' + (0.4 \times 0.7') = 0.9' + 0.3' = 1.2'$. The correct value by solution of the formula is 1.156'. The value for 6.8 minutes is 4.6' by interpolation and 4.624' by computation.

Section 204 (Nonlinear Interpolation) addresses the nonlinear interpolation used when the curve representing tabular values under consideration is not a close approximation to a straight line. However, such instances are infrequent in navigation, and generally occur at a part of the navigation table that is not commonly used, or for which special provisions are made. For example, in *Pub. No. 229* nonlinear interpolation *may* be required only when the altitude is above 60°. Even when the altitude is above 60°, the need for nonlinear interpolation is infrequent. When it is needed, such fact is indicated by the altitude difference being printed in italic type followed by a small dot.

202. Double Interpolation

In a double-entry table it may be necessary to interpolate for each entering argument. Table 202a is an extract from Table 22 (amplitudes). If one entering argument is an exact tabulated value, the amplitude can be found by single interpolation. For instance, if latitude is 45° and declination is 21.8°, amplitude is $31.2° + \left(\frac{3}{5} \times 0.8°\right) = 31.2° + 0.5° = 31.7°$. However, if neither entering argument is a tabulated value, double interpolation is needed. This may be accomplished in any of several ways:

Lat.	*Declination*	
	21.5°	22.0°
°	°	°
45	31.2	32.0
46	31.8	32.6

Table 202a. Excerpts from amplitude table.

"Horizontal" method. Use single interpolation for declination for each tabulated value of latitude, followed by single interpolation for latitude. Suppose latitude is 45.7° and declination is 21.8°. First, find the amplitude for latitude 45°, declination 21.8°, as above, 31.7°. Next, repeat the process for latitude 46°: $31.8° + \left(\frac{3}{5} \times 0.8°\right) = 32.3°$. Finally, interpolate between 31.7° and 32.3° for latitude

45.7°: $31.7° + (0.7 \times 0.6°) = 32.1°$. This is the equivalent of first inserting a new column for declination 21.8°, followed by single interpolation in this column, as shown in Table 202b.

Lat.	*Declination*		
	21.5°	*21.8°*	22.0°
°	°	°	°
45	31.2	*31.7*	32.0
45.7		***32.1***	
46	31.8	*32.3*	32.6

Table 202b. "Horizontal" method of double interpolation.

"Vertical" method. Use single interpolation for latitude for each tabulated value of declination, followed by single interpolation for declination. Consider the same example as above. First, find the amplitude for declination 21.5°, latitude 45.7°: $31.2° + (0.7° \times 0.6°) = 31.6°$. Next, repeat the process for declination 22.0°: $32.0° + (0.7° \times 0.6°) = 32.4°$. Finally, interpolate between 31.6° and 32.4° for declination 21.8°: $31.6° + \left(\frac{3}{5} \times 0.8°\right) = 32.1°$. This is the equivalent of first inserting a new line for latitude 45.7°, followed by single interpolation in this line, as shown in Table 202c.

Lat.	*Declination*		
	21.5°	*21.8°*	22.0°
°	°	°	°
45	31.2		32.0
45.7	*31.6*	***32.1***	*32.4*
46	31.8		32.6

Table 202c. "Vertical" method of double interpolation.

"Combined" method. Select a tabulated "base" value, preferably that nearest the given tabulated entering arguments. Next, find the correction to be applied, with its sign, for single interpolation of this base value both horizontally and vertically. Finally, add these two corrections algebraically and apply the result, in accordance with its sign, to the base value, In the example given above, the base value is 32.6°, for declination 22.0° (21.8° is nearer 22.0° than 21.5°) and latitude 46° (45.7° is nearer 46° than 45°). The correction for declination is $\frac{2}{5} \times (-)0.8° = (-)0.3°$. The correction for latitude is $0.3° \times (-)0.6° = (-)0.2°$. The algebraic sum is $(-)0.3° + (-)0.2° = (-)0.5°$. The interpolated value is then $32.6° - 0.5° = 32.1°$. This is the method customarily used by navigators, however, it is also less precise. If more accuracy is required more tedium must be exercised using the horizontal or vertical methods.

203. Triple Interpolation

With three entering arguments, the process is similar to that for double interpolation. It would be possible to perform double interpolation for the tabulated value on each side of the given value of one argument, and then interpolate for that argument, but the method would be tedious. The only method commonly used by navigators is that of selecting base value and applying corrections.

204. Nonlinear Interpolation

When the curve representing the values of a table is nearly a straight line, or the portion of the curve under consideration is nearly a straight line, linear interpolation suffices. However, when the successive tabular values are so nonlinear that a portion of the curve under consideration is not a close approximation to a straight line, it is necessary to include the effects of second differences, and possibly higher differences, as well as first differences in the interpolation.

The plot of Table 204a data in Figure 204b indicates that the altitude does not change linearly between declination values of 51° and 52°. If the first difference only were used in the interpolation, the interpolated value of altitude would lie on the straight line between points on the curve for declination values of 51° and 52°.

LHA 38°, Lat. 45° (Same as Dec.)			
Dec.	ht (Tab. Hc)	*First Difference*	Second Difference
50°	64°08.2'		
		+2.8'	
51°	64°11.0'		-2.3'
		+0.5'	
52°	64°11.5'		-2.1'
		-1.6'	
53°	64°09.9'		

Table 204a. Data from Pub. No. 229.

If the altitude for declination 51°30' is obtained using only the **first difference**, i.e., the difference between successive tabular altitudes in this case, $Hc = 64°11.0' + \frac{30'}{60'} \times 0.5' = 64°11.3'$. However, inspec-

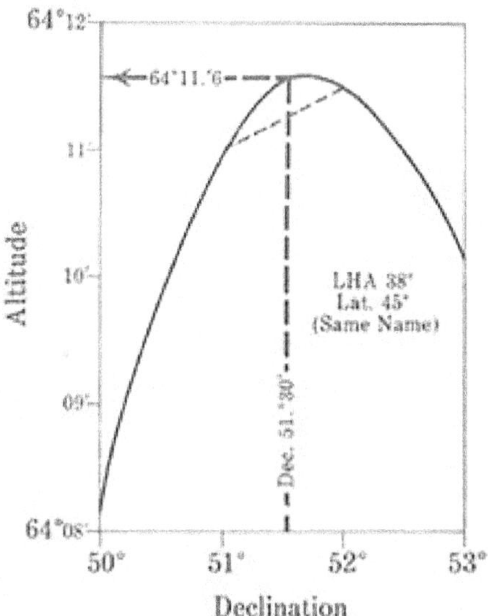

Figure 204b. Altitude curve.

tion of Figure 204b reveals that this interpolated altitude is 0.3' low. If the tabular data were such that the differences between successive first differences, the **second differences**, were nearly zero, interpolation using the first difference only would provide the correct altitude. In this case, however, second differences are significant and must be included in the interpolation.

Function	*First Difference*	Second Difference
f_{-2}		δ^2_{-2}
	$\delta_{-3/2}$	
f_{-1}		δ^2_{-1}
	$\delta_{-1/2}$	

Table 204c. Notation used with Bessel's Formula.

Function	*First Difference*	Second Difference
f_0		δ^2_0
	$\delta_{1/2}$	
f_{+1}		δ^2_1
	$\delta_{3/2}$	
f_{+2}		δ^3_2

Table 204c. Notation used with Bessel's Formula.

Table 204c shows the format and notation used to distinguish the various tabular quantities and differences when using Bessel's formula for the nonlinear interpolation. The quantities $f_{-2}, f_{-1}, f_0, f_{+1}, f_{+2}, f_{+3}$ represents represent successive tabular values.

Allowing for first and second differences only, Bessel's formula is stated as:

$$f_p = f_0 + p\delta_{1/2} + B_2\left(\delta_0^2 + \delta_1^2\right)$$

In this case, f_p is the computed altitude; f_0 is the tabular altitude; p is the fraction of the interval between tabular values of declination. The quantity B_2 is a function of p and is always negative. This coefficient is tabulated in Table 204d. The quantity $\left(\delta_0^2 + \delta_1^2\right)$ is the **double second difference (DSD)**, which is the sum of successive second differences.

Applying Bessel's formula to the data of Table 204a to obtain the altitude for a declination of 51°30',

$$f_p = f_0 + p\delta_{1/2} + B_2\left(\delta_0^2 + \delta_1^2\right)$$

$$Hc = 64°11.0' + \left(\frac{30'}{60'}\right)(0.5') + (-0.062)[-2.3' + (-2.1')]$$

$$Hc = 64°11.0' + 0.3' + 0.3' = 64°11.6'$$

p	B_2	*p*	B_2	*p*	B_2	*p*	B_2	*p*	B_2
0.0000	.000	0.1101	.025	0.2719	.050	0.7280	.049	0.8898	.024
.0020	.001	.1152	.026	.2809	.051	.7366	.048	.8949	.023
.0060	.002	.1205	.027	.2902	.052	.7449	.047	.9000	.022

Table 204d. Bessel's Coefficient B_2. In critical cases ascend. B_2 is always negative.

p	B_2	p	B_2	p	B_2	p	B_2	p	B_2
.0101	.003	.1258	.028	.3000	.053	.7529	.046	.9049	.021
.0142	.004	.1312	.029	.3102	.054	.7607	.045	.9098	.020
.0183	.005	.1366	.030	.3211	.055	.7683	.044	.9147	.019
.0225	.006	.1422	.031	.3326	.056	.7756	.043	.9195	.018
.0267	.007	.1478	.032	.3450	.057	.7828	.042	.9242	.017
.0309	.008	.1535	.033	.3585	.058	.7898	.041	.9289	.016
.0352	.009	.1594	.034	.3735	.059	.7966	.040	.9335	.015
.0395	.010	.1653	.035	.3904	.060	.8033	.039	.9381	.014
.0439	.011	.1713	.036	.4105	.061	.8098	.038	.9427	.013
.0483	.012	.1775	.037	.4367	.062	.8162	.037	.9472	.012
.0527	.013	.1837	.038	.5632	.061	.8224	.036	.9516	.011
.0572	.014	.1901	.039	.5894	.060	.8286	.035	.9560	.010
.0618	.015	.1966	.040	.6095	.059	.8346	.034	.9604	.009
.0664	.016	.2033	.041	.6264	.058	.8405	.033	.9647	.008
.0710	.017	.2101	.042	.6414	.057	.8464	.032	.9690	.007
.0757	.018	.2171	.043	.6549	.056	.8521	.031	.9732	.006
.0804	.019	.2243	.044	.6673	.055	.8577	.030	.9774	.005
.0852	.020	.2316	.045	.6788	.054	.8633	.029	.9816	.004
.0901	.021	.2392	.046	.6897	.053	.8687	.028	.9857	.003
.0950	.022	.2470	.047	.7000	.052	.8741	.027	.9898	.002
.1000	.023	.2550	.048	.7097	.051	.8794	.026	.9939	.001
.1050	.024	.2633	.049	.7190	.050	.8847	.025	0.9979	.000
0.1101		0.2719		0.7280		0.8898		1.0000	

Table 204d. Bessel's Coefficient B_2. In critical cases ascend. B_2 is always negative.

205. Interpolation Tables

A number of frequently used navigation tables are provided with auxiliary tables to assist in interpolation. Table 1 (Logarithms of Numbers) provides columns of "d" (difference between consecutive entries) and auxiliary "proportional parts" tables. The auxiliary table for the applicable difference "d" is selected and entered with the digit of the additional place in the entering argument. The value taken from the auxiliary table is *added* to the base value for the next *smaller* number from the main table. Suppose the logarithm (mantissa) for 32747 is desired. The base value for 3274 is 51508, and "d" is 13. The auxiliary table for 13 is entered with 7, and the correction is found to be 9. If this is added to 51508, the interpolated value is found to be 51517. This is the same result that would be obtained by subtracting 51508 from 51521 (the logarithm for 3275) to obtain 13, multiplying this by 0.7, and adding the result (9) to 51508.

Table 1 (Logarithms of Numbers) and Table 2 (Natural Trigonometric Functions) provide the difference between consecutive entries, but no proportional parts tables.

The *Nautical Almanac* "Increments and Corrections" are interpolation tables for the hourly entries of Greenwich Hour Angle (GHA) and declination. The increments are the products of the constant value used as the change of GHA in 1 hour and the fractional part of the hour. The corrections provide for the difference between the actual change of GHA in 1 hour and the constant value used. The corrections also provide the product of the change in declination in 1 hour and the fractional part of the hour.

The main part of the four-page interpolation table of *Pub. No. 229* is basically a multiplication table providing tabulations of:

$$\text{Altitude Difference} \times \frac{\text{Declination Increment}}{60'}$$

The design of the table is such that the desired product must be derived from component parts of the altitude difference. The first part is a multiple of 10' (10', 20', 30', 40', or 50') of the altitude difference; the second part is the remainder in the range 0.0' to 9.9'. For example, the component parts of altitude difference 44.3' are 40' and 4.3'.

In the use of the first part of the altitude difference, the table arguments are declination increment (Dec. Inc.) and the integral multiple of 10' in the altitude difference, d. As shown in Figure 205a, the respondent is:

$$\text{Tens} \times \frac{\text{Dec. Inc.}}{60'}.$$

In the use of the second part of the altitude difference, the interpolation table arguments are the nearest Dec. Inc. ending in 0.5' and Units and Decimals. The respondent is:

$$\text{Units and Decimals} \times \frac{\text{Dec. Inc.}}{60'}.$$

In computing the table, the values in the Tens part of the multiplication table were modified by small quantities varying from -0.042' to +0.033' before rounding to the tabular precision to compensate for any difference between the actual Dec. Inc. and the nearest Dec. Inc. ending in 0.5' when using the Units and Decimals part of the table.

INTERPOLATION TABLE

Dec. Inc.	Altitude Difference (d): Tens 10'	20'	30'	40'	50'	Decimals	Units 0'	1'	2'	3'	4'	5'	6'	7'	8'	9'
45.0						.0										
45.1						.1										
45.2						.2										
45.3						.3	0.2	1.0	1.7	2.5	3.3	4.0	4.8	5.5	6.3	7.1
45.4						.4										
45.5	7.6	15.2	22.8	30.3	37.9	.5										
45.6						.6										
45.7						.7										
45.8						.8										
45.9						.9										

Tens × Dec. Inc. / 60'

40' × 45'.5 / 60' = 30'.3

Units & Decimals × Dec. Inc. / 60'

4'.3 × 45'.5 / 60' = 3'.3

Double Second Diff.	and Corr.
	0.8
18.1	
	0.9
20.3	
	1.0
22.4	
	1.1
24.5	
	1.2
26.7	
	1.3
28.8	
	1.4
30.9	
	1.5
33.1	
	1.6
35.2	

Figure 205a. Interpolation table.

Using the interpolation table shown in Figure 205b to obtain the altitude for 51°30' from the data of Table 204a (*Data from Pub. No. 229*), the linear correction for the first difference (+0.5') is +0.3'. This correction is extracted from the Units and Decimals block opposite the Dec. Inc. (30.0'). The correction for the **double second difference (DSD)** is extracted from the DSD subtable opposite the block in which the Dec. Inc. is found. The argument for entering this critical table is the DSD (-4.4'). The DSD correction is +0.3'. Therefore,

$$\begin{aligned} Hc &= \text{ht} + \text{first difference correction} + \text{DSD correction} \\ &= 64°11.0' + 0.3' + 0.3' = 64°11.6'. \end{aligned}$$

INTERPOLATION TABLE

Dec. Inc.	Altitude Difference (d): Tens 10'	20'	30'	40'	50'	Decimals	Units 0'	1'	2'	3'	4'	5'	6'	7'	8'	9'
30.0	5.0	10.0	15.0	20.0	25.0	.0	0.0	0.5	1.0	1.5	2.0	2.5	3.0	3.6	4.1	4.6
30.1	5.0	10.0	15.0	20.0	25.1	.1	0.1	0.6	1.1	1.6	2.1	2.6	3.1	3.6	4.1	4.6
30.2	5.0	10.0	15.1	20.1	25.1	.2	0.1	0.6	1.1	1.6	2.1	2.6	3.2	3.7	4.2	4.7
30.3	5.0	10.1	15.1	20.2	25.2	.3	0.2	0.7	1.2	1.7	2.2	2.7	3.2	3.7	4.2	4.7
30.4	5.1	10.1	15.2	20.3	25.3	.4	0.2	0.7	1.2	1.7	2.2	2.7	3.3	3.8	4.3	4.8
30.5	5.1	10.2	15.3	20.3	25.4	.5	0.3	0.8	1.3	1.8	2.3	2.8	3.3	3.8	4.3	4.8
30.6	5.1	10.2	15.3	20.4	25.5	.6	0.3	0.8	1.3	1.8	2.3	2.8	3.4	3.9	4.4	4.9
30.7	5.1	10.3	15.4	20.5	25.6	.7	0.4	0.9	1.4	1.9	2.4	2.9	3.4	3.9	4.4	4.9
30.8	5.2	10.3	15.4	20.6	25.7	.8	0.4	0.9	1.4	1.9	2.4	2.9	3.5	4.0	4.5	5.0
30.9	5.2	10.3	15.5	20.6	25.8	.9	0.5	1.0	1.5	2.0	2.5	3.0	3.5	4.0	4.5	5.0

Double Second Diff.	and Corr.
0.8	
	0.1
2.4	
	0.2
4.0	
	0.3
5.6	
	0.4
7.2	
	0.5
8.8	
	0.6
10.4	
	0.7
12.0	
	0.8
13.6	
	0.9
15.2	
	1.0
16.8	

Figure 205b. Interpolation table.

More on Second Differences using Pub 229. The accuracy of linear interpolation usually decreases as the altitude increases. At altitudes above 60° it may be necessary to include the effect of second differences in the interpolation. When the altitude difference, d, is printed in italic type followed by a small dot, the second-difference correction may exceed 0.25', and should normally be applied. The need for a second-difference correction is illustrated by the graph of Table 205c data in Figure 205d.

LHA 28°, Lat. 15° (Same as Dec.)			
Dec.	ht (Tab. Hc)	*First Difference*	Second Difference
15°	62°58.4'		
		+2.8'	
16°	63°01.2'		-2.0'
		+0.8'	
17°	63°02.0'		-2.1'
		-1.3'	
18°	63°00.7'		

Table 205c. Data from Pub. No. 229.

Other than graphically, the required correction for the effects of second differences is obtained from the appropriate subtable of the Interpolation Table. However, before the Interpolation Table can be used for this purpose, what is known as the double-second difference (DSD) must be formed.

Forming the Double-Second Difference (DSD). The double-second difference is the sum of two successive second differences. Although second differences are not tabulated, the DSD can be formed readily by subtracting,

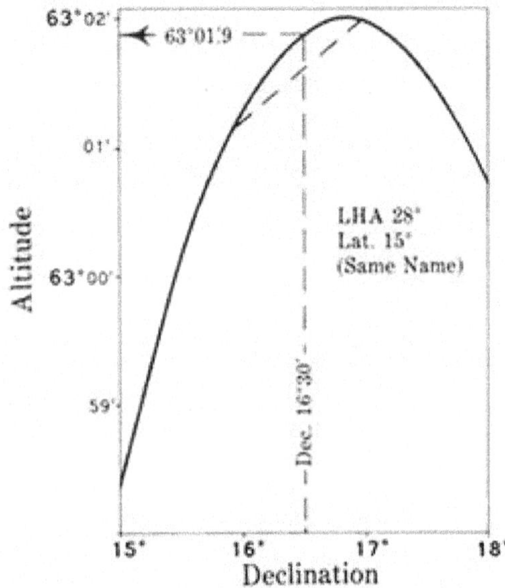

Figure 205d. Graph of Table 205c Data.

algebraically, the tabular altitude difference immediately above the respondent altitude difference from the tabular altitude difference immediately below. The result will always be a negative value.

The Double-Second Difference Correction. As shown in Figure 205a, that compartment of the DSD table opposite the block in which the Dec. Inc. is found is entered with the DSD to obtain the DSD correction to the altitude. The correction is always plus. Therefore, the sign of the DSD need not be recorded. When the DSD entry corresponds to an exact tabular value, always use the upper of the two possible corrections.

Example of the Use of the Double-Second Difference. As an example of the use of the double-second difference (DSD) the computed altitude and true azimuth are determined for Lat. 15°N, LHA 28°, and Dec. 16°30.0'N. Data are exhibited in Figure 205a.

The respondents for the entering arguments (Lat. 15° Same Name as Declination, LHA 28°, and Dec. 16°) are:

tabular altitude,	ht	63°01.2'
altitude difference,	d	(+)0.8'
azimuth angle,	Z	84.1°

Table 205e.

The linear interpolation correction to the tabular altitude for Dec. Inc. 30.0' is (+)0.4'.

$$Hc = ht + \text{linear correction} + \text{DSD correction}$$

However, by inspection of Figure 205d, illustrating this solution graphically, the computed altitude should be 63°01.9'. The actual change in altitude with an increase in declination is nonlinear. The altitude value lies on the curve between the points for declination 16° and declination 17° instead of the straight line connecting these points.

The DSD is formed by subtracting, algebraically, the tabular altitude difference immediately above the respondent altitude difference from the tabular altitude difference immediately below. Thus, the DSD is formed by algebraically subtracting (+)2.8' from (-)1.3'; the result is (-)4.1'.

As shown in Figure 205f, that compartment of the DSD table opposite the block in which the Dec. Inc. (30.0') is found is entered with the DSD (4.1') to obtain the DSD correction to the altitude. The correction is 0.3'. The correction is always plus.

$$Hc = ht + \text{linear correction} + \text{DSD correction}$$

$$Hc = 63°01.2' + 0.4' + 0.3' = 63°01.9'$$

Extrapolation.-The extending of a table is usually performed by assuming that the difference between the last few tabulated entries will continue at the same rate. This assumption is strictly correct only if the change is truly linear, but in most tables the assumption provides satisfactory results for a *slight* extension beyond tabulated values. The extent to which the assumption can be used reliably can often be determined by noting the last few differences. If the "second differences" (differences between consecutive differences) are nearly zero, the curve is nearly a straight line, for a short distance. But if consecutive second differences are appreciable, extrapolation is not reliable. For examples of linear and nonlinear relationships, refer to the first page of Table 3 (Common Logarithms of Trigonometric Functions) and compare the tabulated differences of the logarithms of secant (approximately linear on this page) and sine (nonlinear on this page).

As an example of extrapolation, consider Table 22 (Amplitudes). Suppose the amplitude for latitude 45°, declination 24.3° is desired. The last declination entry is 24.0°. The amplitude for declination 23.5° is 34.3°, and for declination 24.0° it is 35.1°. The difference is (+) 0.8°. Assuming this same difference between declinations 24.0° and 24.5°, one finds the value for 24.3° is $35.1° + \left(\frac{3}{5} \times 0.8°\right) = 35.6°$. Below latitude 50° this table is so nearly linear that extrapolation can be carried to declination 30° without serious error.

For double or triple extrapolation, differences are found as in single interpolation.

206. General Comments

As a general rule, the final answer should not be given to greater precision than tabulated values. A notable exception to this rule is the case where

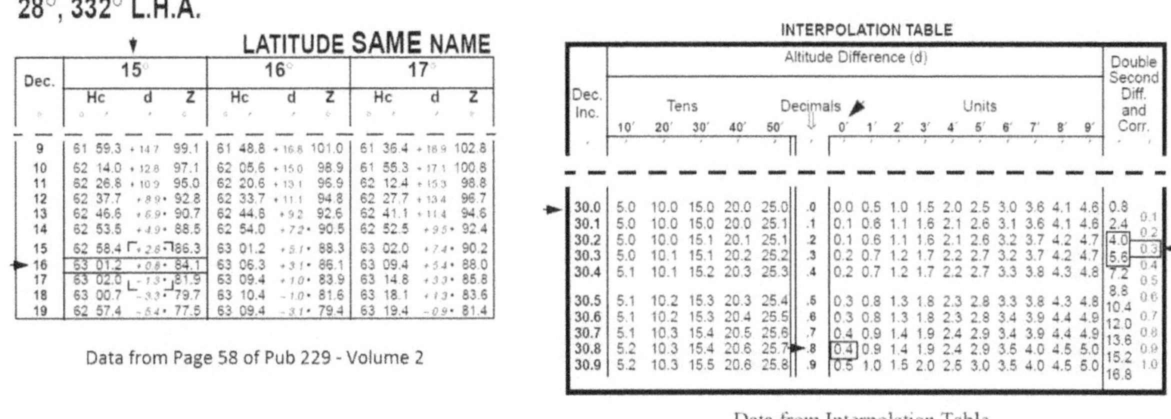

28°, 332° L.H.A. — LATITUDE SAME NAME

Dec.	15° Hc	15° d	15° Z	16° Hc	16° d	16° Z	17° Hc	17° d	17° Z
°	° ′	′	°	° ′	′	°	° ′	′	°
9	61 59.3	+14.7	99.1	61 48.8	+16.8	101.0	61 36.4	+18.9	102.8
10	62 14.0	+12.8	97.1	62 05.6	+15.0	98.9	61 55.3	+17.1	100.8
11	62 26.8	+10.9	95.0	62 20.6	+13.1	96.9	62 12.4	+15.3	98.8
12	62 37.7	+8.9•	92.8	62 33.7	+11.1	94.8	62 27.7	+13.4	96.7
13	62 46.6	+6.9•	90.7	62 44.8	+9.2	92.6	62 41.1	+11.4	94.6
14	62 53.5	+4.9•	88.5	62 54.0	+7.2•	90.5	62 52.5	+9.5•	92.4
15	62 58.4	+2.8•	86.3	63 01.2	+5.1•	88.3	63 02.0	+7.4•	90.2
16	63 01.2	+0.8•	84.1	63 06.3	+3.1•	86.1	63 09.4	+5.4•	88.0
17	63 02.0	-1.3•	81.9	63 09.4	+1.0•	83.9	63 14.8	+3.3•	85.8
18	63 00.7	-3.3•	79.7	63 10.4	-1.0•	81.6	63 18.1	+1.3•	83.6
19	62 57.4	-5.4•	77.5	63 09.4	-3.1•	79.4	63 19.4	-0.9•	81.4

Data from Page 58 of Pub 229 - Volume 2

INTERPOLATION TABLE

Altitude Difference (d)

Dec. Inc.	Tens 10′	20′	30′	40′	50′	Decimals	Units 0′	1′	2′	3′	4′	5′	6′	7′	8′	9′
30.0	5.0	10.0	15.0	20.0	25.0	.0	0.0	0.5	1.0	1.5	2.0	2.5	3.0	3.6	4.1	4.6
30.1	5.0	10.0	15.0	20.0	25.1	.1	0.1	0.6	1.1	1.6	2.1	2.6	3.1	3.6	4.1	4.6
30.2	5.0	10.0	15.1	20.1	25.1	.2	0.1	0.6	1.1	1.6	2.1	2.6	3.2	3.7	4.2	4.7
30.3	5.0	10.1	15.1	20.2	25.2	.3	0.2	0.7	1.2	1.7	2.2	2.7	3.2	3.7	4.2	4.7
30.4	5.1	10.1	15.2	20.3	25.3	.4	0.2	0.7	1.2	1.7	2.2	2.7	3.3	3.8	4.3	4.8
30.5	5.1	10.2	15.3	20.3	25.4	.5	0.3	0.8	1.3	1.8	2.3	2.8	3.3	3.8	4.3	4.8
30.6	5.1	10.2	15.3	20.4	25.5	.6	0.3	0.8	1.3	1.8	2.3	2.8	3.4	3.9	4.4	4.9
30.7	5.1	10.3	15.4	20.5	25.6	.7	0.4	0.9	1.4	1.9	2.4	2.9	3.4	3.9	4.4	4.9
30.8	5.2	10.3	15.4	20.6	25.7	.8	0.4	0.9	1.4	1.9	2.4	2.9	3.5	4.0	4.5	5.0
30.9	5.2	10.3	15.5	20.6	25.8	.9	0.5	1.0	1.5	2.0	2.5	3.0	3.5	4.0	4.5	5.0

Double Second Diff.	and Corr.
0.8	
	0.1
2.4	
	0.2
4.0	
	0.3
5.6	
	0.4
7.2	
	0.5
8.8	
	0.6
10.4	
	0.7
12.0	
	0.8
13.6	
	0.9
15.2	
	1.0
16.8	

Data from Interpolation Table

Figure 205f. Interpolation blocks from Pub No. 229.

tabulated values are known to be exact, as in Table 201a. A slight increase in accuracy can sometimes be attained by retaining one additional place in the solution until the final answer. Suppose, for instance, that the corrections for triple interpolation are (+)0.2, (+)0.3, and (-)0.3. The total correction is (+)0.2. If the total correction, rounded to tenths, had been obtained from the sum of (+)0.17, (+)0.26, and (-)0.34, the correct total would have been (+)0.09 = (+)0.1. The retaining of one additional place may be critical if the correction factors end in 0.5. Thus, in double interpolation, one correction value might be say (+)0.15, and the other one (-)0.25. The correct total is (-)0.1. But if the individual differences are rounded to (+)0.2 and (-)0.2, the total is 0.0.

The difference used for establishing the proportion is also a matter subject to some judgment. Thus, if the latitude is 17°14.6', it might be rounded to 17.2° for many purposes. Slightly more accurate results can sometimes be obtained by retaining the minutes, using $\frac{14.6}{60}$ instead of 0.2. If the difference to be multiplied by this proportion is small, the increase in accuracy gained by using the more exact value is small, but if the difference is large, the gain might be considerable. Thus, if the difference is 0.2°, the correction by using either $\frac{14.6}{60}$ or 0.2 is less than 0.05°, or 0.0° to the nearest 0.1°. But if the difference is 3.2°, the value by $\frac{14.6}{60}$ is 0.8°, and the value by 0.2 is 0.6°.

If the tabulated entries involved in an interpolation are all positive or all negative, the interpolation can be carried out on either a numerical or an algebraic basis. Most navigators prefer the former, carrying out the interpolation as if all entries were positive, and giving to the interpolated value the common sign of all entries. When both positive and negative entries are involved, all differences and corrections should be on an algebraic basis, and careful attention should be given to signs. Thus, if single interpolation is to be performed between values of (+)0.9 and (-)0.4, the difference is $0.9 - (-0.4) = 0.9 + 0.4 = 1.3$ 0. If the correction is 0.2 of this difference, it is (-)0.3 if applied to (+)0.9, and (+)0.3 if applied to (-)0.4. In the first case, the interpolated value is $(+)0.9 - 0.3 = (+)0.6$. In the second case, it is $(-)0.4 + 0.3 = (-)0.1$. If the correction had been 0.4 of the difference, it would have been (-)0.5 in the first case, and (+)0.5 in the second. The interpolated value would have been $(+)0.9 - 0.5 = (+)0.4$, or $(-)0.4 + 0.5 = (+)0.1$, respectively.

Because of the variety in methods of interpolation used, solutions by different persons may differ slightly.

CHAPTER 3

NAVIGATIONAL ERRORS

DEFINING NAVIGATIONAL ERRORS

300. Introduction

As commonly practiced, navigation is not an exact science. A number of approximations which would be unacceptable in careful scientific work are used by the navigator, because greater accuracy may not be consistent with the requirements or time available, or because there is no alternative.

Thus, when the navigator uses his latitude graduations as a mile scale or computes a great-circle course and distance, s/he neglects the flattening of the earth at the poles, a practice that is not acceptable to the geodetic surveyor. When the navigator plots a visual bearing or an azimuth line for a celestial line of position, s/he uses a rhumb line to represent a great circle on a Mercator chart. When s/he plots the celestial line of position, s/he substitutes a rhumb line for a small circle. When the navigator interpolates in sight reduction or lattice tables, s/he assumes a linear (constant-rate) change between tabulated values. When s/he measures distance by radar or depth by echo sounder, s/he assumes that the radio- or sound-wave has constant speed under all conditions. When the navigator applies dip and refraction corrections to his or her sextant altitude, s/he generally assumes standard atmospheric conditions. These are only a few of the approximations commonly applied by a navigator.

There are so many that there is a natural tendency for some of them to cancel others. Thus, under favorable conditions, a position at sea determined from celestial observation by an experienced observer should seldom be in error by more than 2 miles. However, if the various small errors in a particular observation all have the same sign (all plus or all minus), the error might be several times this amount without any mistake having been made by the navigator.

Greater accuracy could be attained, but at a price. The navigator is a practical individual. In the course of ordinary navigation, s/he would rather spend 10 minutes determining a position having a probable error of plus or minus 2 miles, than to spend several hours learning where s/he was to an accuracy of a few meters. But if the navigator can determine a recent or present position to greater accuracy, the decrease in error is attractive. The various navigational aids have been designed with this in mind. Greater accuracy in plotting could be achieved by increasing the scale of the chart or plotting sheet. This has been done for confined waters where a higher degree of accuracy is needed, but a large scale plotting sheet would be a nuisance at sea. The hand-held marine sextant is not sufficiently accurate for use in determining an astronomical position in a geodetic survey. But, it is much more satisfactory at sea than the surveyor's astrolabe or theodolite, which require stable platforms if their potential accuracy is to be realized.

An understanding of the kinds of errors involved in navigation, and of the elementary principles of probability, should be of assistance to a navigator in interpreting his or her results.

301. Definitions

The following definitions apply to the discussions of this chapter:

Error is the difference between a specific value and the correct or standard value. As used here it does not include mistakes, but is related to lack of perfection. Thus, an altitude determined by marine sextant is corrected for a standard amount of refraction, but if the actual refraction at the time of observation varies from the standard, the value taken from the table is in error by the difference between standard and actual refraction. This error will be compounded with others in the observed altitude. Similarly, depth determined by echo sounder is in error, among other things, by the difference between the actual speed of sound waves in the water and the speed used for calibration of the instrument. The depth will also be in error if an echo is returned from a phantom bottom instead of from the actual bottom. This chapter is concerned primarily with the deviation from standards. Thus, while variation of the compass is an error when referred to true directions, the difference between the assumed variation and that actually existing is an error with reference to magnetic direction. Corrections can be applied for standard values of error. It is the deviation from standard, as well as mistakes, that produce inaccurate results in navigation. Various kinds of errors are discussed in the following articles.

Mistake is a blunder, such as an incorrect reading of an instrument, the taking of a wrong value from a table, or the plotting of a reciprocal bearing. The mistake is discussed in more detail in Section 312.

Standard is something established by custom, agreement, or authority as a basis for comparison. It is customary to use nautical miles for measuring distances between ports. By international agreement the nautical mile is defined as exactly 1852 meters. By authority of various countries which are parties to the agreement, this length is translated to the linear units adopted by that country. It is the fact of establishment or general acceptance that determines whether a given quantity or condition has become a standard of measure or quality.

Thus, in 1960, the standard unit of length agreed upon at the Eleventh General (International) Conference on Weights and Measures to redefine the meter was 1,650,763.73 wavelengths of the orange-red radiation in vacuum of krypton 86 corresponding to the unperturbed transition between the 2p10 and 5d5 levels. This established standard of length now serves as a basis for measurement of any physical magnitude, as the length of the meridian. Multiples and submultiples of a standard are exact. In 1959, the U.S. adopted the exact relationships of 1 yard as equal to 0.9144 meter and 1 inch as equal to 2.54 centimeters. Hence, 39.37 U.S. inches are approximately equal to 1 meter. Because 1 foot equals 12 inches by definition, and the international nautical mile has been defined as 1852 meters, the international nautical mile is equal to 6,076.11549 U.S. feet (approximately). The previous U.S. foot (6,076.10333 . feet equals 1 nautical mile) has been re-designated as the U.S. survey foot.

Frequently, a standard is chosen so that it serves as a model which approximates a mean or average condition. However, the distinction between the standard value and the actual value at any time should not be forgotten. Thus, a standard atmosphere has been established in which the temperature, pressure, density, etc., are precisely specified for each altitude. Actual conditions, however, are generally different from those defined by the standard atmosphere. Similarly, the values for dip given in the almanacs are considered standard by those who use them, but actual dip may be appreciably different from that tabulated.

Accuracy is the degree of conformance with the correct value, while **precision** is the degree of refinement of a value. Thus, an altitude determined by a marine sextant might be stated to the nearest 0.1', and yet be accurate only to the nearest 1.0' if the horizon is indistinct.

302. Systematic Errors

Systematic errors are those which follow some law by which they can be predicted. The accuracy with which a systematic error can be predicted depends upon the accuracy with which the governing law is understood. An error which can be predicted can be eliminated, or compensation can be made for it.

The simplest form of systematic error is one of unchanging magnitude and sign. This is called a **constant error**. Examples are the index error of a marine sextant, watch error, or the error resulting from a lubber's line not being accurately aligned with the longitudinal axis of the craft. In each of these cases, all readings are in error by a constant amount as long *as the adjustment remains unchanged*, and can be removed by applying a correction of equal magnitude and opposite sign. Index error and watch error can be removed by adjustment of the instrument. Lubber's line error can be removed by aligning the lubber's line with the longitudinal axis of the craft.

Another type of systematic error results from a non-standard rate. If a watch is gaining 4 seconds per day, its readings will be in error by 1 second after an interval of 6 hours, 8 seconds at the end of 2 days, etc. This principle is used in establishing a chronometer rate (Section 1608, Volume 1, 2019 edition) for determination of chronometer error between comparisons of the chronometer with time signals. It can be eliminated by adjusting the rate. If a current is running and no allowance for it is made in the dead reckoning, the DR position is in error by an amount proportional to elapsed time. The error introduced by maintaining heading by means of an inaccurate compass is proportional to distance, as is the lateral error in a line of position plotted from an inaccurate bearing.

One of the causes of equation of time (Section 1601, Volume 1, 2019 edition) is the fact that the ecliptic, around which annual motion occurs, is not parallel to the celestial equator, around or parallel to which apparent daily motion takes place. The same type of systematic error is involved in other measurements. Consider the measurement of bearing with a tilted compass card. Bearing is measured by a system of uniform graduations (degrees) of a circle (such as a compass card) in the horizontal plane. If the card is tilted, and its graduations are projected onto the horizontal plane, the circle becomes an ellipse with the graduations unequally spaced. Along the axis of tilt and a line perpendicular to it, directions are correct. But near the axis of tilt the graduations are too close together, and near the perpendicular they are too widely spaced.

The error thus introduced is similar to that which would arise if a watch face were tilted but the motion of the hands remained horizontal. If it were tilted around the "3-9" line, it would appear to run slow near the hour and half hour, and fast near the quarter and three-quarter hours. If the direction to be observed is of an object above or below the horizontal, as the azimuth of a celestial body, measurement is made to the foot of the perpendicular through the object.

The sight vanes of a compass move in a plane perpendicular to the compass card. Hence, if the card is tilted, measurement is made to the foot of a perpendicular to the card, rather than to the foot of a perpendicular to the horizontal, introducing an error which increases with the angle of tilt and also with the angle of elevation (or depression) of the object. This error is greatest along the axis of tilt, and zero along the perpendicular to it. Both of these tilt errors can be corrected by leveling the compass card.

A different type of tilt error occurs when a reflection takes place from a tilted surface, such as the ionosphere, the error being proportional to the angle of tilt. In some respects, this error is similar to coastal refraction of a radio wave.

Additional examples of systematic error are uncorrected deviation of the compass, error due to a position in a pattern of hyperbolas, error due to incorrect location of a Loran transmitter, uncorrected parallax, and uncorrected personal error.

303. Random Errors

Random errors are chance errors, unpredictable in magnitude or sign. They are governed by the laws of probability. If the altitude of a celestial body is observed, the reading may be (1) too great, (2) correct, or (3) too small. If a number of observations are made, and there is no systematic error, the probability of a positive error is exactly equal to the probability of a negative error. This does not mean that every second observation having an error will be too great. However, the greater the number of observations, the greater is the probability that the percentage of positive errors will equal the percentage of negative ones, and that their magnitudes will correspond.

Error	No. of obs.	Percent of obs.
- 10′	0	0. 0
- 9′	1	0. 2
- 8′	2	0. 4
- 7′	4	0. 8
- 6′	9	1. 8
- 5′	17	3. 4
- 4′	28	5. 6
- 3′	40	8. 0
- 2′	53	10. 6
- 1′	63	12. 6
0	66	13. 2
+ 1′	63	12. 6
+ 2′	53	10. 6
+ 3′	40	8. 0
+ 4′	28	5. 6
+ 5′	17	3. 4
+ 6′	9	1. 8
+ 7′	4	0. 8
+ 8′	2	0. 4
+ 9′	1	0. 2
+10′	0	0. 0
0	500	100. 0

Table 303. Normal distribution of random errors.

Suppose that 500 observations are made, with the results shown in Table 303. A close approximation of the plot of these errors is shown in Figure 303a. The plot has been modified slightly to constitute the normal curve of random errors, which is the same as the actual curve except that the normal curve approaches zero as the error increases, while the actual curve reaches zero at (+)10' and (-)10'. The height of the curve at any point represents the percentage of observations that can be expected to have the error indicated at that point. The probability of any similar observation having any given error is the proportion of the number of observations having this error to the total number of observations, or the percentage expressed as a decimal. Thus, the probability of an observation having an error of -3' is

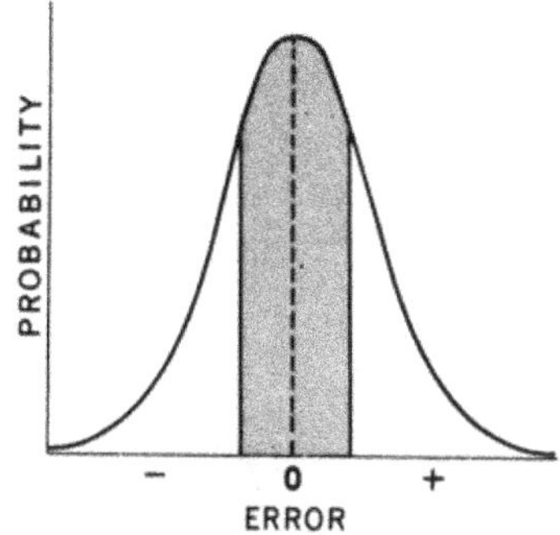

Figure 303a. Normal curve of random error with 50 percent of area shaded. Limits of shaded area indicate probable error.

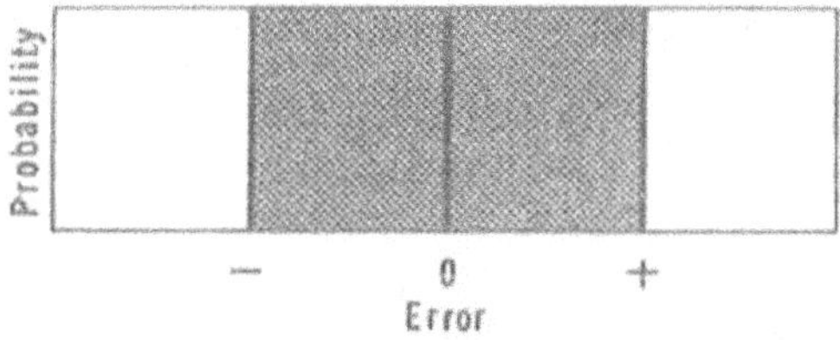

Figure 303b. Rectangular error, with 50 percent area shaded.

$$\frac{40}{500} = \frac{1}{12.5} = 0.08(8\%)$$

If the area under the curve represents 100 percent of the observations, half the area (the shaded portion of Figure 303c) represents 50 percent of the observations. The value of the error at the limits of this shaded portion is often called the "50 percent error," or **probable error**, meaning that 50 percent of the observations can be expected to have less error, and 50 percent greater error. Similarly, the limits which contain the central 95 percent of the area denote the 95 percent error. The percentage of error is found mathematically. For a normal curve, each error is squared, the sum of the squares is divided by one less than the number of observations, and the square root of the quotient is determined. This value is called the **standard deviation** or **standard error** (σ, the Greek letter sigma). In the illustration, the standard deviation is the square root of:

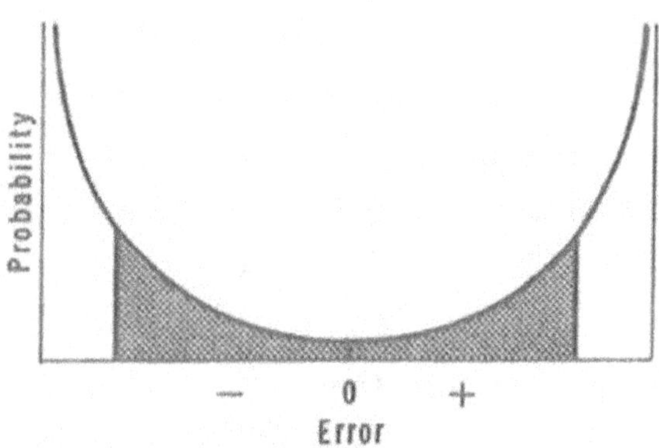

Figure 303c. Periodic error, with 50 percent area shaded.

$$0 \times (-10)^2 + 1 \times (-9)^2 + 2 \times (-8)^2 + 4 \times (-7)^2 + 9 \times (-6)^2, \text{ etc}$$

divided by 499 or

$$\frac{4474}{\sqrt{499}} = \sqrt{8.966} = 2.99 \text{ (about 3)}$$

The standard deviation is the 68.27 percent error. The probability of the occurrence of an error of or less than a specific magnitude may be approximately determined by the following relationship (with the answers for the illustration given):

50% error = 2/3 x σ = 2' (approx.)

68% error = 1 x σ = 3' (approx.)

95% error = 2 x σ = 6' (approx.)

99% error = 2 2/3 x σ = 8' (approx.)

99.9% error =3 1/3 x σ = 10' (approx.)

Many of the errors of navigation do not follow the normal distribution discussed above. *Pub. No. 229* values of altitude can be taken only to the nearest 0.1'. The error in tabular altitude might have any value from (+) 0. 05' to (-) 0.05', and any value within these limits is as likely to occur as any other of the same precision. The same is true of a sextant that cannot be read more precisely than 0.1', and of a time-difference that cannot be measured more precisely than 1 µs. These values refer to the single errors indicated, and not to the total error that might be involved. This is a **rectangular error**, so called because of the shape of its plot, as shown in Figure 303b. The 100 percent error is half the difference between readings. The 50 percent error is half this amount, the 95 percent error is 0.95 times this amount, etc. In some cases it may be more meaningful to refer to the rectangular error as the **resolution error**.

Still another type random error is encountered in navigation. If a compass is fluctuating periodically due to yaw of a ship, its motion slows as the end of a swing is approached, when the error approaches maximum value. If readings were taken continuously or at equal intervals of time, the interval being a small percentage of the total period of oscillation, the curve of errors would have a characteristic U-shape, as shown in Figure 303c. The same type error is involved in measurement of altitude of a celestial body from a wing of the bridge of a heavily rolling vessel, when the roll causes large changes in the height of eye. This type of error is called a **periodic error**. The effect is accentuated by the tendency of the observer to make readings near one of the extreme values because the instrument appears steadiest at this time. If it is impractical to make a reading at the center of the period, the error can be eliminated or reduced by averaging readings taken continuously or at short intervals, as indicated above. This is the method used in averaging type artificial-horizon sextants. Generally, better results can be obtained by taking maximum positive and maximum negative readings, and averaging the results.

The curve of any type of random error is symmetrical about the line representing zero error. This means that in the ideal plot every point on one side of the curve is error of the same magnitude. The average of all readings, considering signs, is zero. The larger the number of readings made, the greater the probability of the errors fitting the ideal curve. Another way of stating this is that as the number of readings increases, the error of the average can be expected to decrease

304. Combinations of Errors

Many of the results obtained in navigation are subject to more than one error. Chapter 19, Volume 1, lists 19 errors applicable to sextant altitudes. Some of these have several components. A number of possible errors are involved in the determination of computed altitude and azimuth. A rectangular error is possible in finding the altitude difference. Several additional errors may affect the accuracy of plotting. Thus, the line of position as finally plotted may include 30 errors or more. Corrections are applied for some of the larger ones, so that in each of these cases the applicable error is the difference between the applied correction and the actual error. Thus, a dip correction may be applied for a height of eye of 30 feet, while the actual height at the moment of observation may be 31 feet 6 inches. Even if the height of eye is exactly 30 feet, a rectangular error may be involved in taking the dip correction from the table

If two or more errors are applicable to a given result, the total error is equal to the algebraic sums of all errors. Thus, if a given number is subject to errors of (+) 4, (-) 2, (-) 1, (+) 3, (+) 2, 0, and (-) 2, the total error is (+) 4. Systematic errors can be combined by adding the curves of

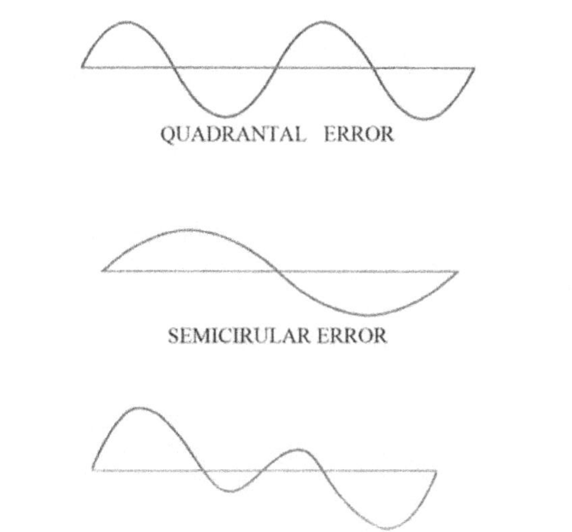

Figure 304. Combining systemic error.

individual errors. Thus, a magnetic compass may have a quadrantal error as shown by the top curve of Figure 304, and a semicircular error as shown by the second curve. The sum of these two errors is shown in the bottom curve. If, in addition, the compass has a constant error, the bottom curve is moved vertically upward or downward by the amount of the constant error, without undergoing a change of form. If the constant error is greater than the maximum value of the combined curves, all errors are positive or all are negative, but of varying magnitude.

If a number of random errors are combined, the result tends to follow a normal curve regardless of the shape of the individual errors, and the greater the number, the more nearly the result can be expected to approach the normal curve (Figure 303a). If a given result is subject to errors of plus or minus 3, 2, 1, 2, 4, 2, 1, 8, 1, and 2, the total error could be as much as 26 if all errors had the same sign. However, if these are truly random, the probability of them all having the same sign is only 1 in 1024. This is so because the chance of any one being positive (or negative) is one half. By the same reasoning, approximately half of the positive (or negative) results will have any one particular additional correction positive (or negative). Thus, the probability of any two particular corrections having a positive (or negative) sign is $1/2 \times 1/2 = (1/2)^2 = \frac{1}{4}$. The probability of all 10 corrections having a positive (or negative) sign is $(1/2)^{10} = \frac{1}{1024}$. If there were 20 corrections, the probability of all having a positive (or negative) sign would be $(1/2)^{20} = \frac{1}{1048576}$.

When both systematic and random errors are present in a process, both effects are present. An increase in the number of readings decreases the residual random error, but regardless of the number of readings, a systematic error is present in its entirety. Thus, if a number of phase-difference readings are made at a fixed point, the average should be a good approximation of the true value if there is no systematic error. But if the equipment is out of adjustment to the extent that the lane is incorrectly identified, no number of readings will correct this error. In this illustration, a constant error is combined with a normal random error. The normal curve has the correct shape, but is offset from the zero value.

Under some conditions, systematic errors can be eliminated from the results even when the magnitude is not determined. Thus, if two celestial bodies differ in azimuth by 180°, and the altitude of each is observed, the line midway between the lines of position resulting from these observations is free from any *constant* error in the *altitude* (such as abnormal refraction or dip, or incorrect IC). It would *not* be free from such a constant error as one in time (unless the bodies were on the celestial meridian). Similarly, a fix obtained by observations of three stars differing in azimuth by 120°, or four stars differing by 90° is free from constant error in the altitude, if the center of the figure made by the lines of position is used. The center of the figure formed by circles of position from distances of objects equally spaced in azimuth is free from a constant error in range. A constant error in bearing lines does not introduce an error in the fix if the objects are equally spaced in azimuth. In all of these examples, the correct position is *outside* the figure formed by the lines of position if all objects observed are on the same side of the observer (that is, if they lie within an arc of less than 180°).

305. Navigation Accuracy

Navigation accuracy is normally expressed in terms of the probability of being within a specified distance of a desired point during the navigation process.

If the accuracy of only a single line of position is being considered, the specified distance may be stated as the standard deviation (Section 303) or some multiple thereof, assuming that the errors of the line of position follow a **single-axis normal distribution.** The distance as stated for the standard deviation of a line of position is measured from the arithmetic mean of the positions which could be established from a large number of observations at a given place and time. Therefore, this distance does not indicate the separation between the line of position and the observer's actual position, except by chance. If the error is stated as 1 σ, 68.27 percent of the cases should result in line of position displacements from the arithmetic mean in any direction not exceeding the distance specified for 1 σ. If the error is stated as 2 σ, 95.45 percent of the lines of position should not be displaced from the arithmetic mean in any direction by more than the distance specified for 2 σ. If the error is stated as the probable error, 50 percent of the lines

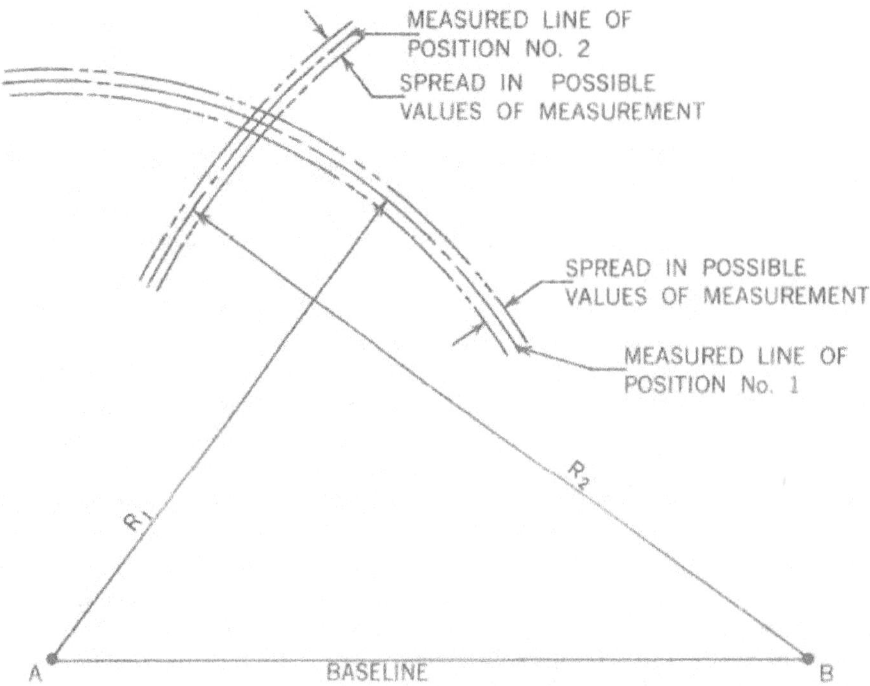

Figure 305a. Fix established at intersection of two lines of position having different values of error.

of position should not be displaced from the arithmetic mean in any direction by more than the distance specified for 0.6745σ.

The standard deviation is also employed in developing expressions for the probability of a fix position being within a specified distance of the mean of the positions which could be established from a large number of observations at a given place and time by means of the system used to establish the fix.

In the following discussion, the fix is established by the intersection of two lines of position, each of which may be in error. The lines of position (Figure 305a) are range measurements from two points at the extremities of a baseline of known length. Because of inaccuracies in measurement, the actual ranges differ from the measured values and may lie somewhere between the limits which are shown as additional arcs either side of the measured arc.

The intersection of the two lines of position together with the standard deviations associated with each is drawn to an expanded scale in Figure 305b. It can be shown that the *contours of equal probability density* about such an intersection are ellipses with their center at the intersection. Thus, the ellipse shown in Figure 305b might be the 75 percent probability ellipse, meaning that there are three chances in four that a fix will lie within such ellipse centered upon the mean of the positions which would be established from a large number of observations at a given place and time by means of the system used to establish the fix.

For simplicity in this discussion of navigation accuracy, the following assumptions are made:

1. All constant errors or **bias errors** have been removed, leaving only the random errors. Thus, the mean or average error is assumed to be zero.
2. These random errors are assumed to be normally distributed.
3. The errors associated with the two intersecting lines of position are assumed to be independent. This assumption implies that a change in the error of one line of position has no effect upon the other.
4. The lines of position are assumed to be straight lines in the small area in the immediate vicinity of their intersection. This assumption is valid so long as the standard deviation is small compared to the radius of curvature of the line of position.
5. Errors of position are limited to the two-dimensional case. As shown in Figure 305b, the general case of the intersection of two lines of position at any angle of cut and with different values of error associated with each line of position results in an elliptical error figure. Figure 305c shows the ellipse simplified to geometrical terms.

One may readily surmise from Figure 305c that the exact shape of the error figure varies with the magnitudes of the two one-dimensional input errors, $\sigma 1$ and $\sigma 2$ as well as with the angle of cut, α. The angle α is also the angle between the two values of sigma because the standard

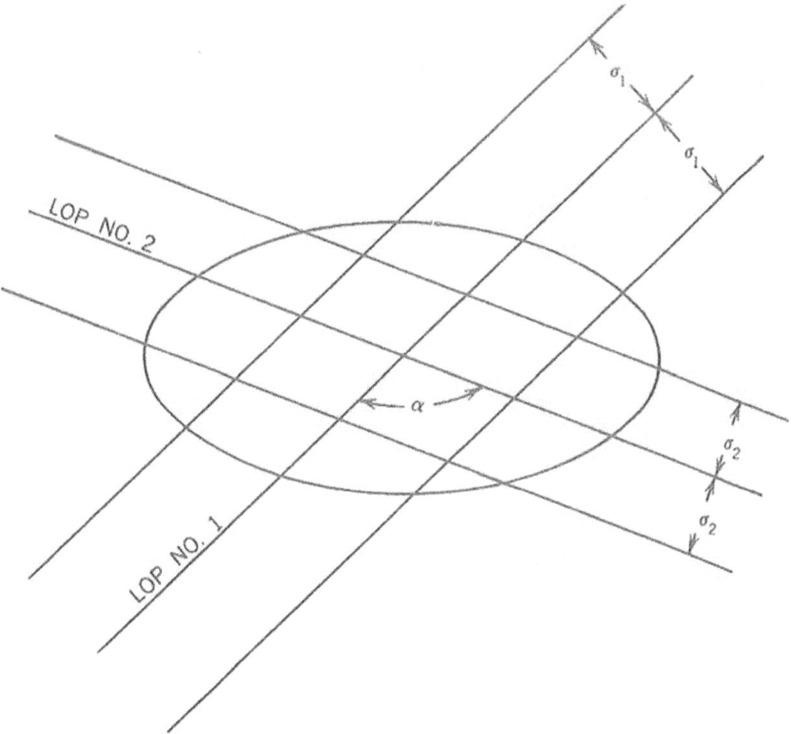

Figure 305b. Expanded view of intersection of two lines of position.

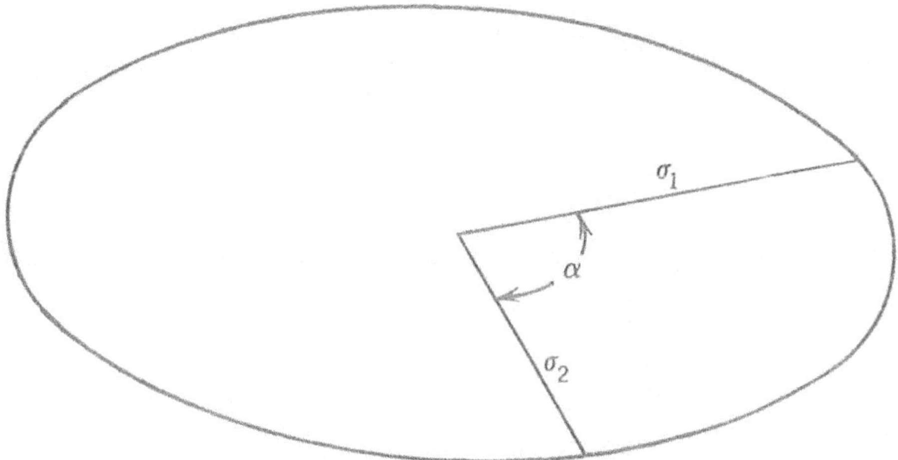

Figure 305c. Basic error ellipse.

deviations are mutually perpendicular to their corresponding lines of position. These variations can be calculated to provide the probability that a point is located within a circle of stated radius.

When this is done, the error is stated in terms more meaningful to the practicing navigator. The basis of this concept may best be seen by first considering the special case when the two errors are equal, and the angle of intersection of the lines of position is a right angle. In this case, *and in this case alone*, the error figure becomes a circle and is described by the circular normal distribution. A plot of this special function is given in Figure 305d. In this plot, the horizontal axis is measured in terms of R/σ, R being the stated radius of the circle and σ being the measure of error. The error measure is given simply as σ, for in this circular case $\sigma 1 = \sigma 2$. To illustrate, a measurement system gives a circular error figure and has a value of $\sigma = 100$ meters; the probability of actually being located within a circle of 100 meters radius when $R/\sigma = 1.0$ may be read from the verti-

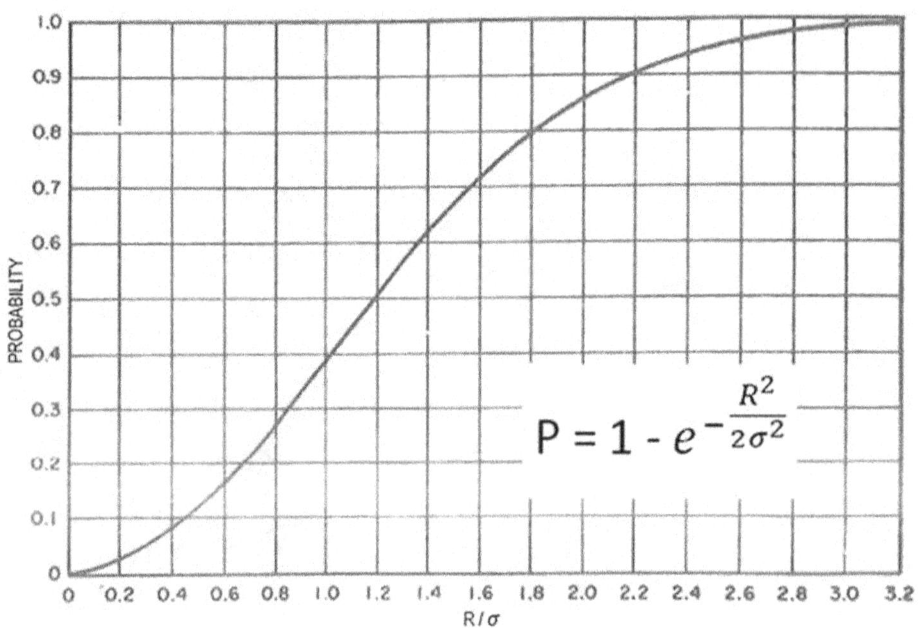

Figure 305d. Circular normal distribution.

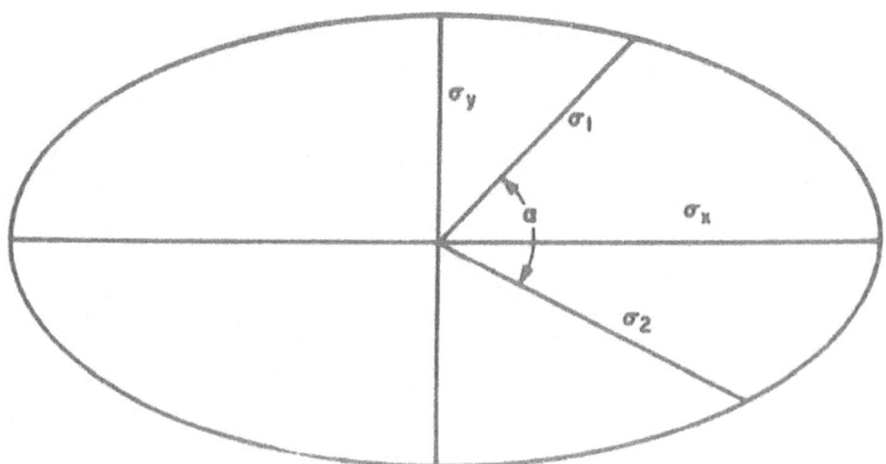

Figure 305e. Transformation to standard deviations along ellipse axes.

cal axis to be 39.3 percent. To obtain the radius of a circle within which a 50 percent probability results, the corresponding value of R/σ is seen to be 1.18 from the graph. Thus, for this example, the **circular probable error** (**CPE** or **CEP** or circle of 50% probability) would be 118 meters..

In one method of using error ellipses to obtain the radii of **circles of equivalent probability**, new values of σ are found along the major and minor axes of the ellipse (Figure 305e) using the following equations:

$$\sigma x^2 = \frac{1}{2\sin^2\alpha}\left[\sigma 1^2 + \sigma 2^2 + \sqrt{(\sigma 1^2 + \sigma 2^2)^2 - 4\sin^2\alpha\sigma_1^2\sigma_2^2}\right]$$

$$\sigma y^2 = \frac{1}{2\sin^2\alpha}\left[\sigma 1^2 + \sigma 2^2 - \sqrt{(\sigma 1^2 + \sigma 2^2)^2 - 4\sin^2\alpha\sigma_1^2\sigma_2^2}\right].$$

Then the ratio $c = \frac{\sigma_y}{\sigma_z}$ where σ_x is the larger of the two new standard deviations, is used in entering Table 305a which relates ellipses of varying values of ellipticity to the radii of circles of equivalent probability.

For a numerical example to illustrate the method of calculation, assume that the angle of cut α is 50°, σ 1 is 15 meters, and σ 2 is 20 meters to determine the probability of location within a circle of 30 meters radius.

For the computation the following numbers are needed:

$$\sigma_1^2 = 225$$

$$\sigma_2^2 = 400$$

$$\sin 2\sigma = 0.5868$$

Substituting in the equations for σ_x^2 and σ_y^2, σ_x and σ_y are calculated as 29.9 meters and 13.1 meters, respectively. Since the function *K* multiplied by the larger of the two standard deviations obtained by the transformation method gives the value of the radius of the circle of the corresponding value of probability shown in Table 305a, *K*=1.003. On entering Table 305a with *K*=1.0 and c= 0.44, the probability is found to be 62 percent.

Table 305b and Figure 305g provide ready information about the sizes of circles of specific probability value associated with ellipses of varying eccentricities.

In another method, fictitious values of sigma of identical value, indicated by σ *, are assumed to replace the two unequal values originally given (σ 1and σ 2). A fictitious angle of cut α * is also assumed to replace the angle of cut (α) originally given (Figure 305f).

The method utilizes a set of probability curves, with a separate curve for each value of angle of cut (Figure 305h). These curves can be used only when the two error measures are equal, hence the need for making the transformation to the fictitious σ *.

The values of σ * and α * needed to utilize the probability curves may either be determined from Figure 305j and Figure 305i or by means of the following equations:

$$\sigma^* = \frac{\sin\beta\sqrt{\sigma_1^2 + \sigma_2^2}}{\sqrt{2}}$$

$$\alpha^* = arc\sin(\sin 2\beta \sin\alpha)$$

where

$$\beta = arc\tan(\sigma_1/\sigma_2)$$

Thus,

$$\sin 2\beta = \frac{2\sigma_1\sigma_2}{\sigma_1^2 + \sigma_2^2}.$$

To use the curve and nomogram for obtaining σ * and α *, one must first calculate the ratio σ_2/σ_1. The value σ_1, is always taken as the larger of the two in the ratio so that the ratio is always less than 1.0. With this ratio, enter the curve of Figure 305j and obtain the σ *factor. Multiply σ_1 by this factor to obtain the fictitious function σ *. The nomogram of Figure 305i is entered with the same ratio to obtain the fictitious angle of cut α *.

For a numerical example to illustrate the method of calculation, assume that the angle of cut of 50°, σ_1, is 20 meters, and σ_2 is 15 meters to determine the probability of location within a circle of 30 meters radius.

Calculate the ratio $\sigma_2/\sigma_1 = \frac{15}{20} = 0.75$.

Enter the curve of Figure 305j with this ratio and obtain the σ * factor (0.845). Multiply this factor by σ_1 to obtain σ * equals 16.9 meters. Calculate the ratio

$$R/\sigma^* = 30/16.9 = 1.78.$$

Enter the nomogram of Figure 305i with the ratio σ_2/σ_1, and with the given angle α to obtain the fictitious angle of cut α * = 47°.

The values $R/\sigma^* = 1.78$ and α^* =47° are then used to enter the probability curves of to obtain P= 0.62 or 62 percent, interpolating between the 40° and 50° curves for α^* = 47°.

GEOMETRIC ERROR CONSIDERATIONS

306. Geometric Error Considerations

From the information that can be derived using the two methods of transformation of elliptical error data, one can develop curves which show for constant values of initial error that the size of a circle of fixed value of probability varies as a function of the angle of cut of the lines of position.

To simplify the investigation of geometrical factors, it is initially desirable to consider the special case of $\sigma_1 = \sigma_2 = \sigma$. Under this special condition, the long equations for σ_x and σ_y can be simplified to facilitate computation as follows:

$$\sigma_x = \frac{\sqrt{2}}{2\sin\frac{1}{2}\alpha}\sigma \qquad (\sigma_1 = \sigma_2)$$

$$\sigma_y = \frac{\sqrt{2}}{2\cos\frac{1}{2}\alpha}\sigma \qquad (\sigma_1 = \sigma_2)$$

Taking the ratio of these two values, a simple equation is found for the ratio *c*

$$c = \frac{\sigma_y}{\sigma_x} = \tan\frac{1}{2}\alpha$$

K \ c	0.0	0.1	0.2	0.3	0.4	0.5	0.6	0.7	0.8	0.9	1.0
0.1	.0796557	.0443987	.0242119	.0164176	.0123875	.0099377	.0082940	.0071157	.0062299	.0055400	.0049875
0.2	.1585194	.1339783	.0884533	.0628396	.0482413	.0390193	.0327123	.0281415	.0246824	.0219757	.0198013
0.3	.2358228	.2213804	.1739300	.1318281	.1039193	.0851535	.0719102	.0621386	.0546598	.0487639	.0440025
0.4	.3108435	.3010228	.2635181	.2139084	.1742045	.1451808	.1237982	.1076237	.0950495	.0850326	.0768837
0.5	.3829249	.3755884	.3481790	.3003001	.2532953	.2152886	.1857448	.1620829	.1443941	.1296286	.1175031
0.6	.4514938	.4457708	.[illegible]255605	.3846374	.3357384	.2914682	.2548177	.2251114	.2009797	.1811783	.1647298
0.7	.5160727	.5115048	.4960683	.4633258	.4170862	.3699305	.3280302	.2925654	.2629373	.2381583	.2172955
0.8	.5762892	.5725957	.5604457	.5349387	.4941882	.4474207	.4025628	.3627122	.3283453	.2989700	.2738510
0.9	.6318797	.6288721	.6191354	.5993140	.5651564	.5213998	.4759375	.4333628	.3953279	.3620135	.3330232
1.0	.6826895	.6802325	.6723586	.6568242	.6291249	.5900953	.5461319	.5025790	.4621421	.4257553	.3934693
1.1	.7286679	.7266597	.7202682	.7079681	.6859367	.6524489	.6116316	.5687467	.5272462	.4887873	.4539256
1.2	.7698607	.7682215	.7630305	.7532175	.7359558	.7079973	.6714269	.6306168	.5893494	.5498736	.5132477
1.3	.8063990	.8050648	.8008554	.7929968	.7793550	.7567265	.7249673	.6873122	.6474394	.6079822	.5704426
1.4	.8384867	.8374049	.8340018	.8277048	.8169851	.7989288	.7720889	.7383089	.7007900	.6623035	.6216889
1.5	.8663856	.8655127	.8627728	.8577362	.8493071	.8350816	.8129287	.7833962	.7489500	.7122546	.6753475
1.6	.8904014	.8897008	.8875060	.8834914	.8768644	.8657559	.8478393	.8226246	.7917194	.7574708	.7219627
1.7	.9108691	.9103102	.9085619	.9053766	.9001746	.8915536	.8773116	.8562471	.8291137	.7977882	.7462539
1.8	.9281394	.9276964	.9263125	.9237989	.9197275	.9130680	.9019110	.8846624	.8613238	.8332175	.8021013
1.9	.9425669	.9422182	.9411299	.9391586	.9359855	.9308615	.9222277	.9083609	.8886731	.8639149	.8355255
2.0	.9544997	.9542272	.9533775	.9518415	.9493815	.9454546	.9388418	.9278799	.9115762	.8901495	.8646647
2.1	.9642712	.9640598	.9634011	.9622127	.9603170	.9573205	.9522999	.9437668	.9305013	.9122714	.8897495
2.2	.9721931	.9720304	.9715237	.9706109	.9691597	.9668845	.9631017	.9565522	.9459386	.9306821	.9110784
2.3	.9785518	.9784275	.9780408	.9773450	.9762419	.9745239	.9716934	.9667306	.9583739	.9458085	.9289946
2.4	.9836049	.9835108	.9832180	.9826918	.9818594	.9805703	.9784661	.9747495	.9682698	.9580804	.9438652
2.5	.9875807	.9875100	.9872900	.9868953	.9862720	.9853112	.9837569	.9810035	.9760522	.9679136	.9560631
2.6	.9906776	.9906249	.9904612	.9901674	.9897045	.9889934	.9878527	.9858331	.9821023	.9756969	.9659525
2.7	.9930661	.9930271	.9929062	.9926894	.9923483	.9918260	.9909944	.9895268	.9867530	.9817837	.9738786
2.8	.9948897	.9948612	.9947727	.9946141	.9943649	.9939842	.9933821	.9923249	.9902888	.9864876	.9801589
2.9	.9962684	.9962477	.9961834	.9960684	.9958878	.9956126	.9951798	.9944246	.9929482	.9900803	.9850792
3.0	.9973002	.9972853	.9972391	.9971564	.9970266	.9968294	.9965205	.9959854	.9949274	.9927925	.9888910
3.1	.9980648	.9980542	.9980212	.9979622	.9978699	.9977296	.9975109	.9971348	.9963851	.9948168	.9918113
3.2	.9986257	.9986182	.9985949	.9985533	.9984880	.9983892	.9982356	.9979733	.9974478	.9963105	.9940240
3.3	.9990332	.9990279	.9990116	.9989824	.9989368	.9988677	.9987607	.9985792	.9982147	.9974004	.9956822
3.4	.9993261	.9993225	.9993112	.9992909	.9992593	.9992115	.9991376	.9990129	.9987626	.9981868	.9969113
3.5	.9995347	.9995323	.9995245	.9995105	.9994888	.9994559	.9994053	.9993204	.9991502	.9987480	.9978125
3.6	.9996818	.9996801	.9996748	.9996653	.9996505	.9996281	.9995938	.9995364	.9994218	.9991442	.9984662
3.7	.9997844	.9997832	.9997797	.9997733	.9997633	.9997482	.9997251	.9996867	.9996102	.9994208	.9989352
3.8	.9998553	.9998545	.9998522	.9998478	.9998412	.9998311	.9998157	.9997902	.9997396	.9996119	.9992682
3.9	.9999038	.9999033	.9999018	.9998989	.9998945	.9998878	.9998776	.9998608	.9998276	.9997426	.9995020
4.0	.9999367	.9999363	.9999353	.9999334	.9999305	.9999261	.9999195	.9999085	.9998870	.9998309	.9996645
4.1	.9999587	.9999585	.9999578	.9999566	.9999547	.9999519	.9999475	.9999404	.9999266	.9998900	.9997763
4.2	.9999733	.9999732	.9999727	.9999720	.9999707	.9999689	.9999661	.9999616	.9999527	.9999292	.9998523
4.3	.9999829	.9999828	.9999826	.9999821	.9999813	.9999801	.9999783	.9999754	.9999698	.9999548	.9999034
4.4	.9999892	.9999891	.9999889	.9999886	.9999881	.9999874	.9999863	.9999845	.9999809	.9999715	.9999375
4.5	.9999932	.9999932	.9999931	.9999929	.9999925	.9999921	.9999914	.9999902	.9999881	.9999822	.9999599
4.6	.9999958	.9999957	.9999957	.9999955	.9999954	.9999951	.9999947	.9999939	.9999926	.9999889	.9999746
4.7	.9999974	.9999974	.9999973	.9999973	.9999971	.9999970	.9999967	.9999963	.9999955	.9999932	.9999840
4.8	.9999984	.9999984	.9999984	.9999983	.9999983	.9999982	.9999980	.9999977	.9999972	.9999959	.9999901
4.9	.9999990	.9999990	.9999990	.9999990	.9999990	.9999989	.9999988	.9999986	.9999983	.9999975	.9999939
5.0	.9999994	.9999994	.9999994	.9999994	.9999994	.9999993	.9999993	.9999992	.9999990	.9999985	.9999963
5.1	.9999997	.9999997	.9999997	.9999996	.9999996	.9999996	.9999996	.9999995	.9999994	.9999991	.9999978
5.2	.9999998	.9999998	.9999998	.9999998	.9999998	.9999998	.9999998	.9999997	.9999997	.9999995	.9999987
5.3	.9999999	.9999999	.9999999	.9999999	.9999999	.9999999	.9999999	.9999998	.9999998	.9999997	.9999992
5.4	.9999999	.9999999	.9999999	.9999999	.9999999	.9999999	.9999999	.9999999	.9999999	.9999998	.9999995
5.5	1.0000000	1.0000000	1.0000000	1.0000000	1.0000000	1.0000000	1.0000000	.9999999	.9999999	.9999999	.9999997
5.6								1.0000000	1.0000000	.9999999	.9999998
5.7										1.0000000	.9999999
5.8											1.0000000
5.9											
6.0											

Table 305a. Circular error probability. Argument c is the ratio of the smaller standard deviation to the larger standard deviation. For the argument c and K, the table provides the probability that a point lies within a circle whose center is at the origin and whose radius is K times the larger standard deviation.

P \ c	0. 0	0. 1	0. 2	0. 3	0. 4	0. 5	0. 6	0. 7	0. 8	0. 9	1. 0
.5000	0. 67449	0. 68199	0. 70585	0. 74993	0. 80785	0. 87042	0. 93365	0. 99621	1. 05769	1. 11807	1. 17741
.7500	1. 15035	1. 15473	1. 16825	1. 19246	1. 23100	1. 28534	1. 35143	1. 42471	1. 50231	1. 58271	1. 66511
.9000	1. 64485	1. 64791	1. 65731	1. 67383	1. 69918	1. 73708	1. 79152	1. 86253	1. 94761	2. 04236	2. 14597
.9500	1. 95996	1. 96253	1. 97041	1. 98420	2. 00514	2. 03586	2. 08130	2. 14598	2. 23029	2. 33180	2. 44775
.9750	2. 24140	2. 24365	2. 25053	2. 26255	2. 28073	2. 30707	2. 34581	2. 40356	2. 48494	2. 58999	2. 71620
.9900	2. 57583	2. 57778	2. 58377	2. 59421	2. 60995	2. 63257	2. 66533	2. 71515	2. 79069	2. 89743	3. 03485
.9950	2. 80703	2. 80883	2. 81432	2. 83289	2. 83830	2. 85894	2. 88859	2. 93347	3. 00431	3. 11073	3. 25525
.9975	3. 02334	2. 02500	3. 03010	3. 03898	3. 05234	3. 07144	3. 09871	3. 13969	3. 20586	3. 31099	3. 46164
.9990	3. 29053	3. 29206	3. 29673	3. 30489	3. 31715	3. 33464	3. 35949	3. 39647	3. 45698	3. 55939	3. 71692

Table 305b. Factors for conversion of probability ellipse to circle of equivalent probability.

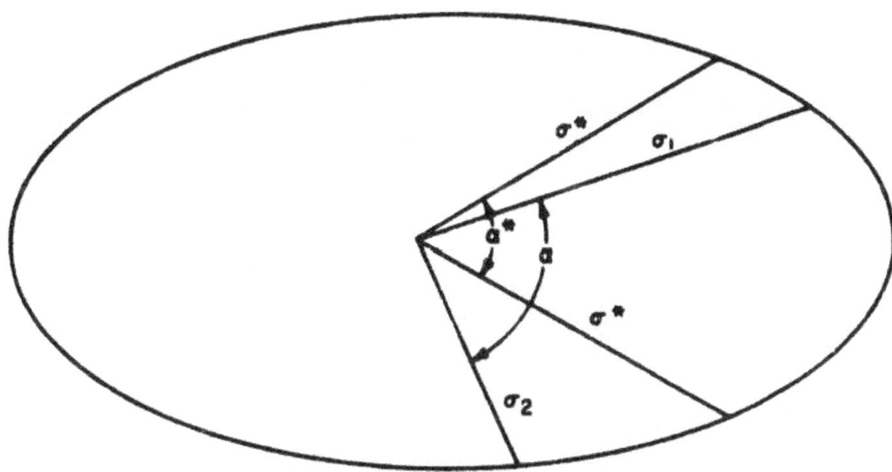

Figure 305f. Transformed parameters of error ellipse.

Utilizing these simplified equations, significant parameters of error ellipses are tabulated in Table 306a as a function of the angle of cut α. Using the CEP curve of Figure 305g, values of the CEP are calculated for each angle, showing that the CEP increases as the angle of cut decreases. The last column in the table gives the factor by which the CEP for angles less than 90° is greater than the CEP for a right angle. This magnification of error curve is plotted in Figure 306b. The curve for the 90 percent probability circle has a slightly differing shape from the CEP curve as shown in Figure 306b. Values for the 90 percent probability circle are given in table Table 306c. Figure 306b indicates the magnitude of the growth of error as the angle of cut varies from 90°.

It is also of interest to consider what values of probability result if the radius of the circle is held constant at the minimum value corresponding to that obtained for the 90° angle of cut. These values may be obtained from the probability versus angle of cut curves in

Along the ordinate $R/\sigma = 1.177$ which corresponds to the CEP for the circular case, one may read the lesser values of probability corresponding to the various angles of cut. Likewise, one may also obtain the probability values corresponding to holding a circle the size of the 90 percent probability circle for the circular case by using the ordinate $R/\sigma = 2.15$ (also equivalent to 1.82 times the CEP). These two curves are plotted in Figure 306e and the numerical values are given in Table 306d. It is to be noted that the probability values are not inversely related to the error factors plotted in the preceding curves. The geometric error factor is a simple trigonometric function; the probability curves are exponential functions.

307. Clarification of Terminology

The following discussion is presented to insure that there is no misunderstanding with respect to the use of terms having one meaning when discussing one-dimensional errors and another when discussing two-dimensional errors.

Although the basic problem of position location is concerned with the two dimensions necessary to describe an area, one-dimensional error measures are commonly applied to each of the two dimensions involved. As demonstrated in article 305, the use of the one-dimensional standard deviation of each line of position permitted a general approach to the consideration of the error ellipse.

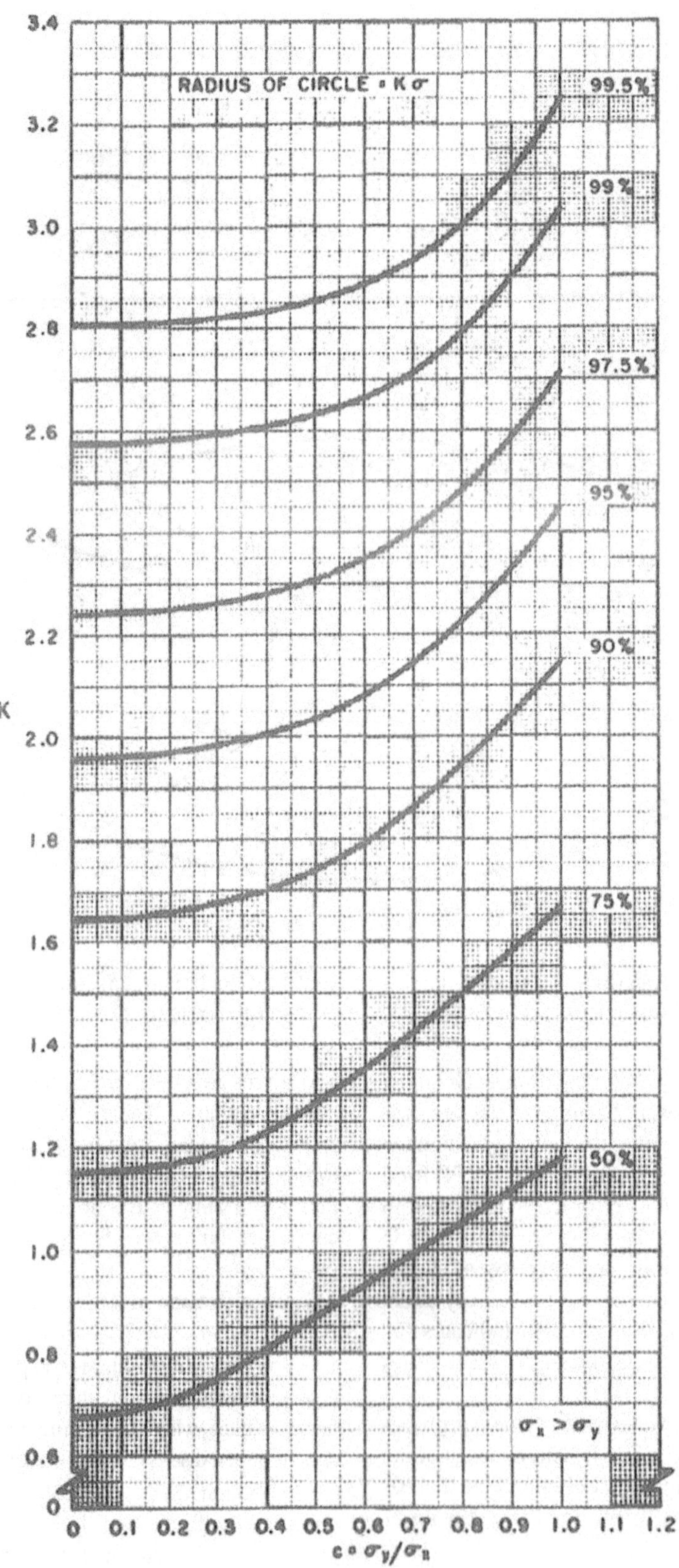

Figure 305g. Factors for conversion of probability ellipse to circle of equivalent probability.

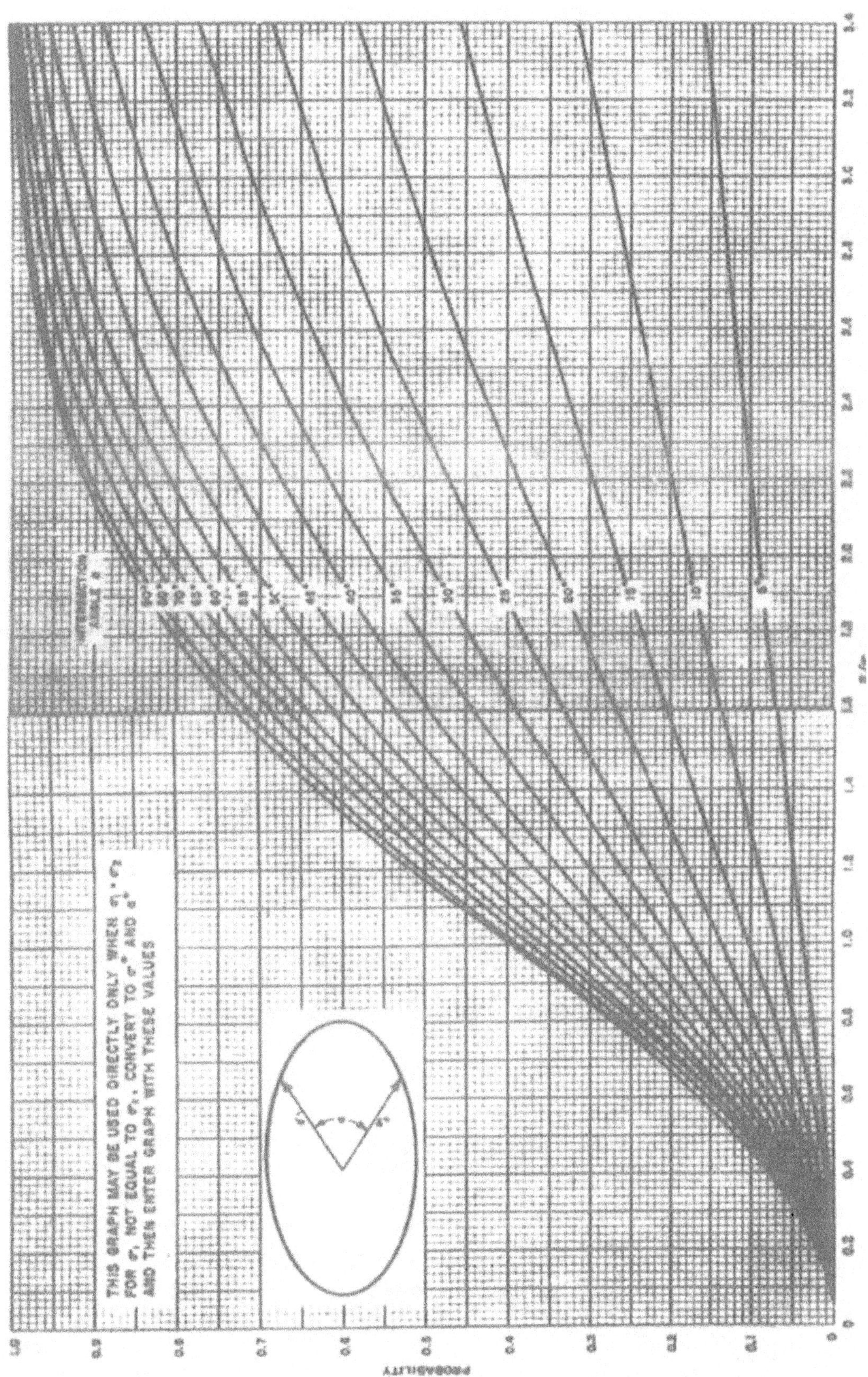

Figure 305h. Probability versus the radius of the circle divided by the standard error and the angle of cut for elliptical bivariate distributions with two equal standards deviations.

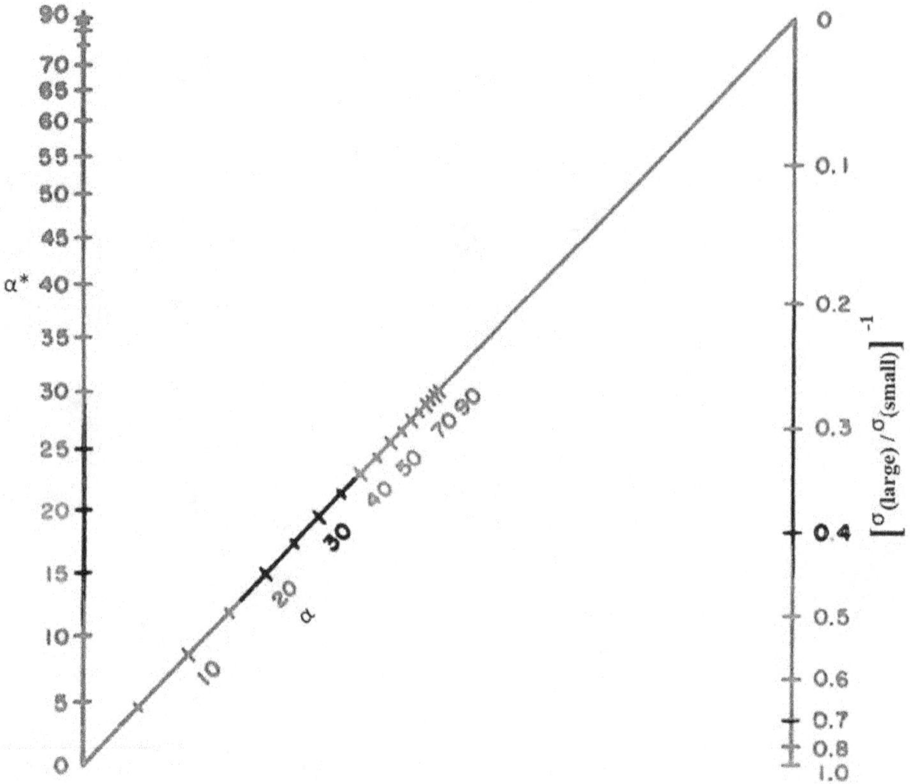

*Figure 305i. Nomogram to obtain α *.*

308. One-Dimensional Errors

The terms **standard deviation, sigma** (σ), and **root mean square (RMS) error** have the same meaning in reference to one-dimensional errors. The basic equation of the normal (Gaussian) distribution indicates the use of the Greek letter sigma, σ, from which its use for standard deviation arises:

$$f(x) = \frac{1}{\sigma\sqrt{2\pi}}e^{-\frac{(x-\mu)^2}{2\sigma^2}} \qquad -\infty < x < \infty$$

where the Greek letter μ is the mean of the distribution.

Standard deviation of a measurement system is a property that may be determined experimentally. If a large number of measurements of the same quantity, a length for example, are made and compared with their mean value, the standard deviation is the square root of the sum of the squares of the differences (deviations) of the measurements from the mean value divided by one less than the number of measurements taken. The mean, or average value, is the sum of the measurements divided by the number of the measurements. Symbolically this operation is represented as:

$$\sigma = \sqrt{\frac{\sum_{i=1}^{n}(x_i-\mu)^2}{n-1}}, \quad \mu = \frac{\sum_{i=1}^{n}x_i}{n}$$

The term root-mean-square (RMS) error comes from this latter method of computation.

Numerically, the values between the mean plus or minus one sigma (one standard deviation) corresponds to 68.27 percent of the distribution. That is, if a large number of measurements were made of a given quantity, 68.27 percent of the errors would be within the value of the mean plus or minus one standard deviation, or within $\mu \pm 1\sigma$. Likewise, errors within $\mu \pm 2\sigma$ correspond to 95.45 percent of the total errors and errors within $\mu \pm 3\sigma$ correspond to 99.73 percent of the total errors. Colloquially, these conditions are described as not exceeding the one-, two-, and three-sigma values, respectively.

The term probable error is identical in concept to standard deviation. The term differs from standard deviation in that it refers to the median error; that is, no more than half the errors in the measurement sample are greater than the value of the probable error. Linear probable error is related to standard deviation by a multiplication factor (Table 308a). One probable error equals 0.6745 times one standard deviation.

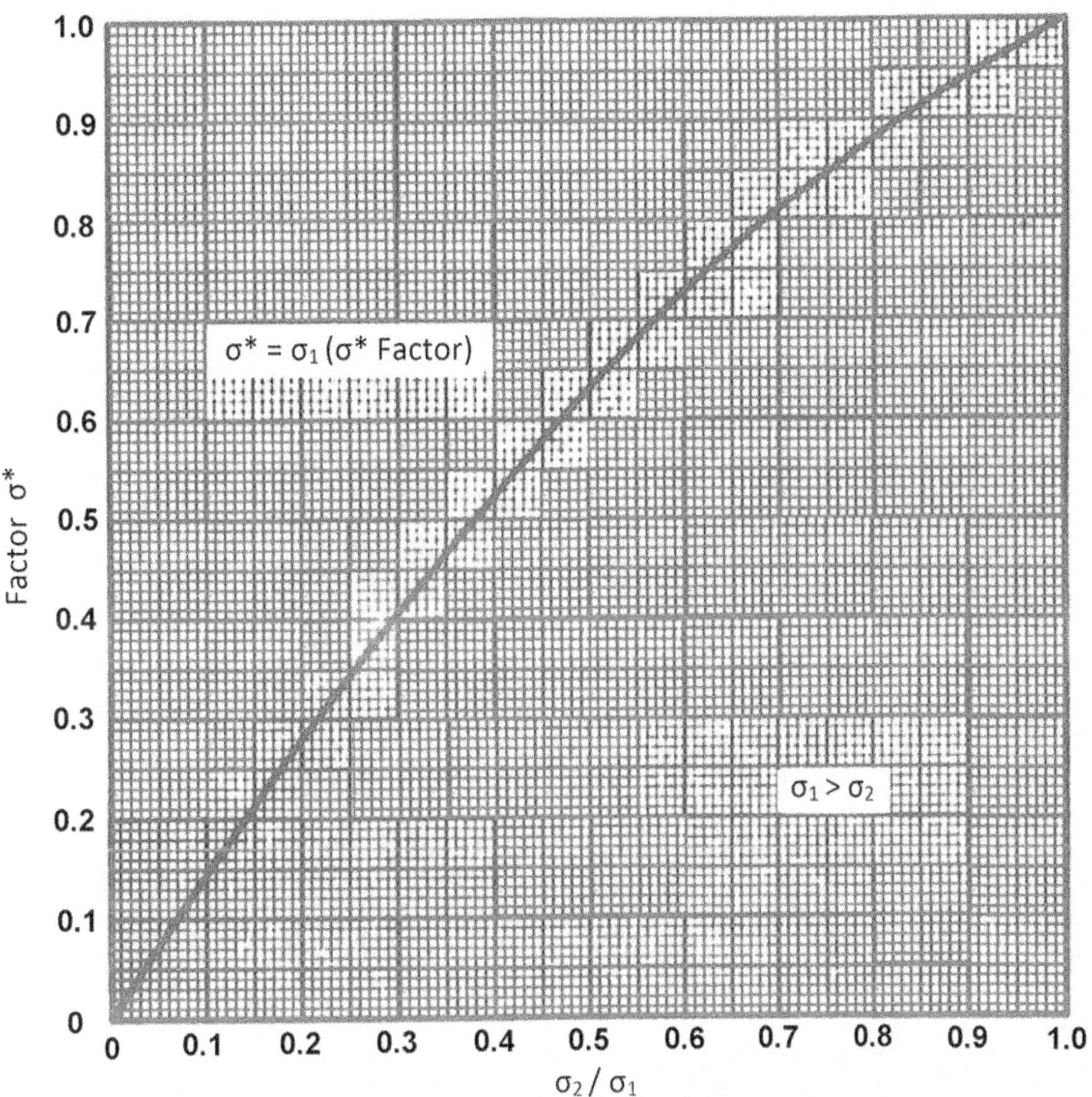

*Figure 305j. σ * factors versus / σ_2/σ_1 ratio.*

α	σ_x	σ_y	c	K	CEP	Error Factor
90	1.0	1.0	1.0	1.177	1.177	1.00
80	1.10	0.924	0.839	1.078	1.186	1.01
70	1.234	0.865	0.700	0.996	1.228	1.042
60	1.414	0.817	0.577	0.914	1.292	1.099
50	1.672	0.782	0.466	0.847	1.420	1.206
45	1.847	0.766	0.414	0.815	1.508	1.281
40	2.06	0.753	0364	0.783	1.620	1.376
30	2.74	0.733	0.268	0.734	2.01	1.710
20	4.06	0.718	0.176	0.700	2.85	2.42
10	8.11	0.710	0.087	0.680	5.52	4.69

Table 306a. Significant parameters of error ellipses when $\sigma_1 = \sigma_2$

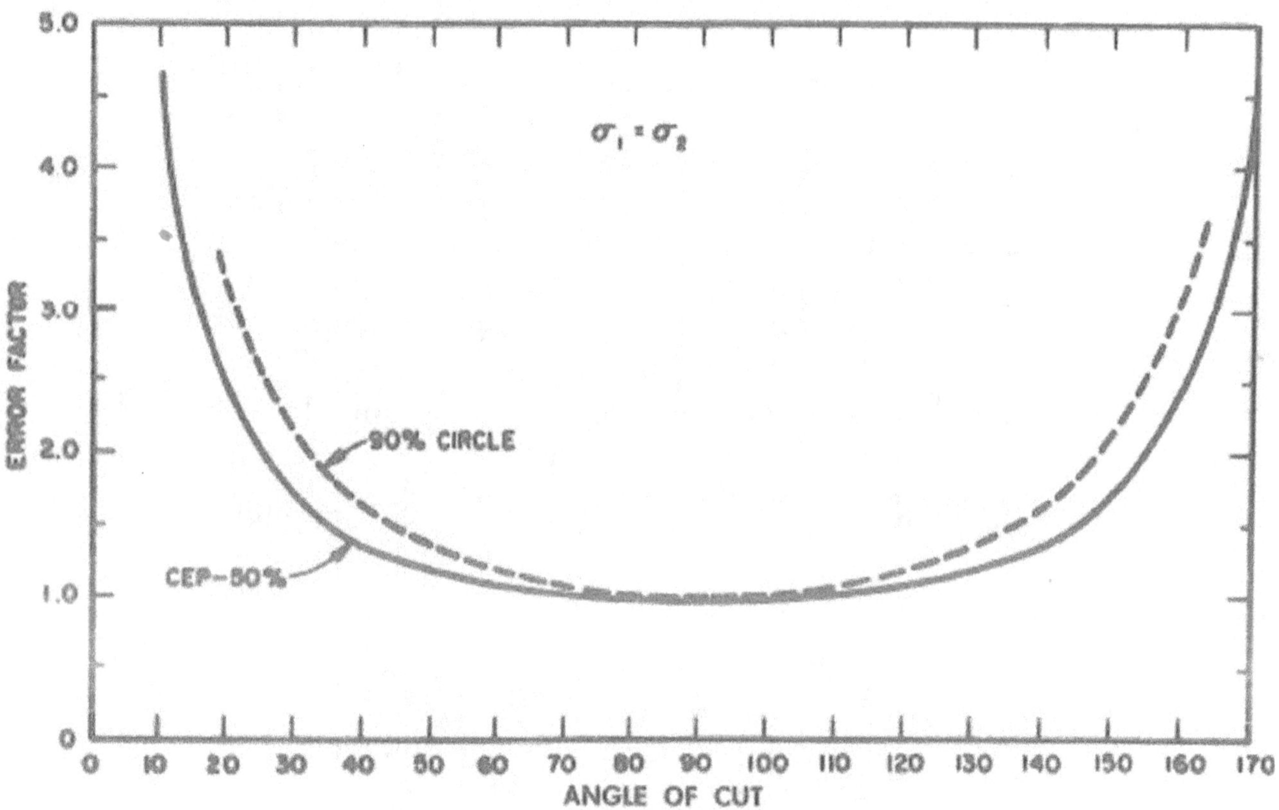

Figure 306b. CEP magnification versus angle of cut.

α	c	K	90% R	Error Factor
90	1.0	2.145	2.145	1.00
80	0.839	1.98	2.18	1.015
70	0.700	1.86	2.30	1.07
60	0.577	1.775	2.51	1.7
50	0.466	1.72	2.88	1.34
45	0.414	1.702	3.15	1.47
40	0.364	1.687	3.47	1.615
30	0.268	1.665	4.53	2.11
20	0.176	1.652	6.72	3.13
10	0.087	1.645	13.35	6.22

Table 306c. 90 percent error factor

α	P	P
90	50	90
80	49.4	89.2
70	47.5	86.9
60	44.0	82.4
50	39.5	76
40	37	66
30	25	53
20	17	37
10	8	19

Table 306d. Probability decrease with decreasing angle of cut for a circle of constant radius

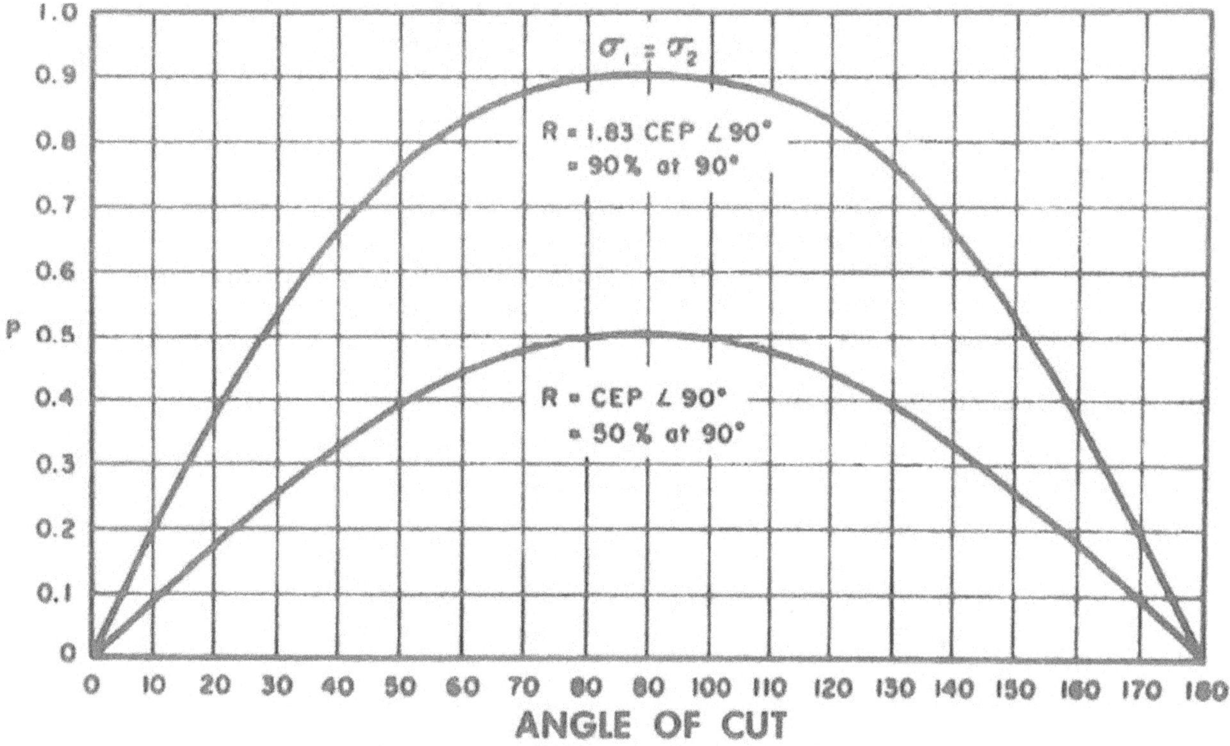

Figure 306e. Decrease in probability for a circle of constant radius versus angle of cut.

The term **variance** is met most frequently in detailed mathematical discussions.

From/To	50.00%	68.27%	95.00%	99.73%
50.00%	1.0000	1.4826	2.9059	4.4475
68.27%	0.6745	1.0000	1.9600	3.0000
95.00%	0.3441	0.5102	1.0000	1.5307
99.73%	0.2248	0.3333	0.6533	1.0000

Table 308a. Linear error conversion factors.

309. Two-Dimensional Error

Terms similar or identical in words to those used for one-dimensional error descriptions are also used with two-dimensional or **bivariate error** descriptions. However, in the two-dimensional case, not all of these terms have the same meaning as before; considerable care is needed to avoid confusion.

Standard deviation or **sigma** has a definable meaning only in the specific case of the circular normal distribution where $\sigma_x = \sigma_y$:

$$P_R = 1 - e\frac{R^2}{2\sigma^2}$$

In the case of the circular normal distribution, the standard deviation σ is equivalent to the standard deviation along both orthogonal axes. Because of concern with a radial distribution, the total distribution of errors involves numbers different from those of the linear case (Table 308a and Table 309a). In the circular case, 1σ error indicates that 39.35 percent of the errors would not exceed the value of the 1σ error; 86.47 percent would not exceed the 2σ error; 98.89 percent would not exceed the 3σ error; and 99.78 percent would not exceed the 3.5σ error.

From/To	39.35%	50.00%	63.21%	95.00%	99.78%
39.35%	1.0000	1.1774	1.4142	2.4477	3.5000
50.00%	0.8493	1.0000	1.2011	2.0789	2.9726
63.21%	0.7071	0.8325	1.0000	1.7308	2.4749
95.00%	0.4085	0.4810	0.5778	1.0000	1.4299

Table 309a. Circular error conversion factors.

From/To	39.35%	50.00%	63.21%	95.00%	99.78%
99.78%	0.2857	0.3364	0.4040	0.6993	1.0000

Table 309a. Circular error conversion factors.

Because the usual case where there are two-dimensional distributions is that the standard deviations are different, resulting in an elliptical distribution, the circular standard deviation is less useful than the linear standard deviation. It is more common to describe two-dimensional distributions by the two separate one-dimensional standard deviations associated with each error axis. References, however, often do not make this distinction, referring to the position accuracy of a system as 600 feet (2σ), for example. Such a description should leave the reader wondering whether the measure is circular error, in which case the numbers describe the 86 percent probability circle, or whether the number are to be interpreted as one-dimensional sigmas along each axis, in which case the 95 percent probability circle is indicated (assuming the distribution to be circular, which actually it may not be).

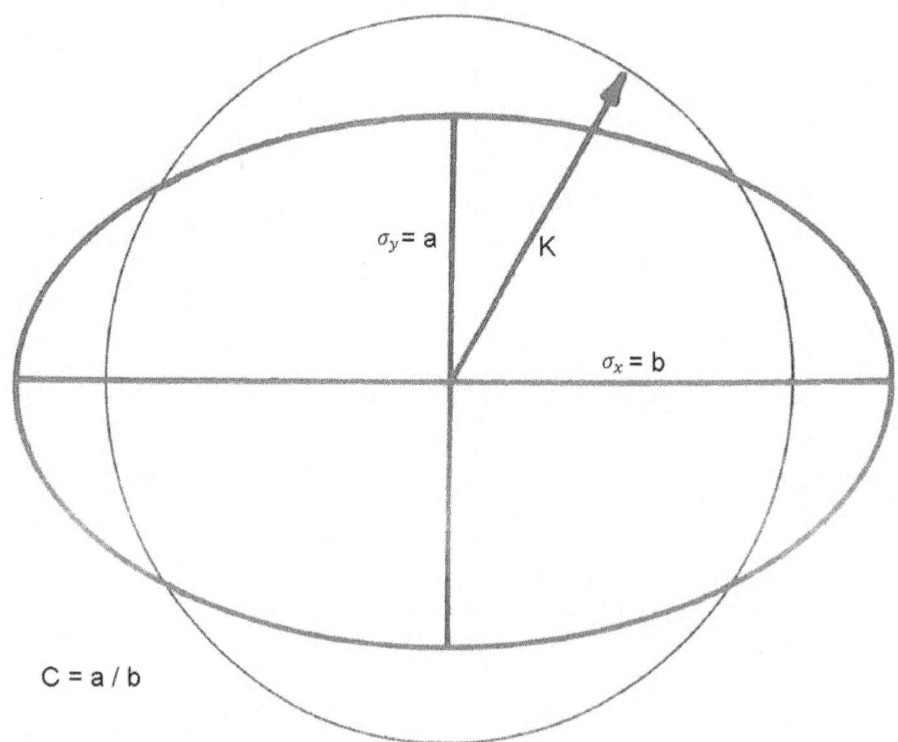

Figure 309b. Error ellipse and circle of equivalent probability.

The term **RMS (root mean square) error** when applied to two-dimensional errors does not have the same meaning as standard deviation. The term has the same meaning as radial error or d_{rms}, discussed later. Such use of the term is deprecated.

In a circular normal distribution, the term **circular probable error (CPE)** or **circular error probable (CEP)** refers to the radius of the circle inside of which there is a 50 percent probability of being located.

The term CEP is also used to indicate the radius of a circle inside of which there is a 50 percent probability of being located, even though the actual error figure (Figure 309b) is an ellipse. Article 305 describes one of the methods of obtaining such CEP equivalents when given ellipses of varying eccentricities. Curves and tables are available for performing this calculation. Despite the availability of these curves and tables, approximations are often made for this calculation of a CEP when the actual error distribution is elliptical. Several of these approximations are indicated and plotted for comparison with the exact curve in Figure 309c. Of the various approximations shown, the top curve, the one which diverges the most rapidly, appears to be the most commonly used.

Another factor of interest concerning the relationship of the CEP to various ellipses is that the area of the CEP circle is always greater than the basic ellipse. Table 309d indicates that the divergence between the actual area of the ellipse of interest and the circle of equivalent probability increases as the ellipse becomes thinner and more elongated.

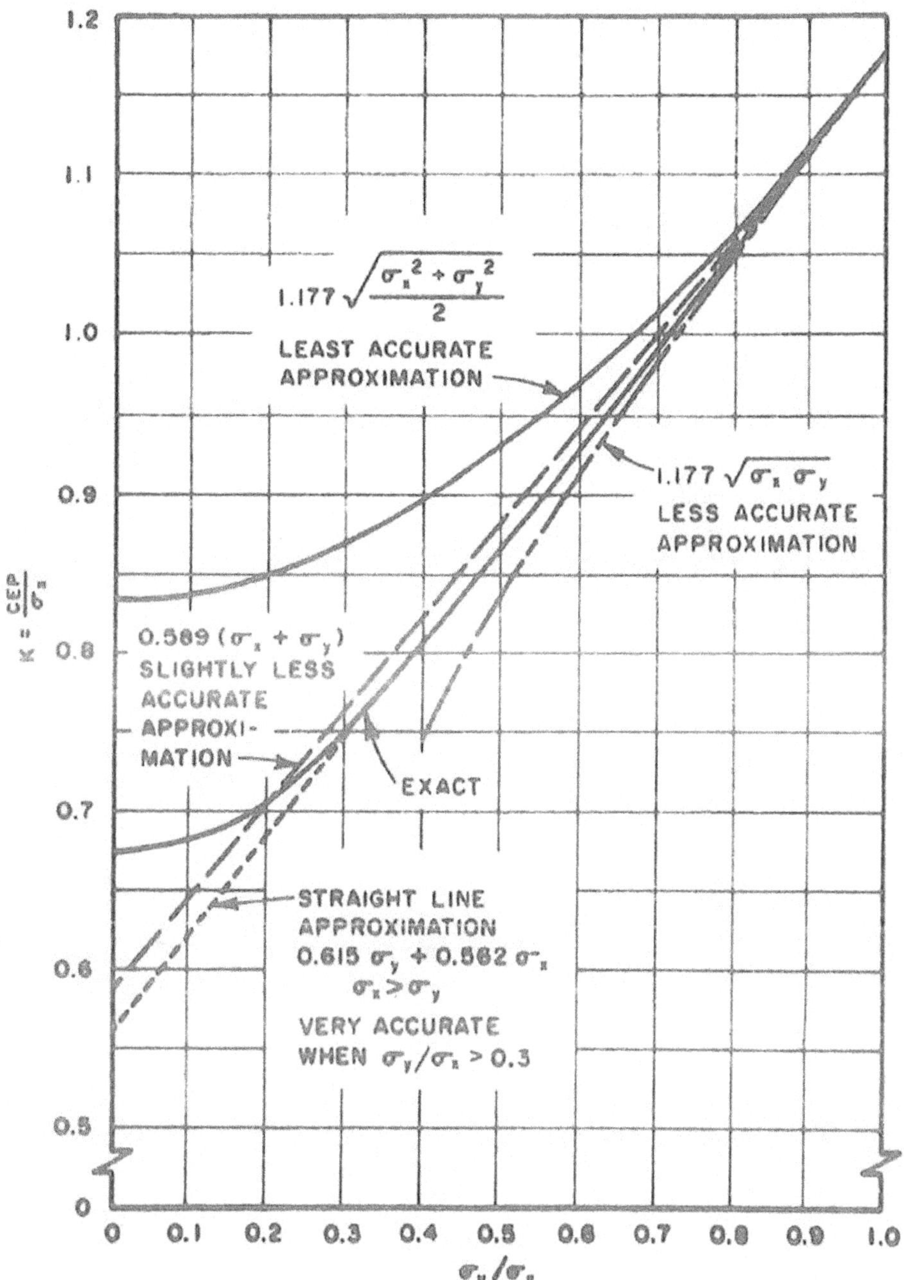

Figure 309c. CEP for elliptical error distribution approximations.

C = a / b	Area of 50% ellipse	Area of equivalent circle
0.0	0	1.43
0.1	0.437	1.46
0.2	0.874	1.56
0.3	1.31	1.76
0.4	1.75	2.06

Table 309d. Comparison of areas of 50% ellipses of varying eccentricities with areas of circles of equivalent probabilities.

C = a / b	Area of 50% ellipse	Area of equivalent circle
0.5	2.08	2.37
0.6	2.62	2.74
0.7	3.06	3.12
0.8	3.49	3.52
0.9	3.93	3.94
1.0	4.37	4.37

Table 309d. Comparison of areas of 50% ellipses of varying eccentricities with areas of circles of equivalent probabilities.

The value of the CEP may be related to the radius of other values of probability circles analytically for the case of the circular normal distribution by solving the basic equation for various values of probability. For this special case of the circular normal distribution, these relationships are shown drawn to scale in Figure 309e with the associated values tabulated in Table 309f.

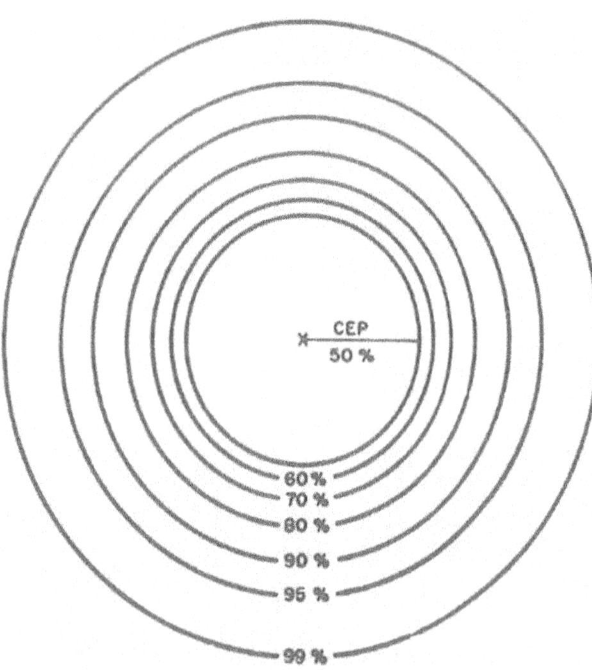

Figure 309e. Relationship between CEP and other probability circles.

Multiply values of CEP by	To obtain radii of circle of probability
1.150	60%
1.318	70%

Table 309f. Relationship between CEP and radii of other probabilities circles of the circular normal distribution.

Multiply values of CEP by	To obtain radii of circle of probability
1.414	75%
1.524	80%
1.655	85%
1.823	90%
2.079	95%
2.578	99%

Table 309f. Relationship between CEP and radii of other probabilities circles of the circular normal distribution.

The derivation of these values is shown in the following analysis. First, the factor relating the CEP to the circular sigma is derived, then, as a second example, the relationship between the 75 percent probability circle and the circular sigma is derived. The ratio of these two values is then the value shown in Table 309f for the 75 percent value.

The circular normal distribution equation is:

$$P_R = 1 - e - \frac{R^2}{2\sigma^2} ,$$

and

$$CEP = P(R) = 0.5$$

$$1 - e - \frac{R^2}{2\sigma^2} = 0.5$$

$$e - \frac{R^2}{2\sigma^2} = 0.5 .$$

Take the natural logarithm of both sides

$$\ln\left(e - \frac{R^2}{2\sigma^2}\right) = \ln 0.5$$

$$\frac{R^2}{2\sigma^2} = \ln 2 \qquad (\ln 0.5 = -\ln 2)$$

$$R = 1.1774\sigma .$$

For the 75 percent probability circle,

$$1 - e^{-\frac{R^2}{2\sigma^2}} = 0.75$$

$$e^{-\frac{R^2}{2\sigma^2}} = 0.25$$

$$\ln\left(e^{-\frac{R^2}{2\sigma^2}}\right) = \ln 0.25$$

$$\frac{R^2}{2\sigma^2} = \ln 4$$

$$R = 1.665\sigma$$

$$\frac{R(75\%)}{R(50\%)} = \frac{1.665\sigma}{1.177\sigma} = 1.414 .$$

The factors tabulated in Table 309f are sometimes used to relate varying probability circles when the basic distribution is not circular, but elliptical. That such a procedure is inaccurate may be seen by the curves of . It can be seen that the errors involved are small when the eccentricities are small. But the errors increase significantly when both high values of probability are desired and when the ellipticity increases in the direction of long, narrow distributions.

The terms **radial error, root mean square error,** and $\boldsymbol{d_{rms}}$ are identical in meaning when applied to two-dimensional errors. Figure 309h illustrates the definition of d_{rms}. It is seen to be the square root of the sum of the square of the 1 sigma error components along the major and minor axes of a probability ellipse. The figure details the definition of 1 d_{rms}. Similarly, other values of d_{rms} can be derived by using the corresponding values of sigma. The measure d_{rms} is not equal to the square root of the sum of the squares of σ_1 and σ_2 that are the basic errors associated with the lines of position of a particular measuring system. The procedures described in section 305 must first be utilized to obtain the values shown as σ_x and σ_y.

The three terms (radial error, root-mean-square error, and d_{rms}) used as a measure of error are somewhat confusing because they do not correspond to a fixed value of probability for a given value of the error measure. The terms can be conveniently related to other error measures only when $\sigma_x = \sigma_y$, and the probability figure is a circle. In the more common elliptical cases, the probability associated with a fixed value of d_{rms} varies as a function of the eccentricity of the ellipse. One d_{rms} is defined as the radius of the circle obtained when $\sigma_x = 1$, in Figure 309h, and σ_y varies from 0 to 1. Likewise, 2 d_{rms} is the radius of the circle obtained when $\sigma_x = 2$, and σ_y varies from 0 to 2. Values of the length of the radius d_{rms} can be calculated as shown in Table 309j. From these values the associated

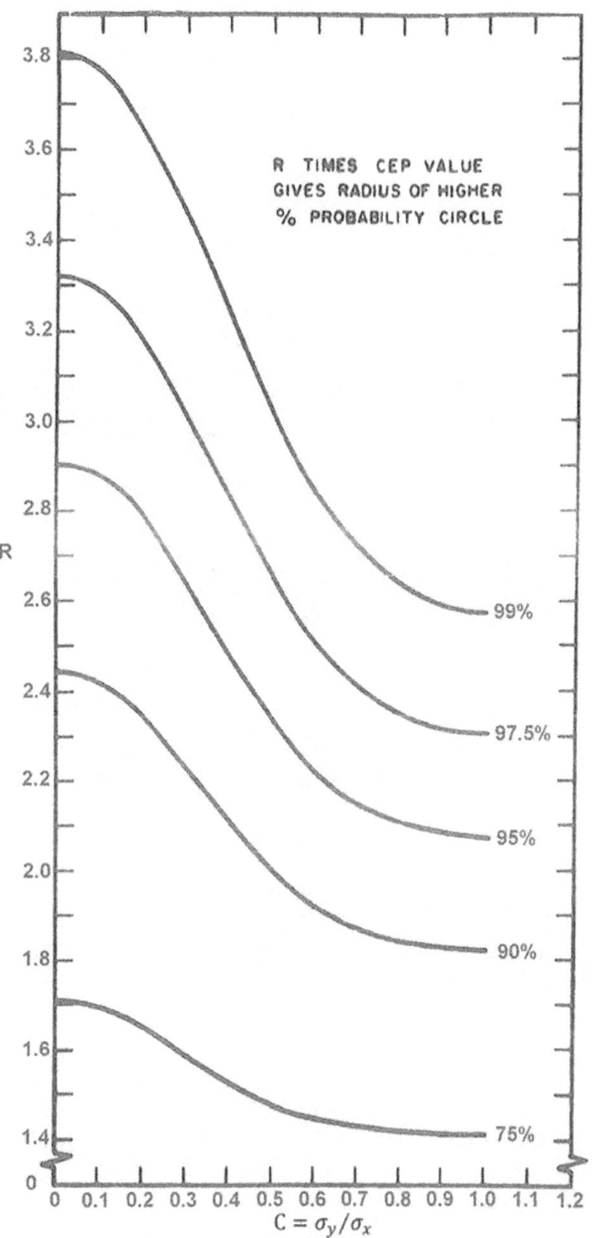

Figure 309g. Relation of probability circles to CEP versus ellipticity.

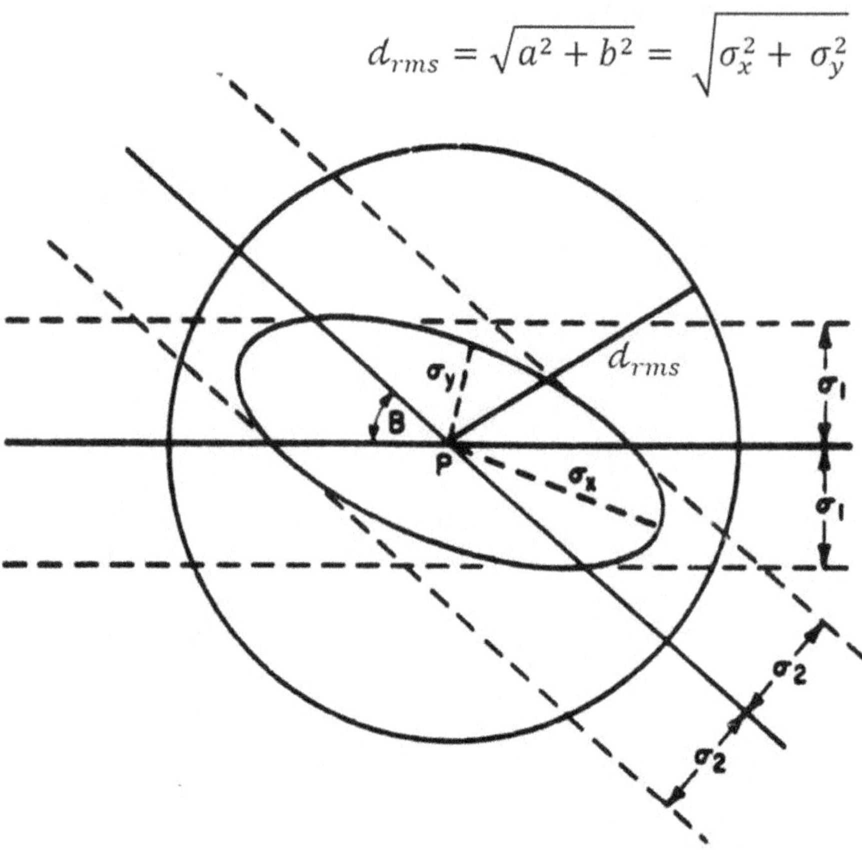

Figure 309h. CEP for elliptical error distribution approximations.

probabilities can be determined from the tables of section 305. The variations of probability associated with the values of 1 d_{rms} and 2 d_{rms} are shown in the curves of and . shows the lack of a constant relationship in a slightly different way. Here the ratio d_{rms}/CEP is plotted against the same measure of ellipticity. The three figures show graphically that there is not a constant value of probability associated with a single value of d_{rms}.

Figure 309i shows the substitution of the circular form for elliptical error distributions. When σ_x and σ_y are equal, the probability represented by 1 d_{rms} is 63.21 percent. When σ_x and σ_y are unequal (σ_x being the greater value), the probability varies from 64 percent when $\sigma_y/\sigma_x = 0.8$ to 68 percent when $\sigma_y/\sigma_x = 0.3$.

310. Navigation System Accuracy

In a navigation system, **predictability** is the measure of the accuracy with which the system can define the position in terms of geographical coordinates; **repeatability** is the measure of the accuracy with which the system permits the user to return to a position as defined only in terms of the coordinates peculiar to that system. **Predictable accuracy**, therefore, is the accuracy of positioning with respect to geographical coordinates; **repeatable accuracy** is the accuracy with which the user can return to a position whose coordinates have been measured previously with the same system. For example, the distance specified for the repeatable accuracy of a system such as GPS is the distance between two GPS positions established using the same satellites at different times. The correlation between the geographical coordinates and the system coordinates may or may not be known.

Relative accuracy is the accuracy with which a user can determine their position relative to that of another user of the same navigation system at the same time. Hence, a system with high relative accuracy provides good rendezvous capability for the users of the system. The correlation between the geographical coordinates and the system coordinates is not relevant.

311. Most Probable Position

Some navigators, particularly those of little experience, have been led by the simplified definitions and explanations usually given in texts to conclude that the line of position is infallible, and that a fix is without error, overlooking the frequent incompatibility of these two notions. Too often the idea has prevailed that information is either all right or all

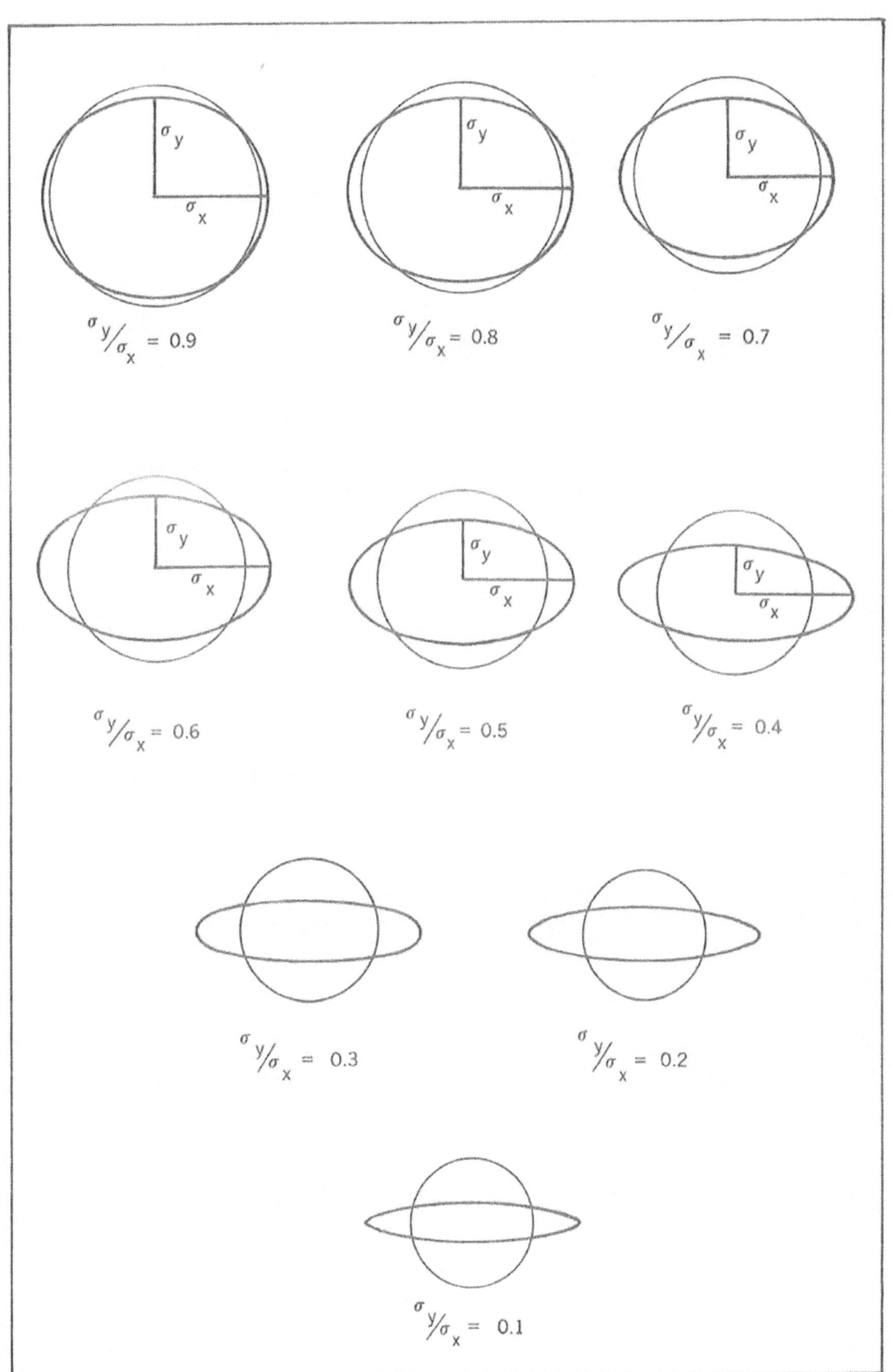

Figure 309i. Substitution of the circular form for elliptical error distributions.

σ_y	σ_x	LENGTH OF 1 d_{rms}	PROBABILITY	
			1 d_{rms}	2 d_{rms}
0.0	1.0	1.000	0.683	0.954
0.1	1.0	1.005	0.682	0.955
0.2	1.0	1.020	0.682	0.957
0.3	1.0	1.042	0.676	0.961
0.4	1.0	1.077	0.671	0.966
0.5	1.0	1.118	0.662	0.969
0.6	1.0	1.166	0.650	0.973
0.7	1.0	1.220	0.641	0.977
0.8	1.0	1.280	0.635	0.980
0.9	1.0	1.345	0.632	0.981
1.0	1.0	1.414	0.632	0.982
$d_{rms} = \sqrt{\sigma_x^2 + \sigma_y^2}$ when σ_x and σ_y are at right angles to each other.				

Table 309j. Calculations of d_{rms}.

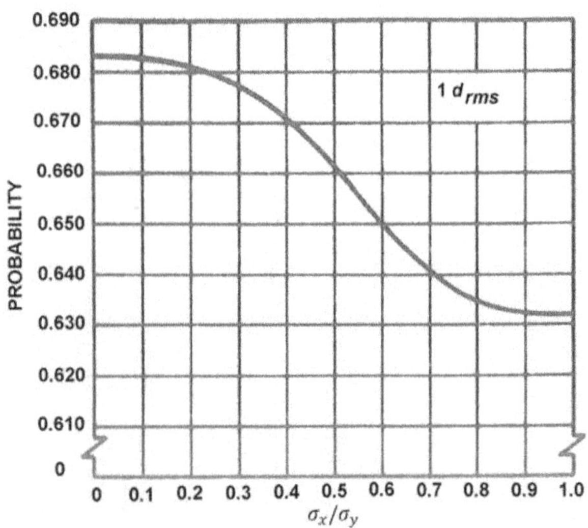

Figure 309k. Variation in d_{rms} with ellipticity (1 d_{rms})..

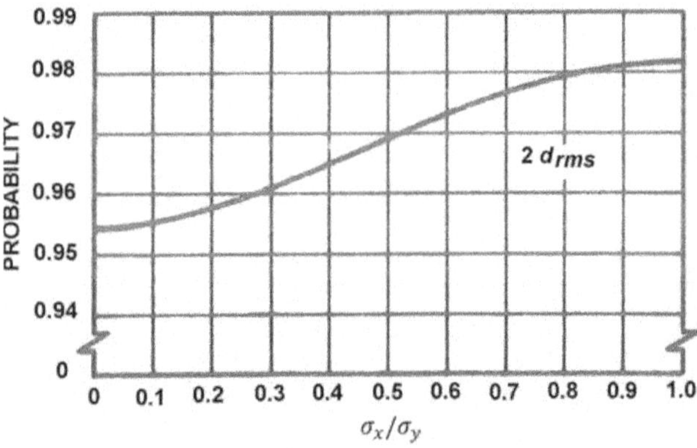

Figure 309l. Variation in d_{rms} with ellipticity (2 d_{rms}).

wrong. An example is the practice of establishing an estimated position at the foot of the perpendicular from a dead reckoning position to a line of position. The assumption is that the vessel *must* be somewhere on the line of position. The limitations of this often valuable practice are not understood by these inexperienced navigators.

A more realistic concept is that of the **most probable position (MPP)**, which recognizes the probability of error in *all* navigational information, and determines position by an evaluation of all available information, using the principles of errors.

Suppose a vessel were to start from a completely accurate position and proceed on dead reckoning. If course and speed over the bottom were of equal accuracy, the uncertainty of dead reckoning positions would increase equally in all directions with either distance or elapsed time (for any one speed these would be directly proportional and therefore either could be used). Therefore, a circle of uncertainty would grow around the dead reckon-

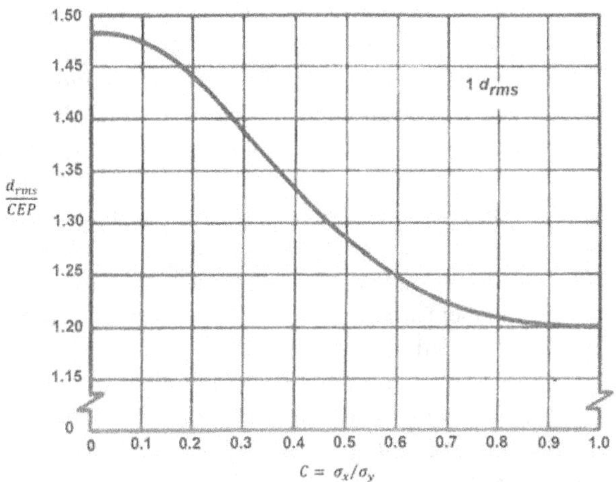

Figure 309m. Ellipticity versus d_{rms} /CEP (1 d_{rms}).

ing position as the vessel proceeded. If the navigator had full knowledge of the distribution and nature of the errors of course and speed, and the necessary knowledge of statistical analysis, s/he could compute the radius of the circle of uncertainty, using the 50 percent, 95 percent, or other probabilities.

In ordinary navigation, this is not practicable, but based upon experience and judgment, the navigator might estimate at any time the likely error of his or her dead reckoning or estimated position. With practice, navigators might acquire considerable skill in making this estimate. They would take into account, too, the fact that the area of uncertainty might be better represented by a circle, the major axis being along the course line if the estimated error of the speed were greater than that of the course, and the minor axis being along the course line if the estimated error of the course were greater. They would recognize, too, that the size of the area of uncertainty would not grow in direct proportion to the distance or elapsed time, because disturbing factors such as wind and current could not be expected to remain of constant magnitude and direction. Also, they would know that the starting point of the dead reckoning would not be completely free from error.

At some future time additional positional information would be obtained. This might be a line of position from a celestial observation. This, too, would be accompanied by an estimated error which might be computed for a certain probability if the necessary information and knowledge were available. If the dead reckoning had started from a good position obtained by means of landmarks, the likely error of the initial position would be very small. At first the dead reckoning or estimated position would probably be more reliable than a line of position obtained by celestial observation. But at *some* distance the two would be equal, and beyond this the line of position might be more accurate.

The determination of most probable position does depend upon *which* information is more accurate. In Figure 311a a dead reckoning position, $\mu_1 = 0.6$, is shown surrounded by a circle of uncertainty with one-sigma error σ_1. A line of position is also shown, with its area of uncertainty with one-sigma error σ_2. The most probable position is within the overlapping area, and if the uncertainty of the dead reckoning position and that of the line of position are about equal, it might be taken at the center of the line perpendicular to the line of position that runs through the dead reckoning position. The intersection of the line of position with the perpendicular is position $\mu_2 = 0.5$. The most probable position means are taken to have only components on the perpendicular. If the overall errors are considered normal, and they are probably approximately, *the effect of each error is proportional to its square, acting on the other position measurement.* Thus, if the likely error of the dead reckoning position is $\sigma_1 = 3$ miles, and that of a line of position is $\sigma_2 =$ 2 miles, the most probable position is nearer the line of position, being given by

$$\mu = \frac{\sigma_2^2}{\sigma_1^2 + \sigma_2^2}\mu_1 + \frac{\sigma_1^2}{\sigma_1^2 + \sigma_2^2}\mu_2 =$$

$$\frac{3^2}{3^2 + 2^2}0.5 + \frac{2^2}{3^2 + 2^2}0.6 = \frac{9}{13}0.5 + \frac{4}{13}0.6 \approx 0.53$$

with an uncertainty given by

$$\frac{1}{\sigma^2} = \frac{1}{\sigma_1^2} + \frac{1}{\sigma_2^2}$$

or

$$\sigma = \sqrt{\frac{\sigma_1^2 + \sigma_2^2}{\sigma_1^2\sigma_2^2}} = \sqrt{\frac{2^2 + 3^2}{2^2 3^2}} = \sqrt{\frac{13}{36}} \approx 0.60$$

showing that the uncertainty of combining the two position estimates results in a position error smaller than that of either of the two contributing errors.

If a fix is obtained from two lines of position, the area of uncertainty is a circle if the lines are perpendicular, have equal likely errors, and these errors can be considered normal. If one is considered more accurate than the other, the area is an ellipse, the two axes being proportional to the standard deviations of the two lines of position. As shown in Figure 311b, it is also an ellipse if the likely error of each is equal and the lines cross at an oblique angle. If the errors are unequal, the major axis of the ellipse is more nearly in line with the line of position having the smaller likely error.

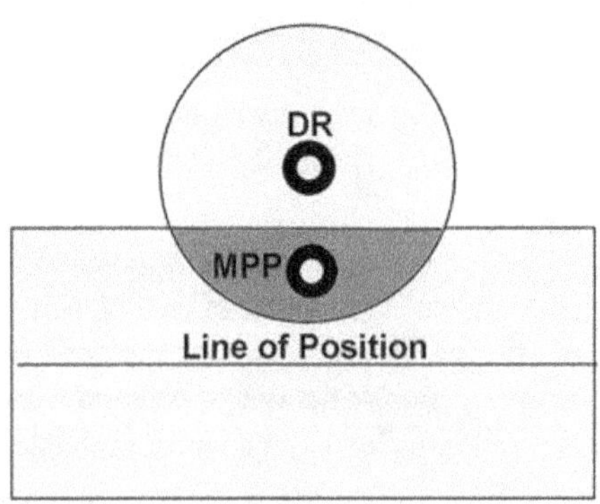

Figure 311a. A most probable position based upon a dead reckoning position and line of position having equal probable errors.

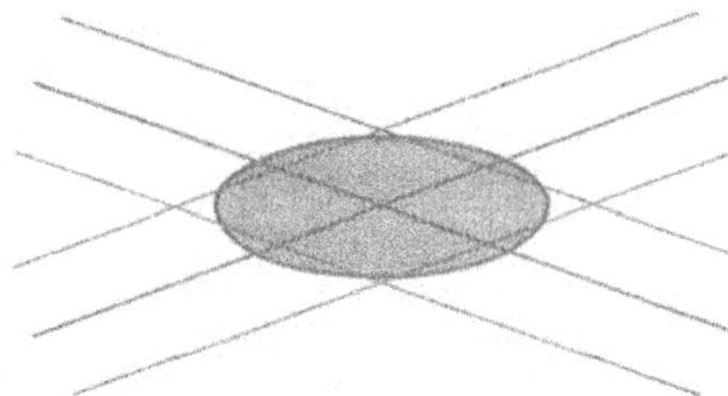

Figure 311b. Ellipse of uncertainty with line of positions of equal probable errors crossing at an oblique angle.

If a fix is obtained from three or more lines of position spread in azimuth by more than 180°, and the error of each line is normal and equal to that of the others, the most probable position is the center of the figure. By "center" is meant that point within the figure which is equidistant from the sides. If the lines are of unequal likely error, the distance of the most probable position from each line of position is proportional to the *square* of the likely error of that line times the sine of the angle formed by the other two lines.

In the discussion of most probable position from lines of position, it has been assumed that no other positional information is available. Usually, this is an incorrect assumption, for there is nearly always a dead reckoning or estimated position. This can be considered in any of several ways. The square of its likely error can be used in the same manner as the square of the likely error of each line of position. A most probable position based upon the dead reckoning or estimated position and the most reliable line of position might be determined as explained above, and that line of position replaced with a new one parallel to it but passing through the most probable position just determined. This adjusted line of position can then be assigned a smaller likely error and used with the other lines of position to determine the overall most probable position. A third way is to establish a likely error for the fix, and consider the most probable position as that point along the straight line joining the fix and the dead reckoning or estimated position, the relative distances being equal to the square of the likely error of each position.

The value of the most probable position determined as suggested above depends upon the degree to which the various errors are in fact normal, and the accuracy with which the likely error of each is established. From a practical standpoint, the second factor is largely a matter of judgment based upon experience. It might seem that interpretation of results and establishment of most probable position is a matter of judgment anyway, and that the procedure outlined above is not needed. If a person will follow this procedure while gaining experience, and evaluate his or her results, the judgment developed should be more reliable than if developed without benefit of knowledge of the principles that are involved. The important point to remember is that the relative effects of normal random errors in any one direction are proportional to their *squares*.

Systematic errors are treated differently. Generally, an attempt is made to discover the errors and eliminate them or compensate for them. In the case of a position determined by three or more lines of position resulting from readings with constant error, the error might be eliminated by finding and applying that correction (including sign) which will bring all lines through a common point.

312. Mistakes

The recognition of a mistake, as contrasted with an error (Section 301), is not always easy, since a mistake may have any magnitude, and may be either positive or negative. A large mistake should be readily apparent if the navigator is alert and has an understanding of the size of error to be reasonably expected. A small mistake is usually not detected unless the work is checked.

If results by two methods are compared, as a dead reckoning position and a line of position, exact agreement is not to be expected. But if the discrepancy is unreasonably large, a mistake is logically suspected. The definition of "unreasonably large" is a matter of opinion. If the 99.9 percent areas of the two results just touch, it is *possible* that no mistake has been made. However, the *probability* of either one having so great an error is remote if the errors are normal. The probability of both having 99.9 percent error of opposite sign at the same instant is very small indeed. Perhaps a reasonable standard is that unless the most accurate result lies within the 95 percent area of the least accurate result, the possibility of a mistake should be investigated. Thus, if the areas of uncertainty shown in Figure 311a represent the 95 percent areas, it is probable that a mistake has been made.

As in other matters pertaining to navigation, judgment is important. The use to be made of the results is certainly a consideration. In the middle of an ocean passage a mistake is usually not serious, and will undoubtedly be corrected before it jeopardizes the safety of the vessel. But if landfall is soon to be made, or if search and rescue operations are to be based upon the position, almost any mistake is intolerable.

313. Conclusion

The correct identification of the nature of an error is important if the error is to be handled intelligently. Thus, the statement is sometimes made that a radio bearing need not be corrected if the receiver is within 50 miles of the transmitter.

The need for a correction arises from the fact that radio waves are assumed to follow great circles, and if radio bearings are to be plotted on a Mercator chart, the equivalent rhumb line is needed. The statement regarding 50 miles implies that the size of the correction is proportional to distance only. It overlooks the fact that latitude and direction of the bearing line are also important factors, and is therefore a dangerous statement unless its limitations are understood.

The recognition of the type of error is also important. A systematic error has quite a different effect than a random error, and cannot be reduced by additional readings unless some method or procedure is instituted which will cause the errors to cancel each other.

The errors for various percentage probabilities are usually of greater interest than the "average" value. The average of a large number of normal errors approaches zero, but the probable (50 percent) error might be quite large.

A person who understands the nature of errors avoids many pitfalls. Thus, the magnitude of the errors of individual lines of position is not a reliable indication of the size of the error of the fix obtained from them. The size of the ·triangle formed by three lines of position has often been used as a guide to the accuracy of the fix, although a large triangle might be the result of a large constant error if the objects observed are equally spaced in azimuth. On the other hand, two lines of position with small errors might produce a fix having a much larger error if the lines cross at a small angle.

314. References

Burt, W. A., Kaplan, D. J., Keenly, R. R., et al. (1965). *Mathematical Considerations Pertaining to the Accuracy of Position Location and Navigation Systems.* Naval Warfare Research Center Research Memorandum NWRC-RM 34, Stanford Research Institute, Menlo Park, California.

Greenwalt, C. R. and Shultz, M. E. (1962). *Principles of Error Theory and Cartographic Applications.* Aeronautical Chart and Information Center Technical Report No. 96, St. Louis, Missouri.

CHAPTER 4

CALCULATIONS AND CONVERSIONS

INTRODUCTION

400. Purpose and Scope

This chapter discusses the use of calculators and computers in navigation and summarizes the formulas the navigator depends on during voyage planning, piloting, celestial navigation, and various related tasks. To fully utilize this chapter, the navigator should be competent in basic mathematics including algebra and trigonometry (see Chapter 1 - Mathematics in Volume II) and be familiar with the use of a basic scientific calculator. The navigator should choose a calculator based on personal needs, which may vary greatly from person to person according to individual abilities and responsibilities.

401. Use of Calculators in Navigation

Any common calculator can be used in navigation, even one providing only the four basic arithmetic functions of addition, subtraction, multiplication, and division. Any good scientific calculator can be used for sight reduction, sailings, and other tasks. However, the use computer applications and handheld calculators specifically designed for navigation will greatly reduce the workload of the navigator, reduce the possibility of errors, and assure accuracy of the results calculated.

Calculations of position based on celestial observations have become increasingly uncommon since the advent of GPS as a dependable position reference for all modes of navigation. This is especially true since GPS units provide worldwide positioning with far greater accuracy and reliability than celestial navigation.

However, for those who use celestial techniques, a celestial navigation calculator or computer application can improve celestial position accuracy by easily solving numerous sights, and by reducing mathematical and tabular errors inherent in the manual sight reduction process. They can also provide weighted plots of the LOP's from any number of celestial bodies, based on the navigator's subjective analysis of each sight, and calculate the best fix with latitude/longitude readout.

In using a calculator for any navigational task, it is important to remember that the accuracy of the result, even if carried out many decimal places, is only as good as the least accurate entry. If a sextant observation is taken to an accuracy of only a minute, that is the best accuracy of the final solution, regardless the calculator's ability to solve to 12 decimal places. See Chapter 3 - Navigational Error in Volume II for a discussion of the sources of error in navigation.

Some basic calculators require the conversion of degrees, minutes and seconds (or tenths) to decimal degrees before solution. A good navigational calculator, however, should permit entry of degrees, minutes and tenths of minutes directly, and should do conversions automatically. Though many non-navigational computer programs have an on-screen calculator, they are generally very simple versions with only the four basic arithmetical functions. They are thus too simple for complex navigational problems. Conversely, a good navigational computer program requires no calculator per se, since the desired answer is calculated automatically from the entered data.

The following articles discuss calculations involved in various aspects of navigation.

402. Calculations of Piloting

- **Hull speed in knots** is found by:

  $$S = 1.34\sqrt{\text{waterline length}}\ \text{(in feet)}.$$

  This is an approximate value which varies with hull shape.

- **Nautical and U.S. survey miles** can be interconverted by the relationships:

  1 nautical mile = 1.15077945 U.S. survey miles.

  1 U.S. survey mile = 0.86897624 nautical miles.

- **The speed of a vessel over a measured mile** can be calculated by the formula:

  $$S = \frac{3600}{T}$$

  where S is the speed in knots and T is the time in seconds.

- **The distance traveled at a given speed** is computed

by the formula:

$$D = \frac{ST}{60}$$

where D is the distance in nautical miles, S is the speed in knots, and T is the time in minutes.

- **Distance to the visible horizon in nautical miles** can be calculated using the formula:

$$D = 1.17\sqrt{h_f}\text{ , or}$$

$$D = 2.07\sqrt{h_m}$$

depending upon whether the height of eye of the observer above sea level is in feet (h_f) or in meters (h_m).

- **Dip of the visible horizon in minutes of arc** can be calculated using the formula:

$$D = 0.97'\sqrt{h_f}\text{ , or}$$

$$D = 1.76'\sqrt{h_m}$$

depending upon whether the height of eye of the observer above sea level is in feet (h_f) or in meters (h_m)

- **Distance to the radar horizon** in nautical miles can be calculated using the formula:

$$D = 1.22\sqrt{h_f}\text{ , or}$$

$$D = 2.21\sqrt{h_m}$$

depending upon whether the height of the antenna above sea level is in feet (h_f) or in meters (h_m).

- **Dip of the sea short of the horizon** can be calculated using the formula:

$$Ds = 60\tan^{-1}\left(\frac{h_f}{6076.1\,d_s} + \frac{d_s}{8268}\right)$$

where Ds is the dip short of the horizon in minutes of arc; h_f is the height of eye of the observer above sea level, in feet and d_s is the distance to the waterline of the object in nautical miles.

- **Distance by vertical angle between the waterline and the top of an object** is computed by solving the right triangle formed between the observer, the top of the object, and the waterline of the object by simple trigonometry. This assumes that the observer is at sea level, the Earth is flat between observer and object, there is no refraction, and the object and its waterline form a right angle. For most cases of practical significance, these assumptions produce no large errors.

$$D = \sqrt{\frac{\tan^2 a}{0.0002419^2} + \frac{H-h}{0.7349}} - \frac{\tan a}{0.0002419}$$

where D is the distance in nautical miles, a is the corrected vertical angle, H is the height of the top of the object above sea level, and h is the observer's height of eye in feet. The constants (0.0002419 and 0.7349) account for refraction.

403. Tide Calculations

- **The rise and fall of a diurnal tide** can be roughly calculated from the following table, which shows the fraction of the total range the tide rises or falls during flood or ebb.

Hour	Amount of flood/ebb
1	1/12
2	2/12
3	3/12
4	3/12
5	2/12
6	1/12

404. Calculations of Celestial Navigation

Unlike sight reduction by tables, sight reduction by calculator permits the use of nonintegral values of latitude of the observer, and LHA and declination of the celestial body. Interpolation is not needed, and the sights can be readily reduced from any assumed position. Simultaneous, or nearly simultaneous, observations can be reduced using a single assumed position. Using the observer's DR or MPP for the assumed longitude usually provides a better representation of the circle of equal altitude, particularly at high observed altitudes.

- **The dip correction** is computed in the *Nautical Almanac* using the formula:

$$D = 0.97\sqrt{h}$$

where dip is in minutes of arc and h is height of eye in feet. This correction includes a factor for refraction. The *Air Almanac* uses a different formula intended for air navigation. The differences are of no significance in practical navigation.

- **The computed altitude** (Hc) is calculated using the basic formula for solution of the undivided navigational triangle:

$$\sin h = \sin L \sin d + \cos L \cos d \cos LHA,$$

in which h is the altitude to be computed (Hc), L is the latitude of the assumed position, d is the declination of the celestial body, and LHA is the local hour angle of the body. Meridian angle (t) can be substituted for LHA in the basic formula.

Restated in terms of the inverse trigonometric function:

$$Hc = \sin^{-1}[(\sin L \ \sin d) + (\cos L \cos d \ \cos LHA)].$$

When latitude and declination are of contrary name, declination is treated as a negative quantity. No special sign convention is required for the local hour angle, as in the following azimuth angle calculations.

- **The azimuth angle** (Z) can be calculated using the altitude azimuth formula if the altitude is known. The formula stated in terms of the inverse trigonometric function is:

$$Z = \cos^{-1}\left(\frac{\sin d - (\sin L \sin Hc)}{(\cos L \cos Hc)}\right)$$

If the altitude is unknown or a solution independent of altitude is required, the azimuth angle can be calculated using the time azimuth formula:

$$Z = \tan^{-1}\left(\frac{\sin LHA}{(\cos L \tan d) - (\sin L \cos LHA)}\right)$$

The sign conventions used in the calculations of both azimuth formulas are as follows: (1) if latitude and declination are of contrary name, declination is treated as a negative quantity; (2) if the local hour angle is greater than 180°, it is treated as a negative quantity.

If the azimuth angle as calculated is negative, add 180° to obtain the desired value.

- **Amplitudes** can be computed using the formula:

$$A = \sin^{-1}(\sin d \sec L)$$

this can be stated as

$$A = \sin^{-1}\left(\frac{\sin d}{\cos L}\right)$$

where A is the arc of the horizon between the prime vertical and the body, L is the latitude at the point of observation, and d is the declination of the celestial body.

405. Calculations of the Sailings

- **Plane sailing** is based on the assumption that the meridian through the point of departure, the parallel through the destination, and the course line form a plane right triangle, as shown in Figure 405.

From this: $\cos C = \frac{l}{D}$, $\sin C = \frac{p}{D}$, and $\tan C = \frac{p}{l}$.

From this: $l = D \cos C$, $D = l \sec C$, and $p = D \sin C$.

From this, given course and distance (C and D), the difference of latitude (l) and departure (p) can be found, and given the latter, the former can be found, using simple trigonometry. See Chapter 12 - The Sailings, Volume I.

- **Traverse sailing** combines plane sailings with two or more courses, computing course and distance along a series of rhumb lines. See Chapter 12 - The Sailings, Volume I.

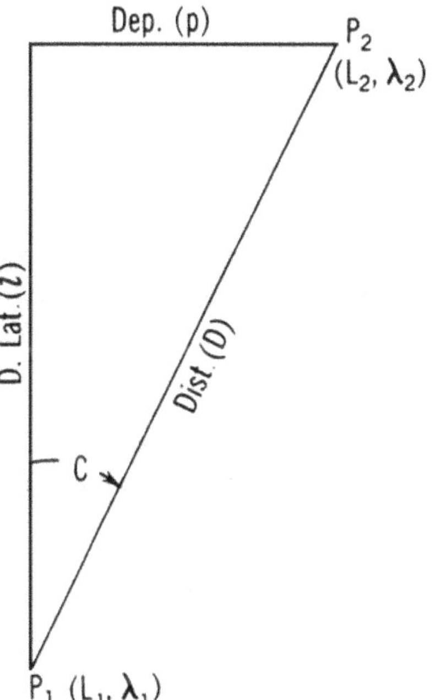

Figure 405. The plane sailing triangle.

- **Parallel sailing** consists of interconverting departure and difference of longitude. Refer to Figure 405.

$$DLo = p \sec L, \text{ and } p = DLo \cos L$$

- **Mid-latitude sailing** combines plane and parallel sailing, with certain assumptions. The mean latitude (Lm) is half of the arithmetical sum of the latitudes of two places on the same side of the equator. For places on opposite sides of the equator, the N and S portions are solved separately.

In mid-latitude sailing:

$$DLo = p \sec Lm, \text{ and } p = DLo \cos Lm$$

- **Mercator Sailing** problems are solved graphically on a Mercator chart. For mathematical Mercator solutions the formulas are:

$$\tan C = \frac{DLo}{m} \text{ or } DLo = m \tan C$$

where m is the meridional part from Table 6 in the Tables Part of this volume. Following solution of the course angle by Mercator sailing, the distance is by the plane sailing formula:

$$D = l \sec C.$$

- **Great-circle solutions for distance and initial course angle** can be calculated from the formulas:

$$D = \cos^{-1}[(\sin L_1 \sin L_2 + \cos L_1 \cos L_2 \cos DLo)],$$

and

$$C = \tan^{-1}\left(\frac{\sin DLo}{(\cos L_1 \tan L_2) - (\sin L_1 \cos DLo)}\right)$$

where D is the great-circle distance, C is the initial great-circle course angle, L_1 is the latitude of the point of departure, L_2 is the latitude of the destination, and DLo is the difference of longitude of the points of departure and destination. If the name of the latitude of the destination is contrary to that of the point of departure, it is treated as a negative quantity.

- **The latitude of the vertex,** L_v, is always numerically equal to or greater than L_1 or L_2. If the initial course angle C is less than 90°, the vertex is toward L_2, but if C is greater than 90°, the nearer vertex is in the opposite direction. The vertex nearer L_1 has the same name as L_1.

The latitude of the vertex can be calculated from the formula:

$$L_v = \cos^{-1}(\cos L_1 \sin C)$$

The difference of longitude of the vertex and the point of departure (DLo_v) can be calculated from the formula:

$$DLo_v = \sin^{-1}\left(\frac{\cos C}{\sin L_v}\right).$$

The distance from the point of departure to the vertex (D_v) can be calculated from the formula:

$$D_v = \sin^{-1}(\cos L_1 \sin DLo_v).$$

- **The latitudes of points on the great-circle track** can be determined for equal DLo intervals each side of the vertex (DLo_{vx}) using the formula:

$$L_x = \tan^{-1}(\cos DLo_{vx} \tan L_v)$$

The DLo_v and D_v of the nearer vertex are never greater than 90°. However, when L_1 and L_2 are of contrary name, the other vertex, 180° away, may be the better one to use in the solution for points on the great-circle track if it is nearer the mid point of the track.

The method of selecting the longitude (or DLo_{vx}), and determining the latitude at which the great-circle crosses the selected meridian, provides shorter legs in higher latitudes and longer legs in lower latitudes. Points at desired distances or desired equal intervals of distance on the great-circle from the vertex (D_{vx}) can be calculated using the formulas:

$$L_x = \sin^{-1}[\sin L_v \cos D_{vx}],$$

and

$$DLo_{vx} = \sin^{-1}\left(\frac{\sin D_{vx}}{\cos L_x}\right).$$

A calculator which converts rectangular to polar coordinates provides easy solutions to plane sailings. However, the user must know whether the difference of latitude corresponds to the calculator's X-coordinate or to the Y-coordinate.

406. Calculations of Meteorology and Oceanography

- **Converting thermometer scales** between centigrade, Fahrenheit, and Kelvin scales can be done using the following formulas:

$$C° = \frac{5(F° - 32°)}{9},$$

$$F° = \frac{9}{5}C° + 32°, \text{ and}$$

$$K° = C° + 273.15°.$$

- **Maximum length of sea waves** can be found by the formula:

  $$W = 1.5\sqrt{\text{fetch in nautical miles}}\ .$$

- **Wave height** = 0.026 S^2 where S is the wind speed in knots.

- **Wave speed** in knots

  $$= 1.34\sqrt{\text{wavelength in feet}}, \text{ or}$$

  $$= 3.03 \times \text{wave period in seconds.}$$

UNIT CONVERSION

Use the conversion tables that appear on the following pages to convert between different systems of units. Conversions followed by an asterisk * are exact relationships.

MISCELLANEOUS DATA

Area

1 square inch	= 6.4516 square centimeters*
1 square foot	= 144 square inches*
	= 0.09290304 square meter*
	= 0.000022957 acre
1 square yard	= 9 square feet*
	= 0.83612736 square meter
1 square (statute) mile	= 27,878,400 square feet*
	= 640 acres*
	= 2.589988110336 square kilometers*
1 square centimeter	= 0.1550003 square inch
	= 0.00107639 square foot
1 square meter	= 10.76391 square feet
	= 1.19599005 square yards
1 square kilometer	= 247.1053815 acres
	= 0.38610216 square statute mile
	= 0.29155335 square nautical mile

Astronomy

1 mean solar unit	= 1.00273791 sidereal units
1 sidereal unit	= 0.99726957 mean solar units
1 microsecond	= 0.000001 second*
1 second	= 1,000,000 microseconds*
	= 0.01666667 minute
	= 0.00027778 hour
	= 0.00001157 day
1 minute	= 60 seconds*
	= 0.01666667 hour
	= 0.00069444 day
1 hour	= 3,600 seconds*
	= 60 minutes*
	= 0.04166667 day
1 mean solar day	= $24^h03^m56^s.55536$ of mean sidereal time
	= 1 rotation of Earth with respect to Sun (mean)*
	= 1.00273791 rotations of Earth with respect to vernal equinox (mean)
	= 1.0027378118868 rotations of Earth with respect to stars (mean)
1 mean sidereal day	= $23^h56^m04^s09054$ of mean solar time
1 sidereal month	= 27.321661 days
	= $27^d07^h43^m11^s.5$
1 synodical month	= 29.530588 days
	= $29^d12^h44^m02^s.8$

1 tropical (ordinary) year	= 31,556,925.975 seconds
	= 525,948.766 minutes
	= 8,765.8128 hours
	= $365^{d}.24219879 - 0^{d}.0000000614(t-1900)$, where t = the year (date)
	= $365^{d}05^{h}48^{m}46^{s}$ (–) $0^{s}.0053(t-1900)$
1 sidereal year	= $365^{d}.25636042 + 0.0000000011(t-1900)$, where t = the year (date)
	= $365^{d}06^{h}09^{m}09^{s}.5$ (+) $0^{s}.0001(t-1900)$
1 calendar year (common)	= 31,536,000 seconds*
	= 525,600 minutes*
	= 8,760 hours*
	= 365 days*
1 calendar year (leap)	= 31,622,400 seconds*
	= 527,040 minutes*
	= 8,784 hours*
	= 366 days
1 light-year	= 9,460,000,000,000 kilometers
	= 5,880,000,000,000 statute miles
	= 5,110,000,000,000 nautical miles
	= 63,240 astronomical units
	= 0.3066 parsecs
1 parsec	= 30,860,000,000,000 kilometers
	= 19,170,000,000,000 statute miles
	= 16,660,000,000,000 nautical miles
	= 206,300 astronomical units
	= 3.262 light years
1 astronomical unit	= 149,600,000 kilometers
	= 92,960,000 statute miles
	= 80,780,000 nautical miles
	= $499^{s}.012$ light-time
	= mean distance, Earth to Sun
Mean distance, Earth to Moon	= 384,400 kilometers
	= 238,855 statute miles
	= 207,559 nautical miles
Mean distance, Earth to Sun	= 149,600,000 kilometers
	= 92,957,000 statute miles
	= 80,780,000 nautical miles
	= 1 astronomical unit
Sun's diameter	= 1,392,000 kilometers
	= 865,000 statute miles
	= 752,000 nautical miles
Sun's mass	= 1,987,000,000,000,000,000,000,000,000,000,000 grams
	= 2,200,000,000,000,000,000,000,000,000 short tons
	= 2,000,000,000,000,000,000,000,000,000 long tons
Speed of Sun relative to neighboring stars	= 19.4 kilometers per second
	= 12.1 statute miles per second
	= 10.5 nautical miles per second
Orbital speed of Earth	= 29.8 kilometers per second
	= 18.5 statute miles per second
	= 16.1 nautical miles per second
Obliquity of the ecliptic	= $23°27'08''.26 - 0''.4684\ (t-1900)$, where t = the year (date)
General precession of the equinoxes	= $50''.2564 + 0''.000222\ (t-1900)$, per year, where t = the year (date)
Precession of the equinoxes in right ascension	= $46''.0850 + 0''.000279\ (t-1900)$, per year, where t = the year (date)
Precession of the equinoxes in declination	= $20''.0468 - 0''.000085\ (t-1900)$, per year, where t = the year (date)

Magnitude ratio	= 2.512
	= $\sqrt[5]{100}$*

Charts

Nautical miles per inch	= reciprocal of natural scale ÷ 72,913.39
Statute miles per inch	= reciprocal of natural scale ÷ 63,360*
Inches per nautical mile	= 72,913.39 × natural scale
Inches per statute mile	= 63,360 × natural scale*
Natural scale	= 1:72,913.39 × nautical miles per inch
	= 1:63,360 × statute miles per inch*

Earth

Acceleration due to gravity (standard)	= 980.665 centimeters per second per second
	= 32.1740 feet per second per second
Mass-ratio—Sun/Earth	= 332,958
Mass-ratio—Sun/(Earth & Moon)	= 328,912
Mass-ratio—Earth/Moon	= 81.30
Mean density	= 5.517 grams per cubic centimeter
Velocity of escape	= 6.94 statute miles per second
Curvature of surface	= 0.8 foot per nautical mile

World Geodetic System (WGS) Ellipsoid of 1984

Equatorial radius (a)	= 6,378,137 meters
	= 3,443.918 nautical miles
Polar radius (b)	= 6,356,752.314 meters
	= 3432.372 nautical miles
Mean radius (2a + b)/3	= 6,371,008.770 meters
	= 3440.069 nautical miles
Flattening or ellipticity (f = 1 – b/a)	= 1/298.257223563
	= 0.003352811
Eccentricity ($e = (2f - f^2)^{1/2}$)	= 0.081819191
Eccentricity squared (e^2)	= 0.006694380

Length

1 inch	= 25.4 millimeters*
	= 2.54 centimeters*
1 foot (U.S.)	= 12 inches*
	= 1 British foot
	= $^1/_3$ yard*
	= 0.3048 meter*
	= $^1/_6$ fathom*
1 foot (U.S. Survey)	= 0.30480061 meter
1 yard	= 36 inches*
	= 3 feet*
	= 0.9144 meter*
1 fathom	= 6 feet*
	= 2 yards*
	= 1.8288 meters*
1 cable	= 720 feet*
	= 240 yards*
	= 219.4560 meters*
1 cable (British)	= 0.1 nautical mile
1 statute mile	= 5,280 feet*
	= 1,760 yards*
	= 1,609.344 meters*
	= 1.609344 kilometers*
	= 0.86897624 nautical mile
1 nautical mile	= 6,076.11548556 feet
	= 2,025.37182852 yards
	= 1,852 meters*
	= 1.852 kilometers*

	= 1.150779448 statute miles
1 meter	= 100 centimeters*
	= 39.370079 inches
	= 3.28083990 feet
	= 1.09361330 yards
	= 0.54680665 fathom
	= 0.00062137 statute mile
	= 0.00053996 nautical mile
1 kilometer	= 3,280.83990 feet
	= 1,093.61330 yards
	= 1,000 meters*
	= 0.62137119 statute mile
	= 0.53995680 nautical mile

Mass

1 ounce	= 437.5 grains*
	= 28.349523125 grams*
	= 0.0625 pound*
	= 0.028349523125 kilogram*
1 pound	= 7,000 grains*
	= 16 ounces*
	= 0.45359237 kilogram*
1 short ton	= 2,000 pounds*
	= 907.18474 kilograms*
	= 0.90718474 metric ton*
	= 0.8928571 long ton
1 long ton	= 2,240 pounds*
	= 1,016.0469088 kilograms*
	= 1.12 short tons*
	= 1.0160469088 metric tons*
1 kilogram	= 2.204623 pounds
	= 0.00110231 short ton
	= 0.0009842065 long ton
1 metric ton	= 2,204.623 pounds
	= 1,000 kilograms*
	= 1.102311 short tons
	= 0.9842065 long ton

Mathematics

π	= 3.1415926535897932384626433832795028841971
π^2	= 9.8696044011
$\sqrt{\pi}$	= 1.7724538509
Base of Naperian logarithms (e)	= 2.718281828459
Modulus of common logarithms ($\log_{10}e$)	= 0.4342944819032518
1 radian	= 206,264.″80625
	= 3,437′.7467707849
	= 57°.2957795131
	= 57°17′44″.80625
1 circle	= 1,296,000″*
	= 21,600′*
	= 360°*
	= 2π radians*
180°	= π radians*
1°	= 3600″*
	= 60′*
	= 0.0174532925199432957666 radian
1′	= 60″*
	= 0.000290888208665721596 radian
1″	= 0.000004848136811095359933 radian
Sine of 1′	= 0.00029088820456342460
Sine of 1″	= 0.00000484813681107637

Meteorology

Atmosphere (dry air)

Nitrogen	= 78.08%	99.99%
Oxygen	= 20.95%	
Argon	= 0.93%	
Carbon dioxide	= 0.03%	
Neon	= 0.0018%	
Helium	= 0.000524%	
Krypton	= 0.0001%	
Hydrogen	= 0.00005%	
Xenon	= 0.0000087%	
Ozone	= 0 to 0.000007% (increasing with altitude)	
Radon	= 0.0000000000000000006% (decreasing with altitude)	

Standard atmospheric pressure at sea level	= 1,013.250 dynes per square centimeter
	= 1,033.227 grams per square centimeter
	= 1,033.227 centimeters of water
	= 1,013.250 hectopascals (millibars)*
	= 760 millimeters of mercury
	= 76 centimeters of mercury
	= 33.8985 feet of water
	= 29.92126 inches of mercury
	= 14.6960 pounds per square inch
	= 1.033227 kilograms per square centimeter
	= 1.013250 bars*
Absolute zero	= (–)273.16°C
	= (–)459.69°F

Pressure

1 dyne per square centimeter	= 0.001 hectopascal (millibar)*
	= 0.000001 bar*
1 gram per square centimeter	= 1 centimeter of water
	= 0.980665 hectopascal (millibar)*
	= 0.07355592 centimeter of mercury
	= 0.0289590 inch of mercury
	= 0.0142233 pound per square inch
	= 0.001 kilogram per square centimeter*
	= 0.000967841 atmosphere
1 hectopascal (millibar)	= 1,000 dynes per square centimeter*
	= 1.01971621 grams per square centimeter
	= 0.7500617 millimeter of mercury
	= 0.03345526 foot of water
	= 0.02952998 inch of mercury
	= 0.01450377 pound per square inch
	= 0.001 bar*
	= 0.00098692 atmosphere
1 millimeter of mercury	= 1.35951 grams per square centimeter
	= 1.3332237 hectopascals (millibars)
	= 0.1 centimeter of mercury*
	= 0.04460334 foot of water
	= 0.039370079 inch of mercury
	= 0.01933677 pound per square inch
	= 0.001315790 atmosphere
1 centimeter of mercury	= 10 millimeters of mercury*
1 inch of mercury	= 34.53155 grams per square centimeter
	= 33.86389 hectopascals (millibars)
	= 25.4 millimeters of mercury*
	= 1.132925 feet of water
	= 0.4911541 pound per square inch
	= 0.03342106 atmosphere
1 centimeter of water	= 1 gram per square centimeter
	= 0.001 kilogram per square centimeter
1 foot of water	= 30.48000 grams per square centimeter
	= 29.89067 hectopascals (millibars)
	= 2.241985 centimeters of mercury
	= 0.882671 inch of mercury
	= 0.4335275 pound per square inch
	= 0.02949980 atmosphere

1 pound per square inch	= 68,947.57 dynes per square centimeter
	= 70.30696 grams per square centimeter
	= 70.30696 centimeters of water
	= 68.94757 hectopascals (millibars)
	= 51.71493 millimeters of mercury
	= 5.171493 centimeters of mercury
	= 2.306659 feet of water
	= 2.036021 inches of mercury
	= 0.07030696 kilogram per square centimeter
	= 0.06894757 bar
	= 0.06804596 atmosphere
1 kilogram per square centimeter	= 1,000 grams per square centimeter*
	= 1,000 centimeters of water
1 bar	= 1,000,000 dynes per square centimeter*
	= 1,000 hectopascals (millibars)*

Speed

1 foot per minute	= 0.01666667 foot per second
	= 0.00508 meter per second*
1 yard per minute	= 3 feet per minute*
	= 0.05 foot per second*
	= 0.03409091 statute mile per hour
	= 0.02962419 knot
	= 0.01524 meter per second*
1 foot per second	= 60 feet per minute*
	= 20 yards per minute*
	= 1.09728 kilometers per hour*
	= 0.68181818 statute mile per hour
	= 0.59248380 knot
	= 0.3048 meter per second*
1 statute mile per hour	= 88 feet per minute*
	= 29.33333333 yards per minute
	= 1.609344 kilometers per hour*
	= 1.46666667 feet per second
	= 0.86897624 knot
	= 0.44704 meter per second*
1 knot	= 101.26859143 feet per minute
	= 33.75619714 yards per minute
	= 1.852 kilometers per hour*
	= 1.68780986 feet per second
	= 1.15077945 statute miles per hour
	= 0.51444444 meter per second
1 kilometer per hour	= 0.62137119 statute mile per hour
	= 0.53995680 knot
1 meter per second	= 196.85039340 feet per minute
	= 65.6167978 yards per minute
	= 3.6 kilometers per hour*
	= 3.28083990 feet per second
	= 2.23693632 statute miles per hour
	= 1.94384449 knots
Light in vacuum	= 299,792.5 kilometers per second
	= 186,282 statute miles per second
	= 161,875 nautical miles per second
	= 983.570 feet per microsecond
Light in air	= 299,708 kilometers per second
	= 186,230 statute miles per second
	= 161,829 nautical miles per second
	= 983.294 feet per microsecond
Sound in dry air at 59°F or 15°C and standard sea level pressure	= 1,116.45 feet per second
	= 761.22 statute miles per hour
	= 661.48 knots
	= 340.29 meters per second

Sound in 3.485 percent saltwater at 60°F _ _ _ = 4,945.37 feet per second
= 3,371.85 statute miles per hour
= 2,930.05 knots
= 1,507.35 meters per second

Volume

1 cubic inch _ _ _ = 16.387064 cubic centimeters*
= 0.016387064 liter*
= 0.004329004 gallon

1 cubic foot _ _ _ = 1,728 cubic inches*
= 28.316846592 liters*
= 7.480519 U.S. gallons
= 6.228822 imperial (British) gallons
= 0.028316846592 cubic meter*

1 cubic yard _ _ _ = 46,656 cubic inches*
= 764.554857984 liters*
= 201.974026 U.S. gallons
= 168.1782 imperial (British) gallons
= 27 cubic feet*
= 0.764554857984 cubic meter*

1 milliliter _ _ _ = 0.06102374 cubic inch
= 0.0002641721 U.S. gallon
= 0.00021997 imperial (British) gallon

1 cubic meter _ _ _ = 264.172035 U.S. gallons
= 219.96878 imperial (British) gallons
= 35.31467 cubic feet
= 1.307951 cubic yards

1 quart (U.S.) _ _ _ = 57.75 cubic inches*
= 32 fluid ounces*
= 2 pints*
= 0.9463529 liter
= 0.25 gallon*

1 gallon (U.S.) _ _ _ = 3,785.412 milliliters
= 231 cubic inches*
= 0.1336806 cubic foot
= 4 quarts*
= 3.785412 liters
= 0.8326725 imperial (British) gallon

1 liter _ _ _ = 1,000 milliliters
= 61.02374 cubic inches
= 1.056688 quarts
= 0.2641721 gallon

1 register ton _ _ _ = 100 cubic feet*
= 2.8316846592 cubic meters*

1 measurement ton _ _ _ = 40 cubic feet*
= 1 freight ton*

1 freight ton _ _ _ = 40 cubic feet*
= 1 measurement ton*

Volume-Mass

1 cubic foot of seawater _ _ _ = 64 pounds

1 cubic foot of freshwater _ _ _ = 62.428 pounds at temperature of maximum density (4°C = 39°.2F)

1 cubic foot of ice _ _ _ = 56 pounds

1 displacement ton _ _ _ = 35 cubic feet of seawater*
= 1 long ton

Prefixes to Form Decimal Multiples and Sub-Multiples of International System of Units (SI)

Multiplying factor		Prefix	Symbol
1 000 000 000 000	$= 10^{12}$	tera	T
1 000 000 000	$= 10^{9}$	giga	G
1 000 000	$= 10^{6}$	mega	M
1 000	$= 10^{3}$	kilo	k
100	$= 10^{2}$	hecto	h
10	$= 10^{1}$	deka	da
0. 1	$= 10^{-1}$	deci	d
0. 01	$= 10^{-2}$	centi	c
0. 001	$= 10^{-3}$	milli	m
0. 000 001	$= 10^{-6}$	micro	μ
0. 000 000 001	$= 10^{-9}$	nano	n
0. 000 000 000 001	$= 10^{-12}$	pico	p
0. 000 000 000 000 001	$= 10^{-15}$	femto	f
0. 000 000 000 000 000 001	$= 10^{-18}$	atto	a

NGA MARITIME SAFETY INFORMATION NAUTICAL CALCULATORS

NGA's Maritime Safety Office website offers a variety of online Nautical Calculators for public use. These calculators solve many of the equations and conversions typically associated with marine navigation. See Figure 406.

Figure 406. Link to NGA Nautical Calculators.
https://msi.nga.mil/NGAPortal/MSI.portal?_nfpb=true&_st=&_pageLabel=msi_portal_page_145

List of NGA Maritime Safety information Nautical Calculators https://msi.nga.mil

Celestial Navigation Calculators
Compass Error from Amplitudes Observed on the Visible Horizon
Altitude Correction for Air Temperature
Table of Offsets
Latitude and Longitude Factors
Altitude Corrections for Atmospheric Pressure

List of NGA Maritime Safety information Nautical Calculators https://msi.nga.mil

Altitude Factors & Change of Altitude
Pub 229
Compass Error from Amplitudes observed on the Celestial Horizon
Conversion Calculators
Chart Scales and Conversions for Nautical and Statute Miles
Conversions for Meters, Feet and Fathoms
Distance Calculators
Length of a Degree of Latitude and Longitude
Speed for Measured Mile and Speed, Time and Distance
Distance of an Object by Two Bearings
Distance of the Horizon
Distance by Vertical Angle Measured Between Sea Horizon and Top of Object Beyond Sea Horizon
Traverse Table
Geographic Range
Distance by Vertical Angle Measured Between Waterline at Object and Top of Object
Dip of Sea Short of the Horizon
Distance by Vertical Angle Measured Between Waterline at Object and Sea Horizon Beyond Object
Meridional Parts
Log and Trig Calculators
Logarithmic and Trigonometric Functions
Sailings Calculators
Great Circle Sailing
Mercator NGA Sailing
Time Zones Calculators
Time Zones, Zone Descriptions and Suffixes
Weather Data Calculators
Direction and Speed of True Wind
Correction of Barometer Reading for Height Above Sea Level
Correction of Barometer Reading for Gravity
Temperature Conversions
Relative Humidity and Dew Point
Corrections of Barometer Reading for Temperature
Barometer Measurement Conversions

CHAPTER 5

COMPASS CONVERSIONS

INTRODUCTION

500. Magnetic Compass Error

Directions relative to the northerly direction along a geographic meridian are **true**. In this case, true north is the **reference direction**. If a compass card is horizontal and oriented so that a straight line from its center to 000° points to true north, any direction measured by the card is a true direction and has no error (assuming there is no calibration or observational error). If the card remains horizontal but is rotated so that it points in any other direction, the amount of the rotation is the **compass error**. Stated differently, compass error is the angular difference between true north and **compass north** (the direction north as indicated by a magnetic compass). It is named east or west to indicate the side of true north on which compass north lies.

If a magnetic compass is influenced by no other magnetic field than that of the earth, and there is no instrumental error, its magnets are aligned with the magnetic meridian at the compass, and 000° of the compass card coincides with **magnetic north**. All directions indicated by the card are **magnetic**. As stated in volume I, the angle between geographic and magnetic meridians is called **variation** (**V** or **Var.**). Therefore, if a compass is aligned with the magnetic meridian, compass error and variation are the same.

When a compass is mounted in a vessel, it is generally subjected to various magnetic influences other than that of the earth. These arise largely from induced magnetism in metal decks, bulkheads, masts, stacks, boat davits, guns, etc., and from electromagnetic fields associated with direct current in electrical circuits. Some metal in the vicinity of the compass may have acquired permanent magnetism. The actual magnetic field at the compass is the vector sum, or resultant of all individual fields at that point. Since the direction of this resultant field is generally not the same as that of the earth's field alone, the compass magnets do not lie in the magnetic meridian, but in a direction that makes an angle with it. This angle is called **deviation** (**D** or **Dev.**). Thus, deviation is the angular difference between magnetic north and compass north. It is expressed in angular units and named east or west to indicate the side of magnetic north on which compass north lies. Thus, deviation is the error of the compass in pointing to magnetic north, and all directions measured with compass north as the reference direction are **compass directions**. Since variation and deviation may each be either east or west, the effect of deviation may be to either increase or decrease the error due to variation alone. The algebraic sum of variation and deviation is the total compass error.

For computational purposes, deviation and compass error, like variation, may be designated positive· (+) if east and negative (-) if west.

Variation changes with location. Deviation depends upon the magnetic latitude and also upon the individual vessel, its trim and loading, whether it is pitching or rolling, the heading (orientation of the vessel with respect to the earth's magnetic field), and the location of the compass within the vessel. Therefore, deviation is not published on charts. The effects of variation and deviation on the compass card is depicted in Figure 500.

501. Deviation Table

In practice aboard ship, the deviation is reduced to a minimum through adjustment of the compass. The remaining value, called **residual deviation**, is determined on various headings and recorded in some form of **deviation table**. Figure 502 shows the form used by the United States Navy. This table is entered with the magnetic heading, and the deviation on that heading is determined from the tabulation, separate columns being given for degaussing (DG) equipment off and on. If the deviation is not more than about 2° on any heading, satisfactory results may be obtained by entering the values at intervals of 45° only.

If the deviation is small, no appreciable error is introduced by entering the table with either magnetic or compass heading. If the deviation on some headings is large, the desirable action is to reduce it, but if this is not practicable, a separate deviation table for compass heading entry may be useful. This may be made by applying the tabulated deviation to each entry value of magnetic heading, to find the corresponding compass heading, and then interpolating between these to find the value of deviation at each 15° compass heading.

502. Applying Variation and Deviation

As indicated in Section 500, a single direction may have any of several numerical values depending upon the reference direction used. One should keep clearly in mind the relationship between the various expressions of a direction. Thus, true and magnetic directions differ by the

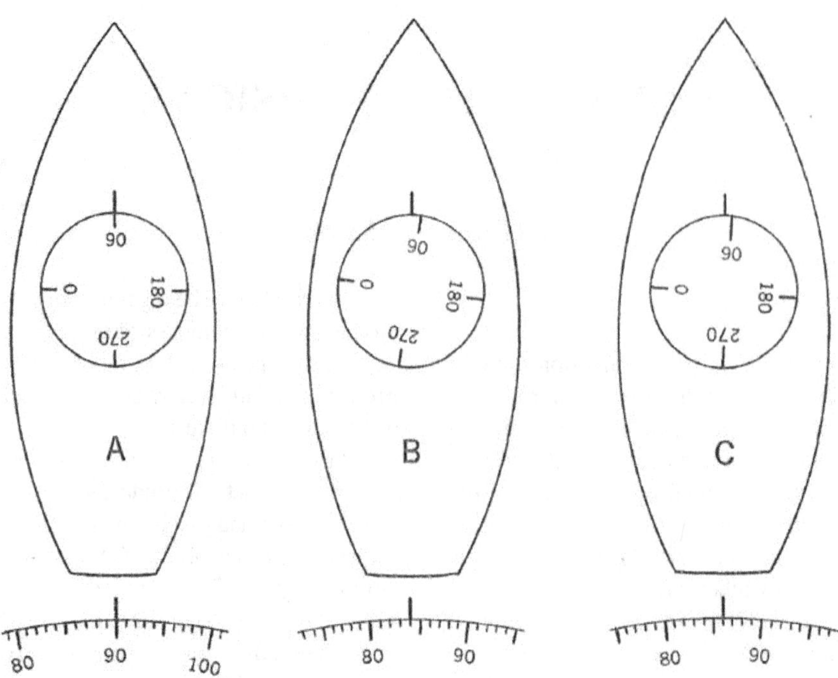

Figure 500. Effects of variation and deviation on the compass card.

variation, magnetic and compass directions differ by the deviation, and true and compass directions differ by the compass error.

If variation or deviation is easterly, the compass card is rotated in a clockwise direction. This brings smaller numbers opposite the lubber's line. Conversely, if either error is westerly, the rotation is counterclockwise and larger numbers are brought opposite the lubber's line. Thus, if the heading is 090° true (Figure 500, A) and variation is 6°E, the magnetic heading is 090°- 6°= 084° (Figure 500, B). If the deviation on this heading is 2°W, the compass heading is 084°+ 2°= 086° (Figure 500, C). Also, compass error is 6°E-2°W= 4°E, and compass heading is 090°- 4°= 086°. If compass error is easterly, the compass reads too low (in comparison with true directions), and if it is westerly, the reading is too high. Many rules-of-thumb have been devised as an aid to the memory, and any which assist in applying compass errors in the right direction are of value. However, one may forget the rule or its method of application, or may wish to have an independent check. If they understand the explanation given above, they can determine the correct sign without further information. The same rules apply to the use of gyro error. Since variation and deviation are compass errors, the process of removing either from an indication of a direction (converting compass to magnetic or magnetic to true) is often called **correcting**. Conversion in the opposite direction (inserting errors) is then called **uncorrecting**.

Example. - A vessel is on course 215° true in an area where the variation is 7°W. The deviation is as shown in Figure 502. Degaussing is off. The gyro error (GE) is 1° E. A lighthouse bears 306.5° by magnetic compass.

Required.- (1) Magnetic heading (MH).
(2) Deviation.
(3) Compass heading (CH).
(4) Compass error.
(5) Gyro heading.
(6) Magnetic bearing of the lighthouse.
(7) True bearing of the lighthouse.
(8) Relative bearing of the lighthouse.

Solution. -

	TH	215°
	V	7°W
(1)	MH	222°
(2)	D	1.5°W
(3)	CH	223.5°

The deviation is taken from the deviation table (Figure 502) to the nearest half degree.

(4) Compass error is 7° W + 1.5° W = 8.5° W.

	TH	215°
	GE	1°E
(5)	Hpgc	214°
	CB	306.5°
	D	1.5°W
(6)	MB	305°
	V	7°W
(7)	TB	298°

(8) RB=TB-TH=298°-215°= 083°.

Answers -

(1) MH 222°
(2) D 1.5W°
(3) CH 223.5°
(4) CE 8.5°W
(5) Hpgc 214°
(6) MB 305°
(7) TB 298°
(8) RB 083°

Problem 1 - Fill in the blanks to this table						
	TC	V	MC	D	CC	CE
	°	°	°	°	°	°
(1)	105	15 E	-	5W	-	-
(2)	-	-	-	4 E	215	14 E
(3)	-	12 W	-	-	067	7 W
(4)	156	-	166	-	160	-
(5)	222	-	216	3 W	-	-
(6)	009	-	357	-	-	10 E
(7)	-	2 W	-	6 E	015	-
(8)	-	-	210	-	214	1 W

Answers to Problem 1.- (1) MC 090°, CC 095°, CE 10°E; (2) TC 229°, V 10°E, MC 219°; (3) TC 060°, MC 072°, D 5°E; (4) V 10°W, D 6°E, CE 4°W; (5) V 6°E, CC 219°, CE 3°E; (6) V 12°E, D 2°W, CC 359°; (7) TC 019°, MC 021°, CE 4°E; (8) TC 213°, V 3°E, D 4°W.

Problem 2: A vessel is on course 150° by compass in an area where the variation is 19°E. The deviation is as shown in Figure 502. Degaussing is on.

Required. - (1) Deviation.

(2) Compass error.

(3) Magnetic heading.

(4) True heading.

Answers to Problem 2. - (1) D 1° E, (2) XE 20° E, (3) MH 151°, (4) TH 170°.

Problem 3: A vessel on a course of 055° by gyro and 041° by magnetic compass. The gyro error is 1° W. The variation is 15° E.

Required. - The deviation on this heading.

Answer to Problem 3. - 2° W.

Problem 4: A vessel is on course 177° by gyro. The gyro error is 0.5° E. A beacon bears 088° by magnetic compass in an area where variation is 11° W. The deviation is as shown in Figure 502. degaussing off.

Required. - The true bearing of the beacon.

Answer to Problem 4. - TB 076°.

MAGNETIC COMPASS TABLE NAVSHIPS RPT. 3530-2
NAVSHIPS 3120/4 (REV. 8-67) (FRONT) *(Formerly NAVSHIPS 1104)*
S/N 0105-601-9520

U.S.S. Truckee NO. AO 147 *(BB, CL, DD, etc.)*

[X] PILOT HOUSE [ ] SECONDARY CONNING STATION [ ] OTHER

BINNACLE TYPE: [X] NAVY ST'D [ ] OTHER

COMPASS 7 1/2 MAKE Lionel SERIAL NO. 1592

TYPE CC COILS "K" DATE

READ INSTRUCTIONS ON BACK BEFORE STARTING ADJUSTMENT

SHIPS HEAD MAGNETIC	DEVIATIONS		SHIPS HEAD MAGNETIC	DEVIATIONS	
	DG OFF	DG ON		DG OFF	DG ON
0	0.5E	0.5E	180	0.5W	0.0
15	1.0E	1.0E	195	1.0W	0.5W
30	1.5E	1.5E	210	1.0W	1.0W
45	2.0E	1.5E	225	1.5W	1.5W
60	2.0E	2.0E	240	2.0W	2.0W
75	2.5E	2.5E	255	2.0W	2.5W
90	2.5E	3.0E	270	1.5W	2.0W
105	2.0E	2.5E	285	1.0W	1.5W
120	1.5E	2.0E	300	1.0W	1.0W
135	1.5E	1.5E	315	0.5W	0.5W
150	1.0E	1.0E	330	0.5W	0.5W
165	0.0	0.5E	345	0.0	0.0

DEVIATIONS DETERMINED BY: [ ] SUN'S AZIMUTH [X] GYRO [ ] SHORE BEARINGS

B 4 MAGNETS RED [ ] FORE [X] AFT AT 14" FROM COMPASS CARD

C 4 MAGNETS RED [ ] PORT [X] STBD AT 10" FROM COMPASS CARD

D 2-7" [X] SPHERES [ ] CYLS AT 12" [X] ATHWARTSHIP [ ] SLEWED ---° [ ] CLOCKWISE [ ] CTR. CLOCKWISE

HEELING MAGNET: [ ] RED UP [X] BLUE UP 10" FROM COMPASS CARD FLINDERS BAR: [X] FORE [ ] AFT 14"

[X] LAT [ ] H 36°10' N [X] LONG [ ] Z 75° 20' W

SIGNED *(Adjuster or Navigator)*	APPROVED *(Commanding)*
T. PARRISH	R. MOSS

Figure 502. Deviation table.

CHAPTER 6

COMPASS ERROR

DETERMINING COMPASS ERROR USING (PUB. NO. 229) SIGHT REDUCTION TABLES FOR MARINE NAVIGATION

600. Compass Error

One of the more frequent applications of sight reduction tables is their use in computing the azimuth of a celestial body for comparison with an observed azimuth in order to determine the error of the compass. In computing the azimuth of a celestial body, for the time and place of observation, it is normally necessary to interpolate the tabular azimuth angle as extracted from the tables for the differences between the table arguments and the actual values of declination, latitude, and local hour angle. The required triple interpolation of the azimuth angle is effected as follows:

1. The main tables are entered with the nearest integral values of declination, latitude, and local hour angle; for these arguments, a base azimuth angle is extracted.
2. The tables are reentered with the same latitude and LHA arguments but with the declination argument 1° greater or less than the base declination argument depending upon whether the actual declination is greater or less than the base argument. The difference between the respondent azimuth angle and the base azimuth angle establishes the azimuth angle difference (Z Diff.) for the increment of declination.
3. The tables are reentered with the base declination and LHA arguments but with the latitude argument 1° greater or less than the base latitude argument depending upon whether the actual (usually DR) latitude is greater or less than the base argument to find the Z Diff. for the increment of latitude.
4. The tables are reentered with the base declination and latitude arguments, but with the LHA argument 1° greater or less than the base LHA argument depending upon whether the actual LHA is greater or less than the base argument to find the Z Diff. for the increment of LHA.
5. The correction to the base azimuth angle for each increment is $\text{Z Diff.} \times \frac{\text{Inc.}}{60'}$.

Example.-In DR Lat. 13°24.0'N, the azimuth of the Sun is observed as 070.3° pgc. At the time of the observation, the declination of the Sun is 20°13.8'N; the local hour angle of the Sun is 276°41.2'. The error of the gyrocompass is found as follows:

Actual		Base Arguments	Base Z	Tab* Z	Z Diff	Increments	Correction (Z Diff × Inc. ÷ 60)
Dec.	20°13.8′N	20°	71.8°	70.8°	−1.0°	13.8′	−0.2°
DR Lat.	13°24.0N	13° (Same)	71.8°	71.9°	+0.1°	24.0′	0.0°
LHA	276°41.2′	277°	71.8°	71.6°	−0.2°	18.8′	−0.1°
						Total Corr.	-0.3°

Base Z	71.8°
Corr.	(-) 0.3°
Z	N71.5°E
Zn	071.5°
Zn pgc	070.3°
Gyro Error	1.2°E

* Respondent for two base arguments and 1° change from third base argument, in vertical order of Dec., DR Lat., and LHA.

APPENDIX B

Haversines

′	0°		1°		2°		3°		4°		′
	Log Hav	Nat. Hav	Log Hav	Nat. Hav	Log Hav	Nat. Hav	Log Hav	Nat. Hav	Log Hav	Nat. Hav	
0	Inf. Neg	0. 00000	5. 88168	0. 00008	6. 48371	0. 00030	6. 83584	0. 00069	7. 08564	0. 00122	60
1	2. 32539	. 00000	. 89604	. 00008	. 49092	. 00031	. 84065	. 00069	. 08925	. 00123	59
2	2. 92745	. 00000	. 91016	. 00008	. 49807	. 00031	. 84543	. 00070	. 09284	. 00124	58
3	3. 27963	. 00000	. 92406	. 00008	. 50516	. 00032	. 85019	. 00071	. 09642	. 00125	57
4	. 52951	. 00000	. 93774	. 00009	. 51219	. 00033	. 85492	. 00072	. 09999	. 00126	56
5	3. 72333	0. 00000	5. 95121	0. 00009	6. 51916	0. 0003.3	6. 85963	0. 00072	7. 10354	0. 00127	55
6	3. 88169	. 00000	. 96447	. 00009	. 52608	. 00034	. 86431	. 00073	. 10708	. 00128	54
7	4. 01559	. 00000	. 97753	. 00009	. 53295	. 00034	. 86897	. 00074	. 11060	. 00129	53
8	. 13157	. 00000	5. 99040	. 00010	. 53976	. 00035	. 87360	. 00075	. 11411	. 00130	52
9	. 23388	. 00000	6. 00308	. 00010	. 54652	. 00035	. 87821	. 00076	. 11760	. 00131	51
10	4. 32539	0. 00000	6. 01557	0. 00010	6. 55323	0. 00036	6. 88279	0. 00076	7. 12108	0. 00132	50
11	. 40818	. 00000	. 02789	. 00011	. 55988	. 00036	. 88735	. 00077	. 12455	. 00133	49
12	. 48375	. 00000	. 04004	. 00011	. 56649	. 00037	. 89188	. 00078	. 12800	. 00134	48
13	. 55328	. 00000	. 05202	. 00011	. 57304	. 00037	. 89639	. 00079	. 13144	. 00135	47
14	. 61765	. 00000	. 06384	. 00012	. 57955	. 00038	. 90088	. 00080	. 13486	. 00136	46
15	4. 67757	0. 00000	6. 07550	0. 00012	6. 58600	0. 00039	6. 90535	0. 00080	7. 13827	0. 00137	45
16	. 73363	. 00001	. 08700	. 00012	. 59241	. 00039	. 90979	. 00081	. 14167	. 00139	44
17	. 78629	. 00001	. 09836	. 00013	. 59878	. 00040	. 91421	. 00082	. 14506	. 00140	43
18	. 83594	. 00001	. 10956	. 00013	. 60509	. 00040	. 91860	. 00083	. 14843	. 00141	42
19	. 88290	. 00001	. 12063	. 00013	. 61136	. 00041	. 92298	. 00084	. 15179	. 00142	41
20	4. 92745	0. 00001	6. 13155	0. 00014	6. 61759	0. 00041	6. 92733	0. 00085	7. 15513	0. 00143	40
21	4. 96983	. 00001	. 14234	. 00014	. 62377	. 00042	. 93166	. 00085	. 15846	. 00144	39
22	5. 01024	. 00001	. 15300	. 00014	. 62991	. 00043	. 93597	. 00086	. 16178	. 00145	38
23	. 04885	. 00001	. 16353	. 00015	. 63600	. 00043	. 94026	. 00087	. 16509	. 00146	37
24	. 08581	. 00001	. 17393	. 00015	. 64205	. 00044	. 94453	. 00088	. 16839	. 00147	36
25	5. 12127	o.00001	6. 18421	0. 00015	6. 64806	0. 00044	6. 94877	0. 00089	7. 17167	0. 00148	35
26	. 15534	. 00001	. 19437	. 00016	. 65403	. 00045	. 95300	. 00090	. 17494	. 00150	34
27	. 18812	. 00002	. 20441	. 00016	. 65996	. 00046	. 95720	. 00091	. 17820	. 00151	33
28	. 21971	. 00002	. 21433	. 00016	. 66585	. 00046	. 96139	. 00091	. 18144	. 00152	32
29	. 25019	. 00002	. 22415	. 00017	. 67170	. 00047	. 96555	. 00092	. 18468	. 00153	31
30	5. 27963	0. 00002	6. 23385	0. 00017	6. 67751	0. 00048	6. 96970	0. 00093	7. 18790	0. 00154	30
31	. 30811	. 00002	. 24345	. 00018	. 68328	. 00048	. . 97382	. 00094	. 19111	. 00155	29
32	. 33569	. 00002	. 25294	. 00018	. 68901	. 00049	. 97793	. 00095	. 19430	. 00156	28
33	. 36242	. 00002	. 26233	. 00018	. 69470	. 00050	. 98201	. 00096	. 19749	. 00158	27
34	. 38835	. 00002	. 27162	. 00019	. 70036	. 00050	. 98608	. 00097	. 20066	. 00159	26
35	5. 41352	0. 00003	6. 28081	0. 00019	6. 70598	0. 00051	6. 99013	0. 00098	7. 20383	0. 00160	25
36	. 43799	. 00003	. 28991	. 00019	. 71157	. 00051	. 99416	. 00099	. 20698	. 00161	24
37	. 46179	. 00003	. 29891	. 00020	. 71712	. 00052	6. 99817	. 00100	. 21012	. 00162	23
38	. 48496	. 00003	. 30781	. 00020	. 72263	. 00053	7. 00216	. 00100	. 21325	. 00163	22
39	. 50752	. 00003	. 31663	. 00021	. 72811	. 00053	. 00613	. 00101	. 21636	. 00165	21
40	5. 52951	0. 00003	6. 32536	0. 00021	6. 73355	0. 00054	7. 01009	0. 00102	7. 21947	0. 00166	20
41	. 55095	. 00004	. 33400	. 00022	. 73896	. 00055	. 01403	. 00103	. 22256	. 00167	19
42	. 57189	. 00004	. 34256	. 00022	. 74434	. 00056	. 01795	. 00104	. 22565	. 00168	18
43	. 59232	. 00004	. 35103	. 00022	. 74969	. 00056	. 02185	. 00105	. 22872	. 00169	17
44	. 61229	. 00004	. 35943	. 00023	. 75500	. 00057	. 02573	. 00106	. 23178	. 00171	16
45	5. 63181	0. 00004	6. 36774	0. 00023	6. 76028	0. 00058	7. 02960	0. 00107	7. 23483	0. 00172	15
46	. 65090	. 00004	. 37597	. 00024	. 76552	. 00058	. 03345	. 00108	. 23787	. 00173	14
47	. 66958	. 00005	. 38412	. 00024	. 77074	. 00059	. 0372	. 00109	. 24090	. 00174	13
48	. 68787	. 00005	. 39220	. 00025	. 77592	. 00060	. 04110	. 00110	. 24392	. 00175	12
49	. 70578	. 00005	. 40021	. 00025	. 78108	. 00060	. 04490	. 00111	. 24693	. 00177	11
50	5. 72332	0. 00005	6. 40814	0. 00026	6. 78620	0. 00061	7. 04869	0. 00112	7. 24993	0. 00178	10
51	. 74052	. 00006	. 41600	. 00026	. 79129	. 00062	. 05245	. 00113	. 25292	. 00179	9
52	. 75739	. 00006	. 42379	. 00027	. 79636	. 00063	. 05620	. 00114	. 25590	. 00180	8
53	. 77394	. 00006	. 43151	. 00027	. 80139	. 00063	. 05994	. 00115	. 25886	. 00181	7
54	. 79017	. 00006	. 43916	. 00027	. 80640	. 00064	. 06366	. 00116	. 26182	. 00183	6
55	5. 80611	0. 00006	6. 44675	0. 00028	6. 81137	0. 00065	7. 06736	0. 00117	7. 26477	0. 00184	5
56	. 82176	. 00007	. 45427	. 00028	. 81632	. 00066	. 07105	. 00118	. 26771	. 00185	4
57	. 83713	. 00007	. 46172	. 00029	. 82124	. 00066	. 07472	. 00119	. 27064	. 00186	3
58	. 85224	. 00007	. 46911	. 00029	. 82614	. 00067	. 07837	. 00120	. 27355	. 00188	2
59	. 86709	. 00007	. 47644	. 00030	. 83100	. 00068	. 08201	. 00121	. 27646	. 00189	1
60	5. 88168	0. 00008	6. 48371	0. 00030	6. 83584	0. 00069	7. 08564	0. 00122	7. 27936	0. 00190	0
	359°		358°		357°		356°		355°		

Haversines

′	5° Log Hav	5° Nat. Hav	6° Log Hav	6° Nat. Hav	7° Log Hav	7° Nat. Hav	8° Log Hav	8° Nat. Hav	9° Log Hav	9° Nat. Hav	′
0	7. 27936	0. 00190	7. 43760	0. 00274	7. 57135	0. 00373	7. 68717	0. 00487	7. 78929	0. 00616	60
1	. 28225	. 00192	. 44001	. 00275	. 57341	. 00374	. 68897	. 00489	. 79089	. 00618	59
2	. 28513	. 00193	. 44241	. 00277	. 57547	. 00376	. 69077	. 00491	. 79249	. 00620	58
3	. 28800	. 00194	. 44480	. 00278	. 57752	. 00378	. 69257	. 00493	. 79409	. 00622	57
4	. 29086	. 00195	. 44719	. 00280	. 57957	. 00380	. 69437	. 00495	. 79568	. 00625	56
5	7. 29371	0. 00197	7. 44957	0. 00282	7. 58162	0. 00382	7. 69616	0. 00497	7. 79728	0. 00627	55
6	. 29655	. 00198	. 45194	. 00283	. 58366	. 00383	. 69794	. 00499	. 79886	. 00629	54
7	. 29938	. 00199	. 45431	. 00285	. 58569	. 00385	. 69972	. 00501	. 80045	. 00632	53
8	. 30220	. 00201	. 45667	. 00286	. 58772	. 00387	. 70150	. 00503	. 80203	. 00634	52
9	. 30502	. 00202	. 45903	. 00288	. 58974	. 00389	. 70328	. 00505	. 80361	. 00636	51
10	7. 30782	0. 00203	7. 46138	0. 00289	7. 59176	0. 00391	7. 70505	0. 00507	7. 80519	0. 00639	50
11	. 31062	. 00204	. 46372	. 00291	. 59378	. 00392	. 70682	. 00509	. 80677	. 00641	49
12	. 31340	. 00206	. 46605	. 00292	. 59579	. 00394	. 70858	. 00511	. 80834	. 00643	48
13	. 31618	. 00207	. 46838	. 00294	. 59779	. 00396	. 71034	. 00513	. 80991	. 00646	47
14	. 31895	. 00208	. 47071	. 00296	. 59979	. 00398	. 71210	. 00515	. 81147	. 00648	46
15	7. 32171	0. 00210	7. 47302	0. 00297	7. 60179	0. 00400	7. 71385	0. 00517	7. 81303	0. 00650	45
16	. 32446	. 00211	. 47533	. 00299	. 60378	. 00402	. 71560	. 00520	. 81459	. 00653	44
17	. 32720	. 00212	. 47764	. 00300	. 60577	. 00403	. 71735	. 00522	. 81615	. 00655	43
18	. 32994	. 00214	. 47994	. 00302	; 60775	. 00405	. 71909	. 00524	. 81771	. 00657	42
19	. 33266	. 00215	. 48223	. 00304	. 60973	. 00407	. 72083	. 00526	. 81926	. 00660	41
20	7. 33538	0. 00216	7. 48452	0. 00305	7. 61170	0. 00409	7. 72257	0. 00528	7. 82081	0. 00B62	40
21	. 33809	. 00218	. 48680	. 00307	. 61367	. 00411	. 72430	. 00530	. 82235	. 00664	39
22	. 34079	. 00219	. 48907	. 00308	. 61564	. 00413	. 72603	. 00532	. 82390	. 00667	38
23	. 34348	. 00221	. 49134	. 00310	. 61760	. 00415	. 72775	. 00534	. 82544	. 00669	37
24	. 34616	. 00222	. 49360	. 00312	. 61955	. 00416	. 72948	. 00536	. 82698	. 00671	36
25	7. 34884	0. 00223	7. 49586	0. 00313	7. 62151	0. 00418	7. 73119	0. 00539	7. 82851	0. 00674	35
26	. 35150	. 00225	. 49811	. 00315	. 62345	. 00420	. 73291	. 00541	. 83004	. 00676	34
27	. 35416	. 00226	. 50036	. 00316	. 62540	. 00422	. 73462	. 00543	. 83157	. 00679	33
28	. 35681	. 00227	. 50259	. 00318	. 62733	. 00424	. 73633	. 00545	. 83310	. 00681	32
29	. 35945	. 00229	. 50483	. 00320	. 62927	. 00426	. 73803	. 00547	. 83463	. 00683	31
30	7. 36209	0. 00230	7. 50706	0. 00321	7. 63120	0. 00428	7. 73974	0. 00549	7. 83615	0. 00686	30
31	. 36471	. 00232	. 50928	. 00323	. 63312	. 00430	. 74143	. 00551	. 83767	. 00688	29
32	. 36733	. 00233	. 51149	. 00325	. 63504	. 00432	. 74313	. 00554	. 83918	. 00691	28
33	. 36994	. 00234	. 51370	. 00326	. 63696	. 00433	. 74482	. 00556	. 84070	. 00693	27
34	. 37254	. 00236	. 51591	. 00828	. 63887	. 00435	. 74651	. 00558	. 84221	. 00695	26
35	7. 37514	0. 00237	7. 51811	0. 00330	7. 64078	0. 00437	7. 74819	0. 00560	7. 84372	0. 00698	25
36	. 37773	. 00239	. 52030	. 00331	. 64269	. 00439	. 74988	. 00562	. 84522	. 00700	24
37	. 38030	. 00240	. 52249	. 00333	. 64458	. 00441	. 75155	. 00564	. 84672	. 00703	23
38	. 38288	. 00241	. 52467	. 00335	. 64648	. 0044,3	. 75323	. 00567	. 84822	. 00705	22
39	. 38544	. 00243	. 52685	. 00336	. 64837	. 00445	. 75490	. 00569	. 84972	. 00707	21
40	7. 38800	0. 00244	7. 52902	0. 00338	7. 65026	0. 00447	7. 75657	0. 00571	7. 85122	0. 00710	20
41	. 39054	. 00246	. 53119	. 00340	. 65214	. 00449	. 75824	. 00573	. 85271	. 00712	19
42	. 39309	. 00247	. 53335	. 00341	. 65402	. 00451	. 75990	. 00575	. 85420	. 00715	18
43	. 39562	. 00249	. 53550	. 00343	. 65590	. 00453	. 76156	. 00578	. 85569	. 00717	17
44	. 39815	. 00250	. 53766	. 00345	. 65777	. 00455	. 76321	. 00580	. 85717	. 00720	16
45	7. 40067	0. 00252	7. 53980	0. 00347	7. 65964	0. 00457	7. 76487	0. 00582	7. 85866	0. 00722	15
46	. 40318	. 00253	. 54194	. 00348	. 66150	. 00459	. 76652	. 00584	. 86014	. 00725	14
47	. 40568	. 00255	. 54407	. 00350	. 66336	. 00461	. 76816	. 00586	. 86161	. 00727	13
48	. 40818	. 00256	. 54620	. 00352	. 66521	. 00463	. 76981	. 00589	. 86309	. 00730	12
49	. 41067	. 00257	. 54833	. 00353	. 66706	. 00465	. 77145	. 00591	. 86456	. 00732	11
50	7. 41315	0. 00259	7. 55045	0. 00355	7. 66891	0. 00467	7. 77308	0. 00593	7. 86603	0. 00735	10
51	. 41563	. 00260	. 55256	. 00357	. 67075	. 00469	. 77472	. 00595	. 86750	. 00737	9
52	. 41810	. 00262	. 55467	. 00359	. 67259	. 00471	. 77635	. 00598	. 86896	. 00740	8
53	. 42056	. 00263	. 55677	. 00360	. 67443	. 00473	. 77798	. 00600	. 87042	. 00742	7
54	. 42301	. 00265	. 55887	. 00362	. 67626	. 00475	. 77960	. 00602	. 87188	. 00745	6
55	7. 42546	0. 00266	7. 56096	0. 00364	7. 67809	0. 00477	7. 78122	0. 00604	7. 87334	0. 00747	5
56	. 42790	. 00268	. 56305	. 00366	. 67991	. 00479	. 78284	. 00607	. 87480	. 00750	4
57	. 43034	. 00269	. 56513	. 00367	. 68173	. 00481	. 78446	. 00609	. 87625	. 00752	3
58	. 43277	. 00271	. 56721	. 00369	. 68355	. 00483	. 78607	. 00611	. 87770	. 00755	2
59	. 43519	. 00272	. 56928	. 00371	. 68536	. 00485	. 78768	. 00613	. 87915	. 00757	1
60	7. 43760	0. 00274	7. 57135	0. 00373	7. 68717	0. 00487	7. 78929	0. 00616	7. 88059	0. 00760	0
	354°		353°		352°		351°		350°		

Haversines

′	10°		11°		12°		13°		14°		′
	Log Hav	Nat. Hav	Log Hav	Nat. Hav	Log Hav	Nat. Hav	Log Hav	Nat. Hav	Log Hav	Nat. Hav	
0	7. 88059	0. 00760	7. 96315	0. 00919	8. 03847	0. 01093	8. 10772	0. 01281	8. 17179	0. 01485	60
1	. 88203	. 00762	. 96446	. 00921	. 03967	. 01096	. 10883	. 01285	. 17282	. 01489	59
2	. 88348	. 00765	. 96577	. 00924	. 04087	. 01099	. 10993	. 01288	. 17384	. 01492	58
3	. 88491	. 00767	. 96707	. 00927	. 04207	. 01102	. 11104	. 01291	. 17487	. 01496	57
4	. 88635	. 00770	. 96838	. 00930	. 04326	. 01105	. 11214	. 01295	. 17590	. 01499	56
5	:7. 88778	0. 00772	7. 96968	0. 00933	8. 04446	0. 01108	8. 11324	0. 01298	8. 17692	0. 01503	55
6	. 88921	. 00775	. 97098	. 00935	. 04565	. 01111	. 11435	. 01301	. 17794	. 01506	54
7	. 89064	. 00777	. 97228	. 00938	. 04684	. 01114	. 11544	. 01305	. 17896	. 01510	53
8	. 89207	. 00780	. 97358	. 00941	. 04803	. 01117	. 11654	. 01308	. 17998	. 01513	52
9	. 89349	. 00783	. 97487	. 00944	. 04922	. 01120	. 11764	. 01311	. 18100	. 01517	51
10	7. 89491	0. 00785	7. 97617	0. 00947	8. 05041	0. 01123	8. 11873	0. 01314	8. 18202	0. 01521	50
11	. 89633	. 00788	. 97746	. 00949	. 05159	. 01126	. 11983	. 01318	. 18303	. 01524	49
12	. 89775	. 00790	. 97875	. 00952	. 05277	. 01129	. 12092	. 01321	. 18405	. 01528	48
13	. 89916	. 00793	. 98003	. 00955	. 05395	. 01132	. 12201	. 01324	. 18506	. 01531	47
14	. 90057	. 00795	. 98132	. 00958	. 05513	. 01135	. 12310	. 01328	. 18607	. 01535	46
15	7. 90198	0. 00798	7. 98260	0. 00961	8. 05631	0. 01138	8. 12419	0. 01331	8. 18709	0. 01538	45
16	. 90339	. 00801	. 98389	. 00964	. 05749	. 01142	. 12528	. 01334	. 18810	. 01542	44
17	. 90480	. 00803	. 98517	. 00966	. 05866	. 01145	. 12636	. 01338	. 18910	. 01546	43
18	. 90620	. 00806	. 98644	. 00969	. 05984	. 01148	. 12745	. 01341	. 19011	. 01549	42
19	. 90760	. 00808	. 98772	. 00972	. 06101	. 01151	. 12853	. 01344	. 19112	. 01553	41
20	7. 90900	0. 00811	7. 98899	0. 00975	8. 06218	0. 01154	8. 12961	0. 01348	8. 19212	0. 01556	40
21	. 91039	. 00814	. 99027	. 00978	. 06335	. 01157	. 13069	. 01351	. 19313	. 01560	39
22	. 91179	. 00816	. 99154	. 00981	. 06451	. 01160	. 13177	. 01354	. 19413	. 01564	38
23	. 91318	. 00819	. 99281	. 00984	. 06568	. 01163	. 13285	. 01358	. 19513	. 01567	37
24	. 91457	. 00821	. 99407	. 00986	. 06684	. 01166	. 13392	. 01361	. 19613	. 01571	36
25	7. 91596	0. 00824	7. 99534	0. 00989	8. 06800	0. 01170	8. 13500	0. 01365	8. 19713	0. 01574	35
26	. 91734	. 00827	. 99660	. 00992	. 06917	. 01173	. 13607	. 01368	. 19813	. 01578	34
27	. 91872	. 00829	. 99786	. 00995	. 07032	. 01176	. 13714	. 01371	. 19913	. 01582	33
28	. 92010	. 00832	7. 99912	. 00998	. 07148	. 01179	. 13822	. 01375	. 20012	. 01585	32
29	. 92148	. 00835	8. 00038	. 01001	. 07264	. 01182	. 13928	. 01378	. 20112	. 01589	31
30	7. 92286	0. 00837	8. 00163	0. 01004	8. 07379	0. 01185	8. 14035	0. 01382	8. 20211	0. 01593	30
31	. 92423	. 00840	. 00289	. 01007	. 07494	. 01188	. 14142	. 01385	. 20310	. 01596	29
32	. 92560	. 00843	. 00414	. 01010	. 07610	. 01192	. 14248	. 01388	. 20410	. 01600	28
33	. 92697	. 00845	. 00539	. 01012	. 07725	. 01195	. 14355	. 01392	. 20509	. 01604	27
34	. 92834	. 00848	. 00664	. 01015	. 07839	. 01198	. 14461	. 01395	. 20608	. 01607	26
35	7. 92970	0. 00851	8. 00788	0. 01018	8. 07954	0. 01201	8. 14567	0. 01399	8. 20706	0. 01611	25
36	. 93107	. 00853	. 00913	. 01021	. 08069	. 01204	. 14673	. 01402	. 20805	. 01615	24
37	. 93243	. 00856	. 01037	. 01024	. 08183	. 01207	. 14779	. 01405	. 20904	. 01618	23
38	. 93379	. 00859	. 01161	. 01027	. 08297	. 01211	. 14885	. 01409	. 21002	. 01622	22
39	. 93514	. 00861	. 01285	. 01030	. 08411	. 01214	. 14991	. 01412	. 21100	. 01626	21
40	7. 93650	0. 00864	8. 01409	0. 01033	8. 08525	0. 01217	8. 15096	0. 01416	8. 21199	0. 01629	20
41	. 93785	. 00867	. 01532	. 01036	. 08639	. 01220	. 15201	. 014HI	. 21297	. 01633	19
42	. 93920	. 00869	. 01656	. 01039	. 08752	. 01223	. 15307	. 01423	. 21395	. 01637	18
43	. 94055	. 00872	. 01779	. 01042	. 08866	. 01226	. 15412	. 01426	. 21493	. 01640	17
44	. 94189	. 00875	. 01902	. 01045	. 08979	. 01230	. 15517	. 01429	. 21590	. 01644	16
45	7. 94324	0. 00877	8. 02025	0. 01048	8. 09092	0. 01233	8. 15622	0. 01433	8. 21688	0. 01648	15
46	. 94458	. 00880	. 02148	. 01051	. 09205	. 01236	. 15726	. 01436	. 21785	. 01651	14
47	. 94592	. 00883	. 02270	. 01054	. 09318	. 01239	. 15831	. 01440	. 21883	. 01655	13
48	. 94726	. 00886	. 02392	. 01057	. 09431	. 01243	. 15935	. 01443	. 21980	. 01659	12
49	. 94859	. 00888	. 02515	. 01060	. 09543	. 01246	. 16040	. 01447	. 22077	. 01663	11
50	7. 94992	0. 00891	8. 02637	0. 01063	8. 09656	0. 01249	8. 16144	0. 01450	8. 22175	0. 01666	10
51	. 95126	. 00894	. 02758	. 01066	. 09768	. 01252	. 16248	. 01454	. 22272	. 01670	9
52	. 95259	. 00897	. 02880	. 01069	. 09880	. 01255	. 16352	. 01457	. 22368	. 01674	8
53	. 95391	. 00899	. 03001	. 01072	. 09992	. 01259	. 16456	. 01461	. 22465	. 01677	7
54	. 95524	. 00902	. 03123	. 01075	. 10104	. 01262	. 16559	. 01464	. 22562	. 01681	6
55	7. 95656	0. 00905	8. 03244	0. 01078	8. 10216	0. 01265	8. 16663	0. 01468	8. 22658	0. 01685	5
56	. 95788	. 00908	. 03365	. 01081	. 10327	. 01268	. 16766	. 01471	. 22755	. 01689	4
57	. 95920	. 00910	. 03486	. 01084	. 10439	. 01272	. 16870	. 01475	. 22851	. 01692	3
58	. 96052	. 00913	. 03606	. 01087	. 10550	. 01275	. 16973	. 01478	. 22947	. 01696	2
59	. 96183	. 00916	. 03727	. 01090	. 10661	. 01278	. 17076	. 01482	. 23044	. 01700	1
60	7. 96315	0. 00919	8. 03847	0. 01093	8. 10772	0. 01281	8. 17179	0. 01485	8. 23140	0. 01704	0
	349°		348°		347°		346°		345°		

Haversines

′	15° Log Hav	15° Nat. Hav	16° Log Hav	16° Nat. Hav	17° Log Hav	17° Nat. Hav	18° Log Hav	18° Nat. Hav	19° Log Hav	19° Nat. Hav	′
0	8. 23140	0. 01704	8.·28711	0. 01937	8. 33940	0. 02185	8. 38867	0. 02447	8. 43522	0. 02724	60
1	. 23235	. 01707	. 28801	. 01941	. 34025	. 02189	. 38946	. 02452	. 43597	. 02729	59
2	. 23331	. 01711	. 28891	. 01945	. 34109	. 02193	. 39026	. 02456	. 43673	. 02734	58
3	. 23427	. 01715	. 28980	. 01949	. 34194	. 02198	. 39105	. 02461	. 43748	. 02738	57
4	. 23523	. 01719	. 29070	. 01953	. 34278	. 02202	. 39185	. 02465	. 43823	. 02743	56
5	8. 23618	0. 01723	8. 29159	0. 01957	8. 34362	0. 02206	8. 39264	0. 02470	8. 43899	0. 02748	55
6	. 23713	. 01726	. 29249	. 01961	. 34446	. 02210	. 39344	. 02474	. 43974	. 02753	54
7	. 23809	. 01730	. 29338	. 01965	. 34530	. 02215	. 39423	. 02479	. 44049	. 02757	53
8	. 23904	. 01734	. 29427	. 01969	. 34614	. 02219	. 39502	. 02483	. 44124	. 02762	52
9	. 23999	. 01738	. 29516	. 01973	. 34698	. 02223	. 39581	. 02488	. 44199	. 02767	51
10	8. 24094	0. 01742	8. 29605	0. 01977	8. 34782	0. 02227	8. 39660	0. 02492	8. 44273	0. 02772	50
11	. 24189	. 01745	. 29694	. 01981	. 34865	. 02232	. 39739	. 02497	. 44348	. 02776	49
12	. 24283	. 01749	. 29783	. 01985	. 34949	. 02236	. 39818	. 02501	. 44423	. 02781	48
13	. 24378	. 01753	. 29872	. 01989	. 35032	. 02240	. 39897	. 02506	. 44498	. 02786	47
14	. 24473	. 01757	. 29960	. 01993	. 35116	. 02245	. 39976	. 02510	. 44572	. 02791	46
15	8. 24567	0. 01761	8. 30049	0. 01998	8. 35199	0. 02249	8. 40055	0. 02515	8. 44647	0. 02796	45
16	. 24661	. 01764	. 30137	. 02002	. 35282	. 02253	. 40133	. 02520	. 44721	. 02800	44
17	. 24755	. 01768	. 30226	. 02006	. 35365	. 02258	. 40212	. 02524	. 44796	. 02805	43
18	. 24850	. 01772	. 30314	. 02010	. 35449	. 02262	. 40290	. 02529	. 44870	. 02810	42
19	. 24944	. 01776	. 30402	. 02014	. 35532	. 02266	. 40369	. 02533	. 44944	. 02815	41
20	8. 25037	0. 01780	8. 30490	0. 02018	8. 35614	0. 02271	8. 40447	0. 02538	8. 45018	0. 02820	40
21	. 25131	. 01784	. 30578	. 02022	. 35697	. 02275	. 40525	. 02542	. 45093	. 02824	39
22	. 25225	. 01788	. 30666	. 02026	. 35780	. 02279	. 40603	. 02547	. 45167	. 02829	38
23	. 25319	. 01791	. 30754	. 02030	. 35863	. 02284	. 40681	. 02552	. 45241	. 02834	37
24	. 25412	. 01795	. 30842	. 02034	. 35945	. 02288	. 40760	. 02556	. 45315	. 02839	36
25	8. 25505	0. 01799	8. 30929	0. 02038	8. 36028	0. 02292	8. 40837	0. 02561	8. 45388	0. 02844	35
26	. 25599	. 01803	. 31017	. 02043	. 36110	. 02297	. 40915	. 02565	. 45462	. 02849	34
27	. 25692	. 01807	. 31104	. 02047	. 36193	. 02301	. 40993	. 02570	. 45536	. 02853	33
28	. 25785	. 01811	. 31192	. 02051	. 36275	. 02305	. 41071	. 02575	. 45610	. 02858	32
29	. 25878	. 01815	. 31279	. 02055	. 36357	. 02310	. 41149	. 02579	. 45683	. 02863	31
30	8. 25971	0. 01818	8. 31366	0. 02059	8. 36439	0. 02314	8. 41226	0. 02584	8. 45757	0. 02868	30
31	. 26064	. 01822	. 31453	. 02063	. 36521	. 02319	. 41304	. 02588	. 45830	. 02873	29
32	. 26156	. 01826	. 31540	. 02067	. 36603	. 02323	. 41381	. 02593	. 45904	. 02878	28
33	. 26249	. 01830	. 31627	. 02071	. 36685	. 02327	. 41459	. 02598	. 45977	. 02883	27
34	. 26341	. 01834	. 31714	. 02076	. 36767	. 02332	. 41536	. 02602	. 46050	. 02887	26
35	8. 26434	0. 01838	8. 31800	0. 02080	8. 36849	0. 02336	8. 41613	0. 0260.7	8. 46124	0. 02892	25
36	. 26526	. 01842	. 31887	. 02084	. 36930	. 02340	. 41690	. 02612	. 46197	. 02897	24
37	. 26618	. 01846	. 31974	. 02088	. 37012	. 02345	. 41767	. 02616	. 46270	. 02902	23
38	. 26710	. 01850	. 32060	. 02092	. 37093	. 02349	. 41845	. 02621	. 46343	. 02907	22
39	. 26802	. 01854	. 32147	. 02096	. 37175	. 02354	. 41921	. 02626	. 46416	. 02912	21
40	8. 26894	0. 01858	8. 32233	0. 02101	8. 37256	0. 02358	8. 41998	0. 02630	8. 46489	0. 02917	20
41	. 26986	. 01861	. 32319	. 02105	. 37337	. 02363	. 42075	. 02635	. 46562	. 02922	19
42	. 27078	. 01865	. 32405	. 02109	. 37419	. 02367	. 42152	. 02639	. 46634	. 02926	18
43	. 27169	. 01869	. 32491	. 02113	. 37500	. 02371	. 42229	. 02644	. 46707	. 02931	17
44	27261	. 01873	. 32577	. 02117	. 37581	. 02376	. 42305	. 02649	. 46780	. 02936	16
45	8. 27352	0. 01877	8. 32663	0. 02121	8. 37662	0. 02380	8. 42382	0. 02653	8. 46852	0. 02941	15
46	. 27443	. 01881	. 32749	. 02126	. 37742	. 02385	. 42458	. 02658	. 46925	. 02946	14
47	. 27534	. 01885	. 32834	. 02130	. 37823	. 02389	. 42535	. 02663	. 46998	. 02951	13
48	. 27626	. 01889	. 32920	. 02134	. 37904	. 02394	. 42611	. 02668	. 47070	. 02956	12
49	. 27717	. 01893	. 33006	. 02138	. 37985	. 02398	. 42687	. 02672	. 47142	. 02961	11
50	8. 27807	0. 01897	8. 33091	0. 02142	8. 38065	0. 02402	8. 42764	0. 02677	8. 47215	0. 02966	10
51	. 27898	. 01901	. 33176	. 02147	. 38146	. 02407	. 42840	. 02682	. 47287	. 02971	9
52	. 27989	. 01905	. 33262	. 02151	. 38226	. 02411	. 42916	. 02686	. 47359	. 02976	8
53	. 28080	. 01909	. 33347	. 02155	. 38306	. 02416	. 42992	. 02691	. 47431	. 02981	7
54	. 28170	. 01913	. 33432	. 0215	. 38387	. 02420	. 43068	. 02696	. 47503	. 02986	6
55	8. 28260	0. 01917	8. 33517	0. 02164	8. 38467	0. 02425	8. 43144	0. 02700	8. 47575	0. 02991	5
56	. 28351	. 01921	. 33602	. 02168	. 38547	. 02429	. 43219	. 02705	. 47647	. 02996	4
57	. 28441	. 01925	. 33686	. 02172	. 38627	. 02434	. 43295	. 02710	. 47719	. 03000	3
58	. 28531	. 01929	. 33771	. 02176	. 38707	. 02438	. 43371	. 02715	. 47791	. 03005	2
59	. 28621	. 01933	. 33856	. 02181	. 38787	. 02443	. 43446	. 02719	. 47862	. 03010	1
60	8. 28711	0. 01937	8. 33940	0. 02185	8. 38867	0. 02447	8. 43522	0. 02724	8. 47934	0. 03015	0
	344°		343°		342°		341°		340°		

Haversines

′	20°		21°		22°		23°		24°		′
	Log Hav	Nat. Hav	Log Hav	Nat. Hav	Log Hav	Nat. Hav	Log Hav	Nat. Hav	Log Hav	Nat. Hav	
0	8. 47934	0. 03015	8. 52127	0. 03321	8. 56120	0. 03641	8. 59931	0. 03975	8. 63576	0. 04323	60
1	. 48006	. 03020	. 52195	. 03326	. 56185	. 03646	. 59993	. 03980	. 63635	. 04329	59
2	. 48077	. 03025	. 52263	. 03331	. 56250	. 03652	. 60055	. 03986	. 63695	. 04335	58
3	. 48149	. 03030	. 52331	. 03337	. 56315	. 03657	. 60117	. 03992	. 63754	. 04340	57
4	. 48220	. 03035	. 52399	. 03342	. 56379	. 03663	. 60179	. 03998	. 63813	. 04346	56
5	8. 48292	0. 03040	8. 52467	0. 03347	8. 56444	0. 03668	8. 60241	0. 04003	8. 63872	0. 04352	55
6	. 48363	.·03045	. 52535	. 03352	. 56509	. 03674	. 60303	. 04009	. 63932	. 04358	54
7	. 48434	. 03050	. 52602	. 03358	. 56574	. 03679	. 60365	. 04015	. 63991	. 04364	53
8	. 48505	. 03055	. 52670	. 03363	. 56638	. 03685	. 60426	. 04020	..64050	. 04370	52
9	. 48576	. 03060	. 52738	. 03368	. 56703	. 03690	. 60488	. 04026	. 64109	. 04376	51
10	8. 48648	0. 03065	8. 52806	0.03373	8. 56767	0. 03695	8. 60550	0. 04032	8. 64168	0. 04382	50
11	. 48719	. 03070	. 52873	. 03379	. 56832	. 03701	. 60611	. 04038	. 64227	. 04388	49
12	. 48789	. 03075	. 52941	. 03384	. 56896	. 03706	. 60673	. 04043	. 64286	. 04394	48
13	. 48860	. 03080	. 53008	. 03389	. 56960	. 03712	. 60734	. 04049	. 64345	. 04400	47
14	. 48931	. 03085	. 53076	. 03394	. 57025	. 03717	. 60796	. 04055	. 64404	. 04406	46
15	8. 49002	0 .03090	8. 53143	0. 03400	8. 57089	0. 03723	8. 60857	0. 04060	8. 64463	0. 04412	45
16	. 49073	. 03095	. 53210	. 03405	. 57153	. 03728	. 60919	. 04066	. 64521	. 04418	44
17	. 49143	. 03101	. 53277	. 03410	. 57217	. 03734	. G0980	. 04072	. 64580	. 04424	43
18	. 49214	. 03106	. 53345	. 03415	. 57282	. 03740	. 61041	. 04078	. 64639	. 04430	42
19	. 49284	. 03111	. 53412	. 03421	. 57346	. 03745	. 61103	. 04083	. 64697	. 04436	41
20	8. 49355	0.03116	8. 53479	0.03426	8. 57410	0. 03751	8. 61164	0. 04089	8. 64756	0. 04442	40
21	. 49425	. 03121	. 53546	. 03431	. 57474	. 03756	. 61225	. 04095	. 64815	. 04448	39
22	. 49496	. 03126	. 53613	. 03437	. 57538	. 03762	. 61286	. 04101	. 64873	. 04454	38
23	'49566	. 03131	. 53680	. 03442	. 57601	. 03767	. 61347	. 04106	. 64932	. 04460	37
24	'49636	'03136	. 53747	. 03447	. 57665	. 03773	. 61408	. 04112	. 64990	. 04466	36
25	8. 49706	0. 03141	8. 53814	0. 03453	8. 57729	0. 03778	8. 61469	0. 04118	8. 65049	0. 04472	35
26	. 49777	. 03146	. 53880	. 03458	. 57793	. 03784	. 61530	. 04124	. 65107	. 04478	34
27	. 49847	. 03151	. 53947	. 03463	. 57856	. 03789	. 61591	. 01130	. 65165	. 04484	33
28	. 49917	. 03156	. 54014	. 03468	. 57920	. 03795	. 61652	. 04135	. 65224	. 04490	32
29	. 49987	. 03161	. 54080	. 03474	. 57984	. 03800	. 61713	. 04141	. 65282	. 04496	31
30	8. 50056	0. 03166	8. 54147	0. 03479	8. 58047	0. 03806	8. 61773	0. 04147	8. 65340	0. 04502	30
31	. 50126	. 03171	. 54214	. 03484	. 58111	. 03812	. 61834	. 04153	. 65398	. 04508	29
32	. 50196	. 03177	. 54280	. 03490	. 58174	. 03817	. 61895	. 04159	. 65456	. 04514	28
33	. 50266	. 03182	. 54346	. 03495	. 58238	. 03823	. 61955	. 04164	. 65514	. 04520	27
34	. 50335	. 03187	. 54413	. 03500	. 58301	. 03828	. 62016	. 04170	. 65572	. 04526	26
35	8. 50405	0. 03192	8. 54479	0. 03506	8. 58364	0. 03834	8. 62077	0. 04176	8. 65630	0. 04532	25
36	. 50475	. 03197	. 54545	. 03511	. 58427	. 03839	. 62137	. 04182	. 65688	. 04538	24
37	. 50544	. 03202	. 54612	. 03517	. 58491	. 03845	. 62197	. 04188	. 65746	. 04544	23
38	. 50614	. 03207	. 54678	. 03522	. 58554	. 03851	. 62258	. 04194	. 65804	. 04550	22
39	. 50683	. 03212	. 54744	. 03527	. 58617	. 03856	. 62318	. 04199	. 65862	. 04556	21
40	8. 50752	0. 03218	8. 54810	0. 03533	8. 58680	0. 03862	8. 62379	0.04205	8. 65920	0. 04562	20
41	. 50821	'03223	. 54976	. 03538	. 58743	. 03867	. 62439	. 04211	. 65978	. 04569	19
42	. 50891	'03228	. 54942	. 03543	. 58806	. 03873	. 62499	. 04217	. 66035	. 04575	18
43	. 50960	. 03233	. 55008	. 03549	. 58869	. 03879	. 62559	. 04223	. 66093	. 04581	17
44	. 51029	'03238	'55073	. 03554	. 58932	. 03884	. 62619	. 04229	. 66151	. 04587	16
45	8. 51098	0. 03243	8. 55139	0. 03560	8. 58994	0. 03890	8. 62680	0. 04234	8. 66208	0. 04593	15
46	. 51167	. 03248	. 55205	. 03565	. 59057	. 03896	. 62740	. 04240	. 66266	. 04599	14
47	. 51236	. 03254	. 55271	. 03570	. 59120	. 03901	. 62800	. 04246	66323	. 04605	13
48	. 51305	. 03259	. 55336	. 03576	. 59183	. 03907	. 62860	. 04252	. 66381	. 04611	12
49	. 51374	. 03264	. 55402	. 03581	. 59245	. 03912	. 62919	. 04258	. 66438	. 04617	11
50	8. 51442	0. 03269	8. 55467	0. 03587	8. 59308	0. 03918	8. 62979	0. 04264	8. 66496	0. 04623	10
51	. 51511	. 03274	. 55533	. 03592	. 59370	. 03924	. 63039	. 04270	. 66553	. 04629	9
52	. 51580	. 03279	. 55598	. 03597	. 59433	. 03929	. 63099	. 04276	. 66610	. 04636	8
53	. 51648	. 03285	. 55664	. 03603	. 59495	. 03935	. 63159	. 04281	. 66668	. 04642	7
54	. 51717	. 03290	. 55729	. 03608	. 59558	. 03941	. 63218	. 04287	. 66725	. 04648	6
55	8. 51785	0. 03295	8. 55794	0. 03614	8. 59620	0. 03946	8. 63278	0. 04293	8. 66782	0. 04654	5
56	. 51854	. 03300	. 55859	. 03619	. 59682	. 03952	. 63338	. 04299	. 66839	. 04660	4
57	. 51922	. 03305	. 55925	. 03624	. 59745	. 03958	. 63397	. 04305	. 66896	. 04666	3
58	. 51990	. 03311	. 55990	. 03630	. 59807	. 03963	. 63457	. 04311	. 66953	. 04672	2
59	. 52058	. 03316	. 56055	. 03635	. 59869	. 03969	. 63516	. 04317	. 67010	. 04678	1
60	8. 52127	0. 03321	8. 56120	0. 03641	8. 59931	0. 03975	8. 63576	0. 04323	8. 67067	0. 04685	0
	339°		338°		337°		336°		335°		

Haversines

′	25°		26°		27°		28°		29°		′
	Log Hav	Nat. Hav	Log Hav	Nat. Hav	Log Hav	Nat. Hav	Log Hav	Nat. Hav	Log Hav	Nat. Hav	
0	8. 67067	0. 04685	8. 70418	0. 05060	8. 73637	0. 05450	8. 76735	0. 05853	8. 79720	0. 06269	60
1	. 67124	. 04691	. 70472	. 05067	. 73690	. 05456	. 76786	. 05859	. 79769	. 06276	59
2	. 67181	. 04697	. 70527	. 05073	. 73742	. 05463	. 76836	. 05866	. 79818	. 06283	58
3	. 67238	. 04703	. 70582	. 05079	. 73795	. 05469	. 76887	. 05873	. 79866	. 06290	57
4	. 67295	. 04709	. 70636	. 05086	. 73847	. 05476	. 76938	. 05880	. 79915	. 06297	56
5	8. 67352	0. 04715	8. 70691	0. 05092	8. 73900	0. 05483	8. 76988	0. 05887	8. 79964	0. 06304	55
6	. 67409	. 04722	. 70745	. 05099	. 73952	. 05489	. 77039	. 05894	. 80013	. 06311	54
7	. 67465	. 04728	. 70800	. 05105	. 74005	. 05496	. 77089	. 05901	. 80061	. 06318	53
8	. 67522	. 04734	. 70854	. 05111	. 74057	. 05503	. 77139	. 05907	. 80110	. 06326	52
9	. 67579	. 04740	. 70909	. 05118	. 74109	. 05509	. 77190	. 05914	. 80158	. 06333	51
10	8. 67635	0. 04746	8. 70963	0. 05124	8. 74162	0. 05516	8. 77240	0. 05921	8. 80207	0. 06340	50
11	. 67692	. 04752	. 71017	. 05131	. 74214	. 05523	. 77291	. 05928	. 80256	. 06347	49
12	. 67748	. 04759	. 71072	. 05137	. 74266	. 05529	. 77341	. 05935	. 80304	. 06354	48
13	. 67805	. 04765	. 71126	. 05144	. 74318	. 05536	. 77391	. 05942	. 80353	. 06361	47
14	. 67861	. 04771	. 71180	. 05150	. 74371	. 05542	. 77441	. 05949	. 80401	. 06368	46
15	8. 67918	0. 04777	8. 71234	0. 05156	8. 74423	0. 05549	8. 77492	0. 05955	8. 80449	0. 06375	45
16	. 67974	. 04783	. 71289	. 05163	. 74475	. 05556	. 77542	. 05962	. 80498	. 06382	44
17	. 68030	. 04790	. 71343	. 05169	. 74527	. 05562	. 77592	. 05969	. 80546	. 06389	43
18	. 68087	. 04796	. 71397	. 05176	. 74579	. 05569	. 77642	. 05976	. 80595	. 06397	42
19	. 68143	. 04802	. 71451	. 05182	. 74631	. 05576	. 77692	. 05983	. 80643	. 06404	41
20	8. 68199	0. 04808	8. 71505	0. 05189	8. 74683	0. 05582	8. 77742	0. 05990	8. 80691	0. 06411	40
21	. 68256	. 04815	. 71559	. 05195	. 74735	. 05589	. 77792	. 05997	. 80739	. 06418	39
22	. 68312	. 04821	. 71613	. 05201	. 74787	. 05596	. 77842	. 06004	. 80788	. 06425	38
23	. 68368	. 04827	. 71667	. 05208	. 74839	. 05603	. 77892	. 06011	. 80836	. 06432	37
24	. 68424	. 04833	. 71721	. 05214	. 74890	. 05609	. 77942	. 06018	. 80884	. 06439	36
25	8. 68480	0. 04839	8. 71774	0. 05221	8. 74942	0. 05616	8. 77992	0. 06024	8. 80932	0. 06446	35
26	. 68536	. 04846	. 71828	. 05227	. 74994	. 05623	. 78042	. 06031	. 80980	. 06454	34
27	. 68592	. 04852	. 71882	. 05234	. 75046	. 05629	. 78092	. 06038	. 81028	. 06461	33
28	. 68648	. 04858	. 71936	. 05240	. 75097	. 05636	. 78142	. 06045	. 81076	. 06468	32
29	. 68704	. 04864	. 71989	. 05247	. 75149	. 05643	. 78191	. 06052	. 81124	. 06475	31
30	8. 68760	0. 04871	8. 72043	0. 05253	8. 75201	0. 05649	8. 78241	0. 06059	8. 81172	0. 06482	30
31	. 68815	. 04877	. 72097	. 05260	. 75252	. 05656	. 78291	. 06066	. 81220	. 06489	29
32	. 68871	. 04883	. 72150	. 05266	. 75304	. 05663	. 78341	. 06073	. 81268	. 06497	28
33	. 68927	. 04890	. 72204	. 05273	. 75355	. 05670	. 78390	. 06080	. 81316	. 06504	27
34	. 68983	. 04896	. 72257	. 05279	. 75407	. 05676	. 78440	. 06087	. 81364	. 06511	26
35	8. 69038	0. 04902	8. 72311	0. 05286	8. 75458	0. 05683	8. 78490	0. 06094	8. 81412	0. 06518	25
36	. 69094	. 04908	. 72364	. 05292	. 75510	. 05690	. 78539	. 06101	. 81460	. 06525	24
37	. 69149	. 04915	. 72418	. 05299	. 75561	. 05697	. 78589	. 06108	. 81508	. 06532	23
38	. 69205	. 04921	. 72471	. 05305	. 75613	. 05703	. 78638	. 06115	. 81555	. 05540	22
39	. 69260	. 04927	. 72525	. 05312	. 75664	. 05710	. 78688	. 06122	. 81603	. 06547	21
40	8. 69316	0. 04934	8. 72578	0. 05318	8. 75715	0. 05717	8. 78737	0. 06129	8. 81651	0. 06554	20
41	. 69371	. 04940	. 72631	. 05325	. 75767	. 05724	. 78787	. 06136	. 81699	. 06561	19
42	. 69427	. 04946	. 72684	. 05331	. 75818	. 05730	. 78836	. 06143	. 81746	. 06568	18
43	. 69482	. 04952	. 72738	. 05338	. 75869	. 05737	. 78885	. 06150	. 81794	. 06576	17
44	. 69537	. 04959	. 72791	. 05345	. 75920	. 05744	. 78935	. 06157	. 81841	. 06583	16
45	8. 69593	0. 04965	8. 72844	0. 05351	8. 75972	0. 05751	8. 78984	0. 06164	8. 81889	0. 06590	15
46	. 69648	. 04971	. 72897	. 05358	. 76023	. 05757	. 79033	. 06171	. 81937	. 06597	14
47	. 69703	. 04978	. 72950	. 05364	. 76074	. 05764	. 79082	. 06178	. 81984	. 06605	13
48	. 69758	. 04984	. 73003	. 05371	. 76125	. 05771	. 79132	. 06185	. 82032	. 06612	12
49	. 69814	. 04990	. 73056	. 05377	. 76176	. 05778	. 79181	. 06192	. 82079	. 06619	11
50	8. 69869	0. 04997	8. 73109	0. 05384	8. 76227	0. 05785	8. 79230	0. 06199	8. 82126	0. 06626	10
51	. 69924	. 05003	. 73162	. 05390	. 76278	. 05791	. 79279	. 06206	. 82174	. 06633	9
52	. 69979	. 05009	. 73215	. 05397	. 76329	. 05798	. 79328	. 06213	. 82221	. 06641	8
53	. 70034	. 05016	. 73268	. 05404	. 76380	. 05805	. 79377	. 06220	. 82269	. 06648	7
54	. 70089	. 05022	. 73321	. 05410	. 76431	. 05812	. 79426	. 06227	. 82316	. 06655	6
55	8. 70144	0. 05028	8. 73374	0. 05417	8. 76481	0. 05819	8. 79475	0. 06234	8. 82363	0. 06662	5
56	. 70198	. 05035	. 73426	. 05423	. 76532	. 05825	. 79524	. 06241	. 82410	. 06670	4
57	. 70253	. 05041	. 73479	. 05430	. 76583	. 05832	. 79573	. 06248	. 82458	. 06677	3
58	. 70308	. 05048	. 73532	. 05436	. 76634	. 05839	. 79622	. 06255	. 82505	. 06684	2
59	. 70363	. 05054	. 73584	. 05443	. 76684	. 05846	. 79671	. 06262	. 82552	. 06691	1
60	8. 70418	0. 05060	8. 73637	0. 05450	8. 76735	0. 05853	8. 79720	0. 06269	8. 82599	0. 06699	0
	334°		333°		332°		331°		330°		

Haversines

′	30°		31°		32°		33°		34°		′
	Log Hav	Nat. Hav	Log Hav	Nat. Hav	Log Hav	Nat. Hav	Log Hav	Nat. Hav	Log Hav	Nat. Hav	
0	8. 82599	0. 06699	8. 85380	0. 07142	8. 88068	0. 07598	8. 90668	0. 08066	8. 93187	0. 08548	60
1	. 82646	. 06706	. 85425	. 07149	. 88112	. 07605	. 90711	. 08074	. 93228	. 08556	59
2	.·82694	. 06713	. 85471	. 07157	. 88156	. 07613	. 90754	. 08082	. 93270	. 08564	58
3	. 82741	. 06721	. 85516	. 07164	. 88200	. 07621	. 90796	. 08090	. 93311	. 08573	57
4	. 82788	. 06728	. 85562	. 07172	. 88244	. 07628	. 90839	. 08098	. 93352	. 08581	56
5	8. 82835	0. 06735	8. 85607	0. 07179	8. 88288	0. 07636	8. 90881	0. 08106	8. 93393	0. 08589	55
6	. 82882	. 06742	. 85653	. 07187	. 88332	. 07644	. 90924	. 08114	. 93435	. 08597	54
7	. 82929	. 06750	. 85698	. 07194	. 88375	' 07652	. 90966	. 08122	. 93476	. 08605	53
8	. 82976	. 06757	. 85743	' 07202	. 88419	. 07659	. 91009	. 08130	. 93517	. 08613	52
9	. 83023	. 06764	. 85789	. 07209	. 88463	. 07667	. 91051	. 08138	. 93558	. 08621	51
10	8. 83069	0. 06772	8. 85834	0. 07217	8. 88507	0. 07675	8. 91094	0. 08146	8. 93599	0. 08630	50
11	. 83116	. 06779	. 85879	. 07224	. 88551	. 07683	. 91136	. 08154	. 93640	. 08638	49
12	. 83163	. 06786	. 85925	. 07232	. 88595	. 07690	. 91179	. 08162	. 93681	. 08646	48
13	. 83210	. 06794	. 85970	. 07239	. 88638	. 07698	. 91221	. 08170	. 93722	. 08654	47
14	. 83257	. 06801	. 86015	. 07247	. 88682	. 07706	. 91263	. 08178	. 93764	. 08662	46
15	8. 83303	0. 06808	8. 86060	0. 07254	8. 88726	0. 07714	8.91306	0. 08186	8. 93805	0. 08671	45
16	. 83350	. 06816	. 86105	. 07262	. 88769	. 07721	. 91348	. 08194	. 93846	. 08679	44
17	. 83397	. 06823	. 86151	. 07270	. 88813	. 07729	. 91390	. 08202	. 93886	. 08687	43
18	. 83444	. 06830	. 86196	. 07277	. 88857	. 07737	. 91432	. 08210	. 93927	. 08695	42
19	. 83490	. 06838	. 86241	. 07285	. 88900	. 07745	. 91475	. . 08218	. 93968	. 08703	41
20	8. 83537	0. 06845	8. 86286	0. 07292	8. 88944	0. 07752	8. 91517	0. 08226	8. 94009	0. 08711	40
21	. 83583	. 06852	. 86331	. 07300	. 88988	. 07760	. 91559	. 08234	. 94050	. 08720	39
22	. 83630	. 06860	. 86376	. 07307	. 89031	. 07768	. 91601	. 08242	. 94091	. 08728	38
23	. 83676	. 06867	. 86421	. 07315	. 89075	. 07776	. 91643	. 08250	. 94132	. 08736	37
24	. 83723	. 06874	. 86466	. 07322	. 89118	. 07784	. 91685	. 08258	. 94173	. 08744	36
25	8. 83769	0. 06882	8. 86511	0. 07330	8. 89162	0. 07791	8. 91728	0. 08266	8. 94213	0. 08753	35
26	. 83816	. 06889	. 86556	. 07338	. 89205	. 07799	. 91770	. 08274	. 94254	. 08761	34
27	. 83862	. 06896	. 86600	. 07345	. 89248	. 07807	. 91812	. 08282	. 94295	. 08769	33
28	. 83909	. 06904	. 86645	. 07353	. 89292	. 07815	. 91854	. 08290	. 94336	. 08777	32
29	. 83955	. 06911	. 86690	. 07360	. 89335	. 07823	. 91896	. 08298	. 94376	. 08785	31
30	8. 84002	0. 06919	8. 86735	0. 07368	8. 89379	0. 07830	8. 91938	0. 08306	8. 94417	0. 08794	30
31	. 84048	. 06926	. 86780	. 07376	. 89422	. 07838	. 91980	. 08314	. 94458	. 08802	29
32	. 84094	. 06933	. 86825	. 07383	. 89465	. 07846	. 92022	. 08322	. 94498	. 08810	28
33	. 84140	. 06941	. 86869	. 07391	. 89509	. 07854	. 92064	. 08330	. 94539	. 08818	27
34	. 84187	. 06948	. 86914	. 07398	. 89552	. 07862	. 92105	. 08338	. 94580	. 08827	26
35	8. 84233	0. 06955	8. 86959	0. 07406	8. 89595	0. 07870	8. 92147	0. 08346	8. 94620	0. 08835	25
36	. 84279	. 06963	. 87003	. 07414	. 89638	. 07877	. 92189	. 08354	. 94661	. 08843	24
37	. 84325	. 06970	. 87048	. 07421	. 89681	. 07885	. 92231	. 08362	. 94701	. 08851	23
38	. 84371	. 06978	. 87093	. 07429	. 89725	. 07893	. 92273	. 08370	. 94742	. 08860	22
39	. 84417	. 06985	. 87137	. 07437	. 89768	. 07901	. 92315	. 08378	. 94782	. 08868	21
40	8. 84464	0. 06993	8. 87182	0. 07444	8. 89811	0. 07909	8. 92356	0. 08386	8. 94823	0. 08876	20
41	. 84510	. 07000	. 87226	. 07452	. 89854	. 07917	. 92398	. 08394	. 94863	. 08885	19
42	. 84556	. 07007	. 87271	. 07459	. 89897	. 07924	. 92440	. 08402	. 94904	. 08893	18
43	. 84602	. 07015	. 87315	. 07467	. 89940	. 07932	. 92482	. 08410	. 94944	. 08901	17
44	. 84648	. 07022	. 87360	. 07475	. 89983	. 07940	. 92523	. 08418	. 94985	. 08909	16
45	8. 84694	0. 07030	8. 87404	0. 07482	8. 90026	0. 07948	8. 92565	0. 08427	8. 95025	0. 08918	15
46	. 84740	. 07037	. 87448	. 07490	. 90069	. 07956	. 92607	. 08435	. 95065	. 08926	14
47	. 84785	. 07045	. 87493	. 07498	. 90112	. 07964	. 92648	. 08443	. 95106	. 08934	13
48	. 84831	. 07052	. 87537	. 07505	. 90155	. 07972	. 92690	. 08451	. 95146	. 08943	12
49	. 84877	. 07059	. 87582	. 07513	. 90198	. 07980	. 92731	. 08459	. 95186	. 08951	11
50	8. 84923	0. 07067	8. 8762'6	0. 07521	8. 90241	0. 07987	8. 92773	0. 08467	8. 95227	0. 08959	10
51	. 84969	. 07074	. 87670	. 07528	. 90284	. 07995	. 92814	. 08475	. 95267	. 08967	9
52	. 85015	. 07082	. 87714	. 07536	. 90326	. 08003	. 92856	. 08483	. 95307	. 08976	8
53	. 85060	. 07089	. 87759	. 07544	. 90369	. 08011	. 92897	. 08491	. 95347	. 08984	7
54	. 85106	. 07097	. 87803	. 07551	. 90412	. 08019	. 92939	. 08499	. 95388	. 08992	6
55	8. 85152	0. 07104	8. 87847	0. 07559	8. 90455	0. 08027	8. 92980	0. 08507	8. 95428	0. 09001	5
56	. 85197	. 07112	. 87891	. 07567	. 90498	. 08035	. 93022	. 08516	. 95468	. 09009	4
57	. 85243	. 07119	. 87935	. 07574	. 90540	. 08043	. 93063	. 08524	. 95508	. 09017	3
58	. 85289	. 07127	. 87980	. 07582	. 90583	. 08051	. 93104	. 08532	. 95548	. 09026	2
59	. 85334	. 07134	. 88024	. 07590	. 90626	. 08059	. 93146	. 08540	. 95588	. 09034	1
60	8. 85380	0. 07142	8. 88068	0. 07598	8. 90668	0. 08066	8. 93187	0. 08548	8. 95628	0. 09042	0
	329°		328°		327°		326°		325°		

Haversines

′	35°		36°		37°		38°		39°		′
	Log Hav	Nat. Hav	Log Hav	Nat. Hav	Log Hav	Nat. Hav	Log Hav	Nat. Hav	Log Hav	Nat. Hav	
0	8.95628	0.09042	8.97997	0.09549	9.00295	0.10068	9.02528	0.10599	9.04699	0.11143	60
1	.95668	.09051	.98035	.09558	.00333	.10077	.02565	.10608	.04735	.11152	59
2	.95709	.09059	.98074	.09566	.00371	.10086	.02602	.10517	.04770	.11161	58
3	.95749	.09067	.98113	.09575	.00408	.10094	.02638	.10626	.04806	.11170	57
4	.95789	.09076	.98152	.09583	.00446	.10103	.02675	.10635	.04842	.11179	56
5	8.95828	0.09084	8.98191	0.09592	9.00484	0.10112	9.02712	0.10644	9.04877	0.11189	55
6	.95868	.09093	.98229	.09601	.00522	.10121	.02748	.10653	.04913	.11198	54
7	.95908	.09101	.98268	.09609	.00559	.10130	.02785	.10662	.04948	.11207	53
8	.95948	.09109	.98307	.09618	.00597	.10138	.02821	.10671	.04984	.11216	52
9	.95988	.09118	.98346	.09626	.00634	.10147	.02858	.10680	.05019	.11225	51
10	8.96028	0.09126	8.98384	0.09635	9.00672	0.10156	9.02894	0.10689	9.05055	0.11234	50
11	.96068	.09134	.98423	.09643	.00710	.10165	.02931	.10698	.05090	.11244	49
12	.96108	.09143	.98462	.09652	.00747	.10174	.02967	.10707	.05126	.11253	48
13	.96148	.09151	.98500	.09661	.00785	.10182	.03004	.10716	.05161	.11262	47
14	.96187	.09160	.98539	.09669	.00822	.10191	.03040	.10725	.05197	.11271	46
15	8.96227	0.09168	8.98578	0.09678	9.00860	0.10200	9.03077	0.10734	9.05232	0.11280	45
16	.96267	.09176	.98616	.09686	.00897	.10209	.03113	.10743	.05268	.11290	44
17	.96307	.09185	.98655	.09695	.00935	.10218	.03150	.10752	.05303	.11299	43
18	.96346	.09193	.98693	.09704	.00972	.10226	.03186	.10761	.05339	.11308	42
19	.96386	.09202	.98732	.09712	.01009	.10235	.03222	.10770	.05374	.11317	41
20	8.96426	0.09210	8.98770	0.09721	9.01047	0.10244	9.03259	0.10779	9.05409	0.11326	40
21	.96465	.09218	.98809	.09729	.01084	.10253	.03295	.10788	.05445	.11336	39
22	.96505	.09227	.98847	.09738	.01122	.10262	.03331	.10797	.05480	.11345	38
23	.96545	.09235	.98886	.09747	.01159	.10270	.03368	.10806	.05515	.11354	37
24	.96584	.09244	.98924	.09755	.01196	.10279	.03404	.10815	.05551	.11363	36
25	8.96624	0.09252	8.98963	0.09764	9.01234	0.10288	9.03440	0.10824	9.05586	0.11373	35
26	.96663	.09260	.99001	.09773	.01271	.10297	.03476	.10833	.05621	.11382	34
27	.96703	.09269	.99039	.09781	.01308	.10306	.03513	.10842	.05656	.11391	33
28	.96742	.09277	.99078	.09790	.01345	.10315	.03549	.10851	.05692	.11400	32
29	.96782	.09286	.99116	.09799	.01383	.10323	.03585	.10861	.05727	.11410	31
30	8.96821	0.09294	8.99154	0.09807	9.01420	0.10332	9.03621	0.10870	9.05762	0.11419	30
31	.96861	.09303	.99193	.09816	.01457	.10341	.03657	.10879	.05797	.11428	29
32	.96900	.09311	.99231	.09824	.01494	.10350	.03694	.10888	.05832	.11437	28
33	.96940	.09320	.99269	.09833	.01531	.10359	.03730	.10897	.05867	.11447	27
34	.96979	.09328	.99307	.09842	.01569	.10368	.03766	.10906	.05903	.11456	26
35	8.97018	0.09336	8.99346	0.09850	9.01606	0.10377	9.03802	0.10915	9.05938	0.11465	25
36	.97058	.09345	.99384	.09859	.01643	.10386	.03838	.10924	.05973	.11474	24
37	.97097	.09353	.99422	.09868	.01680	.10394	.03874	.10933	.06008	.11484	23
38	.97136	.09362	.99460	.09876	.01717	.10403	.03910	.10942	.06043	.11493	22
39	.97176	.09370	.99498	.09885	.01754	.10412	.03946	.10951	.06078	.11502	21
40	8.97215	0.09379	8.99536	0.09894	9.01791	0.10421	9.03982	0.10960	9.06113	0.11511	20
41	.97254	.09387	.99575	.09903	.01828	.10430	.04018	.10969	.06148	.11521	19
42	.97294	.09396	.99613	.09911	.01865	.10439	.04054	.10978	.06183	.11530	18
43	.97333	.09404	.99651	.09920	.01902	.10448	.04090	.10988	.06218	.11539	17
44	.97372	.09413	.99689	.09929	.01939	.10457	.04126	.10997	.06253	.11549	16
45	8.97411	0.09421	8.99727	0.09937	9.01976	0.10466	9.04162	0.11006	9.06288	0.11558	15
46	.97450	.09430	.99765	.09946	.02013	.10474	.04198	.11015	.06323	.11567	14
47	.97489	.09438	.99803	.09955	.02050	.10483	.04234	.11024	.06358	.11577	13
48	.97529	.09447	.99841	.09963	.02087	.10492	.04270	.11033	.06393	.11586	12
49	.97568	.09455	.99879	.09972	.02124	.10501	.04306	.11042	.06428	.11595	11
50	8.97607	0.09464	8.99917	0.09981	9.02161	0.10510	9.04341	0.11051	9.06462	0.11604	10
51	.97646	.09472	.99955	.09990	.02197	.10519	.04377	.11060	.06497	.11614	9
52	.97685	.09481	8.99993	.09998	.02234	.10528	.04413	.11070	.06532	.11623	8
53	.97724	.09489	9.00031	.10007	.02271	.10.537	.04449	.11079	.06567	.11632	7
54	.97763	.09498	.00068	.10016	.02308	.10546	.04485	.11088	.06602	.11642	6
55	8.97802	0.09506	9.00106	0.10025	9.02345	0.10555	9.04520	0.11097	9.06637	0.11651	5
56	.97841	.09515	.00144	.10033	.02381	.10564	.04556	.11106	.06671	.11660	4
57	.97880	.09524	.00182	.10042	.02418	.10573	.04592	.11115	.06706	.11670	3
58	.97919	.09532	.00220	.10051	.02455	.10582	.04628	.11124	.06741	.11679	2
59	.97958	.09541	.00258	.10059	.02492	.10591	.04663	.11134	.06776	.11688	1
60	8.97997	0.09549	9.00295	0.10068	9.02528	0.10599	9.04699	0.11143	9.06810	0.11698	0
	324°		323°		322°		321°		320°		

Haversines

′	40°		41°		42°		43°		44°		′
	Log Hav	Nat. Hav	Log Hav	Nat. Hav	Log Hav	Nat. Hav	Log Hav	Nat. Hav	Log Hav	Nat. Hav	
0	9. 06810	0. 11698	9. 08865	0. 12265	9. 10866	0. 12843	9. 12815	0. 13432	9. 14715	0. 14033	60
1	. 06845	. 11707	. 08899	. 12274	. 10899	. 12852	. 12847	. 13442	. 14746	. 14043	59
2	. 06880	. 11716	. 08933	. 12284	. 10932	. 12862	. 12879	. 13452	. 14778	. 14053	58
3	. 06914	. 11726	. 08966	. 12293	. 10965	. 12872	. 12911	. 13462	. 14809	. 14063	57
4	. 06949	. 11735	. 0900,0	. 12303	. 10997	. 12882	. 12943	. 13472	. 14840	. 14073	56
5	9. 06984	0. 11745	9. 09034	0. 12312	9. 11030	0. 12891	9. 12975	0. 13482	9. 14871	0. 14084	55
6	. 07018	. 11754	. 09068	. 12322	. 11063	. 12901	. 13007	. 13492	. 14902	. 14094	54
7	. 07053	. 11763	. 09101	. 12331	. 11096	. 12911	. 13039	. 13502	. 14934	. 14104	53
8	. 07088	. 11773	. 09135	. 12341	. 11129	. 12921	. 13071	. 13512	. 14965	. 14114	52
9	. 07122	. 11782	. 09169	. 12351	. 11161	. 12930	. 13103	. 13522	. 14996	. 14124	51
10	9. 07157	0. 11791	9. 09202	0. 12360	9. 11194	0. 12940	9. 13135	0. 13532	9. 15027	0. 14134	50
11	. 07191	. 11801	. 09236	. 12370	. 11227	. 12950	. 13167	. 13542	. 15058	. 14144	49
12	. 07226	. 11810	. 09269	. 12379	. 11260	. 12960	. 13199	. 13552	. 15089	. 14154	48
13	. 07260	. 11820	. 09303	. 12389	. 11292	. 12970	. 13231	. 13562	. 15120	. 14165	47
14	. 07295	. 11829	. 09337	. 12398	. 11325	. 12979	. 13263	. 13571	. 15152	. 14175	46
15	9. 07329	0. 11838	9. 09370	0. 12408	9.11358	0. 12989	9. 13295	0. 13581	9. 15183	0. 14185	45
16	. 07364	. 11848	. 09404	. 12418	. 11391	. 12999	. 13326	. 13591	. 15214	. 14195	44
17	. 07398	. i1857	. 09437	. 12427	. 11423	. 13009	. 13358	. 13601	. 15245	. 14205	43
18	. 07433	. 11867	. 09471	. 12437	. 11456	. 13018	. 13390	. 13611	. 15276	. 14215	42
19	. 07467	. 11876	. 09504	. 1244!3	. 11489	. 13028	. 13422	. 13621	. 15307	. 14226	41
20	9. 07501	0. 11885	9. 09538	0. 12456	9. 11521	0. 13038	9. 13454	0. 13631	9. 15338	0. 14236	40
21	. 07536	. 11895	. 09571	. 12466	. 11554	. 13048	. 13486	. 13641	. 15369	. 14246	39
22	. 07570	. 11904	. 09605	. 12475	. 11586	. 13058	. 13517	. 13651	. 15400	. 14256	38
23	. 07605	. 11914	. 09638	. 12485	. 11619	. 13067	. 13549	. 13661	. 15431	. 14266	37
24	. 07639	. 11923	. 09672	. 12494	. 11652	. 13077	. 13581	. 13671	. 15462	. 14276	36
25	9. 07673	0. 11933	9. 09705	0. 12504	9. 11684	0. 13087	9. 13613	0. 13681	9. 15493	0. 14287	35
26	. 07708	. 11942	. 09739	. 12514	. 11717	. 13097	. 13644	. 13691	. 15524	. 14297	34
27	. 07742	. 11951	. 09772	. 12523	. 11749	. 13107	. 13676	. 13701	. 15555	. 14307	33
28	. 07776	. 11961	. 09805	. 12533	. 11782	. 13116	. 13708	. 13711	. 15585	. 14317	32
29	. 07810	. 11970	. 09839	. 12543	. 11814	. 13126	. 13739	. 13721	. 15616	. 14327	31
30	9. 07845	0. 11980	9. 09872	0. 12552	9. 11847	0. 13136	9. 13771	0. 13731	9. 15647	0. 14337	30
31	. 07879	. 11989	. 09905	. 12562	: 11879	. 13146	. 13803	. 13741	. 15678	. 14348	29
32	. 07913	. 11999	. 09939	. 12571	. 11912	. 13156	. 13834	. 13751	. 15709	. 14358	28
33	. 07947	. 12008	. 09972	. 12581	. 11944	. 13166	. 13866	. 13761	. 15740	. 14368	27
34	. 07981	. 12018	. 10005	. 12591	. 11977	. 13175	. 13898	. 13771	. 15771	. 14378	26
35	9. 08016	0. 12027	9. 10039	0. 12600	9. 12009	0. 13185	9. 13929	0. 13781	9. 15802	0. 14388	25
36	. 08050	. 12036	. 10072	. 12610	. 12041	. 13195	. 13961	. 13791	. 15832	. 14399	24
37	. 08084	. 12046	. 10105	. 12620	. 12074	. 13205	. 13992	. 13801	. 15863	. 14409	23
38	. 08118	. 12055	. 10138	. 12629	. 12106	. 13215	. 14024	. 13811	. 15894	. 14419	22
39	. 08152	. 12065	. 10172	. 12639	. 12139	. 13225	. 14056	. 13822	. 15925	. 14429	21
40	9. 08186	0. 12074	9. 10205	0. 12649	9. 12171	0. 13235	9. 14087	0. 13832	9. 15955	0. 14440	20
41	. 08220	. 12084	. 10238	. 12658	. 12203	. 13244	. 14119	. 13842	. 15986	. 14450	19
42	. 08254	. 12093	. 10271	. 12668	. 12236	. 13254	. 14150	. 13852	. 16017	. 14460	18
43	. 08288	. 12103	. 10304	. 12678	. 12268	. 13264	. 14182	. 13862	. 16048	. 14470	17
44	. 08323	. 12112	. 10337	. 12687	. 12300	. 13274	. 14213	. 13872	. 16078	. 14480	16
45	9. 08357	0. 12122	9. 10371	0. 12697	9. 12332	0. 13284	9. 14245	0. 13882	9. 16109	0. 14491	15
46	. 08391	. 12131	. 10404	. 12707	. 12365	. 13294	. 14276	. 13892	. 16140	. 14501	14
47	. 08425	. 12141	. 10437	. 12717	. 12397	. 13304	. 14307	. 13902	. 16170	. 14511	13
48	. 08459	. 12150	. 10470	. 12726	. 12429	. 13314	. 14339	. 13912	. 16201	. 14521	12
49	. 08492	. 12160	. 10503	. 12736	. 12461	. 13323	. 14370	. 13922	. 16232	. 14532	11
50	9. 08526	0. 12169	9. 10536	0. 12746	9. 12494	0. 13333	9. 14402	0. 13932	9. 16262	0. 14542	10
51	. 08560	. 12179	. 10569	. 12755	. 12526	. 13343	. 14433	. 13942	. 16293	. 14552	9
52	. 08594	. 12188	. 10302	. 12765	. 12558	. 13353	. 14465	. 13952	. 16324	. 14562	8
53	. 08628	. 12198	. 10635	. 12775	. 12590	. 13363	. 14496	. 13962	. 16354	. 14573	7
54	. 08662	. 12207	. 10668	. 12784	. 12622	. 13373	. 14527	. 13972	. 16385	. 14583	6
55	9. 08696	0. 12217	9. 10701	0. 12794	9. 12655	0. 13383	9. 14559	0. 13983	9. 16415	0. 14593	5
56	. 08730	. 12226	. 10734	. 12804	. 12687	. 13393	. 14590	. 13993	. 16446	. 14604	4
57	. 08764	. 12236	. 10767	. 12814	. 12719	. 13403	. 14621	. 14003	. 16476	. 14614	3
58	. 08797	. 12245	. 10800	. 12823	. 12751	. 13412	. 14653	. 14013	. 16507	. 14624	2
59	. 08831	. 12255	. 10833	. 12833	. 12783	. 13422	. 14684	. 14023	. 16537	. 14634	1
60	9. 08865	0. 12265	9. 10866	0. 12843	9. 12815	0. 13432	9. 14715	0. 14033	9. 16568	0. 14645	0
	319°		318°		317°		316°		315°		

Haversines

′	45°		46°		47°		48°		49°		′
	Log Hav	Nat. Hav	Log Hav	Nat. Hav	Log Hav	Nat. Hav	Log Hav	Nat. Hav	Log Hav	Nat. Hav	
0	9. 16568	0.14645	9. 18376	0. 15267	9. 20140	0. 15900	9. 21863	0. 16543	9. 23545	0. 17197	60
1	. 16598	. 14655	. 18405	. 15278	. 20169	. 15911	. 21891	. 16554	. 23573	. 17208	59
2	. 16629	. 14665	. 18435	. 15288	. 20198	. 15921	. 21919	. 16565	. 23601	. 17219	58
3	. 16659	. 14676	. 18465	. 15298	. 20227	. 15932	. 21948	. 16576	. 23629	. 17230	57
4	. 16690	. 14686	. 18495	. 15309	. 20256	. 15943	. 21976	. 16587	. 23656	. 17241	56
5	9. 16720	0. 14696	9. 18524	0. 15319	9. 20285	0. 15953	9. 22004	0. 16598	9. 23684	0. 17252	55
6	. 16751	. 14706	. 18554	. 15330	. 20314	. 15964	. 22033	. 16608	. 23712	. 17263	54
7	. 16781	. 14717	. 18584	. 15340	. 20343	. 15975	. 22061	. 16619	. 23739	. 17274	53
8	. 16812	. 14727	. 18613	. 15351	. 20372	. 15985	. 22089	. 16630	. 23767	. 17285	52
9	. 16842	. 14737	. 18643	. 15361	. 20401	. 15996	. 22118	. 16641	. 23794	. 17296	51
10	9. 16872	0. 14748	9. 18673	0. 15372	9. 20430	0. 16007	9. 22146	0. 16652	9. 23822	0. 17307	50
11	. 16903	. 14758	. 18702	. 15382	. 20459	. 16017	. 22174	. 16663	. 23850	. 17318	49
12	. 16933	. 14768	. 18732	. 15393	. 20488	. 16028	. 22202	. 16673	. 23877	. 17329	48
13	. 16963	. 14779	. 18762	. 15403	. 20517	. 16039	. 22231	. 16684	. 23905	. 17340	47
14	. 16994	. 14789	. 18791	. 15414	. 20546	. 16049	. 22259	. 16695	. 23932	. 17351	46
15	9. 17024	0. 14799	9. 18821	0. 15424	9. 20574	0. 16060	9. 22287	0. 16706	9. 23960	0. 17362	45
16	. 17054	. 14810	. 18850	. 15435	. 20603	. 16071	. 22315	. 16717	. 23988	. 17373	44
17	. 17085	. 14820	. 18880	. 15445	. 20632	. 16081	. 22343	. 16728	. 24015	. 17384	43
18	. 17115	. 14830	. 18909	. 15456	. 20661	. 16092	. 22372	. 16738	. 24043	. 17395	42
19	. 17145	. 14841	. 18939	. 15466	. 20690	. 16103	. 22400	. 16749	. 24070	. 17406	41
20	9. 17175	0. 14851	9. 18968	0. 15477	9. 20719	0. 16113	9. 22428	0. 16760	9. 24098	0. 17417	40
21	. 17206	. 14861	. 18998	. 15487	. 20748	. 16124	. 22456	. 16771	. 24125	. 17428	39
22	. 17236	. 14872	. 19027	. 15498	. 20776	. 16135	. 22484	. 16782	. 24153	. 17439	38
23	. 17266	. 14882	. 19057	. 15508	. 20805	. 16145	. 22512	. 16793	. 24180	. 17450	37
24	. 17296	. 14892	. 19086	. 15519	. 20834	. 16156	. 22540	. 16804	. 24208	. 17461	36
25	9. 17327	0. 14903	9. 19116	0. 15530	9. 20863	0. 16167	9. 2.2569	0. 16815	9. 24235	0. 17472	35
26	. 17357	. 14913	. 19145	. 15540	. 20891	. 16178	. 22597	. 16825	. 24263	. 17483	34
27	. 17387	. 14923	. 19175	. 15551	. 20920	. 16188	. 22625	. 16836	. 24290	. 17494	33
28	. 17417	. 14934	. 19204	. 15561	. 20949	. 16199	. 22653	. 16847	. 24317	. 17505	32
29	. 17447	. 14944	. 19234	. 15572	. 20978	. 16210	. 22681	. 16858	. 24345	. 17517	31
30	9. 17477	0. 14955	9. 19263	0. 15582	9. 21006	0. 16220	9. 22709	0. 16869	9. 24372	0. 1,7528	30
31	. 17507	. 14965	. 19292	. 15593	. 21035	. 16231	. 22737	. 16880	. 24400	. 17539	29
32	. 17538	. 14975	. 19322	. 15603	. 21064	. 16242	. 22765	. 16891	. 24427	. 17550	28
33	. 17568	. 14986	. 19351	. 15614	. 21092	. 16253	. 22793	. 16902	. 24454	. 17561	27
34	. 17598	. 14996	. 19381	. 15624	. 21121	. 1,6263	. 22821	. 16913	. 24482	. 17572	26
35	9. 17628	0. 15006	9. 19419	0. 15635	9. 21150	0. 16274	9. 22849	0. 16923	9. 24509	0. 17583	25
36	. 17658	. 15017	. 19439	. 15646	. 21178	. 16285	. 22877	. 16934	. 24536	. 17594	24
37	. 17688	. 15027	. 19469	. 15656	. 21207	. 16296	. 22905	. 16945	. 24564	. 17605	23
38	. 17718	. 15038	. 19498	. 15667	. 21236	. 16306	. 22933	. 16956	. 24591	. 17616	22
39	. 17748	. 15048	. 19527	. 15677	. 21264	. 16317	. 22961	. 16967	. 24618	. 17627	21
40	9. 17778	0. 15058	9, 19557	0. 15688	9. 21293	0. 16328	9. 22989	0. 16978	9. 24646	0. 17638	20
41	. 17808	. 15069	, 19586	. 15698	. 21322	. 16339	. 23017	. 16989	. 24673	. 17649	19
42	. 17838	. 15079	. 19615	. 15709	. 21350	. 16349	. 23045	. 17000	. 24700	. 17661	18
43	. 17868	. 15090	. 19644	. 15720	. 21379	. 16360	. 23073	. 17011	. 24728	. 17672	17
44	. 17898	. 15100	. 19674	. 15730	. 21407	. 16371	. 23100	. 17022	. 24755	. 17683	16
45	9. 17928	0. 15110	9. 19703	0. 15741	9. 21436	0. 16382	9. 23128	0. 17033	9. 24782	0. 17694	15
46	. 17958	. 15121	. 19732	. 15751	. 21464	. 16392	. 23156	. 17044	. 24809	. 17705	14
47	. 17988	. 15131	. 19761	. 15762	. 21493	. 16403	. 23184	. 17055	. 24837	. 17716	13
48	. 18018	. 15142	. 19790	. 15773	. 21521	. 16414	. 23212	. 17066	. 24864	. 17727	12
49	. 18048	. 15152	. 19820	. 15783	. 21550	. 16425	. 23240	. 17076	. 24891	. 17738	11
50	9. 18077	0. 15163	9. 19849	0. 15794	9. 21578	0. 16436	9. 23268	0. 17087	9. 24918	0. 17749	10
51	. 18107	. 15173	. 19878	. 15804	. 21607	. 16446	. 23295	. 17098	. 24945	. 17760	9
52	. 18137	. 15183	. 19907	. 15815	. 21635	. 16457	. 23323	. 17109	. 24973	. 17772	8
53	. 18167	. 15194	. 19936	. 15826	. 21664	. 16468	. 23351	. 17120	. 25000	. 17783	7
54	. 18197	. 15204	. 19965	. 15836	. 21692	. 16479	. 23379	. 17131	. 25027	. 17794	6
55	9. 18227	0. 15215	9. 19995	0. 15847	9. 21721	0. 16489	9. 23407	0. 17142	9. 25054	0. 17805	5
56	. 18256	. 15225	. 20024	. 15858	. 21749	. 16500	. 23434	. 17153	. 25081	. 17816	4
57	. 18286	. 15236	. 20053	. 15868	. 21778	. 16511	. 23462	. 17164	. 25108	. 17827	3
58	. 18316	. 15246	. 20082	. 15879	. 21806	. 16522	. 23490	. 17175	. 25135	. 17838	2
59	. 18346	. 15257	. 20111	. 15889	. 21834	. 16533	. 23518	. 17186	. 25163	. 17849	1
60	9. 18376	0. 15267	9. 20140	0. 15900	9. 21863	0. 16543	9. 23545	0. 17197	9. 25190	0. 17861	0
	314°		313°		312°		311°		310°		

Haversines

′	50°		51°		52°		53°		54°		′
	Log Hav	Nat. Hav	Log Hav	Nat. Hav	Log Hav	Nat. Hav	Log Hav	Nat. Hav	Log Hav	Nat. Hav	
0	9. 25190	0. 17861	9. 26797	0. 18534	9. 28368	0. 19217	9. 29906	0. 19909	9. 31409	0. 20611	60
1	. 25217	. 17872	. 26823	. 18545	. 28394	. 19228	. 29931	. 19921	. 31434	. 20623	59
2	. 25244	. 17883	. 26850	. 18557	. 28420	. 19240	. 29956	. 19932	. 31459	. 20634	58
3	. 25271	. 17894	. 26876	. 18568	. 28446	. 19251	. 29981	. 19944	. 31484	. 20646	57
4	. 25298	. 17905	. 26903	. 18579	. 28472	. 19263	. 30007	. 19956	. 31508	. 20658	56
5	9. 25325	0. 17916	9. 26929	0. 18591	9. 28498	0. 19274	9. 30032	0. 19967	9. 31533	0. 20670	55
6	. 25352	. 17928	. 26956	. 18602	. 28524	. 19286	. 30057	. 19979	. 31558	. 20681	54
7	. 25379	. 17939	. 26982	. 18613	. 28549	. 19297	. 30083	. 19991	. 31583	. 20693	53
8	. 25406	. 17950	. 27008	. 18624	. 28575	. 19309	. 30108	. 20002	. 31607	. 20705	52
9	. 25433	. 17961	. 27035	. 18636	. 28601	. 19320	. 30133	. 20014	. 31632	. 20717	51
10	9. 25460	0. 17972	9. 27061	0. 18647	9. 28627	0. 19332	9. 30158	0. 20026	9. 31657	0. 20729	50
11	. 25487	. 17983	. 27088	. 18658	. 28653	. 19343	. 30184	. 20037	. 31682	. 20740	49
12	. 25514	. 17995	. 27114	. 18670	. 28679	. 19355	. 30209	. 20049	. 31706	. 20752	48
13	. 25541	. 18006	. 27140	. 18681	. 28704	. 19366	. 30234	. 20060	. 31731	. 20764	47
14	. 25568	. 18017	. 27167	. 18692	. 28730	. 19378	. 30259	. 20072	. 31756	. 20776	46
15	9. 25595	0. 18028	9. 27193	0. 18704	9. 28756	0. 19389	9. 30285	0. 20084	9. 31780	0. 20788	45
16	. 25622	. 18039	. 27219	. 18715	. 28782	. 19401	. 30310	. 20095	. 31805	. 20799	44
17	. 25649	. 18050	. 27246	. 18727	. 28807	. 19412	. 30335	. 20107	. 31830	. 20811	43
18	. 25676	. 18062	. 27272	. 18738	. 28833	. 19424	. 30360	. 20119	. 31854	. 20823	42
19	. 25703	. 18073	. 27298	. 18749	. 28859	. 19435	. 30385	. 20130	. 31879	. 20835	41
20	9. 25729	0. 18084	9. 27325	0. 18761	9. 28885	0. 19447	9. 30410	0. 20142	9. 31903	0. 20847	40
21	. 25756	. 18095	. 27351	. 18772	. 28910	. 19458	. 30436	. 20154	. 31928	. 20858	39
22	. 25783	. 18106	. 27377	. 18783	. 28936	. 19470	. 30461	. 20165	. 31953	. 20870	38
23	. 25810	. 18118	. 27403	. 18795	. 28962	. 19481	. 30486	. 20177	. 31977	. 20882	37
24	. 25837	. 18129	. 27430	. 18806	. 28987	. 19493	. 30511	. 20189	. 32002	. 20894	36
25	9. 25864	0. 18140	9. 27456	0. 18817	9. 29013	0. 19504	9. 30536	0. 20200	9. 32026	0. 20906	35
26	. 25891	. 18151	. 27482	. 18829	. 29039	. 19516	. 30561	. 20212	. 32051	. 20918	34
27	. 25917	. 18162	. 27508	. 18840	. 29064	. 19527	. 30586	. 20224	. 32076	. 20929	33
28	. 25944	. 18174	. 27535	. 18852	. 29090	. 19539	. 30611	. 20235	. 32100	. 20941	32
29	. 25971	. 18185	. 27561	. 18863	. 29116	. 19550	. 80636	. 20247	. 32125	. 20953	31
30	9. 25998	0. 18196	9. 27587	0. 18874	9. 29141	0. 19562	9. 30662	0. 20259	9. 32149	0. 20965	30
31	. 26025	. 18207	. 27613	. 18886	. 29167	. 19573	. 30687	. 20271	. 32174	. 20977	29
32	. 26051	. 18219	. 27639	. 18897	. 29192	. 19585	. 30712	. 20282	. 32198	. 20989	28
33	. 26078	. 18230	. 27666	. 18908	. 29218	. 19597	. 30737	. 20294	. 32223	. 21000	27
34	. 26105	. 18241	. 27692	. 18920	. 29244	. 19608	. 30762	. 20306	. 32247	. 21012	26
35	9. 26132	0. 18252	9. 27718	0. 18931	9. 29269	0. 19620	9. 30787	0. 20317	9. 32272	0. 21024	25
36	. 26158	. 18263	. 27744	. 18943	. 29295	. 19631	. 30812	. 20329	. 32296	. 21036	24
37	. 26185	. 18275	. 27770	. 18954	. 29320	. 19643	. 30837	. 20341	. 32321	. 21048	23
38	. 26212	. 18286	. 27796	. 18965	. 29346	. 19654	. 30862	. 20352	. 32345	. 21060	22
39	. 26238	. 18297	. 27822	. 18977	. 29371	. 19666	. 30887	. 20364	. 32370	. 21072	21
40	9. 26265	0. 18308	9. 27848	0. 18988	9. 29397	0. 19677	9. 30912	0. 20376	9. 32394	0. 21083	20
41	. 26292	. 18320	. 27875	. 19000	. 29422	. 19689	. 30937	. 20388	. 32418	. 21095	19
42	. 26319	. 18331	. 27901	. 19011	. 29448	. 19701	. 30962	. 20399	. 32443	. 21107	18
43	. 26345	. 18342	. 27927	. 19022	. 29473	. 19712	. 30987	. 20411	. 32467	. 21119	17
44	. 26372	. 18353	. 27953	. 19034	. 29499	. 19724	. 31012	. 20423	. 32492	. 21131	16
45	9. 26398	0. 18365	9. 27979	0. 19045	9. 29524	0. 19735	9. 31036	0. 20435	9. 32516	0. 21143	15
46	. 26425	. 18376	. 28005	. 19057	. 29550	. 19747	. 31061	. 20446	. 32541	. 21155	14
47	. 26452	. 18387	. 28031	. 19068	. 29575	. 19758	. 31086	. 20458	..32565	. 21167	13
48	. 26478	. 18399	. 28057	. 19080	. 29601	. 19770	. 31111	. 20470	. 32589	. 21178	12
49	. 26505	. 18410	. 28083	. 19091	. 29626	. 19782	. 31136	. 20481	. 32614	. 21190	11
50	9. 26532	0. 18421	9. 28109	0. 19102	9. 29652	0. 19793	9. 31161	0. 20493	9. 32638	0. 21202	10
51	. 26558	. 18432	. 28135	. 19114	. 29677	. 19805	. 31186	. 20505	. 32662	. 21214	9
52	. 26585	. 18444	. 28161	. 19125	. 29703	. 19816	. 31211	. 20517	. 32687	. 21226	8
53	. 26611	. 18455	. 28187	. 19137	. 29728	. 19828	. 31236	. 20528	. 32711	. 21238	7
54	. 26638	. 18466	. 28213	. 19148	. 29753	. 19840	. 31260	. 20540	. 32735	. 21250	6
55	9. 26664	0. 18477	9. 28239	0. 19160	9. 29779	0. 19851	9. 31285	0. 20552	9. 32760	0. 21262	5
56	. 26691	. 18489	. 28265	. 19171	. 29804	. 19863	. 31310	. 20564	. 32784	. 21274	4
57	. 26717	. 18500	. 28291	. 19183	. 29829	. 19874	. 31335	. 20575	. 32808	. 21285	3
58	. 26744	. 18511	. 28317	. 19194	. 29855	. 19886	. 31360	. 20587	. 32833	. 21297	2
59	. 26770	. 18523	. 28342	. 19205	. 29880	. 19898	. 31385	. 20599	. 32857	. 21309	1
60	9. 26797	0. 18534	9. 28368	0. 19217	9. 29906	0. 19909	9. 31409	0. 20611	9. 32881	0. 21321	0
	309°		308°		307°		306°		305°		

Haversines

′	55°		56°		57°		58°		59°		′
	Log Hav	Nat. Hav	Log Hav	Nat. Hav	Log Hav	Nat. Hav	Log Hav	Nat. Hav	Log Hav	Nat. Hav	
0	9. 32881	0. 21321	9. 34322	0. 22040	9. 35733	0. 22768	9. 37114	0. 23504	9. 38468	0. 24248	60
1	. 32905	. 21333	. 34346	. 22052	. 35756	. 22780	. 37137	. 23516	. 38490	. 24261	59
2	. 32930	. 21345	. 34369	. 22064	. 35779	. 22792	. 37160	. 23529	. 38512	. 24273	58
3	. 32954	. 21357	. 34393	. 22077	. 35802	. 22805	. 37183	. 23541	. 38535	. 24286	57
4	. 32978	. 21369	. 34417	. 22089	. 35826	. 22817	. 37205	. 23553	. 38557	. 24298	56
5	9. 33002	0. 21381	9. 34441	0. 22101	9. 35849	0. 22829	9. 37228	0. 23566	9. 38579	0. 24310	55
6	. 33027	. 21393	. 34464	. 22113	. 35872	. 22841	. 37251	. 23578	. 38602	. 24323	54
7	. 33051	. 21405	. 34488	. 22125	. 35895	. 22853	. 37274	. 23590	. 38624	. 24335	53
8	. 33075	. 21417	. 34512	. 22137	. 35918	. 22866	. 37296	. 23603	. 38646	. 24348	52
9	. 33099	. 21429	. 34535	. 22149	. 35942	. 22878	. 37319	. 23615	. 38668	. 24360	51
10	9. 33123	0. 21440	9. 34559	0. 22161	9. 35965	0. 22890	9. 37342	0. 23627	9. 38691	0. 24373	50
11	. 33148	. 21452	. 34583	. 22173	. 35988	. 22902	. 37364	. 23640	. 38713	. 24385	49
12	. 33172	. 21464	. 34606	. 22185	. 36011	. 22915	. 37387	. 23652	. 38735	. 24398	48
13	. 33196	. 21476	. 34630	. 22197	. 36034	. 22927	. 37410	. 23665	. 38757	. 24410	47
14	. 33220	. 21488	. 34654	. 22209	. 36058	. 22939	. 37433	. 23677	. 38780	. 24423	46
15	9. 33244	0. 21500	9. 34677	0. 22221	9. 36081	0. 22951	9. 37455	0. 23689	9. 38802	0. 24435	45
16	. 33268	. 21512	. 34701	. 22234	. 36104	. 22964	. 37478	. 23702	. 38824	. 24448	44
17	. 33292	. 21524	. 34725	. 22246	. 36127	. 22976	. 37501	. 23714	. 38846	. 24460	43
18	. 33317	. 21536	. 34748	. 22258	. 36150	. 22988	. 37523	. 23726	. 38868	. 24473	42
19	. 33341	. 21548	. 34772	. 22270	. 36173	. 23000	. 37546	. 23739	. 38891	. 24485	41
20	9. 33365	0. 21560	9. 34795	0. 22282	9. 36196	0. 23012	9. 37569	0. 23751	9. 38913	0. 24498	40
21	. 33389	. 21572	. 34819	. 22294	. 36219	. 23025	. 37591	. 23764	. 38935	. 24510	39
22	. 33413	. 21584	. 34843	. 22306	. 36243	. 23037	. 37614	. 23776	. 38957	. 24523	38
23	. 33437	. 21596	. 34866	. 22318	. 36266	. 23049	. 37636	. 23788	. 38979	. 24535	37
24	. 33461	. 21608	. 34890	. 22330	. 36289	. 23061	. 37659	. 23801	. 39002	. 24548	36
25	9. 33485	0. 21620	9. 34913	0. 22343	9. 36312	0. 23074	9. 37682	0. 23813	9. 39024	0. 24560	35
26	. 33509	. 21632	. 34937	. 22355	. 36335	. 23086	. 37704	. 23825	. 39046	. 24573	34
27	. 33533	. 21644	. 34960	. 22367	. 36358	. 23098	. 37727	. 23838	. 39068	. 24585	33
28	. 33557	. 21656	. 34984	. 22379	. 36381	. 23110	. 37749	. 23850	. 39090	. 24598	32
29	. 33581	. 21668	. 35007	. 22391	. 36404	. 23123	. 37772	. 23863	. 39112	. 24611	31
30	9. 33605	0. 21680	9. 35031	0. 22403	9. 36427	0. 23135	9. 37794	0. 23875	9. 39134	0. 24623	30
31	. 33629	. 21692	. 35054	. 22415	. 36450	. 23147	. 37817	. 23887	. 39156	. 24636	29
32	. 33653	. 21704	. 35078	. 22427	. 36473	. 23160	. 37840	. 23900	. 39178	. 24648	28
33	. 33677	. 21716	. 35101	. 22440	. 36496	. 23172	. 37862	. 23912	. 39201	. 24661	27
34	. 33701	. 21728	. 35125	. 22452	. 36519	. 23184	. 37885	. 23925	. 39223	. 24673	26
35	9. 33725	0. 21740	9. 35148	0. 22464	9. 36542	0. 23196	9. 37907	0. 23937	9. 39245	0. 24686	25
36	. 33749	. 21752	. 35172	. 22476	. 36565	. 23209	. 37930	. 23950	. 39267	. 24698	24
37	. 33773	. 21764	. 35195	. 22488	. 36588	. 23221	. 37952	. 23962	. 39289	. 24711	23
38	. 33797	. 21776	. 35219	. 22500	. 36611	. 23233	. 37975	. 23974	. 39311	. 24723	22
39	. 33821	. 21788	. 35242	. 22512	. 36634	. 23246	. 37997	. 23987	. 39333	. 24736	21
40	9. 33845	0. 21800	9. 35266	0. 22525	9. 36657	0. 23253	9. 38020	0. 23999	9. 39355	0. 24749	20
41	. 33869	. 21812	. 35289	. 22537	. 36680	. 23270	. 38042	. 24012	. 39377	. 24761	19
42	. 33893	. 21824	. 35312	. 22549	. 36703	. 23282	. 38065	. 24024	. 39399	. 24774	18
43	. 33917	. 21836	. 35336	. 22561	. 36726	. 23295	. 38087	. 24036	. 39421	. 24786	17
44	. 33941	. 21848	. 35359	. 22571	. 36749	. 23307	. 38110	. 24049	. 39443	. 24799	16
45	9. 33965	0. 21860	9. 35383	0. 22585	9. 36772	0. 23319	9. 38132	0. 24061	9. 39465	0. 24811	15
46	. 33988	. 21872	. 35406	. 22598	. 36794	. 23332	. 38154	. 24074	. 39487	. 24824	14
47	. 34012	. 21884	. 35429	. 22610	. 36817	. 23344	. 38177	. 24086	. 39509	. 24836	13
48	. 34036	. 21896	. 35453	. 22622	. 36840	. 23356	. 38199	. 24099	. 39531	. 24849	12
49	. 34060	. 21908	. 35476	. 22634	. 36863	. 23368	. 38222	. 24111	. 39553	. 24862	11
50	9. 34084	0. 21920	9. 35500	0. 22646	9. 36886	0. 23381	9. 38244	0. 24124	9. 39575	0. 24874	10
51	. 34108	. 21932	. 35523	. 22658	. 36909	. 23393	. 38267	. 24136	. 39597	. 24887	9
52	. 34132	. 21944	. 35546	. 22671	. 36932	. 23405	. 38289	. 24148	. 39619	. 24899	8
53	. 34155	. 21956	. 35570	. 22683	. 36955	. 23418	. 38311	. 24161	. 39641	. 24912	7
54	. 34179	. 21968	. 35593	. 22695	. 36977	. 23430	. 38334	. 24173	. 39663	. 24924	6
55	9. 34203	0. 21980	9. 35610	0. 22707	9. 37000	0. 23442	9. 38356	0. 24186	9. 39685	0. 24937	5
56	. 34227	. 21992	. 35639	. 22719	. 37023	. 23455	. 38378	. 24198	. 39706	. 24950	4
57	. 34251	. 22004	. 35663	. 22731	. 37046	. 23467	. 38401	. 24211	. 39728	. 24962	3
58	. 34274	. 22016	. 35686	. 22744	. 37069	. 23479	. 38423	. 24223	. 39750	. 24975	2
59	. 34298	. 22028	. 35709	. 22756	. 37091	. 23492	. 38445	. 24236	. 39772	. 24987	1
60	9. 34322	0. 22040	9. 35733	0. 22768	9. 37114	0. 23504	9. 38468	0. 24248	9. 39794	0. 25000	0
	304°		303°		302°		301°		300°		

Haversines

′	60°		61°		62°		63°		64°		′
	Log Hav	Nat. Hav	Log Hav	Nat. Hav	Log Hav	Nat. Hav	Log Hav	Nat. Hav	Log Hav	Nat. Hav	
0	9. 39794	0. 25000	9. 41094	0. 25760	9. 42368	0. 26526	9. 43617	0. 27300	9. 44842	0. 28081	60
1	. 39816	. 25013	. 41115	. 25772	. 42389	. 26539	. 43638	. 27313	. 44862	. 28095	59
2	. 39838	. 25025	. 41137	. 25785	. 42410	. 26552	. 43658	. 27326	. 44882	. 28108	58
3	. 39860	. 25038	. 41158	. 25798	. 42431	. 26565	.43679	. 27339	. 44903	. 28121	57
4	. 39881	. 25050	. 41180	. 25810	. 42452	. 26578	. 43699	. 27352	. 44923	. 28134	56
5	9. 39903	0. 25063	9. 41201	0. 25823	9. 42473	0. 26591	9. 43720	0. 27365	9. 44943	0. 28147	55
6	. 39925	. 25076	. 41222	. 25836	. 42494	. 26604	. 43741	. 27378	. 44963	. 28160	54
7	. 39947	. 25088	. 41244	. 25849	. 42515	. 26616	. 43761	. 27391	. 44983	. 28173	53
8	. 39969	. 25101	. 41265	. 25861	. 42536	. 26629	. 43782	. 27404	. 45003	. 28186	52
9	. 39991	. 25113	. 41287	. 25874	. 42557	. 26642	. 43802	. 27417	. 45024	. 28199	51
10	9. 40012	0. 25126	9. 41308	0. 25887	9. 42578	0. 26655	9. 43823	0. 27430	9. 45044	0. 28212	50
11	. 40034	. 25139	. 41329	. 25900	. 42599	. 26668	. 43843	. 27443	. 45064	. 28225	49
12	. 40056	. 25151	. 41351	. 25912	. 42620	. 26681	. 43864	. 27456	. 45084	. 28238	48
13	. 40078	. 25164	. 41372	. 25925	. 42641	. 26694	. 43884	. 27469	. 45104	. 28252	47
14	. 40100	. 25177	. 41393	. 25938	. 42662	. 26706	. 43905	. 27482	. 45124	. 28265	46
15	9. 40121	0. 25189	9. 41415	0. 25951	9. 42682	0. 26719	9. 43926	0. 27495	9. 45144	0. 28278	45
16	. 40143	. 25202	. 41436	. 25963	. 42703	. 26732	. 43946	. 27508	. 45165	. 28291	44
17	. 40165	. 25214	. 41457	. 25976	. 42724	. 26745	. 43967	. 27521	. 45185	. 28304	43
18	. 40187	. 25227	. 41479	. 25989	. 42745	. 26758	. 43987	. 27534	. 45205	. 28317	42
19	. 40208	. 25240	. 41500	. 26002	. 42766	. 26771	. 44008	. 27547	. 45225	. 28330	41
20	9. 40230	0. 25252	9. 41521	0. 26014	9. 42787	0. 26784	9. 44028	0. 27560	9. 45245	0. 28343	40
21	. 40252	. 25265	. 41543	. 26027	. 42808	. 26797	. 44048	. 27573	. 45265	. 28356	39
22	. 40274	. 25278	. 41564	. 26040	. 42829	. 26809	. 44069	. 27586	. 45285	. 28369	38
23	. 40295	. 25290	. 41585	. 26053	. 42850	. 26822	. 44089	. 27599	. 45305	. 28383	37
24	. 40317	. 25303	. 41606	. 26065	. 42870	. 26835	. 44110	. 27612	. 45325	. 28396	36
25	9. 40339	0. 25316	9. 41628	0. 26078	9. 42891	0. 26848	9. 44130	0. 27625	9. 45345	0. 28409	35
26	. 40360	. 25328	. 41649	. 26091	. 42912	. 26861	. 44151	. 27638	. 45365	. 28422	34
27	. 40382	. 25341	. 41670	. 26104	. 42933	. 26874	. 44171	. 27651	. 45385	. 28435	33
28	. 40404	. 25354	. 41692	. 26117	. 42954	. 26887	. 44192	. 27664	. 45405	. 28448	32
29	. 40425	. 25366	. 41713	. 26129	. 42975	. 26900	. 44212	. 27677	. 15426	. 28461	31
30	9. 40447	0. 25379	9. 41734	0. 26142	9. 42996	0. 26913	9. 44232	0. 27690	9. 45446	0. 28474	30
31	. 40469	. 25391	. 41755	. 26155	. 43016	. 26925	. 44253	. 27703	. 45466	. 28488	29
32	. 40490	. 25404	. 41776	. 26168	. 43037	. 26938	. 44273	. 27716	. 45486	. 28501	28
33	. 40512	. 25417	. 41798	. 26180	. 43058	. 26951	. 44291	. 27729	. 45506	. 28514	27
34	. 40534	. 25429	. 41819	. 26193	. 43079	. 26964	. 44314	. 27742	. 45526	. 28527	26
35	9. 40555	0. 25442	9. 41840	0. 26206	9. 43100	0. 26977	9. 44334	0. 27755	9. 45546	0. 28540	25
36	. 40577	. 25455	. 41861	. 26219	. 43120	. 26990	. 44355	. 27768	. 45566	. 28553	24
37	. 40599	. 25467	. 41882	. 26232	. 43141	. 27003	. 44375	. 27781	. 45586	. 28566	23
38	. 40620	. 25480	. 41904	. 26244	. 43162	. 27016	. 44396	. 27794	. 45606	. 28580	22
39	. 40642	. 25493	. 41925	. 26257	. 43183	. 27029	. 44416	. 27807	. 45625	. 28593	21
40	9. 40663	0. 25506	9. 41946	0. 26270	9..43203	0. 27042	9. 44436	0. 27820	9. 45645	0. 28606	20
41	. 40685	. 25518	. 41967	. 26283	. 43224	. 27055	. 44457	. 27833	. 45665	. 28619	19
42	. 40707	. 25531	. 41988	. 26296	. 43245	. 27068	. 44477	. 27846	. 45685	. 28632	18
43	. 40728	. 25544	. 42009	. 26308	. 43266	. 27080	. 44497	. 27859	. 45705	. 28645	17
44	. 40750	. 25556	. 42031	. 26321	. 43286	. 27093	. 44518	. 27873	. 45725	. 28658	16
45	9. 40771	0. 25569	9. 42052	0. 26334	9. 43307	0. 27106	9. 44538	0. 27886	9. 45745	0. 28672	15
46	. 40793	. 25582	. 42073	. 26347	. 43328	. 27119	. 44558	. 27899	. 45765	. 28685	14
47	. 40814	. 25594	. 42094	. 26360	. 43348	. 27132	. 44579	. 27912	. 45785	. 28698	13
48	. 40836	. 25607	. 42115	. 26372	. 43369	. 27145	. 44599	. 27925	. 45805	. 28711	12
49	. 40858	. 25620	. 42136	. 26385	. 43390	. 27158	. 44619	. 27938	. 45825	. 28724	11
50	9. 40879	0. 25632	9. 42157	0. 26398	9. 43411	0. 27171	9. 44639	0. 27951	9. 45845	0. 28737	10
51	. 40900	. 25645	. 42178	. 26411	. 43431	. 27184	. 44660	. 27964	. 45865	. 28751	9
52	. 40922	. 25658	. 42199	. 26424	. 43452	. 27197	. 44680	. 27977	. 45884	. 28764	8
53	. 40943	. 25671	. 42221	. 26437	. 43473	. 27210	. 44700	. 27990	. 45904	. 28777	7
54	. 40965	. 25683	. 42242	. 26449	. 43493	. 27223	. 44721	. 28003	. 45924	. 28790	6
55	9. 40986	0. 25696	9. 42263	0. 26462	9. 43514	0. 27236	9. 44741	0. 28016	9. 45944	0. 28803	5
56	. 41008	. 25709	. 42284	. 26475	. 43535	. 27249	. 44761	. 28029	. 45964	. 28816	4
57	. 41029	. 25721	. 42305	. 26488	. 43555	. 27262	. 44781	. 28042	. 45984	. 28830	3
58	. 41051	. 25734	. 42326	. 26501	. 43576	. 27275	. 44801	. 28055	. 46004	. 28843	2
59	. 41072	. 25747	. 42347	. 26514	. 43596	. 27288	. 44822	. 28068	. 46023	. 28856	1
60	9. 41094	0. 25760	9. 42368	0. 26526	9. 43617	0. 27300	9. 44842	0. 28081	9. 46043	0. 28869	0
	299°		298°		297°		296°		295°		

Haversines

′	65°		66°		67°		68°		69°		′
	Log Hav	Nat. Hav	Log Hav	Nat. Hav	Log Hav	Nat. Hav	Log Hav	Nat. Hav	Log Hav	Nat. Hav	
0	9. 46043	0. 28869	9. 47222	0. 29663	9. 48378	0. 30463	9. 49512	0. 31270	9. 50626	0. .32082	60
1	. 46063	. 28882	. 47241	. 29676	. 48397	. 30477	. 49531	. 31283	. 50644	. 32095	59
2	. 46083	. 28895	. 47261	. 29690	. 48416	. 30490	. 49550	. 31297	. 50662	. 32109	58
3	. 46103	. 28909	. 47280	. 29703	. 48435	. 30504	. 49568	. 31310	. 50681	. 32122	57
4	. 46123	. 28922	. 47300	. 29716	. 48454	. 30517	. 49587	. 31324	. 50699	. 32136	56
5	9. 46142	0. 28935	9. 47319	0. 29730	9. 48473	0. 30530	9. 49606	0. 31337	9. 50717	0. 32150	55
6	. 46162	. 28948	. 47338	. 29743	. 48492	. 30544	. 49625	. 31351	. 50736	. 32163	54
7	. 46182	. 28961	. 47358	. 29756	. 48511	. 30557	. 49643	. 31364	. 50754	. 32177	53
8	. 46202	. 28975	. 47377	. 29770	. 48530	. 30571	. 49662	. 31378	. 50772	. 32190	52
9	. 46222	. 28988	. 47397	. 29783	. 48549	. 30584	. 49681	. 31391	. 50791	. 32204	51
10	9. 46241	0. 29001	9. 47416	0. 29796	9. 48568	0. 30597	9. 49699	0. 31405	9. 50809	0. 32217	50
11	. 46261	. 29014	. 47435	. 29809	. 48587	. 30611	. 49718	. 31418	. 50827	. 32231	49
12	. 46281	. 29027	. 47455	. 29823	. 48607	. 30624	. 49737	. 31432	. 50846	. 32245	48
13	. 46301	. 29041	. 47474	. 29836	. 48626	. 30638	. 49755	. 31445	. 50864	. 32258	47
14	. 46320	. 29054	. 47493	. 29849	. 48645	. 30651	. 49774	. 31459	. 50882	. 32272	46
15	9. 46340	0. 29067	9. 47513	0.29863	9.48664	0. 30664	9. 49793	0. 31472	9. 50901	0. 32285	45
16	. 46360	. 29080	. 47532	. 29876	. 48683	. 30678	. 49811	. 31486	. 50919	. 32299	44
17	. 46380	. 29093	. 47552	. 29889	. 48702	. 30691	. 49830	. 31499	. 50937	. 32313	43
18	. 46399	. 29107	. 47571	. 29903	. 48720	. 30705	. 49849	. 31513	. 50956	. 32326	42
19	. 46419	. 29120	. 47590	. 29916	. 48739	. 30718	. 49867	. 31526	. 50974	. 32340	41
20	9. 46439	0. 29133	9. 47610	0. 29929	9. 48758	0. 30732	9. 49886	0. 31540	9. 50992	0. 32353	40
21	. 46458	. 29146	. 47629	. 29943	. 48777	. 30745	. 49904	. 31553	. 51010	. 32367	39
22	. 46478	. 29160	. 47648	. 29956	. 48796	. 30758	. 49923	. 31567	. 51029	. 32381	38
23	. 46498	. 29173	. 47668	. 29969	. 48815	. 30772	. 49942	. 31580	. 51047	. 32394	37
24	. 46517	. 29186	. 47687	. 29983	. 48834	. 30785	. 49960	. 31594	. 51065	. 32408	36
25	9. 46537	0. 29199	9. 47706	0. 29996	9. 48853	0. 30799	9. 49979	0. 31607	9. 51083	0. 32422	35
26	. 46557	. 29212	. 47725	. 30009	. 48872	. 30812	. 49997	. 31621	. 51102	. 32435	34
27	. 46576	. 29226	. 47745	. 30023	. 48891	. 30826	. 50016	. 31634	. 51120	. 32449	33
28	. 46596	. 29239	. 47764	. 30036	. 48910	. 30839	. 50034	. 31648	. 51138	. 32462	32
29	. 46616	. 29252	. 47783	. 30049	. 48929	. 30852	. 50053	. 31661	. 51156	. 32476	31
30	9. 46635	0. 29265	9. 47803	0. 30063	9. 48948	0. 30866	9. 50072	0. 31675	9. 51174	0. 32490	30
31	. 46655	. 29279	. 47822	. 30076	. 48967	. 30879	. 50090	. 31688	. 51193	. 32503	29
32	. 46675	. 29292	. 47841	. 30089	. 48986	. 30893	. 50109	. 31702	. 51211	. 32517	28
33	. 46694	. 29305	. 47860	. 30103	. 49004	. 30906	. 50127	. 31716	. 51229	. 32531	27
34	. 46714	. 29318	. 47880	. 30116	. 49023	. 30920	. 50146	. 31729	. 51247	. 32544	26
35	9. 46733	0. 29332	9. 47899	0. 30129	9. 49042	0. 30933	9. 50164	0. 31743	9. 51265	0. 32558	25
36	. 46753	. 29345	. 47918	. 30143	. 49061	. 30946	. 50183	. 31756	. 51284	. 32571	24
37	. 46773	. 29358	. 47937	. 30156	. 49080	. 30960	. 50201	. 31770	. 51302	. 32585	23
38	. 46792	. 29371	. 47957	. 30169	. 49099	. 30973	. 50220	. 31783	. 51320	. 32599	22
39	. 46812	. 29385	. 47976	. 30183	. 49118	. 30987	. 50238	. 31797	. 51338	. 32612	21
40	9. 46831	0. 29398	9. 47995	0. 30196	9. 49137	0. 31000	9. 50257	0. 31810	9. 51356	0. 32626	20
41	. 46851	. 29411	. 48014	. 30209	. 49155	. 31014	. 50275	. 31824	. 51374	. 32640	19
42	. 46871	. 29424	. 48033	. 30223	. 49174	. 31027	. 50294	. 31837	. 51393	. 32653	18
43	. 46890	. 29438	. 48053	. 30236	. 49193	. 31041	. 50312	. 31851	. 51411	. 32667	17
44	. 46910	. 29451	. 48072	. 30249	. 49212	. 31054	. 50331	. 31865	. 51429	. 32681	16
45	9. 46929	0. 29464	9. 48091	0. 30263	9. 49231	0. 31068	9. 50349	0. 31878	9. 51447	0. 32694	15
46	. 46949	. 29477	. 48110	. 30276	. 49250	. 31081	. 50368	. 31892	. 51465	. 32708	14
47	. 46968	. 29491	. 48129	. 30290	. 49268	. 31094	. 50386	. 31905	. 51483	. 32721	13
48	. 46988	. 29504	. 48148	. 30303	. 49287	. 31108	. 50405	. 31919	. 51501	. 32735	12
49	. 47007	. 29517	. 48168	. 30316	. 49306	. 31121	. 50423	. 31932	. 51519	. 32749	11
50	9. 47027	0. 29530	9. 48187	0. 30330	9. 49325	0. 31135	9. 50442	0. 31946	9. 51538	0. 32762	10
51	. 47046	. 29544	. 48206	. 30343	. 49344	. 31148	. 50460	. 31959	. 51556	. 32776	9
52	. 47066	. 29557	. 48225	. 30356	. 49362	. 31162	. 50478	. 31973	. 51574	. 32790	8
53	. 47085	. 29570	. 48244	. 30370	. 49381	. 31175	. 50497	. 31987	. 51592	. 32803	7
54	. 47105	. 29583	. 48263	. 30383	. 49400	. 31189	. 50515	. 32000	. 51610	. 32817	6
55	9. 47124	0. 29597	9.48282	0. 30397	9. 49419	0. 31202	9. 50534	0. 32014	9. 51628	0. 32831	5
56	. 47144	. 29610	. 48302	. 30410	. 49437	. 31216	. 50552	. 32027	. 51646	. 32844	4
57	. 47163	. 29623	. 48321	. 30423	. 49456	. 31229	. 50570	. 32041	. 51664	. 32858	3
58	. 47183	. 29637	. 48340	. 30437	. 49475	. 31243	. 50589	. 32054	. 51682	. 32872	2
59	. 47202	. 29650	. 48359	. 30450	. 49494	. 31256	. 50607	. 32068	. 51700	. 32885	1
60	9. 47222	0. 29663	9. 48378	0. 30463	9. 49512	0. 31270	9. 50626	0. 32082	9. 51718	0. 32899	0
	294°		293°		292°		291°		290°		

Haversines

′	70°		71°		72°		73°		74°		′
	Log Hav	Nat. Hav	Log Hav	Nat. Hav	Log Hav	Nat. Hav	Log Hav	Nat. Hav	Log Hav	Nat. Hav	
0	9. 51718	0. 32899	9. 52791	0. 33722	9. 53844	0. 34549	9. 54878	0. 3538i	9. 55893	0. 36218	60
1	. 51736	. 32913	. 52809	. 33735	. 53861	. 34563	. 54895	. 35395	. 55909	. 36232	59
2	. 51754	. 32926	. 52826	. 33749	. 53879	. 34577	. 54912	. 35409	. 55926	. 36246	58
3	. 51772	. 32940	. 52844	. 33763	. 53896	. 34591	. 54929	. 35423	. 55943	. 36260	57
4	. 51790	. 32954	. 52862	. 33777	. 53913	. 34604	. 54946	. 35437	. 55960	. 36274	56
5	9. 51808	0. 32967	9. 52879	0. 33790	9. 5393	0. 34618	9. 54963	0. 35451	9. 55976	0. 36288	55
6	. 51826	. 32981	. 52897	. 33804	. 53948	. 34632	. 54980	. 35465	. 55993	. 36302	54
7	. 51844	. 32995	. 52915	. 33818	. 53966	. 34646	. 54997	. 35479	. 56010	. 36316	53
8	. 51862	. 33008	. 52932	. 33832	. 53983	. 34660	. 55014	. 35493	. 56027	. 36330	52
9	. 51880	. 33022	. 52950	. 33845	. 54000	. 34674	. 55031	. 35507	. 56043	. 36344	51
10	9. 51898	0. 33036	9. 52968	0. 33859	9. 54017	0. 34688	9. 55048	0. 35521	9. 56060	0. 36358	50
11	. 51916	. 33049	. 52985	. 33873	. 54035	. 34701	. 55065	. 35534	. 56077	. 36372	49
12	. 51934	. 33063	. 53003	. 33887	. 54052	. 34715	. 55082	. 35548	. 56093	. 36386	48
13	. 51952	. 33077	. 53021	. 33900	. 54069	. 34729	. 55099	. 35562	. 56110	. 36400	47
14	. 51970	. 33090	. 53038	. 33914	. 54087	. 34743	. 55116	. 35576	. 56127	. 36414	46
15	9. 51988	0. 33104	9. 53056	0. 33928	9. 54104	0. 34757	9. 55133	0. 35590	9. 56144	0. 36428	45
16	. 52006	. 33118	. 53073	. 33942	. 54121	. 34771	. 55150	. 35604	. 56160	. 36442	44
17	. 52024	. 33132	. 53091	. 33956	. 5'4139	. 34784	. 55167	. 35618	. 56177	. 36456	43
18	. 52042	. 33145	. 53109	. 33969	. 54156	. 34798	. 55184	. 35632	. 56194	. 36470	42
19	. 52060	. 33159	. 53126	. 33983	. 54173	. 34812	. 55201	. 35646	. 56210	. 36484	41
20	9. 52078	0. 33173	9. 53144	0. 33997	9. 54190	0. 34826	9. 55218	0. 35660	9. 56227	0. 36498	40
21	. 52096	. 33186	. 53162	. 34011	. 54208	. 34840	. 55235	. 35674	. 56244	. 36512	39
22	. 52114	. 33200	. 53179	. 34024	. 54225	. 34854	. 55252	. 35688	. 56260	. 36526	38
23	. 52132	. 33214	. 53197	. 34038	. 54242	. 34868	. 55269	. 35702	. 56277	. 36540	37
24	. 52150	. 33227	. 53214	. 34052	. 54260	. 34882	. 55286	. 35716	. 56294	. 36554	36
25	9. 52168	0. 33241	9. 53232	0. 34066	9. 54277	0. 34895	9. 55303	0. 35730	9. 56310	0. 36568	35
26	. 52185	. 33255	. 53249	. 34080	. 54294	. 34909	. 55320	. 35743	. 56327	. 36582	34
27	. 52203	. 33269	. 53267	. 34093	. 54311	. 34923	. 55337	.·35757	. 56343	. 36596	33
28	. 52221	. 33282	. 53285	. 34107	. 54329	. 34937	. 55354	. 35771	. 56360	. 36610	32
29	. 52239	. 33296	. 53302	. 34121	. 54346	. 34951	. 55370	. 35785	. 56377	. 36624	31
30	9. 52257	0. 33310	9. 53320	0. 34135	9. 54363	0. 34965	9. 55387	0. 35799	9. 56393	0. 36638	30
31	. 52275	. 33323	. 53337	. 34149	. 54380	. 34979	. 55404	. 35813	. 56410	. 36652	29
32	. 52293	. 33337	. 53355	. 34162	. 54397	. 34992	. 55421	. 35827	. 56426	. 36666	28
33	. 52311	. 33351	.·53372	. 34176	. 54415	. 35006	. 55438	. 35841	. 56443	. 36680	27
34	. 52328	. 33365	. 53390	. 34190	. 54432	. 35020	. 55455	. 35855	. 56460	. 36694	26
35	9. 52346	0. 33378	9. 53407	0. 34204	9. 54449	0. 35034	9. 55472	0. 35869	9. 56476	0. 36708	25
36	. 52364	. 33392	. 53425	. 34218	. 54466	. 35048	. 55489	. 35883	. 56493	. 36722	24
37	. 52382	. 33406	. 53442	. 34231	. 54483	. 35062	. 55506	. 35897	. 56509	. 36736	23
38	. 52400	. 33419	. 53460	. 34245	. 54501	. 35076	. 55523	. 35911	. 56526	. 36750	22
39	. 52418	. 33433	. 53477	..34259	. 54518	. 35090	. 55539	. 35925	. 56543	. 36764	21
40	9. 52436	0. 33447	9. 53495	0. 34273	9. 54535	0. 35103	9. 5.5556	0. 35939	9. 56559	0. 36778	20
41	. 52453	. 33461	. 53512	. 34287	. 54552	. 35117	. 55573	. 35953	. 56576	. 36792	19
42	. 52471	. 33474	. 53530	. 34300	. 54569	. 35131	. 55590	. 35967	. 56592	. 36806	18
43	. 52489	. 33488	. 53547	. 34314	. 54587	. 35145	. 55607	. 35981	. 56609	. 36820	17
44	. 52507	. 33502	. 53565	. 34328	. 54604	. 35159	. 55624	. 35995	. 56625	. 36834	16
45	9. 52525	0. 33515	9. 53582	0. 34342	9. 54621	0. 35173	9. 55641	0. 36009	9. 56642	0. 36848	15
46	. 52542	. 33529	. 53600	. 34356	. 54638	. 35187	. 55657	. 36023	. 56658	. 36862	14
47	. 52560	. 33543	. 53617	. 34369	. 54655	. 35201	. 55674	. 36036	. 56675	. 36877	13
48	. 52578	. 33557	. 53635	. 34383	. 54672	. 35215	. 55691	. 36050	. 56692	. 36891	12
49	. 52596	. 33570	. 53652	. 34397	. 54689	. 35228	. 55708	. 36064	. 56708	. 36905	11
50	9. 52613	0. 33584	9. 53670	0. 34411	9. 54707	0. .35242	9. 55725	0. 36078	9. 56725	0. 36919	10
51	. 52631	. 33598	. 53687	. 34425	. 54724	. 35256	. 55742	. 36092	. 96741	. 36933	9
52	. 52649	. 33612	. 53704	. 34439	. 54741	. 35270	. 55758	. 36106	. 56758	. 36947	8
53	. 52667	. 33625	. 53722	. 34452	. 54758	. 35284	. 55775	. 36120	. 56774	. 36961	7
54	. 52684	. 33639	. 53739	. 34466	. 54775	. 35298	. 55792	. 36184	. 56791	. 36975	6
55	9. 52702	0. 33653	9. 53757	0. 34480	9. 54792	0. 35312	9. 55809	0. 36148	9. 56807	0. 36989	5
56	. 52720	. 33667	. 53774	. 34494	. 54809	. 35326	. 55826	. 36162	. 56824	. 37003	4
57	. 52738	. 33680	. 53792	. 34508	. 54826	. 35340	. 55842	. 36176	. 56840	. 37017	3
58	. 52755	. 33694	. 53809	. 34521	. 54843	. 35354	. 55859	. 36190	. 56856	. 37031	2
59	. 52773	. 33708	. 53826	. 34535	. 54860	. 35368	. 55876	. 36204	. 56873	. 37045	1
60	9. 52791	0. 33722	9. 53844	0. 34549	9. 54878	0. 35381	9. 55893	0. 36218	9. 56889	0. 37059	0
	289°		288°		287°		286°		285°		

Haversines

′	75°		76°		77°		78°		79°		′
	Log Hav	Nat. Hav	Log Hav	Nat. Hav	Log Hav	Nat. Hav	Log Hav	Nat. Hav	Log Hav	Nat. Hav	
0	9. 56889	0. 37059	9. 57868	0. 37904	9. 58830	0. 38752	9. 59774	0. 39604	9. 60702	0. 40460	60
1	. 56906	. 37073	. 57885	. 37918	. 58846	. 38767	. 59790	. 39619	. 60717	. 40474	59
2	. 56922	. 37087	. 57901	. 37932	. 58862	. 38781	. 59806	. 39633	. 60733	. 40488	58
3	. 56939	. 37101	. 57917	. 37946	. 58878	. 38795	. 59821	. 39647	. 60748	. 40502	57
4	. 56955	. 37115	. 57933	. 37960	. 58893	. 38809	. 59837	. 39661	. 60763	. 40517	56
5	9. 56972	0. 37129	9. 57949	0. 37974	9. 58909	0. 38823	9. 59852	0. 39676	9. 60779	0. 40531	55
6	. 56988	. 37143	. 57965	. 37989	. 58925	. 38837	. 59868	. 39690	. 60794	. .40545	54
7	. 57005	. 37157	. 57981	. 38003	. 58941	. 38852	. 59883	. 39704	. 60809	. 40560	53
8	. 57021	. 37171	. 57998	. 38017	. 58957	. 38866	. 59899	. 39718	. 60825	. 40574	52
9	. 57037	. 37186	. 58014	. 38031	. 58973	. 38880	. 59915	. 39732	60840	. 40588	51
10	9. 57054	0. 37200	9. 58030	0. 38045	9. 58989	0. 38894	9. 59930	0. 39747	9. 60855	0. 40602	50
11	. 57070	. 37214	. 58046	. 38059	. 59004	. 38908	. 59946	. 39761	. 60870	. 40617	49
12	. 57087	. 37228	. 58062	. 38073	. 59020	. 38923	. 59961	. 39775	. 60886	. 40631	48
13	. 57103	. 37242	. 58078	. 38087	. 59036	. 38937	. 59977	. 39789	. 60901	. 40645	47
14	. 57119	. 37256	. 58094	. 38102	. 59052	. 38951	. 59992	. 39804	. 60916	. 40660	46
15	9. 57136	0. 37270	9. 58110	0. 38116	9. 59068	0. 38965	9. 60008	0. 39818	9. 60931	0. 40674	45
16	. 57152	. 37284	. 58126	. 38130	. 59083	. 38979	. 60023	. 39832	. 60947	. 40688	44
17	. 57169	. 37298	. 58143	. 38144	. 59099	. 38994	. 60039	. 39846	. 60962	. 40702	43
18	. 57185	. 37312	. 58159	. 38158	. 59115	. 39008	. 60054	. 39861	. 60977	. 40717	42
19	. 57201	. 37326	. 58175	. 38172	. 59131	. 39022	. 60070	. 39875	. 60992	. 40731	41
20	9. 57218	0. 37340	9. 58191	0. 38186	9. 59147	0. 39036	9. 60085	0. 39889	9. 61008	0. 40745	40
21	. 57234	. 37354	. 58207	. 38200	. 59162	. 39050	. 60101	. 39903	. 61023	. 40760	39
22	. 57250	. 37368	. 58223	. 38215	. 59178	. 39064	. 60116	. 39918	. 61038	. 40774	38
23	. 57267	. 37382	. 58239	. 38229	. 59194	. 39079	. 60132	. 39932	. 61053	. 40788	37
24	. 57283	. 37397	. 58255	. 38243	. 59210	. 39093	. 60147	. 39946	. 61069	. 40802	36
25	9. 57299	0. 37411	9. 58271	0. 38257	9. 59225	0. 39107	9. 60163	0. 39960	9. 61084	0. 40817	35
26	. 57316	. 37425	. 58287	. 38271	. 59241	. 39121	. 60178	. 39975	. 61099	. 40831	34
27	. 57332	. 37439	. 58303	. 38285	. 59257	. 39135	. 60194	. 39989	. 61114	. 40845	33
28	. 57348	. 37453	. .58319	. 38299	. 59273	. 39150	. 60209	. 40003	. 61129	. 40860	32
29	. 57365	. 37467	. 58335	. 38314	. 59289	. 39164	. 60225	. 40017	. 61145	. 40874	31
30	9. 57381	0. 37481	9. 58351	0. 38328	9. 59304	0. 39178	9. 60240	0. 40032	9. 61160	0. 40888	30
31	. 57397	. 37495	. 58367	. 38342	. 59320	. 39192	. 60256	. 40046	. 61175	. 40903	29
32	. 57414	. 37509	. 58383	. 38356	. 59336	. 39206	. 60271	. 40060	. 61190	. .40917	28
33	. 57430	. 37523	. 58399	. 38370	. 59351	. 39221	. 60287	. 40074	. 61205	. 40931	27
34	. 57446	. 37537	. 58415	. 38384	. 59367	. 39235	. 60302	. 40089	. 61221	. 40945	26
35	9. 57463	0. 37551	9. 58431	0. 38398	9. 59383	0. 39249	9. 60318	0. 40103	9. 61236	0. 40960	25
36	. 57479	. 37566	. 58447	. 38413	. 59399	. 39263	. 60333	. 40117	. 61251	. 40974	24
37	. 57495	. 37580	. 58463	. 38427	. 59414	. 39277	. 60348	. 40131	. 61266	. 40988	23
38	. 57511	. 37594	. 58479	. 38441	. 59430	. 39292	. 60364	. 40146	. 61281	. 41003	22
39	. 57528	. 37608	. 58495	. 38455	. 59446	. '39306	. 60379	. 40160	. 61296	. 41017	21
40	9. 57544	0. 37622	9. 58511	0. 38469	9. 59461	0. 39320	9. 60395	0. 40174	9. 61312	0. 41031	20
41	. 57560	. 37636	. 58527	. 38483	. 59477	. 39334	. 60410	. 40188	. 61327	. 41046	19
42	. 57577	. 37650	. 58543	. 38498	. 59493	. 39348	. 60426	. 40203	. 61342	. 41060	18
43	. 57593	. 37664	. 58559	. 38512	. 59508	. 39363	. 60441	. 40217	. 61357	. 41074	17
44	. 57609	. 37678	. 58575	. 38526	. 59524	·. 39377	. 60456	. 40231	. 61372	. 41089	16
45	9. 57625	0. 37692	9. 58591	0. 38540	9. 59540	0. 39391	9. 60472	0. 40245	9. 61387	0. 41103	15
46	. 57642	. 37706	. 58607	. 38554	. 59556	. 39405	. 60487	. 40260	. 61402	. 41117	14
47	. 57658	. 37721	. 58623	. 38568	. 59571	. 39420	. 60502	. 40274	. 61417	. 41131	13
48	. 57674	. 37735	. 58639	. 38582	. 59587	. 39434	. 60518	. 40288	. 61433	. 41146	12
49	. 57690	. 37749	. 58655	. 38597	. 59602	. 39448	. 6053.3	. 40303	. 61448	. 41160	11
50	9. 5706	0. 37763	9. 58671	0. 38611	9. 59618	0. 39462	9. 60549	0. 40317	9. 61463	0. 41174	10
51	. 57723	. 37777	. 58687	. 38625	. 59634	. 39476	. 60564	. 40331	. 61478	. 41189	9
52	. 57739	. 37791	. 58703	. 38639	. 59649	. 39491	. 60579	. 40345	. 61493	. 41203	8
53	. 57755	. 37805	. 58719	. 38653	. 59665	. 39505	. 60595	. 40360	. 61508	. 41217	7
54	. 57771	. 37819	. 58735	. 38667	. 59681	. 39519	. 60610	. 40374	. 61523	. 41232	6
55	9. 57787	0. 37833	9. 58750	0. 38682	9. 59696	0. 39533	9. 60625	0. 40388	9. 61538	0. 41246	5
56	. 57804	. 37847	. 58766	. 38696	. 59712	. 39548	. 60641	. 40402	. 61553	. 41260	4
57	. 57820	. 37862	. 58782	. 38710	. 59728	. 39562	. 60656	. 40417	. 61568	. 41275	3
58	. 57836	. 37876	. 58798	. 38724	. 59743	. 39576	. 60671	. 40431	. 61583	. 41289	2
59	. 57852	. 37890	. 58814	. 38738	. 59759	. 39590	. 60687	. 40445	. 61598	. 41303	1
60	9. 57868	0. 37904	9. 58830	0. 38752	9. 59774	0. 39604	9. 60702	0. 40460	9. 61614	0. 41318	0
	284°		283°		282°		281°		280°		

Haversines

′	80°		81°		82°		83°		84°		′
	Log Hav	Nat. Hav	Log Hav	Nat. Hav	Log Hav	Nat. Hav	Log Hav	Nat. Hav	Log Hav	Nat. Hav	
0	9. 61614	0. 41318	9. 62509	0. 42178	9. 63389	0. 43041	9. 64253	0. 43907	9. 65102	0. 44774	60
1	. 61629	. 41332	. 62524	. 42193	. 63403	. 43056	. 64267	. 43921	. 65116	. 44788	59
2	. 61644	. 41346	. 62538	. 42207	. 63418	. 43070	. 64281	. 43935	. 65130	. 44803	58
3	. 61659	. 41361	. 62553	. 42221	. 63432	. 43085	. 64296	. 43950	. 65144	. 44817	57
4	. 61674	. 41375	. 62568	. 42236	. 63447	. 43099	. 64310	. 43964	. 65158	. 44831	56
5	9. 61689	0. 41389	9. 62583	0. 42250	9. 63461	0. 43113	9. 64324	0. 43979	9. 65172	0. 44846	55
6	. 61704	. 41404	. 62598	. 42264	. 63476	. 43128	. 64339	. 43993	. 65186	. 44860	54
7	. 61719	. 41418	. 62612	. 42279	. 63490	. 43142	. 64353	. 44008	. 65200	. 44875	53
8	. 61734	. 41432	. 62627	. 42293	. 63505	. 43157	. 64367	. 44022	. 65214	. 44889	52
9	. 61749.	. 41447	. 62642	. 42308	. 63519	. 43171	. 64381	. 44036	. 65228	. 44904	51
10	9. 61764	0. 41461	9. 62657	0. 42322	9. 63534	0. 43185	9. 64396	0. 44051	9. 65242	0. 44918	50
11	. 61779	. 41475	. 62671	. 42336	. 63548	. 43200	. 64410	. 44065	. 65256	. 44933	49
12	. 61794	. 41490	. 62686	. 42351	. 63563	. 43214	. 64424	. 44080	. 65270	. 44947	48
13	. 61809	. 41504	. 62701	. 42365	. 63577	. 43229	. 64438	. 44094	. 65284	. 44962	47
14	. 61824	. 41518	. 62716	. 42379	. 63592	. 43243	. 64452	. 44109	. 65298	. 44976	46
15	9. 61839	0. 41533	9. 62730	0. 42394	9. 63606	0..43257	9. 64467	0. 44123	9. 65312	0. 44991	45
16	. 61854	. 41547	. 62745	. 42408	. 63621	. 43272	. 64481	. 44138	. 65326	. 45005	44
17	. 61869	. 41561	. 62760	. 42423	. 63635	. 43286	. 64495	. 44152	. 65340	. 45020	43
18	. 61884	. 41576	: 62774	. 42437	. 63649	. 43301	. 64509	. 44166	. 65354	. 45034	42
19	. 61899	. 41590	. 62789	. 42451	. 63664	. 43315	. 64523	. 44181	. 65368	. 45048	41
20	9. 61914	0. 41604	9. 62804	0. 42466	9. 63678	0. 43330	9. 64538	0. 44195	9. 65382	0. 45063	40
21	. 61929	. 41619	. 62819	. 42480	. 63693	. 43344	. 64552	. 44210	. 65396	. 45077	39
22	. 61944	. 41633	. 62833	. 42494	. 63707	. 43358	. 64566	. 44224	. 65410	. 45092	38
23	. 61959	. 41647	. 62848	. 42509	. 63722	. 43373	. 64580	. 44239	. 65424	. 45106	37
24	. 61974	. 41662	. 62863	. 42523	. 63736	. 43387	. 64594	. 44253	. 65438	. 45121	36
25	9. .61989	0. 41676	9. 62877	0. 42538	9. 63751	0. 43402	9. 64609	0. 44268	9. 65452	0. 45135	35
26	. 62003	. 41690	. 62892	. 42552	. 63765	. 43416	. 64623	. 44282	. 65466	. 45150	34
27	. 62018	. 41705	. 62907	. 42566	. 63779	. 43430	. 64637	. 44296	. 65480	. 45164	33
28	. 62033	. 41719	. 62921	. 42581	. 63794	. 43445	. 64651	. 44311	. 65493	. 45179	32
29	. 62048	. 41733	. 62936	. 42595	. 63808	. 43459	. 64665	. 44325	. 65507	. 45193	31
30	9. 62063	o. 41748	9. 62951	0. 42610	9. 63823	0. 43474	9. .64679	0. 44340	9. 65521	0. 45208	30
31	. 62078	. 41762	. 62965	. 42624	. 63837	. 43488	. 64694	. 44354	. 65535	. 45222	29
32	. 62093	. 4:1776	. 62980	. 42638	. 63851	. 43503	. 64708	. 44369	. 65549	. 45237	28
33	. 62108	. 41791	. 62995	. 42653	. 63866	. 43517	. 64722	. 44383	. 65563	. 45251	27
34	. 62.123	. 41805	. 63009	. 42667	. 63880	. 43531	. 64736	. 44398	. 65577	. 45266	26
35	9. 62138	0. 41819	9. 63024	0. 42681	9. 63895	0. 43546	9. 64750	0. 44412	9. 65591	0. 45280	25
36	. 62153	. 41834	. 63039	. 42696	. 63909	. 43560	. 64764	. 44427	. 65605	. 45295	24
37	. 62168	. 41848	. 63053	. 42710	. 63923	. 43575	. 64778	. 44441	. 65619	. 45309	23
38	. 62182	. 41862	. 63068	. 42725	. 63938	. 43589	. 64793	. 44455	. 65632	. 45324	22
39	. 62197	. 41877	. 63082	. 42739	. 63952	. 43603	. 64807	. 44470	. 65646	. 45338	21
40	9. 62212	0. 41891	9. 63097	0. 42753	9. 63966	0. 43618	9. 64821	0. 44484	9. 65660	0. 45353	20
41	. 62227	. 41905	. .63112	. 42768	. 63981	. 43632	. 64835	. 44499	. 65674	. 45367	19
42	. 62242	. 41920	. 63126	. 42782	. 63995	. 43647	. 64849	. 44513	. 65688	. 45381	18
43	. 62257	. 41934	. 63141	:42797	. 64010	. 43661	. 64863	. 44528	. 65702	. 45396	17
44	. 62272	. 41949	. 63156	. 42811	. 64024	. 43676	. 64877	. 44542	. 65716	. 45410	16
45	9. 62287	0. 41963	9. 63170	0. 42825	9. 64038	0. 43690	9. 64891	0. 44557	9. 65729	0. 45425	15
46	. 62301	. 41977	. 63185	. 42840	. 64053	. 43704	. 64905	. 44571	. 65743	. 45439	14
47	. 62316	. 41992	. 63199	. 42854	. 64067	. 43719	. 64919	. 44586	. 65757	. 45454	13
48	. 62331	. 42006	. 63214	..42869	. 64081	. 43733	. 64934	. 44600	. 65771	. 45468	12
49	. 62346	. 42020	. 63228	. 42883	. 64096	. 43748	. 64948	. 44614	. 65785	. 45483	11
50	9. 62361	0. 42035	9. 63243	0. 42897	9. 64110	0. 43762	9. 64962	0. 44629	9. 65799	0. 45497	10
51	. 62376	. 42049	. 63258	. 42912	. 64124	. 43777	. 64976	. 44643	. 65812	. 45512	9
52	. 62390	. 42063	. 63272	. 42926	. 64139	. 43791	. 64990	. 44658	. 65826	. 45526	8
53	. 62405	. 42078	. 63287	. 42941	. 64153	. 43805	. 65004	. 44672	. 65840	. 45541	7
54	. 62420	. 42092	. 63301	. 42955	. 64167	. 43820	. 65018	. 44687	. 65854	. 45555	6
55	9. 62435	0. 42106	9. 63316	o; 42969	9. 64181	0. 43834	9. 65032	0. 44701	9. 65868	0. 45570	5
56	. 62450	. 42121	. 63330	. 42984	. 64196	. 43849	. 65046	. 44716	. 65881	. 45584	4
57	. 62464	. 42135	. 63345	. 42998	. 64210	. 43863	. 65060	. 44730	. 65895	. 45599	3
58	. 62479	. 42150	. 63360	. 43013	. 64224	. 43878	. 65074	. 44745	. 65909	. 45613	2
59	. 62494	. 42164	. 63374	. 43027	. 64239	. 43892	. 65088	. 44759	. 65923	. 45628	1
60	9. 62509	0. 42178	9. 63389	0. 43041	9. 64253	0. 43907	9. 65102	0. 44774	9. 65937	0. 45642	0
	279°		278°		277°		276°		275°		

Haversines

′	85°		86°		87°		88°		89°		′
	Log Hav	Nat. Hav	Log Hav	Nat. Hav	Log Hav	Nat. Hav	Log Hav	Nat. Hav	Log Hav	Nat. Hav	
0	9. 65937	0. 45642	9. 66757	0. 46512	9. 67562	0. 47383	9. 68354	0. 48255	9. 69132	0. 49127	60
1	. 65950	. 45657	. 66770	. 46527	. 67576	. 47398	. 68367	. 48270	. 69145	. 49142	59
2	. 65964	. 45671	. 66784	. 46541	. 67589	. 47412	. 68380	. 48284	. 69158	. 49156	58
3	. 65978	. 45686	. 66797	. 46556	. 67602	. 47427	. 68393	. 48299	. 69171	. 49171	57
4	. 65992	. 45700	. 66811	. 46570	. 67616	. 47441	. 68407	. 48313	. 69184	. 49186	56
5	9. 66006	0. 45715	9. 66824	0. 46585	9. 67629	0. 47456	9. 68420	0. 48328	9. 69197	0. 49200	55
6	. 66019	. 45729	. 66838	. 46599	. 67642	. 47470	. 68433	. 48342	. 69209	. 49215	54
7	. 66033	. 45744	. 66851	. 46614	. 67656	. 47485	. 68446	. 48357	. 69222	. 49229	53
8	. 66047	. 45758	. 66865	. 46628	. 67669	. 47499	. 68459	. 48371	. 69235	. 49244	52
9	. 66061	. 45773	. 66878	. 46643	. 67682	. 47514	. 68472	. 48386	. 69248	. 49258	51
10	9. 66074	0. 45787	9. 66892	0. 46657	9. 67695	0. 47528	9. 68485	0. 48400	9. 69261	0. 49273	50
11	. 66088	. 45802	. 66905	. 46672	. 67709	. 47543	. 68498	. 48415	. 69274	. 49287	49
12	. 66102	. 45816	. 66919	. 46686	. 67722	. 47558	. 68511	. 48429	. 69286	. 49302	48
13	. 66116	. 45831	. 66932	. 46701	. 67735	. 47572	. 68524	. 48444	. 69299	. 49316	47
14	. 66129	. 45845	. 66946	. 46715	. 67748	. 47587	. 68537	. 48459	. 69312	. 49331	46
15	9. 66143	0. 45860	9. 66959	0. 46730	9. 67762	0. 47601	9. 68550	0. 48473	9. 69325	0. 49346	45
16	. 66157	. 45874	. 66973	. 46744	. 67775	. 47616	. 68563	. 48488	. 69338	. 49360	44
17	. 66170	. 45889	. 66986	. 46759	. 67788	. 47630	. 68576	. 48502	. 69350	. 49375	43
18	. 66184	. 45903	. 67000	. 46773	. 67801	. 47645	. 68589	. 48517	. 69363	. 49389	42
19	. 66198	. 45918	. 67013	. 46788	. 67815	. 47659	. 68602	. 48531	. 69376	. 49404	41
20	9. 66212	0. 45932	9. 67027	0. 46802	9. 67828	0. 47674	9. 68615	0. 48546	9. 69389	0. 49418	40
21	. 66225	. 45947	. 67040	. 46817	. 67841	. 47688	. 68628	. 48560	. 69402	. 49433	39
22	. 66239	. 45961	. 67054	. 46831	. 67854	. 47703	. 68641	. 48575	. 69414	. 49447	38
23	. 66253	. 45976	. 67067	. 46846	. 67868	. 47717	. 68654	. 48589	. 69427	. 49462	37
24	. 66266	. 45990	. 67081	. 46860	. 67881	. 47732	. 68667	. 48604	. 69440	. 49476	36
25	9. 66280	0. 46005	9. 67094	0. 46875	9. 67894	0. 47746	9. 68680	0. 48618	9. 69453	0. 49491	35
26	. 66294	. 46019	. 67108	. 46890	. 67907	. 47761	. 68693	. 48633	. 69465	. 49505	34
27	. 66307	. 46034	. 67121	. 46904	. 67920	. 47775	. 68706	. 48648	. 69478	. 49520	33
28	. 66321	. 46048	. 67134	. 46919	. 67934	. 47790	. 68719	. 48662	. 69491	. 49535	32
29	. 66335	. 46063	. 67148	. 46933	. 67947	. 47804	. 68732	. 48677	. 69504	. 49549	31
30	9. 66348	0. 46077	9. 67161	0. 46948	9. 67960	0. 47819	9. 68745	0. 48691	9. 69516	0. 49564	30
31	. 66362	. 46092	. 67175	. 46962	. 67973	. 47834	. 68758	. 48706	. 69529	. 49578	29
32	. 66376	. 46106	. 67188	. 46977	. 67986	. 47848	. 68771	. 48720	. 69542	. 49593	28
33	. 66389	. 46121	. 67202	. 46991	. 68000	. 47863	. 68784	. 48735	. 69555	. 49607	27
34	. 66403	. 46135	. 67215	. 47006	. 68013	. 47877	. 68797	. 48749	. 69567	. 49622	26
35	9. 66417	0. 46150	9. 67228	0. 47020	9. 68026	0. 47892	9. 68810	0. 48764	9. 69580	0. 49636	25
36	. 66430	. 46164	. 67242	. 47035	. 68039	. 47906	. 68823	. 48778	. 69593	. 49651	24
37	. 66444	. 46179	. 67255	. 47049	. 68052	. 47921	. 68836	. 48793	. 69605	. 49665	23
38	. 66458	. 46193	. 67269	. 47064	. 68066	. 47935	. 68849	. 48807	. 69618	. 49680	22
39	. 66471	. 46208	. 67282	. 47078	. 68079	. 47950	. 68862	. 48822	. 69631	. 49695	21
40	9. 66485	0. 46222	9. 67295	0. 47093	9. 68092	0. 47964	9. 68875	0. 48837	9. 69644	0. 49709	20
41	. 66499	. 46237	. 67309	. 47107	. 68105	. 47979	. 68887	. 48851	. 69656	. 49724	19
42	. 66512	. 46251	. 67322	. 47122	. 68118	. 47993	. 68900	. 48866	. 69669	. 49738	18
43	. 66526	. 46266	. 67336	. 47136	. 68131	. 48008	. 68913	. 48880	. 69682	. 49753	17
44	. 66539	. 46280	. 67349	. 47151	. 68144	. 48022	. 68926	. 48895	. 69694	. 49767	16
45	9. 66553	0. 46295	9. 67362	0. 47165	9. 68158	0. 48037	9. 68939	0. 48909	9. 69707	0. 49782	15
46	. 66567	. 46309	. 67376	. 47180	. 68171	. 48052	. 68952	. 48924	. 69720	. 49796	14
47	. 66580	. 46324	. 67389	. 47194	. 68184	. 48066	. 68965	. 48938	. 69732	. 49811	13
48	. 66594	. 46338	. 67402	. 47209	. 68197	. 48081	. 68978	. 48953	. 69745	. 49825	12
49	. 66607	. 46353	. 67416	. 47223	. 68210	. 48095	. 68991	. 48967	. 69758	. 49840	11
50	9. 66621	0. 46367	9. 67429	0. 47238	9. 68223	0. 48110	9. 69004	0. 48982	9. 69770	49855	10
51	. 66635	. 46382	. 67443	. 47252	. 68236	. 48124	. 69017	. 48997	. 69783	. 49869	9
52	. 66648	. 46396	. 67456	. 47267	. 68249	. 48139	. 69029	. 49011	. 69796	. 49884	8
53	. 66662	. 46411	. 67469	. 47282	. 68263	. 48153	. 69042	. 49026	. 69808	. 49898	7
54	. 66675	. 46425	. 67483	. 47296	. 68276	. 48168	. 69055	. 49040	. 69821	. 49913	6
55	9. 66689	0. 46440	9. 67496	0. 47311	9. 68289	0. 48182	9. 69068	0. 49055	9. 69834	49927	5
56	. 66702	. 46454	. 67509	. 47325	. 68302	. 48197	. 69081	. 49069	. 69846	. 49942	4
57	. 66716	. 46469	. 67522	. 47340	. 68315	. 48211	. 69094	. 49084	. 69859	. 49956	3
58	. 66730	. 46483	. 67536	. 47354	. 68328	. 48226	. 69107	. 49098	. 69872	. 49971	2
59	. 66743	. 46498	. 67549	. 47369	. 68341	. 48240	. 69120	. 49113	. 69884	. 49985	1
60	9. 66757	0. 46512	9. 67562	0. 47383	9. 68354	0. 48255	9. 69132	0. 49127	9. 69897	0. 50000	0
	274°		273°		272°		271°		270°		

Haversines

′	90°		91°		92°		93°		94°		′
	Log Hav	Nat. Hav	Log Hav	Nat. Hav	Log Hav	Nat. Hav	Log Hav	Nat. Hav	Log Hav	Nat. Hav	
0	9. 69897	0. 50000	9. 70648	0. 50873	9. 71387	0. 51745	9. 72112	0. 52617	9. 72825	0. 53488	60
1	. 69910	. 50015	. 70661	. 50887	. 71399	. 51760	. 72124	. 52631	. 72837	. 53502	59
2	. 69922	. 50029	. 70673	. 50902	. 71411	. 51774	. 72136	. 52646	. 72849	. 53517	58
3	. 69935	. 50044	. 70686	. 50916	. 71123	. 51789	. 72148	. 52660	. 72861	. 53531	57
4	. 69948	. 500.58	. 70698	. 50931	. 71436	. 51803	. 72160	. 52675	. 72873	. 53546	56
5	9. 69960	0. 50073	9. 70710	0. 50945	9. 71448	0. 51818	9. 72172	0. 52689	9. 72884	0. 53560	55
6	. 69973	. 50087	. 70723	. 50960	. 71460	. 51832	. 72184	. 52704	. 72896	. 53575	54
7	. 69985	. 50102	. 70735	. 50974	. 71472	. 51847	. 72196	. 52718	. 72908	. 53539	53
8	. 69998	. 50116	. 70748	. 50989	. 71484	. 51861	. 72208	. 52733	. 72920'	. 53604	52
9	. 70011	. 50131	. 70760	. 51003	. 71496	. 51876	. 72220	. 52748	. 72931	. 53618	51
10	9. 70023	0. 50145	9. 70772	0. 51018	9. 71509	0. 51890	9. 72232	0. 52762	9. 72943	0. 53633	50
11	. 70036	. 50160	. 70785	. 51033	. 71521	. 51905	. 72244	. 52777	. 72955	. 53647	49
12	. 70048	. 50175	. 70797	. 51047	. 71533	. 51919	. 72256	. 52791	. 72967	. 53662	48
13	. 70061	. 50189	. 70809	. 51062	. 71545	. 51934	. 72268	. 52806	. 72978	. 53676	47
14	. 70074	. 50204	. 70822	. 51076	. 71557	. 51948	. 72280	. 52820	. 72990	. 53691	46
15	9. 70086	0. 50218	9. 70834	0. 51091	9. 71569	0. 51963	9. 72292	0. 52835	9. 73002	0. 53705	45
16	. 70099	. 50233	. 70847	. 51105	. 71582	. 51978	. 72304	. 52849	. 73014	. 53720	44
17	. 70111	. 50247	. 70859	. 51120	. 71594	. 51992	. 72316	. 52864	. 73025	. 53734	43
18	. 70124	. 50262	. 70871	. 51134	. 71606	. 52007	. 72328	. 52878	. 73037	. 53749	42
19	. 70136	. 50276	. 70884	. 51149	. 71618	. 52021	. 72340	. 52893	. 73049	. 53763	41
20	9. 70149	0. 50291	9. 70896	0. 51163	9. 71630	0. 52036	9. 72352	0. 52907	9. 73060	0. 53778	40
21	. 70161	. 50305	. 70908	. 51178	. 71642	. 52050	. 72363	. 52922	. 73072	. 53792	39
22	. 70174	. 50320	. 70921	. 51193	. 71654	. 52065	. 72375	. 52936	. 73084	. 53807	38
23	. 70187	. 50335	. 70933	. 51207	. 71666	. 52079	. 72387	. 52951	. 73096	. 53821	37
24	. 70199	. 50349	. 70945	. 51222	. 71679	. 52094	. 72399	. 52965	. 73107	. 53836	36
25	9. 70212	0. 50364	9. 70958	0. 51236	9. 71691	0. 52108	9. 72411	0. 52980	9. 73119	0. 53850	35
26	. 70224	. 50378	. 70970	. 51251	. 71703	. 52123	. 72423	. 52994	. 73131	. 53865	34
27	. 70237	. 50393	. 70982	. 51265	. 71715	. 52137	. 72435	. 53009	. 73142	. 53879	33
28	. 70249	. 50407	. 70995	. 51280	. 71727	. 52152	. 72447	. 53023	. 73154	. 53894	32
29	. 70262	. 50422	. 71007	. 51294	. 71739	. 52166	. 72459	. 53038	. 73166	. 53908	31
30	9. 70274	0. 50436	9. 71019	0. 51309	9. 71751	0. 52181	9. 72471	0. 53052	9. 73177	0. 53923	30
31	. 70287	. 50451	. 71032	. 51323	. 71763	. 52195	. 72482	. 53067	. 73189	. 53937	29
32	. 70299	. 50465	. 71044	. 51338	. 71775	. 52210	. 72494	. 53081	. 73201	. 53952	28
33	. 70312	. 50480	. 71056	. 51352	. 71787	. 52225	. 72506	. 53096	. 73212	. 53966	27
34	. 70324	. 50495	. 71068	. 51367	. 71800	. 52239	. 72518	. 53110	. 73224	. 53981	26
35	9. 70337	0. 50509	9. 71081	0. 51382	9. 71812	0. 52254	9. 72530	0. 53125	9. 73236	0. 53995	25
36	. 70349	. 50524	. 71093	. 51396	. 71824	. 52268	. 72542	. 53140	. 73247	. 54010	24
37	. 70362	. 50538	. 71105	. 51411	. 71836	. 52283	. 72554	. 53154	. 73259	. 54024	23
38	. 70374	. 50553	. 71118	. 51425	. 71848	. 52297	. 72565	. 53169	. 73271	. 54039	22
39	. 70387	. 50567	. 71130	. 51440	. 71860	. 52312	. 72577	. 53183	. 73282	. 54053	21
40	9. 70399	0. 50582	9. 71142	0. 51454	9. 71872	0. 52326	9. 72589	0. 53198	9. 73294	0. 54068	20
41	. 70412	. 50596	. 71154	. 51469	. 71884	. 52341	. 72601	. 53212	. 73306	. 54082	19
42	. 70424	. 50611	. 71167	. 51483	. 71896	. 52355	. 72613	. 53227	. 73317	. 54097	18
43	. 70437	. 50625	. 71179	. 51498	. 71908	. 52370	. 72625	. 53241	. 73329	. 54111	17
44	. 70449	. 50640	. 71191	. 51512	. 71920	. 52384	. 72637	. 53256	. 73341	. 54126	16
45	9. 70462	0. 50654	9. 71203	0. 51527	9. 71932	0. 52399	9. 72648	0. 53270	9. 73352	0. 54140	15
46	. 70474	. 50669	. 71216	. 51541	. 71944	. 52413	. 72660	. 53285	. 73364	. 54155	14
47	. 70487	. 50684	. 71228	. 51556	. 71956	. 52428	. 72672	. 53299	. 73375	. 54169	13
48	. 70499	. 50698	. 71240	. 51571	. 71968	. 52442	. 72684	. 53314	. 73387	. 54184	12
49	. 70512	. 50713	. 71252	. 51585	. 71980	. 52457	. 72696	. 53328	. 73399	. 54198	11
50	9. 70524	0. 50727	9. 71265	o. 51600	9. 71992	0. 52472	9. 72708	0. 53343	9. 73410	0. 54213	10
51	. 70537	. 50742	. 71277	. 51614	. 72004	. 52486	. 72719	. 53357	. 73422	. 54227	9
52	. 70549	. 50756	. 71289	. 51629	. 72016	. 52501	. 72731	. 53372	. 73433	. 54242	8
53	. 70561	. 50771	. 71301	. 51643	. 72028	. 52515	. 72743	. 53386	. 73445	. 54256	7
54	. 70574	. 50785	. 71314	. 51658	. 72040	. 52530	. 72755	. 53401	. 73457	. 54271	6
55	9.70586	0. 50800	9. 71326	0. 51672	9. 72052	0. 52544	9. 72767	0. 53415	9. 73468	0. 54285	5
56	. 70599	. 50814	. 71338	. 51687	. 72064	. 52559	. 72778	. 53430	. 73480	. 54300	4
57	. 70611	. 50829	. 71350	. 51701	. 72076	. 52573	. 72790	. 53444	. 73491	. 54314	3
58	. 70624	. 50844	. 71362	. 51716	. 72088	. 52588	. 72802	. 53459	. 73503	. 54329	2
59	. 70636	. 50858	. 71375	. 51730	. 72100	. 52602	. 72814	. 53473	. 73515	. 54343	1
60	9. 70648	0. 50873	9. 71387	0. 51745	9. 72112	0. 52617	9. 72825	0. 53488	9. 73526	0. 54358	0
	269°		268°		267°		266°		265°		

Haversines

′	95°		96°		97°		98°		99°		′
	Log Hav	Nat. Hav	Log Hav	Nat. Hav	Log Hav	Nat. Hav	Log Hav	Nat. Hav	Log Hav	Nat. Hav	
0	9. 73526	0. 54358	9. 74215	0. 55226	9. 74891	0. 56093	9. 75556	0. 56959	9. 76209	0. 57822	60
1	. 73538	. 54372	. 74226	. 55241	. 74902	. 56108	. 75567	. 56973	. 76220	. 57836	59
2	. 73549	. 54387	. 74237	. 55255	. 74914	. 56122	. 75578	. 56987	. 76231	. 57850	58
3	. 73561	. 54401	. 74249	. 55270	. 74925	. 56137	. 75589	. 57002	. 76241	. 57865	57
4	. 73572	. 54416	. 74260	. 55284	. 74936	. 56151	. 75600	. 57016	. 76252	. 57879	56
5	9. 73584	0. 54430	9. 71272	0. 55299	9. 74947	0. 56166	9. 75611	0. 57031	9. 76263	0. 57894	55
6	. 73596	. 54445	. 74283	. 55313	. 74958	. 56180	. 75622	. 57045	. 76274	. 57908	54
7	. 73607	. 54459	. 74294	. 55328	. 74969	. 56195	. 75633	. 57059	. 76285	. 57922	53
8	. 73619	. 54474	. 74306	. 55342	. 74981	. 56209	. 75644	. 57074	. 76296	. 57937	52
9	. 73630	. 54488	. 74317	. 55357	. 74992	. 56223	. 75655	. 57088	. 76306	. 57951	51
10	9. 73642	0. 54503	0. 74323	0. 55371	9. 75003	0. 56238	9. 75666	0. 57103	9. 76317	0. 57965	50
11	. 73653	. 54517	. 74340	. 55386	. 75014	. 56252	. 75677	. 57117	. 76328	. 57980	49
12	. 73665	. 54532	. 74351	. 55400	. 75025	. 56267	. 75688	. 57131	. 76338	. 57994	48
13	. 73676	. 54546	. 74362	. 55414	. 75036	. 56281	. 75698	. 57146	. 76349	. 58008	47
14	. 73688	. 54561	. 74374	. 55429	. 75047	. 56296	. 75709	. 57160	. 76360	. 58023	46
15	9. 73699	0. 54575	9. 74385	0.55443	9. 75059	0. 56310	9. 75720	0. 57175	9. 76371	0. 58037	45
16	. 73711	. 54590	. 74396	. 55458	. 75070	. 56324	. 75731	. 57189	. 76381	. 58051	44
17	. 73722	. 54604	. 74408	. 55472	. 75081	. 56339	. 75742	. 57203	. 76392	. 58066	43
18	. 73734	. 54619	. 74419	. 55487	. 75092	. 56353	. 75753	. 57218	. 76403	. 58080	42
19	. 73746	. 54633	. 74430	. 55501	. 75103	. 56368	. 75764	. 57232	. 76414	. 58095	41
20	9. 73757	0. 54647	9. 74442	0. 55516	9. 75114	0. 56382	9. 75775	0. 57247	9. 76424	0. 58109	40
21	. 73769	. 54662	. 74453	. 55530	. 75125	. 56397	. 75786	. 57261	. 76435	. 58123	39
22	. 73780	. 54676	. 74464	. 55545	. 75136	. 56411	. 75797	. 57275	. 76446	. 58138	38
23	. 73792	. 54691	. 74475	. 55559	. 75147	. 56425	. 75808	. 57290	. 76456	. 58152	37
24	. 73803	. 54705	. 74487	. 55573	. 75159	. 56440	. 75819	. 57304	. 76467	. 58166	36
25	9. 73815	0. 54720	9. 74498	0. 55588	9. 75170	0. 56454	9. 75830	0. 57319	9. 76478	0. 58181	35
26	. 73826	. 54734	. 74509	. 55602	. 75181	. 56469	. 75840	. 57333	. 76489	. 58195	34
27	. 73838	. 54749	. 74521	. 55617	. 75192	. 56483	. 75851	. 57347	. 76499	. 58209	33
28	. 73849	. 54763	. 74532	. 55631	. 75203	. 56497	. 75862	. 57362	. 76510	. 58224	32
29	. 73860	. 54778	. 74543	. 55646	. 75214	. 56512	. 75873	. 57376	. 76521	. 58238	31
30	9. 73872	0. 54792	9. 74554	0. 55660	9. 75225	0. 56526	9. 75884	0. 57390	9. 76531	0. 58252	30
31	. 73883	. 54807	. 74566	. 55675	. 75236	. 56541	. 75895	. 57405	. 76542	. 58267	29
32	. 73895	. 54821	. 74577	. 55689	. 75247	. 56555	. 75906	. 57419	. 76553	. 58281	28
33	. 73906	. 54836	. 74588	. 55704	. 75258	. 56570	. 75917	. 57434	. 76563	. 58295	27
34	. 73918	. 54850	. 74600	. 55718	. 75269	. 56584	. 75927	. 57448	. 76574	. 58310	26
35	9. 73929	0. 54865	9. 74611	0. 55732	9. 75280	0. 56598	9. 75938	0. 57462	9. 76585	0. 58324	25
36	. 73941	. 54879	. 74622	. 55747	. 75291	. 56613	. 75949	. 57477	. 76595	. 58338	24
37	. 73952	. 54894	. 74633	. 55761	. 75303	. 56627	. 75960	. 57491	. 76606	. 58353	23
38	. 73964	. 54908	. 74645	. 55776	. 75314	. 56642	. 75971	. 57506	. 76617	. 58367	22
39	. 73975	. 54923	. 74656	. 55790	. 75325	. 56656	. 75982	. 57520	. 76627	. 58381	21
40	9. 73987	0.54937	9. 74667	0. 55805	9. 75336	0.5667	9. 75993	0. 57534	9. 76638	0. 58396	20
41	. 73998	. 54952	. 74678	. 55819	. 75347	. 56685	. 76004	. 57549	. 76649	. 58410	19
42	. 74009	. 54966	. 74690	. 55834	. 75358	. 56699	. 76014	. 57563	. 76659	. 58424	18
43	. 74021	. 54980	. 74701	. 55848	. 75369	. 56714	. 76025	. 57577	. 76670	. 58439	17
44	. 74032	. 54995	. 74712	. 55862	. 75380	. 56728	. 76036	. 57592	. 76681	. 58453	16
45	9. 74044	0. 55009	9. 74723	0. 55877	9. 75391	0. 56743	9. 76047	0. 57606	9. 76691	0. 58467	15
46	. 74055	. 55024	. 74734	. 55891	. 75402	. 56757	. 76058	. 57621	. 76702	. 58482	14
47	. 74067	. 55038	. 74746	. 55906	. 75413	. 56771	. 76069	. 57635	. 76713	. 58496	13
48	. 74078	. 55053	. 74757	. 55920	. 75424	. 56786	. 76079	. 57649	. 76723	. 58510	12
49	. 74089	. 55067	. 74768	. 55935	. 75435	. 56800	. 76090	. 57664	. 76734	. 58525	11
50	9. 74101	0. 55082	9. 74779	0. 55949	9. 75446	0. 56815	9. 76101	0. 57678	9. 76745	0. 58539	10
51	. 74112	. 55096	. 74791	. 55964	. 75457	. 56829	. 76112	. 57692	. 76755	. 58553	9
52	. 74124	. 55111	. 74802	. 55978	. 75468	. 56843	. 76123	. 57707	. 76766	. 58568	8
53	. 74135	. 55125	. 74813	. 55992	. 75479	. 56858	. 76134	. 57721	. 76777	. 58582	7
54	. 74146	. 55140	. 74824	. 56007	. 75490	. 56872	. 76144	. 57736	. 76787	. 58596	6
55	9. 74158	0. 55154	9. 7483.5	0. 56021	9. 75501	0. 56887	9. 76155	0. 57750	9. 76798	0. 58611	5
56	. 74169	. 55169	. 74846	. 56036	. 75512	. 56901	. 76166	. 57764	. 76808	. 58625	4
57	. 74181	. 55183	. 74858	. 56050	. 75523	. 56915	. 76177	. 57779	. 76819	. 58639	3
58	. 74192	. 55197	. 74869	. 56065	. 75534	. 56930	. 76188	. 57793	. 76830	. 58654	2
59	. 74203	. 55212	. 74880	. 56079	. 75545	. 56944	. 76198	. 57807	. 76840	. 58668	1
60	9. 74215	0. 55226	9. 74891	0. 56093	9. 75556	0. 56959	9. 76209	0. 57822	9. 76851	0. 58682	0
	264°		263°		262°		261°		260°		

Haversines

′	100°		101°		102°		103°		104°		′
	Log Hav	Nat. Hav	Log Hav	Nat. Hav	Log Hav	Nat. Hav	Log Hav	Nat. Hav	Log Hav	Nat. Hav	
0	9. 76851	0. 58682	9. 77481	0. 59540	9. 78101	0. 60396	9. 78709	0. 61248	9. 79306	0. 62096	60
1	. 76861	. 58697	. 77492	. 59555	. 78111	. 60410	. 78719	. 61262	. 79316	. 62110	59
2	. 76872	. 58711	. 77502	. 59569	. 78121	. 60424	. 78729	. 61276	. 79326	. 62124	58
3	. 76883	. 58725	. 77512	. 59583	. 78131	. 60438	. 78739	. 61290	. 79336	. 62138	57
4	. 76893	. 58740	. 77523	. 59598	. 78141	. 60452	. 78749	. 61304	. 79'346	. 62153	56
5	9. 76904	0. 58754	9. 77533	0. 59612	9. 78152	0. 60467	9. 78759	0. 61318	9. 79356	0. 62167	55
6	. 76914	. 58768	. 77544	. 59626	. 78162	. 60481	. 78769	. 61333	. 79366	. 62181	54
7	. 76925	. 58783	. 77554	. 59640	. 78172	. 60495	. 78779	. 61347	. 79376	. 62195	53
8	. 76936	. 58797	. 77564	. 59655	. 78182	. 60509	. 78789	. 61361	. 79385	. 62209	52
9	. 76946	. 58811	. 77575	. 59669	78192	. 60524	. 78799	. 61375	. 79395	. 62223	51
10	9. 76957	0. 58826	9. 77585	0. 59683	9. 78203	0. 60538	9. 78809	0. 61389	9. 79405	0. 62237	50
11	. 76967	. 58840	. 77596	. 59697	. 78213	. 60552	. 78819	. 61403	.. 79415	. 62251	49
12	. 76978	. 58854	. 77606	. 59712	. 78223	. 60566	. 78829	. 61418	. 79425	. 62265	48
13	. 76988	. 58869	. 77616	. 59726	· 78233	. 60580	. 78839	. 61432	. 79434	. 62279	47
14	. 76999	. 58883	. 77627	. 59740	. 78243	. 60595	. 78849	. 61446	. 79444	. 62294	46
15	9. 77009	0. 58897	9. 77637	0. 59755	9. 78254	0. 60609	9. 78859	0. 61460	9. 79454	0. 62308	45
16	. 77020	. 5891.1	. 77647	. 59769	. 78264	. 60623	. 78869	. 61474	. 79464	. 62322	44
17	. 77031	. 58926	. 77658	. 59783	. 78274	. 60637	. 78879	. 61488	. 79474	. 62336	43
18	. 77041	. 58940	. 77668	. 59797	. 78284	. 60652	. 78889	. 61502	. 79484	. 62350	42
19	. 77052	. 58954	. 77679	. 59812	. 78294	. 60666	. 78899	. 61517	. 79493	. 62364	41
20	9. 77062	0. 58969	9. 77689	0. 59826	9. 78305	0. 60680	9. 78909	0. 61531	9. 79503	0. 62378	40
21	. 77073	. 58983	. 77699	. 59840	. 78315	. 60694	. 7.8919	. 61545	. 79513	. 62392	39
22	. 77083	. 58997	. 77710	. 59854	. 78325	. 60708	. 78929	. 61559	. 79523	. 62406	38
23	. 11094	. 59012	. 77720	. 59869	. 78335	. 60723	. 78939	. 61573	. 79533	. 62420	37
24	. 77104	. 59026	. 77730	. 59883	. 78345	. 60737	. 78949	. 61587	. 79542	. 62434	36
25	9. 77115	0. 59040	9. 77741	0. 59897	9. 78355	0. 60751	9. 78959	0. 61602	9. 79552	0. 62449	35
26	. 77125	. 59055	. 7775.1	. 59911	. 78365	. 60765	. 78969	. 61616	. 79562	. 62463	34
27	. 77136	. 59069	. 77761	. 59926	. 78376	. 60779	. 78979	. 61630	. 79572	. 62477	33
28	. 77146	. 59083	. 77772	. 59940	. 78386	. 60794	. 78989	. 61644	. 79582	. 62491	32
29	. 77157	. 59097	. 77782	. 59954	. 78396	. 60808	. 78999	. 61658	. 79591	. 62505	31
30	9. 77167	0. 59112	9. 77792	0. 59968	9. 78406	0. 60822	9. 79009	0. 61672	9. 79601	0. 62519	30
31	. 77178	. 59126	. 77803	. 59983	. 78416	. 60836	. 79019	. 61686	. 79611	. 62533	29
32	. 77188	. 59140	. 77813	. 59997	. 78426	. 60850	. 79029	. 61701	. 79621	. 62547	28
33	. 77199	. 59155	. 77823	. 60011	. 78436	. 60865	. 79039	. 61715	. 79631	. 62561	27
34	. 77209	. 59169	. 77834	. 60025	. 78447	. 60879	. 79049	. 61729	. 79640	. 62575	26
35	9. 77220	0. 59183	9. 77844	0. 60040	9. 78457	0. 60893	9. 79059	0. 61743	9. 79650	0. 62589	25
36	. 77230	. 59198	. 77854	. 60054	. 78467	. 60907	. 79069	. 61757	. 79660	. 62603	24
37	. 77241	. 59212	. 77864	. 60068	. 78477	. 60921	. 79079	. 61771	. 79670	. 62618	23
38	. 77251	. 59226	. 77875	. 60082	. 78487	. 60936	. 79089	. 61785	. 79679	. 62632	22
39	. 77262	. 59240	. 77885	. 60097	. 78497	. 60950	. 79099	. 61800	. 79689	. 62646	21
40	9. 77272	0. 59255	9. 77895'	0. 60111	9. 78507	0. 60964	9. 79108	0. 61814	9. 79699	0. 62660	20
41	. 77283	. 59269	. 77906	. 60125	. 78517	. 60978	. 79118	. 61828	. 79709	. 62674	19
42	. 77293	. 59283	. 77916	. 60139	. 78528	. 60992	. 79128	. 61842	. 79718	. 62688	18
43	. 77304	. 59298	. 77926	. 60154	. 78538	. 61006	. 79138	. 61856	. 79728	. 62702	17
44	. 77314	. 59312	. 77936	. 60168	. 78548	. 61021	. 79148	. 61870	. 79738	. 62716	16
45	9. 77325	0. 59326	9. 77947	0. 60182	9. 78558	0. 61035	9. 79158	0. 61884	9. 79748	0. 62730	15
46	. 77335	. 59340	. 77957	. 60196	. 78568	. 61049	. 79168	. 61898	. 79757	. 62744	14
47	. 77346	. 59355	. 77967	. 60211	. 78578	. 61063	. 79178	. 61913	. 79767	. 62758	13
48	. 77356	. 59369	.'77978	. 60225	. 78588	. 61077	. 79188	. 61927	. 79777	. 62772	12
49	. 77366	. 59383	. 77988	. 60239	. 78598	. 61092	. 79198	. 61941	. 79787	. 62786	11
50	9. 77377	0. 59398	9. 77998	0. 60253	9. 78608	0. 61106	9. 79208	0. 61955	9. 79796	0. 62800	10
51	. 77387	. 59412	. 78008	. 60268	. 78618	. 61120	. 79217	. 61969	. 79806	. 62814	9
52	. 77398	. 59426	. 78019	. 60282	. 78628	. 61134	. 79227	. 61983	. 79816	. 62829	8
53	. 77408	. 59440	. 78029	. 60296	. 78638	. 61148	. 79237	. 61997	. 79825	. 62843	7
54	. 77419	. 59455	. 78039	. 603io	. 78649	. 61163	. 79247	. 62011	. 79835	. 62857	6
55	9. 77429	0. 59469	9. 78049	0. 60324	9. 78659	0. 61177	9. 79257	0. 62026	9. 79845	0. 62871	5
56	. 77440	. 59483	. 78060	. 60339	. 78669	. 61191	. 79267	. 62040	. 79855	. 62885	4
57	. 77450	. 59498	. 78070	. 60353	. 78679	. 61205	. 79277	. 62054	. 79864	. 62899	3
58	. 77460	. 59512	. 78080	. 60367	. 78689	. 61219	. 79287	. 62068	. 79874	. 62913	2
59	. 77471	. 59526	. 78090	. 60381	. 78699	. 61233	. 79297	. 62082	. 79884	. 62927	1
60	9. 77481	0. 59540	9. 78101	0. 60396	9. 78709	0. 61248	9. 79306	0. 62096	9. 79893	0. 62941	0
	259°		258°		257°		256°		255°		

Haversines

′	105°		106°		107°		108°		109°		′
	Log Hav	Nat. Hav	Log Hav	Nat. Hav	Log Hav	Nat. Hav	Log Hav	Nat. Hav	Log Hav	Nat. Hav	
0	9. 79893	0. 62941	9. 80470	0. 63782	9. 81036	0. 64619	9. 81592	0. 65451	9. 82137	0. 66278	60
1	. 79903	. 62955	. 80479	. 63796	. 81045	. 64632	. 81601	. 65465	. 82146	. 66292	59
2	. 79913	. 62969	. 80489	. 63810	. 81054	. 64646	. 81610	. 65479	. 82155	. 66306	58
3	. 79922	. 62983	. 80498	. 63824	. 81064	. 64660	. 81619	. 65492	. 82164	. 66320	57
4	. 79932	. 62997	. 80508	. 63838	. 81073	. 64674	. 81628	. 65506	. 82173	. 66333	56
5	9. 79942	0. 63011	9. 80517	0. 63852	9. 81082	0. 64688	9. 81637	0. 65520	9. 82182	0. 66347	55
6	. 79951	. 63025	. 80527	. 63866	. 81092	. 64702	. 81647	. 65534	. 82191	. 66361	54
7	. 79961	. 63039	. 80536	. 63880	. 81101	. 64716	. 81656	. 65548	. 82200	. 66375	53
8	. 79971	. 63053	. 80546	. 63894	. 81110	. 64730	. 81665	. 65561	. 82209	. 66388	52
9	. 79980	. 63067	. 80555	. 63908	. 81120	. 64744	. 81674	. 65575	. 82218	. 66402	51
10	9. 79990	0. 63081	9. 80565	0. 63922	9. 81129	0. 64758	9. 81683	0. 65589	9. 82227	0. 66416	50
11	. 80000	. 63095	. 80574	. 63936	. 81138	. 64772	. 81692	. 65603	. 82236	. 66430	49
12	. 80009	. 63109	. 80584	. 63950	. 81148	. 64785	. 81701	. 65617	. 82245	. 66443	48
13	. 80019	. 63123	. 80593	. 63964	. 81157	. 64799	. 81711	. 65631	. 82254	. 66457	47
14	. 80029	. 63138	. 80603	. 63977	. 81166	. 64318	. 81720	. 65644	. 82263	. 66471	46
15	9. 80038	0. 63152	9. 80612	0. 63991	9. 81176	0. 64827	9. 81729	0. 65658	9. 82272	0. 66485	45
16	. 80048	. 63166	. 80622	. 64005	. 81185	. 64841	. 81738	. 65672	. 82281	. 66498	44
17	. 80058	. 63180	. 80631	. 64019	. 81194	. 64855	. 81747	. 65686	. 82290	. 66512	43
18	. 80067	. 63194	. 80641	. 64033	. 81204	. 64869	. 81756	. 65700	. 82299	. 66526	42
19	. 80077	. 63208	. 80650	. 64047	. 81213	. 64883	. 81765	. 65713	. 82308	. 66539	41
20	9. 80087	0. 63222	9. 80660	0. 64061	9. 81222	0. 64897	9. 81775	0. 65727	9. 82317	0. 66553	40
21	. 80096	. 63236	. 80669	. 64075	. 81231	. 64910	. 81784	. 65741	. 82326	. 66567	39
22	. 80106	. 63250	. 80678	. 64089	. 81241	. 64924	. 81793	. 65755	. 82335	. 66581	38
23	. 80116	. 63264	. 80688	. 64103	. 81250	. 64938	. 81802	. 65769	. 82344	. 66594	37
24	. 80125	. 63278	. 80697	. 64117	. 81259	. 64952	. 81811	. 65782	. 82353	. 66608	36
25	9. 80135	0. 63292	9. 80707	0. 64131	9. 81269	0. 64966	9. 81820	0. 65796	9. 82362	0. 66622	35
26	. 80144	. 63306	. 80716	. 64145	. 81278	. 64980	. 81829	. 65810	. 82371	. 66635	34
27	. 80154	. 63320	. 80726	. 64159	. 81287	. 64994	. 81838	. 65824	. 82380	. 66649	33
28	. 80164	. 63334	. 80735	. 64173	. 81296	. 65008	. 81847	. 65838	. 82388	. 66663	32
29	. 80173	. 63348	. 80745	. 64187	. 81306	. 65021	. 81857	. 65851	. 82397	. 66677	31
30	9. 80183	0. 63362	9. 80754	0. 64201	9. 81315	0. 65035	9. 81866	0. 65865	9. 82406	0. 66690	30
31	. 80192	. 63376	. 80763	. 64215	. 81324	. 65049	. 81875	. 65879	. 82415	. 66704	29
32	. 80202	. 63390	. 80773	. 64229	. 81333	. 65063	. 81884	. 65893	. 82424	. 66718	28
33	. 80212	. 63404	. 80782	. 64243	. 81343	. 65077	. 81893	. 65907	. 82433	. 66731	27
34	. 80221	. 63418	. 80792	. 64257	. 81352	. 65091	. 81902	. 65920	. 82442	. 66745	26
35	9. 80231	0. 63432	9. 80801	0. 64270	9. 81361	0. 65105	9. 81911	0. 65934	9. 82451	0. 66759	25
36	. 80240	. 63446	. 80811	. 64284	. 81370	. 65118	. 81920	. 65948	. 82460	. 66773	24
37	. 80250	. 63460	. 80820	. 64298	. 81380	. 65132	. 81929	. 65962	. 82469	. 66786	23
38	. 80260	. 63474	. 80829	. 64312	. 81389	. 65146	. 81938	. 65976	. 82478	. 66800	22
39	. 80269	. 63488	. 80839	. 64326	. 81398	. 65160	. 81947	. 65989	. 82487	. 66814	21
40	9. 80279	0. 63502	9. 80848	0. 64340	9. 81407	0. 65174	9. 81956	0. 66003	9. 82495	0. 66827	20
41	. 80288	. 63516	. 80858	. 64354	. 81417	. 65188	. 81965	. 66017	. 82504	. 66841	19
42	. 80298	. 63530	. 80867	. 64368	. 81426	. 65202	. 81975	. 66031	. 82513	. 66855	18
43	. 80307	. 63544	. 80876	. 64382	. 81435	. 65216	. 81984	. 66044	. 82522	. 66868	17
44	. 80317	. 63558	. 80886	. 64396	. 81444	. 65229	. 81993	. 66058	. 82531	. 66882	16
45	9. 80327	0. 63572	9. 80895	0. 64410	9. 81454	0. 65243	9. 82002	0. 66072	9. 82540	0. 66896	15
46	. 80336	. 63586	. 80905	. 64424	. 81463	. 65257	. 82011	. 66086	. 82549	. 66910	14
47	. 80346	. 63600	. 80914	. 64438	. 81472	. 65271	. 82020	. 66100	. 82558	. 66923	13
48	. 80355	. 63614	. 80923	. 64452	. 81481	. 65285	. 82029	. 66113	. 82567	. 66937	12
49	. 80365	. 63628	. 80933	. 64466	. 81490	. 65299	. 82038	. 66127	. 82575	. 66951	11
50	9. 80374	0. 63642	9. 80942	0. 64479	9. 81500	0. 65312	9. 82047	0. 66141	9. 82584	0.66964	10
51	. 80384	. 63656	. 80952	. 64493	. 81509	. 65326	. 82056	. 66155	. 82593	. 66978	9
52	. 80393	. 63670	. 80961	. 64507	. 81518	. 65340	. 82065	. 66168	. 82602	. 66992	8
53	. 80403	. 63684	. 80970	. 64521	. 81527	. 65354	. 82074	. 66182	. 82611	. 67005	7
54	. 80413	. 63698	. 80980	. 64535	. 81536	. 65368	. 82083	. 66196	. 82620	. 67019	6
55	9. 80422	0. 63712	9. 80989	0. 64549	9. 81546	0. 65382	9. 82092	0. 66210	9. 82629	0. 67033	5
56	. 80432	. 63726	. 80998	. 64563	. 81555	. 65396	. 82101	. 66223	. 82638	. 67046	4
57	. 80441	. 63740	. 81008	. 64577	. 81564	. 65409	. 82110	. 66237	. 82646	. 67060	3
58	. 80451	. 63754	. 81017	. 64591	. 81573	. 65423	. 82119	. 66251	. 82655	. 67074	2
59	. 80460	. 63768	. 81026	. 64605	. 81582	. 65437	. 82128	. 66265	. 82664	. 67087	1
60	9. 80470	0. 63782	9. 81036	0. 64619	9. 81592	0. 65451	9. 82137	0. 66278	9. 82673	0. 67101	0
	254°		253°		252°		251°		250°		

Haversines

′	110°		111°		112°		113°		114°		′
	Log Hav	Nat. Hav	Log Hav	Nat. Hav	Log Hav	Nat. Hav	Log Hav	Nat. Hav	Log Hav	Nat. Hav	
0	9. 82673	0. 67101	9. 83199	0. 67918	9. 83715	0. 68730	9. 84221	0. 69537	9. 84718	0. 70337	60
1	. 82682	. 67115	. 83207	. 67932	. 83723	. 68744	. 84230	. 69550	. 84726	. 70350	59
2	. 82691	. 67128	. 83216	. 67946	. 83732	. 68757	. 84238	. 69563	. 84735	. 70363	58
3	. 82699	. 67142	. 83225	. 67959	. 83740	. 68771	. 84246	. 69577	. 84743	. 70377	57
4	. 82708	. 67156	. 83233	. 67973	. 83749	. 68784	. 84255	. 69590	. 84751	. 70390	56
5	9. 82717	0. 67169	9. 83242	0. 67986	9. 83757	0. 68798	9. 84263	0. 69603	9. 84759	0. 70403	55
6	. 82726	. 67183	. 83251	. 68000	. 83766	. 68811	. 84271	. 69617	. 84767	. 70417	54
7	. 82735	. 67197	. 83259	. 68013	. 83774	. 68825	. 84280	. 69630	. 84776	. 70430	53
8	. 82744	. 67210	. 83268	. 68027	. 83783	. 68838	. 84288	. 69644	. 84784	. 70443	52
9	. 82752	. 67224	. 83277	. 68041	. 83791	. 68852	. 84296	. 69657	. 84792	. 70456	51
10	9. 82761	0. 67238	9. 83285	0. 68054	9. 83800	0. 68865	9. 84305	0. 69670	9. 84800	0. 70470	50
11	. 82770	. 67251	. 83294	. 68068	. 83808	. 68879	. 84313	. 69684	. 84808	. 70483	49
12	. 82779	. 67265	. 83303	. 68081	. 83817	. 68892	. 84321	. 69697	. 84817	. 70496	48
13	. 82788	. 67279	. 83311	. 68095	. 83825	. 68906	. 84330	. 69710	. 84825	. 70509	47
14	. 82796	. 67292	. 83320	. 68108	. 83834	. 68919	. 84338	. 69724	. 84833	. 70523	46
15	9. 82805	0. 67306	9. 83329	0. 68122	9. 83842	0. 68932	9. 84346	0. 69737	9. 84841	0. 70536	45
16	. 82814	. 67319	. 83337	. 68135	. 83851	. 68946	. 84355	. 69751	. 84849	. 70549	44
17	. 82823	. 67333	. 83346	. 68149	. 83859	. 68959	. 84363	. 69764	. 84857	. 70562	43
18	. 82832	. 67347	. 83355	. 68163	. 83868	. 68973	. 84371	. 69777	. 84866	. 70576	42
19	. 82840	. 67360	. 83363	. 68176	. 83876	. 68986	. 84380	. 69791	. 84874	. 70589	41
20	9. 82849	0. 67374	9. 83372	0. 68190	9. 83885	0. 69000	9. 84388	0. 69804	9. 84882	0. 70602	40
21	. 82858	. 67388	. 83380	. 68203	. 83893	. 69013	. 84396	. 69817	. 84890	. 70615	39
22	. 82867	. 67401	. 83389	. 68217	. 83902	. 69027	. 84405	. 69831	. 84898	. 70629	38
23	. 82876	. 67415	. 83398	. 68230	. &3910	. 69040	. 84413	. 69844	. 84906	. 70642	37
24	i 82884	. 67429	. 83406	. 68244	. 83919	. 69054	. 84421	. 69857	. 84914	. 70655	36
25	9. 82893	0. 67442	9. 83415	0. 68257	9. 83927	o.69067	9. 84430	0. 69871	9. 84923	0. 70668	35
26	. 82902	. 67456	. 83424	. 68271	. 83935	. 69080	. 84438	. 69884	. 84931	. 70682	34
27	; 82911	. 67469	. 83432	. 68284	. 83944	. 69094	. 84446	. 69897	. 84939	. 70695	33
28	. 82920	. 67483	. 83441	. 68298	. 83952	. 69107	. 84454	. 69911	. 84947	. 70708	32
29	. 82928	. 6749·7	. 83449	. 68312	. 83961	. '69121	. 84463	. 69924	. 84955	. 70721	31
30	9. 82937	0. 67510	9. 83458	0. 68325	9. 83969	0. 69134	9. 84471	0. 69937	9. 84963	0. 70735	30
31	. 82946	. 67524	. 83467	. 68339	. 83978	. 69148	. 84479	. 69951	. 84971	. 70748	29
32	. 82955	. 67538	. 83475	. 68352	. 83986	. 69161	. 84488	. 69964	. 84979	. 70761	28
33	. 82963	. 67551	. 83484	. 68366	. 83995	. 69174	. 84496	. 69977	. 84988	. 70774	27
34	. 82972	. 67565	. 83492	. 683.79	. 84003	. 69188	. 84504	. 69991	. 84996	. 70788	26
35	9. 82981	0. 67578	9. 83501	0. 68393	9. 84011	0. 69201	9. 84512	0. 70004	9. '85004	0. 70801	25
36	. 82990	. 67592	. 83510	. 68406	. 84020	. 69215	. 84521	. 70017	. 85012	. 70814	24
37	. 82998	. 67606	. 83518	. 68420	. 84028	. 69228	. 84529	. 70031	. 85020	. 70827	23
38	. 83007	. 67619	. 83527	. 68433	. 84037	. 69242	. 84537	. 70044	. 85028	. 70840	22
39	. 83016	. 67633	. 83535	. 68447	. 84045	. 69255	. 84545	. 70057	. 85036	. 70854	21
40	9. 83025	0. 67647	9. 83544	0. 68460	9. 84054	0. 69268	9. 84554	0. 70071	9. 85044	0. 70867	20
41	. 83033	. 67660	. 83552	. 68474	. 84062	. 69282	. 84562	. 70084	. 85052	. 70880	19
42	. 83042	. 67674	. 83561	. 68487	. 84070	. 69295	. 84570	. 70097	. 85061	. 70893	18
43	. 83051	. 67687	. 83570	. 68501	. 84079	. 69309	. 84578	. 70111	. 85069	. 70907	17
44	. 83059	. 67701	. 83578	. 68514	. 84087	. 69322	. 84587	. 70124	. 85077	.·70920	16
45	9. 83068	0. 67715	9. 83q87	0. 68528	9. 84096	0. 69336	9. 84595	0. 70137	9. 85085	0. 70933	15
46	. 83077	. 67728	. 83595	. 68541	. 84104	. 69349	. 84603	. 70151	. 85093	. 70946	14
47	. 83086	. 67742	. 83604	. 68555	. 84112	. 69362	. 84611	. 70164	. 85101	. 70959	13
48	. 83094	. 67755	. 83612	. 68568	. 84121	. 69376	. 84620	. 70177	. 85109	. 70973	12
49	. 83103	. 67769	. 83621	. 68582	. 84129	. 69389	. 84628	. 70191	. 85117	. 70986	11
50	9. 83112	0. 67783	9. 83630	0. 68595	9. 84138	0. 69403	9. 84636	0. 70204	9. 85125	0. 70999	10
51	. 83120	. 67796	. 83638	. 68609	. 84146	. 69416	. 84644	. 70217	. 85133	. 71012	9
52	. 83129	. 67810	. 83647	. 68622	. 84154	. 69429	. 84653	. 70230	. 85141	. 71025	8
53	. 83138	. 67823	. 83655	. 68636	. 84163	. 69443	. 84661	. 70244	. 85149	. 71039	7
54	. 83147	. 6783.7	. 83664	. 6864.9	. 84171	. 69456	. 84669	. 70257	. 85158	. 71052	6
55	9. 83155	0. 67850	9. 83672	0. 68663	9. 84179	0. 69470	9. 84677	0. 70270	9. 85166	0. 71065	5
56	. 83164	. 67864	. 83681	. 68676	. 84188	. 69483	. 84685	. 70284	. 85174	. 71078	4
57	. 83173	. 67878	. 83689	. 68690	. 84196	. 69496	. 84694	. 70297	. 85182	. 71091	3
58	. 83181	. 67891	. 83698	. 68703	. 84205	. 69510	. 84702	. 70310	. 85190	. 71105	2
59	. 83190	. 67905	. 83706	. 68717	. 84213	. 69523	. 84710	. 70324	. 85198	. 71118	1
60	9. 83199	0. 67918	9. 83715	0. 68730	9. 84221	0. 69537	9. 84718	0. 70337	9. 85206	0. 71131	0
	249°		248°		247°		246°		245°		

Haversines

′	115°		116°		117°		118°		119°		′
	Log Hav	Nat. Hav	Log Hav	Nat. Hav	Log Hav	Nat. Hav	Log Hav	Nat. Hav	Log Hav	Nat. Hav	
0	9. 85206	0. 71131	9. 85684	0. 71919	9. 86153	0. 72700	9. 86613	0. 73474	9. 87064	0. 74240	60
1	. 85214	. 71144	. 85692	. 71932	. 86161	. 72712	. 86621	. 73486	. 87072	. 74253	59
2	. 85222	. 71157	. 85700	. 71945	. 86169	. 72725	. 86628	. 73499	. 87079	. 74266	58
3	. 85230	. 71170	. 85708	. 71958	. 86176	. 72738	. 86636	. 73512	. 87086	. 74279	57
4	. 85238	. 71184	. 85716	. 71971	. 86184	. 72751	. 86643	. 73525	. 87094	. 74291	56
5	9. 85246	0. 71197	9. 85724	0. 71984	9. 86192	0. 72764	9. 86651	0. 73538	9. 87101	0. 74304	55
6	. 85254	. 71210	. 85731	. 71997	. 86200	. 72777	. 86659	. 73551	. 87109	. 74317	54
7	. 85262	. 71223	. 85739	. 72010	. 86207	. 72790	. 86666	. 73563	. 87116	. 74329	53
8	. 85270	. 71236	. 85747	. 72023	. 86215	. 72803	. 86674	. 73576	. 87124	. 74342	52
9	. 85278	. 71249	. 85755	. 72036	. 86223	. 72816	. 86681	. 73589	. 87131	. 74355	51
10	9. 85286	0. 71263	9. 85763	0. 72049	9. 86230	0. 72829	9. 86689	0. 73602	9. 87138	0. 74368	50
11	. 85294	. 71276	. 85771	. 72062	. 86238	. 72842	. 86696	. 73615	. 87146	. 74380	49
12	. 85302	. 71289	. 85779	. 72075	. 86246	. 72855	. 86704	. 73628	. 87153	. 74393	48
13	. 85310	. 71302	. 85787	. 72088	. 86254	. 72868	. 86712	. 73640	. 87161	. 74406	47
14	. 85318	. 71315	. 85794	. 72101	. 86261	. 72881	. 86719	. 73653	. 87168	. 74418	46
15	9. 85326	0. 71328	9. 85802	0. 72114	9. 86269	0. 72894	9. 86727	0. 73666	9. 87175	0. 74431	45
16	. 85334	. 71342	. 85810	. 72127	. 86277	. 72907	. 86734	. 73679	. 87183	. 74444	44
17	. 85342	71355	. 85818	. 72141	. 86284	. 72920	. 86742	. 73692	. 87190	. 74456	43
18	. 85350	. 71368	. 85826	. 72154	. 86292	. 72932	. 86749	. 73704	. 87198	. 74469	42
19	. 85358	. 71381	. 85834	. 72167	. 86300	. 72945	. 86757	. 73717	. 87205	. 74482	41
20	9. 85366	0. 71394	9. 85841	0. 72180	9. 86307	0. 72958	9. 86764	0. 73730	9. 87212	0. 74494	40
21	. 85374	. 71407	. 85849	. 72193	. 86315	. 72971	. 86772	. 73743	. 87220	. 74507	39
22	. 85382	. 71420	. 85857	. 72206	. 86323	. 72984	. 86780	. 73756	. 87227	. 74520	38
23	. 85390	. 71434	. 85865	. 72219	. 86331	. 72997	. 86787	. 73768	. 87235	. 74533	37
24	. 85398	. 71447	. 85873	. 72232	. 86338	. 73010	. 86795	. 73781	. 87242	. 74545	36
25	9. 85406	0. 71460	9. 85881	0. 72245	9. 86346	0. 73023	9.86802	0. 73794	9. 87249	0. 74558	35
26	. 85414	. 71473	. 85888	. 72258	. 86354	. 73036	. 86810	. 73807	. 87257	. 74571	34
27	. 85422	. 71486	. 85896	. 72271	. 86361	. 73049	. 86817	. 73820	. 87264	. 74583	33
28	. 85430	. 71499	. 85904	. 72284	. 86369	. 73062	. 86825	. 73832	. 87271	. 74596	32
29	. 85438	. 71512	. 85912	. 72297	. 86377	. 73075	. 86832	. 73845	. 87279	. 74609	31
30	9, 85446	0. 71526	9. 85920	0. 72310	9. 86384	0. 73087	9. 86840	0. 73858	9. 87286	0. 74621	30
31	. 85454	. 71539	. 85928	. 72323	. 86392	. 73100	. 86847	. 73871	. 87294	. 74634	29
32	. 85462	. 71552	. 85935	. 72336	. 86400	. 73113	. 86855	. 73883	. 87301	. 74646	28
33	. 85470	. 71565	. 85943	. 72349	. 86407	. 73126	. 86862	. 73896	. 87308	. 74659	27
34	. 85478	. 71578	. 85951	. 72362	. 86415	. 73139	. 86870	. 73909	. 87316	. 74672	26
35	9. 85486	0. 71591	9. 85959	0. 72375	9. 86423	0. 73152	9. 86877	0. 73922	9. 87323	0. 74684	25
36	. 85494	. . 71604	. 85967	. 72388	. 86430	. 73165	. 86885	. 73935	. 87330	. 74697	24
37	. 85502	. 71617	. 85974	. 72401	. 86438	. 73178	. 86892	. 73947	. 87338	. 74710	23
38	. 85510	. 71631	. 85982	. 72414	. 86446	. 73191	. 86900	. 73960	. 87345	. 74722	22
39	. 85518	. 71644	. 85990	. 72427	. 86453	. 73203	. 86907	. 73973	. 87352	. 74735	21
40	9. 85526	0. 71657	9. 85998	0. 72440	9. 86461	0. 73216	9. 86915	0. 73986	9. 87360	0. 74748	20
41	. 85534	. 71670	. 86006	. 72453	. 86468	. 73229	. 86922	. 73998	. 87367	. 74760	19
42	. 85542	. 71683	. 86013	. 72466	. 86476	. 73242	. 86930	. 74011	. 87374	. 74773	18
43	. 85550	. 71696	. 86021	. 72479	. 86484	. 73255	. 86937	. 74024	. 87382	. 74786	17
44	. 85557	. 71709	. 86029	. 72492	. 86491	. 73268	. 86945	. 74037	. 87389	. 74798	16
45	9. 85565	0. 71722	9. 86037	0. 72505	9. 86499	0. 73281	9. 86952	0. 74049	9. 87396	0. 74811	15
46	. 85573	. 71735	. 86045	. 72518	. 86507	. 73294	. 86960	. 74062	. 87404	. 74823	14
47	. 85581	. 71748	. 86052	. 72531	. 86514	. 73306	. 86967	. 74075	. 87411	. 74836	13
48	. 85589	. 71762	. 86060	. 72544	. 86522	. 73319	. 86975	. 74088	. 87418	. 74849	12
49	. 85597	. 71775	. 86068	. 72557	. 86529	. 73332	. 86982	. 74100	. 87426	. 74861	11
50	9. 85605	0. 71788	9. 86076	0. 72570	9. 86537	0. 73345	9. 86990	0. 74113	9. 87433	0. 74874	10
51	. 85613	. 71801	. 86083	. 72583	. 86545	. 73358	. 86997	. 74126	. 87440	. 74887	9
52	. 85621	. 71814	. 86091	. 72596	. 86552	. 73371	. 87004	. 74139	. 87448	. 74899	8
53	. 85629	. 71827	. 86099	. 72609	. 86560	. 73384	. 87012	. 74151	. 87455	. 74912	7
54	. 85637	. 71840	. 86107	. 72622	. 86568	. 73396	. 87019	. 74164	. 87462	. 74924	6
55	9. 85645	0. 71853	9. 86114	0. 72635	9. 86575	0. 73409	9. 87027	0. 74177	9. 87470	0. 74937	5
56	. 85653	. 71866	. 86122	. 72648	. 86583	. 73422	. 87034	. 74190	. 87477	. 74950	4
57	. 85660	. 71879	. 86130	. 72661	. 86590	. 73435	. 87042	. 74202	. 87484	. 74962	3
58	. 85668	. 71892	. 86138	. 72674	. 86598	. 73448	. 87049	. 74215	. 87492	. 74975	2
59	. 85676	. 71905	. 86145	. 72687	. 86606	. 73461	. 87057	. 74228	. 87499	. 74987	1
60	9. 85684	0. 71919	9. 86153	0. 72700	9. 86613	0. 73474	9. 87064	0. 74240	9. 87506	0. 75000	0
	244°		243°		242°		241°		240°		

Haversines

′	120°		121°		122°		123°		124°		′
	Log Hav	Nat. Hav	Log Hav	Nat. Hav	Log Hav	Nat. Hav	Log Hav	Nat. Hav	Log Hav	Nat. Hav	
0	9. 87506	0. 75000	9. 87939	0. 75752	9. 88364	0. 76496	9. 88780	0. 77232	9. 89187	0. 77960	60
1	. 87513	. 75013	. 87947	. 75764	. 88371	. 76508	. 88787	. 77244	. 89194	. 77972	59
2	. 87521	. 75025	. 87954	. 75777	. 88378	. 76521	. 88793	. 77256	. 89200	. 77984	58
3	. $7528	. 75038	. 87961	. 75789	. 88385	. 76533	. 88800	. 77269	. 89207	. 77996	57
4	. 87535	. 75050	. 87968	. 75802	. 88392	. 76545	. 88807	. 77281	. 89214	. 78008	56
5	9. 87543	0. 75063	9. 87975	0. 75814	9. 88399	0. 76558	9. 88814	0. 77293	9. 89221	0. 78020	55
6	. 87550	. 75076	. 87982	. 75827	. 88406	. 76570	. 88821	. 77305	. 89227	. 78032	54
7	. 87557	. 75088	. 87989	. 75839	. 88413	. 76582	. 88828	. 77317	. 89234	. 78044	53
8	. 87564	. 75101	. 87996	. 75852	. 88420	. 76595	. 88835	. 77329	. 89241	. 78056	52
9	. 87572	. 75113	. 88004	. 75864	. 88427	. 76607	. 88841	. 77342	. 89247	. 78068	51
10	9. 87579	0. 75126	9. 88011	0. 75876	9. 88434	0. 76619	9. 88848	0. 77354	9. 89254	0. 78080	50
11	. 87586	. 75138	. 88018	. 75889	. 88441	. 76632	. 88855	. 77366	. 89261	. 78092	49
12	. 87593	. 75151	. 88025	. 75901	. 88448	. 76644	. 88862	. 77378	. 89267	. 78104	48
13	. 87601	. 75164	. 88032	. 75914	. 88455	. 76656	. 88869	. 77390	. 89274	. 78116	47
14	. 87608	. 75176	. 88039	. 75926	. 88462	. 76668	. 88876	. 77402	. 89281	. 78128	46
15	9. 87615	0. 75189	9. 88046	0. 75939	9..88469	0. 76681	9. 88882	0. 77415	9. 89287	0. 78140	45
16	. 87623	. 75201	. 88053	. 75951	. 88476	. 76693	. 88889	. 77427	. 89294	. 78152	44
17	. 87630	. 75214	. 88061	. 75964	. 88483	. 76705	. 88896	. 77439	. 89301	. 78164	43
18	. 87637	. 75226	. 88068	. 75976	. 88490	. 76718	. 88903	. 77451	. 89308	. 78176	42
19	. 87644	. 75239	. 88075	. 75988	.. 88496	. 76730	. 88910	. 77463	. 89314	. 78188	41
20	9. 87652	0. 75251	9. 88082	0. 76001	9. 88503	0. 76742	9. 88916	0. 77475	9. 89321	0. 78200	40
21	. 87659	. 75264	. 88089	. 76013	. 88510	. 76754	. 88923	. 77488	. 89328	. 78212	39
22	. 87666	. 75277	. 88096	. 76026	. 88517	. 76767	. 88930	. 77500	. 89334	. 78224	38
23	. 87673	. 75289	. 88103	. 76038	. 88524	. 76779	. 88937	. 77512	. 89341	. 78236	37
24	. 87680	. 75302	. 88110	. 76050	. 88531	. 76791	. 88944	. 77524	. 89348	. 78248	36
25	9. 87688	0. 75314	9. 88117	0. 76063	9. 88538	0. 7680{	9. 88950	0. 77536	9. 89354	0. 78260	35
26	. 87695	. 75327	. 88124	. 76075	. 88545	. 76816	. 88957	. 77548	. 89361	. 78272	34
27	. 87702	. 75339	. 88131	. 76088	. 88552	. 76828	. 88964	. 77560	. 89368	. 78284	33
28	. 87709	. 75352	. 88139	. 76100	. 88559	. 76840	. 88971	. 77573	. 89374	. 78296	32
29	. 87717	. 75364	. 88146	. 76113	. 88566	. 76853	. 88978	. 77585	. 89381	. 78308	31
30	9. 87724	0. 75377	9. 88153	0. 76125	9. 88573	0. 76865	9. 88984	0. 77597	9. 89387	0. 78320	30
31	. 87731	. 75389	. 88160	. 76137	. 88580	. 76877	. 88991	. 77609	. 89394	. 78332	29
32	. 87738	. 75402	. 88167	. 76150	. 88587	. 76890	. 88998	. 77621	. 89400	. 78344	28
33	. 87745	. 75415	. 88174	. 76162	. 88594	. 76902	. 89005	. 77633	. 89407	. 78356	27
34	. 87753	. 75427	. 88181	. 76175	. 88600	. 76914	. 89012	. 77645	. 89414	. 78368	26
35	9. 87760	0. 75440	9. 88188	0. 76187	9. 88607	0. 76926	9. 89018	0. 77657	9. 89421	0. 78380	25
36	. 87767	. 75452	. 88195	. 76199	. 88614	. 76939	. 89025	. 77670	. 89427	. 78392	24
37	. 87774	. 75465	. 88202	. 76212	. 88621	. 76951	. 89032	. 77682	. 89434	. 78404	23
38	. 87782	. 75477	. 88209	. 76224	. 88628	. 76963	. 89039	. 77694	. 89441	. 78416	22
39	. 87789	. 75490	. 88216	. 76236	. 88635	. 76975	. 89045	. 77706	. 89447	. 78428	21
40	9. 87796	0. 75502	9. 88223	0. 76249	9. 88642	0. 76988	9..89052	0. 77718	9. 89454	0. 78440	20
41	. 87803	. 75515	. 88230	. 76261	. 88649	. 77000	. 89059	. 77730	. 89460	. 78452	19
42	. 87810	. 75527	. 88237	. 76274	. 88656	. 77012	. 89066	. 77742	. 89467	. 78464	18
43	. 87818	. 75540	. 88244	. 76286	. 88663	. 77024	. 89072	. 77754	. 89474	. 78476	17
44	. 87825	. 75552	. 88252	. 76298	. 88670	. 77036	. 89079	. 77766	. 89480	. 78488	16
45	9. 87832	0. 75565	9. 88259	0. 76311	9. 88677	0. 77049	9. 89086	0. 77779	9. 89487	0. 78500	15
46	. 87839	. 75577	. 88266	. 76323	. 88683	. 77061	. 89093	. 77791	. 89493	. 78512	14
47	. 87846	. 75590	..88273	. 76335	. 88690	. 77073	. 89099	. 77803	. 89500	. 78524	13
48	. 87853	. 75602	. 88280	. 76348	. 88697	. 77085	. 89106	. 77815	. 89507	. 78536	12
49	..87861	. 75615	. 88287	. 76360	. 88704	. 77098	. 89113	. 77827	. 89513	. 78548	11
50	9. 87868	0. 75627	9. 88294	0. 76373	9. 88711	0. 77110	9 89120	0. 77839	9. 89520	0. 78560	10
51	. 87875	. 75640	. 88301	. 76385	. 88718	. 77122	. 89126	. 77851	. 89527	78571	9
52	. 87882	. 75652	. 88308	. 76397	. 88725	. 77134	. 89133	. 77863	. 89533	. 78583	8
53	. 87889	. 75665	. 88315	. 76410	. 88732	. 77147	. 89140	. 77875	. 89540	. 78595	7
54	. 87896	. 75677	. 88322	. 76422	. 88739	. 77159	. 89147	. 77887	. 89546	. 78607	6
55	9. 87904	0. 75690	9. 88329	0. 76434	9. 88745	0. 77171	9. 89153	0. 77899	9. 89553	0. 78619	5
56	. 87911	. 75702	. 88336	. 76447	. 88752	. 77183	. 89160	. 77911	. 89559	. 78631	4
57	. 87918	. 75714	. 88343	. 76459	. 88759	. 77195	. 89167	. 77923	. 89566	. 78643	3
58	. 87925	. 75727	. 88350	. 76471	. 88766	. 77208	. 89174	. 77936	. 89573	. 78655	2
59	. 87932	. 75739	. 88357	. 76484	. 88773	. 77220	. 89180	. 77948	. 89579	. 78667	1
60	9. 87939	0. 75752	9. 88364	0. 76496	9. 88780	0. 77232	9. 89187	0. 77960	9. 89586	0. 78679	0
	239°		238°		237°		236°		235°		

Haversines

′	125°		126°		127°		128°		129°		′
	Log Hav	Nat. Hav	Log Hav	Nat. Hav	Log Hav	Nat. Hav	Log Hav	Nat. Hav	Log Hav	Nat. Hav	
0	9. 89586	0. 78679	9. 89976	0. 79389	9. 90358	0. 80091	9. 90732	0. 80783	9. 91098	0. 81466	60
1	. 89592	. 78691	. 89983	. 79401	. 90365	. 80102	. 90738	. 80795	. 91104	. 81477	59
2	. 89599	. 78703	. 89989	. 79413	. 90371	. 80114	. 90744	. 80806	. 91110	. 81489	58
3	. 89606	. 78715	. 89995	. 79425	. 90377	. 80126	. 90751	. 80817	. 91116	. 81500	57
4	. 89612	. 78726	. 90002	. 79436	. 90383	. 80137	. 90757	. 80829	. 91122	. 81511	56
5	9. 89619	0. 78738	9. 90008	0. 79448	9. 90390	0. 80149	9. 90763	0. 80840	9. 91128	0. 81523	55
6	. 89625	. 78750	. 90015	. 79460	. 90396	. 80160	. 90769	. 80852	. 91134	. 81534	54
7	. 89632	. 78762	. 90021	. 79472	. 90402	. 80172	. 90775	. 80863	. 91140	. 81545	53
8	. 89638	. 78774	. 90028	. 79483	. 90409	. 80184	. 90781	. 80875	. 91146	. 81556	52
9	. 89645	. 78786	. 90034	. 79495	. 90415	. 80195	. 90787	. 80886	. 91152	. 81568	51
10	9. 89651	0. 78798	9. 90040	0. 79.507	9. 90421	0. 80207	9. 90794	0. 80898	9. 91158	0. 81579	50
11	. 89658	. 78810	. 90047	. 79519	. 90428	. 80218	. 90800	. 80909	. 91164	. 81590	49
12	. 89665	. 78822	. 90053	. 79530	. 90434	. 80230	. 90806	. 80920	. 91170	. 81601	48
13	. 89671	. 78833	. 90060	. 79542	. 90440	. 80242	. 90812	. 80932	. 91176	. 81613	47
14	. 89678	. 78845	. 90066	. 79554	. 90446	. 80253	. 90818	. 80943	. 91182	. 81624	46
15	9. 89684	0. 78857	9. 90072	0. 79565	9. 90452	0. 80265	9. 90824	0. 80955	9. 91188	0. 81635	45
16	. 89691	. 78869	. 90079	. 79577	. 90459	. 80276	. 90830	. 80966	. 91194	. 81647	44
17	. 89697	. 78881	. 90085	. 79589	. 90465	. 80288	. 90836	. 80978	. 91200	. 81658	43
18	. 89704	. 78893	. 90092	. 79601	. 90471	. 80299	. 90843	. 80989	. 91206	. 81669	42
19	. 89710	. 78905	. 90098	. 79612	. 90478	. 80311	. 90849	. 81000	. 91212	. 81680	41
20	9. 89717	0. 78917	9. 90104	0. 79624	9. 90484	0. 80323	9. 90855	0. 81012	9. 91218	0. 81692	40
21	. 89723	. 78928	. 90111	. 79636	. 90490	. 80334	. 90861	. 81023	. 91224	. 81703	39
22	. 89730	. 78940	. 90117	. 79648	. 90496	. 80346	. 90867	. 81035	. 91230	. 81714	38
23	. 89736	. 78952	. 90124	. 79659	. 90503	. 80357	. 90873	. 81046	. 91236	. 81725	37
24	. 89743	. 78964	. 90130	. 79671	. 90509	. 80369	. 90879	. 81057	. 91242	. 81737	36
25	9. 89749	0. 78976	9. 90136	0. 79683	9. 90515	0. 80380	9. 90885	0. 81069	9. 91248	0. 81748	35
26	. 89756	. 78988	. 90143	. 79694	. 90521	. 80392	. 90892	. 81080	. 91254	. 81759	34
27	. 89763	. 79000	. 90149	. 79706	. 90527	. 80403	. 90898	. 81092	. 91260	. 81770	33
28	. 89769	. 79011	. 90156	. 79718	. 90534	. 80415	. 90904	. 81103	. 91265	. 81781	32
29	. 89776	. 79023	. 90162	. 79729	. 90540	. 80427	. 90910	. 81114	. 91271	. 81793	31
30	9. 89782	0. 79035	9. 90168	0. 79741	9. 90546	0. 80438	9. 90916	0. 81126	9. 91277	0. 81804	30
31	. 89789	. 79047	. 90175	. 79753	. 90552	. 80450	. 90922	. 81137	. 91283	. 81815	29
32	. 89795	. 79059	. 90181	. 79765	. 90559	. 80461	. 90928	. 81148	. 91289	. 81826	28
33	. 89802	. 79071	. 90187	. 79776	. 90565	. 80473	. 90934	. 81160	. 91295	. 81838	27
34	. 89808	. 79082	. 90194	. 79788	. 90571	. 80484	. 90940	. 81171	. 91301	. 81849	26
35	9. 89815	0. 79094	9. 90200	0. 79800	9. 90.577	0. 80496	9. 90946	0. 81183	9. 91307	0. 81860	25
36	. 89821	. 79106	. 90206	. 79811	. 90584	. 80507	. 90952	. 81194	. 91313	. 81871	24
37	. 89828	. 79118	. 90213	. 79823	. 90590	. 80519	. 90958	. 81205	. 91319	. 81882	23
38	. 89834	. 79130	. 90219	. 79835	. 90596	. 80530	. 90965	. 81217	. 91325	. 81894	22
39	. 89840	. 79142	. 90225	. 79846	. 90602	. 80542	. 90971	. 81228	. 91331	. 81905	21
40	9. 89847	0. 79153	9. 90232	0. 79858	9. 90608	0. 80553	9. 90977	0. 81239	9. 91337	0. 81916	20
41	. 89853	. 79165	. 90238	. 79870	. 90615	. 80565	. 90983	. 81251	. 91343	. 81927	19
42	. 89860	. 79177	. 90244	. 79881	. 90621	. 80576	. 90989	. 81262	. 91349	. 81938	18
43	. 89866	. 79189	. 90251	. 79893	. 90627	. 80588	. 90995	. 81273	. 91355	. 81950	17
44	. 89873	. 79201	. 90257	. 79905	. 90633	. 80599	. 91001	. 81285	. 91361	. 81961	16
45	9. 89879	0. 79212	9. 90264	0. 79916	9. 90639	0. 80611	9. 91007	0. 81296	9. 91367	0. 81972	15
46	. 89886	. 79224	. 90270	. 79928	. 90646	. 80622	. 91013	. 81308	. 91372	. 81983	14
47	. 89892	. 79236	. 90276	. 79940	. 90652	. 80634	. 91019	. 81319	. 91378	. 81994	13
48	. 89899	. 79248	. 90282	. 79951	. 90658	. 80645	. 91025	. 81330	. 91384	. 82005	12
49	. 89905	. 79260	. 90289	. 79963	. 90664	. 80657	. 91031	. 81342	. 91390	. 82017	11
50	9. 89912	0. 79271	9. 90295	0. 79974	9. 90670	0. 80668	9. 91037	0. 81353	9. 91396	0. 82028	10
51	. 89918	. 79283	. 90301	. 79986	. 90676	. 80680	. 91043	. 81364	. 91402	. 82039	9
52	. 89925	. 79295	90308	. 79998	. 90683	. 80691	. 91049	. 81376	. 91408	. 82050	8
53	. 89931	. 79307	. 90314	. 80009	. 90689	. 80703	. 91055	. 81387	. 91414	. 82061	7
54	. 89938	. 79319	. 90320	. 80021	. 90695	. 80714	. 91061	. 81398	. 91420	. 82072	6
55	9. 89944	0. 79330	9. 90327	0. 80033	9. 90701	0. 80726	9. 91067	0. 81409	9. 91426	0. 82084	5
56	. 89950	. 79342	. 90333	. 80044	. 90707	. 80737	. 91074	. 81421	. 91432	. 82095	4
57	. 89957	. 79354	. 90339	. 80056	. 90714	. 80749	. 91080	. 81432	. 91437	. 82106	3
58	. 89963	. 79366	. 90346	. 80068	. 90720	. 80760	. 91086	. 81443	. 91443	. 82117	2
59	. 89970	. 79377	. 90352	. 80079	. 90726	. 80772	. 91092	. 81455	. 91449	. 82128	1
60	9. 89976	0. 79389	9. 90358	0. 80091	9. 90732	0. 80783	9. 91098	0. 81466	9. 91455	0. 82139	0
	234°		233°		232°		231°		230°		

Haversines

′	130°		131°		132°		133°		134°		′
	Log Hav	Nat. Hav	Log Hav	Nat. Hav	Log Hav	Nat. Hav	Log Hav	Nat. Hav	Log Hav	Nat. Hav	
0	9.91455	0.82139	9.91805	0.82803	9.92146	0.83457	9.92480	0.84100	9.92805	0.84733	60
1	.91461	.82151	.91810	.82814	.92152	.83467	.92485	.84111	.92811	.84743	59
2	.91467	.82162	.91816	.82825	.92157	.83478	.92491	.84121	.92816	.84754	58
3	.91473	.82173	.91822	.82836	.92163	.83489	.92496	.84132	.92821	.84764	57
4	.91479	.82184	.91828	.82847	.92169	.83500	.92502	.84142	.92827	.84775	56
5	9.91485	0.82195	9.91833	0.82858	9.92174	0.83511	9.92507	0.84153	9.92832	0.84785	55
6	.91490	.82206	.91839	.82869	.92180	.83521	.92512	.84164	.92837	.84796	54
7	.91496	.82217	.91845	.82880	.92185	.83532	.92518	.84174	.92843	.84806	53
8	.91502	.82228	.91851	.82891	.92191	.83543	.92523	.84185	.92848	.84817	52
9	.91508	.82240	.91856	.82902	.92197	.83554	.92529	.84196	.92853	.84827	51
10	9.91514	0.82251	9.91862	0.82913	9.92202	0.83564	9.92534	0.84206	9.92859	0.84837	50
11	.91520	.82262	.91868	.82924	.92208	.83575	.92540	.84217	.92864	.84848	49
12	.91526	.82273	.91874	.82934	.92213	.83586	.92545	.84227	.92869	.84858	48
13	.91532	.82284	.91879	.82945	.92219	.83597	.92551	.84238	.92875	.84869	47
14	.91537	.82295	.91885	.82956	.92225	.83608	.92556	.84249	.92880	.84879	46
15	9.91543	0.82306	9.91891	0.82967	9.92230	0.83618	9.92562	0.84259	9.92885	0.84890	45
16	.91549	.82317	.91896	.82978	.92236	.83629	.92567	.84270	.92891	.84900	44
17	.91555	.82328	.91902	.82989	.92241	.83640	.92573	.84280	.92896	.84910	43
18	.91561	.82339	.91908	.83000	.92247	.83651	.92578	.84291	.92901	.84921	42
19	.91567	.82351	.91914	.83011	.92253	.83661	.92584	.84302	.92907	.84931	41
20	9.91573	0.82362	9.91919	0.83022	9.92258	0.83672	9.92589	0.84312	9.92912	0.84942	40
21	.91578	.82373	.91925	.83033	.92264	.83683	.92594	.84323	.92917	.84952	39
22	.91584	.82384	.91931	.83044	.92269	.83694	.92600	.84333	.92923	.84962	38
23	.91590	.82395	.91936	.83055	.92275	.83704	.92605	.84344	.92928	.84973	37
24	.91596	.82406	.91942	.83066	.92280	.83715	.92611	.84354	.92933	.84983	36
25	9.91602	0.82417	9.91948	0.83077	9.92286	0.83726	9.92616	0.,84365	9.92939	0.84994	35
26	.91608	.82428	.91954	.83087	.92292	.83737	.92622	.84376	.92944	.85004	34
27	.91613	.82439	.91959	.83098	.92297	.83747	.92627	.84386	.92949	.85014	33
28	.91619	.82450	.91965	.83109	.92303	.83758	.92633	.84397	.92955	.85025	32
29	.91625	.82461	.91971	.83120	.92308	.83769	.92638	.84407	.92960	.85035	31
30	9.91631	0.82472	9.91976	0.83131	9.92314	0.83780	9.92643	0.84418	9.92965	0.85045	30
31	.91637	.82483	.91982	.83142	.92319	.83790	.92649	.84428	.92970	.85056	29
32	.91643	.82495	.91988	.83153	.92325	.83801	.92654	.84439	.92975	.85066	28
33	.91648	.82506	.91993	.83164	.92330	.83812	.92660	.84449	.92981	.85077	27
34	.91654	.82517	.91999	.83175	.92336	.83822	.92665	.84460	.92986	.85087	26
35	9.91660	0.82528	9.92005	0.83185	9.92342	0.83833	9.92670	0.84470	9.92992	0.85097	25
36	.91666	.82539	.92010	.83196	.92347	.83844	.92676	.84481	.92997	.85108	24
37	.91672	.82550	.92016	.83207	.92353	.83855	.92681	.84492	.93002	.85118	23
38	.91677	.82561	.92022	.83218	.92358	.83865	.92687	.81502	.93007	.85128	22
39	.91683	.82572	.92027	.83229	.92364	.83876	.92692	.84513	.93013	.85139	21
40	9.91689	0.82583	9.92033	0.83240	9.92369	0.83887	9.92698	0.84523	9.93018	0.85149	20
41	.91695	.82594	.92039	.83251	.92375	.83897	.92703	.84534	.93023	.85159	19
42	.91701	.82605	.92044	.83262	.92380	.83908	.92708	.84544	.93029	.85170	18
43	.91706	.82616	.92050	.83272	.92386	.83919	.92714	.84555	.93034	.85180	17
44	.91712	.82627	.92056	.83283	.92391	.83929	.92719	.84565	.93039	.85190	16
45	9.91718	0.82638	9.92061	0.83294	9.92397	0.83940	9.92725	0.84576	9.93044	0.85201	15
46	.91724	.82649	.92067	.83305	.92402	.83951	.92730	.84586	.93050	.85211	14
47	.91730	.82660	.92073	.83316	.92408	.83961	.92735	.84597	.93055	.85221	13
48	.91735	.82671	.92078	.83327	.92413	.83972	.92741	.84607	.93060	.85232	12
49	.91741	.82682	.92084	.83337	.92419	.83983	.92746	.84618	.93065	.85242	11
50	9.91747	0.82693	9.92090	0.83348	9.92425	0.83993	9.92751	0.84628	9.93071	0.85252	10
51	.91753	.82704	.92095	.83359	.92430	.84004	.92757	.84639	.93076	.85263	9
52	.91758	.82715	.92101	.83370	.92436	.84015	.92762	.84649	.93081	.85273	8
53	.91764	.82726	.92107	.83381	.92441	.84025	.92768	.84660	.93086	.85283	7
54	.91770	.82737	.92112	.83392	.92447	.84036	.92773	.84670	.93092	.85294	6
55	9.91776	0.82748	9.92118	0.83402	9.92452	0.84047	9.92778	0.84681	9.93097	0.85304	5
56	.91782	.82759	.92124	.83413	.92458	.84057	.92784	.84691	.93102	.85314	4
57	.91787	.82770	.92129	.83424	.92463	.84068	.92789	.84702	.93107	.85324	3
58	.91793	.82781	.92135	.83435	.92469	.84079	.92794	.84712	.93113	.85335	2
59	.91799	.82792	.92140	.83446	.92474	.84089	.92800	.84722	.93118	.85345	1
60	9.91805	0.82803	9.92146	0.83457	9.92480	0.84100	9.92805	0.84733	9.93123	0.85355	0
	229°		228°		227°		226°		225°		

Haversines

′	135°		136°		137°		138°		139°		′
	Log Hav	Nat. Hav	Log Hav	Nat. Hav	Log Hav	Nat. Hav	Log Hav	Nat. Hav	Log Hav	Nat. Hav	
0	9. 93123	0. 85355	9. 93433	0. 85967	9. 93736	0. 86568	9. 94030	0. 87157	9. 94318	0. 87735	60
1	. 93128	. 85366	. 93438	. 85977	. 93741	. 86578	. 94035	. 87167	. 94322	. 87745	59
2	. 93134	. 85376	. 93443	. 85987	. 93746	. 86588	. 94040	. 87177	. 94327	. 87755	58
3	. 93139	. 85386	. 93448	. 85997	. 93751	. 86597	. 94045	. 87186	. 94332	. 87764	57
4	. 93144	. 85396	. 93454	. 86007	. 93755	. 86607	. 94050	. 87196	. 94336	. 87774	56
5	9. 93149	0. 85407	9. 93459	0. 86017	9. 93760	0. 86617	9. 94055	0. 87206	9. 94341	0. 87783	55
6	. 93154	. 85417	. 93464	. 86028	. 93765	. 86627	. 94059	. 87216	. 94346	. 87793	54
7	. 93160	. 85427	. 93469	. 86038	. 93770	. 86637	. 94064	. 87225	. 94351	. 87802	53
8	. 93165	. 85438	. 93474	. 86048	. 93775	. 86647	. 94069	. 87235	. 94355	. 87812	52
9	. 93170	. 85448	. 93479	. 86058	. 93780	. 86657	. 94074	. 87245	. 94360	. 87821	51
10	9. 93175	0. 85458	9. 93484	0.86068	9. 93785	0. 86667	9. 94079	0. 87254	9. 94365	0. 87831	50
11	. 93181	. 85468	. 93489	. 86078	. 93790	. 86677	. 94084	. 87264	. 94369	. 87840	49
12	. 93186	. 85479	. 93494	. 86088	. 93795	. 86686	. 94088	. 87274	. 94374	. 87850	48
13	. 93191	. 85489	. 93499	. 86098	. 93800	. 86696	. 94093	. 87283	. 94379	. 87859	47
14	. 93196	. 85499	. 93504	. 86108	. 93805	. 86706	. 94098	. 87293	. 94383	. 87869	46
15	9. 93201	0. 85509	9. 93509	0. 86118	9. 93810	0.86716	9. 94103	0. 87303	9. 94388	0. 87878	45
16	. 93207	. 85520	. 93515	. 86128	. 93815	. 86726	. 94108	. 87313	. 94393	. 87888	44
17	. 93212	. 85530	. 93520	. 86138	. 93820	. 86736	. 94112	. 87322	. 94398	. 87897	43
18	. 93217	. 85540	. 93525	. 86148	. 93825	. 86746	. 94117	. 87332	. 94402	. 87907	42
19	. 93222	. 85550	. 93530	. 86158	. 93830	. 86756	. 94122	. 87342	. 94407	. 87916	41
20	9. 93227	0. 85560	9. 93535	0. 86168	9. 93835	0. 86765	9. 94127	0. 87351	9. 94412	0. 87926	40
21	. 93232	. 85571	. 93540	. 86178	. 93840	. 86775	. 94132	. 87361	. 94416	. 87935	39
22	. 93238	. 85581	. 93545	. 86189	. 93845	. 86785	. 94137	. 87371	. 94421	. 87945	38
23	. 93243	. 85591	. 93550	. 86199	. 93849	. 86795	. 94141	. 87380	. 94426	. 87954	37
24	. 93248	. 85601	. 93555	. 86209	. 93854	. 86805	. 94146	. 87390	. 94430	. 87964	36
25	9. 93253	0. 85612	9. 93560	0. 86219	9. 93859	0. 86815	9. 94151	0. 87400	9. 94435	0. 87973	35
26	. 93258	. 85622	. 93565	. 86229	. 93864	. 86825	. 94156	. 87409	. 94440	. 87982	34
27	. 93264	. 85632	. 93570	. 86239	. 93869	. 86834	. 94161	. 87419	. 94444	. 87992	33
28	. 93269	. 85642	. 93575	. 86249	. 93874	. 86844	. 94165	. 87429	. 94449	. 88001	32
29	. 93274	. 85652	. 93580	. 86259	. 93879	. 86854	. 94170	. 87438	. 94454	. 88011	31
30	9. 93279	0. 85663	9. 93585	0.86269	9. 93884	0. 86864	9. 94175	0. 87448	9. 94458	0. 88020	30
31	. 93284	. 85673	. 93590	. 86279	. 93889	. 86874	. 94180	. 87457	. 94463	. 88030	29
32	. 93289	. 85683	. 93595	. 86289	. 93894	. 86884	. 94184	. 87467	. 94468	. 88039	28
33	. 93295	. 85693	. 93600	. 86299	. 93899	. 86893	. 94189	. 87477	. 94472	. 88049	27
34	. 93300	. 85703	. 93605	. 86309	. 93904	. 86903	. 94194	. 87486	. 94477	. 88058	26
35	9. 93305	0. 85713	9. 93611	0. 86319	9. 93908	0. 86913	9. 94199	0. 87496	9. 94482	0. 88067	25
36	. 93310	. 85724	. 93616	. 86329	. 93913	. 86923	. 94204	. 87506	. 94486	. 88077	24
37	. 93315	. 85734	. 93621	. 86339	. 93918	. 86933	. 94208	. 87515	. 94491	. 88086	23
38	. 93320	. 85744	. 93626	. 86349	. 93923	. 86942	. 94213	. 87525	. 94496	. 88096	22
39	. 93326	. 85754	. 93631	. 86359	. 93928	. 86952	. 94218	. 87534	. 94500	. 88105	21
40	9. 93331	0. 85764	9. 93636	0. 86369	9. 93933	0. 86962	9. 94223	0. 87544	9. 94505	0. 88115	20
41	. 93336	. 85774	. 93641	. 86379	. 93938	. 86972	. 94227	. 87554	. 94509	. 88124	19
42	. 93341	. 85785	. 93646	. 86389	. 93943	. 86982	. 94232	. 87563	. 94514	. 88133	18
43	. 93346	. 85795	. 93651	. 86399	. 93948	. 86991	. 94237	. 87573	. 94519	. 88143	17
44	. 93351	. 85805	. 93656	. 86409	. 93952	. 87001	. 94242	. 87582	. 94523	. 88152	16
45	9. 93356	0. 85815	9. 93661	0.86419	9. 93957	0. 87011	9. 94246	0. 87592	9. 94528	0.88162	15
46	. 93362	. 85825	. 93666	. 86429	. 93962	. 87021	. 94251	. 87602	. 94533	. 88171	14
47	. 93367	. 85835	. 93671	. 86438	. 93967	. 87030	. 94256	. 87611	. 94537	. 88180	13
48	. 93372	. 85846	. 93676	. 86448	. 93972	. 87040	. 94261	. 87621	. 94542	. 88190	12
49	. 93377	. 85856	. 93681	. 86458	. 93977	. 87050	. 94265	. 87630	. 94546	. 88199	11
50	9. 93382	0. 85866	9. 93686	0. 86468	9. 93982	0. 87060	9. 94270	0. 87640	9. 94551	0. 88209	10
51	. 93387	. 85876	. 93691	. 86478	. 93987	. 87070	. 94275	. 87649	. 94556	. 88218	9
52	. 93392	. 85886	. 93696	. 86488	. 93991	. 87079	. 94280	. 87659	. 94560	. 88227	8
53	. 93397	. 85896	. 93701	. 86498	. 93996	. 87089	. 94284	. 87669	. 94565	. 88237	7
54	. 93403	. 85906	. 93706	. 86508	. 94001	. 87099	. 94289	. 87678	. 94570	. 88246	6
55	9. 93408	0.85916	9. 93711	0.86518	9. 94006	0.87109	9. 94294	0. 87688	9. 94574	0. 88255	5
56	. 93413	. 85927	. 93716	. 86528	. 94011	. 87118	. 94299	. 87697	. 94579	. 88265	4
57	. 93418	. 85937	. 93721	. 86538	. 94016	. 87128	. 94303	. 87707	. 94583	. 88274	3
58	. 93423	. 85947	. 93726	. 86548	. 94021	. 87138	. 94308	. 87716	. 94588	. 88284	2
59	. 93428	. 85957	. 93731	. 86558	. 94026	. 87148	. 94313	. 87726	. 94593	. 88293	1
60	9. 93433	0. 85967	9. 93736	0. 86568	9. 94030	0. 87157	9. 94318	0. 87735	9. 94597	0. 88302	0
	224°		223°		222°		221°		220°		

Haversines

′	140°		141°		142°		143°		144°		′
	Log Hav	Nat. Hav	Log Hav	Nat. Hav	Log Hav	Nat. Hav	Log Hav	Nat. Hav	Log Hav	Nat. Hav	
0	9.94597	0.88302	9.94869	0.88857	9.95134	0.89401	9.95391	0.89932	9.95641	0.90451	60
1	.94602	.88312	.94874	.88866	.95138	.89409	.95396	.89941	.95645	.90459	59
2	.94606	.88321	.94878	.88876	.95143	.89418	.95400	.89949	.95649	.90468	58
3	.94611	.88330	.94883	.88885	.95147	.89427	.95404	.89958	.95654	.90476	57
4	.94616	.88340	.94887	.88894	.95151	.89436	.95408	.89967	.95658	.90485	56
5	9.94620	0.88349	9.94892	0.88903	9.95156	0.89445	9.95412	0.89975	9.95662	0.90494	55
6	.94625	.88358	.94896	.88912	.95160	.89454	.95417	.89984	.95666	.90502	54
7	.94629	.88368	.94901	.88921	.95164	.89463	.95421	.89993	.95670	.90511	53
8	.94634	.88377	.94905	.88930	.95169	.89472	.95425	.90002	.95674	.90519	52
9	.94638	.88386	.94909	.88940	.95173	.89481	.95429	.90010	.95678	.90528	51
10	9.94643	0.88396	9.94914	0.88949	9.95177	0.89490	9.95433	0.90019	9.95682	0.90536	50
11	.94648	.88405	.94918	.88958	.95182	.89499	.95438	.90028	.95686	.90545	49
12	.94652	.88414	.94923	.88967	.95186	.89508	.95442	.90037	.95690	.90553	48
13	.94557	.88423	.94927	.88976	.95190	.89517	.95446	.90045	.95694	.90562	47
14	.94661	.88433	.94932	.88985	.95195	.89526	.95450	.90054	.95699	.90570	46
15	9.94666	0.88442	9.94936	0.88994	9.95199	0.89534	9.95454	0.90063	9.95703	0.90579	45
16	.94670	.88451	.94941	.89003	.95203	.89543	.95459	.90071	.95707	.90587	44
17	.94675	.88461	.94945	.89012	.95208	.89552	.95463	.90080	.95711	.90596	43
18	.94680	.88470	.94950	.89022	.95212	.89561	.95467	.90089	.95715	.90604	42
19	.94684	.88479	.94954	.89031	.95216	.89570	.95471	.90097	.95719	.90613	41
20	9.94689	0.88489	9.94958	0.89040	9.95221	0.89579	9.95475	0.90106	9.95723	0.90621	40
21	.94693	.88498	.94963	.89049	.95225	.89588	.95480	.90115	.95727	.90630	39
22	.94698	.88507	.94967	.89058	.95229	.89597	.95484	.9012.4	.95731	.90638	38
23	.94702	.88516	.94972	.89067	.95234	.89606	.95488	.90132	.95735	.90647	37
24	.94707	.88526	.94976	.89076	.95238	.89614	.95492	.90141	.95739	.90655	36
25	9.94711	0.88535	9.94981	0.89085	9.95242	0.89623	9.95496	0.90150	9.95743	0.90664	35
26	.94716	.88544	.94985	.89094	.95246	.89832	.95501	.90158	.95747	.90672	34
27	.94721	.88553	.94989	.89103	.95251	.89641	.95505	.90167	.95751	.90680	33
28	.94725	.88563	.94994	.89112	.95255	.89650	.95509	.90176	.95755	.90689	32
29	.94730	.88572	.94998	.89121	.95259	.89659	.95513	.90184	.95759	.90697	31
30	9.94734	0.88581	9.95003	0.89130	9.95264	0.89668	9.95517	0.90193	9.95763	0.90706	30
31	.94739	.88590	.95007	.89139	.95268	.89677	.95521	.90201	.95768	.90714	29
32	.94743	.88600	.95011	.89149	.95272	.89685	.95526	.90210	.95772	.90723	28
33	.94748	.88609	.95016	.89158	.95276	.89694	.95530	.90219	.95776	.90731	27
34	.94752	.88618	.95020	.89167	.95281	.89703	.95534	.90227	.95780	.90740	26
35	9.94757	0.88627	9.95025	0.89176	9.95285	0.89712	9.95538	0.90236	9.95784	0.90748	25
36	.94761	.88637	.95029	.89185	.95289	.89721	.95542	.90245	.95788	.90756	24
37	.94766	.88646	.95033	.89194	.95294	.89730	.95546	.90253	.95792	.90765	23
38	.94770	.88655	.95038	.89203	.95298	.89738	.95550	.90262	.95796	.90773	22
39	.94774	.88664	.95042	.89212	.95302	.89747	.9'5555	.90271	.95800	.90782	21
40	9.94779	0.88674	9.95047	0.89221	9.95306	0.89756	9.95559	0.90279	9.95804	0.90790	20
41	.94784	.88683	.95051	.89230	.95311	.89765	.95563	.90288	.95808	.90798	19
42	.94788	.88692	.95055	.89239	.95315	.89774	.95567	.90296	.95812	.90807	18
43	.94793	.88701	.95060	.89248	.95319	.89782	.95571	.90305	.95816	.90815	17
44	.94797	.88710	.95064	.89257	.95323	.89791	.95575	.90314	.95820	.90824	16
45	9.94802	0.88720	9.95069	0.89266	9.95328	0.89800	9.95579	0.90322	9.95824	0.90832	15
46	.94806	.88729	.95073	.89275	.95332	.89809	.95584	.90331	.95828	.90840	14
47	.94811	.88738	.95077	.89284	.95336	.89818	.95588	.90339	.95832	.90849	13
48	.94815	.88747	.95082	.89293	.95340	.89826	.95592	.90348	.95836	.90857	12
49	.94820	.88756	.95086	.89302	.95345	.89835	.95596	.90357	.95840	.90866	11
50	9.94824	0.88766	9.95090	0.89311	9.95349	0.89844	9.95600	0.90365	9.95844	0.90874	10
51	.94829	.88775	.95095	.89320	.95353	.89853	.95604	.90374	.95848	.90882	9
52	.94833	.88784	.95099	.89329	.95357	.89862	.95608	.90382	.95852	.90891	8
53	.94838	.88793	.95104	.89338	.95362	.89870	.95613	.90391	.95856	.90899	7
54	.94842	.88802	.95108	.89347	.95366	.89879	.95617	.90399	.95860	.90907	6
55	9.94847	0.88811	9.95112	0.89356	9.95370	0.89888	9.95621	0.90408	9.95864	0.90916	5
56	.94851	.88821	.95117	.89365	.95374	.89897	.95625	.90417	.95868	.90924	4
57	.94856	.88830	.95121	.89374	.95379	.89906	.95629	.90425	.95872	.90933	3
58	.94860	.88839	.95125	.89383	.95383	.89914	.95633	.90434	.95876	.90941	2
59	.94865	.88848	.95130	.89392	.95387	.89923	.95637	.90442	.95880	.90949	1
60	9.94869	0.88857	9.95134	0.89401	9.95391	0.89932	9.95641	0.90451	9.95884	0.90958	0
	219°		218°		217°		216°		215°		

Haversines

′	145°		146°		147°		148°		149°		′
	Log Hav	Nat. Hav	Log Hav	Nat. Hav	Log Hav	Nat. Hav	Log Hav	Nat. Hav	Log Hav	Nat. Hav	
0	9. 95884	0. 90958	9. 96119	0. 91452	9. 96347	0. 91934	9. 96568	0. 92402	9. 96782	0. 92858	60
1	. 95888	. 90966	. 96123	. 91460	. 96351	. 91941	. 96572	. 92410	. 96786	. 92866	59
2	. 95892	. 90974	. 96127	. 91468	. 96355	. 91949	. 96576	. 92418	. 96189	. 92873	58
3	. 95896	. 90983	. 96131	. 91476	. 96359	. 91957	. 96579	. 92426	. 96793	. 92881	57
4	. 95900	. 90991	. 96135	. 91484	. 96362	. 91965	. 96583	. 92433	. 96796	. 92888	56
5	9. 95904	0. 90999	9. 96139	0. 91493	9. 96366	0. 91973	9. 96586	0. 92441	9. 96800	0. 92896	55
6	. 95908	. 91008	. 96142	. 91501	. 96370	. 91981	. 96590	. 92449	. 96803	. 92903	54
7	. 95912	. 91016	. 96146	. 91509	. 96374	. 91989	. 96594	. 92456	. 96807	. 92911	53
8	. 95916	. 91024	. 96150	. 91517	. 96377	. 91997	. 96597	. 92464	. 96810	. 92918	52
9	. 95920	. 91033	. 96154	. 91525	. 96381	. 92005	. 96601	. 92472	. 96814	. 92926	51
10	9. 95924	0. 91041	9. 96158	0. 91533	9. 96385	0. 92013	9. 96604	0. 92479	9. 96817	0. 92933	50
11	. 95928	. 91049	. 96162	. 91541	. 96388	. 92020	. 96608	. 92487	. 96821	. 92941	49
12	. 95932	. 91057	. 96165	. 91549	. 96392	. 92028	. 96612	. 92495	. 96824	. 92948	48
13	. 95936	. 91066	. 96169	. 91557	. 96396	. 92036	. 96615	. 92502	. 96827	. 92955	47
14	. 95939	. 91074	. 96173	. 91565	. 96400	. 92044	. 96619	. 92510	. 96831	. 92963	46
15	9. 95943	0. 91082	9. 96177	0. 91573	9. 96403	0. 92052	9. 96622	0. 92518	9. 96834	0. 92970	45
16	. 95947	. 91091	. 96181	. 91582	. 96407	. 92060	. 96626	. 92525	. 96837	. 92978	44
17	. 95951	. 91099	. 96185	. 91590	. 96411	. 92068	. 96630	. 92533	. 96841	. 92985	43
18	. 95955	. 91107	. 96188	. 91598	. 96414	. 92076	. 96633	. 92541	. 96845	. 92993	42
19	. 95959	. 91115	. 96192	. 91606	. 96418	. 92083	. 96637	. 92548	. 96848	. 93000	41
20	9. 95963	0. 91124	9. 96196	0. 91614	9. 96422	0. 92091	9. 96640	0. 92556	9. 96852	0. 93007	40
21	. 95967	. 91132	. 96200	. 91622	. 96426	. 92099	. 96644	. 92563	. 96855	. 93015	39
22	. 95971	. 91140	. 96204	. 91630	. 96429	. 92107	. 96648	. 92571	. 96859	. 93022	38
23	. 95975	. 91149	. 96208	. 91638	. 96433	. 92115	. 96651	. 92579	. 96862	. 93030	37
24	. 95979	. 91157	. 96211	. 91646	. 96437	. 92123	. 96655	. 92586	. 96866	. 93037	36
25	9. 95983	0. 91165	9. 96215	0. 91654	9. 96440	0. 92130	9. 96658	0. 92594	9. 96869	0. 93045	35
26	. 95987	. 91173	. 96219	. 91662	. 96444	. 92138	. 96662	. 92602	. 96873	. 93052	34
27	. 95991	. 91182	. 96223	. 91670	. 96448	. 92146	. 96665	. 92609	. 96876	. 93059	33
28	. 95995	. 91190	. 96227	. 91678	. 96451	. 92154	. 96669	. 92617	. 96879	. 93067	32
29	. 95999	. 91198	. 96230	. 91686	. 96455	. 92162	. 96673	. 92624	. 96883	. 93074	31
30	9. 96002	0. 91206	9. 96234	0. 91694	9. 96459	0. 92170	9. 96676	0. 92632	9. 96886	0. 93081	30
31	. 96006	. 91215	. 96238	. 91702	. 96462	. 92177	. 96680	. 92640	. 96890	. 93089	29
32	. 96010	. 91223	. 96242	. 91710	. 96466	. 92185	. 96683	. 92647	. 96894	. 93096	28
33	. 96014	. 91231	. 96246	. 91718	. 96470	. 92193	. 96687	. 92655	. 96897	. 93104	27
34	. 96018	. 91239	. 96249	. 91726	. 96473	. 92201	. 96690	. 92662	. 96900	. 93111	26
35	9. 96022	0. 91247	9. 96253	0. 91734	9. 96477	0. 92209	9. 96694	0. 92670	9. 96904	0. 93118	25
36	. 96026	. 91256	. 96257	. 91742	. 96481	. 92216	. 96697	. 92678	. 96907	. 93126	24
37	. 96030	. 91264	. 96261	. 91750	. 96484	. 92224	. 96701	. 92685	. 96910	. 93133	23
38	. 96034	. 91272	. 96265	. 91758	. 96488	. 92232	. 96705	. 92693	. 96914	. 93140	22
39	. 96038	. 91280	. 96268	. 91766	. 96492	. 92240	. 96708	. 92700	. 96917	. 93148	21
40	9. 96042	0. 91289	9. 96272	0. 91774	9. 96495	0: 92248	9. 96712	0. 92708	9. 96921	0. 93155	20
41	. 96046	. 91297	. 96276	. 91782	. 96499	. 92255	. 96715	. 92715	. 96924	. 93162	19
42	. 96049	. 91305	. 96280	. 91790	. 96503	. 92263	. 96719	. 92723	. 96928	. 93170	18
43	. 96053	. 91313	. 96283	. 91798	. 96506	. 92271	. 96722	. 92730	. 96931	. 93177	17
44	. 96057	. 91321	. 96287	. 91806	. 96510	. 92279	. 96726	. 92738	. 96934	. 93184	16
45	9. 96061	0. 91329	9. 96291	0. 91814	9. 96514	0. 92286	9. 96729	0. 92746	9. 96938	0. 93192	15
46	. 96065	. 91338	. 96295	. 91822	. 96517	. 92294	. 96733	. 92753	. 96941	. 93199	14
47	. 96069	. 91346	. 96299	. 91830	. 96521	. 92302	. 96736	. 92761	96945	. 93206	13
48	. 96073	. 91354	. 96302	. 91838	. 96525	. 92310	. 96740	. 92768	. 96948	. 93214	12
49	. 96077	. 91362	. 96306	. 91846	. 96528	. 92317	. 96743	. 92776	. 96951	. 93221	11
50	9. 96081	0. 91370	9. 96310	0. 91854	9. 96532	0. 92325	9. 96747	0. 92783	9. 96955	0. 93228	10
51	. 96084	. 91379	. 96314	. 91862	. 96536	. 92333	. 96750	. 92791	. 96958	. 93236	9
52	. 96088	. 91387	. 96317	. 91870	. 96539	. 92341	. 96754	. 92798	. 96962	. 93243	8
53	. 96092	. 91395	. 96321	. 91878	. 96543	. 92348	. 96758	. 92806	. 96965	. 93250	7
54	. 96096	. 91403	. 96325	. 91886	. 96547	. 92356	. 96761	. 92813	. 96968	. 93258	6
55	9. 96100	0. 91411	9. 96329	0. 91894	9. 96550	0. 92364	9. 96765	0. 92821	9. 96972	0. 93265	5
56	. 96104	. 91419	. 96332	. 91902	. 96554	. 92372	. 96768	. 92828	. 96975	. 93272	4
57	. 96108	. 91427	. 96336	. 91910	. 96557	. 92379	. 96772	. 92836	. 96979	. 93279	3
58	. 96112	. 91436	. 96340	. 91918	. 96561	. 92387	. 96775	. 92843	. 96982	. 93287	2
59	. 96115	. 91444	. 96344	. 91926	. 96565	. 92395	. 96779	. 92851	. 96985	. 93294	1
60	9. 96119	0. 91452	9. 96347	0. 91934	9. 96568	0. 92402	9. 96782	0. 92858	9. 96989	0. 93301	0
	214°		213°		212°		211°		210°		

Haversines

′	150°		151°		152°		153°		154°		′
	Log Hav	Nat. Hav	Log Hav	Nat. Hav	Log Hav	Nat. Hav	Log Hav	Nat. Hav	Log Hav	Nat. Hav	
0	9.96989	0.93301	9.97188	0.93731	9.97381	0.94147	9.97566	0.94550	9.97745	0.94940	60
1	.96992	.93309	.97192	.93738	.97384	.94154	.97569	.94557	.97748	.94946	59
2	.96996	.93316	.97195	.93745	.97387	.94161	.97572	.94564	.97751	.94952	58
3	.96999	.93323	.97198	.93752	.97390	.94168	.97575	.94570	.97754	.94959	57
4	.97002	.93330	.97201	.93759	.97393	.94175	.97578	.94577	.97756	.94965	56
5	9.97006	0.93338	9.97205	0.93766	9.97397	0.94181	9.97581	0.94583	9.97759	0.94972	55
6	.97009	.93345	.97208	.93773	.97400	.94188	.97584	.94590	.97762	.94978	54
7	.97012	.93352	.97211	.93780	.97403	.94195	.97587	.94596	.97765	.94984	53
8	.97016	.93359	.97214	.93787	.97406	.94202	.97591	.94603	.97768	.94991	52
9	.97019	.93367	.97218	.93794	.97409	.94209	.97594	.94610	.97771	.94997	51
10	9.97022	0.93374	9.97221	0.93801	9.97412	0.94215	9.97597	0.94616	9.97774	0.95003	50
11	.97026	.93381	.97224	.93808	.97415	.94222	.97600	.94623	.97777	.95010	49
12	.97029	.93388	.97227	.93815	.97418	.94229	.97603	.94629	.97780	.95016	48
13	.97033	.93395	.97231	.93822	.97422	.94236	.97606	.94636	.97783	.95022	47
14	.97036	.93403	.97234	.93829	.97425	.94243	.97609	.94642	.97785	.95029	46
15	9.97039	0.93410	9.97237	0.93836	9.97428	0.94249	9.97612	0.94649	9.97788	0.95035	45
16	.97043	.93417	.97240	.93843	.97431	.94256	.97615	.94655	.97791	.95041	44
17	.97046	.93424	.97244	.93850	.97434	.94263	.97618	.94662	.97794	.95048	43
18	.97049	.93432	.97247	.93857	.97437	.94270	.97621	.94669	.97797	.95054	42
19	.97052	.93439	.97250	.93864	.97440	.94276	.97624	.94675	.97800	.95060	41
20	9.97056	0.93446	9.97253	0.93871	9.97443	0.94283	9.97627	0.94682	9.97803	0.95066	40
21	.97059	.93453	.97257	.93878	.97447	.94290	.97630	.94688	.97806	.95073	39
22	.97063	.93460	.97260	.93885	.97450	.94297	.97633	.94695	.97808	.95079	38
23	.97066	.93468	.97263	.93892	.97453	.94303	.97636	.94701	.97811	.95085	37
24	.97069	.93475	.97266	.93899	.97456	.94310	.97639	.94708	.97814	.95092	36
25	9.97073	0.93482	9.97269	0.93906	9.97459	0.94317	9.97642	0.94714	9.97817	0.95098	35
26	.97076	.93489	.97273	.93913	.97462	.94324	.97645	.94721	.97820	.95104	34
27	.97079	.93496	.97276	.93920	.97465	.94330	.97647	.94727	.97823	.95110	33
28	.97083	.93503	.97279	.93927	.97468	.94337	.97650	.94734	.97826	.95117	32
29	.97086	.93511	.97282	.93934	.97471	.94344	.97653	.94740	.97829	.95123	31
30	9.97089	0.93518	9.97285	0.93941	9.97474	0.94351	9.97656	0.94747	9.97831	0.95129	30
31	.97093	.93525	.97289	.93948	.97478	.94357	.97659	.94753	.97834	.95136	29
32	.97096	.93532	.97292	.93955	.97481	.94364	.97662	.94760	.97837	.95142	28
33	.97099	.93539	.97295	.93962	.97484	.94371	.97665	.94766	.97840	.95148	27
34	.97103	.93546	.97298	.93969	.97487	.94377	.97668	.94773	.97843	.95154	26
35	9.97106	0.93554	9.97301	0.93976	9.97490	0.94384	9.97671	0.94779	9.97846	0.95161	25
36	.97109	.93561	.97305	.93982	.97493	.94391	.97674	.94786	.97849	.95167	24
37	.97113	.93568	.97308	.93989	.97496	.94397	.97677	.94792	.97851	.95173	23
38	.97116	.93575	.97311	.93996	.97499	.94404	.97680	.94799	.97854	.95179	22
39	.97119	.93582	.97314	.94003	.97502	.94411	.97683	.94805	.97857	.95185	21
40	9.97123	0.93589	9.97317	0.94010	9.97505	0.94418	9.97686	0.94811	9.97860	0.95192	20
41	.97126	.93596	.97321	.94017	.97508	.94424	.97689	.94818	.97863	.95198	19
42	.97129	.93603	.97324	.94024	.97511	.94431	.97692	.94824	.97866	.95204	18
43	.97132	.93611	.97327	.94031	.97514	.94438	.97695	.94831	.97868	.95210	17
44	.97136	.93618	.97330	.94038	.97518	.94444	.97698	.94837	.97871	.95217	16
45	9.97139	0.93625	9.97333	0.94045	9.97521	0.94451	9.97701	0.94844	9.97874	0.95223	15
46	.97142	.93632	.97337	.94051	.97524	.94458	.97704	.94850	.97877	.95229	14
47	.97146	.93639	.97340	.94058	.97527	.94464	.97707	.94856	.97880	.95235	13
48	.97149	.93646	.97343	.94065	.97530	.94471	.97710	.94863	.97883	.95241	12
49	.97152	.93653	.97346	.94072	.97533	.94477	.97713	.94869	.97885	.95248	11
50	9.97156	0.93660	9.97349	0.94079	9.97536	0.94484	9.97716	0.94876	9.97888	0.95254	10
51	.97159	.93667	.97352	.94086	.97539	.94491	.97718	.94882	.97891	.95260	9
52	.97162	.93674	.97356	.94093	.97542	.94497	.97721	.94889	.97894	.95266	8
53	.97165	.93682	.97359	.94099	.97545	.94504	.97724	.94895	.97897	.95272	7
54	.97169	.93689	.97362	.94106	.97548	.94511	.97727	.94901	.91899	.95278	6
55	9.97172	0.93696	9.97365	0.94113	9.97551	0.94517	9.97730	0.94908	9.97902	0.95285	5
56	.97175	.93703	.97368	.94120	.97554	.94524	.97733	.94914	.97905	.95291	4
57	.97179	.93710	.97371	.94127	.97557	.94531	.97736	.94921	.97908	.95297	3
58	.97182	.93717	.97375	.94134	.97560	.94537	.97739	.94927	.97911	.95303	2
59	.97185	.93724	.97378	.94141	.97563	.94544	.97742	.94933	.97914	.95309	1
60	9.97188	0.93731	9.97381	0.94147	9.97566	0.94550	9.97745	0.94940	9.97916	0.95315	0
	209°		208°		207°		206°		205°		

Haversines

′	155°		156°		157°		158°		159°		′
	Log Hav	Nat. Hav	Log Hav	Nat. Hav	Log Hav	Nat. Hav	Log Hav	Nat. Hav	Log Hav	Nat. Hav	
0	9. 97916	0. 95315	9. 98081	0. 95677	9. 98239	0. 96025	9. 98389	0. 96359	9. 98533	0. 96679	60
1	. 97919	. 95322	. 98084	. 95683	. 98241	. 96031	. 98392	. 96365	. 98536	. 96684	59
2	. 97922	. 95328	. 98086	. 95689	. 98244	. 96037	. 98394	. 96370	. 98538	. 96689	58
3	. 97925	. 95334	. 98089	. 95695	. 98246	. 96042	. 98397	. 96376	. 98540	. 96695	57
4	. 97927	. 95340	. 98092	. 95701	. 98249	. 96048	. 98399	. 96381	. 98543	. 96700	56
5	9. 97930	0. 95346	9. 98094	0. 95707	9. 98251	0. 96054	9. 98402	0. 96386	9. 98545	0. 96705	55
6	. 97933	. 95352	. 98097	. 95713	. 98254	. 96059	. 98404	. 96392	. 98547	. 96710	54
7	. 97936	. 95358	. 98100	. 95719	. 98256	. 96065	. 98406	. 96397	. 98550	. 96715	53
8	. 97939	. 95364	. 98102	. 95724	. 98259	. 96071	. 98409	. 96403	. 98552	. 96721	52
9	. 97941	. 95371	. 98105	. 95730	. 98262	. 96076	. 98411	. 96408	. 98554	. 96726	51
10	9. 97944	0. 95377	9. 98108	0. 95736	9. 98264	0. 96082	9. 98414	0. 96413	9. 98557	0. 96731	50
11	. 97947	. 95383	. 98110	. 95742	. 98267	. 96088	. 98416	. 96419	. 98559	. 96736	49
12	. 97950	. 95389	. 98113	. 95748	. 98269	. 96093	. 98419	. 96424	. 98561	. 96741	48
13	. 97953	. 95395	. 98116	. 95754	. 98272	. 96099	. 98421	. 96430	. 98564	. 96746	47
14	. 97955	. 95401	. 98118	. 95760	. 98274	. 96104	. 98424	. 96435	. 98566	. 96752	46
15	9. 97958	0. 95407	9. 98121	0. 95766	9. 98277	0. 96110	9. 98426	0. 96440	9. 98568	0. 96757	45
16	. 97961	. 95413	. 98124	. 95771	. 98279	. 96116	. 98428	. 96446	. 98570	. 96762	44
17	. 97964	. 95419	. 98126	. 95777	. 98282	. 96121	. 98431	. 96451	. 98573	. 96767	43
18	. 97966	. 95425	. 98129	. 95783	. 98285	. 96127	. 98433	. 96457	. 98575	. 96772	42
19	. 97969	. 95431	. 98132	. 95789	. 98287	. 96133	. 98436	. 96462	. 98577	. 96777	41
20	9. 97972	0. 95438	9. 98134	0. 95795	9. 98290	0. 96138	9. 98438	0. 96467	9. 98580	0. 96782	40
21	. 97975	. 95444	. 98137	. 95801	. 98292	. 96144	. 98440	. 96473	. 98582	. 96788	39
22	. 97977	. 95450	. 98139	. 95806	. 98295	. 96149	. 98443	. 96478	. 98584	. 96793	38
23	. 97980	. 95456	. 98142	. 95812	. 98297	. 96155	. 98445	. 96483	. 98587	. 96798	37
24	. 97983	. 95462	. 98145	. 95818	. 98300	. 96161	. 98448	. 96489	. 98589	. 96803	36
25	9. 97986	0. 95468	9. 98147	0. 95824	9. 98302	0. 96166	9. 98450	0. 96494	9. 98591	0. 96808	35
26	. 97988	. 95474	. 98150	. 95830	. 98305	. 96172	. 98453	. 96500	. 98593	. 96813	34
27	. 97991	. 95480	. 98153	. 95836	. 98307	. 96177	. 98455	. 96505	. 98596	. 96818	33
28	. 97994	. 95486	. 98155	. 95841	. 98310	. 96183	. 98457	. 96510	. 98598	. 96823	32
29	. 97997	. 95492	. 98158	. 95847	. 98312	. 96188	. 98460	. 96516	. 98600	. 96829	31
30	9. 97999	0. 95498	9. 98161	0. 95853	9. 98315	0. 96194	9. 98462	0.96521	9. 98603	0. 96834	30
31	. 98002	. 95504	. 98163	. 95859	. 98317	. 96200	. 98465	. 96526	. 98605	. 96839	29
32	. 98005	. 95510	. 98166	. 95865	. 98320	. 96205	. 98467	. 96532	. 98607	. 96844	28
33	. 98008	. 95516	. 98168	. 95870	. 98322	. 96211	. 98469	. 96537	. 98609	. 96849	27
34	. 98010	. 95522	. 98171	. 95876	. 98325	. 96216	. 98472	. 96542	. 98612	. 96854	26
35	9. 98013	0. 95528	9. 98174	0. 95882	9. 98327	0. 96222	9. 98474	0. 96547	9. 98614	0. 96859	25
36	. 98016	. 95534	. 98176	. 95888	. 98330	. 96227	. 98476	. 96553	. 98616	. 96864	24
37	. 98019	. 95540	. 98179	. 95894	. 98332	. 96233	. 98479	. 96558	. 98619	. 96869	23
38	. 98021	. 95546	. 98182	. 95899	. 98335	. 96238	. 98481	. 96563	. 98621	. 96874	22
39	. 98024	. 95552	. 98184	. 95905	. 98337	. 96244	. 98484	. 96569	. 98623	. 96879	21
40	9. 98027	0. 95558	9. 98187	0. 95911	9. 98340	0. 96249	9. 98486	0. 96574	9. 98625	0.96884	20
41	. 98030	. 95564	. 98189	. 95917	. 98342	. 96255	. 98488	. 96579	. 98628	. 96889	19
42	. 98032	. 95570	. 98192	. 95922	. 98345	. 96260	. 98491	. 96585	. 98630	. 96894	18
43	. 98035	. 95576	. 98195	. 95928	. 98347	. 96266	. 98493	. 96590	. 98632	. 96899	17
44	. 98038	. 95582	. 98197	. 95934	. 98350	. 96272	. 98496	. 96595	. 98634	. 96905	16
45	9. 98040	0. 95588	9. 98200	0. 95940	9. 98352	0. 96277	9. 98498	. 96600	9. 98637	0. 96910	15
46	. 98043	. 95594	. 98202	. 95945	. 98355	. 96283	. 98500	. 96606	. 98639	. 96915	14
47	. 98046	. 95600	. 98205	. 95951	. 98357	. 96288	. 98503	. 96611	. 98641	. 96920	13
48	. 98049	. 95606	. 98208	. 95957	. 98360	. 96294	. 98505	. 96616	. 98643	. 96925	12
49	. 98051	. 95612	. 98210	. 95962	. 98362	. 96299	. 98507	. 96621	. 98646	. 96930	11
50	9. 98054	0. 95618	9. 98213	0. 95968	9. 98365	0. 96305	9. 98510	0. 96627	9. 98648	0. 96935	10
51	. 98057	. 95624	. 98215	. 95974	. 98367	. 96310	. 98512	. 96632	. 98650	. 96940	9
52	. 98059	. 95630	. 98218	. 95980	. 98370	. 96315	. 98514	. 96637	. 98652	. 96945	8
53	. 98062	. 95636	. 98221	. 95985	. 98372	. 96321	. 98517	. 96642	. 98655	. 96950	7
54	. 98065	. 95642	. 98223	. 95991	. 98375	. 96326	. 98519	. 96648	. 98657	. 96955	6
55	9. 98067	0. 95648	9. 98226	0. 95997	9. 98377	0. 96332	9. 98521	0. 96653	9. 98659	0. 96960	5
56	. 98070	. 95654	. 98228	. 96002	. 98379	. 96337	. 98524	. 96658	. 98661	. 96965	4
57	. 98073	. 95660	. 98231	. 96008	. 98382	. 96343	. 98526	. 96663	. 98664	. 96970	3
58	. 98076	. 95665	. 98233	. 96014	. 98384	. 96348	. 98529	. 96669	. 98666	. 96975	2
59	. 98078	. 95671	. 98236	. 96020	. 98387	. 96354	. 98531	. 96674	. 98668	. 96980	1
60	9. 98081	0. 95677	9. 98239	0. 96025	9. 98389	0. 96359	9. 98533	0. 96679	9. 98670	0. 96985	0
	204°		203°		202°		201°		200°		

Haversines

′	160°		161°		162°		163°		164°		′
	Log Hav	Nat. Hav	Log Hav	Nat. Hav	Log Hav	Nat. Hav	Log Hav	Nat. Hav	Log Hav	Nat. Hav	
0	9.98670	0.96985	9.98801	0.97276	9.98924	0.97553	9.99041	0.97815	9.99151	0.98063	60
1	.98673	.96990	.98803	.97281	.98926	.97557	.99043	.97819	.99152	.98067	59
2	.98675	.96995	.98805	.97285	.98928	.97562	.99044	.97824	.99154	.98071	58
3	.98677	.97000	.98807	.97290	.98930	.97566	.99046	.97828	.99156	.98075	57
4	.98679	.97004	.98809	.97295	.98932	.97571	.99048	.97832	.99158	.98079	56
5	9.98681	0.97009	9.98811	0.97300	9.98934	0.97575	9.99050	0.97836	9.99159	0.98083	55
6	.98684	.97014	.98813	.97304	.98936	.97580	.99052	.97841	.99161	.98087	54
7	.98686	.97019	.98815	.97309	.98938	.97584	.99054	.97845	.99163	.98091	53
8	.98688	.97024	.98817	.97314	.98940	.97589	.99056	.97849	.99165	.98095	52
9	.98690	.97029	.98819	.97318	.98942	.97593	.99058	.97853	.99166	.98099	51
10	9.98692	0.97034	9.98822	0.97323	9.98944	0.97598	9.99059	0.97858	9.99168	0.98103	50
11	.98695	.97039	.98824	.97328	.98946	.97602	.99061	.97862	.99170	.98107	49
12	.98697	.97044	.98826	.97332	.98948	.97606	.99063	.97866	.99172	.98111	48
13	.98699	.97049	.98828	.97337	.98950	.97611	.99065	.97870	.99173	.98115	47
14	.98701	.97054	.98830	.97342	.98952	.97615	.99067	.97874	.99175	.98119	46
15	9.98703	0.97059	9.98832	0.97347	9.98954	0.97620	9.99069	0.97879	9.99177	0.98123	45
16	.98706	.97064	.98834	.97351	.98956	.97624	.99071	.97883	.99179	.98127	44
17	.98708	.97069	.98836	.97356	.98958	.97629	.99072	.97887	.99180	.98131	43
18	.98710	.97074	.98838	.97361	.98960	.97633	.99074	.97891	.99182	.98135	42
19	.98712	.97078	.98840	.97365	.98962	.97637	.99076	.97895	.99184	.98139	41
20	9.98714	0.97083	9.98842	0.97370	9.9894	0.97642	9.99078	0.97899	9.99186	0.98142	40
21	.98717	.97088	.98845	.97374	.989 6	.97646	.99080	.97904	.99187	.98146	39
22	.98719	.97093	.98847	.97379	.98968	.97651	.99082	.97908	.99189	.98150	38
23	.98721	.97098	.98849	.97384	.98970	.97655	.99084	.97912	.99191	.98154	37
24	.98723	.97103	.98851	.97388	.98971	.97660	.99085	.97916	.99193	.98158	36
25	9.98725	0.97108	9.98853	0.97393	9.98973	0.97664	9.99087	0.97920	9.99194	0.98162	35
26	.98728	.97113	.98855	.97398	.98975	.97668	.99089	.97924	.99196	.98166	34
27	.98730	.97117	.98857	.97402	.98977	.97673	.99091	.97929	.99198	.98170	33
28	.98732	.97122	.98859	.97407	.98979	.97677	.99093	.97933	.99200	.98174	32
29	.96734	.97127	.98861	.97412	.98981	.97681	.99095	.97937	.99201	.98178	31
30	9.98736	0.97132	9.98863	0.97416	9.98983	0.97686	9.99096	0.97941	9.99203	0.98182	30
31	.98738	.97137	.98865	.97421	.98985	.97690	.99098	.97945	.99205	.98185	29
32	.98741	.97142	.98867	.97425	.98987	.97695	.99100	.97949	.99206	.98189	28
33	.98743	.97147	.98869	.97430	.98 89	.97699	.99102	.97953	.99208	.98193	27
34	.98745	.97151	.98871	.97435	.98991	.97703	.99104	.97957	.99210	.98197	26
35	9.98747	0.97156	9.98873	0.97439	9.98993	0.97708	9.99106	0.97962	9.99212	0.98201	25
36	.98749	.97161	.98875	.97444	.98995	.97712	.99107	.97966	.99213	.98205	24
37	.98751	.97166	.98877	.97448	.98997	.97716	.99109	.97970	.99215	.98209	23
38	.98754	.97171	.98880	.97453	.98999	.97721	.99111	.97974	.99217	.98212	22
39	.98756	.97176	.98882	.97458	.99001	.97725	.99113	.97978	.99218	.98216	21
40	9.98758	0.97180	9.98884	0.97462	9.99003	0.97729	9.99115	0.97982	9.99220	0.98220	20
41	.98760	.97185	.98886	.97467	.99004	.97734	.99116	.97986	.99222	.98224	19
42	.98762	.97190	.98888	.97471	.99006	.97738	.99118	.97990	.99223	.98228	18
43	.98764	.97195	.98890	.97476	.99008	.97742	.99120	.97994	.99225	.98232	17
44	.98766	.97200	.98892	.97480	.99010	.97747	.99122	.97998	.99227	.98236	16
45	9.98769	0.97204	9.98894	0.97485	9.99012	0.97751	9.99124	0.98002	9.99229	0.98239	15
46	.98771	.97209	.98896	.97490	.99014	.97755	.99126	.98007	.99230	.98243	14
47	.98773	.97214	.98898	.97494	.99016	.97760	.99127	.98011	.99232	.98247	13
48	.98775	.97219	.98900	.97499	.99018	.97764	.99129	.98015	.99234	.98251	12
49	.98777	.97224	.98902	.97503	.99020	.97768	.99131	.98019	.99235	.98255	11
50	9.98779	0.97228	9.98904	0.97508	9.99022	0.97773	9.99133	0.98023	9.99237	0.98258	10
51	.98781	.97233	.98906	.97512	.99024	.97777	.99135	.98027	.99239	.98262	9
52	.98784	.97238	.98908	.97517	.99026	.97781	.99136	.98031	.99240	.98266	8
53	.98786	.97243	.98910	.97521	.99027	.97785	.99138	.98035	.99242	.98270	7
54	.98788	.97247	.98912	.97526	.99029	.97790	.99140	.98039	.99244	.98274	6
55	9.98790	0.97252	9.98914	0.97530	9.99031	0.97794	9.99142	0.98043	9.99245	0.98277	5
56	.98792	.97257	.98916	.97535	.99033	.97798	.99143	.98047	.99247	.98281	4
57	.98794	.97262	.98918	.97539	.99035	.97802	.99145	.98051	.99249	.98285	3
58	.98796	.97266	.98920	.97544	.99037	.97807	.99147	.98055	.99250	.98289	2
59	.98798	.97271	.98922	.97548	.99039	.97811	.99149	.98059	.99252	.98293	1
60	9.98801	0.97276	9.98924	0.97553	9.99041	0.97815	9.99151	0.98063	9.99254	0.98296	0
	199°		198°		197°		196°		195°		

Haversines

′	165°		166°		167°		168°		169°		′
	Log Hav	Nat. Hav	Log Hav	Nat. Hav	Log Hav	Nat. Hav	Log Hav	Nat. Hav	Log Hav	Nat. Hav	
0	9.99254	0.98296	9.99350	0.98515	9.99440	0.98719	9.99523	0.98907	9.99599	0.99081	60
1	.99255	.98300	.99352	.98518	.99441	.98722	.99524	.98910	.99600	.99084	59
2	.99257	.98304	.99353	.98522	.99443	.98725	.99526	.98913	.99602	.99087	58
3	.99259	.98308	.99355	.98525	.99444	.98728	.99527	.98916	.99603	.99090	57
4	.99260	.98311	.99356	.98529	.99446	.98732	.99528	.98919	.99604	.99092	56
5	9.99262	0.98315	9.99358	0.98532	9.99447	0.98735	9.99529	0.98922	9.99605	0.99095	55
6	.99264	.98319	.99359	.98536	.99448	.98738	.99531	.98925	.99606	.99098	54
7	.99265	.98323	.99361	.98539	.99450	.98741	.99532	.98928	.99608	.99101	53
8	.99267	.98326	.99362	.98543	.99451	.98745	.99533	.98931	.99609	.99103	52
9	.99269	.98330	.99364	.98546	.99453	.98748	.99535	.98934	.99610	.99106	51
10	9.99270	0.98334	9.99366	0.98550	9.99454	0.98751	9.99536	0.98937	9.99611	0.99109	50
11	.99272	.98337	.99367	.98553	.99456	.98754	.99537	.98940	.99612	.99112	49
12	.99274	.98341	.99369	.98557	.99457	.98757	.99539	.98943	.99614	.99114	48
13	.99275	.98345	.99370	.98560	.99458	.98761	.99540	.98946	.99615	.99117	47
14	.99277	.98349	.99372	.98564	.99460	.98764	.99541	.98949	.99616	.99120	46
15	9.99278	0.98352	9.99373	0.98567	9.99461	0.98767	9.99543	0.98952	9.99617	0.99123	45
16	.99280	.98356	.99375	.98571	.99463	.98770	.99544	.98955	.99618	.99125	44
17	.99282	.98360	.99376	.98574	.99464	.98774	.99545	.98958	.99620	.99128	43
18	.99283	.98363	.99378	.98577	.99465	.98777	.99546	.98961	.99621	.99131	42
19	.99285	.98367	.99379	.98581	.99467	.98780	.99548	.98964	.99622	.99133	41
20	9.99287	0.98371	9.99381	0.98584	9.99468	0.98783	9.99549	0.98967	9.99623	0.99136	40
21	.99288	.98374	.99382	.98588	.99470	.98786	.99550	.98970	.99624	.99139	39
22	.99290	.98378	.99384	.98591	.99471	.98789	.99552	.98973	.99626	.99141	38
23	.99291	.98382	.99385	.98595	.99472	.98793	.99553	.98976	.99627	.99144	37
24	.99293	.98385	.99387	.98598	.99474	.98796	.99554	.98979	.99628	.99147	36
25	9.99295	0.98389	9.99388	0.98601	9.99475	0.98799	9.99555	0.98982	9.99629	0.99149	35
26	.99296	.98393	.99390	.98605	.99477	.98802	.99557	.98985	.99630	.99152	34
27	.99298	.98396	.99391	.98608	.99478	.98805	.99558	.98988	.99631	.99155	33
28	.99300	.98400	.99393	.98612	.99479	.98808	.99559	.98990	.99633	.99157	32
29	.99301	.98404	.99394	.98615	.99481	.98812	.99561	.98993	.99634	.99160	31
30	9.99303	0.98407	9.99396	0.98618	9.99482	0.98815	9.99562	0.98996	9.99635	0.99163	30
31	.99304	.98411	.99397	.98622	.99484	.98818	.99563	.98999	.99636	.99165	29
32	.99306	.98415	.99399	.98625	.99485	.98821	.99564	.99002	.99637	.99168	28
33	.99308	.98418	.99400	.98629	.99486	.98824	.99566	.99005	.99638	.99171	27
34	.99309	.98422	.99402	.98632	.99488	.98827	.99567	.99008	.99639	.99173	26
35	9.99311	0.98426	9.99403	0.98635	9.99489	0.98830	9.99568	0.99011	9.99641	0.99176	25
36	.99312	.98429	.99405	.98639	.99490	.98834	.99569	.99014	.99642	.99179	24
37	.99314	.98433	.99406	.98642	.99492	.98837	.99571	.99016	.99643	.99181	23
38	.99316	.98436	.99408	.98646	.99493	.98840	.99572	.99019	.99644	.99184	22
39	.99317	.98440	.99409	.98649	.99495	.98843	.99573	.99022	.99645	.99186	21
40	9.99319	0.98444	9.99411	0.98652	9.99496	0.98846	9.99575	0.99025	9.99646	0.99189	20
41	.99320	.98447	.99412	.98656	.99497	.98849	.99576	.99028	.99648	.99192	19
42	.99322	.98451	.99414	.98659	.99499	.98852	.99577	.99031	.99649	.99194	18
43	.99324	.98454	.99415	.98662	.99500	.98855	.99578	.99034	.99650	.99197	17
44	.99325	.98458	.99417	.98666	.99501	.98858	.99580	.99036	.99651	.99199	16
45	9.99327	0.98462	9.99418	0.98669	9.99503	0.98862	9.99581	0.99039	9.99652	0.99202	15
46	.99328	.98465	.99420	.98672	.99504	.98865	.99582	.99042	.99653	.99205	14
47	.99330	.98469	.99421	.98676	.99505	.98868	.99583	.99045	.99654	.99207	13
48	.99331	.98472	.99422	.98679	.99507	.98871	.99584	.99048	.99655	.99210	12
49	.99333	.98476	.99424	.98682	.99508	.98874	.99586	.99051	.99657	.99212	11
50	9.99335	0.98479	9.99425	0.98686	9.99510	0.98877	9.99587	0.99053	9.99658	0.99215	10
51	.99336	.98483	.99427	.98689	.99511	.98880	.99588	.99056	.99659	.99217	9
52	.99338	.98487	.99429	.98692	.99512	.98883	.99589	.99059	.99660	.99220	8
53	.99339	.98490	.99430	.98695	.99514	.98886	.99591	.99062	.99661	.99223	7
54	.99341	.98494	.99431	.98699	.99515	.98889	.99592	.99065	.99662	.99225	6
55	9.99342	0.98497	9.99433	0.98702	9.99516	0.98892	9.99593	0.99067	9.99663	0.99228	5
56	.99344	.98501	.99434	.98705	.99518	.98895	.99594	.99070	.99664	.99230	4
57	.99345	.98504	.99436	.98709	.99519	.98898	.99596	.99073	.99666	.99233	3
58	.99347	.98508	.99437	.98712	.99520	.98901	.99597	.99076	.99667	.99235	2
59	.99349	.98511	.99438	.98715	.99522	.98904	.99598	.99079	.99668	.99238	1
60	9.99350	0.98515	9.99440	0.98719	9.99523	0.98907	9.99599	0.99081	9.99669	0.99240	0
	194°		193°		192°		191°		190°		

Haversines

′	170°		171°		172°		173°		174°		′
	Log Hav	Nat. Hav	Log Hav	Nat. Hav	Log Hav	Nat. Hav	Log Hav	Nat. Hav	Log Hav	Nat. Hav	
0	9. 99669	0. 99240	9. 99732	0. 99384	9. 99788	0. 99513	9. 99838	0. 99627	9. 99881	0. 99726	60
1	. 99670	. 99243	. 99733	. 99387	. 99789	. 99515	. 99839	. 99629	. 99882	. 99728	59
2	. 99671	. 99245	. 99734	. 99389	. 99790	. 99517	. 99839	. 99631	. 99882	. 99729	58
3	. 99672	. 99248	. 99735	. 99391	. 99791	. 99519	. 99840	. 99633	. 99883	. 99731	57
4	. 99673	. 99250	. 99736	. 99393	. 99792	. 99521	. 99841	. 99634	. 99884	. 99732	56
5	9. 99674	0. 99253	9. 99737	0. 99396	9. 99793	0. 99523	9. 99842	0. 99636	9. 99884	0. 99734	55
6	. 99675	. 99255	. 99738	. 99398	. 99793	. 99525	. 99842	. 99638	. 99885	. 99735	54
7	. 99677	. 99258	. 99739	. 99400	. 99794	. 99527	. 99843	. 99640	. 99885	. 99737	53
8	. 99678	. 99260	. 99740	. 99402	. 99795	. 99529	. 99844	. 99641	. 99886	. 99738	52
9	. 99679	. 99263	. 99741	. 99405	. 99796	. 99531	. 99845	. 99643	. 99887	. 99740	51
10	9. 99680	0. 99265	9. 99742	0. 99407	9. 99797	0. 99533	9. 99845	0. 99645	9. 99887	0. 99741	50
11	. 99681	. 99268	. 99743	. 99409	. 99798	. 99535	. 99846	. 99647	. 99888	. 99743	49
12	. 99682	. 99270	. 99744	. 99411	. 99799	. 99537	. 99847	. 99648	. 99889	. 99744	48
13	. 99683	. 99273	. 99745	. 99414	. 99800	. 99539	. 99848	. 99650	. 99889	. 99746	47
14	. 99684	. 99275	. 99746	. 99416	. 99800	. 99541	. 99848	. 99652	. 99890	. 99747	46
15	9. 99685	0. 99278	9. 99747	0. 99418	9. 99801	0. 99543	9. 99849	0. 99653	9. 99891	0. 99748	45
16	. 99686	. 99280	. 99748	. 99420	. 99802	. 99545	. 99850	. 99655	. 99891	. 99750	44
17	. 99687	. 99283	. 99748	. 99422	. 99803	. 99547	. 99851	. 99657	. 99892	. 99751	43
18	. 99688	. 99285	. 99749	. 99425	. 99804	. 99549	. 99851	. 99659	. 99893	. 99753	42
19	. 99690	. 99288	. 99750	. 99427	. 99805	. 99551	. 99852	. 99660	. 99893	. 99754	41
20	9. 99691	0. 99290	9. 99751	0. 99429	9. 99805	0. 99553	9. 99853	0. 99662	9. 99894	0. 99756	40
21	. 99692	. 99293	. 99752	. 99431	. 99806	. 99555	. 99854	. 99664	. 99894	. 99757	39
22	. 99693	. 99295	. 99753	. 99433	. 99807	. 99557	. 99854	. 99665	. 99895	. 99759	38
23	. 99694	. 99297	. 99754	. 99436	. 99808	. 99559	. 99855	. 99667	. 99896	. 99760	37
24	. 99695	. 99300	. 99755	. 99438	. 99809	. 99561	. 99856	. 99669	. 99896	. 99761	36
25	9. 99696	0. 99302	9. 99756	0. 99440	9. 99810	0. 99563	9. 99857	0. 99670	9. 99897	0. 99763	35
26	. 99697	. 99305	. 99757	. 99442	. 99811	. 99565	. 99857	. 99672	. 99897	. 99764	34
27	. 99698	. 99307	. 99758	. 99444	. 99811	. 99567	. 99858	. 99674	. 99898	. 99766	33
28	. 99699	. 99309	. 99759	. 99446	. 99812	. 99568	. 99859	. 99675	. 99899	. 99767	32
29	. 99700	. 99312	. 99760	. 99449	. 99813	. 99570	. 99859	. 99677	. 99899	. 99768	31
30	9. 99701	0. 99314	9. 99761	0. 99451	9. 99814	0. 99572	9. 99860	0. 99679	9. 99900	0. 99770	30
31	. 99702	. 99317	. 99762	. 99453	. 99815	. 99574	. 99861	. 99680	. 99901	. 99771	29
32	. 99703	. 99319	. 99763	. 99455	. 99815	. 99576	. 99862	. 99682	. 99901	. 99773	28
33	. 99704	. 99321	. 99764	. 99457	. 99816	. 99578	. 99862	. 99684	. 99902	. 99774	27
34	. 99705	. 99324	. 99765	. 99459	. 99817	. 99580	. 99863	. 99685	. 99902	. 99775	26
35	9. 99706	0. 99326	9. 99766	0. 99461	9. 99818	0. 99582	9. 99864	0. 99687	9. 99903	0. 99777	25
36	. 99707	. 99329	. 99766	. 99464	. 99819	. 99584	. 99864	. 99688	. 99904	. 99778	24
37	. 99708	. 99331	. 99767	. 99466	. 99820	. 99585	. 99865	. 99690	. 99904	. 99779	23
38	. 99710	. 99333	. 99768	. 99468	. 99820	. 99587	. 99866	. 99692	. 99905	. 99781	22
39	. 99711	. 99336	. 99769	. 99470	. 99821	. 99589	. 99867	. 99693	. 99905	. 99782	21
40	9. 99712	0. 99338	9. 99770	0. 99472	9. 99822	0. 99591	9. 99867	0. 99695	9. 99906	0. 99784	20
41	. 99713	. 99340	. 99771	. 99474	. 99823	. 99593	. 99868	. 99696	. 99906	. 99785	19
42	. 99714	. 99343	. 99772	. 99476	. 99824	. 99595	. 99869	. 99698	. 99907	. 99786	18
43	. 99715	. 99345	. 99773	. 99478	. 99824	. 99597	. 99869	. 99700	. 99908	. 99788	17
44	. 99716	. 99347	. 99774	. 99480	. 99825	. 99598	. 99870	. 99701	. 99908	. 99789	16
45	9. 99717	0. 99350	9. 99774	0. 99483	9. 99826	0. 99600	9. 99871	0. 99703	9. 99909	0. 99790	15
46	. 99718	. 99352	. 99775	. 99485	. 99827	. 99602	. 99871	. 99704	. 99909	. 99792	14
47	. 99719	. 99354	. 99776	. 99487	. 99828	. 99604	. 99872	. 99706	. 99910	. 99793	13
48	. 99720	. 99357	. 99777	. 99489	. 99828	. 99606	. 99873	. 99708	. 99911	. 99794	12
49	. 99721	. 99359	. 99778	. 99491	. 99829	. 99608	. 99874	. 99709	. 99911	. 99796	11
50	9. 99722	0. 99361	9. 99779	0. 99493	9. 99830	0. 99609	9. 99874	0. 99711	9. 99912	0. 99797	10
51	. 99723	. 99364	. 99780	. 99495	. 99831	. 99611	. 99875	. 99712	. 99912	. 99798	9
52	. 99724	. 99366	. 99781	. 99497	. 99832	. 99613	. 99876	. 99714	. 99913	. 99799	8
53	. 99725	. 99368	. 99782	. 99499	. 99832	. 99615	. 99876	. 99715	. 99913	. 99801	7
54	. 99726	. 99371	. 99783	. 99501	. 99833	. 99617	. 99877	. 99717	. 99914	. 99802	6
55	9. 99727	0. 99373	9. 99784	0. 99503	9. 99834	0. 99618	9. 99878	0. 99718	9. 99915	0. 99803	5
56	. 99728	. 99375	. 99785	. 99505	. 99835	. 99620	. 99878	. 99720	. 99915	. 99805	4
57	. 99729	. 99378	. 99786	. 99507	. 99836	. 99622	. 99879	. 99722	. 99916	. 99806	3
58	. 99730	. 99380	. 99786	. 99509	. 99836	. 99624	. 99880	. 99723	. 99916	. 99807	2
59	. 99731	. 99382	. 99787	. 99511	. 99837	. 99626	. 99880	. 99725	. 99917	. 99808	1
60	9. 99732	0. 99384	9. 99788	0. 99513	9. 99838	0. 99627	9. 99881	0. 99726	9. 99917	0. 99810	0
	189°		188°		187°		186°		185°		

Haversines

′	175°		176°		177°		178°		179°		′
	Log Hav	Nat. Hav	Log Hav	Nat. Hav	Log Hav	Nat. Hav	Log Hav	Nat. Hav	Log Hav	Nat. Hav	
0	9.99917	0.99810	9.99947	0.99878	9.99970	0.99931	9.99987	0.99970	9.99997	0.99992	60
1	.99918	.99811	.99948	.99879	.99971	.99932	.99987	.99970	.99997	.99993	59
2	.99918	.99812	.99948	.99880	.99971	.99933	.99987	.99971	.99997	.99993	58
3	.99919	.99814	.99948	.99881	.99971	.99934	.99987	.99971	.99997	.99993	57
4	.99919	.99815	.99949	.99882	.99972	.99934	.99988	.99972	.99997	.99993	56
5	9.99920	0.99816	9.99949	0.99883	9.99972	0.99935	9.99988	0.99972	9.99997	0.99994	55
6	.99921	.99817	.99950	.99884	.99972	.99936	.99988	.99973	.99997	.99994	54
7	.99921	.99819	.99950	.99885	.99973	.99937	.99988	.99973	.99997	.99994	53
8	.99922	.99820	.99951	.99886	.99973	.99937	.99988	.99973	.99998	.99994	52
9	.99922	.99821	.99951	.99887	.99973	.99938	.99989	.99974	.99998	.99994	51
10	9.99923	0.99822	9.99951	0.99888	9.99973	0.99939	9.99989	0.99974	9.99998	0.99995	50
11	.99923	.99823	.99952	.99889	.99974	.99940	.99989	.99975	.99998	.99995	49
12	.99924	.99825	.99952	.99890	.99974	.99940	.99989	.99975	.99998	.99995	48
13	.99924	.99826	.99953	.99891	.99974	.99941	.99989	.99976	.99998	.99995	47
14	.99925	.99827	.99953	.99892	.99975	.99942	.99990	.99976	.99998	.99996	46
15	9.99925	0.99828	9.99953	0.99893	9.99975	0.99942	9.99990	0.99977	9.99998	0.99996	45
16	.99926	.99829	.99954	.99894	.99975	.99943	.99990	.99977	.99998	.99996	44
17	.99926	.99831	.99954	.99895	.99976	.99944	.99990	.99978	.99998	.99996	43
18	.99927	.99832	.99954	.99896	.99976	.99944	.99990	.99978	.99998	.99996	42
19	.99927	.99833	.99955	.99897	.99976	.99945	.99991	.99978	.99998	.99996	41
20	9.99928	0.99834	9.99955	0.99898	9.99976	0.99946	9.99991	0.99979	9.99999	0.99997	40
21	.99928	.99835	.99956	.99899	.99977	.99947	.99991	.99979	.99999	.99997	39
22	.99929	.99837	.99956	.99900	.99977	.99947	.99991	.99980	.99999	.99997	38
23	.99929	.99838	.99957	.99900	.99977	.99948	.99991	.99980	.99999	.99997	37
24	.99930	.99839	.99957	.99901	.99978	.99949	.99992	.99981	.99999	.99997	36
25	9.99931	0.99840	9.99958	0.99902	9.99978	0.99949	9.99992	0.99981	9.99999	0.99997	35
26	.99931	.99841	.99958	.99903	.999'8	.99950	.99992	.99981	.99999	.99998	34
27	.99932	.99842	.99958	.99904	.99978	.99950	.99992	.99982	.99999	.99998	33
28	.99932	.99844	.99959	.99905	.99979	.99951	.99992	.99982	.99999	.99998	32
29	.99933	.99845	.99959	.99906	.99979	.99952	.99992	.99982	.99999	.99998	31
30	9.99933	0.99846	9.99959	0.99907	9.99979	0.99952	9.99993	0.99983	9.99999	0.99998	30
31	.99934	.99847	.99960	.99908	.99980	.99953	.99993	.99983	.99999	.99998	29
32	.99934	.99848	.99960	.99909	.99980	.99954	.99993	.99984	.99999	.99998	28
33	.99935	.99849	.99961	.99909	.99980	.99954	.99993	.99984	.99999	.99998	27
34	.99935	.99850	.99961	.99910	.99980	.99955	.99993	.99984	.99999	.99999	26
35	9.99935	0.99852	9.99961	0.99911	9.99981	0.99956	9.99993	0.99985	9.99999	0.99999	25
36	.99936	.99853	.99962	.99912	.99981	.99956	.99994	.99985	9.99999	.99999	24
37	.99936	.99854	.99962	.99913	.99981	.99957	.99994	.99985	0.00000	.99999	23
38	.99937	.99855	.99963	.99914	.99981	.99957	.99994	.99986	.00000	.99999	22
39	.99937	.99856	.99963	.99915	.99982	.99958	.99994	.99986	.00000	.99999	21
40	9.99938	0.99857	9.99963	0.99915	9.99982	0.99959	9.99994	0.99986	0.00000	0.99999	20
41	.99938	.99858	.99964	.99916	.99982	.99959	.99994	.99987	.00000	.99999	19
42	.99939	.99859	.99964	.99917	.99983	.99960	.99994	.99987	.00000	.99999	18
43	.99939	.99860	.99964	.99918	.99983	.99960	.99995	.99987	.00000	.99999	17
44	.99940	.99861	.99965	.99919	.99983	.99961	.99995	.99988	.00000	.99999	16
45	9.99940	0.99863	9.99965	0.99920	9.99983	0.99961	9.99995	0.99988	0.00000	1.00000	15
46	.99941	.99864	.99965	.99920	.99983	.99962	.99995	.99988	.00000	.00000	14
47	.99941	.99865	.99966	.99921	.99984	.99963	.99995	.99989	.00000	.00000	13
48	.99942	.99866	.99966	.99922	.99984	.99963	.99995	.99989	.00000	.00000	12
49	.99942	.99867	.99966	.99923	.99984	.99964	.99995	.99989	.00000	.00000	11
50	9.99943	0.99868	9.99967	0.99924	9.99984	0.99964	9.99996	0.99990	0.00000	1.00000	10
51	.99943	.99869	.99967	.99924	.99985	.99965	.99996	.99990	.00000	.00000	9
52	.99943	.99870	.99968	.99925	.99985	.99965	.99996	.99990	.00000	.00000	8
53	.99944	.99871	.99968	.99926	.99985	.99966	.99996	.99991	.00000	.00000	7
54	.99944	.99872	.99968	.99927	.99985	.99966	.99996	.99991	.00000	.00000	6
55	9.99945	0.99873	9.99969	0.99928	9.99986	0.99967	9.99996	0.99991	0 .00000	1.00000	5
56	.99945	.99874	.99969	.99928	.99986	.99967	.99996	.99991	.00000	.00000	4
57	.99946	.99875	.99969	.99929	.99986	.99968	.99996	.99992	.00000	.00000	3
58	.99946	.99876	.99970	.99930	.99986	.99969	.99996	.99992	.00000	.00000	2
59	.99947	.99877	.99970	.99931	.99987	.99969	.99997	.99992	.00000	.00000	1
60	9.99947	0.99878	9.99970	0.99931	9.99987	0.99970	9.99997	0.99992	0.00000	1.00000	0
	184°		183°		182°		181°		180°		

APPENDIX C

CONVERSION OF COMPASS POINTS TO DEGREES

Conversion of Compass Points to Degrees					
	Points	Angular measure		Points	Angular measure
NORTH TO EAST		° ′ ″	SOUTH TO WEST		° ′ ″
North	0	0 00 00	South	16	180 00 00
N1/4E	1/4	2 48 45	S1/4W	16 1/4	182 48 45
N1/2E	1/2	5 37 30	S1/2W	16 1/2	185 37 30
N3/4E	3/4	8 26 15	S3/4W	16 3/4	188 26 15
N by E	1	11 15 00	S by W	17	191 15 00
N by E1/4E	1 1/4	14 03 45	S by W1/4W	17 1/4	194 03 45
N by E1/2E	1 1/2	16 52 30	S by W1/2W	17 1/2	196 52 30
N by E3/4E	1 3/4	19 41 15	S by W3/4W	17 3/4	199 41 15
NNE	2	22 30 00	SSW	18	202 30 00
NNE1/4E	2 1/4	25 18 45	SSW1/4W	18 1/4	205 18 45
NNE1/2E	2 1/2	28 07 30	SSW1/2W	18 1/2	208 07 30
NNE3/4E	2 3/4	30 56 15	SSW3/4W	18 3/4	210 56 15
NE by N	3	33 45 00	SW by S	19	213 45 00
NE3/4N	3 1/4	36 33 45	SW3/4S	19 1/4	216 33 45
NE1/2N	3 1/2	39 22 30	SW1/2S	19 1/2	219 22 30
NE1/4N	3 3/4	42 11 15	SW1/4S	19 3/4	222 11 15
NE	4	45 00 00	SW	20	225 00 00
NE1/4E	4 1/4	47 48 45	SW1/4W	20 1/4	227 48 45
NE1/2E	4 1/2	50 37 30	SW1/2W	20 1/2	230 37 30
NE3/4E	4 3/4	53 26 15	SW3/4W	20 3/4	233 26 15
NE by E	5	56 15 00	SW by W	21	236 15 00
NE by E1/4E	5 1/4	59 03 45	SW by W1/4W	21 1/4	239 03 45
NE by E1/2E	5 1/2	61 52 30	SW by W1/2W	21 1/2	241 52 30
NE by E3/4E	5 3/4	64 41 15	SW by W3/4W	21 3/4	244 41 15
ENE	6	67 30 00	WSW	22	247 30 00
ENE1/4E	6 1/4	70 18 45	WSW1/4W	22 1/4	250 18 45
ENE1/2E	6 1/2	73 07 30	WSW1/2W	22 1/2	235 07 30
ENE3/4E	6 3/4	75 56 15	WSW3/4W	22 3/4	255 56 15

Conversion of Compass Points to Degrees					
E by N	7	78 45 00	W by S	23	258 45 00
E3/4N	7 1/4	81 33 45	W3/4S	23 1/4	261 33 45
E1/2N	7 1/2	84 22 30	W1/2S	23 1/2	264 22 30
E1/4N	7 3/4	87 11 15	W1/4S	23 3/4	267 11 15
EAST TO SOUTH			WEST TO NORTH		
East	8	00 00 00	West	24	270 00 00
E1/4S	8 1/4	92 48 45	W1/4N	24 1/4	272 48 45
E1/2S	8 1/2	95 37 30	W1/2N	24 1/2	275 37 30
E3/4S	8 3/4	98 26 15	W3/4N	24 3/4	278 26 15
E by S	9	101 15 00	W by N	25	281 15 00
ESE3/4E	9 1/4	104 03 45	WNW3/4W	25 1/4	284 03 45
ESE1/2E	9 1/2	106 52 30	WNW1/2W	25 1/2	286 52 30
ESE1/4E	9 3/4	109 41 15	WNW1/4W	25 3/4	289 41 15
ESE	10	112 30 00	WNW	26	292 30 00
SE by E3/4E	10 1/4	115 18 45	NW by W3/4W	26 1/4	295 18 45
SE by E1/2E	10 1/2	118 07 30	NW by W1/2W	26 1/2	298 07 30
SE by E1/4E	10 3/4	120 56 15	NW by W1/4W	26 3/4	300 56 15
SE by E	11	123 45 00	NW by W	27	303 45 00
SE3/4E	11 1/4	126 33 45	NW3/4W	27 1/4	306 33 45
SE1/2E	11 1/2	129 22 30	NW1/2W	27 1/2	309 22 30
SE1/4E	11 3/4	132 11 15	NW1/4W	27 3/4	312 11 15
SE	12	135 00 00	NW	28	315 00 00
SE1/4S	12 1/4	137 48 45	NW1/4N	28 1/4	317 48 45
SE1/2S	12 1/2	140 37 30	NW1/2N	28 1/2	320 37 30
SE3/4S	12 3/4	143 26 15	NW3/4N	28 3/4	323 26 15
SE by S	13	146 15 00	NW by N	29	326 15 00
SSE3/4E	13 1/4	149 03 45	NNW3/4W	29 1/4	329 03 45
SSE1/2E	13 1/2	151 52 30	NNW1/2W	29 1/2	331 52 30
SSE1/4E	13 3/4	154 41 15	NNW1/4W	29 3/4	334 41 15
SSE	14	157 30 00	NNW	30	337 30 00
S by E3/4E	14 1/4	160 18 45	N by W3/4W	30 1/4	340 18 45
S by E1/2E	14 1/2	163 07 30	N by W1/2W	30 1/2	343 07 30
S by E1/4E	14 3/4	165 56 15	N by W1/4W	30 3/4	345 56 15
S by E	15	168 45 00	N by W	31	348 45 00
S3/4E	15 1/4	171 33 45	N3/4W	31 1/4	351 33 45
S1/2E	15 1/2	174 22 30	N1/2W	31 1/2	354 22 30

Conversion of Compass Points to Degrees					
S1/4E	15 3/4	177 11 15	N1/4W	31 3/4	357 11 15
South	16	180 00 00	North	32	360 00 00

GLOSSARY
OF
MARINE NAVIGATION

A

abaft., *adv.* In a direction farther aft in a ship than a specified reference position, such as abaft the mast. See also ABAFT THE BEAM, AFT, ASTERN.

abaft the beam.. Any direction between broad on the beam and astern. See also FORWARD OF THE BEAM.

abampere., *n.* The unit of current in the centimeter-gram-second electromagnetic system. The abampere is 10 amperes.

abeam., *adv.* In a line approximately at right angle to the ship's keel or centerline - opposite the waist or middle part of a ship. See also BROAD ON THE BEAM.

aberration., *n.* 1. The apparent displacement of a celestial body in the direction of motion of the earth in its orbit caused by the motion of the earth combined with the finite velocity of light. When, in addition to the combined effect of the velocity of light and the motion of the earth, account is taken of the motion of the celestial body in space during the interval that the light is traveling to the earth from the luminous body, as in the case of planets, the phenomenon is termed planetary aberration. The aberration due to the rotation of the earth on its axis is termed diurnal aberration or daily aberration. The aberration due to the revolution of the earth about the sun is termed annual aberration. The aberration due to the motion of the center of mass of the solar system in space is termed secular aberration but is not taken into account in practical astronomy. See also CONSTANT OF ABERRATION. 2. The convergence to different foci, by a lens or mirror, of parallel rays of light. In a single lens having spherical surfaces, aberration may be caused by differences in the focal lengths of the various parts of the lens: rays passing through the outer part of the lens come to a focus nearer the lens than do rays passing through its central part. This is termed spherical aberration and, being due to the faulty figure of the lens, is eliminated by correcting that figure. A lens so corrected is called an aplanatic lens. Aberration may also result from differences in the wavelengths of light of different colors: light of the shorter wavelengths (violet end of the spectrum) comes to a focus nearer the lens than light of the longer wavelengths (red end of the spectrum). This is termed chromatic aberration, and is practically eliminated over a moderate range of wavelengths by using a composite lens, called an achromatic lens, composed of parts having different dispersive powers.

aberration constant.. See CONSTANT OF ABERRATION.

ablation., *n.* Wasting of snow or ice by melting or evaporation.

abnormal., *adj.* Deviating from normal.

abrasion., *n.* Rubbing or wearing away, or the result of such action.

abroholos., *n.* A squall frequent from May through August between Cabo de Sao Tome and Cabo Frio on the coast of Brazil.

abrupt., *adv.* Steep, precipitous. See also BOLD.

abscissa., *n.* The horizontal coordinate of a set of rectangular coordinates. Also used in a similar sense in connection with oblique coordinates.

absolute.. Pertaining to measurement relative to a universal constant or natural datum.

absolute accuracy.. The ability of a navigation or positioning system to define an exact location in relation to a coordinate system.

absolute gain.. See ISOTROPIC GAIN (of an antenna).

absolute humidity.. The mass of water vapor per unit volume of air.

absolute motion.. Motion relative to a fixed point. If the earth were stationary in space, any change in the position of another body, relative to the earth, would be due only to the motion of that body. This would be absolute motion, or motion relative to a fixed point. Actual motion is motion of an object relative to the earth.

absolute temperature.. Temperature measured from absolute zero which is 0°K on the Kelvin scale, -459.69°F on the Fahrenheit scale, and -273.16°C on the Celsius scale. The sizes of the Kelvin and Celsius degree are equal. The size of a degree on the Fahrenheit scale equals that on the Rankine scale.

absolute value.. The value of a real number without regard to sign. Thus, the absolute value of +8 or -8 is $|8|$. Vertical lines on each side of a number indicate that its absolute value is intended.

absorption.. The process by which radiant energy is absorbed and converted to other forms of energy. See ATTENUATION.

absolute zero.. The theoretical temperature at which molecular motion ceases, -459.69°F or -273.16°C.

abyss., *n.* A very deep area of the ocean. The term is used to refer to a particular deep part of the ocean, or to any part below 300 fathoms.

abyssal plain.. See under PLAIN.

accelerate., *v., t.* To move or cause to move with increasing velocity.

acceleration., *n.* 1. The rate of change of velocity. 2. The act or process of accelerating, or the state of being accelerated. Negative acceleration is called DECELERATION.

acceleration error.. The error resulting from change in velocity (either speed or direction); specifically, deflection of the apparent vertical, as indicated by an artificial horizon, due to acceleration. Also called BUBBLE ACCELERATION ERROR when applied to an instrument using a bubble as an artificial horizon.

accelerometer., *n.* A device used to measure the accelerations of a craft, resulting from the craft's acceleration with respect to the earth, acceleration of gravity, and Coriolis acceleration.

accidental error.. See RANDOM ERROR. An error of accidental nature. (Not to be confused with MISTAKE.)

accretion., *n.* Accumulation of material on the surface of an object.

accuracy., *n.* 1. In navigation, a measure of the difference between the position indicated by measurement and the true position. Some expressions of accuracy are defined in terms of probability. 2. A measure of how close the outcome of a series of observations or measurements approaches the true value of a desired quantity. The degree of exactness with which the true value of the quantity is determined from observations is limited by the presence of both systematic and random errors. Accuracy should not be confused with PRECISION, which is a measure of the repeatability of the observations. Observations may be of high precision due to the quality of the observing instrument, the skill of the observer and the resulting small random errors, but inaccurate due to the presence of large systematic errors. Accuracy implies precision, but precision does not imply accuracy. See also ERROR, RADIAL ERROR, ABSOLUTE ACCURACY, PREDICTABLE ACCURACY, RELATIVE ACCURACY, REPEATABLE ACCURACY.

achromatic lens.. See under ABERRATION, definition 2.

aclinal., *adj.* Without dip; horizontal.

aclinic., *adj.* Without magnetic dip.

aclinic line.. The magnetic equator; the line on the surface of the earth connecting all points of zero magnetic dip.

acoustic depth finder.. See ECHO SOUNDER.

acoustic navigation.. See SONIC NAVIGATION.

acoustics., *n.* 1. That branch of physics dealing with sound. 2. The sound characteristics of a room, auditorium, etc., which determine its quality with respect to distinct hearing.

acoustic sounding.. See ECHO SOUNDING.

acquisition., *n.* The selection of those targets or satellites requiring a tracking procedure and the initiation of their tracking.

acre., *n.* A unit of area equal to 43,560 square feet.

across-the-scope echo. . See CLASSIFICATION OF RADAR ECHOES.

active satellite. . 1. An artificial satellite which transmits an electromagnetic signal. A satellite with the capability to transmit, repeat, or retransmit electromagnetic information, as contrasted with PASSIVE SATELLITE. 2. As defined by International Telecommunications Union (ITU), an earth satellite carrying a station intended to transmit or retransmit radio communication signals.

active tracking system. . A satellite tracking system which operates by transmission of signals to and receipt of responses from the satellite.

actual motion. . Motion of an object relative to the earth. See also MOTION.

acute angle. . An angle less than 90°.

acute triangle. . A triangle with three acute angles.

additional secondary phase factor correction. A correction in addition to the secondary phase factor correction for the additional time (or phase delay) for transmission of a low frequency signal over a composite land-water path when the signal transit time is based on the free-space velocity.

ADF reversal. . The swinging of the needle on the direction indicator of an automatic direction finder through 180°, indicating that the station to which the direction finder is tuned has been passed.

adiabatic. , *adj.* Referring to a thermodynamic change of state of a system in which there is no transfer of heat or mass across the boundaries of the system. In an adiabatic process, compression causes warming, expansion causes cooling.

adjacent angles. . Two angles having a common vertex and lying at opposite ends of a common side.

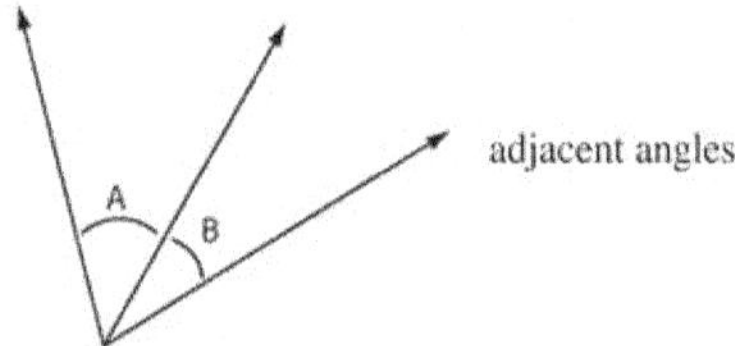

adjustment, *n.* The determination and application of corrections to observations, for the purpose of reducing errors or removing internal inconsistencies in derived results.

admiralty. . Pertaining to the body of law that governs maritime affairs.

adrift. , *adj.* & *adv.* Afloat and unattached to the shore or the sea bottom, and without propulsive power. See also UNDERWAY.

advance. , *n.* 1. The distance a vessel moves in its initial direction from the point where the rudder is started over until the heading has changed 90°. 2. The distance a vessel moves in the initial direction for heading changes of less than 90°. See also TRANSFER.

advance. , *v., t.* & *i.* To move forward, as to move a line of position forward, parallel to itself, along a course line to obtain a line of position at a later time. The opposite is RETIRE.

advanced line of position. . A line of position which has been moved forward along the course line to allow for the run since the line was established. The opposite is RETIRED LINE OF POSITION.

advection. , *n.* Transport of atmospheric properties solely by mass motion of the atmosphere. WIND refers to air motion, while advection refers more specifically to the transfer of any property of the atmosphere (temperature, humidity, etc.) from one area to another.

advection fog. . A type of fog caused by the advection of moist air over a cold surface, and the consequent cooling of that air to below its dew point. SEA FOG is a very common advection fog that is caused by moist air in transport over a cold body of water.

aero light. . Short for AERONAUTICAL LIGHT.

aeromarine light. . A marine light having part of its beam deflected to an angle of 10° to 15° above the horizon for use by aircraft.

aeromarine radiobeacon. . A radiobeacon established for use by both mariners and airmen.

aeronautical. , *adj.* Of or pertaining to the operation or navigation of aircraft.

aeronautical beacon. . A visual aid to navigation, displaying flashes of white or colored light or both, used to indicate the location of airports, landmarks, and certain points of the Federal airways in mountainous terrain and to mark hazards.

aeronautical chart. . See under CHART.

aeronautical light. . A luminous or lighted aid to navigation intended primarily for air navigation. Often shortened to AERO LIGHT.

aeronautical radiobeacon. . A radiobeacon whose service is intended primarily for aircraft.

aestival. , *adj.* Pertaining to summer. The corresponding adjectives for fall, winter, and spring are autumnal, hibernal and vernal.

affluent. , *n.* A stream flowing into a larger stream or lake; a tributary.

afloat. , *adj.* & *adv.* Floating on the water; water-borne. See also SURFACED, UNCOVERED, AGROUND, ASHORE.

aft. , *adv.* Near, toward, or at the stern of a ship. See also ABAFT, ASTERN.

afterglow. , *n.* 1. The slowly decaying luminescence of the screen of the cathode-ray tube after excitation by an electron beam has ceased. See also PERSISTENCE. 2. A broad, high arch of radiance or glow seen occasionally in the western sky above the highest clouds in deepening twilight, caused by the scattering effect of very fine particles of dust suspended in the upper atmosphere.

aged ridge. . A ridge of ice forced up by pressure which has undergone considerable weathering.

age of diurnal inequality. . The time interval between the maximum semimonthly north or south declination of the moon and the maximum effect of the declination upon the range of tide or the speed of the tidal current; this effect is manifested chiefly by an increase in the height or speed difference between the two high (low) waters or flood (ebb) currents during the day. The tides occurring at this time are called TROPIC TIDES. Also called DIURNAL AGE.

age of parallax inequality. . The time interval between perigee of the moon and the maximum effect of parallax upon the range of tide or the speed of the tidal current. See also PARALLAX INEQUALITY.

age of phase inequality. . The time interval between new or full moon and the maximum effect of these phases upon the range of tide or the speed of the tidal current. Also called AGE OF TIDE.

age of the moon. . The elapsed time, usually expressed in days, since the last new moon. See also PHASES OF THE MOON.

age of tide. . See AGE OF PHASE INEQUALITY.

Ageton. . *n.* 1. A divided triangle method of sight reduction in which a perpendicular is dropped from the GP of the body to the meridian of the observer. 2. Rear Admiral Arthur A. Ageton, USN, inventor of the Ageton method.

agger. , *n.* See DOUBLE TIDE.

agonic line. . A line joining points of no magnetic variation, a special case of an isogonic line.

agravic. , *adj.* Of or pertaining to a condition of no gravitation.

aground. , *adj.* & *adv.* Resting or lodged on the bottom.

Agulhas Current. . A generally southwestward flowing ocean current of the Indian Ocean, one of the swiftest ocean currents. To the south of latitude 30°S the Agulhas Current is a well-defined and narrow current that extends less than 100 kilometers from the coast of South Africa. To the south of South Africa the greatest volume of its water bends sharply to the south and then toward the east, thus returning to the Indian Ocean.

ahead. , *adv.* Bearing approximately 000° relative. The term is often used loosely for DEAD AHEAD or bearing exactly 000° relative. The opposite is ASTERN.

ahead reach. . The distance traveled by a vessel proceeding ahead at full power from the time the engines are reversed until she is at full stop.

ahull. . The condition of a vessel making no way in a storm, allowing wind and sea to determine the position of the ship. Sailing vessels lying ahull lash the helm alee, and may carry storm sails.

aid. , *n.* Short for AID TO NAVIGATION.

aid to navigation. . A device or structure external to a craft, designed to assist in determination of position, to define a safe course, or to warn of dangers or obstructions. If the information is transmitted by light waves, the device is called a visual aid to navigation; if by sound waves, an audible aid to navigation; if by radio waves; a radio aid to navigation. Any aid to navigation using electronic equipment, whether or not radio waves are involved, may be called an electronic aid to navigation. Compare with NAVIGATIONAL AID, meaning an instrument, device, chart, method, etc., intended to assist in the navigation of a craft.

air. , *n.* 1. The mixture of gases comprising the earth's atmosphere. It is composed of about 78% nitrogen, 21% oxygen, 1% other gases, and a variable amount of impurities such as water vapor, suspended dust particles, smoke, etc. See also ATMOSPHERE. 2. Wind of force 1 (1-3 knots or 1-3 miles per hour) on the Beaufort wind scale, called LIGHT AIR.

air almanac. . 1. A periodical publication of astronomical data designed primarily for air navigation, but often used in marine navigation. 2. *Air Almanac*, a joint publication of the U.S. Naval Observatory and H. M. Nautical Almanac Office, Royal Greenwich Observatory, designed primarily for air navigation. In general the information is similar to that of the *Nautical Almanac*, but is given to a precision of 1' of arc and 1 second of time, at intervals of 10 meters (values for the sun and Aries are given to a precision of 0.1').

air defense identification zone (ADIZ). . Airspace of defined dimensions within which the ready identification, location, and control of aircraft are required.

air mass. . An extensive body of air with fairly uniform (horizontal) physical properties, especially temperature and humidity. In its incipient stage the properties of the air mass are determined by the characteristics of the region in which it forms. It is a cold or warm air mass if it is colder or warmer than the surrounding air.

air-mass classification. . Air masses are classified according to their source regions. Four such regions are generally recognized - equatorial (E), the doldrum area between the north and south trades; tropical (T), the trade wind and lower temperate regions; polar (P), the higher temperate latitudes; and Arctic or Antarctic (A), the north or south polar regions of ice and snow. This classification is a general indication of relative temperature, as well as latitude of origin. Air masses are further classified as maritime (m) or continental (c), depending upon whether they form over water or land. This classification is an indication of the relative moisture content of the air mass. A third classification sometimes applied to tropical and polar air masses indicates whether the air mass is warm (w) or cold (k) relative to the underlying surface. The w and k classifications are primarily indications of stability, cold air being more stable.

air temperature correction. . A correction due to nonstandard air temperature, particularly the sextant altitude correction due to changes in refraction caused by difference between the actual temperature and the standard temperature used in the computation of the refraction table. The *Nautical Almanac* refraction table is based upon an air temperature of 50°F (10°C) at the surface of the earth. Refraction is greater at lower temperatures, and less at higher temperatures. The correction for air temperature varies with the temperature of the air and the altitude of the celestial body, and applies to all celestial bodies, regardless of the method of observation. It is not applied in normal navigation.

AIS. , *n.* See AUTOMATED INFORMATION SYSTEM.

alarm. . In ECDIS a device or system which alerts by audible means, or audible and visual means, a condition requiring attention.

Alaska Current. A North Pacific Ocean current flowing counterclockwise in the Gulf of Alaska. It is the northward flowing division of the Aleutian Current.

Alaska-Hawaii standard time. . See STANDARD TIME.

albedo. , *n.* The ratio of radiant energy reflected to that received by a surface, usually expressed as a percentage; reflectivity. The term generally refers to energy within a specific frequency range, as the visible spectrum. Its most frequent application in navigation is to the light reflected by a celestial body.

alert. , *n.* See ALERT TIME CALCULATIONS.

alert time calculations. . Computations of times and-altitudes of available satellite passes in a given period of time at a given location, based on orbital data transmitted from satellite memory. Sometimes called ALERT.

Aleutian Current. . An eastward flowing North Pacific Ocean current which lies north of the North Pacific Current. As it approaches the coast of North America it divides to form the northward-flowing ALASKA CURRENT, and the southward-flowing CALIFORNIA CURRENT. Also called SUBARCTIC CURRENT.

alga. *(pl. algae)*, *n.* A plant of simple structure which grows chiefly in water, such as the various forms of seaweed. It ranges in size from a microscopic plant, large numbers of which sometimes cause discoloration of water, to the giant kelp which may extend for more than 600 feet in length. The Red Sea owes its name to red algae, as does the "red tide."

algorithm. . A defined procedure or routine used for solving a specific mathematical problem.

alidade. , *n.* The part of an optical measuring instrument comprising the optical system, indicator, vernier, etc. In modern practice the term is used principally in connection with a bearing circle fitted with a telescope to facilitate observation of bearings. Also called TELESCOPIC ALIDADE.

align. , *v., t.* To place objects in line.

alignment. , *n.* 1. The placing of objects in a line. 2. The process of orienting the measuring axes of the inertial components of inertial navigation equipment with respect to the coordinate system in which the equipment is to be used.

Allard's law. . A formula relating the illuminance produced on a normal surface at a given distance from a point source of light, the intensity of the light, and the degree of transparency of the atmosphere, assumed to be uniform. See OMNIDIRECTIONAL LIGHT.

allision. . In the context of maritime law, the term allision means the act of striking of a moving vessel against a stationary object. Allision is different from collision. The term collision signifies the running of two vessels against each other.

all other information. In ECDIS used to describe information additional to the STANDARD DISPLAY. Also called ON-DEMAND INFORMATION.

all-weather, *adj.* Designed or equipped to perform by day or night under any weather conditions.

almanac. , *n.* A periodical publication of ephemeral astronomical data. If information is given in a form and to a precision suitable for marine navigation, it is called a nautical almanac. See also NAUTICAL ALMANAC; if designed primarily for air navigation, it is called an AIR ALMANAC. See also EPHEMERIS, ASTRONOMICAL ALMANAC.

almucantar. , *n.* A small circle on the celestial sphere paralleled to the horizon. Also called CIRCLE OF EQUAL ALTITUDE, PARALLEL OF ALTITUDE.

almucantar staff. . An ancient instrument formerly used for amplitude observations.

alnico. , *n.* An alloy composed principally of aluminum, nickel, cobalt, and iron; used for permanent magnets.

aloft. . Up in the rigging of a ship.

alongshore current. . See LONGSHORE CURRENT.

alphanumeric. . Referring to a set of computer characters consisting of alphabetic and numeric symbols.

alphanumeric grid. . See ATLAS GRID.

alternate blanking. . See under DUAL-RATE BLANKING.

alternating current. . An electric current that continually changes in magnitude and periodically reverses polarity.

alternating. . Referring to periodic changes in color of a lighted aid to navigation.

alternating fixed and flashing light. . A fixed light varied at regular intervals by a single flash of greater luminous intensity, with color variations in either the fixed light or flash, or both. See ALTERNATING LIGHT.

alternating fixed and group flashing light. . A fixed light varied at regular intervals by a group of two or more flashes of greater luminous intensity, with color variations in either the fixed light or flashes or both.

alternating flashing light. . A light showing a single flash with color variations at regular intervals, the duration of light being shorter than that of darkness. See also FLASHING LIGHT.

alternating group flashing light. . A group flashing light which shows periodic color change.

alternating group occulting light. . A group occulting light which shows periodic color change.

alternating occulting light. . A light totally eclipsed at regular intervals, the duration of light always being longer than the duration of darkness, which shows periodic color change. See also ALTERNATING LIGHT.

alternating light. . A light showing different colors alternately.

altitude. , *n.* Angular distance above the horizon; the arc of a vertical circle between the horizon and a point on the celestial sphere, measured upward from the horizon. Angular distance below the horizon is called negative altitude or depression. Altitude indicated by a sextant is called sextant altitude. Sextant altitude corrected only for inaccuracies in the reading (instrument, index, and personal errors, as applicable) and inaccuracies in the reference level (principally dip) is called apparent or rectified altitude. After all corrections are applied, it is called corrected sextant altitude or observed altitude. An altitude taken directly from a table, before interpolation, is called tabulated altitude. After interpolation, or if determined by calculation, mechanical device, or graphics, it is called computed altitude. If the altitude of a celestial body is computed before observation, and sextant altitude corrections are applied with reversed sign, the result is called precomputed altitude. The difference between computed and observed altitudes (corrected sextant altitudes), or between precomputed and sextant altitudes, is called altitude intercept or altitude difference. An altitude determined by inexact means, as by estimation or star finder, is called an approximate altitude. The altitude of a celestial body on the celestial meridian is called meridian altitude. The expression ex-meridian altitude is applied to the altitude of a celestial body near the celestial meridian, to which a correction is to be applied to determine the meridian altitude. A parallel of altitude is a circle of the celestial sphere parallel to the horizon, connecting all points of equal altitude. See also EQUAL ALTITUDES.

altitude azimuth. . An azimuth determined by solution of the navigational triangle with altitude, declination, and latitude given. A time azimuth is computed with meridian angle, declination, and latitude given. A time and altitude azimuth is computed with meridian angle, declination, and altitude given.

altitude circle. . See PARALLEL OF ALTITUDE.

altitude difference. . 1. See ALTITUDE INTERCEPT. 2. The change in the altitude of a celestial body occurring with change in declination, latitude, or hour angle, for example the *first difference* between successive tabulations of altitude in a latitude column of *Pub. No. 229, Sight Reduction Tables for Marine Navigation.*

altitude intercept. . The difference in minutes of arc between the computed and the observed altitude (corrected sextant altitude), or between precomputed and sextant altitudes. It is labeled T (toward) or A (away) as the observed (or sextant) altitude is greater or smaller than the computed (or precomputed) altitude. Also called ALTITUDE DIFFERENCE, INTERCEPT.

altitude intercept method. . See ST. HILAIRE METHOD.

altitude of the apogee. . As defined by the International Telecommunication Union (ITU), the altitude of the apogee above a specified reference surface serving to represent the surface of the earth.

altitude of the perigee. . As defined by the International Telecommunication Union (ITU), the altitude of the perigee above a specified reference surface serving to represent the surface of the earth.

altitude tints. . See HYPSOMETRIC TINTING.

alto-. . A prefix used in cloud classification to indicate the middle level (mean height 6,500-20,000 ft.). See also CIRRO-.

altocumulus. , *n.* Clouds within the middle level composed of flattened globular masses, the smallest elements of the regularly arranged layers being fairly thin, with or without shading. These elements are arranged in groups, in lines, or waves, following one or two directions, and are sometimes so close together that their edges join. See also CLOUD CLASSIFICATION.

altostratus. , *n.* A sheet of gray or bluish cloud within the middle level. Sometimes the sheet is composed of a compact mass of dark, thick, gray clouds of fibrous structure; at other times the sheet is thin and through it the sun or moon can be seen dimly. See also CLOUD CLASSIFICATION.

A.M. . Abbreviation for Ante Meridian; before noon in zone time.

ambient temperature. . The temperature of the air or other medium surrounding an object. See also FREE-AIR TEMPERATURE.

ambiguity. , *n.* In navigation, the condition obtained when a given set of observations defines more than one point, direction, line of position, or surface of position.

ambiguous. , *adj.* Having two or more possible meanings or values.

American Ephemeris and Nautical Almanac. . See ASTRONOMICAL ALMANAC.

American Practical Navigator, The. . A navigational text and reference book published by the National Geospatial-Intelligence Agency (NGA); originally by Nathaniel Bowditch (1773-1838). Popularly called BOWDITCH.

amidships. , *adv.* At, near, or toward the middle of a ship.

ampere. , *n.* The base unit of electric current in the International System of Units; it is that constant current which, if maintained in two straight parallel conductors of infinite length, of negligible circular cross section, and placed 1 meter apart in vacuum, would produce between these conductors a force equal to 2×10^{-7} newton per meter of length.

ampere per meter. . The derived unit of magnetic field strength in the International System of Units.

amphidromic point. . Point on a tidal chart where the cotidal lines meet.

amphidromic region. . An area surrounding a no-tide point from which the radiating cotidal lines progress through all hours of the tidal cycle.

amplification. , *n.* 1. An increase in signal magnitude from one point to another, or the process causing this increase. 2. Of a transducer, the scalar ratio of the signal output to the signal input.

amplifier. , *n.* A device which enables an input signal to control power from a source independent of the signal and thus be capable of delivering an output which is greater than the input signal.

amplitude. , *n.* 1. Angular distance of a celestial body north or south of the prime vertical circle; the arc of the horizon or the angle at the zenith between the prime vertical circle and a vertical circle through the celestial body measured north or south from the prime vertical to the vertical circle. The term is customarily used only with reference to bodies whose centers are on the celestial horizon, and is prefixed E or W, as the body is rising or setting, respectively; and suffixed N or S to agree with the declination. The prefix indicates the origin and the suffix the direction of measurement. Amplitude is designated as true, magnetic, compass, or grid as the reference direction is true, magnetic, compass, or grid east or west, respectively. 2. The maximum value of the displacement of a wave, or other periodic phenomenon, from the zero position. 3. One-half the range of a constituent tide. By analogy, it may be applied also to the maximum speed of a constituent current.

amplitude compass. . A compass intended primarily for measuring amplitude. It is graduated from 0° at east and west to 90° at north and south. Seldom used on modern vessels.

amplitude distortion. . Distortion occurring in an amplifier or other device when the output amplitude is not a linear function of the input amplitude.

amplitude modulation. . The process of changing the amplitude of a carrier wave in accordance with the variations of a modulating wave. See also MODULATION.

AMVER System. . See Automated Mutual-assistance Vessel Rescue System.

anabatic wind. . Any wind blowing up an incline. A KATABATIC WIND blows down an incline.

analemma. , *n.* A graduated scale of the declination of the sun and the equation of time for each day of the year located in the Torrid Zone on the terrestrial globe.

analemma

analog, *adj.* Referring to the processing and/or transfer of information via physical means such as waves, fluids, or mechanical devices.

analog computer. . A computer in which quantities are represented by physical variables. Problem parameters are translated into equivalent mechanical or electrical circuits as an analog for the physical phenomenon being investigated without the use of a machine language. An analog computer measures continuously; a digital computer counts discretely. See DIGITAL.

anchorage. , *n.* An area where vessels may anchor, either because of suitability or designation.

anchorage buoy. . A buoy which marks the limits of an anchorage; not to be confused with a MOORING BUOY.

anchorage chart. . A nautical chart showing prescribed or recommended anchorages.

anchorage mark. . A navigation mark which indicates an anchorage area or defines its limits.

anchor. , *n.* A device used to secure a ship to the sea floor.

anchor. , *v,t.* To use the anchor to secure a ship to the sea floor. If more than one anchor is used the ship is moored.

anchor buoy. . A buoy marking the position of an anchor on the bottom, usually painted green for the starboard anchor and red for the port anchor, and secured to the crown of the anchor by a buoy rope.

anchor ice. . Submerged ice attached or anchored to the bottom, irrespective of the nature of its formation.

anchor light. . A light shown from a vessel or aircraft to indicate its position when riding at anchor. Also called RIDING LIGHT.

anemometer. , *n.* An instrument for measuring the speed of the wind. Some instruments also indicate the direction from which it is blowing. See also VANE, definition 1; WIND INDICATOR.

aneroid barometer. . An instrument which determines atmospheric pressure by the effect of such pressure on a thin-metal cylinder from which the air has been partly exhausted. See also MERCURIAL BAROMETER.

angel. . A radar echo caused by a physical phenomenon which cannot be seen.

angle. , *n.* The inclination to each other of two intersecting lines, measured by the arc of a circle intercepted between the two lines forming the angle, the center of the circle being the point of intersection. An acute angle is less than 90°; a right angle, 90°; an obtuse angle, more than 90° but less than 180°; a straight angle 180°; a reflex angle, more than 180° but less than 360°; a perigon, 360°. Any angle not a multiple of 90 is an oblique angle. If the sum of two angles is 90°, they are complementary angles; if 180°, supplementary angles; if 360°, explementary angles. Two adjacent angles have a common vertex and lie on opposite sides of a common side. A dihedral angle is the angle between two intersecting planes. A spherical angle is the angle between two intersecting great circles.

angle of cut. . The smaller angular difference of two bearings or lines of position.

angle of depression. . The angle in a vertical plane between the horizontal and a descending line. Also called DEPRESSION ANGLE. See ANGLE OF ELEVATION.

angle of deviation. . The angle through which a ray is bent by refraction.

angle of elevation. . The angle in a vertical plane between the horizontal and an ascending line, as from an observer to an object. A negative angle of elevation is usually called an ANGLE OF DEPRESSION. Also called ELEVATION ANGLE.

angle of incidence. . The angle between the line of motion of a ray of radiant energy and the perpendicular to a surface, at the point of impingement. This angle is numerically equal to the ANGLE OF REFLECTION.

angle of reflection. . The angle between the line of motion of a ray of reflected radiant energy and the perpendicular to a surface, at the point of reflection. This angle is numerically equal to the ANGLE OF INCIDENCE.

angle of refraction. . The angle between a refracted ray and the perpendicular to the refracting surface.

angle of roll. . The angle between the transverse axis of a craft and the horizontal. Also called ROLL ANGLE.

angle of uncertainty. . The horizontal angle of the region of indefinite characteristic near the boundaries of a sector of a sector light. Also called ARC OF UNCERTAINTY.

angstrom. , *n.* A unit of length, used especially in expressing the length of light waves, equal to one ten-thousandth of a micron or one hundred millionth of a centimeter.

angular. , *adj.* Of or pertaining to an angle or angles.

angular distance. . 1. The angular difference between two directions, numerically equal to the angle between two lines extending in the given directions. 2. The arc of the great circle joining two points, expressed in angular units. 3. Distance between two points, expressed in angular units of a specified frequency. It is equal to the number of waves between the points multiplied by 2π if expressed in radians, or multiplied by 360° if measured in degrees.

angular distortion. . Distortion in a map projection because of non-conformity.

angular momentum. . The quantity obtained by multiplying the moment of inertia of a body by its angular speed.

angular rate. . See ANGULAR SPEED.

angular rate of the earth's rotation. . Time rate of change of angular displacement of the earth relative to the fixed stars equal to 0.729211×10^{-4} radian per second.

angular resolution. . See BEARING RESOLUTION.

angular speed. . Change of direction per unit time. Also called ANGULAR RATE. See also LINEAR SPEED.

anneal. , *v., t.* To heat to a high temperature and then allow to cool slowly, for the purpose of softening, making less brittle, or removing permanent magnetism. When Flinders bars or quadrantal correctors acquire permanent magnetism which decreases their effectiveness as compass correctors, they are annealed.

annotation. , *n.* Any marking on illustrative material for the purpose of clarification such as numbers, letters, symbols, and signs.

annual. , *adj.* Of or pertaining to a year; yearly.

annual aberration. . See under ABERRATION, definition 1.

annual inequality. . Seasonal variation in water level or tidal current speed, more or less periodic due chiefly to meteorological causes.

annual parallax. . See HELIOCENTRIC PARALLAX.

annular. , *adj.* Ring-shaped.

annular eclipse. . An eclipse in which a thin ring of the source of light appears around the obscuring body. Annular solar eclipses occur, but never annular lunar eclipses.

annulus. , *n.* A ring-shaped band.

anode. , *n.* 1. A positive electrode; the plate of a vacuum tube; the electrode of an electron tube through which a principal stream of electrons leaves the inter-electrode space. 2. The positive electrode of an electrochemical device, such as a primary or secondary cell, toward which the negative ions are drawn. See also CATHODE.

anomalistic. , *adj.* Pertaining to the periodic return of the moon to its perigee, or of the earth to its perihelion.

anomalistic month. . The average period of revolution of the moon from perigee to perigee, a period of 27 days, 13 hours, 18 minutes, and 33.2 seconds in 1900. The secular variation does not exceed a few hundredths of a second per century.

anomalistic period. . The interval between two successive passes of a satellite through perigee. Also called PERIGEE-TO-PERIGEE PERIOD and RADIAL PERIOD. See also ORBITAL PERIOD.

anomalistic year. . The period of one revolution of the earth around the sun, from perihelion to perihelion, averaging 365 days, 6 hours, 13 minutes, 53.0 seconds in 1900, and increasing at the rate of 0.26 second per century.

anomaly. , *n.* 1. Departure from the strict characteristics of the type, pattern, scheme, etc. 2. An angle used in the mathematical description of the orbit of one body about another. It is the angle between the radius vector of the body and the line of apsides and is measured from pericenter in the direction of motion. When the radius vector is from the center of the primary to the orbiting body, the angle is called true anomaly. When the radius vector is from the center of the primary to a fictitious body moving with a uniform angular velocity in such a way that its period is equal to that of the actual body, the angle is called mean anomaly. When the radius vector is from the center of the elliptical orbit to the point of intersection of the circle defined by the semimajor axis with the line perpendicular to the semimajor axis and passing through the orbiting body, the angle is called eccentric anomaly or eccentric angle. 3. Departure of the local mean value of a meteorological element from the mean value for the latitude. See also MAGNETIC ANOMALY.

antarctic. , *adj.* referring to the Antarctic region.

Antarctic. , *n.* The region within the Antarctic Circle, or, loosely, the extreme southern regions of the earth.

antarctic air. . A type of air whose characteristics are developed in an antarctic region. Antarctic air appears to be colder at the surface in all seasons, and at all levels in fall and winter, than ARCTIC AIR.

Antarctic Circle. . The parallel of latitude at about 66°33'S, marking the northern limit of the south Frigid Zone. This latitude is the complement of the sun's greatest southerly declination, and marks the approximate northern limit at which the sun becomes circumpolar. The actual limit is extended somewhat by the combined effect of refraction, semidiameter of the sun, parallax, and the height of the observer's eye above the surface of the earth. A similar circle marking the southern limit of the north Frigid Zone is called ARCTIC or NORTH POLAR CIRCLE. Also called SOUTH POLAR CIRCLE.

Antarctic Circumpolar Current. . See WEST WIND DRIFT.

antarctic front. . The semi-permanent, semi-continuous front between the antarctic air of the antarctic continent and the polar air of the southern oceans; generally comparable to the ARCTIC FRONT of the Northern Hemisphere.

antarctic whiteout. . The obliteration of contrast between surface features in the Antarctic when a covering of snow obscuring all landmarks is accompanied by an overcast sky, resulting in an absence of shadows and an unrelieved expanse of white, the earth and sky blending so that the horizon is not distinguishable. A similar occurrence in the Arctic is called ARCTIC WHITEOUT.

ante meridian (A.M.). . Before noon in zone time, or the period of time between midnight (0000) and noon (1200). The period between noon and midnight is called POST MERIDIAN or P.M.

antenna. , *n.* A structure or device used to collect or radiate electromagnetic waves.

antenna array. . A combination of antennas with suitable spacing and with all elements excited to make the radiated fields from the individual elements add in the desired direction, i.e., to obtain directional characteristics.

antenna assembly. . The complete equipment associated with an antenna, including, in addition to the antenna, the base, switches, lead-in wires, revolving mechanism, etc.

antenna bearing. . The generated bearing of the antenna of a radar set, as delivered to the indicator.

antenna coupler. . 1. A radio-frequency transformer used to connect an antenna to a transmission line or to connect a transmission line to a radio receiver. 2. A radio-frequency transformer, link circuit, or tuned line used to transfer radio-frequency energy from the final plate-tank circuit of a transmitter to the transmitter to the transmission line feeding the antenna.

antenna directivity diagram. . See DIRECTIVITY DIAGRAM.

antenna effect. . A spurious effect, in a loop antenna, resulting from the capacitance of the loop to ground.

antenna feed. . The component of an antenna of mirror or lens type that irradiates, or receives energy from, the mirror or lens. See also HORN ANTENNA.

antenna radiation pattern. . See RADIATION PATTERN.

anthelion. , *n.* A rare kind of halo, which appears as a bright spot at the same altitude as the sun and 180° from it in azimuth. See also PARHELION.

anti-clutter gain control. . See SENSITIVITY TIME CONTROL.

anti-clutter rain. . See FAST TIME CONSTANT CIRCUIT.

anti-clutter sea. . See SENSITIVITY TIME CONTROL.

anticorona. , *n.* A diffraction phenomenon very similar to but complementary to the corona, appearing at a point directly opposite to the sun or moon from the observer. Also called BROKEN BOW, GLORY.

anti-crepuscular arch. . See ANTITWILIGHT.

anti-crepuscular rays. . Extensions of crepuscular rays, converging toward a point 180° from the sun.

anticyclone. , *n.* An approximately circular portion of the atmosphere, having relatively high atmospheric pressure and winds which blow clockwise around the center in the Northern Hemisphere and counterclockwise in the Southern Hemisphere. An anticyclone is characterized by good weather. Also called HIGH. See also CYCLONE.

anticyclonic winds. . The winds associated with a high pressure area and constituting part of an anticyclone.

Antilles Current. . This current originates in the vicinity of the Leeward Islands as part of the Atlantic North Equatorial Current. It flows along the northern side of the Greater Antilles. The Antilles Current eventually joins the Florida Current (north of Grand Bahama Island) to form the Gulf Stream.

antilogarithm. , *n.* The number corresponding to a given logarithm. Also called INVERSE LOGARITHM.

antinode. , *n.* Either of the two points on an orbit where a line in the orbit plane, perpendicular to the line of nodes, and passing through the focus, intersects the orbit.

antipodal effects. . See as LONG PATH INTERFERENCE under MULTIPATH ERROR.

antipode. , *n.* Anything exactly opposite to something else. Particularly, that point on the earth 180° from a given place.

antisolar point. . The point on the celestial sphere 180° from the sun.

antitrades. , *n., pl.* The prevailing western winds which blow over and in the opposite direction to the trade winds. Also called COUNTERTRADES.

anti-TR tube. . See TR TUBE.

antitwilight. , *n.* The pink or purplish zone of illumination bordering the shadow of the earth in the dark part of the sky opposite the sun after sunset or before sunrise. Also called ANTI-CREPUSCULAR ARCH.

anvil cloud. . Heavy cumulus or cumulonimbus having an anvil-like upper part.

apastron. , *n.* The point of the orbit of one member of a double star system at which the stars are farthest apart. That point at which they are nearest together is called PERIASTRON.

aperiodic. , *adj.* Without a period; of irregular occurrence.

aperiodic compass. . Literally "a compass without a period," or a compass that, after being deflected, returns by one direct movement to its proper reading without oscillation. Also called DEADBEAT COMPASS.

aperture. , *n.* 1. An opening; particularly, the opening in the front of a camera through which light rays pass when a picture is taken. 2. The diameter of the objective of a telescope or other optical instrument, usually expressed in inches, but sometimes as the angle between lines from the principal focus to opposite ends of a diameter of the objective. 3. Of a directional antenna, that portion of nearby plane surface that is perpendicular to the direction of maximum radiation and through which the major part of the radiation passes.

aperture antenna. . An antenna in which the beam width is determined by the dimensions of a horn, lens, or reflector.

aperture ratio. . The ratio of the diameter of the objective to the focal length of an optical instrument.

apex. , *n.* The highest point of something, as of a cone or triangle, or the maximum latitude (vertex) of a great circle.

aphelion. , *n.* That point in the elliptical orbit of a body about the sun farthest from the sun. That point nearest the sun is called PERIHELION.

aphylactic map projection. . A map projection which is neither conformal nor equal area. Also called ARBITRARY MAP PROJECTION.

aplanatic lens. . See under ABERRATION, definition 2.

apoapsis. , *n.* See APOCENTER.

apocenter. , *n.* In an elliptical orbit, the point in the orbit which is the farthest distance from the focus, where the attracting mass is located. The apocenter is at one end of the major axis of the orbital ellipse. The opposite is PERICENTER, PERIFOCUS, PERIAPSIS. Also called APOAPSIS, APOFOCUS.

apofocus. , *n.* See APOCENTER.

apogean range. . The average semidiurnal range of the tide occurring at the time of apogean tides. It is smaller than the mean range, where the type of tide is either semidiurnal or mixed, and is of no practical significance where the type of tide is diurnal.

apogean tidal currents. . Tidal currents of decreased speed occurring monthly as the result of the moon being at apogee (farthest from the earth).

apogean tides. . Tides of decreased range occurring monthly as the result of the moon being at apogee (farthest from the earth).

apogee. , *n.* That orbital point of a non-circular orbit farthest from the center of attraction. Opposite is PERIGEE. See APOCENTER, PERICENTER.

app. , *n.* an application, typically a small, specialized program downloaded onto mobile devices. See APPLICATION PROGRAM.

apparent altitude. Sextant altitude corrected for inaccuracies in the reading (instrument, index, and personal errors) and inaccuracies in the reference level (principally dip or Coriolis/acceleration), but not for other errors. Apparent altitude is used in obtaining a more accurate refraction correction than would be obtained with an uncorrected sextant altitude. Also called RECTIFIED ALTITUDE. See also OBSERVED ALTITUDE, SEXTANT ALTITUDE.

apparent horizon. . See VISIBLE HORIZON.

apparent motion. . Motion relative to a specified or implied reference point which may itself be in motion. The expression usually refers to movement of celestial bodies as observed from the earth. Usually called RELATIVE MOVEMENT when applied to the motion of one vessel relative to that of another. Also called RELATIVE MOTION.

apparent noon. . Twelve o'clock apparent time, or the instant the apparent sun is over the upper branch of the meridian. Apparent noon may be either local or Greenwich depending upon the reference meridian. High noon is local apparent noon.

apparent place. . The position on the celestial sphere at which a celestial body would be seen if the effects of refraction, diurnal aberration, and geocentric parallax were removed; the position at which the object would actually be seen from the center of the earth. Also called APPARENT POSITION.

apparent position. . See APPARENT PLACE.

apparent precession. . Apparent change in the direction of the axis of rotation of a spinning body, such as a gyroscope, due to rotation of the earth. As a result of gyroscopic inertia or rigidity in space, to an observer on the rotating earth a gyroscope appears to turn or precess.

apparent secular trend. . The non-periodic tendency of sea level to rise, fall and/or remain stationary with time. Technically, it is frequently defined as the slope of a least-squares line of regression through a relatively long series of yearly mean sea level values. The word apparent is used since it is often not possible to know whether a trend is truly non-periodic or merely a segment of a very long oscillation.

apparent shoreline. . A line drawn on the chart in lieu of the mean high water line or the mean water level line in areas where either may be obscured by marsh, mangrove, cypress, or other marine vegetation. This line represents the intersection of the appropriate datum with the outer limits of vegetation and appears to the navigator as the shoreline.

apparent sidereal time. . See under SIDEREAL TIME.

apparent solar day. . The duration of one rotation of the earth on its axis, with respect to the apparent sun. It is measured by successive transits of the apparent sun over the lower branch of a meridian. The length of the apparent solar day is 24 hours of apparent time and averages the length of the mean solar day, but varies somewhat from day to day.

apparent sun. . The actual sun as it appears in the sky. Also called TRUE SUN. See also MEAN SUN, DYNAMICAL MEAN SUN.

apparent time. . Time based upon the rotation of the earth relative to the apparent or true sun. This is the time shown by a sun dial. Apparent time may be designated as either local or Greenwich, as the local or Greenwich meridian is used as the reference. Also called TRUE SOLAR TIME. See also EQUATION OF TIME.

apparent wind. . The speed and direction from which the wind appears to blow with reference to a moving point. Sometimes called RELATIVE WIND. See also TRUE WIND.

application profile. . In ECDIS used in reference to data structure. An application profile is defined for a specific purpose, such as the transfer of ENC DATA.

application program. A computer program designed to do a specific task or group of tasks. See APP.

applier. . In ECDIS used for an entity controlling the application of the UPDATE INFORMATION, e.g. the mariner keying in update information, or software inside ECDIS automatically processing the ENC update information.

approach chart. A chart used to approach a harbor. See CHART CLASSIFICATION BY SCALE.

approximate altitude. . An altitude determined by inexact means, as by estimation or by a star finder or star chart.

approximate coefficients. . The six coefficients used in the analysis of the magnetic properties of a vessel in the course of magnetic compass adjustment. The values of these coefficients are determined from deviations of an unadjusted compass. See also COEFFICIENT A, COEFFICIENT B, COEFFICIENT C, COEFFICIENT D, COEFFICIENT E, COEFFICIENT J.

appulse. , *n.* 1. The near approach of one celestial body to another on the celestial sphere, as in occultation, conjunction, etc. 2. The penumbral eclipse of the moon.

apron. , *n.* 1. On the sea floor a gentle slope, with a generally smooth surface, particularly as found around groups of islands or sea mounts. Sometimes called ARCHIPELAGIC APRON. 2. The area of wharf or quay for handling cargo. 3. A sloping underwater extension of an iceberg. 4. An outwash plain along the front of a glacier.

apse line. . See LINE OF APSIDES.

apsis. *(pl. apsides), n.* Either of the two orbital points nearest or farthest from the center of attraction, the perihelion and aphelion in the case of an orbit about the sun, and the perigee and apogee in the case of an orbit about the earth. The line connecting these two points is called LINE OF APSIDES.

aqueduct. , *n.* A conduit or artificial channel for the conveyance of water, often elevated, especially one for the conveyance of a large quantity of water that flows by gravitation.

arbitrary map projection. . See APHYLACTIC MAP PROJECTION.

arc. , *n.* 1. A part of a curved line, as of a circle. See also ANGULAR DISTANCE. 2. The semi-circular graduated scale of an instrument for measuring angles. See also EXCESS OF ARC.

arched squall. . A squall which is relatively high in the center, tapering off on both sides.

archipelagic apron. . See APRON, definition 1.

archipelago. , *n.* 1. A sea or broad expanse of water containing many islands or groups of islands. 2. A group of such islands.

arc of uncertainty. . See ANGLE OF UNCERTAINTY.

arc of visibility. . The arc of a light sector, designated by its limiting bearings as observed from seaward.

Arcs of Lowitz. . Oblique, rare, downward extensions of the parhelia of 22°, concave toward the sun, and with red inner borders. They are formed by refraction by ice crystals oscillating about the vertical, such as with snowflakes.

arctic. , *adj.* Of or pertaining to the arctic, or intense cold.

Arctic. , *n.* The region within the Arctic Circle, or, loosely, northern regions in general, characterized by very low temperatures.

arctic air. . A type of air which develops mostly in winter over the Arctic. Arctic air is cold aloft and extends to great heights, but the surface temperatures are often higher than those of POLAR AIR. For two or three months in summer, arctic air masses are shallow and rapidly lose the characteristics as they move southward. See also ANTARCTIC AIR.

Arctic Circle. . The parallel of latitude at about 66°33'N, marking the southern limit of the north Frigid Zone. This latitude is the complement of the sun's greatest northerly declination and marks the approximate southern limit at which the sun becomes circumpolar. The actual limit is extended somewhat by the combined effect of refraction, semi-diameter of the sun, parallax, and the height of the observer's eye above the surface of the earth. A similar circle marking the northern limit of the south Frigid Zone is called ANTARCTIC or SOUTH POLAR CIRCLE. Also called NORTH POLAR CIRCLE.

arctic front. . The semi-permanent, semi-continuous front between the deep, cold arctic air and the shallower, generally less cold polar air of northern latitudes; generally comparable to the ANTARCTIC FRONT of the Southern Hemisphere.

arctic sea smoke. . Steam fog, but often specifically applied to steam fog rising from small areas of open water within sea ice. See also FROST SMOKE.

arctic smoke. . See STEAM FOG.

arctic whiteout. . The obliteration of contrast between surface features in the Arctic when a covering of snow obscuring all landmarks is accompanied by an overcast sky, resulting in an absence of shadows and an unrelieved expanse of white, the earth and sky blending so that the horizon is not distinguishable. A similar occurrence in the Antarctic is called ANTARCTIC WHITEOUT.

arc to chord correction. . See CONVERSION ANGLE.

area. In ECDIS the 2-dimensional GEOMETRIC PRIMITIVE of an OBJECT that specifies location.

area to be avoided. A ship routing measure comprising an area with defined limits which should be avoided by all ships, or certain classes of ships; instituted to protect natural features or to define a particularly hazardous area for navigation. See also PRECAUTIONARY AREA, ROUTING SYSTEM.

areal feature. . A topographic feature, such as sand, swamp, vegetation, etc., which extends over an area. It is represented on the published map or chart by a solid or screened color, by a prepared pattern of symbols, or by a delimiting line.

argument, *n.* One of the values used for entering a table or diagram.

argument of latitude. . The angular distance measured in the orbital plane from the ascending node to the orbiting body; the sum of the argument of pericenter and the true anomaly.

argument of pericenter. . The angle at the center of attraction from the ascending node to the pericenter point, measured in the direction of motion of the orbiting body. Also called ARGUMENT OF PERIFOCUS.

argument of perifocus. . See ARGUMENT OF PERICENTER.

argument of perigee. . The angle at the center of attraction from the ascending node to the perigee point, measured in the direction of motion of the orbiting body.

Aries. , *n.* 1. Vernal equinox. Also called FIRST POINT OF ARIES. 2. The first sign of the zodiac.

arithmetic mean. . See MEAN.

arm. , *v., t.* To place tallow or other substance in the recess at the lower end of a sounding lead for obtaining a sample of the bottom.

Armco., *n.* The registered trade name for a high purity, low carbon iron, used for Flinders bars, quadrantal correctors, etc., to correct magnetic compass errors resulting from induced magnetism.

arming., *n.* Tallow or other substance placed in the recess at the lower end of a sounding lead, for obtaining a sample of the bottom.

array., *n.* See ANTENNA ARRAY.

articulated light.. An offshore aid to navigation consisting of a pipe attached to a mooring by a pivoting or universal joint; more accurate in position than a buoy but less than a fixed light.

artificial antenna.. See DUMMY ANTENNA.

artificial asteroid.. A man-made object placed in orbit about the sun.

artificial earth satellite.. A man-made earth satellite, as distinguished from the moon. Often shortened to ARTIFICIAL SATELLITE.

artificial harbor.. A harbor where the desired protection from wind and sea is obtained from breakwaters, moles, jetties, or other man-made works. See also NATURAL HARBOR.

artificial horizon.. A device for indicating the horizontal, such as a bubble, gyroscope, pendulum, or the surface of a liquid.

artificial magnet.. A magnet produced by artificial means, either by placing magnetic material in the field of another magnet or by means of an electric current, as contrasted with a NATURAL MAGNET occurring in nature.

artificial range.. A range formed by two objects such as buildings, towers, etc., not designed as aids to navigation. See also NATURAL RANGE.

artificial satellite.. See ARTIFICIAL EARTH SATELLITE.

ascending node.. That point at which a planet, planetoid, or comet crosses the ecliptic from south to north, or a satellite crosses the plane of the equator of its primary from south to north. Also called NORTHBOUND NODE. The opposite is called DESCENDING NODE.

ASCII.. Acronym for American Standard Code for Information Interchange, a standard method of representing alphanumeric characters with numbers in a computer.

ash breeze.. Expression referring to rowing a sailing vessel in a calm, usually from ship's boats which tow the ship. (Oars are commonly made of ash wood.)

ashore., *adj. & adv.* On the shore; on land; aground. See also AFLOAT.

aspect., *n.* The relative bearing of own ship from the target ship, measured 0° to 180° port (red) or starboard (green). See also TARGET ANGLE.

aspects., *n., pl.* The apparent positions of celestial bodies relative to one another; particularly the apparent positions of the moon or a planet relative to the sun.

assigned frequency.. The center of the frequency band assigned to a radio station. Sometimes called CENTER FREQUENCY.

assigned frequency band.. The frequency band whose center coincides with the frequency assigned to the station and whose width equals the necessary bandwidth plus twice the absolute value of the frequency tolerance.

assumed latitude.. The latitude at which an observer is assumed to be located for an observation or computation, as the latitude of an assumed position or the latitude used for determining the longitude of time sight.

assumed longitude.. The longitude at which an observer is assumed to be located for an observation or computation, as the longitude of an assumed position or the longitude used for determining the latitude by meridian altitude.

assumed position.. A point at which a craft is assumed to be located, particularly one used as a preliminary to establishing certain navigational data, as that point on the surface of the earth for which the computed altitude is determined in the solution of a celestial observation.

astern., *adv.* Bearing approximately 180° relative. The term is often used loosely for DEAD ASTERN, or bearing exactly 180° relative. The opposite is AHEAD.

asteroid., *n.* A MINOR PLANET, one of the many small celestial bodies revolving around the sun, most of the orbits being between those of Mars and Jupiter. Also called PLANETOID. See under PLANET.

astigmatism., *n.* A defect of a lens which causes the image of a point to appear as a line, rather than a point.

astigmatizer., *n.* A lens which introduces astigmatism into an optical system. Such a lens is so arranged that it can be placed in or removed from the optical path at will. In a sextant, an astigmatizer may be used to elongate the image of a celestial body into a horizontal line.

astre fictif.. Any of several fictitious stars which are assumed to move along the celestial equator at uniform rates corresponding to the speeds of the several harmonic constituents of the tide producing force. Each astre fictif crosses the meridian at a time corresponding to the maximum of the constituent that it represents.

astro.. A prefix meaning *star* or *stars* and sometimes used as the equivalent of *celestial.*

astrodynamics., *n.* The practical application of celestial mechanics, astroballistics, propulsion theory, and allied fields to the problem of planning and directing the trajectories of space vehicles.

astrograph., *n.* A device for projecting a set of precomputed altitude curves onto a chart, the curves moving with time such that if they are properly adjusted, they will remain in the correct position on the chart.

astrolabe., *n.* An instrument which measures altitudes of celestial bodies, used for determining an accurate astronomical position, usually while ashore in survey work. Originally, the astrolabe consisted of a disk with an arm pivoted at the center, the whole instrument being hung by a ring at the top to establish the vertical.

astrometry., *n.* The branch of astronomy dealing with the geometrical relations of the celestial bodies and their real and apparent motions.

astronomical., *adj.* Of or pertaining to astronomy.

Astronomical Almanac, The.. An annual publication prepared jointly by the Nautical Almanac Office, U.S. Naval Observatory, and H.M. Nautical Almanac Office, Royal Greenwich Observatory. With the exception of certain introductory pages, the publication as printed in the United Kingdom is identical to that printed in the United States. This ephemeris gives high precision, detailed information on a large number of celestial bodies. It is arranged to suit the convenience of the astronomer for whom it is primarily intended and is not intended for ordinary purposes of navigation. But it does contain some information of general interest to the navigator, such as various astronomical constants, details of eclipses, information on planetary configurations, and miscellaneous phenomena. Prior to 1981 this publication was entitled *American Ephemeris and Nautical Almanac*. See also NAUTICAL ALMANAC.

astronomical day.. Prior to January 1, 1925, a mean solar day which began at mean noon, 12 hours later than the beginning of the calendar day of the same date. Since 1925 the astronomical day agrees with the civil day.

astronomical equator.. A line connecting points having 0° astronomical latitude. Because the deflection of the vertical varies from point to point, the astronomical equator is not a plane curve. But since the verticals through all points on it are parallel, the zenith at any point on the astronomical equator lies in the plane of the celestial equator. When the astronomical equator is corrected for station error, it becomes the GEODETIC EQUATOR. Sometimes called TERRESTRIAL EQUATOR.

astronomical latitude.. Angular distance between the plumb line at a station and the plane of the celestial equator. It is the latitude which results directly from observations of celestial bodies, uncorrected for deflection of the vertical which, in the United States, may amount to as much as 25". Astronomical latitude applies only to positions on the earth, and is reckoned from the astronomical equator (0°), north and south through 90°. Also called ASTRONOMIC LATITUDE and sometimes GEOGRAPHIC LATITUDE. See also GEODETIC LATITUDE.

astronomical longitude.. Angular distance between the plane of the celestial meridian at a station and the plane of the celestial meridian at Greenwich. It is the longitude which results directly from observations of celestial bodies, uncorrected for deflection of the vertical, the prime vertical component of which, in the United States, may amount to more than 18". Astronomical longitude applies only to positions on the earth, and is reckoned from the Greenwich meridian (0°) east and west through 180°. Also called ASTRONOMIC LONGITUDE and sometimes GEOGRAPHIC LONGITUDE. See also GEODETIC LONGITUDE.

astronomical mean sun.. See MEAN SUN.

astronomical meridian. . A line connecting points having the same astronomical longitude. Because the deflection of the vertical (station error) varies from point to point, the astronomical meridian is not a plane curve. When the astronomical meridian is corrected for station error, it becomes the GEODETIC MERIDIAN. Also called TERRESTRIAL MERIDIAN and sometimes called GEOGRAPHIC MERIDIAN.

astronomical parallel. . A line connecting points having the same astronomical latitude. Because the deflection of the vertical varies from point to point, the astronomical parallel is an irregular line not lying in a single plane. When the astronomical parallel is corrected for station error, it becomes the GEODETIC PARALLEL. Sometimes called GEOGRAPHIC PARALLEL.

astronomical position. . 1. A point on the earth whose coordinates have been determined as a result of observation of celestial bodies. The expression is usually used in connection with positions on land determined with great accuracy for survey purposes. 2. A point on the earth, defined in terms of astronomical latitude and longitude.

astronomical refraction. . Atmospheric refraction of a ray of radiant energy passing through the atmosphere from outer space, as contrasted with TERRESTRIAL REFRACTION of a ray emanating from a point on or near the surface of the earth. See also REFRACTION.

astronomical tide. . The tide without constituents having their origin in the daily or seasonal variations in weather conditions which may occur with some degree of periodicity. See also METEOROLOGICAL TIDES.

astronomical time. . Time used with the astronomical day which prior to 1925 began at noon of the civil day of same date. The hours of the day were numbered consecutively from 0 (noon) to 23 (11 A.M. of the following morning).

astronomical triangle. . The navigational triangle, either terrestrial or celestial, used in the solution of celestial observations.

astronomical twilight. . The period of incomplete darkness when the center of the sun is more than 12° but not more than 18° below the celestial horizon. See also CIVIL TWILIGHT, NAUTICAL TWILIGHT.

astronomical unit. . 1. The mean distance between the earth and the sun, approximately 92,960,000 miles. 2. The astronomical unit is often used as a unit of measurement for distances within the solar system. In the system of astronomical constants of the International Astronomical Union the adopted value for it is 1 AU = $149{,}600 \times 10^6$ meters.

astronomical year. . See TROPICAL YEAR.

astronomic latitude. . See ASTRONOMICAL LATITUDE.

astronomic longitude. . See ASTRONOMICAL LONGITUDE.

astronomy. , *n.* The science which deals with the size, constitution, motions, relative position, etc. of celestial bodies, including the earth. That part of astronomy of direct use to a navigator, comprising principally celestial coordinates, time, and the apparent motions of celestial bodies is called navigational or nautical astronomy.

astro-tracker. . A navigation equipment which automatically acquires and continuously tracks a celestial body in azimuth and altitude.

asymmetrical. , *adj.* Not symmetrical.

asymptote. , *n.* A straight line or curve which a curve of infinite length approaches but never quite reaches.

Atlantic Equatorial Counter Current. . An ocean current that flows eastward between the westward flowing Atlantic North and South Equatorial Currents. The counter current is most prominent during August and September, when it extends from about 52°W to 10°W and joins the GUINEA CURRENT. In October it narrows and separates into two parts at about latitude 7°N, longitude 35°W. The western part, which appears to be a region where the counter current probably sinks and flows eastward beneath the equatorial currents, gradually diminishes in size to the west-northwest, while the eastern part diminishes to the east-southeast. The greatest separation occurs during March; during April the western part of the counter current disappears, but in May it reappears in the vicinity of latitude 0°, longitude 40°W. The two segments progress west-northwestward without much change in size. They merge at about latitude 6°N, longitude 43°W during August and continue their flow eastward uninterrupted through September.

Atlantic North Equatorial Current. . A broad, slow, westward flowing ocean current generated mainly by the northeast trade winds. The current originates near longitude 26°W between about latitude 15°N and 30°N and flows across the ocean past longitude 60°W. It forms the ANTILLES CURRENT in the vicinity of the Leeward Islands. The part of the current between 12°N and 15°N joins the Guiana Current and forms the CARIBBEAN CURRENT.

Atlantic South Equatorial Current. . The major part of this westward flowing ocean current is located south of the equator, the central portion extending to about latitude 20°S. The northern part expands northward during January, February, and March when the Atlantic Equatorial Counter Current dissipates and is least evident. On approaching the coast of South America one part turns northwestward as the GUIANA CURRENT; the other part turns below Natal and flows southwestward along the coast of Brazil as the BRAZIL CURRENT. Of the two equatorial currents in the Atlantic, the Atlantic South Equatorial Current is the stronger and more extensive.

Atlantic standard time. . See STANDARD TIME.

atlas. , *n.* A collection of charts or maps kept loose or bound in a volume.

atlas grid. . A reference system that permits the designation of the location of a point or an area on a map, photograph, or other graphic in terms of numbers and letters. Also called ALPHANUMERIC GRID.

atmosphere. , *n.* 1. The envelope of air surrounding the earth and bound to it more or less permanently by gravity. The earth's atmosphere extends from the surface of the earth to an indefinite height, its density asymptotically approaching that of interplanetary space. At heights of the order of 80 kilometers (50 miles) the atmosphere is barely dense enough to scatter sunlight to a visible degree. The atmosphere may be subdivided vertically into a number of atmospheric layers, but the most common basic subdivision is that which recognizes a troposphere from the surface to about 10 kilometers, a stratosphere from about 10 kilometers to about 80 kilometers, and an ionosphere above 80 kilometers. See also STANDARD ATMOSPHERE. 2. The gaseous envelope surrounding any celestial body, including the Earth.

atmospheric absorption. . The loss of power in transmission of radiant energy by dissipation in the atmosphere.

atmospheric drag. . A major cause of perturbations of close artificial satellite orbits caused by the resistance of the atmosphere. The secular effects are decreasing magnitudes of eccentricity, major axis, and period. Sometimes shortened to DRAG.

atmospheric noise. . See ATMOSPHERIC RADIO NOISE.

atmospheric pressure. . The pressure exerted by the weight of the earth's atmosphere, about 14.7 pounds per square inch. See also STANDARD ATMOSPHERE, definition 1; BAROMETRIC PRESSURE.

atmospheric radio noise. . In radio reception, noise or static due to natural causes such as thunderstorm activity. Sometimes shortened to ATMOSPHERIC NOISE. See also MAN-MADE NOISE, RADIO INTERFERENCE.

atmospheric refraction. . Refraction resulting when a ray of radiant energy passes obliquely through the atmosphere. It may be called astronomical refraction if the ray enters the atmosphere from outer space, or terrestrial refraction if it emanates from a point on or near the surface of the earth.

atoll. , *n.* A ring-shaped coral reef which has closely spaced islands or islets on it enclosing a central area or lagoon. The diameter may vary from less than a mile to 80 or more.

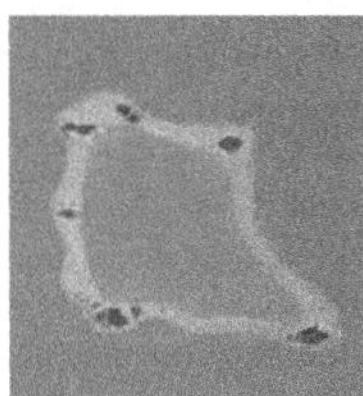

atoll

atollon, *n.* A large reef ring in the Maldive Islands consisting of many smaller reef rings. The word ATOLL was derived from this name.

atomic clock. . A precision clock that depends for its operation upon an electrical oscillator regulated by an atomic system. The basic principle of the clock is that electromagnetic waves of a particular frequency are emitted when an atomic transition occurs.

atomic second. . See SECOND, definition 1.

Atomic Time.. A fundamental kind of time based on transitions in the atom. International Atomic Time (TAI) is the time reference coordinate established by the Bureau International de l'Heure (BIH) on the basis of the readings of atomic clocks functioning in various establishments in accordance with the definition of the atomic second, the unit of time in the International System of Units. The Atomic Time scales maintained in the United States by the National Institute of Standards and Technology and the U.S. Naval Observatory constitute approximately 37.5%of the stable reference information used in maintaining a stable TAI scale by the BIH.

A-trace.. The first trace of an oscilloscope having more than one displayed.

attenuation., *n.* 1. A lessening in amount, particularly the reduction of the amplitude of a wave with distance from the origin. 2. The decrease in the strength of a radar wave resulting from absorption, scattering, and reflection by the medium through which it passes (wave guide, atmosphere) and by obstructions in its path. Also attenuation of the wave may be the result of artificial means, such as the inclusion of an attenuator in the circuitry or by placing an absorbing device in the path of the wave.

attitude., *n.* The position of a body as determined by the inclination of the axes to some other frame of reference. If not otherwise specified, this frame of reference is fixed to the earth.

atto-.. A prefix meaning one-quintillionth (10^{-18}).

attribute.. In ECDIS a characteristic of an OBJECT, usually of a charted feature. It is implemented by a defined ATTRIBUTE LABEL/CODE, acronym, definition and applicable values. In the DATA STRUCTURE, the attribute is defined by its LABEL/CODE. Attributes are either qualitative or quantitative.

attribute label/code. In ECDIS, a fixed length numeric label or a 2-byte unsigned integer code of an ATTRIBUTE.

attribute value. In ECDIS, a defined characteristic of an ATTRIBUTE LABEL/CODE.

audible, *adj.* Capable of being translated into sound by the human ear.

audible aid to navigation.. An aid to navigation which uses sound waves.

audio frequency.. A frequency within the audible range, about 20 to 20,000 hertz. Also called SONIC FREQUENCY.

augmentation., *n.* The apparent increase in the semidiameter of a celestial body as its altitude increases, due to the reduced distance from the observer. The term is used principally in reference to the moon.

augmentation correction.. A correction due to augmentation, particularly that sextant altitude correction due to the apparent increase in the semidiameter of a celestial body as its altitude increases.

augmenting factor.. A factor used in connection with the harmonic analysis of tides or tidal currents to allow for the difference between the times of hourly tabulation and the corresponding constituent hours.

aural., *adj.* Of or pertaining to the ear or sense of hearing.

aural null.. A null detected by listening for the minimum or the absence of an audible signal.

aureole., *n.* A poorly developed corona, characterized by a bluish-white disk immediately around the luminary and a reddish-brown outer edge. An aureole, rather than a corona, is produced when the cloud responsible for this diffraction effect is composed of droplets distributed over a wide size-range. The diffracted rays approach the observer from a wide variety of angles, in contrast to the relative uniform diffraction produced by a cloud of more limited drop-size range. In as much as most clouds exhibit rather broad drop-size distributions, aureoles are observed much more frequently than coronas.

aurora., *n.* A luminous phenomenon due to electrical discharges in the atmosphere, probably confined to the thin air high above the surface of the earth. It is most commonly seen in high latitudes where it is most frequent during periods of greatest sunspot activity. If it occurs in the Northern Hemisphere, it is called aurora borealis or northern lights; and if in the Southern, aurora Australis.

aurora Australis.. The aurora in the Southern Hemisphere.

aurora borealis.. The aurora in the Northern Hemisphere. Also called NORTHERN LIGHTS.

auroral zone.. The area of maximum auroral activity. Two such areas exist, each being a 10° wide annulus centered at an average distance of 23° from a geomagnetic pole.

aurora polaris.. A high-latitude aurora borealis.

austral., *adj.* Of or pertaining to south.

authalic map projection.. See EQUAL-AREA MAP PROJECTION.

Automated Information System. 1. A shipboard broadcast system that acts like a transponder, operating in the VHF Maritime Band, that is capable of handling well over 4,500 reports per minute and updates as often as every two seconds. It uses Self-Organizing Time Division Multiple Access (SOTDMA) technology to meet this high broadcast rate and ensure ship to ship operation. 2. An automatic tracking system used on ships and by vessel traffic services (VTC) for identifying and locating vessels by electronically exchanging data with other nearby ships.

Automated Mutual-assistance Vessel Rescue System (AMVER).. Operated by the United States Coast Guard, the AMVER System is a maritime mutual-assistance program that aids coordination of search and rescue efforts in the oceans of the world, by maintaining a worldwide computerized dead-reckoning plot of participating vessels.

automatic direction finder. A radio direction finder in which the bearing to the transmitter is indicated automatically and continuously, in contrast with a MANUAL RADIO DIRECTION FINDER which requires manual operation. Also called AUTOMATIC RADIO DIRECTION FINDER.

automatic frequency control.. The technique of automatically maintaining, or a circuit or device which automatically maintains, the frequency of a receiver within specified limits.

automatic gain control.. A feature involving special circuitry designed to maintain the output of a radio, radar, or television receiver essentially constant, or to prevent its exceeding certain limits, regardless of variations in the strength of the incoming signal.

Automatic Identification System (AIS).. 1. An internationally adopted radio communications protocol that enables the autonomous and continuous exchange of navigation safety related messages amongst vessels, lifeboats, aircraft, shore stations, and aids to navigation (AIS ATON). AIS ATON variants include *real*, *virtual*, or *synthetic* systems.

automatic radar plotting aid. A computer-assisted radar data processing system which generates predicted ship vectors based on the recent plotted positions. For such a system to meet the specifications of the Inter Governmental Maritime Consultative Organization (IMCO), it must satisfy requirements with respect to detection, acquisition, tracking, display, warnings, data display, and trial maneuvers.

automatic radio direction finder.. See AUTOMATIC DIRECTION FINDER.

automatic tide gage.. An instrument that automatically registers the rise and fall of the tide. In some instruments, the registration is accomplished by recording the heights at regular intervals in digital format, in others by a continuous graph in which the height versus corresponding time is recorded.

automatic updating.. In ECDIS, either the SEMI-AUTOMATIC or the FULLY AUTOMATIC means of updating the ENC/SENC.

auto pilot, *n.* A device which steers a vessel unattended along a given bearing. See GYRO PILOT.

autumn., *n.* The season between summer and winter. In the Northern Hemisphere autumn begins astronomically at the autumnal equinox and ends at the winter solstice. In the Southern Hemisphere the limits are the vernal equinox and the summer solstice. The meteorological limits vary with the locality and the year. Also called FALL.

autumnal., *adj.* Pertaining to fall (autumn). The corresponding adjectives for winter, spring, and summer are *hibernal, vernal,* and *aestival.*

autumnal equinox.. 1. That point of intersection of the ecliptic and the celestial equator occupied by the sun as it changes from north to south declination, on or about September 23. Also called SEPTEMBER EQUINOX, FIRST POINT OF LIBRA. 2. The instant the sun reaches the point of zero declination when crossing the celestial equator from north to south.

auxiliary lights.. See under VERTICAL LIGHTS.

average., *adj.* Equaling or approximating a mean.

average., *n.* See MEAN.

average., *v., t.* To determine a mean.

avoirdupois pound.. See POUND.

avulsion., *n.* The rapid erosion of shore land by waves during a storm.

awash. , *adj. & adv.* Situated so that the top is intermittently washed by waves or tidal action. The term applies both to fixed objects such as rocks, and to floating objects with their tops flush with or slightly above the surface of the water. See also ROCK AWASH, SUBMERGED, UNCOVERED.

axial. , *adj.* Of or pertaining to an axis.

axis. , *n. (pl. axes).* 1. A straight line about which a body rotates, or around which a plane figure may rotate to produce a solid; a line of symmetry. A polar axis is the straight line connecting the poles of a body. The major axis of an ellipse or ellipsoid is its longest diameter; the minor axis, its shortest diameter. 2. One of a set of reference lines for certain systems of coordinates. 3. The principal line about which anything may extend, as the axis of a channel or compass card axis. 4. A straight line connecting two related points.

axis of freedom. . An axis about which the gimbal of a gyro provides a degree-of-freedom of movement.

azimuth. , *n.* The horizontal direction or bearing of a celestial point from a terrestrial point, expressed as the angular distance from a reference direction. It is usually measured from 000° at the reference direction clockwise through 360°. An azimuth is often designated as true, magnetic, compass grid, or relative as the reference direction is true, magnetic, compass, or grid north, or heading, respectively. Unless otherwise specified, the term is generally understood to apply to true azimuth, which may be further defined as the arc of the horizon, or the angle at the zenith, between the north part of the celestial meridian or principal vertical circle and a vertical circle, measured from 000° at the north part of the principal vertical circle clockwise through 360°. Azimuth taken directly from a table, before interpolation, is called tabulated azimuth. After interpolation, or, if determined by calculation, mechanical device, or graphics, it is called computed azimuth. When the angle is measured in either direction from north or south, and labeled accordingly, it is properly called azimuth angle; when measured either direction from east or west, and labeled accordingly, it is called amplitude. An azimuth determined by solution of the navigational triangle with altitude, declination, and latitude then is called an altitude azimuth; if meridian angle, declination, and latitude are given, it is called a time azimuth; if meridian angle, declination and altitude are given, it is called a time and altitude azimuth. See also BACK AZIMUTH, BEARING.

azimuthal. , *adj.* Of or pertaining to azimuth.

azimuthal chart. . A chart on an azimuthal map projection. Also called ZENITHAL CHART.

azimuthal equidistant chart. . A chart on the azimuthal equidistant map projection.

azimuthal equidistant map projection. . An azimuthal map projection on which straight lines radiating from the center or pole of projection represent great circles in their true azimuths from that center, and lengths along those lines are of exact scale. This projection is neither equal-area nor conformal. If a geographic pole is the pole of projection, meridians appear as radial straight lines and parallels of latitude as equally spaced concentric circles.

azimuthal map projection. . A map projection on which the azimuths or directions of all lines radiating from a central point or pole are the same as the azimuths or directions of the corresponding lines on the ellipsoid. This classification includes the gnomonic, stereographic, orthographic, and the azimuthal equidistant map projections. Also called ZENITHAL MAP PROJECTION.

azimuthal orthomorphic projection. . See STEREOGRAPHIC MAP PROJECTION.

azimuth angle. . Azimuth measured from 0° at the north or south reference direction clockwise or counterclockwise through 90° or 180°. It is labeled with the reference direction as a prefix and the direction of measurement from the reference direction as a suffix. When azimuth angle is measured through 180°, it is labeled N or S to agree with the latitude and E or W to agree with the meridian angle.

azimuth bar. . An instrument for measuring azimuths, particularly a device consisting of a slender bar with a vane at each end, and designed to fit over a central pivot in the glass cover of a magnetic compass. See also BEARING BAR.

azimuth circle. . A ring designed to fit snugly over a compass or compass repeater, and provided with means for observing compass bearings and azimuths. A similar ring without the means for observing azimuths of the sun is called a BEARING CIRCLE.

azimuth instrument. . An instrument for measuring azimuths, particularly a device which fits over a central pivot in the glass cover of a magnetic compass. See also BEARING BAR.

azimuth stabilized display. . See as STABILIZED IN AZIMUTH under STABILIZATION OF RADARSCOPE DISPLAY.

azimuth tables. . Publications providing tabulated azimuths or azimuth angles of celestial bodies for various combinations of declination, latitude and hour angle. Great circle course angles can also be obtained by substitution of values.

Azores Current. . A slow but fairly constant southeast branch of the North Atlantic Current and part of the Gulf Stream System. Its mean speed is only 0.4 knot, and the mean maximum speed computed from all observations above 1 knot in the prevailing direction is 1.3 knots. There is no discernible seasonal fluctuation. The speed and direction of the current is easily influenced for short periods by changing winds. The Azores Current is an inner part of the general clockwise oceanic circulation of the North Atlantic Ocean. Also called SOUTHEAST DRIFT CURRENT.

B

back. , *adj.* Reciprocal.

back. , *v., i.* 1. A change in wind direction in reverse of the normal pattern, or counterclockwise in the Northern Hemisphere and clockwise in the Southern Hemisphere. Change in the opposite direction is called VEER. See also HAUL. 2. To go stern first, or to operate the engines in reverse. 3. To brace the yard of a square sail so as to bring the wind on the forward side.

back azimuth. . An azimuth 180° from a given azimuth.

back echo. . The effect on a radar display produced by a back lobe of a radar antenna. See also SIDE ECHO.

backlash. , *n.* 1. The amount which a gear or other part of a machine, instrument, etc., can be moved without moving an adjoining part, resulting from loose fit. See also LOST MOTION. 2. The tangle resulting when a reel of line or cable revolves faster than line is being stripped off.

back lobe. . The lobe of the radiation pattern of a directional antenna which makes an angle of approximately 180° with the direction of the axis of the main lobe.

back range. . A range observed astern, particularly one used as guidance for a craft moving away from the objects forming the range.

backrush. , *n.* The seaward return of water following the uprush onto the foreshore. See also RIP CURRENT, UNDERTOW.

backshore. , *n.* That part of a beach which is usually dry, being reached only by the highest tides, and by extension, a narrow strip of relatively flat coast bordering the sea. See also FORESHORE.

back sight. . A marine sextant observation of a celestial body made by facing away from the body, measuring an angle of more than 90°.

backstaff. , *n.* A forerunner of the sextant, consisting essentially of a graduated arc and a single mirror. To use the instrument it was necessary to face away from the body being observed. Also called QUADRANT WITH TWO ARCS, SEA QUADRANT.

backstays of the sun. . Crepuscular rays extending downward toward the horizon.

back-up arrangement. ,. In ECDIS, facilities enabling safe take-over of ECDIS functions and measures facilitating means for safe navigation of the remaining part of the voyage in case of ECDIS failure.

backwash, *n.* Water or waves thrown back by an obstruction such as a seawall, breakwater, cliff, etc.

backwater. , *n.* Water held back from the main flow, as that which overflows the land and collects in low places or that forms an inlet approximately parallel to the main body and connected thereto by a narrow outlet.

bad-bearing sector. . Relative to a radio direction finder station or radiobeacon, a sector within which bearings are known to be liable to significant errors of unknown magnitudes.

baguio. , *n.* Local term in the Philippines for a tropical cyclone.

balancer. , *n.* A device used with a radio direction finder to balance out antenna effect and thus produce a sharper reading.

balancing. , *n.* The process of neutralizing antenna effect in order to improve the definition of the observed bearing. See also BALANCER.

Bali wind. . A strong east wind at the eastern end of Java.

ball. , *n.* 1. A spherical identifying mark placed at the top of a perch. 2. A time ball.

ballast ground. . A designated area for discharging solid ballast before entering a harbor.

ballistic damping error. . A temporary oscillatory error of a gyrocompass introduced during changes of course or speed as a result of the means used to damp the oscillations of the spin axis.

ballistic deflection error. . A temporary oscillatory error of a gyrocompass introduced when the north-south component of the speed changes, as by speed or course change. An accelerating force acts upon the compass, causing a surge of mercury from one part of the system to another in the case of the non pendulous compass, or a deflection (along the meridian) of a mass in the case of a pendulous compass. In either case, a precessing force introduces a temporary ballistic deflection error in the reading of the compass unless it is corrected.

band. , *n.* A specific section or range of anything. See also FREQUENCY BAND.

band of error. . An area either side of a line of position, within which, for a stated level of probability, the true position is considered to lie.

bandwidth. , *n.* 1. The range of frequencies of a device within which its performance, in respect to some characteristic, conforms to a specified standard. 2. The range within the limits of a frequency band.

bank. , *n.* 1. An elevation of the sea floor typically located on a shelf, over which the depth of water is relatively shallow. Reefs or shoals, dangerous to surface navigation, may rise above the general depths of a bank. 2. A shallow area of shifting sand, gravel, mud, etc., such as a *sand bank, mud bank,* etc. 3. A ridge of any material such as earth, rock, snow, etc., or anything resembling such a ridge, as a *fog bank* or *cloud bank.* 4. The edge of a cut or fill. 5. The margin of a watercourse. 6. A number of similar devices connected so as to be used as a single device in common.

bank cushion. . In a restricted channel, especially one with steep banks, bank cushion tends to force the bow away from the bank due to the increase in the bow wave on the near side.

bank suction. . The bodily movement of a ship toward the near bank due to a decrease in pressure as a result of increased velocity of flow of water past the hull in a restricted channel.

banner cloud. . A banner like cloud streaming off from a mountain peak in a strong wind. See also CAP CLOUD.

bar. , *n.* 1. A ridge or mound of sand, gravel, or other unconsolidated material below the high water level, especially at the mouth of a river or estuary, or lying a short distance from and usually parallel to the beach, and which may obstruct navigation. 2. A unit accepted temporarily for use with the International System of Units; 1 bar is equal to 100,000 pascals.

barat. , *n.* A heavy northwest squall in Manado Bay on the north coast of the island of Celebes, prevalent from December to February.

barber. , *n.*1. A strong wind carrying damp snow or sleet and spray that freezes upon contact with objects, especially the beard and hair. 2. See FROST SMOKE, definition 2.

bar buoy. . A buoy marking the location of a bar at the mouth of a river on approach to a harbor.

bare ice. . Ice without snow cover.

bare rock. . A rock that extends above the mean high water datum in tidal areas or above the low water datum in the Great Lakes. See also ROCK AWASH, SUBMERGED ROCK.

barogram. , *n.* The record made by a barograph.

barograph. , *n.* A recording barometer. A highly sensitive barograph may be called a microbarograph.

barometer. , *n.* An instrument for measuring atmospheric pressure. A **mercurial barometer** employs a column of mercury supported by the atmosphere. An aneroid barometer has a partly exhausted, thin metal cylinder somewhat compressed by atmospheric pressure.

barometric pressure. . Atmospheric pressure as indicated by a barometer.

barometric pressure correction. . A correction due to nonstandard barometric pressure, particularly the sextant altitude correction due to changes in refraction caused by difference between the actual barometric pressure and the standard barometric pressure used in the computation of the refraction table.

barometric tendency. . See PRESSURE TENDENCY.

barothermogram. , *n.* The record made by a barothermograph.

barothermograph. , *n.* An instrument which automatically records pressure and temperature.

barothermohygrogram. , *n.* The record made by a barothermohygrograph.

barothermohygrograph. , *n.* An instrument which automatically records pressure, temperature and humidity of the atmosphere.

barrel. , *n.* A unit of volume or weight, the U.S. petroleum value being 42 U.S. gallons.

barrel buoy. . A buoy having the shape of a barrel or cylinder floating horizontally, usually for special purposes, including mooring.

barrier beach. . A bar essentially parallel to the shore, the crest of which is above high water.

barrier reef. . A coral reef which roughly parallels land but is some distance offshore, with deeper water adjacent to the land, as contrasted with a FRINGING REEF closely attached to the shore.

bar scale. . A line or series of lines on a chart, subdivided and labeled with the distances represented on the chart. Also called GRAPHIC SCALE. See also SCALE.

barycenter. , *n.* The center of mass of a system of masses; the common point about which two or more celestial bodies revolve.

base chart. . See BASE MAP.

base course up. . One of the three basic orientations of display of relative or true motion on a radarscope. In the base course up orientation, the target pips are painted at their measured distances and in their directions relative to a preset base course of own ship maintained up in relation to the display. This orientation is most often used with automated radar plotting aids. Also called COURSE UP. See also HEAD UP, NORTH UP.

base data. . In ECDIS, the S-57 conforming data at the data producer's site that does not contain any UPDATE RECORDS. Once this data is exchanged, it becomes TARGET DATA at the APPLIER's site.

baseline. 1. The reference used to position limits of the territorial sea and the contiguous zone. 2. One side of a series of connected survey triangles, the length of which is measured with prescribed accuracy and precision, and from which the lengths of the other triangle sides are obtained by computation. Important factors in the accuracy and precision of base measurements are the use of standardized invar tapes, controlled conditions of support and tension, and corrections for temperatures, inclination, and alignment. Baselines in triangulation are classified according to the character of the work they are intended to control, and the instruments and methods used in their measurement are such that prescribed probable errors for each class are not exceeded. These probable errors, expressed in terms of the lengths, are as follows: first order, 1 part in 1,000,000; second order, 1 part in 500,000; and third order, 1 part in 250,000. 3. The line along the surface of the earth between two radio navigation stations operating in conjunction for the determination of a line of position.

baseline delay. . The time interval needed for the signal from a master station of a hyperbolic radionavigation system to travel the length of the baseline, introduced as a delay between transmission of the master and slave (or secondary) signals to make it possible to distinguish between the signals and to permit measurement of time differences.

baseline extension. . The extension of the baseline in both directions beyond the transmitters of a pair of radio stations operating in conjunction for determination of a line of position.

base map. . 1. A map or chart showing certain fundamental information, used as a base upon which additional data of specialized nature are compiled or overprinted. 2. A map containing all the information from which maps showing specialized information can be prepared. Also called BASE CHART in nautical charting.

base map symbol. . A symbol used on a base map or chart as opposed to one used on an overprint to the base map or chart. Also called BASE SYMBOL.

base symbol. . See BASE MAP SYMBOL.

base units. . See under INTERNATIONAL SYSTEM OF UNITS.

basin. , *n.* 1. A depression of the sea floor approximately equidimensional in plan view and of variable extent. 2. An area of water surrounded by quay walls, usually created or enlarged by excavation, large enough to receive one or more ships for a specific purpose. See also GRAVING DOCK, HALF. TIDE BASIN, NON-TIDAL BASIN, SCOURING BASIN, TIDAL BASIN, TURNING BASIN. 3. An area of land which drains into a lake or sea through a river and its tributaries. 4. A nearly land-locked area of water leading off an inlet, firth, or sound.

bathyal. , *adj.* Pertaining to ocean depths between 100 and 2,000 fathoms; also to the ocean bottom between those depths, sometimes identical with the continental slope environment.

bathymeter. , *n.* An instrument for measuring depths of water.

bathymetric. , *adj.* Of or pertaining to bathymetry.

bathymetric chart. . A topographic chart of the seabed of a body of water, or a part of it. Generally, bathymetric charts show depths by contour lines and gradient tints.

bathymetry. , *n.* The science of measuring water depths (usually in the ocean) in order to determine bottom topography.

bathysphere. , *n.* A spherical chamber in which persons are lowered for observation and study of ocean depths.

bathythermogram. , *n.* The record made by a bathythermograph.

bathythermograph. , *n.* An instrument which automatically draws a graph showing temperature as a function of depth when lowered in the sea.

batture. , *n.* An elevation of the bed of a river under the surface of the water; sometimes used to signify the same elevation when it has risen above the surface.

baud. . A measure of the speed of computer data transmission in bits per second.

bay. , *n.* A recess in the shore, on an inlet of a sea or lake between two capes or headlands, that may vary greatly in size but is usually smaller than a gulf but larger than a cove.

bayamo. , *n.* A violent blast of wind, accompanied by vivid lightning, blowing from the land on the south coast of Cuba, especially near the Bight of Bayamo.

Bayer's letter. . The Greek (or Roman) letter used in a BAYER'S NAME.

Bayer's name. . The Greek (or Roman) letter and the possessive form of the Latin name of a constellation, used as a star name.

baymouth bar. . A bar extending partially or entirely across the mouth of a bay.

bayou. , *n.* A minor, sluggish waterway or estuaries creek, generally tidal or with a slow or imperceptible current, and with its course generally through lowlands or swamps, tributary to or connecting with other bodies of water. Various specific meanings have been implied in different parts of the southern United States. Sometimes called SLOUGH.

beach. , *n.* The zone of unconsolidated material that extends landward from the low water line to the place where there is a marked change in material or physiographic form, or to the line of permanent vegetation (usually the effective limit of storm waves). A beach includes foreshore and backshore. The beach along the margin of the sea may be called SEABEACH. Also called STRAND, especially when the beach is composed of sand. See also TIDELAND.

beach. , *v., t. & i.* To intentionally run a craft ashore.

beach berm. . See BERM.

beach erosion. . The carrying away of beach materials by wave action, tidal or littoral currents, or wind.

beacon. , *n.* A fixed artificial navigation mark. See also MARK, definition l; DAYBEACON; DAYMARK; LIGHTED BEACON; RADIOBEACON.

beaconage. , *n.* A system of fixed aids to navigation comprised of beacons and minor lights. See also BUOYAGE.

beacon buoy. . See PILLAR BUOY.

beacon tower. . A beacon which is a major structure, having a support as distinctive as the topmark. See also LATTICE BEACON, REFUGE BEACON.

beam. , *n.* 1. A directed flow of electromagnetic radiation from an antenna. See also MAIN BEAM under LOBE, BEAM WIDTH. 2. A group of nearly parallel rays, as a *light beam.*

beam compass. . Compass for drawing circles of large diameter. In its usual form it consists of a bar with sliding holders for points, pencils, or pens which can be set at any desired position.

beam sea. . Waves moving in a direction approximately 90° from the vessel's heading. Those moving in a direction approximately opposite to the heading are called HEAD SEA, those moving in the general direction of the heading are called FOLLOWING SEA, and those moving in a direction approximately 135° from the heading (striking the quarter) are called QUARTERING SEA. See also CROSS SEA.

beam tide. . A tidal current setting in a direction approximately 90° from the heading of a vessel. One setting in a direction approximately 90° from the course is called a CROSS TIDE. In common usage, these two expressions are usually used synonymously. One setting in a direction approximately opposite to the heading is called a HEAD TIDE. One setting in such a direction as to increase the speed of a vessel is called a FAIR TIDE.

beam width. . The angular measure of the transverse section of a beam (usually in the main lobe). Lying within directions corresponding to specified values of field strength relative to the maximum (e.g., half field strength beam width and half power beam width). The beam width is usually measured in one or more specified planes containing the axis of the beam. See also HORIZONTAL BEAM WIDTH, VERTICAL BEAM WIDTH.

beam-width error. . An azimuth or bearing distortion on a radar display caused by the width of the radar beam. See also BEAM WIDTH, PULSE LENGTH ERROR.

beam wind. . Wind blowing in a direction approximately 90° from the heading. One blowing in a direction approximately 90° from the course is called a CROSS WIND. In common usage these two expressions are usually used synonymously, BEAM WIND being favored by mariners and CROSS WIND by aviators. One blowing from ahead is called a HEAD WIND. One blowing from astern is called a FOLLOWING WIND by mariners and a TAIL WIND by aviators. See also FAIR WIND, FAVORABLE WIND, UNFAVORABLE WIND.

bear. , *v., i.* To be situated as to direction, as, the light bears 165°.

bear down. . To approach from windward.

bearing. , *n.* The horizontal direction of one terrestrial point from another, expressed as the angular distance from a reference direction. It is usually measured from 000° at the reference direction clockwise through 360°. The terms BEARING and AZIMUTH are sometimes used interchangeably, but in navigation the former customarily applies to terrestrial objects and the latter to the direction of a point on the celestial sphere from a point on the earth. A bearing is often designated as true, magnetic, compass, grid, or relative as the reference direction is true, magnetic, compass, or grid north, or heading, respectively. The angular distance between a reference direction and the initial direction of a great circle through two terrestrial points is called great circle bearing. The angular distance between a reference direction and the rhumb line through two terrestrial points is called rhumb or Mercator bearing. A bearing differing by 180°, or one measured in the opposite direction, from a given bearing is called a reciprocal bearing. The maximum or minimum bearing of a point for safe passage of an off-lying danger is called a danger bearing. A relative bearing of 045° or 315° is sometimes called a four-point bearing. Successive relative bearings (right or left) of 45° and 90° taken on a fixed object to obtain a running fix are often called bow and beam bearings. Two or more bearings used as intersecting lines of position for fixing the position of a craft are called cross bearings. The bearing of a radio transmitter from a receiver, as determined by a radio direction finder, is called a radio bearing. A bearing obtained by radar is called a radar bearing. A bearing obtained by visual observation is called a visual bearing. A constant bearing maintained while the distance between two craft is decreasing is called a collision bearing. See also CURVE OF EQUAL BEARING.

bearing angle. . Bearing measured from 0° at the reference direction clockwise or counterclockwise through 90° or 180°. It is labeled with the reference direction as a prefix and the direction of measurement from the reference direction as a suffix. Thus, bearing angle N37°W is 37° west of north, or true bearing 323°.

bearing bar. . An instrument for measuring bearings, particularly a device consisting of a slender bar with a vane at each end, and designed to fit over a central pivot in the glass cover of a magnetic compass. See also AZIMUTH BAR.

bearing book. . A log for the recording of visual bearings.

bearing calibration. . The determination of bearing corrections of a radio direction finder by observations of a radiobeacon, particularly a calibration radiobeacon, of known visual bearing, observations being taken over 360° of swing of the observing vessel.

bearing circle. . A ring designed to fit snugly over a compass or compass repeater, and provided with vanes for observing compass bearings. A similar ring provided with means for observing azimuths of the sun is called an AZIMUTH CIRCLE.

bearing compass. . A compass intended primarily for use in observing bearings.

bearing cursor. . The radial line on a radar set inscribed on a transparent disk which can be rotated manually about an axis coincident with the center of the Planned Position Indicator. It is used for bearing determination. Also called MECHANICAL BEARING CURSOR.

bearing light. . A navigation light using two superimposed optical systems which provides an approximate bearing without the use of a compass.

bearing line. . A line extending in the direction of a bearing.

bearing repeater. . A compass repeater used primarily for observing bearings.

bearing resolution. . See as RESOLUTION IN BEARING under RESOLUTION, definition 2. Also called ANGULAR RESOLUTION.

beat frequency. . Either of the two additional frequencies obtained when signals of two frequencies are combined, equal to the sum or difference, respectively, of the original frequencies.

Beaufort wind scale. . A numerical scale for indicating wind speed, devised by Admiral Sir Francis Beaufort in 1805. Beaufort numbers (or forces) range from force 0 (calm) to force 12 (hurricane).

bed. , *n.* The ground upon which a body of water rests. The term is usually used with a modifier to indicate the type of water body, as river bed or sea bed. See also BOTTOM.

before the wind. . In the direction of the wind. The expression applies particularly to a sailing vessel having the wind well aft. See also DOWNWIND.

bell. , *n.* A device for producing a distinctive sound by the vibration of a hollow, cup-shaped metallic vessel which gives forth a ringing sound when struck.

bell book. . The log of ordered engine speeds and directions.

bell buoy. . A buoy with a skeleton tower in which a bell is fixed.

belt. , *n.* A band of pack ice from 1 kilometer to more than 100 kilometers in width.

bench. , *n.* On the sea floor, a small terrace.

bench mark. . A fixed physical object used as reference for a vertical datum. A tidal bench mark is one near a tide station to which the tide staff and tidal datums are referred. A primary tidal bench mark is the principal (or only) mark of a group of tidal bench marks to which the tide staff and tidal datums are referred. A geodetic bench mark identifies a surveyed point in the National Geodetic Vertical Network. Geodetic bench mark disks contain the inscription VERTICAL CONTROL MARK, NATIONAL GEODETIC SURVEY with other individual identifying information. Bench mark disks of either type may, on occasion, serve simultaneously to reference both tidal and geodetic datum's. Numerous bench marks, both tidal and geodetic, still bear the inscription U.S. COAST & GEODETIC SURVEY.

beneaped. , *adj.* See NEAPED.

Benguela Current. . A slow-moving ocean current flowing generally northwestward along the west coast of Africa. It is caused mainly by the prevailing southeast trade winds. Near the equator the current flows westward and becomes the ATLANTIC SOUTH EQUATORIAL CURRENT.

benthic. . The bottom of the sea or lake.

bentu de soli. An east wind on the coast of Sardinia.

berg. , *n.* Short for ICEBERG.

bergy bit. . A large piece of floating glacier ice, generally showing less than 5 meters above sea level but more than 1 meter and normally about 100 to 300 square meters in area. It is smaller than an ICEBERG but larger than a GROWLER. A typical bergy bit is about the size of a small house.

Bering Current. . A northward flowing current through the eastern half of the Bering Sea, through Bering Strait, and in the eastern Chukchi Sea. The current speed in the Bering Sea is estimated to be usually 0.5 knot or less but at times as high as 1.0 knot. In the Bering Strait, current speeds frequently reach 2 knots. However, in the eastern half of the strait, currents are even stronger and usually range between 1.0 and 2.5 knots. Strong southerly winds may increase current speeds in the strait to 3 knots, and up to 4 knots in the eastern part. Persistent, strong northerly winds during autumn may cause the current to reverse direction for short periods. During winter a southward flow may occur in the western part of the strait. After flowing through Bering Strait, the current widens, and part continues toward Point Barrow, where it turns northwestward. Along the Alaska coast, current speeds have been observed to range between 0.1 and 1.5 knots and increase to 2.0 or 2.5 knots with southerly winds. In the western part of the Chukchi Sea, currents are considerably weaker and do not usually exceed 0.5 knots.

berm. , *n.* A nearly horizontal portion of a beach or backshore having an abrupt fall and formed by wave deposition of material and marking the limit of ordinary high tides. Also called BEACH BERM.

berm crest. . The seaward limit of a berm. Also called BERM EDGE.

berm edge. . See BERM CREST.

berth. , *n., v., t.* 1. A place for securing a vessel. 2. To secure a vessel at a berth. See also FOUL BERTH, MUD BERTH.

beset. , *adj.* State of a vessel surrounded by ice and unable to move. If the ice forcibly squeezes the hull, the vessel is said to be NIPPED.

Bessel ellipsoid of 1841. . The reference ellipsoid of which the semimajor axis is 6,377,397.155 meters, the semiminor axis is 6,356,078.963 meters and the flattening or ellipticity equals 1/299.1528. Also called BESSEL SPHEROID OF 1841.

Besselian year. . See FICTITIOUS YEAR.

Bessel spheroid of 1841. . See BESSEL ELLIPSOID OF 1841.

bias error. . See CONSTANT ERROR.

bifurcation. , *n.* A division into two branches.

bifurcation buoy. . A buoy which indicates the place at which a channel divides into two. See also JUNCTION BUOY.

bifurcation mark. . A navigation mark which indicates the place at which the channel divides into two. See also JUNCTION MARK.

big floe. . See under FLOE.

bight. , *n.* 1. A long and gradual bend or recess in the coastline which forms a large open receding bay. 2. A bend in a river or mountain range. 3. An extensive crescent-shaped indentation in the ice edge.

Bilateral Chart. , *n.* A chart which is produced by a home country but, via formal agreement between the two countries, is re-numbered, printed, and disseminated by another nation. In the U.S., the National Geospatial-Intelligence Agency oversees bi-lateral chart dissemination and correction.

bill, *n.* A narrow promontory.

bi-margin format. . The format of a map or chart on which the cartographic detail is extended to two edges of the sheet, thus leaving only two margins. See also BLEED.

binary notation. . Referring to a system of numbers with a base of 2; used extensively in computers, which use electronic on-off storage devices to represent the numbers 0 and 1.

binary star. . A system of two stars that revolve about their common center of mass. See also DOUBLE STAR.

binnacle. , *n.* The stand in which a compass is mounted. For a magnetic compass it is usually provided with means of mounting various correctors for adjustment and compensation of the compass.

binocular. , *n., adj.* 1. An optical instrument for use with both eyes simultaneously. 2. Referring to vision with two eyes.

bioluminescence. , *n.* The production of light by living organisms in the sea. Generally, these displays are stimulated by surface wave action, ship movement, subsurface waves, up welling, eddies, physical changes in sea water, surfs, and rip tides.

bisect. , *v., t.* To divide into two equal parts.

bit. *(from binary digit).* The smallest unit of information in a computer. Bits are grouped together into bytes, which represent characters or other information.

bit-map. . A type of computerized display which consists of a single layer of data; individual elements cannot be manipulated. See VECTOR, RASTER.

bivariate error distribution. . A two-dimensional error distribution.

blackbody. , *n.* An ideal emitter which radiates energy at the maximum possible rate per unit area at each wavelength for any given temperature. A blackbody also absorbs all the radiant energy in the near visible spectrum incident upon it. No actual substance behaves as a true blackbody.

black light. . Ultraviolet or infrared radiant energy. It is neither black nor light.

blanket. , *v, t.* To blank out or obscure weak radio signals by a stronger signal.

blanketing. , *n.* The blanking out or obscuring of weak radio signals by a stronger signal.

blank tube. . A marine sextant accessory consisting of a tubular sighting vane, the function of which is to keep the line of vision parallel to the frame of the instrument when observing horizontal sextant angles.

blather. , *n.* Very wet mud of such nature that a weight will rapidly sink into it. See also QUICKSAND.

bleed. , *n.* The edge of a map or chart on which cartographic detail is extended to the edge of the sheet. Also called BLEEDING EDGE.

bleeding edge. . See BLEED.

blind lead. . A lead with only one outlet.

blind pilotage. . *British terminology.* The task of conducting the passage of a ship in pilot waters using means available to the navigator in low visibility.

blind rollers. . Long, high swells which have increased in height, almost to the breaking point, as they pass over shoals or run in shoaling water. Also called BLIND SEAS.

blind seas. . See BLIND ROLLERS.

blind sector. . A sector on the radarscope in which radar echoes cannot be received because of an obstruction near the antenna. See also SHADOW SECTOR.

blink. , *n.* A glare on the underside of extensive cloud areas, created by light reflected from snow or ice-covered surfaces.

snow blink. . Blink caused by a snow-covered surface, which is whitish and brighter than the yellowish-white glare of ice blink. See also LAND SKY, WATER SKY, SKY MAP.

blinking. , *n.* A means of providing information in radionavigation systems of the pulse type by modifying the signal at its source so that the signal presentation alternately appears and disappears or shifts along the time base. In Loran, blinking is used to indicate that a station is malfunctioning.

blip. , *n.* On a radarscope, a deflection or spot of contrasting luminescence caused by an echo, i.e., the radar signal reflected back to the antenna by an object. Also called PIP, ECHO, RETURN.

blip scan ratio. . The ratio of the number of paints from a target to the maximum possible number of paints for a given number of revolutions of the radar antenna. The maximum number of paints is usually equivalent to the number of revolutions of the antenna.

blister. , *n.* See BORDER BREAK.

blizzard. , *n.* A severe weather condition characterized by low temperatures and by strong winds bearing a great amount of snow (mostly fine, dry snow picked up from the ground). The National Weather Service specifies the following conditions for a blizzard: a wind of 32 miles per hour or higher, low temperatures, and sufficient snow in the air to reduce visibility to less than 500 feet; for a severe blizzard, it specifies wind speeds exceeding 45 miles per hour, temperature near or below 10°F, and visibility reduced by snow to near zero. In popular usage in the U.S., the term is often used for any heavy snowstorm accompanied by strong winds.

block. , *n.* See CHARTLET.

block correction. . See CHARTLET.

blocky iceberg. . An iceberg with steep sides and a flat top. The length-to-height ratio is less than 5:1. See also TABULAR ICEBERG.

Blondel-Rey effect. . The effect that the flashing of a light has on reducing its apparent intensity as compared to the intensity of the same light when operated continuously or fixed.

blooming. , *n.* Expansion of the spot produced by a beam of electrons striking the face of a cathode-ray indicator, caused by maladjustment.

blowing snow. . Snow raised from the ground and carried by the wind to such a height that both vertical and horizontal visibility are considerably reduced. The expression DRIFTING SNOW is used when only the horizontal visibility is reduced.

blue ice. . The oldest and hardest form of glacier ice, distinguished by a slightly bluish or greenish color.

blue magnetism. . The magnetism displayed by the south-seeking end of a freely suspended magnet. This is the magnetism of the earth's north magnetic pole.

bluff. , *n.* A headland or stretch of cliff having a broad nearly perpendicular face. See also CLIFF.

blunder. , *n.* See MISTAKE.

Board of Geographic Names. . An agency of the U.S. Government, first established by Executive Order in 1890 and currently functioning under Public Law 242-80, 25 July 1947. Twelve departments and agencies have Board membership. The board provides for "uniformity in geographic nomenclature and orthography throughout the Federal Government." It develops policies and romanization systems under which names are derived and it standardizes geographic names for use on maps and in textual materials.

boat. , *n.* A small vessel. The term is often modified to indicate the means of propulsion, such as motorboat, rowboat, steamboat, sailboat, and sometimes to indicate the intended use, such as lifeboat, fishing boat, etc. See also SHIP.

boat compass. . A small compass mounted in a box for small craft. use.

boat harbor. . A sheltered area in a harbor set aside for the use of boats, usually with docks, moorings, etc.

boat sheet. . The work sheet used in the field for plotting details of a hydrographic survey as it progresses.

bobbing a light. . Quickly lowering the height of eye and raising it again when a navigational light is first sighted to determine if the observer is at the geographic range of the light.

bold. , *adj.* Rising steeply from the sea; as a bold coast. See also ABRUPT.

bolide. , *n.* A meteor having a magnitude brighter than 4 magnitude. Bolides are observed with much less frequency than shooting stars. Light bursts, spark showers, or splitting of the luminous trail are sometimes seen along their trails. The luminous trails persist for minutes and may persist up to an hour in exceptional cases. Also called FIREBALL. See also METEOR.

bollard. , *n.* A post (usually steel or reinforced concrete) firmly secured on a wharf, quay, etc., for mooring vessels with lines.

bombing range. . An area of land or water, and the air space above, designated for use as a bombing practice area.

boom. , *n.* A floating barrier used for security, shelter, or environmental cleanup.

boot. . To start a computer, which initiates a series of internal checks and programs which ready the computer for use.

bora. , *n.* A cold, northerly wind blowing from the Hungarian basin into the Adriatic Sea. See also FALL WIND.

borasco. , *n.* A thunderstorm or violent squall, especially in the Mediterranean.

border break. . A cartographic technique used when it is required to extend cartographic detail of a map or chart beyond the neatline into the margin, which eliminates the necessity of producing an additional sheet. Also called BLISTER.

borderland. , *n.* A region bordering a continent, normally occupied by or bordering a shelf that is highly irregular with depths well in excess of those typical of a shelf.

bore. , *n.* See TIDAL BORE.

boring. , *n.* Forcing a vessel under power through ice, by breaking a lead.

borrow. , *v., t.* To approach closer to the shore or wind.

bottom. , *n.* The ground under a body of water. The terms FLOOR, and BOTTOM have nearly the same meaning, but BED refers more specifically to the whole hollowed area supporting a body of water, FLOOR refers to the essential horizontal surface constituting the principal level of the ground under a body of water, and BOTTOM refers to any ground covered with water.

bottom characteristics. . Designations used on surveys and nautical charts to indicate the consistency, color, and classification of the sea bottom. Also called NATURE OF THE BOTTOM, CHARACTER OF THE BOTTOM.

bottom contour chart. . A chart designed for surface and sub-surface bathymetric navigation seaward of the 10 fathom contour. Bottom configuration is portrayed by depth contours and selected soundings.

bottom sample. . A portion of the material forming the bottom, brought up for inspection.

bottom sampler. . A device for obtaining a portion of the bottom for inspection.

Bouguer's halo. . An infrequently observed, faint, white. circular arc or complete ring of light which has a radius of about 39°, and is centered on the antisolar point. When observed, it usually is in the form of a separate outer ring around an anticorona. Also called ULLOA'S RING. See also FOGBOW.

Bouguer's halo

boulder, *n.* A detached water-rounded stone more than 256 millimeters in diameter, i.e., larger than a man's head. See also COBBLE.

boundary disclaimer. . A statement on a map or chart that the status and/or alignment of international or administrative boundaries is not necessarily recognized by the government of the publishing nation.

boundary lines of inland waters. . Lines dividing the high seas from rivers, harbors, and inland waters. The waters inshore of the lines are "inland waters" and upon them the Inland Rules of the Road or Pilot Rules apply. The waters outside of the lines are the high seas and upon them the International Rules apply.

boundary monument. . A material object placed on or near a boundary line to preserve and identify the location of the boundary line on the ground.

bow. , *n.* The forward part of a ship, craft, aircraft, or float.

bow and beam bearings. . Successive relative bearings (right or left) of 45° and 90° taken on a fixed object to obtain a running fix. The length of the run between such bearings is equal to the distance of the craft from the object at the time the object is broad on the beam., neglecting current.

Bowditch. , *n.* Popular title for *Pub. No. 9, The American Practical Navigator.*

bow wave. . 1. The wave set up by the bow of a vessel moving through the water. Also called WAVE OF DISPLACEMENT. 2. A shock wave in front of a body such as an airfoil.

boxing the compass. . Stating in order the names of the points (and sometimes the half and quarter points) of the compass.

brackish. , *adj.* Containing salt to a moderate degree, such as sea water which has been diluted by fresh water, such as near the mouth of a river. The salinity values of brackish water range from approximately 0.50 to 17.00 parts per thousand.

branch. , *n.* 1. A creek or brook, as used locally in the southern U.S. 2. One of the bifurcations of a stream.

brash ice. . Accumulations of floating ice made up of fragments not more than 2 meters across, the wreckage of other forms of ice.

brave west winds. . The strong, often stormy, winds from the west-northwest and northwest which blow at all seasons of the year between latitudes 40°S and 60°S. See also ROARING FORTIES.

Brazil Current. . The ocean current flowing southwestward along the Brazilian coast. Its origin is in the westward flowing Atlantic South Equatorial Current, part of which turns south and flows along the South American coast as the Brazil Current. The mean speed of the current along its entire length is about 0.6 knots. Off Uruguay at about 35° S, it meets the Falkland Current, the two turning eastward to join the South Atlantic Current.

break-circuit chronometer. . A chronometer equipped with an electrical contact assembly and program wheel which automatically makes or breaks an electric circuit at precise intervals, the sequence and duration of circuit-open circuit-closed conditions being recorded on a chronograph. The program sequence is controlled by the design of the program wheel installed. Various programs of make or break sequence, up to 60 seconds, are possible. In some chronometers the breaks occur every other second, on the even seconds, and a break occurs also on the 59th second to identify the beginning of the minute; in other chronometers, breaks occur every second except at the beginning of the minute. By recording the occurrence of events (such as star transits) on a chronograph sheet along with the chronometer breaks, the chronometer times of those occurrences are obtained.

breaker. , *n.* A wave which breaks, either because it becomes unstable, usually when it reaches shallow water, or because it dashes against an obstacle. Instability is caused by an increase in wave height and a decrease in the speed of the trough of the wave in shallow water. The momentum of the crest, often aided by the wind, causes the upper part of the wave to move faster than the lower part. The crest of a wave which becomes unstable in deep water and topples over or "breaks" is called a WHITECAP.

breakwater. , *n.* A line of rocks, concrete, pilings, or other material which breaks the force of the sea at a particular place, forming a protected area. Often an artificial embankment built to protect the entrance to a harbor or to form an artificial harbor. See also JETTY.

breasting float. . See CAMEL.

breeze. , *n.* 1. Wind of force 2 to 6 (4-31 miles per hour or 4-27 knots) on the Beaufort wind scale. Wind of force 2 (4-7 miles per hour or 4-6 knots) is classified as a light breeze; wind of force 3 (8-12 miles per hour or 7-10 knots), a gentle breeze; wind of force 4 (13-18 miles per hour or 11-16 knots), a moderate breeze; wind of force 5 (19-24 miles per hour or 17-21 knots), a fresh breeze; and wind of force 6 (25-31 miles per hour or 22-27 knots), a strong breeze. See also LIGHT AIR. 2. Any light wind.

bridge. , *n.* 1. An elevated structure extending across or over the weather deck of a vessel, or part of such a structure. The term is sometimes modified to indicate the intended use, such as *navigating bridge* or *signal bridge*. 2. A structure erected over a depression or an obstacle such as a body of water, railroad, etc. to provide a roadway for vehicles or pedestrians. See also CAUSEWAY, VIADUCT.

bridge resource management. The study of the resources available to the navigator and the exploitation of them in order to achieve the goal of safe and efficient voyages.

Briggsian logarithm. . See COMMON LOGARITHM.

bright display. . A radar display capable of being used under relatively high ambient light levels.

brisa, briza. , *n.* 1. A northeast wind which blows on the coast of South America or an east wind which blows on Puerto Rico during the trade wind season. 2. The northeast monsoon in the Philippines.

brisote. , *n.* The northeast trade wind when it is blowing stronger than usual on Cuba.

Broadcast Notice to Mariners. . Notices to mariners disseminated by radio broadcast, generally of immediate interest to navigators.

broad on the beam. . Bearing 90° relative *(broad on the starboard beam)* or 270° relative *(broad on the port beam)*. If the bearings are approximate, the expression ON THE BEAM or ABEAM should be used.

broad on the bow. . Bearing 45° relative *(broad on the starboard bow)* or 315° relative *(broad on the port bow)*. If the bearings are approximate, the expression ON THE BOW should be used.

broad on the quarter. . Bearing 135° relative *(broad on the starboard quarter)* or 225° relative *(broad on the port quarter)*. If the bearings are approximate, the expression ON THE QUARTER should be used.

broadside on. . Beam on, such as to the wind or sea.

broad tuning. . Low selectivity, usually resulting in simultaneous reception of signals of different frequencies (spill-over). The opposite is SHARP TUNING.

Broken bow. . See ANTICORONA.

broken water. . An area of small waves and eddies occurring in what otherwise is a calm sea.

brook. , *n.* A very small natural stream; a rivulet. Also called RUN, RUNNEL. See also CREEK, definition 2.

brubu. , *n.* A name for a squall in the East Indies.

B-trace. . The second trace of an oscilloscope having more than one displayed.

bubble acceleration error. . The error of a bubble sextant observation caused by displacement of the bubble by acceleration or deceleration resulting from motion of a craft. Also called ACCELERATION ERROR.

bubble horizon. . An artificial horizon parallel to the celestial horizon, established by means of a bubble level.

bubble sextant. . A sextant with a bubble or spirit level to indicate the horizontal.

bucket temperature. . Temperature of surface sea water trapped and measured in a bucket or similar receptacle.

buffer. . In computers, a temporary storage area used when incoming data cannot be processed as fast as it is transmitted.

building. , *n.* A label on a nautical chart which is used when the entire structure is the landmark, rather than an individual feature of it. Also labeled HOUSE.

bull's eye squall. . A squall forming in fair weather, characteristic of the ocean off the coast of South Africa. It is named for the peculiar appearance of the small isolated cloud marking the top of the invisible vortex of the storm.

bull the buoy. . To bump into a buoy.

bummock. , *n.* A downward projection from the underside of an ice field; the counterpart of a HUMMOCK.

bund. , *n.* An embankment or embanked thoroughfare along a body of water. The term is used particularly for such structures in the Far East.

buoy. , *n.* An unmanned floating device moored or anchored to the bottom as an aid to navigation. Buoys may be classified according to shape, as spar, cylindrical or can, conical, nun, spherical, barrel, or pillar buoy. They may also be classified according to the color scheme as a red, green, striped, banded, or checkered buoy. A buoy fitted with a characteristic shape at the top to aid in its identification is called a topmark buoy. A sound buoy is one equipped with a characteristic sound signal, and may be further classified according to the manner in which the sound is produced, as a bell, gong, horn, trumpet, or whistle buoy. A lighted buoy is one with a light having definite characteristics for detection and identification during darkness. A buoy equipped with a marker radiobeacon is called a radiobeacon buoy. A buoy with equipment for automatically transmitting a radio signal when triggered by an underwater sound signal is called a sonobuoy. A combination buoy has more than one means of conveying information; it may be called a lighted sound buoy if it is a lighted buoy provided with a sound signal. Buoys may be classified according to location, as channel, mid channel, middle ground, turning, fairway junction, junction, or sea buoy. A bar buoy marks the location of a bar. A buoy marking a hazard to navigation may be classified according to the nature of the hazard, such as obstruction, wreck, telegraph, cable, fish net, dredging, or spoil ground buoys. Buoys used for particular purposes may be classified according to their use, as anchor, anchorage, quarantine, mooring, marker, station, watch, or position buoy. A light-weight buoy especially designed to withstand strong currents is called a river buoy. An ice buoy is a sturdy one used to replace a more easily damaged buoy during a period when heavy ice is anticipated.

buoyage., *n.* A system of buoys. One in which the buoys are assigned shape, color, and number distinction in accordance with location relative to the nearest obstruction is called a cardinal system. One in which buoys are assigned shape, color, and number distinction as a means of indicating navigable waters is called a lateral system. See also IALA MARITIME BUOYAGE SYSTEM.

buoy station.. The established (charted) location of a buoy.

buoy tender.. A vessel designed for, and engaged in, servicing aids to navigation, particularly buoys.

butte., *n.* An isolated flat-topped hill, similar to but smaller than a MESA.

Buys Ballot's Law.. A rule useful in locating the center of cyclones and anticyclones. It states that, facing away from the wind in the northern hemisphere, the low pressure lies to the left. Facing away from the wind in the southern hemisphere, it is to the right; named after Dutch meteorologist C. H. D. Buys Ballot, who published it in 1857.

byte.. Basic unit of measurement of computer memory. A byte usually consists of 8 BITS; each ASCII character is represented by 1 byte.

by the head.. See DOWN BY THE HEAD.

by the stern.. See DOWN BY THE STERN.

C

C/A code., *n.* The coarse acquisition, or "civilian code," modulated on the GPS L1 signal.

cable., *n.* 1. A unit of distance equal to one-tenth of a nautical mile. Sometimes called CABLE LENGTH. 2. A chain or very strong fiber or wire rope used to anchor or moor vessels or buoys. 3. A stranded conductor or an assembly of two or more electric conductors insulated from each other, but laid up together with a strong, waterproof covering. A coaxial cable consists of two concentric conductors insulated from each other.

cable buoy.. 1. A buoy used to mark one end of a cable being worked by a cable ship. 2. A floating support of a submarine cable.

cable length.. See CABLE, definition 1.

cage., *n.* The upper part of the buoy built on top of the body of the buoy and used as a daymark or part thereof, usually to support a light, topmark and/or radar reflector. Also called SUPERSTRUCTURE.

cage., *v., t.* To erect a gyro or lock it in place by means of a caging mechanism.

caging mechanism.. A device for erecting a gyroscope or locking it in position.

cairn., *n.* A mound of rough stones or concrete, particularly one intended to serve as a landmark or message location. The stones are customarily piled in a pyramidal or beehive shape.

caisson., *n.* A watertight gate for a lock, basin, etc.

calcareous., *adj.* Containing or composed of calcium or one of its compounds.

calculated altitude.. See under COMPUTED ALTITUDE, definition 2.

calculator.. A device for mathematical computations; originally mechanical, modern ones are exclusively electronic, and able to run simple programs, as compared to a computer, which can be used for many other applications and run complex programs. A navigational calculator contains ephemeral data and algorithms for the solution of navigation problems.

caldera., *n.* A volcanic crater.

calendar., *n.* A graphic or printed record of time, usually of days, weeks, months, etc., used to refer to future events. The Gregorian calendar is in common use today. See also JULIAN DAY.

calendar day.. The period from midnight to midnight. The calendar day is 24 hours of mean solar time in length and coincides with the civil day unless a time change occurs during a day.

calendar line.. *British terminology.* See DATE LINE.

calendar month.. The month of the calendar, varying from 28 to 31 days in length.

calendar year.. The year of the calendar. Common years have 365 days and leap years 366 days. Each year exactly divisible by 4 is a leap year, except century years (1800, 1900, etc.), which must be exactly divisible by 400 (2000, 2400, etc.) to be leap years. The calendar year is based on the TROPICAL YEAR. Also called CIVIL YEAR.

calibrate., *n.* To determine or rectify the scale graduations of an instrument.

calibration card.. See under CALIBRATION TABLE.

calibration correction.. The value to be added to or subtracted from the reading of an instrument to obtain the correct reading.

calibration error.. The error in an instrument due to imperfection of calibration or maladjustment of its parts. Also called SCALE ERROR.

calibration radiobeacon.. A special radiobeacon operated primarily for calibrating shipboard radio direction finders. These radiobeacons transmit either continuously during scheduled hours or upon request.

calibration table.. A list of calibration corrections or calibrated values. A card having such a table on it is called a CALIBRATION CARD.

California Current.. A North Pacific Ocean current flowing southeastward along the west coast of North America from a point west of Vancouver Island to the west of Baja (Lower) California where it gradually widens and curves southward and southwestward, to continue as the westerly flowing PACIFIC NORTH EQUATORIAL CURRENT. The California Current is the southern branch of the Aleutian Current, augmented by the North Pacific Current, and forms the eastern part of the general clockwise oceanic circulation of the North Pacific Ocean. Although usually described as a permanent ocean current, the California Current is actually a poorly defined and variable flow easily influenced by the winds. See also MEXICO CURRENT.

California Norther.. See NORTHER.

Callipic cycle.. A period of four Meteoric cycles equal to 76 Julian years or 27,759 days. Devised by Callipus, a Greek astronomer, about 350 B.C., as a suggested improvement on the Meteoric cycle for a period in which new and full moon would recur on the same day of the year. Taking the length of the synodical month as 29.530588 days, there are 940 lunations in the Callipic cycle with about 0.25 days remaining.

calm., *adj.* In a state of calm; without motion.

calm., *n.* 1. Absence of appreciable wind; specifically, force 0 (less than 1 mile per hour or 1 knot) on the Beaufort wind scale. 2. The state of the sea when there are no waves.

calm belt.. 1. The doldrum sides of the trade winds, called calms of Cancer and calms of Capricorn.

calving., *n.* The breaking away of a mass of ice from an ice wall, ice front, or iceberg.

camanchaca., *n.* See GARUA.

camel., *n.* A float used as a fender. Also called BREASTING FLOAT.

canal., *n.* 1. An artificial waterway for navigation. 2. A long, fairly straight natural channel with steep sloping sides. 3. Any watercourse or channel. 4. A sluggish coastal stream, as used locally on the Atlantic coast of the U.S.

Canary Current, Canaries Current.. The southern branch of the North Atlantic Current (which divides on the eastern side of the ocean); it moves south past Spain and southwestward along the Northwest coast of Africa and past the Canary islands. In the vicinity of the Cape Verde Islands, it divides into two branches, the western branch augmenting the Atlantic North Equatorial Current and the

Eastern branch curving southward and continuing as the GUINEA CURRENT. The Canary Current forms the southeastern part of the general clockwise oceanic circulation of the North Atlantic Ocean. Also called the Canaries Current.

can buoy. . An unlighted buoy of which the upper part of the body (above the waterline), or the larger part of the superstructure has the shape of a cylinder or nearly so. Also called CYLINDRICAL BUOY.

candela. , *n.* The base unit of luminous intensity in the International System of Units. It is the luminous intensity, in the perpendicular direction, of a surface of 1/600,000 square meter of a blackbody at the temperature of freezing platinum, under a pressure of 101,325 newtons per square meter. The definition was adopted by the Thirteenth General Conference on Weights and Measures (1967).

candela per square meter. . The derived unit of luminance in the International System of Units.

candlepower. , *n.* Luminous intensity expressed in candelas.

canyon. , *n.* On the sea floor, a relatively narrow, deep depression with steep sides, the bottom of which generally has a continuous slope.

cap cloud. . 1. A cloud resting on the top of an isolated mountain peak. The cloud appears stationary, but actually is being continually formed to windward and dissipated to leeward. A similar cloud over a mountain ridge is called a CREST CLOUD. See also BANNER CLOUD. 2. False cirrus over a towering cumulus, in the form of a cap or hood. See also SCARF CLOUD.

cape. , *n.* A relatively extensive land area jutting seaward from a continent, or large island, which prominently marks a change in or interrupts notably the coastal trend.

Cape Breton Current. . Originating in the Gulf of St. Lawrence, the Cape Breton Current flows southeastward in the southwestern half of Cabot Strait, and merges with the Labrador Current Extension. It may be augmented by a branch of the constant but tide influenced Gaspe Current to the northwest.

cape doctor. . The strong southeast wind which blows on the South African coast. Also called DOCTOR.

Cape Horn Current. . An ocean current that flows continuously eastward close to the tip of South America. It enters Drake Passage, at about longitude 70°W, in a 150-mile-wide band, with observed surface speeds to 2.4 knots. The current veers north-northeastward; when it crosses longitude 65°W, the current has narrowed to a width of about 85 miles, and its speed has decreased considerably. The current continues as the FALKLAND CURRENT.

card. . An element of a computer consisting of the hard surface on which components are mounted. A completed card performs one or more specific functions, such as graphics.

cardinal heading. . A heading in the direction of any of the cardinal points of the compass. See also INTERCARDINAL HEADING.

cardinal mark. . An IALA aid to navigation intended to show the location of a hazard to navigation based on its position relative to the danger. Its distinguishing features are black double-cone topmarks and black and yellow horizontal bands.

cardinal point. . Any of the four principal directions; north, east, south, or west. Directions midway between cardinal points are called INTERCARDINAL POINTS.

cardinal system. . A system of aids to navigation in which the shape, color, and number distinction are assigned in accordance with location relative to the nearest hazard to navigation. The cardinal points delineate the sectors for aid location. The cardinal system is particularly applicable to a region having numerous small islands and isolated dangers. In a LATERAL SYSTEM, such as is used in U.S. waters, the aids are assigned shape, color, and number distinction as a means of indicating navigable waters.

cardioid. , *n.* The figure traced by a point on a circle which rolls around an equal fixed circle.

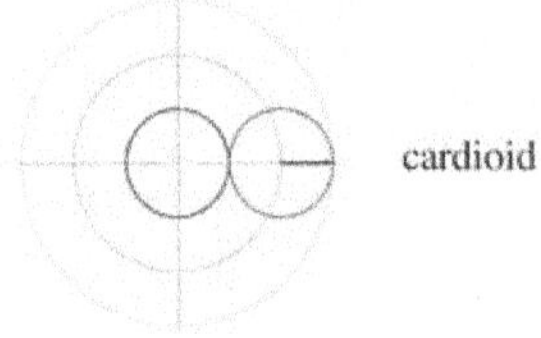

cargo transfer area. See under CARGO TRANSSHIPMENT AREAS.

cargo transshipment area. . An area generally outside port limits that is specifically designated as suitable for the transshipment of oil or other materials from large ships to smaller ones. As the purpose of transshipment is usually to reduce the draft of the larger vessel to allow her to proceed to port, the operation is often known as lightening and the area may be called lightening area or cargo transfer area.

Caribbean Current. . An ocean current flowing westward through the Caribbean Sea to the Yucatan Channel. It is formed by the co-mingling of part of the waters of the Atlantic North Equatorial Current with those of the Guiana Current.

carrier. , *n.* 1. A radio wave having at least one characteristic which may be varied from a known reference value by modulation. 2. The part of a modulated wave that corresponds in a specified manner to the unmodulated wave. 3. In a frequency stabilized system, the sinusoidal component of a modulated wave; or the output of a transmitter when the modulating wave is made zero; or a wave generated at a point in the transmitting system and subsequently modulated by the signal; or a wave generated locally at the receiving terminal which, when combined with the sidebands in a suitable detector, produces the modulating wave. Also called CARRIER WAVE.

carrier frequency. . 1. The frequency of the unmodulated fundamental output of a radio transmitter. 2. In a periodic carrier, the reciprocal of its period. The frequency of a periodic pulse carrier often is called PULSE REPETITION FREQUENCY.

carrier power. . See under POWER (OF A RADIO TRANSMITTER).

carrier wave. . See CARRIER.

cartesian coordinates. . Magnitudes defining a point relative to two intersecting lines, called AXES. The magnitudes indicate the distance from each axis, measured along a parallel to the other axis. If the axes are perpendicular, the coordinates are rectangular; if not perpendicular, they are oblique coordinates.

cartographer. , *n.* One who designs and constructs charts or maps.

cartographic feature. . A natural or cultural object shown on a map or chart by a symbol or line. See also TOPOGRAPHY.

cartographic object. , *n.* In ECDIS, a FEATURE OBJECT which contains information about the cartographic representation (including text of real world entities).

cartography, *n.* The art and science of making charts or maps.

cartometer. , *n.* A device consisting of a small wheel and a calibrated dial used to measure distances on a map by following the desired route.

cartouche. , *n.* A panel of a map, often with decoration enclosing the title, scale, publishing information, and other notes.

cask buoy. . A buoy in the shape of a cask.

Cassegrainian telescope. . A reflecting telescope in which the incoming light is reflected from the primary mirror onto a secondary mirror and back through a small central aperture in the primary mirror. See also NEWTONIAN TELESCOPE.

cast. , *v., t.* 1. To turn a ship in her own length. 2. To turn a ship to a desired direction without gaining headway or sternway. 3. To take a sounding with the lead.

catamaran. , *n.* 1. A double-hulled vessel. 2. A raft consisting of a rectangular frame attached to two parallel cylindrical floats and which may be used for working alongside a ship. See also CAMEL.

catenary. , *n.* The curve formed by a uniform cable supported only at its ends. Navigators are concerned with the catenary of overhead cables which determines clearance underneath, and the catenary of the anchor rode, which in part determines holding power and swing circle.

cathode. , *n.* 1. The electrode through which a primary stream of electrons enters the interelectrode space. 2. The general term for a negative electrode. See also ANODE.

cathode ray. . A stream of electrons emitted from the cathode of any vacuum tube, but normally used in reference to special purpose tubes designed to provide a visual display.

cathode-ray tube (CRT). . A vacuum tube in which the instantaneous position of a sharply focused electron beam, deflected by means of electrostatic or electromagnetic fields, is indicated by a spot of light produced by impact of the electrons on a fluorescent screen at the end of the tube opposite the cathode. Used in radar displays.

catoptric light. . A light concentrated into a parallel beam by means of one or more reflectors. One so concentrated by means of refracting lenses or prisms is a DIOPTRIC LIGHT.

cat's paw. . A puff of wind; a light breeze affecting a small area, as one that causes patches of ripples on the surface the water.

causeway. , *n.* A raised earthen road across wet ground or water. See also BRIDGE definition 2; VIADUCT.

cautionary characteristic. . Of a light, a unique characteristic which can be recognized as imparting a special cautionary significance e.g., a quick flashing characteristic phase indicating a sharp turn in a channel.

cautionary note. . Information calling special attention to some fact, usually a danger area, shown on a map or chart.

caver, kaver. , *n.* A gentle breeze in the Hebrides.

cavitation. . The formation of bubbles in a liquid which occurs when the static pressure becomes less than the fluid vapor pressure; it usually occurs from rotating propellers and is acoustically very noisy.

cay, kay. , *n.* A low, flat, tropical or sub-tropical island of sand and coral built up on a reef lying slightly above high water. Also called KEY.

C-band. . A radiofrequency band of 3,900 to 6,200 megahertz. This band overlaps the S- and X-bands. See also FREQUENCY.

ceiling. , *n.* The height above the earth's surface of the lowest layer of generally solid clouds, not classified as thin or partial.

celestial. , *adj.* Of or pertaining to the heavens.

celestial body. . Any aggregation of matter in space constituting a unit for astronomical study, as the sun, moon, a planet, comet, star, nebula, etc. Also called HEAVENLY BODY.

celestial concave. . See CELESTIAL SPHERE.

celestial coordinates. . Any set of coordinates used to define a point on the celestial sphere. The horizon, celestial equator, and the ecliptic systems of celestial coordinates are based on the celestial horizon, celestial equator, and the ecliptic, respectively, as the primary great circle.

celestial equator. . The primary great circle of the celestial sphere, everywhere 90° from the celestial poles; the intersection of the extended plane of the equator and the celestial sphere. Also called EQUINOCTIAL.

celestial equator system of coordinates. . A set of celestial coordinates based on the celestial equator as the primary great circle. Also called EQUINOCTIAL SYSTEM OF COORDINATES.

celestial fix. . A fix established by means of two or more celestial bodies.

celestial globe. . See STAR GLOBE.

celestial horizon. . That circle of the celestial sphere formed by the intersection of the celestial sphere and a plane through the center of the earth and perpendicular to the zenith-nadir line. Also called RATIONAL HORIZON. See also HORIZON.

celestial latitude. . Angular distance north or south of the ecliptic; the arc of a circle of latitude between the ecliptic and a point on the celestial sphere, measured northward or southward from the ecliptic through 90°, and labeled N or S indicate the direction of measurement.

celestial line of position. . A line of position determined by means of a celestial body.

celestial longitude. . Angular distance east of the vernal equinox, along the ecliptic; the arc of the ecliptic or the angle at the ecliptic pole between the circle of latitude of the vernal equinox at the circle of latitude of a point on the celestial sphere, measured eastward from the circle of latitude of the vernal equinox, through 360°.

celestial mechanics. . The study of the motions of celestial bodies under the influence of gravitational fields.

celestial meridian. . A great circle of the celestial sphere, through the celestial poles and the zenith. The expression usually refers to the upper branch, that half from pole to pole which passes through the zenith; the other half being called the lower branch. The celestial meridian coincides with the hour circle through the zenith and the vertical circle through the elevated pole.

celestial navigation. . Navigation by celestial bodies.

celestial observation. . Observation of celestial phenomena. The expression is applied in navigation principally to the measurement of the altitude of a celestial body, and sometimes to measurement of azimuth, or to both altitude and azimuth. The expression may also be applied to the data obtained by such measurement. Also called SIGHT in navigation usage.

celestial parallel. . See PARALLEL OF DECLINATION.

celestial pole. . Either of the two points of intersection section of the celestial sphere and the extended axis of the earth, labeled N or S to indicate whether the north celestial pole or the south celestial pole.

celestial sphere. . An imaginary sphere of infinite radius concentric with the earth, on which all celestial bodies except the earth are imagined to be projected.

celestial triangle. . A spherical triangle on the celestial sphere, especially the navigational triangle.

cell. . In ECDIS the basic unit of ENC DATA covering a defined geographical area bounded by two meridians and two parallels.

Celsius temperature. The designation given to the temperature measured on the International Practical Temperature Scale with the zero taken as 0.01° below the triple point of water. Normally called CENTIGRADE TEMPERATURE, but the Ninth General Conference of Weights and Measures, held in October 1948, adopted the name *Celsius* in preference to *Centigrade,* to be consistent with naming other temperature scales after their inventors, and to avoid the use of different names in different countries. On the original Celsius scale, invented in 1742 by a Swedish astronomer named Andres Celsius, the numbering was the reverse of the modern scale, 0°C representing the boiling point of water, and 100°C its freezing point.

center frequency. . See ASSIGNED FREQUENCY.

centering control. . On a radar indicator, a control used to place the sweep origin at the center of the plan position indicator.

centering error. . Error in an instrument due to inaccurate pivoting of a moving part, as the index arm of a marine sextant. Also called ECCENTRIC ERROR.

center line. . 1. The locus of points equidistant from two reference points or lines. 2. *(Usually centerline)* The line separating the port and starboard sides of a vessel, center of buoyancy. The geometric center of the immersed portion of the hull and appendages of a floating vessel All buoyant forces may be resolved into one resultant force acting upwards at this point.

center of gravity. . The point in any body at which the force of gravity may be considered to be concentrated. Same as CENTER OF MASS in a uniform gravitational field.

center of mass. . The point at which all the given mass of a body or bodies may be regarded as being concentrated as far as motion is concerned. Commonly called CENTER OF GRAVITY.

Centesimal system. , *n.* Used chiefly in France, a system of dividing a circle into 400 centesimal degrees (sometimes called grades) each of which is divided into 100 centesimal minutes of 100 centesimal seconds each.

centi-. A prefix meaning one-hundredth.

centibar. , *n.* One-hundredth of a bar; 10 millibars.

centigrade temperature. . See under CELSIUS TEMPERATURE.

centimeter. , *n.* One-hundredth of a meter.

centimeter-gram-second system. . A system of units based on the centimeter as the unit of length, the gram as the unit of mass, and the mean solar second as the unit of time. Its units with special names include the erg, the dyne, the gauss, and the oersted. See also INTERNATIONAL SYSTEM OF UNITS.

centimetric wave. . A super high frequency radio wave, approximately 0.01 to 0.1 meter in length (3 to 30 gigahertz). See also ULTRA SHORT WAVE.

central force. . A force which for purposes of computation can be considered to be concentrated at one central point with its intensity at any other point being a function of the distance from the central point. Gravitation is considered as a central force in celestial mechanics.

central force field. . The spatial distribution of the influence of a central force.

central force orbit. . The theoretical orbit achieved by a particle of negligible mass moving in the vicinity of a point mass with no other forces acting; an unperturbed orbit.

central processing unit (CPU). . The computer chip which is the brain of a computer, which runs PROGRAMS and processes DATA; also the container in which the CPU is located, along with many other associated devices such as the power supply, disk drives, etc., distinct from the MONITOR and other peripherals.

central standard time. . See STANDARD TIME.

centrifugal force. . The force acting on a body or part of a body moving under constraint along a curved path, tending to force it outward from the center of revolution or rotation. The opposite is CENTRIPETAL FORCE.

centripetal force. . The force directed toward the center of curvature, which constrains a body to move in a curved path. The opposite is CENTRIFUGAL FORCE.

chain. , *n.* A group of associated stations of a radionavigation system.

chain node.. In ECDIS the data structure in which the geometry is described in terms of EDGES, ISOLATED NODES and CONNECTED NODES. Edges and connected nodes are topologically linked. NODES are explicitly coded in the DATA STRUCTURE.

chains. The platform or station from which soundings are taken with a hand lead.

chain signature.. See under GROUP REPETITION INTERVAL.

chalk., *n.* Soft earthy sandstone of marine origin, composed chiefly of minute shells. It is white, gray, or buff in color. Part of the ocean bed and shores and composed of chalk, notably the "white cliffs of Dover," England.

challenge., *n.* A signal transmitted by a interrogator.

challenge., *v. t.* To cause an interrogator to transmit a signal which puts a transponder into operation.

challenger., *n.* See INTERROGATOR.

chance error.. See RANDOM ERROR.

change of the moon.. The time of new moon. See also PHASES OF THE MOON.

change of tide.. A reversal of the direction of motion (rising or falling) of a tide. The expression is also sometimes applied somewhat loosely to a reversal in the set of a tidal current. Also called TURN OF THE TIDE.

channel., *n.* 1. The part of a body of water deep enough for navigation through an area otherwise not suitable. It is usually marked by a single or double line of buoys and sometimes by ranges. 2. The deepest part of a stream, bay, or strait, through which the main current flows. 3. A name given to certain large straits, such as the English Channel. 4. A hollow bed through which water may run. 5. A band of radio frequencies within which a radio station must maintain its modulated carrier frequency to prevent interference with stations on adjacent channels. Also called FREQUENCY CHANNEL.

channel buoy.. A buoy marking a channel.

channel light.. A light either on a fixed support or on a buoy, marking the limit of a navigable channel. In French, the term "feu de rive" is commonly used for a channel light on a fixed support.

characteristic., *n.* 1. The color and shape of a daymark or buoy or the color and period of a light used for identifying the aid. See also CHARACTERISTIC COLOR, CHARACTERISTIC PHASE. 2. The identifying signal transmitted by a radiobeacon. 3. That part of a logarithm (base 10) to the left of the decimal point. That part of a logarithm (base 10) to the right of the decimal point is called the MANTISSA. 4. A quality, attribute, or distinguishing property of anything.

characteristic color.. The unique identifying color of a light.

characteristic frequency.. A frequency which can be easily identified and measured in a given emission.

characteristic phase.. Of a light, the sequence and length of light and dark periods and the color or colors by which a navigational light is identified, i.e., fixed, flashing, interrupted quick flashing, etc. See also CAUTIONARY CHARACTERISTIC.

characteristics of a light.. The sequence and length of light and dark periods and the color or colors by which a navigational light is identified.

character of the bottom.. See BOTTOM CHARACTERISTICS.

chart., *n.* A map or geospatial database intended primarily for navigation of aircraft or vessels.

chart amendment patch.. See CHARTLET.

chart catalog.. A list or enumeration of navigational charts, sometimes with index charts indicating the extent of coverage of the various navigational charts.

chart cell.. See CELL.

chart classification by scale. 1. Charts are constructed on many different scales, ranging from about 1:14,000,000 (and even smaller for some world charts) to 1:2,500. Small-scale charts are used for voyage planning and offshore navigation and may contain generalized soundings and minimal detail. Charts of larger scale are used as the vessel approaches land and contain greater detail and specificity. Several methods of classifying charts according to scale are in use in various nations. 2. The following classifications of nautical charts are used by the National Ocean Survey: Sailing, General, Coast, and Harbor. Sailing charts are the smallest scale charts used for planning, fixing position at sea, and for plotting while proceeding on a long voyage; the scale is generally smaller than 1:600,000. The shoreline and topography are generalized and only offshore soundings, the principal navigational lights, outer buoys, and landmarks visible at considerable distances are shown. General charts are intended for coastwise navigation outside of outlying reefs and shoals; scales range from about 1:600,000 to 1:150,000. Coast (coastal) charts are intended for inshore coastwise navigation where the course may lie inside outlying reefs and shoals, for entering or leaving bays and harbors of considerable width, and for navigating large inland waterways; scales range from about 1:150,000 to 1:50,000. Harbor charts are intended for navigation and anchorage in harbors and small waterways; the scale is generally larger than 1:50,000. 3. The classification system used by the National- Geospatial-Intelligence Agency differs from the system in definition 2 above in that the Sailing-scale charts are incorporated in the General-scale classification (smaller than about 1:150,000); those Coastal-scale charts especially useful for approaching more confined waters (bays, harbors) are classified as Approach charts. DNC libraries are based on the following scales: General: (<1:500K), Coastal: (1:500K - 1:75K), Approach: (1:75K - 1:25K), Harbor: (>1:50K).

chart comparison unit.. An optical device used to superimpose the plan position indicator radar picture on a navigational chart.

chart convergence.. Convergence of the meridians as shown on a chart.

chart datum.. See CHART SOUNDING DATUM.

chart desk.. A flat surface on which charts are spread out, usually with stowage space for charts and other navigating equipment below the plotting surface. One without stowage space is called a CHART TABLE.

charted depth.. The vertical distance from the chart sounding datum to the bottom.

charthouse.. A room, usually adjacent to or on the bridge, where charts and other navigational equipment are stored, and where navigational computations, plots, etc., may be made. Also called CHARTROOM.

chartlet., *n.* A corrected reproduction of a small area of a nautical chart which is pasted to the chart for which it is issued. These chartlets are disseminated in *Notice to Mariners* when the corrections are too numerous or of such detail as not to be feasible in printed form. Also called BLOCK, BLOCK CORRECTION, CHART AMENDMENT PATCH.

chart portfolio.. A systematic grouping of nautical charts covering a specific geographical area.

chart projection.. See MAP PROJECTION.

chart reading.. Interpretation of the symbols, lines, abbreviations, and terms appearing on charts. May be called MAP READING when applied to maps generally.

chartroom., *n.* See CHARTHOUSE.

chart scale.. The ratio between a distance on a chart and the corresponding distance represented as a ratio such as 1:80,000 (natural scale), or 30 miles to an inch (numerical scale). May be called MAP SCALE when applied to any map. See also REPRESENTATIVE FRACTION.

chart sounding datum.. The tidal datum to which soundings and drying heights on a chart are referred. It is usually taken to correspond to a low water stage of the tide. Often shortened to CHART DATUM, especially when it is clear that reference is not being made to a geodetic datum.

chart symbol.. A character, letter, or similar graphic representation used on a chart to indicate some object, characteristic, etc. May be called MAP SYMBOL when applied to any map.

chart table.. A flat surface on which charts are spread out, particularly one without stowage space below the plotting surface. One provided with stowage space is usually called a CHART DESK.

Charybdis., *n.* See GALOFARO.

chasm., *n.* A deep breach in the earth's surface; an abyss; a gorge; a deep canyon.

check bearing.. An additional bearing, using a charted object other than those used to fix the position, observed and plotted in order to insure that the fix is not the result of a blunder.

cheese antenna.. An antenna consisting of a mirror in the shape of part of a parabolic cylinder bounded by two parallel plates normal to the cylinder axis, and of an antenna feed placed on or near the focal point.

Chile Current.. See under PERU CURRENT.

chimney., *n.* A label on a nautical chart which indicates a relatively small smokestack.

chip. , *n.* 1. An integrated circuit. 2. The length of time to transmit a "0" or "1" in a binary pulse code.

chip log. . A historical speed measuring device consisting of a weighted wooden quadrant (quarter of a circle) attached to a bridle in such a manner that it will float in a vertical position, and a line with equally spaced knots, usually each 47 feet 3 inches apart. Speed is measured by casting the quadrant overboard and counting the number of knots paid out in a unit of time, usually 28 seconds.

chip rate. , *n.* The number of chips per second. See CHIP.

chopped response. . See CHOPPING.

chopping. , *n.* The rapid and regular on and off switching of a transponder, for recognition purposes.

choppy. , *adj.* description of short, breaking waves.

chord. , *n.* A straight line connecting two points on a curve.

chromatic aberration. . See under ABERRATION, definition 2.

chromosphere. , *n.* A thin layer of relatively transparent gases above the photosphere of the sun.

chromospheric eruption. . See SOLAR FLARE.

chronograph. , *n.* An instrument for producing a graphical record of time as shown by a clock or other device. The chronograph produces a double record: the first is made by the associated clock and forms a continuous time scale with significant marks indicating periodic beats of the time keepers; the second is made by some external agency, human or mechanical, and records the occurrence of an event or a series of events. The time interval of such occurrences are read on the time scale made by the clock. See also BREAK-CIRCUIT CHRONOMETER.

chronogram. , *n.* The record of a chronograph.

chronometer. , *n.* A timepiece with a nearly constant rate. It is customarily used for comparison of watches and clocks to determine their errors. A chronometer is usually set approximately to Greenwich mean time and not reset as the craft changes time zones. A hack chronometer is one which has failed to meet the exacting requirements of a standard chronometer, and is used for timing observations of celestial bodies. Hack chronometers are seldom used in modern practice, any chronometer failing to meet the requirements being rejected. See also CHRONOMETER WATCH.

chronometer correction. . The amount that must be added algebraically to the chronometer time to obtain the correct time. Chronometer correction is numerically equal to the chronometer error, but of opposite sign.

chronometer error. . The amount by which chronometer time differs from the correct time to which it was set, usually Greenwich mean time. It is usually expressed to an accuracy of 1s and labeled fast (F) or slow (S) as the chronometer time is later or earlier, respectively, than the correct time. CHRONOMETER ERROR and CHRONOMETER CORRECTION are numerically the same, but of opposite sign. See also WATCH ERROR.

chronometer rate. . The amount gained or lost by a chronometer in a unit of time. It is usually expressed in seconds per 24 hours, to an accuracy of 0.1s, and labeled gaining or losing, as appropriate, when it is sometimes called DAILY RATE.

chronometer time. . The hour of the day as indicated by a chronometer. Shipboard chronometers are generally set to Greenwich mean time. Unless the chronometer has a 24-hour dial, chronometer time is usually expressed on a 12-hour cycle and labeled A.M. or P.M.

chronometer watch. . A small chronometer, especially one with an enlarged watch-type movement.

chubasco. , *n.* A very violent wind and rain squall attended by thunder and vivid lightning often encountered during the rainy season along the west coast of Central America.

churada. , *n.* A severe rain squall in the Mariana Islands during the northeast monsoon. It occurs from November to April or May, especially from January through March.

cierzo. , *n.* See MISTRAL.

cinders. , *n., pl.* See SCORIAE.

circle. , *n.* 1. A plane closed curve all points of which are equidistant from a point within, called the center. A great circle is the intersection of a sphere and a plane through its center; it is the largest circle that can be drawn on a sphere. A small circle is the intersection of a sphere and a plane which does not pass through its center. See also PARALLEL OF ALTITUDE, PARALLEL OF DECLINATION, PARALLEL OF LATITUDE; AZIMUTH CIRCLE, BEARING CIRCLE, DIURNAL CIRCLE, EQUATOR, HOUR CIRCLE, PARASELENIC CIRCLES, POSITION CIRCLE, SPEED CIRCLE, VERTICAL CIRCLE. 2. A section of a plane, bounded by a curve all points of which are equidistant from a point within, called the center.

circle of declination. . See HOUR CIRCLE.

circle of equal altitude. . A circle on the surface of the earth, on every point of which the altitude of a given celestial body is the same at a given instant. The center of this circle is the geographical position of the body, and the great circle distance from this pole to the circle is the zenith distance of the body. See PARALLEL OF ALTITUDE.

circle of equal declination. . See PARALLEL OF DECLINATION.

circle of equivalent probability. . A circle with the same center as an error ellipse of specified probability and of such radius that the probability of being located within the circle is the same as the probability of being located within the ellipse. See also CIRCULAR ERROR PROBABLE.

circle of latitude. . A great circle of the celestial sphere through the ecliptic poles and along which celestial latitude is measured.

circle of longitude. . See PARALLEL OF LATITUDE, definition 2.

circle of perpetual apparition. . The circle of the celestial sphere, centered on the polar axis and having a polar distance from the elevated pole approximately equal to the latitude of the observer, within which celestial bodies do not set. The circle within which bodies do not rise is called the CIRCLE OF PERPETUAL OCCULTATION.

circle of perpetual occultation. . The circle of the celestial sphere, centered on the polar axis and having a polar distance from the depressed pole approximately equal to the latitude of the observer, within which celestial bodies do not rise. The circle within which bodies do not set is called the CIRCLE OF PERPETUAL APPARITION.

circle of position. . A circular line of position. The expression is most frequently used with reference to the circle of equal altitude surrounding the geographical position of a celestial body. Also called POSITION CIRCLE.

circle of right ascension. . See HOUR CIRCLE.

circle of uncertainty. . A circle having as its center a given position and as its radius the maximum likely error of the position—a circle within which a vessel is considered to be located. See also CIRCLE OF EQUAL PROBABILITY, CIRCLE OF POSITION, POSITION CIRCLE.

circle of visibility. . The circle surrounding an aid to navigation in which the aid is visible. See also VISUAL RANGE OF A LIGHT.

circle sheet. . A chart with curves enabling a graphical solution of the three-point problem rather than using a three-arm protractor. Also called SEXTANT CHART, STANDARD CIRCLE SHEET.

circuit. , *n.* 1. An electrical path between two or more points. 2. Conductors connected together for the purpose of carrying an electric current. 3. A connected assemblage of electrical components, such as resistors, capacitors, and inductors.

circular error probable. . 1. In a circular normal distribution (the magnitudes of the two one-dimensional input errors are equal and the angle of cut is 90°), the radius of the circle containing 50 percent of the individual measurements being made, or the radius of the circle inside of which there is a 50 percent probability of being located. 2. The radius of a circle inside of which there is a 50 percent probability of being located even though the actual error figure is an ellipse. That is, it is the radius of a circle of equivalent probability when the probability is specified as 50 percent. See also ERROR ELLIPSE, CIRCLE OF EQUIVALENT PROBABILITY. Also called CIRCULAR PROBABLE ERROR.

circular fix. . The designation of any one of the erroneous fix positions obtained with a revolver or swinger.

circularly polarized wave. . An electromagnetic wave which can be resolved into two plane polarized waves which are perpendicular to each other and which propagate in the same direction. The amplitudes of the two waves are equal and in time-phase quadrature. The tip of the component of the electric field vector in the plane normal to the direction of propagation describes a circle. See also ELLIPTICALLY POLARIZED WAVE.

circular normal distribution. . A two-dimensional error distribution defined by two equal single axis normal distributions, the axes being perpendicular. The error figure is a circle.

circular probable error. . See CIRCULAR ERROR PROBABLE.

circular radiobeacon. . See under RADIOBEACON.

circular velocity. . The magnitude of the velocity required of a body at a given point in a gravitational field which will result in the body following a circular orbital path about the center of the field. With respect to circular velocities characteristic of the major bodies of the solar system, this is defined for a circular orbit at the surface of the body in question. Circular velocity equals escape velocity divided by the square root of 2.

circumference. , *n.* 1. The boundary line of a circle or other closed plane curve or the outer limits of a sphere or other round body. 2. The length of the boundary line of a circle or closed plane curve or of the outer limits of a sphere or other rounded body. The circumference of a sphere is the circumference of any great circle on the sphere.

circumlunar. , *adj.* Around the moon, generally applied to trajectories.

circummeridian altitude. . See EX-MERIDIAN ALTITUDE.

circumpolar. , *adj.* Revolving about the elevated pole without setting. A celestial body is circumpolar when its polar distance is approximately equal to or less than the latitude of the observer. The actual limit is extended somewhat by the combined effect of refraction, semidiameter parallax, and the height of the observer's eye above the horizon.

circumscribed halo. . A halo formed by the junction of the upper and lower tangent arcs of the halo of 22°.

circumzenithal arc. . A brilliant rainbow-colored arc of about a quarter of a circle with its center at the zenith and about 46° above the sun. It is produced by refraction and dispersion of the sun's light striking the top of prismatic ice crystals in the atmosphere. It usually lasts for only a few minutes. See also HALO.

cirriform. , *adj.* Like cirrus; more generally, descriptive of clouds composed of small particles, mostly ice crystals, which are fairly widely dispersed, usually resulting in relative transparency and whiteness, and often producing halo phenomena not observed with other cloud forms. Irisation may also be observed. Cirriform clouds are high clouds. As a result, when near the horizon, their reflected light traverses a sufficient thickness of air to cause them often to take on a yellow or orange tint even during the midday period. On the other hand, cirriform clouds near the zenith always appear whiter than any other clouds in that part of the sky. With the sun on the horizon, this type of cloud is whitish, while other clouds may be tinted with yellow or orange; when the sun sets a little below the horizon, cirriform clouds become yellow, then pink or red and when the sun is well below the horizon, they are gray. All species and varieties of cirrus, cirrocumulus, and cirrostratus clouds are cirriform in nature. See also CUMULIFORM, STRATIFORM.

cirro-. . A prefix used in cloud classification to indicate the highest of three levels generally recognized. See also ALTO-.

cirrocumulus. , *n.* A principal cloud type (cloud genus), appearing as a thin, white patch of cloud without shadows, composed of very small elements in the form of grains, ripples, etc. The elements may be merged or separate, and more or less regularly arranged; they subtend an angle of less than 1° when observed at an angle of more than 30° above the horizon. Holes or rifts often occur in a sheet of cirrocumulus. Cirrocumulus may be composed of highly super cooled water droplets, as well as small ice crystals, or a mixture of both; usually, the droplets are rapidly replaced by ice crystals. Sometimes corona or irisation may be observed. Mamma may appear. Small virga may fall, particularly from cirrocumulus castellanus and floccus. Cirrocumulus, as well as altocumulus, often forms in a layer of cirrus and/or cirrostratus. In middle and high latitudes, cirrocumulus is usually associated in space and time with cirrus and/or cirrostratus; this association occurs less often in low latitudes. Cirrocumulus differs from these other cirriform clouds in that it is not on the whole fibrous, or both silky and smooth; rather, it is rippled and subdivided into little cloudlets. Cirrocumulus is most often confused with altocumulus. It differs primarily in that its constituent elements are very small and are without shadows. The term cirrocumulus is not used for incompletely developed small elements such as those on the margin of a sheet of altocumulus, or in separate patches at that level. See also CIRRIFORM, CLOUD CLASSIFICATION.

cirrostratus. , *n.* A principal cloud type (cloud genus), appearing as a whitish veil, usually fibrous but sometimes smooth, which may totally cover the sky, and which often produces halo phenomena, either partial or complete. Sometimes a banded aspect may appear, but the intervals between the bands are filled with thinner cloud veil. The edge of a veil of cirrostratus may be straight and clear-cut, but more often it is irregular and fringed with cirrus. Some of the ice crystals which comprise the cloud are large enough to fall, and thereby produce a fibrous aspect. Cirrostratus occasionally may be so thin and transparent as to render it nearly indiscernible, especially through haze or at night. At such times, the existence of a halo may be the only revealing feature. The angle of incidence of illumination upon a cirrostratus layer is an important consideration in evaluating the identifying characteristics. When the sun is high (generally above 50° altitude), cirrostratus never prevents the casting of shadows by terrestrial objects, and a halo might be completely circular. At progressively lower altitudes of the sun, halos become fragmentary and light intensity noticeably decreases. Cirrostratus may be produced by the merging of elements of cirrus; from cirrocumulus; from the thinning of altostratus; or from the anvil of cumulonimbus. Since cirrostratus and altostratus form from each other, it frequently is difficult to delineate between the two. In general, altostratus does not cause halo phenomena, is thicker than cirrostratus, appears to move more rapidly, and has a more even optical thickness. When near the horizon, cirrostratus may be impossible to distinguish from cirrus. See also CIRRIFORM, CLOUD CLASSIFICATION.

cirrus. , *n.* A principal cloud type (cloud genus) composed of detached cirriform elements in the form of delicate filaments or white (or mostly white) patches, or of narrow bands. These clouds have a fibrous aspect and/or a silky sheen. Many of the ice crystal particles of cirrus are sufficiently large to acquire an appreciable speed of fall; therefore, the cloud elements have a considerable vertical extent. Wind shear and variations in particle size usually cause these fibrous trails to be slanted or irregularly curved. For this reason, cirrus does not usually tend, as do other clouds, to appear horizontal when near the horizon. Because cirrus elements are too narrow, they do not produce a complete circular halo. Cirrus often evolves from virga of cirrocumulus or altocumulus, or from the upper part of cumulonimbus. Cirrus may also result from the transformation of cirrostratus of uneven optical thickness, the thinner parts of which dissipate. It may be difficult at times to distinguish cirrus from cirrostratus (often impossible when near the horizon); cirrostratus has a much more continuous structure, and if subdivided, its bands are wider. Thick cirrus (usually cirrus spissatus) is differentiated from patches of altostratus by its lesser extension and white color. The term *cirrus* is frequently used for all types of cirriform clouds. See also CIRRIFORM, CLOUD CLASSIFICATION.

cirrus spissatus. . See FALSE CIRRUS.

cislunar. , *adj.* Of or pertaining to phenomena, projects, or activity in the space between the earth and moon, or between the earth and the moon's orbit.

civil day. . A mean solar day beginning at midnight. See also CALENDAR DAY.

civil noon. . U.S. terminology from 1925 through 1952. See MEAN NOON.

civil time. . U.S. terminology from 1925 through 1952. See MEAN TIME.

civil twilight. . The period of incomplete darkness when the upper limb of the sun is below the visible horizon, and the center of the sun is not more than 6° below the celestial horizon.

civil year. . A year of the Gregorian calendar of 365 days in common years, or 366 days in leap years. see CALENDAR YEAR.

clamp screw. . A screw for holding a moving part in place, as during an observation or reading, particularly such a device used in connection with the tangent screw of a marine sextant.

clamp screw sextant. . A marine sextant having a clamp screw for controlling the position of the tangent screw.

clapper. , *n.* A heavy pendulum suspended inside a bell which sounds the bell by striking it.

Clarke ellipsoid of 1866. . The reference ellipsoid adopted by the U.S. Coast and Geodetic Survey (now the National Geodetic Survey) in 1880 for charting North America. This ellipsoid is not to be confused with the Clarke ellipsoid of 1880, which was the estimate of the size and shape of the earth at that time by the English geodesist Alexander Ross Clarke. For the Clarke ellipsoid of 1866, the semimajor axis is 6,378,206.4 meters, the semiminor axis is 6,356,583.8 meters, and the flattening or ellipticity is 1/294.98. Also called CLARKE SPHEROID OF 1866.

Clarke ellipsoid of 1880.. The reference ellipsoid of which the semimajor axis is 6,378,249.145 meters, the semiminor axis is 6,356,514.870 meters and the flattening or ellipticity is 1/293.65. This ellipsoid should not be confused with the CLARKE ELLIPSOID OF 1866. Also called CLARKE SPHEROID OF 1880.

Clarke spheroid of 1866.. See CLARKE ELLIPSOID OF 1866.

Clarke spheroid of 1880.. See CLARKE ELLIPSOID OF 1880.

classification of radar echoes.. When observing a radarscope having a stabilized relative motion display, the echoes (targets) may be classified as follows as an aid in rapid predictions of effects of evasive action on the compass direction of relative movement: an up-the-scope echo is an echo whose direction of relative movement differs by less than 90° from own ship's heading; a down-the-scope echo is an echo whose direction of relative movement differs by more than 90° from own ship's heading; an across-the scope (limbo) echo is an echo whose direction of relative movement differs by 90° from own ship's heading, i.e., the echo's tail is perpendicular to own ship's heading flasher.

clay., *n.* See under MUD.

clean., *adj.* Free from obstructions, unevenness, imperfections, as a clean anchorage.

clear., *v., t.* To leave port or pass safely by an obstruction.

clearance., *n.* The clear space between two objects, such as the nearest approach of a vessel to a navigational light, hazard to navigation, or other vessel.

clear berth.. A berth in which a vessel may swing at anchor without striking or fouling another vessel or an obstruction. See also FOUL BERTH.

cliff., *n.* Land arising abruptly for a considerable distance above water or surrounding land. See also BLUFF.

climate., *n.* The prevalent or characteristic meteorological conditions of a place or region, in contrast with weather, the state of the atmosphere at any time. A marine climate is characteristic of coastal areas, islands, and the oceans, the distinctive features being small annual and daily temperature range and high relative humidity, in contrast with continental climate, which is characteristic of the interior of a large land mass, and the distinctive features of which are large annual and daily temperature range and dry air with few clouds.

climatology., *n.* 1. The study of climate. 2. An account of the climate of a particular place or region.

clinometer., *n.* An instrument for indicating the degree of the angle of heel, roll, or pitch of a vessel; may be of the pivot arm or bubble type, usually indicating in whole degrees.

clock., *n.* A timepiece not meant to be carried on the person. See also CHRONOMETER.

clock speed.. The speed with which a computer performs operations, commonly measured in mega- or gigahertz.

clockwise., *adv.* In the direction of rotation of the hands of a clock.

close., *v., i.* To move or appear to move together. An order is sometimes given by a flagship for a vessel to close to yards, or miles. When a craft moves onto a range, the objects forming the range appear to move closer together, or close. The opposite is OPEN.

close aboard.. Very near.

closed., *adj.* Said of a manned aid to navigation that has been temporarily discontinued for the winter season. See also COMMISSIONED, WITHDRAWN.

closed sea.. 1. A part of the ocean enclosed by headlands, within narrow straits, etc. 2. A part of the ocean within the territorial jurisdiction of a country. The opposite is OPEN SEA. See also HIGH SEAS, INLAND SEA.

close pack ice.. Pack ice in which the concentration is 7/10 to 8/10, composed of floes mostly in contact.

closest approach.. 1. The event that occurs when two planets or other bodies are nearest to each other as they orbit about the primary body. 2. The place or time of the event in definition 1. 3. The time or place where an orbiting earth satellite is closest to the observer. Also called CLOSEST POINT OF APPROACH.

cloud., *n.* 1. A hydrometeor consisting of a visible aggregate of minute water and/or ice particles in the atmosphere above the earth's surface. Cloud differs from fog only in that the latter is, by definition, in contact with the earth's surface. Clouds form in the free atmosphere as a result of condensation of water vapor in rising currents of air, or by the evaporation of the lowest stratum of fog. For condensation to occur at the point of saturation or a low degree of supersaturation, there must be an abundance of condensation nuclei for water clouds, or ice nuclei for ice-crystal clouds. The size of cloud drops varies from one cloud to another, and within any given cloud there always exists a finite range of sizes. In general, cloud drops range between 1 and 100 microns in diameter and hence are very much smaller than rain drops. See also CLOUD CLASSIFICATION. 2. Any collection of particulate matter in the atmosphere dense enough to be perceptible to the eye, such as a dust cloud or smoke cloud.

cloud bank.. A fairly well defined mass of clouds observed at a distance; it covers an appreciable portion of the horizon sky, but does not extend overhead.

cloud base.. For a given cloud or cloud layer, that lowest level in the atmosphere at which the air contains a perceptible quantity of cloud particles.

cloudburst., *n.* In popular terminology, any sudden and heavy fall of rain. An unofficial criterion sometimes used specifies a rate of fall equal to or greater than 100 millimeters (3.94 inches) per hour. Also called RAIN GUSH, RAIN GUST.

cloud classification.. 1. A scheme of distinguishing and grouping clouds according to their appearance and, where possible, to their process of formation. The one in general use, based on a classification system introduced by Luke Howard in 1803, is that adopted by the World Meteorological Organization and published in the *International Cloud Atlas*. This classification is based on the determination of (a) genera, the main characteristic forms of clouds; (b) species, the peculiarities in shape and differences in internal structure of clouds; (c) varieties, special characteristics of arrangement and transparency of clouds; (d) supplementary features and accessory clouds, appended and associated minor clouds forms; and (e) mother-clouds, the origin of clouds if formed from other clouds. The ten cloud genera are cirrus, cirrocumulus, cirrostratus, altocumulus, altostratus, nimbostratus, stratocumulus, stratus, cumulus, and cumulonimbus. The fourteen cloud species are fibratus, uncinus, spissatus, castellanus, floccus, stratiformis, nebulous, lenticularis, fractus, humilis, mediocris, congestus, calvus, and capillatus. The nine cloud varieties are intortus, vertebratus, undulatus, radiatus, lacunosis, duplicatus, translucidus, perlucidus, and opacus. The nine supplementary features and accessory clouds are inclus, mamma, virga, praecipitatio, arcus, tuba, pileus, velum, and pannus. Note that although these are Latin words, it is proper convention to use only the singular endings, e.g., more than one cirrus cloud are, collectively, cirrus, not cirri. 2. A scheme of classifying clouds according to their usual altitudes. Three classes are distinguished: high, middle, and low. High clouds include cirrus, cirrocumulus, cirrostratus, occasionally altostratus and the tops of cumulonimbus. The middle clouds are altocumulus, altostratus, nimbostratus, and portions of cumulus and cumulonimbus. The low clouds are stratocumulus, stratus, most cumulus and cumulonimbus bases, and sometimes nimbostratus. 3. A scheme of classifying clouds according to their particulate composition; namely water clouds, ice-crystal clouds, and mixed clouds. The first are composed entirely of water droplets (ordinary and/or super cooled), the second entirely of ice crystals, and the third a combination of the first two. Of the cloud genera, only cirrostratus and cirrus are always ice-crystal clouds; cirrocumulus can also be mixed; and only cumulonimbus is always mixed. Altostratus nearly always is mixed, but occasionally can be ice-crystal. All the rest of the genera are usually water clouds, occasionally mixed: altocumulus, cumulus, nimbostratus and stratocumulus.

cloud cover.. That portion of the sky cover which is attributed to clouds, usually measured in tenths of sky covered.

cloud deck.. The upper surface of a cloud.

cloud height.. In weather observations, the height of the cloud base above local terrain.

cloud layer.. An array of clouds, not necessarily all of the same type, whose bases are at approximately the same level. It may be either continuous or composed of detached elements.

club., *v., i.* To drift in a current with an anchor dragging to provide control. Usually used with the word down, ie. club down.

clutter., *n.* 1. Unwanted radar echoes reflected from heavy rain, snow, waves, etc., which may obscure relatively large areas on the radarscope. See also RAIN CLUTTER, SEA RETURN. 2. In ECDIS excess information or noise data on a DISPLAY or CHART, reducing legibility.

co-. . A prefix meaning 90° minus the value with which it is used. Thus, if the latitude is 30° the colatitude is 90° - 30° = 60°. The cofunction of an angle is the function of its complement.

coalsack. , *n.* Any of several dark areas in the Milky Way, especially, when capitalized, a prominent one near the Southern Cross.

coaltitude. , *n.* Ninety degrees minus the altitude. The term has significance only when used in connection with altitude measured from the celestial horizon, when it is synonymous with ZENITH DISTANCE.

coast. , *n.* The general region of indefinite width that extends from the sea inland to the first major change in terrain features. Sometimes called SEACOAST. See also SEABOARD.

coastal aid. . See COASTAL MARK.

coastal area. . The land and sea area bordering the shoreline.

coastal boundary. . A general term for the boundary defined as the line (or measured from the line or points thereon) used to depict the intersection of the ocean surface and the land at an elevation of a particular datum, excluding one established by treaty or by the U.S. Congress.

coastal chart. . See under CHART CLASSIFICATION BY SCALE.

coastal current. . An ocean current flowing roughly parallel to a coast, outside the surf zone. See also LONGSHORE CURRENT.

coastal mark. . A navigation mark placed on the coast to assist coastal navigation. Particularly used with reference to marks placed on a long straight coastline devoid of many natural landmarks. Also called COASTAL AID.

coastal marsh. . An area of salt-tolerant vegetation in brackish and/or salt-water habitats subject to tidal inundation.

coastal plain. . Any plain which has its margin on the shore of a large body of water, particularly the sea, and generally represents a strip of recently emerged sea bottom.

coastal refraction. . The bending of the wave front of a radio wave traveling parallel to a coastline or crossing it at an acute angle due to the differences in the conducting and reflective properties of the land and water over which the wave travels. This refraction affects the accuracy of medium frequency radio direction finding systems. Also called COAST REFRACTION.

Coast and Geodetic Survey. . Name of the mapping, charting, and surveying arm of the National Ocean Service (NOS), a component of the National Oceanic and Atmospheric Administration (NOAA), which has reorganized and renamed at various times. The organization was known as: The Survey of the Coast from its founding in 1807 to 1836, Coast Survey from 1836 to 1878, and Coast and Geodetic Survey from 1878 to 1970, when it became the Office of Charting and Geodetic Services under the newly formed NOAA. In 1991 the name Coast and Geodetic Survey was reinstated. In 1995 the topographic and hydrographic parts of the Coast and Geodetic Survey were split and became the National Geodetic Survey (NGS) and the Office of Coast Survey (OCS). The Center for Operational Oceanographic Products and Services (CO-OPS) was also established. All three of these organizations are now part of NOS. Today OCS compiles onto nautical charts, and also maintains the National Geodetic Reference System. CO-OPS provides tides, water levels, currents and other oceanographic information that are used directly by mariners, as well as part of the hydrographic surveys and chart production processes that OCS carries out.

Coast Earth Station (CES). . A station which receives communications from an earth orbiting satellite for retransmission via landlines, and vice versa.

coast chart. . See under CHART CLASSIFICATION BY SCALE.

coasting. , *n.* Proceeding approximately parallel to a coastline (headland to headland) in sight of land, or sufficiently often in sight of land to fix the ship's position by observations of land features.

coasting lead. . A light deep sea lead (30 to 50 pounds), used for sounding in water 20 to 60 fathoms.

coastline. , *n.* The configuration made by the meeting of land and sea.

Coast Pilot. . See UNITED STATES COAST PILOT.

coast refraction. . See COASTAL REFRACTION.

coastwise. , *adv. & adj.* By way of the coast; moving along the coast. coastwise navigation. Navigation in the vicinity of a coast, in contrast with OFFSHORE NAVIGATION at a distance from a coast. See also COASTING.

coastwise navigation. . Navigation in the vicinity of a coast, in contrast with OFFSHORE NAVIGATION at a distance from a coast. See also COASTING.

coaxial cable. . A transmission cable consisting of two concentric conductors insulated from each other.

cobble. , *n.* A stone particle between 64 and 256 millimeters (about 2.5 to 10 inches) in diameter. See also STONE.

cocked hat. . Error triangle formed by lines of position which do not cross at a common point.

cockeyed bob. . A colloquial term in western Australia for a squall, associated with thunder, on the northwest coast in Southern Hemisphere summer.

code beacon. . A beacon that flashes a characteristic signal by which it may be recognized.

codeclination. , *n.* Ninety degrees minus the declination. When the declination and latitude are of the same name, codeclination is the same as POLAR DISTANCE measured from the elevated pole.

coding delay. . An arbitrary time delay in the transmission of pulse signals. In hyperbolic radionavigation systems of the pulse type, the coding delay is inserted between the transmission of the master and slave (or secondary) signals to prevent zero or small readings, and thus aid in distinguishing between master and slave (or secondary) station signals.

coefficient. , *n.* 1. A number indicating the amount of some change under certain specified conditions, often expressed as a ratio. For example, the coefficient of linear expansion of a substance is the ratio of its change in length to the original length for a unit change of temperature, from a standard. 2. A constant in an algebraic equation. 3. One of several parts which combine to make a whole, as the maximum deviation produced by each of several causes. See also APPROXIMATE COEFFICIENTS.

coefficient A. . A component of magnetic compass deviation of constant value with compass heading resulting from mistakes in calculations, compass and pelorus misalignment, and unsymmetrical arrangements of horizontal soft iron. See also APPROXIMATE COEFFICIENTS.

coefficient B. . A component of magnetic compass deviation, varying with the sine function of the compass heading, resulting from the fore-and-aft component of the craft's permanent magnetic field and induced magnetism in unsymmetrical vertical iron forward or abaft the compass. See also APPROXIMATE COEFFICIENTS.

coefficient C. . A component of magnetic compass deviation, varying with the cosine function of the compass heading, resulting from the athwartship component of the craft's permanent magnetic field and induced magnetism in unsymmetrical vertical iron port or starboard of the compass. See also APPROXIMATE COEFFICIENTS.

coefficient D. . A component of magnetic compass deviation, varying with the sine function of twice the compass heading, resulting from induced magnetism in all symmetrical arrangements of the craft's horizontal soft iron. See also APPROXIMATE COEFFICIENTS.

coefficient E. . A component of magnetic compass deviation, varying with the cosine function of twice the compass heading, resulting from induced magnetism in all unsymmetrical arrangements of the craft's horizontal soft iron. See also APPROXIMATE COEFFICIENTS.

coefficient J. . A change in magnetic compass deviation, varying with the cosine function of the compass heading for a given value of J, where J is the change of deviation for a heel of 1° on compass heading 000°. See also APPROXIMATE COEFFICIENTS.

coercive force. . The opposing magnetic intensity that must be applied to a magnetic substance to remove the residual magnetism.

COGARD. , *n.* Acronym for U.S. Coast Guard usually used in radio messages.

coherence. , *n.* The state of there being correlation between the phases of two or more waves, as is necessary in making phase comparisons in radionavigation.

coincidence. , *n.* The condition of occupying the same position as regards location, time, etc.

col. , *n.* 1. A neck of relative low pressure between two anticyclones. 2. A depression in the summit line of a mountain range. Also called PASS.

colatitude. , *n.* Ninety degrees minus the latitude, the angle between the polar axis and the radius vector locating a point.

cold air mass. . An air mass that is colder than surrounding air. The expression implies that the air mass is colder than the surface over which it is moving.

cold core system. . A cyclonic system where at any given level of atmosphere, the center of the low is colder than the environment surrounding it. Extra-tropical cyclones and winter lows are examples of normally cold core weather systems.

cold front. Any non-occluded front, or portion thereof, that moves so that the colder air replaces the warmer air, i.e., the leading edge of a relatively cold air mass. While some occluded fronts exhibit this characteristic, they are more properly called COLD OCCLUSIONS.

cold occlusion. . See under OCCLUDED FRONT.

cold wave. . Unseasonably low temperatures extending over a period of a day or longer, particularly during the cold season of the year.

collada. , *n.* A strong wind (35 to 50 miles per hour or stronger) blowing from the north or northwest in the northern part of the Gulf of California and from the northeast in the southern part of the Gulf of California.

collection object. . In ECDIS a FEATURE OBJECT describing the RELATIONSHIP between other OBJECTS.

collimate, *v., t.* 1. To render parallel, as rays of light. 2. To adjust the line of sight of an optical instrument, such as a theodolite, in proper relation to other parts of the instrument.

collimation error. . The angle by which the line of sight of an optical instrument differs from its collimation axis. Also called ERROR OF COLLIMATION.

collimator. , *n.* An optical device which renders rays of light parallel. One of the principal navigational uses of a collimator is to determine the index error of a bubble sextant.

collision bearing. . A constant bearing maintained while the distance between two craft is decreasing.

collision course. . A course which, if followed, will bring two craft together.

cologarithm. , *n.* The logarithm of the reciprocal of a number, or the negative logarithm. The sum of the logarithm and cologarithm of the same number is zero. The addition of a cologarithm accomplishes the same result as the subtraction of a logarithm.

colored light. . An aid to navigation exhibiting a light of a color other than white.

color calibration. In ECDIS, in order to reproduce the standard colors for ECDIS, a color calibration at the monitor must be performed to transform the CIE-specified colors for ECDIS into the color coordinate system of the screen. Calibration will ensure correct color transfer at the time a DISPLAY leaves the manufacturer's plant.

color differentiation test diagrams. In ECDIS - screen diagrams supplied in the PRESENTATION LIBRARY for use by the mariner to check brightness and contrast settings and to find out whether the screen still has the capability of distinguishing the important colors.

color fill. 1. In ECDIS the use of color to fill the interior area of a chart symbol to make it more readily recognizable. 2. In ECDIS a method of distinguishing different area features by filling areas with color. "Transparent" color fill is used to allow information to show through the fill, e.g., soundings in a traffic separation zone.

color gradients. See HYPSOMETRIC TINTING.

COLREGS. , *n.* Acronym for International Regulations for Prevention of Collisions at Sea.

COLREGS Demarcation Lines. . Lines delineating the waters upon which mariners must comply with the International Regulations for Preventing Collisions at Sea 1972 (72 COLREGS) and those waters upon which mariners must comply with the Navigation Rules for Harbors, Rivers, and Inland Waters (Inland Rules). The waters outside the lines are COLREGS waters. For specifics concerning COLREGS Demarcation Lines, see *U.S. Code of Federal Regulations*, Title 33, Navigation and Navigable Waters; Part 82, COLREGS Demarcation Lines.

column. , *n.* A vertical line of anything, such as a column of air, a column of figures in a table, etc.

colure. , *n.* A great circle of the celestial sphere through the celestial poles and either the equinoxes or solstices, called, respectively, the equinoctial colure or the solstitial colure.

coma. , *n.* The foggy envelope surrounding the nucleus of a comet.

combat chart. . A special-purpose chart of a land-sea area using the characteristics of a map to represent the land area and a chart to represent the sea area, with special features to make the chart useful in naval operations, particularly amphibious operations. Also called MAP CHART.

comber. , *n.* A deep water wave whose crest is pushed forward by a strong wind and is much larger than a whitecap. A long spilling breaker. See ROLLER.

comet. , *n.* A luminous member of the solar system composed of a head or coma, at the center of which a nucleus of many small solid particles is sometimes situated, and often with a spectacular gaseous tail extending a great distance from the head. The orbits of comets are highly elliptical and present no regularity as to their angle to the plane of the ecliptic.

command and control. . The facilities, equipment, communications, procedures, and personnel essential to a commander for planning, locating, directing, and controlling operations of assigned forces pursuant to the missions assigned. In many cases, a locating or position fixing capability exists in, or as a by-product to, command and control systems.

commissioned. , *adj.* Officially placed in operation. In navigation, most commonly used to describe seasonal aids to navigation, which are *decommissioned* in the fall or winter, *commissioned* in spring.

Commission on the Promulgation of Radio Navigation Warnings. . International commission that monitors and guides the Worldwide Navigation Warning Service (WWNWS). Facilitates major changes and or studies to enhance navigational warning dissemination, encourages bilateral agreements, prepares and reviews WWNWS guidance documents.

common establishment. . See under ESTABLISHMENT OF THE PORT.

common logarithm. A logarithm to the base 10. Also called BRIGGSIAN LOGARITHM.

common-user. , *adj.* Having the characteristics of being planned, operated or used to provide services for both military and civil applications. The availability of a system having such characteristics is not dependent on tactical military operations or use.

common year. . A calendar year of 365 days. One of 366 days is called a LEAP YEAR.

communication. , *n.* The transfer of intelligence between entities. If by wire, radio, or other electromagnetic means, it may be called telecommunication; if by radio, radiocommunication.

commutation. , *n.* A method by means of which the transmissions from a number of stations of a radionavigation system are time shared on the same frequency.

compact disk. . A type of computer storage media which records data using bubbles melted into the surface of a disk.

compacted ice edge. . A close, clear-cut ice edge compacted by wind or current. It is usually on the windward side of an area of pack ice.

compacting. , *adj.* Pieces of sea ice are said to be compacting when they are subjected to a converging motion, which increases ice concentration and/or produces stresses which may result in ice deformations.

compact pack ice. . Pack ice in which the concentration is 10/10 and no water is visible.

comparing watch. . A watch used for timing observations of celestial bodies. Generally its error is determined by comparison with a chronometer, hence its name. A comparing watch normally has a large sweep second hand to facilitate reading time to the nearest second. Sometimes called HACK WATCH. See also SPLIT-SECOND TIMER.

comparison frequency. . In the Decca Navigator System, the common frequency to which the incoming signals are converted in order that their phase relationships may be compared.

comparison of simultaneous observations. . A reduction process in which a short series of tide or tidal current observations at any place is compared with simultaneous observations at a control station where tidal or tidal current constants have previously been determined from a long series of observations. For tides, it is usually used to adjust constants from a subordinate station to the equivalent of that which would be obtained from a 19-year series.

compass. , *adj.* Of or pertaining to a compass or related to compass directions.

compass. , *n.* An instrument for indicating a horizontal reference direction relative to the earth. Compasses used for navigation are equipped with a graduated compass card for direct indication of any horizontal direction. A magnetic compass depends for its directive force upon the attraction of the magnetism of the earth for a magnet free to turn in any horizontal direction. A compass having one or more gyroscopes as the directive element, and tending to indicate true north is called a gyrocompass. A compass intended primarily for use in observing bearings is called a bearing compass; one intended primarily for measuring amplitudes, an amplitude compass. A directional gyro is a gyroscopic device used to indicate a selected horizontal direction for a limited time. A remote-indicating compass is equipped with one or more indicators, called compass repeaters, to repeat at a distance the readings of a master compass. A compass designated as the standard for a vessel is called a standard compass; one by which a craft is steered is called a steering compass. A liquid, wet, or spirit compass is a magnetic compass having a bowl completely filled with liquid; a magnetic compass without liquid is called a dry compass. An aperiodic or deadbeat compass, after being deflected, returns by one direct movement to its proper reading, without oscillation. A small compass mounted in a box for convenient use in small water craft is called a boat compass. A pelorus is sometimes called a dumb compass. A radio direction finder was formerly called a radio compass.

compass adjustment. . The process of neutralizing undesired magnetic effects on a magnetic compass. Permanent magnets and soft iron correctors are arranged about the binnacle so that their effects are about equal and opposite to the magnetic material in the craft, thus reducing the deviations and eliminating the sectors of sluggishness and unsteadiness. See also COMPASS COMPENSATION.

compass adjustment buoy. . See SWINGING BUOY.

compass amplitude. . Amplitude relative to compass east or west.

compass azimuth. . Azimuth relative to compass north.

compass bearing. . Bearing relative to compass north.

compass bowl. . The housing in which the compass card is mounted, usually filled with liquid.

compass card. . The part of a compass on which the direction graduations are placed. It is usually in the form of a thin disk or annulus graduated in degrees, clockwise from 000° at the reference direction to 360°, and sometimes also in compass points. A similar card on a pelorus is called a PELORUS CARD.

compass card axis. . The line joining 000° and 180° on a compass card. Extended, this line is sometimes called COMPASS MERIDIAN.

compass compensation. . The process of neutralizing the effects of degaussing currents on a marine magnetic compass. The process of neutralizing the magnetic effects the vessel itself exerts on a magnetic compass is properly called COMPASS ADJUSTMENT, but the expression compass compensation is often used for this process, too.

compass course. . Course relative to compass north.

compass direction. . Horizontal direction expressed as angular distance from compass north.

compass error. . The angle by which a compass direction differs from the true direction; the algebraic sum of variation and deviation; the angle between the true meridian and the compass card axis, expressed in degrees east or west to indicate the direction of compass north with respect to true north. See also ACCELERATION ERROR, GAUSSIN ERROR, GYRO ERROR, HEELING ERROR, LUBBER'S LINE ERROR, QUADRANTAL ERROR, RETENTIVE ERROR, SWIRL ERROR.

compasses. , *n.* An instrument for drawing circles. In its most common form it consists of two legs joined by a pivot, one leg carrying a pen or pencil and the other leg being pointed. An instrument for drawing circles of large diameter, usually consisting of a bar with sliding holders for points, pencils, or pens is called beam compasses. If both legs are pointed, the instrument is called DIVIDERS and is used principally for measuring distances or coordinates.

compass heading. . Heading relative to compass north.

compass meridian. . A line through the north-south points of a magnetic compass. The COMPASS CARD AXIS lies in the compass meridian.

compass north. . The direction north as indicated by a magnetic compass; the reference direction for measurement of compass directions.

compass points. . The 32 divisions of a compass, at intervals of 11.25°. Each division is further divided into quarter points. Stating in order the names of the points (and sometimes the half and quarter points) is called BOXING THE COMPASS.

compass prime vertical. . The vertical circle through the compass east and west points of the horizon.

compass repeater. . That part of a remote-indicating compass system which repeats at a distance the indications of the master compass. One used primarily for observing bearings may be called a bearing repeater. Also called REPEATER COMPASS. See also GYRO REPEATER.

compass rose. . A circle graduated in degrees, clockwise from 000° at the reference direction to 360°, and sometimes also in compass points. Compass roses are placed at convenient locations on the Mercator chart or plotting sheet to facilitate measurement of direction. See also PROTRACTOR.

compass track. . The direction of the track relative to compass north.

compass transmitter. . The part of a remote-indicating compass system which sends the direction indications to the repeater compass.

compensate. , *v., t.* To counteract an error; to counterbalance.

compensated loop radio direction finder. . A loop antenna radio direction finder for bearing determination, which incorporates a second antenna system designed to reduce the effect of polarization and radiation error.

compensating coils. . The coils placed near a magnetic compass to neutralize the effect of the vessel's degaussing system on the compass. See also COMPASS COMPENSATION.

compensating error. . An error that tends to offset a companion error and thus obscure or reduce the effect of each.

compensator. , *n.* 1. A corrector used in the compensation of a magnetic compass. 2. The part of a radio direction finder which applies all or part of the necessary correction to the direction indication.

compilation scale. . In ECDIS the SCALE at which the DATA was compiled.

compilation update. In ECDIS the CORRECTION INFORMATION which has been issued since the last new edition of the ENC or since the last OFFICIAL UPDATE applied to the SENC, compiled into a single, comprehensive ENC UPDATE.

compile. To assemble various elements of a system into a whole.

compiler. . 1. One who compiles. 2. Computer software which translates programs into machine language which a computer can use.

complement. , *n.* An angle equal to 90° minus a given angle. See also EXPLEMENT, SUPPLEMENT.

complementary angles. . Two angles whose sum is 90°.

component. , *n.* 1. See CONSTITUENT. 2. The part of a tidal force of tidal current velocity which, by resolution into orthogonal vectors, is found to act in a specified direction. 3. One of the parts into which a vector quantity can be divided. For example, the earth's magnetic force at any point can be divided into *horizontal* and *vertical components*.

composite. , *adj.* Composed of two or more separate parts.

composite group flashing light. . A light similar to a group flashing light except that successive groups in a single period have different numbers of flashes.

composite group occulting light. . A group occulting light in which the occultations are combined in successive groups of different numbers of occultations.

composite sailing. . A modification of great circle sailing used when it is desired to limit the highest latitude. The composite track consists of a great circle from the point of departure and tangent to the limiting parallel, a course line along the parallel, and a great circle tangent to the limiting parallel to the destination. Composite sailing applies only when the vertex lies between the point of departure and destination.

composite track. . A modified great circle track consisting of an initial great circle track from the point of departure with its vertex on a limiting parallel of latitude, a parallel-sailing track from this vertex along the limiting parallel to the vertex of a final great circle track to the destination.

composition of vectors. . See VECTOR ADDITION.

compound harmonic motion. . The projection of two or more uniform circular motions on a diameter of the circle of such motion. The projection of a simple uniform circular motion is called SIMPLE HARMONIC MOTION.

compound tide. . A tidal constituent with a speed equal to the sum or difference of the speeds of two or more elementary constituents. Compound tides are usually the result of shallow water.

compressed-air horn. . See DIAPHRAGM HORN.

compression. , *n.* See FLATTENING.

computed altitude. . 1. Tabulated altitude interpolated for increments of latitude, declination, or hour angle. If no interpolation is required, the tabulated altitude and computed altitude are identical. 2. Altitude determined by computation, table, mechanical computer, or graphics, particularly such an altitude of the center of a celestial body measured as an arc on a vertical circle of the celestial sphere from the celestial horizon. Also called CALCULATED ALTITUDE.

computed azimuth. . Azimuth determined by computation, table, mechanical device, or graphics for a given place and time. See also TABULATED AZIMUTH.

computed azimuth angle. . Azimuth angle determined by computation, table, mechanical device, or graphics for a given place and time. See also TABULATED AZIMUTH ANGLE.

computed point. . In the construction of the line of position by the Marcq St. Hilaire method, the foot of the perpendicular from the assumed position to the line of position. Also called SUMNER POINT.

concave. , *adj.* Curving and hollow, such as the inside of a circle or sphere. The opposite is CONVEX.

concave. , *n.* A concave line or surface.

concentration. , *n.* The ratio, expressed in tenths, of the sea surface actually covered by ice to the total area of sea surface, both ice-covered and ice-free, at a specific location or over a defined area.

concentration boundary. . The transition between two areas of pack ice with distinctly different concentrations.

concentric. , *adj.* Having the same center. The opposite is ECCENTRIC.

concurrent line. . A line on a map or chart passing through places having the same current hour.

condensation. , *n.* The physical process by which a vapor becomes a liquid or solid. The opposite is EVAPORATION.

conduction. , *n.* Transmission of electricity, heat, or other form of energy from one point to another along a conductor, or transference of heat from particle to particle through a substance, such as air, without any obvious motion. Heat is also transferred by CONVECTION and RADIATION.

conductivity. , *n.* The ability to transmit, as electricity, heat, sound, etc. Conductivity is the opposite of RESISTIVITY.

conductor. , *n.* A substance which transmits electricity, heat, sound, etc.

cone. , *n.* 1. A solid having a plane base bounded by a closed curve and a surface formed by lines from every point on the circumference of the base to a common point or apex. 2. A surface generated by a straight line of indefinite length, one point of which is fixed and another point of which follows a fixed curve. Also called a CONICAL SURFACE.

configuration. , *n.* 1. The position or disposition of various parts, or the figure or pattern so formed. 2. A geometric figure, usually consisting principally of points and connecting lines.

conformal. , *adj.* Having correct angular representation.

conformal chart. . A chart using a conformal map projection; also called orthomorphic chart.

conformal map projection. . A map projection in which all angles around any point are correctly represented, In such a projection the scale is the same in all directions about any point. Very small shapes are correctly represented, resulting in an orthomorphic projection. The terms *conformal* and *orthomorphic* are used synonymously since neither characteristic can exist without the other.

confusion region. . The region surrounding a radar target within which the radar echo from the target cannot be distinguished from other echoes.

conic. , *adj.* Pertaining to a cone.

conical buoy. . See NUN BUOY.

conical surface. . See CONE, definition 2.

conic chart. . A chart on a conic map projection.

conic chart with two standard parallels. . A chart on the conic map projection with two standard parallels. Also called SECANT CONIC CHART. See also LAMBERT CONFORMAL CHART.

conic map projection. . A map projection in which the surface of a sphere or spheroid, such as the earth, is conceived as projected onto a tangent or secant cone which is then developed into a plane. In a simple conic map projection the cone is tangent to the sphere or spheroid, in a conic map projection with two standard parallels the cone intersects the sphere or spheroid along two chosen parallels, and in a polyconic map projection a series of cones are tangent to the sphere or spheroid. See also LAMBERT CONFORMAL CONIC MAP PROJECTION, MODIFIED LAMBERT CONFORMAL MAP PROJECTION.

conic map projection with two standard parallels. . A conic map projection in which the surface of a sphere or spheroid is conceived as developed on a cone which intersects the sphere or spheroid along two standard parallels, the cone being spread out to form a plane. The Lambert conformal map projection is an example. Also called SECANT CONIC MAP PROJECTION.

conic section. . Any plane curve which is the locus of a point which moves so that the ratio of its distance from a fixed point to its distance from a fixed line is constant. The ratio is called the eccentricity; the fixed point is the focus; the fixed line is the directrix. When the eccentricity is equal to unity, the conic section is a parabola; when less than unity an ellipse; and when greater than unity, a hyperbola. They are so called because they are formed by the intersection of a plane and a right circular cone.

conjunction. , *n.* The situation of two celestial bodies having either the same celestial longitude or the same sidereal hour angle. A planet is at superior conjunction if the sun is between it and the earth; at inferior conjunction if it is between the sun and the earth. The situation of two celestial bodies having either celestial longitudes or sidereal hour angles differing by 180° is called OPPOSITION.

conjunction

conn, *v., t.* 1. To direct the course and speed of a vessel. The person giving orders to the helmsman (not just relaying orders) is said to have the conn or to be conning the ship. 2. *n.* Control of the maneuvering of a ship.

connected node. . In ECDIS a NODE referred to as a beginning and/or end node by one or more EDGE. Connected nodes are defined only in the CHAIN-NODE, PLANAR GRAPH and FULL TOPOLOGY data structures.

Consol, *n.* A long range, obsolete azimuthal radionavigation system of low accuracy operated primarily for air navigation.

console. , *n.* The housing of the main operating unit of electronic equipment, in which indicators and general controls are located. The term is popularly limited to large housings resting directly on the deck, as contrasted with smaller cabinets such as rack or bracket-mounted units.

consolidated pack ice. . Pack ice in which the concentration is 10/10 and the floes are frozen together.

consolidated ridge. . A line or wall of ice forced up by pressure in which the base has frozen together.

Consol station. . A short baseline directional antenna system used to generate Consol signals.

constant. , *n.* A fixed quantity; one that does not change.

constant bearing, decreasing range. . See STEADY BEARING.

constant deviation. . Deviation which is the same on any heading, as that which may result from certain arrangements of asymmetrical horizontal soft iron.

constant error. . A systematic error of unchanging magnitude and sign throughout a given series of observations. Also called BIAS ERROR.

constant of aberration. . The measure of the maximum angle between the true direction and the apparent direction of a celestial body as observed from earth due to aberration. It has a value of 20.496 seconds of arc. The aberration angle depends upon the ratio of the velocity of the earth in its orbit and the velocity of light in addition to the angle between the direction of the light and the direction of motion of the observing telescope. The maximum value is obtained when the celestial body is at the pole of the ecliptic. Also called ABERRATION CONSTANT.

constant of the cone. . The chart convergence factor for a conic projection. See also CONVERGENCE FACTOR.

constant-pressure chart. . The synoptic chart for any constant-pressure surface, usually containing plotted data and analyses of the distribution of, e.g., height of the surface, wind, temperature, and humidity. Constant-pressure charts are most commonly known by their pressure value; for example the 1000-millibar chart. Also called ISOBARIC CHART.

constant-pressure surface. . In meteorology, an imaginary surface along which the atmospheric pressure is everywhere equal at a given instant. Also called ISOBARIC SURFACE.

constellation. , *n.* A group of stars which appear close together, regardless of actual distances, particularly if the group forms a striking configuration. Among astronomers a constellation is now considered a region of the sky having precise boundaries so arranged that all of the sky is covered, without overlap. The ancient Greeks recognized 48 constellations covering only certain groups of stars. Modern astronomers recognize 88 constellations.

constituent. , *n.* One of the harmonic elements in a mathematical expression for the tide-producing force and in corresponding formulas for the tide or tidal current. Each constituent represents a periodic change or variation in the relative positions of the earth, moon, and sun. Also called HARMONIC CONSTITUENT, TIDAL CONSTITUENT, COMPONENT.

constituent day. . The duration of one rotation of the earth on its axis, with respect to an astre fictif, a fictitious star representing one of the periodic elements in tidal forces. It approximates the length of a lunar or solar day. The expression is not applicable to a long period.

constituent, constituent hour. . One twenty-fourth part of a constituent day.

contact. , *n.* Any echo detected on the radarscope and not evaluated as clutter or as a false echo. Although the term *contact is* often used interchangeably with *target,* the latter term specifically indicates that the echo is from an object about which information is being sought.

conterminous U.S. . Forty-eight states and the District of Columbia, i.e., the United States before January 3, 1959 (excluding Alaska and Hawaii).

contiguous zone. . The band of water outside or beyond the territorial sea in which a coastal nation may exercise customs control and enforce public health and other regulations.

continent. , *n.* An expanse of continuous land constituting one of the major divisions of the land surface of the earth.

continental borderland. . A region adjacent to a continent, normally occupied by or bordering a shelf, that is highly irregular with depths well in excess of those typical of a shelf. See also INSULAR BORDERLAND.

continental climate. . The type of climate characteristic of the interior of a large land mass, the distinctive features of which are large annual and daily temperature range and dry air with few clouds, in contrast with MARINE CLIMATE.

continental polar air. . See under AIR-MASS CLASSIFICATION.

continental rise. . A gentle slope rising from oceanic depths toward the foot of a continental slope.

continental shelf. . A zone adjacent to a continent that extends from the low water line to a depth at which there is usually a marked increase of slope towards oceanic depths. See also INSULAR SHELF.

continental tropical air. . See under AIR-MASS CLASSIFICATION.

Continental United States. . United States territory, including the adjacent territorial waters, located within the North American continent between Canada and Mexico. See also CONTERMINOUS U.S.

continuous carrier radiobeacon. . A radiobeacon whose carrier wave is unbroken but which is modulated with the identification signal. The continuous carrier wave signal is not audible to the operator of an aural null direction finder not having a beat frequency oscillator. The use of the continuous carrier wave improves the performance of automatic direction finders. The marine radiobeacons on the Atlantic and Pacific coasts of the U.S. are of this type. See also DUAL CARRIER RADIOBEACON.

continuous quick light. . A quick flashing light (flashing 50-80 times per minute) which operates continuously with no eclipses.

continuous system. . A classification of a navigation system with respect to availability. A continuous system gives the capability to determine position at any time.

continuous ultra quick light. . An ultra quick light (flashing not less than 160 flashes per minute) with no eclipses.

continuous very quick light. . A very quick light (flashing 80-160 times per minute) with no eclipses.

continuous wave. . 1. Electromagnetic radiation of a constant amplitude and frequency. 2. Radio waves, the successive sinusoidal oscillations of which are identical under steady-state conditions.

contour. , *n.* The imaginary line on the ground or seafloor, all points of which are at the same elevation above or below a specified datum.

contour interval. . The difference in elevation between two adjacent contours.

contour line. . A line connecting points of equal elevation or equal depth. One connecting points of equal depth is usually called a depth contour, but if depth is expressed in fathoms, it may be called a fathom curve or fathom line. See also FORM LINES.

contour map. . A topographic map showing relief by means of contour lines.

contrary name. . A name opposite or contrary to that possessed by something else, as declination has a name *contrary* to that of latitude if one is north and the other south. If both are north or both are south, they are said to be of SAME NAME.

contrastes. , *n., pl.* Winds a short distance apart blowing from opposite quadrants, frequent in the spring and fall in the western Mediterranean.

contrast threshold. . The minimum contrast at the eye of a given observer at which an object can be detected. The contrast threshold is a property of the eye of the individual observer. See METEOROLOGICAL VISIBILITY, VISUAL RANGE.

control. , *n.* 1. The coordinated and correlated dimensional data used in geodesy and cartography to determine the positions and elevations of points on the earth's surface or on a cartographic representation of that surface. 2. A collective term for a system of marks or objects on the earth or on a map or a photograph, whose positions and/or elevations have been or will be determined.

control current station. . A current station at which continuous velocity observations have been made over a minimum of 29 days. Its purpose is to provide data for computing accepted values of the harmonic and nonharmonic constants essential to tidal current predictions and circulatory studies. The data series from this station serves as the control for the reduction of relatively short series from subordinate current stations through the method of comparison of simultaneous observations. See also CURRENT STATION, SUBORDINATE CURRENT STATION.

controlled air space. . An airspace of defined dimensions within which air traffic control service is provided.

controlling depth. . 1. The least depth in the approach or channel to an area, such as a port or anchorage, governing the maximum draft of vessels that can enter. 2. The least depth within the limits of a channel; it restricts the safe use of the channel to drafts of less than that depth. The center line controlling depth of a channel applies only to the channel center line; lesser depths may exist in the remainder of the channel. The mid-channel controlling depth of a channel is the controlling depth of only the middle half of the channel. See also FEDERAL PROJECT DEPTH.

control station. . See PRIMARY CONTROL TIDE STATION, SECONDARY CONTROL TIDE STATION, CONTROL CURRENT STATION.

convection. , *n.* Circulation in a fluid of nonuniform temperature, due to the differences in density and the action of gravity. In the atmosphere, convection takes place on a large scale. It is essential to the formation of many clouds, especially those of the cumulus type. Heat is transferred by convection and also by ADVECTION, CONDUCTION, and RADIATION.

convention. , *n.* A body of regulations adopted by the International Maritime Organization (IMO) which regulate an aspect of maritime affairs. See also GEOGRAPHIC SIGN CONVENTIONS.

conventional direction of buoyage. . 1. The general direction taken by the mariner when approaching a harbor, river, estuary or other waterway from seaward, or 2. The direction determined by the proper authority. In general it follows a clockwise direction around land masses.

converge. , *v., i.* To tend to come together.

converged beam. . See under FAN BEAM.

convergence constant. . The angle at a given latitude between meridians 1° apart. Sometimes loosely called CONVERGENCY. On a map or chart having a convergence constant of 1.0, the true direction of a straight line on the map or chart changes 1° for each 1° of longitude that the line crosses; the true direction of a straight line on a map or chart having a convergence constant of 0.785 changes 0.785° for each 1° of longitude the line crosses. Also called CONVERGENCE FACTOR. See also CONVERGENCE OF MERIDIANS.

convergence factor.. See CONVERGENCE CONSTANT.

convergence of meridians. . The angular drawing together of the geographic meridians in passing from the Equator to the poles, At the Equator all meridians are mutually parallel; passing from the Equator, they converge until they meet at the poles, intersecting at angles that are equal to their differences of longitude. See also CONVERGENCE CONSTANT.

convergency. , *n.* See under CONVERGENCE CONSTANT.

conversion. , *n.* Determination of the rhumb line direction of one point from another when the initial great circle direction is known, or vice versa. The difference between the two directions is the conversion angle, and is used in great circle sailing.

conversion angle. . The angle between the rhumb line and the great circle between two points. Also called ARC TO CHORD CORRECTION. See also HALF-CONVERGENCY.

conversion scale. . A scale for the conversion of units of one measurement to equivalent units of another measurement. See NOMOGRAM.

conversion table. . A table for the conversion of units of one measurement to equivalent units of another measurement. See NOMOGRAM.

convex. , *adj.* Curving away from, such as the outside of a circle or sphere. The opposite is CONCAVE.

convex. , *n.* A convex line or surface.

coordinate. , *n.* One of a set of magnitudes defining a point in space. If the point is known to be on a given line, only one coordinate is needed; if on a surface, two are required; if in space, three. Cartesian coordinates define a point relative to two intersecting lines, called AXES. If the axes are perpendicular, the coordinates are rectangular; if not perpendicular, they are oblique coordinates. A three-dimensional system of Cartesian coordinates is called space coordinates. Polar coordinates define a point by its distance and direction from a fixed point called the POLE. Direction is given as the angle between a reference radius vector and a radius vector to the point. If three dimensions are involved, two angles are used to locate the radius vector. Space-polar coordinates define a point on the surface of a sphere by (1) its distance from a fixed point at the center, called the POLE (2) the COLATITUDE or angle between the POLAR AXIS (a reference line through the pole) and the RADIUS VECTOR (a straight line connecting the pole and the point)- and (3) the LONGITUDE or angle between a reference plane through the polar axis and a plane through the radius vector and the polar axis. Spherical coordinates define a point on a sphere or spheroid by its angular distances from a primary great circle and from a reference secondary great circle. Geographical or terrestrial coordinates define a point on the surface of the earth. Celestial coordinates define a point on the celestial sphere. The horizon, celestial equator and the ecliptic systems of celestial coordinates are based on the celestial horizon, celestial equator, and the ecliptic, respectively, as the primary great circle.

coordinate conversion. . Changing the coordinate values from one system to those of another.

Coordinated Universal Time (UTC). . The time scale that is available from most broadcast time signals. It differs from International Atomic Time (TAI) by an integral number of seconds. UTC is maintained within 1 second of UT1 by the introduction of 1-second steps (leap seconds) when necessary, normally at the end of December. DUT1, an approximation to the difference UT1 minus UTC, is transmitted in code on broadcast time signals.

coordinate paper. . Paper ruled with lines to aid in the plotting of coordinates. In its most common form, it has two sets of parallel lines, usually at right angles to each other, when it is also called CROSS-SECTION PAPER. A type ruled with two sets of mutually-perpendicular, parallel lines spaced according to the logarithms of consecutive numbers is called logarithmic coordinate paper or semilogarithmic coordinate paper as both or only one set of lines is spaced logarithmically. A type ruled with concentric circles and radial lines from the common center is called polar coordinate paper. Also called GRAPH PAPER.

coplanar. , *adj.* Lying in the same plane.

coprocessor. . A microprocessor chip which performs numerical functions for the Central Processing Unit (CPU), freeing it for other tasks.

coral. , *n.* The hard skeleton of certain tiny sea animals or the stony, solidified mass of a number of such skeletons.

coral head. . A large mushroom or pillar shaped coral growth.

coral reef. . A reef made up of coral, fragments of coral and other organisms, and the limestone resulting from their consolidation. Coral may constitute less than half of the reef material.

corange line. . A line passing through places of equal tidal range.

cordillera. , *n.* On the sea floor, an entire mountain system including all the subordinate ranges, interior plateaus, and basins.

cordonazo. , *n.* The "Lash of St. Francis." Name applied locally to southerly hurricane winds along the west coast of Mexico. The cordonazo is associated with tropical cyclones in the southeastern North Pacific Ocean. These storms may occur from May to November, but ordinarily affect the coastal areas most severely near or after the Feast of St. Francis, on October 4.

Coriolis acceleration. . An acceleration of a body in motion in a relative (moving) coordinate system. The total acceleration of the body, as measured in an inertial coordinate system, may be expressed as the sum of the acceleration within the relative system, the acceleration of the relative system itself, and the Coriolis acceleration. In the case of the earth, moving with angular velocity Ω, a body moving relative to the earth with velocity V has the Coriolis acceleration 252 × Ω. If Newton's laws are to be applied in the relative system, the Coriolis acceleration and the acceleration of the relative system must be treated as forces. See also CORIOLIS FORCE.

Coriolis correction. . 1. A correction applied to an assumed position, celestial line of position, celestial fix, or to a computed or observed altitude to allow for Coriolis acceleration. 2. In inertial navigation equipment, an acceleration correction which must be applied to measurements of acceleration with respect to a coordinate system in translation to compensate for the effect of any angular motion of the coordinate system with respect to inertial space.

Coriolis force. . An inertial force acting on a body in motion, due to rotation of the earth, causing deflection to the right in the Northern Hemisphere and to the left in the Southern Hemisphere. It affects air (wind), water (current), etc. and introduces an error in bubble sextant observations made from a moving craft due to the liquid in the bubble being deflected, the effect increasing with higher latitude and greater speed of the craft.

corner reflector. . A radar reflector consisting of three mutually perpendicular flat reflecting surfaces designed to return incident electromagnetic radiation toward its source. The reflector is used to render objects such as buoys and sailboats more conspicuous to radar observations. Since maximum effectiveness is obtained when the incident beam coincides with the axis of symmetry of the reflector, clusters of reflectors are sometimes used to insure that the object will be a good reflector in all directions. See also RADAR REFLECTOR. Also called TRIHEDRAL REFLECTOR.

coromell. , *n.* A night land breeze prevailing from November to May at La Paz, near the southern extremity of the Gulf of California.

corona. , *n.* 1. The luminous envelope surrounding the sun but visible only during a total eclipse. 2. A luminous discharge due to ionization of the air surrounding an electric conductor. 3. A set of one or more rainbow-colored rings of small radii surrounding the sun, moon, or other source of light covered by a thin cloud veil. It is caused by diffraction of the light by tiny droplets in the atmosphere, and hence the colors are in the reverse order to those of a HALO caused by refraction. 4. A circle of light occasionally formed by the apparent convergency of the beams of the aurora.

corona discharge. . Luminous and often audible discharge of electricity intermediate between a spark and a point discharge. See ST. ELMO'S FIRE.

corposant. , *n.* See CORONA DISCHARGE, ST. ELMO'S FIRE.

corrasion. , *n.* The wearing away of the earth's surface by the abrasive action of material transported by glacier, water, or air; a process of erosion.

corrected compass course. . Compass course with deviation applied; magnetic course.

corrected compass heading. . Compass heading with deviation applied; magnetic heading.

corrected current. . A relatively short series of current observations from a subordinate station to which a factor is applied to adjust the current to a more representative value, based on a relatively long series from a nearby control station. See also CURRENT, TOTAL CURRENT.

corrected establishment. . See under ESTABLISHMENT OF THE PORT.

corrected sextant altitude. . Sextant altitude corrected for index error, height of eye, parallax, refraction, etc. Also called OBSERVED ALTITUDE, TRUE ALTITUDE.

correcting. , *n.* The process of applying corrections, particularly the process of converting compass to magnetic direction, or compass, magnetic, or gyro to true direction. The opposite is UNCORRECTING.

correction. , *n.* That which is added to or subtracted from a reading, as of an instrument, to eliminate the effect of an error, or to reduce an observation to an arbitrary standard.

correction information. . See UPDATE INFORMATION.

correction of soundings. The adjustment of soundings for any departure from true depth because of the method of sounding or any fault in the measuring apparatus. See also REDUCTION OF SOUNDINGS.

corrector. , *n.* A magnet, piece of soft iron, or device used in the adjustment of a magnetic compass. See also FLINDERS BAR, HEELING MAGNET, QUADRANTAL CORRECTORS.

corrosion. , *n.* The wearing or wasting away by chemical action, usually by oxidation. A distinction is usually made between corrosion and EROSION, the latter referring to the wearing away of the earth's surface primarily by non-chemical action. See also CORRASION.

cosecant. , *n.* The ratio of the hypotenuse of a plane right triangle to the side opposite one of the acute angles of the triangle, equal to l/sin. The expression NATURAL COSECANT is sometimes used to distinguish the cosecant from its logarithm (called LOGARITHMIC COSECANT).

cosine. , *n.* The ratio of the side adjacent to an acute angle of a plane right triangle to the hypotenuse. The expression NATURAL COSINE is sometimes used to distinguish the cosine from its logarithm (called LOGARITHMIC COSINE).

COSPAS/SARSAT. . A cooperative search and rescue satellite system operated by the U.S. and Russia which provides worldwide coverage by sensing the signals of Emergency Position Indicating Radiobeacons (EPIRBs).

cotangent. , *n.* The ratio of the shorter side adjacent to an acute angle of a plane right triangle to the side opposite the same angle, equal to l/tan. The expression NATURAL COTANGENT is sometimes used to distinguish the cotangent from its logarithm (called LOGARITHMIC COTANGENT).

cotidal. , *adj.* Having tides occurring at the same time.

cotidal chart. . A chart showing COTIDALlines.

cotidal hour. . The average interval between the moon's transit over the meridian of Greenwich and the time of the following high water at any place, expressed in either mean solar or lunar time units. When expressed in solar time, it is the same as the Greenwich high water interval. When expressed in lunar time, it is equal to the Greenwich high water interval multiplied by the factor 0.966.

cotidal line. . A line on a map or chart passing through places having the same cotidal hour.

coulomb. , *n.* A derived unit of quantity of electricity in the International System of Units; it is the quantity of electricity carried in 1 second by a current of 1 ampere.

counterclockwise. , *adv.* In a direction of rotation opposite to that of the hands of a clock.

countercurrent. , *n.* A current usually setting in a direction opposite to that of a main current.

counterglow. , *n.* See GEGENSCHEIN.

countertrades. , *n., pl.* See ANTITRADES.

coupler. , *n.* See as ANTENNA COUPLER.

course. , *n.* The direction in which a vessel is steered or intended to be steered, expressed as angular distance from north, usually from 000° at north, clockwise through 360°. Strictly, the term applies to direction through the water, not the direction intended to be made good over the ground. The course is often designated as true, magnetic, compass, or grid as the reference direction is true, magnetic compass, or grid north, respectively. TRACK MADE GOOD is the single resultant direction from the point of departure to point of arrival at any given time. The use of this term to indicate a single resultant direction is preferred to the use of the misnomer course made good. A course line is a line, as drawn on a chart, extending in the direction of a course. See also COURSE ANGLE, COURSE OF ADVANCE, COURSE OVER GROUND. HEADING. TRACK.

course angle. . Course measured from 0° at the reference direction clockwise or counterclockwise through 90° or 180°. It is labeled with the reference direction as a prefix and the direction of measurement from the reference direction as a suffix.

course beacon. . A directional radiobeacon which gives an "on course" signal in the receiver of a vessel which is on, or in close proximity to, the prescribed course line and "off course" signals in sectors adjacent to this line.

course board. . A board located on the navigation bridge used to display the course to steer, track, drift angle, leeway angle, compass error, etc.

course line. . 1. The graphic representation of a ship's course, usually with respect to true north. 2. A line of position approximately parallel to the course line (definition 1), thus providing a check as to deviating left or right of the track. See also SPEED LINE.

course made good. . A misnomer indicating the resultant direction from a point of departure to a point of arrival at any given time. See also COURSE, COURSE OVER GROUND, TRACK MADE GOOD.

course of advance. . An expression sometimes used to indicate the direction intended to be made good over the ground. The preferred term is TRACK, definition 1. This is a misnomer in that courses are directions steered or intended to be steered through the water with respect to a reference meridian. See also COURSE, COURSE OVER GROUND.

course over ground. . The direction of the path over the ground actually followed by a vessel. The preferred term is TRACK, definition 1. It is normally a somewhat irregular line. This is a misnomer in that courses are directions steered or intended to be steered through the water with respect to a reference meridian. See also COURSE, COURSE MADE GOOD.

course recorder. . A device which makes an automatic graphic record of the headings of a vessel vs. time. See also DEAD RECKONING TRACER.

course up. . See BASE COURSE UP.

course up display. . In ECDIS (or radar) the information shown on the DISPLAY with the direction of the vessel's course upward.

cove, *n.* A small sheltered recess or indentation in a shore or coast, generally inside a larger embayment.

crab. , *v., t.* To drift sideways while in forward motion.

crack line. , *n.* Any fracture (in ice) which has not parted.

creek. , *n.* 1. A stream of less volume than a river but larger than a brook. 2. A small tidal channel through a coastal marsh. 3. A wide arm of a river or bay, as used locally in Maryland and Virginia.

crepuscular rays. . Literally, "twilight rays," alternating lighter and darker bands (rays and shadows) which appear to diverge in fanlike array from the sun's position at about twilight. This term is applied to two quite different phenomena: a. It refers to shadows cast across the purple light, a true twilight phenomenon, by cloud tops that are high enough and far enough away from the observer to intercept some of the sunlight that would ordinarily produce the purple light. b. A more common occurrence is that of shadows and rays made visible by haze in the lower atmosphere. Towering clouds produce this effect also, but they may be fairly close to the observer and the sun need not be below the horizon. The apparent divergence of crepuscular rays is merely a perspective effect. When they continue across the sky to the antisolar point, these extensions are called ANTI-CREPUSCULAR RAYS. Also called SHADOW BANDS.

crescent. , *adj.* Bounded by a convex and a concave curve. Originally, the term applied only to the "increasing" moon, from which the word was derived. By extension, it is now generally applied to the moon between last quarter and new as well as between new and first quarter, and to any other celestial body presenting a similar appearance, or any similarly shaped object. See also PHASES OF THE MOON.

crest. , *n.* The highest part of a wave or swell; or terrestrially, a hill or ridge.

crest cloud. . A type of cloud over a mountain ridge, similar to a cap cloud over an isolated peak. The cloud is apparently stationary, but actually is continually being formed to windward and dissipated to leeward.

crevasse. , *n.* A deep fissure or rift in a glacier.

critical angle. . 1. The maximum angle at which a radio wave may be emitted from an antenna, in respect to the plane of the earth, and still be returned to the earth by refraction or reflection by an ionospheric layer. 2. The angle at which radiation, about to pass from a medium of greater density into one of lesser density, is refracted along the surface of the denser medium.

critical table. . A single entering argument table in which values of the quantity to be found are tabulated for limiting values of the entering argument. In such a table interpolation is avoided through dividing the argument into intervals so chosen that successive intervals correspond to successive values of the required quantity, called the respondent. For any value of the argument within these intervals, the respondent can be extracted from the table without interpolation. The lower and upper limits (critical values) of the argument correspond to half-way values of the respondent and, by convention, are chosen so that when the argument is equal to one of the critical values, the respondent corresponding to the preceding (upper) interval is to be used.

critical temperature. . The temperature above which a substance cannot exist in the liquid state, regardless of pressure.

cross-band Racon. . A Racon which transmits at a frequency not within the marine radar frequency band. To be able to use this type of Racon, the ship's radar receiver must be capable of being tuned to the frequency of the crossband Racon, or special accessory equipment is required. In either case, normal radar echoes will not be painted on the radarscope. This is an experimental type of Racon. See also INBAND RACON.

cross-band transponder. . A transponder which responds on a frequency different from that of the interrogating signal.

cross bearings. . Two or more bearings used as intersecting lines of position for fixing the position of a craft.

cross hair. . A hair, thread, or wire constituting part of a reticle.

cross sea. . A series of waves imposed across the prevailing waves. It is called CROSS SWELL when the imposed waves are the longer swell waves.

cross-section paper. . Paper ruled with two sets of parallel lines, useful as an aid in plotting Cartesian coordinates. Usually, the two sets are mutually perpendicular. See also COORDINATE PAPER.

cross-staff. , *n.* A forerunner of the modern sextant used for measuring altitudes of celestial bodies, consisting of a wooden rod with one or more perpendicular cross pieces free to slide along the main rod. Also called FORESTAFF, JACOB'S STAFF.

cross swell. . See under CROSS SEA.

cross tide. . A tidal current setting in a direction approximately 90° from the course of a vessel. One setting in a direction approximately 90° from the heading is called a BEAM TIDE. In common usage these two expressions are usually used synonymously. One setting from ahead is called a HEAD TIDE. One setting from aft is called a FAIR TIDE.

cross wind. . See under BEAM WIND.

cruising radius. . The distance a craft can travel at cruising speed without refueling. Also called CRUISING RANGE.

cruising range. . See CRUISING RADIUS.

cryogenics. , *n.* 1. The study of the methods of producing very low temperatures. 2. The study of the behavior of materials and processes at cryogenic temperatures.

cryogenic temperature. . In general, a temperature range below the boiling point of nitrogen (-320.4°F or-195.8°C); more particularly, temperatures within a few degrees of absolute zero.

crystal. , *n.* A crystalline substance which allows electric current to pass in only one direction.

crystal clock. . See QUARTZ CRYSTAL CLOCK.

cube. , *n.* 1. A solid bounded by six equal square sides. 2. The third power of a quantity.

cubic meter. . The derived unit of volume in the International System of Units.

cul-de-sac. , *n.* An inlet with a single small opening.

culmination. , *n.* See MERIDIAN TRANSIT.

culture. , *n.* 1. The man-made features of a map or chart, including roads, rails, cables, etc.; boundary lines, latitude and longitude lines, isogonic lines, etc. are also properly classified as culture.

cumulative update. . In ECDIS, the collection of all sequential CORRECTION INFORMATION which has been issued since the last new edition of the ENC or since the last OFFICIAL UPDATE applied to the SENC.

cumuliform, *adj.* Like cumulus; generally descriptive of all clouds, the principal characteristic of which is vertical development in the form of rising mounds, domes, or towers. This is the contrasting form to the horizontally extended STRATIFORM types. See also CIRRIFORM.

cumulonimbus. , *n.* An exceptionally dense cloud of great vertical development, occurring either as an isolated cloud or one of a line or wall of clouds with separated upper portions. These clouds appear as mountains or huge towers, at least a part of the upper portions of which are usually smooth, fibrous, striated, and almost flattened. This part often spreads out in the form of an anvil or plume. Under the base of cumulonimbus, which often is very dark, there frequently exists virga, precipitation, and low, ragged clouds, either merged with it or not. Its precipitation is often heavy and always of a showery nature. The usual occurrence of lightning and thunder within or from this cloud leads to its being popularly called THUNDERCLOUD and THUNDERHEAD. The latter term usually refers to only the upper portion of the cloud. See also CLOUD CLASSIFICATION.

cumulus. , *n.* A cloud type in the form of individual, detached elements which are generally dense and possess sharp non-fibrous outlines. These elements develop vertically, appearing as rising mounds, domes, or towers, the upper parts of which often resemble a cauliflower. The sunlit parts of these clouds are mostly brilliant white; their bases are relatively dark and nearly horizontal. Near the horizon the vertical development of cumulus often causes the individual clouds to appear merged. If precipitation occurs, it is usually of a showery nature. Various effects of wind, illumination, etc. may modify many of the above characteristics. Strong winds may shred the clouds, often tearing away the cumulus tops to form the species *fractus.* See also CLOUD CLASSIFICATION.

cupola. , *n.* A label on a nautical chart which indicates a small dome-shaped tower or turret rising from a building.

current. , *n.* A horizontal movement of water. Currents may be classified as tidal and nontidal. Tidal currents are caused by gravitational interactions between the sun, moon, and earth and are a part of the same general movement of the sea that is manifested in the vertical rise and fall, called TIDE. Tidal currents are periodic with a net velocity of zero over the tidal cycle. Nontidal currents include the permanent currents in the general circulatory systems of the sea as well as temporary currents arising from more pronounced meteorological variability. The SET of a current is the direction toward which it flows; the DRIFT is its speed. In British usage, tidal current is called TIDAL STREAM, and nontidal current is called current.

current chart. . A chart on which current data are graphically depicted. See also TIDAL CURRENT CHARTS.

current constants. . Tidal current relations that remain practically constant for any particular locality. Current constants are classified as harmonic and nonharmonic. The harmonic constants consist of the amplitudes and epochs of the harmonic constituents, and the nonharmonic constants include the velocities and intervals derived directly from the current observations.

current curve. . A graphic representation of the flow of the current. In the reversing type of tidal current, the curve is referred to rectangular coordinates with time represented by the abscissas and the speed of the current by the ordinates, the flood speeds being considered as positive and the ebb speeds as negative. In general, the current curve for a reversing tidal current approximates a cosine curve.

current cycle. . A complete set of tidal current conditions, as those occurring during a tidal day, lunar month, or Metonic cycle.

current diagram. . A graphic table showing the speeds of the flood and ebb currents and the times of slack and strength over a considerable stretch of the channel of a tidal waterway, the times being referred to tide or tidal current phases at some reference station.

current difference. . The difference between the time of slack water (or minimum current) or strength of current in any locality and the time of the corresponding phase of the tidal current at a reference station, for which predictions are given in the *Tidal Current Tables*.

current direction. . The direction toward which a current is flowing, called the SET of the current.

current ellipse. . A graphic representation of a rotary current in which the velocity of the current at different hours of the tidal cycle is represented by radius vectors and vectorial angles. A line joining the extremities of the radius vectors will form a curve roughly approximating an ellipse. The cycle is completed in one half tidal day or in a whole tidal day according to whether the tidal current is of the semidiurnal or the diurnal type. A current of the mixed type will give a curve of two unequal loops each tidal day.

current hour. . The mean interval between the transit of the moon over the meridian of Greenwich and the time of strength of flood, modified by the times of slack water (or minimum current) and strength of ebb. In computing the mean current hour an average is obtained of the intervals for the following phases: flood strength, slack (or minimum) before flood increased by 3.10 hours (one-fourth of tidal cycle), slack (or minimum) after flood decreased by 3.10 hours, and ebb strength increased or decreased by 6.21 hours (one-half of tidal cycle). Before taking the average, the four phases are made comparable by the addition or rejection of such multiples of 12.42 hours as may be necessary. The current hour is usually expressed in solar time, but if the use of lunar time is desired the solar hour should be multiplied by the factor 0.966.

current line. . A graduated line attached to a CURRENT POLE, used in measuring the velocity of the current. The line is marked so that the speed of the current, expressed in knots and tenths, is indicated directly by the length of line carried out by the current pole in a specified interval of time. When marked for a 60 second run, the principal divisions for the whole knots are spaced 101.33 feet and the subdivisions for tenths of knots are spaced at 10.13 feet. Also called LOG LINE.

current meter. . An instrument for measuring the speed and direction or just speed of a current. The measurements are usually Eulerian since the meter is most often fixed or moored at a specific location.

current pole. . A pole used in observing the velocity of the current. In use, the pole, which is weighted at one end so as to float upright, is attached to the current line but separated from the graduated portion by an ungraduated section of approximately 100 feet, known as the *stray line*. As the pole is carried out from an observing vessel by the current, the amount of line passing from the vessel during a specific time interval indicates the speed of the current. The set is obtained from a bearing from the vessel to the pole.

current rips. . See RIPS.

current sailing. . The process of allowing for current when predicting the track to be made good or of determining the effect of a current on the direction of motion of a vessel. The expression is better avoided, as the process is not strictly a sailing.

current station. . The geographic location at which current observations are conducted. Also, the facilities used to make current observations. These may include a buoy, ground tackle, current meters, recording mechanism, and radio transmitter. See also CONTROL CURRENT STATION, SUBORDINATE CURRENT STATION.

current tables. . See TIDAL CURRENT TABLES.

cursor. , *n.* A device used with an instrument to provide a movable reference. A symbol indicating the location in a file of the data entry point of a computer.

cursor-pick, *n.* In ECDIS, the process of querying a point, symbol, line or area for further information from the database which is not represented by the SYMBOL.

curve of constant bearing. . See CURVE OF EQUAL BEARING.

curve of equal bearing. . A curve connecting all points at which the great circle bearing of a given point is the same. Also called CURVE OF CONSTANT BEARING.

curvilinear. , *adj.* Consisting of or bounded by a curve.

curvilinear triangle. . A closed figure having three curves as sides.

cusp. , *n.* One of the horns or pointed ends of the crescent moon or other luminary.

cut. , *n.* 1. A notch or depression produced by excavation or erosion. 2. The intersection of lines of position, constituting a fix, with particular reference to the angle of intersection.

cut in. . To observe and plot lines of position locating an object or craft, particularly by bearings.

cut-off. , *n.* 1. A new and relatively short channel formed when a stream cuts through the neck of an oxbow or horseshoe bend. 2. An artificial straightening or short-cut in a channel.

cycle. , *n.* One complete train of events or phenomena that recur sequentially. When used in connection with sound or radio the term refers to one complete wave, or to a frequency of one wave per second. See also KILOCYCLE, MEGACYCLE, CALLIPIC CYCLE, CURRENT CYCLE, DUTY CYCLE, LUNAR CYCLE, METONIC CYCLE, TIDAL CYCLE.

cycle match. . The comparison, in time difference, between corresponding carrier cycles contained in the rise times of a master and secondary station pulse. The comparison is refined to a determination of the phase difference between these two cycles. See also ENVELOPE MATCH.

cyclic. , *adj.* Of or pertaining to a cycle or cycles.

cyclogenesis. , *n.* A development or strengthening of cyclonic circulation in the atmosphere. The opposite is CYCLOLYSIS. The term is applied to the development of cyclonic circulation where previously it did not exist, as well as to the intensification of existing cyclonic flow. While cyclogenesis usually occurs with a deepening (a decrease in atmospheric pressure), the two terms should not be used synonymously.

cyclolysis. , *n.* Any weakening of cyclonic circulation in the atmosphere. The opposite is CYCLOGENESIS. While cyclolysis usually occurs with a filling (an increase in atmospheric pressure), the two terms should not be used synonymously.

cyclone. , *n.* 1. A meteorological phenomena characterized by relatively low atmospheric pressure and winds which blow counterclockwise around the center in the Northern Hemisphere and clockwise in the Southern Hemisphere. 2. The name by which a tropical storm having winds of 34 knots or greater is known in the South Indian Ocean. See TROPICAL CYCLONE.

cyclonic storm. . See under TROPICAL CYCLONE.

cyclonic winds. . The winds associated with a low pressure area and constituting part of a CYCLONE.

cylinder. , *n.* 1. A solid figure having two parallel plane bases bounded by closed congruent curves, and a surface formed by parallel lines connecting similar points on the two curves. 2. A surface formed by a straight line moving parallel to itself and constantly intersecting a curve. Also called CYLINDRICAL SURFACE.

cylindrical. , *adj.* Of or pertaining to a cylinder.

cylindrical buoy. . See CAN BUOY.

cylindrical chart. . A chart on a CYLINDRICAL MAP PROJECTION.

cylindrical map projection. . A map projection in which the surface of a sphere or spheroid, such as the earth, is conceived as developed on a tangent cylinder, which is then spread out to form a plane. See also MERCATOR MAP PROJECTION, RECTANGULAR MAP PROJECTION, EQUATORIAL MAP PROJECTION, OBLIQUE MAP PROJECTION, OBLIQUE MERCATOR MAP PROJECTION, TRANSVERSE MAP PROJECTION.

cylindrical surface. . A surface formed by a straight line moving parallel to itself and constantly intersecting a curve. Also called a CYLINDER.

D

daily aberration. . See under ABERRATION, definition 1.

Daily Memorandum. . An electronic file of the National Geospatial-Intelligence Agency's Maritime Safety Information System web site, containing HYDROLANTS, HYDROPACS, HYDROARCS and NAVAREAS IV and XII Warnings issued during the last 24 hours or since the last Daily Memorandum was issued.

daily rate. . See CHRONOMETER RATE, WATCH RATE.

dale. , *n.* A vale or small valley.

dam. , *n.* A barrier to check or confine anything in motion; particularly a bank of earth, masonry, etc., across a watercourse to keep back moving water.

damped wave. . 1. A wave such that, at every point, the amplitude of each sinusoidal component is a decreasing function of time. 2. A wave in which the amplitudes of successive peaks (crests) progressively diminish.

damp haze. . See under HAZE.

damping. , *n.* 1. The reduction of energy in a mechanical or electrical system by absorption or radiation. 2. The act of reducing the amplitude of the oscillations of an oscillatory system; hindering or preventing oscillation or vibration; diminishing the sharpness of resonance of the natural frequency of a system.

damping error. . See BALLISTIC DAMPING ERROR.

dan buoy. . A buoy consisting of a ballasted float carrying a staff which supports a flag or light. Dan buoys are used principally in minesweeping, and by fisherman to mark the position of deepsea fishing lines or nets.

danger angle. . The maximum or minimum angle between two points, as observed from a craft indicating the limit of safe approach to an offlying danger. A horizontal danger angle is measured between points shown on the chart. A vertical danger angle is measured between the top and bottom of an object of known height.

danger area. . A specified area above, below, or within which there may exist potential danger. See also PROHIBITED AREA, RESTRICTED AREA.

danger bearing. . The maximum or minimum bearing of a point for safe passage of an off-lying danger. As a vessel proceeds along a coast, the bearing of a fixed point on shore, such as a lighthouse, is measured frequently. As long as the bearing does not exceed the limit of the predetermined danger bearing, the vessel is on a safe course.

danger buoy. . A buoy marking an isolated danger to navigation, such as a rock, shoal or sunken wreck.

danger line. . 1. A line drawn on a chart to indicate the limits of safe navigation for a vessel of specific draft. 2. A line of small dots used to draw the navigator's attention to a danger which would not stand out clearly enough if it were represented on the chart solely by the specific symbols. This line of small dots is also used to delimit areas containing numerous dangers, through which it is unsafe to navigate.

dangerous semicircle. . The half of a cyclonic torm in which the rotary and forward motions of the storm reinforce each other and the winds tend to blow a vessel into the storm track. In the Northern Hemisphere this is to the right of the storm center (when facing the direction the storm is moving) and in the Southern Hemisphere it is to the left. The opposite is the LESS DANGEROUS or NAVIGABLE SEMICIRCLE.

danger sounding. . A minimum sounding chosen for a vessel of specific draft in a given area to indicate the limit of safe navigation.

dark nilas. . NILAS which is under 5 centimeters in thickness and is very dark in color.

dark-trace tube. . A cathode-ray tube having a specially coated screen which changes color but does not necessarily luminesce when struck by the electron beam. It shows a dark trace on a bright background.

data. . Factual information.

data-acquisition station. . A ground station used for performing the various functions necessary to control satellite operations and to obtain data from the satellite.

database. . A uniform, organized set of data.

data dictionary. In ECDIS, conveys the meaning of entities and ATTRIBUTES, the RELATIONSHIP between entities and attributes and the relationship between attribute and value domains.

data model. . In ECDIS a conceptual specification of the sets of components and the RELATIONSHIPS among the components pertaining to the specific phenomena defined by the model reality. A data model is independent of specific systems or DATA STRUCTURES.

data processing. Changing data from one form or format to another by application of specified routines or algorithms.

data quality indicator. . In ECDIS an indication of reliability and ACCURACY of surveys of a particular area provided through relevant ATTRIBUTE of the quality of data META OBJECT in the IHO TRANSFER STANDARD.

data reduction. The process of transforming raw data into more ordered data.

data smoothing. . The process of fitting dispersed data points to a smooth or uniform curve or line.

data structure. In ECDIS a computer interpretable format used for storing, accessing, transferring, and archiving data.

date. , *n*. A designated mark or point on a time scale.

date line. . The line coinciding approximately with the 180th meridian, at which each calendar day first begins; the boundary between the -12 and +12 time zones. The date on each side of this line differs by 1 day, but the time is the same in these two zones. When crossing this line on a westerly course, the date must be advanced 1 day; when crossing on an easterly course, the date must be put back 1 day. Sometimes called INTERNATIONAL DATE LINE.

datum. , *n*. Any numerical or geometrical quantity or set of such quantities which may serve as reference or base for other quantities. In navigation, two types of datums are used: horizontal and vertical. See also HORIZONTAL GEODETIC DATUM, VERTICAL GEODETIC DATUM. CHART SOUNDING DATUM, VERTICAL DATUM.

datum-centered ellipsoid. . The reference ellipsoid that gives the best fit to the astrogeodetic network of a particular datum, and hence does not necessarily have its center at the center of the earth.

datum plane. . A misnomer for collection of datums used in mapping, charting, and geodesy which are not strictly planar. This term should not be used.

datum transformation. . The systematic elimination of discrepancies between adjoining or overlapping triangulation networks from different datums by moving the origins, rotating, and stretching the networks to fit each other.

Davidson Current. . A seasonal North Pacific Ocean countercurrent flowing northwestward along the west coast of North America from north of 32°N to at least latitude 48°N, inshore of the southeasterly-flowing California Current. This current occurs generally between November and April, but is best established in January. Strong opposing winds may cause the current to reverse. Also called WINTER COASTAL COUNTERCURRENT.

Davidson Inshore Current. . See DAVIDSON CURRENT.

dawn. , *n*. The first appearance of light in the eastern sky before sunrise; DAYBREAK. See also DUSK, TWILIGHT.

day. , *n*. 1. The duration of one rotation of a celestial body on its axis. It is measured by successive transits of a reference point on the celestial sphere over the meridian, and each type takes its name from the reference used. Thus, for a solar day on earth the reference is the sun; a mean solar day uses the mean sun; and an apparent solar day uses the apparent sun. For a lunar day the reference is the moon; for a sidereal day the vernal equinox; for a constituent day an astre fictif or fictitious star representing one of the periodic elements in the tidal forces. The expression lunar day refers also to the duration of one rotation of the moon with respect to the sun. A JULIAN DAY begins at Greenwich mean noon and the days are consecutively numbered from January 1, 4713 B.C. 2. A period of 24 hours beginning at a specified time, as the civil day beginning at midnight, or the astronomical day beginning at noon, which was used up to 1925 by astronomers. 3. A specified time or period, usually of approximately 24-hours duration. A CALENDAR DAY extends from midnight to midnight, and is of 24-hours duration unless a time change occurs during the day. A tidal day is either the same as a lunar day (on the earth), or the period of the daily cycle of the tides, differing slightly from the lunar day because of priming and lagging. 4. The period of daylight, as distinguished from night.

daybeacon. , *n*. An unlighted beacon. A daybeacon is identified by its color and the color, shape and number of its daymark. The simplest form of daybeacon consists of a single pile with a daymark affixed at or near its top. See also DAYMARK.

daybreak. , *n*. See DAWN.

daylight control. . A photoelectric device that automatically lights and extinguishes a navigation light, usually lighting it at or about sunset and extinguishing it at or about sunrise. Also called SUN RELAY, SUN SWITCH, SUN VALVE.

daylight saving meridian. . The meridian used for reckoning daylight saving time. This is generally 15° east of the ZONE or STANDARD MERIDIAN.

daylight saving noon. . Twelve o'clock daylight saving time, or the instant the mean sun is over the upper branch of the daylight saving meridian. Also called SUMMER NOON, especially in Europe. See also MEAN NOON.

daylight saving time. . A variation of standard time in order to make better use of daylight. In the U.S. the *Energy Policy Act of 2005* (Public Law 109-58) establishes the annual advancement and retardation of standard time by 1 hour at 2 A.M. on the second Sunday of March and first Sunday of November, respectively, except in those states which have by law exempted themselves from the observance of daylight saving time. This change from previous policy went into effect in 2007. Also called SUMMER TIME, especially in Europe.

daylight signal light. . A signal light exhibited by day and also, usually with reduced intensity by night. The reduction of intensity is made in order to avoid glare. Daylight signals may be used to indicate whether or not the entrance to a lock is free.

daymark. , *n.* 1. The daytime identifying characteristics of an aid to navigation. See also DAYBEACON. 2. An unlighted navigation mark. 3. The shaped signals used to identify vessels engaged in special operations during daytime, more properly known as day shapes.

day's run. . The distance traveled by a vessel in 1 day, usually reckoned from noon to noon.

dead ahead. . Bearing exactly 000° relative. If the bearing is approximate, the term AHEAD should be used.

dead astern. . Bearing 180° relative. If the bearing is approximate, the term ASTERN should be used. Also called RIGHT ASTERN.

deadbeat. , *adj.* APERIODIC, or without a period.

deadbeat compass. . See APERIODIC COMPASS.

deadhead. , *n.* 1. A block of wood used as an anchor buoy. 2. A bollard, particularly one of wood set in the ground.

deadman. . Timber or other long sturdy object buried in ice or ground to which a ship's mooring lines are attached.

dead reckoning. . Determining the position of a vessel by adding to the last fix the ship's course and speed for a given time. The position so obtained is called a DEAD RECKONING POSITION. Comparison of the dead reckoning position with the fix for the same time indicates the sum of currents, winds, and other forces acting on the vessel during the intervening period.

dead reckoning equipment. . A device that continuously indicates the dead reckoning position of a vessel. It may also provide, on a dead reckoning tracer, a graphical record of the dead reckoning. See also COURSE RECORDER.

dead reckoning plot. . The graphic plot of the dead reckoning, suitably labeled with time, direction, and speed. See also NAVIGATIONAL PLOT.

dead reckoning position. . See under DEAD RECKONING.

dead reckoning tracer. . A device that automatically provides a graphic record of the dead reckoning. It may be part of dead reckoning equipment. See also COURSE RECORDER.

dead water. . The water carried along with a ship as it moves through the water. It is maximum at the waterline and decreases with depth. It increases in a direction towards the stern.

deca-. . A prefix meaning ten.

decameter. , *n.* Ten meters.

Decca. , *n.* See as DECCA NAVIGATOR SYSTEM.

Decca chain. . A group of associated stations of the Decca Navigator System. A Decca chain normally consists of one master and three slave stations. Each slave station is called by the color of associated pattern of hyperbolic lines as printed on the chart, i.e., red slave, green slave, purple slave. See also CHAIN.

Decca Navigator System. . A short to medium range low frequency (70-130 kilohertz) radionavigation system which yields a hyperbolic line of position of high accuracy. The system is an arrangement of fixed, phase locked, continuous wave transmitters operating on harmonically related frequencies and special receiving and display equipment carried on a vessel or other craft. The operation of the system depends on phase comparison of the signals from the transmitters brought to a common comparison frequency within the receiver.

decelerate. , *v., t.* To cause to move slower. *v. i.* To decrease speed.

deceleration. , *n.* Negative acceleration.

December solstice. . Winter solstice in the Northern Hemisphere.

deci-. . A prefix meaning one-tenth. decibar, *n.* One-tenth of a bar; 100 millibars.

decibar. , *n.* One-tenth of a bar; 100 millibars.

decibel. , *n.* A dimensionless unit used for expressing the ratio between widely different powers. It is 10 times the logarithm to the base 10 of the power ratio.

decimeter. , *n.* One-tenth of a meter.

deck log. . See LOG, definition 2.

declination. , *n.* 1. Angular distance north or south of the celestial equator; the arc of an hour circle between the celestial equator and a point on the celestial sphere, measured northward or southward from the celestial equator through 90°, and labeled N or S (+ or -) to indicate the direction of measurement. 2. Short for MAGNETIC DECLINATION.

declinational inequality. . See DIURNAL INEQUALITY.

declinational reduction. . A processing of observed high and low waters or flood and ebb tidal currents to obtain quantities depending upon changes in the declination of the moon; such as tropic ranges or speeds, height or speed inequalities, and tropic intervals.

declination difference. . The difference between two declinations, particularly between the declination of a celestial body and the value used as an argument for entering a table.

declinometer. , *n.* An instrument for measuring magnetic declination. See also MAGNETOMETER.

Decometer. , *n.* A phase meter used in the Decca Navigator System.

decrement. , *n.* 1. A decrease in the value of a variable. 2. *v.* To decrease a variable in steps. See also INCREMENT.

deep. , *n.* 1. An unmarked fathom point on a lead line. 2. A relatively small area of exceptional depth found in a depression of the ocean floor. The term is generally restricted to depths greater than 3,000 fathoms. If it is very limited in area, it is referred to as a HOLE. 3. A relatively deep channel in a strait or estuary.

deepening. , *n.* Decrease in atmospheric pressure, particularly within a low. Increase in pressure is called FILLING. See also CYCLOGENESIS.

deep sea lead. . A heavy sounding lead (about 30 to 100 pounds), usually having a line 100 fathoms or more in length. A light deep sea lead is sometimes called a COASTING LEAD. Sometimes called DIPSEY LEAD.

deep water route. . A route for deep draft vessels within defined limits which has been accurately surveyed for clearance of sea bottom and submerged obstacles as indicated on the chart. See also ROUTING SYSTEM.

definition. , *n.* The clarity and fidelity of the detail of radar images on the radarscope. A combination of good resolution and focus is required for good definition.

definitive orbit. . An orbit that is defined in a highly precise manner with due regard taken for accurate constants and observational data, and precision computational techniques including perturbations.

deflection of the plumb line. . See under DEFLECTION OF THE VERTICAL.

deflection of the vertical. . The angular difference at any place, between the direction of a plumb line (the vertical) and the perpendicular to the reference ellipsoid. This difference seldom exceeds 30". Often expressed in two components, meridian and prime vertical. Also called STATION ERROR.

deflection of the vertical correction. . The correction due to deflection of the vertical resulting from irregularities in the density and form of the earth. Deflection of the vertical affects the accuracy of sextant altitudes.

deflector. , *n.* An instrument for measuring the directive force acting on a magnetic compass. It is used for adjusting a compass when ordinary methods of determining deviation are not available, and operates on the theory that when the directive force is the same on all cardinal headings, the compass is approximately adjusted.

deformed ice. . A general term for ice which has been squeezed together and in places forced forwards (and downwards). Subdivisions are RAFTED ICE, RIDGED ICE, and HUMMOCKED ICE.

degaussing. , *n.* Neutralization of the strength of the magnetic field of a vessel, using electric coils permanently installed in the vessel. See also DEPERMING.

degaussing cable. . A cable carrying an electric current for degaussing a vessel.

degaussing range. . An area for determining magnetic signatures of ships and other marine craft. Such signatures are used to determine required degaussing coil current settings and other required corrective actions. Sensing instruments and cables are installed on the sea bed in the range, and there are cables leading from the range to a control position ashore.

degree. , *n.* 1. A unit of circular measure equal to 1/360th of a circle. 2. A unit of measurement of temperature.

degree-of-freedom. . The number of orthogonal axes of a gyroscope about which the spin axis is free to rotate, the spin axis freedom not being counted. This is not a universal convention. For example, the free gyro is frequently referred to as a three-degree-of-freedom gyro, the spin axis being counted.

deka-. . A prefix meaning ten.

delayed plan position indicator. . A plan position indicator on which the start of the sweep is delayed so that the center represents a selected range. This allows distant targets to be displayed on a larger-scale presentation.

delayed sweep. . Short for DELAYED TIME BASE SWEEP.

delayed time base. . Short for DELAYED TIME BASE SWEEP.

delayed time base sweep. . A sweep, the start of which is delayed, usually to provide an expanded scale for a particular part. Usually shortened to DELAYED SWEEP, and sometimes to DELAYED TIME BASE.

delta. , *n.* 1. The low alluvial land, deposited in a more or less triangular form, as the Greek letter delta, at the mouth of a river, which is often cut by several distributaries of the main stream. 2. A change in a variable quantity, such as a change in the value of the declination of a celestial body.

demagnetize. , *v., t.* To remove magnetism. The opposite is MAGNETIZE.

demodulation. , *n.* The process of obtaining a modulating wave from a modulated carrier. The opposite is MODULATION.

density. , Quantity of mass per unit of volume.

departure, *n.* 1. The distance between two meridians at any given parallel of latitude, expressed in linear units, usually nautical miles; the distance to the east or west made good by a craft in proceeding from one point to another. 2. The point at which reckoning of a voyage begins. It is usually established by bearings of prominent landmarks as the vessel clears a harbor and proceeds to sea. When a navigator establishes this point, he is said to take departure. Also called POINT OF DEPARTURE. 3. Act of departing or leaving. 4. The amount by which the value of a meteorological element differs from the normal value.

dependent surveillance. . Position determination requiring the cooperation of the tracked craft.

deperming. , *n.* The process of changing the magnetic condition of a vessel by wrapping a large conductor around it a number of times in a vertical plane, athwartships, and energizing the coil thus formed. If a single coil is placed horizontally around the vessel and energized, the process is called FLASHING if the coil remains stationary, and WIPING if it is moved up and down. See also DEGAUSSING.

depressed pole. . The celestial pole below the horizon, of opposite name to the latitude. The celestial pole above the horizon is called ELEVATED POLE.

depression. , *n.* 1. See NEGATIVE ALTITUDE. 2. A developing cyclonic area, or low pressure area.

depression angle. . See ANGLE OF DEPRESSION.

depth. , *n.* The vertical distance from a given water level to the sea bottom. The charted depth is the vertical distance from the tidal datum to the bottom. The least depth in the approach or channel to an area, such as a port or anchorage, governing the maximum draft of vessels that can enter is called the controlling depth. See also CHART SOUNDING DATUM.

depth contour. . A line connecting points of equal depth below the sounding datum. It may be called FATHOM CURVE or FATHOM LINE if depth is expressed in fathoms. Also called DEPTH CURVE, ISOBATH.

depth curve. . See DEPTH CONTOUR.

depth finder. . See ECHO SOUNDER.

depth of water. . The vertical distance from the surface of the water to the bottom. See also SOUNDING.

depth perception. . The ability to estimate depth or distance between points in the field of vision.

derelict. , *n.* Any property abandoned at sea, often large enough to constitute a menace to navigation; especially an abandoned vessel. See also JETTISON, WRECK.

derived units. . See under INTERNATIONAL SYSTEM OF UNITS.

descending node. . The point at which a planet, planetoid, or comet crosses the ecliptic from north to south, or a satellite crosses the plane of the equator of its primary from north to south. Also called SOUTHBOUND NODE. The opposite is ASCENDING NODE.

destination. , *n.* The port of intended arrival. Also called POINT OF DESTINATION. See also POINT OF ARRIVAL.

detection. , *n.* 1. The process of extracting information from an electromagnetic wave. 2. In the use of radar, the recognition of the presence of a target.

detritus. , *n.* An accumulation of the fragments resulting from the disintegration of rocks.

developable. , *adj.* Capable of being flattened without distortion. The opposite is UNDEVELOPABLE.

developable surface. . A curved surface that can be spread out in a plane without distortion, e.g., the cone and the cylinder.

deviascope. , *n.* A device for demonstration of various forms of deviation and compass adjustment, or compass compensation.

deviation. , *n.* 1. The angle between the magnetic meridian and the axis of a compass card, expressed in degrees east or west to indicate the direction in which the northern end of the compass card is offset from magnetic north. Deviation is caused by disturbing magnetic influences in the immediate vicinity of the compass. Semicircular deviation changes sign (E or W) approximately each 180° change of heading; quadrantal deviation changes sign approximately each 90° change of heading; constant deviation is the same on any heading. Deviation of a magnetic compass after adjustment or compensation is RESIDUAL DEVIATION. Called MAGNETIC DEVIATION when a distinction is needed to prevent possible ambiguity. 2. Given a series of observations or measurements of a given quantity, the deviation of a single observation is the algebraic difference between the single observation and the mean or average value of the series of observations. See also RANDOM ERROR.

deviation table. . A table of the deviation of a magnetic compass on various headings, magnetic or compass. Also called MAGNETIC COMPASS TABLE. See also NAPIER DIAGRAM.

dew point. . The temperature to which air must be cooled at constant pressure and constant water vapor content to reach saturation. Any further cooling usually results in the formation of dew or frost.

DGPS. . Differential Global Positioning System; a method of increasing the accuracy of GPS positions by transmitting corrections generated by precisely surveyed reference stations.

diagram on the plane of the celestial equator. . See TIME DIAGRAM.

diagram on the plane of the celestial meridian. . A theoretical orthographic view of the celestial sphere from a point outside the sphere and over the celestial equator. The great circle appearing as the outer limit is the local celestial meridian; other celestial meridians appear as ellipses. The celestial equator appears as a diameter 90° from the poles. Parallels of declination appear as straight lines parallel to the equator. The celestial horizon appears as a diameter 90° from the zenith.

diagram on the plane of the equinoctial. . See TIME DIAGRAM.

diameter. , *n.* Any chord passing through the center of a figure, as a circle, ellipse, sphere, etc., or the length of such chord. See also RADIUS.

diaphone. , *n.* A sound signal emitter operating on the principle of periodic release of compressed air controlled by the reciprocating motion of a piston operated by compressed air. The diaphone usually emits a powerful sound of low pitch which often concludes with a brief sound of lowered pitch called the GRUNT. The emitted signal of a TWO-TONE DIAPHONE consists of two tones of different pitch, in which case the second tone is of lower pitch.

diaphragm horn. . A sound signal emitter comprising a resonant horn excited at its throat by impulsive emissions of compressed air regulated by an elastic diaphragm. Duplex or triplex horn units of different pitch produce a chime signal. Also called COMPRESSED-AIR HORN.

diatom. , *n.* A microscopic alga with an external skeleton of silica, found in both fresh and salt water. Part of the ocean bed is composed of a sedimentary ooze consisting principally of large collections of the skeletal remains of diatoms.

dichroic mirror. . A glass surface coated with a special metallic film that permits some colors of light to pass through the glass while reflecting certain other colors of light. Also called SEMIREFLECTING MIRROR.

dichroism. , *n.* The optical property of exhibiting two colors, as one color in transmitted light and another in reflected light. See also DICHROIC MIRROR.

dielectric reflector. . A device composed of dielectric material which returns the greater part of the incident electromagnetic waves parallel to the direction of incidence. See also RADAR REFLECTOR.

difference of latitude. . The shorter arc of any meridian between the parallels of two places, expressed in angular measure.

difference of longitude. . The smaller angle at the pole or the shorter arc of a parallel between the meridians of two places, expressed in angular measure.

difference of meridional parts. . See MERIDIONAL DIFFERENCE.

differential. . Relating to the technology of increasing the accuracy of an electronic navigation system by monitoring the system error from a known, fixed location and transmitting corrections to vessels using the system. Differential GPS is in operation. Differential Loran has been in an experimental phase.

differentiator. , *n.* See FAST TIME CONSTANT CIRCUIT.

diffraction. , *n.* 1. The bending of the rays of radiant energy around the edges of an obstacle or when passing near the edges of an opening, or through a small hole or slit, resulting in the formation of a spectrum. See also REFLECTION REFRACTION. 2. The bending of a wave as it passes an obstruction.

diffuse ice edge. . A poorly defined ice edge limiting an area of dispersed ice. It is usually on the leeward side of an area of pack ice.

diffuse reflection. . A reflection process in which the reflected radiation is sent out in many directions usually bearing no simple relationship to the angle of incidence. It results from reflection from a rough surface with small irregularities. See also SPECULAR REFLECTION.

diffusion. , *n.* See DIFFUSE REFLECTION.

digit. , *n.* A single character representing an integer.

digital. . Referring to the use of discreet expressions to represent variables. See ANALOG.

digital calculator. . In navigation, a small electronic device which does arithmetical calculations by applying mathematical formulas (ALGORITHMS) to user-entered values. A navigational calculator has preloaded programs to solve navigational problems.

digital nautical chart (DNC). . The electronic chart data base used in the U.S. Navy's Navigation Sensor System Interface (NAVSSI).

digital selective calling (DSC). . A communications technique using coded digitized signals which allows transmitters and receivers to manage message traffic, accepting or rejecting messages according to certain variables.

digital tide gage. . See AUTOMATIC TIDE GAGE.

digitize. . To convert analog data to digital data.

digitizing conventions. . See ENCODING CONVENTIONS.

dihedral angle. . The angle between two intersecting planes.

dihedral reflector. . A radar reflector consisting of two flat surfaces intersecting mutually at right angles. Incident radar waves entering the aperture so formed with a direction of incidence perpendicular to the edge, are returned parallel to their direction of incidence. Also called RIGHT ANGLE REFLECTOR.

dike. , *n.* A bank of earth or stone used to form a barrier, which restrains water outside of an area that is normally flooded. See LEVEE.

dioptric light. . A light concentrated into a parallel beam by means of refracting lenses or prisms. One so concentrated by means of a reflector is a CATOPTRIC LIGHT.

dip. , *n.* 1. The vertical angle, at the eye of an observer, between the horizontal and the line of sight to the visible horizon. Altitudes of celestial bodies measured from the visible sea horizon as a reference are too great by the amount of dip. Since dip arises from and varies with the elevation of the eye of the observer above the surface of the earth, the correction for dip is sometimes called HEIGHT OF EYE CORRECTION. Dip is smaller than GEOMETRICAL DIP by the amount of terrestrial refraction. Also called DIP OF THE HORIZON. 2. The angle between the horizontal and the lines of force of the earth's magnetic field at any point. Also called MAGNETIC DIP, MAGNETIC LATITUDE, MAGNETIC INCLINATION. 3. The first detectable decrease in the altitude of a celestial body after reaching its maximum altitude on or near meridian transit.

dip. , *v., i.* To begin to descend in altitude after reaching a maximum on or near meridian transit.

dip circle. . An instrument for measuring magnetic dip. It consists of a DIP NEEDLE, or magnetic needle, suspended in such manner as to be free to rotate about a horizontal axis.

dip correction. . The correction to sextant altitude due to dip of the horizon. Also called HEIGHT OF EYE CORRECTION.

dip needle. . A magnetic needle suspended so as to be free to rotate about a horizontal axis. An instrument using such a needle to measure magnetic dip is called a DIP CIRCLE. A dip needle with a sliding weight that can be moved along one of its arms to balance the magnetic force is called a HEELING ADJUSTER.

dip of the horizon. . See DIP, *n.*, definition 1.

dipole antenna. , *n.* A straight center-fed one-half wavelength antenna. Horizontally polarized it produces a figure eight radiation pattern, with maximum radiation at right angles to the plane of the antenna. Also called DOUBLET ANTENNA.

dip pole. . See MAGNETIC POLE, definition 1.

dipsey lead. . See DEEP SEA LEAD.

direct indicating compass. . A compass in which the dial, scale, or index is carried on the sensing element.

direction. , *n.* The position of one point in space relative to another without reference to the distance between them. Direction may be either three-dimensional or two-dimensional, the horizontal being the usual plane of the latter. Direction is not an angle but is often indicated in terms of its angular distance from a reference directions. Thus, a horizontal direction may be specified as compass, magnetic, true, grid or relative. A Mercator or rhumb direction is the horizontal direction of a rhumb line, expressed as angular distance from a reference direction, while great circle direction is the horizontal direction of a great circle, similarly expressed. See also CURRENT DIRECTION, SWELL DIRECTION, WAVE DIRECTION, WIND DIRECTION.

directional antenna. . An antenna designed so that the radiation pattern is largely concentrated in a single lobe.

directional gyro. . A gyroscopic device used to indicate a selected horizontal direction for a limited time.

directional gyro mode. . The mode of operation of a gyrocompass in which the compass operates as a free gyro with the spin axis oriented to grid north.

directional radiobeacon. . See under RADIOBEACON. Also see as COURSE BEACON.

direction finder. . See RADIO DIRECTION FINDER.

direction finder deviation. . The angular difference between a bearing observed by a radio direction finder and the correct bearing, caused by disturbances due to the characteristics of the receiving craft or station.

direction finder station. . See RADIO DIRECTION FINDER STATION.

direction light. . A light illuminating a sector of very narrow angle and intended to mark a direction to be followed. A direction light bounded by other sectors of different characteristics which define its margins with small angles of uncertainty is called a SINGLE STATION RANGE LIGHT.

direction of current. . The direction toward which a current is flowing, called the SET of the current.

direction of force of gravity. . The direction indicated by a plumb line. It is perpendicular (normal) to the surface of the geoid. Also called DIRECTION OF GRAVITY.

direction of gravity. . See DIRECTION OF FORCE OF GRAVITY.

direction of relative movement. . The direction of motion relative to a reference point, itself usually in motion.

direction of waves or swell. . The direction from which waves or swell are moving.

direction of wind. . The direction from which a wind is blowing.

directive force. . The force tending to cause the directive element of a compass to line up with the reference direction. Also, the value of this force. Of a magnetic compass, it is the intensity of the horizontal component of the earth's magnetic field.

directive gain. . Four times the ratio of the radiation intensity of an antenna for a given direction to the total power radiated by the antenna. Also called GAIN FUNCTION.

directivity. , *n.* 1. The characteristic of an antenna which makes it radiate or receive more efficiently in some directions than in others. 2. An expression of the value of the directive gain of an antenna in the direction of its maximum gain. Also called POWER GAIN (OF AN ANTENNA).

directivity diagram. . See RADIATION PATTERN.

direct motion. . The apparent motion of a planet eastward among the stars. Apparent motion westward is called RETROGRADE MOTION. The usual motion of planets is direct.

directory. . A list of files in a computer.

direct wave. , 1. A radio wave that travels directly from the transmitting to the receiving antenna without reflections from any object or layer of the ionosphere. The path may be curved as a result of refraction. 2. A radio wave that is propagated directly through space; it is not influenced by the ground. Also called SPACE WAVE.

discontinued., *adj.* Said of a previously authorized aid to navigation that has been removed from operation (permanent or temporary).

discontinuity., *n.* 1. A zone of the atmosphere within which there is a comparatively rapid transition of any meteorological element. 2. A break in sequence of continuity of anything.

discrepancy., *n.* 1. Failure of an aid to navigation to maintain its position or function exactly as prescribed in the *List of Lights*. 2. The difference between two or more observations or measurements of a given quantity.

discrepancy buoy.. An easily transportable buoy used to temporarily replace a buoy which is missing, damaged or otherwise not working properly.

disk.. A type of computer data storage which consists of a plastic or metallic disk which rotates to provide access to the stored data. Data is stored in discreet areas of the disk known as tracks and sectors.

dismal., *n.* A swamp bordering on, or near the sea. Also called POCOSIN.

dispersion., *n.* The separation of light into its component colors by its passage through a diffraction grating or by refraction such as that provided by a prism.

display., *n.* 1. The visual presentation of radar echoes or electronic charts. 2. The equipment for the visual display.

display base, . See DISPLAY CATEGORY.

display category, 1. In ECDIS, three categories for SENC objects are established in the ECDIS PERFORMANCE STANDARDS: display base, permanently retained on the display; standard display, displayed at switch-on, recalled by single operator action; ALL OTHER INFORMATION, displayed individually (by class) on demand.

display generator, . In ECDIS the manufacturer's software which takes an OBJECT from the SENC, assigns a symbol and color, and presents it appropriately on the DISPLAY, using the tools and procedures provided in the PRESENTATION LIBRARY.

display priority.. In ECDIS, detailed rules to decide which line or point SYMBOL is to be shown when two OBJECTS overlap. Priority 2 overwrites priority 1. Display priority is given in the LOOKUP TABLE.

display priority layer, *n.* In ECDIS, layers to establish the priority of information on the DISPLAY. Lower priority information must not obscure higher priority information.

display scale, *n.* In ECDIS the ratio between a distance on the display and a distance on the ground, normalized and expressed for example 1/10,000 or 1:10,000.

disposal area.. Area designated by the U.S. Army Corps of Engineers for depositing dredged material where existing depths indicate that the intent is not to cause sufficient shoaling to create a danger to surface navigation. Disposal areas are shown on nautical charts. See also DUMPING GROUND, DUMP SITE, SPOIL AREA.

disposition of lights.. The arrangement, order, etc., of navigational lights in an area.

distance circles.. Circles concentric to the center of a formation of ships, designated by their radii in thousands of yards.

distance finding station.. An attended light station or lightship emitting simultaneous radio and sound signals as a means of determining distance from the source of sound, by measuring the difference in the time of reception of the signals. The sound may be transmitted through either air or water or both and either from the same location as the radio signal or a location remote from it. Very few remain in use.

distance of relative movement.. The distance traveled relative to a reference point, itself usually in motion.

distance resolution.. See RANGE RESOLUTION.

Distances Between Ports.. See PUB. 151.

Distances Between United States Ports.. A reference published by the National Ocean Service (NOS) which provides distances in nautical miles over water areas between U.S. ports. A similar publication published by the National Geospatial-Intelligence Agency for foreign waters is entitled *Pub. No. 151, Distances Between Ports.*

diurnal., *adj.* Having a period or cycle of approximately 1 day. The tide is said to be diurnal when only one high water and one low water occur during a tidal day, and the tidal current is said to be diurnal when there is a single flood and single ebb period in the tidal day. A rotary current is diurnal if it changes its direction through 360° once each tidal day. A diurnal constituent is one which has a single period in the constituent day. See also STATIONARY WAVE THEORY, TYPE OF TIDE.

diurnal aberration.. See under ABERRATION, definition 1.

diurnal age.. See AGE OF DIURNAL INEQUALITY.

diurnal circle.. The apparent daily path of a celestial body, approximating a PARALLEL OF DECLINATION.

diurnal current.. Tidal current in which the tidal day current cycle consists of one flood current and one ebb current, separated by slack water; or a change in direction of 360° of a rotary current. A SEMIDIURNAL CURRENT is one in which two floods and two ebbs, or two changes of 360°, occur each tidal day.

diurnal inequality.. The difference in height of the two high waters or of the two low waters of each tidal day; the difference in speed between the two flood tidal currents or the two ebb tidal currents of each tidal day. The difference changes with the declination of the moon and to a lesser extent with declination of the sun. In general, the inequality tends to increase with an increasing declination, either north or south. Mean diurnal high water inequality is one-half the average difference between the two high waters of each day observed over a specific 19-year Metonic cycle (the National Tidal Datum Epoch). It is obtained by subtracting the mean of all high waters from the mean of the higher high waters. Mean diurnal low water inequality is one-half the average difference between the two low waters of each day observed over a specific 19-year Metonic cycle (the National Tidal Datum Epoch). It is obtained by subtracting the mean of the lower low waters from the mean of all low waters. Tropic high water inequality is the average difference between the two high waters of the day at the times of the tropic tides. Tropic low water inequality is the average difference between the two low waters of the day at the times of the tropic tides. Mean and tropic inequalities as defined above are applicable only when the type of tide is either semidiurnal or mixed. Sometimes called DECLINATIONAL INEQUALITY.

diurnal motion.. The apparent daily motion of a celestial body.

diurnal parallax.. See GEOCENTRIC PARALLAX.

diurnal range.. See GREAT DIURNAL RANGE.

diurnal tide.. See under TYPE OF TIDE; DIURNAL, *adj.*

dive., *n.* Submergence with one end foremost.

dive., *v., i.* To submerge with one end foremost.

diverged beam.. See under FAN BEAM.

dividers., *n.* An instrument consisting of two pointed legs joined by a pivot, used principally for measuring distances or coordinates on charts. If the legs are pointed at both ends and provided with an adjustable pivot in the middle of the legs, the instrument is called proportional dividers. An instrument having one pointed leg and one leg carrying a pen or pencil is called COMPASSES.

dividers

D-layer, *n.* The lowest of the ionized layers in the upper atmosphere, or ionosphere. It is present only during daylight hours, and its density is proportional to the altitude of the sun. The D-layer's only significant effect upon radio waves is its tendency to absorb their energy, particularly at frequencies below 3 megahertz. High angle radiation and signals of a frequency greater than 3 megahertz may penetrate the D-layer and be refracted or reflected by the somewhat higher E-layer.

DNC Library, *n.* The working unit of a geographic area on a Digital Nautical Chart (DNC). DNC is divided into scale-based libraries that fall into one of four (4) categories: General (1:500,000 and smaller), Coastal (1:75,000 to 1:500,000), Approach (1:25,000 to 1:100,000), and Harbor (1:50,000 and larger). The geographic limits and scale of the library are determined by the Regional Data Manager based on U.S. Navy Requirements.

dock, *n.* 1. The slip or waterway between two piers, or cut into the land for the berthing of ships. A PIER is sometimes erroneously called a DOCK. Also called SLIP. See also JETTY; LANDING, definition 1; QUAY; WHARF. 2. A basin or enclosure for reception of vessels, provided with means for controlling the water level. A wet dock is one in which water can be maintained at various levels by closing a gate when the water is at the desired level. A dry dock is a dock providing support for a ship, and means of removing the water so that the bottom of the ship can be exposed. A dry dock consisting of an artificial basin is called a graving dock; one consisting of a floating structure is called a floating dock. 3. Used in the plural, a term used to describe area of the docks, wharves, basins, quays, etc.

dock. , *v., t.* To place in a dock.

docking signals. . See TRAFFIC CONTROL SIGNALS.

dock sill. . The foundation at the bottom of the entrance to a dry dock or lock against which the caisson or gates close. The depth of water controlling the use of the dock or lock is measured from the sill to the surface.

dockyard. , *n. British terminology.* Shipyard.

doctor. , *n.* 1. A cooling sea breeze in the Tropics. 2. See HARMATTAN. 3. The strong southeast wind which blows on the south African coast. Usually called CAPE DOCTOR.

dog days. . The period of greatest heat in the summer.

doldrums. , *n., pl.* The equatorial belt of calms or light variable winds, lying between the two trade wind belts. Also called EQUATORIAL CALMS.

dolphin. , *n.* A post or group of posts, used for mooring or warping a vessel. The dolphin may be in the water, on a wharf, or on the beach. See PILE DOLPHIN.

dome. , *n.* A label on a nautical chart which indicates a large, rounded, hemispherical structure rising from a building or a roof.

dome-shaped iceberg. . A solid type iceberg with a large, round, smooth top.

doppler effect. . First described by Christian Johann Doppler in 1842, an effect observed as a frequency shift which results from relative motion between a transmitter and receiver or reflector of acoustic or electromagnetic energy. The effect on electromagnetic energy is used in doppler satellite navigation to determine an observer's position relative to a satellite. The effect on ultrasonic energy is used in doppler sonar speed logs to measure the relative motion between the vessel and the reflective sea bottom (for bottom return mode) or suspended particulate matter in the seawater itself (for volume reverberation mode). The velocity so obtained and integrated with respect to time is used in doppler sonar navigators to determine position with respect to a start point. The doppler effect is also used in docking aids which provide precise speed measurements. Also called DOPPLER SHIFT.

doppler navigation. . The use of the doppler effect in navigation. See also DOPPLER SONAR NAVIGATION, DOPPLER SATELLITE NAVIGATION.

doppler radar. . Any form of radar which detects radial motion of a distant object relative to a radar apparatus by means of the change of the radio frequency of the echo signal due to motion.

doppler satellite navigation. . The use of a navigation system which determines positions based on the doppler effect of signals received from an artificial satellite.

doppler shift. . See DOPPLER EFFECT.

doppler sonar navigation. . The use of the doppler effect observed as a frequency shift resulting from relative motion between a transmitter and receiver of ultrasonic energy to measure the relative motion between the vessel and the reflective sea bottom (for bottom return mode) or suspended particulate matter in the seawater itself (for volume reverberation mode) to determine the vessel's velocity. The velocity so obtained by a doppler sonar speed log may be integrated with respect to time to determine distance traveled. This integration of velocity with time is correlated with direction of travel in a doppler sonar navigator to determine position with respect to a start point. The doppler effect is also used in docking aids to provide precise speed measurements.

double. , *v., t.* To travel around with a near reversal of course. See also ROUND.

double altitudes. . See EQUAL ALTITUDES.

double ebb. . An ebb tidal current having two maxima of speed separated by a lesser ebb speed.

double flood. . A flood tidal current having two maxima of speed separated by a lesser flood speed.

double interpolation. . Interpolation when there are two arguments or variables.

double sextant. . A sextant designed to enable the observer to simultaneously measure the left and right horizontal sextant angles of the three-point problem.

double stabilization. . See under STABILIZATION Of RADARSCOPE DISPLAY.

double star. . Two stars appearing close together. If they appear close because they are in nearly the same line of sight but differ greatly in distance from the observer, they are called an optical double star; if in nearly the same line of sight and at approximately the same distance from the observer, they are called a physical double star. If they revolve about their common center of mass, they are called a binary star.

double summer time. . See under SUMMER TIME.

doublet antenna. . See DIPOLE ANTENNA.

double tide. . A high water consisting of two maxima of nearly the same height separated by a relatively small depression, or a low water consisting of two minima separated by a relatively small elevation. Sometimes called AGGER. See also GULDER.

doubling the angle on the bow. . A method of obtaining a running fix by measuring the distance a vessel travels on a steady course while the relative bearing (right or left) of a fixed object doubles. The distance from the object at the time of the second bearing is equal to the run between bearings, neglecting drift.

doubly stabilized. . See under STABILIZATION OF RADARSCOPE DISPLAY.

doubtful. , *adj.* Of questionable accuracy. Approximate or second class may be used with the same meaning.

doubtful sounding. . Of uncertain depth. The expression, as abbreviated, is used principally on charts to indicate a position where the depth may be less than indicated, the position not being in doubt.

down. , *n.* 1. See DUNE. 2. An area of high, treeless ground, usually undulating and covered with grass.

down by the head. . Having greater draft at the bow than at the stern. The opposite is DOWN BY THE STERN or BY THE STERN. Also called BY THE HEAD.

down by the stern. . Having greater draft at the stern than at the bow. The opposite is DOWN BY THE HEAD or BY THE HEAD. Also called BY THE STERN. See DRAG *n.*, definition 3.

downstream. , *adj. & adv.* In the direction of flow of a current or stream. The opposite is UPSTREAM.

down-the-scope echo. . See CLASSIFICATION OF RADAR ECHOES.

downwind. , *adj. & adv.* In the direction toward which the wind is blowing. The term applies particularly to the situation of moving in this direction, whether desired or not. BEFORE THE WIND implies assistance from the wind in making progress in a desired direction. LEEWARD applies to the direction toward which the wind blows, without implying motion. The opposite is UPWIND.

draft. , *n.* The depth to which a vessel is submerged. Draft is customarily indicated by numerals called DRAFT MARKS at the bow and stern. It may also be determined by means of a DRAFT GAUGE.

draft gauge. . A hydrostatic instrument installed in the side of a vessel, below the light load line, to indicate the depth to which a vessel is submerged.

drafting machine. . See PARALLEL MOTION PROTRACTOR.

draft marks. . Numerals placed on the sides of a vessel, customarily at the bow and stern, to indicate the depth to which a vessel is submerged.

drag. , *n.* 1. See SEA ANCHOR. 2. Short for WIRE DRAG. 3. The designed difference between the draft forward and aft when a vessel is down by the stern. See also TRIM, definition 1. 4. The retardation of a ship when in shallow water. 5. Short for ATMOSPHERIC DRAG.

drag. , *v., t.* 1. To tow a line or object below the surface, to determine the least depth in an area or to ensure that a given area is free from navigational dangers to a certain depth. DRAG and SWEEP have nearly the same meanings. DRAG refers particularly to the location of obstructions, or the determination that obstructions do not exist. SWEEP may include, additionally, the removal of any obstructions located. 2. To pull along the bottom, as in dragging anchor.

dragging. , *n.* 1. The process of towing a wire or horizontally set bar below the surface, to determine the least depth in an area or to insure that a given area is free from navigational dangers to a certain depth. 2. The process of pulling along the bottom, as in dragging anchor.

draw. , *v., i.* 1. To be immersed to a specified draft. 2. To change relative bearing forward or aft, or to port or starboard.

drawing sequence, . In ECDIS the implementation of DISPLAY PRIORITY.

dredge. , *n.* A vessel used to dredge an area.

dredge. , *v., t.* To remove solid matter from the bottom of a water area.

dredging area. . An area where dredging vessels may be encountered dredging material for construction. Channels dredged to provide an adequate depth of water for navigation are not considered as dredging areas.

dredging buoy. . A buoy marking the limit of an area where dredging is being performed. See also SPOIL GROUND BUOY.

dried ice. . Sea ice from the surface of which meltwater has disappeared after the formation of cracks and thaw holes. During the period of drying, the surface whitens.

drift. , *n.* 1. The speed of a current as defined in CURRENT. 2. The distance a craft is moved by current and wind. 3. Downwind or downcurrent motion of airborne or waterborne objects due to wind or current. 4. Material moved from one place and deposited in another, as sand by a river, rocks by a glacier, material washed ashore and left stranded, snow or sand piled up by wind. Rock material deposited by a glacier is also called ERRATIC. 5. The horizontal component of real precession or apparent precession, or the algebraic sum of the two. When it is desired to differentiate between the sum and its components, the sum is called total drift.

drift. , *v., i.* To move by action of wind or current without control.

drift angle. . 1. The angle between the tangent-to the turning circle and the centerline of the vessel during a turn. 2. The angular difference between a vessel's ground track and the water track. See also LEEWAY ANGLE.

drift axis. . On a gyroscope, the axis about which drift occurs. In a directional gyro with the spin axis mounted horizontally the drift axis is the vertical axis. See also SPIN AXIS, TOPPLE AXIS.

drift bottle. An identifiable float allowed to drift with ocean currents to determine their sets and drifts.

drift current. . A wide, slow-moving ocean current principally caused by prevailing winds.

drifting snow. . Snow raised from the ground and carried by the wind to such a height that the horizontal visibility is considerably reduced but the vertical visibility is not materially diminished. The expression BLOWING SNOW is used when both the horizontal and vertical visibility are considerably reduced.

drift lead. . A lead placed on the bottom to indicate movement of a vessel. At anchor the lead line is usually secured to the rail with a little slack and if the ship drags anchor, the line tends forward. A drift lead is also used to indicate when a vessel coming to anchor is dead in the water or when it is moving astern. A drift lead can be used to indicate current if a ship is dead in the water.

drilling rig. . A term used solely to indicate a mobile drilling structure. A drilling rig is not charted except in the rare cases where it is converted to a permanent production platform.

drizzle. , *n.* Very small, numerous, and uniformly dispersed water drops that may appear to float while following air currents. Unlike fog droplets, drizzle falls to the ground. It usually falls from low stratus clouds and is frequently accompanied by low visibility and fog. See also MIST.

drogue. , *n.* 1. See SEA ANCHOR. 2. A current measuring assembly consisting of a weighted parachute and an attached surface buoy.

drought. , *n.* A protracted period of dry weather.

droxtal. , *n.* A very small ice particle (about 10 to 20 microns in diameter) formed by the direct freezing of supercooled water droplets at temperatures below –30°C. Droxtals cause most of the restriction to visibility in ice fog.

dry-bulb temperature. . The temperature of the air, as indicated by the dry-bulb thermometer of a PSYCHROMETER.

dry-bulb thermometer. . A thermometer with an uncovered bulb, used with a wet-bulb thermometer to determine atmosphere humidity. The two thermometers constitute the essential parts of a PSYCHROMETER.

dry compass. . A compass without a liquid-filled bowl, particularly a magnetic compass having a very light compass card. Such a magnetic compass is seldom, if ever, used in marine applications. See also LIQUID COMPASS.

dry dock. . A dock providing support for a vessel, and means for removing the water so that the bottom of the vessel can be exposed. A dry dock consisting of an artificial basin is called a graving dock; one consisting of a floating structure is called a floating dock. See also MARINE RAILWAY.

dry-dock. , *v., t.* To place in a dry dock.

drydock iceberg. . An iceberg eroded in such manner that a large U-shaped slot is formed with twin columns. The slot extends into or near the waterline.

dry fog. . A fog that does not moisten exposed surfaces.

dry harbor. . A small harbor which either dries at low water or has insufficient depths to keep vessels afloat during all states of the tide. Vessels using it must be prepared to take the ground on the falling tide.

dry haze. . See under HAZE.

drying heights. . Heights above chart sounding datum of those features which are periodically covered and exposed by the rise and fall of the tide.

dual-carrier radiobeacon. . A continuous carrier radiobeacon in which identification is accomplished by means of a keyed second carrier. The frequency difference between the two carriers is made equal to the desired audio frequency. The object of the system is to reduce the bandwidth of the transmission.

duct. , *n.* See as TROPOSPHERIC RADIO DUCT.

dumb compass. . See PELORUS.

dummy antenna. . A substantially non-radiating device used to simulate an antenna with respect to input impedance over some specified range of frequencies. Also called ARTIFICIAL ANTENNA.

dumping ground. . An area used for the disposal of dredge spoil. Although shown on nautical charts as dumping grounds in U.S. waters, the Federal regulations for these areas have been revoked and their use for dumping discontinued. These areas will continue to be shown on nautical charts until they are no longer considered to be a danger to navigation. See also DUMP SITE, SPOIL AREA, DISPOSAL AREA.

dump site. . Area established by Federal regulation in which dumping of dredged and fill material and other nonbuoyant objects is allowed with the issuance of a permit. Dump sites are shown on nautical charts. See also DISPOSAL AREA, DUMPING GROUND, SPOIL AREA.

dune. , *n.* A mound, ridge, or hill of sand piled up by the wind on the shore or in a desert. Also called SAND DUNE.

duplex. . Concurrent transmission and reception of radio signals, electronic data, or other information.

duplexer. , *n.* A device which permits a single antenna system to be used for both transmitting and receiving.

duration of flood, duration of ebb. . Duration of flood is the interval of time in which a tidal current is flooding, and the duration of ebb is the interval in which it is ebbing; these intervals being reckoned from the middle of the intervening slack waters or minimum currents. Together they cover, on an average, a period of 12.42 hours for a semidiurnal tidal current or a period of 24.84 hours for a diurnal current. In a normal semidiurnal tidal current, the duration of flood and duration of ebb will each be approximately equal to 6.21 hours, but the times may be modified greatly by the presence of a nontidal flow. In a river, the duration of ebb is usually longer than the duration of flood because of the fresh water discharge, especially during the spring months when snow and ice melt are the predominant influences. See also DURATION OF RISE, DURATION OF FALL.

duration of rise, duration of fall. . Duration of rise is the interval from low water to high water, and duration of fall is the interval from high water to low water. Together they cover, on an average, a period of 12.42 hours for a semidiurnal tide or a period of 24.84 hours for a diurnal tide. In a normal semidiurnal tide, the duration of rise and duration of fall will each be approximately equal to 6.21 hours, but in shallow waters and in rivers there is a tendency for a decrease in the duration of rise and a corresponding increase in the duration of fall. See also DURATION OF FLOOD, DURATION OF EBB.

dusk. , *n.* The darker part of twilight; that part of twilight between complete darkness and the darker limit of civil twilight, both morning and evening.

dust devil. . A well-developed dust whirl, a small but vigorous whirlwind, usually of short duration, rendered visible by dust, sand, and debris picked up from the ground. Diameters of dust devils range from about 10 feet to greater than 100 feet; their average height is about 600 feet, but a few have been observed as high as several thousand feet. They have been observed to rotate anticyclonically as well as cyclonically. Dust devils are best developed on a hot, calm afternoon with clear skies, in a dry region when intense surface heating causes a very steep lapse rate of temperature in the lower few hundred feet of the atmosphere.

dust storm. , *n.* An unusual, frequently severe weather condition characterized by strong winds and dust-filled air over an extensive area. Prerequisite to a dust storm is a period of drought over an area of normally arable land, thus providing very fine particles of dust which distinguish it from the much more common SANDSTORM.

dust whirl. . A rapidly rotating column of air, or WHIRLWIND, over a dry and dusty or sandy area, carrying dust, leaves, and other light material picked up from the ground. When well developed it is called a DUST DEVIL.

Dutchman's log. . A buoyant object thrown overboard to determine the speed of a vessel. The time required for a known length of the vessel to pass the object is measured.

duty cycle. . An expression of the fraction of the total time of pulse radar that radio-frequency energy is radiated. It is the ratio of pulse length to pulse repetition time.

dynamical mean sun. . A fictitious sun conceived to move eastward along the ecliptic at the average rate of the apparent sun. The dynamical mean sun and the apparent sun occupy the same position when the earth is at perihelion in January. See also MEAN SUN.

dyne. , *n.* A force which imparts an acceleration of 1 centimeter per second to a mass of 1 gram. The dyne is the unit of force in the CENTIMETER-GRAM-SECOND SYSTEM. It corresponds to 10^{-5} newton in the International System of Units.

E

earth-centered ellipsoid. . A reference ellipsoid whose geometric center coincides with the earth's center of gravity and whose semiminor axis coincides with the earth's rotational axis.

earth-fixed coordinate system. . Any coordinate system in which the axes are stationary with respect to the earth. See also INERTIAL COORDINATE SYSTEM.

earthlight. , *n.* The faint illumination of the dark part of the moon by sunlight reflected from the earth. Also called EARTHSHINE.

earth rate. . The angular velocity or rate of the earth's rotation. See also EARTH-RATE CORRECTION, HORIZONTAL EARTH RATE, VERTICAL EARTH RATE.

earth-rate correction. . A rate applied to a gyroscope to compensate for the apparent precession of the spin axis caused by the rotation of the earth. See also EARTH RATE, HORIZONTAL EARTH RATE, VERTICAL EARTH RATE.

earth satellite. . A body that orbits about the earth. See also ARTIFICIAL EARTH SATELLITE.

earthshine. , *n.* See EARTHLIGHT.

earth tide. . Periodic movement of the earth's crust caused by the gravitational interactions between the sun, moon, and earth.

east. , *n.* The direction 90° to the right of NORTH. See also CARDINAL POINT.

East Africa Coastal Current. . An Indian Ocean current which originates mainly from the part of the Indian South Equatorial Current which turns northward off the northeast coast of Africa in the vicinity of latitude 10°S. The current appears to vary considerably in speed and direction from month to month. The greatest changes coincide with the period of the opposing northeast monsoon during November through March. This coastal current is most persistent in a north or northeast direction and strongest during the southwest monsoon from May through September, particularly during August. Speed and frequency begin to decrease during the transition month of October. In November at about latitude 4°N a part of the current begins to reverse; this part expands northward and southward until February. The region of reverse flow begins to diminish in March and disappear in April, when the northward set again predominates. Also called SOMALI CURRENT. See also MONSOON.

East Australia Current. . A South Pacific Ocean current flowing southward along the east coast of Australia, from the Coral Sea to a point northeast of Tasmania, where it turns to join the northeastward flow through the Tasman Sea. It is formed by that part of the Pacific South Equatorial Current that turns south east of Australia. In the southern hemisphere summer, a small part of this current flows westward along the south coast of Australia into the Indian Ocean. The East Australia Current forms the western part of the general counterclockwise oceanic circulation of the South Pacific Ocean.

eastern standard time. . See STANDARD TIME.

East Greenland Current. . An ocean current flowing southward along the east coast of Greenland carrying water of low salinity and low temperature. The East Greenland Current is joined by most of the water of the Irminger Current. The greater part of the current continues through Denmark Strait between Iceland and Greenland, but one branch turns to the east and forms a portion of the counterclockwise circulation in the southern part of the Norwegian Sea. Some of the East Greenland Current curves to the right around the tip of Greenland, flowing northward into Davis Strait as the WEST GREENLAND CURRENT. The main discharge of the Arctic Ocean is via the East Greenland Current.

easting. , *n.* The distance a craft makes good to the east. The opposite is WESTING.

East Siberian Coastal Current. . An ocean current in the Chukchi Sea which joins the northward flowing Bering Current north of East Cape.

ebb. , *n.* Tidal current moving away from land or down a tidal stream. The opposite is FLOOD. Sometimes the terms ebb and flood are also used with reference to vertical tidal movement, but for this vertical movement the expressions FALLING TIDE and RISING TIDE are preferable. Also called EBB CURRENT.

ebb axis. . The average direction of current at strength of ebb.

ebb current. . The movement of a tidal current away from shore or down a tidal river or estuary. In the mixed type of reversing tidal current, the terms *greater ebb* and *lesser ebb* are applied respectively to the ebb tidal currents of greater and lesser speed of each day. The terms *maximum ebb* and *minimum ebb* are applied to the maximum and minimum speeds of a current running continuously. Maximum ebb is also applicable to any ebb current at the time of greatest speed. The opposite is FLOOD CURRENT.

ebb interval. . Short for STRENGTH OF EBB INTERVAL. The interval between the transit of the moon over the meridian of a place and the time of the following strength of ebb. See also LUNICURRENT INTERVAL.

ebb strength. . Phase of the ebb tidal current at the time of maximum velocity. Also, the velocity at this time. Also called STRENGTH OF EBB.

eccentric. , *adj.* Not having the same center. The opposite is CONCENTRIC.

eccentric angle. . See under ANOMALY, definition 2.

eccentric anomaly. . See under ANOMALY, definition 2.

eccentric error. . See CENTERING ERROR.

eccentricity. , *n.* 1. Degree of deviating from a center. 2. The ratio of the distance between foci of an ellipse to the length of the major axis, or the ratio of the distance between the center and a focus to the length of the semimajor axis. 3. The ratio of the distances from any point of a conic section to a focus and the corresponding directrix.

eccentricity component. . That part of the equation of time due to the ellipticity of the orbit and known as the eccentricity component is the difference, in mean solar time units, between the hour angles of the apparent (true) sun and the dynamical mean sun. It is also the difference in the right ascensions of these two suns.

ECDIS. . See ELECTRONIC CHART DISPLAY AND INFORMATION SYSTEM.

ECDIS Chart 1. An ECDIS version of IHO INT 1, including all SYMBOLS, line styles and color coding used for chart and navigation symbols, contained in the PRESENTATION LIBRARY.

echo, *n.* 1. A wave which has been reflected or otherwise returned with sufficient magnitude and delay to be perceived. 2. A signal reflected by a target to a radar antenna. Also called RETURN. 3. The deflection or indication on a radarscope representing a target. Also called PIP, BLIP, RETURN.

echo box.. A resonant cavity, energized by part of the transmitted pulse of a radar set, which produces an artificial target signal for tuning or testing the overall performance of a radar set. Also called PHANTOM TARGET.

echo box performance monitor.. See under PERFORMANCE MONITOR.

echogram., *n.* A graphic record of depth measurements obtained by an echo sounder. See also FATHOGRAM.

echo ranging.. The determination of distance by measuring the time interval between transmission of a radiant energy signal and the return of its echo. Since echo ranging equipment is usually provided with means for determining direction as well as distance, both functions are generally implied. The expression is customarily applied only to ranging by utilization of the travel of sonic or ultrasonic signals through water. See also RADIO ACOUSTIC RANGING, SONAR.

echo sounder.. An instrument used to determine water depth by measuring the time interval for sound waves to go from a source of sound near the surface to the bottom and back again. Also called DEPTH FINDER, ACOUSTIC DEPTH FINDER.

echo sounding.. Determination of the depth of water by measuring the time interval between emission of a sonic or ultrasonic signal and the return of its echo from the bottom. The instrument used for this purpose is called an ECHO SOUNDER. Also called ACOUSTIC SOUNDING.

eclipse., *n.* 1. Obscuring of a source of light by the intervention of an object. When the moon passes between the earth and the sun, casting a shadow on the earth, a SOLAR ECLIPSE takes place within the shadow. A solar eclipse is partial if the sun is partly obscured, total if the entire surface is obscured, or annular if a thin ring of the sun's surface appears around the obscuring body. When the moon enters the earth's shadow, a LUNAR ECLIPSE occurs. When the moon enters only the penumbra of the earth's shadow, a PENUMBRAL LUNAR ECLIPSE occurs. A lunar eclipse can be either total or partial. 2. An interval of darkness between flashes of a navigation light.

eclipse year.. The interval between two successive conjunctions of the sun with the same node of the moon's orbit, averaging 346 days, 14 hours, 52 minutes 50.7 seconds in 1900, and increasing at the rate of 2.8 seconds per century.

ecliptic., *n.* The apparent annual path of the sun among the stars; the intersection of the plane of the earth's orbit with the celestial sphere. This is a great circle of the celestial sphere inclined at an angle of about 23°27' to the celestial equator. See also ZODIAC.

ecliptic diagram.. A diagram of the ZODIAC, indicating the positions of certain celestial bodies in this region.

ecliptic pole.. On the celestial sphere, either of the two points 90° from the ecliptic.

ecliptic system of coordinates.. A set of celestial coordinates based on the ecliptic as the primary great circle; celestial latitude and celestial longitude.

eddy., *n.* A quasi-circular movement of water whose area is relatively small in comparison to the current with which it is associated. Eddies may be formed between two adjacent currents flowing counter to each other and where currents pass obstructions, especially on the downstream side. See also WHIRLPOOL.

edge.. In ECDIS, a one-dimensional SPATIAL OBJECT, located by two or more coordinate pairs (or two CONNECTED NODES) and optional interpolation parameters. If the parameters are missing, the interpolation is defaulted to straight line segments between the coordinate pairs. In the CHAIN-NODE, PLANAR GRAPH and FULL TOPOLOGY data structures, an edge must reference a connected node at both ends and must not reference any other NODES.

effective radiated power. The power supplied to the antenna multiplied by the relative gain of the antenna in a given direction.

effective radius of the earth.. The radius of a hypothetical earth for which the distance to the radio horizon, assuming rectilinear propagation, is the same as that for the actual earth with an assumed uniform vertical gradient of a refractive index. For the standard atmosphere, the effective radius is 4/3 that of the actual earth.

Ekman spiral.. A logarithmic spiral (when projected on a horizontal plane) formed by current velocity vectors at increasing depth intervals. The current vectors become progressively smaller with depth. They spiral to the right (looking in the direction of flow) in the Northern Hemisphere and to the left in the Southern with increasing depth. Theoretically, the surface current vector sets 45° from the direction toward which the wind is blowing. Flow opposite to the surface current occurs at the depth of frictional resistance. The phenomenon occurs in wind drift currents in which only the Coriolis and frictional forces are significant. Named for Vagn Walfrid Ekman who, assuming a constant eddy viscosity, steady wind stress, and unlimited depth and extent, published the effect in 1905.

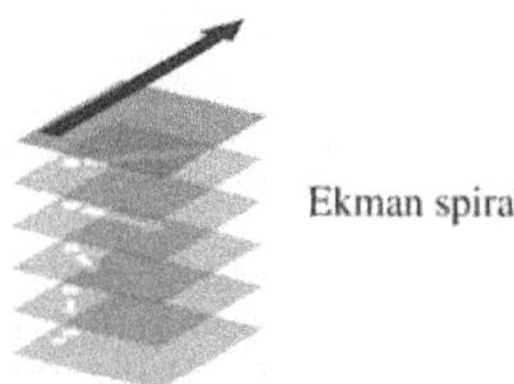

Ekman spiral

E-layer, *n.* From the standpoint of its effect upon radio wave propagation, the lowest useful layer of the Kennelly-Heaviside radiation region. Its average height is about 70 miles, and its density is greatest about local apparent noon. For practical purposes, the layer disappears during the hours of darkness.

elbow., *n.* A sharp change in direction of a coast line, a channel, river, etc.

electrical distance.. A distance expressed in terms of the duration of travel of an electromagnetic wave in a given medium between two points.

electrically suspended gyro.. A gyroscope in which the main rotating element is suspended by a magnetic field or any other similar electrical phenomenon. See also GYRO, ELECTROSTATIC GYRO.

electrical storm.. See THUNDERSTORM.

electric field.. That region in space which surrounds an electrically charged object and in which the forces due to this charge are detectable. See also ELECTRIC VECTOR.

electric tape gage.. A tide gage consisting of a monel metal tape on a metal reel (with supporting frame), voltmeter, and battery. The tape is graduated with numbers increasing toward the unattached end. Tidal heights can be measured directly by unreeling the tape into its stilling well. When contact is made with the water's surface, the circuit is completed and the voltmeter needle moves. At that moment, the length of tape is read against an index mark, the mark having a known elevation relative to the tidal bench marks. Used at many long term control stations in place of the tide staff.

electric vector.. The component of the electromagnetic field associated with electromagnetic radiation which is of the nature of an electric field. The electric vector is considered to coexist with, but to act at right angles to, the magnetic vector.

electrode., *n.* A terminal at which electricity passes from one medium into another. The positive electrode is called the ANODE; the negative electrode is called the CATHODE.

electromagnetic., *adj.* Of, pertaining to, or produced by electromagnetism.

electromagnetic energy.. All forms of radiant energy, such as radio waves, light waves, X-rays, heat waves, gamma rays, and cosmic rays.

electromagnetic field.. 1. The field of influence which an electric current produces around the conductor through which it flows. 2. A rapidly moving electric field and its associated magnetic field located at right angles to both electric lines of force and to their direction of motion. 3. The magnetic field resulting from the flow of electricity.

electromagnetic log.. A log containing an electromagnetic sensing element extended below the hull of the vessel, which produces a voltage directly proportional to speed through the water.

electromagnetic waves.. Waves of associated electric and magnetic fields characterized by variations of the fields. The electric and magnetic fields are at right angles to each other and to the direction of propagation. The waves are propagated at the speed of light and are known as radio (Hertzian) waves, infrared rays, light, ultraviolet rays, X-rays, etc., depending on their frequencies.

electromagnetism., *n.* 1. Magnetism produced by an electric current. 2. The science dealing with the physical relations between electricity and magnetism.

electron., *n.* A negatively-charged particle of matter constituting a part of an atom. Its electric charge is the most elementary unit of negative electricity.

electron gun. . A group of electrodes which produces an electron beam of controllable intensity. By extension, the expression is often used to include, also, the elements which focus and deflect the beam.

electronic aid to navigation. . An aid to navigation using electronic equipment. If the navigational information is transmitted by radio waves, the device may be called a RADIO AID TO NAVIGATION.

electronic bearing cursor. . The bright rotatable radial line on the display of a marine radar set, used for bearing determination.

electronic chart (EC). . A chart displayed on a video terminal, usually integrated with other navigational aids.

electronic chart data base (ECDB). . The master electronic chart data base for the electronic navigation chart held in digital form by the hydrographic authority.

electronic chart display and information system (ECDIS). . An electronic chart system which complies with IMO guidelines and is the legal equivalent of a paper chart. ECDIS is the only equipment on the bridge that provides an overall view of all navigational sensors simultaneously with nautical charts. Displaying multiple information feeds on one screen enhances the navigating officer's situational awareness.

Electronic Chart System (ECS). . Navigation information system that electronically displays vessel position and relevant nautical chart data and information from the ECS database on a display screen, but does not meet all IMO requirements for ECDIS, and does not satisfy SOLAS Chapter V requirements to carry a navigational chart.

Electronic Navigational Chart (ENC). The data base, standardized as to content, structure and format, issued for use with ECDIS on the authority of government authorized hydrographic offices. The ENC contains all the chart information necessary for safe navigation and may contain supplementary information in addition to that contained in the paper chart (e.g. sailing directions) which may be considered necessary for safe navigation.

electronic cursor. . Short for ELECTRONIC BEARING CURSOR.

electronic distance measuring devices. . Instruments that measure the phase differences between transmitted and reflected or retransmitted electromagnetic waves of known frequency, or that measure the round-trip transit time of a pulsed signal, from which distance is computed.

electronic navigation. . Navigation by means of electronic equipment. The expression electronic navigation is more inclusive than RADIONAVIGATION, since it includes navigation involving any electronic device or instrument.

electronics. , *n.* The science and technology relating to the emission, flow, and effects of electrons in a vacuum or through a semiconductor such as a gas, and to systems using devices in which this action takes place.

electronic telemeter. . An electronic device that measures the phase difference or transit time between a transmitted electromagnetic impulse of known frequency and speed and its return.

electrostatic gyro. . A gyroscope in which a small ball rotor is electrically suspended within an array of electrodes in a vacuum inside a ceramic envelope. See also GYRO, ELECTRICALLY SUSPENDED GYRO.

elements of a fix. . The specific values of the coordinates used to define a position.

elephanta. , *n.* A strong southerly or southeasterly wind which blows on the Malabar coast of India during the months of September and October and marks the end of the southwest monsoon.

elevated duct. . A TROPOSPHERIC RADIO DUCT of which the lower boundary is above the surface of the earth.

elevated pole. . The celestial pole above the horizon, agreeing in name with the latitude. The celestial pole below the horizon is called DEPRESSED POLE.

elevation. , *n.* 1. Vertical distance of a point above a datum, usually mean sea level. Elevation usually applies to a point on the surface of the earth. The term HEIGHT is used for points on or above the surface. See also SPOT ELEVATION. 2. An area higher than its surroundings, as a hill.

elevation angle. . See ANGLE OF ELEVATION.

elevation tints. . See HYPSOMETRIC TINTING.

elimination. , *n.* One of the final processes in the harmonic analysis of tides in which preliminary values of the harmonic constants of a number of constituents are cleared of residual effects of each other.

E-link. . A bracket attached to one of the arms of a binnacle to permit the mounting of a quadrantal corrector in an intermediate position between the fore-and-aft and athwartship lines through a magnetic compass.

ellipse. , *n.* A plane curve constituting the locus of all points the sum of whose distances from two fixed points called FOCI is constant; an elongated circle. The orbits of planets, satellites, planetoids, and comets are ellipses with the center of attraction at one focus. See also CONIC SECTION, CURRENT ELLIPSE.

ellipsoid. , *n.* A surface whose plane sections (cross-sections) are all ellipses or circles, or the solid enclosed by such a surface. Also called ELLIPSOID OF REVOLUTION, SPHEROID.

ellipsoidal height. . The height above the reference ellipsoid, measured along the ellipsoidal outer normal through the point in question. Also called GEODETIC HEIGHT.

ellipsoid of reference. . See REFERENCE ELLIPSOID.

ellipsoid of revolution. . A term used for an ellipsoid which can be formed by revolving an ellipse about one of its axes. Also called ELLIPSOID OF ROTATION.

ellipsoid of rotation. . See ELLIPSOID OF REVOLUTION.

elliptically polarized wave. . An electromagnetic wave which can be resolved into two plane polarized waves which are perpendicular to each other and which propagate in the same direction. The amplitudes of the waves may be equal or unequal and of arbitrary time-phase. The tip of the component of the electric field vector in the plane normal to the direction of propagation describes an ellipse. See also CIRCULARLY POLARIZED WAVE.

ellipticity. , *n.* The amount by which a spheroid differs from a sphere or an ellipse differs from a circle, found by dividing the difference in the lengths of the semiaxes of the ellipse by the length of the semimajor axis. See also FLATTENING.

elongation. , *n.* The angular distance of a body of the solar system from the sun; the angle at the earth between lines to the sun and another celestial body of the solar system. The greatest elongation is the maximum angular distance of an inferior planet from the sun before it starts back toward conjunction. The direction of the body east or west of the sun is usually specified, as greatest elongation east (or west).

embayed. , *adj.* l. Formed into or having bays. 2. Unable to put to sea safely because of wind, current, or sea conditions.

embayment. , *n.* Any indentation of a coast regardless of width at the entrance or depth of penetration into the land. See also ESTUARY.

emergency light. . A light put into service in an emergency when the permanent or standby light has failed. It often provides reduced service in comparison with the permanent light.

Emergency Position Indicating Radiobeacon (EPIRB). . A small portable radiobeacon carried by vessels, aircraft, or personnel which transmits radio signals which can be used by search and rescue authorities to locate a marine emergency.

emergency position indicating radiobeacon station. . As defined by the International Telecommunication Union, a station in the mobile service whose emissions are intended to facilitate search and rescue operations.

emission delay. . 1. A delay in the transmission of a pulse signal from a slave (or secondary) station of a hyperbolic radionavigation system, introduced as an aid in distinguishing between master and slave (or secondary) station signals.

empirical. , *adj.* Derived by observation or experience rather than by rules or laws.

e-Navigation. , *n.* The harmonized collection, integration, exchange, presentation and analysis of maritime information on board and ashore by electronic means to enhance berth-to-berth navigation and related services for safety and security at sea and protection of the marine environment.

ENC. . See ELECTRONIC NAVIGATIONAL CHART.

ENC cell structure, See CELL.

ENC product specification. , In ECDIS the IHO Standard which specifies the content, structure and other mandatory aspects of an ENC.

ENC test data set. , In ECDIS a standardized data set supplied on behalf of the INTERNATIONAL HYDROGRAPHIC ORGANIZATION (IHO) that is necessary to accomplish all IEC testing requirements for ECDIS.

encapsulation. In ECDIS the identification of FIELDS and RECORDS and the grouping of fields and records and the data syntax rules used.

encoding conventions. In ECDIS a set of rules to be followed when encoding data for a particular purpose.

endless tangent screw. A tangent screw which can be moved over its entire range without resetting.

endless tangent screw sextant. A marine sextant having an endless tangent screw for controlling the position of the index arm and the vernier or micrometer drum. The index arm may be moved over the entire arc without resetting, by means of the endless tangent screw.

enhanced group call (EGC). . A global automated satellite communications service capable of addressing messages to specific areas or specific groups of vessels.

ensonify, insonify. To fill the ocean or any fluid medium with acoustic radiation, which is then observed and analyzed to study the medium or to locate or image objects with it.

entrance. , *n.* The seaward end of a channel, harbor, etc.

entrance lock. . A lock between the tideway and an enclosed basin when their water levels vary. By means of the lock, which has two sets of gates vessels can pass either way at all states of the tide. Also called TIDAL LOCK. See also NONTIDAL BASIN.

ephemeris . *(pl. ephemerides), n.* 1. A periodical publication tabulating the predicted positions of celestial bodies at regular intervals, such as daily, and containing other data of interest to astronomers and navigators. The *Astronomical Almanac* is an ephemeris. See also ALMANAC. 2. A statement, not necessarily in a publication, presenting a correlation of time and position of celestial bodies or artificial satellites.

ephemeris day. . See under EPHEMERIS SECOND.

ephemeris second. . The ephemeris second is defined as 1/31,556,925.9747 of the tropical year for 1900 January 0^d 12^h ET. The ephemeris day is 86,400 ephemeris seconds. See also EPHEMERIS TIME.

Ephemeris Time. . The time scale used by astronomers as the tabular argument of the precise fundamental ephemerides of the sun, moon and planets. It is the independent variable in the gravitational theories of the solar system. It is determined in arrears from astronomical observations and extrapolated into the future, based on International Atomic Time.

epicenter. , *n.* The point on the earth's surface directly above the focus of an earthquake.

epoch. , *n.* 1. A particular instant of time or a date for which values of data, which vary with time, are given. 2. A given period of time during which a series of related acts or events takes place. 3. Angular retardation of the maximum of a constituent of the observed tide behind the corresponding maximum of the same constituent of the hypothetical equilibrium. Also called PHASE LAG, TIDAL EPOCH. 4. As used in tidal datum determinations, a 19-year Metonic cycle over which tidal height observations are meaned in order to establish the various datums.

equal altitudes. . Two altitudes numerically the same. The expression applies particularly to the practice of determining the instant of local apparent noon by observing the altitude of the sun a short time before it reaches the meridian and again at the same altitude after transit, the time of local apparent noon being midway between the times of the two observations, if the second is corrected as necessary for the run of the ship. Also called DOUBLE ALTITUDES.

equal-area map projection. . A map projection having a constant area scale. Such a projection is not conformal and is not used for navigation. Also called AUTHALIC MAP PROJECTION, EQUIVALENT MAP PROJECTION.

equal interval light. . A navigation light having equal periods of light and darkness. Also called ISOPHASE LIGHT.

equation of time. . The difference at any instant between apparent time and local mean time. It is a measure of the difference of the hour angles of the apparent (true) sun and the mean (fictitious) sun. The curve drawn for the equation of time during a year has two maxima: February 12 (+14.3^m) and July 27 (+6.3^m) and two minima: May 15 (-3.7^m) and November 4 (-16.4^m). The curve crosses the zero line on April 15, June 14, September 1, and December 24. The equation of time is tabulated in the *Nautical Almanac*, without sign, for 00^h and 12^h GMT on each day. To obtain apparent time, apply the equation of time to mean time with a positive sign when GHA sun at 00^h GMT exceeds 180°, or at 12^h exceeds 0°, corresponding to a meridian passage of the sun before 12^h GMT; otherwise apply with a negative sign.

equator. , *n.* The primary great circle of a sphere or spheroid, such as the earth, perpendicular to the polar axis, or a line resembling or approximating such a circle. The terrestrial equator is 90° from the earth's geographical poles, the celestial equator or equinoctial is 90° from the celestial poles. The astronomical equator is a line connecting points having 0° astronomical latitude, the geodetic equator connects points having 0° geodetic latitude. The expression terrestrial equator is sometimes applied to the astronomical equator. The equator shown on charts is the geodetic equator. A fictitious equator is a reference line serving as the origin for measurement of fictitious latitude. A transverse or inverse equator is a meridian the plane of which is perpendicular to the axis of a transverse projection. An oblique equator is a great circle the plane of which is perpendicular to the axis of an oblique projection. A grid equator is a line perpendicular to a prime grid meridian at the origin. The magnetic equator or aclinic line is the line on the surface of the earth connecting all points at which the magnetic dip is zero. The geomagnetic equator is the great circle 90° from the geomagnetic poles of the earth.

equatorial. , *adj.* Of or pertaining to the EQUATOR.

equatorial air. . See under AIR-MASS CLASSIFICATION.

equatorial bulge. . The excess of the earth's equatorial diameter over the polar diameter.

equatorial calms. . See DOLDRUMS.

equatorial chart. . 1. A chart of equatorial areas. 2. A chart on an EQUATORIAL MAP PROJECTION.

equatorial countercurrent. . An oceanic current flowing between and counter to the EQUATORIAL CURRENTS. See ATLANTIC EQUATORIAL COUNTERCURRENT, PACIFIC EQUATORIAL COUNTERCURRENT, INDIAN EQUATORIAL COUNTERCURRENT.

equatorial current. . See NORTH EQUATORIAL CURRENT, SOUTH EQUATORIAL CURRENT.

equatorial cylindrical orthomorphic chart. . See MERCATOR CHART.

equatorial cylindrical orthomorphic map projection. . See MERCATOR MAP PROJECTION.

equatorial gravity value. . The mean acceleration of gravity at the equator, approximately equal to 978.03 centimeters per second per second.

equatorial map projection. . A map projection centered on the equator.

equatorial node. . Either of the two points where the orbit of the satellite intersects the equatorial plane of its primary.

equatorial satellite. . A satellite whose orbital plane coincides, or almost coincides, with the earth's equatorial plane.

equatorial tidal currents. . Tidal currents occurring semimonthly as a result of the moon being over the equator. At these times the tendency of the moon to produce a diurnal inequality in the tidal current is at a minimum.

equatorial tides. . Tides occurring semimonthly as the result of the moon being over the equator. At these times the tendency of the moon to produce a diurnal inequality in the tide is at a minimum.

equiangular. , *adj.* Having equal angles.

equilateral. , *adj.* Having equal sides.

equilateral triangle. . A triangle having all of its sides equal. An equilateral triangle is necessarily equiangular.

equilibrium. , *n.* A state of balance between forces. A body is said to be in equilibrium when the vector sum or all forces acting upon it is zero.

equilibrium argument. . The theoretical phase of a constituent of the equilibrium tide.

equilibrium theory. . A model under which it is assumed that the waters covering the face of the earth instantly respond to the tide-producing forces of the moon and sun, and form a surface of equilibrium under the action of these forces. The model disregards friction and inertia and the irregular distribution of the land masses of the earth. The theoretical tide formed under these conditions is called EQUILIBRIUM TIDE.

equilibrium tide. . Hypothetical tide due to the tide producing forces under the equilibrium theory. Also called GRAVITATIONAL TIDE.

equinoctial. , *adj.* Of or pertaining to an EQUINOX or the equinoxes.

equinoctial. , *n.* See CELESTIAL EQUATOR.

equinoctial colure. . The great circle of the celestial sphere through the celestial poles and the equinoxes; the hour circle of the vernal equinox. See also SOLSTITIAL COLURE.

equinoctial point. . One of the two points of intersection of the ecliptic and the celestial equator. Also called EQUINOX.

equinoctial system of coordinates. . See CELESTIAL EQUATOR SYSTEM OF COORDINATES.

equinoctial tides. . Tides occurring near the times of the equinoxes, when the spring range is greater than average.

equinoctial year. . See TROPICAL YEAR.

equinox. , *n.* 1. One of the two points of intersection of the ecliptic and celestial equator, occupied by the sun when its declination is 0°. The point occupied on or about March 21, when the sun's declination changes from south to north, is called vernal equinox, March equinox, or first point of Aries; the point occupied on or about September 23, when the declination changes from north to south, is called autumnal equinox, September equinox, or first point of Libra. Also called EQUINOCTIAL POINT. 2. The instant the sun occupies one of the equinoctial points.

equiphase zone. . The region in space within which there is no difference in phase between two radio signals.

equipotential surface. . A surface having the same potential of gravity at every point. See also GEOID.

equisignal. , *adj.* Pertaining to two signals of equal intensity.

equisignal zone. . The region in space within which the difference in amplitude of two radio signals (usually emitted by a signal station) is indistinguishable.

equivalent echoing area. . See RADAR CROSS SECTION.

equivalent map projection. . See EQUAL-AREA MAP PROJECTION.

erect image. . See under IMAGE, definition 1.

erecting telescope. . A telescope with which the observer sees objects right side up as opposed to the upside down view provided by the INVERTING TELESCOPE. The eyepiece in the optical system of an erecting telescope usually has four lenses, and the eyepiece in the optical system of an inverting telescope has two lenses.

erg. , *n.* The work performed by a force of 1 dyne acting through a distance of 1 centimeter. The erg is the unit of energy or work in the centimeter-gram-second system. It corresponds to 10^{-7} joule in the International System of Units.

ergonomics. . The science of making mechanical and electronic devices easily usable by humans; human factors engineering.

error. , *n.* The difference between the value of a quantity determined by observation, measurement or calculation and the true, correct, accepted, adopted or standard value of that quantity. Usually, the true value of the quantity cannot be determined with exactness due to insufficient knowledge of the errors encountered in the observations. Exceptions occur (1) when the value is mathematically determinable, or (2) when the value is an adopted or standard value established by authority. In order to analyze the exactness with which the true value of a quantity has been determined from observations, errors are classified into two categories, random and systematic errors. For the purpose of error analysis, blunders or mistakes are not classified as errors. The significant difference between the two categories is that random errors must be treated by means of statistical and probability methods due to their accidental or chance nature whereas systematic errors are usually expressible in terms of a unique mathematical formula representing some physical law or phenomenon. See also ACCURACY.

error budget. . A correlated set of individual major error sources with statements of the percentage of the total system error contributed by each source.

error ellipse. . The contour of equal probability density centered on the intersection of two straight lines of position which results from the one-dimensional normal error distribution associated with each line. For the 50% error ellipse, there is a 50% probability that a fix will lie within such ellipse. If the angle of cut is 90° and the standard deviations are equal, the error figure is a circle.

error of collimation. . See COLLIMATION ERROR.

error of perpendicularity. . That error in the reading of a marine sextant due to non-perpendicularity of the index mirror to the frame.

escape velocity. , *n.* The minimum velocity required of a body at a given point in a gravitational field which will permit the body to escape from the field. The orbit followed is a parabola and the body arrives at an infinite distance from the center of the field with zero velocity. With respect to escape velocities characteristic of the major bodies of the solar system, this is defined as escape from the body's gravitational field from the surface of the body in question. Escape velocity equals circular velocity times the square root of 2. Also called PARABOLIC VELOCITY.

escarpment. , *n.* An elongated and comparatively steep slope separating flat or gently sloping areas. Also called SCARP.

established direction of traffic flow. . A traffic flow pattern indicating the directional movement of traffic as established within a traffic separation scheme. See also RECOMMENDED DIRECTION OF TRAFFIC FLOW.

establishment of the port. . Average high water interval on days of the new and full moon. This interval is also sometimes called the COMMON or VULGAR ESTABLISHMENT to distinguish it from the CORRECTED ESTABLISHMENT, the latter being the mean of all high water intervals. The latter is usually 10 to 15 minutes less than the common establishment. Also called HIGH WATER FULL AND CHANGE.

estimate. , *v., t.* To determine roughly or with incomplete information.

estimated position. . The most probable position of a craft determined from incomplete data or data of questionable accuracy. Such a position might be determined by applying a correction to the dead reckoning position, as for estimated current; by plotting a line of soundings; or by plotting lines of position of questionable accuracy. If no better information is available, a dead reckoning position is an estimated position, but the expression *estimated position* is not customarily used in this case. The distinction between an estimated position and a fix or running fix is a matter of judgment.

estimated time of arrival. . The predicted time of reaching a destination or waypoint.

estimated time of departure. . The predicted time of leaving a place.

estimation. , *n.* A mathematical method or technique of making a decision concerning the approximate value of a desired quantity when the decision is weighted or influenced by all available information.

estuarine sanctuary. . A research area which may include any part or all of an estuary, adjoining transitional areas, and adjacent uplands, constituting to the extent feasible a natural unit, set aside to provide scientists and students the opportunity to examine over a period of time the ecological relationships within the area. See also MARINE SANCTUARY.

estuary. , *n.* 1. An embayment of the coast in which fresh river water entering at its head mixes with the relatively saline ocean water. When tidal action is the dominant mixing agent, it is usually called TIDAL ESTUARY. 2. The lower reaches and mouth of a river emptying directly into the sea where tidal mixing takes place. Sometimes called RIVER ESTUARY. 3. A drowned river mouth due to sinking of the land near the coast.

etesian. , *n.* A refreshing northerly summer wind of the Mediterranean, especially over the Aegean Sea.

Eulerian current measurement. . The direct observation of the current speed or direction, or both, during a period of time as it flows past a recording instrument such as the Ekman or Roberts current meter. See also LAGRANGIAN CURRENT MEASUREMENT.

Eulerian motion. . A slight wobbling of the earth about its axis of rotation, often called POLAR MOTION, and sometimes WANDERING OF THE POLES. This motion, which does not exceed 40 feet from the mean position, produces slight variation of latitude and longitude of places on the earth.

European Datum. . The origin of this datum is at Potsdam, Germany. Numerous national systems have been joined in a large datum based upon the International Ellipsoid 1924 which was oriented by a modified astrogeodetic method. European, African, and Asian triangulation chains were connected. African arc measurements from Cairo to Cape Town were completed. Thus, all Europe, Africa, and Asia are molded into one great system. Through common survey stations, it was possible to convert data from the Russian Pulkovo 1932 system to the European Datum, and as a result the European Datum includes triangulation as far east as the 84th meridian. Additional ties across the Middle East have permitted connection of the Indian and European Datums.

evaporation. , *n.* The physical process by which a liquid or solid is transformed to the gaseous state. The opposite is CONDENSATION. In meteorology, the term evaporation is usually restricted in use to the change of water from liquid to gas, while SUBLIMATION is used for the change from solid to gas as well as from gas to solid. Energy is lost by an evaporating liquid, and when no heat is added externally, the liquid always cools. The heat thus removed is called LATENT HEAT OF VAPORIZATION.

evection., *n.* A perturbation of the moon depending upon the alternate increase or decrease of the eccentricity of its orbit, which is always a maximum when the sun is passing the moon's line of apsides and at minimum when the sun is at right angles to it.

evening star.. The brightest planet appearing in the western sky during EVENING TWILIGHT.

evening twilight.. The period of time between sunset and darkness.

everglade., *n.* 1. A tract of swampy land covered mostly with tall grass. 2. A swamp or inundated tract of low land, as used locally in the southern U.S.

excess of arc.. That part of a sextant arc beginning at zero and extending in the direction opposite to that part usually considered positive. See also ARC, definition 2.

exchange format.. In ECDIS a specification for the structure and organization of data to facilitate exchange between computer systems.

exchange set.. In ECDIS the set of FILES representing a complete, single purpose (i.e. product specific) data transfer. The ENC PRODUCT SPECIFICATION defines an exchange set which contains one Catalogue file and at least one data set file.

existence doubtful. Of uncertain existence. The expression is used principally on charts to indicate the possible existence of a rock, shoal, etc., the actual existence of which has not been established.

ex-meridian altitude.. An altitude of a celestial body near the celestial meridian of the observer to which a correction must be applied to determine the meridian altitude. Also called CIRCUMMERIDIAN ALTITUDE.

ex-meridian observation.. Measurement of the altitude of a celestial body near the celestial meridian of the observer, for conversion to a meridian altitude; or the altitude so measured.

expanded center PPI display.. A plan position indicator display on which zero range corresponds to a ring around the center of the display.

expanded sweep.. Short for EXPANDED TIME BASE SWEEP.

expanded time base.. A time base having a selected part of increased speed. Particularly an EXPANDED TIME BASE SWEEP.

expanded time base sweep.. A sweep in which the sweep speed is increased during a selected part of the cycle. Usually shortened to EXPANDED SWEEP, and sometimes to EXPANDED TIME BASE.

explement., *n.* An angle equal to 360° minus a given angle. See also COMPLEMENT, SUPPLEMENT.

explementary angles.. Two angles whose sum is 360°.

explosive fog signal.. A fog signal consisting of short reports produced by detonating explosive charges.

exponent., *n.* A number which indicates the power to which another number is to be raised.

external noise.. In radio reception, atmospheric radio noise and man-made noise, singly or in combination. Internal noise is produced in the receiver circuits.

extragalactic nebula.. An aggregation of matter beyond our galaxy, large enough to occupy a perceptible area but which has not been resolved into individual stars.

extrapolation., *n.* The process of estimating the value of a quantity beyond the limits of known values by assuming that the rate or system of change between the last few known values continues.

extratropical cyclone.. Any cyclonic-scale storm that is not a tropical cyclone, usually referring only to the migratory frontal cyclones of middle and high latitudes. Also called EXTRATROPICAL LOW.

extratropical low.. See EXTRATROPICAL CYCLONE.

extreme high water.. The highest elevation reached by the sea as recorded by a tide gage during a given period. The National Ocean Survey routinely documents monthly and yearly extreme high waters for its control stations. See also EXTREME LOW WATER.

extreme low water.. The lowest elevation reached by the sea as recorded by a tide gage during a given period. The National Ocean Survey routinely documents monthly and yearly extreme low water for its control stations. See also EXTREME HIGH WATER.

extremely high frequency (EHF).. Radio frequency of 30,000 to 300,000 megahertz.

eye guard.. A guard or shield on an eyepiece of an optical system, to protect the eye from stray light, wind, etc., and to maintain proper eye distance. Also called EYE SHIELD, EYE SHADE, SHADE.

eye of the storm.. The center of a tropical cyclone marked by relatively light winds, confused seas, rising temperature, lowered relative humidity, and often by clear skies. The general area of lowest atmospheric pressure of a cyclone is called STORM CENTER.

eye of the wind.. Directly into the wind; the point or direction from which the wind is blowing.

eyepiece., *n.* In an optical device, the lens group which is nearest the eye and with which the image formed by the preceding elements is viewed.

eye shade.. See EYE GUARD.

eye shield.. See EYE GUARD.

F

face., *n.* In ECDIS a two dimensional SPATIAL OBJECT. A face is a continuous area defined by a loop of one or more EDGES which bound it. A face may contain interior holes, defined by closing loops of EDGES. These interior boundaries must be within the outer boundary. No boundary may cross itself or touch itself other than at the beginning/end NODE. None of the boundaries may touch or cross any other boundary. Faces are defined only in the FULL TOPOLOGY data structure.

facsimile, *n.* A system for transmitting images electronically. A fax, or the hard-copy result of a facsimile transmission.

fading., *n.* The fluctuation in intensity or relative phase of any or all of the frequency components of a received radio signal due to changes in the characteristics of the propagation path. See also SELECTIVE FADING.

Fahrenheit temperature.. Temperature based on a scale in which, under standard atmospheric pressure, water freezes at 32° and boils at 212° above zero.

fair., *adj.* Not stormy; good; fine; clear.

fair tide.. A tidal current setting in such a direction as to increase the speed of a vessel. One setting in a direction approximately opposite to the heading is called a HEAD TIDE. One abeam is called a BEAM TIDE. One approximately 90° from the course is called a CROSS TIDE.

fairway., *n.* 1. The main thoroughfare of shipping in a harbor or channel. 2. The middle of a channel.

fairway buoy.. A buoy marking a fairway, with safe water on either side. Its color is red and white vertical stripes. Also called MID-CHANNEL BUOY.

fair wind.. A wind which aids a craft in making progress in a desired direction. Used chiefly in connection with sailing vessels, when it refers to a wind which permits the vessel to proceed in the desired direction without tacking. See also FOLLOWING WIND.

Falkland Current.. Originating mainly from the Cape Horn Current in the north part of Drake Passage, the Falkland Current flows northward between the continent and the Falkland Islands after passing through the strait. The current follows the coast of South America until it joins the BRAZIL CURRENT at about latitude 36°S near the entrance to Rio de la Plata. Also called MALVIN CURRENT.

fall., *n.* 1. See AUTUMN. 2. Decrease in a value, such as a fall of temperature. 3. Sinking, subsidence, etc., as the rise and fall of the sea due to tidal action or when waves or swell are present. See also WATERFALL.

fall equinox.. See AUTUMNAL EQUINOX.

falling star.. See METEOR.

falling tide.. The portion of the tide cycle between high water and the following low water in which the depth of water is decreasing. Sometimes the term EBB is used as an equivalent, but since ebb refers primarily to horizontal rather than vertical movement, falling tide is considered more appropriate. The opposite is RISING TIDE.

fall streaks. . See VIRGA.

fall streaks

fall wind. A cold wind blowing down a mountain slope. It is warmed by its descent, but is still cool relative to surrounding air. A warm wind blowing down a mountain slope is called a FOEHN. The bora, mistral, papagayo, and vardar are examples of fall winds. See also KATABATIC WIND.

false cirrus. . A cloud species unique to the genus cirrus, of such optical thickness as to appear grayish on the side away from the sun, and to veil the sun, conceal its outline, or even hide it. These often originate from the upper part of a cumulonimbus, and are often so dense that they suggest clouds of the middle level. Also called THUNDERSTORM CIRRUS, CIRRUS SPISSATUS.

false echo. . See INDIRECT ECHO, PHANTOM TARGET.

false horizon. . A line resembling the VISIBLE HORIZON but above or below it.

false light. . A light which is unavoidably exhibited by an aid to navigation and which is not intended to be a part of the proper characteristic of the light. Reflections from storm panes come under this category.

false relative motion. . False indications of the movement of a target relative to own ship on a radar display that is unstabilized in azimuth due to continuous reorientation of the display as own ship's heading changes. See also STABILIZATION OF RADARSCOPE DISPLAY.

fan. , *n.* On the sea floor, a relatively smooth feature normally sloping away from the lower termination of a canyon or canyon system.

fan beam. . A beam in which the radiant energy is concentrated in and about a single plane. The angular spread in the plane of concentration may be any amount to 360°. This type beam is most widely used for navigational lights. A converged beam is a fan beam in which the angular spread is decreased laterally to increase the intensity of the remaining beam over all or part of its arc; a diverged beam is a fan beam formed by increasing the divergence of a pencil beam in one plane only.

farad. , *n.* A derived unit of capacitance in the International System of Units; it is the capacitance of a capacitor between the plates of which there appears a potential difference of 1 volt when it is charged by a quantity of electricity of 1 coulomb.

far vane. . That instrument sighting vane on the opposite side of the instrument from the observer's eye. The opposite is NEAR VANE.

fast ice. . Sea ice which forms and remains attached to the shore, to an ice wall, to an ice front, between shoals or grounded icebergs. Vertical fluctuations may be observed during changes of sea level. Fast ice may be formed in situ from the sea water or by freezing of pack ice of any age to the shore, and it may extend a few meters or several hundred kilometers from the coast. Fast ice may be more than 1 year old and may then be prefixed with the appropriate age category (old, second-year or multi-year). If it is thicker than about 2 meters above sea level, it is called an ICE SHELF.

fast-ice boundary. . The ice boundary at any given time between FAST ICE and PACK ICE.

fast-ice edge. . The demarcation at any given time between FAST ICE and open water.

fast-sweep racon. . See under SWEPT-FREQUENCY RACON.

fast time constant circuit. . A type of coupling circuit, with high pass frequency characteristics used in radar receivers to permit discrimination against received pulses of duration longer than the transmitted pulse. With the fast time constant (FTC) circuit in operation, only the leading edge of an echo having a long time duration is displayed on the radarscope. The use of this circuit tends to reduce saturation of the scope which could be caused by clutter. Also called ANTI-CLUTTER RAIN, or RAIN CLUTTER DIFFERENTIATOR.

fata morgana. . A complex mirage, characterized by marked distortion, generally in the vertical. It may cause objects to appear towering, magnified, floating in air, and at times even multiplied.

fathogram. , *n.* A graphic record of depth measurements obtained by a fathometer. See also ECHOGRAM.

fathom. , *n.* A unit of length equal to 6 feet. This unit of measure is used principally as a measure of depth of water and the length of lead lines, anchor chains, and cordage.

fathom curve, fathom line. . A depth contour, with depths expressed in fathoms.

Fathometer. , *n.* The registered trade name for a widely-used echo sounder.

favorable current. . A current flowing in such a direction as to increase the speed of a vessel over the ground. The opposite is UNFAVORABLE CURRENT.

favorable wind. . A wind which aids a craft in making progress in a desired direction. Usually used in connection with sailing vessels. A wind which delays the progress of a craft is called an UNFAVORABLE WIND. Also called FAIR WIND. See also FOLLOWING WIND.

feasibility orbit. . An orbit that can be rapidly and inexpensively computed on the basis of simplifying assumptions (e.g., two-body motion, circular orbit, rectilinear orbit, three-body motion approximated by two two-body orbits, etc.) and yields an indication of the general feasibility of a system based upon the orbit without having to carry out a full-blown definitive orbit computation.

feature. . In ECDIS a representation of a real world phenomenon.

feature object. . In ECDIS an OBJECT which contains the non-locational information about real world entities.

feature record. In ECDIS a feature record is the implemented term used in the S-57 data structure for a FEATURE OBJECT (i.e. a feature object as defined in the DATA MODEL is encoded as a feature record in the DATA STRUCTURE). There are four types of feature records: GEO, META, COLLECTION, and CARTOGRAPHIC.

federal project depth. The design dredging depth of a channel constructed by the U.S. Army Corps of Engineers; the project depth may or may not be the goal of maintenance dredging after completion of the channel. For this reason federal project depth must not be confused with CONTROLLING DEPTH.

feel the bottom. . The effect on a ship underway in shallow water which tends to reduce her speed, make her slow in answering the helm, and often make her sheer off course. The speed reduction is largely due to increased wave making resistance resulting from higher pressure differences due to restriction of flow around the hull. The increased velocity of the water flowing past the hull results in an increase in squat. Also called SMELL THE BOTTOM.

femto-. . A prefix meaning one-quadrillionth (10^{-15}).

fen. , *n.* A low-lying tract of land, wholly or partly covered with water at times.

fetch. , *n.* 1. An area of the sea surface over which seas are generated by a wind having a constant direction and speed. Also called GENERATING AREA. 2. The length of the fetch area, measured in the direction of the wind, in which the seas are generated.

fiber optic gyro (FOG). . A type of compass that senses changes in orientation using the Sagnac effect, thus performing the function of a mechanical gyroscope. However its principle of operation is instead based on the interference of light which has passed through a coil of optical fiber which can be as long as 5 kilometers. The development of diode (semiconductor) lasers and low-loss single-mode optical fiber in the early 1970s for the telecommunications industry enabled Sagnac effect fiber optic gyros to be developed as practical devices. Sometimes call a fiber optic gyro/navigator (FOG-N).

fictitious equator. . A reference line serving as the origin for measurement of fictitious latitude. A transverse or inverse equator is a meridian the plane of which is perpendicular to the axis of a transverse map projection. An oblique equator is a great circle the plane of which is perpendicular to the axis of an oblique map projection. A grid equator is a line perpendicular to a prime grid meridian, at the origin.

fictitious graticule. The network of lines representing fictitious parallels and fictitious meridians on a map, chart, or plotting sheet. It may be either a transverse graticule or an oblique graticule depending upon the kind of projection; a fictitious graticule may also be a GRID. See also OBLIQUE GRATICULE, TRANSVERSE GRATICULE.

fictitious latitude. . Angular distance from a fictitious equator. It may be called transverse, oblique, or grid latitude depending upon the type of fictitious equator.

fictitious longitude. . The arc of the fictitious equator between the prime fictitious meridian and any given fictitious meridian. It may be called transverse, oblique, or grid longitude depending upon the type of fictitious meridian.

fictitious loxodrome. . See FICTITIOUS RHUMB LINE.

fictitious loxodromic curve. . See FICTITIOUS RHUMB LINE.

fictitious meridian. . One of a series of great circles or lines used in place of a meridian for certain purposes. A transverse meridian is a great circle perpendicular to a transverse equator; an oblique meridian is a great circle perpendicular to an oblique equator; a grid meridian is one of the grid lines extending in a grid north-south direction. The reference meridian (real or fictitious) used as the origin for measurement of fictitious longitude is called prime fictitious meridian.

fictitious parallel. . A circle or line parallel to a fictitious equator, connecting all points of equal fictitious latitude. It may be called transverse, oblique, or grid parallel depending upon the type of fictitious equator.

fictitious pole. . One of the two points 90° from a fictitious equator. It may be called the transverse or oblique pole depending upon the type of fictitious equator.

fictitious rhumb. . See FICTITIOUS RHUMB LINE.

fictitious rhumb line. . A line making the same oblique angle with all fictitious meridians. It may be called transverse, oblique, or grid rhumb line depending upon the type of fictitious meridian. The expression OBLIQUE RHUMB LINE applies also to any rhumb line, real or fictitious, which makes an oblique angle with its meridians; as distinguished from parallels and meridians real or fictitious, which may be consider special cases of the rhumb line. Also called FICTITIOUS RHUMB, FICTITIOUS LOXODROME, FICTITIOUS LOXODROMIC CURVE.

fictitious ship. . An imaginary craft used in the solution of certain maneuvering problems, as when a ship to be intercepted is expected to change course or speed during the interception run.

fictitious sun. . An imaginary sun conceived to move eastward along the celestial equator at a rate equal to the average rate of the apparent sun or to move eastward along the ecliptic at the average rate of the apparent sun. See also DYNAMICAL MEAN SUN, MEAN SUN.

fictitious year. . The period between successive returns of the sun to a sidereal hour angle of 80° (about January 1). The length of the fictitious year is the same as that of the tropical year, since both are based upon the position of the sun with respect to the vernal equinox. Also called BESSELIAN YEAR.

fidelity. , *n.* The accuracy to which an electrical system, such as a radio, reproduces at its output the essential characteristics of its input signal.

field. . In ECDIS, a named collection of labeled subfield(s). For example, IHO ATTRIBUTE LABEL/CODE and IHO ATTRIBUTE VALUE are collected into a field named Feature Record Attribute.

field glass. . A telescopic binocular.

field lens. . A lens at or near the plane of a real image, to collect and redirect the rays into another part of the optical system; particularly, the eyepiece lens nearest the object, to direct the rays into the eye lens.

field of view. . The maximum angle of vision, particularly of an optical instrument.

figure of the earth. . See GEOID.

file. , *n.* In ECDIS, an identified set of S-57 records collected together for a specific purpose. The file content and structure must be defined by a PRODUCT SPECIFICATION.

filling. , *n.* Increase in atmospheric pressure, particularly within a low. Decrease in pressure is called DEEPENING.

final diameter. . The diameter of the circle traversed by a vessel after turning through 360° and maintaining the same speed and rudder angle. This diameter is always less than the tactical diameter. It is measured perpendicular to the original course and between the tangents at the points where 180° and 360° of the turn have been completed.

final great circle course. . The direction, at the destination, of the great circle through that point and the point of departure, expressed as the angular distance from a reference direction, usually north, to that part of the great circle extending beyond the destination. See also INITIAL GREAT CIRCLE COURSE.

finger rafted ice. . The type of rafted ice in which floes thrust "fingers" alternately over and under the other.

finger rafting. . A type of rafting whereby interlocking thrusts are formed, each floe thrusting "fingers" alternately over and under the other. Finger rafting is common in NILAS and GRAY ICE.

finite. , *adj.* Having limits. The opposite is INFINITE.

fireball. , *n.* See BOLIDE.

firn. , *n.* Old snow which has recrystallized into a dense material. Unlike snow, the particles are to some extent joined together; but, unlike ice, the air spaces in it still connect with each other.

first estimate-second estimate method. . The process of determining the value of a variable quantity by trial and error. The expression applies particularly to the method of determining time of meridian transit (especially local apparent noon) at a moving craft. The time of transit is computed for an estimated longitude of the craft, the longitude estimate is then revised to agree with the time determined by the first estimate, and a second computation is made. The process is repeated as many times as necessary to obtain an answer of the desired precision.

first light. . The beginning of morning nautical twilight, i.e., when the center of the morning sun is 12° below the horizon.

first point of Aries. . See VERNAL EQUINOX.

first point of Cancer. . See SUMMER SOLSTICE.

first point of Capricornus. . See WINTER SOLSTICE.

first point of Libra. . See AUTUMNAL EQUINOX.

first quarter. . The phase of the moon when it is near east quadrature, when the western half of it is visible to an observer on the earth. See also PHASES OF THE MOON.

first-year ice. . Sea ice of not more than one winter's growth, developing from young ice, with a thickness of 30 centimeters to 2 meters. First-year ice may be subdivided into THIN FIRST-YEAR ICE, WHITE ICE, MEDIUM FIRST-YEAR ICE, and THICK FIRST-YEAR ICE.

firth. , *n.* A long, narrow arm of the sea.

Fischer ellipsoid of 1960. . The reference ellipsoid of which the semimajor axis is 6,378,166.000 meters, the semiminor axis is 6,356,784.298 meters, and the flattening or ellipticity is 1/298.3. Also called FISCHER SPHEROID OF 1960.

Fischer ellipsoid of 1968. . The reference ellipsoid of which the semimajor axis is 6,378,150 meters, the semiminor axis is 6,356,768.337 meters, and the flattening or ellipticity is 1/298.3. Also called FISCHER SPHEROID OF 1968.

Fischer spheroid of 1960. . See FISCHER ELLIPSOID OF 1960.

Fischer spheroid of 1968. . See FISCHER ELLIPSOID OF 1968.

fish. , *n.* Any towed sensing device.

fishery conservation zone. . See under FISHING ZONE.

fish havens. . Areas established by private interests, usually sport fishermen, to simulate natural reefs and wrecks that attract fish. The reefs are constructed by dumping assorted junk in areas which may be of very small extent or may stretch a considerable distance along a depth contour. Fish havens are outlined and labeled on charts.

fishing zone. The offshore zone in which exclusive fishing rights and management are held by the coastal nation. The U.S. fishing zone, known as the fishery conservation zone, is defined under P.L. 94-265. The law states, "The inner boundary of the fishery conservation zone is a line conterminous with the seaward boundary of catch of the coastal states, and the outer boundary of such zone is a line drawn in such manner that each point on it is 200 nautical miles from the baseline from which the territorial sea is measured."

fish lead. . A type of sounding lead used without removal from the water between soundings.

fish stakes. . Poles or stakes placed in shallow water to outline fishing grounds or to catch fish.

fish trap areas. . Areas established by the U.S. Army Corps of Engineers in which traps may be built and maintained according to established regulations. The fish stakes which may exist in these areas are obstructions to navigation and may be dangerous. The limits of fish trap areas and a cautionary note are usually charted.

fix. , *n.* A position determined without reference to any former position; the common intersection of two or more lines of position obtained from simultaneous observations. Fixes obtained from electronic systems are often given as lat./long. coordinates determined by algorithms in the system software. See also RUNNING FIX.

fixed. . A light which is continuously on.

fixed and flashing light. . A light in which a fixed light is combined with a flashing light of higher luminous intensity. The aeronautical light equivalent is called UNDULATING LIGHT.

fixed and group flashing light. . A fixed light varied at regular intervals by a group of two or more flashes of greater intensity.

fixed and variable parameters of satellite orbit. . The fixed parameters are those parameters which describe a satellite's approximate orbit and which are used over a period of hours. The variable parameters describe the fine structure of the orbit as a function of time and are correct only for the time at which they are transmitted by the satellite.

fixed antenna radio direction finder. . A radio direction finder whose use does not require the rotation of the antenna system.

fixed light. . A light which appears continuous and steady. The term is sometimes loosely used for a light supported on a fixed structure, as distinct from a light on a floating support.

fixed mark. . A navigation mark fixed in position.

fixed satellite. . See GEOSTATIONARY SATELLITE.

fixed star. . A star whose apparent position relative to surrounding stars appears to be unvarying or fixed for long periods of time.

fjord. , *n.* A long, deep, narrow arm of the sea between high land. A fjord often has a relatively shallow sill across its entrance.

fjord

flag alarm. . A semaphore-type flag in the indicator of an instrument, to serve as a signal, usually to warn that the indications are unreliable.

flagpole. , *n.* A label on a nautical chart which indicates a single pole from which flags are displayed. The term is used when the pole is not attached to a building. The label flagstaff is used for a flagpole rising from a building.

flagstaff. , *n.* See under FLAGPOLE.

Flamsteed's number. . A number sometimes used with the possessive form of the Latin name of the constellation to identify a star.

flash. , *n.* A relatively brief appearance of a light, in comparison with the longest interval of darkness in the period of the light. See also OCCULTATION.

flasher. , *n.* An electrical device which controls the characteristic of a lighted aid to navigation by regulating power to the lamp according to a certain pattern.

flashing. , *n.* The process of reducing the amount of permanent magnetism in a vessel by placing a single coil horizontally around the vessel and energizing it. If the energized coil is moved up and down along the sides of the vessel, the process is called WIPING. See also DEPERMING.

flashing light. . A navigation light in which the total duration of light in a cycle is shorter than the total duration of darkness. The term is commonly used for a SINGLE-FLASHING LIGHT, a flashing light in which a flash is regularly repeated at a rate of less than 50 flashes per minute. See also GROUP FLASHING LIGHT, COMPOSITE GROUP FLASHING LIGHT, LONG FLASHING LIGHT, QUICK LIGHT.

flat. , *n.* 1. A large flat area attached to the shore consisting usually of mud, but sometimes of sand and rock. Also called TIDAL FLATS. See also SALT MARSH, SLOUGH, TIDAL MARSH. 2. On the sea floor, a small level or nearly level area.

flattening. , *n.* The ratio of the difference between the equatorial and polar radii of the earth to its equatorial radius. The flattening of the earth is the ellipticity of the spheroid. The magnitude of the flattening is sometimes expressed as the numerical value of the reciprocal of the flattening. Also called COMPRESSION.

flaw. , *n.* A narrow separation zone between pack ice and fast ice, where the pieces of ice are in a chaotic state. The flaw forms when pack ice shears under the effect of a strong wind or current along the fast-ice boundary. See also SHEARING.

flaw lead. . A passage-way between pack ice and fast ice which is navigable by surface vessels.

flaw polynya. . A POLYNYA between pack ice and fast ice.

F-layer. , *n.* The second principal layer of ionization in the Kennelly-Heaviside region (the E-layer is the first principal layer; the D-layer is of minor significance except for a tendency to absorb energy from radio waves in the medium frequency range). Situated about 175 miles above the earth's surface, the F-layer exists as a single layer only during the hours of darkness. It divides into two separate layers during daylight hours.

F1-layer. , *n.* The lower of the two layers into which the F-layer divides during daylight hours. Situated about 140 miles above the earth's surface, it reaches its maximum density at noon. Since its density varies with the extent of the sun's radiation, it is subject to daily and seasonal variations. It may disappear completely at some point during the winter months.

F2-layer. , *n.* The higher of the two layers into which the F-layer divides during daylight hours. It reaches its maximum density at noon and, over the continental U.S., varies in height from about 185 miles in winter to 250 miles in the summer. The F2-layer normally has a greater influence on radio wave propagation than the F1-layer.

FleetNET. . INMARSAT broadcast service for commercial traffic.

Fleet Guide. . One of a series of port information booklets for U.S. naval bases prepared for U.S. Navy use only.

Flinders bar. . A bar of soft unmagnetized iron placed vertically near a magnetic compass to counteract deviation caused by magnetic induction in vertical soft iron of the craft.

float chamber. . A sealed, hollow part attached to the compass card of a magnetic compass as part of the compass card assembly, to provide buoyancy to reduce the friction on the pivot bearing.

floating aid. . A buoy serving as an aid to navigation secured in its charted position by a mooring.

floating breakwater. . A moored assembly of floating objects used for protection of vessels riding at anchor.

floating dock. . A form of dry dock consisting of a floating structure of one or more sections, which can be partly submerged by controlled flooding to receive a vessel, then raised by pumping out the water so that the vessel's bottom can be exposed. See also GRAVING DOCK.

floating ice. . Any form of ice found floating in water. The principal kinds of floating ice are lake ice, river ice and sea ice which form by the freezing of water at the surface, and glacier ice (ice of land origin) formed on land or in an ice shelf. The concept includes ice that is stranded or grounded.

floating mark. . A navigation mark carried on a floating body such as a lightship or buoy.

float pipe. . A pipe used as a float well.

float well. . A vertical pipe or box with a relatively small opening (orifice) in the bottom. It is used as a tide gage installation to dampen the wind waves while freely admitting the tide to actuate a float which, in turn, operates the gage. Also called STILLING WELL.

floe. , *n.* Any relatively flat piece of sea ice 20 meters or more across. Floes are subdivided according to horizontal extent. A giant flow is over 5.4 nautical miles across; a vast floe is 1.1 to 5.4 nautical miles across; a big floe is 500 to 2000 meters across; a medium floe is 100 to 500 meters across; and a small floe is 20 to 100 meters across.

floeberg. , *n.* A massive piece of sea ice composed of a hummock, or a group of hummocks frozen together, and separated from any ice surroundings. It may float showing up to 5 meters above sea level.

flood. , *n.* Tidal current moving toward land or up a tidal stream. The opposite is EBB. Also called FLOOD CURRENT.

flood axis. . Average direction of tidal current at strength of flood.

flood current. . The movement of a tidal current toward the shore or up a tidal river or estuary. In the mixed type of reversing current, the terms *greater flood* and *lesser flood* are applied respectively to the flood currents of greater and lesser speed of each day. The terms *maximum flood* and *minimum flood* are applied to the maximum and minimum speeds of a flood current, the speed of which alternately increases and decreases without coming to a slack or reversing. The expression maximum flood is also applicable to any flood current at the time of greatest velocity. The opposite is EBB CURRENT.

flooded ice. . Sea ice which has been flooded by melt-water or river water and is heavily loaded by water and wet snow.

floodgate. , *n.* A gate for shutting out, admitting, or releasing a body of water; a sluice.

flood interval. . Short for STRENGTH OF FLOOD INTERVAL. The interval between the transit of the moon over the meridian of a place and the time of the following strength of flood. See also LUNICURRENT INTERVAL.

flood plain.. The belt of low flat ground bordering a stream or river channel that is flooded when runoff exceeds the capacity of the stream channel.

flood strength.. Phase of the flood current at time of maximum speed. Also, the speed at this time. Also called STRENGTH OF FLOOD.

floor., *n.* The ground under a body of water. See also BOTTOM.

Florida Current.. A swift ocean current that flows through the Straits of Florida from the Gulf of Mexico to the Atlantic Ocean. It shows a gradual increase in speed and persistency as it flows northeastward and then northward along the Florida coast. In summer, the part of the surface current south of latitude 25°N moves farther south of its mean position, with a mean speed of 2.0 knots and a maximum speed of about 6.0 knots; the part of the current north of latitude 25°N moves farther west of its mean position, with a mean speed of 2.9 knots and a maximum speed of 6.5 knots. In winter the shift of position is in the opposite direction, and speeds are somewhat less by about 0.2 to 0.5 knots. The flow prevails throughout the year, with no significant changes in direction; the speed, however, varies slightly from one season to another. North of Grand Bahama Island, it merges with the Antilles Current to form the GULF STREAM. The Florida Current is part of the GULF STREAM SYSTEM.

flotsam.. *n.* Floating articles, particularly those that are thrown overboard to lighten a vessel in distress. See also JETSAM, JETTISON, LAGAN.

flow., *n. British terminology.* Total current or the combination of tidal current and nontidal current. In British usage, tidal current is called TIDAL STREAM and nontidal current is called CURRENT.

fluorescence., *n.* Emission of light or other radiant energy as a result of and only during absorption of radiation from some other source.

fluorescent chart.. A chart reproduced with fluorescent ink or on fluorescent paper, which enables the user to read the chart under ultraviolet light.

flurry., *n.* See SNOW FLURRY.

flux-gate.. The magnetic direction-sensitive element of a flux-gate compass. Also called FLUX VALVE.

fluxmeter., *n.* An instrument for measuring the intensity of a magnetic field.

flux valve.. See FLUX-GATE.

focal length.. The distance between the optical center of a lens, or the surface of a mirror, and its focus.

focal plane.. A plane parallel to the plane of a lens or mirror and passing through the focus.

focal point.. See FOCUS.

focus. *(pl. foci), n.* 1. The point at which parallel rays of light meet after being refracted by a lens or reflected by a mirror. Also called FOCAL POINT. 2. A point having specific significance relative to a geometrical figure. See under ELLIPSE, HYPERBOLA, PARABOLA. 3. The true center of an earthquake, within which the strain energy is first converted to elastic wave energy.

focus., *v., t.* The process of adjusting an optical instrument, projector, cathode-ray tube, etc., to produce a clear and well-defined image.

foehn., *n.* A warm, dry, wind blowing down the leeward slope of a mountain and across a valley floor or plain.

fog., *n.* A visible accumulation of tiny droplets of water, formed by condensation of water vapor in the air, with the base at the surface of the earth. It reduces visibility below 1 kilometer (0.54 nautical miles). If this is primarily the result of movement of air over a surface of lower temperature, it is called advection fog. If this is primarily the result of cooling of the surface of the earth and the adjacent layer of atmosphere by radiational cooling, it is called radiation fog. An advection fog occurring as monsoon circulation transports warm moist air over a colder surface is called a monsoon fog. A fog that hides less than six-tenths of the sky, and does not extend to the base of any clouds is called a ground fog. Fog formed at sea, usually when air from a warm-water surface moves to a cold-water surface, is called sea fog. Fog produced by apparent steaming of a relatively warm sea in the presence of very cold air is called steam fog, steam mist, frost smoke, sea smoke, arctic sea smoke, arctic smoke, or water smoke. A rare simulation of true fog by anomalous atmospheric refraction is called mock fog. A dry fog is a fog that does not moisten exposed surfaces. Ice fog is composed of suspended ice crystals (20-100 microns in diameter) and droxtals (12-20 microns in diameter). In dense ice fog, the lower visibility is chiefly due to the presence of the droxtals, rather than the crystals.

fog bank.. A well-defined mass of fog observed at a distance, most commonly at sea.

fogbound., *adj.* Surrounded by fog. The term is used particularly with reference to vessels which are unable to proceed because of the fog.

fogbow., *n.* A faintly colored circular arc similar to a RAINBOW but formed on fog layers containing drops whose diameters are of the order of 100 microns or less. See also BOUGUER'S HALO.

fog detector.. A device used to automatically determine conditions of visibility which warrant sounding a fog signal.

fog signal.. See under SOUND SIGNAL.

following sea.. A sea in which the waves move in the general direction of the heading. The opposite is HEAD SEA. Those moving in a direction approximately 90° from the heading are called BEAM SEA, and those moving in a direction approximately 45° from the heading (striking the quarter) are called QUARTERING SEA.

following wind.. Wind blowing in the general direction of a vessel's course. The equivalent aeronautical expression is TAIL WIND. Wind blowing in the opposite direction is called a HEAD WIND. Wind blowing in a direction approximately 90° from the heading is called a BEAM WIND. One blowing in a direction approximately 90° from the course is called a CROSS WIND. See also FAIR WIND, FAVORABLE WIND, UNFAVORABLE WIND.

foot., *n.* Twelve inches or 30.48 centimeters. The latter value was adopted in 1959 by Australia, Canada, New Zealand, South Africa, the United Kingdom, and the United States. See also U.S. SURVEY FOOT. 2. The bottom of a slope, grade, or declivity.

foraminifera., *n., pl.* Small, single-cell, jellylike marine animals with hard shells of many chambers. In some areas the shells of dead foraminifera are so numerous they cover the ocean bottom.

Forbes log.. A log consisting of a small rotator in a tube projecting below the bottom of a vessel, and suitable registering devices.

forced wave.. A wave generated and maintained by a continuous force, in contrast with a FREE WAVE that continues to exist after the generating force has ceased to act.

foreland., *n.* See PROMONTORY, HEADLAND.

foreshore., *n.* That part of the shore or beach which lies between the low water mark and the upper limit of normal wave action. See also BACKSHORE.

forestaff., *n.* See CROSS-STAFF.

fork., *n.* On the sea floor, a branch of a canyon or valley.

format., *v., t.* To prepare a computer disk for data storage; formatting defines tracks and sectors, sets up a directory, and performs other functions before a new disk can be used.

form lines.. Broken lines resembling contour lines but representing no actual elevations, which have been sketched from visual observation or from inadequate or unreliable map sources, to show collectively the shape of the terrain rather than the elevation.

formation axis.. An arbitrarily selected direction within a formation of ships from which all bearings used in the designation of station are measured; bearings are always expressed in true direction from the center.

formation center.. An arbitrary point around which a formation of ships is centered, designated "station zero."

formation guide.. A ship designated by the officer of tactical command (OTC) as the reference vessel upon which all ships in a formation maintain position.

forward., *adj.* In a direction towards the bow of a vessel. See also AHEAD, ABAFT.

forward of the beam.. Any direction between broad on the beam and ahead. See also ABAFT THE BEAM.

foul berth.. A berth in which a vessel cannot swing to her anchor or moorings without fouling another vessel or striking an obstruction. See also FOUL GROUND, CLEAR BERTH.

foul bottom.. A term used to describe the bottom of a vessel when encrusted with marine growth.

foul ground.. An area unsuitable for anchoring or fishing due to rocks, boulders, coral, or other obstructions. See also FOUL BERTH.

four-point bearing.. A relative bearing of 045° or 315°. See also BOW AND BEAM BEARINGS.

fractional scale.. See REPRESENTATIVE FRACTION.

fracto-.. A prefix used with the name of a basic cloud form to indicate a torn, ragged, and scattered appearance caused by strong winds. See also SCUD.

fracture. , *n.* A break or rupture through very close pack ice, compact pack ice, consolidated pack ice, fast ice, or a single floe resulting from deformation processes. Fractures may contain brash ice and/or be covered with NILAS and/or young ice. The length of a fracture may vary from a few meters to many miles. A large fracture is more than 500 meters wide, a medium fracture is 200 to 500 meters wide, a small fracture is 50 to 200 meters wide, and a very small fracture is up to 50 meters wide.

fracture zone. . 1. An extensive linear zone of irregular topography of the sea floor characterized by steep-sided or asymmetrical ridges, troughs, or escarpments. 2. An ice area which has a great number of fractures. See also FRACTURE.

fracturing. , *n.* The pressure process whereby ice is permanently deformed, and rupture occurs. The term is most commonly used to describe breaking across very close pack ice, compact pack ice, and consolidated pack ice.

Franklin continuous radar plot technique. . A method of providing continuous correlation of a small fixed radar-conspicuous object with own ship's position and movement relative to a planned track. Named for QMCM Byron Franklin, USN.

Franklin piloting technique. . A method of finding the most probable position of a ship from three lines of position which do not intersect in a point.

frazil ice. . Fine spicules or plates of ice, suspended in water.

free-air temperature. . Temperature of the atmosphere, obtained by a thermometer located so as to avoid as completely as practicable the effects of extraneous heating. See also AMBIENT TEMPERATURE, WET-BULB TEMPERATURE.

freeboard. , *n.* The vertical distance from the uppermost complete, watertight deck of a vessel to the surface of the water, usually measured amidships. Minimum permissible freeboards may be indicated by LOAD LINE MARKS.

free gyro. . A two-degree-of-freedom gyro or a gyro the spin axis of which may be oriented in any specified altitude. The rotor of this gyro has freedom to spin on its axis, freedom to tilt about its horizontal axis, and freedom to turn about its vertical axis. Also called FREE GYROSCOPE. See also DEGREE-OF-FREEDOM.

free gyroscope. . See FREE GYRO.

free wave. . A wave that continues to exist after the generating force has ceased to act, in contrast with a FORCED WAVE that is generated and maintained by a continuous force.

freezing drizzle. . Drizzle that falls in liquid form but freezes upon impact to form a coating of glaze upon the ground and exposed objects.

freezing fog. . A fog whose droplets freeze upon contact with exposed objects and form a coating of rime and/or glaze. See also FREEZING PRECIPITATION.

freezing precipitation. . Precipitation which falls to the earth in a liquid state and then freezes to exposed surfaces. Such precipitation is called freezing rain if it consists of relatively large drops of water, and freezing drizzle if of smaller drops. See also GLAZE.

freezing rain. . Rain that falls in liquid form but freezes upon impact to form a coating of ice on the ground and exposed objects.

frequency. , *n.* The rate at which a cycle is repeated. See also AUDIO FREQUENCY, RADIO FREQUENCY.

frequency band. . 1. A specified segment of the frequency spectrum. 2. One of two or more segments of the total frequency coverage of a radio receiver or transmitter, each segment being selectable by means of a band change switch. 3. Any range of frequencies extending from a specified lower to a specified upper limit. See ASSIGNED FREQUENCY BAND.

frequency channel. . The assigned frequency band commonly referred to by number, letter, symbol, or some salient frequency within the band.

frequency-modulated radar. . A type of radar in which the radiated wave is frequency modulated and the frequency of an echo is compared with the frequency of the transmitted wave at the instant of reception, thus enabling range to be measured.

frequency modulation. . Angle modulation of a sinewave carrier in which the instantaneous frequency of the modulated wave differs from the carrier frequency by an amount proportional to the instantaneous value of the modulating.

frequency tolerance. . The maximum permissible departure by the center frequency of the frequency band occupied by an emission from the assigned frequency, or by the characteristic frequency of an emission from the reference frequency. The frequency tolerance is expressed in parts per million or in hertz.

fresh breeze. . Wind of force 5 (17 to 21 knots or 19 to 24 miles per hour) on the Beaufort wind scale.

freshen. , *v., i.* To become stronger, applied particularly to wind.

Freshet. ,n. A sudden increased flow of fresh water, as from a flood, emptying from a river into a larger body of salt or brackish water.

fresh gale. A term once used by seamen for what is now called GALE on the Beaufort wind scale.

fresh-water marsh. . A tract of low, wet ground, usually miry and covered with rank vegetation.

friction. , *n.* Resistance to motion due to interaction between the surface of a body and anything in contact with it.

friction error. . The error of an instrument reading due to friction in the moving parts of the instrument.

friction layer. . See SURFACE BOUNDARY LAYER.

friendly ice. . From the point of view of the submariner, an ice canopy containing many large skylights or other features which permit a submarine to surface. There must be more than 10 such features per 30 nautical miles along the submarine's track.

frigid zones. . Either of the two zones between the polar circles and the poles, called the north frigid zone and the south frigid zone.

fringing reef. . A reef attached directly to the shore of an island or continental landmass. Its outer margin is submerged and often consists of algal limestone, coral rock, and living coral. See also BARRIER REEF.

front. , *n.* Generally, the interface or transition zone between two air masses of different density. Since the temperature distribution is the most important regulator of atmospheric density, a front almost invariably separates air masses of different temperature. Along with the basic density criterion and the common temperature criterion, many other features may distinguish a front, such as a pressure trough, a change in wind direction, a moisture discontinuity, and certain characteristic cloud and precipitation forms. The term front is used ambiguously for: frontal zone, the three-dimensional zone or layer of large horizontal density gradient, bounded by frontal surfaces across which the horizontal density gradient is discontinuous (frontal surface usually refers specifically to the warmer side of the frontal zone); and surface front, the line of intersection of a frontal surface or frontal zone with the earth's surface or less frequently, with a specified constant-pressure surface. See also POLAR FRONT, ARCTIC FRONT, COLD FRONT, WARM FRONT, OCCLUDED FRONT.

frontal. , *adj.* Of or pertaining to a front.

frontal cyclone. . In general, any cyclone associated with a front; often used synonymously with WAVE CYCLONE or with EXTRATROPICAL CYCLONE (as opposed to tropical cyclones, which are non-frontal).

frontal occlusion. . See OCCLUDED FRONT; OCCLUSION, definition 2.

frontal surface. . See under FRONT.

frontal zone. . See under FRONT.

front light. . The closer of two range lights. It is the lowest of the lights of an established range. Also called LOW LIGHT.

frontogenesis. , *n.* 1. The initial formation of a front or frontal zone. 2. In general, an increase in the horizontal gradient of an air mass property, principally density, and the development of the accompanying features of the wind field that characterize a front.

frontolysis. , *n.* 1 The dissipation of a front or frontal zone. 2. In general, a decrease in the horizontal gradient of an air mass property, principally density, and the dissipation of the accompanying features of the wind field.

frost. , *n.* 1. A deposit of interlocking ice crystals formed by direct sublimation on objects, usually those of small diameter freely exposed to the air. The deposition is similar to the process in which dew is formed, except that the temperature of the object must be below freezing. It forms when air with a dew point below freezing is brought to saturation by cooling. It is more fluffy and feathery than rime which in turn is lighter than glaze. Also called HOAR, HOARFROST. 2. The condition which exists when the temperature of the earth's surface and earthbound objects falls below 0°C or 32°F. Temperatures below the freezing point of water are sometimes expressed as "degrees of frost."

frost smoke. . 1. Fog-like clouds due to contact of cold air with relatively warm water, which can appear over openings in the ice, or leeward of the ice edge, and which may persist while ice is forming. 2. A rare type of fog formed in the same manner as a steam fog but at lower temperatures. It is composed of ice particles or droxtals instead of liquid water as is steam fog. Thus, it is a type of ice fog. Sometimes called BARBER. 3. See STEAM FOG.

frozen precipitation. . Any form of precipitation that reaches the ground in frozen form; i.e., snow, snow pellets, snow grains, ice crystals, ice pellets, and hail.

frustum. , *n.* That part of a solid figure between the base and a parallel intersecting plane; or between any two intersecting planes, generally parallel.

full depiction of detail. . Since even on charts of the largest scale full depiction of detail is impossible because all features are symbolized to an extent which is partly determined by scale and partly by the conventions of charting practice, the term *full depiction of detail* is used to indicate that over the greater part of a chart nothing essential to navigation is omitted. See also GENERALIZATION, MINIMAL DEPICTION OF DETAIL.

full moon. . The moon at opposition, when it appears as a round disk to an observer on the earth because the illuminated side is toward him. See also PHASES OF THE MOON.

full topology. . In ECDIS a 2-dimensional DATA STRUCTURE in which the geometry is described in terms of NODES, EDGES and FACES which are all TOPOLOGICALLY linked. A PLANAR GRAPH with faces.

fully automatic updating. . In ECDIS the application of corrections to ENC DATA in the SENC in a fully integrated state, without human intervention.

function. , *n.* A magnitude so related to another magnitude that for any value of one there is a corresponding value of the other. See also TRIGONOMETRIC FUNCTIONS.

fundamental circle. . See PRIMARY GREAT CIRCLE.

fundamental frequency. . In the Decca Navigator System, the frequency from which other frequencies in a chain are derived by harmonic multiplication.

funnel cloud. . A cloud column or inverted cloud cone, pendant from a cloud base. This supplementary feature occurs mostly with cumulus and cumulonimbus; when it reaches the earth's surface, it constitutes a tornado or waterspout. Also called TUBA, TORNADO CLOUD.

furrow. , *n.* On the sea floor, a closed, linear, narrow, shallow depression.

fusion. , *n.* The phase transition of a substance passing from the solid to the liquid state; melting. In meteorology, fusion is almost always understood to refer to the melting of ice, which, if the ice is pure and subjected to l standard atmosphere of pressure, takes place at the ice point of 0°C or 32°F. Additional heat at the melting point is required to fuse any substance. This quantity of heat is called LATENT HEAT OF FUSION; in the case of ice, it is approximately 80 calories per gram.

G

G. , *n.* An acceleration equal to the acceleration of gravity, approximately 32.2 feet per second per second at sea level.

gain. , *n.* The ratio of output voltage, current, or power to input voltage, current, or power in electronic instruments.

gain control. . See RECEIVER GAIN CONTROL.

gain function. . See DIRECTIVE GAIN.

gain of an antenna. . An expression of radiation effectiveness, it is the ratio of the power required at the input of a reference antenna to the power supplied to the input of the given antenna to produce, in a given direction, the same field at the same distance. When not specified otherwise, the figure expressing the gain of an antenna refers to the gain in the direction of the radiation main lobe. In services using scattering modes of propagation, the full gain of an antenna may not be realizable in practice and the apparent gain may vary with time.

gain referred to a short vertical antenna. . The gain of an antenna in a given direction when the reference antenna is a perfect vertical antenna, much shorter than one quarter of the wavelength, placed on the surface of a perfectly conducting plane earth.

gal. , *n.* A special unit employed in geodesy and geophysics to express the acceleration due to gravity. The gal is a unit accepted temporarily for use with the International System of Units; 1 gal is equal to 1 centimeter per second, per second.

galactic nebula. . An aggregation of matter within our galaxy but beyond the solar system, large enough to occupy a perceptible area but which has not been resolved into individual stars.

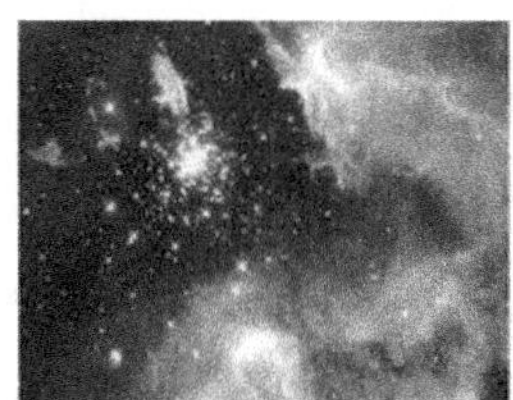
galactic nebula

galaxy, *n.* A vast assemblage of stars, planets, nebulae, and other bodies composing a distinct group in the universe. The sun and its family of planets are part of a galaxy commonly called the MILKY WAY.

gale. , *n.* Wind of force 8 on the Beaufort wind scale (34 to 40 knots or 39 to 46 miles per hour) is classified as a gale. Wind of force 9 (41 to 47 knots or 47 to 54 miles per hour) is classified as a strong gale. Wind of force 7 (28 to 33 knots or 32 to 38 miles per hour) is classified as a near gale. See also MODERATE GALE, FRESH GALE, WHOLE GALE.

gallon. , *n.* A unit of volume equal to 4 quarts or 231 cubic inches.

Galofaro. , *n.* A whirlpool in the Strait of Messina; formerly called CHARYBDIS.

galvanometer. , *n.* An instrument for measuring the magnitude of a small electric current or for detecting the presence or direction of such a current by means of motion of an indicator in a magnetic field.

gap. , *n.* On the sea floor, a narrow break in a ridge or rise.

garua. , *n.* A thick, damp fog on the coasts of Ecuador, Peru, and Chile. Also called CAMANCHACA.

gas. , *n.* A fluid without shape or volume, which tends to expand indefinitely, or to completely fill a closed container of any size.

gas buoy. . A buoy having a gas light. See also LIGHTED BUOY.

gat. , *n.* A natural or artificial passage or channel extending inland through shoals or steep banks. See also OPENING.

gather way. . To begin to move.

gauge, gage. , *n.* An instrument for measuring the size or state of anything.

gauge, gage. , *v., t.* To determine the size or state of anything.

gauss. , *n.* The centimeter-gram-second electromagnetic unit of magnetic induction. It corresponds to 10^{-4} tesla in the International System.

Gaussian distribution. . See NORMAL DISTRIBUTION.

Gaussin error. . Deviation of a magnetic compass due to transient magnetism caused by eddy currents set up by a changing number of lines of force through soft iron as the ship changes heading. Due to these eddy currents, the induced magnetism on a given heading does not arrive at its normal value until about 2 minutes after change to the heading. This error should not be confused with RETENTIVE ERROR.

gazeteer. , *n.* An alphabetical list of place names giving geographic coordinates.

Gegenschein. , *n.* A faint light area of the sky always opposite the position of the sun on the celestial sphere. It is believed to be the reflection of sunlight from particles moving beyond the earth's orbit. Also called COUNTERGLOW.

general chart. . See CHART CLASSIFICATION BY SCALE.

generalization. . The process of selectively removing less-important features of charts as scale becomes smaller, to avoid over-crowding charts. See also FULL DEPICTION OF DETAIL, MINIMAL DEPICTION OF DETAIL.

general precession. . The resultant motion of the components causing precession of the equinoxes westward along the ecliptic at the rate of about 50.3" per year, completing the cycle in about 25,800 years. The effect of the sun and moon, called lunisolar precession, is to produce a westward motion of the equinoxes along the ecliptic. The effect of other planets, called planetary precession, tends to produce a much smaller motion eastward along the ecliptic. The component of general precession along the celestial equator, called precession in right ascension, is about 46.1" per year; and the component along a celestial meridian, called precession in declination, is about 20.0" per year.

General Prudential Rule. . Rule 2(b) of the International Rules (COLREGS) as well as the Inland Navigation and Inland Rules. Rule 2(b) states "In construing and complying with these Rules due regard shall be had to all dangers of navigation and collision and to any special circumstances, including the limitations of the vessels involved, which may make a departure from these Rules necessary to avoid immediate danger."

generating area. . The area in which ocean waves are generated by the wind. Also called FETCH.

gentle breeze. . Wind of force 3 (7 to 10 knots or 8 to 12 miles per hour) on the Beaufort wind scale.

geo. , *n.* A narrow coastal inlet bordered by steep cliffs. Also called GIO.

geo-. . A prefix meaning earth.

geocentric. , *adj.* Relative to the earth as a center; measured from the center of the earth.

geocentric latitude. . The angle at the center of the reference ellipsoid between the celestial equator and a radius vector to a point on the ellipsoid. This differs from the geographic latitude by a maximum of 11.6' of arc at Lat. 45°.

geocentric parallax. . The difference in apparent direction of a celestial body from a point on the surface of the earth and from the center of the earth. This difference varies with the body's altitude and distance from the earth. Also called DIURNAL PARALLAX. See also HELIOCENTRIC PARALLAX.

geodesic. , *adj.* Of or pertaining to geodesy; geodetic.

geodesic. , *n.* See GEODESIC LINE.

geodesic line. . A line of shortest distance between any two points on any mathematically defined surface. A geodesic line is a line of double curvature and usually lies between the two normal section lines which the two points determine. If the two terminal points are in nearly the same latitude, the geodesic line may cross one of the normal section lines. It should be noted that, except along the equator and along the meridians, the geodesic line is not a plane curve and cannot be sighted over directly. Also called GEODESIC, GEODETIC LINE.

geodesy. , *n.* The science of the determination of the size and shape of the earth.

geodetic. , *adj.* Of or pertaining to geodesy; geodesic.

geodetic bench mark. . See under BENCH MARK.

geodetic datum. . See DATUM, HORIZONTAL GEODETIC DATUM, VERTICAL GEODETIC DATUM.

geodetic equator. . The line of zero geodetic latitude; the great circle described by the semimajor axis of the reference ellipsoid as it is rotated about the minor axis. See also ASTRONOMICAL EQUATOR.

geodetic height. . See ELLIPSOIDAL HEIGHT.

geodetic latitude. . The angle which the normal to the ellipsoid at a station makes with the plane of the geodetic equator. It differs from the corresponding astronomical latitude by the amount of the meridional component of the local deflection of the vertical. Also called TOPOGRAPHICAL LATITUDE and sometimes GEOGRAPHIC LATITUDE.

geodetic line. . See GEODESIC LINE.

geodetic longitude. . The angle between the plane of the geodetic meridian at a station and the plane of the geodetic meridian at Greenwich. A geodetic longitude differs from the corresponding astronomical longitude by the amount of the prime vertical component of the local deflection of the vertical divided by the cosine of the latitude. Sometimes called GEOGRAPHIC LONGITUDE.

geodetic meridian. . A line on a reference ellipsoid which has the same geodetic longitude at every point. Sometimes called GEOGRAPHIC MERIDIAN.

geodetic parallel. . A line on a reference ellipsoid which has the same geodetic latitude of every point. A geodetic parallel, other than the equator, is not a geodesic line. In form, it is a small circle whose plane is parallel with the plane of the geodetic equator. See also ASTRONOMICAL PARALLEL.

geodetic position. . A position of a point on the surface of the earth expressed in terms of geodetic latitude and geodetic longitude. A geodetic position implies an adopted geodetic datum.

geodetic satellite. . Any satellite whose orbit and payload render it useful for geodetic purposes.

geodetic survey. . A survey that takes into account the shape and size of the earth. It is applicable for large areas and long lines and is used for the precise location of basic points suitable for controlling other surveys.

geographic, geographical. , *adj.* Of or pertaining to geography.

geographical coordinates. . Spherical coordinates defining a point on the surface of the earth, usually latitude and longitude. Also called TERRESTRIAL COORDINATES.

geographical mile. . The length of 1 minute of arc of the equator, or 6,087.08 feet. This approximates the length of the nautical mile.

geographical plot. . A plot of the movements of one or more vessel relative to the surface of the earth. Also called TRUE PLOT. See also NAVIGATIONAL PLOT.

geographical pole. . Either of the two points of intersection of the surface of the earth with its axis, where all meridians meet, labeled N or S to indicate whether the north geographical pole or the south geographical pole.

geographical position. . 1. That point on the earth at which a given celestial body is in the zenith at a specified time. The geographical position of the sun is also called the sub solar point, of the moon the sublunar point, and of a star the substellar or subastral point. 2. Any position on the earth defined by means of its geographical coordinates either astronomical or geodetic.

geographic graticule. . The system of coordinates of latitude and longitude used to define the position of a point on the surface of the earth with respect to the reference ellipsoid.

geographic information system. . An approach to modeling the world that allows for data in a wide variety of forms to be linked to geographic positioning to aid in decision-making, intelligence, and safety of navigation applications. Database, analysis, and display are separate aspects that multiply the power and usefulness in a digital environment.

geographic latitude. . A general term applying to astronomic and geodetic latitudes.

geographic longitude. A general term applying to astronomic and geodetic longitudes.

geographic meridian. . A general term applying to astronomical and geodetic meridians.

geographic number. . The number assigned to an aid to navigation for identification purposes in accordance with the lateral system of numbering.

geographic parallel. . A general term applying to astronomical and geodetic parallels.

geographic range. . The maximum distance at which the curvature of the earth and terrestrial refraction permit an aid to navigation to be seen from a particular height of eye without regard to the luminous intensity of the light. The geographic range sometimes printed on charts or tabulated in light lists is the maximum distance at which the curvature of the earth and terrestrial refraction permit a light to be seen from a height of eye of 15 feet above the water when the elevation of the light is taken above the height datum of the largest scale chart of the locality. Therefore, this range is a nominal geographic range. See also VISUAL RANGE OF A LIGHT.

geographic sign conventions. . In mapping, charting, and geodesy, the inconsistent application of algebraic sign to geographical references and the angular reference of azimuthal systems is a potential trouble area in scientific data collection. The following conventions have wide use in the standardization of scientific notation: Longitude references are positive eastward of the Greenwich meridian to 180°, and negative westward of Greenwich. Latitude references are positive to the north of the equator and negative to the south. Azimuths are measured clockwise, using South as the origin and continuing to 360°. Bearings are measured clockwise, using North as the origin and continuing to 360°. Tabulated coordinates, or individual coordinates, are annotated N, S, E, W, as appropriate.

geoid. , *n.* The equipotential surface in the gravity field of the earth; the surface to which the oceans would conform over the entire earth if free to adjust to the combined effect of the earth's mass attraction and the centrifugal force of the earth's rotation. As a result of the uneven distribution of the earth's mass, the geoidal surface is irregular. The geoid is a surface along which the gravity potential is everywhere equal (equipotential surface) and to which the direction of gravity is always perpendicular. Also called FIGURE OF THE EARTH.

geoidal height. . The distance of the geoid above (positive) or below (negative) the mathematical reference ellipsoid. Also called GEOIDAL SEPARATION, GEOIDAL UNDULATION, UNDULATION OF THE GEOID.

geoidal horizon. . The circle of the celestial sphere formed by the intersection of the celestial sphere and a plane through a point on the sea level surface of the earth, and perpendicular to the zenith-nadir line. See also HORIZON.

geoidal separation. . See GEOIDAL HEIGHT.

geoidal undulation. . See GEOIDAL HEIGHT.

geological oceanography. . The study of the floors and margins of the oceans, including description of submarine relief features, chemical and physical composition of bottom materials, interaction of sediments and rocks with air and seawater, and action of various forms of wave energy in the submarine crust of the earth.

geomagnetic. , *adj.* Of or pertaining to geomagnetism.

geomagnetic equator. . The terrestrial great circle everywhere 90° from the geomagnetic poles. The geomagnetic equator is not the same as the MAGNETIC EQUATOR, the line connecting all points of zero magnetic dip.

geomagnetic latitude. . Angular distance from the geomagnetic equator, measured northward or southward on the geomagnetic meridian through 90° and labeled N or S to indicate the direction of measurement. The geomagnetic latitude should not be confused with MAGNETIC LATITUDE.

geomagnetic pole. . Either of two antipodal points marking the intersection of the earth's surface with the extended axis of a bar magnet assumed to be located at the center of the earth and approximating the source of the actual magnetic field of the earth. The pole in the Northern Hemisphere (at about 78.5°N 69°W) is designated north geomagnetic pole, and the pole in the Southern Hemisphere (at about 78°S 111°E) is designated south geomagnetic pole. The great circle midway between these poles is called GEOMAGNETIC EQUATOR. The expression GEOMAGNETIC POLE should not be confused with MAGNETIC POLE, which relates to the actual magnetic field of the earth. See also GEOMAGNETIC LATITUDE.

geomagnetic pole. . The great circle midway between these poles is called GEOMAGNETIC EQUATOR. The expression GEOMAGNETIC POLE should not be confused with MAGNETIC POLE, which relates to the actual magnetic field of the earth. See also GEOMAGNETIC LATITUDE.

geomagnetism. , *n.* Magnetic phenomena, collectively considered, exhibited by the earth and its atmosphere. Also called TERRESTRIAL MAGNETISM.

geometric dilution. . See GEOMETRIC DILUTION OF PRECISION.

geometric dilution of precision. . All geometric factors that degrade the accuracy of position fixes derived from externally referenced navigation systems. Often shortened to GEOMETRIC DILUTION.

geometric map projection. . See PERSPECTIVE MAP PROJECTION.

geometric primitive. . In ECDIS one of the three basic geometric units of representation: POINT, LINE, and AREA.

geometric projection. . See PERSPECTIVE PROJECTION.

geometrical dip. The vertical angle between the horizontal and a straight line tangent to the surface of the earth. It is larger than DIP by the amount of terrestrial refraction.

geometrical horizon. . Originally, the celestial horizon; now more commonly the intersection of the celestial sphere and an infinite number of straight lines tangent to the earth's surface, and radiating from the eye of the observer. If there were no terrestrial refraction, GEOMETRICAL and VISIBLE HORIZONS would coincide. See also RADIO HORIZON.

geometry, *n.* A branch of mathematics dealing with the properties, relations, and measurement of points, lines, surfaces, solids, and angles.

geomorphology, *n.* A branch of both geography and geology that deals with the form of the earth, the general configuration of its surface, and the changes that take place in the evolution of land forms.

geo-navigation, *n.* Navigation by means of reference points on the earth. The term is obsolete.

geo object. , *n.* In ECDIS a FEATURE OBJECT which carries the descriptive characteristics of a real world ENTITY.

geophysics, *n.* The study of the composition and physical phenomena of the earth and its liquid and gaseous envelopes; it embraces the study of terrestrial magnetism, atmospheric electricity, and gravity; and it includes seismology, volcanology, oceanography, meteorology, and related sciences.

geopotential. , *n.* The gravity potential of the actual earth. It is the sum of the gravitational (attraction) potential and the potential of the centrifugal force.

Georef. , *n.* See WORLD GEOGRAPHIC REFERENCE SYSTEM.

geosphere. , *n.* The portion of the earth, including land (lithosphere) and water (hydrosphere), but excluding the atmosphere.

geostationary satellite. . An earth satellite moving eastward in an equatorial, circular orbit at an altitude (approximately 35,900 kilometers) such that its period of revolution is exactly equal to and synchronous with the rotational period of the earth. Such a satellite will remain fixed over a point on the earth's equator. Although geostationary satellites are frequently called GEOSYNCHRONOUS or SYNCHRONOUS SATELLITES, the orbit of an eastward moving synchronous satellite must be equatorial if the satellite is to remain fixed over a point on the equator. Otherwise, the satellite moves daily in a figure eight pattern relative to the earth. Also called FIXED SATELLITE. See also STATIONARY ORBIT.

geostrophic equilibrium. , *n.* The state of motion in which the Coriolis force exactly balances the horizontal pressure force. Also called geostrophic balance. See also GEOSTROPHIC WIND, GRADIENT CURRENT.

geostrophic wind. The horizontal wind velocity for which the Coriolis force exactly balances the horizontal pressure force. See also GRADIENT WIND.

geosynchronous satellite. . An earth satellite whose period of rotation is equal to the period of rotation of the earth about its axis. The orbit of a geosynchronous satellite must be equatorial if the satellite is to remain fixed over a point on the earth's equator. Also called TWENTY-FOUR HOUR SATELLITE. See also SYNCHRONOUS SATELLITE, GEOSTATIONARY SATELLITE.

ghost. , *n.* 1. An unwanted image appearing on a radarscope caused by echoes which experience multiple reflections before reaching the receiver. See also SECOND-TRACE ECHO, MULTIPLE ECHOES, INDIRECT ECHO. 2. An image appearing on a radarscope the origin of which cannot readily be determined.

giant floe. . See under FLOE.

gibbous. , *adj.* Bounded by convex curves. The term is used particularly in reference to the moon when it is between first quarter and full or between full and last quarter, or to other celestial bodies when they present a similar appearance. See also PHASES OF THE MOON.

giga-. . A prefix meaning one billion (10^9).

gigahertz. , *n.* One thousand megahertz, or one billion cycles per second.

gimbal freedom. . The maximum angular displacement of a gyro about the output axis of a gimbal.

gimballess inertial navigation equipment. . See STRAPPED-DOWN INERTIAL NAVIGATION EQUIPMENT.

gimballing error. . That error introduced in a gyro-compass by the tilting of the gimbal mounting system of the compass due to horizontal acceleration caused by motion of the vessel, such as rolling.

gimbal lock. . A condition of a two-degree-of-freedom gyro wherein the alignment of the spin axis with an axis of freedom deprives the gyro of a degree-of-freedom and therefore its useful properties.

gimbals. , *n., pl.* A device for supporting anything, such as an instrument, in such a manner that it will remain horizontal when the support tilts. It consists of a ring inside which the instrument is supported at two points 180° apart, the ring being similarly supported at two points 90° from the instrument supports.

gio. , *n.* See GEO.

glacial. , *adj.* Of or pertaining to a glacier.

glacier. , *n.* A mass of snow and ice continuously moving from higher to lower ground or, if afloat, continuously spreading. The principal forms of glaciers are ICE SHELVES, ICE STREAMS, ICE CAPS, inland ice sheets, ice piedmonts, cirque glaciers, and various types of mountain (valley) glaciers.

glacier berg. . An irregularly shaped iceberg. Also called WEATHERED BERG.

glacier ice. . Ice in, or originating from, a glacier, whether on land or floating on the sea as icebergs, bergy bits, or growlers.

glacier tongue. . The seaward projecting extension of a glacier, usually afloat. In the Antarctic, glacier tongues may extend many tens of kilometers.

glare. , *n.* Dazzling brightness of the atmosphere caused by excessive reflection and scattering of light by particles in the line of sight.

glaze. , *n.* A coating of ice, generally clear and smooth but usually containing some air pockets, formed on exposed objects by the freezing of a film of super cooled water deposited by rain, drizzle, fog, or possibly condensed from super cooled water vapor. Glaze is denser, harder and more transparent than either rime or hoarfrost Also called GLAZE ICE, GLAZED FROST VERGLAS.

glazed frost. . See GLAZE.

glaze ice. . See GLAZE.

glint. , *n.* The pulse-to-pulse variation in amplitude of reflected radar signals due to rapid change of the reflecting surface, as in the case of the propeller of an aircraft in flight.

Global Navigation Satellite System (GNSS). . A system of satellites that provides time- referenced position information that can be received by particular radio systems, and used to calculate the position of the receiver in latitude, longitude, and elevation. One such GNSS system used in the United States is known as GPS.

Global Positioning System (GPS). . A satellite navigation system developed by the U.S. Department of Defense. The system provides highly accurate position and velocity information in three dimensions and precise time and time intervals on a global basis continuously, to an unlimited number of users. It is unaffected by weather and provides a worldwide common grid reference system. The objective of the program is to provide very precise position information for a wide spectrum of military missions, although its use has expanded broadly in civilian sectors. Also called NAVSTAR GLOBAL POSITIONING SYSTEM.

globigerina *(pl. globlgerinae), n.* A very small marine animal of the foraminifera order, with a chambered shell; or the shell of such an animal. In large areas of the ocean the calcareous shells of these animals are very numerous, being the principal constituent of a soft mud or globigerina *ooze* forming the ocean bed.

GLONASS. . Stands for Global Navigation Satellite System. A satellite navigation system operated by Russia, analogous to the U.S. Global Positioning System (GPS).

gloom. , *n.* The condition existing when daylight is very much reduced by dense cloud or smoke accumulation above the surface, the surface visibility not being materially reduced.

glory. , *n.* See ANTICORONA.

gnomon. , *n.* Any object the shadow of which serves as an indicator, as the SHADOW PIN on a sun.

gnomonic. , *adj.* Of or pertaining to a gnomon.

gnomonic chart. . A chart constructed on the gnomonic projection and often used as an adjunct for transferring a great circle to a Mercator chart. Commonly called GREAT CIRCLE CHART.

gnomonic map projection. . A perspective azimuthal map projection in which points on the surface of a sphere or spheroid, such as the earth, are conceived as projected by radials from the center to a tangent plane. Great circles project as straight lines. For this reason the projection is used principally for charts for great circle sailing. The projection is neither conformal nor equal area.

gong. , *n.* A sound signal produced by the vibration of a resonant disc struck by a clapper.

gong buoy. . A buoy fitted with a group of saucer shaped bells of different tones, used as an audible signal.

goniometer. , 1. An instrument for measuring angles. 2. A pick-up coil which eliminates the necessity of having to rotate a radio direction finder antenna to determine direction.

gore. , *n.* A lune-shaped map which may be fitted to the surface of a globe with a negligible amount of distortion.

gorge. , *n.* 1. A narrow opening between mountains, especially one with steep, rocky walls. 2. A collection of solid matter obstructing a channel, river, etc., as *ice gorge.*

GPS. , See GLOBAL POSITIONING SYSTEM.

gradient. , *n.* 1. A rate of rise or fall of a quantity against horizontal distance expressed as a ratio, decimal, fraction, percentage, or the tangent of the angle of inclination. 2. The rate of increase or decrease of one quantity with respect to another. 3. A term used in radionavigation to refer to the spacing between consecutive hyperbolas. If the gradient is high, a relatively small time-difference error in determining a hyperbolic line of position will result in a relatively high position error. See also GEOMETRIC DILUTION OF PRECISION.

gradient current. . An ocean current associated with horizontal pressure gradients in the ocean and determined by the condition that the pressure force due to the distribution of mass balances the Coriolis force due to the earth's rotation. See also OCEAN CURRENT.

gradient tints. . See HYPSOMETRIC TINTING.

gradient wind. . Any horizontal wind velocity tangent to the contour line of a constant pressure surface (or to the isobar of a geopotential surface) at the point in question. At such points where the wind is gradient, the Coriolis force and the centrifugal force together exactly balance the horizontal pressure force. See also GEOSTROPHIC WIND.

graduation error. . Inaccuracy in the graduations of the scale of an instrument.

graduations. , *n., pl.* The marks on a scale.

grain noise. . See SNOW, definition 2.

gram. , *n.* One one-thousandth of a kilogram.

granular snow. . See SNOW GRAINS.

graph. , *n.* A diagram indicating the relationship between two or more variables.

graph. , *v., t.* To represent by a graph.

graphic scale. . See BAR SCALE.

graticule. , *n.* 1. The network of lines representing parallels and meridians on a map, chart, or plotting sheet. A fictitious graticule represents fictitious parallels and fictitious meridians. See also GRID, *n.* 2. A scale at the focal plane of an optical instrument to aid in the measurement of objects. See also RETICLE.

graupel. , *n.* See SNOW PELLETS.

gravel. , *n.* See under STONES.

graving dock. . A form of dry dock consisting of an artificial basin fitted with a gate or caisson, into which vessels can be floated and the water pumped out to expose the vessels' bottoms. The term is derived from the term used to describe the process of burning barnacles and other accretions from a ship's bottom. See also FLOATING DOCK.

gravisphere. , *n.* The spherical extent in which the force of a given celestial body's gravity is predominant in relation to that of other celestial bodies.

gravitation. , *n.* 1. The force of attraction between two bodies. According to Newton, gravitation is directly proportional to the product of the masses of two bodies and inversely proportional to the square of the distance between them. 2. The acceleration produced by the mutual attraction of two masses, directed along the line joining their centers of mass, and of magnitude inversely proportional to the square of the distance between the two centers of mass.

gravitational disturbance. . See GRAVITY DISTURBANCE.

gravitational gradient. . The change in the gravitational acceleration per unit distance.

gravitational perturbations. . Perturbations caused by body forces due to nonspherical terrestrial effects, lunisolar effect, tides, and the effect of relativity.

gravitational tide. . See EQUILIBRIUM TIDE.

gravity. , *n.* The force of attraction of the earth, or another body, on nearby objects.

gravity anomaly. . The difference between the observed gravity value properly reduced to sea level and the theoretical gravity obtained from gravity formula. Also called OBSERVED GRAVITY ANOMALY.

gravity anomaly map. . A map showing the positions and magnitudes of gravity anomalies. Also, a map on which contour lines are used to represent points at which the gravity anomalies are equal.

gravity data. . Information concerning that acceleration which attracts bodies and is expressed as observations or in the form of gravity anomaly charts or spherical harmonics for spatial representation of the earth and other celestial bodies.

gravity disturbance. . The difference between the observed gravity and the normal gravity at the same point (the vertical gradient of the disturbing potential) as opposed to GRAVITY ANOMALY which uses corresponding points on two different surfaces. Because the centrifugal force is the same when both are taken at the same point, it can also be called GRAVITATIONAL DISTURBANCE.

gravity field of the earth. . The field of force arising from a combination of the mass attraction and rotation of the earth. The field is normally expressed in terms of point values, mean area values, and/or series expansion for the potential of the field.

gravity network. . A network of gravity stations.

gravity reduction. . A combination of gravity corrections to obtain reduced gravity on the geoid.

gravity reference stations. . Stations which serve as reference values for a gravity survey, i.e., with respect to which the differences at the other stations are determined in a relative survey. The absolute value of gravity may or may not be known at the reference stations.

gravity station. . A station at which observations are made to determine the value of gravity.

gravity wind. . A wind blowing down an incline. Also called KATABATIC WIND.

gray ice. . A subdivision of YOUNG ICE 10 to 15 centimeters thick. Gray ice is less elastic than nilas and breaks in swells. It usually rafts under pressure.

gray-white ice. . A subdivision of YOUNG ICE 15 to 30 centimeters thick. Gray-white ice under pressure is more likely to ridge than to raft.

grease ice. Ice at that stage of freezing when the crystals have coagulated to form a soupy layer on the surface. Grease ice is at a later stage of freezing than FRAZIL ICE and reflects little light, giving the sea a matte appearance.

great circle. . The intersection of a sphere and a plane through its center. The intersection of a sphere and a plane which does not pass through its center is called a small circle. Also called ORTHODROME, ORTHODROMIC CURVE.

great circle bearing. . The initial direction of a great circle through two terrestrial points, expressed as angular distance from a reference direction. It is usually measured from 000° at the reference direction clockwise through 360°. Bearings obtained by any form of radiant energy are great circle bearings.

great circle chart. . A chart on which a great circle appears as a straight line or approximately so, particularly a chart on the gnomonic map projection.

great circle course. . The direction of the great circle through the point of departure and the destination, expressed as the angular distance from a reference direction, usually north, to the direction of the great circle. The angle varies from point to point along the great circle. At the point of departure it is called initial great circle course; at the destination it is called final great circle course.

great circle direction. . Horizontal direction of a great circle, expressed as angular distance from a reference direction.

great circle distance. . The length of the shorter arc of the great circle joining two points. It is usually expressed in nautical miles.

great circle sailing. . Any method of solving the various problems involving courses, distance, etc., as they are related to a great circle track.

great circle track. . The track of a vessel following a great circle, or a great circle which a vessel intends to follow.

great diurnal range. . The difference in height between mean higher high water and mean lower low water. Often shortened to DIURNAL RANGE. The difference in height between mean lower high water and mean higher low water is called SMALL DIURNAL RANGE.

greater ebb. . See under EBB CURRENT.

greater flood. . See under FLOOD CURRENT.

greatest elongation. . The maximum angular distance of an inferior planet from the sun before it starts back toward conjunction, as observed from the earth. The direction of the body east or west of the sun is usually specified, as *greatest elongation east* (or *west*). See also ELONGATION.

great tropic range. . The difference in height between tropic higher high water and tropic lower low water. Often shortened to TROPIC RANGE. See also MEAN TROPIC RANGE, SMALL TROPIC RANGE.

great year. . The period of one complete cycle of the equinoxes around the ecliptic, about 25,800 years. Also called PLATONIC YEAR. See also PRECESSION OF THE EQUINOXES.

green flash. . A brilliant green coloring of the upper edge of the sun as it appears at sunrise or disappears at sunset when there is a clear, distinct horizon. It is due to refraction by the atmosphere, which disperses the first (or last) spot of light into a spectrum and causes the colors to appear (or disappear) in the order of refrangibility. The green is bent more than red or yellow and hence is visible sooner at sunrise and later at sunset.

green house effect. . The heating phenomenon due to shorter wavelengths of insolation passing through the atmosphere to the earth, which radiates longer wavelength infrared radiation, which is trapped by the atmosphere. Some of this trapped radiation is re-radiated to the earth. This causes a higher earth temperature than would occur from direct insolation alone.

Greenwich apparent noon. . Local apparent noon at the Greenwich meridian; 12 o'clock Greenwich apparent time, or the instant the apparent sun is over the upper branch of the Greenwich meridian.

Greenwich apparent time. . Local apparent time at the Greenwich meridian; the arc of the celestial equator, or the angle at the celestial pole between the lower branch of the Greenwich celestial meridian and the hour circle of the apparent or true sun, measured westward from the lower branch of the Greenwich celestial meridian through 24 hours; Greenwich hour angle of the apparent or true sun, expressed in time units, plus 12 hours.

Greenwich civil time. . United States terminology from 1925 through 1952. See GREENWICH MEAN TIME.

Greenwich hour angle. . Angular distance west of the Greenwich celestial meridian; the arc of the celestial equator, or the angle at the celestial pole, between the upper branch of the Greenwich celestial meridian and the hour circle of a point on the celestial sphere, measured westward from the Greenwich celestial meridian through 360°; local hour angle at the Greenwich meridian.

Greenwich interval. . An interval based on the moon's transit of the Greenwich celestial meridian, as distinguished from a local interval based on the moon's transit of the local celestial meridian.

Greenwich lunar time. . Local lunar time at the Greenwich meridian; the arc of the celestial equator, or the angle at the celestial pole, between the lower branch of the Greenwich celestial meridian and the hour circle of the moon, measured westward from the lower branch of the Greenwich celestial meridian through 24 hours; Greenwich hour angle of the moon expressed in time units, plus 12 hours.

Greenwich mean noon. . Local mean noon at the Greenwich meridian, 12 o'clock Greenwich mean time, or the instant the mean sun is over the upper branch of the Greenwich meridian.

Greenwich mean time. . Local mean time at the Greenwich meridian; the arc of the celestial equator, or the angle at the celestial pole, between the lower branch of the Greenwich celestial meridian and the hour circle of the mean sun, measured westward from the lower branch of the Greenwich celestial meridian through 24 hours; Greenwich hour angle of the mean sun expressed in time units, plus 12 hours. Also called UNIVERSAL TIME, or ZULU.

Greenwich meridian. . The meridian through Greenwich, England, serving as the reference for Greenwich time, in contrast with LOCAL MERIDIAN. It is accepted almost universally as the PRIME MERIDIAN, or the origin of measurement of longitude.

Greenwich noon. . Noon at the Greenwich meridian.

Greenwich sidereal noon. . Local sidereal noon at the Greenwich meridian; zero hour Greenwich sidereal time, or the instant the vernal equinox is over the upper branch of the Greenwich meridian.

Greenwich sidereal time. . Local sidereal time at the Greenwich meridian; the arc of the celestial equator, or the angle at the celestial pole, between the upper branch of the Greenwich celestial meridian and the hour circle of the vernal equinox, measured westward from the upper branch of the Greenwich celestial meridian through 24 hours; Greenwich hour angle of the vernal equinox expressed in time units.

Greenwich time. . Time based upon the Greenwich meridian as reference.

gregale. , *n.* A strong northeast wind of the central Mediterranean.

Gregorian calendar. . The calendar now in almost universal use for civil purposes in which each year has 365 days, except leap years which have 366 days. Leap years are those years which are divisible by 4, and in the case of centurial years, those years divisible by 400. This calendar, a modification of the Julian calendar, was not adopted in Great Britain and the English colonies in North America until 1752. The calendar was instituted in 1582 by Pope Gregory XIII to keep calendar days in adjustment with the tropical year for the purpose of regulating the date of Easter and the civil and ecclesiastical calendars.

gray ice. . A subdivision of YOUNG ICE 10 to 15 centimeters thick. Gray ice is less elastic than nilas and breaks in swells. It usually rafts under pressure.

gray-white ice. . A subdivision of YOUNG ICE 15 to 30 centimeters thick. Gray-white ice under pressure is more likely to ridge than to raft.

grid. , *adj.* Pertaining to a grid or related to grid north.

grid. , *n.* 1. A series of lines, usually straight and parallel, superimposed on a chart or plotting sheet to serve as a directional reference for navigation. See also FICTITIOUS GRATICULE, GRATICULE, definition 1. 2. Two sets of mutually perpendicular lines dividing a map or chart into squares or rectangles to permit location of any point by a system of rectangular coordinates. Also called REFERENCE GRID. See also MILITARY GRID, UNIVERSAL POLAR STEREOGRAPHIC GRID, UNIVERSAL TRANSVERSE MERCATOR GRID, WORLD GEOGRAPHIC REFERENCE SYSTEM.

grid amplitude. . Amplitude relative to grid east or west.

grid azimuth. . Azimuth relative to grid north.

grid bearing. . Bearing relative to grid north.

grid convergence. . The angular difference in direction between grid north and true north. It is measured east or west from true north.

grid course. . Course relative to grid north.

grid declination. . The angular difference between grid north and true north.

grid direction. . Horizontal direction expressed as angular distance from grid north. Grid direction is measured from grid north, clockwise through 360°.

grid equator. . A line perpendicular to a prime grid meridian, at the origin. For the usual orientation in polar regions the grid equator is the 90°W - 90°E meridian forming the basic grid parallel, from which grid latitude is measured. See also FICTITIOUS EQUATOR.

grid heading. . Heading relative to grid north.

grid latitude. . Angular distance from a grid equator. See also FICTITIOUS LATITUDE.

grid line. . One of the lines of a grid.

grid longitude. . Angular distance between a prime grid meridian and any given grid meridian. See also FICTITIOUS LONGITUDE.

grid magnetic angle. . Angular difference in direction between grid north and magnetic north. It is measured east or west from grid north. Grid magnetic angle is sometimes called GRID VARIATION or GRIVATION.

grid meridian. . One of the grid lines extending in a grid north-south direction. The reference grid meridian is called prime grid meridian. In polar regions the prime grid meridian is usually the 180° - 0° geographic meridian. See also FICTITIOUS MERIDIAN.

grid navigation. . Navigation by the use of grid directions.

grid north. . 1. An arbitrary reference direction used with grid navigation. The direction of the 180th geographical meridian from the north pole is used almost universally as grid north. 2. The northerly or zero direction indicated by the grid datum of directional reference.

grid parallel. . A line parallel to a grid equator, connecting all points of equal grid latitude. See also FICTITIOUS PARALLEL.

grid prime vertical. . The vertical circle through the grid east and west points of the horizon.

grid rhumb line. . A line making the same oblique angle with all grid meridians. Grid parallels and meridians may be considered special cases of the grid rhumb line. See also FICTITIOUS RHUMB LINE.

grid track. . The direction of the track relative to grid north.

grid variation. . See GRID MAGNETIC ANGLE.

grivation. , *n.* See GRID MAGNETIC ANGLE.

groin. , *n.* A structure (usually one of a group) extending approximately perpendicular from a shore to protect the shore from erosion by tides, currents, or waves or to trap sand for making a beach. See also JETTY, definition 1.

ground. , *n.* A conducting connection between an electric circuit and the earth or some other conducting body of zero potential with respect to the earth.

ground. , *v., t. & i.* 1. To touch bottom or run aground. *v., t.* 2. To connect an electric circuit with the earth or some other conducting body, such that the earth or body serves as part of the circuit.

ground absorption. . The dissipation of energy in radio waves because of absorption by the ground over which the waves are transmitted.

ground-based duct. . See SURFACE DUCT.

ground chain. . Heavy chain used with permanent moorings and connecting the various legs or bridles.

grounded hummock. . Hummocked grounded ice formation. There are single grounded hummocks and lines (or chains) of grounded hummocks. A hummock refers to a mound.

grounded ice. . Floating ice which is aground in shoal water. See also STRANDED ICE, FLOATING ICE.

ground fog. . A fog that obscures less than six tenths of the sky, and does not extend to the base of any clouds.

grounding. , *n.* The touching of the bottom by a vessel. A serious grounding is called a stranding.

ground log. . A device for determining the course and speed over the ground in shallow water consisting of a lead or weight attached to a line. The lead is thrown overboard and allowed to rest on the bottom. The course over ground is indicated by the direction the line tends and the speed by the amount of line paid out in a unit of time.

ground stabilization. . In ECDIS a display whereby own ship position is referenced to the ground. It is usually performed in conjunction with radar/ARPA, it can be determined by computing set and drift or by the use of GPS/DGPS.

ground swell. A long, deep swell or undulation of the ocean often caused by a long-continued gale and sometimes a seismic disturbance and felt even at a remote distance. In shallow water the swell rises to a prominent height. See SWELL.

ground tackle. . The anchors, anchor chains, fittings etc., used for anchoring a vessel.

ground track. . 1. See under TRACK, definition 2. 2. See under TRUE TRACK OF TARGET.

groundwave. . A radio wave that is propagated over the earth and is ordinarily influenced by the presence of the ground and the troposphere. Except for ionospheric and tropospheric waves, the groundwave includes all components of a radio wave.

group flashing light. . A flashing light in which the flashes are combined in groups, each group having the same number of flashes, and in which the groups are repeated at regular intervals. The eclipses separating the flashes within each group are of equal duration and this duration is clearly shorter than the duration of the eclipse between two successive groups.

group occulting light. . An occulting light in which the occultations are combined in groups, each group including the same number of occultations, and in which the groups are repeated at regular intervals. The intervals of light separating the occultations within each group are of equal duration and this duration is clearly shorter than the duration of the interval of light between two successive groups.

group quick light. . A quick flashing light in which a specified group of flashes is regularly repeated. See also CONTINUOUS QUICK LIGHT, INTERRUPTED QUICK LIGHT.

group very quick light. . A very quick flashing light in which a specified group of flashes is regularly repeated. See also CONTINUOUS VERY QUICK LIGHT, INTERRUPTED VERY QUICK LIGHT.

growler. , *n.* A piece of ice smaller than a BERGY BIT or FLOEBERG, often transparent but appearing green or almost black in color. It extends less than 1 meter above the sea surface and its length is less than 20 feet (6 meters). A growler is large enough to be a hazard to shipping but small enough that it may escape visual or radar detection.

grunt. , *n.* See under DIAPHONE.

Guiana Current. . An ocean current flowing northwestward along the northeast coast of South America. The Guiana Current is an extension of the Atlantic South Equatorial Current, which crosses the equator and approaches the coast of South America. Eventually, it is joined by part of the Atlantic North Equatorial Current and becomes, successively, the CARIBBEAN CURRENT, and the FLORIDA CURRENT. Also called NORTH BRAZIL CURRENT.

Guinea Current. . A North Atlantic Ocean current flowing eastward along the south coast of northwest Africa into the Gulf of Guinea. The Guinea Current is the continuation of the Atlantic Equatorial Countercurrent augmented by the eastern branch of the Canary Current.

gulder. , *n.* Local name given to double low water occurring on the south coast of England. See DOUBLE TIDE.

gulf. , *n.* A major indentation of the sea into the land, usually larger than a bay.

Gulf Coast Low Water Datum.. Gulf Coast Low Water Datum (GCLWD) is defined as mean lower low water when the type of tide is mixed, and mean low water when the type of tide is diurnal. GCLWD was used as chart tidal datum from November 14, 1977, to November 28, 1980, for the coastal waters of the gulf coast of the United States.

Gulf Stream.. A warm, well defined, swift, relatively narrow ocean current which originates where the Florida Current and the Antilles Current meet north of Grand Bahama Island. It gains its impetus from the large volume of water that flows through the Straits of Florida. Near the edge of the Grand Banks of Newfoundland - extensions of the Gulf Stream and the Labrador Current continue as the NORTH ATLANTIC CURRENT, which fans outward and widens in a northeastward to eastward flow across the ocean. The Florida Current, the Gulf Stream, and the North Atlantic Current together form the GULF STREAM SYSTEM. Sometimes the entire system is referred to as the Gulf Stream. The Gulf Stream forms the western and northwestern part of the general clockwise oceanic circulation of the North Atlantic Ocean.

Gulf Stream System.. A system of ocean currents comprised of the Florida Current, the Gulf Stream, and the North Atlantic Current.

gulfweed., *n.* See SARGASSUM.

gully., *n.* 1. A small ravine, especially one cut by running water, but through which water flows only after a rain. 2. On the sea floor, a small valley-like feature.

gust., *n.* 1. A sudden brief increase in the speed of the wind of more transient character than a squall, and followed by a lull or slackening of the wind. 2. The violet wind or squall that accompanies a thunderstorm.

gut., *n.* A narrow passage or contracted strait connecting two bodies of water.

guyot., *n.* See TABLEMOUNT.

gyre., *n.* A closed circulatory system, but larger than a whirlpool or eddy.

gyro., *n.* Short for GYROSCOPE.

gyrocompass., *n.* A compass having one or more gyroscopes as the directive element, and which is north-seeking. Its operation depends upon four natural phenomena, namely gyroscopic inertia, gyroscopic precession, the earth's rotation, and gravity. When such a compass controls remote indicators, called GYRO REPEATERS, it is called a master gyrocompass. See also DIRECTIONAL GYRO MODE.

gyro error.. The error in the reading of the gyrocompass, expressed in degrees east or west to indicate the direction in which the axis of the compass is offset from true north. See also BALLISTIC DAMPING ERROR, BALLISTIC DEFLECTION ERROR, COMPASS ERROR, GIMBALLING ERROR, INTERCARDINAL ROLLING ERROR, LUBBER'S LINE ERROR, SPEED ERROR.

gyro log.. A written record of the performance of a gyrocompass.

Gyro pilot., *n.* An automatic device for steering a vessel by means of control signals received from a gyrocompass. Also called AUTO PILOT.

gyro repeater.. A device which displays at a different location the indications of the master gyrocompass. See also COMPASS REPEATER.

gyroscope., *n.* A rapidly rotating mass free to move about one or both axes perpendicular to the axis of rotation and to each other. It is characterized by GYROSCOPIC INERTIA and PRECESSION. Usually shortened to GYRO. The term also refers colloquially to the GYROCOMPASS. See also DIRECTIONAL GYRO, FREE GYRO.

gyroscopic drift.. The horizontal rotation of the spin axis of a gyroscope about the vertical axis.

gyroscopic inertia.. The property of a gyroscope of resisting any force which tends to change its axis of rotation. A gyroscope tends to maintain the direction of its axis of rotation in space. Also called RIGIDITY IN SPACE.

gyro sextant.. A sextant provided with a gyroscope to indicate the horizontal.

H

haar., *n.* A wet sea fog or very fine drizzle which drifts in from the sea in coastal districts of eastern Scotland and northeast England, especially in summer.

habitat sanctuary.. A marine sanctuary established for the preservation, protection, and management of essential or specialized habitats representative of important marine systems. See also MARINE SANCTUARY.

hachures., *n. pl.* 1. Short lines on topographic maps or nautical charts to indicate the slope of the ground or the submarine bottom. They usually follow the direction of the slope. 2. Inward-pointing short lines or "ticks" around the circumference of a closed contour indicating a depression or a minimum.

hack., *n.* A chronometer which has failed to meet the exacting requirements of a standard chronometer, and is used for timing observations of celestial bodies, regulating ship's clocks, etc. A comparing watch, which may be of high quality, is normally used for timing celestial observations, the watch being compared with the chronometer, preferably both before and after observations. Sometimes called HACK CHRONOMETER.

hack chronometer.. See HACK.

hack watch.. See COMPARING WATCH.

hail., *n.* Frozen precipitation consisting of ice balls or irregular lumps of ice of varying size, ranging from that of a raindrop to an inch or considerably more. They are composed of clear ice or of alternate layers of ice and snow, and may fall detached or frozen together into irregular lumps. Hail is usually associated with thunderstorms. A hailstone is a single unit of hail. Small hail consists of snow pellets surrounded by a very thin ice covering. See also SNOW PELLETS.

hailstone., *n.* See under HAIL.

hail storm.. See under STORM, definition 2.

half-power points.. Power ratios used to define the angular width of a radar beam. One convention defines beam width as the angular width between points at which the field strength is 71 percent of its maximum value. Expressed in terms of power ratio, this convention defines beam width as the angular width between half-power points. A second convention defines beam width as the angular width between points at which the field strength is 50 percent of its maximum value. Expressed in terms of power ratio, the latter convention defines beam width as the angular width between quarter-power points.

half tide.. The condition or time of the tide when midway between high and low.

half-tide basin.. A lock of very large size and usually of irregular shape, the gates of which are kept open for several hours after high tide so that vessels may enter as long as there is sufficient depth over the sill. Vessels remain in the half-tide basin until the ensuing flood tide before they may pass through the gate to the inner harbor. If entry to the inner harbor is required before this time, water must be admitted to the half-tide basin from some external source. See also TIDAL BASIN, NON-TIDAL BASIN.

half-tide level.. A tidal datum midway between mean high water and mean low water. Mean sea level may coincide with half-tide level, but seldom does; the variation is generally about 3 centimeters and rarely exceeds 6 centimeters. Also called MEAN TIDE LEVEL. See also MID-EXTREME TIDE.

halo., *n.* Any of a group of optical phenomena caused by refraction or reflection of light by ice crystals in the atmosphere. The most common form is a ring of light of radius 22° or 46° around the sun or moon. See also CORONA, PARHELION, CIRCUMSCRIBED HALO, PARHELIC CIRCLE, SUN CROSS, SUN PILLAR, CIRCUMZENITHAL ARC, ANTHELION, PARANTHELION, HAVELIAN HALO, TANGENT ARC.

halving., *n.* The process of adjusting magnetic compass correctors so as to remove half of the deviation on the opposite cardinal or adjacent intercardinal headings to those on which adjustment was originally made when all deviation was removed. This is done to equalize the error on opposite headings.

***Handbook of Magnetic Compass Adjustment*.**. See PUB. NO. 226. (No longer in print, but available on the NGA Maritime Safety Information website)

hand lead. . A light sounding lead (7 to 14 pounds), usually having a line of not more than 25 fathoms.

hanging compass. . See INVERTED COMPASS.

harbor. , *n.* 1. A body of water providing protection for vessels and, generally, anchorage and docking facilities. 2. A haven or space of deep water so sheltered by the adjacent land as to afford a safe anchorage for ships. See also NATURAL HARBOR, ARTIFICIAL HARBOR.

harbor chart. . See under CHART CLASSIFICATION BY SCALE.

harbor line. . The line beyond which wharves and other structures cannot be extended.

harbor reach. . See REACH.

hard beach. . A portion of a beach especially prepared with a hard surface extending into the water, employed for the purpose of loading or unloading directly into landing ships or landing craft.

hard iron. . Iron or steel which is not readily magnetized by induction, but which retains a high percentage of the magnetism acquired. The opposite is SOFT IRON.

hardware. . The physical parts of a computer system; compare with SOFTWARE, the programs which accomplish work.

harmattan. , *n.* The dry, dusty trade wind blowing off the Sahara Desert across the Gulf of Guinea and the Cape Verde Islands. Sometimes called the DOCTOR, because of its supposed healthful properties.

harmful interference. . Any emission, radiation, or induction which endangers the functioning of a radionavigation service or of other safety services or seriously degrades, obstructs, or repeatedly interrupts a radio-communication service operating in accordance with the International Telecommunications Union Regulations.

harmonic. , *n.* 1. A sinusoidal quantity having a frequency that is an integral multiple of the frequency of a periodic quantity to which it is related. 2. A signal having a frequency which is an integral multiple of the fundamental frequency.

harmonic analysis. . The process by which the observed tide or tidal current at any place is separated into basic harmonic constituents. Also called HARMONIC REDUCTION.

harmonic analyzer. . A machine designed for the resolution of a periodic curve into its harmonic constituents. Now performed by computer.

harmonic component. . Any of the simple sinusoidal components into which a periodic quantity may be resolved.

harmonic constants. . The amplitudes and epochs of the harmonic constituents of the tide or tidal current at any place.

harmonic constituent. . See CONSTITUENT.

harmonic expressions. . Trigonometric terms of an infinite series used to approximate irregular curves in two or three dimensions.

harmonic function. . Any real function that satisfies a certain equation. In its simplest form, as used in tide and tidal current predictions, it is a quantity that varies as the cosine of an angle that increases uniformly with time.

harmonic motion. . The projection of circular motion on a diameter of the circle of such motion. Simple harmonic motion is produced if the circular motion is of constant speed. The combination of two or more simple harmonic motions results in compound harmonic motion.

harmonic prediction. *(tidal).* Method of predicting tides and tidal currents by combining the harmonic constituents into a single tide curve, usually performed by computer.

harmonic reduction. . See HARMONIC ANALYSIS.

harmonic tide plane. . See INDIAN SPRING LOW WATER.

harpoon log. . A log which consists of a rotator and distance registering device combined in a single unit, which is towed through the water. The TAFFRAIL LOG is similar except that the registering device is located at the taffrail, with only the rotator in the water.

harvest moon. . The full moon occurring nearest the autumnal equinox. See also PHASES OF THE MOON.

haul. , *v., i.* 1. A counterclockwise change in direction of the wind. 2. A shift in the direction of the wind forward. The opposite is to VEER. 2. *v., t.* To change the course of a sailing vessel to bring the wind farther forward, usually used with up, such as *haul up*.

haven. , *n.* A place of safety for vessels.

haze. , *n.* Fine dust or salt particles in the air, too small to be individually apparent but in sufficient number to reduce horizontal visibility and give the atmosphere a characteristic hazy appearance which casts a bluish or yellowish veil over the landscape, subduing its colors. This is sometimes called a dry haze to distinguish it from damp haze, small water droplets or very hygroscopic particles in the air, smaller and more scattered than light fog.

head. , *n.* See HEADLAND.

heading. , *n.* The horizontal direction in which a ship actually points or heads at any instant, expressed in angular units from a reference direction, usually from 000° at the reference direction clockwise through 360°. Heading is often designated as true, magnetic, compass, or grid. Heading should not be confused with COURSE, which is the intended direction of movement through the water. At a specific instant the heading may or may not coincide with the course. The heading of a ship is also called SHIP'S HEAD.

heading angle. . Heading measured from 0° at the reference direction clockwise or counterclockwise through 90° or 180°. It is labeled with the reference direction as a prefix and the direction of measurement from the reference direction as a suffix.

heading flasher. . An illuminated radial line on the radar for indicating own ship's heading on the bearing dial. Also called HEADING MARKER.

heading line. . The line extending in the direction of a heading.

heading marker. . See HEADING FLASHER.

headland. , *n.* A comparatively high promontory having a steep face. Usually called HEAD when coupled with a specific name. Also called FORELAND.

head sea. . A sea in which the waves move in a direction approximately opposite to the heading. The opposite is FOLLOWING SEA.

head tide. . A tidal current setting in a direction approximately opposite to the heading of a vessel. One setting in such a direction as to increase the speed of a vessel is called a FAIR TIDE. One abeam is called a BEAM TIDE. One approximately 90° from the course is called a CROSS TIDE.

head up, heading upward. . One of the three basic orientations of display of relative or true motion on a radarscope. In the HEAD UP orientation, the target pips are painted at their measured distances and in their directions relative to own ship's heading maintained UP in relation to the display and so indicated by the HEADING FLASHER. See also NORTH UP, BASE COURSE UP.

head-up display. . In ECDIS information shown on a display in such a fashion so that the vessel's HEADING is always pointing upward. This ORIENTATION corresponds to the visual view from the bridge in the direction of the ship's heading. This orientation may require frequent rotations of the display contents. Changing the ship's course or yawing of the vessel may render this non stabilized orientation mode unreadable. (See COURSE-UP DISPLAY).

headwaters. , *n., pl.* The source of a stream or river.

headway, *n.* Motion in a forward direction. Motion in the opposite direction is called STERNWAY.

head wind. . Wind from ahead of the vessel.

heat lightning. . A flash of light from an electric discharge, without thunder, believed to be the reflection by haze or clouds of a distant flash of lightning, too far away for the thunder to be audible.

heat wave. . Unseasonably high temperatures extending over a period of a day or longer, particularly during the warm season of the year.

heave. , *n.* The oscillatory vertical rise and fall due to the entire hull being lifted by the force of the sea. Also called HEAVING. See also SHIP MOTIONS.

heavenly body. . See CELESTIAL BODY.

heave the lead. . To take a sounding with a lead.

heaving. , *n.* See HEAVE.

Heaviside layer. . See under KENNELLY-HEAVISIDE REGION.

hecto-. . A prefix meaning one hundred (10^2).

hectometer, *n.* One hundred meters.

heel. , *n.* Lateral inclination of a vessel. See also LIST, *n.*

heel. , *v., t., i.* To incline or be inclined to one side. See also LIST, *n.*

heeling adjuster. . A dip needle with a sliding weight that can be moved along one of its arms to balance magnetic force, used to determine the correct position of a heeling magnet. Also called HEELING ERROR INSTRUMENT, VERTICAL FORCE INSTRUMENT. See also HEELING ERROR.

heeling error. . The change in the deviation of a magnetic compass when a craft heels due to the change in the position of the magnetic influences of the craft relative to the earth's magnetic field and to the compass.

heeling error instrument. . Heeling adjuster. Also called VERTICAL FORCE INSTRUMENT.

heeling magnet. . A permanent magnet placed vertically in a tube under the center of a marine magnetic compass, to correct for heeling error.

height. , *n.* Vertical distance above a datum.

height of eye correction. . The correction to sextant altitude due to dip of the horizon. Also called DIP CORRECTION.

height of tide. . Vertical distance from the chart sounding datum to the water surface at any stage of the tide. It is positive if the water level is higher than the chart sounding datum. The vertical distance from the chart sounding datum to a high water datum is called RISE OF TIDE.

heliocentric. , *adj.* Relative to the sun as a center.

heliocentric parallax. . The difference in the apparent direction or positions of a celestial body outside the solar system, as observed from the earth and sun. Also called STELLAR PARALLAX, ANNUAL PARALLAX. See also GEOCENTRIC PARALLAX.

helm. , *n.* The apparatus by which a vessel is steered; the tiller or wheel.

hemisphere. , *n.* Half of a sphere.

hemispheric resonating gyro (HRG). , *n.* Also called wine-glass gyroscope, mushroom gyro or hemispheric resonating gryro/navigator (HRG-N), is made using a thin solid-state hemispherical shell, anchored by a thick stem. This shell is driven to a flexural resonance by electrostatic forces generated by electrodes which are deposited directly onto separate fused-quartz structures that surround the shell. Gyroscopic effect is obtained from the inertial property of the flexural standing waves. HRG has no moving parts and is extremely reliable and accurate.

henry, *n.* A derived unit of electric inductance in the International System of Units; it is the inductance of a closed circuit in which an electromotive force of one volt is produced when the electric current in the circuit varies uniformly at a rate of one ampere per second.

hertz. , *n.* The special name for the derived unit of frequency in the International System of Units, it is one cycle per second.

Hertzian waves. . See RADIO WAVES.

heterodyne reception. . Radio reception in which an audio frequency is derived by beating the signal frequency with that produced by a local oscillator, followed by detection. Also called BEAT RECEPTION.

Hevelian halo. . A faint white halo consisting of a ring occasionally seen 90° from the sun, and probably caused by the refraction and internal reflection of the sun's light by bi-pyramidal ice crystals.

hexagon. , *n.* A closed plane figure having six sides.

hibernal. , *adj.* Pertaining to winter. The corresponding adjectives for spring, summer, and fall are vernal, aestival, and autumnal.

high. , *n.* An area of high pressure. Since a high is, on a synoptic chart, always associated with anticyclonic circulation, the term is used interchangeably with ANTICYCLONE. See also LOW.

high altitude method. . The establishing of a circular line of position from the observation of the altitude of a celestial body by means of the geographical position and zenith distance of the body. The line of position is a circle having the geographical position as its center and a radius equal to the zenith distance. The method is normally used only for bodies at high altitudes having small zenith distances. See also SAINT HILAIRE METHOD, SUMNER METHOD LONGITUDE METHOD.

high clouds. . Types of clouds the mean lower level of which is above 20,000 feet. The principal clouds in this group are cirrus, cirrocumulus, and cirrostratus.

higher high water. . The higher of the two high waters of any tidal day.

higher high water interval. . See under LUNITIDAL INTERVAL.

higher lower water. . The higher of the two low waters of any tidal day.

higher low water interval. . See under LUNITIDAL INTERVAL.

high fidelity. . The ability to reproduce modulating waves at various audio frequencies without serious distortion.

high focal plane buoy. . A type of lighted buoy in which the light is mounted exceptionally high above the surface of the sea.

high frequency. . Radio frequency of 3 to 30 megahertz.

high light. . The rear light of a lighted range. See REAR LIGHT.

high noon. . See LOCAL APPARENT NOON.

high sea, high seas. . All water beyond the outer limit of the territorial sea. Although the high seas are in part coextensive with the waters of the contiguous zone, the fishing zone, and those over the continental shelf, freedom of the seas is not invalidated by the zonal overlap.

high tide. . See under HIGH WATER.

high water. . The maximum height reached by a rising tide. The height may be due solely to the periodic tidal forces or it may have superimposed upon it the effects of prevailing meteorological conditions. Use of the synonymous term HIGH TIDE is discouraged.

high water full and change. . See ESTABLISHMENT OF THE PORT.

high water inequality. . The difference between the heights of the two high waters during a tidal day. See under DIURNAL INEQUALITY.

high water interval. . See under LUNITIDAL INTERVAL.

high water line. . 1. The intersection of the land with the water surface at an elevation of high water. 2. The line along the shore to which the waters normally reach at high water.

high water mark. . A line or mark left upon tide flats, beach, or alongshore objects indicating the elevation of the intrusion of high water. It should not be confused with the MEAN HIGH WATER LINE or MEAN HIGHER HIGH WATER LINE.

high water neaps. . See under NEAP TIDES.

high water springs. . Short for MEAN HIGH WATER SPRINGS.

high water stand. . The condition at high water when there is no sensible change in the height of the water. A similar condition at low water is called LOW WATER STAND. See also STAND.

hill. , *n.* 1. A relatively low, rounded elevation of the earth's surface. 2. On the sea floor, an elevation rising generally less than 500 meters.

hillock. , *n.* A small hill.

hoar. , *n.* See FROST, definition 1.

hoarfrost. , *n.* See FROST, definition 1.

HO-information. , *n.* In ECDIS, the information content of the SENC originated by hydrographic offices. It consists of the ENC content and UPDATES to it.

holding ground. The bottom ground of an anchorage. The expression is usually used with a modifying adjective to indicate the quality of the holding power of the material constituting the bottom.

hole. , *n.* 1. A small depression of the sea floor. 2. An opening through a piece of sea ice, or an open space between ice cakes. 3. A small bay, particularly in New England.

homing. , *n.* Navigation toward a point by following a signal from that point. Radiobeacons are commonly used for homing.

homogenous. , *adj.* Uniform throughout, or composed of parts which are similar in every detail.

hood. , *n.* A shield placed over a radarscope, to eliminate extraneous light and thus make the radar picture appear clearly.

hook. , *n.* A feature resembling a hook in shape, particularly, a. a spit or narrow cape of sand or gravel which turns landward at the outer end; or b. a sharp bend or curve, as in a stream.

hooked spit. . See RECURVED SPIT.

hop. , *n.* Travel of a radio wave to the ionosphere and back to earth. The number of hops a radio signal has experienced is usually designated by the expression one-hop, two-hop, multihop, etc.

horizon. , *n.* The great circle of the celestial sphere midway between the zenith and nadir, or a line resembling or approximating such a circle. The line where earth and sky appear to meet, and the projection of this line upon the celestial sphere, is called the visible or apparent horizon. A line resembling the visible horizon but above or below it is called a false horizon. The circle of the celestial sphere-formed by the intersection of the celestial sphere and a plane perpendicular to the zenith-nadir line is called a sensible horizon if the plane is through any point, such as the eye of an observer; geoidal horizon if through any sea-level point; and celestial or rational horizon if through the center of the earth. The geometrical horizon was originally considered identical with the celestial horizon, but the expression is now more commonly used to refer to the intersection of the celestial sphere and an infinite number of straight lines tangent to the earth's surface, and radiating from the eye of the observer. If there were no terrestrial refraction, GEOMETRICAL AND VISIBLE HORIZONS would coincide. An artificial horizon is a device for indicating the horizontal. A radio horizon is the line at which direct rays from a transmitting antenna become tangent to the earth's surface. A radar horizon is the radio horizon of a radar antenna.

horizon glass. . The glass of a marine sextant, attached to the frame, through which the horizon is observed. The half of this glass nearer the frame is silvered to form the HORIZON MIRROR for reflecting the image of a celestial body; the other half is clear.

horizon mirror. . The mirror part of the horizon glass. The expression is sometimes used somewhat loosely to refer to the horizon glass.

horizon prism. . A prism which can be inserted in the optical path of an instrument, such as a bubble sextant, to permit observation of the visible horizon.

horizon system of coordinates. . A set of celestial coordinates based on the celestial horizon as the primary great circle; usually altitude and azimuth or azimuth angle.

horizontal. , *adj*. Parallel to the plane of the horizon; perpendicular to the direction of gravity.

horizontal. , *n*. A horizontal line, plane, etc. horizontal beam width. The beam width measured in a horizontal plane.

horizontal beam width. , *n*. The beam width measured in a horizontal plane.

horizontal control datum. See HORIZONTAL GEODETIC DATUM.

horizontal danger angle. . The maximum or minimum angle between two points on a chart, as observed from a vessel, indicating the limit of safe approach to an off-lying danger. See also DANGER ANGLE.

horizontal datum. . See HORIZONTAL GEODETIC DATUM.

horizontal earth rate. . The rate at which the spin axis of a gyroscope must be tilted about the horizontal axis to remain parallel to the earth's surface. Horizontal earth rate is maximum at the equator, zero at the poles, and varies as the cosine of the latitude. See also EARTH RATE, VERTICAL EARTH RATE.

horizontal force instrument. . An instrument used to make a comparison between the intensity of the horizontal component of the earth's magnetic field and the magnetic field at the compass location on board. Basically, it consists of a magnetized needle pivoted in a horizontal plane, as a dry card compass. It will settle in some position which will indicate the direction of the resultant magnetic field. If the needle is started swinging, it will be damped down with a certain period of oscillation dependent upon the strength of the magnetic field. Also called HORIZONTAL VIBRATING NEEDLE. See also DEFLECTOR.

horizontal geodetic datum. . The basis for computations of horizontal control surveys in which the curvature of the earth is considered. It consists of the astronomical and geodetic latitude and the astronomical and geodetic longitude of an initial point (origin); an azimuth of a line from this point; the parameters (radius and flattening) of the reference ellipsoid; and the geoidal separation at the origin. A change in any of these quantities affects every point on the datum. For this reason, while positions within a system are directly and accurately relatable, those points from different datums must be transformed to a common datum for consistency. The horizontal geodetic datum may extend over a continent or be limited to a small area. See also DATUM. Also called HORIZONTAL DATUM, HORIZONTAL CONTROL DATUM.

horizontal intensity of the earth's magnetic field. . The strength of the horizontal component of the earth's magnetic field.

horizontally polarized wave. . A plane-polarized electromagnetic wave in which the electric field vector is in a horizontal plane.

horizontal parallax. . The geocentric parallax when a body is on the horizon. The expression is usually used only in connection with the moon, for which the tabulated horizontal parallax is given for an observer on the equator. The parallax at any altitude is called PARALLAX IN ALTITUDE.

horizontal vibrating needle. . See HORIZONTAL FORCE INSTRUMENT.

horn. , *n*. 1. A flared tube designed to match the acoustic impedance to the impedance of the atmosphere; it can behave as a resonator and can influence the directivity; the narrow end is called the throat and the large end the mouth. Also called TRUMPET. 2. See HORN ANTENNA.

horn antenna. . An antenna consisting of a waveguide, the cross-sectional area of which increases toward the open end. Often shortened to HORN.

horse latitudes. . The regions of calms and variable winds coinciding with the subtropical high pressure belts on the poleward sides of the trade winds. The expression is generally applied only to the northern of these two regions in the North Atlantic Ocean, or to the portion of it near Bermuda.

hostile ice. . An ice canopy containing no large sky lights or other features which permit a submarine to surface.

hour. , *n*. 1. A 24th part of a day. 2. A specified interval. See also COTIDAL HOUR, CURRENT HOUR.

hour angle. . Angular distance west of a celestial meridian or hour circle; the arc of the celestial equator, or the angle at the celestial pole, between the upper branch of a celestial meridian or hour circle and the hour circle of a celestial body or the vernal equinox, measured westward through 360°. It is usually further designated as local, Greenwich, or sidereal as the origin of measurement is the local or Greenwich celestial meridian or the hour circle of the vernal equinox. See also MERIDIAN ANGLE.

hour angle difference. . See MERIDIAN ANGLE DIFFERENCE.

hour circle. . On the celestial sphere, a great circle through the celestial poles. An hour circle through the zenith is called a celestial meridian. Also called CIRCLE OF DECLINATION, CIRCLE OF RIGHT ASCENSION.

hour-glass effect. . A radarscope phenomenon which appears as a constriction or expansion of the display near the center of the plan position indicator, which can be caused by a nonlinear time base or the sweep plot starting on the radar indicator at the same instant as the transmission of the pulse. The phenomenon is most apparent when in narrow rivers or close to shore.

hug. , *v., t*. To remain close to, as to *hug the land*.

Humboldt Current. . See PERU CURRENT.

humidity. , *n*. The amount of water vapor in the air. The mass of water vapor per unit volume of air is called absolute humidity. The mass of water vapor per unit mass of moist air is called specific humidity. The ratio of the actual vapor pressure to the vapor pressure corresponding to saturation at the prevailing temperature is called relative humidity.

hummock. , *n*. 1. A hillock of broken ice which has been forced upwards by pressure. It may be fresh or weathered. The submerged volume of broken ice under the hummocks, forced downwards by pressure, is called a BUMMOCK; 2. A natural elevation of the earth's surface resembling a hillock, but smaller and lower.

hummocked ice. . Sea ice piled haphazardly one piece over another to form an uneven surface. When weathered, hummocked ice has the appearance of smooth hillocks.

hummocking. , *n*. The pressure process by which sea ice is forced into hummocks. When the floes rotate in the process, it is called SCREWING.

hunter's moon. . The full moon following the harvest moon. See also PHASES OF THE MOON.

hunting. , *n*. Fluctuation about a mid-point due to instability, as oscillations of the needle of an instrument about the zero point.

hurricane. , *n*. 1. See under TROPICAL CYCLONE. 2. Wind of force 12 (64 knots and higher or 73 miles per hour and higher) on the Beaufort wind scale.

hydraulic current. . A current in a channel caused by a difference in the surface level at the two ends. Such a current may be expected in a strait connecting two bodies of water in which the tides differ in time or range. The current in the East River, N.Y., connecting Long Island Sound and New York Harbor, is an example.

HYDROARC. , *n*. A report containing details about maritime hazards to surface ships and submarines in the international waters of the Arctic Ocean and adjacent northern seas. Any person who physically collects data, or has an interest in data collected in the Arctic region should refer to these reports

hydrographer, *n*. One who studies and practices the science of hydrography.

hydrographic. , *adj*. Of or pertaining to hydrography.

hydrographic datum. . A datum used for referencing depths of water or the heights of predicted tides. See also DATUM.

hydrographic sextant. . A surveying sextant similar to those used for celestial navigation but smaller and lighter, constructed so that the maximum angle that can be read on it is slightly greater than that on the navigating sextant. Usually the angles can be read only to the nearest minute by means of a vernier. It is fitted with a telescope with a large object glass and field of view. Although the ordinary navigating sextant may be used in place of the hydrographic sextant, it is not entirely satisfactory for use in observing objects ashore which are difficult to see. Hydrographic sextants are either not provided with shade glasses or they are removed before use. Also called SOUNDING SEXTANT, SURVEYING SEXTANT.

hydrographic survey. . The survey of a water area, with particular reference to submarine relief, and any adjacent land. See also OCEANOGRAPHIC SURVEY.

hydrography. , *n.* The science that deals with the measurement and description of the physical features of the oceans, seas, lakes, rivers, and their adjoining coastal areas, with particular reference to their use for navigation.

HYDROLANT. , *n.* A radio message disseminated by the National Geospatial-Intelligence Agency and restricted to important marine incidents or navigational changes which affect navigational safety. The HYDROLANT broadcast covers those water areas outside and eastward of NAVAREA IV in the Atlantic Ocean. HYDROLANT messages constitute part of the U.S. long range radio navigational warning system. The text of effective HYDROLANT is available through NAVINFONET and printed in the weekly *Notice to Mariners.*

hydrology. , *n.* The scientific study of the waters of the earth, especially with relation to the effects of precipitation and evaporation upon the occurrence and character of ground water.

hydrometeor. , *n.* Any product of the condensation or sublimation of atmospheric water vapor whether formed in the free atmosphere or at the earth's surface; also any water particles blown by the wind from the earth's surface. See also LITHOMETEOR.

HYDROPAC. , *n.* A radio message disseminated by the National Geospatial-Intelligence Agency and restricted to important marine incidents or navigational changes which affect navigational safety. The HYDROPAC broadcast covers those water areas outside of NAVAREA XII in the Pacific Ocean. HYDROPAC messages constitute part of the U.S. long-range radio navigational warning system. The text of effective HYDROPAC messages is available through NAVINFONET and is printed in the weekly *Notice to Mariners.*

hydrophone. , *n.* A listening device for receiving underwater sounds.

hydrosphere. , *n.* The water portion of the earth as distinguished from the solid part, called the LITHOSPHERE, and from the gaseous outer envelope, called the ATMOSPHERE.

hyetal. , *adj.* Of or pertaining to rain.

hygrometer. , *n.* An instrument for measuring the humidity of the air. The most common type is a psychrometer consisting of drybulb and wet-bulb thermometers.

hygroscope. , *n.* An instrument which indicates variation in atmospheric moisture.

hygroscopic. , *adj.* Able to absorb moisture.

hyperbola. , *n.* An open curve with two parts, all points of which have a constant difference in distance from two fixed points called FOCI.

hyperbolic. , *adj.* Of or pertaining to a hyperbola.

hyperbolic lattice. . A pattern formed by two or more families of intersecting hyperbolas.

hyperbolic line of position. . A line of position in the shape of a hyperbola, determined by measuring the difference in distance to two fixed points. Those who remember Loran C lines of position are familiar with those lines as an example.

hyperbolic navigation. . Radionavigation based on the measurement of the time differences in the reception of signals from several pairs of synchronized transmitters. For each pair of transmitters the isochrones are substantially hyperbolic. The combination of isochrones for two or more pairs of transmitters forms a hyperbolic lattice within which position can be determined according to the measured time differences.

hypersonic. , *adj.* Of or pertaining to high supersonic speed, of the order of five times the speed of sound, or greater.

hypotenuse. , *n.* The side of a plane right triangle opposite the right angle; the longest side of a plane right triangle.

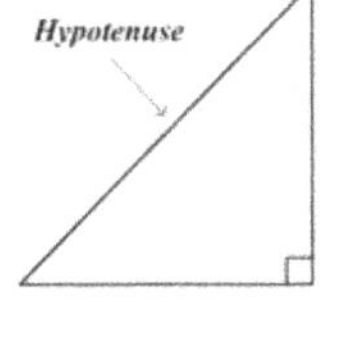

right triangle

hypsographic detail. The features pertaining to relief or elevation of terrain.

hypsographic map. . A map showing land or submarine bottom relief in terms of height above, or below, a datum by any method, such as contours, hachures, shading, or hypsometric tinting. Also called HYPSOMETRIC MAP, RELIEF MAP.

hypsography. , *n.* 1. The science or art of describing elevations of land surfaces with reference to a datum, usually sea level. 2. That part of topography dealing with relief or elevation of terrain.

hypsometer. , *n.* An instrument for measuring height by determining the boiling temperature of a liquid. Its operation depends on the principle that boiling temperature is dependent on pressure, which normally varies with height.

hypsometric map. . See HYPSOGRAPHIC MAP.

hypsometric tinting. . A method of showing relief on maps and charts by coloring, in different shades, those parts which lie between different levels. Also called ALTITUDE TINTS, COLOR GRADIENTS, ELEVATION TINTS, GRADIENT TINTS, LAYER TINTS. See also HYPSOMETRIC TINT SCALE.

hypsometric tint scale. . A graphic scale in the margin of maps and charts which indicates heights or depths by graduated shades of color. See also HYPSOMETRIC TINTING.

hysteresis. , *n.* The lagging of the effect caused by change of a force acting on anything.

hysteresis error. . That error in the reading of an instrument due to hysteresis.

I

IALA Maritime Buoyage System. . A uniform system of maritime buoyage, organized by the International Association of Marine Aids to Navigation and Lighthouse Authorities, which is now implemented by most maritime nations. Within the system there are two buoyage *regions*, designated as Region A and Region B, where lateral marks differ only in the colors of port and starboard hand marks. In Region A, red is to port on entering; in Region B, red is to starboard on entering. The system is a combined cardinal and lateral system, and applies to all fixed and floating marks, other than lighthouses, sector lights, leading lights and marks, lightships, and large navigational buoys.

ice. , *n.* Frozen water, the solid form of H_2O.

ice anchor. . An anchor designed for securing a vessel to ice.

ice atlas. . A publication containing a series of ice charts showing geographic distribution of ice, usually by seasons or months.

iceberg. , *n.* A massive piece of ice greatly varying in shape, showing more than 5 meters above the sea surface, which has broken away from a glacier, and which may be afloat or aground. Icebergs may be described as blocky, dome shaped, dry dock, glacier, pinnacled, tabular, tilted, or weathered. For reports to the International Ice Patrol they are described with respect to size as small, medium, or large icebergs.

iceberg tongue. . A major accumulation of icebergs projecting from the coast, held in place by grounding, and joined together by fast ice.

ice blink. . A whitish glare on low clouds above an accumulation of distant ice.

ice blink

icebound, *adj.* Pertaining to a harbor, inlet, etc. when entry or exit is prevented by ice, except possibly with the assistance of an icebreaker.

ice boundary. . The demarcation at any given time between fast ice and pack ice or between areas of pack ice of different concentrations. See also ICE EDGE.

ice breccia. . Ice pieces of different age frozen together.

ice bridge., *n.* 1. Surface river ice of sufficient thickness to impede or prevent navigation. 2. An area of fast ice between the mainland and nearby inhabited islands used in winter as a means of travel.

ice buoy.. A sturdy buoy, usually a metal spar, used to replace a more easily damaged buoy during a period when heavy ice is anticipated.

ice cake.. Any relatively flat piece of sea ice less than 20 meters across. See also SMALL ICE CAKE.

ice canopy.. From the point of view of the submariner, PACK ICE.

ice cap.. A perennial cover of ice and snow over an extensive portion of the earth's surface. The largest ice caps are those in Antarctica and Greenland. Arctic Ocean ice is seasonal and in motion, and is not considered an ice cap.

ice cover.. The ratio, expressed in tenths, of the amount of ice to the total area of sea surface in a defined area; this locale may be global, hemispheric, or a specific geographic entity.

ice crystal.. Any one of a number of macroscopic crystalline forms in which ice appears.

ice-crystal haze.. A type of very light ice fog composed only of ice crystals (no droxtals). It is usually associated with precipitation of ice crystals.

ice crystals.. A type of precipitation composed of slowly falling, very small, unbranched crystals of ice which often seem to float in the air. It may fall from a cloud or from a cloudless sky. It is visible only in direct sunlight or in an artificial light beam, and does not appreciably reduce visibility. The latter quality helps to distinguish it from ice fog, which is composed largely of droxtals.

ice edge.. The demarcation at any given time between the open sea and sea ice of any kind, whether fast or drifting. See also COMPACTED ICE EDGE, DIFFUSE ICE EDGE, ICE BOUNDARY.

ice field.. An area of pack ice consisting of floes of any size, which is greater than 10 kilometers (5.4 nautical miles) across. Ice fields are subdivided according to areal extent. A large ice field is over 11 nautical miles across; a medium ice field is 8 to 11 nautical miles across; a small ice field is 5.4 to 8 nautical miles across.

ice fog.. Fog composed of suspended particles of ice, partly ice crystals 20 to 100 microns in diameter, but chiefly, especially when dense, droxtals 12 to 20 microns in diameter. It occurs at very low temperatures, and usually in clear, calm weather in high latitudes. The sun is usually visible and may cause halo phenomena. Ice fog is rare at temperatures warmer than -30° C or -20°F. Also called RIME FOG. See also FREEZING FOG.

ice foot., *n.* A narrow fringe of ice attached to the coast, unmoved by tides and remaining after the fast ice has moved away.

ice-free., *adj.* Referring to a locale with no sea ice; there may be some ice of land origin present.

ice front.. The vertical cliff forming the seaward face of an ice shelf or other floating glacier varying in height from 2 to 50 meters above sea level. See also ICE WALL.

ice island.. A large piece of floating ice showing about 5 meters above the sea surface, which has broken away from an ice shelf, having a thickness of 30 to 50 meters and an area of from a few thousand square meters to 150 square nautical miles or more; usually characterized by a regularly undulating surface which gives it a ribbed appearance from the air.

ice jam.. An accumulation of broken river ice or sea ice caught in a narrow channel.

ice keel.. A downward projecting ridge on the underside of the ICE CANOPY, the counterpart of a RIDGE. An ice keel may extend as much as 50 meters below sea level.

ice limit.. The climatological term referring to the extreme minimum or extreme maximum extent of the ice edge in any given month or period based on observations over a number of years. The term should be preceded by minimum or maximum, as appropriate. See also MEAN ICE EDGE.

ice massif.. A concentration of sea ice covering an area of hundreds of kilometers, which is found in the same region every summer.

ice needle.. A long, thin ice crystal whose cross-section is typically hexagonal.

ice of land origin.. Ice formed on land or in an ice shelf, found floating in water, including ice that is stranded or grounded.

ice patch.. An area of pack ice less than 5.4 nautical miles (10 kilometers) across.

ice pellets.. A type of precipitation consisting of transparent or translucent pellets of ice, 5 millimeters or less in diameter. The pellets may be spherical, irregular, or (rarely) conical in shape. They usually bounce when hitting hard ground, and make a sound upon impact. The term includes two basically different types of precipitation, those which are known in the United States as SLEET and SMALL HAIL. Sleet is generally transparent, globular, solid grains of ice which have formed from the freezing of raindrops or the refreezing of largely melted snowflakes when falling through a below-freezing layer of air near the earth's surface. Small hail is generally translucent particles, consisting of snow pellets encased in a thin layer of ice. The ice layer may form either by the accretion of droplets upon the snow pellet, or by the melting and refreezing of the surface of the snow pellet.

ice port.. An embayment in an ice front, often of a temporary nature, where ships can moor alongside and unload directly onto the ice shelf.

ice rind.. A brittle, shiny crust of ice formed on a quiet surface by direct freezing or from grease ice, usually in water of low salinity. Of thickness to about 5 centimeters, ice rind is easily broken by wind or swell, commonly breaking into rectangular pieces.

ice sheet.. Continuous ice overlaying a large land area.

ice shelf.. A floating ice sheet attached to the coast and of considerable thickness, showing 20 to 50 meters or more above sea level. Usually of great horizontal extent and with a level or gently undulating surface, the ice shelf is augmented by annual snow accumulation and often also by the seaward extension of land glaciers. Limited areas of the ice shelf may be aground. The seaward edge is called ICE FRONT.

ice storm. A storm characterized by a fall of freezing precipitation with significant buildup of ice on exposed surfaces.

ice stream.. The part of an inland ice sheet in which the ice flows more rapidly and not necessarily in the same direction as the surrounding ice. The margins are sometimes clearly marked by a change in direction of the surface slope, but may be indistinct.

ice under pressure.. Ice in which deformation processes are actively occurring; hence the ice is a potential impediment or danger to shipping.

ice wall.. An ice cliff forming the seaward margin of a glacier which is not afloat. An ice wall is aground with the underlying land at or below sea level. See also ICE FRONT.

ice-worn., *adj.* Abraded by ice.

icicle., *n.* A hanging mass of ice, usually conical, formed by the freezing of dripping water.

IHO Transfer Standard for Digital Hydrographic Data., *n.* In ECDIS a "THEORETICAL DATA MODEL", "DATA STRUCTURE", "OBJECT CATALOGUE", "ENC PRODUCT SPECIFICATION", "USE OF THE OBJECT CATALOGUE for ENC" and an "Object Catalogue DATA DICTIONARY Product Specification" for use in the exchange or transfer of digital hydrographic data.

illuminance., *n.* The luminous flux per unit of area. The derived unit of illuminance in the International System of Units is the LUX.

IHO test data set., *n.* See ENC test data set.

image, *n.* 1. The optical counterpart of an object. A real image is actually produced and is capable of being shown on a surface, as in a camera; while a virtual image cannot be shown on a surface, but is visible, as in a mirror. 2. A visual representation, as on a radarscope.

improved channels.. Dredged channels under the jurisdiction of the U.S Army Corps of Engineers, and maintained to provide an assigned CONTROLLING DEPTH. Symbolized on National Ocean Survey charts by black, broken lines to represent side limits, with the controlling depth and date of the survey given together with a tabulation of more detailed information.

impulse train.. See PULSE TRAIN.

in-band racon.. A racon which transmits in the marine radar frequency band. There are two types of in-band racons, swept-frequency racons and experimental fixed-frequency racons. The transmitter of the swept-frequency racon sweeps through a range of frequencies within the band to ensure that a radar receiver tuned to a particular frequency within the band will be able to detect the signal. The fixed-frequency racon transmits on a fixed frequency at the band edge. It is therefore necessary that the radar set be tuned to the racon's transmitting frequency or that auxiliary receiving equipment be used. When the radar is tuned to the fixed-frequency racon, normal radar echoes are not painted on the radarscope. See also CROSS-BAND RACON.

incandescence., *n.* Emission of light due to high temperature. Any other emission of light is called LUMINESCENCE.

inch. , *n.* A unit of length equal to one-twelfth of a foot, or 2.54 centimeters.

incidence. , *n.* 1. Partial coincidence, as a circle and a tangent line. 2. The impingement of a ray on a surface.

incident ray. . A ray impinging on a surface.

incineration area. . An officially designated offshore area for the burning of chemical waste by specially equipped vessels. The depiction of incineration areas on charts (in conjunction with radio warnings) is necessary to ensure that passing vessels do not mistake the burning of waste for a vessel on fire.

inclination. , *n.* 1. The angle which a line or surface makes with the vertical, horizontal, or with another line or surface. 2. One of the orbital elements (parameters) that specifies the orientation of an orbit. It is the angle between the orbital plane and a reference plane, the plane of the celestial equator for geocentric orbits and the ecliptic for heliocentric orbits. See also ORBITAL ELEMENTS, ORBITAL PARAMETERS OF ARTIFICIAL EARTH SATELLITES.

inclination of an orbit. . 1. See INCLINATION, definition 2. 2. As defined by the International Telecommunication Union (ITU), the angle determined by the plane containing an orbit and the plane of the earth's equator.

increment. , *n.* A change in the value of a variable. A negative increment is also called DECREMENT.

independent surveillance. , Position determination by means requiring no cooperation from the craft or vehicle.

index. *(pl. indices or indexes), n.* 1. A mark on the scale of an instrument, diagram, etc., to indicate the origin of measurement. 2. A pointer or part of an instrument which points to a value, like the needle of a gauge. 3. A list or diagram serving as a guide to a book, set of charts, etc. 4. A ratio or value used as a basis for comparison of other values.

index arm. . A slender bar carrying an index; particularly the bar which pivots at the center of curvature of the arc of a marine sextant and carries the index and the vernier or micrometer.

index chart. . An outline chart showing the limits and identifying designations of navigational charts, volumes of sailing directions, etc.

index correction. . The correction due to index error.

index error. . The error in the reading of an instrument equal to the difference between the zero of the scale and the zero of the index. In a marine sextant it is due primarily to lack of parallelism of the index mirror and the horizon glass at zero reading.

index glass. . See INDEX MIRROR.

index mirror. . The mirror attached to the index arm of a marine sextant. The bubble or pendulum sextant counterpart is called INDEX PRISM. Also called INDEX GLASS.

index prism. . A sextant prism which can be rotated to any angle corresponding to altitudes between established limits. It is the bubble or pendulum sextant counterpart of the INDEX MIRROR of a marine sextant.

Indian Equatorial Countercurrent. . A complex Indian Ocean current which is influenced by the monsoons and the circulations of the Arabian Sea and the Bay of Bengal. At times it is easily distinguishable; at other times it is not evident. During December through March, the countercurrent has a marked tendency to migrate southward and to become narrower. In December the northern and southern boundaries are at 2°N and 4°S, respectively, moving southward to 3°S and 6°S by February. The northern boundary of Indian Equatorial Countercurrent is easily discernible at this time due to the generally westward current flow in the region immediately north. During May through July the cell, within which the Indian Equatorial Countercurrent and the Monsoon Drift flow clockwise, moves toward the west side of the region. In June and July the southeastward flowing currents prevail in the region between the Bay of Bengal and the Indian South Equatorial Current; only traces of the countercurrent remain. During August through November eastward flowing currents prevail north of the Indian Equatorial Countercurrent. As a result, the northern boundary of the countercurrent is difficult to distinguish from the eastward drift currents. See also MONSOON.

Indian South Equatorial Current. . An Indian Ocean current that flows westward throughout the year, controlled by the southeast trade winds. Its northern and southern boundaries are at approximately 10°S and 25°S, respectively. The northern boundary of the current fluctuates seasonally between 9°S and 11°S, being at its northernmost limit during the southwest monsoon and at its southernmost limit during the northeast monsoon. The current flows westward toward the east coast of Madagascar to the vicinity of Tamatave and Ile Sainte-Marie, where it divides; one part turns northward, flows past the northern tip of the island with speeds up to 3.3 knots, and then flows westward and northwestward toward the African coast. The northern branch of the current divides upon reaching the coast of Africa near Cabo Delgado; one part turns and flows northward, the other turns and flows southward in the western part of the Mozambique Channel and forms the AGULHAS CURRENT. See also MONSOON.

Indian spring low water. . A tidal datum originated by G.H. Darwin when investigating the tides of India. It is an elevation depressed below mean sea level by an amount equal to the sum of the amplitudes of certain harmonic constituents. Also called INDIAN TIDE PLANE, HARMONIC TIDE PLANE.

Indian summer. . An indefinite and irregular period of mild, calm, hazy weather often occurring in autumn or early winter, especially in the United States and Canada.

Indian tide plane. . See INDIAN SPRING LOW WATER.

indicator. , *n.* See RADAR INDICATOR.

indirect echo. . A radar echo which is caused by the electromagnetic energy being transmitted to the target by an indirect path and returned as an echo along the same path. An indirect echo may appear on the radar display when the main lobe of the radar beam is reflected off part of the structure of the ship (the stack for example) from which it is reflected to the target. Returning to own ship by the same indirect path, the echo appears on the PPI at the bearing of the reflecting surface. Assuming that the additional distance by the indirect path is negligible, the indirect echo appears on the PPI at the same range as the direct echo received. Also called FALSE ECHO.

indirect wave. . A radio wave which reaches a given reception point by a path from the transmitting point other than the direct line path between the two. An example is the SKYWAVE received after reflection from one of the layers of the ionosphere.

induced magnetism. . The magnetism acquired by soft iron while it is in a magnetic field. Soft iron will lose its induced magnetism when it is removed from a magnetic field. The strength and polarity of the induced magnetism will alter immediately as its magnetic latitude, or its orientation in a magnetic field, is changed. The induced magnetism has an immediate effect upon the magnetic compass as the magnetic latitude or heading of a craft changes. See also PERMANENT MAGNETISM, SUBPERMANENT MAGNETISM.

induced precession. . See REAL PRECESSION.

inequality . *(tidal), n.* A systematic departure from the mean value of a tidal quantity.

inertia. , *n.* The tendency of a body at rest to remain at rest and of a body in motion to remain in motion, unless acted upon by another force. See also GYROSCOPIC INERTIA.

inertial alignment. . The process of orienting the measuring axes of the inertial components of inertial navigation equipment with respect to the coordinate system in which the equipment is to be used.

inertial coordinate system. . A coordinate system in which the axes do not rotate with respect to the "fixed stars" and in which dynamic behavior can be described using Newton's laws of motion. See also EARTH-FIXED COORDINATE SYSTEM.

inertial force. . A force in a given coordinate system arising from the inertia of a mass moving with respect to another coordinate system.

inertial navigation. . The process of measuring a craft's velocity, attitude, and displacement from a known start point through sensing the accelerations acting on it in known directions using devices that mechanize Newton's laws of motion. Inertial navigation is described as self-contained because it is independent of external aids to navigation, and passive because no energy is emitted to obtain information. The basic principle of inertial navigation is the measurement of the accelerations acting on a craft, other than those not associated with its orientation or motion with respect to the earth, and the double integration of these accelerations along known directions to obtain the displacement from the start point. Due to increasing position errors with time, an inertial system must be reset from time to time using another navigation system.

in extremis. . Condition in which changes in course and/or speed are required on the part of both ships if the ships are to avoid collision.

inferior conjunction. . The conjunction of an inferior planet and the sun when the planet is between the earth and the sun.

inferior planets.. The planets with orbits smaller than that of the earth; Mercury and Venus. See also PLANET.

inferior transit.. See LOWER TRANSIT.

infinite., *adj.* Without limits. The opposite is FINITE.

infinitesimal., *adj.* 1. Immeasurably small. 2. Approaching zero as a limit.

infinity., *n.* Beyond finite limits. In navigation, a source of light is regarded as at infinity if it is at such a great distance that rays from it can be considered parallel. The sun, planets, and stars can be considered at infinity without serious error. See also PARALLAX.

inflection, inflexion., *n.* Reversal of direction of curvature. A point at which reversal takes place is called POINT OF INFLECTION.

infrared., *adj.* Having a frequency immediately beyond the red end of the visible spectrum; rays of longer wavelength than visible light, but shorter than radio waves.

infrasonic., *adj.* Having a frequency below the audible range. Frequencies above the audible range are called ULTRASONIC.

initial great circle course.. The direction, at the point of departure, of the great circle through that point and the destination, expressed as the angular distance from a reference direction, usually north, to that part of the great circle extending toward the designation. Also called INITIAL GREAT CIRCLE DIRECTION. See also FINAL GREAT CIRCLE COURSE.

initial great circle direction.. See INITIAL GREAT CIRCLE COURSE.

injection messages.. Messages periodically transmitted to artificial satellites for storage in satellite memory.

Inland Rules of the Road.. Officially the Inland Navigation Rules; Rules to be followed by all vessels while navigating upon certain defined inland waters of the United States. See also COLREGS DEMARCATION LINES, RULES OF THE ROAD.

inland sea.. A body of water nearly or completely surrounded by land, especially if very large or composed of salt water. If completely surrounded by land, it is usually called a LAKE. This should not be confused with CLOSED SEA, that part of the ocean enclosed by headlands, within narrow straits, etc., or within the territorial jurisdiction of a country.

inlet., *n.* A narrow body of water extending into the land from a larger body of water. A long, narrow inlet with gradually decreasing depth inward is called a RIA. Also called TONGUE.

inner harbor.. The part of a harbor most remote from the sea, as contrasted with the OUTER HARBOR. These expressions are usually used only in a harbor that is clearly divided into two parts by a narrow passageway or man-made structures.

inner planets.. The four planets nearest the sun; Mercury, Venus, Earth, and Mars.

inoperative., *adj.* Said of a sound signal or radionavigation aid out of service due to a malfunction.

in phase.. The condition of two or more cyclic motions which are at the same part of their cycles at the same instant. Two or more cyclic motions which are not at the same part of their cycles at the same instant are said to be OUT OF PHASE.

input axis.. The axis of applied torque of a gyroscope. See also OUTPUT AXIS, PRECESSION.

inshore., *adj., adv.* Near or toward the shore.

inshore., *n.* The zone of variable width between the shore face and the seaward limit of the breaker zone.

inshore traffic zone.. A routing measure comprising a designated area between the landward boundary of a traffic separation scheme and the adjacent coast, intended for local traffic.

in situ.. A Latin term meaning “in place”; in the natural or original position.

insolation., *n.* Solar radiation received, or the rate of delivery of such radiation.

instability., *n.* The state or property of submitting to change or of tending to increase the departure from original conditions after being disturbed. The opposite is STABILITY.

instability line.. Any non-frontal line or band of convective activity in the atmosphere. This is the general term and includes the developing, mature, and dissipating stages. However, when the mature stage consists of a line of active thunderstorms, it is properly called SQUALL LINE; therefore, in practice, *instability line* often refers only to the less active phases. Instability lines are usually hundreds of miles long (not necessarily continuous), 10 to 50 miles wide, and are most often formed in the warm sectors of wave cyclones. Unlike true fronts, they are transitory in character, ordinarily developing to maximum intensity in less than 12 hours and then dissipating in about the same time. Maximum intensity is usually attained in late afternoon.

instrument correction.. That correction due to instrument error.

instrument error.. The inaccuracy of an instrument due to imperfections within the instrument. See CALIBRATION ERROR, CENTERING ERROR, FRICTION ERROR, GRADUATION ERROR, HYSTERESIS ERROR, LAG ERROR, PRISMATIC ERROR, SECULAR ERROR, TEMPERATURE ERROR, VERNIER ERROR.

instrument shelter.. A cage or screen in which a thermometer and sometimes other instruments are placed to shield them from the direct rays of the sun and from other conditions that would interfere with registration of true conditions. It is usually a small wooden structure with louvered sides.

insular., *adj.* Of or pertaining to an island or islands.

insular borderland.. A region around an island normally occupied by or bordering a shelf, that is highly irregular with depths well in excess of those typical of a shelf. See also CONTINENTAL BORDERLAND.

insular shelf.. A zone around an island that extends from the low water line to a depth at which there is usually a marked increase of slope towards oceanic depths. See also CONTINENTAL SHELF.

insulate., *v., t.* To separate or isolate a conducting body from its surroundings, by means of a nonconductor, as to prevent transfer of electricity, heat, or sound.

insulator., *n.* A non-conducting substance or one offering high resistance to passage of energy.

integer., *n.* A whole number; a number that is not a fraction.

integral., *adj.* Of or pertaining to an integer.

integral Doppler navigation.. Navigation by means of integrating the Doppler frequency shift that occurs over a specific interval of time as the distance between a navigational satellite and navigator is changing to determine the time rate of change of range of the satellite from the navigator for the same interval. See also DOPPLER SATELLITE NAVIGATION.

integrated navigation system.. A navigation system which comprises two or more positioning systems combined in such manner as to achieve performance better than each constituent system.

integrating accelerometer.. An instrument which senses the component of specific acceleration along an axis known as the sensitive axis of the accelerometer, and produces an output equal to the time integral of that quantity. Also called VELOCITY METER.

intended track.. See TRACK, definition 2.

intercalary day.. A day inserted or introduced among others in a calendar, such as February 29 during leap years.

intercardinal heading.. A heading in the direction of any of the intercardinal points. See also CARDINAL HEADING.

intercardinal point.. Any of the four directions midway between the cardinal points; northeast, southeast, southwest, or northwest. Also called QUADRANTAL POINT.

intercardinal rolling error.. See under QUADRANTAL ERROR.

intercept., *n.* See ALTITUDE INTERCEPT, ALTITUDE INTERCEPT METHOD.

interference., *n.* 1. Unwanted and confusing signals or patterns produced by nearby electrical equipment or machinery, or by atmospheric phenomena. 2. The variation of wave amplitude with distance or time, caused by superposition of two or more waves. Sometimes called WAVE INTERFERENCE.

interferometer., *n.* An apparatus used to produce and measure interference from two or more coherent wave trains from the same source. Used to measure wavelengths, to measure angular width of sources, to determine the angular position of sources (as in satellite tracking), and for other purposes. See also RADIO INTERFEROMETER.

interlaced.. Referring to a computer monitor which displays data by scanning alternate lines instead of each line sequentially.

intermediate frequency.. In super heterodyne reception, the frequency which is derived by mixing the signal-carrying frequency with the local oscillator frequency. If there is more than one such mixing process, the successive intermediate frequencies are known as the first, second, etc. intermediate frequency.

intermediate light.. The middle light of the three-light range.

intermediate orbit.. A central force orbit that is tangent to the real (or disturbed) orbit at some point. A fictitious satellite traveling in the intermediate orbit would have the same position, but not the same velocity, as the real satellite at the point of tangency.

internal noise.. In radio reception, the noise which is produced in the receiver circuits. Internal noise is in addition to external noise.

internal tide.. A tidal wave propagating along a sharp density discontinuity, such as at a thermocline, or in an area of gradual changing density (vertically).

International Atomic Time.. See under ATOMIC TIME.

International Bureau of Weights and Measures.. The International Bureau of Weights and Measures (BIPM) ensures worldwide unification of physical measurements. It is responsible for establishing the fundamental standards and scales for measurement of the principal physical quantities, maintaining the international prototypes, carrying out comparisons of national and international standards, ensuring coordination of corresponding measuring techniques, and carrying out and coordinating the determinations relating to the fundamental physical constants.

international call sign.. An alpha-numeric symbol assigned in accordance with the provisions of the International Telecommunications Union to identify a radio station. The nationality of the radio station is identified by the first three characters; also referred to as call letters or signal letters.

international chart.. One of a coordinated series of small-scale charts for planning and long range navigation. The charts are prepared and published by different Member States of the International Hydrographic Organization using the same specifications.

International Code of Signals., See PUB. NO. 102.

international date line.. See DATE LINE.

International ellipsoid of reference.. The reference ellipsoid of which the semimajor axis is 6,378,388.0 meters, the semiminor axis is 6,356,911.946 meters, and the flattening or ellipticity is 1/297. Also called INTERNATIONAL SPHEROID OF REFERENCE.

International Great Lakes Datum (1955).. Mean water level at Pointe-au-Pere, Quebec, on the Gulf of St. Lawrence over the period 1941-1956, from which dynamic elevations throughout the Great Lakes region are measured. The term is often used to mean the entire system of dynamic elevations rather than just the referenced water level.

International Hydrographic Bulletin.. A publication, published monthly by the International Hydrographic Bureau for the International Hydrographic Organization, which contains information of current hydrographic interest.

International Hydrographic Bureau (IHB).. The Directors and administrative staff of the International Hydrographic Organization, based in Monaco.

International Hydrographic Organization (IHO).. An institution formed in 1921, consisting of representatives of maritime nations organized for the purpose of coordinating the hydrographic work of the participating governments.

International Maritime Organization (IMO).. A Specialized Agency of the United Nations responsible for maritime safety and efficiency of navigation. The IMO enables cooperation among governments in matters affecting shipping and international trade. It encourages the general adoption of the highest practicable standards in matters concerning maritime safety, efficiency of navigation, and the prevention and control of marine pollution.

International Nautical Mile.. A unit of length equal to 1,852 meters, exactly. See also NAUTICAL MILE.

international number.. An alpha-numeric designation given to navigational lights to facilitate the exchange of light information between maritime offices of different countries. The United Kingdom Hydrographic Office (UKHO) is responsible for the designation of an international number for a light. Both the national and the international light numbers are given in the light list, with the international number shown in italic type under the national number. See LIGHT LIST NUMBER.

International spheroid of reference.. See INTERNATIONAL ELLIPSOID OF REFERENCE.

International System of Units (SI).. A modern form of the metric system adopted in 1960 by the General Conference of Weights and Measures (CGPM). The units of the International System of Units (SI) are divided into three classes. The first class of SI units are the base units or the seven well defined units which by convention are regarded as dimensionally independent: the meter the kilogram, the second, the ampere, the kelvin, the mole, and the candela. The second class of SI units are the derived units, i.e., the units that can be formed by combining base units according to the algebraic relations linking the corresponding quantities. Several of these algebraic expressions in terms of base units can be replaced by special names and symbols which can themselves be used to form other derived units. The third class of SI units are the supplementary units, those units not yet classified by the CGPM as either base units or derived units. In 1969 the International Committee of Weights and Measures (CIPM) recognized that users of SI units will wish to employ with it certain units not part of SI, but which are important and widely used. These are the minute, the hour, the day, the degree of arc, the minute of arc, the second of arc, the liter, and the tonne. Outside the International System are some other units useful in specialized fields. Their value expressed in SI units must be obtained by experiment, and are therefore not known exactly These are the electron-volt, the unified atomic mass unit, the astronomical unit, and the parsec. Other temporary units are the nautical mile, the knot, the angstrom, the arc, the hectare, the barn, the bar, the standard atmosphere, the gal, the curie, the röntgen, and the rod.

interpolation., *n.* The process of determining intermediate values between given values in accordance with some known or assumed rate or system of change. Linear interpolation assumes that changes of tabulated values are proportional to changes in entering arguments. Interpolation is designated as single, double, or triple if there are one, two, or three arguments or variables respectively. The extension of the process of interpolation beyond the limits of known value is called EXTRAPOLATION.

interpolation table.. An auxiliary table used for interpolating. See also PROPORTIONAL PARTS.

interrogating signal.. The signal emitted by an interrogator to trigger a transponder.

interrogation., *n.* The transmission of a radio frequency pulse, or combination of pulses, intended to trigger a transponder or group of transponders.

interrogator., *n.* A radar transmitter which sends out a pulse that triggers a transponder. An interrogator may be combined in a single unit with a responsor, which receives the reply from a transponder and produces an output suitable for feeding a display system; the combined unit is called INTERROGATOR-RESPONSOR. Also called CHALLENGER.

interrogator-responsor., *n.* A radar transmitter and receiver combined to interrogate a transponder and display the resulting replies. Often shortened to INTERROGATOR and sometimes called CHALLENGER.

interrupted quick flashing light.. A quick flashing light (50-80 flashes per minute) that is interrupted at regular intervals by eclipses of long duration. See also QUICK FLASHING LIGHT, VERY QUICK FLASHING LIGHT.

interrupted quick light.. A quick light in which the sequence of flashes is interrupted by regularly repeated eclipses of constant and long duration. See also CONTINUOUS QUICK LIGHT, GROUP QUICK LIGHT.

interrupted very quick light.. A very quick light (80-160 flashes per minute) in which the sequence of flashes is interrupted by regularly repeated eclipses of long duration. See also CONTINUOUS VERY QUICK LIGHT, GROUP VERY QUICK LIGHT.

inter scan., *n.* See INTER-TRACE DISPLAY.

intersect., *v., t. & i.* To cut or cross. For example, two non parallel lines in a plane intersect in a point, and a plane intersects a sphere in a circle.

inter-trace display.. A technique for presenting additional information, in the form of alphanumerics, markers, cursors, etc., on a radar display, by using the intervals between the normal presentation scans. Also called INTER-SCAN.

Intracoastal Waterway.. An inland waterway for small craft and small commercial vessels extending, in three non-contiguous segments, from Brownsville, Texas to Norfolk, Virginia. through New Jersey; Segments stretch from Brownsville, Texas to Carrabelle, Florida; Tarpon Springs, Florida to Fort Myers, Florida; and Key West, Florida to Norfolk, Virginia. Some portions of the waterway are in exposed waters, and some portions are very limited in depth.

Invar. , *n.* The registered trade name for an alloy of nickel and iron, containing about 36% nickel. Its coefficient of expansion is extremely small over a wide range of temperature.

inverse chart. . See TRANSVERSE CHART.

inverse cylindrical orthomorphic chart. . See TRANSVERSE MERCATOR CHART.

inverse cylindrical orthomorphic map projection. . See TRANSVERSE MERCATOR MAP PROJECTION.

inverse equator. . See TRANSVERSE EQUATOR.

inverse latitude. . See TRANSVERSE LATITUDE.

inverse logarithm. . See ANTILOGARITHM.

inverse longitude. . See TRANSVERSE LONGITUDE.

inverse Mercator chart. . See TRANSVERSE MERCATOR CHART.

inverse Mercator map projection. . See TRANSVERSE MERCATOR MAP PROJECTION.

inverse meridian. . See TRANSVERSE MERIDIAN.

inverse parallel. . See TRANSVERSE PARALLEL.

inverse rhumb line. . See TRANSVERSE RHUMB LINE.

inversion. , *n.* In meteorology, a departure from the usual decrease or increase with altitude of the value of an atmospheric property. This term is almost always used to refer to a temperature inversion, an atmospheric condition in which the temperature increases with increasing altitude.

inverted compass. . A marine magnetic compass designed and installed for observation from below the compass card. Frequently used as a telltale compass. Also called HANGING COMPASS, OVERHEAD COMPASS.

inverted image. . An image that appears upside down in relation to the object.

inverter. , *n.* A device for changing direct current to alternating current. A device for changing alternating current to direct current is called a CONVERTER if a rotary device and a RECTIFIER if a static device.

inverting telescope. . An instrument with the optics so arranged that the light rays entering the objective of the lens meet at the crosshairs and appear inverted when viewed through the eyepiece without altering the orientation of the image. See also ERECTING TELESCOPE.

inward bound. . Heading toward the land or up a harbor away from the open sea. The opposite is OUTWARD BOUND.

ion. , *n.* An atom or group of atoms which has become electrically charged, either positively or negatively, by the loss or gain of one or more electrons.

ionization. , *n.* The process by which neutral atoms or groups of atoms become electrically charged either positively or negatively, by the loss or gain of electrons; or the state of a substance whose atoms or groups of atoms have become thus charged.

ionized layers. . Layers of charged particles existing in the upper reaches of the atmosphere as a result of solar radiation.

ionosphere. , *n.* 1. The region of the atmosphere extending from about 40 to 250 miles above the earth's surface, in which there is appreciable ionization. The presence of charged particles in this region profoundly affects the propagation of certain electromagnetic radiation. 2. A region composed of highly ionized layers at varying heights above the surface of the earth which may cause the return to the earth of radio waves originating below these layers. See also D-LAYER, E-LAYER, F-LAYER, F1-LAYER, F2-LAYER.

ionospheric correction. . A correction for ionospheric refraction, a major potential source of error in all satellite radionavigation systems. Navigation errors can result from the effect of refraction on the measurement of the doppler shift and from the errors in the satellite's orbit if refraction is not accurately accounted for in the satellite tracking. The refraction contribution can be eliminated by the proper mixing of the received Doppler shift from two harmonically related frequencies to yield an accurate estimate of the vacuum doppler shift. Also called REFRACTION CORRECTION.

ionospheric delay. . The delay experienced by a wave or signal as it passes through the ionosphere.

ionospheric disturbance. . A sudden outburst of ultraviolet light on the sun, known as a SOLAR FLARE or CHROMOSPHERIC ERUPTION, which produces abnormally high ionization in the region of the D-layer. The result is a sudden increase in radio wave absorption, with particular severity in the upper medium frequencies and lower high frequencies. It has negligible effects on the heights of the reflecting/refracting layers and, consequently, upon critical frequencies, but enormous transmission losses may occur. See also SUDDEN IONOSPHERIC DISTURBANCE.

ionospheric error. . The total systematic and random error resulting from the reception of a navigation signal after ionospheric reflections. It may be due to variations in transmission paths, non-uniform height of the ionosphere, or non-uniform propagation within the ionosphere. Also called IONOSPHERIC-PATH ERROR, SKYWAVE ERROR.

ionospheric-path error. . See IONOSPHERIC ERROR.

ionospheric storm. . An ionospheric disturbance characterized by wide variations from normal in the state of the ionosphere, such as turbulence in the F-region, absorption increase, height increase, and ionization density decreases. The effects are most marked in high magnetic latitudes and are associated with abnormal solar activity.

ionospheric refraction. . Change in the propagation speed of a signal as it passes through the ionosphere.

ionospheric wave. . See SKYWAVE.

iridescence. , *n.* Changing-color appearance, such as of a soap bubble, caused by interference of colors in a thin film or by diffraction.

iridescent clouds. . Ice-crystal clouds which exhibit brilliant spots or borders of colors, usually red and green, observed up to about 30° from the sun.

iridescent clouds

irisation, *n.* The coloration exhibited by iridescent clouds.

Irminger Current. . A North Atlantic Ocean current, one of the terminal branches of the Gulf Stream System (part of the northern branch of the North Atlantic Current); it flows toward the west off the southwest coast of Iceland. A small portion of the water of the Irminger Current bends around the west coast of Iceland but the greater amount turns south and becomes more or less mixed with the water of the East Greenland Current.

ironbound. , *adj.* Rugged, rocky, as an *ironbound coast.*

irradiation. , *n.* The apparent enlargement of a bright surface against a darker background.

irradiation correction. . A correction due to irradiation, particularly that sextant altitude correction caused by the apparent enlargement of the bright surface of a celestial body against the darker background of the sky.

irregular error. . See RANDOM ERROR.

irregular iceberg. . See PINNACLED ICEBERG.

isallobar. , *n.* A line of equal change in atmospheric pressure during a specified time interval.

isallotherm. , *n.* A line connecting points having the same anomalies of temperature, pressure, etc.

isanomal. , *n.* A line connecting points of equal variations from a normal value.

island. , *n.* An area of land not a continent, surrounded by water.

islet. , *n.* A very small and minor island.

iso-. . A prefix meaning equal.

isobar. , *n.* A line connecting points having the same atmospheric pressure reduced to a common datum, usually sea level.

isobaric. , *adj.* Having the same pressure.

isobaric chart. . See CONSTANT-PRESSURE CHART.

isobaric surface. . See CONSTANT-PRESSURE SURFACE.

isobath. , *n.* See DEPTH CONTOUR.

isobathic. , *adj.* Having equal depth.

isobathytherm. , *n.* A line on the earth's surface connecting points at which the same temperature occurs at some specified depth.

isobront. , *n.* A line connecting points at which some specified phase of a thunderstorm occurs at the same time.

isoceraunic, isokeraunic. , *adj.* Indicating or having equal frequency or intensity of thunderstorms.

isochasm. , *n.* A line connecting points having the same average frequency of auroras.

isochronal., *adj.* Of equal time; recurring at equal intervals of time. Also called ISOCHRONOUS.

isochrone., *n.* A line connecting points having the same time or time difference relationship, as a line representing all points having the same time difference in the reception of signals from two radio stations such as the master and slave stations of a Loran rate.

isochronize., *v., t.* To render isochronal.

isochronon., *n.* A clock designed to keep very accurate time.

isochronous., *adj.* See ISOCHRONAL.

isoclinal., *adj.* Of or pertaining to equal magnetic dip.

isoclinal., *n.* See ISOCLINIC LINE.

isoclinal chart.. See ISOCLINIC CHART.

isoclinic chart.. A chart of which the chief feature is a system of isoclinic lines. Also called ISOCLINAL CHART.

isoclinic line.. A line drawn through all points on the earth's surface having the same magnetic dip. The particular isoclinic line drawn through points of zero dip is called ACLINIC LINE. Also called ISOCLINAL.

isodynamic chart.. A chart showing isodynamic lines. See also MAGNETIC CHART.

isodynamic line.. A line connecting points of equal magnetic intensity, either the total or any component.

isogonal., *adj.* Having equal angles; isogonic.

isogonic., *adj.* Having equal angles; isogonal.

isogonic., *n.* A line connecting points of equal magnetic variation. Also called ISOGONIC LINE, ISOGONAL.

isogonic chart.. A chart showing magnetic variation with isogonic lines and the annual rate of change in variation with isoporic lines. See also MAGNETIC CHART.

isogonic line.. See ISOGONIC, *n.*

isogram., *n.* That line, on a chart or diagram, connecting points of equal value of some phenomenon.

isogriv., *n.* A line drawn on a map or chart joining points of equal grivation.

isogriv chart.. A chart showing isogrivs. See also MAGNETIC CHART.

isohaline, isohalsine., *n.* A line connecting points of equal salinity in the ocean.

isolated danger mark (or buoy).. An IALA navigation aid marking a danger with clear water all around; it has a double ball topmark and is black with at least one red band. If lighted its characteristic is Fl(2).

isolated node.. In ECDIS an isolated zero-dimensional SPATIAL OBJECT that represents the geometric location of a point FEATURE.

isosceles, *adj.* Having two equal sides.

isosceles triangle.. A triangle having two of its sides equal.

isomagnetic., *adj;*. Of or pertaining to lines connecting points of equality in some magnetic element *t.*

isomagnetic., *n.* A line connecting points of equality in some magnetic element. Also called ISOMAGNETIC LINE.

isomagnetic chart.. A chart showing isomagnetics. See also MAGNETIC CHART.

isomagnetic line.. See ISOMAGNETIC, *n.*

isometric., *n.* Of or pertaining to equal measure.

isophase., *adj.* Referring to a light having a characteristic of equal intervals of light and darkness.

isopleth., *n.* 1. An isogram indicating the variation of an element with respect to two variables, one of which is usually the time of year. The other may be time of day, altitude, or some other variable. 2. A line on a map depicting points of constant value of a variable. Examples are contours, isobars, and isogons.

isopor., *n.* See ISOPORIC LINE.

isoporic chart.. A chart with lines connecting points of equal annual rate of change of any magnetic element. See also ISOPORIC LINE.

isoporic line.. A line connecting points of equal annual rate of change of any magnetic element. Also called ISOPOR. See also ISOGONIC.

isostasy., *n.* A supposed equality existing in vertical sections of the earth, whereby the weight of any column from the surface of the earth to a constant depth is approximately the same as that of any other column of equal area, the equilibrium being maintained by plastic flow of material from one part of the earth to another.

isotropic antenna.. A hypothetical antenna which radiates or receives equally well in all directions. Although such an antenna does not physically exist, it provides a convenient reference for expressing the directional properties of actual antennas. Also called UNIPOLE ANTENNA.

isotropic gain.. The gain of an antenna in a given direction when the reference antenna is an isotropic antenna isolated in space. Also called ABSOLUTE GAIN (of an antenna).

isthmus., *n.* A narrow strip of land connecting two larger portions of land. A submarine elevation joining two land areas and separating two basins or depressions by a depth less than that of the basins is called a submarine isthmus.

Issuing Authority., *n.* In ECDIS the official agency which issues nautical chart and updates including ENC's and ENC UPDATES.

J

Jacob's staff.. See CROSS-STAFF.

jamming., *n.* Intentional transmission or re-radiation of radio signals in such a way as to interfere with reception of desired signals by the intended receiver.

Janus configuration.. A term describing orientations of the beams of acoustic or electromagnetic energy employed with doppler navigation systems. The Janus configuration normally used with doppler sonar speed logs, navigators, and docking aids employs four beams of ultrasonic energy, displaced laterally 90° from each other, and each directed obliquely (30° from the vertical) from the ship's bottom, to obtain true ground speed in the fore and aft and athwartship directions. These speeds are measured as doppler frequency shifts in the reflected beams. Certain errors in data extracted from one beam tend to cancel the errors associated with the oppositely directed beam.

Japan Current.. See KUROSHIO.

jetsam., *n.* Articles that sink when thrown overboard, particularly those jettisoned for the purpose of lightening a vessel in distress. See also FLOTSAM, JETTISON, LAGAN.

jet stream.. Relatively strong winds (50 knots or greater) concentrated in a narrow stream in the atmosphere. It usually refers only to a quasi-horizontal stream of maximum winds imbedded in the middle latitude westerlies, and concentrated in the high troposphere.

jettison., *n.* To throw objects overboard, especially to lighten a craft in distress. Jettisoned objects that float are termed FLOTSAM; those that sink JETSAM; and heavy articles that are buoyed for future recovery, LAGAN. See also DERELICT.

jetty., *n.* A structure built out into the water to restrain or direct currents, usually to protect a river mouth or harbor entrance from silting, etc. See also GROIN; MOLE, definition 1.

jitter., *n.* A term used to describe the short-time instability of a signal. The instability may be in amplitude, phase, or both. The term is applied especially to signals reproduced on the screen of a cathode-ray tube.

joule., *n.* A derived unit of energy of work in the International System of Units; it is the work done when the point of application of 1 newton (that force which gives to a mass of 1 kilogram an acceleration of 1 meter per second, per second) moves a distance of 1 meter in the direction of the force.

Julian calendar.. A revision of the ancient calendar of the city of Rome, instituted in the Roman Empire by Julius Caesar in 46 B.C., which reached its final form in about 8 A.D. It consisted of years of 365 days, with an intercalary day every fourth year. The current Gregorian calendar is the same as the Julian calendar except that October 5, 1582, of the Julian calendar became October 15, 1582 of the Gregorian calendar. Furthermore, in the Gregorian calendar, only those centurial years which are divisible by 400 are leap years.

Julian day.. The number of each day, as reckoned consecutively since the beginning of the present Julian period on January 1, 4713 B.C. It is used primarily by astronomers to avoid confusion due to the use of different calendars at different times and places. The Julian day begins at noon, 12 hours later than the corresponding civil day. The day beginning at noon January 1, 2017, was Julian day 2,457,755.000000.

junction buoy. . A buoy which, when viewed from a vessel approaching from the open sea or in the same direction as the main stream of flood current, or in the direction established by appropriate authority, indicates the place at which two channels meet. See also BIFURCATION BUOY.

junction mark. . A navigation mark which, when viewed from a vessel approaching from the open sea or in the same direction as the main stream of flood current, or in the direction established by appropriate authority, indicates the place at which two channels meet. See also BIFURCATION MARK.

June solstice. . Summer solstice in the Northern Hemisphere.

Jupiter. , *n.* The navigational planet whose orbit lies between those of Mars and Saturn. Largest of the known planets.

Jutland Current. . A narrow and localized nontidal current off the coast of Denmark between longitudes 8°30'E and 10°30'E. It originates partly from the resultant counterclockwise flow in the tidal North Sea. The main cause, however, appears to be the winds which prevail from south through west to northwest over 50 percent of the time throughout the year and the transverse flows from the English coast toward the Skaggerak. The current retains the characteristics of a major nontidal current and flows northeastward along the northwest coast of Denmark at speeds ranging between 1.5 to 2.0 knots 75 to 100 percent of the time.

K

Kaléma. , *n.* A very heavy surf breaking on the Guinea coast during the winter, even when there is no wind.

Kalman filtering. . A statistical method for estimating the parameters of a dynamic system, using recursive techniques of estimation, measurement, weighting, and correction. Weighting is based on variances of the measurements and of the estimates. The filter acts to reduce the variance of the estimate with each measurement cycle. In navigation, the technique is used to refine the positions given by one or more electronic systems.

katabatic wind. . Any wind blowing down an incline. If the wind is warm, it is called a foehn; if cold, a fall wind. An ANABATIC WIND blows up an incline. Also called GRAVITY WIND.

kaver. , *n.* See CAVER.

kay. , *n.* See CAY.

K-band. . A radio-frequency band of 10,900 to 36,000 megahertz. See also FREQUENCY, FREQUENCY BAND.

kedge. , *v., t.* To move a vessel by carrying out an anchor, letting it go, and winching the ship to the anchor. See also WARP.

keeper. , *n.* A piece of magnetic material placed across the poles of a permanent magnet to assist in the maintenance of magnetic strength.

kelp. , *n.* 1. A family of seaweed found in cool to cold waters along rocky coasts, characterized by its extreme length. 2. Any large seaweed. 3. The ashes of seaweed.

kelvin. , *n.* The base unit of thermodynamic temperature in the International System of Units; it is the fraction 1/273.16 of the thermodynamic temperature of the triple point of water.

Kelvin temperature. . Temperature based upon a thermodynamic scale with its zero point at absolute zero (-273.16°C) and using Celsius degrees. Rankine temperature is based upon the Rankine scale starting at absolute zero (-459.69° F) and using Fahrenheit degrees.

Kennelly-Heaviside layer. . See under KENNELLY-HEAVISIDE REGION.

Kennelly-Heaviside region. . The region of the ionosphere, extending from approximately 40 to 250 miles above the earth's surface within which ionized layers form which may affect radio wave propagation. The E-layer, which is the lowest useful layer from the standpoint of wave propagation, is sometimes called KENNELLY-HEAVISIDE LAYER or, in some instances, simply the HEAVISIDE LAYER.

Kepler's laws. . The three empirical laws describing the motions of the planets in their orbits. These are: (1) The orbits of the planets are ellipses, with the sun at a common focus; (2) As a planet moves in its orbit, the line joining the planet and sun sweeps over equal areas in equal intervals of time; (3) The squares of the periods of revolution of any two planets are proportional to the cubes of their mean distances from the sun. Also called KEPLER'S PLANETARY LAWS.

Kepler's planetary laws. . See KEPLER'S LAWS.

key. , *n.* 1. See CAY. 2. In ECDIS, an identifier which establishes linkages, e.g. between different LAYERS, or FEATURES and ATTRIBUTES.

Keyhole Markup Language (KML). , *n.* A file format used to specify a set of geographical features for display in Google Earth, Google Maps, and Google Mobile, or any other 3D Earth browser. KML is one of a number of extended versions of XML (Extensible Markup Language).

Keyhole Markup Language Zipped (KMZ). A zipped KML file with a ".kmz" extension. When a KMZ file is unzipped, a single "doc.kml" is found along with any overlay and icon images referenced in the KML.

kick, *n.* 1. The distance a ship moves sidewise from the original course away from the direction of turn after the rudder is first put over. 2. The swirl of water toward the inside of the turn when the rudder is put over to begin the turn.

kilo-. . A prefix meaning one thousand (10^3).

kilobyte. . One thousand bytes of information in a computer.

kilocycle. , *n.* One thousand cycles, the term is often used as the equivalent of one thousand cycles per second.

kilogram. , *n.* 1. The base unit of mass in the International System of Units; it is equal to the mass of the international prototype of the kilogram, which is made of platinum-iridium and kept at the International Bureau of Weights and Measures. 2. One thousand grams exactly, or 2.204623 pounds, approximately.

kilometer. , *n.* One thousand meters; about 0.54 nautical mile, 0.62 U.S. Survey mile, or 3,281 feet.

kinetic energy. . Energy possessed by a body by virtue of its motion, in contrast with POTENTIAL ENERGY, that possessed by virtue of its position.

klaxon. , *n.* A diaphragm horn similar to a nautophone, but smaller, and sometimes operated by hand.

knik wind. A strong southeast wind in the vicinity of Palmer, Alaska, most frequent in the winter.

knoll, *n.* 1. On the sea floor, an elevation rising generally more than 500 meters and less than 1,000 meters and of limited extent across the summit. 2. A small rounded hill.

knot. , *n.* A unit of speed equal to 1 nautical mile per hour.

Kona storm. . A storm over the Hawaiian Islands, characterized by strong southerly or southwesterly winds and heavy rains.

Krassowski ellipsoid of 1938. . A reference ellipsoid of which the semimajor axis is 6,378,245 meters and the flattening of ellipticity equals 1/298.3.

Kuroshio. , *n.* A North Pacific Ocean current flowing northeastward from Taiwan to the Ryukyu Islands and close to the coast of Japan. The Kuroshio is the northward flowing part of the Pacific North Equatorial Current (which divides east of the Philippines). The Kuroshio divides near Yaku Shima, the weaker branch flowing northward through the Korea Strait and the stronger branch flowing through Tokara Kaikyo and then along the south coast of Shikoku. There are light seasonal variations in speed; the Kuroshio is usually strongest in summer, weakens in autumn, strengthens in winter, and weakens in spring. Strong winds can accelerate or retard the current but seldom change its direction. Beyond latitude 35°N on the east coast of Japan, the current turns east-northeastward to form the transitional KUROSHIO EXTENSION. The Kuroshio is part of the KUROSHIO SYSTEM. Also called JAPAN CURRENT.

Kuroshio Extension. . The transitional, eastward flowing ocean current that connects the Kuroshio and the North Pacific Current.

Kuroshio System. . A system of ocean currents which includes part of the Pacific North Equatorial Current, the Tsushima Current, the Kuroshio, and the Kuroshio Extension.

kymatology. , *n.* The science of waves and wave motion.

L

L-1 Signal. , The primary L-band signal transmitted by each GPS satellite at 1572.42 MHz. It is modulated with the C/A and P codes and the navigation message.

L-2 Signal. , The second L-band signal of the GPS satellite, transmitted at 1227.60 MHz, modulated with the P-code and navigation message.

label/code., In ECDIS, a group of related information displayed as a whole.

labor., *v., i.* To pitch and roll heavily under conditions which subject the ship to unusually heavy stresses caused by confused or turbulent seas or unstable stowage of cargo.

Labrador Current. Originating from cold arctic water flowing southeastward through the Davis Strait at speeds of 0.2 to 0.5 knot and from a westward branching of the warmer West Greenland Current, the Labrador Current flows south eastward along the shelf of the Canadian coast. Part of the current flows into Hudson Strait along its north shore. The outflow of fresh water along the south shore of the strait augments the part of the current flowing along the Labrador coast. The current also appears to be influenced by surface outflow from inlets and fjords along the Labrador coast. The mean speed is about 0.5 knot, but current speed at times may reach 1.5 to 2.0 knots.

Labrador Current Extension.. A name sometimes given to the nontidal current flowing southwestward along the northeast coast of the United States. This coastal current originates from part of the Labrador Current flowing clockwise around the southeastern tip of Newfoundland. Its speeds are fairly constant throughout the year and average about 0.6 knot. The greatest seasonal fluctuation appears to be in the width of the current. The current is widest during winter between Newfoundland and Cape Cod. Southwest of Cape Cod to Cape Hatteras the current shows very little seasonal change. The current narrows considerably during summer and flows closest to shore in the vicinity of Cape Sable, Nova Scotia and between Cape Cod and Long Island in July and August. The current in some places encroaches on tidal regions.

lagan., *n.* A heavy object thrown overboard and buoyed to mark its location for future recovery. See also JETTISON.

lag error.. Error in the reading of an instrument due to lag.

lagging of tide.. The periodic retardation in the time of occurrence of high and low water due to changes in the relative positions of the moon and the sun. See also PRIMING OF TIDE.

lagoon., *n.* 1. A shallow sound, pond, or lake generally separated from the open sea. 2. A body of water enclosed by the reefs and islands of an atoll.

Lagrangian current measurement.. The direct observation of the current speed or direction, or both, by a recording device such as a parachute drogue which follows the movement of a water mass through the ocean. See also EULERIAN CURRENT MEASUREMENT.

lake., *n.* 1. A standing body of inland water, generally of considerable size. There are exceptions such as the lakes in Louisiana which are open to or connect with the Gulf of Mexico. Occasionally a lake is called a SEA, especially if very large and composed of salt water. 2. An expanded part of a river.

lake ice.. Ice formed on a lake.

Lambert conformal chart.. A chart on the Lambert conformal projection. See also CONIC CHART WITH TWO STANDARD PARALLELS, MODIFIED LAMBERT CONFORMAL CHART.

Lambert conformal map projection.. A conformal map projection of the conic type, on which all geographic meridians are represented by straight lines which meet in a common point outside the limits of the map, and the geographic parallels are represented by a series of arcs of circles having this common point for a center. Meridians and parallels intersect at right angles, and angles on the earth are correctly represented on the projection. This projection may have one standard parallel along which the scale is held exact; or there may be two such standard parallels, both maintaining exact scale. At any point on the map, the scale is the same in every direction. The scale changes along the meridians and is constant along each parallel. Where there are two standard parallels, the scale between those parallels is too small; beyond them, too large. See also MODIFIED LAMBERT CONFORMAL MAP PROJECTION.

laminar flow.. See under STREAMLINE FLOW.

land., *v., t. & i.* To bring a vessel to a landing.

land breeze.. A breeze blowing from the land to the sea. It usually blows by night, when the sea is warmer than the land, and alternates with a SEA BREEZE, which blows in the opposite direction by day. See also OFFSHORE WIND.

landfall., *n.* The first sighting of land when approached from seaward. By extension, the term is sometimes used to refer to the first contact with land by any means, as by radar.

landfall buoy.. See SEA BUOY.

landfall light.. See PRIMARY SEACOAST LIGHT.

landing., *n.* 1. A place where boats receive or discharge passengers, freight, etc. See also LANDING STAGE, WHARF. 2. Bringing of a vessel to a landing.

landing compass.. A compass taken ashore so as to be unaffected by deviation. If reciprocal bearings of the landing compass and the magnetic compass on board are observed, the deviation of the latter can be determined.

landing stage.. A platform attached to the shore for landing or embarking passengers or cargo. In some cases the outer end of the landing stage is floating. Ships can moor alongside larger landing stages.

landmark., *n.* A conspicuous artificial feature on land, other than an established aid to navigation, which can be used as an aid to navigation. See also SEA MARK.

land mile.. See MILE.

land sky.. Dark streaks or patches or a grayness on the underside of extensive cloud areas, due to the absence of reflected light from bare ground. Land sky is not as dark as WATER SKY. The clouds above ice or snow covered surfaces have a white or yellowish white glare called ICE BLINK. See also SKY MAP.

lane., *n.* In any continuous wave phase comparison system, the distance between two successive equiphase lines, taken as 0°–360°, in a system of hyperbolic or circular coordinates.

lane count.. An automatic method of counting and totaling the number of hyperbolic or circular lanes traversed by a moving vessel.

language.. A set of characters and rules which allow human interface with the computer, allowing PROGRAMS to be written.

lapse rate.. The rate of decrease of temperature in the atmosphere with height, or, sometimes, the rate of change of any meteorological element with height.

large fracture.. See under FRACTURE.

large iceberg.. For reports to the International Ice Patrol, an iceberg that extends more than 150 feet (45 meters) above the sea surface and which has a length of more than 400 feet (122 meters). See also SMALL ICEBERG, MEDIUM ICEBERG.

large ice field.. See under ICE FIELD.

large navigational buoy (LNB).. A large buoy designed to take the place of a lightship where construction of an offshore light station is not feasible. These buoys may show secondary lights from heights of about 30–40 feet above the water. In addition to the light, they may mount a radiobeacon and provide sound signals. A station buoy may be moored nearby.

large scale.. A scale involving a relatively small reduction in size. A large-scale chart is one covering a small area. The opposite is SMALL SCALE. See also REPRESENTATIVE FRACTION.

last quarter.. The phase of the moon when it is near west quadrature, when the eastern half of it is visible to an observer on the earth. See also PHASES OF THE MOON.

latent heat of fusion.. See under FUSION.

latent heat of vaporization.. See under EVAPORATION.

lateral., *adj.* Of or pertaining to the side, such as lateral motion.

lateral drifting.. See SWAY.

lateral mark.. A navigation aid intended to mark the sides of a channel or waterway. See CARDINAL MARK.

lateral sensitivity.. The property of a range which determines the rapidity with which the two lights of the range open up as a vessel moves laterally from the range line, indicating to the mariner that he is off the center line.

lateral system.. A system of aids to navigation in which the shape, color, and number are assigned in accordance with their location relative to navigable waters. When used to mark a channel, they are assigned colors to indicate the side they mark and numbers to indicate their sequence along the channel. In the CARDINAL SYSTEM the aids are assigned shape, color, and number distinction in accordance with location relative to obstructions.

latitude., *n.* Angular distance from a primary great circle or plane. Terrestrial latitude is angular distance from the equator, measured northward or southward through 90° and labeled N or S to indicate the direction of measurement; astronomical latitude at a station is angular distance between the plumb line and the plane of the celestial equator; geodetic or topographical latitude at a station is angular distance between the plane of the geodetic equator and a normal to the ellipsoid; geocentric latitude is the angle at the center of the reference ellipsoid between the celestial equator and a radius vector to a point on the ellipsoid. Geodetic and sometimes astronomical latitude are also called geographic latitude. Geodetic latitude is used for charts. Assumed (or chosen) latitude is the latitude at which an observer is assumed to be located for an observation or computation. Observed latitude is determined by one or more lines of position extending in a generally east-west direction. Fictitious latitude is angular distance from a fictitious equator. Grid latitude is angular distance from a grid equator. Transverse or inverse latitude is angular distance from a transverse equator. Oblique latitude is angular distance from an oblique equator. Middle or mid-latitude is the latitude at which the arc length of the parallel separating the meridians passing through two specific points is exactly equal to the departure in proceeding from one point to the other by middle-latitude sailing. Mean latitude is half the arithmetical sum of the latitude of two places on the same side of the equator. The mean latitude is usually used in middle-latitude sailing for want of a practical means of determining middle latitude. Difference of latitude is the shorter arc of any meridian between the parallels of two places, expressed in angular measure. Magnetic latitude, magnetic inclination, or magnetic dip is angular distance between the horizontal and the direction of a line of force of the earth's magnetic field at any point. Geomagnetic latitude is angular distance from the geomagnetic equator. A parallel of latitude is a circle (or approximation of a circle) of the earth, parallel to the equator, and connecting points of equal latitude - or a circle of the celestial sphere, parallel to the ecliptic. Celestial latitude is angular distance north or south of the ecliptic. See also VARIATION OF LATITUDE.

latitude factor. . The change in latitude along a celestial line of position per 1' change in longitude. The change in longitude for a 1' change in latitude is called LONGITUDE FACTOR.

latitude line. . A line of position extending in a generally east-west direction. Sometimes called OBSERVED LATITUDE. See also LONGITUDE LINE; COURSE LINE, definition 2; SPEED LINE.

lattice. , *n.* A pattern formed by two or more families of intersecting lines, such as that pattern formed by two or more families of hyperbolas representing, for example, curves of equal time difference associated with a hyperbolic radionavigation system. Sometimes the term *pattern* is used to indicate curves of equal time difference, with the term *lattice* being used to indicate its representation on the chart. See also PATTERN, definition 2.

lattice beacon. . A beacon or daymark in the form of a lattice. See also BEACON TOWER.

laurence. , *n.* A shimmering seen over a hot surface on a calm, cloudless day, caused by the unequal refraction of light by innumerable convective air columns of different temperatures and densities.

lava. , *n.* Rock in the fluid state, or such material after it has solidified. Lava is formed at very high temperature and issues from the earth through volcanoes. Part of the ocean bed is composed of lava.

law of equal areas. . Kepler's second law.

layer tints. . See HYPSOMETRIC TINTING.

L-band. . A radio-frequency band of 390 to 1,550 megahertz. See also FREQUENCY, FREQUENCY BAND.

lead. , *n.* A fracture or passageway through ice which is navigable by surface vessels.

lead. , *n.* A weight attached to a line. A sounding lead is used for determining depth of water. A hand lead is a light sounding lead (7 to 14 pounds), usually having a line of not more than 25 fathoms. A deep sea lead is a heavy sounding lead (about 30 to 100 pounds), usually having a line 100 fathoms or more in length. A light deep sea lead (30 to 50 pounds), used for sounding depths of 20 to 60 fathoms is called a coasting lead. A type of sounding lead used without removal from the water between soundings is called a fish lead. A drift lead is one placed on the bottom to indicate movement of a vessel.

leader cable. . A cable carrying an electric current, signals from or the magnetic influence of which indicates the path to be followed by a craft equipped with suitable instruments.

leading lights. . See RANGE LIGHTS.

leading line. . On a nautical chart, a straight line drawn through leading marks. A ship moving along such line will clear certain dangers or remain in the best channel. See also RANGE, definition, *n.* 1.

leading marks. . See RANGE, *n.* definition 1.

lead line. . A line, graduated with attached marks and fastened to a sounding lead, used for determining the depth of water when making soundings by hand. The lead line is usually used in depths of less than 25 fathoms. Also called SOUNDING LINE.

leadsman. , *n.* A person using a sounding lead to determine depth of water.

leap second. . A step adjustment to Coordinated Universal Time (UTC) to maintain it within 0.95^s of UT1. The 1 second adjustments, when necessary, are normally made at the end of June or December. Because of the variations in the rate of rotation of the earth, the occurrences of the leap second adjustments are not predictable in detail.

leap year. . A calendar year having 366 days as opposed to the COMMON YEAR having 365 days. Each year exactly divisible by 4 is a leap year, except century years (1800, 1900, etc.) which must be exactly divisible by 400 (2000, 2400, etc.) to be leap years.

least squares adjustment. . A statistical method of adjusting observations in which the sum of the squares of all the deviations or residuals derived in fitting the observations to a mathematical model is made a minimum.

ledge. , *n.* On the sea floor, a rocky projection or datum outcrop, commonly linear and near shore.

lee. , *adj.* Referring to the downwind, or sheltered side of an object.

lee. , *n.* The sheltered area on the downwind side of an object.

lee shore. . As observed from a ship, the shore towards which the wind is blowing. See also WEATHER SHORE.

lee side. . That side of a craft which is away from the wind and therefore sheltered.

lee tide. . See LEEWARD TIDAL CURRENT.

leeward. , *adj. & adv.* Toward the lee, or in the general direction toward which the wind is blowing. The opposite is WINDWARD.

leeward. , *n.* The lee side. The opposite is WINDWARD.

leeward tidal current. . A tidal current setting in the same direction as that in which the wind is blowing. Also called LEE TIDE, LEEWARD TIDE.

leeward tide. . See LEEWARD TIDAL CURRENT.

leeway. , *n.* The leeward motion of a vessel due to wind. See also LEEWAY ANGLE.

leeway angle. . The angular difference between a vessel's course and the track due to the effect of wind in moving a vessel bodily to leeward. See also DRIFT ANGLE, definition 2.

left bank. . The bank of a stream or river on the left of an observer facing downstream.

leg. , *n.* 1. A part of a ship's track line that can be represented by a single course line. 2. In ECDIS a line connecting two WAYPOINTS.

legend. , *n.* A title or explanation on a chart, diagram, illustration, etc.

lens. , *n.* A piece of glass or transparent material with plane, convex, or concave surfaces adapted for changing the direction of light rays to enlarge or reduce the apparent size of objects. See also EYEPIECE; FIELD LENS, MENISCUS, definition 2. OBJECTIVE.

lenticular, lenticularis. , *adj.* In the shape of a lens, used to refer to an apparently stationary cloud resembling a lens, being broad in its middle and tapering at the ends and having a smooth appearance. Actually, the cloud continually forms to windward and dissipates to leeward.

lesser ebb. . See under EBB CURRENT.

lesser flood. . See under FLOOD CURRENT.

leste. , *n.* A hot, dry, easterly wind of the Madeira and Canary Islands.

levanter. , *n.* A strong easterly wind of the Mediterranean, especially in the Strait of Gibraltar, attended by cloudy, foggy, and sometimes rainy weather especially in winter.

levantera. , *n.* A persistent east wind of the Adriatic, usually accompanied by cloudy weather.

levanto. , *n.* A hot southeasterly wind which blows over the Canary Islands.

leveche. , *n.* A warm wind in Spain, either a foehn or a hot southerly wind in advance of a low pressure area moving from the Sahara Desert. Called a SIROCCO in other parts of the Mediterranean area.

levee. , *n.* 1. An artificial bank confining a stream channel or limiting adjacent areas subject to flooding. 2. On the sea floor, an embankment bordering a canyon, valley, or sea channel.

levee

level ice. Sea ice which is unaffected by deformation.

leveling. , *n.* A survey operation in which heights of objects are determined relative to a specified datum.

libration. , *n.* A real or apparent oscillatory motion, particularly the apparent oscillation of the moon, which results in more than half of the moon's surface being revealed to an observer on the earth, even though the same side of the moon is always toward the earth.

light. , *adj.* 1. Of or pertaining to low speed, such as light air, force 1 (1-3 knots or 1-3 miles per hour) on the Beaufort scale or light breeze, force 2 (4-7 knots or 4-7 miles per hour) on the Beaufort scale. 2. Of or pertaining to low intensity, as light rain, light fog, etc.

light. , *n.* 1. Luminous energy. 2. An apparatus emitting light of distinctive character for use as an aid to navigation.

light air. . Wind of force 1 (1-3 knots or 1-3 miles per hour) on the Beaufort wind scale.

light attendant station. . A shore unit established for the purpose of servicing minor aids to navigation within an assigned area.

light-beacon. , *n.* See LIGHTED BEACON.

light breeze. . Wind of force 2 (4-6 knots or 4-7 miles per hour) on the Beaufort wind scale.

lighted beacon. . A beacon exhibiting a light. Also called LIGHT-BEACON.

lighted buoy. . A buoy exhibiting a light.

lighted sound buoy. . See SOUND BUOY.

lightering area. . An area designated for handling ship's cargo by barge or lighter.

light-float. , *n.* A buoy having a boat-shaped body. Light-floats are usually unmanned and are used instead of smaller lighted buoys in waters where strong currents are experienced.

lighthouse. , *n.* A distinctive structure exhibiting a major navigation light.

light list. . 1. A publication giving detailed information regarding lighted navigational aids and fog signals. In the United States, light lists are published by the U.S. Coast Guard and the National Geospatial-Intelligence Agency.

light list number. . The sequential number used to identify a navigational light in the light list. This may or may not be the same as the INTERNATIONAL NUMBER.

light nilas. . Nilas which is more than 5 centimeters in thickness and somewhat lighter in color than dark nilas.

light sector. . As defined by bearings from seaward, the sector in which a navigational light is visible or in which it has a distinctive color different from that of adjoining sectors, or in which it is obscured. See also SECTOR LIGHT.

lightship. , *n.* A distinctively marked vessel providing aids to navigation services similar to a light station, i.e., a light of high intensity and reliability, sound signal, and radiobeacon are moored at a station where erection of a fixed structure is not feasible. Most lightships are anchored to a very long scope of chain and, as a result, the radius of their swinging circle is considerable. The chart symbol represents the approximate location of the anchor. Also called LIGHT VESSEL. See also LIGHT-FLOAT.

lights in line. . Two or more lights so situated that when observed in transit they define the alignment of a submarine cable, the limit of an area, an alignment for use in anchoring, etc. Not to be confused with RANGE LIGHTS which mark a direction to be followed. See also RANGE, definition 1.

light station. . A manned station providing a light usually of high intensity and reliability. It may also provide sound signal and radiobeacon services.

light vessel. . See LIGHTSHIP.

light-year. , *n.* A unit of length equal to the distance light travels in 1 year, equal to about 5.88 x 10^{12} miles. This unit is used as a measure of stellar distances.

liman. , *n.* A shallow coastal lagoon or embayment with a muddy bottom; also a region of mud or slime deposited near a stream mouth.

Liman Current. . Formed by part of the Tsushima Current and river discharge in the Tatar Strait, the coastal Liman Current flows southward in the western part of the Sea of Japan. During winter, it may reach as far south as 35°N. See also under TSUSHIMA CURRENT.

limb. , *n.* 1. The graduated, curved part of an instrument for measuring angles, such as the part of a marine sextant carrying the altitude scale, or ARC. 2. The circular outer edge of a celestial body, usually referred to with the designation upper or lower.

limbo echo. . See CLASSIFICATION OF RADAR ECHOES.

line. , *n.* 1. A series of related points, the path of a moving point. A line has only one dimension, which is length. 2. A row of letters, numbers, etc. 3. A mark of division or demarcation, as a *boundary line*. 4. In ECDIS, a one-dimensional GEOMETRIC PRIMITIVE of an OBJECT.

linear. , *adj.* 1. Of or pertaining to a line. 2. Having a relation such that a change in one quantity is accompanied by an exactly proportional change in a related quantity.

linear interpolation. . Interpolation in which changes of tabulated values are assumed to be proportional to changes in entering arguments.

linear light. . A luminous signal having perceptible length, as contrasted with a POINT LIGHT, which does not have perceptible length.

linearly polarized wave. . A transverse electromagnetic wave, the electric field vector of which lies along a fixed line at all times.

linear scale. . A scale graduated at uniform intervals.

linear speed. . Rate of motion in a straight line. See also ANGULAR SPEED.

linear sweep. . Short for LINEAR TIME BASE SWEEP.

linear time base. . A time base having a constant speed, particularly a linear time base sweep.

linear time base sweep. . A sweep having a constant sweep speed before retrace. Usually shortened to LINEAR SWEEP, and sometimes to LINEAR TIME BASE.

line blow. . A strong wind on the equator side of an anticyclone, probably so called because there is little shifting of wind direction during the blow, as contrasted with the marked shifting which occurs with a cyclonic windstorm.

line of apsides. . The line connecting the two points of an orbit that are nearest and farthest from the center of attraction, such as the perigee and apogee of the moon or the perihelion and aphelion of a planet. Also called APSE LINE.

line of force. . A line indicating the direction in which a force acts, as in a magnetic field.

line of nodes. . The straight line connecting the two points of intersection of the orbit of a planet, planetoid, or comet and the ecliptic; or the line of intersection of the planes of the orbits of a satellite and the equator of its primary.

line of position. . A plotted line on which a vessel is located, determined by observation or measurement. Also called POSITION LINE.

line of sight. . The straight line between two points, which does not follow the curvature of the earth.

line of soundings. . A series of soundings obtained by a vessel underway, usually at regular intervals. In piloting, this information may be used to determine an estimated position, by recording the soundings at appropriate intervals (to the scale of the chart) along a line drawn on transparent paper or plastic to represent the track, and then fitting the plot to the chart, by trial and error. A vessel obtaining soundings along a course line, for use in making or improving a chart, is said to run *a line of soundings*.

line of total force. . The direction of a freely suspended magnetic needle when acted upon by the earth's magnetic field alone.

line squall. . A squall that occurs along a squall line.

lipper. , *n.* 1. Slight ruffling or roughness on a water surface. 2. Light spray from small waves.

liquid compass. . A magnetic compass of which the bowl mounting the compass card is completely filled with liquid. Nearly all modern magnetic compasses are of this type. An older liquid compass using a solution of alcohol and water is sometimes called a SPIRIT COMPASS. Also called WET COMPASS. See also DRY COMPASS.

list. , *n.* Inclination to one side. LIST generally implies equilibrium in an inclined condition caused by uneven distribution of mass aboard the vessel itself, while HEEL implies either a continuing or momentary inclination caused by an outside force, such as the wind. The term ROLL refers to the oscillatory motion of a vessel rather than its inclined condition.

list. , *v., t. & i.* To incline or be inclined to one side.

lithometeor. , *n.* The general term for dry atmospheric suspensoids, including dust, haze, smoke, and sand. See also HYDROMETEOR.

little brother. . A secondary tropical cyclone sometimes following a more severe disturbance.

littoral. , *adj. & n.* 1. A littoral region. 2. The marine environment influenced by a land mass. 3. Of or pertaining to a shore, especially a seashore. See also SEABOARD.

load line marks. . Markings stamped and painted amidships on the side of a vessel, to indicate the minimum permissible freeboard. Also called PLIMSOLL MARKS. See also DRAFT MARKS.

lobe. , *n.* 1. The portion of the overall radiation pattern of a directional antenna which is contained within a region bounded by adjacent minima. The main beam is the beam in the lobe containing the direction of maximum radiation (main lobe) lying within specified values of field strength relative to the maximum field strength. See also BACK LOBE, SIDE LOBE, BEAM WIDTH 2. The radiation within the region of definition 1.

local apparent noon. . Twelve o'clock local apparent time, or the instant the apparent sun is over the upper branch of the local meridian. Local apparent noon at the Greenwich meridian is called Greenwich apparent noon. Sometimes called HIGH NOON.

local apparent time. . The arc of the celestial equator, or the angle at the celestial pole, between the lower branch of the local celestial meridian and the hour circle of the apparent or true sun, measured westward from the lower branch of the local celestial meridian through 24 hours; local hour angle of the apparent or true sun, expressed in time units, plus 12 hours. Local apparent time at the Greenwich meridian is called Greenwich apparent time.

local attraction. . See LOCAL MAGNETIC DISTURBANCE.

local civil noon. . *United States terminology from 1925 through 1952.* See LOCAL MEAN NOON.

local civil time. . United States terminology from 1925 through 1952. See LOCAL MEAN TIME.

local hour angle (LHA). . Angular distance west of the local celestial meridian; the arc of the celestial equator, or the angle at the celestial pole, between the upper branch of the local celestial meridian and the hour circle of a point on the celestial sphere, measured westward from the local celestial meridian through 360°. The local hour angle at longitude 0° is called Greenwich hour angle.

local knowledge. . The term applied to specialized, detailed knowledge of a port, harbor, or other navigable water considered necessary for safe navigation. Local knowledge extends beyond that available in charts and publications, being more detailed, intimate, and current.

local lunar time. . The arc of the celestial equator, or the angle at the celestial pole, between the lower branch of the local celestial meridian and the hour circle of the moon, measured westward from the lower branch of the local celestial meridian through 24 hours; local hour angle of the moon, expressed in time units, plus 12 hours. Local lunar time at the Greenwich meridian is called Greenwich lunar time.

local magnetic disturbance. An anomaly of the magnetic field of the earth, extending over a relatively small area, due to local magnetic influences. Also called LOCAL ATTRACTION, MAGNETIC ANOMALY.

local mean noon. Twelve o'clock local mean time, or the instant the mean sun is over the upper branch of the local meridian. Local mean noon at the Greenwich meridian is called Greenwich mean noon.

local mean time. The arc of the celestial equator, or the angle at the celestial pole, between the lower branch of the local celestial meridian and the hour circle of the mean sun, measured westward from the lower branch of the local celestial meridian through 24 hours; local hour angle of the mean sun, expressed in time units, plus 12 hours. Local mean time at the Greenwich meridian is called Greenwich mean time, or Universal Time.

local meridian. The meridian through any particular place of observer, serving as the reference for local time, in contrast with GREENWICH MERIDIAN.

local noon. Noon at the local meridian.

***Local Notice to Mariners*.** A notice issued by each U.S. Coast Guard District to disseminate important information affecting navigational safety within the District. The *Local Notice* reports changes to and deficiencies in aids to navigation maintained by and under the authority of the U.S. Coast Guard. Other information includes channel depths, new charts, naval operations, regattas, etc. Since temporary information, known or expected to be of short duration, is not included in the weekly *Notice to Mariners* published by the National Geospatial-Intelligence Agency, the appropriate *Local Notice to Mariners* may be the only source of such information. Much of the information contained in the *Local Notice to Mariners* is included in the weekly *Notice to Mariners*. The *Local Notice to Mariners* is published as often as required; usually weekly and available on the USCG Navigation Center (NAVCEN) website.

local oscillator. An oscillator used to drive an intermediate frequency by beating with the signal carrying frequency in superheterodyne reception.

local sidereal noon. Zero hours local sidereal time, or the instant the vernal equinox is over the upper branch of the local meridian. Local sidereal noon at the Greenwich meridian is called Greenwich sidereal noon.

local sidereal time. Local hour angle of the vernal equinox, expressed in time units; the arc of the celestial equator, or the angle at the celestial pole, between the upper branch of the local celestial meridian and the hour circle of the vernal equinox, measured westward from the upper branch of the local celestial meridian through 24 hours. Local sidereal time at the Greenwich meridian is called Greenwich sidereal time.

local time. 1. Time based upon the local meridian as reference, as contrasted with that based upon a standard meridian. Local time was in general use in the United States until 1883, when standard time was adopted. 2. Any time kept locally.

local update. In ECDIS a generic term used to indicate all update information other than OFFICIAL UPDATES, regardless of source; for application as a MANUAL UPDATE only as opposed to automatic updates.

local vertical. The direction of the acceleration of gravity as opposed to the normal to the reference ellipsoid. It is in the direction of the resultant of the gravitational and centrifugal accelerations of the earth at the location of the observer. Also called PLUMB-BOB VERTICAL. See also MASS ATTRACTION VERTICAL.

loch, *n.* 1. A lake. 2. An arm of the sea, especially when nearly landlocked.

lock, *n.* 1. A basin in a waterway with caissons or gates at each end by means of which vessels are passed from one water level to another.

lock

lock, *v. t.* To pass through a lock, referred to as *locking through.*

lock on. To identify and begin to continuously track a target in one or more coordinates (e.g., range, bearing, elevation).

locus, *n.* All possible positions of a point or curve satisfying stated conditions.

log, *n.* 1. An instrument for measuring the speed or distance or both traveled by a vessel. A chip log (ancient) consists essentially of a weighted wooden quadrant (quarter of a circle) attached to a bridle in such a manner that it will float in a vertical position, and a line with equally spaced knots. A mechanical means of determining speed or distance is called a patent log. A harpoon log consists essentially of a combined rotator and distance registering device towed through the water. This has been largely replaced by the taffrail log, a somewhat similar device but with the registering unit secured at the taffrail. A Pitometer log consists essentially of a Pitot tube projecting into the water, and suitable registering devices. An electromagnetic log consists of suitable registering devices and an electromagnetic sensing element, extended below the hull of a vessel, which produces a voltage directly proportional to speed through the water. A Forbes log consists of a small rotator in a tube projecting below the bottom of the vessel, and suitable registering devices. A Dutchman's log is a buoyant object thrown overboard, the speed of a vessel being determined by noting the time required for a known length of the vessel to pass the object. 2. A written record of the movements of a craft, with regard to courses, speeds, positions, and other information of interest to navigators, and of important happenings aboard the craft. The book in which the log is kept is called a LOG BOOK. Also called DECK LOG. See also NIGHT ORDER BOOK 3. A written record of specific related information, as that concerning performance of an instrument. See GYRO LOG.

logarithm, *n.* The power to which a fixed number, called the base, usually 10 or *e* (2.7182818), must be raised to produce the value to which the logarithm corresponds. A logarithm (base 10) consists of two parts: the characteristic is that part to the left of the decimal point and the mantissa is that part to the right of the decimal point. An ANTILOGARITHM or INVERSE LOGARITHM is the value corresponding to a given logarithm. Logarithms are used to multiply or divide numbers, the sum or difference of the logarithms of two numbers being the logarithm of the product or quotient, respectively, of the two numbers. A COLOGARITHM is the logarithm of the reciprocal of a number. Logarithms to the base 10 are called common or Briggsian and those to the base *e* are called natural or Napierian logarithms.

logarithmic, *adj.* Having to do with a logarithm, used with the name of a trigonometric function to indicate that the value given is the logarithm of that function, rather than the function itself which is called the natural trigonometric function.

logarithmic coordinate paper. Paper ruled with two sets of mutually-perpendicular, parallel lines spaced according to the logarithms of consecutive numbers, rather than the numbers themselves. On SEMILOGARITHMIC COORDINATE PAPER one set of lines is spaced logarithmically and the other set at uniform intervals.

logarithmic scale. A scale graduated in the logarithms of uniformly-spaced consecutive numbers.

logarithmic tangent. See under TANGENT, definition 1.

logarithmic trigonometric function. See under TRIGONOMETRIC FUNCTIONS.

log book. See LOG, definition 2.

log chip. The wooden quadrant forming part of a chip log. Also called LOG SHIP.

log file. In ECDIS a record of nautical information, including time of application and identification parameters.

log glass. A small hour glass used to time a chip log. The period most frequently used is 28 seconds.

log line. 1. A graduated line used to measure the speed of a vessel through the water or to measure the speed of a current, the line may be called a CURRENT LINE. 2. The line secured to a log.

long flashing light. A navigation light with a duration of flash of not less than 2 seconds.

longitude, *n.* Angular distance, along a primary great circle, from the adopted reference point. Terrestrial longitude is the arc of a parallel, or the angle at the pole, between the prime meridian and the meridian of a point on the earth measured eastward or westward from the prime meridian through 180°, and labeled E or W to indicate the direction of measurement. Astronomical longitude is the angle between the plane of the prime meridian and the plane of the celestial meridian; geodetic longitude is the angle between the plane of the geodetic meridian and a station and the plane of the geodetic meridian at Greenwich. Geodetic and sometimes astronomical longitude are also called geographic longitude. Geodetic longitude is used in charting. Assumed longitude is the longitude at which an observer is assumed to be located for an observation or computation. Observed longitude is determined by one or more lines of position extending in a generally north-south direction. Difference of longitude is the smaller angle at the pole or the shorter arc of a parallel between the meridians of two places, expressed in angular measure. Fictitious longitude is the arc of the fictitious equator between the prime fictitious meridian and any given fictitious meridian. Grid longitude is angular distance between a prime grid meridian and any given grid meridian. Oblique longitude is angular distance between a prime oblique meridian and any given oblique meridian. Transverse or inverse longitude is angular distance between a prime transverse meridian and any given meridian. Celestial longitude is angular distance east of the vernal equinox, along the ecliptic.

longitude factor. The change in longitude along a celestial line of position per 1' change in latitude. The change in latitude for a 1' change in longitude is called LATITUDE FACTOR.

longitude line. A line of position extending in a generally north-south direction. Sometimes called OBSERVED LONGITUDE. See also LATITUDE LINE; COURSE LINE, definition 2; SPEED LINE.

longitude method. The establishing of a line of position from the observation of the latitude of a celestial body by assuming a latitude (or longitude), and calculating the longitude (or latitude) through which the line of position passes, and the azimuth. The line of position is drawn through the point thus found, perpendicular to the azimuth. See also ST. HILAIRE METHOD, SUMNER METHOD, HIGH ALTITUDE METHOD.

longitude of Greenwich at time of perigee. See RIGHT ASCENSION OF GREENWICH AT TIME OF PERIGEE.

longitude of pericenter. An orbital element that specifies the orientation of an orbit; it is a broken angle consisting of the angular distance in the ecliptic from the vernal equinox to the ascending node of the orbit plus the angular distance in the orbital plane from the ascending node to the pericenter, i.e. the sum of the longitude of the ascending node and the argument of pericenter.

longitude of the ascending node. 1. The angular distance in the ecliptic from the vernal equinox to the ascending node of the orbit. See also LONGITUDE OF PERICENTER, RIGHT ASCENSION OF THE ASCENDING NODE. 2. The angular distance, always measured eastward, in the plane of the celestial equator from Greenwich through 360°.

longitude of the moon's nodes. The angular distance along the ecliptic of the moon's nodes from the vernal equinox; the nodes have a retrograde motion, and complete a cycle of 360° in approximately 19 years.

longitudinal axis. The fore-and-aft line through the center of gravity of a craft, around which it rolls.

longitudinal wave. A wave in which the vibration is in the direction of propagation, as in sound waves. This is in contrast with a TRANSVERSE WAVE, in which the vibration is perpendicular to the direction of propagation.

long path interference. See under MULTIPATH ERROR.

long period constituent. A tidal or tidal current constituent with a period that is independent of the rotation of the earth but which depends upon the orbital movement of the moon or of the earth. The principal lunar long period constituents have periods approximating the month and half-month, and the principal solar long period constituents have periods approximating the year and half-year.

long period perturbations. Periodic eccentricities in the orbit of a planet or satellite which require more than one orbital period to execute one complete periodic variation.

long range systems. Radionavigation systems providing positioning capability on the high seas. See also SHORT RANGE SYSTEMS.

longshore current. A current paralleling the shore largely within the surf zone. It is caused by the excess water brought to the zone by the small net mass transport of wind waves. Longshore currents feed into rip currents.

look angles. The elevation and azimuth at which a particular satellite is predicted to be found at a specified time.

lookout station. A label on a nautical chart which indicates a tower surmounted by a small house from which a watch is kept regularly.

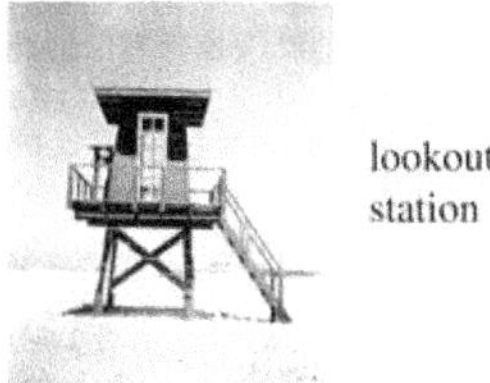

lookout station

look-up table. In ECDIS, a table giving symbology instructions to link SENC objects to point, line or area symbolization, and providing DISPLAY PRIORITY, radar priority, IMO category and optional viewing group.

loom, *n.* The diffused glow observed from a light below the horizon, due to atmospheric scattering.

looming, *n.* 1. An apparent elevation of distant terrestrial objects by abnormal atmospheric refraction. Because of looming, objects below the horizon are sometimes visible. The opposite is SINKING. 2. The appearance indistinctly of an object during a period of low visibility.

loop antenna. A closed circuit antenna in the form of a loop, lying in the same plane, or of several loops lying in parallel planes.

loop of stationary wave. See under STATIONARY WAVE.

Loran, *n.* The general designation of a type of radionavigation system by which a hyperbolic line of position is determined through measuring the difference in the times of reception of synchronized signals from two fixed transmitters. The name Loran is derived from the words long range navigation.

Loran A, *n.* A long range medium frequency (1850 to 1950 kHz) radionavigation system by which a hyperbolic line of position of medium accuracy was obtained. System operation in U.S. waters was terminated on 31 December 1980. See also LORAN, HYPERBOLIC NAVIGATION.

Loran C, *n.* A long range, low frequency (90-110 kHz) radionavigation system by which a hyperbolic line of position of high accuracy was obtained by measuring the difference in the times of arrival of signals radiated by a pair of synchronized transmitters (master station and secondary station) which are separated by several hundred miles. The U.S. Coast Guard terminated the transmission of all U.S. LORAN-C signals on 08 Feb 2010. See also LORAN, HYPERBOLIC NAVIGATION.

Lorhumb line. A line along which the rates of change of the values of two families of hyperbolae are constants.

lost motion. Mechanical motion which is not transmitted to connected or related parts, due to loose fit. See also BACKLASH.

low, *n.* Short for area of low pressure. Since a low is, on a synoptic chart, always associated with cyclonic circulation, the term is used interchangeably with CYCLONE. See also HIGH.

low clouds. Types of clouds the mean level of which is between the surface and 6,500 feet. The principal clouds in this group are stratocumulus, stratus, and nimbostratus.

lower branch. The half of a meridian or celestial meridian from pole to pole which passes through the antipode or nadir of a place. See also UPPER BRANCH.

lower culmination. See LOWER TRANSIT.

lower high water. The lower of the two high waters of any tidal day.

lower high water interval. See under LUNITIDAL INTERVAL.

lower limb. The lower edge (closest to the horizon) of a celestial body having measurable diameter; opposite is the UPPER LIMB, or the upper edge.

lower low water. The lower of the two low waters of any tidal day.

lower low water datum. An approximation of mean lower low water that has been adopted as a standard reference for a limited area, and is retained for an indefinite period regardless of the fact that it may differ slightly from a better determination of mean lower low water from a subsequent series of observations. Used primarily for river and harbor engineering purposes. Columbia River lower low water datum is an example.

lower low water interval. See under LUNITIDAL INTERVAL.

lower transit. Transit of the lower branch of the celestial meridian. Transit of the upper branch is called UPPER TRANSIT. Also called INFERIOR TRANSIT, LOWER CULMINATION.

low frequency. Radio frequency of 30 to 300 kilohertz.

low light. See FRONT LIGHT.

low tide. See under LOW WATER.

low water. The minimum height reached by a falling tide. The height may be due solely to the periodic tidal forces or it may have superimposed upon it the effects of meteorological conditions.

low water datum. 1. The dynamic elevation for each of the Great Lakes, Lake St. Clair, and the corresponding sloping surfaces of the St. Marys, St. Clair, Detroit, Niagara, and St. Lawrence Rivers to which are referred the depths shown on the navigation charts and the authorized depths for navigation improvement projects. Elevations of these planes are referred to International Great Lakes Datum (1955) and are: Lake Superior - 600.0 feet, Lakes Michigan and Huron - 576.8 feet, Lake St. Clair - 571.7 feet, Lake Erie - 568.6 feet, and Lake Ontario- 242.8 feet. 2. An approximation of mean low water that has been adopted as a standard reference for a limited area and is retained for an indefinite period regardless of the fact that it may differ slightly from a better determination of mean low water from a subsequent series of observations. Used primarily for river and harbor engineering purposes.

low water equinoctial springs. Low water spring tides near the times of the equinoxes. Expressed in terms of the harmonic constituents, it is an elevation depressed below mean sea level by an amount equal to the sum of the amplitudes of constituents M_2, S_2 and K_2.

low water inequality. See under DIURNAL INEQUALITY.

low water interval. See under LUNITIDAL INTERVAL.

low water line. The intersection of the land with the water surface at an elevation of low water.

low water neaps. See under NEAP TIDES.

low water springs. Short for MEAN LOW WATER SPRINGS.

low water stand. The condition at low water when there is no sensible change in the height of the tide. A similar condition at high water is called HIGH WATER STAND. See also STAND.

loxodrome, *n.* See RHUMB LINE. See also ORTHODROME.

loxodromic curve. See RHUMB LINE.

lubber's line. A reference line on a compass marking the reading which coincides with the heading.

lubber's line error. The angular difference between the heading as indicated by a lubber's line, and the actual heading; the horizontal angle, at the center of an instrument, between a line through the lubber's line and one parallel to the keel.

lull, *n.* A momentary decrease in the speed of the wind.

lumen, *n.* The derived unit of luminous flux in the International System of Units; it is the luminous flux emitted within unit solid angle (1 steradian) by a point source having a uniform luminous intensity of 1 candela.

luminance, *n.* In a given direction, at a point on the surface of a source or receptor, or at a point on the path of a beam, the quotient of the luminous flux leaving, arriving at, or passing through an element of surface at this point and propagated in directions defined by an elementary cone containing the given directions, by the product of the solid angle of the cone and the area of the orthogonal projection of the element of surface on a plane perpendicular to the given direction. The derived unit of luminance in the International System of Units is the CANDELA PER SQUARE METER.

luminescence, *n.* Emission of light other than incandescence, as in bioluminescence; emission as a result of and only during absorption of radiation from some other source is called FLUORESCENCE; continued emission after absorption of radiation has ceased is called PHOSPHORESCENCE.

luminous, *adj.* Emitting or reflecting light.

luminous flux. The quantity characteristic of radiant flux which expresses its capacity to produce a luminous sensation, evaluated according to the values of spectral luminous efficiency. Unless otherwise indicated, the luminous flux relates to photopic vision, and is connected with the radiant flux in accordance with the formula adopted in 1948 by the International Commission on Illumination. The derived unit of luminous flux in the International System of Units is the LUMEN.

luminous range. See under VISUAL RANGE (OF A LIGHT).

Luminous Range Diagram. A diagram used to convert the nominal range of a light to its luminous range under existing conditions.

lunar, *adj.* Of or pertaining to the moon.

lunar cycle. An ambiguous expression which has been applied to various cycles associated with the moon's motion, including CALLIPPIC CYCLE, METONIC CYCLE, NODE CYCLE, SYNODICAL MONTH or LUNATION.

lunar day. 1. The duration of one rotation of the earth on its axis, with respect to the moon. Its average length is about $24^h\ 50^m$ of mean solar time. Also called TIDAL DAY. 2. The duration of one rotation of the moon on its axis, with respect to the sun.

lunar distance. The angle, at an observer on the earth, between the moon and another celestial body. This was the basis of a method formerly used to determine longitude at sea.

lunar eclipse. An eclipse of the moon. When the moon enters the shadow of the earth, it appears eclipsed to an observer on the earth. A lunar eclipse is penumbral when it enters only the penumbra of the earth's shadow, partial when part of its surface enters the umbra of the earth's shadow, and total if its entire surface is obscured by the umbra.

lunar inequality. 1. Variation in the moon's motion in its orbit, due to attraction by other bodies of the solar system. See also EVECTION, PERTURBATIONS. 2. A minute fluctuation of a magnetic needle from its mean position, caused by the moon.

lunar interval. The difference in time between the transit of the moon over the Greenwich meridian and a local meridian. The lunar interval equals the difference between the Greenwich and local intervals of a tide or current phase.

lunar month. The period of revolution of the moon about the earth, especially a synodical month.

lunar node. A node of the moon's orbit. See also LINE OF NODES.

lunar noon. The instant at which the sun is over the upper branch of any meridian of the moon.

lunar parallax. Parallax of the moon.

lunar rainbow. See MOON BOW.

lunar tide. That part of the tide due solely to the tide-producing force of the moon. That part due to the tide-producing force of the sun is called SOLAR TIDE.

lunar time. Time based upon the rotation of the earth relative to the moon. Lunar time may be designated as local or Greenwich according to whether the local or Greenwich meridian is used as the reference.

lunation, *n.* See SYNODICAL MONTH.

lune, *n.* The part of the surface of a sphere bounded by halves of two great circles.

lunicurrent internal. The interval between the moon's transit (upper or lower) over the local or Greenwich meridian and a specified phase of the tidal current following the transit. Examples are strength of flood interval and strength of ebb interval, which may be abbreviated to flood interval and ebb interval, respectively. The interval is described as local or Greenwich according to whether the reference is to the moon's transit over the local or Greenwich meridian. When not otherwise specified, the reference is assumed to be local. See also LUNITIDAL INTERVAL.

lunisolar effect. Gravitational effects caused by the attractions of the moon and of the sun.

lunisolar perturbation. Perturbations of the orbits of artificial earth satellites due to the attractions of the sun and the moon. The most important effects are secular variations in the mean anomaly, in the right ascension of the ascending node, and in the argument of perigee.

lunisolar precession. That component of general precession caused by the combined effect of the sun and moon on the equatorial protuberance of the earth, producing a westward motion of the equinoxes along the ecliptic. See also PRECESSION OF THE EQUINOXES.

lunitidal interval. The interval between the moon's transit (upper or lower) over the local or Greenwich meridian and the following high or low water. The average of all high water intervals for all phases of the moon is known as mean high water lunitidal interval and is abbreviated to high water interval. Similarly the mean low water lunitidal interval is abbreviated to low water interval. The interval is described as local or Greenwich according to whether the reference is to the transit over the local or Greenwich meridian. When not otherwise specified, the reference is assumed to be local. When there is considerable diurnal inequality in the tide separate intervals may be obtained for the higher high waters, the lower high waters, the higher low waters and the lower low waters. These are designated respectively as higher high water interval, lower high water interval higher low water interval, and lower low water interval. In such cases, and also when the tide is diurnal, it is necessary to distinguish between the upper and lower transit of the moon with reference to its declination.

lux, *n.* The derived unit of illuminance in the International System of Units; it is equal to 1 lumen per square meter.

M

mackerel sky. An area of sky with a formation of rounded and isolated cirrocumulus or altocumulus resembling the pattern of scales on the back of a mackerel.

macroscopic, *adj.* Large enough to be seen by the unaided eye.

madrepore, *n.* A branching or stag-horn coral, or any perforated stone coral.

maelstrom, *n.* A powerful often violent whirlpool.

maestro, *n.* A northwesterly wind with fine weather which blows, especially in summer, in the Adriatic. It is most frequent on the western shore. This wind is also found on the coasts of Corsica and Sardinia.

magnet, *n.* A body which produces a magnetic field around itself. It has the property of attracting certain materials capable of being magnetized. A magnet occurring in nature is called a natural magnet in contrast with a man-made artificial magnet. See also HEELING MAGNET, KEEPER.

magnetic, *adj.* Of or pertaining to a magnet or related to magnetic north.

magnetic amplitude. Amplitude relative to magnetic east or west.

magnetic annual change. The amount of secular change in the earth's magnetic field which occurs in 1 year. magnetic annual variation; the small systematic temporal variation in the earth's magnetic field which occurs after the trend for secular change has been removed from the average monthly values.

magnetic anomaly. See LOCAL MAGNETIC DISTURBANCE.

magnetic azimuth. Azimuth relative to magnetic north.

magnetic bay. A small magnetic disturbance whose magnetograph resembles an indentation of a coastline. On earth, magnetic bays occur mainly in the polar regions and have duration of a few hours.

magnetic bearing. Bearing relative to magnetic north; compass bearing corrected for deviation.

magnetic chart. A chart showing magnetic information. If it shows lines of equality in one or more magnetic elements, it may be called an isomagnetic chart. It is an isoclinal or isoclinic chart if it shows lines of equal magnetic dip, an isodynamic chart if it shows lines of equal magnetic intensity, an isogonic chart if it shows lines of equal magnetic variation, an isogriv chart if it shows lines of equal grid variation, an isoporic chart if it shows lines of equal rate or change of a magnetic element.

magnetic circle. A sphere of specified radius about the magnetic compass location to be kept free of any magnetic or electrical equipment which would interfere with the compass.

magnetic compass. A compass depending for its directive force upon the attraction of the horizontal component of the earth's magnetic field for a magnetized needle or sensing element free to turn in a horizontal direction.

magnetic course. Course relative to magnetic north; compass course corrected for deviation. magnetic daily variation. See MAGNETIC DIURNAL VARIATION.

magnetic declination. See VARIATION, definition 1.

magnetic deviation. See DEVIATION, definition 1.

magnetic dip. Angular distance between the horizontal and the direction of a line of force of the earth's magnetic field at any point. Also called DIP, MAGNETIC INCLINATION.

magnetic dip pole. See MAGNETIC POLE, definition 1.

magnetic direction. Horizontal direction expressed as angular distance from magnetic north. magnetic diurnal variation. Oscillations of the earth's magnetic field which have a periodicity of about a day and which depend to a close approximation only on local time and geographic latitude. Also called MAGNETIC DAILY VARIATION.

magnetic element. 1. Variation, dip, or magnetic intensity. 2. The part of an instrument producing or influenced by magnetism.

magnetic equator. The line on the surface of the earth connecting all points at which the magnetic dip is zero. Also called ACLINIC LINE. See also GEOMAGNETIC EQUATOR.

magnetic field. Any space or region in which magnetic forces are present, as in the earth's magnetic field, or in or about a magnet, or in or about an electric current. See also MAGNETIC VECTOR.

magnetic force. The strength of a magnetic field. Also called MAGNETIC INTENSITY.

magnetic heading. Heading relative to magnetic north; compass heading corrected for deviation.

magnetic inclination. See MAGNETIC DIP.

magnetic induction. The act or process by which material becomes magnetized when placed in a magnetic field.

magnetic intensity. The strength of a magnetic field. Also called MAGNETIC FORCE.

magnetic latitude. Angular distance north or south of the magnetic equator. The angle is equal to an angle, the tangent of which is equal to half the tangent of the magnetic dip at the point.

magnetic lines of force. Closed lines indicating by their direction the direction of magnetic influence.

magnetic meridian. A line of horizontal magnetic force of the earth. A compass needle without deviation lies in the magnetic meridian.

magnetic moment. The quantity obtained by multiplying the distance between two magnetic poles by the average strength of the poles.

magnetic needle. A small, slender, magnetized bar which tends to align itself with magnetic lines of force.

magnetic north. The direction indicated by the north seeking pole of a freely suspended magnetic needle, influenced only by the earth's magnetic field.

magnetic observation. Measurement of any of the magnetic elements.

magnetic parallel. An isoclinal; a line connecting points of equal magnetic dip.

magnetic pole. 1. Either of the two places on the surface of the earth where the magnetic dip is 90°, that in the Northern Hemisphere being designated north magnetic pole, and that in the Southern Hemisphere being designated south magnetic pole. Also called MAGNETIC DIP POLE. See also MAGNETIC LATITUDE, GEOMAGNETIC POLE, MAGNETIC LATITUDE. 2. Either of those two points of a magnet where the magnetic force is greatest.

magnetic prime vertical. The vertical circle through the magnetic east and west points of the horizon.

magnetic range. A range oriented in a given magnetic direction and used to assist in the determination of the deviation of a magnetic compass.

magnetic retentivity. The ability to retain magnetism after removal of the magnetizing force.

magnetic secular change. The gradual variation in the value of a magnetic element which occurs over a period of years.

magnetic storm. A disturbance in the earth's magnetic field, associated with abnormal solar activity, and capable of seriously affecting both radio and wire transmission.

magnetic temporal variation. Any change in the earth's magnetic field which is a function of time.

magnetic track. The direction of the track relative to magnetic north.

magnetic variation. See VARIATION, definition 1.

magnetic vector. The component of the electromagnetic field associated with electromagnetic radiation which is of the nature of a magnetic field. The magnetic vector is considered to coexist with, but to act at right angles to, the electric vector.

magnetism, *n*. The phenomena associated with magnetic fields and their effects upon magnetic materials, notably iron and steel. The magnetism of the north-seeking end of a freely suspended magnet is called red magnetism; the magnetism of the south-seeking end is called blue magnetism. Magnetism acquired by a piece of magnetic material while it is in a magnetic field is called induced magnetism. Permanent magnetism is retained for long periods without appreciable reduction, unless the magnet is subjected to a demagnetizing force. The magnetism in the intermediate iron of a ship which tends to change as the result of vibration, aging, or cruising in the same direction for a long period but does not alter immediately so as to be properly termed induced magnetism is called sub permanent magnetism. Magnetism which remains after removal of the magnetizing force may be called residual magnetism. The magnetism of the earth is called terrestrial magnetism or geomagnetism.

magnetize, *v., t.* To produce magnetic properties. The opposite is DEMAGNETIZE.

magnetometer, *n*. An instrument for measuring the intensity and direction of the earth's magnetic field. See also DECLINOMETER.

magnetron, *n*. An electron tube characterized by the interaction of electrons with the electric field of circuit element in crossed steady electric and magnetic fields to produce an alternating current power output. It is used to generate high power output in the ultra-high and super-high frequency bands.

magnification, *n*. The apparent enlargement of anything.

magnifying power. The ratio of the apparent length of a linear dimension as seen through an optical instrument to that seen by the unaided eye. See POWER.

magnitude, *n*. 1. Relative brightness of a celestial body. The smaller (algebraically) the number indicating magnitude, the brighter the body. The expression first magnitude is often used somewhat loosely to refer to all bodies of magnitude 1.5 or brighter, including negative magnitudes. 2. Amount; size; greatness.

magnitude ratio. The ratio of relative brightness of two celestial bodies differing in magnitude by 1.0. This ratio is 2.512, the 5th root of 100. A body of magnitude 1.0 is 2.512 times as bright as a body of magnitude 2.0, etc.

main beam. See under LOBE.

mainland, *n*. The principal portion of a large land area. The term is used loosely to contrast a principal land mass from outlying islands and sometimes peninsulas.

main light. The principal light of two or more lights situated on the same support or neighboring supports.

main lobe. The lobe of the radiation pattern of a directional antenna which contains the direction of maximum radiation.

major axis. The longest diameter of an ellipse or ellipsoid. Opposite is MINOR AXIS.

major datum. See PREFERRED DATUM.

major light. A light of high intensity and reliability exhibited from a fixed structure or on marine site (except range lights). Major lights include primary seacoast lights and secondary lights. See also MINOR LIGHT.

major planets. See under PLANET.

make the land. To sight and approach or reach land from seaward.

make way. To progress through the water.

making way. Progressing through the water. See also UNDERWAY.

Malvin Current. See FALKLAND CURRENT.

mamma, *n*. Hanging protuberances, like pouches on the under surface of a cloud. This supplementary cloud feature occurs mostly with cirrus, cirrocumulus, altocumulus, altostratus. stratocumulus, and cumulonimbus; in the case of cumulonimbus, mamma generally appear on the under side of the anvil.

mammatus, *n*. See MAMMA.

maneuvering board. A polar coordinate plotting sheet devised to facilitate solution of problems involving relative movement.

Maneuvering Board Manual. See PUB. NO. 217.

Manganese nodules. *n*. A small, lumpy rock concretions found on the ocean floor formed by layers of metal which have slowly crystallized around a core.

man-made noise. In radio reception, noise due entirely to unwanted transmissions from electrical or electronic apparatus, which has been insufficiently suppressed.

manned light. A light which is operated and maintained by full-time resident personnel.

mantissa, *n*. The part of a logarithm (base 10) to the right of the decimal point. The part of a logarithm (base 10) to the left of the decimal point is called the CHARACTERISTIC.

manual, *adj*. By hand, in contrast with AUTOMATIC.

manual radio direction finder. A radio direction finder which requires manual operation of the antenna and determination of the aural null by speaker or headphones.

manual update. In ECDIS, the manual application of corrections to ENC DATA in the SENC by human operator, usually based on unformatted UPDATE INFORMATION (such as NtMs, voice radio, verbal communications, etc.) The manual application of hand corrections to nautical charts.

map, *n*. A digital or graphic representation of all or part of the surface of the earth, celestial sphere, or other area; showing relative size and position, according to a given projection, of the features represented. Such a representation intended primarily for navigational use is called a chart. A planimetric map indicates only the horizontal positions of features; a topographic map both horizontal and vertical positions. The pattern on the underside of extensive cloud areas, created by the varying amounts of light reflected from the earth's surface, is called a sky map. A chart which shows the distribution of meteorological conditions over an area at a given moment may be called a weather map.

map accuracy standards. See UNITED STATES NATIONAL MAP ACCURACY STANDARDS.

map chart. See COMBAT CHART.

mapping, charting and geodesy. The collection, transformation, generation, dissemination, and storing of geodetic, geomagnetic, gravimetric, aeronautical, topographic, hydrographic, cultural, and toponymic data. These data may be used for military planning, training, and operations including aeronautical, nautical, and land navigation, as well as for weapon orientation and target positioning. Mapping, charting and geodesy (MC&G) also includes the evaluation of topographic, hydrographic, or aeronautical features for their effect on military operations or intelligence. The data may be presented in the form of topographic, planimetric, relief, or thematic maps and graphics; nautical and aeronautical charts and publications, and in simulated, photographic, digital, or computerized formats.

map projection. A systematic drawing of lines on a plane surface to represent the parallels of latitude and the meridians of longitude of the earth or a section of the earth. A map projection may be established by analytical computation or may be constructed geometrically.

map symbol. A character, letter, or similar graphic representation used on a map to indicate some object, characteristic, etc. May be called a CHART SYMBOL when applied to a chart.

March equinox. See VERNAL EQUINOX.

mare's tails. Long, slender, well-defined streaks of cirrus cloud which resemble horse's tails.

marigram, *n.* A graphic record of the rise and fall of the tide. The record is in the form of a curve, in which time is generally represented on the abscissa and the height of the tide on the ordinate.

marina, *n.* A harbor facility for small boats, yachts, etc., where supplies, repairs, and various services are available.

marine, *adj.* Of or pertaining to the sea. See also NAUTICAL.

marine chart. See NAUTICAL CHART.

marine climate. The type of climate characteristic of coastal areas, islands, and the oceans, the distinctive features of which are small annual and daily temperature range and high relative humidity in contrast with CONTINENTAL CLIMATE, which is characteristic of the interior of a large landmass, and the distinctive features of which are large annual and daily temperature range and dry air with few clouds.

Marine Information Object (MIO). In ECDIS an OBJECT which has one or more ATTRIBUTES, the value or values of which vary with time.

marine light. A luminous or lighted aid to navigation intended primarily for marine navigation. One intended primarily for air navigation is called an AERONAUTICAL LIGHT.

marine parade. See MARINE REGATTA.

marine radiobeacon. A radiobeacon whose service is intended primarily for the benefit of ships.

marine railway. A track, a wheeled cradle, and winching mechanism for hauling vessels out of the water so that the bottom can be exposed.

marine railway

marine regatta. An organized race or other public water event, conducted according to a prearranged schedule, noted in the Local Notice to Mariners. Also called MARINE PARADE.

marine sanctuary. An area established under provisions of the Marine Protection, Research, and Sanctuaries Act of 1972, Public Law 92-532 (86 Stat. 1052), for the preservation and restoration of its conservation, recreational, ecological, or esthetic values. Such an area may lie in ocean waters as far seaward as the outer edge of the continental shelf, in coastal waters where the tide ebbs and flows, or in the Great Lakes and connecting waters, and may be classified as a habitat, species, research, recreational and esthetic, or unique area.

marine sextant. A sextant designed primarily for marine navigation. On a clamp screw sextant the position of the tangent screw is controlled by a clamp screw; on an endless tangent screw sextant the position of the index arm and the vernier or micrometer drum is controlled by an endless tangent screw. A vernier sextant provides a precise reading by means of a vernier used directly with the arc, and may have either a clamp screw or an endless tangent screw for controlling the position of the tangent screw or the index arm. A micrometer drum sextant provides a precise reading by means of a micrometer drum attached to the index arm, and has an endless tangent screw for controlling the position of the index arm. See also SEXTANT.

mariner's information. In ECDIS, the information is entered to the SENC, e.g. area of strong currents. Information originated by and added by the mariner.

mariner's navigational objects. In ECDIS features other than chart objects, such as the ownship symbol and velocity vector, planned route, bearing line, etc.

maritime, *adj.* Bordering on, concerned with, or related to the sea. See also NAUTICAL.

maritime polar air. See under AIR-MASS CLASSIFICATION.

maritime position. The location of a seaport or other point along a coast.

Maritime Safety Information (MSI). Designation of the IHO/IMO referring to navigational information of immediate importance to mariners, affecting the safety of life and/or property at sea.

maritime tropical air. See under AIR-MASS CLASSIFICATION.

mark, *n.* 1. An artificial or natural object of easily recognizable shape or color, or both, situated in such a position that it may be identified on a chart. A fixed artificial navigation mark is often called a BEACON. This may be lighted or unlighted. Also called NAVIGATION MARK; SEAMARK. See also CLEARING MARKS. 2. A major design or redesign of an instrument, denoted by a number. Minor changes are designated MODIFICATIONS. 3. One of the bits of leather, cloth, etc., indicating a specified length of a lead line. 4. An indication intended as a datum or reference, such as a bench mark.

mark, *v., i.* "Now" or "at this moment." A call used when simultaneous observations are being made, to indicate to the second person the moment a reading is to be made, as when the time of a celestial observation is to be noted; or the moment a reading is a prescribed value, as when the heading of a vessel is exactly a desired value.

marker beacon. 1. See MARKER RADIOBEACON. 2. As defined by the International Telecommunication Union (ITU), a transmitter in the aeronautical radionavigation service which radiates vertically a distinctive pattern for providing position information to aircraft.

marker buoy. A small, brightly painted moored float used to temporarily mark a location on the water while placing a buoy on station.

marker radiobeacon. A low powered radiobeacon used primarily to mark a specific location such as the end of a jetty. Usually used primarily for homing bearings. Also called MARKER BEACON.

marl, *n.* A crumbling, earthy deposit, particularly one of clay mixed with sand, lime, decomposed shells, etc. Sometimes a layer of marl becomes quite compact.

Mars, *n.* The navigational planet whose orbit lies between the orbits of the Earth and Jupiter.

marsh, *n.* An area of soft wet land. Flat land periodically flooded by salt water is called a salt marsh. Sometimes called SLOUGH.

marsh

mascaret, *n.* See TIDAL BORE.

mass, *n.* The measure of a body's inertia, or the amount of material it contains. This term should not be confused with WEIGHT.

mass attraction vertical. The normal to any surface of constant geopotential. On the earth this vertical is a function only of the distribution of mass and is unaffected by forces resulting from the motions of the earth.

master, *n.* Short for MASTER STATION.

master compass. The main part of a remote-indicating compass system which determines direction for transmission to various repeaters.

master gyrocompass. See under GYROCOMPASS.

master station. In a radionavigation system, the station of a chain which provides a reference by which the emissions of other (slave or secondary) stations are controlled.

masthead light. A fixed running light placed on the centerline of a vessel showing an unbroken white light over an arc of the horizon from dead ahead to 22.5° abaft the beam on either side of the vessel.

Matanuska wind. A strong, gusty, northeast wind which occasionally occurs during the winter in the vicinity of Palmer, Alaska.

matrix. In ECDIS an array of regularly spaced locations.

maximum ebb. See under EBB CURRENT.

maximum flood. See under FLOOD CURRENT.

maximum thermometer. A thermometer which automatically registers the highest temperature occurring since its last setting. One which registers the lowest temperature is called a MINIMUM THERMOMETER.

mean, *adj*. Occupying a middle position.

mean, *n*. The average of a number of quantities, obtained by adding the values and dividing the sum by the number of quantities involved. Also called AVERAGE, ARITHMETIC MEAN. See also MEDIAN.

mean anomaly. See under ANOMALY, definition 2.

mean diurnal high water inequality. See under DIURNAL INEQUALITY.

mean diurnal low water inequality. See under DIURNAL INEQUALITY.

mean elements. Elements of an adopted reference orbit that approximates the actual, perturbed orbit. Mean elements serve as the basis for calculating perturbations. See also ORBITAL ELEMENTS.

mean higher high water. A tidal datum that is the average of the highest high water height of each tidal day observed over the National Tidal Datum Epoch. For stations with shorter series, simultaneous observational comparisons are made with a control tide station in order to derive the equivalent of a 19-year datum. See also HIGH WATER.

mean higher high water line. The intersection of the land with the water surface at the elevation of mean higher high water.

mean high tide. See under MEAN HIGH WATER.

mean high water. A tidal datum, the average of all the high water heights observed over the National Tidal Datum Epoch. For stations with shorter series, simultaneous observational comparisons are made with a control tide station in order to derive the equivalent of a 19-year datum. See also HIGH WATER.

mean high water line. The intersection of the land with the water surface at the elevation of mean high water. See also SHORELINE.

mean high water lunitidal interval. See under LUNITIDAL INTERVAL. mean high water neaps. See as NEAP HIGH WATER or HIGH WATER NEAPS under NEAP TIDES.

mean high water springs. See under SPRING TIDES.

mean ice edge. The average position of the ice edge in any given month or period based on observations over a number of years. Other terms which may be used are mean maximum ice edge and mean minimum ice edge. See also ICE LIMIT.

mean latitude. Half the arithmetical sum of the latitudes of two places on the same side of the equator. Mean latitude is labeled N or S to indicate whether it is north or south of the equator. The expression is occasionally used with reference to two places on opposite sides of the equator, but this usage is misleading as it lacks the significance usually associated with the expression. When the places are on opposite sides of the equator, two mean latitudes are generally used, the mean of each latitude north and south of the equator. The mean latitude is usually used in middle-latitude sailing for want of a practicable means of determining the middle latitude. See also MIDDLE LATITUDE, MIDDLE-LATITUDE SAILING.

mean lower low water. A tidal datum that is the average of the lowest low water height of each tidal day observed over the National Tidal Datum Epoch. For station with shorter series, simultaneous observational comparisons are made with a control tide station in order to derive the equivalent of a 19-year datum. See also LOW WATER.

mean lower low water line. The intersection of the land with the water surface at the elevation of mean lower low water.

mean low water. A tidal datum that is the average of all the low water heights observed over the National Tidal Datum Epoch. For stations with shorter series, simultaneous observational comparisons are made with a control tide station in order to derive the equivalent of a 19-year datum. See also LOW WATER.

mean low water line. The intersection of the land with the water surface at the elevation of mean low water.

mean low water lunitidal interval. See under LUNITIDAL INTERVAL.

mean low water neaps. See as NEAP LOW WATER or LOW WATER NEAPS under NEAP TIDES.

mean low water springs. 1. A tidal datum that is the arithmetic mean of the low waters occurring at the time of the spring tides observed over a specific 19-year Metonic cycle (the National Tidal Datum Epoch). It is usually derived by taking an elevation depressed below the halftide level by an amount equal to one-half the spring range of tide, necessary corrections being applied to reduce the result to a mean value. This datum is used, to a considerable extent, for hydrographic work outside of the United States and is the level of reference for the Pacific approaches to the Panama Canal. Often shortened to SPRING LOW WATER. See also DATUM. 2. See under SPRING TIDES.

mean motion. In undisturbed elliptic motion, the constant angular speed required for a body of a specified mass to complete one revolution in an orbit of a specified semimajor axis.

mean noon. Twelve o'clock mean time, or the instant the mean sun is over the upper branch of the meridian. Mean noon may be either local or Greenwich depending upon the reference meridian. Zone, standard, daylight saving or summer noon are also forms of mean noon, the mean sun being over the upper branch of the zone, standard, daylight saving or summer reference meridian, respectively.

mean power. See under POWER (OF A RADIO TRANSMITTER).

mean range. The average difference in the extreme values of a variable quantity, as the mean range of tide.

mean range of tide. The difference in height between mean high water and mean low water.

mean rise interval. The average interval between the meridian transit of the moon and the middle of the period of the rise of the tide. It may be computed by adding the half of the duration of rise to the mean low water interval, rejecting the semidiurnal tidal period of 12.42 hours when greater than this amount. The mean rise interval may be either local or Greenwich according to whether it is referred to the local or Greenwich meridian.

mean rise of tide. The height of mean high water above the reference or chart sounding datum.

mean river level. A tidal datum that is the average height of the surface of a tidal river at any point for all stages of the tide observed over a 19-year Metonic cycle (the National Tidal Datum Epoch) usually determined from hourly height readings. In rivers subject to occasional freshets, the river level may undergo wide variations, and for practical purposes certain months of the year may be excluded in the determination of tidal datums. For charting purposes, tidal datums for rivers are usually based on observations during selected periods when the river is at or near low water state. See also DATUM.

mean sea level. A tidal datum that is the arithmetic mean of hourly water elevations observed over a specific 19-year Metonic cycle (the National Tidal Datum Epoch). Shorter series are specified in the name, e.g., monthly mean sea level and yearly mean sea level. See also DATUM; EPOCH, definition 2.

mean sidereal time. See under SIDEREAL TIME.

mean solar day. The duration of one rotation of the earth on its axis, with respect to the mean sun. The length of the mean solar day is 24 hours of mean solar time or $24^h\ 03^m\ 56.555^s$ of mean sidereal time. See also CALENDAR DAY.

mean solar time. See MEAN TIME, the term usually used.

mean sun. A fictitious sun conceived to move eastward along the celestial equator at a rate that provides a uniform measure of time equal to the average apparent time. It is used as a reference for reckoning mean time, zone time, etc. Also called ASTRONOMICAL MEAN SUN. See also DYNAMICAL MEAN SUN.

mean tide level. See HALF-TIDE LEVEL.

mean time. Time based upon the rotation of the earth relative to the mean sun. Mean time may be designated as local or Greenwich as the local or Greenwich meridian is the reference. Greenwich mean time is also called UNIVERSAL TIME. Zone, standard, daylight saving or summer time are also variations of mean time, specified meridians being used as the reference. See also EQUATION OF TIME, MEAN SIDEREAL TIME.

mean tropic range. The mean between the great tropic tidal range and the small tropic range. The small tropic range and the mean tropic range are applicable only when the type of tide is semidiurnal or mixed. See also GREAT TROPIC RANGE.

mean water level. The mean surface elevation as determined by averaging the heights of the water at equal intervals of time, usually hourly.

mean water level line. The line formed by the intersection of the land with the water surface at an elevation of mean water level.

measured mile. A length of 1 nautical mile, the limits of which have been accurately measured and are indicated by ranges ashore. It is used by vessels to calibrate logs, engine revolution counters, etc., and to determine speed.

measured-mile buoy. A buoy marking the end of a measured mile.

mechanical scanning. Scanning effected by moving all or part of the antenna.

median, *n*. A value in a group of quantities below and above which fall an equal number of quantities. Of the group 60, 75, 80, 95, and 100, the median is 80. If there is no middle quantity in the group, the median is the value interpolated between the two middle quantities. The median of the group 6, 10, 20, and 31 is 15. See also MEAN.

median valley. The axial depression of the midoceanic ridge system.

medium. A method of electronic data storage and physical transfer, commonly relying on the properties of electromagnetic coatings on tape, disks, or other surfaces, or on the effects of laser light on light-sensitive surfaces.

medium first-year ice. First-year ice 70 to 120 centimeters thick.

medium floe. See under FLOE.

medium fracture. See under FRACTURE.

medium frequency. Radio frequency of 300 to 3,000 kilohertz.

medium iceberg. For reports to the International Ice Patrol, an iceberg that extends 51 to 150 feet (16 to 45 meters) above the sea surface and which has a length of 201 to 400 feet (61 to 122 meters). See also SMALL ICEBERG, LARGE ICEBERG.

medium ice field. See under ICE FIELD.

medium range systems. Those radionavigation systems providing positioning capability beyond the range of short range systems, but their use is generally limited to ranges permitting reliable positioning for about 1 day prior to making landfall; Decca is an example.

mega-. A prefix meaning one million (10^6).

megabyte. One million bytes of information in a computer.

megacycle, *n*. One million cycles; one thousand kilocycles. The term is often used as the equivalent of one million cycles per second.

megahertz, *n*. One million hertz or one million cycles per second.

megaripple, *n*. See SAND WAVE.

meniscus, *n*. 1. The curved upper surface of a liquid in a tube. 2. A type of lens.

mensuration, *n*. 1. The act, process, or art of measuring. 2. That branch of mathematics dealing with determination of length, area, or volume.

Mentor Current. Originating mainly from the easternmost extension of the South Pacific Current at about 40°S 90°W, the Mentor Current flows first northward and then northwestward. It has the characteristic features of a WIND DRIFT in that it is a broad, slow-moving flow that extends about 900 miles westward from the Peru Current to about longitude 90°W at its widest section and tends to be easily influenced by winds. It joins the westward flowing Pacific South Equatorial Current and forms the eastern part of the general counterclockwise oceanic circulation of the South Pacific Ocean. The speed in the central part of the current at about 26°S 80°W, may at times reach about 0.9 knots. Also called PERU OCEANIC CURRENT.

Mercator bearing. See RHUMB BEARING.

Mercator chart. A chart on the Mercator projection. This is the chart commonly used for marine navigation. Also called EQUATORIAL CYLINDRICAL ORTHOMORPHIC CHART.

Mercator course. See RHUMB-LINE COURSE.

Mercator direction. Horizontal direction of a rhumb line, expressed as angular distance from a reference direction. Also called RHUMB DIRECTION.

Mercator map projection. A conformal cylindrical map projection in which the surface of a sphere or spheroid, such as the earth, is developed on a cylinder tangent along the equator. Meridians appear as equally spaced vertical lines and parallels as horizontal lines drawn farther apart as the latitude increases, such that the correct relationship between latitude and longitude scales at any point is maintained. The expansion at any point is equal to the secant of the latitude of that point, with a small correction for the ellipticity of the earth. The Mercator is not a perspective projection. Since rhumb lines appear as straight lines and directions can be measured directly, this projection is widely used in navigation. If the cylinder is tangent along a meridian. a transverse Mercator map projection results; if the cylinder is tangent along an oblique great circle, an oblique Mercator map projection results. Also called EQUATORIAL CYLINDRICAL ORTHOMORPHIC MAP PROJECTION.

Mercator sailing. A method of solving the various problems involving course, distance, difference of latitude, difference of longitude, and departure by considering them in the relation in which they are plotted on a Mercator chart. It is similar to plane sailing, but uses meridional difference and difference of longitude in place of difference of latitude and departure, respectively.

mercurial barometer. An instrument which determines atmospheric pressure by measuring the height of a column of mercury which the atmosphere will support. See also ANEROID BAROMETER.

mercury ballistic. A system of reservoirs and connecting tubes containing mercury used with a type of non-pendulous gyrocompass. The action of gravity on this system provides the torques and resultant precessions required to convert the gyroscope into a compass.

meridian, *n*. A north-south reference line, particularly a great circle through the geographical poles of the earth. The term usually refers to the upper branch, the half, from pole to pole, which passes through a given place; the other half being called the lower branch. An astronomical (terrestrial) meridian is a line connecting points having the same astronomical longitude. A geodetic meridian is a line connecting points of equal geodetic longitude. Geodetic and sometime astronomical meridians are also called geographic meridians. Geodetic meridians are shown on charts. The prime meridian passes through longitude 0°. Sometimes designated TRUE MERIDIAN to distinguish it from magnetic meridian, compass meridian, or grid meridian, the north-south lines relative to magnetic, compass, or grid direction, respectively. A fictitious meridian is one of a series of great circles or lines used in place of a meridian for certain purposes. A transverse or inverse meridian is a great circle perpendicular to a transverse equator. An oblique meridian is a great circle perpendicular to an oblique equator. Any meridian used as a reference for reckoning time is called a time meridian. The meridian used for reckoning standard zone, daylight saving, or war time is called standard, zone, daylight saving, or war meridian respectively. The meridian through any particular place or observer, serving as the reference for local time, is called local meridian, in contrast with the Greenwich meridian, the reference for Greenwich time. A celestial meridian is a great circle of the celestial sphere, through the celestial poles and the zenith. Also called CIRCLE OF LATITUDE. See also ANTE MERIDIAN, POST MERIDIAN.

meridian altitude. The altitude of a celestial body when it is on the celestial meridian of the observer, bearing 000° or 180° true.

meridian angle. Angular distance east or west of the local celestial meridian; the arc of the celestial equator, or the angle at the celestial pole, between the upper branch of the local celestial meridian and the hour circle of a celestial body measured eastward or westward from the local celestial meridian through 180°, and labeled E or W to indicate the direction of measurement. See also HOUR ANGLE.

meridian angle difference. The difference between two meridian angles, particularly between the meridian angle of a celestial body and the value used as an argument for entering a table. Also called HOUR ANGLE DIFFERENCE.

meridian observation. Measurement of the altitude of a celestial body on the celestial meridian of the observer, or the altitude so measured.

meridian passage. See MERIDIAN TRANSIT.

meridian sailing. Following a true course of 000° or 180°, sailing along a meridian. Under these conditions the dead reckoning latitude is assumed to change 1 minute for each mile run and the dead reckoning longitude remains unchanged.

meridian transit. The passage of a celestial body across a celestial meridian. Upper transit, the crossing of the upper branch of the celestial meridian, is understood unless lower transit, the crossing of the lower branch, is specified. Also called TRANSIT, MERIDIAN PASSAGE, CULMINATION.

meridional difference. The difference between the meridional parts of any two given parallels. This difference is found by subtraction if the two parallels are on the same side of the equator and by addition if on opposite sides. Also called DIFFERENCE OF MERIDIONAL PARTS.

meridional parts. The length of the arc of a meridian between the equator and a given parallel on a Mercator chart, expressed in units of 1 minute of longitude at the equator.

mesoscale. Typically a spatial scale between 10 and 1000 kilometers.

metacenter, *n*. For small angles of inclination of a ship, the instantaneous center of a very small increment of the curved path of the center of buoyancy locus. Or, for small angles of inclination, the point of intersection of the lines of action of the buoyant force and the original vertical through the center of buoyancy.

meta object. In ECDIS a FEATURE OBJECT containing information about other OBJECTS.

meteor, *n*. The phenomenon occurring when a solid particle from space enters the earth's atmosphere and is heated to incandescence by friction of the air. A meteor whose brightness does not exceed that of Venus (magnitude -4) is popularly called SHOOTING STAR or FALLING STAR. A shooting star results from the entrance into the atmosphere of a particle having a diameter between a few centimeters and just visible to the naked eye. Shooting stars are observed first as a light source, similar to a star, which suddenly appears in the sky and moves along a long or short path to a point where it just as suddenly disappears. The brighter shooting stars may leave a trail which remains luminous for a short time. Meteors brighter than magnitude -4 are called BOLIDES or FIREBALLS. Light bursts, spark showers, or splitting of the trail are sometimes seen along their luminous trails which persist for minutes and for an hour in exceptional cases. The intensity of any meteor is dependent upon the size of the particle which enters the atmosphere. A particle 10 centimeters in diameter can produce a bolide as bright as the full moon. See also METEORITE.

meteorite, *n*. 1. The solid particle which causes the phenomenon known as a METEOR. 2. The remnant of the solid particle, causing the meteor, which reaches the earth.

meteorological optical range. The length of path in the atmosphere required to reduce the luminous flux in a collimated beam from an incandescent lamp at a color temperature of 2,700°K to 0.05 of its original value, the luminous flux being evaluated by means of the curve of spectral luminous efficiencies for photopic vision given by the International Commission on Illumination. The quantity so defined corresponds approximately to the distance in the atmosphere required to reduce the contrast of an object against its background to 5 percent of the value it would have at zero distance, for daytime observation. See also METEOROLOGICAL VISIBILITY.

Meteorological Optical Range Table. A table from the International Visibility Code which gives the code number of meteorological visibility and the meteorological visibility for several weather conditions.

meteorological tide. A change in water level caused by local meteorological conditions, in contrast to an ASTRONOMICAL TIDE, caused by the attractions of the sun and moon. See also SEICHE, STORM SURGE.

meteorological tides. Tidal constituents having origin in the daily or seasonal variations in weather conditions which may occur with some degree of periodicity. See also STORM SURGE.

meteorological visibility. The greatest distance at which a black object of suitable dimensions can be seen and recognized by day against the horizon sky, or, in the case of night observations, could be seen and recognized if the general illumination were raised to the normal daylight level. It has been established that the object may be seen and recognized if the contrast threshold is 0.05 or higher. The term may express the visibility in a single direction or the prevailing visibility in all directions. See also VISIBILITY, METEOROLOGICAL OPTICAL RANGE, CONTRAST THRESHOLD.

meteor swarm. The scattered remains of comets that have broken up.

meter, *n*. 1. The base unit of length in the International System of Units, equal to 1,650,763.73 wavelengths in vacuum of the radiation corresponding to the transition between the levels $2p_{10}$ and $5p_5$ of the krypton-86 atom. It is equal to 39.37008 inches, approximately, or approximately one ten-millionth of the distance from the equator to the North or South Pole. The old international prototype of the meter is still kept at the International Bureau of Weights and Measures under the conditions specified in 1889. 2. A device for measuring, and usually indicating, some quantity.

method of bisectors. As applied to celestial lines of position, the movement of each of three or four intersecting lines of position an equal amount, in the same direction toward or away from the celestial bodies, so as to bring them as nearly as possible to a common intersection. When there are more than four lines of position, the lines of position in the same general direction are combined to reduce the data to not more than four lines of position. See also OUTSIDE FIX.

Metonic cycle. A period of 19 years or 235 lunations, devised by Meton, an Athenian astronomer who lived in the fifth century B.C., for the purpose of obtaining a period in which new and full moon would recur on the same day of the year. Taking the Julian year of 365.25 days and the synodic month as 29.53058 days, we have the 19-year period of 6939.75 days as compared with the 235 lunations of 6939.69 days, a difference of only 0.06 days. See also CALLIPPIC CYCLE.

meter per second. The derived unit of speed in the International System of Units.

meter per second squared. The derived unit of acceleration in the International System of Units.

metric system. A decimal system of weights and measures based on the meter as the unit of length and the kilogram as a unit mass. See also INTERNATIONAL SYSTEM OF UNITS.

Mexico Current. From late October through April an extension of the California Current, known as the Mexico Current, flows southeastward along the coast to the vicinity of longitude 95°W where it usually turns west, but at times extends southward as far as Honduras with speeds from 0.5 to 1 knot. During the remainder of the year, this current flows northwestward along the Mexican coast as far as Cabo Corrientes, where it turns westward and becomes a part of the Pacific North Equatorial Current.

micro-. A prefix meaning one-millionth (10^{-6}).

micrometer, *n*. An auxiliary device to provide measurement of very small angles or dimensions by an instrument such as a telescope.

micrometer drum. A cylinder carrying an auxiliary scale and sometimes a vernier, for precise measurement, as in certain type sextants.

micrometer drum sextant. A marine sextant providing a precise reading by means of a micrometer drum attached to the index arm, and having an endless tangent screw for controlling the position of the index arm. The micrometer drum may include a vernier to enable a more precise reading. On a vernier sextant the vernier is directly on the arc.

micron, *n*. A unit of length equal to one-millionth of a meter.

microprocessor. An integrated circuit in a computer which executes machine-language instructions.

microsecond, *n*. One-millionth of a second.

microwave, *n*. A very short electromagnetic wave, usually considered to be about 30 centimeters to 1 millimeter in length. While the limits are not clearly defined, it is generally considered as the wavelength of radar operation.

microwave frequency. Radio frequency of 1,000 to 300,000 megahertz, having wavelengths of 30 centimeters to 1 millimeter.

mid-channel buoy. See FAIRWAY BUOY.

mid-channel mark. A navigation mark serving to indicate the middle of a channel, which can be passed on either side safely.

middle clouds. Types of clouds the mean level of which is between 6,500 and 20,000 feet. The principal clouds in this group are altocumulus and altostratus.

middle ground. A shoal in a fairway having a channel on either side.

middle ground buoy. One of the buoys placed at each end of a middle ground. See BIFURCATION BUOY, JUNCTION BUOY.

middle latitude. The latitude at which the arc length of the parallel separating the meridians passing through two specific points is exactly equal to the departure in proceeding from one point to the other by middle-latitude sailing. Also called MID-LATITUDE. See also MEAN LATITUDE, MIDDLE-LATITUDE SAILING.

middle-latitude sailing. A method that combines plane sailing and parallel sailing. Plane sailing is used to find difference of latitude and departure when course and distance are known, or vice versa. Parallel sailing is used to inter-convert departure and difference of longitude. The mean latitude is normally used for want of a practicable means of determining the middle latitude, the latitude at which the arc length of the parallel separating the meridians passing through two specific points is exactly equal to the departure in proceeding from one point to the other. See also MEAN LATITUDE.

mid-extreme tide. An elevation midway between the extreme high water and the extreme low water occurring in any locality. See also HALFTIDE LEVEL.

mid-latitude. See MIDDLE LATITUDE.

midnight, *n*. Twelve hours from noon, or the instant the time reference crosses the lower branch of the reference celestial meridian.

midnight sun. The sun when it is visible at midnight. This occurs during the summer in high latitudes, poleward of the circle at which the latitude is approximately equal to the polar distance of the sun.

mill, *n*. 1. A unit of angular measurement equal to an angle having a tangent of 0.001. 2. A unit of angular measurement equal to an angle subtended by an arc equal to 1/6,400th part of the circumference of a circle.

mile, *n*. A unit of distance. The nautical mile, or sea mile, is used primarily in navigation. Nearly all maritime nations have adopted the International Nautical Mile of 1,852 meters proposed in 1929 by the International Hydrographic Bureau. The U.S. Departments of Defense and Commerce adopted this value on July 1, 1954. Using the yard-meter conversion factor effective July 1, 1959, (1 yard = 0.9144 meter, exactly) the International Nautical Mile is equivalent to 6076.11549 feet, approximately. The geographical mile is the length of 1 minute of arc of the equator considered to be 6,087.08 feet. The U.S. Survey mile or land mile (5,280 feet in the United States) is commonly used for navigation on rivers and lakes, notably the Great Lakes of North America. See also CABLE, MEASURED MILE.

mileage number. A number assigned to aids to navigation which gives the distance in sailing miles along the river from a reference point to the aid. The number is used principally in the Mississippi and other river systems.

miles of relative movement. The distance, in miles, traveled relative to a reference point which is usually in motion.

military grid. Two sets of parallel lines intersecting at right angles and forming squares; the grid is superimposed on maps, charts, and other similar representations of the earth's surface in an accurate and consistent manner to permit identification of ground locations with respect to other locations and the computation of direction and distance to other points. See also MILITARY GRID REFERENCE SYSTEM, UNIVERSAL POLAR STEREOGRAPHIC GRID, UNIVERSAL TRANSVERSE MERCATOR GRID, WORLD GEOGRAPHIC REFERENCE SYSTEM.

military grid reference system. A system which uses a standard-scaled grid square, based on a point of origin on a map projection of the earth's surface in an accurate and consistent manner to permit either position referencing or the computation of direction and distance between grid positions. See also MILITARY GRID.

Milky Way. The galaxy of which the sun and its family of planets are a part. It appears as an irregular band of misty light across the sky. Through a telescope, it is seen to be composed of numerous individual stars. See also COALSACK.

milli-. A prefix meaning one-thousandth.

millibar, *n*. A unit of pressure equal to 1,000 dynes per square centimeter, or 1/1,000th of a bar. The millibar is used as a unit of measure of atmospheric pressure, a standard atmosphere being equal to 1,013.25 millibars or 29.92 inches of mercury.

milligal, *n*. A unit of acceleration equal to 1/1,000th of a gal, or 1/1,000 centimeter per second per second. This unit is used in gravity measurements, being approximately one-millionth of the average gravity at the earth's surface.

millimeter, *n*. One thousandth of a meter- one tenth of a centimeter;.03937008 inch.

millisecond, *n*. One-thousandth of a second.

minaret, *n*. A tall, slender tower attached to a mosque and surrounded by one or more projecting balconies; frequently charted as landmarks.

minaret

minimal depiction of detail. A term used to indicate the extreme case of generalization of detail on a chart. In the extreme case most features are omitted even through there is space to show at least some of them. The practice is most frequently used for semi-enclosed areas such as estuaries and harbors on smaller-scale charts, where use of a larger scale chart is essential.

minimum distance (of a navigational system). The minimum distance at which a navigational system will function within its prescribed tolerances.

minimum ebb. See under EBB CURRENT.

minimum flood. See under FLOOD CURRENT.

minimum signal. The smallest signal capable of satisfactorily operating an equipment, e.g., the smallest signal capable of triggering a racon.

minimum thermometer. A thermometer which automatically registers the lowest temperature occurring since its last setting. One which registers the highest temperature is called a MAXIMUM THERMOMETER.

minor axis. The shortest diameter of an ellipse or ellipsoid.

minor light. An automatic unmanned light on a fixed structure usually showing low to moderate intensity. Minor lights are established in harbors, along channels, along rivers, and in isolated locations. See also MAJOR LIGHT.

minor planets. See under PLANET.

minute, *n*. 1. The sixtieth part of a degree of arc. 2. The sixtieth part of an hour.

mirage, *n*. An optical phenomenon in which objects appear distorted, displaced (raised or lowered), magnified, multiplied, or inverted due to varying atmospheric refraction when a layer of air near the earth's surface differs greatly in density from surrounding air. See also TOWERING, STOOPING, LOOMING, SINKING, FATA MORGANA.

mirror reelection. See SPECULAR REFLECTION.

missing, *adj*. Said of a floating aid to navigation which is not on station with its whereabouts unknown.

mist, *n*. An aggregate of very small water droplets suspended in the atmosphere. It produces a thin, grayish veil over the landscape. It reduces visibility to a lesser extent than fog. The relative humidity with mist is often less than 95 percent. Mist is intermediate in all respects between haze (particularly damp haze) and fog. See also DRIZZLE.

mistake, *n*. The result of carelessness or of a mistake. For the purpose of error analysis, a mistake is not classified as an error. Also called BLUNDER.

mistral, *n*. A cold, dry wind blowing from the north over the northwest coast of the Mediterranean Sea, particularly over the Gulf of Lions. Also called CIERZO. See also FALL WIND.

mixed current. Type of tidal current characterized by a conspicuous speed difference between the two floods and/or ebbs usually occurring each tidal day. See also TYPE OF TIDE.

mixed tide. Type of tide with a large inequality in either the high and/or low water heights, with two high waters and two low waters usually occurring each tidal day. All tides are mixed, but the name is usually applied to the tides intermediate to those predominantly semidiurnal and those predominantly diurnal. See also TYPE OF TIDE.

moat, *n*. An annular depression that may not be continuous, located at the base of many sea mounts, islands, and other isolated elevations of the sea floor, analogous to the moat around a castle.

mobile service. As defined by the International Telecommunication Union (ITU), a service of radiocommunication between mobile and land stations, or between mobile stations.

mobile offshore drilling unit (MODU). A movable drilling platform used in offshore oil exploration and production. It is kept stationary by vertically movable legs or by mooring with several anchors. After drilling for oil it may be replaced by a production platform or a submerged structure.

mock fog. A rare simulation of true fog by anomalous atmospheric refraction.

mock moon. See PARASALENE.

mock sun. See PARHELION.

mock-sun ring. See PARHELIC CIRCLE.

modal interference. Omega signals propagate in the earth-ionosphere wave guide. This waveguide can support many different electromagnetic field configurations, each of which can be regarded as an identifiable signal component or mode having the same signal frequency, but with slightly different phase velocity. Modal interference is a special form of signal interference wherein two or more waveguide modes interfere with each other and irregularities appear in the phase pattern. This type of interference occurs predominantly under nighttime conditions when most of the propagation path is not illuminated and the boundary conditions of the waveguide are unstable. It is most severe for signals originating at stations located close to the geomagnetic equator. During all daylight path conditions, the only region of modal interference is a more-less circular area of radius 500-1000 kilometers immediately surrounding a transmitting station.

model atmosphere. Any theoretical representation of the atmosphere, particularly of vertical temperature distribution. See also STANDARD ATMOSPHERE.

modem. An electronic device which converts digital information to analog signals and vice-versa, used in computer file transfer over telephone lines; derived from MOdulator-DEModulator.

moderate breeze. Wind of force 4 (11 to 16 knots or 13 to 18 miles per hour) on the Beaufort wind scale.

moderate gale. A term once used by seamen for what is now called NEAR GALE on the Beaufort wind scale.

modification, *n*. An instrument design resulting from a minor change, and indicated by number. A design resulting from a major change is called a MARK.

modified Julian day. An abbreviated form of the Julian day which requires fewer digits and translates the beginning of each day from Greenwich noon to Greenwich midnight; obtained by subtracting 2400000.5 from Julian days.

modified Lambert conformal chart. A chart on the modified Lambert conformal map projection. Also called NEY'S CHART.

modified Lambert conformal map projection. A modification of the Lambert conformal projection for use in polar regions, one of the standard parallels being at latitude 89°59'58" and the other at latitude 71° or 74°, and the parallels being expanded slightly to form complete concentric circles. Also called NEY'S MAP PROJECTION.

modified refractive index. For a given height above sea level, the sum of the refractive index of the air at this height and the ratio of the height to the radius of the earth.

modulated wave. A wave which varies in some characteristic in accordance with the variations of a modulating wave. See also CONTINUOUS WAVE.

modulating wave. A wave which modulates a carrier wave.

modulation, *n*. A variation of some characteristic of a radio wave, called the CARRIER WAVE in accordance with instantaneous values of another wave called the MODULATING WAVE. These variations can be amplitude, frequency, phase, or pulse.

modulator, *n*. The component in pulse radar which generates a succession of short pulses of energy which in turn cause a transmitter tube to oscillate during each pulse.

mole, *n*. 1. A structure, usually massive, on the seaward side of a harbor for its protection against current and wave action, drift ice, wind, etc. Sometimes it may be suitable for the berthing of ships. See also JETTY, definition 1; QUAY. 2. The base unit of amount of substance in the International System of Units; it is the amount of substance of a system which contains as many elementary entities as there are atoms in 0.012 kilogram of carbon atom 12. When the mole is used, the elementary entities must be specified and may be atoms, molecules, ions, electrons, other particles, or specified groups of such particles.

moment, *n*. The tendency or degree of tendency to produce motion about an axis. Numerically it is the quantity obtained by multiplying the force, speed, or mass by the distance from the point of application or center of gravity to the axis. See also MAGNETIC MOMENT.

moment of inertia. The quantity obtained by multiplying the mass of each small part of a body by the square of its distance from an axis, and adding all the results.

momentum, *n*. The quantity of motion. Linear momentum is the quantity obtained by multiplying the mass of a body by its linear speed. Angular momentum is the quantity obtained by multiplying the moment of inertia of a body by its angular speed.

monitor, *v. t*. In radionavigation, to receive the signals of a system in order to check its operation and performance.

monitor, *n*. The video display portion of a computer system.

monitoring, *n*. In radionavigation, the checking of the operation and performance of a system through reception of its signals.

monsoon, *n*. A name for seasonal winds first applied to the winds over the Arabian Sea, which blow for 6 months from the northeast (northeast monsoon) and for 6 months from the southwest (southwest monsoon). The primary cause is the much greater annual variation of temperature over large land areas compared with the neighboring ocean surfaces, causing an excess of pressure over the continents in winter and a deficit in summer, but other factors such as the relief features of the land have a considerable effect. In India the term is popularly applied chiefly to the southwest monsoon and by extension, to the rain which it brings.

monsoon current. A seasonal wind-driven current occurring in the northern part of the Indian Ocean and the northwest Pacific Ocean. See also MONSOON DRIFT.

Monsoon Drift. A drift current of the northeast Indian Ocean located north of the Indian Equatorial Countercurrent and south of the Bay of Bengal. During February and March when the northeast monsoon decreases in intensity, the monsoon drift is formed from the outflow of the Strait of Malacca and a small amount of northwestward flow along the upper southwest coast of Sumatra. Off the southwest coast of Sumatra, a current generally sets southeast during all months. It is strongest during October through April. The monsoon drift broadens as it flows westward and divides off the east coast of Sri Lanka, part joining the circulation of the Bay of Bengal and part joining the flow from the Arabian Sea. During April, the transition period between monsoons, the monsoon drift is ill-defined. A counterclockwise circulation exists between Sumatra and Sri Lanka. During May through October, the monsoon drift flows east to southeast. During November and December part of the monsoon drift is deflected into the Bay of Bengal and the remainder turns clockwise and flows southeastward. See also MONSOON.

monsoon fog. An advection fog occurring as a monsoon circulation transports warm moist air over a colder surface.

month, *n*. 1. The period of the revolution of the moon around the earth. The month is designated as sidereal, tropical, anomalistic, nodical or synodical, according to whether the revolution is relative to the stars, the vernal equinox, the perigee, the ascending node, or the sun. 2. The calendar month, which is a rough approximation to the synodical month.

month of the phases. See SYNODICAL MONTH.

moon, *n*. The astronomical satellite of the earth.

moonbow, *n*. A rainbow formed by light from the moon. Colors in a moonbow are usually very difficult to detect. Also called LUNAR RAINBOW.

moon dog. See PARASELENE.

moonrise, *n*. The crossing of the visible horizon by the upper limb of the ascending moon.

moonset, *n*. The crossing of the visible horizon by the upper limb of the descending moon.

moor, *v., t*. To secure a vessel to land by tying to a pier, wharf or other land-based structure, or to anchor with two or more anchors.

moor

mooring, *n*. 1. The act of securing a craft to the ground, a wharf, pier, quay, etc., other than anchoring with a single anchor. 2. The place where a craft may be moored. 3. Chains, bridles, anchors, etc. used in securing a craft to the ground.

mooring buoy. A buoy secured to the bottom by permanent moorings and provided with means for mooring a vessel by use of its anchor chain or mooring lines.

morning glory. A spectacular propagating roll cloud, which frequents the sparsely populated southern margin of the Gulf of Carpentaria. Morning Glories are frequently observed during the spring months near dawn over the southern Gulf area between Sweers Island and the remote community of Burketown in northern Queensland. They often appear in the form of one or more, rapidly advancing, rather formidable roll cloud formations, which extend from horizon to horizon in an arc as far as the eye can see.

morning star. The brightest planet appearing in the eastern sky during morning twilight.

morning twilight. The period of time between darkness and sunrise.

Morse code light. A navigation light which flashes one or more characters in Morse code.

motion, *n*. The act, process, or instance of change of position. Absolute motion is motion relative to a fixed point. Actual motion is motion of an object relative to the earth. Apparent or relative motion is change of position as observed from a reference point which may itself be in motion. Diurnal motion is the apparent daily motion of a celestial body. Direct motion is the apparent motion of a planet eastward among the stars; retrograde motion, the apparent motion westward among the stars. Motion of a celestial body through space is called space motion, which is composed of two components: proper motion, that component perpendicular to the line of sight; and radial motion, that component in the direction of the line of sight. Also called MOVEMENT, especially when used in connection with problems involving the motion of one vessel relative to another.

mound, *n.* On the sea floor, a low, isolated, rounded hill.

mountain breeze. A breeze that blows down a mountain slope due to the gravitational flow of cooled air. See also KATABATIC WIND, VALLEY BREEZE.

mountains, *n., pl.* On the sea floor, a well delineated subdivision of a large and complex positive feature, generally part of a cordillera.

movement, *n.* See MOTION.

moving havens. Moving restricted areas established to prevent mutual interference of Naval vessels in transit.

moving target indication. A radar presentation in which stationary targets are wholly or partially suppressed.

Mozambique Current. The part of the Indian South Equatorial Current that turns and flows along the African coast in the Mozambique Channel. It is considered part of the AGULHAS CURRENT.

mud, *n.* A general term applied to mixtures of sediments in water. Where the grains are less than 0.002 millimeter in diameter, the mixture is called clay. Where the grains are between 0.002 and 0.0625 millimeter in diameter, the mixture is called silt. See also SAND; STONES; ROCK, definition 2.

mud berth. A berth where a vessel rests on the bottom at low water.

mud flat. A tidal flat composed of mud.

mud pilot. A person who pilots a vessel by visually observing changes in the color of the water as the depth of the water increases or decreases.

multihop transmission. See MULTIPLE-HOP TRANSMISSION.

multipath error. Interference between radio waves which have traveled between the transmitter and the receiver by two paths of different lengths, which may cause fading or phase changes at the receiving point due to the vector addition of the signals, making it difficult to obtain accurate information.

multipath propagation. Radio propagation from the transmitter to the receiver by two or more paths simultaneously. Also called MULTIPATH TRANSMISSION.

multipath transmission. See MULTIPATH PROPAGATION.

multiple echoes. Radar echoes which may occur when a strong echo is received from another ship at close range. A second or third or more echoes may be observed on the radarscope at double triple, or other multiples of the actual range of the radar target, resulting from the echo's being reflected by own ship back to the target and received once again as an echo at a multiple of the preceding range to the target. This term should not be confused with MULTIPLE-TRACE ECHO. See also SECOND-TRACE ECHO.

multiple-hop transmission. Radio wave transmission in which the waves traveling between transmitter and receiver undergo multiple reflections and refractions between the earth and ionosphere. Also called MULTIHOP TRANSMISSION.

multiple ranges. A group of two ranges, having one of the range marks (either front or rear) in common.

multiple star. A group of three or more stars so close together that they appear as a single star, whether through physical closeness or as a result of lying in approximately the same direction. See also STAR CLUSTER.

multiple tide staff. A succession of tide staffs on a sloping shore so placed that the vertical graduations on the several staffs will form a continuous scale referred to the same datum.

multiple-trace echo. See SECOND-TRACE ECHO.

multi-year ice. Old ice up to 3 meters or more thick which has survived at least two summer's melt. Hummocks are even smoother than in second-year ice. The ice is almost salt-free. The color, where bare, is usually blue. The melt pattern consists of large interconnecting irregular puddles and a well-developed drainage system.

Mumetal, *n.* The registered trade name for an alloy of about 75% nickel and 25% iron, having high magnetic permeability and low hysteresis.

N

nadir, *n.* The point on the celestial sphere vertically below the observer, or 180° from the zenith.

name, *n.* The label of a numerical value, used particularly to refer to the N (north) or S (south) label of latitude and declination. When latitude and declination are both N or both S, they are said to be of same name, but if one is N and the other S, they are said to be of contrary name.

nano-. A prefix meaning one-billionth (10^{-9}).

nanosecond, *n.* One-billionth of a second.

Napier diagram. A diagram on which compass deviation is plotted for various headings, and the points connected by a smooth curve, permitting deviation problems to be solved quickly without interpolation. It consists of a vertical line, usually in two parts, each part being graduated for 180° of heading, and two additional sets of lines at an angle of 60° to each other and to the vertical lines. See also DEVIATION TABLE.

Napierian logarithm. A logarithm to the base e (2.7182818). Also called NATURAL LOGARITHM. See also COMMON LOGARITHM.

Napier's Rule of Circular Parts. *n.* A series of mathematical rules which aid in solving right spherical triangles.

narrows, *n.* A navigable narrow part of a bay, strait, river, etc.

nashi, n'aschi, *n.* A northeast wind which occurs in winter on the Iranian coast of the Persian Gulf, especially near the entrance to the gulf, and also on the Makran coast. It is probably associated with an outflow from the central Asiatic anticyclone which extends over the high land of Iran. It is similar in character but less severe than the BORA.

National Geodetic Vertical Datum. A fixed reference once adopted as a standard geodetic datum for heights in the United States. The geodetic datum now in use in the United States is the North American Vertical Datum of 1988. The geodetic datum is fixed and does not take into account the changing stands of sea level. Because there are many variables affecting sea level, and because the geodetic datum represents a best fit over a broad area, the relationship between the geodetic datum and local mean sea level is not consistent from one location to another in either time or space. For this reason the National Geodetic Vertical Datum should not be confused with MEAN SEA LEVEL.

National Tidal Datum Epoch. The specific 19-year cycle adopted by the National Ocean Survey as the official time segment over which tide observations are taken and reduced to obtain mean values (e.g., mean lower low water, etc.) for tidal datums. It is necessary for standardization because of apparent periodic and apparent secular trends in sea level. The present National Tidal Datum Epoch is 1960 through 1978.

National Water Level Observation Network. (National Tidal Datum Control Network). A network composed of the primary control tide stations of the National Ocean Service. This network of coastal observation stations provides the basic tidal datums for coastal boundaries and chart datums of the United States. Tidal datums obtained at secondary control tide stations and tertiary tide stations are referenced to the Network.

natural, *adj.* 1. Occurring in nature; not artificial. 2. Not logarithmic-used with the name of a trigonometric function to distinguish it from its logarithm (called LOGARITHMIC TRIGONOMETRIC FUNCTION).

natural frequency. The lowest resonant frequency of a body or system.

natural harbor. A harbor where the configuration of the coast provides the necessary protection See also ARTIFICIAL HARBOR.

natural logarithm. See NAPIERIAN LOGARITHM.

natural magnet. A magnet occurring m nature, as contrasted with an ARTIFICIAL MAGNET, produced by artificial means.

natural period. The period of the natural frequency of a body or system.

natural range. A range formed by natural objects such as rocks, peaks, etc. See also ARTIFICIAL RANGE.

natural scale. See REPRESENTATIVE FRACTION.

natural tangent. See under TANGENT, definition 1.

natural trigonometric function. See under TRIGONOMETRIC FUNCTIONS.

natural year. See TROPICAL YEAR.

nature of the bottom. See BOTTOM CHARACTERISTICS.

nautical, *adj*. Of or pertaining to ships, marine navigation, or seamen.

nautical almanac. 1. A periodical publication of astronomical data designed primarily for marine navigation. Such a publication designed primarily for air navigation is called an AIR ALMANAC. 2. *Nautical Almanac*; a joint annual publication of the U.S. Naval Observatory and the Nautical Almanac Office, Royal Greenwich Observatory listing the Greenwich hour angle and declination of various celestial bodies to a precision of 0.1' at hourly intervals; time of sunrise, sunset, moon rise, moonset; and other astronomical information useful to navigators.

nautical astronomy. See NAVIGATIONAL ASTRONOMY.

nautical chart. A representation of a portion of the navigable waters of the earth and adjacent coastal areas on a specified map projection, designed specifically to meet requirements of marine navigation.

nautical day. Until January 1, 1925, a day that began at noon, 12 hours earlier than the calendar day, or 24 hours earlier than the astronomical day of the same date.

nautical mile. A unit of distance used principally in navigation. For practical consideration it is usually considered the length of 1 minute of any great circle of the earth, the meridian being the great circle most commonly used. Because of various lengths of the nautical mile in use throughout the world, due to differences in definition and the assumed size and shape of the earth, the International Hydrographic Bureau in 1929 proposed a standard length of 1,852 meters, which is known as the International Nautical Mile. This has been adopted by nearly all maritime nations. The U.S. Departments of Defense and Commerce adopted this value on July 1, 1954. With the yard-meter relationship then in use, the International Nautical Mile was equivalent to 6076.10333 feet, approximately. Using the yard-meter conversion factor effective July 1, 1959, (1 yard = 0.9144 meter, exactly) the International Nautical Mile is equivalent to 6076.11549 feet, approximately. See also SEA MILE.

nautical twilight. The time of incomplete darkness which begins (morning) or ends (evening) when the center of the sun is 12° below the celestial horizon. The times of nautical twilight are tabulated in the *Nautical Almanac*; at the times given the horizon is generally not visible and it is too dark for marine sextant observations. See also FIRST LIGHT.

nautophone, *n*. A sound signal emitter comprising an electrically oscillated diaphragm. It emits a signal similar in power and tone to that of a REED HORN.

Naval Vessel Lights Act. Authorized departure from the rules of the road for character and position of navigation lights for certain naval ships. Such modifications are published in *Notice to Mariners*.

NAVAREA. A geographical subdivision of the Long Range Radio Broadcast Service.

NAVAREA Warnings. Broadcast messages containing information which may affect the safety of navigation on the high seas. In accordance with international obligations, the National Geospatial-Intelligence Agency (NGA) is responsible for disseminating navigation information for ocean areas designated as NAVAREAS IV and XII of the World Wide Navigational Warning Service. NAVAREA IV broadcasts cover the waters contiguous to North America from the Atlantic coast eastward to 35°W and between latitudes 7°N and 67°N. NAVAREA XII broadcasts cover the waters contiguous to North America extending westward to the International Date Line and from 67°N to the equator east of 120°W, south to 3°25′S, thence east to the coast. Other countries are responsible for disseminating navigational information for the remaining NAVAREAS.

navigable, *adj*. Affording passage to a craft; capable of being navigated.

navigable semicircle (less dangerous semicircle). The half of a cyclonic storm area in which the rotary and forward motions of the storm tend to counteract each other and the winds are in such a direction as to tend to blow a vessel away from the storm track. In the Northern Hemisphere this is to the left of the storm center and in the Southern Hemisphere it is to the right. The opposite is DANGEROUS SEMICIRCLE.

navigable waters. Waters usable, with or without improvements, as routes for commerce in the customary means of travel on water.

navigating sextant. A sextant designed and used for observing the altitudes of celestial bodies, as opposed to a hydrographic sextant.

navigation, *n*. The process of planning, recording, and controlling the movement of a craft or vehicle from one place to another. The word navigate is from the Latin navigatus, the past participle of the verb navigere, which is derived from the words navis, meaning "ship," and agere meaning "to move" or "to direct." Navigation of water craft is called marine navigation to distinguish it from navigation of aircraft, called air navigation. Navigation of a vessel on the surface is sometimes called surface navigation to distinguish it from navigation of a submarine. Navigation of vehicles across land or ice is called land navigation. The expression polar navigation refers to navigation in the regions near the geographical poles of the earth, where special techniques are employed.

navigational aid. An instrument, tool, system, device, chart, method, etc., intended to assist in navigation. This expression is not the same as AID TO NAVIGATION, which refers to devices external to a craft such as lights and buoys.

navigational astronomy. Astronomy of direct use to a navigator, comprising principally celestial coordinates, time, and the apparent motions of celestial bodies. Also called NAUTICAL ASTRONOMY.

navigational information. In ECDIS the information contained in MARINER'S NAVIGATIONAL OBJECTS.

navigational planets. The four planets commonly used for celestial observations: Venus, Mars Jupiter, and Saturn.

navigational plot. A graphic plot of the movements of a craft. A dead reckoning plot is the graphic plot of the dead reckoning, suitably labeled with respect to time, direction, and speed; a geographical plot is one relative to the surface of the earth.

navigational purpose. In ECDIS, the specific purpose for which an ENC has been compiled. There are six such purposes; berthing, harbor, approach, coastal, general, and overview.

navigational symbol. See MARINERS' NAVIGATIONAL OBJECTS

navigational triangle. The spherical triangle solved in computing altitude and azimuth and great circle sailing problems. The celestial triangle is formed on the celestial sphere by the great circles connecting the elevated pole, zenith of the assumed position of the observer, and a celestial body. The terrestrial triangle is formed on the earth by the great circles connecting the pole and two places on the earth; the assumed position of the observer and geographical position of the body for celestial observations, and the point of departure and destination for great circle sailing problems. The expression astronomical triangle applies to either the celestial or terrestrial triangle used for solving celestial observations.

navigation, head of. A transshipment point at the end of a waterway where loads are transferred between water carriers and land carriers; also the point at which a river is no longer navigable due to rapids or falls.

navigation lights. Statutory, required lights shown by vessels during the hours between sunset and sunrise, in accordance with international agreements.

navigation mark. See MARK.

navigation/positioning system. A system capable of being used primarily for navigation or position fixing. It includes the equipment, its operators, the rules and procedures governing their actions and, to some extent, the environment which affects the craft or vehicle being navigated.

navigation satellite. An artificial satellite used in a system which determines positions based upon signals received from the satellite.

Navigation Sensor System Interface (NAVSSI). The U.S. Naval version of the electronic chart display and information system (ECDIS). It is integrated with command and control, weapons, and other systems.

Navigation Tables for Mariners and Aviators. See H.O. PUB. NO. 208.

navigator, *n*. 1. A person who navigates or is directly responsible for the navigation of a craft. 2. A book of instructions on navigation, such as the *The American Practical Navigator (Bowditch)*.

NAVSTAR Global Positioning System. See GLOBAL POSITIONING SYSTEM.

NAVTEX. A medium frequency radiocommunications system intended for the broadcast of navigational information up to 200 miles at sea, which uses narrow band direct printing technology to print out MSI and safety messages aboard vessels, without operator monitoring.

Navy Navigation Satellite System. A satellite navigation system of the United States conceived and developed by the Applied Physics Laboratory of the Johns Hopkins University. It is an all-weather, worldwide, and passive system which provides two-dimensional positioning from low-altitude satellites in near-polar orbits. The Transit launch program ended in 1988, and the system is scheduled for termination in 1996, replaced by GPS.

neaped, *adj*. Left aground following a spring high tide. Also called BENEAPED.

neap high water. See under NEAP TIDES.

neap low water. See under NEAP TIDES.

neap range. See under NEAP TIDES.

neap rise. The height of neap high water above the elevation of reference or datum of chart.

neap tidal currents. Tidal currents of decreased speed occurring semimonthly as the result of the moon being in quadrature. See also NEAP TIDES.

neap tides. Tides of decreased range occurring semimonthly as the result of the moon being in quadrature. The neap range of the tide is the average semidiurnal range occurring at the time of neap tides and is most conveniently computed from the harmonic constants. It is smaller than the mean range where the type of tide is either semidiurnal or mixed and is of no practical significance where the type of tide is diurnal. The average height of the high waters of the neap tides is called neap high water or high water neaps and the average height of the corresponding low waters is called neap low water or low water neaps.

nearest approach. The least distance between two objects having relative motion with respect to each other.

near gale. Wind of force 8 (28 to 33 knots or 32 to 38 miles per hour) on the Beaufort wind scale. See also GALE.

nearshore current system. The current system caused by wave action in or near the surf zone. The nearshore current system consists of four parts: the shoreward mass transport of water; longshore currents; rip currents; the longshore movement of expanding heads of rip currents.

near vane. That instrument sighting vane on the same side of the instrument as the observer's eye. The opposite is FAR VANE.

neatline, *n*. That border line which indicates the limit of the body of a map or chart. Also called SHEET LINE.

nebula *(pl. nebulae), n*. 1. An aggregation of matter outside the solar system, large enough to occupy a perceptible area but which has not been resolved into individual stars. One within our galaxy is called a galactic nebula and one beyond is called an extragalactic nebula. If a nebula is resolved into numerous individual stars, it is called a STAR CLUSTER. 2. A galaxy.

necessary bandwidth. As defined by the International Telecommunication Union (ITU) for a given class of emission, the minimum value of the occupied bandwidth sufficient to ensure the transmission of information at the rate and with the quality required for the system employed, under specified conditions. Emissions useful for the good functioning of the receiving equipment as, for example, the emission corresponding to the carrier of reduced carrier systems, shall be included in the necessary bandwidth.

neck, *n*. 1. A narrow isthmus, cape or promontory. 2. The land areas between streams flowing into a sound or bay. 3. A narrow strip of land which connects a peninsula with the mainland. 4. A narrow body of water between two larger bodies; a strait.

negative altitude. Angular distance below the horizon. Also called DEPRESSION.

Network Coordinating Station. An INMARSAT COAST EARTH STATION (CES) equipped to process messages in the EGC SafetyNET system.

neutral occlusion. See under OCCLUDED FRONT.

new ice. A general term for recently formed ice which includes frazil ice, grease ice, slush, and shuga. These types of ice are composed of ice crystals which are only weakly frozen together (if at all) and have definite form only while they are afloat.

new moon. The moon at conjunction, when little or none of it is visible to an observer on the earth because the illuminated side is away from him. Also called CHANGE OF THE MOON. See also PHASES OF THE MOON.

new ridge. A newly formed ice ridge with sharp peaks, the slope of the sides usually being about 40°. Fragments are visible from the air at low altitude.

newton, *n*. The special name for the derived unit of force in the International System of Units; it is that force which gives to a mass of 1 kilogram an acceleration of 1 meter per second, per second.

Newtonian telescope. A reflecting telescope in which a small plane mirror reflects the convergent beam from the speculum to an eyepiece at one side of the telescope. After the second reflection the rays travel approximately perpendicular to the longitudinal axis of the telescope. See also CASSEGRAINIAN TELESCOPE.

newton per square meter. The derived unit of pressure in the International System of Units. See also PASCAL.

Newton's laws of motion. Universal laws governing all motion, formulated by Isaac Newton. These are: (1) Every body continues in a state of rest or of uniform motion in a straight line unless acted upon by a force; (2) When a body is acted upon by a force, its acceleration is directly proportional to the force and inversely proportional to the mass of the body, and the acceleration takes place in the direction in which the force acts; (3) To every action there is always an equal and opposite reaction; or, the mutual actions of two bodies are always equal and oppositely directed.

Ney's chart. See MODIFIED LAMBERT CONFORMAL CHART.

Ney's map projection. See MODIFIED LAMBERT CONFORMAL MAP PROJECTION.

night, *n*. The part of the solar day when the sun is below the visible horizon, especially the period between dusk and dawn.

night effect. See under POLARIZATION ERROR.

night error. See under POLARIZATION ERROR.

night order book. A notebook in which the commanding officer of a ship writes orders with respect to courses and speeds, any special precautions concerning the speed and navigation of the ship, and all other orders for the night for the officer of the deck.

nilas, *n*. A thin elastic crust of ice, easily bending on waves and swell and under pressure, thrusting in a pattern of interlocking "fingers." Nilas has a matte surface and is up to 10 centimeters in thickness. It may be subdivided into DARK NILAS and LIGHT NILAS. See also FINGER RAFTING.

nimbostratus, *n*. A dark, low shapeless cloud layer (mean upper level below 6,500 ft.) usually nearly uniform; the typical rain cloud. When precipitation falls from nimbostratus, it is in the form of continuous or intermittent rain or snow, as contrasted with the showery precipitation of cumulonimbus.

nimbus, *n*. A characteristic rain cloud. The term is not used in the international cloud classification except as a combining term, as cumulonimbus.

nipped, *adj*. Beset in the ice with the surrounding ice forcibly pressing against the hull.

nipping, *n*. The forcible closing of ice around a vessel such that it is held fast by ice under pressure. See also BESET, ICE-BOUND.

no-bottom sounding. A sounding in which the bottom is not reached.

nocturnal, *n*. An old navigation instrument which consisted of two arms pivoted at the enter of a disk graduated for date, time and arc. The nocturnal was used for determining time during the night and for obtaining a correction to be applied to an altitude observation of Polaris for finding latitude.

nodal, *adj*. Related to or located at or near a node or nodes.

nodal line. A line in an oscillating body of water along which there is a minimum or no rise and fall of the tide.

nodal point. 1. See NODE, definition 1. 2. The no-tide point in an amphidromic region.

node, *n*. 1. One of the two points of intersection of the orbit of a planet, planetoid, or comet with the ecliptic, or of the orbit of a satellite with the plane of the orbit of its primary. That point at which the body crosses to the north side of the reference plane is called the ascending node; the other, the descending node. The line connecting the nodes is called LINE OF NODES. Also called NODAL POINT. See also REGRESSION OF THE NODES. 2. A zero point in any stationary wave system. 3. In ECDIS a zero-dimensional SPATIAL OBJECT, located by a pair of coordinates. A node is either ISOLATED or CONNECTED.

node cycle. The period of approximately 18.61 Julian years required for the regression of the moon's nodes to complete a circuit of 360° of longitude. It is accompanied by a corresponding cycle of changing inclination of the moon's orbit relative to the plane of the earth's equator, with resulting inequalities in the rise and fall of the tide and speed of the tidal current.

node factor. A factor depending upon the longitude of the moon's node which, when applied to the mean coefficient of a tidal constituent, will adapt the same to a particular year for which predictions are to be made.

nodical, *adj*. Of or pertaining to astronomical nodes; measured from node to node.

nodical month. The average period of revolution of the moon about the earth with respect to the moon's ascending node, a period of 27 days, 5 hours, 5 minutes, 35.8 seconds.

nodical period. The interval between two successive passes of a satellite through the ascending node. See also ORBITAL PERIOD.

nominal orbit. The true or ideal orbit in which an artificial satellite is expected to travel. See also NORMAL ORBIT.

nominal range. See under VISUAL RANGE (OF A LIGHT).

nomogram, *n*. A diagram showing, to scale, the relationship between several variables in such manner that the value of one which corresponds to known values of the others can be determined graphically. Also called NOMOGRAPH.

nomograph, *n*. See NOMOGRAM.

non-chart symbol, See MARINERS NAVIGATIONAL OBJECTS.

non-dangerous wreck. A term used to describe a wreck having more than 20 meters of water over it. This term excludes a FOUL GROUND, which is frequently covered by the remains of a wreck and is a hazard only for anchoring, taking the ground, or bottom fishing.

nongravitational perturbations. Perturbations caused by surface forces due to mechanical drag of the atmosphere (in case of low flying satellites), electromagnetism, and solar radiation pressure.

nonharmonic constants. Tidal constants such as lunitidal intervals, ranges, and inequalities which may be derived directly from high and low water observations without regard to the harmonic constituents of the tide. Also applicable to tidal currents.

non-HO information. In ECDIS, the information contained in the SENC provided by non-HO sources (MARINER'S INFORMATION or other sources outside HOs.

non-standard buoys. The general classification of all lighted and unlighted buoys built to specifications other than modern standard designs.

non-tidal basin. An enclosed basin separated from tidal waters by a caisson or flood gates. Ships are moved into the dock near high tide. The dock is closed when the tide begins to fall. If necessary, ships are kept afloat by pumping water into the dock to maintain the desired level. Also called WET DOCK. See also BASIN, definition 2.

nontidal current. See under CURRENT.

noon, *n*. The instant at which a time reference is over the upper branch of the reference meridian. Noon may be solar or sidereal as the sun or vernal equinox is over the upper branch of the reference meridian. Solar noon may be further classified as mean or apparent as the mean or apparent sun is the reference. Noon may also be classified according to the reference meridian, either the local or Greenwich meridian or additionally in the case of mean noon, a designated zone meridian. Standard, daylight saving or summer noon are variations of zone noon. The instant the sun is over the upper branch of any meridian of the moon is called lunar noon. Local apparent noon may also be called high noon.

noon constant. A predetermined value added to a meridian or ex-meridian sextant altitude to determine the latitude.

noon interval. The predicted time interval between a given instant, usually the time of a morning observation, and local apparent noon. This is used to predict the time for observing the sun on the celestial meridian.

noon sight. Measurement of the altitude of the sun at local apparent noon, or the altitude so measured.

normal, *adj*. Perpendicular. A line is normal to another line or a plane when it is perpendicular to it. A line is normal to a curve or curved surface when it is perpendicular to the tangent line or plane at the point of tangency.

normal, *n*. 1. A straight line perpendicular to a surface or to another line. 2. In geodesy, the straight line perpendicular to the surface of the reference ellipsoid. 3. The average, regular, or expected value of a quantity.

normal curve. Short for NORMAL DISTRIBUTION CURVE.

normal distribution. A mathematical law which predicts the probability that the random error of any given observation of a series of observations of a certain quantity will lie within certain bounds. The law can be derived from the following properties of random errors: (1) positive and negative errors of the same magnitude are about equal in number, (2) small errors occur more frequently than large errors, and (3) extremely large errors rarely occur. One immediate consequence of these properties is that the average or mean value of a large number of observations of a given quantity is zero. Also called GAUSSIAN DISTRIBUTION. See also SINGLE-AXIS NORMAL DISTRIBUTION, CIRCULAR NORMAL DISTRIBUTION, STANDARD DEVIATION.

normal distribution curve. The graph of the normal distribution. Often shortened to NORMAL CURVE.

normal orbit. The orbit of a spherical satellite about a spherical primary during which there are no disturbing elements present due to other celestial bodies, or to some physical phenomena. Also called UNPERTURBED ORBIT, UNDISTURBED ORBIT.

normal section line. A line on the surface of a reference ellipsoid, connecting two points on that surface, and traced by a plane containing the normal at one point and passing through the other point.

normal tide. A non technical term synonymous with tide, i.e., the rise and fall of the ocean due to the gravitational interactions of the sun, moon, and earth alone.

norte, *n*. A strong cold northeasterly wind which blows in Mexico and on the shores of the Gulf of Mexico. It results from an outbreak of cold air from the north. It is the Mexican extension of a norther.

north, *n*. The primary reference direction relative to the earth; the direction indicated by 000° in any system other than relative. True north is the direction of the north geographical pole; magnetic north the direction north as determined by the earth's magnetic compass; grid north an arbitrary reference direction used with grid navigation. See also CARDINAL POINT.

North Africa Coast Current. A nontidal current in the Mediterranean Sea that flows eastward along the African coast from the Strait of Gibraltar to the Strait of Sicily. It is the most permanent current in the Mediterranean Sea. The stability of the current is indicated by the proportion of no current observations, which averages less than 1 percent. The current is most constant just after it passes through the Strait of Gibraltar; in this region, west of longitude 3°W, 65 percent of all observations show an eastward set, with a mean speed of 1.1 knots and a mean maximum speed of 3.5 knots. Although the current is weaker between longitudes 3°W and 11°E, it remains constant, the speed averaging 0.7 knot through its length and its maximum speed being about 2.5 knots.

North American Datum of 1927. The geodetic datum the origin of which is located at Meade's Ranch, Kansas. Based on the Clarke spheroid of 1866, the geodetic position of triangulation station Meades Ranch and azimuth from that station to station Waldo are as follows: Latitude of Meades Ranch: 39°13'25.686"N; Longitude of Meades Ranch: 98°32'30.506"W Azimuth to Waldo: 75°28'09.64" The geoidal height at Meades Ranch is assumed to be zero.

North American Datum of 1983. The modern geodetic datum for North America; it is the functional equivalent of the World Geodetic System (WGS). It is based on the GRS 80 ellipsoid, which fits the size and shape of the earth more closely, and has its origin at the earth's center of mass.

North Atlantic Current. An ocean current which results from extensions of the Gulf Stream and the Labrador Current near the edge of the Grand Banks of Newfoundland. As the current fans outward and widens in a northeastward through eastward flow, it decreases sharply in speed and persistence. Some influence of the Gulf Stream is noticeable near the extreme southwestern boundary of the current. The North Atlantic Current is a sluggish, slow-moving flow that can easily be influenced by opposing or augmenting winds. There is some evidence that the weaker North Atlantic Current may consist of separate eddies or branches which are frequently masked by a shallow, wind-driven surface now called the NORTH ATLANTIC DRIFT. A branch of the North Atlantic Current flows along the west coasts of the British Isles at speeds up to 0.6 knot and enters the Norwegian Sea as the NORWAY CURRENT mainly through the east side of the Faeroe–Shetland Channel. A small portion of this current to the west of the Faeroe Islands mixes with part of the southeastward flow from the north coast of Iceland; these two water masses join and form a clockwise circulation around the Faeroe Islands. The very weak nontidal current in the Irish Sea, which averages only about 0.1 knot, depends on the wind. The part of the North Atlantic Current that flows eastward into the western approaches to the English Channel tends to increase or decrease the speed of the reversing tidal currents. The southern branch of the North Atlantic Current turns southward near the Azores to become the CANARY CURRENT.

North Atlantic Drift. See under NORTH ATLANTIC CURRENT.

northbound node. See ASCENDING NODE.

North Brazil Current. See GUIANA CURRENT.

North Cape Current. An Arctic Ocean current flowing northeastward and eastward around northern Norway, and curving northeastward into the Barents Sea. The North Cape Current is the continuation of the northeastern branch of the NORWAY CURRENT.

northeaster, nor'easter, *n*. A northeast wind, particularly a strong wind or gale associated with cold rainy weather. In the U.S., nor'easters generally occur on the north side of late-season low pressure systems which pass off the Atlantic seaboard, bringing onshore gales to the region north of the low. Combined with high tides, they can be very destructive.

northeast monsoon. See under MONSOON.

north equatorial current. See ATLANTIC NORTH EQUATORIAL CURRENT, PACIFIC NORTH EQUATORIAL CURRENT.

norther, *n*. A northerly wind. In the southern United States, especially in Texas (Texas norther) in the Gulf of Mexico, in the Gulf of Panama away from the coast, and in central America (the norte), the norther is a strong cold wind from the northeast to northwest. It occurs between November and April, freshening during the afternoon and decreasing at night. It is a cold air outbreak associated with the southward movement of a cold anticyclone. It is usually preceded by a warm and cloudy or rainy spell with southerly winds. The norther comes as a rushing blast and brings a sudden drop of temperature of as much as 25°F in 1 hour or 50°F in 3 hours in winter. The California norther is a strong, very dry, dusty, northerly wind which blows in late spring, summer and early fall in the valley of California or on the west coast when pressure is high over the mountains to the north. It lasts from 1 to 4 days. The dryness is due to adiabatic warming during descent. In summer it is very hot. The Portuguese norther is the beginning of the trade wind west of Portugal. The term is used for a strong north wind on the coast of Chile which blows occasionally in summer. In southeast Australia, a hot dry wind from the desert is called a norther.

northern lights. See AURORA BOREALIS.

north frigid zone. That part of the earth north o the Arctic Circle.

north geographical pole. The geographical pole in the Northern Hemisphere, at lat. 90°N.

north geomagnetic pole. The geomagnetic pole in the Northern Hemisphere. This term should not be confused with NORTH MAGNETIC POLE. See also GEOMAGNETIC POLE.

northing, *n*. The distance a craft makes good to the north. The opposite is SOUTHING.

north magnetic pole. The magnetic pole in the Northern Hemisphere. This term should not be confused with NORTH GEOMAGNETIC POLE. See also GEOMAGNETIC POLE.

North Pacific Current. Flowing eastward from the eastern limit of the Kuroshio Extension (about longitude 170°E), the North Pacific Current forms the northern part of the general clockwise oceanic circulation of the North Pacific Ocean.

north polar circle. See ARCTIC CIRCLE.

North Pole. 1. The north geographical pole. See also MAGNETIC POLE GEOMAGNETIC POLE. 2. The north-seeking end of a magnet. See also RED MAGNETISM.

north temperate zone. That part of the earth between the Tropic of Cancer and the Arctic Circle.

north up, north upward. One of the three basic orientations of display of relative or true motion on a radarscope or electronic chart. In the NORTH UP orientation, the presentation is in true (gyrocompass) directions from own ship, north being maintained UP or at the top of the radarscope. See also HEAD UP, BASE COURSE UP.

north-up display. In ECDIS information shown on the display (radar or ECDIS) with the north direction upward. The north-up display corresponds with the usual ORIENTATION of the nautical chart.

northwester, nor'wester, *n*. A northwesterly wind.

Norway Coastal Current. Originating mainly from Oslofjord outflow, counterclockwise return flow of the Jutland Current within the Skaggerak, and outflow from the Kattegat, the Norway Coastal Current begins at about 59°N 10°E and follows the coast of Norway, and is about 20 miles in width. Speeds are strongest off the southeast coast of Norway, where they frequently range between 1 and 2 knots. Along the remainder of the coast the current gradually weakens. It may widen to almost 30 miles at about latitude 63°N, where it joins the NORWAY CURRENT. South of latitude 62°N the current speed usually ranges between 0.4 and 0.9 knots. Speeds are generally stronger in spring and summer, when the flow is augmented by increased discharge from fjords.

Norway Current. An Atlantic Ocean current flowing northeastward along the northwest coast of Norway, and gradually branching and continuing as the SPITZBERGEN ATLANTIC CURRENT and the NORTH CAPE CURRENT. The Norway Current is the continuation of part of the northern branch of the North Atlantic Current. Also called NORWEGIAN CURRENT.

Norwegian Current. See NORWAY CURRENT.

notch filter. An arrangement of electronic components designed to attenuate or reject a specific frequency band with a sharp cut-off at either end.

notice board. A signboard used to indicate speed restrictions, cable landings, etc.

notice to mariners. A periodic publication used by the navigator to correct charts and publications.

Notice to Mariners. A weekly publication of the National Geospatial-Intelligence Agency (NGA) prepared jointly with the National Oceanic and Atmospheric Administration (NOAA) and the U.S. Coast Guard giving information on changes in aids to navigation, dangers to navigation, selected items from the *Local Notice to Mariners*, important new soundings, changes in channels, harbor construction, radionavigation information, new and revised charts and publications, special warnings and notices, pertinent HYDROLANT, HYDROPAC, NAVAREA IV and XII messages and corrections to charts, manuals, catalogs, sailing directions (pilots), etc. The *Notice to Mariners* should be used routinely for updating the latest editions of nautical charts and related publications.

nova *(pl. novae), n*. A star which suddenly becomes many times brighter than previously, and then gradually fades. Novae are believed to be exploding stars.

nucleus, *n*. The central, massive part of anything, such as an atom or comet.

numerical scale. A statement of that distance on the earth shown in one unit (usually an inch) on the chart, or vice versa. See also REPRESENTATIVE FRACTION.

nun buoy. An unlighted buoy of which the upper part of the body (above the waterline), or the larger part of the superstructure, has a cone shape with vertex upwards.

nutation, *n*. Irregularities in the precessional motion of the equinoxes due chiefly to regression of the nodes.

object. In ECDIS an identifiable set of information. An object may have ATTRIBUTES and may be related to other objects. See also SPATIAL OBJECT and FEATURE OBJECT.

Object Catalogue. In ECDIS a feature schema which provides a description of real world entities. It contains a list of FEATURE OBJECT classes (each relating to a real world entity), ATTRIBUTES and allowable ATTRIBUTE VALUES.

object class. In ECDIS a generic description of OBJECTS which have the same characteristics.

object description. In ECDIS the definition of which OBJECT CLASS a specific OBJECT belongs to.

object glass. See OBJECTIVE.

objective, *n*. The lens or combination of lenses which receives light rays from an object, and refracts them to form an image in the focal plane of the eyepiece of an optical instrument, such as a telescope. Also called OBJECT GLASS.

oblate spheroid. An ellipsoid of revolution, the shorter axis of which is the axis of revolution. An ellipsoid of revolution, the longer axis of which is the axis of revolution, is called a PROLATE SPHEROID. The earth is approximately an oblate spheroid.

oblique, *adj*. Neither perpendicular nor parallel; slanting.

oblique angle. Any angle not a multiple of 90°.

oblique ascension. The arc of the celestial equator, or the angle at the celestial pole, between the hour circle of the vernal equinox and the hour circle through the intersection of the celestial equator and the eastern horizon at the instant a point on the oblique sphere rises, measured eastward from the hour circle of the vernal equinox through 24h. The expression is not used in modern navigation.

oblique chart. A chart on an oblique map projection.

oblique coordinates. Magnitudes defining a point relative to two intersecting non-perpendicular lines, called AXES. The magnitudes indicate the distance from each axis, measured along a parallel to the other axis. The horizontal distance is called the abscissa and the other distance the ordinate. This is a form of CARTESIAN COORDINATES.

oblique cylindrical orthomorphic chart. See OBLIQUE MERCATOR CHART.

oblique cylindrical orthomorphic map projection. See OBLIQUE MERCATOR MAP PROJECTION oblique equator. A great circle the plane of which is perpendicular to the axis of an oblique projection. An oblique equator serves as the origin for measurement of oblique latitude. On an oblique Mercator map projection, the oblique equator is the tangent great circle. See also FICTITIOUS EQUATOR.

oblique graticule. A fictitious graticule based upon an oblique map projection.

oblique latitude. Angular distance from an oblique equator. See also FICTITIOUS LATITUDE.

oblique longitude. Angular distance between a prime oblique meridian and any given oblique meridian. See also FICTITIOUS LONGITUDE.

oblique map projection. A map projection with an axis inclined at an oblique angle to the plane of the equator.

oblique Mercator chart. A chart on the oblique Mercator map projection. Also called OBLIQUE CYLINDRICAL ORTHOMORPHIC CHART. See also MERCATOR CHART.

oblique Mercator map projection. A conformal cylindrical map projection in which points on the surface of a sphere or spheroid, such as the earth, are developed by Mercator principles on a cylinder tangent along an oblique great circle. Also called OBLIQUE CYLINDRICAL ORTHOMORPHIC MAP PROJECTION. See also MERCATOR MAP PROJECTION.

oblique meridian. A great circle perpendicular to an oblique equator. The reference oblique meridian is called prime oblique meridian. See also FICTITIOUS MERIDIAN.

oblique parallel. A circle or line parallel to an oblique equator, connecting all points of equal oblique latitude. See also FICTITIOUS PARALLEL.

oblique pole. One of the two points 90° from an oblique equator.

oblique rhumb line. 1. A line making the same oblique angle with all fictitious meridians of an oblique Mercator map projection. Oblique parallels and meridians may be considered special cases of the oblique rhumb line. 2. Any rhumb line, real or fictitious, making an oblique angle with its meridians. In this sense the expression is used to distinguish such rhumb lines from parallels and meridians, real or fictitious, which may be included in the expression rhumb line. See also FICTITIOUS RHUMB LINE.

oblique sphere. The celestial sphere as it appears to an observer between the equator and the pole, where celestial bodies appear to rise obliquely to the horizon.

oblique triangle. A triangle with no right angle.

obliquity factor. A factor in an expression for a constituent tide or tidal current involving the angle of the inclination of the moon's orbit to the plane of the earth's equator.

obliquity of the ecliptic. The acute angle between the plane of the ecliptic and the plane of the celestial equator, about 23°27'.

obscuration, *n.* The designation for the sky cover when the sky is completely hidden by obscuring phenomena in contact with, or extending to the surface.

obscuring phenomenon. Any atmospheric phenomenon, not including clouds, which restricts the vertical or slant visibility.

observed altitude. Corrected sextant altitude; angular distance of the center of a celestial body above the celestial horizon of an observer measured along a vertical circle, through 90°. Occasionally called TRUE ALTITUDE. See also ALTITUDE INTERCEPT, APPARENT ALTITUDE, SEXTANT ALTITUDE.

observed gravity anomaly. See GRAVITY ANOMALY.

observed latitude. See LATITUDE LINE.

observed longitude. See LONGITUDE LINE.

obstruction, *n.* Anything that hinders or prevents movement, particularly anything that endangers or prevents passage of a vessel or aircraft. The term is usually used to refer to an isolated danger to navigation, such as a submerged rock or reef in the case of marine navigation, and a tower, tall building, mountain peak, etc., in the case of air navigation.

obstruction buoy. A buoy used to indicate a dangerous obstruction. See ISOLATED DANGER BUOY.

obstruction light. A light indicating a radio tower or other obstruction to aircraft.

obstruction mark. A navigation mark used to indicate a dangerous obstruction. See ISOLATED DANGER MARK.

obtuse angle. An angle greater than 90° and less than 180°.

obtuse triangle. A triangle with an obtuse angle. A plane triangle can have only one obtuse angle.

occasional light. A light put into service only on demand.

occluded front. A composite of two fronts, formed when a cold front overtakes a warm front or stationary front. This is common in the late stages of wave-cyclone development, but is not limited to occurrence within a wave-cyclone. There are three basic types of occluded front, determined by the relative coldness of the air behind the original cold front to the air ahead of the warm (or stationary) front. A cold occlusion results when the coldest air is behind the cold front. The cold front undercuts the warm front and, at the earth's surface, cold air replaces less-cold air. When the coldest air lies ahead of the warm front, a warm occlusion is formed in which case the original cold front is forced aloft at the warm-front surface. At the earth's surface, cold air is replaced by less-cold air. A third and frequent type, a neutral occlusion, results when there is no appreciable temperature difference between the cold air masses of the cold and warm fronts. In this case frontal characteristics at the earth's surface consist mainly of a pressure trough, a wind-shift line, and a band of cloudiness and precipitation. Commonly called OCCLUSION. Also called FRONTAL OCCLUSION.

occlusion, *n.* 1. See OCCLUDED FRONT. 2. The process of formation of an occluded front. Also called FRONTAL OCCLUSION.

occultation, *n.* 1. The concealment of a celestial body by another which crosses the line of view. Thus, the moon occults a star when it passes between the observer and the star. 2. The interval of darkness in the period of the light. See also FLASH.

occulting light. A light totally eclipsed at regular intervals, with the duration of light always longer than the intervals of darkness called OCCULTATIONS. The term is commonly used for a SINGLE OCCULTING LIGHT, an occulting light exhibiting only single occultations which are repeated at regular intervals.

occupied bandwidth. As defined by the International Telecommunication Union (ITU) the frequency bandwidth such that, below its lower and above its upper frequency limits, the mean powers radiated are each equal to 0.5 percent of the total mean power radiated by a given emission. In some cases, for example multichannel frequency-division systems, the percentage of 0.5 percent may lead to certain difficulties in the practical application of the definitions of occupied and necessary bandwidth; in such cases a different percentage may prove useful.

ocean, *n.* 1. The major area of salt water covering the greater part of the earth. 2. One of the major divisions of the expanse of salt water covering the earth.

ocean current. A movement of ocean water characterized by regularity, either of a cyclic nature, or as a continuous stream flowing along a definable path. Three general classes may be distinguished, by cause: (a) currents associated with horizontal pressure gradients, comprising the various types of gradient current; (b) wind-driven currents, which are those directly produced by the stress exerted by the wind upon the ocean surface; (c) currents produced by long-wave motions. The latter are principally tidal currents, but may also include currents associated with internal waves, tsunamis and seiches. The major ocean currents are of continuous, stream-flow character, and are of first-order importance in the maintenance of the earth's thermodynamic balance.

oceanic, *adj.* Of or pertaining to the ocean.

oceanographic, *adj.* Of or pertaining to oceanography, or knowledge of the oceans.

oceanographic survey. The study or examination of conditions in the ocean or any part of it. with reference to zoology, chemistry, geology, or other scientific discipline. See also HYDROGRAPHIC SURVEY.

oceanography, *n*. The study of the sea, embracing and integrating all knowledge pertaining to the sea's physical boundaries, the chemistry and physics of sea water, and marine biology. Strictly, oceanography is the description of the marine environment, whereas OCEANOLOGY is the study of the oceans.

oceanology, *n*. The study of the ocean. See also OCEANOGRAPHY.

Ocean Passages for the World. A British publication relating to the planning and conduct of ocean passages. Published by the Hydrographer of the Navy, *Ocean Passages for the World* addresses those areas which lie mainly out side the areas covered in detail by Admiralty Sailing Directions. It is kept up-to-date by periodical supplements. The publication should not be used without reference to the latest supplement and those *Notices to Mariners* published to correct Sailing Directions.

ocean waters. For application to the provisions of the Marine Protection, Research, and Sanctuaries Act of 1972, those waters of the open sea lying seaward of the base line from which the territorial sea is measured.

octagon, *n*. A closed plane figure having 8 sides.

octahedral cluster. An arrangement of eight corner reflectors with common faces designed to give substantially uniform response in all directions. The octahedral cluster is formed by mounting three rectangular plates mutually at right angles with the geometric centers of the plates coincident. See also PENTAGONAL CLUSTER.

octant, *n*. A double-reflecting instrument for measuring angles, used primarily for measuring altitude of celestial bodies. It has a range of 90°, with the graduated arc subtending 45°, or 1/8 of a circle, hence the term octant; a precursor of the sextant, whose arc subtends 60° or 1/6 of a circle.

octant altitude. See SEXTANT ALTITUDE.

Odessey protractor. A device used in conjunction with a plotting sheet having equally spaced concentric circles (range circles) drawn about two or more stations of a radio determination system being operated in the ranging mode.

oe, *n*. A whirlwind off the Faeroe Islands.

oersted, *n*. The centimeter-gram-second electromagnetic system unit of magnetic field strength. It corresponds to $1000/4\pi$ ampere per meter.

off-center PPI display. A plan position indicator display in which the center about which the sweep rotates is offset from the center of the radarscope.

Office of Coast Survey. The Office of Coast Survey is the oldest U.S. scientific organization, dating from 1807 when President Thomas Jefferson signed "An act to provide for surveying the coasts of the United States." OCS is the charting, surveying, and bathymetric modeling arm of the National Ocean Service (NOS), a component of the National Oceanic and Atmospheric Administration (NOAA). OCS supports safe and efficient navigation by maintaining over 1,000 nautical charts and Coast Pilots for U.S. coasts and the Great lakes, covering 95,000 miles of shoreline and 3.4 million square miles of water. The charts are distributed in a variety of formats, which include electronic navigation charts (ENCs), raster navigational charts (RNCs), print on demand (POD) paper charts, and digital chart tile service.

official HO data. See HO information.

official updates. In ECDIS, updates provided in digital format by the ISSUING AUTHORITY of the ENC being corrected, for integration with the ENC DATA in the SENC. Updates provided by the ISSUING AUTHORITY for application to a chart.

offing, *n*. The part of the visible sea a considerable distance from the shore, or that part just beyond the limits of the area in which a pilot is needed.

offshore, *adj*. & *adv*. Away from the shore.

offshore, *n*. The comparatively flat zone of variable width which extends from the outer margin of the rather steeply sloping shore face to the edge of the shelf.

offshore light stations. Manned light stations built on exposed marine sites to replace lightships.

offshore navigation. Navigation at a distance from a coast, in contrast with COASTWISE NAVIGATION in the vicinity of a coast.

offshore water. Water adjacent to land in which the physical properties are slightly influenced by continental conditions.

offshore wind. Wind blowing from the land toward the sea. An ONSHORE WIND blows in the opposite direction. See also LAND BREEZE.

off soundings. Navigating beyond the 100-fathom curve. In earlier times, said of a vessel in water deeper than could be sounded with the sounding lead.

off station. Not in charted position.

ogival buoy. A buoy with a pointed-arch shaped vertical cross-section. Used in the cardinal system.

ohm, *n*. A derived unit of electrical resistance in the International System of Units; it is the electrical resistance between two points of a conductor when a constant potential difference of 1 volt, applied to these points, produces in the conductor a current of 1 ampere, the conductor not being the seat of an electromotive force.

old ice. Sea ice which has survived at least one summer's melt. Most topographic features are smoother than on first-year ice. Old ice may be subdivided into SECOND-YEAR ICE and MULTI YEAR ICE.

Omega Navigation System. A worldwide. continuous, radionavigation system of medium accuracy which provides hyperbolic lines of position through phase comparisons of VLF (10-14kHz) continuous wave signals transmitted on a common frequency on a time-shared basis. The full system is comprised of eight transmitting stations.

Omega plotting chart. See under PLOTTING CHART.

Omega Table. *See PUB. 224.*

omni-. A prefix meaning all.

omniazimuthal antenna. See OMNIDIRECTIONAL ANTENNA.

omnidirectional antenna. An antenna whose radiating or receiving properties at any instant are the same on all bearings. Also called OMNIAZIMUTHAL ANTENNA. See also DIRECTIONAL ANTENNA.

omnidirectional light. A light which presents the same characteristic over the whole horizon of interest to marine navigation. Also called ALL-ROUND LIGHT.

omnidirectional radiobeacon. A radiobeacon transmitting a signal in all directions. A circular radiobeacon is an omnidirectional beacon which transmits in all horizontal directions simultaneously. A rotating radiobeacon is an omnidirectional beacon with one or more beams that rotate. A DIRECTIONAL RADIOBEACON is a beacon which beams its signals in one or several prescribed directions.

on-demand information. In ECDIS, the SENC information which is not part of the standard display. See also ALL OTHER INFORMATION.

onshore wind. Wind blowing from the sea towards the land. An OFFSHORE WIND blows in the opposite direction. See also SEA BREEZE.

on soundings. Navigating within the 100-fathom curve. In earlier times, said of a vessel in water sufficiently shallow for sounding by sounding lead.

on the beam. Bearing approximately 90° relative (on the starboard beam) or 270° relative (on the port beam). The expression is often used loosely for BROAD ON THE BEAM, or bearing exactly 90° or 270° relative. Also called ABEAM.

on the bow. Bearing approximately 45° relative (on the starboard bow) or 315° relative (on the port bow). The expression is often used loosely for BROAD ON THE BOW, or bearing exactly 45° or 315° relative.

on the quarter. Bearing approximately 135° relative (on the starboard quarter) or 225° relative (on the port quarter). The expression is often used loosely for BROAD ON THE QUARTER, or bearing exactly 135° or 225° relative.

ooze, *n*. A soft, slimy, organic sediment covering part of the ocean bottom, composed principally of shells or other hard parts of minute organisms.

open, *v., i*. To move or appear to move apart, such as when range lights appear to separate as the vessel moves off the channel centerline. The opposite is CLOSE.

open basin. See TIDAL BASIN.

open berth. An anchorage berth in an open roadstead.

open coast. A coast that is not sheltered from the sea.

open harbor. An unsheltered harbor exposed to the sea.

opening, *n*. A break in a coastline or a passage between shoals, etc. See also GAT.

open pack ice. Pack ice in which the concentration is 4/10 to 6/10, with many leads and polynyas, and the floes generally not in contact with one another.

open roadstead. A roadstead with relatively little protection from the sea.

open sea. 1. The part of the ocean not enclosed by headlands, within narrow straits, etc. 2. The part of the ocean outside the territorial jurisdiction of any country. The opposite is CLOSED SEA. See also HIGH SEAS.

open water. A large area of freely navigable water in which sea ice is present in concentration less than 1/10. When there is no sea ice present, the area should be described as ICE FREE, even though icebergs may be present.

operating area chart. A base chart with overprints of various operating areas necessary to control fleet exercise activities. Submarine Transit Lanes, Surface and Sub-surface Operating Areas, Air Space Warning Areas, Controlled Air Spaces, and other restricted areas are portrayed.

operating system. The portion of a computer's software devoted to running programs and providing for operator interface.

opposition, *n*. The situation of two celestial bodies having either celestial longitudes or sidereal hour angles differing by 180°. The term is usually used only in relation to the position of a superior planet or the moon with reference to the sun. The situation of two celestial bodies having either the same celestial longitude or the same sidereal hour angle is called conjunction.

optic, *adj*. Of or pertaining to vision.

optical, *adj*. Of or pertaining to optics or to vision.

optical double star. Two stars in nearly the same line of sight but differing greatly in distance from the observer, as distinguished from a PHYSICAL DOUBLE STAR (two stars in nearly the same line of sight and at approximately the same distance from the observer).

optical glass. Glass of which the composition and molding are carefully controlled in order to insure uniform refractive index and high transmission factor.

optical path. The path followed by a ray of light through an optical system.

optical system. A series of lenses, apertures, prisms, mirrors, etc., so arranged as to perform a definite optical function.

optics, *n*. The science dealing with light, lenses, etc.

Optimum Track Ship Routing. See under SHIP WEATHER ROUTING.

orbit, *n*. 1. The path of a body or particle under the influence of a gravitational or other force. See also CENTRAL FORCE ORBIT, INERTIAL ORBIT, INTERMEDIATE ORBIT, NOMINAL ORBIT, NORMAL ORBIT, OSCULATING ORBIT, PERTURBED ORBIT, POLAR ORBIT, STATIONARY ORBIT.

orbital altitude. The mean altitude of the orbit of a satellite above the surface of the parent body.

orbital elements. Parameters that specify the position and motion of a body in orbit. The elliptical orbit of a satellite attracted by an exactly central gravitational force is specified by a set of six parameters as follows: Two parameters, the semimajor axis and eccentricity of the ellipse, establish the size and shape of the elliptical orbit. A third parameter, time of perifocal passage, enables determination of the location of the satellite in its orbit at any instant. The three remaining parameters establish the orientation of the orbit in space. These are the inclination of the orbital plane to a reference plane, the right ascension of the ascending node of the satellite, and the argument of pericenter. See also ORBITAL PARAMETERS OF ARTIFICIAL SATELLITE, MEAN ELEMENTS, OSCULATING ELEMENTS.

orbital inclination. See as INCLINATION, definition 2.

orbital mode. A method for determining the position of an unknown station position when the unknown position cannot be viewed simultaneously with known positions. The arc of the satellite orbit is extrapolated from the ephemeris of the satellite determined by the known stations which permits the determination of the position of the unknown station dependent completely on the satellite's orbital parameters.

orbital motion. Continuous motion in a closed path about and as a direct result of a source of gravitational attraction.

orbital parameters of artificial earth satellite. The precessing elliptical orbit of an artificial earth satellite is unambiguously specified by the following set of parameters: semimajor axis. eccentricity, time of perigee, inclination of the orbital plane to the plane of the reference plane (celestial equator), the right ascension of the ascending node of the satellite at time of perigee, the argument of perigee at time of perigee, right ascension of Greenwich at time of perigee, mean motion (rate of change of mean anomaly), rate of change of argument of perigee, and rate of change of right ascension of the ascending node at time of perigee. With the inclination expressed as the sine and cosine of the orbital inclination, the parameters number 11. See also ORBITAL ELEMENTS.

orbital path. One of the tracks on a primary body's surface traced by the subpoint of a satellite that orbits about it several times in a direction other than normal to the primary body's axis of rotation. Each track is displaced in a direction opposite and by an amount equal to the degrees of rotation between each satellite orbit and of the nodical precession of the plane of the orbit. Also called SUBTRACK. See also WESTWARD MOTION.

orbital period. If the orbit is unchanging and ideal, the in travel between successive passages of a satellite through the same point in its orbit. If the orbit is not ideal, the point must be specified. When the perigee is specified it is called radial or anomalistic period. When the ascending node is specified, it is called nodical period. When the same geocentric right ascension is specified, it is called sidereal period. Also called PERIOD OF SATELLITE.

orbital plane. The plane of the ellipse defined by a central force orbit.

orbital velocity. The velocity of an earth satellite or other orbiting body at any given point in its orbit.

ordinary, *adj*. With respect to tides, the use of this non technical term has, for the most part, been determined to be synonymous with mean. The use of the term ordinary in tidal terms is discouraged.

ordinate, *n*. The vertical coordinate of a set of rectangular coordinates. Also used in a similar sense in connection with oblique coordinates.

orient, *v., t*. 1. To line up or adjust with respect to a reference. 2. To obtain a mental grasp of the existing situation.

orientability of a sound signal. The property of a sound signal by virtue of which a listener can estimate the direction of the location of the signal.

orientation. In ECDIS, the mode in which information on the ECDIS is being presented. Typical modes include: north-up - as shown on a nautical CHART, north is at the top of the display; Ship's head-up - based on the actual HEADING of the ship, (e.g. Ship's gyrocompass); course-up display - based on the COURSE or ROUTE being taken.

orographic rain. Rain resulting when moist air is forced upward by a mountain range.

orthodrome, *n*. See GREAT CIRCLE.

orthodromic curve. See GREAT CIRCLE.

orthogonal, *adj*. Right angled, rectangular.

orthogonal map projection. See ORTHOGRAPHIC MAP PROJECTION.

orthographic, *adj*. Of or pertaining to right angles or perpendicular lines.

orthographic chart. A chart on the orthographic map projection.

orthographic map projection. A perspective azimuthal projection in which the projecting lines, emanating from a point at infinity, are perpendicular to a tangent plane. The projection is used chiefly in navigational astronomy for inter converting coordinates of the celestial equator and horizon systems. Also called ORTHOGONAL PROJECTION.

orthomorphic, *adj*. Preserving the correct shape. See also CONFORMAL MAP PROJECTION.

orthomorphic chart. A chart on which very small shapes are correctly represented. See also CONFORMAL MAP PROJECTION.

orthomorphic map projection. A projection in which very small shapes are correctly represented. See also CONFORMAL MAP PROJECTION.

oscar satellite. A general term for one of the operational satellites of the Navy Navigation Satellite System, except for satellite 30110 called TRANSAT, placed in orbit prior to 1981. The improved satellites placed in orbit beginning in 1981 are called NOVA.

oscillation, *n*. 1. Fluctuation or vibration to each side of a mean value or position. 2. Half an oscillatory cycle, consisting of fluctuation or vibration in one direction; half a vibration.

oscillator, *n.* A sound signal emitter comprising a resonant diaphragm maintained in vibrating motion by electromagnetic action.

oscillatory wave. A wave in which only the form advances, the individual particles of the medium moving in closed orbits, as ocean waves in deep water; in contrast with a WAVE OF TRANSLATION, in which the individual particles are shifted in the direction of wave travel, as ocean waves in shoal water.

oscilloscope, *n.* An instrument for producing a visual representation of oscillations or changes in an electric current. The face of the cathode-ray tube used for this representation is called a SCOPE or SCREEN.

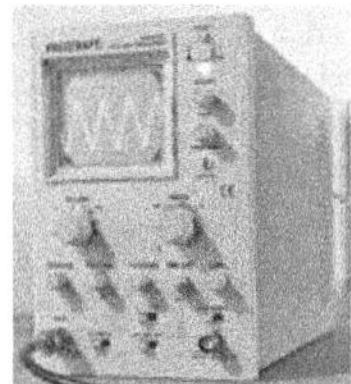
oscilloscope

osculating elements. A set of parameters that specifies the instantaneous position and velocity of a celestial body, or artificial satellite in a perturbed orbit. Osculating elements describe the unperturbed (two-body) orbit (osculating orbit) that the body would follow if perturbations were to cease instantaneously.

osculating orbit. The ellipse that a satellite would follow after a specific time "t" (the epoch of osculation) if all forces other than central force ceased to act from "t" on. An osculating orbit is tangent to the real, perturbed, orbit and has the same velocity at the point of tangency. See also OSCULATING ELEMENTS.

other chart information. See DISPLAY CATEGORY.

other navigational information. In ECDIS, NAVIGATIONAL INFORMATION not contained in the SENC, that may be displayed by an ECDIS, such as radar information.

outage, *n.* The failure of an aid to navigation to function exactly as described in the light list.

outer harbor. See under INNER HARBOR.

outfall, *n.* The discharge end of a narrow street sewer, drain, etc.

outfall buoy. A buoy marking the position where a sewer or other drain discharges.

outline chart. A chart with only a generally presentation of the landmass with little or no culture or relief. See also PLOT CHART.

output axis. The axis of precession of a gyroscope. See also INPUT AXIS, PRECESSION.

outside fix. A term describing the fix position determined by the method of bisectors when the lines of position result from observations of objects or celestial bodies lying within a 180° arc of the horizon. See also METHOD OF BISECTORS.

outward bound. Heading for the open sea. The opposite is INWARD BOUND. See also HOMEWARD BOUND.

overcast, *adj.* Pertaining to a sky cover of 95% or more.

overcast, *n.* A cloud cover.

overfalls, *n. pl.* Breaking waves caused by the meeting of currents or by waves moving against the current. See also RIPS.

overhead cable effect. A radar phenomenon which may occur in the vicinity of an overhead power cable. The echo from the cable appears on the plan position indicator as a single echo, the echo being returned from that part of cable where the radar beam is at right angles to the cable. If this phenomenon is not recognized, the echo can be wrongly identified as the echo from a ship on a steady bearing. Evasive action results in the echo remaining on a constant bearing and moving to the same side of the channel as the ship altering course. This phenomenon is particularly apparent for the power cable spanning the Straits of Messina.

overhead compass. See INVERTED COMPASS.

overhead constraints. The elevation angle limitations between which usable navigation data may be obtained from a satellite in the doppler mode.

overlay, *n.* A printing or drawing on a transparent or translucent medium at the same scale as a map, chart, etc., to show details not appearing on the original.

overprint, *n.* New material printed on a map or chart to show data of importance or special value in addition to that originally printed.

overscale, In ECDIS, to display the chart information at a DISPLAY SCALE larger than the COMPILATION SCALE. Overscaling may arise from a deliberate overscaling by the mariner, or from automatic overscaling by ECDIS in compiling a DISPLAY when the data included is of various NAVIGATIONAL PURPOSES.

overscale area, In, ECDIS, when the data displayed is from data of two different NAVIGATIONAL PURPOSES the chart display will, where drawn at the larger SCALE, include an overscale area of data from the smaller scale CELL in order to complete the DISPLAY. This area should be identified by the "overscale pattern" of the PRESENTATION LIBRARY.

overtide, *n.* A harmonic tidal or tidal current constituent with a speed that is an exact multiple of the speed of one of the fundamental constituents derived from the development of the tide-producing force. The presence of overtides is usually attributed to shallow water conditions.

own ship's safety contour, In ECDIS the contour related to the own ship selected by the mariner from the contours provided for in the SENC, to be used by ECDIS to distinguish on the DISPLAY between the safe and the unsafe water, and for generating anti-grounding ALARMS.

own ship's symbol, In ECDIS (and ARPA) a non-chart symbol used to show the ship's position on the CHART or ARPA display.

own ship, In ECDIS a term identifying the vessel upon which an ECDIS is operating.

Oyashio, *n.* A cold ocean current flowing from the Bering Sea southwestward along the coast of Kamchatka, past the Kuril Islands to meet the Kuroshio off the coast of Honshu. The Oyashio turns and continues eastward, eventually joining the Aleutian Current.

P

Pacific Equatorial Countercurrent. A Pacific Ocean current that flows eastward, counter to and between the westward flowing Pacific North and South Equatorial Currents, between latitudes 3°N and 10°N. East of the Philippines it is joined by the southern part of the Pacific North Equatorial Current.

Pacific North Equatorial Current. A North Pacific Ocean current that flows westward between latitudes 10°N and 20°N. East of the Philippines, it divides, part turning south to join the Pacific Equatorial Counter current and part turning north to flow along the coast of Japan as the KUROSHIO.

Pacific South Equatorial Current. A Pacific Ocean current that flows westward between latitudes 3°N and 10°S. In mid ocean, much of it turns south to form a large whirl. The portion that continues across the ocean divides as it approaches Australia, part flowing north toward New Guinea and part turning south along the east coast of Australia as the EAST AUSTRALIA CURRENT.

Pacific standard time. See STANDARD TIME.

pack ice. The term used in a wide sense to include any area of sea ice, other than fast ice, no matter what form it takes or how it is disposed.

pagoda, *n.* As a landmark, a tower having a number of stories and a characteristic architecture, used as a place of worship or as a memorial, primarily in Japan, China, and India.

paint, *n.* The bright area on the phosphorescent plan position indicator screen resulting from the brightening of the sweep by the echoes.

paint, *v., t & i.* To brighten the phosphorescent plan position indicator screen through the effects of the echoes on the sweep.

painted mark. A navigation mark formed simply by painting a cliff, wall, rock, etc.

pancake ice. Predominantly circular pieces of ice from 30 centimeters to 3 meters in diameter, and up to about 10 centimeters in thickness with raised rims due to pieces striking against one another. It may be formed on a slight swell from grease ice, shuga, or slush or as a result of the breaking of ice rind, nilas, or under severe conditions of swell or waves, of gray ice. It also sometimes forms at some depth, at an interface between water bodies of different physical characteristics, from where it floats to the surface; its appearance may rapidly cover wide areas of water.

pantograph, *n.* An instrument for copying maps, drawings, or other graphics at a predetermined scale.

papagayo, *n.* A violet northeasterly fall wind on the Pacific coast of Nicaragua and Guatemala. It consists of the cold air mass of a *norte* which has overridden the mountains of Central America. See also TEHUANTEPECER.

parabola, *n.* An open curve all points of which are equidistant from a fixed point, called the FOCUS, and a straight line. The limiting case occurs when the point is on the line, in which case the parabola becomes a straight line.

parabolic reflector. A reflecting surface having the cross section along the axis in the shape of a parabola. Parallel rays striking the reflector are brought to a focus at a point, or if the source of the rays is placed at the focus, the reflected rays are parallel. See also CORNER REFLECTION RADAR REFLECTOR, SCANNER.

parabolic velocity. See ESCAPE VELOCITY.

parallactic angle. That angle at the navigational triangle at the celestial body; the angle between a body's hour circle and its vertical circle. Also called POSITION ANGLE.

parallax, *n.* The difference in apparent direction or position of an object when viewed from different points. For bodies of the solar system, parallax is the difference in the direction of the body due to the displacement of the observer from the center of the earth, and is called geocentric parallax, varying with the body's altitude and distance from the earth. The geocentric parallel when a body is in the horizon is called horizontal parallax, as contrasted with the parallax at any altitude, called parallax in altitude. Parallax of the moon is called lunar parallax. In marine navigation it is customary to apply a parallax correction to sextant altitudes of the sun, moon, Venus, and Mars. For stars, parallax is the angle at the star subtended by the semimajor axis of the earth's orbit and is called heliocentric or stellar parallax, which is too small to be significant as a sextant error.

parallax correction. A correction due to parallax, particularly that sextant altitude correction due to the difference between the apparent direction from a point on the surface of the earth to celestial body and the apparent direction from the center of the earth to the same body.

parallax in altitude. Geocentric parallax of a body at any altitude. The expression is used to distinguish the parallax at the given altitude from the horizontal parallax when the body is in the horizon. See also PARALLAX.

parallax inequality. The variation in the range of tide or in the speed of a tidal current due to changes in the distance of the moon from the earth. The range of tide and speed of the current tend alternately to increase and decrease as the moon approaches its perigee and apogee, respectively, the complete cycle being the anomalistic month. There is a similar but relatively unimportant inequality due to the sun; this cycle is the anomalistic year. The parallax has little direct effect upon the lunitidal intervals but tends to modify the phase effect. When the moon is in perigee, the priming and lagging of the tide due to the phase is diminished and when in apogee the priming and lagging is increased.

parallax reduction. Processing of observed high and low waters to obtain quantities depending upon changes in the distance of the moon, such as perigean and apogean ranges.

parallel, *adj.* Everywhere equidistant, as of lines or surfaces.

parallel, *n.* See PARALLEL OF LATITUDE, definition 1.

parallel indexing. The use of rotating parallel lines overlayed on a radar display to aid in piloting.

parallel motion protractor. An instrument consisting of a protractor and one or more arms attached to a parallel motion device, so that the movement of the arms is everywhere parallel. The protractor can be rotated and set at any position so that it can be oriented to a chart. Also called DRAFTING MACHINE.

parallel of altitude. A circle of the celestial sphere parallel to the horizon, connecting all points of equal altitude. Also called ALTITUDE CIRCLE, ALMUCANTAR. See also CIRCLE OF EQUAL ALTITUDE.

parallel of declination. A circle of the celestial sphere parallel to the celestial equator. Also called CELESTIAL PARALLEL, CIRCLE OF EQUAL DECLINATION. See also DIURNAL CIRCLE.

parallel of latitude. 1. A circle (or approximation of a circle) on the surface of the earth, parallel to the equator, and connecting points of equal latitude. Also called a PARALLEL. 2. A circle of the celestial sphere, parallel to the ecliptic, and connecting points of equal celestial latitude. Also called CIRCLE OF LONGITUDE.

parallelogram, *n.* A four-sided figure with both pairs of opposite sides parallel. A right-angled parallelogram is a rectangle; a rectangle with sides of equal length is a square. A parallelogram with oblique angles is a rhomboid; a rhomboid with sides of equal length is a rhombus.

parallel rulers. An instrument for transferring a line parallel to itself. In its most common form it consists of two parallel bars or rulers connected in such manner that when one is held in place, the other may be moved, remaining parallel to its original position.

parallel sailing. A method of converting departure into difference of longitude, or vice versa, when the true course is 090° or 270°.

parallel sphere. The celestial sphere as it appears to an observer at the pole, where celestial bodies appear to move parallel to the horizon.

parameter, *n.* 1. A quantity which remains constant within the limits of a given case or situation. 2. One of the components into which a craft's magnetic field is assumed to be resolved for the purpose of compass adjustment. The field caused by permanent magnetism is resolved into orthogonal components or parameters: Parameter P, Parameter Q, and Parameter R. The field caused by induced magnetism is resolved into that magnetism induced in 9 imaginary soft iron bars or rods. With respect to the axis of a craft, these parameters lie in a fore-and-aft direction, an athwart ships direction, and in a vertical direction. See also ROD, definition 2.

paranthelion, *n.* A phenomenon similar to a PARHELION but occurring generally at a distance of 120° (occasionally 90° or 140°) from the sun.

paraselene *(pl. paraselenae), n.* A form of halo consisting of an image of the moon at the same altitude as the moon and some distance from it, usually about 22°, but occasionally about 46°. Similar phenomena may occur about 90°, 120°, 140°, or 180° from the moon. A similar phenomenon in relation to the sun is called a PARHELION, SUN DOG, or MOCK SUN. Also called MOCK MOON.

paraselenic circle. A halo consisting of a faint white circle through the moon and parallel to the horizon. It is produced by reflection of moonlight from vertical faces of ice crystals. A similar circle through the sun is called a PARHELIC CIRCLE.

parhelic circle. A halo consisting of a faint white circle through the sun and parallel to the horizon. It is produced by reflection of sunlight from vertical faces of ice crystals. A similar circle through the moon is called a PARASELENIC CIRCLE. Also called MOCK SUN RING.

parhelion *(pl. parhelia), n.* A form of halo, consisting of an image of the sun at the same altitude as the sun and some distance from usually about 22°, but occasionally about 40°. A similar phenomenon occurring at a distance of 90°, 120°, or 140° from the sun is called a PARANTHELION, and if occurring at a distance of 180° from the sun, an ANTHELION. A similar phenomenon in relation to the moon is called PARASELENE, MOON DOG, or MOCK MOON. The term PARHELION should not be confused with PERIHELION, the orbital point near the sun when the sun is the center of attraction. Also called SUN DOG, MOCK SUN.

parsec, *n.* The distance at which 1 astronomical unit subtends an angle of 1 second of arc. One parsec equals about 206,265 astronomical units or 30,857 × 10^{12} meters or 3.26 light years. The name parsec is derived from <u>par</u>allax <u>sec</u>ond.

partial eclipse. An eclipse in which only part of the source of light is obscured. See ECLIPSE.

pascal, *n.* The special name for the derived unit of pressure and stress in the International System of Units; it is 1 newton per square meter.

pass, *n.* 1. A navigable channel leading to a harbor or river. Sometimes called PASSAGE. 2. A break in a mountain range, permitting easier passage from one side of the range to the other; also called COL. 3. A narrow opening through a barrier reef atoll, or sand bar. 4. A single circuit of the earth by a satellite. See also ORBIT. 5. The period of time a satellite is within telemetry range of a data acquisition station.

passage, *n.* 1. A navigable channel, especially one through reefs or islands. Also called PASS. 2. A transit from one place to another; one leg of a voyage.

passing light. A low intensity light which may be mounted on the structure of another light to enable the mariner to keep the latter light in sight when he passes out of its beam. See also SUBSIDIARY LIGHT.

passive satellite. 1. A satellite which contains power source to augment the output signal (i.e., reflected only) as contrasted with ACTIVE SATELLITE; a satellite which is a passive reflector. 2. As defined by the International Telecommunications Union (ITU), an earth satellite intended to transmit radiocommunication signals by reflection.

passive system. A term used to describe a navigation system whose operation does not require the user to transmit a signal.

patent log. A mechanical log, particularly a TAFFRAIL LOG.

patent slip. See MARINE RAILWAY.

path, *n*. See as ORBITAL PATH.

pattern, *n*. 1. See under LATTICE. 2. In a hyperbolic radionavigation system, the family of hyperbolas associated with a single pair of stations, usually the master station and a slave (secondary) station.

P-band. A radio-frequency band of 225 to 390 megahertz. See also FREQUENCY, FREQUENCY BAND.

P-code. The precise code of the GPS signal, used by military receivers.

polar cap anomaly. See under POLAR CAP DISTURBANCE.

peak, *n*. 1. On the sea floor, a prominent elevation, part of a larger feature, either pointed or of very limited extent across the summit. 2. A pointed mountain summit. 3. An individual or conspicuous mountain with a single conspicuous summit, as Pikes Peak. 4. The summit of a mountain. 5. A term sometimes used for a headland or promontory.

peak envelope power. See under POWER (OF A RADIO TRANSMITTER).

pebble, *n*. See under STONES.

pelorus, *n*. A dumb compass, or a compass card (called a PELORUS CARD) without a directive element, suitably mounted and provided with vanes to permit observation of relative bearings unless used in conjunction with a compass to give true or magnetic bearings.

pelorus card. The part of a pelorus on which the direction graduations are placed. It is usually in the form of a thin disk or annulus graduated in degrees, clockwise, from 0° at the reference direction to 360°.

pendulous gyroscope. A gyroscope with its axis of rotation constrained by a suitable weight to remain horizontal. The pendulous gyroscope is the basis of one type of gyrocompass.

peninsula, *n*. A section of land nearly surrounded by water. Frequently, but not necessarily, a peninsula is connected to a larger body of land by a neck or isthmus.

pentagon, *n*. A closed plane figure having five sides.

pentagonal cluster. An arrangement of five corner reflectors, mounted so as to give their maximum response in a horizontal direction, and equally spaced on the circumference of a circle. The response is substantially uniform in all horizontal directions. See also OCTAHEDRAL CLUSTER.

penumbra, *n*. 1. That part of a shadow in which light is partly cut off by an intervening object. The penumbra surrounds the darker UMBRA in which light is completely cut off. 2. The lighter part of a sun spot, surrounding the darker UMBRA.

penumbral lunar eclipse. The eclipse of the moon when the moon passes only through the penumbra of the earth's shadow.

performance monitor. A device used to check the performance of the transmitter and receiver of a radar set. Such device does not provide any indication of performance as it might be affected by the propagation of the radar waves through the atmosphere. An echo box is used in one type of performance monitor called an echo box performance monitor.

Performance Standards for ECDIS. Minimum performance requirements for ECDIS, adopted by IMO as Assembly resolution and published as an Annex to IMO resolution MSC.232(82).

per gyrocompass (PGC). Relating to or from the gyrocompass.

periapsis, *n*. See PERICENTER.

periastron, *n*. That point of the orbit of one member of a double star system at which the stars are nearest together. That point at which they are farthest apart is called APASTRON.

pericenter, *n*. In an elliptical orbit, the point in the orbit which is the nearest distance from the focus where the attracting mass is located. the pericenter is at one end of the major axis of the orbital ellipse. The opposite is APOAPSIS, APOCENTER. Also called PERIAPSIS, PERIFOCUS.

perifocus, *n*. See PERICENTER.

perigean range. See under PERIGEAN TIDES.

perigean tidal currents. Tidal currents of increased speed occurring monthly as the result of the moon being in perigee or nearest the earth.

perigean tides. Tides of increased range occurring monthly as the result of the moon being in perigee or nearest the earth. The perigean range of tide is the average semidiurnal range occurring at the time of perigean tides and is most conveniently computed from the harmonic constants. It is larger than the mean range where the type of tide is either semidiurnal or mixed and is of no practical significance where the type of tide is diurnal.

perigee, *n*. The orbital point nearest the earth when the earth is the center of attraction. The orbital point farthest from the earth is called APOGEE. See also APOCENTER, PERICENTER.

perigee-to-perigee period. See ANOMALISTIC PERIOD.

perigon, *n*. An angle of 360°.

perihelion, *n*. That orbital point nearest the sun when the sun is the center of attraction. That point farthest from the sun is called APHELION.

perimeter, *n*. 1. The length of a closed plane curve or the sum of the sides of a polygon. 2. The boundary of a plane figure. Also called PERIPHERY.

period, *n*. 1. The interval needed to complete a cycle. See also NATURAL PERIOD, SIDEREAL PERIOD, SYNODIC PERIOD, WAVE PERIOD). 2. The interval of time between the commencement of two identical successive cycles of the characteristic of the light.

periodic, *adj*. Of or pertaining to a period.

periodic error. An error whose amplitude and direction vary systematically with time.

periodic perturbations. Perturbations to the orbit of a satellite which change direction in regular or periodic manner in time, such that the average effect over a long period of time is zero.

periodic terms. In the mathematical expression of the orbit of a satellite, terms which vary with time in both magnitude and direction in a periodic manner. See also SECULAR TERMS.

period of satellite. 1. See ORBITAL PERIOD. 2. As defined by the International Telecommunication Union (ITU), the time elapsing between two consecutive passages of a satellite or planet through a characteristic point on its orbit.

periphery, *n*. See PERIMETER.

periplus, *n*. The early Greek name for SAILING DIRECTIONS. The literal meaning of the term is "a sailing round."

periscope, *n*. An optical instrument which displaces the line of sight parallel to itself, to permit a view which may otherwise be obstructed.

periscope sextant. A sextant designed to be used in conjunction with the periscope of a submarine.

permafrost, *n*. Permanently frozen subsoil. Any soil or other deposit, including rock, the temperature of which has been below freezing continuously for 2 years or more is considered permafrost.

Permalloy, *n*. The trade name for an alloy of about 80% nickel and 20% iron, which is very easily magnetized and demagnetized.

permanent current. A current that runs fairly continuously and is independent of tides and other temporary causes.

permanent echo. An echo from an object whose position relative to the radar set is fixed.

permanent light. A light used in regular service.

permanent magnetism. The magnetism which is acquired by hard iron, which is not readily magnetized by induction, but which retains a high percentage of magnetism acquired unless subjected to a demagnetizing force. The strength and polarity of this magnetism in a craft depends upon the heading, magnetic latitude, and building stresses imposed during construction. See also INDUCED MAGNETISM, SUBPERMANENT MAGNETISM.

permeability, *n*. 1. The ability to transmit magnetism; magnetic conductivity. 2. The ability to permit penetration or passage. In this sense the term is applied particularly to substances which permit penetration or passage of fluids.

perpendicular, *adj*. At right angles; normal.

perpendicular, *n*. A perpendicular line, plane, etc. A distinction is sometimes made between PERPENDICULAR and NORMAL, the former applying to a line at right angles to a straight line or plane, and the latter referring to a line at right angles to a curve or curved surface.

persistence, *n*. A measure of the time of decay of the luminescence of the face of the cathode ray tube after excitation by the stream of electrons has ceased. Relatively slow decay is indicative of high persistence. Persistence is the length of time during which phosphorescence takes place. See also AFTERGLOW, definition 1.

personal correction. A correction due to personal error. Also called PERSONAL EQUATION.

personal equation. A term used for both PERSONAL ERROR and PERSONAL CORRECTION.

personal error. A systematic error in the observation of a quantity due to the personal idiosyncrasies of the observer. Also called PERSONAL EQUATION.

perspective chart. A chart on a perspective map projection.

perspective map projection. A map projection produced by the direct projection of the points of the ellipsoid (used to represent the earth) by straight lines drawn through them from some given point. The projection is usually made upon a plane tangent to the ellipsoid at the end of the diameter joining the point of projection and the center of the ellipsoid. The plane of projection is usually tangent to the ellipsoid at the center of the area being mapped. he analytical expressions that determine the elements of the projection. If the point of projection is at the center of the ellipsoid, a gnomonic map projection results; if it is at the point opposite the plane's point of tangency a stereographic map projection; and if at infinity (the projecting lines being parallel to each other), an orthographic map projection. Most map projections are not perspective. Also called GEOMETRIC MAP PROJECTION.

perspective map projection upon a tangent cylinder. A cylindrical map projection upon a cylinder tangent to the ellipsoid produced by perspective projection from the ellipsoid's center. The geographic meridians are represented by a family of equally spaced parallel straight lines, perpendicular to a second family of parallel straight lines which represent the geographic parallels of latitude. The spacing, with respect to the equator of the lines which represent the parallels of latitude, increases as the tangent function of the latitude; the line representing 90° latitude is at an infinite distance from the line which represents the equator. Not to be confused with MERCATOR MAP PROJECTION to which it bears a general resemblance.

perspective projection. The representation of a figure on a surface, either plane or curved, by means of projecting lines emanating from a single point, which may be infinity. Also called GEOMETRIC PROJECTION. See also PERSPECTIVE MAP PROJECTION.

per standard compass. Relating to the standard magnetic compass.

per steering compass. Relating to the magnetic steering compass.

perturbations, *n. (pl.)*. In celestial mechanics differences of the actual orbit from a central force orbit, arising from some external force such as a third body attracting the other two; a resisting medium (atmosphere); failure of the parent body to act as a point mass, and so forth. Also the forces that cause differences between the actual and reference (central force) orbits. See also GRAVITATIONAL PERTURBATIONS, LONG PERIOD PERTURBATIONS, LUNISOLAR PERTURBATIONS, NONGRAVITATIONAL PERTURBATIONS, PERIODIC PERTURBATIONS, SECULAR PERTURBATIONS, SHORT PERIOD PERTURBATIONS, TERRESTRIAL PERTURBATIONS.

perturbed orbit. The orbit of a satellite differing from its normal orbit due to various disturbing effects, such as nonsymmetrical gravitational effects, atmospheric drag, radiation pressure, and so forth. See also PERTURBATIONS.

perturbing factor. In celestial mechanics, any factor that acts on an orbiting body to change its orbit from a central force orbit. Also called PERTURBING FORCE.

perturbing force. See PERTURBING FACTOR.

Peru Coastal Current. See PERU CURRENT.

Peru Current. A narrow, fairly stable ocean current that flows northward close to the South American coast. It originates off the coast of Chile at about latitude 40°S and flows past Peru and Ecuador to the southwest extremity of Colombia. The southern portion of the Peru Current is sometimes called the CHILE CURRENT. It has sometimes been called the HUMBOLDT CURRENT because an early record of its temperature was taken by the German scientist Alexander von Humboldt in 1802. The name Corriente del Peru was adopted by a resolution of the Ibero-American Oceanographic Conference at its Madrid-Malaga meeting in April 1935. Also called PERU COASTAL CURRENT.

Peru Oceanic Current. See MENTOR CURRENT.

phantom, *n*. That part of a gyrocompass carrying the compass card.

phantom bottom. A false bottom indicated by an echo sounder, some distance above the actual bottom. Such an indication, quite common in the deeper parts of the ocean, is due to large quantities of small organisms.

phantom echo. See PHANTOM TARGET.

phantom target. 1. An indication of an object on a radar display that does not correspond to the presence of an actual object at the point indicated. Also called PHANTOM ECHO. 2. See ECHO BOX.

phase, *n*. The amount by which a cycle has progressed from a specified origin. For most purposes it is stated in circular measure, a complete cycle being considered 360°. See also PHASES OF THE MOON.

phase angle. The angle at a celestial body between the sun and earth.

phase inequality. Variations in the tides or tidal currents due to changes in the phase of the moon. At the times of new and full moon the tide-producing forces of the moon and sun act in conjunction, causing the range of tide and speed of the tidal current to be greater than the average, the tides at these times being known as spring tides. At the time of quadrature of the moon these forces are opposed to each other, causing the neap tides with diminished range and current speed.

phase lag. See EPOCH, definition 3.

phase lock. The technique whereby the phase of an oscillator signal is made to follow exactly the phase of a reference signal by first comparing the phases of the two signals and then using the resulting phase difference signal to adjust the reference oscillator frequency to eliminate phase difference when the two signals are next compared.

phase meter. An instrument for measuring the difference in phase of two waves of the same frequency.

phase modulation. The process of changing the phase of a carrier wave in accordance with the variations of a modulating wave. See also MODULATION.

phase reduction. Processing of observed high and low waters to obtain quantities depending upon the phase of the moon, such as the spring and neap ranges of tide. Formerly this process was known as SECOND REDUCTION. Also applicable to tidal currents.

phases of the moon. The various appearances of the moon during different parts of the synodical month. The cycle begins with new moon or change of the moon at conjunction. The visible part of the waxing moon increases in size during the first half of the cycle until full moon appears at opposition, after which the visible part of the waning moon decreases for the remainder of the cycle. First quarter occurs when the waxing moon is at east quadrature; last quarter when the waning moon is at west quadrature. From last quarter to new and from new to first quarter the moon is crescent; from first quarter to full and from full to last quarter it is gibbous. The elapsed time, usually expressed in days, since the last new moon is called age of the moon. The full moon occurring nearest the autumnal equinox is called harvest moon; the next full moon, hunter's moon.

phase synchronized. A term used to indicate that radio wave transmissions have the same phase at their sources at any instant of time.

phenomenon *(pl. phenomena), n*. 1. An occurrence or event capable of being explained scientifically, particularly one relating to the unusual. 2. A rare or unusual event.

phonetic alphabet. A list of standard words used to identify letters in a message transmitted by radio or telephone.

phosphor, *n*. A phosphorescent substance which emits light when excited by radiation, as on the scope of a cathode-ray tube.

phosphorescence, *n*. Emission of light without sensible heat, particularly as a result of but continuing after absorption of radiation from some other source. PERSISTENCE is the length of time during which phosphorescence takes place. The emission of light or other radiant energy as a result of and only during absorption of radiation from some other source is called FLUORESCENCE.

photogrammetry, *n*. 1. The science of obtaining reliable measurements from photographic images. 2. The science of preparing charts and maps from aerial photographs using stereoscopic equipment and methods.

photosphere, *n*. The bright portion of the sun visible to the unaided eye.

physical double star. Two stars in nearly the same line of sight and at approximately the same distance from the observer, as distinguished from an OPTICAL DOUBLE STAR (two stars in nearly the same line of sight but differing greatly in distance from the observer). If they revolve about their common center of mass, they are called a **binary star**.

pico-. A prefix meaning one-trillionth (10^{-12}).

piedmont, *n*. An area of hills situated at the base of a range of mountains.

pier, *n*. 1. A structure extending into the water from a shore or a bank which provides berthing for ships, or use as a promenade or fishing pier. See also WHARF. 2. A support for the spans of a bridge.

pierhead, *n*. The outer end of a pier or jetty.

pile, *n*. A long, heavy timber or section of steel, concrete, etc., forced into the earth to serve as a support, as for a pier, or to resist lateral pressure.

pile beacon. A beacon formed of one or more piles.

pile dolphin. A minor light structure consisting of a number of piles driven into the bottom in a circular pattern and drawn together with or without a light mounted at the top. Referred to in the *Light List* as a DOLPHIN.

pile dolphin

pillar buoy. A buoy composed of a tall central structure mounted on a broad flat base.

pilot, *n*. 1. A person who directs the movement of a vessel through pilot waters, usually a person who has demonstrated extensive knowledge of channels, aids to navigation, dangers to navigation, etc., in a particular area and is licensed in that area. See also LOCAL KNOWLEDGE. 2. A book of sailing directions. For waters the United States and its possessions, They are prepared by the National Ocean Survey, and are called COAST PILOTS.

pilotage, *n*. 1. The services of especially qualified navigators having local knowledge who assist in the navigation of vessels in particular areas. Also called PILOTAGE SERVICE. 2. A term loosely used for piloting.

pilotage service. See PILOTAGE, definition 1.

pilotage waters. See PILOT WATERS.

pilot boat. A small vessel used by the pilot to go or from a vessel employing his services. Also called PILOT VESSEL.

pilot chart. A chart of a major ocean area which presents in graphic form averages obtained from weather, wave, ice, and other marine data gathered over many years in meteorology and oceanography to aid the navigator in selecting the quickest and safest routes; published by the Defense Mapping Agency Hydrographic/Topographic Center from data provided by the U.S. Naval Oceanographic Office and the Environmental Data and Information Service of the National Oceanic and Atmospheric Administration.

piloting, *n*. Navigation involving frequent or continuous determination of position relative to observed geographical points, to a high order of accuracy; directing the movements of a vessel near a coast by means of terrestrial reference points is called coast piloting. Sometimes called PILOTAGE. See also PILOTAGE, definition 1.

pilot rules. Regulations supplementing the Inland Rules of the Road, superseded by the adoption of the Inland Navigation Rules in 1980 (1983 on the Great Lakes).

pilot station. The office or headquarters of pilots; the place where the services of a pilot may be obtained.

pilot vessel. See PILOT BOAT.

pilot waters. 1. Areas in which the services of a marine pilot are essential. 2. Waters in which navigation is by piloting. Also called PILOTAGE WATERS.

pinnacle, *n*. A high tower or spire-shaped pillar of rock or coral on the sea floor, alone or cresting a summit. It may or may not be a hazard to surface navigation. Due to the steep rise from the sea floor no warning is given by sounding.

pinnacled iceberg. An iceberg weathered in such manner as to produce spires or pinnacles. Also called PYRAMIDAL ICEBERG, IRREGULAR ICEBERG.

pip, *n*. See BLIP.

pitch, *n*. 1. Oscillation of a vessel about the transverse axis due to the vessel's bow and stern being raised or lowered on passing through successive crests and troughs of waves. Also called PITCHING. See also SHIP MOTIONS. 2. The distance a propeller would advance longitudinally in one revolution if there were no slip.

pitch, *v., i*. To oscillate about the transverse axis. See also SHIP MOTIONS.

pitching, *n*. See PITCH, definition 1.

pivot point. The point on the centerline between the bow and the center of gravity at which the resultant of the velocities of rotation and translation is directed along the centerline, after a ship has assumed its drift angle in a turn. To an observer on board, the ship appears to rotate about this point.

pixel. The smallest area of phosphors on a video terminal that can be excited to form a picture element.

place name. See TOPONYM.

plain, *n*. On the sea floor, a flat, gently sloping or nearly level region. Sometimes called ABYSSAL PLAIN in very deep water.

plan, *n*. 1. An orthographic drawing or view on a horizontal plane, as of an instrument, a horizontal section, or a layout. 2. A large-scale map or chart of a small area, generally showing at increased scale a portion of the chart on which it is placed.

planar, *adj*. Lying in a plane.

planar graph, In ECDIS a 2-dimensional data structure in which the geometry is described in terms of NODES and EDGES which are TOPOLOGICALLY linked. A special case of a CHAINNODE data structure in which edges must not cross. CONNECTED NODES are formed at all points where edges meet.

plane, *n*. A surface without curvature, such that a straight line joining any two of its points lies wholly on the surface.

plane of polarization. With respect to a plane polarized wave, the plane containing the electric field vector and the direction of propagation.

plane polarized wave. An electromagnetic wave the electric field vector of which lies at all times in a fixed plane which contains the direction of propagation.

plane sailing. A method of solving the various problems involving a single course and distance, difference of latitude, and departure, in which the earth, or that part traversed. is considered as a plane surface.

planet, *n*. A celestial body of a solar system, in orbit around the sun or a star and shining by reflected light. The larger of such bodies are sometimes called major planets to distinguish them from minor planets (asteroids) which are very much smaller. Larger planets may have satellites. In the solar system an inferior planet has an orbit smaller than that of the earth; a superior planet has an orbit larger than that of the earth. The four planets commonly used for celestial observations are called navigational planets. The word planet is of Greek origin, meaning, literally, wanderer, applied because the planets appear to move relative to the stars.

planetary, *adj*. Of a planet or the planets; terrestrial; worldwide.

planetary aberration. See under ABERRATION definition 1.

planetary configurations. Apparent positions of the planets relative to each other and to other bodies of the solar system, as seen from the earth.

planetary precession. The component of general precession caused by the effect of other planets on the equatorial protuberance of the earth producing an eastward motion of the equinoxes along the ecliptic. See also PRECESSION OF THE EQUINOXES.

planetoid, *n*. See ASTEROID.

plane triangle. A closed plane figure having three straight lines as sides.

planimetric map. A map indicating only the horizontal positions of features, without regard to elevation, in contrast with a TOPOGRAPHIC MAP, which indicates both horizontal and vertical positions.

planisphere, *n*. A representation on a plane of the celestial sphere, especially one on a polar projection, with means provided for making certain measurements such as altitude and azimuth. See also STAR FINDER.

plankton, *n*. Floating, drifting, or feebly swimming plant and animal organisms of the sea. These are usually microscopic or very small, although jellyfish are included.

planning chart. A chart designed for use in planning voyages or flight operations or investigating areas of marine or aviation activities.

plan position indicator. An intensity-modulated radar display in which the radial sweep rotates on the cathode-ray tube in synchronism with the rotating antenna. The display presents a maplike representation of the positions of echo-producing objects. It is generally one of two main types: RELATIVE MOTION DISPLAY or TRUE MOTION DISPLAY.

plastic relief map. A topographic map printed on plastic and molded into a three-dimensional form.

plateau, *n*. On the sea floor, a comparatively flat-topped feature of considerable extent, dropping off abruptly on one or more sides.

plate glass. A fine quality sheet glass obtained by rolling, grinding, and polishing.

platform erection. In the alignment of inertial navigation equipment, the alignment of the stable platform vertical axis with the local vertical.

platform tide. See STAND.

Platonic year. See GREAT YEAR.

Plimsoll mark. A special marking (positioned amidships) that indicates the draft of the ship and the legal limit to which a ship may be loaded for specific water types and temperatures in order to safely maintain buoyancy, particularly with regard to the hazard of waves that may arise.

Plimsoll mark

plot, *n*. A drawing consisting of lines and points representing certain conditions graphically, as the progress of a craft. See also NAVIGATIONAL PLOT.

plot, *v., t*. To draw lines and points to represent certain conditions graphically, as the various lines and points on a chart or plotting sheet representing the progress of a vessel, a curve of magnetic azimuths vs. time or of altitude vs. time, or a graphical solution of a problem, such as a relative motion solution.

plotter, *n*. An instrument used for plotting straight lines and measuring angles on a chart or plotting sheet. See also PROTRACTOR.

plotting chart. An outline chart on a specific scale and projection, usually showing a graticule and compass rose, designed to be used ancillary to a standard nautical chart, and produced either as an independent chart or part of a coordinated series. See also POSITION PLOTTING SHEET.

plotting head. See REFLECTION PLOTTER.

plumb bob. A conical device, usually of brass and suspended by a chord, by means of which a point can be projected vertically into space over relatively short distances.

plumb-bob vertical. See LOCAL VERTICAL.

plumb line. 1. A line in the direction of gravity. 2. A cord with a weight at one end for determining the direction of gravity.

pluvial, *adj*. Of or pertaining to rain. The expression pluvial period is often used to designate an extended period or age of heavy rainfall.

P.M. Abbreviation for Post Meridian; after noon in zone time.

pocosin, *n*. See DISMAL.

point, *n*. 1. A place having position, but no extent. 2. A tapering piece of land projecting into a body of water. It is generally less prominent than a CAPE. 3. One thirty-second of a circle, or 11.25°. Also called COMPASS POINT when used in reference to compass directions. See also FOUR-POINT BEARING.

point designation grid. A system of lines, having no relation to the actual scale or orientation, drawn on a map, chart, or air photograph, dividing it into squares so that points can be more readily located.

point light. A luminous signal without perceptible length, as contrasted with a LINEAR LIGHT which has perceptible length.

point of arrival. The position at which a craft is assumed to have reached or will reach after following specified courses for specified distance from a point of departure. See also DESTINATION.

point of departure. The point from which the initial course to reach the destination begins. It is usually established by bearings of prominent landmarks as the vessel clears a harbor and proceeds to sea. When a person establishes this point, he is said to take departure. Also called the DEPARTURE.

point of destination. See DESTINATION.

point of inflection. The point at which a reverse in direction of curvature takes place.

polar, *adj*. Of or pertaining to a pole or the poles.

polar air. A type of air whose characteristics are developed over high latitudes, especially Within the subpolar highs. Continental polar air has low surface temperature, low moisture content, and especially in its source regions, has great stability in the lower layers. It is shallow in comparison with arctic air. Maritime polar air initially possesses similar properties to those of continental polar air, but in passing over warmer water it becomes unstable with a higher moisture content.

polar axis. 1. The straight line connecting the poles of a body 2. A reference line for one of the spherical coordinates.

polar cap absorption. See under POLAR DISTURBANCE.

polar cap disturbance. An ionospheric disturbance (which does not refer to the ice cap in the polar regions). It is a result of the focusing effect that the earth's magnetic field has on particles released from the sun during a solar proton event. The effect concentrates high-energy particles in the region of the magnetic pole with the result that normal very low frequency Omega propagation is disrupted. The effect on radio waves is known as POLAR CAP ABSORPTION (PCA). Historically, polar cap disturbances (PCDs) produced large or total absorption of high frequency radio waves crossing the polar region, hence the term POLAR CAP ABSORPTION. A transmission path which is entirely outside the polar region is unaffected by a PCD. The PCDs, often called PCA EVENTS (PCAs), may persist for a week or more, but duration of only a few days is more common. The PCD can cause line of position errors about 6 to 8 nautical miles. The *Omega Propagation Correction Tables* make no allowance for this phenomenon since it is not predictable. However, the frequency of the phenomenon increases during those years of peak solar activity. See also SUDDEN IONOSPHERIC DISTURBANCE, MODAL INTERFERENCE.

polar chart. 1. A chart of polar areas. 2. A chart on a polar projection. The projections most used for polar charts are the gnomonic, stereographic, azimuthal equidistant, transverse Mercator, and modified Lambert conformal.

polar circles. The minimum latitudes, north and south, at which the sun becomes circumpolar.

polar continental air. Air of an air mass that originates over land or frozen ocean areas in polar regions. Polar continental air is characterized by low temperature, stability, low specific humidity, and shallow vertical extent.

polar coordinates. A system of coordinates defining a point by its distance and direction from a fixed point, called the POLE. Direction is given as the angle between a reference radius vector and a radius vector to the point. If three dimensions are involved, two angles are used to locate the radius vector. See also SPACE-POLAR COORDINATES.

polar distance. Angular distance from a celestial pole; the arc of an hour circle between a celestial pole, usually the elevated pole, and a point on the celestial sphere, measured from the celestial pole through 180°. See also CODECLINATION.

polar front. The semi-permanent, semi-continuous front separating air masses of tropical and polar origin. This is the major front in terms of air mass contrast and susceptibility to cyclonic disturbance.

Polaris correction. A correction to be applied to the corrected sextant altitude of Polaris to obtain latitude. This correction for the offset of Polaris from the north celestial pole varies with the local hour angle of Aries, latitude, and date. See Q-CORRECTION.

polarization, *n*. The attribute of an electromagnetic wave which describes the direction of the electric field vector.

polarization error. An error in a radio direction finder bearing or the course indicated by a radiobeacon because of a change in the polarization of the radio waves between the transmitter and receiver on being reflected and refracted from the ionosphere. Because the medium frequency radio direction finder normally operates with vertically polarized waves, a change to horizontal polarization in the process of reflection and refraction of the waves from the ionosphere can have a serious effect on bearing measurements. If the horizontally polarized skywaves are of higher signal strength than the vertically polarized groundwaves, the null position for the loop antenna cannot be obtained. If the skywaves are of lower signal strength than the groundwaves, the null position is made less distinct. Before the cause of the error was understood, it was called NIGHT EFFECT or NIGHT ERROR because it occurs principally during the night, and especially during twilight when rapid changes are occurring in the ionosphere.

polar map projection. A map projection centered on a pole.

polar maritime air. An air mass that originates in the polar regions and is then modified by passing over a relatively warm ocean surface. It is characterized by moderately low temperature, moderately high surface specific humidity, and a considerable degree of vertical instability. When the air is colder than the sea surface, it is further characterized by gusts and squalls, showery precipitation, variable sky, and good visibility between showers.

polar motion. See EULERIAN MOTION.

polar navigation. Navigation in polar regions, where unique considerations and techniques are applied. No definite limit for these regions is recognized but polar navigation techniques are usually used from about latitude 70°N.

polar orbit. An earth satellite orbit that has an inclination of about 90° and, hence, passes over or near the earth's poles.

polar orthographic map projection. An orthographic map projection having the plane of the projection perpendicular to the axis of rotation of the earth, in this projection, the geographic parallels are full circles, true to scale, and the geographic meridians are straight lines.

polar regions. The regions near the geographic poles. No definite limit for these regions is recognized.

polar satellite. A satellite that passes over or near the earth's poles, i.e., a satellite whose orbital plane has an inclination of about 90° to the plane of the earth's equator.

polar stereographic map projection. A stereographic map projection having the center of the projection located at a pole of the sphere.

pole, *n*. 1. Either of the two points of intersection of the surface of a sphere or spheroid and its axis, labeled N or S to indicate whether the north pole or south pole. The two points of intersection of the surface of the earth with its axis are called geographical poles. The two points of intersection of the celestial sphere and the extended axis of the earth are called celestial poles. The celestial pole above the horizon is called the elevated pole; that below the horizon the depressed pole. The ecliptic poles are 90° from the ecliptic. Also, one of a pair of similar points on the surface of a sphere or spheroid, as a magnetic pole, definition l; a geomagnetic pole; or a fictitious pole. 2. A magnetic pole, definition 2. 3. The origin of measurement of distance in polar or spherical coordinates. 4. Any point around which something centers.

pole beacon. A vertical spar fixed in the ground or in the sea bed or a river bed to show as a navigation mark. Sometimes called SPINDLE BEACON or SINGLE-PILE BEACON in the United States.

polyconic, *adj*. Consisting of or related to many cones.

polyconic chart. A chart on the polyconic map projection.

polyconic map projection. A conic map projection in which the surface of a sphere or spheroid, such as the earth, is conceived as developed on a series of tangent cones, which are then spread out to form a plane. A separate cone is used for each small zone. This projection is widely used for maps but seldom used for charts, except for survey purposes. It is not conformal.

polygon, *n*. A closed plane figure bounded by straight lines. See also HEXAGON, OCTAGON, PARALLELOGRAM, PENTAGON, QUADRILATERAL, RECTANGLE, SQUARE, TRAPEZOID, TRIANGLE.

polynya, *n*. A non-linear shaped area of water enclosed by ice. Polynyas may contain brash ice and/or be covered with new ice, nilas, or young ice; submariners refer to these as SKYLIGHTS. Sometimes the POLYNYA is limited on one side by the coast and is called a SHORE POLYNYA or by fast ice and is called a FLAW POLYNYA. If it recurs in the same position every year, it is called a RECURRING POLYNYA.

polyzoa, *n., pl*. Very small marine animals which reproduce by budding, many generations often being permanently connected by branchlike structures. These animals are often very numerous and in some areas they cover the bottom. Also called BRYOZOA.

pond, *n*. A relatively small body of water, usually surrounded on all sides by land. A larger body of water is called a LAKE.

pontoon, *n*. A float or low, flat-bottomed vessel to float machinery such as cranes, capstans, etc. or to support weights such as floating bridges boat landings, etc.

pool, *n*. 1. A small body of water, usually smaller than a pond, especially one that is quite deep. One left by an ebb tide is called a **tide pool**. 2. A small and comparatively still, deep part of a larger body of water such as a river or harbor.

poop, *n*. A short enclosed structure at the stern of a vessel, extending from side to side. It is covered by the poop deck, which is surrounded by the poop rail.

pooped. To have shipped a sea or wave over the stern.

pororoca, *n*. See TIDAL BORE.

port, *n*. 1. A place provided with moorings and transfer facilities for loading and discharging cargo or passengers, usually located in a harbor. 2. The left side of a craft, facing forward. The opposite is STARBOARD.

portable pilot unit, *n*. A portable, computer-based system that pilots bring aboard a vessel to use as a decision-support tool for navigating in confined waters.

portfolio, *n*. A portable case for carrying papers. See also CHART PORTFOLIO.

port hand buoy. A buoy which is to be left to the port side when approaching from the open sea or proceeding in the direction of the main stream of flood current, or in the direction established by appropriate authority.

port of call. A port visited by a ship.

Portugal Current. A slow-moving current that is the prevailing southward flow off the Atlantic coasts of Spain and Portugal. Its speed averages only about 0.5 knot during both winter and summer. The maximum speed seldom exceeds 2.0 knots north of latitude 40°N and 2.5 knots south of 40°N. It is easily influenced by winds.

Portuguese norther. See under NORTHER.

position, *n*. A point defined by stated or implied coordinates, particularly one on the surface of the earth. A fix is a relatively accurate position determined without reference to any former position. A running fix is a position determined by crossing lines of position obtained at different times and advanced or retired to a common time. An estimated position is determined from incomplete data or data of questionable accuracy. A dead reckoning position is determined by advancing a previous position for courses and distances. A most probable position is a position judged to be most accurate when an element of doubt exists as to the true position. It may be a fix, running fix, estimated position, or dead reckoning position depending upon the information upon which it is based. An assumed position is a point at which a craft is assumed to be located. A geographical position is that point on the earth at which a given celestial body is in the zenith at a specified time, or any position defined by means of its geographical coordinates. A geodetic position is a point on the earth the coordinates of which have been determined by triangulation from an accurately known initial station, or one defined in terms of geodetic latitude and longitude. An astronomical position is a point on the earth whose coordinates have been determined as a result of observation of celestial bodies, or one defined in terms of astronomical latitude and longitude. A maritime position is the location of a seaport or other point along a coast. A relative position is one defined with reference to another position, either fixed or moving. See also PINPOINT, LINE OF POSITION, BAND OF POSITION, SURFACE OF POSITION.

position angle. See PARALLACTIC ANGLE.

position approximate. Of inexact position. The expression is used principally on charts to indicate that the position of a wreck, shoal, etc., has not been accurately determined or does not remain fixed.

position buoy. An object towed astern to assist a following vessel in maintaining the desired or prescribed distance, particularly in conditions of low visibility.

position circle. 1. The chart symbol denoting the position of a buoy. 2. See CIRCLE OF POSITION.

position doubtful. Of uncertain position. The expression is used principally on charts to indicate that a wreck, shoal, etc., has been reported in various positions and not definitely determined in any. See also VIGIA.

positioning, *n*. The process of determining, at a particular point in time, the precise physical location of a craft, vehicle, person or site.

position line. See LINE OF POSITION.

position plotting sheet. A blank chart, usually on the Mercator projection, showing only the graticule and a compass rose. The meridians are usually unlabeled by the publisher so that they can be appropriately labeled when the chart is used in any longitude. It is designed and intended for use in conjunction with the standard nautical chart. See also SMALL AREA PLOTTING SHEET, UNIVERSAL PLOTTING SHEET, PLOTTING CHART.

post meridian (PM). After noon, or the period of time between noon (1200) and midnight (2400). The period between midnight and noon is called ANTE MERIDIAN.

potential, *n*. The difference in voltage at two points in a circuit.

potential energy. Energy possessed by a body by virtue of its position, in contrast with KINETIC ENERGY, that possessed by virtue of its motion.

pound, *n*. A unit of mass equal to 0.45359237 kilograms. Also called AVOIRDUPOIS POUND.

pound, *v*. To strike oncoming waves repeatedly or heavily.

pounding, *n*. A series of shocks received by a pitching vessel as it repeatedly or heavily strikes the water in a heavy sea. The shocks can be felt over the entire vessel and each one is followed by a short period of vibration.

power, *n*. 1. Rate of doing work. 2. Luminous intensity. 3. The number of times an object is magnified by an optical system, such as a telescope. Usually called MAGNIFYING POWER. 4. The result of multiplying a number by itself a given number of times. See also EXPONENT.

power gain (of an antenna). See DIRECTIVITY, definition 2.

power gain (of a transmitter). The ratio of the output power delivered to a specified load by an amplifier to the power absorbed by its input circuit.

power (of a radio transmitter), *n*. The power of a radio transmitter is expressed in one of the following forms: The peak envelope power is the average power supplied to the antenna transmission line by a transmitter during one radio frequency cycle at the highest crest of the modulation envelope, taken under conditions of normal operation. The mean power is the power supplied to the antenna transmission line by a transmitter during normal operation, averaged over a time sufficiently long compared with the period of the lowest frequency encountered in the modulation. The carrier power is the average power supplied to the antenna transmission line by a transmitter during one radio frequency cycle under conditions of no modulation. This definition does not apply to pulse modulated emissions.

PPI display. See as PLAN POSITION INDICATOR.

PPI repeater. See RADAR REPEATER.

precautionary area. A routing measure comprising an area within defined limits where ships must navigate with particular caution and within which the direction of traffic flow may be recommended. See also ROUTING SYSTEM.

precession, *n*. The change in the direction of the axis of rotation of a spinning body, as a gyroscope, when acted upon by a torque. The direction of motion of the axis is such that it causes the direction of spin of the gyroscope to tend to coincide with that of the impressed torque. The horizontal component of precession is called drift, and the vertical component is called topple. Also called INDUCED PRECESSION, REAL PRECESSION. See also APPARENT PRECESSION, PRECESSION OF THE EQUINOXES.

precession in declination. The component of general precession along a celestial meridian, amounting to about 20.0" per year.

precession in right ascension. The component of general precession along the celestial equator, amounting to about 46.1" per year.

precession of the equinoxes. The conical motion of the earth's axis about the vertical to the plane of the ecliptic, caused by the attractive force of the sun, moon, and other planets on the equatorial protuberance of the earth. The effect of the sun and moon, called lunisolar precession, is to produce a westward motion of the equinoxes along the ecliptic. The effect of other planets, called planetary precession, tends to produce a much smaller motion eastward along the ecliptic. The resultant motion, called general precession, is westward along the ecliptic at the rate of about 50.3" per year. The component of general precession along the celestial equator, called precession in right ascension, is about 46.1" per year and the component along a celestial meridian, called precession in declination, is about 20.0" per year.

precipice, *n*. A high and very steep cliff.

precipitation, *n*. 1. Any or all forms of water particles, whether liquid or solid, that fall from the atmosphere and reach the ground. It is distinguished from cloud, fog, dew, rime, frost, etc., in that it must fall; and it is distinguished from cloud and virga in that it must reach the ground. Precipitation includes drizzle, rain, snow, snow pellets, snow grains, ice crystals, ice pellets, and hail. 2. The amount usually expressed in inches of liquid water depth, of the water substance that has fallen at a given point over a specified period of time.

precipitation static. A type of interference experienced in a radio receiver, during snow storms, rain storms, and dust storms, caused by the impact of dust particles against the antenna. It may also be caused by the existence of induction fields created by nearby corona discharges.

precipitation trails. See VIRGA.

precision, *n*. A measure of how close the outcome of a series of observations or measurement cluster about some estimated value of a desired quantity. Precision implies repeatability of the observations within some specified limit and depends upon the random errors encountered due to the quality of the observing instrument, the skill of the observer and randomly fluctuating conditions such as temperature, pressure, refraction, etc. Precision should not be confused with ACCURACY. Observations may be of high precision but inaccurate due to the presence of systematic errors. For a quantity to be accurately measured, both systematic and random errors should be small. For a quantity to be known with high precision, only the random errors due to irregular effects need to be small. See ERROR.

precision graphic recorder. A device used with the standard hydrographic echo sounder in ocean depths where soundings cannot be recorded on the expanded scale of the standard recorder. It provides a sounding record with a scale expansion and high accuracy. Commonly called a PGR.

precision index. A measure of the magnitude of the random errors of a series of observations of some given quantity. If the precision index is large, most of the random errors of the observations are small. The precision index appears as a parameter in the normal (Gaussian) distribution law. While making a series of observations, the standard deviation can be calculated. The precision index is then calculated using a formula and a measure of the precision of the observing instrument is obtained. See also RANDOM ERROR, NORMAL DISTRIBUTION, PRECISION, STANDARD DEVIATION.

Precise Positioning Service. The most accurate military positioning service of the Global Positioning System.

precomputation, *n*. The process of making navigational solutions in advance; applied particularly to the determination of computed altitude and azimuth before making a celestial observation for a line of position. When this is done, the observation must be made at the time used for the computation, or a correction applied.

precomputed altitude. The altitude of a celestial body computed before observation, and with the sextant altitude corrections applied with reversed sign. When a precomputed altitude has been calculated, the altitude difference can be determined by comparison with the sextant altitude.

precomputed curve, A graphical representation of the azimuth or altitude of a celestial body plotted against time for a given assumed position, computed for use with celestial observations.

predictability, *n*. In a navigation system, the measure of the accuracy with which the system can define the position in terms of geographical coordinates. See also REPEATABILITY, definition 2.

predicable accuracy. The accuracy of predicting position with respect to precise space and surface coordinates. See also REPEATABLE ACCURACY.

predicted tides. The times and heights of the tide as given in the Tide Tables in advance of their occurrence.

predicting machine. See TIDE PREDICTING MACHINE.

preferred datum. A geodetic datum selected as a base for consolidation of local independent datums within a geographical area. Also called MAJOR DATUM.

Presentation Library. In ECDIS a set of mostly digital specifications, composed of SYMBOL libraries, color schemes, LOOK-UP TABLES and rules, linking every OBJECT CLASS and ATTRIBUTE of the SENC to the appropriate presentation of the ECDIS DISPLAY.

preferred datum. A geodetic datum selected as a base for consolidation of local independent datums within a geographical area. Also called MAJOR DATUM.

pressure, *n*. Force per unit area. The pressure exerted by the weight of the earth's atmosphere is called atmospheric or, if indicated by a barometer, barometric pressure. Pressure exerted by the vapor of a liquid is called vapor pressure. The pressure exerted by a fluid as a result of its own weight or position is called static pressure. Pressure exerted by radiant energy is called radiation pressure.

pressure gage. A tide gage that is operated by the change in pressure at the bottom of a body of water due to rise and fall of the tide.

pressure tendency. The character and amount of atmospheric pressure change for a 3-hour or other specified period ending at the time of observation. Also called BAROMETRIC TENDENCY.

prevailing westerlies. The prevailing westerly winds on the poleward sides of the sub-tropical high-pressure belts.

prevailing wind. The average or characteristic wind at any place.

primary, *n*. See PRIMARY BODY.

primary body. The celestial body or central force field about which a satellite orbits, or from which it is escaping, or towards which it is falling. The primary body of the earth is the sun, the primary body of the moon is the earth. Usually shortened to PRIMARY.

primary circle. See PRIMARY GREAT CIRCLE.

primary control tide station. A tide station at which continuous observations have been made over a minimum of a 19-year Metonic cycle. Its purpose is to provide data for computing accepted values of the harmonic and non harmonic constants essential to tide predictions and to the determination of tidal datums for charting and coastal boundaries. The data series from this station serves as a primary control for the reduction of relatively short series from subordinate tide stations through the method of comparisons of simultaneous observations, and for monitoring long-period sea-level trends and variations. See also TIDE STATION; SUBORDINATE TIDE STATION, definition 1; SECONDARY CONTROL TIDE STATION; TEMPORARY TIDE STATION.

primary great circle. A great circle used as the origin of measurement of a coordinate; particularly such a circle 90° from the poles of a SYSTEM of spherical coordinates, as the equator. Also called PRIMARY CIRCLE, FUNDAMENTAL CIRCLE.

primary radar. 1. Radar which transmits a SIGNAL and receives the incident energy reflected from an object to detect the object. 2. As defined by the International Telecommunications Union (ITU), a radio-determination system based on the comparison of reference signals with radio signals reflected from a position to be determined.

primary seacoast light. A light established for purpose of making landfall or coastwise past from headland to headland. Also called LAND FALL LIGHT.

primary tidal bench mark. See under BENCH MARK.

primary tide station. See PRIMARY CONTROL TIDE STATION.

prime fictitious meridian. The reference meridian (real or fictitious) used as the origin for measurement of fictitious longitude. Prime grid meridian is the reference meridian of a grid; prime transverse or prime inverse meridian is the reference meridian of a transverse graticule; prime oblique meridian is the reference fictitious meridian of an oblique graticule.

prime grid meridian. The reference meridian of a grid. In polar regions it is usually the 180°-0° geographic meridian, used as the origin for measuring grid longitude.

prime inverse meridian. See PRIME TRANSVERSE MERIDIAN.

prime meridian. The 0° meridian of longitude, used as the origin for measurement of longitude The meridian of Greenwich, England, is almost universally used for this purpose. See also PRIME FICTITIOUS MERIDIAN.

prime oblique meridian. The reference fictitious meridian of an oblique graticule.

prime transverse meridian. The reference meridian of a transverse graticule. Also called PRIME INVERSE MERIDIAN.

prime vertical. See PRIME VERTICAL CIRCLE.

prime vertical circle. The vertical circle perpendicular to the principal vertical circle. The intersections of the prime vertical circle with the horizon define the east and west points of the horizon. Often shortened to PRIME VERTICAL; Sometimes called TRUE PRIME VERTICAL to distinguish from magnetic, compass, or grid prime vertical, defined as the vertical circle passing through the magnetic, compass, or grid east and west points of the horizon, respectively.

priming of tide. The periodic acceleration in the time of occurrence of high and low waters due changes in the relative positions of the moon and the sun. Priming occurs when the moon between new and first quarter and between full and third quarter. High tide occurs before transit of the moon. Lagging occurs when the moon is between first quarter and full and between third quarter and new. High tide occurs after transit of the moon. See also LAGGING OF TIDE.

principal vertical circle. The vertical circle passing through the north and south celestial poles. The intersection of the principal vertical circle with the horizon defines the north and south points of the horizon.

priority blanking. See DUAL-RATE BLANKING.

prism, *n*. A solid having parallel, similar, equal, plane geometric figures as bases, and parallelograms as sides. By extension, the term is also applied to a similar solid having nonparallel bases, and trapezoids or a combination of trapezoids and parallelograms as sides. Prisms are used for changing the direction of motion of a ray of light and for forming spectra.

prismatic error. That error due to lack of parallelism of the two faces of an optical element, such as a mirror or a shade glass. See also SHADE ERROR.

private aids to navigation. In United States waters, those aids to navigation not established and maintained by the U.S. Coast Guard. Private aids include those established by other federal agencies with prior U.S. Coast Guard approval, aids to navigation on marine structures or other works which the owners are legally obligated to establish, maintain, and operate as prescribed by the U.S. Coast Guard, and those aids which are merely desired, for one reason or another, by the individual corporation, state or local government or other body that has established the aid with U.S. Coast Guard approval.

probable error. A measure of the dispersion or spread of a series of observations about some value, usually the mean or average value of all the observations. See also CIRCULAR ERROR PROBABLE.

processor. The brain of a computer, which executes programs to do work. Also known more correctly as the CENTRAL PROCESSING UNIT (CPU).

production platform. A term used to indicate a permanent offshore structure equipped to control the flow of oil or gas. For charting purposes, the use of the term is extended to include all permanent platforms associated with oil or gas production, e.g. field terminal, drilling and accommodation platforms, and "booster" platforms sited at intervals along some pipelines. It does not include entirely submarine structures.

prognostic chart. A chart showing, principally, the expected pressure pattern of a given synoptic chart at a specified future time. Usually, positions of fronts are also included, and the forecast values of other meteorological elements may be superimposed.

program. A set of instructions which a computer executes to perform work. Programs are written in one of many LANGUAGES, which translate the instructions into MACHINE LANGUAGE used by the PROCESSOR.

progressive wave. In the ocean, a wave that advances in distance along the sea surfaces or at some intermediate depth. Although the wave form itself travels significant distances, the water particles that make up the wave merely describe circular (in relatively deep water) or elliptical (in relatively shallow water) orbits. With high, steep, wind waves, a small overlap in the orbit motion becomes significant. This overlapping gives rise to a small net transport.

prohibited area. 1. An area shown on nautical charts within which navigation and/or anchoring is prohibited except as authorized by appropriate authority. 2. A specified area within the land areas of a state or territorial waters adjacent thereto over which the flight of aircraft is prohibited. See also DANGER AREA, RESTRICTED AREA.

projection, *n*. The extension of lines or planes to intersect a given surface; the transfer of a point from one surface to a corresponding position on another surface by graphical or analytical means. See also MAP PROJECTION.

projector compass. A magnetic compass in which the lubber's line and compass card, or a portion thereof, are viewed as an image projected through a system of lenses upon a screen adjacent to the helmsman's position. See also REFLECTOR COMPASS.

prolate cycloid. See TROCHOID.

prolate spheroid. An ellipsoid of revolution, the longer axis of which is the axis of revolution. An ellipsoid of revolution, the shorter axis of which is the axis of REVOLUTION, is called an OBLATE SPHEROID.

promontory, *n*. High land extending into a large body of water beyond the line of the coast. Called HEADLAND when the promontory is comparatively high and has a steep face. Also called FORELAND.

propagation, *n*. The travel of waves of energy through or along a medium other than a specially constructed path such as an electrical circuit.

proper motion. The component of the space motion of a celestial body perpendicular to line of sight, resulting in the change of a stars apparent position relative to other stars. Proper motion is expressed in angular units.

proportional dividers. An instrument consisting in its simple form of two legs pointed at both ends and provided with an adjustable pivot, so that for any given pivot setting, the distance between one set of pointed ends always bears the same ratio to the distance between the other set. A change in the pivot changes the ratio. The dividers are used in transferring measurements between charts or other graphics which are not the same scale.

proportional dividers

proportional parts. Numbers in the same proportion as a set of given numbers. Such numbers are used in an auxiliary interpolation table based on the assumption that the tabulated quantity and entering arguments differ in the same proportion. For each intermediate argument a "proportional part" or number is given to be applied the preceding tabulated value in the main table.

protractor, *n*. An instrument for measuring angles on a surface; an angular scale. In its most usual form it consists of a circle or part of one (usually a semicircle) graduated in degrees. See also COMPASS ROSE, THREE-ARM PROTRACTOR.

province, *n*. On the sea floor, a region identifiable by a group of similar physiographic features whose characteristics are markedly in contrast with surrounding areas.

pseudo-independent surveillance. Position determination that relies on craft or vehicle cooperation but is not subject to craft or vehicle navigational errors (e.g., secondary radar).

pseudo-random noise. An apparently random but reproducible sequence of binary code used in the GPS signal.

pseudo-range. Measure of distance from GPS satellite to receiver, uncorrected for synchronization errors between satellite and receiver clocks.

psychrometer, *n*. A type of hygrometer (an instrument for determining atmospheric humidity) consisting of dry-bulb and wet-bulb thermometers. The dry-bulb thermometer indicates the temperature of the air, and the wet bulb thermometer the lowest temperature to which air can be cooled by evaporating water into it at constant pressure. With the information obtained from a psychrometer, the humidity, dew point, and vapor pressure for any atmospheric pressure can be obtained by means of appropriate tables.

psychrometric chart. A nomogram for graphically determining relative humidity, absolute humidity, and dew point from wet- and dry-bulb thermometer readings.

pteropod *(pl. pteropoda), n*. A small marine animal with or without a shell and having two thin, winglike feet. These animals are often so numerous they may cover the surface of the sea for miles. In some areas, their shells cover the bottom.

Pub. No. 9. The American Practical Navigator. A publication of the National Geospatial-Intelligence Agency, originally by Nathaniel Bowditch (1773-1838) and first published in 1802, comprising a complete manual of navigation with tables for solution of navigational problems. Popularly called BOWDITCH.

Pub. No. 102. International Code of Signals. A publication of the National Geospatial-Intelligence Agency intended primarily for communication at sea in situations involving safety of life at sea and navigational safety, especially when language difficulties arise between ships or stations of different nationalities. The Code is suitable for transmission by all means of communication, including radiotelephony, radiotelegraphy, sound, flashing light, and flags.

Pub. 117. Radio Navigational Aids. A publication of the National Geospatial-Intelligence Agency which contains data on radio aids to navigation services provided to mariners. Information on radio direction finder and radar stations, radio time signals, radio navigational warnings, distress signals, stations transmitting medical advice, long range radionavigation systems, emergency procedures and communications instructions, listed in text and tabular format.

Pub. 150. World Port Index. A publication of the National Geospatial-Intelligence Agency listing the location, characteristics, known facilities, and available services of ports, shipping facilities and oil terminals throughout the world. The applicable chart and Sailing Direction volume is given for each place listed. A code indicates certain types of information.

Pub. 151. Distances Between Ports. A publication of the National Geospatial-Intelligence Agency providing calculated distances in nautical miles over water areas between most of the seaports of the world. A similar publication published by the National Ocean Service of United States waters is entitled *Distances between United States Ports*.

Pub. 217. Maneuvering Board Manual. A publication of the National Geospatial-Intelligence Agency providing explanations and examples of various problems involved in maneuvering and in relative movement.

Pub. No. 226. Handbook of Magnetic Compass Adjustment. A publication of the National Geospatial-Intelligence Agency, providing information for adjustment of marine magnetic compasses.

Pub. No. 229. Sight Reduction Tables for Marine Navigation. A publication of the National Geospatial-Intelligence Agency, in six volumes each of which includes two 8° zones of latitude. An overlap of 1° of latitude occurs between volumes. The six volumes cover latitude bands 0°-15°, 15°-30°, 30°-45°, 45°-60°, 60°-75°, and 75°-90°. For entering arguments of integral degrees of latitude, declination, and local hour angle, altitudes and their differences are tabulated to the nearest tenth of a minute, azimuth angles to the nearest tenth of a degree. The tables are designed for precise interpolation of altitude for declination only by means of interpolation tables which facilitate linear interpolation and provide additionally for the effect of second differences. The data are applicable to the solutions of sights of all celestial bodies; there are no limiting values of altitude, latitude, hour angle, or declination.

Pub. No. 249. Sight Reduction Tables for Air Navigation. A publication of the National Geospatial-Intelligence Agency, in three volumes, with volume 1 containing tabulated altitudes and azimuths of selected stars, the entering arguments being latitude, local hour angle of the vernal equinox, and the name of the star; and volumes 2 and 3 containing tabulated altitudes and azimuth angles of any body within the limits of the entering arguments, which are latitude, local hour angle, and declination (0°-29°) of the body.

Pub. 1310. Radar Navigation Manual. A publication of the National Geospatial-Intelligence Agency which explains the fundamentals of shipboard radar, radar operation collision avoidance, radar navigation, and radar-assisted vessel traffic systems in the U.S.

puddles *n.* An accumulation of melt-water on ice, mainly due to melting snow, but in the more advanced stages also due to the melting of ice.

pulse, *n.* A short burst of electromagnetic energy, such as emitted by a radar.

pulse decay time. The interval of time required for the trailing edge of a pulse to decay from 90 percent to 10 percent of the pulse amplitude.

pulse duration. The time interval during which the amplitude of a pulse is at or greater than a specified value, usually stated in terms of a fraction or percentage of the maximum value.

pulse duration error. A range distortion of a radar return caused by the duration of the pulse. See also SPOT-SIZE ERROR.

pulse group. See PULSE TRAIN.

pulse interval. See PULSE SPACING.

pulse length. See PULSE DURATION.

pulse-modulated radar. The type of radar generally used for shipboard navigational applications. The radio-frequency energy transmitted by a pulse-modulated radar consists of a series of equally spaced short pulses having a pulse duration of about 1 microsecond or less. The distance to the target is determined by measuring the transmit time of a pulse and its return to the source as a reflected echo. Also called PULSE RADAR.

pulse modulation. 1. The modulation of a carrier wave by a pulse train. In this sense, the term describes the process of generating carrier-frequency pulses. 2. The modulation of one or more characteristics of a pulse carrier. In this sense, the term describes methods of transmitting information on a pulse carrier.

pulse radar. See PULSE-MODULATED RADAR.

pulse repetition frequency. The pulse repetition rate of a periodic pulse train.

pulse repetition rate. The average number pulses per unit of time. See also PULSE REPETITION FREQUENCY.

pulse rise time. The interval of time required for the leading edge of a pulse to rise from 10 to 90 percent of the pulse amplitude.

pulse spacing. The interval between corresponding points on consecutive pulses. Also called PULSE INTERVAL.

pulse train. A series of pulses of similar characteristics. Also called PULSE GROUP, IMPULSE TRAIN.

pulse width. See PULSE DURATION.

pumice, *n.* Cooled volcanic glass with a great number of minute cavities caused by the expulsion of water vapor at high temperature, resulting in a very light rocky material.

pumice

pumping, *n.* Unsteadiness of the mercury in a barometer, caused by fluctuations of the air pressure produced by a gusty wind or due to the motion of a vessel.

pure sound. See PURE TONE.

pure tone. A sound produced by a sinusoidal acoustic oscillation. Also called PURE SOUND.

purple light. The faint purple glow observed on clear days over a large region of the western sky after sunset and over the eastern sky before sunrise.

put to sea. To leave a sheltered area and head out to sea.

pyramidal iceberg. See PINNACLED ICEBERG.

Q

Q-band. A radio-frequency band 36 to 46 gigahertz. See also FREQUENCY, FREQUENCY BAND.

Q-correction. The Polaris correction as tabulated in the *Air Almanac*.

Q signals. Conventional code signals used in radiotelegraphy, each signal of three letters beginning with Q and representing a complete sentence.

quadrant, *n.* 1. A quarter of a circle; either an arc of 90° or the area bounded by such an arc and two radii. 2. A double-reflecting instrument for measuring angles used primarily for measuring altitudes of celestial bodies.

quadrantal correctors. Masses of soft iron placed near a magnetic compass to correct for quadrantal deviation. Spherical quadrantal correctors are called quadrantal spheres.

quadrantal deviation. Deviation which changes its sign (E or W) approximately each 90° change of heading. It is caused by induced magnetism in horizontal soft iron.

quadrantal error. An error which changes sign (plus or minus) each 90°. Also called INTERCARDINAL ROLLING ERROR when related to a gyrocompass.

quadrantal point. See INTERCARDINAL POINT.

quadrantal spheres. Two hollow spheres of soft iron placed near a magnetic compass to correct for quadrantal deviation. See also QUADRANTAL CORRECTORS.

quadrant with two arcs. See BACKSTAFF.

quadrature, *n.* An elongation of 90° usually specified as east or west in accordance with the direction of the body from the sun. The moon is at quadrature at first and last quarters.

quadrilateral, *adj.* Having four sides.

quadrilateral, *n.* A closed plane figure having four sides. See also PARALLELOGRAM, TRAPEZOID.

quarantine anchorage. An area where a vessel anchors while satisfying quarantine regulations.

quarantine buoy. A buoy marking the location of a quarantine anchorage. In U.S. waters a quarantine buoy is yellow.

quarantine mark. A navigation mark indicating a quarantine anchorage area for shipping, or defining its limits.

quartering sea. Waves striking the vessel on the quarter, or relative bearings approximately 045°, 135°, 225°, and 315°.

quarter-power points. See under HALF-POWER POINTS.

quartz, *n.* Crystalline form of silica. In its most common form it is colorless and transparent, but it takes a large variety of forms of varying degrees of opaqueness and color. It is the most common solid mineral.

quartz clock. See QUARTZ CRYSTAL CLOCK.

quartz crystal clock. A precision timepiece, consisting of a current generator of constant frequency controlled by a resonator made of quartz crystal with suitable methods for producing continuous rotation to operate time-indicating and related mechanisms. See also QUARTZ CRYSTAL MARINE CHRONOMETER.

quartz crystal marine chronometer. A quartz crystal clock intended for marine use. The degree of accuracy is such that it requires no chronometer rate, but can be reset electrically if necessary.

quasi-stationary front. See STATIONARY FRONT.

quay, *n.* A structure of solid construction along a shore or bank which provides berthing for ships and which usually provides cargo handling facilities. A similar facility of open construction is called WHARF. See also MOLE, definition 1.

quick flashing light. A light flashing 50-80 flashes per minute. See also CONTINUOUS QUICK LIGHT, GROUP QUICK LIGHT, INTERRUPTED QUICK LIGHT.

quick light. See QUICK FLASHING LIGHT.

quicksand, *n.* A loose mixture of sand and water that yields to the pressure of heavy objects. Such objects are difficult to extract once they begin sinking.

quiet sun. The sun when it is free from unusual radio wave or thermal radiation such as that associated with sun spots.

quintant, *n.* A double-reflecting instrument for measuring angles, used primarily for measuring altitudes of celestial bodies, having an arc of 72°.

R

race, *n.* A rapid current or a constricted channel in which such a current flows. The term is usually used only in connection with a tidal current, when it may be called a TIDE RACE.

racon, *n.* As defined by the International Telecommunication Union (ITU), in the maritime radionavigation service, a receiver-transmitter device which, when triggered by a surface search radar, automatically returns a distinctive signal which can appear on the display of the triggering radar, providing range, bearing and identification information. See also IN-BAND RACON, CROSS BAND RACON, SWEPT-FREQUENCY RACON, RAMARK. Also called RADAR TRANSPONDER BEACON.

radar, *n.* 1. (from radio detection and ranging) A radio system which measures distance and usually direction by a comparison of reference signals with the radio signals reflected or retransmitted from the target whose position is to be determined. Pulse-modulated radar is used for shipboard navigational applications. In this type of radar the distance to the target is determined by measuring the time required for an extremely short burst or pulse of radio-frequency energy to travel to the target and return to its source as a reflected echo. Directional antennas allow determination of the direction of the target echo from the source. 2. As defined by the International Telecommunication Union (ITU) a radiodetermination system based on the comparison of reference signals with radio signals reflected, or re-transmitted, from the position to be determined.

radar beacon. A radar transmitter whose emissions enable a ship to determine its direction and frequently position relative to the transmitter using the ship's radar equipment. There are two general types of radar beacons: one type, the RACON, must be triggered by the ship's radar emissions; the other type, the RAMARK transmits continuously and provides bearings only. See also TRANSPONDER.

radar bearing. A bearing obtained by radar.

radar buoy. A buoy having corner reflectors designed into the superstructure, the characteristic shape of the buoy being maintained. This is to differentiate from a buoy on which a corner reflector is mounted.

radar conspicuous object. An object which return a strong radar echo which can be identified with a high degree of certainty.

radar cross section. The area of a plane element situated at the position of an object and normal to the direction of the radar transmitter, which would be traversed by a power such that, if the power were re-radiated equally in all directions with suitable polarization, it would give an echo of the same power as that given by the object itself. Also called EQUIVALENT ECHOING AREA.

radar echo. See ECHO, definition 3.

radar fix. A fix established by means of radar.

radar horizon. The sensible horizon of a radar antenna.

radar indicator. A unit of a radar set which provides a visual indication of radar echoes received using a cathode-ray tube or video monitor. Besides the cathode-ray tube, the radar indicator is comprised of sweep and calibration circuit; and associated power supplies. Often shortened to INDICATOR.

radar link. A means by which the information from a radar set is reproduced at a distance by use of a radio link or cable. Also called RADAR RELAY SYSTEM.

radar nautical mile. The time interval required for the electromagnetic energy of a radar pulse to travel 1 nautical mile and the echo to return; approximately 12.4 microseconds.

radar picture. See DISPLAY, definition 1.

radar range. 1. The distance of a target as measured by radar. 2. The maximum distance at which a radar is effective in detecting targets. Radar range depends upon variables such as the weather, transmitted power, antenna height, pulse duration, receiver sensitivity, target size, target shape, etc.

radar receiver. A unit of a radar set which demodulates received radar echoes, amplifies the echoes and delivers them to the radar indicator. A radar receiver differs from the usual superheterodyne communications receiver in that its sensitivity is much greater; it has a better signal noise ratio, and it is designed to pass a pulse-type signal.

radar reference line. A mid-channel line on a chart which corresponds to a line incorporated in harbor radar display for the purpose of providing a reference for informing a vessel of its position. In some cases the line may be coincident with the recommended track. The line may be broken into sections of specified length having assigned names or numbers.

radar reflector. A device arranged so that incident electromagnetic energy reflects back to its source. See also CORNER REFLECTOR, PENTAGONAL CLUSTER, OCTAHEDRAL CLUSTER, DIHEDRAL REFLECTOR, DIELECTRIC REFLECTOR, REFLECTOR.

radar relay system. See RADAR LINK.

radar repeater. A unit which duplicates the radar display at a location remote from the main radar indicator installation. Also called PPI REPEATER, REMOTE PPI.

radar return. See ECHO, definition 2.

radar scan. The motion of a radar beam through space in searching for an echo.

radar scanning. The process or action of directing a radar beam through a search pattern.

radarscope, *n.* The cathode-ray tube or video monitor in the indicator of a radar set which displays the received echo to indicate range and bearing. Often shortened to SCOPE. See also PLAN POSITION INDICATOR.

radar set. An electronic apparatus consisting of a transmitter, antenna, receiver, and indicator for sending out radio-frequency energy and receiving and displaying reflected energy so as to indicate the range and bearing of the reflecting object. See also RADAR.

radar shadow. The area shielded from radar signals because of an intervening obstruction or absorbing medium. The shadow region appears as an area void of targets.

radar target. See as TARGET.

radar transponder beacon. See RACON.

radial, *adj.* Of or pertaining to a ray or radius; extending in a straight line outward from a center.

radial, *n.* A straight line extending outward from a center.

radial error. In a two-dimensional or elliptical error distribution, the measure of error as the radius of a circle of equivalent probability derived from the error ellipse. The error, expressed as 1 d_{rms}, is the square root of the sum of the error components along the major and minor axes of the probability ellipse. The use of radial error or d_{rms} error as a measure of error is somewhat confusing because the term does not correspond to a fixed value of probability for a given value of the error measure.

radial motion. Motion along a radius, or a component in such a direction, particularly the component of space motion of a celestial body in the direction of the line of sight.

radial period. See ANOMALISTIC PERIOD.

radian, *n.* The supplementary unit of plane angle in the International System of Units; it is the plane angle subtended at the center of a circle by an arc equal in length to the radius of the circle. It is equal to 360 Ö 2π, or approximately 57°17'48.8".

radian per second. The derived unit of angular velocity in the International System of Units.

radian per second squared. The derived unit of angular acceleration in the International System of Units.

radiant, *adj.* Of, pertaining to, or transmitted by radiation.

radiant energy. Energy consisting of electromagnetic waves.

radiate, *v., t. & i.* To send out in rays or straight lines from a center.

radiation, *n.* 1. The process of emitting energy in the form of electromagnetic waves. 2. The energy radiated in definition 1 above.

radiational cooling. The cooling of the earth's surface and adjacent air, occurring mainly at night whenever the earth's surface suffers a net loss of heat due to terrestrial radiation.

radiational tides. Periodic variations in sea level primarily related to meteorological changes such as the semi-daily (solar) cycle in barometric pressure, daily (solar) land and sea breezes, and seasonal (annual) changes in temperature. Only changes in sea level due to meteorological changes that are random in phase are not considered radiational tides.

radiation fog. A major type of fog, produced over land when radiational cooling reduces the temperature to or below its dew point. Radiation fog is a nighttime occurrence although it may begin to form by evening twilight and often does not dissipate until aft sunrise.

radiation pattern. A curve representing, in polar or Cartesian coordinates, the relative amounts of energy radiated in various directions. Also called DIRECTIVITY DIAGRAM.

radiatus, *adj.* Radial. A term used to refer to clouds in parallel bands which, owing to perspective, appear to converge toward a point on the horizon, or two opposite points if the bands cross the sky.

radio, *n.* A general term applied to the use of radio waves.

radio acoustic ranging. Determining distance by a combination of radio and sound, the radio being used to determine the instant of transmission or reception of the sound, and distance being determined by the time of transit of sound usually in water. See also ECHO RANGING.

radio aid to navigation. An aid to navigation transmitting information by radio waves. See also ELECTRONIC AID TO NAVIGATION.

radio altimeter. As defined by the International Telecommunications Union (ITU), a radionavigation device for aircraft, which uses reflected radio waves from the ground to determine the height of the aircraft above the ground.

radiobeacon, *n.* A radio transmitting station which emits a distinctive or characteristic signal so a navigator can determine the direction of the source using a radio direction finder, providing a line of position. The most common type of marine radiobeacon transmits radio waves of approximately uniform strength in all directions. These omnidirectional beacons are called circular radiobeacons. A radiobeacon some or all of the emissions of which are directional so that the signal characteristic changes according to the vessel's bearing from the beacon is called a directional radiobeacon. A radiobeacon all or part of the emissions of which is concentrated in a beam which rotates is called a rotating radiobeacon. See also CONTINUOUS CARRIER RADIOBEACON, DUAL-CARRIER RADIOBEACON, SEQUENCED RADIOBEACON, ROTATING PATTERN RADIOBEACON, COURSE BEACON.

radiobeacon characteristic. The description of the complete cycle of transmission of a radiobeacon in a given period of time, inclusive of any silent period.

radiobeacon station. As defined by the International Telecommunications Union (ITU), a station in the radionavigation service the emissions of which are intended to enable a mobile station to determine its bearing or direction from the radiobeacon station.

radio bearing. The bearing of a radio transmitter from a receiver, as determined by a radio direction finder.

radio compass. The name by which the radio direction finder was formerly known.

radiodetermination, *n.* As defined by the International Telecommunication Union (ITU), the determination of position using propagation properties of radio waves.

radiodetermination-satellite service. As defined by the International Telecommunication Union (ITU), a radiocommunication service involving the use of radiodetermination and the use of one or more space stations.

radio direction finder. A radio receiver system used for radio direction finding. Also called DIRECTION FINDER. Formerly called RADIO COMPASS. See also AUTOMATIC DIRECTION FINDER.

radio direction finder station. A radio station equipped with special apparatus for determining the direction of radio signals transmitted by ships and other stations. The bearing taken by a radio direction finder station, and reported to a ship, is corrected for all determinable errors except conversion angle. Also called DIRECTION FINDER STATION.

radio direction finding. As defined by the International Telecommunication Union (ITU), radiodetermination using the reception of radio waves to determine the direction of a station or object.

radio direction-finding station. As defined by the International Telecommunication Union (ITU), a radiodetermination station using radio direction finding.

radio fix. A navigational position determined by radio direction finder.

radio frequency. Any electromagnetic wave occurring within that segment of the spectrum normally associated with some form of radio propagation.

radio guard. A ship, aircraft, or radio station designated to listen for and record transmissions, and to handle traffic on a designated frequency for a certain unit or units.

radio horizon. The locus of points at which direct rays from a transmitting antenna become tangent to the earth's surface, taking into account the curvature due to refraction. Its distance from the transmitting antenna is greater than that of the visible horizon, and increases with decreasing frequency.

radio interference. Interference due to unwanted signals from other radio transmitting stations operating on the same or adjacent frequencies.

radio interferometer. An interferometer operating at radio frequencies; used in radio astronomy and in satellite tracking.

radiolarian *(pl. radiolaria), n.* A minute sea animal with a siliceous outer shell. The skeletons of such animals are very numerous, covering the ocean bottom in certain areas, principally in the tropics.

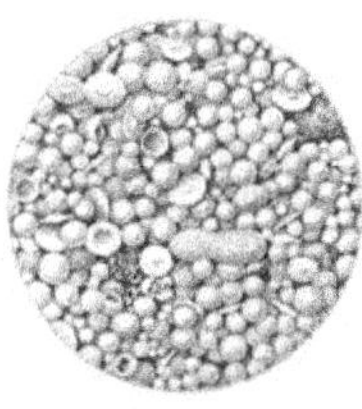

radiolarian

radiolocation, *n.* As defined by the International Telecommunication Union (ITU), radiodetermination used for purposes other than navigation.

radio mast. A label on a nautical chart which indicates a pole or structure for elevating radio antennas, usually found in groups.

radionavigation, *n.* 1. The determination of position, or the obtaining of information relating to position, for the purposes of navigation by means of the propagation properties of radio waves. 2. As defined by the International Telecommunication Union (ITU), radiodetermination used for the purposes of navigation, including obstruction warning. See also RADIODETERMINATION, RADIOLOCATION.

Radio Navigational Aids. See *PUB. 117.*

radio navigational warning. A radio-transmitted message affecting the safe navigation of vessels or aircraft. See also HYDROLANT, HYDROPAC, NAVAREA WARNINGS, WORLD WIDE NAVIGATIONAL WARNING SERVICE.

radionavigation-satellite service. As defined by the International Telecommunication Union (ITU) a radiodetermination-satellite service used for the same purposes as the radionavigation service; in certain cases this service includes transmission or retransmission of supplementary information necessary for the operation of radionavigation systems.

radio receiver. An electronic device connected to an antenna or other receptor of radio signals which receives and processes the signals for use.

radio silence. A period during which all or certain radio equipment capable of radiation is kept inoperative.

radio spectrum. The range of electromagnetic radiation useful for communication by radio (approximately 10 kilohertz to 300,000 megahertz).

radio station. A place equipped with one or more transmitters or receivers and accessory equipment for carrying on a radiocommunication service.

radio tower. A label on a nautical chart which indicates a tall pole or structure for elevating radio antennas.

radio transmitter. Equipment for generation and modulation of radio-frequency energy for the purpose of radiocommunication.

radio wave propagation. The transfer of energy by electromagnetic radiation at radio frequencies.

radio waves. Electromagnetic waves of frequencies lower than 3,000 gHz propagated in space without artificial guide. The practicable limits of radio frequency are approximately 10 kHz to 100 GHz. Also called HERTZIAN WAVES.

radius, *n.* A straight line from the center of a circle, arc, or sphere to its circumference, or the length of such a line. Also called SEMIDIAMETER for a circle or sphere. See also DIAMETER.

radius of action. The maximum distance a ship, aircraft, or vehicle can travel away from its base along a given course with normal combat load and return without refueling, allowing for all safety and operating factors.

radius vector. A straight line connecting a fixed reference point or center with a second point, which may be moving. In astronomy the expression is usually used to refer to the straight line connecting a celestial body with another which revolves around it. See also POLAR COORDINATES, SPHERICAL COORDINATES.

radome, *n.* A dome-shaped structure used to enclose radar apparatus.

rafted ice. A type of deformed ice formed by one piece of ice overriding another. See also FINGER RAFTING.

rain, *n.* Liquid precipitation consisting of drops of water larger than those which comprise DRIZZLE. Orographic rain results when moist air is forced upward by a mountain range. See also FREEZING RAIN.

rainbow, *n.* A circular arc of concentric spectrally colored bands formed by the refraction of light in drops of water. One seen in ocean spray is called a marine or sea rainbow. See also FOGBOW, MOONBOW.

rain clutter. Clutter on the radarscope which is the result of the radar signal being reflected by rain or other forms of precipitation.

rain gush. See CLOUDBURST.

rain gust. See CLOUDBURST.

rain shadow. The condition of diminished rainfall on the lee side of a mountain or mountain range, where the rainfall is noticeably less than on the windward side.

rain storm. See under STORM, definition 2.

raise. To cause to appear over the horizon or higher above the horizon by approaching closer.

ram, *n.* An underwater ice projection from an ice wall, ice front, iceberg, or floe. Its formation is usually due to a more intensive melting and erosion of the unsubmerged part.

ramark, *(from radar marker) n.* A radar beacon which continuously transmits a signal appearing as a radial line on the radar display, indicating the direction of the beacon from the ship. For identification purposes, the radial line may be formed by a series of dots or dashes. The radial line appears even if the beacon is outside the range for which the radar is set, as long as the radar receiver is within the power range of the beacon. Unlike the RACON, the ramark does not provide the range to the beacon.

ramming, *n.* In ice navigation, the act of an icebreaker at full power striking ice to break a track through it.

ramming

ramp, *n.* On the sea floor, a gentle slope connecting areas of different elevations.

random access memory (RAM). Type of computer memory used for temporary storage and processing of data, as opposed to permanent storage of data. RAM is volatile, meaning it is unable to store data without a constant source of power. See READ ONLY MEMORY(ROM).

random error. One of the two categories of errors of observation and measurement, the other category being systematic error. Random errors are the errors which occur when irregular, randomly occurring conditions affect the observing instrument, the observer and the environment, and the quantity being observed so that observations of the same quantity made with the same equipment and observer under the same observing conditions result in different values of the observed quantity. Random errors depend upon (1) the quality of the observing instrument. (2) the skill of the observer, particularly, the ability to estimate the fraction of the smallest division or graduation on the observing instrument, and (3) randomly fluctuating conditions such as temperature, pressure, refraction, etc. For many types of observations, random errors are characterized by the following properties: (1) positive and negative errors of the same magnitude are about equal in number, (2) small errors occur more frequently than large errors. and (3) extremely large errors rarely occur. These properties of random errors permit the use of a mathematical law called the Gaussian or normal distribution of errors to calculate the probability that the random error of any given observation of a series of observations will lie within certain limits. Random error might more properly be called deviation since mathematically, the random error of an individual observation is calculated as the difference or deviation between the actual observation and an improved or adjusted value of the observation obtained by some mathematical technique such as averaging all the observations. Also called ACCIDENTAL ERROR, CHANCE ERROR, IRREGULAR ERROR, STATISTICAL ERROR. See also ERROR, PRECISION, PRECISION INDEX, STANDARD DEVIATION.

range, *n.* 1. Two or more objects in line. Such objects are said to be in range. An observer having them in range is said to be on the range. Two beacons are frequently located for the specific purpose of forming a range to indicate a safe route or the centerline of a channel. See also BACK RANGE, LEADING LINE, MAGNETIC RANGE, MULTIPLE RANGES. 2. Distance in a single direction or along a great circle. 3. The extreme distance at which an object or light can be seen is called VISUAL RANGE. When the extreme distance is limited by the curvature of the earth and the heights of the object and the observer, this is called geographic range; when the range of a light is limited only by its intensity, clearness of the atmosphere, and sensitiveness of the observer's eyes, it is called luminous range. 4. The extreme distance at which a signal can be detected or used. The maximum distance at which reliable service is provided is called operating range. The spread of ranges in which there is an element of uncertainty of interpretation is called critical range. 5. The distance a vessel can travel at cruising speed without refueling is called CRUISING RADIUS. 6. The difference in extreme values of a variable quantity. See also RANGE OF TIDE. 7. A series of mountains or mountain ridges is called MOUNTAIN RANGE. 8. A predetermined line along which a craft moves while certain data are recorded by instruments usually placed below the line, or the entire station at which such information is determined. See also DEGAUSSING RANGE. 9. An area where practice firing of ordnance equipment is authorized is a firing range. See also BOMBING RANGE. 10. On the sea floor, a series of ridges or seamounts.

range, *v., t.* 1. To place in line. 2 To determine the distance to an object. 3 To move along or approximately parallel to something, as to range along coast.

range daymark. 1. One of a pair of unlighted structures used to mark a definite line of bearing. See also RANGE, definition 1. 2. A daymark on a range light.

range finder. An optical instrument for measuring the distance to an object. See also STADIMETER.

range lights. Two or more lights at different elevations so situated to form a range (leading line) when brought into transit. The one nearest the observer is the front light and the one farthest from the observer is the rear light. The front light is at a lower elevation than the rear light.

range marker. A visual presentation on a radar display for measuring the range or for calibrating the time base. See also VARIABLE RANGE MARKER, RANGE RING.

range (of a light). See VISUAL RANGE (OF A LIGHT).

range of tide. The difference in height between consecutive high and low waters. The mean range is the difference in height between mean high water and mean low water. The great diurnal range or diurnal range is the difference in height between mean higher high water and mean lower low water. Where the type of tide is diurnal the mean range is the same as the diurnal range. For other ranges see APOGEAN TIDES, NEAP TIDES, PERIGEAN TIDES, SPRING TIDES, TROPIC TIDES.

range-range mode. See RANGING MODE.

range rate. Rate of change in range between satellite and receiver, measured by determining the Doppler shift of the satellite carrier signal.

range resolution. See as RESOLUTION IN RANGE under RESOLUTION, definition 2. Also called DISTANCE RESOLUTION.

range ring. One of a set of equally spaced concentric rings, centered on own ship's position, providing a visual presentation of range on a radar display. See also VARIABLE RANGE MARKER.

ranging mode. A mode of operation of a radio navigation system in which the times for the radio signals to travel from each transmitting station to the receiver are measured rather than their *differences* as in the HYPERBOLIC MODE. Also called RHO-RHO MODE, RANGE-RANGE MODE.

Rankine temperature. Temperature based upon a scale starting at absolute zero (–459.69°F) and using Fahrenheit degrees.

rapids, *n.* A portion of a stream in swift, disturbed motion, but without cascade or waterfall.

raster. 1. A type of computerized display which consists of a single undifferentiated data file, analogous to a picture. See BIT-MAP, VECTOR. 2. In ECDIS a regular array with information pertaining to each element (PIXEL) or group of elements. See also RASTER DATA PRESENTATION.

Raster Chart Display System (RCDS). In ECDIS, a navigation information system displaying RNCs with positional information from navigation sensors to assist the mariner in route planning and route monitoring, and if required, display additional navigation-related information.

Raster Navigational Chart (RNC). A facsimile of a paper chart originated by, or distributed on the authority of, a government-authorized hydrographic office. It is either a single chart or a collection of charts.

ratan, *n*. An experimental short-range aid to navigation, not operational, in which radar harbor surveillance information is transmitted to the user by television.

rate, *n*. 1. Quantity or amount per unit of something else, usually time. See also ANGULAR RATE, CHRONOMETER RATE, PULSE REPETITION RATE, REPETITION RATE, WATCH RATE.

rate gyro. A single-degree-of-freedom gyro having primarily elastic restraint of its spin axis about the output axis. In this gyro, an output signal is produced by gimbal angular displacement, relative to the base, which is proportional to the angular rate of the base about the input axis. See also RATE INTEGRATING GYRO.

rate integrating gyro. A single-degree-of-freedom gyro having restraint of its spin axis about the output axis. In this gyro an output signal is produced by gimbal angular displacement, relative to the base, which is proportional to the integral of the angular rate of the base about the input axis. See also RATE GYRO.

ratio, *n*. The relation of one magnitude to another of the same kind, the quotient obtained by dividing one magnitude by another of the same kind. See also MAGNITUDE RATIO.

rational horizon. See CELESTIAL HORIZON.

ratio of ranges. The ratio of the ranges of tide at two places. It is used in the tide tables where the times and heights of all high and low tides are given for a relatively few places, called REFERENCE STATIONS. The tides at other places called SUBORDINATE TIDE STATIONS, are found by applying corrections to the values given for the reference stations. One of these corrections is the ratio of ranges, or the ratio between the height of the tide at the subordinate station and its reference station.

ratio of rise. The ratio of the height of tide at two places.

ravine, *n*. 1. A gulch; a small canyon or gorge, the sides of which have comparatively uniform slopes. 2. On the sea floor, a small canyon.

RCDS. See RASTER CHART DISPLAY SYSTEM.

read only memory (ROM). Computer memory used for permanent storage of data. It retains the data without a source of power. See RANDOM ACCESS MEMORY (RAM).

reach, *n*. A comparatively straight segment of a river or channel between two bends.

reach, *v*. To travel approximately perpendicular to the wind.

reach ahead. The distance traveled from the time a new speed is ordered to the time the new speed is being made.

real image. An image actually produced and capable of being shown on a surface, as in a camera.

real precession. Precession of a gyroscope resulting from an applied torque such as that resulting from friction and dynamic unbalance as opposed to APPARENT PRECESSION. Also called INDUCED PRECESSION, PRECESSION.

rear-light. The range light which is farthest from the observer. It is the highest of the lights of an established range. Also called HIGH LIGHT.

receiver, *n*. A person who or a device which receives anything, particularly a radio receiver.

receiver gain control. An operating control on a radar indicator used to increase or decrease the sensitivity of the receiver. The control regulates the intensity of the echoes displayed on the radarscope.

receiver monitor. See under PERFORMANCE MONITOR.

reciprocal, *adj*. In a direction 180° from a given direction. Also called BACK.

reciprocal, *n*. 1. A direction 180° from a given direction 2. The quotient of 1 divided by a given number.

reciprocal bearing. A bearing differing by 180° or one measured in the opposite direction, from a given bearing.

recommended direction of traffic flow. A traffic flow pattern indicating a recommended directional movement of traffic in a routing system within which it is impractical or unnecessary to adopt an established direction of traffic flow.

recommended track. A route which has been examined to ensure that it is free of dangers and along which vessels are advised to navigate. See also ROUTING SYSTEM.

record. In ECDIS, a TRANSFER STANDARD construct which is comprised of one or more tagged FIELDS and identified by a KEY.

rectangle, *n*. A four-sided figure with its opposite sides parallel and its angles 90°, a -right-angle parallelogram.

rectangular chart. A chart on the rectangular projection.

rectangular coordinates. Magnitudes defining a point relative to two perpendicular lines, called AXES. The magnitudes indicate the perpendicular distance from each axis. The vertical distance is called the ordinate and the horizontal distance the abscissa. This is a form of CARTESIAN COORDINATES.

rectangular error. An error which results from rounding off values prior to their inclusion in table or which results from the fact that an instrument cannot be read closer than a certain value The error is so called because of the shape of its plot. For example: if the altitudes tabulated in a sight reduction table are stated to the nearest 01', the error in the altitude as extracted from the table might have any value from (+) 0.05' to (-) 0.05', and any value within these limits is as likely to occur as another value having similar decimals. See also SIMILAR DECIMALS.

rectangular projection. A cylindrical map projection with uniform spacing of the parallels. This projection is used for the star chart in the *Air Almanac*.

rectified altitude. See APPARENT ALTITUDE.

rectilinear, *adj*. Moving in or characterized by straight line.

rectilinear current. See REVERSING CURRENT.

recurring decimal. See REPEATING DECIMAL.

recurring polynya. See under POLYNYA.

recurved spit. A hook developed when the end or spit is turned toward the shore by current deflection or by opposing action of two or more currents. Also called HOOK, HOOKED SPIT.

red magnetism. The magnetism of the northseeking end of a freely suspended magnet. This is the magnetism of the earth's south magnetic pole.

red sector. A sector of the circle of visibility of a navigational light in which a red light is exhibited. Such sectors are designated by their limiting bearings, as observed from a vessel. Red sectors are often located to warn of dangers.

red shift. In astronomy, the displacement of observed spectral lines toward the longer wavelengths of the red end of the spectrum. The red shift in the spectrum of distant galaxies has been interpreted as evidence that the universe is expanding.

red snow. Snow colored red by the presence in it either of minute algae or of red dust particles.

reduction, *n*. The process of substituting for an observed value one derived from it; often referring specifically to the adjustment of soundings to the selected chart datum. Usually the term reduction of soundings does not pertain to corrections other than those for height of tide. See also CORRECTION OF SOUNDINGS.

reduction of tidal current. The processing of observed tidal current data to obtain mean values of tidal current constants. See also REDUCTION OF TIDES.

reduction of tides. The processing of observed tidal data to obtain mean values of tidal constants. See also REDUCTION OF TIDAL CURRENTS.

reduction tables. See SIGHT REDUCTION TABLES.

reduction to the meridian. The process of applying a correction to an altitude observed when a body is near the celestial meridian of the observer, to find the altitude at meridian transit. The altitude at the time of such an observation is called an EX-MERIDIAN ALTITUDE.

reed, *n*. A steel tongue which is designed to vibrate when air is passed across its unsupported end.

reed horn. A sound signal emitter comprising a resonant horn excited by a jet of air which is modulated by a vibrating reed. The signal is a high-pitched note. See also REED, HORN.

reef, *n*. 1. An offshore consolidated rock hazard to navigation with a depth of 16 fathoms (or 30 meters) or less over it. See also SHOAL. 2. Sometimes used as a term for a low rocky or coral area some of which is above water. See BARRIER REEF, CORAL REEF, FRINGING REEF.

reef flat. A flat expanse of dead reef rock which is partly or entirely dry at low tide. Shallow pools, potholes, gullies, and patches of coral debris and sand are features of the reef flat.

reference datum. A general term applied to any datum, plane, or surface used as a reference or base from which other quantities can be measured.

reference ellipsoid. A theoretical figure whose dimensions closely approach the dimensions of the geoid; the exact dimensions of the ellipsoid are determined by various considerations of the section of the earth's surface of concern. Also called REFERENCE SPHEROID, SPHEROID OF REFERENCE, ELLIPSOID OF REFERENCE.

reference frequency. A frequency having a fixed and specified position with respect to the assigned frequency. The displacement of this frequency, with respect to the assigned frequency, has the same absolute value and sign that the displacement of the characteristic frequency has with respect to the center of the frequency band occupied by the emission.

reference grid. See GRID, definition 2.

reference orbit. An orbit, usually but not exclusively, the best two-body orbit available, on the basis of which the perturbations are computed.

reference ship. The ship to which the movement of other ships is referred.

reference spheroid. See REFERENCE ELLIPSOID.

reference station. A tide or current station for which independent daily predictions are given in the Tide Tables and Tidal Current Tables, and from which corresponding predictions obtained for subordinate stations by means differences and ratios. Also called STANDARD STATION. See also SUBORDINATE CURRENT STATION, SUBORDINATE TIDE STATION.

reflecting prism. A prism that deviates a light beam by internal reflection.

reflecting telescope. A telescope which collects light by means of a concave mirror. All telescopes more than 40 inches in diameter arc of this type. See also CASSEGRAINIAN TELESCOPE, NEWTONIAN TELESCOPE.

reflection, *n*. The return or the change in direction of travel of radiation by a surface without change of frequency of the monochromal components of which the radiation is composed. The radiation does not enter the substance providing the reflecting surface. If reflecting surface is smooth, specular reflection occurs; if the reflecting surface is rough with small irregularities, diffuse reflection occurs.

reflection plotter. An attachment fitted to a radar display which provides a plotting surface permitting plotting without parallax errors. Marks made on the plotting surface are reflected on the radarscope directly below. Also called PLOTTING HEAD.

reflectivity, *n*. The ratio of the radiant energy reflected by a surface to that incident upon it.

reflector, *n*. A reflecting surface situated behind the primary radiator, an array of primary radiators or a feed for the purpose of increasing forward and reducing backward radiation from antenna. See also RADAR REFLECTOR.

reflector compass. A magnetic compass in which the image of the compass card is viewed by direct reflection in a mirror adjacent to helmsman's position. See also PROJECTOR COMPASS.

reflex angle. An angle greater than 180° and less than 360°.

reflex reflection. See RETRO-REFLECTION.

reflex-reflector, *n*. See RETRO-REFLECTOR.

refracted ray. A ray extending onward from point of refraction.

refracting prism. A prism that deviates a beam light by refraction. The angular deviation is function of the wavelength of light; therefore if the beam is composed of white light, the prism will spread the beam into a spectrum.

refracting telescope. A telescope which collects light by means of a lens or system of lenses.

refraction, *n*. The change in direction of motion of a ray of radiant energy as it passes obliquely from one medium into another in which the speed of propagation is different. Atmospheric refraction is caused by the atmosphere and may be further designated astronomical refraction if the ray enters from outside the atmosphere or terrestrial refraction if it emanates from a point on or near the surface of the earth. Super-refraction is greater than normal and sub-refraction is less than normal. See also DIFFRACTION, REFLECTION.

refraction correction. 1. A correction due to refraction, particularly such a correction to a sextant altitude, due to atmospheric refraction. 2. See IONOSPHERIC CORRECTION.

refractive index. The ratio of the velocity of light in vacuum to the velocity of light in a medium. This index is equal to the ratio of the sines of the angles of incidence and refraction when a ray crosses the surface separating vacuum and medium.

refractive modulus. One million times the amount by which the modified refractive index exceeds unity.

refrangible, *adj*. Capable of being refracted.

regelation, *n*. The melting of ice under pressure and the subsequent refreezing when the pressure is reduced or removed.

region. One of the major subdivisions of the earth based on the NGA chart numbering system.

Regional ENC Coordinating Center (RENC). An organizational entity where IHO Member States have established cooperation amongst each other to guarantee a world-wide consistent level of high quality data, for bringing about coordinated services with official ENCs and updates to ENCs.

regression of the nodes. Precessional motion of a set of nodes. The expression is used principally with respect to the moon, the nodes of which make a complete westerly revolution in approximately 18.6 years.

regular error. See SYSTEMATIC ERROR.

regular reflection. See SPECULAR REFLECTION.

relationship. In ECDIS, a logical link between two elements from the DATA MODEL which may be spatial (e.g. TOPOLOGICAL relationship) and/or non-spatial. In general a relationship is implemented in the data structure as a POINTER.

relative, *adj*. Having relationship. In navigation the term has several specific applications: a. related to a moving point; apparent, as relative wind, relative movement; b. related to or measured from the heading, as relative bearing; c. related or proportional to a variable, as relative humidity. See also TRUE.

relative accuracy. The accuracy with which a user can measure current position relative to that of another user of the same navigation system at the same time. Hence, a system with high relative accuracy provides good rendezvous capability for the users of the system. The correlation between the geographical coordinates and the system coordinates is not relevant. See also PREDICTABLE ACCURACY, REPEATABLE ACCURACY.

relative azimuth. Azimuth relative to heading.

relative bearing. Bearing relative to heading of a vessel, expressed as the angular difference between the heading and the direction. It is usually measured from 0° at the heading clockwise through 360°, but is sometimes measured from 0° at the heading either clockwise or counterclockwise through 180°, when it is designated right or left.

relative course. Misnomer for DIRECTION OF RELATIVE MOVEMENT.

relative direction. Horizontal direction expressed as angular distance from heading.

relative distance. Distance relative to a specified reference point, usually one in motion.

relative gain of an antenna. The gain of an antenna in a given direction when the reference antenna is a half-wave loss-free dipole isolated in space, the equatorial plane of which contains the given direction.

relative humidity. See under HUMIDITY.

relative motion. See RELATIVE MOVEMENT.

relative motion display. 1. A type of radarscope display in which the position of own ship is fixed, usually at the center of the display, and all detected targets move relative own ship. 2. In ECDIS, a DISPLAY in which OWN SHIP remains stationary, while all other charted information and targets move relative to own ship's position. See also TRUE MOTION DISPLAY.

relative movement. Motion of one object relative to another. The expression is usually used in connection with problems involving motion of one vessel to another, the direction such motion being called DIRECTION RELATIVE MOVEMENT and the speed of the motion being called SPEED OF RELATIVE MOVEMENT or RELATIVE SPEED. Distance relative to a specified reference point, usually one in motion, is called RELATIVE DISTANCE.

Usually called APPARENT MOTION applied to the change of position of a celestial body as observed from the earth. Also called RELATIVE MOTION.

relative plot. A plot of the successive positions of a craft relative to a reference point, which is usually in motion. A line connecting successive relative positions of a maneuvering ship relative to a reference ship is called a RELATIVE MOVEMENT LINE. A relative plot includes relative movement lines and the position of the reference ship.

relative position. A point defined with reference to another position, either fixed or moving coordinates of such a point are usually between true or relative, and distance from an identified reference point.

relative speed. See SPEED OF RELATIVE MOVEMENT.

relative wind. The wind with reference to a moving point. Sometimes called APPARENT WIND. See also APPARENT WIND, TRUE WIND.

release, *n*. A device for holding or releasing a mechanism, particularly the device by which the tangent screw of a sextant is engaged or disengaged from the limb.

relief, *n*. 1. The elevations of a land surface; represented graphics by contours, hypsometric tints, spot elevations, hachures, etc. Similar representation of the ocean floor is called SUBMARINE RELIEF. 2. The removal of a buoy (formerly also referred to lightships) from station and provision of another buoy having the operating characteristics authorized for that station.

relief map. See HYPSOGRAPHIC MAP.

relief model. Any three-dimensional representation of an object or geographic area, modeled in any size or medium. See also PLASTIC RELIEF MAP.

relieved, *adj*. Said of a buoy that has been removed from a station and replaced by another having the proper operating characteristics.

relighted, *adj*. Said of an extinguished aid to navigation returned to its advertised light characteristic.

relocated, *adj*. Said of aid to navigation that has been permanently moved from one position to another.

reluctance, *n*. Magnetic resistance.

remanence, *n*. Ability to retain magnetism after removal of the magnetizing force. Also See RETENTIVITY.

remote-indicating compass. A compass equipped with one or more indicators to repeat at a distance the readings of the master compass. The directive element and controls are called a master compass to distinguish this part of the system from the repeaters, or remote indicators. Most marine gyrocompass installations are of this type. Also called REMOTE-READING COMPASS.

remotely controlled light. A light which is operated by personnel at a considerable distance from the light, through electrical or radio links.

remote PPI. See RADAR REPEATER.

remote-reading compass. See REMOTE-INDICATING COMPASS.

repaired, *adj*. Said of a sound signal or radionavigation aid previously INOPERATIVE, placed back in operation, or of a structure previously DAMAGED, that has been restored as an effective aid to navigation.

repeatability, *n*. 1. A measure of the variation in the accuracy of an instrument when identical tests are made under fixed conditions. 2. In a navigation system, the measure of the accuracy with which the system permits the user to return to a specified point as defined only in terms of the coordinates peculiar to that system. See also PREDICTABILITY.

repeatable accuracy. In a navigation system, the measure of the accuracy with which the system permits the user to return to a position as defined only in terms of the coordinates peculiar to that system. The correlation between the geographical coordinates and the system coordinates may or may not be known. See also PREDICTABLE ACCURACY, RELATIVE ACCURACY.

repeater, *n*. A device for repeating at a distance the indications of an instrument or device. See also COMPASS REPEATER, GYRO REPEATER, RADAR REPEATER, STEERING REPEATER.

repeating decimal. A decimal in which all the digits after a certain digit consist of a set of one or more digits repeated and infinitum. Also called RECURRING DECIMAL.

replaced, *adj*. Said of an aid to navigation previously OFF STATION, ADRIFT or MISSING that has been restored by another aid of the same type and characteristic.

representative fraction. The scale of a map or chart expressed as a fraction or ratio that relates unit distance on the map to distance measured in the same unit on the ground. Also called NATURAL SCALE, FRACTIONAL SCALE. See also NUMERICAL SCALE.

reradiation, *n*. 1. The scattering of incident radiation. Reradiation from metallic objects in proximity to either the transmitting or receiving antennas can introduce unwanted effects. This is particularly true on a vessel having a number of metallic structures or wires in the vicinity of an antenna. Where such structures are permanent, the effects can sometimes be allowed for by calibration. Also called SECONDARY RADIATION. 2. Radiation from a radio receiver due to poor isolation between the antenna circuit and the local oscillator within the receiver, causing unwanted interference in other receivers.

research sanctuary. A marine sanctuary established for scientific research in support of management programs, and to establish ecological baselines. See also MARINE SANCTUARY.

reset, *adj*. Said of a floating aid to navigation previously OFF STATION, ADRIFT, or MISSING that has been returned to its station.

residual deviation. Deviation of a magnetic compass after adjustment or compensation. The values on various headings are called RESIDUALS.

residual magnetism. Magnetism which remains after removal of the magnetizing force.

residuals, *n., pl*. The remaining deviation of a magnetic compass on various headings after adjustment or compensation. See also DEVIATION TABLE.

resistance, *n*. Opposition, particularly to the flow of electric current.

resistivity, *n*. The amount of resistance in a system. Resistivity is the reciprocal of CONDUCTIVITY.

resolution, *n*. 1. The ability of an optical system to distinguish between individual objects; the degree of ability to make such a separation, called RESOLVING POWER, is expressed as the minimum distance between two objects that can be separated. 2. The degree of ability of a radar set to indicate separately the echoes of two targets in range, bearing, and elevation. Resolution in range is the minimum range difference between separate targets at the same bearing which will allow both to appear separately; Resolution in bearing is the minimum horizontal angular separation between two targets at the same range which will allow both to appear separately. Resolution in elevation is the minimum separation in the vertical plane between two contacts at the same range and bearing which will allow both to appear as distinct echoes. 3. In ECDIS, it is the capability of depicting detail, represented by the smallest distance apart at which two objects can be seen to be separate. The separation is called the RESOLVING POWER. In ECDIS, it is dependent on PIXEL size.

resolution of vectors. The resolving of a vector into two or more components. The opposite is called VECTOR ADDITION.

resolving power. The degree of ability of an optical system to distinguish between objects close together. See also RESOLUTION.

resolving time. 1. The minimum time interval between two events which permits one event to be distinguishable from the other. 2. In computers, the shortest permissible period between trigger pulses for reliable operation of a binary cell.

resonance, *n*. Re-enforcement or prolongation any wave motion, such as sound, radio waves etc., resulting when the natural frequency of a body or system in vibration is equal to that of an impressed vibration.

resonant frequency. Any frequency at which a body or system vibrates most readily. The lowest resonant frequency is the natural frequency of the body or system.

responsor, *n*. A unit which receives the response emitted by a transponder.

restricted area. 1. An area (land, sea, or air) in which there are special restrictive measures employed to prevent or minimize interference between friendly forces. 2. An area under military jurisdiction in which special security measures are employed to prevent unauthorized entry. See also DANGER AREA, PROHIBITED AREA.

restricted waters. Areas which for navigational reasons such as the presence of shoals or other dangers confine the movements of shipping within narrow limits.

resultant, *n*. The sum of two or more vectors.

retard, *v., t & i*. To delay. This term is sometimes used as the equivalent of RETIRE (meaning "to move back"), but this usage is not appropriate.

retarded line of position. See RETIRED LINE OF POSITION.

retentive error. Deviation of a magnetic compass due to the tendency of a vessel's structure to retain some of the induced magnetic effects for short periods of time. For example, a vessel on a northerly course for several days, especially if pounding in heavy seas, will tend to retain some fore-and-aft magnetism gained through induction. Although this effect is not large and generally decays within a few hours, it may cause incorrect observations or adjustments, if neglected. This error should not be confused with GAUSSIN ERROR.

retentivity, *n*. See REMANENCE.

reticle, *n*. A system of lines, wires, etc., placed in the focal plane of an optical instrument to serve as a reference. A cross hair is a hair, thread, or wire constituting part of a reticle. See also GRATICULE, definition 2.

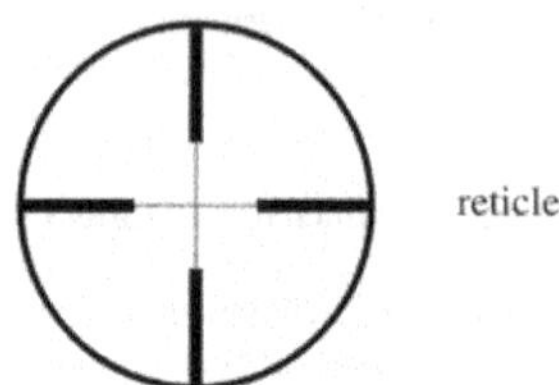

reticle

retire, *v., t. & i.* To move back, as to move a line of position back, parallel to itself, along a course line to obtain a line of position at an earlier time. The term RETARD (meaning "to delay") is sometimes used as an equivalent, but the term RETIRE (meaning "to move back") is more appropriate. The opposite is ADVANCE.

retired line of position. A line of position which has been moved backward along the course line to correspond with a time previous to that at which the line was established. The opposite is ADVANCED LINE OF POSITION.

retrace, *n*. The path of the visible dot from the end of one sweep to the start of the next sweep across the face of a cathode-ray tube.

retract, *v., t. & i.* The opposite of BEACH, *v., t & i.*

retrograde motion. The apparent motion of a planet westward among the stars. Apparent motion eastward, called DIRECT MOTION, is more common. Also called RETROGRESSION.

retrogression, *n*. See RETROGRADE MOTION.

retro-reflecting material. A material which produces retro-reflection over a wide range of angles of incidence of a light beam, by use of a large number of very small reflecting and refracting elements, usually very small beads.

retro-reflection, *n*. Reflection in which light is returned in directions close to the direction from which it came over wide variations of the direction of the incident light. Also called REFLEX REFLECTION.

retro-reflector, *n*. A device intended to produce retro-reflection. It may comprise one or more retro-reflecting optical units, for example, comer reflectors or special lens units of glass or plastic. Such devices may be installed generally on unlighted buoys or other aids to navigation to increase the range at which they may be seen at night. Also called REFLEX REFLECTOR.

return, *n*. See BLIP; ECHO, definition 2.

reverberation, *n*. Continuation of radiant energy, particularly sound, by multiple reflection.

reversing current. A tidal current which flows alternately in approximately opposite directions with a slack water at each reversal of direction. Currents of this type usually occur in rivers and straits where the direction of flow is somewhat restricted to certain channels. When the movement is towards the shore or up a stream the current is said to be flooding, and when in the opposite direction it is said to be ebbing. The combined flood and ebb movement including the slack water covers, on an average, 12.4. hours for the semidiurnal current. If unaffected by a nontidal flow, the flood and ebb movements will each last about 6 hours, but when combined with such a flow, the durations of flood and ebb may be quite unequal. During the low in each direction the speed of the current will vary from zero at the time of slack water to a maximum about midway between the slacks. Also called RECTILINEAR CURRENT.

reversing falls. Falls which flow alternately in opposite directions in a narrow channel in the St. John River, New Brunswick, Canada, due to the large range of tide and a constriction in the river. The direction of flow is upstream or downstream according to whether it is high or low water on the outside, the falls disappearing at the half-tide level.

revolution, *n*. Circular motion about an axis usually external to the body. The terms REVOLUTION and ROTATION are often used interchangeably but, with reference to the motions of a celestial body, REVOLUTION refers to the motion in an orbit or about an axis external to the body while ROTATION refers to motion about axis within the body. Thus, the earth revolves about the sun annually and rotates about its axis daily.

revolution counter, revolution indicator. An instrument for registering the number of revolutions of a shaft, particularly a propeller shaft of a vessel (when it may be called ENGINE REVOLUTION COUNTER). This information is useful in estimating a vessel's speed through the water.

revolution table. A table listing the number of shaft revolutions corresponding to various speeds of a vessel.

revolver, *n*. The pair of horizontal angles between three points, as observed at any place on the circle defined by the three points. This is the only situation in which such angles do not establish a fix. Also called SWINGER.

revolving light. See ROTATING LIGHT.

revolving storm. A cyclonic storm, or one in which the wind revolves about a central low pressure area.

rheostat, *n*. A variable resistor for changing the amount of current in an electrical circuit.

rhomboid, *n*. A parallelogram with oblique angles. A rhomboid with sides of equal length is rhombus.

rhombus, *n*. A rhomboid with sides of equal length.

Rho-Rho mode. See RANGING MODE.

rho-theta navigation. Navigation by means measuring ranges and bearings of a known position.

rhumb, *n*. Short for RHUMB LINE.

rhumb bearing. The direction of a rhumb line through two terrestrial points, expressed angular distance from a reference direction. It is usually measured from 0° at the reference direction clockwise through 360°. Also called MERCATOR BEARING.

rhumb direction. See MERCATOR DIRECTION.

rhumb line. A line on the surface of the earth making the same oblique angle with all meridians; a loxodrome or loxodromic curve spirals toward the poles in a constant true direction. Parallels and meridians, which also maintain constant true directions, may be considered special cases of the rhumb line. A rhumb line is a straight line on a Mercator projection. Sometimes shortened to RHUMB. See also FICTITIOUS RHUMB LINE.

rhumb-line course. The direction of the rhumb line from the point of departure to the destination, expressed as the angular distance from a reference direction, usually north. Also called MERCATOR COURSE.

rhumb-line distance. Distance point to point along a rhumb line, usually expressed in nautical miles.

rhumb-line sailing. Any method of solving the various problems involving course, distance, difference of latitude, difference of longitude, and departure as they are related to a rhumb line.

rhythmic light. A light showing intermittently with a regular periodicity.

ria, *n*. A long, narrow inlet with gradually decreasing depth inward.

ridge, *n*. 1. On the sea floor, a long, narrow elevation with steep sides. 2. A line or wall of broken ice forced up by pressure. The ridge may be fresh or weathered. See also AGED RIDGE. 3. In meteorology, an elongated area of relatively high atmospheric pressure, almost always associated with and most clearly identified as an area of maximum anticyclonic curvature of wind flow. The opposite of a ridge is called TROUGH. Sometimes called WEDGE.

ridged ice. Ice piled haphazardly one piece over another in the form of ridges or walls; usually found in first-year ice.

ridged ice

ridged-ice zone. An area in which much ridged ice with similar characteristics has formed.

ridging, *n*. The pressure process by which sea ice is forced into ridges.

riding light. See ANCHOR LIGHT.

rift, *n*. An opening made by splitting; a crevasse; usually in the earth.

right angle. An angle of 90°.

right angle reflector. See DIHEDRAL REFLECTOR.

right ascension. Angular distance east of the vernal equinox; the arc of the celestial equator, or the angle at the celestial pole, between the hour circle of the vernal equinox and the hour circle of a point on the celestial sphere, measured eastward from the hour circle of the vernal equinox through 24 hours. Angular distance west of the vernal equinox, through 360°, is SIDEREAL HOUR ANGLE.

right astern. See DEAD ASTERN.

right bank. The bank of a stream or river on the right of the observer when he is facing in the direction of flow, or downstream. See also LEFT BANK.

right circular cone. A cone having a circular base perpendicular to the axis of the cone. Often shortened to RIGHT CONE.

right cone. Short for RIGHT CIRCULAR CONE.

right sphere. The celestial sphere as it appears to an observer at the equator, where celestial bodies appear to rise vertically above the horizon.

right spherical triangle. A spherical triangle with a right angle.

right triangle. A triangle one angle of which is 90°.

rigidity in space. See GYROSCOPIC INERTIA.

rime, *n*. A white or milky and opaque granular deposit of ice formed by the rapid freezing of supercooled water drops as they impinge on an exposed object. It is denser and harder than frost, but lighter, softer, and less transparent than glaze.

rime fog. See ICE FOG.

ring time. The time, reckoned from the end of pulse transmitted by a radar set, during which the output of an echo box produces a visible signal on the display.

rip current. A narrow intense current setting seaward through the surf zone. It removes excess water brought to the zone by the small net mass transport of waves, and is fed by longshore currents. Rip currents usually occur at points groins, jetties, etc., of irregular beaches, and at regular intervals along straight, uninterrupted beaches. See also RIPS.

riprap, *n*. Stones or broken rock thrown together without order to provide a revetment.

riprap mounds. Mounds of riprap maintained at certain light structures to protect the structures against ice damage and scouring action. Submerged portions present a hazard to vessels attempting to pass very close aboard.

rips, *n. pl*. Agitation of water caused by the meeting of currents or by a rapid current setting over an irregular bottom. Called TIDE RIPS when the tidal current is involved. See also OVERFALLS, RIP CURRENT.

rise, *n*. A broad elevation that rises gently and generally smoothly from the sea floor. See also CONTINENTAL RISE.

rise, *v., i*. To ascend past the visible horizon. The opposite is SET.

rise of tide. Vertical distance from the chart sounding datum to a higher water datum. Mean rise of tide is the height of mean high water above the chart sounding datum. Spring rise and neap rise are the heights of spring high water and neap high water, respectively, above the chart sounding datum; while mean spring rise and mean neap rise are the heights of mean high water springs and mean high water neaps, respectively above the chart sounding datum. Also called TIDAL RISE. See also HEIGHT OF TIDE.

rising tide. A tide in which the depth of water is increasing. Sometimes the term FLOOD is used as an equivalent, but since flood refers primarily to horizontal rather than vertical movement RISING TIDE is more appropriate. The opposite is FALLING TIDE.

river, *n*. A natural stream of water, of greater volume than a creek or rivulet, flowing in a more or less permanent bed or channel, between defined banks or walls, with a current which may either be continuous in one direction or affected by the ebb and flow of the tidal current.

river buoy. A lightweight nun or can buoy especially designed to withstand strong currents.

river estuary. See ESTUARY, definition 2.

river ice. Ice formed on a river, regardless of observed location.

river radar. A marine radar set especially designated for river pilotage, generally characterized by high degree of resolution and a wide selection of range scales.

rivulet, *n*. A small stream; a brook.

RNC. See RASTER NAVIGATIONAL CHART.

road, *n*. An open anchorage affording less protection than a harbor. Some protection may be afforded by reefs, shoals, etc. Often used in the plural. Also called ROADSTEAD.

roadstead, *n*. See ROAD.

roaring forties. The area of the oceans between 40° and 50° south latitude, where strong westerly winds prevail. See also BRAVE WEST WIND.

roche moutonnée. A rock worn into a rounded shape by a glacier.

rock, *n*. 1. An isolated rocky formation or single large stone, usually one constituting a danger navigation. It may be always submerged, always uncovered, or alternately covered and uncovered by the tide. A pinnacle is a sharp-pointed rock rising from the bottom. 2. The naturally occurring material that forms the firm, hard, and solid masses of the ocean floor. Also, rock is a collective term for hard material generally not smaller than 256 millimeters.

rock awash. A rock that becomes exposed, or nearly so, between chart sounding datum and mean high water. In the Great Lakes, the rock awash symbol is used on charts for rocks that are awash, or nearly so, at low water datum. See also BARE ROCK, SUBMERGED ROCK.

rocking the sextant. See SWINGING THE ARC.

rod, *n*. 1. A unit of length equal to 5.5 yards or 16.5 feet. Also called POLE, PERCH. 2. One of the imaginary slender soft iron bars which are assumed to be components or parameters of a craft's magnetic field caused by magnetism induced in soft iron.

roll, *n*. Oscillation of a craft about its longitudinal axis. Also called ROLLING. See also LIST, *n*.; SHIP MOTIONS.

roll, *v., t. & i*. To oscillate or be oscillated about the longitudinal axis.

roll angle. See ANGLE OF ROLL.

rollers, *n*. Amongst the islands of the West Indies, the South Atlantic and the South Indian Ocean, swell waves which after moving into shallow water have grown to such height as to be destructive. See also COMBER.

rolling, *n*. See ROLL, *n*.

root mean square. The square root of the arithmetical mean of the squares of a group of numbers.

root mean square error. For the one-dimensional error distribution, this term has the same meaning as STANDARD DEVIATION or STANDARD ERROR. For the two-dimensional error distribution, this term has the same meaning as RADIAL (d_{rms}) ERROR. However, such use of the term is deprecated. Root mean square error is commonly called RMS ERROR.

rotary current. A tidal current that flows continually, with the direction of flow changing through 360° during the tidal period. Rotary currents are usually found offshore where the direction of flow is not restricted by any barriers. The tendency for rotation is due to the Coriolis force and, unless modified by local conditions, is clockwise in the Northern Hemisphere and counterclockwise in the Southern Hemisphere. The speed of the current usually varies throughout the tidal cycle, passing through the two maxima in approximately opposite directions and the two minima with the direction of the current at approximately 90° from the direction at time of maximum speed.

rotating light. A light with one or more beams that rotate. Sometimes called REVOLVING LIGHT.

rotation, *n*. Turning of a body about an axis within the body, such as the daily rotation of the earth. See also REVOLUTION.

rotten ice. Sea ice which has become honeycombed and is in an advanced state of disintegration.

round, *v., t.* To pass and alter direction of travel, as a vessel ROUNDS A CAPE. If the course is nearly reversed, the term DOUBLE may be used.

roundabout, *n.* A routing measure comprising a separation point or circular separation zone and a circular traffic lane within defined limits. Traffic within the roundabout moves in a counterclockwise direction around the separation point or zone. See also ROUTING SYSTEM, TRAFFIC SEPARATION SCHEME.

round of bearings. A group of bearings observed together for plotting as a fix.

round of sights. A group of celestial observations made together for plotting a fix.

round wind. A wind that gradually changes direction through approximately 180° during the daylight hours. See also LAND BREEZE.

route. In ECDIS, a sequence of WAYPOINTS and LEGS.

route chart. A chart showing routes between various places, usually with distances indicated.

route monitoring. In ECDIS, the operational navigational function in which the chart information is displayed, under control of the positioning sensor input, according to the vessel's present position (either in TRUE MOTION or RELATIVE MOTION DISPLAY mode).

route planning. In ECDIS, the pre-determination of COURSE, speed, and WAYPOINTS in relation to the waters to be navigated. Designed to plan a route between two geographical locations using computational software specialized for the purpose of ocean navigation. In addition, it provides, ETA, fuel burn rate information and numerous other data once the vessel's operating parameters are set in the system.

routing system. Any system of one or more defined tracks and/or traffic control measures for reducing the risk of casualties; it includes traffic separation schemes, two-way routes, recommended tracks, areas to be avoided, inshore traffic zones, roundabouts, precautionary areas, and deep water routes.

rubble, *n.* 1. Fragments of hard sea ice, roughly spherical and up to 5 feet in diameter, resulting from the disintegration of larger ice formations. When afloat, commonly called BRASH ICE. 2. Loose angular rock fragments.

Rude Star Finder. A star finder named for Captain Gilbert T. Rude, U.S. Coast and Geodetic Survey.

rugged, *adj.* Rock-bound; craggy.

rules of navigation. Rules of the road.

rules of the road. The *International Regulations for Prevention of Collisions at Sea*, commonly called *International Rules of the Road*, and the *Inland Navigation Rules*, to be followed by all vessels while navigating upon certain inland waters of the United States. Also called RULES OF NAVIGATION.

run, *n.* 1. A brook, or small creek. 2. A small, swift watercourse. 3. The distance traveled by a craft during any given time interval, or since leaving a designated place. See also DAY'S RUN.

run a line of soundings. To obtain soundings along a course line, for use in making or improving a chart.

run before the wind. To steer a course downwind, especially under sail.

run down a coast. To sail approximately parallel with the coast.

runnel, *n.* The smallest of natural streams; a brook or run.

running fix. A position determined by crossing lines of position obtained at different times and advanced or retired to a common time. However in celestial navigation or when using long-range electronic aids, a position determined by crossing lines of position obtained within a few minutes is considered a FIX; the expression RUNNING FIX is applied to a position determined by advancing or retiring a line over a considerable period of time. There is no sharp dividing line between a fix and a running fix in this case.

running light. See NAVIGATION LIGHTS.

run-off, *n.* That portion of precipitation which is discharged from the area of fall as surface water in streams.

run of the coast. The directional trend of a coast.

run-up. The rush of water up a structure on the breaking of a wave. The amount of run-up is the vertical height above the still water level that the rush of water reaches. Also called UPRUSH.

S

saddle, *n.* A low part of the sea floor resembling in shape a saddle, in a ridge or between contiguous seamounts.

safety contour. See OWN SHIP's SAFETY CONTOUR.

safety depth. In ECDIS, the depth defined by the mariner, e.g. the ship's draft plus under keel clearance, to be used by ECDIS to emphasize soundings on the DISPLAY equal to or less than this value.

safety lanes. Specified sea lanes designated for use by submarines and surface ships in transit to prevent attack by friendly forces. They may be called SUBMARINE SAFETY LANES when designated for use by submarines in transit.

safe water mark. See under IALA MARITIME BUOYAGE SYSTEM.

SafetyNET. The INMARSAT broadcast service for MARITIME SAFETY INFORMATION (MSI).

sailing, *n.* A method of solving the various problems involving course, distance, difference of latitude, difference of longitude, and departure. The various methods are collectively spoken of as the sailings. Plane sailing considers the earth as a plane. Traverse sailing applies the principles of plane sailing to determine the equivalent course and distance made good by a craft following a track consisting of a series of rhumb lines. Any of the sailings which considers the spherical or spheroidal shape of the earth is called spherical sailing. Middle-latitude sailing is a method of converting departure into difference of longitude, or vice versa, by assuming that such a course is steered at the middle or mean latitude; if the course is 090° or 270° true, it is called parallel sailing. Mercator sailing applies when the various elements are considered in their relation on a Mercator chart. Meridian sailing is used when the course is 000° or 180° true. Rhumb-line sailing is used when a rhumb line is involved; great-circle sailing when a great circle track is involved. Composite sailing is a modification of great circle sailing used when it is desired to limit the highest latitude. The expression current sailing is occasionally used to refer to the process of allowing for current in determining the predicted course made good, or of determining the effect of a current on the direction of motion of a vessel.

sailing chart. See under CHART CLASSIFICATION BY SCALE.

sailing directions. 1. A descriptive book for the use of mariners, containing detailed information of coastal waters, harbor facilities, etc. of an area. For waters of the United States and its possessions, they are published by the National Ocean Survey and are called UNITED STATES COAST PILOTS. Sailing directions, as well as light lists, provide the information that cannot be shown graphically on the nautical chart and that is not readily available elsewhere. See also UNITED STATES COAST PILOT.

St. Elmo's fire. A luminous discharge of electricity from pointed objects such as the masts and arms of ships, lightning rods, steeples, etc. occurring when there is a considerable atmospheric difference in potential. Also called CORPOSANT, CORONA DISCHARGE.

St. Hilaire method. Establishing a line position from observation of the altitude of a celestial body by using an assumed position, the difference between the observed and computed altitudes, and the azimuth. The method was devised by Marcq St. Hilaire, a French naval officer, in 1874. See also SUMNER METHOD, LONGITUDE METHOD, HIGH ALTITUDE METHOD. Also see ALTITUDE INTERCEPT METHOD.

salinity marsh. A measure of the amount of dissolved solid material in water.

sallying ship. Producing rolling motion of a ship by having the crew run in unison from to side. This is usually done to help float a ship which is aground or to assist it to make way when it is beset by ice.

salt marsh. A flat coastal area flooded by most high tides, characterized by various species of marsh grasses and animal life.

salt-water wedge. The intrusion of a tidal estuary by sea water in the form of a wedge underneath the less dense fresh water.

same name. A name the same as that possessed by something else, as declination has the same name as latitude if both are north or both south. They are of CONTRARY NAME if one is north and the other south.

sand, *n.* Sediment consisting of small but distinguishable separate grains between 0.0625 and 2.0 millimeters in diameter. It is called very fine sand if the grains are between 0.0625 and 0.125 millimeter in diameter, fine sand between 0.125 and 0.25 millimeter, medium sand if between 0.25 and 0.50 millimeters, coarse sand if between 0.50 and 1.0 millimeters, and very coarse sand if between 1.0 and 2.0 millimeters. See also MUD, STONES, ROCK definition 2.

sand bar. *n.* A ridge of sand built up by currents such that the top is near or just above the surface of the water.

sand dune. See DUNE.

sandstorm, *n.* A strong wind carrying sand through the air, the diameter of most of the particles ranging from 0.08 to 1.0 millimeter. In contrast to a DUST STORM, the sand particles are mostly confined to the lowest 10 feet, and rarely rise more than 50 feet above the ground.

sandwave, *n.* A large wavelike sea-floor sediment feature in very shallow water and composed of sand. The wavelength may reach 100 meters, the amplitude is about 0.5 meter. Also called MEGARIPPLE.

Santa Ana. A strong, dust-laden foehn occurring in Southern California near the mouth of the Santa Ana pass and river.

Sargasso Sea. The west central region of the subtropical gyre of the North Atlantic Ocean. It is bounded by the North Atlantic, Canary, Atlantic North Equatorial, and Antilles Currents, and the Gulf Stream. It is characterized by the absence of well-marked currents and by large quantities of drifting Sargassum, or gulfweed.

sargasso weed. See SARGASSUM.

sargassum, *n.* A genus of brown algae characterized by a bushy form, a substantial holdfast when attached, and a yellowish brown, greenish yellow, or orange color. Species of the group have a large variety of forms and are widely distributed in warm seas as attached and free floating plants. Two species (*S. fluitans* and *S. matans)* make up 99 percent of the macroscopic vegetation in the Sargasso Sea. Also called SARGASSO WEED, GULFWEED.

sargassum

Saros, *n.* A period of 223 synodic months corresponding approximately to 19 eclipse years or 18.03 Julian years, and is a cycle in which solar and lunar eclipses repeat themselves under approximately the same conditions.

sastrugi, *(sing. sastruga), n., pl.* Sharp, irregular ridges formed on a snow surface by wind erosion and deposition. On mobile floating ice, the ridges are parallel to the direction of the prevailing wind at the time they were formed.

satellite, *n.* 1. A body, natural or man-made, that orbits about another body, the primary body. The moon is a satellite of the earth, the primary body. 2. As defined by the International Telecommunication Union (ITU), a body which revolves around another body of preponderant mass and which has a motion primarily and permanently determined by the force of attraction of that other body. See also ACTIVE SATELLITE, EARTH SATELLITE, EQUATORIAL SATELLITE, GEODETIC SATELLITE, NAVIGATION SATELLITE, PASSIVE SATELLITE, POLAR SATELLITE, SNYCHRONOUS SATELLITE, TWENTY-FOUR HOUR SATELLITE.

satellite geodesy. The discipline which employs observations of an earth satellite to extract geodetic information.

satellite triangulation. The determination of the angular relationships between two or more stations by the simultaneous observation of an earth satellite from these stations.

satellite triangulation stations. Triangulation stations whose angular positions relative to one another are determined by the simultaneous observations of an earth satellite from two or more of them.

saturable system. A term used to describe a navigation system whose use is limited to a single user or a limited number of users on a time-shared basis.

saturation, *n.* Complete impregnation under given conditions, such as the condition that exists in the atmosphere when no additional water vapor can added at the prevailing temperature without condensation or supersaturation occurring.

Saturn, *n.* The navigational planet whose orbit lies outside that of Jupiter.

santanna, *n.* A plain with low vegetation, especially in the sub-tropical latitudes.

S-band. A radio-frequency band of 1,550 to 5,200 megahertz. See also FREQUENCY, FREQUENCY BAND.

scalar, *adj.* Having magnitude only.

scalar, *n.* Any physical quantity whose field can be described by a single numerical value at each point in space. A scalar quantity is distinguished from a VECTOR quantity by the fact that scalar quantity possesses only magnitude, where as, a vector quantity possesses both magnitude and direction.

scale, *n.* 1. A series of marks or graduations at definite intervals. A linear scale is a scale graduated at uniform intervals; a logarithmic scale is graduated in the logarithms of uniformly-spaced consecutive numbers. 2. The ratio between the linear dimensions of chart, map drawing, etc. and the actual dimensions. See also CONVERSION SCALE, BAR SCALE, REPRESENTATIVE FRACTION, SMALL SCALE, LARGE SCALE.

scale bar. A graduated line on a MAP, PLAN, PHOTOGRAPH, or MOSAIC, by means of which actual ground distances may be determined. Also called GRAPHIC SCALE or LINEAR SCALE. In ECDIS, a vertical bar scale of 1 nautical mile divided into 1/10ths, intended to convey an immediate sense of distance.

scale error. See CALIBRATION ERROR.

scalene triangle. A triangle that has three unequal sides. In such a triangle, no two angles are equal.

scan, *v., t.* In the use of radar, to search or investigate an area or space by varying the direction of the radar antenna and thus the beam. Normally scanning is done by continuous rotation of the antenna.

scanner, *n.* 1. A unit of a radar set consisting of the antenna and drive assembly for rotating the antenna. 2. A computerized electronic device which digitizes printed images.

scarf cloud. A thin cirrus-like cloud sometimes observed above a developing cumulus. See also CAP CLOUD.

scarp, *n.* See ESCARPMENT.

scatter reflections. Reflections from portions of the ionosphere having different virtual height which mutually interfere and cause rapid fading.

Schuler frequency. The natural frequency of simple pendulum with a length equal to the earth's radius. The corresponding period is 84 minutes.

Schuler loop. The portion of the inertial navigator in which the instrumental local vertical is established.

Schuler tuned. The condition wherein gyroscopic devices should be insensitive to applied accelerations. M. Schuler determined that if gyroscopic devices were not to be affected by the motions of the craft in which installed, the devices should have a natural period of oscillation of about 84.4 minutes. This period is equal to the product of 2π and the square root of the quotient: radius of the earth divided by the acceleration of gravity.

scintillation, *n.* Twinkling; emission of sparks or quick flashes; shimmer.

scope, *n.* Short for RADARSCOPE.

scoria *(pl. scoriae), n.* Volcanic rock fragments usually of basic composition, characterized by marked vesicularity, dark color, high density and a partly crystalline structure. Scoria is a constituent of certain marine sediments.

scouring basin. A basin containing impounded water which is released at about low water in order to maintain the desired depth in the entrance channel by scouring the bottom. Also called SLUICING POND.

screen, *n.* The chemically coated inside surface of the large end of a cathode-ray tube which becomes luminous when struck by an electron beam.

scud, *n.* Shreds or small detached masses of cloud moving rapidly before the wind, often below a layer of lighter clouds. See also FRACTO.

scud, *v., i.* To run before a storm.

sea, *n.* 1. A body of salt water more or less confined by continuous land or chains of islands and forming a distinct region. 2. A body of water nearly or completely surrounded by land, especially if very large or composed of salt water. Sometimes called INLAND SEA. See also LAKE. 3. Ocean areas in general, including major indentations in the coast line, such as gulfs. See also CLOSED SEA, OPEN SEA, HIGH SEA. 4. Waves generated or sustained by winds within their fetch as opposed to SWELL. 5. The character of a water surface, particularly the height, length (period), and direction of travel of waves generated locally. A smooth sea has waves no higher than ripples or small wavelets. A short sea has short, irregular, and broken waves. A confused sea has a highly disturbed surface without a single, well-defined direction of travel, as when waves from different directions meet following a sudden shift in the direction of the wind. A cross sea is a series of waves imposed across the prevailing waves. A sea may be designated as head, beam, quartering, or following. See also SWELL definition 1.

Sea Area. A defined area under the Global Maritime Distress and Safety System (GMDSS) which regulates certain safety and communication equipment necessary according to the area of the ship's operations. Sea Area A-1 is within coverage of VHF coast radio stations (25-30 miles) providing digital selective calling. Sea Area A-2 is within range of the medium frequency coast radio stations (to approximately 300 miles). Sea Area A-3 is within the footprint of the geostationary INMARSAT communications satellites, covering the rest of the open seas except the poles. Sea Area A-4 covers the rest of the earth, chiefly the polar areas. The areas do not overlap.

sea-air temperature difference correction. A correction due to a difference in the temperature of the sea and air, particularly the sextant altitude correction caused by abnormal terrestrial refraction occurring when there is a nonstandard density lapse rate in the atmosphere due to a difference in the temperature of the water and air at the surface.

sea anchor. An object towed by a vessel, usually a small one, to keep the vessel end-on to a heavy sea or surf or to reduce the drift. Also called DRAG, DROGUE.

seabeach, *n*. See under BEACH.

seaboard, *n*. The region of land bordering the sea. The terms SEABOARD, COAST, and LITTORAL have nearly the same meanings. SEABOARD is a general term used somewhat loosely to indicate a rather extensive region bordering the sea. COAST is the region of indefinite width that extends from the sea inland to the first major change in terrain features. LITTORAL applies more specifically to the various parts of a region bordering the sea, including the coast, foreshore, backshore, beach, etc.

sea breeze. A breeze blowing from the sea to adjacent land. It usually blows by day, when the land is warmer than the sea, and alternates with a LAND BREEZE, which blows in the opposite direction by night. See also ONSHORE WIND.

sea buoy. The outermost buoy marking the entrance to a channel or harbor.

seachannel, *n*. On the sea floor, a continuously sloping, elongated depression commonly found in fans or plains and usually bordered by levees on one or two sides.

sea clutter. See SEA RETURN.

seacoast, *n*. See COAST.

sea fog. A type of advection fog formed when air that has been lying over a warm water surface is transported over colder water, resulting in cooling of the lower layer of air below its dew point. See also HAAR.

sea gate. 1. A gate which serves to protect a harbor tidal basin from the sea, such as one of a pair of supplementary gates at the entrance to a tidal basin exposed to the sea. 2. A movable gate which protects the main deck of a ferry from waves and sea spray.

seagirt, *adj*. Surrounded by sea. Also called SEA BOUND.

sea ice. Any form of ice found at sea which has originated from the freezing of sea water.

sea-ice nomenclature. See WMO SEA-ICE NOMENCLATURE.

sea kindliness. A measure of the ease of motion of a vessel in heavy seas, particularly in regard to rolling, pitching, and shipping water. It is not to be confused with seaworthiness which implies that the vessel is able to sustain heavy rolling, pitching, etc., without structural damage or impaired stability.

sea level. Height of the surface of the sea at any time.

sea manners. Understood by seamen to mean consideration for the other vessel and the exercise of good judgment under certain condition when vessels meet.

seaman's eye. To estimate your position without navigational instruments by utilizing distances and angles obtained from instinctive knowledge and experience of the local maritime environment.

seamark, *n*. See MARK, *n*., definition 1.

sea mile. An approximate mean value of the nautical mile equal to 6,080 feet; the length of a minute of arc along the meridian at latitude 48°.

sea mist. See STEAM FOG.

seamount, *n*. On the sea floor, an elevation rising generally more than 1,000 meters and of limited extent across the summit.

sea quadrant. See BACKSTAFF.

search and rescue chart. A chart designed primarily for directing and conducting search and rescue operations.

search and rescue radar transponder (SART). An electronic device which transmits a homing signal on the radar frequency used by rescue ships and aircraft.

sea reach. The reach of a channel entering a harbor from seaward.

sea return. Clutter on the radarscope which is the result of the radar signal being reflected from the sea, especially near the ship. Also called SEA CLUTTER. See also CLUTTER.

sea room. Space in which to maneuver without danger of grounding or colliding.

seashore, *n*. A loose term referring to the general area in close proximity to the sea.

season, *n*. 1. One of the four principal divisions of the year: spring, summer, autumn, and winter. 2. An indefinite part of the year, such as the rainy season.

seasonal current. An ocean current which changes in speed or direction due to seasonal winds.

sea-temperature difference correction. A correction due to a difference in the temperature of the sea and air, particularly the sextant altitude correction caused by abnormal terrestrial refraction occurring when there is a nonstandard density lapse rate in the atmosphere due to a difference in the temperature of the water and air at the surface.

seaward, *adj*. In a direction away from the land; toward the sea.

seaward, *adv*. Away from the land; toward the sea.

seaward boundary. Limits of any area or zone offshore from the mean low, or mean lower low water line and established by an act of the U.S. Congress.

seaway, *n*. 1. A moderately rough sea. Used chiefly in the expression in a seaway. 2. The sea as a route of travel from one place to another; a shipping lane.

secant, *n*. 1. The ratio of the hypotenuse of a plane right triangle to the side adjacent to one of the acute angles of the triangle, equal to 1/cos. The expression NATURAL SECANT is sometimes used to distinguish the secant from its logarithm (called LOGARITHMIC SECANT). 2. A line that intersects another, especially a straight line intersecting a curve at two or more points.

secant conic chart. See CONIC CHART WITH TWO STANDARD PARALLELS.

secant conic map projection. See CONIC MAP PROJECTION WITH TWO STANDARD PARALLELS.

Secchi disk, *n*. A metal disk used for measuring water clarity. Users lower the disk into the water and record the depth at which it is no longer visible.

second, *n*. 1. The base unit of time in the International System of Units. In 1967 the second was defined by the Thirteenth General Conference on Weights and Measures as the duration of 9,192,631,770 periods of the radiation corresponding to the transition between two hyperfine levels of the ground state of the cesium-133 atom. This value was established to agree as closely as possible with the ephemeris second. Also called ATOMIC SECOND. See also ATOMIC TIME. 2. A sixtieth part of a minute in either time or arc.

secondary, *n*. A small low pressure area accompanying a large or primary one. The secondary often grows at the expense of the primary, eventually replacing it.

secondary circle. See SECONDARY GREAT CIRCLE.

secondary control tide station. A tide station at which continuous observations have been made over a minimum period of 1 year but less than a 19-year Metonic cycle. The series is reduced by comparison with simultaneous observations from a primary control tide station. This station provides for a 365-day harmonic analysis including the seasonal fluctuation of sea level. See also PRIMARY CONTROL TIDE STATION; SUBORDINATE TIDE STATION, definition 1; TERTIARY TIDE STATION; TIDE STATION.

secondary great circle. A great circle perpendicular to a primary great circle, as a meridian. Also called SECONDARY CIRCLE.

secondary light. A major light, other than a primary seacoast light, established at harbor entrances and other locations where high intensity and reliability are required. See also MINOR LIGHT.

secondary phase factor correction. A correction for additional time (or phase delay) for transmission of a low frequency signal over an all seawater path when the signal transit time is based on the free-space velocity. See also ADDITIONAL SECONDARY PHASE FACTOR CORRECTION.

secondary radar. 1. Radar in which the target is fitted with a transponder and in which the target retransmits automatically on the interrogating frequency, or a different frequency. The response may be coded. See also PRIMARY RADAR, RACON, RAMARK. 2. As defined by the International Telecommunication Union (ITU), a radiodetermination system based on the comparison of reference signals with radio signals re-transmitted from the position to be determined.

secondary radiation. See RERADIATION, definition 2.

secondary station. In a radionavigation system, the station of a chain whose emissions are made with reference to the emissions of a master station without being triggered by the emissions of such station. See also SLAVE STATION.

secondary tide station. See as SECONDARY CONTROL TIDE STATION.

second reduction. See PHASE REDUCTION.

second-trace echo. A radar echo received from a target after the following pulse has been transmitted. Second-trace echoes are unusual except under abnormal atmospheric conditions, or conditions under which super-refraction is present, and are received from targets at actual ranges greater than the radar range scale setting. They may be recognized through changes in their position on the radarscope on changing the pulse repetition rate; their hazy, streaky or distorted shape; and their erratic movements on plotting. Also called MULTIPLE-TRACE ECHO.

second-year ice. Old ice which has survived only one summer's melt. Because it is thicker and less dense than first-year ice, it stands higher out of the water. In contrast to multi-year ice, summer melting produces a regular pattern of numerous small puddles. Bare patches and puddles are usually greenish-blue.

sector, *n*. 1. Part of a circle bounded by two radii and an arc. See also RED SECTOR. 2. Something resembling the sector of a circle, as a warm sector between the warm and cold fronts of a cyclone.

sector display. A radar display in which a high persistence screen is excited only when the radar beam is within a narrow sector which can be selected at will.

sector light. A light having sectors of different colors or the same color in specific sectors separated by dark sectors.

sector scanning. In the use of radar, the process of scanning within a sector as opposed to scanning around the horizon.

secular, *adj*. Of or pertaining to a long period of time.

secular aberration. See under ABERRATION, definition 1.

secular error. That error in the reading of an instrument due to secular change within the materials of the instrument.

secular perturbations. Perturbations of the orbit of a planet or satellite that continue to act in one direction without limit, in contrast to periodic perturbations which change direction in a regular manner.

secular terms. In the mathematical expression of the orbit of a satellite, terms which are proportional to time, resulting in secular perturbations. See also PERIODIC TERMS.

secular trend. See APPARENT SECULAR TREND.

seiche, *n*. A stationary wave usually caused by strong winds and/or changes in barometric pressure. It is usually found in lakes and semi-enclosed bodies of water. It may also be found in areas of the open ocean. See also STANDING WAVE.

Seismic sea wave. See as TSUNAMI.

selective availability. A Department of Defense program which degrades the accuracy of the pseudorange measurement of the GPS signal by dithering the clock time and ephemerides data, providing a less accurate fix for civilian users. It can be turned on or off at will by DoD.

selective fading. 1. Fading of the skywave in which the carrier and various sideband frequencies fade at different rates, causing audio-frequency distortion. 2. Fading that affects the different frequencies within a specified band unequally. 3. Fading in which the variation in the received signal strength is not the same for all frequencies in the frequency band of the received signal. See also FADING.

selectivity, *n*. 1. The characteristic of a radio receiver which enables it to differentiate between the desired signal and those of other frequencies. 2. The ability of a receiver to reject transmissions other than the one to which tuned. 3. The degree to which a radio receiver can accept the signals of one station while rejecting those of stations on adjacent channels. See also SENSITIVITY.

selenographic, *adj*. Of or pertaining to the physical geography of the moon.

semaphore, *n*. A device using visual signals, usually bodies of defined shapes or positions or both, by which information can be transmitted.

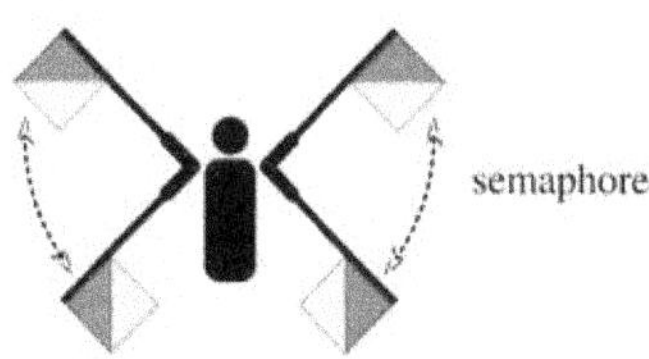

semi-. A prefix meaning half.

semi-automatic updating. In ECDIS, the application of CORRECTIONS to ENC DATA in the SENC updating in a fully integrated state, by hard media or telecommunications transfer in a manner which requires human intervention at the ECDIS interface.

semicircle, *n*. Half of a circle. See also DANGEROUS SEMICIRCLE, LESS DANGEROUS SEMICIRCLE, NAVIGABLE SEMICIRCLE.

semicircular deviation. Deviation which changes sign (E or W) approximately each 180° change of heading.

semidiameter, *n*. 1. Half the angle at the observer subtended by the visible disk of a celestial body. Sextant altitudes of the sun and moon should be corrected for semidiameter unless the center is observed. 2. The radius of a circle or sphere.

semidiameter correction. A correction due to semidiameter, particularly that sextant altitude correction, when applied to the observation of the upper or lower limb of a celestial body, determines the altitude of the center of that body.

semidiurnal, *adj*. Having a period or cycle of approximately one-half of a day. The predominating type of tide throughout the world is semidiurnal, with two high waters and two low waters each tidal day. The tidal current is said to be semidiurnal when there are two flood and two ebb periods each tidal day. A semidiurnal constituent has two maxima and minima each constituent day. See also TYPE OF TIDE.

semidiurnal current. Tidal current in which tidal day current cycle consists of two flood currents and two ebb currents, separated by slack water; or two changes in direction, 360° of a rotary current. This is the most common type of tidal current throughout the world.

semidiurnal tide. See under TYPE OF TIDE, SEMIDIURNAL, *adj*.

semilogarithmic coordinate paper. Paper ruled with two sets of mutually-perpendicular parallel lines, one set being spaced according to the logarithms of consecutive numbers, and the other set uniformly spaced.

semimajor axis. One-half of the longest diameter of an ellipse.

semiminor axis. One-half of the shortest diameter of an ellipse.

semi-reflecting mirror. See DICHROIC MIRROR.

SENC. See SYSTEM ELECTRONIC NAVIGATIONAL CHART.

sense, *n*. The solution of the 180° ambiguity present in some radio direction finding systems.

sense antenna. An antenna used to resolve a 180° ambiguity in a directional antenna.

sense finding. The process of eliminating 180° ambiguity from the bearing indication some types of radio direction finder.

sensibility, *n*. The ability of a magnetic compass card to align itself with the magnetic meridian after deflection.

sensible horizon. The circle of the celestial sphere formed by the intersection of the celestial sphere and a plane through any point, such as the eye of an observer, and perpendicular to the zenith-nadir line. See also HORIZON.

sensitive axis. 1. The axis Of an accelerometer along which specific acceleration is measured. 2. See also INPUT AXIS.

sensitivity, *n*. The minimum input signal required to produce a specified output signal from a radio or similar device, having a specific signal-to-noise ratio. See also SELECTIVITY.

sensitivity time control. An electronic circuit designed to reduce automatically the sensitivity of the radar receiver to nearby targets. Also called SWEPT GAIN, ANTI-CLUTTER GAIN CONTROL, ANTI-CLUTTER SEA.

separation line. A line separating the traffic lanes in which ships are proceeding in opposite or nearly opposite directions, or separating a traffic lane from the adjacent inshore traffic zone. See also ROUTING SYSTEM, SEPARATION ZONE.

separation zone. A defined zone which separates traffic lanes in which ships are proceeding in opposite directions, or which separates traffic lanes from the adjacent inshore traffic zone. See also ROUTING SYSTEM, SEPARATION LINE.

September equinox. See AUTUMNAL EQUINOX.

sequenced radiobeacon. One of a group of marine radiobeacons in the same geographical area, except those operating continuously, that transmit on a single frequency. Each radiobeacon transmits for 1 minute of each period in sequence with other beacons of the group. If less than six radiobeacons are assigned to a group, one or more of the beacons may transmit during two 1-minute periods.

sequence of current. The order of occurrence of the four tidal current strengths of a day, with special reference as to whether the greater flood immediately precedes or follows the greater ebb.

sequence of tide. The order in which the four tides of a day occur, with special reference as to whether the higher high water immediately precedes or follows the lower low water.

service area. The area within which a navigational aid is of use. This may be divided into primary and secondary service areas having different degrees of accuracy.

service area diagram. See RELIABILITY DIAGRAM.

service period. The number of days that an automatic light or buoy is expected to operate without requiring recharging.

set, *n*. The direction towards which a current flows.

set, *v., i*. Of a celestial body, to cross the visible horizon while descending. The opposite is RISE.

set, *v., t*. To establish, as to set a course.

set screw. A screw for locking a movable part of an instrument or device.

setting a buoy. The act of placing a buoy on station in the water.

settled, *adj*. Pertaining to weather, devoid of storms for a considerable period. See also UNSETTLED.

seven-eighths rule. A rule of thumb which states that the approximate distance to an object broad on the beam equals 7/8 of the distance traveled by a craft while the relative bearing (right or left) changes from 30° or 60° or from 120° to 150°, neglecting current and wind.

seven seas. Figuratively, all the waters or oceans of the world. Applied generally to the seven oceans - Arctic, Antarctic, North Atlantic, South Atlantic, North Pacific, South Pacific, and Indian.

seven-tenths rule. A rule of thumb which states that the approximate distance to an object broad on the beam equals 7/10 of the distance traveled by a craft while the relative bearing (right or left) changes from 22.5° to 45° or from 135° to 157.5°, neglecting current and wind.

seven-thirds rule. A rule of thumb which states that the approximate distance to an object broad on the beam equals 7/3 of the distance traveled by a craft while the relative bearing (right or left) changes from 22.5° to 26.5°, 67.5° to 90°, 90° to 112.5°, or 153.5° to 157.5°, neglecting current and wind.

sexagesimal system. A system of notation by increments of 60°, such as the division of the circle into 360°, each degree into 60 minutes, and each minute into 60 seconds.

sextant, *n*. A double-reflecting instrument for measuring angles, primarily altitudes of celestial bodies. As originally used, the term applied only to instruments having an arc of 60°, a sixth of a circle, from which the instrument derived its name. Such an instrument had a range of 120°. In modern practice the term applies to a similar instrument, regardless of its range, very few modern instruments being sextants in the original sense. Thus, an octant, having a range of 90°; a quintant, having a range of 144°; and a quadrant, having a range of 180°, may be called sextants. A marine sextant is designed primarily for marine navigation. See also MARINE SEXTANT.

sextant adjustment. The process of checking the accuracy of a sextant and removing or reducing its error.

sextant altitude. Altitude as indicated by a sextant or similar instrument, before corrections are applied. See also OBSERVED ALTITUDE, APPARENT ALTITUDE.

sextant altitude correction. Any of several corrections applied to a sextant altitude in the process of converting it to observed altitude. See also ACCELERATION CORRECTION, AIR TEMPERATURE CORRECTION, AUGMENTATION CORRECTION, BAROMETRIC PRESSURE CORRECTION, CORIOLIS CORRECTION, DEFLECTION OF THE VERTICAL CORRECTION, DIP CORRECTION, HEIGHT OF EYE CORRECTION, INDEX CORRECTION, INSTRUMENT CORRECTION, IRRADIATION CORRECTION, PARALLAX CORRECTION, PERSONAL CORRECTION, REFRACTION CORRECTION, SEA-AIR TEMPERATURE DIFFERENCE CORRECTION, SEMI-DIAMETER CORRECTION, TIDE CORRECTION, TILT CORRECTION, WAVE HEIGHT CORRECTION.

sextant chart. See CIRCLE SHEET.

sextant error. The error in reading a sextant, due either to lack of proper adjustment or imperfection of manufacture. See CALIBRATION ERROR, CENTERING ERROR, COLLIMATION ERROR, ERROR OF PERPENDICULARITY, GRADUATION ERROR, INDEX ERROR, INSTRUMENT ERROR, PRISMATIC ERROR, SHADE ERROR, SIDE ERROR, VERNIER ERROR.

shade, *n*. See SHADE GLASS.

shaded relief. A cartographic technique that provides an apparent three-dimensional configuration of the terrain on maps and charts by the use of graded shadows that would be cast if light were shining from the northwest. Shaded relief is usually used in combination with contours.

shade error. The error of an optical instrument due to refraction in the shade glasses. If this effect is due to lack of parallelism of the faces it is usually called PRISMATIC ERROR.

shade glass. A darkened transparent glass that can be moved into the line of sight of an optical instrument, such as a sextant, to reduce the intensity of light reaching the eye. Also called SHADE.

shadow, *n*. 1. Darkness in a region, caused by an obstruction between the source of light and the region. By extension, the term is applied to similar condition when any form of radiant energy is cut off by an obstruction, as in a radar shadow. The darkest part of a shadow in which light is completely cut off is called the UMBRA; the lighter part surrounding the umbra in which the light is only partly cut off is called the PENUMBRA. 2. A region of diminished rainfall on the lee side of a mountain or mountain range, where the rainfall is noticeably less than on the windward side. Usually called RAIN SHADOW.

shadow bands. See CREPUSCULAR RAYS.

shadow bar. A rod or bar used to cast a shadow, such as on the sighting assembly of an astro compass.

shadow pin. A small rod or pin used to cast a shadow on an instrument, such as a magnetic compass or sun compass, to determine the direction of the luminary; a GNOMON.

shadow region. A region shielded from radar signals because of an intervening obstruction or absorbing medium. This region appears as an area void of targets on a radar display such as a plan position indicator. The phenomenon is called RADAR SHADOW. See also SHADOW SECTOR, BLIND SECTOR.

shadow sector. A sector on the radarscope in which the appearance of radar echoes is improbable because of an obstruction near the antenna. While both blind and shadow sectors have the same basic cause, blind sectors generally occur within the larger angles subtended by the obstruction. See also SHADOW REGION.

shallow, *adj*. Having little depth; shoal.

shallow, *n*. An area where the depth of water is relatively slight.

shallow water constituent. A short-period harmonic term introduced into the formula of tidal (or tidal current) constituents to take account of the change in the form of a tide wave resulting from shallow water conditions. Shallow water constituents include the overtides and compound tides.

shallow water wave. A wave is classified as a shallow water wave whenever the ratio of the depth (the vertical distance of the still water level from the bottom) to the wave length (the horizontal distance between crests) is less than 0.04. Tidal waves are shallow water waves.

shamal, *n*. A northwesterly wind blowing over Iraq and the Persian Gulf, in summer, often strong during the day, but decreasing during the night.

sharki, *n*. A southeasterly wind which sometimes blows in the Persian Gulf.

shearing, *n.* An area of pack ice is subject to shear when the ice motion varies significantly in the direction normal to the motion, subjecting the ice to rotational forces. These forces may result in phenomena similar to a FLAW.

sheet line. See NEATLINE.

shelf, *n.* A zone adjacent to a continent, or around an island, that extends from the low water line to a depth at which there is usually a marked increase of slope towards oceanic depths.

shelf valley. A valley on the shelf, generally the shoreward extension of a canyon.

shield, *n.* A metal housing around an electrical or magnetic element to eliminate or reduce the effect of its electric or magnetic field, or to reduce the effect of an exterior field on the element.

shielding factor. The ratio of the strength of the magnetic field at a compass to the strength if there were no disturbing material nearby; usually expressed as a decimal. Because of the metal of a vessel, the strength of the earth's magnetic field is reduced somewhat at a compass location aboard ship. The shielding factor is one minus the percentage of reduction.

shimmer, *v., i.* To appear tremulous or wavering due to varying atmospheric refraction in the line of sight.

shingle, *n.* See under STONES.

ship, *n.* Originally a sailing vessel with three or more masts, square-rigged on all. The term is now generally applied to any large, ocean-going vessel, except submarines which are called boats regardless of size.

ship earth station (SES). An INMARSAT satellite system installed aboard a vessel.

ship error. The error in radio direction finder bearings due to reradiation of radio waves by the metal of the ship.

ship motions. Surge is the bodily motion of a ship forward and backward along the longitudinal axis, caused by the force of the sea acting alternately on the bow and stern; heave is the oscillatory rise and fall due to the entire hull being lifted by the force of the sea; sway is the side-to-side bodily motion, independent of rolling caused by uniform pressure being exerted all along one side of the hull; yaw is the oscillation about a vertical axis approximately through the center of gravity of the vessel; roll is the oscillation about the longitudinal axis; and pitch is oscillation about the transverse axis, due to the bow and stern being raised or lowered on passing through successive crests and troughs of waves.

shipping lane. An established route traversed by ocean shipping.

ship's emergency transmitter. As defined by the International Telecommunication Union (ITU) a ship's transmitter to be used exclusively on a distress frequency for distress, urgency or safety purposes.

ship's head. Heading of a vessel.

ship simulator. A computerized system which uses video projection techniques to simulate navigational and shiphandling situations. A full capability system includes a completely equipped ship's bridge and can duplicate almost any aspect of ship operation; partial systems focus on a particular function, such as radar collision avoidance or nighttime navigation.

Ships' Routeing. A publication of the International Maritime Organization (IMO) which describes the general provisions of ships' routing, traffic separation schemes, deep water routes and areas to be avoided, which have been adopted by IMO. All details of routing systems are promulgated through *Notices to Mariners* and *Sailing Directions* and are depicted on charts.

ship weather routing. A procedure whereby an optimum route is developed based on the forecasts of weather and seas and the ship's characteristics for a particular transit. Within specified limits of weather and sea conditions, ship weather routing seeks maximum safety and crew comfort, minimum fuel consumption, minimum time underway, or any desired combination of these factors.

shoal, *adj.* Shallow.

shoal, *n.* An offshore hazard to navigation on which there is a depth of 16 fathoms or 30 meters or less, composed of unconsolidated material. See also REEF.

shoal, *v., i.* To become less deep.

shoal, *v., t.* To cause to become less deep.

shoaling, A process wherein waves encounter shallow water resulting in reduced wave speed. As the wave speed slows, the period remains the same, so the wavelength becomes shorter. Since the energy in the waves remains the same, the shortening of wavelengths results in increased heights.

shoal patches. Individual and scattered elevations of the bottom, with depths of 16 fathoms (or 30 meters) or less, but composed of any material except rock or coral.

shoal water. Shallow water; water over a shoal.

shoot, *v., t.* To observe the altitude of (a celestial body).

shooting star. See METEOR.

shore, *n.* That part of the land in immediate contact with a body of water including the area between high and low water lines. The term SHORE is usually used with reference to the body of water and COAST with reference to the land, as the east coast of the United States is part of the western shore of Atlantic Ocean. The term SHORE usually refers to a narrow strip of land in immediate contact with any body of water, while COAST refers to a general region in proximity to the sea. A shore bordering the sea may be called a SEASHORE. See also FORESHORE, BACKSHORE.

shoreface, *n.* The narrow zone seaward from the low tide shoreline, permanently covered by water, over which the beach sands and gravels actively oscillate with changing wave conditions.

shore lead. A lead between pack ice and the shore or between pack ice and an ice front.

shoreline, *n.* The intersection of the land with the water surface. The shoreline shown on charts represents the line of contact between the land and a selected water elevation.

shore polynya. See under POLYNYA.

short period perturbations. Periodic perturbations in the orbit of a planet or satellite which execute one complete periodic variation in the time of one orbital period or less.

short range systems. Radionavigation systems limited in their positioning capability to coastal regions, or those systems limited to making landfall. See also MEDIUM RANGE SYSTEMS, LONG RANGE SYSTEMS.

short sea. A sea in which the waves are short, irregular, and broken.

short wave. A radio wave shorter than those of the standard broadcast band. See also WAVE, definition 2.

shower, *n.* Precipitation from a convective cloud. Showers are characterized by the suddenness with which they start and stop, by the rapid changes of intensity, and usually by rapid changes in the appearance of the sky. In weather observing practice, showers are always reported in terms of the basic type of precipitation that is falling, i.e., rain showers, snow showers, sleet showers.

shuga, *n.* An accumulation of spongy white ice lumps, a few centimeters across, the lumps are formed from grease ice or slush and sometimes from anchor ice rising to the surface.

side echo. The effect on a radar display by a side lobe of a radar antenna. See also ECHO.

side error. The error in the reading of a sextant due to nonperpendicularity of horizon glass to the frame.

side lights. Running lights placed on the sides of a vessel, green to starboard and red to port, showing an unbroken light over an arc of the horizon from dead ahead to 22.5° abaft the beam.

side lobe. Any lobe of the radiation pattern of a directional antenna other than the main or lobe.

sidereal, *adj.* Of or pertaining to the stars, though SIDEREAL generally refers to the stars and TROPICAL to the vernal equinox, sidereal time and the sidereal day are based upon position of the vernal equinox relative the meridian. The SIDEREAL YEAR is based on the stars.

sidereal day. See under SIDEREAL TIME.

sidereal hour angle. Angular distance west of the vernal equinox; the arc of the celestial equator or the angle at the celestial pole between the hour circle of the vernal equinox and the hour circle of a point on the celestial sphere, measured westward from the hour circle of the equinox through 360°. Angular distance east of the vernal equinox, through 24 hours, is RIGHT ASCENSION.

sidereal month. The average period of revolution of the moon with respect to the stars, a period of 27 days, 7 hours, 43 minutes, 11.5 seconds.

sidereal noon. See under SIDEREAL TIME.

sidereal period. 1. The length of time required for one revolution of a celestial body about a primary, with respect to the stars. 2. The interval between two successive returns of an artificial earth satellite in orbit to the same geocentric right ascension.

sidereal time. Time defined by the daily rotation of the earth with respect to the vernal equinox of the first point of Aries. Sidereal time is numerically measured by the hour angle of the equinox, which represents the position of the equinox in the daily rotation. The period of one rotation of the equinox in hour angle, between two successive upper meridian transits, is a sidereal day. It is divided into 24 sidereal hours, reckoned at upper transit which is known as sidereal noon. The true equinox is at the intersection of the true celestial equator of date with the ecliptic of date; the time measured by its daily rotation is apparent sidereal time. The position of the equinox is affected by the nutation of the axis of rotation of the earth, and the nutation consequently introduces irregular periodic inequities into the apparent sidereal time and the length of the sidereal day. The time measured by the motion of the mean equinox of date, affected only by the secular inequalities due to the precession of the axis, is mean sidereal time. The maximum difference between apparent mean sidereal times is only a little over a second and its greatest daily change is a little more than a hundredth of a second. Because of its variable rate, apparent sidereal time is used by astronomers only as a measure of epoch; it is not used for time interval. Mean sidereal time is deduced from apparent sidereal time by applying the equation of equinoxes.

sidereal year. The period of one apparent rotation of the earth around the sun, with relation to a fixed point, or a distant star devoid of proper motion, being 365 days, 6 hours, 9 minutes and 9.5 seconds in 1900, and increasing at a rate of rate of 0.0001 second annually. Because of the precession of the equinoxes this is about 20 minutes longer than a tropical year.

sight, *n*. Observation of the altitude, and sometimes also the azimuth, of a celestial body for a line of position; or the data obtained by such observation. An observation of a celestial body made by facing 180° from the azimuth of the body is called a back sight. See also NOON SIGHT, TIME SIGHT.

sighting vane. See VANE, definition 2.

sight reduction. The process of deriving from a sight the information needed for establishing a line of position.

sight reduction tables. Tables for performing sight reduction, particularly those for comparison with the observed altitude of a celestial body to determine the altitude difference for establishing a line of position.

Sight Reduction Tables for Air Navigation. See *PUB. NO. 249*.

Sight Reduction Tables for Marine Navigation. See *PUB. NO. 229*.

signal, *n*. 1. As applied to electronics, any transmitted electrical impulse 2. That which conveys intelligence in any form of communication, such as a time signal or a distress signal.

signal-to-noise ratio. The ratio of the magnitude of the signal to that of the noise, often expressed in decibels.

signature, *n*. The graphic record of the magnetic or acoustic properties of a vessel.

sign conventions. See as GEOGRAPHIC SIGN CONVENTIONS.

significant digits. Those digits of a number which have a significance, zeros at the left and sometimes those at the right being excluded.

sikussak, *n*. Very old ice trapped in fjords. Sikussak resembles glacier ice, since it is formed partly from snow.

sill, *n*. On the sea floor, the low part of a gap or saddle separating basins. See also DOCK SILL.

sill depth. The depth over a sill.

silt, *n*. See under MUD.

similar decimals. Decimals having the same number of decimal places, as 3.141 and 0.789. Decimals can be made similar by adding the appropriate number of zeros. For example, 0.789 can be made similar to 3.1416 by stating it as 0.7890. See also REPEATING DECIMAL, SIGNIFICANT DIGITS.

simple conic chart. A chart on a simple conic projection.

simple conic map projection. A conic map projection in which the surface of a sphere or spheroid, such as the earth, is conceived as developed on a tangent cone, which is then spread out to form a plane.

simple harmonic motion. The projection of uniform circular motion on a diameter of the circle of such motion. The combination of two or more simple harmonic motions results in COMPOUND HARMONIC MOTION.

simplified symbols. In ECDIS, SYMBOLS designed specifically for fast draw and to give the maximum clarity under all conditions of viewing the CRT. They are less complex than the equivalent paper CHART SYMBOLS.

simultaneous altitudes. Altitudes of two or more celestial bodies observed at the same time.

simultaneous observations (of a satellite). Observations of a satellite that are made from two or more distinct points or tracking stations at exactly the same time.

sine, *n*. The ratio of the side opposite an angle of a plane right triangle to the hypotenuse. The expression NATURAL SINE is used to distinguish the sine from its logarithm (called LOGARITHMIC SINE).

sine curve. Characteristic simple wave pattern; a curve which represents the plotted values of sines of angles, with the sine as the ordinate and the angle as the abscissa. The curve starts at 0 amplitude at the origin, increases to a maximum at 90°, decreases to 0 at 180°, increases negatively to a maximum negative amplitude at 270°, and returns to 0 at 360°, to repeat the cycle. Also called SINUSOID.

sine wave. A simple wave in the form of curve.

single astronomic station datum orientation. Orientation of a geodetic datum by accepting the astronomically determined coordinates of the origin and the azimuth to one other station without any correction.

single-axis normal distribution. A one-time normal distribution along an axis perpendicular to a line of position. Two single-axis normal distributions may be used to establish the error ellipse and the corresponding circle of equivalent probability when the error distribution is two-dimensional or bivariate.

single-degree-of-freedom gyro. A gyroscope, the spin axis of which is free to rotate about one of the orthogonal axes, the spin axis not being counted. See also DEGREE-FREEDOM, RATE GYRO.

single-flashing light. See under FLASHING LIGHT.

single interpolation. Interpolation with only one argument or variable.

single-occulting light. See under OCCULTING LIGHT.

single-sideband transmission. A method of transmission in which the frequencies produced by the process of modulation on one side of the carrier are transmitted and those on the other side are suppressed. The carrier frequency may either be transmitted or suppressed. With this method, less power is required for the effective signal at the receiver, a narrower frequency band can be used, and the signal is less subject to man-made interference or selective fading.

single station range light. A directional light bound by other sectors of different characteristic which define its margins with small angular uncertainty. Most commonly the bounding sectors are of different colors (red and green).

sinking, *n*. An apparent lowering of distant terrestrial objects by abnormal atmospheric refraction. Because of sinking, objects normally visible near the horizon sometimes disappear below the horizon. The opposite is LOOMING.

sinusoid, *n*. See SINE CURVE.

sinusoidal, *adj*. Of or pertaining to a sine wave or sinusoid.

siren, *n*. A sound signal emitter using the periodic escape of compressed air through a rotary shutter.

sirocco, *n*. A warm wind of the Mediterranean area, either a foehn or a hot southerly wind in advance of a low pressure area moving from the Sahara or Arabian deserts. Called LEVECHE in Spain.

skeleton tower. A tower, usually of steel and often used for navigation aids, constructed of open legs with various horizontal and diagonal bracing members.

skip distance. The least distance from a transmitting antenna at which a skywave can normally be received at a given frequency.

skip zone. The area between the outer limit of reception of groundwaves and the inner limit of reception of skywaves, where no signal is received.

sky diagram. A diagram of the heavens, indicating the apparent position of various celestial bodies with reference to the horizon system of coordinates.

skylight, *n*. Thin places in the ice canopy, usually less than 1 meter thick and appearing from below as relatively light, translucent patches in dark surroundings. The under-surface of a skylight is normally flat, but may have ice keels below. Skylights are called large if big enough for a submarine to attempt to surface through them, or small if not.

sky map. The pattern on the underside of extensive cloud areas, created by the varying amounts of light reflected from the earth's surface. Snow surfaces produce a white glare (SNOW BLINK) and ice surfaces produce a yellowish-white glare (ICE BLINK). Bare land reflects relatively little light (LAND SKY) and open water even less (WATER SKY).

skywave, *n.* A radio wave that is propagated by way of the ionosphere. Also called IONOSPHERIC WAVE.

skywave correction. The correction to be applied to the time difference reading of signals received via the ionosphere to convert it to the equivalent groundwave reading. The correction for a particular place is established on the basis of an average height of the ionosphere.

skywave error. See IONOSPHERIC ERROR.

skywave transmission delay. The amount by which the time of transit from transmitter to receiver of a pulse carried by skywaves reflected once from the E-layer exceeds the time of transit of the same pulse carried by groundwaves.

slack water. The state of a tidal current when its speed is near zero, especially the moment when a reversing current changes direction and its speed is zero. The term is also applied to the entire period of low speed near the time of turning of the current when it is too weak to be of any practical importance in navigation. The relation of the time of slack water to the tidal phases varies in different localities. For standing tidal waves, slack water occurs near the times of high and low water, while for progressive tidal waves, slack water occurs midway between high and low water.

slant range. The line-of-sight distance between two points not at the same elevation.

slave, *n.* Short for SLAVE STATION.

slaved gyro magnetic compass. A directional gyro compass with an input from a flux valve to keep the gyro oriented to magnetic north.

slave station. In a radionavigation system, the station of a chain whose emissions are made with reference to the emissions of a master station, its emissions being triggered by the emissions of the master station. See also SECONDARY STATION.

sleet, *n.* See under ICE PELLETS; colloquially some parts of the United States, precipitation the form of a mixture of rain and snow.

slewing, *n.* In ice navigation, the act of forcing a ship through ice by pushing apart adjoining ice floes.

slick, *n.* A smooth area of water, such as one caused by the sweep of a vessel's stern during a turn, or by a film of oil on the water.

slime, *n.* Soft, fine, oozy mud or other substance of similar consistency.

slip, *n.* 1. A berthing space between two piers. Also called DOCK. 2. The difference between the distance a propeller would travel longitudinally in one revolution if operating in a solid and the distance it travels through a fluid.

slope, *n.* On the sea floor, the slope seaward from the shelf edge to the beginning of a continental or insular rise or the point where there is a general reduction in slope.

slot radiator. A slot in the wall of a slotted wave guide antenna which acts as a radiating element.

slotted guide antenna. See SLOTTED WAVE GUIDE ANTENNA.

slotted wave guide antenna. An antenna consisting of a metallic waveguide in the walls of which are cut one or more slot radiators.

slough (sloo), *n.* A minor marshland or tidal waterway which usually connects other tidal areas; often more or less equivalent to a bayou occasionally applied to the sea level portion of a creek on the U.S. West Coast.

slow-sweep racon. See under SWEPT-FREQUENCY RACON.

slue, *n.* A slough or swamp.

sluice, *n.* A floodgate. sluicing pond. See SCOURING BASIN.

slush, *n.* Snow which is saturated and mixed with water on land or ice surfaces, or which is viscous floating mass in water after a heavy snow fall.

small area plotting sheet. For a relatively small area, a good approximation of a Mercator position plotting sheet, constructed by the navigator by either of two methods based upon graphical solution of the secant of the latitude which approximates the expansion. A partially completed small area plotting sheet printed in advance for later rapid completion according to requirements is called UNIVERSAL PLOTTING SHEET.

small circle. The intersection of a sphere and plane which does not pass through its center.

small diurnal range. The difference in height between mean lower high water and mean higher low water. Applicable only when the type of tide is either semidiurnal or mixed. See also TROPIC RANGES.

small floe. See under FLOE.

small fracture. See under FRACTURE.

small hail. See under ICE PELLETS.

small iceberg. For reports to the International Ice Patrol, an iceberg that extends 4 to 50 feet (1 to 15 meters) above the sea surface and which has a length of 20 to 200 feet (6 to 60 meters). See also MEDIUM ICEBERG, LARGE ICEBERG.

small ice cake. A flat piece of ice less than 2 meters across.

small ice field. See under ICE FIELD.

small scale. A scale involving a relatively large reduction in size. A small-scale chart usually covers a large area. The opposite is LARGE SCALE, which covers a small area. See also REPRESENTATIVE FRACTION.

small-scale chart. See under CHART. See also SMALL SCALE.

small tropic range. The difference in height between tropic lower high water and tropic higher low water. Applicable only when the type of tide is either semidiurnal or mixed. See also MEAN TROPIC RANGE, GREAT TROPIC RANGE.

smell the bottom. See FEEL THE BOTTOM.

smog, *n.* Originally a natural fog contaminated by industrial pollutants, or a mixture of smoke and fog. Today, smog is a common term applied to visible air pollution with or without fog.

smoke, *n.* Small particles of carbon and other solid matter, resulting from incomplete combustion, suspended in the air. When it settles, it is called SOOT.

smokes, *n., pl.* Dense white haze and dust clouds common in the dry season on the Guinea coast of Africa, particularly at the approach of the harmattan.

smooth sea. Sea with waves no higher than ripples or small wavelets.

snow, *n.* 1. Frozen precipitation consisting of translucent or white ice crystals which fall either separately or in loose clusters called snowflakes. Very fine, simple crystals, or minute branched, star-like snowflakes are called snow grains. Snow pellets are white, opaque, roundish grains which are crisp and easily compressible, and may rebound or burst when striking a hard surface. Snow is called brown, red, or yellow when it is colored by the presence of brown dust, red dust or algae, or pine or cypress pollen, respectively. See also BLOWING SNOW, DRIFTING SNOW. 2. The speckled background on the plan position indicator or video display due to electrical noise.

snow barchan. See under SNOWDRIFT.

snow blink. A white glare on the underside of extensive cloud areas, created by light reflected from snow-covered surfaces. Snow blink is brighter than the yellowish-white glare of ICE BLINK. Clouds above bare land or open water have no glare. See also LAND SKY, WATER SKY, SKY MAP.

snowdrift, *n.* An accumulation of wind-blown snow deposited in the lee of obstructions or heaped by wind eddies. A crescent-shaped snowdrift, with ends pointing downwind, is called a SNOW BARCHAN.

snowflake, *n.* A loose cluster if ice crystals, or rarely, a single crystal.

snow flurry. A popular term for SNOW SHOWER, particularly of a very light and brief nature.

snow grains. Frozen precipitation consisting of very fine, single crystals, or of minute, branched star-like snowflakes. Snow grains are the solid equivalent of drizzle. Also called GRANULAR SNOW.

snow pellets. Frozen precipitation consisting of small, white, opaque, roundish grains of snowlike structure which are crisp and easily compressible, and may rebound or burst when striking a hard surface. Also called SOFT HAIL, GRAUPEL. See also SMALL HAIL.

snow storm. See under STORM, definition 2.

soft hail. See SNOW PELLETS.

soft iron. Iron or steel which is easily magnetized by induction, but loses its magnetism when the magnetic field is removed. The opposite is HARD IRON.

solar, *adj.* Of or pertaining to the sun.

solar day. 1. The duration of one rotation of the earth on its axis, with respect to the sun. This may be either a mean solar day, or an apparent solar day, as the reference is the mean or apparent sun, respectively. 2. The duration of one apparent rotation of the sun.

solar eclipse. An eclipse of the sun. When the moon passes between the sun and the earth, the sun appears eclipsed to an observer in the moon's shadow. A solar eclipse is partial if the sun is partly obscured; total if the entire surface is obscured, or annular if a thin ring of the sun's surface appears around the obscuring body.

solar eclipse

solar flare. A bright eruption from the sun's chromosphere. Solar flares may appear within minutes and fade within an hour.

solar noon. Twelve o'clock solar time, or the instant the sun is over the upper branch of the reference meridian. Solar noon may be classified as mean if the mean sun is the reference, or as apparent if the apparent sun is the reference. It may be further classified according to the reference meridian, either the local or Greenwich meridian or additionally in the case of mean noon, a designated zone meridian. Standard, daylight saving or summer noon are variations of zone noon. Local apparent noon may also be called high noon.

solar-radiation pressure. A cause of perturbations of high flying artificial satellites of large diameter. The greater part is directly from the sun, a minor part is from the earth, which is usually divided into direct (reflected) and indirect terrestrial (radiated) radiation pressures.

solar system. The sun and other celestial bodies within its gravitational influence, including planets, planetoids, satellites, comets, and meteors.

solar tide. 1. The part of the tide that is due to the tide-producing force of the sun. See also LUNAR TIDE. 2. The observed tide in areas where the solar tide is dominant. This condition provides for phase repetition at about the same time each solar day.

solar time. Time based upon the rotation of the earth relative to the sun. Solar time may be classified as mean if the mean sun is the reference; or as apparent if the apparent sun is the reference. The difference between mean and apparent time is called EQUATION OF TIME. Solar time may be further classified according to the reference meridian, either the local or Greenwich meridian or additionally in the case of mean time, a designated zone meridian. Standard and daylight saving or summer time are variations of zone time. Time may also be designated according to the timepiece, as chronometer time or watch time, the time indicated by these instruments.

solar year. See TROPICAL YEAR.

solid color buoy. A buoy which is painted only one color above the water line.

solitary wave. A wave of translation consisting of a single crest rising above the undisturbed water level, without any accompanying trough, in contrast with a WAVE TRAIN. The rate of advance of a solitary wave depends upon the depth of water.

solstice, *n*. 1. One of the two points of the ecliptic farthest from the celestial equator; one of the two points on the celestial sphere occupied by the sun at maximum declination. That in the Northern Hemisphere is called the summer solstice and that in the Southern Hemisphere the winter solstice. Also called SOLSTITIAL POINT. 2. That instant at which the sun reaches one of the solstices about June 21 (summer solstice) or December 22 (winter solstice).

solstitial colure. The great circle of the celestial sphere through the celestial poles and the solstices.

solstitial point. One of the two points on the ecliptic at the greatest distance from the celestial equator. Also called SOLSTICE.

solstitial tides. Tides occurring near the times of the solstices. The tropic range may be expected to be especially large at these times.

Somali Current. See EAST AFRICA COASTAL CURRENT.

sonar, *n*. A system which determines distance and/or direction of an underwater object by measuring the interval of time between transmission of an underwater sonic or ultrasonic signal and the return of its echo. The name sonar is derived from the words sound navigation and ranging. See also ECHO RANGING.

sonic, *adj*. Of, or pertaining to, the speed of sound.

sonic depth finder. A direct-reading instrument which determines the depth of water by measuring the time interval between the emission of a sound and the return of its echo from the bottom. A similar instrument utilizing signals above audible range is called an ULTRASONIC DEPTH FINDER. Both instruments are also called ECHO SOUNDERS.

sonic frequency. See AUDIO FREQUENCY.

sonic navigation. Navigation by means of sound waves whether or not they are within the audible range. Also called ACOUSTIC NAVIGATION.

sonne, *n*. A German forerunner of the CONSOL navigation system.

sonobuoy, *n*. A buoy with equipment for automatically transmitting a radio signal when triggered by an underwater sound signal.

sound, *n*. 1. A relatively long arm of the sea or ocean forming a channel between an island and a mainland or connecting two larger bodies of water, as a sea and the ocean, or two parts of the same body but usually wider and more extensive than a strait. The term has been applied to many features which do not fit the accepted definition. Many are very large bodies of water such as Mississippi Sound and Prince William Sound, others are mere salt water ponds or small passages between islands. 2. A vibratory disturbance in air or some other elastic medium, capable of being heard by the human ear, and generally of a frequency between about 20 and 20,000 cycles per second.

sound, *v., i*. To measure the depth of the water.

sound, *v., t*. For a whale or other large sea mammal to dive for an extended period of time.

sound buoy. A buoy equipped with a gong, bell, whistle, or horn.

sounding, *n*. Measured or charted depth of water, or the measurement of such depth. A minimum sounding chosen for a vessel of specific draft in a given area to indicate the limit of safe navigation is called a danger sounding. See also ECHO SOUNDING, LINE OF SOUNDINGS.

sounding datum. Short for CHART SOUNDING DATUM.

sounding lead. See under LEAD.

sounding machine. An instrument for measuring depth of water, consisting essentially of a reel of wire to one end of which is attached a weight which carries a device for recording the depth. A crank or motor is provided for reeling in the wire.

sounding sextant. See HYDROGRAPHIC SEXTANT.

sound signal. A sound transmitted in order to convey information.

sound signal station. An attended station whose function is to operate a sound signal.

sound wave. An audio-frequency wave in any material medium, in which vibration is in the direction of travel, resulting in alternate compression and rarefaction of the medium, or, by extension, a similar wave outside the audible range.

south, *n*. The direction 180° from north. See also CARDINAL POINT.

South Atlantic Current. An eastward flowing current of the South Atlantic Ocean that is continuous with the northern edge of the WEST WIND DRIFT. It appears to originate mainly from the Brazil Current and partly from the northernmost flow of the West Wind Drift west of longitude 40°W. The current is under the influence of the prevailing westerly trade winds; the constancy and speed increase from the northern boundary to about latitude 40°S, where the current converges with the West Wind Drift. The mean speed varies from about 0.5 to 0.7 knots.

southbound node. See DESCENDING NODE.

Southeast Drift Current. See AZORES CURRENT.

southeaster, sou'easter, *n*. A southeasterly wind, particularly a strong wind or gale.

south equatorial current. See ATLANTIC SOUTH EQUATORIAL CURRENT, PACIFIC SOUTH EQUATORIAL CURRENT, INDIAN SOUTH EQUATORIAL CURRENT.

south frigid zone. That part of the earth south of the Antarctic Circle.

south geographical pole. The geographical pole in the Southern Hemisphere, at lat. 90°S.

south geomagnetic pole. The geomagnetic pole in the Southern Hemisphere. This term should not be confused with SOUTH MAGNETIC POLE. See also GEOMAGNETIC POLE.

South Indian Current. An eastward flowing current of the Indian Ocean that is continuous with the northern edge of the WEST WIND DRIFT.

southing, *n*. The distance a craft makes good to the south. The opposite is NORTHING.

south magnetic pole. The magnetic pole in the Southern Hemisphere. This term should not be confused with SOUTH GEOMAGNETIC POLE. See also GEOMAGNETIC POLE.

South Pacific Current. An eastward flowing current of the South Pacific Ocean that is continuous with the northern edge of the WEST WIND DRIFT.

south polar circle. See ANTARCTIC CIRCLE.

South Pole. 1. The south geographical pole. See also MAGNETIC POLE, GEOMAGNETIC POLE. 2. The south-seeking end of a magnet. See also BLUE MAGNETISM.

south temperate zone. The part of the earth between the Tropic of Capricorn and the Antarctic Circle.

southwester, sou'wester, *n*. A southwest wind, particularly a strong wind or gale.

southwest monsoon. See under MONSOON.

space coordinates. A three-dimensional system of Cartesian coordinates by which a point is located by three magnitudes indicating distance from three planes which intersect at a point.

spacecraft, *n*. Devices, manned and unmanned which are designed to be placed into an orbit about the earth or into a trajectory to another celestial body.

space motion. Motion of a celestial body through space. The component perpendicular to the line of sight is called proper motion and that component in the direction of the line of sight is called radial motion.

space-polar coordinates. A system of coordinates by which a point on the surface of a sphere is located in space by (1) its distance from a fixed point at the center, called the POLE; (2) the COLATITUDE or angle between the POLAR AXIS (a reference line through the pole) and the RADIUS VECTOR (a straight line connecting the pole and the point); and (3) the LONGITUDE or angle between a reference plane through the polar axis and a plane through the radius vector and polar axis. See also POLAR COORDINATES, SPHERICAL COORDINATES.

space wave. See DIRECT WAVE, definition 2.

spaghetti data. In ECDIS, a DATA STRUCTURE in which all lines and points are unrelated to each other (i.e. no topological RELATIONSHIPS exist in the data structure).

spar buoy. A buoy in the shape of a spar, or tapered pole, floating nearly vertically. See also SPINDLE BUOY.

spatial object. In ECDIS, an OBJECT which contains locational information about real world ENTITIES.

spatial record. In ECDIS, the implemented term used in the IHO transfer standard data structure for a spatial object (i.e. a SPATIAL OBJECT as defined in the data model is encoded as a spatial record in the data structure). There are three types of spatial records: VECTOR, RASTER and MATRIX.

special mark. See under IALA MARITIME BUOYAGE SYSTEM.

Special Notice To Mariners. These notices contain important information of interest to all mariners such as cautions on the use of foreign charts; warning on use of floating aids; use of the Automated Mutual-Assistance Vessel Rescue (AMVER) system; rules, regulations, and proclamations issued by foreign governments; oil pollution regulations, etc. *Special Notice to Mariners* is published annually in *Notice to Mariners No. 1* by the National Geospatial-Intelligence Agency.

special purpose buoy. A buoy used to indicate a special meaning to the mariner and having no lateral significance, such as one used to mark a quarantine or anchorage area.

Special Warnings. Messages originated by the U.S. government which promulgate official warning of dangers to navigation, generally involving political situations. They remain active until canceled, and are published in *Notice to Mariners No. 1* issued by NGA.

species of constituent. A classification depending upon the period of a constituent. The principal species are semidiurnal, diurnal, and long period.

species sanctuary. A sanctuary established for the conservation of marine life. See also MARINE SANCTUARY.

specific humidity. See HUMIDITY.

spectral, *adj*. Of or pertaining to a spectrum.

spectroscope, *n*. An optical instrument for forming spectra, very useful in studying the characteristics of celestial bodies.

spectrum *(pl. spectra)*, *n*. 1. A series of images formed when a beam of radiant energy is separated into its various wavelength components. 2. The entire range of electromagnetic radiation, or any part of it used for a specific purpose, such as the radio spectrum (10 kilohertz to 300 gigahertz).

specular reflection. Reflection without diffusion in accordance with the laws of optical reflection, such as in a mirror. Also called REGULAR REFLECTION, MIRROR REFLECTION.

speculum, *n*. An optical instrument reflector of polished metal or of glass with a film of metal.

speed, *n*. Rate of motion. The terms SPEED and VELOCITY are often used interchangeably but SPEED is a scalar, having magnitude only while VELOCITY is a vector quantity, having both magnitude and direction. Rate of motion in a straight line is called linear speed, while change of direction per unit time is called angular velocity. Subsonic, sonic, and supersonic refer to speeds respectively less than, equal to, greater than the speed of sound in standard air at sea level. Transonic speeds are those in the range in which flow patterns change from subsonic to supersonic, or vice versa.

speed circle. A circle having a radius equal to a given speed and drawn about a specified center. The expression is used chiefly in connection with relative movement problems.

speed-course-latitude error. See SPEED ERROR.

speed error. An error in both pendulous and nonpendulous type gyrocompasses resulting from movement of the gyrocompass in other than an east-west direction. The error is westerly if any component of the ship's course is north, and easterly if south. Its magnitude is proportional to the course, speed, and latitude of the ship. Sometimes called SPEED-COURSE-LATITUDE ERROR.

speed line. A line of position approximately perpendicular to the course line, thus providing a check on the speed of advance. See also COURSE LINE.

speed made good. The speed estimated by dividing the distance between the last fix and an EP by the time between the fix and the EP.

speed of advance. 1. The speed intended to be made good along the track. 2. The average speed in knots which must be maintained during a passage to arrive at a destination at an appointed time.

speed of relative movement. Speed relative to a reference point, usually itself in motion.

speed over ground. The vessel's actual speed, determined by dividing the distance between successive fixes by the time between the fixes.

speed triangle. See under VECTOR DIAGRAM.

spending beach. In a wave basin, the beach on which the entering waves spend themselves, except for the small remainder entering the inner harbor.

sphere, *n*. 1. A curved surface all points of which are equidistant from a fixed point within, called the center. The celestial sphere is an imaginary sphere of infinite radius concentric with the earth, on which all celestial bodies except the earth are imagined to be projected. The celestial sphere as it appears to an observer at the equator, where celestial bodies appear to rise vertically above the horizon, is called a right sphere; at the pole, where bodies appear to move parallel to the horizon, it is called a parallel sphere; between the equator and pole, where bodies appear to rise obliquely to the horizon, it is called an oblique sphere. Half a sphere is called a HEMISPHERE. 2. A body or the space bounded by a spherical surface. For most practical problems of navigation, the earth is considered a sphere, called the terrestrial sphere.

spherical, *adj.* Of or pertaining to a sphere.

spherical aberration. See under ABERRATION, definition 2.

spherical angle. The angle between two intersecting great circles.

spherical buoy. A buoy of which the upper part of the body (above the waterline), or the larger part of the superstructure, is spherical.

spherical coordinates. A system of coordinates defining a point on a sphere or spheroid by its angular distances from a primary great circle and from a reference secondary great circle, as latitude and longitude. See also CELESTIAL COORDINATES, POLAR COORDINATES.

spherical excess. The amount by which the sum of the three angles of a spherical triangle exceeds 180°.

spherical harmonics. Trigonometric terms of an infinite series used to approximate a two- or three-dimensional function of locations on or above the earth.

spherical sailing. Any of the sailings which solve the problems of course, distance, difference of latitude, difference of longitude, and departure by considering the spherical or spheroidal shape of the earth.

spherical triangle. A closed figure having arcs of three great circles as sides.

spherical wave. A wave with a spherical wave front.

spheroid, *n.* An ellipsoid; a figure resembling a sphere. Also called ELLIPSOID or ELLIPSOID OF REVOLUTION, from the fact that it can be formed by revolving an ellipse about one of its axes. If the shorter axis is used as the axis of revolution, an oblate spheroid results, and if the longer axis is used, a prolate spheroid results. The earth is approximately an oblate spheroid.

spheroidal excess. The amount by which the sum of the three angles on the surface of a spheroid exceeds 180°.

spheroid of reference. See REFERENCE ELLIPSOID.

spin axis. The axis of rotation of a gyroscope.

spindle buoy. A buoy having a spindle-like shape floating nearly vertically. See also SPAR BUOY.

spire, *n.* A pointed structure extending above a building, often charted with the symbol of a position circle. The spire is seldom less than two-thirds of the entire height of the structure, and its tines are rarely broken by stages or other features.

spirit compass. A magnetic compass of which the bowl mounting the compass card is filled with a solution of alcohol and water.

spit, *n.* A small tongue of land or a long narrow shoal (usually sand) extending from the shore into a body of water. Generally the tongue of land continues in a long narrow shoal for some distance from the shore.

Spitzbergen Atlantic Current. An ocean current flowing northward and westward from a point south of Spitzbergen, and gradually merging with the EAST GREENLAND CURRENT in the Greenland Sea. The Spitzbergen Atlantic Current is the continuation of the northwestern branch of the NORWAY CURRENT. Also called SPITZBERGEN CURRENT.

Spitzbergen Current. See SPITZBERGEN ATLANTIC CURRENT.

split fix. A fix by horizontal sextant angles obtained by measuring two angles between four charted features, with no common center object observed.

split-second timer. A watch with two sweep second hands which can be started and stopped together with one push button.

spoil area. Area for the purpose of disposing dredged material, usually near dredged channels. Spoil areas are usually a hazard to navigation and navigators should avoid crossing these areas. Spoil areas are shown on nautical charts. See also DISPOSAL AREA, DUMPING GROUND DUMP SITE. Also called SPOIL GROUND.

spoil ground. See SPOIL AREA.

spoil ground buoy. A buoy which marks a spoil ground.

spoil ground mark. A navigation mark indicating an area used for deposition of dredge spoil.

sporadic E-ionization. Ionization that appears at E-layer heights, is more noticeable toward the polar regions, and is caused by particle radiation from the sun. It may occur at any time of day. A sporadic E-layer sometimes breaks away from the normal E-layer and exhibits especially erratic characteristics.

spot elevation. A point on a map or chart where height above a specified datum is noted, usually by a dot and the height value.

spot-size error. The distortion of the radar return on the radarscope caused by the diameter of the electron beam which displays the returns on the scope and the lateral radiation across the scope of part of the glow produced when the electron beam strikes the phosphorescent coating of the cathode-ray tube. See also PULSE-DURATION ERROR.

spring, *n.* The season in the Northern Hemisphere which begins astronomically at the vernal equinox and ends at the summer solstice. In the Southern Hemisphere the limits are the autumnal equinox and the winter solstice.

spring high water. See under SPRING TIDES.

spring low water. See under SPRING TIDES.

spring range. See under SPRING TIDES.

spring tidal currents. Tidal currents of increased speed occurring semimonthly as the result of the moon being new or full. See also SPRING TIDES.

spring tides. Tides of increased range occurring semimonthly as the result of the moon being new or full. The spring range of tide is the average semidiurnal range occurring at the time of spring tides and is most conveniently computed from the harmonic constants. It is larger than the mean range where the type of tide is either semidiurnal or mixed, and is of no practical significance where the type of tide is diurnal. The average height of the high waters of the spring tides is called spring high water or mean high water springs and the average height of the corresponding low waters is called spring low water or mean low water springs. See also SPRING TIDAL CURRENTS.

spur, *n.* A terrestrial or bathymetric feature consisting of a subordinate elevation, ridge, or rise projecting outward from a larger feature.

spurious disk. The round image of perceptible diameter of a star as seen through a telescope, due to diffraction of light in the telescope.

spurious emission. Emission on a frequency or frequencies which are outside the necessary band, the level of which may be reduced without affecting the corresponding transmission of information. Spurious emissions include harmonic emissions, parasitic emissions and intermodulation products, but exclude emissions in the immediate vicinity of the necessary band, which are a result of the modulation process for the transmission of information.

squall, *n.* A wind of considerable intensity caused by atmospheric instability. It forms and dissipates relatively quickly, and is often accompanied by thunder, lightning, and precipitation, when it may be called a thundersquall. An arched squall is one relatively high in the center, tapering off on both sides. A bull's eye squall is one formed in fair weather, characteristic of the ocean off the coast of South Africa. See also GUST, LINE SQUALL, SQUALL LINE, WHITE SQUALL.

squall cloud. A small eddy cloud sometimes formed below the leading edge of a thunderstorm cloud, between the upward and downward currents.

squall line. A non-frontal line or narrow band of active thunderstorms (with or without squalls); a mature instability line.

squally, *adj.* Having or threatening numerous squalls.

squamish, *n.* A strong and often violent wind occurring in many of the fjords of British Columbia. Squamishes occur in those fjords oriented in a northeast-southwest or east-west direction where cold polar air can be funneled westward. They are notable in Jervis, Toba, and Bute inlets and in Dean Channel and Portland Canal. Squamishes lose their strength when free of the confining fjords and are not noticeable 15 to 20 miles offshore.

square, *n.* 1. A four-sided geometrical figure with all sides equal and all angles 90°; a rectangle or right-angled parallelogram with sides of equal length. 2. The second power of a quantity.

square meter. The derived unit of area in the International System of Units.

squat, *n.* For a vessel underway, the bodily sinkage and change of trim which are caused by the pressure distribution on the hull due to the relative motion of water and hull. The effect begins to increase significantly at depth-to-draft ratios less than 2.5. It increases rapidly with speed and is augmented in narrow channels.

SRNC. See SYSTEM RASTER NAVIGATIONAL CHART DATABASE.

stability, *n.* The state or property of resisting change or of tending to return to original conditions after being disturbed. The opposite is INSTABILITY.

stabilization of radarscope display. Orientation of the radar display to some reference direction. A radarscope display is said to be STABILIZED IN AZIMUTH when the orientation of the display is fixed to an unchanging reference (usually north). The NORTH UP orientation is an example. A radarscope display is said to be UNSTABILIZED IN AZIMUTH when the orientation of the display changes with changes in own ship's heading. The HEAD UP orientation is an example. A radarscope display is said to be DOUBLY STABILIZED or to have DOUBLE STABILIZATION when the basic orientation of the display is fixed to an unchanging reference (usually north) but the radarscope is rotated to keep own ship's heading or heading flasher up on the radarscope.

stabilized in azimuth. See under STABILIZATION OF RADARSCOPE DISPLAY.

stabilized platform. A gimbal-mounted platform, usually containing gyros and accelerometers, the purpose of which is to maintain a desired orientation in inertial space independent of craft motion. Also called STABLE PLATFORM.

stable platform. See STABILIZED PLATFORM.

stack, *n*. A label on a nautical chart which indicates a tall smokestack or chimney. The term is used when the stack is more prominent as a landmark than the accompanying buildings.

stadimeter, *n*. An instrument for determining the distance to an object of known height by measuring the vertical angle subtended by the object. The instrument is graduated directly in distance. See also RANGE FINDER.

stand, *n*. The state of the tide at high or low water when there is no sensible change in the height of the tide. The water level is stationary at high and low water for only an instant, but the change in level near these times is so slow that it is not usually perceptible. In general, the duration of the apparent stand will depend upon the range of tide, being longer for a small range than for a large range, but where there is a tendency for a double tide the stand may last for several hours, even with a large range of tide. It may be called high water stand if it occurs at the time of high water, and low water stand if it occurs at low water. Sometimes called PLATFORM TIDE.

standard, *n*. 1. Something established by custom, agreement, or authority as a basis for comparison. 2. A physical embodiment of a unit. In general it is not independent of physical conditions, and it is a true embodiment of the unit only under specified conditions.

standard acceleration of gravity. The value adopted in the International Service of Weights and Measures for the standard acceleration due to gravity is 980.665 centimeters per second, per second. See also WEIGHT.

standard atmosphere. 1. A unit accepted temporarily for use with the International System of Units; 1 standard atmosphere is equal to 101,325 pascals. 2. A hypothetical vertical distribution of atmospheric temperature, pressure, and density which is taken to be representative of the atmosphere for various purposes.

standard chronometer. See CHRONOMETER.

standard circle sheet. See CIRCLE SHEET.

standard compass. A magnetic compass designated as the standard for a vessel. It is normally located in a favorable position with respect to magnetic influences.

standard deviation. A measure of the dispersion of random errors about the mean value. If a large number of measurements or observations of the same quantity are made, the standard deviation is the square root of the sum of the squares of deviations from the mean value divided by the number of observations less one. The square of the standard deviation is called the VARIANCE. Also called RMS ERROR. See also ROOT MEAN SQUARE ERROR.

standard display. See DISPLAY CATEGORY.

standard error. See under STANDARD DEVIATION.

standard meridian. 1. The meridian used for reckoning standard time. Throughout most of the world the standard meridians are those whose longitudes are exactly divisible by 15°. The DAYLIGHT SAVING MERIDIAN is usually 15° east of the standard meridian. 2. A meridian of a map projection, along which the scale is as stated.

standard noon. Twelve o'clock standard time, or the instant the mean sun is over the upper branch of the standard meridian. DAYLIGHT SAVING or SUMMER NOON usually occurs 1 hour later than standard noon.

standard parallel. 1. A parallel of latitude which is used as a control line in the computation of a map projection. 2. A parallel of latitude on a map or chart along which the scale is as stated for that map or chart.

standard propagation. The propagation of radio waves over a smooth spherical earth of uniform electrical characteristics, under conditions of standard refraction in the atmosphere.

standard positioning service (SPS). GPS service provided to non-military users using the single-frequency C/A code. Accuracy is 100 meters 95% (2 drms) of the time with SA turned on.

standard radio atmosphere. An atmosphere having the standard refractive modulus gradient.

standard radio horizon. The radio horizon corresponding to propagation through the standard radio atmosphere.

standard refraction. The refraction which would occur in a standard atmosphere.

standard refractive modulus gradient. The uniform variation of refractive modulus with height above the earth's surface which is regarded as a standard for comparison. The gradient considered as normal has a value of 0.12M unit per meter. The M unit is the unit in terms of which the refractive modulus is expressed.

standard station. Use of this term is discouraged. See REFERENCE STATION.

standard tactical diameter. A prescribed tactical diameter used by different types of vessels, or by vessels of the same formation in maneuvers.

standard time. The legally established time for a given zone. The United States and its possessions are, by law, divided into eight time zones. The limits of each time zone are defined by the Secretary of Transportation in Part 71, Title 49 of the *Code of Federal Regulations*. The standard time within each zone is the local mean time at the standard meridian that passes approximately through the center of the zone. Since the standard meridians are the same as those used with ZONE TIME, standard time conforms generally with the zone time for a given area. The standard time zone boundary may vary considerably from the zone time limits (7.5° in longitude on each side of the standard meridian) to conform to political or geographic boundaries or both. The standard times used in various countries and places are tabulated in the *Air Almanac* and the *Nautical Almanac* and are displayed on Chart 76, *Standard Time Zone Chart of the World*.

standard type buoy. The general classification of lighted and unlighted buoys in U.S. waters built to modern (1962) specifications.

standby lamp. A lamp brought into service in the event of failure of the lamp in regular service.

standby light. A permanently installed navigation light used in the event of failure of the main light; it is usually of lesser intensity.

standing floe. A separate floe standing vertically or inclined and enclosed by rather smooth ice.

standing wave. See STATIONARY WAVE.

stand on. To proceed on the same course.

standpipe, *n*. A label on a nautical chart which indicates a tall cylindrical structure in a waterworks system.

star, *n*. A large self-luminous celestial body. Stars are generally at such great distances from the earth that they appear to the eye to be fixed in space relative to each other. Comets, meteors, and nebulae may also be self-luminous, but are much smaller. Two stars appearing close together are called a double star, an optical double star if they appear close because they are in nearly the same line of sight but differ greatly in distance from the observer, a physical double star if in nearly the same line of sight and at approximately the same distance from the observer. A system of two stars that revolve about their common center of mass is called a binary star. A group of three or more stars so close together that they appear as a single star is called a multiple star. A group of stars physically close together is called a star cluster. A variable star changes in magnitude. A star which suddenly becomes many times brighter than previously, and then gradually fades, is called a nova. The brightest planet appearing in the western sky during evening twilight is called evening star, and the brightest one appearing in the eastern sky during morning twilight is called morning star. A shooting star or meteor is a solid particle too small to be seen until it enters the earth's atmosphere, when it is heated to incandescence by friction of the air. See also GALAXY, MILKY WAY.

starboard, *n.* The right side of a craft, facing forward. The opposite is PORT.

starboard hand buoy. A buoy which is to be left to the starboard side when approaching from seaward or in the general direction of buoyage, or in the direction established by the appropriate authority.

star chain. A radionavigation transmitting system comprised of a master station about which three (or more) slave (secondary) stations are more or less symmetrically located.

star chart. A representation, on a flat surface, of the celestial sphere or a part of it, showing the positions of the stars and sometimes other features of the celestial sphere.

star cloud. A large number of stars close together, forming a congested part of a galaxy.

star cluster. A group of stars physically close together. See also MULTIPLE STAR.

star cluster

star finder. A device to facilitate the identification of stars. Sometimes called a STAR IDENTIFIER. See also PLANISPHERE.

Star Finder and Identifier (No. 2102-D). A circular star finder and identifier, which consists of a white opaque base with an azimuthal equidistant projection of most of the celestial sphere on each side, one side having the north celestial pole at the center and the other side having the south celestial pole at the center, and a series of transparent templates, at 10° intervals of latitude, each template having a family of altitude and azimuth curves.

star globe. A small globe representing the celestial sphere, on which the apparent positions of the stars are indicated. It is usually provided with graduated arcs and a suitable mount for determining the approximate altitude and azimuth of the stars, to serve as a star finder. Star globes are more commonly used by the British than by Americans. Also called CELESTIAL GLOBE.

star identifier. See STAR FINDER.

star telescope. An accessory of the marine navigational sextant designed primarily for star observations. It has a large object glass to give a greater field of view and increased illumination. It is an erect telescope, i.e., the object viewed is seen erect as opposed to the inverting telescope in which the object viewed is inverted. The latter type telescope requires one less lens than the erect telescope, consequently for the same size object glass, it has greater illumination. The telescope may be used for all observations.

static, *adj.* Having a fixed, nonvarying condition.

static, *n.* 1. Radio wave interference caused by natural electrical disturbances in the atmosphere, or the electromagnetic phenomena capable of causing such interference 2. Noise heard in a radio receiver caused by electrical disturbances in the atmosphere, such as lightning, northern lights, etc.

station, *n.* 1. The authorized location of an aid to navigation. 2. One or more transmitters or receivers, or a combination of transmitters and receivers, including the accessory equipment necessary at one location, for carrying on a radiocommunication service.

stationary front. A front which is stationary or nearly so. A front which is moving at a speed less than about 5 knots is generally considered to be stationary. In synoptic chart analysis, a stationary front is one that has not moved appreciably from its position on the last previous synoptic chart (3 or 6 hours before). Also called QUASI-STATIONARY FRONT.

stationary orbit. An equatorial orbit in which the satellite revolves about the primary at the angular rate at which the primary rotates on its axis. From the primary, the satellite appears to be stationary over a point on the primary's equator. See also GEOSTATIONARY SATELLITE.

stationary wave. A wave that oscillates without progressing. One-half of such a wave may be illustrated by the oscillation of the water in a pan that has been tilted. Near the axis, which is called the node or nodal line, there is no vertical rise and fall of the water. The ends of the wave are called loops and at these places the vertical rise and fall is at a maximum. The current is maximum near the node and minimum at the loops. The period of a stationary wave depends upon the length and depth of the body of water. A stationary wave may be resolved into two progressive waves of equal amplitude and equal speeds moving in opposite directions. Also called STANDING WAVE.

stationary wave theory. An assumption that the basic tidal movement in the open ocean consists of a system of stationary wave oscillations, any progressive wave movement being of secondary importance except as the tide advances into tributary waters. The continental masses divide the sea into irregular basins, which, although not completely enclosed, are capable of sustaining oscillations which are more or less independent. The tide-producing force consists principally of two parts, a semidiurnal force with a period approximating the half-day and a diurnal force with a period of a whole day. Insofar as the free period of oscillation of any part of the ocean, as determined by its dimensions and depth, is in accord with the semidiurnal or diurnal tide producing forces, there will be built up corresponding oscillations of considerable amplitude which will be manifested in the rise and fall of the tide. The diurnal oscillations, superimposed upon the semidiurnal oscillations, cause the inequalities in the heights of the two high and the two low waters of each day. Although the tidal movement as a whole is somewhat complicated by the overlapping of oscillating areas, the theory is consistent with observational data.

station buoy. An unlighted buoy established in the vicinity of a lightship or an important lighted buoy as a reference point in case the lightship or buoy should be dragged off station. Also called WATCH BUOY.

station error. See DEFLECTION OF THE VERTICAL.

statistical error. See RANDOM ERROR.

steady bearing. A bearing line to another vessel or object, which does not change over time. An approaching or closing craft is said to be on a steady bearing if the compass bearing does not change and risk of collision therefore exists. Also called CONSTANT BEARING, DECREASING RANGE (CBDR).

steam fog. Fog formed when water vapor is added to air which is much colder than the source of the vapor. It may be formed when very cold air drifts across relatively warm water. At temperatures below about-20°F, ice particles or droxtals may be formed in the air producing a type of ice fog known as frost smoke. See also ARCTIC SEA SMOKE, FROST SMOKE. Also called ARCTIC SMOKE, SEA MIST, STEAM MIST, WATER SMOKE, ARCTIC SEA SMOKE, FROST SMOKE.

steam mist. See STEAM FOG.

steep-to, *adj.* Precipitous. The term is applied particularly to a shore, bank, or shoal that descends steeply to the sea.

steerage way, *n.* The condition wherein a ship has sufficient way on to respond to rudder movements to maintain a desired course.

steering compass. A compass by which a craft is steered, generally meaning the magnetic compass at the helm. See STEERING REPEATER.

steering repeater. A compass repeater by which a craft is steered. Sometimes loosely called a STEERING COMPASS.

stellar, *adj.* Of or pertaining to stars.

stellar observation. See CELESTIAL OBSERVATION.

stellar parallax. See HELIOCENTRIC PARALLAX.

stem, *v., t.* To make headway against a current.

steradian, *n.* The supplementary unit of solid angle in the International System of Units, which, having its vertex in the center of a sphere, cuts off an area on the surface of the sphere equal to that of a square with sides of length equal to the radius of the sphere.

stereographic, *adj.* Of or pertaining to stereography, the art of representing the forms of solid bodies on a plane.

stereographic chart. A chart on the stereographic map projection.

stereographic map projection. A perspective, conformal, azimuthal map projection in which points on the surface of a sphere or spheroid, such as the earth, are conceived as projected by radial lines from any point on the surface to a plane tangent to the antipode of the point of projection. Circles project as circles except for great circles through the point of tangency, which project as straight lines. The principal navigational use of the projection is for charts of the polar regions. Also called AZIMUTHAL ORTHOMORPHIC MAP PROJECTION.

sternboard, *n.* Making way through the water in a direction opposite to the heading. Also called STERNWAY, though the term STERNBOARD is sometimes used to refer to the beginning of motion astern and STERNWAY is used as the vessel picks up speed. Motion in the forward direction is called HEADWAY.

stern light. A running light placed on the centerline of a vessel showing a continuous white light from dead astern to 67.5° to either side.

sternway, *n.* Making way through the water in a direction opposite to the heading. Motion in the forward direction is called HEADWAY. See also STERNBOARD.

stilling well. See FLOAT WELL.

still water level. The level that the sea surface would assume in the absence of wind waves not to be confused with MEAN SEA LEVEL or HALF TIDE LEVEL.

stippling, *n.* Graduation of shading by numerous separate dots or marks. Shallow areas on charts, for instance, are sometimes indicated by numerous dots decreasing in density as the depth increases.

stones, *n., pl.* A general term for rock fragments ranging in size from 2 to 256 millimeters. An individual water-rounded stone is called a cobble if between 64 to 256 millimeters (size of clenched fist to size of man's head), a pebble if between 4 and 64 millimeters (size of small pea to size of clenched fist), and gravel if between 2 and 4 millimeters (thickness of standard pencil lead to size of small pea). An aggregate of stones ranging from 16 to 256 millimeters is called shingle. See also MUD; SAND; ROCK, definition 2.

stooping, *n.* Apparent decrease in the vertical dimension of an object near the horizon, due to large inequality of atmospheric refraction in the line of sight to the top and bottom of the object. The opposite is TOWERING.

stop watch. A watch that can be started, stopped, and reset at will, to indicate elapsed time.

storm, *n.* 1. Wind of force 10 (48 to 55 knots or 55 to 63 miles per hour) on the Beaufort wind scale. See also VIOLENT STORM. 2. Any disturbed state of the atmosphere implying severe weather. In synoptic meteorology, a storm is a complete individual disturbance identified on synoptic charts as a complex of pressure, wind, clouds, precipitation, etc., or identified by such means as radar. Thus, storms range in scale from tornadoes and thunderstorms, through tropical cyclones, to widespread extra tropical cyclones. From a local and special interest viewpoint, a storm is a transient occurrence identified by its most destructive or spectacular aspect. Examples are rain storms, wind storms, hail storms, snow storms, etc. Notable special cases are blizzards, ice storms, sandstorms, and dust storms. 3. A term once used by seamen for what is now called VIOLENT STORM on the Beaufort wind scale.

storm center. The area of lowest atmospheric pressure of a cyclone. This is a more general expression than EYE OF THE STORM, which refers only to the center of a well-developed tropical cyclone, in which there is a tendency of the skies to clear.

storm surge. Increase or decrease in sea level by strong winds such as those accompanying a hurricane or other intense storm. Reduced atmospheric pressure often contributes to the decrease in height during hurricanes. It is potentially catastrophic, especially in deltaic regions with onshore winds at the time of high water and extreme wind wave heights. Also called STORM TIDE, STORM WAVE, TIDAL WAVE.

storm tide. See STORM SURGE.

storm track. The horizontal component of the path followed or expected to be followed by a storm CENTER.

storm track

storm wave. See STORM SURGE.

straight angle. An angle of 180°.

strait, *n.* A relatively narrow waterway connecting two larger bodies of water.

strand, *n.* See BEACH.

strand, *v., t. & i.* To run hard aground. The term STRAND usually refers to a serious grounding, while the term GROUND refers to any grounding, however slight.

stranded ice. Ice which has been floating and has been deposited on the shore by retreating high water.

stranding, *n.* The grounding of a vessel so that it is not easily refloated; a serious grounding.

strapped-down inertial navigation equipment. Inertial navigation equipment in which a stable platform and gimbal system are not utilized. The inertial devices are attached or strapped directly to the carrier. A computer utilizing gyro information resolves accelerations sensed along the carrier axes and refers these accelerations to an inertial frame of reference. Also called GIMBALLESS INERTIAL NAVIGATION EQUIPMENT. See also INERTIAL NAVIGATION.

stratiform, *adj.* Descriptive of clouds of extensive horizontal development, as contrasted to the vertically developed CUMULIFORM types. See also CIRRIFORM.

stratocumulus, *n.* A principal cloud type (cloud genus), predominantly stratiform, in the form of a gray and/or whitish layer or patch, which nearly always has dark parts and is non-fibrous (except for virga). Its elements are tessellated, rounded, roll-shaped, etc.; they may or may not be merged, and usually are arranged in orderly groups, lines or undulations, giving the appearance of a simple (or occasionally a cross-pattern) wave system. These elements are generally flat-topped, smooth and large; observed at an angle of more than 30° above the horizon, the individual stratocumulus element subtends an angle of greater than 5°. Stratocumulus is composed of small water droplets, sometimes accompanied by larger droplets, soft hail, and (rarely) by snowflakes. When the cloud is not very thick, the diffraction phenomena corona and irisation appear. Precipitation rarely occurs with stratocumulus. Stratocumulus frequently forms in clear air. It may also form from the rising of stratus, and by the convective or undulatory transformation of stratus, or nimbostratus, with or without change of height. Since stratocumulus may be transformed directly from or into altocumulus, stratus, and nimbostratus, all transitional stages may be observed. When the base of stratocumulus is rendered diffuse by precipitation, the cloud becomes nimbostratus. See also STRATIFORM, CLOUD CLASSIFICATION.

stratosphere, *n.* The atmospheric shell extending upward from the tropopause to the height where the temperature begins to increase in the 20- to 25-kilometer region.

stratus, *n.* A low cloud (mean upper level below 6,500 ft.) in a uniform layer, resembling fog but not resting on the surface.

stray line. Ungraduated portion of line connected with a current pole used in taking current observations The stray line is usually about 100 feet long and permits the pole to acquire the velocity of the current at some distance from the disturbed waters in the immediate vicinity of the observing vessel before the current velocity is read from the graduated portion of the current line.

stream, *v., t.* To place overboard and tow, as to stream a log or stream a sea anchor.

stream current. A relatively narrow, deep, fast-moving ocean current. The opposite is DRIFT CURRENT.

streamline, *n.* The path followed by a particle of fluid flowing past an obstruction. The term generally excludes the path of a particle in an eddy current.

streamline flow. Fluid motion in which the fluid moves uniformly without eddies or turbulence. If it moves in thin layers, it is called laminar flow. The opposite is TURBULENT FLOW.

stream the log. To throw the log overboard and secure it in place for taking readings.

strength of current. Phase of tidal current in which the speed is a maximum; also the speed at this time.

strength of ebb. See EBB STRENGTH.

strength of ebb interval. See EBB INTERVAL. See also LUNICURRENT INTERVAL.

strength of flood. See FLOOD STRENGTH.

strength of flood interval. See FLOOD INTERVAL. See also LUNICURRENT INTERVAL.

strip, *n.* A long narrow area of pack ice, about 1 kilometer or less in width, usually composed of small fragments detached from the main mass of ice, and run together under the influence of wind, swell, or current.

stripes, *n.* In navigation terminology, stripes are vertically arranged areas of color, such as the red and white stripes on a safe-water buoy. Horizontal areas are called bands.

strong breeze. Wind of force 6 (22 to 27 knots or 25 to 31 miles per hour) on the Beaufort wind scale.

strong fix. A fix determined from horizontal sextant angles between objects so situated as to give very accurate results.

strong gale. Wind of force 9 (41 to 47 knots or 47 to 54 miles per hour) on the Beaufort wind scale See also GALE.

sub-. A prefix meaning under, less, or marginal. The opposite is SUPER-.

Subarctic Current. See ALEUTIAN CURRENT.

subastral point. See SUBSTELLAR POINT.

sublimation, *n.* The transition of a substance directly from the solid state to the vapor state, or vice versa, without passing through the intermediate liquid state. See also CONDENSATION, EVAPORATION, FUSION.

sublunar point. The geographical position of the moon; the point on the earth at which the moon is in the zenith.

submarine bell. See under BELL.

submarine cable. A submarine conductor or fiber-optic conduit for electric current or communications.

submarine havens. Specified sea areas for submarine operations established by the submarine commander in which no friendly ASW attack may be launched. Compare with MOVING HAVENS, which are designed to prevent collisions.

submarine relief. Variations in elevation of the sea bed, or their representation by depth contours, hypsometric tints, or soundings.

submarine safety lanes. See SAFETY LANES.

submarine site. The site of a structure when located below the surface of the water.

submerge, *v., i.* To descend below the surface The opposite is SURFACE. See also DIVE.

submerged, *adj. & adv.* 1. Under water. The opposite is UNCOVERED. See also AWASH. 2. Having descended below the surface. The opposite is SURFACED.

submerged breakwater. A breakwater with its top below the still water level. When this structure is struck by a wave, part of the wave energy is reflected seaward. The remaining energy is largely dissipated in a breaker, transmitted shoreward as a multiple crest system, or as a simple wave system.

submerged lands. Lands covered by water at any stage of the tide, as distinguished from tidelands which are attached to the mainland or an island and cover and uncover with the tide. Tidelands presuppose a highwater line as the upper boundary; submerged lands do not.

submerged production well. An oil or gas well that is a seabed installation only, i.e., the installation does not include a permanent production platform. See also WELLHEAD.

submerged rock. A rock covered at the chart sounding datum and considered to be potentially dangerous to navigation. See also BARE ROCK, ROCK AWASH.

submerged screw log. A type of electric log which is actuated by the flow of water past a propeller.

subordinate current station. 1. A current station from which a relatively short series of observations is reduced by comparison with simultaneous observations from a control current station. 2. A station listed in the *Tidal Current Tables* for which predictions are to be obtained by means of differences and ratios applied to the full predictions at a reference station. See also CURRENT STATION, CONTROL CURRENT STATION. REFERENCE STATION.

subordinate tide station. 1. A tide station from which a relatively short series of observations is reduced by comparison with simultaneous observations from a tide station with a relatively long series of observations. 2. A station listed in the *Tide Tables* for which predictions are to be obtained by means of differences and ratios applied to the full predictions at a reference station. See also PRIMARY CONTROL TIDE STATION, REFERENCE STATION, SECONDARY CONTROL TIDE STATION, TERTIARY TIDE STATION.

subpermanent magnetism. The magnetism in the intermediate iron of a ship which tends to change as a result of vibration, aging, or cruising in the same direction for a long period, but does not alter immediately so as to be properly termed induced magnetism. This magnetism is the principal cause of deviation changes of a magnetic compass. At any instant this magnetism is recognized as part of the ship's permanent magnetism, and consequently must be corrected as such by means of permanent magnet correctors. See also MAGNETISM.

sub-refraction, *n.* Less-than-normal refraction, particularly as related to the atmosphere. Greater than normal refraction is called SUPER-REFRACTION.

subregion. One of the subdivisions of the earth based on the NGA chart numbering system.

subsatellite point. The point at which a line from the satellite perpendicular to the ellipsoid intersects the surface of the earth.

subsidence, *n.* Decrease in the elevation of land without removal of surface material due to tectonic, seismic, or artificial forces.

subsidiary light. A light placed on or near the support of a main light and having a special use in navigation. See also PASSING LIGHT.

subsolar point. The geographical position of the sun; the point on the earth at which the sun is in the zenith at a specified time.

substellar point. The geographical position of a star; that point on the earth at which the star is in the zenith at a specified time. Also called SUBASTRAL POINT.

substratosphere, *n.* A region of indefinite lower limit just below the stratosphere.

subsurface current. An underwater current which is not present at the surface. See also SURFACE CURRENT, UNDERCURRENT, UNDERTOW.

subtend, *v., t.* To be opposite, as an arc of a circle subtends an angle at the center of the circle, the angle being formed by the radii joining the ends of the arc with the center.

subtrack, *n.* See ORBITAL PATH.

subtropical anticyclones. High pressure belts which prevail on the poleward sides of the trade winds characterized by calms, light breezes, and dryness.

sudden ionospheric disturbances (SID's). Sudden increases in the ionization density in the lower part of the ionosphere caused by very sudden and large increases in X-ray flux emitted from the sun, usually during a solar flare. SID's also occur during flares called X-ray flares that produce large X-ray flux, but which have no components in the visible light spectrum. The effect, which is restricted to sunlit propagation paths, causes a phase advance in certain radionavigation systems and is known as a SUDDEN PHASE ANOMALY (SPA). The SID effects are related to solar zenith angle, and consequently, occur mostly in lower latitude regions. Usually there is a phase advance over a period of 5 to 10 minutes followed by a recovery over a period of 30 to 60 minutes. See also POLAR CAP DISTURBANCE, MODAL INTERFERENCE.

sudden phase anomaly. See under SUDDEN IONOSPHERIC DISTURBANCES.

Suestado, *n.* A storm with southeast gales, caused by intense cyclonic activity off the coasts of Argentina and Uruguay, which affects the southern part of the coast of Brazil in the winter.

sugarloaf sea. A sea characterized by waves that rise into sugarloaf (conical) shapes, with little wind, resulting from intersecting waves.

sugg, *v., i.* To roll with the action of the sea when aground.

sumatra, *n.* A squall with violent thunder, lightning, and rain, which blows at night in the Malacca Straits, especially during the southwest monsoon. It is intensified by strong mountain breezes.

Summary of Corrections. A cumulative summary of corrections to charts, *Sailing Directions,* and *United States Coast Pilots* previously published in *Notice to Mariners,* published by the National Geospatial-Intelligence Agency.

summer, *n.* In the Northern Hemisphere summer begins astronomically at the summer solstice and ends at the autumnal equinox. In the Southern Hemisphere the limits are the winter solstice and the vernal equinox. The meteorological limits vary with the locality and the year. See also INDIAN SUMMER.

summer noon. Daylight saving noon. The expression applies where summer time is used, particularly in Europe.

summer solstice. 1. The point on the ecliptic occupied by the sun at maximum northerly declination. Sometimes called JUNE SOLSTICE, FIRST POINT OF CANCER. 2. That instant at which the sun reaches the point of maximum northerly declination, about June 21.

summer time. A variation of standard time in which the clocks are advanced 1 hour. The variation when the clocks are advanced 2 hours is called double summer time. The expression is used principally in Europe. See also DAYLIGHT SAVING TIME.

Sumner line. A line of position established by the Sumner method or, loosely, any celestial line of position.

Sumner method. The establishing of a line of position from the observation of the altitude of a celestial body by assuming two latitudes (or longitudes) and calculating the longitudes (or latitudes) through which the line of position passes. The line of position is the straight line connecting these two points (extended if necessary). This method, discovered by Thomas H. Sumner, an American sea captain, is seldom used by modern navigators, an adaptation of it, called ST. HILAIRE METHOD, being favored. See also LONGITUDE METHOD, HIGH ALTITUDE METHOD.

Sumner point. See COMPUTED POINT.

sun, *n*. The luminous celestial body at the center of the solar system, around which the planets asteroids, and comets revolve. It is an average star in terms of size and age. The sun visible in the sky is called apparent or true sun. A fictitious sun conceived to move eastward along the celestial equator at a rate that provides a uniform measure of time equal to the average apparent time is called mean sun or astronomical mean sun; a fictitious sun conceived to move eastward along the ecliptic at the average rate of the apparent sun is called dynamical mean sun. When the sun is observable at midnight, in high latitudes, it is called midnight sun.

sun cross. A rare halo phenomenon in which horizontal and vertical shafts of light intersect at the sun. It is probably due to the simultaneous occurrence of a sun pillar and a parhelic circle.

sun dog. See PARHELION.

sun line, *n*. A line of position determined from a sextant observation of the sun.

sun pillar. A glittering shaft of light, white or reddish, extending above and below the sun, most frequently observed at sunrise or sunset. If a parhelic circle is observed at the same time, a SUN CROSS results. See also HALO.

sun relay. See DAYLIGHT CONTROL.

sunrise, *n*. The crossing of the visible horizon by the upper limb of the rising sun.

sunset, *n*. The crossing of the visible horizon by the upper limb of the setting sun.

sunspot, *n*. Dark spots on the sun's surface. These spots are apparently magnetic in character and exert a disturbing influence on radio propagation on the earth.

sun's way. The path of the solar system through space.

sun switch. See DAYLIGHT CONTROL.

super-. A prefix meaning over, more, greater. The opposite is SUB-.

super-buoy. A very large buoy, generally more than 5 meters in diameter, used for navigation, offshore mooring, or data acquisition.

superheterodyne receiver. A receiver in which the incoming radio frequency signals are normally amplified before being fed into a mixer (first detector) for conversion into a fixed, lower carrier (the intermediate frequency). The intermediate frequency signals undergo very high amplification in the intermediate frequency amplifier stages and are then fed into a detector (second detector) for demodulation. The resulting audio or video signals are then usually further amplified before use.

super high frequency. Radio frequency of 3,000 to 30,000 megahertz.

superior conjunction. The conjunction of an inferior planet and the sun when the sun is between the earth and the other planet.

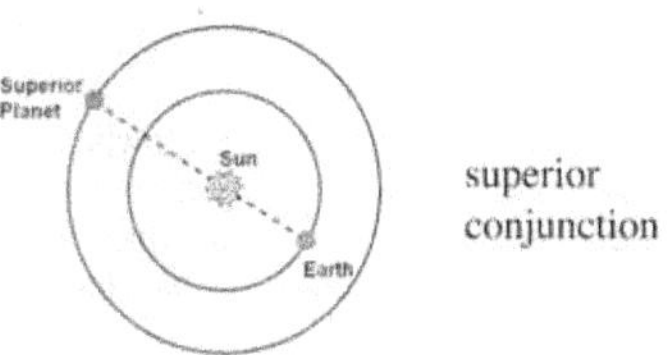

superior planets. The planets with orbits outside that of the Earth: Mars, Jupiter, Saturn Uranus, Neptune, and Pluto. See also PLANET.

superior transit. See UPPER TRANSIT.

super-refraction, *n*. Greater than normal refraction, particularly as related to the atmosphere. Less than normal refraction is called SUB-REFRACTION.

supersaturation, *n*. Beyond the usual point of saturation. As an example, if saturated air is cooled, condensation takes place only if nuclei are present. If they are not present, the air continues to hold more water than required for saturation until the temperature is increased or until a nucleus is introduced.

supersonic, *adj*. Faster than sound. Formerly this term was also applied to a frequency above the audible range, but in this usage it has been replaced by the term ULTRASONIC.

superstructure, *n*. See CAGE.

supplement, *n*. An angle equal to 180° minus a given angle. Two angles which equal 180° supplementary. See also COMPLEMENT, EXPLEMENT.

supplementary angles. Two angles whose sum is 180°.

supplementary information. In ECDIS, non-chart hydrographic office information, such as SAILING DIRECTIONS, TIDE TABLES, and LIGHT LISTS.

supplementary units. See under INTERNATIONAL SYSTEM OF UNITS.

surf, *n*. The region of breaking waves near a beach or over a detached reef.

surface, *v., i.* To rise to the surface. The opposite is SUBMERGE.

surface boundary layer. That thin layer of air adjacent to the earth's surface extending up to a level of about 10 to 100 meters. Within this layer the wind distribution is determined largely by the vertical temperature gradient and the nature and contours of the underlying surface; shearing stresses are approximately constant. Also called FRICTION LAYER.

surface chart. Short for SYNOPTIC SURFACE CHART.

surface current. A current which does not extend more than about 3 meters below the surface. See also SUBSURFACE CURRENT, UNDERCURRENT, UNDERTOW.

surfaced, *adj*. & *adv*. Having come to the surface from below the water. The opposite is SUBMERGED. See also AFLOAT, UNCOVERED.

surface duct. A tropospheric radio duct in which the lower boundary is the surface of the earth. Also called GROUND-BASED DUCT.

surface front. See under FRONT.

surface of position. A surface on some point of which a craft is located. See also LINE OPPOSITION, FIX.

surface wave. A radio wave which is propagated along the boundary between two media in a manner determined by the properties of the two media in the vicinity of the boundary.

surf zone. The area between the outermost limit of breakers and the limit of wave uprush.

surge, *n*. 1. The bodily motion of a vessel in a seaway forward and backward along the longitudinal axis, caused by the force of the sea acting alternately on the bow and stern. Also called SURGING. See also SHIP MOTIONS. 2. See as STORM SURGE.

surging, *n*. See SURGE, *n*., definition.

surveillance, *n*. The observation of an area or space for the purpose of determining the position and movements of craft or vehicles in that area or space. Surveillance can be either dependent, independent, or pseudo-independent.

surveillance radar. A primary radar installation at a land station used to display at that station the position of vessels within its range, usually for advisory purposes.

survey, *n.* 1. The act or operation of making measurements for determining the relative positions of points on, above, or beneath the earth's surface. 2. The results of operations as in definition 1. 3. An organization for making surveys. See also GEODETIC SURVEY, HYDROGRAPHIC SURVEY, OCEANOGRAPHIC SURVEY, TOPOGRAPHIC SURVEY.

surveying, *n.* The branch of applied mathematics which teaches the art of determining accurately the area of any part of the earth's surface, the lengths and directions of bounding lines, the contour of the surface, etc., and accurately delineating the whole on a map or chart for a specified datum.

survey mile (U.S.). A unit of distance equal to 5,280 feet. This mile is generally used on land, and is sometimes called LAND MILE. It is commonly used to express navigational distances by navigators of river and lake vessels, particularly those navigating the Great Lakes.

surveying sextant. See HYDROGRAPHIC SEXTANT.

swamp, *n.* An area of spongy land saturated with water. It may have a shallow covering of water, usually with a considerable amount of vegetation appearing above the surface. Sometimes called SLOUGH.

swash, *n.* 1. A narrow channel or sound within a sand bank, or between a sand bank and the shore. 2. A bar over which the sea washes. 3. The rush of water up onto the beach following the breaking of a wave.

sway, *n.* The side-to-side bodily motion of a vessel in a seaway, independent of rolling, caused by uniform pressure being exerted all along one side of the hull. Also called LATERAL DRIFTING, SWAYING. See also SHIP MOTIONS.

swaying, *n.* See SWAY.

sweep, *v., t.* To tow a line or object below the surface, to determine the least depth in an area or to insure that a given area is free from navigational dangers to a certain depth; or the removal of such dangers. See also DRAG, *v., t.*

sweep (of radarscope), *n.* As determined by the time base or range calibration, the radial movement of the stream of electrons impinging on the face of the cathode-ray tube.

sweeping, *n.* 1. The process of towing a line or object below the surface, to determine whether an area is free from isolated submerged dangers to vessels and to determine the position of any dangers that exist, or to determine the least depth of an area. 2. The process of clearing an area or channel of mines or other dangers to navigation.

sweep rate. The number of times a radar radiation pattern rotates during 1 minute of time. Sometimes expressed as the duration of one complete rotation in seconds of time.

swell, *n.* A relatively long wind wave, or series of waves, that has traveled out of the generating area. In contrast the term SEA is applied to the waves while still in the generating area. As these waves travel away from the area in which they are formed, the shorter ones die out. The surviving waves exhibit a more regular and longer period with flatter crests. When these waves reach shoal water, they become more prominent in height and of decreased wave length and are then known as ground swell.

swell direction. The direction from which swell is moving.

swept-frequency racon. An in-band racon which sweeps through the marine radar band (2920-3100 MHz in the 10-centimeter band and 9220-9500 MHz in the 3-centimeter band) in order that it may be triggered at the frequency of the interrogating radar transmitting at a given frequency within the band. Almost all such racons operate in the 3-centimeter band only. There are two types of swept-frequency racons: the slow-sweep racon sweeps through the 180 MHz frequency band in 10s of seconds (1.5 to 3.0 MHz per second); the fast-sweep racon sweeps through the band in microseconds.

swept gain. See SENSITIVITY TIME CONTROL.

swinger, *n.* See REVOLVER.

swinging buoy. A buoy placed at a favorable location to assist a vessel to adjust its compass or swing ship. The bow of the vessel is made fast to one buoy and the vessel is swung by means of lines to a tug or to additional buoys. Also called COMPASS ADJUSTMENT BUOY.

swinging ship. The process of placing a vessel on various headings and comparing magnetic compass readings with the corresponding magnetic directions, to determine deviation. This usually follows compass adjustment or compass compensation, and is done to obtain information for making a deviation table.

swinging the arc. The process of rotating a sextant about the line of sight to the horizon to determine the foot of the vertical circle through a body being observed. Also called ROCKING THE SEXTANT.

swirl error. The additional error in the reading of a magnetic compass during a turn, due to friction in the compass liquid.

symmetrical, *adj.* Being equal or identical on each side of a center line or middle value. The opposite is ASYMMETRICAL.

synchronism, *n.* The relationship between two or more periodic quantities of the same frequency when the phase difference between them is zero or constant at a predetermined value.

synchronization error. In radionavigation, the error due to imperfect timing of two operations.

synchronize, *v., t.* To bring into synchronization.

synchronous, *adj.* Coincident in time, phase, rate, etc.

synchronous lights. Two or more lights the characteristics of which are in synchronism.

synchronous satellite. A satellite whose period of rotation is equal to the period of rotation of the primary about its axis. The orbit of a synchronous satellite must be equatorial if the satellite is to remain fixed over a point on the primary's equator. See also GEOSYNCHRONOUS SATELLITE, GEOSTATIONARY SATELLITE.

synodical month. The average period of revolution of the moon about the earth with respect to the sun, a period of 29 days, 12 hours, 44 minutes, 2.8 seconds. This is sometimes called the MONTH OF THE PHASES, since it extends from new moon to the next new moon. Also called LUNATION.

synodical period. See SYNODIC PERIOD.

synodic period. The interval of time between any planetary configuration of a celestial body, with respect to the sun, and the next successive same configuration of that body, as from inferior conjunction to inferior conjunction. Also called SYNODICAL PERIOD.

synoptic chart. In meteorology, any chart or map on which data and analyses are presented that describe the state of the atmosphere over a large area at a given moment of time. A synoptic surface chart is an analyzed synoptic chart of surface weather observations.

synoptic surface chart. See under SYNOPTIC CHART.

system accuracy. The expected accuracy of a navigation system expressed in d_{rms} units, not including errors which may be introduced by the user, or geodetic or cartographic errors.

systematic error. One of the two categories of errors of observation, measurement and calculation, the other category being random error. Systematic errors are characterized by an orderly trend, and are usually predictable once the cause is known. They are divided into three classes: (1) errors resulting from changing or nonstandard natural physical conditions, sometimes called theoretical errors, (2) personal (nonaccidental) errors, and (3) instrument errors. Also called REGULAR ERROR. See also ERROR.

System Electronic Navigation Chart (SENC). 1. The electronic chart data base actually accessed aboard ship for the display of electronic charts. It is developed from the ENC provided by hydrographic authorities, but is specific to the shipboard system. When corrected, it is the equivalent of a paper chart. 2. In ECDIS, a database in the manufacturer's internal ECDIS format, resulting from the errorless transformation of the entire ENC contents and its updates. It is this database that is accessed by ECDIS for the display generation and other navigational functions, and is equivalent to an up-to-date paper chart. The SENC may also contain information added by the mariner and information from other sources.

System Raster Navigation Chart (SRNC). In ECDIS, a database resulting from the transformation of the RNC by the RCDS to include updates to the RNC by appropriate means.

syzygy, *n.* 1. A point of the orbit of a planet or satellite at which it is in conjunction or opposition. The term is used chiefly in connection with the moon at its new and full phase. 2. A west wind on the seas between New Guinea and Australia preceding the summer northwest monsoon.

T

table, *n.* An orderly, condensed arrangement of numerical or other information, usually in parallel rows or columns. A table in which values of the quantity to be found are tabulated for limiting values of the entering argument is called critical table. See also CALIBRATION TABLE, CONVERSION TABLE, CURRENT TABLES, TIDE TABLES, TRAVERSE TABLE.

tablemount, *n.* A seamount having a comparatively smooth, flat top. Also called GUYOT.

tabular altitude. See TABULATED ALTITUDE.

tabular azimuth. See TABULATED AZIMUTH.

tabular azimuth angle. See TABULATED AZIMUTH ANGLE.

tabular iceberg. A flat-topped iceberg with length-to-height ratio greater than 5:1. Most tabular bergs form by calving from an ice shelf and show horizontal banding. See also ICE ISLAND, BLOCKY ICEBERG.

tabulated altitude. In navigational sight reduction tables, the altitude taken directly from a table for the entering arguments. After interpolation for argument increments, i.e., the difference between each entering argument and the actual value, it is called COMPUTED ALTITUDE. Also called TABULAR ALTITUDE.

tabulated azimuth. Azimuth taken directly from a table, before interpolation. After interpolation, it becomes COMPUTED AZIMUTH.

tabulated azimuth angle. Azimuth angle taken directly from a table, before interpolation. After interpolation, it becomes COMPUTED AZIMUTH ANGLE.

Tacan, *n.* An ultra high frequency aeronautical radionavigation system which provides a continuous indication of bearing and distance to a Tacan station. The term is derived from Tactical Air Navigation.

tactical diameter. The distance gained to the right or left of the original course when a turn of 180° with a constant rudder angle has been completed. See also STANDARD TACTICAL DIAMETER.

taffrail, *n.* The after rail at the stern of a vessel.

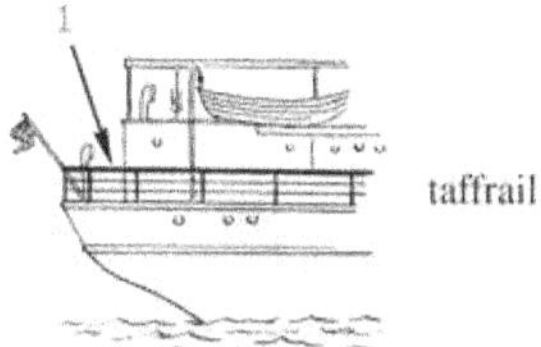

taffrail

taffrail log. A log consisting of a rotator towed through the water by a braided log line attached to a distance-registering device usually secured at the taffrail. Also called PATENT LOG.

tail wind. A wind from behind the vessel. See FOLLOWING WIND.

take departure. See under DEPARTURE, definition 2.

take the ground. To become stranded by the tide.

Taku wind. A strong, gusty, east-northeast wind, occurring in the vicinity of Juneau, Alaska, between October and March. At the mouth of the Taku River, after which it is named, it sometimes attains hurricane force.

tangent, *adj.* Touching at a single point.

tangent, *n.* 1. The ratio of the side opposite an acute angle of a plane right triangle to the shorter side adjacent to the same angle. The expression NATURAL TANGENT is sometimes used to distinguish the tangent from its logarithm (called LOGARITHMIC TANGENT). 2. A straight line, curve, or surface touching a curve or surface at one point.

tangent arc. 1. An arc touching a curve or surface at one point. 2. A halo tangent to a circular halo.

tangent latitude error. On a nonpendulous gyrocompass where damping is accomplished by offsetting the point of application of the force of a mercury ballistic, the angle between the local meridian and the settling position or spin axis. Where the offset of the point of application of a mercury ballistic is to the east of the vertical axis of the gyrocompass, the settling position is to the east of the meridian in north latitudes and to the west of the meridian in south latitudes. The error is so named because it is approximately proportional to the tangent of the latitude in which the gyrocompass is operating. The tangent latitude error varies from zero at the equator to a maximum at high northern and southern latitudes.

tank, *n.* An elevated water tank, indicated on a chart by a position circle.

tape gage. See ELECTRIC TAPE GAGE.

tapper, *n.* A heavy pendulum suspended outside a bell which rings it.

target, *n.* In navigation, an object observed on a radar screen. See also CONTACT.

target angle. The relative bearing of own ship from a target vessel, measured clockwise through 360°. See also ASPECT.

target tail. The display of diminishing luminance seen to follow a target on a radar display which results from afterglow and the progress of the target between successive scans of the radar. Also called TARGET TRAIL.

target trail. See TARGET TAIL.

tehuantepecer, *n.* A violent squally wind from north or north-northeast in the Gulf of Tehuantepec (south of southern Mexico) in winter. It originates in the Gulf of Mexico as a norther which crosses the isthmus and blows through the gap between the Mexican and Guatamalan mountains. It may be felt up to 100 miles out to sea. See also PAPAGAYO.

telecommunication, *n.* Any transmission, emission, sound, or intelligence of any nature by wire, radio, or other electromagnetic system. If the transfer is by radio, it may be called radiocommunication.

telegraph buoy. A buoy used to mark the position of a submarine telegraph cable.

telemeter, *n.* The complete equipment for measuring any quantity, transmitting the results electrically to a distant point, and there recording the values measured.

telemetry, *n.* The science of measuring a quantity or quantities, transmitting the measured value to a distant station, and there interpreting, indicating, or recording the quantities measured.

telemotor, *n.* A device for controlling the application of power at a distance, especially one by which the steering gear of a vessel is controlled from the wheel house.

telescope, *n.* An optical instrument used as an aid in viewing or photographing distant objects, particularly celestial objects. A reflecting telescope collects light by means of a concave mirror; a refracting telescope by means of a lens or system of lenses. A Cassegrainian telescope is a reflecting telescope in which the immergent light is reflected from the main mirror onto a secondary mirror, where it is reflected through a hole in the main mirror to an eyepiece; a Newtonian telescope is a reflecting telescope in which the immergent beam is reflected from the main mirror onto a small plane mirror, and from there to an eyepiece at the side of the telescope.

telescopic alidade. See ALIDADE.

telescopic alidade

telescopic meteor. See under METEOR.

telltale compass. A marine magnetic compass, usually of the inverted type, frequently installed in the master's cabin for his convenience.

temperate zone. Either of the two zones between the frigid and torrid zones, called the north temperate zone and the south temperate zone.

temperature, *n.* Intensity or degree of heat. Fahrenheit temperature is based upon a scale in which water freezes at 32°F and boils at about 212°F; Celsius temperature upon a scale in which water freezes at 0°C and boils at 100°C. Absolute temperature is measured from absolute zero which is zero on the Kelvin scale, –273.16° on the Celsius scale, and 459.69°F on the Fahrenheit scale. Absolute temperature based upon degrees Fahrenheit is called Rankine temperature and that based upon degrees Celsius is called Kelvin temperature.

temperature error. That instrument error due to nonstandard temperature of the instrument.

temperature inversion. An atmospheric condition in which the usual lapse rate is inverted, i.e., the temperature increases with increasing altitude.

temporal, *adj.* Pertaining to or limited by time.

temporary light. A light put into service for a limited period.

temporary units. See under INTERNATIONAL SYSTEM OF UNITS.

tend, *v., i.* To extend in a stated direction, as an anchor cable.

tera-. A prefix meaning one trillion (10^{12}).

terdiurnal, *adj.* Occurring three times per day. A terdiurnal tidal constituent has three periods in a constituent day.

terminator, *n.* The line separating illuminated and dark portions of a non-self-luminous body, as the moon.

terrace, *n.* On the sea floor, a relatively flat horizontal or gently inclined surface, sometimes long and narrow, which is bounded by a steeper ascending slope on one side and by a steeper descending slope on the opposite side.

terrestrial, *adj.* Of or pertaining to the earth.

terrestrial coordinates. See GEOGRAPHICAL COORDINATES.

terrestrial equator. 1. The earth's equator, 90° from its geographical poles. 2. See ASTRONOMICAL EQUATOR.

terrestrial latitude. Latitude on the earth; angular distance from the equator, measured northward or southward through 90° and labeled N or S to indicate the direction of measurement. See also LATITUDE.

terrestrial longitude. Longitude on the earth, the arc of a parallel, or the angle at the pole, between the prime meridian and the meridian of a point on the earth, measured eastward or westward from the prime meridian through 180°, and labeled E or W to indicate the direction of measurement. See also LONGITUDE.

terrestrial magnetism. See GEOMAGNETISM.

terrestrial meridian. See ASTRONOMICAL MERIDIAN.

terrestrial perturbations. The largest gravitational perturbations of artificial satellites which are caused by the fact that the gravity field of the earth is not spherically symmetrical.

terrestrial pole. One of the poles of the earth. See also GEOGRAPHICAL POLE, GEOMAGNETIC POLE, MAGNETIC POLE.

terrestrial radiation. The total infrared radiation emitted from the earth's surface.

terrestrial refraction. Atmospheric refraction of a ray of radiant energy emanating from a point on or near the surface of the earth, as contrasted with ASTRONOMICAL REFRACTION of a ray passing through the earth's atmosphere from outer space.

terrestrial sphere. The earth.

terrestrial triangle. A triangle on the surface of the earth, especially the navigational triangle.

territorial sea. The zone off the coast of a nation immediately seaward from a base line. Sovereignty is maintained over this coastal zone by the coastal nation, subject to the right of innocent passage to the ships of all nations. The United States recognizes this zone as extending 4.8 kilometers from the base line. See also FISHING ZONE, FISHERY CONSERVATION ZONE.

tertiary tide station. A tide station at which continuous observations have been made over a minimum period of 30 days but less than 1 year. The series is reduced by comparison with simultaneous observations from a secondary control tide station. This station provides for a 29-day harmonic analysis. See also PRIMARY CONTROL TIDE STATION; SECONDARY CONTROL TIDE STATION; SUBORDINATE TIDE STATION, definition 2; TIDE STATION.

tesla, *n.* The derived unit of magnetic flux density in the International System of Units; it is equal to 1 weber per square meter.

Texas norther. See under NORTHER.

textual HO information. In ECDIS, information presently contained in separate publications (e.g. SAILING DIRECTIONS) which may be incorporated in the ENC and also textual information contained in explanatory attributes of specific objects.

thaw holes. Vertical holes in sea ice formed when surface puddles melt through to the underlying water.

thematic map. See TOPICAL MAP.

theoretical error. See under SYSTEMATIC ERROR.

thermocline. A transition layer between warmer mixed water at the ocean's surface and cooler deep water below in which temperature decreases more rapidly with depth than it does in the layers above or below.

thermometer, *n.* An instrument for measuring temperature. A maximum thermometer automatically registers the highest temperature and a minimum thermometer the lowest temperature since the last thermometer setting.

thermostat, *n.* A device for automatically regulating temperature or detecting temperature changes.

thick first-year ice. First-year ice over 120 centimeters thick.

thick weather. Condition of greatly reduced visibility, as by fog, snow, rain, etc.

thin first-year ice. First-year ice 30 to 70 centimeters thick. Also called WHITE ICE.

thin overcast. An overcast sky cover which is predominantly transparent.

thorofare, *n.* This shortened form of thoroughfare has become standard for a natural waterway in marshy areas. It is the same type of feature as a slough or bayou.

thoroughfare, *n.* A public waterway such as a river or strait. See also THOROFARE.

three-arm protractor. An instrument consisting of a circle graduated in degrees, to which is attached one fixed arm and two arms pivoted at the center and provided with clamps so that they can be set at any angle to the fixed arm, within the limits of the instrument. It is used for finding a ship's position when the horizontal angles between three fixed and known points are measured.

three-point problem. From the observation of two horizontal angles between three objects or points of known (charted) positions, to determine the position of the point of observation. The problem is solved graphically by means of the three-arm protractor and analytically by trigonometrical calculation.

threshold signal. The smallest signal capable of being detected above the background noise level.

threshold speed. The minimum speed of current at which a particular current meter will measure at its rated reliability.

thundercloud, *n.* See CUMULONIMBUS.

thunderhead, *n.* See CUMULONIMBUS.

thundersquall, *n.* Strictly, the combined occurrence of a thunderstorm and a squall, the squall usually being associated with the downrush phenomenon typical of a well-developed thunderstorm.

thunderstorm, *n.* A local storm invariably produced by a cumulonimbus cloud and always accompanied by lightning and thunder, usually with strong gusts of wind, heavy rain, and sometimes with hail. It is usually of short duration. Sometimes called ELECTRICAL STORM.

thunderstorm cirrus. See FALSE CIRRUS.

thundery sky. A sky with an overcast and chaotic aspect, a general absence of wind except during showers, a mammatus appearance of the lower clouds, and dense cirrostratus and altocumulus above.

tick, *n.* A short, audible sound or beat, as that of a clock. A time signal in the form of one or more ticks is called a TIME TICK.

tickle, *n.* A narrow channel, as used locally in the Arctic and Newfoundland.

tidal, *adj.* Of or pertaining to tides.

tidal amplitude. One-half the range of a constituent tide.

tidal basin. A basin without a caisson or gate in which the level of water rises and falls with the tides. Also called OPEN BASIN. See also TIDAL HARBOR, NON-TIDAL BASIN.

tidal bench mark. See under BENCH MARK.

tidal bench mark description. A published, concise description of the location, stamped number of designation, date established, and elevation (referred to a tidal datum) of a specific bench mark.

tidal bench mark state index map. A state map which indicates the locations for which tidal datums and tidal bench mark descriptions are available.

tidal bore. A tidal wave that propagates up a relatively shallow and sloping estuary or river in a solitary wave. The leading edge presents an abrupt rise in level, frequently with continuous breaking and often immediately followed by several large undulations. An uncommon phenomenon, the tidal bore is usually associated with very large ranges in tide as well as wedge-shaped and rapidly shoaling entrances. Also called EAGRE, EAGER, MASCARET, POROROCA, BORE.

tidal constants. Tidal relations that remain practically constant for any particular locality. Tidal constants are classified as harmonic and nonharmonic. The harmonic constants consist of the amplitudes and epochs of the harmonic constituents, and the nonharmonic constants include the ranges and intervals derived directly from the high and low water observations.

tidal constituent. See CONSTITUENT.

tidal current. A horizontal movement of the water caused by gravitational interactions between the sun, moon, and earth. The horizontal component of the particulate motion of a tidal wave. Part of the same general movement of the sea that is manifested in the vertical rise and fall, called tide. Also called TIDAL STREAM. See also CURRENT, TIDAL WAVE, TIDE.

tidal current charts. 1. Charts on which tidal current data are depicted graphically. 2. *Tidal Current Chart,* as published by the National Ocean Survey, part of a set of charts which depict, by means of arrows and figures, the direction and velocity of the tidal current for each hour of the tidal cycle. The charts, which may be used for any year, present a comprehensive view of the tidal current movement in the respective waterways as a whole and also supply a means for readily determining for any time the direction and velocity of the current at various localities throughout the water area covered.

tidal current constants. See CURRENT CONSTANTS.

tidal current diagrams. Monthly diagrams which are used with tidal current charts to provide a convenient method to determine the current flow on a particular day.

tidal current station. See CURRENT STATION.

tidal current tables. 1. Tables which give the predicted times of slack water and the predicted times and velocities of maximum current flood and ebb for each day of the year at a number of reference stations, together with time differences and velocity ratios for obtaining predictions at subordinate stations. 2. *Tidal Current Tables,* published annually by the National Ocean Survey.

tidal cycle. A complete set of tidal conditions as those occurring during a tidal day, lunar month, or Metonic cycle.

tidal datum. See VERTICAL DATUM.

tidal day. See LUNAR DAY, definition 1.

tidal difference. Difference in time or height of a high or low water at a subordinate station and at a reference station for which predictions are given in the *Tide Tables*. The difference, when applied according to sign to the prediction at the reference station, gives the corresponding time or height for the subordinate station.

tidal epoch. See EPOCH, definition 3.

tidal estuary. See under ESTUARY, definition 1.

tidal flats. See FLAT.

tidal harbor. A harbor affected by the tides, distinct from a harbor in which the water level is maintained by caissons or gates. See also NON-TIDAL BASIN.

tidal lights. Lights shown at the entrance of a harbor, to indicate tide and tidal current conditions within the harbor.

tidal lock. See ENTRANCE LOCK.

tidal marsh. Any marsh the surface of which is covered and uncovered by tidal flow. See also FLAT.

tidal platform ice foot. An ice foot between high and low water levels, produced by the rise and fall of the tide.

tidal quay. A quay in an open harbor or basin with sufficient depth alongside to enable ships lying alongside to remain afloat at any state of the tide.

tidal range. See RANGE OF TIDE.

tidal rise. See RISE OF TIDE.

tidal stream. See TIDAL CURRENT.

tidal water. Any water subject to tidal action. See also TIDEWATER.

tidal wave. 1. A wave caused by the gravitational interactions between the sun, moon and earth. Essentially, high water is the crest of a tidal wave and low water is the trough. Tide is the vertical component of the particulate motion and tidal current is the horizontal component. The observed tide and tidal current can be considered the result of the combination of several tidal waves, each of which may vary from nearly pure progressive to nearly pure standing and with differing periods, heights, phase relationships, and directions. 2. Any unusually high and destructive water level along a shore. It usually refers to either a storm surge or tsunami.

tide, *n*. The periodic rise and fall of the water resulting from gravitational interactions between the sun, moon, and earth. The vertical component of the particulate motion of a tidal wave. Although the accompanying horizontal movement of the water is part of the same phenomenon, it is preferable to designate this motion as TIDAL CURRENT. See also TIDAL WAVE definition 1.

tide-bound, *adj*. Unable to proceed because of insufficient depth of water due to tidal action.

tide crack. A crack at the line of junction between an immovable icefoot or ice wall and fast ice the latter subject to rise and fall of the tide.

tide curve. A graphic representation of the rise and fall of the tide in which time is usually represented by the abscissa and height by the ordinate of the graph. For a normal tide the graphic representation approximates a cosine curve. See also MARIGRAM.

tide datum. See VERTICAL DATUM.

tide gage. An instrument for measuring the rise and fall of the tide. See also AUTOMATIC TIDE GAGE, ELECTRIC TAPE GAGE, PRESSURE GAGE, TIDE STAFF.

tide gate. 1. A restricted passage through which water runs with great speed due to tidal action. 2. An opening through which water may flow freely when the tide sets in one direction, but which closes automatically and prevents the water from flowing in the other direction when the direction of flow is reversed.

tidehead, *n*. Inland limit of water affected by a tide.

tide hole. A hole made in ice to observe the height of the tide.

tide indicator. The part of a tide gage which indicates the height of tide at any time. The indicator may be in the immediate vicinity of the tidal water or at some distance from it.

tideland, *n*. Land which is under water at high tide and uncovered at low tide.

tidemark, *n*. 1. A high water mark left by tidal water. 2. The highest point reached by a high tide. 3. A mark placed to indicate the highest point reached by a high tide, or, occasionally, any specified state of tide.

tide notes. Notes included on nautical charts which give information on the mean range or the diurnal range of the tide, mean tide level, and extreme low water at key places on the chart.

tide pole. A graduated spar used for measuring the rise and fall of the tide. Also called TIDE STAFF.

tide pool. A pool left by an ebb tide.

tide predicting machine. A mechanical analog machine especially designed to handle the great quantity of constituent summations required in the harmonic method. William Ferrel's Maxima and Minima Tide Predictor was the first such machine used in the United States. Summing only 19 constituents, but giving direct readings of the predicted times and heights of the high and low waters, the Ferrel machine was used for the predictions of 1885 through 1914. A second machine was used for the predictions of 1912 through 1965. Predictions are now prepared using a computer.

tide-producing force. The part of the gravitational attraction of the moon and sun which is effective in producing the tides on the earth. The force varies approximately as the mass of the attracting body and inversely as the cube of its distance. The tide-producing force exerted by the sun is a little less than one-half as great as that of the moon.

tide producing potential. Tendency for particles on the earth to change their positions as a result of the gravitational interactions between the sun, moon, and earth. Although the gravitational attraction varies inversely as the square of the distance of the tide-producing body, the resulting potential varies inversely as the cube of the distance.

tide race. A very rapid tidal current through a comparatively narrow channel. Also called RACE.

tide rips. Small waves formed on the surface of water by the meeting of opposing tidal currents or by a tidal current crossing an irregular bottom. Vertical oscillation, rather than progressive waves, is characteristic of tide rips. See also RIPS.

tide rode. The condition of a ship at anchor heading into the tidal current. See also WIND RODE.

tide signals. Signals showing to navigators the state or change of the tide according to a prearranged code, or by direct display on a scale.

tide staff. A tide gage consisting of a vertical graduated staff from which the height of the tide can be read directly. See also ELECTRIC TAPE GAGE.

tide station. The geographic location at which tidal observations are conducted. Also, the facilities used to make tidal observations. These may include a tide house, tide gage, tide staff, and tidal bench marks. See also PRIMARY CONTROL TIDE STATION, SECONDARY CONTROL TIDE STATION, SUBORDINATE TIDE STATION, TERTIARY TIDE STATION.

tide tables. 1. Tables which give the predicted times and heights of high and low water for every day in the year for a number of reference stations, and tidal differences and ratios by which additional predictions can be obtained for subordinate stations. From these values it is possible to interpolate by a simple procedure the height of the tide at any hour of the day. See also TIDAL CURRENT TABLES.

tidewater, *n*. Water affected by tides or sometimes that part of it which covers the tideland. The term is sometimes used broadly to designate the seaboard. See also TIDAL WATER.

tide wave. See TIDAL WAVE, definition 1.

tideway, *n*. A channel through which a tidal current runs.

tilt, *n*. The angle which anything makes with the horizontal.

tilted blocky iceberg. A blocky iceberg which has tilted to present a triangular shape from the side.

tilt correction. The correction due to tilt error.

tilt error. The error introduced in the reading of an instrument when it is tilted, as a marine sextant held so that its frame is not perpendicular to the horizon.

time, *n*. 1. The interval between two events. 2. The date or other designated mark on a time scale. See also TIME SCALE, APPARENT TIME MEAN TIME, SIDEREAL TIME.

time and altitude azimuth. An azimuth determined by solution of the navigational triangle with meridian angle, declination, and altitude given. A TIME AZIMUTH is computed with meridian angle, declination, and latitude given. An ALTITUDE AZIMUTH is computed with altitude, declination, and latitude given.

time azimuth. An azimuth determined by solution of the navigational triangle, with meridian angle, declination, and latitude given. An ALTITUDE AZIMUTH is computed with altitude, declination, and latitude given. A TIME AND ALTITUDE AZIMUTH is computed with meridian angle, declination, and altitude given.

time ball. A visual time signal in the form of a ball. Before the widespread use of radio time signals, time balls were dropped, usually at local noon, from conspicuously-located masts in various ports. The accuracy of the signal was usually controlled by a telegraphic time signal from an observatory.

time base. A motion, of known but not necessarily of constant speed, used for measuring time intervals, particularly the sweep of a cathode-ray tube. In a linear time base the speed is constant in an expanded time base a selected part is of increased speed, and in a delayed time base the start is delayed. See also SWEEP.

time diagram. A diagram in which the celestial equator appears as a circle, and celestial meridians and hour circles as radial lines; used to facilitate solution of time problems and others involving arcs of the celestial equator or angles at the pole, by indicating relations between various quantities involved. Conventionally the relationships are given as viewed from a point over the south pole westward direction being counterclockwise. Also called DIAGRAM ON THE PLANE OF THE CELESTIAL EQUATOR, DIAGRAM ON THE PLANE OF THE EQUINOCTIAL.

time line. A line joining the heads of two vectors which represent successive courses and speeds of a ship in passing from one point to another in a known time via a specified intermediate point.

time meridian. Any meridian used as a reference for reckoning time, particularly a zone or standard meridian.

timepiece, *n*. An instrument for measuring time. See also CHRONOMETER, CLOCK, WATCH.

time scale. A system of assigning dates to events. There are three fundamental scales: Ephemeris Time, time based upon the rotation of the earth, and atomic time or time obtained by counting the cycles of a signal in resonance with certain kinds of atoms. Ephemeris Time (ET), the independent variable in the gravitational theories of the solar system, is the scale used by astronomers as the tabular argument of the precise, fundamental ephemerides of the sun, moon, and planets. Universal Time (UT1), time based on the rotation of the earth, is the scale used by astronomers as the tabular argument for most other ephemerides, e.g., the *Nautical Almanac*. Although ET and UT1 differ in concept, both are determined in arrears from astronomical observations and are extrapolated into the future based on International Atomic Time (TAI). Coordinated Universal Time (UTC) is the scale disseminated by most broadcast time services; it differs from TAI by an integral number of seconds.

time sight. Originally, an observation of the altitude of a celestial body, made for the purpose of determining longitude. Now, the expression is applied primarily to the common method of reducing such an observation.

time signal. An accurate signal marking a specified time or time interval. It is used primarily for determining errors of timepieces; usually sent from an observatory by radio. As defined by the International Telecommunications Union (ITU), a radiocommunication service for the transmission of time signals of stated high precision, intended for general reception.

time switch. A device for lighting or extinguishing a light at predetermined times, controlled by a timing device.

time tick. A time signal consisting of one or more short audible sounds or beats.

time varying object. In ECDIS, an OBJECT which has one or more ATTRIBUTES, the value or values of which vary with time.

time zone. An area in all parts of which the same time is kept. In general, each zone is 15° of longitude in width with the Greenwich meridian (0° longitude) designated as the central meridian of zone 0 and the remaining zones centered on a meridian whose longitude is exactly divisible by 15. The zone boundary may vary considerably to conform to political and geographic boundaries. See also STANDARD TIME.

Tokyo datum. A geodetic datum that has its origin in Tokyo. It is defined in terms of the Bessel ellipsoid and is oriented by means of a single astronomic station. Using triangulation ties through Korea, the Tokyo datum is connected with the Manchurian datum. Unfortunately, since Tokyo is situated on a steep geoidal slope, the single station orientation has resulted in large systematic geoidal separations as the system is extended from its initial point.

tombolo, *n*. An islet and a shoal connecting it to a larger land area.

tombolo

tonnage. A measure of the weight, size or capacity of a vessel. Deadweight tonnage refers to the number of tons of 2240 lbs. that a vessel will carry in salt water loaded to summer marks. It may also be considered the difference between loaded and light displacement tonnage. Displacement tonnage refers to the amount of water displaced by a vessel afloat, and is thus a measure of actual weight. Gross tonnage or gross register tonnage refers to the total measured cubic volume (100 cubic feet per ton of 2240 lbs.), based on varying formulas. Net tonnage or net registered tonnage refers to the gross tonnage minus spaces generally not used for cargo, according to varying formulas. Register tonnage is the tonnage listed on the ship's registration certificate, usually gross and/or net. Cargo tonnage refers to the weight of the cargo, independent of the vessel. Merchant ships are normally referred to by their gross or deadweight tonnage, warships by their displacement tonnage.

tongue, *n*. 1. A projection of the ice edge up to several kilometers in length, caused by wind or current. 2. An elongated extension of flat sea floor into an adjacent higher feature.

topical map. A map portraying a special subject. Also called SPECIAL SUBJECT MAP, THEMATIC MAP.

topmark, *n*. One or more objects of characteristic shape and color placed on top of a beacon or buoy to aid in its identification.

topographical latitude. See GEODETIC LATITUDE.

topographic feature. See under TOPOGRAPHY definition 1.

topographic map. A map which presents the vertical position of features in measurable form as well as their horizontal positions.

topography, *n*. 1. The configuration of the surface of the earth, including its relief and the position of features on it; the earth's natural and physical features collectively. 2. The science of delineation of natural and man-made features of a place or region especially in a way to show their positions and elevations.

topology. In ECDIS and digital data, the set of properties of geometric forms (such as connectivity, neighborhood) which is defined with the DATA MODEL remaining invariant when subject to a continuous transformation.

toponym, *n*. A name applied to a physical or cultural topographic feature. For U.S. Government usage, policies and decisions governing place names on earth are established by the Board on Geographic Names. Also called PLACE NAME.

toponymy, *n*. 1. The study and treatment of toponyms. 2. A body of toponyms.

topple, *n*. 1. The vertical rotation of the spin axis of a gyroscope about the topple axis. 2. The vertical component of real precession or apparent precession, or the algebraic sum of the two. See also DRIFT, *n*. definition 6; TOTAL DRIFT.

topple axis. Of a gyroscope, the horizontal axis perpendicular to the horizontal spin axis, around which topple occurs. See also DRIFT AXIS, SPIN AXIS.

tornado, *n*. A violently rotating column of air, pendant from a cumulonimbus cloud, and nearly always observable as a funnel cloud. On a local scale, it is the most destructive of all atmospheric phenomena. Its vortex, commonly several hundreds of yards in diameter, whirls usually cyclonically with wind speeds estimated at 100 to more than 200 miles per hour. Its general direction of travel is governed by the motion of its parent cloud. Tornadoes occur on all continents, but are most common in Australia and the United States where the average number is 140 to 150 per year. They occur throughout the year and at any time of day, but are most frequent in spring and in middle and late afternoon. In the United States, tornadoes often develop several hundred miles southeast of a deep low centered in the central or north-central states. However, they may appear in any sector of the low, and/or be associated with fronts, instability lines, troughs, and even form within high-pressure ridges. A distinction sometimes is made between cyclonic tornadoes and convective tornadoes, the former occurring within the circulation of a well-developed parent cyclone, and the latter referring to all others. A tornado over water is called WATERSPOUT.

tornado cloud. See FUNNEL CLOUD.

torque, *n*. That which effects or tends to effect rotation or torsion and which is measured by the product of the applied force and the perpendicular distance from the line of action of the force to the axis of rotation.

torrid zone. The region of the earth between the Tropic of Cancer and the Tropic of Capricorn. Also called the TROPICS.

total current. The combination of the tidal and nontidal current. See also CURRENT.

total drift. The algebraic sum of drift due to real precession and that due to apparent precession.

total eclipse. An eclipse in which the entire source of light is obscured.

tower, *n*. A tall, slender structure, which may be charted with a position circle.

towering, *n*. Apparent increase in the vertical dimension of an object near the horizon, due to large inequality of atmospheric refraction in the line of sight to the top and bottom of the object. The opposite is STOOPING.

towing light. A yellow light having the same characteristics as a STERN LIGHT.

trace, *n*. The luminous line resulting from the radial movement of the points of impingement of the electron stream on the face of the cathode-ray tube of a radar indicator. See also SWEEP.

track, *n*. 1. The intended or desired horizontal direction of travel with respect to the earth. The track as expressed in degrees of the compass may be different from the course due to such factors as making allowance for current or sea or steering to resume the TRACK, definition 2. 2. The path of intended travel with respect to the earth as drawn on the chart. Also called INTENDED TRACK, TRACK-LINE. 3. The actual path of a vessel over the ground, such as may be determined by tracking.

track, *v., t*. To follow the movements of an object such as by radar or an optical system.

track angle. See TRACK, definition 1.

track chart. A chart showing recommended, required, or established tracks, and usually indicating turning points, courses, and distances. A distinction is sometimes made between a TRACK CHART and a ROUTE CHART, the latter generally showing less specific information, and sometimes only the area for some distance each side of the great circle or rhumb line connecting two terminals.

tracking, *n*. In the operation of automated radar plotting aids, the process of observing the sequential changes in the position of a target to establish its motion.

track-line, *n*. See TRACK, definition 2.

track made good. The single resultant direction from a point of departure to a point of arrival at any given time. The use of this term to indicate a single resultant direction is preferred to the use of the misnomer course made good. See also COURSE, TRACK.

trade winds. Relatively permanent winds on each side of the equatorial doldrums, blowing from the northeast in the Northern Hemisphere and from the southeast in the Southern Hemisphere. See also ANTI-TRADES.

traffic control signals. Visual signals placed in a harbor or waterway to indicate to shipping the movements authorized or prohibited at the time at which they are shown. Also called DOCKING SIGNALS.

traffic lane. An area of defined limits in which one-way traffic is established. See also TWO-WAY ROUTE, ROUTING SYSTEM.

traffic separation scheme. A routing measure designed for separating opposing streams of traffic in congested areas by the establishment of traffic lanes, precautionary areas, and other measures. See also ROUTING SYSTEM.

train, *v., t*. To control motion in bearing.

training wall. A wall, bank, or jetty, often submerged, built to direct or confine the flow of a river or tidal current.

tramontana, *n*. A northeasterly or northerly wind occurring in winter off the west coast of Italy. It is a fresh wind of the fine weather mistral type.

transceiver, *n*. A combination transmitter and receiver in a single housing, with some components being used by both parts. See also TRANSPONDER.

transducer, *n*. A device that converts one type of energy to another, such as the part of a depth sounder that changes electrical energy into acoustical energy.

transfer, *n*. 1. The distance a vessel moves perpendicular to its initial direction in making a turn of 90° with a constant rudder angle. 2. The distance a vessel moves perpendicular to its initial direction for turns of less than 90°. See also ADVANCE.

transit, *n*. 1. The passage of a celestial body across a celestial meridian, usually called MERIDIAN TRANSIT. 2. The apparent passage of a celestial body across the face of another celestial body or across any point, area, or line. 3. An instrument used by an astronomer to determine the exact instant of meridian transit of a celestial body. 4. A reversing instrument used by a surveyor for accurately measuring horizontal and vertical angles; a theodolite which can be reversed in its supports without being lifted from them.

transit, *v., t*. To cross. In navigation the term is generally used with reference to the passage of a celestial body over a meridian, across the face of another celestial body, or across the reticle of an optical instrument.

TRANSIT, *n*. See NAVY NAVIGATION SATELLITE SYSTEM.

transition buoy. A buoy indicating the transition between the lateral and cardinal systems of buoyage.

transition mark. A navigation mark indicating the transition between the lateral and cardinal systems of marking.

translocation, *n*. The determination of the relative positions of two points by simultaneous Doppler satellite observations from each point.

translunar, *adj*. Of or pertaining to space outside the moon's orbit about the earth.

transmit-receive tube. See as TR TUBE.

transponder, *n*. A component of a secondary radar system capable of accepting the interrogating signal, received from a radar set or interrogator, and in response automatically transmitting a signal which enables the transponder to be identified by the interrogating station. Also called TRANSPONDER BEACON. See also RADAR BEACON, RACON.

transponder beacon. See TRANSPONDER.

transpose, *v., t*. To change the relative place or position of, as to move a term from one side of an equation to the other with a change of sign.

transverse bar. A bar which extends approximately normal to the shoreline.

transverse chart. A chart on a transverse map projection. Also called INVERSE CHART.

transverse cylindrical orthomorphic chart. See TRANSVERSE MERCATOR CHART.

transverse cylindrical orthomorphic projection. See TRANSVERSE MERCATOR MAP PROJECTION.

transverse equator. The plane which is perpendicular to the axis of a transverse map projection. Also called INVERSE EQUATOR. See also FICTITIOUS EQUATOR.

transverse graticule. A fictitious graticule based upon a transverse map projection.

transverse latitude. Angular distance from a transverse equator. Also called INVERSE LATITUDE. See also FICTITIOUS LATITUDE.

transverse longitude. Angular distance between a prime transverse meridian and any given transverse meridian. Also called INVERSE LONGITUDE. See also FICTITIOUS LONGITUDE.

transverse map projection. A map projection with its axis in the plane of the equator.

transverse Mercator chart. A chart on the transverse Mercator projection. Also called TRANSVERSE CYLINDRICAL ORTHOMORPHIC CHART, INVERSE MERCATOR CHART, INVERSE CYLINDRICAL ORTHOMORPHIC CHART. See also MERCATOR CHART.

transverse Mercator map projection. A conformal cylindrical map projection, being in principle equivalent to the regular Mercator map projection turned (transversed) 90° in azimuth. In this projection, the central meridian is represented by a straight line, corresponding to the line which represents the equator on the regular Mercator projection. Neither the geographic meridians (except the central meridian) nor the geodetic parallels (except the equator) are represented by straight lines. Also called INVERSE MERCATOR MAP PROJECTION, TRANSVERSE CYLINDRICAL ORTHOMORPHIC MAP PROJECTION, INVERSE CYLINDRICAL ORTHOMORPHIC MAP PROJECTION. See also MERCATOR MAP PROJECTION.

transverse meridian. A great circle perpendicular to a transverse equator. The reference transverse meridian is called prime transverse meridian. Also called INVERSE MERIDIAN. See also FICTITIOUS MERIDIAN.

transverse parallel. A circle or line parallel to a transverse equator connecting all points of equal transverse latitude. Also called INVERSE PARALLEL. See also FICTITIOUS PARALLEL.

transverse pole. One of the two points 90° from a transverse equator.

transverse rhumb line. A line making the same oblique angle with all fictitious meridians of a transverse Mercator map projection. Transverse parallels and meridians may be considered special cases of the transverse rhumb line. Also called INVERSE RHUMB LINE. See also FICTITIOUS RHUMB LINE.

transverse wave. A wave in which the vibration is perpendicular to the direction of propagation, as in light waves. This is in contrast with a LONGITUDINAL WAVE, in which the vibration is in the direction of propagation.

trapezoid, *n*. A quadrilateral having two parallel sides and two nonparallel sides.

traverse, *n*. A series of directions and distances, such as when a sailing vessel beats into the wind, a steam vessel zigzags, or a surveyor makes measurements for determination of position.

traverse sailing. A method of determining the equivalent course and distance made good by a craft following a track consisting of a series of rhumb lines. The solution is usually made by means of traverse tables.

traverse table. A table giving relative values of various parts of plane right triangles, for use in solving such triangles, particularly in connection with various sailings.

TR box. See TR SWITCH.

trench, *n*. A long, narrow, characteristically very deep and asymmetrical depression of the sea floor, with relatively steep sides. See also TROUGH.

triad, *n*. Three radionavigation stations operated as a group for the determination of positions. Also called TRIPLET. See also STAR CHAIN.

triangle, *n*. A closed figure having three sides. The triangle is plane, spherical, or curvilinear as the sides are straight lines, arcs of great circles, or curves, respectively. See also EQUILATERAL TRIANGLE, ISOSCELES TRIANGLE, NAVIGATIONAL TRIANGLE, RIGHT TRIANGLE.

triangulation, *n*. A method of surveying in which the stations are points on the ground, located on the vertices of a chain or network of triangles. The angles of the triangles are measured instrumentally, and the sides are derived by computation from selected sides which are called BASE LINES, the lengths of which are obtained from direction measurements on the ground. See also TRILATERATION.

triaxial ellipsoid. A reference ellipsoid having three unequal axes; the shortest is the polar axis, and the two longer ones lie in the plane of the equator.

triaxial ellipsoid

tributary. Any body of water that flows into a larger body, i.e., a creek in relation to a river, or a river in relation to a bay.

trigger, *n*. In a radar set, a sharp voltage pulse which is applied to the modulator tubes to fire the transmitter, applied simultaneously to the sweep generator to start the electron beam moving radially from the sweep origin to the edge of the face of the cathode-ray tube.

triggering, *n*. The process of causing a transponder to respond.

trigonometric functions. The ratios of the sides of a plane right triangle, as related to one of its angles. If a is the side opposite an acute angle, b the adjacent side, and c the hypotenuse the trigonometric functions are: sine = a/c, cosine = b/c, tangent = a/b, cotangent = b/a, secant = c/b, cosecant = c/a. The expression NATURAL TRIGONOMETRIC FUNCTION is sometimes used to distinguish a trigonometric function from its logarithm (called LOGARITHMIC TRIGONOMETRIC FUNCTION).

trigonometry. A branch of mathematics dealing with the relations among the angles and sides of triangles.

trihedral reflector. See CORNER REFLECTOR.

trilateration, *n*. A method of surveying wherein the lengths of the triangle sides are measured, usually by electronic methods, and the angles are computed from the measured lengths. See also TRIANGULATION.

trim, *n*. The relation of the draft of a vessel at the bow and stern. See also DOWN BY THE HEAD; DOWN BY THE STERN; DRAG, *n*., definition 3; SQUAT, *n*.

triple interpolation. Interpolation when there are three arguments or variables.

triples, *n*. See TRIAD.

trochoid, *n*. In relation to wave motion, a curve described by a point on a radius of a circle that rolls along a straight line. Also called PROLATE CYCLOID.

tropic, *adj*. Of or pertaining to a tropic or the tropics.

tropic, *n*. Either of the two parallels of declination (north or south), approximately 23°27' from the celestial equator, reached by the sun at its maximum declination, or the corresponding parallels on the earth. The northern of these is called the TROPIC OF CANCER and the southern, the TROPIC OF CAPRICORN. The region of the earth between these two parallels is called the TORRID ZONE, or often the TROPICS.

tropical, *adj*. 1. Of or pertaining to the vernal equinox. See also SIDEREAL. 2. Of or pertaining to the Tropics.

tropical air. Warm air of an air mass originating in subtropical anticyclones, further classified as tropical continental air and tropical maritime air, as it originates over land or sea, respectively.

tropical continental air. Air of an air mass originating over a land area in low latitudes, such as the Sahara desert. Tropical continental air is characterized by high surface temperature and low specific humidity.

tropical cyclone. The general term for cyclones originating in the tropics or subtropics. These cyclones are classified by form and intensity as follows: A tropical disturbance is a discrete system of apparently organized convection generally 100 to 300 miles in diameter, having a nonfrontal migratory character, having maintained its identity for 24 hours or more. It may or may not be associated with a detectable perturbation of the wind field. It has no strong winds and no closed isobars, i.e., isobars that completely enclose the low. In successive stages of intensification, the tropical cyclone are classified as tropical disturbance, tropical depression, tropical storm, and hurricane or typhoon. The tropical depression has one or more closed isobars and some rotary circulation at the surface. The highest sustained (l-minute mean) surface wind speed is 33 knots. The tropical storm has closed isobars and a distinct rotary circulation. The highest sustained (1-minute mean) surface wind speed is

34 to 63 knots. The hurricane or typhoon has closed isobars, a strong and very pronounced rotary circulation, and a sustained (1-minute mean) surface wind speed of 64 knots or higher. Tropical cyclones occur almost entirely in six rather distinct areas, four in the Northern Hemisphere and two in the Southern Hemisphere. The name by which the tropical cyclone is commonly known varies somewhat with locality as follows: North Atlantic: A tropical cyclone with winds of 64 knots or greater is called a HURRICANE. Eastern North Pacific: The name HURRICANE is used as in the North Atlantic. Western North Pacific: A fully developed storm with winds of 64 knots or greater is called a TYPHOON or, locally in the Philippines, a BAGUIO. North Indian Ocean: A tropical cyclone with winds of 34 knots or greater is called a CYCLONIC STORM. South Indian Ocean: A tropical storm with winds of 34 knots or greater is called a CYCLONE. Southwest Pacific and Australian Area: The name CYCLONE is used as in the South Indian Ocean. A severe tropical cyclone originating in the Timor Sea and moving southwestward and then southeastward across the interior of northwestern Australia is called a WILLY-WILLY. Tropical cyclones have not been observed in the South Atlantic Ocean or in the South Pacific Ocean east of longitude 140°W.

tropical depression. See under TROPICAL CYCLONE.

tropical disturbance. See under TROPICAL CYCLONE.

tropical maritime air. Air of an air mass originating over an ocean area in low latitudes. Tropical maritime air is characterized by high surface temperature and high specific humidity.

tropical month. The average period of the revolution of the moon about the earth with respect to the vernal equinox, a period of 27 days, 7 hours, 43 minutes, 4.7 seconds. This is almost the same length as the sidereal month.

tropical storm. See under TROPICAL CYCLONE.

tropical year. The period of one revolution of the earth around the sun, with respect to the vernal equinox. Because of precession of the equinoxes, this is not 360° with respect to the stars, but 50.3" less. A tropical year is about 20 minutes shorter than a sidereal year, averaging 365 days, 5 hours, 48 minutes, and 46 seconds in 1900, decreasing at the rate of 0.00530 second annually. Also called ASTRONOMICAL, EQUINOCTIAL, NATURAL, or SOLAR YEAR.

tropic currents. Tidal currents occurring semimonthly when the effect of the moon's maximum declination is greatest. At these times the tendency of the moon to produce a diurnal inequality in the current is at a maximum.

tropic higher high water. The higher high water of tropic tides. See also TROPIC TIDES.

tropic higher high water interval. The lunitidal interval pertaining to the higher high waters at the time of the tropic tides. See also TROPIC LOWER LOW WATER INTERVAL.

tropic higher low water. The higher low water of tropic tides. See also TROPIC TIDES.

tropic high water inequality. The average difference between the two high waters of the day at the times of the tropic tides. Applicable only when the tide is semidiurnal or mixed. See also TROPIC TIDES, TROPIC LOW WATER INEQUALITY.

tropic inequalities. See TROPIC HIGH WATER INEQUALITY, TROPIC LOW WATER INEQUALITY.

tropic intervals. See TROPIC HIGH WATER INTERVAL, TROPIC LOWER LOW WATER INTERVAL.

tropic lower high water. The lower high water of tropic tides. See also TROPIC TIDES.

tropic lower low water. The lower low water of tropic tides. See also TROPIC TIDES.

tropic lower low water interval. The lunitidal interval pertaining to the lower low waters at the time of tropic tides. See also TROPIC HIGHER HIGH WATER INTERVAL.

tropic low water inequality. The average difference between the two low waters of the day at the times of the tropic tides. Applicable only when the type of tide is semidiurnal or mixed. See also TROPIC TIDES, TROPIC HIGH WATER INEQUALITY.

Tropic of Cancer. The northern parallel of declination, approximately 23°27' from the celestial equator, reached by the sun at its maximum northerly declination, or the corresponding parallel on the earth. It is named for the sign of the zodiac in which the sun reached its maximum northerly declination at the time the parallel was so named.

Tropic of Capricorn. The southern parallel of declination, approximately 23°27' from the celestial equator, reached by the sun at its maximum southerly declination, or the corresponding parallel on the earth. It is named for the sign of the zodiac in which the sun reached its maximum southerly declination at the time the parallel was so named.

tropic ranges. See GREAT TROPIC RANGE, MEAN TROPIC RANGE, SMALL TROPIC RANGE.

tropics, *n*. See TORRID ZONE.

tropic speed. The greater flood or greater ebb speed at the time of tropic currents.

tropic tides. Tides occurring semimonthly when the effect of the moon's maximum declination is greatest. At these times there is a tendency for an increase in the diurnal range. The tidal datums pertaining to the tropic tides are designated as tropic higher high water, tropic lower high water, tropic higher low water, and tropic lower low water.

tropopause, *n*. The boundary between the troposphere and the stratosphere.

troposphere, *n*. The portion of the atmosphere from the earth's surface to the tropopause, i.e., the lowest 10 to 20 kilometers of the atmosphere. It is characterized by decreasing temperature with height, appreciable vertical wind motion, appreciable water vapor content, and variable weather.

tropospheric radio duct. A quasi-horizontal layer in the troposphere between the boundaries of which radio energy of sufficiently high frequency is substantially confined and propagated with abnormally low attenuation. The duct may be formed in the lower portion of the atmosphere when there is a marked temperature inversion or a sharp decrease in water vapor with increased height. See also SURFACE DUCT, ELEVATED DUCT.

tropospheric wave. A radio wave traveling between points on or near the surface of the earth by one or more paths lying wholly within the troposphere. The propagation of this wave is determined primarily by the distribution of the refractive index in the troposphere.

trough, *n*. 1. A long depression of the sea floor, characteristically flat bottomed and steep sided, and normally shallower than a trench. 2. In meteorology, an elongated area of relatively low pressure. The opposite of a trough is called RIDGE. The term trough is commonly used to distinguish the above elongated area from the closed circulation of a low (or cyclone). But a large-scale trough may include one or more lows. 3. The lowest part of a wave between two crests.

TR switch *(from transmit/receive)*. A switch used to automatically decouple the receiver from the antenna during transmission when there is a common transmitting and receiving antenna. Also called TR BOX.

TR tube. An electronic switch capable of rapid switching between transmit and receive functions, used to protect the receiver from damage from energy generated by the transmitter. Another device called the anti-TR tube is used to block the passage of echoes to the receiver during the relatively long periods when the transmitter is inactive. See also TR SWITCH, ATR TUBE.

true, *adj*. 1. Related to true north. 2. Actual, as contrasted with fictitious, such as the true sun. 3. Related to a fixed point, either on the earth or in space, such as true wind, in contrast with RELATIVE, which is related to a moving point. 4. Corrected, as in the term true altitude.

true altitude. See OBSERVED ALTITUDE.

true amplitude. Amplitude relative to true east or west.

true anomaly. See under ANOMALY, definition 2.

true azimuth. Azimuth relative to true north.

true bearing. Bearing relative to true north; compass bearing corrected for compass error.

true course. Course relative to true north.

true direction. Horizontal direction expressed as angular distance from true north.

true heading. Heading relative to true north.

true meridian. A meridian through the geographical pole; compare with MAGNETIC MERIDIAN, COMPASS MERIDIAN, or GRID MERIDIAN, the north-south lines according to magnetic, compass, or grid direction, respectively.

true motion display. 1. A type of radarscope display in which own ship and other moving targets move on the plan position indicator in accordance with their true courses and speeds. All fixed targets appear as stationary echoes. However, uncompensated set and drift of own ship may result in some movement of the echoes of stationary targets. This display is similar to a navigational (geographical) plot. 2. In ECDIS, a DISPLAY in which OWN SHIP and each target moves with its own true motion, while the position of all charted information remains fixed. See also RELATIVE MOTION DISPLAY.

true motion radar. A radar set which provides a true motion display as opposed to the relative motion display most commonly used. The true motion radar requires own ship's speed input, either log or manual, in addition to own ship's course input.

true north. The direction of the north geographical pole; the reference direction for measurement of true directions.

true plot. See GEOGRAPHICAL PLOT.

true prime vertical. See under PRIME VERTICAL CIRCLE.

true solar time. See APPARENT TIME.

true sun. The actual sun as it appears in the sky. Usually called APPARENT SUN. See also MEAN SUN, DYNAMICAL MEAN SUN.

true track of target. The motion of a radar target on a true motion display. When the true motion display is ground stabilized, i.e., allowance is made for the set and drift of current, the motion displayed is called GROUND TRACK. Without such stabilization the motion displayed is called WATER TRACK.

true wind. Wind relative to a fixed point on the earth. Wind relative to a moving point is called APPARENT or RELATIVE WIND.

trumpet, *n*. See HORN.

tsunami, *n*. A long-period sea wave, potentially catastrophic, produced by a submarine earthquake or volcanic eruption. It may travel unnoticed across the ocean for thousands of miles from its point of origin, building up to great heights over shoal water. Also called SEISMIC SEA WAVE, TIDAL WAVE.

Tsushima Current. That part of the Kuroshio flowing northeastward through Korea Strait and along the Japanese coast in the Japan Sea; it flows strongly eastward through Tsugaru Strait at speeds to 7 knots. The Tsushima Current is strong most of the time, averaging about 1 knot; however, it may weaken somewhat during autumn. In Western Channel, between Tsushima and southeastern Korea, tidal currents retard the general northeastward flowing Tsushima Current during the southwest-setting flood and reinforce it during the northeast-setting ebb. Resultant current speeds range from 1/4 knot during flood to 3 knots during ebb. In the strait between Tsushima and Kyushu, the current flows northeastward throughout the year. Current speeds in Korea Strait also are affected by the seasonal variations of the monsoons. The strongest currents usually occur from July through November. The Tsushima Current divides after flowing through Korea Strait, a small branch flowing northward along the east coast of Korea as far as Vladivostok in summer. During this season the current is strongest and overcomes the weak southward flowing, coastal Liman Current. When the current combines with the ebb current, the resultant speed may reach 2 knots. During winter this branch of the Tsushima Current is weakest and is influenced by the stronger southward flowing Liman Current which normally extends as far south as 39°N, with speeds from 1/4 to 3/4 knot. The main body of the Tsushima Current flows northeastward off the northeast coast of Honshu. In summer, after entering the Japan Sea, its speed is about 1/2 to 1 knot. In winter the current is relatively weak, although near the islands and headlands speeds may exceed 1 knot, especially after northwesterly gales.

tuba, *n*. See FUNNEL CLOUD.

tufa, *n*. A porous rocky deposit formed in streams and in the ocean near the mouths of rivers.

tumble, *v., i*. The tendency of a gyroscope to precess suddenly and to an extreme extent as a result of exceeding its operating limits of bank or pitch.

tune, *v., t*. To adjust the frequency of a circuit or system to obtain optimum performance, commonly to adjust to resonance.

turbidity, *n*. A measure of the amount of suspended material in water.

turbulent, *n*. Agitated or disturbed fluid motion, not flowing smoothly or uniformly.

turbulent flow. Fluid motion in which random motions of parts of the fluid are superimposed upon a simple pattern of flow. All or nearly all fluid flow displays some degree of turbulence. The opposite is STREAMLINE FLOW.

turning basin. A water area, usually dredged to well-defined limits, used for turning vessels.

turning buoy. A buoy marking a turn in a channel.

turning circle. The path described by the pivot point of the vessel as it makes a turn of 360° with constant rudder and speed.

turn of the tide. See CHANGE OF TIDE.

twenty-four hour satellite. See GEOSYNCHRONOUS SATELLITE.

twilight, *n*. The period of incomplete darkness following sunset (evening twilight) or preceding sunrise (morning twilight). Twilight is designated as civil, nautical, or astronomical, as the darker limit occurs when the center of the sun is 6°, 12°, or 18° below the celestial horizon, respectively. See also DAWN, DUSK.

twinkle, *v., i*. To flicker randomly, or vary in intensity.

two-body orbit. The motion of a point mass in the presence of the gravitational attraction of another point mass, and in the absence of other forces. This orbit is usually an ellipse, but may be a parabola or hyperbola.

two-degree-of-freedom gyro. A gyroscope the spin axis of which is free to rotate about two orthogonal axes, not counting the spin axis. See also DEGREE-OF-FREEDOM.

two-tone diaphone. See under DIAPHONE.

two-way route. A route within defined limits in which two-way traffic is established, aimed at providing safe passage of ships through waters where navigation is difficult or dangerous. See also ROUTING SYSTEM.

tyfon, *n*. See TYPHON.

type of tide. A classification based on characteristic forms of a tide curve. Qualitatively, when the two high waters and two low waters of each tidal day are approximately equal in height, the tide is said to be semidiurnal; when there is a relatively large diurnal inequality in the high or low waters or both, it said to be mixed; and when there is only one high water and one low water in each tidal day, it is said to be diurnal.

typhon, *n*. A diaphragm horn which operates under the influence of compressed air or steam. Also called TYFON.

typhoon, *n*. See under TROPICAL CYCLONE.

U

Ulloa's ring. See BOUGUER'S HALO.

ultra high frequency. Radio frequency of 300 to 3,000 megahertz.

ultra quick light. A navigation light flashing at a rate of not less than 160 flashes per minute. See also CONTINUOUS ULTRA QUICK LIGHT, INTERRUPTED ULTRA QUICK LIGHT.

ultrashort wave. A radio wave shorter than 10 meters. A wave shorter than 1 meter is called a MICROWAVE. See also WAVE.

ultrasonic, *adj*. Having a frequency above the audible range. Frequencies below the audible range are called INFRASONIC. See also SUPERSONIC.

ultrasonic depth finder. A direct-reading instrument which determines the depth of water by measuring the time interval between the emission of an ultrasonic signal and the return of its echo from the bottom. A similar instrument utilizing signals within the audible range is called a SONIC DEPTH FINDER. Both instruments are also called ECHO SOUNDERS.

umbra, *n*. 1. The darkest part of a shadow in which light is completely cut off by an intervening object. A lighter part surrounding the umbra, in which the light is only partly cut off, is called the PENUMBRA. 2. The darker central portion of a sun spot, surrounded by the lighter PENUMBRA.

uncorrecting, *n*. The process of converting true to magnetic, compass, or gyro direction, or magnetic to compass direction. The opposite is CORRECTING.

uncovered, *adj. & adv*. Above water. The opposite is SUBMERGED. See also AFLOAT; AWASH.

undercurrent, *n*. A current below the surface, particularly one flowing in a direction or at a speed differing from the surface current. See UNDERTOW, SUBSURFACE CURRENT, SURFACE CURRENT.

underscale. In ECDIS, the condition where data displayed is not the largest scale NAVIGATIONAL PURPOSE data available for that area.

under the lee. To leeward.

undertow, *n*. Receding water below the surface of breakers on a beach. See also UNDERCURRENT, SUBSURFACE CURRENT, SURFACE CURRENT, BACKRUSH, RIP CURRENT.

underway, under way, *adv*. Not moored or anchored. See also ADRIFT. See also MAKING WAY.

undevelopable, *adj*. A surface not capable of being flattened without distortion. The opposite is DEVELOPABLE.

undisturbed orbit. See NORMAL ORBIT.

undulating, *adj*. Having the form of more or less regular waves.

undulating light. See under FIXED AND FLASHING LIGHT.

undulation of the geoid. See GEOIDAL HEIGHT.

undulatus, *adj*. Having undulations, referring to a cloud composed of elongated and parallel elements resembling ocean waves.

undulatus

unfavorable current. A current flowing in such a direction as to decrease the speed of a vessel over the ground. The opposite is FAVORABLE CURRENT.

unfavorable wind. A wind which delays the progress of a craft in a desired direction. Usually used in plural and chiefly in connection with sailing vessels. A wind which aids the progress of a craft is called a FAIR or FAVORABLE WIND. See also FOLLOWING WIND, HEAD WIND.

Uniform State Waterway Marking System. An aids to navigation system developed jointly by the U.S. Coast Guard and state boating administrators to assist the small craft operator in inland state waters marked by states. It consists of two categories of aids to navigation. One is a system of aids to navigation, generally compatible with the Federal lateral system of buoyage, to supplement the federal system in state waters The other is a system of regulatory markers to warn the small craft operator of dangers or to provide general information and directions.

unipole antenna, *n*. See ISOTROPIC ANTENNA.

unique sanctuary. A marine sanctuary established to protect a unique geologic, oceanographic, or living feature. See also MARINE SANCTUARY.

unit, *n*. A value, quantity, or magnitude in terms of which other values, quantities, or magnitudes are expressed. In general, a unit is fixed by definition and is independent of such physical conditions as temperature. See also STANDARD, definition 2; INTERNATIONAL SYSTEM OF UNITS.

United States Coast Pilot. One of a series of SAILING DIRECTIONS published by the National Ocean Service, that cover a wide variety of information important to navigators of U.S. coastal and intracoastal waters, and waters of the Great Lakes. Most of this information cannot be shown graphically on the standard nautical charts and is not readily available elsewhere. This information includes navigation regulations, outstanding landmarks, channel and anchorage peculiarities, dangers, weather, ice, currents, and port facilities. Each *Coast Pilot* is corrected through the dates of *Notices to Mariners* shown on the title page and should not be used without reference to the *Notices to Mariners* issued subsequent to those dates.

United States National Map Accuracy Standards. A set of standards which define the accuracy with which features of U.S. maps are to be portrayed. 1. Horizontal accuracy: For maps at publication scales larger than 1:20,000, 90 percent of all well-defined features, with the exception of those unavoidably displaced by exaggerated symbolization, will be located within 0.85 mm of their geographic positions as referred to the map projection; for maps at publication scales of 1:20,000 or smaller, 0.50 mm. 2. Vertical accuracy: 90 percent of all contours will be accurate within one-half of the basic contour interval. Discrepancies in the accuracy of contours and elevations beyond this tolerance may be decreased by assuming a horizontal displacement within 0.50 mm. Also called MAP ACCURACY STANDARDS.

universal plotting sheet. See under SMALL AREA PLOTTING SHEET.

Universal Polar Stereographic grid. A military grid system based on the polar stereographic map projection, applied to maps of the earth's polar regions north of 84°N and south of 80°S.

Universal Time. Conceptually, time as determined from the apparent diurnal motion of a fictitious mean sun which moves uniformly along the celestial equator at the average rate of the apparent sun. Actually, Universal Time (UT) is related to the rotation of the earth through its definition in terms of sidereal time. Universal Time at any instant is derived from observations of the diurnal motions of the stars. The time scale determined directly from such observations is slightly dependent on the place of observation; this scale is designated UT0. By removing from UT0 the effect of the variation of the observer's meridian due to the observed motion of the geographic pole, the scale UT1 is established. A scale designated UT2 results from applying to UT1 an adopted formula for the seasonal variation in the rate of the earth's rotation. UT1 and UT2 are independent of the location of the observer. UT1 is the same as Greenwich mean time used in navigation. See also TIME SCALE.

Universal Transverse Mercator (UTM) grid. A military grid system based on the transverse Mercator map projection, applied to maps of the earth's surface extending to 84°N and 80°S.

unlighted buoy. A buoy not fitted with a light, whose shape and color are the defining features; may have a sound signal.

unlighted sound buoy. See under SOUND BUOY.

unmanned light. A light which is operated automatically and may be maintained in service automatically for extended periods of time, but with routine visits for maintenance purposes. Also called UNWATCHED LIGHT.

unperturbed orbit. See NORMAL ORBIT.

unsettled, *adj*. Pertaining to fair weather which may at any time become rainy, cloudy, or stormy. See also SETTLED.

unstabilized display. A radarscope display in which the orientation of the relative motion presentation is set to the ship's heading and changes with it.

unstabilized in azimuth. See under STABILIZATION OF RADARSCOPE DISPLAY.

unwatched light. See UNMANNED LIGHT.

update. See UPDATE INFORMATION. (Verb) applying the UPDATE MECHANISM. See also OFFICIAL UPDATES.

update information. In ECDIS, the data which is needed to update the TARGET DATA automatically. Update information is comprised of one or more UPDATE RECORDS.

update mechanism. In ECDIS, the defined sequence of update operations necessary to update the TARGET DATA by applying the UPDATE INFORMATION to the content of the TARGET DATA so that no operator interaction is involved.

update record. In ECDIS, a generic term for FEATURE or SPATIAL RECORDS containing update instructions.

upper branch. That half of a meridian or celestial meridian from pole to pole which passes through a place or its zenith.

upper culmination. See UPPER TRANSIT.

upper limb. The upper edge of a celestial body, in contrast with the LOWER LIMB, the lower edge.

upper transit. Transit of the upper branch of the celestial meridian. Transit of the lower branch is called LOWER TRANSIT. Also called SUPERIOR TRANSIT, UPPER CULMINATION.

uprush, *n*. 1. The rush of the water onto the foreshore following the breaking of a wave. 2. See RUN-UP.

upstream, *adj*. & *adv*. Toward the source of a stream. The opposite is DOWNSTREAM.

up-the-scope echo. See CLASSIFICATION OF RADAR ECHOES.

upwelling, *n*. The process by which water rises from a lower to a higher depth, usually as a result of divergence and offshore currents. Upwelling is most prominent where persistent wind blows parallel to a coastline so that the resultant wind-driven current sets away from the coast. Over the open ocean, upwelling occurs whenever the wind circulation is cyclonic, but is appreciable only in areas where that circulation is relatively permanent. It is also observable when the southern trade winds cross the equator.

upwind, *adj*. & *adv*. In the direction from which the wind is blowing. The opposite is DOWNWIND.

U.S. Survey foot. The foot used by the National Ocean Service in which 1 inch is equal to 2.540005 centimeters. The foot equal to 0.3048 meter, exactly, adopted by Australia, Canada, New Zealand, South Africa, the United Kingdom, and the United States in 1959 was not adopted by the National Ocean Service because of the extensive revisions which would be necessary to their charts and measurement records.

UTC, *n*. See under COORDINATED UNIVERSAL TIME.

UT0., *n.* See under UNIVERSAL TIME.

UT1., *n.* See under UNIVERSAL TIME.

UT2., *n.* See under UNIVERSAL. TIME.

V

vacuum., *n.* A space containing no matter.

valley., *n.* On the sea floor, a relatively shallow, wide depression, the bottom of which usually has a continuous gradient. This term is generally not used for features that have canyon-like characteristics for a significant portion of their extent.

valley breeze. . A gentle wind blowing up a valley or mountain slope in the absence of cyclonic or anticyclonic winds, caused by the warming of the mountainside and valley floor before the sun. See also KATABATIC WIND, MOUNTAIN BREEZE.

Van Allen Radiation Belts. . Popular term for regions of high energy charged particles trapped in the earth's magnetic field. Definition of size and shape of these belts depends on selection of an arbitrary standard of radiation intensity and the predominant particle component. Belts known to exist are: a proton region centered at about 2,000 miles altitude at the geomagnetic equator; an electron region centered at about 12,000 miles altitude at the geomagnetic equator; overlapping electron and proton regions centered at about 20,000 miles altitude at the geomagnetic equator. Trapped radiation regions from artificial sources also exist. These belts were first reported by Dr. James A. Van Allen of Iowa State University.

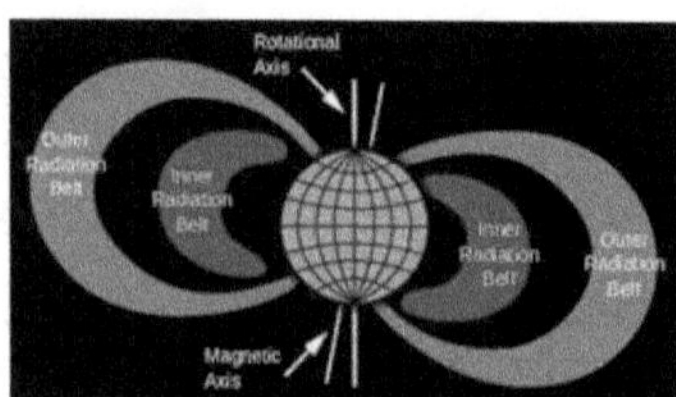

Van Allen Radiation Belt

vane., *n.* 1. A device to sense or indicate the direction from which the wind blows. Also called WEATHER VANE, WIND VANE. See also ANEMOMETER. 2. A sight on an instrument used for observing bearings, as on a pelorus, azimuth circle, etc. That vane nearest the observer's eye is called near vane and that on the opposite side is called far vane. Also called SIGHTING VANE. 3. In current measurements, a device to indicate the direction toward which the current flows.

vanishing tide. . In a mixed tide with very large diurnal inequality, the lower high water (or higher low water) frequently becomes indistinct (or vanishes) at time of extreme declinations. During these periods the diurnal tide has such overriding dominance that the semidiurnal tide, although still present, cannot be readily seen on the tide curve.

vapor pressure. . 1. The pressure exerted by the vapor of a volatile liquid. Each component of a mixed-gas vapor has its own pressure, called partial pressure.

vardar., *n.* A cold fall wind blowing from the northwest down the Vardar valley in Greece to the Gulf of Salonica. It occurs when atmospheric pressure over eastern Europe is higher than over the Aegean Sea, as is often the case in winter. Also called VARDARAC.

vardarac., *n.* See VARDAR.

variable., *n.* A quantity to which a number of values can be assigned.

variable parameters of satellite orbit. . See under FIXED AND VARIABLE PARAMETERS OF SATELLITE ORBIT.

variable range marker. An adjustable range ring on the radar display.

variable star. A star which is not of constant magnitude.

variance, *n.* The square of the standard deviation.

variation, *n.* 1. The angle between the magnetic and geographic meridians at any place, expressed in degrees and minutes east or west to indicate the direction of magnetic north from true north. The angle between magnetic and grid meridians is called GRID MAGNETIC ANGLE, GRID VARIATION, or GRIVATION. Called MAGNETIC VARIATION when a distinction is needed to prevent possible ambiguity. Also called MAGNETIC DECLINATION. 2. Change or difference from a given value.

variation of latitude. A small change in the astronomical latitude of points on the earth due to polar motion.

variation of the poles. See POLAR MOTION.

variometer, *n.* An instrument for comparing magnetic forces, especially of the earth's magnetic field.

vast floe. See under FLOE.

V-band. A radio-frequency band of 46.0 to 56.0 kilomegahertz. See also FREQUENCY, FREQUENCY BAND.

vector, *n.* Any quantity, such as a force, velocity, or acceleration, which has both magnitude and direction, as opposed to a SCALAR which has magnitude only. Such a quantity may be represented geometrically by an arrow of length proportional to its magnitude, pointing in the given direction.

vector, *adj.* A type of computerized display which consists of layers of differentiated data, each with discreet features. Individual data files can be independently manipulated. See RASTER, BIT-MAP.

vector addition. The combining of two or more vectors in such manner as to determine the equivalent single vector. The opposite is RESOLUTION OF VECTORS. Also called COMPOSITION OF VECTORS.

vector diagram. A diagram of more than one vector drawn to the same scale and reference direction and in correct position relative to each other. A vector diagram composed of vectors representing the actual courses and speeds of two craft and the relative motion vector of either one in relation to the other may be called a SPEED TRIANGLE.

vector quantity. A quantity having both magnitude and direction and hence capable of being represented by a vector. A quantity having magnitude only is called a SCALAR.

veer, *v., i.* 1. For the wind to change direction in a clockwise direction in the Northern Hemisphere and a counterclockwise direction in the Southern Hemisphere. Change in the opposite direction is called BACK. 2. Of the wind, to shift aft. The opposite motion is to HAUL forward.

veer, *v., t.* To pay or let out, as to veer anchor chain.

vehicle location monitoring. A service provided to maintain the orderly and safe movement of platforms or vehicles. It encompasses the systematic observation of airspace, surface, or subsurface areas by electronic, visual, and other means to locate, identify, and control the movement of vehicles.

velocity, *n.* A vector quantity equal to speed in a given direction.

velocity meter. See INTEGRATING ACCELEROMETER.

velocity of current. Speed and set of the current.

velocity ratio. The ratio of two speeds, particularly the ratio of the speed of tidal current at a subordinate station to the speed of the corresponding current at the reference station.

Venus, *n.* The planet whose orbit is next nearer the sun than that of the earth.

verglas, *n.* See GLAZE.

vernal, *adj.* Pertaining to spring. The corresponding adjectives for summer, fall, and winter are aestival, autumnal, and hibernal.

vernal equinox. 1. The point of intersection of the ecliptic and the celestial equator, occupied by the sun as it changes from south to north declination, on or about March 21. Also called MARCH EQUINOX, FIRST POINT OF ARIES. 2. That instant the sun reaches the point of zero declination when crossing the celestial equator from south to north.

vernier, *n.* A short, auxiliary scale situated alongside the graduated scale of an instrument, by which fractional parts of the smallest division of the primary scale can be measured with greater accuracy by a factor of ten. If 10 graduations on a vernier equal 9 graduations on the micrometer drum of a sextant, when the zero on the vernier lies one-tenth of a graduation beyond zero on the micrometer drum, the first graduation beyond zero on the vernier coincides with a graduation on the micrometer drum. Likewise, when the zero on the vernier lies five-tenths of a graduation beyond zero on the micrometer drum, the fifth graduation beyond zero on the vernier coincides with a graduation on the micrometer drum.

vernier error. Inaccuracy in the graduations of the scale of a vernier.

vernier sextant. A marine sextant providing a precise reading by means of a vernier used directly with the arc, and having either a clamp screw or an endless tangent screw for controlling the position of the index arm. The micrometer drum on a micrometer drum sextant may include a vernier to enable a more precise reading.

vertex. *(pl. vertices), n.* 1. The highest point. See also APEX. 2. The point at which tow lines meet to form an angle.

vertical. , *adj.* In the direction of gravity, or perpendicular to the plane of the horizon.

vertical. , *n.* A vertical line, plane, etc.

vertical axis. . The line through the center of gravity of a craft, perpendicular to both the longitudinal and lateral axes, around which it yaws.

vertical beam width. . The beam width measured in a vertical plane.

vertical circle. . A great circle of the celestial sphere through the zenith and nadir. Vertical circles are perpendicular to the horizon. The prime vertical circle or prime vertical passes through the east and west points of the horizon. The principal vertical circle passes through the north and south points of the horizon and coincides with the celestial meridian.

vertical control datum. . See VERTICAL GEODETIC DATUM.

vertical danger angle. . The maximum or minimum angle between the top and bottom of an object of known height, as observed from a craft, indicating the limit of safe approach to an offlying danger. See also DANGER ANGLE.

vertical datum. . 1. A base elevation used as a reference from which to reckon heights or depths. It is called TIDAL DATUM when defined by a certain phase of the tide. Tidal datums are local datums and should not be extended into areas which have differing topographic features without substantiating measurements. In order that they may be recovered when needed, such datums are referenced to fixed points known as bench marks. See also CHART SOUNDING DATUM. 2. See VERTICAL GEODETIC DATUM.

vertical earth rate. . To compensate for the effect of earth rate, the rate at which a gyroscope must be turned about its vertical axis for the spin axis to remain in the meridian. Vertical earth rate is maximum at the poles, zero at the equator and varies as the sine of the latitude. See also EARTH RATE, HORIZONTAL EARTH RATE.

vertical force instrument. . See HEELING ADJUSTER.

vertical geodetic datum. . A surface derived by geodetic means and taken as a surface of reference from which to reckon geodetic elevations. See also DATUM. Also called VERTICAL DATUM, VERTICAL CONTROL DATUM.

vertical intensity of the earth's magnetic field. . The strength of the vertical component of the earth's magnetic field.

vertical lights. . Two or more lights disposed vertically, or geometrically to form a triangle, square or other figure. If the individual lights serve different purposes, those of lesser importance are called AUXILIARY LIGHTS.

vertically polarized wave. . A plane polarized electromagnetic wave in which the electric field vector is in a vertical plane.

very close pack ice. . Pack ice in which the concentration is 9/10 to less than 10/10.

very high frequency. . Radio frequency of 30 to 300 megahertz.

very low frequency. . Radio frequency below 30 kilohertz.

very open pack ice. . Pack ice in which the concentration is 1/10 to 3/10.

very quick flashing light. . A navigation light flashing 80-160 flashes per minute. See also CONTINUOUS VERY QUICK LIGHT, GROUP VERY QUICK LIGHT, INTERRUPTED VERY QUICK LIGHT.

very small fracture. . See under FRACTURE.

very weathered ridge. . A ridge with tops very rounded, the slopes of the sides usually being about 20° to 30°.

vessel, *n.* Any type of craft which can be used for transportation on water.

Vessel Traffic Services. . A system of regulations, communications, and monitoring facilities established to provide active position monitoring, collision avoidance services, and navigational advice for vessels in confined and busy waterways. There are two main types of VTS, surveilled and non-surveilled. Surveilled systems consist of one or more land-based radar sites which output their signals to a central location where operators monitor and to a certain extent control traffic flows. Non-surveilled systems consist of one or more calling-in points at which ships are required to report their identity, course, speed, and other data to the monitoring authority.

viaduct. , *n.* A type of bridge which carries a roadway or railway across a ravine; distinct from an aquaduct, which carries water over a ravine. See also BRIDGE, definition 2; CAUSEWAY.

vibrating needle. . A magnetic needle used in compass adjustment to find the relative intensity of the horizontal components of the earth's magnetic field and the magnetic field at the compass location. Also called HORIZONTAL FORCE INSTRUMENT.

vibration. , *n.* 1. Periodic motion of an elastic body or medium in alternately opposite directions from equilibrium; oscillation. 2. The motion of a vibrating body during one complete cycle; two oscillations.

video. , *n.* In the operation of a radar set, the demodulated receiver output that is applied to the indicator. Video contains the relevant radar information after removal of the carrier frequency.

violent storm. . Wind of force 11 (56 to 63 knots or 64 to 72 miles per hour) on the Beaufort wind scale. See also STORM, definition 1.

virga. , *n.* Wisps or streaks of water or ice particles falling out of a cloud but evaporating before reaching the earth's surface as precipitation. Virga is frequently seen trailing from altocumulus and altostratus clouds, but also is discernible below the bases of high-level cumuliform clouds from which precipitation is falling into a dry subcloud layer. It typically exhibits a hooked form in which the streaks descend nearly vertically just under the precipitation source but appear to be almost horizontal at their lower extremities. Such curvature of virga can be produced simply by effects of strong vertical windshear, but ordinarily it results from the fact that droplet or crystal evaporation decreases the particle terminal fall velocity near the ends of the streaks. Also called FALL STREAKS, PRECIPITATION TRAILS.

virtual image. . An image that cannot be shown on a surface but is visible, as in a mirror.

virtual meridian. . The meridian in which the spin axis of a gyrocompass will settle as a result of speed-course-latitude error.

viscosity. , The property of resistance to flow.

visibility. , *n.* A measure of the ability of an observer to see objects at a distance through the atmosphere. A measure of this property is expressed in units of distance. This term should not be confused with VISUAL RANGE. See also METEOROLOGICAL VISIBILITY.

visible horizon. . The line where earth and sky appear to meet, and the projection of this line upon the celestial sphere. If there were no terrestrial refraction, VISIBLE and GEOMETRICAL HORIZONS would coincide. Also called APPARENT HORIZON.

visual aid to navigation. . An aid to navigation which transmits information through its visible characteristics. It may be lighted or unlighted.

visual bearing. . A bearing obtained by visual observation.

visual range. . The maximum distance at which a given object can be seen, limited by the atmospheric transmission. The distance is such that the contrast of the object with its background is reduced by the atmosphere to the contrast threshold value for the observer. This term should not be confused with VISIBILITY. See also CONTRAST THRESHOLD, VISUAL RANGE OF A LIGHT.

visual range of light. . The predicted range at which a light can be observed. The predicted range is the lesser of either the luminous range or the geographic range. If the luminous range is less than the geographic range, the luminous range must be taken as the limiting range. The luminous range is the maximum distance at which a light can be seen under existing visibility conditions. This luminous range takes no account of the elevation of the light, the observer's height of eye, the curvature of the earth, or interference from background lighting. The luminous range is determined from the nominal range and the existing visibility conditions, using the Luminous Range Diagram. The nominal range is the maximum distance at which a light can be seen in clear weather as defined by the International Visibility Code (meteorological visibility of 10 nautical miles). The geographic range is the maximum distance at which the curvature of the earth and terrestrial refraction permit a light to be seen from a particular height of eye without regard to the luminous intensity of the light. The geographic range sometimes printed on charts or tabulated in light lists is the maximum distance at which the curvature of the earth and refraction permit a light to be seen from a height of eye of 15 feet above the water when the elevation of the light is taken above the height datum of the largest scale chart of the locality.) See also VISUAL RANGE, CONTRAST THRESHOLD.

volcano. , *n.* An opening in the earth from which hot gases, smoke, and molten material issue, or a hill or mountain composed of volcanic material. A volcano is characteristically conical in shape with a crater in the top.

volt. , *n.* A derived unit of electric potential in the International System of Units, it is the difference of electric potential between two points of a conducting wire carrying a constant current of 1 ampere, when the power dissipated between these points is equal to 1 watt.

volt per meter. . The derived unit of electric field strength in the International System of Units.

volume. , *n.* 1. A measure of the amount of space contained within a solid. 2. Loudness of a sound, usually measured in decibels.

voyage. , *n.* 1. A trip by sea.

vulgar establishment. . See under ESTABLISHMENT OF THE PORT.

W

wandering of the poles. . See EULERIAN MOTION.

waning moon. . The moon between full and new when its visible part is decreasing. See also PHASES OF THE MOON.

warble tone. . A tone whose frequency varies periodically about a mean value.

warm air mass. . An air mass that is warmer than surrounding air. The expression implies that the air mass is warmer than the surface over which it is moving.

warm braw. . A foehn in the Schouten Islands north of New Guinea. A foehn is a type of dry, warm, down-slope wind that occurs in the lee or downwind side of a mountain range.

warm front. . Any non-occluded front, or portion thereof, which moves in such a way that warmer air replaces colder air. While some occluded fronts exhibit this characteristic, they are more properly called WARM OCCLUSIONS.

warm occlusion. . See under OCCLUDED FRONT.

warm sector. . An area at the earth's surface bounded by the warm and cold fronts of a cyclone.

warning. . In ECDIS, an ALARM or INDICATION.

warning beacon. . See WARNING RADIOBEACON.

warning radiobeacon. . An auxiliary radiobeacon located at a lightship to warn vessels of their proximity to the lightship. It is of short range and sounds a warbling note for 1 minute immediately following the main radiobeacon on the same frequency. Also called WARNING BEACON.

warp. , *v., t.* To move, as a vessel, from one place to another by means of lines fastened to an object, such as a buoy, wharf, etc., secured to the ground. See also KEDGE.

warp. , *n.* A heavy line used in warping or mooring.

warping buoy. . A buoy located so that lines to it can be used for the movement of ships.

wash. , *n.* The dry channel of an intermittent stream.

watch. , *n.* A small timepiece of a size convenient to be carried on the person. A hack or comparing watch is used for timing observations of celestial bodies. A stop watch can be started, stopped, and reset at will, to indicate elapsed time. A chronometer watch is a small chronometer, especially one with an enlarged watch-type movement.

watch buoy. . See STATION BUOY.

watch error. . The amount by which watch time differs from the correct time. It is usually expressed to an accuracy of 1 second and labeled fast (F) or slow (S) as the watch time is later or earlier, respectively, than the correct time. See also CHRONOMETER ERROR.

watching properly. . The state of an aid to navigation on charted position and exhibiting its proper characteristics.

watch rate. . The amount gained or lost by a watch or clock in a unit of time. It is usually expressed in seconds per 24 hours, to an accuracy of 0.1^s, and labeled gaining or losing, as appropriate, when it is sometimes called DAILY RATE.

watch time. . The hour of the day as indicated by a watch or clock. Watches and clocks are generally set approximately to zone time. Unless a watch or clock has a 24-hour dial, watch time is usually expressed on a 12-hour cycle and labeled AM or PM.

watch tower. . See LOOKOUT STATION.

water-borne. , *adj.* Floating on water; afloat. See also SEA-BORNE.

watercourse. , *n.* 1. A stream of water. 2. A natural channel through which water runs. See also GULLY, WASH.

waterfall. , *n.* A perpendicular or nearly perpendicular descent of river or stream water.

waterline. , *n.* The line marking the junction of water and land. See also HIGH WATER LINE, LOW WATER LINE, SHORELINE.

water sky. . Dark streaks on the underside of low clouds, indicating the presence of water features in the vicinity of sea ice.

water smoke. . See STEAM FOG.

water stabilization. . In ECDIS, the reference system relative to the water based on course and speed-through-water sensors.

waterspout. , *n.* 1. A tornado occurring over water; most common over tropical and subtropical waters. 2. A whirlwind over water comparable in intensity to a dust devil over land.

water tower. . A structure erected to store water at an elevation above the surrounding terrain; often charted with a position circle and label.

water track. . 1. See under TRACK, definition 2. 2. See under TRUE TRACK OF TARGET.

waterway. , *n.* A water area providing a means of transportation from one place to another, principally one providing a regular route for water traffic, such as a bay, channel, passage, or the regularly traveled parts of the open sea. The terms WATERWAY, FAIRWAY, and THOROUGHFARE have nearly the same meanings. WATERWAY refers particularly to the navigable part of a water area. FAIRWAY refers to the main traveled part of a waterway. A THOROUGHFARE is a public waterway. See also CANAL.

watt. , *n.* A derived unit of power in the International System of Units; it is that power which in 1 second gives rise to energy of 1 joule.

wave. , *n.* 1. An undulation or ridge on the surface of a fluid. See also STORM SURGE, TIDAL WAVE, TSUNAMI. 2. A disturbance propagated in such a manner that it may progress from point to point. See also ELECTROMAGNETIC WAVES, RADIO WAVES, SKYWAVE, GROUNDWAVE, DIRECT WAVE, INDIRECT WAVE, MODULATED WAVE, MICROWAVE, SPHERICAL WAVE, TRANSVERSE WAVE, LONGITUDINAL WAVE.

wave basin. . A basin close to the inner entrance of a harbor in which the waves from the outer entrance are absorbed, thus reducing the size of the waves entering the inner harbor. See also WAVE TRAP.

wave crest. . The highest part of a wave.

wave cyclone. . A cyclone which forms and moves along a front. The circulation about the cyclone center tends to produce a wavelike deformation of the front. The wave cyclone is the most frequent form of extratropical cyclone (or low). Also called WAVE DEPRESSION. See also FRONTAL CYCLONE.

wave depression. . See WAVE CYCLONE.

wave direction. . The direction from which waves are coming.

waveguide. , *n.* A transmission line for electromagnetic waves consisting of a hollow conducting tube within which electromagnetic waves may be propagated; or a solid dielectric or dielectric-filled conductor designed for the same purpose.

wave height. . The distance from the trough to the crest of a wave, equal to double the amplitude, and measured perpendicular to the direction of advance.

wave height correction. . A correction due to the elevation of parts of the sea surface by wave action, particularly such a correction to a sextant altitude because of altered dip.

wave interference. . See INTERFERENCE, definition 2.

wavelength. , *n.* The distance between corresponding points in consecutive cycles in a wave train, measured in the direction of propagation at any instant.

wave of translation. . A wave in which the individual particles of the medium are shifted in the direction of wave travel, as ocean waves in shoal waters; in contrast with an OSCILLATORY WAVE, in which only the form advances, the individual particles moving in closed orbits, as ocean waves in deep water.

wave period. . The time interval between passage of successive wave crests at a fixed point.

wave train. . A series of waves moving in the same direction. See also SOLITARY WAVE.

wave trap. . Breakwaters situated close within the entrance used to reduce the size of waves from sea or swell which enter a harbor before they penetrate into the harbor. See also WAVE BASIN.

wave trough. . The lowest part of a wave form between successive wave crests.

waxing moon. . The moon between new and full when its visible part is increasing. See also PHASES OF THE MOON.

waypoint. , *n.* 1. A reference point on the track. 2. In ECDIS, in conjunction with ROUTE PLANNING, a geographical location (e.g. latitude and longitude) indicating a significant event on a vessel's planned route (e.g. course alteration point, calling in point, etc).

weak fix. . A fix determined from horizontal sextant angles between objects poorly located.

weather. , *adj.* Pertaining to the windward side, or the side in the direction from which the wind is blowing. LEE pertains to the leeward or sheltered side.

weather. , *n.* 1. The state of the atmosphere as defined by various meteorological elements, such as temperature, pressure, wind speed and direction, humidity, cloudiness, precipitation, etc. This is in contrast with CLIMATE, the prevalent or characteristic meteorological conditions of a place or region. 2. Bad weather. See also THICK WEATHER.

weathered. , *adj.* Eroded by action of the weather.

weathered berg. . An irregularly shaped iceberg. Also called GLACIER BERG.

weathered ridge. . An ice ridge with peaks slightly rounded, the slopes of the sides usually being about 30° to 40°. Individual fragments are not discernible.

weathering. , *n.* Processes of ablation and accumulation which gradually eliminate irregularities in an ice surface.

weather map. . See under SYNOPTIC CHART.

weather shore. . As observed from a vessel, the shore lying in the direction from which the wind is blowing. See also LEE SHORE.

weather side. . The side of a ship exposed to the wind or weather.

weather vane. . A device to indicate the direction from which the wind blows. Also called WIND DIRECTION INDICATOR, WIND VANE. See also ANEMOMETER.

weber. , *n.* A derived unit of magnetic flux in the International System of Units; it is that magnetic flux which, linking a circuit of one turn, would produce in it an electromotive force of 1 volt if it were reduced to zero at a uniform rate in 1 second.

wedge. . See RIDGE, definition 3.

weight. , *n.* A quantity of the same nature as a force; the weight of a body is the product of its mass and the acceleration due to gravity; in particular, the standard weight of a body is the product of its mass and the standard acceleration due to gravity. The value adopted in the International Service of Weights and Measures for the standard acceleration due to gravity is 980.665 centimeters per second, per second.

weighted mean. . A value obtained by multiplying each of a series of values by its assigned weight and dividing the sum of those products by the sum of the weights. See also WEIGHT OF OBSERVATION.

weight of observation. . The relative value of an observation, source, or quantity when compared with other observations, sources, or quantities of the same or related quantities. The value determined by the most reliable method is assigned the greatest weight. See also WEIGHTED MEAN.

wellhead. , *n.* A submarine structure projecting some distance above the seabed and capping a temporarily abandoned or suspended oil or gas well. See also SUBMERGED PRODUCTION WELL.

west. , *n.* The direction 90° to the left or 270° to the right of north. See also CARDINAL POINT.

West Australia Current. . An Indian Ocean current which generally first flows northward and then northwestward off the west coast of Australia. This current varies seasonally with the strength of the wind and is most stable during November, December, and January, and least stable during May, June, and July, when it may set in any direction. North of 20°S the main part of this current flows northwestward into the Indian South Equatorial Current.

westerlies. , *n., pl.* Winds blowing from the west on the poleward sides of the subtropical high-pressure belts.

West Greenland Current. . The ocean current flowing northward along the west coast of Greenland into Davis Strait. It is a continuation of the East Greenland Current. Part of the West Greenland Current turns around when approaching the Davis Strait and joins the Labrador Current; the rest rapidly loses its character as a warm current as it continues into Baffin Bay.

westing. , *n.* The distance a craft makes good to the west. The opposite is EASTING.

westward motion. . The motion in a westerly direction of the subtrack of a satellite, including the motion due to the earth's rotation and the nodical precession of the orbital plane.

West Wind Drift. . An ocean current that flows eastward through all the oceans around the Antarctic Continent, under the influence of the prevailing west winds. On its northern edge it is continuous with the South Atlantic Current, the South Pacific Current, and the South Indian Current. Also called ANTARCTIC CIRCUMPOLAR CURRENT.

wet-bulb temperature. . The lowest temperature to which air can be cooled at any given time by evaporating water into it at constant pressure, when the heat required for evaporation is supplied by the cooling of the air. This temperature is indicated by a well-ventilated wet-bulb thermometer. See also FREE-AIR TEMPERATURE.

wet-bulb thermometer. . A thermometer having the bulb covered with a cloth, usually muslin or cambric, saturated with water. See also PSYCHROMETER.

wet compass. . See LIQUID COMPASS.

wet dock. . See NON-TIDAL BASIN.

wharf. , *n.* A structure of open pilings covered with a deck along a shore or a bank which provides berthing for ships and which generally provides cargo-handling facilities. A similar facility of solid construction is called QUAY. See also PIER, definition 1; DOCK; LANDING; MOLE, definition 1.

whirlpool. , *n.* Water in rapid rotary motion. See also EDDY.

whirlwind. , *n.* A general term for a small-scale, rotating column of air. More specific terms include DUST WHIRL, DUST DEVIL, WATERSPOUT, and TORNADO.

whirly. , *n.* A small violent storm, a few yards to 100 yards or more in diameter, frequent in Antarctica near the time of the equinoxes.

whistle. , *n.* A sound signal emitter comprising a resonator having an orifice of suitable shape such that when a jet of air is passed through the orifice the turbulence produces a sound.

whistle buoy. . A sound buoy equipped with a whistle operated by wave action. The whistle makes a loud moaning sound as the buoy rises and falls in the sea.

whitecap. , *n.* A crest of a wave which becomes unstable in deep water, toppling over or "breaking." The instability is caused by the too rapid addition of energy from a strong wind. A wave which becomes unstable due shallow water is called a BREAKER.

white ice. See THIN FIRST-YEAR ICE.

white squall. . A sudden, strong gust of wind coming up without warning, noted by whitecaps or white, broken water; usually seen in whirlwind form in clear weather in the tropics.

white water. . 1. Frothy water as in whitecaps or breakers. 2. Light-colored water over a shoal.

whole gale. . A term once used by seamen for what is now called STORM on the Beaufort wind scale.

wide berth. . A generous amount of room given to a navigational danger.

williwaw. , *n.* A sudden blast of wind descending from a mountainous coast to the sea, especially in the vicinity of either the Strait of Magellan or the Aleutian Islands.

willy-willy. , *n.* See under TROPICAL CYCLONE.

wind. . Air in horizontal motion over the earth.

wind cone. . See WIND SOCK.

wind direction. . The direction from which wind blows.

wind direction indicator. . See WEATHER VANE.

wind drift current. . See DRIFT CURRENT.

wind driven current. . A current created by the action of the wind.

wind indicator. . A device to indicate the direction or speed of the wind. See also ANEMOMETER.

wind rode. . A ship riding at anchor is said to be wind rode when it is heading into the wind. See also TIDE RODE.

wind rose. . A diagram showing the relative frequency and sometimes the average speed of the winds blowing from different directions in a specified region.

winds aloft. . Wind speeds and directions at various levels beyond the domain of surface weather observations.

wind shear. . A change in wind direction or speed in a short distance, resulting in a shearing effect. It can act in a horizontal or vertical direction and, occasionally, in both. The degree of turbulence increases as the amount of wind shear increases.

wind-shift line. . In meteorology, a line or narrow zone along which there is an abrupt change of wind direction.

wind sock. . A tapered fabric sleeve mounted so as to catch and swing with the wind, thus indicating the wind direction. Also called WIND CONE.

wind speed. . The rate of motion of air. See also ANEMOMETER.

wind storm. . See under STORM, definition 2.

wind vane. . See WEATHER VANE.

wind velocity. . The speed and direction of wind.

windward. , *adj.* & *adv.* In the general direction from which the wind blows; in the wind; on the weather side. The opposite is LEEWARD.

windward. , *n.* The weather side. The opposite is LEEWARD.

windward tide. A tidal current setting to windward. One setting in the opposite direction is called a LEEWARD TIDE or LEE TIDE.

wind wave. . A wave generated by friction between wind and a fluid surface. Ocean waves are produced principally in this way.

winged headland. . A seacliff with two bays or spits, one on either side.

winter. , *n.* The coldest season of the year. In the Northern Hemisphere, winter begins astronomically at the winter solstice and ends at the vernal equinox. In the Southern Hemisphere the limits are the summer solstice and the autumnal equinox. The meteorological limits vary with the locality and the year.

winter buoy. . An unlighted buoy which is maintained in certain areas during winter months when other aids to navigation are temporarily removed or extinguished.

Winter Coastal Countercurrent. . See DAVIDSON CURRENT.

winter light. . A light which is in service during the winter months when the regular light is out of service. It has lower intensity than the regular light but usually has the same characteristic.

winter marker. . An unlighted buoy or small lighted buoy which is established as a replacement during the winter months when other aids are out of service or withdrawn.

winter solstice. . The point on the ecliptic occupied by the sun at maximum southerly declination. During the winter solstice the northern regions of the earth remain dark, while the southern regions bathe though 24 hours of sunshine. Sometimes called DECEMBER SOLSTICE, FIRST POINT OF CAPRICORNUS.

winter solstice

wiping. , *n.* The process of reducing the amount of permanent magnetism in a vessel by placing a single coil horizontally around the vessel and moving it, while energized, up and down along the sides of the vessel. If the coil remains stationary, the process is called FLASHING. See also DEPERMING.

wire drag. , An apparatus for surveying rock areas where the normal sounding methods are insufficient to insure the discovery of all existing obstructions above a given depth, or for determining the least depth of an area. It consists of a buoyed wire towed at the desired depth by two vessels. Often shortened to DRAG. See also DRAG, *v., t.*

withdrawn. , *adj.* Removed from service during severe ice conditions or for the winter season. Compare with the term disestablished, which means permanently removed. See also CLOSED, COMMISSIONED.

WMO Sea-Ice Nomenclature (WMO/OMM/BMO No. 259. TP. 145). A publication of the World Meteorological Organization which is comprised of sea-ice terminology, ice reporting codes, and an illustrated glossary. This publication results from international cooperation in the standardization of ice terminology.

working, *n.* In sea ice navigation, making headway through an ice pack by boring, breaking, and slewing.

World Geographic Reference System. . A worldwide position reference system that may be applied to any map or chart graduated in latitude and longitude (with Greenwich as prime meridian) regardless of projection. It is a method of expressing latitude and longitude in a form suitable for rapid reporting and plotting. Commonly referred to by use of the acronym GEOREF.

World Geodetic System. . A consistent set of parameters describing the size and shape of the earth, the positions of a network of points with respect to the center of mass of the earth, transformations from major geodetic datums, and the potential of the earth (usually in terms of harmonic coefficients). It forms the common geodetic reference system for modern charts on which positions from electronic navigation systems can be plotted directly without correction.

Worldwide Electronic Navigational Chart Data Base (WEND). In ECDIS, a common worldwide network of ENC datasets, based on IHO standards, designed specifically to meet the needs of international maritime traffic using ECDIS which conform to the IMO PERFORMANCE STANDARDS.

Worldwide Marine Radiofacsimile Broadcasts Schedules. . A publication of the National Weather Service that provides information on marine weather broadcasts in all areas of the world. In general, English language broadcasts (or foreign language broadcasts repeated in English) are included in the publication. For areas where English language broadcasts are not available foreign language transmissions are also included.

World Meteorological Organization. . A specialized agency of the United Nations which seeks to facilitate world-wide cooperation in the establishment of stations for meteorological and related geophysical observations of centers providing meteorological services, of systems of rapid exchange of weather information; and to promote the standardization and publication of meteorological and hydrometeorological observations and statistics; to further the application of meteorology to aviation, shipping, agriculture, and other related activities; to encourage research and training in meteorology and their international coordination.

World Port Index. . See *PUB. 150.*

World Wide Navigational Warning Service. . Established through the joint efforts of the International Hydrographic Organization (IHO) and the Intergovernmental Maritime Consultative Organization (IMCO) now called the International Maritime Organization (IMO), the World Wide Navigational Warning Service (WWNWS) is a coordinated global service for the promulgation by radio of information on hazards to navigation which might endanger international shipping. The basic objective of the WWNWS is the timely promulgation by radio of information of concern to the ocean-going navigator. Such information includes failure and or changes to major navigational aids, newly discovered wrecks or natural hazards in or near main shipping lanes; areas where search and rescue, antipollution operations, cable-laying or other underway activities are taking place. For WWNWS purposes, the world is divided into 21 NAVAREAS. Within each NAVAREA one national authority, designated the Area Coordinator, has assumed responsibility for the coordination and promulgation of warnings. Designated "National Coordinators" of other coastal states in a NAVAREA are responsible for collecting and forwarding information to the Area Coordinator. In the Baltic, a Sub-Area Coordinator has been established to filter information prior to passing to the Area Coordinator. Coordinators are responsible for the exchange of information as appropriate with other coordinators, including that which should be further promulgated by charting authorities in *Notice to Mariners*. The language used is English, although warnings may also be transmitted in one or more of the official languages of the United Nations. Broadcast schedules appear in an Annex to the International Telecommunication Union *List of Radiodetermination and Special Service Stations Volume II,* and in the lists of radio signals published by various hydrographic authorities (for the U.S., *Pub 117, Radio Navigational Aids.*) Transmissions usually occur frequently enough during day to fall within at least one normal radio watch period, and the information is repeated with varying frequency as time passes until either the danger has passed or the information on it has appeared as a notice to mariners.

worldwide system. . A term used to describe a navigation system providing positioning capability wherever the observer may be located. Also called GLOBAL SYSTEM.

wreck. , *n.* The ruined remains of a vessel which has been rendered useless, usually by violent action by the sea and weather, on a stranded or sunken vessel. In hydrography the term is limited to a wrecked vessel, either submerged or visible, which is attached to or foul of the bottom or cast up on the shore. In nautical cartography wrecks are designated visible, dangerous, or non-dangerous according to whether they are above tidal datum, less than, or more than 20 meters (66 feet; 11 fathoms) below tidal datum, respectively.

wreck buoy. . A buoy marking the position of a wreck. It is usually placed on the seaward or channel side of the wreck and as near to the wreck as conditions will permit. To avoid confusion in some situations, two buoys may be used to mark the wreck.

wreck mark. . A navigation mark which marks the position of a wreck.

X-Y-Z

X-band. . A radio-frequency band of 5,200 to 10,900 megahertz. See also FREQUENCY, FREQUENCY BAND.

yard. , *n.* A unit of length equal to 3 feet, 36 inches, or 0.9144 meter.

yaw. , *n.* The oscillation of a vessel in a seaway about a vertical axis approximately through the center of gravity.

Y-code. , *n.* The encrypted version of the P-code.

yawing. , *n.* See YAW.

year. , *n.* A period of one revolution of a planet around the sun. The period of one revolution of the earth with respect to the vernal equinox, averaging 365 days, 5 hours, 48 minutes, 46 seconds in 1900, is called a tropical, astronomical, equinoctial, or solar year. The period with respect to the stars, averaging 365 days, 6 hours, 9 minutes, 9.5 seconds in 1900, is called a sidereal year. The period of revolution from perihelion to perihelion, averaging 365 days, 6 hours, 13 minutes, 53.0 seconds in 1900, is an anomalistic year. The period between successive returns of the sun to a sidereal hour angle of 80° is called a fictitious or Besselian year. A civil year is the calendar year of 365 days in common years, or 366 days in leap years. A light-year is a unit of length equal to the distance light travels in 1 year, about 5.88×10^{12} miles. The term year is occasionally applied to other intervals such as an eclipse year, the interval between two successive conjunctions of the sun with the same node of the moon's orbit, a period averaging 346 days, 14 hours, 52 minutes, 50.7 seconds in 1900, or a great or Platonic year, the period of one complete cycle of the equinoxes around the ecliptic, about 25,800 years.

young coastal ice. . The initial stage of fast ice formation consisting of nilas or young ice, its width varying from a few meters up to 100 to 200 meters from the shoreline.

young ice. . Ice in the transition stage between nilas and first-year ice, 10 to 30 centimeters in thickness. Young ice may be subdivided into GRAY ICE and GRAY-WHITE ICE.

zenith. , *n.* The point on the celestial sphere vertically overhead. The point 180° from the zenith is called the NADIR.

zenithal. , *adj.* Of or pertaining to the zenith.

zenithal chart. . See AZIMUTHAL CHART.

zenithal map projection. . See AZIMUTHAL MAP PROJECTION.

zenith distance. . Angular distance from the zenith; the arc of a vertical circle between the zenith and a point on the celestial sphere, measured from the zenith through 90°, for bodies above the horizon. This is the same as COALTITUDE with reference to the celestial horizon.

zephyr. , *n.* A warm, gentle breeze, especially one from the west.

zodiac. , *n.* The band of the sky extending 9° either side of the ecliptic. The sun, moon, and navigational planets are always within this band, with the occasional exception of Venus. The zodiac is divided into 12 equal parts, called signs, each part being named for the principal constellation originally within it.

zodiacal light. . A faint cone of light which extends upward from the horizon along the ecliptic after sunset or before sunrise, seen best in the tropics and believed to be the reflection of sunlight by extraterrestrial particles in the zodiac.

zodiacal light

zone. , *n.* 1. A defined area or region. The surface of the earth is divided into climatic zones by the polar circles and the tropics; the parts between the poles and polar circles are called the north and south frigid zones; the parts between the polar circles and the tropics are the north and south temperate zones; the part between the two tropics is the torrid zone. 2. A time zone, within which the same time is kept.

zone description. . The number, with its sign, that must be added to or subtracted from the zone time to obtain the Greenwich mean time. The zone description is usually a whole number of hours.

zone meridian. . The meridian used for reckoning zone time. This is generally the nearest meridian whose longitude is exactly divisible by 15°. The DAYLIGHT SAVING MERIDIAN is usually 15° east of the zone meridian.

zone noon. . Twelve o'clock zone time, or the instant the mean sun is over the upper branch of the zone meridian. Standard noon is 12 o'clock standard time.

zone time. . The local mean time of a reference or zone meridian whose time is kept throughout a designated zone. The zone meridian is usually the nearest meridian whose longitude is exactly divisible by 15°. Standard time is a variation of zone time with irregular but well-defined zone limits. Daylight saving or summer time is usually 1 hour later than zone or standard time. See ZONE DESCRIPTION.

Zones of Confidence. . An assessment of the limitations of the hydrographic data from which a chart was compiled and used to assess the associated risk to navigate in a particular area.

zoom. . In ECDIS, a method of enlarging (zoom in) or reducing (zoom out) graphics displayed on a SCREEN.

zulu. . See GREENWICH MEAN TIME.

GLOSSARY OF ABBREVIATIONS AND ACRONYMS

A

A	amplitude; augmentation; away (altitude intercept); Arctic/Antarctic (air mass).
a	semimajor axis.
a	altitude intercept (Ho~Hc); altitude factor (change of altitude in 1 minute of time from meridian transit); assumed.
ABAND	abandoned.
AC	alternating current; altocumulus.
ACC	Antarctic Circumpolar Current.
add'l	additional.
ADF	automatic direction finder.
ADIZ	air defense identification zone.
ADLL	Admiralty Digital List of Lights.
AEB	acquisition exclusion boundary.
AERO	aeronautical.
AF	audio frequency.
AFC	automatic frequency control.
AGC	automatic gain control.
AIS-SART	AIS Search And Rescue Transmitter.
AIS	Automatic Identification System.
AISM	Association Internationale de Signalisation Maritime (International Association of Lighthouse Authorities).
aL	assumed latitude.
Al., Alt,	alternating (light).
A.L.R.S.	*Admiralty List of Radio Signals.*
am	amber.
AM	amplitude modulation.
AM	ante meridian (before noon).
AMHS	Automated Message Handling System.
AMSL	Above Mean Sea Level.
Anch	anchorage.
antilog	antilogarithm.
AP	assumed position.
approx.	approximate, approximately.
ARCS.	Admiralty Raster Chart System.
ARPA	automatic radar plotting aid.
ASAM	anti-ship activity message.
ASF	Additional Secondary Phase Factor.
ASM	Application Specific Message.
ASP	Application Service Provider.
AT	atomic time.
ATON (AtoN)	Aid(s) To Navigation.
AUSREP	Australian Ships Reporting System.
al	assumed longitude.

B

B	atmospheric pressure correction (altitude); bearing, bearing angle.
BC	Bathymetric Contour Chart.
Bdy Mon	boundary monument.
BFO	beat frequency oscillator.
BIH	Bureau Internationale de l'Heure.
BIPM	International Bureau of Weights and Measures.
bk	broken.
bkw	breakwater.
bl	blue.
BM	bench mark.
Bn	beacon.
BNPC	Bathymetric Navigation Planning Chart.
Bpgc	bearing per gyrocompass.
br	breakers.
Brg.	bearing (as distinguished from bearing angle).
bu	blue.

C

C	Celsius (centigrade); chronometer time; compass (direction); correction; course, course angle; can; cylindrical; cove.
CALM	catenary anchor leg mooring.
CB	compass bearing.
CBDR	constant bearing, decreasing range.
CC	compass course; chronometer correction.
CCIR	International Radio Consultative Committee.
CCU	Consultative Committee for Units of the International Committee of Weights and Measures (CIPM).
CCZ	Coastal Confluence Zone.
cd	candela, candelas.
CD	chart datum.
CD-ROM	compact disk-read only memory.
CG	Coast Guard.
CE	chronometer error- compass error.
CFR	Code of Federal Regulations.
cec	centicycle.
cel	centilane.
CEP	circular probable error.
CES	coast earth station.
CFR	Code of Federal Regulations.
CGPM	General Conference of Weights and Measures.
CH	Channel.

CH compass heading.
CIPM International Committee of Weights and Measures.
Cl clearance.
cm centimeter(s).
CMG course made good.
Cn course (as distinguished from course angle).
CNO Chief of Naval Operations, US Navy.
co coral.
co- the complement of (90° minus).
COA course of advance.
COE Committee on ECDIS (IHO).
COG course over ground.
coL colatitude.
colog cologarithm.
corr. correction.
cos cosine.
cot cotangent.
COTP Captain of the Port.
cov coversine.
CPA closest point of approach.
CPE circular probable error.
Cpgc course per gyrocompass.
CPRNW Commission on the Promulgation of Radio Navigational Warnings.
cps cycles per second.
Cpsc course per standard compass.
Cp stg c course per steering compass.
CPU central processing unit.
crs course.
CRT cathode-ray tube.
csc cosecant.
CSP Communications Service Provider.
CSTDMA Carrier-sense Time Division Multiple Access.
cup cupola.
Cus Ho customs house.
CW continuous wave.
CZn compass azimuth.

D

D deviation; dip (of horizon); distance; destroyed.
d declination (astronomical); altitude difference.
d declination change in 1 hour.
dA difference of longitude (time units).
DAAS Defense Automatic Addressing System.
DAC Designated Area Code.
DC direct current.
deg. degree(s).
Dec. declination.
Dec. Inc. declination increment.
Dep. departure.
destr destroyed.
Dev. deviation.
DG degaussing.
DGIWG Digital Geographic Information Working Group.
DGNSS Differential Global Navigation Satellite Service.
DGPS differential global positioning system.
DHQ mean diurnal high water inequality.
DHS Department of Homeland Security.
Dia diaphone.
diff. difference.
Dist. distance.
DLA. Defense Logistics Agency.
D. Lat. difference of latitude.
DLo difference of longitude (arc units).
DLQ mean diurnal low water inequality.
dm decimeters.
DNC digital navigation chart.
dol dolphin.
DOT Department of Transportation.
DR dead reckoning; dead reckoning position.
DRE dead reckoning equipment.
DRM direction of relative movement.
DRT dead reckoning tracer.
Ds dip short of horizon.
DSC digital selective calling.
DSD double second difference.
DSVL doppler sonar velocity log.
dur. duration.
DW Deep Water Route.
DZ danger zone.

E

E east.
e base of Naperian logarithms; origin of own ship's true vector.
e eccentricity.
EBL electronic bearing line.
ECD envelope to cycle difference; envelope to cycle discrepancy.
EC electronic chart.
ECC electronic chart correction.
ECDB electronic chart data base.
ECDIS electronic chart display and information system.
ECS electronic chart system.
ED existence doubtful.
EDD estimated date of departure.
EEZ exclusive economic zone.
EGC enhanced group calling.
EHF extremely high frequency.
E. Int. equal interval; isophase.
EM electromagnetic (underwater log).
em other ship's true vector.
ENC electronic navigation chart.
ENCDB electronic navigation chart data base.
EP estimated position.
EPFS Electronic Position Fixing System.
EPIRB Emergency Position Indicating Radio Beacon.
EPIRB-AIS Emergency Position Indicating Radio Beacon - AIS enabled.
ePODS electronic Product On Demand.

EPROM	erasable programmable read only memory.
Eq.T	equation of time.
er	own ship's true vector.
ET	Ephemeris Time.
ETA	estimated time of arrival.
ETD	estimated time of departure.
Exting	extinguished.

F

F	Fahrenheit; fast; longitude factor; phase correction (altitude); fixed (light)
f	latitude factor.
f	flattening or ellipticity.
FATDMA	Fixed Access Time Division Multiple Access.
F.Fl.	fixed and flashing.
FI	Function Identifier.
Fl.	flashing (light).
Fl. (2)	group flashing (light).
Fl. (2+1)	composite group flashing (light).
FLO	Fleet Liaison Officer - a civilian NGA analyst of Navy Quartermaster (QM).
fm(s)	fathom(s).
FM	frequency modulation.
Fog Det.	fog detector.
Fog Sig.	fog signal.
ft.	foot, feet.
FTC	fast time constant.

G

G	Greenwich; Greenwich meridian (upper branch); grid (direction); gravel; green.
g	acceleration due to gravity; Greenwich meridian (lower branch).
GAT	Greenwich apparent time.
GB	grid bearing.
GC	grid course.
GCLWD	Gulf Coast Low Water Datum.
GDOP	geometric dilution of precision.
GE	gyro error.
GEOINT	Geospatial Intelligence.
GH	grid heading.
GHA	Greenwich hour angle.
GIS	Geographic Information System.
GMDSS	Global Maritime Distress and Safety System.
GMT	Greenwich mean time.
GNSS	Global Navigation Satellite System.
Gp. Fl.	group flashing.
GP	geographical position.
GPS	Global Positioning System.
Gr.	Greenwich.
GRI	group repetition interval.
GST	Greenwich sidereal time.
GV	grid variation.
GZn	grid azimuth.

H

h	altitude (astronomical); height above sea level; hours.
ha	apparent altitude.
Hc	computed altitude.
Hdg.	heading.
HE	heeling error; height of eye.
HF	high frequency.
hf	height above sea level in feet.
HFL	Hydrographic Feature Layer.
HHW	higher high water.
HHWI	higher high water interval.
Hk	hulk.
HLW	higher low water.
HLWI	higher low water interval.
hm	height above sea level in meters.
Ho	observed altitude.
Hor	horizontal.
Hor Cl	horizontal clearance.
HP	horizontal parallax.
Hp	precomputed altitude.
Hpgc	heading per gyrocompass.
Hpsc	heading per standard compass.
Hp stg c	heading per steering compass.
hr	rectified (apparent) altitude.
hr.	hour, hrs., hours.
hs	sextant altitude.
HSD	high speed data.
ht	tabulated altitude.
HW	high water.
H.W.F.&C.	high water full and change.
HWI	high water interval, mean high water lunitidal interval.
HWQ	tropic high water inequality.
Hz	hertz.

I

I	instrument correction.
i	inclination (of satellite orbit).
IALA	International Association of Lighthouse Authorities.
IAU	International Astronomical Union.
IC	index correction.
ICC	Intelligence Coordination Center.
ICW	Intracoastal Waterway.
IDC	International Data Center.
IEC	International Electrotechnical Commission.
IDE	International Data Exchange.
IGLD	International Great Lakes Datum.
IHB	International Hydrographic Bureau.
IHO	International Hydrographic Organization.
IIP	International Ice Patrol.
IMO	International Maritime Organization.
in.	inch, inches.
INM	International Nautical Mile.

INMARSAT International Maritime Satellite Organization.
INS inertial navigation system.
int. interval.
Int. Qk. Interrupted quick flashing.
ION Institute of Navigation.
I.Q. interrupted quick flashing.
IR interference rejection.
IRP image-retaining panel.
ISLW Indian spring low water.
ISO International Order of Standardization, International Organization for Standards; isophase (light).
ITDMA Incremental Time Division Multiple Access.
ITU International Telecommunications Union.
IUGG International Union of Geodesy and Geophysics.
I.U.Q. interrupted ultra quick flashing.
I.V.Q. interrupted very quick flashing.
IWW Intracoastal Waterway.

J – K – L

J irradiation correction (altitude).
JRCC Joint Rescue Coordination Center.
K Kelvin (temperature).
kHz kilohertz.
km kilometer, kilometers.
KML Keyhole Markup Language
KMZ Keyhole Markup Language Zipped
kn knot, knots.
L latitude; lower limb correction for moon.
l difference of latitude; logarithm, logarithmic.
LAN local apparent noon.
LANBY large automatic navigational buoy.
LASH lighter aboard ship.
LAT local apparent time.
lat. latitude.
LF low frequency.
L.Fl. long flashing.
LHA local hour angle.
LHW lower high water.
LHWI lower high water interval.
LL Light List.
LL lower limb.
LLW lower low water.
LLWD lower low water datum.
LLWI lower low water interval.
Lm middle latitude; mean latitude.
LMT local mean time.
LNB large navigational buoy.
LNG liquified natural gas.
LPC Littoral Planning Chart.
LPG liquified petroleum gas.
Log logarithm, logarithmic.
Loge natural logarithm (to the base e).
Log10 common logarithm (to the base 10).
LoL List of Lights.
Long. longitude.
LOP line of position.
LRIT Long-Range Identification and Tracking.
LSS Logical AIS Shore Station.
LST local sidereal time.
Lt. light.
Lt Ho light house.
Lt V light vessel.
LW low water.
LWD low water datum.
LWI low water interval; mean low water lunitidal interval.
LWQ tropic low water inequality.

M

M celestial body; meridian (upper branch); magnetic (direction); meridional parts; nautical mile, miles; other ship.
m meridian (lower branch); meridional difference; meter,(s); U.S. survey mile, miles; end of other ship's true vector; minutes.
MA. Marine Analyst.
mag. magnetic; magnitude.
MARAD United States Maritime Administration.
MB magnetic bearing.
mb millibar(s).
MC magnetic course.
mc megacycle, megacycles; megacycles per second.
MC&G mapping, charting and geodesy.
MCPA minutes to closest point of approach.
MDA Maritime Domain Awareness.
Mer. Pass. meridian passage.
MF medium frequency.
MGRS military grid reference system.
MH magnetic heading.
MHHW mean higher high water.
MHHWL mean higher high water line.
MHW mean high water.
MHWI mean high water lunitidal interval.
MHWL mean high water line.
MHWN neap high water or high water neaps.
MHWS mean high water springs.
MHz megahertz.
mi. mile, miles.
MID Maritime Identification Digit.
mid middle.
min. minute(s).
MISLE Marine Information for Safety and Law Enforcement.
MLLW mean lower low water.
MLLWL mean lower low water line.
MLW mean low water.
MLWI mean low water lunitidal interval.
MLWL mean low water line.
MLWN neap low water or low water neaps.
MLWS mean low water springs.
mm millimeters.

MMSI	Maritime Mobile Service Identity.
Mn	mean range of tide.
mo(s)	month(s).
MOB-AIS	Man Overboard AIS device.
MODU	mobile offshore drilling unit.
Mon	monument.
Mo.(U)	Morse Uniform (light).
mph	miles per hour.
MPP	most probable position.
MRCC	Maritime Rescue Coordination Center.
MRI	mean rise interval.
MRM	miles of relative movement.
ms	millisecond(s).
MSC	IMO Maritime Safety Committee.
MSC	Military Sealift Command.
MSI	maritime safety information.
MSIWG	Maritime Safety Information Working Group.
MSL	mean sea level.
MSO	Maritime Safety Office (NGA).
MTI	moving target indication.
MTL	mean tide level.
MWL	mean water level.
MWLL	mean water level line.
MZn	magnetic azimuth.

N

N	north; nun.
n	natural (trigonometric function).
Na	nadir.
NAD	North American Datum.
NASA	National Aeronautics and Space Administration.
NATO	North Atlantic Treaty Organization.
NAUTO	nautophone.
NAVAREA	Navigation Area.
NAVEX	Naval Exercise Chart.
NAVSAT	Navy Navigation Satellite System.
NAVSSI	navigation sensor system interface.
NAVO	Naval Oceanographic Office.
NBDP	narrow band direct printing.
NBS	National Bureau of Standards.
NCS	network coordination station.
NEPA	National Environmental Policy Act.
NESS	National Earth Satellite Service.
NGA	National Geospatial-Intelligence Agency.
NGVD	National Geodetic Vertical Datum.
NLT	not less than (used with danger bearing).
n. mi.	nautical mile(s).
NM	nautical mile, miles; notice to mariners.
NMEA	National Marine Electronics Association.
NMT	not more than (used with danger bearing).
NNSS	Navy Navigation Satellite System.
NOA	Notice of Arrival.
NOAA	National Oceanic and Atmospheric Administration.
NOS	National Ocean Service.
NPRM	Notice of Proposed Rule Making.
NRML	new relative movement line.
NtM	notice to mariners.
NTTAA	National Technology Transfer and Advancement Act.
NVMC	National Vessel Movement Center.
NWS	National Weather Service.

O

Obsc	obscured.
Obs Spot	Observation spot.
Obstr	obstruction.
Oc.	occulting.
Oc.(2)	group occulting.
Oc.(2+1)	composite group occulting.
Occas	occasional.
OCS	Outer Continental Shelf.
ODAS	oceanographic data acquisition systems.
OMB	Office of Management and Budget.
ONI	Office of Naval Intelligence.
OPAREA	US Navy Operating Area Chart.
Or	orange.
OTC	officer in tactical command.
OTSR	Optimum Track Ship Routing.

P

P	atmospheric pressure; parallax; planet; pole; pillar.
p	departure; polar distance.
PA	position approximate.
PC	personal correction; personal computer.
PD	position doubtful.
PCA	polar cap absorption.
PCD	polar cap disturbance.
PCP	potential point of collision.
pgc	per gyrocompass.
PI	Presentation Interface.
P in A	parallax in altitude.
PM	pulse modulation.
PM	post meridian (after noon).
PMP	parallel motion protractor.
Pn	north pole; north celestial pole.
PPC	predicted propagation correction.
PPDB	point positioning data base.
PPI	plan position indicator.
PRF	pulse repetition frequency.
Priv	private; privately.
PROHIB	prohibited.
PRR	pulse repetition rate.
Ps	south pole; south celestial pole.
psc (p stg c)	per standard compass.
PSS	Physical AIS Shore Station.
Pub.	publication.
PV	prime vertical.
Pyl	pylon.

Q

Q quick flashing.
Q(3) group quick flashing (3 flashes).
Q(6)+L.Fl. group quick flashing (6 flashes) plus a long flash.
Q Polaris correction.
QM US Navy Quartermaster.
QQ' celestial equator.

R

r end of own ship's true vector.
R Rankine (temperature); refraction; own ship; red; rocky; coast radio station.
RA right ascension.
RACON radar transponder beacon.
rad radian(s).
RATDMA Random Access Time Division Multiple Access.
RB relative bearing.
R Bn radiobeacon.
RCC Rescue Coordination Center.
RCDS raster chart display system.
RDF radio direction finder, RDF station.
Rep. reported.
rev. reversed.
RF (rf) radio frequency.
R Fix running fix.
rk rock, rocky.
RLG ring laser gyro.
rm relative DRM-SRM vector.
R Mast radio mast.
RORO roll-on/roll-off.
ROT Rate of Turn.
RML relative movement line.
RMS root mean square.
RNC raster navigation chart.
RSS root sum square.
RTCM Radio Technical Commission for Maritime Services.
Rx reception.
RZn relative azimuth.

S

s second(s).
S sea-air temperature difference correction; slow; south; set; speed; sand.
SAIS Synthetic AIS.
SALM single anchor leg mooring.
SAM system area monitor.
SAR search and rescue.
SART search and rescue radar transponder.
SBM single buoy mooring.
SCP SafetyNET Coordinating Panel.
SD semidiameter; sounding doubtful.
sec secant.
sec. second, seconds.
semidur. semiduration.
SENC system electronic navigation chart.
SERS Sea Floor Earth Data System.
SES ship earth station.
SF Secondary Phase Factor.
SH ship's head (heading).
SHA sidereal hour angle.
SHF super high frequency.
SI International System of Units.
SID sudden ionospheric disturbance.
sin sine.
SINS Ships Inertial Navigation System.
SLD sea level datum.
SME Subject Matter Expert.
SMG speed made good.
SNC Standard Nautical Chart.
SNR signal-to-noise ratio.
SOA speed of advance.
SOG speed over ground.
SoN Safety of Navigation.
SOLAS Safety of Life at Sea Convention.
SOTDMA Self-Organizing Time Division Multiple Access.
SP spire; spherical.
SPA sudden phase anomaly.
SPM single point mooring.
SRM speed of relative movement.
SS signal station.
SSAS Ship Security Alert System.
sub, subm submerged.
SVC Sound Velocity Correction.

T

T air temperature correction (altitude); table; temperature; time; toward (altitude intercept); true (direction).
t dry-bulb temperature; elapsed time; meridian angle.
t' wet-bulb temperature.
tab. table.
TAI International Atomic Time.
tan tangent.
TB true bearing; turning bearing; air temperature atmospheric pressure correction (altitude).
TC true course.
TCA time of satellite closest approach.
TCPA time to closest point of approach.
TcHHW tropic higher high water.
TcHHWI tropic higher high water interval.
TcHLW tropic higher low water.
TcLHW tropic lower high water.
TcLLW tropic lower low water.
TcLLWI tropic lower low water interval.
TD time difference (Loran C).
TDMA Time Division Multiple Access.
Tel telephone; telegraph.

TG	time difference of groundwaves from master and secondary (slave) stations (Loran).
TGS	time difference of groundwave from master and skywave from secondary (slave) station (Loran).
TH	true heading.
TMG	track made good.
TOD	time of day (clock), Tactical Ocean Data
Tk	tank.
TR	track.
Tr	transit; tower.
TRANSCOM	U.S. Transportation Command.
Ts	time difference of skywaves from master and secondary (slave) stations (Loran).
TSG	time difference of skywave from master and groundwave from secondary (slave) station (Loran).
TSS	traffic separation scheme.
TZn	true azimuth.

U

U	upper limb correction for moon.
UHF	ultra high frequency.
UK	United Kingdom.
UL	upper limb.
Uncov	uncovers.
UPS	Universal Polar Stereographic.
U.Q.	ultra quick flashing.
USGS	United States Geodetic Survey.
U.S. Sur M	U.S. Survey mile(s).
USWMS	Uniform State Waterway Marking System.
UT	Universal Time.
UT0	Universal Time 0.
UTl	Universal Time 1.
UT2	Universal Time 2.
UTC	Coordinated Universal Time or Universal Time Coordinated.
UTM	Universal Transverse Mercator.

V

V	variation; vertex.
v	excess of GHA change from adopted value for 1 hour.
VAIS.	Virtual AIS.
var.	variation.
VDE	VHF Data Exchange.
VDES	VHF Data Exchange System.
VDU	Vector Product Format Database Update.
VDL	VHF Data Link.
vel	velocity.
Ver	vertical.
VHF	very high frequency.
VHSD	very high speed data.
Vi	violet.
VLCC	very large crude carrier.
VLF	very low frequency.
VMS	Voyage Management System.
VPF	vector product format.
vol	volcano; volcanic.
VPF	vector product format.
V.Q.	very quick flashing.
V.Q.(3)	group very quick flashing.
VRM	variable range marker.
VTS	vessel traffic service.

W

W	west; white.
WARC	World Administrative Radio Council.
WE	watch error.
WG	Working Group.
WGS	World Geodetic System.
Wk	wreck.
WMO	World Meteorological Organization.
WPI	World Port Index.
WT	watch time.
WTS	Worldwide Threat to Shipping.
WWNWS	World Wide Navigational Warning Service.

X – Y – Z

X	parallactic angle.
XMTR	transmitter.
y.	yellow.
yd(s).	yard(s).
yr(s).	year(s).
z	zenith distance.
Z	azimuth angle; zenith; Zulu.
ZD	zone description.
Z Diff.	azimuth angle difference.
Zn	azimuth.
Znpgc	azimuth per gyrocompass.
ZOC	Zones of Confidence.

INDEX

V

W

www.ingramcontent.com/pod-product-compliance
Lightning Source LLC
Chambersburg PA
CBHW080128270326
41926CB00021B/4391

* 9 7 8 1 9 5 1 1 1 6 1 9 4 *